The Official Sotheby Parke Bernet Price Guide to Antiques and Decorative Arts

EDITED BY

Charles C. Colt, Jr.

A FIRESIDE BOOK

PUBLISHED BY

Simon and Schuster/New York

A Fireside Book

Published by Simon and Schuster
A Division of Gulf & Western Corporation
Simon & Schuster Building
Rockefeller Center
1230 Avenue of the Americas
New York, New York 10020

SIMON AND SCHUSTER and colophon are trademarks of Simon & Schuster

FIRESIDE and colophon are trademarks of Simon & Schuster

Manufactured in the United States of America

1 2 3 4 5 6 7 8 9 10

1 2 3 4 5 6 7 8 9 10 (pbk.)

Library of Congress Cataloging in Publication Data

Main entry under title:

The Official Sotheby Parke Bernet price guide to antiques and decorative arts.

   1. Art objects—Prices. 2. Antiques—Prices.
3. Sotheby Parke Bernet Inc. I. Colt, Charles C.
II. Sotheby Parke Bernet Inc.
NK1125.036   707'.5   80-13886
ISBN 0-671-25024-8
ISBN 0-671-25025-6 (pbk.)

Acknowledgments

This book could not have been produced without the help of many people with a wide variety of skills. The staff of Sotheby Parke Bernet created the catalogues from which the entries and photographs have been taken. A team from the Infoconversion Division of CallData Inc., a Grumman Company, stored the entries in a computer which was programmed to sort them into chapters and subchapters. Finally, Simon and Schuster has stayed with the project despite difficult delays.

At each office dozens of people helped to write entries, programmed the computer and assisted in many other ways. A number of free-lancers also contributed to the project. To name them all would be impossible. I shall always be grateful for the help they gave to this demanding endeavor.

Special thanks are due to Robert C. Woolley of Sotheby Parke Bernet, who understood how difficult the project would be and provided generously from Sotheby Parke Bernet staff and resources. Without his support the guide could not have been completed.

The opportunity to review a year's activity in the antiques and fine arts markets has been most pleasurable for me. Any mistakes in the text are mine, whether of fact, emphasis, meaning or other nature. At the end I am fortunate to have spent this time studying so many beautiful objects from man's past.

—CHARLES C. COLT, JR.
New York, May 1980

A Message from Sotheby's

Our primary objective in undertaking this project has been to provide a frame of reference which collectors can use in approaching the often difficult and confusing question of "value" for tangible property.

Many readers may be surprised by the diversity of categories and the range of prices which our business encompasses: cast-iron mechanical banks and cast-bronze Rodins, Dior dresses and Chinese court robes, Currier & Ives prints and Monet oils, primitive American tavern tables and sophisticated French furniture. Approximately 80 percent of all the objects sold by Sotheby's in the United States have fetched under $1,000; approximately 60 percent of these fetched under $500. Nevertheless, our firm holds the vast majority of the world-record prices at auction, many of which were achieved in the United States and are included here. We feel that this very broad experience, in types as well as in values of objects, makes our business a valid and important statistical sample of American auction activity. It is this experience which we are pleased to make available to the general public for the first time in an organized format.

In using this book, it is essential to keep in mind one very important *caveat:* no two objects are completely identical in all their elements of value. Therefore, the descriptions and prices published here should be viewed as guides, as indicators of what was paid for objects and paintings at specific moments in time. It is most important to remember that these are auction prices, achieved by competitive bidding in an open marketplace. Prices asked anywhere else may reflect a different set of dynamics and therefore may not be comparable. Even at auction, a particular object may attract bidding motivated by factors not wholly attributable to a dispassionate perception of value. Fortunately, the underlying concept of comparability of objects on which this book is based more than adequately offsets such infrequent occurrences, which in their turn are instructive in depicting the upper limits to which the market will go for an object which is seen by more than one participant to be especially desirable. With a fundamental understanding of components of value, such as quality, condition, age, rarity, fashion, size, provenance and historical importance, this book can serve as a very useful tool in understanding the worth of your own possessions, and in making decisions about buying, selling, financial management, estate planning and related activities.

We have produced this book because we have felt a very strong demand for well-organized facts about performance in our many and diverse markets. We believe that the better informed collectors are, the more effective they will be as participants in the marketplace. We hope you will be encouraged to take thorough account of your tangible possessions, and that you will seek expert guidance in their management. We also hope that you may find a thing or two of unexpected value—in your present collection as well as in the future. Above all, we hope you have fun.

A Note on How to Use This Guide

For convenience, the complete description of each item in this guide is called an entry, and each entry usually includes at least the following information: what the item is, a brief description of what it is made of or its main characteristics, its size, condition, date and the price for which it was sold. Immediately preceding the price are two figures separated by a slash, 4109/345, for example. The first number, 4109, is the number of the Sotheby Parke Bernet sale at which the item was sold to the highest bidder, and the next number, 345, is the number the item had in that sale: its lot number.

The entries have been arranged in chapters, subchapters and frequently under headings. Within headings, entries are arranged alphabetically. Because antiques can be described or categorized in so many different ways, objects may have been assigned to chapters or subchapters the reader would not anticipate. Those who make use of the extensive Table of Contents and turn to all likely references will benefit from the full variety of antiques and fine arts in ths volume.

The Table of Contents lists in considerable detail the subjects covered in each of the twenty-four chapters of the guide. The first chapter is devoted to American furniture and decorative objects, and the next six chapters contain European entries sorted into various specialties. Then comes a chapter composed of collectible categories. Oriental, Islamic and Russian entries are next, followed by African, American Indian, Oceanic and Pre-Columbian works of art. Antiquities from Egypt, Greece and Rome round out the works of art entries. Chapters on books, carpets and photographic images come before the final section of the guide which is devoted to fine arts, paintings, drawings and sculpture, arranged by chapter in chronological order.

Every picture in the guide illustrates an actual item on the same page as the picture or on a facing page. The sale and lot number of the item is included in each caption to identify which items are pictured. As a further aid, the price of an item for which there is a picture is printed in italics.

In converting the descriptions of items in the Sotheby Parke Bernet catalogues to entries in this guide, a number of conventions have been followed and abbreviations have been used, particularly for dimensions, date, condition and authorship.

Dimensions: All dimensions are given in inches: height first, width second, depth, if needed, third. For example a picture described as "48 x 27" means a picture forty-eight inches high and twenty-seven inches wide. A chest which is "29 x 72 x 36" is twenty-nine inches high, six feet wide and three feet deep. If only one dimension is shown, it is the logical one; e.g. height for a candlestick. When needed, an initial is added before the dimension: H for height, W for width, L for length, D for depth and Diam for diameter.

Date: If a specific year is included in the description, the reader may assume the date is imprinted, marked, derived from a code on the item or has been established by an expert. Otherwise, an approximate date is shown, such as E18c, 1810–25 or ca1810. The initials E, M and L are used for early, middle and late, and c stands for century. Thus, E18c means early eighteenth century and ca1810 means circa (about) 1810. Chinese porcelain and certain other works of art are identified by dynasty or period as "Ming Dynasty" or "Warring States Period."

Authorship: The identity of the "author" of an item is stated in different ways to show varying degrees of certainty of authenticity. These ways of stating authorship are used primarily in the fine arts chapters; however, they also apply when authorship is stated for objects in other chapters.

Starting with the highest statement of authenticity and descending, examples of these descriptions are:

Bellini, Giovanni: The work is ascribed to the named artist either by an outside expert or by the Sotheby Parke Bernet staff, and such ascription is accepted as reliable by the galleries. While this is the highest category of authenticity and is assigned only upon the exercise of Sotheby Parke Bernet's best judgment, no unqualified statement as to authorship is made or intended.

Bellini, Giovanni; attrib.: In the best judgment of Sotheby Parke Bernet, the work can be ascribed to the named artist on the basis of style, but less certainty of authorship is expressed than in the preceding category.

Bellini, Giovanni; circle of: In the judgment of Sotheby Parke Bernet, a work by an unknown hand closely associated with the named artist.

Bellini, Giovanni; studio of: In the best judgment of Sotheby Parke Bernet, a work by an unknown hand executed in the style of the artist under his direct supervision.

Bellini, Giovanni; school of...follower of: In the best judgment of Sotheby Parke Bernet, a work by a pupil or follower of the artist.

Bellini, Giovanni; manner of: In the best judgment of Sotheby Parke Bernet, a work in the style of the artist but not by him and probably of a later period.

Bellini, Giovanni; after: In the best judgment of Sotheby Parke Bernet, a copy of a known work of the artist.

The Asterisk: An asterisk is used after a word in this book to show that although an item was not definitely identified as to author, place of origin or other significant fact, it is probably of a certain origin. Example: "probably Connecticut" in the catalogue would be abbreviated to "Conn.*" in the book.

Condition: In general, subject to the "Conditions of Sale," notice is given in the Sotheby Parke Bernet catalogues of any condition of an item which would be detrimental to its value. In the case of many objects, notably furniture, as virtually all of them have been subject to use over a considerable period of time, no mention is made of age cracks, scratches, chips or other minor damages, imperfections or restorations. On the other hand, descriptions of porcelain and glass objects do mention cracks, chips and other imperfections even though they may be caused by normal wear and tear. Items which, in the opinion of Sotheby Parke Bernet, have been significantly restored or altered are not included in this book.

For brevity, these comments on the condition of items have been shortened as follows:

General Usage

    res = restored
    rep = repaired
    imp = imperfect
    def = defective, defects, slight defects
    dam = damaged
    pcs = pieces
    insc = inscribed (with a name, date, etc.)

Islamic Miniatures
    fla = flaking, flaked
    sta = staining, stained
    rub = rubbing, rubbed
    disc = discoloration

Paintings
    All paintings are assumed to be oil on canvas and framed unless otherwise stated.

Porcelain and Ceramics
    hc = hairline crack
    chip = chipping, chipped
    cr = cracked, cracks

Silver Items
    ozs = ounces
    dwts = pennyweights

Contents

CHAPTER 2
European Furniture and Decorations   105

ENGLISH DECORATIONS   107

ENGLISH DECORATIVE OBJECTS   109

ENGLISH FURNITURE *(arranged chronologically)*   112

FRENCH DECORATIONS   145

FRENCH FURNITURE *(arranged chronologically)*,   150

GERMAN DECORATIONS   160

CHAPTER 3

European Porcelain, Ceramics and Glass 178

CERAMICS 179

CHAPTER 4

European Silver   223

CHAPTER 5

European Renaissance, Medieval and Later Works of Art   247

CHAPTER 6

American and European Works of Art, 19th and 20th Century: Works of the Victorian, Art Nouveau, Art Deco and Art Moderne Periods 272

ART POTTERY 274

CHAPTER 7
Objects of Virtu   328

CHAPTER 8
Items of Special Interest   354

CHAPTER 9

Chinese Works of Art

388

CHAPTER 10
Japanese Works of Art

CHAPTER 13

Ethnological Works of Art 543

Introduction

Over the past decade, the art and antiques market has soared. People have discovered that collections, large and small, are not only a source of aesthetic satisfaction but a sound investment, a hedge against the shrinking dollar.

Yet, with all this attention, no reference work exists that discusses the full range of current activity or contains complete—and reliable—price information. Everyone involved, in whatever way, with the auction market, has long been in need of a systematic and up-to-date guide to values for collectibles. *The Sotheby Parke Bernet Guide* answers that need.

With it, the beginning collector can decide whether local art and antique prices are reasonable or search out fields in which quality objects are still available at moderate prices. With it, the established collector can check his value judgments against the current state of the market, estimate the worth of his own collection, and watch for trends in volatile areas.

Professional people such as lawyers, tax authorities and executors can use this book to judge whether valuations supplied by others are reasonable. Investment advisers as well as decorators can use the book to recommend purchases at various price levels, while insurers will find it helpful in determining appropriate amounts of coverage. This book will aid museum curators and university professors in estimating the value of holdings and donated works. Whether for insurance purposes, estate and tax considerations or simply setting a figure for buying or selling, this book provides a means to obtain current prices in almost every category of antiques, decorative objects and fine arts.

The prices listed in *The Sotheby Parke Bernet Guide* are the result of competitive bidding among experts—museum representatives, dealers and collectors from around the world—at the world's best-known and most prestigious auction house. These values represent the combined judgments of a broad, thoroughly knowledgeable and sophisticated group. The book covers almost every category of quality collectibles. Only Sotheby Parke Bernet handles such a wide variety of works.

This guide contains prices for some 32,000 items sold recently at Sotheby Parke Bernet, arranged in 24 chapters, with numerous subchapters and subheadings within subchapters. This breakdown follows the structure of the marketplace, corresponding to the way dealers and collectors specialize. The entry for each item is an abbreviated version of the description printed in the Sotheby Parke Bernet sales catalogue for the auction at which the piece was sold. Comments on the condition of the item have been included. The sale number and the lot number of each item have also been retained, so that readers will be able to refer to the catalogue for the complete description. This book is thus a partial index to the catalogues.

The price given in each entry is in every case the winning bid on the item. Most of the entries describe a single item: a chair, a lamp, a print. The remainder describe items normally sold in units: a pair of candlesticks, a set of plates, a tea-and-coffee service. There are no miscellaneous lots or prices extrapolated from miscellaneous lots.

The more than 1000 illustrations in this book—photographs of actual items listed in this guide—have been chosen both to provide as much help as possible in the identification process and to show characteristic examples of a certain period or style. An identification made solely from comparison with photographs cannot be absolutely reliable, of course, but the wealth of illustrations in this book should enable its users to identify antiques and works of art with a high degree of accuracy.

For any item, the reader should consult the Contents for the relevant chapter, subchapter and subheading. Turning to the page that deals with any particular category of object, the reader is likely to find four or five pieces listed, in a wide price range. The reader should then compare the item in question with those listed in the book, measuring it against the descriptions of others in terms of age, condition, size and other criteria which determine value. With this book, one can quickly make a rough estimate of a work's value or, with a more detailed evaluation, fix a state-of-the-market price for almost any piece.

This book cannot and is not intended to replace the services of qualified experts. Only specialists can certify a work's authenticity. All the elements of value—age, condition, rarity and quality—are impossible for the nonprofessional to judge with certainty. Nowhere else, however, can one find the abundance of information this book contains; nowhere else can one survey the entire range of auction activity. The world of art and antiques is now at your fingertips.

Chapter 1
Americana

Sales of Americana established new highs last season, pushed up by a strong surge of public interest in all aspects of the American experience.

In furniture, pieces of true distinction or those showing unusual features brought substantially higher prices than the more ordinary. In the search for outstanding pieces, collectors paid well for examples of cabinetwork from rural centers, especially for those pieces whose maker and point of origin were known. Shaker, Windsor and primitive items like blanket chests sold steadily but did not increase dramatically in price as they have done over the past few years. Rural pieces, which tend to be not heavily carved, may increase in value if tastes change toward the simpler designs.

The preference for the more elaborate style was reflected in sales of American silver, where many collectors sought out the heavily ornamented work of nineteenth-century artisans. Water pitchers with heavy decoration sold well. Lavishly decorated Kirk silver from Baltimore increased over previous years. On the other hand, American tea sets of conventional design remain bargains at costs below that of new ones. Silver by eighteenth-century craftsmen brought dramatic prices.

Buyers of Chinese export porcelain showed special interest in items manufactured for the American market. Standard export porcelain items showed no weakening in price, but neither did they command a premium.

In folk art as in other areas, more and more weight is given by collectors to identification of the item and its significance in history. A signed and dated quilt, for example, will bring as much as five times the price of one equally handsome but sewn by an unknown hand. Similarly, crocks bring substantially more when imprinted with the name of a famous maker or user. And weathervanes, though highly prized, generally sell in the thousands of dollars only if they have unusual design features or historical association.

A generation of Americana collectors have become more sophisticated, more educated in the history of the items and more discerning in its taste. Whether one is buying or selling, then, ordinary pieces may provide a steady base, but it's the unusual that will command attention and a substantial rise in value.

Note: See Chapter 23, "American Painting and Sculpture," for more formal American art; Chapter 6, "Nineteenth and Twentieth-Century Works of Art," for works by American art-pottery and art-glass manufacturers, with a special section on the Tiffany studios; and Chapter 8, "Items of Special Interest," for American-manufactured collectibles like dolls, toys and musical instruments, which, for convenience, are grouped with their European counterparts.

Pitcher (4211/993)

Figure of a cat (4211/1013)

American Ceramics and Glass

CERAMICS OF AMERICAN INTEREST

Assorted patterns and styles

Cup, commemorative, glazed pottery, The Chicago Pioneer Railroad, cream pink glaze, 2¾, cr, 1832 (4211/1010)	$600
Dinner service, Vieux Paris, arms of Ward, motto 'Truth', 157 pcs, 1825-35 (4211/992)	6000
Harvest ring, glazed, circular, molded, American, Southern*, H10¼, 19c (4076/45)	275
Jug, baluster, glazed green-black, American Southern*, ca1850, H16, M19c (4076/47)	125
Milk jug, Wedgwood, 'Liberty China', fluted lozenge shaped body gilt edged rim, (4268/629)	125
Pitcher, pear shaped with putti, glazed, John Bell, Waynesboro, Pa., H8⅞, 19c (4076/13)	850
Pitcher, presentation, Charles Cartlidge & Co., Brooklyn, 8½, 1848-56 (4211/993)	*1400*
Pitcher, Trenton white ware, relief, death of Colonel Ellsworth, eagle, 9, star cr, ca1861 (4268/612)	325
Pitchers, pair, Tucker porcelain, vase shaped buildings with a hilly landscape, 9¼, 1825-38 (4268/614)	*1600*
Plate, glazed, circular, Conrad K. Raininger, Montgomery, Pa., D9⅝, June 23, 1838, rare (4076/71)	8250
Plate, Lenox, by B. Geyer, portrait smiling maiden, ruby red ground, gilt, 10¼, ca1900 (649/143)	900
Whippet, semi matte black glaze, Solomon Bell, Winchester, Va., H6¾ x 10, E19c, rare (4076/19)	*3250*

Bennington

Figure of a lion, flint enamel, beast with a brown tufted mane, 11, rep, 1849-58 (4268/613)	*1200*
Spaniel, large, glazed pottery, greenish-brown, oval pedestal base with chip, H16½, L19c (654/90)	225
Spaniels, two, seated, glazed, dark brown, greenish-brown, L9, 7¾, L19c (654/89)	200
Vases, cottage type, rare, molded, lady in pink and blue dress, 7½, rep, 1850-58 (4180/206)	450

Boehm

Meadowlark, rock base, flowering branch, mushroom, H20¼ (649/26)	*1500*

Whippet (4076/19)

Pitchers (4268/614)

Figure of a lion (4268/613)

Meadowlark (649/26)

Mourning Doves, group, two birds perched on a gnarled tree stump, 13½, 20c (669/22)	475
Wuen, Jenny, perched on rocky base, H5½ (649/23)	200

Boehm malvern

Plaque, flowers with enameled crane vase, floral still life, 11 x 14, framed (631/33)	2000
Plaque, sulphur crested cockatoo and flowers, framed, 11 x 14, limited edition (631/37)	2000
Plaque, Coach and Four, coaching party stopping by an inn, 14 x 11, framed (631/32)	1400
Plaque, Finches in Harmony, six finches in a setting with Chinese inscription, 14 x 11, framed (631/30)	1400

Plaque, Nature's Bounty, still life of fruit and flowers, 11 x 14, framed (631/36)   2000
Plaque, The Drummer, outside Buckingham Palace, 14¼ x 11½, framed, limited edition, 15 (631/31)   1000
Plaque, The Glories of Spring, two swans in a Chinese garden setting, 11½ x 14, framed (631/29)   1300
Plaque, floral still life, 11 x 14, framed (631/34)   1800

Chalkware

Bust, Pa.*, gentleman, hollow-mold, 19c, H9¾ (4209/119)   750
Figure of a cat, painted, light yellow, black whiskers, 13, ca1850 (4211/1013)   *950*
Kitten, yellow painted body, valley of Va., H7½, 19c (4076/69)   425

Creamware

Charger, English transfer-printed, half-rigged ship, D15½, ca1800 (4076/446)   150
Jug, probably Liverpool, masonic, poem 'Poor Jack', hc, H10⅝, large, ca1805 (4076/468)   250
Jug, English transfer-printed, apotheosis of George Washington, hc, H9, ca1810 (4076/443)   300
Jug, English transfer-printed, enamelled, Hope leaning on an anchor, H8, ca1810 (4076/439)   200

Delftware

Barber's bowl, Dutch, polychrome, with 4 putti, rep, D9⅞, rare, 18c (4076/420)   425
Bowl, Bristol, blue and white with a floral spray, hc, D9, 1760-70 (4076/401)   400
Bowl, Lambeth, blue and white, inscribed 'one bowl more & then', D10¾, rare, 1760-80 (4076/399)   425
Bowl, London, blue and white, floral sprays and a twig, hc, D11⅝, ca1770 (4076/402)   450
Bowl, London, blue and white, with willow tree, hc, D7⅝, ca1760 (4076/404)   225
Figure of a cow, Dutch, polychrome, blue sponged spots, r., L4⅜, 18c (4076/416)   *400*
Figure of a sheep, polychrome, sponged body, Dutch, H3¾, M18c (4076/417)   *200*
Figures, pair of chinoiserie, faces and robes in blue, Dutch, 4¼, M18c (4076/418)   *150*
Flower brick, probably Liverpool, blue & white, L6, ca1760 (4076/400)   400
Plate, polychrome, plant near a pagoda, D12¾, ca1730 (4076/398)   400
Plate, 'Peacock Pattern', polychrome, blue and yellow vase, c, D10, 1785-1811 (4076/422)   175
Plate, probably Frisian, blue & white, painted equestrian figure, r, D12⅝, E18c (4076/411)   325
Plate, Bristol, blue and white, lady fanning herself, large, D11½, ca1760 (4076/407)   200
Plate, Dutch, blue and white, willow near river bank, D13¼, 18c (4076/414)   225
Plate, Dutch, blue and white, Christ talking to Rebecca, D10, 18c (4076/413)   125
Plates, pair, Bristol or Liverpool, blue & white, insect flying near shrubbery, r, D11¾, ca1750
(4076/403)   375
Plates, set of six, blue & white, Bristol, D8¾, ca1760 (4076/406)   350
Plates, set of six, Bristol, blue and white, with lady fanning herself, D8¾, ca1760 (4076/405)   375
Posset pot and cover, polychrome, colored scrollwork border, r, H7⅝, ca1725 (4076/396)   2600
Teabowl and saucer, Dutch, blue & white, central floral sprig, D2½ & 4⅜, fine, rare, 18c (4076/421)   375
Vases, covered, pair, Dutch, blue and, H13⅛, M18c (4076/410)   900

Ironstone

Dinner service, 105 pcs, panels of oriental pagodas, discoloration, rim chip, 19c (654/50)   900

Liverpool

Jug, transfer-printed creamware, apotheosis of George Washington, hair cracked, H9¼, good,
ca1805 (4076/423)   550
Jug, transfer-printed creamware, eagle, names of 16 states, chip, H8⅛, ca1800 (4076/424)   450
Jug, transfer-printed creamware, eagle, names of 16 states, Success to America, r., H9⅛, ca1800
(4076/425)   425
Jug, transfer-printed creamware, enamelled, figure of Hope, hc, H8¾, ca1805 (4076/436)   375
Jug, transfer-printed creamware, enamelled, with an American ship, H7¾, ca1805-15 (4076/442)   325
Jug, transfer-printed creamware, inscribed, 'Peace, Plenty and Independence', r., H7⅞, ca1800
(4076/430)   450

Figure of a cow   (4076/416)
Figure of a sheep   (4076/417)
Figures   (4076/418)

Jug (4076/434)   Jug (4076/433)

Jug, transfer-printed creamware, inscribed with original, states' names, damages, H10⅝, ca1800
(4076/437) — 450
Jug, transfer-printed creamware, inscribed, with a soldier, rep, H8, ca1800 (4076/427) — 650
Jug, transfer-printed creamware, inscribed, The Boston Frigate, discolored, r., H10½, ca1800
(4076/432) — 225
Jug, transfer-printed creamware, inscribed, The Macedonian & the United States, H9, ca1800
(4076/431) — 650
Jug, transfer-printed creamware, map, George Washington, other figures, r, H10¾, ca1805
(4076/434) — *800*
Jug, transfer-printed creamware, masonic, chip, H11⅛, ca1800 (4076/445) — 600
Jug, transfer-printed creamware, masonic, imperfections, H9, ca1805 (4076/449) — 175
Jug, transfer-printed creamware, masonic, rim repaired, H9⅜, ca1805 (4076/448) — 425
Jug, transfer-printed creamware, portrait of George Washington, imperfections, H11½, ca1800
(4076/447) — 375
Jug, transfer-printed creamware, American naval engagement, r., H8⅞, ca1805 (4076/426) — 450
Jug, transfer-printed creamware, George Washington and other figures imperfect, H13⅛, rare,
ca1800 (4076/433) — *900*
Jug, transfer-printed creamware, George Washington and others, imperfections, H8⅞, ca1800
(4076/438) — 325

Liverpool creamware

Jug, 'The Farmers Arms', figures merrymaking, 7⅞, ca1800 (4180/170) — 350
Jug, 'United we stand', with JD under spout, 11, disc, ca1800 (4180/169) — 700
Jug, 'Washington in Glory, America in Tears', 9, ca1800 (4180/171) — 650

Lustreware

Jug, pink, American Eagle, hc discoloration, H6½, rare, ca1810 (4076/452) — 600
Plate, probably Cambrian Pottery, copper lustre, 10, 1820-30 (4180/192) — 100
Tea cups and saucers, six, pink, floral vine border, ca1810 (4076/456) — 125
Tea service, part, 'Strawberry' pattern, 19 pcs, ca1810 (4076/454) — 375

Mochaware

Bowl, blue and dark brown, D6¼, fine, E19c (4076/465) — 250
Bowl, herringbone border, D6¼, fine, E19c (4076/466) — 225
Pitcher, swelling body, brown and blue stripes, H7¼, E19c, rim chip (654/80) — 90

Pearlware

Bowl, variegated, Leeds, marbleized in brown, imperfections, D8⅝, ca1805 (4076/461) — 150
Plate, American Eagle decoration, 7¼, dam, 1805-20 (4211/987) — 150
Plates, set of twelve, and a platter, Chinaman holding parasol, (4076/460) — 475

Pottery

Pitcher, glazed, applied strap handle, N. Carolina, H9½, 19c (4076/49) — 175

Presidential china

Bowls, soup, pair, President Rutherford B. Hayes, 9, ca1880 (4268/622) — 650
Bowls, soup, pair, Haviland & Co., President Rutherford B. Hayes service, 9, ca1880 (4211/997) — 800
Bowls, soup, pair, Haviland & Co., President Rutherford B. Hayes service, 9, ca1880 (4211/998) — 800
Bowls, soup, pair, Haviland & Co., President Rutherford B. Hayes service, 9, ca1880 (4211/996) — 1300

Bowls, soup, set of 8, Haviland & Co., President Rutherford, B. Hayes, service, 9, ca1880 (4211/995)	3900
Cake stand, 3 tier, Edouard Honore, President James K. Polk service, 17½, imp, 1846 (4211/994)	2800
Dessert plate, reorder, Lincoln dinner service, Limoges, 8¼, rep, ca1873 (4180/207)	350
Fish dish, President Rutherford B. Hayes, molded as scallop shell, 8⅞, ca1880 (4268/625)	550
Plate, Harrison breakfast service, Limoges, 8½, fine, ca1892 (4180/210)	800
Plate, President Rutherford B. Hayes, 'snowshoe' service, 7¼, 1879-80 (4268/620)	1100
Plate, dinner, President Rutherford B. Hayes, tones, grey and brown, 10 ca1880 (4268/624)	425
Plate, Order of Cincinnati, from George Washington's service, 9¾, 1784-85 (4180/168)	8000
Plates, dinner, pair, Haviland & Co., President Rutherford B. Hayes service, 10, ca1880 (4211/1002)	1300
Plates, game bird, pair, Haviland & Co., President Rutherford B. Hayes service, 9, ca1880 (4211/1001)	700
Plates, game bird, set of 8, Haviland & Co., President Rutherford B. Hayes service, 9, ca1880 (4211/1000)	2000
Plates, pair, President Rutherford B. Hayes, 'Indian' basket form, 8⅞, 1879-80 (4268/621)	1400
Plates, pair, game bird, President Rutherford B. Hayes, 9, ca1880 (4268/623)	700
Plates, tea set of 3, President Benjamin Harrison, with American Eagle, 7¼, 1892 (4268/626)	1400
Plates, tea, pair, President Benjamin Harrison, with American Eagle, 7¼, 1897-1901 (4268/627)	375
Platter, turkey, Haviland & Co., President Rutherford B. Hayes service, 19⅞, ca1880 (4211/999)	1400
Soup bowl, Hayes service designed by Davis, Limoges, 9, fine, ca1880 (4180/208)	500

Redware

Bank, beehive, glazed, probably Pa., 4¼, 19c (4146/28)	60
Bowl, glazed green and brown, 10¼, hc, 19c (4146/31)	40
Bowl, glazed, circular body, D14¼, 19c (4076/26)	225
Bowl decorated with white slip, S. Bell & Son, Strasburg, Va., D15, L19c (4076/7)	425
Bowl incised with zig-zag band, S. Bell & Son, Strasburg, Va., D10, L19c (4076/8)	550
Boy with basket of apples, glazed, John Bell*, Waynesboro, Pa., H6, M19c (4076/11)	800
Charger, Norwalk, Conn., glazed, slip decorated, D14, chip (4209/140)	750
Churn, butter, baluster glazed green, N.C., H18½, 19c (4076/46)	300
Covered jar, Norcross*, Me. 19c, baluster, standup lip, lid, ch, 10 (4180/701)	150
Cuspidors, glazed, pair, S. Bell & Son*, Strasburg, Va., H3¼, D6¼, 19c (4076/22)	225
Dish, deep, incised ring, Upton Bell, Waynesboro, Pa., D9¼, L19c (4076/32)	150
Dish, glazed, circular, notched rim, yellow and orange, Conn.*, 11, slip missing, 19c (4211/1019)	325
Dish, sgraffito decorations, glazed, Pa., D11½, 19c (4076/39)	2700
Dish, slip decorated, centering a stylized reindeer, D13⅝, 19c (4076/43)	350
Dish, yellow slip, red orange ground, Christ,* N.C., D11¾, E19c (4076/40)	1000
Figural group, commemorative, Eberly Potters, Strasburg, Va. 1894, 15¼ x 15⅛, 19c (4076/33)	2500
Flowerpot, 2, Bell*, Shenandoah, Va., yellow glaze with brown splotches, 19c, H8½-8¾, chip (4209/138)	550
Flowerpot, baluster form, S. Bell & Son, Strasburg, Va., H8¼, L19c (4076/24)	300
Flowerpot, glazed, New England, possibly Me., 6, 19c (4146/30)	*75*
Flowerpot and saucer, attached, glazed, S. Bell & Sons, Strasburg, Va., H8, M19c (4076/25)	150
Flowerpot and saucer, glazed, South Western Conn.*, H8½, 19c (4076/79)	300
Jar, covered, glazed black brown, N.Eng., Mass.*, H10½, 19c (4076/80)	250
Jars, 2, Bell, S. & Son, Va., glazed, baluster form, molded lip, 19c, H7½-8½, chip (4209/137)	550
Jug, bubous, olive green glaze, N.Eng.* Gonic, N.H., H8½, E19c (4076/76)	850
Jug, ovoid, brown glaze, Mass.*, H11¾, ca1800 (4076/61)	200
Jug, ovoid, dark green glaze, N.Eng., H9¾, 19c (4076/73)	225
Jug, ovoid, moss green glaze, Mass.*, H7½, 19c (4076/75)	325
Jug, ovoid, with strap handle, glazed, Mass.*, H11¾, 19c (4076/74)	200
Jug, sgraffito, puzzle, glazed, baluster, pierced neck, James Ryers, 9 chip, 1825 (4211/1018)	700
Jug, Merrimacport*, Mass. 19c, ovoid with incised double ring, 10½ (4180/702)	300
Lafayette, slip-decorated plate, probably Conn., rectangular, 9⅛ x 11¼, 19c (4146/27)	*700*
Lamb, sleeping, glazed, molded fleece, S. Bell & Son, Strasburg, Va., 3½ x 12, L19c (4076/28)	1750
Lion glazed yellow and brown, John Bell, Waynesboro, Pa., 7½ x 8½, M19c, rare (4076/1)	18000
Mug, glazed, slip-decorated, S. Bell & Son, Va., stylized leaves, 4½, L19c (4268/972)	800
Pan, glazed, probably Pa., H4, 19c (4146/29)	150

Pitcher (4076/15)

Flowerpot (4146/30)

Whimsey (4146/26)
Lafayette (4146/27)

Plate
(4156/242)

Pitcher (4146/32)

Pitcher, baluster form, glazed green, John Bell, Waynesboro, Pa., H10, 19c (4076/20) 550
Pitcher, baluster form, molded decor, Solomon Bell, H8, M19c (4076/15) *400*
Pitcher, baluster shape, glazed, *J. Eberly & Co., Strasburg, Va., H7¼, L19c (4076/35) 275
Pitcher, baluster, form, glazed, Bell Family, American, 5, 19c (4076/29) 225
Pitcher, baluster, glazed, C.J. Meaders, Cleveland, Ga., H10, 19c (4076/54) 250
Pitcher, baluster, glazed, N.C., H10, 19c (4076/52) 75
Pitcher, baluster, glazed brown, *N.C., grey glaze interior, H14, 19c (4076/50) 175
Pitcher, baluster, glazed green, H13½, 19c (4076/51) 250
Pitcher, baluster, yellow glaze, Pa. or Va., 1876, H8¾, 19c (4076/55) 225
Pitcher, baluster, celadon glazed, John Bell, H7½, 19c (4076/14) 950
Pitcher, covered, bulbous body, glazed, *Pa., H7½, 19c (4076/81) 125
Pitcher, covered, fine glazed, N.Eng., Conn.*, 8, 19c (4146/32) *275*
Pitcher, covered, glazed, N.Eng., H7½, 19c (4076/83) 225
Pitcher, glazed, molded, streaky, John Bell*, Waynesboro, Pa., H6¼, M19c (654/88) 250
Pitcher, ovoid body, glazed, N.Eng., H8, E19c (4076/82) 225
Pitcher, water, cylindrical body, J. Eberly & Co.*, Strasburg, Va., H9⅛, L19c (4076/34) 250
Plate, glazed, inscribed Lemon Pie, N.Eng., D9⅛, 19c (4076/77) 850
Plate, glazed, slip-decorated, Conn.*, finely notched rim, linear motif, 10, ch, 19c (4268/974) 300
Plate, initials WB in yellow slip, N.Eng., D9⅛, 19c (4076/78) 475
Plate, sgraffito decorated, glazed, Pa., D11¾, E19c, rare & fine (4076/70) 5750
Plate, slip decorated glazed, circular, notched rim, N.Eng.*, 11, some slip missing, 19c (4211/1017) 300
Plate, slip decorated, glazed, Pa., D9¾, 1882 (4076/72) 1750
Plate, slip-glazed, Long Island or Conn., 11½, 19c (4149/67) 250
Plate, slipware, glazed, N.Eng., inscribed 'St. Rose of Lima', 19c., chip (4156/242) *325*
Rooster, glazed, free standing, orange glaze, Pa.*, 13¾, 19c (4211/1020) 325
Spaniel, glazed streaky brown, Solomon Bell, Strasburg, Va., H8¾, M19c (4076/3) 1000
Spaniel, painted yellow and black, John Bell, Waynesboro, Pa., H9, M19c (4076/2) 1000
Storage jar, Southern, 19c, baluster form, streaky white glaze, 16 (4180/704) 75
Trivet, surface with grapes, on feet, John Bell, Waynesboro, Pa., D8½, M19c (4076/9) 475
Vase, baluster form, brown glaze, Samuel Bell*, Va., H6¼, M19c (4076/23) 750
Vase, baluster, glazed green & orange, H6¾, 19c (4076/56) 150
Vase, ornamental, Beecher, Va., scrolled ear handles, 9½, L19c (4268/973) 850
Vessels, 3, Bell*, Shenandoah, Va., vase, bowl, flower pot, glazed, 19c, H6⅛-8½ (4209/139) 650
Wall pocket, cylindrical, glazed, J. Eberly & Co.*, Strasburg, Va., H7¼, L19c (4076/36) 325
Wall pocket, glazed green and brown, Bell Family*, Shenandoah Valley, H8½, 19c (4076/21) 275
Washbowl and pitcher, glazed, S. Bell & Son, Strasburg, Va., H11¾, D14½, L19c (4076/18) 1000
Whimsey, glazed pottery hat, Pa.*, 6½, 1897 (4146/26) *200*

Samson, modern

Plates, set 6, tightrope walker above juggler and drummer, 8⅜, imp (4180/39) 175

Slipware

Plate, green and yellow, N.C., D12½, 19c (4076/37) 700

Spatterware

Plates, six, peacock perched on green spattered ground, 9¼ (4180/175) 600

Teabowls and saucers, 5 and 6, underglaze blue, American eagle, purple spatter, Diam 3⅞ x 5⅞, ca1840 (4211/989) 400

Staffordshire

Basket and stand, creamware, oval, pierced wavy rim, imp, L9½, 10, ca1810 (654/65) 80
Bowl, yellow glaze, russet rim, 6⅜, ca1820 (4180/179) 300
Bowl, Single rose pattern, russet rim, 6⅜, ca1820 (4180/184) 475
Bowl and stand, fruit, blue and white, 'Landing of Gen. Lafayette', 11, cr, ca1825 (684/78) 900
Coffeepot and cover, gaudy Dutch 'Butterfly' pattern, H10⅞, 1820-30 (4076/458) 1900
Coffeepot and cover, blue and white, exotic birds, scrolling flowers and foliage, 11¾, ca1815 (684/85) 325
Dish, meat, blue and white, 'Landing of Gen. Lafayette,' J. & R. Clews, 17, ca1825 (684/94) 600
Dish, vegetable, blue and white, 'A Ship of the Line in the Downs', Enoch Wood & Sons, 9½, ca1830 (684/79) 375
Doll's dinner service, blue & white, 20 pcs, Pearlware, rare, ca1810 (4076/459) 275
Figure of Benjamin Franklin, wearing blue coat, base labeled Washington, 15½, M19c (4268/609) 475
Flowerpots and stands, yellow glaze, flowering vine border, 4½, var mks (4180/176) 650
Jug, single rose pattern, russet rim, 6⅜, ca1820 (4180/181) 1000
Jug, single rose pattern, russet rim, 6⅞, ca1820 (4180/180) 1100
Jug, blue and white, 'N.Y. City Hall and Insane Asylum' J. & R. Clews, 7¾, ca1830 (684/100) *450*

Plate (684/72)
Plate (684/73)

Plate (684/77)

Plate (684/99)
Jug (684/100)

Jug, transfer-printed canary-yellow, masonic, imperfections, H8½, rare, ca1800 (4076/451) 500
Knobs, mirror, pair, enamel, oval, bust portraits, 2 x 1½, cr, L18c (4211/1123) 600
Milk jug, print of gentleman beneath tree, 3¼, ca1820 (4180/190) 175
Milk jug, single rose pattern, russet rim, 3⅝, ca1820 (4180/182) 325
Mirror knobs, pair, transfer printed, American eagle, brass frames, Diam 1⅞, E19c (4268/1098) 600
Plate, blue and white, 'Winter View of Pittsfield, Mass.' J. & R. Clews, 10½, ca1825 (684/86) 225
Plate, blue and white, 'Baltimore & Ohio R.R. Incline Plane', Enoch Wood & Sons, 9¼, ca1830 (684/73) *425*
Plate, blue and white, 'City Hall, New York', J. & W. Ridgway, 9¾, ca1830 (684/101) 125
Plate, blue and white, 'Commodore MacDonough's Victory', Enoch Wood & Sons, (684/84) 300
Plate, blue and white, 'Commodore MacDonough's Victory', Enoch Wood & Sons, 10, ca1825 (684/83) 300
Plate, blue and white, 'Dr. Syntax Taking Possession of His Living', J. & R. Crews, 10, ca1830 (684/75) 130
Plate, blue and white, 'Erie Canal Aqueduct Bridge at Rochester', Enoch Wood, 7¾, ca1830 (684/106) 375
Plate, blue and white, 'Erie Canal Inscription', 10¼, ca1830 (684/102) 275
Plate, blue and white, 'Fall of Montmorenci near Quebec' Enoch Wood & Sons, 9, ca1835 (684/69) 125
Plate, blue and white, 'Gilpins Mills', Enoch Wood & Sons, 9, ca1830 (684/66) 175
Plate, blue and white, 'Landing of Gen. Lafayette at Castle Garden, N.Y.', J. & R. Clews, 10, ca1825 (684/72) *200*
Plate, blue and white, 'Landing of Gen. Lafayette', J. & R. Clews, 7¾, ca1825 (684/97) 150
Plate, blue and white, 'Peace and Plenty', J. & R. Clews, 10¼, ca1830 (684/88) 125

Plate, blue and white, 'St. Paul Church, New York', 6¼, ca1820 (684/107) 600
Plate, blue and white, 'Table Rock, Niagara', Enoch Wood & Sons, 10, ca1835 (684/67) 200
Plate, blue and white, 'The Holme, Regent's Park' London views E. Wood & Sons, 10, ca1825 (684/80) 60
Plate, blue and white, 'The Kent East Indian', Enoch Wood, 9¼, ca1830 (684/99) *150*
Plate, blue and white, 'Upper Ferry Bridge over the River Schuylkill', Joseph Stubbs, 8¾, ca1825 (684/96) 150
Plate, blue and white, Profile of Washington, American Eagle, J. Heath*, 9½, chip, ca1800 (684/77) *425*
Plate, meat, blue and white, 'The Advertisement for a Wife', J. & R. Clews, 15, ca1830 (864/95) 450
Plate, soup, blue, 'Baltimore & Ohio R.R.' Enoch Wood & Sons, 10, ca1835 (684/68) 450
Plate, soup, blue and white, 'Octagon Church, Boston', J. & W. Ridgways, 9¾, ca1820 (684/103) 125
Plate, soup, blue and white, 'Table Rock, Niagara', Enoch Wood & Sons, 10, ca1835 (684/70) 225
Plates, set of 4, blue and white, 'Landing of Gen. Lafayette', J. & R. Clews, 8¾, ca1825 (684/104) 650
Plates, set of 4, blue and white, 'Landing of Gen. Lafayette', J. & R. Clews, 10, ca1825 (684/105) 800
Platter, topographical blue and white, 'Newburg, Hudson River', 17¾, ca1840 (684/76) 180
Portrait figure of Napoleon, blue coat, green jacket, striped waistcoat, 21¼, ca1850 (684/120) 300
Spill vase, yellow glaze, flowering vine border, 4⅞, ca1820 (4180/177) 250
Tea set, part lustre decorated, floral, pink borders, ca1815, 15 pcs (684/114) 90
Teapot, blue and white, transfer, two ladies, gentleman, H7, ca1830, chip (654/56) 75
Tureen sauce and cover, 'Landing of Gen. Lafayette at Castle Garden, N.Y.', J. & R. Crews, 8¼, ca1825 (684/74) 125
Vases, pair, lustre, pink, campana-shaped bodies with bouquet, 5¾, ca1815 (4180/196) 200

Staffordshire, historical

Bowl, Clews, 'Peace and Plenty', 10, ca1830 (654/63) 275
Egg cup, blue, rare, 'Washington Standing at Tomb,' Enoch Wood & Sons, 2⅜, chip, 1819-30 (4156/55) 325
Plate, blue, variation of arms of the United States, 6½, ca1830, chip (654/53) 275
Plate, blue, James and Ralph Clews, depicting 'University Building', 8⅝, 1819-36 (4156/61) 200
Plate, blue, Joseph Stubbs, depicting 'Fair Mount Near Philadelphia', 10¼, ca1820, fine (4156/60) 225
Plate, Stevenson and Williams, City Hotel, N.Y., and Aqueduct Bridge, 8⅝, ca1830, chip (654/52) 325
Plates, blue, pair, 'Harvard College,' Ralph Stevenson and Williams, D10, ca1820 (4156/59) 500
Plates, two, Clews, depicting 'Landing of Lafayette', 10, ca1825 (654/60) 400
Platter, View of West Point, black printed, chip rep., L17½, ca1840 (654/59) 125
Saucer, blue, fine, 'Washington Standing at Tomb', Enoch Wood & Sons, D5¾, 1819-30 (4156/58) 125
Tea service, blue, 20 pieces, 'Washington Standing at Tomb,' Enoch Wood & Sons, 1819-30, rare (4156/54) 4500
Teabowls and saucers, pair, blue, 'Washington Standing at Tomb', Enoch Wood & Sons, 1819-30, D3⅞, 5¾, fine (4156/57) 500

Stoneware

Bottle, ash glazed, with snake, American, S.C., H9½, 19c (4076/48) 1600
Crock, cylindrical, salt glazed, Cowden & Wilcox, Harrisonburg, Pa., H11, 19c (4076/64) 250
Crock, cylindrical, salt glazed, N.Y.*, H11, M19c (4076/63) 225
Crock, double handle glazed, impressed Commeraw, Coerlears Hook, N.Y., 9⅝, age cr, L18/E19c (4211/1004) 800
Crock, salt glaze, cobalt bird on flowering branch, E.S. White & Son, Utica, 18½, 19c (684/140) 425
Crock, salt glazed, floral spray, Norton & Fenton, E. Bennington, Vt., 13½, cr (684/139) 150
Crock, salt glazed, inscribed in underglaze blue, 1839, 9, 1839 (684/138) 100
Doorstop, spaniel, molded and glazed, cream colored, 21½, 1860-70 (4211/1006) 200
Figure, recumbent spaniel, molded and glazed, gray glazed, 6¾, 1840-50 (4211/1007) 325
Flask, salt glazed, Albany*, near pint size, deep beige, checkerboard motif, 7½, cr, ca1820 (4211/1008) 200
Jar, baluster, salt glazed, American*, 9¾, 19c (4076/65) 200
Jar, open, baluster, American*, May 3, 1885, H11, L19c (4076/62) 175
Jar, Brewer, Clark & Son, Boston, salt-glazed, 19c, H27, D15, rare (4209/136) 3500
Jug, Clark, N.Y. 1843-92, baluster form, prancing horse, 14 (4180/699) 1300
Jug, cylindrical, salt glazed, Ballard Brothers, Burlington, Vt., H11½, 19c (4076/66) 125
Jug, elliptical, salt glazed, Hamilton & Jones, Greensboro, Pa., H18, 19c (4076/57) 225
Jug, salt glazed, D. Roberts, Binghamton, N.Y., H20, 19c (4076/67) 325
Jug, Ulbridge*, N.J., 19c, baluster form, incised fish on shoulder, 17¼ (4180/706) 425
Pitcher, Bell, Solomon, Strasburg, Va., 15¾, 19c (4076/6) 375
Pitcher, baluster, elongated neck, N.C., H10½, 19c (4076/60) 250
Pitcher, 3-quart, beer, Carl Wingender*, N.J., baluster body, pewter lid, 14¾, 19c (4268/977) 450
Salt-glazed covered jar, 14 (4146/25) 150
Water cooler, cylindrical, glazed, front and shoulders with a flowering vine, H16½, 19c (4076/58) 350

Sunderland

Plaques, 3, similar, Peace and Plenty, pink and copper lustre borders, H7⅜, 8⅜, ca1840 (654/77)	300
Plaques, 4, apricot lustre borders, H7⅜, 8⅜, ca1870 (654/79)	200
Plaques, 4, similar, pink lustre borders, religious themes, H5⅞, 8½, M19c (654/78)	175

Tucker

Pitcher, vase shape, floral spray, 9¼, fine, Philadelphia 1825-38 (4180/202)	550

Union Porcelain Works

Teacups and saucers, pair, white, trellis pattern, quilting panels, imp, mkd, 1877-87 (4180/205)	75
Teacups and saucers, pair, white, trellis pattern, quilting panels, imp, mkd, 1877-87 (4180/204)	150
Teacups and saucers, pair, white, trellis pattern, quilting panels, fine, mkd, 1877-87 (4180/203)	425

Vieux Paris

Matchbox and cover, with view of Baltimore, Md., L3⅞, fine, rare, 19c (4076/473)	450
Teacup and saucer, with a view of Philadelphia, fine, rare, 1820-40 (4076/474)	275

CHINESE EXPORT PORCELAIN

An assortment of patterns and styles

Baskets, reticulated, oval, pair, with 'L'Urne Mysterieuse' medallions, L10⅞, rare, 1793-95 (4211/917)	1800
Bottles, pair, flower-encrusted, red-crested pheasants, H15¼, ca1830 (4076/360)	700
Bowl, clusters of flowers within scrolls, 11¼, cr, ca1775 (4180/50)	225
Bowl, shipping motifs, en grisaille, D10⅛, fine, ca1775 (4076/298)	700
Bowl, painted with masonic symbols, D11½, ca1795 (4076/320)	1200
Bowl, 'cabbage leaf', enamelled in green and white, 10⅞, 1830-50 (4268/534)	275
Bowl, cabbage leaf pattern, with shou character medallion, D13¼, 1830-50 (4076/348)	475
Bowl, fish, dignitary and 21 boys, 6¾, 19c (4211/942)	450
Bowl, large, decorated in blue enamel and gilding, D12⅜, ca1790 (4076/321)	300
Bowl, made for the American market, field of butterflies, birds, fruit, flowers, D9, 1820-50 (4076/344)	250
Bowl, Mandarin palette, two panels of figures on a terrace, 7¾, fine, ca1775 (4211/893)	325
Bowl, scalloped, animal handles, serpentine floral swags, diameter 9, ca1780 (4148/24)	200
Bowl, shipping, black, yellow and iron red, British flags, 9, hc, rep, ca1785 (4268/476)	375
Bowl, small, American market, with stylized eagle and 16 gold stars, D5½, fine, 1796-1810 (4076/334)	500
Bowl, square, floral bouquet and sprigs, 10½, crack, ca1780 (4260/238)	500
Bowl, Mandarin palette, diameter 11½, rep., ca1780 (4148/33)	650
Bowls, pair, shallow, floral cluster, for Persian market, 9, cr, 1790-1820 (4180/75)	250
Bowls, pair, lotus pattern, Chia Ch'ing, Tao Kuang seal marks, D9¼, fine, 19c (4076/370)	800
Box, double butterfly, Canton, formed as 2 butterflies, L9⅝, unusual, 18c/19c (4076/377)	550
Cachepot, Batavian, 4 leaf shaped panels, 7¾, ca1745 (4268/453)	350
Candlestick figures of court ladies, pair, painted with 'Mandarin' palette, H16½ & 16⅛, ca1775 (4076/294)	600
Charger, colored flowers, hair crack, 14¾, ca1750 (654/34)	200
Charger, cabbage leaf, with shou character medallion, chip, D14⅝, 1830-50 (4076/349)	175
Charger, scalloped, sprays of flowers, 15, ca1760 (4260/217)	700
Chocolate pot and cover, initialled MR, gilt sprig under spout, 9, ca1790 (4211/911)	300
Coffeepot and cover, gilding, fluted body, 8, ca1740 (4268/446)	300
Coffeepot and cover, lighthouse form, gilt sprig within pendant, 9¼, ca1790 (4180/74)	450
Coffeepot and cover, lighthouse, model, with American Eagle, 9⅜, 1795-1805 (4211/912)	950
Coffeepot and cover, 'Valentine' motif, handle riveted, 9¾, ca1750 (4211/884)	275
Cuspidor and cover, blue and white, foliage and tight scrolls, 8¼, 19c (4211/922)	375
Dish, quatrefoil, crested, brown eagle crest, 11, chip, hc, ca1805 (4260/246)	200
Dish, reticulated, oriental figures and landscape, 13¾, ca1820 (4260/248)	500
Dish, shell shaped, 4 floral bouquets and a sprig, 9, ca1785 (4260/242)	325
Dish, turquoise ground, painted in famille-rose enamels with quail, D9⅛, ca1750 (4076/274)	325
Dishes, pair, leaf shaped, figures on terrace, celadon, 8¼, ca1830 (4180/141)	400
Dishes, pair of oval, reticulated, painted in famille-rose palette, ladies, L9¼, fine, ca1780 (4076/296)	600
Dishes, pair, lotus, cluster of oriental flowers, 9, rep, ca1745 (4260/202)	1100
Dishes, saucer, pair, iron red, thick blue enamel and gilding, 10⅞, hc ca1805 (4268/513)	225
Ewers, initialled, pair, molded with scrollwork, floral sprays, 9¼, fine, ca1790 (4180/68)	225
Figure of a Dutch lady, in colorful Dutch costume, neck repaired, H16⅜, rare, 1730-50 (4076/272)	15500
Figure of a peacock, brilliantly enamelled, H19⅝, good, 19c (4076/382)	800
Figure Pu Tai, god of happiness, 11¼, chip, 1820-50 (4211/947)	700
Figures of cockerels, pair, red, yellow, on black rockwork, 1 chip, H8, 19c (4076/383)	600
Figures of cocks, pair, greenish glaze, pierced rockwork bases, 12⅛, dam, 19c (4211/949)	750
Figures of elephants now candlesticks, iron red, heightened in gilding, 4¾, imp, 19c (4268/517)	600

Fish bowl, flowering tree peony, green rockwork, 18⅝, 19c (4268/565)	3100
Fish bowl, pheasant and songbird, floral, 13¾, 19c (4268/519)	1400
Garden seats, pair, blue and white, 2 rows of bosses, foliage, 18⅝, hc (4180/143)	1000
Garden seats, pair, celadon, 2 rows of molded bosses, 18¼, fine (4180/142)	2000
Ginger jar, blue and white, flowering peony, stylized rockwork, 19c (4268/555)	400
Ginger jar, famille-rose enamels, flowering tree peonies, H9⅛, L18c/E19c (4076/368)	300
Ginger jar and a cover, famille-rose enamels, phoenix bird perched, H9⅝, 19c (4076/369)	300
Hot water dish, central floral medallion, W11, ca1800 (4076/342)	375
Hot water dish, painted in brown tones, sepia, iron-red, W11, fine, ca1800 (4076/341)	260
Hot water dish, octagonal, brown cornucopia, W11⅛, fine, ca1780 (4076/311)	250
Hot water dishes, pair, flower filled cornucopia, Greek key rim, 10⅞, fine, ca1800 (4180/85)	500
Jar, covered, millefleurs, blue ground, with a profusion of blossoms, 10 (4268/553)	400
Jar and cover, large, painted in famille-rose, elderly man teaching, H17⅛, 1820-50 (4076/353)	*1300*
Jar and cover sweetmeat 4 parts, 4, circular stacking bowls, 6⅛ (4268/562)	125
Jardiniere, pale blue, bird in a flowering tree, 11¾, hc, 19c (4180/144)	275
Jardiniere, oblong, octagonal, peacocks, floral sprays, 8¾, 19c (4211/939)	275
Jardiniere, oblong, octagonal, 4 feet, 2 peacocks, rockwork, 8⅝, 19c (4211/938)	450
Jardinieres, pair, enamel and gilding with oriental figures, pine tree, 7⅛ (4268/550)	375
Jardinieres, pair, painted, faux bois, shades of brown to resemble wooden buckets, 19½, 19c (4268/511)	2700
Jars, and covers, pair, rose ground, green gourds and white flowers, 17¾, 19c (4268/520)	1200
Joss stick holders, pair, carp-form, iron-red, unusual, L8½, ca1820 (4076/381)	*1100*
Jug, initialled, gilt and green bowknot, molding, 9¼, rep, ca1785 (4180/66)	500
Jug and cover, gilding with pair of cornucopias, 8½, rep, ca1745 (4268/445)	250
Kylin groups, pair, pink, turquoise, red, unusual, H4½, 19c (4076/380)	700
Mantel garniture, 3 vases and a pair of beaker vases, 14, 16¾, mi, ca1775 (4180/26)	3600
Mantel garniture, 5-piece, famille-rose, H9¾ - 11¼, imp, ca1780 (4148/28)	4000
Marriage plate, mythological marriage, gilt cyphers, 9, rep, ca1745 (4180/13)	300
Milk jug, Helmet, American market, with stylized eagle and 16 gold stars, H5⅜, fine, 1796-1810 (4076/333)	600
Milk jug and cover, pear shaped, spray of sprigs and flowers, 5½, rep cover rim (4268/467)	60
Mug, barrel shaped, sprays and sprigs of flowers, 5¼, ca1780 (4260/230)	575
Mug, cylindrical, birds on branch and rockwork, 5⅜, ca1775 (4260/228)	400
Mug, cylindrical, butterflies, flowers, 5⅛, ca1780 (4260/227)	650
Mug, cylindrical, oriental ladies and children, 4⅞, ca1780 (4260/231)	550
Oval stand, reticulated, psuedo tobacco leaf, basketwork, 9¼, L18c (4180/80)	275
Plaques, pair, 'Aesop's Fable' motifs, sepia background, oval shape, 10¾ x 13⅜, ca1740, fine (4211/879)	2500
Plaques, pair, 'Aesop's Fable' motifs, wolf in trap and farm scene, rare, 13¾ x 10⅜, ca1740, fine (4211/878)	3750
Plate, painted center in thick enamels, pink, blue, D9, fine, ca1740 (4076/271)	600
Plate, Masonic, grisaille brown and gold, initials 'GWC', 7¾, ca1800 (4268/488)	100
Plate, 'Pronck' pattern, with 'La Dame au Parasol', abrasion to rim, D10¼, 1736-47 (4076/278)	2000
Plates, deep, octagonal, 4, serpentine floral swags, diameter 9, chip, ca1780 (4148/25)	200
Plates, dinner, rose-medallion, diameter 9⅝, imp, 1820-50 (4148/39)	1600
Plates, dinner, 12, diameter 9¼, chip, ca1780 (4148/20)	325
Plates, dinner, 13, octagonal, serpentine floral swags, diameter 9¼, chip, ca1780 (4148/27)	800
Plates, large, pair, blue and white, with central kylin, D13, 33¼, 19c (4076/347)	450
Plates, octagonal, 14, serpentine floral swags, diameter 9¼, chip, ca1780 (4148/26)	950
Plates, pair, flowers, pomegranates, insects and scrolls, 9, ch, ca1775 (4180/49)	225
Plates, pair, 'Pronck', blue, iron red and gilding, with 7 insects, 9½. 1736-47 (4268/436)	2400
Plates, pair, Judgment of Paris, D9, ca1750, hc (4076/280)	700
Plates, pair, Judgment of Paris, painted with Greek Gods, D9, fine, ca1750 (4076/279)	1100
Plates, set of six, shield initialled JAB in center, D9¼, minor imp, ca1790 (4076/331)	300

Chocolate pot
and cover
(4211/911)

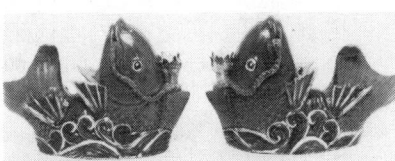

Joss stick holders (4076/381)

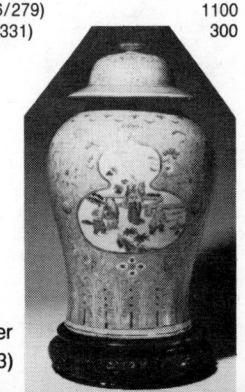

Jar and cover
(4076/353)

Soup tureen (4076/288)

Plates, set of six, crested, central bouquet of flowers, imperfections, D8⅞, ca1770 (4076/387)	200
Plates, set of 9, oriental river landscape in centers, 9, chip, ca1750 (4211/890)	650
Plates, twelve, mantled shield center with blue, gilt border, 9¾, ca1790 (4180/72)	750
Plates, nine, two rows of lotus petals, peony blossom, 8⅛, hc, 19c, T'ai Chi mk (4180/138)	600
Platter, deep, flowers in a basket, 14⅝, ca1790 (4180/70)	325
Platter, from DeWitt Clinton service, oriental river, 10, 1796-1810 (4180/88)	2000
Platter, for the Indian market, a mahout riding an elephant, L16⅝, ca1785 (4076/314)	850
Platter, oblong, octagonal, 11 figures, cluster of flowers, 13, ca1770 (4260/224)	650
Platter, octagonal, oblong, large, with scattered floral sprays, L17⅝, ca1775 (4076/301)	200
Platter, oval, central bouquet, 10⅛, ca1780 (4268/471)	350
Platter, oval, central vignette of water birds, 18⅛, ca1745 (4268/456)	581
Platter, oval, iron-red, green and aubergine, L14⅞, ca1780 (654/43)	225
Platter, oval, crested, stag's head crest of green, 14¾, ca1790 (4260/245)	250
Platters, pair, octagonal, serpentine floral swags, l 16½, chip, ca1780 (4148/23)	750
Punch bowl, figures at various pursuits, D15¾, very fine, ca1775 (4076/303)	2700
Punch bowl, pair to preceeding, rim chip, D16⅜, ca1780 (4076/310)	1300
Punch bowl, paneled with songbirds and butterflies, 15¼, hc, 1775 (4180/23)	1600
Punch bowl, with figures at various pursuits, D16⅜, ca1780 (4076/309)	*1300*

Punch bowl
(4076/309)

Teapot and cover (4211/899)
Teapot and cover (4211/900)

Punch bowl, hunting, 'Mandarin' palette, D15½, good, ca1780 (4076/318)	3000
Punch pot and cover, ladies and attendants, 7¾, ca1775 (4260/226)	450

Punch pot stand, hexafoil, scrollwork and floral garlands, 6⅝, ca1775 (4260/225)   225
Sauce tureen and cover, all over pattern, for American market, 8, ca1810 (4180/86)   450
Sauceboat, American market, initialled medallion, chip, L6⅜, 1833 (4076/345)   75
Saucer dishes, pair, painted in famille-rose enamels, fluted, D8⅞, ca1740 (4076/270)   375
Saucers, pair, bouquet and spray of flowers, 7⅛, ch, ca1765 (4180/16)   225
Serving dish, from DeWitt Clinton service, oriental river, 12¾, 1796-1810 (4180/87)   4000
Serving dish, deep, famille-rose enamels, oriental lady, crane, L16½, ca1770 (4076/292)   325
Soup plates, set of 10, oriental river landscape in centers, 9, chip, ca1750 (4211/892)   800
Soup plates, set of 8, oriental river landscape in centers, 9, chip, ca1750 (4211/891)   600
Soup plates, Jefferson Crest, pair, blue enamel, grisaille, gilding, small chip, D9¾ (4076/394)   400
Soup tureen, cover and stand, rabbit's head handles, L13⅞ & 15⅝, good, ca1765 (4076/288)   *2250*
Soup tureen, cover and stand, rabbit's head handles, floral bouquets, L13⅝ & 14¾, ca1775 (4076/300)   750
Spoon trays, pair, quatrefoil, spray and sprigs of flowers, 7½, ca1780 (4260/240)   550
Tankard, lightly molded blossoms and gilded fruit, 6⅛, fine, ca1750 (4180/11)   275
Tankard, with 5 oriental figures, H5¼, fine, ca1750 (4076/277)   375
Tankard, barrel-shaped, painted with green floral sprays, H5⅝, fine, ca1785 (4076/317)   300
Tapersticks, pair, in the form of elephants, grisaille, chip, H6⅛, rare, 18c/19c (4076/378)   2200
Tea and coffee service, brown monochrome with central rose sprig, 20 pcs, imp, ca1790 (4268/493)   125
Tea and coffee service, part, Juno and the peacock, imp, 6 pcs, ca1750 (4260/207)   425
Tea and coffee service, part, 15 pcs, miniature, AM initialled in shield, ca1790 (4211/905)   550
Tea caddy and cover, ovoid body, oriental figures and attendants, 5¼, res, ca1780 (4268/469)   150
Tea caddy and cover, 'Juno and the Peacock' motif, 5, ca1745 (4211/880)   250
Tea service, part, border 7 gilded brown scallop shell, 7 pcs, chips, ca1800 (4268/496)   100
Tea service, part, child's, 14 pcs, floral sprigs, imp., ca1790 (4148/30)   550
Tea service, part, 17 pcs, 'Martin Luther' pattern, rare, ca1745 (4211/877)   4500
Teabowl and saucer, rare, 'Le Pecheur' motif, young man fishing, D2⅞, 4⅝, chip, ca1750 (4211/881)   175
Teabowls and saucers, pair, made for American market, hc, 1796-1810 (4076/335)   375
Teapot and cover, bouquets and sprigs, 5¼, ca1755 (4260/214)   75
Teapot and cover, cupid holding floral wreath, 5⅝, res, ca1775 (4268/470)   425
Teapot and cover, fields of flowers, for Persian market, 5⅞, ca1810 (4180/79)   225
Teapot and cover, figures on terrace at river edge, 5⅛, ch, ca1780 (4180/45)   200
Teapot and cover, globular body applied with flowers, H4¼, ca1740 (4076/266)   375
Teapot and cover, globular body, 2 iron red birds, 5, ca1745 (4268/460)   125
Teapot and cover, partially fluted body, 5⅛, ca1775 (4268/472)   225
Teapot and cover, pear-shaped body, H4⅜, ca1730 (4076/264)   200
Teapot and cover, three oriental figures in a garden, 6¼, ca1780 (4180/34)   150
Teapot and cover, flowering shrubbery, neoclassical borders, 5¾, ca1780 (4211/900)   *225*
Teapot and cover, orange peel glaze, Buddha's hand citrous, 5⅛, ca1750 (4211/887)   150
Teapot and cover, ship flying British flag above green sea, 5, ca1790 (4211/903)   *550*

Teapot and cover   (4211/902)
Teapot and cover   (4211/903)

Teapot and cover, ship flying 2 British flags, borders, 5¾, ca1785 (4211/902) *400*
Teapot and cover, straight spout, entwined strap handles, 6, ca1790 (4211/915) 150
Teapot and cover, 'Mandarin palette', crabstock spout, handle, 6½, ca1780 (4211/899) *350*
Teapot and cover, ovoid, Mandarin palette, H6½, ca1775 (4076/302) 125
Teapot stand, lobed hexagonal, floral spray and sprigs, 5¾, ca1785 (4260/244) 125
Toddy jug, initials on either side, H8⅛, ca1795 (4076/340) 450
Toddy jug and cover, with a mantled shield containing initials, c, H11⅜, 1790-1810 (4076/337) 425
Tureen, covered soup, platter, octagonal, serpentine floral swags, ca1780 (4148/22) 2100
Tureen and cover, oval, flowers within coral, gilt, blue border, 13¾, rep, ca1790 (4180/69) 475
Urn, pistol handled, molded oval medallion, base, 14⅛, hc, ca1800 (4180/65) 275
Vase, baluster shaped, figures on riverside terrace, 9⅜, hc, ca1780 (4180/31) 200
Vase, baluster, mounted as lamp, ladies, animals and mountain views, 16¾, L18/E19c (4260/247) 2000
Vase, baluster, mounted as lamp, scrolling foliate and floral design, 16, 19c (4260/256) 1300
Vase, millefleurs, black ground, 11⅞, 19c (4268/554) 375
Vase, mounted as lamp, hexagonal, oriental figures, 15, ca1775 (4260/223) 1600
Vase, turquoise ground, baluster body, floral motifs, 11¼, rep, ca1780 (4268/452) 275
Vase and cover, floral vines and flowers, 14¼, ca1780 (4260/239) 1000
Vase and cover, hexagonal, panels of figures and birds, 23, rep, ca1775 (4268/465) 800
Vase and cover, mounted as lamp, oriental figures, 12¾, ca1775 (4260/221) 1000
Vase mounted as lamp, 'Mandarin' palette with figures, H10, ca1780 (4076/306) 500
Vases, baluster, fabulous beasts, gilt dragon handles, H9¾, 19c (4076/366) 400
Vases, covered pair, mounted as lamps, dragon handles, oriental figures, 13⅜, ca1780 (4260/233) 2800
Vases, covered pair, mounted as lamps, dragon handles, oriental views, 14, imp, ca1780 (4260/236) 2000
Vases, pair, baluster, brown with oval landscape, 10, hc, ca1790 (4180/84) 525
Vases, pair carp, modelled with brown eyes, iron red bodies, 11⅜ (4268/556) 700
Vases, pair mounted as lamps, 'Mandarin palette', flower-filled urns, 11½, ca1780 (4211/901) 1400
Vases, pair, mounted as lamps, allover lotus pattern, 16, 19c (4260/255) 2100
Vases, yellow ground, Chia Ch'ing seal marks in iron-red, H9¾, ca1820 (4076/367) 400
Vases and covers, pair, clobbered, baluster form, flowers, rockwork, 10⅞, 19c (4268/512) 175
Vases and stands, pair, famille-rose enamels with figural views, r, H13¼, 19c (4076/363) 475
Watch stand and a cover, quatrefoil form with applied flowers, leaves, H7⅛, ca1775 (4076/295) 850
Wine cooler, brightly painted with floral sprays, 6⅝, mi, ca1765 (4180/24) 1100
Wine pot and cover, sprigs and sprays of flowers, 7¾, cr, ca1750 (4268/441) 275
Wine pot and cover, octagonal, floral sprays, insects, (4211/886) 200

Armorial

Basin, Beckford, pheasant on rockwork, flowers, 15, ca1745 (4211/952) 500
Bowl, arms of Horbury, 11⅛, ca1750 (4260/212) 850
Bowl, shield of Webster of St. Martin, 10¼, ca1750 (4260/209) 800
Bowl, bouillon, arms of Daniel Seton, 4½, ca1795 (4268/591) 150
Bowl, bouillon, arms of N.Y., 4¼, hc, ca1795 (4211/973) 150
Bowl, square, crest and arms of Robert Charnock, 9⅝, ca1785 (4268/594) 700
Chamber pot and cover, arms of Falconer of Halkerton, 8¼, ca1785 (4211/967) 400
Chamberstick, rare, Earle, pink bow knots, 5⅝, res, ca1775 (4180/155) 850
Charger, arms of Daniel Giles of Bowden in Devon, 15, ca1745 (4268/568) 550
Charger, arms of Daniel Giles of Bowden in Devon, 12¾, hc, ca1745 (4268/570) 200
Charger, arms of Spanish or French ducal house, 17¾, hc, ca1750 (4260/208) 900
Chargers, pair, arms of Daniel Giles of Bowden in Devon, 12¾, 12⅝, ca1745 (4268/569) 700
Chargers, pair, crest and arms of Robert Charnock, 14¾, 1785 (4268/593) 500
Coffee cups and saucers, pair, arms of N.Y., 1 saucer, hc, ca1795 (4211/971) 450
Coffeepot and cover, arms of N.Y., 9⅝, cover rep, ca1790 (4211/968) 1100
Cups and saucers, coffee set of 6, arms of Gyllenborgs, chip, ca1785 (4268/589) 300
Cutlery handles, 2 Continental coat of arms, 3⅜, 1 reduced, 1720-30 (4211/956) 600
Dinner service, part, arms of DaCosta, 31 pcs, some imperfect, M19c (4076/395) 3250
Dish, blue enamel shield, gold fleurs-de-lis, 9½, ca1720 (4268/567) 1200
Dish, saucer, crest and arms of Robert Charnock, 8½, ca1785 (4268/595) 275
Dishes, berry, octagonal, birds and insects, arms of Hardwicke, 6¼, rep, ca1760 (4260/219) 650
Dishes, berry, set of 10, arms of MacKenzie, quartering Chisholm, 6¼, chip, ca1760 (4211/959) 800
Dishes, saucer, arms of Daniel Giles of Bowden in Devon, 10, hc, ca1745 (4268/572) 275
Dishes, saucer, pair, crested, 2 phoenix birds, 8½, ca1755 (4268/583) 500
Guglets, pair, Sir Thomas Bootle, 9¾, fine, ca1730 (4180/148) 3000
Mugs, pair, Montgomerie quartering Eglinton, 5⅜, cr, ca1785 (4180/164) 225
Plate, arms, van Herzeele, impaling another, 11⅜, ca1740 (4211/951) 450
Plate, arms, Braithwaite impaling Tayleur, 11⅛, ca1735 (4211/950) 800
Plate, Fort St. George, and Plymouth Sound, 9, hc, ca1745 (4268/585) 325
Plate, Goold above initials GG, 9⅝, fine, ca1775 (4180/154) 175
Plate, Harries of Cructon, Ludlow and Tonge Castle, 11, fine, ca1735 (4180/150) *900*

Plates, pair, arms of Daniel Giles of Bowden in Devon, 11⅜, ca1745 (4268/571) — 275
Plates, pair, arms of Daniel Giles of Bowden in Devon, 9, ca1745 (4268/574) — 425
Plates, pair, arms of Fenton with Weldon in pretence, 8¾, ca1755 (4211/961) — 450
Plates, pair, Catherine the Great, with Imp. Russian eagle, 9⅞, mi, ca1785 (4180/158) — 1800
Plates, pair, Catherine the Great, with Imp. Russian eagle, 9⅞, rep, ca1785 (4180/157) — 1500
Plates, pair, Catherine the Great, with Imp. Russian eagle, 9⅞, mi, ca1785 (4180/159) — 1300
Plates, pair, Imari palette, Continental coat of arms hc, D8¾, ca1715 (4076/384) — 550
Plates, pair, Rudge of Evesham quartering Chalmers, 8½, ca1740 (4180/149) — 650
Plates, pair, Saunders within border of wreaths, 9, imp, ca1745 (4180/152) — 650
Plates, pair, 2 Continental coats of arms, floral bouquet, 9, ca1750 (4268/579) — 450
Plates, pair, crested, 2 phoenix birds, 8¾, ca1755 (4268/584) — 400
Plates, pair, octagonal, arms of Archer impaling Meares, 8⅝, ca1760 (4211/965) — 350
Plates, pair, octagonal, arms of Archer impaling Meares, 8¾, chip, ca1755 (4211/963) — 1000
Plates, set of 12, arms of Daniel Giles of Bowden in Devon, 9, imp, ca1745 (4268/575) — 650
Plates, set of 12, arms of Taswell, 8⅞, imp, ca1775 (4260/210) — 1900
Plates, set of 8, arms of Daniel Giles of Bowden in Devon, 9, ca1745 (4268/573) — 800
Plates, set of 8, octagonal, arms of Archer impaling Meares, 8¾, chip, ca1775 (4211/962) — 2600
Plates, six, Montgomerie quartering Eglinton, 9⅝, cr, ca1785 (4180/165) — 850
Plates, soup, crested, 2 phoenix birds, 8¾, ca1755 (4268/582) — 450
Plates, soup, pair, arms of Taswell, 8⅞, rep, ca1775 (4260/211) — 175
Plates, soup, set of 12, arms of Daniel Giles of Bowden in Devon, 9, cr, ca1745 (4268/577) — 850
Plates, soup, set of 8, arms of Daniel Giles of Bowden in Devon, 9, ca1745 (4268/576) — 1000
Plates, soup, set of 8, crested, 2 phoenix birds, 8¾, ca1755 (4268/581) — 1400
Plates, soup, set of 9, 2 Continental coats of arms, floral bouquet, 9, ca1750 (4268/580) — 800
Platter, arms of Allott impaling Allott, 13, ca1755 (4211/966) — 400
Platter, arms of MacDonald of St. Martin's, restored, L14¾, ca1780 (4076/393) — 310
Platter, arms of Robert Nugent of Carlanstown, 14¾, ca1760 (4260/215) — 475
Platter, oval, iron, red and gold, flowers, 14¼, ca1780 (684/37) — 250
Platters, pair, Montgomerie quartering Eglinton, 10⅝, cr, ca1785 (4180/163) — 475
Platters, pair, large, arms of Roberts impaling Carter, L17¼ & 17⅜, ca1780 (4076/392) — 700
Sauce tureens, covers, stands, pair, Montgomerie quartering Eglinton, 7⅛, 7⅞, mi, ca1785 (4180/161) — 1600
Sauceboats, pair, Saunders, 8½, rep, ca1745 (4180/153) — 200
Saucer dishes, pair, large, arms of Grimaldi di Castro, D11⅛, rim chip, ca1730 (4076/385) — 1750
Soup plates, six, Montgomerie quartering Eglinton, 9¾, ca1785 (4180/166) — 800
Soup tureens, covers, stands, pair, Montgomerie quartering Eglinton, 13⅛, 14¼, imp, ca1785 (4180/160) — 4000
Stand, teapot, arms, Shepherd of Kent and Peasmarsh in Sussex, 5⅜, ca1750 (4211/955) — 350

Plate (4180/150)

Platters (4076/322)

Tankard, arms of Danne, glaze cracked, H4⅝, ca1755 (4076/390) — 450
Tankard, arms of Newland, handle restored, H4⅝, ca1745 (4076/388) — 325
Tankard, arms, Fauntleroy, floral sprays, stand, 6⅛, 1755 (4211/954) — 800
Tankard, arms, Wingfield impaling Franklyn, stand, 6, chip, ca1745 (4211/953) — 550

Tea caddy and cover, arms of Sir Lambert Blackwell, 4⅝, chip, ca1755 (4211/957) 350
Teabowl and saucer, arms of N.Y., 3½ x 5½, saucer, hc, ca1795 (4211/972) 175
Teabowl and saucer, blue and gold, with the Arms of New York State, ca1800 (4149/115) 500
Teapot and cover, arms of Stracey, 5⅜, imp, ca1755 (4211/958) 500
Teapot and cover, painted in famille-rose, grisaille, r, H5, ca1750 (4076/389) 250
Teapot and cover, two Continental coats of arms, grisaille, H5⅜, ca1750 (4076/386) 125
Tureen and cover, soup, crest and arms of Robert Charnock, 12⅜, ca1785 (4268/592) 1200
Vase, 'Soldier', arms of Texeira quartering Sampaio, 42½, ca1710 (4268/566) 3200

Batavian ware

Teapot and cover, floral sprays on cafe au lait ground, 4¾, M18c (4180/29) 150

Blue and white

Bowls, oval, pair of, molded with basketwork, rope handle, L8, unusual, ca1770 (4076/289) 550
Dish, hotwater, blue and white, variation of the 'Willow Pattern', 10½, rep, 19c (4268/557) 200
Dish, figures, pavilions, mountainous riverscape, 15¾, 19c (684/6) 150
Jardiniere on stand, hexagonal, 2 pcs, H8, E19c, rim chip (654/42) 200
Plate, willow tree, stylized cloud border, 12⅝, L18c (654/41) 160
Plates, dinner set of 21, Willow pattern, 10¼, dam, 19c (684/8) 700
Platter, river landscape, trellis diaper border, 16⅛, 1780-95 (4268/510) 225
Platter, with jars placed on stylized rockwork, 14⅝, ca1770 (4268/461) 250
Platter, meat, fitted with pierced mazarine, river landscape, L17, ca1780 (654/40) 400
Platters, pair, large, with pagodas and a junk, L17⅝, L18c (4076/322) *375*
Sauceboats, pair, underglaze river landscape, chip, L8¾, 1800-20 (654/29) 100
Stands, pair, oval, reticulated, version of Willow pattern, trellis diaper border, 10⅞, ca1810 (4268/509) 300
Teapot and cover, man in a sampan, another crossing bridge, 6¼, ca1785 (4268/508) 250
Tureen and cover, rabbit's head handles, L13⅜, ca1775 (4076/290) 375
Tureen and cover, rectangular, animal's head handles, 12, ca1800 (684/1) 700
Vase, tulip, cinquefoil body, tall neck, H9⅝, 19c (654/30) 225

Blue and white, Canton

Basket and Stand, blue and white, Willow pattern, L10⅞, 11⅛, 19c (4156/95) 500
Bowls, soup, 5, octagonal, all with hair cracks, Willow pattern, 9, 19c (654/4) 70
Coffeepot, and cover, barrel form, strap handles, Willow pattern, H8, 19c (654/22) 325
Coffeepot and cover, lighthouse, with eagle standing on blue and black bar, (4156/90) 650
Cups, egg, 4, rare, Willow pattern, cr, ch, H2⅜, 19c (654/17) 150
Dinner service, part, 54 pcs, Willow pattern variants, chip, 19c (4156/93) *2800*

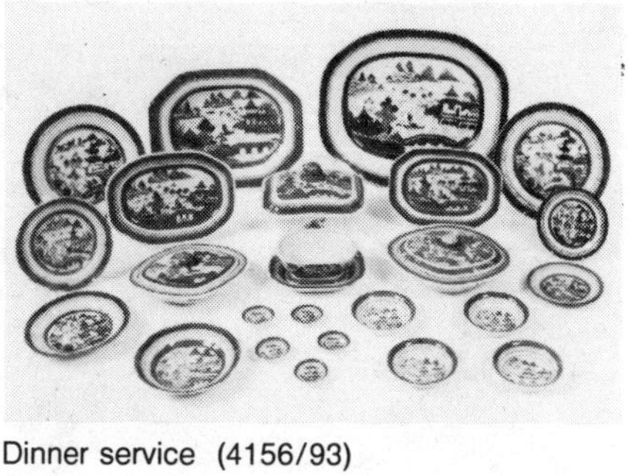
Dinner service (4156/93)

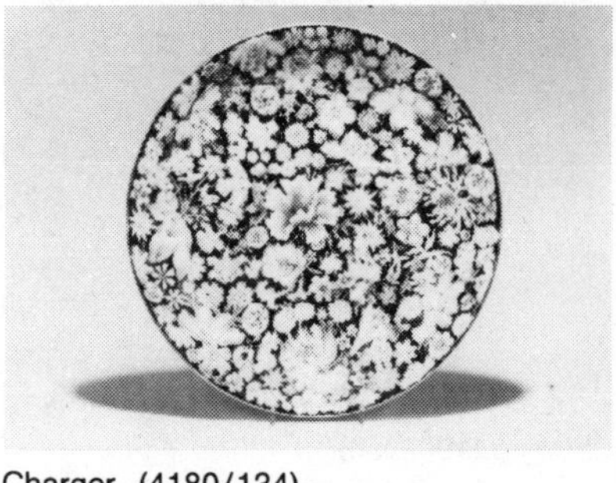
Charger (4180/134)

Dish, serving, and cover, rectangular, gourd knop, Willow pattern, L9¾, 19c (654/25) 200
Dishes, leaf, pair, Willow pattern, hc, L7¾, 19c (654/16) 325
Ewer, rare, cylindrical, tall neck, Willow pattern, H10½, 19c (654/1) 450
Hot water dish, octagonal, oblong, variation of Willow pattern, minor chip, L13⅜, 19c (4076/361) 250
Jug, toddy, and cover, barrel shape, kylin knop, Willow pattern, H8¾, 19c, spout chip (654/2) 500

Mug, large, blue and white, oriental river view, 5⅝, ca1800 (4156/89) — 400
Mug, small, blue and white, Willow pattern, H3⅜, 19c (4156/98) — 150
Plate, hot water, octagonal, Willow pattern, L10¼, 19c (654/21) — 175
Plates, dessert, set of 12, Willow pattern, imp, 7½, L19c (654/13) — 175
Plates, dinner, set of 6, Willow pattern, hc, 10⅛, L19c (654/14) — 200
Plates, dinner, twelve, octagonal, 7 with hair cracks, Willow pattern, D9, 19c (654/3) — 200
Platter, large, octagonal, Willow pattern, L17¼, rim chip (654/6) — 200
Salad Bowl, square, blue and white, Willow pattern, W9½, 19c (4156/96) — 350
Shell dish, blue and white, Willow pattern, L10½, 19c (4156/97) — 325
Tea service, 36 pcs, Willow pattern variants, 19c (4156/94) — 1000
Teapot, covered, hexagonal stand, floral Rice pattern, H7¼, L19c (654/28) — 350
Tureen, sauce, covered, and stand, scroll knop, Willow pattern, L7¾ (stand) (654/12) — 300
Tureen, soup, covered, oblong, boar's head handles, Willow pattern, L12½, 19c (654/5) — 650

Canton

Mug, procelain, blue, white, interlaced strap handle, 5¼, chip, crack, 19c (4149/109) — 85
Pitcher, milk, rim with gothic arches, 4¾, ca1860 (684/58) — 150
Plates, set of 6, figures, floral panels, insects and fruits, 8, ca1900 (684/62) — 175
Platter, porcelain octagonal, blue, white, 18¾, 19c (4149/108) — 375

Famille-noire

Charger, millefleurs decoration, black ground, 15¾, fine, 19c (4180/134) — *600*

Famille-rose

Basin, rose-robed lady, turquoise-robed lady, chip, D16⅛, 19c (4076/365) — 275
Basin, Canton, Rose Medallion pattern, 19⅛, repaired, 1820-50 (4211/934) — 800
Bottle and cover, Canton, oriental warriors and maidens, 14⅝, chip, 19c (4268/543) — 700
Bowl, Rose Medallion pattern, 13, 1 foot rep, 19c (684/45) — 700
Bowl, Rose Medallion pattern, 11⅝, 19c (684/46) — 450
Bowl, Judgment of Paris, with lotus sprays, 10¼, res, ca1760 (4180/15) — 275
Bowl, punch, Canton, Rose Medallion pattern, 16⅛, 1820-50 (4211/932) — 1700
Bowls, pair, peonies and blossoms, 10, ca1750 (4180/9) — 1000
Butter tub and cover, pastel shades, iron-red and gilding, D4⅜, fine, 1735-50 (4076/267) — 350
Butter tubs, covers, stands pair, Canton, figures on terrace, fruit, flowers, 5¾, 6½, 1820-50 (4268/526) — 550
Charger, cluster of flowers, 15, ca1760 (4260/218) — 375
Charger, flowers behind landscape, 15, ca1745 (4260/203) — 800
Charger, octagonal, D13⅛, 1735-45 (4076/263) — 300
Charger, two white sheep in green meadow, 13⅝, mi, ca1750 (4180/7) — 500
Charger, Canton, Rose Medallion pattern, 19, 1820-50 (4211/933) — 850
Charger, Canton, with characteristic Rose Medallion pattern, 16, 19c (4268/548) — 175
Cups and saucers, set of three, Canton, oriental figures, ca1815 (4260/251) — 400
Dish, square, Canton, oriental dignitaries seated on terrace, 9¼, ca1815 (4260/250) — 550
Dishes, hotwater and covers, 4 ladies on terrace, strong colors, 10⅞, ca1820 (4268/514) — 800
Ecuelles, covers and stands, pair Canton, oriental figures, 8⅜, hc, 19c (4260/249) — 800
Fish bowl, Canton, 2 peacocks amidst colorful flowers, 8⅞, 19c (4268/546) — 300
Garden seat, Canton, Rose Medallion pattern, 17⅞, 19c (4211/944) — 1750
Garden seat, Canton, Rose Medallion pattern, 18⅜, rubbed, 19c (4211/945) — 1600
Garden seats, pair, phoenix bird amidst peonies, H18¾, fine, 19c (4076/355) — *3600*

Garden seats (4076/355)

Dishes (4211/928)

Umbrella stand (4076/354)

Garden seats, pair, hexagonal, Canton, birds and butterflies, shrubbery, fruit, 18¾, 19c (4211/943)	3400
Jars, ginger, pair, ovoid, floral sprays, H8¾, 19c (4148/40)	600
Jugs, covers, on stands, Chinese ladies playing instruments, 15½, imp, ca1755 (4180/18)	1200
Mug, five oriental figures in river landscape, 3⅞, fine, ca1830 (4180/135)	325
Mug, cylindrical, Canton, dignitary flanked by attendants, 4⅞, ca1830 (4260/252)	375
Plate, dignitary astride a pink horse, D8¾, ca1750 (4076/275)	200
Plate, painted with a rooster, star cracked, D8⅞, ca1740 (4076/276)	150
Plate, painted with boy beside a lady on a bench, D9⅜, ca1730 (4076/273)	400
Plate, rim with 6 sprays of fruit and flowers, 10⅛, 1735-40 (4268/439)	350
Plates, pair, bouquet within a lappet border, 8⅞, hc, ca1740 (4180/2)	300
Plates, pair, dignitary with 7 attendants, 9½, fine, ca1830 (4180/139)	250
Plates, pair, multi-colored with peony spray, 9, hc, ca1740 (4180/1)	175
Plates, pair, rim with 6 sprays of fruit and flowers, 9⅛, 1735-40 (4268/438)	500
Plates, set of 6, centers with oriental river landscape, 9, ca1750 (4211/889)	550
Plates, set of 6, songbirds on a branch of peonies, 8⅞, 1740 (4268/440)	1000
Plates, set thirteen, bouquet with gilding, shaped rim, 9¼, hc, ch, ca1755 (4180/17)	800
Plates, set twelve, bearded swordsman confronting a lady, 8⅞, hc, ca1760 (4180/19)	1200
Platter, two ladies in pavilion watching gentleman, 16¾, ca1760 (4180/22)	550
Platter oval, Canton, Rose Medallion pattern, 18⅛, 19c (4268/537)	300
Platter oval, Canton, Rose Medallion pattern, 16¾, 19c (4268/536)	250
Punch bowl, hunting theme with 4 hunters and pack, 15¾, hc, ca1780 (4180/27)	2200
Punch bowl, hunting theme with 4 hunters and pack, 15¾, hc, ca1780 (4180/28)	2300
Soup plates, pair, deer on turquoise leaf, 8⅞, fine, ca1740 (4180/4)	525
Soup plates, pair, pink peonies and green leaves, 9, 1 riv, ca1740 (4180/3)	150
Sugar bowl, and cover, Canton, figures on terrace, fruit, flowers, 5, 1820-50 (4268/528)	200
Tea service, part, Canton, Rose Medallion pattern, hc, L19c, 20 pcs (4211/937)	850
Teapot and cover, gentleman smoking a pipe as 2 ladies talk, 5⅜, hc, ca1775 (4180/48)	150
Tureen and cover, soup, two Chinese ladies carrying fishing poles, L14, ca1750 (4211/888)	1300
Umbrella stand, Canton, Rose Medallion pattern, 24¾, star cr, 19c (4268/539)	1600
Vase, ovoid shaped with figures in a garden, 10⅝, ca1780 (4180/43)	550
Vase, ku form, Canton now as lamp, Rose Medallion pattern, 14¾, cr, 19c (4211/936)	450
Vase, mounted as lamp, two pheasants on rockwork, 10⅜, ca1735 (4211/873)	800
Vase, beaker, mounted as lamp, pheasants on rockwork, 13, ca1750 (4260/216)	750
Vase, bottle form, figures of a woman and Peking Opera actors, 16¼, 19c (684/47)	600
Vase, ku form, Canton, now as lamp, Rose Medallion pattern, 15⅜, 19c (4211/935)	550
Vase, lamp, baluster, figures within scrollwork panel, 9⅜, drilled, ca1785 (4180/53)	475
Vase, Canton, Rose Medallion pattern, 13½, 19c (4268/542)	350

Vase, Canton, front and back panels of ladies on terrace, 9½, L19c (4268/532) — 125
Vases, ku form, pair, Rose Medallion pattern, 13, 19c (684/44) — 850
Vases, pair doublegourd, field of flowers, fruit, butterflies and figures, 13⅛, cr, 1820-50 (4268/518) — 1100
Vases, pair, Canton, Rose Medallion pattern, 13⅝, 19c (4268/541) — 900
Vases, pair, Canton, pear shape body, warriors and other figures, 25⅜, cr, 19c (4268/533) — 2100
Vegetable dishes and covers, pair Canton, Rose Medallion pattern, 10½, 19c (4268/535) — 500
Vegetable dishes and covers, pair, Canton, oval panel of figures, 10¾, 1820-50 (4268/530) — 450
Vegetable dishes and covers, pair, Canton, oval panel of figures, 10⅝, 1820-50 (4268/531) — 375
Vegetable dishes and covers, pair, Canton, panel of flowers, 9½, 1820-50 (4268/525) — 550

Famille-rose, Canton

Bowl, Rose Medallion, 11, 19c (4180/133) — 250
Bowl, Rose Medallion decoration, D11⅝, fine, 1820-50 (4076/358) — 450
Bowl, birds and butterflies, gilt ground, D11½, 1820-50 (4211/923) — 550
Box and cover, rare, square with Rose Medallion pattern, 7⅛, 19c (4180/125) — 425
Dessert plates, set 6, bowl of fruit in center, with birds, 8½, M19c (4180/124) — 450
Dishes, kidney-shaped pair, scenes with dignitaries, 11⅜, ca1830, fine (4211/928) — *700*
Dishes, kidney-shaped pair, scenes with figures, 11⅜, ca1830, fine (4211/927) — *700*
Dishes, scalloped oval pair, scenes with figures, 10¼, ca1830, fine (4211/926) — 650
Dishes, square, pair, figures on a terrace, 9¼, ca1830, fine (4211/929) — 650
Garden seat, pierced medallions, 2 rows of gilt bosses, 18⅝, fine, 19c (4180/132) — 1900
Hot water dishes, pair, groups on terraces, 10⅞, fine, ca1830 (4180/117) — 325
Hot water dishes, pair, scenes in gardens, 11, ca1830 (4180/119) — 225
Hot water dishes, pair, scenes near a pagoda and chariot, 10¾, rep, ca1830 (4180/121) — 200
Hot water dishes, pair, scenes of daily life, 10⅞, ch, ca1830 (4180/118) — 225
Hot water dishes, pair, scenes on terraces, 10¾, ca1830 (4180/120) — 200
Hot water dishes, pair, three ladies on terrace, 10⅝, fine, ca1830 (4180/116) — 350
Plates, set of 12, initialled, vases of flowers, D9¾, fine, ca1820 (4076/371) — 900
Plates, Dessert, set of 10, figures at various pursuits, 7¾, chip, ca1830, good (4211/930) — 930
Platter, oval, warrior, 2 attendants, 4 maidens, 15¾, fine, ca1830 (4180/112) — 375
Platter, oval, 2 dignitaries, 2 ladies on terrace, 14½, fine, ca1830 (4180/113) — 325
Platter, oval, 8 figures and horse on terrace, 17¼, ca1830 (4180/111) — 425
Punch bowl, field of birds, fruit, flowers, 16⅛, rep, ca1830 (4180/123) — 400
Punch bowls, mammoth pair, ormolu mounted, brilliantly enamelled, 37¾, fine, ca1830 (4180/122) — 13000
Soup plates, pair, butterfly, flower and fruit border, 7⅞, ca1830 (4180/136) — 250
Tureen, cover and stand, soup, figures in a lotus garden, (4211/924) — 2300
Umbrella stand, cylindrical body painted with warriors, H24, fine, 19c (4076/354) — *1700*
Umbrella stand, Rose Medallion pattern, r on foot rim, H24¼, 19c (4076/362) — *1200*
Vase, baluster shaped, Rose Medallion, wood stand, 18⅛, ch, 19c (4180/128) — *550*
Vase mounted as lamp, Rose Medallion decoration, rim chip, H11½, 19c (4076/364) — 200
Vase, Ku Form, Rose Medallion decoration, H15½, fine, 1820-50 (4076/357) — 425
Vase, Ku-form, Rose Medallion, panels of figures and birds, 15½, fine, 19c (4180/129) — 750
Vase, Ku-form, Rose Medallion, panels of figures and birds, 15⅝, ch, 19c (4180/130) — 650
Vases, Ku-form, pair, Rose Medallion, gilt dragons applied, 13⅞, fine, 19c (4180/131) — 1500
Vegetable dish liner, servant holding tripod burner, 11½, fine, ca1830 (4180/114) — 300

Umbrella stand (4076/362)   Vase (4180/128)

Dish (4211/918)   Platter (4211/919)

Famille-verte

Bottles, pair, mounted as lamps, peacocks and pheasants, 9⅝, 1 hc, L17/E18c (4260/201)   2100
Charger, diaper border, panels of flowering plants, diameter 14½, chip, E18c (4148/19)   850
Jardiniere, with huang huali stand, overall flowers, buds, W7⅝ (4180/146)   475
Vase mounted as lamp, panels of beasts, birds, 73⅝, E18c (4211/872)   1400

Fitzhugh, blue

Basin, 'clobbered', butterflies and sprigs of flowers, 16½, ca1830 (4268/505)   425
Butter tub, cover and stand, four clusters of flowers around medallion, 5¼, 6⅜, fine, ca1820
  (4180/109)   500
Dish, hot water, very large, L18½, E19c (4211/920)   500
Dish, warming and cover, blue and white, 14¼, 19c (684/32)   375
Ecuelle, cover and saucer, enhanced with floral clusters, 7⅛, 8⅜, ca1820 (4180/110)   500
Fruit coolers, covers and liners, pair, after Derby originals, 1 chip, H10⅞, rare, 1790-1820
  (4076/329)   4250
Platter, oval, well and tree, central 'pine cone' medallion, 17½, 1790-1810 (4268/506)   375
Teapot and cover, pine cone and 4 beast medallions, 5, ca1800 (4268/507)   350
Tureen, cover and platter, clusters of flowers and precious objects, L14, 14½, 1790-1820
  (4076/328)   900
Vegetable dish, cover and liner, Fitzhugh-type pine cone medallions, L11⅞, E19c (4211/921)   550
Vegetable dish, covered, underglaze-blue, L9⅝, 1790-1810 (4076/330)   375

Fitzhugh, brown

Milk jug, helmet shaped, gilt rim beneath spout, 5, hc, ca1820 (4180/103)   275

Fitzhugh, green

Plates, pair, American eagle decoration, initialled AF, 6⅜, ca1810 (4268/503)   800

Fitzhugh, orange

Dish, scalloped, oval, with American eagle, 10⅛, hc, ca1800 (4180/89)   3700
Dish, hot water, American Eagle decoration, W10¾, rare, 1800-10 (4211/918)   *4300*
Plate, American eagle, red, white and blue shield, 9¾, rep, ca1800 (4180/100)   600
Plate, American eagle, red, white and blue shield, 9¾, mi, ca1800 (4180/91)   1700
Plate, American eagle, red, white and blue shield, 7¾, hc, ca1800 (4180/96)   1100
Plates, pair, American eagle, red, white and blue shield, 7¾, ca1800 (4180/92)   1700
Plates, pair, American eagle, red, white and blue shield, 7¾, mi, ca1800 (4180/95)   1200
Plates, pair, American eagle, red, white and blue shield, 7¾, ch, ca1800 (4180/94)   4100
Platter, oval, American eagle, red, white and blue shield, 12, rep, ca1800 (4180/99)   3400
Platter, oval, deep, pine cone and 4 beast medallion centered, L14⅛, 19c (4211/919)   550
Sauce tureen stand, American eagle, red, white and blue shield, 7⅞, ca1800 (4180/98)   425
Soup plate, American eagle, red, white and blue shield, 9¾, mi, ca1800 (4180/90)   2300
Vase, Ku-form, lamp, acanthus leaves and peony medallions, 13, drilled, 19c (4180/101)   600
Vegetable dish, no cover, American eagle, red, white and blue shield, 9⅜, ca1800 (4180/97)   700

Fitzhugh, yellow

Soup plates, pair, peony and beast medallion, with yellow enamel, 7⅞, 19c (4180/105) 1300
Soup plates, pair, peony and beast medallion, with yellow enamel, 7⅞, fine, 19c (4180/104) 1800
Soup plates, pair, peony and beast medallion, with yellow enamel, 7⅞, 19c (4180/106) 2100
Soup plates, pair, peony and beast medallion, with yellow enamel, 7⅞, cr, 19c (4180/107) 1400
Soup plates, three, peony and beast medallion, with yellow enamel, 7⅞, imp, 19c (4180/108) 1300

Imari

Bottles, pair, square section with landscape panels, 10, ca1725 (4211/871) 1800
Ecuelle, covered, continuous river landscape, W7⅛, ca1740 (4211/870) 500
Garden seat, pair, English ironstone, swelling hexagonal shape, 19¾, imp, ca1820 (4268/564) 1600
Plate, 2 birds perched on flowering tree, 12¼, 18c (4268/459) 150
Tankard, flowers flanked by cornucopias, 6⅜, M18c (4260/204) 500
Tankard, 2 carp swimming, 6⅜, M18c (4260/205) 650

Lotus

Bowl, painted with 3 rows of lotus petals, D11, ca1760 (4076/286) 1000
Dishes, pair of, shaded pink lotus petals, D10¾, ca1760 (4076/285) 1700

Mandarin palette

Bowl, peony blossoms beneath bamboo border, 10¼, riv, ca1785 (4180/44) 100
Bowl, 2 panels of figures, 10¼, ca1785 (4268/478) 650
Bowl, 3 floral clusters, 11⅜, hc, rim rep, ca1775 (4268/466) 225
Dish, two cornucopias with flowers, s-scroll border, 14⅛, ca1785 (4180/36) 475
Dish, deep serving, landscape, 14½, chip, ca1780 (684/41) 300
Ecuelle and bowl, floral sprays within scrollwork border, 6¾, ca1785 (4180/35) 350
Plates, set nine, ribbon-tied floral bouquet, 9⅛, ca1770 (4180/40) 650
Punch bowl, four panels of oriental figures, 16, hc, ca1785 (4180/63) 1100
Teapot and cover, five figures on a terrace, 5¾, ca1780 (4180/33) 250
Tureen and cover, butterflies and floral sprigs, 12, chip, ca1780 (684/40) 750
Tureen sauce and cover, riverscape setting, 7¼, chip, ca1780 (684/39) 400
Vase, lamp, baluster, figures on a terrace, 9½, drilled, ca1780 (4180/52) 575
Vase and cover, lamp, figures on a terrace, 10½, pcs married, ca1780 (4180/54) 475
Vases, lamps, pair, baluster, figures on a terrace, 9½, drilled, ca1780 (4180/51) 1100
Vases, pair, baluster shaped with painted vases of flowers, 10⅛, ca1785 (4180/42) 550

Nanking

Cider jug and cover, variation of Willow pattern, 9⅛, ca1800 (4211/909) *450*
Tea and coffee service, part, 22 pcs, blue and white, variation of Willow pattern, ca1790 (4211/908) 800

Pseudo Tobacco Leaf

Platter, 2 iron red mandarin ducks, 10, ca1785 (4268/483) 650
Teapot and cover, globular pot, 6⅛, ca1770 (4268/484) 550

Rockefeller Pattern

Plates, pair, 2 ladies wearing robes, little boy, 2 chickens, 9¼, 1790-1810 (4268/481) 350
Plates, pair, 2 ladies wearing robes, little boy, 2 chickens, 9⅜, 1790-1810 (4268/480) 525

Rose Mandarin

Plateaux pair, Canton, terrace view of dignitaries, 14½ x 14¾, ca1830 (4211/925) 950

Rose-verte

Jars and covers, pair, continuous scene of the 'Boys' Festival', 16½, ca1725 (4211/867) 2600
Soup plates, pair, underglaze multi-colors, central peony, 9, ca1725 (4211/868) 300

Cider jug and cover
(4211/909)

Pitcher (4180/247)   Vase (4180/233)   Bowls (4219/41)

GLASS OF AMERICAN INTEREST

Assorted patterns and styles

Curtain tie back, set of 6, N. Eng. flower form, opalescent, Diam 3, M19c (4149/40)	110
Curtain tie backs, glass, American*, set of 6, turned mahogany, Diam 4, 19c (4149/61)	80
Decanter set, inlaid walnut, hinged lid opens to fitted interior, 11 bottles, 10¼, E19c (4156/183)	275
Flip, Continental engraved, colorless glass, scrolling flowers and leaves, 6, 19c (4211/1022)	50

Blown glass

Basket, fruit, clear, wrought, fine, H4¾, ca1730 (4076/1178)	200
Bottle, green, baluster-form, spiral ring on neck, H10 (654/134)	20
Bottle, Ludlow, deep green, H9, 19c (4076/1064)	75
Bottles, two, George Washington figural, aquamarine, sea-green, similar, H10 (654/140)	20
Bowl, lily-pad, S. Jersey*, fine, H3¾, Diam 9⅝, 19c (4076/1079)	375
Bowls, 2, lt. green, H2¾, H3, 19c (4076/1078)	150
Candlestick, blown-mold, lt. green, rare, S. Jersey*, H6½, 19c (4076/1176)	350
Decanter, pint, Keene, N.H.*, rare, olive-amber, 3-mold, H7¾, M19c (4076/1075)	325
Decanters, masonic, three, elongated bell shape, dissimilar stoppers, 11, L18c (4180/231)	550
Decanters, quart, colorless, mushroom stoppers, applied tooled rings, 10⅝, E19c (4156/127)	200
Dishes, sweet-meat, pair, knobbed baluster stem, H7⅞, 18/19c (4076/1174)	250
Flask, whiskey, olive green, molded designs, H6¾, 19c (654/132)	150
Free-blown, lily-pad, 2, N.Y.*, pitcher, vase, rare, H6⅞, H8¼, dam, 19c (4076/1151)	1100
Free-blown, settling bowl, rare, aqua, H4½, Diam 10¾, 19c (4076/1162)	400
Glass, blown-mold, flip, apple-green, H5¾, rare, ca1820 (4076/1065)	160
Glass, flip, 3-mold, N.Eng.*, clear, H5¾, M19c (4076/1070)	75
Ink wells, 2, 3-mold, deep, Keene, N.H., amber-green, H1½, H2, E19c (4076/1074)	150
Lamps, fluid, pair brown swirl-glass, inverted trumpet form, red glass-white opaque swirls, 10½, 1 imp, 19c (4268/652)	225
Lamps, fluid, pair, colorless, Boston and Sandwich Glass Co.*, 11½, M19c (4156/121)	400
Lamps, oil, pair, frosted globes, Boston and Sandwich Glass Co.*, 19¾, M19c (4156/120)	800
Lamps, oil, pair, N.Eng.*, each font with brass collar, square base, M19c (4156/119)	200
Mugs, 3, enameled, Bristol*, H2¾, ca1800 (4076/1066)	75
Pitcher, applied handle, etched with band of leaves, flower heads, 10, fine, L18c (4180/247)	375
Pitcher, aquamarine, N.Y.*, good, baluster-form, H7¾, 19c (4076/1081)	400
Pitcher, good, curvaceous body, H9¾, 19c (4076/1082)	325

Bohemian glass

Box, covered, ruby-flash, cylindrical etched body, leaping stag, H4⅝ (4156/132)	120

Cut glass

Bowl, boat shape, hobstar border, diamond foot, 15, L19c (684/170)	190
Bowl, rare, saw-tooth rim, D9, ca1900 (654/190)	375

Fruit bowl, stand, George III, oval, lozenge-cut sides, L11⅜, E19c (4156/128) 160
Jars, pair, regency, covered, clear, H10, 1900-25 (4076/1071) 250
Platter, circular J. Hoare & Co., split vessicas, hobstars, strawberry diamond, cane, 14, ca1900 (669/225) 950
Punch bowl, 2 piece, hobstar and strawberry diamond designs, 12, ca1910 (631/229) 250
Punch bowl, 2 piece and 9 punch cups, 44 point hobstars, 14, ca1910, American (619/226) 1100
Vase, squat vase cut with hobstars and festoons, 6½ ca1910 American (619/225) 225
Vase, intaglio carved, wild flowers, butterflies, 16, L19c, Joseph Locke* (631/223) 400
Vase, yellow-olive, baluster form, probably Sandwich, 10, fine, 19c (4180/233) *125*

End of Day

Bowls, pair, in pink, blue, iron-red, yellow, Diam 10, L19c (4219/41) *250*
Whimsey, light green, form long pipe, trumpet bowl, twisted stem, 38¼, 19c (4211/1026) 175

Glass bottles

Bar, blown, 3-mold, green, rare, Sandwich*, H8¾, crack, 19c (4076/1148) 600
Calabash, mold-blown, 2, mid-west, aquamarine, golden-amber, H7½, H8¼, 19c (4076/1158) 425
Calabash, 2, hunter-fisherman, amber, aquamarine, 19c (4076/1137) 200
Calabash, 3, aquamarine, 2 inscribed Jenny Lind, 1 inscr. Kossuth, 19c (4076/1136) 175
Ludlow, set of 14, graduated, rare, free-blown,N.Eng.*, H5-13, 19c (4076/1173) 750
Scent, cobalt-blue, engraved, flattened ovoid with initials JW and crown, L4⅜, silver top, L18c (4180/217) *160*

Glass flasks

American Eagle Whiskey, very rare, aquamarine, half-pint, with eagle, 19c (4180/213) *475*
Calabash, sapphire-blue, rare, Jenny Lind, Ohio Glass Works, Ravenna, quart-40, 19c (4076/1138) 1700
Cider, hard, very rare, aquamarine, Monongahela/early Pittsburgh, pint-12, 19c (4076/1144) 4250
Commemorative, initialed T.U., flattened baluster form, sprigs of wheat, 9, fine, mkd, 1792 (4180/234) *750*
Cornucopia, olive-green, two, pint and half-pint, Conn.*, 19c (4146/84) 125
Eagle, American, emerald-green, pint, chip, 19c (4076/1104) 425
Eagle, American, Coffin & Hay, N.J., Hammonton, pint, 19c (4076/1109) 225
Eagle, American, Kensington, Philadelphia Glass Works*, pint-11, scarce, 19c (4076/1114) 150

Scent (4180/217)

American Eagle Whiskey (4180/213)

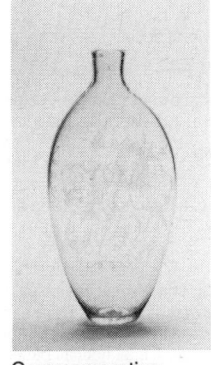

Commemorative (4180/234)

Eagle, American, Louisville*, emerald-green, quart-19, 19c (4076/1107) 950
Eagle, American, Louisville*, pint, rare, 19c (4076/1100) 800
Eagle, American, Monongahela, early Pittsburgh, pint, scarce, 19c (4076/1102) 325
Eagle, American, Monongahela, early Pittsburgh district, pint, scarce, 19c (4076/1101) 475
Eagle, American, Monongahela, early Pittsburgh, pint, very rare, 19c (4076/1115) 6750
Game, good, lt. aquamarine, Coffin & Hay, N.J., Hammonton*, pint-14, 19c (4076/1147) 275
Masonic, amber, rare, Keene/Marlboro St.*,½ pint, chip, 19c (4076/1133) 375
Masonic, olive-amber, rare, Conn. glass-works, coventry,½ pint-4, cracked, 19c (4076/1135) 200
Masonic, sapphire-blue, rare, Keene/Marlboro St., pint-8, 19c (4076/1131) 400
Pike's Peak, rare, yellow-green, 19c (4076/1145) 800

Portrait, American, aquamarine, pint-9, chip, 19c (4076/1099)   125
Portrait, Jackson, James Taylor & Co., pint-12, scarce, 19c (4076/1097)   900
Portrait, Jackson/flowers, Monongahela, pint-12, rare, 19c (4076/1085)   1900
Portrait, Jackson, aquamarine, rare, pint-12, hole, 19c (4076/1080)   600
Portrait, Lafayette, Stebbins, Thomas, Coventry Glass Works, pint-4, scarce, 19c (4076/1094)   325
Portrait, Washington, green-aquamarine, pint-12, rare, 19c (4076/1098)   750
Portrait, Washington, Kensington Glass Works, pint-11, 19c (4076/1091)   200
Portrait, Washington/Jackson, Keene/Marlboro St., pint-11, 19c (4076/1092)   200
Portrait, Washington, rare, pint-12, chip, 19c (4076/1090)   750
Portrait, Washington, scarce, pint-11, chip, 19c (4076/1089)   400
Portrait, Washington, Kimber, attrib., Pa. Glass Works, rare, pint, hole, 19c (4076/1087)   1300
Railroad, 'Success to', Keene/Marlboro St., 3 pieces, 2 pint-11,½ pint-11, 19c (4076/1142)   675
Railroad, 'Success to', clear, green, N.Y. Glass Works, pint-11, chip, crack, 19c (4076/1140)   450
Scroll, aquamarine, quart-36, chip, 19c (4076/1124)   80
Scroll, aquamarine, scarce, quart-35, 19c (4076/1125)   1100
Scroll, brilliant sapphire-blue, pint-36, chip, 19c (4076/1121)   900
Scroll, emerald-green, scarce, Pittsburgh, Pa., pint-35, 19c (4076/1122)   2300
Scroll, golden-amber, heart shaped devices, pint-36, 19c (4076/1116)   400
Scroll, golden-yellow, eight pointed stars, pint-36, chip, 19c (4076/1117)   550
Scroll, lt. blue, rare, pint-36, 19c (4076/1119)   300
Scroll, lt. emerald-green, irregularly shaped star, pint-36, 19c (4076/1118)   475
Scroll, sapphire-blue, brilliant, N.Y. Glass Works*, pint-36, chip, 19c (4076/1123)   2000
Sunburst, 2, good, gold-amber, olive-amber,½ pint,½ pint-4, 19c (4076/1128)   550
Sunburst, 2, good, bottle-green, blue-aquamarine, pint-3,¾ pint, 19c (4076/1129)   650
Whiskey, pictoral, aquamarine, mechanic glass works, Philadelphia, rare, 19c (4076/1077)   300

Lacy glass

Dish, deep, Boston & Sandwich Co., tapestry pattern, H2, rare, 19c (4076/1076)   175

Mold-blown glass

Plates, small, pair, radiating ribs, dark blue rim, D5¼ (654/135)   10

Molded glass

Bottle, calabash, mold-blown, amber bottle with fine ribs, 8, 19c (4268/643)   375
Compotes, sapphire-blue, pair, probably Bakewell and Co., Pittsburgh, 4½ x 6, ch, 19c (4180/215)   *40*
Lamp, oil, clear, knopped columnar base, above an octagonal base, 19c (684/165)   30
Punch set, clear, bowl, 8 cups, with stellate devices, 13½, bowl, E20c (684/161)   75
Salts, colorless, double-ogee form, group of four, mid-western*, H2½ - 3¼, 19c (4146/81)   100

Pattern glass

Cake stand, colorless, pressed coin, baluster form stem, W. Va., 6¼, ca1893 (4180/254)   300
Plates, set of 4, campaign, contenders in the 1884 presidential election, 11¾, 1884 (4211/1021)   1100

Pressed glass

Compote, 'Three-face' pattern, frosted and clear, H14¾, Pittsburgh*, L19c (654/178)   70
Compote, clear and frosted, 'Dog and Deer' pattern, H13, Pittsburgh, L19c (654/179)   50
Compotes, 'Westward Ho,' 6, H2½, 19c (654/177)   100
Compotes, lion-pattern, covered, 2, frosted lion's-head knops, H10½, 12½ (654/147)   80
Compotes, pair, thumbprint pattern, H6, L19c (654/180)   30
Dish, oblong and 5 small compotes, lion-pattern, frosted bases, L8¾, dish, H 2⅜ (654/142)   40
Dishes, dessert, amber, 16, square, hobnail, 6 with amberina rims, L4½, L19c (654/159)   50
Pitcher, 6 cups, clear, opalescent, foliage, flowerheads, rim chip on cups, H8⅝, pitcher (654/174)   40
Tumblers, blue, 23, all hobnail pattern, similar, H4 (654/153)   90

Sandwich glass

Candlesticks, dolphin, Boston and Sandwich Glass Co.*, H10¾, ca1840 (4156/113)   550
Candlesticks, pressed clear, pair, H8, 19c (4076/1069)   275
Lamps, whale oil, vaseline, Boston and Sandwich Glass Co.*, H9, ca1840 (4156/114)   *500*

Compotes (4180/215)

Connecticut
(4180/944)

Tumblers, set 5 colorless glass, N. Lutz*, cylindrical, turquoise glass threading, 4, L19c (4211/1028) 100
Vases, pair, vaseline, each with scalloped lip in Printie-Block pattern, H11½, ca1840 (4156/112) 475

Steuben

Arctic fisherman, model, glass and silver, mounted, Eskimo spearing fish through crevice in ice, 6½
(649/258) 1300
Goblets, set of 12, 5¼, chip, 20c (649/254) 325
Ice hunter, model, glass and silver, mounted, an Eskimo in a kayak, beneath an ice arch, 6 (649/257) 1600

Stiegel type glass

Bottle, amethyst, blown, diamond-daisy pattern, 5½, fine, 19c (4180/248) 550
Bottle, amethyst, blown, expanded diamond pattern, 5½, fine, 19c (4180/249) 700
Vase, cobalt-blue, vase-form, H8, 19c (4076/1073) 325

American Decorations

BAROMETERS

Barometer, brass and carved mahogany, rectangular dial, L.C. Francis, Philadelphia, 36¾, 19c
(4211/1124) 1500
Barometer, carved mahogany and brass, rectangular, G. Tagliabue, N.Y., 4, 19c (4211/1113) 1300
Barometer, stick, inlaid mahogany, Queen Anne style, H38¼, M19c (4076/1203) 425
Barometer, stick, mahogany, Boston, Widdifidd & Co., H35¾, 19c (4148/165) 500

CLOCKS

Ansonia Clock Co., steeple, finials, H20,Ansonia, Conn., M19c (654/300) 350
Atkins Clock Co., Conn., mahogany, steeple case, eglomise panel, H19½, 19c (4146/186) 100
Barnes, Edward M., empire, mahogany, dial with floral spandrels, 36, 1834-35 (684/284) 125
Black marble, gilt-bronze, Mantel, with elephant's head each side, architectural, 13, ca1870
(649/377) 75
Chelsea Clock Co., bronze mantel, sold by Tiffany & Co., 2 train movement, 15¾ x 12, ca1900
(4180/941) 850
Chelsea Clock Co., gilt-metal, mantel, beveled glass sides, retailed by Tiffany & Co., M10½, ca1910
(4238/326) 200
Connecticut, pillar-scroll, mantel, Federal, slender feet, 31½ x 16½, ca1830 (4180/944) *1200*
Double-dial, walnut-cased, broken pediment, Ithaca Calendar Co., H25½, ca1866 (654/314) 900
DuBuc, Paris, American eagle, ball feet with figure of George Washington, 19¾ x 14¼, ca1805
(4076/1250) 8000

Federal rosewood, Seth Thomas Clock Co., gilt eglomise panels, H32⅜, ca1866 (654/325)   500
Mark Leavenworth, Waterbury, Conn., pillar and scroll, swan's neck cresting, H31½, ca1835
(4076/1248)   1100
Mulliken*, Samuel, carved pine, Chippendale, circular brass dial, 48 x 10½, ca1810 (4180/940)   2000
New Haven Clock Co., steeple clock, inlaid rosewood, H19¾, W10, M19c (4076/1247)   325
O. Brackett, Vassalboro, Maine, cherrywood, carved, 1810-20, 29¾ x 9¼ (4209/296)   6500
Parker, Thomas, inscription, Philadelphia, inlaid mahogany, Federal, H15, ca1815 (4076/1255)   550
Seth Thomas Clock Co., box-on-box, 15 day regulator clock, mahogany, H31½, ca1870 (654/307)   700
Terry, E. & Sons, mahogany, Federal, pillar and scroll, (4180/937)   1100
Terry, Eli and Samuel, pillar-scroll, Federal, inlaid mahogany, 28¾ x 17½, ca1825 (4180/935)   1300
Terry, Samuel, pillar-scroll, mantel, Federal, mahogany, 31½ x 16½, res, ca1835 (4180/942)   1200
Tiffany and Co., black and green marble, Mantel, fluted columns, H8, ca1910, N.Y.C. (654/304)   300
Wadsworths, Lounsbury, Turners Litchfield, bracket base, shaped apron, Conn., H24½, 19c
(4146/187)   250
Willard, Aaron, inlaid mahogany, Federal, white painted dial, pierced cresting, 40¼ x 14¼, 19c
(4180/931)   1800
Willard, Simon, 'Lighthouse' clock, mahogany and brass, fine, columnar stand, H26½, Roxbury,
ca1825 (4076/1252)   15000
Wood, David, Newburyport, Mass., carved, inlaid mahogany, flat top hood, H24⅛, ca1800
(4156/284)   13000

Tall-case clocks

Bulkley, Joseph, Fairfield, bonnet hood, silvered dial, 81 x 17¾, 1779 (4156/285)   7250
Federal, inlaid mahogany, dwarf, tapering case, bracket feet, 53½ x 11¾, 1810-20 (4076/1253)   3500
Federal pine, bonnet hood, bracket feet, Pa.*, H83, W17, E19c (4146/190)   *750*
Fisher, J., Yorktown, Pa., rare, sulfur-inlaid walnut, bonnet hood, waisted case, H99, 1773
(4076/1257)   9500
Hadwen, cherrywood, brass dial, Chippendale, phases of moon, date register, 91 x 21¼, 18c
(4180/934)   2600
Hill, Joachim, bonnet hood, Federal, phases of moon, minute, date register, 96½ x 18½, ca1815
(4180/933)   3500
Hoadley, Silas, bonnet hood, Federal, painted and grained case, 84 x 15¼, E19c (4180/938)   1000
Huston, Wm., Philadelphia , carved walnut, Chippendale, bonnet top, molded feet, H92, ca1770
(4076/1249)   3500
Massey, E. Newcastle, mahogany, bonnet hood, bracket feet, H89, W21 (4076/1256)   900
Painted, grained, Conn.*, molded cornice, painted, 83½ x 15⅝ (4209/297)   1900
Rogers, John, Newton, Mass., carved, turned cherrywood, coffered bonnet, H88, W19 (4076/1254)   3200
Terry, Eli, cherrywood, bonnet hood, Federal, moon, minute, date registers., 78¾ x 17¾, E19c
(4180/936)   *1800*
Thompson, William, mahogany, Baltimore, seconds and calendar dial, 2 train movement, Federal,
96½, 1799 (4159/122)   7000

Wall clocks

Banjo, mahogany, eagle and ship eglomise panels, H30¾ (654/293)   250
Banjo, Aaron Willard, Boston, white dial, Roman numerals, landscape, 29, res, ca1830 (4211/1151)   1500
Banjo, Federal mahogany, eglomise panels, H33½, ca1800-50 (654/320)   *750*

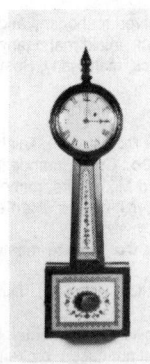

Federal pine   Terry (4180/936)   Banjo (654/320)
(4146/190)

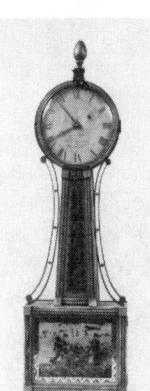

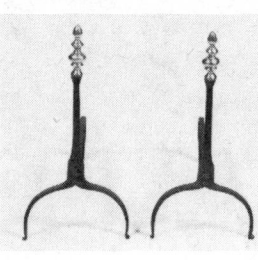

Andirons (4180/924)

English burl walnut
(654/309)

E. Howard and Co.
(654/310)

Curtis & Dunning
(4156/288)

Andirons
(4180/911)

Banjo, Federal, mahogany, eagle finial, H32¼, 19c (654/294)   250
Banjo, Wm. Grant & Co., Boston, Federal, stenciled mahogany, 32¼, rep, ca1820 (4211/1157)   3000
Black and giltwood, Jerome, C., octagonal, New Haven lever movement, H13¼, L19c (654/319)   300
Curtis & Dunning, Burlington, Vt., Banjo, Drum case, white-painted dial, naval battle, 32¼ x 9⅝,
  ca1815 (4156/288)   *7000*
E. Howard and Co., banjo, mahogany, No. 3, carved scrolls, H33½, ca1860, Boston (654/310)   1500
English burl walnut, carved foliage, Seth Thomas movement, H30, L19c (654/309)   400
New Haven Clock Co., rectangular, hinged, glass door, dial above, view below, H25¾ (684/291)   600
Regulator bank, walnut-cased, large, Ithaca Calendar Co., H48, ca1866 (654/327)   1900
Regulator, mahogany-cased, carved leaves on sides, H23 (654/295)   75
Steeple, mahogany, white painted dial, Gilbert, Winsted, Conn., 16 x 9¼, L19c (4149/44)   120
Time, oak, face reads General Time Recorder Exchange, 47½ x 13¾ x 9¾, N.Y.C., ca1910
  (654/297)   150
Walnut, inlaid octagon face, carved foliage, H31 (654/296)   150
Willard, Aaron, Banjo, mahogany, Federal, white painted dial, 38 x 10¼ (4180/932)   1900
Willard, Aaron, Boston, Banjo, mahogany, Federal, giltwood and gesso, 29 x 10, ca1830, res
  (4156/286)   2600

HEARTH EQUIPMENT

Andirons, bell-metal, lemon-top, Boston, tapering standard, snake foot, ca1810, H12½ (4076/894)   275
Andirons, brass, Davis, J., snake feet, 23, ca1800 (4180/929)   1200
Andirons, brass, John Molineux ball finials and log guards, 15½, E19c (4180/930)   400
Andirons, brass and wrought-iron, arched supports, 19½, rep, L18c (4180/924)   *225*
Andirons, brass, double lemon-top, Bailey, N.Y., ring turned standard, ca1800, H22 (4076/895)   400
Andirons, brass, double urn finials, Chippendale, claw and ball feet, 17¾, ca1780 (4180/914)   900
Andirons, brass, pair, scroll feet, H26½ (654/234)   550
Andirons, brass, pair, Wittingham, N.Y., ball finial, columnar stand., ball feet, ca1800, H16 sgd
  (4076/887)   900
Andirons, brass, pr, steeple top, Federal, N.Y., ca1800, 19½ (4209/280)   500
Andirons, brass, Federal, steeple top, ball feet, 22¼, ca1800 (4180/928)   650
Andirons, brass, Wittingham, N.Y., sphere finial, ball ft., screen, 3 pcs., ca1800, H18 sgd (4076/896) 1100
Andirons, brass, Wittingham, Richard, spurred arch supports, ball feet, 17¾, sgd, fine, ca1800
  (4180/910)   1500
Andirons, cast-iron, each a black youth in plumed skirt, leggings, 12, M19c (4180/911)   *400*
Andirons, cast-iron Hessian soldiers, marching in step, 20, 19c (4180/927)   *425*
Andirons, chippendale brass urn-top, spurred-arch, penny feet, inscribed, pair, H17¼, 1781
  (4146/177)   700
Andirons, double-lemon-tops, ball feet, 19, ca1800 (4180/923)   250

Andirons (4180/927)

Andirons (4156/223)

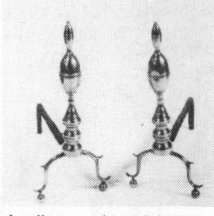

Andirons (4146/178)

Lamp
(4180/894)

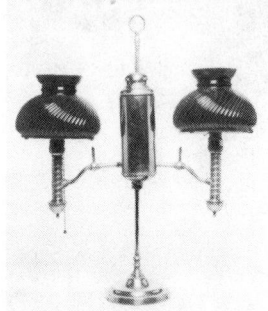

Lamp (4180/899)

Fireback (4180/922)

Andirons, double-lemon-top brass, N.Eng.*, arch supports, ball feet, H21¾, ca1800 (4156/218)   650
Andirons, iron and brass, English, with spit hooks and melon finials, 23, ca1675 (4180/916)   200
Andirons, painted wrought iron, standard fitted with 3 brackets, 27 1/, 18c (4156/221)   2750
Andirons, pair, Chippendale, brass, columnar standard, spurred arch supports, 27, res, L18c
   (4211/1140)   1100
Andirons, penny-foot, brass, R.I., ball finial, rectangular base, ca1750, H17¼, fine (4076/891)   1400
Andirons, screen, brass and wirework, Federal, L48¾, ca1800 (4156/216)   425
Andirons, steeple-top pair, Federal, brass, beaded decoration, rectangular base, 17½, ca1800
   (4211/1144)   900
Andirons, steeple-top brass, Federal, Molineux, with 4 matching tools, H22, ca1800 (4156/223)   *1700*
Andirons, steeple-top, brass, N.Y., hex base, trivet, tongs, 4 pcs, H18, ca1810 (4076/890)   275
Andirons, urn top pair, Chippendale, bell metal, tapering columnar, shaft, 29, ca1780 (4211/1143)   1900
Andirons, urn top pair, Chippendale, brass, columnar standard, spurred arch supports, 28, ca1780
   (4211/1136)   1000
Andirons, urn top, brass, pair, columnar standard, ball and claw feet, 18, ca1780 (684/661)   275
Andirons, urn top, pair, brass, columnar shaft, engraved American eagle, 20, L18c (4211/1142)   900
Andirons, urn top, penny foot, pair, brass, beaded border, columnar standard, 24⅛, 1780-1800
   (4211/1145)   750
Andirons, wrought-iron, brass, knife blade standard, E18c, H18¼ (4076/888)   400
Andirons, wrought-iron, brass,N.Eng., knife blade, urn finial, H20½, insc.I.C., ca1780 (4076/900)   420
Andirons, wrought-iron, brass,N.Eng., knife-blade stand, urn finial, 1770-90, H24½ (4076/897)   475
Andirons, wrought-iron, pair, loop finial, knife-blade standard, scroll toe, 18c, H20 (4076/885)   150
Andirons, Federal, brass ball-top, spurred-arch supports, H14¾, ca1820 (4146/175)   150
Andirons, Federal, brass double-lemon, spurred-arch supports, ball feet, N.Eng., H17¾, ca1810
   (4146/178)   *225*
Andirons, Federal, brass, pair, conical standard, penny feet, H12, E19c (4146/182)   350
Andirons and firescreen, Federal, brass ball-top, H14¾, E19c (4180/919)   450
Andirons and tools, 4 pieces, steeple top finials, 22¾, ca1800 (4180/921)   1300
Andirons and tools, 5 pieces, Federal, brass acorn top, 16, E19c (4180/912)   800
Andirons and tools, 6 pieces, Chippendale, lemon-tops, bell-metal, 16¾, ca1780 (4180/913)   850
Bedwarmer, American or English, engraved brass, copper, walnut handle, ca1800, L42½
   (4076/884)   175
Bedwarmer, brass and wrought-iron, L41¼, ca1800 (4156/222)   225
Bedwarmer, brass, copper, turned maple, engraved with flowers, L40, ca1800 (4156/219)   200

Bedwarmer, brass, turned wood, L43, ca1800 (4156/214) 300
Bedwarmer, copper and turned wood, engraved lid, L42¼, ca1800 (4156/217) 200
Bedwarmer, engraved and pierced brass, hinged lid, baluster turned handle, 48¾, ca1800 (4211/1146) 250
Fender, wirework and brass, Federal, L49½, ca1800 (4180/918) 300
Fender, wirework. brass, N.Y.*, D-shape fender, hex. finials, ca1810, 15½ x 52½ (4076/892) 500
Fire grate, engraved brass, serpentine grate, beaded borders, 31 x 39, L18c (4076/899) 475
Fireback, cast-iron, arched crest, tulips, 22½ x 14¼, 1794 (4180/922) *400*
Fireback, cast-iron, 2 piece, Whitehead and Law, Gothic Revival, 34½ x 40, 1843 (4180/926) 1600
Stove, cast-iron and brass, Jones and Wardell, 2 ball-turned finials, 21¾ x 20 x 18¼, ca1840 (4180/920) 275
Tongs, pipe, wrought-iron, engraved, N.Eng.*, double scroll terminals, L18c, L20¾, very fine (4156/180) 850

LIGHTING DEVICES AND DECORATIONS

Bronze lamps, pair, Lewis Varon & Co., Philadelphia, fonts, 2 burners, glass shades, H21¼, ca1840 (4268/1068) 650
Candelabra, cast-brass, lustre pair, three stylized eagleheads on standard, 13¾, 19c (4180/901) 550
Candelabra, 2 light, pair, ormolu, cut-glass, oval bobeche, scall. feet, H12¼, E19c (4076/1209) 400
Candelabrum, gilded bronze eagle, three lights, E19c (4180/900) 425
Candelamps, pair, pewter, each with a removable bobeche, 7¾, unmarked, M19c (4268/161) 100
Candlestand, tinned sheet iron, 2 light, rectangular drip pan, conical base, N.Eng.*, H31, E19c (4146/165) 450
Candlestand, wrought-iron and brass, single light, tripod base, 56 (4180/897) 325
Candlestand, wrought-iron, brass, adjustable, N.Eng.*, 48¼, 18c (4156/181) 1700
Candlestick, brass, domed foot, engraved letter 'EC', 6½, 17/18c (4076/518) 425
Candlestick, brass, high domical foot, 9¼, Dutch, E18c (4076/529) 350
Candlestick, brass, spiral standard, 6, 17c (4076/506) 100
Candlesticks, brass, octagonal, foot, 6¼, 17/18c (4076/500) 160
Candlesticks, brass, pair, hexagonal, capstan, domed feet, 4½, 17c (4076/496) 600
Candlesticks, brass, pair, octagonal foot, 9⅛, M18c (4076/526) 325
Candlesticks, brass, two, flattened domed feet, 8¾ & 9¼, fine 17c (4076/497) 700
Candlesticks, brass push-up, pair, squared bobeche and base, 9½, 19c (4076/501) 200
Candlesticks, brass, Federal, pair, push-up, squre foot, H9¾, E19c (4146/161) 175
Candlesticks, brass, pair, square foot, 5¾, 17c (4076/507) 90
Candlesticks, brass, pair, William and Mary, mid-drip pan, 9½, fine, ca1700 (4211/256) 125
Candlesticks, brass, set, four, English, domed foot with scalloped border, 10⅛, fine, M18c (4211/255) 1300
Candlesticks, brass, single-light, faceted lustres, marble base, 16, ca1850 (4149/43) 140
Candlesticks, brass, Federal, pair, circular base with headed borders, 8⅜, E19c (4180/895) 275
Candlesticks, brass, Queen Anne, English, ring-turned standard, shaped foot, pair, H7¼, M18c (4146/160) 400
Candlesticks, cut-glass, lustre, George III, pair, vasiform standard, H10¼, ca1810 (4148/173) 250
Candlesticks, gilt-metal, pair, scrolled arms hung with pear shaped lustres, 10, M19c (4180/893) 200
Candlesticks, painted tole, pair, Corinthian capital, square foot, 11⅝, L18c (4076/523) 150
Candlesticks, Sheffield plated, pair, hurricane shades, H23½, 19c (4148/169) 425
Candlesticks, William & Mary, brass, prickett, tapered column, domed foot, 9½, ca1700 (4211/258) 1000
Chamberstick, brass, saucer base, with a snuffer, 4¾, E19c (4076/511) 200
Chamberstick, brass, engraved, repousee, L10½, 18c (4146/1) 60
Chandelier, painted and gilded, 20 light, sawtooth border, N.Eng.*, H37, 18/19c (4146/162) 375
Chandelier, pressed tinware, 6 light, turned wood standard, 14½ x 29¼, 1750-1800 (4149/68) 375
Chandelier, 10 light, tinware, N.Eng., L18, E19c (4156/184) 1600
Chandeliers, pair, painted and decorated, tinware, yellow and orange, 4 light, 22½, electrified, ca1825 (4211/1083) 950
Chandeliers, pair, 12 light, pressed brass, central standard, tiered base, 26½ x 13¼, E19c (4211/1077) 400
Clock garniture, champleve enamel, gilt metal, with 5 branch candelabra pair, Tiffany & Co., H15⅛, L19c (649/388) 6500
Girandole group, 3 pieces, Archer & Garner, mother, father, 2 babes, H17½-19½, 1851 (4180/908) 300
Girandole group, 3 pc, gilt metal, 3 light candelabra, single light candelabrum, 13½, 19c (4211/1116) 200
Hurricane shades, pair, blown glass, cobalt blue, baluster form, 21¾, 19c (4076/487) 1000
Lamp, grease, four wick, iron, suspended, 21, 17/18c (4076/482) 325
Lamp, oil, bull's eye, pewter, drum shaped font, 8¾, one bull's eye broken, ca1835 (4268/157) 325
Lamp, oil, etched glass and brass, stylized wisteria sprays, electrified, 22, M19c (4180/894) *250*
Lamp, sparking, Dyott & Kent, brass, 9¼, 19c (4180/903) 400
Lamp, student, 2 brass arms on, brass standard, domed foot, dark green shades, 29, 19c (4180/899) *525*

Lantern
(4146/163)

Lamp, Betty, wrought iron, suspended with reflector, 7¾, American*, E18c (4076/484)	80
Lamps, empire, bronze, etched glass, argand, pair, Philadelphia, Veron & Co., H14, ca1840 (4148/162)	600
Lamps, single-light, painted tinware, two, H19½ and 18¾ (4209/285)	300
Lamps, table candle, pair, tinware, single light, black painted, brass mounted, 16½, E19c (4211/1074)	700
Lantern, blown glass, globular body, repousse brass collar, 16, 19c (4076/492)	325
Lantern, painted toleware, yellow, chinoiserie scenes, French*, H15¼, ca1810 (4146/163)	*275*
Lantern, repousse brass, blown, etched clear glass, brass collar, 12, N.Eng., ca1830 (4076/488)	250
Lanterns, brass, pair, ship's, Perkins Marine Lamp Co., N.Y., electrified, 17½ (4268/1095)	325
Lanterns, coach, painted iron, pair, each with beveled glass sides, 14½, 19c (4149/28)	80
Lanterns, Federal brass and blown glass, cylindrical form, matching smoke bell, pair, H8¼ - 14, 19c (4146/164)	375
Lanterns, hanging, tin, glass, pair, domed doors, H14 (654/241)	90
Light, loom, wrought iron, rod standard, adjustable loop, rushlight below, 30, 18c (4211/1078)	550
Oil lamps, pressed blue glass, pair, diamond pattern shades, H22½ (654/265)	200
Rush-light, wrought-iron, carved wood, 8¾, 18c (4156/179)	130
Rush-light stand, wrought iron, crossed ash base, 21, 18/19c (4076/483)	175
Sconce, wall, tinware, single light, crimped border, N. Eng., H17, 19c (4156/209)	300
Sconces, pair, tin, circular back, mirrored tiles, 11, L18c/E19c (4076/489)	500
Sconces, pressed tinware, pair, mirrored tiles, single candlearm, 10, 19c (4180/906)	700
Sconces, pressed tinware, pair, mirrored tiles, single candlearm, 9, 19c (4180/907)	300
Sconces, single-light, pair, N.Eng.*, circular pressed tin backplate, mirror, 9, 19c (4149/92)	200
Sconces, tin single-light wall, pair, concave circular mirrored backplates, 9½ (4149/53)	250
Sconces, tinware single-light, pair, N.Eng.*, pressed, 10, 19c (4149/55)	90
Sconces, wall, pair, 2-light, with carved, ebonized eagle, scrolling arms, H25½, E19c (4268/1085)	4100
Sconces, wall, 2-light, carved wood, painted, pair, H13½, Conn., ca1825 (654/258)	250
Shelves, hanging, three-tier, pair, pine, H22, W29¾, E19c (4076/1229)	350
Table lamp, tin ware, painted, electrified, L18c, H19⅝ (4209/282)	700
Taper sticks, brass, pair, ring-turned standards, rectangular bases, 4, 19c (4268/1106)	150
Tole lamps, painted, pair, bell-form, made into table lamps, H11½ (654/232)	150
Tray on stand, papier mache inlaid mother of, pearl, Victorian, oblong, floral, leaf, 18, 19c (4211/1100)	250
Vase, Chinese export procelain, now as lamp, baluster, body, Chinese figures, 28, 19c (4142/22)	600
Vase, Chinese porcelain, now as lamp, bulbous, body with flambe glaze, 31 (4142/30)	500
Vase, Chinese porcelain, now as lamp, circular crackled beige body, flared neck, 26¼, 19c (4142/60)	250
Vase, Chinese porcelain, now as lamp, green celadon, foliate handles, 22, L19c (4142/3)	175
Vase, Chinese porcelain, now as lamp, pale blue tapered body, 22, painted to simulate cracks (4142/5)	275

American Folk Art: Objects
CARVINGS

Assorted carvings

American eagle figure, gilded, spread eagle, 19c, 12 x 41½ (4209/271)	1900
Angel, painted, naive, metal wings, H12½ (654/289)	75

Arrow directional, carved pine, shaped devices, 19c, L35 (4209/231) — 700
Barber figure, free standing, carved, painted wood, 19c, H23¼ (4209/184) — 3500
Barn ornament, wood, painted, 5-pointed star, green, 19c, D37½ (4209/107) — 3750
Bird house, wood, pillared porch, red and white paint, H72 x W21, E20c (4180/793) — 350
Birds in tree made from bent twigs, H14½, 19c (4211/703) — 700
Bracket, wall, eagle carved and gilded pine, D shaped, spreadwinged eagle, 29¼ x 11¾, ca1800 (4211/1091) — 1200
Captain M. Starbuck bust, Nantucket, carved painted wood, important, 1838, H13¾ (4209/182) — *30000*
Circus wagon model, carved and painted wood, rectangular, tableaus scenes, in case, case, 18 x 25½, L19c (4211/1057) — 2900
Civil war toy of marching soldiers, carved wood, sheet metal, rachet mechanism, rare, ca1860, 15¼ x 30 (4209/200) — *11000*

Civil war toy of marching soldiers
(4209/200)

Captain M. Starbuck
bust (4209/182)

Pelican mounted as
umbrella stand
(4180/774)

Hops worker figure (4209/180)

Dog, painted composition, white, seated, H36 (4211/700) — 350
Eagle carved wood, spread wings on scrollwork, 2 winged griffins, 16½ x 36, 19c (4211/1108) — 700
Eagle figure, carved pine, 19c, 14 x 22 (4209/234) — 850
Eagle plaque, giltwood, gesso, 19c, 10¼ (4209/274) — 650
Eagles wood, carved and painted, black and, white, wings spread, H6¼ (4211/708) — 250
Figure, circus pony, carved wood, wearing red and gold, painted blanket, bisque figure, 10¼ x 13⅝, M19c (4211/1056) — 325
Fireboard, painted pine, urn with blossoms, 1830-40, 24½ x 33¾ (4209/270) — 3750
Flying goose wood figure, carved, painted, Ira Hudson, Va., E20c, L42½ (4209/195) — 14000
Gentleman figure, carved, painted wood, mustachioed man, 19c, H18 (4209/183) — 2400
Giraffe's head of wood, carved, painted, glass eyes inset, 19c, H24½ (4209/197) — 2200
Hobby horse, carved and painted, gray horsehair tail, 20½, 19c (4211/1058) — 350
Hops worker figure, wood, reclining, with jug, dated 1840, rare, H12 x L45 (4209/180) — *9000*
Horses, miniature, carved and painted yellow and black, pair, 5, 19c (4211/728) — 225
Man, dancing, amusing, wood, painted, 19c, 19 (4209/96) — 3250
Musicians, wood, painted, 2 violins, trumpet, cello, H5½-7 (4209/77) — 1900
Pelican mounted as umbrella stand, Continental*, H40, 19c (4180/774) — *550*
Punch figure, cigars in hand, John Campbell, Md., huge hat, red jacket, 81, ca1860 (4268/1048) — 12000
Ram figure, wood, painted, stylized carving, unusual, 19c, 11¼ x 17¼ (4209/201) — 3400
Rearing horse, wood, H13½ (654/278) — 75
Robin figure, wood, painted, Conn.*, 19c, H4 (4209/202) — 1700
Rooster figure, carved, painted wood, good, Pa., 19c, H20 (4209/181) — 3400
Rooster figure, wood, carved, painted, 19c, H6 (4209/199) — 475
Rooster figure, wood, painted, stylized, H5½ (4209/118) — 650

Seagulls, pair, carved, painted, mounted on bases, 19c, H15¼ (4209/122)   2600
Soldier, wood, painted, Revolutionary War, raising flag, L19c, H29 (4209/73)   850
Sternboard, wood, American eagle, painted with shield, flags carved, fine, rare, 19c, 22½ x 112 (4209/203)   13000
Woman figure, wood, carved, painted, wearing pleated dress, boots, ca1890, H19½ (4209/193)   3400

Cigar Store figures

Full length figure, gold highlights, Samuel Robb, attrib., N.Y., 72¼, 1880 (4268/1030)   23000
Indian princess, carrying box of, cigars, 62½, fine, 19c (4180/796)   5750
Princess, carved, painted wood, holding cigars, ca1870, fine, H57 (4209/191)   5000
Squaw, full length figure, Samuel Robb, attrib., N.Y., with box of cigars, 66, ca1880 (4268/1031)   12000

Decoys

American Brant, Stick-up, Lobb type, Virginia, (4211/641)   125
Black-bellied plover, Long Island origin, N carved on base, (4268/943)   175
Brant, snake-head, Harry V. Shourds, N.J., hollow-cedar construction, 1976 (4268/958)   100
Brant, American, North Carolina origin, mule shoe weight, (4180/839)   75
Broadbills, pair, Cranmer, made for Ducks Unlimited Selection, 1976 (4268/955)   125
Canada goose, composition cork with white pine, factory mark, 34 (684/274)   40
Canada goose, Barnegat Bay style, hollow-cedar, (4268/949)   100
Canada goose, Hurley Conklin, Manahawkin, N.J., (4211/638)   650
Canada goose, Hurley Conklin, Manahawkin, N.J., (4211/639)   300
Canada goose, South Jersey, Seabrook brand on bottom, (4268/950)   200
Canada goose, pair, hollow construction, (4268/968)   400
Canvasback, cast-iron, painted, black, white, (4209/142)   300
Canvasback, mammoth drake, North Carolina origin, (4180/838)   50
Curlew, Hurley Conklin, N.J., branded H.C., (4268/961)   75
Dowitcher, early Va. origin, Mackey Collection stamp, (4268/946)   260
Drake canvasback, Evens McKenny, Md., solid cedar, original paint, ca1940 (4268/953)   100
Drake canvasback, Madison R. Mitchell, Md., no weight, ca1935 (4268/954)   75
Drake Mallard Miniature, A.E. Crowell, Harwichport, Mass., (4211/640)   450
Drake Mallard, with hen Broadbill, Mid-western, (4211/642)   *200*

Goose (4209/148)   Gull (4209/147)

Duck, black, hollow cedar, Seabrook, (4268/959)   50
Duck, black, weighted, Capt. Harry Jobes, Aberdeen, Md., cedar, (4268/938)   75
Duck, black, Cobb Island, H carved in bottom, ca1880 (4268/957)   150
Goose, Canada,N.Eng., extremely fine, hollow construction, (4209/148)   12500
Goose, Canada,N.Eng., extremely fine, hollow construction, (4209/149)   *10000*
Greater, Long Island origin, Mackey Collection stamp, (4268/945)   40
Green-winged teal, pair, Frederick Brown, hollow-cedar construction, 1978 (4268/952)   100
Gull, Carter, John W., N.Y., Jamaica Bay, iron weight, (4209/147)   *2600*
Hudsonian curlew, Assawaman Island, Va., 2 piece construction, pegged, (4268/942)   175
Long-billed curlew, Long Island origin, wood base, ca1880 (4268/947)   600
Merganser, hen, Harry V. Shourds, N.J., preening position, (4268/956)   125
Merganser, primitive, Maine origin, Mackey Collection stamp, (4268/948)   275

Pintails, hen, drake, pair, Ward, Lem, Md., Crisfield, (4209/146)   4500
Plover, black-bellied, Crowell, Elmer, Mass., Harwichport, (4209/144)   3250
Plover, black-breasted, pair, Shourds, N.J., driftwood base, (4268/970)   175
Snipe, roothead, N.J., wood base, ca1860, (4209/143)   1600
Snipe, Va.*, carved winged-tail, Mackey Collection stamp, (4268/944)   325
Wood fish, two, metal fins, tails, nail head eyes, L7½, 8½ (4211/637)   *350*
Yellowlegs, greater, feeding, metal stand, (4209/145)   900
Yellowlegs, lesser, Va., Berlin, in silhouette, 1896, (4209/141)   475

Dioramas

Civil War, wood, carved, painted, 22 union soldiers standing at attention, H7, 12 x 20, rare, 19c (4209/54)   1500
Civil War, wood, carved, painted, 23 soldiers engaged in battle, H6½, 11½ x 61, rare, 19c (4209/48)   1000
Civil War, wood, carved, painted, 9 union soldiers at camp, H7, 12 x 30, rare, 19c (4209/51)   *1000*

Eagles

Eagle, carved, fierce expression, wings upraised, glass eyes, 38¾ x 22¼, 19c (4268/1067)   3800
Eagle, sternboard, pine, spread-winged, vigorous carving, 35 x 82¾, 19c (4268/1021)   6500

Prisoners of war

Card set, ivory in wooden box, L8½ (4211/652)   750
Mechanical toy, mother and daughter, spinning wheel, activated by hand gear, ivory, H8, 19c (4211/650)   *1300*

Wood fish (4211/637)

Mechanical toy (4211/650)

Civil War (4209/51)

Schimmel, W.

American eagle figure, carved, painted wood, Cumberland Valley, Pa., fine, ca1870, H15 x W20 (4209/185)   14000
Eagle, painted wood figure, attrib. Wilhelm Schimmel, Pa., res to paint, H10, wing span 18, 19c (654/280)   3500
Parrot figure, carved, painted, Cumberland, Pa., 19c, H5 (4209/187)   1900
Rooster figure, carved, painted wood, Cumberland Valley, Pa., 19c, H4 (4209/186)   1800
Rooster figure, carved, painted, Cumberland Valley, Pa., 19c, H4¾ (4209/188)   2200

Ship's figureheads

Nantucket captain figure, repainted, 19c, H59 (4209/179)   3750
Wood figure of a woman, acanthus leaves, N.Eng.*, 19c, H16½ (4209/178)   5000

Whirligigs

Dutchman, wood, painted, yellow tunic & gaiters, red arm baffles, 19c, H10½, unusual (4209/85)   1200
Farm house, red and white, horses and men revolve in wind, 34 x 33 (4211/695)   350
Fireman, carved, painted, wood base, H12, 19c (4209/8)   1700
Man, wood, painted, stylized, top hat, arms wind activated, H18½, some paint loss (4209/76)   2600
Revolutionary War, painted, wood, H29, fine, 19c (4209/17)   5000

Soldier, carved, painted, arms fitted with gilt-painted blades, H20½, fine, 19c (4209/66)   3250

Wood figures

Alligator, open jaws, L41 (4180/809)   325
Alten, Fred K., brown bear, Wyandotte, Mich., H7, E20c (4146/46)   125
Alten, Fred K., oxen, Wyandotte, Mich., H7, E20c (4146/47)   75
Alten, Fred K., pheasant, Wyandotte, Mich., H13½, E20c (4146/45)   325
Alten, Fred K., prehistoric reptile, Wyandotte, Mich., H5, E20c (4146/49)   250
Carousel, complete, Md.*, six pairs of horses, 2 carts, hand-made, horses, H46L53, overall D26 ft.
   (4211/680)   14500
Civil War Infantryman, anonymous, 8, 19c (4211/682)   350
Uncle Sam painted, carved from flat plank of wood, H132 (4180/783)   750

PAINTED OBJECTS

Butler holding cigarette cup, ashtray, cast-iron, red, white, black, 34 1/5, ca1930 (4268/988)   800
Carousel horse, wooden, carved and painted, American, 39, repainted, ca1910 (659/624)   750
Collage picture of a steamship, ground in oil, ship embroided, frames, 23¾ (684/273)   70
Milliner's stand, painted, papier mache, young woman's head, brown hair, 14, 19c (4211/1042)   400
Mirror, dressing table, cast and painted, metal framed, oval glass, pivoted between 2 figures, 21,
   ca1890 (684/316)   500
Owl figure, glass eyes, on triangular sheet plaque, 19c, 22½ x 52 (4209/238)   1700
Rocking horse, carved and painted, American, 42, ca1900 (659/625)   80
Smoke stand, painted metal, Negro in butler's uniform holding ashtray, 35 (684/313)   110
Swordfish bill, painted farm scene, farmer, boys, ducks, case, glass panel, 4¼ x 32½ (4268/921)   400

SCRIMSHAW

Ostrich egg, engraved with black slaves, 6½ (4146/19)   225
Powder horn, Canadian, with pewter mounts, 9 (4146/18)   425
Walrus tusk, sailor embracing woman, her skirt raised, L16 (4268/918)   1100
Wart hog's tusk, 'Aaron Pratt, Harpoonman, 1804', sailing vessels, 7½ (4180/716)   550
Whale's teeth, set of 3, New Bedford, William Perry, whaling scenes, 6-6½, 20c (4268/916)   2500
Whale's tooth, carved, L6½, 1861 (4149/50)   110
Whale's tooth, depiction of Patterson Park, Md., and ship, 8¼ (4146/16)   1400
Whale's tooth, sailing ship inscribed Peace, 5 (684/248)   100
Whale's tooth, carved eagle head, New Bedford, William Perry, L6, 20c (4268/917)   800
Whale's tooth, dance hall girl, C. Covil, Oxford, Mass., H5 (4211/654)   450
Whale's tooth, engraved, inscribed, 3 masted clipper ship in full sail, 4, 1851 (684/247)   250
Whale's tooth, engraved young woman, baring her breasts, hole in crown of tooth, L4½ (4268/919)   375
Whale's tooth, extremely rare, 'Susan', engraved by Fredk. Myrick, fine, 1829 (4211/644)   21000
Whale's tooth, harpoon man, fully-rigged ship, H7¼ (4211/645)   800
Whale's tooth, harpooning whale, A. Young, 1852, L6 (4268/915)   250
Whale's tooth, men in longboats, maiden in 18th century garb, L6½ (4211/648)   850
Whale's tooth, polar bear, seal, fully-rigged ship, (4211/646)   650
Whale's tooth, young woman on one side, men in long boats on back, 6½ (4180/717)   2200
Whale's tooth, American eagle, young maiden on reverse, 8 (4146/17)   1400
Whale's tooth, Nile, full rigged, with little girl in 19th century dress, L6 (4268/913)   400
Whale's tooth, On Board the Susan, Dec. 22, 1828, cutting blubber, L6½, 1828 (4268/911)   29000
Whale's tooth, Tropic Bird, 1878, men in long boats pursuing whales, L6, 1878 (4268/912)   1100

SCULPTURES

American School, Zachary Taylor, marble bust, 17½, 19c (4268/1096)   375
Anonymous, Daniel Webster, realistic, modeled, gray to white clay, H18½ (654/290)   275
Anonymous, 19-20c, baseball player, young man seated on stump, H11 (4211/722)   850
Black man sitting, smoking a pipe, H22, 20c (4211/709)   250
Bust gentleman in frock coat, b,Bell*, pottery, H5¼, 19c (4076/10)   400
Bust of Benjamin Franklin, bronze, wearing fur coat, open waistcoat, after J.J. Boyle, 5¾ (684/300) 150
Bust of George Washington, cast-bronze, Henry-Bonnard Bronze Co., N.Y., H18, 1898
   (4076/1232)   800
Bust of Washington, bronze, reduction of original, by Jean Antoine Hudson, 8½, 1899 (684/301)   175
Cat, seated, yellow glaze, H11¼, 19c (4076/30)   300
Decoupage Cigar Store Urn, cigar bands on green framework, 34¼, 1912'100 (4211/683)   300
Eagle, cast iron, rockwork base, 13¼ x 30½, 1915 (4180/807)   250
Figure, 'Sportsman' painted cast iron, holding gun, slain deer on shoulder, 31 (684/315)   60
Figure, young black girl terra cotta, painted, long white dress, carrying hat, 9¼, 19c (684/236)   150
Garden ornament, cast-iron, painted, Indian princess and sunflower form, 19c, 29 x 40 (4209/237) 3300
George Washington figure, molded zinc, free-standing, fine, 19c, H58 (4209/236)   3250

Group, 'Union Refugees', cast metal, forlorn family, Rogers, 23, L19c (684/314) — 350
Group, painted plaster, young boy, dog scrambling into a burrow, John Rogers, 15, chip, ca1880 (684/232) — 150
Group, American plaster, 'Coming to the Parson', John Rogers, 21½, ca1870 (684/233) — 200
Group, American plaster, 'Going for the Cows', John Rogers, 10½, chip, ca1880 (684/230) — 200
Group, American plaster, 'Taking the Oath and Drawing Rations', John Rogers, 23, rep, ca1870 (684/231) — 200
Group, American plaster figure, 'One More Shot', John Rogers, 24, ca1870 (684/234) — 200
Horses heads, cast iron, hitching posts with ring, 14, 19c (4180/812) — 225
Indian figure, molded zinc, W. Demuth & Co., N.Y., seated on tobacco bale, ca1850, rare, 32 x 29 (4209/235) — 5500
Pig and piglets, stone, realistic, H5, L7¼ (4268/980) — 375
Plaster figural group, 'Chess', painted grey-brown, John Rogers, H21¼, ca1890 (654/291) — 700
Rush, William*, Phila, John Dickinson, life size, carved, painted, 70, res, 1787-90 (4180/845) — 10000
Volk, Leonard Wells, attrib. to, 'President Lincoln-Emancipation Proclamation', H20¼, white metal (654/362) — 375
Whippets, pair, cast-iron, L38, 19c (4180/877) — 1600

SHIP MODELS

Bedford whale boat, by Capt. H.L. Hall, Mass., H7, L23, L19c (4076/1246) — 2300
'Endeavor', detailed, fully-rigged, three masts, plexiglass case, 25½ x 27 (4180/720) — 1200
Half-ship, carved, painted wood, framed, 24 x 34, 19c (4211/664) — 325
Half-ship model in wood, painted, fully rigged, 19c, 18 x 24⅜ (4209/196) — 850
'Kaiulani', detailed, fully-rigged, modern, glass and wood case, (4180/723) — 1400
Naval Ship, carved wood, 3 masts, black with red details, 43 x 57 (4268/928) — 350
'Phantom' American clipper ship, fully rigged, deck housings, black, green, L18½, L19c (4156/208) — 400
'Sea Witch', detailed, fully rigged, modern, glass and wood case, fine, 25 x 35 (4180/722) — 3000
Ship model, carved and painted wood, East Indiaman, John and Elizabeth, 42½ x 58, 19c (4211/1126) — 1200
Ship model, carved and painted wood, Ship of the line 'Exeter', 42 x 49, 19c (4211/1128) — 1500
Sloop, wood, hull built of thin strips, Art Deco ornament, 75 x 49½, ca1920 (4268/1078) — 1000
The Royal Louis, ship of the line, 100-guns, 3 fully rigged masts, French, 47½ x 59½, 1760-80 (4268/927) — 900
Three-masted, wood, canvas sails, H32½ (654/263) — 200
'U.S.S. Constitution', detailed, fully rigged, modern, glass and wood case, fine, 30 x 42¼ (4180/721) — *2000*
Wood model of a sail boat, painted in cream and green with a red stripe, 57 (684/249) — 100

TRADE SIGNS

Bouve, S.R., painter, oil on wood, 3 masted vessel, 19c, 23 x 28, fine,N.Eng.* (4209/24) — 5250
Consulate sign, with eagle and motto, L19c, 16¾ x 21 (4211/723) — 800
Gunmaker's wood, painted, carved, double-barreled rifle, gilt, L153, 19c (4209/4) — 2700
Indian, sheet iron, painted, shooting arrow, 48½ x 21½, 19c (4209/22) — 3000
Inn, carved, painted, bunches of red grapes with green leaves, H19, paint loss, 19c (4209/67) — 800
Key, wood, painted, carved, yellow, 19c, L30 (4209/108) — 2600
Livery, wood, painted, carved, horse's head, L19c, H15 (4209/37) — 900
Milliner's trade sign, painted tinware, form of top hat, dark green with black band, 9¼, 19c (4211/1035) — 400
Sheep, carved, painted, 19c, rod standard, wood base, 37½ x 36 (4209/14) — 6250
Ship's chandler, Little Navigator, top hat, red jacket, carrying a sextant, H27½ (4268/924) — 450
Shoe Shop, carved and painted wood, old iron repairs, 54 x 22 (4180/824) — 500

Whale's tooth
(4211/645)

'U.S.S. Constitution' (4180/721)

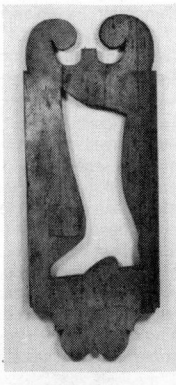

Shoe Shop (4180/824)

Shoemaker's shop, pair of tin shoes, 5½ x 10½, 19c (4076/204)   700
Sign, barbershop, painted pinewood, blue on white, 19c (684/761)   50
Sign, apothecary, gold painted tole, mortar and pestle surrounded by eagle, 27, L19c (684/240)   250
Stage coach sign, wood, painted, single ball, gold, 19c, D15 (4209/99)   900
Tavern sign, inscribed S. Akin, with American eagle and shield, 28¼ x 40¾, 19c (4076/224)   2750
Tea canister, painted and decorative tin, cylindrical with band of red, yellow and green flowers, 8¼,
19c (4211/1037)   250
Tinmaker's sign, boy's cap with conical peak, 17¼, L19c (4268/1011)   250
Whale, Mass., New Bedford, wood, carved, painted, 19c, 9¼ x 29 (4209/28)   2000
Woman with plaited hair and skirt, hand pierced for holding flag, 35½, L19c (4180/833)   *550*
Wood fish with flag, trade sign, 48½ x 46¼, L19c (4211/685)   2600
Wood sign board, painted, inscribed 'Vulcan Hillside Plows', 71 (684/253)   50

WEATHERVANES

American flag, carved, painted, shaped wood base, M19c, H76 (4209/216)   4250
Angel Gabriel, molded copper, blowing his trumpet, 19c, fine, 18 x 24 (4209/223)   16000
Angel Gabriel, molded copper, chubby, wings raised, trumpet bell missing, 12 x 36 (4268/986)   375
Arrow, wrought iron, zinc head, painted wood finials, 19c, 108 x 94 (4209/218)   1000
Blacksmith, painted sheet-metal, two men working at an anvil, 19c, 21 x 16½ (4209/226)   1200
Bull, molded copper, original color traces, 19c, 26 x 40 (4209/209)   2300
Bull, sheet-metal, stylized, paint traces, 19c, H36 x 53½ (4209/205)   3750
Cannon model, molded copper, gilt-painted, 19c, 14 x 17 (4209/232)   1000
Carp, painted, molded copper, open jaws, 19c, 27½ x 35½ (4209/228)   1500
Cock, molded copper, yellow paint, 19c, 24 x 24 (4209/233)   1000
Columbia figure, molded copper, carrying painted flag of sheet metal, fine, rare, 19c, H31
(4209/221)   12000
Copper horse and rider, rounded on both sides, H20½, ca1840 (4180/754)   1500
Copper, cast-iron rooster, with directional indicators below, H37 (654/222)   325
Eagle, molded copper, spread winged, orb mounted on arrow, 19c, 34½ x 39½ (4209/212)   2100
Eagle, molded copper, spread-winged, perched on an orb, H29 (4180/818)   150
Fire engine, cast metal, good 3 dimensional detail, H19 x L52, fine (4211/687)   3750
Fireman, sheet-metal, Md.*, dated 1882, 40½ (4211/690)   3250
Fish, carved, painted wood, 19c, H20 (4209/208)   1300
Fish, carved, painted wood, painted details, driftwood base, H20 (654/271)   150
Fish, molded copper, sheet iron fins, 19c, 9½ x 18 (4209/211)   700
Flying man, carved, painted wood, 19c, 20 x 18 (4209/215)   2800
Grasshopper, molded and gilded copper, fine, rare, 19c, 17 x 44½ (4209/219)   23000
Grasshopper, cast-iron, on directionals, painted green, 19c, 97 x 36 (4209/227)   1500
Grasshopper, molded copper, stylized body, 15¼ x 29 (4268/1023)   800
Horse, double-sheet metal, mane flowing, 19c, fine, L35 (4209/230)   950
Horse, running, above directionals, 60 x 30 (654/253)   250
Horse, running, molded copper, powerful, brass standard, 18½ x 37 (4268/1045)   1800
Horse and jockey, molded copper, gilded, stylized, 16 x 32, 19c (4268/1022)   1900
Horse and jockey, molded copper, with directionals, 19 x 33½ (4180/778)   700
Horse and rider, sheet-tin, painted, on arrow directional, wind wheel, 19c, H98 (4209/206)   3000
Hunting dog perched on rifle, carved, painted wood, following a scent, 19c, 13 x 28¼ (4209/225)   1200
Indian, molded, gilded copper, head in profile, on directional arrow, 19c, fine, rare, 28 x 29½
(4209/217)   17000
Jockey and horse 'Dexter', molded, copper, red, yellow, black silks, 24 x 31 (4180/782)   1200
Leaping stag and hound, gilded copper, rod standard, extremely fine, 19c, 26 x 62 (4209/214)   17000
Mallards, 3, flying, sheet-metal, painted black, 34 x 53½ (4268/1043)   1100
Mashamoquet the Indian, molded copper, headdress, mounted on arrow, important, rare, 19c, 45 x
58 (4209/207)   *25000*
Molded copper, running horse, stylized, flowing mane, 18 x 18 (654/221)   400
Peacock, molded, gilded copper, stylized, mounted on orb, 19c, fine, rare, 25½ x 35 (4209/222)   9500
Pig, molded copper, directional, L28, 19c (4211/691)   400
Quill pen, Washburne Co.*, N.Y.C, molded copper, unusual, ca1890, 79 x 37½ (4209/210)   1400
Rooster, carved, painted wood, 19c, 16½ x 12 (4209/229)   1300
Rooster, flat, sheet iron, 7⅜ x 11¼, E19c (4180/755)   400
Rooster, cast metal, vigorous modeling, fine, 34 x 35 (4211/679)   900
Rooster, molded metal, melon body, fine, 19c, H19¼ x 32½ (4209/204)   1300
Rooster, sheet metal, tail feathers silhouetted, H20, 19c (4180/792)   650
Rooster, sheet-iron, flat with, pierced comb and tail, H23½, 19c (4211/726)   *500*
Running horse, fine molded copper, vigorously modeled, 19 x 38 (654/279)   900
Running horse, molded copper, cast zinc head, H21 x L43 (4211/720)   2400
Running horse, molded copper, flowing mane and tail, H20 (4180/835)   275
Running horse, molded copper, flowing mane and tail, wood base, 17 x 30 (4211/658)   *550*
Schooner, wood, 4 masts, full sails painted white, 37 x 44 (4268/1051)   150

Ship, molded copper, three-masted frigate, fine, rare, 19c, 31½ x 36 (4209/220) 3250
Stag, leaping, molded copper, traces of gilding, 23 x 30 (4268/1049) 1200
Stork, molded copper, traces of paint, rare, 19c, H28 (4209/224) 4750
Weathervane, galloping horse above directionals, 60 x 30 (684/310) 300
Whale, molded copper, upturned tail, sheet copper fins, 17¾ x 37½ (4268/995) 200
Wind toy, wood, painted, carved, miniature weathervane, 19c, H20 (4209/113) 1500

Woman with
plaited hair
and skirt
(4180/833)

Mashamoquet the Indian (4209/207)

Valentine (4146/43)

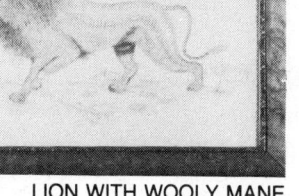

LION WITH WOOLY MANE
(4211/701)

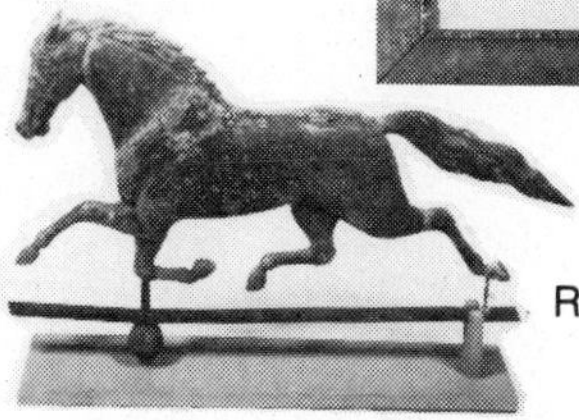

Running horse (4211/658)

Rooster (4211/726)

American Folk Art: Pictorial

CALLIGRAPHIC ITEMS

Bookplate, 6¾ x 4, Pa., 19c (4076/222) 650
Bookplate, a large tulip with diamond designs, 5⅞ x 3/3/8, Pa., 19c (4076/221) 550
Leaping Stag, M.F. Blackman, 1833, 31¼ x 45¼ (4211/725) 500
LION WITH WOOLY MANE, fine, 15 x 23 (4211/701) *550*
Swank, John E., calligraphy, THE INDIAN OSCEOLA, 23¾ x 18, M19c (4180/784) 1000

CUT WORK

Anonymous, charcoal and sandpaper, classical building, 20 x 30 (4180/826) 225
Anonymous, Cutout monument with profile of Washington, 10½ x 11⅝, ca1820 (4211/732) 350
Anonymous, inscribed 'Eliza', black and white cutouts on orange ground, 7¾ x 10 (4180/825) 275
Rocking horse, carved and painted, pony with stick legs, leather saddle, 24½ x 45 (4180/828) 150
Valentine, with keys and hearts, anonymous, probably N.Eng., 13¾ x 13¼, 19c (4146/43) *275*

EARLY PRINTS

Anonymous, AN EMBLEM OF WALES, 14 x 10 (4156/260) 75
Anonymous, JAMES WOLFE ESQR., mezzotint, 13 x 9⅛ (4156/255) 225
Barometer, wheel inlaid stainwood, 'COTTONUS MATHERUS,' mezzotint, first in colonies*, 13¾ x 9¾, 1728 (4156/253) 600
Collet, John, (after), PAUL JONES SHOOTING A SAILOR, mezzotint, 12½ x 10, 1779 (4156/256) 1100

De St.-Memin, C.B. Julien, after, A VIEW FROM BROOKLYN HEIGHTS, etching, 7¼ x 58, imp, 1861 (4211/268) 150
Doolittle, Amos, THE PRODIGAL SON, set of four, 12⅝ x 9⅞, 1814 (4156/257) 2000
Edwards, S. Arlent, GEORGE WASHINGTON, mezzotint, 12 x 9⅛, proof before letters (4156/254) 175
Houston, Richard, MAJOR GENERAL JAMES WOLFE, mezzotint, 14 x 9⅞ (4156/262) 250
Houston, Richard, MAJOR GENERAL JAMES WOLFE, mezzotint, 13⅞ x 10 (4156/263) 250
Sergent, A.L.F., LOUIS-JOSEPH, MARQUIS DE MONTCALM, 9½ x 6½, 1790 (4156/259) 200
Wall, William Guy, after, BAKER'S FALLS, plate 8, aquatint, 17⅞ x 24¼, imp, 1823-24 (4211/277) 475
Wall, William Guy, after, GLENNS FALLS, plate 6, aquatint, 17⅞ x 24¼, imp, 1822 (4211/275) 475
Wall, William Guy, after, Hudson, plate 13, aquatint, 18⅛ x 28¼, imp, 1825 (4211/282) 650
Wall, William Guy, after, JUNCTION OF THE SACANDAGA AND HUDSON RIVERS, plate 2, aquatint, 18½ x 24⅝, imp, 1821-22 (4211/271) 350
Wall, William Guy, after, LITTLE FALLS AT LUZERNE, plate 1, aquatint, 18 x 24¼, imp, 1822-23 (4211/270) 250
Wall, William Guy, after, NEWBURGH, plate 14, aquatint, 17⅞ x 24⅜, imp, 1825 (4211/283) 650
Wall, William Guy, after, PALISADES, plate 19, aquatint, 17¾ x 24⅛, imp, 1823-24 (4211/288) 1400
Wall, William Guy, after, RAPIDS ABOVE HADLEYS FALL, plate 4, aquatint, 17⅞ x 24¼, imp, 1822-23 (4211/273) 500
Wall, William Guy, after, TROY FROM MOUNT IDA, plate 12, aquatint, 18¼ x 25, imp, 1822 (4211/280) 550
Wall, William Guy, after, VIEW FROM FISHKILL LOOKING TO WEST POINT, plate 15, aquatint, 17⅞ x 24½, imp, 1825 (4211/284) 1000
Wall, William Guy, after, VIEW NEAR FORT MILLER, plate 10, aquatint, 17⅞ x 24, imp, 1822-23 (4211/278) 375
Wall, William Guy, after, VIEW NEAR FORT MONTGOMERY, plate 22, aquatint, 17⅞ x 24⅜, imp, 1812 (4211/287) 625
Wall, William Guy, after, VIEW NEAR HUDSON, plate 15, aquatint, 17⅞ x 24¼, imp, 1825 (4211/281) 650
Wall, William Guy, after, VIEW NEAR JESSUPS LANDING, plate 3, aquatint, 18¼ x 24⅜, imp, 1821-22 (4211/272) 425
Wall, William Guy, after, VIEW NEAR SANDY HILL, plate 18, aquatint, 17⅞ x 24¼, imp, 1822 (4211/286) 850
Wall, William Guy, after, VIEW NEAR SANDY HILL, plate 7, aquatint, 17⅞ x 24¼, imp, 1822-23 (4211/276) 575
Wall, William Guy, after, WEST POINT, plate 16, aquatint, 18 x 24⅝, imp, 1825 (4211/285) 1800
Wilkinson, Bowles, & Carver, A VIEW OF THE TAKING OF QUEBEC, 14⅜ x 19⅛ (4156/258) 700
Young, John, LE MARQUIS DE LA FAYETTE, mezzotint, 8¾ x 6¾, 1759 (4156/261) 175

FRAKTUR

Bauman, Pa.*, Timoclea before king, 13 x 15, 1802 (4268/1026) 325
Bestling, John T., printer, printed and watercolor, Harrisburg, Pa., 15½ x 13, 19c (4146/36) 150
Birth records, pair,N.Eng.*, Brown, Simeon, Susanna, 1770-77, 6¾ x 8½ (4209/9) 750
Petermann, calligraphy, watercolor, vital statistics, German sayings, Pa., 12 x 14, 1828 (4268/1041) 3400
Strooh, Nicholas, birth and christening certificate, 13½ x 15½, 1808 (4146/72) 500

MAPS

Delaware Bay and River, engraved, Paris, 1777 21 x 29 (4158/20) 225
Evans, Lewis, Map of Middle British Colonies, engraved, partly colored, Philadelphia , 1755 20 x 26 (4158/24) 6750
Faden, William, Plan of the Town of Boston, engraved, Oct. 1777, 18 x 12½, borders frayed (4158/1) 350
Homann, Johann Baptist, engraved colored map - Virginia, Md., Carolina, from Homann's Atlas 1759 (4158/32) 175
Lay, Amos, Map of Northern N.Y., engraved, July, 1812, 30 x 50 (4158/38) 175
N.Y. City, new and accurate plan of the city, engraved, 1797 (4158/57) 2000
Plan of the Siege of Savannah, for Stedman's History of the American War, 1779, 18 x 24 (4158/28) 160
Regni Mexicani, Novae Hisparia, colored, printed, L18c, 22 x 26 (4076/876) 250
Seutter, Matheus, map of New England, etching, 19 x 22¼, imp (4211/267) 700
Terre-Marie Nova et Virginie, tabula, colored, 18c, 15½ x 17½ (4076/875) 350
Topographical, Ipswich, Barres, J.F.W., 41½ x 29¼, 1781 (4148/176) 750

MEMORIAL PICTURES

Anonymous, Overmantel Painting - Landscape, 32½ x 63 19c (4211/602) 3000
Anonymous, hairwork, mourning for Sarah C. Winne, fine black stitchery, 13¼ x 18¼, 1796 (4180/842) 250
Anonymous, mourning pictures, pair, silk and chenile, anon., 11 x 14¾, 19c (4076/1216) 850
Anonymous, N.Eng.*, for Capt. John Carnes, watercolor on velvet, 19 x 22¼, ca1830 (4268/1012) 275

Anonymous, N.Eng.*, mourning picture, urn under large tree, 11½ x 11¼ (4180/837) — 125
Hair bracelets, gold, pair, each with locket, M19c (4076/555) — 175
Hair bracelets, snake, with turquoises, pair, M19c (4076/556) — 225
Hairwork on silk, to Mrs. Elizabeth Gibbons and Mr. Thomas Cock, 17 x 23¼, ca1820 (4076/214) — 350
Lawton, C., N.Y.*, TO THE MEMORY OF MRS. MARY HEBARD, ca1825, 16¾ x 21¼, rep
    (4209/71) — 9500
Maentel, Jacob, S.E. Pa., portrait, THE IRONMASTER'S WIFE, 1810, 9⅝ x 7⅛, creases (4209/69) — 3250
Pratt, Catherine H.B., John & Mary Foot, 2 urn-topped monuments, 7½ x 10⅞, 1828 (4211/731) — 225
Sacred to the memory of Esther Shaw, two women at monument, 15 x 17, 19c (4076/209) — 400

NAIVE PAINTINGS AND PICTURES

American School, MR., MRS. JOSEPH MARTIN, pair portraits, 9⅝ x 7¾, 19c (4209/255) — 2200
American School, THE EGAR OF YARMOUTH, N.S. BROWN CAPT., 24¼ x 36¼, 19c (4268/932) — 750
American School, THREE CHILDREN IN AN INTERIOR, 17¼ x 19½, 1853 (4076/711) — 1500
American School, TWO BOYS WITH THE AMERICAN FLAG, 34 x 28 (4076/705) — 17000
American School, 18c, PORTRAIT OF CATALINA VAN DUSEN, 30¼ x 25 (4156/275) — *4000*
American School, 18c, PORTRAIT OF HUGH HENDERSON, 23 x 18 (4156/273) — 1400
American School, 18c, PORTRAIT OF SAMUEL BURLING, oval, pastel, 17½ x 14 (4156/276) — *1200*
American School, 19c, A CHILD OF THE TAYLOR FAMILY, 32 x 16 (4268/201) — 26000
American School, 19c, A COUNTRY KITCHEN, 24 x 30 (654/337) — 850
American School, 19c, A GENTLEMAN, 16 x 12 (4268/202) — 1200
American School, 19c, A HUDSON RIVER VIEW, 18 x 24 (654/412) — 300
American School, 19c, A MOTHER AND CHILD, 30¼ x 25¼ (4268/195) — 2300
American School, 19c, A SNOWY LANDSCAPE, 22 x 26 (654/348) — 325
American School, 19c, A WOMAN, 14 x 10, tempera on board (4268/203) — 1000
American School, 19c, BOY WITH A HORN and GIRL WITH ROSES, two pictures, 33¾ x 29
    (4268/197) — 2500
American School, 19c, CHILD WITH TOY SOLDIERS, 24 x 20 (4076/703) — 2100
American School, 19c, DOG IN A LANDSCAPE, 18 x 22 (654/353) — 175
American School, 19c, FIRE FIGHTING SCENE, 18½ x 24, oil on board (4209/260) — 2000
American School, 19c, FISHING, 1884, 10 x 13¾, watercolor (654/385) — 200
American School, 19c, HUSBAND AND WIFE, PAIR OF PORTRAITS, 25 x 22 (654/390) — 350
American School, 19c, LANDING OF THE PILGRIMS, ca1850, 34¾ x 53 (4209/259) — 4000
American School, 19c, LITTLE GIRL IN A RED DRESS, 48¼ x 38 (4076/712) — 3250
American School, 19c, M. BRYANT, 22 x 34 (4268/265) — 2100
American School, 19c, MOTHER AND CHILD, 40½ x 32½ (654/366) — 550
American School, 19c, PAIR OF PORTRAITS, HUSBAND & WIFE, 30 x 24 (654/396) — 175
American School, 19c, PORTRAIT OF A GENTLEMAN, 16½ x 13½ (4156/282) — 250

onymous (4180/837)

American School (4156/275)

American School (4156/276)

American School, 19c, PORTRAIT OF A GENTLEMAN, 19c, 23½ x 18½ (4209/263) — 3250
American School, 19c, PORTRAIT OF A LADY, 30 x 25 (654/395) — 70
American School, 19c, PORTRAIT OF A LADY, 40 x 30 (654/377) — 175
American School, 19c, PORTRAIT OF A LADY, 36 x 28 (654/401) — 750
American School, 19c, PORTRAIT OF A LADY, 30 x 25 (654/359) — 75

American School, 19c, PORTRAIT OF CAPTAIN THOMAS FLENDER, 8 x 6 oval, watercolor
(4149/147)   147
American School, 19c, PORTRAIT OF JOHN C. GIFFORD, 20 x 16, on board (654/365)   50
American School, 19c, SUR LE BORD DE LA MER, BESOIN, 8 x 16 (654/375)   850
American School, 19c, THE BARK AMY TURNER, 23½ x 32 (4268/269)   3400
American School, 19c, THE SHIP LIZZIE WILSON, 22 x 28, pastel (654/381)   1500
American School, 19c, THE SHOE SHINE BOY, 1802, 16 x 11 (654/407)   500
American School, 19c, THE WATERMILL, 10 x 13, paper on board (654/338)   125
American School, 19c, UNION SOLDIER GUARDING A CEMETERY, 10 x 11½, on masonite
(654/363)   75
American School, 19c, WATCH HILL, R.I., 19c, 24¼ x 33½ (4209/257)   11000
American School, 19c, YOUNG LADY WITH PINK BOW, ca1835, 21⅞ x 17¾ (4209/256)   1700
American School, 19c, YOUNG WOMAN AT A PIANO, 50 x 39¾ (4076/713)   3750
American School, L19c, THE STEAMBOAT HIGHLANDER, 20 x 28 (654/335)   950
Anderson, Oscar, AT DUSK, 9 x 12 (654/344)   40
Anonymous, FASHIONABLE LADIES, pair, watercolor on paper, 7 x 5⅝, N.Eng.*, ca1815
(4268/1003)   250
Anonymous, Painted mirror, Pelicans on a tropic shore, 19 x 27, L19c (4180/769)   375
Anonymous, RURAL TOWN SCENE WITH STROLLERS, 13¼ x 16¾, 19c (4076/223)   650
Anonymous, SURRENDER OF GEN. BURGOYNE, Saratoga, N.Y., 1777, 7¾ x 11 (4146/42)   *500*
Anonymous, YOUNG CHILD, 8 x 5¾, M19c (4180/813)   250
Anonymous, N.Eng.*, FASHIONABLE LADY, full-length, ca1840, 5¾ x3½, discolor (4209/103)   900
Anonymous, N.Eng.*, ca1830, VIEW OF AN INN, oval, fine, 12 x 15 (4211/699)   450
Bacrett, A.A., THE BARK ADELIA CARLETON, 21 x 31 (654/408)   175
Bartlett, M., attrib. to, HANGING DUCK, 17 x 11¼, on board (654/391)   90
Bear, B.W., THE STORM, oxen sense fallen bridge, 40 x 29¾, 1861 (4180/758)   600
Belknap, Zedekiah, attrib (1781-1858), A LADY AND A GENTLEMAN, pair, each 27½ x 23½, oil on
panel (4076/693)   1200
Belknap, Zedekiah, 1781-1858, A GENTLEMAN AND HIS WIFE, portraits, pair, 26¾ x 20¾, oil on
panel (4268/198)   1600
Bliss, Colonel, CIVIL WAR SCENE, Blacks in open wagon, 11 x 16, M19c (4180/760)   500
Bradley, J. 1832-47, CHILD IN A GREEN DRESS, 33 x 26 (4209/253)   43000
Brewster, John Jr., CHARLES MUSSEY PORTRAIT, ca1806, 29½ x 24½ (4209/244)   3300
Brewster, John Jr., CHILD PORTRAIT, mounted on aluminum (1766-1854), 38 x 25⅛ (4209/243)   67500
Brewster, John Jr., MR. AND MRS. RICHARD GILPATRICK, pair, 1805, 29½ x 24 (4209/245)   9000
Briscoe, Franklin D., TAKING IN THE NETS, 1890, 14 x 20 (654/351)   425
Brown, Harrison B., A COASTAL INLET, 9 x 18 (654/387)   350
Brown, J. 1802-35, CLARISSA INGERSOL, age 31, portrait, 29½ x 25 (4209/242)   7500
Brown, J., attrib., A LADY AND A GENTLEMAN, portraits, pair, 26 x 21, 19c (4268/181)   3500
Brown, Joseph Randolf, COWS GRAZING IN THE SNOW, 1893, 14 x 17 (654/379)   150
Champney, Benjamin, MOUNT CHOCUPHA, 16 x 24 (654/410)   900
Chinese School, A clipper ship, fully rigged, American ensign, 15½ x 21¼, oil on board, 19c
(4211/1089)   1800
Cohen, Frederick E., GETTING BACK TO CAMP, 1857, 26 x 48 (654/336)   600
Coombs, Delbert D., A BASKET OF APPLES, 11 x 14¾ (654/409)   475
Coulter, William A., PAIR OF COASTAL SCENES, STORMY WEATHER & CALM, 12 x 24, on panel
(654/384)   650
Coverly, N., E19c, REVOLUTIONARY WAR BATTLE, 10¼ x 16 (4211/696)   550
De St.-Memin, Charles B.F.J., Philadelphia, MR. AND MRS. JOHN WELLS, pair, crayon, 21 x 16¾,
1799-1800 (4180/874)   5750
Duplessis, Joseph S. after, PORTRAIT OF BENJAMIN FRANKLIN, 23½ x 19¼ (4156/272)   2250
Earl, Ralph (1751-1801), PORTRAIT OF MR. LOGANBACK, 36½ x 30¼ (4076/689)   2100
Fairman, James, AFTER THE STORM, 1873, 26½ x 44½ (654/406)   275
Field, E.S., DEACON HARLOW PEASE, portrait, 34½ x 28 (4209/250)   10000
Field, E.S., FANNY SMITH, portrait, ca1836, 35 x 28½ (4209/251)   5500
Field, E.S., HENRY PEASE, portrait, 34½ x 28 (4209/249)   11500
Finch, E.E., fl. 1833-50, A LADY AND A GENTLEMAN, portraits, pair, 29¾ x 25 (4268/189)   600
Folsom, Mrs. F.J., M19c, CONWAY CASTLE, charcoal on sandpaper, 22 x 27½ (4211/721)   *850*
Frothingham, James, attrib, LADY WITH LACE COLLAR, 23½ x 14⅝, 1808-09 (4180/763)   800
Georgius, K., THREE FOXES AND A MOUSE, 1867, 19 x 26 (654/340)   1600
Gignoux, Regis Francois, WINTER LANDSCAPE, 14¼ x 23½ (4156/274)   1600
Giles, Howard P., BEACH, 15¼ x 27 (654/398)   150
Hamilton, James, ARCTIC SCENERY-SUN SETTING, 1856, 30 x 20 (654/352)   1100
Hart, James M, A FARMYARD, 15½ x 24 (654/383)   1100
Helmick, Howard, CAUGHT IN THE ACT, 16½ x 24½, gouache, ink (654/404)   275
Herzog, Hermann, GRAZING COWS, 22½ x 29 (654/397)   1000
Howe, K.L., RIVER LANDSCAPE, 1871, 17 x 21 (654/367)   225

Hunt, M.P., FISHING, 14 x 20, 1857 (4156/279) — 700
Jarvis, John Wesley, attrib., 1770-1840, DE WITT CLINTON, 30¼ x 25¼ (4268/194) — 1400
Jennys, William, YOUNG WOMAN OF THE HEWINS FAMILY, NEWBURYPORT, 30 x 24¾, ca1783-98 (4209/240) — 20000
Jennys, William (fl. 1790-1800), PORTRAIT OF MOSES KIMBALL, JR., 30¼ x 25 (4156/271) — 9000
Kitchell, H.M., AN AUTUMN LANDSCAPE, 20 x 30 (654/382) — 200
Kitchell, H.M., AUTUMN DUSK, 16 x 20 (654/370) — 100
Knight, A.M., RIVER VIEW, 17 x 23, chalk on board (654/354) — 175
Lehr, Adam, BASKETFUL OF APPLES,1900, 20 x 30 (654/378) — 350
McAuliff, James (1848-1921), RED CAPE, 25 x 30, 1872 (4076/717) — 1200
McCallion, GEORGE WASHINGTON'S HATCHET, trompe-l'oeil, 12 x 10, 1890 (4180/757) — 800
McClory, A., THE SICKNESS OF AN ODDFELLOW, 1845, 25 x 30 (654/380) — 325
Moses, Anna M.R., 'Grandma' (1860-1961), IN THE ADIRONDACKS, 16 x 20 (4180/612) — 4250
Oertel, Johannes Adam, HEAD OF ST. PAUL, 30 x 20 (654/386) — 175
Parker, G., GREEN WOOD COTTAGE, 1870, 8¼ x 10½ (654/355) — 60
Peale, Sarah, attrib, A PLATTER OF FRUIT, melons, peaches and grapes, 15¼ x 20, ca1830 (4180/797) — 900
Phillips, Ammi, ELIZABETH MYGANS, portrait, ca1834, 31¾ x 26¾ (4209/247) — 18000
Phillips, Ammi, MAN HOLDING LARGE BIBLE, ca1815, 32 x 27¼ (4209/248) — 7000
Phillips, Ammi 1788-1865, LADY AND GENTLEMAN, portraits, pr, ca1836, 31¼ x 26¼ (4209/246) — 62500
Pinney, Conn, 1825, MOTHER AND CHILDREN, oval, 11½ x 9¼ (4211/704) — 550
Poole, T. L., SHIP PAINTING, 18 x 15 (4211/609) — *500*
Portrait of young girl, pastel on paper, half length profile, 13⅜ x 9½, ca1800 (4211/1064) — 2000
Prior, W.M. 1806-73, TWO CHILDREN, portrait, ca1830, 11¼ x 15¼ (4209/252) — 13000
Pudor, Heinrich, 19c, THE DAYAN CHILDREN, 26½ x 32½, 1873 (4076/710) — 800
River with fields, townscape, charcoal on sandpaper, anonymous, 21 x 27 (4211/693) — 650
Ryder, Albert Pinkham, after, SAILING UNDER MOONLIGHT, 15 x 19¾, panel (654/339) — 250
Sawin, J.G., Mass., MOUNT VERNON, side-long view, 18⅝ x 27, 1849 (4180/756) — 500
Senat, Prosper Louis, SHIPPING OFF CORSICA, 1890, 18 x 30 (654/372) — 275
Shapleigh, Frank H., VIEW ON HIGHLAND ST., SCITUATE, MASS., 22 x 36 (654/411) — 1500
Sharples, James, after, PROFILE PORTRAIT OF GEORGE WASHINGTON, 9¾ x 7¾, ovoid (654/364) — 75
Shute, R.W. and S.A., MISS ADELINE BARTLETT OF LOWELL, MASS., ca1832, 23¾ x 19¾ (4209/264) — 32000
Stock, Joseph Whiting, 1815-55, A WOMAN, 30 x 25 (4268/200) — 3500
Taylor, Jay C., FOREST SCENE, 15 x 18 (654/369) — 100
Theus, Jeremiah, in the manner of 18c, A LADY AND A GENTLEMAN, 2 portraits, each 30 x 20 (4076/686) — 2300
Turner, Harriet French, MABRY MILL, oil on pressed wood, 24¼ x 17⅞, 1962 (4180/766) — 475
Unknown (19c), THE BARQUE DANIEL OF BOSTON, 20 x 27 (4076/762) — 700
Wales, Nathaniel F., CAPTAIN AND MRS. NATHAN SAGE, 24 x 20¾, 1803-15 (4209/241) — 12000
Waters, George W., STREAM IN THE WOODS, 4¾ x 9¾ (654/346) — 550
Webber, W., THE HAY GATHERERS, 9¾ x 17 (654/349) — 375
Weide, MOUNTAINOUS LANDSCAPES, a pair, 7½ x 9¼, pastel on paper (654/392) — 30
Williams, Micah, LADY AND GENTLEMAN, pair portraits, 24¾ x 20 (4209/262) — 6000
Young,Harvey, SOLITUDE, 30 x 40 (654/357) — 950

PAINTINGS ON GLASS

Amorous scenes, pair, young man peering out window, couple embracing, 10½ x 8, E19c (4268/1086) — 2100
Anonymous, ABRAHAM LINCOLN, 23¾ x 17¾, 19c (4180/810) — 375
Anonymous, YOUNG BOY, blond-haired little boy, 9½ x 6½, ca1840 (4180/801) — 650
Anonymous, Silhouette, YOUNG GIRL, full length, holding bird, 19c, 4⅝ x 3⅝ (4209/112) — 700
August, women and children harvesting wheat, fine, 23¾ x 19, E19c (4180/729) — 700
Bishop, THE CHRYSTENAM, Hudson River steamer sign, 11 x 19, L19c (4180/795) — 425
Chinese export, reclining court lady, 9½ x 10½, M19c (4146/141) — 725
December, men and women, Christmas celebration, fine, 14 x 11¾, E19c (4180/731) — 800
Ellsworth,N.Eng., portrait, CALISTA HOWARD, miniature, ca1840, 4¼ x 3⅜, fine (4209/68) — 1100
Hunter's Return, country scene, pair, rope twist gilded frames, 14 x 11, E19c (4268/1087) — 2100
January, 2 ladies standing on the shore of a frozen pond, fine, 14 x 11¾, E19c (4180/732) — 650
July, two maidens shearing sheep, 14 x 11¾, E19c (4180/730) — 600
Lady in a ribboned hat, seated figure of young girl, circular, fine, D8½ E19c (4180/728) — 1300
Landscape with pine trees, mountains, primitive style landscape, H15½, L19c (654/287) — 50
The Apotheosis of Washington, allegorical figures weep, L8 x 20½, E19c (4180/727) — 950

The Sailor's Farewell, sailor bidding farewell to sobbing sweetheart, fine, 9¾ x 7⅝, E19c
(4180/734)   1200
The Weary Hunter, woman serves glass of port to hunter, circular, D13½, E19c (4180/735)   1500

PASTELS

American School, 19c, LADY AND GENTLEMAN, portraits, pr pastel on paper, ca1810, 15 x 11½
(4209/266)   3500
American School, 19c, VIEW OF RIKER'S ISLAND, charcoal, chalk on sandpaper, 19c, 15½ x 19¼
(4209/269)   1300
Anonymous, PERRY'S VICTORY AT LAKE ERIE, 12½ x 29½ (4180/790)   700
Anonymous, PORTRAIT OF A GENTLEMAN, Micah Williams*, 13½ x 10¼, 19c (4076/217)   750
Bascom, Ruth H. 1772-1848, JOEL WOOD FAY, LUCY D. FAY, portraits, pastel on paper, ca1829,
18½ x 13⅜ (4209/265)   7000
Delanoy, Abraham, MARY BRADLEY, portrait, pastel on paper, ca1790, 20¾ x 13¼ (4209/267)   1000
Sharples family, attributed to, PORTRAIT OF MARY PIXTON, 8¼ x 6¼, pastel on paper (4076/704)   700
Williams, Micah, N.J., MR. AND MRS. WILLIAM PRATT, pair, 25¼ x 21¼, res, ca1824 (4180/779)   3500

PENCIL PORTRAITS

Anonymous, Empire chairs showing, GENTLEMAN AND LADY, 8½ x 11½, 19c (4180/791)   100
De St.-Memin, Charles, ca1800, PAUL BACOT, crayon and chalk portrait, 22 x 16½ (4268/1093)   6250
Levitt, Huld, N.H., VIEW OF MEREDITH BAY, N.H., 13 x 17¼, ca1830 (4180/840)   150
Pencil drawing of a sailing ship, anonymous, probably American, 3¼ x 4¼, 19c (4146/62)   100
Plunkett, Jos., civil war encampment, Delaware, 9 x 13½, 19c (4146/51)   175

SILHOUETTES

Assorted works

Adams family, Williams, John, Abigail, John, Quincy, Louise Catherine, 12⅛ x 10¼, 1809
(4180/429)   3250
Anonymous, group of 3, hollow-cut bust portraits, 2 gentlemen, young woman, 4 x 3¼, details in blk.
ink (4209/110)   275
Conversation group, room setting in crayon and pencil, 6¾ x 8¾, M19c (4180/453)   600
Drummer boy, watercolor landscape background, 7½ x 5½, 1840 (4180/454)   *550*

Poole (4211/609)

Folsom (4211/721)

Esther Isaacs, hollow cut silhouette, Aunt of John Howard Payne, 6½ x 5¼, framed, 18/19c
(4149/155)   275
Horse throwing rider, reverse label 'Exhibited at Phil. Expo. 1876', L3¼ (654/275)   150

Edouart, Auguste

ABERCROMBIE SISTERS, 3 figures, 9⅞ x 13⅞, Dec. 27, 1830 (4180/451)   250
AGNEW AND LINDSAY, double portrait, two young girls, H4½, 5¾, Feb. 9, 1831 (4180/445)   *425*
BENNET FAMILY, with figures of 4 gentlemen on reverse, 10 x 14, Nov. 21, 1831 (4180/433)   350
BLACKBURN SISTERS WITH MISS CALLEN, 10 x 14¼, April 4, 1832 (4180/442)   200
BROWN, JOHN AND ROBERT DAGLISH, Brown wearing spectacles, 10 x 7, Jan. 30, 1832
(4180/435)   200
FORBES FAMILY, mother and son, with Miss Moir, 9⅞ x 13⅞, May 26, 1832 (4180/452)   300

GRATTNAY FAMILY, 9¾ x 13¾, Oct. 16, 1830 (4180/440) — 175
LINGHAM FAMILY, two figures, 7⅛ x 8¼, March 20, 1837 (4180/436) — 325
MACDOUGALL, brother and sister, 6⅞ x 9, June 25, 1837 (4180/447) — 450
MACDOUGALL, PATRICK AND ALEXANDER, young boys in pinafores, 8¼ x 14, June 25, 1832 (4180/449) — 250
MCCLURE FAMILY, four figures with silhouettes on reverse, 10 x 14, Mar. 3, 1832 (4180/437) — 500
MONRO, ELIZABETH AND ALEXANDER, H8, July 4,5, 1831 (4180/439) — 200
MONTEITH BROTHERS, 9⅞ x 13¾, Jan. 30, 1831 (4180/443) — 200
OITHEY, Dr. Robert, with Finlay, Dr. David, 9½ x 8, April 21, 1832 (4180/450) — 150
SITTERS LIST BOOK, alphabetized list of American subjects, L13⅜, 1840-44 (4180/434) — 1000
WEMYSS, CAP'N AND SON, child playing with father, 13¾ x 9⅞, Jan. 10, 1831 (4180/438) — 400

THEOREM PAINTINGS

Allen, P.A.,N.Eng.*, watercolor, THE BLUE & WHITE BOWL, ca1830, 15 x 17¾, on velvet (4209/46) — 1700
Anonymous, BLUE BOWL WITH FRUIT, foxed, 10½ x 12½, ca1830 (4180/808) — 700
Anonymous, BASKET FILLED WITH FRUITS, 8½ x 11⅜ (4209/6) — 850
Anonymous, GARDEN FLOWERS, green, yellow, pink, blue, 16¼ x 14¼ (4211/667) — *600*

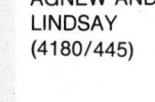

AGNEW AND
LINDSAY
(4180/445)

Drummer boy (4180/454)

Anonymous
(4211/667)

Anonymous, THE THEOREM BOWL, N.Eng.*, on velvet, 19½ x 24, ca1830 (4268/994) — 700
Anonymous, velvet,N.Eng.*, ca1830, BASKET WITH BIRD & FRUIT, 19 x 23½, fine (4209/12) — 2100
Anonymous, watercolor, on velvet, THE FULL BASKET, ca1835, 16¾ x 16½, stains, foxing (4209/87) — 800
Anonymous,N.Eng.*, BASKET FILLED WITH FRUIT, ca1830, 11⅝ x 14½, good, on velvet (4209/30) — 950
Anonymous,N.Eng.*, on velvet, double slab heaped with fruits, ca1830, 17 x 23¼, good (4209/75) — 950
Anonymous,N.Eng.*, watercolor, on velvet, basket with fruits, vines, 12⅜ x 14¼, foxing, discolor (4209/61) — 1800
Anonymous,N.Eng.*, 2, Basket filled with fruit, 9⅞ x 13, 5⅛ x 6⅜, good (4209/44) — 4500
Anonymous, N.Eng., THE BLUE COMPOTE, with variety of fruit, 16¾ x 19, ca1840 (4268/1046) — 900
Anonymous, N.Eng.*, A SLICE OF WATERMELON, watercolor on paper, 18¾ x 21, ca1830 (4268/1025) — 500
Anonymous, N.Eng.* ca1830, footed compote, watercolor on paper, 11¼ x 13¼ (4211/705) — 450
Clark, E.M., Chatham, Adelina, THE CLEAR BOWL, ca1830, 10⅛ x 13¼, unusual (4209/36) — 2100
Cole, Maria O.,N.Eng.*, watercolor, on velvet, basket with fruits, ca1835, 15 x 15¼, foxing (4209/82) — 950
Jones, Mary Carpenter, BASKET OF FLOWERS, watercolor on paper, 18 x 21¼, 1825 (4268/1024) — 550
Yellow woven basket, flowers, W.P. Eaton, 1843, 25 5/12 x 28 (4211/729) — 1400

WALL PAINTINGS

Porter, Rufus 19c, East Jaffrey, N.H., Scene of Boston Harbor, wall fresco, 72 x 180, rare, ca1825
(4211/655)   10000

WATERCOLORS

Anonymous, Coat of Arms, Barber and Drake Families, American, 23¾ x 18¼, 19c (4146/63)   200
De St.-Memin, Charles B.F.J., Philadelphia, A GENTLEMAN, engraving with watercolor, 9 x 7,
ca1800 (4180/875)   400
Albright, D., AMERICAN SAILING SHIPS, cliffs in background, 9 x 10¼, May 21, 1814 (4180/803)   200
American School, 19c, S.S. VIRGINIAN, 15¼ x 21¼, watercolor (654/388)   350
Anonymous, YOUNG BOY, 5⅛ x 4¼, 19c (4180/843)   150
Anonymous, abstract arrangement of houses, trees, 11½ x 12¼ (4180/823)   950
Anonymous, A GIRL WEARING A BLACK DRESS, watercolor, 5¼ x 6¾, 19c (4076/220)   350
Anonymous, BATTLE OF NEW ORLEANS, 1815, 15½ x 25¼, rare (4209/23)   6750
Anonymous, BIRDS AND FLOWERS, brilliant tones, watercolor, 12¼ x 8½, 19c (4268/990)   250
Anonymous, CAPITOL OF THE UNITED STATES, 12½ x 16½, on velvet, holes (4209/29)   1100
Anonymous, HESSIAN SOLDIER, holding a hatchet, 9¾ x 7 (4180/794)   250
Anonymous, Portraits, pair, miniature, oval, 4 x 3⅛, M19c (4180/761)   650
Anonymous, PORTRAIT OF A GENTLEMAN, full length, 19c, 11 x 74, discolor (4209/117)   500
Anonymous, PORTRAIT OF A GENTLEMAN, ¾ view, ca1830, 6¼ x 5¼ (4209/98)   400
Anonymous, River scenes, pair, 14¼ x 19 (4180/830)   350
Anonymous, THE UNITED STATES CAPITOL, 19c, 14½ x 17, on velvet (4209/102)   550
Anonymous, THREE BIRDS, stellate designs, Pa.*, 13 x 15¾, 19c (4268/1000)   350
Anonymous, TURKEY, TWO STAGS, etc., watercolor on paper, 13½ x 14¾, E19c (4268/999)   325
Anonymous, VIEW FROM PAWCATUCK ACADEMY, 8¾ x 11½ (4180/836)   150
Anonymous, watercolor, FILM CITY, SHARK RIVER, N.J., aerial view, 36 1/5 x 59, E20c (4268/997) 800
Anonymous, Continental*, Cavalry Officers, brilliant uniforms, 5½ x 8½, E19c (4180/827)   400
Anonymous, Lancaster County*, Flowers in a vase, 9½ x 7¼, ca1830 (4180/773)   475
Anonymous, MOURNING PICTURE, MEMORY OF ELIZABETH & ALEXANDER, ca1820, 17 x 22½
(4209/5)   650
Anonymous, M19c, MOTHER AND CHILD, M19c, 23½ x 18 (4211/724)   550
Anonymous, N.Eng.*, PICTURE OF A YOUNG GIRL, ca1830, 4¾ x 7⅜ (4209/95)   1100
Anonymous, N.Eng.*, PORTRAIT OF A LADY, CHAIR, CAT, ca1830, 8½ x 6¾, creases (4209/91)   750
Anonymous, N.Eng.*, TWELVE DIFFERENT STAGES OF LIFE, L18-E19, 13 x 15, rare (4209/81)   1000
Anonymous, N.Eng.*, TWO LADIES IN A LANDSCAPE, ca1830, 10 x 17⅜, foxing, stains (4209/63)   650
Anonymous, N.Eng.*, watercolor, THE BASKET OF FLOWERS, ca1830, 9 x 11¼ (4209/97)   900
Anonymous, N.Eng.*, watercolor, THE FLUTED BOWL, ca1830, 9¾ x 13½, discolor (4209/88)   550
Anonymous, N.Eng.*, 1778-1821, family record, Jonathan & Sarah S. Hannah, 9 x 10¾, discolor,
tear (4209/105)   1300
Anonymous, N.Eng.*, 2, PICTURES OF CONTEMPLATION, woman, shepherd, 8 x 10, ca1830
(4209/114)   550
Anonymous, N.Eng.*, FAMILY IN A LANDSCAPE, mother, 3 small children, 14 x 18, ca1820
(4268/1034)   450
Anonymous, N.Eng.*, HAGAR AND ISHMAEL, in wilderness, waterfall, 15½ x 19, ca1820
(4268/1035)   650
Anonymous, N.Eng.*, MOSES IN BULL RUSHES, vivid tones, contemporary, costumes, 16 x 19,
ca1820 (4268/1033)   950
Anonymous, N.Eng.*, THE AGONY IN THE GARDEN, Christ with Angel, 14 x 18½, ca1830
(4268/1036)   1900
Anonymous, N.Eng.*, THE CASTLE GATE, with cows, bridge over river, 10½ x 13½, ca1830
(4268/1037)   650
Anonymous, Pa.*, Commodore Deladore and Die Gute Mutter, pair, 6 x 5⅞, E19c (4180/822)   1600
Anonymous, Pennsylvania*, E19c, Napoleon, on horseback, lush background, 11 x 9½ (4211/713)   550
Anonymous, N.Eng.*, PICTURE OF AN INN, ca1830, 10 x 12½, creases, foxing (4209/13)   1500
Bredel, A., CAMP CONVALESCENT, VA., Union soldiers, 19c, 9½ x 13⅜, paper loss (4209/89)   450
Citizenship document, Elisha Snow, sketches of Boston, slave ship Polly in border, 13 x 10⅝, 1827
(4268/935)   800
Cunningham, Wm. A., 13th U.S. Inf., JACKSON BARRACKS, LA., rare watercolor, 13½ x 16½, L19c
(654/254)   *900*
Davis, J.A., Mass., PORTRAIT OF A LADY, ¾ view, ca1830, 4½ x 4¼, fine (4209/74)   1300
Davis, J.A., N.Eng., PORTRAIT Of A GENTLEMAN, ca1830, 5⅛ x 4⅛, fine (4209/18)   1100
Davis, J.A., N.Eng., PORTRAIT OF A YOUNG BOY, ca1830, 4 x 4⅝, fine (4209/40)   900
Davis, J.H., attrib., THE FESSENDEN FAMILY, in living room, 9 x 14¼, ca1835 (4268/1027)   2200
Davis, J.H., N.H., portrait, GILBERT GUSTAVUS KNOWLTON, full-length, 1836, 9¾ x 6¾ (4209/65) 3750
Davis, Joseph, PORTRAIT OF A CHILD, John A. Adams, 1834, 4 x 5½, fine (4209/34)   *2600*
Davis, Joseph, PORTRAIT, ALMIRA CLARK, ca1835, 9½ x 6½, discloration (4209/15)   2300

Cunningham (654/254)

Davis (4209/34)

Dyer, Candace, Conn., Simsbury, SCHOOLGIRL'S SENTIMENT, 1797, 16 x 21¾, foxing, tears (4209/32) — 2500

Ellsworth, James S.,N.Eng., PORTRAIT OF A YOUNG GIRL, ca1830, 3⅝ x 2⅜, fine (4209/47) — 1200

Fay, Capt. John G., N.Y., group, 6, Civil War, Union Army, S.C., ca1863, 5¼ x 8½, sketches (4209/56) — 950

Fay, Capt. John G., N.Y., group, 6, Civil War, Union Army, Va. ca1863, 6¾ x 9, sketches (4209/55) — 750

Goldsmith, Deborah, N.Y., Oneida, FAMILY GROUP, Lyman Day, 9 x 8¾, fine, rare (4209/10) — 29000

Hayes, Sarah M.,N.Eng.*, MOUNT VERNON & WASHINGTON'S TOMB, ca1830, 13¾ x 17½ (4209/86) — 950

Hodge, W.H., Mass., Newburyport, TREE OF LIFE, L18c, 9¾ x 7⅜, discolor (4209/42) — 400

Hosier, BROADWAY, TRINITY AND GRACE CHURCH, 16½ x 21¼ (4156/248) — 300

Landes, Johannes, Pa., ADAM AND EVE AND THE SERPENT, creased, 11¼ x 15½, ca1815 (4180/752) — 1200

Landes, Johannes, Pa., FARM SCENE, creased, 12¼ x 15½, ca1820 (4180/753) — 175

Lange, E., LONG ISLAND SOUND, house on a bluff, 13¼ x 20, 1877 (4180/780) — 700

Lenher, Levi, S.E. Pa., set of 2, AMERICAN EAGLE, 1832, 6 x 8 (4209/64) — 1400

Maentel, Jacob, attrib, HENRY PETER STICHER, 6 x 5¼, 19c (4076/215) — 40760

Maentel, Jacob, watercolor, ca 1830, YOUNG MOTHER AND CHILD, 9½ x 14½ (4211/686) — 11000

Maentel, Jacob, S.E. Pa., PORTRAIT OF YOUNG GENTLEMAN, 1810, 11½ x 7⅜, discolor (4209/31) — 7250

Marble, Polley, Mass.*, 1739, VALENTINE, THE LADY CHOICE, 14½ x 13, unusual (4209/2) — 400

Noel, N.P., OUR OLD HOME IN ST. CLOUD, MINN., watercolor on paper, 19c, 15¾ x 20 (4209/268) — 4200

Parsons, Charles, attrib., 1821-1910, THE CLIPPER SHIP FLYING CLOUD, 19¼ x 28, watercolor on paper (4268/934) — 800

Pinney, Eunice, Conn., THE FOND FAREWELL, ca1815, 12½ x 13, fine (4209/72) — 3500

Rademacher, C., FISHING FROM AN ISLAND,1813, 3 x 4, watercolor (654/399) — 40

Rawell, S.,N.Eng.*, portraits, pair, E.A. Johnson, watercolor ca1840, 3⅛ x 2⅝ (4209/21) — 450

Richardson, W.,N.Eng., 1796-1836, FAMILY TREE, 16⅝ x 13, fine (4209/3) — 2200

Richardson, William,N.Eng., family tree, 19c, 8½ x 6¾ (4209/83) — 550

Rowell, Sam'l, Mass., Amesbury, PORTRAIT OF A GENTLEMAN, profile, bust, 184-, 4 x 2⅞, watercolor (4209/104) — 250

Suplee, Thomas, THE PELICAN, watercolor on paper, gray, beige, Pa., 14¾ x 13½, E19c (4268/998) — 200

Walber, T.B., POTOMAC ARMY INTO RICHMOND, ca1864, 8¾ x 12½, rare (4209/11) — 4250

Walton, Henry, N.Y.*, PORTRAIT OF A LADY, ca1840, 7½ x 5½ (4209/109) — 1300

Weber, Carl, BY A POND, 11½ x 19, watercolor (654/371) — 200

Weber, Carl, RIVER LANDSCAPE & WATERING COWS, A PAIR, 13½ x 26, watercolor (654/361) — 275

Woodside, Joseph A., attrib., MR. AND MRS. FANSEEN HOUSE, pair, 6¼ x 4½, ca1810 (4180/873) — 825

American Furniture

Pilgrim Century

Armchair, turned maple, rush-seat, ring-and-vase-turned posts, ball feet, Conn.*, 1680-1700 (4076/1391) — 550

Armchair, carver, ash and oak, mushroom finials, N.Eng., ca1670 (4156/318)   300

Armchair, carver, Mass.*, turned cross member and spindles now on, rockers, 1690-1710 (4268/757)   250

Blanket chest with drawer, lift-top, carved oak and pine, painted, rep, Conn., 1690-1710, 33½ x 45¾ (4209/324)   20000

Box, Bible, carved pine and oak, molded, cleated top, initials 'HS 1716', Conn. Valley*, ca1716 (4156/315)   5500

Box, Bible, carved, painted pine, with stylized tulips, initials 'RC 1685', L28½, E.Mass.* (4156/306)   3250

Candlestand, single-light adjustable, ash, Long Island*, stick legs, 35½, ca1700 (4149/230)   *800*

Candlestand
(4149/230)

Chairs (4156/341)

Chest (4180/1051)

Chair, wainscot, oak, carved, 1650-1700 (4076/1043)   450

Chest, Hadley, carved oak and pine, case with 3 reserves, 37½ x 44, ca1680 (4076/1337)   9000

Chest, Hadley, oak and pine, carved with stylized leafage and scrolls, 36 x 45¾, Mass., 1680-1710 (4076/1288)   17000

Chest, lift-top, cleated oak, front and stiles carved sunbursts, fans, 28 x 53¼, 17c (4180/1051)   *2400*

Chest, lift-top, oak, pine, carved, stylized leafage, scrolls, 30 x 44¾, E.Mass., ca1680 (4156/304)   7500

Chest, pine, oak, painted, carved, with scrolls, flowers, initials 'RS 1685', 31¾ x 53¼ (4156/326)   18000

Chest, sunflower, oak and maple, carved with stylized tulips, scrolls, 36½ x 48, Conn., 1690 (4156/322)   12000

Chest over drawers, lift-top, oak, Mass., carving, 2 long drawers, 46 x 44 x 19¼, res, 1680-1710 (4268/1256)   10000

William and Mary

Armchair, banister-back, cherrywood, Conn., heart, crown crest, 4 uprights, res, 1700-40 (4268/1293)   500

Armchair, banister-back, maple, Conn.*, painted black, splint seat, 1730-60 (4268/748)   250

Armchair, bannister back, painted, N.Eng., black, splint seat, turned legs, E18c (654/579)   400

Armchair, carved cane-back, scrolling arched crest, res, L17-E18c (4211/840)   700

Armchair, carved cherrywood, banister back, N.Eng., 1720 (4211/783)   800

Armchair, carved walnut, cane back within molded frame, Flemish*, ca1700 (4156/329)   3750

Armchair, ladder-back, turned, painted maple, ball feet, legs restored, N.Eng., 18c (4209/368)   800

Armchair, maple banister-back, turned and painted, Conn. or R.I., ca1725 (4156/313)   950

Armchair, rush-seat banister-back, painted with arum lilies, turned, Mass., ca1710 (4209/320)   2750

Armchair, turned maple, bannister back, 4 splats, M18c (684/705)   275

Armchair, R.I.*, banister-back, pine, maple, turned, res., 1720-40 (654/716)   225

Blanket chest, painted pine, lift-top, incised ball feet, 25 x 46, 18c (684/785)   200

Blanket chest, lift-top, Pa.*, walnut, 26½ x 44, E18c (4076/968)   1100

Bureau, slant-front, carved mahogany, fitted interior, ball feet, 40 x 36, ca1780 (684/609)   1000

Candlestand, octagonal-top, painted pine, chamfered stand, cruciform base, 26¼ x 13½, E18c
(4209/308)   1100
Candlestand, turned and ptd. pine, maple, circ. top, cruciform base, H25¼, D15, ca1710
(4076/1309)   275
Candlestand, two-light, adjustable, walnut, cruciform trestle base, 34½, 18c (4076/1298)   550
Chair, rocking, turned maple, ladder-back, rush-seat, 18c (684/726)   400
Chair, side, grained banister-back, pierced, scrolled cresting, Mass., ca1720, rare (4156/321)   4250
Chair, side, painted, cupid bow crestrail, vase shaped splat, ca1750 (684/776)   100
Chair, side, rush-seat, banister back, Mass., pierced crestrail double-ball feet, res, 1690-1720
(4268/822)   1200
Chair, side, rush-seat, banister-back, Mass., pierced crestrail, vase-turned legs, 1690-1720
(4268/818)   1600
Chair, side, turned maple and oak, rare, uphol., baluster-turned legs, stretcher, 1680-1710
(4076/1335)   2400
Chairs, side, banister back, pair, N.Eng., 3 uprights, splint seats, painted black, E18c (4268/858)   450
Chairs, side, banister-back, maple, pair, rush-seat, N. Eng., ca1730 (4156/341)   *900*
Chest, blanket, carved walnut, lift-top, Pa., res, E18c, 23 x 47¼ (4211/773)   325
Chest of drawers, ball-foot, pine, painted, 2 small drawers, 3 long drawers, Conn., 39 x 37¾ x 21
(4209/326)   5000
Chest-over-drawers, lift-top, painted pine, ball-turned feet, 45½ x 39, E18c (4209/345)   1300
Desk, table, pine, slant-front, four pigeon holes, single long drawer, 17 x 24⅜, N.Eng., E18c
(4156/298)   1700
Desk on frame, slant-front, walnut, Germantown*, 2 parts, Herpster brand, 38⅛ x 34¾ x 20¾, rep,
ca1710 (4268/816)   7000
Desk on frame, slant-top, rare, ring-and-baluster turned legs, ball feet, 33½ x 32¾, 1700-20
(4076/1386)   5500
Highboy, flat-top, burl walnut, Mass., 2 parts, graduated drawers, 62½ x 37½ x 20, res, ca1720
(4268/763)   2100
Highboy, flat top, cherry, 2 parts, 8 drawers, 62½ x 37, M18c (684/798)   1200
Highboy, inlaid burl walnut flat-top, two parts, restoration, 67 x 39¼, E. Mass., 1700-20 (4156/328)   15000
Lift-top chest, painted, grained, N.Eng., ball feet, 2 drawers, 40¾ x 37, ca1700 (4209/309)   3500
Lowboy, inlaid walnut, oblong top, Victorian backboard, 34 x 30½ x 20¼, ca1710 (4211/1252)   5000
Side chairs, set of 6, assembled, turned, painted, maple, banister-back, rush-seat, some restorations
(4209/319)   5000
Table, drop-leaf, walnut, 2 parts, cabriole legs, pad feet, 69 x 39, ca1760 (684/642)   200
Table, gate-leg, walnut, large, N.Eng., 2 D-shaped drop leaves, 28½ x 62 x 70, res, 18c (4268/772)   2500
Table, gate-leg, turned walnut, sausage turned legs, long drawer, 30 x 53, Diam 52, Mass.*, ca1710
(4156/336)   3250
Table, trestle-base butterfly, sycamore and maple, drop leaves, 24½ x 37½, R.I.*, ca1700
(4156/317)   13500
Table, trestle-base, pine, rect. cleated top, Hudson River Valley*, 30¾ x 96, E18c (4076/1293)   5000

Queen Anne

Armchair, carved elm, arched crest, cabriole legs, E18c (4156/332)   1400
Armchair, carved maple, rush-seat, Spanish feet, 1730-50, Mass. (4211/799)   2000
Armchair, carved, walnut, serpentine crest, solid splat, Philadelphia, 1750-60 (4211/1277)   18000
Armchair, ladder-back, maple, Pa., 5 arched slats, painted dark green, ca1740 (4268/855)   3100
Armchair, maple, rush-seat, spooned back, solid vase-form splat, 1720-40 (4076/1367)   2500
Armchair, rush-seat, maple, N.Eng., solid splat, Spanish feet, ca1740 (4268/821)   2000
Armchair, turned maple painted black, splint seat, N.Y.*, res, 1750-1800 (4211/861)   450
Armchair, turned painted maple, rush-seat, Mass., 1740-50 (4156/320)   2400
Armchair, walnut, cupid bow crestrail, John Elliott*, Philadelphia, ca1750 (4211/1272)   30000
Armchair, wing, slipper foot, walnut, canted back, scrolled wings, Philadelphia, 1730-40 (4211/1267)   32500
Candlestand, cherrywood, ring and baluster-turned standard, tripod legs, 27 x 16½, N.Eng., ca1750
(4156/338)   600
Candlestand, cherrywood, N.Eng. circular top, pestle-turned standard, 27¾ x 16¾, res, ca1780
(4268/726)   350
Candlestand, cherrywood, birdcage, N.Y.*, 26½ x 19, M18c (4211/808)   450
Candlestand, dish-top, walnut, arched tripod, snake feet, 27 x 20¾, ca1750 (4211/1266)   5000
Candlestand, inlaid cherrywood, Conn.*, square top, tripod, snake feet, 26 x 15½, ca1780
(4268/832)   900
Candlestand, maple, turned, painted, N.Eng., with gilding, 26½ x 16, 1770-90 (4209/343)   700
Candlestand, painted and decorated, circular top with stellate device, H25½, 17, 18c (4211/796)   500
Candlestand, painted and grained, N.Eng.*, res, 1770-90 (4211/778)   275
Candlestand, tilt-top, cherrywood, N.Eng., ring and spirally carved standard, 29 x 21¾, res, ca1780
(4268/727)   450
Candlestand, tilting dish-top, Philadelphia, vase-turned standard, tripod, 28¼ x 19¼, 1740-60
(4268/1220)   2200

Candlestand, turned cherrywood, arched tripod, snake feet, 24¼ x 16¼, res (4149/266)   400
Candlestand, turned cherrywood, circular top, N.Eng. 19c, 27½ x 19, 18c (4211/849)   450
Candlestand, turned cherrywood, tripod ending in carved toes, 23 x 17, ca1760 (4149/238)   *750*
Candlestand, N.Eng., cherry, circular, pestle standard, snake feet, H28, Diam 14¾, 1750-80 (654/595)   450
Chair, arm, ladder-back, turned, curly maple, 5 arched slats, ball feet, Pa. 1730-40 (4076/1292)   1400
Chair, arm, ladder-back, turned, maple, 5 arched slats, mushroom feet, Pa., 1730-40 (4076/1294)   2500
Chair, arm, maple, N.Eng., inverted and carved crestrail, turned support, 1730-50 (4076/1346)   1800
Chair, arm, ptd. and grained, rare, spooned back, vase-form splat, Spanish feet, Mass., 1725-40 (4076/1344)   2500
Chair, arm, turned maple mushroom, N.Eng., 1720-40 (4076/1303)   1000
Chair, arm, turned maple, rush-seat, shaped crestrail, beed and reel stretcher, 1740-50 (4076/1354)   1700
Chair, arm, walnut, rare, Wm. Savery, spooned back, vase-form splat, balloon seat, Phila., ca1740 (4076/1289)   40000
Chair, arm, wing, walnut, fine, arched back, balloon seat, cabriole legs, 1730-50 (4076/1329)   13000
Chair, corner, carved walnut, Md., horseshoe-shaped backrest, 2 solid splats, ca1790 (4268/1186)   2700
Chair, corner, cherrywood, Conn.*, horseshoe backrest, molded crest, ca1750 (4268/1161)   7000
Chair, corner, high-back, rare, carved cherrywood, vase-form splat, R.I., 1740-50 (4076/1274)   5000
Chair, corner, mahogany, horseshoe backrest, Newport, res, ca1750 (4211/1280)   6500
Chair, corner, maple rush-seat, horseshoe backrest, N.Eng., ca1750, fine (4156/323)   7250
Chair, rocking, painted and decorated, ladder-back, splint seat, 18c (684/558)   75
Chair, rocking, turned and painted, maple ladder-back, splint-seat, ca1800 (684/568)   75
Chair, side, balloon seat, walnut, N.Eng., Mass.*, spooned back, 1740-60 (4180/988)   3000
Chair, side, carved walnut, baluster splat, cabriole legs, pad feet, 1750-70 (4076/1313)   400
Chair, side, carved walnut, Pa., 1740-60, vase form splat, (4211/752)   1600
Chair, side, carved walnut, Philadelphia, cupid's bow crestrail, ca1750 (4180/1003)   1500
Chair, side, carved walnut, Philadelphia, vase form splat, trifid feet, ca1750 (4180/1010)   2500
Chair, side, carved walnut, pad feet, Philadelphia, cupid's bow crestrail, ca1740-50 (4180/1042)   1100
Chair, side, cherrywood, spooned back, solid vase-form splat, Conn., 1740-50 (4076/1403)   1500
Chair, side, cherrywood rush-seat, reed and trumpet legs, N. East, 1750-1800 (4156/309)   650
Chair, side, curly maple, rush-seat, bead and reel frontal stretcher, Mass.*, 1740-60 (4156/297)   5500
Chair, side, maple, yoked crestrail, solid baluster splat, Conn., 1720-50 (4076/1383)   2000
Chair, side, maple ladder-back, turned finials, 5 slats, rush-seat, Delaware, 1750-75 (4156/290)   475
Chair, side, maple, leather covered, Mass., owned by William Williams, Decl., of Ind. (4180/965)   3500
Chair, side, rush-seat, maple, ash, yoked cresting, N. East, 1750-1800 (4156/300)   550
Chair, side, solid vase-form splat, R.I. or Mass., block, ring-turned stretchers, ca1750 (4180/1012)   4250
Chair, side, walnut, Mass., solid vase-form splat, ca1750 (4211/815)   *1400*

Candlestand (4149/238)

Chair (4211/815)

Chair, slipper, rush-seat, turned, painted, vase-form splat, Conn., 1750-80 (4209/362)   450
Chairs, set of 10, turned maple, rush-seat, spoon back, solid vase-form splat, 1730-50 (4076/1365)   11000
Chairs, side, pair, cedarwood, arched crestrail, carved brush feet, Bermudian, M18c (4076/1305)   1900
Chairs, side, pair, cherrywood, maple, spooned back, vase-form splat, pad feet, 1730-80 (4076/1333)   2100
Chairs, side, pair, Mass., maple, carved, fine, 1740-50 (4076/1053)   3500
Chairs, side, pr, N.Eng. carved walnut and cherry wood, solid splat, rep and res, 1730-60 (4268/717)   1600

Chairs, side, set of 3, Philadelphia, curly walnut, carved, fine, 1750-70 (4076/973)   12000

Chairs, side, set of 4, walnut, cupid's bow crest, solid splat, Philadelphia, 1740-60 (4211/1276)   20000

Chairs, side, set of 4, walnut, John Elliott*, Philadelphia, ca1750 (4211/1271)   19000

Chest of drawers, carved early maple, Mass., 4 graduated drawers, 38½ x 37½ x 19¼, res, 1750-1800 (4268/779)   1400

Chest of drawers, cherrywood, lower drawer carved with concave shell, fine, 32 x 32¾, Conn., 1750-70 (4156/340)   4000

Chest of drawers, inlaid walnut, N.Eng., H36¼, L38¼, 18c (4146/193)   750

Chest of drawers, inlaid walnut, N.Eng., upper section of a highboy, 36¼ x 38¼, 18c (4180/962)   700

Chest on frame, carved walnut, 3 short, 4 long drawers, frame with drawer, ca1750 (684/744)   3000

Chest on frame, flat-top, maple, N.Eng., 5 graduated drawers, frame later, 50¾ x 41½ x 19¾, ca1780 (4268/854)   750

Chest on frame, maple, N.Eng., oblong top, scallop apron, cabriole leg, 55¼ x 41, altered, ca1750 (4076/901)   650

Chest on frame, walnut, flat-top, Philadelphia, 5 small drawers over 3 long, 62¼ x 41, ca1760 (4180/1014)   3500

Chest on frame with drawers, flat-top, walnut, 2 sections, 76 x 40 x 22½, 1750-70 (4211/1223)   11500

Corner chair, rush-seat, turned, painted, maple, bead-and-reel stretcher, Conn. (4209/328)   3000

Corner chair, turned and painted, maple, rush-seat, N.Eng., M18c (4211/803)   900

Corner cupboard, barrel-back, carved and painted, exterior red, inside blue, 88½ x 32½, 18c, N.Eng. (4211/746)   800

Corner cupboard, barrel-back, pine, carved, painted, N.Eng., H85, W49 ca1750 (4146/290)   1700

Cupboard, carved and painted pine, painted blue-green, 52⅜ x 29 x 15½, N.Eng., 18c (4211/800)   900

Cupboard, corner, N.Eng.*, pine, barrel-back, 6' 9½ x 39½, res, 1725-50 (4076/954)   1300

Cupboard, hanging wall, walnut, rare, molded cornice, scalloped apron, lower shelf, 38½ x 26½, Pa. (4076/1404)   3900

Daybed, cherrywood, solid baluster splat, cabriole legs, pad feet, 66½, 1740-50 (4076/1327)   4250

Desk, block front, mahogany, hinged lid, fitted interior, Mass., 42¼ x 36, ca1750 (4211/1269)   50000

Desk, slant-front, walnut, Mass., inlaid lid, 4 graduated drawers, 40 x 36 x 19, res, E19c (4268/1168)   1600

Desk, slant-front, walnut, Mass., stepped interior, 4 graduated drawers, 43 x 39¼ x 20¾, 1750-60 (4268/1154)   5500

Desk on frame, slant-front, miniature, carved cherrywood, chestnut, rare, 39½ x 24¾, N. Eng., ca1740 (4156/330)   9500

Desk on frame, slant-front, cherrywood, Conn., valanced pigeon-holes, drawers, 43 x 38 x 21, rep, 1740-80 (4268/741)   8250

Desk on stand, curly maple, slant-front, miniature, 2 parts, 38½ x 24, alt, ca1760 (684/693)   1600

Highboy, bonnet top, mahogany, two parts, removable legs, 90½ x 40½ x 21¼, res, 1750-60 (4211/1245)   *15000*

Highboy, flat-top, Mass. or N.H., maple, carved, carved fan, 74 x 38¼ x 19, 1740-70 (654/655)   6500

Highboy (4211/1245)

Highboy, bonnet-top, cherrywood, swan's neck cresting, cabriole legs, pad feet, 88 x 39, 1750-80
(4076/1321)   7500

Highboy, bonnet-top, cherrywood, Conn., 2 married parts, swan's neck cresting, 83 x 36½ x 20,
ca1750 (4268/1229)   4000

Highboy, bonnet-top, mahogany, N.Eng., 2 parts, swan's neck cresting, carved, 73 x 40 x 20½,
ca1750 (4268/1285)   31000

Highboy, carved cherrywood, Conn., bonnet-top, flower, shell carvings, 89½ x 41¼, fine, 1740-80
(4180/1075)   19000

Highboy, flat-top, burl walnut, rare, molded cornice, herringbone cross-banding, 65½ x 40¼, ca1736
(4076/1373)   16000

Highboy, flat-top, carved maple, N.Eng., 5 graduated drawers in upper, 75¼ x 39 x 19¼, ca1750
(4268/817)   8500

Highboy, flat-top, carved walnut, N.Eng. or Pa., 2 parts, different origins, 70½ x 39½ x 21¾, res, 18c
(4268/771)   1700

Highboy, flat-top, carved, curly maple, 2 parts, pierced skint, 72 x 36 x 20, res, 1750-75 (4211/1167)   5250

Highboy, flat-top, cherrywood, Conn., carved sunburst, 66¼ x 37½, 1760-90 (4180/981)   9500

Highboy, flat-top, cherrywood, Conn., 2 parts, upper with 4 graduated drawers, 71 x 39 x 20½,
ca1740 (4268/1296)   9000

Highboy, flat-top, cherrywood, N.Eng., 2 parts, base fan-carved, married parts, 72½ x 39¼ x 21, res,
ca1740 (4268/853)   2000

Highboy, flat-top, cherrywood, 2 parts, angular cabriole legs, N.Eng., 72¼ x 38¼ x 21¼, res, 1750-
80 (4211/1214)   3000

Highboy, flat-top, maple, 2 parts, molded cornice, cabriole legs, N.H., 70¼ x 38½ x 19¼, 1760-90
(4211/1191)   7000

Highboy, flat-top, maple and cherrywood, 2 married parts, N.H., 73 x 39½ x 18¾, res, 1760-80
(4211/1195)   2200

Highboy, flat-top, maple, cherrywood, Conn. or R.I., 5 drawers over 3 drawers, 67 x 37 x 18, rep,
1740-70 (4268/1309)   8500

Highboy, flat-top, maple, cherrywood, N.Eng. top of different origin, 62½ x 38¼ x 21½, ca1750
(4268/742)   2500

Highboy, flat-top, walnut, molded cornice, scalloped skirt, Spanish feet, Pa. or N.J., 1740-60
(4076/1387)   4750

Highboy, flat-top, Conn., curly maple, cherrywood, 68¼ x 39, 1740-60 (4076/957)   4400

Highboy, flat-top, Dunlap, N.H., curly maple, carved, 72¼ x 38¼, 1750-1800 (4076/986)   *9000*

Highboy, slip foot, curly maple, 2 parts, concealed lock device, 67½ x 38¼ x 21½, res, ca1750
(4211/1241)   4500

Highboy, slipper-foot, C. Townsend, carved walnut, molded cornice, cabriole legs, 70 x 38½, ca1750
(4076/1276)   20000

   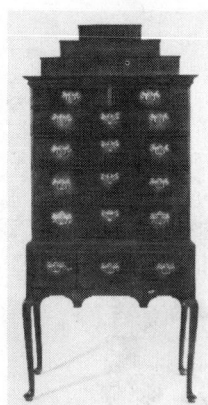   

Highboy (4076/986)   Highboy (4211/1257)   Table (4211/844)

Highboy, step-top, carved mahogany, 2 parts, shaped skirt, cabriole legs, 80½ x 38, res, 1740-60 (4211/1257) *4250*

Highboy, step-top, rare, important, carved walnut, molded cornice, shaped skirt, H80½, W38, Mass., 1740-60 (4076/1268) 13000

Highboy, walnut, maple flat-top, 2 parts, deep cornice, very fine, 69½ x 37¾, E Mass.*, 1750 (4156/324) 19000

Linen press, carved cherrywood, pine, 3 long drawers, cabriole legs, Conn., H74 12, W40¼, M18c (4146/224) 1900

Linen press, cherrywood, Conn., cavetto cornice, door, 3 graduated drawers, 74 x 41½ x 22, M18c (4159/156) 3200

Lowboy, carved maple, oblong top, valanced skirt, 29 x 32, 18c (684/786) 2750

Lowboy, carved walnut, oblong, notched corners, Mass.*, 31¼ x 34 x 20, res, 1740-60 (4211/1297) 5750

Lowboy, carved walnut, Delaware River Valley, paneled trifid feet, 29 x 33¾, ca1750 (4180/998) 12000

Lowboy, fine, carved walnut, notched corners, cabriole legs, 29 x 36, Philadelphia , ca1760 (4076/1273) 15000

Lowboy, inlaid burl walnut, oblong top, 5 drawers, carved feet, 31¼ x 33¾ x 18¾, res, 1740-50 (4211/1170) 3000

Lowboy, inlaid crotch, walnut, cabriole legs with pad feet, very fine, 29½ x 32, E. Mass.*, ca1750 (4156/325) 14000

Lowboy, mahogany, oblong, notched corners, shaped apron, Mass., 30 x 34 x 20½, ca1750 (4211/1270) 26000

Lowboy, mahogany, Philadelphia, notched corner top, shell-carved legs, 28¼ x 34 x 19½, top reset, 1750-60 (4268/1248) 10500

Lowboy, rare, small, inlaid walnut, oblong top, blocked apron, cabriole legs, 28½ x 29¾, ca1730 (4076/1320) 8250

Lowboy, walnut, notched corners, 6 drawers, Philadelphia, 30 x 33½ x 20¾, ca1740 (4211/1268) 15000

Lowboy, walnut, N.J., oblong top, 4 drawers, Spanish feet, 29½ x 33¾ x 21¼, 1730-50 (4268/1255) 11000

Lowboy, Mass., walnut, carved, fine, 30¾ x 35, 1740-60 (4076/958) 5000

Lowboy, Pa. or N.J., walnut, carved, 30 x 33, res, 1740-60 (4076/950) 7000

Mirror, carved pine and glass, shaped cresting, painted panels, 18 x 13, E18c, N.Eng.* (4156/185) 1700

Mirror, courting, painted wood, floral painted glass panel in crest, 17¾ x 11¾, fine, ca1750 (4180/851) 1600

Mirror, giltwood and gesso, rectangular, molded slip, 22 x 9½, E18c (4211/1090) 1500

Mirror, inlaid walnut parcel-gilt, scrolled cresting with gilded shell, 41¼ x 16¼, E18c (4156/319) 2700

Mirror, inlaid, parcel-gilded wood, applied gilt scrolls, 18¼ x 11¾, 18c (4156/296) 125

Mirror, wall, inlaid and parcel gilded walnut, rectangular, 55 x 22½, 18c (4211/1196) 2200

Mirror, wall, inlaid walnut, parcel-gilt applied flowers, scrolls, 34¼ x 14¼, ca1720 (4156/310) 900

Mirror, wall, inlaid walnut, shaped cresting, 57¾ x 20½, 1725-50 (4076/1302) 1300

Mirror, wall, inlaid walnut, 2 part beveled plate, molded framework, 53 x 20¾, 18c (4211/1287) 850

Mirror, wall, inlaid, walnut, rectangular, 39¼ x 23¼, res, 18c (4211/1187) 1100

Mirror, wall, walnut, scrolled cresting, 24½, ca1750 (4076/1316) 450

Mirror, wall, walnut, parcel-gilded, shaped cresting, shaped pendant below, 34½ x 14, ca1740 (4076/1349) 400

Octagonal top, snake feet, N.Eng., rep, H27, W18½, 1760-90 (4146/284) 325

Rocker, early maple, ladder-back, 5 slats in back, bead-and-reel stretcher, Pa., ca1750, res (4156/342) 900

Secretary bookcase-on-frame, rare, cherrywood, Conn. River, 83 x 42, ca1750 (4211/818) 5000

Shelf, hanging, graduated shelves, carved and painted green and red, 28 x 30½ x 5, N.Eng.*, 18c (4211/794) 600

Slipper chair, rush-seat, turned and painted maple, probably Conn., repairs, 1740-70 (4209/304) 1000

Spice cabinet-on-frame, rare, Philadelphia, walnut, 18 spice drawers, 46¼ x 19½, ca1750 (4180/1068) 74000

Stool, walnut, carved, rectangular, cabriole, L19½, M18c (4076/997) 1800

Table, card, carved walnut, (Southern) hinged top, drawer, cabriole legs, 29¼ x 35¾ x 17½, rep, 1740-70 (4268/732) 2000

Table, card, mahogany, rectangular, hinged top, Newport, 28 x 34¾ x 17, ca1750 (4211/1282) 18000

Table, center, inlaid mahogany, rectangular cleated top, 2 drawers, 30¼ x 49½ x 30¾, res, L18c (4268/1207) 1000

Table, center, two-drawer, walnut, Hudson River Valley, 30 x 53½ x 29⅜, 1750-1800 (4211/844) *1300*

Table, center, walnut, Pa., 2 molded drawers, box stretcher, 31 x 48½ x 32¼, res, ca1750 (4268/774) 600

Table, center, walnut, Pa., rounded corner top, cleated, 28½ x 65 x 35¼, rep, 18c (4268/761) 400

Table, dining, drop-leaf, oak, Irish*, carved, oblong top, stockinged trifid feet, res, 28¾ x 53¼ x 51½, M18c (4146/312) 950

Table, dining, drop-leaf, Pa., walnut, carved, trifid feet, 28½ x 47½, res, 1750-70 (654/617) 700

Table, drop-leaf, mahogany, oblong, half round leaves, R.I., 26¾ x 34¼ x 37¾, ca1750 (4211/1275) 36000

Table, drop-leaf, walnut, 2 half round leaves, scalloped apron, 28½ x 41¼ x 39½, res, 1750-70 (4211/1190)   1300

Table, drop-leaf, turned walnut, single drawer, 28¾ x 41½ x 46, M18c (4211/777)   *1750*

Table (4211/777)

Table (4211/805)

Armchair (4211/774)

Blanket chest (4211/747)

Table, drop-leaf, walnut, small, R.I.*, half round leaves, claw-and-ball-feet, 27¾ x 40¾ x 40½, rep, ca1750 (4268/864)   4500

Table, drop-leaf, walnut, N.Eng.*, 29 x 41½, res, 1740-60 (4076/921)   900

Table, drop-leaf, N.Y. or Pa., walnut, oblong top, pad feet, 26¾ x 37¾ x 44, res, 1740-60 (654/616)   500

Table, drop-leaf, turned curly maple, oval top, pad feet, N.Eng., res, 271/3 x 43½ x 41 ca1750 (4146/327)   1000

Table, gate-leg, oblong top, baluster-turned legs, ball feet, 26¼ x 34¼ x 40, Mass., 1720-40 (4076/1295)   4500

Table, gate-leg, turned walnut, oblong top, ring-and-baluster-turned legs, 29 x 48½ x 58, 1720-40 (4076/1306)   4250

Table, serving or dressing, carved fan in lower drawer, N.Eng., 33⅛ x 42¼ x 21¼, 1750-80 (4211/805)   *3300*

Table, side, block front, marble top, mahogany, serpentine, Newport, 33 x 49½, ca1750 (4211/1284)   32000

Table, side, carved cherrywood, pad feet, single long drawer, 29½ x 32¾ x 22½, N.Eng., 18c (4211/760)   900

Table, tavern turned curly maple, oval top, arched apron, Conn.*, H26, L35¼ 1740-60 (4146/325)   1400

Table, tavern, maple, oblong top, long drawer, Conn., 25 x 41, ca1750 (4156/314)   1700

Table, tavern, pine and turned maple, rectangular, single drawer, button feet, 27½ x 42½, 18c (684/544)   600

Table, tavern, walnut, Pa. oblong top, drawer, ball feet, 28¾ x 28 x 21¾, res, ca1750 (4268/806)   950

Table, tea or mixing, slate-top, ptd. cherrywood, oblong top, shaped skirt, 26 x 23¼, Conn. 1730-50 (4076/1284)   16500

Table, tea, cherrywood, Mass., molded top, cabriole legs, pad feet, 25¾ x 30¾ x 26, res, 1730-50 (4268/828)   2100

Table, tea, drop-leaf, walnut, Mass., oblong top, bowed ends, cabriole legs, 26 x 28¼ x 30, ca1750 (4268/1246)   14000

Table, tea, porringer-top, walnut, slightly-shaped skirt, round tapering legs, 25¾ x 36¼, 1740-60 (4076/1371)   3750

Table, tea, tray-top, N.Eng., cherrywood, carved, 26¾ x 27½, res, 1740-60 (4076/996)   1700

Table, tea, walnut, oblong top, scalloped apron, pad feet, 28½ x 34⅝, 18c (4076/1300)   500

Table, turned cherrywood, oval drop-leaf, shaped apron, pad feet, 26¾ x 40½ x 46½, 1750-70 (4149/283)   1300

Tall-chest of drawers-on-frame, painted, grained maple, N.H., 5 drawers, 56 x 39¾ x 20, 1770-1800 (4209/315)   5750

Tavern table, turned cherrywood, single thumb-molded drawer, N.Eng., 26¾ x 31 x 24¾, 18c (4211/758)   375

Tavern table, turned maple, N.Eng., base painted blue, 29½ x 39, ca1750 (4211/852)   2750

Tea table, oval top, maple, button feet, N.Eng., ca1750 (4211/769)   650

Tea table, pine and maple, turned, painted, pad feet, N.Eng., 27¾ x 36¼ x 23½, 1740-70 (4209/327)   3500

Tea table, tilt-top, cherrywood, N.Eng., 30¼ x 30¼, ca1770 (4211/830)   700

Wall mirror, carved walnut, good, 18c, 13½ x 7½ (4209/279)   800
Work table, turned birch and pine, cleated rectangular top, button feet, 27 x 95¼ x 30½, 18c
(4209/307)   4750

Chippendale

Armchair, carved mahogany, trumpet-form splat, cabriole legs, Prob. N.Y., 1760-80 (4076/1264)   850
Armchair, carved mahogany, Phila., pierced, gothic splat, 'knuckle' arms, ca1760-80 (4180/1040)   1600
Armchair, carved mahogany, open, canted back, upholstered back seat, Mass., ca1780 (4156/333)   3750
Armchair, carved mahogany, wing, canted back, loose cushion, upholstered, ca1780 (4149/281)   1700
Armchair, carved maple, rush-seat, pierced splat, N.Eng., ca1780 (4211/774)   *300*
Armchair, mahogany, shaped crest, pierced splat, flaring seat, Philadelphia, 1770-80 (4211/1299)   500
Armchair, open, mahogany, carved, L18c (4076/929)   500
Armchair, wing, carved mahogany, canted back, scrolled wings, ca1780 (4211/1247)   2000
Armchair, wing, carved mahogany, canted back, scrolled wings and arms, Mass., 1760-70
(4211/1278)   18000
Armchair, wing, mahogany, scrolled crest, shaped wings, ca1770 (4211/1219)   2700
Armchair, wing, mahogany, scrolled wings, scrolling arms, ca1780 (4211/1209)   2000
Armchair, wing, mahogany, serpentine crest, scrolled wings and arms, ca1780 (4211/1260)   3500
Armchair, wing, mahogany, Mass., canted back, shaped crest, scroll arms, rep, 1760-80
(4268/1222)   1600
Armchair, wing, mahogany, upholstered, arched crest, flared wings, scrolled arms, ca1790
(4268/1212)   1300
Bedstead, tester, pine, arched headboard, chintz hangings, Conn., 81 x 80 x 55½, 1750-1800
(4209/318)   5250
Blanket chest, carved and stained pine, lift-top, dummy front of drawers, 2 long drawers, 47¼ x
42¼, 19c (684/793)   175
Blanket chest, lift-top, stained pine, deep well, 2 drawers, 43 x 37½, ca1800 (684/623)   400
Blanket chest, lift-top, stained pine, 2 short drawers, brass bale handles, 28½ x 49, ca1800
(684/648)   450
Blanket chest, lift-top, painted, decorated pine, N.Y.*, 21 x 44¾ x 17½, 1817 (4209/341)   2800
Blanket chest, lift-top, miniature, painted, decorated, N.Y. State*, L19, 1810-40 (4209/344)   2400
Blanket chest, painted pine, Pa., deep well, drawers, blue, green paint, 27 x 50¾ x 22½, res, L18c
(4268/1162)   500
Blanket chest, painted pine, Pa., deep well, 3 drawers, orange, yellow paint, 26½ x 48¾ x 22½, res,
E19c (4268/1163)   650
Blanket chest, pine, painted, Pa., hinged top, breadboard ends, 26 x 54½ x 23, ca1800 (4268/1209)   250
Blanket chest, Pa., top, front and sides painted with birds, etc., 23 x 47, ca1780 (4211/747)   *750*
Bureau, slant-front, cherrywood, pigeon-holes and drawers above 4 drawers, 41 x 35½, ca1780
(684/799)   1500
Bureau, tiger maple and chestnut, slant-front, fitted interior, 4 drawers, 42½ x 36, ca1770 (684/756)   2500
Cabinet, corner, carved maple, pair fielded doors, cupboard, 82 x 45, ca1800 (684/783)   550
Candlestand, birdcage support, Philadelphia, top tilts and revolves, 27 x 21¼, rep, 1760-80
(4180/1058)   2800
Candlestand, carved cherrywood, square top, tripod standard, 27½ x 15, E19c (684/541)   275
Candlestand, dish-top, mahogany, birdcage support, tripod, Philadelphia, 29½ x 21⅝, ca1760
(4211/1281)   10000
Candlestand, dish-top, mahogany, birdcage, 27 x 25½, rep., 1760-80 (4076/1000)   375
Candlestand, dish-top, mahogany, Philadelphia, 28½ x 22, top res, 1760-80 (4148/250)   900
Candlestand, dish-top, mahogany, Philadelphia, birdcage support, 29¼ x 23½, 1760-80
(4180/1060)   3400
Candlestand, dish-top, mahogany, Philadelphia, tapering standard, 30¼ x 18, rep, 1750-70
(4268/1223)   950
Candlestand, dish-top, Philadelphia, walnut, carved, 29 x 21⅛, 1770-80 (4076/971)   2300
Candlestand, mahogany, Mass., circular top, spirally turned standard, 28½ x 15½, ca1770
(4268/1276)   1000
Candlestand, mahogany, tilt-top, Philadelphia, circular, tripod, 28¼ x 20½, 1760-90 (4268/1210)   1000
Candlestand, tilt-top, mahogany, carved, oval top, snake feet, Mass., 427¼, L21½ ca1770
(4146/318)   325
Candlestand, tilt-top, mahogany, circular, revolving, snake feet, 26½ x 24¾, res, ca1770
(4211/1173)   1400
Candlestand, tilt-top, mahogany, Mass., circular top above ring and vase, 27½ x 20¼, res, 1760-80
(4180/989)   400
Candlestand, tilt-top, mahogany, N.Eng., oblong top, notched corners, tripod, 24 x 21¼, ca1770
(4268/1272)   550
Candlestand, tilt-top, Pa., birdcage, support, 27¾ x 19½, 1760-80 (4076/992)   2700
Candlestand, tilt-top, Pa., inlaid mahogany, oval top, snake feet, 28¾ x 21¾, ca1780 (4076/1281)   2000
Candlestand, tilt-top, Pa., mahogany, carved, fine, 28 x 22½, 1760-80 (4076/990)   3250

Candlestand, turned maple, cherrywood, circ. top, snake feet, 26½ x 16, 1760-80 (4076/1315)   250
Cellarette, carved walnut, molded top, chamfered legs, Marlboro feet, H33¾, W22, Philadelphia ,
    1760-80 (4076/1265)   8000
Cellarette, curly walnut, Md., hinged lid to case above 2 drawers, 34¾ x 20½ x 17, ca1770
    (4268/1264)   7250
Chair, arm, ladder-back, mahogany, pretzel splats, square legs, Philadelphia, 1760-80 (4076/1286) 4000
Chair, corner, Conn.*, maple, carved, 1750-1800 (4076/976)   950
Chair, corner, N.Eng., walnut, horseshoe backrest, 1760-80 (4148/248)   2000
Chair, side, carved cherrywood, cupid's bow crestrail with carved fan, Mass., 1760-80 (4156/339) 850
Chair, side, carved cherrywood, leather upholstery original*, Conn., ca1770 (4211/832)   650
Chair, side, carved cherrywood, Mass., cupid's bow crestrail, pierced splat, 1770-80 (4180/1009) 650
Chair, side, carved mahogany, cupid's bow crestrail, pierced splat, Mass., res, 1760-70 (4211/1201) 1300
Chair, side, carved mahogany, Thomas Tufft, attrib., pierced, flaring splat, ca1770 (4180/1028) 1600
Chair, side, carved walnut, cupid's bow crestrail, pierced splat, rep, ca1770 (4211/1228)   200
Chair, side, carved walnut, Philadelphia, baluster splat, ca1770 (4180/1002)   2300
Chair, side, carved walnut, Philadelphia, baluster splat, seat rail lacks shell, ca1770 (4180/1000) 1300
Chair, side, fine, carved walnut, serpentine crestail, scrolling splat, Phila., 1750-70 (4076/1283) 7500
Chair, side, mahogany, cupid's bow crestrail, cabriole legs, Philadelphia, ca1760 (4076/1396)   5500
Chair, side, mahogany, shaped crest, upholstered seat, 1760-80 (4211/1262)   2750
Chair, side, mahogany, shell, leaf-carved top rail, baluster splat, M18c (4159/163)   225
Chair, side, rush-seat, cherrywood,N.Eng., cupid's bow, 1770-1800 (4076/1019)   275
Chair, side, Conn., cherry, carved, pierced baluster splat, rep., ca1780 (654/652)   225
Chair, side,N.Eng.*, cherrywood, carved, baluster splat, res., 1770-1800 (4076/1006)   500
Chair, side, Pa., mahogany, carved, Gothic splat, cabriole, 1760-80 (4076/994)   1700
Chairs, dining, set of 7, walnut, arm and 6 side chairs, pierced splats, res, 1770-80 (4211/1237) *3750*
Chairs, dining, set of 8, mahogany, 2 arm chairs, pierced splats, ca1770 (4211/1259)   8000
Chairs, side, carved cherrywood, pair, rush-seat, N.Eng., ca1760 (4211/810)   700
Chairs, side, carved mahogany, pair, baluster splat, cabriole legs, N.Y.*, rep, 1760-80 (4146/319) 650
Chairs, side, carved walnut, pair, Philadelphia, cupid's bow crestrail, ca1770 (4180/1069)   11500
Chairs, side, carved walnut, pair, Philadelphia, vase-form splat, 1760-80 (4180/995)   4500
Chairs, side, carved walnut, pair, Philadelphia, vase-form splat, 1760-80 (4180/996)   4000
Chairs, side, cherrywood, maple, pair, Conn.*, shaped crestrail, pierced splat, ca1780 (4268/838) 1900
Chairs, side, fine, pair, mahogany, 'Gothic' splat, square legs, Philadelphia, 1760-80 (4076/1359) 1500
Chairs, side, ladder-back, set of 3, Philadelphia, mahogany, carved, ca1780 (4076/988)   1100
Chairs, side, ladder-back, pair, Pa., shaped crestrail, pretzel slats, cherrywood, ca1780 (4268/804) 550
Chairs, side, mahogany, set of eight, cupid's bow crestrail, scrolled ears, Conn.*, 1760-80,
    (4156/345)   5750
Chairs, side, pair, mahogany, carved, cupid's bow crestrail, pierced splat, res., 1760-80 (654/590) 900
Chairs, side, pair, walnut, Gothic splat, bracketed square legs, Phila., 1760-70 (4076/1393)   2250
Chairs, side, pair, Pa., mahogany, carved, Gothic splat, cabriole, fine, 1760-80 (4076/993)   3500
Chairs, side, pair, Pa., walnut, carved, pretzel splat, 1760-80 (4076/991)   900
Chairs, side, pr., carved mahogany, gothic splat, square legs, res., 1760-80 (4076/906)   350
Chairs, side, set of six, Mass.*, mahogany, carved, cupid bow crestrail, 1760-80 (4076/983)   4100
Chairs, side, set of 3, pierced splat, claw and ball feet, N.Y., 1760-80 (4156/335)   7000
Chairs, side, set of 5, Mass.*, walnut, cupid crestrail, cabriole leg, 1750-70 (4076/908)   *2500*

Chairs (4211/1237)

Chairs (4076/908)

Chest of drawers
(4146/208)

Chest of drawers
(4146/207)

Chest of drawers (4156/343)

Chairs, side, 6, transitional, cherrywood, pierced vase-form splat, 1760-70 (4076/1336) 15000
Chest, blanket, lift-top, poplar, carved, painted, Pa., H27, L50, 1780-1800 (4146/200) 1300
Chest, blanket, painted and grained, lift-top, 19¾ x 37¼, res, ca1800 (4211/819) 350
Chest, blanket, Pa., carved walnut, molded hinged lid, bracket ft, 18c, 10 x 17½, res (4076/859) 700
Chest of drawers, birch, N.Eng., 4 beaded graduated drawers, 32½ x 41¼, res, ca1780 (4180/957) 1000
Chest of drawers, block front, mahogany, ogee bracket feet, 31¼ x 36¼ x 20¾, res, 1760-80 (4211/1261) 14000
Chest of drawers, block-front, fine, mahogany, oblong top, blocked bracket feet, 31¾ x 36¼, 1760-80 (4076/1328) 14000
Chest of drawers, block-front, fine, mahogany, oblong top, claw-and-ball feet, H32½, L35½, Mass., 1760-80 (4076/1290) 57000
Chest of drawers, blockfront, walnut, Boston, 4 blocked, graduated drawers, 29¾ x 35¾, ca1770 (4180/1072) 30000
Chest of drawers, carved birch, thumb-molded top, bracket feet, Mass., 36½ x 41, 1760-80 (4146/208) *1500*
Chest of drawers, carved cherrywood, Philadelphia, 4 graduated long drawers, 34 x 37¼, rep, 1770-80 (4180/997) 3500
Chest of drawers, carved curly maple, Theophilus Shove, Boston, 4 long drawers, 35 x 37¼, ca1760, (4156/343) *10000*
Chest of drawers, carved mahogany, molded top, 4 cockbeaded, graduated drawers, 35 x 39 x 22½, rep, ca1780 (4268/731) 1800
Chest of drawers, carved mahogany, Pa., rectangular top, 4 graduated drawers, 33 x 37 x 22½, res, ca1780 (4268/1188) 2400
Chest of drawers, carved mahogany, 4 graduated long drawers, molded base, 34 x 41 x 19¾, res, ca1780 (4268/720) 700
Chest of drawers, carved maple, cabriole legs, claw and ball feet, N.Eng., 37½ x 39, 1760-80 (4146/207) *650*
Chest of drawers, carved walnut, molded cornice, flaring bracket feet, 62¾ x 42¼ x 23, res, 1760-80 (4211/1163) 1700
Chest of drawers, carved walnut, Pa., Chester County*, 4 drawers, 34¾ x 38¼, 1760-80 (4180/1063) 2100
Chest of drawers, cherrywood, pine, N.Eng., 5 long, graduated drawers, 41¾ x 36¾ x 17½, res, ca1780 (4268/833) 700
Chest of drawers, curly cherrywood, rectangular top, 3 graduated drawers, 38¾ x 48¾ x 20, res, 1770 (4268/1240) 600
Chest of drawers, flat top, maple, 5 drawers, wooden pulls, was highboy top, 44 x 40, 18c (684/750) 650
Chest of drawers, mahogany, Philadelphia, top with applied molded edge, 35¼ x 41¼ x 22¼, res, 1750-80 (4268/826) 3000
Chest of drawers, mahogany, 4 serpentine drawers, claw and ball feet, 32¼ x 38¾, res, 1770 (4211/1242) 7000
Chest of drawers, mahogany, 7 drawers flanked by columns, 51 x 45, rep, ca1790 (684/566) 850

Chest of drawers, rare small size, Philadelphia, carved walnut, original brasses, 33½ x 36¼, 1760-70 (4180/1045) — 8750

Chest of drawers, reverse serpentine, Mass., carved birch, claw and ball feet, 33½ x 39½ x 20½, res, ca1770 (4268/729) — 2200

Chest of drawers, serpentine-front, carved, inlaid mahogany, graduated drawers, H33, W39¼, Mass, ca1780 (4146/231) — *4000*

Chest of drawers, serpentine-front, carved, inlaid mahogany, oblong top, RI*, 33¾ x 39 1770-80 (4146/233) — 1750

Chest of drawers, serpentine-front, cherrywood or applewood, oblong, bracket feet, 35 1/3 x 39, ca1780 (4076/1319) — 11000

Chest of drawers, tall, carved birch, N.Eng., molded cornice, 6 drawers, 55½ x 41½ x 19½, res, 1760-80 (4268/825) — 1400

Chest of drawers, tall, carved birch, N.H.*, 6 graduated drawers, fan-carved, 60½ x 40 x 19¾, res, 1770-90 (4268/765) — 900

Chest of drawers, tall, walnut, Pa., 3 small, 5 long drawers, fluted columns, 65 x 44 x 23¾, 1793 (4268/1247) — 16000

Chest of drawers, tall, Pa. 1760-70, fluted quarter columns, 58 x 44, res (4211/753) — 950

Chest of drawers, walnut, molded cornice and base, ogee bracket feet, 61 x 41¾ x 22, res, 1760-80 (4211/1231) — *3750*

Chest of drawers, walnut, Pa., fluted quarter columns, 4 drawers, 35½ x 39½ x 19¼, ca1770 (4268/1155) — 2800

Chest of drawers, walnut, Southern*, pull-out slide, fluted corners, 32 x 36½ x 21¼, 1760-80 (4268/831) — 3500

Chest of drawers, walnut, 7 drawers, columns, ball feet, 52 x 43½, ca1770 (684/649) — 1100

Chest of drawers, carved walnut, Pa., oblong top, ogee bracket ft., 38 x 37⅝, res, 1760-80 (4076/907) — 2000

Chest of drawers, Conn.*, cherrywood, 38½ x 43¼, res, 1760-80 (4076/1008) — 1600

Chest of drawers, Mass., bow-front, mahogany, carved, inlaid, 40¼ x 24¾ x 23¾, res, ca1780 (654/654) — 950

Chest of drawers, N.Eng. or N.Y., mahogany, 37½ x 43¼, 1760-80 (4076/1013) — 1200

Chest of drawers, N.Eng.*, maple, exotic wood, inlaid, scalloped apron, 37½ x 39½, rest., 1770-90 (654/591) — 350

Chest of drawers, N.Eng., cherry, oblong top, scroll-cut bracket feet, 35 x 43½, rest., ca1780 (654/581) — 700

Chest of drawers, N.Eng., maple, pine, 45 x 38, res, 1770-90 (4076/1035) — 950

Chest of drawers, Pa., walnut, carved, 61 x 39½, 1760-80 (654/721) — 2900

Chest on chest, bonnet top, mahogany, Blockfront form, 11 drawers, 84 x 38, ca1875 (684/698) — 5250

Chest on chest, bonnet-top, mahogany, Philadelphia, 2 parts, carved finials, drawer front, 90 x 44 x 22¾, 1760-80 (4268/1249) — 20000

Chest on chest, bonnet top, mahogany, 2 parts, cabriole legs, claw and ball feet, 91½ x 39½ x 21, res, 1760-80 (4211/1207) — 5750

Chest on chest, carved mahogany, Philadelphia, removable cornice, important, 99¼ x 46, 1766-80 (4180/1043) — 12000

Chest on chest, cherrywood, Marvin family, block-front, bonnet-top 2 parts, 89 x 44½, Conn., 1760-90 (4156/327) — 45000

Chest on chest, flat-top, carved walnut, 2 parts, molded cornice, ogee bracket feet, 78½ x 41¾, 1770-80 (4211/1225) — 6750

Chest on chest, flat-top, carved mahogany, coved cornice, bracket feet, 80 x 43, Philadelphia, 1760-80 (4076/1263) — 6000

Chest on chest, flat-top, mahogany, attrib. to Janvier, dentiled cornice, 68 x 43, 1795-1800 (4076/1338) — 3500

Chest on chest, flat-top, mahogany, Phila., carved, 86½ x 45½, fine, 1760-80 (4180/1008) — 10000

Chest on chest, flat-top, maple, cherrywood, molded cornice, bracket feet, 76¼ x 38, 1770-90 (4076/1399) — 4500

Chest of drawers
(4146/231)

Chest on frame, Pa., walnut, carved, valanced apron, 1760-80, 60½ x 39½ x 21½, later frame (654/713) — 1100

Chest on stand, Pa., walnut, molded top cornice, frame later date, 68 x 33¼ x 24, ca1760 (654/528) — 1400

Clothes press, maple, 3 drawers, cupboard, 56 x 46, ca1800 (684/651) — 200

Cupboard, bedside, inlaid mahogany, galleried top, 2 muck drawers, 3¼ x 21¼, L18c (4180/1065) — 350

Cupboard, corner mahogany, 2 parts, cupboard, top and bottom, 100 x 39 x 21½, altered, 18c (4211/1301) — 1400

Cupboard, corner, barrel back, pine, N.Eng., arched opening, 82 x 49 x 32½, painted, ca1770 (4268/1237) — 1600

Cupboard, corner, carved and painted pine, breakfront outline, Pa., 100 x 59½ x 21½, 1760-80 (4211/1286) — 2300

Cupboard, corner, carved walnut, 2 parts, glazed doors, cupboard, Pa., 93 x 53 x 27½, res, ca1770 (4211/1293) — *1900*

Cupboard (4211/1293)

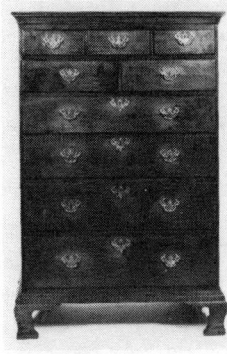

Chest of drawers
(4211/1231)

Cupboard, corner, painted pine, Md., glazed door, 2 paneled doors, 91 x 49 x 31½, ca1780 (4268/1278) — 1300

Cupboard, corner, painted pine, 2 parts, pair glazed doors, pair of fielded doors, 84½ x 60, ca1780 (684/550) — 850

Cupboard, corner, pine, 2 parts, glazed door, white painted interior, 84 x 41¼ x 22¼, res, ca1800 (4268/769) — 900

Cupboard, corner, pine, carved, glazed door, 78 x 42¼, ca1780 (654/715) — 1100

Cupboard, corner, pine, painted, grained, projecting molded cornice, 96 x 56½, 1775-1800 (4076/1394) — 5000

Cupboard, corner, walnut, Pa., 2 parts, glaze door over paneled door, 91 x 53 x 29¼, ca1770 (4268/1275) — 6000

Cupboard, corner, Pa.*, pine, stained, miniature, glazed door, 48 x 29, 19c (654/651) — 750

Cupboard, press, walnut, carved, Pa.*, 56 x 43, res, 1750-1800 (4076/1042) — 600

Cupboard, wall, cherrywood, 2-part, Pa., glazed doors, drawers, 84 x 50¾ x 18¾, res, L18/E19c (4268/810) — 2900

Cupboards, corner, pair, cherrywood, pine, dentiled cornice, flaring bracket feet, 62½ x 33, 1775-1800 (4076/1384) — 3750

Daybed, carved mahogany, canted back, shaped crestrail, L76, Conn.*, 1770-80 (4156/312) — 3000

Desk, block-front, mahogany, Mass., hinged lid, carved fan, 45¼ x 41¾, res, 1760-80 (4180/990) — 5250

Desk, ox-bow and bookcase, Mass., carved, inlaid mahogany, ogee bracket feet, 101¾ x 42, ca1780 (4146/228) — 11500

Desk, slant-front, carved cherrywood, hinged lid, cabriole legs, 35 x 38¾ x 19¼, res, 1760-80 (4211/1175) — 2500

Desk, slant-front, carved mahogany, serpentine, fitted interior, 44 x 42 x 23½, 1760-80 (4211/1189) — 4250

Desk, slant-front, carved walnut, hinged top, fitted interior, 43½ x 42¾, res, ca1780 (4211/1178) — 1600

Desk, slant-front, mahogany, hinged lid, fitted interior, Mass., 44 x 42 x 21½, 1760-80 (4211/1302) — 2600

Desk, slant-front, mahogany, reverse serpentine, stepped interior fitted, Mass., 43 x 40¼ x 21¾, res, 1760-80 (4211/1194) — 4250

Desk, slant-front, N.Eng., maple, carved, 42½ x 38, res, 1760-80 (4076/944) — 2000

Desk, slant-front, birch, serpentine, Mass., 4 graduated drawers, 41 x 41¾ x 20⅝, res, 1760-80 (4268/813) — 2900

Desk, slant-front, carved cherrywood, S.E. Conn. or R.I., 43 x 35¾, ca1770 (4211/768) — 5250

Desk, slant-front, carved curly maple, pigeon holes, ogee bracket feet, R.I., 39 x 33¾, 1760-80 (4146/254) — *1500*

Desk, slant-front, carved mahogany, Pa., pigeon holes, 4 long drawers, 41¾ x 39 x 21, res, 1760-80 (4268/815) — 2500

Desk, slant-front, carved walnut, Pa., molded lid, serpentine small drawers, 45¼ x 38½ x 19½, rep, ca1770 (4268/1198) — 5500

Desk, slant-front, carved walnut, Pa., shell-carved prospect door, 43¼ x 41 x 21¾, rep, ca1770 (4268/770) — 4000

Desk, slant-front, carved walnut, Va.* molded lid, arched pigeon-holes, 4 drawers, 43¼ x 36 x 19¼, res, 1750-80 (4268/733) — 3000

Desk, slant-front, cherrywood, N.Eng., diamond shaped medallions in lid, 43 x 42¾ x 19, res ca1780 (4268/1165) — 1200

Desk, slant-front, cherrywood, N.Eng., valanced pigeon holes, 4 long drawers, 41½ x 39½ x 18½, 18c (4268/1214) — 1000

Desk, slant-front, cherrywood, Pa., hinged lid above 4 graduated drawers, 45 x 40½ x 21¾, 1760-80 (4268/843) — 3500

Desk, slant-front, curly maple, N.Eng., hinged top, 4 graduated drawers, 41½ x 35½ x 18, M18c (4268/1261) — 4250

Desk, slant-front, curly maple, R.I., fitted interior, 4 long drawers, 40¼ x 37¼ x 17½, ca1770 (4268/1156) — 5500

Desk, slant-front, inlaid mahogany, Pa.*, pigeon holes, small drawers, 44 x 46¾ x 22½, ca1780 (4268/753) — 800

Desk, slant-front, mahogany, thumb-molded lid, gadrooned apron, N.Y., 43 x 45¼, 1760-80 (4076/1390) — 4000

Desk, slant-front, mahogany, N.Y., fitted interior, 7 graduated drawers, 43¾ x 44½ x 22¾, ca1770 (4268/1228) — 3500

Desk, slant-front, maple, numerous pigeon-holes, N.Eng., 41⅝ x 34½ x 19½, 1750-1800 (4211/780) — 2400

Desk, slant-front, walnut, Mass.*, valanced pigeon-holes, 4 drawers, 42¼ x 39¾ x 19½, M18c (4268/1231) — 4000

Desk, slant-front, walnut, Pa., shell, flowerhead carvings, 4 long drawers, 43 x 39 x 41¾, rep, ca1770 (4268/1305) — 8000

Desk, slant-front, walnut, Philadelphia, blocked serpentine, small drawers, 46¼ x 38 x 20½, res, 1760-80 (4268/1245) — 7500

Desk, slant-front, walnut, Philadelphia, shell-carved drawers, 45¼ x 38¼ x 21¾, res, ca1770 (4268/1172) — 5750

Desk, slant-front, N.Y., mahogany, claw and ball feet, 43¼ x 42, 1760-80 (4076/925) — 2800

Desk, slant-front, R.I.*, curly maple, 42¾ x 40, 1770-80 (4076/917) — 2100

Dressing glass, parcel gilded, mahogany, label of John Elliott, 24¼ x 16½, ca1760 (4180/872) — *500*

Dressing glass, walnut and parcel-gilt, rectangular, molded supports, 18⅛ x 11¾, L18c (4146/136) — 175

Highboy, bonnet top, mahogany, swan's neck crest, shell apron, Newport, 88 x 40¾ x 20¾, ca1760 (4211/1283) — 42500

Highboy, bonnet top, mahogany, 2 parts, swan neck cresting, 3 flame finials, 80 x 40½, ca1770 (684/685) — 2750

Highboy, carved cherrywood, 2 parts, Eliphalet Chapin, attrib., open fretwork, 84 x 38¼, ca1780 (4180/1006) — 35000

Highboy, carved curly maple, flat-top, molded cornice, very fine, N.H., 73 x 38, 1770-80 (4146/234) — *13500*

Highboy, carved mahogany bonnet-top, Goddard, John, Newport, attrib., important, 82¾ x 39¾, res, ca1770 (4180/1073) — 32000

Highboy, cherrywood, bonnet-top, Conn. River Valley, fan carved, 89 x 42, 1760-90 (4180/1080) — 14000

Lowboy, carved cherrywood, Conn., oblong top, cabriole legs, claw-and-ball feet, H30¼, W36¾, res 1770-80 (4146/266) — 5000

Lowboy, carved curly maple, rare, Philadelphia, claw and ball feet, 28½ x 36, 1760-80 (4180/1071) — 1800

Lowboy, carved mahogany, oblong, scalloped skirt, 29 x 34·x 21⅛, 19c (4211/1233) — 2000

Lowboy, carved walnut, scall. skirt, claw and ball feet, Philadelphia, 30 x 34½, ca1770 (4076/1339) — 15000

Lowboy, Pa., walnut, carved, cabriole leg, 27¾ x 33, res, 1770-80 (4076/989) — 3000

Mirror, carved mahogany wall, scroll-carved cresting, 20½ x 14, res (4149/289) — 200

Mirror, carved mahogany, wall, scroll carved cresting, 21 x 12½, ca1780 (4156/293) — 275

Mirror, carved, inlaid, mahogany, shaped cresting and pendant, partial label, 41 x 20½, rep, 1784-1804 (4268/800) — 800

Mirror, inlaid mahogany wall, scroll carved cresting, 26¼ x 14¼, ca1790 (4149/279) — 425

Mirror, inlaid, parcel-gilded, gilt eagle, fruit, leaf, floral fillets, 51½ x 24¼, res (4180/1001) — 1300

Mirror, swan's neck cresting, walnut, inlaid and parcel-gilded, 54 x 22½ (4180/1024) — 1800

Mirror, wall, carved, scroll-carved cresting, inlaid conch shell, 39 x 19½, 1780-1800 (4076/1361) — 600

Mirror, wall, carved and inlaid mahogany, scroll cresting, oval medallion, 32¾ x 17¾, res, ca1780 (4211/1169) — 500

Mirror, wall, carved mahogany, scroll-cut cresting, centering phoenix, gilt, 45 x 23¾, ca1770 (4156/302) 2600
Mirror, wall, inlaid mahogany, parcel gilded, scroll-carved cresting, 38¼ x 20½, ca1780 (4146/293) 500
Mirror, wall, inlaid mahogany, parcel-gilded, swan's neek cresting, 36¾ x 17¾, ca1765 (4146/220) 900
Mirror, wall, mahogany, parcel-gilded, molded swan's neck cresting, 56 x 26½, ca1770 (4076/1330) 3100
Mirror, wall, mahogany, scrolled cresting, conforming pendant below, 18½ x 11¼, 1770-1800 (4076/1343) 200
Mirror, wall, mahogany, carved, parcel-gilded, 25 x 15, res, L18c (4148/249) 425
Mirror, wall, mahogany, inlaid, parcel-gilded, 36½ x 20, res, L18c (4076/984) 600
Mirror, wall, mahogany, parcel-gilded, American eagle, H27¾, res, L18c (4076/909) 325
Mirror, wall, mahogany, parcel-gilded, cluster of Prince of Wales feathers, 49, 1760-80 (4076/1351) 1000
Mirror, wall, mahogany, parcel-gilded, scrolled cresting with phoenix, H39, 1780-90 (4076/1380) 750
Mirror, wall, mahogany, parcel-gilded, shaped cresting, pierced and gilded shell, 32 x 16½, ca1770 (4146/287) 500
Mirror, wall, mahogany, parcel-gilt, scroll-carved cresting, 50¾ x 25½, L18c (4180/1062) 1800
Mirror, wall, parcel-gilded, mahogany, leaf-carved swan's neck cresting, 50½ x 24¾, 1760-80 (4076/1407) 2200
Mirror, wall, Elliot, J., Philadelphia, mahogany, carved, 40¾ x 21¼, ca1780 (4076/972) 1600
Mirror, wall, Smith, George, Md., mahogany, inlaid, 33½ x 17¼, rep., ca1800 (4076/966) 1200
Mirrors, miniature wall, mahogany, carved, scroll-cut cresting, pair, H18½, L18c (4146/127) 400
Open dresser, 2 parts, walnut, 3 shelves over 2 doors, Pa., 84¾ x 63½, 1760-80 (4211/837) *2300*

Desk (4146/254)

Highboy (4146/234)

Dressing glass (4180/872)

Open dresser (4211/837)

Pole screen, carved mahogany, octagonal screen with needlework, 56¾ (4149/265) 125
Schrank, carved walnut, Pa., doors opening to shelves, 5 drawers below, 87 x 68 x 20½, 1786 (4268/1297) 15000
Secretary-bookcase, walnut, paneled cupboard, writing flap, drawers, 96 x 39¼ x 23¼, res, 1760-70 (4211/1258) 10000
Secretary-bookcase, bonnet-top, cherrywood, Conn. or R.I., 2 parts, carved, 91½ x 37 x 20, rep, 1760-90 (4268/740) 18000
Secretary-bookcase, carved mahogany, Mass., 2 parts, paneled doors, serpentine, 95 x 40½ x 22½, ca1770 (4268/1250) 22500
Secretary-bookcase, cherrywood, Va.*, 2 parts, swan's neck cresting, carving, 101 x 41 x 23½, res, ca1770 (4268/1213) 9500
Secretary-bookcase, flat-top, Conn., cherrywood, carved, 80¾ x 39, 1760-90 (4076/980) 3250
Secretary-bookcase, inlaid walnut, cherrywood, John Shearer, egg-and-dart molding, 106 x 41, ca1801 (4076/1341) 40000
Secretary-bookcase, painted blue, carved with shells, N.Eng., L18c (4211/809) 3000
Secretary-bookcase, walnut, swan's neck cresting, ogee bracket feet, 98¾ x 40¼, 1760-80 (4076/1340) 10000

Secretary-bookcase, walnut, Philadelphia, 2 married parts, paneled doors, 92½ x 38 x 21, 1760-80
(4268/1273)   8500
Secretary-bookcase, curly maple, N.Eng., 2 parts, married, pendant res, 91½ x 38, 1770
(4180/1020)   7000
Secretary, cabinet, mahogany, 2 parts, glazed doors, flip top writing surface, 80 x 42, M19c
(684/525)   175
Secretary, tambour-front, mahogany, 2 parts, sliding doors, drawers, 47 x 48, L19c (684/666)   900
Settee 3 chair back, walnut, crestrail, 3 elements, pierced splats, 73½, res, 1770 (4211/1232)   2750
Sidechair, carved mahogany, Mass., Cupid's bow crestail, trumpet-form splat, 1760-80 (4076/1267)   900
Sofa, camel back, carved mahogany, upholstered back, bowed front, scrolled arms, 88½, res
(4211/1251)   3750
Sofa, camel back, walnut, cutswept arms, square legs, Philadelphia, 95½, 1760-80 (4076/1342)   15000
Table, card, 5 legged, mahogany, serpentine, fitted interior, N.Y., 27¾ x 34 x 16½, ca1770
(4211/1274)   55000
Table, card, carved mahogany, John Goddard, Newport, attrib., important, 27 x 34, ca1770
(4180/1074)   40000
Table, card, cherrywood, hinged, rectangular, single drawer, N.Eng., 29¾ x 35¼ x 16⅜, res, ca1780
(4211/1288)   325
Table, tea, carved walnut tilt-top, bird cage supports, claw-ball feet, 28 x 33¾ 1770-80 (4146/215)   2000
Table, breakfast, drop-leaf, rare, cherrywood, serpentine, pierced brackets, 27¾ x 34½, ca1775
(4076/1334)   6000
Table, dining, deep drop leaves, Philadelphia, claw and ball feet, 28¼ x 53½ x 54⅛, 1760-80
(4180/1032)   4250
Table, dining, drop-leaf, carved mahogony, oblong top, claw and ball feet, 28½ x 47½ x 45, res,
1760-80 (4211/1165)   1600
Table, dining, drop-leaf, mahogany, oblong, half round leaves, 28 x 50½ x 66, 1760-80 (4211/1263)   8000
Table, dining, drop-leaf, Pa., claw and ball feet, 28½ x 40½ x 56, rep, 1760-80 (4268/762)   800
Table, dining, drop-leaf, mahogany, Philadelphia, notched leaves, claw and ball feet, 28 x 48 x 54,
ca1770 (4268/1262)   3000
Table, dining, drop-leaf, walnut, Van Kleek family, shell carved cabriole legs, 28¼ x 60¼ x 58¾,
1760-70 (4076/1398)   10000
Table, dressing, kneehole, mahogany, Boston, blocked front, secret drawer, 30½ x 35¼ x 21¾,
ca1770 (4268/1254)   41000
Table, drop-leaf mahogany, raised on square legs, 28 x 45, ca1800 (684/538)   200
Table, drop-leaf, mahogany, Pa., oblong top, cabriole legs, claw-ball feet, 28¾ x 41½ x 49½, 1750-
90 (4268/1269)   1400
Table, drop-leaf, walnut, Mass., deep drop leaves, scalloped skirt, 28¼ x 44¾ x 42½, ca1770
(4268/1203)   4000
Table, low, carved mahogany, Pa., single drawer, 17¾ x 13¾, M18c (4180/1056)   400
Table, side, mahogany, King of Prussia marble top, Philadelphia, 31½ x 37¼ x 22¼, ca1760
(4211/1279)   40000
Table, single drop-leaf, mahogany, webbed chaw and ball feet, Mass., 26½ x 30½ x 28, 1750-60
(4211/1273)   20000
Table, tea, birdcage, mahogany, Pa., circular top tips, revolves, claw-ball feet, 28 x 33, res, ca1780
(4268/1238)   900
Table, tea, dish-top, mahogany, revolving, birdcage support, 28½ x 33, res, ca1770 (4211/1256)   1900
Table, tea, dish-top, mahogany, Pa., molded, tilting top, birdcage support, 29½ x 30, ca1770
(4268/805)   1100
Table, tea, mahogany, N.Y.*, circular top, birdcage supports, club feet, 28½ x 32¼, 1760-80
(4146/251)   350
Table, tea, tilt-top, circular top, turned standard, pad feet, H27½, Diam 31, L18c (654/572)   500
Table, tea, tilt-top, cherrywood, Philadelphia, dished top, birdcage support, 29¾ x 34¼, ca1770
(4268/730)   3000
Table, tea, tilt-top, curly maple, circular molded top, snake feet, 27¼ x 31, 1760-80 (4076/1357)   2500
Table, tea, tilt-top, mahogany, circular top, ring-turned shaft, snake feet, 27½ x 35¼, 18c
(4268/1202)   400
Table, tea, tilt-top, mahogany, Pa., circular top, birdcage support, 27½ x 31⅝, res, ca1770
(4268/849)   1000
Table, tea, N.Y.*, mahogany, birdcage, 28½ x 32¼, 1760-80 (654/619)   350
Table, tilt-top, mahogany, circular top, birdcage support, pad feet, 27¾ x 22½ (654/576)   650
Table, tilt-top, walnut, circular top, bell-shaped standard, tripod, 28 x 35¾, res, ca1770 (4268/722)   475
Table, Pembroke, carved walnut, good, oblong top, square tapering molded legs, Pa.*, H28¼, L31¼,
W41 1770-90 (4146/310)   *1100*
Table, Pembroke, short drop leaves, Philadelphia, square legs, X-stretcher, 28¾ x 31¼, rep, 1760-
80 (4180/1016)   1000
Table, Pembroke, walnut, drop-leaf, Pa. or Va., oblong top, 1 drawer, X-stretcher, 27¾ x 35¾ x 42½,
ca1770 (4268/1268)   1400
Table, Pembroke, Philadelphia, mahogany, carved, 28¾ x 30¼, res, 1760-80 (4076/969)   1100

Tea table, serpentine-top, cherrywood, snake feet, repairs, 28½ x 30½, 1750-80 (4209/313) — 1200
Tea table, tilt-top, turned walnut, Pa., ca1780 (4211/776) — 650
Tea table, turned walnut, dish-top, bird-cage support, 28 x 32¾, Pa., 1760-80 (4211/798) — 3100
Tea Table, pie crust, mahogany, Mass., Salem*, tilt-top, claw and ball feet, 28¾ x 37, 1760-80 (4180/1077) — 4000
Urn stand, cherrywood, single drawer, Pa., chamfered square legs, 22¼ x 12½, ca1780 (4180/1054) — 175
Wall mirror, mahogany, scroll carved cresting, 24 x 14¼ (4211/787) — 200

Classical

Bed, gilt-wood, gesso, brass-mounted, Charles H. Lannuier, N.Y., labeled, 42½ x 96 x 57¼, ca1815 (4180/1004) — 19000
Chair, side, brass-mounted, gilded, mahogany, sabre legs, N.Y., 19c (4211/797) — 350
Chest of drawers, ebonized mahogany, N.Y., splashboard stenciled with leaves, 60½ x 46½ x 20½, ca1830 (4268/1263) — 275
Dressing glass, carved mahogany, School of Duncan Phyfe, N.Y., mirror, 39½ x 20½, 1815 (4180/1027) — 650
Mirror, girandole, giltwood, gesso, convex mirror, standing lion crest, H54 x W33½, ca1820 (4180/1036) — 3750
Recamier, mahogany, gilt-metal mounted, L74, E19c (4076/1010) — 1800
Settee, carved mahogany, N.Y., cylindrical crest, S-scroll arms, L87, ca1820 (4146/196) — 700
Settee, mahogany, Boston, scrolled arms, fluted square tapering legs, L83, ca1815 (4076/1360) — 1600
Side chairs, painted and stenciled cane seat, set of 6, ca1830, N.Eng. (4149/293) — 375
Sideboard, mahogany, rectangular top, 2 frieze drawers, cupboards, hairy paw feet, 44½ x 66 x 20, E19c (4159/138) — 1300
Sofa, carved mahogany, paw feet, School of Duncan Phyfe, N.Y., winged eagles., L85, ca1815 (4180/1037) — *3000*

Sofa (4180/1037)

Table (4146/310)

Table (4146/295)

Sofa, carved, brass mounted mahogany, Boston, paneled crestrail, brass casters, L78½, ca1820 (4268/820) — 850
Table, card, rosewood and mahogany, N.Y., gilt-brass mounts, paw feet, 30 x 35¾, ca1815 (4180/978) — 3200
Table, dressing, mahogany lyre-base, School of Duncan Phyfe, N.Y., 57½ x 36, ca1810 (4180/982) — 2500
Table, dressing, mahogany, N.Y., inlaid, curule-base, 32½ x 32½, ca1810 (4076/923) — 2250
Table, drop-leaf, library, N.Y., mahogany, carved, inlaid, castered paw feet, 29½ x 36 x 46¾, ca1820 (654/584)
Table, library, school of Duncan Phyfe, mahogany, carved, painted, oblong top, N.Y., H28¼, W35, L45¼, ca1815 (4146/295) — *750*
Table, pier, brass-mounted, mahogany, N.Y., gilt-stenciled leaves, marble-top, 34⅝ x 42 x 18, ca1820 (4268/1190) — 1100
Table, writing, mahogany, rectangular top, kneehole, spirally turned legs, 32½ x 38 x 19, E19c (4159/132) — 425

Wardrobe, carved, gilded mahogany, N.Y., shelves, dressing slides, drawers, 96 x 62½, ca1815 (4180/1005)   12500

Federal

Armchair, cane-seat, mahogany, Haines-Connelly School, Philadelphia, ca1800 (4180/1057)   3100
Armchair, carved, mahogany, Martha Washington, upholstered seat, rep, 1790-1800 (4211/1213)   1300
Armchair, open, mahogany, Mass., canted back, shaped crest, res, 1780-1800 (4268/862)   450
Armchair, rush-seat, painted, decorated, ball feet, ca1820 (4209/311)   550
Armchair, wing, carved mahogany, arched crest, square arms, loose cushion, N. Eng.*, ca1810 (4156/344)   550
Armchair, wing, curly maple, canted back, arched cresting, scrolled wings, res, ca1790 (4211/1216)   2200
Armchair, wing, mahogany, N.Y., canted back, arched cresting, in muslin, ca1815 (4268/1191)   600
Armchair, Conn., mahogany, leaf-carved urn splat, 1790-1800 (4076/1009)   700
Armchairs, carved mahogany, pair, N.Y., upholstered seat, shield-back, fine, 1800 (4180/1007)   3100
Armchairs, pr, rush-seat, painted, N.Eng., (4209/323)   1000
Armchairs, shield-back, mahogany, pair, Philadelphia, carvings of flowers, leafage, ca1800 (4180/993)   *650*
Basin stand, mahogany, quarter round top, stretcher, 38¾ x 25, ca1800 (4149/231)   200
Basin stand, mahogany, single drawer, square tapering legs, 28¾ x 13¾, ca1800 (684/774)   125
Basin stand, corner, inlaid mahogany, shaped splashboard, quarter round top, 46 x 25½, Mass., 1800 (4156/308)   1100
Bedstead, curly maple, 4-post, shaped headboard, headposts H65, W54½, E19c (4268/777)   600
Bedstead, four-post tester, mahogany, prob. Mass., 103 x 75, ca1810 (4076/1408)   3500
Bedstead, high-post tester, N.Eng., turned cherrywood, scroll-cut headboard, 86 x 54 x 78½, ca1830 (4146/265)   900
Bedstead, pencil-post tester, Pa.*, carved walnut, and pine, octagonal head, 75½ x 55¼ x 73, ca1800 (4146/323)   1400
Bedstead, tester, mahogany, shaped headboard, figure of eagle, posts 65, 44 x 78, res, ca1815 (4211/1204)   1100
Bedstead, tester, maple, pine, turned posts, has hangings, 86 x 78 x 55, N. Eng., ca1810 (4156/307)   1900
Bedstead, tester, turned maple, Roberts and Hoar, 60 x 52, E19c (684/792)   425
Bedstead, turned curly maple, scrolled head and foot boards, 60 x 55, E19c (684/628)   1500
Bedstead, N.Eng., painted and grained, 50¾ x 51½, 1815-30 (4076/953)   500
Bench, bamboo-turned, painted, grained, N.Eng., L75¾, ca1820 (4209/348)   5500
Blanket chest, lift-top, painted and grained, ball feet, prob. N.Eng., 41¾ x 40½, 1820-35 (4076/1317)   800
Blanket chest, lift-top, painted, grained, thumb-molded drawers, 38¾ x 44¼ x 17¼, 1780-1820 (4209/349)   700
Blanket chest, pine, 2 drawers, valenced apron, 40¾ x 41¾, ca1780 (4149/260)   300
Blanket chest, N.Eng., pine, painted & grained, 33 x 37¾, 1800-30 (4076/952)   500
Bookcase, desk, Mass., mahogany, 3 parts, glazed doors, tambour slides, 83 x 35¼ x 17½, 19c (654/674)   1140
Bookcase, inlaid mahogany, N.Y., bracket feet, mullioned cupboard doors, 51¼ x 32, ca1815 (4076/1363)   600

Armchairs (4180/993)   Bookcase (654/558)   Card table (4146/191)

Bookcase, lady's desk, N.Eng., mahogany, inlaid, 28¼ x 22, ca1815 (4076/1024)   500
Bookcase, lady's writing desk, mahogany, inlaid, Mass., top-different origin, 84 x 49¼, ca1800 (4148/232)   3700
Bookcase, secretary, cylinder front, mahogany, Baltimore*, 100 x 46 x 23, ca1800 (654/558)   *3000*
Bookcase, walnut, 2 glazed doors, interior with shelves, 53¼ x 42¼, ca1800 (4211/1227)   500
Bookcase, Lady's desk, Pa. or Md., mahogany, carved, inlaid, 83 x 32¾, 1810-20 (4076/960)   1100
Bookcase, Mass., N. Shore*, library, carved, mahogany, inlaid, 100 x 75 x 26, ca1800 (4148/263)   16000
Butler's desk, pull-out drawer, with pigeon holes, Conn., 45 x 40⅛ x 20⅛, ca1800 (4211/829)   900
Candlestand, carved, inlaid mahogany, N.Y.*, 28¾ x 25⅞ x 18⅝, ca1800 (4211/839)   450
Candlestand, cherrywood, maple, almost square top, snake feet, 25 x 15¼, ca1800 (4076/1347)   325
Candlestand, circular, maple, molded top, flat cabriole legs, snake feet, 22½ x Diam 15, L18c (4159/127)   350
Candlestand, inlaid cherrywood, ring and double vase-turned standard, 26¾ x 12½ (4076/1366)   900
Candlestand, inlaid mahogany, N.Eng., tilt-top, ring-vase standard, tripod, 27¼ x 21, ca1800 (4268/1271)   1400
Candlestand, inlaid mahogany, Dunlap, oval top, pattern stringing, spade feet, 29¼ x 18, ca1800 (4076/1372)   5500
Candlestand, mahogany, Pa.*, octagonal top, ring and vase standard, 29 x 23½ x 17½, ca1810 (4268/1179)   275
Candlestand, mahogany tilt-top, 28 x 22, 19c (4211/828)   600
Candlestand, mahogany, cherrywood, rectangular top, arched tripod, 29¾ x 15½, ca1810 (4149/284)   400
Candlestand, maple, cherrywood, (N. Eng.) circular top, tripod, 26 x 16, ca1810 (4268/747)   450
Candlestand, octagonal, mahogany, tilt-top, baluster, tripod, legs, 29½ x 22, 16½, res, L18c (4159/129)   300
Candlestand, octagonal, tilt-top, Mass., 28¼ x 20¾ x 15¾, ca1780 (4268/1227)   1800
Candlestand, painted cherrywood, top with notched corners, snake feet, 27 x 19¼, ca1810 (4149/256)   800
Candlestand, serpentine-top, arched tripod, tapering feet, 26½ x 18¾, ca1800 (4076/1381)   550
Candlestand, tilt-top mahogany, N.Y.*, arched, reeded tripod, 27½ x 24, ca1810 (4180/951)   450
Candlestand, tilt-top, cherrywood, N.Eng., octagonal top, ring-vase standard, 28¾ x 22 x 16, ca1800 (4268/1294)   175
Candlestand, tilt-top, mahogany, oval top, birdcage support, vase-turned shaft, 29 x 29¼, 1780-1800 (4076/1312)   650
Candlestand, tilt-top, mahogany, Mass.*, inlaid top, 30½ x 21½ x 14¾, rep, ca1800 (4268/1251)   650
Candlestand, tilt-top, mahogany, N.Y., octagonal top, casters, 28½ x 24 x 19¼, ca1810 (4268/1217)   600
Candlestand, tilt-top, turned cherrywood, shaped top, arched tripod, 26¾ x 22½, res, ca1800 (4211/1176)   225
Candlestand, tilt-top, N.Eng., mahogany, inlaid, 30 x 19½, rep., ca1800 (4076/955)   325
Candlestand, tilt-top, N.Y.*, carved mahogany, pestle-shaped standard, 30 x 23 5/2 ca1800 (4146/303)   200
Candlestand, tilt-top, inlaid mahogany, oval top, tapering spade feet, 32½ x 23, ca1790 (4076/1345)   1300
Candlestand, turned cherrywood, pestle-shaped standard, 26½ x 16½, ca1780 (4149/280)   625
Candlestand, turned cherrywood, ring and vase turned standard, 28 x 17½, ca1810 (4149/261)   650
Candlestand, N.Eng., cherrywood, turned, snake ft., 28 x 18¼, res, 1780-1800 (4076/1051)   550
Card table, carved mahogany, serpentine-top, attributed McIntyre, Salem, H31½, ca1815 (4146/191)   *750*
Card table, cherrywood, pine, hinged top, plain skirt, bow-front, 29¾ x 36¼, ca1800 (4149/254)   400
Chair, arm, carved mahogany, molded arched crestrail, tapering legs, ca1800 (4076/1348)   200
Chair, side, carved mahogany, 3 pierced splats, spade feet, N.Y., ca1800 (4156/303)   650
Chair, side, mahogany shield-back, upholstered seat, serpentine, Mass., 1790-1810 (4156/305)   800
Chair, side, shield back, mahogany, pierced splat, reeded, square legs, N.Y., res, ca1800 (4211/1289)   275
Chair, side, shield-back, mahogany, carved, Samuel McIntire*, Salem, ca1790 (4146/236)   *650*
Chair, side, shield-back, mahogany, Philadelphia*, arched back, carved urn, tapering legs, ca1800 (4268/1215)   1400
Chairs, dining, set of 10, Federal, 2 armchairs, 8 side, shield back, spade feet, rest., ca1800 (654/522)   2600
Chairs, set of 4, side, cherrywood, solid splat, 4 spindles, 19c (684/747)   250
Chairs, side, balloon-seat, pair, Pa., painted, decorated, baluster splat, ca1815 (4076/913)   425
Chairs, side, cane-seat, set, four, crestings painted with scenes, N.Y., ca1815 (4211/767)   *1300*
Chairs, side, carved mahogany, Pa. - N.Y., concave crestrail, sabre legs, ca1810 (4180/1052)   1200
Chairs, side, carved mahogany, 6, Baltimore, shield-backs, molded crests, spade feet, rep, L18c (4268/1281)   3000
Chairs, side, four, painted, crestrail painted with roses and leaves, N.Y., ca1810 (4076/1379)   750
Chairs, side, ladder-back, N.H.*, set of 4, painted, flaring stiles, ca1800 (4076/942)   1600

Chairs (4211/767)

Chair (4146/236)

Chest of drawers (4146/300)

Chairs, side, mahogany, shield-back, Philadelphia, serpentine, carved splat, ca1800 (4180/1044)	1400
Chairs, side, painted, five, N.Y., crestrail painted, colorful flowers, ca1810 (4180/1834)	1000
Chairs, side, pair, mahogany, Baltimore, shielD-shaped back, serpentine, rep, 1790-1810 (4268/1185)	800
Chairs, side, pair, painted, Md., Baltimore*, caned seat, turned legs, E19c (654/533)	250
Chairs, side, pair, shield-back, serpentine seat, tapering legs, Philadelphia, ca1790 (4076/1362)	2000
Chairs, side, racquet-back, pair, Philadelphia, mahogany, rectangular back, rep, ca1800 (4268/1243)	650
Chairs, side, racquet-back, pair, Philadelphia, rectangular backs, 4-stretchers, ca1800 (4268/1244)	1300
Chairs, side, rush-seat, pair, painted and decorated, N.Eng., ca1820 (4211/791)	250
Chairs, side, rush-seat, set of six, painted light green, decorated, N.Eng., ca1815 (4211/757)	750
Chairs, side, set of 6, Hepplewhite, mahogany, carved, ca1790 (4148/241)	2700
Chairs, side, set of 6, Hitchcock, painted, stenciled, rush-seat, 1832-43 (4076/931)	450
Chairs, 3 side, 1 armchair, Seymour, John, attrib, Mass., curly maple, owned by John Hancock, fine (4180/980)	15000
Chest and cabinet, inlaid mahogany, 2 parts, glazed doors, 4 drawers, N.Eng., 97½ x 51¼ x 21¼, res, ca1800 (4211/1296)	2700
Chest of drawers, birch, N.Eng. 4 graduated drawers, 34¾ x 41½ x 17¾, res, ca1800 (4268/750)	700
Chest of drawers, bird's eye, curly maple, brass pulls depicting Benjamin Franklin, 39 x 44, ca1810 (684/614)	850
Chest of drawers, bow-front, cherrywood, inlaid curly maple, scal. apron, H42¾, L41½, ca1790 (4076/1308)	1400
Chest of drawers, bow-front, birch, Mass.*, 4 graduated legs, bracket feet, 35¼ x 41 x 22¼, res, ca1800 (4268/824)	1400
Chest of drawers, bow-front, mahogany, N.Eng., 4 graduated drawers, 36½ x 41¾ x 23¾, rep, ca1790 (4268/1265)	1500
Chest of drawers, bow-front, Mass*, inlaid mahogany, cherrywood, valanced apron, 37¾ x 41¾ ca1800 (4146/300)	*950*
Chest of drawers, carved birch, N.Eng. 4 long drawers, shaped apron, 40¾ x 42 x 20, ca1810 (4268/744)	500
Chest of drawers, carved curly maple, 7 drawers, flaring French feet, 45½ x 42½, ca1800 (4149/291)	525
Chest of drawers, carved mahogany, cockbeaded drawers, ring-turned legs, Mass., 45¼ x 43½ ca1815 (4146/314)	325
Chest of drawers, carved maple and cherry, flaring bracket feet, 43 x 42½, ca1800 (4211/1166)	900
Chest of drawers, cherry and curly maple, freestanding columns, plinth base, 46 x 45, ca1830 (684/598)	275
Chest of drawers, cherrywood, maple, 3 graduated drawers, 35 x 37¼ x 15¾, ca1820 (654/506)	750
Chest of drawers, curly maple, Pa., 4 graduated long drawers, 38¼ x 43, ca1800 (4180/1067)	1100
Chest of drawers, inlaid early maple, N.Eng., 4 graduated long drawers, 41½ x 41⅜ x 22, res, ca1800 (4268/773)	800
Chest of drawers, inlaid mahogany, bow-front, 4 drawers, French feet, 37 x 40¼, 1790-1810 (4211/1224)	2100
Chest of drawers, inlaid mahogany, curly maple, bow-front, 4 drawers, 35 x 39, 19c (684/515)	650
Chest of drawers, inlaid mahogany, 4 cockbeaded, graduated drawers, 41¼ x 45, ca1815 (4149/227)	525
Chest of drawers, inlaid mahogany, 4 graduated long drawers, 39¾ x 44½ x 21¼, rep, ca1800 (4268/783)	300

Chest of drawers, inlaid, mahogany, bow-fronted, 4 drawers, 38 x 40, ca1800 (684/564)	700
Chest of drawers, mahogany, bow-fronted, brass pulls, circular turned legs, 40 x 40, ca1880 (684/597)	300
Chest of drawers, mahogany, N.Eng., bowed, 4 graduated long drawers, 37¾ x 39¾ x 21, rep, ca1800 (4268/1289)	1200
Chest of drawers, mahogany, N.Y., rectangular top, inlaid upper drawer, 47½ x 46½ x 21¾, 1800-15 (4268/1260)	500
Chest of drawers, mahogany, 4 drawers, glass pulls, 37 x 43, ca1820 (684/620)	200
Chest of drawers, mahogany, 4 drawers, wooden pulls, circular fluted legs, 39 x 42, ca1820 (684/595)	200
Chest of drawers, mahogany, 5 drawers, reeded balusters, ring turned legs, 40½ x 41½, ca1815 (684/739)	75
Chest of drawers, mahogany bow-front, 4 graduated drawers, shaped skirt, 37 x 41½ x 22½, ca1800 (4268/734)	1200
Chest of drawers, mahogany, bow-front, Pa. or N.Y., 4 graduated drawers, 40¼ x 41 x 22¼, ca1810 (4268/814)	500
Chest of drawers, mahogany, maple, N.H., bow-front, bamboo-turned colonnettes, 38½ x 44 x 23½, rep, ca1815 (4268/1171)	3250
Chest of drawers, maple, 4 drawers, French feet, 42½ x 37½, E19c (684/513)	400
Chest of drawers, pine, bow-front, N.Eng., all over painted and grained, 38¾ x 41⅛, 1800-15 (4180/977)	2300
Chest of drawers, Pa., walnut, mahogany, inlaid, 62 x 44½, 1780-1800 (4148/260)	2400
Chest of drawers, bow-front, mahogany, shell-inlaid, 38½ x 43 x 23, ca1800 (654/624)	500
Chest of drawers, bow-front, mahogany,N.Eng., 34½ x 42, ca1790 (4148/227)	
Chest of drawers, bow-front, Mass., plum pudding mahogany, satin-wood, 37 x 42, ca1800 (4076/1004)	1200
Chest of drawers, cherry, interior with hinged writing flap, 32¼ x 36¾, E19 (654/660)	150
Chest of drawers, cherry, rectangular top, turned outset legs, 47 x 14 x 20½, 1800-25 (654/557)	700
Chest of drawers, cherry, maple, rectangular top, 4 drawers, turned legs, 39½ x 40¾ x 21½, ca1810 (654/514)	500
Chest of drawers, inlaid cherrywood, 4 graduated drawers, black and white stringing, 37 x 40½ x 18, res, ca1800 (4268/760)	850
Chest of drawers, mahogany, Mass., carved, inlaid, bow-front, 42 x 43, 1800-15 (4076/920)	425
Chest of drawers, walnut, inlaid, cross-banded top, valanced apron, 38½ x 37½, res, ca1800 (654/682)	900
Chest of drawers, Conn.*, cherrywood, inlaid, 37 x 42¼, res, ca1800 (4076/1001)	750
Chest of drawers, Mass.*, mahogany, curly maple, inlaid, 37⅛ x 39¾, res, 1790-1810 (4076/1038)	875
Chest of drawers,N.Eng., cherry, valanced apron, 40 x 44½, ca1800 (654/672)	600
Chest of drawers,N.Eng.*, bow-front, mahogany, inlaid, 37¼ x 45, ca1800 (654/670)	450
Chest of drawers,N.Eng., cherry, inlaid, 38½ x 43½ x 19½, ca1790 (654/626)	500
Chest of drawers,N.Eng., mahogany, inlaid, curly maple, rectangular top, 40½ x 41¾ x 19¾, ca1810 (654/599)	450
Chest of drawers, N.Y., mahogany, inlaid, 39 x 45, res, 1800-10 (4076/1044)	350
Chest of drawers, N.Y., mahogany, inlaid, 39 x 42, 1790-1810 (4076/1040)	600
Chest of drawers, Pa.*, curly maple, two-tier top, bracket base, 1780-1820, 13½ x 15, res (4076/854)	375
Crib, turned walnut, prob. southern, mushroom finials, ring-turned supports, E19c (4076/1299)	325
Cupboard, corner, hanging, mahogany, inlaid, broken cornice, 2 doors, 53¼ x 39, E19 (654/695)	275
Desk, bookcase lady's, painted, grained, cupboard doors, 77½ x 31¼ x 15¾, ca1820-30 (4209/305)	3300
Desk, bookcase, lady's, inlaid mahogany, rosewood, shaped cresting, writing flap, 80 x 40½, ca1800 (4076/1395)	4000
Desk, butler's inlaid mahogany, rectangular, ball front, fitted interior, 45¼ x 46¾ x 24¼ (4211/1179)	1100
Desk, butler's, inlaid mahogany, fitted secretaire drawer, 3 long drawers, 41½ x 42½ x 20½, E19c (4159/164)	800
Desk, butler's, inlaid mahogany, N.Y.*, pull-out butler's drawer, 3 long drawers, 44 x 43 x 22½, rep, ca1810 (4268/803)	450
Desk, butler's, inlaid mahogany, N.Y., fall-front open to pigeon holes, 42 x 47¼, ca1800 (4180/985)	1000
Desk, cylinder-front, mahogany, Haines-Connelly School, Philadelphia, 42½ x 42, ca1800 (4180/1059)	4250
Desk, lady's, inlaid mahogany, hinged fall-front, square double tapering legs, 34¼ x 29, N.H., ca1800 (4076/1389)	900
Desk, lady's, inlaid mahogany, birch, Mass. or N.H., 2 parts, writing flap, 48½ x 40 x 20½, 1790-1810 (4268/725)	3300
Desk, lady's, inlaid, mahogany, Mass., tambour shutters, 44 x 42¼, ca1800 (4148/246)	3800
Desk, lady's, tambour, inlaid mahogany, Mass., 2 parts, valanced pigeon-holes, 46 x 36¼ x 18, L19c (4268/768)	800
Desk, slant-front, curly walnut, hinged lid, fitted interior, drawers, 41½ x 39, ca1800 (4211/1226)	1800
Desk, slant-front, Va.*, walnut, inlaid, 42¼ x 42, 1800-15 (4076/962)	2700

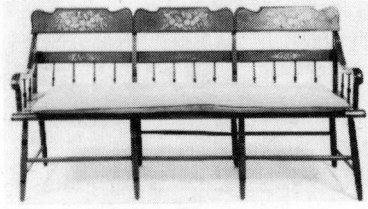

Long bench (4146/322)

Mantel (4076/1015)

Piano stool
(4180/1029)

Desk and bookcase
(4180/972)

Desk, slope front, painted blue, square tapering legs, N.Eng., 37½ x 35 1/3, ca1800 (4211/854)	650
Desk and bookcase, butler's, mahogany, 2 married parts, glazed doors, pull-out drawer, 76 x 43¼ x 21, res, ca1800 (4268/1201)	1600
Desk and bookcase, lady's, inlaid mahogany, shaped ped., apron, Salem, 79½ x 40¾, ca1800 (4076/1287)	4500
Desk and bookcase, lady's mahogany, N.Eng., two parts, glazed doors over 3 drawers, 79 x 38 x 19, 19c (4268/1166)	1300
Desk and bookcase, lady's, inlaid mahogany, 2doors, cupboards, writing flap, 81 x 41½, E19c (4211/1248)	2500
Desk and bookcase, lady's, mahogany, N.Eng., 2 parts, glazed doors, tambour slides, 74 x 36¼ x 18½, 19c (4268/1189)	1100
Desk and bookcase, lady's, mahogany, N.Eng., 2 parts, glazed doors, writing flap, 82 x 41 x 18¾, ca1800 (4268/1224)	1400
Desk and bookcase, lady's, mahogany, N.H., 2 parts, glazed doors, tambour slides, 82 x 41 x 17¾, ca1800 (4268/1177)	2000
Desk and bookcase, lady's, 2 part, Mass., mahogany and satinwood, 68 x 40¾, feet res, ca1800 (4180/972)	*2500*
Desk on frame, slant-top, inlaid, N.Eng.*, walnut, cherrywood, 38½ x 24½ x 18¾, ca1800 (4268/860)	650
Dressing glass, carved mahogany, rectangular, domed ball feet, H15¾, W14¾, E19c (4146/130)	75
Dressing glass, inlaid mahogany, bow-front, rectangular, N.Y.*, H24¾, W22, ca1810 (4146/146)	250
Dressing glass, inlaid mahogany, rectangular, 2 drawers, ball ft, E19c, 20 x 17¾ (4076/857)	125
Dressing glass, mahogany bow-front, secret compartments, ball feet, 26 x 23, ca1800 (4149/86)	150
Dressing glass, mahogany, bow-front, N.Eng., pivoting mirror, 2 drawers, 18¾ x 19, lacks feet, E19c (4268/1090)	90
Dressing table, painted, grained pine, ball feet, 36 x 28¾ x 16½, ca1825 (4209/338)	400
Dressing table, painted, decorated pine, Salem, Mass., fine, ca1820 (4209/302)	5250
Dressing table, pine, painted, grained, shaped splashboard, 40 x 32 x 16½, ca1825 (4209/333)	950
Long bench, pine, painted, decorated, shaped crestrail, plane seat, Pa., L71¼ E19c (4146/322)	*800*
Mantel, carved, painted pine, dentilled frieze, reeded pillasters, Pa., 60 x 70½, ca1800 (4146/229)	750
Mantel, carved, painted, N.Eng., punch-carved frieze, fluted pillasters, 58¼ x 799, ca1800 (4146/232)	*1100*
Mantel, pine, N.J.*, 55¾ x 78½, ca1800 (4076/1015)	950
Mirror, convex, carved giltwood, circular plate, 36, ca1820 (684/682)	150
Mirror, dressing, inlaid mahogany, oval, lyre supports, 3 drawers, 21¾, E19c (4211/1104)	350
Mirror, dressing, inlaid, rectangular, bow-front case, ball feet, H18¼, W17¼, E19c (4146/156)	225
Mirror, ebonized, eglomise, wall, giltwood, N.Eng.*, 20½ x 11, E19c (4149/287)	150
Mirror, eglomise, giltwood, broken cornice, rectangular, 33½ x 17, ca1825 (654/569)	150

Mirror, giltwood, upper panel with view of Mount Vernon, 49½ x 25¼, res, E19c (4268/719) — 150

Mirror, giltwood and gesso, 'broken' cornice, N.Eng.*, 38¾ x 22½ 19c (4146/210) — 175

Mirror, giltwood, gesso, panel depicting a naval engagement, 39¼ x 20¾, E19c (4180/987) — 450

Mirror, giltwood, gesso girandole, circular convex mirror, eagle, E19c (4156/347) — 950

Mirror, giltwood, wall, crested with spread-winged American Eagle, 19c (4156/294) — 150

Mirror, girandole, convex, gilded, vigorously carved eagle, candlearms, 55 x 34, E19c (4268/1218) — 1900

Mirror, mahogany, parcel-gilded, rectangular, gilt basket, flowerheads, 49½ x 24¾ (4180/992) — 650

Mirror, shaving, inlaid mahogany, bow-front, rectangular plate, 2 drawers, 20, ca1800 (4211/1105) — 175

Mirror, wall, carved, gilded wood, gesso, 43 x 19⅜, E19c (4148/229) — 300

Mirror, wall, convex, gilded, small, with carved eagle holding chain in beak, 24 x 15¼, ca1820 (4268/1176) — 700

Mirror, wall, convex, giltwood, gesso, rookwood cresting, 40¼ x 23½, ca1820 (4076/1355) — 600

Mirror, wall, fine, parcel-gilded, inlaid mahogany, swan's neck cresting, 54 x 22¾, N.Y., ca1790 (4076/1282) — 5000

Mirror, wall, gilded wood, 31 x 20, E19c (4148/206) — 150

Mirror, wall, giltwood, broken cornice, 31¼ x 18¾, ca1815 (4076/1025) — 75

Mirror, wall, giltwood and gesso, broken cornice, above a shaped frieze, 35 x 34½, ca1830 (684/509) — 100

Mirror, wall, giltwood and gesso, broken cornice, rectangular plate, 43½ x 25¾, E19c (684/508) — 125

Mirror, wall, giltwood and gesso, rectangular frame, 28 x 18¾, 19c (4211/825) — 100

Mirror, wall, giltwood, gesso, 42 x 25½, E19c (4076/978) — 375

Mirror, wall, giltwood, gesso, 'broken' cornice, gilt spherules, N.Eng.*, 32 x 20½, E19c (4146/279) — 275

Mirror, wall, giltwood, gesso, 'Washington Memorial', broken cornice, 44½ x 23, ca1810 (4076/1358) — 1300

Mirror, wall, giltwood, gesso, broken cornice, eglomise, 44 x 23¾, res, E19c (654/661) — 125

Mirror, wall, giltwood, gesso, broken cornice, gilt-stenciled panel, 39¼ x 21½, ca1820 (4268/1173) — 175

Mirror, wall, giltwood, gesso, cresting, eglomise panel, N.Y., 50½ x 27, 1790-1800 (4076/1405) — 1900

Mirror, wall, giltwood, gesso, eglomise, 49¼ x 28½, ca1815 (4076/933) — 250

Mirror, wall, giltwood, gesso, eglomise, 39½ x 23, E19c (4076/999) — 300

Mirror, wall, giltwood, gesso, eglomise, 39 x 21¼, 1815 (4076/1021) — 400

Mirror, wall, giltwood, gesso, Mass., eglomise, 32¾ x 19, ca1815 (4076/918) — 375

Mirror, wall, giltwood, gesso, 2 part mirror plate, gilt decorations, 40 x 23¼, E19c (4268/819) — 150

Mirror, wall, inlaid mahogany, parcel-gilded, swan's neck cresting, 50½ x 23¼, 19c (4076/1304) — 1600

Mirror, wall, parcel-gilded, swan's neck cresting, scrolled pendant below, 55½ x 21½, ca1790 (4076/1370) — 1400

Mirror, wall, parcel-gilded, mahogany, scrolled cresting, N.Eng., 20⅛ x 12, ca1790 (4076/1397) — 200

Mirror, wall, N.Y.*, giltwood, gesso, 44¾ x 26¾, res, ca1800 (4076/1032) — 350

Mirror,N.Eng., wall, giltwood, gesso, spherules, rinceaux, colonettes, 39¾ x 21½, E19c (654/613) — 100

Night stand, mahogany,N.Eng., serpentine top, 28 x 19¾, ca 1810 (4148/224) — 450

Night stand, Mass. or N.H., painted, decorated, curly maple, 30 x 20¾, ca1800 (4148/258) — 3600

Piano stool, upholstered top, adjustable on a screw standard, 19¼, ca1815 (4180/1029) — *350*

Rocker, ptd. and dec., baluster splat, ring-turned tapering legs, ca1820 (4076/1296) — 225

Screen, pole, N.Y.*, maple, mahogany, carved, rectangular, H59¼, E19c (4076/1011) — 200

Secretary cabinet, walnut, fitted interior, 3 drawers, 47½ x 49½, ca1820 (684/800) — 250

Secretary-bookcase, mahogany, Md., swan's neck cresting, inlaid American eagle, H96, W41, 1790-1800 (4146/244) — 2850

Settee, carved mahogany, upright arms, reeded top rail, 78½, ca1810 (4211/1188) — 1300

Settee, carved mahogany, Pa., square back, molded square legs, rep., L74 1775-90 (4146/311) — 1200

Settee, N.Y.,* mahogany, carved, sabre legs, claw feet, L69¾, ca1815 (4148/256) — 3900

Settee, Pa., mahogany, carved, square back, recessed stretchers, L74, rep., 1775-90 (654/711) — 1300

Settee, Southern*, walnut, carved, L47¼, 19c (4076/963) — 1100

Settee, 2-chair back, mahogany, Philadelphia, racquet-form splats, bell flowers, L48¼, res, 19c (4268/1239) — 1000

Side chairs, pair, cane-seat, painted, grained, N.Y. State, restoration, ca1830 (4209/301) — 400

Side chairs, pair, rush-seat, Mass., painted, decorated, 1805-20 (4209/347) — 3250

Side chairs, set of six, rush-seat, painted with landscapes, tapering legs, Conn.*, ca1825 (4209/330) — 16000

Side table, pine, painted, grained, single drawer, tapering legs, 27¼ x 30½ x 21, ca1820 (4209/361) — 650

Sideboard, birch, N.Eng., rectangular top, frieze drawer, 39¼ x 38 x 21¾, top reset, ca1800 (4268/1235) — 2300

Sideboard, bow-front, mahogany, N.Y., 3 bowed frieze drawers, oval medallions, 44¼ x 71½ x 29¾, rep, 1790-1810 (4268/1230) — 2800

Sideboard, bow-front, N.Y., mahogany, inlaid, fan spandrels, 42½ x 73¼, res, 1790-1820 (654/696) — 1000

Sideboard, butler's, Mass. or N.Y., mahogany, inlaid, 53 x 45⅝, ca1815 (4076/975) — 800

Sideboard, butler's, Philadelphia, mahogany, carved, inlaid, rear gallery, 53 x 48½, ca1810 (654/677) — 500

Sideboard, carved and inlaid mahogany, drawers, cupboards, tapering legs, 39 x 71 x 25, ca1810 (4211/1205) — 2200

Sideboard, carved and inlaid mahogany, rectangular top,¾ gallery, drawers, cupboard, 47 x 73½, ca1815 (684/510) — 325

Sideboard, hollow front, inlaid mahogany, shaped top, drawer and cupboards, 38½ x 68 x 24¾, res, ca1800 (4211/1234) — 2100

Sideboard, inlaid mahogany, cockbeaded drawers, cupboard doors, 41¾ x 69¼ x 27¼, reps, ca1800 (4268/746) — 950

Sideboard, inlaid mahogany, oblong, 5 drawers, square legs, 32½ x 51, 19c (4211/1197) — 650

Sideboard, inlaid mahogany, rectangular with projecting front, cupboards, 38¼ x 70 x 24¾, ca1800 (4268/735) — 2500

Sideboard, inlaid mahogany, shaped top, drawers, cupboards, 41½ x 75⅜ x 28¼, res, 1790-1810 (4211/1174) — 1700

Sideboard, inlaid mahogany, Mass., bowed oblong top, bowed drawers, 6 legs, 402/3 x 72 x 28¾, ca1800 (4268/1225) — 4250

Sideboard, inlaid mahogany, Md., shaped top, bowed side drawers, 39 x 56½ x 23½, 1790-1810 (4268/1280) — 8750

Sideboard, inlaid mahogany, N.Eng., oblong top, bowed front, bottle drawers, 40½ x 75½ x 24½, 1800-15 (4268/1216) — 650

Sideboard, inlaid mahogany, 3 cockbeaded drawers, spade feet, 32½ x 51, 19c (4149/239) — 375

Sideboard, inlaid walnut, Va.*, 'broken' front, bellflowers, H38, L62, D24, ca1810 (4146/209) — *2500*

Sideboard, inlaid, mahogany, serpentine-front, 3 drawers, cupboard doors, 39 x 65, ca1800 (684/684) — 1300

Sideboard, mahogany, inlaid, N.Y., 3 drawers, 51 x 70½, ca1815 (4076/1048) — 425

Sideboard, mahogany, serpentine, Conn., lily of vally inlays, bottle drawer, 36½ x 71¾ x 29¾, 1790-1810 (4180/1076) — *2100*

Sideboard (4146/209)

Stand (4156/295)

Sideboard (4180/1076)

Sideboard, mahogany, Southern*, shallow frieze drawer, square tapering legs, res. 34 x 60½ x 22¼, ca1800 (4146/241) — 900

Sideboard, serpentine-front, mahogany, gallery, cupboard, bottle drawers, 49 x 75, ca1810 (684/680) — 650

Sideboard, serpentine-front, inlaid mahogany, frieze drawer, square legs, 40 x 75, 1790-1810 (4076/1270) — 3000

Sideboard, serpentine-front, mahogany, inlaid, 42 x 60 x 20½, ca1800 (4076/1052) — 2500

Sideboard, serpentine-front, N.Y., mahogany, inlaid, 51¾ x 74½, res, 1790-1810 (4076/1034) — 950

Sideboard, serpentine, mahogany, frieze, drawer and doors conform to top, inlay, 37¾ x 82¼ x 27, ca1800 (4168/1175) — 1600

Sideboard, serpentine, mahogany, Baltimore, drawer inlaid with medallions, 38½ x 77¼ x 31½, res, ca1800 (4268/1301) — 8250

Sideboard, serpentine, N.Y., inlaid, mahogany, 39¾ x 69, res, 1790-1810 (4076/939) — 1600

Sideboard, two-tier, inlaid mahogany, bird's-eye maple, attrib. to J. Seymour, 46 x 73, Mass., ca1800 (4076/1406) — 5500

Sideboard, James Young, N.Y., serpentine-front, mahogany, inlaid, rare, 39¼ x 69¾, ca1810 (4076/934) — 3000

Sideboard, Mass., mahogany, inlaid, marble-top, 41½ x 54, rare, 1790-1810 (4076/977) — 3250

Sofa, carved inlaid mahogany, arms and supports inlaid with curly maple, L57, Mass., 19c (4156/337) — 2600
Sofa, carved mahogany, Mass., canted back, reeded crestrail, upholstered, L71½, ca1800 (4268/1307) — 3400
Sofa, carved mahogany, N.Y. or R.I., molded arms, tapered supports, and legs, L74¾, 1790-1810 (4268/1195) — 1200
Sofa, carved mahogany, Slover and Taylor, N.Y.*, 78½, res, ca1800 (4211/1202) — 2100
Sofa, carved mahogany and curly maple, arched top, curving arms, 71½, res, 1790-1810 (4211/1193) — 10500
Sofa, carved mahogany, reeded frame, School of Duncan Phyfe, N.Y., L87½, rep, ca1815 (4180/1019) — 6500
Sofa, country, upholstered, painted, grained base, N.Eng., L72¾, ca1825 (4209/321) — 1700
Sofa, country, upholstered, tapering legs, L80, 19c (4209/329) — 1300
Sofa, curly maple, N.Eng., upholstered, tall back, L74½, res, 1800-15 (4268/827) — 1600
Sofa, school of Duncan Phyfe, N.Y., carved mahogany, crestrail with reeded panels, L78, ca1810 (4146/294) — 2250
Sofa, square, mahogany, molded crestrail, upholstered, reeded legs, L79½, 1800-10 (4268/1242) — 650
Sofa, N.Y., mahogany, carved, bow-knot drapery swags, bowed seat, casters, L77¼, res, ca1810 (654/583) — 2500
Stand, basin, mahogany, inlaid, quarter-round top, splashboard, drawer, 37½ x 22, E19 (654/687) — 325
Stand, basin, Pa., mahogany, carved, 29¾ x 13, ca1790 (654/667) — 150
Stand, cherrywood, rectangular, 27¼ x 18, res, 1790-1810 (4076/1036) — 150
Stand, cherrywood, one-drawer, splayed, ring-turned tapering legs, 27 x 16¼, N.Eng., 1790 (4156/299) — 1100
Stand, corner basin, mahogany, 37½ x 25, ca1800 (4076/924) — 375
Stand, corner basin, turned cherrywood, quarter round top, splashboard, 40 x 25¾ x 18½, E19c (4211/1222) — 175
Stand, curly maple, Pa., medial shelf with drawer, 32¼ x 16, ca1800 (4180/1064) — 1000
Stand, inlaid mahogany, cherrywood, medial shelf, turned legs, 27 x 22¾, ca1820 (4146/218) — 100
Stand, maple, 1 drawer, square tapering legs, 27 x 17¾, E19c (4156/291) — 150
Stand, maple, 1 drawer, N.Eng., rectangular top, square tapering legs, 26¾ x 16¾, E19c (4156/289) — 300
Stand, painted pine, turned, curly maple, N.Eng., 28¾ x 20¾, ca1810 (4076/1297) — 450
Stand, stained pine, rectangular top, N.Eng., 27¾ x 18⅜ x 17⅞, 19c (4211/845) — 60
Stand, turned cherrywood, N.Eng., 27½ x 16¾ x 16¾, ca1815 (4211/820) — 400
Stand, N.Y.*, cherrywood, curly maple, one-drawer, 27½ x 19¾, ca1825 (654/644) — 175
Stand, 1 drawer, cherrywood, delicate, ring-turned reeded legs, 28¾ x 18⅛, Conn.*, ca1810 (4156/295) — *1000*
Stand, 1 drawer, cherrywood, N.Eng., square, legs slightly tapered, 26 x 17½, ca1800 (4180/953) — 275
Table, breakfast, drop-leaf, mahogany, oblong, D-shaped leaves, 29½ x 41¾ x 46¼, ca1810 (4211/1180) — 850
Table, breakfast, carved mahogany, brass-inlaid, tri-lobed drop leaves, N.Y., 29¼ x 39 x 50¼, ca1820 (4146/222) — *275*
Table, breakfast, drop-leaf, mahogany, oblong, short leaves, drawer, 28¾ x 37¾ x 49¼, res, ca1810 (4211/1218) — 600
Table, breakfast, drop-leaf, mahogany, lobed drop leaves, leaf-carved standard, 29 x 48¾, ca1810 (4076/1400) — 1400
Table, card, carved and inlaid mahogany, D shaped hinged top, 28½ x 35¼ x 34½, res, ca1800 (4211/1192) — 1200
Table, card, carved mahogany, McIntire, Samuel F., attrib., hinged top, 31¾ x 36¾, ca1815 (4180/1031) — 1000
Table, card, carved mahogany, N.Y., hinged top, reeded, tapered legs, 29¼ x 35¾, ca1810 (4180/1035) — 400
Table, card, carved mahogany, Pa. half-round, hinged, molded top, square legs, 30 x 38 x 18, rep, 1790-1810 (4268/736) — 650
Table, card, cherrywood, rectangular, shaped corners, Conn.*, 30¼ x 37⅝ x 18¼, res, ca1800 (4211/1292) — 250
Table, card, cherrywood, birch, Conn., shaped skirt with inlaid American eagle, 28¾ x 36¼ x 17½, warped, ca1800 (4268/1299) — 9500
Table, card, flip-top, mahogany, Shaped top, drawer, taper legs, 28½ x 35 x 16½, ca1800 (654/507) — 800
Table, card, inlaid cherrywood, D-shaped hinged top, 28¼ x 36 x 35¼, res, ca1800 (4268/758) — 550
Table, card, inlaid mahogany, bowed front, oval medallions, crossbanded cuffs, 30¾ x 35,¾ 19c (4146/317) — 450
Table, card, inlaid mahogany, hinged D shape, N.Eng., 29½ x 41½ x 19⅜, ca1800 (4211/1300) — 200
Table, card, inlaid mahogany, hinged, half-round top, tapering legs, 29¾ x 36 x 17¾, 1790-1810 (4268/738) — 700
Table, card, inlaid mahogany, oblong top, 30 x 36 x 16¾, ca1800 (4211/831) — 550
Table, card, inlaid mahogany, shaped top, square tapered legs, 29 x 36¾ x 19, res, ca1810 (4211/1240) — 3000

Table, card, inlaid mahogany, D-shaped hinged top, square tapering legs, 28 x 33¼ x 16½, ca1800 (4268/718)	750
Table, card, inlaid mahogany, D-shaped top, Mass., 1790-1810, 30⅜ x 36¼ (4156/346)	850
Table, card, inlaid mahogany, birch, Mass. or N.H., oblong top with bowed front, 31½ x 45 x 21, ca1800 (4268/1169)	4250
Table, card, inlaid mahogany, cherrywood, half-round top, apron inlaid, Conn., 28½ x 35⅞, 1790-1810 (4146/206)	*1300*

Table (4146/222)    Table (4146/230)

Table (4146/206)

Table, card, mahogany, inlaid, Mass., Salem, serpentine contour, 29¼ x 36¾ (4148/253)	1600
Table, card, mahogany, satinwood, inlaid, Mass. or N.H., 30½ x 36¾, 1790-1810 (4076/919)	900
Table, card, serpentine, Mass., mahogany, inlaid, 29¼ x 37, ca1800 (4076/1005)	500
Table, card, serpentine inlaid, Mass., Salem, 29½ x 36, ca1800 (4148/230)	2200
Table, card, serpentine-front,N.Eng., mahogany, inlaid, 29¾ x 36½, 1790-1810 (4076/1003)	750
Table, card, serpentine, mahogany, inlaid, Mass. or N.H., 28¼ x 35¼, res, 1790-1810 (4076/1033)	1300
Table, card, serpentine, mahogany, shaped top, reeded tapering legs, Mass., 29¼ x 36¾, ca1810 (4146/258)	250
Table, card, serpentine, Mass., mahogany, curly maple, inlaid, 29¾ x 37¼, 1790-1810 (4076/995)	1000
Table, card, serpentine, Mass., mahogany, inlaid, 29½ x 34½, 1790-1810 (4148/257)	650
Table, card, serpentine, Mass. or, N.H., mahogany, curly maple, 30¼ x 37¼, ca1800 (4076/956)	1100
Table, card, swivel-top, mahogany, N.Y., canted corners, paw feet, 28¾ x 36¾ x 18½, res, 1810 (4268/1241)	1300
Table, card, swivel-top, mahogany, N.Y., top on 4 fluted uprights, acanthus carving, 28⅞ x 35¾ x 36, res, ca1810 (4268/1300)	1100
Table, card, Mass. or N.H., mahogany, cherrywood, inlaid, 28¾ x 36, ca1800 (4076/1030)	800
Table, card,N.Eng., cherry, birch, inlaid, conch shell, 28 x 36 x 17½, res, ca1800 (654/653)	750
Table, card, N.Y., mahogany, carved, inlaid, clover-leaf top, 29½ x 36, 1800-10 (4076/927)	500
Table, card, Pa., mahogany, inlaid, 29¼ x 36, ca1800 (4076/935)	325
Table, card, Philadelphia or Baltimore, hollow front, mahogany, inlaid, 29 x 35½, res, 1780-1810 (654/631)	450
Table, cherrywood and pine Pembroke, plain skirt, tapering legs, 28½ x 34½, ca1800 (4149/226)	375
Table, cherrywood, pine drop-leaf, square tapering legs, painted, 28¾ x 40, res, E19c (4149/192)	125
Table, console, drop-leaf, Md.*, mahogany, carved, 29 x 54, ca1815 (4076/959)	450
Table, console, inlaid mahogany, D shaped top, square tapered legs, N.Eng., 28 x 46½ x 22, ca1800 (4211/1304)	225
Table, console, mahogany, serpentine form, 30 x 59, ca1820 (684/652)	100
Table, curly and bird's eye maple, drop-leaf, on square tapering legs, 28½ x 42, ca1800 (684/608)	400
Table, curly maple and mahogany, Mass., 2 drawer, 28½ x 19¾, 19c (4211/827)	400
Table, dining, cherrywood, N.Eng. 2 D-shaped ends, drop leaves, 29 x 75¼ x 42¼, 19c (4268/745)	950
Table, dining, drop-leaf mahogany, oblong beaded apron, 30 x 48, ca1800 (684/500)	500
Table, dining, drop-leaf, turned walnut, oblong top, 6 legs, 29½ x 44½ x 60½, ca1810 (4211/1177)	300
Table, dining, drop-leaf, mahogany, oblong top, square tapering legs N.Eng., 29 x 53½ x W54¼, E19c (4146/259)	475
Table, dining, drop-leaf,N.Eng., walnut, 30⅛ x 61, 1790-1810 (4076/1018)	500

Table, dining, drop-leaf, gate-leg, cherry, pine, 8 legs, 29 x 53, ca1800 (684/748) 550

Table, dining, gate-leg, drop-leaf, mahogany, 30½ x 68, ca1820 (684/601) 175

Table, dining, inlaid mahogany, N.Eng.*, 3 part, D-shaped ends, drop leaves, 29 x 47⅞ x 123¼, ca1800 (4268/1200) 5750

Table, dining, inlaid mahogany, 3 parts, drop-leaf with 2 console legs, 28¼ x 90¼, 19c (684/733) 1300

Table, dining, 2 parts, Pa.,*, cherrywood, D shape top, H29, ex. L75, ca1800 (4076/914) 800

Table, dining, 3 part, mahogany, carved, 2 D-ends, reeded tapering legs, 29 x 134, W53¼ (4146/270) 2750

Table, dressing, stenciled pine, N.Eng., 2-tiered top, splashboard, 39¼ x 32 x 18½, M19c (4268/781) 300

Table, dressing, N.Y., mahogany, inlaid, 2 pedestal sideboard, 36¼ x 48, rare, ca1810 (4076/938) 1700

Table, drop-leaf, cherry and maple, turned legs with gate supports, 30 x 65, ca1830 (684/505) 250

Table, drop-leaf breakffast, inlaid, cherrywood, square tapering legs, N.Eng., H27¾, L45¾, 1780-1810 (4146/204) 450

Table, drop-leaf, breakfast, mahogany, carved, D-shaped leaves, tapering legs, N.Y., 29 x 41¾ x 51¾, ca1820 (4146/226) 275

Table, drop-leaf, maple and pine, rectangular top and leaves, painted red-brown, 29½ x 41 x 39½ (4268/787) 375

Table, drop-leaf, maple, birch, N.Eng., D-shaped drop leaves, tapering legs, 28½ x 38 x 47, res, ca1810 (4268/1158) 275

Table, drop-leaf, painted, pine, oblong top, ring-turned legs, child's, 19c, 19 x 21⅝, res (4076/852) 200

Table, drop-leaf, turned cherrywood, D-shaped leaves, turned legs, 27½ x 36, E19c (4146/219) 150

Table, gaming, inlaid, satin wood, hinged top, fitted interior, 29½ x 35⅝ x 17¾, 1790-1810 (4211/1249) 9000

Table, harvest, pine, turned cherrywood, oblong top, pear-shaped feet, N.Eng.*, 30½ x 71 x 45, 19c (4146/292) 950

Table, harvest, pine, Pa.*, oblong top, square tapering legs, res, 28¾ x 76 x 37¼, 19c (4146/309) 900

Table, harvest, turned birch, oblong top, tapering legs, N.Eng., 29 x 60 x 41¾, 19c (4146/298) 700

Table, inlaid mahogany work, 2 drawers, ball feet, 28¾ x 21, ca1820 (4149/267) 125

Table, lady's writing, mahogany and cherry, circular turned legs, ball feet, 31 x 54, ca1820 (684/521) 250

Table, library, carved mahogany, N.Y., drop-leaf, drawer, lion's heads feet, 28½ x 38 x 50¾, 1810 (4180/1026) 2100

Table, library, drop-leaf, mahogany, rectangular, single drawer, N.Y., 29¼ x 38 x 47⅛, ca1815 (4211/1290) 900

Table, library, drop-leaf, N.Y., mahogany, carved, reeded tetrapod, 29¼ x 44, E19c (654/646) 275

Table, mahogany breakfast, lobed drop leaves, 29 x 36, ca1815 (4149/235) 250

Table, occasional, mahogany, rectangular top, 2 drawers, 28½ x 19 x 15½, E19c (4159/167) 350

Table, occasional, walnut, lobed top, single drawer, 27 x 19, ca1800 (684/699) 250

Table, pembroke, breakfast, N.Y., mahogany, carved, inlaid, 28½ x 41½, ca1815 (4076/1063) 325

Table, pembroke, cherrywood, oblong top, drawer, tapering legs, 28¼ x 34¾ x 35, ca1810 (654/618) 275

Table, pembroke, inlaid cherrywood, N.Eng., Conn.*, rectangular top, D-shaped leaves, 28½ x 32¾, rep, 1790-1810 (4268/728) 700

Table, pembroke, maple, D-shape, tapered legs, x-stretcher, 28½ x 35 x 32, 1800-25 (654/551) 650

Table, pine, cherrywood, breakfast, drop-leaf, 28¼ x 40, ca1830 (4149/290) 140

Table, pine, D-shaped console, N.Eng.*, 34½ x 36 x 19¼, 19c (4211/842) 70

Table, side, curly maple, bow-front, Pa., single drawer, 27½ x 29½, ca1800 (4180/1066) 900

Table, side, painted and marbleized, graining, 30 x 24¼, N.Eng., 19c (4211/762) 1000

Table, sofa, mahogany, brass casters, D-shaped leaves, 29 x 66, rep, ca1800 (4180/949) 1300

Table, work, painted, decorated, single drawer, N.Eng., 29½ x 17½ x 17½, ca1825 (4209/350) 700

Table, work, painted, grained pine, paint restoration, 29¼ x 22¾ x 20½, ca1820 (4209/369) 950

Table, work, painted, grained pine, single drawer, 28¾ x 18 x 17¾, ca1830 (4209/367) 450

Table, work, painted, grained pine, single drawer, 28½ x 18 x 16½, ca1825 (4209/365) 325

Table, work, carved birch, inlaid, mahogany, bowed front, tapering legs, Mass*, 27½ x 20½, ca1815 (4146/235) 600

Table, work, carved mahogany, oblong top, outset rounded colonettes, N.Eng., 29 x 22¼, ca1800 (4146/306) 300

Table, work, carved mahogany, upper drawer fitted, swiveling standard, paw feet, 28 x 21¾, ca1825 (4211/1203) 1500

Table, work, carved, inlaid mahogany, Philadelphia - N.Y., hinged top, reeded legs, 30 x 26¾, 1790-1810 (4180/1046) 1500

Table, work, cherrywood, Pa.*, medial shelf with cockbeaded drawer, 32 x 17½, ca1800 (4180/1030) 350

Table, work, curly and bird's eye maple, single drawer, 27½ x 18, ca1800 (684/610) 300

Table, work, drop-leaf, painted, grained, D-shaped leaves, 2 drawers, glass pulls, 29 x 34, ca1815 (684/615) 250

Table, work, inlaid mahogany, feather birch, serpentine, oblong top, Salem, 30 x 17¼, fine, ca1800-10 (4146/230) *3750*

Table, work, inlaid mahogany, writing flap, Mass., 30½ x 20½, 1800-10 (4076/1401) 1400
Table, work, inlaid satinwood, oblong top with canted corners, Seymour, 28¼ x 19¾, ca1805
(4156/334) 6500
Table, work, inlaid, mahogany, hinged leather top, ratchet support, 30¼ x 18½ x 14¼, E19c
(4211/1171) 1200
Table, work, inlaid, mahogany, oblong, D shaped leaves, N.Y., 29 x 34½, ca1810 (4211/1200) 600
Table, work, mahogany, octagonal case, round tapering legs, Mass, 28 x 20¾, ca1810 (4146/237) 450
Table, work, mahogany, rectangular top, 2 drawers, 27 x 22, top replaced, ca1815 (684/697) 175
Table, work, mahogany, cherrywood, rectangular top, 2 drawers, 28½ x 21, 1820, N.Eng.*
(4149/292) 120
Table, work, mahogany, 1 drawer, N.Y. or N.Eng., reeded tapering legs, 28 x 21½, ca1815
(4180/970) 175
Table, work, maple and birch, ptd., dec., square tapering legs, 28½ x 15½, ca1800 (4076/1375) 1600
Table, work, painted and decorated, octagonal top, turned X-stretcher, Salem, H29, W15¾, 1800-10
(4076/1285) 1000
Table, work, painted, rare, Boston*, octagonal top, neoclassical vignettes, 29 x 19¼ 1800-15
(4146/212) 800
Table, work, square top, single, drawer, turned legs, 27 x 20 x 19½, 1825-50 (654/553) 300
Table, work, Mass., mahogany, inlaid, 28¼ x 22, 1815 (4076/1023) 750
Table, writing, inlaid mahogany, top opening to writing surface, 28 x 26, ca1820 (684/590) 600
Table, writing, maple, 3 quarter gallery, single drawer, 33½ x 30, ca1810 (684/604) 125
Table, drop-leaf, mahogany, end drawer, ball feet, 29 x 48, ca1815 (684/647) 175
Table, Pembroke, carved mahogany, Pa.*, bowed ends, D-shaped leaves, 28½ x 35½ x 43¼,
ca1800 (4268/751) 750
Table, Pembroke, cherrywood, oblong top, square tapering legs, H28¼, L34¾, W35 ca1810
(4146/253) 175
Table, Pembroke, drop-leaf cherry, square tapering legs, 27 x 36, E19c (684/613) 300
Table, Pembroke, inlaid cherrywood, fine, Conn. or N.Y., 27¾ x 37¾, 1790-1810 (4076/1331) 1400
Table, Pembroke, inlaid mahogany, N.Y., rectangular top, shaped drop leaves, 20¼ x 32 x 38¾,
ca1800 (4268/1234) 1800
Table, Pembroke, mahogany, N.Y., D-shaped drop leaves, tapering legs, 28¾ x 36 x 45¼, ca1810
(4268/1292) 450
Table, Pembroke, satinwood, mahogany, Md., J. Shaw, inlays, drop leaves, spade feet, 27¾ x 30¼ x
39, 1790-1800 (4268/1258) 20000
Table, 2 tier chamber, mahogany, drawers, tapered legs, ball feet, 43¼ x 36 x 22¼, ca1815
(4211/1217) 550
Table, 2-part, cherrywood, inlaid, Conn.*, 29¼ x 103¼, 1790-1810 (4076/1045) 2100
Tables, card, pair, mahogany, carved, Mass., 29¼ x 35¾, ca18l5 (4148/236) 2800
Wall cupboard, child's, painted, pine, molded cornice, 2 drawers, 19c, 28½ x 15¾ (4076/856) 225
Washstand, mahogany, rectangular, backboard, pierced for basin, 38¼ x 22⅞ x 17⅛, ca1810
(4211/1182) 400
Washstand, pine and cherrywood, ring turned uprights, 29⅛ x 18, E19c (4149/207) 180
Washstand, turned ash and chestnut, shaped splashboard, towel rest, 32¾ x 29, 19c (4149/229) 130
Washstand, pine, splashboard, shelf with drawer, 33 x 17, E19c (4149/210) 160
Washstand, turned maple and tulip, single drawer, ball feet, 33 x 29¼, ca1820 (4149/218) 110
Washstand, 2 tier, stained pine, high splashboard, corner candlestand, 2 drawers, 43 x 46, ca1820
(684/534) 200
Window bench, mahogany, outscrolled arm, outswept legs, brass paw feet, 55, M19c (684/536) 500
Window seat, carved mahogany, S-scroll arms, Mass*, L66, ca1815 (4146/727) 1300
Work table, painted, decorated, Salem, Mass., 28 x 17¼ x 15¾, ca1820 (4209/303) 3500
Writing desk, slant-front, painted, grained pine, tapering legs, 35 x 30¼ x 17½, ca1825 (4209/340) 450
Writing table, slope top, mahogany, N.Y., leather-lined writing surface, 31¾ x 27, ca1800
(4180/1023) 1000

Empire

Armchair, mahogany, carved, eagle head terminals, ca1825 (4076/1012) 550
Bed, brass-mounted mahogany, scrolled feet, N.Y., H35¾, W58, L78 ca1830 (4146/268) 400
Book-cabinet, inlaid mahogany, molded cornice, bracket feet, N.Y.*, H69, W44¾, M19c (4146/248) *700*
Bookcase, lady's desk,N.Eng., mahogany, cherrywood, 69½ x 39, res, ca1815 (4076/1027) 400
Bookcase, secretary, mahogany, molded cornice, slant-front, convex drawer, 93 x 44 x 20, ca1825
(654/509) 500
Breakfront-bookcase, mahogany, N.Eng.*, 3 parts, cornice, glazed door case, 81½ x 64 x 23, res,
ca1815 (4268/848) 1000
Bureau, slant-front, mahogany, fitted interior, 3 drawers, 40 x 42, 19c (684/704) 425
Cabinet, side, carved mahogany, gallery, 2-frieze drawers, cupboards doors, 51¼ x 48, ca1830
(684/735) 75
Chairs, side set of 4, N.Y., mahogany, inlaid, barrel-shaped back, res., ca1830 (654/698) 1000
Chairs, side set of 6, maple, cane seat, carved crestrail, vase splat, ca1840 (684/518) 600

Chairs, side, set of six, walnut, carved, Gothic back, ca1850 (4076/961)   950
Chest of drawers, carved, painted, spirally-turned columns, 49¼ x 41¾ x 20¾, ca1830 (4209/332)   1900
Chest of drawers, carved curly maple, oblong top, turned legs, 48 x 41¾, ca1820 (4211/1164)   225
Chest of drawers, mahogany, convex frieze drawer, 3 drawers, columns, 39 x 41, ca1830 (684/596)   *375*

Chest of drawers (684/596)

Book-cabinet (4146/248)

Chest of drawers, mahogany, wooden pulls, scroll feet, 46 x 43, ca1840 (684/599)   75
Chest of drawers, mahogany, 2small, 3 long drawers, 42 x 43, ca1820 (684/757)   500
Chest of drawers, ormolu mounted, mahogany, dressing mirror, candle branches, 82 x 46½ x 21,
 ca1830 (4211/1168)   1100
Chest of drawers, tall, brass-mounted, mahogany, leaf-carved paw feet, 48½ x 46¾ ca1825
 (4146/267)   100
Chest of drawers, N.Y.*, mahogany, scrolled uprights, ca1820, 19½ x 19½ (4076/883)   475
Chest of drawers, mahogany, veneered, now fitted as secretary, 44¾ x 45, ca1830 (654/589)   150
Chest of drawers, maple, 3 drawers, spool turned pilasters, 41 x 43 x 18½, 1825-50 (654/605)   175
Chest of drawers, serpentine, mahogany, inlaid, scalloped skirt, 38½ x 40½, ca1825 (654/582)   175
Cupboard, Pa.*, pine, painted, grained in yellow, brown, 55¼ x 42½ x 21, ca1840 (654/645)   300
Day bed, turned curly maple, turned arms, tapering feet, N.Y.*, res, L66½ ca1825 (4146/282)   150
Desk-bookcase, lady's, painted, decorated, pine, cupboard doors, tapering feet, 67¾ x 37¾ x 19¾,
 ca1825 (4209/312)   4000
Desk, bookcases, mahognay, inlaid, glazed doors, butler's drawer, 88 x 42¼, ca1825 (654/621)   475
Dressing table, mirror, mahogany, carved, rectangular top, turned legs, 59 x 39½ x 18¾, ca1825
 (654/517)   400
Loveseat, carved, S-shaped back, serpentine-front seat, L42, ca1830 (654/625)   300
Mirror, carved and gilded, overmantel, leaves on punchwork ground, 29¼ x 44, ca1825 (4211/1181) 175
Mirror, inlaid mahogany ogee wall, 34½ x 23⅜, 19c (4149/212)   90
Mirror, overmantel, giltwood, 28 x 64, ca1830 (684/701)   200
Mirror, shaving, mahogany, brass, animal-paw feet, 25½ x 22, 19c (4180/859)   325
Mirror, wall, curly maple, molded framework, painted panel, 43¾ x 23¾, 1820 (4180/1053)   300
Mirror, wall, N.Y., Williams, J.W., mahogany, parcel-gilded, 48½ x 25¼, 19c (4076/928)   225
Secretary, bookcase, cherry, 2 glazed doors, slant-front, 2 drawers, 80 x 48, ca1830 (684/514)   150
Secretary cabinet, butler's mahogany, gallery, secretary drawer, bottle drawers, 56 x 46, ca1825
 (684/767)   500
Secretary cabinet, butler's, carved, mahogany, 2 drawers, secretary drawer, cupboards, 51 x 48,
 ca1820 (684/765)   1700
Secretary cabinet, mahogany, 2 parts, glazed doors, flip top writing surface, 79 x 42, ca1820
 (684/524)   225
Settee, carved mahogany, baluster crestrail, massive paw feet, 70, ca1830 (684/565)   125
Settee, carved mahogany, paneled crestrail, downward curving arms, N.Y., 72½, res, ca1825
 (4211/1199)   1200
Settee, mahogany, upholstered, 80, ca1820 (684/722)   500
Settee, mahogany, cylindrical crest, N.Y.*, S-scroll fronts, leafage, cross-hatch, L93½, ca1820
 (4180/968)   500
Settee, mahogany, N.Y., carved, stenciled, L77, ca1825 (4076/947)   2500
Shaving mirror, mahogany, rectangular panel, columnar standards, 30 x 22, ca1820 (684/780)   50
Side chair, mahogany fiddle back, slip seat, sabre legs, ca1845 (4149/185)   140

Sideboard, inlaid, maple and cherry, 3 drawers, 4 fielded cupboard doors, 42 x 66, ca1820 (684/563)   175
Sofa, carved mahogany, stuffed seat, back, arms, green plush, paw feet, 70, ca1820 (684/740)   *550*

Sofa   (684/740)

Sofa, mahogany, cornucopia-carved arms and legs, L88, ca1825 (654/627)   400
Sofa, mahogany, Mass., crestrail, upholstered, acanthus carving, L71, rep, ca1825 (4268/1252)   650
Stand, 2 drawer, empire, mahogany, square top, 2 drop leaves, 28½ x 33 x 18, ca1830 (654/525)   200
Stand, 2-drawer, mahogany, rectangular top, 2 convex drawers, turned leg, 29 x 42 x 22½, mid 19c
(654/559)   75
Stand, 2-drawer, mahogany, square top, tapered standard, turned feet, 28½ x 34½ x 17, 1825-50
(654/562)   250
Table, breakfast, flip top, mahogany, swiveling flip top, brass paw feet, 28 x 49, M19c (684/567)   250
Table, breakfast, drop-leaf, tetrapod, paw feet, 29½ x 39, ca1825 (654/665)   200
Table, card, birch and inlaid burlwood, D shape, trestle shaped feet, 30 x 35, ca1825 (684/516)   300
Table, card, carved mahogany, D-shaped, paw feet, N.Y., H29½, ca1830 (4146/216)   200
Table, card, flip top, carved mahogany, D-shaped, paw feet, 28 x 36, M19c (684/632)   325
Table, center drop-leaf, carved mahogany, lobed drop leaves, paw feet, 28 x 50, ca1840 (684/692)   200
Table, center, gothic revival, N.Y. or Newark, marble-top, mahogany, 29¼ x 42¾, rep, ca1855
(4268/1199)   1700
Table, center, N.Y., pine, painted and grained, 29½ x 41¼, ca1825 (4076/941)   650
Table, dining, drop-leaf, carved mahogany, 2 pedestal, cylindrical standard, 29 x 88, ca1830
(684/644)   3500
Table, dining, drop-leaf, mahogany, 1 real, 1 dummy drawer, paw feet, 28 x 51, ca1820 (684/639)   225
Table, drop-leaf, mahogany, D shape leaves, 1 swing leg, 27½ x 62, ca1840 (684/569)   150
Table, drum, inlaid mahogany, circular, 3 drawers, Baltimore*, 28¾ x 25, ca1825 (4211/1285)   700
Table, game, mahogany, carved, convex shape platform base, 30½ x 36 x 18¼, warp, ca1825
(654/620)   150
Table, library drop-leaf, carved mahogany, Allison, N.Y., label, 28¾ x 39¼ x 48 (4211/1198)   1600
Table, library, mahogany, rectangular, D shaped leaves, N.Y.*, 28¾ x 37⅞ x 47, ca1820
(4211/1303)   500
Table, work, carved mahogany, rectangular, 2 real, 2 dummy drawers, 31 x 25½, ca1825 (684/517)   300
Table, work, mahogany, 2 drawers, 26½ x 18, ca1820 (684/736)   175
Table, work, Mass.*, mahogany, carved, inlaid, lyre support, 28½ x 19½ x 17¼, 19c (654/629)   225
Tables, pair, console, mahogany, marble top, trestle supports, mirrored back, 35 x 36, ca1830
(684/681)   600

Chinese Export

Candlestand, gold, black lacquer, octagonal, top tilting, 31 x 22⅜, M19c (4211/1215)   550
Tables, nest of four, black-lacquer, serpentine contour, lyre-form trestle, H28, W20, 19c (4076/1243)   400
Work table, black lacquer, gold deco, oblong top, lyre-form supports, M19c (4076/851)   500

Country

Armchair, horn, open, back, arms, legs formed from steer horn, 19c (654/544)   250
Armchair, ladder-back, turned maple, painted 4 shaped splats, N.Eng., res, ca1750 (4146/328)   1200
Armchair, ladder-back, N.Eng., maple, turned, painted, black, 1740-80 (654/656)   3000
Armchair, ladder-back, oak and ash, Canadian*, 4 shaped slates, 18-19c (4180/963)   650

Armchair, turned maple and pine, inversely arched crestrail, rockers, ca1780 (4149/257)	500
Armchair, windsor, wheel-back, English yewwood, shaped seat, turned legs, ca1800 (654/515)	400
Armchairs, ladder-back, pair, turned maple, rush-seat French Canadian, 18/19c (4076/1050)	2600
Bed, cast-iron, painted, stamped J. Bagnall and Sons, Boston, 33 x 78½ x 39, 19c (4209/331)	1200
Beds, cast-iron single, pair, crossed bar foot and headboards, 19c, 36½ x 76 x 32½ (4209/317)	850
Bedstead, low-post, turned, N.Eng.*, painted blue, 35¼ x 56½, 19c (4211/857)	125
Bedsteads, pair,cherrywood, urn-finials, 74½ x 82½, 19c (4148/111)	450
Bench/table, pine, primitive, hinged top, trestle supports, seat stretcher, 60 x 20, res, 19c (4159/158)	600
Bench, carved and painted, bootjack feet, 37½ x 71, 19c (4211/826)	325
Bench, cobbler's, pine, leather seat, 2 drawers, 19 x 44 x20 (654/502)	225
Bench, pail, painted pine, bootjack feet, traces of red-orange paint, 18¼ x 68, 19c (684/507)	125
Bench, pail, pine, green paint, bootjack feet, 17 x 90¾, 19c (4211/863)	125
Bench, pine cobbler's, work surface fitted with drawers, L47, 19c (4149/243)	250
Bench, pine two-tier pail, painted green, 34½ x 53¾, 19c (4211/858)	250
Bench, pine, pair, Pa.*, L78, 19c (4149/181)	140
Bench, plank-seat, long, Pa.*, turned, L84, 19c (654/639)	300
Bench, rush-seat, double back, walnut, traces of red paint, 33, 19c (684/631)	425

Blanket chest   (4211/865)

Bench, turned and painted wood long, L120, E19c (4149/245)	200
Benches, pine wagon, pair, with loose cushions, L38, 19c (4149/180)	175
Blanket chest, carved Schwenkfelder, Montgomery County, Pa., 24¾ x 51 x 22, ca1780 (4211/865)	*3250*
Blanket chest, lift-top, painted, decorated oak, rectangular, iron bale handles, 33½ x 73, 19c (684/749)	900
Blanket chest, lift-top, painted pinewood, domed top, 29 x 49, 1862 (684/645)	125
Blanket chest, lift-top, carved pine, bracket feet and bootjack feet, 30¼ x 44, 18c (4209/359)	500
Blanket chest, lift-top, pine, painted, decorated, 23½ x 37, res, 1780-1820 (4076/1041)	200
Blanket chest, lift-top, tulip, poplar, grained, bracket feet, Pennsylvania, 24½ x 41⅝ x 19¾, 1820-40 (4209/352)	950
Blanket chest, lift-top, carved, painted with vessel flying American flag, 16 x 42, E19c (684/679)	125
Blanket chest, painted and grained, lift-top, Pa.*, 24¾ x 50, ca1820 (4211/856)	450
Blanket chest, painted with flower, grained, initials B.T., N.Eng., 37 x 39¾ x 18¾, ca1810 (4211/804)	1000
Blanket chest, pine lift-top, bracket feet, H42, L42½, L18c/E19c (4146/308)	100
Blanket chest, pine lift-top, single thumb, painted blue-black, 37 x 36¼, 18c (4149/183)	1000
Blanket chest, pine, painted, paneled front, red, black graining, 21 x 41¾ x 18⅛, res, 18c (4268/809)	550
Blanket chest, poplar, Pa., wrought-iron lock, strap hinges, painted red, 25¼ x 53½ x 23, res, ca1800 (4268/790)	200
Blanket chest, stained pinewood, lift-top enclosing till and well, 24 x 43, E19c (684/794)	225
Blanket chest, well with till and, drawer, bootjack feet, red, 26¾ x 52 x 18 (4211/790)	400
Bottle rack, 12 crossarms, with pegs, cruciform base, H77, 19c (4211/712)	400
Box, writing, pilgrim century carved oak, hinged slant-front, interior with drawers, 11 x 28 x 15, 17c (4211/1098)	650

Box, Pa., painted and decorated, tulip, poplar, Maria Brandin, 10 x 18, 1832 (684/592)   450
Cabinet, paneled pine 2-door storage, 47¼ x 43¾, 19c (4149/196)   225
Cabinet secretary, wooton, burl walnut, bird's eye maple, Standard Grade, 52 x 40, 1874 (684/650)   5000
Candlestand, adjustable, walnut, wrought-iron, circ. top, birdcage support, 25½ x 17½, ca1800 (4076/1378)   600
Candlestand, dish-top, maple, N.Eng., tilt-top, platform base, 3 legs, 27½ x 18¾, 18c (4268/1208)   750
Chair, arm, ladder-back, turned, maple and ash, 4 splats, turned legs, 1730-80 (4076/1301)   1400
Chair, corner, maple with comb crest, splint seat, N. Eng., ca1750 (4156/316)   2900
Chair table, pine and chestnut, top lifting to a seat, 30 x 42, 1750-1800 (4149/242)   400
Chairs, side, rare, set of six, ladder-back, turned and painted, 5 slats, Delaware Valley, 1750-1800 (4076/1291)   18000
Chairs, side, set, six, N.Eng., maple, splint seat, painted black over red, (4211/789)   1500
Chairs, side, turned maple, ladder-back, rush-seats, E19c (4211/743)   125
Chest, blanket, pine, tulip-poplar, Pa.*, deep well, 2 drawers, grained, 27½ x 42 x 21, res, E19c (4268/844)   400
Chest, lift-top, painted, grained pine, bracket base, 25 x 42¾ x 18, 1810-40 (4209/355)   3750
Chest, lift-top, grained pine, hinged lid, valanced apron, bracket feet, 20¼ x 36½ x 15¾, res, E19c (4268/1160)   150
Chest, lift-top, primitive, pine, oblong top, on molded base, 26 x 37¾, 19c (4146/288)   70
Chest, painted, grained pine lift-top, turned feet, Pa., H24¼, M19c (4146/217)   275
Chest, pine apothecary, upright, many thumb molded drawers, 40 x 35¼, E19c (4149/189)   1000
Chest of drawers, cherrywood, pine, sides forming bootjack feet, 33 x 31½, ca1800 (4149/248)   2000
Chest of drawers, painted birds, Mahantango Valley, Pa., 52 x 39¼ x 20½, ca1830 (4211/866)   10000
Chest of drawers, Pa., painted and grained pine, 37¾ x 39¾, ca1830 (4211/749)   500
Chest of drawers, cherry, maple, rectangular top, 3 inlaid drawers, turned leg, 54 x 23 x 18½, ca1830 (654/519)   400
Chest over drawers, carved pine, N.Eng., hinged top, 2 working drawers, 39¾ x 37½ x 17⅛, 1750-80 (4268/794)   450
Corner cupboard, carved pine, 2 parts, glazed doors over cupboard doors, 88½ x 42 x 26½, ca1800 (4268/752)   1000
Corner cupboard, pine, painted, grained, bracket feet, cupboard doors, 86 x 42¼ x 27, E19c (4209/325)   10000
Corner stand, carved, painted pine, N.Eng., 56 x 19 x 13½, E19c (4211/813)   300
Cradle, carved and painted green, slatted bottom, N.Eng.*, L36, L18-E19c (4211/848)   175
Cradle, painted and grained pine, sponge decoration, L42½, 18-19c (4211/824)   375
Cradle, pine and turned maple, inward tapering posts, L35¾, ca1750 (4149/249)   300
Cradle, walnut, primitive, shaped sides, pierced ends, 41½, 19c (4159/154)   400
Cupboard, pine, press, 2 paneled cupboard doors, painted blue, red, 70 x 54 x 16¼, 18/19c (4268/796)   450
Cupboard, primitive painted pine, molded cornice, 2 panelled cupboard doors, 74 x 43½, 18c (4076/1353)   850
Cupboard, wall, cherrywood, 2-part, Pa.*, glazed doors, 3 drawers, cupboard, 85 x 53½ x 21, altered, E19c (4268/829)   2000
Cupboard, wall, painted, Pa., recessed upper part, boot-jack feet, 71½ x 49¼, ca1820 (4076/1325)   3000
Cupboard, wall, panelled pine, bracket base, 66¼ x 43¼, ca1800 (4211/862)   300
Cupboard, wall, pine, 64½ x 35¾, 19c (654/649)   100
Cupboard, wall, pine, Pa.*, panelled door, drawer, 27¼ x 17¾, 19c (4211/859)   500
Cupboard, 2-part, pine, Pa., 2 glazed doors, painted red and white, 74 x 51½ x 19½, res, 1780-1820 (4268/846)   1800
Desk, counting house, pine, Mass., from 'Old manse', historical house, 52½ x 31½, ca18c (4180/966)   *900*
Desk, inlaid walnut ball-foot, crossbanded edge, stepped interior, ball feet, 43½ x 36, 1710-30 (4076/1260)   3500
Dry sink, pine, rectangular top with gallery, 26 x 28½, E19c (684/691)   250
Dry sink, primitive, pine, rectangular top, 2 drawers, 2 cupboard doors, 36½ x 43¼ x 19¼ (654/532)   250
Dry sink, Amish, maple, painted, rectangular top, single drawer, 2 doors, 30½ x 60½x 19 (654/571)   650
Headboard, maple, spool-turned double, 34¾ x 84, 19c (4149/209)   150
Headboards, turned maple, pair, spool turned crests, 37½ x 40, 19c (4149/220)   175
Highchair, child's, walnut, splint seat, E19c (684/797)   50
Highchair, painted pine, child's, ring and bamboo-turned, 19c (4180/863)   300
Lift-top chest, painted, decorated, pine bootjack feet, restored, 27¼ x 41¾ x 17¾, 1710-40 (4209/314)   4500
Lift-top chest, painted, grained pine, ball feet, plain case, fine, ca1820, 23¼ x 39¼ x 18¼ (4209/346)   5500
Linen press, inlaid mahogany, N.Y., removable cornice, valanced apron, French feet, H87, ca1800 (4146/197)   1600

Desk   (4180/966)

Mantel, carved and white-painted, pine, H45¾ x 47, E19c (4211/811)	150
Meeting house bench, pine, carved, painted, bootjack feet, L78 (4211/788)	450
Mirror, courting, eglomise, pine, angular arched cresting, eglomise panels, 16¼ x 11¼, ca1790 (4076/1392)	600
Mirror, courting, Continental, painted glass and pine, cresting, H16, W10⅝, M18c (4076/1217)	500
Panel, painted pinewood, semi-circular fan form, with radiating panels, 27½ x 54, 19c (684/690)	125
Panel, rectangular, architectural, pine, carved and painted, 22 x 145, E19c (4211/744)	550
Rocker, arrow-back, painted, decorated, bamboo-turned legs, N.Eng., ca1825 (4209/306)	900
Rocker, arrow-back rush-seat, painted, grained, tapering legs, ca1820, Fairfield* (4209/372)	1100
Rocker, ladder-back, child's, Pa., maple, rush-seat, turned supports, L18c (4076/860)	275
Rocker, plank-seat, painted, decorated, concave crestrail, ca1825, N.Eng. (4209/358)	3000
Rocker, stencilled and grained, red on yellow graining, all over decoration, N. Eng., ca1825 (4156/311)	700
Safe, pie, pine, straight cornice, 2 pierced tin doors, drawer, 2 cupboard doors, 71½ x 40 x 14½ (654/530)	425
Settee, ash, caned seat, back, adjustable to daybed, L60, 10½ (4149/253)	250
Settee, pine plank seat, carved and painted, Pa.*, L78, ca1830 (4211/779)	375
Settle, hooded, paneled pine, Pa., 6 panels, shaped sides, dark green, 61 x 64½ x 23, alt, 1750-80 (4268/1308)	2400
Shelf, carved pine, 4 shelves, red stain, 38 x 34½ x 9, E19c (4211/814)	250
Shelves, pine, walnut, scrolled sides, 35 x 34½ x 8½ (654/564)	225
Side chair, pine, maple, rush-seat, solid vase-form splat, L18c (4149/259)	400
Side chairs, plank-seat, set of six, white-painted, decorated, ca1825 (4209/360)	2100
Sofa, country, carved pine and oak, upholstered, 19c, L74 (4209/337)	2100
Stand, pine and turned maple, on turned tapered legs, 1 drawer, 26½ x 23½, 19c (4149/190)	60
Stand, 1 drawer, carved pine, Pa.*, tapering legs, 28 x 17, ca1815 (4211/836)	150
Stool, joint, oak, sycamore, turned, 23¼ x 21½, 1710-30 (654/712)	500
Stool, plank top, painted green, Pa.*, H9, L8, 19c (4146/158)	70
Stool, rush-seat, turned and painted, N.Eng., L 11½, E19c (4146/139)	200
Stove, open grate, painted cast iron, N. Winslow, Portland, 30 x 27, ca1820 (684/723)	350
Swan bench, cast-iron, with original paint, 37¼ x 76, 19c (4209/239)	5250
Table, center, walnut, turned cherrywood, oblong cleated top, tapering legs, Pa., H28¼, L59½, ca1750 (4146/240)	450
Table, chair, painted blue, pine, rectangular top above seat, hinged lid, 28¾ x 66½ x 36¼, 1760-90 (4211/1264)	2400
Table, dining, drop-leaf, mahogany, D-shape leaves, turned legs, 28½ x 58 x 42 (654/510)	150
Table, drop-leaf, carved and painted, pine, H26¾ x 42 x 40, ca1820 (4211/792)	250
Table, drop-leaf, occasional, rectangular top, turned legs, 29 x 42 x 30½ (654/549)	200
Table, drop-leaf, cherry, maple, rectangular top, 2 end drawers, turned legs, 30 x 60 x 45 (654/527)	325

Table, harvest, drop-leaf, plank top, traces of blue paint, 28 x 84, ca1820 (684/549)   425
Table, pine harvest, N.Eng., oblong top, x-form legs, 28½ x 156, 19c (4076/1311)   1700
Table, pine, maple, square top, splayed tapered legs, 28 x 17½ x 17½, 1800-25 (654/566)   75
Table, tavern, maple, pine, primitive, rectangular top, turned legs, 26 x 35 x 25½, E19c (4159/160)   600
Table, tavern, oval, maple, pine, Conn.*, molded apron, tapering legs, 29½ x 30¼, rep, 18c
(4268/836)   425
Table, tavern, pine and maple, oblong top, breadboard ends, turned legs, 24½ x 28 x 20, res, M18c
(4268/1167)   300
Table, tavern, pine, cherrywood, rect. top, turned legs, button feet, 26¼ x 46¾, M18c (4076/1350)   950
Table, tavern, pine, cherrywood, N.Eng., oval top, box stretcher, 26¼ x 32½, 1740-70 (4180/1011)   800
Table, tavern, pine, turned maple, skirt with single drawer, 24 x 38¼, 1750-1800 (4149/246)   1500
Table, tavern, turned walnut, Pa., single drawer, baluster-turned leg, H29, L47, D32, M18c
(4146/199)   350
Table, tavern, turned, painted maple, oval top, ball feet, 25¾ x 31, 1740-80 (4076/1318)   2600
Table, tavern,N.Eng., pine, primitive, oblong, octagonal legs, 25¾ x 31¼ x 22½ (654/596)   400
Table, tilt-top, mahogany, circular top, turned tripod, H29, Diam 29 (654/539)   375
Table, Tavern, oval top, cherrywood, N.Eng., button feet, 28 x 33¾, 1750-1800 (4180/955)   750
Tea caddy, Chippendale, mahogany, rect., bracket feet, L9, 1775-1800 (4076/1198)   150
Tray, cutlery, walnut, heart-shaped handhold, 6 x 15¼, 19c (4180/871)   *225*
Trestle table, carved and painted, oblong cleated top, bootjack feet, Hudson River*, 29½ x 50,
ca1750 (4076/1258)   1000
Wagon bench, maple, ash rush-seat, N.Eng., 19c (4211/823)   300
Wall mirror, stenciled pine, flower devices, ca1840, N.Eng., 16¼ x 13¼ (4209/286)   350

Country, Shaker

Cupboard, wall, pine, carved,N.Eng., 3 parts, 3 glazed doors, 2 cupboard doors, 97 x 73¾ x 15½,
E19 (654/575)   *3000*
Footstool, painted and cushioned, oblong top, 5½ x 11½, 19c (684/665)   175

Country, Windsor

Armchair, bamboo-turned, incised saddle seat, N.Eng. ca1800, (4211/745)   *450*
Armchair, bamboo-turned, R.I.*, res., ca1790 (4211/771)   *450*
Armchair, bow-back, ring-and-baluster-turned tapering legs, good, 1780-1800, Conn. (4209/366)   1300
Armchair, bow-back, turned, painted green, res., ca1780 (654/678)   400
Armchair, bow-back,N.Eng., turned, painted, saddle seat, 1780-1800, rep. (654/630)   300
Armchair, bow-back, N.Eng., saddle seat, baluster-turned legs, 1780-1800 (4146/324)   *1200*

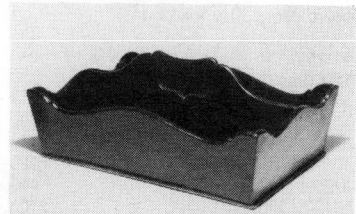

Tray (4180/871)

Cupboard (654/575)

Armchair (4211/745)

Armchair (4146/324)

Armchair (4076/967)

Armchair, bow-back, turned spindles, saddle seat, red stain, 1780-1800 (4268/1159)	375
Armchair, brace-back, turned, painted black over red, R.I., fine, ca1790 (4209/351)	2000
Armchair, brace-back, 8 turned spindles, saddle seat, ca1780 (4149/288)	2200
Armchair, child's, painted black, N.Eng., saddle seat, ca1790 (4180/1038)	1300
Armchair, continuous, comb crest, above hoop back, ca1800 (4211/835)	550
Armchair, fan-back, bamboo-turned spindles, saddle seat, ca1790 (684/545)	550
Armchair, fan-back, carved, painted, Pa., 1780-1800 (4209/310)	6250
Armchair, fan-back, scrolled ears, tapering legs, Conn.*, ca1790 (4209/354)	1100
Armchair, fan-back, Philadelphia, fan-shaped crest, 7 spindles, provenance, ca1760 (4268/812)	3000
Armchair, fan-back, Philadelphia, 9 spindles, bobbin stretchers, painted black, res, 1770-80 (4268/861)	1600
Armchair, fan-back, painted black, N.Eng.*, fan shaped cresting, L18c (4180/961)	1000
Armchair, fan-back, saddle seat, N.Eng., ca1780 (4211/770)	1000
Armchair, fan-back, scroll carved, crest, N.Eng., ca1780 (4211/821)	1700
Armchair, hoop-back, N.Eng., saddle seat, res, L18/E19 (4146/195)	400
Armchair, hoop-back, 7 spindles, knuckle arms, saddle seat, turned legs, E19c (654/601)	400
Armchair, low-back, turned, painted, horseshoe back, Philadelphia, 1770-80 (4076/1278)	3750
Armchair, low-back, Philadelphia, good, ca1770 (4076/967)	2750
Armchair, lowback, Philadelphia, horseshoe back, saddle seat, turned, legs, 1750-70 (4268/1211)	3250
Armchair, painted and bamboo-turned, 7 turned spindles, incised seat, E19c (684/788)	325
Armchair, painted black, yellow, Conn.*, cupid bow crestrail, red rooster, ca1790, fine (4180/1078)	2100
Armchair, painted, fan-back, horseshoe back, Conn.*, ca1800 (4076/1326)	2600
Armchair, sack-back, N.Eng., spindles, saddle seat, raking legs, ca1780 (4268/1164)	350
Armchair, sack-back, N.Eng., 7 spindles, knuckle terminals, res, 1780 (4268/764)	700
Armchair, sack-back, Tracy, E., Conn., ca1800 (4076/970)	1000
Armchair, sack-back, Pa., ring and baluster turned legs, res., ca1780 (654/683)	450
Armchair, sackback, N.Eng., 7 spindles, carved saddle seat, painted black, ca1800 (4268/857)	750
Armchair, sackback, N.Eng., 7 spindles, plank seat, dark green, 1790-1800 (4268/863)	650
Armchair, turned and painted, N.Eng., R.I.*, shaped seat, ca1800 (4180/1050)	950
Armchair, turned and painted green, fan-back, N.Eng., ca1780 (4211/801)	1400
Armchair, turned oak bow-back, back with 8 turned spindles, seat res, ca1800 (4149/255)	575
Armchair, writing, painted black-green, N.Eng., horsebshoe backrest, writing arm, drawer, ca1790 (4268/1303)	2300
Armchair, N.Eng., 7 spindles, bowed back, painted red-brown, ca1780, rep (4211/750)	700
Armchair, R.I.*, continuous back, 7 spindles, saddle seat, ca1780 (4268/754)	850
Armchairs, continuous, pair, turned, painted with original black paint, fine, Rhode sland (4209/335)	6250
Armchairs, 2, Pa.*, turned, bamboo, rectangular back, res., E19 (654/684)	600
Bench, turned, painted, Conn., fine, 1780-1800, L80 (4209/334)	3750
Bench, bamboo-turned, pine, Pa., birdcage back, plank seat, painted green, L73, res, 1800-15 (4268/845)	1700
Chair, hoop-back, slipper, Conn., baluster leg, 1770-1800 (4076/1062)	175
Chair, rocking, arrow back, rectangular crestrail, 4 splats, E19c (684/589)	75
Chair, rocking, painted and decorated, rush-seat, ca1800 (684/801)	150

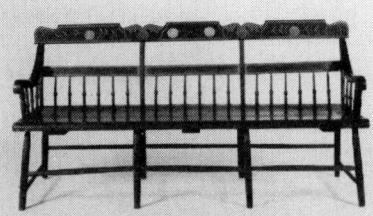

Rocker (4149/252)   Chair (4146/301)   Settee (684/547)

Chair, side, bamboo-turned, Philadelphia, I. Henzey, bowed crest, 9 spindles, ca1785 (4268/1266)	1000
Chair, side, bamboo-turned bow-back, shaped seat, raking legs, N.Eng., E19c (4156/292)	250
Chair, side, bamboo-turned hoopback, incised saddle seat, N.Eng., ca1800 (4211/740)	150
Chair, side, bow-back, painted, N.Eng., incised crest, 9 spindles, saddle, seat, ca1780 (4268/1206)	450
Chair, side, brace-back, Conn.*, deeply scooped saddle seat, 1780-1800, good (4180/1079)	2000
Chair, side, fan-back, incised saddle seat, good, Conn. ca1780 (4211/775)	550
Chair, side, fan-back, saddle seat, branded E.B. Tracy, Lisbon, Conn., ca1780 (4211/759)	650
Chair, side, fan-back, saddle seat, painted black, N.Eng., ca1780 (4211/765)	350
Chair, side, fan-back, scroll-carved ears, Conn.*, ca1780 (4211/855)	1500
Chair, side, fan-back, Conn*, bamboo-turned legs, ca1800 (4146/301)	*325*
Chair, side, fan-back,N.Eng., painted black, ca1790 (654/676)	400
Chair, side, hoop-back, saddle seat, turned, painted black, RI*, 1780-1800 (4146/247)	275
Chair, side, painted fan-back, seven turned spindles, Conn., ca1780 (4076/1310)	1900
Chair, slipper, turned and painted, N.Eng., ca1780 (4211/851)	225
Chairs, side, bamboo-turned, pair, bow-back, painted, Conn*, E19c (4146/256)	275
Chairs, side, hoop-back, saddle seat, painted white, R.I.*, pair, 1780-1800 (4146/263)	1300
Chairs, side, hoop-back,N.Eng., 2, saddle seat, bamboo-turned legs, ca1800 (654/598)	400
Chairs, side, pair, Pa., bamboo-turned, ca1810 (654/647)	375
Chairs, side, set of 6, N. Eng.* painted black over white, birdcage crests, E19c (4268/737)	2000
Chairs, side, three, bamboo-turned, N.Eng., hoop backs, 1 painted brown, ca1800 (4180/967)	450
Cradle, child's, wooden, arched head and foot board, shaped rockers, 38, ca1800 (684/588)	250
Highchair, child's, bamboo-turned, horseshoe crest, 10 spindles, 19c (684/582)	75
Highchair, child's, bamboo-turned, horseshoe crest, 8 spindles, 19c (684/583)	150
Highchair, turned and painted, red with gilt decoration, 1820 (684/561)	425
Rocker, bamboo-turned, painted, branded A. Hagget, Charlestown, E19c (4211/763)	1000
Rocker, child's plank-seat, painted, decorated, ca1825 (4209/299)	600
Rocker, comb-back, bamboo-turned, rectangular crest, 6 spindles, painted red, black, ca1820 (4268/778)	375
Rocker, comb-back, Conn., painted dark green, 1780-1800 (4076/946)	1200
Rocker, hoop-back, fan-shaped crest, N.Eng., seat with incised edge, black, ca1810 (4180/1081)	800
Rocker, painted comb-back, painted with fruit, leaves, red ground, ca1810 (4149/252)	*500*
Settee, bamboo-turned, painted and, decorative scrolled arms, plank seat, 72, E19c (684/547)	*550*
Settee, bamboo-turned, 22 spindle back, incised apron, L68¾, ca1800 (4076/1374)	1300
Settee, bamboo-turned and painted, Conn.*, ca1800, rare size, L35 3/5 (4209/342)	1900
Settee, Pa., turned, bamboo, rectangular crestrail, plank seat, L80, res, E19 (654/680)	1600
Side chairs, bamboo-turned bow-back, each with brass brace, ca1810 (4149/244)	650
Stool, turned maple and pine, painted red, N.Eng., L18-19c (4211/834)	1700
Stool, N.Eng., two, turned, brown paint traces, 18-19c (4209/298)	550

American Household Objects

BOXES, CHESTS

Bandboxes, pasteboard, two, New England, printed paper, wear, 19c, 10½ x 15 and 10¼ x 15 (4209/293)	700
Bandboxes, two, N.Eng., pineapple print, inscribed, ca1835, 12½ - 16¼ (4209/290)	700
Bandboxes, N.Eng., two, oblong, wear, ca1835 (4209/291)	1000

'Beever' hat box, pasteboard, worn, 19c, 9½ x 12½ (4209/294)	300
Bible box, Pa.*, chip carved, hinged lid, L19¾, 19c (4180/860)	200
Box, desk, painted and grained pine and oak, slope front, interior fitted, 7 x 10¾, 19c (4211/1076)	125
Box, desk, traveling, brass mounted mahogany, rectangular, hinged top, fitted interior, 6⅜ x 17⅞, M19c (4211/1114)	200
Box, desk, traveling, mahogany, hinged lid, writing flap, drawer, brass handles, 6¼, 19c (4211/1110)	175
Box, document, inlaid, mahogany Federal, hinged lid, plain interior, bracket feet, 8¾, ca1800 (4211/1079)	600
Box, document, painted tinware, domed lid, Pa., L9⅜, E19c (4076/1189)	175
Box, document, Pa.*, painted, decorated, flowers, bail handle, ca1820, 7⅝ x 9⅞ (4209/134)	2100
Box, gold decorated black lacquer, Chinese, export, octagonal, hinged lid, 8⅛, M19c (4211/1102)	325
Box, patch, engraved brass, oval, figure on seashore, L4½, Dutch*, 18c (654/261)	90
Box, pipe, carved walnut, shaped and pierced cresting, drawer, 17½ x 5¼, N. Eng., 18c (4156/186)	1500
Box, sailor's, poplar, inlaid with hearts and anchors, 6½ x 11, 19c (4076/206)	100
Box, tea, inlaid mahogany, George III, ivory finial, inlaid all over, 5 x 5⅜, ca1800 (4211/1111)	500
Box, wood, carved, decorated as a book, pullout drawer, 19c, 2¾ x 12 (4209/190)	800
Box, writing, papier-mache, enameled with song birds, 14¾, L19c (4148/127)	170
Box,N.Eng.*, painted, decorated, dome-fitted cover, bail handle, ca1820, H11½, good (4209/133)	1600
Bride's Box, Pa.*, oval, with fitted lid, painted, L16¾, 19c (4180/816)	150
Candlebox, carved and painted pine, sliding cover, initials RNS, date 1773, L13¾ (4156/196)	600
Candlebox, hanging, Pa., carved mahogany, angular sides, L13½, ca1800 (4076/1191)	325
Captain's chest, dome-top, inscribed, painted, grained pine, Continental*, H27, 19c (4146/194)	200
Chest, painted pine seaman's, cedar lined, green, L43¾, 19c (4149/198)	160
Chest, painted seaman's, rope handles, 2 bottles, L46, 19c (4149/194)	375
Chest, seaman's, painted and decorated wood, rectangular, dome lid 8¼ x 16⅝, 1823 (4211/1118)	275
Chest, small, Federal, Mass.*, inlaid mahogany, curly maple, apron, L12, ca1800 (4076/1190)	275
Coffrette, Federal, inlaid mahogany, probably Mass., carrying handles, H28¾, W16, ca1800 (4076/1228)	1600
Coffrette, N.Eng., Federal, curly maple, dome-top, L7⅜, E19c (4076/1197)	200
Desk, pine and oak, painted, N.Eng., H15½, L29¼, 1670-1700 (4146/135)	500
Deed box, American, parquetry lid, various Masonic symbols, 10 x 9 x 5½, ca1850 (684/279)	225
Desk box, painted, decorated pine, E19c, N.Eng., L12 (4209/288)	450
Desk box, painted, decorated maple, Federal, ca1800, Mass., L12½ (4209/287)	950
Document box, painted tinware, domed, hinged lid, 3½ x 7, 19c (4180/891)	150
Document box, Pa.*, scrolled crest pierced with a heart, 10¼ x 14⅛, E19c (4180/852)	450
Dough box, carved pine, covered, tapering sides, 9 x 23, 19c (4180/831)	250
Knife, pair, inlaid mahogany, serpentine, beaded base, L18c, 14¼ x 8¾ (4076/858)	850
Knifebox, serpentine, mahogany, brass handles, 13¾, ca1800 (4180/861)	175
Lectern box, N.Eng., painted wood book decoration, P.F. Coist, fine, rare, 1860-75, 6 x 13½ x 10 (4209/189)	17000
Letter box, travelling, carved, engraved walnut, rosewood in 17c style, L21, 19c (4156/192)	375
Milliner's bandbox, labeled S.M. Harlbert's Boston, wear, rare, ca1820, 9 x 12 (4209/292)	700
Papier-mache, painted, unusual, 19c, 2 x 5¾ (4209/277)	350
Papier-mache and leather, painted, view of resevoirs, N.Y.*, 2¾ x 5½, E19 (4146/150)	250
Patchbox, Dutch, oval box with engraved lid, L5', 18c (4180/865)	150
Pipe box, pine carved,N.Eng., scallop sides, painted dark green, E19c, H19 (4076/878)	1000
Sewing box, gold decorated, Chinese export, black lacquer, L14¼, 19c (4076/1193)	225
Small box, painted decorated, domed lid, 19c, 5 x 8 (4209/275)	300
Snuff box, painted tin, silver mounted, L4, ca1790 (4076/1210)	90
Tea box, plain pine, wrought iron, hinges on lid, initials A&L, 11 x 16 x 16, 1796 (4180/820)	*400*
Tobacco box, engraved gilded copper, 17c, L5¼ (4076/869)	350
Tobacco box, brass, engraved eagle, oval, hinged lid, L3⅜, ca1800 (4268/1126)	375
Tobacco box, brass, engraved eagle, rectangular, hinged lid, L3½, ca1800 (4268/1116)	350
Traveling box, mahogany, rectangular, ball feet, metal-mount, 19c, 117¾ (4076/855)	125
Wood, grained and painted, black and red spongework, 8, American, 19c (4146/71)	80
Work box, decoupage decorated wood, landscape views, L10½, 1837 (4076/1194)	175

HOUSEHOLD EQUIPMENT

Apple peeler, cast iron, wood handle, 7 gears to peel, 3 gears to core, 11¾, 19c (684/241)	50
Basket, painted, decorated, filled with marble fruit, 19c, H11 (4209/135)	2100
Baskets, 8 Nantucket nesting, ash rim, swing handles, H3¼ - 8¼, L19c (4076/1181)	3500
Bellows set, carved wood and leather, allegorical depiction of the wind, 33½, 19c (4211/1109)	90
Boot scraper, wrought iron, stylized horse, twisted tail, 6¾, 19c (4211/1039)	300
Bowl, circular, carved and red painted pine, broad rim beaded edge, short foot, 21, 19c (4211/1073)	250
Bowl, good treenware, small, covered, turned finial, footed body, D4⅛, L18/E19c (4076/1199)	125
Bowl, turned burl, deep circular form, H6, Diam 18¼, 19c (4146/134)	450
Bowls, 2 turned burl, 18/19c, L16½ (4076/865)	950

Bucket, copper, circular, brass handle, 12, E19c (4156/199) 90
Bucket, fire, leather, 1735, H10 (4076/877) 225
Bucket, George III, mahogany, brass bound, H11½, L13½, ca1800 (4076/1230) 150
Bucket, Geroge III, mahogany, brass bound, brass liner, 14 x 15, ca1800 (4076/1226) 350
Buckets, fire, pair, painted leather, insc. John A. Tucker, Dorchester, H12¼, ca1800 (4076/1215) 1100
Candlemold, pewter and pine, 24 light, unmarked, rare, American, H18, E19c (4146/93) *525*

Tea box (4180/820)

Candlemold (4146/93)

Coffee urn (654/256)

Canister, tea, Pa.*, painted, decorated, flowers, black ground, ca1820, H8¼, good (4209/128) 375
Clock jack, Balter, Geo. & Co., brass, H15¾, ca1825 (4076/1202) 125
Coal scuttle, cover and liner, pierced metal, oval, ring handle, 71, 19c (684/257) 150
Coffeepot, Pa.*, painted, decorated, flowers, gooseneck spout, ca1820, H12, fine (4209/131) 1900
Coffeepot, painted tinware, conical lid straight-tapering side, H11, 19c (4076/1235) 150
Coffeepot, Pa.*, painted, decorated, flower motif, ca1825, H9, fine (4209/126) 1700
Coffeepot, Whitlock, Troy, N.Y., double scroll handle, gooseneck spout, H11½, ca1840 (4156/145) 450
Coffee urn, painted tinware, pyriform on cabriole legs, paint restored, H15¼, 19c (654/256) *125*
Dutch oven, cast iron, on 3 peg feet, H11, 19c (4076/477) 250
Griddle, wrought and cast iron, circular, arched hangar, H16, 19c (4076/478) 100
Jar, turned treenware, covered, squat body, circular, American*, H8¾, 19c (4146/147) 325
Jenny wheel, wood, turned, 40, 19c (4149/186) 100
Jug, syrup, Pa.*, painted, decorated, flowers, dark brown ground, ca1820, H4, rare (4209/132) 800
Kettle, cast iron, gooseneck spouts, domed cover, H10, 19c (4076/479) 175
Kettle, spun bell-metal, molded lip, H6⅛, 19c (4076/480) 225
Mortar and pestle, treenware, H7¾, 19c (4146/128) 100
Pipe rack, English, pierced brass, scrolled back, L12, M18c (4076/1196) 175
Spinning wheel, pine, on peg legs, 37¾, 19c (4149/187) 120
Spinning wheel, small, turned and painted wood, applied carved hearts, ca1800 (4076/1227) 175
Spinning wheel, turned wood, N.Eng.*, H36¼, 19c (4146/129) 150
Teapot, brass, pyriform body, 7½, 19c (4076/510) 150
Teapot, English, painted tole, oval, domed lid, scrolled handle, H7¾, ca1800 (4076/1201) 80
Traveling toilet box, rosewood, three, yellow green blown glass bottles, 6 x 9, 19c (4180/867) 100
Tray, apple,N.Eng.*, painted, decorated, flowers, black ground, ca1820, 3⅛ x 12 (4209/125) 700
Tray, painted and decorated wood, hand holds, 18c figures, 19¾ x 27, 19c (654/255) 70
Tray, painted tinware, octagonal, fruits, vines, 21¼ x 30¼ (654/260) 50
Tray, Pa.*, painted, decorated, flower motif, ca1820, 2½ x 12⅝ (4209/130) 375
Tray, Pa.*, painted, decorated, oval, flowers, vines, ca1820, 4 x 13¼, good (4209/127) 600
Tray, painted tinware, N. Eng.*, handholds, peacocks, L28, 19c (4156/210) 275
Urn, hot water, Regency, brass and copper, H12¾, E19c (4076/1195) 60
Urn, hot water, Regency, brass, copper, pistol handles, fluted legs, ball feet, H16½, E19c
(4076/1200) 150
Yarn winder, carved oak and ash, 38, 19c (4149/193) 90
Yarn winder, oak and turned maple, on peg legs, 37, 19c (4149/182) 90

IMPLEMENTS

Airplane propeller, wooden, trade mark Paragon, reinforced with sheet metal, 108 (684/254) 200
Airplane propeller, wooden, Curtis, #432R, H. Oriele, reinforced with sheet metal, 98 (684/255) 200

Bedwarmer, brass and wrought-iron, stamped IST, engraved flowers on hinged lid, 40¾, 18c (4180/917) — 450

Candlemold, pewter and pine, twenty-four light, bootjack feet, H18 x L23¼, E19c (4180/886) — 575

Cane, fruitwood, carved with various American motifs, 35½, M19c (684/244) — 70

Chopper, tobacco, carved wood, wrought-iron, leaf-shaped, 18/19c, L12 (4076/871) — 325

Fan, Chinese export, paper, painted, scenes of Hong Kong, Canton, 19½ x 27¼, ca1850 (4268/1091) — 1200

Fan, Chinese export, paper, painted, scenes of Whampoa Reach, mother-of-pearl, ca1840 (4268/1092) — 250

Hand truck, carved wood, turned and fitted with wood pegs and pin, 42, 19c (4180/802) — 225

Hatchels, iron spikes in breadboard, with wood flax comb, H5-8, 19c* (4180/798) — 100

Mortar and pestle, treen, good, lignum vitae, 18/19c (4076/874) — 375

Skimmer, brass, pierced handle, eagle engraved on pan, L22, ca1760 (4180/885) — *600*

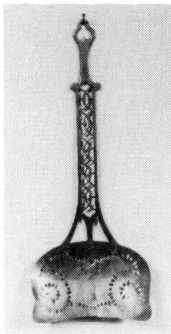
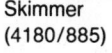
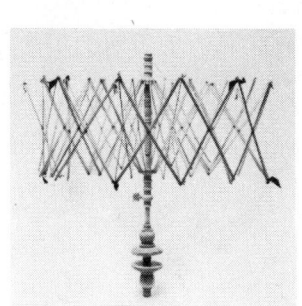

Skimmer (4180/885)

Swifts (4146/20)

Coffeepot (4180/775)

Skimmer, brass, Richard Lee, 15 (4180/915) — 750

Swifts, carved whalebone, pair, H20-21 (4146/20) — *275*

Two wheel cart, carved and painted wood, rectangular, traces of original paint, 30½ x 48½, 19c (4211/1041) — 650

Walking stick, Abraham Lincoln, gold-mounted ebony, L36¼, ca1857 (4076/1238) — 9000

METAL WARES

Bell, brass, ship's, with brass link chain, H15 (654/226) — 75

Bell, cast-iron school, painted gray-green, stand, H28 (654/227) — 175

Casters, 14 karat gold, set of 6, baluster shape, Shreve & Co., H5⅝, 19 ozs, c1900 (4076/633) — 2300

Coal scuttle or log box, painted, flared body, 2 scenes of shipping, 19½, L19c (684/351) — 600

Coffeepot, tinware, Pa.*, gooseneck spout, domed lid, painted, 11½, M19c (4180/775) — *600*

Coffee urn and stand, 'ponty pool', tinware, black-body with matching stand, 19¼, 19c (4180/887) — 450

Horn, brass, copper and wood ship's, L24¾ (654/228) — 75

Lighter, 18 karat gold, circular shape, Tiffany & Co., H2, 4 ozs 10 dwts, c1920 (4076/636) — 575

Merchant's spice cabinet, tole, fitted with 2 tiers of hatches, 34, 19c (684/297) — 200

Scales, brass, wrought iron, cast foliate scroll work, H38 (654/225) — 225

Tazzas, 14 karat gold, trumpet shaped bases, Shreve & Co., D9, 30 ozs 10 dwts, c1900 (4076/631) — 3300

Tray, tinware, painted and decorated, now on stand, peacock on branch, 31¼, 19c (4211/1121) — 750

Tray, tinware, painted and decorated, seated figure before a pagoda, 29¾, 19c (4211/1101) — 400

Warmer, plate, painted tinware, Victorian, bailhandle, hinged door, 3 shelves, 24½ x 12¾, M19c (4211/1068) — 175

MINIATURE FURNITURE

Bedstead, pencil post, doll's carved, shaped head and foot boards, arched tester, 19 x 21, 19c (4211/1088) — 275

Blanket chest, painted wood, N.Eng., 4 feet, black, red and green, 20⅝, res, 19c (684/282) — 450

Blanket chest, rare Chippendale, molded base, ogee feet, Pa. Chester*, 10¼ x 18½, 1760-80 (4076/1207) — 2300

Chest, lift-top, painted, grained, N.Eng., ca1820, 9½ x 21 x 7⅛ (4209/276)   600
Chest of drawers, N.Eng.*, Empire, curly maple and mahogany, 13 x 11, 19c (4180/869)   225
Chest of drawers miniature, carved mahogany, Empire, oblong, 4 drawers, brass pulls, 14 x 11½, ca1840 (4211/1099)   450
Cradle, doll's carved mahogany, rectangular, turned posts, scrimshaw rockers, 9¾, 19c (4211/1062)   150
Cupboard, corner, miniature, Queen Anne, carved and painted, barrel pack, 26½ x 18 x 5¾, L18/E19c (4211/1066)   1300
Desk, slant-front, Chippendale style, 27¼ x 23 (4180/864)   *1000*

Desk (4180/864)   Scale (4180/884)

High chair, child's, turned and painted maple, splint seat, green with yellow striping, L18/E19c (4211/1107)   400
Recamier, S-scroll back, pine, Empire, L28 (4180/868)   200

SCIENTIFIC INSTRUMENTS

Draughting instruments set, retailed by Keuffel and Esser, N.Y., 12½, L19c (4141/152)   250
Globe-on-stand, celestial, rare, Gilman Joslin & Son, Boston, H18½, E19c (4076/1244)   550
Globe-on-stand, celestial, rare, Merriam & Co., Troy, N.Y., H18½, E19c (4076/1245)   500
Globe-on-stand, terrestial, published David Felt, N.Y. and Boston, D12, H18, 1829 (654/239)   200
Register, trolley car, brass, cord pull, mounted on board, D10¾, ca1900 (654/318)   200
Scale, plotting, brass, stated to belong to George Washington, 6½ (4141/146)   425
Scale, wrought iron and brass beam, J.L. Fulton & Co., N.Y. with numeral 83, H17½, 19c (4180/884)   *225*
Scales, apothecary, two brass weighing pans, 8 x 14, 19c (4180/862)   275
Surveying instrument, brass, R. Patten N.Y., 15¾, E19c (4141/145)   350
Terrestial, celestial, pair, Wilson's, Albany, N.Y., calibrated meridians, stands, Diam 18½, ca1850 (4268/1089)   1100

TOYS

'Alabama coon jigger', Lehman, dancing figure in blue jacket, H9½, ca1920 (690/739)   300
American Speedboat, Lindstrom, 2 helmeted passengers, L18½, ca1950 (690/742)   50
Animals, barnyard, group of 8, papier-mache, colorfully painted, H3 to 4¼, 19c (4209/62)   1200
Animals, group, carved, painted, Pa., ca1850, fine (4209/7)   7750
Beer Hall Dance, automated toy, people and furniture made from cigarette tins, 6½ x 13½, ca1890 (4268/1002)   1700
'B.O. Plenty', Marx, ca1930 (690/725)   80
Carriage, Phila*, painted chestnut and walnut, carved, 28½ x 72, L18c (4180/854)   *2100*
Cash register, tin, with scrollwork, Benjamin Franklin, Kam Kap, N.Y., H7½ (690/711)   20
Charleston trio, Marx wind-up, H9¾, 1920's (690/721)   250
Christmas Wind Toy, Pa., animals on 4 tiers turned by candle heat, 36 x 20, ca1870 (4268/1010)   1200
Clock, birdcage, American, yellow bird ticks to mark seconds, H7½ (690/776)   75
'Dancing Joe', articulated toy, black man mounted in metal base, 15 (4180/718)   1000
Delivery wagon, Howard's Special, delivery, scale rendering, 14 x 20 (4180/844)   *300*
Disney lithographed ferris wheel, by J. Chein, H17, ca1950 (690/719)   200
Donkey cart with Happy Hooligan, Wilkins*, L10, ca1925 (690/714)   175
'Felix on a Scooter', Orange scooter, H6, ca1930 (690/730)   180

Figure of a pony hide covered, brown and white, horsehair mane and tail, 28¼, 19c (4211/1044)   325
Good Ives Walking Toy, bald head, original clothes, H9½, ca1875, very good condition (690/743)   850
Gottlieb pinball machine, people playing pool, dancing, 51 x 69, ca1960, Ill. (690/690)   100
'Ham and Sam', the Minstrel team, Ferdinand Strauss, H8, 1920's (690/724)   275
Horse, pull-toy, wood, carved, painted, 19c, H21 (4209/123)   1700
Horse, pull-toy, wood, painted, chestnut, 19c, H15 (4209/106)   500
Hubley Harley Davidson Motorcycle, cast iron, L10, ca1930 (690/740)   350
Ingersoll Mickey Mouse watch, D2, ca1935 (690/748)   125
'Jazzbo-Jim', wind-up, Ferdinand Strauss, N.Y., H10, 1920's (690/723)   175

Carriage   (4180/854)

Delivery wagon   (4180/844)

Joe Penner, Walking Tin Toy, wind-up, Joe carrying ducks for sale, H8, 1930's (690/731)   150
'Kingsbury' bi-plane, tin, wind-up, ca1925, single propeller, maroon wings, L16 (690/735)   170
'L'il Abner and his Dogpatch Band', wind-up toy, Unique Art Manufacturing Co., H5½, ca1945
   (690/753)   50
'L'il Abner and the Dogpatch Band', tin wind-up, H6, ca1945 (690/720)   300
Lionel Mickey-Minnie Mouse Handcar, L9¾, ca1933 (690/741)   325
Locomotive 'Union', American, painted tin, G. Brown*, L10, ca1875 (690/757)   500
Lone Ranger Toy, Marx, Lone Ranger on Silver, H7½, ca1940 (690/734)   60
Magic Latern Set, marked E.P., red painted projector, 15 slides, (690/749)   70
P and L Locomotive and Tender, L19c, L9½ (690/763)   125
Painted tin/wood, Velo-King, locomotive, black body, yellow trim, L51, #67, ca1890 (690/691)   225
'Popeye Express', Marx, wind-up, wheelbarrow, parrot, H8½, ca1930 (690/729)   150
Popeye Figure, Chien, H11, ca1935 (690/745)   300
Puzzle Blocks, large set, original wood box, 87 blocks, 1 missing, 21 x 16, ca1920 (690/775)   200
Q.R.S. Playasax, marked, gold painted metal, 6 paper music rolls, L12 (690/747)   175
Rocking horse, carved and painted, shaped rockers, 29½ x 56 (4180/811)   175
Rocking horse, on stand, printed wood, mottled gray, H39 (654/246)   475
Rocking horse, tin 'poney-bike', one rocker broken, 33 x 30, L19/E20c (4180/800)   375
Sheep pull toy, painted, American, George Brown*, H6¼, (ca1890) (690/694)   100
'Siren Fire Chief' car, battery powered, Louis Marx, L15, ca1930 (690/715)   50
Sled, wood, painted, red and green inscribed in gold 'Jumper Harbor', 47 (684/251)   110
Snakes, pair of, wood, painted, entwined, red, green, 19c, L16 (4209/115)   900
'Spic and Span', wind-up, Marx, fiddler and drummer, H10, 1920's (690/722)   475
Stick-toy, monkey, wood, carved, painted, 19c, L24¾ (4209/124)   700
'The Butter and Eggs Man', tin, yellow checkered jacket, H7½, ca1930 (690/732)   125
Tin, 2, painted, man driving auto, man driving ambulance, H5, L5¼, ca1890 (4209/93)   300
Toy, jump, carved and painted wood, articulated figure of black man, 13 x 18½, L19c (4211/1053)   500
Train Set, cast iron, Wilkins, 4 pieces, L12½, ca1890 (690/761)   225
Train, tinware, painted, decorated, wind-up, engine, 2 cars, 8 x 28½, rare (4209/101)   1500
Train, cast iron, five pcs, Wilkins, L10¼, ca1890 (690/762)   150
Trick pony bell-ringer, cast iron, Gong Bell Co., 1839, H5¼, #39 (690/692)   250
Tut-Tut toy, Lehmann, H7, ca1910, missing forearm (690/737)   250
Wagon, carved wood, American*, H15½, L27, 19c (4146/76)   100
Walking Man, American, Wind-up, ca1925, red top hat, revolving head, H9½, ca1925 (690/727)   300

Wood, tricycle, painted, orange and yellow, black trim, 41, ca1866 (684/252)   800

TRUNKS
Chinese export, painted leather, brass mounted lid, brass interior, 12½ x 29 x 15, M19c (4268/1079)   225
Dome-top, brass-studded, miniature, newspaper lined interior, L13½, E19c (4180/858)   225
Dome-top, nesting, set of 4, covered in printed paper, 12 x 23½ (largest) (654/247)   60

American Pewter and Silver

AMERICAN PEWTER
Basin, 'Love Bird', incised decoration, molded edge, 11½, 1750-1800 (4211/215)   750
Basin, Daniel Curtiss, incised, center and rim, 6⅝, ca1830 (4211/200)   350
Basin, English, incised edge, Diam. 12, E19c (4146/104)   60
Basin, H.N. Rust, circular, shallow rim, 8, 19c (4211/206)   275
Basin, O. Nichols, circular, incised edge, 8, E19c (4211/204)   150
Basin, Peter Young, deep, molded rim, 10⅞, 1775-1795 (4211/203)   1400
Basin, Richard Lee, circular, incised decoration, 6⅝, 1790-1816 (4211/199)   900
Basin, Spencer Stafford, circular, incised decorations, 8, 1794-1800 (4211/198)   1000
Beaker, straight tapering sides, N.Eng.*, 2⅞, 19c (4211/138)   70
Bowl, baptismal, Oliver Trask, broad scooped rim, domed foot, 10¾, ca1835 (4211/170)   2900
Bowl, baptismal, Roswell Gleason, deep, wide flaring lip, circular foot, 11½, ca1830 (4211/220)   550
Box, tobacco, oval, lid crested with eagle, H7, E19c (4076/1188)   800
Candlesticks, baluster push-up, pair, unmarked, English*, H12, E19c (4146/117)   275
Candlesticks, baluster standard, domed foot, unmarked, pair, English*, H10¾, E19c (4146/114)   150
Candlesticks, baluster standard, domed foot, unmarked, pair, H8, E19c (4146/113)   175
Candlesticks, baluster standard, domed foot, unmarked, two, H10, E19c (4146/111)   150
Candlesticks, chamber, pair, Mark H.T., saucer base, finger holder, 3⅛, E19c (4211/157)   275
Candlesticks, pair, saucer base, short standard, finger holder, Ostander & Norris, 4⅛, ca1850
   (4211/147)   550
Candlesticks, pair, Henry Hopper, tapered standard, domed base, 10, 1842-47 (4211/168)   600
Candlesticks, pair, Rufus Dunham, baluster standard, domed foot, 1837-61 (4211/153)   1100
Candlesticks, pair, Thomas Wildes, removable bobeche, tapered standard, domed base, 10, ca1833
   (4211/169)   1500
Candlesticks, ring-turned standard, unmarked, pair, N.Eng.*, H6½, M19c (4146/119)   120
Candlesticks, ring-turned standard, unmarked, two, N.Eng.*, H6½, M19c (4146/118)   100
Caster frame, Oliver Trask, loop handle, fitted for 5 bottles, domed foot, 9, ca1835 (4211/135)   50
Chalices, pair, knopped stem on a molded domed foot, 6¾, unmarked, 19c (4268/167)   200
Chalices, pair, T.M. Buckley, molded rim, conical vessel, circular foot, 6⅛, 19c (4211/171)   375
Coffeepot, A. Portes, pear shape body, groups of concentic bands, 11½, ca1840 (684/321)   250
Coffeepot, Sellow & Co., baluster body, oricular scroll handle, hinged cover, 10, M19c (684/322)   150
Commode, Mark, I.F., broad rim, molded lip, John Fryers*, Newport, 8½, M18c (4211/132)   450
Dish, deep 'Love Bird', molded rim, incised edge, Philadelphia*, 13, 1750-1800 (4211/189)   475
Dish, deep, Robert Palethrop, Jr., broad rim, molded edge, 13, 1817-21 (4211/190)   600
Dish, William Kirby, broad rim, incised decoration, 13½, 1760-93 (4211/211)   1500
Flagon, Boardman & Co., domed lid, straight tapering sides, 11⅛, 1825-27 (4268/156)   1100
Flagon, Boardman & Co., N.Y., domed lid, molded thumbpiece, H8, ca1825 (4156/140)   800
Flagon, Leonard, Reed, and Barton, cove molded hinged lid, 11, 1837-40 (4268/164)   425
Flagon, Roswell Gleason, domed lid, shaped thumbpiece, 10, ca1840 (4211/144)   700
Flagon, William Calder, domed lid, molded banding, covered spout, 11¾, ca1835 (4211/172)   700
Lamp, oil, single bull's eye, Roswell Gleason*, drum shaped font, domed base, 9¼, ca1835
   (4211/155)   350
Lamp, swing oil, 2 light top, ribbed, trumpet form font finger hold, 7¼, 19c (4211/141)   250
Lamp, swing oil, Capon & Molineux, N.Y., 2 light, saucer base, finger hold, brass hanger, 7¾, 1848-
   54 (4211/142)   375
Lamp, whale oil, single burner, scrolled handle, ribbed domed base, 6, 19c (4211/126)   250
Lamp, whale oil, Allen Porter, turned standard, domed base, 8⅜, ca1835 (4211/148)   200
Lamp, whale oil, Smith & Co, Boston, conical font, 2 lights above stepped foot, 7, 1847-49
   (4211/128)   225
Lamps, oil, double bull's eyes, pr, drum shaped font, domed foot, Roswell Gleason, 11, ca1840
   (4211/240)   850
Lamps, whale oil, pair, I. Neal, bulbous font, 2 lights, loop handle, 6¼, ca1842 (4211/143)   450
Mug, cylindrical, pint, Jacob Whitmore, flaring lip, molded base, scroll handle, 4½, 1780 (4211/226)   1100
Mug, cylindrical, pint, Robert Bonynge*, tapering sides, scrolled handle, 4¾, ca1760 (4211/159)   1600
Mug, cylindrical, quart, Samuel Hamlin, banded body, flaring lip, scroll handle, 6, 1771-1801
   (4211/224)   1800
Mug, shaving, George Richardson, outward flaring body, scroll handle, 4½, ca1820 (4211/218)   500

Mug, Parks Boyd, barrel-shaped body, molded banding, 4⅜, 1795-1819 (4268/169) 3250

Pewter mug, large, Wm. Eddon, London, cyl. body, scrolled handle, molded base, H5⅞, E17c (4076/1182) 500

Pewter tea and coffee service, 5 pcs, Sheldon and Felton, Albany, N.Y., H10½ (coffee pot) ca1848 (4076/1183) 600

Pewter teapot, oct. panelled body, scrolled feet, Reed and Barton, H4⅜, M19c (4076/1187) 60

Pewter urn, hot water, baluster body, domed foot, Roswell Gleason, H13¾, M19c (4076/1186) 700

Pitcher, baluster, Boardman & Co., banded neck and spout, flaring foot, 6½, dam, 1825-27 (4211/247) 225

Pitcher, quart, Rufus Dunham, baluster, flaring spout, domed foot, 6⅝, ca1840 (4211/146) 375

Pitcher, unmarked, American, N.Eng.*, 6½, M19c (4146/106) 125

Plate, marked on the reverse, Bassett, Diam 8½, 1770 (4149/133) 2400

Plate, marked on the reverse, Bassett, Diam 8½, ca1770 (4149/132) 475

Plate, marked on the reverse, Bassett, Diam 8½, ca1770 (4149/131) 450

Plate, shallow rim, 9, ca1880 (4211/238) 50

Plate, Blakeslee Barns, 7⅞, 1812-17 (4268/154) 175

Plate, Blakeslee Barns, 8, 1812-17 (4268/151) 350

Plate, George Lightner, 7¾, 1806-15 (4268/150) 200

Plate, Parks Boyd, 7⅞ 1795-1819 (4268/148) 200

Plate, Parks Boyd, 9½, 1795-1819 (4268/152) 200

Plate, Stephen Barns, 8¾, 1791-1800 (4268/149) 250

Plate, 'semper eadem', Boston*, 8½, ca1770 (4211/175) 400

Plate, 'Love Birds', Philadelphia*, 7¾, 1750-1800 (4268/153) 275

Plate, broad concave rim, molded edge, marked on reverse, Diam. 13½, 1787-1815 (4146/125) 375

Plate, butter, 'Love Birds', Philadelphia, 6, 1750-1800 (4211/192) 500

Plate, butter, B and J. Harbeson, Philadelphia, 6, ca1800 (4211/193) 350

Plate, butter, J.H. Putnam, Malden, 5¼, ca1840 (4211/191) 230

Plate, deep with broad shaped rim, Hartford, Diam 13, 1805-20 (4146/126) 150

Plate, deep, Gershom Jones, molded rim, incised edge, 15, L18c (4211/188) 800

Plate, molded edge, incised center, Middletown, Conn., Diam. 12¼, 1780-88 (4146/124) 300

Plate, David Melville, Newport, 8¼, 1776-84 (4211/183) 300

Plate, Francis Bassett I-II, N.Y., 8½, 1718-58, 1755-99 (4211/182) 700

Plate, Frederick Basset, incised decoration and edge molded rim, 8, ca1770 (4211/195) 450

Plate, Frederick Bassett, incised banding, 14¾, ca1770 (4211/205) 1200

Plate, George Lightner, Baltimore, 7¾, 1800-15 (4211/177) 425

Plate, George Lightner, Baltimore, 7¾, 1800-15 (4211/194) 300

Plate, Parks Boyd, Philadelphia, 8½, 1785-1819 (4211/186) 425

Plate, Parks Boyd, Philadelphia, 7¾, 1795-1819 (4211/178) 425

Plate, Richard Austin, Boston, 8½, 1793-1817 (4211/176) 300

Plate, Samuel and Thomas Melville, Newport, 8½, 1793-1800 (4211/184) 550

Plate, Samuel Kilbourn, Baltimore, 7¾, 1814-30 (4211/179) 350

Plate, Samuel Pierce, Greenfield, 11¼, 1792-1830 (4211/181) 400

Plate, Thomas Byles, Philadelphia, 9, ca1750 (4211/180) 500

Plate, William Billings, Providence, 8, 1791-1806 (4211/185) 500

Porringer, crown handled, Mark S.G., circular, upright lip, 8, 18c (4211/160) 400

Porringer, crown handled, Mark I.C., circular, domed foot, 6¼, 18c (4211/151) 200

Porringer, crown handled, Mark I.G., circular, flaring lip, 6⅛, 18c (4211/152) 350

Porringer, crown handled, Mark W.W., circular upright lip, 6¾, 18c (4211/150) 325

Porringer, geometric handled, circular, upright flaring lip, 7¼, M18c (4211/161) 400

Porringer, pierced handle, Gershom Jones, circular, flaring lip, 7½, ca1790 (4211/162) 1500

Porringer, scroll handled, trilobed handle, baluster, upright lip, 7, 18c (4211/209) 250

Porringer, scroll handled, Mark E.C., circular, 6⅜, 18c (4211/163) 425

Porringer, scroll handled, Samuel Hamlin, baluster body, upright lip, 7¾, ca1800 (4211/208) 1050

Porringer, scroll handled, Samuel Hamlin, circular upright rim, 7⅞, E19c (4211/214) *800*

Porringer, scroll handled, Samuel Hamlin, circular, upright rim, 7⅞, E19c (4211/213) *500*

Porringer (4211/213) (4211/214)

Tankard (4211/222)

Basket (4268/56)

Teapot (4211/145)

Porringer, scroll handled, Samuel Hamlin, handle pierced, upright lip, 7¾, ca1800 (4211/207)   750
Porringer, scroll handled, body with flaring lip, N.Eng., L6¼, ca1800 (4156/143)   275
Porringer, scrolled handle, pierced and scrolling handle, 6¼, unmarked, ca1800 (4268/155)   300
Porringer, tab handle, Samuel Pennock*, circular bowl, beaded lip, 7¼, L18c (4211/149)   450
Porringer, David Melville, pierced handle, upright rim, 6⅝, L18c (4211/216)   1200
Porringer, Richard Lee*, pierced handle, circular, upright lip, 4¾, L18/E19c (4211/164)   225
Porringer, William Ellsworth, shell handle, circular, short foot, 6, 1767-98 (4211/210)   2400
Sugar bowl, covered, and cream pitcher, Cincinnati Sellew & Co., H6 and 6½, M19c (4146/121)   300
Tankard, cylindrical, pint, domed corner, banded sides, molded foot, 7, M18c (4211/174)   400
Tankard, cylindrical, quart, domed lid, hollow cast handle, banded body, R.I.*, 8¼, ca1750
  (4211/229)   1500
Tankard, cylindrical, quart, domed lid, scroll handle, 7, M18c (4211/173)   600
Tankard, cylindrical, quart, William Will, double domed lid, scroll handle, 7¾, ca1770 (4211/222)   *5500*
Tankard, flat top, Peter Young, cylindrical molded base, scrolled handle, 6¾, ca1780 (4211/230)   4500
Teapot, oval body, ball feet, Mass., 6¾, res, ca1815 (4146/100)   150
Teapot, oval, Lee & Creesy, wood finial and handle, 4 ball feet, 6¾, ca1810 (4211/217)   1000
Teapot, oval, W. Potter, wood finial, scrolled handle, ball feet, 7¼, ca1830 (4211/145)   *1000*
Teapot, pear shape, George Richardson, domed lid, scroll handle, gooseneck spout, 7½, ca1820
  (4211/219)   1500
Tray, English, rectangular, inscribed Lord Ward, L22, 19c (4146/110)   350

AMERICAN SILVER

Assorted periods and manufacturers

Basket, cake, oval, lobed sides, double beaded handle, 11⅛, 23 ozs, M19c (4268/92)   500
Basket, cake, sides pierced with scrolls, grapevine borders The Gorham Co., 11, ca1900, 19 ozs, 10
  dwts (4160/211)   220
Basket, cake, oval scrolls, foliage Frank W. Smith Silver Co., ca1915, 14¼ (4182/41)   300
Basket, cake, Bailey & Kitchen, circular form, gardroon rim, 12½, 48 ozs, ca1840 (4268/56)   *850*
Basket, cake, C and I.W. Forbes, rectangular with rounded angles, 13, 35 ozs, ca1820 (4268/45)   1300
Basket, cake, Gerardus Boyce, circular form, fluted rim, 10½, 44 ozs, ca1845 (4268/70)   *600*
Basket, cake, S. Kirk & Son Co., shallow circular form, 11⅜, 24 ozs, ca1910 (4268/27)   400
Basket, cake, Thibault & Bros, circular with everted rim, 10, 36 ozs, ca1830 (4268/57)   650
Basket, sweetmeat, with flowers and foliage S. Kirk & Son, 5⅝, ca1880, 7 ozs, 10 dwts (4160/214)   175
Beaker, bombe tapered form, 3⅜, 3 ozs, ca1800 (4180/374)   300
Beaker, molded border with cording, 3⅛, ca1840, S.P. Bailey, 3 ozs (4238/138)   350
Beaker, A.E. Warner, slightly bulbous tapered form, 3⅝, 3 ozs, ca1810 (4268/126)   200
Beaker, Charles A. Burnett, straight sided, reeded lip, 3¼, 4 ozs, ca1830 (4268/130)   550
Beaker, Charles Farley, slightly bulbous tapered form, 3¾, 5 ozs, 1830 (4268/131)   500
Beaker, E. Stebbins & Co., plain tapered form, rounded sides, 3⅛, 3 ozs, ca1840 (4268/101)   200
Beakers, pair, Tiffany & Co., tapered cylindrical form, 3¾, 13 ozs, modern (4259/108)   225
Beakers, pair, tapered, engraved with monogram 'PRD', 2½, ca1800 (4211/99)   *750*
Beakers, pair, William Gale, plain barrel form, 3½, 7 ozs, ca1860 (4268/86)   250
Bells, Christmas, eighteen, 2½, 20 ozs (619/155)   200

Bottle vinaigrette/scent, silver, Tiffany and Co., shape M. Amphora, 3¼, 1880, American (4141/76) — 175
Bouillion cup holders, twelve, laurel decorated rims and loop handles, Diam3⅝, 41 ozs, ca1930 (4211/11) — 700
Bowl, circular body, wide everted rim, pierced with foliate scrolls, 50, ca1920, Howard & Co. 35 ozs (669/351) — 300
Bowl, circular with openwork, monogrammed Tiffany & Co., 13, ca1910, 28 ozs (4160/221) — 300
Bowl, fluted hemispherical form, flared rim, pedestal foot Stone, 9⅝, ca1930, 25 ozs, 5 dwts (4160/222) — 275
Bowl, hemispherical form, Tiffany & Co., D6, 13 ozs, ca1865 (4076/584) — 160
Bowl, Kirk & Sons, D11½, 18 ozs, modern (4076/583) — 120
Bowl, Tiffany & Co., D9½, 27 ozs 10 dwts, c1900 (4076/619) — 290
Bowl, Tiffany & Co., circular, initials, 27 ozs, 5 dwts, Diam 12¾, ca1900 (4194/29) — 250
Bowl, armorials, circular with molded lip, D8, 20 ozs 5 dwts, ca1730 (4180/404) — 13500

Basket (4268/70)

Beakers (4211/99)

Bowl, footed, chased with scrolling roses, 12, Jacobi & Co., good, 40 ozs (669/352) — 650
Bowl, footed, silver, repousse, chased, Kirk, S. and Son, H7½, ca1885, 32 ozs. (654/101) — 850
Bowl, hemispherical, pedestal foot, 5½, 19 ozs 10 dwts, 1820 (4211/88) — 425
Bowl, landscapes with romantic lake, pedestal foot, Diam6, 6 ozs, ca1905 (4211/17) — 200
Bowl, plate and mug, matching, with flowering foliage, 21 ozs, modern (4076/611) — 170
Bowl, punch, oval shape grapes and leaves The Gorham Co., ca1910 (4182/36) — 3750
Bowl, punch, Hugh Wishart, for Capt. Wm. Seton, 13½, 94 ozs, ca1799 (4268/102) — 105000
Bowl, punch, The Gorham Co., oval, incurved neck, rim chased grapevines, 18½, 140 ozs, 1913 (4268/16) — 2200
Bowl, Gerardus Boyce, hemispherical, molded rim, 5⅝, 11 ozs, ca1830 (4268/132) — 600
Bowl, sugar, oval form, foliate strapwork at shoulders, L6¾, 17 ozs 5 dwts, ca1855 (4211/61) — 150
Bowl, 2 handled, chased and engraved, 13, ca1880, S. Kirk and Son, 23 ozs (669/364) — 550
Bowl, 4 claw supports, ferns and flowerheads, 9⅜, 25 ozs, ca1920 (4180/296) — 275
Butter dish, cover and stand, circular bowl, domed cover, Gale & Willis, D7, 14 ozs, 1858 (4076/591) — 225
Butter dish, cover with cow finial, four hoof supports, D5½, 20 ozs, ca1875 (4180/324) — 325
Cake basket, openwork, corded handle, Hyde & Goodrich, L13, 25 ozs, ca1840 (4180/365) — 1000
Cake basket, oval form with strawberries and leafage, Tiffany & Co., L15½, 44 ozs (4076/653) — 550
Cake basket, 2 foliate handles, pedestal base, flowers, L15¾, 45 ozs 10 dwts, mkd, ca1825 (4180/369) — 1500
Cake stand, Black, Starr & Frost, 3 tiered, arched framework, 17⅞, 26 ozs, 1924 (4260/477) — 350
Candelabra, pair, 5 light, silverplated, square knops cast with eagle's heads, 24, L19c (649/313) — 500
Candelabra, 3 light, gadroon borders, detachable nozzles Blackington & Co., 18¼, ca1930, weighted (4160/228) — 275
Candelabra, 5 light silver pair, scrolls and flowers, Dominick & Haff, ca1905, 20¼ (4182/30) — 1300
Candelabra, 5 light, pair, chrysanthemum pattern, Tiffany & Co., H19, 237 ozs, 1900 (4076/600) — 5500
Candle snuffer, tray, Sheffield plated, elaborately wrought with leaves, scrolling, L11, 19c (4156/157) — 50
Candlesticks, plated, pair table, said to have belonged to General Washington, H10, ca1790 (4156/146) — 625

Candlesticks, set of four, circular base, floral sprays, shellwork Durgin Co., 10, ca1910, weighted (4160/220) 450

Candlesticks, small, set of four, ribbed baluster stems, Sheffield plated, H7½, E19c (4156/150) 170

Candlesticks, table, pair, telescopic, circular bases, tapered stems, Roberts, John & Co., 8¼, George III (4076/574) 450

Candlesticks, table, pair, fluted octagonal stems, H11¾ (4156/149) 70

Candlesticks, table, pair, Sheffield plated, ribbed tapering stem, 10, ca1800 (4156/154) 200

Candlesticks, weighted bases, four, fluted tapered stems, reeded bands, 11, mkd H, ca1925 (4180/290) 900

Cann, baluster shape, spreading foot, 5⅛, 12 ozs 10 dwts, ca1770 (4076/678) 375

Cann, baluster shape, Pelletreau, William S., 6, 13 ozs 10 dwts, ca1810 (4076/679) 800

Cann, angular handle, two reeded bands, 4⅜, 9 ozs 10 dwts, mkd, E19c (4180/372) 375

Cann, baluster form, molded lip, double-scroll handle, 4 4/8, ca1769 (4211/105) 5750

Cann, molded lip, pedestal foot, scroll handle, 5⅛, 11 ozs, ca1745 (4211/107) 2000

Cann, Joseph Downes, tapered barrel form, 3¾, 9 ozs, ca1810 (4268/128) 550

Cann, L. Allen, tapered, monogram, running foliage and berries, 4½, 10 ozs, E19c (4268/98) 325

Cann, Samuel Kirk, baluster form, double scroll handle, 3¾, 5 ozs, ca1820 (4268/127) 375

Cann, Samuel Minott, baluster form, molded lip, 4, 4 ozs, ca1760 (4268/140) 1500

Cann, William A. Williams, slightly bulbous form, 4⅛, 8 ozs, ca1825 (4268/129) 700

Card case, depicting a view of the U.S. Capitol, 3½, M19c (4268/106) 200

Card case, view of Trinity Church, Wall Street, 3½, M19c (4268/108) 250

Card case, view of U.S. Capitol, portrait of Hebe and Zeus, 3½, M19c (4268/107) 200

Card case, silver, rectangular form chased, with flowers, view U.S. Capital, 3½, ca1845 (4141/40) 120

Card case, 2 scenes, Schuylkill Water Works and Christ Church, Philadelphia, 3½, ca1850 (4268/111) 425

Card Case, Leonard and Wilson, depicting U.S. Capitol, 3⅝, ca1850 (4268/110) 125

Caster, for mustard, with 'EP', 'Stephenson' and '1750-1868', Jacob Hurd, 5⅜, ca1735 (4211/108) 1300

Caster, lacks finial, baluster form, domed cover, 5⅝, 5 ozs 15 dwts, ca1720 (4180/400) 1400

Casters, pair, Samuel Minott, baluster form, 5⅜, 7 ozs, ca1760 (4268/135) 2200

Caviar knives, silver, mother-of-pearl, husk ornament, ca1900, dam, set of 12 (4194/17) 190

Centerpiece, circular, openwork decoration, Starr, Theodore B., D11½, 55 ozs, c1910 (4076/624) 600

Centerpiece, oval shape, flowers and sprays The Gorham Co., ca1910, 17⅛ (4182/38) 2000

Centerpiece, rectangular shape, leaves and flowers The Gorham Co., ca1910, 14¾ (4182/37) 1800

Centerpiece, simulating ice encrusted rock, Gorham & Co., L10¾, 31 ozs, 1894 (4076/582) 750

Centerpiece, circular with flowers, foliage, Diam11½, 23 ozs 5 dwts, ca1925 (4211/13) 350

Centerpiece, silver-gilt, circular form, gadroon rim, 13¾, 28 ozs, ca1935 (4180/295) 150

Centerpiece, The Gorham Co., shallow bowl, crouching cherubs, 12⅜, 48 ozs, 1872 (4268/53) 1100

Chambersticks, pressed brass, pair, molded sides and fingerhold, L8¾ (4211/261) 175

Chambersticks, Molded brass, pair, boat shaped form with ring fingerhold, H3 L8½, E19c (4211/265) 350

Child's set, 3 pieces, scenes and verses of nursery rhymes, D7⅛, 18 ozs, ca1900 (4180/283) 450

Coasters, 18 karat gold, set of 12, circular, with liners, Tiffany & Co., D3⅝, c1920 (4076/635) 5600

Cocktail shaker, The Gorham Co., girdled body and cover, applied handle, 9, 18 ozs, 1925 (684/360) 200

Coffeepot, bulbous body repousse, Warner, A.E., H13, 39 ozs 10 dwts, ca1860 (4076/629) 850

Coffeepot, inverted pear shape, 11½, ca1840, Bailey & Kitchen, 46 ozs 10 dwts (4238/139) 675

Coffeepot, swan neck spout, domed cover Cartier, 8½, modern, 18 ozs (4160/217) 225

Coffeepot, 'oriental movement', sprays of chased holly and copper berries, 8⅜, 18 ozs 5 dwts, ca1875 (4211/35) 600

Coffeepot, hemispherical, knop finial Shepherd, Robert, 10⅛, 36 ozs 5 dwts, ca1805 (4211/89) 1650

Coffeepot, monograms, domed cover with bud finial, 11½, 11 ozs 5 dwts, ca176 (4180/409) 2600

Coffeepot, J. & A. Gardiner, baluster form, fluted and lobed, 12, 37 ozs, ca1840 (4268/61) 600

Coffeepot, Thomas Fletcher, vase shape form, leaf tip rim, 11¼, 50 ozs, ca1825 (4268/69) 950

Coffee set, 3 piece, baluster form, Arthur J. Stone, 7¼, 22 ozs 15 dwts, mkd H, ca1920 (4180/293) 350

Coffee set, 3 piece, plain vase shape, Arthur J. Stone, H9½, 35 ozs 10 dwts, mkd H, ca1920 (4180/288) 800

Coffee set, 3 pieces, oval section, fluted at the angles, H11, 22 ozs 10 dwts, ca1910 (4180/282) 225

Coffee set, 4 pcs, cast with flower heads and foliate swags, Gorham & Co., 91 ozs, ca1900 (649/323) 650

Coffee set, 4 piece, engraved scrolls and festoons, 9¾, coffee pot, ca1875, 72 ozs (669/361) 550

Coffee set and tray, 4 piece, tray chased with flowers and foliage, H9¼, L14½, 70 ozs 5 dwts, ca1905 (4180/309) 850

Compotes, twelve, shallow, circular, domed pedestal bases, Diam3⅞, 54 ozs, ca1930 (4211/12) 700

Creamer, baluster shape, Warner, 6¾, ca1850, 9 ozs (4160/227) — 175
Creamer, bombe oval form, Gale, Wood & Hughes, 4, 4 ozs, 1835 (4076/658) — 100
Creamer, bulbous form, reeded handle, Moulton, Ebenezer, 5⅜, 4 ozs 15 dwts, ca1800 (4076/665) — 200
Creamer, helmet shape, 6½, 5 ozs, L18c (4076/661) — 125
Creamer, vase shape on square foot, maker's mark J.D., 6⅜, 5 ozs, ca1785 (4076/668) — 375
Creamer, vase shape, Wiltberger, Christian, H6½, 6 ozs, ca1795 (4076/657) — 350
Creamer, angular handle, Joseph Shoemaker, 6, 6 ozs, 1810 (4180/384) — 250
Creamer, hemispherical, with continuous band of flowers, 4¾, 8 ozs 10 dwts, ca1830 (4211/68) — 500
Creamer, strap handle, partly fluted oval form, 5¾, 5 ozs 15 dwts, mkd, ca1800 (4180/382) — 300
Creamer, waved rim, wide spout, double scroll handle, 4½, 4 ozs 10 dwts, ca1770 (4211/102) — 1900
Creamer, Att. to David Griffeth, inverted pear shape, 5¼, 4 ozs, ca1770 (4268/143) — 800
Creamer, Benjamin Burt, pear shape, scalloped rim, 3⅝, 3 ozs, ca1760-70 (4268/133) — 2600
Creamer, F.G. att. to Frances Garden, pear shape, beaded lip, 4⅞, 3 ozs, ca1770 (4268/142) — 850
Creamer, Gale & Willis, pear shape, molded rim, 5¼, 7 ozs, 1859 (4268/89) — 150
Creamer, Nathaniel Vernon, rectangular, applied gadroon rim, initials, 3½, 7 ozs, ca1815 (4268/93) — 850
Creamer, 3 double scroll legs, scrolls and thistle, 4¼, 3 ozs 5 dwts, ca1760 (4180/405) — 1100
Cruet, with 7 cut glass bottles, circular base raised on 4 paw feet, D9¼, 43 ozs, ca1815 (4180/380) — 4750
Cup, bell form, 1 side with a foliate monogram, 5⅞, ca1790, 7 ozs (4238/124) — 325
Cup, engraved with monogram and date 1853 Eoff & Shepherd, 5⅝, ca1853, 19 ozs, 10 dwts (4160/212) — 200
Cup, three handled, blossoms and leaves The Gorham Co., ca1910, 9¾ (4182/35) — 1700
Cup, presentation, two handled, silver, grape cluster and vines The Gorham Co., ca1917, 15⅝ (4182/40) — 350
Cup, presentation, vase shape, with engraving, 5½, ca1820, 7 ozs (4238/126) — 150
Cup, presentation, 3 handle, Tiffany & Co., high relief with overlapping grapevines, 9, 63 ozs, ca1902 (4268/11) — 900
Cup, saucer and waiter, waiter engraved 'Lora' Bailey & Kitchen, Diam 5¼, 7, ca1845 (4211/52) — 300
Cup, vase shaped bowl, tapered stem, 6½, 8 ozs 10 dwts, ca1800 (4211/97) — 700
Decanter, Bacchus head stopper, scrolling grapevine all over pearshaped body, 12, 30 ozs, ca1885 (4211/18) — 2700
Demi Tasse 3 piece set, pot, 2 handled sugar and creamer Wanamaker, 10, 1920, 22 ozs, 5 dwts (4160/219) — 275
Dish, asparagus, Chester Billings & Son, rectangular, removable insert, 17⅛, 43 ozs, 1905 (4268/14) — 375
Dish, entree, regency style, shells and foliage reversible cover, L10¾, modern (4211/3) — 450
Dish, grape, composed of a large grapeleaf, L12, H13, 32 ozs 5 dwts, c1900 (4076/617) — 300
Dish, meat, oval, Dominick & Haff, N.Y., 61 ozs, 10 dwts, 20¼, ca1900 (4159/53) — 450
Dish, serving, Stone Associates, circular, monogram, Diam 10, 19 ozs, ca1920 (4194/23) — 200
Dish, serving, Lebkuecher & Co., circular, chased with fruiting vines, initialed, 14¾, 39 ozs, ca1900 (684/357) — 325
Dish, sweatmeat, George Rideout, circular, fluted border, 5, 3 ozs, ca1745 (4268/136) — 2200
Dish, vegetable, circular, Eoff & Shepherd, stamped laurel and beaded border, 9⅛, 17 ozs, ca1850 (4268/79) — 375
Dish, venison, oval, foliate cartouches containing bands of roses, L22½, Bailey, Banks & Biddle, 109 ozs, ca1890 (649/327) — 1000
Dish, 2 compartment vegetable, mat ground, dome cover, Gorham & Co., L18¾, 76 ozs 5 dwts, ca1870 (4076/616) — 1500
Dishes, entree and cover, pair, Wm., Forbes, laurel band rim, 12¼, 78 ozs, ca1840 (4268/76) — 1500
Dishes, entree and covers, pair, profuse flowers and foliage, L10½, 68 ozs 5 dwts, ca1930 (4211/14) — 1350
Dishes, meat, pair, E.G. & B., plain, oval form, 15, 71 ozs, ca1850 (4268/74) — 1500
Dishes, meat, 2 matching, twelve sided borders, scrolled initial M, L17⅞, 20⅛, 136 ozs 10 dwts, ca1930 (4211/2) — 1100
Dishes, sweetmeat, pair, Dominick & Hoff, circular with latticework, 6¾, 13 ozs, 1888 (4260/482) — 150
Dishes, sweetmeat, pair, Howard & Co., circular with latticework, 5, 8 ozs, 1888 (4260/483) — 150
Dishes, vegetables, covered, pair, oval, with flowerheads and foliage, 15, ca1900, Gorham & Co. 78 ozs (669/372) — 1400
Entree dish, with cable handles, rectangular, armorials, L14½, 31 ozs 5 dwts, mkd, ca1835 (4180/383) — *500*

Entree dish   (4180/383)

Epergne, stand with 4 baskets, octagonal form, foliage and scrollwork, L18, 74 ozs 10 dwts, ca1905
   (4180/297)   1300
Ewer, baluster form, with bacchanal putti, Tiffany & Co., H21¾, 91 ozs 10 dwts, c1900 (4076/606)   3600
Ewer, inverted pear shape, Caldwell & Co., H14⅛, 44 ozs, 1897 (4076/609)   650
Ewer, retailed by J.E. Caldwell, Philadelphia, engraved with armorials, 41 ozs, M19c (4076/578)   850
Fish servers, scrolling foliage, blade has monster head, 8 ozs, ca1850 (4211/58)   175
Fish servers, stylized foliage, handles shaped like oriental houses, etc., 11 ozs 10 dwts, ca1870
   (4211/40)   300
Fish servers, N.Y., by Gerardus Boyce and Albert Coles, ca1850 (4211/63)   150
Flatware, colonial pattern, monogrammed, Tiffany & Co., 125 pcs., 125 ozs (4238/135)   1600
Flatware, reeded and foliate border, initialed, ca1900, 285 pcs, Dominick & Haft, 352 ozs (4238/144)   3100
Flatware, Fiddle Thread pattern, mostly monogrammed, 85 pcs, 160 ozs, ca1865 (4268/42)   1700
Flatware, Renaissance pattern, Dominick & Haft, 206 pcs., 302 ozs (4238/123)   3750
Flatware, service, Schofield Co., Old English pattern, 111 pcs, 137 ozs, 10 dwts, ca1905 (4194/18)   1000
Flatware, service, Tiffany & Co., Colonial pattern, 146 ozs, ca1900, 116 pcs (4194/27)   2100
Flatware, service, 83 pcs, oak case, Renaissance pattern, 120 ozs, ca1895 (4211/25)   1400
Flatware, set, 141 pcs, Copenhagen pattern, wooden case, 115 ozs, modern (4211/8)   1500
Flatware, 117 pcs, Clinton pattern, Tiffany & Co., 146 ozs 10 dwts, modern (4076/607)   1900
Flatware, 37 pcs, retailed by Tiffany's, Gorham & Co., 48 ozs., L19c (4076/601)   800
Flatware, 73 pcs, with rose sprays and scrolls, The Gorham Co., 78 ozs (619/171)   750
Forks, table, six, Michael Gibney, fiddle pattern, 18 ozs, 1844 (4260/480)   150
Forks, table, 8, The Gorham Co., Imperial Queen pattern, 13 ozs, ca1895 (4268/22)   125
Fruit basket, swing handle, gadroon rim, D11½, ca1840 (4180/336)   525
Glasses, cocktail silver, female figures Udall & Ballou, ca1920 (4182/31)   800
Goblet, pedestal foot, pearshaped body, 5¼, 6 ozs, ca1850 (4180/360)   175
Jug, glass body cut with poppies, inverted flowerhead cover, 14, ca1900 (4211/31)   2200
Kettle on lampstand, spherical, classical masks on open-work supports, 12½, 53 ozs 5 dwts,
   ca1870 (4211/27)   475
Knives, dessert set of twelve, with lobed and fluted handles and silver blades, ca1850, N.Y.*
   (4238/131)   175
Lemon strainer, bowl pierced, flowerhead pattern, Diam 4, ca1770 (4211/95)   225
Lemon strainer, shallow bowl, peirced in flowerhead pattern, Diam3¼, 1 oz 10 dwts, ca1830
   (4211/85)   150
Log Cabin, pcd linsey-Woolsey, T-square pattern, red, green striped border, (4180/683)   400
Mug, baluster form, scroll handle, Hurd, Jacob, 5⅛, 12 ozs 5 dwts, ca1750 (4076/667)   2300
Mug, baluster shape, domed foot, 5, 8 ozs 10 dwts, 1810 (4076/660)   225
Mug, tapered cylindrical, Bailey Co., 4¾, 13 ozs, ca1850 (4076/659)   300
Mug, child's, Peter L. Krider, engraved 'Anna', 2 reeded hoop bands, 3¾, 4 ozs, ca1860 (4268/47)   125

Mug, double scroll handle, cylindrical, foliage and scrolls, 4½, 6 ozs, ca1860 (4180/363) 200
Mug, oval reserve, slightly tapered form, foliate swags, 3⅞, 3 ozs 15 dwts, ca1845 (4180/368) 125
Mug, pedestal foot, faceted cylindrical shape, 4¾, 5 ozs 10 dwts, ca1840 (4180/356) 150
Pap boat, Stephen Richard, plain oval form, elongated spout, 5½, 20 ozs, ca1820 (4268/99) 400
Pepper box, William Simpson, straight sided octagonal shape, 3⅞, 2 ozs, ca1735 (4268/134) 1600
Pillbox, H.P., rectangular, hinged lid, 'Dr. F. Howes', 2¾, E19c (4268/100) 400
Pitcher, bulbous body repousse, Kirk, S. & Son, H8, 22 ozs, c1905 (4076/623) 350
Pitcher, baluster form, beaded rim, circular pedestal, 4⅞, 6 ozs 5 dwts, ca1770 (4211/104) 1300
Pitcher, vase shaped body, initials, handle cast as eagle's head, 12¼, 19 ozs 10 dwts, 1825
(4211/87) *800*
Pitcher, water, chased with flowering, foliage on a matted ground, 8¾, ca1904, S. Kirk & Co., 29 ozs
(669/365) 650

Pitcher (4211/87)

Pitcher, water, baluster body, Tiffany & Co., H8¾, 37 ozs, ca1867 (4076/589) 850
Pitcher, water, border of shells, H10¾, 25 ozs, 1900 (4076/597) 230
Pitcher, water, bulbous body repousse, Kirk, S. & Son, H7⅞, 23 ozs, c1900 (4076/643) 390
Pitcher, water, bulbous body repousse, Kirk, S. & Son, 23 ozs 10 dwts, modern (4076/640) 300
Pitcher, water, bulbous circular form leaves The Gorham Co., ca1900, 8¾ (4182/34) 1000
Pitcher, water, oval shape, Tiffany & Co., H8¼, 28 ozs 10 dwts, c1900 (4076/652) 275
Pitcher, water, Tiffany & Co., tapered circular body, 29 ozs, 10¼, ca1900 (4194/31) 325
Pitcher, water, bulbous body, eagle's head handle, Harvey Lewis, 10½, 40 ozs, ca1820 (4211/69) 1900
Pitcher, water, bulbous shape, engraved with foliage, 6⅜, 50 ozs, 1902-07 (4211/5) 200
Pitcher, water, foliate handle, horseman, dog, flowers and foliage, 17½, 54 ozs 15 dwts, ca1850
(4211/16) 1600
Pitcher, water, ovoid form, foliate monogram, 14¼, 19 ozs 15 dwts, ca1850 (4211/50) 400
Pitcher, water, pear form, landscape scenes with dog, 2 deer, 11¼, 31 ozs, ca1850 (4211/43) 2500
Pitcher, water, pear shape, flared lip, 11¾, 45 ozs 10 dwts, modern (4211/4) 475
Pitcher, water, silver, chased, engraved, Kirk, S. and Son, H9½, ca1910, 23 ozs. (654/98) 550
Pitcher, water, Black, Starr and Frost, inverted pear shape, 10½, 25 ozs, ca1900 (4268/12) 360
Pitcher, water, E.G. & B., baluster form, floral and scrollwork cartouches, 10⅜, 24 ozs, ca1869
(4268/88) 475
Pitcher, water, J. Cook, vase shape, stamped foliate rim, 13, 35 ozs, ca1860 (4268/81) 400
Pitcher, water, J.E. Caldwell, inverted pear shape, chased in Kirk style, 10⅝, 32 ozs, ca1900
(4268/15) 500
Pitcher, water, Joseph Foster, bulbous form, molded rim, 8¼, 23 ozs, ca1820 (4268/124) 500
Pitcher, water, S. Kirk & Son, vase shaped, in curved neck, 12, 41 ozs, modern (4268/23) 750
Pitcher, water, Tiffany & Co., vase shape, angular handle, 9¾, 31 ozs, ca1865 (4268/80) 375
Pitcher, water, Watson & Hildeburn, vase shape, guilloche rim, 14⅛, 52 ozs, ca1840 (4268/87) 950
Pitcher, E.G. & B., ovoid form body, 12¾, 22 ozs, ca1859 (4268/71) 350
Pitcher, Walter S. Kirk & Co., bulbous circular form, chased all over with flowers and foliage, 7¾, 23
ozs, ca1905 (4268/8) 525
Pitchers, covered, pair, Eoff & Shepherd, flower sprays, scrolls, foliage, 13, 83 ozs, ca1850
(4268/72) 2300
Pitchers, water, pair, Gerardus Boyce, baluster form with leaf tip borders, 9¾, 68 ozs, ca1840
(4268/73) 1700

Plate, bread and butter, set of twelve, Gorham & Co., 50 ozs (619/156)   350

Plates, bread and butter, six, centers engraved with bees, 6⅜, 26 ozs 10 dwts, ca1910 (4211/24)   150

Plates, dinner, set of 12, Watson Co., Attleboro Co., monograms, Diam 11, 188 ozs, 15 dwts, ca1910 (4194/21)   1000

Plates, service, set of six, with flowering foliage, 11, ca1925, S. Kirk & Son, 131 ozs (669/366)   2100

Plates, 14 karat gold, set of 18, molded rims and strapwork, Shreve & Co., D9, c1900 (4076/630)   19500

Plates, 15 silver-gilt side, Towle silversmith, D6¼, 56 ozs, c1900 (4076/639)   375

Plates, 18 silver-gilt, borders chased with shells, Tiffany & Co., D11, 360 ozs, c1900 (4076/638)   4500

Platter, meat, oval form, gadroon border, with 'Q', 20¾, 53 ozs, M20c (4180/303)   450

Platter, serving, Chester Billings & Son, oval, with scrollwork rim, 20, 53 ozs, 1905 (4268/13)   425

Platter, Samuel Kirk and Son, circular, flower and foliage in a granulated ground, 13, 30 ozs, ca1905 (4268/54)   375

Porringer, pierced, keyhole handle, Burt, Benjamin, 8¼, 9 ozs 15 dwts, ca1770 (4076/674)   1000

Porringer, flat keyhole handle, bulbous sides, 5, 8 ozs 10 dwts, mkd, ca1820 (4180/387)   600

Porringer, Benjamin Burt, circular, open keyhole handle, 8¼, 7 ozs, ca1760 (4268/144)   1600

Pot, chocalate, plain pear shape, turned wood handle, 9, L18/E19c, South American, 28 ozs gross (4238/23)   550

Salt cellar and spoons 4 sets, Sayre, Joel, H2, 9 ozs 15 dwts, Victorian (4076/603)   170

Salt cellars, standing, pair, tapered cylindrical bowl, base, 3¾, 7 ozs 10 dwts, ca1860 (4180/370)   150

Salt cellars, 14 karat gold, set of 6, circular bowls, 6 matching spoons, Shreve & Co., D2¾, c1900 (4076/632)   1650

Salt spoons, pair, twist stems, belonged to Thomas Jefferson, 14 dwts, M18c (4076/577)   425

Salts, pair, William Gale & Son, straight sided circular form, 2⅞, 4 ozs, 1851 (4268/62)   90

Salver, border repousse, Kirk, S. & Son, Diam 14¼, 42 ozs, c1900 (4076/646)   425

Salver, circular with sprays, scrolling poppies, Reed and Barton, 21¼, ca1910, 119 ozs 10 dwts (4238/137)   950

Salver, engraved with a steam train, Boyce, Gerardus, L17¼, 38 ozs, ca1849 (4076/627)   800

Salver, Gorham Co., circular, applied shell work, Diam 12⅞, 26 ozs, 10 dwts, 1901 (4194/25)   260

Salver, oval, key-pattern border, scroll feet, Gale, William & Son, L14, 26 ozs, 1862 (4076/592)   250

Salver, James Morison, London, with pie-crust border and crest, Diam 11¾, 1756 (4156/148)   *1350*

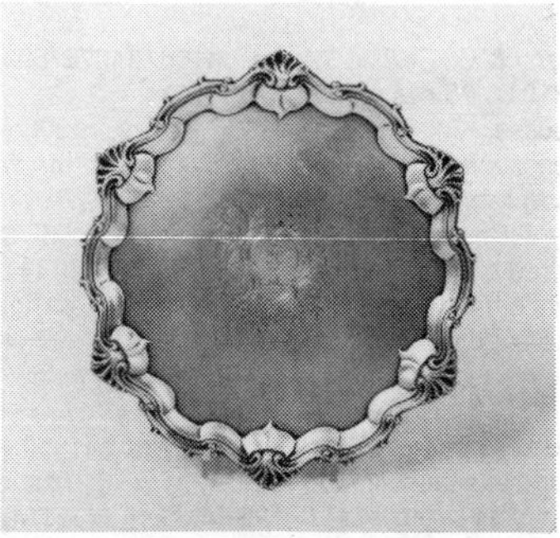

Salver (4156/148)

Sauce boat, early George II style, double scroll handle, 8½, ca1930, Peter Guille, 10 ozs 10 dwts (4238/140)   225

Sauce boat, leaf borders, oval pedestal foot, Marquand, Frederick, 7¼, 15 ozs, ca1820 (4076/672)   800

Sauce boat, oval shape, scallop rim, W. Hollingshead, L7⅞, 13 ozs 5 dwts, ca1770 (4211/103)   4000

Sauce boat, Fredrick Marquand, slightly bulbous boat form, 7⅜, 14 ozs, ca1835 (4268/68)   400

Saucepan, turned wood handle, Richard Humphreys, 3⅝, 7 ozs, ca1780 (4211/101)   2300

Saucepans, brandy, pair, circular, wood handles, 6⅝, Modern, Ensko, 19 ozs 10 dwts (4238/149)   175

Sculpture, Steuben, intaglio etched figure of a naked man, 11¼, fitted box (669/227)   1600

Serving dish, circular, Arthur J. Stone, 14½, 35 ozs 5 dwts, mkd T, ca1920 (4180/289)   400

Soup ladle, with slightly pointed end, makers mark C.C., L15¼, 6 ozs, Philadelphia*, E19c (4076/608)   200

Soup ladle, Onslow pattern, belonged to Thomas Jefferson, Timberlake, Joseph, George III, London 1766 (4076/575) — 6100
Soup tureen, cover, boat shape, with ladle by Ball, Black & Co., L14, 54 ozs, ca1865 (4180/323) — 750
Spoons, silver, basting, pair, Old English Pattern, L12¼, ca1790, 7 ozs. (654/104) — 250
Sportsman, figure, silver gilt, holding shotgun, 7, R. Wallace & Sons, 11 ozs, L19c (649/314) — 250
Stands, oval, 2 handled pair, Wm. Forbes, laurel band rim, 16⅛, 60 ozs, ca1840 (4268/77) — 850
Strainer, 2 bell-shaped handles, pierced bowl, 4 ozs, L10¼, ca1750-60 (4194/38) — 200
Sugar basket, swing handle, William Gale & Son, L6, 7 ozs, 1862 (4180/320) — 190
Sugar bowl, covered, inverted pear shape, domed cover, H7¼, 15 ozs, Philadelphia*, ca1775 (4076/663) — 2300
Sugar bowl, silver covered, bulbous, floral sprays, 6⅞, 14 ozs, ca1810 (4180/390) — 650
Sugar bowl, vase shape, beaded border, scroll handles, 8¾, 19 ozs, ca1850 (4180/345) — 200
Sugar bowl and creamer, cover, foliage and flower sprays, H8¾, 7¼, 22 ozs 5 dwts, ca1825 (4180/351) — 150
Sugar nips, scissor, shell grip, flowerheads on central boss, 5⅛, 1 oz 5 dwts, ca176 (4180/399) — 300
Sugar tongs, shell-shaped grips, Revere, Paul Jr., 5¾, 1 oz 15 dwts, ca1795 (4076/685) — 2300
Sugar vase, silver covered, Joseph Richardson Jr., 8½, 13 ozs 5 dwts, mkd, ca1800 (4180/389) — 1200
Sugar vase with cover, vase shape, square pedestal shape, 9¼, 14 ozs 10 dwts, L18c (4076/662) — 425
Sugar vase and creamer, J. Richardson, vase form with beaded rim, 9⅞ - 7¼, 10 ozs, ca1795 (4268/139) — 2500
Sweetmeat basket, oval shape, Wood & Hughes, L7, 9 ozs, ca1850 (4076/615) — 150
Sweetmeat basket, oval, grapevine, Ball, Black & Co., L6, 10 ozs, ca1865 (4076/585) — 130
Tablespoon, initials SBM, belonged to Thomas Jefferson, Elizabeth Taylor, 2 ozs 5 dwts, 1768 (4076/576) — 1800
Tablespoon, Old English pattern, handle engraved, 1 oz 15 dwts, ca1780 (4211/106) — 1000
Tablespoons, six, Old English pattern, 10 ozs, mkd, ca1800 (4180/393) — 175
Tablespoons, 6, J. & W. Catlin, Fiddle pattern, engraved with initials I.A., 14 ozs, ca1830 (4268/94) — 325
Tankard, cylindrical shape, 8¾, 28 ozs, ca1770 (4076/677) — 1400
Tankard, tapered cylindrical form, domed cover, Burt, Benjamin, 7¾, 22 ozs, ca1780 (4076/666) — 2000
Tankard, tapered cylindrical form, domed cover, Syng, Philip Jr., 7½, 33 ozs 10 dwts, fine, ca1770 (4076/684) — 13500
Tankard, tapered cylindrical shape, domed cover, Soumaien, Samuel, 7½, M18c (4076/670) — 1100
Tankard, double scroll handle, engraved with ship, domed cover, 11, 42 ozs 5 dwts, ca1775 (4180/408) — 2500
Tankard, silver gilt and carved ivory, moose eating and wounded by hunters, 21¾, ca1905 (4160/573) — 10500
Tankard, Benjamin Burt, tapered, molded girdle, domed cover, 8, 21 ozs, ca1760 (4268/145) — 4500
Tazza, Tiffany & Co., chased in Kirk style with flowers, 10½, 32 ozs, ca1880 (4268/20) — 500
Tazze, pair, pierced sides, engraved flowers The Sweetser Co., ca1910, 11¼ (4182/42) — 325
Tazze, pair, Dominick & Haff, vase shape, multiple beaded borders, 11¼, 78 ozs, 1906 (4268/26) — 950
Tazze, pair, T. Hausmann & Sons, shaped circular form, waved grapevine rim, 9, 26 ozs, ca1900 (4268/9) — 350
Tea and coffee service, 5 pcs, chased and engraved with foliate scrolls, Wood & Hewes, 108 ozs, ca1800 (649/318) — 1700
Tea and coffee service, 7 pcs, plain oval bulbous bodies with urn shaped finials, Gorham & Co., 249 ozs, E20c (649/319) — 2000
Tea and coffee service, 7 pieces, repousse flowers, 32¾, tray, 362 ozs., Mexican (631/194) — 1700
Tea and coffee set, 3 piece, ribbed bodies of baluster form, knop finials, 10⅝, 81 ozs, ca1840 (4211/54) — 900
Tea and coffee set, 5 pcs, hammered surface Lebolt & Co., ca1920 (4182/48) — 1700
Tea and coffee set, 5 pcs, with a frieze of satyr masks, Starr and Marcus, 103 ozs, c1900 (4076/614) — 1100
Tea and coffee set, 5 pcs, S. Hammond & Co., chased with sprays of flowers, coffee pot 10½, 107 ozs, ca1850 (4268/41) — 1800
Tea and coffee set, 5 pcs, Tiffany, Young & Ellis, baluster form, 11, 99 ozs, ca1855 (4268/40) — 1500
Tea and coffee set, 5 piece, assembled, scenes and figures, 13, 11 ozs 5 dwts, ca1925 (4211/15) — 2200
Tea and coffee set, 5 piece, with matching Gorham Co. tray, all over flowers, H8½, 91 ozs 10 dwts, ca1880 (4180/312) — 2100
Tea and coffee set, 5 pieces, chased with fruit and floral sprays, H13, 119 ozs, ca1900 (4180/280) — 1700
Tea and coffee set, 5 pieces, four scroll feet, 94 ozs 15 dwts, modern (4211/9) — 1600
Tea and coffee set, 5 pieces, rectangular vase shaped bodies, H10¼, 70 ozs, ca1915 (4180/281) — 525
Tea and coffee set, 6 pcs, bulbous shape repousse, Kirk, S. & Son, 182 ozs., c1900 (4076/641) — 3600
Tea and coffee set, 6 pieces, chased with flowering foliage, ca1904, S. Kirk & Son, 195 ozs (669/367) — 4250
Tea and coffee set, 6 pieces, monogrammed, swan neck spouts, mahogany case, 12¾, 121 ozs gross, ca1920 (4180/307) — 1100

Tea and coffee set, 6 pieces, with silver and mahogany tray, by Durgin Co., H13 3/16, 113 ozs gross, ca1920 (4180/306) — 1400

Tea and coffee set, 6 pieces, hammered surface The Kalo Company, ca1925 (4182/47) — 950

Tea and coffee set, 6 pieces, tray, scrolling flowers, foliage, H12½, 266 ozs, 1923 (4211/21) — 3400

Tea caddy, eagle on hinged cover, claw and ball feet, L6¼, 23 ozs, ca1820 (4180/373) — 1000

Tea kettle, warming stand, chased initials, Gorham and Co., H13, 1913, 45 ozs. (654/93) — 375

Tea kettle on stand, circular, fluted neck, 74 ozs, 5 dwts, 15¼, ca1850 (4194/32) — 550

Tea service, scroll work shells, Black, Starr & Frost, 7 pcs, 368 ozs (649/332) — 5500

Tea service and tray, with scrolls and foliage, Reed & Barton, 30, tray, 6 pcs, 302 ozs (619/169) — 4750

Tea set, 3 pcs, Gerardus Boyce, circular form, flowers and shells, teapot, 10, 77 ozs, ca1830 (4268/44) — 1000

Tea set, 3 piece, bulbous, wriggle-work borders, 8, 38 ozs 15 dwts, ca1810 (4180/391) — 2400

Tea set, 3 piece, chased with flowering foliage, 50 ozs, 1824 (4180/375) — 160

Tea set, 3 piece, monogrammed, domed covers, 10½, 1840 (4211/53) — 900

Tea set, 4 pcs, Cann & Dunn, vase form bodies, Greek key, teapot 11, 61 ozs, ca1860 (4268/52) — 1300

Tea set, 4 pc, decorated with flowering foliage, North, William B. & Co., h. of teapot 8½, 77 ozs 15 dwts, ca1830 (4076/622) — 1550

Tea set, 4 piece, lobed lower body, bands of roses, Shepherd & Boyd foliage, 9½, 82 ozs, ca1825 (4211/91) — *1900*

Tea set, 4 pieces, paneled oval shape, Sayre, Joel, teapot, H7½, 44 ozs 15 dwts, ca1800 (4076/683) — 2600

Tea tray, James Dixon & Sons, London, Sheffield plated, 2 handles, L33½, E19c (4156/153) — 250

Tea tray, rectangular, monogram, cut out handles, 26¼, 128 ozs, ca1900 (4211/23) — 1100

Tea tray, 2 handled, Lafayette silver, oval form, 26¼, ca1910, Towle, 112 ozs 15 dwts (4238/122) — 850

Tea urn, vase shape, presentation inscription, 'w', 16¼, 49 ozs, mkd AGT, ca1865 (4180/315) — 700

Teapot, fluted pear shape, scroll handle, 8½, 29 ozs 10 dwts, mkd, ca1840 (4180/349) — 325

Teapot, pear shape, domed cover, Van Dyck, Peter, H7½, 22 ozs, important, ca1720-40 (4076/669) — 47000

Teapot, rectangular bombe form, ball feet, 'A.M.', 7, 16 ozs, ca1810 (4180/316) — 250

Teapot, bulbous body, foliage sprays, bud finial, pedestal foot, 11, 38 ozs 10 dwts, ca1825 (4211/70) — 950

Teapot, bulbous oval form, flowers, foliage, 9¾, 32 ozs, ca1825 (4211/71) — 350

Teapot, bulbous oval form, fluted at angles, wood handle, 7½, 19 ozs 10 dwts, ca1805 (4211/96) — *950*

Teapot, bulbous rectangular section, hinged dome, urn finial, 9½, 27 ozs, ca1805 (4211/78) — 500

Teapot, by Connor and Eoff, N.Y., bulbous circular shape, foliage, 10, 32 ozs 10 dwts, mkd, ca1835 (4180/317) — 400

Teapot, straight-sided, oval form, drapery hung shields, 6⅞, 22 ozs, ca1790 (4211/100) — 1150

Teapot, swan-neck spout, hinged lid, Jacob Hurd, 5⅜, 15 ozs 10 dwts, ca1735 (4211/109) — 5750

Teapot, wood handle and knop, reeded borders, tapered spout, 6⅜, 19 ozs 15 dwts, mkd, ca1800 (4180/388) — 1600

Teapot, Joseph Richardson, inverted pear shape, 5¾, 21 ozs, ca1760 (4268/138) — 11500

Teapot and hot water kettle, Bailey, Banks & Biddle, H13, 8½, 78 ozs 10 dwts, ca1900 (4211/20) — 500

Teapot and sugar bowl, bombe, raised on ball feet, H7½, 34 ozs 10 dwts, ca1810 (4180/386) — 550

Teapot on lampstand, Tiffany, Young & Ellis, H12⅜, 51 ozs 10 dwts, ca1850 (4076/628) — 1100

Teapots, pair, oval, harp handles, Crosby, Morse, Foss, 7, 48 ozs, ca1875 (4180/318) — 450

Teaspoon, old English pattern, engraved with initials, L4⅞, 33 ozs 10 dwts, mkd, ca1775 (4180/410) — 6000

Teaspoons, 8, Nicholas Hayden, single King's pattern, engraved monogram, 5 ozs, ca1835 (4268/95) — 250

Teaspoons, set of twelve, fiddle pattern, monogrammed HC A & G Welles, 7 ozs 10 dwts, ca1810 (4211/81) — 250

Teaspoons, 5, bright-cut and pricked decoration, Woodcock, Bancroft, 2 ozs., ca1780 (4076/604) — 250

Toast rack, Lincoln & Reed, 6 bars, crest, 7 ozs, 5 dwts, L6¼, ca1840 (4194/33) — 250

Tray, Sheffield plated, 2 handled engraved with armorials, L23, ca1820 (4076/563) — 225

Tray, footed, oval shape, crest, armorials, 118 ozs, 15 dwts, L24, ca1850 (4194/34) — 1400

Tray, oval, repousse with foliate cartouches, bands of roses, ca1890 (649/331) — 800

Tray, oval, repousse with foliate cartouches, bands of roses, 18½, 51 ozs, ca1890 (649/330) — 600

Tray, oval, rim chased with daisies, roses other flowers, 18½, 1896, Gorham & Co., 55 ozs (669/371) — 700

Tray, square, reeded rim, brightcut border, 13, 35 ozs, ca1910 (4259/110) — 250

Tray, tea, 2 handled, Reed and Barton, oval, with cased shell and scrollwork, 27½, 116 ozs, ca1900 (4268/18) — 1150

Tray, 2 handled, oval, gadroon rim and handles, L29, 120 ozs, ca1900 (649/324) — 1300

Trays, pair, circular, bodies repousse with foliate cartouches, 15, 86 ozs, ca1890 (649/329) — 1000

Tureen, 2 handled, oval, bulbous sides, handles, 4 feet, L13, 1896, Gorham Co., 60 ozs (669/370) — 800

Tureens, vegetable, covered, pair, foliate cartouches containing bands of roses, Bailey, Banks & Biddle, 70 ozs, ca1890 (649/326) — 1500

Urn, hot-water, Sheffield plated, reeded body and handles, 14½, ca1790 (4156/151) — 600

Urn, tea, beaded border, foliate sprays and bands Bailey, Banks & Biddle, 19¼, ca1850, 72 ozs (4160/208) — 1200

Urn, tea, monogram, reeded loop handle Ball, Black & Co., 16¾, ca1850, 51 ozs, 10 dwts (4160/216) — 900

Urn, tea, reeded borders, engraved shoulders Tuttle, 19, ca1925, 62 ozs, 15 dwts (4160/218) — 550

Vase, amphora shape, wreaths of flowers and foliage, 12, 13 ozs, ca1839 (4268/64)   300
Vase, slender, cylindrical shape The Gorgan Co., ca1920, 15¼ (4182/44)   375
Vase, flower, trumpet shape, engraved with shields, scrolling foliage, 20, 45 ozs 10 dwts, ca1900
(4180/294)   450
Vase, silver, floral George Shiebler & Co., ca1890, 14½ (4182/26)   400
Vase, three handled, baluster shape loop handles The Gorham Co., ca1900, 7⅜ (4182/39)   1000
Vase, two-handled, amphora shape, twin swan head handles, 11 1/16, 26 ozs 10 dwts, ca1920
(4211/1)   350
Vases, flower, pair, flowers, baluster form, 8¼, 24 ozs, ca1920 (4211/19)   300
Vases, pair, trumpet shape, swags of flowers, 10, ca1910, Redlich & Co., 27 ozs 10 dwts (4238/125)   320
Vegetable dishes, pair, oval form, foliate scrolled edges, 12, 48 ozs 15 dwts, ca1890 (4180/314)   400
Waiter, George III, with arms of Charles Carroll of Carrollton, 12 ozs 10 dwts, L18c (4211/113)   *1100*

Tea set (4211/91)

Waiter (4211/113)

Teapot (4211/96)

Waiter, S. Kirk & Co., circular form, chased with flowers and foliage, 6½, 7 ozs, ca1915 (4268/7)   300
Waiter, S. Kirk & Son Co., circular form, scrollwork rim, 6, 5 ozs, ca1910 (4268/48)   100
Waiter, The Gorham Co., rectangular, rounded ends, 8⅞, 9 ozs, 1873 (4268/85)   275
Water pitcher, engraved with oviform medal lions, flowers, 14½, ca1850 (4180/338)   600
Water pitcher, on pedestal base, Howard & Co., 12¾, 1895, 45 ozs. (631/186)   500
Water pitcher, pedestaled base, Forbes & Sons, 14½, 1840, 38 ozs. (631/187)   650
Water pitcher, anthemion borders, engraved, Baldwin Gardiner, scroll handle, 14¼, 47 ozs, Feb 4,
1844 (4180/366)   650
Water pitcher, embossed foliage, acanthus leaves, 13, 55 ozs, ca1830 (4180/367)   850
Water pitcher, scroll handle, baluster shape, domed foot, 11½, 21 ozs, ca1840 (4180/376)   750
Water pitcher, scroll handle, Fletcher & Gardiner, 12, 42 ozs 15 dwts, ca1820 (4180/381)   1000
Water pitcher, with Lowndes arms, baluster form, 11¾, 27 ozs 10 dwts, ca1825 (4180/350)   525
Water pitcher, Kirk style, flowers and scrolls, Dominick & Haff, 9, 34 ozs, 1886 (4180/310)   600

The Gorham Co.

Centerpiece, florenz pattern, circular bowl, scrolling foliage, 13¼, 1927, 40 ozs 15 dwts (4238/121)   375
Cups, eight, tulip shape, supported by 3 dogfish linked by waves, 3¼, 38 ozs 10 dwts, ca1900
(4211/32)   2600
Pitcher, covered, fluted baluster form, cartouches and floral swags, 11¼, 1873, 36 ozs gross
(4238/136)   475
Tea and coffee service, 5 pieces, repousse floral and scroll decoration, 7¾, 5⅜, 45 ozs (619/159)   500
Tea and coffee service, 6 pieces, Plymouth pattern, 1929-33, 115 gross ozs. (631/188)   1500
Tea and coffee set, tray, tongs, eight pcs, Art Nouveau, monogrammed, 329 ozs 10 dwts, ca1900
(4211/30)   7750
Tea set, 5 pieces, Plymouth pattern, 13, 91 ozs, 1926 (4211/22)   850

Tiffany & Co.

Bowl, footed, shallow circular form, stamped floral garland Tiffany & Co., D12, 38 ozs 5 dwts, ca1875
(4180/339)   450

Bowl, oval, wide fluted band, below border of scrolled foliage flowers, 12, ca1890, 32 ozs (669/379)   550

Jardinieres, pair, rectangular, shaped sides, cartouches, flanked by griffins, 9⅝, ca1880, 39 ozs (669/377)   1000

Kettle, tea on lamp stand, boat shaped, swing handles, 13, 1891-1902, 51 ozs (4238/128)   550

Table service vermeil flatware, 72 pcs, Olympian pattern, 20c, 103 ozs (669/381)   3500

Tea and coffee service, 7 piece, bulbous lobed body, beaded, 26¼, tray, ca1902, 364 ozs (669/376)   5750

Tea and coffee service, 8 pieces, oval bodies, bead and kernel borders, 28 tray, 307 ozs. (631/189)   3250

American Textiles

COVERLETS

Assorted patterns

Appliqued calico and chintz, floral center, double calico borders with hangings, E19c, fine (4156/227)   2000

Crewel, embroidered, N.Eng., white linen, vine and leaf motif, four poster size, 18c, fine (4156/226)   2000

Jacquard, blue and white, by David Haring, Dec. 18, 1834 (4076/230)   1500

Jacquard, blue and white, inscribed for Elizabeth White, 1840 (4146/4)   350

Jacquard, blue and white, single weave, center seam, eagles in corners, (4180/685)   300

Jacquard, blue and white, B. Talcott, double woven with center seam, 1835, unusual, N.Y.* (4076/237)   1500

Jacquard, blue and white, E. Davis, 1832, rosettes, leaves, snowflakes, (4180/688)   375

Jacquard, blue and white, Initialed T.T. Bethany, Genessee County, N.Y., 1834 (654/194)   *350*

Jacquard, blue and white, Marian Spalding, 1851, fine, 1851, N.Eng.* (4076/239)   1200

Jacquard Blue and white woven   Jacquard (654/194)
(4211/634)

Jacquard, blue and white, N.Y., center seam, double woven, Harry Tyler, 72 x 88, 1836 (4268/890)   1800

Jacquard, red and white, floral, dated 1848 at corners (654/193)   350

Jacquard, red and white, portraits of George Washington, 1869 (4076/250)   *550*

Jacquard, red, green and white, Samuel Dornbach, Luzerne Co., Pa., 1846, (4076/234)   600

Jacquard, red, green, white, single woven, oak leaf and flowers, P. Schurn, 19c (654/195)   150

Lady of the Lake variation, silk, multicolored triangular patches, imp, 104 x 101 (4268/907)   550

Pieced, linsey-Woolsey, multi-colored squares, brown quilted border, (4156/233)   1200

Trapunto, all-white, initialed D.C., N.Eng., tasseled fringe, dated 1808, fine, rare (4156/224)   2750

Tulip, pcd cotton, white sawtooth border, (4180/689)   550

Calamanco

Bright pink glazed, floral vines, L18-E19c (4209/177)   1350

Dark-indigo-blue, fine, L18-E19c (4209/173)   1400

Linsey-Woolsey

Floral vine, central pineapple, extremely fine, L18-E19c (4209/174) 3000
Green field, concentric shell motifs, fine, L18-19c (4209/175) 900
Meandering trapunto motifs, L18c (4209/176) 450

FLAGS

American flag banner, thirty-five stars, holes and tears., L168 (4180/750) 425
American thirteen star flag, holes, and fraying, framed, 22 x 35½ (4180/749) 1000
Civil War, American, hand sewn, 13 star, embroidered, F. Garland, Ft. Fisher, 46 x 72, 1865 (4268/1094) 2600

HOOKED RUGS

Centennial theme with 1776-1876, Stars and the United States shield, 23½ x 36 (4211/734) 150
Clusters of flowers, brown ground, 29¼ x 55, fine, E19c,N.Eng.* (4209/172) 700
Couple pointing to steamship, verse, ca1920, 45 x 33 (4076/258) 750
Crazy quilt pattern, red, blue, green tan, 50 x 100 (4209/163) 950
Dog, brown and tan, in landscape, Ebeneser Ross*, 31¼ x 55, L19c (4268/1063) 600
Elephant, trees, scrolling flowers, leaves, ca1800,N.Eng., 31½ x 75¼, needs res, rare (4209/150) 1900
Floral sprays, dark navy-blue ground, 30 x 55 (4268/1062) 275
Fully rigged sailing vessel, Ship Albert, 4 American flags, 32¾ x 46, ca1920 (4076/259) 500
Fully rigged ship, on open seas, with American ensign, 29¼ x 45 (4211/736) *500*

Jacquard (4076/250)

Fully rigged ship (4211/736)

Geometric and leaf design, gray, blue, pink, yellow, green, 144 x 108 (4180/849) 150
Geometric pattern, green field with orange and green circles, 19 x 36½ (4268/1064) 30
Horse, seated, dog, leaf border, 32½ x 57¾, 19c (4209/161) 2100
Lady and gentleman in sleigh, by Christine Wuerpel after N. Currier print, 22 x 33 (4268/1066) 200
Lamb, floral sprays, 23¼ x 37¾ (4211/733) 300
Lion, recumbent, grey, red, blue, yellow, 19c, 30 x 56¼,N.Eng.* (4209/152) 950
Lions, scrolling flowers, sawtooth border, 19c, 30½ x 61½ (4209/158) 1200
Loomed, cotton,N.Eng., floor, stripes, E19c, 162 x 180 (4209/151) 1300
Rooster and chicks, multi-colored, 24 x 39, 1944 (654/219) 150
Runner, animals, birds, lavender ground, 252 x 190½ (4209/155) 600
Runner, clustered flowers, leaves, geometric squares, 25 x 240 (4209/166) 950
Stag, lake, mountains, textile threads, 20 x 46 (654/220) 40
Tulips, pinwheels, Pa.*, olive-green, red, yellow, 93 x 38, 19c (4180/850) 1500
Village street scene, houses, horse and cart, 30½ x 59 (4076/256) 950
Welcome, 2 cats, 19c, L30 (4209/171) 700

NEEDLEWORK

American Eagle; American flags, gray, white, silver eagle, oriental origin*, 23 x 27⅝, E20c (4268/989) 150
American Eagle over navy battleship, embroidered on silk, oriental origin, 42 x 25½, E20c (4268/1017) 200
Anonymous, Spring, embroidered and painted on silk, 16½ x 18, L18/E19c (4268/1083) 400
Anonymous, ca1800, silk embroidered picture of mother and boy, 28 x 21 (4211/698) 600

Coffin drapery, Abraham Lincoln, knitted wool with presidential eagle, ca1865 (4076/1239)   1700
Counterpane, appliqued chintz, large pomegranate tree with peacocks, L18c, fine (4156/225)   1300
Embroidery, Chinese silk, framed, American eagle, H19¼, M19c (654/285)   125
Floor cover, jacquard florally-woven, red and white, 72 x 108, 19c (4149/42)   225
Flower picture, Maria Hoffman, spray of garden flowers, crewel embroidery, 17¾ x 14, fine
(4180/743)   500
Flower pictures, pair, crewel, embroidered floral sprays, 14 x 11½, fine, 18c (4180/744)   450
Lewis, Sarah, Country Scene, Fishing, Pa.*, embroidered silk, 16 x 18¾, stains, E19c (4268/1006)   1000
Patterns, 27 watercolor on paper, with leather box, rare, (4211/636)   500
Pillow, charity sheltering two small children, 7½ x 12, fine (4180/740)   450
Pocketbook, Irish stitch, red and pink, green ground, initialed AB, L7, W6½, 1766 (4146/138)   750
Sampler, 'Jane Pullyn, wrought in, the year 1742, Aged thirteen years', 15¾ x 10¾, fine (4180/741)   1200
Ship Golden West, Boston, oil on canvas with silk, velvet, 21 x 32¼, initialed PW, 1858 (4268/930)   850
Silkwork American eagle, Chinese, inscribed E. Pluribus Unum, 21½ x 25, 19c (4146/140)   200
The Barnard Family Group, portrait, embroidered by Amelia Wright Barnard*, 27½ x 39¼, ca 1800
(4211/681)   1200
Tree of life embroidered panel, 120 x 52¾ (4211/630)   *500*
Woolwork picture of ship, fully rigged, Union Jack, 22½ x 24, 19c (4268/929)   900
Yacht with shore boats, cabins, curtains, figures, flags in textiles, 15¾ x 25½, 19c (4268/931)   175

PRINTED TEXTILES

A memorial to George Washington, copper-printed cotton panel, 25 x 19, ca1820 (4156/252)   200
Counterpane, stenciled, Mass.*, four large trees bearing stenciled blossoms, ca1840 (4156/230)   2200
Linsey-Woolsey, orange, 120 x 62, 18c (4076/251)   350
Punch bowl, with figures and animals, D15¼, very fine, ca1775 (4076/299)   2200
Washington standing beside his horse, red, navy-blue and brown, 23½ x 17, 19c (4180/748)   200

QUILTS

Album, pieced and appliqued calico, Lexington, Va.*, 1845-50, fine (4180/686)   1000
Amish, Ohio, quatrefoil and wreath motif, blue band, 66 x 71, ca1920 (684/196)   250
Applique, cotton, Dresden plate pattern, pink center, E20c (684/217)   125
Appliqued and trapunto cotton quilts, pair, red, white rose blossoms, fraying, 100 x 100
(4268/895)   500
Appliqued calico, red, yellow, green flowers, fine (4076/254)   275
Appliqued orange and green flowers, good (4211/628)   *425*
Appliques, green red and orange, on white quilted ground, (4076/232)   225
Basket pattern, blue and black patches, 1918, Amish (4076/245)   425
Basket pattern, Wool and cotton patches, Amish, (4076/241)   400
Birds in the Air, pieced red, white, triangular patches, faded, 74 x 85 (4268/891)   300
Bow-tie, calico, (4146/7)   200
Bride's all-white trapunto, elaborately stitched, ca1835 (4070/236)   1200
Bride's quilt, all white, pineapple motif, blossoms, diamond quilting, 82 x 41 (4268/906)   450

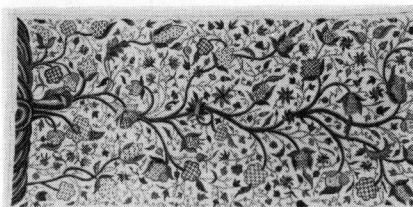

Tree of life embroidered panel   (4211/630)

Appliqued orange and green
flowers   (4211/628)

Crib   (654/208)

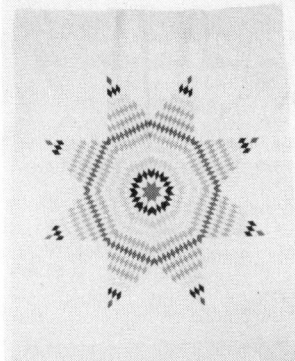

Star of Le Moyne (4146/12)

Star of Bethlehem (4146/5)

Calico and chintz, multicolored octagonal and triangular patches, 94 x 96 (4268/908)	550
Compass star, pieced calico, elaborate quilting on white field, fine (4180/698)	450
Crazy quilt of pieced silk, satin, velvet, Victorian, triangle pattern, (4180/696)	75
Crib, calico, appliqued, pcd, fine, red, green on white cotton, John Lyon, 1876, N.Y.* (654/208)	*3500*
Double Irish chain, red and green, white ground, (4076/235)	150
Duck's foot in the mud, pieced calico, cube quilting, (4180/695)	150
Feathered star, vari-colored calico, with line and cube quilting, (4076/231)	150
Four Roses, flowers, red and green, double border, 72 x 72, L19c (684/199)	175
Friendship, calico flower basket, each basket by seamstress, (4076/228)	400
Friendship, pieced and appliqued, each square by stitcher, fine 1853 (4180/694)	500
Friendship, pieced calico and chintz, Squares with Indian ink signatures of stitcher, 1844 (4211/635)	500
Friendship, pieced cotton, each square by stitcher, (4180/684)	250
Lone Star, pieced calico crib quilt, Lancaster County, Pa., fine, rare, ca1880 (4211/622)	550
Lone Star, Pennsylvania Amish, dark blue, red, pink and yellow on blue ground, 72 x 72, ca1910 (684/203)	425
Mariner's Compass, calico and chintz, N.Y.*, multicolored patches, floral chintz, 90 x 90, ca1820 (4268/893)	2200
Mosaic, pieced calico, top only, Conn.*, octagonally-shaped patches, minor, stains, 96 x 88 (4268/901)	1100
Nine Patch, circle and diamonds, red foliate printed cotton, 72 x 73, L19c (684/198)	150
North Carolina lily, pieced cotton, red, green, white patches, meandering vine, border, 82 x 74 (4268/903)	225
Nursery, all white cotton, red thread, each square, (654/192)	20
Ocean waves, calico and cotton patches, Mennonite, fine, (4076/244)	125
Patchwork, bightly colored panels, 1,860 patches, 76 x 84, ca1900 (684/187)	300
Patchwork, pink and white, triangular and square motifs, tulip pattern, 72 x 85, ca1900 (684/197)	125
Patchwork crazy Victorian, Sopha Boilleau, Riddletown, Md., 1890 (4076/233)	550
Philadelphia pavement, calico, (4146/9)	150
Pieced cotton quilt, red cut-outs on white ground, stains, 82 x 80 (4268/899)	100
Pinwheel, calico, (4146/8)	120
Star, all-silk, multicolor patches enhanced with cube quilting, 94 x 80 (4268/909)	500
Star, pieced and appliqued cotton, Beale sisters, Philadelphia, 19c (4076/253)	200
Star, pieced calico, sawtooth border, cube quilting, (4180/687)	300
Star, pieced cotton, Ohio, Amish, light brown central star, quilting, 80 x 82, 20c (4268/889)	500
Star of Bethlehem, calico, (4146/5)	*225*
Star of East, calico, (4146/15)	60
Star of Le Moyne, pieced and appliqued, (4146/12)	*475*
Star of Le Moyne, pieced crib quilt, N.Eng., fine, ca1830 (4211/623)	425
Starburst, pieced cotton, brilliant colors, irregular spacing, red sawtooth border (4180/692)	• 700
Sunburst, pieced calico, Cornelia Ann Schenck, 1851, fine (4180/682)	2400
Trip around the world pattern, cotton and wool, Amish, crib size (4076/247)	250
Triple Irish Chain, pieced cotton, Ohio, Amish, multicolored patches, 69 x 79, 1920 (4268/886)	400
Variable star, cotton and sateen, Amish (4076/246)	275
Washington's Plume, red, green and yellow, (4180/693)	350
Wild Goose Chase, cotton and calico, Vt., triangular multicolored patches, 85½ x 83, fading, ca1890 (4268/885)	300

Zig-zag, calico, (4146/6)   250

SAMPLERS

A Negro's prayer, with enchained, black slave, verse and floral border, 25¾ x 29½, 1838 (4211/688)	500
Allen, Elizabeth Ann, Long Island, in 10th year, verse and border, 17 x 12½, ca1820 (4268/993)	200
Alphabets, floral border, Sally Sanborn, Pa., 16½ x 13¼, 1799 (4211/660)	2100
Beall, Hariot, Md.*, Map of Maryland, points of compass, 13 x 17½, ca1800 (4268/1032)	2100
Carver, Anne G., alphabet and verse, little girl in bonnet holding flowers, 17 x 15¾, E19c (4268/1050)	550
Four story brick house, verse, Elizabeth Newby, 12¼ x 12, M19c (4211/689)	425
Hoff, Ann*, Pa., family record, dates, picture of brick house, 17¼ x 15½, 1826 (4268/1038)	200
Hotchkin-Hubbard family record, N.Eng.*, family names and birth dates, 17 x 17, 1769-1800 (4076/207)	130
Letters and numerals by Fanny Smither, 13, 17, 1800, (684/180)	150
Mary Frost, pair, flowers and alphabets, 12½ x 13, 13 x 11, 1814 (4180/770)	600
Nancy Thompson, alphabets, sayings, 15½ x 12¼, dated 1783 (4156/250)	350
Needlework, map, England, Wales, Foxwell, F.E., 21 x 19¼, 1803 (4148/164)	600
Needlework, Grant, Mary, trees, animals, alphabets, 12¾ x 12, 1773 (4148/148)	650
Needlework, MacColloch, Mary, plants, pious verses, 13¼ x 10¼, 1740 (4148/149)	350
Needlework, Mary Graham Moyemee, 17 x 12, 1814 (4146/65)	*275*
Needlework, Sherman, letters, flowers, 12 x 8¼, 1736 (4148/146)	325
Sampler, figures, flowers, birds, 18, 17¾, maple frame, 1812 (4149/82)	330
Verse, alphabets, plants, Caroline Hubbard, N.J. 1825, (4211/711)	400

Needlework (4146/65)

Chapter 2

European Furniture and Decorations

Sales of European furniture and decorative objects enjoyed another strong season. Though portions of the French and Continental market behaved erratically, traditionally strong areas remained solid, and several others showed promising growth.

Queen Anne and early eighteenth-century items sold well. Walnut pieces proved especially strong, being generally earlier in origin than similar pieces in mahogany. Pieces from the early nineteenth century, however, in Regency, William IV and early-Victorian styles, also showed strength. Nineteenth-century sofa tables, usually with trestle legs and drop leaves, were especially popular, while the Canterbury, frequently found with a small drawer, also rose in price.

The contradictory nature of the English market showed itself with respect to long-case clocks. But collectors had some excellent opportunities. Walnut clocks sold for as much as 3 times what similar mahogany pieces brought, probably because collectors thought walnut was of earlier manufacture. Chandeliers and hall lanterns especially sold at reasonable prices.

In the French and Continental market, case and seat furniture brought particularly good prices throughout the season. Empire seat furniture also sold well. The high prices for early-nineteenth century seat furniture consolidated and built on the strong gains of the previous season; this relatively new demand was also reflected in strong prices for other types of neoclassical and Empire furniture. In general, French furniture has enjoyed a tremendous surge in popularity and price.

Wooden commodes of the eighteenth-century, either of plain wood, simply veneered or decorated with marquetry or parquetry panels, are one of the most stable portions of the market. Another entirely reliable aspect of the market for French furniture is the continuing demand for small tables and other small pieces. Pieces with fitted drawers, with slides or incorporating a shelved cupboard of some sort are particularly sought after.

Lacquered commodes proved unexpectedly strong. While they have enjoyed spells of popularity in the North American market, as recently as 1977 they were exceptionally difficult to sell. But recent sales indicate that these items are returning to public favor. Dutch furniture with its elaborate marquetry and ornate appearance was popular.

Decorative objects, such as lighting devices, mirrors, clocks and chenets, consistently appeal to collectors, and these items posted another season of high prices. Eighteenth-century clocks were in particular demand.

Most areas of French and Continental furniture and decoration showed the consistent strength characteristic of this field. Early nineteenth-century furniture is likely to make further gains, with certain other areas, such as lacquer commodes, offering more speculative opportunities. In the field of English furniture and decoration, prices within each category of object depend largely upon the characteristics of the piece itself—its date and the quality of its design and workmanship. Public taste, however, is growing more knowledgeable in the search for the distinctive item, and unusual pieces are always highly sought after.

English Decorations

ENGLISH BAROMETERS

Barometer, carved wood, Louis XVI style, octagonal, carved bird and foliage group, 36 French* (619/266) — $200

Barometer, cistern, mahogany, England, Storr, B., 41, L18c (4111/54) — 1200

Barometer, cistern, mahogany, Muston, Bristol, ivory dial, 36, Victorian (4134/206) — 575

Barometer, gilt wood, French, circular dial, oval frame, 33, L18c (4232/66) — 500

Barometer, gilt wood, Louis XVI, circular blue and grey dial, oval frame, 33½ x 19, restorations (4218/42) — 425

Barometer, mahogany, inlaid, George III, 38 x 10, El9c (654/505) — 300

Barometer, mahogany, Davis, Cheltenham, swan's neck cresting, urn finial, 39, L18c (4111/9) — 1300

Barometer, nautical, brass inlaid mahogany, England, ivory dial, 36 (4134/216) — 900

Barometer, portable, carved walnut, Daniel Quare, 38½, L17c (4189/4) — 4100

Barometer, wheel inlaid mahogany, 38 cresting replaced, M19c (4216/63) — *450*

Barometer, wheel, inlaid mahogany, Donegan Co, London, 38½ 19c (4216/57) — 325

Barometer, wheel, inlaid mahogany, F. Somalvico, Hatton Garden, 38, July 11, 1818 (4134/205) — *450*

Barometer, wheel, inlaid mahogany, J. Fagioli, Clerkenwell, swan's neck cresting, 42, Victorian (4134/241) — 500

Barometer, wheel, inlaid mahogany, P. Gago built, with hygrometer dial, 44½, M19c (4189/55) — 475

Barometer, wheel, inlaid mahogany, Victorian, A. Carioli, Sheffield, 38, L19c (4165/250) — 600

Barometer, wheel, inlaid, mahogany, C. Realini, Preston, 38 M19c (4189/58) — 250

Barometer, wheel, mahogany, King, Bristol, silvered dials, 38, E19c (4111/42) — 500

Barometer, wheel, shell inlaid mahogany, Jennings, Ipswich, 39 M19c (4216/8) — 175

ENGLISH CLOCKS

Assorted shelf clocks

Brass, inlaid mahogany, 8 inch painted dial, 2 train movement, 18½, E19c (4239/206) — 550

Bright, Henry, movement, 2 barrels, anchor escapement, for church*, 37 ca1800 (4165/132) — 2100

Carriage, repeating (small), gilt metal, dial Dent, London, French, 5½ (4165/244) — 850

Clock, lantern, brass, William and Mary, William Cattell, London, engraved dial, bun feet, 19½, L17c (4159/187) — 2600

Cockburn, mahogany, arched hood, 12 inch arched dial, 2 train movement, 85, L18c (4239/186) — 1200

Cox, J. Architectural, gold-mounted, miniature, reverse paintings on glass, London, ca1765, H5¾ (4086/32) — 25000

Inlaid mahogany, George III, 14 in. painted dial, seconds & phase of the moon, 97, E19c (4159/245) — 1700

Klaftenberger, bracket time piece, brass inlaid mahogany, 6 inch dial, ring handles, 15, E19c (4239/32) — 400

Mahogany, Finney, Liverpool, George III, 13 in. brass dial, silver chapter ring, seconds dial, 96½, L18c (4159/327) — 2900

Nicholas, W, 8 inch painted arched dial, 2 train movement, 17, ca1800 (4272/19) — 1200

Orbital, musical, silver gilt and enamel, pedestal set on carved rosewood base, 11 (4165/238) — 5500

Ormolu and patinated bronze, circular dial, striking on half and hour, 15¼ x 12, E19c (4272/315) — 900

Regency, brass, rosewood, inlaid, Mantel, H15½, 19c (4148/157) — 275

Signed Vacciho & Co., time pc, formerly wheel barometer, 40 (4152/37) — 325

Skeleton time pc, brass, Victorian, 13½, L19c (4165/249) — 1100

Bracket clocks

Brass inlaid, Regency style, mahogany, silvered dial, 2 train movement, 14½ 19c (4152/62) — 500

Farquar, London, seven inch painted dial, stepped hood, 19½, movement not original (4079/46) — 350

Gilt metal mounted mahogany, Robert Henderson, London, George III, 21½, L18c (4165/252) — 4500

Goodhugh, London, inlaid rosewood, with matching bracket, brass dial, 28½ E19c (4189/49) — *1900*

Green, Thos., Liverpool, loop handle, enamelled dial, engraved backplate, 22½, L18c (4111/25) — 750

Harlow, Ashborn, gilt metal mounted, mahogany, brass carrying handles, 23 L18c (4189/23) — *1700*

Kelly, P., London, gilt metal corners, dated 1790, 20, finials, bracket feet later (4111/46) — 750

Mahogany, 2 train movement, gilt metal ogee bracket feet, 17 F19c, 6¾ dial (4152/31) — 700

McCabe, James, London, mahogany, silvered dial, 3 train movement not original, 22½, Regency (4216/61) — 1000

Quarter repeating gilt, mounted ebonized, chiming, George III, 21, L18c (4165/251) — 2600

Richardson, gilt metal mounted, mahogany, two-train movement, 16, L18c (4189/22) — 425

Robert Henderson, London, gilt metal mounted maogany, George III, 18, L18c (4165/248) — 3000

Storr, Marmaduke, London, time pc, silvered dial, 1 train movement, 16½, M18c (4216/34) — 425

Swannell, Robert, London, calendar, ebonized, foliate engraved back plate, 23, L18c (4189/24) — *1350*

Toulmin, Strand, gilt metal, mounted, painted enamelled dial, 20½, L18c (4111/8)   1900
Turnbull, London, red japanned, seven-inch brass dial, 20, George III (4152/7)   1600
Two train movement, carved mahogany, silvered dial, strike-silent in arch, 25, M19c (4216/52)   550
Webster, Wm., London, alarm, brass, arched dial, 6½, E18c (4189/3)   3500

S

Tall-case clocks

Angus, George, Aberdeen, anchor escapement, arched topped oak case, 84, L18c (4079/28)   550
Bracegirdle, London, brass dial, cherub-spandrels, George III style, 5' 1½ (4189/30)   1400
Bradley, London, burr walnut, engraved brass dial, 91, restoration (4189/8)   3250
Brown, W. Birmingham, Inlaid mahogany, George III, date register, 75¾ x 17½, L18c (4156/287)   1200
Buddely, Albrighton, silvered dial, seconds and calendar dials in arch, 93 (4111/21)   1500
Cleland, Edinburgh, silvered dial, calendar aperture, strike-silent, George III, 78½ (4189/42)   1600
Clock, musical, mahogany, broken arched hood, glazed front and sides, paw feet, H84, Elliott, London (631/348)   1900
Coles, Michael, Scarborough, oak, seconds and calendar dials, 87 L18c (4189/43)   1700
Doriell, Fra, London, subsidiary seconds dial and calendar, aperture, 88½ (4079/30)   1900
Drury, John, inlaid mahogany, 12 inch brass dial, 2 train movement, 91, L18c (4272/5)   1500
Garone, Peter, inlaid walnut, leafy spandrels, two-train movement, 85½, L17-E18c (4189/1)   *3750*
Hall, Thos, black lacquer, brass dial, seconds and calendar, chinoiserie, 7' 11 restorations L18c (4152/36)   3200
Hemings, Thos., mahogany, 12 inch brass dial, 2 train movement, 85, ca1765 (4272/16)   2100
Hughes, David, Festonig, 2 train movement, arched hood, 90½, E19c (4079/23)   800

Barometer (4216/63)

Barometer (4134/205)

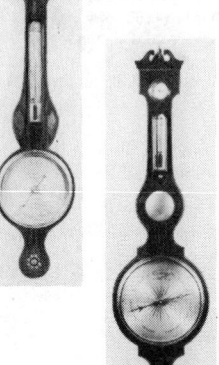

Barometer (4189/55)

Goodhugh (4189/49)

Harlow (4189/23)

Hunter, John, London, musical quarter repeating, brass inlaid mahogany, 93 (4079/25)   2000
Inlaid mahogany, seconds dial, calendar aperture, 96, 19c (4189/35)   1200
Inlaid mahogany, swan's neck crest, subsidiary seconds, calendar dial, 85, E19c (4189/39)   1000
Inlaid oak and mahogany, 12 inch painted dial, anchor escapement, 85, L18c (4239/27)   1000
Laurie, Arch, Edinborough, walnut, foliate spandrels, phase of the moon, M18c (4189/36)   3600
Lee, John, Lougborough, chinoiserie, pineapple finials, seconds dial, 95½ L18c (4189/34)   *2000*

Massey, William, painted dial, 2 train movement, 83½, E19c (4239/15) — 1000
Mereman, Henry, inlaid walnut, 11 inch brass dial, 2 train movement, 82, L17c (4239/178) — *10500*
Miller, Aaron, brass dial, calendar aperture, pierced cresting, 93, L18c (4134/14) — 5250
Miller, John, London, time pc, gilt chinoiserie on red ground, 78½, George III (4216/35) — 700
Osbourne, Edward, Chene Prior, 2 train movement, arched dial, 95, reduced in height, L18c (4152/1) — 750
Pyke, John, London, burr walnut, brass dial, seconds dial, 89 L18c (4189/21) — 3800
Rimbault, Stepn, London, green lacquer, twelve inch brass dial, seconds and calendar, 92, L18c (4152/27) — 2600
Rogger, Isaal, London, mahogany, brass dial, eagle finial, 89 base altered L18c (4134/32) — 2250
Rudkin, Thomus, inlaid mahogany, brass dial glued over original painted dial, 78 (4152/38) — 800
Scott, John, gilt-decorated, japanned, 12 inch brass dial, 2 train movement, 98, L18c (4239/180) — 1700
Townsend, Robert, Greenock, brass dial, calendar aperture, 6' 10½, L18c (4189/41) — 1900
Whitaker, William, marquetry, mahogany, phase of the moon in the arch, 85½ 19c (4189/40) — 1800
Wilson, J., miniature, arched brass dial, column with waist door, 60 movement later (4111/34) — 2000

Wall clocks

Brass, inlaid mahogany, 14 inch circular dial, anchor encasement, 23½, E19c (4239/207) — 350
Mother of pearl, inlaid and ebonized, 26 x 21, M19c (4272/281) — 150
Picture of River Thames, inset with circular clock, swiss watch movements, 21½ x 27½ (4111/28) — 650
Torin, Dan, 3 train movement with pull repeater, 40½ x 16¼, L18c (4272/38) — *5750*

ENGLISH DECORATIVE OBJECTS

Brackets, wall, gilt wood and gilt gesso, semi circular shaped, leaf carved scroll, 16½ x 13½ L18c (4134/12) — 3600
Brackets, wall, pair, mahogany, 3 leaf and carved supports, George III, 16 x 13½ x 9, L18c (4111/13) — 1300
Bucket, brass bound mahogany, bailhandle, 16 E19c (4216/60) — 850

Garone (4189/1)

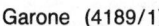

Lee (4189/34)

Mereman (4239/178)

Swannell (4189/24)

Torin (4272/38)

Bucket, oval, brass bound, mahogany, bail handle, dipped sides, 12, E19c (4216/53) — 750
Coal scuttle, brass, Victorian, helmet shaped, wooden and brass bail handle, 20½, 19c (4260/895) — 700
Coal scuttle, brass, Victorian, horizontal, hinged oval front, conical base, 16, 19c (4260/832) — 800
Ewers and pedestals, pair, monumental, pieta dura inlaid black Belgian marble, 67, L19c (649/418) — 3750
Milk churns, pair, brass, tall conical bodies, dished lids, 19½, L19c (4260/835) — 3500
Pot and cover, hexagonal, ormolu mounted, blanc de chine, molded figures, H9⅞, M18c (4086/61) — 11000

Tea caddies, pair, pedestal, mahogany, 7 E19c (4152/11)	200
Toby jug, leather, 10, L18-E19c (4216/49)	80
Tray, painted tinware, Victorian, exotic birds, flowers on olive-green, L30½ (4156/202)	500
Trivet, brass, engraved, George I, serpentine, cabriole legs, 9½, ca1725 (4260/811)	1000
Trivet, brass, pierced, engraved, George III, elmwood handle, 3 cabriole legs, 12 x 15½, ca1790 (4260/807)	375
Trivet, brass, George III, rectangular top, on tapering cabriole legs, 19½, E19c (4260/801)	650
Trivets, pair, brass, George II, pierced, serpentine, 24, M18c (4260/856)	3500
Urn, covered, ponty pool, George III, bell shaped lid, cabriole legs, ball feet, 20, L18c (4079/22)	300
Urn, marble, ormolu mounted, George III, manner of Matthew Boulton ram's head handles, 12½, L18c (4079/14)	700
Urn, Derbyshire Spar, Regency, 10½, E19c (4239/189)	475
Water kettle, brass, George III, domed rectangular form, ebony handle, 11, E19c (4260/825)	800
Weights, set of 6, brass, English, dumbbell shape, 56 lbs to 1 lb (14 lbs missing), 13¾, 3½, 19c (4260/813)	2600
Weights, set of 5, brass, dumbbell shape, handle at top, 14 lbs to 1 lb, 3½, 9, 19c (4260/861)	600

ENGLISH HEARTH EQUIPMENT

Andirons, pair, brass, George II, trestle foot, 22½, 18c (4260/890)	500
Brass fender, 2 bars on baluster supports, George III, 77, E19c (4239/29)	250
Chimney piece, inlaid hardwood, 51 x 62 reduced in depth, L18c (4134/28)	1700
Chimney piece, marble, inverted breakfront form, carvings, George II, 60 x 75 x 12, ca1740 (4239/181)	3000
Fender, bow-front pierced, engraved steel, Regency, L50, E19c (4216/45)	125
Fender, bow-front, pierced brass, on paw feet, George III, 44½, E19c (4272/24)	250
Fender, brass, George III, bow-front, pierced, paw feet, 37½, E19c (4260/855)	1000
Fender, serpentine, 1, brass pierced and engraved, George III, 56 L18c (4134/240)	650
Fender, steel serpentine, engraved with flowers and leaves, George III, 59½ L18c (4134/207)	200
Footwarmer, brass, octagonal, pierced and engraved with masks, 6, English or Dutch, E18c (4076/534)	275
Grate, fire, engraved brass, serpentine, 34 x 35½, L18c (4165/264)	325
Grate, fire, engraved brass and steel, flowerhead and oval medallions, 26 x 31½, L18c (4165/271)	550
Grate, fire, engraved steel, serpentine front, 32 x 31½ (4165/261)	250
Jug, hot-water, brass, baluster body, 3 shaped foot, 7¾, English, L18c (4076/508)	125
Trivet, steel, George III, serpentine pierced front, 13 x 12, L18c (4159/190)	90

ENGLISH LIGHTING DEVICES

Assorted styles

Candelabra, pair, cut glass, gilt metal, urn finial, 4 branches, George III, 35½, dam, L18c (4239/191)	4000
Candelabra, 2 light, cut glass, 19½ L18c (4216/9)	375
Candelabra, 2 light, cut glass, ormolu, 2 candle branches, 2 tiers, prisms, 14, M19c (4111/27)	400
Candelabra, pair, gilt, ebonized bronze, form of a blackamoor holding 2 candles, branches, 19, E19c (4165/280)	5250
Candlestand, brass, wrought-iron, two-light, standing, modern, 63¾ (4209/289)	250
Candlestick, bell-metal, flaring foot, 6¼, Dutch*, 17c (4076/531)	450
Candlestick, brass, hexagonal foot, 6, English, M17c (4076/516)	175
Candlestick, brass, square molded base on paw feet, 7, English or Continental, E18c (4076/528)	350
Candlesticks, bell metal, 2, molded square base, 10¾, English, L18c (4076/533)	450
Candlesticks, bell-metal, pair, molded square foot, 12, English, L18c (4076/525)	250
Candlesticks, bell-metal, pair, square molded foot, 9½, English, L18c (4076/536)	175
Candlesticks, brass, 4, petal form bobeche, 8½, English, rare, fine, M18c (4076/515)	2000
Candlesticks, brass, pair, flaring standard, 8⅜, English, M18c (4076/539)	300
Candlesticks, brass, pair, molded square foot, 7, English*, 18c (4076/532)	400
Candlesticks, brass, pair, English, 6¼, M18c (4076/505)	550
Candlesticks, brass, trumpet form standard, pair, 7, English*, M18c (4076/538)	325
Candlesticks, brass and mahogany, pair, fluted and turned stems, 14½ L18c (4152/13)	650
Candlesticks, brass, pair, English, animal paw feet, E19c, 8½ (4209/278)	550
Candlesticks, brass, petal base, pair, incised bobeche, 8½, English, M18c (4076/514)	900
Candlesticks, brass, pr, William and Mary, Dutch or English, drip pan, electrified, 17c, 5¾ x 6¾ (4209/272)	1000
Candlesticks, pair, brass, flared socket, baluster stem, dished square base, 6½, 18c (4260/806)	850
Candlesticks, pair, silvered metal, baluster shaped stem, William IV, 22¾, L19c (4219/66)	600
Candlesticks, pair, William IV, brass, inverte D-shaped stems, rectangular bases, 12, 19c (4260/834)	600
Candlesticks, pr, William and Mary, English, domed foot, 1 repaired, electrified, 17c, 6 to 9 inches (4209/273)	750
Candlesticks, set of 4, brass, bee hive stem, canted square bases, 10, 19c (4260/833)	950

Candlesticks, silvered brass, 4, English, octagonal foot, 7½, E18c (4076/513) — 650
Canister, (mounted as lamp) tole peinte, rectangular, gilt chinoiserie figures, 24½ 19c (4134/45) — 200
Chamberstick, brass, waisted turned socket, dished drip pan, 9, E18c (4260/849) — 400
Chandelier, brass and glass, frame incorporating female masks and scallop shells, 21 x 22, L19c (649/427) — 650
Girandoles, pair, gilt wood, shaped mirror plate, candle branches, 35½ x 18 (4165/272) — 10500
Girandoles, 2 light, gilt wood, pair, shaped mirror plate, scrolling leaf border, 34¾ x 17, M18c (4216/48) — 8250
Hogscraper candlesticks, 2, tinware, 6, English*, E19c (4076/517) — 80
Lamps, pair of double argand, cut glass and brass, William Brookes, London, 24, L19c (4076/493) — 2200
Lamps, urn-form, terra-cotta, pair, continental, H24½, l9c (4148/154) — 175
Lantern, hall, gilt metal and blown glass, 26 L18c (4152/22) — 550
Lantern, hall, gilt metal and blown glass, circular, shade, from chain, 27, L18c (4165/260) — 450
Pedestal vases, pair Vieux Paris, fitted as lamps, swan's head handles, H19½, ca1815 (4086/54) — 3300
Sconces, brass, 2 light, pair, oval mirrored backplates, electrified, 12, L18c (4149/78) — 250
Urn, tole, gilt chinoiserie decorated, black, mounted as lamp, 25, 19 (4216/54) — 200
Vase, mounted as lamp, mason's ironstone, Japan ware, gilt decoration, 23¼, E19c (4111/50) — 400
Vase, Samson, porcelain-covered, mounted as lamp, baluster-shaped body pierced, H16½ (4168/4) — 275
Wall lights, brass, pair, Queen Anne, engraved, pierced with tree of life, 11½, E18c (4111/2) — 1500
Wall lights, gilt gesso, pair, ribbon tied doves, scrolled candle branches, 41, L18c (4111/23) — 3750
Wall lights, gilt metal and cut glass, candle branches leaf 'S' scrolled supports, 18, res, L18c (4134/13) — 650
Wall sconces, single light, brass pair, mirrored glass backs, Queen Anne, 16¾, E18c (4156/205) — 1500

William and Mary

Chandelier, 24 light, brass, bulbous baluster stem supporting 3 tiers, 49 x 47½, 19c (4272/51) — 3750
Torchere, tripod, marquetry inlaid, 41 x 14½, L17c (4165/296) — 425
Torcheres, pair, octagonal mahogany, tripod, scrolled feet, 35½ x 11½ (4216/101) — 275

Queen Anne

Candlesticks, brass, baluster stem on a stepped circular base, 8¼, E18c (4272/1) — 125

George III

Candelabra, 3 light, pair, cut glass, gilt metal and Jasperware, lion's head feet, 33, L18c (4079/29) — 1800
Candelabra, 4 light cut glass, 21½ L18c (4216/37) — 1000
Candelabra, 2 light, gilt wood and gilt metal, 22½ (4152/29) — 650
Candelabra, 2 light, cut glass and, gilt metal, mounted, Jasperware, 29 (4134/233) — 650
Candelabrum, 2 light brass, with drip dish, pierce D-shaped arms, H8, ca1780 (4272/7) — 350
Chandelier, 10 light, cut glass, prism hung canopy, 41 (4111/38) — 1300
Chandelier, 4 light, cut glass and, bronze, double canopy hung reeded column, 26 (4134/11) — 450
Chandelier, 6 light, cut glass, 36 x 11½ (4134/43) — 650
Chandelier, 6 light, cut glass, 3 circular tier, 40 (4079/26) — 300
Chandelier, 6 lights, gilt wood and, gilt metal, octagonal baluster stem, 23 (4134/21) — 900
Girandoles, pair gilt wood, mirror plate, within leaf carved border, 40 x 19, L18c (4111/45) — 9500
Girandoles, pair, gilt wood, 28 (4189/46) — 600
Girandoles, pair, Jasperware mounted, gilt gesso, 39 (4189/26) — 1100
Lamps, alabaster, gilt metal, pair, swag hung urn on paw feet, 26 (4111/41) — 650

Regency

Candlesticks, pair, cut glass, gilt, metal and gilt decorated, green glass, 10 E19c (4134/217) — 525
Chandelier, gilt metal and cut glass, pierced corona, cut glass swags, 8 candle branches, 42, E19c (4272/60) — 3200
Chandelier, 16 light carved, wood and gilt gesso, 34½, E19c (4216/55) — 2400
Chandelier, 6 light, cut glass and brass, downswept beaded waist, circular corona, 27, E19c (4272/55) — 550
Girandole, convex, gilt wood, ebonized, ball hung borders, pair candle branches, 46 x 25, E19c (4272/58) — 850
Girandole, convex, gilt wood, ebonized, circular plate, pair tassel, hung scrolled candle branches, 42 x 28, E19c (4239/25) — 1800
Lamps, coach, pair, stamped brass, painted metal, eagle finial, 32 E19c (4134/8) — 900
Lamps, oil, gilt metal and steel, pair, shaded lamp with bamboo stem, tripod legs, 70, electrified, E19c (4111/15) — 2250

William IV

Girandole, gilt decorated, ebonized, convex, 55, M19c (4152/49) — 1800

Chinese export

Lamp, mounted from vase, porcelain, stippled ground, baluster, mandarin palette scenes, (4079/35) — 400

Vases, now mounted as lamps, famille rose, Chinese figures, 26, M19c (4165/288)   1500

Nineteenth Century

Lamp, Tole, gilt decorated and painted, now wired for electricity, 29 M19c (4216/36)   300
Lanterns, wall, gilt decorated red, painted tole, set of 4, 18 electrified 19c (4152/21)   700

ENGLISH NEEDLEWORK

Assorted needlework

Panel, needlepoint, kneeling, gentlemen, 28½ x 24½ M17 (4134/5)   400
Panels, needlepoint pair, fruiting trees, flowers, butterflies, birds, 15½ x 66 L17c (4134/237) 650
Picture, needlework, depicting marriage, Margaret Hear, 12½, 1683 (4165/256)   950
Picture, silk and woolwork, farmer and daughter, barn yard setting, framed, 26½ x 23½, 19c
(4216/27)   250
Picture, silkwork, Shepherd and His Flock, framed, 15 x 19-E19c E19c (4216/30)   800
Picture, silkwork (Charles II), court presentation with birds, flowers and animals, 16¼ x 20½ L17c
framed (4079/2)   1100
Pictures, pair, Italian painted silk, wolf in sheep's clothing, seascape framed, 12½ x 15½ L18c
(4216/26)   225
Pictures, pair, silkwork, regency, frolicking child, gilt wood frames, 11 x 9½, E19c (4079/38)   275
Pictures, pair, silkwork, regency, one a shepherd, 1 lady sowing, gilt wood frames, 17 x 15, E19c
(4079/39)   250
Wall hanging, crewell (Charles II), birds on flowering leafy branches, 91½ x 92 L17c (4079/1)   1700

George II

Picture, needlework, lady musicians, framed, 29 x 27 restoration M18c (4134/2)   325
Picture, stumpwork/beadwork, lady in courtly dress, castle background, 16 x 18, frame (4165/255) 700

Regency

Picture, painted silk and woolwork, boy and dog, framed, 19 x 14½, E19c (4216/25)   110
Picture, silkwork, garden and young woman, framed, 16½ x 19 E19c (4216/29)   600
Picture, silkwork, shepherd playing flute, framed, 18½ x 14¼ E19c (4134/4)   140
Pictures, pair silkwork, lady in woodland setting, framed, 17 x 14½, E19c (4216/22)   275

English Furniture

James I

Chair, turner's, oak, E17c (4189/62)   350
Chair, turner's, Elmwood, triangular plane seat, E17c (4189/60)   *3800*

Chair (4189/60)

Chest (4189/71)

Cupboard (4189/63)

Chairs, pair, turner's, oak, feet tipped, E17c (4189/61)	700
Chest, carved and inlaid oak, 27 x 46 x 21, E17c (4189/71)	*4000*
Chest, small oak, hinged top, wrought iron lock plate, shaped feet, 21½ x 32 x 12½, E17c (4272/77)	450
Cupboard, court, carved oak, 51½ x 47¼ x 16½, res, E17c (4189/63)	*2300*
Cupboard, court, carved oak, interlacing geometric patterns, 49 x 51½ x 18¾, E17c (4189/64)	3100
Cupboard, court, inlaid and carved oak, leaf carved cornice, lower 3 cupboards, 71 x 59 x 20, E17c (4239/36)	1500
Table, refectory carved oak, 32 x 150 x 31, res E17c (4216/175)	9000

Charles I

Stool, joint, carved oak, molded top, frieze and turned, columnar legs, 17¼, res, L17c (4239/65)	450
Stool, joint, walnut, L17c (4189/65)	350

Charles II

Armchair, caned, walnut, oval backrest and seat caned carving, L17c (4157/159)	900
Chest of drawers, elmwood, oak, yewwood, 2 short, 3 long drawers, 39 x 40½ x 24, M17c (4111/57)	850
Chest of drawers, oak, 31 x 34 x 22, feet rep, L17c (4189/70)	1400
Chest of drawers, oak, 4 long graduated panelled drawers, on bun feet, 37 x 37 x 23, ca1665 (4272/78)	1700
Chest of drawers, oak and pine, 2 parts, 2 short, 3 long drawers, 34 x 37½ x 23½, M17c (4111/56)	1100
Mirror, carved walnut, parcel-gilt, broken triangular pediment, 42½ x 27 M18c (4216/2)	2000

James II

Chest, oak, hinged top, 3 panels, 27¼ x 51½ x 20½, M17c (4255/401)	800
Cupboard, court carved oak, fret-carved cornice, 2 panel doors, 60½ x 56½ x 23, res, ca1670 (4239/37)	1300
Cupboard, court, oak, frieze carved with scrolls and leaves, 2 doors, 64½ x 61½ x 24, E17c (4272/71)	1000
Table, refectory, oak, 3 plank top, 6 baluster legs, 31¾ x 110½ x 28¾, 17c (4255/399)	3250

William and Mary

Armchair, reclining, adjustable caned backrest, leaf carved armrest, L17c (4079/70)	1300
Armchair, reclining wing, walnut, upholstered, restoration L17c (4216/68)	3100
Armchair tub, mahogany, revolving, upholstered, L19c (4165/357)	400
Armchairs, pair, stained walnut, carving, upholstered L17c, one stretcher partly replaced (4134/247)	1000
Bureau book case, inlaid walnut, 2 parts, mirrored doors, candle slides, 89½ x 44 x 23½, ca1700 (4272/88)	9000
Bureau cabinet, inlaid burr walnut, 82½ x 40½, res, L17c (4216/69)	7500

Cabinet, coromandel lacquer, decorated with birds, flowers, 65 x34 x 19½, L17c (4111/115)	3000
Cabinet on stand, inlaid walnut, 2 sections, 54 x 32 x 15½, res, L17c (4189/73)	1900
Chair, child's, elmwood and beechwood, spindle construction with plank seat, L17c (4239/215)	125
Chair, library, metamorphic, carved mahogany, E17c (4216/206)	1400
Chair, side, walnut caned, free standing column support, L17c (4079/75)	275
Chairs, side, 3, caned walnut, backrest carved, with foliate motifs, L17c (4157/167)	400
Chair table, oak, flower and leaf carved, oval backrest, 44 L17c (4134/246)	1700
Chest, blanket, hinged top with fielded panels, carved front, 26½ x 48½ x 25, L17c (4239/33)	450
Chest, oak, hinged panelled top, 22½ x 39½ x 18, L17c (4216/71)	500
Chest, oak, hinged top, 26 x 47 x 20½, L17c, res (4119/37)	650
Chest of drawers, oak, panelled long drawers (four), 32½ x 36½ x 22, L18c (4152/68)	950
Chest of drawers, oak, 2 short, 3 long, panelled drawers, bun feet, 36 x 35½ x 21, L17c (4239/50)	500
Chest of drawers, secretaire, burr walnut, fall front, 68 x 44 x 19, pulls later E17c (4189/88)	2600
Chest of drawers, walnut, parquetry, 2 short, 3 graduated drawers, 32½ x 39 x 24, feet replaced, L17c (4239/51)	*2300*
Chest on stand, inlaid walnut, 38¼ x 40½ x 21¼ res, L17c (4216/66)	*3100*

Chest of drawers (4239/51)

Secretaire (4134/252)

Chest on stand   (4152/64)

Chest on stand   (4216/66)

Chest on stand, inlaid walnut, veneered, feather and cross banded, 5 drawers, 47½ x 40½ x 22½, res, ca1690 (4239/217)	1600
Chest on stand, oyster veneered, walnut, bun feet, 50½ x 37 x 22½, res (4152/64)	*2800*
Chest on stand, walnut and oak, 52½ x 40 x 22, res L17c (4152/69)	1900
Chest on stand, walnut and oak, 2 parts, 5 drawers lower, 3 drawers, 63 x 38½ x 20½, rep, ca1690 (4272/83)	1800
Cupboard, court, oak, rectangular, cornice, flower carved frieze, recessed, 62½ x 78½ x 24, L17c (4079/71)	1600
Cupboard, oak, front with 2 cupboards carving, 55 x 25 x 17½ altered, L17c (4134/352)	400
Desk, lap, carved oak, 11 x 25½ x 18½, L17c (4216/70)	225
Dresser, oak, 3 geometrically panelled frieze drawers, 31 x 76½ x 20½, L18c (4152/67)	2800
Dresser, oak, 3 geometrically panelled frieze drawers, 32½ x 82½ x 19½ (4079/62)	1000
Drop leaf table, oval, oak, 2 drawers, 29½ x 54 x 45½, res, L17c (4152/70)	950
Mirror, walnut, cushion-molded, rectangular, 20 x 18 L17c (4134/1)	650
Mirror, walnut, cushion molded, bevelled rectangular plate, 28, L17c (4152/5)	700
Secretaire, fall front, black japanned, fitted interior above 3 drawers, 58 x 38 x 18½ L17c (4134/252)	*2100*
Settee, 2 chair back, walnut, double arched backrest, upholstered, 52½, L17c (4079/69)	3500
Stool, oak joint, fluted frieze and turned legs, 19 L17c (4134/251)	800
Stool, turned walnut, circular caned, 15, L17c (4260/1655)	4000

Table, dressing, oak, rectangular top, frieze drawer, turned legs, 29½ x 29½ x 20, ca1700 (4239/213) — 1600
Table, dressing, walnut, drawer bobbin turned legs, 29 x 35 x 22½, res, L17c (4111/67) — 650
Table, drop-leaf, oak, oval top, 2 frieze drawers, 28 x 41 x 51, ca1685 (4260/1294) — 1000
Table, drop-leaf, oval, oak, 2 drawers, 28 x 49 x 19 L17c (4152/77) — 1200
Table, drop-leaf, oval, oak, walnut, hinged oval, top frieze drawer, bobbin turned legs, 28½ x 36 x 16, ca1685 (4239/216) — 400
Table, drum, inlaid fruitwood, leather inset, 4 drawers, 28½ x 24, L19c (4165/356) — 500
Table, gate-leg, elmwood, rectangular top, spirally turned legs, 23 x 21, ca1680 (4260/1295) — 1600
Table, oak and walnut, hinged oval top, spirally turned legs, 30½ x 71 x 50, res, L17c (4111/71) — 1500
Table, writing, pedestal, mahogany, leather inset, 3 drawers, 28½ x 48 x 26, L19c (4111/144) — 1100
Tables, games, pair, rosewood, gilt decorated, with pedestals, 29 x 36 x 18, E19c (4111/216) — 2250
Torcheres, bone inlaid, walnut, spirally turned stem tripod legs, 35 x 11½, L17c (4152/74) — 2600

Queen Anne

Bookcase double dome bureau, inlaid burr walnut, 99½ x 43½ x 25, res, E18c (4189/74) — 8000
Bureau, bookcase, inlaid, burr walnut, 82 x 41½ x 14½, E18c (4189/91) — *13000*

Bureau (4189/91)

Chairs (4189/77)

Armchair (4189/85)

Chairs, side, pair, walnut, one with stretcher replaced, E18c (4189/77) — *4750*
Chairs, side, pair, burr walnut, shaped backrest, drop in seat, res, ca1710 (4260/1658) — 18000
Chairs, side, set of 8, gilt, japanned, upholstered seat, chinoiserie, res, ca1710 (4272/125) — 13500
Chest of drawers, walnut, 3 short and long drawers on bun feet, 31½ x 31½ x 19½, E18c (4111/217) — 3000
Mirror, overmantel, black japanned, triple divided, bevelled, 19 x 55, E18c (4165/257) — 900
Mirror, toilet, black japanned, free standing, block fronted with drawer, 33 x 16 E18c (4134/30) — 850
Table, estate, burr walnut, hinged top, candle slides, 32½ x 35½ x 22½, ca1710 (4260/1659) — 26000

George I

Armchair, carved walnut, solid backrest, upholstered seat, ca1720 (4260/1662) — 8000
Armchair, mahogany, solid back, upholstered seat, ca1725 (4260/1673) — 8500
Armchair, set of 4, walnut, pierced fluted splats, solid seat, ca1730 (4260/1675) — 15000
Armchair, walnut, shaped top rail, drop in seat, back legs tipped, E18c (4111/118) — 600
Armchair, walnut, shepherd crook armrests, E18c (4189/85) — *3250*
Armchair, walnut, upholstered, shepherds crook armrest, restorations, E18c (4165/298) — 2500
Armchair, wing walnut, upholstered, E18c (4152/90) — 5000
Armchair, wing walnut, upholstered, E18c (4152/88) — 2400
Armchair, wing walnut, upholstered, E18c (4134/308) — 800
Armchair, wing, carved walnut, arched, upholstered, res, ca1730 (4260/1668) — 2750
Armchairs, pair, gilt decorated, red lacquer, 19c (4189/78) — 2900
Bureau, walnut, sloping front, with writing surface, 30 x 30 x 17, E18c (4111/215) — 4000
Bureau, walnut inlaid, sloping front, 2 short, 3 long drawers, 39 x 36 x 21½, ca1720 (4239/224) — 4200
Bureau bookcase, small, inlaid walnut, 2 parts, mirrored doors, drawers and pigeon holes, 83½ x 39 x 21, ca1720 (4239/270) — 8000
Cabinet, corner, needlework inset, black japanned, arched cornice, 35 x 23 (4165/301) — 900
Cabinet, miniature, inlaid walnut, rectangular top, field door, bracket feet, 15 x 14 x 8½, ca1720 (4260/1301) — 800

Chair, side, walnut, dipped top rail solid baluster splat, rush seat, rep, E18c (4111/218) 800
Chair, side, walnut, shell carved top rail, E18c, rep (4111/154) 400
Chairs, dining, walnut, set of 4, solid baluster splat, drop in seat, E18c (4079/76) 2000
Chairs, side walnut, solid baluster splat, drop in seat, restoration E18c (4134/66) 1000
Chairs, side, inlaid burr walnut, rectangular splat, drop in seat, res, ca1720 (4260/1680) 3750
Chairs, side, pair, carved walnut, dipped top rail, solid vase shape splat, drop in seat, res, ca1720
(4239/220) 3750
Chairs, side, pair, carved walnut, scrolled top, baluster splat, drop in seat, ca1720 (4239/60) 2400
Chairs, side, pair, walnut, solid baluster splat, drop in seat, cabriole legs, res, ca1720 (4239/229) 1800
Chest of drawers, walnut, 5 drawers, bracket feet, 30 x 29 x 17, ca1720 (4260/1679) 6000
Chest on chest inlaid walnut, 2 parts, 71 x 42 x 21, E18c (4216/94) 2600
Chest on stand, inlaid walnut, 2 parts, 64½ x 39½ x 22, res, E18c (4216/64) 4000
Chest on stand, inlaid walnut, 2 parts, back legs replaced, 59 x 38 x 20½, E18c (4189/79) 2750
Chest on stand, inlaid walnut, 2 parts, top 5 drawers, lower 3 drawers, 65 x 39 x 20, res, ca1720
(4239/230) 4500
Chest on stand, inlaid walnut, 2 parts, top 5 drawers, lower 3 drawers, 60½ x 33½ x 20, L18c
(4239/55) 2300
Mirror, gilt gesso, 33½ x 16½, M18c (4189/7) 750
Mirror, gilt gesso, swan neck cresting, leaf carved border, 42 x 21½ E18c (4134/222) 1200
Mirror, toilet, silver gilt gess, arched cresting, sloped, fitted interior, 40 x 17¾ x 11¾, E18c (4079/6) 650
Mirror, toilet, walnut, free standing supports, base with drawer, 25 x 14 restoration E18c (4134/227) 375
Mirror, walnut parcel-gilt, plate within egg and dart corbelled sides, 51 x 27 L18c (4134/17) 1300
Settee, 2 chair back, walnut, double arched backrest, solid splat, drop in seat, 49½, res, ca1725
(4239/222) 3600
Stool, carved walnut, drop in seat, claw and ball feet, 20, ca1725 (4260/1664) 2200
Stool, carved walnut, rectangular, drop in seat, 20, ca1720 (4260/1672) 2200
Stool, close, burr walnut, removable top, 21 x 16½, ca1725 (4260/1670) 1300
Stools, pair, elmwood, rectangular drop in seat, upholstered, 18, ca1725 (4260/1299) 1900
Stools, pair, walnut, rectangular, drop in seat, 22½, ca1725 (4260/1676) 18000
Table, center walnut, cross band top, drawer, 27 x 29½ x 19½, ca1720 (4260/1677) 9500
Table, center, mahogany, dished top, deep frieze, cabriole legs, 28 x 17 x 14½, ca1725 (4260/1302) 850
Table, center, walnut, cross band top, drawer, 27 x 28 x 18, ca1720 (4260/1663) 3250
Table, dressing walnut, 27½ x 31 x 20½, E18c (4189/105) 2400
Table, dressing, inlaid walnut, 28 x 29½ x 19½, E19c (4189/80) 3250
Table, dressing, inlaid walnut, rectangular top, 4 drawers, 28½ x 30½ x 19, 2 feet spliced, E18c
(4239/225) 2000
Table, dressing, kneehole, inlaid walnut, feather and cross banded, rectangular top, frieze drawer, 31
x 34 x 19, res, ca1725 (4239/231) 4000
Table, dressing, oak, rectangular top, frieze drawer, shaped apron, 28 x 28½ x 20, ca1720
(4239/226) 750
Table, games, carved, padouk wood, hinged top, drawers each end, 28 x 31 x 12½, rep, ca1725
(4260/1661) 5250
Table, patience, walnut, triangle hinged top, cavetto frieze, 28 x 26 x 13½, from 18c table
(4260/1304) 750
Table, side, inlaid burr walnut, rectangular top, 3 drawers, 27 x 30 x 19½, ca1720 (4260/1303) 5250
Table, side, inlaid walnut, veneered, feather and crossed banded top, 27½ x 31 x 20, res, ca1715
(4239/344) 4500
Table, side, walnut, marble top, 28½ x 46½ x 25½, E18c (4152/87) 2400
Table, dressing, inlaid walnut, quartered veneered, 2 short 1 long drawers, 29 x 30 x 18½, res,
ca1730 (4239/47) 1850
Trumeau, gilt wood, triple divided mirror, below oil painting, 43 x 47½, E18c (4165/258) 1000

George II

Andirons, pair, spherical finial, baluster stem and ball and claw feet, 23¾, 19c (4272/37) 275
Armchair, carved mahogany, M18c (4189/198) 1100
Armchair, carved mahogany, ram's heads and hoof feet on front legs, M18c (4189/200) 1400
Armchair, carved walnut, dipped top rail, solid baluster splats, solid seat, ca1730 (4239/78) 350
Armchair, corner mahogany, scrolled top rail, drop in seat, restorations, L18c (4165/389) 1400
Armchair, corner, carved mahogany, L18c (4189/112) 800
Armchair, corner, carved mahogany, U-shaped back, solid splat, drop in seat, ca1735 (4260/1715) 4250
Armchair, corner, elmwood, res L18c (4189/103) 650
Armchair, corner, mahogany, U-shaped top rail, double pierced vase splat, M18c (4079/78) 950
Armchair, corner, walnut, U-shaped top rail, double solid baluster splat, M18c (4239/237) 600
Armchair, corner, walnut, 2 splats, upholstered seat, M18c (4260/1704) 4250
Armchair, library, carved mahogany, res, M18c (4189/106) 2000
Armchair, library, walnut, seat, upholstered, C scroll carved legs, M18c (4079/95) 1600
Armchair, mahogany, cartouche, shaped backrest oval drop in seat, L18c (4165/392) 1700
Armchair, mahogany, in Chinese taste, open lattice work back and arms, M18c (4239/242) *2200*

Armchair (4239/242)

Armchair (4152/110)

Chair (4152/83)

Armchair, mahogany, scrolled bow knotted top rail, M18c (4111/86)	1400
Armchair, walnut, pierced splat, drop in seat, ca1735 (4260/1701)	4500
Armchair, walnut, scrolled armrests, drop in seat, L18c (4152/110)	*3250*
Armchair, windsor, beechwood, elmwood, rep, M18c (4189/100)	1300
Armchair, wing, carved fruitwood, double arched panelled backrest, ca1760 (4260/1693)	11000
Armchair, wing, mahogany, shaped wings, M18c (4260/1703)	1700
Armchair, wing, mahogany, upholstered, claw and ball feet, M18c (4165/304)	3500
Armchair, wing, walnut, upholstered, scrolling, M18c (4111/124)	2750
Armchairs, library, pair, mahogany, upholstered, serpentine shaped top rail, L18c (4111/76)	9250
Armchairs, set of 4, mahogany, pierced backs, solid dished seat, ca1735 (4260/1700)	9000
Bed tester, mahogany, carved, cluster, column foot posts, 93½ x 68 x 80, ca1760 (4260/1706)	15500
Bench, window, mahogany, scrolled arms and legs, 60, ca1760 (4260/1696)	3250
Benches, hall, carved mahogany, rectangular, fluted frieze, 18 x 36½ x 21, ca1731 (4260/1681)	21000
Breakfront, bookcase, mahogany, 2 sections, cupboard, drawers, 99 x 92 x 25, ca1760 (4260/1699)	10000
Bureau, mahogany, sloping front 5 drawers, 44½ x 45 x 21, L18c (4111/92)	2800
Bureau, slant front, inlaid walnut, interior pigeon holes, center cupboard door, drawers, 39½ x 36½ x 20¼, L18c (4272/109)	2600
Bureau bookcase, brass inlaid, mahogany, rare, manner of John Channon, 86 x 40 x 23½, ca1740 (4216/96)	19000
Bureau on chest, mahogany, 2 sections, sloping from top, 49 x 46 x 23½, M18c (4189/110)	1300
Bureau on stand, oak, sloping front, 37½ x 32 x 19, M18c (4152/107)	1150
Cabinet, bookcase, carved mahogany, 2 sections, 83 x 46 x 15, L18c (4216/127)	4000
Cabinet, carved mahogany, portico cresting, corbelled supports, 45½ x 34, ca1745 (4260/1684)	1500
Cabinet, hanging, Chinese chippendale, mahogany, pagoda roof, pair glazed doors, 58 x 41 x 8, E19c (4111/209)	1700
Cabinet, medal, hanging, padouk wood, gilt-decorated, broken triangular pediment, 49¾ x 32, M18c (4159/221)	11500
Cabinet, side, Chinoiserie, black, japanned, 73½ x 36 x 10 M18c (4152/86)	6500
Cabinet, vitrine, hanging, walnut, arched crest, glazed doors, 28 x 19¾, ca1740 (4260/1690)	2100
Cabinet, Japanese gilt decorated, black lacquer on George II carved gilt wood stand, 67½ x 43 x 23, M18c (4216/106)	8500
Candlestand, mahogany, piecrust, circular top, tripod legs, 26 x 19¼, M18c (4165/390)	1200
Chair, arm, mahogany, baluster splat, S-shaped arms, square legs, M18c (4159/233)	600
Chair, arm, mahogany, pierced baluster splat, square legs, M18c (4159/235)	550
Chair, arm, mahogany, pierced beaker splat, scrolled arms, cabriole legs, M18c (4159/217)	3100
Chair, corner pot, carved walnut, E18c (4216/131)	850
Chair, corner, carved walnut, U-shaped backrest, drop in seat, res, ca1730 (4260/1688)	1900
Chair, corner, mahogany, U-shaped top rail, hoof feet, M18c (4152/83)	*900*
Chair, corner, mahogany, U-shaped top, rail and armrests, pierced splats, ca1750 (4239/67)	1400
Chair, corner, walnut, U-shaped rail, double baluster splats, pad feet, ca1740 (4272/105)	1200
Chair, hall, carved mahogany, pierced back, solid seat, ca1740 (4260/1713)	1300

Chair, hall, carved yewwood, sgabello form, solid seat, M18c (4260/1685)	1600
Chair, side, carved walnut, L18c (4189/123)	1700
Chair, side, carved walnut, res L18c (4189/121)	1300
Chair, side, walnut, L18c (4189/116)	700
Chair, side, library, mahogany, shaped upholstered backrest, seat, scrolled toes, M18c (4159/227)	1700
Chair, side, mahogany, beaker splat, cabriole legs, ball/claw feet, M18c (4159/239)	200
Chair, side, walnut, pierced interlaced baluster splat, pad feet, M18c (4159/232)	550
Chair, side, walnut and elmwood, shaped top rail, pierced beaker splat, pad feet, ca1740 (4272/93)	700
Chairs, dining, mahogany, set of 4, upholstered in needlepoint, M18c (4165/387)	6000
Chairs, dining, set of five, oak, elmwood, dipped top rail, solid splat, rushed seat, res, ca1740 (4272/94)	2300
Chairs, dining, set of 4, mahogany, leaf carved top rail, some rails, restored, L18c (4111/81)	2250
Chairs, dining, set of 3, mahogany, 1 armchair, scrolled armrests and top rail, ca1733 (4239/233)	1200
Chairs, dining, set 4, mahogany, dipped top rail, solid splat, drop in seat, ca1740 (4239/251)	2500
Chairs, hall, pair, mahogany, pierced circular backrest solid seat, L18c (4165/391)	1000
Chairs, set 6, dining mahogany, M18c, some with rails replaced (4189/96)	3500
Chairs, side pair, carved mahogany, M18c (4189/126)	1200
Chairs, side pair, carved mahogany, shaped top rail, pierced Gothic splat, res, ca1760 (4272/186)	1100
Chairs, side pair, mahogany, upholstered backrest, seat carved legs, M18c (4079/88)	450
Chairs, side, pair walnut, dipped top rail, solid baluster splat, drop in seat, ca1735 (4272/107)	1400
Chairs, side, pair, carved mahogany, carved top rail, interlaced splat, ca1760 (4272/187)	1700
Chairs, side, pair, carved mahogany, dipped top rail, pierced baluster splat, C scroll legs, res, ca1750 (4239/81)	*750*
Chairs, side, pair, mahogany, carving, drop in seat, M18c (4134/267)	2100
Chairs, side, pair, walnut, arched top rail, pierced beaker and splat, cabriole legs, ca1730 (4239/249)	1300
Chairs, side, pair, walnut, open cartouche shaped backrest, claw and ball feet, ca1735 (4239/232)	21000
Chairs, side, set of 3, carved walnut, shaped top rail, pierced interlaced splat scroll legs, ca1745 (4239/274)	5250
Chairs, side, walnut, solid baluster splat, shell carved legs, E18c (4079/94)	2800
Chairs, side, walnut, pair, backrest and seats upholstered, L18c (4165/303)	4500
Chest, brass bound mahogany, lidded compartment, brass, studs, mounts, lock plate, 22 x 42½ x 21, M18c (4111/85)	950
Chest, elmwood, hinged rectangular top on shaped plinth, 22½ x 49½ x 17, plinth res, M18c (4239/99)	275
Chest, mule, inlaid mahogany, hinged top, enclosed well, false drawer front, 43 x 82 x 22, ca1750 (4239/70)	850
Chest, mule, oak, 4 arched panels, 5 drawers, 45 x 55½ x 22½, M18c (4111/61)	950
Chest, mule, oak, hinged top, enclosed well, 35 x 38 x 20½ (4152/97)	*425*
Chest, mule, oak, panelled front 3 drawers, 35 x 60 x 21½, L18c (4152/105)	1500
Chest of drawers, bookcase, mahogany, broken arch pediment, 81 x 49, L18c (4111/141)	3000
Chest of drawers, inlaid walnut, veneered 4 drawers, on bracket feet, 32 x 34 x 19½, ca1710 (4239/271)	6000
Chest of drawers, mahogany, rectangular, 3 drawers, bracket feet, 28 x 24 x 14, ca1760 (4260/1308)	1400
Chest on chest, inlaid walnut, 3 short 3 long graduated drawers, 69 x 44 x 22½, L18c (4111/212)	2600
Chest on stand, inlaid mahogany, 4 drawers, turned legs, 38 x 17 stand of later date (4134/51)	450

Chairs (4239/81)

Chest (4152/97)

Dresser (4189/122)

Mirror (4152/14)

Clothes press, carved mahogany, 2 part, doors with mirrors, lower 3 drawers, 83 x 50 x 25, ca1750 (4239/244) 1700
Console mahogany, claw and ball feet, carvings, 33 x 23¼ x 14 M18c (4134/263) 1600
Cupboard, carved and ebonized oak, 2 parts, panelled doors, lower 5 drawers, 60½ x 52 x 20, L18c (4239/240) 1000
Cupboard, carved oak, 2 sections, apron and feet replaced, 72 x 51½ x 20, M18c (4216/111) 1200
Cupboard, corner oak, molded cornice, 2 pair of panelled doors, 82½ x 45, L18c (4239/93) 800
Cupboard, corner, carved mahogany, fluted arch, 3 shelves, 92 x 48, formerly with doors, ca1760 (4260/1691) 3750
Dining chairs, set of eight, mahogany, 2 armchairs, upholstered seat, (4152/94) 2800
Dresser, inlaid oak, 86½ x 84½ x 19, res M18c (4216/122) 3400
Dresser, oak, rectangular top, 3 frieze drawers, 30 x 72 x 19 L18c (4134/79) 2400
Dresser, oak, 3 drawers above 2 drawers, 33½ x 60½ x 20, res, L18c (4216/103) 900
Dresser, oak, 3 open shelves, 3 drawers, 85½ x 72 x 18 restoration M18c (4134/76) 1500
Dresser, oak, molded cornice, 3 shelves over 2 doors at sides, 70½ x 71 x 18½, res, M18c (4189/122) *3200*
Mirror, gilt cesso, flowerhead, bellflower, trellis border, 47 x 24½, M18c (4216/3) 1900
Mirror, gilt decorated mahogany, leaf carving and molded, borders, 26 x 15½, restoration, M18c (4134/192) 150
Mirror, gilt decorated mahogany, HoHo bird, 50 x 21 M18c (4216/4) 4000
Mirror, gilt decorated, carved mahogany, rectangular plate, pierced cresting, shaped apron, 41 x 23, res, ca1740 (4272/39) 850
Mirror, gilt dectored mahogany, leaf carved and molded borders, 36½ x 19½ M18c (4134/191) 175
Mirror, gilt wood, carved borders, sides hung with fruit, candle branches, 64, L18c (4152/14) *5000*
Mirror, inlaid burr, yewwood and walnut, 49 (4134/234) 525
Mirror, overmantel, carved gilt wood, 3 divide D-shaped plates, scrolling and pierced border, 24 x 53, ca1760 (4239/210) 1200
Mirror, parcel-gilt mahogany, rectangular plate, pierced eagle cresting, 26 x 26, M18 (4079/9) 325
Mirror, parcel-gilt, walnut, bevelled rectangular plate, leaftip molded borders, 26 x 16, ca1740 (4239/187) 600
Mirror, parcel-gilt, walnut, rectangular plate, carved borders, scrolled ears, 48 x 22½, ca1735 (4239/182) 1900
Mirror, parcel-gilt mahogany, gilt wood molded borders, 41, restorations, M18c (4152/17) 500
Mirror, parcel-gilt mahogany, leaf carved border, scrolling crest, HoHo bird, 28½ M18c (4152/16) 475
Mirror, small carved mahogany, rectangular plate within moulded borders, 26 x 12, ca1740 (4239/5) 275
Mule chest on stand, mahogany, 2 parts, hinged lid, well above 2 drawers, 42¾ x 52 x 26½, ca1740 (4272/102) 900
Reading stand, mahogany, adjustable hinged top, tripod support, 19, ca1740 (4260/1320) 1600
Reading stand, mahogany, each side with candle slide, 27½ x 24 x 16½, ca1750 (4260/1314) 2400
Reading stand, mahogany, hinged top, with fitted bookrest, 27 x 20 x 15¾, ca1750 (4260/1305) 1100
Settee, carved mahogany, upholstered, 79, restoration M18c (4216/168) 2000
Settee, double chair back mahogany, shell shaped top rail drop in seat, L52, M18c (4111/214) 4750
Settee, 2 chair mahogany, leaf carved top rail, upholstered seat, 38½ (4134/74) 600
Settle, oak, arched panelled rectangular backrest, upholstered, 72½, M18c (4272/106) 800

Shelf hanging, oak, rectangular cornice above 3 shelves, 39 x 34, 18c (4111/60)   350
Stand, carved mahogany, verde antico inset top, tapered legs, 25½ x 15 x 12, ca1735 (4260/1325)   1000
Stand, mahogany, verde antico inset top, plain frieze, apron, 27 x 20 x 12½, ca1735 (4260/1319)   1700
Stand, tripod, mahogany, circular, gallery, cabriole legs, 24 x 9, ca1745 (4260/1310)   550
Stand, tripod, walnut, circular, turned stem, 27 x 8½, ca1725 (4260/1313)   850
Stand, tripod, walnut, circular, turned stem, 21½ x 9, ca1725 (4260/1716)   2000
Stool, carved walnut, rectangular, drop in seat, ca1735 (4260/1692)   3000
Stool, carved walnut, upholstered seat shell and bell, flower carved legs, 28½, ca1740 (4272/97)   950
Stool, oval, mahogany, upholstered seat, cabriole legs, pad feet, 22, M18c (4159/222)   3200
Stool, oval, walnut, upholstered, seat on shell, L23½, M18c (4152/109)   375
Stool, walnut, drop in seat, curved cabriole legs, hairy paw feet, W21, M18c (4159/242)   1400
Stool, walnut, upholstered seat, cabriole legs, hairy paw feet, W24½, M18c (4159/236)   1500
Stools, pair, walnut, square, cabriole legs, pad feet, 13, ca1730 (4260/1311)   2300
Table, architects, mahogany, hinged folding adjustable top, gate-leg support, 30 x 36 x 21, res, ca1760 (4272/98)   1000
Table, card, mahogany, green leather inset playing surface, 28½ x 31 x 15, M18c (4189/128)   2800
Table, card, mahogany, hinged leather top, leaf carved legs, 28½ x 36 x 17, ca1740 (4260/1318)   2000
Table, center, carved mahogany, rectangular, paw feet, 28 x 32½ x 22, ca1735 (4260/1712)   3750
Table, center, carved walnut, rectangular, claw and ball feet, 26 x 36 x 23½, ca1745 (4260/1683)   4500
Table, center, mahogany, rectangular top, blind fret decoration, 27½ x 21½ x 15, ca1755 (4260/1316)   600
Table, center, carved mahogany, dished rectangular top, paw feet, 27 x 29½ x 19½, ca1735 (4260/1719)   2300
Table, drop-leaf, mahogany, hinged rectangular top, turned top, 27 x/1/2 x 41 x 15 M18c (4134/264)   500
Table, dressing, carved oak, 28½ x 30 x 19, M18c (4189/113)   300
Table, dressing, inlaid oak, one long, 2 short drawers, aroun D-shaped apron, 28½ x 33 x 19 M18c (4134/268)   800
Table, dressing, kneehole mahogany, recessed cupboard, bracket feet, 31 x 36 x 21¾, M18c (4079/83)   650
Table, dressing, mahogany, 28 x 30 x 17½, M18c (4189/109)   1200
Table, dressing, oak, rectangular, frieze drawer, turned legs, pad feet, 27½ x 36 x 22½ (4159/240)   350
Table, dressing, stained oak, rectangular top, frieze drawer, 28 x 31 x 19½ M18c (4134/80)   175
Table, drop-leaf carved mahogany, 28 x 42 x 15½, res M18c (4216/104)   550
Table, drop-leaf, carved mahogany, carving of later date, 28 x 36 x 15, M18c (4216/135)   750
Table, drop-leaf, carved mahogany, hinged top, scroll carved cabriole legs, 28 x 48½ x 36, ca1745 (4239/250)   *2500*
Table, drop-leaf, mahogany, hinged oval top, scroll carved, cabriole legs, 29 x 40 x 15, M18c (4111/91)   2100
Table, drop-leaf, mahogany, hinged top, cabriole legs, claw and ball feet, 27 x 42 x 40, ca1740 (4260/1328)   2100
Table, drop-leaf, mahogany, oval top, 6 turned legs, 27 x 47 x 22, M18c (4111/119)   400
Table, drop-leaf, mahogany, shaped, molded top, carved cabriole legs, 28 x 25½ x 15, M18c (4165/305)   1800
Table, drop-leaf, oval, mahogany, oval top, frieze drawer, cabriole legs, hoof feet, 28½ x 51½ x 42, M18c (4159/225)   4300
Table, game, double top, mahogany, 29½ x 31½ x 15½, M18c (4189/119)   3250
Table, game, triple top, carved mahogany, hinged tops, 1 leather inset surface, claw and ball feet, 29½ x 35½ x 17, ca1750 (4239/246)   2200
Table, game, walnut, hinged top, frieze drawer on lappet carved turned legs, 29 x 29½ x 13½, ca1735 (4239/241)   1600
Table, games table, triple top, mahogany, D-shaped, turned legs, pad feet, 29 x 32 x 15¾, M18c (4159/230)   1300
Table, games, carved mahogany, needlepoint inset, hinged top, rounded corners, 28 x 41½ x 13½, ca1745 (4272/96)   2600
Table, games, D-shaped carved mahogany, rear leg replaced, 28½ x 29½ x 14½, M18c L18c (4216/130)   1400
Table, gate-leg, carved mahogany, six legged, rectangular top, claw and ball feet, 28 x 40 x 21½, M18c (4272/114)   800
Table, gate-leg, mahogany, hinged folding top, flap 1 side, 27 x 27 x 32, M18c (4260/1705)   2750
Table, gate-leg, spider, mahogany, rectangular, 2 flaps, drawer, 27½ x 36 x 36½, ca1760 (4260/1686)   4000
Table, gate-leg, spider, mahogany, top with 1 flap, turned legs, 27 x 33 x 26½, M18c (4260/1317)   3250
Table, library, gilt metal mounted, carved mahogany, manner of William Vile, 30½ x 56½ x 37½, ca1745 (4216/126)   *15000*
Table, mahogany drop-leaf dining, oblong top, pad feet, 28 x 35½ x 35¾, M18c (4149/286)   600
Table, octagonal tripod mahogany, needlepoint inset, 27½ x 33, M18c (4111/226)   1200
Table, oval drop-leaf, carved mahogany, on leaf and 'C' scroll carved cabriole legs, 29½ x 62 x 40½, ca1750 (4272/110)   3000

Table, oval dropleaf mahogany, hinged top on 6 turned legs, 29 x 52½ x 43½, M18c (4239/94)	950
Table, reading, mahogany, hinged top, with reading support, 27½ x 20 x 16, ca1730 (4260/1315)	3250
Table, side carved walnut, 31 x 51 x 24, M18c (4216/129)	2100
Table, supper, brass inlaid mahogany, manner of Abraham Roentgen, 28½ x 21¾, M18c (4189/114)	2250
Table, supper, brass, and mother-of-pearl, inlaid mahogany, Abraham Roentgen*, 28¾ x 24½ M18c (4189/102)	8500
Table, tea, mahogany, dished rectangular top, cabriole legs, pad feet, 28 x 33 x 22½, L18c (4239/96)	*1500*
Table, tilt-top, carved mahogany, circular top, tripod legs, 28½ x 28½, rep, ca1750 (4272/101)	700
Table, tilt-top, carved mahogany, spirally turned columnar step, tripod, 28 x 28, ca1750 (4272/190)	850
Table, tilt-top piecrust tripod, mahogany, 29 x 31 M18c (4134/353)	775
Table, tilt-top tripod, fluted column support, 21 x 28½, M18c (4165/313)	1600
Table, tilt-top tripod, mahogany, flared turned support, 28 x 32, M18c (4165/311)	375
Table, tilt-top, carved mahogany, circular, baluster stem, cabriole legs, pad feet, 29 x 32, res, M18c (4239/71)	300
Table, tilt-top, mahogany, bird cage support, claw and ball feet, 28½ x 32½, feet res, ca1750 (4239/57)	500
Table, tilt-top, piecrust, tripod, mahogany, 28½ x 28, M18c (4165/310)	1100
Table, tilt-top, tripod mahogany, 28½ x 29½, L18c (4152/102)	400
Table, tilt-top, tripod mahogany, circular flower carved, bird cage supports, 27 x 29½, M18c (4111/193)	2500
Table, tilt-top, tripod, brass, inlaid, carved, mahogany, bird cage support, 29½ x 25¼ x 21, M18c (4189/107)	*1500*
Table, tilt-top, tripod, carved mahogany, circular, revolving, 28 x 36½, ca1745 (4260/1711)	4000
Table, tilt-top, tripod, carved mahogany, piecrust, 25 x 28, M18c (4189/201)	1000
Table, tilt-top, tripod, mahogany, 28 x 27, M18c (4189/124)	1300
Table, tilt-top, tripod, mahogany, bird cage support, carved legs, 28½ x 28, M18c (4165/309)	400
Table, tilt-top, tripod, mahogany, circular dishtop, bird cage supports, 27½ x 23½, M18c (4165/306)	850
Table, tripod, carved mahogany, circular, gallery top, 29 x 25½, ca1755 (4260/1695)	5250
Table, tripod, tilt-top, mahogany, circular, spirally turned stem, cabriole legs, 27½, Diam 29½, M18c (4159/234)	600
Table, writing, carved walnut, folding library, leather inset, 31½ x 69½ x 19, ca1740 (4260/1720)	40000
Table, writing, pedestal, mahogany, leather inset, drawers, 29 x 44 x 23, ca1760 (4260/1717)	2750

George III

Armchair, carved mahogany, shaped top rail, pierced splat, scrolled armrests, L18c (4239/308)	800
Armchair, carved mahogany, upholstered, L18c (4189/167)	3200
Armchair, carved mahogany, upholstered seat, L18c (4216/146)	1500
Armchair, child's, mahogany, back rest, serpentine shaped cresting, L18c (4111/78)	425
Armchair, child's, mahogany, serpentine top rail, L18c, formerly with fittings (4111/79)	275
Armchair, corner elmwood, U-shaped top rail, double pierced splats, chamfered legs, ca1750 (4239/90)	450
Armchair, corner, elmwood, U-shaped top rail, pierced splats, 1 foot tipped, L18c (4239/253)	1100
Armchair, corner, mahogany, U-shaped backrest, drop in seat, M18c (4152/118)	1100
Armchair, elmwood and oak, ladder back, rush seat, pad feet, L18c (4079/142)	150

Table (4239/250)

Table (4239/96)

Table (4216/126)

Table (4189/107)

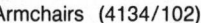

Armchairs (4134/102)

Armchair (4152/128)

Armchair (4165/321)

Armchair (4216/176)

Armchair, gilt wood, molded voluted frame upholstered, L18c (4152/128)	*1800*
Armchair, gilt, dec back painted, solid top rail, double X form pierced splat, ca1800 (4272/119)	800
Armchair, high back, mahogany, upholstered, L18c (4152/134)	850
Armchair, large, provincial oak and pine, rectangular slatted back, plank seat, square legs, M18c (4239/149)	500
Armchair, library, fret carved, mahogany upholstered, one seat rail replaced L18c (4216/176)	*2300*
Armchair, library, mahogany, L18c (4189/170)	600
Armchair, library, mahogany, pad armrest, upholstered seat, L18c (4165/321)	*2000*
Armchair, library, mahogany, serpentine upholstered backrest, chamfered legs, res, L18c (4079/111)	750
Armchair, mahogany, L18c (4189/177)	650
Armchair, mahogany, arched backrest upholstered, L18c (4152/127)	350
Armchair, mahogany, leaf carved rail, scrolled armrests, L18c (4134/243)	700
Armchair, mahogany, shield-shaped open backrest, upholstered, L18c (4111/161)	550
Armchair, mahogany, spindle back, solid dipped seat, L18c (4134/122)	1800
Armchair, mahogany, upholstered (one leg tipped), restorations, L18c (4165/402)	650
Armchair, mahogany, Chinese chippendale style upholstered seat, L18c (4152/114)	2000
Armchair, mahogany, carved, cabriole legs, claw and ball, L18c (4148/266)	1200
Armchair, mahogany, shield-back, pierced beaker splat, L18c (4111/94)	650
Armchair, tub back wing, carved, mahogany, upholstered, res, L18c (4189/168)	600
Armchair, wing, scrolled wings and arms, upholstered, L18c (4111/99)	1500
Armchair, wing mahogany, arched upholstered backrest, L18c (4152/120)	950
Armchair, wing mahogany, upholstered, L18c (4216/79)	900
Armchair, wing, mahogany, serpentine top rail, square chamfered legs, (not upholstered) L18c (4079/132)	600
Armchair, wing, mahogany, shaped backrest, square molded legs, restoration seat rail, L18c (4079/99)	450
Armchair, wing, mahogany, upholstered, L18c (4134/358)	750
Armchair, wing, mahogany, upholstered on square tapered legs, ca1770 (4272/113)	850
Armchair, wing, mahogany, upholstered, chamfered legs, L18c (4111/126)	900
Armchair, wing, mahogany, upholstered, scrolled armrests, L18c (4134/279)	1000
Armchair, wing, mahogany, upholstered, scrolled armrests, L18c (4111/120)	450
Armchair, winged, mahogany, serpentine shaped, upholstered backrest, scrolled arms, back legs tipped, L18c (4239/121)	700
Armchairs, pair, backrest painted with Prince of Wales plume, repainted, ca1790 (4272/152)	1800
Armchairs, pair, mahogany, oval upholstered backrest, L18c (4111/168)	1000
Armchairs, pair, stained, beechwood, oval upholstered backrest, L18c (4134/114)	3500

Armchairs, pair, carved gilt wood, upholstered, padded armrests, turned legs, ca1775 (4239/304) — 1400

Armchairs, pair, carved mahogany, serpentine shaped molded top rail, tapered legs, ca1780 (4239/328) — 800

Armchairs, pair, carved mahogany, French style oval back, upholstered, ca1790 (4239/295) — 1800

Armchairs, pair, mahogany, shield-back, Prince of Wales plume, block toes, L18c (4079/51) — 1600

Armchairs, pair, mahogany, shield-back, beaker splat, dipped seat, shaped arms, L18c (4159/337) — 1200

Armchairs, pair, painted shield-back, upholstered seat, decoration later L18c (4134/102) — *1500*

Armchairs, set of 5, painted, caned seats, L18c (4189/171) — 3750

Armchairs, set of 8, mahogany, panelled top rail, downswept armrests, square legs, ca1810 (4239/314) — 4500

Armchairs, wing, mahogany, upholstered, square chamfered legs, res, ca1780 (4239/326) — 900

Basin stand, carved mahogany, 32 x 11½, L18c (4189/152) — 175

Bed steps, caned mahogany, 3 treads, caned front and sides, 37 x 19 x 28½, ca1810 (4260/1732) — 1100

Bench, library, mahogany, converting to steps, 21 x 25, L18c (4111/165) — 1800

Bench, window mahogany, upholstered seat, 39½ L18c (4216/83) — 700

Bergere, carved beechwood, fluted frame, tub shaped upholstered backrest, ca1790 (4239/292) — 2000

Billiard board, portable, mahogany, rectangular top, fitted baize lined interior, 30, 19c (4260/1369) — 1300

Bookcase, breakfront carved mahogany, swan's neck cresting, 107 x 104 x 18½, L18c (4189/133) — 14500

Bookcase, breakfront mahogany, 4 glazed doors, gothic astragals, 100 x 110 x 22, L18c (4216/98) — 10000

Bookcase, bureau, inlaid mahogany, 2 sections, glazed door, sloping front, 5 drawers, 102 x 42 x 21, L18c (4165/343) — 3000

Bookcase, bureau, mahogany, pair mirrored doors, slant front, 4 drawers, 84 x 41 x 24½ res L18c (4134/307) — 4100

Bookcase, inlaid mahogany, 2 sections, pair glazed doors, panelled doors lower, 84 x 51½ x 14½, ca1790 (4239/321) — 5250

Bookcase, inlaid mahogany, urn finial above pair glazed doors, 43½ x 13½, L18c (4111/113) — 3750

Bookcase, secretaire inlaid mahogany, 96 x 49 x 22½, L18c (4189/186) — 3000

Bookcase, secretaire, carved mahogany, 81 x 40 x 20 L18c (4189/160) — 4500

Bookcase, secretaire, inlaid mahogany, 95½ x 46 x 22, L18c (4216/164) — 2600

Bookcase, secretaire, mahogany, 86 x 43 x 22½, rep, L18c (4189/159) — 3000

Bookcase, secretaire, mahogany, 2 parts, glazed doors over secretaire, 3 drawers, 87 x 41½ x 19½, ca1810 (4272/131) — 2000

Bookcase, secretaire, breakfront, mahogany, glazed doors, lower cupboards, 10 drawers, 100 x 76 x 75½, ca1790 (4272/148) — 7750

Bookshelf, open, fret carved, 4 shelves, pierced and strapwork sides, 45 x 43½ x 8, E19c (4260/1333) — 1600

Bookshelves, pair, Gothic mahogany, 3 graduated shelves, 50½ x 15, E19c (4260/1742) — 6250

Bookstand, breakfront, mahogany, adjustable shelves, 3 drawers, 46 x 37 x 8½, ca1790 (4260/1334) — 1800

Box, octagonal, inlaid satinwood, colored engraving, with oval wood samples, 11, L18c (4111/10) — 275

Boxes, knife, inlaid pollard, oak, pair, serpentine, 16 L18c (4189/47) — 1400

Boxes, knife, pair serpentine, inlaid mahogany, 14½ L18c (4152/20) — 950

Boxes, knife, pair, mahogany, hinged, sloping top, shaped front, 15 x 9 x 11½, interior removed, L18c (4159/198) — 675

Boxes, knife, pair, serpentine, flower inlaid mahogany, 14 interiors removed, L18c (4152/30) — 450

Boxes, knife, pair, silver mounted, inlaid satinwood, hinged sloping front, 14½, ca1790 (4272/20) — 3500

Breakfront, inlaid mahogany, satinwood, 4 glazed doors above fitted doors, 81 x 98 x 20½, L18c (4216/117) — 13500

Breakfront, mahogany, pierced fret, carved leaf, flower and scroll, 112 x 99½ x 25, L18c (4111/228) — 48000

Breakfront bookcase, carved mahogany, 2 parts, 3 glazed doors, cupboards and drawers, 99 x 70½ x 26, ca1770 (4239/281) — 16000

Breakfront bookcase, inlaid, mahogany, 99 x 127 x 21, L18c (4216/162) — 14000

Breakfront bookcase, mahogany, 4 glazed doors above 4 oval doors, 116 x 110 x 23, L18c (4152/160) — 8750

Breakfront bookcase, mahogany, 4 glazed, 2 panelled doors, 4 drawers, 105 x 96 x 24, L18c (4165/315) — 28000

Breakfront bookcase, mahogany, 2 parts, fret-carved swan's neck cresting, 108 x 89 x 21½, L18c (4216/118) — 11500

Bureau, bookcase, mahogany, arched arcade, tall front 4 drawers, 86 x 43, L18c (4111/163) — 5000

Bureau, bookcase, mahogany, swan neck cresting, mirrored doors, 85 x 40 x 22, L18c (4152/152) — 4250

Bureau, cylinder, inlaid mahogany, tambour-fronted, fitted interior, square legs, 39 x 35½, 28, L18c (4159/286) — 3300

Bureau, inlaid mahogany, slope front, fitted interior, 4 long drawers, 44 x 39 x 22, res, ca1770 (4272/136) — 1000

Bureau, inlaid mahogany, sloping front, fitted interior, 4 drawers, 43½ x 40 x 19½, L18c (4159/248) — 1050

Bureau, inlaid mahogany, sloping front, fitted interior, 4 drawers, 41 x 35 x 20, L18c (4159/317) — 1700

Bureau, mahogany, hinged sloping front, fitted interior, 40 x 30 x 18, ca1775 (4260/1721) — 1900

Bureau, mahogany, slope front, fitted interior, 4 drawers, 44 x 39 x 19½ L18c (4134/276) — *1900*

Bureau, mahogany, slope front, fitted interior, 4 drawers, 42½ x 39 x 21, res, ca1780 (4239/254)   1500

Bureau, mahogany, slope front, fitted interior, 4 long drawers, 40½ x 33½ x 18½, ca1770 (4272/147)   3200

Bureau, mahogany, slope front, fitted interior, 4 long drawers, 42½ x 37½ x 20, ca1790 (4272/153)   1200

Bureau, mahogany, sloping front, 39½ x 30 19½, L18c (4216/114)   1600

Bureau, mahogany, sloping front enclosing fitted interior, 41½ x 41½ x 20, feet replaced, L18c (4165/345)   850

Bureau, mahogany, sloping front, fitted interior, 4 drawers, 44 x 42 x 21½, L18c (4159/260)   1900

Bureau, mahogany, sloping front, over 4 graduated drawers, 41 x 36 x 20, L18c (4216/154)   1900

Bureau, mahogany, 2 short, 2 long drawers sloping front, 42 x 38 x 21, L18c (4152/156)   *1500*

Bureau (4134/276)

Bureau (4152/156)

Cabinet (4168/81)

Bureau, mahogany sloping front, 43½ x 41 x 22, M18c (4216/90)   2000

Bureau, mahogany, slope front, pigeon holes and drawers, 4 long drawers, 41½ x 36 x 20½, res, ca1780 (4272/118)   1000

Bureau, mahogany, small, sloping front enclosing fitted interior, 37 x 23 x 19, L18c (4111/108)   1500

Bureau, oak, slope front, fitted interior, 4 long drawers, 40 x 32½ x 19½, ca1780 (4272/154)   800

Cabinet, bookcase mahogany, molded cornice, pair glazed doors, bracket feet, L18c (4079/102)   2500

Cabinet, bookcase, mahogany, pair glaze doors, and 2 panelled doors, 97 x 67 x 20½, L18c (4165/326)   3200

Cabinet, bookcase, mahogany, pair glazed doors, 2 short, 3 long drawers, 86 x 49 x 22, res, L18c (4111/146)   800

Cabinet, bookcase, mahogany, harewood, pierced swan's neck cresting, fan medallions, 108 x 54 x 17, L18c (4111/137)   12000

Cabinet, bookshelf, mahogany, 3 open shelves frieze drawer, pair panelled doors, 64 x 28 x 9½, res, ca1810 (4239/133)   600

Cabinet, bureau, mahogany, 2 parts, panelled doors, sloping front, 7 drawers, 89 x 45 x 23, panels replaced, ca1780 (4239/107)   1300

Cabinet, corner, hanging, mahogany, molded cornice, glazed door, 47 x 32½, L18c (4159/292)   1050

Cabinet, corner, hanging, mahogany, molded cornice, glazed door, 3 drawers, 48 x 32, L18c (4159/295)   1050

Cabinet, corner, mahogany, glazed door, panelled door below, 77½ x 35, ca1800 (4260/1351)   1700

Cabinet, oak, upper doors, lower 2 drawers, later cornice, 82½ x 73 x 25¼, L18c (4168/81)   *3100*

Cabinet, serpentine mahogany, front enclosed by doors, 37 x 58 x 25, ca1790 (4272/179)   1000

Cabinet, side, mahogany, pair doors, oval and rectangular panels, 36 x 39 x 15, ca1790 (4260/1746)   2750

Cabinet, side, mahogany, serpentine front, arched cupboard, 4 drawers, 36 x 69½ x 18½, ca1780 (4260/1340)   6500

Cabinet, side, mahogany, 4 doors panelled to resemble 8 doors, 36½ x 50½ x 15, ca1765 (4260/1356)   1300

Cabinet, vitrine, hanging, mahogany, double sided, 45 x 25 x 8, ca1810 (4260/1344)   1900

Cabinets, semicircular, pair, inlaid satinwood, 33 x 42 x 21, res, L18c (4216/167)   6000

Candlestand, mahogany, pierced brass gallery, candle slide, 24 x 11, ca1760 (4272/195)   2800

Candlestand, octagonal, inlaid mahogany, star inlaid, galleried top, turned stem, cabriole legs, 27 x 15½, L18c (4159/313)   350

Candlestand, tripod, mahogany, rectangular top, baluster stem, downswept legs, 28 x 18½ x 13½, L18c (4239/120)	150
Candlestands, pair, octagonal, inlaid mahogany, 28 L18c (4152/167)	950
Canterbury, gilt dec, rosewood, 4 slatted dipped divisions, drawer on scrolled legs, 20½ x 21 x 14½, ca1810 (4239/357)	*3900*
Canterbury, mahogany, 4 dipped slatted divisions, 20 x 18, L18c (4152/142)	800
Canterbury, turned mahogany, dipped top, 4 slatted divisions, base drawer, 20½ x 20 x 13½, ca1815 (4239/282)	550
Casket, mahogany, hinged lid, panelled body, chamfered feet, 17 x 19½ x 13½, ca1765 (4260/1378)	650
Cellaret, brass bound mahogany, octagonal, metal interior lining, 27 x 17¾ L18c (4134/300)	1300
Cellaret, mahogany, hinged lid, carrying handles, 29½ x 15½ x 16, ca1765 (4260/1727)	1100
Cellaret, mahogany, hinged rounded top, lead lined fitted interior, 16½ x 29½ x 13, ca1810 (4272/165)	300
Cellaret, mahogany, hinged, galleried tray top, 23 x 22 x 14½, ca1770 (4272/116)	550
Cellaret, inlaid mahogany, hinged top, brass loop handles, 26 x 15½ x 11, L18c (4152/125)	325
Cellaret, inlaid mahogany, hinged top, fitted interior, stand, 27 x 16 x 10¾, L18c (4159/269)	650
Cellaret on stand, mahogany, octagonal, hinged top, brass bound, 28 x 20, L18c (4111/132)	1200
Chair, arm, elmwood, rectangular backrest, molded spindles, reeded arms, L18c (4159/244)	200
Chair, arm, mahogany, Chinese Chippendale style, upholstered seat, L18c (4159/311)	1500
Chair, arm, mahogany, 4 pierced crossbars, dipped upholstered seat, L18c (4159/329)	350
Chair, arm, wing, stained oak, upholstered, arched back, loose cushion, square legs, L18c (4159/330)	1250
Chair, arm, wing, mahogany, arched back, upholstered, out-scrolled arms, res, L18c (4159/300)	850
Chair, arm, wing, mahogany, arched backrest, scrolled arms, upholstered, re-railed, ca1780 (4239/134)	850
Chair, child, elmwood, shaped top rail, solid baluster splat, solid seat, ca1730 (4239/252)	300
Chair, child's, mahogany, arched top rail, pierced splat, restraining bar, L18c (4272/127)	500
Chair, hall, wheelback, carved, mahogany, L18c (4216/161)	1300
Chair, library side, mahogany, L18c (4189/179)	650
Chair, porter's, leather upholstered, 67½ L18c (4134/306)	*850*
Chair, reading, inlaid mahogany, upholstered U-shaped top rail, adj reading stand, ca1820 (4272/193)	1500
Chair, side mahogany, Gothic, pierced beaker splat, upholstered seat, L18c (4165/395)	425
Chair, side, carved mahogany, L18c (4189/182)	250
Chair, side, mahogany, bow knotted ribbon arched top rail, L18c (4152/130)	150
Chair, side, mahogany, pierced beaker splat, square legs, L18c (4159/256)	110
Chair, side, mahogany, rectangular back, 3 pierced spindle splats, L18c (4159/318)	150
Chair, side, shield-back, mahogany, carved pierced splat, upholstered seat, L18c (4239/164)	175
Chair, tub, mahogany, arched backrest, upholstered bow-front seat, 1 front leg replaced, ca1790 (4239/311)	850
Chair, tub, mahogany, upholstered seat, square tapered legs, L18c (4079/124)	950
Chair, wing, mahogany, upholstered, on square chamfered logs, ca1770 (4272/197)	1300
Chairs, dining set of sixteen, inlaid mahogany, upholstered seats, 2 armchairs, L18c (4216/95)	2500
Chairs, dining set of 12, mahogany, Two armchairs, serpentine shape top rail, 19c (4152/124)	6250

Canterbury (4239/357)

Chair (4134/306)

Chairs, dining set of 4 fruitwood, pierced beaker splat, drop in seat, restoration L18c (4134/110)	700
Chairs, dining shield-backs, carved, mahogany, upholstered seats, L18c (4216/116)	1200
Chairs, dining, set of eight, mahogany, 2 armchairs, turned top rail, pierced splat, ca1880 (4272/196)	4900
Chairs, dining, set of eight, mahogany, 2 armchairs, wheat and bell flower carved pendant, L18c (4111/102)	6250
Chairs, dining, set of 4, mahogany, serpentine shaped tops, columnar spindle splats, ca1790 (4272/124)	1100
Chairs, dining, set of 6, mahogany, oval backrest, serpentine, tapered legs, L18c (4079/104)	1500
Chairs, dining, set of 12, mahogany upholstered seats, ca1800 (4152/168)	6750
Chairs, dining, set of 12, mahogany, 2 armchairs, pierced beaker, carved, ca1790 (4239/297)	10000
Chairs, dining, set of 3, mahogany, 1 armchair, shield-backrest, pierced splat, L18c (4239/125)	3600
Chairs, dining, set of 4, mahogany, shield-backs, L18c (4134/129)	600
Chairs, dining, set of 8, mahogany, 2 armchairs, 3 pierced splats, upholstered seats, L18c (4239/289)	5100
Chairs, pair, hall, mahogany, panelled and waisted backs, solid seats, ca1815 (4260/1360)	550
Chairs, reading, pair, mahogany, caned backrest, top rail hinged and fitted, E19c (4272/178)	300
Chairs, set of 6, carved mahogany, shield-back, pierced upholstered seat, ca19c (4239/104)	1300
Chairs, side carved mahogany, pair, L18c (4189/185)	350
Chairs, side, pair, painted satinwood, panelled top rail, turned legs, L18c (4079/138)	325
Chairs, side, pair, carved mahogany, arched back, urn pierced splat, upholstered seat, ca1775 (4239/108)	500
Chairs, side, pair, mahogany, shaped toprail, baluster splat, square legs, L18c (4159/316)	550
Chairs, side, pair, painted shield-back, pierced backrest, upholstered seat, ca1790 (4239/302)	600
Chairs, tub, pair, arched backs, upholstered, L18c (4111/96)	2700
Chairs, tub, pair, mahogany small, upholstered seat, L18c (4216/165)	1900
Chairs, tub, pair, painted, upholstered, L18c (4189/137)	1900
Chest of drawers, 5 drawers, bracket feet, 35 x 36 x 17¾, L18c (4111/224)	1100
Chest of drawers, bachelor's, mahogany, 2 short, 3 long drawers, 29 x 30 x 13½, L18c (4111/97)	3000
Chest of drawers, bow-front, mahogany, 41¼ x 42¼ x 20, E19c (4152/143)	500
Chest of drawers, bow-front mahogany, 2 short and 3 long drawers, bracket feet, 40½ x 42 x 20½, E19c (4239/105)	475
Chest of drawers, bow-front, mahogany, 2 short, 3 long drawers on shaped bracket feet, 38½ x 42½ x 22½, ca1810 (4239/280)	1300
Chest of drawers, bow-front, mahogany, 2 short, 3 long drawers, splayed bracket feet, 41½ x 41½ x 20, E19c (4239/268)	350
Chest of drawers, inlaid mahogany, bow-front, 2 short, 3 long drawers, 41½ x 20½ L18c (4134/165)	550
Chest of drawers, inlaid mahogany, bow-front, 3 drawers, bracket feet, 34½ x 34 x 18½ L18c (4134/294)	900
Chest of drawers, inlaid mahogany, bow-front, 5 drawers, 4½ x 42 x 21 M19c (4134/317)	500
Chest of drawers, inlaid mahogany, bow-front, 3 long drawers, 38 x 43 x 21 L19c (4134/312)	650
Chest of drawers, inlaid mahogany, bow-front, 4 graduated drawers, 34 x 43 x 22½, L18c (4165/319)	1000
Chest of drawers, inlaid mahogany, checker, cross bande D-shaped top, 4 drawers, 34½ x 40½ x 23, ca1780 (4239/317)	3100
Chest of drawers, inlaid mahogany, 4 long drawers, splayed bracket feet, 34½ x 37 x 20, ca1790 (4272/201)	2700
Chest of drawers, inlaid mahogany, serpentine 4 drawers, shaped apron, 41½ x 45 x 22, E19c (4272/120)	1100
Chest of drawers, inlaid mahogany, 4 drawers, bracket feet, 34 x 55 x 18½, E19c (4260/1345)	1000
Chest of drawers, mahogany, bow-front, 2 short, 2 long drawers, bracket feet, 34½ x 36½ x 21, E19c (4239/142)	500
Chest of drawers, mahogany, brushing slide above 4 drawers, bracket feet, 28 x 26 x 15½, ca1765 (4260/1385)	2700
Chest of drawers, mahogany, molded top, 2 short, 3 long drawers, 35½ x 37½ x 20, L18c (4159/326)	1400
Chest of drawers, mahogany, molded top, 2 short, 3 long drawers, 32½ x 41 x 19½, L18c (4159/324)	1950
Chest of drawers, mahogany, rectangular, bracket feet, 28½ x 31 x 13½, ca1770 (4260/1730)	3100
Chest of drawers, mahogany, serpentine, 4 drawers, bracket feet, 36½ x 40 x 21, L18c (4159/335)	3400
Chest of drawers, mahogany, serpentine, 4 drawers, 33 x 33, L18c (4111/164)	1600
Chest of drawers, mahogany, serpentine, 4 drawers, bracket feet, 32½ x 44 x 22½, ca1765 (4260/1741)	6500
Chest of drawers, mahogany, 2 short, 3 long graduated drawers, 37½ x 32 x 18, L18c (4216/156)	750
Chest of drawers, mahogany, 2 short and 3 long drawers, on ogee bracket feet, 34 x 37 x 21, ca1780 (4272/174)	1100
Chest of drawers, mahogany, 5 drawers, bracket feet, 33 x 34, L18c (4149/268)	650
Chest of drawers, miniature, mahogany, 4 long drawers, 17 x 12, L18c (4216/12)	425
Chest of drawers, miniature, mahogany, 2 short, 3 long drawers, 13 x 13 x 6½, E19c (4272/150)	150

Chest of drawers, serpentine, carved mahogany, 34½ x 45 x 27, L18c (4216/149)   *1600*

Chairs (4152/168)

Chest of drawers
(4189/191)

Chest of drawers (4216/149)

Chest of drawers, serpentine, inlaid mahogany, 39½ x 39½ x 23, L18c (4189/193)	2500
Chest of drawers, serpentine, mahogany, 36 x 38 x 24, pulls replaced L18c (4189/191)	*1900*
Chest of drawers, serpentine, mahogany, 4 long drawers, 30½ x 37½ x 22, L18c (4111/114)	2000
Chest on chest, 8 drawers on ogee bracket feet, 68 x 42 x 20½, L18c (4165/352)	3250
Chest on chest, 2 section, 8 drawers, 73 x 51 x 22 L18c (4165/351)	4500
Chest on chest, carved mahogany, 2 parts, 70½ x 42 x 18, M18c (4189/176)	2300
Chest on chest, carved mahogany, 2 parts, 70½ x 41 x 19½, L18c (4216/155)	1500
Chest on chest, mahogany, 2 section, 75 x 40 x 21½, L18c (4189/192)	1700
Chest on chest, carved mahogany, 2 sections, 73 x 44 x 22, L18c (4216/151)	1600
Chest on chest, carved mahogany, 2 sections, 5 drawers, lower 3 drawers, 76½ x 44 x 22½, L18c (4239/320)	1800
Chest on chest, inlaid oak, 2 short 3 long drawers, 75½ x 43 x 23, L18c (4152/135)	1000
Chest on chest, inlaid oak, upper 5 drawers, lower 3 drawers, bracket legs, 69½ x 43 x 19½ L18c (4134/90)	1800
Chest on chest, mahogany, serpentine, dentil cornice, reeded corners, 72½ x 48 x 21, L18c (4079/121)	4000
Chest on chest, mahogany, 2 sections, 73 x 41½ x 22, L18c (4189/188)	850
Chest on chest, mahogany and pine, 2 parts, top 5 drawers, lower 3 drawers, 70 x 41½ x 19½, ca1770 (4239/318)	1200
Coaching stand, turned mahogany, hinged rectangular form, block and turned legs, 29½ x 31½ x 22, E19c (4239/301)	400
Coffer on stand, inlaid mahogany, small, domed top, brass handles, 20½ x 12 x 8½ L18c (4134/320)	525
Commode, inlaid mahogany, 3 drawers, 3 oval inlaid fronted cupboards, 32½ x 55½ x 21½, ca1790 (4260/1747)	2800
Commode, inlaid mahogany, serpentine, 4 drawers, panelled sides, 35½ x 58 x 22, ca1790 (4260/1736)	5000
Commode, mahogany, serpentine, 4 drawers, 32 x 42 x 23½, L18c (4165/405)	18500
Commode, serpentine, marquetry, inlaid ormolu mounted tulipwood, and harewood, 33½ - 5½ x 2¼ L18c (4189/132)	14000
Commode, serpentine, carved mahogany, 35½ x 43 x 23, M18c (4189/173)	8000
Commodes, pair, serpentine, marquetry inlaid tulipwood and harewood, 33 x 41, M18c (4189/158)	18000
Cupboard, bedside, mahogany, galleried top, tambour front compartments, 32 x 21½ x 18½ L18c (4134/135)	525
Cupboard, bedside, mahogany, tambour fronted, 32 x 21½ x 18, L18c (4152/115)	500
Cupboard, bedside, mahogany, 30 x 21 x 18½ L18c (4216/153)	750
Cupboard, bedside, mahogany, serpentine, tambour cupboard, drawer, 29 x 19 x 17, ca1770 (4260/1726)	650
Cupboard, bedside, mahogany, ¾ gallery, trifyd feet, 30 x 15 x 14, ca1760 (4260/1338)	1500

Cupboard, corner, hanging mahogany, molded cornice, panelled doors, 39½, res, caL18c
(4239/119)   150
Cupboard, corner, dec. black japanned, front with pair doors, with gilt chinoiserie figures, 38½ x 24,
L18c (4239/288)   350
Cupboard, corner, gilt, black japanned, bow-front, with pair of doors, 36½ x 24, ca1770 (4272/128)   850
Cupboard, corner, hanging, inlaid, mahogany, glazed door enclosing shelves, 44 x 29½ L18c
(4134/281)   450
Cupboard, corner, hanging, mahogany, inlaid oak, feather band cornice, panelled door, 39½ x 32,
ca1770 (4260/1330)   500
Cupboard, corner, mahogany, bowed front, drawer, 35 x 17, altered, ca1790 (4260/1336)   600
Cupboard, corner, mahogany, pair glazed doors, lower 2 panelled doors, 83 x 40, L18c (4111/83)   1600
Cupboard, corner, mahogany inlaid oak, 2 pairs of panelled doors, 80 x 51, L18c (4216/108)   1600
Cupboard, corner, pollard oak, bow-front with 2 doors, now with marble top, 37½ x 27, ca1780
(4260/1353)   450
Cupboard, hanging corner, inlaid mahogany, broken arch crest, 52 x 35, L18c (4111/153)   550
Cupboard, hanging mahogany, dentil molded cornice above glazed doors, 45 x 31½ x 19¼, ca1770
(4272/129)   800
Cupboard, pedestal, mahogany, hinged domed top, enclosing humidor, 28½ x 15½ x 16, ca1800
(4260/1383)   425
Cupboard, pedestal, mahogany, rectangular panelled door, cellaret drawer, 30 x 19½ x 16, ca1780
(4260/1382)   800
Cupboard, pedestal, mahogany, square stepped top, front enclosed by carved door, 38 x 14, L18c
(4165/396)   650
Cupboards, pair, pedestal, mahogany, fielded panelled door, lead lined interior, 43 x 23 x 17½,
ca1780 (4272/169)   1500
Decanter, set 'six' inlaid mahogany, 8½ x 10 L18c (4189/17)   450
Desk, cylinder, inlaid mahogany, tambour fronted, 38 x 36½ x 26, L18c (4216/86)   1300
Desk, cylinder, tambour fronted, mahogany, 37 x 34½ x 26½, L18c (4216/172)   1100
Desk, partner's, mahogany, leather inset, drawers, brass carrying handles, 29½ x 63½ x 42,
L18/E19c (4260/1743)   8500
Desk, partner's, mahogany, leather inset, drawers, cupboard, 29½ x 60 x 39, E19c (4260/1735)   4500
Desk, partner's, mahogany, leather inset, drawers, cupboard, 30 x 59 x 41, ca1795 (4260/1724)   5000
Desk box, brass bound mahogany, baize lined, fitted drawer, L18, L18c (4149/81)   375
Dresser, applewood, splashboard, 2 drawers, 39 x 50 x 18½, L18c (4111/70)   900
Dresser, oak, molded cornice, 3 shelves, 5 drawers, 80 x 57½ x 15, L18c (4111/69)   2750
Dresser, oak, open shelves and pair cupboard, 3 drawers, 77 x 73 x 16½ L18c (4134/309)   3400
Dresser, oak, 2 part, top open, lower, drawers and cupboards, 81 x 63½ x 19½, ca1790 (4272/134)   3300
Dressing glass, inlaid mahogany, bow-front, plate pivoting between uprights, 19½ x 18½, E19c
(4156/194)   300
Dumbwaiter, mahogany, 2 tier, circular, 36 x 25½, L18c (4079/141)   450
Dumbwaiter, 2 tier, mahogany, 36 x 30, L18c (4152/82)   450
Dumbwaiter, 3 tier, circular tiers, tripod legs, 39 x 23½, L18c (4079/58)   650
Dumbwaiter, 3 tier, mahogany, 46 x 23, L18c (4165/342)   300
Dumbwaiter, 3 tier, mahogany, circular, graduated tiers, spirally turned supports, 44, Diam 24, L18c
(4159/307)   450
Dumbwaiter, 3 tier, mahogany, circular, graduated tiers, turned supports, tripod, legs, H43, Diam
23½, L18c (4159/273)   550
Etagere, mahogany, 4 shelves on square chamfered legs, 48½ x 13 x 13, E19c (4239/106)   295
Etagere, turned, rectangular gallery top, stretcher with drawer, 25 x 20 x 15½, E19c
(4239/276)   300
Etagere, 2 tier mahogany, rectangular top, shaped apron, square chamfered legs, 30 x 14 x 13¾,
ca1790 (4239/79)   225
Frames, pair carved, gilt decoration, white painted, 73½ x 54, ca1760 (4189/29)   8750
Frames, pair, gilt decorated white, painted, 133 x 88, 1 res ca1760 (4189/27)   3200
Frames, pair, gilt decoration, white, painted, 133 x 88, ca1760 (4189/28)   3100
Globes-on-stands, terrestial, celestial, by I & W Newton, London, compass, 36, 1801-10 (4149/276)   2700
Knife boxes, inlaid mahogany, hinged sloping top, fitted interior, 15½ x 9 L18c (4134/195)   900
Knife boxes, mahogany, serpentine, pair, fitted interior, 14½ x 9, L18c (4149/64)   550
Knife boxes, serpentine, shell, inlaid, mahogany, fitted interior, 14½ L18c (4134/224)   1100
Library steps, mahogany, folding, 3 treads, 38½, E19c (4260/1723)   800
Linen press, oak, 60½ x 34 x 22 res E19c (4216/109)   950
Mirror, bow-front, inlaid mahogany, 23½ x 18, L18c (4189/45)   225
Mirror, bow-front, inlaid mahogany, 19 x 14, L18c (4216/18)   150
Mirror, carved gilt wood, pair, oval plate, border form interlaced branches, 37 x 19¾, new plates, res,
ca1770 (4239/188)   6750
Mirror, carved gilt wood, oval plate, S scroll borders, flanked by Hoho birds, 60 x 36, ca1765
(4272/14)   3100

Mirror, dressing, mahogany, inlaid, oval, ogee bracket feet, 22 x 14½, ca1800 (4148/129) 525
Mirror, gilt gesso, 40 L18c (4189/31) 1200
Mirror, gilt mirror, with subsidiary plates, border carved, 75 x 39, L18c (4111/19) 4000
Mirror, gilt wood, bevelled plate, pierced leafy C-scroll border, 53 x 25, L18c (4165/293) 2100
Mirror, gilt wood, column, scroll, flowering border, HoHo bird cresting, 65 x 28 L18c (4134/220) 2000
Mirror, gilt wood, oval, surmounted 3 HoHo birds, 40½, L18c (4079/33) 850
Mirror, gilt wood, rusticated columns and scrolling border, 52 x 25, L18c (4134/35) 1050
Mirror, gilt wood, scroll, flower border HoHo bird cresting, 69 x 33 L18c (4134/221) 2300
Mirror, gilt wood, shaped plate, pierced leafy scrolled borders, 52 x 27 L18c (4134/19) 800
Mirror, gilt wood, pierced borders, 51 x 27½ L18c (4189/38) 1100
Mirror, gilt wood, 40 x 22, L18c (4189/33) 750
Mirror, gilt wood, shaped plate, leaf border, 53 x 37½ L18c (4189/32) *2200*
Mirror, inlaid mahogany wall, crest inlaid with fan patera, 40½ x 17⅝ (4149/251) 350
Mirror, oval, free standing uprights and trestle feet, 23½ restorations L18c (4216/42) 200
Mirror, oval, gilt wood, 63 x 41 L18c (4189/37) 5750
Mirror, oval, gilt wood, beaded gadrooned border, anthemion cresting, 56, L18c (4159/196) 1600
Mirror, overmantel, gilt wood, triple divided plate, 31 x 56 L18c (4134/9) 650
Mirror, overmantle, gilt wood, triple divided, 39 x 36, L18c (4165/284) 3600
Mirror, pair, carved gilt wood, oval plate pierced and scrolling borders, 41½ x 24½, res, ca1770 (4239/192) *3800*

Mirror (4189/32)

Mirror (4239/192)

Mirror, parcel-gilt mahogany, 24 x 15, L18c (4189/48) 200
Mirror, parcel-gilt walnut, rectangular plate, carved and molded borders, 36½ x 20, ca1745 (4272/30) 900
Mirror, small dressing table, oval mirror, inlaid mahogany, 3 drawers, 16 x 9⅝, ca1800 (4149/84) 235
Mirror, toilet, bone inlaid mahogany, rectangular plate, reeded uprights, 3 drawers, 19¼ x 20½, mirror replaced, E19c (4239/12) 225
Mirror, wall, carved, gilt wood, 2 parts, cartouche, oblong, 88x 57, 1850-75 (4148/281) 6000
Mirrors, gilt wood and gilt gesso, pair, oval, flowerhead, mounted frame, 51 x 10, L18c (4111/1) 900
Mirrors, pair, gilt wood, divided mirror plate leafy scroll border, 31 x 20, L18c (4134/18) 1500
Mirrors, pair, gilt wood, leafy C scroll icicle borders, 48, L18c (4152/23) 1400
Mirrors, pair, gilt wood, C scroll leafy and flower carved borders, 45 x 24, L18c (4134/20) 2200
Mirrors, pair, gilt wood, 53 (4189/25) 1600
Mirrors, pair, oval, gilt wood, beaded border, 48 x 21, L18c (4165/267) 3500
Pedestals, pair, mahogany, panelled door, lead lined interior, 37 x 16½ x 14, ca1790 (4260/1346) 800
Pedestals, pair, simulated carved marble, glass globes on metal supports, cupboard, 78, res, ca1790 (4272/146) 1500
Press, clothes, inlaid mahogany, 2 parts, pair oval panelled doors, 3 drawers, 76½ x 48 x 22½, ca1790 (4239/87) 1600
Reading stand, mahogany, hinged adjustable top, brass arms, columnar supports, 29½ x 12½ x 12, ca1810 (4260/1376) 600
Screens, pole, pair, painted and gilded, adjustable dual screen inset with Chinese wallpaper, 54½ x 15, E19c (4239/345) 300

Secretaire, bookcase, inlaid mahogany, 2 parts, pair glazed doors, fitted drawer, 87½ x 42 x 20, ca1810 (4239/293)	2500
Secretaire, bookcase, mahogany, 2 parts, pair glazed doors, writing surface, 85 x 38½ x 18½, ca1800 (4239/137)	2000
Secretaire, bookcase, mahogany, 2 parts, glazed doors, fitted interior, drawers, 86 x 42½ x 22½, ca1790 (4272/204)	4250
Secretaire, bookcase, breakfront, mahogany 4 doors, pair cupboards, 94½ x 73 x 18 L18c (4134/286)	4250
Secretaire, bookcase, inlaid mahogany, swan's neck cresting, 4 glazed doors, 100 x 97½ x 19½, L18c (4079/108)	5750
Secretaire, bookcase, inlaid mahogany, arched inlaid cornice, 84 x 36 x 18½, L18c (4111/223)	2400
Secretaire, bookcase, mahogany, 4 doors, fitted secretaire drawer, 91 x 85 x 20, L18c (4165/350)	9250
Secretaire, bookcase, mahogany, pair of doors on top and bottom, 1 drawer, 87 x 31 x 17 L18c (4134/134)	2000
Secretaire, bookcase, small, mahogany, 2 parts, glazed doors, secretaire fitted drawer, 81 x 31 x 19½, ca1810 (4239/172)	*3000*
Secretaire, chest on chest, inlaid, mahogany, 7 drawers, fitted interior, 77 x 42 x 20½, L18c (4165/328)	5100
Secretaire, mahogany, fitted drawer, pair cupboard doors, 41 x 49½ x 20, altered, ca1790 (4260/1347)	1500
Secretaire, mahogany, 2 tier lattice work, 62½ x 28 x 12¼, M18c (4152/119)	6750
Settee, carved and stained, beechwood, L70, L18c (4216/15)	13000
Settee, gilt wood, in French manner, carved frame, upholstered, L18c (4239/306)	1900
Settee, gilt wood, reeded top rail, upholstered fluted legs, L85, L18c (4111/202)	2500
Settee, mahogany, arched backrest, scrolled armrest, upholstered, 97, ca1770 (4239/265)	2200
Settee, mahogany, arched backrest, upholstered, 65½, legs res, ca1790 (4239/83)	800
Settee, mahogany, rectangular backrest, upholstered, 76½, L18c (4152/121)	1600
Settee, mahogany, rectangular molded frame, L78 ca1800 (4189/187)	1100
Settee, mahogany, upholstered, 59 L18c (4134/274)	1000
Settee, mahogany, upholstered, 80½ seat rails reinforced L18c (4134/171)	2100
Settee, mahogany, upholstered, 84, L18c (4165/323)	2400
Settee, mahogany, upholstered, L78, L18c (4216/81)	2100
Settee, mahogany, upholstered, arched back, bow-front, square legs, 72, L18c (4159/278)	2100
Settee, mahogany, upholstered, arched back, loose cushion, bow-front, 78, L18c (4159/320)	1400
Settee, mahogany, upholstered, serpentine back, loose cushion seat, 71, res, L18c (4159/291)	1000
Settee, painted, upholstered, L69, L18c (4189/136)	2000
Shaving stand, divided top enclosing 5 apertures, 34½ x 16 x 16 L18c (4134/166)	300
Shelves, hanging, mahogany, 2 shelves on bracket swanneck cresting, 49 x 27 x 10 (4134/226)	425
Sideboard, D-shaped, inlaid mahogany, 4 drawers, 2 cupboards, 38 x 70.8 x 35 some res L18c (4134/112)	1000
Sideboard, bow-front, mahogany, 3 drawers, arched apron, 34 x 41½ x 21, L18c (4152/139)	1400
Sideboard, bow-front, mahogany, 35½ x 44½ x 23, L18c (4152/153)	2400
Sideboard, bow-front, mahogany, cellaret drawer, 37 x 43 x 26½, L18c (4216/121)	1400
Sideboard, bow-front, satinwood, inlaid mahogany, 36 x 60 x 27½, 19c (4189/199)	*3100*
Sideboard, bow-front, mahogany with inlay of later date, 35 x 42 x 21½ (4152/141)	1200
Sideboard, bow-front, inlaid mahogany, drawer, arched apron, cellaret drawer, square legs, 38 x 56 x 27, L18c (4159/280)	2400
Sideboard, concave fronted, mahogany, drawer, arched apron, cellaret drawers, 36 x 77½ x 27½, E19c (4272/177)	2200
Sideboard, inlaid mahogany, bow-front, brass, splashed board, 36 x 65 x 31½ restorations, L18c (4134/302)	3400
Sideboard, inlaid mahogany, bow-front, 5 drawers, arched apron, block toes, 33 x 73 x 31, res, 19c (4239/135)	1000
Sideboard, inlaid mahogany, center drawer flanked by cellarets, 36 x 53 x 22, L18c (4111/220)	1100
Sideboard, inlaid mahogany, serpentine front, concave tambour front, 40 x 63 x 27½, L18c (4111/104)	1600
Sideboard, inlaid mahogany, serpentine front, frieze drawer, cellaret drawers, 37½ x 54½ x 26, L18c (4239/169)	2300
Sideboard, inlaid mahogany, serpentine, 36 x 54 x 21½ L18c (4134/100)	1400
Sideboard, inlaid mahogany, serpentine, drawer above arched apron, 36 x 66 x 27½, L18c (4111/110)	2500
Sideboard, mahogany, carved and inlaid, frieze drawer, apron, 33½ x 52 x 24, ca1790 (4260/1745)	8250
Sideboard, mahogany, serpentine, concaved, cupboard, 36½ x 75 x 29 L18c (4134/117)	*1900*

Sideboard
(4189/199)

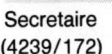

Secretaire
(4239/172)

Sideboard
(4134/117)

Sideboard, mahogany, bow-front, drawer above arched apron, cellaret at each side, 57 x 55 x 19½, ca1810 (4272/121)	1700
Sideboard, serpentine, inlaid satinwood and mahogany, 36½ x 73 x 24, E19c (4216/123)	2400
Sideboard, serpentine mahogany, pair, tambour doors, cellaret drawer, fluted legs, 38 x 79, L18c (4079/133)	800
Sideboard, serpentine, fronted, inlaid mahogany, 38½ x 72 x 28½, L18c (4216/152)	3250
Sideboard, serpentine, mahogany, drawer and 2 cellaret drawers on each side, 37 x 72 x 29, res, ca1790 (4272/137)	4400
Small chest on stand, inlaid mahogany, rectangular form, 1 long and 2 short drawers, 27½ x 11½, ca1810 (4239/128)	175
Stand, basin, corner, mahogany, bow-front, hinged top and enclosing apertures, 32½ x 28, E18c (4165/403)	900
Stand, basin, corner, inlaid mahogany, bow-front, 45½ x 21, L18c (4111/148)	300
Stand, basin, corner, inlaid mahogany, hinged wedge shaped top, 3 basin apertures, 32½ x 26½, altered, ca1790 (4260/1749)	1600
Stand, basin, mahogany, circular molded top, tripod cabriole legs, 31½ x 12, L18c (4079/119)	475
Stand, folio mahogany, 2 open compartments, 32 x 35½ x 19½ L18c (4134/314)	650
Stand, wash, inlaid mahogany, rectangular, splashboard, 2 drawers, square legs, 34½ x 29 x 15, L18c (4159/287)	800
Stand, wine, mahogany, full gallery, ends pierced for handles, 18 x 26 x 14, L18c (4111/222)	550
Stool, hall, mahogany, dished seat on chamfered legs, 21, ca1760 (4260/1348)	950
Stool, mahogany, rectangular drop in seat, square molded legs, ca1770 (4239/118)	250
Stool, mahogany, rectangular upholstered seat, square legs, 15, ca1790 (4239/103)	150
Stool, mahogany, rectangular, upholstered, square tapered legs, W22, L18c (4159/299)	325
Stool, mahogany, rectangular, upholstered, square tapered legs, 18, 1 leg spliced, ca1780 (4239/148)	225
Stool, mahogany, upholstered seat carved legs, 16½ x 24, L18c (4111/156)	4250
Stool, mahogany, upholstered top, square tapered legs, 12, ca1790 (4272/198)	125
Stool, mahogany, L17, L18c (4189/183)	275
Stool, tall, mahogany, oval, square tapering legs, 28, ca1790 (4260/1352)	450
Stools, pair, inlaid mahogany, upholstered, seat, 19 L18c (4216/82)	650
Stools, pair, mahogany, dipped rectangular seat, from Leeds Cloth Hall, 24½ x 19, L18c (4152/140)	1000
Stools, pair, mahogany, kidney shaped, 16½ x 15, ca1790 (4260/1729)	1700
Stools, pair, mahogany, solid tops, square tapering legs, 17½ x 20, ca1780 (4260/1355)	1200
Stools, pair, mahogany, upholstered seats, 25, L18c (4165/330)	1000
Table, architect's, drop-leaf mahogany, fitted adjustable work surface, 29½ x 27 x 30 L18c (4134/277)	1800
Table, architect's, mahogany, adjustable top on double ratchet supports, 29½ x 30 x 21, L18c (4111/206)	1600

Table, architect's, mahogany, adjustable top, writing slide, 33 x 59½ x 24, rep feet later, L18c (4111/98) — 3500

Table, breakfast, circular, rosewood, inlaid mahogany, tilting top, 28 x 51, ca1800 (4272/180) — 2600

Table, breakfast, inlaid mahogany, octagonal, tilting top, 28½ x 53, L18c (4111/203) — 1000

Table, breakfast, mahogany, circular tilting top, 28 x 41, L18c (4219/155) — 850

Table, breakfast, mahogany, oval, 4 down curved legs, 26½ x 64½ x 47, ca1785 (4260/1738) — 6750

Table, breakfast, mahogany, rectangular reeded tilting top, tripod legs, 27 x 37 x 29, E19c (4239/136) — 225

Table, dining, fruitwood, drawer, tapered legs, 29 x 59 x 26½, L18c (4111/66) — 1100

Table, dining, inlaid mahogany, 3 parts, gate-leg supports, 28½, 119 x 58¾ L18c (4134/127) — 1300

Table, dining, inlaid mahogany, 2 pedestal rounded ends, baluster supports, 28½ x 86½ x 44½ (4134/86) — 650

Table, dining, mahogany, central drop-leaf section, 2 D-shaped ends, 28½ x 126 x 53, ca1800 (4239/43) — 2200

Table, dining, oak, rectangular top, frieze drawer, square legs, 25½ x 13½ x 19, L18c (4111/59) — 700

Table, dining, D end, mahogany, central drop-leaf section, square tapered legs, 128 x 44½, ca1800 (4272/139) — 1200

Table, dining, D-end, mahogany, 2 D-shaped ends, drop-leaf, square legs, 29½ x 154 x 47, res, L18c (4159/305) — 1400

Table, dining, 3 pedestal, mahogany, reeded divided top, tripod downswept reeded legs, 28½ x 118 x 50½, ca1810 (4272/140) — 3800

Table, dressing, inlaid mahogany, leather inset top, 4 drawers, 30 x 41 x 18½, E19c (4111/189) — 1100

Table, dressing, inlaid mahogany, 3 drawers, arched apron tapered legs, 30 x 34½ x 17½, L18c (4111/192) — 400

Table, dressing, inlaid mahogany, 2 short, 1 long drawer, 29 x 28½ x 16, L18c (4216/72) — 650

Table, dressing, mahogany, knee hole flanked each side, 3 drawers, 30 x 30½ x 17, ca1770 (4260/1341) — 1600

Table, dressing, mahogany, molded rectangular top, frieze drawer, chamfered legs, 28 x 30 x 19½, ca1770 (4239/141) — 300

Table, dressing, mahogany, rectangular, drawer, square tapered legs, 29 x 34 x 20, rep, L18c (4159/334) — 425

Table, dressing, mahogany, tambour fronted, fitted interior, toilet mirror, 34½ x 29½ x 20½, L18c (4272/172) — 1400

Table, dressing, oak, drawer, shaped apron, chamfered legs, 29 x 32½ x 17¾, L18c (4111/65) — 400

Table, drop-leaf, mahogany, 2 drawers, brass casters, 30 x 43½ x 54¾, L18c (4216/115) — 600

Table, drum, inlaid mahogany, 'small', circular, revolving, leather inset top, 29 x 19 L18c (4134/162) — 550

Table, drum, circular, inlaid mahogany, leather inset top, revolving top, 4 drawers, 27½ x 32½, ca1810 (4239/285) — 1200

Table, drum, inlaid mahogany, leather inset, circular, 4 drawers, 29 x 36, ca1815 (4260/1751) — 2600

Table, drum, mahogany, leather inset, 4 drawers, turned pedestal, 78 x 44, ca1820 (4239/355) — 1800

Table, folding, mahogany, hinged, reeded top, rectangular, 30 x 30 x 18, L18c (4239/300) — 450

Table, game, mahogany, hinged top, frieze drawer, square tapered legs, 30 x 35 x 17½, ca1790 (4239/255) — 650

Table, game, mahogany, hinged top, lined interior, square chamfered legs, 29 x 36 x 17½, ca1765 (4239/139) — 550

Table, game, D shape, inlaid, mahogany, 29½ x 35 x 17½, res, L18c (4189/165) — 1100

Table, games semicircular inlaid, mahogany, 29 x 36 x 17½, L18c (4152/157) — 750

Table, games, D-shaped, mahogany, hinged open to smooth playing surface, 29 x 36 x 17, L18c (4239/150) — 550

Table, games, inlaid mahogany, rectangular top, square tapered legs, block feet, 29 x 35 x 17½, L18c (4079/52) — 750

Table, games, inlaid mahogany, semicircular, 29 x 36 x 17¾, L18c (4165/394) — 900

Table, games, inlaid mahogany, serpentine front, baize lined top, 28½ x 36 x 17½, L18c (4111/221) — 600

Table, games, inlaid mahogany, serpentine, 28½ x 36 x 17½, L18c (4165/349) — 1500

Table, games, inlaid mahogany, D-shaped, 28½ x 35½ x 17½, L18c (4152/133) — 850

Table, games, inlaid satinwood, canted corners, lined interior, 29 x 36 x 17 L18c (4134/315) — 1250

Table, games, mahogany, hinged top, drawer on side, 28 x 26 x 13¾, L18c (4111/95) — 350

Table, games, mahogany, hinged top, frieze drawer, square chamfered legs, 29 x 33½ x 14½, ca1770 (4272/170) — 600

Table, games, mahogany, hinged, rectangular, carved, edge, legs, square, 29 x 32½ x 15½, res, L18c (4159/309) — 450

Table, games, mahogany, rounded corners, candle recesses, money wells, 28 x 35½ x 17½, L18c (4111/88) — 2700

Table, games, mahogany, serpentine, 29 x 36 x 17½, L18c (4165/398) — 1000

Table, games, mahogany, serpentine, hinged top, tapered legs, 28½ x 36½, L18c (4165/325) — 1400

Table, games, mahogany, carved, serpentine, 28¼ x 32¼, L18c (4148/259) — 2200

Table, games, painted satinwood, semicircular, 30½ x 59½ x 39, L18c (4165/333) — 1700

Table, games, semicircular, mahogany, inlaid, hinged top, frieze drawer, square tapered legs, 30 x 47½ x 20, ca1790 (4239/256) — 1300

Table, games, serpentine, mahogany, hinged top and frieze on square molded legs, 29½ x 36 x 19, supports replaced, ca1790 (4239/257) — 750

Table, gate-leg, spider, mahogany, hinged, rectangular, turned legs, pad feet, 38½ x 29 x 8½, L18c (4159/308) — 500

Table, gate-leg, spider, mahogany, rectangular, turned legs, stretchers, top feet, 28 x 30 x 13, L18c (4159/314) — 1275

Table, gate-leg, spider, mahogany, top with 2 flaps, drawer, 26 x 27, ca1765 (4260/1349) — 950

Table, gate-leg, mahogany, 27½ x 39½ x 19, rep, L18c (4189/150) — 425

Table, hunt, mahogany, hinged oval top, gate-leg supports, 28½ x 95 x 56½, ca1770 (4260/1733) — 7500

Table, hunt, mahogany, hinged oval top, on gate-leg supports, 28½ x 73 x 45, res, ca1770 (4260/1363) — 2200

Table, hunt, mahogany, oval, 2 flaps, 8 legs, 28½ x 63 x 46½, rep, L18c (4260/1748) — 8000

Table, hunt, mahogany, oval, 2 shallow drop leaves, 28 x 91 x 59, 19c (4260/1739) — 3750

Table, hunt, mahogany, oval, 2 shallow leaves, 8 legs, 29 x 108 x 58, L18c (4260/1722) — 13000

Table, low, from butler's tray, pierced, hinged sides, 19 x 28 x 18, L18c (4165/265) — 575

Table, mahogany, folding extensions, 31 x 42 E19c (4134/293) — 1000

Table, occasional, inlaid mahogany, front with 2 drawers, ivory escutcheons, 30 x 17 x 13, ca1815 (4272/182) — 550

Table, occasional, inlaid satinwood, hinge lid, enclosing well, octagonal, 27 x 20½ x 14½, L18c (4239/307) — 650

Table, occasional, mahogany, small, 27½ x 23¾ x 17, L18c (4216/76) — 550

Table, octagonal, mahogany, ivory top, baluster stem, tripod legs, 25½ x 18½, res, L18c (4272/171) — 700

Table, oval, occasional, inlaid, mahogany, 29½ x 26½ x 17½, L18c (4216/77) — 650

Table, rent, mahogany, circular, leather inset, 12 drawers, 30½ x 55, ca1760 (4260/1750) — 32000

Table, rent, small, mahogany, leather inset, revolving circular top, 4 drawers, 30 x 34, E19c (4239/258) — *2000*

Table (4239/258)

Table, secretaire, inlaid mahogany, open compartment, enclosed front, 52 x 34 x 22½, ca1810 (4272/181) — 2900

Table, shell inlaid mahogany, hinged top, frieze, drawer square tapered legs, 27 x 29½ x 17½ L18c (4134/95) — 850

Table, side satinwood inlaid mahogany, D-shaped, 29 x 37 x 14½, L18c (4111/101) — 550

Table, side serpentine, fluted frieze on square tapered legs, 65 x 23 L18c (4134/163) — 800

Table, side, bow-front, inlaid mahogany, 2 false drawer fronts, center drawer, reeded legs, 37 x 66 x 25½, ca1790 (4239/262) — 1800

Table, side, inlaid mahogany, bow-front drawer on square tapered legs, 29 x 84 x 29, E18c (4111/205) — 3100

Table, side, mahogany, molded top 2 drawers, square tapered legs, 36 x 63 x 18 L18c (4134/94) — 500

Table, side, mahogany, serpentine front, square tapered legs, 28 x 52½ x 20, altered, ca1790 (4260/1337) — 1000

Table, side, marquetry and parquetry, inlaid, semicircular, tapered legs, 31½ x 52½ x 21, ca1790 (4239/315) — 1700

Table, side, semicircular, satinwood and mahogany, marquetry inlaid, square tapered legs, 33½ x 71½ x 19, L18c (4272/115) — 4000

Table, side, serpentine, carved mahogany, 34½ x 60½ x 28½, L18c (4189/147) — 2500

Table, sofa, inlaid mahogany, hinged top, 2 drawers, trestle support, 28 x 51 x 22, ca1810 (4260/1725) — 3600

Table, spider gate-leg, mahogany, hinged top, turned legs and stretcher, 26 x 30¼ x 12¼, L18c (4165/397) — 900

Table, spider gate-leg, mahogany, rectangular top, gate-leg supports, 27½ x 33½ x 11, restoration L18c (4079/145) — 500

Table, supper, tripod, mahogany, tilting top, bird cage support, 27½ x 27½, L18c (4165/400) — 1000

Table, tavern oak circular, 3 chamfered legs, 25 x 30 L18c (4134/104) — 250

Table, tea, carved mahogany, gallery missing, 27½ x 32½ x 22 M18c (4189/163) — 1200

Table, tea, mahogany, oblong top, deep gallery, snake feet, 28 x 24, L18c (4148/274) — 1150

Table, tilt-top tripod, circular dish top with molded border, 27½ x 19, L18c (4111/170) — 400

Table, tilt-top, tripod, mahogany, 30½ x 30, gallery replaced (4152/150) — 1200

Table, tilt-top, tripod, mahogany, circular top, 26 x 24, L18c (4079/55) — 750

Table, toilet, inlaid mahogany, toilet mirror in central compartment, 33 x 30 x 20, L18c (4189/155) — 1200

Table, trestle, mahogany, rectangular, rounded corners, trestle supports, 30 x 30 x 14, E19c (4260/1362) — 600

Table, tripod, mahogany, circular gallery top, S-scroll tripod legs, 30 x 18, L18c (4079/109) — 325

Table, tripod, mahogany, tilting top, bird cage supports, 29 x 22, L18c (4165/399) — 1400

Table, tripod, carved mahogany, gallery later, 27½ x 32½ M18c L18c (4216/166) — 400

Table, tripod, penwork decorated, rectangular top, canted corners, warrior, chariot, 24½ x 22½ x 16½, reduced, ca1810 (4239/298) — 700

Table, tripod, tilt-top mahogany, circular top, cabriole legs, pad feet, 26½ x 23 restoration, L18c (4079/116) — 500

Table, tripod, tilt-top, mahogany, circular, vase shape stem, pad feet, 28, Diam 23½, res, L18c (4159/252) — 450

Table, tripod, tilt-top, mahogany, circular, vase shape support, pad feet, H28, Diam 20, L18c (4159/276) — 275

Table, tripod, tilt-top, mahogany, rectangular, turned support, cabriole legs, 28 x 29½ x 22½, L18c (4159/312) — 700

Table, tripod, tilt-top, mahogany, shaped balustraded tilt-top, spiral supports, 28 x 27½, L18c (4239/294) — *1500*

Table, tripod, tilt-top, mahogany, shaped top, bird cage support, baluster stem, 27½ x 25, L18c (4159/251) — 1100

Table, work, leather inset top, 30 x 29½, E19c (4111/167) — 800

Table, work, inlaid mahogany, molded rectangular top, 2 drawers, square tapered legs, 27 x 19½ x 13¾, ca1800 (4239/350) — 800

Table, work, inlaid mahogany, rectangular top, end with drawer, above work basket, 27½ x 21 x 15¾, ca1820 (4239/110) — 200

Table, work, inlaid rosewood, end with fitted drawer, simulating 2 drawer fronts, 30 x 22 x 15, ca1800 (4239/319) — 1500

Table, work, inlaid satinwood, hinged adjustable reading surface, 29½ x 20 x 14½, L18c (4165/353) — 950

Table, work, mahogany, reeded rectangular hinged top, frieze drawer, 30 x 33 x 21½, E19c (4239/140) — 300

Table, writing, leather inset, reeded top, drawer, panelled doors, 30 x 49 x 25, ca1810 (4272/162) — 550

Table, writing, games, inlaid satinwood, divided folding top, fitted interior, leather inset, 30½ x 44 x 20, ca1790 (4272/123) — 2700

Table, writing, mahogany, green leather inset, 2 pedestals, 29½ x 47¾ x 23½ res L18c (4216/143) — 2000

Table, writing, mahogany unusual, hinged top encloses 3 wells, 29 x 35 x 14½, L18c (4189/178) — 750

Table, writing, inlaid satinwood and kingwood, kidney shaped, 30½ x 42 x 26, 19c (4134/283) — 2000

Table, writing, carved mahogany, leather inset top, pedestal, ea 3 drawers, frieze drawers, 30½ x 53 x 24½, E19c (4239/145) — *3200*

Table, writing, cylinder, painted and inlaid satinwood, fitted interior, 39½ x 35 x 21, E19c (4079/105) — 1600

Table, writing, inlaid mahogany, leather inset, concave fronted fitted frieze drawer, 32 x 60 x 31, ca1800 (4272/142) — 12000

Table, writing, inlaid mahogany and harewood, tambour, 33½ x 30 x 22, L18c (4216/87) — 2400

Table, writing, inlaid mahogany small, front with slide, drawer with inkwell, 28 x 29 x 20½, L18c (4111/190) — 1000

Table, writing, kneehole, mahogany, reeded rectangular leather inset top, 31 x 51 x 26, E19c (4239/132) — 1600

Table, writing, mahogany, inset leather top, frieze 2 drawers, 30 x 55 x 35, ca1770 (4260/1357) — 4500

Table, writing, mahogany, leather inset, 3 drawers, 32 x 38 x 25 - L18c (4134/301) — 1700

Table, writing, mahogany, leather inset top, 3 frieze drawers, 6 drawers, 28½ x 48 x 25½, E19c (4239/143) — 650

Table, writing, mahogany, leather inset, 2 drawers, tapered legs, 29 x 48 x 31½, ca1790 (4260/1740) — 10500

Table, writing, mahogany, leather inset, 2 pedestals, 3 drawers each, 29½ x 60½ x 38, E19c
(4239/316)   5000
Table, writing, mahogany, leather inset top, adjustable reading surface, 30 x 53 x 27½ L18c
(4134/287)   3400
Table, writing, mahogany, library steps enclosed in hinged top, 6' open L18c (4152/112)   2600
Table, writing, mahogany, semicircular, drawers, panelled doors, 29½ x 63 x 26, ca1800
(4260/1737)   6500
Table, writing, partner's, mahogany, green leather top, drawers front and back, 30½ x 59½ x 33½,
L18c (4165/332)   *4500*

Table (4165/332)

Table (4239/145)

Table (4239/294)

Table, writing, pedestal, mahogany, leather inset top, 6 drawers, 31 x 68 x 37 E19c (4134/356)   5000
Table, writing, pedestal, mahogany, leather inset, 6 drawers on raised plinth, 29½ x 48 x 26½, 19c
(4272/135)   1700
Table, writing, pedestal, mahogany, leather inset, 3 drawers each pedestal, 31 x 49½ x 28, E19c
(4239/325)   3000
Table, Pembroke, inlaid harewood, oval, 28½ x 28 x 18½, L18c (4189/164)   6750
Table, Pembroke, inlaid mahogany, 28½ x 31 x 19, L18c (4189/169)   1100
Table, Pembroke, inlaid mahogany, 27 x 30 x 18½, L18c (4216/91)   900
Table, Pembroke, inlaid mahogany, oval inlaid top, frieze drawer, square legs, 28½ x 28 x 17, legs
rep, ca1790 (4239/130)   900
Table, Pembroke, oval inlaid mahogany, frieze drawer on square tapered legs, 28 x 30 x 18½ L18c
(4134/167)   950
Table, Pembroke, carved mahogany, hinged top, frieze drawer, chamfered legs, 28 x 29 x 20, ca1760
(4260/1384)   3250
Table, Pembroke, fruitwood, hinged top, drawer, square tapered legs, 28 x 29 x 17¼, L18c (4111/62)   600
Table, Pembroke, inlaid mahogany, 28½ x 24 x 19, L18c (4216/88)   850
Table, Pembroke, inlaid mahogany, 27½ x 31½ x 19½, L18c (4216/145)   700
Table, Pembroke, inlaid mahogany, hinged oval top, bow-front drawer, 28½ x 39½ x 32, L18c
(4165/347)   2300
Table, Pembroke, inlaid mahogany, hinged reeded top, frieze drawer, square tapered legs, 27½ x
29½ x 18, ca1800 (4239/266)   550
Table, Pembroke, inlaid mahogany, hinged serpentine shaped top drawer, 27½ x 29½ x 20½, L18c
(4111/191)   900
Table, Pembroke, inlaid mahogany, hinged top, frieze drawer, square tapered legs, 28 x 30 x 19½,
ca1790 (4239/138)   500
Table, Pembroke, inlaid mahogany, hinged top, frieze drawers, square tapered legs, 28½ x 44 x 25,
drawer relined, ca1790 (4239/85)   800
Table, Pembroke, inlaid mahogany, oval top, turned legs, 27 x 31, L18c (4079/56)   550
Table, Pembroke, inlaid satinwood, hinged oval top, drawer, square tapered legs, 27 x 31½ x 21½,
L18c (4159/258)   2600
Table, Pembroke, inlaid satinwood, hinged top, drawer square tapered legs, 29½ x 31 x 39½, L18c
(4165/341)   4000
Table, Pembroke, mahogany, 27½ x 33 x 23½, L18c (4216/75)   500
Table, Pembroke, mahogany, drawer square tapered legs, 38 x 31 x 19½ L18c (4134/313)   600

Table, Pembroke, mahogany, hinged top, drawer at end, square tapered legs, 28½ x 32 x 21, ca1790 (4272/163) 750
Table, Pembroke, mahogany, hinged top, drawer, square tapered legs, 28 x 20½ x 24, L18c (4159/328) 650
Table, Pembroke, mahogany, hinged top, frieze drawers, ring turned legs, 28½ x 36 x 20, ca1820 (4239/323) 400
Table, Pembroke, mahogany, oval top, bow-front, frieze drawer, tapered legs, 28 x 32 x 19, ca1790 (4272/133) 850
Table, Pembroke, mahogany, serpentine, drawer, square legs, X-stretcher, 28½ x 20 x 29, L18c (4159/332) 1600
Table, Pembroke, mahogany, D-shaped, 1 end with drawer, 27½ x 30, L18c (4111/166) 3100
Table, Pembroke, oval, mahogany, drawer, square tapered legs, 27½ x 21 x 28, L18c (4159/293) 1000
Table, Pembroke, serpentine mahogany, shaped top, frieze drawer, chamfered legs, 27 x 30 x 22, ca1770 (4272/189) 850
Table, 3 pedestal, mahogany, reeded top, turned supports, tripod legs, 28½ x 96 x 52½, E19c (4272/176) 4800
Tables, side, inlaid mahogany, semicircular, 33½ x 44½ x 21, L18c (4165/334) 5800
Tables, side, pair, shell inlaid, mahogany, D-shaped, 30 x 6 x 12½ L18c (4134/288) 2200
Tables, side, pair, D-shaped mahogany, leaf carved border, bell, and flower pendant, 31½ x 41 x 20 (4134/111) 600
Tea caddy, burr yewwood, hinged domed lid, interior 2 removable canisters, 12, ca1790 (4239/199) 150
Tea caddy, inlaid harewood, 2 lidded compartments, inlaid shells, 5½ x 9¼, L18c (4111/53) 325
Tea caddy, inlaid mahogany, hinged lid, ivory escutcheon, 4½ x 5, L18c (4111/40) 100
Tea caddy, inlaid satinwood, domed top, inlaid with ovals, animals and leaves, 5½ x 7¼, L18c (4079/12) 200
Tea caddy, inlaid satinwood, hinged lid, 2 removable lidded compartments, W10, L18c (4111/11) 225
Tea caddy, inlaid satinwood, 2 removable lidded compartments, 6½ x 9, L18c (4134/209) 200
Tea caddy, mahogany, 6¾ x 10, M18c (4189/44) 150
Tea caddy, mahogany, compartmented interior, 12¼, 18c (4149/89) 160
Tea caddy, mahogany, inlaid, satinwood, small, 4¼ wide L18c (4216/11) 150
Tea caddy, marquetry, inlaid mahogany, rectangular form with canted sides, hinged lid, 7, ca1790 (4239/190) 250
Tea caddy, octagonal, shell inlaid, harewood, 5½, L18c (4152/35) 400
Tea caddy, oval, inlaid harewood, marquetry, 5 x 7¼, ca1790 (4239/184) 350
Tea caddy, oval, shell inlaid, satinwood, 5¼ L18c (4152/34) 200
Tea caddy, oval, silver mt. tortoiseshell, hinged lid, bun feet, 8½, ca1790 (4272/17) 425
Tea caddy, rectangular tortoiseshell, hinged lid, enclosing 2 lidded compartments, 10, E19c (4272/18) 300
Tea caddy, rectangular, shell, inlaid satinwood, 5, L18c (4152/25) 300
Tea caddy, shell inlaid mahogany, octgonal, 5 x 5 L18c (4134/214) 300
Tea caddy, silver mounted and tortoiseshell inlaid octagonal ivory, medallion, ca1790 (4272/26) 750
Tea caddy, silver mounted, inlaid, tortoiseshell, 5¼, L18c (4152/33) 500
Tea caddy, stepped hinged top, bail handle, bracket feet, 5 x 8¼, L18c (4079/16) 125
Tray, butler's, mahogany, rectangular form, pierced sides with handles, 27½ x 21½, E19c (4239/198) 225
Tray, butler's, on stand, carved mahogany, carrying handles, 35 x 32½ x 18, E19c (4260/1343) 900
Tray, coaching and stand, mahogany, carved and pierced, 29 x 14½, ca1790 (4260/1380) 1200
Tray, now as low table, mahogany, full gallery, tapered legs, 22½ x 20½, L18c (4239/346) 425
Tray, oval, mahogany, full gallery, shaped handles, fan medallion, L29, L18c (4111/7) 325
Tray, oval, mahogany, now table, inlaid and brass bound, gallery, 19½ x 32 x 23, ca1780 (4260/1731) 1900
Tray, oval, mahogany, scroll handle, brass bound gallery, now on stand, 20 x 36, ca1765 (4260/1368) 2800
Tray, oval, now as low table, mahogany, full gallery, brass handles, square tapered legs, L18c (4239/340) 250
Tray, oval, shell inlaid mahogany, shaped gallery and brass handles, 28½, L18c (4079/32) 350
Tray, shell inlaid mahogany, oval with full gallery, 23, L18c (4079/17) 100
Wardrobe, mahogany, 2 parts, pair panelled doors, 3 drawers, 72 x 49½ x 23½ , E19c (4239/124) 750
Wardrobe chest of drawers, inlaid mahogany, bow-front, pair shell inlaid doors, 5 drawers, 85½ x 50 x 20, res, L18c (4239/100) 1300
Window seat, mahogany, upholstered armrests and seat, 52½ L18c (4165/327) 1400
Wine cistern on stand, mahogany, brass bound, now with oval top, 20½ x 38 x 26, ca1800 (4260/1379) 1000
Wine cistern, mahogany, oval, brass carrying handles, brass bound body, 25½ x 23, ca1765 (4260/1359) 1900
Wine cooler, mahogany, oval, brass bound, brass handles, 26 x 22, ca1780 (4260/1728) 1900
Wine cooler, octagonal, inlaid mahogany, brass turned, 26 x 18¼, L18c (4152/144) 1000
Wine pedestal, brass and mahogany, 2 parts, bucket with lid, lower with drawer, 48½ x 16½ x 16½, ca1780 (4260/1734) 2900

Writing desk, mahogany, cylinder-top, brass handles, square tapering legs, 39¾ x 40¼, L18c (4149/232) — 1500

Regency

Armchair, child's, Regency, mahogany, H34¾, E19c (4076/974) — 300
Armchair, painted black, E19c (4216/78) — 500
Armchair, inlaid mahogany, panelled top rail, E19c (4152/166) — 200
Armchair, library steps, mahogany, solid seat, folding with 4 steps, E19c (4165/385) — 2000

Breakfront
(4079/164)

Cabinet
(4165/378)

Armchair, painted, backrest, pierced trellis splat caned seat, E19c (4111/169) — 350
Armchairs, pair, painted and grained, block and turned top rail, caned seat, turned legs, decoration later, E19c (4239/334) — 1300
Armchairs, pair, mahogany, panelled top rail, reeded armrests, upholstered, res, E19c (4111/194) — 900
Armchairs, pair, mahogany, serpentine front upholster, E19c (4134/345) — 525
Armchairs, pair, gilt decorated, black painted, E19c (4134/331) — 1600
Armchairs, pair, inlaid mahogany, panelled top rail, scrolled armrests, E19c (4111/135) — 1000
Armchairs, pair, painted, decorated, ca1815 (4148/280) — 1400
Armchairs, stencil decorated, black painted, E19c (4189/142) — 1900
Bookcase, rosewood, brass inlaid, top with brass inset border, 37¼ x 25 x 13, L19c (4219/163) — 400
Bookcase, secretaire, mahogany, pair glazed doors, secretaire drawer, 3 drawers, 92½ x 45 x 21, E19c (4159/348) — 3000
Bookcase cabinet, black painted, 2 sections, 3 open shelves, panel doors, 65 x 32 x 12 (4239/309) — 450
Bookshelf, concave, brass inlaid rosewood, 3 quarter, gallery, adjustable shelves, 34½ x 31 x 11½, E19c (4079/169) — 650
Bookshelves, open pair, pine, 3 graduated compartments, trimmed in lime green, 36 x 19½ x 9, E19c (4272/205) — 500
Breakfront, bookcase, inlaid mahogany, secretaire drawer, 3 drawers, 96 x 48½ x 24, E19c (4079/164) — *1400*
Breakfront, inlaid mahogany, 4 glass doors, 4 panelled doors, 89 x 76½ x 21, E19c (4165/380) — 3100
Buckets, pair, brass bound mahogany, bail handler, removable liner, 19 E19c (4134/223) — 1500
Bureau, cylinder lap, sloping front, fitted interior, 31½ x 18 x 11¾, E19c (4079/174) — 275
Cabinet, bookcase, gilt metal, rosewood, 2 open shelves, grill-work doors, 60 x 36 x 14, E19c (4165/378) — *850*
Cabinet, bookcase, mahogany, 3 glazed doors over 3 panelled doors, 89 x 60½ x 18, E19c (4152/433) — 3100
Cabinet, bookcase, open, grillwork doors, inlaid mahogany, 69 x 36 x 12, E19c (4189/229) — 1200
Cabinet, bookshelf, mahogany painted, 3 graduated shelves above cupboard, 50½ x 20 x 11½ E19c (4134/343) — 325
Cabinet, dwarf, inlaid rosewood, rectangular form with adjustable shelf, 28½ x 42 x 11, ca1810 (4239/40) — 400
Cabinet, hanging inlaid mahogany, 3 quarter gallery, 27½ x 48, E19c (4216/205) — 900
Cabinet, side, gilt metal mounted rosewood, breakfront form, 36 x 61 x 17¾ E19c (4134/155) — 1300

Cabinet, side, lacquer and gilt, decorated black painted, 36½ x 36½ x 11¾, E19c (4216/89) — 450
Cabinet, side, brass mounted, carved rosewood, 63 x 90 x 14, M19c (4216/192) — 900
Cabinet, side, brass mounted rosewood, marble top above pair of cupboard doors, E19c (4165/363) — 1000
Cabinet, side, ebonized columns, mahogany, grillwork doors, 61 x 34½ x 13, E19c (4189/230) — 650
Cabinet, side, gilt decorated rosewood, marble top, 3 doors, 46 x 92 x 18½, E19c (4111/184) — 4500
Cabinet, side, gilt metal mounted, rosewood, bow-front, 36 x 72 x 23, E19c (4079/155) — 800
Cabinet, side, inlaid mahogany, serpentine top, 35½ x 59 x 26, E19c (4216/189) — 650
Cabinet, side, painted and gilded, pair drawers above grillwork doors, 32½ x 42 x 16½, E19c (4111/196) — 1700
Cabinet, side, rosewood, concave front, 4 drawers, 4 grillwork doors, 37 x 89½ x 16, E19c (4272/211) — 2400
Cabinet, side, rosewood, gilt dec, gilt metal, marble top, 3 grillwork cupboard doors, 34½ x 61½ x 18½, ca1820 (4239/332) — 2200
Cabinet, vitrine, carved mahogany, semicircular, glazed front, 4 shelves, 108 x 33 x 16½, res, ca1825 (4260/1762) — 12000
Cabinet, writing, inlaid mahogany, 3 quarter gallery, pigeon holes, 49½ x 45 x 22½ E19c (4134/153) — 1800
Canterbury, mahogany, 5 slatted divisions, 21½ x 24 E19c (4134/326) — 525
Canterbury, turned and inlaid mahogany, L17½, E19c (4149/272) — 575
Canterbury, 4 dividers, drawer, mahogany, H17½, E19c (4156/200) — 400
Cellaret inlaid mahogany, sarcophagus, shaped, 21 x 27 x 22 feet later (4134/359) — 400
Cellaret on stand, oval brass bound, hinged top, fitted interior, lion mask handles, 28 x 25½ x 19 E19c (4134/144) — 700
Chair, hall, gilt metal mounted, mahogany, backrest arched with lion mask, rings, E19c (4152/180) — *450*
Chair, invalid's, caned mahogany, tub shaped backrest and sides, padded armrests, ca1815 (4239/341) — *500*
Chair, master's, inlaid mahogany, carved with Prince of Wales plume, E19c (4152/186) — *1500*

Chair (4152/180)   Chair (4239/341)   Chair (4152/186)   Secretaire cabinet (4134/147)

Chair, piano, rosewood, solid top rail, pierced lyre splat, upholstered seat, ca1820 (4272/226) — 950
Chair, side, inlaid mahogany, rosewood, ring-turned legs, E19c (4152/188) — 50
Chair, side, mahogany, solid top rail, upholstered, E19c (4111/183) — 100
Chair, tub, gilt decorated, black painted upholstered backrest, E19c (4189/235) — 1400
Chair, tub, gilt decorated, painted black, spindled backrest, E19c (4189/236) — 1300
Chairs, dining, set of 6, carved rosewood, L19c (4189/231) — 1700
Chairs, dining, mahogany set seven, one armchair, upholstered seats, E19c (4134/361) — 800
Chairs, dining, set 4, rosewood, mahogany, 1 armchair, scrolled armrests, panelled top rail, ca1810 (4272/212) — 1200
Chairs, dining, set of eight, beechwood, bamboo turned, L19c (4189/141) — 2700
Chairs, dining, set of eight, mahogany, 2 armchairs, with downswept armrest, ca1810 (4272/221) — 2900
Chairs, dining, set of 6, fruitwood, E19c (4152/173) — 1400
Chairs, dining, set of 6, mahogany, brass inlaid, upholstered, E19c (4134/337) — 1400
Chairs, dining, set of 6, mahogany, scrolled panelled top rail, drop in seat, E19c (4111/136) — 2000

Chairs, dining, set of 7, mahogany, 1 armchair, ring turned supports, E19c (4239/310) — 1400
Chairs, hall, pair, waisted backs, inlaid with ebony and painted, ca1815 (4260/1758) — 800
Chairs, set of 4, gilt decorated, black painted, formerly cane seats, L19c (4111/130) — 550
Chairs, set of 4, painted, including 2 armchairs, pierced backs, upholstered, E19c (4239/165) — 1200
Chairs, side, gilt metal mounted, black, painted, caned seat and sabre legs, E19c (4079/171) — 300
Chairs, side, pair, beechwood, turned top rail, drop in seat, E19c (4079/167) — 100
Chairs, side, pair, inlaid mahogany, panelled top rail, solid crossbar, sabre legs, ca1810 (4239/339) — 250
Chairs, side, pair, mahogany, panelled top rail, flower carved crossbar, ca1810 (4272/213) — 325
Chairs, side, pair, painted, open backrest, horizontal splat, E19c (4219/106) — 450
Chairs, side, set of 3, painted, turned toprail, pierced crossbars, caned seat, sabre legs, E19c (41594/358) — 550
Chest, secretaire, campaign, thuyuwood, 2 sections, 42½ x 36 x 18½, E19c (4165/381) — 3900
Chest of drawers, secretaire, small, brass inlaid padouk wood, 34 x 28½ x 15, E19c (4189/218) — 2200
Chest on chest, inlaid mahogany, stained pine, 72 x 45 x 21, E19c (4152/202) — 650
Curtain poles, pair painted with geometric designs, 85, M19c (4189/57) — 300
Daybed, gilt metal, mounted caned and, stained pine, upholstered, sabre legs, 82, ca1815 (4272/218) — 500
Dining, chairs, set of 6, mahogany, open backrest, X shaped splat, E19c (4219/124) — 2300
Dining table, extension, mahogany, drop eaves with rounded corners, 27¾ x 47½ x 96, E19c (4219/123) — 1700
Jardiniere, mahogany brass bound, lead lined interior on stand, 22 x 24½ x 16½ E19c (4134/143) — 900
Jardiniere, mahogany, brass bound, oval, 21 x 26½, E19c (4189/234) — 900
Library steps, rosewood, 3 leather treads, 2 with compartments, 24 x 28½, res, E19c (4111/197) — 700
Mirror, over mantel, verre eglomise, decorated, oval, 34 x 46½, E19c (4165/281) — 800
Mirror, carved gilt wood, bevelled rectangular plate, cluster column borders, 47 x 28, ca1815 (4272/50) — 500
Mirror, convex gilt wood, reeded, ebonized and ball hung borders, carved apron, 43 x 34, ca1825 (4239/209) — 1200
Mirror, convex gilt wood, reeded, ebonized, and ball hung borders, scrolling apron, 54 x 38, ca1825 (4239/208) — 1100
Mirror, convex, gilt wood, circular plate, 36 x 23 E19c (4134/23) — 300
Mirror, convex, gilt wood, circular, reeded, ball-hung molded border, Diam 26, E19c (4159/202) — 500
Mirror, convex, gilt wood, ebonized, ball hung borders, eagle cresting carved apron, 43 x 26, E19c (4272/53) — 500
Mirror, convex, gilt wood, reeded, ebonized and molded ball hung borders, 37 x 23½, E19c (4272/52) — 400
Mirror, gilt wood, rectangular, reeded border, inverted corners, 26 x 15, E19c (4079/37) — 175
Mirror, gilt wood, rectangular, split-baluster sides, carved frieze, 43 x 28, E19c (4159/207) — 375
Mirror, gilt wood convex, eagle cresting, 34 E19c (4152/61) — 650
Mirror, overmantel, carved gilt gesso, triple divided plate, flanked by Egyptian figures, 36 x 57, E19c (4239/18) — 350
Mirror, painted and gilt wood, 50, E19c (4152/58) — 800
Mirror, painted and parcel-gilt, oval, foliate border on green ground, 38½ x 23¼, E19c (4232/67) — 375
Mirror, verre eglomise decorated, gilt wood, 41½, E19c (4152/56) — 500
Mirror, verre eglomise inset, gilt wood, 39 x 16½, E19c (4189/52) — 200
Mirrors, pair oval gilt wood, ball hung molded oval borders, 35, E19c (4152/50) — 1100
Mirrors pier, gilt wood painted and verre eglomise, pair, 62 x 21, E19c (4134/22) — 1600
Pail, oval, brass bound mahogany, loop handle, 13, E19c (4111/14) — 450
Seat, window, grained rosewood X-form, scrolled upholstered ends and seat, L38, E19c (4189/214) — 1300
Secretaire, brass inlaid, rosewood, pair grill work doors, pigeon holes, drawers, 80 x 45 x 23, ca1825 (4239/312) — 2000
Secretaire bookcase, mahogany, 2 section, shelves and drawers, 84½ x 36½ x 21, E19c (4165/375) — 2800
Secretaire cabinet, inlaid mahogany, glazed door, drawer, lower cupboard doors, 68 x 37 x 19, E19,c (4134/147) — *2600*
Secretaire chest of drawers, inlaid mahogany, 42 x 41 x 22½, E19c (4216/194) — 850
Secretary bookcase, ebony, mahogany, 2 parts, glazed doors, cupboard, drawers, 100 x 51 x 23½, ca1810 (4272/224) — 4600
Secretary bookcase, inlaid mahogany, pair glazed doors, fitted secretaire drawer, 87 x 43 x 21½ E19c (4134/55) — 1900
Settees, pair, 4 chair back, beechwood, turned top rail, X-form slats, bow-front, caned seat, 70, res, ca1810 (4239/337) — 1500
Sideboard, carved mahogany, 36½ x 68 x 26, M19c (4216/193) — 800
Sideboard, inlaid mahogany, sepentine, drawer, arched apron, turned legs, 37½ x 72 x 29, E19c (4159/356) — 2800
Sideboard, inlaid mahogany, 3 frieze drawers, cast-iron paw feet, 38 x 49 x 23, E19c (4152/187) — 1600
Sideboard, mahogany, bow-front, 4 drawers, 37 x 43 x 25, E19c (4165/371) — 1100
Sideboard, mahogany bow-front, front with drawer, shaped apron, 31½ x 48 x 23 E19c (4134/182) — 700

Sofa, mahogany, curved backrest, scrolled armrest, 82, E19c (4079/159)   650
Stand, reading, inlaid mahogany, adjustable top, 29 x 23½ x 18½, E19c (4079/162)   550
Stand, music, bone inlaid brass, mahogany, 52, E19c (4152/84)   1600
Table, breakfast, oval, mahogany, tilting, top, flared column support, 27½ x 61 x 46½ E19c
  (4134/56)   1900
Table, breakfast, circular tilting top, tripod legs, 30 x 48, E19c (4079/156)   1500
Table, breakfast, folding, brass, inlaid mahogany, swiveling top, 28 x 53 x 42½, E19c (4189/226)   1300
Table, breakfast, inlaid mahogany, circular, tilting top, 28½ x 43, E19c (4165/382)   1300
Table, breakfast, inlaid mahogany, rectangular top, tripod legs, 28 x 40½ x 34½, E19c (4079/170)   950
Table, breakfast, inlaid mahogany, rectangular, burr elm cross-banded top, 27 x 83½ x 38, E19c
  (4111/201)   1800
Table, breakfast, inlaid rosewood, painted and gilded, 28½ x 60 x 35, E19c (4111/195)   1800
Table, breakfast, inlaid rosewood, tilting top, 28 x 58 x 42 E19c (4134/322)   950
Table, breakfast, mahogany, tilt-top, 28 x 59 x 43 E19c (4134/275)   550
Table, breakfast, mahogany, tilting top, ring turned supports, 28½ x 40½ x 45 (4165/376)   200
Table, breakfast, mahogany, oval, reeded oval tilting top, 28 x 60 x 47½ (4111/185)   350
Table, breakfast, oval, inlaid mahogany, 28 x 53 x 41, E19c (4152/174)   1300
Table, breakfast, oval, mahogany, reeded tilting top, 28 x 60 x 47½ (4189/225)   350
Table, breakfast, rectangular, calamander wood inlaid mahogany, 28 x 48 x 35, E19c (4216/213)   2100
Table, center, calamander wood, circular, flared, support, downswept legs, 28½ x 46, E19c
  (4111/134)   1800
Table, dining D-end carved mahogany, with central drop-leaf section, 28½ x 107 x 40, ca1815
  (4216/184)   950
Table, dining, inlaid mahogany, circular hinged top, 28½ x 59, E19c (4111/210)   4250
Table, dining, inlaid mahogany, 2 pedestal oval cross banded top 3 add. leaves, 29 x 132 x 51, E19c
  (4111/204)   2500
Table, dining, mahogany, 3 pedestal, 2 additional leaves, 28½ x 126½ x 48, E19c (4111/198)   1700
Table, dining, mahogany, 2 pedestal, 28½ x 94 x 54½, E19c (4165/362)   2300
Table, dining, mahogany 2 pedestal, cross banded rectangular top, turned supports, 27 x 115 x 50½
  (4134/175)   900
Table, dining, 2 pedestal mahogany, reeded edges and rounded ends, 28 x 118 x 45, E19c
  (4111/103)   2750
Table, dining, 2 pedestal, mahogany, reeded edge, flared supports, tripod legs, 27½ x 119 x 50, E19c
  (4079/53)   1200
Table, dining, 3 pedestal, mahogany, reeded top, downswept legs, brass casters, 28 x 60, 19c
  (4272/216)   4000
Table, drop-leaf, mahogany, 29 x 45½ x 22½, M19c (4152/192)   400
Table, drop-leaf, pedestal, mahogany, 29 x 36 x 35½, E19C (4216/191)   225
Table, drum, mahogany, circular, green leather inset tripod legs, 29½ x 35 E19c (4134/157)   *1800*

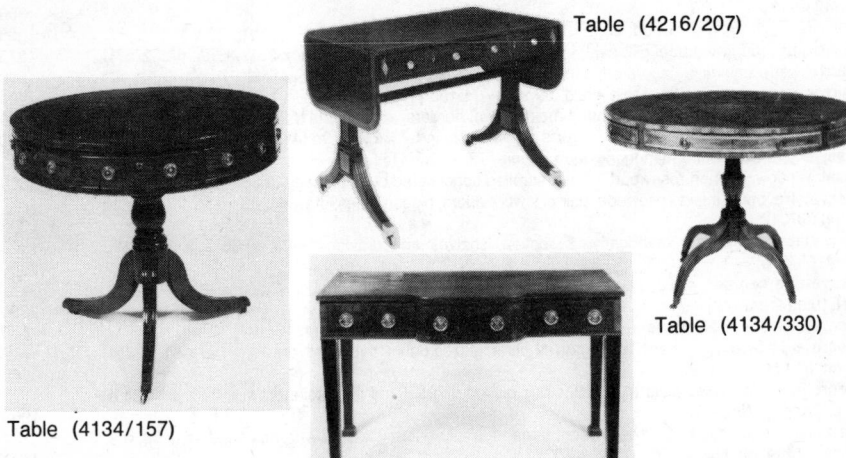

Table (4216/207)

Table (4134/330)

Table (4134/157)

Table (4189/219)

Table, drum, mahogany, circular, leather inset top, 29 x 41 E19c (4134/347)   850
Table, drum, mahogany 'small', circular, leather inset revolving top, 29 x 28½ E19c (4134/174)   850

Table, drum, inlaid mahogany, circular revolving top, leather inset, drawers, 28½ x 38½, E19c (4239/168)	1700
Table, drum, inlaid mahogany, circular, 4 drawers, octagonal support, 21½, Diam 4½, E19c (4159/342)	2500
Table, drum, inlaid rosewood, small, circular top, 4 frieze drawers, 28 E19c (4134/329)	1200
Table, extending, mahogany, divided top, rounded, turned gate-leg trestle, supports, 28 x 98 x 51½, E19c (4159/339)	750
Table, games, brass inlaid rosewood, hinged swivelling top, 30½ x 36 x 17¾ E19c (4134/341)	300
Table, games, brass, ebony inlaid rosewood, green baize-lined top, 28½ x 36 x 17½, E19c (4152/191)	1100
Table, games, calamander, inlaid mahogany, hinged top, 29¼ x 36 x 17¾, E19c (4216/208)	1000
Table, games, calamander wood, hinged top, writing surface, 28½ x 36 x 18, E19c (4111/133)	700
Table, games, inlaid mahogany, U-shaped support, 28 x 35½ x 18, E19c (4111/143)	350
Table, games, inlaid mahogany D-shaped, hinged baize lined top, 28 x 36 x 17½ E19c (4134/333)	350
Table, games, inlaid mahogany, bow-front, polished interior, 30 x 36 x 17½ E19c (4134/54)	300
Table, gentlemen's dressing, adjustable mirror and basin aperture, 36 x 22 x 20, E19c (4165/377)	175
Table, library, brass mounted rosewood, oblong top, lyre supports, 31½ x 43, E19c (4165/365)	3100
Table, library, oval inlaid mahogany, leather inset top 4 drawers, 30 x 42 x 32½ E19c (4134/330)	*1700*
Table, occasional, Pembroke, inlaid mahogany, 28½ x 19½ x 20, E19c (4189/238)	1600
Table, occasional, small, inlaid, mahogany, 28 x 27 x 13¼, E19c (4189/217)	900
Table, rosewood game, sliding games panel, 28¼ x 42 x 18, E19c (4219/144)	1400
Table, side mahogany, cross-banded, 2 drawers, ring turned tapered legs, 31 x 42 x 21 E19c (4134/178)	500
Table, side, brass inlaid, rosewood, top with three quarter gallery, mirrored back, 48½ x 39 x 12½, ca1820 (4272/229)	2100
Table, side, gilt metal, mounted, gilt, dec rosewood, top on reeded, flower carved supports, 36½ x 35 x 14, ca1820 (4272/210)	750
Table, side, inlaid, carved mahogany, projecting bow-front frieze drawer, 35 x 59 x 26½, E19c (4189/219)	*2400*
Table, side, mahogany, bow-front, 2 drawers, 30 x 51½ x 29, E19c (4111/186)	1100
Table, sofa, brass inlaid, mahogany, lyre-form supports, 28½ x 37 x 24, E19c (4189/228)	1500
Table, sofa, ebony inlaid mahogany, divided top, 2 drawers, 28 x 36 x 26½, E19c (4165/406)	1100
Table, sofa, inlaid mahogany, 28¼ x 38 x 25¾, E19c (4216/207)	*1750*
Table, sofa, inlaid mahogany, amboyna wood, cross-banded hinged top, 29 x 39 28½, E19c (4189/208)	2500
Table, sofa, inlaid mahogany, hinged top, 2 drawers, trestle supports, 28 x 39½ x 32, E19c (4159/355)	1050
Table, sofa, inlaid mahogany, hinged top, 2 drawers, trestle supports, 28 x 37 x 26, E19c (4165/411)	2100
Table, sofa, inlaid mahogany, top with flap each side, 2 frieze drawers, 27½ x 32 x 28, ca1810 (4239/335)	1300
Table, sofa, inlaid satinwood, 2 frieze drawers, 28 x 35 x 27, E19c (4189/209)	3000
Table, sofa, mahogany, hinged top above 2 frieze drawers, 29 x 39½ x 27, E19c (4152/177)	950
Table, sofa, satinwood, rectangular top, frieze drawer, bun feet, 28½ x 36 x 22¾, E19c (4219/132)	1300
Table, tilt-top, tripod, penwork decorated, simulated rosewood, adjustable top, 27½ x 15¾ x 12½, E19c (4079/166)	550
Table, toilet, inlaid mahogany, enclosed lidded compartments, 33½ x 46 x 20 E19c (4134/148)	475
Table, tripod black japanned, gilt and red, chinoiserie figures, 27 x 16 x 15, dec. restored (4134/346)	225
Table, work, brass inlaid mahogany, fitted interior, lyre form supports, 29½ x 18½ x 15, E19c (4079/158)	375
Table, work, inlaid mahogany, drawer at each end, 30 x 23 x 16½, E19c (4152/179)	500
Table, writing, brass inlaid risewood, 2 drawers, testle supports, 28½ x 48 x 27 E19c (4134/149)	2400
Table, writing, cylinder inlaid, 3 quarter pierced gallery, 42½ x 39½ x 24 E19c (4134/335)	1300
Table, writing, gilt metal mounted, amboyna and ebony inlaid rosewood, 29 x 45 x 23½, E19c (4189/239)	9250
Table, writing, inlaid mahogany, rectangular, 2 drawers, turned legs, 29½ x 44 x 22, E19c (4159/345)	475
Table, writing, pedestal mahogany, leather inset, 9 drawers, 30 x 48 x 26 E19c (4134/362)	1800
Table, writing, pedestal, mahogany, leather inset, 3 drawers each pedestal, 30 x 48, E19c (4239/161)	1100
Table, writing, rosewood, gold leather inset, 30 x 48 x 34, E19c (4152/201)	1400
Table, writing, small inlaid mahogany, sliding top, inset leather compartments, 29 x 33 x 18, E19c (4189/227)	1400
Table, writing, trestle, mahogany, 2 frieze drawers, brass paw casters, 28 x 45 x 23½, E19c (4189/222)	2700
Table, Pembroke, inlaid mahogany, hinged top, drawer, ring turned legs, 28 x 33 x 19, E19c (4165/373)	325
Table, Pembroke, inlaid mahogany, pedestal, quadruple downswept legs, 28 x 29 x 19½, E19c (4111/105)	650
Table, Pembroke, large pedestal, inlaid rosewood, 28½ x 42 x 24, E19c (4152/163)	950
Table, Pembroke, mahogany, hinged top, drawer ring turned legs, 28 x 32 x 17 E19c (4134/334)	275

Table, Pembroke, pedestal, inlaid mahogany, 30 x 24 x 15¼, E19c (4152/178) 550
Table, Pembroke, pedestal mahogany, frieze drawer on a baluster stem, 29 x 36 x 20, E19c
(4134/176) 600
Table, Pembroke, pedestal, parquetry, inlaid, mahogany 2 drawers, 28 x 30 x 20½, E19c (4134/360) 2600
Table, Pembroke, trestle, mahogany, hinged top, drawer on lyre form supports, 29 x 20½ x 18, E19c
(4111/109) 800
Tables, games, brass, inlaid rosewood, pair, lyre supports, 29½ x 36 x 17½, E19c (4111/131) 2000
Tables, side, pair, gilt metal mounted, green marble, top mirrored, back, 36 x 29½ x 12¾, E19c
(4079/172) 1400
Tea caddy, applewood, hinged lid, round, 4, E19c (4079/40) 275
Tea caddy, inlaid rosewood, hinged domed lid, 7 x 12, E19c (4159/201) 250
Tea caddy, sarcophagus shape, inlaid, rosewood, 2 lidded compartments, 5 x 8 E19c (4079/21) 125
Tea caddy, sarcophagus shape, painted and inlaid mahogany, 9½, E19c (4189/56) 150
Tea poy, inlaid mahogany, sarcophagus form, hinged lid, enclosing canisters, 27 x 18 x 12, ca1815
(4272/228) 800
Torcheres, pair, padouk, calamander wood, gadrooned top, tripod turned legs, 49½ x 15½, ca1815
(4239/333) 7750
Urn, knife, inlaid mahogany, 28½ interior removed E19c (4189/50) 350
Vitrine, gilt metal, mounted, grained, rosewood small sarcophagus form, 16½ x 18½ E19c
(4134/230) 225
Wardrobe, carved mahogany, drawers and shelves enclosed, 75½ x 76 x 22½, E19c (4216/187) 1100
Window seat, gilt dec simulated rosewood, upholstered seat, X form legs, ball feet, 23, ca1810
(4239/354) 400
Wine cooler, brass bound mahogany, oval, interior, removable metal liner, 21½ x 24, E19c
(4165/367) *3750*
Wine cooler, sarcophagus shape carved mahogany, 21½ x 26½ x 19, E19c (4216/180) 900
Writing table, inlaid calamander wood, ebonized, 2 drawers, lyre trestle, 82½ x 39 x 22½, ca1815
(4239/358) 7750
Writing table, mounted brass, inlaid mahogany, hinged top, 36 x 36 x 25½, E19c (4216/183) 2500

Country

Armchairs, pair, Windsor, burr yewwood and, burr elmwood, yoke rail, solid seat, M18c (4260/1694) 25000
Settee, triple back, Windsor Gothic, yewwood, elmwood and beechwood, solid seat, 65, res, L18c
(4260/1702) 20000

Neoclassical

Cupboard, tambour fronted, mahogany, rectangular top, canted corners, pair panelled doors, 31 x 31
x 16½, L18c (4239/356) 350

William IV

Bergere, caned mahogany, tub form, E19c (4111/150) 800
Breakfront, bookcases, mahogany, open shelves, 3 cupboards, 116 x 153 x 19, ca1835
(4260/1760) 16000
Cabinet, breakfront, side, rosewood, pierced gallery, 38 x 78 x 16½, E19c (4152/190) *1300*

Wine cooler (4165/367)

Cabinet (4152/190)

Chair (4239/330)

Cabinet, side, rosewood, top with 2 shelves above 2 drawers, 62 x 37½ x 15, M19c (4152/176)	1000
Cellaret, inlaid mahogany, hinged domed lid, fitted interior, ring handles, 23½ x 24½ x 18, ca1825 (4239/44)	750
Chair, child's on stand, caned, carved mahogany, L19c (4216/197)	325
Chair, reading, carved mahogany, U-shaped top rail, spindle splats, upholstered seat, now with bookstand, ca1830 (4239/330)	*600*
Chairs, dining set of 6, mahogany, including 2 armchairs, M19c (4189/232)	550
Chest of drawers, miniature, mahogany, 13½, M19c (4152/48)	225
Etagere, 4-tier, mahogany, rectangular, turned supports, 2 drawers, 52½ x 21 x 17, M19c (4159/338)	850
Etageres, mahogany, pair, 3 tier, 43 x28½, M19c (4111/155)	850
Mirror, convex, gilt wood, ebonized, leaf molded tubular borders, leafy crest, 42 x 26, E19c (4272/57)	225
Mirror, toilet, turned mahogany, bevelled rectangular plate, 3 drawers in base, 21½ x 23 x 9½, ca1830 (4239/31)	100
Screen, writing, mahogany, trestle form with adjustable, needlepoint screen, 32½ x 15, E19c (4111/200)	150
Seat, hall, mahogany, shaped leaf carved top rail, 19c (4152/205)	1800
Stand, reading, mahogany, adjustable reading surface, 36 x 21, L19c (4165/364)	650
Table, breakfast, circular, mahogany, gadrooned baluster stem, reeded legs, 29 x 49½, ca1830 (4272/231)	1200
Table, center, circular mahogany, reeded flared column supports, 28½ x 32½, M19c (4079/179)	600
Table, circular, rosewood, scroll apron, hexagonal stem, 29½, Diam 48½, M19c (4159/350)	3200
Table, dining, mahogany, 3 pedestal, rectangular top, quadruple legs, 28½ x 96 x 51, ca1830 (4239/158)	2000
Table, drum, mahogany, circular top, black leather inset, 30 x 42, M19c (4189/237)	900
Table, drum, mahogany, leather inset, revolving top, 4 drawers, 30 x 43, L19c (4134/180)	400
Table, occasional, mahogany, kidney shaped, 3 tier, 29½ x 26½, M19c (4111/173)	350
Table, occasional, octagonal, pollard oak, 29 x 23, M19c (4189/212)	500
Table, wine, carved mahogany, hinged C-shaped top, fitted brass rail, 29½ x 96 x 48, ca1830 (4260/1761)	5750
Table, writing, mahogany, leather inset, total 9 drawers, on plinth, 29 x 48 x 26½, ca1830 (4239/349)	1700
Table, Pembroke, pedestal, mahogany, hinged top drawer, leaf carved legs, 29½ x 40, 22½, L19c (4134/177)	450
Tables, games, parcel-gilt, pair, composition and rosewood, 29½ x 36 x 18, M19c (4152/200)	2200
Tea caddy, mahogany, sideboard form, 11 L19c (4152/45)	325
Teapot, gilt metal mounted mahogany, octagonal form, hinged top, 2 tea caddies, 2 bowls, 30 x 14½, ca1830 (4272/217)	425
Writing screen, mahogany, trestle form, adjustable needlepoint screen, 32½ x 15, E19c (4272/236)	150

Chinese export

Altar table, carved rosewood, 32½ x 50, 19c (4111/178)	700
Armchair, carved teakwood, pierced floral form splat, 19c (4111/176)	400

Armchair, carved teakwood, pierced splat, 19c (4111/175)	450
Armchairs, pair, decorated bamboo, tub shaped, caned seat, E19c (4134/332)	3100
BonHeur, DuJour lacquer, oval panelled doors, fitted interior, 59 x 24½ x 24½ M19c (4134/374)	1800
Cabinet on stand, lacquer, Chinese scenes, foliate borders, 62 x 26, M19c (4189/224)	*1900*
Cainet, secretaire, gilt decorated, black lacquer, 64 x 22 x 25, M19c (4216/210)	1500
Coffer, stencil decorations, red and brown on black ground, 14 x 16½, 19c (4216/17)	425
Screen, 12 fold, Coromandel, black lacquer, Chinese scenes, H114, L18c (4189/108)	*19500*

Screen (4189/108)

Table (4152/181)

Cabinet on stand
(4189/224)

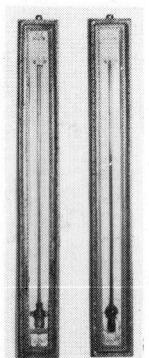

Desk (4216/47)

Tables (4152/199)

Barometer and
thermometer
(4168/34)

Desk (4152/172)

Seats, garden, pair black lacquer, red and yellow chinoiserie figures, W14½, 19c (4152/204)	3100
Sewing box, lacquer, removable fitted interior, above drawer, 5¼ x 12 E19c (4134/239)	150
Stand, black lacquer, octagonal, dec red chinoiserie figures, 34 x 17½, 19c (4165/408)	900
Stand, gilt decorated black lacquer, retangular, pierced scrollwork frieze, 33½ x 17¼ x 13, 19c (4165/410)	1100
Table, games, lacquer, checkerboard surface, 32 x 31, E19c (4111/179)	750
Table, low, decorated lacquer, Chinese figures and pavillion settings, 18½ x 44¾, 19c (4165/384)	1500
Table, low, orange lacquer, top etched with dragon, 16 x 42 x 22, 18c (4189/156)	3400
Table, low, Huang Huali, square legs, scrolled feet, 13 x 60 x 29½, 18c (4165/314)	2000
Table, work, lacquer, chinoiserie figures, shell carved paw feet, 28 x 24 x 16, M19c (4079/180)	650
Table, work, lacquer, fitted interior, trestle support, 29½ x 24½ x 17, L19c (4079/177)	1300
Table, writing, hardwood, top with 3 drawers, pedestals 2 drawers each, 33½ x 63 x 25½ 19c (4134/265)	3100
Tables, nest of 4, 27½ x 19 x 12, M19c (4216/92)	900
Tables, nest of 4, dragonhead feet, 27½ x 20, E19c (4152/199)	*600*
Tables, nest of 4, papier mache and lacquer, 28 x 21, E19c (4111/180)	550
Tables, nest of 4, lacquer, 27½ x 19 x 12, M19c (4189/138)	700
Tea caddy, lacquer, gilt decorated, chinoiserie figures, 5 x 8½, M19c (4165/279)	500

Victorian

Cabinets on stands, pair, black, decorated doors, enclosing drawers, 48 x 20½ x 12½ M19c (4134/185)	1200

Canterbury, mahogany, 4 slatted divisions on turned supports, 20 x 19½, M19c (4189/215)	400
Canterbury, mahogany, 4 slatted divisions on turned supports, L16½, M19c (4189/206)	225
Chair, spoon back rosewood, caned seat, L19c (4134/371)	250
Chairs, pair, painted, spindle backrest, oval caned loose cushioned seat, M19c (4134/141)	325
Chest, campaign, brass, mounted, 2 sections, 4 drawers, 38½ x 32 x 17 19c (4111/128)	650
Chest of drawers, campaign, mahogany, brass-bound, fire drawers, 38 x 36 x 18½ 19c (4134/188)	600
Daybed, mahogany, L61½, L19c (4189/144)	300
Desk, campaign, partner's, brass inlaid, ebonized, hinged flap at each side, 30 x 59½ x 45, L19c (4152/172)	*3100*
Desk, lap, brass mounted, padoukwood, campaign, W25¾, D19, L19c (4216/47)	*1000*
Desk, partner's, mahogany, pedestal, leather inset, reeded quarter columns, 31 x 77½ x 54 19c (4134/179)	*4100*
Desk, pedestal, mahogany, green leather inset top, 29 x 48 x 29, L19c (4152/175)	1200
Etagere, 4 tier mahogany, 54 x 17, L19c (4216/203)	450
Gueridon, papier mache, painted and mother-of-pearl, 29 x 28¾ x 23 M19c (4134/187)	175
Lap desk, brass inlaid, rosewood, rectangular hinged lid, inlaid center, 5 x 13, M19c (4142/58)	125
Mirror, bow-front, inlaid mahogany, free standing, 29 x 33, L19c (4216/58)	225
Screen, writing trestle, inlaid mahogany, 47 x 22, M19c (4216/178)	325
Screen, writing,fall front trestle, marquetry inlaid rosewood, 45 x 21 x 5, M19c (4216/199)	300
Screen, 4 fold, painted tin, decorations of classical figures and still lives, 66 x 108 M19c (4134/370)	1000
Shelf, display, rosewood, 5 tier, pierced and scroll carved back and side, 56½ x 33½ x 12 (631/409)	400
Stool, carved rosewood, upholstered seat, L21 (4189/205)	350
Table, campaign writing, brass, inlaid mahogany, 30½ x 43 x 24½, 19c (4189/221)	1200
Table, from papier mache tray, decorated in flowers, on a black ground, 21 x 32 res (4134/57)	350
Table, gaming, inlaid rosewood, lined playing surface, 28½ x 35 x 19¾, M19c (4079/182)	1700
Table, low, formerly tole peinte tray, tortoise shell ground, 20 x 24, M19c (4111/31)	650
Table, low, from papier mache tray, with mother-of-pearl inlays, 18 x 31 x 23½, M19c (4111/43)	475
Table, low, mounted, papier mache and lacquer tray, bamboo stand, 19½ x 39, M19c (4111/33)	425
Table, occasional, mahogany, mosaic plaque, circular top, carved leafage, plaque of Roman forum, 28½ x 22, L19c (631/379)	350
Table, painted and carved oak, figure of camel base, 27½ x 29½, 19c (4111/177)	2200
Table, wine mahogany, semicircular form, removable center section, 29 x 71½ x 37, M19c (4152/181)	*1400*
Table, writing, pedestal, Amboyna wood, 3 drawers above cupboard, 31½ x 59 x 25 L19c (4134/373)	2500
Table, writing, burr walnut, 2 drawers, 29 x 56½ x 33, res, L19c (4152/194)	2500
Table, writing, mahogany, 30 x 53½ x 29, M19c (4189/135)	2500
Table, writing, mahogany, balustrated superstructure, leather inset top, 46 x 60 x 29½ M19c (4134/186)	2300
Tables, nest of 3, mother-of-pearl, inlaid papier mache, 28 x 22 x 15 M19c (4134/368)	325
Trunk on stand, brass studded black leather, 19, 19c (4165/372)	250
Window seat, rosewood, roll over upholstered ends, 61 L19c (4134/375)	450

French Decorations

FRENCH BAROMETERS

Barometer, gilt wood, frame carved with garlands and pair of doves, 40, L18c, French (4119/172)	400
Barometer and thermometer, pair, gilt wood, Louis XV, 44¼ x 5½, L18c (4168/34)	*5400*

FRENCH CLOCKS

Assorted shelf clocks

Anchor escapement, Roman numbers, bell raised upon 2 plinths, oval base, 16¼ L19c (4165/207)	1100
Athena figure, bronze and marble, owl medallion, 29, L19c, good (669/406)	2100
Boudoir, silver, engine-turned, quadrangular, H1¾ ca1900 (4148/130)	300
Bracket, bronze and tortoiseshell, white dial inset Lenoire a Paris, 33, L19c (619/284)	1600
Brass ball, neoclassical, circular brass dial, Arabic numerals, 6¼, L19c (4218/2)	200
Carriage, gilt, metal and porcelain, repeating, white dial with landscapes, 6½, ca1900 (4141/182)	2900
Carriage, with alarm, repeating, gilt metal, 7, L19c (4165/241)	1000
Carriage clock, brass, alarm, cylinder movement, white enamel dial, 6¾, ca1890, repeat missing (4238/332)	
Carriage clock, brass, alarm, white enamel dial, fitted case, H6¼, ca1890 (4238/329)	275
Cartel, gilt bronze, high relief with foliate scrolls, lattice panels, 20, L19c (669/403)	500
Cartel, gilt bronze, lyre form case, 20 (619/270)	400
Cartel, gilt bronze, striking hours, half-hours, 26½, 19c (4141/174)	425
Chinese porcelain case, ormolu, porcelain of Ch'ien Lung period, 19, ca1780 (4232/29)	10000

Clock, annular, gilt bronze and red marble, horizontal dial, globe, maiden with harp, 19¼, 19c (649/392)   3750
Clock, bleu-de-roi porcelain, gilt bronze, ovoid body, lions mask and ring handles, 18½, L19c (649/384)   500
Clock, bracket, boulle and ebonized, architectural case, gilt bronze 'Justice', 19, L19c (649/389)   750
Clock, bracket, boulle, Balthasar, Paris, face with fowl and foliage, female finial, 32¼, L19c (649/390)   2000
Clock, desk, gilt metal, rectangular case, glazed on all sides, H11, ca1900 (4156/193)   300
Clock, mantel, gilt bronze, shape of maiden leaning against pillar, with lyre, 22, ca1900 (649/378)   750
Clock, mantel, gilt bronze, shell and scroll-work surmounted by scroll finial, 18½, L19c (649/379)   650
Clock, mantel, gilt bronze, grey marble, band glass brilliants inset in lyre form frame, 23, L19c (649/382)   2250
Clock, ormolu and porphyry, obelisk, neptune and a winged putto, 38½ x 12½, 19c (4119/215)   6250
Clock, Empire, gilt bronze and marble, dial inset below 2 lady astronomers, H16, E19c (649/370)   2250
Clock, Mantel, ormolu, Louis XVI, movement within bale-shaped case, half dressed, black youth, 13¼, L18c (4159/189)   2700
Clock and stand, gilt bronze, cast with foliate scrolls surmounted by urn finial, 21½, L19c (649/381)   800
Clock bracket, gilt bronze mounted boulle, marquetry, cartouche shaped case, 33, L19c (669/396)   1200
Clock bracket, ormolu mounted, Boulle marquetry, blue, black numerals, 39½, 19c (4232/21)   3250
Clock garniture, gilt bronze, 3 pcs, embossed with dolphins, bust, 9 light candelabra, clock H27, L19c (649/385)   2000
Compendium silver, with barometer, perpetual calendar, compass, 4½, ca1910 (4141/188)   200
Desk clock, 8 day calendar, silver and enamel, day, date, month, dials, 4½, ca1930 (4238/333)   225
Dial in patinated and gilt bronze, with 2 equestrian soldiers in combat, marble, 35¼, L19c (669/402)   1400
Drum case, gilt bronze, 4 ebonized columns form portico, 19½, L19c (4157/4)   750
Drum form, gilt bronze-mounted marble, set between columns, 23½, L19c (669/405)   1800
Drum shaped case, ormolu mounted, surmounted by figure of Diana, Louis XVI, 15, L18c (4142/23)   2250
Eight day, revolving chapter ring, shellwork cresting, on 4 cabriole legs, 11⅛ M18c (4165/216)   4000
Garniture, gilt bronze, clock and pair 2 light candelabra, signed Susse Freres, H13½ (669/399)   950
Garniture, gilt bronze, pink marble, 2 urns with clock, Leroy, Paris, M16 (619/286)   400
Garniture, gilt bronze, porcelain, clock, with 2 porcelain vases, Raingo, Paris, L19c (619/296)   3250
Garniture, gilt bronze, white marble, clock, Leda and swan, Blanc, Geneve, 2 cassolets (619/290)   950
Miniature, the form of Gothic Arch, glass dome, wood base, 5¼ M19c (4165/208)   550
Ormolu, Charles X, vase shape case flanked by floral sprays, loop handles, 10 x 8¼, M19c (4218/1)   525
Ormolu, Charles X, with standing figure of Francois I, 15, M19c (4218/3)   *1500*
Ormolu, Charles X, Guiton et Cie, white dial, lyre-shaped case, H14 (4168/30)   500
Ormolu, Louis XVI, circular white enamel dial on columns, 23, L18c (4218/10)   650
Ormolu and brass mounted, tortoiseshell, blue enamel Roman numerals, feet later, Louis XIV, 18½, L17c (4218/12)   1700
Ormolu and marble, Louis XVI, circular dial in drum-shaped case, obelisk, 26 x 15, L18c (4218/8)   1200
Ormolu and mother-of-pearl, Charles X, ormolu dial, 12, M19c (4218/4)   600
Ormolu and patinated bronze, Louis XVI, with Leda and the swan group, 23, L18c (4218/7)   *4000*
Ormolu and white marble, white enamel dial, Roman numerals, opera figural scene, 20¼ x 13½ x 9¾, L18c (4272/307)   *3000*
Porcelain champleve and gilt bronze, angular case, maidens amongst scrolls, 15½, L18c (669/389)   3100
Portico, ormolu mounted, rosewood, with day of month and week dials, 23½, L19c (4232/36)   1300
Samson porcelain and gilt bronze, mounted, drum case, putto and flowerhead branches, 18½, L19c (669/385)   1300
Sevres porcelain and gilt, bronze, mounted, architectural form, urn scene, 16½, L19c (669/387)   1200
Signs of Zodiac, ormolu mounted, standing winged female figures, 27½, E19c (4119/193)   2250
Standing female figure, arch case, ormolu mounted, 17½ x 12½, L19c (4119/213)   750
Tower, with alarm and calendar, small, gilt metal, 6½, ca1575 (4165/229)   10000

Mantel clocks

Dial in column, gilt bronze, flanked by winged putti, 14¾, L19c (619/276)   1800
Dial in urn, gilt bronze, swan handles, 16, 19c (619/278)   1000
Dial surmounted by lyre, ormolu, flanked by perfume burner, figure, 18¾, E19c (4232/22)   *850*
Drum shape, ormolu, patinated bronze, wooden marbleized base, H11¼, 19c (4119/176)   475
Drum shaped case between obelisks, ormolu mounted marble, 16 x 12¼, L18c (4119/181)   550
Drum shaped case, ormolu and marble, flanked by standing female, 13, L19c (4142/2)   550
Female figure playing piano, Empire interior, ormolu mounted, 22 x 19¾, rare, E19c (4119/189)   *9000*
Galle faience, column case, painted in pink and grey, 15¼, finial dam, ca1880 (669/388)   450
Gaudron a Paris, ormolu mounted, boulle marquetry, 19¾ x 11, ca1700 (4119/168)   2200
Haulaugeur, Planchon, gilded, bronze, Paris, L19½, 19c (4148/161)   750
Meuron et Compte, ormolu mounted, with standing figure of Apollo, 15½, L19c (4119/175)   300
Ormolu and white marble, Louis XVI, paw feet, Rogue a Paris, 12¾ x 10¾, L18c (4168/42)   2800

Ormolu and patinated
bronze (4218/7)

Ormolu and
white marble
(4272/307)

Ormolu (4218/3)

Dial
surmounted
by lyre
(4232/22)

Female figure
playing piano
(4119/189)

Revolving dials, ormolu mounted, Sevres porcelain, 29, rep, L18c (4232/23) — 17500
Seated figure of pensive maiden, throne form case, ormolu mounted, 20½, E19c (4157/27) — 750
Spherical body, gilt bronze, champleve, putto, 2 columns, 7½, L19c (669/391) — 700
Standing winged figure, ormolu mounted, 11½, 19c (4119/196) — 275
Tiffany & Co., champleve enamel, bronze upright architectural case, urn, 22, L19c (619/281) — 2000
Tortoiseshell, brass mounted, urn and vase shaped finials, 23¾, L19c (4232/18) — 1300
Winged figure seated on square case, ormolu mounted, 17¾, E19c (4119/204) — 1000

Standing clocks

Carriage, gilt metal, retailed, J.E. Caldwell, Philadelphia, French, 5¾ (4165/242) — 125
Carriage repeating, gilt metal, retailed by Tiffany & Co., French, 7, ca1900 (4165/243) — 650
Desk, silver and enamel, E. Dreyfous, Paris, 6⅛, ca1900 (4165/237) — 750
Easel minute repeating - gilt metal, Tiffany & Co., France, 6, ca1920 (4165/236) — 900
Tabernacle, gilt metal, ring for 24 hours, 16¼, ca1600 (4165/230) — 18500
Travel, tripod, gilt metal, case, 2 pendulums, front mounted, rococo ornament, 8⅛, ca1760, unusual
(4165/226) — 5000

Tall-case clocks

Oak, long case, Regence, later white enamel dial and movement, 95½ x 17¼ (4218/13) — 1200
Regulateur, ormolu mounted, kingwood, marquetry, 93 x 23½, L19c (4218/14) — 4000

Wall clocks

Cartel clock, ormolu with scrolls and flowers, insc. gilbert a Paris, 25½, M18c (4119/185) — 4750
Cartel clock, ormolu and patinated bronze, sunray motif, reclining female figure, 26½ x 14½, L19c
(4119/186) — 1000
Gilt bronzes, ovoid form, foliage, swags, ring handles, 16, L19c (669/398) — 1400
Gilt metal, signed Morel a Attignat, two-train movement, 54, M19c (4232/34) — 300
Green horn, ormolu mounted, Louis XV, Cartouche shaped case, Jean Loyers a Paris, 41 x 16, M18c
(4168/38) — 13000
Ormolu, large, Louis XV, elaborate case, figures, branches, scrolls, H46½, M18c (4168/41) — 4750

Picture, Empire, village and clock tower, 34 x 40, M19c, Guyerdet (4168/32) 750
With matching barometer, gilt wood, Louis XVI, lyre-shaped cases, dials later, 42½ (4218/9) 1100

FRENCH DECORATIVE OBJECTS

Baluster vase, Chinese export, famille-rose, octagonal, gilt wood base, H22¼, 18c (4086/58) 4500
Cabinet display, gilt bronze, Mahogany parquetry, open tiers, glass door enclosing shelves, 22 x 47¼ x 15¾, Louis XVI style (619/381) 1600
Caskets, pair painted, with genre scenes, 11½, M18c, Louis XV (4119/174) 700
Chenets, pair, ormolu, Luis XV, winged putti on bases with scrolled feet, H13¼, ca1735 (4168/14) 5750
Cups, 2 handled, ormolu and patinated, bronze, pair, centaurs in relief, 7¼ (4218/28) 250
Lyres, pair, tole peinte, each resting on a globe, pedestal with claw feet, 22, L19c (4119/226) 950
Mantel, white marble, breakfront form above floral carved frieze, L19c (649/417) 1100
Pot pourris, pair, ormolu mounted porcelain, circular tapered bodies, lion's masks, 19½, L19c (4218/65) 3750
Pots, tole peinte, cache, pair, square tapered bodies, painted, neoclassical figures, 12, M19c (4218/34) 500
Vase, enamel on copper, maiden stepping across stream, 9½, ca1900, French (669/274) 700
Vase, enameled and silver mounted, profile portrait of maiden, 8¼, ca1900, French (669/273) 700
Vases, Chinese porcelain ormolu, pair, porcelain of Ch'ien Lung period, 13½, ca1780, rep (4232/28) 22000
Vases and covers, pair, enamel and 'jewelled', ovoid, 18c pastoral lovers, riverscape, 11½, ca1880, French (669/271) 750
Wall paper fragments, pair, painted, fishing scenes, multicolor tones, gilt wood frames, 31, L18c (4157/12) 450
Water jug, brass, baluster, oval lid, scrolled handle, 7¼, 18c (4260/945) 1100
Water jug, brass, baluster, oval lid, scrolled handle, 7¼, 18c (4260/946) 1100
Water jug, brass, baluster, oval lid, scrolled handle, 7¼, 18c (4260/947) 1100

FRENCH HEARTH EQUIPMENT

Coal bucket, brass, helmet shaped, wooden and bail handle, 22, 19c (4260/953) 1200

FRENCH LIGHTING DEVICES

Bras de lumiere, 3 light pair ormolu, 3 intertwined branches, 21¾ (4218/63) 1400

Bras de lumiere (4232/70)

Candelabra (4168/6)

Bras de lumiere, pair 3 light ormolu, fluted branches with leaves, 23½ (4218/43) 700
Bras de lumiere, pair, ormolu 1 light, voluted branch and backplate, leaves and scrolls, 9¾, fitted for electricity (4218/45) 550
Bras de lumiere, 1 light, ormolu, with palmettes, sockets raised on scroll branches, 15¾, L18c (4232/52) 1100
Bras de lumiere, 2 light rock crystal, cut glass, gilt metal, Louis XVI style, 32½ (4218/40) 2000
Bras de lumiere, 2 light, ormolu, pair, voluted branches, backplate, 17¼, L18c (4232/62) 3600
Bras de lumiere, 4 lights, pair, ormolu, chiselled with scrolls, leaves, flowerheads, 23¼, M18c, electrified (4218/58) 2750
Bras de lumiere, 2 light ormolu, foliate sockets and drip pans, winged dragon, 21¾, M18c (4232/70) *14500*
Candelabra pair, gilt brass, voluted sockets, circular bases, 13½, L19c, Louis XV style (4119/198) 400
Candelabra, ormolu and patinated bronze, pair, now lamps, encircled by ormolu snake, 35½, E19c (4218/29) 1200

Candelabra, pair, ormolu mounted, form winged female holding aloft 2 candle arms, 26½, L19c French (619/303) — 1000

Candelabra, pair, 3 light, patinated bronze, winged female, 28½, L18c, now as lamps (4142/35) — 900

Candelabra, pair, 3 light, ormolu and, marble, standing naked winged putto, raised on a globe, 20, L19c (4142/40) — 325

Candelabra, pair, marble mounted gilt and patinated bronze, winged maidens holding aloft wreaths, 46, French (619/304) — 3250

Candelabra, pair, ormolu and patinated bronze, 3 light, figure raised on circular pedestal, 23¾, L19c (4119/224) — 900

Candelabra, pair, silvered bronze, 2 light, Louis XV, mounted as lamps, foliate, H30¼ (4168/25) — 2100

Candelabra, pair, 6 light, ormolu, female figure above a globe, 32, L19c (4119/190) — 1280

Candelabra, pair, 3 light, patinated bronze, cornucopia, 41½, L19c, now lamps (4119/188) — 1100

Candelabra, pair, 5 light, Napoleon III, bronze branches above reeded ormolu stem, 41¾, L19c, now as lamps (669/464) — 550

Candelabra, pair, 6 light, ormolu and patinated, bronze, vase shaped sockets, triangular bases, 31¾, M19c (4119/208) — 750

Candelabra, pr, 3 light, Louis XVI, 3 arms, circular marble base, H17¼, L18c (4168/6) — *4250*

Candelabra, 13 light columnar pair, gilt bronze, 39½ (619/310) — 2600

Candelabra, 2 light pair, with porcelain figures and flowers, 6¾ (619/298) — 275

Candelabra, 2 light, ormolu and marble, satyr and nymph holding floral branches, 17½, L18c (4232/56) — 4800

Candelabra, 2 light, ormolu, pair, lights on foliate arms, Charles X, E19c (4219/60) — 950

Candelabra, 3 light pair, gilt bronze, each scroll molded base, 3 branches, 12, L19c (669/459) — 450

Candelabra, 4 light pair, gilt bronze, scrolled stem and base, 19¼, L19c (669/460) — 1150

Candelabra, 4 lights, gilt bronze mounted, handles in shape of winged putti, 14, ca1870 (631/235) — 400

Candelabra, 5 light, pair, Napoleon III, patinated and gilt brass, female form, 32 (4157/26) — 1500

Candelabra, 6 light, ormolu, vase shape socket, curved branch, circular fluted column, 28, M19c (4218/35) — 1000

Candelabra, 6 light, pair gilt metal, hung with colored glass drops, 21 (619/297) — 175

Candelabra, pair, 2 light, Louis-Phillippe, ormolu and opaline glass, 19½, M19c (4157/34) — 900

Candlestick, ormolu and brass, tapered stem, surmounted by Sphinx heads, 19½, E19c, now as lamp (4119/222) — 150

Candlesticks, pair, ormolu, circular tapered, stem decorated with leaves, 11, L19c (4119/199) — 325

Candlesticks, brass, pair, domed foot, 11¼, French, 1800 (4076/524) — 225

Candlesticks, gilt brass, Charles X, stems of reeded guivers of arrows, 12, M19c (4142/19) — 275

Candlesticks, ormolu, vase shaped sockets, bases dec with laurel leaves, 10½, L18c (4232/54) — 3000

Candlesticks, ormolu mounted opaline glass, rococo, acanthus leafage, 9, L19c, 1 dam (631/234) — 325

Candlesticks, ormolu, white marble, Louis XVI, ovoid stems, circular base, feet, H7¼, L18c (4168/43) — 425

Candlesticks, ormolu, Regence, angular stem, shell motifs, 9½, ca1725 (4218/21) — 1900

Candlesticks, pair, ormolu, Napoleon III, L19c (4219/61) — 1200

Candlesticks, pair, directoire, circular stems, satyr's masks, 11¾, L18c, socket replaced (4142/12) — 750

Candlesticks, pair, gilt brass, with shells and scrolls, 14, L19c, now as lamps (4142/42) — 100

Candlesticks, pair, ormolu, hexagonal socket, tapered stem, ca1725 (4218/16) — 1000

Candlesticks, pair, ormolu and brass, vase shaped socket, Directoire, 21, now lamps, L18c (4219/64) — 500

Candlesticks, pair, ormolu and patinated, bronze, Charles X, 13¼, L19c (4272/302) — 700

Candlesticks, pair, silvered, Louis XVI, vase shape socket, baluster stem, 10¾, L18c (4218/48) — 325

Candlesticks, columnar, pair, gilt bronze, paw footed bases, now table lamps, 39, without fixture (619/312) — 400

Cassollettes, ormolu, Charles X, now as lamps, campana shape, raised on circular bases, 17½, covers now missing (4142/37) — 125

Chandelier, baccarat, 6 light, brass, turned bulbous glass standard, 24 (649/462) — 300

Chandelier, gilt metal and porcelain, six curved branches, multicolor flowers, 24 (4218/54) — 850

Chandelier, gilt metal and porcelain, 3 pairs of foliate voluted, branches, 22½, Louis XV style (4142/7) — 3250

Chandelier, ormolu, 3 pairs of foliate branches, held by angels, 30½, L19c (4218/38) — 500

Chandelier, ormolu and cut glass, 8 light, clear and purple glass, 32, Louis XVI style (4142/10) — 450

Chandelier, 12 light, ormolu, tole peinte, 2 sections, neoclassical, 38, M19c (4232/46) — 1800

Chandelier, 4 light, rock crystal and amethystine, 20 x 12, L19c (649/425) — 100

Chandelier, 8 light, crystal, ormolu branches, 2 row alternating, Empire, 37, L19c (4272/317) — 1900

Chandelier, 8 light, ormolu, cut glass, scalloped circular shape, tear drop pendants, 31 x 22 (4157/19) — 1400

Chandelier, 9 light, gilt metal, bronzed, swans, female figures, 30, French, empire style (619/332) — 500

Chandelier, 9 light, gilt bronze, Acanthus candle branches, 24 x 18, French, Louis XV style (619/333) — 1600

Chandeliers, pair, 18 light, ormolu rock crystal, blue glass, rosettes, fine, H50 x 35½, L18c (4086/71) — 37500

Lamp, ormolu, 3 light, foliate branches, H28½ (4168/9) — 700

Lamp, bouillote, brass and patinated, bronze brass shade, standing female figure, 20½, empire style
(4142/21)   450
Lamp, bouillotte, brass, 3 vase shaped sockets, Directoire, 29, L18c (4219/69)   1200
Lamp, bouillotte, ormolu, acanthus leaves, pierced dished base, 30½, L18c (4232/44)   3250
Lamp, oil, tole peinte, semicircular adjustable shade, 18, electrified, L18c (4219/56)   550
Lamps, bouillotte, ormolu, 3 carved branches, dish base, 26, L18c (4232/47)   4500
Lamps, oil, pair, tole peinte, circular columns, rectangular bases, 29, L19c, now for electricity
(4119/163)   300
Lamps, pair, empire, brass, figure of Victory, circular pedestal, 27¾, L19c (4232/4)   475
Lantern, wall gilt metal, 4 branch light within glazed sides and foliate mounts, 26, 19c, French
(619/331)   800
Perfume burners, ormolu mounted, celadon porcelain, Louis XVI, electrified, 10½, L18c (4219/67)   2800
Prisms, pendants rosettes and beads, 27, 19c (4232/68)   4250
Sconces, pair, Louis XV, ormolu, 2 light, voluted branches and backplate, H15, ca1825-50 (4168/7) *2600*
Sconces, wall, pair 3 light gilt bronze, with acanthus scroll branches, 24, French (619/315)   750
Sconces, wall, 3 light, set of 4, gilt bronze, 20, French, Louis XIV style (619/322)   1500
Sconces, wall, 3 light, set of 4, gilt bronze, 20, French, Louis XIV style (619/323)   1400
Sconces, 2 light, pair, Napoleon III, ormolu, raised on voluted branches, 8, L19c (4157/23)   850
Sconces, 3 light, ormolu, reeded sockets, curved support decorated, 38, L18c, rare, large (4232/75) 13000
Sconces, 3 light, set of 4, gilt bronze, 21, Eighteenth Century style (619/320)   1200
Surtout de table, ormolu porcelain, lidded receptacle, 4 pairs of candles, 17½ x 21½, M18c
(4218/53)   5500
Urns, pair, painted tole, tapering square sections, with mythological scenes, 15¼, now as lamps
(4157/3)   300
Vase, Chinese procelain, now as lamp, baluster, pale green crackle, 35½, 19c (4142/57)   650
Vases, pair, Paris porcelain, now lamps, swan shaped handles, oriental scenes, 27¼, E19c
(4218/25)   700
Wall lights, set of 4, Second Empire, bronze and glass, each with 2 lights, 17, L19c, electrified
(4157/31)   1500

French Furniture

Louis XIV

Armchair, walnut, upholstered backrest, scrolled armrests, L17c (4218/82)   1500

Bureau en pente
(4168/136)

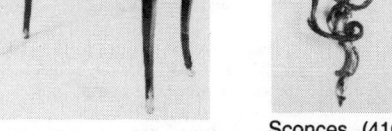

Sconces (4168/7)

Bidet (4168/107)

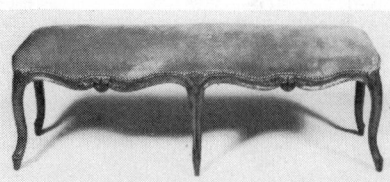

Banquette (4168/129)   Bureau (4168/137)

Bureau, mazarin, brass, red, tortoise shell, bow-front drawers, 28½ x 37¾ x 24½, L17c (4119/326)	12000
Bureau, mazarin, marquetry, ebonized grounds, toupie feet, 32 x 44¾ x 26½, M17c (4168/137)	*22000*
Chair, side, oak and walnut, rectangular open backrest, wooden seat, L17c (4272/398)	350
Chairs side set of 3, walnut, upholstered, serpentine top rail, L17c (4193/381)	2000
Chest of drawers, pair glazed doors, lower 3 drawers, claw feet, 98 x 73 x 26, L18c (4272/399)	5500
Commode, ormolu mounted, boulie, marquetry, foliate birds and dancing figure, 32 x 48¼ x 25¾, L17c (4232/212)	27000
Commode, walnut, 3 drawers, claw feet, 32½ x 48 x 24, E18c (4119/322)	4500
Fauteuil, walnut, tall rectangular backrest, voluted wooden armrests, L17c (4272/362)	1150
Fauteuil, walnut, upholster, back, seat, wooden arms, L17c (4157/67)	2900
Fauteuil, walnut, upholstered backrest, wooden armrests, L17c (4255/416)	1800
Fauteuil a oreilles, walnut, upholstered, backrest, with padded wings, ca1700 (4157/77)	1200
Table, console, painted, voluted stretcher, marble top (broken), 31 x 91 x 30¾, L17c (4168/164)	26000

Regence

Canape a oreilles, gilt wood, upholstered wings, loose cushions, L78, M18c (4168/77)	2500
Canape a oreilles, stained, beechwood, serpentine seat, 87, ca1725 (4119/311)	1300
Chaise a la reine, caned, painted grey, loose cushion, ca1725 (4232/94)	850
Commode, kingwood, parquetry, rouge languedoc top, bombe, later ormolu, 34¼ x 51 x 26½, ca1725 (4168/99)	225
Commode, provincial fruitwood, 4 drawers, 2 short, 2 long, 31½ x 48¾ x 24, ca1725 (4218/156)	2100
Commode, provincial fruitwood, 3 drawers, brass handles, 34 x 50½ x 26¼, ca1720 (4157/82)	3800
Commode walnut, provincial, serpentine front, 2 short and 3 long drawers, 33½ x 50 x 23½, ca1725 (4232/148)	3400
Fauteuil, beechwood, cabriole legs, X-stretcher, ca1725, Tilliard (4168/49)	3250
Fauteuil, caned beechwood, caned backrest, arched top rail, ca1720 (4168/72)	2300
Fauteuil, caned beechwood, serpentine top rail with shell, X-stretcher, ca1720 (4168/105)	1900
Fauteuil a la reine, caned beechwood, caned backrest, wooden armrest, ca1725 (4157/41)	1100
Fauteuil a la reine, walnut, padded armrests, upholsted seat carvings, ca1725 (4232/106)	2000
Fauteuil a la reine, walnut, upholstered, carved, voluted support, ca1725 (4119/285)	2000
Fauteuil a la reine, walnut, arched top rail, wooden armrests, upholstered, legs spliced, ca1725 (4272/322)	1400
Fauteuils a la reine pair, walnut, cartouche shape, backrest, ca1725 (4119/239)	4100
Panel, Savonnerie, trophy, floral cartouche, birds, beige ground, 108 x 25, ca1725 (4168/44)	4500
Screen 4 fold, painted wallpaper, representing London street (Whitehall), 67 x 70, E19c (4218/33)	1600
Tabouret, beechwood, foliate motifs, cabriole legs, scrolled toes, W21½, ca1725 (4168/63)	2100

Louis XV

Armoire, provincial oak, carved with floral sprays, 78¾ x 52½ x 19½, L18c (4218/198)	1900
Banquette, walnut, double serpentine seat, L57½, M18c (4168/129)	*1700*
Bed, beechwood, roll over ends carved, upholestered, Carpentier, 94¼ x 52, M18c, fine (4232/126)	7000
Bergere, beechwood, curved backrest, upholestered, L. Carpentier, L18c, fine (4232/127)	2400
Bergere a la reine, gilt wood, cresting with flowerheads, on cabriole legs, M18c, formerly caned (4232/156)	10000
Bergere en cabriolet, painted, molded cabriole legs, backrest, M18c (4086/84)	4500
Bergere en cabriolet, walnut, short wings, floral damask, beige-white, M18c (4218/111)	1800
Bergeres en cabriolet, pair, painted cream, highlighted with green, M18c (4119/252)	3300
Bibliotheque, purplewood and fruitwood, Marquetry, white marble top, doors enclosing shelves, 51½ x 27¾ x 11¼, L18c (4232/180)	10500
Bidet, kingwood, purplewood, leather removable seat, parquetry, L27, M18c, Migeon (4168/107)	*4200*
Bidet, mahogany, opening to reveal compartments, L18c (4119/254)	650
Bonheur du jour, tulipwood and kingwood, top with 3 drawers, 3 compartments, 40¼ x 25½ x 17, L18c (4232/186)	5250
Bras de lumiere, pair, ormolu, two-light, H18, M18c (4086/65)	3250
Bras de lumiere, pair, ormolu, two-light, chinoiserie, H18, M18c (4086/64)	3500
Brisee, duchese, walnut, tub shaped backrest and end, voluted carved frame, 90, M18c (4157/97)	5000
Buffet oak provincial, rectangular top, cabriole legs, 37½ x 44½ x 21½, M18c (4119/313)	1500
Bureau en pente provincial, fruitwood, slant front, fitted interior, 38 x 40¾ x 17⅝, M18c (4218/163)	1900
Bureau en pente, I. Dubois, JME, ormolu mounted, lacquer, bombe shape, fine, 35½ x 25½ x 15, M18c (4086/90)	47500
Bureau en pente, rosewood, ormolu, veneered with panels, 37½ x 39 x 17½, M18c (4168/136)	*8250*
Bureau plat, ormolu mounted, parquetry, 3 drawers, 30¾ x 57 x 30, M18c (4086/91)	14000
Bureau plat, attributed J. Baumhauer, ormolu mounted, 3 drawers, 30 x 45 x 26½, fine, L18c (4086/85)	82000
Bureau plat, kingwood, parquetry, leather inset, 3 drawers, 29½ z 63½ x 34, M18c (4232/175)	17000
Bureau plat, ormolu mounted kingwood, bois satine marquetry, 29 x 46 x 26, M18c, rare (4119/294)	*20000*

Bureau plat (4119/294)

Commode (4168/128)

Bureau plat, ormolu mounted, tulipwood, parquetry, 3 drawers, 29½ x 35½ x 22¼, M18c (4119/336)   7750
Bureau plat, provincial fruitwood, rectangular top, drawer and slide, cabriole legs, 29½ x 49 x 22, res
  (4142/146)   800
Canape, beechwood, top rail carved, upholstered, 61, M18c (4218/169)   800
Canape, beechwood, upholstered backrest, padded armrests, 78, M18c (4218/89)   900
Canape, beechwood, upholstered, oval seat carved cresting, 79, M18c (4218/179)   1000
Canape, painted, voluted top rail, cabriole legs, L56, M18c (4086/75)   8500
Canape, painted, upholstered blue cut velvet, painted grey with gilding, 78, M18c (4218/125)   2250
Canape a oreilles, beechwood, molded borders, serpentine seat rail, 80½, M18c (4119/265)   1300
Canape a oreilles, beechwood, triple backrest serpentine top rail, 77½, M18c (4232/149)   3000
Candlesticks, pair, ormolu, after Meissonnier, scrolls and roses, fine, h12, M18c (4086/62)   12500
Cartel clock, white enamel dial, scrolls, fine, H24½, M18c (4086/63)   9000
Cartonnier on stand, ormolu mounted, marquetry, 3 compartments, 54 x 36½ x 14¾, M18c
  (4086/93)   22000
Chaise a la reine, caned beechwood, acanthus carved knees, St. George, M18c (4168/133)   3300
Chaise longue, beechwood, voluted frame, upholstered, L78, M18c (4142/143)   1100
Chaise longue, walnut, molded frame, armrests, raised on down curved supports, 82, L18c
  (4157/63)   1000
Chaises a la reine, set of 4, gilt wood, cartouche-shaped backrest, E18c (4086/87)   17500
Chaises en cabriolet, gilt wood, pair, carved with twisted ribbons & beads, L18c (4218/173)   2500
Chaises en cabriolet, set of 3, cartouche-shaped backrest, painted, M18c (4219/154)   2000
Chest, provincial walnut, hinged top, fielded sides, short cabriole legs, 26 x 48 x 16¼, M18c
  (4157/66)   700
Chest of drawers, provincial walnut, serpentine 2 long drawers, wrought iron handles, 30¾ x 38¼ x
  23, L18c (4157/64)   1900
Commode, 3 short and 2 long drawers, scrolls and leaves, 32 x 47 x 26, M18c, I.B. Hedouin
  (4218/115)   6750

Commode (4119/332)

Commode, brass mounted fruitwood, marble top, 5 drawers, brass handles, 35¼ x 51 x 25¾, M18c (4272/445) — 7250

Commode, kingwood marquetry, serpentine border, 2 drawers, marble top, 33 x 46 x 24, millet (619/370) — 4750

Commode, miniature, tulipwood and kingwood, parquetry, serpentine, 13¾ x 18¾ x 10¼, M18c, rare (4218/191) — 3000

Commode, ormolu mounted, parquetry, red and white veined, marble top, 2 drawers, 34 x 61½ x 30½, M18c (4232/168) — 13000

Commode, ormolu mounted black lacquer, marble top, figure in landscape scene, 35 x 58 x 25, M18c (4232/161) — 60000

Commode, ormolu mounted black lacquer, 2 drawer, figures in country landscape, 32½ x 37¾ x 18¼, handles later (4218/190) — 3250

Commode, ormolu mounted kingwood, parquetry, grey and purple marble top, 33 x 51 x 26, ca1730 (4157/79) — 8000

Commode, ormolu mounted tulipwood, parquetry, marble top, (4119/258) — 5250

Commode, ormolu mounted tulipwood and kingwood parquetry, marble top, 34½ x 50½ x 24½, M18c (4232/130) — 10000

Commode, ormolu mounted, amaranthe, bombe front, marble top, sgd L. Boudin, JME, L18c (4086/73) — 31000

Commode, ormolu mounted, kingwood parquetry, serpentine marble top, 32½ x 31 x 18½, M18c (4218/122) — 5000

Commode, ormolu mounted, kingwood parquetry, serpentine 2 short, 1 long drawers, marble top, 22½ x 51 x 6¾ (4218/133) — 14500

Commode, ormolu mounted fruitwood, early for style, bombe shape, 33 x 48¾ x 25¼, M18c (4168/128) — *6500*

Commode, parquetry, bois satine, crowned 'C' on ormolu, 34½ x 50½ x 25, M18c, Migeon (4168/124) — 25000

Commode, petite, fruitwood, 2 panelled drawers, cabriole legs, 24 x 19, L18c (4119/273) — 1200

Commode, provincial brass mounted walnut, 3 long drawers, carved on side, 38½ x 52 x 27, M18c (4218/180) — 4500

Commode, provincial walnut, bow-front wooden top, 3 drawers, scrolled toes, 36½ x 50 x 23, L18c (4142/140) — 5000

Commode, provincial walnut, 3 long drawers, brass handles, 34½ x 45½ x 21, M18c (4218/160) — 4500

Commode, provincial walnut, wooden top, 3 drawers, short cabriole legs, 37 x 54 x 27, M18c (4272/379) — 3500

Commode, provincial walnut, wooden top, 3 long drawers, fitted brass handles, L18c (4272/382) — 5500

Commode, provincial early, oak, molded corners, scrolled feet, 33¾ x 49¼ x 25, M18c (4168/118) — 5250

Commode, serpentine, tulipwood, inlaid, ormolu mounted, marble top, 34½ x 54½, mid18c (4148/265) — 2400

Commode, tulipwood and kingwood, parquetry, serpentine, 4 drawers, 34¾ x 55 x 22, M18c (4119/332) — *5500*

Commode, tulipwood and purplewood, marquetry, with a flower filled basket, 29¾ x 22¾ x 17¼, J. Birkle (4119/264)	4750
Commode, tulipwood, parquetry, marble top, 2 long drawers, raised on cabriole legs, 35½ x 39 x 21¼, L18c (4157/84)	4600
Commode, walnut, 3 drawers, cabriole legs, 32¼ x 49 x 20, M18c, F.C. Franc (4142/139)	1750
Commode, walnut, provincial, brass handles on 3 drawers, 36½ x 50 x 25¾, M18c (4218/162)	4250
Commode, walnut, provincial brass mounted, serpentine, 34¼ x 48 x 25, L18c (4142/92)	4750
Commode, kingwood and tulipwood, parquetry, grey marble top, 2 short, 3 long drawers, 33½ x 39¼ x 21, L18c (4232/134)	6250
Commodes, pair, ormolu mounted black lacquer, chinoiserie landscape, 34 x 56 x 23, L19c (4119/298)	10000
Console, gilt wood, marble top, 34½ x 32½ x 15½, M18c (4119/306)	900
Console, marble, marble top raised on marble pedestals carved, 35 x 84 x 20, L18c (4218/129)	2750
Console, wrought-iron, serpentine breche d' Alep marble top, 34 x 36 x 18¼, M18c (4168/65)	3000
Cupboard, bedside, kingwood and tulipwood, writing surface, drawer, 31¼ x 19½ x 12¼, M18c (4232/178)	10000
Cupboard, provincial painted, pair doors, enclosing shelves, 60 x 51 x 21½, L18c (4157/62)	1500
Dining chairs, suite, fruitwood, 2 armchairs and 8 side chairs, carved backrails, (631/387)	2200
Encoignures, pair, B. van Risenburgh, lacquer, ormolu mounted, serpentine, 37 x 33½ x 24½, magnificent, M18c (4086/78)	105000
Etagere, stained pine and fruitwood, molded cornice, 3 shelves above drawer, 33 x 27 x 10, L18c (4142/184)	325
Etagere en encoignure, tulipwood, fruitwood marquetry, veneered floral sprays, 33½ x 15, M18c (4218/55)	1300
Etagere en encoignure, tulipwood, 3 graduated shelves, 34¼ x 26½ x 17¾, M18c (4232/135)	
Fauteuil, beechwood, cabriole legs, cabochons at knees, M18c (4168/113)	1800
Fauteuil, beechwood, cartouche back, Pere Gourdin, M18c (4168/131)	1000
Fauteuil, carved beechwood, with flowerheads and foliage, M18c (4119/275)	1000
Fauteuil, pair, walnut, carved, cartouche back, molded serpentine frame, M18c (4148/269)	3200
Fauteuil a coiffer, stained beechwood, molded voluted frame, padded armrests, M18c (4157/74)	550
Fauteuil a la reine, beechwood, voluted leaf and ribbon carved frame, M18c, C.L. Burgat (4119/266)	3100
Fauteuil a la reine, painted, cartouche shaped backrest, cabriole legs, L18c (4142/113)	1300

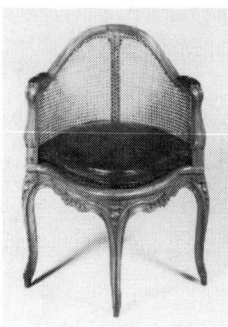

Fauteuil
de cabinet
(4168/130)

Fauteuil a la reine, painted, padded armrests, M18c (4168/156)	2000
Fauteuil a la reine, walnut, padded armrests, voluted suppports, M18c (4193/414)	900
Fauteuil de cabinet, beechwood, caned, E. Meunier, M18c (4168/130)	*6000*
Fauteuil de cabinet, beechwood, caned backrest and seat, padded armrests, M18c (4232/137)	2500
Fauteuil en cabriolet, beechwood, carved with flowerheads, M18c (4119/304)	600
Fauteuil en cabriolet, painted, molded voluted frame, floral silk, M18c (4168/52)	3100
Fauteuil en cabriolet, painted grey, carved cresting, scrolled toes, M18c, Nawroy (4232/203)	1000
Fauteuils a la reine, pair, gilt wood, cabriole legs, cartouche-shaped back, sgd F.R.C. Reuze, M18c (4086/72)	20000
Fauteuils a la reine, pair, caned fruitwood, serpentine seat, L18c (4119/251)	2000
Fauteuils en cabriolet, beechwood, cartouche shaped backrest, padded armrests, M18c (4272/380)	2700
Fauteuils en cabriolet, beechwood, pair, scrolled toes, carved at knees with acanthus leaves, (4157/56)	500

Fauteuils en cabriolet, painted, painted cream, M18c (4218/98)	1700
Fauteuils en cabriolet, pair walnut, molded frames, cartouche shaped backrests, M18c (4157/96)	1900
Fauteuils en cabriolet, pair, painted, oval backrest, with laurel leaves, L18c (4119/282)	1500
Fauteuils en cabriolet, set 6 beachwood, molded voluted frames carved flowerheads, M18L (4157/58)	8750
Fire screen, ormolu, scrolls, scrolled feet, H28½, L19c (4086/70)	1200
Inkstand, ormolu, lacquer, porcelain, glazed biscuit group, mounted as candelabrum, L14¼, ca1740 (4086/60)	15000
Marquise, painted, heart shaped motif, flanked by laurel leaves, 33, M 18c (4232/139)	5250
Mirror, carved gilt wood, mirrored frame, scrolls and flowerheads, 55 x 34, M18c (4119/218)	1700
Mirror, gilt wood, frame, carved, scrolls, leaves, flowerheads, 88 x 52, M18c (4157/16)	2300
Mirror, gilt wood, fruiting grape vine borders, basket of fruit, 68 x 37, L18c (4157/14)	2600
Mirror, gilt wood, framed carved with scrolls and leaves, 27½ x 18¾, M18c (4232/48)	800
Mirror, gilt wood, fruiting grape vine border, 68 x 37, L18c (4232/24)	5250
Mirror, gilt wood, shaped rectangular plate, mirrored and carved borders, 48 x 32, M18c (4272/316)	3250
Mirror, gilt wood, surmounted by a flower filled basket, 51½ x 31, L18c (4218/62)	3250
Mirror, wall, gilt wood, gessoed rococo frame, shell cresting, floral decoration, 47 x 26, 18c (631/332)	1500
Poudreuse, walnut, triple hinged divided top, enclosing mirror, 28 x 31½ x 18, M18c (4119/235)	450
Screen, 2-fold, gilt wood, cartouche-shaped panel, silk floral damask, H45½, W25 panels, M18c (4168/115)	4800
Screen, 4 fold, painted canvas, scenes in tones of grey on beige ground, 83 x 100 (4157/1)	200
Secretaire a abattant, B. van Risenburgh, ormolu mounted, marquetry, important, 53 x 41¾ x 18¼, M18c (4086/82)	195000
Secretaire a abattant, tulipwood and, purplewood parquetry, marble top, 50½ x 27½ x 15, L18c (4157/73)	1000
Settee, upholstered backrest, top rail carved, cabriole legs, 76, M18c (4272/429)	2700
Table, bedside, tulipwood, marquetry, marble top, veneered floral motif, 29 x 19½ x 13¼, M18c (4119/247)	3500
Table, center, boulle and ormolu mounted, serpentine top, cabriole legs, 30½ x 40 x 26 (631/391)	900
Table, center, provincial, fruitwood, breche d' Alep top, hoof feet, 28 x 30 x 17½, M18c (4168/120)	2400
Table, de chevet, tulipwood, parquetry, shaped top with writing surface, wooden gallery, 30 x 20 x 12½, L18c (4119/261)	4000
Table, dressing, fruitwood parquetry, top fitted with adjustable reading stand, 27 x 21¾ x 11½, 19c, top restored (4232/131)	800
Table, game, fruitwood, baize, gaming surface, drawer at each end, 28¼ x 37¾ x 24¾, M18c (44232/202)	1600
Table, occasional, fruitwood, 3 quarter gallery, drawer, cabriole legs, 28 x 22½, M18c (4119/279)	850
Table, side, ormolu mounted, mahogany, leather top with ormolu rim, 28½ x 21 x 16, M19c (4218/126)	1200
Table, tric trac, removable top veneered to reveal chessboard, 29 x 44½ x 24, M18c (4219/173)	6250
Table, writing and reading, tulipwood, marquetry, kidney shaped, 27½ x 38½ x 17¾, L19c (4119/289)	1750
Table, writing, provincial walnut, rounded corners, frieze containing 1 drawer, 28¼ x 25¾ x 18¾, L18c (4232/200)	1300
Table a ecrire, kingwood parquetry, frieze drawer, cabriole leg, 29 x 33 x 17¼, M18c (4086/88)	6000
Table a ecrire, parquetry, cabriole legs, rectangular top, 27¼ x 30¼ x 18¾, M18c (4086/83)	4250
Table a ecrire, ormolu mounted, kingwood parquetry, cabriole legs, 30 x 32 x 19½, M18c (4086/74)	10000
Table de toilette, kingwood and tulipwood, mirror, compartments, 28¾ x 30 x 18, L18c (4218/192)	1700
Table en chiffonniere, fruitwood, marquetry, pierced brass gallery, 29¼ x 16½ x 12¾, M18c (4232/159)	17000
Table en chiffonniere, ormolu mounted, tulipwood and kingwood, 27½ x 16¾ x 12¾, M18c (4119/262)	7750
Table en chiffonniere, 3 drawers, parquetry, ormolu mounted, bombe front, 27¾ x 12 x 10 (4086/99)	6000
Tables, console, pair, silkwood, marble top, frieze centered by lion's mask, 25½ x 26 x 12, L18c (4232/160)	13000
Tables, work, pair, ormolu mounted, fruitwood, purplewood, marquetry, kidney shaped hinged top, 27½ x 16¼ x 12¼, M18c (4232/199)	45000
Tabourets, gilt wood, pair, M18c (4168/155)	8250
Vase, Chinese incised celadon, mounted in ormolu, H21⅛, M18c (4086/57)	11500
Wall panels, 6, mounted as screen, represent months of year, res, 97 x 28, panels, E18c (4168/135)	6500

Louis XV-XVI

Armoire, provincial walnut, molded cornice, pair fielded doors, cabriole legs, 89½ x 56¼ x 23, L18c (4272/430)	2100
Armoire, provincial walnut, molded cornice, pair fielded doors, cabriole legs, 102 x 55 x 24½, L18c (4272/431)	2500

Bonheur du jour, marquetry, 6 drawers, cabriole legs, 37¾ x 26 x 15¼, L18c (4086/97)   10500
Buffet, oak, provincial, wooden top, 2 frieze drawers, pair of doors, 47 x 50 x 21, L18c (4272/401)   1900
Cabinet, 2-part, pine, provincial, upper glazed doors, lower fielded, 91½ x 59 x 20, M18c (4168/74)   1500
Pannetiere, provincial walnut, rectangular body, front centered by a door, 36 x 31½ x 16, L18c
(4272/329)   1500
Table de chevet, M. Carlin, JME, ormolu mounted, parquetry, drawer, cabriole legs, fine, rare, 30¼ x
20¾ x 13, L18c (4086/89)   45000
Table en chiffonniere, ormolu mounted, parquetry, oval top, L18c, 29.5 x 20 x 14.75, Lacroix
(4086/76)   50000
Table en chiffonniere, ormolu mounted, parquetry, L18c, 29¾ x 18 x 14, Lacroix, R.V.L.C.
(4086/77)   40000
Table en chiffonniere, F. Schey, mahogany, 3 drawers, cabriole legs, 28¾ x 21¼ x 15, L18c
(4086/94)   6250

Louis XVI

Armchair, beechwood, carved with leaf tips, bow-front seat, L18c (4157/46)   700
Banquette, painted, baluster shaped supports, painted grey, 76, L18c, unusual (4119/321)   2500
Banquette, painted, upholstered seat, circular tapered legs, 63½, L18c (4157/72)   550
Banquettes, pair, painted, rectangular, spiral twisted legs, L32½, L18c (4086/80)   7500
Bergere, mahogany, bow-front seat, tapered legs, L18c (4119/286)   800
Bergere a la reine, painted, upholstered, stop fluted legs, painted green, L18c (4142/159)   1200
Bergere en cabriolet, painted, curved molded backrest, L18c (4119/250)   800
Bergere en cabriolet, painted, top rails flanked by free standing columns, L18c (4218/139)   2000
Bergere en gondole, gilt wood, circular tapered stop-fluted legs, L18c (4086/95)   4750
Bergeres en cabriolet, painted, molded voluted frame, upholstered, padded armrests, L18c
(4157/93)   4600
Bonheur du jour, mahogany, marble top, glazed doors, 2 drawers, 42 x 31 x 15, L18c (4119/327)   1600
Bonheur du jour, parquetry, tulipwood, purplewood, tambour shutter, 35 x 21½ x 17, L18c
(4168/123)   6250
Buffet, a deux coups, provincial oak, edge carved with egg & dart motifs, 82 x 52 x 19, L18c
(4157/49)   3800
Bureau a cylindre, 3 quarter gallery, 48 x 49½ x 24½, L18c (4218/158)   3500
Bureau plat, rectangular, leather inset, 29 x 50 x 25, L18c (4219/103)   2700
Bureau plat, mahogany, ormolu and brass-mounted, leather top, 30 x 51¼ x 25¼, L18c (4168/139)   *16000*

Canape a encoignure
(4119/253)

Bureau plat (4168/139)

Commode (4168/125)

Canape, gilt wood, canted corners, 44, L18c (4119/257)   3750
Canape, painted, backrest flanked by pomegranate finials, 64, P. Pluvinet, L18c (4218/103)   4250
Canape, painted, painted grey, oval seat, fluted legs, 76, L18c (4119/291)   1100
Canape, walnut, stop-fluted legs, carved with twisted ribbons, L79, L18c (4168/84)   2100
Canape a encoignure, molded frame, curved seat rail, 53, L18c (4119/253)   *1300*
Chair, side, mahogany, panelled top, 5 stick splats, turned reeded legs, L18c (4142/69)   125

Chairs, side, pair, painted, open backrest, lyre shaped splats, fluted columns, (4232/108) — 1800

Chaises a la reine, pair, painted, bow-front seat, stop fluted legs, L18c (4119/335) — 600

Chauffeuses, pair, painted, arched top rail, bow-front seat, L18c (4142/161) — 1600

Chiffonnier, mahogany, marble top, canted, corners, 5 drawers, 37½ x 24¾ x 13½, L18c (4142/129) — 1300

Commode, brass mounted mahogany, marble top, gilt brass molding, 34½ x 40¼ x 18½, L18c (4119/334) — 2400

Commode, mahogany, grey marble top, 3 long drawers, 35 x 38¼ x 19¾ (4219/98) — 1800

Commode, mahogany, marble top above 3 drawers, 35 x 34¼ x 17½, L18c (4219/171) — 1000

Commode, ormolu and brass mounted, mahogany, 3 drawers, grey and white marble, 33½ x 50¾ x 22¾ (4218/128) — 3000

Commode, ormolu mounted mahogany, white marble, 3 drawers, 35 x 45 x 21½, L18c (4232/140) — 2500

Commode, ormolu mounted, bois satine, 3 frieze drawers over 2 drawers, 35½ x 57 x 23½, L18c (4168/125) — *20000*

Commode, ormolu mounted mahogany, veneer, ormolu beading, F. Ratie, 34½ x 43½ x 20, L18c (4168/54) — 11500

Commode, painted, rectangular top, square tapered legs, 34½ x 49 x 26½, L18c (4086/81) — 5000

Commode, tulipwood, purplewood, parquetry, marble top, J. M. Petit, 33 x 24 x 13½, L18c (4168/152) — 4500

Commode, walnut, provincial, 3 drawers flanked by fluted columns, 34½ x 43½ x 23½, L18c (4168/45) — 1600

Commode a encoignures, mahogany, semicircular, marble top, 3 drawers, 33 x 45½ x 24½ (4219/91) — 3000

Commode petite, provincial fruitwood, marble top, 3 drawers, 27½ x 17, L18c (4119/305) — 750

Console, brass mounted mahogany, white marble top, with concave sides, 34 x 40 x 15, L18c (4157/38) — 1200

Console, mahogany, white marble top, frieze with 1 drawer, raised legs, 32 x 31 x 13, L18c (4157/36) — 1300

Console, ormolu mounted mahogany, one drawer, gallery, 33¼ x 24 x 12¼, L18c, J. B. Vassou (4168/51) — 3750

Console, painted, marble top, carved with rosettes, stop fluted legs, 35¾ x 77 x 28½, L18c (4119/281) — 6000

Console desserte, brass mounted mahogany, 3 drawers, gallery, marble top, 35 x 48¾ x 17, L18c (4142/148) — 2100

Consoles, pair, Saunier, parquetry, ormolu mounted, 2 platform stretchers, fine, rare, 38½ x 38 x 14½, L18c (4086/79) — 35000

Consoles, pair, rare, gilt wood, breche d' Alep top, caduceus supports, 34½ x 19 x 9¾, L18c (4168/106) — 11500

Cupboard, bedside, provincial walnut, rectangular top, frieze drawer above cupboard, 29 x 15 x 14½, res, L18c (4272/440) — 375

Cupboard, fruitwood, wooden top above 2 pair doors, outlined with brass, 51½ x 36½ x 15, L18c (4272/331) — 1400

Desserte, console, brass mounted, mahogany, marble top, toupie feet, 31 x 31½ x 12, L18c, res (4142/135) — 1100

Desserte, console, fruitwood, grey marble top gallery, drawer, turned supports, 33¾ x 26 x 13, L18c (4142/119) — 650

Dining table, provincial fruitwood, hinged, semicircular top, plain frieze tapered legs, 31 x 49¼ x 24, L18c (4272/414) — 700

Encoignure, marquetry, tulipwood and, ringwood, molded marble top above a case door, 34 x 29 x 17, ca1770 (4272/365) — 750

Encoignures, pair, tulipwood, parquetry, one with marble top, fluted inlaid stiles, 33 x 25 x 16½, res, L18c (4272/437) — 1300

Fauteuil, painted, grey, rectangular backrest, L18c (4119/248) — 550

Fauteuil, walnut, lyre shaped splat, bow-front seat, upholstered, L18c (4142/112) — 900

Fauteuil, walnut, open backrest with circulat splats, L18c (4157/78) — 1000

Fauteuil, walnut, scrolled terminals carved with flowerheads, L18c (4232/144) — 1800

Fauteuil a la reine, rectangular backrest, painted white, L18c (4119/241) — 1300

Fauteuil de cabinet, caned and painted, tub shape, painted grey, (4142/144) — 2500

Fauteuil en cabriolet, painted, carving, upholstered, oval backrest, L18c (4218/135) — 1000

Fauteuil en cabriolet, painted, grey, carved with intertwined ribbons, L18c (4218/137) — 750

Fauteuil en cabriolet, painted, rectangular tapered backrest, padded armrests, L18c (4272/419) — 2500

Fauteuil en cabriolet, painted grey, oval backrest, L18c (4157/141) — 450

Fauteuils a la reine, painted, molded framed raised on tapered legs, painted white, L18c (4232/192) — 2700

Fauteuils a la reine, painted and parcel-gilt, set of five, painted grey highlightes with gilding, L18c (4232/128) — 3250

Fauteuils a la reine, pair, painted, square backrests, bow-front seat, L18c (4119/333) — 1400

Fauteuils en cabriolet, seat carved with twisted ribbons, upholstered, L18c (4232/142) — 2300

Fauteuils en cabriolet, pair, parcel-gilt, oval backrest, L18c (4119/240) — 2800

Fauteuils en cabriolet, painted pair, oval backrest, white highlighted with yellow, L18c (4142/105)   1300
Fauteuils en cabriolet, painted pair, oval backrest, cresting with cabbage roses L18, (4142/168)   21000
Fauteuils en cabriolet, pair, walnut, tapered backrest, padded armrest, bow-front seat, L18c
   (4272/427)   1600
Fauteuils en cabriolet, set of 4 painted, oval back rest, upholstered, L18c (4232/174)   2250
Fire screen, mahogany, rectangular screen, brass supports, 34¾ x 17½, L18c (4149/282)   185
Gueridon, mahogany, circular marble top, brass rim, fluted pedestal, 27¾ x 30, L18c (4142/157)   550
Gueridon, mahogany, circular white marble top, pierced gallery, 29 x 23, L18c (4218/127)   1600
Gueridon porte-lumiere, mahogany, adjustable marble top, 3 legs, J. Canabas, 29 x 12½, L18c
   (4168/66)   *2100*
Library steps, mahogany, 6 treads, railed banisters, 76½ x 20, 18c (4260/1744)   22000
Mirror, gilt wood, carved leaf tips, surmounted by trophy, 47¼ x 36½, L18c (4232/65)   1600
Screen, gilt wood, 6-fold, fine, carved with leaves, 49½ x 21½, panels, 18c (4168/134)   *3500*

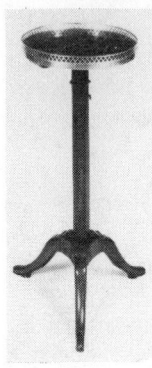
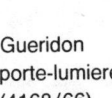

Screen (4168/134)

Gueridon
porte-lumiere
(4168/66)

Screen, 4 fold, painted, harbour scene with figures, 71 x 95, L18c (4232/138)   2600
Secretaire a abattant, brass mounted, mahogany, pierced gallery, fall front, shelves, drawers, 37 x
   38¼ x 16, L18c (4218/194)   2100
Secretaire a abattant, fruitwood, marble top, fall front opening to reveal shelves, drawers, 54 x 37 x
   16 (4157/45)   800
Secretaire a abattant, tulipwood and kingwood, parquetry, shelves, drawer, writing surface, 48½ x
   31½ x 14½, L18c (44232/181)   2500
Secretaire on stand, M. Carlin, black Japanese lacquer, ormolu, fine, rare, 56½ x 21¾ x 10, L18c
   (4086/100)   60000
Serviteur fidele, mahogany, 33½ x 12 x 10, L18c, J. Passmar (4119/323)   6500
Serviteur fidele, ormolu mounted, parquetry, 3 octagonal trays, candle arms, 35½ x 12½, L18c
   (4086/86)   6000
Sofa, provincial carved, beechwood, rectangular backrest, bow-front seat, 73, L18c (4119/297)   500
Table, tric, trac, mahogany, removable leather inset top, revolving, 29¼ x 44¼ x 11¼, L18c
   (4232/91)   2400
Table, bedside, inlaid tulipwood, tambour enclosed front, tapered legs, 29 x 16½ x 12 2/3, L18c
   (4119/287)   900
Table, bedside, provincial fruitwood, 3 quarter gallery, 3 drawers, 29 x 15½ x 11, L18c (4272/444)   550
Table, bedside, provincial oak and fruit, wood parquetry, 3 quarter wooden gallery, drawer, 31 x 20½
   x 13¼, L18c (4232/204)   300
Table, bouillotte, brass mounted mahogany, removable circular top, leather inset, 28¼ x 28, L18c
   (4218/199)   2000
Table, center, ormolu mounted tulipwood, parquetry, oval marble top, square tapered legs, 28 x 45¾
   x 34½, L18c (4272/387)   2000
Table, de chevet, mahogany, white marble top, wooden gallery, L18c (4219/156)   3250
Table, dining, provincial fruitwood, simicircular wooden top to form dining surface, 28¾ x 41, L18c
   (4232/198)   700
Table, dressing, gentleman's, mahogany, hinged top, mirror, compartments, 30¼ x 32 x 20, L18c
   (4218/196)   700
Table, en chiffoniere, tulipwood, parquetry, gallery, marble top, 28 x 16½ x 12¼, L18c (4142/162)   850
Table, games, brass mounted mahogany, hinged top, brass rim, 28½ x 33½ x 16½, L18c
   (4232/169)   1600
Table, games, provincial, hinged swivel top, open to game surface, plain frieze, 27½ x 33½ x 17½,
   L18c (4272/415)   500
Table, tric trac, walnut, removable top with leather writing surface, 30½ x 45 x 23¼, L18c (4218/83)   1200
Table, work, provincial walnut, dished top, drawer, trestle supports, 26 x 17 x 12½, L18c (4272/441)   600

Table, writing, leather inset top, single drawer, 28¾ x 37½ x 21½, L18c (4232/92) — 950

Table, 3-tiered, marquetry, oval tiers, ormolu rims, trellis pattern, 28¾ x 19½ x 10¼, L18c (4168/64) — 3000

Table a ecrire, slightly dished top, drawer at end, 24 x 25 x 15½, L18c (4219/141) — 850

Table a ecrire, mahogany, leather writing surface, 2 drawers, 27¼ x 38 x 20, L18c (4219/169) — 2100

Table a ecrire, kingwood and tulipwood, 3 quarter gallery, white marble, 31¼ x 19¾ x 14¾, L18c (4232/188) — 4750

Table a ecrire, mahogany, gallery, marble top, 29 x 19½ x 15¼, L18c (4142/120) — 4500

Table a ecrire, tulipwood, parquetry, leather inset, 28½ x 38 x 22, L18c (4219/128) — 1900

Table a ecrire, tulipwood, oval top, gallery, parquetry, 28¼ x 27 x 17, L18c (4119/263) — 4750

Table a lire a ecrire, with adjustable reading stand, 27 x 19¼ x 12, L18c (4219/165) — 3800

Table en chiffonniere, veneered with floral motifs, marquetry, 28 x 15 x 11½, L18c, A.P. Jacot (4218/116) — 8000

Table en chiffonniere, mahogany, 3 quarter gallery, marble top, kidney shape, 29 x 19½ x 15, L18c (4142/117) — 2500

Table en rogon, mahogany, kidney shaped, I.S. Rebour, 27¾ x 32 x 15½, L18c (4218/104) — 1600

Tabouret de lit, painted, carved with beads, white with gilding, W22, L18c (4168/53) — 2000

Trumeau, painted and parcel-gilt, grisaille panel, figures of musicians, 67 x 49, L18c (4119/219) — 650

Voyeuse, walnut, upholstered top rail, horseshoe shape seat, L18c (4272/422) — 1200

Directoire

Atheniennes, pair, ormolu, mahogany, brass bowls, columns with sphinx heads, H35 (4168/96) — 3600

Bench, window, rectangular, roll over ends, grey, 51½, L18c (4219/97) — 1000

Bergere, painted, roll over rectangular backrest, L18c (4219/148) — 1300

Bergeres, pair, painted, arm supports with Egyptian busts, H36, E19c (4168/56) — 2200

Chair, side, mahogany, wide curved backrest, L18c (4219/102) — 150

Chairs, side, pair, fruitwood, carved urns, lyre-shaped splats, sabre legs, L18c (4168/48) — 650

Chiffonnier, mahogany, veined white marble, 6 long drawers brass handles, 56 x 35½ x 16¼, L18c (4157/75) — 1500

Fauteuil, mahogany, open back, wide top rail, curved front legs, L18c, fine, rare, Freres (4232/147) — 8000

Fauteuil, painted, open backrest, arched top rail, painted brown, L18c (4142/108) — 650

Fauteuil a la reine, painted, curved seat, sabre legs, ca1795 (4232/125) — 1300

Gueridon, ormolu and marble, marble top circular, 28 x 24, L18c (4232/118) — 5000

Mirror, gilt wood, rectangular, carved frame, 43½ x 31½, ca1795 (4219/77) — 550

Stool, painted, rectangular seat with molded rails, 15¼, L18c (4219/110) — 250

Stools, pair, mahogany, rectangular upholstered seat, 17, L18c (4219/147) — 900

Table, bouillotte, marble top, pierced gallery, 28 x 25½, 19c (4232/120) — 800

Table, dining, mahogany, ormolu mounted, oval divided top, sabots, casters, 3 leaves, 29¼ x 139 (4168/79) — 15000

Table, dining, mahogany, divided oval top, circular tapered legs, 28½ x 57½, L18c (4219/167) — 2700

Tabouret, fruitwood, square upholstered seat, ca1795 (4232/123) — 400

Tabouret de pied, painted, rectangular seat, circular tapered legs, L18c (4218/105) — 225

Empire

Bed, mahogany, head and foot board raised on free standing columns, 41¾ x 46 x 82, E19c (4157/90) — 325

Bergere, mahogany, carved with laurel leaves, E19c (4218/76) — 1700

Bergere, provincial walnut, upholstered, square supports, E19c (4218/157) — 350

Bibliotheque, ormolu mounted, mahogany, black marble top, glazed doors, 62½ x 41½ x 16½, E19c (4157/92) — 1000

Bureau a cylindre, mahogany, rectangular grey marble top, drawers, 48¾ x 57½ x 28½, E19c (4219/159) — 6000

Bureau plat, ormolu mounted, mahogany, top with brass border, writing surface, 32 x 59 x 31½, L18c (4232/145) — 5250

Canape, 2 fauteuils, 2 side chairs, gilt wood set, winged lion supports, L78, E19c (4168/161) — 7000

Chairs, side set of 4, brass mounted, curved open backrest, drop in seat, E19c (4232/112) — 2750

Commode, fruitwood, wooden top, frieze with drawer, above 3 drawers, 36 x 50½ x 25, E19c (4272/411) — 1600

Commode, mahogany, grey marble top, 1 frieze and 3 long drawers, 29¾ x 34¼ x 19¾, E19c (4157/86) — 1000

Commode, mahogany, grey marble top, 3 drawers, 34¾ x 51 x 24, 19c (4219/101) — 1900

Commode, mahogany, one frieze and 3 long drawers, marble top, 37 x 43 x 28¾, E19c (4157/89) — 2100

Commode, ormolu mounted mahogany, marble top, 1 drawer, 3 long drawers, 34½ x 47 x 23, E19c (4219/96) — 700

Commode, ormolu mounted, thuyawood, black marble top, block feet, 37 x 51 x 23½, E19c (4219/162) — 3000

Day bed, ormolu mounted, mahogany, rectangular ends, rounded top rails, block feet, 76, E19c (4272/323) — 1600

Fauteuils, en gondole, mahogany pair, semicircular seat, upholstered, E19c (4232/90) — 2600

Fauteuils, mahogany, upholstered backrest, wooden armrests, E19c (4232/111)   3100
Fauteuils, pair, fruitwood, rectangular backrest, wooden armrests, sabre legs, E19c (4232/196)   1500
Fauteuils, pair, mahogany, parcel-gilt, slightly curved backrest, wooden armrest, E19c (4272/345)   2700
Gueridon, ormolu mounted mahogany, circular marble top, circular pedestal, scrolled feet, 28¾ x 30¾, E19c (4272/421)   1100
Gueridon, mahogany, circular top on circular columns, 26 x 27½, E19c (4219/143)   1100
Gueridon, ormolu, mahogany, bearded heads on monopode legs, attrib. Jacob, 32 x 39½ (4168/153)   13000
Marquise, mahogany, rectangular backrest, wooden armrests, 43½, E19c (4218/154)   1200
Secretaire a abattant, fruitwood, marble top, drawer, fall front, 57½ x 36½ x 17¼, L19c (4193/418)   900
Secretaire a abattant, ormolu mahogany, marble top, fall front, 57 x 37¾ x 17¼, E19c (4142/154)   6500
Shaving stand, brass mounted mahogany, onyx top, drawers, 40¼ x 20 x 15½, E19c (4232/113)   1400
Table, dressing mahogany, marble top, frieze, drawer on either side, 39 x 21¼ x 17¼, E19c (4157/88)   850
Tray, tea, tole on stand, oval top, painted in gold, border of swags, trophies, 19 x 29, E19c (4272/206)   850

Neoclassical

Etagere, walnut provincial, 3 shelves above drawer, 34 x 20½ x 8, E19c (4142/183)   275

Charles X

Chairs, side, set of 3, mahogany, open backrests, L19c (4232/98)   650
Commode, fruitwood, marble top, 4 drawers, square feet, 37¾ x 49¾ x 21¾, ca1830 (4272/412)   1200
Fauteuil, parcel-gilt mahogany, upholstered backrest with gilt metal griffin, M19c (4142/167)   275
Gueridon, mahogany, cabriole legs, H27¼, Diam 18½, M19c (4168/144)   600
Music stand, patinated, bronze and rouge marble, pierced music holder, fluted stem, 18½, L19c (4272/303)   950
Screen, 3 fold, mahogany, clear glass panel above leather inset panel, solid panel, 69 x 69, M19c (4272/339)   850
Screen, 4-fold, wallpaper panels, upper painted country scenes, H63, W23 panel (4168/68)   450
Table, dining, burr fruitwood, triangular pedestal, claw feet, H29½, Diam 47½, E19c (4168/141)   1300

Louis Philippe

Cartonnier, mahogany, twelve drawers, short bracket feet, 62 x 25 x 13½, M19c (4119/230)   950
Daybed, ormolu mounted mahogany, 79, L19c (4142/151)   1300
Gueridon, ormolu, patinated bronze, circular inlaid marble top, tripod, paw feet, 26½ x 26, M19c (4168/58)   5750
Gueridon, ormolu, patinated bronze, circular inlaid marble top, tripod, paw feet, 26½ x 29¼, M19c (4168/57)   5250
Tables, bedside, 2, marble tops, plinth bases, H28, Diam 16, E19c (4168/142)   550

Napoleon III

Bed, cast iron, roll over headboard and footboard, 35½ x 81, L19c (4219/113)   850
Etagere, brass mounted thuyawood, 3 tiers, 3 quarter gallery, 29½ x 16½x 12½, L19c (4232/201)   75
Piano stool, brass, inlaid, L19c (4232/95)   175

German Decorations

GERMAN CLOCKS

Shelf clocks

Biedermeier, walnut-tapestry, movement by L. Louis Violier, embroidered dial, 17½ ca1830 (4165/210)   425
Clock, carriage, hour repeater, bronze, 4 plaques, swing handle, 4¾, ca1910, crack, Viennese (669/295)   1300
Clock, mantel, ebonized, mounted, 2 train movement, glass panels, 14½, E18c (4232/31)   2700
Clock, mantel, ormolu mounted white marble, malachite, base and pedestals, 15, L18/E19c, fine (4232/55)   6250
Clock, mantel, silver gilt and enameled, mannerist style with grotesques, 5, L19c, Viennese (669/294)   1300
Clock, mantel, walnut, Austrian, circular white dial, three-train movement, 16¾, E19c (4232/11)   550
Drum shape, German, standing rack, I.I. Schmidt, Karlsruhe, marble base, 20, ca1810, base later (4165/209)   2700
German gilt, ebonized, musical, 8½ inch dial, 2 train movement, 19½, E18c (4272/254)   5750
Mantel, fruitwood and ebonized, Austrian, white enamel dial in square case, 17, E19c (4218/6)   300
North German, late baroque, rosewood, steel dial, roman numerals, strike repeat cord, 10¼, E18c (4272/243)   3500

Standing clocks

Alarm, silver metal, twin pendulums, dowble bell, German, 8¾, ca1780 (4165/217)   4000
Astronomical tabernacle, gilt metal, calendar and moon phase dials, German, 15¾, ca1600, important (4165/231)   11000
Crucifix, gilt metal, surmounted by revolving globe, German, 12½, ca1600 (4165/228)   5000
Figural, Black Forest, form of watchmaker clock on chest, 14½ ca1800 (4165/215)   *3500*

Figural
(4165/215)

Table (4165/224)

Telleruhr (4165/221)

Zappler small
brass chapter ring
(4165/214)

Table, repeating with alarm, silver, Peter Krenckel, Euchstet, 3¾, ca1710, German (4165/232)   8500
Table, repeating, gilt metal hexagonal, Petitot, Berlin, clock and foot pierced, 5, ca1740 (4165/224)   *9250*
Table, with alarm, gilt metal repeating, applied ram's masks and festoons, German, 3⅜, ca1775 (4165/225)   4000
Travel, repeating, gilt metal, enamel, Grand Sonnerie, Austrian, 10, E19c (4165/245)   1700

Tall-case clocks

Clock, long case, chiming, rococo, gilt-decorated, simulated walnut, Lippert, Berlin, 102½, M18c (4232/7)   1300
Miniature, silver, enamel movement, by Touchon and Co., Austrian, 9¼, ca1900 (4165/247)   1100

Time devices

Rolling drum, gilt metal and silver, Andreas Kraus, Schweidnitz, 4⅛ x 20¼, E18c (4165/227)   21000
Sand clock, brass, 4 quarter hour glasses, German, 9⅛, E18c (4165/223)   2400

Wall clocks

Automation post Gothic painted iron, man's head with moving bearded jaw, 17¼, ca1600 (4165/219)   25000
Black forest painted wood, predominantly wood movements, side panels later, 9¾ lacks hour hand, 18c (4165/218)   3750
Metal and gilt wood, cartouche shaped dial, 27½, L18c, German (4165/212)   1900
Telleruhr, gilt metal, circular, Augsburg*, 18½ ca1700 (4165/222)   4250
Telleruhr, silvered metal and brass, 22¾, ca1740, German (4165/221)   *6000*
Telleruhr, small gilt metal, firmed as a Rococo Cartouche, German, 18c alterations (4165/220)   2200
Zappler small brass chapter ring, front mounted pendulum, front pierced, engraved, 4⅞ L18c, German (4165/214)   *3000*

Wall rack clocks

Hooded, mermaids and ships, Friesland verge movement, single bell and alarm, 24½ M18c, Dutch (4165/213)   1800
White enamel dial, weight movement slides on double saw edge rack, 30¾ alterations, German (4165/211)   8000

GERMAN LIGHTING DEVICES

Candelabra, figural, pair, 3 branch, seated woman, parrot and bird, Bitzendorf, 19¾, L19c, some leafage lacking (631/153)   550

Candelabra, pair, plaue, 5 branch, 4 scrolling arms, 1 upright socket, 21, 20c (619/120) — 400
Candlesticks, pricket pair, bronze, with paterae, masks and scrolls, 17¼, rep, E17c (4193/124) — 2500
Chandelier, 6 light, cranberry overlay glass, 3 tier, scrolled branches and curved glass canes, 32 (631/237) — 950
Chandelier, 8 light, green overlay glass, 3 tier, painted with floral sprays and insects, 41 (631/238) — 1800
Sconces, 4 light, flower, pair, pink and green, encrusted with flowers, 18, damages (631/148) — 650

German Furniture

Assorted styles

Chest, iron strongbox, painted on exterior with birds, flowers, other motifs, 31½, 17c, repair to base (4133/89) — 2700
Chest, painted, Austrian, hinged black painted top, multicolored flowers, 33 x 50½ x 25, 1830 (4232/99) — 700
Coffer, brass and iron engraved, hinged top, loop handles, engraved flowering foliage, 10, L17c, small (4133/87) — 3000
Kas, marquetry inlaid walnut, pair doors flanked by canted sides, bun feet, 77 x 69 x 29½, ca1740 (4232/110) — 8000

Baroque

Armoire, oak and walnut, rectangular, pair of doors, 92 x 78 x 22, res, L17c (4193/384) — 3100
Cabinet, table walnut marquetry, crest with 2 drawers, 12 drawers, center cupboard, 29 x 21½ x 8, ca1740 (4272/285) — 1800
Cabinet, table, inlaid walnut, nine drawers surrounding a cupboard, 29 x 22 x 8, M18c (4119/155) — 950
Cabinet bureau, inlaid walnut, block front, fitted interior, 97 x 42 x 21½, L18c (4119/234) — 9000
Chair, sleeping-porter's, carved mahogany, German, hinged back and seat, L18c (4260/1709) — 6500
Chair, sleeping-porter's, carved mahogany, German, hinged back and seat, L18c (4260/1710) — 6500
Chair, sleeping-porter's, carved mahogany, German, hinged back and seat, L18c (4260/1707) — 9500
Chair, sleeping-porter's, carved mahogany, German, hinged back and seat, L18c (4260/1708) — 9500
Chest, inlaid walnut, hinged, arched lappet, carved border, 22½ x 55½, E17c (4193/430) — 3750
Commode, rosewood, ivory inlaid, serpentine, 5 drawers, 42½ x 52 x 26½, ca1710 (4119/309) — *1700*
Desk, writing, rosewood and pewter, marquetry, chinoiserie scenes, 50¾ x 38, L17c (4119/280) — 16000
Headboard, oak, overhanging cornice with carved panels, 72½ x 61, M17c (4255/428) — 1700
Table, inlaid walnut center, frame inlaid with stellate devices, 29 x 44, 18c (4149/247) — 800
Table, refectory, walnut and brass, plank top, 3 frieze drawers, 32½ x 76 x 30½, E17c (4255/431) — 4000

Rococo

Armchair, painted and parcel-gilt, painted blue with gilder border, L18c (4218/95) — 2000
Bookcase bureau, fruitwood, mirrored doors, writing surface, 3 drawers, 83 x 35 x 18, M18c (4232/114) — 6500
Bureau en pente, burr, fruitwood, slant front to form writing surface, 38 x 39¼ x 21, M18c (4232/189) — 3750
Bureau en pente, fruitwood and kingwood, floral sprays, birds, scrolls, marquetry, 38 x 36 x 20¾, M18c (4232/179) — 12500
Chairs, side, pair, gilt wood, leaf, shell flowerhead and putti, M18c (4119/303) — 3100
Chest of drawers, bureau, walnut, slant front, inlaid with pair of birds, 44 x 52 x 22, M18c (4119/158) — 6000
Chest of drawers, walnut, fruitwood, serpentine top, 2 long drawers, 33½ x 48½ x 21, M18c (4272/351) — 5000
Commode, ormolu mounted fruitwood, bow-front, 2 drawers, pad feet, 30½ x 44¼ x 22½, L18c (4119/157) — *1700*
Console, painted, marble top, carved with cabochons and rinceaux, 32 x 64 x 30¼, ca1725 (4142/128) — 3500
Fauteuil a la reine, painted, carved with foliate motifs, ca1730 (4218/144) — 1600
Games table, parquetry, kingwood, concave-sided removable top, cabriole legs, rare, 30¾ x 42¼, M18c (4086/98) — 47500
Mirror, gilt wood, pierced cresting, frame with arabesques, 47, M18c (4272/273) — 800
Mirror, overmantel, gilt wood, floral wreaths, shell cresting, 48 x 58, M18c (4168/3) — 1200
Mirror, toilet, burr walnut, arched plate, free standing supports, 30 x 18 (4218/50) — 550
Mirrors, pair, gilt wood, frames, surmounted by animal head, carvings, 35 x 18, M18c (4232/5) — 850
Settee, 3 chair, mahogany, leaf and C scroll carved top rail, 77, 18c (4157/145) — 850
Stool, gilt wood, serpentine rails, scrolled toes, W20¼, M18c (4168/86) — 1100
Stool, walnut, rectangular seat, cabriole legs, 24 (4218/91) — 375
Table console, brass mounted, kingwood, top inlaid with oval, 30¾ x 40½ x 19¾, L18c (4232/183) — 1700

Neoclassical

Bergeres, pair, mahogany, upholstered backrest, wooden arms, Austrain, E19c (4232/93) — 2500

Chairs, side, oak, pair, open backrests, horizontal pierced splats, L18c (4232/170)   600
Chest of drawers, burr fruitwood and walnut, parquetry, fitted interior, 47 x 52½ x 26, L18c
(4218/167)   4000
Mirror, gilt wood, rectangular, urn, drapery swag, 44 x 20, L18c (4168/22)   300
Panel, marquetry, inlaid with fruitwood, 43 x 24, L18c (4142/62)   2600

Biedermeier

Cabinet, wood and bois clair ebonized, pair glazed doors enclosing shelves, 68 x 45 x 19, E19c
(4142/98)   800
Chair, side, fruitwood, open backrest, arched top rail, painted splat, L19c (4157/87)   150
Chairs, side, pair, open backrest, ebonized baluster shaped splats, L19c (4272/391)   500
Chairs, side, pair, fruitwood, hoop shaped open backrests, upholstered seats, L19c (4232/105)   750
Chairs, side, 5, fruitwood, carved, lyre splat, square taper legs, res, ca1840 (4148/277)   1000
Chairs, side pair, boisclair and ebonized wood, panelled top rail, upholstered seat, E19c (4142/145)   225

Furniture
(631/365)

Commode (4119/309)

Table (4232/104)

Commode
(4119/157)

Furniture, suite, circular dining table and 6 side chairs, 7 pcs (631/365)   *1700*
Gueridon, mahogany and fruitwood, top with drawer, triangular base, 26¾ x 15, L19c (4232/96)   475
Mirror, gilt mounted fruitwood, molded cornice, panelled frieze, rectangular plate, 60 x 30, E19c
(4272/251)   325
Settee, fruitwood, concave seat on raised block feet, 64½, 19c (4232/101)   950
Table, center, circular, bois claire, frieze drawer, tripod supports, 28 x 18½, res, E19c (4272/439)   500
Table, work, fruitwood, thuyawood, oval dish tray fitted with drawer, lyre shape support, 28 x 21¼ x
13¼, L19c (4232/104)   *800*
Vitrine corner, fruitwood, glazed enclosing shelves, 68¾ x 40 x 19, E19c (4218/166)   650

Italian Decorations

ITALIAN DECORATIVE OBJECTS

Angels, pair gilt wood, rococo, standing figures on clou D-shaped bases, 40, ca1725 (4218/20)   2000
Blackamoors, pair, Venetian, painted, carrying circular tray, 62, 19c (4119/14)   2000
Figure of a blackamoor, carved, painted, gilded, standing woman fully clothed, 37, M19c (4218/49)   1000
Procession ornaments, pair, rococo gilt, papier mache, oval, foliage, flowerheads, 27½, M18c
(4232/19)   550

ITALIAN LIGHTING DEVICES

Candlestickes, figural, pricket pair, wood gilt, standing angels, 24, 18c, arm replaced, Italian
(4133/357)   650
Candlesticks, altar, pair, brass, now electrified, 38, 17c (4260/928)   1800
Candlesticks, pair, brass, baluster and urn shaped knobs, 35, now electrified, 17c (4260/922)   1700
Candlesticks, pair, gilt wood pricket, columnar fluted stem, neoclassical, 22½, L18c (4272/293)   150
Candlesticks, pair, gilt wood, Rococo, baluster stem, carved leaves and scrolls, 27½, E18c
(4272/274)   475

Candlesticks, pricket, pair, wood, carved acanthus, leaves, baluster stems, 30, 18c, Italian (4133/360)   300

Chandelier, 6 light baroque gilt wood, plum carved, stem, scrolling candle branches, 48, L18c (4157/6)   1900

Girandoles, pair, early, ormolu, rock crystal, 7 light, 3 branches, rare, H29¾ x 17, M18c (4086/67)   16500

Lamp, table, silver, bronze figure of mercury supporting spherical lamp, 23, Rome, ca1800 (4141/570)   1850

Lanterns, pair, gilt wood, triangular, glazed sides, on poles and bases, H97, Venetian (4168/28)   *1600*

Lanterns, pair, wood, tall, gilt, curling scroll work around frosted glass panels, 95, 17c, Venetian (4133/350)   1100

Lanterns, pair, wood, tall, gilt, glass panels, poles, 104, L17, E18c, Venetian (4133/351)   650

Sconces, wood, pair, carved and painted, dec. with shells and scrolling acanthus leaves, 71, Italian large (619/316)   400

Sconces, 4 light gilt wood, shape of vases, surmounted by oval mirror, 41, L18c (4218/36)   1700

Wall lights, Venetian baroque, fruitwood, carved backplate, single candle arm, 25, M18c (4157/33)   950

Italian Furniture

Assorted styles

Appliques, pair copper, each figure hollow back, 1 a bishop other martyr, 4¼, 15c (4133/97)   350

Figure of a foot soldier, gilt bronze, striding position Italo-Flemish, H6¼, ca1610 (4086/69)   2100

Mirror, cut glass, venetian, octagonal shape, frame composed bevelled, panels, 25½ x 18¼, 19c (4232/61)   500

Mirror, gilt wood, oval, plate, surmounted by pair of angels, leaves, 68 x 48, M18c (4119/13)   2400

Mirror, Venetian octagonal, bevelled plate, subsidiary mirrored border, 49 x 34 (4157/8)   400

Plaque, Madonna Del Sedia, after Raphael, 5¾, L19c, gilt frame (631/168)   250

Table, center, marble top, black marble, dentil apron with portrait medallions, (631/336)   300

Tables, pair, fruitwood, inlaid top above drawer and a tambour door, 31½ x 15½ x 18 (631/403)   450

Renaissance

Armchair, dante folding, walnut, carved, trestle supports, L16c (4119/53)   2900

Armoire, carved oak, doors carved with male and female busts, 81 x 72 x 25, L19c (4157/40)   1700

Cabinet, side, walnut, friezed drawers, guilloche carved doors, 40½ x 52 x 19, res, L16c (4119/23)   *5000*

Cabinet, walnut, rectangular, panelled doors, flower head pulls, 48 x 57 x 21½, L16c (4119/57)   6000

Cabinets, side, walnut, frieze drawers, guilloche carved doors, 41½ x 70 x 19½, E17c (4119/43)   4250

Prie dieu (4119/39)

Chairs (4119/32)

Lanterns (4168/28)

Scabelli (4119/55)

Table (4119/27)

Cabinet (4119/23)

Cassone, gilt decorated, walnut, compartments, carved, 29 x 68 x 21½, M16c (4119/46)   4500
Cassone, walnut, hinged top enclosing lidded compartment, 25 x 65 x 22, L16c (4142/71)   1300
Cassone, walnut, miniature, hinged top, front carved with coat of arms, 13 x 24¼ x 10¼, restoration (4142/64)   1000
Chair, side, walnut, backrest with 2 scroll carved panelled cross bars, E17c (4157/120)   600
Chairs, dining set of 6, walnut, Studded leather backs, square legs, E17c, res (4119/32)   *3200*
Chairs, savonarola, silver mounted, embroidered with gold, various medals, 19c (4157/129)   2700
Chest of drawers, fruitwood, marquetry, 2 drawers, gilt metal handles, 31 x 49 x 25½ (4157/165)   1200
Cupboard, carved oak, geometrical panelled doors, corinthian columns, 84 x 77 x 31, L16c (4119/58)   22000
Prie dieu, carved walnut, panelled base with lidded compartment, 36½ x 26½ x 22, restorations (4218/140)   2100
Prie dieu, walnut, frieze drawer, above 3 drawers, columns, 35½ x 27 x 24, E17c (4119/39)   1500
Scabelli, walnut, cartouche, shaped backrest, octagonal seat, trestle supports, L16c (4119/55)   *3200*
Table, draw leaf, walnut, plank top, baluster ends, trestle supports, 33 x 59½ x 32¼, L16c (4119/45)   3300
Table, side, walnut, frieze drawer, turned legs, bun feet, 32 x 31 x 20, E17c (4119/22)   2500
Table, side, walnut, rectangular top, 2 drawers, bobbin turned legs, 32½ x 39 x 23, E17c (4119/27)   *1800*
Table, side, walnut and pine, frieze drawers, bobbin turned legs, 34 x 37½ x 16, E17c (4119/31)   1300
Table, writing, walnut, 2 drawers, trestle supports, 30 x 52 x 25, L17c, res (4119/30)   1900

Baroque

Armchair, open backrest, seat open to reveal well, res, E17c (4193/396)   500
Armchair, walnut, upholstered back, wooden armrests ending with lions heads, L17c (4157/133)   600
Armchair, walnut, upholstered backrest, E17c (4255/452)   600
Armchair, walnut, upholstered backrest, wooden armrest, rep, L17c (4272/348)   175
Armchair, walnut, upholstered, wood arms, L17c (4193/391)   450
Armchair, walnut, upholstered, wood arms, L17c (4193/440)   1000
Armchairs, pair, rectangular backrest, voluted wodden armrests, L17c (4255/423)   1000
Armchairs, pair, walnut, upholsted needlepoint backrest and seat, M17c (4255/419)   4000
Armchairs, pair, walnut, upholstered in comtemporary brussel tapestry, 17c (4218/88)   3500
Bench, hall, walnut, rectangular backrest, baluster shaped supports, 53½, M17c (4119/66)   1300
Bench, silvered wood, not upholstered, carved, scrolls and leaves, 49½, E18c (4232/191)   1900
Casket, walnut, with wrought iron plaques, 9¼ x 15¾ x 11, M17c (4119/18)   475
Cassone, baroque walnut, rectangular hinged top, lapped carved border, 22½ x 55 x 21, E17c (4142/80)   375
Cassone, walnut, hinged lid, plinth base, 21½ x 66 x 20, 17c (4193/400)   650
Cassone, walnut fruitwood inlaid, stepped hinged rectangular, inlaid plinth base, 39½ x 88 x 28, E17c (4193/408)   12000
Chair, Savonarola, walnut and fruitwood inlaid, curved armrests, E17c (4193/421)   2600
Chairs, side, set of 6, rectangular, upholstered, voluted legs, L18c (4193/439)   6100
Chest, brass mounted, ebonized, hinged top, fitted interior, 12½ x 28½ x 14½, 17c (4255/447)   600
Credenza, baroque walnut, lappet carved border bracket feet, 42½ x 63½, 17c (4142/97)   1600
Credenza, walnut, lappet border, drawer, cupboard, 36 x 30 x 14, E17c (4255/397)   2500
Credenza, walnut, rectangular, drawer, pair doors, 32¾ x 35¼ x 16¼, 17c (4193/402)   450
Credenza, walnut, 2 drawers, pair doors, rectangular top, 39 x 49½ x 23½, 17c (4142/186)   2300
Mirror, rectangular plate, surrounded by leaf tips, 27½ x 26, E17c (4255/392)   750
Mirror, painted and parcel-gilt, concave sided, floral decoration, 26½ x 20¾, E18c (4119/194)   325
Mirror, painted gilt wood, pierced oval frame with plume cresting, 51½ x 38, 17c (4272/244)   400
Table, center, walnut, rectangular, iron stretchers, 28¼ x 46¾ x 26½, 17c, res (4142/94)   425
Table, writing, rectangular top, frieze drawer, straight legs, 26¾ x 42 x 22, L17c (4119/60)   400

Rococo

Armchair, fruitwood, upholstered, wooden armrest, cabriole legs, M18c (4142/124)   450
Armchair, gilt wood, leaf, shell and scroll carved frame, M18c (4119/302)   500
Armchair, Venetian, painted green, ca1730 (4218/108)   1900
Armchair, walnut caned, cartouche shaped backrest, carved with foliate motifs, L18c (4157/52)   650
Armchairs, pair walnut, cartouche shaped, backrest, cabriole legs, L18c (4119/74)   1300
Bergeres en cabriolet, pair, painted, whole carved with flower heads and leaves, M18c (4232/158)   5000
Bureau, chest of drawers, slant front 3 serpentine drawers, 38 x 42¼ x 22, M18c (4142/125)   2100
Bureau, Plat inlaid walnut, cross band rectangular top, arrangement of 5 drawers, 29½ x 44 x 25, ca1760 (4272/407)   1600
Bureau en pente, tulipwood and kingwood, marquetry, slant front, writing surface, 34½ x 27½ x 16½ (4218/148)   4250
Cabinet, walnut, 4 drawers, flanked by grotesques and putti, 35 x 28 x 14 (4157/166)   650
Chairs, side, pair, painted with foliate, motifs, L18c (4119/292)   1700
Chairs, side, pair, painted, open backrest, with pierced splat, upholstered seat, M18c (4272/321)   900
Chest of drawers, walnut and fruitwood, 3 long drawers, gilt metal handles, 42 x 52 x 25½, L18c (4157/173)   2000

Commode, painted, 2 drawers, cabriole legs, 34 x 43½ x 20½, M18c (4119/88)	1000
Commode, fruitwood, serpentine, 3 drawers, scrolling borders, 34 x 55½ x 26½, M18c (4119/85)	2700
Commode, fruitwood, 2 short over 2 long drawers, inlaid, 30½ x 40½ x 19¾ (4142/149)	1200
Commode, fruitwood parquetry, veined yellow marble top, 3 drawers, 34¾ x 25 x 15¼, M18c (4218/143)	1500
Commode, inlaid walnut, serpentine, 3 long drawers, 34 x 49½ x 22½, M18c (4142/133)	7000
Commode, kingwood parquetry, veneered with stylized flower heads, 36 x 57½ x 25¾, M18c (4119/237)	*4500*

Commode (4119/237)

Commode, walnut, molded canted top, 2 drawers, cabriole legs, 33½ x 42 x 18 (4119/127)	900
Commode, Venetian, lacquer, serpentine, lacquered top, cabriole legs, 35 x 52 x 20½, M18c (4218/77)	4250
Console, gilt wood, serpentine, simulated marble, 31 x 56 x 22¼, M18c (4219/125)	1500
Console, gilt wood, veined yellow marble top, with flowers and scrolls, 28¾ (4157/152)	350
Console, painted, Venetian, painted to simulate yellow marble, 31½ x 50½ x 21¼, M18c (4218/114)	1100
Cupboard, corner, parcel-gilt, painted, arched molded cornice, H81, D24, M18c (4168/116)	750
Fauteuil a la reine, c scroll carved, molded voluted frame, L18c, restorations (4218/97)	800
Fauteuil a la reine, painted, cartouche shaped backrest, M18c (4219/99)	1200
Fauteuils a la reine, set of 4, cartouche shaped backrest, padded armrests, M18c (4219/95)	8000
Fauteuils en cabriolet, painted beige, highlighted gilding, M18c (4218/170)	2750
Headboards, pair, Venetian, not upholstered, carved, 44 x 81 (4218/100)	250
Mirror, gilt decorated green painted, triple divided leaf carved scroll borders, 52½ x 34, M18c (4157/11)	275
Mirror, gilt wood, cartouche-shaped plate, H48, Venetian (4168/16)	300
Mirror, gilt wood, rectangular, surmounted by shell, 30½ x 19, parts missing (4168/27)	300
Mirror, gilt wood, carved at corners, scrolls and shells, 35½ x 40, L18c (4232/25)	1500
Mirror, gilt wood, plate surrounded by scrolls, leaves and grapes, 58 x 41, L18c (4218/32)	1500
Mirror, painted, pierced borders, pale green, yellow, 50 x 35, M18c (4119/7)	1300
Mirror, painted gilt decorated, shaped plate, within leaf, flower and scroll borders, 66 x 33, M18c (4119/20)	1300
Mirror, silvered metal, cartouche shaped frame decorated scrolls, 17 x 20, L18c (4157/21)	100
Mirror, toilet, cartouche frame, stylized fruit basket above, stand, M18c (4219/73)	275
Mirror, Venetian gilt wood, scroll and leaves, foliate cresting, 49½ x 34, M18c (3242/39)	650
Mirror, walnut, carved with heart shaped motifs and floral swags, 37, M18c (4232/43)	650
Mirrors, pair, shaped plate, pierced C scroll flowerhead, mask, 32 x 19½, M18c (4272/311)	750
Mirrors, pair, gilt wood, surmounted by seated figures, canopy naked female, 45, ca1730 (4218/37)	4000
Mirrors, pair, Venetian, shaped panes, 2 scrolling candle arms, 42 x 28 (649/445)	550
Mirrors, pair, Venetian gilt wood and reverse etched, with candle arms, 43¼ x 25, ca1730 (4218/47)	7750
Screen, 2 fold, painted leather, exotic birds on fruiting branches, gilt ground, 77 x 56 (4157/10)	400
Settee, white, painted, arched molded backrest and sides, upholstered, 83, res, M18c (4272/405)	1300
Table, console, Venetian, painted and parcel-gilt dec with rosettes, arabesques, 29½ x 47¾ x 25, M18c (4232/121)	700
Table, side, fruitwood, serpentine front, 31¼ x 42 x 20½, M18c (4119/117)	1200
Table, writing, fruitwood, one drawer, cabriole legs, 28½ x 25½ x 15¾, L18c (4119/115)	900
Table, writing, tulipwood and kingwood parquetry, drawer, cabriole legs, 28 x 33 x 23¾, M18c (4119/86)	1700
Tables, console, pair, gilt wood, red and beige, breccia marble top, 37½ x 65 x 29, M18c, fine (4218/159)	15000

Neoclassical

Armchair, desk, painted, arm supports in form of dolphins, gilt, black, H30½, E19c (4168/62)	900
Armchair, painted, curved open backrest, x shaped splat, tapered legs, E19c (4119/93)	180
Armchair, painted, slightly curved open backrest, L18c (4219/119)	1200

Armchair, stained fruitwood, pierced splat, scrolled armrests, L18c (4255/459) — 225

Armchairs, pair, painted and parcel-gilt, backrest carved with beads, legs with butterflies, L18c (4142/121) — 850

Armchairs, pair, cartouche shaped backrest, fluted legs, L18c (4119/98) — 500

Armchairs, pair, mahogany, scrolled top rail, upholstered, L18c (4218/71) — 1000

Bed, fruitwood, green acanthus carving, 53½ x 44 x 77, L18c (4219/115) — 800

Bed, fruitwood, molded borders, plain rails, stop fluted legs, 49½ x 45 x 73½, L18c (4218/142) — 300

Bed, painted, rectangular headboard, painted scrolls, 59 x 59 x 75, L18c (4219/133) — 800

Bench, window, fruitwood, pierced splats, sabre-less, 50½, E19c (4119/110) — 450

Bracket, painted and parcel-gilt, large, acanthus carved, scrolled, support, 27½ x 30, M18c (4119/76) — 500

Bureau, plat, fruitwood parquetry, writing surface, 5 drawers, square legs, 30½ x 47½ x 25½, L18c (4119/79) — 1400

Bureau chest of drawers, fruitwood, slant front, brass handles, 40½ x 46½ x 21, L18c (4142/86) — 650

Bureau plat, fruitwood, top inlaid to form geometric motifs, 31½ x 51 x 25¾, L18c (4218/141) — 2000

Bureau plat, fruitwood parquetry, 5 drawers, slide, kneehole, 29½ x 40½ x 24, L18c (4142/153) — 2600

Cabinet, hanging, painted, 2 doors, decorated cartouche shaped panels, 47 x 28½ x 12, L18c (4272/342) — 600

Cabinet, painted, semicircular, top painted to simulate marble, 35½ x 48 x 24½, L18c (4119/118) — 1600

Cabinet, side, fruitwood parquetry, marble top, slide above cupboard doors, pair doors, 33½ x 34½ x 13, L18c (4272/319) — 800

Chair, desk, fruitwood, tub shaped, swan shaped supports, E19c (4142/179) — 1000

Chairs, side, fruitwood, roll over top rail, bow-front caned seats, (4157/91) — 350

Chairs, side, painted, pair, backrest painted with grapes, E19c (4219/160) — 500

Chairs, side, painted, set of 4, palmette shaped splat, yellow ground, L18c (4219/164) — 1200

Chairs, side, pair, carved fruitwood, panelled top rail, pierced flowerhead carved splat, ca1790 (4272/406) — 200

Chairs, side set of 4, painted, rectangular seat and back, painted beige with gilding, L18c (4142/131) — 800

Chairs, side, caned and painted, serpentine, painted grey, L18c (4119/107) — 1200

Chairs, side, fruitwood, open back rests, vase shaped splats, fluted sabre legs, E19c (4157/108) — 300

Chairs, side, fruitwood, pierced splats, drop in seat, baluster legs, L18c (4218/149) — 950

Chairs, side, painted, shiel D-shaped backrest, L18c (4157/142) — 475

Chairs, side, painted, set of 4, interlocking circles on back, E19c (4168/160) — 1200

Chairs, side, pair, open backrest, painted green, L18c (4219/117) — 500

Chairs, side, pair, fruitwood, backrest carved with dolphins, tapered legs, E19c (4119/99) — 350

Chairs, side, pair, fruitwood, marquetry, lyre-shaped splat, E19c (4168/150) — 400

Chairs, side, pair, fruitwood, open backrest, bow-front, seat on sabre legs, E19c (4119/102) — 125

Chairs, side, pair, fruitwood, open backrest, upholstered seat, sabre legs, E19c (4272/332) — 275

Chairs, side, pair, painted, curved open back rest, X shaped splat, L18c (4272/358) — 800

Chairs, side, set of 4, fruitwood, open backrest, carved with gilt wood eagle, E19c (4157/127) — 900

Chairs, side, set of 8, backrail painted with trophies, E19c (4219/170) — 4750

Chest of drawers, slant front opening to form writing surface, 43 x 45¼ x 21½ (4157/143) — 750

Chest of drawers, fruitwood, marquetry, 3 long drawers, gilt metal handles, 35 x 47¼ x 23½, L18c (4157/137) — 1600

Chest of drawers, fruitwood, parquetry, 3 long drawers, brass handles, 35 x 47½ x 21, L18c (4157/116) — 850

Chest of drawers, walnut, rectangular top, 2 short, 3 long drawers, 34 x 47½ x 21, L18c (4272/423) — 1300

Commode, fruitwood, 4 drawers, tapering pedestals, Egyptian heads, 34 x 46 x 22½, E19c (4119/92) — 650

Commode, fruitwood, rectangular wooden top, 4 long drawers, bracket feet, 34 x 47½ x 21¾, L19c (4142/150) — 800

Commode, fruitwood, 2 long drawers, brass handles, tapered, fluted legs, 33½ x 49½ x 22 (4157/110) — 1000

Commode, fruitwood inlaid, top inlaid with foliate motifs, 3 drawers, 35½ x 47½ x 22½, L18c (4218/165) — 4250

Commode, fruitwood marquetry, top inlaid neoclassical figure, 3 drawers, 35 x 48½ x 23, L18c (4272/318) — 4500

Commode, fruitwood marquetry, various veneers, 35 x 48½ x 22½, L18c (4168/154) — 2000

Commode, fruitwood, parquetry, marquetry top, 2 long drawers, 33 x 41 x 20, L18c (4157/140) — 2000

Commode, fruitwood parquetry, top veneered to form lozenge design, 33 x 51 x 24¼, L18c (4218/164) — 2600

Commode, fruitwood, parquetry, marble top, chequer borders, brass handles, 35¾ x 49¾ x 22½, L18c (4119/119) — 1500

Commode, fruitwood, parquetry, serpentine grey marble top, 31 x 21½ x 14½, L18c (4219/138) — 950

Commode, fruitwood, parquetry, serpentine wooden top, 30½ x 26 x 13¼, M18c (4219/139) — 1100

Commode, mahogany, black painted, 3 drawers, block feet, 38½ x 55½ x 24½, E19c (4232/206) — 2200

Commode, marquetry, 2 short, 2 long drawers, inlaid to form chequer borders, 35 x 48½ x 23, L18c (4157/134) — 850

Commode, painted, top painted to simulate green marble, 37 x 47 x 24½, L18c (4119/105)	2400
Commode, parquetry, bow-front, front with 3 drawers, shaped apron, 34½ x 34 x 20½, L18c (4272/442)	1900
Commode, parquetry, inlaid, rectangular form above 3 drawers, shaped apron, 35 x 38 x 20½, L18c (4272/336)	1700
Commode, walnut, 2 panelled drawers, shell carved apron, 29½ x 35½ x 16, L18c (4119/70)	*1000*

Commode (4119/70)

Commodes, pair, fruitwood, parquetry, rectangular free standing columns, 38 x 50 x 24½, L19c (4142/91)	1700
Console, gilt wood, neo-Egyptian legs, 35 x 52 x 26 (4168/162)	2500
Console, painted, marble top, painted grey, 31¼ x 32 x 19¼, M18c (4218/93)	450
Consoles, pair gilt wood, marble top, rosettes & trophies, 30 x 39 x 21, L18c (4142/82)	1100
Consoles, pair, painted and parcel-gilt, semicircular, marble top, carved with laurel leaves, 34 x 33 x 17, L18c (4142/160)	1400
Cupboard, enclosed within a door, simulating 2 drawers, 32¾ x 20½ x 12¾ (4157/168)	· 300
Daybed, fruitwood, curved upholstered headboard, footboard, L73, M19c (4168/50)	500
Dining chairs, set of 8, painted and parcel-gilt, carved at cresting, grey, with gilding, L18c (4157/37)	3100
Fauteuil, gilt wood, eagle's heads, carved, beading and rosettes, L18c (4119/87)	550
Fauteuils, pair, painted, arm supports carved as Egyptian busts, E19c (4168/60)	2200
Fauteuils, pair, painted, armrests on swan-neck supports, E19c (4168/55)	2200
Fauteuils, pair, painted, gilt wood, arm supports as winged sphinxes, gilding, H35½, E19c (4168/61)	900
Gueridon, circular, marble top, brass gallery, 28¼ x 19, E19c (4219/114)	1000
Mirror, gilt wood, oval shape, with fruit and flowers, 36 x 31, L18c (4157/2)	600
Mirror, gilt wood, arched top, surmounted by an urn, bird's head, 81 x 44¼, L18c (631/408)	1000
Mirror, gilt wood, divided plate with eagle, trophy, 72½ x 33½, L18c (4219/62)	1900
Mirror, painted, gilt decorated, beaded guilloche carved borders, 51 x 31, L18c (4119/9)	2000
Mirror, parcel-gilt, rectangular plate, red velvet border, gilt wood molding, 41 x 34 (4142/14)	100
Mirrors, pair, gilt wood, rectangular plates, pierced cresting, 70 x 35 (4168/18)	1300
Mirrors, pair, gilt wood and gesso, frames fitted with 2 candle arms, 28, L18c (4232/59)	600
Mirrors, pair, painted, parcel-gilt, rectangular, twisted ribbons, 77 x 47½, L18c (4219/82)	2800
Pedestal, black painted and parcel-gilt, triangular, with plant holder, 61 x 26 x 16 (4157/113)	1000
Seat furniture, suite, painted, pair armchairs and settee, cream ground, L18c (4119/315)	800
Settee, fruitwood, back and sides with swan's heads, later feet, L82, M19c (4168/47)	600
Settee, fruitwood, 5 urn shaped splats, drop in seat, 72, L18c (4232/163)	600
Settee, fruitwood, open backrest, wooden armrests, 67½, E19c (4142/136)	275
Settee, gilt wood, eagle's heads on armrests, L71, L18c (4168/163)	700
Settee, painted grey, carved all around, gilding, 80, L18c (4218/84)	550
Settee, parcel-gilt, fruitwood, triple backrest, voluted armrests, fluted legs, 46½, L18c (4119/90)	250
Settees, pair, walnut, open double backrest with palmette shaped splats, 36, L18c (4157/51)	800
Stools, pair, fruitwood, square upholstered seat, 19, E19c (4219/112)	900
Table, a ecrire, fruitwood, rectangular top, parquetry, 26½ x 27¼ x 21½, L18c (4219/122)	700
Table, bedside, fruitwood, 3 quarter gallery, 2 drawers, 27½ x 18 x 13¾, E19c (4232/119)	700
Table, bedside, fruitwood, wooden gallery, drawer, 34¾ x 18 x 12, E19c (4119/111)	225
Table, center, fruitwood, square veneered top, 28½ x 32¼, L18c (4219/140)	900
Table, center, fruitwood, marquetry, oval, floral motif, sabre legs, 30 x 25 x 18¾, E19c (4119/116)	550
Table, console, gilt wood, marble top, raised on square tapered legs, 36½ x 48½ x 19½, L18c (4272/360)	900
Table, games, fruitwood, hinged swivel top, open gaming surface, 30½ x 35¼ x 17¾, E19c (4272/343)	250

Table, dressing, fruitwood, hinged top open to reveal central recess, compartments, 31¾ x 32¾ x 17¼, L18c (4272/413)	600
Table, dressing, fruitwood parquetry, top with 2 ovals, opening to reveal mirror, 30½ x 22¼ x 17¾, L18c (4272/344)	550
Table, dressing, fruitwood, parquetry, divided top open to reveal mirror, 31¾ x 36 x 18, L18c (4157/171)	850
Table, en rognon, fruitwood, kidney shaped, leather surface, 27 x 38 x 17½, E19c (4219/146)	750
Table, games, fruitwood and burr walnut, veneered with playing cards, 32½ x 32¾ x 16½, L18c (4119/109)	850
Table, games, fruitwood parquetry, rectangular top opening to gaming surface, 30¼ x 37½ x 17¼, L18c (4168/46)	475
Table, games, fruitwood, parquetry, swivel top, 30¼ x 37½ x 17¼, L18c (4218/152)	550
Table, library, fruitwood, rounded corners, draw leaf each end, 30¼ x 120 x 30¼, L18c (4219/174)	2200
Table, occasional, fruitwood, 3 quarter gallery, 3 drawers, 25½ x 15½, ca1780 (4232/84)	375
Table, tripod fruitwood, 33¾ x 13, E19c, (4119/95)	175
Table, writing fruitwood, concaved fronted, drawer, sabre legs, 27¼ x 25½ x 17½, E19c (4119/113)	400
Table, writing, fruitwood, rectangular top above a frieze drawer, 28¾ x 34¼ x 17¾, E19c (4157/139)	450
Table, writing, fruitwood, wooden top, parquetry, 28¼ x 36½ x 29¼, L18c (4219/109)	750
Tables, console pair, painted, gilt, marble top, carved lion's masks, 37 x 52½ x 26, E19c (4219/107)	6000
Tables, side, pair, Italian, painted, parcel-gilt, 35¾ x 44 x 22¾ (4168/83)	3250

Miscellaneous Decorations

MISCELLANEOUS BAROMETERS

Barometer, continental, painted with flowers, green ground, 37½, E19c (4149/88)	150

MISCELLANEOUS CLOCKS

Assorted shelf clocks

Bracket, brass in lacquer case, moveable 'circular' dial, 7, 19c, Japanese (4141/173)	1750
Carriage, with alarm, gilt metal, Grande Sonnerie repeating, retailed Tiffany and Co., 6⅞, ca1900, Swiss (4141/187)	300
Clock, annular, breche violette marble, gilt bronze, flanked by mermaid and merman, 28, L19c (649/393)	7500
Clock, carriage, miniture, gilt metal, enameled scene, Viennese, 3⅛, ca1900 (4259/524)	425
Clock, gilt metal and onyx, D-shaped base, surmounted by a gypsy and goat, 17, L19c (649/374)	200
Clock, globe form standing gilt metal, enamel, cupid, woman musician, Viennese, 13, L19c (4259/533)	3750
Clock, mantel, bronze and marble, with a figure of the Victory Thermopylae, 23¼ (619/283)	300
Clock, mantel, gilt metal, enamel, miniature, Viennese, 4¾, ca1900 (4259/523)	500
Clock, mantel, miniature, gilt metal, white enamel dial, black Roman numerals, 4, ca1900 (4259/522)	550
Clock, silver, lapis, enamel and jeweled, surmounted by knife grinder, 7⅝, L19c, Austrian (4141/53)	3000
Clock, silvered bronze, architectural form, lion's mask, foliate motifs, 21, L19c (649/373)	450
Clock, triptych, gilt metal and enamel, 3 panels of landscapes, 4¾, L19c, Austrian (4141/52)	475
Desk, Art Deco, silver, translucent pink enamel, 3¾, ca1935, Swiss (4141/185)	500
Garniture, gilt bronze, clock, flanking 6 light candelabra, 24, L19c (669/468)	650
Gilt bronzes and painted enamel, dial painted with figure of a cavalier, 20½ (619/274)	650
Glass ball, desk clock, stem wind, spherical glass case, 4, ca1900, Swiss (4141/191)	250
Gold miniature, black, Starr and Frost, engraved case, 2¼, Swiss movement (4141/186)	500
Long case, watch holder miniature, marquetry, arched top, bombe base, 17½, M18c, Dutch (4141/179)	900
Staartklok, stained oak, Dutch, 10½ inch painted arched dial, 41, L18c (4218/11)	1800
Teakwood on stand, back plate engraved with foliage, birds, 13¼, M19c, Chinese (4141/171)	750
Teakwood on stand, back plate engraved, sweep second hand, 19½, M19c, Chinese (4141/169)	950
Teakwood on stand (small), decorative steel hands, 11½, M19c, Chinese (4141/172)	950
Travel clock, grand sonnerie, alarm, gilt metal, green painted, fitted case, 8½, ca1810, Aurstrian (4238/330)	
Vrijthoff, Jan B., 14 inch dial, 2 train movement, Dutch, 101½, E18c (4272/296)	13500

Mantel clocks

Bronze mounted basalt, dial surmounted by figure of a kneeling naked woman, 29, 19c (619/279)	325
Gilt and patinated bronze, with Orpheus seated on throne, Eurydice, 18½, 19c (619/277)	900
Gilt bronze, architectural form, 24½, L19c (669/393)	650
Gilt bronze, cast with figure of Orpheus and wild beasts, 23, 19c (619/275)	400

Gilt bronze, panel of classical figures within formal borders, 20, E19c (669/394)	1650
Gilt bronze, Ionic columns, satyr's masks, 23, L19c (669/397)	1100
Gilt wood, Neoclassical, Austrian, circular dial, figures, on rockwork, 34 x 25½, L18c (4168/33)	1600
Wood frame, carved with birds and foliage, 25, German, 19c (619/271)	600

Tall-case clocks

Clock, long case, Dutch rococo burr walnut, 13" brass dial, arched hood, 89, (reduced in height) (4157/18)	6000
Clock, tall case, carved mahogany, Austrian, carved and turned columns, 99, 19c (649/480)	2800
Du Chesne, Amsterdam, walnut, marquetry, H107½, fine, ca1750 (4148/247)	11000
Paulus, P., Amsterdam, Dutch rococo, inlaid burr walnut, 102, M18c (4111/49)	5750
Straatmans, C., Hage, Dutch rococo, marquetry inlaid walnut, 98, M18c (4111/48)	7250
Van Der Cloese, B, burr walnut, musical, 14 inch dial, 2 train movement, Dutch, 108, E18c (4272/271)	21000

Wall clocks

Inlaid mahogany stoelklok, eleven inch brass dial, anchor encasement, Dutch, 63, E19c (4272/267)	1900
Picture, musical, village, clock tower, gilt wood frame, 31½ x 27, 19c, Desfontaines (4168/40)	1300

MISCELLANEOUS DECORATIVE OBJECTS

Blackamoor, standing, painted gesso, Persian garb, holding urn, electrified, 60, 19c (649/472)	1600
Brule parfums, pair, white marble, ovoid receptacles raised on ormulu ram's head legs, 22½, L19c (669/474)	3600
Bucket, coal, brass, Dutch, truncated conical form, loop handle, bun feet, 15, 18c (4260/826)	600
Bucket, coal, copper, Dutch, truncated conical form, domed lid, swing handle, 14, 18c (4260/817)	550
Casket, tortoiseshell and bone inlaid, hinged domed top, 14 x 16 x 11½, L17c (4218/52)	1300
Churn, brass, Dutch, ovoid, domed lid, copper bands and handles, 27, E19c (4260/906)	850
Churn, brass, Dutch, pear shaped, swing handle, converted to tea urn, 20¾, 18c (4260/939)	350
Coal bucket, brass and copper, Dutch, removable lid, loop handle, flared sides, 16½, ca1800 (4260/892)	1000
Columns, Swedish neoclassical painted and parcel-gilt, circular, rectangular bases, with swags, L18c (4157/35)	1200
Cornucopiae, pair, silvered metal, cut glass, seated draped figure, 18¼, L19c (4119/202)	125
Cup, silver gilt and mounted enamel, boat shape, monster head, Viennese, 9½, ca1900, res (669/297)	1500
Ewers, pair, patinated bronze, bulbous bodies, applied lion masks, pierced panels, 24, renaissance style (649/360)	475
Jardiniere, copper, oval, convex sides, pendant oval handles, 26, 18/19c (4260/803)	350
Jardiniere, copper, oval, paw feet, 20, ca1800 (4260/804)	425
Jars, covered, pair delfware, blue and white, lion shaped, finial, circular bulbous body, 28, M19c (4119/170)	1100
Kettle, brass, Dutch, bulbous shape, domed lid, swing handle, 14, 18c (4260/829)	450
Milk churn, brass, domed cover, loop handle, 16, 19c (4260/902)	325
Tray, basalt, bronze mounted, plaque of classical figures, 25¼, dam, M19c (649/359)	325
Tray, tea, on stand, decorated tole, oval tray, black, city view on a yellow ground, Dutch, 18 x 23¼, 19c (4157/111)	300
Urn stands, pair, white marble, square top, grotesque and swag carved standard, 39 x 14 (649/419)	1500
Urns, marble, pair, gilt bronze, drum form, snake handles, 28, as lamps, ca1900 (649/361)	800
Urns, pair, gilt bronze, circular porphyry base, bacchic handles, 14, ca1900 (669/452)	450
Urns, pair, gilt bronze mounted, marble, inverted pear form, ram's head handles, 24, 19c (669/475)	1000
Urns, pair, porphyry gilt bronze mounted, ribboned, floral swags, satyr-mask handles, 17, L19c (669/454)	1000
Urns and covers, pair, marble and bronze, chalice form, 19¼, ca1860 (649/357)	700
Vase, enamel, lobed body, domed foot, Viennese, 4, ca1900 (669/296)	475
Vase, flambe, gilt bronze mounted, ovoid body, purple and red, hue-gilt, foliate handles, 23, L19c (669/470)	1200
Vase, porcelain, famille verte, now as lamp multicolored, floral sprays, 17, 19c (4232/50)	475
Vase 2 handled, parcel-gilt and jeweled, amphora shape, 19½, M19c, Austrian (4238/569)	3750
Vases, pair, covered cut glass, ovoid body, circular bases, (4119/207)	200
Vases, pair, covered, ormolu mounted, blue Chinese porcelain, Louis XV style, H29, M19c (669/473)	5000

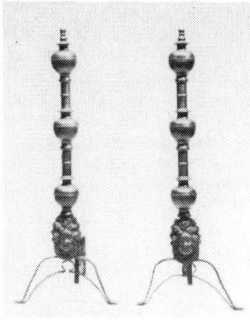

Andirons (4255/396)

MISCELLANEOUS HEARTH EQUIPMENT

Andirons, pair, brass, Dutch, acron finial, trestle toes, 27½, E18c (4260/805)	1300
Andirons, pair, brass, Flemish, baluster shaped stems above masks, barogue, 33½, L17c (4255/396)	*950*
Andirons, pair, brass, Flemish, masks in base, baroque, 20½, L17c (4255/391)	950
Andirons, pair, brass, Flemish, masks in base, Baroque, 21, 17c (4255/394)	750
Andirons, pair, cast-brass, cherub's heads, tripod bases, 43¾, 19c (619/418)	1500
Bed warmer, copper and brass, 19c (4232/40)	150
Irons, pair, bronze, eagle head, finial above armorial cartouche, 35½, baroque style (4142/51)	400

MISCELLANEOUS LIGHTING DEVICES

Alcove lights, set of 4, brass urns, 7 glass hung candle arms, marble stands, 57 x 14 (649/429)	1100
Candelabra, pair, 5 lights, 4 scroll arms, raised on 4 paw feet, 20½, Mexican (4141/564)	1400
Candelabra, pair, 4 light, bronze Mercury holding a branched torch, 38¼, L19c (669/463)	1600
Candelabra, pair, 4 light, silverplate, Bronze Rococo style, 20½ (619/306)	600
Candelabra, pair, 2 light, gilt bronze, circular base, 15, L19c (669/458)	350
Candelabra, pair, 4 light, bronze putto, holding 2 branched lights, 18¼, L19c, after Clodion (669/466)	1200
Candelabra, pair, 4 light gilt bronze, winged goddess holding 2 branched torches, 25¾, L19c (669/462)	1700
Candelabra, pair, 5 branch, barbedienne, part gilt bronze, looped handles, 27¾, L19c, good (669/471)	250
Candelabra, pair, 6 light, bronze, 22½ (619/305)	175
Candelabra, pair, 8 light, brass, Eastern European, 24½, 18c (4260/919)	2500
Candelabra, pair, 8 light, tole, gilt brass, shape of vases, filled with tole, tulips, 21½ (4142/6)	375
Candelabra, 2 light pair, gilt bronze, 4 cut glass columns supporting 2 branches, 13½, ca1900 (669/457)	650
Candelabra, 4 light, pair, patinated, gilt bronze marble-mounted, 3 putti supporting branches, 18½, L19c (649/367)	650
Candelabra, 5 light, pair, bronze, cast as medieval knight, 28½, L19c (649/363)	800
Candelabra, 5 light, pair, painted, wrought iron, form of a flowering tree, 27 (4157/29)	400
Candelabra, 6 light, pair, gilt bronze, square marble bases, foliate motifs, 26, now as lamps, L19c (649/364)	850
Candelabra, 6 light, pair, patinated and gilt bronze, form of a winged maiden, 34, L19c (649/369)	1000
Candelabra, 7 light pair, gilt bronze, urn shaped stem, 3 feet, 26½, L19c (619/307)	250
Candelabra, 7 light, pair, gilt bronze, mounted-marble, urn form body, 27¾, L19c (649/368)	3500
Candelabrum 8 light, bronze cherub seated, holding branch, 33, L19c (669/469)	700
Candle holders, pair, brass, Dutch, reeded stems, stepped bases, 19½, 16/17c (4260/959)	2100
Candlestick, bell-metal, domical base, scalloped edge, 9, Dutch*, L17c, E18c (4076/527)	125
Candlestick, bell-metal, octagonal foot, 5½, Dutch, E18c (4076/537)	100
Candlestick, bell-metal, square foot, 5⅜, Spanish*, L17c (4076/504)	225
Candlestick, pricket, carved wood, a standing angel, now painted, 35, E18c, Flemish (4142/47)	900
Candlesticks, pair, brass, brass pricket, dished drip pan, baluster stem, Baroque, 23, 17c (4272/280)	2400
Candlesticks, pair, brass, Dutch, 3 feet, electrified, 23, 17c (4260/960)	1450
Candlesticks, pair, brass, Eastern European, columnar stem, domed square bases, 13½, 18/19c (4260/932)	400
Candlesticks, pair, brass, Eastern European, columnar stems, scrolled feet, 14, 19c (4260/941)	750
Candlesticks, pair, brass, Eastern European, domed square base, 12, 18/19c (4260/970)	350

Candlesticks, pair, brass, Eastern European, flared socket, dished drip pans, 11½, 19c (4260/930)   475
Candlesticks, pair, brass, Eastern European, ring stem, domed square bases, 11½, 19c (4260/969)   275
Candlesticks, pair, brass, Eastern European, tapered stem, circular bases, 8½, 18c (4260/966)   350
Candlesticks, pair, brass, Mediterranean, turned socket, baluster stem, 11½, 18/19c (4260/893)   375
Candlesticks, pair, brass, Spanish, domed turned bases, now electrified, 24½, 17/18c (4260/964)   850
Candlesticks, pair, iron, massive, shaft surrounded by scrollwork, Spanish, 74, 17/18c (4193/110)   550
Candlesticks, pair, table, pewter, square bases, tapered quadrangular stems, 10¾, ca1791 (4133/119)   150
Candlesticks, pricket, pair, brass, Dutch, dished drip pan, 29, altered, ca1700 (4260/954)   2300
Candlesticks, pricket, pair, brass, Dutch, ribbed, ovoid knop stem, bell base, ball feet, 16, 17c (4260/904)   1900
Candlesticks, set of 4, pricket, gilt, bronze, 48½ (619/313)   1900
Candlesticks, set of 4, brass, Dutch, baluster stems, square bases, 23½, E18c (4260/845)   3750
Chandelier, ormolu and cut glass, six lights, teardrop pendants, 44, Swedish (4218/64)   3750
Chandelier, red glass, cut glass, gilt metal, 2 tier, 8 S-scroll branches, Neoclassical, 41, E19c (4272/261)   2750
Chandelier, 32 light, cut glass, double scrolled, arms, glassdrops, 39 (669/482)   400
Chandelier, Dutch brass, 6-light, 6 scrolling candlearms, 20 x 26½, 18c (4149/63)   1400
Chandelier, 12 light, gilt bronze, scrolling arm cast with foliage, 29, ca1900 (649/350)   1300
Chandelier, 13 light, rock crystal, gilt frame hung with crystal drops, 44 x 42 (649/424)   700
Chandelier, 6 light, brass, glass and rock crystal, each hung with 7 rock crystal drops, 31 x 20 (649/426)   175
Chandelier, 6 light, brass, Eastern European, animal form branches, 21½, 18c (4260/916)   3750
Chandelier, 8 light, brass and glass, 4 scrolling branches above 8 candle arms, 34 x 28 (649/428)   100
Chandelier, 8 light, bronze, alabaster, 42 x 18 (649/435)   250
Chandeliers, brass 5 light, pair, scrolled candle arms, 14, rare, Dutch, 18c (4076/521)   3000
Lamp, standing, polychromed blackamoor, female figure, exotic costume, child on shoulder, 60 (619/363)   600
Lamp base, marble, patinated gilt bronze, cupids, urn containing flowers, 22½, L19c (649/355)   600
Lamps, pair, white metal, goddesses of sailors and of fall harvest, 26, 20c (649/353)   400
Lantern, bronze and glass, with caryatids flanking each pane, 34 x 16 (649/443)   550
Lantern, bronze and glass, with swag draped panes flanked by female terms, 28 x 11 (649/440)   350
Lantern, hanging iron, Near Eastern, spherical body pierced all over, 26, 18c (4255/395)   1000
Lanterns, pair, brass and glass, 42 x 10½ (649/444)   550
Sconce, wall, brass, engraved with circular devices, 26½, Dutch*, E18c (4076/520)   900
Sconce, wall, pair, 3 light, urn form, gilt bronze, 20½ (619/319)   350
Sconce, wall, 2 light, pair, gilt bronze, bacchic merman, 21, L19c, now as lamps (669/455)   800
Sconce, wall, 8 light, gilt bronze, branches entwined with roses, 49½ (619/318)   100
Sconces, wall, pair, gilt bronze, cut-glass, 9 light, classical figure relief, 39½, L19c (649/446)   1000
Sconces, wall, pair, gilt bronze, urn shape, above foliate scrolls, below term masks, 21¾, ca1900 (649/349)   375
Sconces, wall, pair, 7 light gilt bronze and opaque white glass, decorated with flowers, 27½ (619/317)   200
Sconces, wall, set of 3, bronze, vase shape, flame surmounting 2 caryatids, 22 (649/430)   500
Sconces, wall, 2 light, set of 4, brass, vase shape, 17 (649/438)   375
Sconces, wall, 2 light, set of 5, candle arms protruding from a dolphin's mouth, 16 (649/431)   750
Sconces, wall, 2 light, set of 5, bronze, each surmounted by plumed cresting female mask, 21 (649/437)   800
Sconces, wall, 5 light, 6 gilt bronze, surmounted by a figure of a swan outstretched wings, 15½ (619/321)   2100
Sconces, 2 light, set of 4, each centered by a rosette, 14 (649/433)   150
Table lectern, brass, Flemish*, pierced quatrefoil motifs, steel supports, 14¼, L17c (4260/836)   2100
Vases, pair, bluejohn and marble mounted, ovoid form, square base, 13, 19c, now as lamps (669/443)   650
Vases, porcelain, Chinese famille rose, floral and butterflies, 17¼, 19c, mounted as lamps (4232/8)   850

Miscellaneous Furniture

Assorted periods

Armchair, marquetry, open backrest, sabre leg, floral motifs with bird, Dutch, E19c, neoclassical (4119/136)   175
Armchairs, pair, marquetry, cartouche shaped backrest, cabriole legs, Dutch, M19c, Rococo (4119/150)   1100
Armoire, painted, shell shaped cresting, pair of fielded doors, 61 x 39 x 19, 18c, Portuguese (4119/80)   250
Bed, day, marquetry, upholstered, downswept marquetry border, scrolled legs, Dutch, 54, E19c, neoclassical (4119/152)   1200

Bookcase, mahogany, Swedish, upper glazed doors, short tapered legs, 100 x 48 x 18, E19c (4168/67) — 2100

Brackets, carved oak, neoclassical, circular top, egg and dart leaf carved, 23¼ x 19, L18c (4218/22) — 1200

Brackets, pair, carved gilt wood, semicircular top, leaf tip and shell carved, 15¾, E18c (4218/46) — 900

Brackets, wall, pair rococo walnut, shaped top, leaf carved support, 9, M18c, res (4119/4) — 350

Cabinet, display, bronze and glass, hinged top, enclosing mirror back shelf, slant front, 37½ x 34¾ x 28, 19c (619/345) — 500

Cabinet, display, marquetry, molded cornice, 2 drawers, baluster, shaped legs, Dutch, 77½ x 28½ x 13½, ca1700, baroque (4119/147) — 5000

Cabinet (4119/147)

Desk cylinder (4119/160)

Bookcase (4168/67)

Cabinet, miniature, inlaid walnut, star inlaid cupboard doors, 6 drawers, 14½, 18c (4157/25) — 350

Cabinets, side, pair, rectangular top, small drawer, cupboard door, 31 x 19 x 13, 19c (631/359) — 350

Chair, side, fruitwood, cupid's bow cresting rail, ball feet, M18c (4119/268) — 750

Chairs, pair, side, marquetry, cartouche, shaped backrest, claw and ball feet, Dutch, 19c, rococo (4119/156) — 500

Chairs, side, pair, marquetry, open backrest, bow-front, cabriole legs, Dutch, E19c, neoclassical (4119/135) — 300

Chest, oak, rectangular, carved rosettes on bracket feet, 21¼ x 51 x 20, L17c (4119/59) — 500

Chest, oak, rectangular, hinged top, carved rosettes, bracket feet, 19¾ x 53¾ x 17, L17c (4119/61) — 400

Chest, pierced and engraved, brass and leather mounted, 3 drawers in the base, 22 x 49½ x 22, 19c, North African (4119/133) — 1500

Chiffonier, marquetry, architectural cornice, Dutch, 63½ x 40½ x 19¾, E19c, neoclassical (4119/141) — 2500

Chiffonnier, marquetry, 6 drawers, block feet, Dutch, 54½ x 39¼ x 20¼, E19c, neoclassical (4119/134) — 1700

Coffer on stand, rosewood, surmounted by winged figure of Ramses, coffer, 26 x 28 x 16, 19c (631/421) — 4500

Cupboard painted, 2 parts, panelled doors, lower 3 drawers, decorated, 76½ x 48½ x 18½, 18c, Swiss* (4232/85) — 1000

Desk, ladies, writing, mahogany, pair glazed doors, 2 drawers, frieze drawer, 48 x 26, 19c (4142/78) — 325

Desk, varqueno, walnut, dentil cornice, full front, fitted interior, 63½ x 31 x 14, Spanish (631/347) — 1400

Desk cylinder, mahogany, inlaid, fitted interior, 44½ x 52 x 26, L18c, rococo (4119/160) — 3250

Dumb waiter, marquetry, 3 tier, veneered, Dutch, 44½ x 22¾, L19c, Victorian (4119/139) — 800

Mirror, wall, walnut, parcel-gilded, eglomise panel, gilded framework, 20⅜ x 10½, 19c (4076/1376) — 300

Painting, glass, courting couple, boy, and dog, framed, 22½ x 24½, M18c, dam (4165/268) — 1900

Painting, mirror, Chinese, George III, woodland setting, pierced frame, 44 x 27 (4079/34) — 1300

Screen, Coromandel, 6 folds, continuous landscape scene, each fold 72 x 16, 19c (631/423) — 900

Screen, 4 fold, oriental lacquer, courtyard scenes, each fold 72 x 16, 19c (631/422) — 1700

Secretaire, a abattant, marquetry inlaid, mahogany, fall front fitted interior, 61½ x 40 x 20½, E19c, Dutch (4142/70) — 1000

Secretaire, fall front, marquetry, 3 drawers, Dutch, 60 x 37¾ x 20, E19c, neoclassical (4119/143) — 2100

Settee, mahogany, Russian, wooden back rest, armrests, drop in seat, sabre legs, 61, ca1910 (4157/101) — 1400

Stools, mahogany, pair, Russian, rectangular upholstered seats, raised on sabre legs, 23½, E19c (4157/102) — 1100

Stove, ceramic, blue and white, circular top and body, paw feet, 35 x 17½, 19c, top replaced (4119/132) — 550

Stove, brass and white, faience, circular marble top claw feet, 39½ x 21¾, M19c (4232/86) — 1200

Table, dining extension, marquetry, square divided top, circular lobed, pedestal, Dutch, 29 x 51, M19c (4119/148) — 2300

Table, campaign walnut, apron with 2 drawers, on both sides, iron stretcher, 31 x 53 x 31, 18c, Spanish (631/340) — 1600

Table, center, marquetry, circular top, tripod support, 29½ x 31½, M19c (4142/96) — 150

Table, games, mother-of-pearl, hinged top, opens to gaming surface, 32½ x 33 x 17, Near Eastern (619/362) — 1000

Table, occasional, wrought iron, later slate top, 3 curved iron supports, 23 x 21, 18c (4119/270) — 325

Tray, on stand, chinoiserie, decorated, papier mache, bamboo stand, floral border, vignette, 19½ x 30 19c (4157/136) — 700

Trunk, stamped leather, domed cover, stamped with medallions, floral panels, 41½, 17c, Spanish (4133/62) — 650

Renaissance

Table, refectory, walnut, trestle, iron stretcher, 29½ x 94 x 31, E17c, Spanish (4119/36) — 1800

Baroque

Armchair, pine and oak, Spanish, scroll finials, pierced splat, wooden armrests, M17c (4193/426) — 300
Armchair, walnut, arched backrest, scrolled armrest and legs, L17c (4119/124) — 850
Armchair, walnut, leather upholstered backrest, wooden armrest, 17c (4157/123) — 450
Armchair, walnut, upholstered, baluster carved legs, L17c, res (4119/44) — 750

Strongbox (4119/64)

Armchair
(4119/44)

Bureau bookcase
(4119/301)

Secretaire
(4232/193)

Chest of drawers
(4272/372)

Armchair, walnut, upholstered, scrolled armrests, L17c (4193/435) — 150
Armchair, walnut, Flemish, tall rectangular backrest, L17c (4219/104) — 1300
Armchair, walnut, Spanish, rectangular, upholstered wood arms, M17c (4193/385) — 750
Armchair, walnut, Spanish, upholstered, wood armrests, L17c (4193/399) — 600
Armchairs, pair, turned walnut, upholstered, scrolled armrests, spiral turning, L17c (4272/328) — 4000
Armchairs, pair, walnut, Spanish, upholstered back, wood armrest, M17c (4193/395) — 1300
Armchairs, 3, oak, arched pierced backrest, block and turned legs, L17c, res (4119/42) — 900

Bench, oak, wood back and armrests, straight supports, 36½, M17c (4193/388) 600

Cabinet, marquetry, upper pair glaze doors, lower pair fielded doors, 71 x 40 x 10½, L17c/E18c (4272/378) 4500

Cabinet, oyster veneered walnut, doors, 12 drawers, on later stand, 65½ x 52½ x 21, L17c (4255/440) 3750

Cabinet, 2 parts, walnut, 4 doors, 3 drawers, 78 x 68 x 24, L17c (4255/453) 4000

Cabinet on stand, amboyna, inlaid walnut, 2 sections, 50½ x 39 x 13, L17c (4218/70) 3000

Cabinet on stand, rosewood and tortoiseshell, Flemish, 10 drawers, 73 x 56 x 19, part missing, M17c (4193/417) 5500

Cabinet vitrine pine, arched, cypher carved, cornice, panelled doors, 87 x 58 x 14, M18c (4119/122) 2750

Cabinet walnut, Spanish, molded cornice, 2 cupboard doors, 2 drawers, 70 x 44 x 22, E17c (4255/415) 4500

Casket, brass mounted rosewood, compartments and drawers, Dutch, 10½ x 15 x 9, L17c (4119/11) 1400

Cassone, oak, hinged top, front carved with foliate motifs, 24 x 65¼ x 15¾, M17c (4272/346) 400

Cellaret, burr walnut and oak, Dutch, rectangular, hinged, fitted interior, inlaid, 19 x 16½ x 16½, ca1730 (4260/1669) 1700

Chair, side, walnut, upholstered back, baluster legs, res, M17c (4193/433) 200

Chairs, dining, set of 6, walnut, arched toprail, caned back, seat, cabriole legs, E18c (4159/214) 1500

Chairs, side, pair, walnut, open backrest, wooden seat, Spanish, L17c (4232/78) 300

Chairs, side, pair, walnut, upholstered backrest and turned legs, res, L17c (4255/430) 500

Chairs, side, pair, walnut, Flemish, tall backrest, pierced splat, L17c (4255/414) 1000

Chairs, side, pair, Flemish, pierced leaf scroll carved cresting, (4232/164) 850

Chairs, side, pair, Spanish, open curved backrests, L17c (4219/86) 450

Chairs, side, pair, Spanish, rectangular, upholstered, straight legs, M17c (4193/392) 1000

Chairs, set of 4, carved and inlaid, Dutch, M18c, restorations (4218/145) 4250

Chairs, side, set of 3, double arched top rail, caned back and seat, E18c (4157/105) 1050

Chest, walnut, rectangular top, molded edge, deep well, plinth base, 16 x 33¼ x 13¼, 17c (4272/299) 400

Chest of drawers, inlaid burr walnut, cross banded top, 5 drawers, Dutch, 31¼ x 36¼ x 21¼, M18c (4218/72) 2500

Cupboard, food, fruitwood, rectangular cornice, panelled doors, 74½ x 46 x 20, L17c (4119/21) 1200

Cupboard, food, fruitwood, rectangular cornice, latticework doors, 68 x 38 x 17½, E18c (4119/34) 2800

Mirror, gilt wood, oval frame, high relief, bird and floral, 34 x 27½, M17c (4272/290) 1400

Sidetable, walnut, Spanish, block and turned legs, iron supports, 30¾ x 49½ x 16¼, E17c (4255/409) 2500

Strongbox, painted, engraved lockplate, polychrome flowers, 19 x 35½ x 20, L17c (4119/64) *2400*

Strongbox on stand, painted, engraved lockplate, inner strongbox, 34 x 35 x 18, L17c (4119/63) 2500

Table, tray top, inlaid walnut, Dutch, removable dished top, 26 x 30 x 18½, res, ca1720 (4260/1674) 2750

Table, walnut, Spanish, block and turned legs, iron supports, 25 x 26½ x 16¼, 17c (4255/412) 950

Table, walnut, Spanish, shaped, trestle supports, 29½ x 37 x 26, 17c (4255/400) 1400

Table, writing, walnut, Spanish, rectangular, drawer, block legs, 29½ x 32¾ x 21, M17c (4193/412) 1400

Table, center, baroque walnut, frieze, drawer, turned legs, 31 x 40 x 30, L17c res (4142/72) 1800

Table, dressing, walnut, marquetry, one long above 2 short drawers, pad feet, Dutch, Dutch, 29½ x 30½ x 19, altered (4157/95) 1000

Torcheres, pair, carved walnut, molded top, baluster stem, angular cabriole legs, 41½ x 12½, res, M18c (4239/59) 400

Vargueno, walnut, gilt metal mounted, fall front, opening to reveal drawers, cupboard doors, 55½ x 40 x 16½, L17c, Spanish (4142/81) 1900

Rococo

Armchair, walnut, not upholstered, carved shell cresting, L18c, restorations (4218/171) 1800

Armoire, painted, rectangular with canted corners, multicolor, 68 x 52 x 9½, L18c (4157/107) 1000

Bench, walnut, rectangular backrest, turned legs, 77, L17c (4119/49) 750

Bureau bookcase, bombe inlaid burr walnut, arched cornice, fitted interior, 98½ x 43 x 25½, M18c Danish* (4119/301) *16500*

Cabinet, hanging, marquetry, front fitted with glazed doors, glazed panels, 34¾ x 41¾ x 10¼, M18c (4272/374) 700

Chair, side, fruitwood, open backrest with baluster shaped splat, upholstered seat, L18c (4272/354) 150

Chairs, dining, walnut, drop in seat, dipped top rail, pierced baluster splat, M18c (4157/154) 650

Chaise a la reine, fruitwood, carved at cresting, upholstered, L18c (4218/151) 300

Chest of drawers, marquetry, serpentine front, 3 drawers, floral designs, 33 x 35¾ x 20½, L18c (4272/372) *2900*

Commode, lacquer, serpentine marble top, 32 x 43¾ x 25¼, M18c (4219/151) 3000

Commodes, pair, rare, walnut, parquetry, ormolu mounted, 39 x 49½ x 27½, M18c, Vienna (4168/82) 16000

Consoles, pair gilt wood, carvings, marble tops, oval base, 34 x 18 x 13½, L18c (4218/132) 3000

Mirror, gilt wood, frame carved with scrolls and foliate motifs, 17 x 10¼, M18c (4232/1) 110

Panel, framed needlework, oval frame carved and fitted with candle holders, 12¼, L18c (4232/2) 120

Secretaire, chest of drawers, burr walnut, door with mirror, thirteen drawers in all, 82½ x 46½ x 19½, ca1740, Dutch (4232/193)   *9500*

Stool, walnut, rectangular upholstered seat, cabriole legs, 21, M18c (4157/117)   650

Table, center, gallery top, frieze drawer, 29½ x 33 x 20½, M18c, res (4232/151)   750

Table, drop-leaf, provincial carved oak, hinged top, 29½ x 36 x 22½, M18c, restoration (4232/82)   650

Table, side walnut, Dutch, serpentine, with 3 drawers, 30½ x 30½ x 18½, ca1770, res (4232/162)   650

Neoclassical

Armchair, marquetry, open backrest, wooden armrest, with floral sprays, E19c, Dutch (4142/114)   75

Armchair, walnut, turned armrests, upholstered, square tapered legs, E19c (4218/161)   450

Armchairs, pair, mahogany, curved open backrest, semicircular splats, sunflower petals, Russian, ca1810 (4157/99)   4400

Armchairs, set of 3, mahogany, arched backrest, heart-shaped splats, sabre legs, Russian, ca1820 (4157/100)   3800

Armoire, Dutch, 84½ x 78½ x 30, L18c (4218/150)   4500

Bonheur du jour, burr elmwood, pair, glazed door, enclosing shelves, writing surface, 45 x 26 (4157/174)   375

Bonheur du jour, kingwood parquetry, fitted with a tambour shutter, 47½ x 32 x 19¼, E19c (4218/195)   2500

Bookcase chest of drawers, pair glazed doors, enclosing shelves, lower 3 drawers, Dutch, 86½ x 62 x 21½ (4157/112)   4750

Bureau, tortoiseshell inlaid, satinwood, sloping front, 2 parts, 43 x 26½ x 19 (4218/155)   1500

Bureau bookcase, marquetry, Dutch, pair door, slant front, drawers, 72 x 45½ x 25, L18c (4218/178)   10500

Bureau plat, walnut parquetry, leather inset drawer above kneehole, 29½ x 49½ x 24, L18c (4272/448)   5000

Cabinet, bureau painted, 2 sections, sloping front, 80 x 35½ x 19, part 18c (4218/66)   1400

Cabinet, hanging, marquetry, tambour-fronted, 14½ x 37 x 11½, Dutch (619/336)   125

Cabinet on chest, oak, pair of doors flanked by columns, 84½ x 65½ x 23, E19c, Dutch (4232/79)   1300

Chair, desk, revolving, brass mounted, Russian, tub shaped backrest, L18c (4219/116)   2900

Chair, side, walnut, panelled top rail upholstered seat, E19c (4218/67)   225

Chairs, dining, set of 4, marquetry inlaid, panelled top rail, upholstered seats, Dutch, E19c (4157/153)   600

Chairs, dining, set of 6, mahogany, pierced beaker splat, upholstered, E19c, res (4157/131)   1000

Chairs, dining, set of 6, mahogany, urn-carved back, fluted seat rail, legs, square, 19c (4159/294)   1900

Chairs, side, set of five, marquetry inlaid, mahogany, scrolled top rail, panelled cross bar, Dutch, Dutch, E19c (4157/94)   1800

Chest of drawers, walnut, 2 short and 3 drawers, brass handles, bracket feet, 38½ x 38 x 20½, L18c (4157/156)   750

Commode, mahogany and burr walnut, swan-shaped supports at sides, 36½ x 53½ x 26, E19c (4168/149)   3000

Commode, marquetry, 3 drawers, brass handles, Dutch, 34 x 51 x 25¼, L18c (4218/75)   4250

Commode, marquetry and parquetry inlaid, elmwood and fruitwood, 4 drawers, 40 x 49½ x 24½, L18c (4157/163)   850

Commode, marquetry, mahogany, rectangular top, canted corners, 3 long drawers, 32 x 48 x 19¾, L18c (4272/366)   *2200*

Commode, marquetry, mahogany, rectangular top, 4 drawers, floral inlays, 34 x 35 x 21½, L18c (4272/367)   1900

Cradle, pine and walnut, tapered with ball finials, 38½, 19c (4255/411)   175

Cupboard, hanging corner, painted, front enclosed pair doors, allegorical scene, 36½ x 23, L18c (4272/341)   550

Cupboard, D-shaped, fruitwood, frieze drawer above a panelled, fluted pilasters, 32½ x 26 x 15, res, L18c (4272/435)   950

Linen press, fruitwood, molded cornice above 2 pairs of molded doors, 91 x 61 x 23½, rebacked (4157/162)   1600

Mirror, toilet, walnut, free standing rectangular plate, base with drawer, 8½ x 18, L18c (4272/282)   125

Pedestals, pair, bone and marquetry inlaid, rectangular ebonized top, tapered body, 49 x 14½ x 14½, L18c (4272/449)   2000

Secretaire chest of drawers, leather writing surface, 37 x 41 x 21 (4157/155)   550

Settee, fruitwood, arched top rail, upholstered, scrolled feet, 85½, L19c (4232/197)   800

Settee, inlaid walnut, panelled backrest and sides, sabre legs, 48½, E19c (4218/193)   1200

Settee, 2 chairback, stained beechwood, backrest pierced with interlaced tassels and rosettes, 39½ (4157/161)   300

Stand, wash, walnut, gallery, marble top, frieze drawer, 31 x 31 x 15, M19c (4142/147)   125

Stool, rectangular seat, plain rails, on curule legs, 15½, L19c (4218/90)   300

Stools, foot, pair, gilt decorated painted, leaf-tip molded frieze, upholstered top, 12½, L18c (4218/69)   500

Table, center, marquetry, circular top, triangular flared pedestal, 29 x 46, L19c (4272/368)	1700
Table, center, walnut and oak, fluted and guilloche carved frieze, 27½ x 36 x 23 (4157/164)	600
Table, console, mahogany, Dutch, grey marble top, frieze drawer, 30¾ x 37½ x 17, E19c (4168/70)	300
Table, console, D-shaped gilt decorated, mahogany, false drawer, female term legs, 34 x 35½ x 20½, L18c (4218/101)	900
Table, game, mahogany, hinged top, baize lined interior, 28½ x 32, E19c (4218/175)	600
Table, game, marquetry inlaid, mahogany, reserves of flowers and playing cards, 29 x 34 x 17, L18c Dutch (4142/66)	325
Table, occasional, marquetry, mahogany, Dutch, hinged, drawer, 33 x 18½ x 19, E19c (4159/310)	700
Table, pier, neoclassical carved walnut, marble top, carved with laurel swags, 35 x 41 x 20½ (631/404)	550
Table, side, marquetry, inlaid mahogany, 30 x 37 x 23, L18c, Dutch (4142/65)	325
Table, tripod, continental, brass, circular, flared columnar stem, 27 x 15½, 19c (4260/1752)	2300

Commode (4272/366)

Chapter 3

European Porcelain, Ceramics and Glass

During the past season, the European ceramics and porcelain market experienced a dramatic upward shift in value. Not all categories were affected, but many of the items dealt with in this chapter—ceramic, porcelain and glass objects manufactured in Europe from 1600 to approximately 1850—were purchased at prices double what could reasonably have been expected in the United States for the first time, and helped to push prices to these new levels.

Dutch and English Delftware and English saltglaze signaled the surge, followed by English creamware and Whieldon pottery. However, the greatest advances were in early-nineteenth-century examples of the Regency period, especially Worcester "Japan" patterns. Barr, Flight and Barr Imari pieces were especially popular, selling at double their anticipated levels.

One category which was very strong, after decades of dull trading, was Chelsea and "Girl-in-a-Swing" scent bottles and bonbonnieres. These items, highly collectible because of their relatively small size and easy identification, were suddenly in demand.

Ceramics outpaced early European glass in interest and activity. (Much less glass survives, of course, and it may well be that owners are reluctant to dispose of what little they have.) For bargain hunters, the most promising opportunities lay in nineteenth-and twentieth-century ceramics.

After a long spell of stable prices, the market for European ceramics, porcelain and glass has moved out of the doldrums. Its leader was high-quality, sometimes flashy Regency porcelain, the bold design of this early-nineteenth-century style catching the fancy of modern collectors. And, in porcelain, there's every reason to expect that attention will continue to be focused on the lively, colorful item. Meanwhile similar patterns manufactured at a later date were considerably more reasonable in price. Although prices are rising, there are still relatively low-priced opportunities in European porcelain.

Note: See Chapter 5, "European Renaissance, Medieval and Later Works of Art," for a report on a number of important ceramic pieces, notably Italian majolica of the fourteenth and fifteenth centuries.

Ceramics
ENGLISH CERAMICS

Alcock

Vase, transfer printed in black, classical figures, 10⅜, 1840-50 (4262/315) *400*
Vases, pair, flower encrusted, 7¾, rep, ca1830 (4132/91) 300

Armorial

Plates, dessert, set of 12, arms of Haslam impaling Harrison, 8¾, 1 hc, ca1825 (4260/293) 250
Plates, dinner, set of 14, arms of Haslam impaling Harrison, 9⅞, ca1830 (4260/292) 650

Assorted periods and manufacturers

Bonbonniere, gold mounted, Venus and Cupid, ca1751-54 2⅛ (4221/71) 1700
Bust of Clytie, black jasper-dip, H9¼, ca1860 (649/10) $30
Compote, white glazed, bowl, supported by 3 rope-carrying putti, 7½, M19c (631/8) 75
Compotes, oval, pair, apple green, flowering shrubbery, 13⅞, 1 rep, ca1835 (4260/295) 200
Dessert service, blue, gold, 12, Ridgway*, floral medallions, ca1840 (4148/52) 300
Dessert service, part, 23 pcs, butterflies and figures, ca1820-30, minor imp (4190/206) 225
Necessaire, enamel, scene of figures in landscape, 4¼, ca1765, Staffordshire (4141/114) 450
Plaque, circular, painted, W. Mitchell, highland landscape, D14¼, ca1860 (649/13) 400
Plaques, pair, floral, framed, 6½ x 5, L19c (4260/301) 500
Plates, pair, landscape and a figure, 8⅛, ca1830 (4260/294) 75

Vase
(4262/315)

Scent bottle and stopper, girl and Dalmatian gold mounted, ca1755-60 2⅞ (4221/33) 3000
Scent bottle and stopper, Girl In A Swing, Hawk, ca1751-54 2¼ good (4221/30) 3000
Scent bottle and stopper, Chinoiserie gold mounted, ca1755-60 3¾ (4221/35) 3300
Scent bottle and stopper, Chinoiserie gold mounted, ca1751-54 3¾ hc (4221/36) 700
Scent bottle and stoppers, girl and mastiff, ca1755-60 3 chip (4221/37) 3000

Aynsley

Plates, set of thirty-four, Imari pattern, 17 dinner, 17 dessert, (631/1) 225

Barr, Flight & Barr

Coolers, fruit, covers & liners, 'Japan' pattern, 11, 1807-11 (4159/75) 3400
Dish, oval, and stand, armorial, Prendergast, Viscount Gort, 13⅝, 10, 1813-16 (4159/78) 1200
Plates, set of twelve, crested, white flowers, cobalt-blue, 8¼, ca1805 (4262/539) 750
Plates, set of 10, 'Fence' pattern, flowers, gilt leafage, Diam 8, ca1813 (4159/76) 800

Barr Worcester

Tea-coffee service, part, 45 pcs, scattered thistles in gilding, ca1792-1807, hc, rep cr (4190/335) 500

Belleek

Frame, photograph, two oval apertures, intricately modeled rare, 12¼, 1863-1891 (669/13) 1200

Bevington

Bowls, footed pair, flower encrusted, 4¼, imp, ca1872-92 (4132/96)	90

Bloor Derby

Group, cobblers wife and gentleman, ca1830-40, 6½, minor imp (4190/197)	225
Pots and covers, pair, bough, rectangular, colored birds and flowers, L8¾, 1830-40 (4262/487)	650
Shakespeare and John Milton, Milton holds a scroll, 9⅝, 9¾, rep, 1830-40 (4262/462)	400
Teapot and cover, applied florettes, floral sprays, 4, rep, ca1855 (4262/481)	200
Urns, flower filled, 7, chips, ca1825 (4132/31)	150

Bow

Autumn, young girl holding a brown basket, 5, ca1755 (4262/382)	225
Autumn, young man seated, 5, handle missing, ca1775 (4262/379)	550
Bacchus, as autumn, swaggering with a brown hare, 10¼, 1755-60 (4262/387)	325
Candlesticks, groups, pair, spring and summer, 10¼, 10⅝, ca1755 (4190/168)	900
Cellist, seated on a white tree stump, 7, ca1760 (4262/384)	275
Cupid, bird nesting, in blue and puce, 7¼, nest missing, 1760-65 (4262/390)	175
Dish, blue and white, molded with grape clusters, 10½, ca1760 (4262/396)	275
Dish, sweetmeat, shell shaped, with the 'Quail' pattern, 5¼, ca1755 (4262/394)	200
Dish, sweetmeat, shell form, pink edged scallop shell, 4⅜, ca1755 (4262/393)	550
Dish, sweetmeat, triple shell, scallop shell feathered in purple, 7⅝, ca1755 (4262/392)	750
Dishes, blue white, pair, relief molded, underglazed blue, 10½, hc, ca1760 (4132/3)	400
Figure, cellist, ca1758-63 7⅞ chip (4190/169)	600
Figure, oriental boy on tree stump, ca1765, 6 (4190/170)	550
Figure, shepherdess, ca1760-69, 6⅛ (4190/171)	400
'Idylic Musician', playing flute and drum, 9, ca1765 (4262/391)	700
Lady gardener, flower filled apron, 10, ca1765 (4262/389)	450
Plate, powder blue, underglaze-blue, a punting Chinaman, 9, 1755-60 (4262/398)	175
Plate, soup, octagonal, Chinaman and his dog, 8⅞, ca1760 (4262/399)	150
Plates, pair, exotic birds, berries, foliage, 8¾, ca1770 (4262/401)	450
Plates, pair, blue and white, 'Golfer and Caddy' pattern, 8¾, 1755-60 (4262/397)	400
Plates, pair, Famille Rose, green and pink peonies, 9¼, ca1755 (4262/395)	325
Platter, oblong octagonal, powder blue, ca1755-60, 15, chip (4190/175)	275
Platters, oblong octagonal, pair, powder blue, ca1755-60, 14½, chip (4190/174)	600
Pot of flowers, rep chip, 8½, ca1760 (4132/2)	275
Shepherd with bagpipes, flowered waistcoat, 9⅞, 1755-60 (4262/388)	550
Spring, young lady seated, white rockwork base, 5, ca1775 (4262/380)	650
Teacup and saucer, powder blue, ogee shaped, flowers and insects, 5¾, ca1760 (4262/400)	350
Teapot and cover, oriental motifs, ca1755-60, 5¼, hc on cover (4190/176)	275
Winter, old man seated on a pile of logs, 4¾, ca1755 (4262/381)	275
Winter and spring, bocage, bearded man, lady with garland, 8½, ca1765 (4262/386)	475

Bristol

Childs mug, sprigs, flowers, handle, 2⅝, hc, ca1770-81 (4132/6)	100
Plate, scalloped, delft blue and white, scene of Chinamen in small boats, 9, 1760-70 (4262/241)	200
Vases, pair, snowball, pear shaped, scrolling branches hung with fruit, 18½, 19c (631/2)	375

Caughley

Bowl, sugar, and cover, fruit, butterflies, scrollwork, ca1780-90, 4⅝, fine (4190/277)	750
Center dish, fisherman pattern, 12½, fine, ca1780-90 (4132/41)	175
Dish, center, Bengal Tiger pattern, ca1785-90, 12¾, chip (4190/288)	400
Dish, lozenge shaped, Bengal Tiger pattern, ca1785-90, 10½, fine (4190/284)	400
Dish, lozenge shaped, Bengal Tiger pattern, ca1785-90, 10¼, fine (4190/283)	400
Dishes, lozenge shaped pair, Bengal Tiger pattern, ca1785-90, 10⅜, hc (4190/285)	500
Jug, cabbage leaf, blue and white, transfer-printed, mask spout, 'Pine Cone', 11⅝, ca1785 (4262/492)	900
Plate, powder blue, insect, floral spray, 8⅝, ca1775 (4262/495)	300
Tea and coffee service, part, miniature, sailboats and island pavilions, 3⅛, imp, 1785-90 (4262/494)	900
Teapot and cover, gold and white, ca1785-95, 5⅝ (4190/281)	300

Chamberlain's

Cups and saucers, caudle, pair, floral, stars and scrollwork, 2⅞, ca1810 (4260/321)	400
Dessert service, crested, 28 pcs, dam, 1810-15 (4260/320)	4000

Chamberlain's Worcester

Bowl, square, Japan pattern, ca1805, 10¼, hc (4190/304)	500

Coolers, covers and liners, pair, crested, thistles, scroll handles, 13, 13⅜, chip, 1811-20 (4262/563) — 1100
Cups and saucers, pair, Armorial, ca1815 (4190/331) — 375
Dessert service, part, fruit flowers, thirty-one pcs, rep, imp, ca1815 (4132/52) — 3500
Dessert service, part, Japan pattern, central bowl of flowers, 17 pcs, 1830-40 (4262/566) — 450
Dinner plates, set of 12, Japan pattern, ca1805, 9¼, fine (4190/308) — 1500
Dinner service, part, 75 pcs, flowers-vines-archers, ca1840, hc, dam (4190/334) — 2500
Dish, lozenge shaped, Armorial, ca1815, 11¾ (4190/328) — 600
Dish, muffin and cover, Armorial, ca1815, 7⅞, hc (4190/329) — 325

Dish (4190/328)

Dessert
service
(4262/566)

Dish (4190/329)

Cellist (4262/384)

Winter and spring
(4262/386)

Pails (669/16)

Dish, oblong, two travellers, rural landscape, 9¾, ca1800 (4262/559) — 225
Dish, square, Bengal Tiger pattern, ca1795-1810, 8⅞ (4190/289) — 500
Dishes, serving, pair, Japan pattern, ca1805, 11 fine (4190/305) — 550
Dishes, serving, pair, Japan pattern, ca1805, 11 (4190/306) — 850
Dishes, square, pair, Japan pattern, ca1810, 7⅞ (4190/324) — 500
Dishes, vegetable, liners, Japan pattern, ca1805, 13¾, fine (4190/297) — 1100
Fruit cooler, cover, liner, Japan pattern, ca1805, 1 handle miss liner hc (4190/307) — 2000
Fruit coolers, cover, liners crested, 12⅝, rep, ca1815 (4132/54) — 950
Pails, ice covers and liners, with floral panels, gilt and green borders, 12, ca1830 (669/16) — 1100
Plate, Bengal Tiger pattern, ca1811-20, 8½, fine (4190/293) — 350
Plate, Armorial, ca1815, 8¾ (4190/330) — 200
Plate, game bird, brown, green and blue, landscape, 8½, 1814-16 (4262/560) — 200
Plate, soup, Japan pattern, ca1805, 9½, fine (4190/317) — 175
Plates, dinner, pair, Japan pattern, ca1805, 9¼ (4190/312) — 275
Plates, dinner, pair, Japan pattern, ca1805, 9¼ (4190/313) — 250
Plates, pair, Bengal Tiger pattern, ca1795-1810, 7¼, fine (4190/292) — 550
Plates, pair, Bengal Tiger pattern, Kakiemon style, 9¼, 9⅜, ca1800 (4262/554) — 300
Plates, pair, 'Jabberwocky' pattern, flowering oriental shrubbery, 7¼, 1800-10 (4262/552) — 400
Plates, pair, crested, 3 sprays of pink roses, 9⅞, 1811-20 (4262/565) — 300
Plates, set 12, Bengal Tiger pattern, ca1795-1810, 9½, cr (4190/294) — 1400
Plates, set 4, Bengal Tiger pattern, ca1795-1810, 8½ (4190/291) — 600
Plates, set 5, Bengal Tiger pattern, ca1790-95, 8⅜, hc (4190/290) — 600
Plates, small set of 8, Japan pattern, ca1805, 7¼ (4190/319) — 600
Plates, small, set of 12, Japan pattern, ca1805, 7¼, fine (4190/318) — 800
Plates, small, two, Japan pattern, ca1805, 7¼ (4190/320) — 200
Plates, soup, pair, Japan pattern, ca1805, 9⅝ (4190/316) — 200
Plates, soup, pair, Japan pattern, ca1805, 9⅝ (4190/314) — 250

Platter, oval, Japan pattern, ca1805, 13¾, hc (4190/302)   475
Platter, oval large, Japan pattern, ca1805, 18, fine (4190/299)   600
Platter, oval small, Japan pattern, ca1805, 12½, fine (4190/303)   375
Platters, oval, pair, Japan pattern, ca1805, 15⅝, 1 hc (4190/300)   700
Platters, oval, very large, Japan pattern, ca1805, 19½ (4190/298)   1100
Stands, lozenge shaped, Armorial, ca1807 (4190/322)   350
Teacups and saucers, pair, Armorial, ca1815 (4190/332)   375
Teapot and cover, Japan pattern, ca1805, 6⅝ (4190/321)   250
Tureen, cover, stand, Armorial, ca1815 (4132/51)   1000
Tureens, covers and stands, Japan pattern, oval, ca1805, 15¾, miss handle imp (4190/296)   2000
Tureens, sauce and covers, crested, with puce sprays, 8¼, 1811-20 (4262/564)   450

Champion

Dish, lozenge shaped, Bristol, with a bouquet and sprigs, 10, ca1775 (4262/415)   175

Charles Ford

Dessert service, part, Italianate landscape, 8⅞, 18 pcs, 1874-90 (4260/302)   200

Chelsea

Basket, reticulated, circular, green twig handles, Red Anchor Period, 7⅞, res (4190/181)   275
Bonbonniere gold mounted, boy and boar, ca1756-60 2⅛ (4221/70)   1900
Candlestick group, 'The Dog with a Clog', 9¾, Late Gold Anchor Period (4262/444)   325
Coffee cups saucers, pair, spray-sprigs-summer flowers, fine, Red Anchor Period (4132/8)   750
Dish, fruits scroll rim, 9, Brown Anchor Period (4132/10)   350
Dish, fluted, Kakiemon pattern, iron-red and gilt dragon, 8, Raised Anchor Period (4262/418) 550
Dish, leaf, 2 overlapping leaves shaped in green, 11⅞, dam, ca1755 (4260/273)   400
Dish, leaf-shaped, overlapping leaves, 8⅛, Gold Anchor Period (4262/425)   300
Dish, quatrefoil, bouquet, 10¾, Gold Anchor Period (4262/433)   150
Dish, silver-shape, scroll-molded rim, 13, Red Anchor Period (4262/422)   700
Dish, turquoise edged, insect, fruit, 9⅝, Gold Anchor Period, hc (4262/430)   200
Dishes, leaf, pair, overlapping lettuce leaves, 11⅜, Red Anchor Period, rep (4262/416)   300
Dishes, pair, fruits, insects, 9½, Gold Anchor Period, rep (4262/437)   350
Dishes, pair, brown edged, insect, fruit, 9½, Early Gold Anchor Period (4262/429)   550
Dishes, pair, oval, sprigs of flowers, 9⅝, Gold Anchor Period (4262/431)   425
Harvesters, pair, with rake and scythe, 6⅞, Gold Anchor Period, imp (4262/440)   350
Mars, orange plumed helmet, shield, 7⅞, Gold Anchor Period (4262/441)   150
Plate, bouquet, 8⅝, Early Gold Anchor Period (4262/428)   100
Plate, scalloped 'Lady in a Pavilion', Kakiemon pattern, 9⅜, chip, 1750-55 (4262/420)   600
Plates, botanical pair, large green leaf with various fruits, 8½, ca1760 (4260/274)   700
Plates, pair, painted birds, scalloped edges, 1 with rim chip, 8¾, Red Anchor Period (4132/9) 300
Platter, oval, scalloped, fruit, green leaves, 13⅜, Gold Anchor Period (4262/435)   *800*
Scent bottle, fruit cluster, ca1756-60 3½ (4221/66)   500
Scent bottle, Three Graces, 2½ (4221/59)   350
Scent bottle and stopper, basket of fruit, ca1756 4½ repair (4221/62)   3500
Scent bottle and stopper, berry gold mounted, ca1756 2 (4221/60)   4100
Scent bottle and stopper, cat gold mounted, ca1755 2½ rep (4221/31)   3400
Scent bottle and stopper, gardener and dog, ca1760 3½ repair-chip (4221/54)   *2200*
Scent bottle and stopper, gardener, young boy, ca1760 3⅜ chip (4221/56)   *2000*

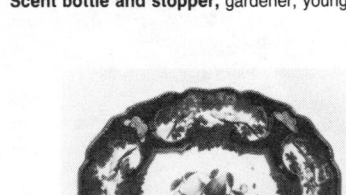

Platter (4262/435)

Scent bottle
and stopper
(4221/54)

Scent bottle
and stopper
(4221/56)

Bulb pot and cover (4262/332)

Scent bottle and stopper, gold mounted, ca1756-60 3½ chip (4221/64)	2000
Scent bottle and stopper, heart shaped gold mounted, ca1756 2¾ hc (4221/65)	1500
Scent bottle and stopper, peacock, gold mounted, ca1755 3⅜ chip (4221/29)	3900
Scent bottle and stopper, pug dog style, 2½ (4221/34)	550
Scent bottle and stopper, tulip, ca1755 2⅜ (4221/57)	4600
Scent bottle and stopper, monkey gold mounted, ca1775 2⅝ rep (4221/51)	1000
Scent bottle and stopper, replaced, Three Graces, 2 (4221/58)	200
Scent bottle and stopper,replaced, wine flask gold mounted, ca1756-60 3⅜ (4221/63)	2500
Scent bottle and stoppers double, cupid gold mounted, ca1756 2¾ rep (4221/46)	400
Scent bottle and 2 stoppers, monk, book, tree trunk, ca1755 3⅛ stoppers replaced (4221/32)	2100
Scent bottle double and stopper, Provender of the Monastery, ca1756 3 chip (4221/52)	3100
Scent bottles and stoppers double, billing doves gold mounted, ca1756 (4221/44)	1600
Tea bowls and saucers, pair, lotus petals, 4⅞, Red Anchor Period, hc (4262/421)	425

Chelsea-Derby

Basket, reticulated, oval, floral sprigs, sprays, 9¾, rep, ca1769-84 (4132/13)	450
Candlesticks, pair, Venus and Mars, 7⅞, 8¼, 1770-85 (4262/447)	200
Figures of four seasons, allegorical, 9¾, ca1775 (4132/16)	1600
Musicians, pair, girl with hurdy gurdy, boy with horn, 5¾, 5⅝, ca1770 (4262/442)	325
Young girl, puce sprigged white capelet, 6, chip, 1770-75 (4262/445)	150

Coalbrookdale

Inkwell, flower-encrusted, urn-form, diameter 6¾ (4148/50)	100
Urns, pair, flower encrusted, vasiform, body, molded with shell and foliage, 19, L19c (631/3)	400
Vases, pair, flower encrusted, 10⅞, imp, ca1835 (4132/86)	100
Vases, pair, pyriform bodies, C-scroll handles, 9½, 19c (619/10)	350

Coalport

Bulb pot and cover, claret ground, bombe body, gilt scrollwork, 11⅛, 2 rep, ca1810 (4262/332)	250
Dessert, service, part, botanical, centers different flowers, 24 pcs, 1800-10 (4262/326)	2000
Dessert service, part, 19 pcs, sprays of mixed flowers, ca1820-30, imp (4190/220)	700
Dessert service, part, 7 pcs., centers with botanical flowers, pattern 2/5961, ca1830 (4148/49)	300
Dinner service, part, 24 pcs, apricot ground, footed serving dishes, ca1845 (4190/222)	1500
Fruit stands, pair, cluster of fruit, 12½, ca1840 (4260/286)	900
Ink well and cover, artichoke form, ca1815-25, 3⅝, rep, chip (4190/207)	250
Plate, soup, 'Yellow Tiger' pattern, tiger curling around bamboo tree, 9⅜, 1805-10 (4262/330)	75
Plates, dessert, set of 12, colorful floral sprays, 9, modern (4260/287)	375
Plates, set of three, Perceval service, initialled, 9¼, ca1809 (4262/329)	300
Plates, set of 5, Bengal Tiger pattern, ca1805-10 8⅜ (4190/208)	200

Plates, ten, painted, spray of fruits within pink border, D9¼, ca1900 (649/5)   200
Tea and coffee service, part (John Rose), pale blue band, green daisies, 32 pcs, cracks, ca1810
  (4262/333)   350
Tea and coffee service, part, 22 pcs, flowers, cobalt blue band, ca1840, imp (4190/223)   350
Tea and coffee service, part, 39 pcs, birds, flowers, ca1820-25 (4190/216)   600
Tea and coffee service, yellow ground, wide yellow border floral sprays, 43 pcs, chip, 1820-25
  (4262/334)   850
Tea and coffee service, 45 pcs, sprays of flowers, ca1820-25 (4190/217)   675
Tea service, John Rose, Imari, 37 pcs., pattern 561, imp., ca1810 (4148/48)   1100
Tureen, sauce, cover and stand, oval, scattered gilt, cornflower sprigs, 7⅛, 8⅜, 1805-10 (4262/331)   125
Tureen, sauce, cover and stand, porcelain, boat shaped, 8⅞ x 9⅛, ca1830 (4219/32)   90
Vase, pair, cornucopia with gilding, encrusted with flowers, 5, chips, ca1835 (4132/87)   150
Vase, royal-blue ground, 'Milady's Garden' by Keeling, H15½, 1906 (649/4)   650
Vases and covers, pair blue ground, still life of ripening fruit on woodland bank, 11½, Ca1910
  (669/11)   700

Coalport, John Rose

Jardiniere and stand, neoclassical pattern, river goddess, 4¾, ca1800-10 (4132/68)   325
Tea and coffee service, part, 21 pcs, Japan pattern, ca1805-10, minor imp (4190/214)   850
Tea and coffee service, 34 pcs, brightly painted flowers, ca1820-30 (4190/215)   375
Tea service, part, 9 pcs, floral sprays, ca1805-10, cr teapot (4190/212)   350

Copeland

Vase, Sevres-style, royal-blue grnd., ovoid body, ptd. flower panels, lamp, H13¼, ca1900 (649/6)   100

Creamware

Bowl, enamelled, Leeds, iron-red, green, black with flower sprays, D6⅞, ca1765 (4156/32)   150
Jug, milk, enamelled, Leeds, baluster body, sprig of flowers, 3¼, 1765 (4156/31)   70
Mug, enamelled, Liverpool*, scroll handle, initialled, 3⅝, 1815 (4156/48)   200
Plaque, scene of nude maiden, Emile Lessore painter, 16¼ x 13½, ca1859-75 (4132/156)   1500
Plate, Dutch-decorated, Leeds, scene from 'Prodigal Son', 8¼, L18c (4156/46)   650
Plate, Dutch-decorated, Leeds, with busts of the House of Orange, 9¾, ca1787 (4156/42)   450
Plate, Dutch-decorated, Leeds, with busts of the House of Orange, 9⅝, ca1787 (4156/43)   400
Plate, Dutch-decorated, Leeds, The Princess and Prince of Orange, 9⅞, ca1787 (4156/44)   325

Crown Derby

Dinner service, part, cobalt blue and gilt, decorated, E19c, 57 pcs, imp and rubbing (631/6)   750
Jar, ginger and cover, gilt scrolls, berry laden flowering branches, 10½, 1886 (631/4)   275
Vase company, ovoid body, designs of Persian inspiration, 6½, ca1880 (669/2)   275

Davenport

Charger, stone china 'Japan' pattern, peonies and bamboo growing from behind stylized rockwork,
  16⅞, ca1825 (4262/284)   225
Dessert service, part, spray of flowers, scalloped rims, 16 pcs, ca1845 (4262/376)   325
Dinner service, part, 17 pcs, Japan pattern, ca1870-86 (4190/253)   1100
Plates, fruit, set of 6, sprays of fruit, 9¼, 1 hc, 1835 (4260/298)   650
Vases, pair, Japan pattern, pot-pourri, pierced rim, paw feet, H6, 1870-86 (649/2)   300

Delft

Bowl, shallow, polychrome, London, flowers and bamboo, 10⅛, imp, ca1770 (4211/978)   275
Dish, 'Queen Mary', lobed center with portrait of Queen Mary, 13½, ca1689 (4156/8)   850
Dish, pickle, blue and white, London, leaf shape, small loop handle, 3¾, ca1770, rare (4156/15)   275
Dish, small, blue and white, London, sailing boat, 7⅝, ca1750, chip (4156/14)   325
Fuddling cup, blue and white, London, three pear shaped cups, strap handles, 4, ca1680 (4156/13)   900
Plate, 'William and Mary', blue and manganese portraits, Bristol or Brislington, D8¾, ca1690
  (4156/12)   1600
Plate, 'William and Mary', blue and ochre portraits, Bristol or Brislington, 8½, 1690-95 (4156/11)   2600
Plate, blue and white Chinoiserie, central figure holding sprig, 8⅝, 1760 (4156/28)   200
Plate, blue and white, Bristol, boats in estuary, 9, ca1760 (4156/23)   200
Plate, blue and white, Bristol, figures in boat in calm estuary, 9⅛, 1750-70, fine (4156/22)   500
Plate, blue and white, Chinoiserie, central figure strolling, 8¼, ca1760 (4156/29)   225
Plate, blue and white, Chinoiserie, with Chinamen and pheasants, London*, 8¾, ca1750 (4156/25)   300
Plate, blue and white, Liverpool, Englishman in oriental dress, 8½, ca1760, fine, unusual (4156/26)   500
Plate, large, polychrome with bird, flowers, 13½, E18c (4156/7)   750
Plate, marriage, blue and white, inscribed, 1722, foliate scroll, 8¾, Bristol* (4156/20)   700
Plate, Bristol, peacock in shrubbery, 9, 1720-30, rep (4156/17)   550
Plate, blue and white, Liverpool, Chinaman smoking, watching 2 roosters, 8½, 1750-60 (4156/24)   350

Plates, assembled pair, Liverpool, Chinaman holding parasol, orange, red edges, 8⅝, 1750-60 (4156/27)   600

Plates, blue and white, London, pair, squirrels perched on grapevine, 8¾, ca1750, good (4156/21)   400

Teapot and cover, London, rare, blue and white, bird and insect on sides, rare, 3¾, ca1740 (4156/16)   1100

Wall pocket, Liverpool, rare, multicolored bird on flowering branch, 7½, ca1760 (4156/18)   500

Derby

Andromache, weeping over the ashes of Hector, 10¼, ca1780 (4262/457)   250

Basket, oval, reticulated, cherries and insects in center, ca1760, 8⅝, rep (4190/189)   275

Butter tub, sprigs of flowers, 5½, rare, ca1770-80 (4132/12)   75

Canaries figures, pair, yellow bird with brown markings, 2⅝, rep, chips, L18c (4132/20)   100

Candlesticks, pair, a gardener and companion, 9¼, rep, ca1765 (4132/17)   575

Candlesticks, musicians, pair, bagpipe, dog, lady playing lute, 8⅝, 8½, ca1770 (4262/455)   400

Cup, stirrup, fox head, inscribed 'Tally Ho', 4¾, ca1820 (4262/461)   500

Cup and saucer, chocolate, bell shape, double C scroll handles, ca1830, 3, fine (4190/200)   175

Dessert plates, pair, botanical, 8½, fine, L18c (4132/22)   300

Dessert service, part, 'Angouleme Sprig' pattern, 16 pcs, ca1820 (4262/486)   400

Dinner service part, 36 pcs, floral, iron-red and gold floral sprays, ca1810-25, dam (4190/193)   850

Dinner service part, 48 pcs, floral, cobalt-blue band on rim, ca1820, rep (4190/195)   800

Dishes, leaf, pair, puce veining, green edges, rare, 7⅛, chips, ca1765 (4132/11)   525

Dishes, lozenge shaped pair 'Imari', gadroon-edged rim, 11¾, ca1820 (4262/482)   150

Figure, Harlequin, ca1760-70, 5⅝, chip, rare (4190/185)   *800*

Figure, Dr. Syntax modelled as bald figure, ca1830 (4190/186)   *300*

Figure (4190/185)   Figure (4190/186)

Figures pair
(4190/188)

Figure, John Milton leaning on books, ca1765, 11⅝ imp (4190/183)	275
Figure, John Wilkes standing, ca1772-75, 12½, chip (4190/184)	350
Figure, white biscuit, Cupid as a falconer, ca1775, 5⅛ minor imp (4190/187)	*150*
Figure, putto, basket and flowers, 4½, ca1785 (4132/18)	90
Figure of musicians, pair, gentleman and lady, 8⅛, rep, chips, ca1825 (4132/19)	300
Figures pair, gardener and companion, ca1760, 9¼, rep chip (4190/188)	*600*
Figures pair, putti seated on stump, ca1775-85, 6¾ imp (4190/182)	100
Harlequin, yellow hat, black mask and shoes, 5½, 1770-80 (4262/450)	700
Jug, squat baluster body, 5⅛, ca1815 (4132/24)	300
Man with a keg, brown keg on stick, 7⅝, imp, ca1765 (4262/453)	250
Milton, John, pink lined cloak, 10⅛, ca1780 (4262/458)	150
Musicians, pair, lady and gentleman playing lutes, 6¼, imp, ca1825 (4262/465)	225
Plate, three putti frolicking around goat, 9⅛, ca1782 (4262/469)	325
Plates, pair, figures near ruins, 8¾, 1795-1800 (4262/474)	400
Plates, set of 8, dinner, blue and iron red, cornflowers, 9¾, ca1825 (4262/478)	325
Plates, soup, set of fifteen, bouquet of flowers and sprigs, 9¾, 2 hc, ca1815 (4260/278)	1500
Plates, 12, garden flowers, molded edge, 25, imp, ca1815-25 (4132/27)	450
Pots, flowering, pair, cluster flowers, 5¼, chips, 1 rep, ca1765 (4132/14)	150
Pug dog, brown muzzle, ears and paws in grey, 2⅜, ca1810 (4262/449)	300
Sauce tureen, cover and stand, bellflowers, eagle heads, scrollwork, ca1815, 6⅝ (4190/194)	200
Sauceboat, blue and white, lobed body, island pavilions, 9, 1756-58 (4262/466)	400
Sheep, pair, russet spotted white coat, 2¾, chip, rep, 1790-1810 (4262/459)	175
Shepherd, wineskin over his shoulder, 8⅛, ca1765 (4262/451)	325
Shepherd and companion, pair, young man playing horn, 9⅛, imp, ca1770 (4262/454)	500
Shepherdess, flower filled apron, 8⅛, 1760-70 (4262/452)	300
Sprinkler, rosewater, flowers, ca1820, 3¾ (4190/260)	275
Sprinkler, rosewater, Japan pattern, ca1820, 3⅝ (4190/259)	250
Tea and coffee service, part, Japan pattern 52 pcs, L19c (4132/23)	825
Tea and coffee service, 31 pcs, scrolling leaves and flowers, imp, ca1820 (4132/29)	600
Tea service, Japan pattern, 12 pieces, transfer printed flowers, 19¼, tray, 19c (619/12)	500
Vase, 2 handled, birds perched and flying near trees, 7⅜, rep, ca1765 (4132/15)	125
Vases, pair, gilt snake handles, 6½, rep, ca1815 (4262/476)	325
Vases, pair, urn-shaped, painted by Thomas Steele*, 9¼, ca1825 (4159/72)	275
Violinist, yellow violin, seated on tree stump, 5⅛, 1756-60 (4262/448)	450

Derbyshire

Tureen, covered, sauce and stand, lozenge shape, views of Derbyshire, 9¾, 8¾, ca1795 (4262/489)	850

Doulton

Vases, pair, Burslem, Luscian ware, scenes from Shakespeare, 18, ca1910, by W. Nunn (669/8)	800
Vases, pair, Lambeth stoneware, frieze of poppies in a moorland setting, 12½, 1879 (669/7)	500

English porcelain

Dessert service, scrolls, yellow and turquoise leaves, rep, ca1830 (4132/82)	400
Figures, 2 swans, seated, arched neck, 3, ca1820 (4132/71)	200
Plate, the old English hound, 8⅝, ca1815 (4132/79)	100
Spirit kegs and covers, gin, rum, hunting scene, spiggots, 9⅛, 19c (4132/78)	100
Sprinkler, rosewater, bouquet of flowers, ca1820 3⅞ (4190/263)	200
Tea service, part, 4 pcs, Japan pattern, ca1810 (4190/204)	275
Tea service, part, 32 pcs, Imari, imp, ca1830 (4132/83)	275
Urn, covered, painted grey, brown, 3 quail, 16⅝, chips, ca1805 (4132/80)	150

Vases, pair, apple green, gold band border, 5⅛, ca1810-20 (4132/67) 300

English Ironstone

Sprinkler, rosewater, Japan pattern, ca1820, 3¾ (4190/258) 225

Flight and Barr

Dessert, service, 'Japan' pattern, initialled JJN, 39 pcs, imp, ca1805 (4262/543) 5500
Dish, shell shaped, 'Queen Charlotte' pattern, white flowers, 73/5, 1792-1804 (4262/535) 225
Plate, 'Lord Henry Thynne' pattern, landscape, man fishing, 8½, 1792-1804 (4262/534) 600

Flight, Barr & Barr

Dessert service, 29 pcs, crested Holgate of Waiden, ca1813-40 (4190/339) 800
Dish, oval, shell decorated, 13½, fine, ca1813 (4132/45) 750
Dishes, shell shape, cream colored band, brown border, 7⅞, fine, ca1813 (4132/43) 150
Dishes, square pair, shell decorated, 8⅝, fine, ca1807-13 (4132/46) 900
Fruit coolers, covers, liners, pair, gilding on white ground, 14, good, ca1815 (4132/42) 1300
Plates, dinner, set of 5, garden flowers, 10½, crack, ca1825 (4260/318) 75
Plates, dinner, set of 6, crested, apple green, 10⅜, chip, ca1815 (4260/312) 400
Plates, pair, shell decorated, 8½, fine, ca1807-13 (4132/47) 900
Plates, pair, shell decorated, 8⅛, fine, ca1807-13 (4132/48) 700
Plates, pair, shell decorated, 8⅛, 1 riveted, ca1807-13 (4132/50) 450
Plates, soup, set of three, apple green, a different view in each, 7¾, 1810-13 (4262/545) 300
Platter, oval, Saracen's head crest, 16, ca1815 (4260/315) 275
Platters, oval, pair, crested, arm holding dagger, 12⅛, ca1815 (4260/314) 250
Tureen, sauce and cover, artichoke knob, pale salmon, 7, ca1820 (4262/549) 250
Tureens, sauce and covers, pair, turquoise ground, pink roses, 6⅝, chip, 1820-25 (4262/548) 450

Grainger & Co.

Vase and cover, pierced, shield-shaped body, square foot, domed cover, H17¼, 1892 (649/20) 1000

Greatbatch

Teapot and cover, transfer printed, enamelled, leaf molded spout, ear shaped handle, inscriptions,
5¼, ca1780 (4262/256) 650

Herculaneum

Tea-coffee service, part, 10 pcs, landscape panels, gilt borders, ca1805, rep, hc (4190/180) 400

Hicks & Meigh

Dinner service, part, 10 pcs, stone china, oriental floral pattern, imp, ca1806-22 (4132/65) 125

Ironstone

Pitcher and basin, John Venables & Co., transfer printed in medium blue, 'Union Pattern', H11⅝,
D13½, ca1853 (4156/64) 150

John Ridgway

Dessert service, part, 21 pcs, apple green, imp, ca1835-40 (4132/94) 500
Tea-coffee service, part, trelliswork, fan-shaped borders, 28 pcs, rep, ca1815-20 (4132/93) 375

Leeds

Cup, satyr head with grapevine wreath, creamware, 4½, chips, ca1760 (4132/102) 175
Jug, enamelled, creamware, swelling body, diamond borders in yellow or blue, 5⅝, 1770 (4262/262) 175
Tea and coffee service, part, enamelled, black floral sprays, strap handles, 8½, 5½, chip, ca1775
(4262/261) 1500

Liverpool

Jug, cream, with spiral molding, 3½, 1770-75 (4262/409) 125

London Delft

Chargers, pair, blue-white, peony, spray, and 2 sprigs, ca1770, 13⅝ (4190/131) 175

Longton Hall

Bracket, wall, shaped top curved slightly downward, 10, ca1755 (4262/402) 650
Plate, 'Strawberry Leaf', hovering insect, bouquets, sprigs, 8⅞, ca1755 (4262/403) 700
Plate, leaf molded, overlapping vine leaves, 8⅛, rare, ca1755 (4132/1) 250
Spring, black haired boy, seated on basket, 5, ca1755 (4262/405) 600
Summer and winter, pair, each a putto standing on a mound base, 4⅜, ca1755 (4262/404) 400
Winter, brown haired boy, heating hands, 4⅜, ca1755 (4262/406) 450

Lowestoft

Baskets, pair, reticulated, blue and white, underglaze blue, 'Pine Cone' pattern, 7¾, 1775-85 (4262/412)   650

Inkstand
(4262/367)

Baskets (4262/412)

Figures (4190/143)

Jardinieres (4190/238)

Dinner service (669/5)

Ewer, oil and vinegar, blue and white, spray of peonies, 6, ca1765 (4262/411)   1100
Lady playing a lute, on flower encrusted base, 6¾, res, ca1780 (4262/413)   450
Sauceboat, blue-white, flowers leaves scrollwork, 8¼, ca1765 (4132/5)   350

Mason, Miles

Jugs, set of 3, transfer printed in black, 5½, 7¼, ca1810 (4262/350)   350
Vases, three, garniture, tapered cylindrical body, landscape, 10⅛, 7⅞, hc, ca1810 (4262/351)   300

Mason's

Jardinieres, pair, ironstone, oriental, ca1820, 5⅛ (4190/238)   400
Sprinkler, Ironstone floral, ca1820 3½ fine (4190/256)   250
Sprinkler, rosewater, Japan pattern, ironstone, ca1820, 3½ fine (4190/257)   275

Minton

Cache pots, pair, hexagonal body scroll handles, 6¼, ca1850 (4132/95)   250
Dessert service, part, green glazed, basketwork, 7 pcs, ca1860 (4219/36)   200
Dessert service, part, apple green, cluster of fruit in centers, 23 pcs, ca1835 (4262/369)   600
Dessert service, part, 8 pcs, realistically painted flowers, ca1853, fine (4190/250)   150
Dishes, pair, rectangular, green ground, white florettes, scrollwork, 9¼, ca1830 (4262/368)   275
Ewer and stand, bisque porcelain, snake handled, molded and painted putti, 19¾, ewer, 18¼ stand, imp (631/17)   450
Inkstand, triple bucket, chamfered rectangular tray, twig handles, 10¾, ca1830 (4262/367)   300
Parian figures, pair, after J. Bell, maiden and Miranda, both cracked, H15½, 1864 and 1865 (649/16)   175
Plaque, rectangular, view of Stokesay Castle, 10 x 11½, ca1880 (4262/371)   600
Plates, pair, by A. Boullemier, head of girl within blue border, foliate scrolls, D9, 1880 (649/18)   325
Plates, six, oval dish, 7 pcs, ptd. by W. Mussill, animals, gilt rim, D9½, 1880, 1881 (649/17)   500
Plates, twelve, pate-sur-pate, classical profile, by Alboine Birks, D9, 1919 (649/19)   700
Tea service part, Japan pattern, ca1830 16 pcs spout dam (4190/249)   150
Teacups and saucers, set of 4, oriental landscape, 1 saucer, rep, 1811-13 (4260/288)   150
Urns and covers, pair, turquoise ground, birds on 2 panels, grapes, flowers, 20½, ca1860-70, chip rep (631/19)   2000
Vase, pate sur pate, bowl shape, rose-pink ground, cupid and Diana, 5¼, ca1910 (669/6)   350
Vase, pate-sur-pate, olive green body, white cupid, 8¾, 1886 (619/14)   1200

Vases, pair, flower encrusted, 7⅜, chips, ca1835 (4132/90)   200
Vases, pair, leaf form, 4⅛, imp, ca1830-35 (4132/88)   100
Vases, small pair, Chelsea bottle style, ruins in a landscape, 6¼, rep, ca1825-30 (4132/89)   175

Nantgarw

Plates, pair, sprays and sprigs of flowers, 8⅜, 1817-20 (4262/377)   325
Plates, pair, sprigs of pink roses, 8⅜, 1817-20 (4262/378)   500

Neale & Co.

Candlesticks, columnar, black basaltes, 7⅝, chips, ca1778-86 (4132/140)   700

Neale Basaltes

Urn, rosette-medallion, L18c, 9½, minor imp (4190/152)   125

New Hall

Coffee service, part, 14 pcs, floral, gilded leaves, white berries, ca1785, imp (4190/202)   425
Dishes, lobed, oval, pair, donkey and man, Italianate ruin, 9¼, 1820-30 (4262/324)   175
Tea-coffee service, part, 25 pcs, transfer printed, figures and butterfly, ca1795-1805 (4132/69)   400

Parianware

Roundels, portrait, pair, profile of a man, framed, 6½, 1847 (4260/300)   100

Parin

Jug, 3 handled, sloping body, pierced flower heads, loop handles, 9, L19c (631/27)   150
Urn, 2 handled, narrow neck, expanding waist, circles and florets, 11½, L19c (631/26)   150

Pearlware

Candelabra, 2 light, pair, figural, one woman playing lyre, 1 man playing instrument, 11¾, 13, E19c (631/9)   250
Jug, puzzle, enamelled, Leeds, inscrip, John Brooks, 1814' 3 nozzles, (4156/47)   500

Plymouth

Musician, playing brown lute, wearing hat, 5⅝, rep, ca1770 (4262/414)   600

Pointon

Plates, dessert, set of 9, blossoms, stems and leaves, 8½, hc, 1883-91 (4260/303)   275

Prattware

Bird nesting, young man in blue coat, with young woman, 5⅝, 1790-1810 (4262/230)   200
Figure, cockerel on tree stump, ca1780, 8⅛ (4190/138)   900
Figures, pair, lions, L18c, 11½ - 11¼, imp (4190/143)   *1300*

Ridgway

Dessert service, part, 18 pcs, cobalt-blue border, gold, white flowers, ca1830 (4190/248)   275

Ridgway, William

Dessert service, ironstone, Imari, 20 pcs., M19c (4148/53)   600

Rockingham

Bottles, large, pair, flower encrusted, 16¾, rep, ca1825 (4132/77)   250
Box and cover, butterfly, floral sprays, gilt borders, 3¼, 1831-42 (4262/358)   1600
Burner and stand, cottage pastille, 2 story octagonal house, 5½, cr, ca1830 (4132/73)   125
Figure, swan, nesting within green moss, 3, ca1830 (4132/72)   110
Figures, pair, giraffes (type), ca1830, 5⅞, ear rep (4190/243)   325
Figures, pair, seated topers, green jackets, brown caps, ca1830, 5, 1 minor imp (4190/245)   125
Frames, oval, flower encrusted, ca1850, 8⅛ chip (4190/246)   200
Figures of lions, pair, standing, 1 forepaw on an orb, 11½, ca1825 (4211/984)   850
Tea service, child's, 16 pcs, sprigs of cornflowers, ca1830, 1 hc (4190/247)   175
Tray, pin, lozenge shaped, view of Wooton Bridge, 4¾, 1831-42 (4262/359)   525
Vases, covered, pair, flower encrusted, cobalt-blue ground, loop handles, 11½, 1830-40 (4262/361)   250

Royal Crown Derby

Dinner service, Imari pattern II26, 10½,dinner plate, 20c, 126 pcs (669/5)   *3750*
Service, Imari pattern 2451, for Tiffany & Co., 48 pc., ca1930 (649/1)   550
Vases, pair, inverted pear shape form, summer flowers, 9, ca1903, by W. Mosley (669/3)   700

Royal Doulton

Plate, games, various wild game birds, 9½, E 20c, Tiffany & Co. retail mark (669/10)   1200

Plates, fish, 18, with various fresh water fish, 9½, E 20c (669/9) 1200
Plates, 12, by S. Hugh, English Shakespeare scenes, D10¼, 1914-16 (649/9) 900
Plates, 12, P. Curnock, flower panel and border, pattern H2147, D8¾, 1923-24 (649/7) 425

Royal Worcester

Bacchante with cymbal figure 'large', green and apricot tunic, 29½, 1919 (669/17) 900
Blackbirds, yellow-headed, pair, on spiderwort sprays after D. Doughty, H10¼, 7 (649/27) 1800
Cactus wren and prickly pear, figure, after Doughty, 10¾, 1958, needles missing (619/19) 700
Dishes, footed, pair, 'Earl Manvers' pattern, 9¾, 1918 (4260/323) 200
Ewer, cherry blossoms and leafage, 6½, ca1887 (619/3) 150
Ewer, parian figural molded, nude female, figure and mermaids, C scroll handle, 9¾, 1884 (631/25) 300
Group, figural, young boy standing before earthenware jug, pitcher, 7, L19c (619/6) 600
Lady and gentleman, Japanese, figure, pair, glazed parian, kimono, book, swords, 16-15½, ca1885 (619/9) 1600
Magnolia warbler figure, bird, large magnolia bloom, 13, after D. Doughty (669/19) *2000*
Mallards, pair, after Ruyckevelt, 17-12, 1967 (619/23) 950
Mocking birds, models, pair, perched amongst sprays of pink blossom, 10½ x 9¾, after D. Doughty (669/20) 3250
Nightingale and honeysuckle, figure, with traveling box, after Doughty, 9½, 1970 (619/16) 1100
Pitcher, gilt orange handle, violets and wild flowers, 5¼ ca1890 (619/1) 100
Plate, bicentennial, American eagle in branches, 10⅝, 1976 (4260/325) 50
Plates, dessert set of 12, cluster of fruit and flowers, 9¼, 1903 (4260/322) 850
Plates, four, ptd. by S. James, game birds, named on reverse, D9¼, 1929 (649/22) 150
Plates, twelve, rare set, painted landscapes by Harry Davis, D10½, 1926 (649/24) 1500
Santa Gertruidis Bull, model, brown shaded coat, standing on oval base, 9¾, 1961 (669/21) 225
Vase, floral sprays, ivory ground, dragon handles, 15¾, 1887 (669/12) 100
Vase, globular body, enamel and gilded dec., mtd as lamp, H10¾, 1883 (649/21) 150
Vase, 2 handled, pine boughs and fruit, 8½, ca1907 (619/5) 275

Salopian

Dish, center, blue and white version of fisherman pattern, ca1775-85, 11½ (4190/280) 200

Samson

Bowl, canoe form, scalloped lip, shell form handles, 11½, L19c (631/43) 275
Figurines, pair, man and woman in eighteenth century costume, 9¾, 19c, res (631/47) 250
Pail, milk, apple green, latticework, sprigs of flowers, 12½, L19c, rep (631/46) 550
Seaux a bouteilles, pair, flaring scalloped lip, spring flowers, 6½, cr (631/41) 500
Seaux a bouteilles, pair, gilt shell shaped handles, apple green, flowers, 6½, L19c, cr (631/39) 550
Seaux a verre, pair, shell shaped gilt handles, latticework, spring bouquets, 4¾, L19c (631/45) 350
Vase, hollandais, large, two parts, medallion with lovers, landscape, 9, L19c, chip (631/38) 300
Vases, hollandais, pair, two parts, putti between vertical banding, sprays of flowers, 7½, L19c, chip (631/40) 300
Vases, hollandais, pair, two parts, scrolling work, spring flowers, 6¼, L19c (631/42) 400

Sherratt, Obadiah

'Grecian and Daughter', Pera suckling her father bound in chains, 9¼, rep, ca1830 (4262/236) 450

Spode

Baskets and covers, potpourri, pair, pattern 1166, ca1807, L4¼, 4c (4190/231) 450
Baskets, covers, stands, potpourri, pair, pattern 1166, ca1807, D5⅜ (4190/230) 750
Bowls and covers, pair, potpourri, gros bleu ground, gilt stars and dots, 5⅛, ca1815 (4262/342) 375
Bowls and covers, potpourri, pattern 1166, ca1807, H2⅝ (4190/232) 325
Dessert service, part, 29 pcs, flowers, rep, fine, ca1821 (4132/63) 1200
Dessert service, 38 pcs, apple green, hc, good, ca1826 (4132/62) 1300
Dessert service, part, mint green borders, peacocks, 25 pcs, ca1825 (4262/348) 750
Dessert set, cornflower pattern, 22 pcs, ca1815 (4132/57) 650
Dish, ornithological, oblong, twig handles, 10⅞, ca1818 (4262/343) 400
Dishes, crested shell shaped, pair, white flowers, 9¾, ca1805 (4262/540) 350
Fruit coolers, covers, liners, apple green, 13⅜, ca1824 (4132/61) 1200
Hoops, beaded, '1166' pattern, pair, gros bleu ground, gilt scalework, 3½, hc, ca1807 (4262/340) 225
Plates, pair dessert, Imari pattern, 8, ca1825 (4132/60) 100
Sprinkler, rosewater, bouquets of flowers, ca1815, 3⅝ imp (4190/262) 175
Tea service, part, 23 pcs, pink rose, colbalt blue border, ca1820-30, cover cr (4190/236) 450
Tea service, 50 pcs, blue gold, ca1815 (4132/58) 225
Urns-stands and covers potpourri, pattern 1166, ca1807, D4½, rep (4190/233) 300
Vases, covered, potpourri, pair, pattern 1166, lush bouquets of flowers, ca1807, H7⅝ (4190/229) 850
Vases-spill, pair, Kakiemon pattern of flowers, ca1805, 3 (4190/234) 150

Staffordshire

Bust of Lord Wellington, black pottery, short curly hair, bare shoulders, 22⅛, 19c (4260/271) — 350
Bust of The Madonna, sepia eyes and eyebrows, brown hair, 15⅝, ca1810 (4219/35) — 425
Butter boat, saltglaze 'scratch blue', each side incised with floral sprig, L4½, ca1750 (4156/36) — 200
Candelsticks, table, pair, enamel, baluster form, fluted domed bases, 11, ca1765 (4259/553) — 1100
Coffee pot, cover, Bargeware, brown glaze, sprays of flowers, 14, 1889, chips (619/13) — 175
Creamers, cow pair, being milked by maiden, 7⅝, M19c (4211/986) — 850
Dish, reticulated, salt glaze, basketwork, foliate scroll borders, 12, ca1760 (4262/243) — 200
Figure, hawk, ca1780, 5¼, chip (4190/139) — 400
Figure, lions, ca1825, 12¼ (4190/144) — 425
Figure of 'Age', old woman wearing, black hat, pearlware, 7⅞, ca1800 (4132/109) — 225
Figures, pair, leopards cream colored, ca1790 8⅛ - 8⅜ fine, rare (4190/142) — *2500*
Group, lion and lamb, M19c, 4¾ (4190/244) — 350
Groups, pair, aperture for pen, parrot on stump, sheep on ground, 5½, L19c (4132/112) — 200
Harlequin and Columbine, pair, Harlequiin holding slapstick, Columbine holding posy, 5¼ x 5⅜, 1790-1810 (4262/225) — 950
Jug, milk, small, saltglaze, white body, 3⅛, ca1750 (4132/99) — 150
Jug, saltglaze 'Scratch Blue', incised with double floral spray, 6⅝, ca1750, res (4156/38) — 400
Jug, toby, Ralph Wood type, 'Martha Gunn', seated holding gin bottle, 11⅝, imp, ca1770-80 (4132/117) — 700
Jug, toby, Ralph Wood type, prattware, tippler with foaming jug, 8⅞, imp, ca1770-80 (4132/116) — 300
Jug, toby, Ralph Wood type, sailor sitting on white chest, blue trim, 11½, rep, ca1770-80 (4132/115) — 700
Pearlware figure, barmaid with blue bottle, ca1780, 8, res, rare (4190/136) — 850
Pearlware pair, figure of musicians on gilt wooden bases, ca1780, 9⅝, minor imp (4190/135) — 275
Salts, pair, enamel, gilt scroll work, on tree hoof feet, 2¾, ca1760 (4238/530) — 275
Sauce boat, saltglaze enamelled, molded with fruiting grapevines, L7¼, ca1750 (4156/37) — 500
Tea service, child's, part, yellowware transfer, printed, English view, 4 pcs, 3¼, teapot imp, ca1815 (4211/985) — 70
Tea service, part, with a woman holding a rake, imp, 33 pcs, 1810-20 (4262/349) — 250
Tea service, part, pink lustre, thirteen pcs, ca1820, dam (4156/66) — 90
Tea service, strawberry luster, berries and leaves, ca1825, 26 pcs (4211/988) — 450
Tea service, strawberry lustre, 26 pieces, 1825, some chip (4156/65) — 350
Teapot, cover, saltglaze, cast-house, three story house with English, Dutch arms, 5¼, ca1745 (4156/35) — 800
Teapot and cover, saltglaze pink ground, 4⅜, rare, cover rep, ca1760 (4132/97) — 800
Teapot and cover, cast house, salt glaze, with Royal Arms of Holland and England, 4¾, ca1745 (4262/242) — 650
Teapot and cover, solid-agate, cream colored body marbleized, 5½, rep, 1745-50 (4262/248) — 500
Vase and cover, flowers, gilt bands, scrollwork, 5¼, 1825-35 (4262/490) — 250
Vases, pair, green dolphin among waves, 7, L18c (4132/110) — 425
Whistle, bird, yellow glazed, perched on tree stump, 3, L19c (4132/106) — 200

Stephen Green

Jug, stoneware, Napoleon, modelled full face with tricorn hat, 8⅞, hc, ca1820-58 (4132/118) — 200

Stoneware

Jug, cobalt-blue decorated, mounted as a lamp, 12, 18c (4149/79) — 450

T.&C. Ford

Service, dessert, 8 pcs, floral spray, blue-ground rim, D9, ca1860 (649/15) — 225

Turner

Jug and cover, hot milk, white stone ware, relief decorations, 6⅞, ca1770-1806 (4132/128) — 175

Magnolia warbler figure
(669/19)

Figures (4190/142)

Turner Basaltes

Teapot and cover, encaustic decorated, L18c, 5⅜, chip, rare, Turner (4190/151)   1150

Walton

The Royal Arms of George IV, as a rampant lion and grey unicorn, 5⅞, ca1820 (4262/237)   375

Wedgwood

American Waltham Watch Co. dish, with 2 platters, transfer-printed factory view, three pcs, 1904
(4238/405)   600
American Waltham Watch Co. plates, set of 48 pcs, transfer-printed factory view, four sizes, 1903
(4238/404)   1200
Baskets and cover, pair, potpourri, blue, white jasper, 4⅛ (4132/153)   225
Black basalts, ewers, wine and water, 'Sacred to Bacchus', 'Sacred to Neptune', 16⅞, 19c
(4159/84)   800
Bottle, scent, jasper, blue and white, dark blue, sacrifice scene, Zeus, 3½, 19c (4262/300)   100
Bowl, hummingbird lustre, dark blue mottled ground, flying geese border, 7½, 1917-32 (4262/318)   425
Bowl, lustre, black fairyland, geisha design, 6¾, ca1916-41 (4132/163)   600
Bowl, lustre, hummingbirds and flying geese border, 5, fine, ca1917-32 (4132/161)   *125*
Bowl, lustre, octagonal, butterfly pattern, 4⅞, ca1914-29 (4132/162)   *150*
Bowl, octagonal, fairyland lustre, painted with 'Dana-Castle on a Road', 11¾, ca1917 (4262/317)   1800
Breakfast set, blue jasperware, classical figures beneath leaf borders, 8 pcs, 20c (649/11)   225
Bust of Charles II, black basaltes, full face, flowing curly hair, 21¾ (4260/269)   1400
Bust of Isaac Newton, black basaltes, 11, L18c (4132/132)   550
Bust of Josiah Wedgwood, black basaltes, head turned right, open coat, ruffled cravat, 15½
(4260/270)   550
Candlestick, moonlight lustre, pink with orange and grey, 3⅝, chip, ca1805-15 (4132/125)   300
Candlestick, figure, black basaltes, Ceres holding a cornucopia, 9⅜, nozzle missing, 19c (4262/291)   225
Coffee service, part, porcelain powdered ruby ground, 11 pcs, imp (4132/159)   500
Dinner service, cream glazed, gilt borders, 119 pcs (631/10)   325
Dishes, pair, sweetmeat creamware, ruffled, shell shaped, snail form feet, 7⅞, 1765-70 (4262/258)   375
Ewer, variegated, snake handle, 12½, L18c (4132/104)   1300
Figures of Sphinxes, pair, black basaltes, head supporting candle nozzle, 12¼, chip, L18c
(4260/268)   2600
Inkstand, black basaltes, enamelled, rectangular, 3 covered inkwells, 8⅛, E19c (4262/288)   *650*
Jug, black basaltes, enamelled, ovoid body, sprays of peonies, chrysanthemums, 6⅜, ca1810
(4262/287)   350
Jug, jasper, crimson and white, crimson dip stoneware body, classical figures, 8¾ (4262/303)   475
Kantharos and cover, jasper, white brown smear glazed, 14, hc, L19c (4132/155)   350
Lamp, oil and cover, Rosso Antico, squat, flat cover, black jasper, 5⅛, ca1810 (4262/285)   350
Medallion, Artemis in a chariot, black, white jasper, 2 1/1, ca1800 (4132/147)   200
Plaque, jasper blue-white mounted on velvet framed, 6¼ (4190/158)   80
Plaque, 'Destruction or Niobes Children', black basaltes, 8¼, L18c-E19c (4132/142)   700
Plaque, 'Sacrifice to Love', blue, white jasper, 9¾ x 23½, L19c (4132/145)   1100
Plaque, black basaltes, 'Death of a Roman Warrior', 10⅞ x 19¾, L18c (4262/293)   3100
Plaque, fairyland lustre, 'Picnic by a River', 4⅞ x 10⅞ (4262/316)   2250
Plaque, jasper, green and white, 'The Judgment of Hercules', 6⅛ x 18½, 19c (4262/295)   275
Plaque, mythological figures, green, white jasper, 6 x 21 (4132/146)   *1600*
Plate bridge, fairyland lustre imps, ca1923, 10⅝ (4190/167)   1500
Plates, botanical, pair, bone china, sprays of flowers, fluted rims, 8½, 1812-29 (4260/261)   500
Plates, botanical, pair, bone china, sprays of flowers, fluted rims, 8½, crack, 1812-29 (4260/265)   300
Plates, botanical, pair, bone china, sprays of flowers, fluted rims, 8½, 1812-29 (4260/260)   600
Plates, botanical, pair, bone china, sprays of flowers, fluted rims, 8½, 1812-29 (4260/263)   650
Plates, set of eleven, creamware, 'Old London Views', 10½, chip, 1941 (4260/267)   50
Plates, set of fourteen, creamware, ivy border, black and sepia, 9⅞, 1890 (4260/266)   700
Plates, set of six, queen's ware, clusters of shells and seaweed, 9, 2 hc, ca1700 (4260/259)   400
Plates, twelve, by A. Holland, ripening fruit within gilt rim, patt. W1021, D9, ca1930 (649/14)   225
Tea coffee service, part, child's, queens ware, pink floral sprays, 5 pcs, imp, L19c (4132/123)   300
Tea coffee service, part, child's, moonlight lustre, 12 pcs, chips, ca1805-15 (4132/124)   1700
Teacup and saucer, black basaltes, reddish brown borders and scrolls, 1780-93 (4262/286)   3000
Teapot and cover, transfer-printed, globular body, entwined strap handle, 5, spout chip, 1775-85
(4262/260)   275
Urns, jasper, blue-white, 19c, 7 discolored rep (4190/157)   110
Vase, Victoriaware portrait medallions, L19c, 7¾, fine (4190/165)   350
Vase, jasper, Portland, blue-white, M19c, 8⅝ (4190/159)   400
Vase, 'Pegasus', black, white jasper, 26½, imp, L19c (4132/151)   2200
Vase, encaustic decoration, black basaltes, reddish brown, figures, (4132/136)   1600

Vase, jasper, crimson and white, crimson dip, 'Sacrifice to Peace' and 'Sacrifice to Love', 4 (4262/306) — 375

Vase, jasper, 3 color, lilac, white relief with lion head, 5⅜, 19c (4262/304) — 750

Vase, large yellow jasper-dip, black classical reliefs, H19, E20c (649/12) — 700

Vase, smear-glazed caneware, flaring cylindrical body 'A Sacrifice to Love', 7½, 19c (4262/311) — 175

Vase, variegated, ovoid body, with mottled glaze, 11, L18c (4262/249) — 150

Vase and cover, black, white jasper, 7, fine, 19c (4132/149) — 200

Vase and cover, jasper, solid white body, green drapery swags, lilac rings, 9⅞, 19c (4262/302) — 350

Vase and cover, jasper green and white, sage green, 6 putti vintners below grapevine border, 12¼, L19c (4262/299) — 500

Vase and cover, jasper, black and white, 10½, minor imp (4190/160) — 450

Vase and cover potpourri, black basaltes, floral swags, 7¼, L19c (4132/138) — 275

Vases, garniture of 3, russet bands, satyr-head handles, 'Dancing Hours', 6⅞, rep, L19c (4262/314) — 700

Vases, garniture of 3, with gilded satyr-head handles, 10, cover missing, ca1895 (4262/313) — 800

Vases, pair, 'Offering To Peace', blue, white jasper, 10¼ (4132/152) — 375

Vases, pair, jasper, yellow and white, 6 putti vintners below grapevine border, 12⅛, 19c (4262/297) — 1800

Wedgwood and Bentley

Bust of Marcus Aurelius, black basaltes, 11¾, rep, ca1774-80 (4132/131) — 1100

Ewer, fish tail handle, rare, black basaltes, 10½, chip, ca1769-80 (4132/139) — 2700

Vase, black basaltes, frieze of 'The Dancing Hours', 14, ca1780 (4132/135) — 3750

Wedgwood basaltes

Bust, Mercury fr model by William Hackwood, 14½ (4190/155) — 200

Candlesticks Triton, flowers-vines-seaweed, ca1790-98, 11 - 11¼ (4190/153) — 2200

Vase, dec high 4 ram's masks, L19c, 11⅝ (4190/154) — 300

Wedgwood pearlware

Dinner service large, Moresque pattern, ca1864, 147 pcs (4190/164) — 2700

Plates soup set five, chrysanthemum, ca1808, 9⅞ (4190/163) — 200

Wedgwood/Whieldon

Sugar bowl, cover, cauliflower ware, 5⅛, imp, ca1770 (4132/100) — 425

Teapot and cover, pineapple molded, 5⅛, imp, ca1770 (4132/101) — 550

Whieldon

Plates, octagonal, pair, mottled tortoiseshell glaze, 8⅜, ca1765 (4156/40) — 550

Plates, pair, rim molded with scrolling basketwork, 8⅝, ca1765 (4156/39) — 425

Plates, small, pair, fine, rice molded and scalloped rim, 7⅝, ca1765 (4156/41) — 650

Teapot and cover, flowering vines, 3 lion paw feet, type, ca1750-60, 3⅞, chip (4190/150) — 350

Teapot and cover, globular body, 3 lion paw feet, 6½, 1765 (4262/251) — 600

Teapot and cover, redware, octagonal, lamprey handle, leaf molded spout, 3½, rep, M18c (4262/247) — 750

Wood, Enoch

Bust of John Wesley, full face with grey hair, black robes, 12⅝, ca1791 (4262/235) — *400*

Wood, Ralph

Hope, allegorical, young woman, brown and green robe leaning on anchor, 5⅞, rep, ca1770 (4262/224) — 450

Vase, spill, 'Goat and Squirrel', brown goat recumbent before green tree trunk, squirrel on branch, 4⅝, ca1770 (4262/223) — 1600

Bowl (4132/161)   Bowl (4132/162)

Bust of John Wesley (4262/235)

Plaque (4132/146)

Inkstand (4262/288)

Worcester

Basket, oval, blue white, 10¾, First Period (4132/33)	300
Coffee cup and saucer, 'Jabberwocky' pattern, with flowering scrollwork, First Period (4262/515)	800
Cup, tea and saucer, Kakiemon style, oriental birds, flowers, First Period, saucer hc (4190/265)	275
Cups, 2, saucer, blue, gold, coat of arms with animal supporters, ca1785 (4148/45)	325
Dish, printed in black, 'The Tea Party', 6⅝, First Period (4262/502)	650
Dish, 'Blind Earl', rose leaves, 2 Chinamen, 6⅜, First Period (4262/508)	1200
Dish, lozenge shape, summer flower, scrollwork, First Period, 10⅜ (4190/274)	275
Dish, lozenge shape, summer flowers, scrollwork, First Period 10⅜ (4190/273)	275
Dish, lozenge shape, summer flowers, scrollwork, First Period 7 fine (4190/272)	375
Dish, lozenge-shaped, apple green, 2 exotic birds, 9¼, First Period (4262/507)	1500
Dish, shell shaped, summer flower, scrollwork, First Period, 7⅝ (4190/275)	275
Dish, square, powder blue, punting Chinaman, landscape, 7¾, First Period (4262/497)	225
Dish, sweetmeat, central floral spray, 3¼, 1752-55 (4262/523)	450
Dish, sweetmeat, scallop shell shape, oriental floral spray, 3¼, 1752-55 (4262/522)	325
Dishes, kidney shaped, Bengal Tiger pattern, Kakiemon style, 10¼, First Period (4262/516)	950
Dishes, leaf pair, blue white, 7½, 1 cr, First Period (4132/34)	400
Dishes, leaf, pair, lettuce leaves, 13¾, 14⅛, First Period, chip (4262/511)	350
Dishes, leaf, pair, lettuce leaves, 10¼, First Period (4262/513)	*300*
Dishes, leaf, pair, overlapping lettuce leaves, 10¼, First Period (4262/510)	500
Dishes, pair, vine leaves, 7¾, First Period (4132/32)	550
Dishes, square, Bengal Tiger pattern, Kakiemon style, 8⅝, First Period (4262/517)	900
Dishes, square, pair, central bouquet and scattered sprigs, 8½, First Period (4262/527)	300
Dishes, square, pair, with floral sprays, 7⅞, First Period (4262/525)	375
Jug, cabbage leaf, blue and white pecking parrot, First Period 7 fine (4190/271)	*550*
Mug, blue white, transfer print, lady fishing, 5¾, cr, First Period (4132/35)	125
Mug, blue and white, parrot and fruit pattern, 5, First Period (4262/496)	375
Plate, armorial, Knox, quartering Flamsted of Ruston, 8¼, First Period (4260/306)	125
Plates, armorial, pair, arms of Knox, quartering Flamsted of Ruston, 8¼, rep, First Period (4260/307)	125
Plates, armorial, set of 6, Knox, quartering, Flamsted of Ruston, 8 1/3, First Period (4260/305)	400
Plates, armorial, set of 8, Knox quartering Flamsted of Ruston, 8¼, ca1785 (4260/304)	1200
Plates, set of 4, central blue tulip, bouquets, sprigs, 9, First Period, imp (4262/528)	225
Pot, bough, apple green, classical figures, ruins, 8⅝, First Period (4262/506)	950
Sauceboat, double end, shell form fluting, 7½, First Period (4262/524)	850
Stand, blue white, flowering branch handles, 10¾, chip, First Period (4132/38)	175
Stand, teapot, diamond shape, sides fluted, 'L'Amour' version, 5½, First Period (4262/500)	475
Stand, teapot, turquoise bordered, clusters of fruit, 5⅞, First Period (4262/514)	800
Tea bowl & saucer, transfer printed with 3 cows, first period, hc (4132/36)	70
Teapot and cover, insect perched on strawberry, First Period, 4⅞, chip, early (4190/266)	1000
Teapot and cover, 'Mandarin' pattern, 5, Late First Period (4262/529)	400
Teapot and cover, blue and white, First Period, 5⅜, rep, early (4190/269)	225
Teapot and cover, blue and white, 'Root' pattern, 4⅝, First Period, chip (4262/498)	750
Teapot and cover, blue scale, Kakiemon palette gilding, 5⅞, First Period (4262/526)	1100
Teapot and cover, early, First Period, 4⅞ chip, (4190/270)	600
Tureen, cover, stand, claret ground, fruits flowers, L6¾, 9⅛, ca1770 (4132/37)	2250
Tureen, sauce and cover, quatrefoil, sprigs and sprays, 6½, First Period (4262/532)	100

Yorkshire

Bovine group, a girl holding basket of flowers, cream-color cow, 6½, 1800-10 (4262/228)	600

FRENCH CERAMICS

Assorted periods and manufacturers

Bust, colored-biscuit, after Carrier, maiden, head turned, ribbon, rose, H15, ca1900 (649/45)	*350*
Card playing group, cavaliers and maiden playing cards, 8¼, L19c, imp (619/74)	175
Centrepiece, gilt-metal mounted, bleu-de-roi, raised on 4 scrolling feet, 12, L19c (619/69)	150
Chinoisserie figures, pair, white bisque, man and woman, 16 (631/83)	225
Figures, pair white, bisque, water seller and a drummer, mounted as lamps, 10½, 12 (631/82)	225
Figures, pair, colored biscuit, gallant and maiden, 18c pastel clothes, 24, ca1900, minor chip (669/30)	600
Group, lady and gentleman seated at a backgammon table, 9¾, E20c (619/76)	400
Group, romantic couple with lady attendant seated at table, 9¾, E20c, imp (619/75)	125
Group, biscuit, La Jeunesse Tourmentee par L' Amour, 12½, L19c (4119/203)	125
Lamps, pair, colored biscuit, young boy and girl, enameled floral costumes, 26, ca1900, chip (669/31)	800
Plaque, battle scene, giltwood frame, 10 x 10, 19c (631/72)	250

Plaque, groupe of French soldiers huddled around fire, 15½ x 12 (631/73) — 450
Plaque, enamelled pottery, circular, octagonal portrait of a young woman, 16, L19c (631/80) — 1000
Plaque, pate-sur-pate, salmon body, with winged figure, 7¾ x 7¾, L19c (619/82) — 175
Plaques, pair, landscape, giltwood frame, 11½ x 7½, 19c (631/71) — 500
Plaques, pair, French soldiers and other group of soldiers playing cards, 15 x 11, framed (631/74) — *1800*
Plaques, pair, oval, painted bisque, relief, young couples running through landscapes, 13 (631/84) — 300
Plate, faience, polychrome, seated peasant woman holding jug, Sceaux, 9, ca1770 (4262/30) — 450
Tete a tete, transfer printed, scenes of Napoleon's life, 19c, 7 pcs (631/79) — 950
Two young girls, plaque, by E.M. Bevridge, in Victorian costume, 10½ x 14½, 1885 (649/48) — 600
Urn and cover, earthenware ormolu mounted, a young woman, 34½, E20c (619/54) — 1900
Urns, earthenware, pair, gilt bronze mounted, maiden, putti and fountain, 33½, L19c (619/81) — 2500
Vase, champleve-mounted, chalice-form body, painted putti, trophies, H12, 1880 (649/28) — 550
Vase, pear shaped, scene of the Madonna, Christ child and Saint John, 20, 19c (631/76) — 200
Vases, covered, pair, glazed pear shaped, portraits of artists, gilt borders, 22, 1860 (631/77) — 1500
Vases, painted, opaline, pair, ovoid bodies, flared necks, multicolored, floral bouquets, 16, L18c (4232/35) — 2100
Vases, pair, champleve, onyx-mtd., ovoid body, scrolls, flowers, as lamps, H9½, L19c (649/29) — 375
Vases, pair, cylindrical, painted porcelain, 13, drilled (619/77) — 120
Vases, pair, gilt, bronze mounted earthware, 18c, lovers in gardens, 23½, L19c, cr (669/32) — 1800

Belle Epoque

Urns, pair, ormolu, mounted, portrait of a young woman, Victorian dress, 47½, L19c (619/64) — 13000

Chantilly

Cup and saucer, floral bouquets and sprigs, M18c (4262/72) — 400
Dinner service, part, 17 pcs, floral sprays, ca1770, rep (4190/1) — 1800
Jars, pair, Kakiemon, green and iron-red wheat sheaves, 2¾, 2⅝, ca1735 (4262/73) — 475
Plates, pair, floral, basketwork rims, ca1760, 9¼ (4190/2) — *325*
Pot and cover, pomade, applied with aubergine branches and leaves, 4⅜, res, ca1735 (4262/74) — 100
Sauce tureens, pair, Kakiemon, quatrefoil, floral sprays, L6¼, ca1735 (4086/49) — 2750

Durlach

Tea service, part, faience, miniature, landscape vignettes, 11⅛ tray, ca1780, 12 pcs (4262/61) — 9500

Jug
(4190/271)

(4190/25)
Group

Group
(4190/26)

Plaques (631/74)

Bust (649/45)

Plates (4190/2)

French faience

Basket, oval, reticulated, purple and yellow tulip, 19, 9⅞, fine (4190/126)   250
Cruet stand, sprays of flowers, insects, 11, imp, E18c (4132/180)   125
Jardiniere large, blue-white with floral swag, 18, L18c (4132/181)   1100

Gille Jeune

Vase, glazed and biscuit, gilt bronze, ovoid body, royal blue, H12¾, ca1860 (649/44)   275

Hesdin

Bowl, faience, polychrome, blue, ochre and manganese, figure of woman holding mirror, 12, E19c
(4262/20)   1300

Jacob Petit

Bottles, pair, modelled as Turks, 13⅛, 13, ca1840 (4132/245)   425
Bottles and stoppers, pineapple, 7¾, ca1840 (4132/247)   600
Tea service, part, turquoise, oval panels enclosing spring flowers, 19c, 26 pcs (619/65)   450
Vase and stand, black ground, scroll-molded body, birds, floral sprays, H16, ca1840 (649/36)   400
Vases, covers, stands, pair, hexagonal potpourri, 9⅝, ca1835 (4132/244)   850
Vases, double cornucopia, pair, blackamoor holding cornucopia, 7½, res rims, ca1840 (4159/93) 190
Vases, potpourri, pair, covers, stands, apple-green, gilded, birds, flowers, 15¾, chip, ca1840
(4159/92)   900

La Courtille

Group, white biscuit, five musicians, L18c, 13, imp (4190/26)   **600**
Group, white biscuit, oak tree surrounded by drinking huntsmen, L18c, 12¾ (4190/25)   425
Group, white biscuit, two couples playing instruments, L18c 10⅞ chip (4190/27)   450
Plate, set of 8, center with a puce rose, 8¾, L18c (4262/93)   225

Le Nove

Coffee cups and saucers, pair, painted with Italian architectural view, 1 cup chip, ca1800 (4219/28)   110

Limoges

Plaque, 2 cardinals, by A.R. Shortland, 12 x 16, L19c (649/30)   800
Service, fish, 7 pcs, salmon dish, 6 plates, L23½, ca1910 (649/34)   200
Vase painted enamel, Young woman holding hand mirror, 6½, ca1900 (619/180)   375

Lyons

Plate, faience, polychrome, chinoiserie, painted in ochre, blue and green with chinaman, shrubs, 8⅝,
18c (4262/23)   150

Marseilles

Coffee cup and saucer, faience, scattered floral bouquets and sprigs, ca1770 (4262/29)   650

Mennecy

Jar and cover, potpourri 'May-blossom', striated flowers, domed cover, floral knob, 4⅜, M18c
(4262/71)   600
Sucrier and cover, silver mounted, white, molded floral sprays, ca1735, 4 (4190/3)   425

Montereau

Plates, creamware transfer-printed, each with a different French poem, 8⅝, E19c (4262/34)   200

Moustiers

Plate, faience, blue and white, center cluster of flowers, wavy rim with stylized flowers, 13⅛, 18c
(4262/22)   475

Nevers faience

Plate polychrome, patriotique, L18c, 9 (4190/125)   300

Nevers-type

Plate, faience, polychrome, house in riverscape, notched rim, florettes and scrolls, 9, ca1800
(4262/19)   125
Plate, faience, polychrome, putto picking flowers, frame of flowers and scrolls, 9, ca1800 (4262/18)   150

Niderville

Jardinieres, pair, yellow quatrefoil lion, landscapes, 10, 19c (4219/27)   950

Pots bulb and covers, pair, faience, multi-colored with floral bouquet, scroll handles, H3¼, 3⅜, 18c (4262/24)   225

Niderviller

Vase-covered with annular clock, applied bieuit floral festoon, L18c 14½ (4221/234)   9000

Nymphenburg

Plate, bouquet of 2 purple roses, edged in gilding, D9¼, 1763-67 (4085/61)   150

Paris

Bowl, gilt bronze, footed, panel 18c lovers, scroll handles, L11½, E20c (649/43)   200
Bowl, pink-ground, gilt bronze, floral sprays, scroll handles, H17, ca1880 (649/42)   500
Service, coffee, part, gold-ground, white band, with flowers, 27 pcs., ca1815 (649/32)   275
Vases and covers, pair, pale blue ground, campana form, mask handles, H22, ca1840 (649/38)   325
Vase, ovoid body, floral panel, bleu-de-roi ground, H14, L19c, neck dam (649/46)   250
Vases, pair, campana form, ptd. scenes, blue, gilt ground, H13¼, ca1840 (649/37)   1100
Vases, pair, cornucopia form, foliate scrolls, 14, M19c (669/28)   325
Vases, pair, gilt-ground, flattened vasiform body, central white panel, H11, L19c (649/33)   250
Vases, pair, large, tapering baluster bodies, gilt foliate handles, H22¾, L19c (649/40)   350

Rouen

Bowl, faience, polychrome, spirally-molded, houses by a stream, floral sprigs, 12¼, ca1800 (4262/17)   475
Ecuelle and cover, faience, painted in shades of blue and iron red, floral vignettes, 9⅝, E18c (4262/14)   1300
Lion, faience, polychrome, nose, mane, tail and legs, yellow, heightened in black, 4¾, Rouen type, 18c (4262/10)   900
Plate, faience, blue and white, center swan amidst flowering shrubbery, rococo border, 9¼, E18c (4262/15)   950
Tray, faience blue and white, painted with stylized flowers and foliate scrolls, 16¼, E18c (4262/12)   500

Samson

Boxes, 2 covered, form of bunches of grapes, H4½, L19c (649/49)   100
Group, conversationed, two ladies, galant, in 18c costume, H8½, L19c (649/50)   400
Neptune, figure, sea king in floral robes, 12½, L19c (669/24)   250
Pan and a Bacchante figure, pair, 8¼, L19c (619/61)   150
Vases, 'Companie des Indes', pair, shield-shaped body, landscapes, H15¼, L19c, as lamps (649/51)   250
Vases, pair, inverted pear-form body, maiden head handles, H17¾, L19c mtd as lamps (649/52)   400

Sceaux

Pots, bulbs, pair, faience, square bodies on raised bracket feet, Sceaux, 3¾, ca1770 (4262/32)   175

Sevres

Basket, oval, gold and white, rope molded rims, 14, 1814-24 (4159/91)   800
Basket on stand, glazed and bisque, pierced basket, supported by 3 caryatids, 14¾, 1804-09 (631/56)   400
Baskets, circular, gold and white, rope molded rims, H5⅞, 1827 (4159/90)   1300
Bowl, deep, everted decangonal rim, scattered pastel floral bouquets, 11¼, ca1770 (4262/80)   300
Bowl, pastel, floral bouquets, dated 1771 9¼ (4190/11)   425
Bowl, shallow, oval, floral bouquets, 12¼, fine, ca1774 (4132/219)   275
Candlesticks, pair, figural, turquoise ground, Bacchus figure holding candle socket, 9, 49c (619/48)   150
Casket, bleu-de-roi ground, oval, domed cover, nymph and a putto, 9½, L19c (669/38)   325
Casket, bleu-de-roi ground, gilt-metal cover, family scene, W8¼, L19c (649/71)   750
Chandelier, 6 branch, ormolu, bleu celeste ground, scrolling ormolu arms, H38, L19c (649/73)   750
Clock garniture, ormolu mounted, clock surmounted by classical urn, H clock 20½, H urns 14½ (649/74)   1500
Clockcase, gilt bronze, bleu celeste ground plaques, circ dial, H17, M19c, cover dam (649/72)   1100
Compote, ormolu, mounted, white ground, rinceau, classical motifs, 7½, M19c (631/48)   375
Compotes, pair, porcelain, rococo style scenes of children at play, 9⅜, L19c (619/40)   700
Confiturier, triangular dish with 3 covered pots, 1773 (4262/78)   500
Cup, saucer coffee, floral medallions, with interlaced L's, chip, dated 1791-92 (4132/229)   125
Cup, saucer, coffee, floral, pink and green rose trellis ground, dated 1780 (4132/226)   226
Cup, saucer, coffee, flowers, green leaves, fine, dated 1773 (4132/225)   350
Cup, saucer, coffee, rows of maroon and gold sprigs, dated 1789 (4132/231)   325
Cup, saucer, coffee, rows of pink and gold sprigs, dated 1786 (4132/230)   375
Cup, saucer, coffee, floral sprigs and small sunbursts, dated 1784 (4132/227)   350
Cup, saucer, coffee, floral medallions, cup 1785 (4132/228)   350

Cup and attached saucer, scene of Napoleon surveying a battle, 3½, 1804-09, decorated in 1848 (631/52) 100
Cup and cover, ormolu mounted, with circular panels, rose buds and leafage, 10, L19c, cover repaired (619/29) 250
Cup and saucer, cylindrical, with black and brown bird, fine, 1773 (4190/19) 425
Cup and saucer, trembleuse, each with bell flower border, 5, ca1767 (4132/215) 900
Cup and saucer, Trembleuse, 2 panels of figures on a quai, 1753 (4190/20) 325
Cups and covers, pair, bleu celeste, with young girl and boy seated in garden, 7½, L19c (619/31) 1600
Cups and Saucers, 6 bleu celeste ground, panels of lovers in a garden, L19c, chip (669/33) 275
Dinner service, part, gilding with initial 'N', 7 pcs, M19c (4219/26) 400
Dish, lozenge shaped, pastel, floral bouquets, ca1780 (4190/8) 225
Dish, oval, gilt bronze, lovers in garden scene Rolti, L15½, L19c (649/70) 400
Dish, yellow-ground, gilt bronze, genre, floral spray, interlaced L's, D13½, L19c (649/66) 500
Dishes, oval, set of 4, pastel, floral bouquets, ca1764-69 8½, 1 hc (4190/14) 300
Dishes, shell, pastel, floral bouquets, ca1764-65, 8¾ (4190/7) 350
Dishes, square, three, pastel floral bouquets, 8½, 18c (4132/224) 300
Ecuelle, cover and stand, floral festoons, fine, W7¾ and 10¼, ca1765 (4086/45) 7500
Ecuelle, cover and stand, rose du Barry, amorous symbols, flowers, fine, W7½ and 10⅞, 1789 (4086/46) 8000
Ecuelle, cover and stand, stylized borders, strap handles, dated 1780, 7⅜, 8⅝ (4190/18) 300
Equestrian figure, horseman in a gray suit of armour, 14¾, ca1830 (631/54) 750
Figure, white biscuit, girl with bird cage, L18c, 8½, dam (4190/22) 150
Figure of La Baigneuse Aux Roseaux, biscuit, modelled by Louis-Simon Boizot, H13⅛, c1774 (4085/45) 1700
Garniture, bleu-de-roi ground, gilt-metal, central bowl, scroll handles, H vases 18¼, L19c (649/82) 2000
Group, biscuit, two children, ca1755-65 6⅝ chip (4221/220) 1400
Louis XVI, bust, turquoise glazed, details of his court dress in tooled gilding, 12½, L19c (669/37) 200
Medallions, small, pair, oval, with musical instruments, 1¾, ca1765 (4132/214) 375
Miniature cup and saucer, yellow-ground, band of maroon C-scrolls, D3, rare, 1788 (4085/46) 825
Muffin dish and cover, black, rims painted w/ chinoiserie vignettes, D6⅞, rare, ca1792 (4085/47) 3100
Orange tubs, pair, bleu celeste, painted art, music symbols, H5⅝, 1756 (4086/40) 5750
Pedestal, gilt bronze and white bisque, marble top, with maidens dancing, 44, L19c (619/59) 2500
Plaque, circular, depicting Louis XIV, cobalt blue border, 20, L19c (619/39) 550
Plaques pair, floral and scrollwork, 4½ (4221/231) 600
Plate, bleu-de-roi ground, jeweled, portrait of Louise de Bourbon, D9½, L19c (649/76) 550
Plate, rose pompador ground, jeweled, scene of Justice A. Dessart, D9½, L19c (649/75) 400
Plate, yellow-ground, floral panels, scene of 18c lovers, D9¾, L19c (649/65) 275
Plates, dinner, set of eighteen, white with gilt laurel wreath, centering 'N', 9¾, 1852-70 (631/57) 500
Plates, dinner, set of 16, floral sprays, 9⅝, fine, 18c (4132/220) 900
Plates, dinner, set 6, pastel, floral bouquets, 18c, 9¾ (4190/5) 400
Plates, dinner, Napoleon III, 18, gilt N within laurel wreath, bee motifs, D9¾, 1852 (649/54) 600
Plates, four, floral, dated 1784-86 (4190/12) 200
Plates, pair, yellow-ground, 18c lovers scene, H. Tessier, H14¼, L19c, as sconces (649/67) 600
Plates, set of twelve, Napoleonic, Napoleonic battle scene, 9⅞, 19c (631/61) 2750
Plates, set of 6, cluster, flowers, fruit, painter's mark, Binet, Diam 9½, 1761 (4159/88) 1200
Platter, oval, blue celeste, medallion of 2 females and gentleman, 16½, ca1840 (631/55) 400
Potpourri vases and covers, pair, Louis XVI ormolu, bleu-du-roi, H10⅝, ca1780 (4086/48) 9000
Potpourri vases and covers, pair, Louis XVI ormolu, bleu-du-roi, neoclassic motif, fine, H9⅝, ca1780 (4086/47) 10000
Pots, cache, pair, bleu celeste, jeweled, painted with putti frolicking,½, L19c (619/42) 450
Pots-on-stand, pair, bleu celeste conserve, Prince de Rohan service, L9¾, 1771 (4086/39) 4000
Sauce tureens, attached stands, pair, pastel floral bouquets, 9¼, 18c (4132/223) 250
Sauceboat and cover on stand, bleu celeste, with birds and flowers, 9⅜ (4132/217) 275
Sauceboat, attached stand, pastel, floral bouquets, dated 1774 (4190/9) 200
Sauceboats and oval stands, pair, gilt, bisque, swan head handles, 1804-09, 4 pcs (631/53) 325
Saucers, five, floral bird decoration, 4¾ x 7½, ca1760-90 (4132/218) 250
Socle circular, bleu du roi, ca1754-59 (4221/233) 1300
Sucrier and cover, a fond vert, green with bouquets in panels, ca1768 3⅞ (4221/225) 1100
Sucriers and covers, pair, bleu-celeste, oval cartouches of winged putti, 4¼, L19c (619/38) 500
Tazze, pair, pastel, floral bouquets, gilt rims, ca1764-65 (4190/6) 800
Tea caddy, apple green with brightly colored birds, 2¾, ca1765 (4132/216) 550
Teacup and saucer, apple green, ca1761 hc-chip repaired (4221/224) 700
Teacup and saucer, petals and scattered floral sprays, rim gilt, 18c (4262/77) 250
Teapot and cover, small, yellow ground, scattered floral sprigs, ca1786 4⅛ fine (4221/226) 1600
Tete a tete, ruby red ground, Napoleonic scene, 18½ tray, M19c, 8 pcs (669/36) 1000
Tray, 2 handled, grapes and plums, flowers, ca1776 14⅝ (4221/229) 1500

Urn, with landscape, cavaliers, maidens, 32¾, ca1900, large (619/45)	1400
Urn, cover and stand, bleu-de-roi, ormolu mounted, ram's head handles, 34½, L19c, rep (619/55)	1800
Urn, cover and stand, bleu-de-roi ormolu, woman and 2 male court figures, 24½, L19c (619/49)	2000
Urn, cover and stand, earthenware, monumental, ormolu mounted, H. Desprez, H urn 25, L19c (649/87)	3500
Urn, cover and stand, gilt bronze mounted, lovers in a garden, spray of spring flowers, 26, L19c (631/50)	900
Urn, cover and stand, ormolu mounted, painted with river landscape, 33, L19c (619/50)	1000
Urn, earthenware, gilt bronze mounted, pastel scene, young Victorian woman, 30¼, L19c (631/49)	1000
Urn and cover, bleu-de-roi, ormolu mounted, ladies and gentlemen in garden, 36, L19c (619/52)	2750
Urn and cover, Napoleonic bleu-de-roi, earthenware, Napoleon and his Generals, 29½, L19c (619/53)	3250
Urn and stand, monumental, ormolu mounted, pastoral scene, with lovers, 36½, L19c (619/51)	2750
Urns, bleu celeste, vasiform vessel, sprays of spring flowers, 11, L19c (631/51)	400
Urns, covered and stands, pair, rustic courting couples in landscape setting, 44, L19c, massive (631/62)	16000
Urns, pair, bleu-de-roi ground gilt-metal, couple in a landscape, 16¾, L19c (669/41)	800
Urns, pair, bleu-celeste, ormolu mounted, jeweled, ovoid vessel, putti in artistic pursuits, 10¼, L19c (619/35)	850
Urns, pair, gilt bronze mounted, bronze handles and bases, 16¾, L19c (619/47)	1300
Urns and covers, pair, jeweled, ormolu, female head handles, landscape, gilt borders, 22½, L19c (619/33)	3000
Urns and covers, pair, bleu-de-roi ormolu, lovers and landscape, 15½, L19c (619/30)	1100
Vase, bleu celeste ground, gilt bronze, 18c ladies and a gallant admiring a baby, 28, L19c (669/46)	1500
Vase, bronze mounted, large, ovoid, nymph playing pipes, 44½, M19c (669/49)	4000
Vase, covered gilt bronzed, courting couple, scrolling gilt borders, 18, L19c (631/60)	300
Vase, covered, gilt bronze mounted, painted with a woman and a putto, 14½, L19c (631/59)	200
Vase, earthenware, gilt bronze mtd, Napoleonic scene, H. Desprez, domed cover, H38, L19c (649/88)	4000
Vase, trumpet form, green ground, scroll handles, H13½, 188¾, res (649/53)	400
Vase and cover, ovoid body, 18c picnic scene, H11½, M19c, as lamp (649/61)	650
Vase and cover, gilt bronze mounted, ovoid, girl emblematic of Autumn, 26½, L19c (669/48)	1300
Vase and cover, gilt bronze, panel of 18c lovers L. Bertren, H23½, L19c (649/84)	900
Vase and cover, gilt bronze mounted, scroll handles, H35, ca1880, Collot (649/78)	2500
Vase and cover, green-ground, ovoid body, girl and putto, H26, L19c, cr (649/69)	1100
Vase aux 'Colombes' or 'Tourterelles', bleu du roi, ca1770 17⅛ (4221/230)	17000
Vase ovale mercure and cover, bleu du roi, ca1768 13½ (4221/232)	9000
Vases, covered, pair, bronze mounted porcelain, picture of cupid and a maiden, 24, E20 (619/43)	1500
Vases, covered, pair, turquoise ground, on expanding curcular base, 12, L19c (619/58)	700
Vases, pair, ormolu-mounted, apple-green, H8¾, ca1770 (4086/43)	10500
Vases, pair, bleu-de-roi ground, 18c scene, snake handles, H12¼, L19c, as lamps (649/85)	800
Vases, pair, gilt bronze mounted, 18c, lovers and landscapes, 20½, L19c, now lamps (669/45)	1200
Vases, pair, gilt bronze, azure-blue, angular handles, H13, L19c, as lamps (649/83)	400
Vases, pair, gilt bronze mounted, ovoid body, Miguel, H23, L19c, as lamps (649/63)	1600
Vases, pair, gilt bronze-mounted, scroll handles, H14½, M19c, mtd as lamps (649/59)	500
Vases, pair, gilt-metal mounted, 18c lovers, E. Lillier, masks, H14½, L19, as lamps (649/80)	250
Vases, pair, L. Bertren, pastoral lovers, H18, L19c, as lamps (649/81)	600
Vases and covers, pair, bleu celeste, pastoral views, H7⅜, 1770-75 (4086/42)	7500
Vases and covers, pair, bleu celeste ground, 18c lovers, H12½, M19c, damage (649/57)	700
Vases and covers, pair, compressed form, musical trophy panel, H9, L19c (649/77)	475
Vases and covers, pair, ovoid body, domed pierced covers, genre, H23¾, L19c, damage (649/64)	1300
Vases and covers, pair, two panels of playful putto, 30½, M19c, covers dam (669/47)	900
Vases and covers, pair, 'jeweled', 18c lovers in landscapes, pierced covers, H10, M19c (649/55)	600
Vases and covers, pair, bleu-de-roi, ovoid body, scroll handles, H14¼, L19c, as lamps (649/86)	700
Vases and covers, pair, genre, bleu celeste ground, H17¾, M19c, as lamps (649/62)	1600
Vases and covers, pair, gilt bronzed mounted, nymph and putti amongst flowers, 16¾, L19c, I cover cracked (669/42)	1400
Vases and covers, pair, Morin, bleu celeste ground, H9, M19c, 1 damaged (649/60)	275
Vases and stands, pair, bleu celeste, panels painted, H7⅜, 1760 (4086/41)	20000
Vases and stands with flowers, pair, apple-green, painted amorous devices, cupids, H18¾, ca1765 (4086/44)	13000

Tournai

Coffee cup, saucer, with insects, scrollwork, ca1787, dam, rare (4190/37)	750
Dinner service, part, 42 pcs, birds and shrubbery, ca1776-90 (4221/237)	6000

Vieux Paris

Cache pots, pair, pocelain, tomato red ground, parrot, 8½, ca1835 (4219/22)   1050
Centerpiece, formed, lozenge-shaped basket, 16⅜, rep, ca1820 (4132/240)   350
Centerpiece, assembled, allegorical of America, kneeling squaws, ca1815 res (4190/30)   1050
Clock, biscuit and glazed, domed case, nymphs, H16, unusual, 1784-89 (4085/48)   6200
Clock case, clock 'Robin', biscuit with muse Erato and cupids, ca1790-1800, 16⅝ (4221/235)   700
Clock case, clock mkd 'Raingo Freres', a Paris white and gold scrollwork, 12¼, M19c (4132/243) 300
Coffee service, part, transfer printed in black with figural subjects, ca1820, 29 pc, dam (4262/100) 500
Coffee service, part, 16 pcs, iron, red and gold, classical figures, imp, ca1815 (4132/239)   350
Dessert service, part, 8 pcs, flowers, scroll, with crest and motto, ca1835, chip (4190/34)   350
Dinner service, part, green bordered, painted in center with a different flower, green rim, ca1825, 22
  pcs (4262/94)   550
Foot bath, bouquets of flowers, M19c, 16½, cr-rep (4190/35)   200
Jardinieres, pair, porcelain, apricot ground, Egyptian figures, 6⅝, ca1815 (4219/24)   175
Jardinieres and stands, pair, porcelain, pale salmon ground, garland, 8⅜, ca1815 (4219/23)   125
Joy and Sorrow bust, white glaze, pair, one woman holding locket, 1 holding dove, 11½, 19c
  (631/70)   225
Plates, pair, painted view of Italy, 9⅝, fine, ca1793-1828 (4132/234)   900
Pots, cache and stands, pair, black ground, bordered at rim, 7½, 19c (4262/98)   *450*

Pots (4262/98)

Plate (4262/76)

Vases (4190/31)

Tea and coffee service, genre scenes highlighted with gilding, 19c, 28 pcs (631/68)   900
Urns, campana shaped, satyr-masked handles, 11¼, gilding rubbed, ca1815 (4132/236)   250
Urns, 2 handled, pair, scenes of Napoleon on horseback, accompainted by generals, 16, ca1820
  (631/67)   400
Vase, gold ground, slender ovoid form, swan shaped handles, 11½, now a lamp, ca1815 (4262/96) 175
Vases, pair, gold ground, military vignettes, ca1820 22½ (4221/236)   6400
Vases, pair, handle roman soldiers, hunting scene, ca1815, 10, rep (4190/31)   *400*
Vases, pair, painted with romantic figures, 12½, L19c, gilding, rubbed (619/67)   100
Vases, pair, Napoleonic, 23, some rubbing, ca1820 (4132/241)   3000
Vases, pair, blue-ground, slender ovoid form, gilt, heightened matte, 11¾, ca1815 (4262/97)   150
Vases, pair, long necked lobed, two flower medallions, pink and blue panels, 19½, 19c (631/66) 175
Vases, pair, neoclassical, mythological, figures against gold ground, 10¾, E19c (631/64)   700
Vases, pair, with covers, potpourri, neoclassical leafage, 5¾, chip, ca1820 (4132/242)   200
Vases, 2 handled, pair, painted with bouquets of flowers, 13¼, L19c, gilding rubbed (619/68)   200

Vincennes

Group, glazed white, L'Astronomie, ca1749-54, 7, chip, rare (4190/4)   950
Plate, floral cluster on gilt edged lobed rim, 9¾, ca1750 (4262/76)   *425*
Tray, triangular, floral panel, fine, W5⅜, 1754 (4086/38)   4000
Wine coolers, pair, bleu celeste, colored fruit, flowers, H5¼, hc on one, ca1754 (4086/36)   2250

White biscuit

Figure of dog, wooly-coated reclining poodle, L18c 6¼ chip (4190/24)   100
Group, maiden and cupid, L18c 15⅛ major imp (4190/23)   100

GERMAN CERAMICS

Assorted periods and manufacturers

Basket on stand, pierced basket encrusted with flowers, painted with bouquets, 19¼, L19c (631/150) 300
Candelabra, pair, five-light, chinoiserie figure, tree trunk stem, H16, L19c, Rudolstadt (649/132) 375
Candlestick, figural, winter and shivering cupid huddled about a fire, Meissen, 11¾, 19c (631/106) 250
Candlesticks, pair, figural, stems supprting boy and girl wearing floral painted costumes, 14½, 19c, Saxe Coburg (631/130) 350
Cane handle, Ludwigsburg*, head of man in hat, L5⅜, rep, c1765 (4085/64) 200
Carriage group, lady alighting from elaborate 2 horse drawn carriage, 11¼, L19c (619/134) 200
Dishes, sweetmeat, pair, gallants, holding bowls, L8¾, ca1900, Potschappel (649/127) 350
Dog band, porcelain, 12 pieces, ten musicians, conductor and music stand, 4¾-6 (619/132) 450
Equestrian figure, white glaze, rearing horse supported by tree trunk, 8½, Nymphenburg (631/141) 125
Figure, equestrian, Napoleon, Sitzendorf, H15, ca1900 (649/135) 325
Figures, military, eleven, Napoleon and officers, Sitzendorf, H8¾ to 9¼, ca1900 (649/136) 800
Figures, pair, seated, one with fish, 1 binding flaming hearts, H5½, L19c, Hochst (649/121) 150
Figures, pair, K.P.M., 19c dress, gilt details, purple dec, H8½, ca1900, Scheibe (649/129) 275
Figurines, pair, blue and white, man and woman in eighteenth century costume, 9½, damage (631/131) 175
Flatware set gilt metal, German porcelain handles, rep, imp, L19c (4132/323) 400
Goblet and cover, engraved with flowers and scrolls, 11⅜, 18c (4133/66) 400
Group of courtship, gallant, girl, maid, Volkstedt, H9¾, ca1900 (649/130) 75
Groups, pair, maiden attended by 2 putti, Volkstedt, H6¼, ca1900, dam (649/134) 300
Hagar and Ishmael, Leaving the House of Abraham, 10 x 8½, M19c (669/102) 2200
Holy Family With Angel, plaque, Nymphenburg, 10¼ x 8¾, L19c (619/121) 850
Jars, potpourri, pair, flowers, vasiform, 2 applied putti, pierced covers, H11⅛, L19c, Sitzendorf (649/133) 500
Jug, beer, large, panels of men drinking and smoking, Villeroy & Boch, 13¾, ca1910 (669/70) 600
Jug, bellarmine, stoneware, ovoid body, dec with bearded mask above medallion, 9, 17c (4133/79) 450
Musical group, two figures seated on a bench, 10, dam (631/152) 375
Pipe bowl, Kelsterbach*, head of man in hat, H1⅞, chip, ca1765 (4085/65) 800
Plaque, young peasant girl kneeling by side road, counting change, 12½ x 10¼, L19c, framed (631/140) 800
Plaque, young woman, flowing hair, red cap, 3¾ x 5¾, framed (631/139) 250
Plaque, of young girl, Turkish garb, pensive, J. Richter, D15½, L19c, Pirkenhammer (649/128) 250
Plaque, oval, Young Boy, with curly hair, in white shirt and red cape, 5, L19c (631/137) 250
Plaque, Cupid and Psyche, floating amidst clouds, 4¾, L19c, framed (631/136) 275
Plaque, Madonna and Child, 6 x 4⅛, L19c, gilt frame (631/138) 325
Plaque, Maiden Seated On A Rock Cliff, 7 x 5, L19c, framed (619/129) 375
Plaque, Noble woman, woman in elegantly dressed French costume, 8½ x 5½, framed (631/135) 550
Plaque, Pope Leo and Nobleman, 15½ x 13½, L19c, Purkenhammer (631/144) 1500
Plaque, Return Of a Barbarian Army, 11⅛ x 14⅞, L19c, framed, (619/130) 1200
Plaque, Young Woman, wearing long hair, red-lined green kimono, 7¼ x 5, L19c, gilt frame (631/133) 550
Plaque of an odalisque, partially clothed, imp MR within circle, 3½ x 5, L19c (649/105) 400
Plaque of captive young maiden, dressed in white robes, seated, 5 x 7, L19c (649/108) 650
Plaque of a young boy smoking, blue work shirt, orange kerchief, 9⅛, E20, framed (619/125) 800
Plaque of a young Spanish girl, red dress and white mantle and mantilla, seated, 9 x 10½, L19c, framed (619/127) 2000
Plaque of Mignon and a Harpist, wearing white flowing robes, standing by harpist, 8½ x 5½, L19c, framed (619/124) 600
Plaque of the Madonna and Child, oval, gilt frame and shadow box,¾, L19c (619/126) 225
Plaques, pair, high relief mythological scenes, 14, L19c, framed (631/147) 600
Plaques, pair, after Makart, Romeo and Juliet, Faust and Gretchen, 5½ x 8½, L19c (649/109) 1300
Plate, mythological scene, gilt, pink and maroon border, 9½, E20, framed (619/128) 275
Plates, pair, faience, cluster of flowers and floral sprigs, 10¼, 1760-80 (4262/60) 950
Platter, oval spray flowers, Crailsheim faience, 14⅞, hc, M18c (4132/212) 200
Scent bottle and stopper, Boy and Goat, M18c, 3 (4221/18) 750
Stand, fruit, pierced, circular basket, domed foot, Potschappel, H7, ca1900 (649/124) 250
Stein, The Sad Radish, pewter hinged cover, 6¾, ca1910 (669/71) 300
Tankard, enamelled glass, blue scroll, traces of inscription, wreath of flowers, 9⅝, 19c (4133/69) 250
Tankard, enamelled glass, painted with a traveller in a landscape, dog and horse, 9½, 19c (4133/70) 150
Tankard, enamelled glass, yellow medallion bearing gilt inscription, 9, 19c (4133/71) 150
Tankard, stylized floral motifs, salt glazed stoneware pewter mounted, 8⅜, hc, 18c (4132/200) 225
Tea service, part, 12 pcs, yellow glazed earthenware, Bayreuth, imp, ca1730-35 (4132/188) 5250

Tureen, cover and stand, apple green ground, spherical, leaf molded scrolled handles, gentlemen
18c dress, H9½, L19c, Helena Wolfsohn (669/108)   600
Urn, scene of young woman, in springtime forest setting, 30¾, ca1910 (631/143)   2750
Urn, cover and stand, flower-encr., campana-form, ptd. myth. figures, H26, L19c, Plaue (649/122)   1300
Vase, woman holding basket of flowers over head, 22 ca1900 (619/133)   325
Vase and cover, potpourri, tree-trunk foot, Proskau faience, chips, ca1783-93 (4132/213)   400

Bayreuth faience

Tankard, large blue bird, pewter mounted, 9⅝, hc, 18c (4132/195)   1200
Tankard, pewter mounted, building flanked by pine trees, 9½, cracks, 1760-88 (4262/62)   1600
Tankard, pewter mounted, Chinaman fishing seated on a knoll, 11¼, 1728-44 (4262/63)   2500
Tankard, standing stag, pewter mounted, 9¾, 18c (4132/194)   1400
Tankard by B.P. Trauer, pewter mounted, pot thrower, dated 1769, imp, rare (4190/122)   1300

Bellarmine

Jug, stoneware, Rhenish, 9½, 17c (4149/90)   225

Berlin

Basket, octagonal, reticulated, center bouquet of flowers, 8¼, ca1800 (4262/160)   300
Bowl and cover, potpourri, oval bowl, ptd. putti in landscape, H10½, L19c (649/162)   375
Cup, cover and stand, scene of figures in garden, mid-blue ground, D saucer 7½, ca1847 (649/160)   900
Cup and saucer, portrait of Napoleon, 19c (619/104)   450
Cups and saucers, pair, cabinet, 18c figures flanked by molded classical figures, 6¾, ca1870
(669/194)   450
Eye wash, with floral sprigs, H1½, fine, rare, ca1770 (4085/69)   325
Figural group, white, Bacchus seated on a cask, with Bacchantes, 10¼, L19c (631/118)   300
Plaque, scrolled cartouche shaped, ribbon tied bouquet of flowers, 30½, 19c (631/117)   600
Plates, twelve, A. Mintschin, Persian-style design, pierced rim, D7¾, 1930's (649/163)   750
Plates, vegetable, twelve, painted with various vegetables, white ground, L19c (619/105)   700
Plates, wall, pair, 18c girls or lovers in garden, gilt, pale green and cream band, 13¾, ca1900
(669/200)   950
Stein, gilt metal mounted, large, with arms of the German empire, 14, L19c (631/116)   700
Tazze, pair, floral and foliate motifs, ca1815, 9¾, fine (4123/329)   1500
Two children, in peasant costume standing in a courtyard, 13⅛ x 7⅞, L19c (619/92)   5000
Urn, gold ground, ca1820, 16⅝, fine (4123/330)   2600
Urn, lapis-lazuli ground, ca1820, 16½ (4123/331)   1800
Urn, 2 handled, covered, painted, roses, daises, violets and petunias, 14, M19c (631/115)   450
Urns and stands, pair, 2 handled, baluster vessel, gentle folks 18c dress, H27, M19c (669/193)   2250
Vase and cover, ovoid body, 18c lovers, 3 scrolled feet, H6, L19c (649/168)   275
Vase and cover, 18c lovers, stepped foot, domed cover, H20, L19c (649/166)   500
Vases, and covers, potpourri, pair, Dresden 18c lovers, mask handles, H13¼, L19c, some damage
(649/165)   325
Vases, covered, pair, paneled vasiform, bodies, sprays of flowers, domed cover, 17, M19c (619/102)   650

Berlin faience

Tankard, ecclesiastical buildings, pewter mounted, 10⅝, ca1747-55 (4132/197)   1300
Tankard, stylized floral motifs, turquoise ground pewter mounted, rare, 9¼, hc, ca1730 (4132/196)   1200

Berlin plaque

Admiration, five maidens around cupid, Wagner, good, 12¼ x 16¼, L19c (649/180)   12000
An amorous couple, printed in Vienna, Austria, 9¾ x 6½, L19c (619/97)   1000
An interesting book, maiden engrossed in book, 8½ x 6¼ (669/215)   2500
C. Melt*, lady nursing child in landscape, 15¼ x 9½, L19c (649/167)   3000
Child Eating Bread, holding peach, 9¼ x 6½, ca1880 (649/173)   5250
Christ in the Temple, 10 x 7½, L19c, K.P.M. (649/171)   1500
Cupid, sleeping beside a shallow pool, 9 x 11¼, L19c (619/99)   2250
Discovery of Moses, pharaoh's daughter at river, 12½ x 10, L19c (631/119)   3750
Dresden-painted, portrait of elderly man, I. Sturm, 18¼ x 13½, 1882 (649/161)   2000
Empress Louise Descending Staircase, signed F. Wagner, K.P.M., 12⅝ x 7¾, L19c (649/181)   13000
Exotic nude with jewels around neck, 12¾ x 6½, L19c, blackwood frame (669/219)   3000
Fisher boy with two maidens, fisher boy leaning out of boat, 13 x 10⅜, L19c, framed (619/94)   4250

Fisherman and maiden, fisherman by riverside with nude woman, 12½ x 10, L19c (631/121) 4000
Hagar and Ishmael Leaving House of Abraham, K.P.M., after Van der Werff, 18 x 22, L19c (649/175) 9500
Hunting scene, German hunter entering beer hall, 7½ x 10, 1900 (631/120) 1500
Judith holding the head of Holofernes, sword in other hand, 19½ x 16, L19c, blank margin 1 side (669/216) 5500
K.P.M., good, naked maidens flee dawn, 12 x 15, L19c (649/179) 16000
Landscape of the ancient ruins of Athens, 11 x 18½, L19c (669/214) 2000
Madonna and child standing amongst clouds, 13 x 7¾ (669/212) 1500
Madonna and child, oval, 6½, L19c, framed (669/196) 400
Maiden comforted, with 4 female companions, 22½ x 18¼, L19c, framed (619/101) 7750
Maternal happiness, young mother and 3 children, (669/211) 5000
Merchant surveying body of murdered nobleman, 15¾ x 19¼, L19c, corner chip, large (669/213) 4250
Mother and Children, K.P.M., 7¼ x 9½, L19c (649/177) 2500
Mother holding sleeping child, 13½, L19c (669/209) 4000
Musician, man playing violin, 16¼ x 12¼, L19c, framed (619/93) 3500
Nun comforting a Maiden, 11¼ x 9, L19c, framed (619/100) 1500
Othello with Desdemona pleading in Venice, 21¾ x 16, L19c, framed (619/96) 12000
Portrait, a long haired girl, 20 58 14½ (619/98) 2500
Portrait of youth in white cap and robe, 6¾, L19c, oval (669/199) 1100
Portrait of Maria Ruthven, seated holding cello, 9¼, L19c (669/208) 1700
Queen Victoria in court dress, 10½, 1897 (669/203) 1200
Saint Jerome, 6¾ x 9½, L19c (619/89) 850
Sistine Madonna, 7, L19c, framed (669/197) 400
St. Cecelia seated at an organ, oval, 6½, L19c (669/198) 550
Summer, seated women, four nudes bathing, Wagner, fine, K.P.M., 16½ x 10½, L19/E20c (649/178) 13000
The penitent Magdalene, 10 x 12½, 1855, rim chip (669/210) 2000
The school room, three children reading or writing, 10¼ x 7½ (669/206) 3500
The Madonna, flanked by St. Sixtus and St. Barbara, 16½ x 12½, L19c (669/207) 3000
The Secret, two young urchins, 1 whispering to other, (669/218) 2500
The 5 senses, female figures, 5 pieces, 14 x 20, L19c, giltwood frames (669/220) 12000
Upper torso of 2 putti looking upwards, 9, L19c, framed (669/202) 400
Winter scene, man standing holding infant, small girl, 12½ x 10, L19c (619/88) 3000
Woman, oval, woman wearing an open white blouse, cummerbund, 6, L19c, framed (619/91) 450
Young woman, standing in 16th century costume, table, flowers, 10 x 11, L19c, framed (619/90) 3000
Young woman seated, reading, K.P.M., after Pickett, 7½ x 10 (649/174) 2750
Young woman with children, in a flower strewn garden setting, 13⅛ x 8, L19c, framed (619/95) 3500
Youth and maiden, running from summer storm, 12½ x 10, L19c, gilt frame (631/122) 4000
17c gentleman, playing lute, companion reads book, circular, 5½, L19c, border repainted, chip (669/204) 400

Bottger porcelain

Figure, pagoda figure with smiling mouth, pierced ears, ca1720 3⅛ (4221/175) 3400
Figure miniature, Mezzetin, ca1720 2⅜ fine rare (4221/10) 2300

Dresden

Bowl, oval, footed, ptd. exterior, hunting scene, snake handles, W18¾, L19c (649/112) 400
Bowls, soup, set of twelve, sprays of summer flowers, scrolling and shell borders, 10, L19c (619/118) 950
Candelabra, pair, seven-light, pierced, scrolled base, H21½, L19c (649/113) 700
Centerpiece, large, floral swags, pierced basket, H25½, L19c, dam (649/117) 800
Centerpierce, three child vintagers pulling cart with vine swags, 19, L19c (669/86) 875
Clock case and card rack, dial below stepped divisions, H9¼, chip (649/116) 250
Coffee service, mythological scenes, gilt formalized borders, 16, tray, L19c, 14 pcs (631/134) 1100
Comports, figures, pair, ovoid basket with loop handles, 2 cupids, 12⅞, L19c (669/83) 400
Ewer and cover, gilt borders, 2 children confiding secret, 6¾, ca1900 (669/84) 400
Figure, Nodding Mandarin, in lotus position, head, tongue articulated, H11, E20c (649/114) 400
Figures and stands, set of four, each a maiden emblematic of the seasons, 17½x 19¼, L19c (669/82) 2250
Plate, slave girl before an Egyptian, gilt rim, 12¼, E20c (619/119) 425
Stand and base, four putti above bulbous base, H17¼, ca1900, mtd as lamp (649/115) 200
Tureen, soup, with stand, white, gold, spherical body, H9, no cover, 19c (4148/59) 200
Vase, ovoid body, portrait of a maiden, gilt and blue, 14¾, L19c (669/85) 800
Vases and covers, pair, Schneeballen, applied fruits and birds, florette ground, H18½, L19c (649/111) 800

Figure (4221/124) (4221/123)

Three quarter length portrait of Anne of Brittany (669/90)

Figure (4221/98)

Dresden plaque

Bacchanal, signed H.G. Poetz, 14¾ x 12, L19c (649/104)	3250
Meleager and Atlanta in landscape with hounds, 8½ x 11¾, L19c, framed (669/93)	1200
Musician holding a swooning maiden, French enameled frame, 9½,L19c (669/97)	800
Peasants in inn, innkeeper offering snuff to a maiden, 6¾ x 8, L19c, framed, reduced (669/94)	1000
Penitent Magdalen, after Rotari, 6¼, L19c (669/92)	300
Portrait of lady, dark brown embroidered dress, 5, L19c (669/95)	300
Psyche, by moonlit pool, 5½ x 3½ (649/103)	550
Three quarter length portrait of Anne of Brittany, 6, L19c (669/90)	*700*
Three sirens seated on rock, white, pink and blue robes, 60½, L19c (669/96)	950
Young maid on a flight of steps, 12½ x 8, L19c (649/102)	2250
Youthful portrait of St.John the Baptist, 7½, L19c (669/89)	425

Erfurt faience

Tankard, harvester, pewter mounted, 9½, ca1768-84 (4132/203)	1500
Tankard, painted with large castle, pewter mounted, 10⅝, fine, 18c (4132/190)	1400
Tankard, pewter mounted, figure in a hilly landscape, 9¾, cracks, 1730-51 (4262/64)	1300
Tankard, sportsman with rifle, pistol, pewter mounted, 10⅞, imp, 18c (4132/191)	1100

Frankenthal

Dejeuner, painted with mythological scenes, 16¼, tray, 1775-80, 6 pcs (4262/147)	5500
Figure, forester, ca1759, 6⅛, rep (4221/94)	700
Figure, Harlequin-slapstick replaced, ca1759, chip repaired (4221/96)	8500
Figure, lady with lilac apron, ca1762-64 5 (4221/98)	*1700*
Figure, rat catcher, ca1756-59 5¼ dam (4190/56)	450
Figure, white Bolognese terrier, ca1767-75 6¼ (4221/95)	2200
Figure, Chinoiserie, musician holding bassoon, ca1773, 5½, tassel missing (4190/57)	1100
Gardener, modelled by Johann Wilhelm Lanz, H5½, rare, 1759-62 (4085/59)	1100
Girl, harvester, yellow straw hat, puce bodice, white blouse, 5¾, rep, 1777 (4262/148)	175
Group, boy w dog-cat, ca1781 (4221/99)	3000
Group, quack doctor with monkey, ca1763, repaired (4221/97)	9000
Hurdy-gurdy player, modelled by Johann Friedrich Luck, H6, chip, 1759-62 (4085/58)	1600
Plates, pair, large, scattered floral spray, banded in gilding, D13¼, 1755-59 (4085/57)	400
Scent bottle and stopper, 'Provender for the Monastery', c1759, 3⅛ (4221/6)	2600

Frankfurt ad Oder

Tankard, faience, rare, pewter mounted, lady with blue green bodice, 9½, hc, ca1763-95 (4132/201)	1200

Frankfurt faience

Vase, blue-white, peacocks and song-birds, 18c, 11½, chip (4190/119)	750

Fulda

Tea caddy, a building amongst hills, scrolls, 4½, dam, 1764-81 (4262/157)	1300

Furstenberg

Dinner service, part, landscape surrounded by sprigs of colorful flowers, 1775-85, 48 pcs (4262/150)	3750
Figure, Hope allegorical, ca1760 7⅜ minor imp (4221/75)	4000
Figure, Venus seated, ca1760-65 7⅞ chip (4221/74)	4000
Plates reticulated pair, man-child-dog-waterfall, ca1757-58 9⅛ (4221/73)	2300
Pot and cover, birds and sprigs, ca1760 2¾ (4190/58)	325
Scent flagon, gallant and sweetheart, H5⅞, c1770 (4085/68)	750

German faience

Tankard, pewter mounted, cartouche with buildings, 18c, 8⅛ hc (4190/121)	750
Tankard, a house flanked by trees, pewter mounted, 6¾, hc, L18c (4132/199)	425
Tankard, church with pine trees, pewter mounted, 9⅛, 18c (4132/192)	*1400*

Tankard (4132/192) (4132/191) (4132/190)   Tankard (4132/193)

Tankard, fanciful floral design, pewter mounted, 8¼, L18c (4132/198)	350
Tankard, large blue bird, pewter mounted, 10⅞, 18c (4132/193)	*900*

German porcelain

Snuffbox and cover, painted all sides, 2⅝, hc, ca1755 (4132/321)	700

Hannoversch Munden

Tankard, 'Trinkt Brader Trinkt', pewter mounted, 8⅝, L18-E19c (4132/202)	350

Helena Wolfsohn

Vases and covers, pair, double-gourd form, 18c travellers, H7½, L19c (649/120)	150
Vases and covers, pair, pink-ground, shield-shaped body, panels of 18c lovers, H13¾, L19c (649/119)	325

Hochst

Autumn, allegorical, as a putto, wreath of purple grapes on head, 5⅜, ca1765 (4262/141)	1100
Box and cover, birds nest, basket supporting 2 finches, ca1765, 4⅝, rep, rare (4190/55)	1700
Boy with flask, with right arm raised, flask by right foot, 4⅝, 1780-85 (4262/140)	475
Chinaman with a horn, as a musician, 7½, horn missing, 1765-70 (4262/138)	3250
Chinese lady with a triangle, with flower arranged in her hair, 7, triangle missing, 1765-70 (4262/139)	2750
Coffee pot and cover (married), gentlemen-horses, ca1765-70 9¾ chip imp (4221/83)	700
Figure, Spring allegorical, ca1750-53 5⅝ rare (4221/76)	1100
Figure, pair, boy and girl, 5⅞, 6⅝, dam, rep, ca1760-70 (4132/322)	3000
Figure, small, The Bowing Chinaman, ca1750-53 3⅝ (4221/78)	*500*

Figure (4221/77) (4221/78)

Tureen and cover (4262/59)

Tea caddy and
cover (4221/81)

Figure, white, Cupid sleeping, ca1775 5⅝ (4221/77)	550
Group, crying over the dead, ca1774 6⅜ (4221/80)	3400
Group, The Adorned Sleeper, ca1770 6½ tail missing (4221/79)	4000
Hot milk pot and cover, painted by Louis-Victor Gerverot, couple, H 7⅛, rare, rep, 1771-73 (4085/56)	3400
Pantaloon, Italian comedy, the actor in a stalking position, 9 (4262/142)	850
Tankard and cover, silver mounted, ca1765-70 5 fine (4221/86)	3000
Tea caddy, rectangular arched, ca1755-60 4½ (4221/82)	450
Tea caddy and cover, rectangular body-domed cover, ca1775 5½ hc cr (4221/81)	*1000*
Teapot and cover, ovoid shape, painted in puce with river scene, H4⅞, 1765-75 (4085/55)	200
The Fencing Lesson, instructor holding arm of the pupil, H6¾, early, rep, c1755 (4085/53)	13000
Tray, lozenge shaped, peasants, landscape, 11⅛, 1765-70 (4262/137)	1300
Tureen and cover, faience, fluted, sprays and sprigs, 10¾, ca1750, cover married* (4262/59)	*600*
Young gardener, yellow straw hat, lavender breeches, H5⅛, rep, c1755 (4085/54)	600

Hochst Rechaud

Bowl and cover, masks and scenes, ca1765-70 7⅝ rep (4221/85)	2000

Hutschenreuther

Plaque, female charioteer riding into a Roman street, 9½ x 12½, framed (669/104)	1900

Hutschenreuther, C.M.

Plaque, Gypsy maiden standing by wall with tambourine, 8¾ x 5¾, L19c (669/105)	1000
Plate, Dresden decorated, Portrait of Clementine, 9½, 1900, framed (669/103)	550

Kellinghusen faience

Plate, large, bird, flowering branches and leaves, L18c, 12⅛, chip (4190/120)	1200

Kloster Veilsdorf

Figure, Doctor Boloardo, Italian comedy, ca1764-65 5⅝ repaired (4221/131)	1600

Limbach

Figure, a fisher boy, ca1770 3⅝ hand missing (4221/130)	200
Figure, a flutist, ca1780 5⅛ dam (4221/128)	400
Figure, winter, ca1780, 5¾ repaired (4221/129)	400
Group, a blackamoor with horse, ca1780, 4¾, reins missing (4221/127)	2400

Ludwigsburg

Bowl, square, bouquet and sprigs, ca1770 9 chip (4190/61)   650
Bowls, square, pair, floral sprays, 8⅜, ca1765-75 (4132/289)   650
Charger, floral sprays, 13⅝, fine, ca1765-70 (4132/293)   400
Charger, small, birds-shrubbery, ca1770, 12¼ (4221/110)   *700*

Chargers (4221/109) (4221/110)

Basket on stand (631/100)

Charger, large, floral sprays, 16¼, fine, ca1765-75 (4132/291)   650
Chargers, pair, birds, shrubbery, ca1770, 14, fine (4221/108)   1300
Chargers, pair, floral sprays, 13½, fine, ca1765-75 (4132/292)   1100
Chargers, pair, painted with birds, insects, 13⅝, fine, ca1770 (4132/305)   1700
Chargers, small pair, birds-shrubbery, ca1770 12 good (4221/109)   *1400*
Dish, oval, birds perched on shrubbery, ca1770 9⅛ fine (4190/69)   600
Dish, oval, birds-shrubbery, ca1770 10½ fine (4221/115)   600
Dish, oval, birds-shrubbery, ca1770, 10, fine (4221/114)   600
Dish, oval, painted with birds, insects, 8¼, ca1770 (4132/315)   275
Dishes, oval, pair, birds perched on shrubbery, 1770 8¾ - 9⅛ fine (4190/67)   900
Dishes, oval, pair, birds perched on shrubbery, ca1770 10¼ (4190/66)   950
Dishes, oval, pair, birds perched on shrubbery, ca1770 8¾ (4190/68)   700
Dishes, oval, pair, painted with birds, insects, 8⅞, ca1770 (4132/314)   450
Dishes, oval, pair, painted with birds, insects, 8⅞, fine, ca1770 (4132/313)   650
Dishes, oval, two, painted with birds, insects, 10½, 1 chip, ca1770 (4132/312)   425
Dishes, pair, birds perched on shrubbery, ca1760 9⅛ fine (4190/64)   950
Dishes, pair, painted with birds, insects, 9⅛, fine, ca1770 (4132/309)   600
Dishes, sauce, painted with birds, insects, 8, fine, ca1770 (4132/310)   700
Dishes, sauce, pair, birds perched on shrubbery, ca1770 8 (4190/65)   850
Dishes, sauce, pair, painted with birds, insects, 7⅝, fine, ca1770 (4132/311)   475
Figure, a lyre player, ca1765 6⅛ lyre miss (4221/103)   500
Figure, a toping shepherd, ca1770 6⅛ chip repaired (4221/101)   1100
Figure, a vestal virgin, ca1780 13¾ grittiness (4221/106)   1400
Figure, harvester, ca1765-70 4⅝ repaired (4221/102)   600
Figure, miniature, butcher's girl, 2½, chips, ca1765-70 (4132/320)   500
Figure, miniature, man carrying a reel of rope, by J.C.W. Beyer, ca1765, 2½, chip, rep (4221/4)   550
Figure, miniature, woman with pail, 2⅜, rare, dam, ca1765-70 (4132/319)   550
Figure, miniature, Wheelwrights' Companion, by J.L.W. Beyer, ca1765, 2⅜ (4221/2)   900
Girl carrying wood, stooped by weighty bundle of brown logs carried in both hands, 4⅝, ca1762 (4262/154)   1300
Girl with a letter, satchel on left hip, a letter held in left hand, 4⅛, chip, ca1765 (4262/155)   950
Group, fortune teller, ca1770 8⅛ hc (4221/105)   1200
Group miniature, three figures at table, woman, 2 men, ca1765, 3, chip, rep (4221/3)   2300
Group-4 Figures, of the seasons allegorical, ca1775 6⅞ repaired (4221/104)   900
Harvester, holding in her right arm a sheaf of yellow wheat and sickle, 4⅝, 1760-65 (4262/153)   1600
Plate, floral sprays, 9½, fine, ca1765-70 (4132/303)   175
Plate, large, birds perched on shrubbery, ca1770 10⅛ fine (4190/74)   800
Plates, large pair, floral sprays, 11¼, fine, ca1765-70 (4132/294)   550

Plates, large pair, painted with birds, insects, 11⅜, ca1770 (4132/307) 1200
Plates, large, 2 pairs, birds on shrubbery, ca1770 11⅜ - 11⅛ (4190/63) 2200
Plates, pair, birds-shrubbery, ca1770, 9⅝, 1 hc (4221/121) 350
Plates, pair, birds-shrubbery, ca1770, 8⅞, fine (4221/119) 900
Plates, pair, painted with birds, insects, 11⅜, ca1770 (4132/306) 1300
Plates, set 12, birds-shrubbery, ca1770, 9⅞ (4221/118) 4800
Plates, set 12, painted with birds, insects, 9⅞, ca1770 (4132/316) 3100
Plates, set 6, painted with birds, insects, 9⅞, ca1770 (4132/317) 1100
Plates, set 8, birds-shrubbery, ca1770, 9¾ (4221/117) 3200
Plates, soup, painted with birds, insects, 9⅝, ca1770 (4132/318) 2500
Plates, soup, pair, birds-shrubbery, ca1770 8¾ fine (4221/111) 1000
Plates, soup, set of 6, birds perched on shrubbery, ca1770, 9, fine (4190/72) 2700
Plates, soup, set 3, floral sprays, 9⅛, fine, ca1765-70 (4132/300) 375
Plates, three, birds-shrubbery, ca1770, 9½ (4221/120) 1300
Platter, oval, birds perched on shrubbery, ca1760 17 fine (4190/62) 1150
Platter, oval, birds-shrubbery, ca1770 13⅛ fine (4221/112) 800
Platter, oval, birds-shrubbery, ca1770, 15⅜ (4221/116) 600
Salt cellars set, four, oval, floral sprays, 4½, fine, ca1765-75 (4132/290) 1400
Sauceboats, pair, floral sprays, 8¾, fine, ca1765-75 (4132/288) 350
Tureen, cover and a stand, circular, birds perched on shrubbery, ca1770 13-13½ good (4190/59) 5000
Tureen, cover, stand, oval body floral sprays, L13½, 16½, chips, ca1765-75 (4132/284) 1300
Tureen, sauce, oval, floral sprays, 6¼, fine, ca1765-70 (4132/304) 250
Tureen and cover, small, floral spray, 8, ca1765-75 (4132/286) 950
Tureens, covers, stands, pair, oval, floral sprays, L10½, 13¾, chips, ca1765-75 (4132/285) 2400

Meissen

Amazon parrot, modelled by Johann Joachim Kaendler, H6, rare, rep, c1740 (4085/141) 16000
An incident group, donkey stumbles into man seated with dog, 6, L19c (669/163) 550
Autumn, four putti amongst sheaves of wheat, 7½, L19c (669/186) 600
Autumn, maiden wearing lilac colored robe, 7¼, L19c, chip (669/166) 350
Bacchus and a satyr, naked god holding chalice, 7¼, L19c, minor chip (669/167) 300
Bases, candelabra, pair, colorful bird perched on branch, 6¼, now as lamps, ca1760 (4262/185) 400
Basins, pair large, fruit, flowers-vegetables, Marcolini Period, 17⅜ (4221/173) 2000
Basket on stand, pierced basket painted with bunches of fruit, 19, L19c (631/100) *1100*
Beaker, painted, manner of Johann Gregor Horoldt, H3⅛, fine, ca1725 (4085/86) 1000
Beaker, painted, manner of Johann Gregor Horoldt, H3, hc, ca1725 (4085/87) 500
Beaker, Augsburg-decorated, painted by Abraham Seuter, H3¼, rare, chip, 1720-35 (4085/78) 3500
Beaker and cover, frieze of chinoiserie figures, H6½, fine, ca1730 (4085/84) 3750
Beaker and saucer, yellow-ground, octagonal shape, c1735 (4085/109) 300
Beaker vases, powder blue, ca1725 12 1 dam (4221/132) 5000
Bolognese, terrier figure, alert expression, 5½, L19c (669/132) 375
Bottle, Kakiemon, oriental figure and a floral spray, H8⅜, fine, ca1730 (4085/93) 12500
Bottle and stopper, quadrangle body with 2 chinoiserie figures, H9, cracked, rep, 1723-24 (4085/80) 1000
Bottles, pair, flower encrusted, mounted with putti holding garland of flowers, 14, dam (631/97) 550
Bottles and stoppers, Kakiemon, Dutch-decorated, guadrangular body, H8⅝, rep, 1720-30 (4085/92) 5500
Bound putto, seated on molded and rocky base, H4¼, L19c (649/226) 325
Bowl, hausmaler, shepherdess and gallant, ca1745, 6⅝, fine (4221/157) 2100
Bowl, puce-ground, chinoiserie figures, ca1740-45 6¾ (4221/144) 3200
Bowl, Watteau figures, ca1745 6⅝ (4221/154) 1300
Bowl, Hausmaler, painted by F.J. Ferner, gallant seated, D6⅞, 1730-45 (4085/124) 2400
Bowl, 2 handled, oval shape, interior painted with birds and chipmunk, 13, E19c (631/103) 375
Bowls, pair, shallow, central floral spray, 12, ca1900 (669/113) 400
Box, sugar oval, river landscape, 5, 1730-35 (4262/164) 200
Boxes and covers, pair of peach, shading from puce to chartreuse, L2⅞, 1 stem missing, ca1760 (4085/129) 800
Boxes and covers, pair of rose, each flower with puce-edged petals, H4⅛, imperfections, ca1760 (4085/131) 1200
Boy playing a flute, standing by barrel of grapes, 4¾, L19c, minor chip (669/176) 225
Boys, pair, young boy feeding dog, companion holding bird, 4, L19c (669/157) 500
Bracket, wall, flower encrusted, ca1760, 8¼ (4221/163) 900
Candelabra, pair, ormolu-mounted, ornithological, canary on nest, H10⅝, ca1750 (4086/52) 15500
Candelabra, 5 light, pair, putti seated before scrolled stem, H18, L19c, dam (649/188) 1200
Candelabrum, 4 light figural, rococo scrolled base with scroll and leafage, 21½, L19c (669/127) 525
Candlesticks, pair, porcelain, baluster stem, scrollwork, gilding, 11½, 1 chip, L19c (4219/21) 375
Cane handle, Lady's Head, Thumb Piece, ca1745 4½ (4221/20) 950
Card player, figure, young lady, cards on tripod table, 6¼, chip, L19c (649/237) 650
Cardinal, perched on rocky base, H8¼, ca1900 (649/212) 225

Casket, gilt, bronze mounted, scenes of Perseus, gilt scrollwork, 9⅜, L19c (669/130)   1300
Celebration, groups, pair, several peasants making music, dancing, 18¼ x 19¾, dam, L19c (649/245)   3000
Celebration, group, several peasants frolicking about leafy tree, 19½, L19c, (losses) (669/192)   1100
Chargers, pair, Zwiebelmuster Pattern, ca1780, 17-16¾, 1 chip, 1 rep (4190/111)   550
Child, Harlequin, yellow hat, costume in iron-red, green and yellow, 4⅞, chip, ca1755 (4262/203)   1400
Child's bust, bedecked with flowers and leaves, 10¾, ca1850 (631/92)   400
Children figures, pair, 1 firing a crossbow, the other riding hobby horse, 6¼ x 6½, res, L19c (649/236)   750
Children groups, pair, making music or dancing with flowers, 10, chip, res, L19c (649/246)   1800
Children's band group, 4 young musicians, 7¼, chip, L19c (649/244)   800
Chocolate pot and cover, samson yellow-ground, cylindrical body, H6⅜, rep, 19th century (4085/111)   2425
Classical maiden, Harvest, floral drapery, holding sheaves of wheat, H15, L19c (649/221)   175
Clock, mantle, and stand, applied floral swags and putti, H20½, L19c (649/189)   2250
Cockatoo, modelled by Johann Joachim Kaendler, H13¼, fine, rare, ca1734 (4085/143)
Cockatoos, pair, white with rose head feathers, perched on tree trunk, 9¼, 19c (631/94)   1000
Cockerel, modelled by Johann Joachim Kaendler, H9⅞, rep, 1742-50 (4085/140)   4500
Coffee cups, saucers, set 6, flowers scrollwork, Dot Period, saucers chip (4132/278)   900
Coffee pot and cover, pear shaped body, 9¼, imp, Dot Period (4132/281)   325
Coffee set, floral-encrusted, applied sprays, insects, L of tray 17, L19c (649/199)   6490
Coffee set, 15 pcs., floral sprays, sprigs below molded rim, H coffee pot 8½, E20c (649/198)   6490
Country gentleman, standing, hand in pocket, dog, 6¼, L19c (669/181)   450
Cup, quatrefoil mocha, with a gallant approaching his sweetheart, W3, fine, ca1745 (4085/123)   300
Cup and saucer, coffee, bataillenmalerei, scenes of skirmishes, ca1740 fine (4221/148)   1400
Cup and saucer large, green Watteau, figures in a park setting, ca1745 3 (4221/153)   850
Cup coffee and saucer, Kakiemon decoration, ca1730, fine (4221/137)   1000
Cupid, naked god searching in bushes for flaming hearts, 4½, L19c, minor chip (669/133)   275
Cupid figure, winged figure with pink drapery at his wrist, standing, L19c (619/109)   225
Cupid preparing for love, sharpening his arrow at grinding wheel, 7½, L19c (669/147)   425
Cupids, two, one bound with garlands, 1 feeding birds, H7½, 7, L19c (649/222)   750
Dancing couple, back to back, 5½, L19c (669/160)   475
Dancing couple, back to back holding hands, 5½, L19c (669/159)   425
Dancing man, yellow coat with flying sleeves, black hat left hand, 3¾, rep, 1750-55 (4262/199)   300
Dinner service, part, scrolling border, spring flowers, L19c, 31 pcs, 2 riveted, 7 with chip (619/116)   1400
Dinner service, part 49 pcs, ornithological, brightly painted colorful birds, 19c (4221/174)   11500
Dish, scene of peasant woman, floral sprays, D11¾, M19c (649/196)   425
Dish, Yellow Tiger pattern with a gold eye, D8⅝, fine, ca1725 (4085/94)   1800
Dish, leaf, 2 overlapping leaves, molded veins, 14½, ca1850 (4262/176)   250
Dish, leaf, Schmetterling pattern, has 2 overlapping leaves, 15, ca1740 (4262/169)   300
Dish, sauce, armorial, the Polish arms of Augustus the Strong, ca1730 4¼ fine (4221/135)   4300
Dish, two-handled, gilt-decorated, scroll-molded, oval shape, flower panel, L13¾, ca1880 (649/195)   175
Dishes, oval, pair, bouquet and sprays, ca1745, 10⅛ (4190/99)   850
Dishes, pair, sprigs, bouquets, brass footings, 9⅝, ca1750 (4132/275)   425
Dishes, pair, sprigs, bouquets, brass footings, 9½, ca1750 (4132/276)   225
Ecuelle, cover and stand, painted manner of Johann Gregor Horoldt, W5⅝, D6⅝, rep, c1735 (4085/85)   5000
Ecuelle, cover and stand, quatrefoil panels surrounded by gold, purple, W6¼, D7, ca1740 (4085/118)   2000
Ecuelle, cover and stand, with green, blue, yellow and iron-red birds, W10¼, D9¼, ca1730 (4085/105)   3400
Ecuelle, cover and underplate, iron red and puce trellis diaper vignettes, W8⅝, D8¾, ca1730 (4085/106)   2800
Eighteenth century lady, floral painted costume, basket of flowers, 18½, L19c, res (669/173)   750
Eighteenth century lady, standing reading letter, 7½, L19c, minor chip (669/180)   550
Europa and the bull, group, Europa atop flower bedecked bull, 2 children, 8¾, 19c (631/114)   900
Family group, gentlemen showing rattle to child, wife at side, 6½, L19c (669/171)   900
Figural clock, three figures, flowers, playing musical instruments, 15, 19c (631/102)   1600
Figural group, three children, 9¼, L19c (631/89)   900
Figural group, young man seated by a covered urn, woman and girl, 9, L19c, repair to urn cover (631/88)   600
Figural group, Bacchus on barrel with nymph and putti, H8½, L19c (649/216)   750
Figural group, 'The Kiss', kneeling man about to kiss hand of lady, 11¼, 19c (631/87)   750
Figural group, pair, fall and winter in form of 2 putti beside a fire, 9½, 10¼, L19c, repairs (631/86)   1000
Figural group, putti fisher boys, three putti around shell salt, H5¾, L19c (649/223)   1200
Figural group, Bacchus and Silenas, Bacchus on donkey, with nymph and putto, H8, L19c, minor rest. (649/215)   700
Figural group of amorous putti, two draped children, scrolled base, H4¼, L19c (649/224)   450

Figural group of Amphitrite, naked goddess in shill-boat, nymphs, putti, H8, L19c, rest. (649/217) — 800

Figural group of 'Love Restrained', two maidens clipping wings, breaking arrow, H 12¾, L19c (649/230) — 1900

Figural groups, pair, courting couples with children seated, 10, dam, L19c (631/90) — 1100

Figure, a dancer, ca1740-50 6⅞ (4221/180) — 1800

Figure, a janissary, ca1743 6½ (4221/186) — *800*

Figure, a Turkish lady, ca1745 5⅝ repair (4221/187) — *700*

Figure, allegcrical, 12¾, rare, ca1745 (4132/271) — 1600

Figure, allegorical, summer, Dot Period 5¼ (4190/84) — 400

Figure, beltrame, ca1744 5¼ (4221/195) — 3200

Figure, court jester Joseph Frohlich, ca1741 9¼ (4221/178) — 8500

Figure, court jester Joseph Frolich, Kaendler, H9⅞, rep, 18c (4085/137) — 4200

Figure, fruit seller, ca1740-50, 5⅞ rep (4190/80) — 1000

Figure, gardener, Dot Period, 5¼ (4190/88) — 350

Figure, girl musician, Dot Period 4⅞ (4190/86) — 450

Figure, grape seller, ca1753, 5½, imp (4190/81) — 650

Figure, Harlequin, ca1744 5¾ restored chip (4221/192) — 6500

Figure, Harlequin playing the bagpipes, ca1745, 5⅛, horn chip (4221/189) — 4000

Figure, Harlequin with a lorgnon, ca1740-46, 7⅛, fingers chip (4221/191) — 34000

Figure, Harlequin with birdcage, ca1740-45 4⅞ (4221/190) — 7000

Figure, narzisin, ca1744 5⅝ repaired (4221/199) — 1200

Figure, pagoda figure with nodding head, 18c 7¾ (4221/177) — 5000

Figure, pagoda figure with open mouth, pierced ears, ca1720-25, 3⅞ (4221/176) — 9000

Figure, pantaloon, ca1744 5⅜ chip (4221/196) — 4000

Figure, parrot mounted in ormolu, 6½, ca1741-45 (4132/270) — 1600

Figure, Pierrot, ca1744 6 repaired (4221/198) — 4400

Figure, Scapin, ca1744 5¼ (4221/194) — 4200

Figure, the captain, ca1744 5½ handle repaired (4221/197) — 3000

Figure, water carrier, 5½, ca1750 (4132/269) — 750

Figure, young boy eating grapes, seated on straw bench, H5, L19c (649/232) — 175

Figure, Augustus the Strong, 4⅛, rare, res, ca1728 (4132/267) — 2800

Figure, Cupid disguised as pandor, ormolu mounted, the porcelain 18c 3⅜ (4221/183) — 450

Figure, Cupid in disguise, ormolu mounted, the porcelain 18c 3⅜ imp (4221/182) — 800

Figure, Doctor Boloardo, ca1744 5½ (4221/193) — 4600

Figure, gold mounted miniature, Turk, ca1750 2⅛ (4221/12) — 350

Figure, Harlequin and pug, mounted in Louis XV ormolu as clock, 11⅜, ca1735-55 (4132/266) — 2750

Figure, white, gallant offering snuff, 8⅛, ca1750 (4132/272) — 200

Figures, boy and girl, L18c, 5⅝, rep (4190/93) — 650

Figures pair, malabars, ca1749-55 7⅛ - 6⅞ (4221/188) — *5600*

Figures, miniature, lady and gentleman, ca1750 2⅜ - 2½ chip (4221/13) — 650

Figures, pair, gallant and a maiden, eighteenth century costume, 16½, ca1900 (649/214) — 425

Figures, pair, gallant and companion, 18c clothes, 13¾, dam, L19c (649/239) — 350

Figures, pair, gallant and girl dressed in pastel colored clothes, 6¼ x 6½, chip, res, L19c (649/238) — 750

Figures, pair, small, swans, ca1740-50 2¾ - 2⅝ rep (4221/16) — 650

Figures, Mandarin nodding, pair, legs crossed, flowered robes, H6⅛, L19c (649/191) — 1500

Figures, Mandarin nodding, pair, seated in lotus position, printed robes, H5¾, L19c (649/190) — 1500

Figures, 2 animal, fox on rocky base, recumbent spaniel, H10, 7, E20c (649/211) — 275

Figurines, pair, fashionably dressed couple on rock bases, H8½, 9, ca1910 (649/231) — 425

Flask miniature, gold mounted, form of a gallant, ca1750, 2⅝ (4221/11) — 1300

Four children playing, 18c dress, holding hands, 5¾, L19c (669/161) — 650

Fruit seller, young woman standing, 5½, L19c, minor chip (669/168) — 250

Gallant, pastel colored clothes, holding posy, 13½, L19c, sword hilt replaced (669/182) — 500

Gallant and companion, pair, hat full of flowers, grapes in apron, 6½, L19c (669/183) — 750

Ganymede, on eagle above clouds, H11, L19c, rest. (649/218) — 325

Gardener and companion, with spade, basket of flowers, 7¼, 7½, L19c (669/177) — 750

Gardening group, 6 peasant figures gardening, 7¼, dam, L19c (649/247) — 1200

Gentleman and lady, pair, gentleman holding staff, companion holding flowers, 6, M19c (669/178) — 800

Girl, holding a basket, 18c peasant costume, 5, L19c, minor chip (669/149) — 300

Girl with watering can, wearing 18c style dress, H5¼, L19c (649/233) — 250

Goblet and cover, hunting vignettes, hunter, tree support cup, ca1741-45 14⅛ rare imp (4221/147) — *8000*

Grape seller, open mouth young man wearing tricorn hat, 5½, ca1753 (4262/200) — 350

Group, flute lesson, ca1760, 5½, major imp (4190/85) — 150

Group, gardener and companion, 7¾, imp, Marcolini Period (4132/282) — 600

Group, gardeners, Marcolini Period 7¾ miss (4221/202) — 1100

Group, gardeners, 5 children, Dot Period, 9⅛, rep, imp (4190/89) — 450

Group, lady stroking the beard of her suitor, 6¾, now lamp base, L19c (649/235) — 750

Group, Gellert memorial monument, Marcolini ca1776 11⅜ imp (4221/200) — 2000

Figure (4221/186)
(4221/187)

Figures pair (4221/188)

Goblet and cover
(4221/147)

Lovers
(4262/206)

Meat cover (4262/178)

Group, Japanese lovers, ca1745 4½ chip-cr (4221/185)	3400
Group, Te Les Ramene, cupid seated amongst clouds, 6, L19c (649/241)	500
Group, 2 pastoral children, 5½, chip, L19c (649/240)	600
Group, musical, boy and girl playing a flute duet, ca1755 major imp (4190/82)	300
Group, musical, four children, Marcolini Period (4190/91)	700
Group, musical, four children playing instruments, Marcolini Period (4221/201)	800
Gypsy girl, holding tambourine, wearing striped skirt, 7¼, E20c, minor chip (669/179)	350
Harlequin with a jug, modelled by Johann Joachim Kaendler, H6½, rep, c1738 (4085/133)	23000
Harvesters, pair, man and woman dressed in eighteenth century costume, 6¾, 19c (631/85)	650
Huntsman, seated, holding rifle with a dog, 5, M19c (669/155)	500
Jardiniere, sprays of spring flowers, butterflies and lady bugs, 21¼, L19c (669/125)	350
Jars and covers, pair, pate surpate, potpourri, medallion in white slip, with nude infant, 11½, L19c (631/96)	2250
Jug, milk, green shaded into grey, Watteau scenes, 4⅝, chip, ca1750 (4262/183)	200
Jug and cover, 'Bataillenmaleri', Camaieu scene of 2 equestrian soldiers, H5⅞, ca1740 (4085/121)	850
Jug hot water, green Watteau, figures in a park setting, ca1745 4½ (4221/152)	550
Jug water and cover, flowers and insects, ca1725-30 9⅛ chip (4190/96)	900
Lady, pastel colored and lace eddged 18c clothes, playing cards, 6, L19c, minor chip (669/143)	550
Lady, pastel colored lace trimmed clothes, 4½, L19c, minor chip (669/153)	450
Lady, seated at table, smelling flower, 5¼, L19c, mirror chip (669/146)	525
Lady, seated in armchair, holding book, 6, L19c (669/189)	300
Lady, seated shoes kicked off, 7¼, L19c, chip and minor dam. (669/185)	400
Lady, 18c floral and yellow paniered dress, flowers, 5¼, L19c, minor chip (669/139)	350
Lady playing spinet, wearing floral dress, 4¾, L19c (669/152)	625
Lady seated by a table, listening to bird in gilded cage, 5½, L19c, minor chip (669/144)	700
Lovers, around urn, both hold wreath of flowers, 8¼, Marcolini period, cover missing (4262/206)	*1300*
Maiden, in a lilac and gilt tunic, 5¼, L19c, minor chip (669/138)	275
Malabar, figures, pair, man playing lute, woman playing hand organ*, 12¾, 13, ca1880 (669/190)	950
Marie Antoinette, bust, ruffled collar, hair topped by roses, 15, 19c (631/111)	425
Meat cover, Mollendorff service, iron-red camieu, gilding, ormulu, Diam 12¾, ca1761 (4262/178)	*1000*
Mercury, young god leaning on tree trunk, 7½, L19c (669/165)	275
Mirror, porcelain, encrusted with putti representing 4 seasons, 66 x 35, massive, L19c (619/110)	2500
Monkey, pale brown animal chained to tree trunk, 7½, ca1750 (4262/196)	500
Monkey and her young, grey-brown monkey, black paws, flesh tone face, 6⅞, rep, ca1750 (4262/195)	1400
Nymph, emblematic of Autumn, 5¼, L19c, minor chip (669/140)	350

Nymph, maiden wearing draped robe, 7¼, L19c, minor chip (669/169)   250
Pantaloon, modelled by Johann Joachim Kaendler, H6, rare, ca1736 (4085/135)   7000
Paperweight, putto with love letter, 7, L19c, res (669/158)   225
Paperweight, seated dog, oblong base, painted with floral arrangements, 7¾, 19c (631/108)   175
Parrot, painted in blue, green, yellow and orange on tree trunk, 14¼, 19c (631/112)   *800*
Parrot mounted in clock, Louis XV ormolu, Johann Joachim Kaendler, H11¾, 1741-49 (4085/142)   14000
Pastoral children, playing with garland of flowers, 5½, chip, L19c (649/243)   850
Pastoral group, man with basket of flowers, hand to lady, 12¼, L19c, (losses) (669/191)   1100
Peasant, woman, violet coat and floral dress, 5½, L19c (669/156)   325
Plaques pair, bull, sheep landscape, ca1760, 5⅝ x 8 (4221/162)   6000
Plate, 'Eichhornchen' pattern, red flying fox, D11¾, fine, ca1735 (4085/97)   1100
Plate, hausmaller, flowers, fruit, ca1770-80 8¾ (4221/172)   400
Plate, Kakiemon decoration, ca1740 9⅛ (4221/141)   300
Plate, ornithological, bird with blue and black wing, ca1750 9½ (4221/166)   900
Plate, red bird in tree, ca1745, 9¾, fine, rare (4221/158)   900
Plate, two country figures, landscape and flowers, 9½, L18c (619/107)   275
Plate, yellow tiger pattern, ca1735-40 9¼ chip (4190/94)   900
Plate, Fliegender Hund pattern, D9¼, fine, 1735-40 (4085/104)   350
Plate, large, central bouquet and 4 sprays, ca1745 12⅛ fine (4190/100)   500
Plate, large, with 4 flower sprays, floral, ca1745 11 (4190/101)   400
Plate, reticulated, flower filled, Dot Period, 10 (4132/279)   1300
Plates, ornithological, set of fifteen, bird perched on tree, 9¾, M19c (4260/339)   3100
Plates, ornithological, set of 23, each with different bird on branch, 10, imp, 19c (4260/341)   4400
Plates, ornithological, set of 8, bird, perched on tree, 9⅜, M19c (4260/340)   1700
Plates, reticulated, set of 12, pierced, scroll molded cartouches, 9¼, 1 hc, 19c (4260/342)   1100
Plates, set of five, scene of 18c lovers, lattice-pierced border, D9½, L19c (649/200)   6490
Plates, set of four, Fliegender Hund pattern, winged kglin, bird, D9¼, 1 damage, ca1735-40 (4085/103)   1200
Plates, set of twelve, fruit within gilt-lined rim, D8¼, L19c (649/201)   6490
Plates, set of 12, birds and shrubbery, Dot Period, 9⅛, chip (4190/106)   3800
Plates, set of 12, central bouquet, 4 sprays, ca1745, 9⅝ (4190/102)   2200
Plates, set of 14, sprays of flowers, 9⅜, rep, ca1830 (4260/338)   1500
Plates, set of 4, gilt scroll edges, bouquets, 9⅝, Dot Period (4262/186)   850
Plates, set of 6, molded decorative borders, bouquets in center, ca1761-62, 10¼ (4221/164)   *6000*
Plates, soup, pair, central bouquet and 4 sprays, ca1745 9½ (4190/103)   450
Plates, twelve, blue and white onion pattern, pierced border, L19c (649/208)   1000
Plates pair, ornithological, chickadee and purple finch, Dot Period 9½ (4221/171)   1600
Plates pair, ornithological, flycatcher and canary, ca1750-65 9⅝ (4221/169)   1700
Plates pair, ornithological, goldfinch, ca1760 9½ (4221/167)   1600
Plates pair, ornithological, goldfinches on chrysanthemum, ca1750 9½ repaired (4221/168)   1300
Plates pair, ornithological, pairs of birds, Dot Period 9½ (4221/170)   1900
Plates soup, set of 6, molded decorative borders, bouquets in center, ca1761-62, 9¾ (4221/165)   1300
Pot, chocolate, floral, twig handle, ca1755, 6¼ (4190/98)   500
Pot and cover, chocolate, with 2 elegant gentleman in river landscape, H7¼, c, ca1745 (4085/125)   500

Parrot
(631/112)

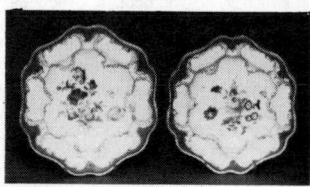

Plates (4221/164)

Pots and cover
(4221/140)

Sauceboat (4221/159)

Pots and cover, mustard pair, Kakiemon decoration, ca1740 4⅛ rare (4221/140) — *2600*
Poulterers, pair of, man with cockerel, companion with a hen, H5¾, 5⅜, mid-18c (4085/136) — 1600
Proposal, gallant and lady and another young man, 12, L19c, cracked to base (669/172) — 950
Proposal, group gallant inviting maiden to cross bridge, 9½, chip, L19c (649/234) — 1300
Proposal, group, gallant approaching lady, 6¾, L19c, chip (669/162) — 500
Pugs, pair, wearing a blue collar, 5¼, 19c (631/93) — 550
Pugs, pair of, modelled by Johann Joachim Kaendler, H5⅛, imp, ca1750 (4085/139) — 5500
Pugs, pair of, Johann Joachim Kaendler and Peter Reinicke, H6, rep, c1744-45 (4085/138) — 3800
Putto, dressed as smith forging heart on anvil, H7, ca1900 (649/227) — 500
Putto as St. George, dressed in armor, waving, sword, on dragon, H9¼, L19c (649/229) — 600
Putto gardener, digging with spade, gilt-scroll base, H4¾, L19c (649/225) — 375
Recumbent cow, grey spotted beast, right legs tucked under her, 4⅝, ca1745 (4262/198) — 250
Roman warrior, holding sword and shield, H8¼, L19c (649/219) — 150
Sauceboat, painted with manierblumen, ca1745-55 8⅝ (4221/159) — *450*
Sauceboat, Kakiemon, double-lipped with female masks, L9½, 1735-40 (4085/96) — 1400
Saucer, painted with men and boats, D4⅞, fine, ca1740 (4085/126) — 400
Saucer, quail pattern, ca1730 5¾ (4221/139) — 750
Saucer, hausmaler, center in iron-red and green with a tulip, 5, ca1745, by Ferner (4262/166) — 275
Saucers, pair, yellow ground, 5⅛, ca1730-35 (4132/273) — 600
Scaramouche and Columbine, modelled by Johann Joachim Kaendler, H7⅞, chip, ca1741 (4085/134) — 7000
Scent bottle, painted, manner of Christian Friedrich Herold, H4, fine, rare, ca1730 (4085/89) — 4200
Scent bottle, painted, manner of Johann Gregor Horaldt, H3⅜, rep, c1725 (4085/90) — 1800
Scent bottle, Provender for the Monastery, ca1750, 3¼, chip (4221/17) — 1000
Scent bottle, gold mounted, ca1725, 3½ (4221/8) — 3000
Scent bottle and stopper, Harlequin, ca1750 3⅜ chip (4221/9) — 3800
Scent bottle and stopper, Columbine, c1750, 3, minor imp (4221/7) — 2600
Scent bottle and stopper, swan, gold mounted, M18c, 3½ rep (4221/15) — 2900
Scent bottle with double stoppers, stoppers formed by monkey's heads, ca1765, 3⅛ fine (4221/5) — 2700
Service, dinner, part, 21 pcs, flowers, gilt rim, 16 plates, 5 bowls, L19c (649/204) — 850
Service, dinner, part, 34 pcs, blue and white onion pattern, L19c (649/207) — 1900
Service, dinner, 51 pcs, iron red, gilded, dragons, birds, E20c (649/206) — 3000
Service, dinner, 75 pcs, ptd. floral sprigs, latticework, D plated 6-9½, L19c (649/210) — 4500
Service, fish, bleu-de-roi grnd, floral sprays, panel border, 21 pc., L salmon dish 23¾, L19c (649/202) — 6490
Service, 112 pcs, petal shaped panels, 9¾, ca1900, minor chip (669/120) — 1300
Shepherd, grey tricorn hat, pink striped coat, holding bagpipe, 5¾, Marcolini period, chip (4262/207) — 450
Snuff box and cover, rococo scrollwork, Watteau scene, 2¾, dam, 1755-60 (4262/182) — 1300
Snuff box and cover, gold mounted, grosbleu ground, portrait, D3, fine, rare, ca1770 (4085/132) — 4500
Soup plates, pair, decorated with birds at later date, Diam 8⅞, M18c (4262/179) — 375
Spring, allegorical, young woman scantily clad, holding posy, 9, res, ca1760 (4262/205) — 1300
Stand and base, 18c lovers dancing, H17¾, L19c, mtd as lamp (649/187) — 550
Stands, fruit, pair, blue and white onion pattern, figure-mounted, H22, L19c (649/209) — 1000
Stands, tureen, oval, pair, bouquet and sprigs, rims edged in gilding, 15½ x 16½ (4262/177) — 800

Sugar box and cover, painted by Philipp Emanuel Schindler*, H4⅞, 1723-24 (4085/83)	5000
Sweetmeat figure, lady reclining on a shaped gilt scrolled base, 12¾, L19c (631/91)	400
Tankard, hausmaler armorial mounted silver gilt, ca1750, 7⅛, important (4211/156)	14500
Tankard, painted by Adam Friedrich von Lowenfinck, H6½, fine, rare, ca1735 (4085/88)	16000
Tankard with silver-gilt cover, by Johann Gregor Horoldt, H6⅞, fine, rare, ca1724 (4085/81)	14000
Tankard with silver-gilt mounts, Bottger, white, cylindrical body, H5⅝, fine, ca1715 (4085/76)	5000
Teabowl, octagonal, quail pattern, ca1730 2¼ (4221/138)	1200
Teabowl and saucer, river views with figures, ca1735 3⅛ - 5⅛ (4221/143)	1400
Teabowl and saucer, with travellers on foot and horseback, fine, ca1725 (4085/114)	2000
Teabowl and saucer, Augsburg-decorated, painted by Abraham Seuter, fine, 1720-35 (4085/79)	1100
Tea caddy, painted with peasant figures, 4, ca1755 (4132/277)	475
Tea caddy, rectangular body, peasant figures, ca1750 4 (4221/160)	300
Tea caddy, yellow ground, Indianische Blumen, H4, ca1730 (4085/100)	800
Tea caddy, Tischenmuster pattern, rectangular, H4⅛, chip, 1730-55 (4085/107)	150
Tea caddy and cover, 'phoenix' pattern, H4⅝, rep, c1735 (4085/102)	1000
Tea caddy and cover, arched angular body and cover, 5¼, ca1750 (4262/171)	1200
Tea caddy and cover, rectangular shape with dog in a landscape, H5, d, ca1740 (4085/113)	650
Tea caddy and cover, turquoise ground, travellers in a landscape, ca1745 4¼ (4221/146)	1900
Tea caddy and cover, Kapuzinerbraun, cafe-au-lait ground, H5¼, fine, ca1730 (4085/77)	2200
Teacup and saucer, bataillenmalerei, scenes of skirmishes, ca1740 fine (4221/149)	1300
Teacup and saucer, green Watteau, figures in park setting, ca1745 (4221/151)	1100
Teacup and saucer, with Dulong molding, fruit and flowers, ca1750 (4262/172)	325
Teapot, bleu-de-roi ground, two oval panels of farmers, putti-form spout, L19c (649/197)	6490
Teapot and cover, bullet-shaped body with river landscapes, H4⅜, redecoration, ca1740 (4085/112)	600
Teapot and cover, globular body with 2 putti, H4¼, chip, ca1755 (4085/128)	500
Teapot and cover, green Watteau, figures in park setting, ca1745 4½ (4221/150)	2300
Teapot and cover, Kakiemon decoration, ca1730 3⅞ (4221/136)	3200
Teapot and cover, light relief, nymphs and swans in a lake, 5½, L19c (669/118)	475
Teapot and cover, painted by Johann Gregor Horoldt, H4½, fine, 1723-24 (4085/82)	13000
Teapot and cover, painted on either side with an estuary view, H4⅛, rep, c1735 (4085/117)	700
Teapot and cover, painted, manner of Christian Freidrich Herold, fine, ca1735 (4085/116)	1000
Teapot and cover, yellow-ground, with a hilly river landscape, H4⅛, ca1740 (4085/110)	2400
Teapot and cover, minature, couple conversing, large building, ca1745 3⅛ (4190/97)	300
Teapot stand, pea green ground, 2 men on riverbank, ca1740-45 6⅛ hc (4221/145)	1200
Teapots and covers, formed as a cockerel and a hen, Kaendeler, L8⅜, 6⅞, chip, ca1734 (4085/144)	10500
Tray, German ice skating scene, 14¾, L19c (619/111)	650
Tray, oval, bouquets, sprays, gilt rim, ca1760 21⅝ chip (4190/105)	550
Tray, oval, painted in pink with floral sprigs, scroll border, 36 x 17½, M19c (631/98)	175
Tray, oval, three eighteenth century figures, landscape, 17¾, 19c (631/107)	550
Tureen, cover, stand, soup, oval, female head handles, 12½, 12¾, ca1740 (4132/274)	1600
Tureen, soup and cover, oval, bombe body, scroll handles, 13⅜, ca1750 (4262/181)	75
Tureen and cover, 'phoenix' pattern ram's head, scroll handles, H12⅝, L12⅛, chip, ca1735 (4085/98)	3000
Tureen and cover, Yellow Tiger pattern, cylindrical body, H11⅝, c, ca1730 (4085/95)	1000
Tureen and cover, circular, floral, decoration with applied florettes, ca1750-60 10⅞ (4221/161)	1100
Tureen and cover, circular, knop formed as orange, 10½, rep, ca1750 (4260/335)	1200
Tureens and covers, pair, circular, knop formed as orange, 8⅞, 1 crack, ca1750 (4260/336)	1000
Two children, seated on gilt scrolled base, L19c, minor chip (669/188)	400
Two young children, boy holding hat full of flowers, 4¼, L19c (669/134)	300
Urn, 2 handled, painted with a continuous bacchic frieze, 11¾, ca1900 (631/104)	2500
Urns, covered, pair, bleu-de-roi enamelled, mythological figures, domed covers, 6, L19c, covers restored, miniature (631/95)	1200
Vase, tapering white body, floral festoons, 8⅝, L19c (619/115)	50
Vase, trumpet-form body, ptd. floral sprays, H6½, ca1900 (649/192)	100
Vase, small, pear-shaped scroll handles, Dot Period, 4 (4132/280)	225
Vase and cover, potpourri, floral sprays, branch handles, H7¾, E19c (649/193)	500
Vases, pair, floral bouquets, fluted, chained borders, H19⅛, L19c (649/186)	1900
Vases, pair, white ovoid body, snake handles, 25½, now lamps, L19c (4219/52)	1000
Vases, pair, flower encrusted, slender body, applied blooms and fruits, H9¼, L19c, mtd as lamps (649/182)	175
Vases, pair, Pate Sur Pate, blue ground, in white with a nymph bearing flowers, 13½, ca1880 (669/131)	4250
Vases and covers, pair, applied fruits, flowers, 2 putti, H11½, L19c, dam (649/184)	450
Vintager, barefooted boy, basket of grapes on his back, 4¾, L19c, minor chip (669/135)	275
Vintager, figure, lady holding grapes in apron, 6½, L19c (669/170)	400
Violinist, man dressed in pink jacket, 4½, L19c (669/154)	200

War, group, two putti, banging drum, trying on helmet, 5¼, L19c, dam. (669/148) — 425
Winter group, 2 peasant children sitting on a sleigh, 5½, res, L19c (649/242) — 550
Woman figure, elegantly clad holding feather muff, 8, L19c (619/108) — 500
Young barefooted boy, peasant costume, posy in right hand, 4½, L19c, minor chip (669/137) — 325
Young boy, peasant costume, grapes in his hat, 4¾, L19c, minor chip (669/136) — 275
Young boy playing bagpipes, wearing rustic clothes, 4½, L19c, minor dam. (669/174) — 200
Young gallant and companion, 6¼, 6½, L19c, minor chip (669/164) — 700
Young girl, on rocky base with basket of flowers, 4½, L19c, minor chip (669/150) — 325
Young girl, plumed bonnet, holding toy dog, 6,L19c, chip and cracked (669/142) — 450
Young girl holding a violin, seated, 4¾, L19c, bow missing (669/175) — 300
Young god, wearing purple drape, 5, 1910, minor chip (669/151) — 225
Young lady, yellow bodice and floral painted skirt, flowers, 5, L19c, minor chip (669/141) — 300
Young lady looking into mirror, seated, 5½, L19c, minor chip (669/145) — 525
Youth, classical, carrying deer, H7½, L19c (649/228) — 250
3 children, gilt-winged cupid, gesturing, 5⅞, wing missing, ca1750 (4262/202) — 1200

Stein
(669/62)

Teapot and cover
(4221/142)

Stein
(669/61)

Stein
(669/63)

Teabowl Hausmaler (4221/134)

Meissen crinoline

Group, lovers, ca1746 4½ imp (4221/184) — 2200
Group, the kiss, ca1740-45 7⅞ cr (4221/181) — 8500
Group, the Spanish lovers, ca1741 7⅛ (4221/179) — 15500

Meissen, early

Teabowl Hausmaler, figures preparing tea-smoking pipes, ca1725 3 fine (4221/134) — *1200*
Teapot and cover, figures, buildings in a river landscape, ca1725-30 5 chip cover (4221/142) — *3200*

Meissen, Kaendler, J.

Crinoline group mounted as clock, Louis XV ormolu, superb, H17⅞, M18c (4086/51) — 42500
Potpourri group, ormolu, and Chinese Batavian ware, pheasants, H10, ca1750 (4086/53) — 10500

Mettlach

Plaques, pair, lovers by castle, figures in white relief on aquamarine ground, H15¾, W8, 1902 (649/140) — 1800
Plate, glazed stoneware, castle on rocky cliff, D17¼, 1907 (649/137) — 600
Plates, pair, a bearded man and his companion, 16½, ca1910 (669/69) — 725
Stein, youth pointing to a cautionary inscription, 9, ca1910 (669/60) — 600
Stein, a portrait of George Ehret, inscriptions, 7, ca1910, cover and mounts missing (669/65) — 175
Stein, cream and blue, inscription, 6¾, ca1910, glaze chip (669/64) — 175
Stein, gentleman at club, wife at home with broom, 7, ca1910 (669/63) — 360
Stein, huntsman amongst boars and hounds, cover with American Eagle, 7¼, ca1910 (669/61) — 400
Stein, students carousing, 8¼, ca1910 (669/62) — 300

Tankard
(631/167)

Stein, George Ehret within hops and inscriptions, 8¾, ca1910 (669/58)   325
Stein, St. Florian pouring beer on raging fire, 9¼, ca1910 (669/59)   550
Stein, knights raising their glasses, 16, ca1910 (669/66)   700
Stein, glazed stoneware, alpine scenes, pewter lid, eagle thumbpiece, H8¼, 1902 (649/138)   450
Stein, half litre black forest, molded pottery top, 9, 1903 (631/125)   950
Stein, pewter mounted, etched, drinking scene inside castle, 8, 1903 (669/68)   600
Stein, pewter mounted, several German officers, woman and peasant girl, 8, 1908 (669/67)   250
Stein, Siegfried, etched, mounts and apostle thumbpiece of pewter, life of Siegfried, 9 (631/123)   400
Vase, earthenware, rare and large, high relief with a winged maiden and flowering vines, 26, 1893
(631/129)   1100

Nuremberg

Jug, spiralling molded, pewter mounted, Hafner, 8¼, chips, E18c (4132/189)   325

Nymphenburg

Bust of Summer, allegorical, young woman's head turned right, 5¾, rep, ca1760 (4262/143)   1200
Coffee cups, miniature, set of 6, chintz pattern, ca1765-80, 1⅛, rare (4190/76)   400
Figure, seated mastiff, ca1760 4⅛ dam (4221/91)   2300
Figure, Chinaman with teacup, (4221/89)   11500
Figure, Chinese lady with pineapples, 1785 4⅜ rep (4221/90)   7000
Figure, Putto as Neptune holding blue dolphin, ca1766 4 part miss (4221/93)   2100
Group of the Impetuous Lover, modelled by Franz Anton Bustelli, H5½, imp, rep, c1756 (4085/60)   7000
Medallion, biscuit, portrait, by Johann Peter Melchior, ca1810, 5⅜ (4123/326)   250
Plate, rim molded with ornithological vignettes, D9¼, ca1765 (4085/63)   1100
Plates, set of three, cluster of fruit, scalloped rims, D9⅜, ca1760 (4085/62)   475
Saucer, puce, iron-red, yellow, blue and green bouquet, 5, ca1770 (4262/145)   200
Tankard, silver mounted, ca1765-70 6½ (4221/87)   1800
Tea and coffee service, part, 13 pcs, gold urns and scrollwork, ca1815, rep (4190/77)   3400
Tea and coffee service, part, 24 pcs, chintz pattern, ca1780-1810 (4190/75)   2500
Tureen, cover, stand, circular figure, building, river landscape, ca1760-65, 11⅝ - 15⅛, imp (4221/88)   5500

Schlaggenwald

Tete-a-tete, ovoid form, ground sprinkled with gilding, 7 pc, cover missing, 1823 (4262/162)   75

Schrezheim faience

Jug, central flower-filled basket, pewter mounted, 8⅛, L18c (4132/206)   300
Tankard, a melon, a gourd, flowers, pewter mounted, 9⅛, imp, L18c (4132/209)   500
Tankard, pewter mounted, cluster of a melon, gourd and flowers, 9, L18c (4262/65)   375
Tankard, spray of flowers, pewter mounted, 9½, hc, ca1760 (4132/208)   425
Tankard, stylized flowers, pewter mounted, 9½, ca1775 (4132/207)   750

South German faience

Figure, dog with yellow collar, 7¼, chips, L18c (4132/210)   700
Figures, pair of lions, shaded yellow coats, 3⅝, 18c (4132/211)   500

Jug, speckled manganese glaze, pewter mounted, 8⅛, 18c (4132/204)   375
Tankard, blue with a large residence, pewter mounted, 8¼, hc, 18c (4132/205)   700

Thuringian

Tea Caddy, arched rectangular body, ca1780 (4262/158)   800

Volkstedt

Figure, a gallant, ca1770-75, 7, restored (4221/125)   300
Group, a gardener and companion, ca1770-75, 8⅝, chip, rare (4221/126)   1800

Wallendorf

Dish, oval, bear in landscape setting, 6, chip, ca1775 (4132/325)   325
Figures, pair, one representing Mars, the other, the Sun, res, rare, ca1770 (4085/72)   1600
Salt cellar, floral, high domed foot, 3⅜, ca1765 (4132/324)   225

Wegely

'Lisette et le Petit Berger', young girl seated by a tree, companion, 9¾, 1755-77, Berlin (4262/159)   1600

ITALIAN CERAMICS

Assorted periods and manufacturers

Bottles, pair, enamelled glass, rectangular form, cold in colorful tones, 12½, L18c (4133/67)   375
Charger, large, with an assembly of the gods on Mt. Olympus, majolica, 20½, 19c (631/172)   200
Coffee service, part, 22 pcs, views of Italy, Le Nove, res, L18c-E19c (4132/255)   320
Figure, modelled as Apollo, white biscuit, L18c, 11¼, imp (4190/53)   1000
Figure, winter allegorical, Naples, ca1771-80 5½ rare (4221/216)   900
Figures pair, summer and autumm allegorical, Buen Retiro, ca1765-71 6⅜ (4221/217)   800
Group allegorical, four peasants possibly representing autumn, L18c, 12⅝, chip (4190/130)   150
Jar, drug, castel durante majolica, tones, yellow, blue and ochre, 13⅜, ca1580 (4133/73)   1700
Jar, drug, wet, ovoid body, long spout, entwined rope handle, 9, 17c (4133/74)   250
Jar, wet drug, blue scrolling foliage, inscription, 8¼, 1590-95, rep (4133/77)   900
Plate, painted with a sybil after Raphael Fresco, 9½, 1872 (631/169)   125
Teabowl, vignettes - flowerheads, Vezzi Venice, ca1725 3¼ fine (4221/212)   1100
Urn, cover and stand, Viennese, gilded with grapes, vines and 3 women, 24, L19c, Wagner (631/173)   2750
Vase, Urbino majolica, three tall grotesque handles, 3 musicians, 12½, L16, E17c, repaired (4133/76)   950

Capo-Di-Monte

Figure, biscuit, of pulcinella, 5⅛, ca1750 (4132/251)   600
Group figural, two nymphs, clothed in gilt drapery, oval base, 12½, L19c (619/85)   200
Group, 2 putti, on rock base, basket of flowers, H19¼, ca1900 (649/99)   300
Plaque, oval, high relief, mythological scene, H17, L19c (649/100)   350
Plate, service, set of twelve, mythological scenes, 10½, L19c (619/87)   500
Saucer, center w lady, ca1750 5¼ fine (4221/213)   2300
Tankard, frieze of Venus, Cupid and Nymphs, caryatid handle, 18, L19c (631/167)   *650*
Vases, bud, pair, high relief with mythological figures, 9, L19c (669/78)   125

Castelli

Plaque, oval, ochre, blue, green and brown, woman on horseback, 9⅜, E18c (4262/3)   1000
Plate, majolica, woman wearing blue and ochre dress, sleeping, 6⅞, E18c (4262/2)   350
Plates, pair, majolica, multi-colors, sunset view of figures, landscape, 9⅛, M18c (4262/1)   2500

Castelli faience

Plaque, St. Ursula, 10 x 13⅛, ca1760-90 (4132/184)   1200

Cozzi Venice

Figure, white, dwarf modelled as lady, ca1775 2⅝ (4221/23)   700
Figures, white, pair, boy and girl, ca1775 4 - 4¼, chip, rare (4221/211)   1600

Doccia

Cup and a saucer, quatrefoil, medallion, lady with muscial instrument, ca1770-80 5¼ (4221/214)   300
Ecuelle and cover, painted with peasants, ca1780 7⅛ covered riveted (4190/51)   225
Figure, oriental woman, ca1765 5¾ fine (4221/215)   1400
Snuff box and cover, shell form, ca1755 3⅛ imp (4221/25)   1000
Teacup and saucer, 2 figures in a landscape, 1770-80 (4262/106)   325

Basket of flowers
(4190/39)

MISCELLANEOUS CERAMICS

Assorted periods and manufacturers

Basket, reticulated, circular, grapevines and leaves, Baranowka, ca1825-40, 10, hc (4221/204)   600
Basket of flowers, openwork basket, twig handles, Copenhagen, ca1790 9¾ chip (4190/39)   *1200*
Bonbonniere and cover, pug's head, Copenhagen*, ca1795 2¾ (4190/38)   950
Box and cover, modeled to resemble asparagus, dark green, Sceaux faience, 7⅞, rep, ca1775 (4132/177)   600
Bust, of Spring, earthenware, Hautin & Boulenger, choisy-le-roy, H30¼, after Belleuse (649/101)   650
Bust, white, of gentleman, rare, Tournai, 6½, L18c (4132/249)   650
Cane Handle, form of a Turk, ca1765-70 3¾ (4221/21)   200
Centerpiece, lovers in 18c costume, seated in a wooden glade, 12¼, L19c, Vienna (619/146)   325
Coffee service, part, painted with peasant figures, 1810-20, 29 pcs (4262/109)   750
Cup and saucer, two rectangular panels with tool gilt decoration, 19c, Vienna (619/147)   325
Figure, girl playing hurdy-gurdy, faience, L18c, 7¼, chip (4190/129)   30
Figurines, pair, porcelain, couple in eighteenth century costume, 11, L19c (619/79)   175
Glass, wine, engraved, coat of arms, 6 pointed star, cipher, D.E. India Trading Co., 6¾, Dutch (4133/65)   400
Goblet and cover, armorial, engraved with coat of arms, 7 provinces of Holland, 11, 18c, Dutch (4133/64)   350
Group of hound and puppy, Blanc de Chine, painted by Ignaz Preissler, H6¼, rare, rep, c1730 (4085/49)   2600
Monkey, as artist, brown shaded monkey holding palette, 7¾, chip, ca1835 (4262/108)   450
Panel, stained glass, armorial, coat of arms, stag, deer and a motto, 25¼ x 16, 17c, Dutch (4133/63)   125
Panels, pair, polychrome tile square, geometric patterns, blue and green, 12¾, E16c, framed, Spanish (4133/72)   275
Plaque, Chariot of the Sun, drawn over coastal landscape, 17, L19c, framed, oval, Vienna (619/142)   1100
Plaque, Discovery of Moses, oval, 16¾, L19c (619/145)   1500
Plaque, Family of Bacchantes, disporting themselves, 10 x 12, L19c, framed, Vienna (619/144)   2750
Plaque, Mandolin Player, circular, half portrait of young woman playing mandolin, 19¾, E20c, Vienna (619/139)   1600
Plaque, Schner, circular, family scene, pink ground, D18½, L19c, Austrian* (649/89)   1500
Plaque, Three Heroic Figures In a Landscape, Circular, 14½, L19c (619/140)   850
Plaque, Ullysses Discovering Achilles, in women's quarters, 15, L19c, circular, Vienna (619/141)   800
Plaque, Venus Blindfolding Cupid, Diana watching, 10¼ x 12½, L19c, framed, Vienna (619/143)   2750
Plaques, circular, pair, landscape scenes, 7¾, fine, ca1830 (4132/256)   1000
Plate, brown glaze, tree, 2 stags, Swiss slipware, E19c, 8¾, chip (4190/123)   500
Plate, Biblical scene, gilt and maroon border, 9¼, L19c, Vienna (619/151)   350
Plate, large, blue and white, oriental trees and flowers, Dutch, D14, E18c (4156/5)   375
Plate, wall, earthenware, Montereau, signed L. Malpass, Japanese girl, D20, ca1880 (649/94)   550
Scent bottle gold mounted, fox and bird, 2⅝ (4221/19)   400
Solitaire, 6 pcs, battle scenes of infantry, cavalry soldiers, Korzec, c1790-97 (4190/49)   5600
Tureen and cover, soup, flowers in blue-feathered rim, Pesaro faience, 15½, res, ca1763-65 (4132/183)   425
Urn, covered, figures, building, river landscape, Talauera, M18c, 14¼, hc, rare (4190/127)   600

Urn, covered, two classical scenes, cobalt blue ground, 27, ca1900, Vienna (619/153) 1400
Urns, 2 handled, classical, pair, white, bisque, now table lamps, 18 (619/84) 325
Vases, covered, landscape scene, Amstel, 10½, ca1785-95 (4132/250) 850

Brussels

Tureen, chicken, and attached stand, covered, faience, hen seated, 6 chicks, 2 eggs, 15, E19c (4262/38) *600*

Continental faience

Box and cover, formed as a bunch of grapes, 7, 18c (4132/187) 225

Delft

Bowl, punch, polychrome, flower filled vases, Dutch, diameter 11¾, 18c (4148/62) 650
Cats, pair, polychrome, sponged yellow coats, blue eyes, Dutch, 3⅝, chip, 18c (4262/43) 850
Dish, 'Queen Mary', bust-length portrait of Queen, 2 tulips, Dutch, D8¾, L18c (4156/10) 325
Jars, covered, pair, Dutch, blue and white, ribbed, ovoid, floral sprays, 16½, repaired, M18c (4211/980) 2000
Plate, blue and white 'Peacock' pattern, cobalt blue, Dutch, 9, 1702-19 (4262/54) 250
Plate, large, central flowerhead, blue flowers, leaves, Dutch, D12, M18c (4156/9) 500
Plate, large, blue and white, peacock pattern, bowl of blossoms, Dutch, 12⅝, ca1730 (4156/6) 400
Plate, polychrome, Chinaman in a sampan, Dutch, 8¾, 1691-1721 (4262/57) 1300
Plate, polychrome, 2 oriental vases, Dutch, 9, 18c (4262/56) 300
Plate, polychrome, 'Peacock' pattern, vase of flowers, Dutch, 7⅜, ca1691 (4262/48) 450

Tureen (4262/38)

Plates, pair, polychrome, 'Peacock' pattern, vase of flowers, Dutch, 7⅜, ca1691 (4262/47) 1600
Plates, set of four, blue and white, 'Peacock' pattern, cobalt blue, Dutch, 9, 1734-64 (4262/50) 1000
Plates, set of four, blue and white, 'Peacock' pattern, cobalt blue, Dutch, 9, 1 cracked, 1731-60 (4262/51) 900
Slippers, pair, polychrome, yellow heels, Dutch, 5⅜, M18c (4262/44) 425
Trencher, salt, rare, polychrome, floral sprays, Dutch, L3⅜, 18c (4156/4) 250
Vase and cover, blue and white, house, fisherman, landscape, Dutch, 13¾, 1763-77 (4262/46) 225

Delft, Dutch

Box and cover, polychrome cauliflower pattern, 6¼, 18c (4132/176) 1700
Jug, blue-white peacock on rockwork, 8, 18c (4132/170) 450
Jug, silver mounted, blue-white bird and shrubbery, 9⅛, 18c (4132/171) 325
Mantel garniture, 5 pieces, blue and white floral bouquets, H12¼, 10⅛, ca1775 (4190/115) *800*
Pilgrim bottles, pair, rare, blue and white, with flowers and foliage, 15¼, rep, chips, ca1687-1701 (4132/169) 4000
Plaque, blue-white, biblical, Abraham sending Hagar awy, M17c, 13⅞ - 19⅞, rare (4190/112) 9000
Plate, large, 'Peacock' pattern blue-white, M18c, 12⅜ (4190/117) 400
Plate, polychrome, iron-red and ochre bird, 13⅝, E18c (4132/172) 700

Plates, blue and white, assembled pair, 'Peacock' pattern, D10½, 10¾, M18c (4190/116)   700
Plates, blue and white, set of 10, scenes of herring fishing, 9, ca1775, chip in one (4190/114)   7500
Plates, pair, polychrome, 8¾, 18c (4132/175)   750
Saucer, peacock pattern, polychrome, 6¼, ca1706 (4132/174)   400
Tile picture, set of twelve, manganese, vase of flowers, 20¼ x 15, 1 cr, framed, L18c (4132/164)   450
Tureens, covers and stands, pair, rare melon shape, yellow fruit, rare, ca1759-1803 (4132/168)   9500

Doccia

Ice cups, set of 4, fruit - flowers, 3⅜, chips, ca1760 (4132/253)   325
Ice cups, set of 4, fruit - flowers, 3⅜, ca1760 (4132/252)   350

Friesland

Tiles, set of six, delft, blue and white, each spider's head corners, genre scene, 5⅛, L17-E18c
(4262/40)   300

'Girl-in-a-Swing'

Bonbonniere, Venus and Cupid, gold mounted, ca1751-54 2 repaired (4221/72)   650
Bonbonniere, gold mounted, Putti and goat, ca1751-54, 1½, fine (4221/69)   1600

'Girl-in-a-Swing' type

Scent bottle, basket of flowers, gold mounted, ca1755-60 2⅛ (4221/61)   3800
Scent bottle and stopper, shepherd boy, ca1755-60, 3¾, stopper rep (4221/43)   3000
Scent bottle and stopper (replaced), Cupid and urn, ca1755-60 3⅛ (4221/48)   800
Scent bottle and stopper, Harlequin and Columbine, ca1755-60 3¾ chip (4221/41)   3500
Scent bottle and stopper, Dalmatian, ca1755-60 2⅞ chip (4221/55)   2000
Scent bottle and stopper, lovers, gold mounted, ca1755-60 4 chip (4221/42)   2800
Scent bottle and stopper, Putti and fountain, ca1755-60 3¾ imp (4221/38)   2500
Scent bottle and stoppers, double, billing doves gold mounted, ca1751-54, 2½, large chip
(4221/45)   175
Scent bottle stopper, Harlequin, gold mounted, ca1751-54 3⅜ (4221/40)   2200
Seal, gold mounted, modelled as young lady, ca1756, 1½, fine (4221/67)   650
Seal, gold mounted, modelled as lady, ca1756 1⅜ (4221/68)   550

Hispano

Dish, Hispano moresque, copper lustre, flowers, D16½, riveted, L16c (4081/30)   200
Dish, Hispano moresque, copper-gold lustre, Aragon, D13¼, rep, 16c (4081/37)   100
Dish, Hispano moresque, copper-gold lustre, Aragon, D15¾, 16c (4081/32)   150
Dish, Hispano moresque, copper-gold lustre, Aragon, D13½, 16c (4081/31)   325

Luxembourg

Plates, set of four, faience, blue and white, scattered floral sprigs, 9½, L18c (4262/37)   175
Platters, pair oval, faience, blue and white, scattered floral sprigs, 11⅞, L18c (4262/36)   150

Mennecy

Bonbonniere and cover, modelled drapery enclosed snare drum, ca1750 1/58 (4221/28)   950
Figure, hearing, allegorical, M18c 6⅛ dam (4221/219)   250
Group, two children, M18c 6¾ minor imp (4221/218)   800
Sabot Bonbonniere and cover, modelled as buckled shoe, ca1740 3⅜ (4221/26)   850

Royal Copenhagen

Coffee cups and saucers, 'Flora Danica', painted with different flowers, modern, set of 12
(4262/115)   1700
Dessert plates, set of 12, 'Flora Danica', each with different flower, 8¾, modern (4262/114)   1900
Dish, leaf, 'Flora Danica', painted with a botanical flower, 8¾, modern (4262/113)   275
Dish, leaf, 'Flora Danica', painted with a botanical flower, 9¾, modern (4262/112)   225
Plates, set of four, 'Flora Danica', painted with different flowers, 8¾, modern (4262/116)   550
Pots-de-creme, covers and stands, pair, 'Flora Danica', botanical flowers, modern (4262/117)   400
Tazze, pair, 'Flora Danica', each with different flower, 4⅞, modern (4262/111)   500

Sorgenthal Vienna

Cup and saucer, coffee, flowers and leaves, ca1805 (4190/44)   375
Cup and saucer, coffee, laurel swag on white scalloped band, ca1805 (4190/45)   375
Cup and saucer, coffee, painted with puce and green motifs, gilt panels, ca1805 (4190/43)   375

Vienna

Centerpiece, quatrefoil tray flowers, 15¾, ca1750-60 (4132/261)   300
Coffee cup and saucer, apricot ground, gilt edged panel, brown bird, yellow cage, colorful flowers,
1823 (4262/132)   600

Coffee cup and saucer, purple ground, flaming urn and grape motifs, gold ground panel, yellow wheat, 1819 (4262/130) 450
Dinner service, floral sprays within green borders, 103 pcs, 1817 (649/159) 2200
Figure, Bacchus with yellow and purple drapery, 9¼, imp, ca1765 (4132/258) *200*

Figure
(4132/258)

Group
(4132/259)

Mantel garniture (4190/115)

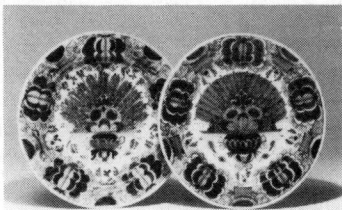

Plates (4190/116)

Figure of a recumbent cow, white body, russet and grey, L4, rare, rep, c1750 (4085/50) 1700
Figure of girl, ca1760 8 rep (4190/40) 400
Figure of shepherd boy, ca1765 5½ rep (4190/42) 225
Figure of Vintner's boy, c1765 6¼ (4190/41) 450
Figures, pair, putti as young boys on scroll bases, 3¾, 3⅜, ca1750 (4132/257) 75
Gardener, wearing black hat, standing against a stump, 8¼, ca1840 (4262/119) 850
Girl harvester, wearing a blue bodice, white blouse and coral skirt, 4⅞, imp, ca1760 (4262/120) 150
Group, putti at a forge, 8½, chips, ca1765-85 (4132/259) *300*
Group of a gallant and companion, gentleman, puce jacket, yellow skirt, baby, H8¼, imp, 1755-60 (4085/51) 1300
Lady with a birdcage, wearing a puce green hat, gilt edged bodice, white apron, 7¼, ca1770 (4262/118) 1200
Plaque, man in grey coat and black hat, ca1760-70 6¾ x 9¾ fine rare (4221/206) 1500
Plaque, circular, jeweled, 'Triumphant Lovers', tooled gilt surround and maroon ground, 14, L19c (649/146) 1300
Plate, center seated nymph punishing the sleeping Cupid, 9¾, 1806 (4262/134) 900
Plate, center, 3 of Diana's nymphs, 9¾, 1806 (4262/135) 850
Plate, painted with Mary Magdalene, 9⅝, dated 1822 (4132/265) 600
Plate, botanical, Sorgenthal, deep brown ground, rose, purple, yellow green, flowers, 9¼, 1805 (4262/133) 250
Plate, by C.M. Hutschreuther, young gypsy maiden, ruby red ground, 9½, 1910 (649/142) 850
Plate, octagonal, by C. Herr, Dido seated in a temple with ladies in attendance, 13½, L19c (649/145) 1200
Plate, octagonal, by C. Herr, 4 graces in a landscape, 13½, L19c (649/144) 950
Plate, wall, large, scene of the death of Tristan and Isolde grieving, 18, ca1900 (649/147) 1300
Plates, pair, brown edged, sprigs of flowers, puce, green, red and yellow, 9½, ca1765 (4262/123) 375
Tea caddies, pair, flowers, sprigs, ca1770 4⅝ (4221/205) 205
Vase, enameled, mythological panels within foliate scrolls, 13¼, ca1900 (649/303) 5000
Vases, pair, 1 with young, other with maiden, pale green ground, 9½, ca1910 (649/148) 550
Vases, pair, enamel, basket form on slender knopped stem, panels of lovers in garden, 10½, chip, ca1905 (649/302) 4250

Zsolnay

Bowl, iridescent pottery, shallow, short circular foot, Diam 6½, L19c (4159/97) 350

Zurich

Figure, a shepherdess, blue-brimmed yellow straw hat, ca1767 7¼ (4221/210)   3200
Figure, the builder, young man with sledge hammer, ca1770 6½ (4221/209)   3500
Figure, the painter, young woman holding pallette, ca1770 6⅜ (4221/208)   8000
Figure, miniature, tradesman, modelled by Josef Nees, c1770, 3⅜, imp (4221/1)   1050

Glass

ENGLISH GLASS

Assorted periods and manufacturers

Compotes, covered, cut, knopped finial, faceted, hexagonal base, 11¼, 19c (4159/101)   250
Decanters, pair, cut glass and engraved, bell formed, disc stoppers, 10½, L18c (4216/41)   650

Regency

Decanters, pair, cut glass, ovoid form with stoppers, 9½ 1 stopper replaced E19c (4152/54)   200

Stevens and Williams

Bowl, engraved, Rock Crystal oval, scrolling foliage, bats, Chinese figures, 8½, ca1884 (649/248)   400

FRENCH GLASS

Vase, ormolu and cut glass, ovoid, ormolu neck, swan handles, 13, L19c (4142/38)   275

GERMAN GLASS

Bowl, cut glass, gilt bronze mounted, resting on 4 Egyptian figures, pedestal base, (631/222)   550
Lusters, pair, Bohemian enameled, overlay, pale ruby ground, painted floral sprays, L19c (649/249)   600
Table service, engraved 84 pcs, Bohemian clear glass, wild animals and birds, L19c, some minor
  chip (669/229)   3750
Table service, engraved, 191 pcs, Bohemian amber flashed, animals in woodland, setting, L19c
  (669/231)   5000
Vase and cover, Bohemian enameled, gilt green glass, chalice form, 17, L19c (649/250)   1000

ITALIAN GLASS

Table service, Venetian enamelled, gilt rims, painted polychrome foliage, ca1900, 152 pcs (669/232)   2750

MISCELLANEOUS GLASS

Candlesticks, pair, baccarat amberina, glass, 2 tier stems, hurricane shades, etched, 29¾, E20c
  (631/225)   750
Table service, engraved, armorial glass, light vaseline colour, ca1900, minor chip, 56 pcs (669/230)   750
Wine glasses, set of 12, ruby overlay, cut with star motifs between fruiting vines, 8¼, E20c
  (649/252)   400

Chapter 4
European Silver

The market for silver items produced in England and Europe between 1600 and approximately 1850, the period reviewed in this chapter, was less affected by the sharp increase in the price of silver bullion recently than might have been expected. The new collectors who entered the market in the search for alternate investments brought an overall strengthening of price levels, if few sensational advances. Apparently silver's rise in value had been anticipated in the slow but steady price increases of the past few years.

No area of English silver has fallen recently, with the possible exception of the work of Hester Bateman, whose reputation may have been overinflated in comparison to her male contemporaries; recently, five lots of her work failed to find buyers at prices comparable to previous levels.

A good deal of collector interest focused on Paul Storr, regarded as England's finest silvermaker of the Regency Period. Reflecting a shift in attention from the late eighteenth century to the more ornate early nineteenth, prices for his work soared.

The rise in prices has extended, though not to the same degree, to work by other English silversmiths such as Digby Scott, Benjamin Smith, Philip Rundell and John Rundell. Their work is often equal to that of Storr, and frequently they executed the same designs for the Royal Goldsmiths Rundell, Bridge and Rundell.

The Victorian period also climbed in value as collectors explored its variety and inventiveness. Function is often subordinated to fantasy or whim in these pieces, whether the silver is massive and intended for display or small enough for the pocket. Interest in the period is so high that a Victorian teakettle can sell for the same price as a Georgian one.

Prices of German silver kept pace with the general rise, but in the field of Continental silver it has been the Dutch market which has proved remarkable, its astonishing prices holding for items which were not of the highest quality and, on occasion, were in less than perfect condition. Today, Dutch silver may be considered the most expensive of all the European silver, exclusive of the finest French examples.

Still, prices for silver from other countries all showed increases, and a minor surprise was the interest in Mexican products, previously regarded as largely derivative of European styles.

In contrast to the high prices paid for pieces fashioned by seventeenth-, eighteenth- and early-nineteenth-century craftsmen, hundreds of silver objects produced in the late nineteenth and early twentieth centuries sold for considerably less; here, prices fluctuated between the hundreds, not thousands, of dollars. Flatware, tea services and candelabra sold for multiples as low as twenty and twenty-five times the number of ounces they weighed. As the bullion price of silver increases, these pieces must surely gain in value. And it's here, in relatively modern silver, particularly with those pieces that have distinctive design features, that opportunities will continue to exist for the investor and the collector.

Note: See Chapter 6 for review of silver of the Victorian era, together with that of the Art Nouveau and Art Deco periods.

Argyle
(4238/232)

Basket (4259/296)

Basket (4194/223)

Basket (4259/154)

ENGLISH SILVER

Assorted periods and manufacturers

Argyle, loose cover, beaded border, 4¾, 1777, 14 ozs gross (4238/232)	*$800*
Argyle, Sheffield plated, cylindrical, ball finial, 4½, ca1790 (4159/49)	375
Argyle, Sheffield plated, vase shape, domed cover, urn finial, 8½, ca1790 (4194/8)	260
Basket, cake, Benjamin Smith II, oblong, George III, 12¼, 42 ozs, 1817 (4259/296)	*1700*
Basket, cake, George III, Robert Makepeace, 17 ozs, 15 dwts, L12¼, 1776 (4194/223)	550
Basket, cake, George III, Henry Chawner, boat shape, reeded rim, 15¼, 24 ozs, 1788 (4259/154)	*1200*
Basket, cake, George III, Smith, Tate & Co., circular, ribbed sides, 10½, 28 ozs, 1814 (4260/514)	1600
Basket, cake, Sheffield plated, boat shape, sides pierced, 13⅛, ca1780 (4259/7)	250
Basket, cake, Sheffield plated, boat shape, wirework side, 13½, ca1800 (4259/6)	100
Basket, sugar, boat shape, pedestal foot, reeded rim, 6⅜, 1794, 9 ozs (4238/238)	325
Basket, sugar, fluted boat shape, reeded rim, swing handle, 5½, 1795, 6 ozs, 10 dwts (4160/254)	300
Basket, sugar, vase shape, pierced sides, Hester Bateman, 5¾, 1778, 6 ozs (4160/278)	800
Basket, sugar, vase shape, with trelliswork and scrolls, 8, 1775, 7 ozs 15 dwts (4238/203)	300
Basket, sweetmeat, oval boat shape, pierced with scrolls, swing handle, 6¾, 1786, 8 ozs (4238/270)	475
Basket, sweetmeat, George III, H. Bateman, oval, swing handle, 6⅝, 5 ozs, 1785 (4260/536)	1000
Basket, sweetmeat, George III, Mark S.B., oval, 6¼, 3 ozs, 1770 (4259/222)	300
Basket, sweetmeat, Wakelin & Garrard, boat shaped, George III, 4⅞, 40 ozs, 1795 (4159/2)	275
Basket, George III, rectangular, gadroon rim, 28 ozs, 10 dwts, L12½, 1808 (4194/167)	600
Basket, George III, sugar, Hester Bateman, swing handle, 3 ozs, 10 dwts, 5¾, 1783 (4194/189)	550
Basket, Sheffield plated cake, boat shape, swing handle, L12¾, ca1800 (4194/3)	120
Beaker, George III, cylindrical, gilt interior, 4 ozs, 15 dwts, 3⅛, 1802 (4194/170)	150
Beaker, George III, cylindrical, initial 'S', 3 ozs, 3⅜, 1789 (4194/230)	225
Beakers, pair, George III, Charles Wright, tapered cylindrical, gilt interior, 3½, 11 ozs, 1778 (4260/541)	2100
Beakers, pair, George III, Mark W.B., cylindrical, with crests, 3⅝, 7 ozs, 1784 (4259/238)	700
Bow, monteith, fluted body, scrolled, loose ring lion mark handles, 12, 1878, 85 ozs (669/339)	2250
Bowl, fluted hemispherical form, engraved crest, scalloped rim, 6½, 1737, 11 ozs (4160/299)	900
Bowl, covered, partly lobed, 4 slender paw supports, 7¼,E19c, 24 ozs, Indian* (4160/204)	150
Bowl, sugar, Irish, beaded, everted rim chased with rustic scenes, 5⅛, 1770, 5 ozs 10 dwts (4238/286)	375
Bowl, George II, Irish, William Townsend, hemispherical shape, 6⅛, 8 ozs, ca1750 (4260/552)	450
Bowl, George III, Irish, sugar, James LeBass, rectangular, 19 ozs, 10 dwts, L8¼, 1819 (4194/208)	325
Bowl, Monteith, Victorian, Queen Anne style, lion masks, ring handles, 11¾, 1874, 77 ozs (4238/174)	2300
Bowl, 2 handled, George IV, Paul Storr, vertically fluted, 10⅜, 73 ozs, 1818 (4259/269)	10500
Bowl and cover, George II, sugar, Thomas Whipham, 10 ozs, 15 dwts, 4¼, 1745 (4194/283)	2000
Box, snuff, engraved with bands of flowers and husks, 2, 1811, small (4238/211)	175
Box, cigar, Birmingham, rectangular, hinged cover, 11⅛, 1918 (4260/492)	600
Box, cigar, Edwardian, Goldsmiths & Silversmiths, rectangular, cedar-lining, 11¾, 1903 (4260/491)	600
Box, cigar, Edwardian, William Comyns, rectangular, cedar-lined, 8⅛, 1912 (4260/490)	450
Box, cigarette, Victorian marked W.G., J.L., rectangular, gilt interior, cedar-lined, 7, 1892 (4260/495)	175
Box, covered, oval, shallow body, chased and engraved with panels, foliage, 8, 1917, 26 ozs (669/340)	400
Box, shell form, silver-gilt, box mounted on rock and shell form base, 6¼, 1890, 17½ ozs. (631/175)	475
Box, sponge, silver-gilt, engraved with crest and motto, domed hinged cover, 3¾, 1720, 11·ozs, 10 dwts (4160/418)	950
Box, tobacco, oval form, engraved with armorials and crest, 4, 1797, 9 ozs (4238/236)	1800
Boxes, pair, George IV, Joseph Willmore, rectangular, slip on covers, 4, 13 ozs, 1820 (4260/513)	425
Bread basket, George III, Hester Bateman, boat shape, cutout handles, 13¾, 18 ozs, 1790 (4259/268)	2800
Butter shells, pair, fluted shells, George II, 2¾, 4 ozs, 1756 (4259/266)	300
Cake basket, oval openwork, scrolling, foliate and shellwork rim, 14½, 1775, 36 ozs, 5 dwts (4160/414)	1500
Cake basket, George II, S. Herbert & Co., oval, latticework panels, 14⅜, 48 ozs, 1755 (4260/548)	4300
Cake slice, blade pierced with bird and snake crest, 1776, Irish, 3 ozs, 10 dwts (4160/377)	325
Candelabra, 3 light, pair, Sheffield plated, Matthew Boulton Co., detachable nozzles, 22¾, ca1815 (4259/17)	1600
Candelabra, 3 light, pair, vase shape, engraved with armorials, 22¼, 1810, 36 ozs, 1 dwt (4160/268)	3000
Candelabra, 3 light, pair, on stepped bases, with repoussé work, 13, weighted (619/168)	200
Candelabra, 3 light, pair, Victorian, 2 branches and central light, 24½, 1888 (4238/161)	1600
Candelabra, 3 light, table, with masks, classical profiles, 13½, modern, 97 ozs (4160/231)	1700
Candelabrum, 5 light, Sheffield plated, Matthew Boulton Co., curved branches, 33, ca1815 (4259/18)	1200

Candlestick, chamber, circular pan, 5½, 1770, 7 ozs 10 dwts (4238/228) — 325

Candlestick, chamber, George III, vase shaped scone, R. Cooke, 4¾, 6 ozs, 1801 (4259/264) — 400

Candlestick, George III, chamber, Jonathan Alleine, 2 crests, 7 ozs, 10 dwts, Diam 15, 1780 (4194/211) — 350

Candlestick, Sheffield plated chamber, Matthew Boulton Co., Diam 4¼, ca1810 (4194/2) — 220

Candlesticks, pair, fluted tulip shaped sconces, 11¼, 1784 (4238/220) — 550

Candlesticks, set of 4, George III, John Roberts & Co., Sheffield plated, 12¾, weighted, 1809 (4259/180) — 2250

Candlesticks, set of 4, Sheffield plated, circular bases, vase shaped stem, 11¼, ca1805 (4259/9) — 425

Candlesticks, set of 6, Sheffield plated, Matthew Boulton Co., vase shape, 11¼, ca1815 (4259/16) — 1150

Candlesticks, table pair, recessed centres, engraved, ducal coronets, 6¾, 1734, 26 ozs, 10 dwts (4160/398) — 3500

Candlesticks, table set of 4, circular bases, George II, J. Roberts & Co., 11½, wtd, 1812 (4259/249) — 3300

Candlesticks, table set of 4, George III, R. Calderwood, Irish, 11, wtd, ca1760 (4259/250) — 4500

Candlesticks, table, pair, baluster form, Rococo scrollwork, 12¼, 1746, fine, 83 ozs, 15 dwts (4160/345) — 7500

Candlesticks, table, pair, circular base, scroll and shellwork, 9⅝, 1772, 48 ozs (4160/410) — 2100

Candlesticks, table, pair, circular bases, scroll and shell work, campana sconces, 9⅝, 1740, 43 ozs, 5 dwts (4160/409) — 3000

Candlesticks, table, pair, engraved with crests, 6¾, 1736, 26 ozs, 10 dwts (4160/399) — 3300

Candlesticks, table, pair, recessed wells showing traces of crests, 6¾, 1736, 30 ozs, 15 dwts (4160/300) — 2700

Candlesticks, table, pair, George III, stepped square bases, William Cafe, 10½, 43 ozs, 1763 (4259/220) — 1900

Candlesticks, table, pair, Mark H.E. Ltd., Adam style, square bases, 10⅝, 1907 (4268/6) — 500

Candlesticks, table, 2 matching, circular bases, shells, knopped stems, 10, 1762-4, 36 ozs, 10 dwts (4160/301) — 1600

Candlesticks, George II, pair, square bases, 26 ozs, 15 dwts, 7, 1743 (4194/255) — 1900

Candlesticks, George II, set of 4, John Cafe, 72 ozs, 9, 1753-4 (4194/247) — 3500

Candlesticks, George III table, pair, weighted, 6⅞, ca1790 (4194/216) — 100

Candlesticks, George III table, pair, S.C. Young & Co., weighted, 10¾, 1816 (4194/177) — 600

Candlesticks, George III, pair, Corinthian Columns, dam, 11¼, 1776 (4194/245) — 150

Candlesticks, William and Mary, pair, crests, 16 ozs, 10 dwts, 6, ca1690 (4194/258) — 1200

Caster, baluster form, engraved with 2 crests, 5½, 1754, 4 ozs (4238/316) — 400

Caster, engraved above a molded girdle with armorials, 7⅛, 1709, 9 ozs, 5 dwts (4160/362) — 1150

Caster, engraved with crest and motto, baluster form, 5¾, 1747, 3 ozs 15 dwts (4238/319) — 750

Caster, inverted pear shape, cover, pierced and engraved, 5¾, 1781, 2 ozs, 10 dwts (4160/307) — 400

Caster, inverted pear shape, cyl. neck, corded border, engraved, 7⅛, 1765, 5 ozs, 15 dwts (4160/413) — 275

Caster, pear shape lower body, pedestal foot, domed lid, 6¾, 1754, 6 ozs 15 dwts (4238/231) — 650

Caster, plain baluster form, with inverted pear lower body, 5⅜, 1748, 3 ozs 5 dwts (4238/271) — 150

Caster, with flowers and flutes, domed cover, 5⅜, 1763, 3 ozs 10 dwts (4238/273) — 200

Caster, George I, Isaac Liger, baluster form, molded girdle, 8, 12 ozs, 1714 (4260/582) — 3100

Caster, George I, Mesach Godwin, pear shape, masks, 4¾, 4 ozs, 1723 (4260/577) — 125

Caster, George II, Samuel Wood, baluster form, 6 ozs, 6, 1747 (4194/215) — 150

Caster, George III, baluster form, 20 ozs, 15 dwts, 5¼, 1790 (4194/201) — 600

Caster, George III, baluster form, repousse, 4 ozs, 10 dwts, 6½, 1780 (4194/184) — 150

Casters, pair, baluster form, domed covers, 6, 1746, 13 ozs 10 dwts (4238/307) — 1100

Casters, pair, octagonal baluster form, engraved with crests, 5½, 1719, 9 ozs (4238/318) — 1400

Casters, pair, George I, Pierre Platel, baluster form, 6⅝, 19 ozs, 1717 (4260/581) — 4700

Casters, pair, George II, Paul Crespin, baluster form, 6¼, 19 ozs, 1736 (4260/583) — 4500

Casters, set of 3, George II, baluster form, foliate panels, 8½, 6½, 43 ozs, 1735 (4260/584) — 4100

Casters, set of 3, George II, J. Daniell, pear shape, bud finial, 5¾, 7½, 17 ozs, 1753 (4260/571) — 1900

Casters, set of 3, George III, J. Daniell, pear shape, wrythen finials, 5¾, 6¾, 13 ozs, 1767 (4260/572) — 1900

Cellars, pair, George III, R. & D. Hennell, oval, shaped, sides pierced, 3¼, 4 ozs, 1767 (4259/170) — 250

Cellars, salt, pair, boat shape, beaded borders, oval pedestal bases, 4⅛, 1787, 4 ozs, 5 dwts (4160/303) — 400

Center pc, Victorian, form of an upright grapevine openwork pendant grapes and leaves, 21¾, 1894, 93 ozs, 5 dwts (4160/232) — 800

Centerpiece, incurved square base, 4 paw feet, wirework basket, 14½, 1820, 257 ozs (4160/424) — 12000

Centerpiece, George III, William Pitts & Joseph Preedy, 85 ozs, 14¾, 1792 (4194/168) — 850

Centerpiece, George III, 6-light, Paul Storr, cut-glass bowl, 233 ozs, 14, 1814 (4194/293) — 10500

Child's rattle, George II, S. Drinkwater, octagonal, Rococo ornament, 6, 1750 (4259/291) — 500

Claret jug, form of a Pompeian Acsos, date 1862, 8¼, 1840, 27 ozs (669/337) — *1800*

Coaster, wine, Sheffield plated, form of row boat, simulated planking, 17¾, ca1800 (4259/34) — 1400

Claret jug (669/337)

Coffeepot
(4194/218)

Coffeepot (4238/217)

Cradle (4160/236)

Coaster, George III, pierced with urns, scrolls, Diam 6⅛, ca1790 (4194/138)	300
Coasters, wine, wirework sides, 5¾, 1806 (4238/224)	850
Coasters, wine set of 4, Sheffield plated, T&J Creswick, decorated with grapevines, 6¾, ca1820 (4259/19)	475
Coffeepot, armorials, Rococo ornament, 10¼, 32 ozs, 1774 (4259/203)	1000
Coffeepot, baluster form, chased with flowersprays, shellwork, 11½, 1764, 31 ozs, 10 dwts (4160/358)	1000
Coffeepot, foliate scrolls, 2 matching cartouches, 8¼, 1738, 22 ozs, 10 dwts (4160/391)	1150
Coffeepot, inverted pear shape, chased with a still life, 13¼, 1775, 39 ozs (4160/331)	550
Coffeepot, plain tapered form, monogrammed 1 side, domed cover, 9½, 1930, 21 ozs, 10 dwts (4160/241)	275
Coffeepot, George I, Thomas Partis, swan neck spout, wood scroll handle, 9, 22 ozs, 1725 (4260/574)	3700
Coffeepot, George II, cylindrical, armorials, 24 ozs, 9⅝, 1727 (4194/288)	2100
Coffeepot, George II, John Fosey, London, 20 ozs, 5 dwts, 8, 1736 (4159/69)	2500
Coffeepot, George II, Thomas Farren, London, 19 ozs, 8¼, 1731 (4159/67)	1900
Coffeepot, George II, Edward Pocock, cylindrical, faceted spout, 8½, 21 ozs, 1732 (4259/178)	1900
Coffeepot, George II, Irish, tuck-in base, 32 ozs, 10 dwts, 10, ca1750 (4194/251)	2200
Coffeepot, George III, bulbous rectangular shape, 27 ozs, 10 dwts, 8¾, 1808 (4194/244)	525
Coffeepot, George III, Charles Wright, pear shape, 11¾, 1773 (4194/218)	*2000*
Coffeepot, George III, Daniel Smith & Robert Sharp, 31 ozs, 15 dwts, 11¾, 1771 (4194/149)	2700
Coffeepot, George III, swan-neck, 10½, 1771, 28 ozs gross (4238/217)	*2100*
Coffeepot, George III, Irish, baluster shape, 28 ozs, 10 dwts, 10½, 1760 (4194/174)	550
Coffeepot, George, Richard Bayley, cylindrical, swan neck spout, 9⅝, 22 ozs, 1717 (4259/218)	1600
Coffeepot, Peter & William Bateman, urn shape, George III, 10½, 27 ozs, 1808 (4259/240)	1100
Coffeepot, Queen Anne, David Willaume I, plain, tapered, cylindrical, 9⅛, 23 ozs, 1709 (4259/157)	1300
Coffee urn, vase shape, reed loop handle, 14⅞, 1784, 40 ozs gross (4238/214)	850
Coffee urn, George III, Charles Wright, vase shape, 45 ozs, 14½, 1781 (4194/227)	550
Coolers, wine, pair, Sheffield plated, circular form, rim scrolls, 9¼, ca1820 (4259/2)	575
Cradle, jewelry, parcel-gilt, Victorian, putti playing instruments, L10¾, 1875, 46 ozs, 10 dwts (4160/236)	*1300*
Cream boat, George III, Mark B.M., oval, waved rim, 5¾, 3 ozs, 1766 (4259/225)	275
Cream boat, George III, Mark S.H., boat shape, 6½, 6 ozs, 1810 (4259/195)	325
Creamer, hexagonal helmet shape, reeded rim, loop handle, 6⅛, 1791, 4 ozs, 10 dwts (4160/253)	150
Creamer, oblong form, molded collar, leaf capped reeded handle, 4½, 1817, 6 ozs, 10 dwts (4160/335)	110
Creamer, vase shape, engraved with foliage, 4⅞, 1799, 3 ozs (4160/270)	125

Creamer, covered, Martin Hall & Co., oval, bands of interlaced ribbons, 5½, 8 ozs, 1859 (4260/507)   325
Creamer, George II, Elizabeth Goodwin, S-scroll handles, 2 ozs, 10 dwts, 3¼, 1729 (4194/286)   450
Creamer, George II, Mark D.H., pear shape, 4, 2 ozs, 1757 (4259/224)   125
Creamer, George III, John Carter, London, 6 ozs, 10 dwts, 6½, 1773 (4159/59)   360
Creamer, George III, Irish, John Stoyte, oval, 7 ozs, 5½, 1800 (4194/207)   275
Creamer, George III, Stephen Adams, bombe oval form, 3¾, 2 ozs, 1809 (4259/204)   125
Creamer, George III, Thomas Radcliffe, octagonal, 6¼, 6 ozs, 1809 (4259/197)   275
Cruet, on 4 ball feet, wirework, superstructure, 12, 1809, 34 ozs (4238/266)   550
Cruet bottles, George II, silver mounted, Samuel Wood, top repousse, 7, ca1759 (4194/242)   175
Cruet egg, Story & Elliot, hexafoil shape, George III, 8¼, 33 ozs, 1810 (4259/162)   *1300*
Cruet frame, beaded rim, pierced and engraved with scrolling foliage, 7½, 1786 (4160/334)   225
Cruet frame, circular stand on 3 fluted panel feet, 7½, 1793, 5 ozs 10 dwts (4238/210)   *300*
Cruet frame, gadroon edge, stylized foliage, 4 paw feet, 9¾, 1823, 29 ozs (4238/282)   275
Cruet frame, oval shaped, sides pierced, interlace ribbons, 9½, 1786 (4160/373)   700
Cruet set, George III, Hester Bateman, oval pierced frame, wood base, 6¾, 1781 (4259/280)   400
Cruet set, Georgian, cinquefoil shape with shell and scroll feet, 7⅝, 27 ozs, excluding glass, 1754-69 (4259/214)   900
Cruet stand, two circular containers with pierced scrolling sides, 8¼, 1768, 10 ozs (4160/275)   325
Cup and cover, 2 handle, bell shape, chased, acorns and starbursts, engraved crest, 9¾, 1701, 40 ozs (4160/422)   1800
Cup, caudle, miniature, lower part fluted with upper border of circles, 2 handles, 1⅜, 10 dwts (4160/364)   225
Cup, caudle, miniature, lower part swirl-fluted below band of flower heads, 1⅜, 1706, 10 dwts (4160/363)   300
Cup, coconut, Phipps & Robinson, silver L.P. mount, George III, 7, weighted, ca1790 (4259/294)   300
Cup, spirit, bulbous circular form, 15 dwts, 1¼, 1750 (4194/81)   375
Cup, Channel Islands christening, Guillaume Henry, 3 ozs, 2¼, ca1740 (4194/285)   400
Cup, George II, 2-handed cup, cylindrical, double scroll handles, 7 ozs, 4, 1745 (4194/246)   350
Cup, George III, bell-shaped bowl, crest, 5 ozs, 10 dwts, 1783 (4194/157)   125
Cup, George III, R. & S. Hennell, bell-shaped bowl, 11 ozs, 10 dwts, 7¾, 1808 (4194/158)   200
Cup, Queen Anne caudle, Henry Greene, S-scroll handles, 8 ozs, 4, 1711 (4194/257)   350
Cup, Queen Anne, caudle, embossed, chased, 4 ozs, 3⅛, 1706 (4194/256)   800
Cup, 2 handled, bell shaped, double scroll handle, 5¾, 1793, 12 ozs 10 dwts (4238/207)   425
Cup, 2 handled, engraved with presentation inscription, 5, 1817, 10 ozs (4160/267)   150
Cup, 2 handled, pear shape, scroll handle, engraved, armorials, & motto, 9½, 1793, Irish, 35 dwts (4160/387)   900
Cup, 2 handled, and cover, John Craig, bell shaped bowl, 14½, 49 ozs, Irish, 1772 (4259/248)   1500
Cup, 2 handled, George II, Fuller White, cylindrical form, 4⅝, 8 ozs, 1747 (4260/546)   325
Cup and cover, 2 handled, bell shape, chased with acorns and star bursts, 9¾, 1701, 40 ozs (4238/259)   1000
Cup and cover, 2 handled presentation, elaborately chased, 13, 1912, inscription, 82 ozs (619/163)   950
Cups, pair, Tapered cylindrical form, 2½, 5 ozs, ca1775 (4260/586)   1200
Cups, pair, George III, vase form bowls, raised on trumpet shaped stems, 5⅞, 1802, 14 ozs (4238/262)   700
Cups, 2 handled, pair, George III, Irish, Jacob West, 5½, 28 ozs, ca1765 (4260/550)   1600
Decanter trolley, Sheffield plated, two lobed, circular coasters, ca1830 (4194/6)   325
Dish, cheese, rim border, domed cover, engraved, 9½, 1792, 30 oz 10 dwts (4238/315)   650
Dish, cheese, George III, Joseph Heriot, shallow oval form, reeded border, 9¾, 22 ozs, 1787 (4259/137)   450
Dish, cross, pear shaped burner with spiraling flute & flowers, 13¼, 1769, 22 ozs 10 dwts (4238/248)   900
Dish, cross, George III, Henry Bayley, shell and scroll supports, 9⅞, 11 ozs, 1769 (4260/545)   650
Dish, cross, George III, William Plummer, 15 ozs, 10 dwts, L12¾, 1791 (4194/150)   750
Dish, cross, Sheffield plated, sliding supports, crest, L11¼, ca1765 (4194/7)   275
Dish, cross, George III, Wm. Plummer, swiveling bar, 11, 19 ozs, 1773 (4259/219)   1100
Dish, entree and cover, rectangular form, domed and engraved with armorials, 10¾, 1833, 21 ozs (4160/333)   125
Dish, meat, oval, border engraved both sides, engraved motto, 17¼, 1820, 55 ozs (4160/265)   1300
Dish, meat, oval, borders engraved on both sides, 22⅝, 1819, 102 ozs, 10 dwts (4160/264)   2100
Dish, meat, oval, engraved with armorials and motto on foliate mantles, 26, 1823, 165 ozs, 10 dwts (4160/402)   2750
Dish, meat, plain oval form, border engraved with crest, 20¼, 1803, 84 ozs (4160/261)   1500
Dish, meat and cover, pair, oval domed shape, berry, plain leaf decoration, 14¾, 1820, 127 ozs (4238/260)   2750
Dish, ring, Irish, reel shaped, pierced, chased, sprays of flowers, 7½, 1765, 15 ozs 10 dwts (4238/314)   1600
Dish, ring, Victorian, circular form, embossed with animals, 7½, 1894, 11 ozs 10 dwts (4238/166)   425
Dish, vegetable and cover, oval, sides applied with small acanthus grips, 15, 1794, 89 ozs 10 dwts (4238/251)   4000

Dish, vegetable, circular, molded edges with flowers and scrolls, 10, 1831, 24 ozs (4160/390) 450
Dish, George I, Irish, circular, fluted sides, 4⅜, 2 ozs, 1718 (4260/542) 450
Dishes, entree and cover, two handled circular dishes, 10, 1768, 54 ozs 10 dwts (4238/249) 1400
Dishes, entree and covers, pair, octagonal, engraved, running foliage, 12¼, 1802, 153 ozs 10 dwts, fine (4238/323) 5500
Dishes, entree, covered pair, oval, reeded border and engraved handles, 15, 1804, 66 ozs, 15 dwts (4160/344) 2200
Dishes, entree, covers, pair, Sheffield plated, rectangular, rounded angles, 11½, ca1810 (4259/12) 400
Dishes, entree, pair, George III, T & J Guest & Reid, 4 covers, 196 ozs, 5 dwts, L11¾, 1808 (4194/238) 3750
Dishes, meat, pair, shaped oval form, rim applied and chased with scrolling flowers, 17⅜, 1829, 118 ozs, 5 dwts (4160/404) 3000
Dishes, meat, pair, George IV, John Mewburn, London, 97 ozs, 16⅜, 1825 (4159/63) 2600
Dishes, meat, 2 graduated, George III, William Burwash & Richard Sibley, London, 98 ozs, 16½ x 17, 1805 (4159/61) 1500
Dishes, serving, pair, square, 4 supports, 8⅝, 1921, 55 ozs 15 dwts (4238/150) 900
Dishes, strawberry, pair, circular, scalloped rim, fluted sides, 7⅛, 1936, 16 ozs, 5 dwts (4238/151) 350
Dishes, vegetable, covered, pair, George III, John Green & Co., Sheffield, 74 ozs, 15 dwts, 12¾, 1800 (4159/64) 1800
Dishes, vegetable, pair, covered, with ram's heads and ring handles, 10½, 110 oz, 5 dwts (4160/352) 5750
Dishes, vegetable, pair, covered, Sheffield-plated, 10, ca1800 (4159/46) 425
Dishes, vegetable, pair, covered, Sheffield-plated, lobed domed covers, 11½, ca1800 (4159/47) 600
Dishes, vegetable, 2 matching, square, incurved, 9, 1929-32, 44 ozs, 10 dwts (4160/383) 375
Dishes, George III entree, 4, viscount's coronets, 99 ozs, 5 dwts, Diam 10¾, 1808 (4194/290) 3000
Egg cruet, square form, oval salt basket, 4 egg cups, 7½, 1807-08, 20 ozs 10 dwts (4238/200) 750
Epergne, central shaped oval basket, foliage and scrollwork, 12⅝, 1762, 95 ozs, 15 dwts (4160/266) 3250
Epergne, George III, central basket, 4 branches, 109 ozs, 16¾, 1794 (4194/172) 4500
Epergne, George III, central basket, 4 others, 117 ozs, 5 dwts, 14⅛, 1765 (4194/252) 4500
Epergne, George III, 4teen-basket, 4 supports, 216 ozs, 15 dwts, 17¼, 1769 (4194/228) 13500
Epergne, Sheffield plated frame, central cut glass bowl, 4 branches, 12, ca1830 (649/305) 550
Ewer, covered, Victorian, scroll handle terminating in female mask, 12½, 1855, 24 ozs gross (4238/180) 700
Ewer, wine, Victorian, Pompeian jug form, engraved with initials, date 1867, 1867, 28 ozs, 10 dwts (4160/238) 1500
Ewer, Edwardian, Goldsmiths & Silversmiths Co., inverted pearshape, 19⅞, 75 ozs, 1902 (4259/113) *2800*
Ewer, Victorian, partly fluted, scrolls and flowers, 14¾, 1853, 47 ozs (4238/177) *1800*
Ewers, Victorian, pair, bulbous, engraved with foliage, 35 ozs, 10 dwts, 11, 1884 (4194/106) *1400*

Cruet egg
(4259/162)

Ewer (4238/177)

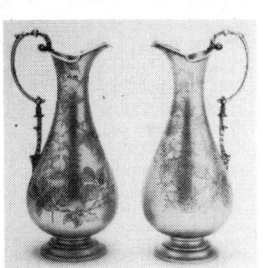

Ewers (4194/106)

Ewer
(4259/113)

Flatware, Hanoverian pattern, Fletcher, London, 1950, 104 pcs, 116 ozs 10 dwts (4238/156) 2000
Fob seal, George III, Hester Bateman, foliate monogram, 1, ca1780 (4194/202) 250
Glove holder, wirework basket, suspended from bracelet, 1825, rare, 2 ozs (4238/185) 350
Goblet, with a cartouche, inscription, 6¼, 1822, 10 ozs (4160/395) 275
Hot water kettle and stand, George II, pear shape, Peze Pilleau, 14, 61 ozs, 1742 (4259/210) 1900
Inkstand, oval tray, reeded rim, ball feet, 7½, 1802, 7 ozs 10 dwts (4238/225) 425
Inkstand, rectangular form, molded rim, applied 1 side of handle, 6⅝, 1748, 10 ozs (4160/255) 700

Inkstand, silver-gilt, rectangular base, lid surmounted by Roman oil lamp, 11, 36 ozs, 1884 (649/308)   550

Inkstand, George III, R. Hennell, rectangular, 4 bottles, 10¾, 24 ozs, 1786 (4260/544)   1600

Inkstand, George III, Samuel Herbert & Co., rectangular, raised gallery, 6⅝, 10 ozs, 1765 (4259/171)   600

Inkstand, Sheffield plated, octagonal, blue glass liners, L11, ca1790 (4194/16)   625

Inkstand, Sheffield plated, oval, blue glass containers, wood base, L8¼, ca1780 (4194/5)   150

Inkstand, Sheffield plated, rectangular form, gadroon rim raised on paw feet, 9½, ca1810 (4259/30)   325

Inkstand, Victorian, rectangular, shell form handles, center with candlesticks, 15, 1840, 53 ozs, 10 dwts (4160/384)   2100

Jug, claret, silver mounted and cut glass, Victorian, oviform, 12, 1865 (4238/170)   300

Jug, cream, double-lipped, Geo. Fox, baluster form, engraved and a crest, 3¾, 6 ozs, 1876 (4260/505)   500

Jug, hot water, baluster form, in 18c style, 10⅜, 23 ozs, 1905 (4259/115)   475

Jug, hot water on stand, lobed lower body, domed lid, burner, 13¼, 1807, 41 ozs gross (4238/201)   900

Jug, hot water, George III, mark I.C., pear shape, domed cover, 7⅛, 17 ozs, 1807 (4260/525)   650

Jug, hot water, George III, Henry C. Hawner, Vase shape, 12¼, 22 ozs, 1790 (4259/196)   700

Jug, shaving, George IV, Robert Garrard II, tapered oval, flat domed lid, 5½, 8 ozs, 1827 (4260/587)   1100

Jug, George III, hot water, raffia-wrapped handle, 30 ozs, 13¼, 1775 (4194/175)   650

Jug water on lampstand, compressed circular form, twin snake handle, 12, 1810, 66 ozs, gross (4160/411)   6000

Jugs, pair, George II, Humphrey Payne, molded girdle, double scroll handles, 11¼, 73 ozs, 1732 (4260/585)   9100

Kettle, (hot water) on lampstand, Chrichton Bros, George I style, 56 ozs, 5 dwts, 12½, 1910 (4194/102)   550

Kettle, tea on lampstand, plain hob shape, curved spout, 12¼, 1930, 54 ozs 10 dwts (4238/153)   500

Kettle, tea on lampstand, circular form, stylized leaf tip base, 3 paw feet, 13½, 1829, 36 ozs (4238/81)   600

Kettle stand, George II, Gabriel Sleath, triangular, rim with foliage, 9½, 17 ozs, 1739 (4259/226)   375

Knives, table, set of 12, Moses Brent, fiddle thread shell pattern, 1807 (4260/521)   550

Knives and forks, dessert, 12, Moses Brent, partly reeded handles, 1804-05 (4260/520)   750

Knives and forks, fish, set of 8, bone handles, wood case, Martin, Hall & Co., 1908 (4260/501)   225

Ladle, soup, Old English pattern, fluted shell bowl, 13½, 1770, 4 ozs 10 dwts (4238/198)   275

Ladle, soup, oval bowl, curved tubular handle, chased eagle's heads, 13, 1737, 8 ozs, 15 dwts (4160/343)   3700

Ladle, soup, Old English pattern, with initialed 'H', 12¾, 1777, 5 ozs (4160/308)   400

Ladle, toddy, ovoid bowl, engraved with foliate monogram, 13⅛, 1733, 3 ozs, 5 dwts (4160/407)   350

Ladle, George III, soup, Hester Bateman, Old English, 5 ozs, 10 dwts, L12⅝, 1783 (4194/199)   300

Mazarin, George III, William Frisbee, London, 53 ozs, 19⅝, 1805 (4159/65)   500

Mirror, dressing table, silver mounted, rectangular pierced scrolls, cupids heads, 21¼, 1904 (669/342)   300

Mug, baluster form, monogram, double scroll handle, 5⅛, 11 ozs, 10 dwts (4160/357)   550

Mug, contemporary monogram, scroll handle, 4⅛, 1794, 7 ozs, 5 dwts (4160/294)   200

Mug, engraved with crest, scroll handle, 3⅞, 1741, 7 ozs, 10 dwts (4160/359)   475

Mug, molded lip and foot, leaf capped scroll handle, 4, 1754, 7 ozs (4160/284)   375

Mug, child's, monogrammed, 'E.C.' reeded band, gilt interior, 2⅝, 1823, 3 ozs 5 dwts (4238/310)   300

Mug, George II, John Swift, crest, 7 ozs, 10 dwts, 3¾, 1736 (4194/254)   800

Mug, William IV, ribbed campana shape, 5 ozs, 10 dwts, 4, 1832 (4194/162)   275

Mustard pot, George III, oval, acorn finial, 3 ozs, 5 dwts, 3⅛, 1802 (4194/273)   150

Mustard pot, George III, oval, loop handle, 3 ozs, 3¼, 1796 (4194/272)   225

Mustard pot, George IV, Emes & Barnard, drum shaped, crest, motto, 2⅝, 3 ozs, 1824 (4259/257)   175

Nutmeg grater, George III, acorn shape top, 3½, ca1750 (4194/205)   550

Nutmeg grater, George III, Phipps & Robinson, upright oval form, 2½, 1807 (4194/204)   290

Pap boat, George III, Peter, Ann, William Bateman, 1 oz, 15 dwts, L4⅝, 1803 (4194/188)   200

Pap boat, George III, mark A.-F., bombe sides, gilt interior, 5¼, 1817 (4260/528)   225

Pap boat, George III, mark W.B., plain, thread border, 4½, 1787 (4260/527)   200

Pepper mills, 6, plain octagonal vase, 3¾, 1938 (4194/262)   1000

Peppers, kitchen pair, mark J.S.B., cylindrical, with a crest, 3½, 5 ozs, 1882 (4260/503)   325

Pitcher, silver-gilt, elaborately repousse with festoons, flowers, masks, 11, 1900, 44 ozs (619/166)   500

Plates, soup, 4, stylized foliage, engraved with armorials, 10½, 1807, 105 ozs, 10 dwts (4160/421)   3000

Plates, George II, dinner, pair, Edward Feline, 37 ozs, 15 dwts, Diam 9½, 1747 (4194/253)   950

Plates, George III, dinner, set of 12, Benjamin Smith III, roses, 328 ozs, Diam 10¾, 1819 (4194/291)   6750

Plates, Victorian dinner, set of 12, circular form, armorials, 197 ozs, 10 dwts, Diam 9⅜, 1894 (4194/110)   2500

Platter, fish, Asprey, oval, rim engraved with leaping salmon, 36, 126 ozs, modern (4259/132)   1500

Pot, chocolate, George I, Irish, John Hamilton, Dublin, 33 ozs, 10 dwts, 10¾, 1715 (4159/68)   4200

Pot, mustard, plain drum shape, flat cover, 2¾, 1764, 4 ozs 5 dwts (4238/226)   200

Pot, mustard, straight sided oval form, pierced and engraved, 3, 1802, 30 ozs 5 dwts (4238/223)	250
Pot, mustard, George IV, R. Emes & E. Barnard, domed lid, 3¼, 6 ozs, 1823 (4260/510)	350
Pot, mustard, Victorian, sides pierced with foliate scrolls, 2½, 1851, 3 ozs 5 dwts (4238/179)	110
Pots, mustard, pair, William IV, Charles Fox II, drum form, hinged cover, 3⅝, 15 ozs, 1834 (4260/511)	2100
Rattle, Victorian child's, whistle, coral teether, L6¼, imp, 1857 (4194/98)	310
Salt cellars, basket form, pair George IV, boat shape, Scottish, 4½, 9 ozs, 1832 (4259/186)	200
Salt cellars, pair, circular with lobed sides, gilt interiors, 3⅛, 1802, 6 ozs (4160/379)	200
Salt cellars, pair, George II, Thomas Heming, circular, short stems, 3½, 18 ozs, ca1760 (4260/592)	1200
Salt cellars, pair, John Robbins, octagonal boat shape, George III, 4, 5 ozs, 1793 (4259/160)	150
Salt cellars, pair, Wm. Hall, oval, reeded rim, George III, 3⅜, 3 ozs, 1807 (4259/267)	225
Salt cellars, set of 4, silver-gilt, circular lion mask, paw feet, 3⅜, 1814, 22 ozs 10 dwts (4238/308)	750
Salt cellars, set of 4, circular with gadroon rim, sloping panels of lobes, beading, 2⅞, 1761, 14 ozs, 5 dwts (4160/415)	650
Salt cellars, set of 4, J. Bridge, George IV, elphinstone crest, 5⅛, 34 ozs, 1807 (4259/289)	*1200*

Salt cellars (4259/289)

Salver (4160/245)

Salt cellars, set of 8, George II, E. Wakelin, circular, with leafage, 3½, 72 ozs, 1746 (4260/591)	9000
Salt cellars, trencher, octagonal form, bases engraved with initials, 3, 1734 (4238/289)	325
Salt cellars, 2 matching, plain boat shape, beaded borders, 4, 1788-87, 4 ozs 10 dwts (4238/192)	175
Salt cellars, 2, George I trencher, octagonal, 2 ozs, 15 dwts, L3, 1725-6 (4194/274)	450
Salt cellars, 2, George II trencher, octagonal, 2 ozs, 15 dwts, L2⅞, 1736-7 (4194/277)	450
Salt cellars, 2, Georgian trencher, octagonal, 5 ozs, L3¼, 1725-32 (4194/275)	500
Salts, pair, circular, on 3 fruit form feet, 3¼, 1822, 8 ozs 10 dwts (4238/272)	200
Salts, set of 4, Carrington & Co., circular, on 4 hoof feet, 21 ozs, 10 dwts, 1927 (4260/502)	350
Salts, George III, set of 6, circular bowls, crests, 20 ozs, 2½, 1794 (4194/236)	600
Salts, 2 matching pairs, circular cord, rims, 3 hoof feet, 2½, 1770-76, 6 ozs 10 dwts (4238/278)	400
Salver, beaded border, foliate motifs, 4 feet, 15, 1776, 47 ozs, 15 dwts (4160/385)	1000
Salver, cast with gadroon and shell rim, 17½, 1919, 72 ozs (669/343)	750
Salver, chased and embossed with rose blossoms and foliage, 1833, 18 ozs (669/336)	225
Salver, circular border set at intervals with cartouches, 13, 1760, 31 ozs, 15 dwts (4160/287)	1000
Salver, circular, armorials, 9, 1802, 18 ozs, 15 dwts (4160/277)	525
Salver, circular, center engraved with crest, 9, 1794, 15 ozs 15 dwts (4238/244)	900
Salver, circular, scroll and shell work rim, 3 hoof supports, 10, 1757, 14 ozs, 10 dwts (4160/408)	325
Salver, circular, shell and scroll work rim, 3 supports, 13⅜, 1755, 32 ozs 10 dwts (4160/405)	1000
Salver, circular, the center engraved with cres, 9, 1794, 16 ozs 10 dwts (4238/243)	700
Salver, clusters of grape & berries, 21½, 1836, 127 ozs (4160/245)	*3500*
Salver, dec. shell and foliage, female heads flanked by eagle, 12½, 1739, 36 ozs (4160/346)	1150
Salver, engraved armorials, crest, inscription, date 1831, 20½, 110 ozs (4160/279)	3500
Salver, molded 'bath' border, 4 scroll feet, engraved, 10¼, 1731, 21 ozs, 10 dwts (4160/397)	1300
Salver, molded bath border, 3 feet, engraved, 10, 1937, 21 ozs, 15 dwts (4160/382)	375
Salver, molded, gadroon border, raised on 3 scroll feet, 14½, 1926, 46 ozs, 15 dwts (4160/381)	600
Salver, shell and scrollwork rim, 3 hoof feet, 9½, 1746, 15 ozs (4238/239)	400
Salver, George II, circular, later crest, 18 ozs, 10 dwts, Diam 10, 1755 (4194/214)	450
Salver, George II, molded Bath border, later ornament, 11¾, 28 ozs, 1734 (4259/215)	475

Salver, George II, pie crust border, crest, 40 ozs, 5 dwts, Diam 14½, 1749 (4194/250)   500

Salver, George II, John Tuite, circular, 12¾, 35 ozs, 1731 (4260/579)   2200

Salver, George II, Robert Abercromby, shaped molded rim, 16¼, 61 ozs, 1736 (4259/262)   1300

Salver, George III, William Peaston, on 3 feet round, 12¾, 32 ozs, 1751 (4260/578)   1400

Salver, George III, John Crouch & Thomas Hannam, oval, 69 ozs, L19½, 1791 (4194/151)   2500

Salver, George III, Richard Rugg, circular, 51 ozs, 10 dwts, Diam 16¼, 1762 (4194/267)   900

Salver, George III, Thomas Hannon & Richard Mills, 29 ozs, 10 dwts, Diam 12, 1763 (4194/219)   700

Salver, George III, Benjamin Smith III, shaped rim, 15, 63 ozs, 1819 (4259/297)   1400

Salver, George III, John Carter, conjoined circles border, 13⅛, 35 ozs, 1770 (4259/138)   1000

Salver, George III, Mark, I.W., center engraved with armorials, hooffeet, 9⅛, 15 ozs, 1772 (4259/174)   350

Salver, George III, Richard Rugg, circular, panel supports, 15⅛, 50 ozs, 1778 (4260/538)   900

Salver, George IV, John Edward Terry, 23 ozs, 5 dwts, Diam 11⅜, 1824 (4194/226)   400

Salver, Octafoil, scalloped and raised border, 4 bracket feet, 27¼, 1913, large, 214 ozs (4238/155)   3500

Salver, Queen Anne, Joseph Ward, molded rim, armorials, 11, 25 ozs, 1707 (4259/263)   800

Salver, Sheffield plated, circular, gadroon, foliate rim, Diam 18⅛, ca1835 (4194/12)   200

Salvers, pair, George III, Timothy Renou, oval, 4 supports, 12¼, 44 ozs, 1798 (4260/530)   2400

Salvers, Sheffield plated, 2 matching, crests, Diams 12 and 10⅛, ca1830 (4194/10)   100

Sauce boat, boat shape, waved rim, engraved initials, 6½, 1759, 6 ozs (4160/360)   400

Sauce boat, oval scalloped rim, leaf capped double scroll handle, 7⅜, 1762, 10 ozs (4238/277)   400

Sauce boat, oval, gadroon rim with foliage, 3 shell capped feet, 9, 1824, 19 ozs (4160/393)   700

Sauce boat, oval, scalloped lip, scroll handle, 8¼, 1746, 12 ozs (4160/392)   550

Sauce boat, oval, with waved rim, scroll handle, 7½,1758, 9 ozs, 10 dwts (4160/304)   475

Sauce boat, wide oval form, engraved with crest, scroll handle, 7¾, 1745, 14 ozs (4160/406)   900

Sauce boat, George II, oval form, waved rim, 6¼, 7 ozs, 1751 (4259/276)   250

Sauce boat, George III, boat shape, crest, monogram, 8 ozs, 7¼, 1789 (4194/155)   800

Sauce boat, George III, bulbous oval form, 13 ozs, L8¼, 1765 (4194/176)   750

Sauce boat, George III, Daniel Smith & Robert Sharp, oval, 9 ozs, 10 dwts, L7, 1780 (4194/210)   475

Sauce boats, pair, oval bodies, waved rim, flying scroll handles, 8, 1750, 27 ozs (4238/304)   650

Sauce boats, pair, oval, gadroon border, scroll handle, 8⅛, 1763, 27 ozs 10 dwts (4238/299)   2000

Sauce boats, pair, plain boat shaped, scrolling handle, 6⅛, 1909, 13 ozs, 5 dwts (4160/258)   250

Sauce boats, pair, Charles Fox, double lipped, circular, scroll handles, 6, 13 ozs, 1830 (4260/509)   1600

Sauce boats, pair, George IV, Paul Storr, fluted shells, 8⅛, 42 ozs, 1828 (4259/270)   12000

Sauce boats, pair, Wm. Galloway, oval, shaped rims, George IV, 8, 20 ozs, 1824 (4259/258)   2300

Sauce pan, bulbous sides, molded rim, wood handle, 3⅜, 1720, 10 ozs, gross (4160/401)   600

Sauce pan, bulbous sides, wood handle, engraved crest, 2⅜, 1730, 4 ozs, gross (4160/400)   375

Sauce pan, plain bulbous shape, short spout with turned wooden handle, 3 1/3, 1821, 8 ozs (4160/380)   575

Sauce pan brandy, molded rim, short spout, turned wood handle, 2⅝, 1726, 3 ozs 15 dwts (4238/258)   325

Saucepan, brandy, George II, mark R.B., wood handle, 2¼, 4 ozs, 1731 (4260/569)   700

Saucepan, George III, cylindrical, wood handle, 7 ozs, 3¾, 1802 (4194/232)   550

Saucepan, George III, later wood handle, 8 ozs, 10 dwts, 3⅝, 1815 (4194/154)   900

Saucepan, George III, Fuller White, baluster form, wood handle, 4⅜, 21 ozs, 1760 (4260/549)   3300

Scent flask and vinaigrette, horn form, Victorian, screw on mouth pc, L3½, 1872 (4238/183)   350

Scissors, grape, pair, shell foliate with lion mask handles, 1819, 4 ozs, 10 dwts (4160/396)   275

Scissors, grape, pair, George III, gilt, Eley, Fearn & Chawner, 1813 (4260/517)   250

Scoop, cheese, rectangular blade with steel knife tip, crest, 10⅛, 1798, rare (4238/189)   425

Scoop, marrow, back engraved with crest, 1789 (4160/315)   225

Scoop, marrow, back of bowl with tongue motif, 1751 (4160/318)   150

Scoop, marrow, pair, with wigglework borders, elongated bowls, 1779 (4160/317)   500

Serving slice, George II, mark J.S., wood handle, 1746 (4260/557)   600

Serving slice, George III, W.L. Dublin, pierced oval blade, ca1780 (4260/539)   350

Shells, butter, fluted, molded handle rim, two feet, 6⅛, 1793, 9 ozs 5 dwts (4238/206)   500

Skewer, modified king pattern, with blackamoor bust crest, 11, 1827 (4238/186)   225

Skewer, ring handle supported by a shaped square panel, 13½, 1812, Irish (4238/188)   225

Snuff box, George III, silver-gilt, Matthew Linwood, 4 ozs, 5 dwts, L3⅛, 1809 (4194/261)   575

Snuff box, George IV, silver-gilt, engine-turned cover, 2 ozs, 15 dwts, L3⅛, 1821 (4194/260)   220

Snuffers and tray, George III, Emes and Barnard, 9 ozs, 10 dwts, L8⅞, 1809-10 (4194/132)   375

Snuffers, pair, stork form, modeled in form of a long beaked stork, on 1 leg, 4¾, 1808, rare (4238/184)   375

Soup ladle, William IV, William Eaton, plain Fiddle pattern, 10 ozs, L13¼, 1836 (4194/161)   160

Spoon, basting, George I, Hanoverian pattern, 14½, 5 ozs, 1723 (4260/553)   350

Spoon, basting, George I, K. McKenzie, Hanoverian pattern rattail bowl, Scottish, 15⅜, 6 ozs, 1768 (4259/169)   550

Spoon, basting, George II, Paul Hanet, Hanoverian pattern, 14¼, 8 ozs, 1731 (4260/555)   550

Spoon, basting, George II, Scottish, A. Ure, Hanoverian pattern, 15¾, 7 ozs, 1740 (4260/556) 550
Spoon, basting, George II, William Young, Hanoverian pattern, 14⅞, 7 ozs, 1739 (4259/165) 700
Spoon, basting, James Gordon, Hanoverian pattern, George III, Scottish, 15, 6 ozs, ca1765 (4259/168) 650
Spoon, basting, Thomas Allen, oval bowl, William III, 14¼, 5 ozs, 1698 (4259/164) 1700
Spoon, basting, Thomas Daniell, Old English pattern, George III, 15, 6 ozs, 1778 (4259/167) 375
Spoon, gravy, George II, James Wilks, Hanoverian pattern, 12½, 3 ozs, 1733 (4260/554) 475
Spoon, marrow, rat-tail bowl, 1699 (4160/324) 200
Spoon, seal-top, pricked with initials T.I., 6½, 1586, 1 oz, 10 dwts (4160/367) 550
Spoon, straining, silver, wood handle, Sheffield plated, large oval bowl, George III, 23, 1804 (4259/163) 600
Spoon, straining, Irish, Old English pattern, 14¾, 1802, 7 ozs 10 dwts (4238/197) 250
Spoon, trefid, oval, rat-tail bowl, initials 'M.D.' with flowering branch, 5½, ca1695, 1 oz (4160/366) 125
Spoon, George II, basting, Maker's Mark J.H., Old English, 5 ozs, 10 dwts, L13¾, 1739 (4194/222) 250
Spoon, Gravy, Old English pattern, back engraved with initials, 1702, 5 ozs, 5 dwts (4160/285) 270
Spoon, James I, seal top, fig-shaped bowl, chased stem, 1 oz, 5 dwts, 1624 (4194/221) 500
Spoons, gravy, pair, Scottish, stylized Kings pattern, stems with blackamoor busts, 11¾, 1827, 11 ozs (4160/247) 225
Spoons, rat tail dessert, set eighteen, Hanoverian pattern, initialed, modern, 34 ozs, 10 dwts (4160/230) 225
Spoons, salt, 4, double shell bowls and serpent entwined ribbed stems, 4, 1819, 3 ozs (4238/309) 250
Spray tea 2 handled, rectangular form, pierced rim, 28¾, 1958, 148 ozs 10 dwts (4238/159) 1700
Stand, dish, George III, John Parsons & Co., Sheffield, 17 ozs, 15 dwts, 11¼, 1811 (4159/66) 275
Stand, teapot, oval, engraved with laurel wreaths, 7⅛, 1789, 4 ozs, 10 dwts (4160/349) 175
Stand, warming, open work stand, 4 s scrolled supports, 11¾, 1808, 19 ozs (4238/297) 300
Strainer, lemon, circular bowl, 8½, 1753, 4 ozs 10 dwts (4238/221) 300
Strainer, lemon, George I, John Albright, pierced in flowerhead design, 6½, 1 oz, 1718 (4260/568) 425
Strainer, lemon, George II, S. Herbert & Co., shallow circular bowl, 4⅛, 8 ozs, 1753 (4259/153) 225
Strainer, lemon, S. Herbert & Co., shallow circular bowl, George II, 8⅞, 3 ozs, 1756 (4259/158) 150
Strainer, tea, bowl pierced with band of foliage, 6⅞, 1735, 4 ozs (4160/417) 475
Strainer, tea, pierced in a geometric flowerhead pattern, 9⅞, 1777, 4 ozs, 10 dwts (4160/350) 325
Strainer, George III, Hester Bateman, circular, 3 ozs, 5 dwts, L6⅞, 1783 (4194/195) 400
Sugar basket, boat shaped, reeded border, swing handles, 6⅝, 1799, 7 ozs, 5 dwts (4160/355) 575
Sugar basket, George III, Michael Plummer, boat shape, 6½, 6 ozs, 1794 (4259/201) 350
Sugar bowl and creamer, panels of scrolling, foliate flowers, 5⅛, 5¼, 1861, 22 ozs, 15 dwts (4160/242) 525
Sugar pail, George III, Thomas Daniell and John Wall, 4, 3 ozs, 1781 (4260/589) 550
Sugar vase and cover, S. Herbert & Co., pear shape, George III, 6, 12 ozs, 1755 (4259/245) 500
Table garniture, Victorian parcel-gilt, Frederick Elkington & Co., 7 pcs, L14¾, 1881 (4194/109) 25000
Tankard, chased with 3 bands of hoops, monogram below a crest, 7½, 1798, 26 ozs 10 dwts (4238/205) 1600
Tankard, cyl form, molded girdle and borders, domed cover, 8⅛, 1701, 27 ozs 5 dwts (4238/253) 1400
Tankard, molded girdle, domed cover, s-scroll handle, 6¾, 1762, 21 ozs (4238/301) 2300
Tankard, parcel-gilt, on 3 ball and claw feet, scrolling foliage, 9¼, ca1720, 57 ozs, 10 dwts (4160/177) 8500
Tankard, Charles II, cylindrical, later armorials, 19 ozs, 5 dwts, 6⅛, 1683 (4194/171) 2000
Tankard, Charles II, mark R.N., flat hinged cover, 6¾, 29 ozs, 1662 (4260/600) 9500
Tankard, Charles II, mark, a Goose, flat domed cover, 7⅝, 37 ozs, 1680 (4260/599) 8500
Tankard, George II, Henry Brind, baluster form, 22 ozs, 15 dwts, 7⅛, 1746 (4194/229) 675
Tankard, George III, mark, I.K., cylindrical, molded girdle, 7⅛, 21 ozs, 1774 (4259/177) 1800
Tankard, Sheffield plated, quart size, tapered cylindrical, 9⅜, ca1780 (4259/8) 300
Taperstick, miniature, C.T. & Geo. Fox, chamber candlestick, 2⅝, 3 ozs, 1844 (4260/497) 375
Taperstock, George II, John Cafe, shaped square base, 4⅝, 4 ozs, 1746 (4259/227) 600
Tazze, pair, silver-gilt, Victorian, fluted shallow circular form, 9, 1878, 33 ozs, 15 dwts (4160/243) 700
Tea and coffeepot, matching, Victorian, S-scroll handles, 9, 47 ozs, 10 dwts (4160/246) 900
Tea and coffee service, 3 piece silver, gilt, tea, coffeepots, 2 handled sugar, 7¾, 5¾, 1878, 38 ozs (669/338) 500
Tea and coffee set, George III, 4 pcs, Thomas Wallace II, 61 ozs, 8, 1807-8 (4194/234) 1800
Tea and coffee set, 4 piece, Victorian, chased with foliate scrolls, 10¼, coffeepot, 1843, 84 ozs 5 dwts (4238/178) 3000
Tea and coffee set, 4 piece, Victorian, engraved with a monogram, sprays fruit and flowers, 11½, 1853, 95 ozs gross (4238/173) 2500
Tea caddies, pair, George I, octagonal scrolled strapwork, 5, 14 ozs, 1725 (4260/595) 1100
Tea caddy, carriage form, raised on 4 scroll feet, 7⅝, 1902, 14 ozs 10 dwt (4238/157) 350
Tea caddy, gadroon rim, locked compartment, 4 balls support, 6¼, 1802, 17 ozs 10 dwts (4238/295) 800
Tea caddy, straight sided oval form, engraved on 1 side, 4⅞, 5 ozs 15 dwts (4238/257) 800

Tea caddy, drum shaped, hinged dome lock, ivory baluster finial, h5¼, 1798, 13 ozs gross (4238/237)   1400

Tea caddy, George I, John Fainell, octagonal, 4⅜, 6 ozs, 1719 (4259/239)   900

Tea caddy, George III, Aldridge & Green, oval, hinged cover, 4⅛, 15 ozs, 1777 (4260/537)   1300

Tea caddy, George III, Henry Chawner, octagonal, 5¾, 13 ozs, 1791 (4259/243)   950

Tea caddy, George III, Henry Chawner, oval, 5¼, 13 ozs, 1792 (4259/244)   800

Tea caddy, George III, R. & S. Hennell, bombe square shape, 6¼, 15 ozs, 1805 (4259/181)   1400

Tea caddy, George III, Thomas Chawner, oval, bright cut, 5¼, 11 ozs, 1785 (4259/242)   1100

Tea caddy, Peter and William Bateman, rectangular, George III, 6½, 17 ozs, 1808 (4259/241)   1200

Tea caddy, William IV Scottish, quadrangular form, 30 ozs, L7, 1835 (4194/148)   1500

Tea caddy, double compartment, oval lock, removable divider, 6½, 1797, 15 ozs gross (4238/234)   *1100*

Tea caddy
(4238/234)

Tea kettle on
lampstand
(4238/208)

Tea kettle on lampstand
(4238/293)

Tea kettle, lampstand, George II, Peter Archambo, 90 ozs, 12¾ x 10, 1734 (4194/281)   1900

Tea kettle and lampstand, George II, pear shape, B. Giglac, 14½, 64 ozs, 1747 (4259/213)   2100

Tea kettle and lampstand, Wm. Fountain, plain hob shape, George III, 14¾, 98 ozs, 1799 (4259/159)   1500

Tea kettle on lampstand, hob shape, raffia covered handle, 13½, 1780, 51 ozs 15 dwts (4238/208)   *700*

Tea kettle on lampstand, inverted pear shape, 15½, 1751, 87 ozs gross (4238/293)   *2500*

Tea kettle on lampstand, oval form with gadroon rim, fixed entwined snake handle, 15⅞, 1804, 106 ozs, gross (4160/403)   2500

Tea kettle on lampstand, George I, Thomas Mason, baluster form, 15½, 104 ozs, 1722 (4260/594)   9500

Tea kettle on lampstand, George II, pear shaped, 13, 54 ozs, 1747 (4259/198)   1900

Tea kettle on lampstand, George II, John Le Sage, melon shape, 13½, 77 ozs, 1734 (4260/575)   3900

Tea set, Victorian 4 pc, Regency style, bombe sides, 48 ozs, 10 dwts, 12½, 1890 (4194/104)   800

Tea set, William IV, 3 pc, John James Keith, 44 ozs, 15 dwts, 6, 1836 (4194/111)   850

Tea set, 3 pc, Maker's Mark C.H., 35 ozs, 5½, 1906 (4194/100)   250

Tea set, 3 pc, George III, Mark I.B., pear shaped, 6⅜, 48 ozs, 1817 (4259/199)   800

Tea set, 3 piece, teapot, 2 handled sugar bowl and creamer, 8½, 1954, 47 ozs (4160/240)   500

Tea set, 3 piece, George III, Mark I.B., pear shaped, 6⅜, 48 ozs, 1817 (4259/202)   1100

Tea Caddy, upright ribbed rectangular shape, chased with leaves, 5⅝, 1776, 9 ozs (4160/281)   425

Teapot, apple shape, flush fitting cover, strapwork, 5, 1728, 11 ozs 15 dwts (4238/256)   1700

Teapot, compressed form, C-scroll handle, 5⅞, 1830, 22 ozs, 10 dwts (4160/248)   325

Teapot, cyl, form, chased with laurel festoon, oval reserves, shield, 5½, 1774, 13 ozs, 5 dwts (4160/356)   600

Teapot, engraved with armorials in a Rococo cartouche, 5½, 1793, 14 ozs, 10 dwts (4160/354)   275

Teapot, oval form with beaded border, 4½, 1780, 14 ozs 15 dwts (4238/213)   450

Teapot, oval form, domed lid, leaf capped handle, 6½, 1817, 28 ozs (4160/249)   550

Teapot, oval form, ivory handle, pineapple finial, 6½, 1792, 18 ozs 10 dwts (4238/227)   575

Teapot, oval, engraved flowers, monogram and crest, 4⅞, 1781, 14 ozs gross (4160/272)   650

Teapot, apple shape, 4½, 13 ozs, 1730 (4259/284)   600

Teapot, Robert & Samuel Hennell, oval, bulbous, George III, 6, 21 ozs, 1805 (4259/205)   325

Teapot, George II, Scottish, John Main, bullet form, fluted spout, scroll handle, 6, 20 ozs, 1734 (4260/573)   1000

Teapot, George III, oblong, harp shaped handle, 6½, 19 ozs, 1815 (4259/144) — 300
Teapot, George III, oval, wood handle, 13 ozs, 10 dwts, 5¾, 1790 (4194/233) — 350
Teapot, George III, partly lobed oblong form, 18 ozs, 5⅝, 1805 (4194/166) — 300
Teapot, George III, Hester Bateman, London, 17 ozs, 5 dwts, 5¾, 1787 (4159/58) — 650
Teapot, George III, Aldridge & Green, oval, loose cover, ivory handle, 4⅞, 11 ozs, 1780 (4259/148) — 550
Teapot, George III, John Emes, bulbous, raised collar, 4⅛, 6 ozs, 1802 (4260/524) — 400
Teapot, George III, Paul Storr, compressed spherical form, 4¾, 18 ozs, 1802 (4259/151) — 1500
Teapot, Irish, George III, James Scott, lobed, circular, matching cover, 6, 23 ozs, 15 dwts, 1805 (4259/152) — 450
Teapot and stand, partly oval shape, engraved scrolls, 6½, 1801, 20 ozs (4160/271) — 1050
Teapot and stand, straight sided oval form, 4 claw and ball feet, 6¼, 1787, 20 ozs 5 dwts (4238/215) — 1900
Teapot and stand, George III, octagonal form, 21 ozs, 10 dwts, 6¾, 1802 (4194/133) — 575
Teapots, pair, George III, R. Garrard I, plain, ivory finials and handles, 5¾, 44 ozs, 1808 (4260/523) — 1200
Toast rack, rectangular gadroon base, 7 double arched rack, 6¾, 1820, 12 ozs, 10 dwts (4160/276) — 200
Toast rack, arts and crafts, J.W.H. & J.T.H., 7 bars, curved, ball feet, 6½, 10 ozs, 1881 (4260/506) — 500
Tobacco box, Queen Anne, B. Bentley, oval, corded and molded borders, rounded cover, 4, 6 ozs, 1703 (4260/598) — 1500
Toilet jars, pair, William & Mary, Anthony Nelme, fluted, 3, 5 ozs, ca1690 (4260/597) — 950
Tray, oval, George I, Jacob Margas, molded border, 6⅜, 5 ozs, 1716 (4259/228) — 1800
Tray, snuffer's, hourglass form, molded rim, engraved crest, 7, 1736, 7 ozs, 5 dwts (4160/361) — 425
Tray, snuffer's, shaped hourglass form, center engraved, 7¼, 1748, 10 ozs, 5 dwts (4160/305) — 700
Tray, snuffer's, hourglass form, hoof feet, scroll handle, 7⅜, 1736, 8 ozs (4238/218) — 475
Tray, tea, George III, Timothy Renou, 2 handled, oval, 25½, 92 ozs, 1801 (4260/531) — 2800
Tray, tea, 2 handled, George IV, Samuel Hennell, rectangular, 24½, 100 ozs, 10 dwts, 1825 (4259/211) — 2400
Tray, 2 handled oval, silver-gilt, for Tiffany & Co., 21¼, 1925, 55 ozs. (619/165) — 650
Tray, 2 handles, oval, handles centered by an anthemion, 26½, 1812, 105 ozs (4238/288) — 2600
Trays, snuffers, pair, John & Thomas Settle, rectangular in curved sides, 9⅝, 14 ozs, 1824 (4259/290) — 900
Trophy, Regatta, silver oars and 6 medallions in box inscription, 1860 (631/176) — 200
Trowel, serving, wood terminal, blade pierced with diaper and scrolling foliage, 13½, ca1770 (4238/195) — 425
Tumbler cup, George II, Edward Wakelin, rounded base, gilt interior, 2⅜, 5 ozs, 1757 (4260/588) — 800
Tumbler cup, George II, Humphrey Payne, cylindrical, rounded base, 2¼, 2 ozs, 1746 (4260/590) — 450
Tureen, soup and cover, gadroon rim, 4 paw feet, 14½, 1812, 151 ozs 10 dwts (4238/281) — 6750
Tureen, soup and cover, oval boat shape, loop handles, 17½, 1794, 76 ozs 5 dwts (4238/261) — 9500
Tureen, soup and cover, oval, cadroon rim, with foliage and shells, 18½, 1821, 144 ozs (4160/347) — 3500
Tureen, soup and cover, plain boat shape, engraved with a 'Marquess', loop handles, 17⅞, 1785, 95 ozs 10 dwts (4238/267) — 4500
Tureen, soup and cover, stand, J. Bridge, boat shaped, William IV, 21¾, 257 ozs, 1829 (4259/287) — *16000*
Tureen, soup, covered, plain boat shape, marquess' coronet, 17⅜, 1785, 95 ozs, 10 dwts (4160/290) — 5500
Tureen sauce and cover, Sheffield plated, lobed and bombe oval form, 8, ca1830 (4259/31) — 275
Tureen soup and cover, J. E. Terrey, spherical, William IV, 16½, 12 ozs, 1831 (4259/285) — *4000*
Tureens, covered, set of 3, Oval, stepped bases with loop handles, 1894, 86 ozs (619/162) — 850
Tureens, sauce and covers, pair, George III, boat shape, reeded loop handles, 8½, 28 ozs, 1793 (4259/156) — 2200
Tureens, sauce and covers, set of 4, boat shape, George IV, John Bridges, 8¾, 146 ozs, 1829 (4259/288) — *11500*

Tureen soup and cover
(4259/285)

Tureen (4259/287)

Tureens (4259/288)

Tureens, sauce and covers, 2 matching, lobed circular form, 4 shell scroll supports, 8½, 1807/11, 53 ozs (4160/257)	1900
Tureens, sauce pair, beaded rim set with flowers, 4 scroll feet, 8¼, 1773, 40 ozs 15 dwts (4238/280)	1000
Tureens, sauce pair, engraved twice with crests, boat shpe, domed covers, 8¾, 1802, 72 ozs, fine (4238/322)	5750
Tureens, sauce, pair, oval, domed cover, urn finials, 9¾, 1788, 33 ozs 15 dwts (4238/265)	2200
Tureens, sauce, covers, pair, Sheffield plated, oval bombe form, armorials, 9½, ca1820 (4259/25)	550
Tureens, sauce, covers, pair, Sheffield plated, plain boatshape, reeded rim, loop handles, 8½, ca1790 (4259/27)	350
Tureens, sauce, pair, engraved with crests, oval form, 8¾, 1771, 24 ozs 10 dwts (4238/302)	1200
Tureens, sauce, pair, oval, gadroon borders, 4 hairy paw feet, lions heads at ends, 6½, 1799, 36 ozs, 10 dwts (4160/289)	2200
Tureens, sauce, pair, rectangular, reeded and faceted handles, 8¼, 1817, 60 ozs 10 dwts (4238/300)	4100
Tureens, soup and covers, pair, partly fluted, oval pedestal bases, domed covers, 9¾, 1788, 33 ozs, 15 dwts (4160/256)	2200
Urn, tea, ovoid form, spigot modeled as snake, floral sprays, 20¼, 1770, 123 ozs (4160/419)	2000
Urn, coffee, Sheffield plated, lobed vase shape with bright cut corners, 15¾, ca1790 (4268/5)	200
Urn, 2-handled, George III, Charles Wright, London, 59 ozs, 10 dwts, 14½, 1780 (4159/62)	600
Vase, sugar, George III, Burrage Davenport, plain, beaded borders, 5⅜, 6 ozs, 1781 (4259/173)	400
Vases, pair, conical form, sides pierced, gothic tracery, 11⅝, 1836, 41 ozs, 10 dwts (4160/235)	1600
Vases, pair of Victorian, Maker's Mark W.W., F.D., 11 ozs, 4½, 1891 (4194/105)	275
Vases, sugar, covered, pair, vase shape, pedestal base, applied 2 handles, 6⅛, 1807, 14 ozs (4238/283)	300
Waiter, circular, beaded rim, feet pierced, engraved, 7, 1777, 9 ozs 15 dwts (4238/245)	550
Waiter, circular, reeded rim, monogram, 3 panel feet, 6, 1791, 5 ozs (4160/332)	175
Waiter, engraved with foliate sprays, 3 hoof feet, 8½, 1766, 12 ozs, 10 dwts (4160/386)	175
Waiter, molded border, scrollwork rim, dec with shells, 6¼, 1766, 7 ozs (4238/252)	475
Waiter, shell and scroll rim on 3 scroll feet, 6¼, 1766, 7 ozs (4160/342)	350
Waiter, shell and scroll rim, 3 hoof feet, 6⅞, 1750, 8 ozs 10 dwts (4238/292)	450
Waiter, George I, square with raised rim, 6¼, 6 ozs, 1726 (4259/261)	600
Waiter, George I, John White, square form, 6½, 11 ozs, 1720 (4259/259)	1200
Waiter, George II, pie-crust border, 7 ozs, Diam 6¾, 1757 (4194/248)	175
Waiter, George II, George Hindmarsh, pie-crust rim, 8 ozs, 5 dwts, Diam 6½, 1737 (4194/156)	225
Waiter, George II, John Tuite, circular, 7 ozs, 10 dwts, Diam 6½, 1737 (4194/282)	400
Waiter, George II, Philips Garden, London, 5 ozs, 10 dwts, Diam 6, 1747 (4159/56)	275
Waiter, George II, Edward Pocock, shaped square form, 10½, 9 ozs, 1730 (4259/221)	800
Waiter, George II, Richard Rugg, with hunting horn crest, 7⅛, 4 ozs, 1756 (4259/176)	350
Waiter, George II, Robert Abercromby, circular, bath border, 6¼, 9 ozs, 1733 (4260/580)	650
Waiter, George II, Robert Abercromby, plain circular form, 6½, 5 ozs, 1742 (4259/147)	200
Waiter, George II, Robert Abercromby, shell and scroll rim, 6½, 6 ozs, 1739 (4259/139)	275
Waiter, George II, Wm. Townsand, armorials, hoof feet, Irish, 6½, 9 ozs, 1775 (4259/260)	750
Waiter, George III, John Beldon, circular, 10 ozs, 15 dwts, Diam 8¼, 1787 (4194/181)	200
Waiter, George III, Edward Capper, 3 claw feet, 7½, 8 ozs, 1763 (4259/252)	275

Waiter, George III, John Schofield, oval, with fluted border, 9, 11 ozs, 1782 (4259/208) — 425
Waiter, George III, Mark R.R., gadroon rim, armorials, 7⅜, 10 ozs, 1771 (4259/175) — 400
Waiter, George III, Richard Rugg, shaped, beaded rim, 8, 12 ozs, 1774 (4259/278) — 450
Waiters, pair, circular form, double beaded border, with engraving, 7⅛, 1780, 15 ozs (4238/321) — 600
Waiters, pair, circular, engraving in shields, 7½, 1780, 19 ozs 15 dwts (4238/320) — 750
Waiters, pair, square shape, engraved with armorials, bracket feet, 6⅛, 1731, 21 ozs (4238/303) — 10000
Waiters, pair, George II, Peter Archambo, circular, strapwork and shellwork, 6, 18 ozs, 1730 (4260/596) — 3500
Waiters, pair, William IV, mark W.E., circular, 8½, 37 ozs, 1836 (4260/551) — 1000
Wax Jack, pierced with trellis, ball and claw feet, 6¾, 1761, 10 os gross (4238/230) — 650
Wax Jack, circular base, reeded lyre shaped holder with chain, 5⅜, 1802, 5 ozs 10 dwts (4238/306) — 550
Wine coaster, shaped border, with scrolls and grapevines, 7¾, 1853 (4160/234) — 225
Wine coaster, George III, P. Roberts, beaded rim, wood base, Scottish, 4⅞, 1789 (4259/265) — 275
Wine coasters, pair, circular, gadroon rims, shellwork, wood base, 6½, 1821 (4160/340) — 575
Wine coasters, pair, ovolo rim with openwork grapevine sides, wood base, 5¾, 1818 (4160/263) — 1200
Wine cooler, campana shape, lobed and fluted, engraved, 10⅞, 1823, 111 ozs 10 dwts (4238/317) — 3200
Wine cooler, William IV, Paul Storr, campana shape, 11½, 67 ozs, 1836 (4259/271) — *3750*
Wine coolers, pair, detachable liners, open lids, 5¾, 1801, 118 0zs, 10 dwts (4160/351) — 8750
Wine coolers, pair, William IV, R. Smith, campana shape, 10⅞, 165 ozs, 1836 (4259/286) — *6500*

Wine coolers (4194/9)

Wine cooler
(4259/271)

Wine coolers
(4259/286)

Wine coolers, Sheffield plated, pair, campana shape, twig handles, 11, ca1810 (4194/15) — 1200
Wine coolers, Sheffield plated, pair, cylindrical, baron's coronet, 7⅜, ca1790 (4194/9) — *1100*
Wine funnel, George III, Peter & Ann Bateman, reeded rim, detachable bowl, 4⅞, 3 ozs, 1793 (4260/534) — 375
Wine labels, George III, set of 6, Paul Storr, silver-gilt, 6 ozs, 10 dwts, L2½, 1817 (4194/292) — 2300

Other Sheffield plated

Argyle, double wall, filled through opening in the top, 4¾, ca1780 (4160/194) — 325
Argyle, straight sided, gadroon foot, domed lid, 5, ca1790 (4238/3) — 200
Basket, cake, double dished circular form, 10⅝, ca1835 (4160/197) — 100
Candelabra, 3 light, pair, with reeded borders, 17 (4160/199) — 225
Candelabra, 5 light, plated, taperd, engraved twice with armorials, 31½, ca1810 (4160/182) — 550
Candlesticks, pair, columnar, campana sconce, 12⅝, ca1775 (4238/6) — 300
Candlesticks, table, pair, bases decorated with urns, foliage at the angles, 13, ca1775 (4238/5) — 250
Candlesticks, table, pair, column form, stems formed with multiple shafts, 12⅜, ca1775 (4238/4) — 300
Coffeepot, oval shape, reeded spout, 13, ca1795 (4238/15) — 250
Coolers, wine, pair, campana shape, detachable liners and rims, 10½, ca1820, good (4238/8) — 1900
Cruet stand, 4 cut-glass cruets, oblong plateau, L11, 19c (4148/83) — 375
Cup, 2 handled, engraved with crest, 9¾, ca1780 (4160/203) — 175
Cups, 2 matching, bell shaped bowls and trumpet shaped stems, 6¼ - 6⅛, ca1775 (4160/193) — 175

Dish, meat, cover plated, domed oval shape, band set with shells and foliage, 18½, ca1825 (4160/180) — 175
Epergne, plated, square base, raised on 4 foliate feet, 14, ca1820 (4160/179) — 475
Garniture table, metal, oval flower holder, 2 circular holders, 27½, ca1880, 3 pcs (669/341) — 900
Inkstand, with scrolling grapevine between gadroon borders, 11¼, ca1800, large (4160/196) — 350
Jug, hot water, octagonal urn shap, reeded border, urn finial, 10, ca1795 (4238/14) — 200
Jug, hot water, oviform body with beaded borders, 11½, ca1780 (4238/13) — 150
Jug, hot water, vase shape, reeded border, ball finial, 12⅜, ca1790 (4238/12) — 225
Tea kettle on lamp stand, fixed handles, fluted spout, 12½ (4160/189) — 125
Tray, serving, two covered vegetable dishes set into warming stand, 23, L19c (631/177) — 250
Tray, tea, 2 handled, raised gallery, engraved, 27¼, ca1880, Hall & Co. (4160/202) — 300
Tray, tea, 2 handled, plated, oval, with egg and foliate border, 34½ (4160/184) — 375
Tureen, soup and cover, leafy scroll feet and handles, 14¾, ca1825, T.&J. Creswick (4160/201) — 800
Tureens, sauce and covers, pair, compressed circular form, engraved, 6⅝, ca1815, Boulton & Co. (4160/198) — 750
Wine coolers, pair, shellwork, banded by grapevines, 11¼, ca1830 (4160/200) — 650

FRENCH SILVER

Beaker, everted molded rim, gadroon pedestal foot, 3¾, 1743, 3 ozs, 5 dwts (4160/99) — 575
Beaker, molded rim, engraved with initials, 3½, ca1760, 3 ozs, 5 dwts (4160/100) — 500
Beaker, tulip shape, stamped with name, 3½, 1754, 3 ozs, 10 dwts (4160/103) — 625
Beaker, Maker's Mark C.T., with Napoleanic arms, 2⅞, 2 ozs, ca1860 (4259/93) — 150
Beaker, Louis XV, Jean Nicholas Hannier, molded lip, 2¼, 2 ozs, 1739 (4259/106) — 450
Beaker, Louis XV, bell form, engraved name P. Perre, 2¼, 1768-70, 20 ozs (4238/47) — 425
Beaker, Louis XV, tulip shape, rococo shells and scrolls, 3⅞, ca1768, 4 ozs 10 dwts (4238/63) — 1900
Beaker, Louis XVI, Boutheroue-Desmarais, molded pedestal foot, 4¾, 4 ozs, 1785 (4259/107) — 175
Bowl sugar,covered, inverted pear shape, 4 double twig feet, 6¼, 1755, 21 ozs, 10 dwts (4238/59) — *3700*
Brazier, circular, rim pierced with vertical pales, 3 feet, 8¼, 1819-38, 21 ozs 10 dwts (4238/41) — 650
Centerpiece, Empire, Jean Baptiste-Claude Odiot, 54 ozs, 10 dwts, L14¼, 1809-19 (4194/60) — *3900*
Coffeepot, pear shape body, wood handle, 8, 1798-1809, Carron, Paris, 12 ozs., 10 dwts. (4141/634) — 550
Coffeepot, bands of acanthus and flowers, 11, ca1820, 23 ozs, 15 dwts (4160/91) — 1400
Coffeepot, bulbous form, fluted spout, turned wood handle, 9¾, 1809-19, 25 ozs, 15 dwts (4160/101) — 950
Coffeepot, oviform, with leaf tip girdle and border, 14, 1809-19, large, 40 ozs gross (4238/42) — *2000*
Coffeepot, Directoire, Jean Baptiste Claude, swan-neck spout, 14, 42 ozs, 1798-1809 (4259/102) — *2300*

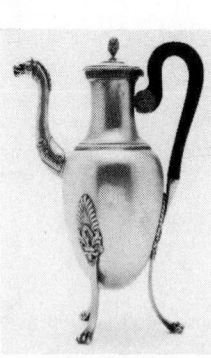

Coffeepot (4238/42)

Beaker (4160/49)

Coffeepot (4259/102)

Bowl sugar covered (4238/59)

Centerpiece (4194/60)

Coffee set, 3 piece, Chinese figure finials, ca1850, M. Fray, 40 ozs. (4141/637) 700
Dish, finials, pair, formed as eagles resting on pedestals, 2¼, 1819-38, 11 ozs. (4160/96) 175
Dish, serving, circular, initials, 12, 1752, Vallieres, Paris, 26 ozs., 10 dwts. (4141/633) 1500
Dish, serving, circular, molded rim, armorials, 11, 1736, Sonlaine, Paris, 24 ozs., 5 dwts. (4141/632) 1600
Dish, vegetable, covered, circular form, branch form handles, 11, ca1850, 40 ozs (4238/40) 1300
Dishes, footed silver-gilt, pair, chased with foliage and scrolls, 7, 1819-38, 19 ozs, 10 dwts (4160/89) 600
Dishes, leafform, pair, overlapping shells and matted vine leaves, 7½, 24 ozs, M19c (4259/96) 650
Dishes, vegetable, stands, pair, Jean-Charles Cahier, Royal Arms of France, 10⅝, 127 ozs, ca1820 (4259/100) 4500
Dressing table set, silver mounted, engraved glass, ribbon swags and floral motifs, ca1900, 12 pcs. (669/345) 1400
Ewer, Louis XVI, baluster form, ivory handle, 33 ozs, 10 dwts, 11, 1788 (4194/62) 6000
Ewers, silver mounted, pair, glass bodies, Maker's Mark H.S., 10½, M19c (4194/51) 850
Flatware, Cardeilhac, Paris, handles engraved with husk pattern, 46 pcs., 64 ozs, ca1890 (4259/89) 600
Flatware, dessert, silver-gilt, Empire, engraved, decorated handles, 1798, 36 pcs., 75 ozs, 1809 (4259/99) 2500
Jug, hot water, compressed circular form, 7¾, 1819-38, 22 ozs 5 dwts (4238/46) 500
Jugs, claret glass and silver mounted pair, with openwork silver floral festoons, 12¾, ca1900, weighted (4160/85) 375
Knives, fruit set of twelve, silver-gilt, mother of pearl handled, leather case, 1798-1809, later marks (4238/44) 500
Lustres, table, pair, starch blue glass, scalloped bobeches, clear prisms, 9⅞, 19c (4219/42) 200
Mostrance, with stones, plaques of saints, crucifix, H29½, 107 gross ozs. (631/185) 1500
Mug, silver-gilt, flared rim, bacchanal masks, 4⅞, 1809-19, Odiot, Paris, 8 ozs., 15 dwts. (4141/631) 475
Platter, meat, oval form, with shaped molded rim, 13¾, ca1880, 27 ozs, 10 dwts (4160/90) 225
Salt cellars, pair, Empire, circular frames, blue glass liners, 3, 4 ozs, 1809-19 (4259/98) 100
Salt cellars, set of 4, pedestal, square base scroll and foliate feet, 3⅝, ca1830, 17 ozs (4238/37) 325
Sugar bowls, covered, pair, Louis XVI, Rene-Pierre Ferrie, festoons of flowers, 6¾, 17 ozs, 1781 (4259/104) 1600
Taster, wine, bowl chased with sloping flutes, punched beading, 3½, ca1800, 30 ozs, 5 dwts (4238/55) 225
Taster, wine, decorated with bosses and flutes, 2¾, ca1780, 1 oz 10 dwts (4238/52) 350
Taster, wine, engraved Bernat, Chirurgien 1743, 3⅛, 1743, 1 oz, 15 dwts (4238/56) 425
Taster, wine, plain circular bowl, engraved J. Besson, snake handle, 2¾, 1772, 2 ozs, 10 dwts (4238/57) 425
Taster, wine, stamped with name M.I. Guitet, coiled snake handle, 2¾, ca1780, 2 ozs, 10 dwts (4238/58) 200
Taster, wine, wide bowl, engraved with flutes, strap handle, 3¼, 1798, later marks, 2 ozs (4238/51) 375
Tea and coffee set, 4 piece, lobed and fluted baluster form, shellwork, H10 pot, 57 ozs, M19c (4259/95) 1000
Tea and coffee set, 4 pieces, baluster shapes, double scroll handles, M19c, 66 ozs. (4160/94) 950
Tea and coffee set, 5 pieces, Puiforcat, Paris, tray, L29¾, modern, 375 ozs (4160/82) 5000
Tea kettle on lampstand, baluster body, with fixed handle, 13¼, ca1900, 41 ozs (4160/93) 225
Tea kettle on lampstand, swirl fluted baluster shape, rococo style, 21¼, M19c, 116 ozs. (4160/95) 1400
Vase, sugar, covered, 3 paw feet, wood harp, shaped handles, 8, 1798-1809, 22 ozs. (4141/584) 375
Vase, sugar, covered, 3 paw feet, bell shape body, 8, 1798-1809, 22 ozs (4160/102) 400
Wine tasters, 2 matching, grape clusters, bosses, lobes, 5 ozs, Diam 3⅜, ca1900 (4194/57) 200

GERMAN SILVER

Altar, wood house, silver and ebonized, 36, L17c, Augsburg (4133/158) 5750
Angel, hollow cast figure, sash over shoulder, stippled engraved cloth, 7¼, E18c (4133/155) 450
Beaker, body embossed with bust, strapwork, fruit and foliage, 5¾, ca1900, 8 ozs (4238/84) 225
Beaker, embossed with fruit and foliage 3 ball feet, 3⅝, ca1680, 3 ozs (4160/54) 1400
Beaker, embossed with large flowers and foliage, 3 ball feet, 2¾, ca1670, 2 ozs, 10 dwts (4160/55) 1100
Beaker, molded rim and gilt interior, 3⅜, ca1700, Wildt, 4 ozs, 10 dwts (4160/60) 1700
Beaker, plain form, gilt interior, 3½, ca1700, 4 ozs, 10 dwts (4160/61) 1600
Beaker, tapered form, chased with large shell and foliage, 3⅝, 1727-37 (4238/92) 1200
Beaker, tapered form, embossed with flowers, 3⅜, ca1670, 3 ozs (4160/56) 800
Beaker, Johan Hoffler, molded rim, 3¼, 4 ozs, L17c (4259/58) 1550
Beaker, Maker's mark I.W., cylindrical, 4 ozs, 10 dwts, 3½, ca1700 (4194/82) 1200
Beaker, double, two halves of a barrel, embossed, hoops and staves, 5, E18c, 6 ozs (4238/95) 2600
Beaker, double, chased to stimulate a barrel, bases engraved, 4⅝, ca1900 (4238/67) 175
Beaker, double, barrel form silver-gilt, with staves and hoops, 6½, ca1660, 7 ozs., 5 dwts. (4141/589) 7750
Beaker, double, barrel form, parcel-gilt, chased with gilded hoops, simulated staves, 5⅞, ca1660, 5 ozs, 10 dwts (4160/49) *4750*
Beaker, double, barrel form, silver-gilt, with staves and hoops, 5¼, M17c, 4 ozs. (4141/590) 6000
Beaker, parcel-gilt, engraved with initials at lip, 3½, L17c, Augsburg, 4 ozs, 10 dwts (4238/62) 1800

Beaker, parcel-gilt, engraved with name and date 1756, 3⅝, M18c, 4 ozs., 10 dwts. (4141/587)   1300
Beaker, parcel-gilt, tapered form, cartouche with pineapple, 4, L18c, 3 ozs 10 dwts (4238/75)   2300
Beaker, parcel-gilt, gilt border top and bottom, molded rim, 3¾, ca1700, 5 ozs, 10 dwt (4160/62)   1800
Beaker, silver-gilt, molded lip, with band of granulation, 3½, L17c, 4 ozs., 10 dwts. (4141/385)   1500
Beaker, silver-gilt, Cylindrical, 1632 coin in base, 3½, L17c (4259/57)   800
Beakers, pair silver-gilt, with a granulated band, 3¾, L17c, 9 ozs, 10 dwts (4160/71)   5250
Bowl, sugar, 2 handled, bowl shape with pedestal foot, loop handles, 8¼, ca1820, 7 ozs (4238/86)   125
Bowl, 2 handled, oval sides, pierced and chased with birds, ca1900, 37 ozs (669/349)   700
Box, sugar, oval, sprays of flowers, raised on 4 shell-scroll feet, 5, ca1765, 7 ozs (4160/70)   2500
Box, oval, parcel-gilt, Otto Friedrick Vollhagen, with crimped rim, 5, 7 ozs, ca1700 (4259/55)   *2400*
Box, seal, silver-gilt, shallow, molded border, slip on cover, 5¼, L18c, 10 ozs (4160/43)   1000
Box, sugar, oval body, bombe sides, 5 ozs, 10 dwts, L4⅜, ca1750 (4194/83)   1900
Candelabra, pair 7 lights, with foliate scrolls and flowers, 24½, ca1840, 102 ozs., 10 dwts. (4141/628)   1800
Candelabra, pair, 4 light, applied female masks, 17, 1828, Kroner, 100 ozs (4160/45)   *3000*
Candlesticks, pair, pestle shaped stems, vase shaped sconces, 13½, 20 ozs, ca1900 (4259/38)   300
Candlesticks, table, pair, slender, applied medallions of foliage, 7⅝, ca1830, 12 ozs, 10 dwts (4160/35)   1000
Candlesticks, table, pair, square bases, tapered stems, 10½, ca1810, 20 ozs. (4141/605)   1300
Candlesticks, table, pair, tapered stems topped by horses' heads, 11½, 1816, 26 ozs, 10 dwts (4160/34)   1400
Centerpiece, oval, scrolled sides, pierced rosette and diaperwork, 24, L19c, 75 ozs. (631/180)   2750
Centerpiece, circular bowl on 4 pilaster supports, 9, ca1900, 35 ozs, 10 dwts (4160/7)   325
Coffeepot B.G.F. Andreack, lobed circular form, ivory handle, 8¾, 25 ozs, ca1840 (4259/61)   275
Coolers, wine, pair parcel-gilt, Brahmfeld und Gutruf, with armorials, 10⅝, 233 ozs, ca1860 (4259/51)   *6750*
Cup, tumbler, silver-gilt, molded rim and rounded base, 3, ca1700, Solanier, 2 ozs, 10 dwts (4160/58)   1400
Cup, silver-gilt, gourd shaped, embossed with foliage and flowers, 6⅝, M17c, 3 ozs, 10 dwts (4160/74)   800
Cup, silver-gilt, half double cup, embossed, 7 ozs, 5 dwts, 5½, ca1580 (4194/89)   2700
Cup, silver-gilt, half of double cup, gourd shaped bowl chased, masks and fruit, 4⅞, c.1680, 7 ozs (4160/73)   1000
Cup and cover, parcel-gilt, engraved with panels of peasants drinking, 10½, 15 ozs, L19c (649/311)   325
Cups, pair silver-gilt, bell shape bowls, banded stems, 6⅛ and 6⅜, 1737-45, 9 ozs, 15 dwts (4160/52)   4500
Dish, oval, parcel-gilt, with armorials, 2 profile busts, 8¼, ca1700, 5 ozs. (4141/588)   1100
Dish, serving, Carl Samuel Betkober, with later armorials, 11⅞, 23 ozs, 1783 (4259/53)   700
Dish, sweetmeat, boat shape, cherub seated on scroll end holding paddle, 7½, ca1900, 9 ozs., 10 dwts. (4141/630)   200
Dish, sweetmeat, oval, parcel-gilt, with Thisbe fleeing from the lioness, 7, ca1640, 11 ozs., 5 dwts. (4141/611)   4750
Dish, sweetmeat, parcel-gilt, chased with flowering plants, scroll handle, 6½, ca1670, 5 ozs., 5 dwts. (4141/615)   1400
Dish, sweetmeat, silver-gilt, oval with waved rim, embossed with flowers, 5, ca1670, 2 ozs., 5 dwts. (4141/612)   1350
Dish, sweetmeat, embossed with a horseman galloping, 6¼, L17c, 3 ozs, 10 dwts (4160/68)   1500
Dish, sweetmeat, parcel-gilt, oval form, with bird, spray of fruit, 6, L17c, 3 ozs, 10 dwts (4160/67)   1700
Dish, sweetmeat, parcel-gilt, oval form, woman seated, urn of flowers, 5, L17c, 3 ozs, 5 dwts (4160/66)   1400
Dish, sweetmeat, parcel-gilt, plain gilt lobes, chased white lobes, 4, ca1665, 2 ozs (4160/72)   2600
Dishes, meat, pair, shaped oval form, with molded rim, 20, modern, 82 ozs, 10 dwts (4160/2)   400
Flatware, pointed terminals over laurel & berry borders, modern, 151 pcs, 127 ozs (4160/15)   850
Flatware, dessert set, silver-gilt, enamel demi-figures, swans, L19c, 36 pcs, Viennese (4141/74)   8500
Knife and fork, enamel and silver-gilt, case, handles dec with flowers in blue and yellow white ground, 6½, E18c, 3 pcs (4133/156)   275
Ladle, fiddle thread pattern, toole border, Judaic inscription, E19c, 5 ozs, 15 dwts (4160/8)   175
Ladle, soup, with a medallion of a deer and boar, 15¼, 1800, 5 ozs, 10 dwts (4160/57)   100
Plate, silver-gilt, Abraham Waremberger, medallions of 3 Romans, 10⅝, 8 ozs, ca1700 (4259/62)   1200
Platters, pair, oval, lobed and fluted sides, chased with shell and scrollwork, 17⅛, 1757-59, large 60 ozs (4238/77)   7250
Salt cellar, Georg Nicolaus Bierfreund, oval, 2 ozs, L4, ca1760 (4194/84)   250
Salt cellars, pair, compressed, circular form, 3 twig and leaf feet, 2½, ca1790, 5 ozs (4238/76)   175
Salver on foot, parcel-gilt, engraved with port scene, ca1780, 12½, Austrian, 24 ozs. (4141/582)   2300
Sauce boats and stands, pair, German*, double-lipped, 18 ozs, L8, 1900 (4194/78)   600
Sauce boats pair, form of cannons decorated with rococo ornament, L10, ca1900, 38 ozs (4238/69)   *1700*
Spoon, parcel, fig. shaped bowl, engraved, terminal as lion rampant, 8⅛, L16c, fine (4141/604)   2200

Spoon, silver-gilt, curved stem, with rat tail rising to a shield, 6¼, L17c (4141/603) — 650
Tankard, chased with putti in landscape, 6¼, ca1700, 22 ozs, 10 dwts (4160/63) — *2200*
Tankard, parcel-gilt, tall hexafoil shaped, engraved with 6 scenes, 13½, ca1630, 55 ozs (4160/64) — 16000
Tankard, parcel-gilt, with merry-making peasants, 9⅛, ca1670, fine, Steinweg, 49 ozs (4160/65) — 13000
Tankard, silver, with strapwork and fruit, figural finial, 6¼, ca1900 (4160/577) — 550
Tankard, silver-gilt, tall dome foot, cover, inset with coins, 8⅝, ca1750, Schlaubitz, 46 ozs, 10 dwts (4160/47) — *5500*
Tazze, pair, bowls pierced with foliage supported on tails of dolphins, 9, ca1900, 24 ozs (4160/32) — 325
Teapot, bulbous circular form, chased flower & foliage, 4, ca1760, Krumstroh, 7 ozs (4160/36) — 1250
Tray, rectangular, cut-out handles, center embossed, 20, ca1900, 36 ozs, 10 dwts (4160/13) — 350
Tray, 2 handled, oval, floral sprays within foliate scrolled cartouches, 31¼, 147 ozs, ca1880 (649/309) — 200
Tureen, covered, 3 hoof feet headed by acanthus, circular, 5¾, 1807, Austrian, 26 ozs., 10 dwts. (4141/583) — 1300
Warmer, muffin, triple, shell form, 10, 64 ozs, ca1900 (4259/46) — 750

Dish cover (4259/77)

Candelabra (4160/45)

Tankard (4160/47)

Tankard (4160/63)

Box (4259/55)

Sauce boats pair (4238/69)

Coolers (4259/51)

ITALIAN SILVER

Ash trays, set of twelve, double shells, on 3 ball feet, 3½, modern, 42 ozs (4160/132) — 650
Beaker, plain cyl. shape with curved base, slip on cover, 2⅝, 18c, 3 ozs, 10 dwts (4160/109) — 200
Bowl, caviar, circular bowl chased with large and small lobes, 7¼, modern, 24 ozs (4160/115) — 450
Bowls and stands, pair, lobed and fluted, strapwork and shell rims, matching stands, 7¾, modern, 28 ozs (4160/136) — 275
Bucket, Italian*, Romanesque style, with seated saints, 9½, 24 ozs, ca1900 (4259/45) — 950
Candlestick, Giusseppe Pocaterra, sconce held by putto, 5½, 5 ozs, ca1870 (4259/73) — 400
Candlestick, hand, cruciform pan and handle, 10¼, M19c, 5 ozs, 5 dwts (4238/35) — 325
Candlesticks, chamber, pair, leaf-shaped pans, Maker's Mark C, 11 ozs, 10 dwts, L7, ca1770 (4194/52) — 650

Dish (4160/137)

Verriere (4238/33)

Candlesticks, set of 4, octagonal bases, standing putti, 7⅛ to 6⅞, modern, 67 ozs, 10 dwts
(4160/108)   600
Coffee percolator, Venice, 2 cylindrical vessels, pierced ends, 7⅛, 21 ozs, M19c (4259/75)   300
Crumb brushes and trays, pair, trays matted scrolling strapwork rims, 7¾, modern, 36 ozs
(4160/131)   425
Dish, entree, circular, boat shape, with reversible cover, detachable handle, 13¼, modern, 87 ozs
(4160/123)   850
Dish, meat and cover, domed cover, shell and scroll handle, 23¾, modern, 194 ozs (4160/137)   *1800*
Dish, well and tree, large, six foliate feet, double shells, 23¾, modern, 136 ozs, 10 dwts (4160/138)   1000
Dish cover, Maker's Mark, B.G., with armorials, leakage, 10⅝, 24 ozs, ca1775 (4259/77)   *800*
Dishes, butter and stands, pair, openwork form, leaf-capped scroll handles, 7¾, modern, 39 ozs
(4160/121)   525
Dishes, entree and covers, pair, oval, strapwork and shell borders, 17¼, modern, 218 ozs
(4160/120)   1900
Dishes, meat, pair, oval, shell and strapwork rim, 19¾, modern, 52 ozs (4160/126)   750
Dishes, meat, pair, oval, shell and strapwork rims, 14, modern, 52 ozs (4160/125)   500
Dishes, roast, pair, centered by well and tree recesses, 23¾, modern, 267 ozs (4160/139)   2250
Dishes, serving, circular, set of 3, shell and strapwork rims, 8¾, modern, 110 ozs, 10 dwts
(4160/127)   1300
Ewer, covered, pear shape with angular handle, pedestal foot, 10, ca1800, 24 ozs (4160/104)   400
Ewers, pair, helmet shape, lobed and fluted, foliate scroll handles, 12¾, modern, 75 ozs, 10 dwts
(4160/116)   1000
Flatware service, French empire pattern, leaf tips and berries, modern, 602 pcs (4160/111)   10500
Lamp, bronze, silver, Pietro Paolo Spagna, Egyptian figure carrying silver lamp, 11¾, ca1830
(4259/78)   650
Lamp, oil, Diana holding urn-shaped lamp, 13½, ca1840 (4194/49)   1300
Paten, dish form with thread border, engraved figure, 7⅜, L17c, 5 ozs (4238/32)   375
Pot mustard, bulbous circular form, domed cover, 3⅜, L18c, 5 ozs (4238/34)   175
Salt and pepper, 12 matching, fluted baluster form, applied with shells, 4½, modern, 72 ozs
(4160/142)   750
Sauce boats on stands, pair, waved rim, leaf capped scroll handle, 11, modern, 62 ozs, 10 dwts
(4160/117)   750
Spoon, egg shaped bowl, faceted and curved, stem, 7⅛ (4238/105)   300
Sugar bowl, covered and creamer, pear shaped and fluted, 6¾, modern, 32 ozs (4160/119)   375
Sugar covered and creamer, pear shape, spirally lobed and fluted, 6¾, modern, 32 ozs (4160/118)   400
Tazza, circular, applied strapwork and shell rim pedestal base, 13¾, modern, 53 ozs (4160/135)   550
Tray, tea, 2 handled, oval, reeded rim and matching handles, 24½, modern, 79 ozs (4160/144)   700
Trays, bread, pair, boat shape, lobed and fluted, strapwork & shell border, 12, modern, 35 ozs
(4160/122)   350
Urn, tea, pear shape, turned wood handles, 17½, modern, 127 ozs, 10 dwts (4160/114)   1000
Urns, cigarette, twelve, cyl. form, molded bases, rims strapwork and shells, 2¾, modern, 36 ozs
(4160/140)   325
Vase, inverted pear shape, bell-form rim, domed circular base, 6¼, M18c, 9ozs. (4141/572)   325
Verriere, oval body, vertical lobes, matted scalework, 11⅜, E19c, 69 ozs (4238/33)   *1400*
Wine cooler, lobed, vase shaped with shell and strapwork border, 13¼, modern, 72 ozs (4160/110)   1100
Wine cooler, tapered cyl. form, pierced and applied with scrollwork, 11½, modern, 59 ozs, 10 dwts
(4160/106)   700
Wine cradles, pair, boat shape, shell mounted scroll handles, 11¾, modern, 57 ozs (4160/124)   900

MISCELLANEOUS SILVER

Basket, cake, boat shape, straight ends, reeded rim, 11¼, 1821, Dutch (4238/110)   1200
Basket, cake, oval basket pierced in a lattice, design, 9¾, ca1820, 21 ozs (4238/85)   325
Basket, Dutch cake, Hoeker & Zoon, Lieshout & Co., 32 ozs, 15 dwts, L15¼, 1887 (4194/67)   450
Basket, sweetmeat, filigree, Austrian, Maker's Mark F.S., 7, 10 ozs, 1807 (4259/50)   400
Basket, 2 handled, oval pierced sides, applied rim and handle, paw feet, 15½, 21.5 ozs, (800), E20c
(649/307)   200
Beaker, romer form, 2 sets of initials, 4⅛, ca1630, rare, Norwegian, 5 ozs 15 dwts (4238/96)   5000
Beaker, trumpet shape, engraved with large house, birds, 4⅞, 1837, Swedish, 3 ozs 5 dwts
(4238/98)   250
Beaker, with strapwork and drapery swags, Norwegian, 4¾, ca1630, 5 ozs, 10 dwts (4160/178)   5750
Beaker, covered, fluted oval shape, domed base, cover, 5, ca1740, Hungarian, 6 ozs, 10 dwts
(4160/51)   2500
Beaker, large, plain, slightly bulbous form, reeded cover, 5, ca1825, Hungarian, 7 ozs (4160/50) 200
Beaker, parcel-gilt, trumpet shape, gilt lip, 6⅞, M18c, Estonian, 10 ozs., 5 dwts. (4141/586)   2000
Beaker, parcel-gilt, trumpet form, monogramed, 7, Swedish, 8 ozs, 15 dwts (4160/175)   750
Beaker, parcel-gilt, trumpet shape, engraved with initials, 3¾, ca1740, Swedish, 2 ozs, 15 dwts
(4160/172)   500
Beaker, Norwegian, Maker's Mark I.A.S., flowers, scrolling foliage, 4⅜, 2 ozs, 15 dwts, ca1830
(4259/65)   150
Bowl, circular, embossed with birds, 4¼, M18c, Dutch, 2 ozs 5 dwts (4238/112)   525
Bowl, brandy, engraved with lobate scrolls and pendant flowers, 2⅞, Dutch, 4 ozs, 18c* (4160/167) 1000
Bowl, brandy, oval, chased with large lobes, scrollwork, initials, 9½, 1776, Dutch, 7 ozs 10 dwts
(4238/115)   2500
Bowl, brandy, oval, flat handles, scroll and foliage, 8⅜, 1742, Dutch, 4 ozs (4238/114)   325
Bowl, brandy, covered, oval chased with foliage and masks, 9, 19c, 11 ozs., 5 dwts., Dutch
(4141/578)   325
Bowl, footed silver-gilt, plique-a-jour enamel, hemispherical form, stylized foliage, 4⅝, ca1910
(4238/547)   1500
Bowl, sugar, covered, rim interlaced with branches and leaves, 5¼, ca1840, Mexican, 9 ozs, 10 dwts
(4160/151)   160
Bowl, Dutch brandy, Casparus Janszonius, circular, 4 ozs, 15 dwts, Diam 5⅝, 1743 (4194/71)   900
Bowl, Jacobus De La Hayze, Dutch, large and small lobes, 9½, 27 ozs, 1807 (4259/85)   3100
Box, spice, heart shape, hinged lid, engraved, 3, ca1780, Scandinavian (4141/623)   300
Box, spice, parcel-gilt, heart shape, foliate strapwork, reeded, reserves, 3, ca1740, Scandinavian
(4141/624)   475
Box, spice, urn shaped, basket weave design, screw on cover and cap, 2¼, E18c (4141/621)   200
Box, Austrian spice, 3 tiers, a filigree tower, 5 ozs, 10 dwts, 10¼, L19c (4194/93)   250
Box, Scandinavian*, plain rectangular form, hinge domed cover, 5⅝, 18c, 9 ozs, 15 dwts (4160/41) 900
Brazier, bowl shape, scrolls, engraved with an inscription, 5½, ca1708, Dutch, 7 ozs 5 dwts
(4238/116)   1100
Brazier, openwork form, 2 molded and shell decorated rings, 5¼, ca1770, Dutch, 4 ozs (4160/158) 1100
Brazier, Mexican, Maker's Mark Agodere, fluted, flared bowl, 9⅞, 12 ozs, ca1830 (4259/69)   375
Candelabra, 3 light, pair, Austrian, branches molded with foliate scrolls, baluster stem, 18¼, 1840,
50 ozs. (631/179)   800
Candlestick, Spanish hand, Barcelona, claw-and-ball feet, 6 ozs, 10 dwts, L11¾, ca1800 (4194/43) 275
Candlesticks, pair of table, circular stems, swans, 30 ozs, 12, ca1825 (4194/80)   *1000*

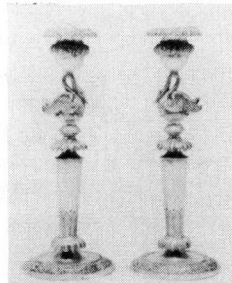

Candlesticks
(4194/80)

Candlesticks
(4259/60)

Caster
(4259/64)

Mustard pot
(4259/86)

Centerpiece
(4194/91)

Salver (4238/113)

Candlesticks, table pair, baluster stems, campana sconces, 9⅝, 1767, Belgian 33 ozs, 15 dwts
(4238/61)   6000
Candlesticks, table pair, domed bases, slender stems, 9¼, ca1810, Portugese, 19 ozs, 10 dwts
(4238/22)   950
Candlesticks, table, pair, square bases, with paw feet chased with foliage, 9, ca1840, 33 ozs
(4160/154)   325
Candlesticks, table, pair, Austrian campana shaped sconces, swags of fruit, 9⅜, ca1900, 14 ozs
(4160/31)   425
Candlesticks, table, set of 4, square bases, chased garland of flowers, 9¼, 33 ozs, ca1810
(4259/60)   *1450*
Caster, baluster shape, pierced slip-on cover, 6⅞, 8 ozs, 15 dwts, Canton*, L18c (4160/205)   225
Caster, Danish, pear shape, spirally ribbed, 6⅛, 4 ozs, 1785 (4259/64)   *1100*
Centerpiece, basket on a tree with a buck, 75 ozs, 10 dwts, 19¾, ca1860 (4194/91)   750
Centerpiece, circular bowl, on openwork leaf and berry stem, 9½, modern, Danish, 40 ozs
(4160/146)   500
Chalice, Plain bell form, gilt interior, 8⅜, 13 ozs, ca1700 (4259/71)   500
Chalice, baroque, bowl gilt on inside, separate pc outer framework, 11, 18c (4133/154)   750
Coffee set with tongs, Danish, Georg Jensen, 3 pcs, 30 ozs, 10 dwts, pot 9⅜, 1925 (4194/74)   750
Coffee urn on lampstand, Austrian pendant ring handles, 12, ca1820, 51 ozs (4160/40)   450
Creamer, ov. form, 3 slender paw feet, entwined snake handle, 8¼, ca1810 (4141/635)   90
Cup, pricked with initals and date 1789, 5½, Norwegian, 3 ozs (4160/173)   950
Cup, covered, baluster form, with grapevine and grapes, 15, M19c (4141/629)   250
Cup, peacock form, rock crystal, silver-gilt and enamel, 9¾, ca1875, Viennese (4238/572)   4500
Cups, pair, silverplate mounted, cornucopia form on circular foot, chased and engraved, 14, L19c, 1
rim split (669/346)   250
Cups, parcel-gilt set of 4, Turkish, vase form, circular feet, 4½, 19 ozs, ca1865 (4259/84)   700
Dish, chariot form, gilt metal and enamel, enameled with classical figures, 7¾, L19c, Viennese
(4160/684)   800
Dish, serving, Hungarian, Carolus Paray, circular, 13¾, 32 ozs, 1844 (4259/47)   325
Dish, sideboard, circular chased with reserves of shell and scroll work, 13¾, Peruvian (4141/561) 225
Dish, sideboard, circular, with hounds attacking stag, 14½, L18c, Spanish, 15 ozs, 15 dwts
(4160/147)   300
Dish, sweetmeat, parcel-gilt, embossed with Putto, 6, ca1680, 4 ozs. (4141/613)   950
Dishes, sweetmeat, pair, plain oval shape, 7⅞, ca1925, Danish, 17ozs (4238/99)   350
Entree dish, 2 handled, covered, with ribbon-tied floral branches, 12½, 31 ozs (649/325)   400
Ewer, covered, baluster body, band of leaves, 10½, ca1780, Spanish, 30 ozs, 10 dwts (4238/30)   1900

Ewer, Austrian, quadrangular baluster form, 9¼, 17 ozs, 1840 (4259/48) — 450

Flask, silver mounted, drop shaped gourd, 4¼, 1792, Scandinavian (4160/169) — 125

Flatware, set, pointed ends, engraved with initial 'E', ca1910, 113 pcs, Swedish, 95 ozs., 10 dwts. (4141/574) — 700

Flatware, set, pyramid pattern, ca1930, 113 pcs, Georg Jensen, Danish, 147 ozs. (4141/575) — 1600

Fruit stands, pair, silver mounted, boat shaped bowls, glass engraved with flwers, 14½, ca1880 (669/347) — 800

Goblet, pierced domed foot supporting an entwined vine stem, 8, L19c, 10 ozs (669/344) — 250

Goblets, set of 12, wood box, 5¼, 38 ozs, 20c (649/320) — 400

Incense burner, Portuguese, Maker's Mark D.C., 3 scroll feet, 6⅝, 15 ozs, ca1800 (4259/70) — 375

Inkstand, filigree, centered by handle, form of flower spray, 5½, M19c, Turkish*, 12 ozs. (4141/609) — 150

Inkwell, agate, pear shaped body, 3 silver ball feet, ring handles, ¼, ca1840, Dutch* (4238/107) — 250

Inkwell, Indian, leaf shaped tray, handles, 11½, 16 ozs, L19c (4259/79) — 150

Ladle, soup, of rounded Fiddle pattern, monogram, 12¾, ca1835, Dutch, 7 ozs, 5 dwts (4160/156) — 175

Mirror, Austrian dressing table, rectangular mirror, 20¼, 1840 (4194/94) — 1000

Mustard pot, Dutch, pear shape, engraved initials and coronet, 4½, 7 ozs, L17c (4259/86) — *950*

Pitcher, water, ovoid chased base with fluted leaf tips, 11½, ca1925, Danish, 29 ozs 10 dwts (4238/100) — 700

Pitcher, Danish water, George Jensen, ovoid, 28 ozs, 10 dwts, 10½, ca1930 (4194/72) — 600

Plates, dinner, set of 12, shaped borders with reeded rim, Czechoslavakian, 10, 192 ozs, (800), ca1930 (649/312) — 1900

Plates, Danish dinner, pair, Nicolai Christensen, 37 ozs, Diam 10¼, 1799 (4194/77) — 675

Platter,meat, Austrian, oval border with grape clusters, 19¼, ca1900, 45 ozs (4160/12) — 275

Platters, set of 3 Austrian, Maker's Mark K.M., 21¾ to 32, 227 ozs, ca1900 (4259/39) — 1500

Pot, coffee, oval pear shape, scroll and floral sprays, monograms, 10¼, M18c, 26 ozs 10 dwts (4238/89) — 4000

Pot, coffee, covered, fluted pear shape, swan neck spout, 10, 1777, Dutch, 24 ozs, 10 dwts (4160/161) — 4000

Reliquary, parcel-gilt silver, holy monograms, cross, 16½, M16c, Spanish, Juan de Castro* (4133/152) — 1400

Salver, Square form, with shells and leaves, 10½, 1753, Dutch, 17 ozs 10 dwts (4238/113) — *1600*

Salver, Portuguese, J.J. Correa, Oporto, 35 ozs, 13½, ca1880 (4159/51) — 300

Salver, Portuguese, Oporto, circular, 28 ozs, Diam 12, M19c (4194/46) — 275

Salvers, pair, with fluted circular dishes, with engraved eagle, 9¾, 1903, Spanish, 27 ozs, 5 dwts (4238/24) — 425

Sauce boats, pair, Austrian, boat shaped with waved molded rims, 8, 44 ozs, L19c (4259/40) — 600

Sauce pan, covered, shallow, circular, ebony handle, 7, modern, Georg Jensen, Danish, 22 ozs. (4141/573) — 475

Server, oval blade, pierced, engraved, inscription, 15⅛, 1778, Dutch, 7 ozs (4160/159) — 1400

Serving set, enamel and silver, Viennese, knife, fork, and spoon, mythological panel, 8½ x 8¼, ca1900 (649/304) — 800

Snuff box, Austrian, engine-turned overall, 3 ozs, L3⅛, 1845 (4194/259) — 175

Snuffers and tray, oblong tray, sprays of flowers, paw feet, 9⅝, ca1830, Portugese, 8 ozs, 15 dwts (4238/31) — 350

Spoon, almost circular bowl, twisted stem, 7, 1640, Dutch (4238/104) — 700

Spoon, fig shaped bowl, engraved, 'Torkel Olversen', L6⅛, E17c, Scandinavian (4238/103) — 475

Spoon, oviform bowl, handle pierced and figure of Ceres, L18c, Dutch (4238/106) — 250

Spoon, basting, Norwegian, N. Tunhe, large egg shaped bowl, 16, 8 ozs, 1858 (4259/66) — 275

Spoon, silver-gilt, fig shape bowl, wriggle work and foliage, L7⅛, ca1625, Norwegian (4238/102) — 450

Spoon, silver-gilt, fig shaped bowl, handle engraved with strapwork, L6⅞, ca1640, Norwegian (4238/101) — 550

Stand, dessert, Austrian, pierced and chased, strawberry plants, 10, 12 ozs, 1840 (4259/49) — 300

Stands, sweetmeat, pair, silver-gilt, boat shaped cut glass bowl, applied swans, 8, ca1800, 29 ozs. (4141/606) — 650

Stirrup, slipper form, chased with scrolling foliage, 9, E19c, South American (4160/150) — 200

Stirrup, South American, slipper form, birds, foliage, a heart, 8¼, 18 ozs, M19c (4259/67) — 600

Table spoons, set of six, fiddle pattern, back pricked with initials, 1771, Norwegian, 10 ozs 15 dwts (4238/97) — 225

Tankard, chased with flowers and foliage, engraved with name, 7¼, ca1890, Swiss, 46 ozs (4238/64) — 1200

Tankard, engraved, initials, date 1832, 6⅞, 1832, Norwegian (4160/176) — 1100

Tankard, raised on 3 claw and ball feet, 8, ca1700, Scandinavian, 26 ozs (4160/174) — 3250

Tea and coffee, tray, panels of flowers and foliage, Austrian, 30¾ tray, ca1900, 314 ozs (4160/17) — 3750

Tea and coffee service, 5 pcs, lobed body, scrolled handle, tray L17½, 24 ozs, 20c (649/322) — 950

Tea and coffee set, 4 piece, chased with foliage, ivory handles, 7⅜, ca1830, Polish, 73 ozs (4238/87) — 1350

Tea caddy, bulbous rectangular form, shield with monogram, 5, 1822, Dutch, 11 ozs 10 dwts (4238/109) 300

Tea caddy, quadrangular shape, lockable hinged cover, 4 ball feet, 4½, 1820, Dutch, 10 ozs (4160/157) 500

Tea caddy, tapered oval form, hinged cover, 4⅞, 1807-09, 9 ozs, 15 dwts (4160/162) 600

Tea caddy, Austrian, bombe form, lock, 12 ozs, 10 dwts, L6½, 1860 (4194/95) 500

Teapot, Dutch, Eise Andeles II, wood handle, 6 ozs, 15 dwts, 4½, 1759 (4194/68) 3300

Teapot, Dutch, Friesland style, mermaid spout, 12 ozs, 10 dwts, 6¼, L19c (4194/64) 425

Tobacco box, Cartouche shape with fluted sides, 5⅞, 5 ozs, 1767 (4259/87) 1900

Tobacco box, Jacob Abram Barbe, cover with couple picniking, 5½, 6 ozs, 1781-88 (4259/88) 2400

Toothpick holder, peacock with fanned tail, 6¾, 8 ozs, 19c (4259/72) 325

Toothpick holder, Portugese*, cupid holding garland over head, 6½, 6 ozs, 10 dwts, ca1870 (4259/74) 300

Tray, engraved robed maiden dancing, 3 female musicians, 8¼, L19c, Persian, 65 ozs (669/384) 600

Tray, Turkish, oval, shaped rim, 19¾, 48 ozs, L19c (4259/83) 600

Tray, 2 handled, rectangular form, raised gallery, Dutch, 20⅜, 1786, 83 ozs, 10 dwts (4160/168) 5250

Tureen, sauce and cover, flowerheads, oval shields, 9½, ca1800, 13 ozs, N. German* (4238/88) 325

Tureens, sauce pair, boat shape, incurved rim, loop handle, 8, ca1800, 10 ozs (4238/83) 300

Turkey, figure, bird with outspread tail, perched on pine branch, 21½, L19c, large (619/172) 1000

Urn, tea, hemispherical, reeded collar, lion finial, 13½, 1820, Dutch, 79 ozs. (4141/577) 2500

Urns, cigarette, twelve, acorn pattern, with flared rim, Danish, 2¼, modern, 26 zs (4160/145) 325

Waiter, circular form engine turned bands, 3 paw feet, 6¾, L19c, 8 ozs (4238/36) 150

Chapter 5

European Renaissance, Medieval and Later Works of Art

As in other areas, sales of works of art reflected the overall rise in the market, with the finer pieces commanding exceptional prices.

Early in the season, an influx of foreign dealers, principally Dutch, German and Italian, drove up prices of wood sculpture. Italian sculpture, however, proved to be a disappointment throughout the season. The market for Italian sculpture seems to be limited to museums and a handful of specialists, while German sculpture, particularly of the Gothic period, is avidly sought by a broad group of collectors.

In contrast to the weakness of Italian sculpture, the price of Italian majolica rose dramatically. More important pieces gained significantly in value, and the relatively ordinary skyrocketed well into the thousands of dollars. (A Castel Durante documentary tazza went for one hundred times what it cost twenty-five years earlier, but the market for bronze mortars was strangely erratic.)

Fifteenth- and sixteenth-century furniture continued to sell for relatively low prices. Italian credenzas, cassones and armchairs sold in the high hundreds and the low thousands. Considering their age and the fine workmanship of their decoration, early French pieces, armoires and chests, seem undervalued and offer excellent opportunities for purchase.

After decades of neglect, interest in tapestries began to revive in the 1960's, and from that time prices have climbed steadily. Despite the upturn of the past decade, however, tapestries remain undervalued, and further dramatic gains are likely as interest in and appreciation of these fine works increase.

Collecting in the field of works of art of the Middle Ages and the Renaissance demands knowledge and sophistication, but few other areas offer a better investment outlook or greater opportunities to own superior examples of craftsmanship for relativly low prices. Though they may be at the moment less widely appreciated than certain other categories, furniture, glass and tapestries seem capable in the future of gains as dramatic as those shown by German Gothic sculpture and Italian majolica.

Note: See also Chapter 6, "Nineteenth- and Twentieth-Century Works of Art."

BRONZES

Assorted periods and localities

Acrobat, naked youth standing on his hands, 11½, added fig leaf (4133/190)	$1700
Applique of an evangelist, gilt, bearded man, 3, E15c (4133/171)	375
Dog, with bared teeth, with left paw raised, 3⅝, ca1600 (4133/184)	750
Figure, from andirons, angel shown playing a flute, 11, ca1600, restored (4133/175)	1500
Figures, pair, seated positions, boy holding mask, girl wearing drapery, 5, 18c, French (4133/210)	225
Finial, eagle, double headed bird with outstretched wings, 4⅝, 16c (4133/179)	1200
Finial, newel post, applied on the side with 3 bees, 8, 17c (4133/192)	*1100*
Hercules Rescuing Deianeira from Centaur, French, 31½, 18c, (4193/135)	14500
Mercury, figure, young naked god flying upwards, 8½, 17c, Flemish* (4133/207)	250
Plaque of the Virgin and Child, holding Child in left knee, German, 5¾, L16c (4255/244)	550
Putto, figure gilt, seated, head to left, holding wreath, Augsburg, 1¾, E17c, wreath part missing (4133/197)	1200
Running putto, figure, young boy shown balanced on ball holding bunches of fruit, 7½, L17c (4133/191)	*1300*
St. John, figure, gilt, bearded saint with left hand to his breast, 4½, ca1600 (4133/188)	1000
Virgin and Child, figure, tall virgin, holding child, 6½, 15/17c, Utrecht (4133/202)	425
Virgin and Child, figure, virgin holding separately cast child, 4½, Flemish (4133/195)	175

Italian

Atlas, figure, Paduan, naked bearded man shown kneeling hand in knee, 5¼, E16c (4133/178)	1400
Busts, pair, maiden gazing, bearded man, 17¾ x 16½, 19c (4255/241)	1200
Case, mirror, gilt, surrounded by putti, beaded border, 8, L17c, Italian (4133/209)	375
Demosthenes, gazing to right, brown patina, 3⅜, L17c (4255/243)	325
Emperor Vitallius, bust, portly emperor with head to the left, armor, 9¼, E17c, Italian (4133/194)	1200
Figure, allegorical, Architecture, naked maiden holding a portractor, 14, 18c (4193/129)	1800
Figure, equestrian, Marcus Aurelius, 14¾, L19c (4193/128)	750
Figure of St. Paul, gilt, holding scroll and sword, 10¾, 18c (4193/131)	350
Knocker, door, Florentine, two confronting dolphins centering on female masks, 4½, 16c (4133/172)	1300
Lion, open mouth, after the antique, 13¾, 17c (4255/239)	2400
Lion of St. Mark, 8½, 15c, dam (4255/240)	*4100*
Man, figure, Florentine, bearded man shown lightly draped, 3¼, M16c (4133/176)	350

Finial (4133/192)

Lion of St. Mark
(4255/240)

Acrobat
(4133/190)

Running
putto
(4133/191)

St Barbara
(4133/325)

Magdalene, Perrata*, kneeling, left hand to breast, 14½, M17c (4255/238)	4000
Ring handle, bronze, form of clenched fist, 2¾, 17/18c (4193/120)	150
St. Agnes, figure, female martyred saint holding palm front in hand, 14½, ca1700, Roman (4133/214)	1500

CARVINGS

Assorted periods and localities

Adam, figure, carved boxwood, holding apple, 7⅛, E16, res, S. German (4133/332)	3000
Altar pc, polychrome wood, Virigin and Child, 2 Gothic towers, 36, 15c, imp, Spanish (4133/320)	3800
Angels, pair wood, polychrome, infants, flying upwards, painted green and pink, 22½, 18c, Austrian (4133/363)	1100
Candlesticks, angel, pair, wood polychrome, kneeling, 31, ca1600, prickets missing, Italian (4133/330)	4000
Cartouche, Armorial, carved wood, polychrome, the Arraya Family, 25¼, 18c, Spanish (4133/354)	800
Door, carved door, entwined monogram below crown, 43¾ x 24¾, ca1775, Swedish (4133/307)	275
Door, carved oak, central panel dated, strapwork, iron keyhole, escutcheon, 17 x 15½, 1598, Flemish (4133/294)	200
Door, carved walnut, eight birds, shield and vase in center, 25¾ x 14½, ca1500, split, Italian (4133/281)	200
Female saint, figure, limewood, with veil over her long tresses, holding book, 32, E16c, Austrian (4133/329)	2000
Female saint, figure, wood, polychrome, with long flowing tresses, crown on head, 51½, 18c, Spanish (4133/369)	1000
Fragment, carved walnut, top ram's head below scroll, 42 x 4¾, ca1590, worm damage, French (4133/302)	100
Group, Virgin and Child, oak, carved and painted, Madonna standing, 41, ca1500 (4193/153)	1800
Lectern, wood gilt, relief of Holy Monogram, scrolls and flowers, 14, 18c, 1 leg replaced, Spanish (4133/356)	300
Man, figure, oak, standing, curly hair to shoulders, 11, E17, part missing, German (4133/337)	400
Mary the Mother of James, oak, wearing long-tressas, turban, 34, ca1490, dam, Rhine (4133/323)	7000
Panel, carved wood, centered with a basket of flowers, strapwork, 31½ x 12, ca1730, French (4133/308)	100
Panel, Gothic carved oak, central florette, spiralling columns, Gothic arch, 14¾ x 9, 15c, Flemish (4133/284)	100
Panel, Gothic carved oak, delicate tracery around spiralling panel, French royal arms, 21½ x 7½, ca1500, French (4133/283)	200
Panel, Gothic carved wood, bold strapwork, 27¾ x 11½, 15c, Spanish (4133/285)	1300
Panel, Gothic oak, carved with a curling grapevine, 3 clusters of grapes, 18¼ x 10¼, L15c, Flemish (4133/296)	150
Panels, pair oak, relief with story of Joseph, 5½, ca1600, Flemish (4133/335)	650
Pieta, group, oak, Virgin with tears, holding body of Christ, 14, E16, rep, Netherlands (4133/333)	3800
Pieta, group, plychrome wood, seated, body of Christ in lap, 20, ca1420, 3 fingers miss, Spanish (4133/319)	4800
Relief, carved limewood, carved with scroll, arabesques, cherub and shells, 25 x 8, L16c, Italian (4133/310)	120
Relief, carved oak, central portrait medallion of a lady, scrollwork, 25¼ x 6¾, M16c, Flemish (4133/304)	100
Relief, coronation of the Virgin, alabaster, with resurrected Christ, Nottingham, 16½ x 10⅛, E15c (4193/359)	7000
Relief, fragment, carved oak, central foliate motif flanked by scrollwork, 34½ x 8¾, 17c French (4133/305)	200
Relief, walnut, Christ on Road to Calvary, 16½, E16c, parts missing, worn dam (4133/328)	4000
Relief, St Peter, oak, with scalloped halo holding key and book, 20¼, M16c, split at base, Flemish (4133/326)	800
Saint bust carved wood, youthful male saint, curly hair, gazing upwards, 12, M18c, French (4133/365)	500
Saint figure, wood, polychrome, male saint wearing cafe, 58¾, 18c, hands lacking (4133/355)	225
Seated Saint, polychrome wood, wearing a papal tiara, outstretched hands, Eastern European, 19, damaged, 18c (4193/156)	325
St Anna Selbdritt group, provincial, polychrome wood, holding the Christ child, 26, 15/16c, Spanish (4133/312)	2600
St Anne, figure, walnut, standing, closed book of gospels in hands, 37, 14c, worn damage, French (4133/314)	5000
St Barbara, figure, oak, heavily draped cloak, jewelled crown, 31, ca1500, restored, Dutch (4133/325)	*6000*
St Elizabeth of Hungary, figure oak, crown, in a nun's habit, Rhine, 37, ca1480, hand missing, crown repainted (4133/315)	3000
St Gregory, figure, oak, old bearded man wearing a papal mitre, 32, ca1490, Rhine (4133/324)	3800
St Mary Magdalene, limewood, holding a skull on open book, 45¾, ca1500, fingers lacking, Rhine (4133/322)	7000
St. Andrew, feet and arms outstretched, 10¾, later wooden cross, 18c (4255/309)	2100
Tankard, Karelian birchroot, body on 3 recumbent lions, Danish, 9, 17-18c (4255/125)	500

The Virgin of the Immaculate Conception, figure, wood, polychrome, 44, 16c, worn damage, Spanish (4133/316)	1400
Virgin and Child, romanesque, walnut, Virgin seated, 31, E13c, worming, French (4133/311)	4000
Virgin and Child, wood, polychrome, standing holding child, 10¾, 18c, Spanish colonial (4133/359)	150
Virgin and Child, wood, polychrome, Malines, 13¾, 1515-20, Malines (4133/331)	10000

Austrian

Cherubs, pair, polychrome wood, gold wings on dark brown clouds, 13, ca1760 (4193/259)	1300
St. James, provincial, painted wood, bearded saint with pilgrim's hat, 33¾, dam, ca1500 (4193/261)	2600
Woman, polychrome wood, left hand above a winged cherub mask, 23½, arm missing, 17c (4193/260)	375

Dutch

Chest, ormolu mounted, veneered tulip wood, bronze strapwork, 17, L17c (4255/126)	650
Figure of Atlas, gilt wood, man in loin cloth, supporting globe, 9½, varnished later, 18c (4193/231)	100
Floral relief, carved oak, vase with flowers, 18½ x 13¼, later frame, L17c (4193/227)	500

Flemish

Cherubs, pair, limewood, reclining position, 22, dam, 18c (4193/230)	1450
Group of the Virgin and Child, boxwood, Virgin standing, Child gesturing, 9½, 17c (4193/226)	1300

St. Anthony Abbot
(4193/244)

St. Barbara
(4193/243)

Archangel Michael
(4193/256)

Group of the Virgin and Child, with St. John, painted wood, 9, 18c (4193/228)	850
Relief figure, carved walnut, man partially covered in drapery, 16, 17c (4193/229)	125
Relief of St. John the evangelist, oak, seated holding open book, 5¾ x 11⅛, 17c (4193/225)	100
The Christ Child, polychrome wood, lying in a recumbent position, hand raised, 15, 17c (4193/232)	600
Venus after the bath, white marble, seated on rock, 17½, ca1700 (4193/370)	3000

French

Chest front, oak, 4 recessed panels, 67, rep, ca1500 (4193/234)	475
Coat of arms, carved and painted, limewood, griffin supports, banners, helmet crest, 38, wing missing, 17c (4193/236)	2800
Crucifix figure, carved wood, head downwards, 35½, E16c (4193/235)	3100
Portrait medallion, Charles Juste, Prince de Beauvau, terracotta, 4¾, 1770 (4193/353)	550
Reliquary bust, carved wood, monk-saint, red clock, 24½, 17c (4193/238)	200
St. Barbara, polychrome wood, hand outstretched, other missing, 21, hand missing, L16c (4193/237)	2100

German

Cherub, polychrome wood, in flight with gilt wings, hands outstretched, 17½, dam, 18c (4193/257)	*450*
Allegorical reliefs, pair, oak, female figures, 19 x 9½, part missing, M16c (4193/247)	1500
Altar, triptych, gilt, polychromed wood, from various elements, 80, res, E16c (4193/246)	34000
Archangel Michael, limewood, wearing a diadem, holding a flaming sword, 12¾, L18c (4193/256)	*650*

Bozetto of 2 putti embracing, dark red, wax, 5½, E18c (4193/356) 600
Bust of a bishop, stone, frowning expression wood base, 19, imp, ca1500 (4193/361) 3500
Candlestick, angel, carved oak, flowing roses, flowing locks, 24, L15c (4193/240) 2800
Chest, marquetry, 3 panels, scrollwork, key, 27¾, E17c (4255/137) 1400
Enthroned Virgin, carved wood, holding Christ Child, 30, res, L15c (4193/241) 2000
Head of a king, Gothic, stone, monumental form, architectural setting, 12¾, L14c (4193/358) 4250
Peasant, polychrome wood, carved as a forester, 22, L17c (4193/249) 3400
Saint, bearded, long flowing robes, 35, dam, 18c (4193/250) 2100
Saints, pair, polychrome wood, St. Michael trampling demon, saint with beggar, 11½ x 12⅛, E18c (4193/258) 1800
Seated, bishop, jewelled mitre, hands holding attributes, 34, dam, L14c (4193/239) 4900
St. Anthony Abbot, book in right hand, 49½, res, E16c (4193/244) *4000*
St. Barbara, standing holding her tower, 39, res, L15c (4193/243) 7000
St. John the Baptist, full length, holding book, Lamb of God, 29, worn, ca1500 (4193/242) 3200
St. John Nepomuk, fur cap, lace trim, flowing robes, 20½, dam, M18c (4193/254) *800*
St. Mary Magdalene, carved limewood, holding a beaker, 24½, L16c (4193/245) *3750*
Virgin of the Annunciation, Virgin kneeling, hand to breast, 33, dam, 16/17c(4193/252) 900

Italian

Adoring, angel, kneeling, hand clasped to breast, 38, wing missing, 18c (4193/209) 700

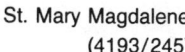

St. Mary Magdalene
(4193/245)

Candlesticks (4255/157)

Apostles Peter and Paul, pair, carved marble, 23½ x 23¾, L15/E16c (4193/360) 6500
Appliques, pair, carved walnut, naked Putto standing within niche, 13, 17c (4193/196) 450
Bozetto, the Adoration, Virgin and Child, king kneeling, terracotta, 8 x 11¾, framed, L16c (4193/350) 1500
Bust of a boy, wearing medallion, head to right, wood base, wax, 12½, L19c (4193/357) 350
Bust of a youth, classical features, wood base, terracotta, 19½, 16c (4193/349) 1500
Bust of the Virgin, head covered by veil, terracotta, 21, ca1500 (4193/348) 2500
Bust Roman emperor, composite white marble, short hair, 15¾, 18c (4193/377) 400
Candlesticks, angel, gilt wood pair, holding scrolling candlestick, 32¼, E17c (4255/157) *2000*
Candlesticks, figural, pair, youths, wearing flamboyant drapery, 35, 18c (4255/164) 900
Candlesticks, pair gilt wood, baluster stems, carved leaves, 30¼, ca1720 (4193/212) 350
Candlesticks, pair, gilt wood, carved acanthus leaves, masks, scrolls, 27, 17c, imp (4255/131) 275
Christ at the column, alabaster, head back, gazing to right, 24⅜, res, 17c (4193/368) 1500
Christ child, standing, right hand in blessing, 21, modern base, 16/17c (4193/193) 550
Coat of arms carved gilt wood, escutcheon surrounded by scrolls, 31, M18c (4193/204) 400
Columns, pair, baroque gilt wood, spiralling form, carved fruiting, vines and birds, 72, M17c (4255/130) 1100
Crucifix figure, fruitwood, Christ wearing a perizonium, 10, 1700 (4193/208) 300
Fragment, marble, pinkish tone, grotesque, mask, 27½, 16/17c (4193/366) 900
Group of the last supper, painted wood, table set with goblets and 2 dishes, 44½, 18c (4193/202) 3000
Head of a man, bearded, curly hair, 21, imp, 17/18c (4193/365) 800
Joseph, creche, standing, hand to breast, 38½, 18c (4193/206) 700

Jupiter, carved and gilt wood, crowned god seated astride his eagle, 20½, dam, base, later, 17c
(4193/195)   225
Lectern, carved wood, heart below cross, St. Catherine of Siena, 14¼, 17c (4193/200)   275
Marquetry panels, pair, bands of cherubs and foliate motifs, 43, ca1835 (4193/214)   1700
Pedestal, white marble, rectangular, waisted sides, 3 cherubs, 29 x 19, 17c (4193/364)   600
Poles, pair, processional, painted green carved with stiff leaves, 93½, 17c, imp (4255/128)   200
Portrait relief, white marble, profile to left on grey marble base, 11, L18c (4193/373)   450
Relief, Roman emperor, white marble, profile to left, laurel wreath frame, 18⅛, 18c (4193/372)   2400
Relief fragment, Genoese white marble, male saint, 19, L17c (4193/371)   2000
Relief of the last supper, carved wood, against architectural interior, 37, L18/E19c (4193/215)   1600
Shrine, rococo, painted and parcel gilt, architectural form, 42 x 28¾ x 12½, L18c (4193/213)   1000
St. Anthony of Padua, carved wood, Saint carrying Christ child, 33, dam, 17/18c (4193/199)   475
Virgin, creche, kneeling, hands in prayer, 34, 18c (4193/205)   550
Virgin and Child, standing position, 36½, dam, 17c (4193/194)   800
Virgin and Child, standing holding Child, 25, 17c (4193/197)   800
Wall plaque, Virgin and Child, carved wood, Virgin holding standing Child on lap, 38, 17c (4193/201) 500
Youth, naked, figure seated on rock, 9¾, rep, L18c (4193/378)   800

Ivory

Crucifix, mounted on wood cross, Indo-Portuguese, H16¼, imp, 18/19c (4081/144)   1500
Medallion, lady with 2 cherubs, French, D2¾, ca1750 (4081/142)   600
Medallion, portrait of a man, profile, oval, German, H2¾, 1715-25 (4081/145)   100
Plaque, The Visitation, South German, 2⅝ x 3⅝, 17c (4081/143)   1300
Plaques, pair, boar hunt, scene near a river, wood frames, 4¼ x 7¾, M19c (4081/146)   650

Malines

Relief, Moses striking the rock, attended by followers, 5¾ x 4⅜, imp, ca1600 (4193/369)   1200

Netherlandish

Group of the entombment, limewood, Christ lowered into the sarcophagus, 21½, res, ca1500
(4193/219)   7200
Putti pair, white marble, leaning against a cartouche, 21, rep, 17c (4193/367)   1500
Relief of the crucifixion, carved oak, with Magdalene, Roman soldiers, 23¾, rep, M16c (4193/222)   2000
Relief of the Virgin and Child, Gothic style, oak, 13¾, inscribed 1510 (4193/217)   350
St. George, fragmentary oak, head downcast, wearing armor, 13, dam, L15c (4193/223)   3000

Scandinavian

Flight into Egypt, oak relief, Mary on donkey, Child on lap, Joseph behind, 14¼, 16-17c (4193/155)   450
Laundry beater, polychrome wood, 5 star motifs, red, yellow, upright handle, 28, 1804 (4193/157)   400
Tankard, Karelian birchroot, cylindrical on 3 lions, lion thumbpiece, 8¼, 17/18c (4193/158)   600

Spanish

Bas reliefs, pair, St. Anne and the Virgin, St. Joseph and Christ child, 33, imp, L16c (4193/164)   2400
Bishops, pair, polychrome wood, seated on a balustrade, holding books, 15½, 16/17c (4193/188)   1000
Bust, carved wood, curly hair, wearing armor, 20¼, 17c (4193/168)   750
Christ child, carved wood, hand raised in blessing, 20, res, 17c (4193/166)   400
Christ child, polychrome wood, standing, hand raised in blessing, 11¾, 18c (4193/181)   275
Figures, pair, polychrome wood, standing holding wheat and grapes, 13¼, 17/18c (4193/178)   575
Head, painted wood, woman, long hair, traces of gilding, 8½, dam, 16c (4193/159)   150
Pediment, gilt wood, winged, cherub mask, flanded by scrollwork, 96, ca1600 (4255/136)   300
Relief, polychrome fruitwood, crucifixion scene, 8½, 17/18c (4193/182)   1400
Relief of the martyrdom of St. Peter, carved and painted wood, 24½ x 30, cr, 16c (4193/169)   1800
Relief of the resurrected Christ, polychrome wood, 18½ x 11, imp, 16c (4193/170)   700
Risen Christ, carved wood, 3 quarter length, hands crossed, 22, 16c (4193/160)   1900
Saint, carved as a bearded man, gilded robes, 12, 16c (4193/163)   600
Saint, polychrome carved wood, holding cloak, 12, imp, 17c (4193/167)   250
St. Anthony of Padua, wood, standing, holding Christ child on book, 31, 18c (4193/179)   175
St. George and the Dragon, polychrome wood, red, black and gold armor, 15, dam, ca1600
(4193/165)   950
St. John and Roman Soldier, Christ nailed to cross, framed, 23¼ x 18¼, ca1600 (4193/172)   2000
St. John bringing Drusiana to life, Saint holding Drusiana's hand, framed, 22¼ x 18, ca1600
(4193/176)   2100
St. John rising from the tomb, stepping from tomb with St. Peter, framed, 22¼ x 18, ca1600
(4193/174)   2900
St. Luke, polychrome wood, holding open book, wood base, 14¾, 18c (4193/187)   600
St. Michael, polychrome wood, wearing red, green and gold armor, 16¾, rep, L16c (4193/162)   650
St. Michael, LaPacho, wood, wearing breast plate, S-scroll belt, colonial, 35, res, E18c (4193/183) 1600

The attempt to boil St. John in oil, surrounded by executioners, framed, 33¼ x 18, dam, ca1600 (4193/175)	2200
The descent from the Cross, Our Lord being lowered by drapery, framed, 23¼ x 18, ca1600 (4193/173)	2200
The revelation of St. John, Island of Patmos, 23¼ x 18, dam, ca1600 (4193/177)	2000
The Nativity, Holy family, St. John and 2 shepherds, 30⅞ x 30½, ca1600 (4193/171)	3400
Vargueno front, inlaid, 3 registers, lockplate hinged straps, 31¾, 17c, later frame (4193/191)	900
Virgin, polychrome wood, glass eyes, hand to her breast, 22¼, hand missing, 18c (4193/180)	500
Virgin of the Immaculate Conception, polychrome wood, 19, fingers missing, 18c (4193/185)	1000

Stone

Alabaster head of a man, North Italian, H11½, L13c (4081/120)	2000
Casket, five porphyry panels, bronze fitted, L16⅜, 19c (4081/136)	2100
Head of a monk with beard, French, H5, d, 15c (4081/122)	550
Relief, boy and a sheep, white marble, Flemish, 8¾ x 12⅛, 18c (4081/133)	500
Relief, mythological scene, marble, Italian, 23¼ x 18¼, ca1500 (4081/124)	1200
Relief, unicorn grazing, oval, marble, Italian, L9¾, c, 17c (4081/127)	2500
Relief, Christ, Road to Calvary, malines alabaster, 5¾ x 4⅜, d, ca1600 (4081/126)	1300
Relief, Immaculate Conception, Malines alabaster, 4¾ x 3¾, c, ca1600 (4081/125)	1200
Relief, Mater Dolorosa, white marble, Italian, 9½ x 6⅞, 1625-50 (4081/128)	1100
Reliefs, pair, a boy and a girl, marble, Italo-Flemish, H14, 1 d, M17c (4081/129)	1000
Reliefs, pair, cupid leaning on a staff, marble, Italian, 14 x 10½, L18/19c (4081/135)	1200
St. Matthew holding an axe, Venetian, H24¾, E14c (4081/121)	3000

Swiss

Saints Gregory and Boniface, pair, painted wood, 38½ x 39½, dam, E16c (4193/262)	14500

Terracotta

Group, nymph with bacchante, Clodion, French, H19¼, 1785 (4081/140)	1000

Wood

Altarpiece, St. Peter and Paul, polychrome, Spanish, H61½, assembled, 16c (4081/82)	6250
Altarpiece, Virgin and Child, polychrome, Spanish, H36, L15c (4081/79)	3000
Angel, flying, polychrome, South German, L12½, M18c (4081/106)	250
Applique, in the form of cherub's head, South German, H15¾, 17c (4081/94)	350
Bust of the Virgin, glass eyes, Spanish, H25, ca1600 (4081/97)	1000
Candlesticks, pair of, formed with angels holding pricket, Italian, H19, d, 15/16c (4081/80)	4250
Cherub, curly hair, polychrome, Spanish, H28, d, 17c (4081/92)	750
Christ, polychrome, North Italian, H43, ca1700 (4081/98)	800
Christ after the Crucifixion, North European, H24½, 15c (4081/73)	2500
Christ at the column, South German, H11, 17c (4081/101)	1200
Crucifix, wearing crown of thorns, Rhenish, H34, 15c (4081/74)	600
Head of a saint, polychrome, Spanish, H12¾, d, ca1600 (4081/91)	300
Hope, left hand on anchor, Italian, H35, d, 17c (4081/102)	600
Monk, polychrome, Spanish Colonial, H19¾, E19c (4081/116)	125
Monk wearing long robes, Spanish, H28½, d, 17/18c (4081/93)	275
Relief, painted gesso, of the Resurrection, Spanish, H23, d, 16c (4081/85)	2500
Relief, with equestrian figures, German, 4⅛ x 7¾, ca1700 (4081/100)	3700
Relief, Flight into Egypt, South Netherlandish, 39½ x 26¼, d, L16c (4081/88)	19000
Relief, Virgin and Child, polychrome, Flemish, H16, rep, M15c (4081/77)	1600
Saint with laurel wreath, polychrome, Austria, H54½, ca1760 (4081/112)	5000
Saint with long flowing beard, South German, H31, d, L17/18c (4081/104)	1600
St. Anthony, polychrome, Spanish, H22¾, imp, 18c (4081/114)	500
St. Barbara, traces of polychrome, French, H12½, d, 16c (4081/84)	3600
St. Benedict, North German, H12¼, M16c (4081/86)	750
St. James the Major, polychrome, Franconian, H51¾, d, 1510-20 (4081/78)	11500
St. John holding a sheep, South German, H4, L17c (4081/99)	400
St. John the Baptist, polychrome, Spanish, H13¼, d, 18c (4081/118)	550
St. John the Baptist, South German, H11⅝, d, L17c (4081/96)	450
St. John with a mournful look, H63, rep, ca1350 (4081/70)	12000
St. Joseph and Virgin, polychrome, Spanish, pair, H12, ca1800 (4081/115)	1400
St. Joseph holding Christ Child, Netherlandish, H13, d, 1600-1650 (4081/87)	1000
St. Philip, polychrome, Spanish, H28¼, 18c (4081/113)	350
The Virgin and Child, gilding, Eastern French, H34⅞, ca1350 (4081/72)	21000
The Virgin and St. John, polychrome, Spanish, H48, ca1300, pair (4081/71)	11000
Virgin and Child, Eastern European, H24½, 18c (4081/107)	550
Virgin and St. John, Spanish, pair, H34½, H33, ca1600 (4081/83)	4000
Virgin gazing downward, provincial, Austrian, H36¼, d, E16c (4081/81)	4750

Virgin standing on orb, polychrome, Austrian, H44½, d, ca1700 (4081/105)   3750
Woman with hand to her breast, Flemish, H9¾, M17c (4081/95)   300

CERAMICS AND GLASS

Assorted periods and localities

Albarelli, pair, winged cherub heads on ochre ground, Sienna Maiolica, 8¾, 1500-10 (4260/355)   16000
Albarelli, pair, Palermo, bearded figures, 6¾, hc, 1606 (4255/369)   1600
Albarello, blue and white, waisted form, rounded base and shoulder, 10, 17/18c (4255/372)   200
Albarello, blue and white, Savona, dumbbell shaped, Spanish, 7, ca1700 (4255/382)   250
Albarello, maiolica, dumbbell shape, Noah, Ark, 8, 17/18c (4255/364)   500
Albarello, miniature, maiolica, geometric pattern, Netherlandish, 3⅜, E17c (4255/377)   600
Albarello, Rouen, with a portrait of a woman, 11, L16c (4255/385)   1600
Albarello, Savona, name of drug, Spanish, blue and white, 7¼, hc, 1650 (4255/386)   125
Albarello, Trapani, maiolica, waisted form, portrait of man, 10, E17c (4255/373)   500
Albarello, Venice, maiolica, cylindrical form, 13½, 1560-70 (4255/363)   *5600*
Basin, oval, Urbina istoriato maiolica, Joseph, Sold by his Brothers, 17, hair crack, L16c (4255/362)   *2600*
Baskets, pair, Faenza, reticulated, Virgilio Calamelli*, 10¾, 1560-70 (4255/366)   *2600*

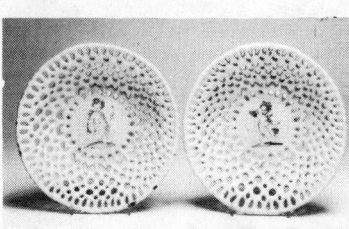

Baskets
(4255/366)

Albarello (4255/363)

Basin
(4255/362)

Beaker, footed, armorial, Silesian, facetted sides, foliate scrollwork, 4¼, chip, M18c (4255/329)   375
Bowl, fruit, 'canoe' cut glass, 'Van Dyck' rim, Irish, 9⅛, chip, ca1810 (4193/302)   350
Crucifixion dish, Our Lord flanked by 2 monks, large, Spanish, D19¾, 1709 (4081/50)   700
Dish, footed, Castel Durante, trefoil, maiolica, naked figures, putto, 6¾, ca1535 (4255/360)   3000
Dish, istoriato, Urbino, David, head of Goliath, Saul, 11, 1540-50 (4255/365)   4800
Dish, Deruta lustred maiolica, bust of warrior, 16½, imp, ca1520 (4255/347)   6500
Glass, wine, engraved, Dutch, round funnel bowl, garden pavillion, 7¼, chip, ca1760 (4255/337)   *500*
Glass, wine, shipping, engraved, Dutch, thistle shaped bowl, sailing ship and mill, 7½, M18c (4255/339)   1050
Goblet, covered, engraved, Silesian, ogee bowl, tall sides, fluted base, 9¼, M18c (4255/333)   1000
Goblet, engraved glass, Bohemian, conical bowl, alternating stars, 8¼, E18c (4255/328)   225
Jar, covered, engraved, Dutch, inverted bell shape, mother and child, 11, chip, L18c (4255/336)   1100
Jar, wet drug, wide strap handle, Neapolitan, 13, 17c (4255/389)   475
Jar, wet drug, Delft, globular, inscribed label, 7¾, L18c (4255/390)   475
Jar, wet drug, Faenza maiolica, strap handle, straight spout, 9, E16c (4255/346)   7200
Jar, wet drug, Savona, Gothic script, Spanish, 7½, L17c (4255/381)   375
Jar, wet drug, Savona, Gothic script, Spanish, 7½, L17c (4255/380)   150
Jar, wet drug, Sicilian, central label, script name of drug, 10¼, rep, ca1600 (4255/383)   1400
Jars, drug, pair, rope handles, 12¾, E18c (4255/388)   4600

Jars, ovoid, Palermo, pair, maiolica, multi-colored with angels, 13½, rep, 1605-10 (4255/352) 3000
Jug, water, glass, French, curved spout, frilled handles, 8, chip, L17c (4255/327) 400
Panel, stained glass, 3 cavaliers, bust portraits, Swiss, 13, 1 cr, 1751 (4193/278) 650
Panel, stained glass, 'Willkommen', Swiss, man and woman, coat of arms, 13½ x 8¾, dam, M16c (4255/325) 900
Panel, stained glass, Swiss, man in armor, coat of arms, 13½ x 9, M16c (4255/326) 900
Panel, stained glass, Swiss, silver wash, man in contemporary dress, 15 x 10, 1539 (4255/324) 1050
Plate, allegorical, Faenza maiolica, naked putto, multi-colors, 11⅝, dam, 1535-40 (4255/349) *3000*
Plate, istoriato, Pesaro, Alcione at the Tomb of Juno, 11½, dam, ca1540 (4255/368) 2000
Plate, Urbino istoriato, David Slaying Goliath, 13¼, L16c (4255/371) 4400
Salt, Faenza maiolica, glazed in white, Virgilio Calamelli*, 5¼, 1565-70 (4255/367) 550
Sauceboat, double, Urbino, maiolica, figure of Venus in center, 7¼, ca1580 (4255/359) 2500
Tazza, documentary, Castel Durante, maiolica, Judith with Holopherne, 10½, M16c (4255/361) *3000*
Tazza, enamelled glass, Venetian, center stylized lion running, multi-colored, 10⅝, M16c (4255/322) 8000
Tazza, istoriato, maiolica, Abraham and Isaac, 10⅞, L16c (4255/354) 3000
Tazza, istoriato, maiolica, Apollo in Pursuit of Daphne, 10⅛, L16c (4255/357) 4000
Tile of Judaic interest, maiolica, central Star of David, Spanish, 2½, 16c (4255/376) 500
Tondino, Urbino istoriato, maiolica, Ovid's Metamorphoses, 8¾, 1545 (4255/353) 1600
Wine glass, engraved, monogram in wreath, facetted stem, Swedish, 6¾, ca1780 (4193/287) 350

Dutch

Glass, 'Friendship' engraved, conical bowl, 2 male figures, 7⅛, M18c (4193/297) 800
Glass, 'Friendship', engraved, bell bowl, 2 shaking hands, 7⅛, M18c (4193/311) 700
Goblet, engraved, funnel bowl, ship and farmer, 8¼, M18c (4193/298) 1300
Goblet, engraved, round funnel bowl, girl, scrollwork, flowers, 8½, M18c (4193/307) 1800
Goblet, shipping, engraved, bell bowl, sailing ship, 7½, M18c (4193/310) 1200
Wine glass, armorial engraved, arms of William IV, 7½, 1766 (4193/299) 1200

English

Glass, 'Friendship', engraved Newcastle, bell bowl, 8¼, chip, ca1750 (4193/296) 325
Rummer, engraved, bucket bowl, squat stem, central knop, flat foot, 5⅞, M19c (4193/301) 200
Wine glass, engraved Newcastle, funnel bowl, arms of George II, 8, ca1750 (4193/294) 1300
Wine glass, engraved Newcastle, round funnel bowl, 7¾, ca1750 (4193/292) 425
Wine glass, engraved Newcastle, English Royal Arms, 7½, ca1750 (4193/295) 700
Wine glass, engraved, Newcastle Dutch, funnel bowl, baluster stem, 7, ca1750 (4193/293) 900

Faenza Maiolica

Albarelli, pair, each with a single figure, 9¾, 1500-20 (4260/356) 32000
Albarello, portrait, profile of a lady, 7¼, chip, 1520-30 (4260/349) 7000

Glass (4255/337)

Plate (4255/349)

Tazza (4255/361)

Bottle   (4255/343)

Dish, profile of young man, 15¼, rep, L15c (4260/358)   15000
Jug, ovoid, pinched spout, 9¼, dam, L15c (4260/351)   12500
Jug, strap handle, pinched spout, 9¼, dam, L15c (4260/353)   4000

German

Beaker, engraved, Bohemian, cylindrical, figure of wolf and crane, 4¾, ca1700 (4193/315)   225
Bottle, pilgrim, blue-glazed grey, circular, straight neck, arms of Saxony, 15⅜, 1588 (4255/343)   4000
Decanter, Bohemian milchglas, mallet shape, allegorical figure of Africa, 9⅛, M18c (4193/291)   1100
Dish, gold lustered, portrait of lady, 13½, cr, ca1520 (4193/268)   2500
Flask, engraved, Bohemian, hexagonal, flowers and leaves, 6½, E18c (4193/316)   350
Goblet, armorial, funnel bowl, coat of arms, 7⅝, E18c (4193/285)   400
Goblet, cutglass, Saxon, funnel bowl, tall panels, domed foot, 9½, ca1710 (4193/286)   400
Goblet, engraved, round funnel bowl, medallion, hollow stem, 8¼, M18c (4193/303)   250
Group of the pieta, red stoneware, Virgin holding dead Christ, 11¼, ca1500 (4193/265)   3250
Jug, Bellarmine, tall ovoid body, small loop handle, 13¼, 17c (4255/344)   600
Jug, Bellarmine stoneware, ovoid, Habsburg eagles, 16½, hc, 1607 (4193/266)   11500
Jug, Bellarmine stoneware, ovoid, tall neck, strap handle, lion rampant, 8¼, 17c (4193/267)   500
Salt cut glass, Silesian, scallop shell form, on stem, 4½, E18c (4193/312)   300
Tankard, enamelled milchglas, medallion with figure, strap handle, 5⅜, M18c (4193/288)   550
Tumblers, set of 4, ruby flash, Bohemian, bell shape, sides etched, 4⅞, rep, L19c (4193/317)   500
Wine glass, Thuringian, facets, engraved, scrollwork, 7, L18c (4193/282)   225

Italian

Albarello, Savona, dumbbell form, bands of gadroons, 7⅛, hc, L17c (4193/276)   450
Jar, wet drug, Savona, blue bands of gadroons, strap handle, portrait, 7¾, L17c (4193/275)   650
Vaso a palla, Venetian polychrome, baluster, landscape, travelers and dog, 15, 16c (4193/272)   5250
Vaso a palla, Venetian polychrome, baluster, warrior with spear, 15, cr, 16c (4193/271)   7500

Majolica

Albarello, inscribed Rad-Cinoglosse, Talavera*, H9⅛, 17/18c (4081/49)   300
Albarello, oval medallion with portrait of Turk, Venice, H5⅛, 1550-60 (4081/44)   1300
Albarello, with portrait of St. Paul, Palermo, H11¾, E17c (4081/48)   950
Dish, lustre, footed, central medallion, Gubbio, D10¼, rep, 1530-40 (4081/40)   650
Dish, lustre, footed, Gubbio, D10⅛, imp, 1530-40 (4081/39)   1500
Dish, Istoriato, Europa and the Bull, Urbino, D11⅛, rep, ca1540 (4081/41)   4000
Drug jar, ovoid, with a coat of arms, Venice*, H13, hc, 1590-1600 (4081/46)   1600
Plate, Istoriato, with a man, maiden, cupid, Urbino, D8⅝, alt., 1570-80 (4081/42)   950
Vase, ovoid, medallion with a Bishop, Venice, H13¾, 1560-70 (4081/45)   2200

Savone Maiolica

Plate, birds and trees, 12⅜, chip, 18c (4260/347) — 650

Sicilian

Albarellos, squat form, flowers and leaves, 7¾, 17c (4193/274) — 350
Albarellos, pair, waisted form, flowers and leaves, 10, 17c (4193/273) — 550

Spanish

Bowl, pottery, center with seated dog, trees and bushes, 12¼, rivetted, L18c (4193/264) — 400
Cantir, loop handle, spiral wreathing, blue-green, 8¼, 18c (4193/280) — 200
Dish, blue and white, butterfly border, center with rampant lion, 12½, 16c (4193/263) — 550

Stoneware

Bellarmine jug, ovoid, grotesque mask, coat-of-arms, Rhenish, H12, 17c (4081/51) — 850
Bellarmine jug, ovoid, with a bearded mask, Rhenish, H7¼, 17c (4081/52) — 650
Tile frieze, with the 12 apostles, Swiss or German, L17¾, d, 16c (4081/54) — 200

Urbino istoriato

Dish, Fontana workshops, Venus defending Aeneus from Diomedes, 10½, res, ca1550 (4193/269) — 4500
Flask and stopper, pilgrim, Fontana workshop, twig handles, myth of Orpheus, 13⅝, res, ca1540 (4193/270) — 8000

Urbino Maiolica

Dish, lustred gubbio, 10½, 1540 (4260/350) — 15500
Dish, Susanna and the Elders, 10¾, ca1545 (4260/348) — 4250
Dish, istoriato, Juno at the forge of Vulcan, 10, rep, ca1545 (4260/352) — 7000

Westerwald

Jug, Raeren*, strap handle with loop terminal, 6¾, E18c (4255/341) — 650
Tankard, maker's monogram I.C., deer, stylized scrollwork, 8½, L18c (4255/342) — 475

ENAMELS

Assorted periods and localities

Cross, parcel-gilt silver and enamel, Spanish, H13½, 15c (4081/62) — 1700
Pax, Limoges, enamel, Virgin and Child, flanked by angels, gilt copper frame, 3, 16c, minor repair on rim (4133/168) — 1500
Plaque, carved ivory, depicting the selling of cupids, carved wood frame, 2¼, E19c, Continental (4160/594) — 150
Plaque, enamel on copper, portrait of a bishop, 6½, ca1900, French easel frame, gilt (669/281) — 100
Plaque, enamel on copper, portrait of gentleman, 7¼, ca1900, French framed (669/279) — 500
Plaque, enamel on copper, portrait of 18c lady, 3¼, ca1900, French framed (669/277) — 250
Plaque, enamel on copper, with a pierrot playing lute, 8¼, ca1900, French frame, gilt (669/284) — 650
Plaque, enamel on copper, circular, profile gypsy maiden, 3¾, ca1900, French framed (669/275) — 400
Plaque, enamel on copper, rectangular, gallant standing, 3¾, ca1900, French frame (669/276) — 300
Plaque, enameled and copper circular, young lady wearing bonnet, 5¼, ca1900, easel frame, gilt (669/280) — 300
Plaque, Limoges enamel, Christ into Jerusalem, 4¾ x 6¼, ca1900, res framed (669/286) — 450
Plaque, Limoges, enamel, angel with lilac wings, wearing white drapery, 8¾ x 6½, M17c (4133/170) — 950
Plaque, Limoges, enamel on copper circular, young girl in profile, 3¾, ca1900, easel frame, gilt (669/282) — 125
Plaque of Britannia, allegorical, enamel, commemorating naval heroes, 13, 1798, English, important (4160/714) — 4500
Plaques, pair, Limoges, enamel on copper, Apollo riding in a chariot, 17½, ca1900, framed (669/283) — 4500
Plate, oval, Limoges, enamel, Rebecca, of the Well*, 12, L19c, chip, unusual (669/290) — 1100
Roundel, Limoges champleve, enamel, copper gilt body, center with lion, prophet St. Mark, 2, L13c (4133/167) — 2000
Vase, enamel gilt ground, ovoid body, mythological figures, 13¾, ca1900, Viennese (669/298) — 4250
Vase, Limoges enamel on copper, hunter and hounds, 5½, ca1910 (669/292) — 225
Vase and cover, mounted enamel, cornucopia form, mythological scenes, 14¾, ca1900, Viennese (669/299) — 4750

French

Chasse, champleve, rectangular, 4 apertures for viewing, 11¼, res, 13c (4193/321) — 7500

Christ in majesty, repousse copper, gilt, hand raised in blessing, book on knee, 9⅜, ca1250 (4193/325)   3000
Crucifix figure, repousse, copper gilt, head to right, bearing crown, 5¼, dam, M13c (4193/323)   850
Incense boat, hinged cover, medallions of angels, 8½, 13c (4193/324)   *3000*
Pax, adoration and God the Father, 5⅞, M16c (4193/326)   4500
Plaque, St. Francis holding a crucifix, 5, later stand, ca1535 (4255/318)   5000
Triptych, Annunciation in center, panel God the Father, 8½ x 11, L19c (4255/320)   200

German

Casket, copper gilt carcass, 9 panels painted with flowers, 7¼, chip, M17c (4255/317)   2600

Limoges

Ciborium, champleve, panels with angels, H12½, fine, 13c (4081/61)   15000
Crucifix, champleve, blue, applied crucifix figure, H10¾, fine, 13c (4081/60)   14000
Plaque, depicting the Pieta, 6⅛ x 4⅞, 16c (4081/63)   1300
Plaque, depicting Christ before Pilate, 6⅛ x 4⅞, 1541 (4081/64)   1300
Plaque, depicting 3 dogs attaching a hare, 3½ x 4½, 16c (4081/66)   1200
Plaque, depicts the Tree of Jesse, exotic figures, H9¼, d, M16c (4081/68)   3000
Tazza, grisaille-decorated, Pierre Reymond, cherubs, D9¼, 1553 (4081/67)   2200

IVORY

Beggar, ivory and fruitwood, provincial, hand raised, clothing in tatters, 9, 18c, So. German (4133/236)   *450*

Beggar
(4133/236)

Incense boat (4193/324)

Figure
(4133/237)

Betrayal of Christ, plaque, Christ being kissed by Judas, 3½ x 2½, hair cracks, German (4133/229)   225
Cabinet, ivory inlaid rosewood, fall front, engraved ivory panels, 15½ x 19¼, M17c (4133/234)   2100
Christ at the column, figure, carved, head downcast, 9¼, L17c, South German (4133/232)   1300
Christ at the flagellation, hands tied with rope, 7¼, 17c, South German, repaired (4133/228)   750
Crucifix figure, Christ with arms outstretched, 14½, E19c, Goanese (4133/230)   1000
Diptych, French ivory, Nativity, 3, L14c (4133/218)   2900
Figure, ivory and fruitwood, provincial, woman, tattered clothing, 9¼, 18c, So. German (4133/237)   *550*
Medallion, double-sided, oval, carved, St. Mary Magdalene addressing Christ, 2¼, Flemish (4133/225)   300
Plaque, carved, Italo Byzantine, case, two apostles St. John and St. Luke, 3¾, 14, 16c, 2 pcs (4133/227)   400
Roundel, St. John the Baptist and St. Anthony of Padua, 2¼, E19c, Spanish (4133/223)   250
Travelers, pair, ivory and fruitwood, beggar holding child, companion, baby, 10, 10½, 18c, fine, So. German (4133/238)   5500
Virgin and Child, child in arm, 3, E17c, 2 pcs, South German (4133/226)   400

PEWTER

Assorted periods and localities

Candlesticks, pricket, pair, Austrian, 28¼, ca1700, fine (4133/117)	1400
Candlsticks, pricket, pair, dec borders of interlaced ribbons, 3 scroll feet, 28½, ca1820 (4133/143)	600
Cannister, cube form, caryatid scroll handles, Austrian, H6, 18c (4081/24)	300
Charger, engraved with armorials and scenes, 19¾ (4133/114)	150
Charger, Michel Hemersam, The Elder, Nuremberg, D18¼, M17c (4081/14)	3100
Coffee pot, pear shape, side hinged domed cover, wood handle with leaf, 9, L18c (4133/123)	450
Ewer, helmet shape, harp handle, vertical lobes and flutes, 8¼, ca1760, Apeller, Austrian (4133/122)	400
Flagon, baluster form and short faceted spout, scroll handle, 10¼, L18c (4133/130)	475
Flagon, baluster form, dolphin finial, Swiss, H13¾, fine, L17c (4081/29)	3250
Flagon, cylindrical form with figure of a soldier, H14⅛, L19c (4081/27)	125
Flagon, cylindrical form, flowering foliage, German, H11¼, E18c (4081/23)	650
Flagon, flat cover with ram's head finial, 11⅜, M18c, Nicolas Paul, Swiss (4133/134)	1800
Flagon, flat cover with rod, thumbpiece, initials, 9⅝, M18c, Charton, Swiss (4133/129)	1100
Flagon, initialed, 1737, scroll handle, mask at end, 11¼, E18c (4133/126)	900
Flagon, initialed flat cover, thumbpiece on chain, 11⅜, M18c, Andre Utin, Vevey, Swiss (4133/135)	1600
Flagon, simple skirt foot, flat cover, molded thumbpiece, 10¾ (4133/142)	100
Flagon, spreading foot, S-scroll handle, short spout, 11, E18c, Irish (4133/127)	400
Measure, bulbous form, narrow neck, molded bandings, 10½, 18c (4133/136)	450
Plates, pair, Continental, with leaves and flowerheads, German*, 9¾, 18c (4211/123)	200
Platter, English*, foliate monogram SDJ, D17½, L18c (4081/5)	275
Tankard, barrel engraved with initials and date, medallion, 9½, ca1720, Reuter (4133/124)	850
Tankard, domed cover, double scroll handle, shell shaped thumbpiece, 8, L18c (4133/131)	200
Tankard, engraved with stork and infant scenes below a rhyme, 10, ca1784, German or Austrian (4133/121)	600
Tankard, scroll handle, initialed, 1738, 8, E18c, Neureitter, Wasserburg (4133/125)	850
Tankard, Johann Gottlieb Klein Goldberg, cylindrical, H7¾, E19c (4081/7)	350
Tureen, covered, circular form, ribbed and fluted, Hebraic initials, 9¾, L18c (4133/137)	425
Urn, two-handled, inverted pear shape, German, H16½, rep, M19c (4081/11)	175

Austrian

Flagon, Thomas Schesser, heart-shaped cover, 11⅜, ca1660 (4255/94)	*1500*

Flagon
(4255/94)

Tankard, cylindrical, flare base, scroll handle, 4¾, ca1770 (4193/63)	425

Continental

Basin, 2 handled, A. Henquin, molded rim, bail handles, 12⅞, 18c (4255/68)	175
Candlesticks, pricket, pair, claw and ball feet, multi-baluster stems, 10, ca1700 (4193/61)	275
Candlesticks, pricket, pair, triform bases, embossed Virgin and Child, 27¾, M19c (4255/75)	1150
Canister, initials W.F., S.W. within foliate spray, 9¾, 18c (4255/82)	400
Canister, octagonal, screw on cover, ring handle, 9, ca1800 (4193/37)	200
Canister, octagonal, engraved with horse, hare and bird, 10⅜, E19c (4255/90)	350

Dish, broad rim, Villette, armorials below foliage, 13¼, ca1700 (4255/111) 800
Dish with Judaic engraving, flat rim with a double scroll, 15¾, 17c (4255/80) 600
Flagon, baluster, domed foot, scroll handle, 11½, ca1815 (4193/19) 500
Flask, flattened circular, screw on cap, 4¾, 18c (4193/17) 175
Flask, gourd shape, body with incised bands, 13, E18c (4255/93) *550*
Flask, screw on cover, bail handle, 10¾, 18c (4255/103) 150
Jug, covered, baluster body, demed lid, shell thumb piece, 10½, ca1760 (4255/69) 225
Jug, covered, baluster form, hinged shell thumb piece, 9½, L18-E19c (4255/87) 250
Lavabo, upright, faceted body, flat back, 8¼, L18c (4193/64) 150
Pitcher, covered, baluster, faceted spout, dome cover, 9, 19c (4193/31) 475
Tureen, soup and cover, domed cover, wood handles and finial, 9, E19c (4255/70) 375
Urn, tea, plain pear shape, double scroll handle, 17, L18c (4255/99) 450
Urn, tea, ring handles, eagle heads, 16¾, E19c (4255/74) 325
Urn hot water and stand, pear shape, s-scroll handle, 20, L18c (4193/34) 800

English

Cup, 2 handled, Georgian, quart capacity, tapered, double scroll handles, 6½, ca1800 (4193/79) 150
Flagon, Commonwealth, tapered 'Beefeater' lid, twin cusped thumbpiece, 9½, ca1655 (4193/91) 1300
Flagon George III, tapered, reeded bands, chairback thumbpiece, 11, ca1760 (4193/81) 650
Flagon James I, tapered, bun cover, notched thumbpiece, 11⅜, 1615-20 (4193/92) 800
Measure, Charles II, hammer head type, quart size, 8⅝, ca1680 (4193/86) 450
Measure, William and Mary, baluster reeded girdle, 1 pint, 6⅜, ca1690 (4193/90) 550
Plates, set of 12, George II with satyr masks, by maxted, London, 9¾, ca1745 (4193/71) 1900
Tankard, Georgian, cylindrical, 'wriggled work', 6⅞, ca1720 (4193/84) 1200
Tankard, Georgian, tapered, reeded foot, bifurcated thumbpiece, 7, ca1720 (4193/83) 700

French

Flagon, Normandy type, twin acorn thumb piece, 10¾, L18c (4255/83) 400
Flagon 'Penquin', barrel form, molded banks, loophandle, 13-19c (4255/100) 600
Measure, lidded, litre capacity, cylindrical, flared rim, 10½, L19c (4193/25) 150
Wine measure, demi-litre, capacity, bulbous, heart shaped cover, 6¾, ca1770 (4193/28) 650
Wine measure, litre capacity, tapered, in curved neck, 8½, 18c (4193/27) 225

German

Clock, oil, lamp form, glass reservoir, pewter mounts, 13⅛, ca1800 (4255/77) 600
Coffee pot, lobed and fluted pear shape, dome cover, 8¾, handle later, L18c (4193/54) 150
Ewer, oviform, flat domed lid, hinged spout, 11¾, ca1820 (4193/36) 325
Flagon, flaring foot, knop and ball finial, name and date, 12, ca1834 (4255/88) 350
Flagon, narrow, tapered, short spout, ball thumbpiece, 11½, ca1820 (4193/51) 300
Flagon, narrow, tapered, short spout, scroll handle, 9¾, ca1847 (4193/52) 200
Flagon, tapered cylindrical, short spout, 11⅝, L18c (4193/18) 500
Flagon, tapered form, flared base, 14, L18c (4255/79) 400
Flagon, H.G.S., tapered form, engraved name and date, 13¾, ca1746 (4255/78) 800
Plate, Kaiser Teller depicting, Kaiser Ferdinand III, by Rumpler, 7⅝, ca1630 (4193/47) 750
Pot, covered, bulbous, molded girdle, swing handle, 8⅞, ca1835 (4193/33) 750
Pot, mustard, cylindrical, domed foot, double scroll handle, 3¾, ca1760 (4193/38) 125
Tankard, plain, baluster, domed cover, acorn handle, 9¾, ca1800 (4193/60) 250
Tankard, straight sided, pedestal foot, scroll handle, 9¾, ca1800 (4255/85) 550
Tankard, straight-sided, pedestal foot, domed cover, 8, ca1800 (4255/84) 650
Vessel, 2 handled, amphora form, circular, 2 strap handles, 10½, ca1800 (4193/35) 550

Irish

Inkstand, George III, rectangular, double flap cover, by Heaney Dublin, 7, ca1790 (4193/89) 300

Scottish

Measure, George III, 'tappithen' shape, 14 gill capacity, 10⅞, ca1800 (4193/87) 675
Measure, George III, 'tappithen' shape, 2 gill capacity, 5⅝, ca1805 (4193/88) 600

Spanish

Candlestand, pricket, wrought iron, tripod feet, octagonal tray, 72, 15c (4193/109) 1200

Swiss

Can, wine, hexagonal, Zimmermann, initialed and dated 1746, 15¼, M18c (4255/123) 1800
Flagon, Baluster, covered spout, 11½, 18c (4193/9) 1300
Flagon, wine, baluster form, 12¾, ca1740 (4255/124) 2500
Wine can, cylindrical, covered spout, 10¾, L18c (4193/8) 750

SCULPTURE

Assorted periods and localities

Angel, head, sandstone, smiling expression, curly hair, 7, 14c, French (4133/264)	800
Archangel Michael, figure, carved marble, head downcast, French, 17, ca1460, part missing, rep (4133/260)	3300
Arm reliquary, wood gilt, carved as an arm with hand raised in blessing, 20¾, 17c, Spanish (4133/344)	100
Blackamoors, pair, rococoo, carved and, painted, kneeling, painted black, with red and white, 33¾, E18c, Continental (4142/17)	4750
Bozzetto of Bacchus and Pan, terracotta, seated satyr feeding infant satyr on lap, 12, 1863, cracked, Italian (4133/253)	300
Cartouche, wood, recoco gilt, now as mirror, 18, 18c, Italian (4133/358)	400
Christ, bust, polychrome, terracotta, wearing robe, modern oak base, 11½, 16c, 2 pcs, No. Italian (4133/248)	1600
Christ, man of sorrows, alabaster, gazing upward, Bohemian, 8½, ca1725, dam (4133/276)	900
Figures, pair, colonial gilt wood, standing attendants, wearing flowing drapery, 30¼, 17c, Spanish (4133/348)	1000
Head of female saint, burgundian stone, turban hairdress fastened below chin, 4½, 4¼, dam (4133/258)	600
Lectern, wood gilt, supported on four, baluster feet, foliate, motifs, 15¾, 17c, Italian (4133/342)	100
Madonna, Immaculata, figure, wood, polychrome, hands clasped in prayer, 15½, 18c, German (4133/381)	700
Panels, pair, gilded wood, Equestrian figure, wooded landscape, 14⅛, E17c, German (4133/339)	1400
Putto, bust, terracotta, gazing left, lips parted, 4, E18c, Flemish (4133/251)	300
Relief, alabaster, head of St. John the Baptist, 12¾, ca1400, restorations, Nottingham (4133/268)	6400
Relief, fragment of the annunciation, marble, Virgin on bench facing the bible, 38, E16c, Italian (4133/269)	1600
Relief, white marble, containing 2 panels, 2 apostles, 23½, 14c, Venetian (4133/261)	3000
Relief, Roman Emperor, marble, middle age man with heavy features, 17, 17c, Italian (4133/278)	2300
Relief, St Catherine, wood carved, polychrome, 30, E18c, German (4133/379)	4000
Relief, The Madonna and Child, Virgin holding child in arms, Malines alabaster, 4¾ x 3¾, ca1600 (4133/271)	1000
Resurrected Christ, figure wood, Baroque, polychrome, 16½, finger missing, Austrian (4133/373)	1400
Saint figure, carved wood, standing wearing gold robe, curly hair, long beard, 36½, M17c, dam, German (4133/341)	850
St. Anne, head, limestone, deeply cut eyes, wearing a wimple overhead, 6, 15c, French, nose restored (4133/265)	450
St. John the Baptist, figure, florentine, terracotta, 26½, 15c, rep (4133/247)	6000
St. Notburga, figure carved limestone, parton of Farming, arms out stretched, 45½, ca1720, Austrian (4133/382)	2000
St. Peter, figure, carved stone, standing, worried expression holding open book, 18, ca1470, res, Dutch (4133/266)	4000
St. Thomas Aquinas, figure, terracotta, saint heavily draped robe, holds open book, 19, ca1700, Roman (4133/250)	2700
Urn on base, decorative, gilt wood, rocaille ornament festooned with flowers, 17½, M18c, German (4133/372)	650
Virgin and Child, alabaster, both fitted for crown, (missing), standing holding child, 20, 16/17c (4133/275)	1400
Virgin and Child, carved marble, virgin wearing long robe, child on left arm, 30½, E14c, res, No. Italian (4133/256)	5800
Virgin and Child, Burgundian limestone, 24½, L15c, res (4133/259)	8000

Austrian

Virgin of Sorrows, hands clasped in prayer, mournful expression, 31, 1510-20 (4255/179)	7500

English

Lame peasant, limestone, left hand holding crutch, 16, 16c rep (4255/276)	200

Flemish

Relief, Master, Dolorosa, alabaster, mournful expression, 12, E16c, rep (4255/279)	1200
Reliefs, set of four, Netherlandish, king and soldiers arresting bishop, 14½ x 22, L16c (4255/169)	5600
Sleeping child, alabaster, long curly hair and arms crossed, 11, 17c (4255/277)	125
Virgin and Child, holding Christ in left hand, 38, ca1600, rep (4255/171)	1600

French

Nymph with Bacchantes, group, signed by Joseph Marin, 11⅛, dam, ca1790 (4255/300)	*9600*
Oval relief, white marble, smiling Bacchante, 12, 17c (4255/286)	800
St. Andrew, stone, hand clasping an X-shaped cross, red polychroming, 33¾, M15c (4255/281)	4000

German

Apostle, polychrome, wearing beard and long wavy hair, holding book, 36, ca1490, dam (4255/175)	700
Sconces, pair, 2 angels in flight, bodies painted white, wings gold, 13½, E18c (4255/186)	1400
St. Adrian, gilt, wearing brown and flowing cloak, 18½, M18c (4255/187)	450
St. Anne, oak, long robes belted at the waist, mantle, 37¾, ca1500, rep (4255/177)	2000
St. Gregory, papal tiara, gilt cloak, 32½, 1630-40, right hand missing (4255/182)	3800
St. Hubert, wood, robes fastened with a morse, 34, E16c (4255/180)	2200
St. John the Baptist, standing wearing sheepskin, a lamb at feet, 18½, L18c (4255/189)	350
St. Leonard, book in right hand, chain in left, 36½, ca1500, rep (4255/176)	*2000*

Nymph with Bacchantes
(4255/300)

St. Leonard
(4255/176)

St. Lucy
(4255/178)

St. Lucy, black robe in elegant folds, Swabian, 40¼, ca1500 (4255/178)	*12000*
Virgin, hands clasped in prayer, 18½, L16c, rep (4255/181)	600
Virgin and Child, limestone, Virgin wearing tall crown, 35¼, ca1420 (4255/280)	15500
Virgin polychrome, right hand outstretched, multi-colored robes, 20½, L17c, dam (4255/183)	2100

Italian

Angels, pair, outspread wings, flowing gilt drapery, 19, 17c (4255/162)	1700
Angels, pair, standing position 1 hand outstretched, 31½, ca1600 (4255/154)	1700
Angels, pair, polychrome, long, flowing hair, robes, red and gold, later wings, 44, ca1600 (4255/156)	2500
Archangel Gabriel, hand raised in blessing, 23⅞, 17c (4255/160)	900
Attendant Neapolitan creche, bald head, hands at sides, 13, L18c, imp (4255/167)	350
Bust of St. John, terracotta, long curly pair, 10¾, res, 16c (4255/297)	1000
Candlestick, gilt wood, putto, outstretched wings, 21, M18c, res (4255/161)	900
Candlesticks, pair, white marble, Dionysus and Ariade, 17¼, 19c (4255/296)	1000
Figures, pair, gilt wood, running, wearing long flowing robes, 41, 17c (4255/163)	900
Figures, pair, Neapolitan creche, buxom woman and stocky man, 19¼, L18c (4255/166)	*800*

Figures (4255/166)

King, head surmounted by a crown, 50, E17c (4255/165)	2600
Lions, pair, white marble, recumbent position, 31, 15c (4255/285)	16000
Male saint, hands outstretched, balding head, beard, 33, L16c (4255/153)	1800
Monk saint, polychrome, holding book, red robes, 37¾, L16c, imp (4255/152)	1000
Peasant, Neapolitan creche, face unshaven, later clothing, 16, L18c, imp (4255/168)	400
Virgin and Child, white marble, Virgin wearing long robes, 19, rep, 14c (4255/284)	1300
Virgin of Trapani, alabaster, long robes with gilt decoration, 12, dam, 17c (4255/289)	350

Malines

Relief, Lot and Daughters, alabaster, seated at table with daughter, 4⅝ x 3½, ca1600 (4255/282)	850
Relief, The Annunciation, alabaster, with the Virgin kneeling, 5 x 3⅞, ca1600 (4255/283)	1800

Spanish

Archangel Raphael, polychrome, right hand raised, 12¼, 18c, dam (4255/151)	850
Crucifix, wood, Our Lord with glass eyes, crown of thorns, 48, L18-E19c (4255/143)	500
Female saint, bust, polychrome wood, reliquary, wearing a red breast plate, 30¾, ca1600 (4255/142)	550
Prophets, pair, polychrome, wearing tall hats, book in 1 hand, 12, ca1700 (4255/144)	225
St. Anne, polychrome, wearing long gilt robes, head covered in a mantle, 11¾, 18c (4255/147)	650
St. Francis, polychrome wood, in monk's robes, cloak, 31, 18c, imp (4255/145)	800
The Virgin, colonial wood relief, wearing flowing robes, 27¼, 18c (4255/149)	400
Virgin and Child, carved Virgin seated, holding Child, 28½, 14-15c (4255/141)	5200
Virgin and St. John pair, polychrome, glass eyes, marbleized bases, 13, 18c, fingers missing (4255/146)	700

Tyrolean

Altarpiece, polychrome, relief with the Virgin holding Christ child, 56¾, L18c (4255/190)	3200

TAPESTRIES

Assorted periods and localities

Aubusson tapestry, nobleman on horseback and hunter in a bucolie scene, 81 x 57 (669/668)	350
Biblical, two woman and gentlemen standing before seated woman, 106 x 98, E17c, Flemish (4133/393)	5250
Chinoiserie, 'The Tea' lady and gentleman seated at table, 114 x 206, M18c, Aubusson, fine (4133/412)	29000
Chouxfleur, birds and flowers, 85 x 59, M16c, Flemish (4133/389)	8000
Courtly romance, late Gothic style, Flemish, 94½ x 82, 16c (4081/249)	13000
Death of Asclepius, Flemish, 79 x 72, E17c (4081/239)	5750
Flemish style tapestry, medieval figures in a castle garden, 68 x 46½, 19c (631/444)	350
Fragment, biblical, Adoration of the Magi, Flemish, 22½ x 27, 16c (4081/236)	600
Fragment, game park, figures and dogs attacking bear, Flemish, 69 x 50, 16c (4081/237)	2400
Game park, stag being pursued by men on horseback, 82 x 74, L16c, Flemish (4133/391)	7500
Gothic, fragment, late, ladies seated, 2 gentlemen in attendance, 37 x 48, E16c, Tournai* (4133/387)	1700
Historical, emperor seated astride horse, parthian spearman, 108 x 137, L17c, Aubusson (4133/403)	5500

Historical, equestrian figure of Henri IV, of France, 75 x 118, ca1600, Qudenarde (4133/392)	9500
Historical, Eygptian Queen and Roman General, at table, 78 x 102, 18c, Aubusson* (4133/413)	2000
Hunting, 'The Wolf Hunt', 136 x 140, M17c, Mortlake (4133/396)	8000
Hunting, hunters on horseback and foot, 74 x 85, L16c, Brussels (4133/390)	5500
Ladies and men in armour, Flemish, 113 x 129, 17c (4081/243)	1200
Millefleurs, coat of arms, family of Pozzo DiBorgo, 112 x 63, E16c (4133/385)	19500
Millefleurs, two large dogs facing each other, 27½ x 96, E16c, French (4133/386)	33000
Mythological, aphrodite and ares conversing with young eros, 111 x 188, M17c, Flemish (4133/395)	4000
Mythological, 'Europa and the Bull', 105 x 108, E18c, Flemish (4133/406)	4200
Mythological, 'The Return of Telemachus', 110 x 130, 17c, Flemish (4133/397)	2600
Mythological, goddess Rhea being drawnin her chariot, 113½ x 164, L17c, Flemish (4133/401)	8000
Panel, bearded man holding garland, Flemish, 90 x 63, E18c (4081/246)	2100
Panel, biblical, Virgin enthroned, angel, Flemish, 77 x 126, M17c (4081/241)	2300
Panel, Teniers type, dancing peasant couples in front of an inn, 90 x 93, 18c, French (4133/414)	2100
Romance, young couple seated together in wooded glade, 128 x 130, 17c, Flemish (4133/398)	5500
Romance, noble couple seated, Flemish, 111 x 100, E18c (4081/252)	5000
Sacrifice of Iphigenia, mythological, Bruges, 147 x 105, 17c (4081/242)	7000
Story of Romulus and Remus*, Brussels, 94 x 233, L16c (4081/238)	*21000*
Tapestry, verdure style, squirrels and parrots in a pastoral landscape, 99 x 60, 19c (619/442)	550
Tapestry, Flemish, Moses and the bronze serpent, 91 x 64, 17c (619/443)	800
Tapestry, Verdure style, two equestrian figures in landscape, 69 x 70, 19c (619/438)	1200
Tapestry,panel, fragment, Brussels, 66 x 22 (619/444)	375
Tapestry fragment, Brussels verdure, 60 x 43, 18c (619/445)	425
Tapestry of a landscape scene, 43 x 36, 19c (619/446)	80
Tapestry panels, pair, Brussels verdure, flora, fauna, small chateau in background, 64 x 42, 19c, framed (619/441)	1800
Teniers, gypsy fortune-teller, V. Leyniers, L.V., Brussels, 114 x 75, M18c (4081/247)	12500
Teniers, woman bringing grapes from vineyard, Brussels, 118 x 98, L18c (4081/251)	14000
Teniers type, three peasant musicians, sheppherd and a cowherd, 86 x 106, E18c, Lille* (4133/405)	5400
Verdure, bird attacking quail, srees, hilly landscape, 92 x 56, 18c, Flemish (4133/409)	2000
Verdure, cockatoo seated in tree branch, Flemish, 179 x 71, M17c (4081/244)	5500
Verdure, hunting dog chasing fox, wooded glade, 102 x 139, L17/18c, Aubusson (4133/404)	4400
Verdure, hunting dog chasing stag, chateau, landscape, 62 x 75, 19c, French (4133/419)	950
Verdure, large tree on the banks of a waterfall, man fishing, 111 x 77, E19c, French (4133/418)	2000
Verdure, noble couple, prancing horse, groom, Brussels, 135 x 152, M17c (4081/240)	3750
Verdure, two game birds, snake, borders, floral, masks and fruits, 101 x 89, L17c, Brussels (4133/399)	4600
Verdure, wooded glade, large chateau floral borders, 114 x 95, L17c, Flemish (4133/402)	4000
Verdure, Dense wooded glade with architectural elements, 49 x 50, L17c, Flemish (4133/400)	600
Verdure, fragment, bird of prey, Flemish, 38 x 76, 18c (4081/245)	550
Verdure, panel, pagoda upon a hill, tree and bird, Flemish, 113 x 45, 18c (4081/248)	600
Verdure, panel, peacock standing before a palm, Flemish, 101 x 49, 18c (4081/250)	1600
Verdure, crane standing within a sparsely wooded glade, 111 x 73, E18c, Flemish (4133/407)	2500

Aubusson

Chinoisserie, 5 men conversing, 92 x 123, M18c (4255/499)	16000
Historical, a scene from Roman history, 105 x 125, L17c (4255/482)	3300
Historical, Alexander, the Battle of Arbela, 135 x 130, E18c (4255/495)	7500
Tapestry, ladies riding asses, two men, 94 x 94, E18c (4193/467)	1500
Verdure, plants, two birds and stream, 102 x 103, M18c (4163/475)	5000

Brussels

Allegorical, lady being crowned by Minerva, 92 x 55, L17c (4193/464)	3000
Allegorical, seated woman holding a scythe, sheep, 113¼ x 72, ca1600 (4255/469)	*3250*
Game park, couple walking in forest, 132 x 172, L16c (4193/446)	20000
Grotesque, nude, Pluto* holding double-pronged fork, 96 x 109, ca1550 (4255/465)	*16000*
Historical, general and troops, 99 x 101, L16/E17c (4193/451)	7500
Mythological, Diana holding bow, 111 x 108, folded back, M18c (4163/474)	9000
Mythological, Vertumnus and Pomona, 140 x 74, 17c (4193/453)	1100
Mythological fragment, goddess holding olive branch, 106 x 44½, M17c (4193/450)	1200
Teniers, the fish quay, 84 x 94, E18c (4193/465)	4300
Verdure fragment, chateau next to a windmill, 85 x 58½, L17/E18c (4255/487)	1100

Story of Romulus and Remus*   (4081/238)

Mythological   (4255/475)

Allegorical   (4255/469)

Grotesque   (4255/465)

Brussels*

Mythological, from the story of Odysseus, 107 x 125½, L17c (4255/475)	8000
Mythological, from the story of Perseus, 107 x 117, L17c (4255/484)	9500
Mythological, fragment, young woman fleeing, 92½ x 25½ (4255/498)	1800
'Feuilles D'Aristoloche', bull butting lion, 103 x 133, M16c (4255/464)	43000
'Feuilles D'Aristoloche', flowering plant flanked by stag, 102 x 155, M16c (4255/463)	40000
'Feuilles D'Aristoloche', rearing horse facing a lion, 92 x 144, M16c (4255/462)	82500

English

Chinoiserie, islands and figures, 89 x 72, 19c (4163/477)	9000
Chinoiserie, islands and figures, 90 x 76, 19c (4163/476)	8500
Chinoiserie, islands and figures, 89 x 48, 19c (4193/478)	6000
Chinoiserie, islands and figures, irregular shape, 89 x 81, 19c (4193/479)	5000

Felletin

Historical fragment, equestrian general, 63 x 72, L17c (4193/458)	1800
Historical fragment, young general and horse in battle, 113 x 72, L17c (4193/457)	2400

Flemish

Biblical, female and angel, landscape, 98 x 122, M17c (4193/452)	900
Biblical, John the Baptist, Herod, 119 x 102, ca1600 (4255/470)	3000
Biblical, fragment, 4 females praying, 93 x 59, E17c (4255/474)	1800
Biblical panel, Eastern king and queen seated, 96 x 67, M17c (4255/481)	1900
Country romance, noblewoman presented jewels, 94½ x 82, 19c (4193/484)	6500
Feuilles De Choux, bull attacked by leopards, 106 x 85, L16c (4255/467)	17000
Feuilles De Choux, many animals in foliage, 90 x 106, L16c (4255/466)	16000

Fragment, two snarling dogs, 28, L16c (4193/447)   450
Game park, panel, figures in a woods, 84 x 55, L16c (4193/445)   2100
Historical, fragment, equestrian group, 90 x 70, L17/E18c (4255/479)   4500
Historical, from the story of Scipio, 117 x 98, 17c (4255/478)   1400
Historical, Fallen warrior on knee, 82 x 135, E17c (4255/472)   5000
Historical, 4 clerical figures, soldiers, 75 x 79, L16c (4255/468)   4250
Mythological, Artemis and Orion*, 135 x 64, 17c (4255/477)   2400
Mythological, Danae and maid, 91 x 58, M17c (4193/455)   1800
Mythological, Juno and two maidens, 100 x 81, L17c (4193/462)   5200
Mythological, 3 dieties seated, 105 x 100, E17c (4255/473)   5000
Mythological fragment, warrior scavenging for food, 95 x 66, E17c (4255/476)   1800
Tapestry panel, bird on tree limb, 82 x 51, E18c (4163/468)   2100
The Story of St. Julian the Hospitator, late Gothic, French*, 121 x 126, ca1525 (4255/461)   52500
Verdure, crane by pool, 101 x 69, E18c (4163/469)   2000
Verdure, dogs chasing stag, 102 x 119, L17/E18c (4193/466)   7000
Verdure, landscape, 102 x 68, E18c (4163/471)   5750
Verdure, landscape, 120 x 147, L17/E18c (4163/470)   5000
Verdure, large aquatic bird, 90 x 101, E18c (4255/490)   8000
Verdure, two birds and trees, 116 x 101, L17c (4193/463)   6250
Verdure, wooded glade, 118 x 141, L17/E18c (4255/494)   15500
Verdure, wooded landscape, 89 x 106, L17c (4193/461)   5500
Verdure, 2 large aquatic birds, 83 x 115, 18c (4255/483)   3000
Verdure panel, large aquatic bird, 88 x 67, E18c (4255/491)   2250
Verdure panel, large bird, wooded surroundings, 90 x 93, L17/E18c (4255/488)   1000
Verdure panel, 2 peahens, large parrot, 73 x 73, L17/E18c (4255/489)   3250

French

Hunting, 2 equestrian hunters and their squire, 76 x 75½, L19/E20c (4255/503)   3500
Millefleurs, warrior saint holding a sword, 77 x 32, L19/E20c (4255/501)   2900
Millefleurs, St. Catherine holding a wheel and flower, 77 x 32, L19/E20c (4255/502)   3100
Pastoral, shepherd and maid, 54½ x 73, L19c (4193/482)   1100
Pastoral, two ladies and gentleman, 77 x 84, 19c (4193/481)   1400
Seasonal, September, hunter astride horse, dogs, 72 x 73, L19-E20c (4255/504)   7250
Verdure, dog stalking game bird, 85 x 84, L19c (4193/480)   1600
Verdure, hilly landscape, 111 x 127, L19c (4193/483)   1750
Verdure, pheasant, plants, stream, 67 x 52, L19c (4193/485)   1400

Gobelins

Mythological, from the triumphs of the gods, 81 x 101, ca1710 (4255/496)   27000

Italian

Silkwork panel, river landscape, framed, 40 x 99, L17c (4193/444)   1800

Lille*

Mythological, from the story of Vertumnus and Pomona, 95 x 53, 17c (4255/486)   6000

Oudenaarde*

Historical, Egyptian queen, Roman general, 108 x 95, 17c (4255/500)   3500

Soho*

Historical, Diogenes contemplating the ruins of Carthage, 106 x 101, E17c (4255/493)   5500
Mythological, Mercury and Argus, 107 x 101, E17c (4255/492)   18000

Swiss

Needlepoint panel, Magdalean and Christ, 26½ x 39½, E17c (4193/443)   2200

TEXTILES

Assorted periods and localities

Altar, frontal, applique velvet, border sewn with jewels, gold thread eagle, 100 x 38, M16c, Spanish
(4133/2)   400
Antinous, figure, naked youth with short curly hair, holding baton, 12, 18c, Florentine (4133/215)   900
Banner, silk appliqued, crimson, strapwork, Florentine, 89 x 62, 16c (4081/216)   350
Cape, green Madonna, bizarre design, Italian*, L123, ca1710-20 (4081/221)   700
Chasuble, brocade and sequined, floral motifs, Russian, L76½, E19c (4081/228)   *150*
Chasuble, embroidered design, tulips, central European, L70, fine, M18c (4081/222)   550
Chasuble, gold brocade, floral patterns, French, L79, 19c (4081/226)   50

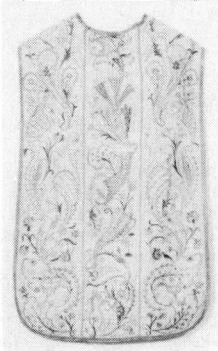

Chasuble (4081/222)

Chasuble (4081/228)

Chasuble (4081/220)

Chasuble, green velvet, cut and uncut, Italian*, L75, M16c (4081/220)	700
Chasuble, metal brocade, foliate and flora, Russian, L74, M19c (4081/224)	200
Cope, red and golt brocade, Spanish, L114, 16c (4081/215)	700
Cope, red cut velvet, pattern, Florentine, L108, 1525-50 (4081/219)	600
Cope, Louis XIV style, floral and foliate, French, W84, 19c (4081/229)	150
Cope, velvet, apricot, edged in yellow and brown woven ribbon, 114, L15/E16c (4133/1)	575
Cover, black velvet, edged in wide ribbon of gold metallic thread, 96 x 72, 17c, Italian (4133/5)	250
Panel, Louis XIII cut velvet, Italy or France, 56 x 48, 17c (4081/217)	150
Panel, biblical embroidered, divided into 3 panels, 32 x 65, L16c (4133/384)	3200
Panel, red silk velvet, 126 x 21½, 17c, Italian (4133/4)	525
Panel, red silk velvet, 108 x 20½, E17c, Italian (4133/3)	200
Panel, Portico, Elaborate floral arrangement within large urn, 85 x 57, 17c, Brussels (4133/394)	2000
Portiere, cut velvet flowers and star motifs, 136 x 50, 19c (4081/230)	150

Flemish

Panel, needlepoint, Biblical, panel work in polychrome, 72 x 47, E18c (4255/27)	1200

French

Brocade, metal, bizarre design, 84 x 22, E18c (4255/28)	125
Cope, satin damask, white floral design, 112, E18c, Italian* (4255/30)	400
Dalmatic, metal brocade, ivory ground, polychrome blossoms, 42, L18c (4255/41)	350
Panel, polychrome and gold, embroidered, architectural scrollwork, 74 x 40, E18c (4255/31)	700

Genoese

Brocade, metal, baroque style, 3 lengths joined, 92 x 72, 19c (4255/49)	350
Panel, cut and uncut red velvet, 71, 19c, after 17c design (4255/50)	100

Italian

Altar, frontal, Immaculata surrounded by blossoms, ribbons, 37 x 95, L17-E18c (4255/23)	1700
Cope, metal brocade, ivory ground, 118, M18c (4255/40)	450
Hanging, armorial, red velvet, silver-gilt thread, 65 x 71, 18c (4255/39)	500
Panel, metal brocade, patterned pale blue satin ground, 115 x 60, E18c (4255/26)	275
Panel, red velvet, embroidered, armorial, kneeling angel, 12½ x 110, 17c (4255/22)	800
Panel, red velvet appliqued, 2 flower filled vases, 10 x 56, L17-E18c (4255/24)	175

Spanish

Chasuble of red velvet, with orphrey, 3 panels, figures, 29½, L16c (4255/16)   250

Swiss

Panel, wool embroidered, S. German*, 30½ x 41½, M16c (4255/12)   5000

WORKS OF ART

Assorted periods and localities

Candlesticks, pair, Nicolo Roccatagliata workshop, urn, satyrs, H6, 16c (4081/198)   1400
Casket, engraved silver mounts, Dutch, East Indian, L7, missing handles, 17c (4081/149)   800
Casket, engraved silver strapwork, Dutch, East Indian, L8¾, imp, 17c (4081/148)   700
Casket, steel, etched with caryatid figures, German, L7⅝, replacements, ca1600 (4081/160)   *1900*
Coffer, leather, iron mounted, cuir bouilli, Spanish, L35¾, 15c (4081/152)   2700
Crucifix, silver, wood cross in low relief with crucifix figure, Roumanian, 8¾, 17c (4255/227)   300
Cup, mate (tea), carved coconut, figures amidst scrollwork, South American, H5⅛, d, 18c (4081/150)   300
Figure of greyhound, after Joseph Gott, recumbent position, English, L6½, 19c (4081/200)   225
Figure of Somnus, Francois Duquesnog workshop, L5¼, 17c (4081/188)   1100
Jewel box, gilt bronze mounts, religious scenes, Italian, H17, 19c (4081/151)   800
Lock, iron, Gothic, 3 figures, angels, French, H8, 15c (4081/157)   2000
Lock, steel, applied with 2 gilt bronze plaques, German, L11¾, M17c (4081/162)   *1200*

Lock
(4081/162)

Casket (4081/160)

Medal, gilt-lead, of Landgraf Augustus, polychrome, German, D3 15/16, rare, E16c (4081/171)   550
Medal, lead, of Antonio Abondio, polychrome, framed, D1¾, M16c (4081/172)   800
Model of Cannon, dolphin form handles, floral, foliate, Flemish, L17⅛, ca1640 (4081/195)   750
Model of Cannon, two dolphin handles with bands, Flemish*, L16¾, 1636 (4081/194)   700
Model of Cannon, two dolphin-form handles, Flemish*, L34, 17/18c (4081/196)   2300
Monstrance, parcel gilt, applied with copper gilt angels, Spanish, H21¼, 18c (4081/178)   350
Monstrance, silver gilt, two cherubs holding hearts, Spanish, H23½, E19c (4081/177)   400
Mortar, angular handles, vertical ribs, Spanish, H4, 17c (4081/203)   450
Mortar, bands contain maidens astride centaur, Italian, H5⅛, M16c (4081/205)   1000
Mortar, molded rims with baluster motifs, Spanish, H4⅝, 17c (4081/204)   450
Mortar, vertical ribs and molded female mask, Spanish, H3¼, corrosion, 17c (4081/202)   150
Mortar, winged cherubs heads, leaf motifs, Flemish, H4⅜, 17c (4081/208)   600
Mortar, bronze, saucer rim, angular handles, rows of florettes, Swiss, 6⅜, 1713 (4193/149)   1600
Mortar, large, stiff leaves, baluster-form handles, Italian, H11, 17c (4081/211)   1800
Mortar, Documentary, Austino De Gilio, oval medallion, Italian, H3½, d, 1566 (4081/206)   500
Mortar, Gothic bronze, 4 buttresses, inscribed 4 times amen, pestle, Netherlands*, H3¾, ca1500 (4255/247)   850
Mortar and Pestle, Gothic tracery with animal heads, Flemish, H5½, 1545 (4081/209)   1700
Plaque, manner of Clodion, embossed putto, French, 6⅜ x 12¼, L18c (4081/156)   225
Sceptre, silver gilt, gold and silver spiralling stripes, S. German, H15, ca1700 (4081/181)   550
Strong box, iron, two shield motifs, scrollwork, German, L11⅜, 17c (4081/161)   900
Writing box, leather, cuir bouilli, scrollwork, Spanish, L14, 16c (4081/154)   1200
Writing box, leather, cuir bouilli, Flemish, L14¾, 16c (4081/153)   650

Brass

Dish, repousse with spiralling gadroons, German, D15¾, rep, 16c (4081/168)	900
Dish, repousse with the Annunciation, German, D16½, rep, 16c (4081/169)	350
Dish, repousse with the Paschal Lamb, German, D16½, and rep, 16c (4081/165)	450
Dish, repousse with Adam and Eve, German, D14¾, d, ca1500 (4081/170)	1100
Dish, repousse with Adam and Eve, German, D14⅞, rep, ca1500 (4081/166)	450
Flask, repousse 2 fighting warriors, German, H4⅞, 16/17c (4081/176)	800

Copper gilt

Chalice and paten, engraved with a cross, Tuscan, H7¼, D5¼, rep, 16c (4081/175)	800
Monstrance, in the form of a tower, Italian or Spanish, H23½, missing pcs, 16c (4081/174)	900
Processional cross, Christ in the Seat of Judgement, Italian, H20⅝, 14/15c (4081/173)	500
Spurs, pair, decorated with flowers, English, L6¼, 17c (4081/179)	600

Dutch

Bed warmer, brass, with brass grips, medallion, 48, 1772 (4255/219)	*1300*
Charger, brass, scene of 2 hunters carrying a grape cluster, 16½, ca1600 (4255/213)	200
Dish, brass, center repousse, with vase full of tulips, 12¾, ca1600 (4255/214)	325

English

Document, legal, parchment, wax seal, King Phillip II & Queen Mary I, ca1556 (4193/340)	375
Mortar, bell metal, bands of scallop shells, scrolls, saucer rim, 8⅛, 17c (4193/152)	1500
Mortar, bronze, flaring, scrollwork reeding, ¼, 17c (4193/146)	200

Flemish

Candlestick, brass, base, knopped stem and engraved moresques, 9¾, L16C (4255/210)	650
Mortar, bell metal, brass, pestle, double brass, mask handles, 4¾, E17c (4255/249)	*750*

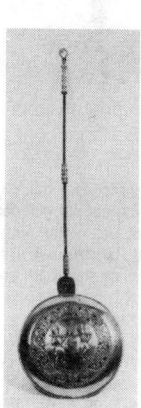

Bed warmer
(4255/219)

Mortar (4255/249)

Strongbox (4255/207)

Mortar, bronze, brass pestle, double dolphin handles, 4¾, E17c (4255/269)	550
Mortar, bronze, double dolphin handles, foliate, scrolls, 4⅜, 1626, with pestle (4255/248)	2100

French

Box, missal, iron, wood core overlaid with iron trelliswork, 12, 15c, Spanish* (4255/205)	3200
Key, iron, straight shaft of square section, 4½, 16c (4255/203)	900
Mortar, bell metal, saucer shaped, buttresses, masks and bosses, 4¼, 16c (4193/138)	75
Mortar, bronze, saucer rim, buttresses, 2 masks, 4½, 16c (4193/139)	600
Mortar, bronze, saucer rim, 6 buttresses, 2 male heads, 4½, 16c (4193/144)	850
Mortar, bronze, 5 females, grotesque busts, 3 medallions, 6¼, 16c (4193/141)	1600
Mortar, bronze, with pestle, cast with male and female portraits, 3¾, 16c (4255/258)	1900
Strongbox, iron, decorative ironwork exterior, handles, 13½, L16c (4255/207)	*1400*

German

Dish, alms, brass, with Virgin, Gothic lettering, Diam 14⅛ (4255/223)	225
Lock and key, iron, shooting 2 bolts, plate engraved, 12¼, L17c (4255/221)	800

Strongbox, chest, painted iron, key and a spike, green, 24½, 16-17c (4255/224)   2800
Strongbox, chest, iron, key, corroded exterior, 30, 16-17c (4255/225)   1300
Strongbox, iron, 4 ball feet, 2 stylized scrolls, key, 14, E17c (4255/220)   1500

Italian

Bell, bronze, bearing the Medici arms, black patina, H6½, 16-17c (4255/237)   1700
Box, document, bone inlaid, rectangular, geometrical pattern, 29, imp, 16c (4193/341)   2100
Casket, gilt bronze and brown jasper, supported by caryatids of naked men, 14½, ca1600 (4193/343)   4000
Casket, ormolu mounted, jasper, tortoiseshell, agate panels, wood carcass, 15, 19c (4193/344)   1100
Casket, work, pastiglia, rectangular, Neptune in chariot, 7¾, imp, 16c (4193/346)   325
Ciborium, covered, copper gilt, repousse bowl, flowerheads, 11½, ca1600 (4255/233)   550
Cross processional, copper gilt, wood core, central crucifix, 25, ca1500 (4255/228)   *2000*

Mortar   (4255/251)

Cross processional
(4255/228)

Mortar   (4255/254)

Cross, processional, copper gilt, wood core, central plaque, 13, 15c, dam (4255/229)   300
Crucifix, copper gilt, base with a cherub mask, 14½, ca1600 (4255/230)   400
Mortar, bell metal, double scroll handles, 4¾, 16c (4255/260)   450
Mortar, bronze, bell shape, double scroll handles, 6⅜, M16c (4193/140)   550
Mortar, bronze, dark brown patina, 4⅝, 16c, handle lacking (4255/257)   800
Mortar, bronze, dolphin handles, saucer rim, 7½, 17c (4193/147)   1400
Mortar, bronze, flaring, protruding handles, 4¼, 17c (4193/143)   600
Mortar, bronze, fleur delys, dark brown patina, pestle, 5, ca1600 (4255/261)   1100
Mortar, bronze, pestle, medallion of John the Baptist, 6⅝, E16c (4255/259)   1100
Mortar, bronze, saucer rim, 3 fleurs de lys, ¼, L16c (4193/142)   750
Mortar, bronze, with pestle, inscription Anno Domini 1619, 8¼, 1619 (4255/262)   2400
Mortar, bronze, single handled, with 4 equestrian figures and shield, 4½, L15c (4193/136)   6750
Mortar and pestle, bronze, 2 horse head handles, brown patina, 5, 16c, dam (4255/256)   500
Saucer rim, molded foot, handles blackamoor heads, 5¼, 17c (4193/148)   2900
Spurs, 2 matching, steel, brass cleats, inlaid silver panels, 10½, 10-17c (4255/231)   450

Spanish

Box, tortoise shell and silver, colonial, rectangular, domed cover, 6¾, 18c (4193/337)   650
Box, writing, cuir, bouilli, medallion shield, lions, scrollwork, 14¼, 16c (4193/342)   1100
Cross, processional, wood core, copper gilt paquettes, 17½, 15c (4255/206)   2600
Cross, processional, copper gilt, curling acanthus leaves, crucifix figure, 19½, 14c (4255/202)   4200
Mortar, bronze, globular Gothic, 4, 16-17c, dark brown patina (4255/253)   1100
Mortar, bell metal, miniature, saucer shaped rim, 1¼, 17c (4255/270)   900
Mortar, bronze, angular handles mounted with rings, 3¾, 15-16c, dam (4255/268)   1100
Mortar, bronze, brass pestle, 6, ca1600 (4255/251)   *1300*
Mortar, bronze, pestle, dark patina, 6½, E17c (4255/254)   *800*
Mortar, bronze, pestle, double straight handles, 3¾ x 16, 1 handle gone (4255/250)   750

Mortar, bronze, saucer rim, 6 baluster form columns, 5⅝, 16c (4193/145)	175
Mortar, bronze, saucer shapes rim, 7, ca1600 (4255/252)	600
Mortar, bronze, with 6 buttresses, 3½, 16c (4255/273)	350
Mortar, bronze, Gothic, band of buttresses, L shaped handles, 4⅞, 15c (4193/137)	1100
Mortar and pestle, bronze, everted rim, sides 5 columns, cherub masks, 6 x 8, 16c (4193/150)	400
Mortar and pestle, bronze, everted rim, 8 form columns, 6 x 7½, 16c (4193/151)	300
Mortar and pestle, bronze, with grotesque masks, brown patina, 4⅛, E17c (4255/255)	*600*

Trapani

Font, holy water, coral, silver base, scrollwork feet, femme figure, 6¾, imp, E18c (4193/339)	750
Relief, God the Father, coral, hand outstretched, other downwards, 4¾, 18c (4193/338)	1100

Chapter 6

American and European Works of Art, 19th and 20th Century: Works of the Victorian, Art Nouveau, Art Deco and Art Moderne Periods

After decades of neglect, Art Nouveau has become in the last few years one of the fastest growing and most competitive areas of collecting. The excitement generated by this spectacular surge has spread throughout the field of nineteenth- and twentieth-century works of art, from the products of the Victorian stylists to Art Deco and Art Moderne. Strong gains in most areas and many record prices were reported last season.

Because the market is so new and the Victorian period so varied, new collectors have exceptional opportunities. (French inkwells, German vases and Viennese silver miniatures all sold in the low hundreds despite their bold design and noteworthy craftsmanship.) Victorian work will probably make strong gains, especially those pieces which foreshadow Art Nouveau or were fashioned by prominent craftsmen of the period.

The products of the Tiffany studios, perhaps the best known of all Art Nouveau works, once again led the surge in prices; Tiffany lamps have doubled in value in less than two years, and as prices rose to record highs collectors turned to related Tiffany items. This year, Tiffany glass was as much sought after as the lamps of this maker.

From Tiffany glass, interest spread to French cameo glass. Prices for the products of Emile Galle's studios reached new highs. Other French manufacturers, such as Burgun & Schrever and Muller, also achieved record prices. There is considerable interest in ceramics, especially the work of regional United States potters, but these products are not as yet prized as highly as glass.

The market for silver was erratic. High prices were paid for the fine-quality reproductions made by Crighton Brothers, but compared to the prices commanded by Art Nouveau glass, bids for silver items of this style seemed low. Much of the silver sold for prices in line with, rather than above, those of the last two years.

Prices for furniture reflected developments in more established markets. Victorian furniture has enjoyed a revival for several years, especially the laminated rosewood pieces made in New York in the mid-nineteenth century. Art Nouveau pieces, especially those by the Galle firm in France, the only manufacturer who can challenge Tiffany, surged more recently. However, the most dramatic movement upward was in Art Moderne. Activity in Art Deco focused primarily on the statuettes and small bronzes of the period. With prices falling short of the Art Nouveau heights, Art Deco continues to be open to investors of moderate means.

After such a strong season, the overall outlook for the entire field is promising, with the market attracting ever greater numbers of interested buyers. With such a wealth of material available, collectors will doubtless find undervalued works and unsung craftsmen whose value will be understood as knowledge and appreciation of this field increases. With new pieces appearing at sales every year, the beginning collector is in a strong position to assemble a significant and valuable collection.

Art Pottery

AMERICAN ART POTTERY

Assorted manufacturers and styles

Bust, gentleman in armor, after Arthur Craco, rep., H24½, L19c (4084/79)	$550
Cache pots, pair, Art Deco, with waves and swimming ducks, 9⅞, ca1930 (4219/40)	500
Ewer, buffalo, with figures of Art Nouveau women, H9, 1907 (4084/81)	200
Jardiniere, possibly Weller, moulded with butterflies, H13½, E20c (4084/93)	100
Ohr pottery vase, red and black glaze, H5, L19/E20c (4084/88)	175
Pottery plate, with two female nude figures and a deer, Diam. 14¾, ca.1925 (4084/111)	125
Vase, Matt Morgan, green and brown bird on leafy branch, ca1880 13 (4182/418)	650

Fulper

Bowl, shallow circular bowl, pale green, gray green glaze, 13, 1910-30, imp factory mark (4230/632)	100
Centerpiece, base in form of 3 monkeys, shallow bowl, H7¾, ca.1915 (4084/83)	125
Jardiniere, bulging vessel, four loop handles, blue glaze, H13½, 1910-30 (4084/84)	800
Vase, short bulbous body, 2 handles blue crystalline glaze, 6¾, painted factory mark, 1910-1930 (4230/633)	150
Vase, large, bulbous, four applied handles, mustard glaze, H11, ca.1900 (4084/82)	1000

George Ohr

Vase, irregular pinched contour, deep green, 8½, 1885-1909 (4266/306)	100

Grueby

Pottery bowl, globular vessel, deep green glaze, Diam. 5½, E20c (4084/87)	225
Tobacco jar, covered, blue mat glaze, H7, ca1907 (4145/103)	600
Vase, ovoid form, leaf molded rim, matt green, 8¼, 1893-1903 (4230/627)	400
Vase, green body, spherical contour, flaring rim, ca1893-1903, 8½ (4182/413)	350

Rookwood

Bowl, pottery, bulbous body waisted neck and flaring rim slip, 7, 1877 (4229/7)	600
Center pc, round basket piled high with flowers and leaves, 10½, 1921 (4213/102)	200
Ewer, painted with sprays of wildflowers, leafage, 12¼, 1890 (4266/314)	300
Ewer, Albert R. Valentien, slip painted with wild roses, 12½, 1890 (4266/313)	500
Ewer, William P. McDonald, trefoil rim, C-scroll handle, 9, 1893 (4266/321)	125
Ewer, (Early), sloping body, ring turnedneck, daisies and leafage, 7½, 1882 (4213/100)	300
Ewer, pottery, long cylindrical neck, applied scrolling handles, 12, 1898 (4229/8)	800
Ewer, sloping vessel, painted, fruiting leafy branches, ca1897 (4182/423)	125
Pitcher, Matthew A. Daly, grasses, swallows, C-scroll handle, 6¾, 1883 (4266/307)	500
Pitcher, cream, globular body, pinched shoulder, applied handle, 2¾, 1894 (4230/624)	150
Pottery vase, pyriform vessel, handles with tulips, mustard, H7, 1898 (4084/90)	200
Pottery vase, tapering vessel with leafy branches, H8½, 1902 (4084/89)	175
Pottery vase, vasiform with autumn foliage, H12¼, 1898 (4084/92)	300
Pottery vase, very fine, gilt neck, bulbous body, morning glory blossoms, H20¼, 1886 (4084/91)	850
Vase, baluster body, green, olive green and brown blossoms and leafage, 10, rose, Fechheimer, 1902 (4230/617)	*450*
Vase, flattened spherical form, flaring rim 3 C scroll handles, 4, Anna Marie Valentien 1891 (4230/619)	*325*
Vase, ovoid body, olive green, golden brown, 46¼, Edward Diers, 1901 (4230/618)	*250*
Vase, ovoid body, 2 applied foliate handles, 13, 1888, very fine (4229/9)	*2500*
Vase, ovoid form plum leaves, olive green, brown, ochre, orange, 8¾, Sallie Toohey (4230/620)	*400*
Vase, ovoid vessel, deep brown and avocado, autumn leafage, 7½, Edith R. Felton 1902 (4230/616)	*200*
Vase, short neck, rose blossoms and leafage, 9½, Edward T. Hurley, 1904 (4230/623)	*150*
Vase, shouldered ovoid form, butterflies, blue-green ground, 6½, Elizabeth N. Lincoln, 1908 (4230/622)	350
Vase, spherical form, three applied C scroll handles, 4½, 1893 (4229/10)	450
Vase, tapering vessel, poppy blossoms and leafage, 9, Lenore Asbury, 1908 (4230/621)	250
Vase, vellum finished expanding cylindrical vessel, 9⅛, 1890 (4266/312)	250
Vase, Elizabeth N. Lincoln, painted with trout lily flowers, 8¾, 1901 (4266/309)	200
Vase, Frederick Rothenbusch*, 8¼, 1900 (4266/317)	150

Vase, Irene Bishop, sperical smokey-blue vessel, 4, 1904 (4266/308) — 75
Vase, Josephine E. Zettel, ovoid vessel, anemones, 8½, 1902 (4266/319) — 125
Vase, Sarah Sax, painted with pansies, leafage, 6¼, 1900 (4266/322) — 100
Vase, baluster vessel, wildflowers and leafage, ca1897 14¾ (4182/427) — 400
Vase, cylindrical vessel, calla lilies and leafage, ca1904 12 (4182/429) — 750
Vase, ovoid form, yellow poppy and green leafage, ca1902 8½ (4182/426) — 325
Vase, pottery, elongated teardrop section, collared neck, 9, 1883 (4229/6) — 550
Vase monumental, painted with roses and leafage, ca1889 (4182/421) — *1900*
Vase with silver overlay, spring flowers and leafage, 2 lug handles, 6¾, 1892, good (4213/103) — 1200

EUROPEAN ART POTTERY

An assortment of manufacturers and styles

Dish, Limoges, enamel, circular, fire-breathing dragon surmounted by a crown, Diam 8½, L19c (4084/4) — 200
Figural group, porcelain, dancing couple 18c dress, blue, chinese red and gilt, 10¾, ca1925, French (4213/122) — 150
Figure, porcelain female, nude, standing in a striding pose, hands raised, German, 11, factory mark, ca1905 (4230/650) — 600
Figures, man and woman, seated, Austrian, H7¼, ca.1925 (4084/116) — 150
Goupy enamelled pottery bowls, pair, panelled sloping form, h5¼, ca.1925 (4084/102) — 125
Lovers, group, polychromed ceramic, reclining female figure, kneeling male, 25¼, 1925 (4213/124) — 1000
Plaque, circular, after Alphonse Mucha design, French, D12¼, ca1900 (4145/94) — 125
Roundel, pate-sur-pate, Art Nouveau, bust portrait of young woman, Diam. 8¾, L19c (4084/95) — 1900
Salt cellars, pair, Arts and Crafts, W. Hutton & Sons, hammered surface, 4 ozs, L5¼, 1903 (4266/120) — 100
Tango, figural group, porcelain, Royal Dux, exotic dancing couple, blue and white, 13, ca1925 (4213/121) — 250
Titania, bust, Art Nouveau, wearing helmet with star at center, dress, blue, green, violet, 21, L19c, French (4213/118) — 1500
Vase, Art Deco pottery, with band of monkeys, H11¼, ca.1925 (4084/103) — 125
Vase, Art Deco, pottery, monumental, landscape with deer, H13¾, ca.1925 (4084/114) — 400
Vases, covered, pair, bronze and marble, circular flattened red griotte, marble bodies, 7¼, M19c (4142/16) — 350
Vases, pottery, two, painted with nude female figures, Austrian, H14⅞, ca.1925 (4084/118) — 650
Wiener Werkstatte pottery figure, woman with ferns in crossed arms, H14¾, ca.1925 (4084/113) — 1100
Wiener Werkstatte pottery vase, frolicking fantastic animals, Vally Wieselthier, H9¼, ca.1925 (4084/115) — 425

Assorted amphoras

Bowl, baluster vessel, four stylized double flower petals, ca1900 8⅝ (4182/437) — 100
Ewer, ovoid, waisted neck, short circular spout, handle, 14½, C.J., factory mark, E20c (4230/642) — 150
Vase, bulbous mouth, waisted neck, dec. cir. opal and blue bosses, 12½, ca1905 (4213/115) — 800
Vase, cylindrical, H6¾, E20c (4145/95) — 300
Vase, elongated teardrop form, orchid blossoms and leafage, 15¼, factory mark, ca1900 (4230/644) — 375
Vase, pale pink and blue body, ca1910 7 (4182/436) — 200
Vase, baluster form, four dove heads, wings terminating base, ca1910 6¾ (4182/442) — 130

Vase
(4230/617)

Vase
(4230/620)

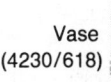

Vase
(4230/618)

Vase
(4230/619)

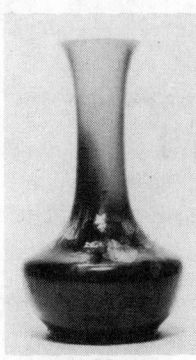

Vase monumental
(4182/421)

Vase
(4182/445)

Vase
(4182/470)

Vase
(4182/440)

Vase, baluster vessel, butterflies and cranes, ca1918 11½ (4182/438) ... 140
Vase, baluster vessel, spider webs, butterflies, ca1905 8½ (4182/444) ... 500
Vase, cylindrical vessel, pink, green floral bosses, ca1900 6¾ (4182/432) ... 60
Vase, double gourd form, black birds in flight, ca1900 6½ (4182/440) ... *300*

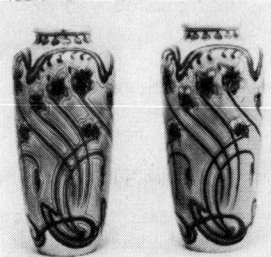

Vases (4182/468)

Vase, double gourd form, four open stem form handles, ca1905 9½ (4182/447) ... 300
Vase, figural, large, gilt figure of woman, 15¼, factory mark, restored, ca1900 (4230/641) ... 550
Vase, modeled as a gourd, textured body, ca1903 6½ (4182/445) ... *550*
Vase, ovoid vessel, colorful rooster, stylized eggs, flowers, ca1915 13½ (4182/448) ... 110
Vase, pyriform vessel, enamelled 1 side, with bust of woman, ca1900 8½ (4182/435) ... 1500
Vase, pyriform vessel, streaked, pink, white, green, stylized leafage, ca1918 10½ (4182/439) ... 90
Vase, waisted gourd form, scrolling handles, ca1915 8½ (4182/433) ... 125
Vase, Art Nouveau, baluster vessel, bust portrait of young woman, H11¾, ca.1920 (4084/97) ... 750
Vase, Art Nouveau, high relief with female heads, H14¼, ca.1920 (4084/96) ... 950
Vase, Art Nouveau, molded lip of sea monster, H11¾, ca.1920 (4084/98) ... 400
Vases, pair, oval, short neck, pattern of circles, 10, factory mark, ca1900 (4230/643) ... 325

Boch Keramis

Vase, pair flattened spherical form, flowers and fruit, ca1925 9½ (4182/476)   200

Galle

Bowl, straight sided, bamboo trees, starfish, waves, ca1890 6¼ (4182/458)   225
Sauce boat, rooster form, flowers and leafage, ca1885, 11 (4182/459)   300

Lamberton

Tall woman, long robes, holding bouquet of flowers, Geza De Vegh, 16½, hairline crack, E20c (4230/655)   225

Longwy

Base lamp, blue, grey, nude female figure with 2 peacocks, ca1925 13¼ (4182/477)   175
Dish, shallow, circular, scene 2 women, landscape, 14¾, pomone bon marche, ca1925 (4230/657)   250
Jardiniere, monumental, ovoid body, cyl foot, pale blue, ochre, brown, roses and leafage, 14½, E20c (4213/120)   375
Plaque, circular, scene of hummingbird on branch, 15½, factory mark, ca1925 (4230/656)   250
Pottery pilgrim flask, azure blue body, H11¾, ca. 1925 (4084/105)   375
Pottery roundel, circular with two horses in center, Diam. 15, ca.1925 (4084/106)   250
Vase, narrow band stylized flowers, ca1925 10½ cr to base (4182/480)   175

Massier

Vase, iridescent, deep red peony blossoms, and leafage, ca1900 9 (4182/466)   125
Vase, tapering body, dragon flies, ca1900 13 large (4182/463)   450
Vases, pair, sloping contour, leafage, elephant head handles, ca1910 15 1, with rim chip (4182/464)   150

Mettlach

Bowl, punch, cover and stand, Art Nouveau, spherical body, bust portrait woman, fruit laden grape vines, 13½, E20c (4213/119)   1500

Primavera

Figure, of woman, standing nude female holding basket, ca1925, 21½ (4182/482)   200
Torchere, flaring conical form, 3 bulging ring turnings, 17, Primaver, ca1925 (4230/658)   75

Quimper

Vases, pair, 2 handles, spherical body, flaring neck, female figure, 10, Quimper/Odetta, ca1925 (4230/659)   400

Reissner Stellmacher

Vase, landscape scene, trees in foreground, ca1905, 6½ (4182/470)   *275*
Vase, landscape scene, trees, greens and blues, dragonflies, 4⅛, factory mark, ca1905 (4230/646)   350

Rosenburg

Vase, eggshell porcelain, bulbous body, sunflowers and other wildflowers, 4⅛, Dec. J.M. Van Rossum 1903 (4230/648)   1100

Rosenthal Porcelain

Exotic dancer figure, H15¼, ca1925 (4145/107)   150
Snake charmer figure, H8, ca1925 (4145/106)   200

Royal Doulton

Bouillon cups and saucers, eight, enamelled porcelain, ca1930 (4145/104)   100
Sung vase, painted by A. Eaton, signed, Good, H9, ca1930 (4145/98)   400

Royal Dux

Bowl, shell form, Art Nouveau, blue iridescent, water lilies, maidens, 6½, ca1900 (619/122)   475

Sevres

Figure of woman in costume, bisque, after M. Guiraud Riviere, H22, ca1920 (4145/105)   400
Vases, pair, Art Nouveau, violets, scrolling leafage, ca1900 (4182/468)   *375*

Zsolnay

Bowl, shallow, fish swimming, ca1900 5¼ (4182/452)   425
Vase, blue and cream ground, four loop handles, flowerheads, ca1900 9¼ (4182/451)   300
Vase, conical body, turquoise and gold swords deep blue ground, ca1900 7¼ (4182/453)   225
Vase, inverted pyriform vessel, blue and gray, green body, ca1900 11¾ (4182/454)   800
Vase, swollen cylindrical neck, green leafage and grasses, ca1900 17⅛ (4182/450)   *400*

Vase
(4182/450)

Cameo Glass

AMERICAN CAMEO GLASS

Assorted manufacturers

Lamp, Art Nouveau, painted glass, patinated metal, river scene, 26½, E20c (4213/232)	425
Shade, Art Nouveau, iridescent, spherical form, opalescent body, greed striated feather devices, 5¾, E20c, Steuben* (4213/229)	60
Shade, Art Nouveau, iridescent glass, bell form shade, amber, green leafage, 5¾, 20c, Fostoria* (4213/234)	175
Shade, Art Nouveau, Tiffany type, domical shade, green, glass, tiles, 14, 20c (4213/230)	700
Vase, iridescent, baluster vessel, opalescent and glass with green heart, 9⅛, ca1920 (4213/231)	50

Durand

Lamps, piano, pair, Egyptian crackle glass, gilt bronze, amber, green and opal shades, 9¼, ca1930, unsigned (4213/214)	550
Vase, glass, amphora form, green, striated feather devices, 9½, 1901-25, unsigned (4213/209)	200
Vase, iridescent, baluster body, waisted neck, amber, 9¾, 1901-25 (4213/210)	150
Vase, iridescent, blue, spherical body, clinging vine motif, 5⅜, 1901-25, unsigned (4213/213)	250
Vase, iridescent, elongated baluster shape, waisted neck, 8⅝, 1901-25 (4213/216)	225
Vase, iridescent, ovoid, waisted neck, gold, blue, amber, 6¾, 1901-25, unsigned (4213/211)	100
Vase, iridescent, spherical body silvery blue, with amber threading, 5¼, 1901-25 (4213/212)	175
Vase, iridescent, spreading, ovoid form, with concentric ring turnings, 6½, 1901-25 (4213/217)	250
Vase, iridescent, trumpet neck, bulbous body, deep green, silvery blue, 6¾, 1901-25, unsigned (4213/218)	160
Vase, iridescent, with incurvate rim, amber, 5⅛, 1901-25 (4213/208)	125

Handel, type

Lamp, painted and frosted glass, domical shades, painted interior, river scene, 23½, E20c (4213/219)	700
Lamp, stained glass and patinated metal, cherry blossom, domical shade, 28¾ x 22, E20c (4213/221)	4250

Pairpoint

Lamp, frosted and painted glass, puffy shade with flowers and leafage, 5¼, E20c, chip (4213/222)	150

Steuben

Vase, vasiform, clear glass, flecked with brown, 7⅛, 1920-30, unsigned (4213/228)	125
Vase, green jade, trumpetform, everted rim, shading to alabaster, 11½, ca1920 (4213/225)	250

Stevens and Williams

Vase, 2-color, trumpet-form neck, bulging waist, globular, 12½, L19c (4159/102)	2600

EUROPEAN CAMEO GLASS

An assortment of manufacturers

Bowl, Art Nouveau, enamelled, silver mounts, shallow circular, 8¾, ca1910, Daum Nancy* (4213/173)	425
Lamp, student, 2 armed, metal and glass, pale green domical shade, 15, E20, Austrian (4213/201)	250
Landscape vase, Richard, overlaid, H7½, ca1905 (4145/135)	325
Liqueure, iridescent Duca de Caranza, sloping vessel, applied C-scroll handle, ca1900 (4084/188)	125
Vase, cameo glass, Louis, landscape, ca1910, 7 (4182/325)	375
Vase, cameo glass, Villeroy and Boch, cut with teazles, ca1900, 10¾ (4182/330)	375
Vase, cameo glass, Weiss, landscape, ca1910, 5⅞ (4182/331)	375
Vase, intaglio-carved glass, Moser, double-waisted cylindrical vessel, applied, decoration, 6¾, ca1920 (4266/206)	250
Vase, Charder Le Verre Francais, cylindrical body, mottled pale lavender, H18¾, ca1925 (4084/145)	225
Vase, Charder Le Verre Francais, trumpet-form, overlaid in orange, H13, ca1925 (4084/143)	175
Vase, Le Verre Francais, bulging cylindrical body, mottled pink, H15¾, ca 1925 (4084/141)	200
Vase, Le Verre Francais, large, green elongated ovoid body, purple base, H17½, ca1925 (4084/142)	175
Vase, Pantin, ovoid, iridescent yellow sides, fuchsia blossoms, 3⅞, ca1910 (4230/506)	425
Vases, pair, decorated peach blow glass, pale pink to deep peach, 5, L19c, T. Webb and Co.* (4213/206)	400
Vases, Charder Le Verre Francais, inverted bell form, mottled pink, pair, H13, ca1925 (4084/144)	400
Veilleuse, light fixture, Sabino, molded as 4 small birds perched on a tree branch, 10, ca1925 (4213/156)	750

Arsall

Vase, cameo glass, landscape, ca1910, 8 (4182/247)	375
Vase, cameo glass, pale pink and green cut with flower pods, ca1910, 14 (4182/248)	625

Austrian

Vase, glass and silvered metal overlay, tooled green sides, meandering blossoms, leafage, 13¾, ca1900 (4230/416)	475

Baccarat

Chandelier, wrought iron and glass, scrolling leaf forms, 4 vertical shafts, 33, ca1925 (4213/155)	1000

Barz

Vase glass, single iris blossom - leafage, ca1900, 8¼ (4182/249)	275

Caranza

Vase, metallic iridescent glass, silver mounts, blossoms and leafage, amber, rust red, 8½, ca1900 (4213/159)	600

Catteau

Vase, cameo glass, Art Deco, frosted, ovoid body, overlay in blue, 9, ca1925, Ch. Catteau (4230/330)	110

Charder

Vase, cameo glass, La Verre Francais, baluster section, flaring circular foot, 17¾, ca1925 (4230/341)	425

Chistallerie DePantin

Bowl, cameo glass, fuschia blossoms and leafage, ca1900, 4¼ (4182/328)	450

D. Christian Meisenthal

Vase, French Art Nouveau, baluster form, deep amber sides, white & yellow spring flowers, 8½, ca1905, very fine (4230/501)	5500

D'Argental

Vase, ovoid, deep amber overlaid in rust red and brown, 12, ca1925 (4213/147)	400

Daum Nancy

Bowl, acid etched mottled pink and blue, bachelor buttons, 12, ca1910 (4230/424)	1400
Bowl, cameo glass, landscape, ca1910, 5 (4182/259)	450

Bowl, intaglio-carved, 2 handled, angular handles, mottled green sky blue, 5⅝, ca1910 (4230/427) — 625
Bowl, landscape, canoe form, mottled yellow, overlaid in green, 7, ca1910 (4213/166) — 450
Box, covered, slightly domed top, gray, pink, green, red, blossoms, leafage,(4230/419) — 550
Box, enamelled, squat, ochre, brown and mustard, 4, ca1915 (4213/162) — 225
Egg, enamelled cameo glass, winter landscape scene, ca1900, 2½, unusual (4182/255) — 550
Ewer, cameo, glass, cylindrical body and neck, elongated spout, 16½, ca1900 (4229/16) — 5000
Lamp, enamelled and wrought iron, Helmut form, H25½ x D11½, ca1920 (4145/62) — 2200
Lamp base, mottled orange sides overlaid in green and red, 12½, ca1915 (4213/168) — 400
Landscape vase, cylindrical, monumental, H19¼, ca1910 (4145/121) — 1100
Scent bottle, enamel, silver-gilt mounts, pale green, 5¼, ca1910 (4213/161) — 150
Tumbler, cameo glass, applied decoration, ca1905, 4 (4182/261) — 650
Tumbler, enamelled, waisted form, frostedsalmon and green sides, 4¾, ca1905 (4213/169) — 275
Vase, applied cabochons, yellow, green and blue,(4084/187) — 250
Vase, enamelled, long neck, H8¾, ca1910 (4145/118) — 350
Vase, etched carved and gilded cameo glass, ca1895, 8½ (4182/253) — 550
Vase, mottled orange, H13¾, ca1915 (4145/119) — 350
Vase, shaded plum sides, dusty lavender, iris blossoms, 19½, ca1900, fine (4230/421) — *1500*
Vase, thick walled vessel, gray, pink, yellow and green, 16½, ca1910, good (4213/165) — 2000
Vase, wheel carved with upright coreus blossoms, leafage, 15¾, ca1900 (4230/420) — *1300*
Vase, acid etched, turquoise cylindrical body, ca1925, 14 (4182/252) — 300
Vase, bud, enamelled cameo glass landscape, 6⅛ (4182/251) — 475
Vase, cameo glass, landscape, ca1915, 10½ (4182/260) — 650
Vase, cameo glass, enamelled, applied decoration, ovoid body, 12, ca1900 (4229/17) — 1100
Vase, enamelled, acid etched orange sides, shading to green, tulips, leafage, 3¾, ca1900
(4230/432) — 250
Vase, enamelled, amber opalescent glass, acid etched, 9¼, ca1900 (4213/171) — 400
Vase, enamelled, flask form, emerald green sides, red enamel, gilding, leafage, 10½, ca1910
(4230/428) — 500
Vase, enamelled, gray, orange sides, red wildflowers, green leafage, 3⅝, ca1910 (4230/433) — 225
Vase, enamelled, slender neck, pale spray, charcoal gray and maroon, thistles, 18⅞, ca1900
(4230/418) — *1000*

Vase
(4230/420)

Vase
(4230/418)

Vase, enamelled, square section white sides, to lavender, blossoms and leafage, 4¾, ca1910
(4230/430) — 400
Vase, enamelled, square section, golden yellow, columbine blossoms, 4¾, ca1910 (4230/429) — 300
Vase, enamelled cameo, leafy vines, ca1915, 6 (4182/264) — 275
Vase, enamelled cameo glass, flower-leafage, ca1905, 12¾ (4182/262) — *750*
Vase, enamelled glass, souvenir de L'Exposition 1900, barrel-form, H5, 1900 (4084/183) — 225
Vase, enamelled with applied decoration, bulging neck, applied scrollwork, acid etched, 5⅛, ca1895
(4230/425) — 600
Vase, enamelled, grotesque, snapdragon form, blossoms, leafage, bee, 8¾ (4230/423) — 2200

Vase, intaglio-carved, aquamarine, with arches and circles, H4⅛, ca.1925 (4084/122)   100
Vase, intaglio-carved, emerald green, with overlapping arcs, H5¾, 1937 (4084/123)   175
Vase, landscape, bulbous, red, yellow, deep brown, river scene, 6½, ca1910 (4230/426)   750
Vase, landscape, mottled gray, blue and green, 4½, ca1915 (4213/164)   350
Vase, mold-blown, landscape, green trees, orange, yellow body, ca1900, 16¼ (4182/266)   2600
Vase, monumental, amethyst and magenta, 22¾, 1908-25 (4213/172)   550
Vase, monumental, baluster form, overlaid in ruby, 19¾, ca1900 (4213/167)   350
Vase, monumental, gray and green body, 2 applied dragonflies, 23, ca1905 (4230/422)   1700
Vase, verre parlant, enamelled, salmon and green sprays, 3¼, ca1900 (4230/435)   425
Vase, 2 handled, baluster vessel, deep green, gray-orange, branches, 10¼, ca1900 (4230/417)   2300
Vases, vasiform, overlaid in transparent avocado, pair, H9¼, ca1910 (4084/185)   400

De Vez

Vase, landscape, pale blue overlaid in green and blue, 4⅞, ca1900 (4213/175)   550

Degue

Vase, frosted grey, baluster, H15½, ca1925 (4145/68)   400
Vase, spherical, H9, ca1925 (4145/69)   200
Vase, vasiform, acid-etched, H17½, ca1925 (4145/70)   250

G. Argy-Rousseau

Veilleuse, pate de verre, wrought iron, bullet form, red blossoms, 7, ca1925 (4213/195)   1500

Galle

Atomizer, cameo glass, landscape, ca1900, 11 (4182/295)   800
Bonbonniere enamelled, cylindrical, with domed lid, smoky glass, H4¼, ca1900 (4084/216)   450
Bottle, pilgrim, cameo glass, violets and leafage canoe form, 5⅞ (4182/284)   475
Bowl, canoe form, iris blossoms, avocado and gray, 6½, ca1900 (4230/489)   500
Bowl, pink and apricot sides, wildflower blossoms, leafage, 5¾, ca1900 (4230/471)   550
Bowl, wide-mouthed, gray overlaid in lavender, H7⅜, after 1904 (4084/202)   450
Bowl, cameo glass, cut with exotic leafage, ca1904, 11¾, minor chip (4182/300)   650
Bowl, cameo glass, sycamore buds, leafage, ca1900, 4¾ (4182/270)   550
Bowl, cameo glass, undulating blossoms-leafage, ca1900, 4¼ (4182/278)   550
Bowl, cameo glass, canoe form, landscape, ca1900 (4182/282)   800
Bowl, enamelled, wide-mouthed with trefoil lip, green, Diam 7, ca1900 (4084/191)   500
Bowl, fish, shallow, mottled yellow, pink and white, truncated base, H5½, ca1900 (4084/193)   2200
Bowl, landscape, pale beige sides, shades of amber and brown, 9¼, ca1900 (4230/476)   3000
Box, covered, cameo glass, nasturtium blossoms, gray body, ca1900, 6 (4182/301)   650
Bud vase, baluster body, H6, ca1900 (4145/128)   225
Bud vase, trumpet-form neck, H9¼, ca1900 (4145/125)   350
Bud vase, cameo glass, fruit laden leafy branches, ca1900, 8 (4182/293)   375
Bud vase, cameo glass, sycamore leafage and buds, ca1900, 6¾ (4182/309)   375
Bud vase, cameo glass, wildflowers - leafage, after 1904, 6¾ (4182/312)   400
Centerpiece, enamelled, mendering peonies pattern, turquoise glass, L13½, ca1900 (4084/199)   800
Cup, ochre, straight-sided, free-form line design in red, H3¼, ca1895 (4084/200)   75
Decanter and stopper, squart bell formed, pale green stripped darker green, ca1895 (4230/483)   1600
Decanter and stopper, enamelled, flattened teardrop form, pale amber, gray rampant lion, 10½, ca1895 (4230/491)   1700
Jar, covered, cameo glass, landscape, amusing, ca1895, 4¼ (4182/280)   1300
Lamp, Figural, bronze, umbrella form, overlaid, H11½ x D8¼, ca1900 (4145/130)   2000
Lamp, wrought iron, domed shade, gray, apricot, poppy blossoms and leafage, 14 x 9½, ca1900 (4230/447)   4750
Lamp, mottled pink and gray, conical shacle, baluster body, H22, ca1900 (4084/222)   5250
Lamp, shade on French pottery base, pink and green helmet form shade, 3 female supports, 18 x 9¼, ca1900 (4230/482)   *3400*
Lamp, wheel carved cameo glass, bronze poppy-stem base, ca1900, 17½, fine, rare (4182/276)   *18000*
Lamp, wrought-iron base, conical shade, blossom laden vines, ca1900, 21 (4182/306)   *5250*
Lamp base, yellow body, streaks, green, blue, pink, 13, ca1900, base drilled (4213/189)   225
Lamp base, vasiform, salmon overlaid in deep ochre, H13⅜, ca1900 (4084/221)   350
Lamp shade, cameo glass, variety of ferns, after 1904, 11 (4182/311)   1600
Perfume vial and stopper, enamelled, with silver mounts, 8, ca1896 (4213/183)   1700
Pilgrim flask, landscape, spherical, H12¾, ca1900 (4145/126)   1400
Tumbler, enamelled, cyl. vessel, 2 dragonflies in red, pink, blue, green, white, 4½, ca1900 (4230/487)   1000

Lamp (4182/306)

Lamp (4182/276)

Lamp (4230/482)

Vase (4182/286)

Vase (4182/296)

Vase, baluster, H6½, ca1900 (4145/127)	400
Vase, baluster section, flaring foot, pink, gray, orchid blossoms, 7, ca1900 (4230/467)	1050
Vase, baluster, amber ground, stalks of delphinium blossoms, 19⅛, ca1900 (4230/473)	1800
Vase, baluster, rolled foot, gray to aquamarine, poppy blossoms, 11½, ca1904 (4230/457)	1200
Vase, baluster, yellow glass overlaid amethyst lilies, leafage, 11¼, ca1900 (4213/184)	400
Vase, cylindrical section yellow, gray, lavender, blossoms, 11⅝, ca1900 (4230/445)	550
Vase, emerald green sides, leafy branches, 14⅛, ca1900 (4213/178)	600
Vase, flattened bulbous base, mottled green, H11¾, ca1900 (4084/219)	350
Vase, flattered expanding vessel, pale brown, after 1904 (4084/189)	375
Vase, gray glass, lavender, iris blossoms, leafage, 5¾, ca1900 (4230/486)	350
Vase, inverted bell form, yellow, red, maroon, rhododendron, 11⅞, ca1900 (4230/455)	900
Vase, lilac overlaid in purple, cut with blossoms,(4084/220)	300
Vase, overlaid in deep purple and cornflower blue, flowers, 13⅞, ca1900 (4230/469)	850
Vase, ovoid, amber and aquamarine sides, poppy blossoms, 6½, ca1900 (4230/484)	375
Vase, ovoid, cyl. neck, yellow, gray, ferns growing, 5¾, ca1900 (4230/446)	500
Vase, ovoid, waisted neck, circular foot, roses, buds, leafage, 16¾, ca1900 (4230/454)	2200
Vase, quatrelube neck, gray body, yellow, amber, daffodils, 13, ca1904 (4230/453)	750
Vase, sloping body in yellow, overlaid in red, H9⅞, ca1900 (4084/203)	450
Vase, spherical body, overlaid, H3½, ca1900 (4145/129)	275
Vase, tapering, H6, after 1904 (4145/124)	500
Vase, tapering body, gray overlaid in deep violet, H17¾, ca 1900 (4084/205)	500
Vase, tapering vessel, avocado, deep red, 7½, ca1900 (4213/179)	550
Vase, tear drop form yellow overlaid in deep blue, lilies of the valley, 7½, ca1900 (4213/186)	650
Vase, triangular yellow glass, sides, deep purple, blossoms, 7¼, ca1900 (4230/490)	475

Vase, applied decoration, taupe glass shading to burnt umber, silver metallic, 17⅛, ca1895 (4230/475)	3900
Vase, bud, banjo form, orange body, 5½, ca1900 (4213/180)	450
Vase, bud, cylindrical, mustard overlaid in red, H6¾, ca.1900 (4084/201)	400
Vase, bud, elongated teardrop section, salmon, blue body, deep purple, 9⅛, ca1900 (4230/443)	550
Vase, bud, flowering blossoms and leafage, ca1900, 6¾ (4182/289)	500
Vase, bud, grey glass, cyl. neck bulging body wild flowers, 4, ca1900 (4230/439)	225
Vase, bud, pale pink sides overlaid, wildflowers, leafage, 6¾, ca1900 (4230/441)	425
Vase, bud, pale salmon glass, overlaid deep salmon, poppy blossoms, 7, ca1900 (4230/488)	650
Vase, bud, slender neck, gray and lavender, anemone blossoms, 8½, ca1900 (4230/438)	450
Vase, bud, tall cylinder, blue overlaid in blue, H15¾, ca1900 (4084/210)	550
Vase, bud, teardrop section, yellow, gray, cherry red, wildflowers, 8, ca1900 (4230/444)	550
Vase, bud cameo glass, tiger lily blossom and leafage, ca1895, 4 (4182/271)	*900*
Vase, bud, baluster form, yellow overlaid in red, H7⅞, ca1900 (4084/217)	300
Vase, bud, cameo glass, inverted pyriform body circular base, 5¼, ca1900 (4182/269)	400
Vase, bud, cameo glass, undulating blossoms and leafage, 5½, ca1900 (4182/305)	375
Vase, bud, cameo glass, wild rose and leafage, ca1900, 6⅝ (4182/285)	375
Vase, bud, teardrop form, yellow overlaid in brown, H48, ca1900 (4084/211)	300
Vase, bullet-form body, mottled yellow overlaid in maroon, H10⅝, ca1900 (4084/212)	300
Vase, cabinet cameo glass, berry laden branches, ca1900, 3¼ (4182/292)	275
Vase, cabinet, cameo glass, sycamore buds-leafage, ca1900, 2¾ (4182/291)	375
Vase, cameo glass, berry laden leafy branches, ca1900, 13¾ (4182/307)	1200
Vase, cameo glass, flowering anemone blossoms-leafage, ca1895, 8 (4182/286)	*1100*
Vase, cameo glass, fuchsia blossoms and leafage, ca1900, 8¾ (4182/283)	300
Vase, cameo glass, fuchsia blossoms, leafage, ca1900, 8½ (4182/304)	425
Vase, cameo glass, fuchsia blossoms, trefoil rim, after 1904, 13½ (4182/303)	700
Vase, cameo glass, nasturtium blossoms and leafage, ca1900, 8 (4182/273)	850
Vase, cameo glass, tear drop vessel, frosted gray glass body, 11¼, ca1900 (4229/14)	1800
Vase, cameo glass, wild flowers, leafage, ca1900, 7½ (4182/274)	1200
Vase, cameo glass, wild lilies and leafage, ca1904, 7¾ (4182/297)	375
Vase, cameo glass, wild rose, leafage and grasses, ca1900, 14¾ (4182/288)	*1300*
Vase, cameo glass, wildflowers - leafage, ca1904, 9⅝ (4182/298)	425
Vase, cameo glass, Nasturtium blossoms-leafage, ca1904, 6 (4182/287)	450
Vase, cameo glass, lyre form, fuchia blossoms and leafage, ca1900, 6¾ (4182/281)	400
Vase, elephant mold-blown, expanding ovoid form, gray, yellow, walking elephants, 15, ca1900, very rare, important (4230/449)	26000
Vase, elongated pyriform, turquoise overlaid in lavender, H15½, ca1900 (4084/214)	1500
Vase, enamelled cameo glass, Islamic portrait, pinwheels, flowers, ca1885, 8½, good (4182/275)	2100
Vase, enamelled, cyl. ring neck, flowers, leafage, rust, cream, green, blue, white, 12, ca1900 (4230/470)	600
Vase, enamelled, cylindrical, clear glass, H12, ca1900 (4084/196)	550
Vase, enamelled, inverted pyriform Vase, deep golden rod, formalized leafage, 5¼, ca1895 (4213/188)	160
Vase, enamelled. mottled pale yellow, cylindrical, H19¾, ca1900 (4084/190)	700
Vase, enamelled, onion-form body, pale yellow, leafage, H7½, ca1900 (4084/213)	300
Vase, enamelled and applied decoration, pale, amber yellow, pink, dusty rose, green flowers, 5½, ca1900 (4230/458)	750
Vase, enamelled cameo glass, iris blossoms, leafage and mushrooms, ca1900, 12½ (4182/296)	*750*
Vase, enamelled, cylindrical, lobed lip, appplied cabochons, emerald green, H8¾, ca1900 (4084/207)	1000
Vase, enamelled, hexagonal, yellow, cross of Lorraine, overlaid green, red, H10, ca1900 (4084/209)	400
Vase, enamelled, trumpet-form, applied cabochons, emerald green, H18, ca1900 (4084/206)	1100
Vase, etched and carved, deep red, grasshopper perched on fern fronds, 8, ca1900, fine (4230/493)	5750
Vase, faience bulbous body, with peony blossoms, H16½, L19c (4084/215)	400
Vase, flattened teardrop body, mottled yellow overlaid in purple, H10, ca1900 (4084/204)	400
Vase, intaglio-carved, enamelled, double gourd salmon glass, pussy willow branch, 6½, ca1900 (4230/442)	1400
Vase, landscape, gray sides, shades of blue, mountain, lake, fir trees, 7½, ca1900 (4230/485)	600
Vase, landscape, spherical vessel, pink and green body, young boy fishing, 10¼, ca1904 (4230/474)	2000
Vase, lozenge form, overlaid pink, mottled gray and green glass, H8½, ca1900 (4084/198)	300
Vase, marquetry-sur-verre, applied decoration, double loop handles, H12½, ca1900 (4084/197)	6000
Vase, mold blown, ovoid contour, cyl. neck, yellow berry laden leafage branches, 11¼, ca1900 (4230/451)	5250
Vase, mold blown, ovoid, salmon, gray, clematis blossoms, buds & leafage, 9¾, ca1900, good (4230/450)	5500
Vase, mold blown, yellow sides to short cyl. foot, clematis blossoms, 9½, ca1900 (4230/452)	4500
Vase, monumental, baluster, gray and pink, overlaid tones of green, 22¾, ca1900, chip to base (4213/191)	1600

Vase, monumental, circular foot, gray glass, green sycamore leafage, 23½, after 1904 (4213/187)   700
Vase, monumental, gray sides, cornflower blue flowers, 28½, ca1900 (4213/176)   850
Vase, monumental, poppies, leafage, yellow blue, 12½, ca1900 (4230/448)   5000
Vase, monumental, trumpet-form, clear glass, splashed in pale spray and lavender, 25½, ca1900
  (4230/468)   3500
Vase, monumental, yellow body, maroon, cherry red, lilac blossoms, leafage, 17¾, ca1900
  (4230/456)   3800
Vase, monumental cameo glass, apple blossoms and leafage, ca1900, 18¼ (4182/313)   1100
Vase, monumental cameo glass, lily pads-blossoms-leafage and a dragonfly, ca1900, 22½
  (4182/290)   *2700*

Vase (4182/290)

Vase (4182/299)

Vase, monumental, cameo glass, fuchsia blossoms, wintergreen body, ca1900, 23½ (4182/302)   1900
Vase, pilgrim cameo glass, landscape, ca1900, 9 (4182/299)   *1300*
Vase, pynform vessel, mustard and opaque glass, chrysanthemums, H15⅝, ca1900 (4084/218)   1300
Vase, solifleur cameo glass, sprays of clematis blossoms, fire polished, ca1895, 14⅛ (4182/294)   *900*
Vase, two-handled, enamelled, double gourd form, H11, ca1900 (4145/123)   1400
Vase, wheel carved, double gourd form, avocado, deep amber, 6½, ca1895, very fine (4230/462)   3900
Vase, wheel carved, flattened baluster section iris blossoms, leafage, 13¾, ca1900, fine (4230/463)   3000
Vase, wheel carved and etched, teardrop vessel, dragonfly, ca1895, 9½, very fine (4182/308)   3500
Vase, wheel carved cameo glass, blossom-laden leafy branches, ca1895, 13¼ (4182/310)   3600
Vase, wheel carved, 2 handled, ovoid form on raised circular foot, avocado sides, 9⅜, 1 handle
  cracked, ca1900 (4230/464)   2000
Vase, 2 handled, pyriform vessel, orange, overlaid in avocado, deep brown, 10, ca1900 (4230/472)   1400
Vase, 2 handles, spherical, gray glass body, streaked, green and lavender,(4213/185)   400
Vases, cabinet, pair, cameo glass, berry laden branches, ca1900, 2½ (4182/279)   550
Vases, enamelled, pair, cylindrical, aquamarine, with stylized flowers, H12¾, ca1900 (4084/194)   1100
Vases, pair enamelled glass, 2 handled, spherical contour, 2 lug handles, good body, enamel thistles,
  10½, ca1900 (4213/182)   2800

George de Feure

Pitcher, acid finished glass, spherical vessel, yellow, orange and deep green, 7, ca1910 (4213/174)   150

Honesdale

Vase, cameo glass, Honesdale, cylindrical, frosted, gilt, green, 8, E20c (4159/104)   300

Lalique

Box, covered, molded glass, short body with florets, washed with blue, 5½, ca1925 (4213/154)   250
Clock, molded glass, Deux-Colombes, ovoid with blue, with 2 doves, 6¾, ca1925 (4213/153)   850
Covered, blue worth, box, glass, spherical, stars against a deep blue ground, 5½, ca1925
  (4213/152)   850
Vase, frosted and molded glass, ovoid, nude male archers hunting birds, 10¾, 20c (4213/149)   1600
Vase, frosted and molded glass, druides, spherical vessel, berry laden, branches, 7, ca1925
  (4213/151)   400
Vase, frosted and molded glass, 4 masques, spherical, grotesque male heads, 11¾, ca1930
  (4213/148)   1150

Le Verre

Vase, flowers, mushrooms, grasses, ca1925, 16¼ (4182/229) 140

Le Verre Francais

Bowl, spherical, H8½, ca1925 (4145/80) 350
Ewer, baluster, c-scroll handle, H12½, ca1925 (4145/79) 225
Vase, spherical lemon yellow body, orange and blue flowers, 12, ca1925 (4230/338) 300
Vase, trumpet-form mottled yellow and orange, 18⅛, ca1925 (4230/340) 475
Vase, two-handled, baluster, H16½, ca1925 (4145/78) 350

Legras

Bowl, rose enamelled cameo glass, landscape, ca1910, 7½ (4182/321) 300
Vase, elongated teardrop form, enamelled, H10, ca1915 (4145/132) 175
Vase, enamelled, three-sided, H10, ca1915 (4145/134) 225
Vase, maroon enamelled, H13¾, ca1915 (4145/71) 250
Vase, mottled pink, H8½, ca1920 (4145/72) 150
Vase, spherical, H9¾, ca1915 (4145/133) 250
Vase, cameo glass enamelled, landscape, ca1915, 10¾ (4182/319) 400
Vase, enamelled, bulbous form, pinched 3 time around waist, brown sides, 7¾, ca1900 (4230/494) 400
Vase, enamelled cameo glass, stylized flowers, ca1915, 12¼ (4182/320) 150
Vase, monumental, beige matt glass, chestnut leafage and fruit, 20, ca1915 (4230/502) 950

Loetz

Vase, cameo glass, opaque ivory sides, coffee brown, blossoms, 4½, ca1900 (4230/403) 160
Vase, cameo glass, variety flowers - fruits and leafage, ca1900, 12 (4182/339) 425
Vase, glass iridescent, baluster form, flaring rim, undulating trails, 12½, ca1900 (4213/198) 400

Mont Joye

Vase, enamelled cameo glass, thistles and leafage, ca1900, 11, unsigned (4182/323) 1000

Muller Freres

Bowl, flurogravure, applied decoration, orange & cream body, oak leafage 2 acorn applied, 4½, ca1900 (4230/504) 775
Bowl, landscape, applied decoration, irregular ovoid shape, owl perched on branch, 12, ca1900, very fine, rare (4230/497) 6500
Lamp base, cameo glass, landscape, ca1900, 18 (4182/327) 350
Vase, double gourd vessel, gray overlaid dusty rose, avocado, 6½, ca1910 (4230/503) 700
Vase, elongated ovoid vessel, streaked gray and salmon, 13⅛, ca1900, good (4213/192) 1200
Vase, inverted trumpet-form, H7, ca1925 (4145/74) 350
Vase, cameo glass, landscape, ca1910, 4¼ (4182/324) 175
Vase, cameo glass, ovoid form, beige sides, golden and silvery foil inclusions, 6½, ca1920 (4230/336) 750
Vase, enamelled, ovoid, orange & yellow sides, exotic flowering, 8¾, ca1915 (4230/505) 1700
Vase, enamelled, landscape, baluster vessel, mottled gray, orange, violet, H7⅛, ca1900 (4084/225) 150
Vase, enamelled, landscape, ovoid form, yellow, orange, autumnal forest landscape, 5¾, ca1910 (4230/460) 900
Vase, flurogravure, applied decoration, raspberry laden leafy branches, 10¼, ca1910 (4230/496) 3500
Vase, flurogravure, landscape, ovoid section, lobed neck, gray and green ground, 17½, ca1900 (4230/499) 3750
Vase flurogravure, 2 handled, gray and green sides, salmon and white, fuchsia blossoms, 8¾, ca1900, very fine (4230/500) 4000
Vases, pair, cameo glass, landscape, ca1905, 8½ (4182/326) 700

Schneider

Lamp, table, glass and wrought iron, sec. pierced wrought with flowers, leafage, 2 shades, 17½, ca1915 (4213/157) 300
Vase, floriform, mottled glass, large, baluster vessel, ochre and mustard and burgundy, 14¾, ca1925 (4213/158) 150

Sevres

Decanter and stopper, clear tooled glass, chrysanthemum leaves, floriform stopper, 15¼, ca1900 (4230/508) 1000

St. Louis

Vase, pale amber baluster vessel, chrysanthemum blossoms, 11, ca1910 (4230/507) 125

Stevens and Williams

Vase, 2 color, cornflower baluster vessel, flowering branches, 4¾, ca1895 (4230/512)   800

Vase   (4230/512)

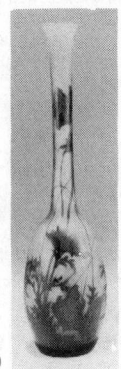

Vase   (4182/288)

Vase, 2-color cameo glass, apple red vessel, overlaid in white, 7, ca1895 (4266/280)   400

Val St. Lambert

Box, covered, cover carved in topaz, gilding against frosted ground, 6, ca1900 (4213/193)   250
Lamp base, wrought iron base - berry ladden leafy branches, ca1925, 14½ HC (4182/227)   175
Vase, baluster form, clear frosted glass, overlaid pale lavender, 8¼, ca1900 (4213/194)   325
Vase, blue, baluster, H23, E20c (4145/136)   300
Vase, bronze overlay, cobalt glass, scrolling foliage, cobalt flowers, 5½, ca1910 (4230/509)   250
Vase, cylindrical contour, flaring neck, blue-green and yellow body, 9¾, ca1910 (4230/511)   240
Vase, landscape, baluster vessel, venetian scene, mottled blue, H12, ca1910 (4084/227)   350

Vallerysthal

Bowl, short squart bowl, raspberry, to gray, berry laden vines, 5, ca1910 (4230/459)   600

Webb

Perfume vial with silver mounts, three color, unsigned, ca1900, 7¼, restored (4182/353)   600
Scent bottle, gold and cloissone enamel, teardrop vial, yellow and white, 10¾, ca1900, unsigned (4213/205)   1300
Vase, three-color, baluster, H10¼, L19c (4145/147)   2000
Vase, vasiform cased glass, aquamarine to mustard, 4½, ca1900, unsigned (4213/203)   1600
Vase, cabinet, 2 color, cherry red, bulbous vessel, morning glory blossoms, 3¾, ca1895, unsigned (4230/513)   850
Vase, cameo glass three-color, yellow, pink, white lily blossoms, ca1890, 10, chip (4182/355)   3800
Vase, cameo glass 3 color, frosted, pink, white flowers - butterflies, ca1895, 9¾ (4182/357)   1800
Vase, cameo glass, 2 color-monumental, cylindrical neck, globular body, 17, 1900 (4229/11)   14000
Vase, cameo glass, 3 color, froste, pink, white flowering wild flowers, ca1890, 10¼ (4182/356)   7000
Vase, cameo glass, 3 color, ovoid flaring rim, unsigned, 10, 1900 (4229/12)   2600
Vase, pair, trumpet-form, overlaid in green, 1 tulip, 1 lily, 9, ca1910 (4230/519)   550
Vase, 2 color, brilliant lemon yellow, teardrop vessel, blossoms & butterfly, 13½, ca1895 (4230/516)   1100
Vase, 2 color, spherical body cherry red sides, prunus blossoms,(4230/514)   1300
Vase, 3 color, neck in frosted glass, pink and white, 14½, ca1900, very fine (4213/204)   10500
Vase, 3 color, pink and white, brilliant yellow baluster vessel, unsigned, 6⅛, ca1895, neck cut down (4230/515)   400
Vase, 3-color cameo glass, grey, overlaid in pink, white, silver mounts, 9¼, ca1900 (4266/282)   800

EUROPEAN ENAMELS

Box, silver-gilt and enamel circular, Viennese, landscapes, Austrian, Diam 2¼, L19c (4194/480)   550
Clock, miniature, enamel, long-case, dial L18c, the movement American, Austrian, 14, L19c (4194/482)   2700
Drinking horn, enamel and silver, Herman Bohm, S-curve, Austrian, 17¾, L19c (4194/481)   3100

Plaque, expressionist, illuminated, plaque A. Jour, enamel, dancer, 2 gentlemen, 7¼, ca1915, German (4141/94) — 600

Plaque, Limoges, The Nativity, 8¾, L19c, wood frame (4213/2) — 850

Plaque, Viennese, country tavern scene, elaborate carved gilt frame, 9¼ x 13, d.1892, Kuttlas (4213/1) — 3000

Plaques, pair, allegorical, barbedienne, enamel on copper, Prudence and Loyalty, 8¼, 1881 (4213/7) — 2250

Triptych, Limoges, of the flagellation of Christ, 10¼, 19c (4213/4) — 750

Urn, barbedienne, cloissoine enamel, and gilt bronze, angular handles, center monogramed, 14½, L19c (619/244) — 900

Wall plaque, ivory and enamel, architecturally modeled, Austrian, 18, L19c (4194/479) — 1400

Furniture

AMERICAN FURNITURE

Assorted periods and manufacturers

Armchair, gentleman's, Victorian, laminated rosewood, pierce-carved scrolls, 19c (649/471) — 1000

Bench, rosewood, satinwood inlaid, gilt decorated, gadrooned legs, L34, L19c (4159/141) — 700

Cabinet, black lacquer burled wood, wood, Donald Deskey, Art Moderne, 30½ x 63½, ca1933 (4230/833) — 4000

Cabinet, harewood, nickel plated chrome, Art Moderne, 47 x 13½, ca1930 (4230/823) — 275

Chair, gentleman's, N.Y., laminated rosewood, carved back, cabriole legs, manner of Belter, M19c (649/467) — 1200

Chair, side, laminated rosewood, carved wood, upholstered seat, ca1860 (669/521) — 250

Chair, side, laminated rosewood, pierce carved back, needlepoint seat, ca1860 (669/523) — 250

Chair, side, lucite upholstered, Lorin Jackson, Art Moderne, ca1940 (4230/828) — 650

Chair, side, rosewood, carved wood, upholstered seat, gilt, ca1870, Renaissance revival (669/591) — *1400*

Chairs, gentleman's, pair, Victorian, laminated, pierce carved, oval back, cabriole legs, 19c (649/465) — 2250

Chairs, pair, upholstered and aluminum, Donald Deskey, Art Moderne, ca1931 (4230/834) — 1700

Chairs, rocking, pair, mahogany, scrolled backrest, upholstered, M19c (4159/142) — 275

Chairs, side, laminated rosewood pair, carved crest rails, backs, stuffed seats, ca1860 (669/518) (4230/826) — 400 / 300

Chest of drawers, inlaid burr walnut, ebonized, gilt decorated, arched mirror, marble top, 97 x 52 x 25¼, L19c (4159/155) — 1100

Chest of drawers, mahogany, top, splash board, oval mirror, turned feet, 54, M19c (4159/145) — 1050

Chest-of-drawers, high, painted, rectangular top, 6 drawers, false graining, Victorian, 49 x 37 x 17, 1850-75 (654/555) — 250

Cupboard, bedside, inlaid burr elm, circular, marble top, frieze drawer, 29½, Diam 19½, L19c (4159/146) — 600

Desk, counting house, carved, ebonized, walnut, slant writing surface, Victorian, 59½ x 60 x 28½, M19c (654/607) — 550

Firescreen, wrought iron and brass, stylized horse against a mesh background, Art Moderne, 41 x 51, ca1927, rare (4230/832) — 3300

Chair
(669/591)

Horn furniture suite, 4 pcs, red plush, horn legs, armrests, backs, ca1880 (669/661)	*2500*
Panel, figural etched glass, young nude woman, 56¼ x 26¼, ca1930 (4230/840)	175
Seat furniture, set, ebonized rosewood, Victorian, 7 pcs, 19c,(649/470)	4000
Seat furniture, set, laminated rosewood, Victorian, 4 pcs, manner of Meeks, M19c (649/466)	5500
Seat furniture, set, laminated rosewood, Victorian, 6 pcs, manner of Meeks, 19c,(649/468)	15000
Servers, pair, pollarded maple, three long drawers, Art Moderne, 39½ x 48 (4230/841)	350
Settee, carved walnut, shaped crestrail, tufted blue silk, L74, ca1860 (4149/219)	450
Sofa, carved walnut, tufted yellow silk fabric, 78, ca1860 (4149/275)	300
Sofa, N.Y., laminated rosewood, backrest and frame, manner of Belter, M19c (649/469)	4500
Table, bedside, black lacquer, Art Moderne, 25 x 13½, ca1935 (4230/831)	300
Table, cadmium-plated iron console, demi-lune top, 3 legs, black lacquer, 30 x 29½ (4266/506)	300
Table, center, glass, lucite and steel, Art Moderne, 26 x 36, ca1940 (4230/827)	500
Table, console, white brass and marble, Art Moderne, 33 x 44, ca1927 (4230/844)	1400
Table, gilt-wood and glass console, semi-circular glass top, 53½ x 31, ca1940 (4266/505)	750
Table, harewood, nickel plated chrome, Art Moderne, 21½ x 21¼, ca1930 (4230/825)	200
Table, low, glass lucite, brushed aluminum, oblong, Art Moderne, 20 x 36, ca1930, unique (4230/838)	*1100*
Table, writing, black lacquer and chrome, W. Hoffman, Art Moderne, 30, ca1930 (4230/837)	700
Table, 2 tier, chrome and glass, Donald Deskey, Art Moderne, 24 x 30, ca1935 (4230/836)	550
Table, 2 tier, occasional, brushed chrome, Gilbert Rohde, Art Moderne, 20½ x 29½, ca1933 (4230/839)	500
Tables, end, pair, chrome and bakelite, Art Moderne, 20 x 28, ca1935 (4230/847)	350
Vitrine, satin monel, white brass, enamel, George Frye, Art Moderne, 68 x 30, ca1932 (4230/845)	3600

Belter

Chair, side, laminated rosewood, elaborate, pierce-carved wood, upholstered seat, ca1860 (669/522)	600
Chairs, side, laminated rosewood, padded backrests, carved stiles and legs, ca1860 (669/516)	350
Parlor suite, laminated rosewood, carved wood, rose pink velvet, attrib to Meeks, ca1860 (669/520)	19000
Parlor suite, laminated rosewood, velvet carved, molded wood, 4 pcs, ca1860, attrib to Meeks (669/524)	12000
Table, laminated rosewood, center, serpentine marble top, carving, 29 x 39½, ca1860 (669/514)	8000

EUROPEAN FURNITURE

Assorted periods and manufacturers

Appliques, wood, painted palm tree, carved, white, ca1935, 89, stylish (4182/722)	3750
Armchairs, pair, rosewood, Art Deco, upright, curved back, arms, upholstered back and seat, 34½, ca1930 (4230/814)	3100
Armchairs, set of three, satinwood and polished brass,(4182/712)	300
Armoire, bamboo, cane and lacquer, mirrored door, panels, 1 long drawer, 72 x 34 x 19, ca1900 (649/464)	800
Bar, satinwood and shagreen, ca1925 61¾ (4182/695)	2400
Bedroom suite, 7 pieces, Art Moderne, ca1930 (4182/721)	1700
Bedstead, inlaid fruitwood, serpentine contour, cresting flower leaves, 60½ x 61, ca1900, School of Nancy (4230/809)	1500
Bookcase, burl walnut and aluminum, ca1930 73½ (4182/693)	2300
Cabinet, parchment covered, ca1935 36¼ (4182/720)	400
Cabinet, hall, fruitwood, Biedermeier, glazed door, ebonized molding, 25½ x 15 x 8, E19c (4260/1388)	800
Cabinet, side oakwood Art Nouveau, two sections, glazed cupboard doors, enclosing shelves, 95 x 65 x 21 (619/396)	2250
Cabinet, side, boulle marquetry, 2 doors, Napoleon III, 45 x 54 x 16, L19c (649/479)	1000
Cabinet, side, carved mahogany, 2 shelves in brass supports, drawers, enclosed doors, 56 x 66 x 22½, ca1850 (4260/1389)	300
Cabinet, side, walnut, Victorian, serpentine marble top, pair, glazed convex doors, 42 x 65 x 17 (649/457)	1300
Cabinet, transitional, carved with basket flowers, open shelf, ca1910, 47½ (4182/692)	175
Cabinets, bedside pair, satinwood, polished brass and glass,(4182/699)	350
Candlestand, turned and carved walnut, brass mozzle, spirally turned stem, H40¼, M19c (4260/1756)	400
Chairs, dining, set of nine, satinwood, ca1925 (4182/697)	600
Chairs, pair, reading, mahogany, U shape, upholstered, ca1840 (4260/1755)	1400
Chairs, pair, reading, mahogany, U shape, upholstered, ca1840 (4260/1754)	800
Chairs, set of fourteen, painted burled, ca1936 (4182/701)	3300
Chairs, side pair, giltwood, Victorian, floral carved crestrail, splat and apron,(649/454)	50
Chairs, side set of four, mahogany, ca1925 (4182/717)	250

Chest of drawers, etched and mirrored glass, polished steel, ca1925,32¼ (4182/718)   *5500*

Chest of drawers, Art Nouveau, two fold mirror, carved iris pulls, stiles, 49 x 49, ca1900 (669/640)   3000

Clock, tall case, mahogany, bronze dial, beveled glass door, ca1925, 18¾ (4182/706)   850

Console, satinwood, red lacquer and polished brass, ca1930, 106 (4182/710)   1400

Daybed, mahogany, Victorian, upholstered back and armrests, L85, L19c (4260/1399)   2500

Desk, writing, Art Nouveau, A. Landry, bleached mahogany and beechwood, pierced legs, H29½, L55, ca1910 (4084/339)   1100

Easel, Art Nouveau bronze figural, cast with a bust portrait of young woman, 69½, ca1895 (4213/290)   *1500*

Hall rack, lacquer and brass, gray lacquered back board, 72 x 61, ca1930, French (4230/818)   150

Lamp, floor, faceted and molded glass, polished brass, ca1930, 68⅛ (4182/713)   300

Lamp, standing, brass-mounted onyx, Victorian, tripod stand incorporating wolves heads, 62½ (649/485)   700

Lamp cabinet, alabaster silvered, metal and black painted, shelves, shade, ca1930, 72 (4182/715)   *2100*

Mirror, cut glass, rectangular, leaf shaped panels, 51 x 34, L19c (4219/79)   1000

Mirror, wood polychromed, Art Deco, oval frame, top bird in flight, plumage encircling frame, 36, ca1925 (4230/813)   375

Piano, baby grand, mahogany, bird's eye, maple, designed by Dominique for Gaveau, Paris, 39 x 61, ca1928 (4230/819)   14000

Rocker, Thonet cane and bentwood, Austrian, ca1880 (4149/217)   650

Screen, 3 fold, frame carved as underwater coral formations (unusual), 64½ x 78, by William Ostrander, ca1926 (4230/815)   950

Screen, 3 fold, nickel plated brass, and mirrored glass, 56 x 64½, ca1930, French (4230/817)   300

Seat, hall, bamboo, cane and lacquer, back with mirror, 2 panels of birds, umbrella stand, 79 x 42 x 14, ca1900 (649/463)   600

Settee, parcel-gilt, carved P. Follot, black-painted, curving crestrail, fluted legs, L55, ca1925 (4084/360)   1800

Shelf, standing corner, Macassar, cubistic form, ca1930 47½ (4182/705)   950

Sideboard, macassar wood, 2 end cabinets, 5 drawers,(4182/702)   1500

Sideboard, satinwood and shagreen, ca1925 44 (4182/694)   550

Stand, plant, black painted, wrought iron, circular veined cream marble top, 39 x 14¾, ca1927 (4230/820)   900

Stand, plant, hammered brass, wrought, iron and glass bead, 35½ x 25¾, possibly Viennese, ca1910 (4230/807)   175

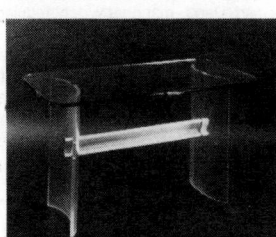

Table (4230/838)

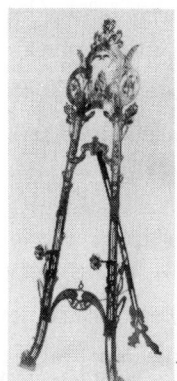

Easel (4213/290)

Lamp cabinet (4182/715)

Horn furniture suite (669/661)

Table, center, boulle, marquetry, circular, raised on tripod legs, Napoleon III, 30 x 38, L19c (649/473)   650
Table, center, carved walnut, Victorian, Circular, raised on quadrupedal pedestal, 31 x 47 (649/482)   800
Table, center, porcelain and 'Sevres', inset with plaque, surrounded by smaller plaques, 24½ x 32½, 19c (649/488)   6000
Table, console, mahogany, classical, marble top, cushion molded frieze, 35 x 38½, 17½, M19c (4159/143)   300
Table, console, Art Deco, wrought iron, marble top, 36 x 39½ x 12 (619/342)   300
Table, console, satinwood and polished brass, ca1930 34½ (4182/709)   400
Table, dining, blondewood, D-shaped leaves, tresle supports, ca1936, 78 (4182/700)   2000
Table, dining, extension, mahogany, Victorian, carved circular, 4 candle slides, 66 x 174½, 11 leaves ex, L19/E20c (4260/1395)   9000
Table, dining, Art Deco, pollarded maple and ebene de Macassar, H30½, L84, ca1930 (4084/344)   1900
Table, dining, D-end, mahogany, Victorian, 2 ends, central gate-leg section, 1 drop-leaf, 28½ x 90½ x 50½, M19c (4159/363)   650
Table, dining, satinwood, U-shaped scrolling supports, ca1925 29¼ (4182/696)   1600
Table, low, zebrawood, oval, inlaid with exotic woods, ca1930 18¼ (4182/704)   475
Table, mahogany drum, Austrian, of octagonal form, inset with beveled glass, 28¾ x 23½, ca1910 (4266/498)   550
Table, majorelle ormolu, mounted, tulipwood and mahogany, 29½ x 19½, ca1900 (4213/289)   2700
Table, wine, carved mahogany, Victorian, semi-circular top, reeded edge, center removable, 27½ x 81 x 42, ca1840 (4260/1400)   3500
Table, writing, mahogany, Victorian, rectangular, drawer, X-formed legs, 27½ x 36 x 18, M19c (4159/364)   900
Table, 2 tier, fruitwood marquetry, top inlaid with fruitwood, blossoms and leafage, 32 x 31¼, ca1900 (4230/804)   4100
Vitrines pair, satinwood, polished brass, shelves, mirror,(4182/711)   1400
Wardrobe, satinwood, polished brass and glass, ca1930 48½ (4182/698)   200

Austria

Cabinet, Art Deco, ebene de macassar and amboine wood, two doors, H25, L30½, ca1930 (4084/354)   150
Cabinet, Art Deco, mahogany, mirrored glass rectangular top, H35, L37½, ca1930 (4084/349)   600
Chair, slipper, Art Deco, mahogany, rectangular back and seat, 2 straight legs, 2, angular legs, ca1930 (4084/351)   50
Chairs, side, Art Deco, pair, walnut and black-stained walnut, shaped back, ca1930 (4084/358)   400
Chairs, side, Art Deco, six, scrolling side supports, ca1930 (4084/348)   1400
Side board, Art Deco, faded mahogany, rectangular top, channelled shaped base, H35¼, L59¾, ca1930 (4084/350)   400
Table, dining, Art Deco, mahogany, alternating grained panels, black-painted base, H30½, L61½, ca1930 (4084/347)   400

French

Breakfront, oak and fruitwood, Bedel & Cie, vineyard scenes, haystacks, 78 x 55, ca1910 (4266/497)   2100
Cabinet, wrought-iron, mirrored glass, in 2 parts, 2 cupboard doors, display, 62¼ x 35½, ca1925 (4266/504)   600
Coiffeuse, mahogany, mirror plate, beveled glass, bronze foliate mounts, 57½, ca1900 (4266/493)   350
Hall rack, chrome-plated brass, skeletal rectangular canopy, mirrored, 71 x 17½, ca1930 (4266/502)   250
Screen, marquetry and Devez cameo glass, inlaid landscape, 3 folds, 59 x 56½, ca1900 (4266/492)   4000
Table, center, two-tier, marquetry, rectangular top, cabriole legs, Majorelle*, H29½, W29¼, ca1900 (4084/336)   300
Table, center, Art Deco, mahogany, circular top, molded apron, trestle supports, H27¾, Diam28¼, ca1925 (4084/343)   500
Table, two-tier, Art Nouveau, marquetry in triangular top, Majorelle School, H31¾, ca1900 (4084/338)   450

Galle

Coffret, marquetry oak, sloping lid, gilt bronze escutcheon, 14 x 11½, ca1900 (4266/491)   6000
Table, marquetry 2-tier, carnation blossoms, leafage inlaid with various woods, 29½ x 22¾, ca1900 (4266/487)   700
Table, oval, marquetry, inlaid, various woods, flowers and leafage, ca1900, 17½ (4182/691)   900

Table, two-tier, marquetry, shaped rectangular top, inlaid, molded legs, H26½, L22½, ca1900 (4084/335) — 350

Tables, nest of four, marquetry, rectangular, trestle supports, tops inlaid, 27½ x 23, L19-E20c (4213/288) — 3700

Tables, nest of two, marquetry, rectangular form, trestle supports, H27½, L22¾, ca1900 (4084/337) — 400

Tray, Marquetry, serpentine sides pierced to form handles, L15¾ (4266/488) — 425

Tray, Marquetry, 2-handled, inlaid with various fruitwoods, L24¼, ca1900 (4266/490) — 850

Vitrine, marquetry, bronze mounts, ca1900,63½, very fine (4182/690) — 26000

Majorelle

Armchairs, marquetry, pair, various woods, iris blossoms, Louis Majorelle, ca1899 (4266/484) — 6250

Settee, walnut, carved, shaped crestrail, pierced central triangular section, L62, before 1900 (4266/486) — 6000

Side chairs, marquetry, pair, Louis Majorelle, upholstered in dusty rose velvet, ca1899 (4266/485) — 4250

Glass

AMERICAN GLASS

Assorted manufacturers

Compote, iridescent glass, shallow ruffled rim, E20c 6⅜ (4182/591) — 130

Cruet and stopper, Wheeling peachblow, Hobbs, Brockunier Co., ca1890 7¼ chip rim stopper (4182/550) — 550

Inkwell, silver-mounted cut glass, possibly by Hawkes, 5, ca1907 (4194/457) — 175

Lamp, decorated oil, Burmese, Mount Washington Glass Co., desert landscapes, 8¾, Diam 10, ca1890 (4266/325) — 3000

Lamp, iris, bronze standard, Freeman, A.H., H23 x D15½, ca1920 (4145/178) — 1800

Lamp, stained glass and bronze, green, pink glass tiles, yellow peony blossoms leafage, 20c 5' 10' (4182/588) — 6250

Lamp, tulip, stained glass and bronze, Duffner & Kimberly, H26 x D19, E20c (4145/186) — 3200

Punch cups, amberina, set of six, maroon to amber, scroll handles, L19c (4182/553) — 200

Vase, iridescent glass, short, amber, ca1910 4 (4182/590) — 100

Windows, stained glass, set of three, Art Nouveau narrow vertical form, field of cattails, 60 x 15 (4230/725) — *4500*

Windows
(4230/725)

Durand

Vase, flashed green glass, baluster vessel with rolled foot, H12¾, ca1910 (4084/252) — 375

Vase, glass, iridescent, silvery blue baluster vessel, stringing (some loose), 7½, 1901-25 (4230/702) — 200

Vase, glass, iridescent, unsigned, ovoid vessel, waisted neck, flaring rim, 7, rim chip, 1901-25 (4230/704) — 150

Vase, iridescent amber, tapering body, H10¼, 1901-25 (4084/250) — 275

Vase, iridescent cylindrical vessel, deep blue, H10, 1901-25 (4084/251) — 250

Handel

Chandelier, painted glass, patinated metal, two exotic parrots, brillant blue, green plumage, E20c 33 unusual (4182/558) — 1700

Lamp, painted glass and bronze, winter snow scene, at sunset, E20c 18 rim cracked (4182/557)   700
Lamp, painted glass and bronze desk, channeled D-form support, C-scroll arm, 15¾, ca1910 (4266/330)   300
Lamp, painted glass and metal, acid-etched shade, circular leaf-molded base, 20¼ (4266/332)   1100
Lamp, stained glass and bronze, bands of green glass tiles, E20c 18 (4182/556)   550
Lamp, stained glass and bronze, domical shade, apple blossoms, pink and white, 22 x 27½, L20c (4230/705)   4500
Lamp, stained glass, cherry blossom, pierced twisted stem, patinated metal, 31, Diam 22, E20c (4266/334)   3250
Shade, lamp, stained glass, bronze, shaped domical shade, pink apple blossoms, Diam 26¾, ca1910 (4084/254)   3750

Handel-type

Lamp, stained glass and bronze, H25½ x 18, E20c (4145/179)   2000
Lamp, stained glass, bronze, apple blossom pattern, 26½ x 24, E20c (4145/177)   2250

Hobbs, Brockunier and Co.

Cruet, wheeling peach blow, glossy finish, bulbous body, H6½, ca1880 (4084/268)   275

Mt. Washington Glass Co.

Sugar shaker, Crown Milano, pink and yellow roses, leafage, L19c 4 (4182/554)   150
Vase, two-handled, Crown Milano, h11¼, L19c (4145/182)   1700
Vase, Royal Flemish, very fine, expanding cylindrical body, lavender ground, H14¼, ca1895 (4084/259)   3800

Nash

Bowls footed pair, green and lavender chintz glass, ca1930 (4182/566)   125
Candlesticks, pair, green and lavender chintz glass, ca1930 (4182/564)   75
Cordials, six, green and lavender chintz glass, ca1930 (4182/561)   175
Goblets, water, seven, green and lavender chintz glass, ca1930 (4182/560)   150
Goblets, wine, seven, green and lavender chintz glass, ca1930 (4182/559)   125
Vase, brass, iridescent, pale aquamarine bulbous neck, leaf tapering stem, 5½, ca1929, unsigned (4230/706)   100

New England Glass Co.

Bowl, plated amberina, flaring, ruffled rim, ribbed body, deep fuchsia red, 5¼, ca1890, good (4230/707)   1100
Bowl, plated amberina, ruffled rim, deep fuchia, lemon yellow, ca1890, 5¼ (4182/552)   1050

Pairpoint

Lamp, painted glass and patinated metal, H22½ x D15, E20c (4145/196)   2100
Lamp, painted glass and painted metal, schooners, canoes, sailboats, E20c, 24 (4182/568)   1100
Lamp, painted glass and painted metal, red and pink poppies, green leafage, E20c (4182/567)   1200
Lamp, patinated metal, red roses and leafage, leaf molded base, 14 x 21, good, E20 (4230/709)   *2100*

Lamp
(4230/709)

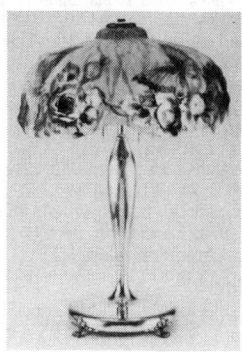

Lamp
(4230/708)

Lamp, patinated metal and painted glass, lobed conical shade pink, orange yellow blossoms, 15¾ x 20, E20 (4230/711) — 1000

Lamp, puffy, silvered metal and painted, glass, leafage, winged butterflies, 14 x 19½, E20c (4230/708) — *2750*

Quezal

Chandelier iridescent glass and brass, six standards, twisted, center, with shades, 26½, 1901-25 (4230/710) — 1700

Globe, iridescent ceiling, amber iridescent interlocking scrollwork, Diam 12¾, 1905-20 (4266/338) — 550

Hocks, two, iridescent, spherical, H8, 1901-25 (4145/187) — 550

Lamp, iridescent glass and gilt-lead, floriform shade, striated green feather devices, 8¼, 1905-20 (4266/339) — 225

Lamp, iridescent, 8-light lily, gadrooned foot, amber shades, ribbed sides, 21¼, 1905-20 (4266/340) — 2800

Shade, glass, iridescent, green-silvery blue, ca1905-1920 9¾ (4182/569) — 950

Shades, lily, two, iridescent amber, 1905-20 (4145/180) — 375

Shades, 5 iridescent glass, amber, green, heart and clinging vine motif, ca1901-1925 (4182/570) — 375

Sherberts, two, iridescent, demi-lune cup, Good, H4, 1901-25 (4145/188) — 750

Vase, floriform, iridescent glass, ruffled flaring rim, all over feathering, 8⅛, 1905-20 (4230/712) — 650

Vase, iridescent blue, vasiform body, rolled circular foot, H11¾, 1900-25 (4084/256) — 325

Vase, iridescent glass, elongated ovoid body, clinging vine motifs, 10½, 1905-20 (4266/343) — 275

Vase, iridescent glass, trumpet-form, ruffled rim, alabaster, green, amber, 6½, 1905-25 (4230/713) — 900

Vase, iridescent with silver overlay, amber, widely ruffled rim, cylindrical body, H7¼, 1901-25 (4084/257) — 1000

Vase, iridescent, baluster vessel, opalescent glass, green striated feather design, H11, 1901-25 (4084/258) — 650

Vase, jack in the pulpit, iridescent glass, green striated feather devices, ca1901-1925 11¾ (4182/572) — 2600

Vase, with silver overlay iridescent, stylied spider, chrysanthemums, ca1905-1920 8 good (4182/571) — 950

Royal Flemish

Ewer, Mount Washington Glass Co., Fourchee crosses, 11½, ca1895 (4266/344) — 1200

Jar, covered with silvered-metal mounts, Mount Washington Glass Co., with rampant eagle, 7½, ca1890 (4266/345) — 700

Steuben

Bowl, green glass, topaz handles, ca1930, 12 (4182/585) — 125

Bowl, iridescent glass, circular, deep curved sides, amber, 4½, E20c, unsigned (4230/719) — 120

Bud vase, Aurene, amber iridescent, ca1904-1925 5½ (4182/577) — 200

Candlestick, Aurene iridescent glass, deep blue, twisted stem, slightly domed foot, ca1905-1925 10 (4182/575) — 225

Candlesticks, pair, verre de soie, iridescent pink threading, unsigned, ca1920, 6 (4182/583) — 150

Comport, rose jade, unsigned, pink jade bowl, white baluster standard, H7¾, ca1925 (4084/267) — 150

Compote, Aurene, deep amber iridescence, ca1904-1925 7¼ (4182/581) — 150

Decanter, stopper and 5 liquers, thumb print indentations, teardrop stopper, decanter, 11, 1904-30 (4230/721) — 800

Flask, pilgrim Cluthra glass, circular section, cylindrical neck, 10, ca1925 (4229/2) — 350

Lamp, aurene iridescent, helmet-form shade, millefiori decorations, Diam 11, E20c (4266/355) — 2100

Lamp, Aurene iridescent, millefiore decorations, unsigned, ca1904-1925 15½ good (4182/582) — *2200*

Perfume bottle and stopper, silvery blue, ribbed teardrop stopper, 7¾, Aurene/F. Carder 1905-30 (4230/722) — 500

Perfume vial and stopper, Aurene, amber iridescent, tear drop stopper, ca1904-1925 6 (4182/579) — 250

Sorbets, set of twelve, iridescent and calcite, unsigned, 1904-30 (4145/184) — 600

Urn, two-handled, green jade, unsigned, H12, ca1920 (4084/264) — 500

Vase, jade green, H9⅜, ca1935 (4145/183) — 150

Vase, acid-cut, unsigned, green, vasiform, chrysanthemum design, H12, ca1920 (4084/262) — 950

Vase, aurene iridescent, amber, baluster vessel, H10, 1904-25 (4084/266) — 225

Vase, aurene iridescent, deep blue, waisted double-lobed body, H6, 1905-25 (4084/260) — 500

Vase, aurene three-prong stick form, deep blue, three panelled cylinders, H6½, 1905-30 (4084/265) — 450

Vase, engraved glass, inverted bell form, conical vase, 11¾ (4266/358) — 225

Vase, fan, french blue glass, applied stringing, ca1930, 8⅝, defective (4182/584) — 80

Vase, fan glass decorated Aurene, iridescent, 8¼, E20c (4229/4) — 650

Vase, glass decorated Aurene, iridescent, baluster body, short waisted neck, 8½, E20c (4229/5) — 950

Vase, glass, Aurene, iridescent blue, ovoid body, waisted neck, flaring rim, 4¼, 1905-30 (4230/718) — 200

Vase, jack in the pulpit, miniature, Aurene, iridescent glass, amber, circular domed foot, 8⅜, 1904-30 (4230/716) — 650

Vase, Aurene iridescent glass, inverted bell form, unsigned, ca1905-1925 5 (4182/576) — 225

Vase, Aurene, iridescent, glass, silvery blue, ovoid vessel, short circular foot, 5¼, 1905-30 (4230/715) — 300

Vase, 3 prong calcite, trumpet-form, 2 calla-lily form receptacles, 12½, ca1915 (4229/3) — 300

EUROPEAN GLASS

Assorted localities and manufacturers

Atomizer, iridescent glass, gilt metal mounts, E20c, 11½ (4182/332) — 350

Bowl, Pate De Cristal Masque (3 males), Decorchemont, ca1930, 3¼ (4182/358) — 750

Chandelier, wrought iron and molded glass, art deco, shade clear, stylized flower, metal base, 25, ca1925, French (4230/348) — 1600

Chandelier, Art Deco frosted glass, three-sided globe, gilt-metal mounts, H32, ca.1925 (4084/125) — 150

Chandelier, Arte Moderne, glass scrolls in glass base, 3 missing, H29, ca1925 (4182/221) — *450*

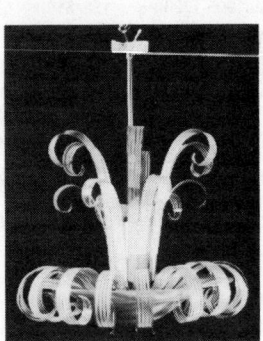

Chandelier (4182/221)

Lamp (4182/582)

Coupe (4182/258)

Chandelier, Sabino, molded glass, patinated metal, 6 lozenge panels, Diam 36, ca1925 (4084/147) — 500

Clock, chrome plated bronze, face set between clear and grey glass plates, Swiss, 8¾, face marked Gorgan, 8 days, ca1930 (4230/334) — 475

Dragonfly vase, molded, frosted, Baccarat, H9, ca1925 (4145/86) — 125

Figure of bird molded glass, clear, ca1930, 5½, ship to break (4182/222) — 70

Lamp, frosted, bell form, wrought-iron, Lorrain, H12xD6¾, ca1925 (4145/73) — 275

Landscape, bowl, rectangular, enamelled, Legras, L7¾, ca1910 (4145/131) — 150
Panel, painted and leaded glass, Woman in classical dress, Art Nouveau,(4229/22) — 750
Panel, stained glass, Art Nouveau, of a woman, 19¼ x 14½, ca1905 (4229/21) — 450
Pate-de-verre figural dish, oval, one end with chameleon, L8, ca1910 (4084/182) — 182
Pate-de-verre figural plaque, rare, Henri Cros, 19 x 8½, ca1885 (4084/181) — 3500
Pin bar, French, gold pique a jour enamel and jewel, ca1890 (4182/131) — 425
Table, dining, satinwood, U-shaped scrolling supports, ca1925 29¼ (4182/696) — 1600
Vase, cut and engraved seated female warrior, ca1950, 10½ chip (4182/231) — 175
Vase, mottled grey, cylindrical, Muller Freres, H17¼, ca1925 (4145/75) — 275
Vase, black glass, carved with 2 rows of chevrons, Jean Luce, ca1925, 6¼ (4182/220) — 500
Vase, cameo glass, opalescent yellow, blossoming wild flowers, Cristallerie D'Art, 8, ca1900 (4266/262) — 325
Vase, clear glass, inlaid gold and silver, inscribed, Barovier & Toso, H14¼, ca.1940 (4084/132) — 200
Vase, enamelled, baluster form, orange and gray sides, berry laden branches, Mado, 11½, ca1900 (4230/495) — 150
Vase, glass, ovoid, etched, standing nude female, figure, Kosta, 12½, ca1930, Kosta lg (4230/347) — 125
Vase, etched glass, pattern of flowers and ferns, Gubisch, ca1910, 11¼ (4182/315) — 175
Vase, glass, enamelled, flattened, spherical body, narrow neck, flaring rim, Brocard, 10, 1876 (4229/19) — 550
Vase, glass, large, bulbous ovoid vessel, fluted neck, Leerdam, ca1950, 13 (4182/219) — 275
Vase, pearl, satin glass, ovoid form, cylindrical neck, Federzeichnung, 7, ca1900 (4229/20) — 1200
Vase, Art Deco, mottled pink, cylindrical vessel, H12½, ca.1925 (4084/130) — 125
Vase, 2 handled molded glass, opalescent, inverted bell form rose blossoms, Etling, 9¼, ca1925 (4230/333) — 225

Austrian

Bowl, acid, etched glass, circular, deep curved sides, green, silvery blue spots, 5, ca1900 (4230/411) — 175
Bowl, iridescent glass, 3-handled, irregular trefoil body, pinched sides, Diam 6½, ca1900 (4266/300) — 125
Comport glass, amber iridescent trumpet-form, short stem, 4¾, ca1900 (4230/415) — 100
Figural cruet stand, glass, form elephant, textured skin, amber iridescent, 11, ca1905 (4230/412) — 475
Vase, cased glass silver overlay, double gourd body streaked, ochre, rust, mint green, 6¼, probably Loetz, ca1900 (4230/410) — 350
Vase, glass, with metal mount, ovoid form, iridescent deep salmon, fitting into stand, 15, ca1900 (4230/414) — 350
Vase, iridescent glass, silver overlay, ovoid, 2 handles, amber-silvery blue, oil spots, 5, crack, ca1900 (4230/398) — 140
Vase, silver overlay, ovoid, yellow iridescent, silver mounts, 3¾, ca1900, possibly Loetz (4230/409) — 325
Vase, silver overlay, iridescent glass, swollen teardrop body, silver foliate mount, 6½, ca1900 (4266/296) — 600
Vase, silver overlay, iridescent glass, Loetz*, tapering ovoid body, 5, ca1900 (4266/295) — 475
Vases, pair, silver overlay, iridescent, tapering cyl. neck, cir. base, deep blue, 4¼, ca1900 (4230/399) — 700

Burgun and Schverer

Vase, internally-decorated cameo glass, amethyst body enameled in dusty rose, 10¼, ca1895 (4266/259) — 6700
Vase, internally-decorated cameo glass, cased, pale lime, acid-cut, gilding, 5¾, ca1895 (4266/258) — 3000
Vase, internally-decorated cameo glass, chocolate brown body, cut medium relief, 7, ca1895 (4266/260) — 4250
Vase, marqueterie sur verre, silver mounts, inverted pyriform frosted glass, 2 handles, 15, ca1900, very fine (4230/498) — 6750

Daum Majorelle

Bowl blue mottled glass, blown into wrought mount, ca1925, 4½ (4182/200) — 110
Footed vase, mottled glass and wrought iron, H7, ca1925 (4145/63) — 800

Daum Nancy

Bowl, mottled blue and orange, gilt inclusions, Diam. 13, ca.1925 (4084/129) — 150
Bowl, cameo glass, bulbous body, waisted neck, flaring rim, 3½, ca1915 (4266/241) — 400
Bowl, cameo glass, wide mouth vessel, streaked emerald green, 6¾, ca1915 (4266/239) — 250
Bowl with metallic inclusions, mottled, H8¼, ca1930 (4145/66) — 175
Box and cover, etched, gilded and enamelled, landscape, ca1875, 4½ (4182/254) — 500
Coupe, mottled glass, applied decoration, ca1910, 8 (4182/258) — 800
Figure, pate-de-verre, a woman in classical dress, 10, ca1915 (4229/15) — 2400
Lamp, acid etched and wrought iron, ca1925, 26½, good (4182/199) — 9250
Lamp, Intaglio carved glass-wrought iron and marble, ca1925, 20½ (4182/197) — 2500
Lamp, acid-etched and wrought iron, cylindrical shade, vertical panels, 19, ca1925 (4266/204) — 3250
Lamp, cameo glass, mushroom shade, 3 arm wrought-iron support, 17, ca1900 (4266/242) — 4000

Pitcher, glass, etched, enamelled and gilded, ca1900, 10½ (4182/257)	400
Torchere, wrought iron and glass, amber shade, 68½, base imp, L. Katona (4230/332)	2600
Vase, four-sided, H6¼, ca1925 (4145/65)	450
Vase, intaglio-carved, H18, ca1930 (4145/64)	300
Vase, mottled, H8, ca1925 (4145/67)	275
Vase, mottled, trumpet-form, H15½, ca1915 (4145/120)	225
Vase, mottled glass, trumpet-form, ca1915, 12¾ (4182/263)	200
Vase, acid-etched glass, ovoid vessel, cased cranberry streaked black, 9, ca1925 (4266/203)	250
Vase, cameo glass, mottled orange, overlaid in deep cherry, 10½, ca1910 (4266/240)	425
Vase, enameled cameo glass, gilt bronze mounts, dragon fly blossoms, 16, ca1915 (4266/238)	725
Vase, 2 handle, mottled glass, spherical vessel, applied with 2 lug handles, 5½, ca1925 (4230/331)	300

G. Argy-Rousseau

Dish, pate-de-verre, figural, center with head of a Bacchante, Diam 6½, ca1910 (4266/274)	1400
Lamp, pate-de-verre, bullet-form shade, scalloped edges, 7½, ca1925 (4266/270)	2500
Liqueur, pate-de-verre, slightly flaring cylindrical contour, 2⅛, ca1905 (4266/271)	175
Vase, pate-de-verre, ovoid form, medial band of lozenge devices, 6½, ca1925 (4266/272)	500

Galle

Bowl, internally decorated, landscape, ca1900, 6, good (4182/267)	1400
Bowl, marqueterie sur verre 2 handled, ovoid form, cyl. neck, pale green, ochre, lavender, gray, 7, ca1900, fine (4230/466)	8000
Bowl, mottled glass, shallow, sloping sides, pale to deep amber, green inclusions, 5¼, ca1890 (4230/465)	900
Ewer, floriform enamelled, pale amber spirally ribbed body, C-scroll handle, 3½, ca1900 (4230/479)	700
Flacons, pair, silver mounts, clear pale topaz enamelled glass, gilding, 6½, ca1885 (4266/245)	1400
Goblet, enameled glass, amber, ovoid cup, conical base, 5⅞, ca1900 (4266/246)	600
Jar, cameo glass bisquit, silver mounts, spherical, repousse with blossoms, 6½, ca1900 (4266/249)	1300
Scent bottle, cameo glass, mottled grey, dusty rose, 4⅜, stopper lacking, ca1895 (4266/252)	175
Scent bottle, enameled glass, ovoid body pressed to a square section, 6, ca1895 (4266/250)	475
Tray, enameled glass, enameled with sprays of thistles, leafage, Diam 12, ca1904 (4266/268)	125
Vase, cameo glass, slender ovoid body, waisted neck, flaring, 14, ca1900 (4266/253)	750
Vase, cameo glass monumental, clear, splashed with white, lilac, maroon overlay, 20, ca1900 (4266/255)	1900
Vase, cameo glass vase, ovoid body pressed to a square section, 5¾, ca1900 (4266/254)	650
Vase, enamelled, clear green glass vessel, sloping sides, short rolled foot, 8¾, ca1900 (4230/481)	750
Vase, enamelled, hexagonal shape, thistle blossoms and leafage, 10, ca1895 (4230/477)	700
Vase, enamelled, applied decoration, amber ribbed body, exotic lily blossoms, leafage, 14¼, ca1895 (4230/478)	2400
Vase, free-form, applied decoration, kidney form, unusual, H3¾, 1900 (4145/122)	275
Vase, mold-blown cameo glass, medium relief of elephants, 13¾, ca1900 (4266/257)	9500
Vase, verre parlant, enamelled, oriental taste, pale gray, water lily blossoms, 6½, ca1895 (4230/480)	1500
Vases, pair, baluster contour, yellow bodies, red, blossoms and leafage,(4213/181)	700

Harrach

Vase, cameo glass, baluster transparent yellow-green body, 10, ca1910 (4266/261)	300

Lalique

Articles, bowl, plate, D14 and 12¼, ca1925 (4145/90)	175
Bottle, scent, molded black glass, female figures holding flowers, 5¼, ca1925 (4230/354)	475
Bowl, frosted, molded, D14½, ca1925 (4145/88)	200
Bowl, glass, molded and enamelled glass, deep circular form, daisy blossoms, 10, 20c (4230/358)	150
Bowl, molded glass, mermaids swimming, M20c, 7½ (4182/212)	400
Bowl, molded glass, Formose, charcoal gray, swimming fish, ca1925, 7¼ (4182/204)	1100
Bowl, molded glass, Formose, swimming fish, ca1925, 7¼ (4182/206)	200
Bowl, molded with sunflowers, bulging body, H4, ca1925 (4084/154)	250
Bowls, berry, ten, hemispherical, 12 sided feet, 3¾, ca1930 (4230/381)	275
Box, covered, molded and frosted glass, flattened lid molded with 3 graces, 3¾, rim chip, ca1925 (4230/377)	175
Box, covered, molded glass cover, circular, curved sides, straight wide rim,(4230/367)	200
Box, molded, with silver figural mounts thistle and beetles, ca1910, 7, rare, important (4182/202)	18000
Carafe, molded glass, teardrop form clear glass silver stopper, ca1925, 12½, chip (4182/214)	750
Centerpiece molded glass, frosted, canoe form bowl, 18½, rim chip, ca1925 (4230/366)	700
Chandelier, molded glass, inverted domical form, patten leaves, pendant, 3 supports, 13½, rim chip, ca1925 (4230/372)	650
Chandelier, molded glass, 3 protruding chrysanthemum blossoms, Diam 12, ca1925 (4266/231)	400
Chardons, molded glass vase, opalescent glass, thistle leaves, 7½, ca1927 (4266/230)	300

Dans La Nuit, Worth perfume bottle, molded with scattered stars, midnight blue, 3, ca1925 (4266/218) — 175

Decanter, glass, molded and stopper, elongated bell form, domed stopper, 8½, ca1930 (4230/380) — 100

Eagle hood ornaments, H4, 20c (4145/92) — 750

Figure, molded glass, rooster, clear glass, running cock, 12¼, ca1930 (4230/363) — 1100

Figures, pair, molded glass, young nude female, upstretched arms, 7½, ca1925 (4230/360) — 4200

Gui, molded glass vase, swelling ovoid vessel, frosted, 7, ca1925 (4266/209) — 175

Inkwell, three-sided, molded with dragonflies, H2¼ (4084/150) — 250

Jar, cire perdue glass covered, rough textured ovoid body, carved at shoulder, 8, ca1905-10 (4266/228) — 3500

Jars, molded glass ginger, pair, molded in medium relief with foliage, flowers, 8, ca1925 (4266/235) — 1000

Medallion, molded glass commemorative, celebrating Exposition Internationale de Paris, 3¾, 1937 (4266/226) — 300

Moissac, molded glass vase, inverted bell-form grey vessel, 5¼, ca1925 (4266/215) — 250

Moissac, molded glass vase, smoky grey conical vessel, high relief, 5¼, ca1925 (4266/221) — 175

Ornament, hood molded, head of rooster with angular ruff, 7½, 20c (4230/379) — *650*

Ornament, molded eagle hood, clear glass, chips, H 5¾, ca1925 (4084/153) — 400

Ornament, molded eagle hood, clear glass, rectangular base, L5¾, ca1925 (4084/152) — 650

Panel, frosted and molded, female face, 4 fish, ca1940, 12½ x 12½ (4182/216) — *2000*

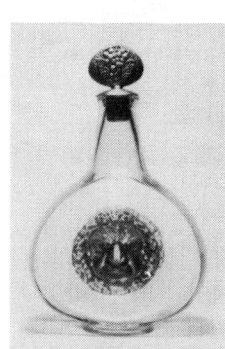

Carafe (4182/214)

Ornament
(4230/379)

Panel (4182/216)

Perfume flacon, two nude figures, flowers, ca1921, 3 (4182/208) — 750

Perfume flacon molded glass, flattened ovoid section, anemone blossoms, 8½, ca1925 (4230/350) — 350

Perfume glass, deep emeraled green, cylindrical with concentric rings at neck, H6, ca1925 (4084/156) — 300

Plate, glass molded, stylized carnations and leafage, ca1925, 14 (4182/215) — 175

Scent bottle, molded glass, deep jade green sides, birds in flight, leafage, 3¼, ca1925 (4266/237) — 1300

Tournai, molded glass vase, ovoid grey vessel, narrow tapering neck, 5¼, ca1925 (4266/214) — 125

Vase, bulbous vessel molded with fern fronds,(4084/151) — 200

Vase, cylindrical, molded, H7½, ca1925 (4145/89) — 175

Vase, molded, clear, H7¾, ca1935 (4145/91) — 250

Vase, blown glass, bronze mounts, smokey gray glass Medusa masks, ca1925, 11, rare (4182/213) — 5500

Vase, cire perdue glass, bulbous vessel with four fantastic fish, H7½, ca1923 (4084/149) — 2000

Vase, frosted and molded glass, flaring rim, interior with leaves, 6¼, ca1925 (4230/373) — 300

Vase, frosted glass, ovoid vessel, pattern of sheaves of wheat, 7, ca1925 (4230/352) — 225

Vase, glass, flaring rim, leafy thorns, stems trailing into body, 8½, ca1925 (4230/351) — 525

Vase, glass, thick walled, lozenge form body, 3 gadroomed handles, 7¼, ca1925, Amiens (4230/356) — 550

Vase, glass molded, inverted bell form, bands of stylized berries, 8, ca1925 (4230/357) — 350

Vase, glass, molded and frosted, conical vessel, opalescent glass, leafage, 5½, ca1925 (4230/369) — 430

Vase, molded amber glass, swollen ovoid vessel, medium relief, 9¼, ca1925 (4266/217) — 1100

Vase, molded and frosted, H5¾, ca1925 (4084/155) — 175

Vase, molded glass, bulbous, opalescent glass, allover relief of fern leaves, 6¾, ca1925 (4230/361) — 275

Vase, molded glass, conical sides, truncated base, frieze of starlings, 11, ca1930 (4266/236) — 600

Vase, molded glass, flattened spherical vessel, molded in medium relief, 7⅝, ca1925 (4266/210) — 500

Vase, molded glass, frieze of cocks, 6¼, ca1925 (4230/364)   250
Vase, molded glass, frosted, ca1925, 7¼ (4182/205)   375
Vase, molded glass, frosted and clear, relief with gourds, branches, 7¼, ca1925 (4230/355)   550
Vase, molded glass, frosted berries and leafage, 7, ca1925 (4230/359)   200
Vase, molded glass, frosted glass, stellate devices, 7¾, ca1935 (4230/349)   350
Vase, molded glass, handles in form of seated female nudes, 8¼, ca1925 (4266/213)   600
Vase, molded glass, inverted bell form, frosted, polished, chevrons, 8½, ca1925 (4230/384)   600
Vase, molded glass, molded roosters, ca1925, 6 (4182/203)   300
Vase, molded glass, opalescent glass, 2 bands of conical shells, Diam 11, ca1925 (4266/212)   900
Vase, molded glass, opalescent, medium relief of swimming fish, 3¾, ca1925 (4266/224)   300
Vase, molded glass, relief of pairs of parakeets, 9¾, ca1925 (4266/216)   450
Vase, molded glass, slightly frosted ovoid vessel, 8¾, ca1925 (4266/234)   300
Vase, molded glass, trumpet-form, sparrows perched on leafy branches, 7¼, ca1925 (4230/353)   425
Vase, molded glass (Amiens), handles, gadrooned sections, 7½, minor chip, ca1925 (4230/374)   400
Vase, molded glass serpent, amber, high relief of coiled snake, 10, chip, ca1925 (4266/222)   5000
Vase, molded glass, cylindrical, frosted vessel, horses, running, 11¼, ca1925 (4230/370)   1200
Vase, molded glass, swimming fish, frosted opalescent glass, 6¾, ca1925 (4230/368)   650
Vase, molded glass, Formose, frosted, exterior with swimming fish, 6¾, ca1925 (4230/378)   575
Vase, molded glass, 2 handled, flaring panel sides, gadrooned, 7¾, major chip, ca1925 (4230/362)   475
Vase, molded green glass, spherical body tapered neck, 9⅛, ca1925 (4230/365)   1600
Wall shade, molded glass, frosted glass of 2 female nudes, 13¼, ca1925 (4266/227)   427

Le Verre Francais

Vase, cameo glass, mottled grey, yellow, upper body mottled red, green, 15¾, ca1925 (4266/208)   175

Loetz

Bowl, iridescent, shell form, amber body, silvery-blue oil spot, H5, ca1900 (4084/240)   125
Footed vase, blue, grey, green iridescent, H7, ca1900 (4145/144)   350
Lamp, iridescent glass, helmet form, avocado glass shade, top & bottom hob nail bands, 11 x 8¾,
   ca1900 (4230/405)   1100
Shell vase, iridescent, L6, ca1900 (4145/146)   150
Vase, iridescent, bulging neck, H8, ca1900 (4145/141)   200
Vase, floriform, iridescent glass, waisted onion form bowl, slender stem, 12¼, 1900, fine (4229/13)   1900
Vase, glass iridescent, elongated tear drop vessel, ruffled rim, amber,(4230/404)   275
Vase, iridescent, silver overlay, ca1900, 4¼, unsigned (4182/342)   150
Vase, iridescent glass, applied decoration, ca1900, 8⅛, unsigned (4182/333)   250
Vase, iridescent glass, baluster clear vessel, random iridescent oil spots, 7, ca1900 (4266/288)   110
Vase, iridescent glass, flaring upper sec - 7 circular flower rec., ca1900, 13⅜, unsigned (4182/335)   550
Vase, iridescent glass, flattened ovoid form, ruby red sides, amber and blue, 7¼, ca1900 (4230/395)   1500
Vase, iridescent glass, flattened spherical base, festoons, diapering, 5⅜, ca1900 (4266/290)   225
Vase, iridescent glass, oil spots, ca1900, 11¾, unsigned (4182/338)   300
Vase, iridescent glass, ovoid body, pinched rim, iridescent, 7¼, ca1900 (4266/284)   300
Vase, iridescent glass, slightly swollen cylindrical vessel, 7, ca1900 (4266/285)   500
Vase, iridescent glass, striated feather devices, ca1900, 7¼, unsigned (4182/344)   75
Vase, iridescent glass, wavy devices, ca1900, 8 (4182/343)   2000
Vase, iridescent glass, with striated feather devices, ca1900, 9¾, good, unsigned (4182/336)   800
Vase, iridescent glass, zig-zags, ca1900, 5 (4182/341)   700
Vase, iridescent glass (good), sloping body with thumb prints, lily pads, 7¼, ca1900 (4230/389)   2200
Vase, iridescent glass floriform, molded in high relief with leaves, 14, ca1900 (4266/289)   300
Vase, iridescent, four-sided vessel, silvery-blue and amber, H9½, ca1900 (4084/232)   500
Vase, iridescent, salmon and blue, H6¼, ca1900 (4084/245)   250
Vase, iridescent, silver overlay, inverted tulip-form, pink, unsigned, H4½, ca1900 (4084/243)   400
Vase, iridescent, silvery-blue, panelled sloping vessel, H8¼, ca1900 (4084/238)   600
Vase, iridescent, silvery-blue, trumpet-formed neck, H8½, ca1900 (4084/234)   1250
Vase, iridescent, unsigned, bulbous body in amber, H13¾, ca1900 (4084/233)   450
Vase, iridescent, unsigned, elongated ovoid body, electric blue ground, H8¼, ca1900 (4084/244)   150
Vase, iridescent, unsigned, flaring flattened rim, silver overlay, H7½, ca1900 (4084/241)   400
Vase, iridescent, unsigned, four-sided balbous vessel, green,(4084/242)   125
Vase, iridescent, unsigned, three-bottle form, green, H8¼, ca1900 (4084/239)   250
Vase, iridescent, unsigned, urn-form, pale salmon, H8, ca1900 (4084/237)   400
Vase, silver overlay iridescent glass, ovoid body, pierced silver mount, 7½, ca1900 (4266/292)   *225*
Vase, Austrian iridescent glass, ribbed, ovoid, everted quatrefoil rim, 8½, ca1900 (4266/287)   200
Vase, Jack in the pulpit, iridescent glass, ca1900, 12⅞ (4182/340)   350

Loetz, unsigned

Lamp, iridescent glass and bronze, salmon, amber silvery blue, base Tiffany, 19½, collar restored,
   ca1900 (4230/386)   *1000*
Vase, iridescent, bulging, H11¼, ca1900 (4145/143)   300

Vase, iridescent, cylindrical, Good, H10, ca1900 (4145/140) 300
Vase, glass, flaring rim, silvery blue oil spots, 12, ca1900 (4230/394) 150
Vase, iridescent glass, flat shouldered globular body, ruby red, 5½, rim chip, ca1900 (4230/396) 475
Vase, iridescent glass, tapering body, clear glass, silvery blue spots, 4½, ca1900 (4230/390) 200
Vase, jack in the pulpit, iridescent glass, green, pulled flower face, 12½, ca1900 (4230/402) 450
Vases, pair, silver overlay iridescent, pinched shoulder, oil spotted amber, 3½, ca1900 (4230/401) 400
Vases, two, iridescent, spherical, H13½ and 9½, ca1900 (4145/142) 250

Mont Joye

Vase, enameled glass, pestle-form, acid-etched, enameled blossoms, 9¾, ca1910 (4266/264) 125

Muller Freres

Bowl, molded glass, flaring cylindrical frosted glass, 9, ca1930 (4266/207) 375

Orrefors

Vase, glass, flaring cyl clear glass, nude figure on skis, 8⅝, ca1930, Orrefors-Lindstrand (4230/346) 150
Vase, glass engraved, mermaid black glass, ca1935, 8½ (4182/236) 700
Vase, Graal glass, air trap pattern - black fish,(4182/246) 325
Vase, Graal glass, fish and reeds,(4182/245) 275

Pallme-Konig & Habel

Jack-in-the-Pulpit vase, knotched rim, Austrian, H16¼, ca1900 (4145/145) 250

Sabino

Bowl, frosted, molded, D17½, ca1925 (4145/85) 275

Sarlandie Limoges

Vase, enamel, ovoid body, flat sloping shoulder, slender neck, 5½, ca1925 (4229/18) 350

Schneider

Cluthra vase, pale blue, bulbous body, H17¾, ca.1925 (4084/126) 125
Vase, four-sided amber, H11½ ca1925 (4145/76) 100
Vase, applied glass, bullet-form, clear to orange, purple foot,(4084/138) 225
Vase, floriform, salmon, double-pyriform, H13, ca.1925 (4084/134) 150
Vase, mottled orange, baluster vessel, H13¾, ca.1925 (4084/135) 100
Vase, overlay, trumpet-form body, blue overlaid base, H8¼, ca.1925 (4084/137) 100
Vase, trumpet-form, mottled purple, orange, pink and yellow, H15½, ca.1925 (4084/136) 100

Stevens and Williams

Vase, intaglio-carved, teardrop form, plum sides, lime yellow thistle buds, 15¾, ca1905 (4230/517) 1800

Val St. Lambert

Bowl, gilt metal encased, griffins and flowers, E20c, 7½ (4182/329) 275
Bowl, molded glass, square, blue, with nude female figures, L8¾, ca.1930 (4084/139) 150

Vedar

Goblets enamelled - clear glass, bouquets of flowers set of 8, ca1930 (4182/228) 200

Venini Vetro Sommerso

Bowl, miniature, circular foot, D3, ca1934 (4145/137) 60

Vestale

Lamp, wrought iron base, coral and waves enamelled on glass globe, ca1930, 6 (4182/230) 200

Walter, pate-de-verre

Box, covered, leafage and berries, grasshopper finial, E20c, 3, finial chip (4182/359) 450
Covered bowl, molded with flowers, D4⅞, ca1920 (4145/148) 300
Dish, relief, bumble bee, ca1920, 4½ (4182/361) 850
Dish, shell-shaped, L6¼, E20c (4145/149) 1000
Vase, frieze of pendant green raspberry leafage, 6¾, ca1910 (4266/276) 725
Woman, flowing drapery, pale gray, lavender, 9¾, A. Walter/Nancy, ca1920 (4230/522) 1800

EUROPEAN IVORY OBJECTS

Ariadne and the panther, ivory, naked goddess seated on the ferocious beast, 4½, M19c, European
(669/235)   800
Box, powder, ivory, carved, in the manner of Pierre Turini, D4, ca1925 (4145/93)   50
Christ figure, wood base, H5½, 19c (4145/8)   150
Crucifix, carved ivory and wood, figure of Christ with well carved details, 17, 19c, European, minor
dam. (669/233)   225
Desk seal, inlaid ivory, set with a citrine, 5, ca1800 (669/236)   325
Dieppe ivory figure, ecclesiastical figure, body opens to reveal 6 scenes, 10½, 19c (669/237)   1600
Diorama, oval, with mother of pearl, figures set within a forest glade, 9, L19c, dam. to frame
(4213/11)   700
Elizabeth I figure, skirt opens to reveal scene, wood base, H7½, L19c, probably Dieppe (4145/4)   750
Maiden figure, standing, carrying basket of flowers and bouquet, 10, ca1890, French (4213/9)   1100
Plaque, ivory, Art Nouveau, carved, oval form, female nude among waves, French, L6, ca1900
(4194/362)   900
Plaque, painted french ivory, triumph of Bacchus, gilt-wood frame, 6 x 9, ca1900 (619/179)   1700
Relief panel, carved, of Baccharalian feast, L17, 19c (4145/7)   1500
Relief panel, carved, Wallenstein's procession through fear, L8, 19c (4145/6)   700
Tankard, carved, medieval bottle scene, handle as a cupid, H13¾, 19c (4084/8)   2000
Triptych, procession of the duke, woodframe, 6¼, 19c French* (4213/8)   425
Urchins, pair figures, one playing horn, other with a fish, 5, 19c, French*, feet res (4213/13)   900
Urn, inlaid copper covered, Paul Mergier, inlaid in brass, silver, 13¾, ca1925 (4266/65)   400
Warriors group, carved ivory, in combat, European, 5, M19c, 1 weapon missing (669/234)   600
Xerxes crossing of the Hellespont, carved relief, 4½ x 5¾, 19c, woodframe (4213/10)   650

Jewelry

AMERICAN JEWELRY

Bracelet, black onyx and green stone, ca1935 (4182/159)   *4500*
Bracelet, platinum diamond, and emerald, ca1930 (4182/158)   2200
Bracelet, platinum, sapphires, diamonds,(4182/151)   *14000*

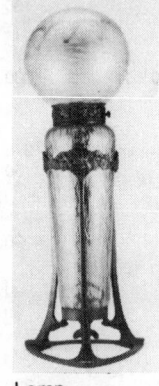

Lamp
(4230/386)

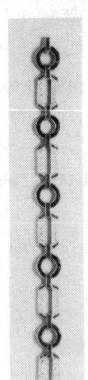

Bracelet
(4182/159)

Bracelet
diamonds,
(4182/151)

Bracelet
(4182/180)

Bracelet, Art Deco, diamond, sapphire and crystal, ca1935 (4182/180)   *6250*
Brooch, platinum and diamond, ca1920 (4182/172)   1800
Brooch, double clip, Art Deco, platinum and diamond, ca1935 (4182/163)   2400
Brooch, gold and citrine, Victorian, 3 oval faceted citrines, 2⅞, M19c (4259/421)   275
Brooch, gold and diamond, mythological god Boreas, ca1900, 1⅛ (4182/115)   700
Brooch, gold and enamel, hinged circle, 5 drops, squares, 2½, ca1875 (4259/417)   325
Brooch, gold mounted shell cameo, Victorian, profile head of classical woman, 3, M19c (4259/422)   300
Brooch, gold, diamond and ruby, Victorian, oval, with rose diamonds, border of rubies, 1⅜, M19c
(4259/425)   450

Brooch, gold, enamel and onyx, Victorian, circular, border of black enamel, 1½, ca1865 (4259/416) — 300
Brooch, gold, American, figural, head of young woman, ca1900, 1⅛ (4182/114) — 225
Brooch, matching bracelet, diamonds in platinum and gold mounts, ca1920 (4182/161) — 1500
Brooch, Art Deco, carved jade and diamond,(4182/170) — 1600
Brooch, Art Deco, diamond and black onyx,(4182/174) — 4500
Brooch, Marrle Bennet & Co., gold and rose quartz, ca1900 (4182/122) — 500
Cigarette case, lighter and watch, gold and enamel, Art Deco, 3¼ (4182/152) — 3100
Clips, pair, platinum-diamond and synthetic ruby,(4182/176) — 1600
Dress set, cufflinks and studs, black onyx and diamonds, Art Deco,(4182/167) — 850
Lorgnette gold, iris blossom and leafage, ca1900 (4180/140) — 600
Pendant, Marrle Bennet & Co., gold and turquoise, ca1910 (4182/124) — 375
Pendant-watch and chain, platinum-diamond and pearl, ca1920 (4182/168) — 4000
Ring, gold and enamel emerald scarab, good, ca1899 (4182/102) — 2100
Ring, platinum-diamond and sapphire, ca1915 (4182/164) — 1100
Ring, gold, diamond and black enamel,(4182/156) — 250
Ring, Art Deco, platinum, diamond and ruby,(4182/154) — 400
Wristwatch, lady's, Art Deco, diamonds and sapphires,(4182/178) — 600

EUROPEAN JEWELRY

Belt, Art Nouveau, gilt metal and felt, clasp cast with female profile, 3 buckel, ca1900, French* (4213/141) — 225
Belt buckle, silver, French, Art Nouveau, oval, blue glass, L4¾, ca1900 (42664/189) — 200
Bracelet, bangle, gold, as buckled belt, chased with flowers and geometric bands, M19c (4141/5) — 250
Bracelet, two-color, gold, Art Deco, yellow gold cartouche links, rose gold bars,(4160/513) — 250
Bracelet, Art Deco gold and enamel, elliptical openwork, links, circular rings, 1920-30 (4141/32) — 400
Brooch, gold, enamel and pear, Art Nouveau, swirling branches, 2½ (4160/507) — 225
Brooch, matching earrings, Victorian, gold and agate with cameos of a lady, 2½, ca1865 (4141/1) — 850
Brooch, silver-gilt and enamel, Art Nouveau, waterlily blossom, locket, 2¾, ca1900, Continental (4213/133) — 225
Brooch, Art Nouveau, silver-gilt, plique a jour enamel, female figure, 2¾, ca1900, French (4213/134) — 425
Brooch, Continental, gold, Egyptian goddess, ca1920, 2⅛ (4182/109) — 425
Brooch, French, gold eagle form, good, ca1910 (4182/103) — 450
Brooch, 2 color gold, French, head of young woman, flowers, ca1900, 1⅜ (4182/116) — 325
Necklace, English*, pendant, turquoise and baroque pearl, standing stork, ca1900 (4182/129) — *2500*

Necklace (4182/129)

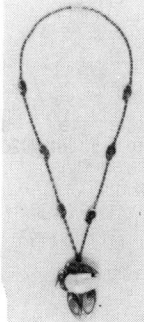

Pendant (4182/112)

Necklace, Intaglio, 2 nude figures, glass and silk, Lalique, ca1925 (4182/144) — 425
Pendant, cameo, gold and hardstone, white and red agate with a gorgoneion head, 2⅝, L19c (4259/454) — 2400
Pendant, enamel and jewel, nine old mine diamonds, pearl drop, ca1905, 2 (4182/112) — *1100*
Pendant, figural, Walter Pate de Verre, rectangular section, mottled blue and green, lizard seated, 2⅜, ca1920 (4213/135) — 450
Pendant, gold, opal and diamond, trefoil outline, Continental, ca1900 (4266/193) — 500
Pendant, silver and enamel, Art Nouveau, Ramsden & Carr, heart shape, L3, 1905 (4266/190) — 500
Pendant, French, diamond, peridot and enamel, ca1900 (4182/105) — 11000
Pendant, French, silver and enamel, ca1900 (4182/118) — 275

Pendant, Lalique, molded and frosted glass, T-form, arched top molded with birds in flight, 2⅛, ca1925 (4213/144) 275

Pin, French, Lalique, gold and molded glass spray daisies, ca1925 (4182/143) 325

Pin, Lalique frosted and molded glass, nude female in landscape, silver metal mounts, 1⅜, ca1925 (4213/143) 175

Pin bar, gold, French, Lalique, molded glass high relief, lovebirds, ca1925 (4182/142) 900

Watch, diamond and jade lapel, Mormac Watch Co., octagonal matte dial, L4¾ (4266/168) 1400

Watch, gold, French, modern, leather-covered steel bangle,(4266/183) 350

Watch, Art Deco gold folding, Swiss, lozenge-shaped watch, W1¼, 1930 (4266/174) 350

Watch, Art Deco gold openface, French, Cartier, enameled back, W1⅝, ca1930 (4266/179) 1600

Watch, Art Deco gold, French, diamond, openface, jump-hour, Cartier, Diam 2, ca1930 (4266/177) 4000

Watch, Art Deco, French, lapis enamel, Cartier, rectangular form, gold, L1⅞, ca1930 (4266/178) 2500

Watch, Gold folding, set with jewels, Swiss, Van Cleef and Arpels, sapphires, diamonds, rubies, L1¾, ca1930 (4266/175) 800

Objects of Virtu

AMERICAN OBJECTS OF VIRTU

Belt, silver, 27 shaped circular, oval medalions, 11 ozs, 10 dwts, L49, ca1910 (4266/142) 550

Cigarette case, gold, sapphire thumb pc, ca1936, 4 (4182/150) 500

Cigarette case, Art Deco, black enamel, sterling silver, bands of gold, dated 1938 (4182/181) 150

Cigarette case, Art Deco, gold and enamel,(4182/177) 1300

Cigarette case, Van Cleet and Arpels, platinum, diamond and ruby monogram, ca1935 (4182/148) 1700

Lamp, 3-light lily, Art Nouveau, bronze, iridescent glass, bronze, 21¼, E20c (4159/105) 750

Lorgnette, gold, 14 karat, form of chased iris, L5 (4266/155) 325

Mantel clock, Art Nouveau, figural, silvered metal, H14, ca1900 (4145/117) 350

Ring, Van Cleet and Arpels, platinum, ruby and diamond, ca1935 (4182/149) 4200

Vanity, fourteen karat gold and sapphire, ca1920 (4182/175) 150

EUROPEAN OBJECTS OF VIRTU

Assorted localities and manufacturers

Banner, silkwork, scene of St. George and the dragon and rampant lion, crest, 52½ x 55 1929 German (619/268) 200

Belt buckle, silver, French, wild lilies and leafage, ca1900 (4182/126) 120

Belt buckle, silver, Liberty & Co., heart shaped leaves, 'Cymric', ca1902 (4182/128) 275

Box, cigarette, Austrian, silver-gilt and enamel, ca1925, 3¼ (4182/85) 175

Box, cigarette, Austrian, silver-gilt and enamel, ca1925, 3⅜ (4182/84) 300

Box, cigarette, Austrian, silver-gilt and enamel, ca1925, 3⅜ (4182/83) 550

Box, covered, Art Deco, champlere enamel, ca1925, 6 x 6 (4182/79) 900

Box, gold cigarette, English, 9 karat gold, shallow rectangular form, 2 ozs, L3⅜ (4266/143) 125

Box, Russian silver cigarette, cabochon green stone thumbpiece, L6⅜, 1908-17 (4266/146) 225

Case, gold cigarette, English, in Russian style, samorodok pattern, 7 ozs, 10 dwts, L5½ (4266/154) 3000

Case, silver cigarette, Austrian, nocturnal stylized city scene, L3½, 1927 (4266/157) 300

Case, vanity Cartier, Art Deco, black enamel silver and gold, ca1935 (4182/182) 750

Case, French agate cigarette, Cartier, mounted in gold and enamel, L3½, ca1930 (4266/147) 1000

Case, German silver cigarette, shallow rectangular form, repousse and chased, L3½, ca1910 (4266/145) 100

Charger, gold, enamel and lapis lazuli, richly enamelled with figured cartouches, 17¾, 1827, magnificent (4141/49) 47000

Clock, desk, Swiss, gilt metal and enamel, ca1930, 4⅜ (4182/94) 400

Clock, dressing table, German, silver-gilt and enamel, ca1930, 4⅜ (4182/93) 300

Clock, easel form, Swiss, silver-gilt and enamel, ca1935, 3⅝ (4182/89) 225

Clock, figural, Art Nouveau, upright, partially clad woman standing on left, 9¾, 1901, Austrian (4213/72) 375

Clock, mantel, glazed pottery, arched case, globe finial, Dutch scenes, 12¾, L19c (4159/107) 225

Clock, mantel, Art Nouveau gilt metal, upright case, pierced whiplash handles, 19¼, ca1900, Meyer and Levy (4213/34) 275

Clock, mantle, miniature, Cartier, silver-gilt and enamel, Art Deco, ca1900, 2½ (4182/99) 250

Clock, French, gilt metal and enamel, ca1930, 6½ (4182/97) 900

Clock, Swiss, gilt metal and ivory screen form, ca1920, 5⅜ (4182/92) 350

Compact, eggshell lacquer, Jean Dunand, circular, Chinese red ground, 4 bronze tassle loops, 2, ca1925 (4213/145) 300

Compact, Cartier, Art Deco, gold-enamel and diamond, 1735 (4182/183) *2500*

Compact ring,
(4182/184)

Watch
(4182/100)

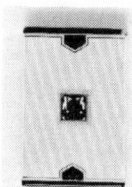

Compact
(4182/183)

Compact, French, black enamel and diamond chain-finger ring,(4182/184)	*1800*
Cup, vodka, Continental silver and enamel, on polychrome enamel, with floral and foliate panels, 2¼, ca1900 (669/264)	750
Cup, 'Napoleonic', Continental silver mounted, spinach jade, deep green bowl supported by tree stem, 5, L19c (669/260)	950
Cup, silver, French, enamelled, very fine, important, ca1905, 6 (4182/91)	4000
Diptych, Limoges enamel, three bishop saints within architecture, 12¼ x 19, L19c (4084/3)	550
Flower holder, champleve, body basket form, central handle and 2 holders, 7, L19c, Elkington & Co. (669/265)	250
Jar, covered gilt bronze mounted, IMARI, painted beasts and flowers, 41½, L18c Mounts 19c (619/267)	6000
Purse, Art Nouveau, silver, leather and silk, rectangular, Gorgonian head, 4½, ca1900 (4213/137)	350
Scent bottle, Continental, silver-gilt and enamel, ca1915, 2¼ (4182/88)	180
Snuff box, French, silver-gilt and enamel, ca1900, 3¼ (4182/87)	275
Vanity, Cartier, gold-enamel and diamond, ca1935, 2¾, mirror cr (4182/147)	1600
Watch, lapel, black onyx and diamond,(4182/155)	1500
Watch, lapel, Cartier, diamond, ca1925 (4182/157)	2700
Watch, open face, Swiss, gold and enamel, Art Deco, ca1930, 1⅝ (4182/100)	*700*
Wristwatch, lady's, diamond and sapphire white enameled dial, ca1930 (4182/166)	950

Limoges

Charger, Joseph interpreting dream, of Pharoah, strapwork surround, D15, 19c (4145/2)	1500
Silhouette plaque of woman, in early 16c costume, probably Limoges, H10⅛, 19c (4145/1)	750

PERIOD PRINTS

Assorted artists

Berthon, Paul, LE LIVRE DE MAGDA, 21¼ x 15, 1898 (4230/663)	700
Berthon, Paul, LES PIPAUX, 16¾ x 22 (4230/664)	275
Carlu, Jean, GRANDES FETES DE PARIS, 34 x 23¼, 1934 (4230/674)	800
Cheret, Jules, DANCING REVELERS, 19¼ x 25¼, 1889 (4230/665)	100
Cheret, Jules, MUSEE GREVIN/THEATRE, 46 x 32⅜, 1900, proof (4230/666)	600
Cheret, Jules, PASTILLES GERAUDEL, 31⅞ x 22¾, 1890 (4230/667)	375
Cheret, Jules, SARAH BERNHARDT, 16⅛ x 32¼, 1890 (4230/668)	450
Coleth, L'ELEGANCE, 34 x 23¼, 1934 (4230/675)	50
De Feure, Georges, AU COMPAINS DU DIABLE AU CORPS, 17¾ x 11¾ (4230/670)	650
De Quelin, Rene, MARSHY LANDSCAPE, 29 x 21, E20c (4230/684)	400
Dupas, Jean, A L'OPERA, 21⅜ x 16⅝, 1932 (4230/680)	2800
French School, LE BAISER, 15 x 12, 20c (4230/683)	275
Icart, Louis, FEMMES AUX FLEURS BLANCS, 23¼ x 19½, 1936 (4230/676)	600
Icart, Louis, NAISSANCE DE VENUS, 19¾ x 15⅛, 1931 (4230/679)	1300

Icart, Louis, SALOME, 20½ x 13⅜, 1919 (4230/678)   325

Butterfly lady
(4213/75)

Tito, VENETIAN ROMANCE, 7½ x 12 (4230/681)   30

Capiello, Leonetto

Le Trait D'Union, lithograph, 53⅛ x 34⅝ (4145/151)   50

Grasset, Eugene

Chocolat Mexicain Masson Paris, lithograph, 46 x 30½, 1892 (4145/166)   100
Encre L. Marquet, lithograph, 45½ x 30½, 1892 (4145/165)   450
Jeanne d'Arc-Sarah Bernhardt, lithograph, 45¼ x 28, 1889-90 (4145/167)   225

Mucha, Alphonse

Head of Boy in Plumed Hat, signed, pastel, 26 x 20, 1898 (4145/176)   5000
Hiver and Ete, two lithographs, 41¼ x 20¼, 1896 (4145/172)   2250
Menus, Cafe Martin, 4 cards, lithographs, 2 x 8⅝, ca1897 (4145/173)   2300
Printemps and Automne, lithographs, two, 41¼ x 20¼, 1896 (4145/171)   2250
Printemps and Automne, two, lithographs, 27⅜ x 11⅝ and 27½ x 11¾, 1900-03 (4145/170)   3250

Rhead, Louis

Peacocks, lithograph, 30⅞ x 59 (4145/175)   2600

SCULPTURE OBJECTS: AMERICAN AND EUROPEAN

An assortment of artists and localities

A clown and a cat group, depatinated, Art Deco, H9, ca1925 (4145/51)   75
A dancing flapper, dark brown patina, green marble base, 17, ca1925 (4213/79)   *1500*
A maiden, nude maiden seated upon tree stump, 28½, L19c (619/220)   900
A smelter, the crucial moment, dark brown patina, 12½, L19c (4213/49)   275
African Princess, Austrian, cold-painted, miniature, foundry stamp Bergmann, 4¾, ca1900 (4230/548)   200
Allegorical figure of knowledge, after Jean-Baptiste Germain, H27½, L19c (4145/27)   800
Allegorical Liberty figure, after Mathurin Moreau, H40, L19c (4145/32)   1900
Amorous group, winged youth whispering in ear of shy maiden, 31½, L19c, French (619/201)   2000
An elegant seated lady, rubbed golden patina, 9⅝, L19/E20c (4213/58)   250
An Arab barber and customer, group, cold painted, Austrian, inscribed Geschutzt, 4¾, L19/E20c (4213/68)   600
Apollo Belvedere, after the classical figure, 40 (619/209)   1100

Archer, figure, lightly clad youth, drawing back his bow, 23 (619/217) — 550
Armorer, figure, youth forging the blade of sword on anvil, by Waltet, 11¼, L19c (649/333) — 650
Artemis and naiad group, parcel gilt, L 16, 19c (4145/13) — 350
Ashtray, colt painted bronze, onyx, supporting ballerina, Lorenzl, 12¾, ca1925, Art Deco (4230/588) — 650
Ashtray, figural gilt bronze, ivory, young woman at water pump, ca1920 (4182/543) — 275
Ashtray, marble and bronze, Art Deco, circular dish, with bronze figure of a walking bear, 9½, ca1925 (4230/601) — 250
Bear hurdy-gurdy player, animal standing, holding hat out, 4½, ca1900, Louchet (669/416) — 300
Beethoven bust, French, by Porsch, 12½, L19c (649/335) — 300
Bell, bronze, Art Nouveau, young curtsying woman, after Tereszczuck, ca1900 2½ (4182/532) — 275
Benjamin Franklin, bust, after Houdon, 18, 19c (619/198) — 650
Bernard Palissy, figure, standing, leather smock, 41, L19c, after E. Barrias (619/203) — 2250
Bison, golden brown patina, 9, L19c (4213/55) — 325
Bloodhound figure, docile animal seated on an oval base, 13, L19c, after Gelibert (669/421) — 600
Borzoi, silvered bronze, Austrian, Art Deco, impressed Hagenauer, 13¾ (4230/575) — 375
Bowl, oval, gilt bronze, mounted red, marble with ram's head handles, 4 feet, l19c (619/247) — 800
Box, in form of a ram, hinged cover, 12¼, L19c (669/413) — 600
Bull, brown patina, inscribed P.J. Mene, 14⅜, L19c (4230/610) — 1400
Bull Figure, after Antoine Louis Barye, L10¾, L19c (4145/58) — 450
Bust, bronze, young woman, after Villanis, L19E20c, 6 (4182/539) — 400
Bust, bronze and ivory, young, Egytian woman, after Tereszczuck, L19E20c 5⅛ (4182/534) — 375
Bust, bronze, French, woman with butterfly wings, L19c 5 (4182/495) — 375
Bust, gilt bronze, Art Nouveau, Woman with Peacock, after Savine, ca1905 6¼ (4182/527) — 500
Bust, Hermes, after the antique, 18½, L19c (649/338) — 300
Bust of Diana, gilt bronze, inscribed A. Falguiere and Thiebaut, 14, ca1890 (4230/552) — 900
Bust of Gentleman, in sixteenth century costume, H10, L19c (4145/26) — 325
Bust of Louis XVIII, bronze, raised on yellow pedestal, 11, L19c (4218/26) — 200
Busts, bronze pair, brown and green patinas, L19c, 5 (4182/503) — 600
Busts of children, pair, H9, l9c (4145/20) — 200
Butterfly lady, fanciful figural, parcel, gilt, brown patina, green marble base, 24½, E20c (4213/75) — *2200*

A dancing flapper
(4213/79)

Candlesticks, pair, form of a bacchante, dressed classical drapery, 18½, 19c (4230/545) — 575
Captive woman in chains figure, H22, L19c (4145/38) — 700
Centerpiece, bronze, molded as a merman holding shell bowl, on sea horse, 9½, L19c (669/445) — 325
Centerpiece, figural, Art Nouveau, gilt, two young embracing children, outstreched legs, 24¼, E20 (4213/71) — 3000
Centerpiece, silvered and gilt, bronze ivory and onyx, caryatids, M. F. Preiss, 8½, ca1925, Art Deco (4230/592) — 4000
Centerpiece, Art Deco, shallow bowl, 2 women, ionic column, Howard, 12½, ca1925 (4230/572) — 650
Centerpiece, Art Nouveau bronze, oval pink and white marble, bowl, male and, female nymphs, 17¾, L19c, French (4213/35) — 600
Charlie Chaplin, Art Deco, green patina, Wittenwuigh, 10¾, ca1935 (4230/596) — 250
Classical figure, insc. Musee Du Louvre, marble base, 18 (619/211) — 300

Classical group Bacchus with a youth perched on his back, 27 (619/213) — 650
Classical maiden, miniature figure, ivory, after Fritz Preiss, kneeling, holding bowl of fruit, 4, ca1925 (4266/70) — 400
Clock, garniture, Art Deco patinated, metal and onyx, flanked by cranes, Bochard, 16¾, ca1930, French (4230/562) — 275
Crowing cockrel, perched on a hemispherical base, 17¾, L19c, after A. Cain (669/419) — 475
Cupid, figure, young boy holding a quiver of flowers, 16¼, 1888, after Waegener (669/426) — 400
Dancer, patinated, bronze, Art Deco, stepped base, A. Kelety & Unis, 14½, ca1925 (4230/570) — 800
Dancing Arab maiden on a windy day, figure, gold painted and gilt, 14¼, ca1900, Austrian (4213/70) — 1400
Dancing females, pair, and cold painted bronze Art Deco, Janle,(4230/585) — 400
Dancing nymph, green patina, black marble base, inscribed Emil, 12½, ca1920 (4230/534) — 400
Dancing woman, brown patina, foundry, Gladenbeck and Son, 12, ca1900, ribbon lacking (4230/560) — 225
Dante bust, golden patina, marble base, inscribed A. Carner, 21, L19c (4230/530) — 400
Diana adjusting her chlamys, brown patina, gilt circular base, 22¼, L19c (4213/24) — 325
Diana the huntress, figure, goddess standing with a stag, reaching for quiver on shoulder, 33½, L19c (669/434) — 1200
Diana, Eros and greyhound, group, parcel-gilt, H19¾, L19c (4145/39) — 700
Diane De Gabies, figure, brown patina, F. Barbedienne, Fondeur, 16½, 19c (4230/527) — 275
Dionysos, figure, youth standing with deerskin over shoulder, 24½ (619/212) — 300
Discus thrower, figure, naked youth preparing his discus throw, 26½, L19c (619/195) — 600
Dish, enamelled in high relief, Faure, D4⅛, ca1925 (4145/115) — 250
Dish, 2 handled, classical style, bronze, classical figures, l19c (619/246) — 75
Dish pedestal, 2 handled, classical, bronze handles applied with panthers,profile of maiden, l19c (619/245) — 225
Donkey, with 2 panniers across back, 6½, L19c, ear dam (669/414) — 300
Duck, bird seated on a fan shaped base, pool with frog,(669/410) — 500
Dying Gaul, after the classical sculpture, 29, L19c (619/199) — 750
Eagle with outspread wings, after Antoine Louis Barye, with open beak, L13½, L19c (4145/59) — 1000
Eastern philosopher, figure, brown patina, 25½, L19c (4213/46) — 600
Egyptian dancer figure, after Demetre Chiparus, gilt bronze, ivory, H13½, cal925 (4147/41) — 1000
Egyptian slaves, pair, patinated and gilt, bronze, holding a spear, 16¼, M19c (649/344) — 750
Equestrian group of a hussar, dark brown patina, 18¾, L19c (4213/48) — 475
Equestrian group of Napoleon, with ivory, after R. Nannani, L24, l9c (4145/35) — 1700
Equestrian group, Arab huntsmen on horseback, white metal, 3/1/2, large, after Guilleman (619/206) — 700
Ewer, bronze, head of woman, thistles, after Jozon, ca1900, 9 (4182/510) — 1300
Exotic dancer, silvered metal, Art Deco, marble base, inscribed, Fayral, 18, ca1925 (4230/569) — 550
Farm worker, green patina, inscribed A. DeWever/Heureux/Presage, 29, L19c (4230/543) — 650
Faun and Lizard group, after F.-M. Charpentier, H17¼, L19c (4145/23) — 600
Female athlete figure, after Pierre le Faguays, H9¾, ca1925 (4145/45) — 800
Female dancer figure, after Bruno Zach, H14, cal925 (4145/44) — 850
Female dancer figure, after Bruno Zach, gilt bronze, ivory, H11, ca1925 (4145/43) — 1100
Female flamenco dancer, wood and silvered bronze, Austrian, Imp. Hagenauer, 10, Art Deco (4230/574) — 300
Female grape harvester, brown patina, 31, L19c, Inc. Tiffany and Co. (4213/53) — 2000
Female swimmer, gilt, polychromed, black marble base, Falkenhagen, 14½, ca1925 (4230/568) — 600
Female water bearer, gilt, green marble base, 15½, ca1925, France (4213/73) — 275
Figural bust gilt bronze and marble, of an Art Nouveau woman, 21½ (4182/500) — 800
Figural group, patinated metal, reclining nude female, seated gazelle, ca1925 25¾ (4182/496) — 550
Figural oil lamp, maiden long, flaring robes, standing Renaa, 11¼, ca1910 (4230/555) — 300
Figural.tray, form nude female oval pond waterlily pads, 13½, ca1900, Maxim (4230/554) — 1200
Figural vase, form of nude female, H9¾, e20c (4145/56) — 375
Figural vase, Art Nouveau, gilt bronze, cylindrical, H8, cal900 (4145/49) — 250
Figure, elegant woman in riding habit, 17¼, ca1925 (4229/23) — 1600
Figure, female athlete, after Schott, E20c 14¼ (4182/528) — 1400
Figure, standing rabbit, after Sandoz, ca1925 4¾ (4182/526) — 275
Figure bronze, walking panther, after August Gaul, dated 1911, 21½ (4182/505) — 1400
Figure gilt bronze and ivory, dancing lady, ca1920 13½ (4182/538) — *1400*
Figure of woman, cold painted bronze, ivory, onyx base, P. Tereszczuk/Austria, 12, E20c (4230/557) — 1200
Figure, bronze, seated chihuahua, after Sandoz, ca1925 (4182/524) — 475
Figure, bronze and composition, Pierrot and Cat, after Omerth, ca1925, 9, rep (4182/521) — 475
Figure, bronze and ivory, young girl knitting, after Tereszczuck, ca1910 12¾ (4182/535) — 700
Figure, bronze and ivory, young girl, after Tereszczuck, ca1920 11½ (4182/536) — *1900*

Figure, bronze and ivory, young sailor, E20c, 9 (4182/508)   375
Figure, bronze and ivory, Flapper, after Zach, ca1925, 14¾ (4182/541)   4750
Figure, bronze, Art Nouveau, kneeling woman, ca1900 13¾ (4182/548)   375
Figure, bronze, Art Nouveau, nude woman, after Slocker, ca1902 21½ (4182/531)   900
Figure, bronze, Art Nouveau, Exotic Dancer, after Seger, L19E20c 12½ (4182/529)   500
Figure, female dancer, the long skirt, after Chiparus, ca1925 21¾ (4182/486)   *2400*
Figure, gilt bronze and ivory, Dancer, green onyx dish tray, after Preiss, ca1925 11½ (4182/522)   *2700*

Figure
(4182/536)

Figure gilt bronze
and ivory
(4182/538)

Figure (4182/522)

Figure (4182/486)

Figure, gilt white metal ivory, Woman in Renaissance Costume, ca1920, 16¾ (4182/540)   450
Figure, gilt bronze and ivory, Young Girl, Playing Musical Instrument, ca1910, 9½ (4182/542)   850
Figure, mechanical, of a female dancer, clothed in drapery golden brown patina, C. Kauba, 8¼, ca1910, parcel gilt (4230/546)   1000
Figure, parcel-gilt bronze, Exotic Egyptian Dancer, after Colinet, ca1925 17¾ (4182/494)   700
Figure, patinated bronze, standing draped naked figure, neoclassical, 19¾, L19c (4142/33)   325
Figure, patinated metal, young girl with hoop, ca1925 17¾ (4182/498)   400
Figure, polychromed, swaying dancer, after Colinet, ca1925 18½ (4182/492)   1000
Figure, polychromed and ivory, dancer, after Chiparus, ca1925 26½ (4182/487)   7750
Figure, silvered bronze and ivory, Elegant Woman, after K. Lorenzl, ca1925 9¾ (4182/517)   725
Figure, wood carved, woman, bathing costume, Jean, Jacques Adnet, ca1925 13½ (4182/484)   650
Figure, Art Deco, Young Woman, ca1925 12 (4182/530)   950
Figures, pair, boy as chimney sweep and girl with broken jug, Lecomey, 19¾, L19c (649/345)   2000
Floor lamps, pair, black nickel plated, brass, bell shaped globe in reeded and tubular support, 64, ca1935 (4230/342)   1500
Florentine singer figure, after Paul Dubois, H24¼, L19c (4145/28)   1000
French, pleasant woman carrying a boy, with basket, Lefeuvre, 24½, L19c (649/348)   1200
French soldier figure, after C. anfrie, gilt bronze, H24, L19c (4145/21)   700
Galileo, brown patina, inscribed Aubert, 16, L19c (4230/529)   350
Gentleman, bust, gilt, green marble socle, 12¾, L19c (4213/60)   175
German soldiers, pair, dark brown patina, marble base, 11½, L19c probably German (4230/525)   350
Glasses, cocktail, set of 6 and tray, Austrian silvered metal, 11½, imp Hagenauer (4230/578)   650
Group, bronze, Victorian Girls, after Marschall, C19c 6⅝ (4182/518)   800
Group, bronze and ivory, pierrot and a lady, ca1925 11¼ (4182/499)   250
Group, parcel-gilt bronze, Pierrot Maitre De Chant, ca1920, 17½ (4182/544)   1200
Guard dog, figure, animal rearing, by Lecourtier, 13¼, ca1880 (649/336)   800
Guillano de Medici, red brown patina, 17, L19c (4213/26)   375
Guinevere figure, depatinated bronze and ivory, H18¼, L19c (4145/29)   1000
Hare, chasse ouverte, golden brown patina J. Moigniez, 9⅛, L19c (4230/612)   500
Hercules and Lichas, group, large, the skin of the Nemean lion below, 54½, L19c (649/342)   2750
Hunter, Art Deco, French, rubbed golden brown patina, black onyx base, 25½, ca1925 (4230/600)   600
Hunting dog, dog crouched low on a rocky base, 12¼, L19c, after Mene (669/423)   325
Icarus, after Schorr, 32 (619/207)   375
Industrial smithie, figure, bearded man reading blue print, hammer on anvil, 11½, L19c (649/334)   650
Ink stand, bronze mounted veined marble, surmounted by cockrel, 2 wells, 15¼, L19c (669/408)   350
Ink stand, gilt bronze, two owls on rocky base beside inkwell, 9¾, 19c, A. Cain (669/409)   550

Inkstand, marble and bronze, surmounted by bust of Napoleon flanked by 2 inkwell, 15½, 19c,
    marble dam (669/448)   250
Inkwell, gilt bronze and marble, mouse leaving home, 5½, L19c, Raphamel (669/417)   500
Isis, Austrian parcel gilt, polychromed, mechanical, foundry stamp, Bergmann, 6, ca1900 (4230/547)   1400
Itinerant, musician, young man with coat and harp, after Bouret, 18¾, L19c, several strings miss.
    (669/430)   950
Lamp, a curio shop, figural, cold painted, inscribed Austria, 12⅛, E20c (4213/67)   900
Lamp, a Moroccan, figural cold painted, foundry,mark of Franz Bergmann, 12¼ ca1900, Austria
    (4213/64)   600
Lamp, chrome and glass, Art Deco, domical grey shade, 8 panelled sides (rim chip), 22, ca1930,
    shade Lautum (4230/343)   800
Lamp, exotic dancer, cold painted, gilt bronze, onyx base Art Deco, Chipaus, 22¾, ca1925
    (4230/566)   1000
Lamp, figural, nude sea nymph with flowing drapery, 31½, L19c (4213/50)   1700
Lamp, figural bronze and onyx, nude female dancer, ca1925 13½ (4182/515)   375
Lamp, figural patinated metal, woman, short sarong, 2 frosted globes, ca1925 18 (4182/497)   850
Lamp, figural, gilt (good, Loie Fuller), as the dancer with swirling robes, arms upheld, 13½, ca1900,
    Raoul Larche (4213/74)   10000
Lamp, floor, 6 light, bronze, Victorian, soldier, wearing chain mail and armor, carved ram's horn, 45,
    L19c (649/351)   1000
Lamp, Art Nouveau, white metal, maiden covered with chestnut leaves, after L Alliot, 37, ca1900,
    French (619/254)   950
Lamp, Art Nouveau, white metal, painted nude maiden, outstreched arms, 38, ca1910 (649/352)   700
Lamps, oil, pair, gilt bronze mounted, painted glass, l19c (619/251)   100
Laquer panel of Josephine Baker, exotic black and white costume, Jean Dunand, 34¾ x 24½,
    ca.1925 (4084/133)   1600
Lights, wall, pair, brass and glass Art Deco, half cylindrical form enamelled in black, 13, ca1925
    (4230/345)   500
Lion, figure, striding forward, on rectangular base, 16 (619/194)   900
Loie Fuller, third figure of six, brown patina after Carabin, 1896-97, very fine (4213/40)   3000
Lorenzo de Medici, red brown patina, 17½, L19c (4213/25)   425
Magyar-nobleman, half length, dark brown patina, inscribed T. Marquet, 18¼, L19c (4230/542)   300
Maiden, figure, draped in loose robe, reclining next to overturned jar, 25½, L19c, French (619/200)   750
Majestic eagle, Art Deco, rubbed green patina, shaped base, Rischmann, 12½, ca1925 (4230/593)   750
Male athlete figure, H13, L19c (4145/25)   200
Marly horse, rearing stallion restrained by naked trainer, 22, L19c, after Coustou (669/433)   800
Marly horses group, pair, after Coustou, H23¾, 19c (4145/16)   950
Marshall Joffer bust, brown patina, inscribed F. Thomasson, 12¼, L19c (4230/541)   200
Match holder, figural gilt bronze, portrait of young woman, after Korschann, ca1900, 5 (4182/511)   450
Mediaeval archer, silver and, patinated bronze and ivory, Art Deco, LeFaguays, 23¾, ca1925
    (4230/580)   3250
Mercury figure, H33½, 19c (4145/19)   400
Mercury figure, after Giovanni de Bologna, black patina, 14¼, 19c (4230/524)   160
Mercury figure, seated in a grey marble rocky base, 19½, 19c (669/431)   600
Moroccan falconer, equestrian, red brown patina, inscribed P.J. Mene, 30½, L19c (4230/611)   3500
Mother and her children reading, black patina, inscribed Mary Yates, 1904, 8½, E20c (4230/544)   700
Muse clio, parcel gilt, brown patina, inscribed Georges-Bareau and F. Barbedienne, 13½, ca1915
    (4230/550)   450
Muse seated, relief of, muse of literature seated beside bust of Athene, 28¼/2, after Chapu
    (619/219)   650
Napoleon, brown patina, 30½, L19c, Tiffany and Co. (4213/56)   2300
Napoleon, bust, after Canova, H11½, 19c (4145/11)   200
Napoleon, bust, marble mounted, head with laurel wreath, 20½ (619/197)   700
Napoleon figure, after Canova, H27½, L19c (4145/12)   850
Napoleon figure, gilt and patinated, bronze and marble, astride galloping horse, 13½, M19c
    (669/425)   750
Narcissus, golden brown patina, 24¼, 19c (4213/23)   400
Nature unveiling herself before science, gilt bronze marble and lapis lazuli, 29½, L19c (4213/37)   4250
Nature unveiling herself before science, green and brown patina, traces of gilding, 28½, L19c
    (4213/36)   4200
Nude female, head and torso, 11½, ca1930 (4230/598)   400
Nude female dancing, bronze, Art Deco, inscribed Lorenzl, 11½, ca1925 (4230/582)   600
Nude woman running with 3 dogs, dogs, Art Deco, onyx base, inscribed Lorenzl, 14¼, ca1925
    (4230/589)   *1700*

Nude woman running with 3 dogs
(4230/589)

Nymph, bust, patinated, bronze, raised on circular base, 13¼, 1794 (4142/13) — 750
Oedipus, figure, youth drawing a cloth from the head of a sphinx, Hebett, 33½, L19c (649/341) — 1000
Olympic athlete figure, H18, L19c (4145/30) — 175
Ottoman warrior, wood base, 12¼, L19c (4213/63) — 200
Owls, pair, inset with glass eyes, perched on a book, 12, L19c (669/420) — 600
Paperweight, parcel-gilt bronze, figural seated nude female,(4182/523) — 475
Partridge and her young, golden brown patina, A. Arson/Admis, 13½, L19c (4230/603) — 1100
Phidias, figure, patinated gilt bronze, sculptor seated in pensive pose, by Hazel, 19¼, L19c (649/340) — 800
Phryne, gilt, after Compagne, 33¾, L19c (4213/39) — 1300
Pierette and a pierrot, amusing, parcel gilt bronze, Lorenzl, 16¾, ca1925 (4230/565) — 750
Pierrot embracing a Pierrete, marble base, 12½, ca1925, Art Deco (4230/602) — 525
Pin tray, after Joaquin Angles, bronze figural, female head, ca1900 9¼ (4182/485) — 850
Pin tray, gilt bronze, nude female, figure, budding trees, after Jouant, L19-E 20c, 6¼ (4182/509) — 150
Plaque, enamel on copper, French, gentleman seated at table, framed, 7, ca1900 (649/300) — 900
Plaque, enamel on copper, French, girl in 18c dress before curtain, steps, 7½, ca1900 (649/301) — 1100
Plaque, enamel, Austrian*, oval, maiden wearing red cloak and hood, framed, 19¼, L19c (649/297) — 750
Plaque, Art Nouveau, young girl, on wood board, 17, 1908, after Crenier (619/215) — 375
Plaque, Electrotype, Elkington*, scene of Diana and maidens attacking water nymphs, 22½, L19c (649/296) — 250
Prancing horse, rubbed black patina, 18½, L19c (4213/42) — 325
Putti, figures, pair, patinated, bronze, emblematic of autumn and spring, 8¼, L19c (4142/20) — 400
Reclining maiden, surrounded by 4 children, goat, 22 L19c (619/221) — 1300
Recumbant husky figure, after Emmanuel Fremiet, L6⅛, L19c (4145/61) — 550
Roman charioteer, bronze, equestrian, green patina Art Deco, A. Kelety, 34¼, ca1930 (4230/586) — 1600
Roman gladiator figures, pair, after Adolph Dressler, H20, L19c (4145/24) — 600
Roman imperial lady, monumental bronze and marble, golden brown patina, 72¼, L19c (4213/27) — 5500
Roman senator, statue, figure cloaked in a toga, 13½, L19c (649/343) — 375
Roundel of a nobleman, brown green patina, inscribed J. Pradier, 10, L19c (4230/538) — 280
Rousseau bust, iron, H19½, 1827 (4145/22) — 300
Royal messenger on horseback group, L29½, L19c (4145/37) — 1200
Salome figure, H10¾, e20c (4145/54) — 500
Sculptor, figure, young man with cloth around waist, 21½, ca1900,Lugerth (669/.427) — 400
Sea nymph, monumental, rubbed golden brown patina, wood base, 34¾ (4213/61) — 1300
Seated classical woman figure, gilt bronze, H12, L19c (4145/33) — 350
Seated Lion figure, after Antoine Louis Barye, L12, 1898 (4145/60) — 1000
Seated woman parcel gilt, bronze, Art Deco, green patina, M. Guiraud-Riviere, 16, ca1925 (4230/571) — 2700
Setter, grout, alert expression standing, 12¾, L19c, after Mene (669/424) — 450
Shakespeare and Pepys figures, pair, H40, L19c (4145/31) — 700
Shepherdess feeding her flock group, after Joseph D'aste, L20½, early 20c (4145/46) — 950
Singing sailors, pair, painted, wood and silvered metal, impressed, Hagenauer, 3½ - 8½, Art Deco (4230/573) — 250
Sleeping woman, in leaves of a poppy plant, Le Pavot, inscribed Angles, 13¼, ca1900 (4230/549) — 550

Small child on a stool, brown and green patina, after Juan Clara, 13⅜, L19/E20c (4213/43)   850

Snake dancer, gilt bronze, Art Deco, columnar marble base, Lorenzl, 24¼, ca1925 (4230/584)   1100

Spanish Dora and her Suitor, dark brown patina, 14¼, L19c (4213/52)   1250

Sphinxes, pair, patinated, bronze, reclining, figure, marble base, 8¾ x 16½, E19c (4119/227)   1100

Staghound and tortoise, dark green patina, A Jacquemart, 6½, L19c (4230/606)   475

Stalking panther, Art Deco, dark brown patina, marble base, M. Prost & Susse, 14⅝, ca1925 (4230/591)   350

Standing and awakening woman, Reveil, French, brown patina, 15, ca1900 (4230/561)   500

Standing nymph, green patina, black marble base, inscribed Emil,(4230/535)   400

Standing panther, golden brown & green patina, T. Cartier, 22½, L19c (4230/604)   850

Strauss, bust, Ene. Benet, 28, 1899 (649/337)   550

Tea service, pewter Art Deco, 5 pieces, C-scroll handles, monogram, The Daughan Co., tray 15¾, ca1930 (4230/266)   350

The Egyptian curio shop, group, cold painted, Austria, 15¼, L19/E20c, inscribed Geschutzt (4213/66)   1200

The rape of the Sabine woman, dark brown patina, French, 17¾, 19c (4230/526)   900

The return of Odysseus, green patina, 18½, 19c (4213/33)   800

Three dancing bacchantes, after clodion, parcel-gilt, H35½, L19c (4145/18)   2200

Three dogs burrowing, dark brown patina, inscribed P.J. Mene,(4230/607)   1000

Three handled vase, C-scroll handles, 3 female heads, 16, ca1900, very fine (4229/24)   4500

Three huntsmen and horses, bronze, Austrian, Art Deco, impressed Hagenauer/Wien, 19¾, ca1930 (4230/576)   *1100*

Tray, bronze, Figural Art Nouveau, picking daisies, ca1900 9¾ (4182/501)   150

Tray, figural gilt bronze, reclining mermaid on 1 end of tray, ca1900 18½ (4182/520)   750

Tray, gilt bronze, Art Deco, center nude female, sloping sides, imp P. Kiss/Paris, 29¼, ca1925 (4230/579)   700

Triumphant warrior figure, after Henri Honore' Ple', H25½, L19c (4145/36)   550

Turkish warrior, figure, turbanned warrior, draped with robe, 55½ L19c, large, after Ple (619/222)   4000

Two Arab merchants, group, cold painted, 8½, E20c, Austrian (4213/69)   550

Two birds, group, gilt bronze, on rocky base, pecking for insects, 5¼, L19c, after F. Pautrot (669/418)   350

Two children, bronze, Pierrot and Pierrette, P. Tereszczuk, 5¼, ca1910, brown patina (4230/558)   400

Two dancing bacchantes and a satyr, golden brown patina, 22½, 19c (4213/44)   2000

Two dancing women, group, H24, 20c (4145/52)   1200

Two maenads, group, two ecstatic maidens and a baby fawn, after Clodion, 30, L19c (619/202)   3000

Two pigs, group, one seated crouched, before other, oval base, 8¾, L19c, Bonheur (669/411)   600

Two rabbits, French, golden patina, 5¼, L19c (4230/613)   160

Vase, enamel on copper, Sarlandie, H5½, ca1925 (4145/116)   100

Vase, figural 2 nudes, German, upright lily pads and blossoms, ca1900, 8 (4182/502)   350

Vase, figural, bronze, female figure, after Tereszczuck, L19E20c 6½ (4182/533)   200

Vase, figural, bronze, Art Nouveau, partially clothed female, French, ca1900 8¾ (4182/549)   350

Vase, gilt bronze, scrolling corn husk handles, ears of corn, ca1900 8½ (4182/516)   225

Vase, 2 grasshopper handles, branches, ca1900 4⅞ (4182/514)   225

Vase, 2 handled, Art Nouveau pewter, ovoid form, female heads, long hair, 6½, ca1900 (4213/129)   600

Vases, pair, bronze and ruby glass, trumpet shaped, fitted into tripod supports, 20⅝, 19c (619/253)   500

Venus figure aubain, after Christophe-Gabriel Allegrain, H20¾, L19c (4145/15)   1000

Walking polar bear, bronze, Art Deco, marble base, inscribed G. Lavroff, 17½ (4230/587)   650

Wall bracket, in form of 3 putti, H17¾, 19c (4145/17)   400

Water goddess, the source figure, H12, ca1925 (4145/50)   600

Whippet, Art Deco, unpatinated, marble base, 6⅛, restored tail, ca1930 (4230/599)   175

Whistling boy, bronzed metal, wearing ragged clothes, 16½, ca1900 (649/346)   275

Woman, bust, parcel gilt, la pensec, gold brown patina, 19, E20c (4213/76)   750

Woman, silvered bronze, Art Deco, standing in full skirt, 1 leg raised, Rischmann, 25½, ca1925 (4230/594)   950

Woman in classical costume, playing ball, black-green patina, inscribed Walter Schott, 18, L19c (4230/539)   425

Woman riding an elephant, gilt bronze, French, stepped onyx & marble base, 424, ca1925 (4230/597)   1500

Woman seated in a canoe, bronze, holding open parasol, M.L. Simard, 27½, ca1925, Art Deco (4230/595)   1000

Woman with a parrot, after K. Lorenzl, painted, H8½, cal925 (4145/48)   300

Wood sprite and a bacchante, allegorical, bronze, base with frieze of harvesting putti, 32¾, 19c (4213/19)   2900

Wounded panther, dark green patina, stone base, Hesteau, 10¼, L19c (4230/605)   200

Young ballerina, bronze, Art Deco, inscribed Lorenzl, 8½, ca1925 (4230/583)   400

Young boy and rooster, winner of the cock fight, brown patina, A. Falguiere, 31½, L19c (4230/533)   900

Young exotic maiden, incense burner, gilt bronze and onyx, Duvernet, 19½, ca1925, French (4230/564)	400
Young fisher maiden with her catch, rubbed light brown patina, black marble base, 13¾, L19/E20c (4213/38)	275
Young girl and dog group, after Samuel-Adolph Cashwan, H10½, 20c (4147/40)	225
Young girl carrying flowers figure, with ivory, H7½, E20c (4145/55)	350
Young girl figure, after Demetre Chiparus, gilt bronze, ivory, H14½, ca1925 (4147/42)	1200
Young girl, bust, her hair bounded by laurel leaf, 11, L19c (619/216)	200
Young maiden holding sheaves, parcel gilt, inscribed H. Moreau, 25½, L19c (4230/537)	900
Young nude maiden, ivory, Art Deco, domed onyx base, Joe Descomps, 5¼, ca1925 (4230/567)	350
Young shepherdess, mustard patina, inscribed H. Moreau, 17¼, E20c (4230/536)	550
Young woman and lamb group, silvered and gilt-metal, L14, ca1925 (4145/57)	125
Young woman in nineteenth century costume, bronze and ivory, 10, ca1910 (4213/78)	700
Young woman standing, an opalescent base, Ice Maiden, J. Causse, 23, ca1900, green patina (4230/551)	4300
Young woman, gilt bronze, ivory, stylish, onyx base, B. Callender, 17, ca1930, finger chip (4230/563)	1700
Young woman, gilt bronze, French, marble, base, Art Deco, Helene Gaunne, 11½, ca1925 (4230/581)	800
Youth, holding basket, Helen Danes, 21 (649/347)	250
Zeus, bust, Errico e Figlio, 19, 19c (649/339)	325

Animalier bronzes, American

A bloodhound on the scent, brown patina, 9, 1905 (4213/92)	*750*
A fallen stag, green patina, 13, L19c (4213/99)	375
A Persian camel, dark green patina, 5⅜, L19c (4213/91)	*250*
A rabbit, dark brown patina, 4⅞, L19c (4213/96)	150
A seated pointer, rubbed brown patina, 14½, L19c (4213/80)	550
A stag browsing, dark brown patina, 15¼, L19c (4213/94)	700
A standing bear, brown green patina, 9⅞, L19c (4213/88)	900
A walking lion, green patina, 15¼, L19c (4213/81)	1000
A walking lion figure, dark brown patina, 15½, L19c (4213/84)	1000
A walking tiger, dark brown patina, 15¼, L19c (4213/85)	625
A walking tiger, rubbed brown green patina, 10¾, L19c (4213/82)	275

Asian
elephant
(4213/90)

A bloodhound on the scent
(4213/92)

Three huntsmen and horses (4230/576)

An Arab scout on camelback, golden brown patina, 12½, gilding added later (4213/98)	950
Asian elephant, dark green patina, 5, L19c (4213/90)	*400*
Cheval turc (autre), green brown patina, 12¼, L19/E20c (4213/87)	4500
Equestrian group of a jockey, brown patina, 17, L19c (4213/93)	1100
Laccolabe, group, brown patina, 21, L19c (4213/95)	2600

Setter with pheasant, rubbed brown patina, 24, L19c (4213/97) — 1200
The elephant of Senegal, rubbed brown-green patina, 3¾, L19c, partialled effaced (4213/89) — *550*

Bronze

Allegorical group, blacksmith and peasant woman, 16¼, E20c (4266/77) — 300
Arab, Austrian, cold-painted, kneeling on a prayer rug, 5¼, ca1900 (4266/24) — 400
Arab and His Cat, Austrian, moveable, cloak opens to reveal nude girl, 4¾, ca1910 (4266/26) — 1100
Arab cobbler, Austrian, cold-painted, seated on a rug, 2¾, ca1900 (4266/34) — 800
Arab Knife Sharpener, Austrian, seated at his barrow-like workplace, 3¼, ca1900 (4266/28) — 500
Arab maiden, Austrian, cold-painted, seated, jeweled halter, diaphanous skirt, 11¼, ca1900 (4266/35) — 800
Arab scribe, Austrian, cold-painted, copying pages from the Koran, 3½, ca1900 (4266/23) — 700
Archer, after Josef Uphues, his back arched, 15¼, ca1900 (4266/74) — 325
Artemis, after Tullio Montini, striding figure, 10¾, 20c (4266/66) — 100
Au But, group of 3 runners, poised on their toes, jockeying for position, L16¼, E20c (4266/45) — 1200
Bull, butting, after Isidore Bonheur, one foreleg raised, L22, L19c (4266/82) — 1600
Bull, figure, after Louis Vidal, dark golden-brown patina, L20, L19c (4266/91) — 900
Bull, standing, treading on sheaves of wheat, L27, L19c (4266/90) — 2700
Bull, standing proudly, after Isidore Bonheur, L22, L19c (4266/84) — 1200
Bull, walking, after Isidore Bonheur, head held erect, L21, L19c (4266/83) — 1500
Bull, walking, dark rubbed brown patina, L21, L19/E20c (4266/81) — 1300
Bull and a man, group, after Isidore Bonheur, rearing bull, L20½, L19c (4266/85) — 1800
Cheval Turc (autre), golden patina, crack to tail, L4⅞, L19c (4266/88) — 800
Classical female athelete, parcel-gilt, French or German, a hoop behind her, 10½, E20c (4266/67) — 350
Clock, pewter and enamel, arched case, enamel dial, 'Tadric', ca1900, 6½ (4182/74) — 550
Dancing fisherman, figure, wearing baggy trunks, black marble base, 17¼, E20c (4266/54) — 550
Dancing Maiden, after Rudolph Kaesbach, wearing a tunic, 16¾, ca1925 (4266/61) — 400
Dancing woman, silvered-bronze, ivory, long skirt hanging from her hips, 10, ca1925 (4266/44) — 650
Desk set, animalier, 4 pcs, each decorated with a stag, L17½, E20c (4266/93) — 650
Discus thrower, figure, after the antique, marbelized base, 10½, E20c (4266/47) — 400
Etoile De Mer, female figure, after Capellaro, young maiden on base with sea life, 31, ca1900 (4266/46) — 1000
Eve, allegorical figure, after Anton Grath, she holding an apple, 19, E20c (4266/57) — 600
Exotic dancer, cold-painted, ivory, after Demetre Chiparus, as a Wagnerian heroine, 17¼, ca1925 (4266/50) — 4250
Exotic dancer, gilt and ivory, young nude Egyptian dancer, 13¾, ca1925 (4266/51) — 2300
Figural lamp, Austrian, cold-painted, a standing water-carrier, 10¾, E20c (4266/15) — 450
Figural lamp, Austrian, cold-painted, a harem girl sits on cushions, 14¾, E20c (4266/20) — 950
Figural lamp, Austrian, cold-painted, an Arab potentate reclines on a couch, 19, E20c (4266/21) — *1500*
Figural lamp, Austrian, cold-painted, nomadic Arab warrior on a rug, 19, E20c (4266/22) — 1800
Figural lamp, Austrian, cold-painted, 2 Arabs in a canteen, 8, E20c (4266/16) — 750
Figure, cold-painted and ivory, after Claire-Jeanne-Roberte Colinet, dancer, 22½, ca1925 (4266/53) — 3750
Flapper in slippers and skirt, on her toes, bare breasts, marble base, 14, ca1920 (4266/76) — 1900
Flying skirt, Austrian, parcel-gilt, after Carl Kauba, dancer's skirt moves, 11, ca1910 (4266/6) — 1900

Figural lamp
(4266/21)

Francois I (4266/3)

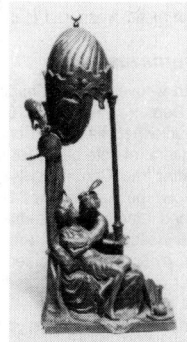

Lamp (4266/30)

Francois I, equestrian group, the monarch seated on his caparisoned mount, L33, L19c (4266/3)   *3750*
Group, Austrian, 2 Arabs, European traveler, 4½, ca1915 (4266/13)   325
Hussar, equestrian group, after Ferruccio Crespi, L18¾, L19c (4266/2)   550
Ida, bust of a young woman, in classical dress, bronze base, 8¼, E20c (4266/75)   225
Joan of Arc, figure, dressed in armour, holding a flag, 29, ca1900 (4266/56)   450
Jockey, equestrian group, after Pierre-Jules Mene, L17, L19/E20c (4266/94)   1700
Just 'Fur' You, Austrian, ashtray, fur coat opens to reveal nude woman, 8¼, ca1920 (4266/8)   950
Lamp, parcel-gilt, moveable, Imperial Eagle atop rocky column, figure underneath, 14¾, E20c (4266/62)   1100
Lamp, Austrian, mechanical, domed stall, opens to reveal standing nude, 12¾, ca1915 (4266/33)   2100
Lamp, moveable, Moor in front of curtained booth, 13¼, ca1920 (4266/32)   1500
Lamp, Moroccan couple, Austrian, cold-painted, beneath a canopy, 13¾, ca1900 (4266/30)   *1000*
Lamp, The Proposition, Austrian, parcel-gilt, polychrome, mechanical, 12¾, ca1915 (4266/31)   2800
Le Froid, figural group, after Roger Bloche, poor couple huddled together, 13¼, E20c (4266/42)   250
Lion, striding, after Antoine-Louis Barye, heavily maned, L10, L19/E20c (4266/87)   350
Little Windy Day, Austrian, moveable, dancing girl, tiara inlaid with glass, 4¾, ca1900 (4266/27)   500
Maiden, with revealing halter dress, marble base, 10¼, ca1900 (4266/64)   450
Mercury, figure, after Giovanni da Bologna, marble base, 43, E20c (4266/1)   650
Naughty alligator, Austrian, moveable, carapace opens to reveal reclining nude female, L9¼, ca1910 (4266/37)   1000
Nude woman, after O. Schmidt, she holding a bocci ball, 12¾, E20c (4266/72)   200
Nymph, figure, drapery about her waist, marble base, 11, L19c (4266/5)   450
On a Windy Day, Austrian, moveable, dancing girl, red marble base, 8, ca1900 (4266/25)   950
Pointer, figure, after Antoine-Louis Barye, L6¾, L19c (4266/92)   300
Riddle of the Sphinx, Austrian, Sphinx opens to reveal seated nude, L6, ca1900 (4266/7)   1700
Rodent's Reward, Austrian, rat on his hindquarters, opens to reveal nude, 3½, ca1910 (4266/19)   550
Roman warrior, figure, standing, black marble base, 8, ca1920 (4266/79)   100
Rug dealer, Austrian, cold-painted, standing on a carpet, looking at another, 4¾, E20c (4266/36)   500
Salome, figure, after Arthur Block, arms outstretched, 12½, ca1920 (4266/43)   450
Satyr with the infant Dionysus, group, after Alfred Raum, marble plinth, 11, L19c (4266/4)   300
Secret of the owl, Austrian, parcel-gilt owl opens to reveal nude, 4¼, ca1900 (4266/18)   750
Shy cigar cutter, Austrian, moveable, reclining nude female, L8½, ca1920 (4266/39)   1600
Sleeping beauty, Austrian, moveable, sleeping maiden, hinged drape reveals total nudity, L9¼, ca1900 (4266/38)   900
Tea and coffee service and tray, pewter leafage and scroll, ca1900, 5 pc (4182/73)   800
The Dragon Killer's Reward, Austrian, after T. Curts, fortress opens to reveal nude, 6⅜, ca1900 (4266/17)   1500
The torch dancer, silvered-bronze, arched backward, onyx and marble pedestal, 11½, ca1925 (4266/69)   1300
Two herons, after Jane LeSoudier, rubbed brown patina, 20, E20c (4266/63)   700
Vase, christofle gilt, patinated, flaring vase, notched lip, 12¼, E20c (4266/48)   500
Vase, 3-footed, after Hans Saint Lerche, pyriform vessel, 4½, ca1900 (4266/71)   500
Vases, pair of 2-handed, inverted baluster form, 6, ca1900 (4266/80)   250
Warrior, bust, after E. Baudet, Minerva*, 16¼, E20c (4266/41)   250
Wolf seizing a stag by the throat, after Antoine-Louis Barye, L18, L19c (4266/86)   1000

Woman and 2 fauns, figural group, green patina, black marble base, 20, ca1925 (4266/49) 850
You Can't Come In, Austrian, after Nam Greb, nude woman on revolving stand, 5⅝, ca1900 (4266/10) 1400
Young fiddler, figure, in rustic dress, red marble base, 9¾, ca1900 (4266/55) 450

Other European bronzes

Bust, female Herme, Art Nouveau, after Charles Korschmann, H12¼, E20c (4084/46) 575
Bust, two lovers, after Demetre Chiparus, L16½, ca1925 (4084/35) 400
Bust, woman, after Meunier, left hand over chest, H27¾, L19c (4084/21) 700
Bust, Diana, after Falguiere, marble base, H6½, L19c (4084/14) 200
Bust, Gertrude Stein, after Paul Cornet, H19¾, E20c (4084/38) 450
Bust, Rosseau, dark brown patina, inscribed Bechu Fondeur, French (4084/13) 600
Candlestick, semi-clothed female, seated, after Auguste-Paul-Gustave Cornu, L6¼, E20c (4084/39) 375
Equestrian group, after Belloc, Arab with female hostage riding camel, H22, L19c (4084/10) 1800
Ewers, gilt bronze, pair, pyriform body molded with flowers, H24, L19c (4084/18) 400
Figure, blacksmith, after boucher, leaning on his hammer, H30¾, E20c (4084/30) 750
Figure, clown playing a lute, gilt and ivory, after Demetre Chiparus, H28½, ca1925 (4084/33) 3450
Figure, dancing woman, gilt, silvered, dressed as a harlequin, H13¼, ca.1925 (4084/25) 400
Figure, elegant lady, after Santiago-Rodriguez Bonome, H26¾, 1929 (4084/51) 800
Figure, female clown, parcel-gilt and ivory, H8½, ca.1925 (4084/42) 325
Figure, female holding butterfly, light brown patina, inscribed Stina Gustafson, H20¼, E20c (4084/43) 375
Figure, female Egyptian dancer, polychromed, after Demetre Chiparus, H28½, ca.1925 (4084/36) 2100
Figure, gilt bronze and ivory, 'La Liseuse', after Belleuse, H12¾, L19c (4084/16) 900
Figure, ivory, nude female, holding a length of drapery, H7½, ca.1925 (4084/37) 800
Figure, nude female dancer, after Phillippe Wolfers, dark green patina, H30, E20c (4084/54) 1000
Figure, nude woman, after Angles, parcel-gilt, brown patina, inscribed, H6, E20c (4084/24) 300
Figure, seated nude woman, black-green patina, inscribed Martini/Roma, H14¾, 1929 (4084/49) 400
Figure, stalking lion, black patina, marble base, inscribed, L23, ca.1925 (4084/48) 375
Figure, woman riding a musk ox, after Hermann haase-Ilsenburg, L15¼, E20c (4084/45) 900
Figure, woman, after Bizett-Lindet, Allegory of Agriculture, 'Ceres', H33½, ca.1925 (4084/27) 1000
Figure, woman, ivory, flowing hair, drapery over shoulder, H12½, E20c (4084/57) 450
Figure, workman, green patina, H13¾, E20c (4084/55) 350
Figure, young girl as a clown, parcel-gilt, ivory, after Demetre Chiparus, H8¾, ca1925 (4084/34) 650
Figure, Napoleon before a column, brown patina, H8¾, L19c (4084/19) 250
Figure, Salome, after Levy, brown patina, H34, L19c (4084/17) 1800
Group, after Pierre Traverse, female figure running aside a gazelle, H71, ca.1925 (4084/53) 13000
Group, two boxers, inscribed A. Bonsaier (?), brown-green patina, L15¼, E20c (4084/29) 500
Group, Allegorical, rich brown patina, inscribed, H30¾, 1906 (4084/40) 1000
Memorial, after Henri Chapu, parcel-gilt, woman clothed in drapery, H29¼, L19c (4084/11) 1000
Pedestals, figural, Art Deco, pair, octagonal marble top, rampart antelopes, H27¼, ca.1925 (4084/52) 1500
Plaque, after charpentier, 'La Maternite', brown patina, 17¾ x 11⅞, L19c (4084/12) 300
Plaque, Bellerton astride Pegasus, parcel-gilt, after Gaetano Cecere, 13¾ x 10¾, ca1930 (4084/32) 175
Tray, figural, man engulfed by water, L9¾, L19c (4084/20) 250
Tray, Art Deco, nude female figure, elongated octagonal contour, L25, ca.1925 (4084/58) 150
Vase, Art Nouveau figural, leafage above 3 female figures, depatinated, H10¾, E20c (4084/26) 350

Various animalier bronzes

Figure, bull, after Gustave Hierholtz, L17, E20c (4084/66) 550
Figure, game bird, after Jules Moigniez, L12¼, L19c (4084/78) 550
Figure, pointer, after Antoine-Louis Barye, L6¾, L19c (4084/61) 425
Figure, rearing bull, after Antoine-Louis Barye, L10¾, L19c (4084/59) 700
Figure, setter, after Pierre Jules Mene, L13, L19c (4084/67) 600
Figure, setter scratching, after Joseph-Victor Chemin, L7½, L19c (4084/74) 500
Figure, walking bull, after Pierre Jules Mene, L14⅜, L19c (4084/70) 700
Figure, walking lion, after Antoine-Louis Barye, L10, L19c (4084/62) 350
Figure, walking tiger, after Antoine-Louis Barye, L10, L19c (4084/63) 300
Figure, whipper with a fan, after Pierre Jules Mene, L7¼, L19c (4084/73) 600
Figure, whippet with a ball, after Pierre Jules Mene, L6¼, L19c (4084/76) 500
Group, boar attacked by hounds, after Pierre Jules Mene, l19, L19c (4084/71) 900
Group, equestrian, jockey, after Pierre Jules Mene, L10, l19c (4084/75) 650
Group, equestrian, picador, after Pierre Jules Mene, H28½, L19c (4084/68) 2300
Group, lion and serpent, after Antoine-Luois Barye, L6½, L19c (4084/60) 750
Group, mare and stallion, after isidore Bonheur, L38, L19c (4084/65) 6000
Group, pointer and hare, after Pierre Jules Mene, L11½, L19c (4084/69) 350
Group, stag and doe, after Pierre Jules Mene, L7¼, L19c (4084/77) 350

Group, Greyhound with dead hare, after Pierre Jules Mene, L7, L19c (4084/72)   450

Silver
AMERICAN SILVER

Bowl, Art Nouveau, circular, flowers, maple and oak leaves, The Gorham Co., 10, ca1910 (4230/234)   650

Candlesticks, pair, Art Nouveau, flaring flattened drip pan, floriform socket, 15¾, ca1920 (4213/126)   950

Centerpiece, silver plate, shallow circular bowl, rising from cyl. stem, Continental, 13⅞, Christofle, 20c (4230/264)   175

Centerpiece, Art Nouveau, oval flowerheads and foliage, 4 short supports, 15¼, 1899, Martele (4230/231)   1500

Cigarette case and match case, sterling silver, enamel, Liberty and Company, ca1905 (4145/111)   200

Cocktail shaker, enamel, of ovoid shape, camel, palm trees, 24 ozs, 5 dwts, 13, ca1930 (4266/102)   550

Coffee pot, The Gorham Co., bulbous gourd shape, ivory ringed, handle, 22 ozs, 10 dwts, 11½, 1898 (4266/97)   550

Cup, ivory, 3 handled silver, silver bamboo, bird, dragon, shield, The Gorham Co., 5⅝, ca1883 (4230/214)   425

Cup, 3-handled, The Gorham Co., baluster form, tendril-like flutes, 31 ozs, 5 dwts, 6, 1898 (4266/96)   1500

Dresser set, Art Nouveau, 5 pieces, maiden with flowers, Webster Co., ca1910 (4230/223)   300

Fish servers, pair, Dominick & Haff, seahorse tail handles, L19c (4266/103)   175

Letter opener, branch form handle, scimitar blade, 5 ozs, 5 dwts, L9½, L19c (4266/104)   60

Letter opener, 'Japanese Style', s-curved shape, overlapping shells, crab, George W. Shiebler, 11⅜ ca1880 (4230/213)   170

Picture frame, Dominick & Haff, on velvet, support, 7½, ca1900 (4266/105)   300

Pitcher, water, Art Nouveau, sprays of grasses and fern, Wm. B. Durgin Co., 8½, ca1900 (4230/217)   400

Pitcher, water, The Gorham Co., inverted pear shape, stylized foliage, 46 ozs, 5 dtws, 10⅝, ca1900 (4266/100)   1600

Place card holders, set of 12, International Silver Co., as animals, 2⅛-2¼, case, modern (4266/98)   250

Sauce boat and stand, Art Nouveau, panels of flowers, stand, The Gorham Co., 9⅛, Martele, ca1910 (4230/233)   1250

Service of flatware, Etruscan pattern, art deco monograms, The Gorham Co., 182 pcs, ca1925 (4230/257)   1300

Tea and coffee set, oriental movement, spreading foliage, Tiffany & Co., ca1890, fine (4182/52)   22000

Tea and coffee set, electroplated, hammered surface and bulbous bodies, Derby Silver Plate Co., ca1915 (4230/236)   175

Tea set, 3 piece, lobed bulbous form, The Gorham Co., teapot 9½, 1887 (4230/224)   900

Vase, Art Nouveau, chased with anemone blossoms, The Gorham Co., 15¼, ca1900, Martele (4230/230)   1100

Vase, 2 handled, copper and silver, The Gorham Co., 16⅝, monogram P.H.C., ca190l (4230/215)   225

EUROPEAN SILVER

Assorted objects

Baskets, Edwardian, shell, pair, after Paul de Lamerie, 74 ozs, 10 dwts, W9⅞, 1909 (4194/115)   3500

Beaker and cover, Arts and Crafts, enamel, bulbous cylindrical form, iridescent enamel, 9¾, ca1900 (4266/118)   2500

Bowl, Arts and Crafts, 2-handled, Ramsden & Carr, fleur-de-lys, handles, 14 ozs, L9⅞, 1916 (4266/119)   200

Bowl, Victorian, Monteith, Elkington & Co., fluted, crest, with ring, 37 ozs, Diam 10¼, 1892 (4194/120)   800

Candelabra, 2 light, pair, Victorian, spreading bases, baluster stems, John l Henry Lias, 17⅛, 1837 (4259/131)   *6000*

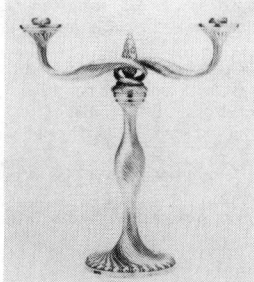

Candelabra (4259/131)

Cup (4213/128)

Centerpiece (4259/126)

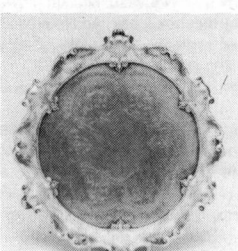

Salver (4259/129)

Candelabrum, 5-light, Georg Jensen, oval domed foot, stylized foliage, 33 ozs, 10 dwts, 9, 1910 (4266/128)	1000
Candlestick, plated chamber, French, Art Nouveau, a mermaid, L6¾ (4266/110)	350
Candlesticks, short, pair, open strapwork stem, green hard stones, Arts and crafts, ca1904, 4¾ (4182/61)	325
Cane handle, Art Nouveau, form couple enbracing, she with long hair, Swedish, C.G. Hallberg, 1903 (4230/219)	500
Case, card, Nathaniel Mills, rectangular, scene from houses of parliament, 3⅝, 1845 (4259/480)	400
Centerpiece, Georg Jensen, circular bowl, grapevine, clusters, 63 ozs, 10 dwts, 12⅛, modern (4266/127)	1900
Centerpiece, E & J Barnard, oval, frosted and cut glass bowl, 13¼, 40 ozs, 1865 (4259/126)	*1700*
Centerpiece, Secessionist, Austrian, oval bowl raised on fluted stem, 10, ca1915 (4266/111)	2000
Coasters, wine, pair, Victorian, sides pierced in a scrolling foliate design, 6¾, ca1845 (4259/33)	200
Creamer, Victorian, Lobed bombe circular form, 5 ozs, 5 dwts, 3½, 1838 (4194/153)	125
Cup, 2 handled, Art Nouveau, bowl with amusing face, 6⅛, 1907, Nathand Hayes, English (4213/128)	*425*
Demi-tasse pot, Austrian, pear shaped, swan-neck spout, 6 ozs, 5 dwts, 5¾, ca1905 (4266/113)	125
Dish, breakfast on lampstand, Sheffield plated, rectangular covered dish, 12½, 67 ozs, 1894 (4259/133)	600
Dish, footed, twin loop, scrolling loop handle set with green agate, ca1901, 11 (4182/58)	1700
Dish, hot water, covered, domed cover with openwork, Diam 9½, E20c (4084/162)	100
Ewer, Victorian, 'Cellini' pattern, Hunt & Roskell, 30 ozs, 12½, 1869 (4194/126)	1100
Ewer, Victorian, Robert Garrard & Co., London, 33 ozs, 11½, 1876 (4194/127)	1250
Flower Vase, German, tapered cylindrical form, knopped base, 24 ozs, 5 dwts, 13, ca1900 (4266/116)	275
Frame, Arts and Crafts, Walker & Hall, stamped with goosegirl and gaggle, 11¼, 1907 (4266/121)	450
Glasses, Desny cocktail, set of 12, plated, conical cup and base, ca1925 (4084/173)	3200
Inkstand, Robert Garrard, rectangular, 2 wells and seal box, 12½, 62 ozs, 1843 (4259/125)	2600
Inkstand, Robinson, Edkins and Aston, oval, shell decorated rim, 13, 24 ozs, 1845 (4259/122)	750
Jug, glass claret, silver mounted, Hands & Son, crested neck, satyr masks, 10⅜, 1860 (4259/124)	200
Jug, hot water, Charles S. Harris, pear shaped, 8¾, 13 ozs, 1882 (4259/123)	325
Liqueur set, silver, 6 cups with tray, iris blossoms and leafage, Armand and Gross, Paris, ca1900 (4182/25)	275
Pairpoint Art Nouveau centerpiece, guadruple plate, repousee, figural, L13, ca1910 (4084/165)	125
Salver, Victorian, Messrs. Barnard, circular, scrolled strapwork rim, 12½, 30 ozs, 1870 (4259/129)	*900*
Scent flask, Art Deco, silver-gilt, oval, enamel, glass, French, 2⅞, ca1930 (4194/366)	275
Service of flatware, Art Deco, flat tapered terminals, beveled edges, monogrammed, German, ca1930, 98 pcs (4230/256)	1000
Soup Tureen and cover, French, octagonal form, chased with volutes, ogees, 46 ozs, 10 dwts, Diam 11¾, ca1930 (4266/131)	900
Tazza, Arts and Crafts, George Edward & Son, shallow bowl, 13 ozs, Diam 8⅝, 1906 (4266/124)	200

Tea and coffee service and tray 6 pieces, circular with c scroll handles, 31¼ tray, 1935, Mexican, 274 ozs. (4213/130) — 1600

Tea and coffee service, with tray, modern, oval form, Mexican, 31' (tray) (4230/258) — 3750

Tea and coffee set, German, 4-piece, each with stylized bud finial, rim support, 68 ozs, 10 dwts, 10, ca1910 (4266/117) — 2500

Tea and coffee set, Victorian, 4 pc, E & J Barnard, bulbous circular bodies, 71 ozs, 11, 1852 (4194/125) — 1700

Tea kettle on lampstand, cylindrical, 3 paw supports, 37 ozs, 11¾, 1884 (4194/264) — 300

Tea kettle on lampstand, W. and G. Sissons, spherical, engraved, strapwork, foliage, 11¾, 41 ozs, 1879 (4259/121) — 800

Tea set, 3 pcs, E.E.J. & W. Barnard, inverted compressed pear shape, 7½, teapot, 52 ozs, 1841 (4259/120) — 1300

Tray, Austrian, oval form, fluted everted rim, 105 ozs, 5 dwts, L31, ca1930 (4266/132) — 1300

Tureen soup and cover, Martin & Hall, oval beaded borders, Victorian, 14, 54 ozs, 1876 (4259/116) — 2200

Tureen soup and cover
(4259/116)

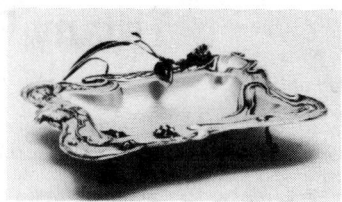

Basket (4182/2)

Vases, bud, pair, cylindrical form with enamel, Arts and crafts, ca1906, 4½ (4182/60) — 225

Wine coaster, English, blue and green enamel, 'Cymric', Liberty & Co., ca1905, 4¾ (4182/62) — 500

Wine cooler, Victorian, John S. Hunt, circular, 141 ozs, 10 dwts, 10½, 1844 (4194/129) — 4750

Austrian

Basket, silver footed, four flower molded feet, flowing leaves, ca1900, 14 (4182/2) — 575

Dish, silver serving, square, berry laden branch, dragonfly, ca1900, 12¾ (4182/3) — 425

Continental

Ice bucket, silver plate Art Deco, cylindrical, incised reeding, angular handle, 10, ca1910 (4230/263) — 425

Vase, flower, hammered surface, 3 stylized flowerheads, foliage, 8d⅞, ca1925, maker's mark, Brilohne (4230/243) — 125

Danish

Bowl, footed, large, bell form, pod and leaf stem, Georg Jensen, ca1930, 6⅝ (4182/11) — 750

Bowl, silver footed, bell form, open work, pod and leaf stem, Georg Jensen, ca1930 (4182/14) — 250

Candelabra, 2 light, pair, bell shaped sconces, leaf forms, Georg Jensen, ca1920, 6½ (4182/10) — 900

Carving set, knife and fork, ovoid handle, stylized flowers, leaves, 12 - 13½, ca1935, Georg Jensen (4230/248) — 125

Dish, entree and cover, circular dish, domed cover, hammered surface, 12½, Georg Jensen (4230/249) — 1100

Dish, meat, oval, stylized flowerheads, inner scalloped band, 19½, ca1930, Georg Jensen (4230/246) — 600

Dish, two-handled, footed, rosewood insets, Georg Jensen, L15¼, ca1925 (4182/20) — 600

Goblet, Art Deco., waisted tapered cyl. form, hammered surface, 4¾, ca1927, Heimbruger (4230/244) — 100

Pitcher, silver water, rounded-tapered cylindrical form, Georg Jensen, ca1925, 5¾ (4182/18) — 275

Platter, silver fish, oval, molded rim, flower pods and tendrils, Georg Jensen, modern, 19½ (4182/15) — 550

Tazza, silver, grape clusters, Georg Jensen, ca1925, 7¼ (4182/9) — 600

Tea and coffee set, hammered surfaces, short spouts, ebonized handles, 7½, ca1930, Georg
Jensen (4230/251)   1400
Tray, oval, rope twist molded border, 11, ca1920, Georg Jensen (4230/247)   150
Tray, silver serving, rectangular form, Georg Jensen, ca1920, 14¾ (4182/13)   550

English

Candlesticks, table, short, Art Deco., 3 openwork panels of diagonal ribbing, 3, ca1930 (4230/240)   250
Dishes, sweetmeat, pair, silver and enamel, form butterflies, hand hammered, 7⅛, ca1913
(4230/237)   250
Jewelry casket, beveled square form, cover set with turquoises, 4⅝, ca1900, Liberty & Co.
(4230/239)   400
Tray, serving, rectangular form, turquoise bosses, 15⅛, ca1908, Liberty & Co. (4230/241)   400

German

Tea, coffee set, matching tray, wood finials, angular handles, ca1930 (4182/5)   1300

Jensen, Georg

Pitcher, sterling, C-scroll handle, designed by Johan Ronde, H9, ca1920 (4084/176)   750

Tiffany Products

Assorted objects

Bowl, flower and frog, Favrile glass, shallow bowl, rolled rim, double frog, 11½, ca1916, frog dam
(4213/237)   425
Bowl, Favrile glass, deep blue iridescent, ruffled lip, ribbed body, 6¾, 1892-1928 (4213/240)   375
Brooch, gold, enamel and diamond, openwork scrolled ribbon, L2, ca1880 (4194/378)   1500
Chandelier, Favrile glass and bronze, bands of yellow streaked opal rippled glass tiles, 12¼, 1899-
1920 (4213/252)   600
Clock, garniture, cloisonne and gilt, bronze, pair urn and clock, colorful foliate cloisonne ground, 14,
clock, 10 urn, L19c (669/395)   2000
Clock, garniture, gilt bronze, enamel, clock's dial set in turtle, with candleabra pair, L19c (619/300)   6750
Clock, gilt bronze, rectangular case, panelled sides, unusual, 5⅞, ca1925, battery operated
(4213/241)   *400*

Vase (4213/239)

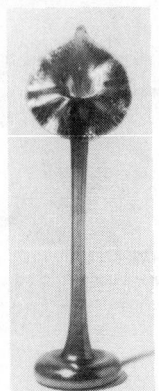

Clock (4213/241)   Bowl (4182/399)

Desk set, gilt bronze, abalone pattern, 1899-1920, 10 pcs, insert lacking (4213/272)   475
Desk set, gilt bronze, modeled design, 1899-1920, 12 pcs (4213/281)   850
Garniture, basalt and veined marble, surmounted with sphinx flanked by pair obelisks, 16½, ca1900,
Tiffany & Co. (669/404)   2000
Jar, jelly, Favrile glass and silver, amber, intaglio, carved with floral swags, 6, 1892-1928 (4213/249)   400
Laburnum lamp, bronze, domical shade, H32½ x D21 1/3, 1899-1920 (4145/215)   32000
Lamp, black eyed Susan, Favrile Glass, bronze, all over design of black-eyed Susan blossoms, 27½
x 16, 1899-1920 (4213/270)   9500
Lamp, bridge, Favrile glass and bronze, domical green damascene shade, 55½ x 10, 1899-1920
(4213/263)   2000

Lamp, bridge, Favrile glass and bronze, with green striated feather devices, and amber, 55 x 1¼, 1899-1920 (4213/283) — 1200

Lamp, candlestick pair, Favrile glass and silvered metal, flaring shade with ruffled rim, 12¾, 1899-1920, 1 res. (4213/286) — 900

Lamp, daffodil, Favrile glass and bronze, conical shade, blooming daffodils and leafage, 24½ x 20, 1899-1920 (4213/282) — 10000

Lamp, desk, Art Nouveau, iridescent glass, Tiffany gilt bronze, shperical shade, amber, 18 x 6, 20c (4213/233) — 700

Lamp, desk, Favrile, glass and bronze, turtleback tile, pivoting shade, 14¾, 1899-1928, protective glass cracked (4213/259) — 2000

Lamp, dragonfly miniature, Favrile glass, gilt bronze on a mushroom base, 17½ x 14, 1899-1920 (4213/264) — 8000

Lamp, floor, Favrile glass and bronze, dome shade, green, amber and opalescent tiles, 77 x 24½ (4213/267) — 8500

Lamp, floor, Favrile glass and bronze, domical shade, bands of mottled green and amber, 77 x 24½, 1899-1920 (4213/244) — *9500*

Lamp, floor, Favrile glass and bronze, geometric domical shade, panels of amber tiles, 77 x 24½, 1899-1920 (4213/257) — 5250

Lamp, floor, Favrile glass and gilt bronze, yellow cabbage rose, blossoms and leafage, 64½, 1899-1920 (4213/287) — 20000

Lamp, student, Favrile glass and bronze, two domical shades, gold iridescent zipper pattern, 29 x 10, ca1900, 1 res. (4213/250) — 1500

Lamp, Favrile glass and bronze, bands of mottled green tiles, 21½, 1899-1920 (4213/245) — 2200

Lamp, Favrile glass and bronze dogwood border, green glass tiles, white and pink blossoms and leafage, 31½ x 20½, 1899-1920 (4213/276) — 7250

Lamp, 3 light lily, Favrile glass, bronze circular base, amber shades, 12¾, 1899-1920 (4213/265) — 1600

Lamp, 3 light lily, Favrile glass, bronze circular base, amber shades, 12¾, 1899-1920 (4213/254) — 1800

Mantel clock, ormolu and marble, trophy raised on sphinxes, 14, Louis XV, style (4142/54) — 750

Planter, gilt bronze, shallow vessel, ring turnings, arabasque devices, 10½, 1899-1920, lacking liner (4213/260) — 125

Smoking stand, bronze bamboo, molder, two holders and match holder, 26½, 1899-1920, dish support dam (4213/262) — 375

Vase, diatreta, Favrile glass, flaring yellow glass Vase, green feathering, 6¼, 1899-1920 (4213/266) — 1000

Vase, floriform, Favrile glass, deep blue, oviform shape, ribbed exterior, 9¼, ca1912 (4213/279) — 475

Vase, floriform, Favrile glass, pyriform bowl, silvery blue, green leafage, 8¾, 1912 (4213/278) — 1200

Vase, jack in the pulpit, Favrile glass, restrained flower head with pointed upper section, 20, ca1908, unusual (4213/239) — *1500*

Vase, red Favrile glass, baluster, deep red with deep blue and amber, 10½, 1918 (4213/280) — 5000

Vase, Favrile glass, amber, outward flaring rim, ribbed body, 9¾, 1892-1928 (4213/277) — 300

Vase, Favrile glass, amber, waisted vessel with flaring lip, flower supports, 4⅛, ca1919 (4213/251) — 400

Vase, Favrile glass, baluster vessel, deep canary yellow iridescent, green, 8¾, ca1904 (4213/247) — 1600

Vase, Favrile glass, transparent opalescent glass, flaring rim, 13⅞, ca1907 (4213/242) — 900

Vase, Favrile glass, trumpet-form, amber and green iridescent, 11¾, ca1915 (4213/256) — 600

Tiffany glass

Base, lamp, bronze, dished circular base, 25, 1899-1920 (4230/733) — 3500

Bowl, flower and frog Favrile glass, and bronze amber iridescence, green leafage, ca1910, 3¼ (4182/671) — 500

Bowl, flower with frog, Favrile glass, amber, green vines, leafage, ca1918, 11¼, rep (4182/595) — 400

Bowl, footed, Favrile glass, amber iridescence, ca1892-1928 (4182/377) — 225

Bowl, footed, Favrile glass, pastel rim, ca1919, 4¾ (4182/390) — 350

Bowl, Favrile, amber iridescent shallow sides, flaring rim, 9⅞, ca1921, original paper label (4230/751) — 300

Bowl, Favrile, classical urn form, scrolling shell handles, 4½, ca1912 (4266/440) — 400

Bowl, Favrile, deep hemispherical bowl, lobed rim, Diam 10, 1899-1920 (4266/413) — 350

Bowl, Favrile glass, amber iridescent, shallow, everted rim, ribbed sides, 9¾, 1892-1928 (4230/753) — 375

Bowl, Favrile glass, pale amber iridescent, everted scalloped rim, 8¾, 1892-1928 (4230/754) — 350

Bowl, Favrile glass, shallow, brillant amber iridescence, ca1892-1928, 12 (4182/628) — 175

Bowl, Favrile glass, wide mouth amber iridescent, waisted neck, 6¾, 1892-1928 (4230/748) — 350

Bowl, Favrile glass, intaglio, millefiore decoration, ca1907, 8 (4182/399) — *2000*

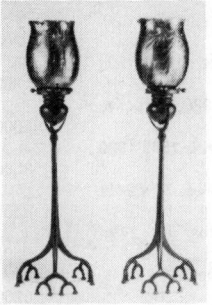

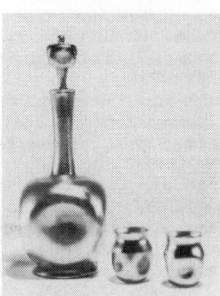

Candlesticks   Desk set (4182/389)   Decanter (4182/373)
(4182/640)

Bowl, Favrile glass, intaglio-carved, meandering leafage, amber, ca1892-1928 9¾ (4182/404)	450
Bowl, Favrile glass, intaglio-carved, ribbed form, amber iridescent, 8½, 1892-1928 (4230/798)	375
Box, enamel-on-copper covered, Favrile, circular, hinged, impressionistic, Diam 6½, after 1900 (4266/463)	2800
Bridge lamp, counter-balance, bronze, Damascene shade, H45 x D10, 1899-1920 (4145/221)	2000
Bud vase, Favrile glass, enameled bronze, H13, ca1920 (4145/229)	300
Bud vase, Favrile glass, enamelled bronze, trumpet-form, ca1899-1920, 11 (4182/393)	225
Bud vase, Favrile glass, gilt bronze, trumpet-form ribbed, ca1899-1920 (4182/387)	275
Cabinet, cameo glass, deep yellow, baluster, Fine, H3, ca1906 (4145/243)	2200
Candelabra, gilt bronze, Favrile, 4 arms, each with 2 candle sockets, 14¼, 1899-1920 (4266/421)	800
Candelabrum, Favrile glass and bronze, three light, green glass extrusions, ca1899-1920, 15⅛ good (4182/615)	1500
Candelabrum, 6 light, Favrile glass, bronze, H15¾, 1899-1920 (4145/202)	5750
Candelabrum, 6 light standing, Favrile glass and bronze, 5 legged support, 49, 1899-1920 (4229/62)	9000
Candlestick, bronze, Favrile glass, H8⅞, 1899-1920 (4145/220)	400
Candlestick, Favrile glass and bronze, green glass, 3 outward flaring legs, ca1892-1920, 10 (4182/651)	550
Candlestick, Favrile, bronze, panelled bell-form shade, 13½, 1899-1920 (4266/405)	900
Candlestick, Favrile, gilt bronze, candle socket cast as a flower pod, 15, 1899-1920 (4266/425)	400
Candlestick, 2 light, Favrile glass, bronze, lily form base, ca1899-1920 (4182/369)	600
Candlestick, 6 arm bronze, spreading dish foot, 20½, 1899-1920 (4230/801)	1000
Candlestick lamp, Favrile, gilt bronze, oval base, short stem, 4 bulbous socket supports, 15½, 1899-1920 (4266/433)	1800
Candlestick paperweight, floriform, Favrile glass, spreading foot, 4¼, ca1921 (4230/756)	750
Candlesticks, pair Favrile glass, and bronze tulip shape green, blue iridescence, ca1892-1928, 17¾ (4182/640)	*2300*
Candlesticks, pair, gilt bronze, shaped leaf form base, scrolling stem, 7½, 1899-1928 (4229/35)	850
Candlesticks, Favrile glass, pair, ovoid candle cup, short knopped, standard, 3¾, ca1920, original paper labels (4230/783)	425
Candlesticks, Favrile, pair, spirally-ribbed contour, ca1892-1928, 5 (4182/384)	350
Candlesticks, Favrile, pair, spirally-ribbed contour, ca1892-1928, 5¼ (4182/385)	175
Chandelier, Favrile glass, mosaic tile, bronze, ca1899-1920 (4182/367)	5500
Chandelier, peony, Favrile glass, bronze, D24½, 1899-1920 (4145/228)	17000
Chandelier, turtle back, Favrile glass, gilt bronze, important, ca1899-1920, 18, rare (4182/363)	26000
Chandelier, Favrile, bronze bouquet, conical shade, beaded border, trumpet blossoms, Diam 28¼, †1899-1920 (4266/386)	40000
Chandelier, Favrile, bronze poinsettia, in deep red, magenta, blue, green, Diam 25½, 1899-1920 (4266/472)	35000
Cigarette box, covered, Favrile glass, with bronze, pine needle pattern, ca1899-1920, 7 (4182/665)	275
Clock, gilt bronze and enamel, 4 ball feet, ca1899-1920 (4182/380)	850
Comport, Favrile, demi-lune body, H5, ca1912 (4145/224)	350
Comport, gilt bronze, circular bowl, opalescent jewels, ca1899-1920, 6½ diameter (4182/364)	110

Comport, Favrile, flaring shallow bowl, spreading foot, 4½, 1892-1928 (4266/476) — 400
Comport, Favrile glass, amber iridescent, ruffled rim, circular foot, 5¼, ca1916 (4230/755) — 475
Comport, Favrile glass, amber, spherical bowl, flaring, ruffled rim, 4¾, ca1909 (4230/789) — 350
Comport, Favrile glass, orange iridescence, ruffled rim, ca1907, 4¼ (4182/391) — 250
Comport, Favrile glass, shallow bowl sloping rim, ca1892-1928, 4½ (4182/664) — 200
Comport, Favrile glass, spherical bowl, amber iridescence, ca1910 (4182/625) — 200
Comport, Favrile glass (unusual), shallow, 9¾, ca1920, inscribed sample approved A.J. Nash
(4230/747) — 325
Counter balance bridge lamp, linen fold shade, bronze, H53 x D9, 1899-1920 (4145/242) — 550
Counter balance lamp, Claflin, bronze, H14 x D7, 1899-1920 (4145/238) — 1500
Cup, 3-handled, Favrile, 3 applied angular C-scroll handles, 5¾, ca1908 (4266/376) — 800
Cups, set of 12 punch, Favrile glass, slightly spherical bowl, amber iridescent, ca1909 (4230/780) — 2100
Daffodil lamp, Favrile glass, gilt bronze, H26 x D19, 1899-20 (4145/199) — 9000
Decanter, eleven sherries, Favrile glass, lily pad bosses, ca1902, 12 pcs (4182/642) — 1400
Decanter, 12 liqueurs, Favrile, amber iridescence, ca1892-1928, decanter 9½ (4182/373) — *1900*
Decanter and stopper, Favrile, applied iridescent lily pads and tendrils, 8¾, res, ca1895 (4266/398) — 750
Decanter and stopper, Favrile glass, double gourd form body, slender tapering neck, 11, ca1904
(4229/41) — 450
Desk articles, Favrile glass, pinecone pattern, 1899-1920 (4145/227) — 200
Desk set, Favrile glass, bronze, grapevine pattern, 9 pcs, 1899-1920 (4145/217) — 375
Desk set, bronze, 12 pcs, Chinese pattern, with lamp (damaged), ca1899-1920 (4182/389) — *3000*
Desk set, grapevine pattern, 11 pcs, Favrile glass, gilt bronze, ca1899-1920, cr (4182/368) — 850
Dish, glass, Favrile glass, shallow circular body, amber iridescent, 9, 1899-1928 (4230/772) — 425
Dragonfly lamp, bronze, circular dish base, H23 x D17, 1899-1920 (4145/213) — 8000
Dragonfly lamp, drop-head, on rare pierced arched base, Favrile glass, H30 x D22, 1899-1920
(4145/210) — 20000
Dragonfly lamp, drop-head, Favrile glass, bronze, domical shade, H32 x D22, 1899-1920
(4145/206) — 21000
Floor lamp, Favrile glass, gilt bronze, laburnum, domical, H75 x D24, 1899-1920 (4145/198) — 42000
Floor lamp, geometric, Favrile glass, gilt bronze, domical shade, H77 x D24½, 1899-1920
(4145/207) — 11000
Flower bowl, Favrile glass, D10½, ca1918 (4145/201) — 950
Flower bowl, Favrile glass, flower frog, D10, ca1919 (4145/239) — 400
Inkstand, Favrile glass, gilt bronze, concentric squares, ca1899-1920, 7½ (4182/637) — 500
Jack-in-pulpit vase, circular base, H19¾, ca1913 (4145/231) — 2100
Lamp, oak leaf with acorn bell, bronze, H24 x 18, 1899-1920 (4145/212) — 6250
Lamp, Favrile glass, bell-form, H14¼ x D7, 1899-1920 (4145/200) — 1600
Lamp, base, bridge, harp-shaped support, H55, 1899-1920 (4145/226) — 450
Lamp, arrowroot, Favrile glass and bronze, ca1899-1920, 25 (4182/376) — 9000
Lamp, base floor, leaf molded cylindrical, raised on 4 petal feet, ca1899-1920 64 (4182/657) — 2600
Lamp, base, bronze, candlestick, bamboo turned cylindrical, ca1900-1920, 10¼ (4182/668) — 300
Lamp, bridge, Favrile glass and bronze, ca1899-1920, 4' 11½' (4182/365) — 2100
Lamp, bridge Favrile glass and bronze, floral pierced banding, counter balance, ca1899-1920 4' 8'
(4182/677) — 750
Lamp, bridge, acorn shade, Favrile glass, and bronze amber, green tiles, ca1899-1920, 4' 10'
(4182/610) — 5250
Lamp, bridge, favrile glass and bronze, green iridescence, with blue amber, ca1899-1920, 4' 8'
(4182/667) — 2000
Lamp, bridge, Favrile glass, bronze, domical blue iridescent damascene shade, 56½ x 8⅛, 1899-
1920 (4230/792) — 4000
Lamp, bridge, Favrile glass and gilt, bronze, 2 butterflies, and dragonfly, 55 x 9¾, 1899-1920
(4230/770) — 2000
Lamp, bridge, Favrile glass, bronze, harp supports, circular base, ca1899-1920, 4' 7', rim chip
(4182/620) — 650
Lamp, candlestick, Favrile glass, H14¾ x 7¾, 1892-1928 (4145/208) — 850
Lamp, candlestick, Favrile glass, gilt bronze, flaring shade, ruffled rim,(4229/46) — 1500
Lamp, cherry blossoms, miniature, Favrile glass and bronze, domical shade, 17, 1899-1920
(4229/48) — 28000
Lamp, daffodil Favrile glass and bronze, conical shade, blooming daffodils, 20, 1925 (4230/797) — 9750
Lamp, dragonfly Favrile glass and, bronze, rare mosaic dragonfly base, 17½, ca1900 (4230/802) — 57000
Lamp, dragonfly, Favrile glass, gilt bronze, shade set randomly with 'jewels', 26¼, 1899-1920
(4229/69) — 11000

Lamp, floor, candlestick, 4 light, Favrile glass and bronze, very rare, 66¼, 1899-1920, important (4229/32) — 8750

Lamp, intaglio-carved, Favrile glass, domical shade, on stepped circular base, 15½, 1892-1928, chip upper rim (4229/47) — 1900

Lamp, linen fold, Favrile glass, gilt, bronze, 10 amber fold panel, ca1899-1920, 22 (4182/669) — 2100

Lamp, linen fold, Favrile glass, gilt bronze, amber American Indian base, ca1899-1920 12½ (4182/612) — 1400

Lamp, linen fold, Favrile glass, gilt bronze, molded at top with berries, ca1892-1920, 16¼ (4182/626) — 1400

Lamp, linen fold, Favrile glass, twelve amber panels, base with abalone shells, 17, 1899-1920 (4229/42) — 2400

Lamp, lotus flowering, Favrile glass, bronze, umbrella form, Extremely fine, rare, H25 (4145/197) — 60000

Lamp, ninth century, Favrile glass, gilt bronze, 12 sided shade, 17¾, 1899-1920 (4229/31) — 13000

Lamp, orange poppy, Favrile glass, bronze, blossoming poppy blossoms, green leafage, 25¼, 1899-1920 (4229/49) — 8000

Lamp, parasol, green, Favrile glass, bronze, domical, mottled green glass tiles, 30¾, 1899-1920 (4229/63) — 12000

Lamp, peony-Favrile glass, bronze, domical shade, circular dish base, lug feet, 22, 1899-1920 (4229/70) — 25000

Lamp, piano 3 light lily, bronze, amber iridescent lily shades, 8, 1899-1920 (4230/785) — 1900

Lamp, prism, Favrile glass, amber, iridescent shade and prisms, 26, 1899-1920 (4229/50) — 5000

Lamp, prism, Favrile glass and bronze, ribbed top, rising to knopped finial, 25½, 1899-1920 (4229/53) — 2500

Lamp, red and pink poppy Favrile glass, filigree decoration, 22½, 1899-1920 (4230/752) — 5500

Lamp, red julip, Favrile glass, bronze, domical shade, raised circular base, 26, 1899-1920 (4229/60) — 30000

Lamp, spreading cherry tree, Favrile glass, bronze, Good, H30½ x D25, 1899-1920 (4145/205) — 38000

Lamp, stained glass, and bronze, acorn, raised on 5 ball feet, has finial, E20c 20 (4182/587) — 2600

Lamp, student lamp, 2 light, bronze, Favrile glass, dart molded, domed, circular base, 20, 1899-1920 (4229/55) — 1600

Lamp, table, Favrile glass and bronze raised on 5 feet, ca1899-1920, 13¾ (4182/386) — 1200

Lamp, table, adjustable, Favrile glass, bronze, ca1899-1920, 22½, rim chip (4182/616) — 2500

Lamp, table, Favrile, domical shade, baluster standard, 16¾, Diam 10, 1899-1920 (4266/406) — 2250

Lamp, table, Favrile glass and bronze, bell form support, 11¾, 1899-1920 (4230/799) — 1700

Lamp, table, Favrile glass and bronze, green damescene shade, amber lappets, ca1899-1920 13¾ good (4182/596) — 1600

Lamp, table, Favrile glass and bronze, green damescene shade, ribbed base, ca1899-1920 (4182/624) — 1500

Lamp, turtle back tile, Favrile glass, gilt bronze, 3 rows amber iridescent tiles, 31½, 1899-1920 (4230/786) — 6000

Lamp, Favrile, bell-form shape, zipper pattern, finial, 14½, Diam 7½, 1899-1920 (4266/439) — 450

Lamp, Favrile glass and bronze, amber, pale green, alabaster damascene shade, 13, 1899-1920 (4230/794) — 950

Lamp, Favrile glass and bronze, domical shade green mottled glass, L19c, 20½, unusual (4182/670) — 3200

Lamp, Favrile glass and bronze, domical, amber, iridescent shade, ca1899-1920, 4' 9½' (4182/411) — 1900

Lamp, Favrile glass and bronze, geometric, leaf molded cir, base, ca188-1920, 22½ (4182/655) — 4250

Lamp, Favrile glass and bronze, geometric, turtle back tile band, ca1899-1920, 23½ (4182/644) — 7000

Lamp, Favrile glass and bronze, green lotus leaf, shade 5 ball feet, ca1899-1920, fine (4182/685) — *18500*

Lamp, Favrile glass and bronze, maple leaf shade, tree trunk base, H34½, 1899-1920 (4182/603) — *33000*

Lamp, Favrile glass and bronze, orange poppy, with filigree overlay, ca1899-1920, 26½ (4182/388) — 9000

Lamp, Favrile glass and bronze, pansy border, ca1899-1920, 21 (4182/649) — *11500*

Lamp (4182/685)

Lamp (4182/603)

Lamp (4182/649)

Lamp, Favrile glass and bronze, poinsettia border, leafage, ca1899-1920, 24 (4182/617)   *13000*
Lamp, Favrile glass and gilt bronze, helmet form shade, ca1899-1920 (4182/666)   32000

Lamp (4182/617)

Lamp, Favrile glass, and gilt bronze, amber, harp shaped support, ca1899-1920, 13½ rim chip (4182/600)   850
Lamp, Favrile glass, bronze, blue ground poinsettia border, ca1899-1920 (4182/408)   12500
Lamp, Favrile, bronze, blown glass shade, spiralling tendrils on standard, 22, Diam 19½, 1892-1920 (4266/424)   3400
Lamp, Favrile, bronze, wisteria blossoms and leafage, tree trunk, standard, 26½, 1899-1920 (4266/404)   69000
Lamp, Favrile, bronze bridge, amber iridescent and green shade, 58, Diam 12, 1899-1920 (4266/407)   2650
Lamp, Favrile, bronze bridge, deep blue, domical, iridescent shade, 57 x 12, 1899-1920 (4266/461)   1700
Lamp, Favrile, bronze bridge, domical green iridescent glass, 54, 1899-1920 (4266/469)   1400
Lamp, Favrile, bronze dogwood, sloping standard molded with ribbon, 25 x 18, 1899-1920 (4266/443)   13500
Lamp, Favrile, bronze dragonfly, 7 dragonflies, sharply conical shade, 25½, 1899-1920 (4266/371)   16500
Lamp, Favrile, bronze geometric, 3 arm serpentine support, 22½ x 16, 1899-1920 (4266/449)   3500
Lamp, Favrile, bronze linenfold, composed of 10 amber linen-fold panels, 23½, Diam 15¾, after 1913 (4266/392)   2800

Lamp, Favrile, bronze nasturtium, shades of mottled pink, orange, green, 25½, Diam 20, 1899-1920 (4266/438) — 10500

Lamp, Favrile, bronze nasturtium, shallow domical shade, circular base, 4 pad feet, Diam 20, 1899-1920 (4266/400) — 8500

Lamp, Favrile, bronze peony, adjustable standard, 5 petal molded feet, 27½, Diam 22 (4266/460) — 25000

Lamp, Favrile, bronze peony border floor, cylindrical standard, 5 pad feet, 78, Diam 24, 1899-1920 (4266/393) — 35000

Lamp, Favrile, gilt bronze, amber iridescent shade, Venetian-style, 17½, 1899-1920 (4266/458) — 2000

Lamp, Favrile, gilt bronze, domical iridescent shade, harp-shaped support, 18½, Diam 8, 1899-1920 (4266/435) — 1000

Lamp, Favrile, gilt bronze, shade of 24 green linen-fold panels, 25, Diam 18¾, ca1915 (4266/453) — 10000

Lamp, Favrile, gilt bronze Harvard, octagonal shade, 4 Virtues base, 25½ x 20, 1899-1920 (4266/467) — 7000

Lamp, Favrile, gilt-metal candlestick, ruffled amber iridescent shade, 12¼, 1898-1928 (4266/462) — 550

Lamp, Russian, Favrile glass, bronze, conical shade, band of 7 roundels, 26, 1899-1920 (4230/761) — 13000

Lamp, 10 light lily, Favrile glass and bronze, ca1899-1920, some chip (4182/379) — *6000*

Lamp, 10 light lily, Favrile glass, circular base with lily pads, 21¼, base regilded, 1899-1920 (4230/736) — 7000

Lamp, 18 light lily, Favrile glass, gilt bronze, base, lily pads and buds, 19½, 1899-1920, 2 shades (4229/52) — 20000

Lamp, 2 light, student lamp, Favrile glass and bronze, 25¾, 1899-1920 (4229/51) — 2200

Lamp, 3 light lily, Art Nouveau, iridescent glass and Tiffany bronze, 13, 1899-1920 (4229/43) — 1500

Lamp, 3 light, lily piano, Favrile glass, amber iridescent lily shade, 8, 1899-1920 (4230/796) — 1700

Lamp, 3-light lily, bronze, Favrile glass, impressed and inscribed, 20½, 1899-1920 (4159/106) — 1400

Lamps, pair, Favrile glass, bell form shade, pale green, deep amber, ca1899-1920 (4182/684) — 2900

Lily floor lamp base, gilt bronze, 12 light, H56, 1899-1920 (4145/209) — 4250

Lily lamp, 18 light, Favrile glass, H20, 1899-1920 (4145/218) — 9000

Nasturtium lamp, bronze, animal paw feet, H31½ x D21¾, 1899-1920 (4145/246) — 39000

Nasturtium lamp, bronze, domical shade, Very fine (4145/214) — 16000

Nut bowl, Favrile, pastel, sloping sides, D5¼ (4145/230) — 100

Panel, mosaic, Favrile glass, two parrots alighting on branch, exotic tree, 44, 1892-1928, very fine (4229/61) — 18000

Paperweight vase, millefiore decoration, H4¼, ca1904 (4145/236) — 2000

Picture frame, gilt bronze, Favrile glass, 12⅜ x 14¼, 1899-1920 (4145/222) — 375

Picture frame, gilt bronze, Favrile, Venetian pattern, 11¾ x 8¾, 1899-1920 (4266/426) — 300

Picture frame, rectangular, bronze and abolone, ca1899-1928, H10¼ (4182/378) — 300

Pitcher, intaglio-carved, Favrile glass, cylindrical contour with short spout, 7⅝, 1892-1928 (4230/737) — 600

Poppy lamp, bronze, orange, conical shade, lacy filigree, H22 x D16½, 1899-1920 (4145/237) — 11000

Salts, four, Favrile glass, amber iridescence, ruffled crimped rims, 2½, 1892-1928 (4230/732) — 500

Salts, six, Favrile, amber iridescence with ruffled rims, 2½, 1892-1928 (4230/759) — 600

Shade, belt, Favrile glass and bronzed dogwood, ca1899-1920, 21½ (4182/362) — 6500

Shade, geometric, Favrile glass, bronze, D16, 1899-1920 (4145/204) — 1100

Shade, Favrile, gilt bronze, irregular border of dragonflies, Diam 22, 1899-1920 (4266/418) — 13000

Shades, Favrile glass, six, lily, ca1899-1920 (4182/634) — 2700

Sherries, set of 6, amber, bell form bowls, Favrile, ca1892-1928 4 (4182/403) — 600

Sketch, watercolor, for a mausoleum, 15 x 22, E20c (4145/233) — 450

Student lamp, 2 light, bronze, waisted shade, H19 x D7, 1899-1920 (4145/216) — 2600

Tazza, intaglio-carved, Favrile glass, shallow circular bowl, ruffled and flaring rim, 10, ca1901 (4229/34) — 550

Tazza, Favrile glass, shallow circular bowl, ruffled flaring rim, 8¼, 1892-1928 (4229/54) — 600

Tray, circular, gilt bronze, D14, 1899-1920 (4145/244) — 100

Vase, sloping vessel, ca1904, 6¼ (4182/673) — 400

Vase, Favrile glass, bottle form, H9⅜, ca1904 (4145/225) — 1000

Vase, Favrile glass, gilt bronze, H25, 1899-1920 (4145/223) — 750

Vase, agate Favrile glass, expanding vessel, yellow, opaque glass, 7⅛, ca1895 (4230/768) — 1800

Vase, black, Favrile glass, bulging ovoid contour, feather devices at base, 6½, ca1902, very fine (4230/745) — 2800

Vase, bud, Favrile, of elongated teardrop form, green feathering, 12, ca1915 (4266/378) — 700

Vase, bud, Favrile glass, alabaster glass, feather devices, ca1919, 10½ (4182/636) — 250

Vase, bud, Favrile glass, amber iridescent, trumpet-form, ca1916 10¼ (4182/594) — 300

Vase, bud, Favrile glass, millefiore decorations, bulbous form, 5⅛, ca1906 (4230/782) — 1300

Vase, bud, Favrile glass, pyriform vessell, deep blue iridescence, ca1917 8 (4182/682) — 300

Vase, bud, Favrile glass and bronze, amber iridescence, green feathers, ca1899-1920, 13¾ (4182/680) — 350

Vase, cabinet, Favrile glass, hemispherical form, amber iridescence, ca1892-1928, 2¾ (4182/646) — *700*

Vase, carved, intaglio, Favrile glass, amber, iridescent, trumpet-form knopped stem, 12¼, ca1917 (4230/735) — 750

Vase, cypriote, decorated, Favrile glass, avocado green baluster vessel, 6¼, ca1916, good (4230/746) — 5750

Vase, cypriote, Favrile glass, flattened gourd form, 4¾, ca1901, original paper label (4230/787) — 1300

Vase, cypriote, Favrile glass, ovoid vessel, short spreading base, 6, ca1919, fine (4230/744) — 2600

Vase, diatreta, Favile glass, flaring, cylindrical body, pierced latticework, 3, 1892-1928 (4229/40) — 2100

Vase, floriform Favrile, glass, waisted bowl, deeply ruffled rim, domed foot, 15½ (4230/730) — 1100

Vase, floriform, Favrile, deep tulip-form cup, pink opalescence, 12¾, ca1903 (4266/383) — 4250

Vase, floriform, Favrile, elongated bowl, ruffled rim, 13½, 1892-1928 (4266/381) — 1800

Vase, floriform, Favrile, elongated onion form, short knoped stem, 9, ca1918 (4266/368) — 1000

Vase, floriform, Favrile, elongated ovoid body, flaring base, 9¼ (4266/446) — 400

Vase, floriform, Favrile, exaggerated tulip-form cup, slender, 19¾, ca1905 (4266/384) — 10500

Vase, floriform, Favrile, midnight blue, elongated teardrop vessel, ca1917 (4182/374) — 350

Vase, floriform, Favrile glass, amber iridescent ruffled, rim circular domed foot, 11¼, ca1902 (4230/795) — 2100

Vase, floriform, Favrile glass, onion form alabaster cup,(4182/643) — *2300*

Vase, floriform, Favrile glass, waisted onion form vessel, slender stem, 12¾, ca1918 (4229/56) — 2500

Vase, gilt bronze trumpet-form, Favrile, silvery-blue iridescence, 15¾, E20c (4266/456) — 275

Vase, glass floriform, Favrile, hemispherical ribbed body, 11, ca1909 (4266/445) — 700

Vase, glass, intaglio-carved Favrile glass, spherical form, carved, flowers, leafage, 4⅛, ca1894, very fine (4230/738) — 2200

Vase, intagio cameo, lilies of the valley, ca1915 8 (4182/395) — 2100

Vase, intaglio-carved, baluster vessel, H9, ca1917 (4145/240) — 1000

Vase, intaglio-carved, Favrile, baluster form, amber iridescence, 8½, ca1916 (4266/441) — 1300

Vase, intaglio-carved, Favrile, teardrop vessel, ribbed sides, 9, ca1919 (4266/477) — 400

Vase, jack in the pulpit, Favrile glass, ruffled rim, ca1890-1928, 14, unsigned (4182/370) — 1800

Vase, jack in the pulpit, sinuous flowerhead in amber iridescense, 18⅛, ca1907, unusual (4230/764) — *4250*

Vase, jack in the pulpit, Favrile glass, flaring ruffled rim, exaggerated pulled flower face, 13¾, ca1905 (4229/58) — 1800

Vase, jack in the pulpit, Favrile glass, slender stem domed foot, 19¾, ca1913, very fine (4230/742) — 17000

Vase (4182/646)

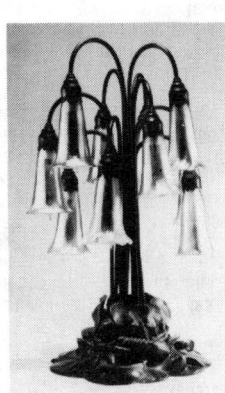

Lamp (4182/379)

Vase cup, (4182/643)

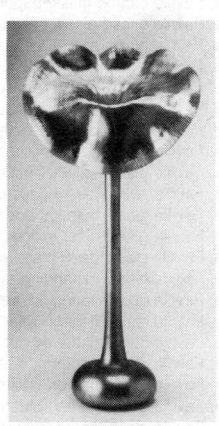

Vase (4230/764)

Vase, jack in the pulpit, Favrile, widely flaring ruffled face, blue-purple iridescence, 21¼, 1897
(4266/363) — 1200

Vase, miniature Favrile glass, amber iridescence, bulging rim, ca1908, 2½ (4182/648) — 300

Vase, miniature, Favrile glass, ovoid green glass vessel, 2¾, ca1902, paper label (4230/750) — 900

Vase, onion-form floriform, Favrile, opalescent, attenuated stem to onion-form base, 16¼, ca1900
(4266/385) — 6500

Vase, paperweight, spherical transparent opalescent vessel, 5, ca1907 (4230/741) — 2100

Vase, paperweight, Favrile, cylindrical vessel, bulbous section below rim, 8⅜, 1899-1928, unsigned
(4230/727) — 1000

Vase, paperweight, Favrile glass, globular opal glass body, short waisted neck, 5¼, ca1907
(4229/29) — 6200

Vase, paperweight, Favrile glass, ovoid body, yellow flowers, 6½, ca1906 (4229/67) — 2500

Vase, peacock, Favrile glass, spherical body, high conical foot, 5¼, 1892-1928 (4229/39) — 2000

Vase, rainbow paperweight, Favrile glass, inverted baluster shape, circular foot, 7½, ca1898
(4229/36) — 800

Vase, red Favrile glass, double gourd shape, deep red, to orange red, ca1910, 6½, very fine
(4182/662) — 4200

Vase, trumpet-form, Favrile, knopped stem, raised scrolling ribbing on base, 10, ca1917 (4266/448) — 600

Vase, trumpet-form, Favrile, amber iridescence, short knopped standard, 9½, ca1917 (4266/471) — 350

Vase, trumpet-form, Favrile, striated feather devices, amber iridescence, 14⅞, 1892-1928
(4266/478) — 500

Vase, with millefiore decoration, Favrile, double gourd form, cased thick bittersweet sides, 8⅞,
ca1913 (4266/365) — 4000

Vase, Cypriote, Favrile glass, amber and green pitted surface, ca1919, 3¼, good (4182/661) — 1800

Vase, Favrile, amber gourd-form vessel, 7, 1892-1928 (4266/401) — 80

Vase, Favrile, amber iridescence, green trailing vines, ca1918, 12 (4182/674) — 1100

Vase, Favrile, amber iridescent sides, green leafage, tendrils, 7, ca1902 (4266/465) — 800

Vase, Favrile, baluster contour, amber iridescent sides, 12, ca1917 (4266/468) — 700

Vase, Favrile, deep blue cylindrical vessel, 4¾, ca1904 (4266/364) — 900

Vase, Favrile, exaggerated baluster form, 10, ca1905 (4266/419) — 1000

Vase, Favrile, gourd-form, blue iridescence, 5¼, ca1900 (4266/409) — 400

Vase, Favrile, ovoid body, green heart, clinging vine motifs, 9, 1892-1928 (4266/417) — 475

Vase, Favrile, pale green globular vessel, neck cut down, 5¼, ca1894 (4266/475) — 550

Vase, Favrile, panelled ovoid body, 5½, ca1906 (4266/408) — 275

Vase, Favrile, pyriform vessel, tapering neck, amber iridescence, 9½, ca1916 (4266/479) — 300

Vase, Favrile, squat teardrop vessel, cruciform handle, 6½, chip, 1899-1920 (4266/410) — 175

Vase, Favrile, trumpet-form, alabaster form, 8¼, ca1898 (4266/416) — 250

Vase, Favrile, wide ruffled lip, truncated body, 3½, ca1916 (4266/459) — 175

Vase, Favrile body, baluster body and mouth, waisted neck, 8½, ca1919 (4229/65) — 2100

Vase, Favrile cameo glass, cylindrical form, frosted glass body, 12, ca1908 (4229/68) — 2500

Vase, Favrile cameo glass, paperweight decoration, ca1899-1920, 12½, very fine (4182/660) — 4400

Vase, Favrile cased glass, baluster form flat shoulder, short flaring rim, 8½, 1892-1928 (4229/59) — 2000

Vase, Favrile glass, amber iridescence, green leafage, ca1916, 12 (4182/683) — 800

Vase, Favrile glass, amber iridescence, irregular contour, ca1910, 5¼ (4182/672) — 550

Vase, Favrile glass, amber iridescence, pyriform vessel, ca1917 9 (4182/678) — 650

Vase, Favrile glass, amber iridescent, green leafage and tendrils, ca1917 (4182/602) — 750

Vase, Favrile glass, baluster body with vertical indentation, 7½, ca1900 (4229/33) — 850

Vase, Favrile glass, baluster vessel amber, blue, green, ca1899, 6¼ (4182/394) — 900

Vase, Favrile glass, baluster vessel, deep amber iridescent, ca1906, 6½ (4182/372) — 325

Vase, Favrile glass, blue iridescence, Egyptianesque motifs, ca1906, 8¾ (4182/663) — 2200

Vase, Favrile glass, bulbous body, lobed sides, short lobed foot, 5⅛, ca1916 (4230/740) — 2400

Vase, Favrile glass, clear yellow vessel, scrollwork, ca1921 9¼ (4182/618) — 300

Vase, Favrile glass, deep blue, urn-form vessel, shell-form handles, ca1917, 4¾ (4182/679) — 650

Vase, Favrile glass, expanding cylindrical form lemon yellow, 6¼, ca1903 (4230/758) — 1700

Vase, Favrile glass, flaring lip, short circular base, 7¼, 1892-1928 (4229/25) — 5250

Vase, Favrile glass, flaring, cylindrical body, flat sloping shoulder, 12, 1892-1928 (4229/44) — 1600

Vase, Favrile glass, flattened spherical vessel, waisted shoulder, 6¾ (4230/749) — 800

Vase, Favrile glass, floriform, amber, ribbed sides, circular foot, ca1905, 6½ (4182/606) — 250

Vase, Favrile glass, floriform, wintergree, feather devices, ca1892-1928 14½ (4182/409) — 800

Vase, Favrile glass, golden blue iridescence, ca1899, 10½ (4182/650) — 625

Vase, Favrile glass, gourd form vessel, waisted neck, thumb prints, 8, ca1907 (4229/57) — 750

Vase, Favrile glass, green glass sides enclosing bubbles, 6, base cracked, ca1904 (4230/773) — 400

Vase, Favrile glass, iridescent, arrowheads, H7¼, ca1909 (4182/382) — 1100

Vase, Favrile glass, iridescent, lappet devices, unsigned, ca1892-1928, 7 (4182/381) — 250

Vase, Favrile glass, millefiore decorations, bulbous, 3, ca1906, fine (4230/739) — 2100

Vase, Favrile glass, ovoid form, alabaster, glass body, 9¾, ca1906 (4229/37) — 700

Vase, Favrile glass, ovoid form, Alabaster, glass body, 9¾, ca1906 (4229/38) — 1700

Vase, Favrile glass, ovoid shaped body, sloping shoulder, waisted neck, 9½, 1892-1928 (4230/788) — 750

Vase, Favrile glass, pyriform vessel, 6, ca1900 (4229/30)   2600
Vase, Favrile glass, shouldered, spherical vessel, with waisted neck, 8½, ca1916, very fine (4229/64)   2000
Vase, Favrile glass, trumpet-form, amber iridescence, ca1916, 17⅞ (4182/647)   275
Vase, Favrile glass, vertical leafage, amber iridescence, ca1892-1928, 8⅜ (4182/598)   375
Vase, Favrile glass and bronze, floriform, feather devices, ca1892-1928, 14½ (4182/410)   550
Vase, Favrile glass and gilt bronze, applied scarabs, amber iridescence, ca1899-1920 17½ unusual (4182/675)   550
Vase, Favrile glass, gilt bronze, amber, base molded, enamelled at top, ca1899-1920, 17¾ (4182/607)   400
Vase, Favrile glass, gilt bronze, trumpet-form, amber, green enamel, ca1899-1920, 19 (4182/406)   700
Vase, Favrile glass, intaglio-carved, amber, baluster, green leafage, ca1910 11¼ (4182/407)   1000
Vase, Favrile red glass, deep red ovoid body, waisted neck, circular foot,(4229/26)   5500
Vase, Favrile, coppered bronze, circular stand, 5 paw-foot supports, 16, 1899 (4266/428)   2250
Vase, Favrile, floriform, stand, ruffled rim, opal glass, silvered metal, 13½, 1892-1902 (4266/420)   550
Vase, Favrile, gilt bronze intaglio, amber iridescent trumpet-form, 16, 1899-1920 (4266/415)   1000
Vase, Floriform, Favrile, triangular amber opalescent neck, 18, ca1900 (4266/380)   3000
Vase, jack in the pulpit, Favrile glass, silvery, amber, iridescence, ca1905, 15 (4182/599)   2600
Vase, Tel el Amarna, Favrile glass, baluster body below bulging, black iridescent neck, 7¼, ca1918, fine (4230/743)   3800
Vase, Tel el Amarna, Favrile glass, baluster vessel, deep turquoise, black foot, 16¾, ca1910, good (4229/66)   2750
Vase, Tel el Amarna, Favrile glass, deep aubergine baluster vessel, 10, foot chip, ca1913 (4230/765)   325
Vase, 2 handle Favrile glass, silvery blue, urn formed, 4¾, 1 handle restored, ca1913 (4230/734)   350
Vase, 2-handled, Favrile, amphora-form vessel, 2 scrolling handles, 8, 1899-1920 (4266/411)   225
Vase, 3 handle, Favrile glass, baluster vessel applied scroll handles, 7¼, ca1912, very fine (4229/27)   4250
Vase, 3-handled, Favrile, amber iridescence, green leaves and vines, 5, ca1908 (4266/412)   550
Vases, pair, iridescent glass and bronze, 16¼, E20c (4145/195)   800
Vases, pair, intaglio-carved Favrile glass, inverted trumpet-form, base with green leaf tops, 11⅝, ca1918-19 (4230/781)   1300
Vases, Favrile glass and gilt bronze, pair, trumpet-form striated feather devices, ca1899-1920 11⅝ (4182/614)   550

Tiffany jewelry

Pendant and chain, plique a jour enamel and black opal, ca1890, pendant 1⅜ (4182/108)   3750
Pin bar, enamel and jewel, ca1925 (4182/133)   475
Pin bar, gold plique a jour enamel and jade, ca1910 (4182/132)   425

Tiffany objects du vertu

Candlestick, bronze, cir base, 5 petal molded candlecups, ca1899-1920 8¾ unusual (4182/619)   600
Desk set, bronze, Saracenic pattern traces of enamelling, four pcs, 1899-1920 (4230/784)   550
Desk set, bronze, Zodiac pattern, ca1899-1920, 7 pcs (4182/638)   300
Desk set, bronze, large, Venetian pattern, thirteen pcs, 1899-1920 (4230/793)   2300
Desk set, gilt bronze, 5 pcs, abalone pattern, ca1899-1920 (4182/613)   500
Desk set, gilt bronze, 6 pieces, Adam pattern, ca1899-1920 (4182/402)   400
Desk set, gilt bronze, 8 pieces, Venetian pattern, 1899-1920 (one well miss) (4230/800)   700
Desk set, 4 piece, signs of zodiac, ca1920 (4145/234)   300
Desk set bronze part, 9 pieces, graduate pattern, ca1899-1920 (4182/653)   350
Dish fern, bronze, wide mouthed, slighly waisted sides, marigolds, ca1899-1920, 10¾, rare (4182/641)   2100
Frames, pair, large, gilt bronze, almost square, with gadrooned borders, 20½ x 42½, 1899-1920 (4230/776)   500
Humidor, enamelled, gilt bronze, rectangular form, hinged lid, 7, 1899-1920 (4230/766)   350
Smoking stand, bronze bamboo molded, dish fitted, ca1899-1920, 26¾ (4182/654)   1100

Tiffany silver

Bread and butter plates, set of twelve, plain circular form, everted border, 5⅜, ca1930 (4230/261)   500
Coffee set, 4 pcs, bulbous hexagonal shape, Art Deco, ca1925 (4182/56)   1000
Flatware service, plain pointed terminals, engraved with monogram, 71 pcs, ca1910 (4230/226)   850
Pitcher, water, silver, oriental movement, ca1890, 7¾ (4182/53)   2600
Vase, baluster shape, swirl, fluted, domed base, 4 supports, 21 ca1900 (4230/227)   475
Vase, flower, silver, trumpet-form, ca1915, 15¾ (4182/54)   350
Vase, silver, female masks and strapwork, ca1900, 12 (4182/45)   375
Vase, silver, trumpet shape, ca1900, 19¾ (4182/50)   350
Vases, silver, pair, Art Nouveau, slender tapering cylindrical form, ca1905, 12½ (4182/51)   325
Wine cups, set of twelve, conical form tuck in base, circular foot, 10, ca1930 (4230/260)   400

Chapter 7

Objects of Virtu

"Objects of Virtue" include antique jewelry, watches, portrait miniatures, music boxes, coins and medals and other items whose appeal lies primarily in their small size, fine detailing and intricate workmanship. Most are made with precious metals, frequently silver. Like gold and diamonds, objects of virtue are prized for their ready negotiability by those who seek a hedge against inflation or anticipate a need to move quickly from one country to another.

The most recent object-of-virtue category to become a prominent sales area is antique jewelry. For the first time, the historical importance of jewelry has become significant in determining price. Collectors seek out those pieces which demonstrate a trend or show the influence of one style or period on another.

Cameos, enamels and precious stones cut in out-of-fashion patterns have become important recently as works of art in their own right. As in other categories, pieces identified as the work of known craftsmen sell at a premium.

Watches have also enjoyed a price rise, with emphasis in three areas: early watches—sixteenth- to seventeenth-century European examples and American watches with low serial numbers; complicated watches—those which do more than tell time; and decorative watches —those of unusual form or decorated with scenes. The ordinary gold-case watch, with standard cylinder or lever movement, even if it was wound with a key and was more than one hundred years old, did little more than keep pace with the value of the gold in its body.

Of these, decorative watches have enjoyed the most spectacular price increases. An Ilberg sold for better than twenty times the price of a comparable piece in 1961. Repeaters by Patek Philippe were also sought after. Though they have not reached the price levels of European watches, interest in American watches is nevertheless strong, and with prices for watches of all types increasing steadily, they should make great gains.

Sales of portrait miniatures have grown dramatically in the last two years, with French miniatures remaining strong but generally slightly behind Austrian, German and Swiss examples in price. Among American miniatures the Peale family continued to dominate sales.

Miniatures portraying known subjects signed by known artists brought the highest prices, but Europeans and the general more cautious Americans have grown increasingly willing to purchase the work of unknown European artists. Collectors are prepared to acknowledge quality even if the miniature is by an unknown artist, and Americans will now buy American miniatures even if they are unsigned.

Objects of virtue allow the beginning collector an opportunity to acquire fine objects for a relatively small investment. For collectors who are limited by space and budget, this field offers a good chance to assemble a significant collection, and the dramatic price rises of recent years show that these works can also provide solid growth opportunities.

BOXES AND CASKETS

Box, form of shoe, enamel, pointed high heel, spray of flowers, 4, ca1760, Staffordshire (4141/108)   350
Box, gilt bronze and porcelain mounted, classical profile, portraits, 6, L19c, French (669/249)   350
Box, jewel, form of piano, gilt metal, after Fragonard, THE SWING, 5, Viennese (4160/685)   500
Box, pentagonal silver-gilt and enamel, filigree, pearls, hinged cover, W2½, ca1900, Austrian*
(4160/606)   350
Box, sewing and writing, ebonized wood, mother pearl and gold, 13, ca1860, Victorian (4141/116)   475
Box, shoe form, enamel, sprays of flowers, 3¼, ca1760, rare, Staffordshire (4160/716)   800
Box, silver and enamel, scene naked girl lying in bed reading, 3½, ca1910, good, French (669/268)   1500
Box, silver and plique a jour enamel, with hinged cover, 1¾, ca1900, Scandinavian (4160/686)   350
Box, singing bird, gilt metal and enamel, rectangular, enameled with pastoral scene, has key, German
(4160/595)   1050
Box, toothpick, gold, narrow rectangular form, hinged cover, waved design, 3⅜, ca1800, Swiss
(4238/552)   500
Box, traveling, red leather, brass mounts, London, L16, 1885 (4148/163)   500
Casket, fruitwood, marquetry, rare, one side a drawer, 8¾ x 17¼ x 12¼, M18c, French (4232/57)   *5750*

Casket (4232/57)

Casket, jewel, gilt metal and mosaic, rectangular doves, sprays of flowers, 7, ca1875 (4238/546)   650
Casket, rosewood, brass and mother of pearl, two scent bottles with views of Paris on lids, 4 x 4½,
M19c (4119/214)   150
Casket, silver and tortoiseshell, dome cover, embossed birds and animals, 7, L17/E18c, Spanish
(4141/563)   900
Casket, with music movement, enamel, ebonized wood doors, reveal 3 drawers, 7½, Viennese
(4141/75)   1200
Chest, iron mounted, wood frame, cloth covered, iron straps, keys, Russian, 18, 18c (4193/111)   500
Coffer, cypress wood, carved with lovers, Italian, 20⅞, lock missing, ca1500 (4193/192)   1500
Tea caddy, tortoiseshell ivory and gilt metal, 2 cut glass bottles, annd a cut glass mixing bowl, 12
ca1830 (619/230)   350

BOXES, MUSIC

Box, singing bird, silver and enamel, top painted with a fruit still life, 3¾, ca1900, German (4238/548)   1400
French singing bird, automaton, feathered bird in a gilt metal cage, circular base, 11, ca1910
(669/439)   250
French singing bird, automaton, two colored feathered bird in gilt metal cage, 20¼, ca1910
(669/440)   500
French singing bird, automaton, two feathered birds perched in gilt metal cage, 20, ca1910
(669/441)   500

Music box and clock, gilt bronze, pagoda base, classical figures in landscape, 17, Viennese (619/186) — 2750

Music box, Swiss, inlaid and, ebonized walnut, fifteen and 1 half inch brass drum, L25½, M19c (4216/32) — 500

Music box, Swiss, Paillard, 33.3 cm. cylinder, 12 tunes, rosewood and tulipwood, 26, L19c (4269/36) — 750

Regina metal disc, wood case, with 27 discs, ca1880 (669/436) — 1800

Singing bird box, gilt-metal, enameled in style of Hondecoeter, L3⅞ (4194/361) — 850

Singing bird box, silver-gilt, rectangular, emeralds, pearls, L3¾, L19c (4194/358) — 1000

Singing bird box, silver-gilt, enamel, rectangular, Alpine lake scene, L3¾, M19c (4194/360) — 4500

Swiss interchangeable cylinder, veneered wood case, 3 cylinders, 42, ca1900 (669/437) — 2000

Wood case, cylinder movement, with Jacot's patented safety check, 19, refurbished (669/438) — 650

BOXES, SNUFF

Assorted manufacturers

Box, snuff, brown and gray agate, 2¾, 1761, French (4160/734) — 4000

Box, snuff, cartouche shape, cover chased with cupid at his forge with Venus, 3, 1727-32, French (4238/556) — 210

Box, snuff, cartouche shape, cover with flowers, 3, ca1750, Scandinavian* (4238/555) — 200

Box, snuff, enamel, oval top painted with a scene of Orpheus, 2⅞, ca1770, English (4160/708) — 500

Box, snuff, enamel, pastoral landscapes, ruins and castles, 3, ca1770, Staffordshire (4141/115) — 550

Box, snuff, enamel, scene of 2 lovers in a garden, 3½, ca1765, Staffordshire, Good (4141/113) — 650

Box, snuff, enamel, with figures in landscape, 3⅜, German (4160/617) — 375

Box, snuff, enamel (unusual), form blue trunk, scrolling bands, inscription, 3½, ca1770, Staffordshire (4141/111) — 500

Box, snuff, gold, key pattern border, 3⅛, 1764, French (4160/737) — 4750

Box, snuff, gold, with foliage and strapwork, 3⅛, M19c, French (4160/736) — 1100

Box, snuff, gold and enamel, oval form, flowerhead in white and turquoise, 2 11/16, ca1795, Swiss (4238/570) — 2700

Box, snuff, gold and enamel, musical, engine turned panels, floral and leaf border, 3¼, M19c, French (669/267) — 6000

Box, snuff, gold and enamel, set with jewels, the Indian market, 3¾, ca1850, fine, French (4160/738) — 14500

Box, snuff, miniature of 3 boys, gold mounted tortoise shell, 3⅜, ca1795, Continental (4238/554) — 800

Box, snuff, oval with watch, silver-gilt, cover mounted with watch, 3⅜, ca1770, Prussian* (4160/647) — 700

Box, snuff, oval, gold, 2 color, raised cable borders, 3⅛, 1780, Swiss (4160/735) — 2800

Box, snuff, silver, flower and scroll decorations, 3⅛, 1836, English (4141/103) — 275

Box, snuff, silver, flower chased thumbpiece, 3¼, 1835, English (4160/650) — 300

Box, snuff, silver, gold plaque with initials, 3½, ca1830, French (4160/652) — 200

Box, snuff, silver, oval form, chased flower and bud clusters, 2⅞, ca1770, Continental (4141/98) — 200

Box, snuff, silver, tall oblong shape, reeded sides, 3½, 1828, English (4160/632) — 500

Box, snuff, silver and niello, retangular quatrefoils gilt interior, 3⅜, ca1830, French (4238/542) — 325

Box, snuff, silver and niello, with the Alexander column, 2⅝, 1851, Russian (4160/644) — 275

Box, snuff, silver mounted, cowrie shell, 3⅜, 18c (4160/636) — 200

Box, snuff, silver mounted, cowrie shell, engraved, 2½, ca1730, English (4160/637) — 250

Box, snuff, silver mounted, cowrie shell, with a reverse cypher EJ, 3, ca1750, English (4160/635) — 175

Box, snuff, silver mounted, cowrie shell, 3¼, 1827, English (4160/638) — 300

Box, snuff, silver mounted, cowrie shell, engraved with monogram SD, 3, ca1780 (4160/639) — 175

Box, snuff, silver mounted, cowrie shell, hinged cover, 3¼, ca1790, Irish (4160/634) — 400

Box, snuff, silver mounted, mother of pearl, basket weave,⅜, ca1760, German* (4160/651) — 300

Box, snuff, silver, mounted tortoiseshell, oval form, chinoiserie scene, 3⅝, ca1760, French (4141/105) — 300

Box, snuff, two-color, gilt metal quadruple, five hinged sections, 3⅛, ca1780, French (4160/649) — 850

Box, snuff, 4 color, Oval, chased trophy of musical instruments, 2⅜, 1776, French (4160/733) — 5750

Box, snuff, 4 color gold, quatre foil, arrangement, scrolls, flowers and foliage, 3¼, 1830, Swiss (4141/96) — 1950

Box, tobacco, engraved with The Quack Dentist, 4, ca1900, Dutch (4238/539) — 350

Box, tobacco, rectangular, hinged lid, bands of running foliage, 5⅝, 1791, Dutch, 6 ozs., 10 dwts. (4141/579) — 1000

Box, tobacco, brass, oblong form, embossed with 4 portraits, 6⅛, ca1758, German (4238/526) — 250

Box, tobacco, brass and copper, double arched ends, engraved with scrolls, 5⅜, M18c, Dutch (4238/525) — 250

Box, tobacco, brass, oval, two confronting oval portraits, nobleman and lady, 4⅞, 18c (4133/96) — 425

Box, tobacco, copper gilt, depicting whaling scene, rhymes, 5¼, E18c, good, Dutch (4160/724) — 1600
Box, tobacco, silver, formal designs, 5¼, 1846, Dutch (4160/633) — 275
Box, tobacco, silver, oval form, scene, a meeting, 7 generals, L3½, ca1700, 2 ozs, 15 dwts (4160/727) — 1500
Case, silver, Engraved with foliate strapwork, 3½, 1863, Victorian (4160/653) — 400
Coffret, Louis XV, silver-gilt, form of a commode, bombe form, French, L3⅛, 1733 (4194/527) — *3000*

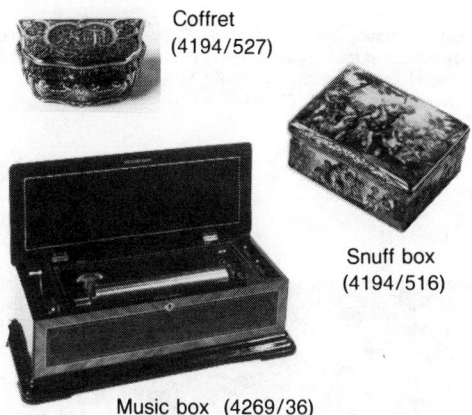

Coffret
(4194/527)

Snuff box
(4194/516)

Music box (4269/36)

Regina metal disc (669/436)

Enamel, boat shape, painted sides, prob. Fromery workshop, Berlin 1750 (4086/22) — 2400
Enamel, gold, rectangular, J.E. Blerzy, diamond-set monogram L.M., Louis XVI, fine, Paris, 1775 (4086/23) — 26000
Gold, agate automaton, James Cox, London watch and shutter-form series lantern, ca1760 (4086/11) — 47500
Gold, enamel oval, Elias Russel London carnations, rare, fine, 1766 (4086/18) — 18000
Gold, enamel, Louis XV, F.G. Tiron, miniatures, fine, Paris, 1768 (4086/2) — 18000
Gold, enamel, Louis XV, P.M. Mothet, oval, miniature of girl, fine, Paris, 1766 (4086/1) — 13000
Gold, enamel, Louis XV, Veuve, circular, Terpsichore playing lute, fine, D3, Paris, ca1765 (4086/12) — 25000
Gold, enamel, Louis XVI, Philippe Le Bourlier, oval, jasper neoclassical plaque, fine, Paris, 1778 (4086/16) — 18000
Gold, four-color, enamel, Louis XV, Jean Ducrollay, important, L3¼, Paris 1759-60 (4086/33) — 32500
Gold, four-color, Louis XV, oval, cover with trophy, fine, Paris, 1773 (4086/9) — 13500
Gold, four-color, Louis XV, oval, D.F. Poitreau chased, fine, Paris, 1766 (4086/30) — 19000
Gold, lacquer, enamel, Louis XV, oval, miniature after Lavreince, fine, Paris, 1765 (4086/15) — 19000
Gold, three-color, Louis XV, J.M. Tiron, oblong, military trophies, fine, Paris, 1756 (4086/14) — 7750
Gold, two-color, Louis XV, oval, arts and sciences trophy, Claude Cherrie, fine, Paris, 1767 (4086/8) — 8000
Snuff box, enamel, Rape of the Sabine Women, German, L3½, ca1760 (4194/516) — *1900*
Snuff box, gold and enamel, octofoil shape, miniature of Venus, cupids, Swiss, Diam 3, ca1800 (4194/530) — 3000
Snuff box, gold and enamel, Madonna Della Sedia, Swiss, L3½, ca1805 (4194/533) — 5000
Snuff box, silver, oval, engraved, mother of pearl, 3¼, L18c (4259/576) — 325
Snuff box, silver, shallow egg shape, molded borders, 2¾, ca1740 (4259/573) — *225*
Snuff box, silver and enamel, rectangular, nude odalisque, 3¼ (4259/497) — 350
Snuff box, silver-gilt and enamel, Viennese, youth playing violin, girl pushing swing, 4⅛, M19c (4259/525) — 900
Snuff box, silver mounted, oval, carved of striated semintranslucent agate, 3½, L18c (4259/591) — 375
Snuff box, silver table, with a Wedgwood classical plaque, English, L4⅞, cr, 1907 (4194/508) — 125
Snuff box, silver, gold mounted, octagonal, hinged cover, Indian*, 4⅜, E19c (4259/586) — 750
Snuff box, enamel, Dresden Venus and Cupid, 3¼, ca1760 (4259/558) — 900
Snuff box, George III, Scottish silver, Robert Keay of Perth, oblong, English, L3, 1810 (4194/504) — 325
Snuff box, Staffordshire enamel, scene of lovers, landscape, English, L3⅛, ca1765 (4194/518) — 125
Snuff box, 2-color gold, bloodstone panels 'en cage', German, L 3¼, ca1760 (4194/534) — 5000
Snuff box, enamel, landscape, shepherd playing pipe, 3 sheep, 3⅜, ca1765, Staffordshire (4141/51) — 200
Snuff box with a miniature, enamel oval box, 2¾, ca1900 (4259/505) — 600

Continental

Snuff box, silver, cover chased with Aphrodite and Adonis, 3¼], ca1720 (4259/571) — *450*
Snuff box, silver, cartouche, chased with shell and scrollwork, landscapes, 3¼, M18c (4259/574) — 500

English

Snuff box, enamel, Staffordshire, fanciful venetain quayside scene, 3½, ca1765 (4259/555)   375
Snuff box, enamel, Staffordshire, pastoral scenes, 3⅛, ca1765 (4259/554)   425
Snuff box, silver, rectangular, engraved armorials, supporter, 2⅞, E18c (4259/572)   *750*
Snuff box, silver, William IV, J. Willmore, sarcophagus shape, 3⅜, 1832 (4259/565)   400
Snuff box, Marshall & Sons, rectangular form, flared sides, 3, ca1845 (4259/601)   1600

French

Snuff box, gilt metal, oval, engine turned, chased leaf tip borders, 2½, ca1780 (4259/592)   200
Snuff box, gold mounted, Louis XV, rectangular, body and cover rock crystal, 2⅝, 1769 (4259/606)   2800
Snuff box, silver, Empire, oblong, with engraved borders of formal ornament, 3, 1809-19 (4259/581)   250
Snuff box, two-color gold, Louis XVI, oval, enamel, scene, N. Marguerit, 2½, 1783 (4259/603)   5500

Spanish

Snuff box, silver, rectangular, chased with profile below a drapery canopy, 3, ca1740 (4259/575)   *325*

Snuff box
(4259/572)

Snuff box
(4259/575)

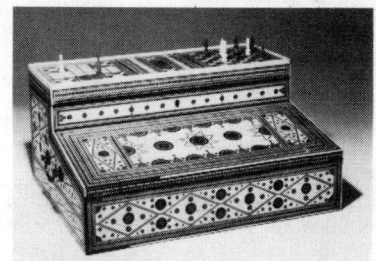

Box (4141/121)

Snuff box, silver and gold, rectangular, reeded sides, engraved name and date, 3¼, ca1830
(4259/587)   300

Swiss

Gold, enamel oval, with musical trophies, ca1770 (4086/17)   6500
Gold, enamel, diamond, oval, oval allegorical plaques, fine, ca1760 (4086/24)   30000
Gold, four-color, oval, cover with lovers, fine, ca1770 (4086/10)   8000
Gold, four-color, enamel, oval, cartouche-shaped paintings after J-F de Troy, important, fine, ca1760
(4086/26)   30000
Gold, four-color, rectangular, chased oval panel bordered half-pearls, fine, circa 1810 (4086/25)   27000
Gold, three-color, rectangular, children, flowers, peacocks, fine, 18c (4086/7)   5500
Gold, three-color, enamel, oval, ca1770 (4086/3)   13000
Gold, three-color, enamel, oval, six painted miniature scenes of Achilles' life, fine, L3⅜, ca1770
(4086/31)   23000
Gold, two-color, oval, chased with arts, sciences trophies, ca1770 (4086/13)   4250
Snuff box, gold and enamel, oval, miniature of 3 classical figures, 3, ca1790 (4259/604)   3400
Snuff box, gold and enamel, shallow rectangular, enameled, 2¾, ca1830 (4259/602)   3800
Snuff box, gold and enamel, shallow rectangular, miniature Holy Family, 3⅜, ca1810 (4259/605)   7000

CHESS SETS

Box, games and writing, ivory and sandlewood, Indian made for English market, L15, E19c, 88 pcs
(4141/121)   *700*

Ivory (4141/122)

Coral, oriental, Kings, Queens in robes, rooks as pagodas, 1⅛ x 2⅛, 32 pcs (4141/117) 400
Dominoes set, ivory and wood, ivory faces, wood bases, Russian, 2½, tile, 45 pcs, woodbox (4259/514) 125
Indian silver-gilt and enamel, green figures against blue, Kings on elephants, 2⅛ x 4¼, 32 pcs (4141/123) 5000
Ivory, carved, acanthus leaves, pierced lattice work, 1½ x 3¾, 32 pcs, North African* (4141/119) 225
Ivory, Indian, wood box, in set with ebony and silver inlaid, 2¼ x 3¾, 20c, 32 pcs (4141/118) 400
Ivory, Russian, Asians vs. Africans, 32 pcs, 2¼ x 3¼, 18c (4141/122) 900
Travelling game set, English, ebony, chess, dice, dominoes, playing cards, 19c, 7 x 12¾, rare (4076/880) 300

COINS AND MEDALS

Plaque, oval bronze, with Virgin and child and St. John, 7⅞, 17c (4133/111) 500
Rouble, Anna Ivanovna, 1731, (4233/89) 75
Rouble, Anna Ivanovna, 1738, (4233/90) 75
Rouble, Elizabeth Petrovna, 1744, (4233/92) 75
Rouble, Elizabeth Petrovna, 1757, coinage struck for Livonia-Esthonia, (4233/96) 150
Rouble, Nicholas II, 1912, (4233/103) 150
Rouble, Nicholas II, 1913, (4233/105) 50
Rouble, Novodel, Peter I, 1707, (4233/80) 125
Rouble,½, Catherine II, 1775, (4233/98) 150
Roubles, 1½, Nicholas I, 1839 Commemorative, (4233/99) 850
Roubles, 15, Nicholas II, 1897, (4233/101) 300
Roubles, 15, Nicholas II, 1912, (4233/102) 750

JEWELRY AND CAMEOS

Badge, gold, arms of N.Y., surmounted by an eagle, 2½, ca1860, American (4160/525) 150
Bangle, gold, of plaited gold wire terminates in Etruscan style gold beads, ca1870 (681/38) 650
Bangle, snake, gold, silver, garnet and diamond, 33 old mine diamonds, ca1820 (681/79) 1700
Bangles, pair, gold, enamel and pearl, engraved with sprays of lilies of the valley, L19c (4160/537) 625
Bar brooch, jeweled, sapphires, diamonds and rubies, pearl terminals, antique (681/90) 300
Bracelet, gold and green enamel, figure eight, loops and ribbons, antique (681/150) 850
Bracelet, gold, green enamel and rose diamond, hinged, ca1840 (681/80) 750
Bracelet, gold, ruby, sapphire and enamel, hinged bangle, antique (681/81) 1300
Bracelet, yellow metal and black mosaic of 3 roses, black ground, antique (681/92) 75
Bracelet, French gold, ca1830 (681/105) 450

Bracelet, bangle, gold, blue enamel and rose diamond, ca1840 (681/82)   1200
Bracelet, bangle, gold, round diamonds and turquoise, antique (681/311)   225
Bracelet, bangle, jeweled and gold, 2 opals and 1 cabochon garnet, antique (681/327)   400
Bracelet, bangle, Indian, gold and jeweled, enamelled flowers and birds, Mogul style, antique
    (681/148)   3000
Bracelet, charm, gold, open link set with 12 charms of vary, gold content (4238/499)   1050
Bracelet, gold, seamless, tubular mesh bracelet, engraved clasp, antique (681/305)   325
Bracelet, gold, diamond and enamel, numerous tapering links, French, ca1860 (4194/420)   5000
Bracelet, gold, silver and mosaic, 5 hexagonal wrought gold plaques, signed Castellani, M19c
    (681/333)   7000
Bracelet, jeweled, bangle, 18 round small diamonds, 1.25* carats, antique (681/257)   500
Bracelet, slide, Victorian, gold, 12 bejeweled slides, antique (681/313)   300
Bracelet, snake motif, gold and turquoise, antique (681/91)   400
Bracelet, Victorian, gold, silver and diamond, hinged, oval quatrefoil panel, ca1845 (681/77)   700
Bracelet, Victorian, gold, silver, rose diamond and pearl, hinged, scrolled, (681/76)   500
Bracelet, 3 color, gold and jeweled, filigree bracelet, openwork domed section, 6, ca1830 (4160/552)   4300
Bracelets, pair, gold mesh, with an engraved panel applied with woman's hand, L19c (4238/491)   325
Bracelets, pair, gold and black enamel, broad hinged gold bangles, ca1860 (681/316)   1100
Bracelets, pair, gold and pearl, thirteen matched pearls on gold chains, 8, 19c (4160/508)   250
Bracelets, pair, gold mesh slide, ca1840 (681/340)   700
Brooch, diamond and pearl, 48 old mine diamonds, .90* carats, 1 pearl, antique (681/177)   550
Brooch, gold and citrine, scrolling cartouche mount, antique (681/134)   125
Brooch, gold and garnet, 3 interlocking circles, ca1830 (681/121)   275
Brooch, gold and rock crystal, ribbon motif engraved with scrollwork, antique (681/128)   300
Brooch, gold, silver and rose diamonds, wild flower, antique (681/20)   650
Brooch, gold, silver, citrine quartz and diamond, ribbon cartouche design, antique (681/13)   500
Brooch, rose, diamond and turquoise bow and heart, antique (681/12)   750
Brooch, 3 round sapphires, rose diamond-set oval, antique (681/179)   1000
Brooch, gold, diamond and enamel, form of flower with 3 leaves, 2, ca1840 (4160/550)   *4000*

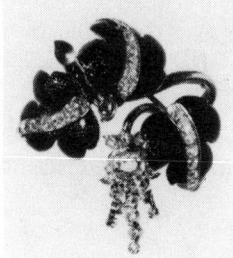

Brooch
(4160/550)

Brooch, bee, gold, silver, emerald, rose diamond and coral, antique (681/200)   800
Brooch, bird in crescent, gold, silver, 27 old mine cut diamonds, 2.25* carats, antique (681/156)   2100
Brooch, bow, gold, silver, pearl and rose diamonds, 12 pearls, antique (681/178)   325
Brooch, bow knot gold, enamel diamond, borders bright cut with waves, 2, M19c (4160/551)   3700
Brooch, butterfly, gold and 1 old mine, .45* carat diamond, rose diamonds, antique (681/241)   700
Brooch, butterfly, gold, pearl, sapphire, ruby and diamond, ca1870 (681/52)   550
Brooch, butterfly, jeweled and gold, diamonds, emeralds and rubies, 2⅛, ca1875 (4238/502)   1500
Brooch, cameo sardonyx, gold and pearl, cameo of young woman, ca1820 (681/252)   400
Brooch, cameo, gold and carnellian, classical portrait bust, in profile, open work frame, 2¼, ca1850
    (4238/503)   450
Brooch, cameo, gold and hardstone, openwork cartouche of strapwork and scrolls, 2½, ca1870
    (4259/443)   425
Brooch, cameo, gold mounted hardstone, agate, classical woman, 2⅞, M19c (4259/459)   1900

Brooch, cameo, gold mounted hardstone, agate, classical woman, 3, L19c (4259/456)   *1600*
Brooch, cameo, gold mounted hardstone, agate, classical woman, 2⅜, L19c (4259/455)   *900*
Brooch, cameo, gold mounted hardstone, agate, Zeus, 2⅛, L19c (4259/457)   *1100*
Brooch, cameo, Art Deco, gold, citrine, neoclassical profile, 1¾, ca1925 (4238/509)   600
Brooch, circular gold enamel and diamond, wreath of rose diamonds, 2⅛ (4238/523)   1300
Brooch, crescent, diamonds, 51 old mine, 5.25* carats, silver and gold, ca1840 (681/158)   1800
Brooch, crescent, platinum, gold and 21 old mine cut diamonds, 2* carats, ca1870 (681/263)   1100
Brooch, cross pendant, gold and diamond, 11 old mine cut diamonds, 11* carats, ca1870 (681/326)   3250
Brooch, diamond, set with 24 old mine cut diamonds, rose diamonds, ca1840 (681/42)   1300
Brooch, diamond, flower spray, form of carnation, 3, 19c (4160/526)   1700
Brooch, dove, diamond, 106 round diamonds, 6 carats, with gold foxtail chain, ca1860 (681/157)   2200
Brooch, flower, gold, silver and rose diamond, antique (681/132)   1000
Brooch, gold and citrine, engraved and set with oval citrine, antique (681/328)   175
Brooch, gold and enamel, circular, head of girl wearing pink scarf, 1⅛, ca1900 (4160/542)   350
Brooch, gold and enamel, rectangular, Alpine lake scene, Swiss, 1¼, ca1840 (4194/388)   500
Brooch, gold and jeweled, with a miniature, frame of old mine diamonds, 1¼, L19c (4259/415)   600
Brooch, gold and rose diamond, a diamond set flower on blue enamel, ca1800 (681/289)   450
Brooch, gold and sard intaglio, depicts a Greek woman warrior, gold frame, ca1870 (681/346)   1000
Brooch, gold and silver, butterfly, 47 round diamonds, 2.75* carats, emerald, ruby and sapphire, antique (681/274)   1900
Brooch, gold mounted, hardstone, depicting farmer walking with a scythe, 1½, L19c (4160/515)   375
Brooch, gold, citrine and enameled brooch, hourglass shape, Swiss, L3½, ca1840 (4194/391)   *900*
Brooch, gold, diamond, ruby and emerald, form of an openwork basket, French, 1⅝, ca1890 (4194/403)   *850*

Brooch
(4259/456)

Brooch
(4259/455)

Brooch
(4259/457)

Brooch
(4194/391)

Brooch
(4194/403)

Brooch, gold, enamel and diamond, centered by star, old mine and rose diamonds, 2, L19c (4141/23)   1300
Brooch, gold, silver, amethyst, border of rose diamonds, ca1840 (681/318)   750
Brooch, insect, emerald and ruby body, eyes and wings set with diamonds, antique (681/292)   1400
Brooch, insect, gold, silver, garnet and rose diamonds, antique (681/203)   550
Brooch, jeweled bee, gold, rose diamond silver body, wings of pearls and rubies, antique (681/53)   600
Brooch, jeweled dragonfly, of numerous colored stones set in silver, antique (681/9)   100
Brooch, pansy, silver-gilt, 1 old mine diamonds .50 carat*, 78 rose diamonds, ca1840 (681/130)   900
Brooch, pendant, gold and silver, sapphire, pendant pearl and diamond, antique (681/191)   2750
Brooch, pendant, gold and silver, French coral wild rose, natural pearl and rose diamond, ca1840 (681/280)   900
Brooch, set with a miniature, gold, fashionable lady, openwork, scrolling frame, 1½, ca1900 (4141/21)   200
Brooch, snake, gold, turquoise and garnet eyes, ca1840 (681/167)   400
Brooch, snake, garnets, pearls, gold, curled body, compartments, 1⅛, L18c (4259/595)   300

Brooch, swallow, silver, 70 old mine cut diamonds, ruby set head, ca1850 (681/131) — 700
Brooch, tade, diamond and platinum, fanciful creatures and scrolls, 2⅜, ca1910 (4238/508) — 1800
Brooch, yellow and green gold, five old mine diamonds 1.25* carats and ruby, flower, antique (681/291) — 800
Brooch, Dragonfly, gold and jeweled, body of mother of pearl, 2 gold feet, 1½, M19c (4259/411) — 275
Brooch, Pietra Dura, depicting a bouquet mounted in gold, antique (681/302) — 150
Brooch, Swiss gold, rectangular panel enameled with a mountain view, 2¼, ca1840 (4259/412) — 625
Brooch, Victorian, gold and enamel, ornamented design blue and black enamel, ca1860 (681/120) — 400
Brooch, Victorian, fifteen karat gold, pearl and blue enamel, antique (681/264) — 225
Buttons, pair, ancient coins, Etruscan style, denarius of Emporer Nero, ca1870 (681/339) — 900
Cameo, carved shell, Apollo on chariot drawn by 4 horses, 3, M19c, Italian, fine (4141/59) — 800
Cameo, hardstone, gold mounted, profile protrait of gentlemen, white on brown, 2⅛, ca1865 (4238/510) — 350
Cameo, of the Dunmore family, four profile heads, 3⅝, 1791, Tassie (4141/58) — 300
Chain, fluted twisted gold links, approximately 60 inches, antique (681/123) — 375
Chain, gold, spiral woven 38 inches, antique (681/245) — 1500
Chain, watch, gold, oblong links joined by fancy links, ca1860 (681/315) — 475
Chain and slide, gold, slide mounted with small enamel miniature, 21, L19c (4238/522) — 650
Charm, wolf's head, gold, silver, diamond and ruby, antique (681/244) — 300
Choker snake, gold, pink sapphire, diamond, enamel and pearl, ca1840 (681/88) — 850
Collar, gold, silver, fire opal, 25 hexagonal opals, rose diamond links, antique (681/357) — 1900
Cross, gold, black enamel and pearl, antique (681/124) — 225
Cuffbuttons, pair, gold and enamel, wreath border, Greek key motif, antique (681/308) — 150
Cufflinks, emerald and diamond, cruciform motif, 16 rose diamonds, antique (681/58) — 550
Drop earrings, Indian gold, turquoise and pearl, antique (681/142) — 200
Drops, gold, silver and diamonds, 42 round and rose cut diamonds, antique (681/22) — 700
Ear clips, pair, silver and numerous old mine cut diamonds, antique (681/242) — 2750
Ear drops, pair, gold and garnets, closed back gold mounts, antique (681/126) — 175
Ear pendants, rose diamonds and silver, of floral motifs, antique (681/19) — 550
Ear pendants, bird, pair, silver-gilt, rose diamond and ruby eyes, antique (681/271) — 400
Ear pendants, fly pair, jeweled, gold, silver, ruby and diamond, seashells, antique (681/201) — 900
Ear pendants, pair, gold, antique (681/27) — 250
Ear pendants, pair, hand in glove, with pinky finger ruby ring, 1 ruby missing, antique (681/270) — 850
Earrings, pair, gold and diamonds, form of pendant, 9 rose cut diamonds, 1, M19c (4141/11) — 400
Earrings, pair, gold and pearl, gold hoops, antique (681/54) — 275
Earrings, pair, diamond, rose and 2 pear shaped diamonds, ca1790 (681/269) — 2400
Earrings, pair, gold and turquoise, oval, corded borders, hung with tassels, (4160/541) — 375
Earrings, pair, gold, diamond and pearl, openwork crowns,⅞ (4160/548) — 600
Flower ornament, silver and rose diamond on gold hinged bangle bracelet, antique (681/59) — 275
Fob, dog, carved agate, diamond set collar, in London box, antique (681/254) — 750
Fob, gold and garnet, ca1850 (681/94) — 300
Fob seal, gold, flutes, foliage, feathers, shells, owlcrest and initials, 1½, ca1825 (4141/84) — 300
Fob seal, gold and carnelian, monogram R.A.S. below the American Eagle, 1½, L18c (4141/71) — 200
Fob seal, musical, Swiss gold, music movement in an oval base, 1⅝, ca1825, Swiss (4141/85) — 1100
Lavaliere, gold, chain of fluted double oval links, panel pendant 1 half, pearl, ca1850 (681/360) — 650
Lavaliere, gold, turquoise and pearl, Tiffany & Co. Union Square N.Y., box, ca1860 (681/165) — 2250
Lavaliere, Victorian, fifteen karat, gold and pearl, chain, heart shaped brooch, antique (681/55) — 750
Locket, gold and enamel, classical profile, 1, ca1780, English (4160/520) — 275
Locket, gold and mosaic, mosaic letters EY in white on blue ground, signed Castellani, antique (681/330) — 1700
Locket, gold and mosaic Etruscan style, domed case, with winged cherub, M19c (681/331) — 800
Locket gold and link chain, Victorian, (681/119) — 750
Necklace, gold and enamel, enamelled with green, red and white floral motif, ca1860 (681/301) — 2500
Necklace, gold and mosaic, classical revival wrought gold urns, signed Castellani, M19c (681/332) — 9000
Necklace, gold, garnet and quartz, rope twisted, 3 jeweled inverted crescents, antique (681/284) — 350
Necklace, pendant, gold, enamel amethyst, oval, openwork filigree, 1⅝, L19c (4160/553) — 2800
Necklace, snake, gold and turquoise, with diamond eyes, antique (681/140) — 2250
Necklace, French gold, bordered by 789 old mine cut diamonds, 26* carats, and 17 amethysts, 20* carats, antique (681/317) — 13000
Necklace, Victorian carved coral, six high relief carved coral portraits on gold bars, (681/336) — 900
Pendant, gold and diamond, open scroll design, fancy link chain, ca1850 (681/129) — 1600
Pendant, gold and emerald, 3 pendant drops, antique (681/240) — 325
Pendant, gold, platinum, natural pearl, 12 x 18 mm., 30 round diamonds, 1* carat, antique (681/260) — 2000
Pendant, gold, silver, emerald and rose diamond, jeweled ribbon, antique (681/10) — 375

Pendant, enameled gold, Orpheus, diamonds, rubies, pearls, emeralds, Italian, 3⅜, L16c (4194/452)   5000
Pendant, gold, drop shape, flutes decorated with turquoise enamel, Swiss, 1, ca1790 (4259/594)   250
Pendant, gold and amethyst, a faceted oval amethyst with three drops, 2⅝, ca1800 (4259/404)   250
Pendant, gold and enamel, cartouche shape, chased with scrolls and trellis, 1⅞, ca1765 (4259/597)   800
Pendant, gold and enamel, oval enamel plaque, peasant in a landscape, pearl drop, 2½, L19c
(669/244)   350

Pendant
(4194/452)

Pendant, gold and jeweled, amethyst, emeralds, sapphire, Spanish, Diam 1⅞, 18c (4194/448)   225
Pendant, gold and jeweled, cameo depicting woman in the classical revival taste, ca1840 (681/250)   75
Pendant, gold and mosaic, hexagonal plaque, signed Castellani, M19c (681/335)   1700
Pendant, gold mask, a bacchanal head, garland of grapevines and grapes, 1¾, ca1860 (4141/20)   500
Pendant, gold, silver, large fire opal bordered by rose diamonds, antique (681/356)   800
Pendant, gold, verre eglomise devotional, St. John and another saint, Italian, 2¾, M18c (4194/450)   800
Pendant, platinum, diamond and enamel, trefoil shape, spider web design, chain, 1¼, ca1900
(4160/547)   1300
Pendant, ruby and diamond, English, formerly a bracelet, 2 stones missing, ca1760 (4194/400)   1300
Pendant, silver gold diamond and enamel, centered by circular enamel of a lady, 3⅞, L18/E19c
(4141/9)   300
Pendant, snake, gold, amethyst, enameled and jeweled, ca1890 (681/166)   1000
Pendant, Etruscan style, with Alexander the Great drachm, signed Pierret, ca1870 (681/338)   3250
Pendant, French 3 color gold and enamel, yellow-gold bird and nest, ca1815 (681/279)   1800
Pendant, St. George and the dragon, silver and jewelered, pearl, emerald and ruby, antique (681/11)   350
Pendant earring pair, gold and carved coral, antique (681/41)   275
Pendant earring pair, black and gold, antique (681/63)   250
Pendant-locket, oriental-style, gold, green, yellow, enamel, French, 2⅛, ca1865-70 (4194/399)   2300
Pendant-locket, double horseshoe, gold, pearl and turquoise, antique (681/139)   225
Pin, butterfly, gold, silver, ruby, diamond and sapphire, antique (681/202)   300
Ring, gold and diamond cluster, antique (681/72)   175
Ring, gold and garnet, chased gold scrolled mount, ca1865 (681/67)   275
Ring, gold, garnet and diamond, styled as a pair of hands, antique (681/66)   350
Ring, gold, platinum, emerald and diamond, engraved mount, antique (681/74)   600
Ring, gold, sapphire, pearl and rose diamond, antique (681/71)   300
Ring, gold, silver, rose diamond and pearl, ca1750 (681/193)   800
Ring, gold, turquoise and diamond, heart and starburst, antique (681/103)   200
Ring, gold, 5 old mine diamonds, .70* carats, 2 diamonds missing, ca1840 (681/102)   425
Ring, pink sapphire and diamond, half hoop, antique (681/73)   750
Ring, sapphire collet, within garland, set with diamonds, antique (681/194)   1200
Ring, diamond, oval mount set with numerous rose diamonds, antique (681/70)   350
Ring, diamond and gold, oval shape, flowerhead arrangement of rose diamonds, E19c (4238/504)   525
Ring, diamond and sapphire, twin circular setting, ca1920 (4160/528)   1000
Ring, gentleman's, three round diamonds in gold, antique (681/174)   450
Ring, gold, with portrait miniature framed by rose diamonds, antique (681/298)   600
Ring, gold and diamond, seven old mine cut diamonds, ca1880 (681/323)   1500
Ring, gold mourning, wreath motif, woven hair ornament, antique (681/267)   225
Ring, gold, ruby, diamond, 2 rubies and 2 old mine cut diamonds, ca1880 (681/275)   2250

Ring, memorial, gold and pearl, woman holding wreath, 1¼, L18c (4160/521)   200
Ring, memorial, gold, elliptical form, underglass ... mother of pearl, 1⅜, 1787 (4141/27)   350
Ring, memorial, gold, marquise shaped, woven hair section, monogram, ca1783 (681/247)   250
Ring, topaz pink, gold, enamel, diamond,⅞, L19c (4160/555)   1200
Rosary, gold, gold balls and filigree beads, 37, 19c, Continental (4160/527)   625
Stick pin, gold mounted Roman coin, formerly a brooch, ca1865 (4238/516)   250
Watch, key - cameo, gilt metal hardstone, agate, Roman Emperor and wife, 2⅛, ca1800 (4259/461)   1750

MINIATURE PORTRAITS

Assorted painters

Allston, Washington, LUCY MARSHALL, three quarter sinister, black dress, rectangular framed, 3⅜,
  1828 (4259/400)   500
American, GENTLEMAN, 2⅝, ca1795 (4141/136)   325
American School, GENTLEMAN, 3¼, ca1810 (4160/443)   70
American School, GEORGE WASHINGTON, 2¾, M19c (4160/437)   80
American School, LADY AND BABY, 3, ca1840 (4160/426)   300
American School, LADY AND GENTLEMAN, 3¼, ca1835 (4160/433)   600
American School, PORTRAITS, pair, watercolor, 4, ca1810 (4160/431)   150
American School, GENTLEMAN, 2¼, ca1810 (4160/428)   225
American School, GIRL, 2¾, ca1810 (4160/427)   110
Anonymous, A GENTLEMAN AND A LADY, 10 x 8¼, 19c (4211/673)   800
Anonymous, A GENTLEMAN AND A LADY, pair of portraits, 8½ x 6¼, 19c (4211/678)   700
Anonymous, A YOUNG BOY, 7 x 5, M19c (4211/672)   400
Anonymous, A YOUNG BOY, holding sword, 8¾ x 8, 19c (4211/671)   350
Anonymous, DIANE DEPOITIERS, 1⅝, 18c (4141/131)   850
Anonymous, MAN AND WOMAN, pair of portraits, 4½ x 3⅝, 19c (4268/1020)   225
Anonymous, possibly J.A. Davis, PORTRAIT OF BLACK MAN, 4⅝ x 3¾, ca1850 (4211/694)   1400
Anonymous, American, A CHILD, on paper, 5¼ x 4½, 19c (4268/984)   275
Anonymous, American, A CHILD, N.Eng.*, on ivory, 3⅜ x 2½, ca1830 (4268/982)   250
Anonymous, American, A CHILD, N.Eng.*, on ivory, ca1830 (4268/985)   275
Anonymous, American, A GENTLEMAN, in black frock coat, 6½ x 5, 19c (4268/1040)   500
Anonymous, American, YOUNG BOY, in brown costume, 8¾ x 6½, 19c (4268/1015)   125
Anonymous, American, N.Eng.*, TWO CHILDREN, pair, dark-haired girl, infant, 6 x 4¾, ca1830
  (4268/1044)   500
Anonymous, N. Eng.*, ANNA JANE AND ELIZABETH ALICE GILL, 3 x 2⅜, ca1840 (4211/674)   425
Anonymous, N.E.*, portraits, watercolor, set of 4, 2⅜ x 1⅞, on ivory (4209/43)   950
Anonymous, N.E., 2, watercolor, ELVIRA COOLIDGE OF BOSTON, 1825-1845, 2¼ x 2½, on ivory
  (4209/45)   600
Anonymous, Penna.*, MOTHER, FATHER AND DAUGHTER, 3 portraits, 4¼ x 3⅜, ca1800
  (4211/675)   475
Aubry, Louis Francois, A YOUNG BOY, blue jacket, oval, rectangular frame, 1⅝, 1829 (4259/347)   1200
Bernhard, E., A GENTLEMAN, seated at table holding bcy, gilt metal oval frame, 1796 (4259/363)   1200
Bertin, LADY, 4¼, E19c (4160/476)   550
Bridport, Hugh, LADY, 2⅞ (4141/141)   300
Brown, George, An Odalisque, nude, blonde hair, oval, leather box frame, 6, 1851 (4259/393)   525
Brown, John Henry, YOUNG GIRL, 3, 1888 (4160/432)   275
Buck, Adam attrib. A LADY, brown hair tied back, oval pendant frame, 1⅝, ca1790 (4259/318)   *200*
Chinese export painting, domestic scene with flowers, 17½ x 23, 19c (4076/1222)   600
Continental School, GENTLEMAN, 2½, L18c (4160/474)   400
Continental School, LADY, 3¼, ca1820 (4160/467)   70
Continental School, GENTLEMAN, brown jacket, 2½, ca1800 (4141/125)   200
Coovelet, Jean Baptiste, LADY AND GENTLEMAN, pair, oval pendant frames, 2¼, 1810 (4259/348)   2000
Cotes, Samuel, attrib. A GENTLEMAN, wearing red jacket, gold oval pendant frame, 1⅛, ca1765
  (4259/322)   250
Crosse, Richard, A Lady, in widow's weeds, oval bracelet mount, 1⅜, ca1780 (4259/319)   *500*
Davis, J.A., N.E., PORTRAIT, George R. Bishop, 1818, 7½ x 5⅝, discolor (4209/26)   800
Davis, J.A., N.E., watercolor, PORTRAIT OF A YOUNG WOMAN, Sarah Lyons, 4¾ x 3⅜, fine
  (4209/39)   1500
De Lauro, AN OFFICER, almost full face, green uniform, oval in rectangular frame, 2¼, 1820
  (4259/334)   325
DeMiervelt, Michael, attrib, ELIZABETH STUART, QUEEN TO FREDERICK V OF BOHEMIA, 4¾,
  1567-1641 (4160/462)   700
DeMiervelt, Michael, attrib, FREDERICK V, KING OF BOHEMIA, 4¾, 1596-1632 (4160/460)   725
DeMiervelt, Michael, attrib, MAURICE DE NASSAU, 4¾, 1567-1625 (4160/461)   550
DeMiervelt, Michael, attrib, WILLIAM THE 1ST OF BOHEMIA, 4¾, 1567-1641 (4160/464)   650
DeMiervelt, Michael, attrib, YOUNG LADY, 4¾, 1567-1641 (4160/463)   800
Dodge, John Wood, GENTLEMAN, 2⅝, ca1840 (4141/137)   350

Dodge, John Woods, GENTLEMAN, 1¾, ca1834 (4160/439) — 370
Doyle, William M.S., GENTLEMAN, 2⅞, ca1825 (4160/442) — 425
Dunlap, William, attrib., GENTLEMAN, 2⅝, ca1795 (4141/138) — 250
English School, GENTLEMAN, 2½, ca1790 (4160/452) — 100
English School, GENTLEMAN, 2¾, ca1835 (4166/453) — 300
English School, LADY AND AN OFFICER, pair, 3¾, ca1840 (4160/451) — 650
Favrin, Louis, A LADY, seated, gilt metal and wood frame, 3⅛, 1810 (4259/355) — 350
Foeyd, Robert, attrib., LADY, 3⅛, ca1800 (4141/140) — 300
Freese, N. A GENTLEMAN, black double breasted jacket, oval pendant frame, 2⅞, ca1795 (4259/320) — 500
French School, GENTLEMAN, 2, ca1790 (4160/483) — 100
French School, GENTLEMAN MOUNTED IN GOLD AND TORTOISE SHELL BOX, 3⅛, ca1780 (4160/486) — 700
French School, LADY, 2¼, ca1800 (4160/477) — 200
French School, LADY, 3¼ (4160/470) — 325
French School, LADY, 2½ (4160/469) — 200
French School, LADY, 3⅝ (4160/468) — 250
French School, LADY, powdered hair, lace cap, 2¾, ca1770 (4141/124) — 275
French School, MARIE ANTOINETTE, 2⅝, ca1780 (4160/478) — 150
French School, NAPOLEON ON TORTOISESHELL BOX, 2½, E19c (4141/130) — *550*
French School, SOLDIER, 3¾, 19c (4141/129) — 200
Green, portrait of A GENTLEMAN, probably N.Eng., 5 x 4½, 1838 (4146/52) — 225
Holbrook, A.M., N.E.*, watercolor, PORTRAIT, LEVI JOHNSON, ca1830, 4⅛ x 5 (4209/100) — 425
Jarvis, John Wesley, A GENTLEMAN, green jacket, black lapels, rectangular, framed, 4¼, 1808 (4259/398) — 250
Jean, Philip, LADY, 1¾, 1775-1802 (4160/449) — 225
Krafft, Joseph, YOUNG LADY, 3⅜ (4141/126) — 250
LeSage, A LADY, full face, crimson dress, oval in rectangular frame, 3¾, 1835 (4259/335) — 700
Military officer, watercolor on paper, 6 x 4½, 19c (654/231) — 125
Mills, Edward, GEORGE WASHINGTON, 2⅛ (4141/133) — 130
Napoleon, executed in hair, 5¾, E19c (4076/542) — 100
Noel, F., attrib, THREE YOUNG-LADIES, 3, ca1810 (4160/481) — 550
Pareato, F.D., LOUIS BONAPARTE, 2½, 1816 (4160/475) — 300
Peale, James, GENTLEMAN, 1¾, ca1780 (4160/447) — 3200
Peale, Raphael, A GENTLEMAN, blue jacket, white waistcoat, red scarf, oval gold frame, 2½, 1799 (4259/401) — *3700*

Buck
(4259/318)

Crosse
(4259/319)

French School
(4141/130)

Peale
(4259/401)

Philippot, Carl Ludwig, A GENTLEMAN, green jacket, black lapels, oval, framed, 2¾, 1834 (4259/383) — 325
Pietrocola R., GENTLEMAN, 3, ca1880 (4160/436) — 100
Plimer, Andrew, LADY, 3⅛, 1763-1837 (4160/459) — 1600
Plimer, Andrew, OFFICER, 3⅛, 1763-1837 (4160/458) — 1700
Porter, Rufus, attrib., N.Eng., PORTRAIT OF A LADY, cut out, mounted, 3⅝ x 2⅞, ca1830 (4268/1039) — 100

Porter, Rufus, N.E.*, portraits, pair, HANNAH G. JOHNSON FLINT, EDWARD JOHNSON, 3⅜ x 2¼,
   ca1820 (4209/78)   1100
Portrait of a gentleman, anonymous, probably American, 5½ x 3½, ca1835 (4146/54)   125
Portrait of a young child, on ivory, three-quarter length, 4½ x 2⅞ (4146/58)   200
Portrait of a young lady on ivory, anonymous, probably Mass., 3½ x 2¾, ca1835 (4146/61)   175
Portrait of a young man, anonymous, probably Mass., 4¾ x 3½, ca1820 (4146/57)   225
Portrait of an infant on ivory, anonymous, probably American, 2¼ x 2, 19c (4146/60)   250
Portraits of husband and wife, pair, anonymous, probably N.Eng., 5½ x 4, ca1840 (4146/56)   125
Portraits of 2 ladies, 1 gentleman, anonymous, Conn.*, each 3¾ x 24, 19c (4146/55)   175
Reverse painting on glass, pair, Chinese export, costumed maidens in garden, 17½ x 25¼, M19c
   (4076/1221)   2800
Rowel, Samuel, N.E.*, PORTRAIT OF YOUNG GIRL, ABBIE J. FIELDEN, ca1820, 3¼ x 2⅜
   (4209/116)   350
Rubens, Peter Paul, ALEXANDER THE GREAT, as Jupiter Ammon, polychrome cameo, 2⅜, ca1606
   (4160/465)   3800
Simes, Mary Jane, attrib. A LADY, blue dress and fur jacket, oval, gold pendant frame, 2½, ca1830
   (4259/399)   300
Smith Sophia, A GENTLEMAN, wearing a mauve jacket and wiast coast, oval frame, 1½, 1765
   (4259/316)   250
Soinsot after Lancret, painting on ivory, 18c lovers in gardens, 4, framed, L19c (649/270)   250
Sullivan, Luke, YOUNG LADY, 1⅝, 1705-71 (4160/448)   425
Theer, Albert, AN OFFICER, blue uniform, white trim, moustache, oval, rectangular frame, 1½,
   ca1840 (4259/385)   1100
Townsend*, pair of portraits, on ivory, 2¾ x 2, 19c (4146/59)   100
Vaslet, Lewis, LADY, 3¼, 1793 (4141/132)   275
Verbryek, Richard, LADY, 2½, 1833 (4160/430)   350
Voiart, Elizabeth, A YOUNG BOY, waist length, oval, velvet frame, 2⅜, ca1845 (4259/346)   400
Voight, Lewis, GENTLEMAN, 2, ca1835 (4160/429)   400

Austrian School

A Gentleman, black double breasted jacket, oval, gold pendant frame, 2⅜, ca1810 (4259/387)   600
A Gentleman, black jacket waistcoat, rectangular frame, 3⅜, ca1835 (4259/384)   350
A Gentleman, black jacket, waxed moustache, oval, framed⅛, 1835, (4259/382)   150
A Gentleman, green jacket, oval, pendant frame, 2¼, ca1820 (4259/378)   275
A Lady, black dress, sky background, oval, framed, 2¼, ca1810 (4259/375)   125
An Officer, blue uniform, green collar, oval, rectangular frame, 2⅞, ca1830 (4259/380)   400
An Officer, red uniform with white braid and black trim, oval, framed, 2¾, ca1830 (4259/379)   475
An Officer, waist length, white uniform, circular, framed, 2⅛, ca1815 (4259/377)   *300*

An Officer   (4259/377)

An Officer
(4259/313)

A Gentleman
(4259/308)

A Gentleman
(4259/315)

An Officer, white uniform, red collar, oval, rectangular leather frame, 2⅞, 1832 (4259/381)		350

Continental School

A Gentleman, blue jacket with gold buttons, oval, framed, 2⅞, ca1800 (4259/368)		325
A Gentleman, blue jacket, oval, framed, 3, ca1810 (4259/366)		225
A Gentleman, dark green jacket, oval, silver pendant frame, 2¼, L18c (4259/370)		150
A Lady, blue dress, coral beads, oval, gilt metal oval frame, 2¼, ca1815 (4259/365)		350
A Lady, white low cut dress, oval, frame ropework border, 2, ca1810 (4259/369)		150
An Officer, blue and red uniform, circular, 2⅛, ca1810 (4259/328)		125

English School

A Gentleman, holding sword, blue military jacket, leather frame, 4⅛, ca1825 (4259/308)		*450*
A Gentleman, red jacket and waist coat, oval bracelet mount, 1½, ca1775 (4259/317)		225
A Gentleman, seated, light brown jacket, oval frame, 4⅝, ca1785 (4259/315)		*375*
A Gentleman, Blue jacket, black lapels, oval, gold pendant frame, 2⅝, ca1795, gold pendant frame (4259/389)		375
A Lady, bust length hair tied back, oval pendat frame, 1⅛, ca1770 (4259/321)		250
A Lady, pink dress with white fichu, oval, framed, 1⅞, ca1780 (4259/388)		375
A Lady, shoulder length hair, oval frame, 1⅝, 19c (4259/314)		275
An Officer, red uniform, oval gold frame, 2½, ca1810 (4259/313)		*250*
Colonel Archibald Cary of Va., brown coat, on blue ground, oval, 1¾, L18c (4259/395)		400
William Penn, standing in front of tree, rectangular, framed, 6⅛, 18c (4259/397)		250

French School

A Gentleman, blue jacket, circular, in open leather case, 2⅜, ca1780 (4259/340)		700
A Gentleman, blue jacket, circular, square wood frame, 2½, 1820 (4259/337)		300
A Gentleman, blue-green jacket, oval in frame, 1½, ca1775 (4259/342)		400
A Gentleman, grey jacket, oval, gold oval frame, 2⅛, ca1800 (4259/358)		350
A Gentleman, grey jacket, powdered hair, oval, framed, 2⅛, ca1780 (4259/360)		325
A Gentleman, mounted in a burrwood box, waist length, circular, 2⅛, ca1780 (4259/324)		350
A Lady, black dress, circular, gold frame, 2¼, ca1800 (4259/357)		200
A Lady, bust length, low cut nauve dress, oval frame, 1⅜, ca1775 (4259/343)		200
A Lady, pink dress, white lace jacket, oval, gilt metal cartouche frame, 2¼, M18c (4259/349)		260
A Lady, standing, white low cut dress, oval, gilt metal frame, 2½, ca1810 (4259/353)		375
A Lady, white dress, green shawl, oval, gilt metal frame, 4⅛, ca1820 (4259/336)		300
A Lady, white dress, oval, gilt metal and wood frame, 2⅜, L18c (4259/362)		225
A Lady, white dress, red shawl, landscape, circular, gilt metal frame, 2⅝, ca1810 (4259/352)		350

A Lady and Two Daughters, in a landscape, circular framed, 3⅛, 1805 (4259/327)   425
A Nude, female, velvet frame, 3¾, 19c (4259/331)   275
An Officer, red uniform, oval, gilt metal oval frame, 1⅝, ca1780 (4259/359)   300

German School

A Gentleman, blue jacket, waistcoat with gold, oval, frame with faceted, 1¼, M18c (4259/373) *425*
A Gentleman, wearing a blue jacket, oval gilt metal frame, 2½, ca1760 (4259/333)   *425*
A Lady, blue dress, oval in oval frame, 2⅝, L18c (4259/371)   *200*
An Officer, navy blue uniform, circular, gold mounted frame, 2⅝, ca1800 (4259/372)   *450*

A Gentleman
(4259/373)

An Officer
(4259/372)

A Gentleman
(4259/364)

Italian School

A Gentleman, standing holding book, oval, framed, 3, ca1810 (4259/364)   *325*

ORNAMENTAL TANKARDS

Pewter mounted blue double overlay, tankard set with a sulphide, of musician%, (4230/94)
Tankard, cast and chased with numerous figures, 8¼, ca1890, 28 ozs (4238/70)   900
Tankard covered, gilt metal, enamel, rock crystal, finial, St. George killing dragon, 6, L19c, Viennese
(4141/54)   3100
Tankard, carved ivory and silver, German, boar hunt, double scroll handle, 13¼, ca1900 (649/264) 3750
Tankard, gilt metal and ivory, German, Neptune holding his trident, 12¾, L19c (649/263)   2250
Tankard, ivory and silver, German, classical battle, foliate handle, 17, L19c (649/262)   4000
Tankard, parcel-gilt, chased with Moses striking the rock, 8¾, ca1670, large, German, 38 ozs
(4238/94)   11000
Tankard, parcel-gilt, high relief with playful tritons, scroll handle, 7½, German, 31 ozs (4238/80) 5100
Tankard, silver-gilt, pineapple pattern, harp shape handle, 6¼, L17c, German, 20 ozs. (4141/600) 7000
Tankard, silver-gilt and serpentine, hunting scene and landscape, 6½, ca1600, fine, German
(4141/601)   7500
Tankard, small, strapwork and fruit, inset with coins, 4¼, 17c, German style, 14 ozs. (4141/608) 425
Tankard, Kirelian Birchroot, carved loop handle, 3 bracket feet, 8, 17/18c, Danish (4133/334) 550

PERSONAL ITEMS

An assortment

Basket, gilt metal, woven wirework with fixed handle, 12½, L19c (4259/512)   175
Beaded pocketbook, gilt embroidery, (690/210)   100
Bell, Spanish, Virgin and child, crucifixation, St. John, 10¾, 1549, rim dam (4133/201)   1600
Bird singing and bird cage, red feathered bird perched in a gilt bronze birdcage, 10¾ (619/176) 250
Bonbonniere, chaffinch, enamel, 3, ca1770, Staffordshire (4160/709)   575

Bottle, perfume, enamel, flattened pear shape, lady smelling rose, 4⅛, ca1765, Staffordshire
(4141/112)   375
Bottle, scent, glass, gold mounted, pear shape, faceted glass, 4, ca1760, English (4160/731)   275
Bowl and cover, circular with triple dome, Continental, 8¼, L19c (4259/545)   250
Box, bronze, seal, chased with arms of Franz Josef, 4⅞, ca1850, Austrian (4160/720)   425
Box, cigarette, jewels, rectangular, mother of pearl, oval citrinc cameo, 3¾, ca1935 (4259/466)   600
Box, cigarette, silver, erotic plaque, engine turned, striped design, 6 (4259/496)   1300
Box, cigarette, French silver, rectangular, reeded thumbpiece set with sapphire, 7⅛, 17 ozs, modern
(4259/463)   275
Box, cigarette, Italian silver, rectangular, tooled in a textured design, 7⅞, 19 ozs (4259/469)   250
Box, circular lacquer with miniature, painted figures by a lake, 2¾, ca1800 (4259/498)   650
Box, circular, gold, Italian, mounted with mosaic of a horse, Marked C.P., 3⅛, E19c (4259/607)   2200
Box, elephant form, silver-gilt, oriental, set with gemstones, tooled flowerheads, L8¼ (4259/515)   700
Box, gold, enamel and diamonds, oval, enameled with Adonis and Aphrodite, 1¾, ca1700
(4259/614)   2700
Box, silver, oval cushion shape, Diana and suitor, L2¾, L17c (4194/528)   800
Box, work, prisoner of war, straw, central floral medallion, amorous, musical devices, 10¾, E19c,
French (4133/242)   200
Bracelet, Art Deco, silver, French paste, flexible, ca1920 (690/237)   50
Cabinet, writing, oak, polychrome, painted birds, animals, 14½, 17c, Spanish (4133/347)   1600
Calendar, pertetual, ormolu and porcelain, surmounted by a winged figure, 15½ L19c French
(619/231)   250
Cane, bamboo sword, stained to simulate rosewood, French, L35½, L19c (4194/466)   300
Cane, carved, presented to King Leopold II of Belgium, L34¾, 1880 (4194/462)   800
Cane, silver-mounted ivory, wood, ivory tip and handle, German, L32¼, ca1884 (4194/461)   250
Cane handle, gold and bloodstone, cylindrical with bulbous top, 2⅜, ca1760 (4259/600)   600
Cane handle, ivory, 17C style, carved from knob, Flemish, 2½ (4259/473)   250
Case, card,silver, Victorian, scene of Windsor Castle, 4, 1854, English (4141/41)   100
Case, card, silver-gilt, Edwardian, Mark C. & N., retangular, chased scrolls and flowers, 4, 1902
(4259/481)   *125*
Case, card, silver, Nathaniel Mills, rectangular, Sir Walter Scott monument, 3½, 1846 (4259/482)   *375*
Case, card, Yapp & Woodward, views of tower of London and Windsor Castle, 3⅜, 1845 (4259/483)   *375*

Case
(4259/481)

Case
(4259/482)

Case
(4259/483)

Case, comb, gold, engraved on both sides with flowers and foliage, 4 (4238/493)   175
Case, vesta, gold and jeweled, chased both sides with lion masks, 2½, ca1890 (4259/468)   950
Casket on stand, Indian silver, long rectangular form, domed lid, stylized floral foliate, 19 (4259/487) 450

Casket, amber and ivory, architectural features, sarcophogus shape, 11 x 18, M17c, fine, North
German (4133/244)   24000
Casket, copper gilt and brass, key, engraved with birds, animals and hunter, 2⅞, E17c (4133/94)   2000
Casket, enamel, lovers in a landscape, sprigs of flowers, 6¼, L19c (4259/540)   475
Casket, gilt metal and carnelian, rectangular, 5⅜, L19c (4259/516)   325
Casket, inlaid staghorn with key, mass of curling vines and birds, figures of Victoria and peace, 19⅜,
16c, 2 pcs, rare, German (4133/239)   13000
Casket, jewel, parcel-gilt, silvered metal, rectangular, domed cover, 6⅝, L19c (4259/503)   700
Chalice, copper gilt, bowl with reeded border, flaring foot with flowering vines, 6½, ca1500 (4133/91)   700
Chest, bronze mounted, wood, painted with 4 enamel plaques, ladies and putti, 8⅛, L19c (619/185)   475
Chest, inlaid wood, foliate scrollwork with in panels, 32, 17c, bark split, Spanish (4133/346)   400
Chest, miniature, wood and pietra dura, two drawers, mounted with 8 panels pietra dura flowers, 7
(619/177)   325
Ciborium and cover, parcel-gilt and enamel, French, etched, stations of cross, 12½, 1875, 49 ozs
(4259/475)   800
Cigarette case, enamel and diamond, shallow rectangular form, 2 Chinese figures, 5½, ca1948
(4160/558)   375
Cigarette case, gold and enamel, cartouche engraved with flowers and scrolls, 3⅛, ca1900
(4160/561)   500
Cigarette case, silver and enamel, sailor and his girl on cover, 3¾, ca1890, Austrian (4160/608)   275
Cigarette case, 18 karat gold, rounded sides, 3½, 6 ozs, 15 dwts gross (4160/560)   1000
Clock, tall case, miniature Dutch silver, bulbous lower body, raised on feet, 9½, L19c (4259/489)   400
Clock, traveling, silver and enamel, French, rectangular case, bands of blue and yellow, 1⅝, ca1900
(649/288)   350
Coach, coronation, gilt metal and enamel, miniature, figures in landscape, 3½, L19c (4259/543)   250
Coffee set, 6 piece, silver-gilt and enamel, tray L14¾,   19c, Viennese (4160/702)   10000
Collar, dog, brass, slip latch and securing loop, engraved, 5¾, E19c, English (4133/103)   175
Column triumphal, red marble classical, surmounted by a bronze eagle, 20¾ (619/237)   225
Columns, pair marble mounted gilt bronze, on triangular bases. Applied with classical marks, 22¼
(619/236)   350
Compact, silver and gold, enamel, French, panel of chased birds, butterflies, 5⅛, ca1940,
Boucheron (4160/569)   1150
Compact, silver-gilt set with jewels, circular, with bird and flowers, 2, ca1900 (4238/566)   400
Compact, Art Deco gold enamel rose diamond, rectangular form, double cover applied with diamond
mounts, 2⅝ (4141/87)   1000
Compact, 14 karat gold and enamel, circular, engine turned red enameled, ring of diamonds, 2¼,
ca1930 (669/243)   700
Crucifix, carved ivory and wood, Continental, 20, 19c (649/260)   375
Crucifix, carved ivory and wood, Continental, 17½, 19c (649/259)   375
Desk seal, mother-of-pearl, silver-gilt, hand below sleeve handle, amethyst, French, 4¼, ca1830
(4194/532)   225
Desk set, ivory and parcel-gilt, inlaid with wood and bronze flowers, leafage, insects, L19c, 8 pcs.
French (619/228)   900
Dish, chariot form, silver-gilt and enamel, lady in a garden with 2 cupids, 5½, ca1900, Viennese
(4160/705)   400
Dish, silver mounted, damascened, Spanish, chased with a bacchanal revel, 16⅜, ca1865
(4259/491)   1000
Etui, enamel, Staffordshire, vignettes, 4¾, ca1770 (4259/547)   150
Etui, gold, agate and diamond, diamond thumbpiece, German, L3½, ca1760 (4194/529)   *1500*
Ewer, coconut, copper gilt, hinged metal mounts, engraved with stylized foliage, 7½, ca1600
(4133/92)   400
Ewer and stand, cabinet, Continental silver, and glass mounted, foliate scrolls, insects, cherubs, 6¼,
ca1880 (669/241)   300
Fan, painted, Chinese export, European courting couples, Chinese scenes in a floral ground, 8,
ca1850 (649/269)   250
Flask, scent glass, gold mounted, vase form, hinged gold cover, 4⅞, ca1840 (4238/550)   400
Flask, scent, gold and glass, drop shape, 4⅝, M19c, French (4160/723)   450
Flask, scent, silver-gilt and hardstone, two handled urn shape, 2, 1890/1, English (4160/722)   350
Flower spray, marble mounted, pporcelain, after Ruyckevelt, 15 (619/229)   150
Frame, miniature, silver, with oval aperture, chased swags, 5⅛, L19c, French (4160/605)   350
Gaming pcs, thirty, ivory, silver-gilt, fitted case, 1⅜ (4160/576)   325
Grater, nutmeg, egg shape, chased with Rococo ornament, 2, ca1760, English* (4160/655)   250
Handle, parasol carved coral, gold mounted, Italian, a seahorse with coiled foil, L19c (4259/501)   550
Inkstand, engraved silver, cut glass, 4 wells, 2 lidded compartments, 3 pentrays, 18 x 12⅛, E19c
(4165/278)   1000
Inkwell, with 3 scroll handles, 3 cherubs masks, 3, 16c (4133/181)   900

Knife, folding, with leather traveling case, curved steel blade, 4½ open, 1574, Dutch (4133/83)	850
Knives and forks, 6 each, and case, steel handles with corinthian capitals, 6¾, 6¼, E17c, rare, Italian (4133/82)	2000
Lorgnette, gold, enamel, rose diamonds and cabochon sapphires, 5⅞, ca1900, French (4141/89)	*800*
Magnifying glass, quadruple, mother of pearl and silver, 4 lenses, 4¾, M18c (4160/729)	200
Miniatures, pair, enamel, Limoges, busts of facing young women in profile, circular frames, 3⅜, ca1900 (4259/537)	325
Mortar, exterior molded with 4 winged cherub masks, ribs, 5, 16/17c, Spanish (4133/211)	100
Mortar, saucer shaped rim, 5 vertical bosses, 5¼, 16c, French (4133/204)	200
Mortar, sides dec with bands of scrollwork, stylized urns, 4, 16c, Italian (4133/199)	350
Mortar, six vertical ribs separating masks, nereids, foliate motifs, 5¼, 16c, Spanish (4133/193)	450
Necessaire, enamel, couple in a pastoral landscape, 4, ca1770, Staffordshire (4160/717)	450
Necessaire, enamel, straight sided taped form, cobalt blue ground, flowers, 3¼, ca1770, Staffordshire (4141/109)	425
Necessaire, enamel, wedge shape, painted, 4 (4160/616)	450
Necessaire, gilt metal and enamel, landscapes and flowers, 3½, ca1790, Swiss (4141/104)	325
Necessaire, gold fittings, mother of pearl, Empire, 4⅞, ca1810 (4259/583)	1250
Necessaire, silver, wedge shape, 3⅝, 1725 (4259/567)	300
Necessaire, silver, wedge shape, chased with female figures, 3¼, ca1770, Dutch* (4160/726)	200
Necessaire, silver, Victorian, rectangular form chased with scrolling foliage, 4¾, 1846, English (4141/42)	325
Necessaire with chatelaine gilt metal, chased with mars and venus, 8¼, M18c (4141/86)	550
Nef, silver-gilt, raised on 4 wheels, axles formed as dolphins, 18½, ca1900, German (4160/575)	1800
Nutmeg box, silver, George III, Mark D.F., acorn shape, 1½, ca1760 (4259/568)	375
Oliphant Ivory, carved with wild beasts, scroll, coat of arms, bust of king, 27, 19c (619/178)	1400
Parasol, black silk satin, (690/224)	40
Parasol, peach silk taffeta, pin stripes, (690/223)	40
Pipe, meerschaum, carved, form of a jockey and a lady on horseback, hounds, 12, L19c (669/240)	750
Placecard holders, set six, Wedgwood mounted, sterling silver, blue, white, classical relief, 1½, 1907 (669/242)	225
Plaque, carved ivory, carved in high relief with homage to Venus, Dieppe*, 4, E19c (4259/517)	250
Plaque, carved mother of pearl, Italian, 2 maidens presenting the baby to mother, 5⅜, ca1820 (4259/492)	475
Plaque, enamel, oval, country party, girl in swing, rectangular frame, 7¼, ca1900 (4259/538)	300
Plaque, enamel, with peacocks on rock and cherry branch, English, 5⅞, ca1760 (4259/551)	2500
Plaque, wall, circular, enamel, Limoges, young woman wearing necklace, 11¾, ca1900 (4259/539)	750
Plate, enamel, Limoges, mounted boar hunt scene, 8½, L19c (4259/536)	500
Purse, evening, gold mesh, rectangular form with pendant ball, clasp ruby, with chain, 5⅛, ca1910 (4238/490)	400
Purse, mesh, gold, neck of criss-cross bars, chain, 3⅜, ca1900, French, 2 ozs (4160/563)	400
Purse mesh, 18 karat gold, chevron design with flap and chain, 4⅞, ca1900, 5 ozs, 10 dwts (4160/562)	900
Salts, set of four, enamel, bulbous circular form painted with pastoral scenes, 1⅜, ca1755, Staffordshire (4141/110)	350
Shears, pair, engraved iron, with foliage, birds and scrollwork, with inscription, 16, 1799, Spanish (4133/86)	650
Spectacles and case, pair, gold, engraved inscription and date 1851, 4½, ca1850 (4238/567)	400
Spice box, silver, Jens Sveistrup, Danish, scroll shape, hinged base, 3¼, 1767 (4259/570)	900
Tea caddy, silver mounted facated overlay, rectangular, band of oval windows, 5, ca1840 (4259/494)	325

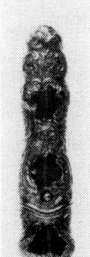

Etui
(4194/529)

Lorgnette
(4141/89)

Tobacco box, brass and copper, portrait of Frederick the Great, 6¼, ca1760 (4259/560)   *900*
Tobacco box, brass and copper, Dutch, brass top with calendar, currency table, 6¾, 18c (4259/559)   425
Toilet set, silver-gilt and enamel, flowers and ribbons, Debain, Paris, ca1920, 23 pcs, French
(4238/488)   725
Toilet set, 10 piece, 14 Karat gold, mounted, Gorham & Co., (619/174)   2000
Toilet set, 14 karat gold, formal foliage and festoons, Gorham Co., ca1910, 14 pcs, American
(4238/489)   2400
Vanity set, traveling, Edward Smith, 11 numbered boxes, covers, English, 4⅝, L19c (4259/127)   *1300*
Vinaigrette, oval blood stone body, hinged gold cover, mounted under glass, 1, ca1800 (4259/593)   650
Vinaigrette, amphora form, pendant, gold and emerald, variegated pattern, 2¼ (4238/507)   400
Vinaigrette, cow form, silver and agate, animal laying on grassy base, agate base, 2¼ (4160/654)   650
Vinaigrette, egg shaped, silver, George III, with rococo ornament, 1¾, ca1760 (4259/569)   125
Vinaigrette, gold and enamel, Swiss, oblong, enameled with bouquet of flowers, 1⅝, ca1840
(4259/580)   1500
Vinaigrette, gold, Swiss, oblong, chased and enameled in multi-color, flowers, 1⅜, ca1840
(4259/579)   1500
Vinaigrette, oval, silver, engraved with garland of leaves, flowers, 1¼, ca1809, English (4160/663)   120
Vinaigrette, silver, basketweave, 3⅞, 1827, English (4160/674)   120
Vinaigrette, silver, engraved with a vase of fruit, 1½, 1809, English (4160/678)   175
Vinaigrette, silver, raised chased border, 1½, 1838, Early Victorian (4160/681)   200
Vinaigrette, silver, rectangular shape, 1⅜, 1830, English (4160/679)   200
Vinaigrette, silver, scrolling tendrils, 1⅞, 1809, English (4160/673)   220
Vinaigrette, silver, with diagonally crossed lines, 1½, 1849, Victorian (4160/680)   200
Vinaigrette, silver-gilt, floral motif, 1⅜, 1814, English (4160/676)   175
Vinaigrette, silver-gilt, pierced grille, 1⅜, 1823, English (4160/675)   200
Vinaigrette, silver-gilt, gold plaque, with initials, 1½, 1838, Victorian (4160/677)   220
Vinaigrette, upright, wedge shape, foliage and flowers, 2¾, ca1850, unusual, Victorian (4160/670)   300
Vinaigrette, Mull shaped, silver, curved horn body, chased with thistles, 2⅛, ca1870, Scottish
(4160/659)   275
Vinaigrette, 3 color gold and jeweled, with rubies and emerald, music trophy, 1¼, ca1820
(4160/671)   1000
Vinaigrette and chain, quatrefoil shape, lobed and fluted sides, 1⅝, ca1840 (4259/578)   1500
Vinaigrette pendant, silver-gilt, Rococo cartouche form, scrolls and flowers, 1½, ca1760, English
(4160/658)   225
Walking stick, carved ivory and wood, ivory handle, Austrian*, 36¼, ca1880 (4194/464)   300
Walking stick, ivory mounted, with a Gallic warrior head, French, L35, ca1890 (4194/465)   375
Water pipe mount, gold mounted, Persian, cylindrical, 5 oval portraits of women, 2½, M19c
(4259/582)   1200

Viennese

Bonbonniere, mandolin form, gilt metal, enamel, couple in a landscape, 4⅞], L19c (4259/541)   450
Casket, jewel, gilt metal and enamel, rectangular on scroll feet, 6¾, ca1900 (4259/527)   1200
Coach, coronation, miniature, silver-gilt and enamel, hinged top, Mark S.G., 4⅜, L19c (4259/518)   1600
Flask, scent, silver-gilt, Mark R.L., lobed and fluted, children playing, 5, L19c (4259/519)   800
Nef, minature, gilt metal and enamel, with couples and maidens, 3½, ca1900 (4259/521)   650
Tazza, gilt metal and enamel, 2 handled oval bowl, 6, L19c (4259/544)   650
Vase covered, 2 handled, enamel, cylindrical, pastoral scenes, 9⅞, ca1900 (4259/534)   1900

STATUETTES

Antoinette, Marie, bust, marble, half length figure on pedestal base, French, 26½, 19c (649/403)   400
Beatrice figure, Lombardi, young girl with hand raised to shield eyes, 39½, 1873 (649/406)   650
Bishop, figure carved ivory, standing holding open bible, 11, L19c, Continental (4160/579)   700
Bonaparte, Napoleon, bust, marble, French, 30½, 19c (649/404)   500
Buccellati, mounted guardsman, silver, 14½, modern (4160/591)   700
Buccellati, Roman warrior, wearing short tunic and cloak, silver, 19½, modern (4160/592)   1300
Bullene, Arab falconer equestrian, silver, with gold details, 11¾, modern (4160/580)   2350
Bullene, Armored Knight, equestrian, silver, 16½, modern (4160/588)   1800
Bullene, Blackbeard, The Pirate, bronze, gold, white marble base, 10, modern (4160/581)   775
Bullene, Don Quixote on Rocinante, silver and bronze, 12½, modern (4160/587)   800
Bullene, Four Horsemen Of Apocalypse, gold, silver and jewels, 17¾, modern (4160/590)   5800
Bullene, Warrior Holding Spear, silver trimmed with gold, 18½, modern (4160/585)   2550
Bullene, Warrior On Rearing Horse, bronze, gold and silver, 10¾, modern (4160/583)   1200
Bust, Italian marble, Garella, of Magurite, her gaze demurely lowered, 24, dam, 19c (649/416)   750
Bust, Russian, marble, Nicholas First, robe around his shoulders, 23, 19c (649/405)   600
Carving of a monkey, agate, reeling, drunken, French, 3⅛, ca1910 (4194/468)   600
Classical maiden, statue, coy pose, right leg crossed over left, hand to chin, 44, ca1900 (649/412)   2250

Cock pheasant statue, parcel-gilt, chased partly gilt plumage, detachable head, 13, ca1900, German (4238/71) — 600

Couple, German silver-gilt and marble, 17c dress, lady playing lute, semi-precious stone, 5¼, L19c (669/262) — 750

Court jester, figure, ivory, jester blowing a horn and dancing, 8¼, 19c (649/266) — 700

Dante, bust, Italian marble, Vich, cap and coat in veined pale brown, 16 (649/402) — 400

French soldier wearing decoration and backpack, 19, M19c, French*, silver (4160/593) — 1200

Tobacco box
(4259/560)

Vanity set
(4259/127)

Frog figure, green nephrite, poised on a quartz rock base, 5½ (649/286) — 350

Garden group, terra-cotta, two children, 30, 19c, French (619/193) — 650

Girl, figure, Italian marble, emblematic of summer, flower and leaves at base, 52¼, 19c (649/414) — 1300

Hercules and the Lion, group, ivory, god wrestling with a ferocious beast, 4, cr, 19c (649/265) — 250

Lucrece, bust, marble, maiden wearing loosely draped robe and tiara, 22½, ca1910, A. Piazza, Carrara (669/485) — 275

Maiden, statue, personifying fall with wheat sheaves at her feet, 31¾, ca1900 (649/407) — 550

Ornament, architectural marble, form of the ruins of the Temple of Jupiter, 30¾ (619/238) — 200

Ornaments, table, pair. Basalt and Bronze, form of temples, containing classical figures, 13 (619/240) — 75

Pedestal, columnar, painted wood, fluted shaft, top set with pink marble, 46 (649/400) — 250

Pedestal, gray marble, in 3 sections, 33¼ (649/396) — 275

Pedestal, green marble, stem with swirling fluted sides, square top, 39½ (649/398) — 600

Pedestal, green marble, stem with swirling fluted sides, square top, 39½ (649/397) — 650

Pedestal, white marble, stem carved with band of 4 lozenges, squared top, 42 (649/399) — 400

Psyche, figure, B. Fausto, winged maiden seated on rocky base, 39, L19c (649/415) — 700

Reclining nude, statue, L. Bolinelly, girl lying on rocky ledge, 16, E20c (649/411) — 2000

Roman emperor, bust, marble, circular base, 22½, ca1872 (649/401) — 325

Roman soldier, painted on marble pedestal, armor and helmet painted gray and black, French*, 46½, L19c (649/395) — 400

Roman warrior bust, citrine quartz, bearded wearing toga and helmet, 6 (4160/732) — 1600

Shell, conch, carved, with cameo scene of putto and maiden, now a lamp, 11, L19c (649/287) — 250

Sophocles, bust, white marble, on circular plinth, 25¾, L19c (649/394) — 450

St. Atuette, enamel and mother of pearl, a harlequin with spiral staff, Viennese, 7½, L19c (4259/528) — 1350

St. Lucy, figure, silver-gilt and ivory, standing holding a salver, 14½, L19c, German (4160/578) — 1400

Statuette, silver, Romulus and Remus, being nursed by the She-Wolf, 6, Italian (4141/571) — 400

Three putti, group, terra cotta, puttis among grape vine, 25 (619/192) — 425

Two children, group, marble, one decorating the others with rose, 21½, 1900, Moreau (669/484) — 650

Venus, statue, Italian marble, standing figure with arms held before her, dolphin, 61, large, 19c (649/410) — 2750

Venus Di Milo, copy white marble, after calendi, 35 (619/191) — 500

Venus Pudenda, statue, goddess holding a drapery, 28¾ (649/409) — 225

Violinist, figure, painted, enamel and, mother of pearl, inset with enamel, plaques, 6½, L19c (619/188) — 450

Young girl sewing, figure, seated on plinth, French*, 28, ca1900 (649/413) — 1600

Young lady bust, wearing lace trimmed hat and bodice, on pedestal, 60, ca1910 (669/487) — 450

WATCHES

American

American Waltham Watch Co., engraved, 14 karat gld, 17 jewels, 2, model 88 (4238/427) — 475

American Waltham Watch Co., four-color, gold hunting case lever movement, 2¼ ca1900
(4165/65) | 1200
American Waltham Watch Co., gold, lady's hunting case, chain, 1⅜ ca1895 (4165/29) | 550
American Waltham Watch Co., gold, lady's 4 color, white enamel dial, 1⅜, model 82 (4238/421) | 450
American Waltham Watch Co., lady's, star and crescent in old mine diamonds, 1⅜, model 90
(4238/429) | 400
American Waltham Watch Co., Art Nouveau, 14 karat gold, 7 jewels, 1⅜, model 1907 (4238/422) | 375
American Waltham Watch, Co., P.S. Bartlett, gold hunting case, 2⅛ ca1883 (4165/66) | 700
American Watch Co., openface, key wind, 15-17 jewels, fall plate lever movement, 2¼, 1870, rare
(4238/403) | 250
American Watch Co., P.S. Bartlett, four-color, gold hunting case, lever movement, 2⅛ ca1889
(4165/67) | 600
Columbus Watch Co., openface watch, 11 jewels, key wind and set, 2¼, ca1883 (4238/380) | 275
E. Howard & Co., gold hunting case, E 3 quarter plate movement, 2⅛ ca1900 (4165/60) | 1000
E. Howard & Co., silver openface, 15 jewels, key wind, 2¼, low number 10860 (4238/408) | 325
Elgin National Watch Co., gold-filled, openface, model 478, 21 jewels, stem wind, 2, ca1924
(4238/397) | 460
Elgin National Watch Co., gold-filled, openface, model 571, 21 jewels, 9 adjustments, 2 (4238/396) | 200
Elgin National Watch Co., hunting case, four-color, lady's, gold cavette, 1⅝, like model 94
(4238/413) | 950
Elgin National Watch Co., hunting case, gold and diamond lady's similar to model 67, 1¾
(4238/415) | 550
Elgin National Watch Co., hunting case, gold and diamond Lady Elgin, 1⅝ (4238/416) | 350
Elgin National Watch Co., hunting case, gold and jeweled lady's model 45, 1⅝ (4238/414) | 900
Elgin National Watch Co., hunting case, 14 karat gold, lady's case engraved, 1⅝, model 94
(4238/412) | 425
Elgin National Watch Co., hunting case, 14 karat gold, stem wind, 1⅝, model 94 (4238/419) | 325
Elgin National Watch Co., hunting case, 14 karat gold, stem wind, 7 jewels, 1⅜ (4238/417) | 325
Elgin National Watch Co., hunting case, 14 Karat lady's, 11 jewels, 1⅝, model 94 (4238/428) | 325
Elgin National Watch Co., 18 karat gold, model 10, 11 jewels, stem wind, engraved, 2, 1882
(4238/393) | 325
Gold lady's hunting case & chain, three quarter plate lever movement, 1¼ ca1905 (4165/64) | 475
Hamden Watch Co., gold hunting case, 2¼ ca1890 (4165/16) | 400
Hamilton Watch Co., gold filled, openface, 21 jewels, model R/R 992B, 2 (4238/387) | 150
Hamilton Watch Co., gold-filled, hunting case, 17 jewels, stem wind, 2, 1906 (4238/385) | 125
Illinois Watch Co., gold thin openface, retailed by Tiffany & Co., 1¾ ca1910 (4165/61) | 325
Illinois Watch Co., lady's hunting case, 14 Karat gold, 15 jewels, 1⅜, model 35 (4238/470) | 200
Waltham Watch Co., gold hunting case, jeweled movement, 2⅛ ca1905 (4165/18) | 325

Continental

Abraham*, Crackow* lady's openface, gold and enamel, 1⅝ hand missing, ca1825 fine (4165/7) | 1300
Astronomical silver and crystal, verge movement, 1¾ ca1650 (4165/119) | 9500
Berthoud a Paris, gold and enamel, openface, verge movement, 1⅝ ca1775, French* (4165/101) | 2500
Chartier a Blois, with alarm, clockwatch verge movement, 1¾ ca1680, French* (4165/114) | 3000
Clockwatch, gilt metal, oval, plague and movement probably of later date, 3 ca1600 (4165/117) | *5000*

Clockwatch (4165/117)

Gilt-metal
and tinted
ivory book
form
(4165/115)

Chronometer
(4194/348)

Dickey
(4165/34)

Concealed watch in parasol handle, silver and enamel, London import marks, L5⅛, 1910 (4238/335)	425
Debary, Henry, with enamel lady, silver pair case, verge movement, 2½ ca1700 (4165/113)	3250
Experimental tourbillon, openface, 2⅜ (4165/58)	1600
Gilt-metal and tinted ivory book form, movement signed, Richard Ledertz, 2⅛ (4165/115)	*2750*
Gilt-metal heart shape, verge movement, 2¾, ca1600 (4165/121)	350
Gilt-metal oval, verge movement, Mary Magdalene before Christ, 2⅜ ca1620 (4165/120)	6000
Hunting case, repeating, gold, Danish, Jules Jurgensen, jeweled movement, 5 minute, Diam 2⅛, ca1900 (4194/315)	3500
Josephson, London, triple case, Dutch, for English market, 2¼ ca1790 (4165/4)	650
L'Epine, Paris, openfaced, repeating, back chased with a love trophy, 1⅝ ca1780 (4165/102)	2300
Mercier, Pierre, silver oignon, large verge movement, 2¼ ca1700 Dutch* (4165/108)	2900
Openface, verge movement, crucifix bridge, angels, 2¼ E19c, Austrian* (4165/19)	275
Openface, ivory, Italian, Filippo Manelli, green, red dots, Diam 2½, ca1790 (4194/336)	5600
Silver melon form, verge movement, 2½ (4165/96)	800
Table clock, calendar, moon phases, Lucas Weidman, cracow, horsemen, W6¼, ca1680 (4194/350)	10500
Triple case, Dutch, verge movement, parcel-gilt bronze stand, 2¼, ca1784 (4194/343)	800
Walnut form, verge movement, 2 (4165/95)	1200

English

Adam Burdess, coventry, lady's gold, openface, key wind, engraved, 1½], 1887 (4238/455)	325
Allen Walker, London silver pair case, enamelled scene on dial, 2, ca1793 (4238/480)	400
Baccuet, London, painted figures, verge movement, 1¾ ca1960 enamel dam (4165/107)	4500
Charter, James, gilt-metal pair-case, bridge engraved with scrolling folige, 1⅞, ca1760 (4165/74)	400
Chronometer, marine, Barraud, Maker to the Royal Navy, W6¾, M19c (4194/348)	*1500*
Dent, London, gold openface, 1⅞ ca1840 (4165/24)	500
Dickey, Andrew, gold pair case, cylinder movement, 2 ca1770 (4165/34)	*1200*
Edward Massey, London, pair case, patent lever movement, gold hands, 2⅛, 1816 (4238/485)	1200
Gay, Charles, London, silver triple case, Continental type bridge, 2¼, ca1772 (4165/110)	650
Gold, hunting case, quarter repeating, erotic automation, 2 ca1900 (4165/77)	5250
Green and Ward, London, gold open face verge movement, 1¾ ca1825 (4165/22)	700
Hughes, William, London, silver hunting case, 2⅛ ca1805 (4165/21)	225
J.B. Yabsley, London, hunting case, gold, key wind and set, 2, 1893 (4238/483)	450
Joseph Johnson & John Harrison, subsidiary seconds, 2, ca1850 (4165/70)	200
M.J. Tobias, Liverpool, openface, 13 jewel movement, key wind, 2⅛, 1850 (4238/484)	275
Openface, gold, W. Farquhar, cylinder movement, key, Diam 1¾, ca1820 (4194/319)	350
Quadruple case, gilt-metal, Edward Prior, Turkish market, 2½, ca1800 (4194/341)	650
Quarter repeating, pair case, Jonathan Pike, silver cock, Diam 1¾, ca1760 (4194/346)	4000
Quarter repeating watch, pair case, verge movement, chased case, Diam 2 (4194/342)	1300
Roskell, Robert, Liverpool, gold dial, gold numerals, gold flowers, 2⅛, ca1837 (4165/75)	1300

Samuel Lowry, London, hunting case, gold, duplix movement, gold hands, 2¼, M19c (4238/482)   900
Samuel Magnus, hunting case, 18 Karat gold, key wind, 2, ca1860 (4238/466)   850
Silver pair case watch, for American market, verge movement, D2-14, ca1810 (4238/370)   225
Silver-gilt and enamel openface, chased gilt movement, 2⅜ M19c (4165/41)   4000
T. Markham, London, pair case, verge movement, Continental bridge, 1⅞, 1784 (4238/473)   1500
Tall case clock, silver miniature, white enamel dial, Edwardian, 11¾, 1903 (4194/359)   425
Triple case quarter repeating, George Prior, verge movement, 4 color gold, Diam 2⅝, ca1820
   (4194/345)   6250

Triple case quarter repeating (4194/345)

Twycross & Son, London, gold openface, 1¾ ca1807 (4165/23)   250
William Stapleton, silver pair case, verge movement, fusee, pierced, 2, 1744, London (4238/478)   440

French

Astronomical, octagonal, gilt metal, Joliuet a Limoges, verge movement, 4 movement ca1620, case
   later (4165/118)   5750
Baltazar, Charles, Paris, coach watch, alarm, silver pair case repeating, 4⅜ ca1770 (4165/98)   9250
Carriage clock, alarm, gilt brass, lever movement, alarm dial, 6½, ca1900 (4194/352)   350
Longines, lady's openface, gold and enamel, 1 3/16 ca1900 (4165/8)   1600
Martinot, Balthazar, Paris, repeating, silver pair case oignon, large verge movement, 2½ ca1690
   (4165/112)   5250
Maubossin, open-face dress watch, circular case carved from Lapis Lazuli, 1⅞, ca1930 (4238/348)   2750
Openface, 3-color gold, J. LeRoy, verge movement, chased, Diam 1⅝, ca1785 (4194/340)   1100
Openface quarter repeating, scroll pierced bridge, hinged dust cover, Diam 2⅛, E19c (4194/339)   1600
Repeating carriage clock, alarm, polished gilt face, 7½, ca1900 (4194/354)   1000
Repeating carriage clock, alarm, Grande Sonnerie, white enamel dial, 6⅞, ca1900 (4194/353)   1700
Repeating coach clockwatch, pair case, calendar and alarm, Diam 5, ca1760, Paris (4194/349)   12500
Silver-gilt, quarter repeating, erotic, automation Willeumier a Paris, 2¼ (4165/69)   3000
Willeamier a Paris, erotic automation scene inside cover, 2¼ (4238/354)   1700

German

A. Lange & Sohne, gold hunting case, case American* 3 quarter plate lever movement, 2⅛] ca1895
   (4165/57)   2100
Bummel, Johan, L., calendar, silver pair case, 2⅜, ca1700 (4165/111)   3250
Gilt-metal and silver oval, movement A Schueder Nurnberg, 3⅛ (4165/116)   2000
Gilt-metal clockwatch, iron verge movement, 3 (4165/122)   1500
Lange & Sohne, gold hunting case, three quarter plate lever movement, 2 ca1910 (4165/27)   1300
Torborch, Goder, quarter repeating, silver pair case, 2¼, ca1720 (4165/109)   1800

Swiss

Agassiz, gold openface, gold cavette, black arabic numerals, 1⅝, ca1900 (4238/447)   225
Andemars Piquet, platinum writwatch, with bracelet, motte white dial, modern, with case (4238/351)   1300
Art deco, gold openface, geometric designs, 1⅞ ca1930 (4165/49)   200
Audemars Piguet, gold openface, 19 jewel movement, 1¾, modern (4238/349)   1000
Beguelin, Edouard, gold openface, lever movement, 2⅛ ca1910 (4165/55)   2300
Bequelin, Henry & Son, hunting case, gold, 21 jewel lever movement, 2⅛ ca1880 (4165/1)   600

Bovet & Rol, lady's hunting case, enamel flowers, gold, 8 jewel movement, 1⅝, ca1860 (4238/437) 550
Boyer, lady's openface, verge movements, gold and enamel, 1⅛ ca1820 (4165/45) 2800
Breitling Gaederich, gold openface, 1⅞ ca1840 (4165/31) 400
C.A. Robert, gold hunting case, cylinder escapement movement, 1¾, M19c (4165/63) 300
Chronograph, minute repeating, calendar and moon phases, 2 ca1910 (4165/40) 1400
Courvoisier Freres, hunting case, silver-gilt, enamel, lever movement, 1¾ ca1870 (4165/44) 475
Desk clocks, silver and enamel, hemispherical dome, 2½, ca1920 (4194/357) 375
Dreyfus Freres, 14 karat gold, hunting case, 19 jewel movement, 2, ca1895 (4238/444) 575
Du Chene & Fils, repeating automation, gold openface, Orpheus and Eurydice, 2⅛ ca1810 (4165/78) 5000
Duchene & Compagne, openfaced, gold and enamel verge movement, 1¾, ca1780 (4165/100) *1700*
Emile Jacot, lady's hunting case, gold, key wind, engraved, 1 3/5, ca1870 (4238/469) 525
Faiver Perrin, hunting case, 18 Karat gold, stem wind, white dial, 2,ca1875 (4238/467) 500
Fob seal, gold musical, oval base containing movements, ca1820 (4165/92) *1700*

Duchene & Compagne
(4165/100)

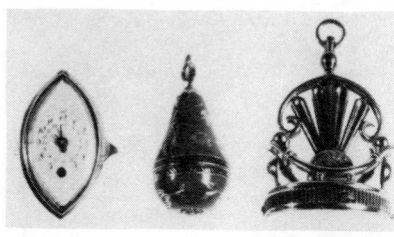

Fob seal
(4165/92)

Gold ring watch
with calendar
(4165/94)

Frederick Nicond, gold hunting case, jeweled lever movement, gold engraved cuvette, 1⅝, ca1865 (4238/368) 550
Freres Bordier, lady's gold, enamel, openface, engraved, 1⅜, 1850 (4238/445) 325
Freres Esquivillon, & de Chaudens, gold and enamel pair case, 1¾, ca1790 (4165/99) 3000
Gilt-metal and enamel 8 day, openfaced, for oriental market, 2 (4165/73) 500
Gold and enamel lady's hunting case, pendant, suspended from brooch, 1½ x 2 L19c (4165/42) 1100
Gold and enamel openface, Gebr, Eppner, Berlin, keyless lever, 2 ca1900 (4165/5) 750
Gold and enamel openface rose form, musical automation, contemporary gold key 2 ca1820 (4165/80) 59000
Gold and enamel openfaced, quarter, repeating erotic automation, 2¼ ca1820 (4165/79) 29000
Gold and enamel pear form, very small verge movement, 1¾ ca1800 (4165/93) 2750
Gold and enamel ring, dials for hours and minutes, bordered with pearls, 1¼ ca1800 (4165/33) 4000
Gold hunting case cover wind watch, white dial, subsidiery seconds, gold hands, 2⅛, ca1895, rare (4238/366) 2750
Gold hunting case, minute repeating, split second chronograph, lever movement, 2⅜ ca1900 (4165/54) 2750
Gold openface, jeweled lever movement, 2 ca1905 (4165/39) 300
Gold openface 5 minute repeating, retailed by Tiffany & Co., 1⅞ ca1900 (4165/59) 3000
Gold openfaced watch, retailed by Tiffany & Co. lever movement 'Swiss', 1 13/16 ca1905 (4165/32) 175
Gold openfaced, quarter repeating, automation, Berthoud a Paris, 2⅛ ca1810 (4165/83) 5750
Gold quarter repeating erotic, automation openface, 2⅜ ca1810 (4165/81) 3250
Gold ring watch with calendar, cylinder movement, 1⅜ ca1800 (4165/94) *1500*
Gruen Watch Co., Art Deco, platinum and enamel, 17 jewel movement, 1¾, ca1925 (4238/345) 2000
Guitar-form watch, parcel-gilt, off-white enamel face, cherubs, key, L6⅛, ca1910 (4238/338) 825
Henry Beguelin, gold hunting case, key wind lever movement, 1¾, ca1875 (4238/448) 225
Henry Sandoz, hunting case chronograph, stem wind, armorial plaque, gold hands, 2⅛, ca1900 (4238/355) 2400
Hunting case quarter repeating, J. Ullman & Co., calendar, moon phases, Diam 2⅛, L19c (4194/331) 1600

Hunting case, gold, M. LeBrun & Co., jeweled lever movement, Diam 1¾, ca1860 (4194/312)   250
Hunting case, gold, South American market, 8 jewels, Diam 1⅞, M19c (4194/321)   375
Hunting case, lady's, oriental market, silver-gilt and enamel, Diam 1⅝, L19c (4194/324)   600
International Watch Co., gold openface, 2 ca1925 (4165/48)   500
J. Assman, glashutte, gold openface, engraved gold cuvette, plain gold case, 2⅛, ca1915, inscript
(4238/361)   2200
J. Uhlman & Co., for oriental market, two tales, 1 with Chinese characters, 2⅛, 1890 (4238/358)   2100
Jurgenson Jules, wrist-watch, white gold, (4165/68)   275
L'Aine, Girardier, verge movement, miniature pictures, dials for day and date, 2⅛ E19c (4165/6)   650
Lady's hunting case, gold, enamel, case with fairy, cupid, flowers, 1½, ca1875 (4238/430)   1250
Lady's openface quarter repeating, highly jeweled lever movement, 1⅜, 1890 (4238/434)   1500
Lady's Art Nouveau hunting case, case enamelled with bird in flight, flowers, 1⅜, ca1900
(4238/435)   800
Laroche, Charles & Fils, hunting case, gold and enamel, detached lever movement, 1⅝ ca1860
(4165/10)   1000
LeCoultre & Co., lady's gold, enamel, openface, cream dial, blue numbers, 1, L19c (4238/446)   390
Monard Brothers, gold hunting case, white dial, Roman numerals, monogram, 2, ca1890 (4238/362)   600
Montandon Freres, lady's hunting case, gold, eamel, pearl-set, key wind, 1⅝, ca1860 (4238/461)   575
Mottu, Geneva, halt hunting case, lady's key wind, flowerhead, 1½, ca1870 (4238/432)   500
Nestor, hunting case, quarter repeating, gold lever movement, 2⅜ ca1905 (4165/15)   1900

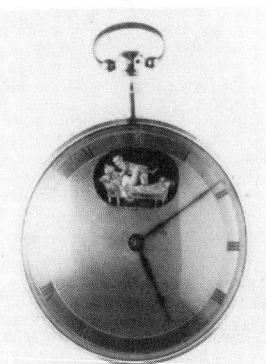

Openface (4194/335)

Openface, calendar, moon phases, gilt dot decoration, Diam 2, 1890 (4194/306)   250
Openface, enamel, Edouard Juvet Fleurier, oriental market, Diam 2¼, ca1830 (4194/327)   3000
Openface, enamel lady's, cylinder movement, engraved flowers, pearls, Diam 1⅜ (4194/325)   1100
Openface, erotic automaton, gold, 4 color gold musical, Diam 2¼, ca1830 (4194/335)   *4750*
Openface, gold, gold dial, key-wind lever movement, Diam 1¾, ca1870 (4194/310)   275
Openface, gold, verge movement, chased foliate border, Diam 1¾, ca1810 (4194/329)   400
Openface, gold, Bovet, oriental market, Diam 2¼, ca1830 (4194/330)   1200
Openface, gold, Vacheron & Constantin, subsidiary seconds, Diam 1⅞, ca1910 (4194/320)   600
Openface, repeating, chronograph, gold, Audemars Piguet, monogrammed, Diam 2, ca1900
(4194/316)   3250
Openface, silver masonic, cylinder movement, triangle case, L2¾, ca1820 (4194/334)   850
Openface, split-second chronograph, gold, gold cuvette, black Arabic numerals, Diam 1⅞, ca1810
(4194/307)   500

Openface, white gold and enamel, retailed by Tiffany & Co., 1⅝, ca1930 (4238/346) 1600
Openface, 5 minute, silver, lady's, Vacheron & Constantin, slide repeat, engraved case, Diam 1⅜, ca1890 (4194/313) 1500
Openface, 8 day, gold, two-train detached lever movement, 1⅞, ca1850 (4194/309) 550
Orssel & Fils, hunting case repeater, fully jeweled stem wind movement, 2, ca1910 (4238/360) 2000
Oscar Fresard, lady's openface, with broach, gold,diamond and enamel, 2¼, 1910 (4238/462) 2100
Patek & Co., gold, enamel, openface, lady's, 10 jewel cylinder movement, 1¼, ca1860 (4238/431) 550
Patek Philippe, gold lady's openface, with chain, 1¼ (4165/53) 425
Patek Philippe, gold openface, minute repeating, retailed by Bailey Bank Biddle, 2, ca1910 (4165/56) 4750
Patek Phillipe Co. gold wristwatch, with 14 karat bracelet, 18 jewels, ca1935 (4238/352) 550
Piaget wristwatch, gold, 18 jewel movement, gold dial in fleck design, modern (4238/350) 650
Qudemars Piquet & Cie, chronograph, openface, minute repeating, calendar, moonphases, 2, 1903, rare (4238/367) 15000
Roger, lady's gold, enamel, hunting case, white dial, D½, 1865 (4238/458) 600
Roulet, Jacques, hunting case, gold and enamel, key wind on chain, 1⅝ ca1860 (4165/35) 1000
Silver and enamel openface, 2 lacks hands, ca1810 (4165/20) 550
Silver gilt, enamel, 20 four hour, openface, for oriental market, 2¼ M19c unusual (4165/43) 2200
Silver openface, quarter repeating, automation, 2¼ ca1840 (4165/82) 2300
Silver openface calendar, dials for time, day of week, days of month, 1⅛ ca1810 (4165/14) 350
Touchon & Co., gold openface, octagonal form, 1¾ ca1910 (4165/38) 350
Two face, gold, matte silver, and skeletonized center, Diam 1¾, ca1880 (4194/333) 750
Ulysse Nardin, repeating wrist watch, white dial, blued hands, 1¼, ca1940 (4238/353) 3500
Voucher, Fleurier, openface, thin, gold, enamel cylinder movement, 1⅝ ca1830 (4165/46) 3200
Watch, lady's, chatelaine, garnets, turquoises, pearls, 3⅞, 1870 (4194/300) 600
Watch back, enameled, blue and white enameled plaque, circle of rhinestones, 1¾, E19c (649/285) 225

WAX PORTRAITS

American*, PORTRAITS, profile, pair, 5, L19c (4160/500) 125
English, PORTRAITS, profile, pair, 3¾, ca1816 (4160/498) 125
English, PORTRAITS, profile, pair, polychrome, 3½, E19c (4160/497) 150
English*, PORTRAITS, profile pair wax, 6¼, ca1765 (4160/501) 160
Mexican*, PORTRAITS, profile Mexican heroes, 8 (two-four each), 2¾, L19c, wax (4160/503) 850
Mexican*, PORTRAITS, profile, Mexican heroes, eight(two, four-each), L19c, wax (4160/502) 900
S. Percy, PORTRAITS, pair, polychrome, 8¼, 1813, unusually large (4160/487) 550

Chapter 8

Items of Special Interest

This chapter covers many miscellaneous categories such as paperweights, dolls, toys, and musical instruments. Generally the pieces are of historic, nostalgic or utilitarian rather than art-historical interest. Items drawn from folk and popular culture, along with those originally designed for a nonadult audience, comprise most of this field.

Paperweights sold at auction are primarily of French and American origin with nineteenth- and twentieth-century dates. American nineteenth-century paperweights have long been undervalued, but recently public appreciation of these pieces has grown, and prices have responded. French antique millefiori paperweights bring the highest prices. In contrast, French antique sulphides bring prices comparable to American paperweights and contemporary French paperweights are also undervalued. The disparity of value among French paperweights offers a good opportunity to collectors.

Dolls, dollhouses and dollhouse furnishings have enjoyed a vogue recently. Dollhouses are valued in proportion to their size, the quality of their construction and the fidelity with which they reflect a style or period of architecture.

Toys have also become extremely popular. For twentieth-century toys, condition is very important; unused toys in their original boxes bring the highest prices. Mechanical banks, Mickey Mouse items and Lionel trains have particularly dedicated followings, with prices for Lionel train sets sometimes reaching into the thousands of dollars.

Memorabilia of the dance, the theater and the opera are a relatively new field and so offer great opportunities for enterprising collectors. Theatrical productions require programs, posters, and designs for costumes and sets. Sketches and studies are treated as original works of art and depend upon an artist's reputation for their value. Other memorabilia are valued for their association with a particular performer, work, dramatist or composer.

Most antique violins and other stringed instruments are purchased to be used by musicians. Unlike other antiques, their value depends upon their utility, which in turn depends upon their tone. Other factors such as the color and grain of the wood have a bearing, but only instruments of fine tone bring high prices. Collectors must be wary of violins with misleading labels. Many nineteenth-century European manufacturers produced copies of the instruments of famous makers, labeled with those makers' names. The poor tone of most of those copies makes them less valuable now than they were when manufactured.

Pianos and harpsichords usually bring disappointingly low prices, the latter frequently being bought for their frames and rebuilt. On the other hand, American-made instruments are attracting considerable attention. Wind instruments—cornets and clarinets—are more prized than American violins, but the greatest activity is in early banjos and guitars.

Because most of the items in it appeal by virtue of nostalgic associations and fine craftsmanship, this field abounds with specialized collectors pursuing narrow ranges of items. The beginning collector can enter a small, well-defined portion of the market and is in an excellent position to acquire an interesting collection with a small budget.

Nijinsky (4183/43)

ANTIQUE CLOTHES

Black net skirt and Bolero jacket, beaded and embroidered, 1910's (690/14)	$90
Bridesmaid dress, slate blue, taffeta, with jacket, repairs (690/292)	30
Cape, black embroidered and beaded, silk, (690/55)	60
Cape, black wool evening, satin lining, 1940's (690/109)	110
Capelet, cream wool, embroidered, (690/56)	70
Chausible, gilt brocade, damaged, (690/291)	40
Coat, black silk taffeta, with black silk pelerine, (690/53)	50
Coat-dress, black silk, embroidered, (690/96)	60
Dress, beaded, blue sequins, 1920's, some damage (690/13)	90
Dress, black beaded, net, 1920's (690/84)	200
Dress, black lace, 1920's (690/88)	60
Dress, black lace, champagne chiffon lining, 1920's (690/89)	100
Dress, black lace, over midnight blue satin, 1920's, labeled (690/80)	125
Dress, black printed 2 piece, silk, 1900's (690/59)	70
Dress, black satin, gold tissue panels, pair of stockings, 1920's (690/86)	275
Dress, black silk chiffon, wrap front, 1920's (690/79)	75
Dress, brown velvet and chiffon, Indian motif, 1920's (690/11)	125
Dress, brown/blue printed wool, floral stripes, 1850's (690/30)	130
Dress, Callot Soeurs, beaded, 1927, labeled (690/85)	350
Dress, champagne silk chiffon, surplus bodice, 1910's (690/70)	200
Dress, convertible neckline, black crepe, 1940's (690/24)	50
Dress, cream silk two-piece, nosegay print, early 1900's, some damage (690/65)	150
Dress, dotted-Swiss and lace, 1900's (690/274)	275
Dress, embroidered and lace-trimmed, 1900's (690/273)	175
Dress, green silk taffeta, tattersoll plaid, 1900's (690/63)	250
Dress, heavy black cotton, two pc with flowers, 1890's/1900's (690/64)	30
Dress, ivory and silk printed, two-piece, 1900's (690/69)	175
Dress, ivory lace, 1920's (690/166)	300
Dress, lace, taupe and gilt, 1920's (690/82)	30
Dress, peach satin, long, embroidered, (690/133)	50
Dress, pink silk organdy, some damages, 1930's (690/97)	250
Dress, plaid heavy cotton, multi-colored woven, 1840's/1850's (690/32)	60
Dress, printed cotton, scalloped sleeves, 1840's/1850's (690/31)	120
Dress, purple and gold cotton, striped, (690/122)	120
Dress, silk champagne, art deco buckle, late 1920's (690/92)	70
Dress, two-piece, watered silk, labeled owner (690/62)	175
Dress and jacket, lilac chiffon, long, 1930's (690/104)	60
Dress and jacket, lilac cotton, 1910's (690/77)	100
Dress and jacket, natural raw silk, 1910's, labeled (690/78)	150
Dress and matching bag, printed lame, 1930's (690/19)	70
Dressing robe and nightgown, white cotton, (690/268)	100
Evening bag, black suede, and rhinestone, (690/187)	40
Evening coat, cream wool, (690/119)	60
Evening dress, changeable taffeta, with roses, 1940's (690/112)	30
Evening dress, pale peach, flowering vines, 1930's (690/21)	100
Evening dress, peach satin damask, two-piece, 1880's (690/71)	275
Evening dress, satin, cream fringe, minor stains (690/116)	30
Evening dress, 2 piece, black velvet and cream lace, 1900's, some damage (690/27)	70
Fortuny dress, black, pleated silk with bill of sale 'Venice', 1930's (690/98)	1100
Frock, organdy plaid, 1950's (690/149)	70
Hattie Carnegie evening coat, black satin, with skirt, 1950's (690/148)	30
Jacket, black braid and net, satin piping, (690/54)	60
Jacket, embroidered, burgundy velvet, (690/120)	425
Jacket, ermine bolero, labeled Bergdorf Goodman, (690/289)	500
Kimono, pale peach, embroidered plum blossoms, (690/163)	60
Kimono, pale peach, with plum blossoms, (690/164)	60
Lawn dress, white cotton lace, some stains, 1900's (690/272)	475
Liberty & Co. dress, gilt, floral silk chiffon, 1920's (690/102)	225
Long dress, gold silk brocade, boat neck, minor stains, 1830's (690/35)	200
Long dress and jacket, lavender grey crepe, labeled, late 1930's (690/107)	200
Mantel, black ribbed silk, (690/52)	70
Peignoir, white sheer, silk crepe, some stains (690/157)	110
Shawl, black wool, with chenille fringe, moth holes (690/235)	20
Shirtwaist, black silk, printed, white dots, 1890's (690/50)	30
Shirtwaist, cream lace net, over pale peach silk, (690/49)	40
Shirtwaist, elaborate, black lace, cream lace and silk, 1900's (690/48)	100

Skirt, white cotton, eyelet, (690/258)	40
Tea gown, navy ribbed silk, damask panel, 19c (690/60)	90
Two-piece dress, brown silk, silk 'fur' trim, early 1880's (690/39)	100
Two-piece dress, cut velvet, deep plum taffeta, 1880's (690/41)	100
Two-piece dress, silk brocade, 1890's (690/40)	100
Wedding dress, ivory satin, and lace, 1900's (690/294)	100
Wedding dress, white lace beaded, 1920's (690/299)	100
Worth jacket, multi-colored floral cut velvet, 1880's, labeled (690/67)	150
Worth tea gown, silk grosgrain, pale beige moive, late 1870's, labeled (690/68)	300

AUTOMATA

An assortment

Acrobatic clown, French, H33, L19c (690/840)	900
American Black, marked Chicago, clockwork in head cause movement, H22 (690/832)	900
Black banjo player, French, seated on back of chair, H26½, (ca1880) (690/850)	2750
Black drinker, musical, French, 6 movements, works in torso, H24, ca1880 (690/844)	3000
Carrousel musical box, automated, Switzerland, with 5 brass rings, H28¾ (case), ca1875 (690/860)	7000
Clock and bird, bird flits from branch to branch, L15¾, French, ca1900 (690/857)	300
Clown, musical, German, composition head, painted tin, ca1900, paint dam (690/718)	450
Cobbler musical, Phalibois*, bearded man, 5 movements, H17, ca1890 (690/831)	2250
Dancing man, French, H25, L19c (690/845)	345
Dancing man, musical, French, 4 movements, H20¾, L19c (690/847)	800
Duck and ducklings nodder, father duck in hat, H19½, ca1900, Austrian* (690/822)	*550*

Duck and ducklings
nodder (690/822)

European Calliope, musical movement, Varetta Bros., Manchester, distressed (690/808)	7500
French musical marotte, Bisque-head, by F. Ganltier, tune plays when whirled, H13, L19c (690/842)	300
French singing bird, H11 (690/863)	175
Girl holding doll, musical, Leopold Lambert, 4 movements, H18½, #1300 dep. L19c (690/846)	1600
Girl holding fan and flowers, musical, French, H19, #1159, L19c (690/827)	75
Girl playing mandolin, bisque head, strums, music, H16, #44, 21 (690/826)	600
Jumeau, bisque head, musical, Lambert*, automation, young girl holding her broken puppet, 15½, dam (659/279)	8500
Monkey Tricyclist, H57, Cook Co., Phila, 1930's (690/805)	800

Musical automaton of a lady, bisque head, closed mouth, blue eyes, H12 (629/172)   550
Musical automaton of a lady, seated at dressing table, closed mouth bisque, socket head H14
  (629/173)   1200
Musical box, Swiss, Mermod Fres., 10 tunes, L28¾ (case), ca1875 (690/862)   800
Musical clock painting, 20x 24½, painting (690/865)   2250
Postal Electric Automaton, airplane propellor spins, train smokes, Cook Co., Philadelphia , 1940's
  (690/796)   400
Rabbit hopping, brown and white, L14½ (690/817)   425
Santa Claus, Cook Co., Philadelphia , H44, 1930's (690/804)   250
Singing Bird, bird in cage, beak, head, tail movement, H10¾, French (690/858)   150
Standing Arab, Cook Co., Philadelphia, H77, 1930's (690/802)   900
The peasant and the pig, musical, Vichy, 10 movements, H30, dam, ca1870 (690/834)   5750
Wax baby in hat, voicebox says 'mama', H9½ (690/839)   150
Witch's head, composition, eyes roll, tongue moves, H7½ (690/833)   *850*
Woman Automaton, head turns, eyes blink, electric, H21, Cook Co., Philadelphia , 1940's (690/801)   750

Decamps

Dog, rears on his hind legs and hops 3 times, L9 (690/811)   100
Laughing man, rocks back and forth, electric, H32, (ca1920) (690/852)   900
Percussionist monkey, shakes gourds, H13 (690/823)   200
Roaring lion, 4 movements, rears and jumps forward, roaring, L17 (690/848)   475
Stalking jaguar, creeps forward, moving side to side, L22½ (690/849)   800
Walking and Mewing Cat, moves 3 times and meows, L20½ (690/812)   350
Walking elephant, trunk raised, L15 (690/821)   325
Walking elephant with sultan, sultan in howdah, H15 (690/851)   375
Walking pig, realistically modeled, winks, L9½ (690/820)   *425*

Witch's head   Walking pig (690/820)   Mickey Mouse
(690/833)   (659/301)

Roullet-Decamps

Cat, fanning herself, H12 (690/815)   350
Cat Cobbler, White fur-covered animal nods as it hammers, H12½ (690/810)   300
Organ grinder monkey, cranks organ, music, H10½ (690/824)   200
Rabbit in cabbage, musical, H10½ (690/838)   425

CELLULOIDS

Comic Strip Art

'**And her Name was Maud**', Sunday, by F. Opper, 7 x 21½, 1931 (659/405)   120
'**Beetle Bailey**', Sunday, by Mort Walker, 11¼ x 15½, 4-18-76 (659/382)   150
'**Blondie**', Sunday, by Chic Young, 15¾ x 17¾, 12-21-1952 (659/372)   200
'**Blondie**', Sunday, by Chic Young, 14 x 17¾, 11-26-1933 (659/408)   150
'**Buck Rogers in the 25th Century**', Sunday by Rick Young, 29½ x 20¼, #1 (659/426)   100
'**Donald Duck**', Sunday, by Walt Disney artist, Al Taliaferro, 15¾ x 22½, 7-22-1962 (659/363)   150
'**Felix**', Sunday panel, by Pat Sullivan, 17¼ x 22, 01-26-1936 (659/402)   100
'**Fritzi Ritz**', Sunday by Ernie Bushmiller, 16½ x 24, 7-28-1957 (659/417)   30
'**Happy Hooligan**', daily, by F. Opper, 22, ca1920 (659/370)   80
'**Howard the Duck**', full page illustration, by Gene Colan, 15¼ x 10¼ (659/367)   30
'**Li'l Abner**', daily, by Al Capp, 23, 01-05-1940 (659/395)   30
'**Li'l Abner**', Sunday by Al Capp, 27¼ x 20¼, 3-16-1941 (659/419)   80
'**Li'l Abner**', Sunday by Al Capp, 22¾ x 20, 8-27-1944 (659/418)   70
'**Li'l Abner**', Sunday by Al Capp, 22 x 19, 8-13-1944 (659/386)   100
'**Little Orphan Annie**', daily, by Harold Gray, 20, 10-2-1967 (659/353)   60

'Moon Beam', panel unpublished, by Al Capp, 22½ x 15¼ (659/390) — 150
'Muggs and Skeeter', 'The Home Run', daily, by Wally Bishop, 22½, 7-24-1930 (659/335) — 30
'One Round Teddy', Sunday, hand colored panel, by Sals Bostwick, 24½ x 16½, 1925 (659/393) — 300
'Peanuts', daily, by Charles Schulz, 27, 05-09-1953 (659/398) — 175
'Pogo', daily, by Walt Kelly, 21¼, 11-17-1970 (659/414) — 250
'Polly and Her Pals', Sunday, panel by Clift Sterrett, 16½ x 25½, 3-24-1957 (659/404) — 50
'Radio Patrol', Sunday, by Eddie Sullivan and Charlie Schmidt, 16¼ x 22, 11-26-1938 (659/403) — 30
'Texas Slim and Dirty Dalton', Sunday by Ferd. Johnson, 23½, 4-7-1946 (659/336) — 30
'The Gumps', Sunday page, by Sidney Smith, 27 x 19½, 1926 (659/409) — 150
'The Gumps', Sunday, by Gus Edson, 27 x 20, 5-18-1941 (659/366) — 175
'Tim Tyler's Luck', Sunday, by Lymon Young, framed, 16½ x 26½, 2-12-1939 (659/401) — 80
'Toots and Casper', Sunday, by Jimmy Murphy, 15¾ x 17, 2-23-1930 (659/364) — 200

Walt Disney

A frog, 'The Old Mill', framed, 4¾ x 6¾, 1937 (659/317) — 90
A King, framed, 6½ (659/333) — 75
Anita from '101 Dalmations', 1961, 11 x 8¼ (690/1002) — 20
'Bambi', framed, 7 x 9⅜, 1942 (659/326) — 475
Bashful from 'Snow White', framed, 1937, H4¾ (690/975) — 75
Carpenter, 'Alice in Wonderland', framed, 8¾ x 7½, 1951 (659/323) — 80
Donald Duck, framed, 7½ x 7½ (659/329) — 350
'Donald Penguin', framed, 8 x 9, 1939 (659/314) — 150
'Donald Penguin', framed, 7¾ x 9, 1939 (659/313) — 200
'Donald Penguin', framed, 4½ x 7½, 1939 (659/312) — 125
'Donald Penguin', framed, 4⅛, 1939 (659/311) — 100
Dopey from 'Snow White', framed, 1937, H3 (690/974) — 150
'Farmyard Symphony', framed, H5½, 1939 (659/300) — 100
Gepetto from 'Pinocchio', framed, 1939, H9½ (690/979) — 150
'Goofy and Wilbur', framed, 6¾ x 10½, 1939 (659/306) — 125
Goofy from 'How to play baseball', 1942, 5¾ x 8⅛ (690/1000) — 75
Grumpy from 'Snow White', framed, 1937, H3¼ (690/973) — 125
Jose Carioca, 'Saludos Amigos', framed, 6½, 1943 (659/310) — 175
Lafayette, 'The Aristocats', framed, 9 x 11¼, 1970 (659/322) — 40
Mickey Mouse, 'The Brave Little Tailor', 7½, 1938 (659/301) — 450
'Pinocchio', 1939, framed, H4⅛ (690/978) — 225
Pluto, 'In Dutch', framed, 4½, 1946 (659/316) — 100
Snow White, 'Snow White and the Seven Dwarfs', framed, 7½ x 9½, 1937 (659/328) — 425
'Society Dog Show', triple, framed, 4½ x 5¼, 7, 1939 (659/325) — 250
'Steamboat Willie', animation drawing, 1928, 7 x 9, #129 (690/1024) — 80
Stepmother, 'Cinderella', framed, 9 x 7 (659/327) — 150
'The Brave Little Tailor', framed, H5, 1938 (659/308) — 120
'The Brave Little Tailor', framed, 6⅞ x 7⅞, 1938 (659/319) — 150
'The Pied Piper', framed, 7¾ x 11, 1933 (659/307) — 125
Timothy Mouse, 'Dumbo', framed, 3½, 1941 (659/315) — 290
Winnie the Pooh and Piglet, 'The Many Adventures of Winnie The Pooh', 10 x 14 (690/1012) — 250

DANCE, THEATRE AND OPERA ITEMS

Ballet material

Alexandre, Arsene, The Decorative Art of Leon Bakst, 77 plates, London, 1913 (4183/48) — 900
Anisfeld, Boris, costume design, Le Roi de Lahore, 9⅞ x 7⅜, ca1924 (4183/22) — 600
Anisfeld, Boris, costume design, Le Roi de Lahore, 9⅞ x 7⅜, ca1924 (4183/21) — 650
Bakst, Leon, costume design for Les Femmes de Bonne Humeur, 19⅛ x 13, 1917 (4183/59) — 6750
Bakst, Leon, costume design for Les Femmes de Bonne Humeur, 19⅛ x 13, 1916 (4183/58) — 7000
Bakst, Leon, La Belle au Bois Dormant, design for decor, 9⅞ x 14, 1916 (4183/65) — 1200
Bakst, Leon, Moskwa, textile design, 18⅜ x 24⅝, ca1922 (4183/35) — 950
Bakst, Leon, Oedipus at Colonus, 6 x 10⅛, 1903 (4183/64) — 1100
Bakst, Leon, San Sebastian, design for 2 bellows, 8⅞ x 11½, 1922 (4183/66) — 800
Bakst, Leon, Caryathis, Poster for dance recital, 90 x 54, ca1919 (4183/49) — 5000
Bakst, Leon, Cleopatra, design for Pavlova costume as Ta-Or, 10⅞ x 8⅛, 1910 (4183/25) — 9250
Bakst, Leon, Helene de Sparte, costume design for Deux Fillets, 10⅝ x 15 11/16, ca1912 (4183/26) — 2600
Bakst, Leon, La Pisanella, costume design for the king, 14¾ x 10¼, ca1913 (4183/27) — 1100
Bakst, Leon, Salome, costume design for St. John the Baptist, 10 11/16 x 7, ca1912 (4183/28) — 900
Benois, Alexandre, design for proscenium arch of Swan Lake, 16½ x 25, ca1945 (4183/19) — 650
Berard Christian, Symphonie Fantastique, costume designs, 13 x 18½, ca1936 (4183/95) — 800
Berman, Eugene, Giselle, design for decor, 9⅛ x 12⅛, ca1940 (4183/91) — 750
Cerrito, Fanny, autograph letter, to Mr. Lumley discussing plans, 1846 (4183/17) — 225

Chirico, Giorgio Di, Bozzetto per un Balleto, 9½ x 12½ (4183/90)   8250
Cocteau, Jean, Karsavina, poster, Spectre de la Rose, lithograph in colors, Paris, 76¾ x 50, ca1911
   (4183/38)   5000
Craig, Edward, Gordon, On the Art of the Theatre, 16 illustrations, Chicago, 1912 (4183/61)   200
Doboujinsky, Mstislau, Petroushka, gouache, dedicated to Alexandre Benois, 9¾ x 7⅞, ca1956
   (4183/23)   1200
Duvernay, Pauline, in The Sleeping Beauty of the Wood, pencil, watercolor, 18 x 14, ca1835
   (4183/7)   400
Exter, Alexandra, Don Juan, costume design for 3 jesters, 23⅛ x 18, ca1929 (4183/70)   6250
Flore et Zephyr, Ballet Mythologique, book with 8 lithographs, hand-colored, London, 1836
   (4183/11)   800
Gontcharova, Natalia, Coq D'Or, costume design for female attendant, 13⅜ x 10, ca1914 (4183/30)   1600
Gontcharova, Natalia, Coq D'Or, set design, Act One, 13 x 17⅞, ca1914 (4183/29)   10500
Hoffman, Malvina, Pavlova the Incomparable, poster, 60¼ x 33⅞, ca1914 (4183/50)   1600
Korovine, Konstantine, floral costume design for Pavlova, 15¼ x 10¾, ca1930 (4183/52)   800
Larionov, Mikhail, drawing, Massine and Diaghilev at Rehearsal, 6¾ x 5½, ca1919 (4183/44)   1700
Les Danseuses de L'Opera, 14 hand-colored lithographs by Bry after, Alophe, Paris, ca1857
   (4183/13)   250
Levinson, Andre, Bakst, The Story of Leon Bakst's Life, London, 1923, (4183/47)   800
Lola Montez as Mariquita, hand-colored lithograph, N. Currier, 11½ x 8½, ca 1850 (4183/14)   *250*
Nijinsky, book by Dorothy Mullock, 7 hand-colored woodcuts, showing ballets, London, ca1910-15
   (4183/40)   800
Nijinsky, photograph, Nijinsky's Wedding in Buenos Aires, 1913, (4183/43)   1900
Nijinsky, Jean Cocteau poster, Spectre de la Rose, lithograph in colors, Paris, 76¾ x 50, ca1911
   (4183/37)   5000
Nijinsky, Six vers de Jean Cocteau, Six Dessins de Paul Iribe, limited edition, no date (4183/41)   350
Nijinsky and Karsavina, 14 prints, set, hand-finished, by Ludwig Kainer, large quarto, Leipzig, 1913
   (4183/39)   750
Nijinsky in Carnaval, Meissen porcelain figure, Paul Scheurich, H10⅜ (4183/42)   800
Pecoar, Louis, Nouveau Recueil de Dance de Bal et Celle de, Ballet, Paris, 1712 (4183/9)   2000
Pogedaieff, Georges de, Hungarian ballet costume design, 18½ x 13¾ (4183/24)   850
Rivera, Diego, H.P., El Official de la Marina, costume design, 17 x 13, 1930 (4183/104)   2200
Roerich, Nicholas, Snegourotchka, costume design, 17¾ x 9½, ca1919 (4183/34)   1500
Roerich, Nicholas, Snegourotchka, scene with 5 figures in costume (Snow Maiden), 18⅞ x 29,
   ca1922 (4183/33)   6500
Soudeikine, Sergei, Balieff's Chauve-Souris, lithograph poster, N.Y., 40¼ x 26½ (4183/32)   275
Svetloff, V., Anna Pavlova, 189 illustrations, French trans., Paris, 1925 (4183/53)   300
Svetlow, V., Le Ballet Contemporain, French version, St. Petersburg, 1912, (4183/46)   400
Taglioni, Madle, lithograph, N. Currier, hand-colored, 14 x 10, discolored, ca1850 (4183/4)   275
Taglioni, Marie, in La Gitana, lithograph, London, hand colored, image 13½ x 9½, 1839 (4183/3)   350
Terry, Ellen, The Russian Ballet, 27 drawings by P.C. Smith, London, 1st Ed., 1913 (4183/60)   475

Fashion drawings

Benito, Chinoiserie, for Vogue Magazine, 16 x 12, 1927 (4183/77)   600
Benito (Eduard Garcia), Apres L'Opera, drawn for Vogue, 9 x 14, 1925 (4183/79)   1100
Benito (Eduard Garcia), Vanity Fair, drawing for and printed cover, 6¼ x 5½, 1927 (4183/78)   1100
Dior, Christian, Album of 81 Fashion Designs, 10¾ x 8¼, 1933-37 (4183/80)   5000
Erte, Croix, design for wrap, 9⅝ x 6⅜ (4183/76)   800

Opera material

Anisfeld, Boris, Tarandot, design for decor, 24¼ x 19¼, ca1926 (4183/71)   600
Berman, Eugene, Rigoletto, costume designs, 11¾ x 8¼, 1951 (4183/102)   750
Buel, James W., editor, The Great Operas, 10 volumes, London, 1899 (4183/56)   150
Caruso, Enrico, silk program for gala performance at Covent, Garden, 1907 (4183/54)   125
Caruso, Enrico, bronze sculpture, self-portrait, caricature, H5¾, 1909 (4183/55)   800
Exter, Alexandra, Revue, decor design, 20 x 23⅞, 1927 (4183/75)   4750
Gontcharova, Natalia, Les Poissons D'Or, gouache, 13½ x 11¾, 1919 (4183/63)   3200
Gontcharova, Natalia, Tsar Saltan, decor design for Act III, 18½ x 21, ca1927 (4183/72)   *2800*
La Fanciulla del West, presentation album to David Belasco, photographs, ca1910 (4183/57)   800

Theatrical material

Benois, Alexandre, La Bien Aimee, design for decor, 17¼ x 24, 1928 (4183/86)   2600
Berman, Eugene, decor design, 15¾ x 21½, 1931 (4183/87)   *500*
Exter, Alexandra, Castle with Figures, study, 23½ x 29½, ca1930 (4183/106)   5000
Gontcharova, Natalia, Petite Catherine, costume design, 18 x 12, ca1930 (4183/82)   700
Mielziner, Jo, A Tree Grows in Brooklyn, decor design, 13¼ x 24½, ca1951 (4183/111)   900
Prampolini, Enrico, Bolero di Ravel, decor design, 13¾ x 20 (4183/92)   900

Gontcharova
(4183/72)

Eight-room dollhouse
(690/593)

Walkowitz (4183/84)

Berman (4183/87)

Lola Montez as Mariquita
(4183/14)

Tchelitchew, Pavel, Acrobats, study, 12⅛ x 8, 1932 (4183/103)	850
Walkowitz, Abraham, Isadora Duncan Dancing, 3 drawings, 1 frame, 7 x 3 each (4183/84)	*650*
Walkowitz, Abraham, Isadora Duncan, 7 drawings framed together, 7 x 2⅝ each (4183/83)	2200

DOLL HOUSES AND FURNISHINGS

American dollhouse, 12 room, large two-story, 75 x 57, dam (690/640)	250
Baby carriage, painted wicker, L43 (690/418)	40
Bed, doll's, white metal, painted, half canopy, (659/261)	90
Bed, doll's, wood, turned post and crossbars, 17 (659/147)	40
Carriage, baby, wicker, painted brown, (659/266)	50
Cradle, rocking, doll, wood, 17 (659/192)	50
Doll's wardrobe trunk, domed, L14 (690/413)	60
Eight-room dollhouse, 18c style, grey, H59 (690/593)	*2750*
Piano, musical, silver gilt filigree, 4 (659/90)	70
Townhouse, 19c style, cream, H39 (690/577)	160
Townhouse, 19c style, green, H40 (690/578)	225
Wicker doll carriage, with parasol, L53 (690/600)	250

DOLLS

An assortment

Alma bisque shoulderhead doll, H21 (690/440)	175

Bisque character doll (690/508)
Bahr and Proschild (690/509)

Bahr and Proschild, bisque character baby, H12½, #585 (690/509) — *300*
Bebe, bisque, socket-head, closed mouth, J. Steiner, Paris, 26, chip, 1889 (659/197) — 2500
Bebe, large jumeau bisque-head, with additional wardrobe, H24 (690/377) — 3000
Bisque character baby, H15½, #3-7 (690/456) — 225
Bisque head doll, marked 1908, 12/0, H11 (690/412) — 60
Bisque shoulderhead doll, German, H24 (690/438) — 325
Bisque socket-head doll, French, painted, L11, #A4/0 (690/408) — 50
Bisque-head-bye-lo baby, marked Copr. Grace Putnam, H13½ (690/458) — 300
Boy doll, bisque-head, possibly French, H17, #227, 6 (690/394) — 650
C.M. Bergmann bisque socket-head, H23¾ (690/474) — 225
China head doll, black-hair-bubble-top, H24½, L19c (690/464) — 70
China head doll, pink lustre blonde, H24½ (690/420) — 350
China head doll, pink tinted, black hair, H19 (690/488) — 70
China head doll, pink-tinted-black hair, H26, L19c (690/463) — 110
China head doll, black hair, flat-top, bisque hands, H16½ (690/389) — 175
Composition-head doll, blonde flat-top, H11⅝ (690/406) — 300
Doll, articulated wood, Joel Ellis type, (690/368) — 400
Doll, composition, American, wearing blanket, moccasins, feather headdress, 36 (684/239) — 40
Doll, early paper-mache-head, vertical curls, H31 (690/390) — 450
Doll, pin cushion, wax shoulderhead, H12 (690/367) — 100
Fashion doll, French, bisque, socket-head, pierced ears, closed mouth, 11¾ (659/262) — 650
French bisque socket-head, marked, S. Bois, DL 13, H19 (690/506) — 225
French bisque-head character, H17 (690/470) — 300
Gebruder Heubach bisque, blue sleep eyes, pouty mouth, H14 (690/491) — 650
German all-bisque child, stationary neck, 5 piece body, H7¼ (690/544) — 60
German bisque doll, solid dome, H14 (690/427) — 550
German bisque shoulderhead, H16½, #148 (690/451) — 175
German bisque shoulderhead, marked D, H14 (690/455) — 100
German bisque shoulderhead doll, H17½, #148 (690/482) — 225
German bisque socket-head, L25, #1910 (690/448) — 200
German bisque socket-head, brown sleep eyes, H20½ (690/481) — 225
German bisque socket-head, glass sleep eyes, H21 (690/480) — 70
German bisque socket-head, marked L½ 15½, H27 (690/473) — 275
German bisque socket-head, Adolf Wislizenus, H23½ (690/533) — 225
German painted all-bisque, black baby, African costume, H7 (690/529) — *250*
Kestner googly-eyed doll, bisque socket head, composition body, 11½, hc (659/276) — 2000

Lady doll, German bisque, shoulderhead, marked indistinctly, H18 (690/379) — 1600
Nippon bisque-head character baby, grey glass eyes, 2 teeth, H12½ (690/490) — 80
Papier-mache blonde-hair doll, H19 (690/478) — 90
Papier-mache-head doll, H19, L19c (690/462) — 175
Parian boy doll, H17½ (690/421) — 600
Peddlar doll, old woman, H15 (690/404) — 175
Peddler, pair, old man, old woman, E19c, mounted on base, H10½, fine (4209/27) — 1300
Portrait China head, painted blue eyes, H4⅛ (690/396) — 425
S.F.B.J. bisque socket-head Bebe, H14 (690/468) — 325
S.F.B.J. bisque socket-head doll, H19, #60 (690/469) — 375
Schoenhut painted wood, boy doll, H14 (690/477) — 175
Schoenhut painted wood doll, H16½ (690/472) — 150
Shoulderhead doll, wax-over papier mache, H22, ca1860 (690/409) — 225
Socket-head doll, bisque, French fashion, H12 (690/397) — 650
Wax-over-composition-head, H22½, ca1900 (690/461) — 50
Wax-over-papier-mache, shoulderhead doll, H17¾ (690/502) — 100
Workmen, black, pair, composition, in wool trousers, 1 carrying stick, on base, 13½ (4268/1053) — 250

Armand Marseille (see Marseille, Armand, p. 364)

Bisque character doll, grey sleep eyes, open mouth, 2 teeth, H16½, #590 (690/508) — 475
Bisque shoulderhead, H20½, #3500 (690/479) — 90
Bisque shoulderhead, H21, #370 (690/476) — 200

German painted
all-bisque
(690/529)

Bisque shoulderhead, blue glass eyes, mouth with teeth, H23½, #370 (690/486) — 130
Bisque shoulderhead doll, H23, #370 (690/450) — 150
Bisque shoulderhead doll, H21½, #370 (690/449) — 160
Bisque socket-head, jointed kid body, bisque hands, H22¼, #370 (690/498) — 150
Bisque socket-head doll, H24, #390n (690/454) — 175
Bisque socket-head doll, composition ball-jointed body, H21, #246/1 (690/495) — 175
Bisque socket-head doll, marked A.M.6 dep., H19 (690/441) — 225
'Floradora' bisque socket-head, dressed as a bride, H19½ (690/444) — 175
'Floradora' doll, bisque socket-head, H20 (690/437) — 130

Averill, Georgene

Bisque head character baby, openmouth with teeth, brown fixed eyes, H15, (629/54) — 6290

China head

Reproduction, cloth body, marked Jenny Lind, (629/3) — 20

F. Gaultier

Bisque shoulderplate fashion doll, (690/398) — 800

Bisque-head Bebe, L19c, H24½ (690/423)   2750

French bisque head

Bru socket head doll, closed mouth, brown-eyes, kid and wood body. H28, (629/127)   2600
Closed mouth, grey paperweight eyes, redressed, inoperative voice box, H23½ (629/42)   800
Fashion doll, closed mouth, fixed eyes, kid body, original clothing. L13, (629/119)   1200
Fashion doll, socket head, closed, mouth , grey paperweight eyes, kid body, H10½, (629/83)   450
Jumeau fashion doll, swivel neck, closed mouth, grey eyes, kid body. H16, (629/143)   1000
Jumeau large doll, closed mouth, blue paperweight eyes, kid body, elaborate, dress, H26 (629/126)   1600
Socket head, open /closed mouth, grey, paperweight eyes, original costumes, head, body, shoes
(629/81)   1100
Socket head fashion doll, closed, mouth, grey fixed eyes, fully-jointed compo-, sition body, H15½
(629/89)   1300
Solid head, closed mouth, fixed, blue eyes, unusual torso, H17, (629/90)   1800

Gebruder, Knoch

Bisque head doll, open mouth, socket head, composition body, felt costume, crossbones H7½
(629/9)   60

Gebruder, Krauss

Bisque socket head doll, open mouth, teeth, composition ball-jointed body, H26½ (629/14)   200

German bisque head

Character baby, closed mouth brown, sleep eyes, composition bent-leg body, L13 (629/50)   500
Character baby, composition body, open mouth, teeth grey fixed eyes, 10, cracked head (629/24)   90
Character baby, socket head, two teeth, grey sleep eyes, composition, bent-leg body. L12 (629/64) 150
Gebruder Heubach 'Whistling Jim', intaglio eyes, voice box inoperative H16 (629/128)   500
Heinrich Handwerck socket head, open mouth, teeth, composition, body, H22 (629/55)   190
Kammer and Reinhart character baby, open-closed mouth, painted hair and intaglio, eyes, L15
(629/66)   6290
Kley and Hahn doll, blue sleep eyes, open mouth, teeth, compostion ball-jointed, body, H26½
(629/15)   150
Open mouth, composition body, (629/8)   120
Open mouth, ball-jointed, composition, body, H12½, (629/7)   70
Open mouth, fixed eyes, wig, cloth body with bisque arms, legs and, shoulders. H13 (629/116)   40
Socket head, open mouth, teeth, brown fixed eyes, composition, body (629/45)   150
Socket head, open mouth with teeth, fixed blue eyes, composition, body. H30 (629/150)   200
Socket head doll, open mouth, teeth, blue fixed eyes, composition body, H17 (629/48)   130

Jules Steiner

Bebe, bisque-head, H10½ (690/376)   1600
Bebe, large bisque-head, marked, H29, d.1889 (690/393)   3000

Kammer and Reinhardt

Bisque 'Kaiser' baby, grey-blue intaglio body, open/closed mouth, H10, #100 (690/516)   375

Kestner

Bisque socket-head doll, H11, #192 o (690/426)   150
Character baby, bisque, H14, #211 (690/366)   200
Kestner socket head character baby, composition bent-leg body, L10 (629/136)   160

Marseille, Armand (see Armand Marseille, p. 363)

Bisque head baby, composition hands, cloth body, brown sleep eyes, L15, (629/30)   225
Bisque head doll, open mouth, composition body, (629/6)   90
Bisque head dream baby, blue sleep eyes, eyes, cloth and composition body, L17, (629/51)   170
Bisque head dream baby, open mouth, two lower teeth, cloth body composition, hands, L10½
(629/57)   100
Bisque shoulder head doll, open, mouth, teeth, brown eyes, kid and cloth body, H21 (629/31)   120
Bisque socket head doll, open mouth with teeth, blue fixed eyes, composition body. H7 (629/146)   160
Black bisque head doll, open mouth, black composition body, H14, (629/10)   170
Indian head doll, red bisque head, with composition ball-jointed body. H13, (629/138)   120

Simon and Halbig

Bisque socket-head doll, brown glass eyes, open mouth, teeth, H21½, #1079 (690/493)   225
Bisque socket-head doll, impressed S&H1009, H15½ (690/419)   275

Bisque socket-head doll, marked S&H-1079 dep. Germany, H19 (690/425) — 225
Doll, bisque turned shoulderhead, H7½, #1010 (690/374) — 100
H. Handwerck bisque socket-head, H24 (690/483) — 300
H. Handwerck bisque socket-head, H23 (690/452) — 300
Handwerck, bisque socket-head, H7½ (690/373) — 120
Kammer and Reinhardt all bisque doll, H6¾ (690/410) — 125
Kammer and Reinhardt character baby, brown glass eyes, open mouth with teeth, H15, #126 (690/517) — 300
Large K. R. bisque doll, H27, #126 (690/446) — 650

JUDAICA

Alms box, architectural form, silver, with leaves and curtains, 8 (605/58) — 1100
Alms box, silver, tankard shape, 3 feet, 4½, ca1850, Austrian (605/55) — 475
Alms box, silver, wooden iron bound chest shape, 3, L19c, German (605/56) — 160
Alms box, synagogue* form, engraved with bricks, window and shingles, 6¾ (605/57) — 900
Amulet, cast silver, heart shaped, harp, commandments tablet, eternal flame, 6½, L19c, Italian (605/144) — 800
Amulet, silver, shape of a hand, Hebraic inscription, 19c, Middle Eastern (605/147) — 60
Amulet container, silver, architectural form, surmounted by 2 dec, 1¾ (605/148) — 100
Astrolabe, persian bronze, engraved with signs of Zodiac, inscriptions, 4 dials, 4 (605/180) — 225
Atarah, framed silver thread, stars and arabesques, 34, 19c, Eastern European (605/119) — 120
Atarah, silver thread, decorated with rosettes, 38½, 19c, Eastern European (605/118) — 225
Becher, covered silver, standing cup, foliated strapwork, 10, ca1830, parts older, Austrian* (605/131) — *500*
Becher, silver, bulbous body, flaring lip, 4 foliate panels, 5½, 1847, Austrian* (605/134) — *140*
Becher, silver, embossed with beadwork above fluting, gilt interior, 7½, Western European, 19c (605/133) — *325*

Becher (605/131)

Becher (605/134)

Becher (605/133)

Becher, silver, tapered bowl, repousse and chased with flowers, 5¼, 1850, American* (605/128) — 70
Becher, silver circumcision ceremonial, Hebraic inscriptiwn on bowl, 5¾, ca1850, Austrian* (605/138) — 200
Becher, silver circumcision ceremonial, Hebrew inscription, 5 34, ca1850, Austrian* (605/137) — 225
Becher, silver, hexagonal, with floral scrolls, Hebrew inscriptions, 4¼, Eastern European (605/125) — 400
Becher, English silver, circular stepped foot, scenes of towers and flowers, 4¾, 1901, London (605/120) — 50
Becher, German silver, engraved with inscriptions, 3¼, 18c (605/†22) — 300
Becher, German silver, on 3 ball feet, leaf and fruit cartouches, 13½, ca1900 (605/124) — 775
Becher, German silver, Chased and repousse flowers and scrolls, 3¼, ca1760, Berlin (605/123) — 300
Becher, Havdalah, Austrian silver, bulbous body, flaring lip, panels of flowers, inscriptions, 8¾, 1857, Austrian (605/132) — 450
Becher, Polish silver, octagon fluted body, festoons and scrolls, inscriptions, 4, E19c (605/126) — 600
Becher, Polish silver, scenes of birds and Hebraic inscriptions, 1¾, E19c (605/130) — 80
Box, brass hinge, lidded, top cut with scene of the Jews going up to Jerusalem, 7½ (605/142) — 500
Box, silver covered, with Hebraic inscription, 2¾, ca1900, Russian (605/139) — 60
Box, silver hinge, lidded, painted oval scene, Judith and Holofernes, 3¼ (605/140) — 350

Box, silver shell shaped, Rococo decoration and repousse floral sprays, 3½, 18c (605/141)   300
Box, silver, Turkish, oval, hinged top, acorn and floral motifs, 7½, L19c (605/52)   225
Breast plate torah, Herbrew inscription between corinthian columns, 9⅝, ca1700 (4238/79)   1100
Candelabra, 7 light brass, baluster stem and circular base, 17, L19c (605/195)   30
Candle holder, Baluster stem on square base, 9¾, L18c, German (605/198)   50
Carved oak panel depicting Adam and Eve, in the Garden of Eden, 29 (605/172)   200
Charoset container silver, shape of a wheelbarrow, 4½ (605/155)   200
Crown, Italian silver, with scrolls, Hebrew inscription, (now Torah crown), 5½, M18c (605/101)   350
Depiction of the Wailing Wall, painted wood, 3 dimensional, 12½, 19c (605/179)   100
Dish, broad rim with Judaic inscription, above a menorah and band of flowering plants, 14⅝ (4133/118)   900
Eternal light, silver, bulbous body with repousse decoratin, 8¾, 18c, Italian (605/164)   100
Ethrog box, silver, hinged top inset with synagogue scene of Shavuoth, 7, ca1900, Austrian (605/47)   450
Ethrog box, silver, oval bombe body, floral decorations, 5¼, M19c, Continental (605/49)   275
Ethrog box, silver, oval, hinged cover, 4 feet, Hebrew inscription, 5½, ca1900, German (605/46)   850
Ethrog box, wooden, painted black, Hebraic inscription, 5¾, ca1900 (605/50)   50
Ethrog box, Israeli, silver, filigree work, glass jewels, 8¼ (605/51)   175
Ethrog container, Turkish silver, octagonal base, inset eith glass stones, 16½, L19c, rare (605/53)   2250
Glass framed fragment, possibly of a marriage contract, 11½, ca1600, Saana, Yemen (605/175)   50
Grager, silver and brass, Cossack figure, Hamen, bound in stocks, 10¼, 20c (605/61)   1600
Grager, Palestinian copper and metal, engraved with branches and Hebrew inscriptions, 5¾, 20c (605/60)   275
Grager, Purim, wood and iron, (noisemaker), 11, E20c (605/59)   120
Hanging lamp brass, has been electrified, 10, 19c, Western European (605/200)   130
Hanukah lamp front pc, silver, lights as jug handles, 10¼, L19c, Eastern European (605/208)   150
Havdalah candle holder, silver, fluted jug with domed cover, 4½, L19c, Pro-Polish (605/177)   160
Hinged box, Turkish silver, oval, 2 handled, repousse with flowers, 11, ca1850 (605/48)   575
Knife, bronze circumcision, 6½ (605/163)   50
Lamp, oil, traveling, Hanukah, silver, oblong shape, lid pierced with 8 holes, 8 (605/216)   600
Lamp, oil, Hanukah, brass, backdrop, Islamic niches, 2 birds, 8,19c, North African (605/210)   150
Lamp, oil, Hanukah, brass and wood, wooden plaque, mother of pearl, 29, 19c, Turkish (605/218)   2000
Lamp, oil, Hanukah, miniature silver, backplate piered with lions and figures, 3 (605/212)   60
Lamp, oil, Hanukah, silver, berainesque strap work enclosing 2 columns, 12, Eastern European (605/217)   550
Lamp, oil, Hanukah, silver, on oblong bases, pierced gallery, 4 feet, 9¼, Continental, marked, 800 (605/222)   850
Lamp, oil, Hanukah, Menorah, silver, bowls in shape of jugs, repousse flowers and scrolls, 12¾, 1841, Austrian (605/223)   1700
Lamp, sabbath brass hanging, seven sconces, ruby glass bowls, 18½, L19c, Western European (605/202)   375
Lamp, sanctuary, Italian silver, base embossed with 9 lobes, with bells, (now Torah crown), 6, ca1700 (605/102)   250
Lamp, Hanukah, brass, backdrop is shape of a crown enclosing a lion, 5½, E19c (605/209)   40
Lamp, Hanukah, brass, Middle stem surmounted by Star of David, 12½ (605/214)   300
Lamp, Hanukah, silver, oval cartouche surmounted by crown, 8½, 19c, German style (605/215)   550
Lamp, Yahrzeit silver filigree, Two headed eagle, 2 talons grasping flowers, 15, E19c, Continental (605/203)   1200
Lamp, 7 light, silver, flanked wooden columns supporting miniature urns, 9¼ (605/207)   175
Lampshade, painted metal, with Star of David and pierced with words, 16½ (605/186)   40
Letter from George Washington, to the Jews of Newport, R.I., framed facsimile, 22½, M19c (605/171)   350
Marriage belt, silver filigree, plaques with beadwork, colored stones, 28, L19c, Russian (605/169)   300
Marriage contract, Italian illuminated, on parchment, tablet shaped, 21, 1826, Siena (605/174)   850
Marriage ring, castle form silver, Four towers enclosing hexagonal gothic structure, 2½ (605/151)   600
Marriage ring, silver parcel gilt, furreted structure with blue roof, inscription, (605/150)   275
Marriage ring, wrought silver, two turrets, set with cabochon amethyst, 19c, Eastern European (605/152)   400
Matchbox, English silver, silver inlaid, tortoise cover, on 4 feet, 3, ca1930 (605/3)   150
Matzah cover, 3 pocket, silk, embroidered floral bouquet, inscriptions, 15¾, 19c, Continental (605/115)   250
Megillah case, silver, with Megillah, case with floral decoration, 16¼, 20c, Eastern European (605/66)   600
Megillah on leather, early wood mounted, 19½, 15c* (605/63)   275
Megillah on leather, early wood mounted, 12½, 18c (605/62)   150
Megillah on vellum, illuminated, handwritten texts surrounded by birds, 11, L18c, Western European (605/65)   1600
Megillah parchment scroll in silver case, pointer, spice box, 12½, 1895, Vienna (605/68)   2100

Memorial plaque to the Warsaw ghetto martyrs, Beaten copper, bearing Hebraic inscription, (605/170) — 60

Menorah, sabbath, 7 light, brass, branches, baluster stem, 20¾, 19c, Eastern European (605/201) — 275

Menorah, Hanukah, silver, bowls on scrolling branches, floral decorations, 25½, L19c, Polish (605/225) — 1200

Menorah, Hanukah, silver, embossed with rampant lions, 9¾, L19c, Western European (605/211) — 600

Menorah, Hanukah, silver, leaf and bell shape ornaments, 29, ca1900, Continental (605/219) — 3000

Menorah, Hanukah, silver, lions rampant, supporting niches and 4 figures, 10½, ca1900, German (605/221) — 1500

Menorah, Hanukah, silver, on circular base, 5, E20, Continental (605/205) — 100

Menorah, Hanukah, silver, on oblong base, 2 lions, palm trees, 9¼, 20c, Continental (605/206) — 225

Menorah, Hanukah, silver, square branches, urn candle holders, 29, ca1900, Polish (605/226) — 1500

Menorah, Hanukah, silver filigree, bowls and shamos supported by American eagle, 9¾ (605/224) — 1700

Mezzuzah, silvered embossed, architectural form with solomonic columns, 5½ (605/157) — 70

Mezzuzah case brass, embossed with Hebrew inscriptions, 8 (605/159) — 175

Mezzuzah case silver and niello, rectangular shape, inscription, 4, 19c, Russian (605/160) — 100

Mezzuzah vase, silver and copper, inset with glass stone, inscription, 13 (605/158) — 300

Mizrach, framed needlepoint, depicting the near sacrifice of Isaac by Abraham, 22½ (605/178) — 75

Nef, silver gilt and enamel, deck applied with numerous figures, Viennese, 8⅜, L19c (4259/530) — 2000

Oil lamp, even light earthenware, sides molded with arabesque, 6 (605/196) — 10

Parrot perched on branch, silver-gilt, Hebrew inscription, 9⅝, ca1690, German (605/45) — 2750

Picture frame, bronze, Star of David on hexagonal pedestal, 6½ (605/187) — 10

Plaque, synagogue scene, worshippers, father and son and torah, 7½ x 6½ (605/193) — 850

Plaque, synagogue scene, bronze, Hasidic Jews at prayer, 11½ x 5½, Schatz (605/189) — 425

Plate, birth, silver, Austro-Hungarian, oval, rim, embossed with Zodiac signs, 4¾, ca1820 (605/81) — 3200

Plate, circular, silver, center embossed with marriage scene, 6½ (605/165) — 200

Plate, metal, Pidyon Haben, Aaron the high priest, scene, 11¾, Middle Eastern* (605/80) — 150

Plate, pewter, rim engraved with a Sabbath song, inscription, 13¾, 1864 (605/79) — 350

Plate, pewter, rim with inscription and a star of David, 10¼, 18c (605/72) — 225

Plate, pewter, Passover, Haggadah excerpts, 14 1809, Western European (605/75) — 950

Plate, Passover, brass, Ten Commandments tablet, 19¼, 1953, North African (605/77) — 250

Plate, Passover, pewter, double headed eagle, 15, 1817, Western European (605/73) — 525

Plate, Passover, silver, shaped border, Seder scene, 13½, ca1900, Continental (605/74) — 500

Plate, Passover, silver, with fruits, Passover scenes, 16½, 20c, Continental (605/76) — 950

Portrait plaque set into a box, bronze, Hasidic boy with side curls, 3½ x 2¾ (605/188) — 70

Remonim, metal, pair, hung with bells, surmounted by crown, 9, Persian (605/99) — 150

Rose water sprinkler, Persian silver, floral decoration, stepped foot, hawk finial, 7 (605/5) — 60

Shivisi, painted wood, Persian, painted with commandments, crown Star of David, 10¾ (605/182) — 150

Shivisi, painted wood, Persian, painted, 10 commandments, torah, Star of David, crown, 10¾ (605/183) — 175

Shivisi (amulets on parchment), Hebrew writing around a menorah, framed, 6½, 18c (605/173) — 100

Spice and incense container, silver, gourd shape, arabesque decoration, 10, ca1800, Turkish (605/54) — 1700

Spice box, double-lidded, hinged, pewter, a fish on 3 feet, 5¾, ca1800 (605/39) — 200

Spice box, hexagonal silver, engraved with processional scenes, 2½, 18c, Middle Eastern (605/143) — 150

Spice box, pear form silver, hinged top, leaf and stem finial, (605/1) — 110

Spice box, pewter, swan shaped, on circular base, 5½ (605/38) — 80

Spice box, silver, engraved with the Wailing Wall, Rachel's Tomb, 7¾, Eastern European (605/37) — 125

Spice box, silver, from mustard pot, snake handle, aquatic creatures, 7, ca1810, German (605/27) — 175

Spice box, silver, tower, chased and pierced decoration, 6¼, 19c, Eastern European (605/20) — 400

Spice box, silver filigree, circular base, pennant, 7, 19c, Eastern European (605/26) — 180

Spice box, silver filigree, shaped covered cup, flowers and foliage, 6¾, 1864, Polish (605/18) — 475

Spice box, silver filigree, square, pyramidal roof with star of David, 5½, M19c (605/23) — 275

Spice box, silver filigree, tower hung with bells, topped with pennants, 14, ca1800, Russian (605/42) — 2100

Spice box, silver filigree, tower, Pyramidal base, pennant, 8, L19c, Continental (605/44) — 900

Spice box, silver filigree, ship form, masts surmounted by pennants, 5½, ca1900, Continental (605/28) — 6050

Spice box, silver plated, Gothic tower, articulated brickwork, 9, 19c, Continental (605/43) — 575

Spice box, silver windmill, base with farmer's horse-drawn cart, 5, M19c, Dutch (605/32) — 1500

Spice box, silver windmill, two tiered galleries, 6, M19c, Dutch (605/31) — 600

Spice box, silver, carriage, four sided pierced body on 4 wheels, 5½ (605/13) — *350*

Spice box, silver, cylindrical, scroll work, 10 commandments tablets, bells, 7¼ (605/34) — 200

Spice box, silver filigree, shape of locomotive on 4 wheels, smokestacks, 3½, 19c, Russian (605/9) — 450

Spice box, silver, rooster, floral decorations, hinged wings, removable head, 7¼, 19c, German (605/14) — *775*

Spice box, silver, tower form, pierced with windows, gallery, lions at corners, 11½, Continental (605/12) — *400*

Spice box
(605/14)

Spice box
(605/12)

Spice box
(605/13)

Spice box, sterling silver, pierced work surmounted by a pennant, 7¼ (605/33)	130
Spice box, Continental silver, floral engravings and stars of David, 9¼ (605/36)	125
Spice box, Dutch silver, windmill with man 3, L19c (605/2)	150
Spice boxes, pair, silverplate, globular, with repousse work, 8¼, ca1830, Polish (605/21)	800
Spice container, ivory, columned bldg., wood base and roof, 4¼, ca1900, Western European (605/153)	200
Spice container, silver and enamel, ostrich shape, wings inset with a stone, 4, 18c, Persian (605/7)	425
Spice container, silver filigree, fish shaped, 'jeweled' eyes, 4¼ (605/35)	150
Spice container, silver filigree, globe and pennant, 6¼, 19c, Eastern European (605/19)	275
Spice container, silver filigree, three tiered tower, bells, 14½, 19c, Continental (605/41)	1100
Spice container, silver gilt, sun flower form, foliate-head base, 9, ca1800, German (605/24)	500
Spice container, silver gourd shape, stem with leaves, 6¾, 19c, Continental (605/30)	400
Spice container, silver, bird, feathers, removable head, 4 3.4, 1841, Vienna (605/11)	375
Spice container, silver, gourd form, floral panels, bird finial with bell, 6, 1847, Vienna (605/15)	800
Spice container, silver, gourd form, rising from stem and leaf base, 3/3/4, ca1900, Continental (605/8)	325
Spice container, silver, tower form, Parrot finial, 6¼, 19c, Palestinian (605/10)	300
Spice container, Persian silver, covered cut, floral decoration 3 (605/4)	150
Spice containers, pair, silver filigree, spherical, with pennants, 6½, ca1850, Austrian (605/22)	400
Spice containers, silver, sunflower shape, foliage, 7, ca1900, Continental (605/29)	800
Table top, brass, Pharoah's daughter taking Moses from bullrushes, 25½, 19c, Persian (605/78)	250
Tallis bag, red velvet, embroidered depicting 2 roosters, 10, ca1900 (605/108)	70
Tefillin bag, black velvet, embroidered flowers, star of David, 11¾, 1907 (605/112)	30
Tefillin bag, black velvet, embroidered silk decorations, Hebrew inscriptions, 9, 1886 (605/111)	60
Tefillin bag, red velvet, embroidered with the owner's name containing 2 tefillin, 7, 1903 (605/113)	30
Torah case and scroll, Sephardic, miniature, on parchment, 21, 19c, Middle Eastern (605/107)	1000
Torah cover, blue velvet, embroidered rendering of Ten Commandments, tablets, 25, 1925, American (605/109)	80
Torah pointer, brass, baluster-shaped stem with chain, 8, middle Eastern (605/93)	100
Torah pointer, silver, beaded spirals and molded flowers, gilt crown, 12 (605/96)	200
Torah pointer, silver, hand holding pointer hand, 6 (605/92)	150
Torah pointer, silver, inset with crown, floral arrangement, Commandments, (605/98)	300
Torah pointer, silver, set with molded tablets of Ten Commandments, 13½ (605/94)	200
Torah pointer, silver 'jewel' inset, jewel inset, silver bands, 13½, L19c (605/97)	550
Torah pointer, silver gilt, scrolling decration and inset with stones, 8½ (605/91)	375
Torah pointer and spice box silver, pointer containing rotating spice box, inscription, 17¼ (605/95)	400
Torah scroll written on parchment, complete miniature, 5¾, 19c*, Eastern European (605/106)	3000
Vase, Middle Eastern brass, Bulbous shape, Hebrew inscriptions, figural scenes, 14 (605/192)	80
Wine labels, pair, silver, one pierced and bunches of grapes, other blssing for the wine, (605/181)	40

MECHANICAL BANKS

Acrobat, cast-iron, paint in good condition, 5, L19c (659/496) — 1500
Bad accident, J. & E. Stevens Co., designed by Charles A. Bailey, 6, L19c (659/525) — 550
Bank, penny, mechanical painted cast iron, figure Uncle Sam, full length, 12, 1886 (4211/1054) — 700
Bull dog, H7¾, L19c (690/961) — 225
Bull dog, H7½, L19c (690/963) — 150
Bull dog, cast-iron, 7½, trap door missing, L19c, (659/514) — 300
Cabin, cast-iron, black man standing in doorway, green and red cabin, 3½ (659/490) — 150
Cabin, with black man in door, H3¾, L19c (690/954) — 150
Cat and dog organ, cast-iron, paint good, 7½, missing trap door, L19c (659/511) — 300
Chief Big Moon, very good condition, J. & E. Stevens Co., 6¾, L19c (659/527) — *600*
Chief Big Moon, cast-iron, 10, paint worn, L19c (659/491) — 300
Circus elephant on wheels, still bank, H4, L19c (690/957) — 125
Clown on globe, very good condition, 9, missing trap door, L19c (659/526) — *650*

Clown on globe
(659/526)

Good tower (still bank)
(659/529)

Eagle and eaglets
(659/522)

Chief Big Moon
(659/527)

Jonah and the whale
(659/523)

Creedmore, cast-iron, J. & E. Stevens Co., 6½, L19c (659/512) — 150
Creedmore cast-iron mechanical bank, good condition, H6½, L19c (690/952) — 225
Darktown battery, very good condition, J. & E. Stevens Co., 7¼, L19c (659/520) — 650
Darktown battery, cast-iron, J. & E. Stevens Co., 7½, L19c (659/498) — 400
'Dinah', yellow dress, silver jewerly, England, John Harper Co., (659/488) — 225
Eagle and eaglets, J. & E. Stevens Co., 6, L19c (659/522) — *150*
Eagle and eaglets, J. & E. Stevens, H6, L19c (690/971) — 300
Elephant, cast-iron, pressure on tail moving trunk, 4¾, L19c (659/510) — 250
Frog on round base, H4½, L19c (690/959) — 300
Good tower (still bank), combination lock, inscription, '1890', 7, 1890 (659/529) — *225*
Hall's excelsior, roof opens to reveal wooden cashier, J. & E. Stevens Co., 5¼, L19c (659/493) — 200
'Humpty Dumpty', H7¾, L19c (690/960) — 360
'I Always Did 'Spise a Mule', J. & E. Stevens Co., 8¼, missing trap door, L19c (659/517) — 250
'I Always Did Spise a Mule', paint good, J. & E. Stevens Co., 6, trap door missing, L19c (659/501) — 325
Jonah and the whale, mfg by Shepard Hardware Co., 5½, L19c (659/523) — *450*
Jolly Nigger, H6¾, L19c (690/966) — 200
Jolly Nigger, cast-iron, 6½, L19c, (659/508) — 125
Jonah and the whale, cast-iron, paint fair, Shepard Hardware Co., 5½, trap door missing, L19c (659/499) — 550
Leap frog, very good condition, Shepard Hardware Co., 4¾, L19c (659/519) — 800
Lion and two monkeys, monkey on trap door, paint worn, Kyser and Rex, 8½, 1 monkey missing, L19c (659/495) — 75
Lion and 2 monkeys, very good condition, Kyser and Rex, 9¼, L19c (659/521) — 400
Magician, cast-iron, paint good, J. & E. Stevens Co., 8, E20c (659/505) — 800
Monkey and organ, H7½, L19c (690/968) — 350
Monkey and organ grinder, modern, H7½ (690/967) — 175

Owl, cast-iron, paint good, turning head, 7½, trap door missing, L19c (659/509)   200
Paddy and the pig, H8½, L19c (690/969)   600
Picture gallery, cast-iron, paint very good, 8¼, trap door missing, L19c (659/506)   1600
Punch and Judy, paint good, Shepard Hardware Co., 7½, missing bottom pc, L19c (659/516)   550
Santa Claus, H6½, L19c (690/953)   550
Speaking dog, good condition, H7, L19c (690/950)   400
Speaking dog, cast-iron, 7, trap door missing, L19c, (659/513)   200
Speaking dog, cast-iron, 8, L19c, (659/492)   275
Still bank resembling 'Capt. Kidd', H5½, L19c (690/970)   175
Stump speaker, cast-iron, paint good, 9½, L19c (659/502)   750
Tammany, J. & E. Stevens Co., 6, L19c (659/507)   90
Tammany, cast-iron, J. & E. Stevens Co., 6, L19c (659/489)   60
Tammany, J. & E. Stevens Co., H6, L19c (690/958)   200
Trick dog, cast-iron, 7¼, (659/531)   175
Uncle Sam, cast-iron, paint fair, Shepard Hardware, 11½, trap door missing, L19c (659/504)   600
Uncle Sam, Shephard Hardware Co., paint fair to good, H11½, L19c (690/951)   475
Uncle Tom, cast-iron, 5½, L19c, (659/530)   150
William Tell, very good condition, J. & E. Stevens Co., 6½, missing trap door, L19c (659/515)   200
World Fair, Columbus and an Indian, 6½, paint worn, E20c (659/518)   550

MILITARY EQUIPMENT

Axe, miner's bone and iron, ceremonial, engraved with St. Peter, 33, 1714, Saxon (4133/42)   850
Belt, gold braid, officer's, emblazoned with silver royal cipher, ca1900, Victorian (4133/25)   80
Belt, gold cross, with silver dispatch case, household cavalry officer's, ca1900 (4133/27)   250
Brayette, steel, with 2 pointed oval raised reserves, 5½, ca1550, German (4133/32)   250
Cannon, miniature bronze, with 2 dolphin handles, barrel with 2 bands of leaves, 9⅝, 17c, Dutch
  East India (4133/43)   70
Cannons, starting pair, cast iron, iron barrels, wood carriages, English, 24, 19c (4193/115)   500
Case, dispatch, gold braid, officer's, centered by a royal monogram within oak sprays, ca1900,
  Victorian (4133/26)   110
Coat, mess guard officer's, Royal Irish, red with black cuffs, (4133/22)   75
Crossbow, hunting, walnut stock, inlaid arrow groove, German, 29½, imp, 18c (4193/116)   1300
Crossbow, target, walnut stock, iron bow, brass facing, Flemish, 40¼, ca1800 (4193/119)   1000
Cutlass, short Austrian, simple blade with plain counter guards, 29¾, 19c (4255/192)   200
Dagger, Malayan, steel, watered steel and iron blade, hilt of ivory, 27¼, 19c (4264/306)   50
Flask, powder, documentary horn, boar hunting scene and stag hunt, 9⅝, 1771, German, Limburg
  (4133/57)   800
Flask, powder, engraved armorial staghorn, Pasini family, 12¾, L16/E17c, Italian (4133/50)   700
Flask, powder, engraved horn, maiden holding sword, soldier, German, 13½, 17c (4255/304)   2000
Flask, powder, engraved horn, three panels, 2 hunts man, letter 'R', 13½, 17c, German (4133/60)   1600
Flask, powder, engraved horn, Adam and Eve, Garden of Eden, letter 'M', 12½, 17c, German
  (4133/61)   1600
Flask, powder, engraved staghorn, archer and a hound, pursuit of a boar, 10¼, L16/E17c, Italian
  (4133/52)   400
Flask, powder, horn, mounted with copper plate at end, mask, trophies of war, 7¾, 17c, German
  (4133/53)   225
Flask, powder, horn, with chamois frolicking on rocks, hunter holding gun, 9¼, 18c, Austrian
  (4133/56)   225
Flask, powder, rococo, horn, naked putto seated and holding gun, 10¾, M18c, Austrian (4133/58)   1300
Flask, powder, stained, staghorn, huntsman and equestrian figures, 6½, L18c, German (4133/51)   550
Gauntlet, steel, with 6 ribs, ropework at cuff, knuckle bend, 10¼, 16c, German, end plate replaced
  (4133/31)   450
Gunstock, fragment, bone inlaid, German, 17, imp, E17c (4193/113)   2900
Halberd, iron, Italian, thin spike, engraved with well worn scrollwork, 26, E17c (4255/201)   200
Halberd, parade, double edge pike, pierced with 3 windows, L16c, Italian (4133/29)   475
Halberd, parade, partial gilt, double edge pike, pierced and worked axe, ca1650, Italian, fine
  (4133/30)   1000
Hanger, 'Hounslow' type, hunting sword, curved blade, 28½, ca1650, English (4133/33)   250
Hanger, hunting sword, curved blade with double narrow channels on either side, 28⅞, L17/E18c
  (4133/34)   200
Hanger, silver mounted, hunting sword, sawtooth back, 27, L18c, English (4133/38)   500
Hat, dress, beaver felt, in black tin case, royal navy officer's gold braid, ca1900, Victorian (4133/18) 100
Kard, Indo Persian, agate and gold mounted, straight blade squared grip, scabbard, 18c* (4133/47)   200
Knife with shagreen scabbard, handle in silver, allegorical figure, Dutch, 12¾, ca1700 (4193/112)   750
Kris, Balinese, serpentine iron blade, handle carved grotesque figure, 15, E19c (4259/502)   250

Mace, battle iron, facetted shaft with spirally twisted finial and grip, 23¾, 16c, Italian (4133/41) — 450
Pouch, metal, caucasion nielloed, equestrian soldier holding cutlass and decapitated head, 5½, ca1800 (4133/54) — 200
Powderhorn, 'Jonathan Barns, his, Horn, May 4th, 1776, Concord', fine (4180/715) — 1600
Powderhorn, with hearts, L8½, E19c (4156/246) — 50
Rapier, silver mounted, mounts pierced in trelliswork, engraved, 42½, 18c, French (4133/37) — 400
Rapier, steel, slender blade, short fuller, hexagonal pommel, 48, 16c (4255/195) — 1300
Rapier, steel mounted, German, narrowing blade, partial fuller, heart pommel, 39⅝, 17c (4255/194) — 750
Rapier, steel, baskethilt, Italian, narrow blade with short fuller, 52½, M17c (4255/196) — 800
Sabre, cavalry, English, curved blade, partially blued, 35½, E19c (4255/193) — 150
Sabre, dress, gilt-mounted, scabbard set with trophies, eagle pommel-grip, L40½, ca1830 (4268/1076) — 1300
Sabre, hussar's, Austrian, curved blade, etched with military trophies, 37⅝, 19c (4255/199) — 400
Schiavona, Venetian, pierced steel basket of characteristic form, 44½, 18c (4255/198) — 1500
Shapska, lancers, officer's, crimson top, rosette cipher, George V, (4133/16) — 1300
Small sword, Meissen porcelain grip, silver mounted, rococo flowers, scrolls, 34⅛, 1750-60, German (4255/197) — 1400
Sporen, Queen's own Cameron Highlanders, ca1900, Victorian (4133/20) — 325
Stiletto, bone and ivory, bone grip carved in lowrelief of acanthu, mounted in iron, 17½, 16c, Italian (4133/40) — 800
Stiletto, iron, Italian, long blade, pommel with ball, 17¾, E17c (4255/200) — 175
Sword, hunting, steel blade, engraved with scrolls, German, 20½, M18c (4193/114) — 300
Sword, short, silver mounted, with repousse, recaille, blade engraved, 33½, English (4133/35) — 300
Sword, European, steel, blade engraved with letters and stars, 37¾, ca1600 (4264/303) — 75
Whistle, Victorian, regimental, Celtic ornaments, L3, 1891 (4194/484) — 170

MINIATURES AND MODELS

An assortment

Cabinet, ebonised wood and enamel, rectangular, domed top, 5½, L19c, Viennese (4160/703) — 850
Cabinet, open bookshelf, inlaid walnut, two shelves open, shaped front with doors, 29¾ x 19, L18c, Continental (4232/81) — 400
Cabinet, porcelain mirrored, August Martin, Mar. 17, 1919, H11¼ (690/602) — 50
Chest of drawers, walnut, miniature, H17½ (690/400) — 175
Child's ladder-back rocking chair, with wicker seat, (629/162) — 40
Coffee pot, miniature, three bun feet with profile busts, groteque masks, 2¼, E18c, Dutch (4238/111) — 250
Commode, tulipwood, serpentine, three drawers on splayed bracket feet, 9½ x 12¼, L18c, Continental (4232/83) — 550
Crib, wood, miniature, various, geometric and other patterns, 7½, 17c, Italian (4133/336) — 1200
Model, carved boxwood, ship of the line, 16, L18c (4165/263) — 3000
Model coach, painted, London to Brighton, Royal Mail GR, IV, 17, E19c (4111/17) — 1050
Schoenhut piano, L10 (690/603) — 30
Screen, musical, miniature, enamel, three hinged fold, H5, ca1910, French (669/269) — 350
Ship model, 'Brig Sloop' type, fully rigged, 75 x 57 L18-E19c (4134/211) — *1800*

Ship model (4134/211)

Tea set, silver gilt, enameled landscapes, tray L4½,   ca1900, Viennese, 13 pcs (4160/700)   1700
Yacht, model, silver gilt, windfilled mainsail and spinnacler, 8, modern (4160/597)   100

Nineteenth Century

Fauteuil en cabriolet, beechwood, Louis XV style, voluted frame, cabriole legs, L19c, miniature
(4142/63)   500

Silver

Coffee set, 4 piece, lightly fluted bodies, 3½, tray (669/308)   150
Knife box inlaid wood, with 6 each of knifes, forks, spoons, tea spoons, 2¾, L18c, style (669/300)   600
Piano and stool, enameled copper and gilt, metal, grand piano with classical motif, scenes, ca1900,
Viennese (669/313)   400
Secretaire, bambay form, hinged pierced doors above 3 drawers, 3¾, L19c, Dutch (669/326)   275
Stand warming, fitted with 4 entree dishes, 3 (669/301)   400
Tazza, circular, pedestal dish with reeded border, central engraved sunburst, 3, 1829, English
(669/322)   150
Tea and coffee set, 6 piece, lobed body, engraved rim, 2¼, tea kettle (669/305)   400

MUSICAL INSTRUMENTS

Assorted instruments

Banjo, 5 strings, open back, wooden hoop with 29 metal tensioners, 10½, L19c (4269/7)   1200
Banjolin, Gibson, wooden hoop, 24 metal tensioners, 10⅝, E20c, dam (4269/9)   125
Bouzouki, Greece, pear shaped, body cut on the slab, inlaid geometric designs, 13⅜, L19c
(4269/32)   200
Clarinet, boxwood 5 key, H. Wrede, ivory mounts, brass keys, square covers, ebony mouthpiece, 23
7/16, E19c (4269/21)   350
Clarinet, composite, boxwood, 4 brass keys, L20⅞, ca1800 (4187/4)   225
Clarinet, Badger, Buffalo, boxwood, 12 brass keys, L20⅜, ca1830 (4187/3)   350
Clarinet, Pourcelle, Henri, boxwood, 10 brass keys, L16¾, M19c (4187/1)   150
Clarinet, Pourcelle, Henri, boxwood, 6 brass keys, L17¼, M19c (4187/2)   180
Flute, rosewood 8 keyed, J. Renton, 5 silver mounts and keys, 2 pewter 3 round cover, 26¼, L19c
(4269/23)   350
Grand pianoforte, Clementi & Co., London, mahogany, 5½ octaves,   11½ x 88¾ x 41¾
(4187/31)   400
Guitar, lyre, French*, bird's eye maple, ivory, 38½, ca1820 (4187/13)   *250*
Guitar, American*, rosewood, mother of pearl, peg machines by Jerome, M19c (4187/16)   *300*

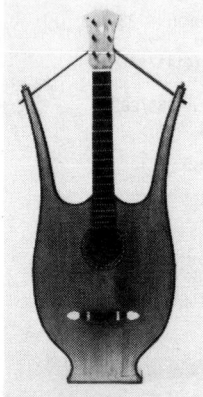  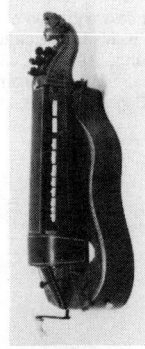

Guitar (4187/13)   Guitar (4187/16)   Hurdy-gurdy (4187/10)

Guitar, French, 2 piece back, small curl, with geometric stringing, 16 15/16 back, ca1800 (4269/34)   700
Guitar, Schmidt & Maal, New York, rosewood, peg machines by Jerome, 18⅞, ca1850 (4187/14)   350
Harp, Irish, John Egan, body, column, and neck painted green, 30 strings, 35½, ca1820-30
(4269/30)   350
Harp-guitar, French, Levien, back medium curl, sound holes, bands of ivory and ebony, 16⅜, E19c
(4269/31)   650
Hurdy-gurdy, Renault & Chatelain, Paris, mahogany, ivory, and ebony, 25⅜, 1775 (4187/10)   *1900*

Mandolin Gibson flat back, inlaid mother of pearl on head, 8 ivory pegs, 18⅝, back, E20c (4269/8) 375
Music stand, duet, mahogany, double desk supported adjustable column, 51, M19c (4269/37) 500
Ophicleide, French, Guichard Prevete, brass body with 9 keys, 44¾, mouthpiece missing, M19c
(4269/26) *650*
Ophicleide, Jules Martin, Paris, serial no. 1001, brass, 11 keys, L41, L19c (4187/6) 250
Pianoforte, federal, mahogany, inlaid, flowers, pierced scrolling devices, 34 x 71, ca1810 (654/577) 300
Serinette, Paris, Thibouville-Lamy, mahogany cabinet, 10 pipes, playing 8 pieces, 10¾, M19c
(4269/35) 500
Serpent, French, leather bound, brass mounts and keys, ivory fingerholes, 79, E19c (4269/25) 1800
Sitar, Karachi, rosewood, ivory, 18 strings, 51½, 1968 (4187/11) 275
Theremini, RCA music desk, 2 antennae, separate speaker, 1929 (4187/18) 200
Timpani, Hawkes & Son, London, military, pair, D22¼, ca1850 (4187/9) 600
Zither, bowed, Vienna, Karl Kiendl, 2 piece back of medium curl, red brown, 13⅜, L19c (4269/33) 100

Books, Reference

Doring, Ernest, How Many Strads, cloth binding, dust jacket, Chicago, 1945 (4269/65) 700
Doring, Ernest, The Guadagnini Family of Violin Makers, Chicago, 1949 (4269/63) 400
Doring, Ernest, The Guadagnini Family of Violin Makers, Chicago, 1949 (4269/64) 425
Hamma, Fridolin, German Violin Makers, 80 plates, cloth binding, London, 1961 (4269/57) 150
Hamma, Walter, Meister Italienischer Geigenbaukunst, New York, 1964 (4269/73) 275
Hart & Son, The Emperor Stradivari, several illustrations, London, 1843 (4269/68) 125
Huggins, Margaret, Gio, Paolo Maggini, His Life and Work, plates, diagrams, London, 1892
(4269/66) 100
Jalovec, Karel, Beautiful Italian Violins, color plates, cloth binding, London, 1963 (4269/62) 60
Jalovec, Karel, German and Austrian Violin Makers, plates, diagrams, London, 1967 (4269/52) 75
Jalovec, Karel, Italian Violin Makers, plates, diagrams, London (4269/53) 50
Jalovec, Karel, Italian Violin Makers, plates, diagrams, cloth binding, London (4269/72) 75
Jalovec, Karel, The Violin Makers of Bohemia, plates, diagrams, London (4269/54) 75
Lyon & Healy, Rare Old Violins, Bound Collection, including, Editions 31, 34 and 35, 1919-29
(4269/45) 300
Lyon & Healy, The Hawley Collection of Violin, plates, cloth bound spine, Chicago, 1904 (4269/69) 175
Millant, Roger, J.B. Vuillaume, Sa Vie et son Oeuvre, first edition, 80 plates, 6 color, London, 1972,
1st edition (4269/70) 50
Millant, Roger, Vuillaume Sa Vie et son Oeuvre, Deluxe Edition, London, 1972, deluxe edition
(4269/47) 75
Moller, Max, The Violin Makers of the Low Countries, plates, cloth binding, Amsterdam, 1955
(4269/58) 300
Poidras, Henri, Dictionary of Violin Makers, 36 plates, Rouen, 1928, binding split (4269/74) 50
Roda, Joseph, Bow for Musical Instruments, numerous plates, Chicago, 1959 (4269/55) 150
Roda, Joseph, Bow for Musical Instruments, numerous plates, Chicago, 1959 (4269/71) 250
Roda, Joseph, Bows for Musical Instruments, Chicago, 1959 (4269/44) 250
Vidal, Antoine, Les Instruments a Archet, Paris, Vols. I, II, III, 1875 (4269/48) 50

Bow, double bass

Fonclause, Paris, round stick stamped, frog of rosewood, 2 silver bands, 113 grams (4269/146) 900
Peccatte, Paris, round out curved, ebony frog and button, 128 grams (4269/147) 1200
Schuster, round stick stamped, half mounted ebony frog, 155 grams (4269/145) 125

Bow, viola

Millant, stick stamped, frog silver rings, silver eyes, 69 grams, 1962 (4269/138) 950
Pajeot, Paris, silver-mounted, 65 grams (4187/110) 3100
Victor Fetique, Paris 1925, silver-mounted, 71 grams (4187/108) 3500

Bow, violin

Albert Nurnberger, silver-mounted, 62.5 grams (4187/85) 225
Albert Nurnberger, Germany, German-silver mounted, 60 grams (4187/67) 325
Albin Hums, gold-mounted, modern, 60.5 (4187/74) 425
Alfred Lamy, round stick stamped, frog, pearl eyes, silver button, 58 grams, L19c (4269/122) 2100
Arthur Bultitude, England, 1976, gold-mounted, 60.5 grams (4187/106) 2600
Bausch, round stick stamped, frog 2 silver circles, abalone eyes, 63 grams, L19c (4269/130) 800
Bernadel, round stick stamped, frog, pearl eyes, button silver bands, 57 grams (4269/121) 700
Bernadel, Paris, octagonal stick stamped, frog with pearl eyes, 2 silver bands, 55 grams, eyes
missing, 19c (4269/113) 1100
Bernadel, Paris, stick stamped, frog with silver rings enclosing pearl eyes, 65 grams (4269/123) 250
Charles Peccate, Paris, silver-mounted, 57.5 grams (4187/96) 3200

Chased gold and tortoiseshell, octagonal stick stamped, C.A. Voigt, Philadelphia, 58 grams, L19c (4269/129) — 600

Dominique Peccatte, Paris, 1826-37, silver-mounted, 60 grams (4187/91) — 8000

Emil Kuehnl, octagonal stick stamped, pearl eyes, gold bands, 62 grams (4269/120) — 1000

Eugene Sartory, Paris, ca1900, silver-mounted, 57 grams (4187/98) — 3400

F.A. Stoess, stick stamped, ebony frog, 2 silver rings, pearl eyes, 62 grams (4269/126) — 200

Francois Lupot, Paris, silver-mounted, 60.5 grams (4187/119) — 3750

Francois Tourt, Paris, gold, pearl, 'ex-Baron de Tremont', 1780-90, 64.5 grams (4187/90) — 19000

Francois-Nicolas Voirin, Paris, gold-mounted, 57.5 grams (4187/104) — 2600

Francois-Nicolas Voirin, Paris, silver-mounted, L19c, 60 grams (4187/99) — 2800

Frank J. Callier, Los Angeles, gold-mounted, 58 grams (4187/105) — 3600

Frank J. Callier, Los Angeles, 1968, gold-mounted, 66 grams (4187/94) — 1800

French, E19c, silver-mounted, 63 grams (4187/109) — 2300

French, E19c, silver-mounted, 55 grams (4187/111) — 3900

French, M19c, silver-mounted, 64 grams (4187/112) — 2600

German, octagonal stick unstamped, frog with pearl eyes, 61 grams (4269/109) — 200

German, round stick stamped Suess, frog of ebony, 2 gold bands, 67 grams, 19c (4269/111) — 650

German, round stick stamped, ebony frog, pearl eyes, 54 grams, eye missing (4269/110) — 125

German, round stick unstamped, ebony frog, button chased silver, 59 grams (4269/112) — 225

Germany, stick stamped Foote, ebony frog with pearl eyes, 2 silver bands, 61 grams (4269/117) — 325

Gustave Bernadel, silver-mounted, 57.5 (4187/75) — 600

H.R. Pfretzschner, nickel-mounted, 55.5 grams (4187/70) — 100

Herrmann, stick stamped, frog 2 silver rings, pearl eyes, 61 grams (4269/131) — 225

J. Tubbs, N.Y. stamp, Nickel mounted, 59.5 grams (4187/78) — 225

J.H. Zimmermann, St. Petersburg, L18c, 58.5 (4187/79) — 150

Jacques Henry, Paris (attrib), silver-mounted, 60.5 grams (4187/114) — 1500

James Tubbs, London, silver-mounted, 55.5 grams (4187/107) — 1800

Jean-Dominique Adam, silver-mounted, 58.5 grams (4187/93) — 2300

John Dodd, London, E19c, gold-mounted, 61.5 grams (4187/115) — 2400

Joseph A. Vigneron, Paris, silver-mounted, L19c (4187/97) — 1500

LaFleur, octagonal stick unstamped, frog modern reproduction, 57 grams, E19c (4269/134) — 2000

Nickel mounted, German, ebony frog, abalone eyes, round stick unstamped, 60 grams (4269/108) — 75

Nicolas Eury, octagonal stick stamped, frog pearl eyes, ebony, 59 grams, rep, E19c (4269/137) — 1600

Nurnberger, octagonal stick stamped, ebony frog with pearl eyes, 60 grams (4269/115) — 450

Nurnberger, octagonal stick stamped, ebony frog, pearl eyes gold button, 55 grams (4269/118) — 800

Nurnberger, octagonal stick stamped, frog and button by another maker, 62 grams (4269/132) — 250

Paesold, octagonal stick stamped, frog with 2 gold rings, 69 grams (4269/133) — 450

Pajeot, Paris, silver-mounted, 59.5 grams (4187/103) — 2600

Paul Mangenot, stick stamped, ebony frog, pearl eyes, button, 3 silver rings, 56 grams (4269/124) — 275

Pfretzschner, round stick stamped, ebony frog 2 silver rings, pearl eyes, 59 grams (4269/116) — 275

Richard Wiechold, nickel-mounted, 19c, 55.5 grams (4187/71) — 100

Roger & Max Millant, Paris, silver mounted, 58.5 grams (4187/69) — 450

Set of 4 matched bows, Arthur Bultitude, England, 1973-4 gold trips, (4187/89) — 7500

Simon Vuillaume, Paris, gold-mounted, 60.5 grams (4187/118) — 4500

Simon/Vuillaume, Paris, silver-mounted, 54 grams (4187/113) — 3700

Tortoiseshell, frog with 2 silver rings, pearl eyes, 60 grams (4269/127) — 425

Unstamped, silver-mounted, 65.5 grams (4187/87) — 200

Van der Meer, Amsterdam, silver, mounted, 63.5 (4187/80) — 600

Victor Fetique, Paris, ca1925, gold-mounted, 62 grams (4187/100) — 4200

Voirin, Paris, stick stamped, frog with pearl eyes, 2 silver bands, 58 grams, rep, L19c (4269/128) — 325

Vuillaume, Paris, silver-mounted, M19c, 56 grams (4187/73) — 525

W.E. Hill & Sons, round stick stamped, frog silver rings, pearl eyes, 55 grams, 1927 (4269/135) — 650

W.E. Hill & Sons, round stick stamped, frog with silver rings, pearl eyes, 63 grams (4269/136) — 1300

W.E. Hill & Sons, stick stamped, ebony frog, silver button, 61 grams, rep (4269/119) — 175

W.E. Hill & Sons, stick stamped, ebony frog, 2 silver rings, pearl eyes, 59 grams (4269/125) — 425

W.E. Hill & Sons, London, silver-mounted, 60 grams (4187/117) — 1600

W.E. Hill & Sons, London, 1926, gold-mounted, 57.5 grams (4187/95) — 3900

W.E. Hill, silver mounted, 58 grams (4187/68) — 375

Wm. Durer, Germany, round stick stamped, ebony frog, pearl eyes, nickel button, 62 grams (4269/114) — 175

Wurlitzer & Co., N.Y., gold-mounted, 62 grams (4187/102) — 850

Bow, violincello

Charles Buthod, Paris, silver-mounted, 73.5 grams (4187/86) — 400

Dodd School, Forster, 76 grams (4187/72) — 700

English, round stick unstamped with pike head, ivory button, 18c (4269/139) — 850

German, stick stamped Bausch, half mounted ebony frog, 77 grams (4269/143) — 75

Pajeot, round stick stamped, ebony frog pearl rings and eyes, 74 grams, E19c (4269/142) — 1800

Stick stamped Peccatte, frog pearl eyes, button silver, 80 grams (4269/140) 2800
W.E. Hill & Sons, round stick stamped, half mounted ebony frog, 79 grams (4269/141) 1000
W.E. Hill & Sons, London, silver-mounted, 67.5 grams (4187/82) 700

Cornet

Klemm & Brother, Phila, in Eb, brass with nickel mounts, 3 rotary values, L25¾, M19c (4187/5) 1500

Keyboard instruments

Clavichord, New York, Hugh Gough, mahogany case, 5 octave keyboard, turned legs, 57 x 17¾, 1767, London (4269/43) *2000*

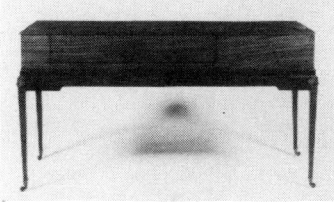

Square piano (4187/26)

Clavichord (4269/43)

Harpsichord, 2-manual, Kirkman, mahogany case, fruitwood stringing, brass hinges, fittings, 93, 1767, London (4269/38) 50000
Melodeon, elbow or rocking, keyboard, 3 octaves and 2 notes, wooden frame, 19, ca1840-50 (4269/6) 175
Melodeon, rosewood veneer, 4 octaves, 6½ x 31 x 17, ca1900 (4187/25) 200
Melodeon, Prince & Co., Buffalo, rosewood, 5 octaves, 9 x 44½ x 23¼, L19c (4187/28) 175
Organ, mechanical, Astor & Co., London, Gothic revival, 3 pegged cylinders, 76 x 25 x 17½, L19c (4187/17) 1800
Piano, baby grand, Louis XVI style, gilt-bronze, satinwood, 26½ x 53 x 84, ca1880, Erard, Paris (669/603) 8000
Piano, grand, Steinway Centennial, rosewood, scroll carved legs, 38 x 86 x 54¾, 1876 (619/410) 2100
Piano, square, Astor & Co., mahogany case, keyboard 5½ octaves, 65 x 23½, ca1795 (4269/41) 850
Piano, Grand, ormolu munted satinwood, inlaid, Erard, L98, 1900 (619/400) 20000
Pianoforte, inlaid mahogany, hinged D shaped top, Gibson & Davis, N.Y., 35 x 70, E19c (4211/1305) 2100
Pianoforte, Geib & Son, N.Y., mahogany, inlaid, 34½ x 65½, ca1790 (4076/943) 3250
Spinet, octave, Arnold Dolmetsch, mahogany case, keyboard 4 octaves, 32 x 21½, ca1940 (4269/42) 475
Square piano, Clementi & Co., London, burl mahogany, 6 octave keyboard, 34½ x 77½ x 27½, ca1830 (4187/19) 700
Square piano, Clementi & Co., London, mahogany, 5½ octaves,   10 x 66 x 23½, 1810 (4187/26) *950*
Square piano, French, painted case, 5 octaves, 1782 (4187/24) 850
Square piano, Geib & Co., N.Y., mahogany, 5½ octaves, 9¼ x 65 x 24, 1820-30 (4187/30) 500
Square piano, John Broadwood, London, mahogany, 5 octaves, 8½ x 61½ x 20½, 1789 (4187/23) 350

Music Stand

Duet, mahogany, double desk, three carved legs, 2 brass candleholders, H47, M19c (4187/32) 41870

Pochette

labelled Antonius Stradivarius, eccentric outline, 9½, 18c (4187/35) 1500

Viola

English school, L18c, no label, of viol outline, 15 3/16 (4187/162)	450
French, labelled J.B. Collin-Mezin...1898, 15 15/16 (4187/155)	1000
French, branded Lambert a Paris, 16, M18c (4187/158)	1300
French, Francis Breton...1831, 15 9/16 (4187/159)	1200
French, Jerome Thibouville, 1 piece back medium curl, orange-brown, case, 15 7/16, L19c (4269/149)	900
German, ca1916, labelled...1916 von Otto Gruber, 15 7/16 (4187/133)	200
Italian, Vittorio Bellarosa, attrib, ca 1935, 16¼ (4187/157)	1700
Italian, Farotto Celestino, 1940, 16⅛ (4187/160)	1200
Modern, no label, 16⅛ (4187/161)	425
Scottish, James W. Briggs, 2 piece back of medium curl, golden brown, case, 16½, 1914 (4269/155)	*4200*

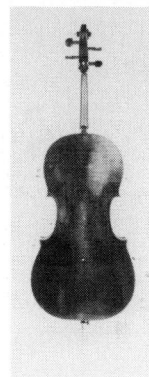 

Scottish
(4269/155)

Antonio Stradivari
(4187/154)

Viola, bass

Da Gamba, 2 piece back, horizontal curl, 28, E18c (4269/157)	6000

Violin

American, August Gemunder & Sons, N.Y., 1903, 14⅛ (4187/185)	200
American, Byron E. Beebe, 2 piece back of faint medium curl, orange-brown, 14 1/16, 1922 (4269/15)	200
American, George Marshall, 2 piece back of medium curl, light orange, 14⅛, 1891 (4269/14)	175
American, Rudolph Wurlitzer Co., 14 3/16 (4187/132)	1100
Antonio Stradivari, Cremona c.1693, Table not original, 14 3/16, important (4187/154)	*33000*
Bohemian, Mathias Heinecke 1924, branded 1924 on 'batton', 14 3/16 (4187/145)	1500
Bohemian, Prague, L18c, labelled Nicolauns Georgus Skomal...17--, 13⅞ (4187/194)	300
English, labelled John Betts...1781, one pc back, with 1 bow, 14 (4187/45)	850
French, 1 piece back of irregular medium curl, golden brown, 13 15/16, 18c (4269/184)	2600
French, 1 piece back, irregular curl, orange brown, 14⅜, E19c (4269/89)	300
French, 1 piece back, medium curl, golden brown, 13 15/16, L18c (4269/87)	950
French, 2 piece back of medium curl, case, orange brown, 14⅛, E20c (4269/81)	600
French, ca1800, branded Tiriot a Paris, 14 1/16 (4187/202)	200
French, ca1880, labelled Nicholas Lupot Luthier...1798, 14⅛ (4187/130)	1400
French, labelled Gand...1844, good, 14 1/16 (4187/61)	5750
French, labelled Joannes Maria, Valenzano...1825, 14⅛ (4187/51)	1500
French, labelled Laurendius Storioni, ...1780, 13 15/16 (4187/52)	700
French, modern, labelled Antonius Stradivarius, 14 3/16 (4187/139)	300
French, Aine, Mirecourt, 1 piece back of medium grain, rich brown, case, 14⅝, E19c (4269/177)	650
French, Augustin Claudot, 19c, 14 1/16 (4187/58)	41870
French, Charles Claudot, 1 piece back of medium curl, golden brown, 14¼, E19c (4269/98)	600
French, Grandjon Pere, 1 piece back of irregular medium curl, 14 5/16, L19c (4269/82)	350
French, Jean B. D. Salomon, 2 piece back, medium curl, golden brown, 14 1/16, L18c (4269/106)	2200
French, Jean Baptiste Vuillaume, Paris, 14⅛, 1844 (4187/127)	1300
French, Louis Pons, 2 piece back medium curl, light orange brown, 13⅞, 1818 (4269/80)	175

French, L18c, branded Salzard a Paris, 14¼ (4187/203) — 800
French, M19c, no label, back decorated with flowers in baskets, 14 (4187/181) — 1100
French, Thibouville-Lamy, 2 piece back faint medium curl, golden brown, case, 14⅛, L19c (4269/161) — 200
French, 19c, labelled Joseph Guarnerius...1740, 14⅛ (4187/168) — 450
German, labelled Johannes Baptista Guadagnini...17--, 14¼ (4187/192) — 100
German, 1 piece back medium curl, golden brown, case, 14, 20c (4269/158) — 400
German, 1 piece back of narrow curl, golden brown, 13 15/16, M18c (4269/91) — 600
German, 2 piece back of medium curl, red brown, 14, 1880 (4269/79) — 400
German, labelled Domenicus Busan..., 17--, 14 (4187/50) — 850
German, labelled Mathias Hornstainer, 14 3/16, 1803 (4187/123) — 275
German, modern, 14 (4187/135) — 400
German, no label, 14 3/16 (4187/197) — 50
German, repair labels 1892, 14 7/16 (4187/131) — 125
German, Berlin School, L19c, labelled Joseph Guarnerius, 14¼ (4187/172) — 550
German, Ernst H. Roth 1927, serial no. B221, 14 3/16 (4187/138) — 300
German, E19c, 14 1/16 (4187/174) — 400
German, G.A. Pfretzschner, labelled...copy of Antonius Stradivarius..., 14 3/16 (4187/137) — 200
German, Joseph Knitl, 2 piece back, faint medium curl, 13¾, 1777 (4269/86) — 1200
German, Kloz, Mittenwald, 2 piece back almost plain, faint medium curl, 13 15/16, 1764 (4269/182) — 2000
German, L. Glasel, 14⅛, 1926 (4187/128) — 800
German, L18c, labelled Joseph Knitl, 1727, 14⅛ (4187/146) — 1250
German, Otto Mockel, 2 piece back, medium curl, orange-brown, case, 13 15/16, 1926 (4269/168) — 1900
German, Wilhelm Durrschmidt, L19c, 14 3/16 (4187/175) — 325
German, 19c, labelled Anno 1754 Carlo Bergonzi..., 14¼ (4187/125) — 350
German, 19c, labelled Casper daSalo...1534, 14 3/16 (4187/124) — 175
German, 19c, labelled Joh. Bapt. Schweitzer, 14¼ (4187/169) — 525
German, 19c, labelled Matthias Kloz...1742, 14 1/16 (4187/170) — 250
German, 19c, labelled...Thibout...1838, 14 1/16 (4187/136) — 200
German, 19c, no label, 14 (4187/193) — 300
Hungarian, no label, one pc back, 14 3/16 (4187/199) — 300
Hungarian, Stowasser, 2 piece back of medium curl, golden brown, 14 3/16, 1910 (4269/171) — 300
Italian, School of Stefano Scarampella, 14 3/16, 1884 (4187/121) — 1200
Italian, labelled Enricus Ceruti, 1845, with 2 bows, 14⅛ (4187/44) — 850
Italian, labelled Ferdinandus, Gagliano...174-, bird's eye maple back, 14⅛ (4187/48) — 1500
Italian, labelled Joseph Guarnerius..., ...1795, 14 (4187/56) — 5300
Italian, labelled Petrus Zianni..., 1752, with 2 silver mounted bows, 14⅛ (4187/60) — 800
Italian, Filippo Brandilioni, 1790, 13⅞, fine (4187/151) — 3300
Italian, Francesco Gofriller, 1739, 13⅞, fine (4187/153) — 12000
Italian, Genigno Saccani, 1 piece back of medium grain, rich orange-red, 14 1/16, 1910 (4269/165) — 3500
Italian, Giambattista Palzini...1946, 14⅛ (4187/180) — 650
Italian, Ginlio Degani M20c, 14 1/16 (4187/182) — 1600
Italian, Giovanni Francesco Celoniato, ca1734, 14 1/16, fine (4187/209) — 5500
Italian, Hannibal Fagnola...1931, 14⅛ (4187/47) — 2200
Italian, Lorenzo Storioni L18c, labelled Giovanni Grancino...1697, 14 (4187/62) — 4750
Italian, Luigi Mozzani, 1939, 14 (4187/143) — 650
Italian, Michele Deconet, Venice, label, 14, fine (4187/210) — 6000
Italian, Michele Deconet, Venice, 1755, 14 1/16, fine (4187/152) — 13000
Jacob Stainer, 2 piece back of medium curl, orange-brown, 13 15/16, 1677 (4269/101) — 24000
Michael Platner, Rome, (attrib), 1745, 14 1/16 (4187/148) — 2900
Miniature, no label, German, with 2 miniature bows, 7 (4187/34) — 450
Mute, American, unlabeled, open figure 8 form, golden brown, 13⅝, L19c (4269/10) — 150
Mute, American C.F. Albert, body anchor form, unpurfled, golden brown, 14, 1877 (4269/11) — 200
Nicolo Amati, Cremona, 1659, original label, 13 13/16, important (4187/212) — 46000
Roth Markneukirchen, 2 piece back of medium curl, dark red, 14 1/16, 1931 (4269/172) — 600
Saxon, labelled Gio. Paolo Maggini..., 14¼4 (4187/196) — 250
Saxon, no label, David Hopf, with silver mounted bow, 14 (4187/53) — 225
Saxon, Conrad Gotz, 2 piece back of medium curl, orange brown, 14, 1962 (4269/88) — 175
Saxon, E.R. Schmidt & Co., 19c, 14 (4187/140) — 175
Saxon, M19c, label not legible, with bow, 13 15/16 (4187/179) — 250
South German, 2 piece back, medium horizontal curl, case, 13⅞, ca1800 (4269/163) — 700
South German, ca1800, labelled Giusseppe Gennari...171-, 14 3/16 (4187/191) — 250
The 'Ovcharov' Stradivari, 1694, with label, 14¼, important (4187/213) — 26000
Tyrolese, L18c, no label, original neck, lengthened, 13 15/16 (4187/198) — 225
Viennese, labelled John Bapt., Schweitzer...1846, 14 1/16 (4187/54) — 200

Violin case

W.E. Hill & Sons, London, double, green Morocco leather, 31 x 12¼, ca1700 (4187/33) — 300

Violincello

English, Barak Norman, 2 piece back nearly horizontal curl, case, 28 5/16, 1715 (4269/156)	14000
French, M19c, labelled Sacquin...1850, 29 (4187/164)	3500
German, ca1900, labelled Luigi Montanari...1893, 30 (4187/165)	1100
German, L19c, labelled Guiseppe Antonio Rocca...1830, 29¾ (4187/166)	1700
Tyrolese, ca1700, labelled Matthias Albanus...1690, 30 1/16 (4187/167)	5000
Tyrolese, labelled Hans Tietgen, N.Y. 1906, 29½ (4187/163)	1700

PAPERWEIGHTS

Assorted manufacturers

Chequer, large, three spaced rows of canes, 3 15/16 (4230/84)	200
Close millefiori, five small silhouettes, profile Queen Victoria, Bacchus, 3¼ (4230/78)	650
Concentric millefiori, centered by a large white and pink florette, Gillinder, 2⅝ (4230/77)	*375*
Concentric millefiori, five rows canes, whole center by a florette, 3 (4230/86)	125
Concentric millefiori, four rows canes, enclosing pink and white rose, 3⅛ (4230/85)	150
Faceted butterfly, small circular top revealing butterfly, 3⅜ (4230/88)	*450*

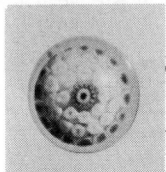

Concentric
millefiori
(4230/77)

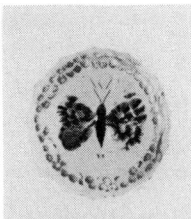

Faceted butterfly
(4230/88)

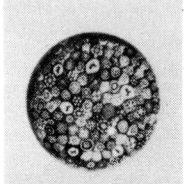

Close millefiori
(4230/153)

Mottled green ground, opaque green, white lizard, Salamander, 3⅝ (4230/44)	250
Patterned millefiori doorknob, silhouetted canes, center pink, florette, 1 13/16 (4230/93)	100
Pedestal rose, rose formed nineteen petals 3 leaves, 3⅝ (4230/48)	900
Rainbow satin glass, swirling pale pink, blue, yellow staves, Mount Washington, 3 9/16 (4230/45)	250
Spaced millefiori, twisted ribbons, numerous florettes, 1 with dog, Bohemian, 2½ (4230/90)	225
Sulphide, cameo profile Robert E. Lee, American, 2 7/16 (4230/103)	150
Sulphide, circular medallion profile Prince Albert, 2 3/16 (4230/104)	100
Sulphide, clear glass, profile of Gentleman, 2¾ (4230/107)	100
Water Lily, flower, yellow and white petals, green leaves, 3½ ca1910 (4230/47)	900

Baccarat

Blue double overlay mushroom, seven windows to reveal upright mushroom, 3⅛ (4230/134)	2200
Butterfly and garlands, alternate stardust and arrow canes, insect, 2 15/16 (4230/175)	950
Butterfly and garlands, pastry mold canes, centered by insect, 3⅛ (4230/176)	1500
Close millefiori, numerous tightly packed canes, 2 (4230/131)	325
Close millefiori, silhouettes of birds, a monkey and squirrel, 2½ B1847 (4230/123)	750
Close millefiori, silhouettes, animals, 2 birds and devil, 3⅛, B 1848 (4230/153)	*1100*
Concentric millefiori, centered bya large star silhouetted florette, 2⅝ (4230/133)	175
Concentric millefiori, setwith an outer garland, green and white florettes, 2½ (4230/124)	175
Concentric millefiori, stardust canes, 2⅝ (4230/163)	225
Concentric millefiori miniature, crowsfoot canes, blue, white and green, 1¾ (4230/138)	75
Double clematis and garland, silhouetted honeycomb center, 2¾ (4230/198)	950

Faceted, double clematis, small, green crows foot center, 7 windows, 2 1/16 (4230/192) — 600
Faceted, double overlay sulphide, five windows and flutes, profile D.Eisenhower, 3⅛ (4230/7) — 350
Faceted, double overlay sulphide, six windows and flutes, profile A.Lincoln, 3⅛ 1953 (4230/16) — 450
Faceted, double overlay-sulphide, green, 6 windows set with profile Martin Luther, 3⅛ 1955 (4230/13) — 325
Faceted, double sulphide, profile Dwight Eisenhower, (4230/19) — 375
Faceted, overlay sulphide, six windows and flutes, profile G. Washington, 3⅛ 1953 (4230/18) — 375
Faceted, overlay sulphide, six windows and flutes, profile Queen Elizabeth, 3⅛ (4230/17) — 350
Faceted, sulphide, seven windows, top and sides, profile D. Eisenhower, 2¾ (4230/10) — 175
Faceted, sulphide, Hunter and Hound, wooded landscape, 3¼ (4230/108) — 650
Faceted, white pom pom, top and sides cut with 6 windows, 2⅝ (4230/191) — 550
Flat bouquet, silhuetted honeycomb center, 2 13/16 (4230/189) — 1800
Mauve double clematis and garland, centered by flower, composed of 2 rows petals, 2¾ (4230/210) — 550
Mushroom, upright tuft of numerous large colored canes, 3⅛ (4230/125) — 425
Pansy, curved stalk with numerous leaves, bi-color bud, 2 9/16 (4230/184) — 375
Pansy, flower formed 2 large petals, 3 lower petals, 2 3/16 (4230/209) — 350
Pansy, flower, 4 leaf tips,short stalk, 5 leaves, (4230/183) — 325
Pansy, leaves and bi-colored bud, 2 7/16 (4230/202) — 325
Pansy, three leaf tips,on s-curved stalk, 2 leaves, 2 3/16 (4230/177) — 275
Pansy, typical flower, starburst, stamens, star cut base, 2½ (4230/181) — 450
Pansy, flower on short curved stalk, 5 leaves, 2 1/16 (4230/178) — 175
Patterned millefiori, centered white and red star florette, 2⅝ (4230/110) — 200
Patterned millefiori, octafoil garland formed of alternating loops, 3 (4230/118) — 250
Patterned millefiori, arrow and stardust canes, 2⅞ (4230/151) — 225
Patterned millefiori, thirteen butterfly silhouette canes, 3⅛ (4230/156) — 2300
Primrose, flower formed 5 red ogee petals, edged in white, 2⅝ (4230/199) — 650
Primrose and garlands, outer row alternative white stardust and red canes, 2⅞ (4230/197) — 1000
Red carpet ground, silhouettes, animals, canes, florettes, 3⅛, 1848 (4230/154) — 4400
Rock, three dimensional, 2 projections, speckled green, 2 13/16 (4230/172) — 100
Scattered, millefiori, random colored ribbons, large canes, animals, 3, 1847 (4230/164) — 900
Spaced millefiori, ribbon ground set with row of 6 colored canes, 1 15/16, 1848 (4230/129) — 600
Spaced millefiori, ribbons, canes, silhouette animals, and shamrock, 3⅛, 1848 (4230/157) — 850
Spaced millefiori, silhouettes of animals and flower shamrock, 2 13/16, 1848 (4230/150) — 900
Spaced millefiori, miniature, seven colored canes, silhouettes of animals, 2 (4230/161) — 350
White camomile, flower, 4 concentric rows of white petals, 2⅞ (4230/201) — 600

Clichy

Blue color ground, closely packed canes, 2 large roses, 3⅛ (4230/159) — 650
Chequer, centered by green and pink rose, 2 rows canes, 2⅝ (4230/141) — 475
Chequer, centered green and pink rose, 2 rows evenly spaced canes, 2⅝ (4230/142) — 800
Chequer, two rows of large florettes in tones of pink, 3¼ (4230/171) — 400
Close millefiori, outer basket of alternate staves, and florettes, 2¾ (4230/121) — *425*
Close millefiori, set in a basket alternate opaque white, pink staves, 2⅞ (4230/152) — 650
Close millefiori, set in basket, numerous tightly packed canes, 2⅞, C with serif (4230/122) — 2700
Concentric millefiori, set in basket white staves, 6 rows of canes, 3¼ (4230/167) — 1000
Concentric millefiori, staves, row of canes, enclosing 3 rows of canes, 2 3/16 (4230/130) — 300
Faceted mushroom, concave windows, upright concentric mushroom, 3 1/16 (4230/165) — 600
Faceted patterned millefiori, seven circular windws, row 6 canes, 2⅝ (4230/119) — 325
Pansy, flower 2 upper and 3 lower petals, 3⅛ (4230/207) — 750
Pansy, flower, curved stalk, 3 green leaves, 2½ (4230/195) — *750*

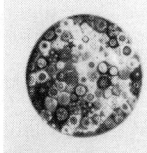

Close millefiori
(4230/121)

Pansy
(4230/195)

Crystal and
sulphide
patch box
(4230/99)

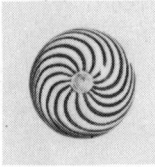

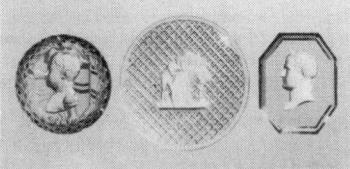

Swirl   (4230/149)

Sulphide
(4230/101)

Patterned millefiori, s-scroll canes, 3 3/16 (4230/117)   475
Patterned millefiori, six large green and pink roses, 2½ (4230/126)   850
Patterned millefiori miniature, five large white pastry cane, (4230/158)   300
Pink flower, composed of 5 rounded petals, green sepals, 2¾ unusual (4230/185)   3600
Posy, two canes, pink and blue, white rose, 2⅛ (4230/182)   425
Red color ground, numerous large spaced canes, 3⅛ C with serif (4230/147)   1100
Scramble, numerous brightly colored cane fragments, 2 1/16 (4230/146)   175
Scramble, numerous large brightly colored canes and fragments, 3 3/16 (4230/112)   250
Scramble, three roses in green, pink, white, 2½' (4230/155)   225
Spaced millefiori, evenly spaced canes, centered, pink-green rose, 2 9/16 (4230/160)   325
Spaced millefiori, three rows of canes, 2 roses, centered by rose, 3¼ (4230/132)   425
Spaced millefiori, three rows spaced canes, center florette, (4230/144)   600
Spaced millefiori, two rows concentric rows florettes, 2 3/16 (4230/115)   350
Spaced millefiori Newel Post, four rows of large florettes, 5¾ (4230/111)   800
Swirl, centered by large white green red pastry, 3 (4230/145)   325
Swirl, closely swirled staves, 2½, good (4230/149)   *2100*
Turquoise color ground, six large canes and 3 small florettes, 2 5/16 (4230/166)   450

French

Crystal and sulphide patch box, circular form, profile Duc de Bordeaux as a child, 2 5/16 (4230/99)   *350*
Sulphide, clear glass, head and shoulder Louis Napoleon Bonaparte, (4230/106)   275
Sulphide, octagonal shape profile Napoleon, Laurel Wreath, 2⅜, Dihl in script (4230/101)   *275*
Sulphide plaque, flattened circular form youthful figure, 3¼ (4230/100)   475
Tumbler, cut glass,set with a sulphide, oval reserve, depicting St. Peter, 3⅞ (4230/98)   275

Kazium, Charles

Pansy, 2 1/16 (4230/34)   550
Pansy, bright blue, set with pansy, bud, leaves and fly, 2⅛ (4230/32)   800
Pansy, Opaque, mauve ground, gold fig, 2⅛ (4230/33)   650
Pedestal, crocus, spherical clear glass, 6 petals, circular foot, 2 1/16 (4230/37)   1100
Pedestal, miniature, blue and white, florette flower, circular foot, 1¼ (4230/39)   425
Pedestal, miniature, pink flower, pale yellow ground, 1 5/18 (4230/41)   275
Pedestal, miniature, yellow flower, pine ground, speckles with gold, 1⅜ (4230/40)   175
Pedestal, rose, yellow rose,twelve pedals, 4 leaves, 1¾ (4230/38)   350
Pedestal, water lily, spherical clear glass, spreading circular foot, 1 15/16 (4230/35)   800
Pedestal rose, fifteen deep red petals, 4 striped green leaves, 2⅛ (4230/31)   1000

New England

Apple, molded apple, opaque yellow to rose pink, circular base, 2 13/16 (4230/54)   300
Apple, shaded, opaque russet to lime green, circular foot, 3 (4230/55)   600
Blue poinsettia, two rows blue petals, florette center, 2⅞ (4230/71)   175
Bouquet, eight pink roses, with trailing green leaves, 2 13/16 unusual (4230/67)   400
Dated patterned millefiori, florettes, 1 with butterfly other 1852, 2½ unusual (4230/76)   650
Faceted crown, two rows, circular windows, and flutes, 2 9/16 (4230/72)   350

Faceted upright bouquet, two rows of 6 windows, spaced by flutes and stars, 2 9/16 (4230/70)   750
Fruit, cluster, 3 pears, 4 cherries, 3 (4230/58)   350
Fruit, eight pears, 3 serrated leaf tips, basket, 2 13/16 (4230/65)   400
Fruit, five apples and 4 cherries, 2 9/16 (4230/66)   475
Fruit, five pears and 4 cherries, 2 13/16 (4230/59)   350
Pear, circular base, realistically molded pear, 2⅞ (4230/53)   225
Pear, opaque green to russet, clear circular base, 3¼ (4230/57)   750
Pear, russet to peach, ruby stem, clear oval base, 2¾ (4230/56)   700
Pink Poinsettia, ten overlapping petals, 5 green leaves, 2¾ good (4230/69)   *275*

Pink Poinsettia
(4230/69)

Fruit (4230/75)

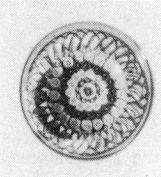

Concentric
mushroom
(4230/169)

Sandwich

Blue double clematis, two overlapping petals, stalk with green leaves, 2¾ (4230/60)   325
Blue poinsettia, ten overlapping petals, curved stalk, 2 leaves, 3 (4230/61)   325
Blue poinsettia, two overlapping rows petals, star-silhouetted cane, 2 15/16 (4230/73)   450
Cross flower, pink, cruciform flower, flanked on base by leaves, 2 15/16 (4230/64)   275
Fruit, five yellow and red apples and tips, 2⅝ (4230/75)   *425*
Pansy, flower, cobalt blue, opaque white, blue markings, 3½ (4230/52)   300
Pink double clematis, two rows of overlapping pointed pink petals, 3⅛ (4230/62)   400
Salmon poinsettia, ten overlapping petals, short curved stalk, leaves, 2⅞ (4230/63)   475
Weedflower, six-petals, 5 leaf tips, short stalk,two leaves, 3 (4230/68)   500

St. Louis

Amber-flash posy, white and salmon canes, posy of 3 florettes, 2¾ (4230/180)   275
Concentric millefiori, five rows of complex canes, 3¼ good (4230/168)   3400
Concentric mushroom, upright turf, 5 rows canes, 3 1/16, SL 1848 (4230/169)   *3400*
Crown, fourteen twisted ribbons, 3 3/16, good (4230/148)   2400
Crown, silhouetted florette, fifteen twisted ribbons, 3 3/16 (4230/114)   1300
Dahlia, two rows overlapping petals, swirling white cushions, 2 15/16 good (4230/190)   800
Dahlia and aventurine ground, centered by dahlia, 2 rows overlapping petals, 3, rare (4230/211)   2700
Faceted amber-flash mushroom, seven windows revealing upright mushroom, 2 13/16 (4230/139)   1000
Faceted blue dahlia, swirling white cushions, 6 circular windows, 3 3/16 (4230/208)   550
Faceted garland and jasper ground, honeycomb facets, 8 circular windows, 2⅝ (4230/205)   1100
Faceted hand cooler, egg shaped, 5 alternate rows windows, 2¾ (4230/193)   1200
Faceted posy, six windows cut around side to reveal center posy, 2⅞ (4230/204)   200
Faceted sulphide, clear,portrait of Queen Elizabeth, 3 1953 (4230/14)   150
Faceted sulphide, translucent blue, white blue line green canes, 3 1953 (4230/15)   200
Fruit, three oranges,and green pears, 4 red cherries, 2 11/16 (4230/173)   700
Jasper ground, five evenly spaced, lime green, white, blue canes, 3¼ (4230/137)   200
Millefiori, hand cooler, plain egg shape, canes and fragments, 2 9/16 (4230/127)   550
Piedouche, concentric, millefiori, seven rows of canes, pedestal foot, 2 15/16 1953 (4230/20)   350
Pink dahlia, large flower formed numerous rows, overlapping petals, 2½ (4230/179)   750
Pink dahlia and aventurine green ground, two rows overlapping petals, twisted blue spiral, 3 rare (4230/188)   5000
Posy miniature, pink and blue canes enclosing posy, 1⅝ (4230/206)   250

Primrose large, flower composed 6 blue and white, 3 3/16 (4230/194)   600
Scramble, numerous brightly colored canes and fragments, 2⅝ (4230/143)   70
Scramble, twisted ribbons, 7 canes, horse silhouette, 3⅛ (4230/170)   250
Strawberry, flower flanked by 2 fruits, 2 7/16 good (4230/186)   1300
Turnip, a cluster of 6 turnips, 2 9/16 (4230/174)   650
Vases, pair, millefiori and etched glass, paperweight bases, pale orange and green canes, 6⅞
(4230/96)   3400
White pom pom, swirling pink ground, 3 1/6 good (4230/187)   2300

Stankard, Paul

Faceted, flower weight, shaped facets, spray of 5 blue forget-me-nots, 2⅜ (4230/43)   250

Walter, pate de verre

Paperweight, modeled dove, seated on yellow, green base, 3¼, chip, A. Walter, ca1925 (4230/521)   700
Paperweight, red and brown lobster perched on rocky yellow-green base, 4¼, ca1920 (4230/520)   2100

Whitefriars

Commemorative contrentic, millefiori, five rows of corrugated canes, 3 1/16 erII 1953 (4230/26)   125
Concentric millefiori inkwell, stopper, six rows of concentric canes, large center florette, 5¾
(4230/82)   250
Dated concentric millefiori ink, well and stopper base set with 6 rows of cane, 6⅛ 1848 (4230/83)   300
Dated millefiori inkwell and stopper, numerous tightly packed corrugated canes, 5½ 1848
(4230/80)   250

Whittemore, Francis

Pedestal rose, mauve rose, 14 petals, 4 leaves, 1 13/16 (4230/42)   175

Ysart, Paul

Flat bouquet, four single clematis, 3 (4230/28)   300
Patterned millefiori, blue ground, five circles of canes, 2⅞ (4230/30)   225
Pink clematis, blue ground, alternategreen and orange canes, 3 1/16 (4230/29)   425

PIPES AND HOLDERS

Meerschaum

Cigar holder, nymph, L6' (690/310)   200
Cigar holder, seated maiden, L5 (690/339)   210
Cigar holder, woman reclining, L7' (690/312)   375
Cigar holder, Roman soldier's head, L3' (690/316)   90
Cigar holder, amber color, H2½' (690/304)   150
Cigar holder, bone, bawdy woman reclining, L5⅜' (690/319)   175
Cigar holder, bone/tan, Turk's head, L7' (690/315)   125
Cigar holder, tan, head of woman, L5¾' (690/303)   125
Cigar holder, tan, lady, L5⅛' (690/313)   140
Cigar holder, tan/amber, H2¾' (690/305)   200
Cigar holder, tan/amber, seated youth, 3¼' (690/320)   325
Cigarette holder, amber, two monkeys, L4¾' (690/308)   110
Cigarette holder, bone color, putto, L4⅜' (690/318)   275
Pipe, maiden with flowers, L7½ (690/337)   150
Pipe, scantily draped lady, L8¾ (690/336)   250
Pipe, wolf's head, L6 (690/331)   325
Pipe, carved, horse's head, L7¾ (690/330)   200
Pipe, carved, lion's head, L6½ (690/328)   100
Pipe, large, hunt scene, L17 (690/340)   2000
Pipe, large carved, tan, Indian shooting lion, H5¼' (690/327)   800
Pipe bowl, dog's head, L4¼ (690/329)   325

SCIENTIFIC INSTRUMENTS

Astrolabe, brass, circular, engraved with navigational aids, 11½, Persian* (4141/158)   200
Belt, chastity, incised with fox running through legs of naked woman, 9½, E17c (4133/165)   5600
Calculus rule, large table, keuffel & Esser, N.Y., 22 ca1900 (4165/129)   250
Calendar, perpetual, gilt and silvered, metal, Austrian, Johann Frantz Nider-Mayr, Salzburg, 1¾
ca1700 (4165/200)   700
Calendar, perpetual, pedometer, parcel gilt, Hager, 2⅞ 1696 (4165/203)   9000
Calendar, perpetual, silver Dutch, 1¾ L17c (4165/202)   750

Chronometer, Marine, Thomas Mercer, St. Albans, No. 21182, 7½ (4141/167) — 650
Chronometer, Marine, Thomas Mercer, St. Albans, No. 22132, 7¼ (4141/165) — 800
Chronometer, Marine, Ulysse, Nardin, Locle, No. 2202, and CIE, 7½, Swiss (4141/164) — 650
Chronometer, Marine, Ulysse, Nardin, Locle, No. 8609, 7½, Swiss (4141/163) — 950
Circumferentor, brass, continental, compass with 6 sighting vanes, 7½ E17c (4165/156) — 6000
Circumferentor, brass, Cave, Dublin, 2 folding vanes, 13½ M18c (4165/157) — 1300
Compass, and sundial, octagonal brass, German, Lorenz Grassl, Augsburg, 2 18c (4165/195) — 400
Compass, marine brass, J. Bassnet & Son, Liverpool, 9½ L19c (4165/142) — 175
Compass, military geometrical, copy of original by Glileo, 15¼ (4165/172) — 175
Compass, mining, mahogany and brass, Whitehurst, Derby, 11¼ - ca1800 (4165/153) — 275
Compass, sundial, brass, Chinese, hinged front, 2½ 19c (4165/190) — 125
Compass, sundial, wood, Chinese, circular dial in square base, (4165/191) — 125
Compass and sundial, brass, 6⅞ (4165/198) — 550
Compass and sundial, gunmetal, Harris, London, 3⅛ E19c (4165/185) — 500
Compass and sundial, wood, 2 ca1800 (4165/197) — 200
Compass and sundial, wood, 3⅝ (4165/193) — 120
Dial, equinoctial, brass, English, T. Wright, with compass, levels, 3⅛ E18c (4165/183) — 3900
Dial, pocket box form, with almanac, latitudes of countries, 3 L18c (4165/184) — 600
Dial, pocket brass German, Andreas Vogler, Augsburg, 2 L18c (4165/199) — 375
Dial, pocket brass, German, 3 M18c (4165/179) — 425
Dial, pocket octagonal parcel gilt, German, (4165/204) — 2100
Dial, pocket octagonal, brass, Butterfield, Paris, 2¾ E18c (4165/177) — 475
Dial, pocket, brass, C. Lerget a Paris Au Butterfield, with compass, 3¼ E18c (4165/178) — 500
Dial, ring brass, English*, central sighting bar, 6⅛ 18c (4165/196) — 1800
Dial, ring, astronomical, brass, English, I. Sisson, Fecit, 6⅞ E18c (4165/181) — *1300*
Dial, tablet, polychrome, ivory, German, Leonhard Miller, with latitudes, 4⅛ ca1640 (4165/206) — *3700*
Dial, wood cube, German, D. Beringer, 7 L18c (4165/182) — 1400
Dial, Butterfield type, silver, Langlois a Paris, Au Galleries du Louvre, 3 ca1700 (4165/194) — 1200
Dial and compass, pocket, wood, with list of towns and latitudes on interior, 3⅞, L18c (4141/159) — 175
Drawing instruments, set, brass and steel, Watkins & Hill London, 7¾ E19c (4165/127) — 225
Dutchmaker's rounding up tool, mahogany base, 19 cutters, 18 collets, L13¼, ca1900 (4238/339) — 260
Fleams, schnapper, pair brass and steel, with case, pistol handles, scrolling leaves, 2, 18c, 3 pcs (4133/162) — 650
Globe, library celestial, mahogany, leaf carved support, tripod legs, 41 Newton and Son 1830 (4079/44) — 375
Globe, terrestrial pocket, 3½ 18c (4165/174) — 700
Globes, library, pair, walnut, celestial and terrestrial, tripod legs, 51, Newtons, London 1860-61 (4079/45) — 1800
Globes, table, turned, molded fruitwood bases, 9½, M19c (4152/12) — 250
Globes, terrestrial and celestial, pair, table, George Adams, London, 22½ 1782 (4165/165) — *4600*

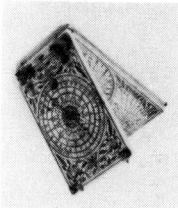

Dial (4165/206)

Dial (4165/181)

Globes (4165/165)

Graphometer brass, French, Meurand, Paris, 10½ L18c (4165/154)	3100
Lathe, Lens polishing, in brass and steel, 10, E19c (4165/131)	400
Microscope, aquatic, brass, small, 5⅜ ca1800 (4165/144)	275
Microscope, aquatic, compound, 17½ - L19c (4165/148)	375
Microscope, binocular, brass, 17 L19c (4165/145)	475
Microscope, brass, Casella, London, 17 ca1900 (4165/146)	700
Microscope, brass 'small', Smith & Beck, London, 11¾ - L19c (4165/147)	250
Microscope, compound brass, attributed to William and Samuel Jones, 17½ ca1800 (4165/151)	800
Microscope, compound, brass, fitted mahogany case with accessories,½ L18c (4165/150)	350
Microscope, compound, brass, large, 17½ L19c (4165/149)	500
Octant, brass and ebony, ivory scale, 14½ L18c (4165/137)	350
Odometer, 'Waywiser', wood and brass, J. Sisson, London, 55 E18c (4165/164)	950
Orrery, portable, fitted wood box, 17 (4165/173)	2000
Pedometer, brass and silvered metal, Jac. Ram. D. Scriba, inventor, 4 E17c (4165/175)	2500
Pedometer, gilt metal and shagreen, Spencer and Perkins, London, 2¼, L18c (4141/155)	350
Pincers, pair iron, dec with stars and hatching, 5½, 17c (4133/160)	225
Prosthetics, flexible, child's, iron, scrolls and hinged, laced at front, 14 bodice, 14 leg, E17c (4133/166)	3000
Scale, brass for coins, two pans, leather case, 2¾ 19c (4165/136)	90
Scale, Continental iron and steel, 27½ L18c (4165/133)	*1400*
Scarificator, blood letter, brass, square with 16 iron blades, trigger mechanism, 1¼, 18c (4133/163)	800
Set of brass weights, 2¾ 19c (4165/134)	125
Sextant, brass, 9¾ M19c (4165/139)	400
Sextant, brass, Troughton & Sims, London, 9½ ca1830 (4165/138)	425
Sextant, engraved brass ivory and, ebony, 1795 - William Curtis (4134/215)	225
Sextant, oxidized brass, G. Rahtjen, Bremen, 9½, L19c (4141/150)	750
Sounding, machine, harpoon, brass, T. Walker, 9½ L19c (4165/141)	300
Sundial, azimuth magnetic, Charles Bloud, Dieppe, 2¾ L17c (4165/205)	1100
Sundial, brass, John Bate, Dublin, 8 ca1750 (4165/176)	450
Sundial, octagonal, brass, S. Saunders, finely engraved compass rose, 9, ca1740, English (4141/160)	700
Sundial, silvered brass, folding chapter ring with Roman numerals, 5⅝, L18c, Italian* (4141/161)	1000
Sundial and compass, miniature, Chinese, rectangular, 2¾ (4165/204)	150
Sundial and compass, pocket, brass, octagonal, 2⅛, 18c, German (4141/162)	475
Surveying instrument, brass, Thomas Hanson Marshall, 14 E19c (4165/186)	275
Telescope, reflecting, brass, large, Gilbert & Sons, London, sighting tube, 39 L18c (4165/166)	*3000*
Telescope, reflecting, brass, large, Newtonian type, 6¾ x 85½ ca1800 (4165/170)	2700
Telescope, refraction mahogany & brass, three sections with brass terminals, 76¾, ca1800 (4165/163)	450
Telescope, refraction, 5 sections, A. Coiffier, Ingr. Opticien, Paris, 11¾, E19c (4165/162)	550
Telescope, universal, achromatic, Jesse Ramsden and Peter Dolland, London, ca1780 (4165/171)	15000
Theodolite, brass, 7 M19c (4165/187)	175
Theodolite, brass, Haiden & Co. Manchester and London, 12, L19c (4165/161)	450
Theodolite, brass, Keuffel & Esser Co. N.Y., 16½ ca1895 (4165/159)	900
Watchmaker's lathe, Perfection 5059, electric motor, collets, wooden case, L13 (4238/340)	100
Wool spinning machine, Good, Brand & Co. Manchester, 27 M19c (4165/128)	1300

TOY SOLDIERS

Britains

Arabs, 8 mounted, 8 on foot, good condition (690/907)	130
Black Watch pipe band, incomplete, 20 pcs, fair condition (690/889)	130
Cameron Highlanders, 4 pipers, 56 pcs, good condition (690/901)	350
Cavalry, Queens' Guards, 27, blue or red uniforms, 3⅛, few cracks, ca1920 (659/579)	225
Circus set, circus ring, tall man, Liberty horses, 20 pcs, incomplete (690/870)	150
Civil War, 23 Confederate, 11 Union Infantry, good condition (690/887)	170
Coldstream Guards, 113 pcs, 1½ x 3, dome paint dam, ca1920 (659/607)	300
Coldstream Guards, 79 pcs, colorfully painted, 1¾ x 3¼, ca1915 (659/598)	425
Early general service wagon, cross bar missing, 5 pcs, (690/936)	150
Early royal field artillery, valises, seated gunners, 12 pcs, good condition (690/933)	*550*
Egyptian Camel Corps., 4 riders, 6 camels, good condition, (690/877)	225
Forty grenadier guards, officer, mounted, marching officer, drummer, good condition (690/884)	150
French cavalry, 16 Turks, 12 horses, 25 officers, in green, 2 x 3⅜, ca1915 (659/588)	*250*

French Foreign Legion, 25 pcs, good condition (690/886) — 140
French infantry, 15 calvary cuirassiers, 29 French infantry, 2-4, ca1915 (659/586) — 250
Guards in greatcoats, twenty Scots guards, 15 grenadiers, good condition (690/882) — 150
Horse-drawn ambulance, 7 pcs, good condition (690/935) — 350
Indian Cavalry, 8 Hodson's horse, 8 Skinner's horse, good condition (690/900) — 200
Infantry set, 84, 40 Gurkha riflemen and 40 Bengal lancers, ca1915 (659/597) — 400
Inniskilling dragoons, 5 pcs, (690/938) — 110
King's African rifles, 21 pcs, good condition (690/898) — 200
Line Infantry, 22 Somerset and 10 Royal West Surrey, good condition (690/883) — 175
Mounted Life Guards, 22, blue, red or grey, 3, 1 deterioration, ca1915 (659/580) — 150
Queen's Guards Band, 104 pcs, 2½, ca1915 (659/599) — *550*

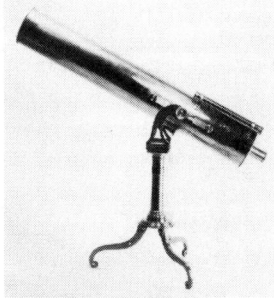

Telescope (4165/166)

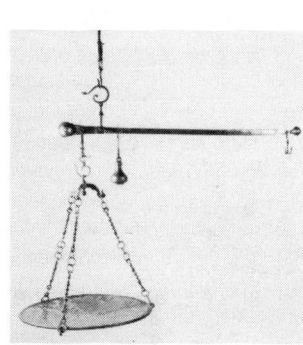

Scale (4165/133)

French cavalry (659/588)

Horse-drawn ambulance
(690/935)

Queen's Guards Band (659/599)

Early royal field artillery
(690/933)

Royal Archers, good condition, 13 pcs (690/876) — 90
Scottish regiments, 125 pcs, Argyle, Sutherland and Blackwatch colors, 1½ x 3, ca1915 (659/589) — 450
Seaforth Highlanders, 46 Infantry, 5 pipers, 5 officers, good condition (690/878) — 275
Sixteen Scot Greys, four officers, good condition (690/888) — 80
State landau, complete, 12 pcs, good condition (690/947) — 190
The Scot's Guards, 79 pcs, 2½, ca1920 (659/606) — 400
Turkish cavalry, 24, blue, yellow or grey uniforns, 3, ca1915 (659/596) — 200
Zouaves, 15 charging infantry, 3 mounted officers, good condition (690/913) — 50
Zouaves, 4 mounted officers, 20 Infantry men, 24 pcs (690/875) — 120
1st Bengal calvary, 17 pcs, flaking, (690/939) — 225
1Foreign Legion, 20 marching troops, 4 mounted officers (690/909) — 120

Frenchal

Alpine figures, 29 in good condition, (690/916) — 60
French Foreign Legion, 97 pcs, assorted, (690/919) — 200

Native African band, 22 bandsmen, 13 marching troops, good condition (690/917)	80
Royal Canadian mounted police, 15 pcs, good condition (690/918)	60

Johillco

Coronation scene, 120 figures, (690/926)	130
Romans, 3 chariots with drivers, 10 footmen, (690/930)	140

Mignot

Box of Chinese Infantry, 12 pcs, good condition (690/867)	100

TOYS

Assorted types

Alabama Coon Jigger, penny toy, tin, 3¼, ca1930, (659/466)	80
Alarm clock, Mickey Mouse, 2 Mickey Mouse subsidiary second dial, Ingersoll Co., 4 (659/477)	50
American Flyer train set, eight pcs, ca1950, (690/716)	50
Amos 'n Andy Fresh Air Taxi Cab, tin wind-up, Marx, 8¼, ca1930 (659/469)	325
Anti-aircraft gun, model, brass, scale model mounted on wooden stand, 4¾ (659/566)	40
Beetle, tin wind-up, black with grey, dotted body, Gunthermann, 7½, ca1911 (659/455)	100
Beetle, tin wind-up, gilt spots on red ground, Lehmann, 3¾, wear, ca1900 (659/454)	50
Billy Goat Bell, painted, tin, Althof Bergmann or Ives, 7½, ca1890 (659/463)	325
Boxing, tin wind-up, American, two boxers, jointed arms and legs, 6, ca1921 (659/453)	140
Buck Rogers Rocket Ship, wind-up, Marx, 12, ca1930 (659/459)	110
Car, three wheel, tin wind-up painted, gentleman steering, servant holding parasol, Lehmann, 5¼, ca1905 (659/434)	200
Clown and Cat, tin wind-up painted, clown playing clarinet, German*, 8½, ca1910 (659/446)	275
Clown on a donkey tin wind-up, painted, 3 wheels, German, 7, 1930 (659/438)	140
Disneyland roller coaster wind-up, lithographed, J. Chein & Co., 10, 1940 (659/548)	80
Doll, Louis Armstrong, wind-up, 10¾, (659/547)	80
Doll, Pinocchio, wind-up composition, painted, moving side to side for French market, 7¾ (659/480)	110
Engine 1912, lithographed tin, Japanese, c1930, L6 (690/7084)	50
Felix the Cat in a roadster, wood model, painted, 11¾, L1920 (659/442)	100
Fire engine, wind-up, L4½, ca1920, German (690/707)	60
Fire Pumper, cast-iron, American, red and grey, Kenton*, 14½, ca1920 (659/452)	190
French Optical Toy, painted wood viewer, 14 prints, L14, M19c (690/784)	125
Friction Trick Jumbo Elephant, moving tusk up and down, Gibbs, 6¼, ca1910 (659/457)	175
Game, marble, turned wood, circular board, Sandwich glass marbles, 9½, 19c (4211/1040)	275
German Horse and Jockey, lithographed wind-up, L. 5¼ (690/756)	20
Horse and jockey, tin, German, 5, ca1920 (659/436)	30
Jonah and the Whale, cast-iron, Jonah popping out of the whale's mouth, 6, bell missing, ca1910 (659/456)	225
Maggs and Jiggs, tin wind-up, seated on 2 wheeled, platform, Nifty, 8, arms missing, 1920 (659/467)	175
Matador and Bull, wind up tin, Gebruder Finfalt, 1930's, L9¼, German (690/693)	50
Mickey Mouse Circus Top, wood and metal, painted, Mickey and Minnie on swing, 11, L1930 (659/448)	130
Minstrel mechanical bank, tin, German, tongue popout, eyes blink, 7, ca1930 (659/472)	200
Model coach, painted, London, Berkely Hotel, Burford Bridge, 15½, E19c (4111/16)	750
New York Central Rail Road Car, Tin, lithographed, American, J. Chein & Co., 4 (659/619)	30
One man band, wooden pole mounted with drum and cymbals, mask of popeye, 69 (659/537)	20
Performing Jumbo, wood body, tin legs, 10, ca1911 (569/458)	60
Popeye and Olive Oyl Dancing on Roof, tin wind-up, Marx, 10, 1930 (569/443)	300
Popeye the Pilot, tin wind-up, Marx, 8¾, 1930 (659/445)	150
Roadster, model, painted, tin, wind-up clockwork, mechanism, rubber wheels, 12½, ca1930 (659/569)	1700
Roadster, wind up, lithographed tin, L9, (ca1925), German (690/705)	150
Skidoodle, tin wind-up, Nifty, 3 characters in roadster, 9½, ca1920 (659/471)	*650*
Sled Ride, tin, American, 2 sled riders, canvas strip, ca1925 (659/461)	100
Smitty on a Scooter, tin wind-up, Marx, 8, ca1930 (659/468)	*450*
Steiff braying donkey, pull toy, (690/717)	50
Stereoscopic viewer, French, 6 cards of photographs, 7⅞ x 4⅞, M19c (690/786)	75
Taxi, wind-up, painted, possibly H. Fisher, L13, ca1910, German (690/709)	1300
Toonerville Trolley, Nifty, tin wind-up, 7¼, ca1922 (659/470)	*450*
Touring Car, tin wind-up, German, 4 wheeled car, 4¾, ca1915 (659/450)	100
Two horse drawn hook and ladder truck, cast-iron, 27½ (659/535)	130
Village, miniature, Czechoslovakian, 1000 pcs, painted, Anton Sippich, ca1935 (659/196)	1000

Wheelbarrow, tin wind-up, painted, porter pulling wheelbarrow, Ferdinand Strauss Corp., 6¼, ca1920 (659/433) 70

Wood horse pull toy, American, leather reins, wood base, cast-iron wheels, 13¼, ca1880 (659/539) 50

Wood shoe shine box, painted, inside lid decorated with print two boys shining boots, 11⅜, L19c (659/540) 30

World War I ambulance, tin, wind-up, L7½, (ca1915), German (690/704) 250

Trains

Lionel, Mickey Mouse hand card, compositoion figure of Mickey and Minnie, original box, 5¼, ca1933 (659/577) *600*

Lionel standard gauge 2 tone green, state set, 6 pcs, 17½, engine, 21½ cars, ca1930 (659/576) *8500*

Lionel (659/577)

Billy Goat Bell (659/463)

Lionel standard gauge 2 tone green (659/576)

Chapter 9

Chinese Works of Art

A worldwide base of support among collectors, dealers and museums makes the market in Chinese art exceptionally stable and dependable. Increasingly, buyers attend or bid by proxy at overseas auctions, bolstering already stiff competition and further insulating the market against local shocks. Though growing demand and rising prices have continued to draw out a reasonable volume of good material, the supply of high-quality items is limited and diminishing. The flow of works of arts from China has all but stopped since the 1949 Revolution; only later decorative wares may now be exported from the mainland. Museum purchases continually deplete the supply of works available for auction. Rising prices are certainly in part a response to this scarcity of material.

The largest sector of the Chinese art market is ceramics, and trends in ceramic prices are the most significant market indicators. Ming ceramics (1368-1643) command the highest prices, and demand continues to be strong. Ch'ing ceramics also find a ready market, particularly among the Hong Kong Chinese. The Sung era (960-1279) is the classic period of Chinese ceramics; American museums and Far Eastern buyers compete heavily in this segment of the market. Among Sung wares a wide price gap exists between lesser pieces and the finest examples.

The recent archaeological work in China has stimulated collecting interest in T'ang (618-907) and earlier wares. Collectors have found the brilliant glazes and bold modeling of T'ang animal figures particularly appealing; outstanding examples now sell in the thousands of dollars. Many early wares, such as Neolithic pottery, which had long been neglected are now much in demand.

Condition is especially important in appraising Chinese ceramics. As prices have risen, the gap in price between perfect and damaged pieces has steadily widened. Buyers are more tolerant of damage in earlier wares, but any defect will significantly reduce the value of a Ming or Ch'ing porcelain.

Archaic bronze vessels have long been recognized as an important part of Chinese art history, but their prices have lagged behind those of ceramics, in large part because of the deterioration most of them have suffered through long burial. Quality and scarcity are the key factors in determining price; fine examples command spectacular bids, while ordinary or damaged pieces are often worth very little despite their great antiquity. Other early bronze objects, such as mirrors, chariot fittings and small shroud weights, being without the significant conservation problems of archaic vessels, have appreciated sharply in the last few years.

Collectors, particularly Americans, continue to seek out good jade carvings, but jade prices have not risen as fast as those of ceramics over the past decade. Archaic and early jades have outpaced those of later date. In the case of Ch'ing and later jade carvings, value often depends most heavily upon the size, quality and color of the stone. White jades are very popular today, and large pieces of pure white stone command high prices, while bright-green jadeite remains the most expensive type of stone on the market.

Increased interest among better-educated and more sophisticated buyers has produced steady growth in the area of Chinese paintings over the last ten years. This is still a relatively new area, however, with a great deal of room for future growth. The only obstacle to a real boom in this field is the problem of attributions. The tradition of painting in China involves much imitation and copying among masters and students, artists and followers, from the earliest period to the present; as a result, it is often difficult to assign a given painting to a specific date or region, much less to a particular artist. Chinese paintings offer the greatest opportunities for price appreciation, but the problem of attributions makes them also the most uncertain and risky market sector; only careful and knowledgeable buyers should invest in this area.

BRONZES

An assortment

Bodhisattva, Sino-Tibetan, seated on a lotus petal molded throne, 6½, LMing Dyasty (4154/318)	$300
Bronze, Food vessel, Li Ting, restored, well cast, Shang Dynasty, 6⅞ (4174/315)	3100
Buddha head, massive, serene expression, tightly curled hair, Ming Dynasty, 18 (4174/156)	5500
Candlesticks, pewter, Fu Lion, crouching with inlaid glass eyes, 19c (4223/432)	500
Censer, deer, prancing on slender legs, 19¾ x 14¼, LMing Dynasty, well cast (4154/323)	1500
Censer, fish-form, bearded immortal cover, supported on its gills, 5¾, Ming (4261/186)	90
Censer, parcel gilt, exotic creatures, ground on frothing waves, 6¼, LMing Dynasty (4154/321)	1100
Censers, bird-form, archaistic, standing, domed petal base, lotus pod, 10½, pitting, 19c (4261/169)	450
Ch'i Lin seal, crouching fantastic beast with scaley body, Ming Dynasty, 3¾, rare (4174/146)	4800
Dignitary figure, well cast, holding a scroll, Ming Dynasty, 19¼ (4214/15)	1000
Elephant figure, parcel-gilt, Ming Dynasty, 2¼ (4174/148)	600
Elephant figure, small, reclining beast heavily cast, Ming Dynasty, 2½ (4174/147)	950
Equestrian censer, figure of a warrior, 17c, 8¼, pcs missing (4214/21)	275
Figure, bronze, Ming Dynasty, of Wen Shu, seated, long robes, beaded chains, 12½ (4223/438)	700
Fu-lion censer, well-cast, 17c, 7½ (4214/20)	800
Gilt lacquered guardian figures, pair, each in warrior costume, Ming Dynasty, 16-17 (4174/155)	400
Guardian figure, animal-form headdress, footed base, Late Ming Dynasty, 12 (4214/14)	550
Ho-Ho boys figure, Ming Dynasty, 6 (4214/9)	300
Imperial seal, fitted hardwood box, square chop, seal 3⅝, box 7, Ch'ien Lung (4154/324)	425
Kuan Ti figure, Ming Dynasty, 8, rep. (4214/12)	225
Kylin censer, late Ming Dynasty, fanciful beast with long horn, 17c, 8 (4214/22)	325
Mirror, barbed, rectangular, carved, low-relief, 4¾, Yuan dynasty (4261/173)	150
Mythical beast figure, archaic style, recumbent winged beast, Ming Dynasty, 3¼ (4214/19)	1200
Official, Realistically modeled, robes with incised floral border, 8¾, Ming Dynasty, unusual, small (4154/319)	625
Puzzle group, Ming Dynasty, circular arrangement of twin boys, 16-17c, 3¼ (4214/18)	620
Ritual bronze, Covered vessel, Fang Yi, Shang Dynasty, 5, repaired (4174/318)	50000
Table screens, onion green, serpentine, wood stands, 13½ (4214/99)	800
Taoist Dignitary, sage seated with a fan held in his raised right hand, 9¾, Ming Dynasty (4154/322)	550
Vessel, ritual food, archaistic, 3 legs, 3 masks, 2 loop handles, 11½, 19c (4261/170)	175
Vessel and cover, ritual, late Ming, chip on cover, Chien Lung Seal Mark, 10½ (4214/23)	350
Waterdropper, water buffalo and boy, recumbant, boy coaxing to rise, 4, Ming (4261/187)	250
Wen Sau figure, seated on lion, Ming Dynasty, 6⅝ (4214/13)	425

Archaic bronzes

Basin, ring handles, Han Dynasty, 10½, cr (4174/288)	400
Beaker, well-cast, Ku, Shang Dynasty, slender trumpet-shaped neck, H12 (4121/16)	21000
Bell, hanging, Chung, eighteen bosses formed by coiled snakes, 6c B.C., 15¾ (4174/303)	18000
Bell, To, eighteen pegs both sides, Early Warring States Period, 18 (4174/301)	2000
Belt hook, cast as mask in rounded relief, 3-2 century B.C., 2⅜ (4174/252)	250
Belt hook, Warring States Period, pattern of linked lozenges, turquoise inlaid, L8½ (4121/12)	1100
Belt hook, 3 longitudinal facets, LWarring States Period, 5¼ (4174/256)	200
Bowl, stem, provincial, Han Dynasty, oval, narrow rib band and 2 loop handles, 5 (4223/427)	650
Bowl, tripod bronze, plain shallow, 3 slender splayed legs, 4¾, flaking, chip, Han Dynasty (4154/326)	200
Cauldron, ritual, Ting, Chou Dynasty, nine dragons in flat relief, D12 (4121/21)	*14000*
Cauldron, tripod, Ting, Shang Dynasty, well cast, stylized dragons, H9¼ (4121/19)	19000
Censer and stand, archaistic stylized dragons, medallions, 17-18c, 7⅜ (4121/89)	575
Chia, large, repaired, Shang Dynasty, 13⅜ (4174/317)	40000
Clapperless bell, Chung, massive, Warring States Period, 25 (4174/300)	3700
Dagger axe, Ko, slender pointed blade with central ridge, L7¾, 3BC (4121/11)	450
Dagger axe, Ko, Shang and Yin Dynasty, slightly carved tapered blade, 8⅝, Early Chou Dynasty* (4121/9)	275
Dagger axe, Ko, Shang Dynasty, chip blade, repaired, 9⅜ (4121/10)	225
'Ear cup' Jen-Lien-Pei, Han Dynasty, thinly cast oval vessel with 'ear' handles, (4121/22)	*1200*
Elephant mask fitting, LEastern Chou Dynasty, 2⅞ (4174/269)	1500
Finial, archaic bronze, Sung Dynasty, phoenix bird, silver, gold decoration, 5 (4223/431)	800
Finial, tapered tube ending in dragon mask, Han Dynasty, 5½ (4174/260)	550
Fittings, pair, T'ang Dynasty, tapered loop and ribbed terminals, 2¼, T'ang Dynasty (4223/429)	50
Food vessel, Kuei, loop handles capped with animal heads, W9¾, 11-10 Century BC (4121/20)	*4000*
Kettle, parcel gilt bronzed cover, globular, vessel raised on tripod animal supports, 7 (4154/325)	250
Kuei plain, simple, widemouthed bowl, Early Chou Dynasty, 10¼, (4121/299)	1300
Lamp, tripod, Warring States, shallow vessel resting on 3 figures, D5 (4121/23)	850
Mirror, astronomical, smooth black patina, touches of rust-brown, D6, fine, 1c (4121/2)	1000
Mirror, bronze, small central knop, 4⅛, L3/2c (4242/264)	1450
Mirror, large, Sung Dynasty, concentric bands enclosing characters, D8½, Yuan Dynasty* (4121/5)	450

Mirror, miniature, small disc with raised ring around knop, Han Dynasty, 2 (417/249) — 170
Mirror, small, 6 Dynasties, four fantastic beasts in relief, D5½ (4121/3) — 100
Mirror, well cast, T'ang Dynasty, small, band of song birds, D3⅝ (4121/4) — 900
Mirror, TLV type, central boss set on quatrefoil motif, D7⅝, L1BC-1c (4121/1) — 1200
Mirror, Wang Mang type, archaic animals interspersed with T, L V motifs, 1st century B.C.-A.D., 5⅜ (4174/247) — 2600
Plaque, rectangular, pierced tab, Han Dynasty* 6⅛ (4174/250) — 175
Plaque, ordos animal-form, Han Dynasty, horse figures, pc missing, D2½ (4121/6) — 800

'Ear cup'
Jen-Lien-Pei
(4121/22)

Plaque (4121/6)

Pole finial
(4121/13)

Plaque (4121/7)

Food vessel
(4121/20)

Cauldron (4121/21)

Plaque, ordos tiger, Han Dynasty, tail broken off, L4¾ (4121/7) — *450*
Pole finial, Shang Dynasty, bovine monster mask, H4½ (4121/13) — *1700*
Ritual foodvessel, Kuei, large, 11-10c B.C., 11⅜ (4174/308) — 10500
Ritual vessel, Lei, restored, Eastern Chou Period, 9¾ (4174/295) — 700
Ritual wine vessel, Ku, Shang Dynasty, 8 (4174/316) — 1700
Tiger Tally, in 2 interlocking pcs, Han Dynasty, 3⅝, rare (4174/257) — 3800
Ting, inlaid, Sung Dynasty, deep vessel. sqiat tripot legs 2 lug handles, 4¾ (4223/430) — 400
Tripod food vessel, Ting, restored, l0c B.C., 8¼, dam (4174/306) — 4000
Vase, globular, T'ang Dynasty, compressed body, wide everted rim, H3½ (4121/24) — 400
Vessel vine, bronze, rounded sides, flared foot, 6½, 11/10c BC (4242/272) — 400
Wine vessel, Chueh, Shang Dynasty, deep body on 3 blade-shaped legs, H8⅛ (4121/15) — 3750
Wine vessel, Ku, Shang Dynasty, flared beaker shape, 11¼ (4121/17) — 6000
Wine vessel and cover (Kuang), with dragons and fretwork in Shang style, 9¾ (4121/87) — 550

Archaic bronzes utensil

Basin, side with band of 3 raised lines, Han Dynasty, 13¼ (4174/290) — 475
Brazier, restored, with animals of 4 quarters, 1-2c A.D., 9½ (4174/293) — 3500
Ceremonial food vessel, Tui, two halves, each with ring, scroll finials, Eastern Chou/Early Warring States Period (4174/297) — 11500
Covered caldron, repaired, Late Eastern Chou Dynasty, 7¾ (4174/296) — 3300
Pilgrim flask and cover, Pien Hu, rare, Late Eastern Chou Dynasty, 14½ (4174/292) — 3900
Steamer, 2 piece, Han Dynasty, 6 (4174/289) — 550
Tripod food vessel and cover (Ting), Han Dynasty, 7½ (4174/287) — 850
Wine vessel and cover, small, Hu, -3c B.C., 6½ (4174/294) — 2100

Bronze

Axe head (Yueh), 6⅞ (4174/273) — 1300
Axe head ritual (Yueh), 7⅝, restored (4174/274) — 1400
Belt hook, inlaid, slender, LWarring States Period, 6 (4174/255) — 125
Belt hook, turquoise, inlaid, curved shaft with 4 lozenges, 3 century B.C, 6⅝ (4174/254) — 475
Drun, Shan, reel shape, herringbone banding, 20 (4174/304) — 3200
Frog fitting, Shan, 4⅞ (4174/270) — 300
Hairpin, archaic, thin shafts joined by trefoil motif, T'ang Dynasty, 9¾ (4174/229) — 80

Mirror, lions and grapevines in double frieze, 4¾ (4174/240)   200
Mirror, with silver and gold decoration, foliate, T'ang Dynasty, 5¼ (4174/239)   1100
Mirror, Taoist scene of a sage with his attendant, Ming Dynasty, 7⅜ (4174/241)   175
Mirror, archaic, small, small ribbed central loop, 4-3c B.C., 2⅞ (4174/245)   800
Mirror, inscribed, raised ring and border of 8 arcs, 1st century B.C.-A.D., 5⅝ (4174/248)   375
Mirror, plain flat six-lobed form, Sung/Yuan Dynasty, 5⅝ (4174/243)   100
Mirror, rare, cast in high relief with 3 winged horses, T'ang Dynasty, 8¾, dam (4174/238) 1300
Mirror, Korean, ship sailing on breaking waves, Koryu Dynasty, 6⅝ (4174/242)   450
Monkeys, pair, miniature, well-cast figures enclose beads which rattle, Yuan Dynasty, 1½
  (4174/235)   1900
Stele, seated Buddha, cast in relief, Sui Dynasty, 4¼ (4174/224)   1200
T'ao T'ieh mask and loose ring handles, pair, Han Dynasty, 2½ (4174/258)   700

Chariot fittings

Archaic bronzes plaque, finely cast, side repaired, Shang Dynasty, 7 (4174/286)   7500
Axle caps, silver inlaid bronze, pair, 5c B.C., rare (4174/276)   *5250*
Beaten gold foil appliques, pair, now mounted behind glass, 5⅛, rare (4174/279)   9500
Double headed appliques, archaic bronze, pair, Chou Dynasty, 5½ (4174/280)   2300
Dragon head, archaic bronze, cast with small loop beneath snout, East Chou Dynasty, 7¼
  (4174/281)   2300
Pierced appliques, pair, archaic bronze, Chou Dynasty, 8¾, restored (4174/282)   3400
Ram mask fitting, archaic bronze, Chou Dynasty, 4⅞ (4174/283)   1200
Silver inlaid bronze, Ko Haft Cap, 3c B.C., 4⅞ (4174/278)   2000
T'ao T'ieh mask, archaic bronze, ca10c, B.C., 8 (4174/285)   19000
T'ao T'ieh mask handles, pair, archaic bronze, Chou Dynasty, 4⅝ (4174/284)   4800

Early bronze sculpture

Avalokitesvara figure, T'ang Dynasty, H3¼ (4121/30)   *800*
Kuan Yin figure, draped with chains and necklaces, H5⅛, 6-7 Centuries (4121/27)   3950
Kuan Yin figure, T'ang Dynasty, details incised through gilding, H3¼ (4121/31)   *500*
Kuan Yin figure, T'ang Dynasty, hips swayed to right, ambrosia in left hand, H5¼, dam (4121/28) 1300
Kuan Yin figure, T'ang Dynasty, loose robes, four-legged bracket support, H3¼ (4121/29)   *750*
Lokapala figure, T'ang Dynasty, quardian figure with left hand upraised, H1⅝, rare (4121/26) 3600
Tiger, boldly cast, stylized figure on powerful legs, 14, 3rd-2nd Century B.C. (4121/25)   4500

Gilt bronzes

Belt fitting, five pcs, 3 plaques, 2 loops, T'ang Dynasty, 6¼, dam (4174/236)   850
Belt hook, turquoise inlaid, rare, Eastern Chou Dynasty, 6/1/4 (4174/251)   1000
Bodhisattva, simple robes, 6c B.C., 4½, repaired, rare (4174/210)   9500
Bodhisattva, small, T'ang Dynasty, 3¾ (4174/222)   950
Bodhisattva figure, T'ang Dynasty, 4, dam (4214/2)   200
Bodhisattva figure, wearing crown, necklace, earrings, Ming Dynasty, 14¼ (4214/17)   2100
Buddha figure, T'ang Dynasty, 6⅝, dam (4174/223)   1600
Buddha figure, Sino-Tibetan, seated on lotus base, L18c, 4¾, rep (4214/16)   450
Buddhist monk figure, small, T'ang Dynasty, 1¾ (4214/3)   200
Buddhist Pantheon, T'ang Dynasty, 3¼ (4174/212)   325
Child Buddha figure, 16-17c, 6½, chip (4214/8)   550
Drummer, rare, kneeling, body swaying, Six Dynasties, 3⅛, dam (4174/217)   4000
Eleven headed Kuan Yin figure, T'ang Dynasty, 8½, very rare (4174/211)   25000
Guardian figures, pair, T'ang Dynasty, 1⅝ (4174/219)   800
Kuan Yin, holding lotus blossom in 1 hand, T'ang Dynasty, 3¼, dam (4174/218)   325
Kuan Yin, legs missing from base, T'ang Dynasty, 3¾ (4174/215)   475
Kuan Yin, seated in rockwork throne, T'ang Dynasty, 2¾ (4174/216)   300
Kuan Yin, small, T'ang Dynasty, 2, dam (4174/220)   250
Kuan Yin on raised base with Lohan attendant, T'ang Dynasty, 2½ (4174/213)   600
Lohan figure, long loose robes, T'ang Dynasty, 3¼ (4174/225)   375
Lohan figure, small, laquer decoration, 17c, 6, chip (4214/10)   130
NOD, Kuan Yin, small, T'ang Dynasty, 2⅝, dam (4174/221)   400
T'ang Dynasty, 3, (4214/4)   300

Ordos bronze

Animal plaque, 2-1c B.C., 2 (4174/266)   200
Boar, probably harness fitting, 3-2c B.C., 1⅝ (4174/263)   1200
Deer, pair, part missing, 4-2c B.C., 2⅛, repair (4174/265)   800
Deer plaques, pair, 4-2c B.C., 1⅝ (4174/264)   650
Knife with Ibex finial, Chou Dynasty, 1½, rare (4174/268)   *2750*
Tiger, small, 4-2c B.C., 1¾ (4174/267)   225

Knife with
Ibex finial
(4174/268)

Animal form
standard
(4242/267)

Axle caps
(4174/276)

Avalokitesvara
figure (4121/30)

Kuan Yin figure
(4121/29)

Kuan Yin figure
(4121/31)

Ritual bronze

Cooking vessel, Li, West Chou Dynasty, 6 (4174/313)	2300
Food vessel, Kuei, heavily cast, whorl bosses, early Chou Dynasty, L11-E10c B.C., 6¼ (4174/305)	9000
Libation cup, Chuen, finely cast, Shang Dynasty, 6⅞ (4174/310)	7500
Vase, small, Lei, flaking in places, *Chou Dynasty, 4⅞ (4174/312)	1400
Vine vessel and cover, Yu, L11-E10c B.C., 10, imp (4174/307)	8000
Wine vessel, Ku, well cast, Shang Dynasty, 11¾ (4174/309)	25000
Wine vessel, Tsun, restored on surface, 11-10c B.C., 9⅞, cr (4174/311)	9500

Silver

Hairpin, gilt, molded in the round with pair of birds, T'ang Dynasty, 10¼, rare (4174/230)	650
Plaque, duck, duck in flight, body and head in relief, T'ang Sung Dynasty, 3½ (4174/233)	4000
Scissors, knife-shaped blades with sharply beveled edges, T'ang Dynasty, 4⅞, rare (4174/231)	1000

Shang Dynasty

Vessel, wine, archaic bronze, 3 blade shaped legs, 7 (4242/270)	1100

Chou Dynasty

Animal form standard, hollow cast, fantastic beast, 11⅜ (4242/267)	*95000*
Axe head, archaic bronze, blade flared at cutting edge, 7 (4242/260)	200

Han Dynasty

Dragon tally, flat plaque cast, round relief, inscribed, 4½ (4242/263)	1600
Finial, pigeon pole, stylized bird on hollow base, 3¼ (4242/262)	1000
Sword, archaic bronze, tapering blade, central rib, 12¼ (4242/258)	300
Vessel, vine miniature, archaic bronze, 2 loose ring handles, 3½ (4242/268)	350
Vessel, vine, archaic bronze, masks and loose ring handles, 11 (4242/273)	425

T'ang Dynasty

Mirror, barbed bronze, domed knop, 2 lions, 2 birds, 6¼ (4242/266)	1500
Mirror, lion and grapevine, 4 leaping lions, 5½ (4242/265)	1200

Ming Dynasty

Censer, covered, 'sunspot' bronze, compressed body, 4 hollow square legs, 17-18c, 5¼, small (4121/91)	1000
Censer, gold splashed, lotus petal, arch shaped panels, 6, late (4121/90)	1200
Censer, Mandarin duck, gold splashed bronze, lotus dec pierced cover, 17-18c, 10½ (4121/86)	1100

CARVINGS

An assortment of materials and periods

Buddha figure, white stone, Wei style, 37, dam-rep (4214/35)	300
Budhisattva, wood, shrine group, Ming Dynasty, 18, chip (4214/32)	750
Fu lions, white marble, pair, each seated on his haunches, 13, chip (4214/39)	375
Inkstone in fitted hardwood case, pinkish-brown stone carved, pine, prunus, bamboo, 19c 9⅝ (4223/449)	1100
Jade archaistic mottled brown-gray, Huang, 4¼, chip (4214/360)	400
Jade gray, figure of carp wood stand, 6½ (4214/295)	400
Jade mottled dark green and brown, vase group double ram, 8¼ (4214/294)	200
Kuan Yin and child, wood small, polychrome, 17c, 8, dam (4214/33)	425
Kuan Yin figure, wood polychrome, standing goddess on rockwork base, Sung style, 23¼, dam (4214/38)	1400
Kuan Yin head, large, black limestone, carved in Sung style with foliate diadem, 15½ (4174/152)	2100
Kuan Yin head, stone, large, fitted wood stand, 18½ (4214/34)	1700
Mountain, amber, small, hut, gate, figures carved on 1 side, 19c, 3¼, chip (4214/44)	325
Mountain, amber, small, woman on a pavillion terrace, wood stand, 19c, 3¼ (4214/46)	550
Mountain, translucent brown amber, long-tailed bird perched beneath branch, 19c, 5 (4214/45)	600
Sceptre, carved fruitwood Ju-l, slender shaft pierced, carved with peaches, bats, 19c (4223/443)	355
Stele, T'ang style stone, figure of Kuan Yin, 26½, dam-rep (4214/36)	1800

Archaic jade

Arc shaped pendant, Western Chou Era, 3½, broken (4121/38)	450
Ceremonial blade, Western Chou Era, dark green, 4 pierced apertures, L14½ (4121/43)	4250
Cicada, Eastern Han Dynasty*, stylized insect with folded wings, 2⅝ (4121/37)	1600
Cicada, Western Han Dynasty*, simply carved with rounded underside, 2 (4121/40)	650
Cicada pendant, Western Chou Dynasty, stylized insect, 2⅛, chip (4121/35)	1200
Cicada pendant, Western Chou Dynasty, wings with D-shaped scales, 1⅞, chip (4121/36)	1100
Fish pendant, Shang Dynasty, carved shape, flattened form, thicker than, usual, L3¼ (4121/32)	5000
Ritual disc, Pi, late Eastern Chou Dynasty, carved with 'grain' pattern, 1⅝ (4121/33)	2200
Scabbard chape, carved with dragon form, 3rd Century B.C. 1 7/16, chip, rare (4121/34)	9000
Ts'ung, ritual vase*, Eastern Chou Era, 3⅝ (4121/39)	300

Coral

Group, pale pink and white, two robed figures of maidens, boy, flower filled basket, 6¼ (4154/90)	425
Group, pale pink and white, woman, tree trunk and phoenix, 7 (4154/89)	275
Woman, standing, robed, hair double topknot, holding scarf, 6 (4154/83)	750

Goldstone

Elephant, standing with upraised trunk, 2 short tusks, 6¼ (4154/97)	200
Incense burner, tripod, covered, oval form, 3 stumps, 2 dragon head handles, 7 (4154/98)	175

Hardstone carvings

Ball on ivory stand, rock crystal, with inlaid mother of pearl, dragons, 7½ (4144/32)	900
Ball on stand, rock crystal, filagree median section, 5¾ (4144/3)	275
Balls on ivory stands, rock crystal, each clear sphere with figures, pair, 7½ (4144/31)	800
Beaker, covered, rock crystal, bat-form handles, loose rings, 5½, repair (4144/27)	700
Brush holder, lapis lazuli, two birds, pine, prunus, bamboo trees, 4¼, minor chip (4144/29)	375
Brush rest, rock crystal, dragon and rockwork, 7 chip (4144/10)	225
Ceremonial axe, calcined serpentine, archaistic, wood stand and case, 8½ (4144/17)	200
Dragon bowl, dragons on exterior, mottled dark green and brown serpentine, 9 (4144/15)	400
Flowering trees, jardinieres, pair, rectangular, gilt-metal, 19¾, imp, L18c (4261/221)	*750*
Fu lion, carnellian agate, ivory stand, cub crawling on back, 19c, 4 (4144/5)	275
Horse figure, carnelian agate, stoutly modeled, downcast head, 5¼ (4214/82)	350
Horse figure, rock cystal, bushy tail, 7¼ (4214/77)	*1800*
Horse figure, small, mottled hardstone, 1¾ (4214/75)	90
Horse figure, tuquoise, small, four square on a rockwork base, 3¾ (4214/85)	175
Horsehead, eyes inset with rubies, 2, chip (4214/78)	175
Incense burner, covered, tripod, onion green, heavily carved, wood stand, 7 (4214/98)	275
Incense burner, gray agate, small, loose ring handles, tripod, 4½, chip (4144/2)	200
Jar, covered, small, Carnellian agate, carved with trailing branches of plum blossoms, 4¼, chip (4144/1)	325
Kuan Yin figure, coral, bare feet resting on ambrosia vase, 7⅛ (4144/9)	650
Kuan Yin figure, green aventurine, hair gressed with tiara, 7⅜, chip (4214/93)	170

Mei Jen figure (4214/57)

Flowering trees
(4261/221)

Horse figure (4214/77)

Mei Jen maidens (4214/91)

Ram figure (4214/79)

Kuan Yin figure, rock crystal, flowing robes, concealed hands, 5¾ (4214/86)	400
Kuan Yin figure, rose quartz, goddess holding vase, 11½, natural flaw, cracks (4214/67)	1100
Kylin figures, pair, quartzite, two dragon-heads, 4¼ (4214/70)	375
Li T'ai-Po figure, rock crystal, reclining, robed drunken poet, 4 (4214/88)	250
Libation cup and cover, rock crystal, dragon handle, ogre mask, wood stand, 7¾, chip (4144/35)	950
Lu Tung-pin figure, rock crystal, elderly immortal, 10½ (4214/68)	850
Maiden and boys figural group, coral, holding peony, wood stand, 8¼ (4214/64)	1300
Maiden with boy, coral, holding a flower basket, 7¾ (4214/72)	1700
Mei Jen and boy, coral, mounted as lamp, 9½ (4214/96)	1300
Mei Jen figure, coral, holding basket, mounted as lamp, 9½ (4214/97)	1000
Mei Jen figure, coral, swaying, robed, wood stand, 5¼ (4214/57)	*600*
Mei Jen figure, cornelian, with a crested bird, wood stand, 5¾, chip (4214/63)	225
Mei Jen figure, rose quartz, hold tasseled lantern, wood stand, 11½ (4214/69)	1600
Mei Jen figure, Lapis lazuli, small wood stand, 4¾ (4214/89)	110
Mei Jen maidens, three, coral, on green jade stand, 11¾ (4214/91)	*2600*
Mountain, lapis lazuli, pine trees and 4 boys crossing bridge, 7½, chip (4214/61)	1600
Mountain as a craggy boulder, soapstone, carved with Eighteen Lohan, 19c, 4½ (4214/90)	200
Mountain shaped as peaked boulder, greenish white, 10½ (4214/66)	600
Pebble carving, brownish serpentine, with flying bat, 3 (4144/14)	200
Praying mantis figure, soapstone, perched on fruiting foliage, 18c, 2 rep (4214/80)	200
Putai figure, carnelian agate, bare bellied god of Happiness, 4½ (4214/81)	150
Ram figure, rock crystal, erect-head, short ears, 6 (4214/79)	*1000*
Ritual ornament, archaistic, brown, green serpentine, 10 (4144/18)	375
Semi-precious mineral plants pair, in cinnabar lacquer jardinieres, 19c, 19¾, repair pcs miss (4144/22)	800
Tortoise figure, gray, black stone, 2⅛ (4214/76)	65
Vase, covered, agate, bronze-form, flattened, wood stand, 5 (4214/62)	100
Vase, covered, rock crystal, bronze-form, wood stand, 7¾ (4214/87)	900
Vase, lapis lazuli, bronze form, 2 dragon fret handles, 4⅜ (4144/26)	225
Vase, lapis lazuli, bronze-form, 5¾, chip (4214/92)	100

Vase, lapis lazuli, bronze-form, wood stand, 7 (4214/94) — 500
Vase, lapis lazuli, double tree trunk wood stand, 6¼, nat flaw cracking (4144/34) — 900
Vase, tree-trunk, lapis lazuli, carved, undercut with small pine trees, 3½ (4144/4) — 175
Water buffalo and boy group, crystal, recumbent animal chewing millet, 5½ (4214/74) — 2300
Woman standing figure, coral, holding a spray of leaves, 4¾ (4214/58) — 375
Woman standing figure, coral, long flowing robes, wood stand, 5 (4214/56) — 500

Jade

Animal, greenish-gray, pale brown small, curly hair, 1¾ (4214/204) — 400
Archer's thumb ring, grayish-white, brown, 1⅛ (4214/327) — 225
Axe blade, archaistic gray-brown, carved with masks, C-scroll, 2½ (4214/162) — 150
Ball figure, greenish-gray-brown, small, T'ang style, 2¾ (4214/222) — 275
Beads, cut, pair, archaic, short cylinders with thick walls, Chou Dynasty,¾ (4174/180) — 1700
Beads, rectangular, archaic, late Eastern Chou Dynasty, 2⅞, chip (4174/192) — 1700
Beaker, mottled gray and pale brown, bronze form, bands of masks and fretted leaves, 5½ (4154/103) — 625
Beaker, mottled gray-pale brown, bronze form, 7¼ (4214/259) — 525
Beaker, white, bronze form wood stand, 5½ (4214/114) — 1100
Beakers, pair, greenish-white, bronze form wood stands-cases fitted, D5¼ (4214/183) — 1300
Bear figure, archaic, seated upright with forepaws on knees, Shang Dynasty, 1⅝, rare (4174/162) — 35000
Belt hook, bird form, white, 3¾ (4214/167) — 325
Belt hook, dragon, 4 (4214/172) — 275
Belt hook, dragon, white, 5¼ (4214/169) — 200
Bird, gray-green finial, compactly carved bird with large beak, six Dynasties, 2¼ (4174/160) — 14000
Bird finial, gray-green-brown, archaistic, 6 dynasties style, 4 (4214/202) — 900
Bird finial mottled gray-green, archaistic, 3¼ (4214/200) — 375
Bitch and puppy, group, reclining, pup playing, W1¾, L19c (4261/291) — 500
Blade, central ridge, small 5, Shang-Early Chou Dynasty (4174/205) — 1300
Book, mottled grayish-white, ten panels, silver mounted, 8⅛ - 3¾, Ch'ien Lung Period (4214/243) — 5500
Bowl, spinach-green, rounded foot, Diam 4½, 19c (4261/270) — 130
Bowl, pale celadon, deep conical form, exterior leafing fish & lotus plants, 5, Ch'ien Lung (4154/129) — 1800
Bowl and cover, gray-green, chrysanthemum, reversible, domed cover, 5¾ (4214/237) — 1800
Bowls, pair, spinach green, 7½, Ch'ien Lung seal (4214/299) — 2200
Bowls, pair, spinach green, wood stands, 7⅞ (4214/307) — 2100
Bowls, pair, white, plain form, 5½ (4214/184) — 2600
Bowls with cover, white, pair, wood stands, 4¾ (4214/238) — 1400
Boy, figure, miniature, grayish-white, standing, chubby, 2 2/1, 19c (4261/303) — 250
Boy, figure, yellow and brown, holding lantern and millet spray, 3 (4214/333) — 3400
Bracelet, gray-green-brown, archaistic, with writhing dragons, 4¼ (4214/359) — 350
Brush washer, dark green, wood stand, 4¾ (4214/137) — 600
Brush washer, lotus form, motted sage, green, open leaf, surrounded by trailing blossoms , stems, 5¼ (4154/127) — 700
Brush washer, lotus leaf, green, blossoms, pods, stems, 4¾ (4214/181) — 300
Brush washer, lotus leaf, greenish gray and, pale brown, carved shallow open leaf, curled edges, 5½ (4154/114) — 425
Brush washer, spinach green, small, inset flat base, 3 feet, 2¾ (4214/241) — 125
Brush washer, Ju-i form, green-gray, wood stand, 18c, 6½, chip (4214/253) — 1600
Buckle, horse-form, pale green-white, recumbent horse gazing at monkey, 3¼ (4214/213) — 650
Buddha figure, gray, 5⅛ (4214/247) — 275
Buddha group, parcel-gilt, lacquered, two Lohans with Buddha, white, 9¾ - 10¼, 19c (4214/310) — 5000
Bull's head Rhyton, greenish-gray, boot-shaped libation cup, 3 (4214/210) — 550
Carving, lotus, gray and russet brown, form, small open lotus, curled stem, 4 legged toad, 2 (4154/101) — 250
Cat, carved, greenish-white, W1⅝, L19c (4261/296) — 425
Cats, groups, pair, gray and white cats playing, 1¾ (4214/135) — 700
Censer, cover, miniature, white, globular, tripod, 1⅜, 19c (4261/300) — 900
'Champion' vase, grayish-white, brown, two vases joined with falcon-like bird, 4 (4214/209) — 1600
Chimera, archaistic, small, well-carved fantastic beast, staring ahead, Sung/Ming Dynasty, 1¾ (4174/163) — 3000
Chimera figure, white and brown, recumbent lion-like beast, wood stand, 18c, 4¾, chip (4214/290) — 3700
Cicada pendant, archaistic yellowish-green and brown, 2 (4214/195) — 500
Coin, disc, black, carved to simulate Spanish silver eight-reales, 1½, 1795 (4214/321) — 275
Cosmetic box, pale yellowish-green, finely incised and carved, Sung Dynasty, rare, 6¾, chip (4214/235) — 75000
Coupe, grayish white, lotus, 4 (4214/120) — 350
Coupe, melon form, oblong hollow melon with undercut branches, 4¼, chip (4214/103) — 450
Coupe or ladle dragon, gray and black, curved spatula form, long neck, horned dragon head, 9¼ (4154/130) — 500

Cup, libation, bronze form, greenish gray, shallow circular form, horned dragon head handles, 4¼, 19c (4154/107)	175
Cup, two-handled, gray-brown, two dragon-head loop handles, 19c, 3½ (4214/201)	400
Deer, pair, green, alert, striding, wood stands, 7 (4214/311)	1300
Deer figure, white, small, 19c, 2½ (4214/219)	350
Discs, cut, miniature, pair, archaic, Chou Dynasty,⅞ (4174/187)	275
Dish, chrysanthemum, white, 'Tibetan style' shallow, fluted petals, 7¾ (4214/239)	800
Dish, white Tibetan style, dish oval w butterfly handles, 7¼ (4214/256)	3700
Dog figure, gray-black, curled tail, outstretched paws, 19c, 1¾ (4214/203)	150
Dog figure, greenish-white, 2¼ (4214/196)	950
Dog figure, moss green small, head turned, erect ears, 3¼ (4214/180)	475
Dogs, group, miniature, grayish-white, playing, W1⅝, 19c (4261/292)	400
Dragon, bottle-horn, archaic, olive green, Shang Dynasty, 1½ (4174/177)	700
Dragon bowl gray and brown, two dragon-form handles, 5¾ (4214/115)	275
Dragon buckle, white, 4¾, chip natural flaws (4214/127)	325
Dragon ornament, archaic, miniature, dragon head on slender drilled shaft, Chou Dynasty, 1⅝ (4174/166)	1100
Dragon plaque, archaistic, calcified cream white jade, Sung Dynasty, 4⅝, rare (4174/161)	9000
Dragon ring, opaque white-brown, archaistic, (4214/231)	150
Dragon-carp, figure, greenish-grey, waves, W8¼, 18c (4261/261)	5250
Duck, small white, holding lotus leaf in beak, 18-19c, 2 (4214/151)	375
Duck and drake group, white, well carved, 2 mandarin ducks swimming, 4½, fine Ch'ien Lung Period (4214/269)	16000
Duck figure, white-brown, archaistic, 4¾ (4214/193)	3400
Ducks, group, grayish-white and brown, trailing stems of Lotus blossoms, 4¼ (4154/128)	475
Ducks, two, group, pale grey, brown, legs tucked beneath bodies, 3½ (4214/214)	1200
Elephant, greenish-gray, small, short trunk, 2 tusks, wood stand, 3½ (4214/160)	500
Elephant and boy group, two boys on elephant's back, wood stand, 3¼ (4214/194)	1000
Elephant and vase, small, vase on elephant's back, 3½ (4214/133)	170
Elephant figures, pair dark green, small, gilt-wood stands, 4, chip (4214/298)	140
Elephant with 3 attendants, greenish white, 3¾ (4214/345)	2100
Fantastic animal, gray, black-brown, small, winged beast on clouds, wood stands, 17-18c, 2½ (4214/348)	2000
Female dancer figure, white, wood stand-case, 5¼ (4214/126)	1500
Finial, archaic bronze and jade, rare, 4½, late Eastern Chou-Han Dynasty (4174/182)	2700
Fish, archaic, olive-brown stone, 2⅜, small, Shang/Western Chou Dynasty (4174/168)	600
Foreigner figure, grayish white, miniature, 2 (4214/148)	275
Foreigner with attendant, boy holds travelling shrine, 3¾, chip, late Ming Dynasty (4214/341)	1500
Fu character plaque, white, small, carved and pierced, 2⅛ (4214/275)	200
Fu lion and cub, greenish-white, W2¼, L19c (4261/294)	500
Fu lion and vase, cover, onion green, 5½ (4214/260)	*500*
Fu lions, small, white, on ivory stand, 1¾ (4214/123)	*500*
Goats, group, white, female, 2 kids, wood stand, fitted case, 19c, 3¾ (4214/186)	1200
Goats, three, spinach green, wood stand, 4¼ (4214/118)	225
Half ring, archaic, Chou Dynasty, 3½ (4174/193)	550
Hare pendant, archaic, simply carved crouching hare, Shang/Western Chou Dynasty (4174/167)	1900

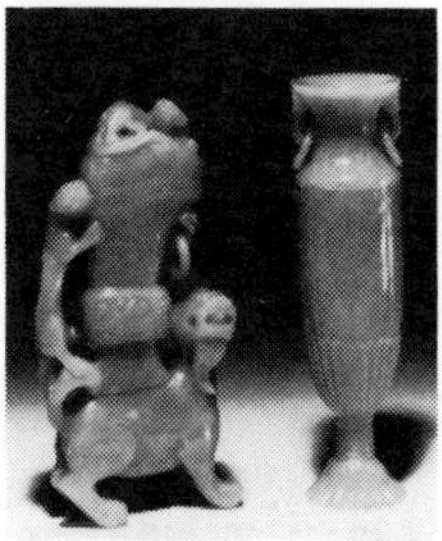

Fu lion and vase
(4214/260)

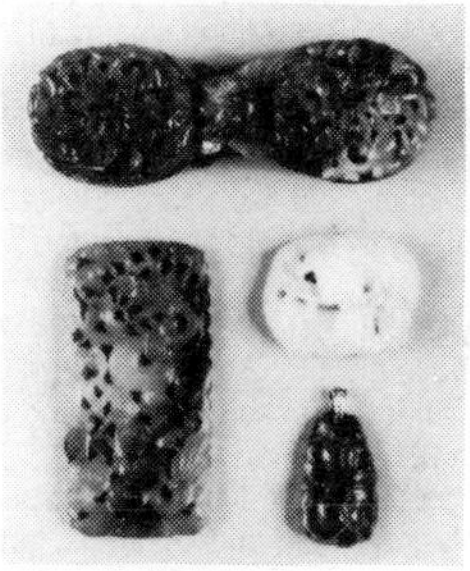

Fu lions
(4214/123)

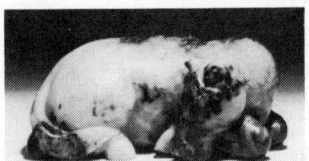

Horse (4214/154)

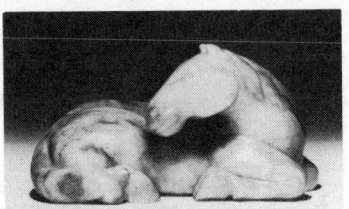

Horse figure (4214/227)

Horse, greenish-gray-brown, head resting on extended forelegs, 5, 17-18c (4214/352)	3400
Horse, yellowish-green and brown, recumbent, wood stand, L9 (4214/154)	4000
Horse figure, greenish-gray, brown, Ming style, short erect ears, 9½ (4214/227)	4500
Horse figure, white, miniature, 1½ (4214/335)	100
Incense burner, covered mottled gray, tripod, dragon head handles, wood stand, 6¾ (4214/297)	3300
Incense burner, covered, large, white, spherical body on lion mask tripod supports, Chien Lung Period 10¼ (4214/356)	47000
Incense burner, covered, tripod, dragon head and loose ring handles, 9½ (4214/308)	3700
Incense burner, covered, white, tripod, loose ring handles, wood stand, case, 6¾, 19c (4214/296)	5000
Incense burner, white, Tibetan style, with reticulated cover, wood stand, 6¾, chip (4214/291)	5800
Ink-stone, mottled brown-gray, archaistic, axe-form, 3¾ (4214/351)	425
Jardiniere, spinach-green, with semi precious mineral plant, 13¾, chip (4214/257)	100
Jardinieres, spinach-green, pair, with semi-precious mineral plants, 15 (4214/300)	750
Ju-I septre, teakwood and grayish white, s curved shaft inset with 3 Jade plaques, 20¼ (4154/115)	375
Kuan Yin, grayish white and pale brown, standing, holding prayer beads, long robes, 8¼ (4154/102)	600
Kylin figure, greenish-white, resting with book, wood stand, 18c, L5 (4214/187)	4000
Lady, figure, miniature, greenish-white, seated, 1⅞, 19c (4261/289)	175
Leaf dish, white, small, carved as cluster of 2 overlapping leaves, 18c, 3½ chip (4214/164)	450
Libation cup, gray, bronze form tripod, Chia 6¾ (4214/289)	1700
Libation cup, grayish white and brown, bronze form wood stand, 3, chip (4214/107)	150
Libation cup, pale-greenish, small, boat-shaped, bronze form, 19c, 4½ (4214/245)	375
Libation cup, white, bronze form, 19c, 4½ (4214/246)	375
Linked pendant with fish, gray-white, 2¾, unusual (4214/343)	250
Lion, small yellowish-green and brown, Buddhist style, 2½ (4214/158)	150
Liu Hai with toad, olive green, 4¾ (4214/336)	450
Lotus carving, white and brown, with crouching frog, 18c, 1¾ (4214/145)	325
Mei Jen figure, wood stand, 7¾, chip (4214/131)	650
Monkey group, grayish-white, brown, 2¾, 18c, finely carved (4214/197)	900
Moon and prunus plaque, white, moon settling behind gnarled prunus tree, 3, 18c (4214/276)	950
Mountain, gray-brown, narrow path beneath pine and willow trees, 9 (4214/252)	450
Mythical animal, gray and brown, 3½, Ming Dynasty (4214/205)	750
Mythical animal figure, white, small, with pierced slot in back, 18c, 2 (4214/199)	475
Ornamental, archaic, miniature, forked shape, Chou Dynasty, 1 3/16 (4174/188)	300
Peaches, four, group, emblem of longevity, 5¼ (4214/134)	2500
Pendant, animal, black, crouching, cat-like figure, 2¼ (4214/346)	475
Pendant, bird, archaic, small, stylized seated bird, folded wings, 1½, Shang/Western Chou Dynasty (4174/172)	1200
Pendant, carved, white, stylized insect, W2⅛, 19c (4261/297)	325
Pendant, carved, white, 2 boys playing, 2, L18/E19c (4261/305)	550
Pendant, fish, archaic, broken in 2 pieces, small, Shang Dynasty, 3⅜ (4174/171)	225
Pendant, white, small, 2½ (4214/191)	200
Pendants, dragon, archaic pair, each broken in two, repaired, Late Chou Dynasty, 4⅞ (4174/183)	1600
Perfume holders, greenish-gray, pair, mountainous landscapes, wood stands, 18c, 10½, chip (4214/330)	8500
Pi, small mottled gray-brown, archaistic, panels of Yin-Yang medallions, 1½ (4214/153)	150
Pig, archaic, small, simply carved reclining figure, Han Dynasty, 2⅞ (4174/164)	300
Pillow in form of boy, gray and black, smiling features, 9 flaw cracks (4214/163)	1700
Plaque, bird, archaic, blunt beak, short tail, Shang Dynasty, 1⅝ (4174/174)	900

Plaque, bottle-horndragon, archaic, slender, brownish green, Shang Dynasty, 2½ (4174/178) — 1700
Plaque, carved, shaped circular, horse, monkey, Diam 2⅛, 18/19c (4261/283) — 275
Plaque, carved, shaped rectangular form, W2⅝, E19c (4261/286) — 300
Plaque, cicada, archaic, stylized wings and body seen from above, Shang Dynasty, 1¾ (4174/170) — 425
Plaque, curved fish, Shang Dynasty, 2½, chip (4174/189) — 1000
Plaque, dragon silhouette, archaic, chip, Western Chou Dynasty, 3 (4174/190) — 1600
Plaque, dragon, archaic, broken from large pc, Late Eastern Chou Dynasty, 3½ (4174/184) — 550
Plaque, dragon, archaic, bottle-horn, dull green, Shang Dynasty, 2½ (4174/176) — 700
Plaque, silhouette, archaic, Late Eastern Chou Dynasty, 3⅞ (4174/185) — 450
Plaque, twin fish, oval, 2 carp together, greenish-white, W2¼, 19c (4261/288) — 200
Quail, carved, grayish-white, seated, W2½, 18c (4261/302) — 2400
Quail group, white, both crouching, 18c, 4½ chip (4214/159) — 2000
Ram, figure, green-brown, incised beard, wood stand, 3¾, 18c (4214/334) — 1400
Ring, archaic, small, 5-4c B.C., 2⅛ (4174/181) — 1600
Ring, archaistic yellowish-green, brown, carved with dragon, animals, 3¾ (4214/212) — 850
Ring, thumb, grayish-white, pine, plum, rock, Diam 1⅜, L18/E19c (4261/277) — 200
Riverboat, grayish white, small, wood stand, 4¼ (4214/129) — 475
Sage and boy, group, greenish-white, 2½, 19c (4261/304) — 200
Saucer, grayish white, small, chrysanthemum wood stand, 3¾ (4214/128) — 650
Screen, table, spinach green, carved, landscape, W7, 18c (4261/252) — 2400
Screens, table, pair gold decorated, spinach green, mountain riverscape, lengthy inscription, 11¾ (4154/137) — 3000
Screens, table, pair, gilt-metal frames, serpentine, carved, grey-white, W9½, crack, 19c (4261/206) — 1300
Spoon, white, small, 4½ (4174/179) — 140
Squirrel and grapes group, white, scattered red, W2, 18/19c (4261/298) — 250
Table screen, grayish-white, sage in pavillion watches 2 boys, 18c, 10½ (4214/331) — 13500
Table screen, spinach green, wood stand, case, 19c, 12¼ (4214/251) — 4000
Table screen, 3 panel, white, large, relief carving, pierced panels above, 16¼-17 (4214/316) — 9000
Table screens, pair, Fei Ts'ui, wood stand-case, 4¾, chip (4214/130) — 1400
Toad figure, gray-green, dark brown, 4½, 17c (4214/206) — 700
Toggle, fish, grayish-white, flat, W3½, 19c (4261/285) — 100
Toggle, gourd, pierced, carved, W2½, 18c (4261/284) — 250
Toggle, white and brown, pebble form, carved and pierced with a cluster of melons, 2⅛, 18c, small (4154/110) — 275
Tortoise shell, gray, miniature, realistic, 1¾ (4214/325) — 150
Tree trunk brush holder, moss green, wood stand-case, 5½ (4214/177) — 900
Tripod censer, white, wood stand, Ch'ien Lung Period 5¼ (4214/138) — 2800
Ts'ung, dark green-brown, archaistic form, 2½ (4214/254) — 375
Two goats, greenish-white, pale, female with kid, 6 (4214/326) — 1400
Vase, bird and bamboo, gray, stalks of bamboo, fungus phoenix rockwork, 5 (4154/119) — 750
Vase, bronze-form, grayish-white, 7¾, 19c (4261/276) — 650
Vase, cover and chain, hanging, bronze, form, pale gray masks, ornaments, loose ring handles, 10 (4154/140) — 2200
Vase, covered bronze form, mottled dark green, body carved with panels of plants and rockwork, 8¾ (4154/113) — 250
Vase, covered, bronzed form, greenish gray, and brown, writhing dragon, 2 pair of dragon heads, 6½ (4154/139) — 1200
Vase, covered, mottled green-brown, 4 (4214/108) — 175
Vase, covered, Fei Ts'ui, large, bronze-form, wood-stand, masks, dragon fret, 13¼ (4214/314) — 14500
Vase, covered, Spinach-green, bronze-form wood stand, 10¾ (4214/139) — 2100
Vase, double fish form, gray, brown, two enjoined carp, wood stand, 6¼, L18-E19c (4214/273) — 1600
Vase, double gourd, carved, 'chicken bone white' fruiting gourds, tendrils, 19c, 7½ (4214/218) — 1800
Vase, gray, bronze-form, 2 floral handles, loose rings, 5½ (4214/261) — 350
Vase, large gray-green, tree trunk, cranes, clouds, figures, wood stand, 10 (4214/266) — 8000
Vase, pair Fei Ts'ui, bronze-form, covered, wood stands, 11¼, rep (4214/301) — 3100
Vase, small grayish white, bronze form, 3¾, chip (4214/111) — 110
Vase, small, greenish gray-brown, bronze-form, wood stand, 5 (4214/112) — 100
Vase, spinach green double, bamboo, wood stand, 4½ (4214/263) — 200
Vase covered, dark green-brown, bronze form, 7½ (4214/250) — 200
Vase with chained couch, bronze form, greenish gray and brown, 2 figures of Fu lions, 5/3/4 (4154/138) — 1650
Vases, covered, pair, celadon, bronze-form wood stand, 5¼, 2 rings missing (4214/142) — 1900
Vases, pair, miniature, lavendar and Fei-Ts'ui jadeite, (4214/102) — 600
Water dropper, Kylin, gray, winged with horned head, 5¼ (4214/262) — 550
Wine cups, pair, grayish-white, 2¼, chip (4214/255) — 130
Wine pot, covered, white camphor, 'Tibetan style' matching cover, 5¾ (4214/240) — 4200
Woman, pale greenish-white, robed maiden, long flowing scarf, holding ornament, 5¾ (4154/124) — 550
Zodiac animals, Chinese, set of twelve, L1½ - 3½, rare (4214/192) — 3100

Jade, ritual

Axe blade, ceremonial, archaic, Western Chou Dynasty, 5¼ (4174/207)   450
Huang, pair, grain pattern, flat arc carved, 3-4c B.C., 8 (4174/196)   600
Pi, flat ring disc, archaic, 3-2c B.C., 6⅛ (4174/195)   3600
Pi, small, archaic, Han Dynasty, 1 11/16, chip (4174/194)   800
Sceptre, archaic, Chou Dynasty, 10¾ (4174/199)   1700
Sceptre, archaic, 14⅞, Eastern Chou Dynasty, chip (4174/198)   4000
Ts'ung calcified, archaic, Chou Dynasty, 3 (4174/200)   650

Jadeite

Belt, hook, dragon, Fei-Ts'ui, curved tapering shaft, dragon-head terminal, 3¾ (4214/175)   800
Belt, hook, dragon, Fei-Ts'ui, pale green with emerald green mottling, 3¾ (4214/168)   6750
Belt, hook, Fei-Ts'ui, plain tapering shaft, 3 (4214/171)   200
Bird-feeder, mottled green-brown, small, D2 (4214/349)   175
Bowls, pair, Fei-Ts'ui, emerald green splashes, wood stands, 6 (4214/188)   2400
Bowls, Fei-Ts'ui pair, 6¾, natural flaw, cracking (4214/249)   850
Brush holder, sea green and brown, hollow peach, treetrunk, wood stand, 6 (4214/117)   1000
Brush-washer, lavender Fei-Ts'ui, scrolled interior, 2 bats in fungus branches, 5¾ (4214/284)   2700
Buckle, Fei-Ts'ui, dragon terminal, lotus scrolls, 4¾ (4214/121)   3000
Carp figure, lavender and Fei-Ts'ui, realistic swimming carp, 1 (4214/281)   *2800*
Cup, wine, pomegranate form, Fei-Ts'ui, hollow with an undercut leafy branch forming handle, 3 (4154/111)   500
Dragon buckle, two sections, 23½ (4214/174)   500
Dragon plaque, Fei-Ts'ui, small, writhing dragons, 3¼ (4214/122)   600
Goats, group, lavender and Fei-Ts'ui, female goat and kid, on pierced rockwork, 6¼ (4214/280)   *3000*
Incense burner, covered, mottled green, loose ring handles, 7 (4214/220)   5200
Incense burner, covered, mottled green, tripod, wood stand, 5¾ (4214/287)   1000
Incense burner, covered, tripod, mottled green, 7, 19c (4214/144)   *2200*

Goats
(4214/280)

Carp figure
(4214/281)

Incense burner
(4214/144)

Incense burner, covered, Fei-Ts'ui, tripod, globose form, dragon head handles, 6¾ (4214/303)   2700
Incense burner, Fei-Ts'ui, Fu lion finial, covered, tripod, 7¼ (4214/248)   2500
Kylin and box groups, pair, Fei-Ts'ui, wood stands-cases, 4¼ (4214/182)   1600
Kuan Yin, Fei-Ts'ui, wood stand, 11¾ (4214/141)   5500
Kuan Yin, Fei-Ts'ui, The Goddess, wearing long robe, holding vase, fly whisk, 7½ (4154/112)   600
Kuan Yin figures, pair, pale green, each holding peony and hanging basket with fish, 17¼ - 17½ (4214/313)   27000
Lohan figure, Fei-Ts'ui, Pu-Tai Ho-Shang holding fly whisk, L4¾ (4214/244)   1300
Mountain, white brown, Shou Lao and small boy, 18c, 4 (4214/109)   1600

Pendant, small mottled apple green, 1½ (4214/124) — 2000
Vase, covered, small Fei-Ts'ui, bronze form, 5 (4214/110) — 250
Vase, gray-green, small, bronze-form, wood stand, 4 (4214/337) — 700
Vase, Fei-Ts'ui, covered bronze form wood stand, 9¼ (4214/309) — 5000
Vase, Fei-Ts'ui, large, bronze form covered wood stand, 13¼ (4214/315) — 18000
Vase, Fei-Ts'ui, bronze form on cloisonne enamel stand, 6¼ (4214/113) — 650
Vase with chained cover, pair, lavender, 2 leaf stalk, loose ring handles, 7, Fei-Ts'ui (4154/116) — 2500
Vases, covered Fei-Ts'ui pair, bronze-form, 8, natural flaws (4214/140) — 3000

Later jades

Animal, fantastic, Ming Dynasty*, calcified jade, reclining cat like beast, 1¾, miniature (4121/51) — 300
Carving of an elephant, Ming Dynasty, buff jade, 4⅞, chip rare (4121/44) — 6500
Cup, 2 handled (Kuei), Ming Dynasty*, mutton-fat jade, bronze form, 5¾ (4121/55) — 1100
Figure, rooster, Ming Dynasty, calcified stone, 2¾ (4121/52) — 450
Figure of ram, small, Ming Dynasty, gray stone, 3¼ (4121/48) — 1100
Figures, pair, water buffalo, sage green, 5 (4121/53) — 800
Group, kneeling chubby boy, Ming, green and brown stone, 1⅞ (4121/49) — 800
Group duck and lotus, pale green stone, 17-18c, 5 (4121/50) — 500
Reclining camel, small, Ming Dynasty*, rudimentary carving, 2½ (4121/46) — 300
Reclining ram, small, Ming Dynasty, brownish-grey, L2 (4121/45) — 400
Ritual disc, Pi, archaistic mottled gray and brown stone, 3⅛ (4121/54) — 175
Waterpot, phoenix, bird biting splayed wing, 4, Sung Dynasty or later (4121/47) — 700

Malachite

Dragon, writhing amid rushing waves, clouds, lotus plants, 4¾ (4154/86) — 625
Ornament, double gourd, large fruiting gourd, with branches, 5½, repaired (4154/84) — 250

Marble

Bull, small, 2½, heavily corroded chip, Shang/Early Chou Dynasty (4174/208) — 1400
T'ao T'ieh mask, archaic, white, Shang Dynasty,¾ (4174/209) — 1400

Ming Dynasty

Boy on a water buffalo, bronze, 8¼ (4121/70) — 650
Figure, court dignitary, cast iron, 16½, casting gaps, cracks (4121/65) — 800
Figure of a warrior immortal, wood, 18 crack, chip, late (4121/66) — 800
Figures, set of four, polychromed ivory, 10-10½, age cracking (4121/69) — 6250

Painted wood

Bodhisattva bust, traces of gesso and fiber, Ming Dynasty, 16½ (4174/157) — 2900

Rose Quartz

Incense burner, covered, stump feet, handles, 6¾, chip and flaws (4154/96) — 500

Steatite (Shou Shan)

Seal, square pillar form, carved dragon, 4, 18c (4154/94) — 225
Seal, mountain form, peaked rocky crag, 3 sages, deer, monkey, 5½, 18c (4154/95) — 300
Seal, mountain form, gray and brown, peaked boulder form, carved with open pavillion, 4¾, 18c (4154/93) — 125

Stone

Blade, ritual, archaic, mottled, 2 conical holes drilled, Chou Dynasty, 7½ (4174/203) — 600
Buddha head, thickly cut figures, heavily lidded eyes, Ming Dynasty, 15 (4174/158) — 1000
Camel, large masks on the saddle bags, traces of buff earth, 16¼ (4154/312) — 900
Head of a Lohan, now sandy beige color, black striations, 3000 (4154/311) — 3000
Head of a Lohan, realistically modeled, now sandy beige color, 16, crack on cheek (4154/310) — 2300
Lohan head, gray limestone, staring eyes, ridged eyebrows, 8 (4174/153) — 550
Stele, limestone,T'ang style, with a pair of Bodhisattvas, lions in relief, 20½ (4174/151) — 900

Sung Dynasty

Head of a female, painted clay, delicate features, inlaid glass eyes, 5½, flaking and cracks (4121/63) — 3700
Kuan figure, large, wood, important, 68, flaking, cracks (4121/58) — 72500
Torso, marble, bodhisattva, dated first year Ching Te, H31, head missing (4121/59) — 5250

Yuan Dynasty

Amitabha figure, lacquered wood, contemplative expression on face, 28, flaking, pcs missing (4121/62) — 2500
Kuan Yin figure, heavily gilded, 12 l hand miss, flaking (4121/60) — 900

Head of a bodhisattva, cast iron, 9½, early (4121/67)   2800
Seated dignitary, gilt-bronze, 8¾ (4121/71)   850
Young cup bearer, parcel, gilt bronze, 5⅞ (4121/72)   550

CERAMICS

An assortment

Bottle, olive brown glazed stoneware, ovoid shape, slender spiral grooved neck, 10¼ lip restored
(4223/538)   90
Bowls, pair, yellow Peking glass, parrot on fruiting branch, 7 (4223/450)   500
Figure, painted, female musican, seated holding drum, 6½ rep, res (4223/477)   210
Jardiniere and stand, 'Famille Rose' pastel enamels, butterflies, praying mantis, 6½ star crack on
base (4223/609)   250
Pillows, pair, Tz'u Chou pottery, kneeling boy cream glaze, 14½ (4223/613)   800
Teapot and cover glazed I-Hsing, reddish brown body, large ear shape handle, 7¾ (4223/584) 500

Chou Dynasty

Vessel, archaic burnished gray pottery, inflated egg shaped, 10, chip (4242/229)   28000

Warring States Period

Bowl, impressed gray pottery, thinly potted sides, linen pattern, 3⅝ x 2¾, chip (4242/227) 750

Han Dynasty

Box, cosmetic, cover, green glazed, cylindrical vessel, 3 cabriole legs, 6¼, crack (4242/219) 2000
Dog, green glazed pottery, tail curled over back, 10 x 12, chip, enc (4242/215)   12000
Flask, green glazed pottery, oval shape, loop handles, 7¼, chip (4242/223)   1300
Gray pottery, covered jar, small, 5⅝, rare (4174/127)   *750*
Horse head, gray pottery, angular forehead, prominent brows, 6¼, crack, enc (4242/214) *900*

Gray pottery
(4174/127)

Horse head
(4242/214)

Iridescent green glazed jar, small, 5¾, chip (4174/125) 1800
Iridescent green glazed pottery scoop, rare, short handle molded with monster mask, 6 chip
(4174/126) 800
Jar, granary, green glazed pottery, tapered cylindrical body, 12, chip (4242/220) 2300
Jar, granary, green glazed pottery, three modeled bear feet, ridge roof, 10¾, dam, repaired chip
(4121/97) 700
Jar, granary, green glazed pottery, three simply modeled bear feet, 11½, chip (4121/96) 1100
Jar, green glazed pottery, squat ovoid body, 4¾, chip (4242/221) 1200
Jar, pottery, streaked red and mottled cucumber green glaze, 14, well molded, restored (4121/93) 1200
Jar, pottery green glazed (Hu), triple band of raised ribs, raised on high foot, 14¼ (4121/92) 5000
Jar, pottery, miniature, green glazed, medial ridge, molded with dragon, 1¾, rare (4154/332) 175
Jar, storage, molded gray pottery, monster mask, mock ring handles, 18, chip (4242/225) 4000
Jar, wine, iridescence, green glazed, supported on splayed foot, 14, rim chip, hole in base (4121/94) 800
Jar, wine, iridescent green glazed, pottery, mask handles, horizontal grooving, 14½, rim repaired
(4121/95) 1700
Jars, covered, early painted pottery, square sectioned shape, 12¾, chip, flaking, very rare
(4121/102) 19000
Kneeling court official, figure, gray, pottery, hands held out in front, 4¼ (4154/335) 225
Mourner, figure, gray pottery, hands across chest, 5½, rare (4154/338) 300
Sow, tomb, figure, pottery, ridged back, slab form joined legs, front and back, 5 (4154/337) 300
Strainer, green glazed pottery, rare, shallow bowl, 5 large holes, 6½, 3 spur marks on rim (4121/98) 2500
Tile, roof, early gray pottery, monster mask medallion, high relief, 4¼, tab on back chip (4121/100) 150
Torso, gray pottery, 2 section mold, seated on horse, 6¼, enc (4242/213) 750
Unglazed gray pottery support, with dwarf decoration, 6, chip% (4174/129) 600
Unglazed gray pottery, figure of ox, traces of white slip and earth encrustation, 8¼ (4174/130) *4200*
Vessel, green glazed pottery, 3 small hemispherical bowls, raised rings, 6½, flaking (4242/224) 2300
Wellhead model, green glazed pottery, sides flared, 13, chip (4242/222) *2000*

Wei Kingdom

Attendant, gray pottery, right arm held at his waist, 7½, rep (4242/212) 400
Attendant, painted gray pottery, standing, 1 hand at his waist, 14¼, chip, enc (4242/211) 2100
Equestrian drummer, painted, gray pottery, rider wearing helmet, 9, res (4242/209) 5000
Equestrian standard bearer, painted gray pottery, high forelock, 8¾, crack, res (4242/210) 6000
Figure of a bullock, gray pottery, reclining with head held up, curling horns, 6¼, 1 ear chip
(4121/108) 1500

Six Dynasties

Jar, proto porcelain, four loop handles, short neck, 5½, chip (4242/216) 400
Jar, proto porcelain, two lug handles, animal head spout, 6, chip (4242/218) 1500
Jar, proto-yueh glazed, wide incised shoulder, lug handles, 6, chip (4242/217) 450
Yueh Yao vessel, rare, almost spherical shape applied handle, 8¼ (4174/124) 2100

Sui Dynasty

Figure of an equestrian drummer, straw glazed pottery, hooded rider, (4121/128) 5000
Jar, stoneware, straw glazed, spherical form, pedestal foot, 5½ (4154/333) 200
Straw glazed earth spirit, T'u Kuai, beast seated on haunches, spiney back, 11¼, chip (4174/136) 1800

T'ang Dynasty

Amphora, pottery, straw glazed, cut shaped mouth, 2 double strand handles, 16½, flaking
(4121/106) 3200
Amphora, straw glazed pottery, double standard loop handles, 17¼, chip (4242/206) *2800*
Attendant, straw glazed pottery, standing, wearing court hat, 8¼, chip (4242/178) 450
Blue splashed San Ts'ai tripod dish, 3 chip rare (4174/121) 6200
Bottle, Kundika, straw glazed pottery, rounded body following metal shape, 10¾, chip (4121/105) 4500
Bullock figure, painted pottery, standing beast, black painted harness, 7 x 8½ (4154/343) 425
Camel, bactrian, pottery, head held high, straw glazed, chestnut splashed, 23¾, rep (4242/170) 13000
Camel, painted pottery, red, standing, head held high, 11, chip (4242/183) *1000*
Camel, pottery, minutely crackled bright amber glaze, baggage, 14¾, res, chip (4242/169) 17000

Chicken, model splash-glazed, small, pale buff on head and tail, 2¾, glaze flaking (4154/344)   275
Court lady, standing, hand concealed by cream glaze shawl, 10½, chip (4242/173)   6750
Court lady, red pottery, elegantly poised figure, 15, chip (4242/195)   13500
Court lady, splash glazed pottery, standing, hand concealed, 10½, rep, chip (4242/174)   2800
Court lady, unglazed pottery, long robe, low neck, 14½, chip (4242/192)   1900
Court lady, unglazed pottery, short sleeved robe with sash, 9½, rep (4242/184)   375
Court lady, unglazed pottery, standing, shawl over long robe, 10¼, chip (4242/185)   575
Dancing lady, painted red pottery, standing, gently swayed body 9¾, rep (4242/179)   1100
Dog, glazed pottery, seated on haunches, 4, chip (4242/164)   1400
Dog, straw glazed pottery, lively model, with incised details, 4⅝, restored (4154/348)   375
Earth spirit, splash glazed pottery, beast, on haunches on rockwork, 11¾, chip (4242/200)   1700
Earth spirit, splash glazed pottery, ferocious beast, 25½, rep, res (4242/191)   4750
Earth spirit, splash glazed pottery, with a fierce human head, 25½, chip (4242/190)   5500
Earth spirit straw glazed pottery, fantastic beast, on haunches, 14, enc (4242/201)   *2100*

Wellhead model
(4242/222)

Amphora
(4242/206)

Unglazed gray pottery
(4174/130)

Earth spirit straw
glazed pottery
(4242/201)

Camel (4242/183)

Equestrian, unglazed pottery, male rider wearing peaked cap, 12½ (4154/342) — 1300

Equestrienne, unglazed pottery, seated with head forward, 14½ (4242/203) — 2400

Ewer, white glazed, well potted ovoid body, flat foot, 2 loop handles, 9¼, flaking rare (4121/104) — 4100

Female attendant figure, glazed pottery, standing wearing short jacket, 8¾ (4154/349) — 425

Figure of a boar, straw glazed, pottery thick mane and long tail, 5½, chip (4121/136) — 500

Figure of a court lady, unglazed, red pottery, plump, elegantly poised, 14, flaking, cracks (4121/117) — 2300

Figure of a dancing lady, unglazed pottery, standing, swaying, arm raised, 8¼, res (4121/120) — 800

Figure of a marton, unglazed red pottery, pump, haughty expression, 18⅛ res, cracking (4121/118) — 7000

Figure of a princess, polychrome, decorated pottery, elaborate court robes, 14¾, res (4121/119) — 6750

Figure of a semitic merchant, unglazed pottery, rare, 10 (4121/114) — 1800

Figure of an earth spirit, San Ts'ai glazed pottery, 14⅛, chip, restored (4121/115) — 1800

Figure of camel, head held high, square base, 13⅞, repaired (4121/133) — 900

Figure of camel unglazed pottery, standing, mouth open, 2 saddle bags, 15¼, repaired (4121/131) — 600

Figure of court lady glazed pottery, standing, arched back and shoulders, 9¾, rep, flaking (4121/122) — 500

Figure of female attendant, glazed pottery standing, hand clasped, 8½ chip (4121/123) — 400

Figure of female dancer, court lady, long robe, hair upswept, 8, arms dam (4121/110) — 475

Figure of groom, painted pottery, hands across chest, long tunic, hunting bag, 10⅛, neck repaired (4121/125) — 1100

Figure of horse unglazed pottery, standing, with saddle and cloth on back, 10⅞, ear restored (4121/129) — 1500

Figure of lady well modeled, unglazed pottery, standing, hands clasped, 15½ (4121/121) — 6250

Figure of ox, standing, pricked ears, bulging eyes, 6½, chip (4121/132) — 500

Figure of ram, unglazed pottery, legs tucked beneath body, head raised, 4⅜, firing cracks (4121/135) — 375

Figure of soldier, painted pottery, standing at attention, hands, folded, 14¾, neck repaired (4121/124) — 850

Figure of supplicant official, unglazed pottery, 5½, chip, dam, rare (4121/107) — 3800

Figure, equestrian brilliantly glazed, rider, facing straight ahead, arms held out, 16¼, repaired (4121/112) — 34000

Figure, equestrienne straw glazed, pottery, hair drawn up, 10¼, chip (4121/127) — 1300

Figure, foreign stable boy, unglazed pottery, leg raised, 7¾, repaired chip (4121/111) — 800

Figure, glazed pottery, saddled horse, 12 rep, res (4223/473) — 3300

Figure, painted pottery, of a court lady slender, long pleated dress, 10⅞ (4223/475) — 550

Figure, painted pottery, DFA court lady, standing, longdress, sash, 11⅜ rep (4223/474) — 650

Figure, San Ts'ai glazed pottery, 10 (4223/479) — 425

Figures, pair straw glazed, pottery, court ladies, standing, hands concealed, long-sleeves, 8, flaking (4223/478) — 700

Figures of guardians, pair, well, modeled pottery standing, hands clasped, 15, res (4121/116) — 2100

Figures of Lokopala, pair, glazed, pottery standing, arm raised, 16-16½, some chip (4121/126) — 11000

Glazed figure of a groom, wood stand, 8¾ (4144/340) — 400

Glazed pottery Lokapala figure, armored tunic with monster mask epaulets, repaired, 32¾ (4174/142) — 5250

Glazed pottery, bactrian camel, powerfully modeled beast, head defiant, 20, repaired (4174/138) — 14000

Glazed pottery, equestrian figure, rider wearing green coat, 15⅜, repaired (4174/140) — 15500

Goose, model, brown glazed, small, simply molded, beak resting on chest, 2¾ (4154/346) — 275

Grooms, pair, figures, red pottery, wearing loose belt, tunic and high boots, 22, large (4154/340) — 2200

Group, equestrienne, glazed pottery, horse standing, head to side, 16, repaired, restored (4121/130) — 2300

Horse, glazed pottery, powerfully molded, head held high, 37½, res (4242/187) — 75000

Horse, unglazed pottery, head, lowered, saddle, 10¼, chip (4242/181) — 3500

Horse, unglazed pottery, standing, head down, red painted body, 9¼, repainting (4242/182) — 3600

Horse and rider, splash glazed pottery, female seated hands raised, 15¾, rep (4242/168) — 18000

Hound, seated, straw glazed pottery, molded 2 section, head, raised, 5 (4121/134) — 700

Hound, unglazed pottery, seated on haunches, rib cage showing, 5, ear chip (4242/165) — 1600

Jar, green glazed pottery, ovoid form, 10, chip (4242/208) — 2500

Jar, ovoid, glazed, rounded sides tapering to solid base, 11½ (4144/339) — 200

Jar, pottery, San Ts'ai, glazed pottery, shallow groove around mouth, 2⅜, chip inside lip, small (4154/345) — 1200

Jar, white glazed pottery, baluster form, flat, 7½, glaze flaking (4242/207) — 3700

Kneeling lady, glazed pottery, bent, both hands on knees, 5¼, chip, rep (4242/198) — 200

Laden camel, unglazed pottery, standing, head slightly turned, 11, imp (4242/186) — 2300

Loka pala splash glazed pottery, warrior guardian standing, 16½, chip (4242/202) — 4100

Polo player, unglazed pottery, female rider of Khorezmian type, 10½, res (4242/204) — 7500

Ram, glazed pottery, hollow modeled, legs tucked under, 4½, chip (4242/166) — 650

Red pottery equestrian, repaired, early, 12¾ (4174/134) — 2400

Red pottery saddled mule figure, small, 6½, (4174/133) — 950

Rooster, straw glaze, with legs astride, incised tail, 4¼, chip (4242/167) — 475

San Ts'ai glazed pottery offering set, shallow dish, 6 cups, jar, splash glazed, 8⅞ (4174/119) — 7200

Seated court lady, elaborate stool, holding stylized flower, 12½, res (4242/197) — 10000

Seated lady and child, pottery, glazed, poised on waisted stool, 11¼, res, rep (4242/175) — 25000

Soldier, painted pottery, standing, right hand across his waist, 15¼, imp (4242/194) — 1500

Splash glazed pottery bowl, small, molded with central florette medallion, 3¾, chip (4174/120) — 120

Splash glazed pottery official figure, hand folded on chest, tablet of rank missing, glaze flaking, 33¾, large (4174/143) — 8000

Splash glazed pottery saddled camel, saddle bags modeled as ogre masks, base rep, 21½ (4174/137) — 11000

Standard bearer, straw-glazed pottery, standing, hooded helmet, 8, imp (4242/176) — 450

Standard bearer, unglazed pottery, standing, hands clasped, hooded helmet, 9 (4242/188) — 210

Straw glazed figure of groom, well modeled, restored, early, 9½ (4174/132) — 600

Straw glazed pottery amphora, 17¼, chip (4174/122) — 4000

Straw glazed pottery stand, galleried rim on keyhole shaped legs, 9⅜, chip (4174/123) — 7000

Vessel pouring, straw glazed pottery, wide mouth globular form, splayed ring foot, 4½ foot chip, flaking (4223/476) — 600

Warrior, painted, glazed pottery, standing, red, black and gold, 16, imp (4242/193) — 3400

Sung Dynasty

Bottle, painted, Honan, rounded body, recessed base, 7½, rim chip (4242/155) — 1900

Bowl, shallow, 6 lobed, Ting type, flared sides divided into 6 shallow lobes, 8, rim chip (4154/386) — 375

Bowl, carved celadon, shallow bowl, overlapping petals, 6½ (4242/131) — 700

Bowl, carved Ying Ch'ing, with pale bluish glaze, 6⅝ (4154/373) — 175

Bowl, conical Northern celadon, plain sides with wheelmarks, 5, glaze, chip (4154/388) — 525

Bowl, glazed white, Ting type, interior with ducks and lotus, 4¼ (4154/384) — 300

Bowl, incised and combed, Ying Ch'ing, duck in flight, 6⅝, res (4242/142) — 1100

Bowl, molded Ting type, phoenix birds in a dense floral scroll, 9½, short crack (4154/385) — 1100
Bowl, petal carved Lung Ch'uan, flared sides, carved with overlapping petals, 5¼ (4223/493) — 375
Bowl, pottery, Ts'u Chou, dark brown over creamy white slip, 7¾, crack (4242/161) — 2600
Bowl, white pottery, carved, ribbed petal motifs, 5 (4154/383) — 2300
Bowl, Honan, oil spot, glazed small, flared sides, broad base, 4¾ (4154/366) — 850
Bowl, Northern celadon, plain conical form, grayish olive glaze, 4⅞, glaze chip (4154/389) — 250
Bowl, Northern celadon, small, carved with motif on the exterior 6 lobes, 4¾, restored, rim chip (4154/387) — 650
Box and cover, cosmetic, inscribed, Ying Ch'ing, chrysanthemum form, 2¼, hc, dam. (4121/145) — 700
Box and cover, molded Ying Ch'ing, flat top, circular, two blossoms, 3¼ (4242/147) — 1700
Brown glazed Honan jar, small, 5 small florette bosses, 3¾ (4174/111) — 1000
Brown glazed teabowl, unusual, 'finger-groove' concave rim, 4¼ (4174/108) — 1100
Brown splash glaze dishes, pair, interior with 6 groups of petal motifs, 6¼, 1 chip (4174/109) — 1300
Carved Tz'u Chou pottery pillow, large, top incised with camelia in blossom, 13½, chip (4174/115) — 4600
Censer, ribbed, tripod, Lung Ch'uan, pale sea green glaze, 5¼, chip (4174/80) — 2000
Censer tripod, brown glazed, unusual, knife cut, supports, 4 (4154/368) — 750
Chu Lu Hsien ewer large, white slip, clear glaze, ll, dam (4174/117) — 1000
Dish, incised, ting yao, shallow interior, lotus blossom, 6¾ (4242/149) — 2100
Dish, ting yao, shallow flared sides, 5⅝, rim chip (4242/150) — 300
Dish, twin fish, Lung Ch'uan celadon, molded in the center 2 fish, 5 (4223/494) — 400
Dish, Northern celadon, shallow notched molded rim, 3⅞, glaze crackled (4242/123) — 1300
Dog, miniature, Ying Ch'ing, reclining, degraded bluish glaze, 1½ (4154/377) — 150
Ewer, celadon, lung ch'uan, small spout, loop handle, 2⅝, chip (4242/128) — 400
Ewer, double gourd Ying Ch'ing, carving strap handle set opposite slender spout, Res - cracking (4223/481) — 425
Ewer, double gourd, celadon, lung ch'uan, applied curved loop handled, 4⅞, chip (4242/125) — 2400
Ewer, Ying Ch'ing, small, with pair of small loops on shoulder, flat base, 3½ (4154/371) — 150
Glazed stoneware box and cover, melon shaped, 2½ (4174/96) — 275
Honan jar, painted, small, mottled olive glaze, 3 (4174/110) — 325
Honan jar, ribbed, five sets of vertical stripes, 4 (4174/107) — 800
Honan teabowl, small, 4 chip (4147/104) — 300
Jar, brown painted Tz'u Chou, three large trefoil motifs, 4⅝, cracks, rim chip (4154/357) — 3200
Jar, painted, Tz'u Chou, painted orangey brown, cream slip, 5¼, chip, flaking, unusual (4154/355) — 225
Jar, Homan, brown glazed, with pair ribbed loop handles, applied, 4½, cracks to lip (4154/369) — 900
Jar and cover, celadon lung ch'uan, ribbed baluster jar, lotus leaf outline, 3 (4242/127) — 650
Jar and cover, funerary, carved celadon, overlapping petals, 12½, dam and repaired (4154/391) — 850
Jar Chi-Chou, splash glazed, brownish, black glaze, 4, rim crack, chip, unusual (4121/152) — 600
Jarlet, spotted Ying Ch'ing, squat, short neck, lug handles, 2⅛ (4242/112) — 550
Jarlet, spotted, Ying Ch'ing, squat rounded, 2 lug handles, 2½ dam (4223/482) — 300
Jarlet, Lobed Yueh, five vertical notches, gray stoneware body, 10c 2¾ small (4223/485) — 160
Kaki-glazed honan dish, glaze with black flecking, 4, chip (4174/106) — 850
Kaki-glazed honan dish, rust-brown glaze, 5¼, res (4174/105) — 550
Lung Ch'uan celadon bowl, flower shaped small, 3½, imp (4174/84) — 325
Lung Ch'uan celadon dish, twin fish, 8¾, chip (4174/85) — 700
Lung Ch'uan celadon jar, baluster shaped, small, 2½, chip (4174/82) — 650
Lung Ch'uan celadon jar and cover, small, 3¼, chip cr (4174/83) — 475
Molded Ying Ch'ing vase, 8⅝ (4174/88) — 750
Sheep, miniature Ying Ch'ing, standing, partially grayish blue glaze, eyes iron brown, 1⅜ (4154/376) — 325
Splashed brown glazed Honan jar, 4½ (4147/112) — 4000
Teabowl, Chien Yao, flared sides, rich brown glaze, 5 (4121/149) — 900
Teabowl, Chien Yao, redddish brown, hare's fur glaze, 5 (4154/364) — 1100
Teabowl, Chien Yao 'hare's fur', lustrous brown glaze, 4¾ (4121/151) — 550
Teabowl, Chien Yao 'hare's fur', thick, lustrous coffee brown glaze, 4⅞ (4121/150) — 700
Teabowl, Chien Yao, conical, covered with a streaked hare's fur glaze, 4⅞ (4154/365) — 325
Teabowl, Kiantemmoku, mottled brownish - black glaze, 4⅜ rim chip (4223/492) — 350
Ting Yao bowl, lobed with thin raised lines, 7⅞, fine (4174/98) — 6200
Ting Yao bowl, plain, rim unglazed, 4⅝ (4174/103) — 1000
Ting Yao carved bowl, lotus sprayon interior, 9 (4174/100) — 2800
Tz'u Chou jar, sgraffiato, large, 13½, res (4174/116) — *2800*
Tz'u Chou pottery lamp unusual, flared sides molded with large petals, 10c, 5⅛, chip (4174/118) — 550
Vase, funerary painted, Ying Ch'ing, iron-red, molded figure, 10½, chip (4242/148) — *1700*
Vase, pear shaped, painted, Honan, speckled olive, brown glaze, 10, neck cut down (4242/157) — 575
Vase, pear shaped, Ying Ch'ing, scrolling lotus, 5⅜, chip (4242/146) — 575
Vase, Chu Lu Hsien, ovoid form, narrow neck, 10, glaze chip, warped (4154/362) — 650
Vase, Lung Ch'uan celadon, covered, well-carved leafy lotus scroll, 8⅝ (4174/81) — 3800
Vase and cover, funerary, carved celadon, five jagged edge spouts, 13½, restored, firing cracks (4154/390) — 1500

Vases, pearshaped, pair, molded Ying Ch'ing, foliate scroll around the shoulder, 7 (4154/372)   200
White bowl, flower shaped, small fitted box, 10c, warped in firing (4174/102)   1100
White bowl, flower shaped, small fitted box, 10c, 6 (4174/101)   2000
Ying Ch'ing bowl, molded with large lotus blossom in center, 7, chip (4174/92)   400
Ying Ch'ing bowl, conical carved, design of boys, peonies, 8⅜, chip (4144/352)   250

Vase (4242/148)

Tz'u Chou jar (4174/116)

Ying Ch'ing ewer and cover (4174/94)

Ying Ch'ing censer miniature, 3⅞, rare (4174/89)   750
Ying Ch'ing dish, incised with lotus leaf, combed details, 5⅝, kilngrit (4174/93)   500
Ying Ch'ing dish molded, small, unusual, 4 fish swimming, 8⅜ (4174/91)   1200
Ying Ch'ing ewer and cover, double gourd, small, 5 (4174/90)   700
Ying Ch'ing ewer and cover, molded, small, 4⅞ (4174/94)   *1600*
Ying Ch'ing funerary vases, two, mounted as lamps, 13¾, chip (4144/359)   900
Ying Ch'ing type bowl, small unusual, 2⅞ (4174/95)   325

Northern Sung Dynasty

Bowl, 6 lobed shallow, carved Ting-Yao, with large lotus spray, 9, crack, chip (4154/378)   1500
Jar, white and brown glazed, ridged lobe, short neck, wide mouth, 4⅜, glaze rubbed, res (4121/148)   375
Vase, Tz'u Chou, five point foliate rim, ivory glaze, white slip, 7 rim chip (4223/486)   1600
Vase, Ying Ch'ing, carved, ovoid, lug handles, erect leaf motifs pale, greenish tint, 5⅞, 1 lug missing, rare (4121/141)   1700

Yuan Dynasty

Bowl, blue and white, early, small, 3 1/3, chip (4174/72)   125
Bowl, blue glaze, Chun, conical, robbin egg blue glaze to beige, 7 (4223/488)   900
Bowl, Chun Yao, rounded sides, milky blue glaze, 7½ (4242/152)   650
Bowl, painted Tz'u Chou, with flower sprays, 4, restored (4154/353)   325
Bowl, splashed, Chun, pale blue glaze to beige, splashed greenish, purple, 7 crack (4223/489)   500
Bowl, Chun Yao, opaque milky grayish glaze, 6¼ (4154/352)   750
Bowl, Chun Yao, widely flared, grayish lavender, blue glaze, 6½ rim restored (4223/490)   500
Bowl, Chun Yao, shallow rounded, sides, knife cut, 6½ (4154/350)   400
Box and cover, Ying Ch'ing molded, shallow circular shape 2 phoenix, 2¾, hc, rim chip (4121/144)   100
Censer, tripod, Chun Yao, Globular body, slab handles, 4½, restored, chip (4154/354)   375
Cover and ewer, Ying Ch'ing, molded with sprays of peony blossoms, 3¾, chip (4242/140)   400
Cup, stand, Ying Ch'ing, rare, shallow dish, with 2 Fu lions, D6, firing cracks (4121/140)   *2100*

Dish, incised celadon, shallow rounded dish, 10¼ (4242/132)   1600
Dish, molded, lung ch'uan celadon, medallion, character shan, 13¼ (4242/66) 700
Dish, shu fu molded, shallow rounded sides, 6⅜, chip (4242/137)   400
Ewer and cover, molded Ying Ch'ing, phoenix bird in flight, lotus petals, 3½, chip (4242/141) 550
Ewer and cover, molded, Ying Ch'ing, pear shaped body, 2 phoenix birds, 9¾ (4242/139) *3100*

Ewer and cover
(4242/139)

Cup (4121/140)

Jar (4242/160)

Ewer molded, Ying Ch'ing, flattened angular pear shaped body, 4, chip (4242/143) 550
Jar, Chun Yao, thick milky grayish blue glaze, 6½, chip and cracks (4154/351) 1000
Jar, dragon-molded celadon, three small lug handles, 1 repaired, 4, crack (4144/376) 275
Jar, molded celadon, pair of dragon above crashing waves, 4⅝ 1 lug restored, crack (4223/497) 200
Jar, stoneware, carved, brown glazed, wide-mounted ovoid form, 7, chip (4242/160) *2500*
Jar, Tz'u Chou, painted, wide mouth, short neck, peony sprays, 9⅞, res, glaze flaking (4121/153) 3200
Jar and cover, black glazed, Honan, heavily potted, wide shoulder, 17½, cover rep, chip (4242/154) 5000
Jar and cover, Ying Ch'ing molded, three bands of linear scrollwork, 3, hc on cover, small (4121/146) 600
Jarlet, blue and white, rounded sides divided into 6 panels, 3, chip (4242/113) 600
Jarlet, blue and white, squat rounded jar, short neck, lug handles, 2 (4242/111) 1400
Lady figure painted, Tz'u Chou, Buff pottery, cream slip, 7, base restored (4154/358) 275
Official figure, T z'u Chou pottery, in long white robe, 9, rep (4144/366) 550
Tz'u Chou pottery jar and cover, 5, chip (4174/114) 2400
Vase, celadon, lung ch'uan, full pear shape, mock loose ring handles, 8½ (4242/134) 7500
Vase, painted Tz'u Chou, pear shape, wide band leafy sprays, 8¼, restored (4154/356) 225
Vase, pottery, carved, brown glazed, slender pear shape, 7¼, chip (4242/159) 2200
White glazed Shu Fu type dish, small, 4⅞, chip (4174/87) 225
Winecup of Shu Fu type molded, band of peony, scroll, rounded sides, 2⅝, hc (4121/147) 300
Ying Ch'ing bowl, spotted, interior impressed with floral medallion, 6¼ (4144/360) 175

Ming Dynasty

Altar vase, blue and white, rare, baluster body, 4 panels, H8½, Wan Li per., chip (4121/186) 12000
Attendant, tomb pottery, glazed figure, standing 1 arm raised, 12⅞, chip (4242/71) 700
Basin, turquoise glazed pottery, shallow circular, convex sides, double row bosses, 8½ (4223/541) 350
Bowl, blue and white, freely drawn floral sprays, L15c (4121/178) 600
Bowl, blue and white, single tree-peony blossom, 4½, hc, Wan Li per. (4121/182) 150
Bowl, blue and white, smudgy underglaze blue with dragons, 16c, 5⅝, glaze chip (4174/48) 250

Bowl, blue and white, attractive, fanciful landscape with oversize peonies, FH17c, 8¾, glaze chip (4174/46) — 1600

Bowl, blue and white, small, exterior with blossoms and emblems, Chia Ching Period, D4⅝, chip (4174/49) — 275

Bowl, bulb incised celadon, heavily potted bowl, tripod feet, 11½ (4242/65) — 1100

Bowl, bulb, carved, Chekiang celadon, pale grayish olive color, II, rim cracks (4154/397) — 375

Bowl, bulb, Chekiang celadon, compressed circular bowl, pale green, 9½, cracks (4154/399) — 150

Bowl, bulb, Chekiang celadon, tripod supports, carved florettes in trellis, 12, large (4121/164) — 1100

Bowl, incised white dragon, two sketchy dragons, glaze chip, 16c, Wan Li per. (4121/183) — 250

Bowl, late Ming blue and white, frieze of songbirds in fruit trees, 14⅛, Chai Ching per. (4121/176) — 4000

Bowl, swatow polychrome, scene of geese, floral landscape, (4223/530) — 200

Bowl, Ming blue and white, dark cobalt, lotus petal medallion, ca1500 (4121/174) — 950

Bowl, Ming blue and white, floral spray, beaded chains, trellis border, L15c, slight chip (4121/177) — 300

Box and cover, Annamese, cracked glaze of greyish green tone, 14c (4121/173) — 125

Box and cover, Annamese, polychrome, 14-15c, 3¼ (4174/78) — 600

Box and cover, blue and white, circular, with continuous floral scroll, 16c, 3⅜, glaze chip (4174/51) — 400

Box and cover, blue and white, coiled dragon, band of flowers, chip, 2½, Wan Li per. (4121/184) — 80

Box and cover, blue and white, octagonal, fleeing crab on cover, 16c, 3½, chip (4174/52) — 325

Box and cover, blue and white, river and mountain scape chip, 4¼, Wan Li per. (4121/179) — 500

Box and cover, circular, lead glazed, domed cover, incised, 3⅛ (4242/67) — 170

Box and cover, Annamese, blue and white, 15c, 3¾, chip (4144/382) — 110

Bulb bowl, tripod, peony scroll, 11½ (4174/79) — 1500

Candlesticks pair, San Ts'ai, elephant head handles, peony blossoms, 9½ chip (4223/537) — 325

Censer, lead glazed pottery, San Ts'ai, tripot supports, dome base, lion masks, 3½ 1 handle repair (4223/532) — 160

Censer, tile work, large peony sprays, Buddhist figures, 19, chip, base restored (4121/191) — 450

Censer and cover, lung ch'uan celadon, rounded sides, incised, tripod, 8¾ (4242/64) — 950

Chen Wu figure, turquoise-glazed, Lord of the Northern Quadrant, 13½, repaired (4174/63) — 900

Chicken waterpot, polychromed enamel, rare, neck set with chicken head for spout, 16c, 3, chip (4174/55) — 850

Cup, libation, tripod, molded Ch'uan, celadon, small mushroom lugs, 15c (4121/166) — 950

Dish, blue and white, boldly painted with duck in flight, L15c, 9¾ (4174/57) — 1400

Dish, blue and white, freely painted with ch'i-lin, ca1500, 9¾ (4174/59) — 2400

Dish, blue and white, Annamese, 14-15c, 7 (4174/77) — 350

Dish, celadon Lung Ch'uan, molded with a floral medallion, wavy lines, 14¼ foot rim ground, large (4223/545) — 900

Dish, celadon Lung Ch'uan, molded with lotus spray, 13rubbing, wear to glaze (4223/551) — 600

Dish, celadon, massive Lung-Chuan, floral spray, 18¼ (4154/394) — 1500

Dish, chrysanthemum molded lung, Ch'uan, large single peony blossoms, 12⅝ (4121/167) — 400

Dish, octagonal, celadon, Chekiang, twin peony spray, sea water green glaze, 14⅞ (4121/165) — 325

Dish, polychrome swatow, pair turquoise birds and iron red flowers, 15½, rim chip, star crack (4154/404) — 325

Dish, sauce, molded, blue and white, panel of deer, garden setting, ca1620, chip 8 (4223/509) — 270

Dish, saucer, celadon, Lung Ch'uan, chrysanthemum blossom, 13 (4223/549) — 600

Dish, saucer, Ming, provincial, blue and, white, chrysanthemum scroll, 12⅜, warped, 16c (4154/408) — 475

Dish, white, blue and white Annamese, peony blossom and leaves, 15c, small cracks, base chip (4223/498) — 1600

Dish, Annamese, blue and white, 15c, 9¼ (4144/381) — 250

Dish, Chekiang celadon, trellis pattern in slightly domed center, 12¾ (4144/379) — 250

Dishes, blue and white, pair, small, interiors with medallions, 16c, 5¼ (4174/47) — 425

Dishes, pair, blue and white, dec, center 1 landscape, 1 fenced garden, 8-8¼ glaze chip rim (4223/507) — 850

Dishes, sauce, late Ming blue and white, pair, fishnet pattern, 5¾, T'ien Ch'i per. (4121/185) — 1700

Dragon ewer, Annamese, blue and white, rare, well-modeled spirited dragon, 14-15c, 9 crack (4174/75) — 14000

Equestrian figure, glazed tileworks, bearded warrior facing right, large, 22½, chip (4174/64) — 5000

Equestrian figure, glazed tileworks, warrior astride a pony, 22½, chip (4174/65) — 5000

Equestrian figure, tileworks pottery, on galloping pony, 13¼, chip, now lamp (4242/73) — 600

Equestrian figure, tileworks pottery, warrior wearing helmet, 15¼, chip, now lamp (4242/74) — 650

Ewer, blue and white, purplish under-glaze blue, Chia Ching Period (4174/54)

Fa Hua garden seat, pierced and molded with lion mask handles, ca1500, 14¾, chip (4174/62) — 2200

Fa Hua Mei P'ing, lotus scroll and sprays, yellow, purple, white, ca1500, 10½, base pierced (4121/193) — 800

Figure glazed, equestrian, 13¾ chip (4223/534) — 1400

Figure of a Buddhist lion, glazed, pottery, roaring beast, curly mane, harness, saddle, 25½, chip, flaking (4121/197) — 2400

Figure of Vajprani, wood stand, 16, arm rep (4144/373) — 550
Figures, pair glazed pottery, attendants, standing, square base, 6¼ chip (4223/539) — 550
Guardian figure, tileworks, celestial warrior, wood pedestal, large, 19¾, chip miss (4174/66) — 2400
Jar, baluster, Wu Ts'ai, dec with slender court ladies and small boys, 12 rim chip, 17c (4154/405) — 1100
Jar, blue and white Ming small, baluster shape, misfired dark 1 side, 16c 3¾ (4223/503) — 125
Jar, incised, green glazed, sprays of lotus, peony, chrysanthemum, 8 hc chip (4121/201) — 1100
Jar, leys, Cha Tou, engraved, green and yellow, dragons, 4¼, hc, Cheng Te per. chip (4121/189) — 8000
Jar, painted, Ts'u Chou, dark brown over cream, 23, chip (4242/163) — 2000
Jar, painted, Ts'u Chou, potted jar, short cylindrical neck, 23, chip (4242/162) — 2000
Jar, rare, blue and white, Annamese, 14-15c, 6¼, firing, cr base (4174/74) — 16000
Jar, slip decorated celadon, small, cluster of chrysanthemum, white slip, 18c, 5⅞, fine (4121/203) — 600
Jar, stoneware, brown, glazed, ovoid body with 4 small loops joining wide mouth, 9 (4154/370) — 225
Jar, storage, massive green glazed, with incised and molded decoration, 32½, chip (4154/437) — 750
Jar, swatow, tw writhing dragons, 10, chip (4223/518) — 550
Jar and cover Wu Ts'ai large, court attendants playing, variety of instruments, 17c, 19½ rim chip (4223/528) — 2300
Kendi, blue and white, freely painted with scrolling blossoms, Wan Li Period, 7¾, glaze, chip (4174/45) — 750
Kendi, elephant, Ming blue and white, square vessel, head high, pierced tusks, 8½, Wan Li per. (4121/188) — 1000
Kendi, late Ming blue and white, rounded body, 6 panel, birds, L16c, 9, chip, firing (4121/187) — 1500
Kuan Ti figure, entwined snake and tortoise at feet, 15, pc missing (4144/368) — 850
Lohan figure, glazed pottery tileworks, holding large fan in 1 hand, 18 chip (4174/68) — 850
Officials, 3 pottery figures, red, standing, robes, high hats, 6½, 1 rep (4242/70) — 550
Pillow, animal form, splash glazed, pottery, crouching cat like beast, 12, chip, early (4121/202) — 1000
Pricket sticks pair, glazed tileworks, snarling beast, 9⅝ x 7⅛, res (4242/75) — 650
Ridgetile, glazed pottery, of a shaman riding, a Ch'i Lin, 16 restored (4223/533) — 2000
Ridgetile, pottery, boy hold animal, 16 - 17c 14½ rep (4223/536) — 1300
Rooftiles, pair, pottery lead glazed, boy seated on winged fish, 12 x 12½, chip (4242/72) — 700
Saucer dish, yellow ground, flowering hibiscus in center repeated on rim, Cheng Te Period, 7⅞ (4174/60) — 28000
Storage jar, green glaze, large, drilled for lamp, 20½ dam-rep (4144/372) — 400
Storage jar, massive, brown-glaze, 27¼, rim rep (4144/371) — 475
Storage jar, ochre glazed, with molded decoration large, 21¼, dam (4144/370) — 350
Storage jar, ochre glazed, with incised decoration large, 14-15c, 24½ crack, rep (4144/367) — 300
Swatow blue and white basin, large, interior with crane amidst pine, bamboo, 17c, 14⅝, rim chip (4174/42) — 750
Swatow blue and white bowl, center with legged bird, 11 (4174/43) — 375
Tile, ridge, pair, turquoise glazed, pottery, crouching kylin, 11½ flaking, retouched (4121/198) — 600
Tileworks, pair glazed, Fu Lions, 13 - 14 restored chip (4223/535) — 550
Tomb figure, court official in heavy robes, 8¼, chip (4144/369) — 375
Vase, celadon, incised on the rounded sides, floral sprays, 10¾ chip (4223/547) — 500
Vase, celadon, carved Chekiang, large blossoming peonies, mounted as lamp, 17½ (4223/550) — 1200
Vase, celadon, incised, rounded sides freely incised with floral sprays, (4223/546) — 300
Vase, lead glazed pottery, pear shape, raised on splayed foot, 6½ (4223/531) — 350
Vase, lung ch'uan celadon, pear shape, sides incised with trellis pattern, 6¼ (4242/63) — 175
Vase, pear shape celadon, Lung Ch'uan, thick olive green glaze, gold lacquer, 7⅝ repair to foot chip (4223/544) — 850
Vase, Chekiang celadon, small, ovoid form, small mouth, 6¼ (4154/401) — 275
Vases, pair double gourd green glazed, pottery, standing on flat foot, 5¼ rim chip restored (4223/542) — 275
Vases, pair pottery, glazed, 2, crawling Chih Lung, loop handles, 7½, chip (4242/69) — 275
Vases, pair turquoise glazed pottery, slender pear shape, 6¾ hc, rim chip (4223/543) — 450
Water dropper, soxt paste Chun, lotus bud shape small mouth, beige, 2⅝ glaze rim chip (4223/540) — 300

Cheng Te Period

Dish, sauce, blue and white, Ming, fierce dragon leaping, 7¾ (4242/100) — 55000

Wan Li Period

Bowl, blue and white, landscape, 8½ cracked (4223/505) — 300
Bowl, blue and white, late Ming, river and mountain landscape, 8¼, rim chip (4242/80) — 1400
Box and cover, Wu Ts'ai ingot shaped, peony blossoms, bird and butterfly, 6½, chip (4223/529) — 800

Censer, blue and white, supported 4 incurved legs, monster mask handles, 3¼ restored, glazed chip (4223/504) — 2800

Censer, slip-decorated, blue glazed, two stylized dragons, blue and white, D8 (4144/384) — 400

Dish, blue and white, late Ming, landscape, 2 figures crossing bridge, 7¾, chip (4223/521) — 225

Dish, blue and white, late Ming, phoenix perched on rockwork, 7⅝, chip (4242/84) — 200

Dish, blue and white, Kraak Porselein, flowers and scroll large, 19½ flaking-restored (4223/523) — 300

Dish, sauce, blue and white, late Ming, 2 peacocks and flowering peony, 7½, kiln grit (4242/90) — 550

Dish, saucer blue and white, late Ming, chrysanthemums and peony, 9½, chip (4242/89) — 300

Jars, pair, blue and white, Ming, heavily potted, hexagonal shape, 14½, chip (4242/103) — 3600

Vase, polychrome, Ming, 4 dragons, 11, neck cut down (4242/95) — 4000

T'ien Ch'i Period

Bowls, shallow, set of 5, blue and white, late Ming, 2 frolicking horses, 5⅜, chip (4242/81) — 1800

Dish, blue and white late Ming, fenced garden, lotus scroll fretwork, 8⅜ glaze chip to lip (4223/514) — 250

Dish, blue and white late Ming, medallion of birds and flowers, 6½ clazed chip to rim (4223/512) — 275

Dish, blue and white late Ming, painted, scene 2 travelers, 8⅝ chip (4223/513) — 300

Dish, blue and white Ming, five petaled flowers, blade shaped leaves, 8½, chip, res (4223/516) — 250

Dish, blue and white, late Ming, bamboo and banana palm, large cricket, 8⅛ rim chip (4223/517) — 425

Dish, blue and white, Ming, official and his attendant, 7⅜ (4242/87) — 450

Dish, blue and white, Ming, two officials and attendants, 7¼, chip (4242/86) — 400

Dish, chrysanthemum petal molded L. Ming, two deer bencath large pine trees, 8⅛ chip (4223/515) — 325

Dish, incised decoration blue and, white, L. Ming, 6 wedge shaped section, (4223/511) — 300

Dish, incised, bue and white L. Ming, blossoming chrysanthemums, and lotus, 8, glaze chip (4223/510) — 375

Dish, 5 lobed, polychrome, late Ming, petal shaped section, 8¼, chip (4242/96) — 700

Dishes, pair, blue and white, late Ming, fisherman poling boat, 6⅛, chip (4242/83) — 600

Dishes, set of 5 blue and white, L. Ming, shallow, wide band of scrolling lotus, 8 - 8½ some glaze chip (4223/508) — 650

Ch'ing Dynasty

Basin enameled blue ground, fruit and 3 leaf medallions, L19c 13 (4223/596) — 250

Batavian ware vases, pair, covered famille rose, 18c chip rey (4174/4) — 2300

Blanc de chine, censer, shoulders set with lion-mask handles, 18c, 6, restored (4144/430) — 175

Blanc de chine, figure of Kuan Yin and child, 18c, 9¾, chip (4144/429) — 400

Blanc de chine, figure of Po T'o-Lo and tiger, L18-E19c, 9¼, hat res (4144/428) — 600

Blanc de chine, censer, squat body on tripod feet, 17-18c 5¼ (4144/424) — 225

Blanc de chine, Fu lion joss stick holder, M17-E18c, 7½, chip (4144/425) — 200

Blanc de chine, cup rhinoceros horn, 18c, 4⅛ (4174/41) — 150

Blanc de chine, figure of Kuan Yin, L17c, 16½, base chip (4174/40) — 1000

Blanc de chine, figure of Kuan Yin well modeled, 18c, 33¼, base cracks (4174/39) — 10500

Bottle, famille rose miniature, two sprays of spider chrysanthemums, E19c, fine (4121/256) — 275

Bottle, famille rose, miniature, white magnolia branches, pink, gold, yellow peonies, E19c (4121/258) — 425

Bottle vase, small, blue and white, dense pattern of lotus scroll, K'ang Hsi period, 6¾ (4174/10) — 800

Bottles, cafe-au-lait, glazed, pair, double gourdshape, miniature, 18c, 2⅜, 1 w chip (4174/33) — 375

Bowl, copper red decoration, two figures seated, large willow tree, 19c 8¾ (4223/564) — 575

Bowl, rare, blue ground, ming style, frieze of four, Yung Cheng Mark, 6⅞, chip (4174/16) — 5250

Bowl, ruby red-underglazed blue, decorated, rare, Kuang Hsu Mark, Period, 8⅝ (4174/2) — 1000

Bowls, pair pierced unusual, floral, and openwork, 18c 3½ (4223/633) — 425

Bowls, pair, Tou Ts'ai, floral scroll, Tho Kuang mark, Period, 5⅝ (4174/3) — 1300

Brushpot, 'Famille Verte' river, mountain landscape, 19c 5¾ (4223/627) — 275

Brushpot, molded 'Famille Verte' four medallions enclosing figures, 19c 6½ slightly rubbed (4223/626) — 400

Brushpot, Pi Tung iron rust, reddish brown glaze, black speckling, E18c, rubbing (4121/221) — 7500

Censer, iron rust, rounded body, 2 loop handles, 18c, 6, small (4223/556) — 400

Chen Wu figure, Blanc de chine, The God of Northern Quadrant, seated on rockwork, 8⅜, 18c (4154/418) — 450

Condiment set enameled I-Hsing, eight fan shaped dishes, central circular dish, 19c (4223/585) — 400

Cup, white porcelain, round sides pierced with chrysanthemum florets, 17c, 3¾, chip (4144/404) — 250

Cup, Blanc de chine, lotus leaf resting on 3 pointed feet, 18c 3⅜ (4223/573) — 175

Cup, Blanc de chine, octagonal, small, flared form, prunus sprays, 4⅜, 18c (4154/416) — 140

Dish, sauce, Ming style blue and white, five lotus blossoms, scrolling stems, E18c, rim chip, restored (4121/287) — 1200

Dish, saucer, petal molded celadon, five large overlapping petals, Hsuan Te mark, 18c (4223/553) — 450

Dish, saucer, rose verte large, scene from Romance of the Western Chambers, ca1725 14⅛ 2 cracks (4223/599) — 425

Dish quatrefoil, blue and white, with long poem in central panel, Chia Ch'ing mark, 6½, crack (4174/12) — *1000*

Dishes, pair, small, biscuit glazed, each with aubergine conch shell, K'ang Hsi Period, 3¾, dam (4174/1) — 275

Dragon bowls, lemon-yellow, pair, each finely incised with 2 fierce dragons, 18-E19c, chip (4144/417) — 175

Famille rose, figures of seated boys, pair, wood stands, 19c, 6½, chip (4144/457) — 275

Famille rose, plates, ruby back semi eggshell, 19c, 9 (4144/459) — 650

Famille rose, vase, attractive, wood stand, 19c, 8⅞ (4144/455) — 300

Famille rose, vases, pair, double ground attractive, M19c, 8¾ (4144/458) — 600

Famille verte, covered baluster jar, mounted as lamp, 19c, 14½ (4144/449) — 275

Famille verte, jardiniere powder blue glazed large stand, 19c, 15¾ (4144/450) — 2200

Famille verte, vase double gourd small, 19c, 6¼, dam (4144/448) — 120

Famille verte basin, with iron-red dragon, K'ang Hsi Period, 15½ (4174/8) — 5600

Famille verte basin, small, with well painted magpies, K'ang Hsi Period, 9⅛, fine (4174/7) — 4000

Famille verte jar, scenes of court ladies and attendants, K'ang Hsi period 8 flake (4174/9) — 800

Figure, blanc de chine, of Ta Mao volouminous robes, cowled headdress, 17c chip (4121/222) — 2500

Figure, blanc de chine, well modeled, of Kuan Ti seated on low throne, drape lion skin, 17c, 14½ dam, chip (4121/223) — 1100

Figure, famille verte, of Lit'ai Po drunken poet, wine jug, 19c, rep (4121/232) — 650

Figure, Blanc de chine, of a Lo Han, clasping scroll, 18 - 19c 4½ (4223/579) — 2000

Figure, Blanc de chine, of Kuan Yin on Throne, with chubby boy, ca1700 chip, repaired 14¾ (4223/576) — 1000

Figure, Blanc de chine, of Kuan Yin, seated, 18 - 19c 6¼ (4223/578) — 550

Figure, Blanc de chine, of Kuan Yin, seated, ca1700 9⅛ hand missing (4223/572) — 700

Figure, Blanc de chine, Ta Mo, holding scroll, 19c 9½ scroll broken (4223/580) — 650

Figure, Ho family, blanc de chine, of Kuan Yin seated on rockwork platform, 18c, dam (4121/224) — 950

Figure, San Ts'ai biscuit, glazed, of Kuan Ti, God of war, 18c (4121/228) — 550

Figures, pair, Blanc de chine, elephants, 19c 3 (4223/582) — 950

Fu lion figure, turquoise glazed, 19c, 9½, chip (4144/422) — 40

Group, blanc de chine, well modeled, Taoist divinity Hsi Wang, 18c, 15¾ (4121/225) — 2900

I-Hsing, covered box, archaistic bronze form, 19c, H2 (4144/431) — 325

I-Hsing, teapot, E20c, 5⅛, chip (4144/439) — 200

I-Hsing, teapot green enameled, 19c, 3 (4144/434) — 325

I-Hsing, teapot rose mallow shape small, 19c, 2¼ (4144/436) — 500

I-Hsing, vessel, animal form, 19c, 4, chip (4144/432) — 550

I-Hsing, Teapot, fruit and nuts, L18-E19c, 5, chip (4144/433) — 375

Jar, blue and white, prunus blossoms on 'cracked ice' ground, K'ang Hsi period, 8½, fine (4174/19) — *1000*

Jar (4174/19)

Dish quatrefoil (4174/12)

Jar, blue and white large, scrolling lotus blossoms, 19c 18 (4223/645) — 375

Jar, blue and white, ovoid, with a mounted official, soldiers, transitional period, 9, imp (4174/24) — 1500

Jar, covered, blue and white, cobalt blue with fans and precious objects, K'ang Hsi, 1½ (4174/21) — 2100

Jar, iron rust, reddish brown glaze, flared rim edged in white, 18c 5 (4223/557) — 450

Jar, red flambe, brilliant deep red tone, 11, chip ground down (4174/35) — 1300

Jardiniere, carved celadon, angular fretwork, pair of dragon heads, 10¾, chip, L18c (4154/424) — 450

Kendi incised decoration, white glaze, two dragons rising above waves, L17 - 18c (4223/570)   375

Kettle and cover, Ho, blue and white, on 4 legs, in 15c style, Tao Kuang seal mark, 8, dam (4174/13)   700

Libation cups, pair, blanc de chine, dragon emerging from clouds, creamy white, 18c (4121/226)   750

Py Tai figure, Blanc de chine, God fo Happiness, leaning on his bag of wind, holding pearl, 5¾, 18c (4154/421)   350

Sacrificial vessel and cover, Kuei, oval bowl raised on pedestal base, 19c, 9½, rep (4144/418)   300

Sauce dish, copper-red glazed, rim and base glazed white, Yung Cheng Period, fine, 8¼ (4147/36)   1300

Stemcups, blue and white, pair, each with Buddhist inscription, K'ang Hsi, 5¼, glaze, chip (4174/22)   1100

Tou Ts'ai bowl, four fruit and flower medallions, 18c, 6, chip (4144/462)   150

Vase, transitional, scene of 6 sages, ca1645, 15 (4174/26)   1800

Vase, baluster, imitation Kuan Yao, pale bluish gray glaze, black stained crackle, 6, L28/E19c (4154/432)   300

Vase, black glazed, miniature, 18c, 4¾ (4144/421)   150

Vase, blue glazed, ovoid shape brigh cobalt blue glaze, wood cover, 19c, small chip rim (4223/558)   180

Vase, bottle shape copper red, deep red tone to white, L18 - 19c (4223/562)   500

Vase, bottle-form, copper-red, underglaze-blue, Yung Cheng mark, 19c, chip, 14½ (4144/402)   300

Vase, bottle-form green glazed, 19c, 10¼ (4144/413)   300

Vase, brown glazed, gold splashed, 19c, 11¾ (4144/419)   175

Vase, coral ground, landscape, pale green andd grayish blue enamel, 7⅛, 18c (4154/445)   425

Vase, coral red, with gilt decoration small, 18c, 6½, hc (4144/409)   175

Vase, famille rose, two of eight, Taoist Immortals, 18c 11½ (4223/598)   325

Vase, flambe glazed, rich, thick red glaze raspberry tones 18c, 7⅛ (4121/215)   700

Vase, flambe glazed, rounded sides, cylindrical neck, 19c 14¼ foot chip (4223/566)   375

Vase, hu, crackle-glazed, pale bluish-grey glaze, Tao Kuang Period, 12 (4174/31)   1500

Vase, incised turquoise glazed, bronze form, pear shape, peony scroll, 18c, H7½ (4121/213)   125

Vase, lobed celadon, eight shaped lobes, 17½, chip, 18c (4154/429)   425

Vase, pear shaped, Sang DeBoeuf, standing on concave pedastal foot, trumpet shaped mouth, 12⅜, 18/19c (4154/439)   700

Vase, powder blue-ground rouleau, with carp and gilt water weeds, K'ang Hsi Period, 18½ (4174/6)   1600

Vase, powder blue-ground rouleau, with 4 large iron-red carp, K'ang Hsi Period, 18½, fine (4174/5)   3000

Vase, purple glaze, pear shaped, slender neck, counter sunk foot, 6, 18c (4154/446)   675

Vase, rare, blue and white, double gourd, 3 boys playing, K'ang Hsi period, 11½, dam (4174/25)   2700

Vase, robin's egg glazed, ovoid form, 18c, 15½, cr (4174/32)   1600

Vase, rouleau, powder blue-glazed, small, K'ang Hsi Period, 7⅞ (4174/27)   1100

Vase, small blue and white, soft paste, phoenix bird in garden landscape, 18c, 10 chip (4174/15)   700

Vase, soft paste, blue and white, continuous river and mountain landscape, 18c, 15 staining (4174/14)   950

Vase, tall slender incised Te'hua, flowerheads and foliage, prlion mask handles, 18c 13⅛ (4223/577)   1600

Vase, tea dust, olive green tone, Ch'ien Lung period, 12¾, chip (4174/34)   4000

Vase, twin fish copper red glazed, two carp standing on their tails, 19c (4223/563)   375

Vase, twin fish, blue glazed, two carp standing on tails, 19c, 9¾ chip at lip (4121/211)   *250*

Vase, Blanc de chine, beaker, bulb flanked by grooved bands, ca1700 (4223/571)   400

Vase, Ju-Yao, pale blue glaze, bronze form imitation, strap handles, Ch'ien Lung Period, 10, res (4174/30)   5200

Vase, Mei P'ing, celadon-glazed, small, translucent pale green glaze, 18c, 7¼ (4174/28)   700

Vase, Yen Yen, blue and white, lotus blossoms on scrolling stems, K'ang Hsi, 17½ (4174/23)   3300

Vase, Yen Yen, mirror black, interior and base glazed white, 19c, 23, chip (4144/420)   475

Vases, blue and white, baluster, pair, each with 6 landscape panels, K'ang Hsi period, 18½, chip (4174/18)   2100

Vases, blue and white, massive pair, scenes of court life, K'ang Hsi Period, 37, chip (4174/17)   *11000*

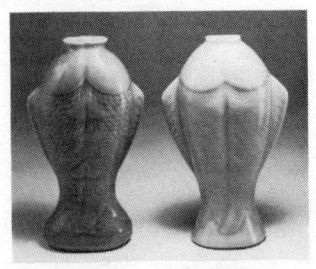

Vase
(4121/211)

Vases
(4174/17)

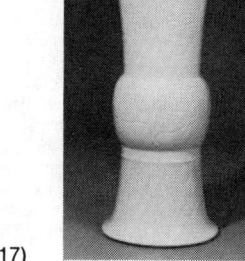

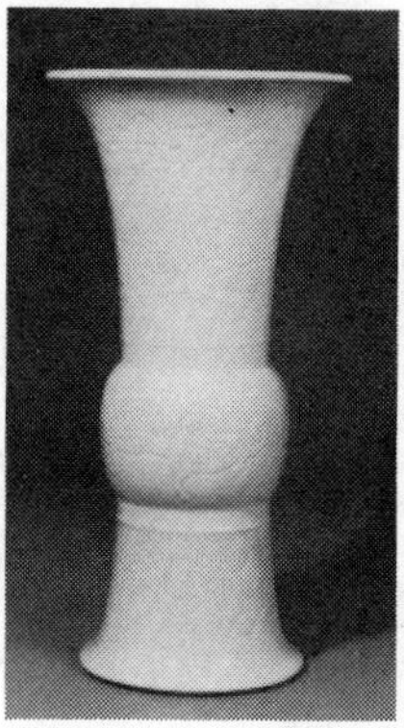

Beaker
(4121/219)

Vases, coral ground, famille rose, elaborate flower filled baskets, L19c 26½ (4223/595) — 3900
Vases, pair 'Famille Verte' Riverboat festival, L19c 23½ each with cracks (4223/605) — 1400
Vases, pair blue ground polychrome, enamelled, 2 panels of court figures, 19c 23½ cracks, rim chip (4223/604) — 375
Vases, pair large gold dragon, pair of dragons, L19c (4223/608) — 1100
Vases, pair polychrome enamel, Eight Immortalsight immortals, L19c 24 (4223/607) — 650
Wen Chang figure, Blanc de chine, The God of Literature, wearing official court dress, 8⅞, 18c, chip (4154/419) — 325
Wine cups, famille rose, floral sprays, E19c, 2⅜ (4121/257) — 450

K'ang Hsi Period

Basin, famille verte painted, decorated, scene of numerous courtesans, 15¼, 2 rim chip (4121/235) — 6700
Beaker, carved porcelain, blue-gray glaze, landscape scenes, 16⅛, glaze chip fine (4121/219) — *5000*
Beaker, octagonal blue and white, panels of flowers, branches, scroll border, 20½ rim chip, drilled (4121/293) — 375
Beakers, pair blue and white large, scene court ladies, 19, chip (4121/291) — 5250
Bottle, blue and white, gold decorated, hanging musical stones, scroll, 8⅝ (4121/284) — 300
Bottles, pear shape, famille verte, decorated with spirited fu dogs, 11 1, res (4121/245) — 4200
Bowl, blue and white 'Kang' five frolicking spotted deer, landscape, 6¾ (4223/640) — 900
Bowl, covered famille verte, rare, deep circular, tripod supports, 7¼, 1 handle repaired (4121/243) — 1000
Bowl, covered, famille verte, large, bright enamels, 2 birds on rockwork, 8½ (4121/247) — 3200
Bowl, covered, Famille Verte, floral sprays, chicken finial, 10 (4154/495) — 900
Bowl, powder blue, gold decorated, deep rounded sides, landscape, 7¼, gilding rubbed (4242/49) — 750
Bowl, Famille-verte, sage on donkey, 2 attendants, landscape, 7½, chip (4242/23) — 400
Box and cover, powder blue glazed, seal paste, circular form, wave scroll on top, 3, fine (4121/214) — 450
Brushpot, (Pi Tung), powder blue, small, jet black glaze showing traces of gilt, landscape, 5⅛ hc (4154/452) — 250
Casket and cover, famille juane, pierced trellis work, translucent yellow glaze, 13¼, chip, rare (4121/240) — 3500
Cha-tou imperial yellow, engraved restored-chip, 3⅜ (4144/405) — 125
Condiment set 8 piece, partial, two song bird perched in flowering branches, 5⅛ - 4⅝ (4223/616) — 750
Cups, pair, Cafe Au Lait famille, verte ground, (4223/623) — 120
Dish, blue and white, camelia blossom in center, 13⅞ (4242/10) — 1300
Dish, blue and white, large stylized lotus blossoms, 15¼, chip (4242/15) — 300
Dish, blue and white, very large, pattern of peonies and daisy like flowers, 19¾ glaze chip (4223/643) — 1800
Dish, dragon, yellow ground, 'flaming pearl' center, 4¼, crack (4242/36) — 425
Dish, famille verte and powder blue, fisherman in boat displaying catch, 16 rim restored large (4121/252) — 850
Dish, famille verte and powder blue, large floral, landscape, 16⅛, rim restored, large (4121/251) — 950
Dish, famille verte, large, enameled, 2 phoenix birds, garden setting, 14, chip (4121/246) — 1400

Dish, famille verte, painted, mythical battle scene, 21⅞, finely, massive (4121/244) 14000
Dish, famille verte, very large, flowers and butterflies, birds, beasts, 20¾, res (4121/248) 4000
Dish, flower shape, blue and white, insect, flowering peonies, 11⅜, chip (4242/14) 450
Dish, iron red, and underglaze, blue dragon, crested waves, 3 dragons, 7⅛ chip, restored, scratching
  (4223/593) 700
Dish, octagonal, enameled gilded, porcelain, flower sprays, 12⅞, rubbed, glaze gaps (4121/270) 450
Dish, saucer, blue and white, deer beneath pine tree, 7¾ rim chip (4223/636) 325
Dish, saucer, copper-red, shallow rounded sides, white edge rim, 6⅛ (4242/44) 1150
Dish, saucer, tou ts'ai, scrolling red berries, green leaves, 8 (4242/31) 2000
Dish, saucer, Famille Verte, Fu lion in center, 15⅛, chip (4154/492) 1300
Dish, Famille-verte, spotted yellow deer, pine tree, 12⅜, chip (4242/26) 1100
Dish, Wu Ts'ai, dragon and phoenix, flowers, 10¾, rim chip (4121/267) 350
Dish, Wu Ts'ai dragon and phoenix, central medalion, 2⅝, chip (4242/27) 2700
Dishes, blue and white, Chinese garden scene, 10⅜, chip (4121/295) 800
Dishes, pair powder blue ground, famille, verte, floral, 11 rim chip 1 broken repaired (4223/592) 175
Dishes, pair, blue and white, petal molded sides, travelers, mountain landscape, 8⅛ (4242/13) 800
Dishes, pair, incised dragon, 'flaming pearl' center, yellow ground, 4¼, cracks (4244/35) 750
Dishes, pair, petal fluted, blue and white, chrysanthemums and peonies, 9¾, chip (4242/12) 550
Dishes, pair, power blue, gold decorated, lobed sides, flat flared rim, 8¼ (4242/48) 1200
Dishes, pair, Famille Verte, central medallion with an equestrian, 8⅞ (4154/493) 450
Dishes, pair, Famille-verte, spotted yellow deer, pine tree, 8⅞, chip (4242/25) *1400*

Vase (4242/16)

Vases (4121/249)

Dishes (4242/25)

Famille verte, cup red, ground unusual, chip, res (4144/442) 170
Famille verte, deep dish octagonal, 12¼ chip (4144/446) 375
Famille verte, dish, garden landscape of pierced rock, chip, res (4144/443) 350
Famille verte, jar ovoid wood stand, 9 (4144/445) 1000
Figure, glazed biscuit, of Li Tai Po, The Drunken T'ang Poet, 7½ (4223/615) 800
Fu Lion, glazed biscuit, glazed green, aubergine, yellow white, 5½ (4223/614) 450
Garniture, 3 piece, famille verte, pr tall neck vases, small mouthed jar, 10¼, 12¾, chip, restored
  (4121/242) 1400
Jar, blue and white, two panel of figures, landscape, 7⅝ crack (4223/637) 250
Jar, blue and white, 3 court ladies, landscape, 5, small chip (4242/11) 170
Jar, blue and white 'Hawthorne' large blossoms on blue, 8⅝ (4223/639) 250
Jar, ginger, blue and white porcelain, mountain landscape, 8¼ (4121/281) 950
Jar, incised white, pattern of chrysanthemum scroll, 10 (4121/218) 2300
Jar, ovoid, blue and white, well painted, magpies on flowering branch, 9¼ (4121/280) 850
Jar, pale lavender glazed, 'hundred rib' rim reduced capped in silver, 6⅞, rim chip (4121/212) 2900

Jar and cover, blue and white 'Hawthorne' decorated with white prunus, 9⅝ (4223/638) — 700

Jar and cover, famille verte, decorated, maiden and her attendants, in garden, 14, enamels restored (4121/250) — 2200

Stand, turquoise glazed, rectangular, 4 upturned feet, 8½ some scratching (4223/559) — 525

Tou Ts'ai dish, two waterfowl with flowering lotus, chip (4144/461) — 225

Vase, 'clobbered' underglazed, copper red decorated, 7 chip rim (4121/273) — 700

Vase, 'noir miroir' shperical body, slender neck, jet black glaze, 14½ (4121/220) — 3600

Vase, baluster, famille verte, panels of 'Hundred Antiques' some repainting, 21¼ neck repaired (4223/622) — 950

Vase, beaker blue and white, floral scrolls, 8⅝ base cracked small (4223/629) — 250

Vase, beaker blue and white, three medallions of court ladies, flowers, 10 (4121/292) — 1900

Vase, beaker shaped blue and white, boatmen on lakes in landscape, 18¼ chip, crack (4223/628) — 1300

Vase, beaker, blue and white, peony sprays, songbirds, 16½, hair cracks (4154/470) — 850

Vase, biscuit ground rouleau, rare, two pheasants in angular rockwork, flowers, 17½, cracks (4121/227) — 5000

Vase, blue and white Yen Yen, mountain landscape, 18 neck restored (4223/632) — 375

Vase, blue glazed, underglaze decorated, song, birds, prunus branches, 8, lip crack (4154/447) — 300

Vase, bronze form, copper red, mask and ring handles, white in coppered ground, 6¼, rare (4154/444) — 1300

Vase, carved celadon, decorated by writhing Chih Lung pale green gray glaze, 16½, lip ground down, star crack (4154/430) — 500

Vase, celadon, carved with 2 dragons, 8 (4144/403) — 800

Vase, double gourd, famille verte, dragon boat festival, 26¾ upper broken restored (4223/618) — 3300

Vase, double gourd, famille verte, well painted flower and stems, 26½ restored, chip (4223/621) — 1800

Vase, enameled rouleau, iron red and green, river landscape, 11 (4121/269) — 2400

Vase, famille verte, decorated with fantastic sea battle, 18, fine (4121/234) — 6000

Vase, famille verte, deer and crane decoration, 9 (4121/237) — 1700

Vase, famille verte, deer and crane decoration, 9, rep (4121/238) — 550

Vase, famille verte, loose ring handles, figural panels, 9¼, res (4121/241) — 400

Vase, famille verte (attractive), ovoid body, blackbird, kingfisher, 17½, chip (4121/239) — 6250

Vase, famille verte, rouleau, scene, 2 figures, wolf-like beast, 17¾ (4121/233) — 5000

Vase, famille verte, Yen Yen, finely, scene of court dignitary, crackle stained, 17½ (4121/236) — 1700

Vase, pear shaped, blue and white, peony scroll on compressed globular body, 8⅛, original glaze cracks (4121/278) — 850

Vase, powder blue glazed, landscape, 9 short crack at lip (4121/285) — 600

Vase, rouleau, blue and white, fisherman seated, mountain landscape, 10⅝, chip (4242/18) — 1800

Vase, rouleau, blue and white, princess and attendants, 17⅜, crackling (4242/19) — 1000

Vase, with gilt metal mount, famille verte, warrior chasing rabbit, 9¾ neck cut down (4223/620) — 350

Vase, yen yen, blue and white, 4 court scenes, 17¾, chip (4242/20) — 950

Vase, yen yen, painted blue and white, court official giving audience, 31, imp (4242/21) — 3600

Vase, yen yen, Famille-verte, painted, fishermen in their boats, 28¼, chip (4242/22) — 4200

Vase, yen-yen, blue and white, 8 Taoist immortals, 17¾ (4242/16) — *1600*

Vase, Rouleau, celadon carved, dense patter of peony, 10 Fire speckling (4223/552) — 700

Vase, Wu Ts'ai well painted, scene courtesan kneeling, front dignitary, 10⅝, lip rim reduced (4121/268) — 700

Vase, Yen Yen, blue and blue, porcelain, birds, flowering trees and shrubs, 27¼, chip (4154/468) — 700

Vase, Yen Yen, blue and white, penciled peony blossoms, scrolling stems, 17⅛ (4121/294) — 1600

Vase, Yen Yen, blue and white porcelain, vivid cobalt, birds in flight, 28¼ (4154/467) — 950

Vase, Yen Yen, blue ground, white plum branches, 17½, restored rim (4154/472) — 400

Vase, Yen Yen, blue ground, prunus decorated, blossoming white plum branches, 17¼ (4154/471) — 1600

Vases, bottle shaped, pair, Dutch decorated, blue, white and copper red, 3 Fu lions, 7½, unusual (4154/490) — 500

Vases, pair, bright enamel and gilt highlight, 10¾ - 11 neck cutoff restuck (4223/619) — 1000

Vases, pair blue and white, pr. gilded dragons scroll handles, 9¾, glaze chip unusual (4121/283) — 600

Vases, pair blue and white, baluster, with covers, river, mountain landscape, 17 crack, chip (4223/642) — 1200

Vases, pair, Ormolu mounted famille, verte' flowers of 4 seasons, 12⅝ crack to one (4223/625) — 925

Vases, pear shaped, pair, famille verte, iron red, flower, butterflies, 10 res (4121/249) — *2000*

Vases, Famille Verte, bulb neck, pair, freize of floral scroll, 7⅞, res (4154/491) — 400

Yung Cheng Period

Bowl, bulb, quatrefoil, imitation Chun Yao, Sung shape, reddish purple, flambe glaze, 11¾, rep (4154/442) — 1000

Bowl, copper red, rounded sides, lipless rim, rimless foot, 5⅛ (4121/217) — 900

Bowl, molded, Clair DeLune, three stylized bat and gourd vine motifs, 6⅛, repaired (4154/451) — 300

Bowl, tou-ts-ai, Buddhist emblems, tied with fluttering ribbons, 5¼ (4242/30) — 3800

Bowl, yellow ground, six archaistic dragons, 9⅛ rim chip (4223/589) — 450

Cup, stem, copper-red glaze, foot glazed white, 4¼ (4242/43) — 3200

Cups, pair, blue glazed, flared sides, interior glazed white, 2⅞ (4242/46) — 3200

Dish, peach, Famille-rose, shallow flared sides, 8⅛, cracks (4242/38) — 4000

Dish, saucer, blue glazed, shallow flared sides, white rim, 6⅞, chip (4242/47) — 450

Dish, saucer, copper-red, shallow flared sides, 5⅞, chip (4242/45) — 300

Dish, saucer, famille rose, painted, scene of seated woman, holding small boy, 7⅞, small hc (4121/261) — 800

Dish, saucer, incised, yellow glazed, floral sprays, pair dragons, 12⅝, chip (4154/454) — 1500

Dish, Famille Rose, with duck and drake swimming, 9, cracked (4154/478) — 275

Dishes, pair Ming style blue and white, bouquet of lotus blossoms, floral scroll, 3½ star crack, ground rim (4121/288) — 700

Flask, moon, flambe glazed, peach shaped panels, downturned loop handles, 9⅞, 1 handle missing (4154/443) — 425

Vase, quadruple, immitation Kuan-Yao, four small vases, pinched mouths, bluish-gray glaze, 3¾, chip and cracks, rare (4154/433) — 525

Vase, sperical, imperial yellow, glazed porcelain, with cylindrical holder, 7½ surface scratching (4223/554) — 3800

Ch'ien Lung Period

Bowl, copper red, 7⅝, chip (4144/406) — 325

Bowl, dragon, blue and white, deep ogee shape, dragons, 6¾, chip (4242/7) — 700

Bowl, famille rose, small, fruit and flowers, butterflies, 4¼, star crack not through (4121/262) — 800

Bowl, tou ts-ai, 2 dragons rising from waves, 13, cracks (4242/29) — 1500

Dish, green dragon, scaley dragon pursuit of the 'flaming pearl' 6⅞ hc rim chip (4121/277) — 400

Dish, green dragon, scaley dragon pursuit of the 'flaming pearl' 6⅞ hc (4121/276) — 550

Famille rose, altar stands, pair, 7½, chip-res (4144/451) — 375

Figures, pair, blue and white, laughing boys, 4¾ (4121/289) — 1500

Pi tung, Famille-rose enamel, 2 partially inrolled, scrolls, 3⅜ (4242/32) — 525

Saucer dishes, copper-red, pair, large, 8¼ (4144/407) — 425

Vase, carved and molded celadon, massive, pedestal foot, scroll handles, 29¾, dam (4121/207) — 1100

Vase, carved celadon, large, Hu shape, butterfly handles, lotus scroll, leaves, 19, fine (4121/206) — 2000

Vase, copper red, compressed body, steeply sloping shoulders, 6⅝, small, unusual (4121/216) — 300

Vase, famille rose, small, chrysanthemum and peony blossoms, 7¼ (4121/260) — 350

Vase, flambe glazed, double loop handles with scroll terminals, 8½ 1 handle repair, chip (4223/565) — 500

Vase, hundred deer, numerous, deer, rocky landscape, 17¾, fine, rare (4121/253) — 60000

Vase, lobed, famille rose, branche of garden, flowers, 12 (4223/597) — 1600

Vase, molded celadon, potted baluster form, writhing dragons, 10 (4242/40) — 6000

Vase, pair double gourd, celadon glaze, spherical lower bulb, pear shaped upper, 12⅞, chip, fine (4121/208) — 18000

Vase, pear shape, copper red, famille rose enamels, insects and flowers, 12 (4223/560) — 800

Vase, tou ts-ai, large exotic flowers on scrolling leafy stems, 21, cracks (4242/28) — 1900

Vase, twin carp celadon, two fish molded side by side, 9⅞, rim chip (4121/210) — 425

Vase, Ming style carved celadon, three bands of raised key-fret, 8¾, small chip (4121/204) — 650

Chia Ch'ing Period

Bowl, turquoise ground enamels, scrolling lotus 11¼ rim restored, (4223/594) — 425

Dishes, pair, yellow ground, 2 dragons, 4 flying cranes, 5⅝ (4242/37) — 1500

Dragon dish, blue and white, with coiled dragon pursuing 'flaming pearl' chip, D10 (4144/400) — 325

Fruit and flowers, butterflies (4121/263) — 250

Vase, bottle form, flambe glaze, 16 (4144/408) — 500

Tao Kuang Period

Bowl, enameled Cafe Au Lait ground, Small bell shape, flower, poem, 4½ (4223/587) — 260

Bowl, famille rose, molded, narrow band of formal peony scroll, 8⅞, unusual (4121/264) — 260

Bowls, pair, celadon ground iron red, decoration 5 stylized phoenix birds, 5¾ (4223/586) — 425

Bowls, Ming style blue and white, pair, lotus blossoms, leaves, 3¾ (4121/290) — 800

Dish, saucer, pair, imperial yellow, clear yellow glazed exterior, 6½ 1 chip, crack (4223/555) — 425

Jar, leys, blue and white 'Cha Tou' floral scroll, 3¼ small (4223/646) — 900

Jar and cover, green dragon, two dragons, pursuit of 'pearls' tapered base, 8⅝, fine (4121/274) — 2300

T'ung Chih Period

Bowls, ruby enameled, pair, T'ung Chih mark 6⅛ (4144/411) — 225

Bowls, ruby red, glazed, pair, 6⅛, 1 dam (4144/410) — 175

Kuang Hsu Period

Bowl, blue and white, band of scrolling blossoms, band of key fret, 16⅝, rim chip, base cracked (4242/1) — 1000

Bowls, pair, Famille Rose, scrolling lotus spray rising from frothy waves, 7 (4154/486)   650
Dish, iron red decoration Cafe Au Lait, ground, 3 grups of 5 bats, 9 (4223/588)   225
Dish, saucer, yellow, ground dragon, dragon pursuing the 'Flaming Pearl' 6¾ (4223/590)   350
Dragon dishes, pair, yellow ground, dragons on interior, cranes on exterior, 5½ (4144/472)   600
Saucers, pair, enameled porcelain, ear of corn, branch of red berries, 5⅞ (4223/611)   200
Wu Ts'ai dragon and phoenix bowl, with coiled dragon on interior, 5¾ (4144/471)   225

ENAMELS

An assortment

Vase, polychrome enamel, historical battle scenes, L19c, 30 (4144/469)   1100
Vases, polychromed enamel, pair, elaborately dressed warrior on each, 19c, 12, 1 hc (4144/468)   275
Wine cups, white enamel, pair, orchid and other flowering sprays, E19c, 2¼, unusual (4144/467)   100

Cloisonne enamels

Basin, late Ming Dynasty, two writhing dragons, 17c, 13⅞, dam (4214/26)   600
Basin, Ming Dynasty, 17c, 13⅞, dam (4214/27)   550
Box and cover, shaped as bat, foliated wings, 12¼, worn, 18c (4242/235)   1300
Brushpots, pair, songbirds perched on peach blossoms, Chia Ching Period, dam (4214/30)   2000
Candlesticks, pair, large, pricket, dark blue, polychrome lotus scroll, 21 12, Ch'ien Lung/Chia Ching (4154/314)
  2000
Four-panel, dragon screen, turquoise, dark blue, red, black, green, 28½, 7½ ea., L19/E20c (4159/38)
  1200
Goose, standing, head turned, beak open, 11¾, rep, pitting, L18/E19c (4261/160)   *1200*
Jardiniere, with semi-precious plant, tree bearing jewel blossoms, 18½, chip, pcs miss (4214/101)   450
Pilgrim flask, Ming Dynasty, 17c, 9¾, rep, part missing (4214/25)   1100
Square bowls, bronze gilt, minor repairs, Chien Lung Period, 4⅞-2⅝ (4214/28)   1000
Tripod censer, two gilt-metal dragon handles, Chien Lung, 4⅛, dam (4214/29)   275
Vase, ovoid shape, fruiting peaches, citron, pomegranates, 18, chip, L18c (4242/234)   *2000*

Goose (4261/160)

Vase (4242/234)

Vases, pair, with birds and butterflies flying around flowers, 12½, 19c (4154/313)   600
Wine vessel, ritual, Chueh, three splayed legs, ca1800, 6¼, res (4214/31)   200

Painted

Basin, Canton, pair Mandarin ducks, pond, lotus, Diam 17¾, L18/E19c (4261/158)   650
Brazier, Canton, 'famille rose' riverscapes, 5½ x 10, E18c (4261/157)   2100
Tray, Canton, rectangular, 4 feet, 3 scholars contemplating, garden, W10¼, res, chip, 18c (4261/159)
  550

Chia Ch'ing Period

Dish, cloisonne, enamel, Ming, red dragon, waves, blossoming magnolia, 19¾, large (4121/74)   1600

Wan Li Period

Vase, fierce dragon and 'pearl' cloud scrolls, 15 (4242/233)   900

Ch'ing Dynasty

Dish, sauce, canton enamel, young scholar and court lady, yellow ground, 19c (4223/437)   225
Dishes, sauce, pair Canton enamel, river, mountain landscape, 18c, 8⅜, both cracks (4121/80)   800
Lanterns, pair reticulated cloisonne, enamel, shells and fish, lotus scroll, drilled, now with frosted
glass, L18c, 15 (4223/436)   4600

Ch'ien Lung Period

Ewer, covered, painted enamel, tall, slender, 2 monster masks, loose ring, handles, 21¼, rim
restored, rubbed (4121/79)   2200
Incense burners, pair, cloisonne, enamel, modeled bird, head 1 side, folded wings, 4½, restored (1)
(4121/75)   1500
Jar, cloisonne enamel, four lotus blossoms, dark blue ground, 4¾, enamel flaked (4121/77)   1100

FURNITURE

Assorted periods

Cabinet-on-stand, hardwood, carved, ebonized, 52⅞ x 29¼,19c (4148/275)   2100
Chairs, arm, pair, red/black lacquer, solid scrolled splat, solid seat, round legs, 19c (4157/186)   6300
Chairs, arm, pair, Huang Huali, yoke-shaped toprail, solid cane seat, turned legs, 17/18c (4159/185)   6500
Sofa, hardwood, scrolled backrest and arms, loose cushions, 7' 5= (4121/311)   600
Stand, hardwood, square top, pierced frieze and stretcher, 38 x 14¾ , 19c (4159/171)   950
Stands, 2-tiered, pair, hardwood, rectangular, pierced frieze, stretcher, square legs, 32 x 17¾ x 13½,
19c (4159/182)   1300
Stands, 2-tiered, pair, hardwood, 2 rectangular tiers, square legs, 31½ x 16½ x 12, L18/E19c
(4159/183)   900
Table, altar, hardwood, rectangular, scrolled pierced ends, trestle supports, 33 x 50½ x 17, 19c
(4159/181)   2600
Table, altar, mother-of-pearl-inlaid, rectangular top, trestle supports, 33¾ x 76 x 19, 18c (4159/175)   4500
Table, altar, Huang Huali, rectangular, pierced frieze, trestle supports, 36½ x 69 x 17½, 18c
(4159/177)   2800
Table, altar, Huang Huali, rectangular, pierced frieze, trestle supports, 41 x 82 x 17½, E19c
(4159/176)   2000
Table, center, hardwood, rectangular, carved frieze, square legs, 34½ x 88½ x 26½, 19c (4159/179)   2800
Table, low, cinnabar laquer, carved with figural and foliate medallions, 19c, 10-18 rep.-pcs miss
(4214/40)   650
Table, side, Huang Huali, rectangular top, scrolled ends, drawer, rounded square, legs, 33½ x 38 x
22, 18c (4159/172)   4000
Table, writing, Huang Huali, rectangular top, 2 frieze drawers, square legs, (4121/312)   5000

Ch'ing Dynasty

Armchair, reclining, rosewood, back, seat, legs, horizontal slats, 19c with restorations (4121/314)   1500
Armchairs, pair, Huang Huali, curved backrest, splat pierced a head, 18c (4121/302)   10000
Cabinet, Chinese walnut (Hu T'ao), panelled doors, inscribed, poem and 2 seals, L17-E18c, 4' 10=
(4121/298)   1100

Stand with marble basin
(4121/297)

Armchairs (4121/300)

Stand
(4121/307)

Screen, table, brass and pewter, 1 side court lady tossing arrow, other peone, 19c (4223/433) 325
Stand, circular, Huang Huali, shaped frieze and cabriole legs, leaf carved foot, 19c (4121/307) *1300*
Stand, red lacquer, rectangular top, pierced apron, scrolled feet, 37, 18c (4121/310) 2000
Stand with marble basin, hardwood, folding X-shaped stand, 19c, 24½ (4121/297) *450*
Stands, pair, hardwood, scroll carved frieze, square molded legs, 19c (4121/309) 500
Table, altar, Huang Huali, rectangular, scrolled top, pierced brackets, supports, 18c (4121/308) 6600
Table, low Chinese hardware, scrolled legs, pierced sides, 18c, 13 (4121/301) 1200
Table, low Chinese hardwood, plain frieze, square legs, 18c, 18 (4121/304) 700
Table, low Huang Huali, rectangular top scrolled ends carved supports, 18c, 31½ (4121/313) 500
Table, scroll, Chinese hardwood, five drawers, cylindrical compartments on end, 18-19c (4121/305) 1200
Table, side hardwood, open work frieze, with 2 drawers, 18c 19¼ (4121/303) 1700

IVORIES

Assorted periods

Ivory, figure of a Mei Jen standing courtesan, 10½ (4223/441) 250
Ivory, figure of Kuan Yin standing, long robe, 19c 10½ (4223/440) 425
Phoenix figures, pair, ivory, 12½ (4214/47) 600
Vases, covered ivory, pair, covered bronze-form, 15¾ (4214/48) 1200

Ming Dynasty

Group, carved, immortal, peach tree, Kuan Yin in clouds, 7½, res, rep (4261/149) 1300
Immortal, figure, holding fan, long flowing robes, 10⅜, cr (4242/237) 1350
Kuan yin figure, godddes of mercy wearing robe, 7⅝, chip (4242/236) 1350

LACQUER ITEMS

Ming Dynasty

Box and cover, painted, rounded basketweave sides, 21 x 4¾, E17c (4242/230) 3100
Panels, set of four, painted laquer, court ladies in the palace gardens, 70, late, rare (4121/81) 2400

Ch'ing Dynasty

Table, screen, rust-red lacquer ground, three court ladies seated on low benches, 17, E18c, 17⅛ age
cracks (4121/82) 850

PAINTINGS

Anonymous, 'BLUE & GREEN' STYLE MOUNTAIN LANDSCAPE, ink, color, silk, 95 x 126, 19c
(4261/54) 2200

Anonymous, ALBUM OF FOUR LANDSCAPE PAINTINGS, 18 x 12¾, Ch'ien Lung Per (4223/260) — 600
Anonymous, ANCESTER PORTRAIT, 19c, 45¾ x 23¾ (4223/307) — 375
Anonymous, ANCESTOR PORTRAIT, 56¾ x 36½, E18c (4154/20) — 3500
Anonymous, ANCESTOR PORTRAIT, 57½ x 34¾, E18c (4154/21) — 3000
Anonymous, ANCESTOR PORTRAIT, 18c, 55¾ x 36¼ (4223/273) — 4250
Anonymous, ANCESTOR PORTRAIT OF FU-LUNG-E, ink, color, paper, 49 x 25, 1846 (4261/31) — 600
Anonymous, ANCESTOR PORTRAIT, ink, color, silk, 32 x 34½, E18c (4261/27) — 750
Anonymous, ANCESTOR PORTRAIT, ink, color, silk, 66½ x 39⅝, 18c (4261/28) — 1700
Anonymous, ARHAT AND DRAGON, 18c 9¾ x 11⅜ (4223/261) — 100
Anonymous, BIRDS AND TREE PEONIES, ink, color, silk, 52½ x 28¾, 18c (4261/22) — *600*
Anonymous, BIRDS, FLOWER AND ROCK, 18c 43 x 33½ (4223/266) — 300
Anonymous, BIRDS, FLOWERS AND ROCK, ink, color, silk, 60½ x 32¼, L18/19c (4261/25) — *350*
Anonymous, BIRDS, ROCKS, AND PEONIES, ink, color, silk, 109 x 56, L19c (4261/38) — 850
Anonymous, BODHISATTVA AND ATTENDANTS, 16c, 68 x 35 (4144/248) — 750
Anonymous, BUTTERFLIES, FLOWER AND ROCK, Ch'ien Lung Period, 63½ x 18¾ (4144/267) — 1300
Anonymous, DUCKS, LOTUS AND MILLET, 17c, 105½ x 59½ (4223/247) — 3100
Anonymous, HERMIT UNDER CLIFFS, 18c, 11½ x 11¾ (4144/292) — 275
Anonymous, HSI WANG MU AND HER ATTENDANTS, K'ang Hsi Period, 71 x 35¾ (4144/256) — 800
Anonymous, HUNDRED CRANES, 70½ x 25, Ch'ien Lung Period (4154/10) — 1200
Anonymous, IMMORTALS AND PALACE LANDSCAPE, Ch'ien Lung Period, 52½ x 29½ (4144/284) — 700
Anonymous, LANDSCAPE, 19c, 51 x 19¾ (4144/315) — 400
Anonymous, LANDSCAPE WITH SCHOLARS ON A BRIDGE, ink, paper, 29 x 13½, 19c (4261/36) — 325
Anonymous, LOHAN, K'ang Hsi Period, 30 x 18½ (4144/250) — 600
Anonymous, LOTUS AND EGRETS, 18c 47½ x 15 (4223/271) — 400
Anonymous, LOTUS, CRANE, BIRD AND FISH, Ch'ien Lung Period, 63½ x 18¾ (4144/266) — 1300
Anonymous, MAGNOLIA PEONY AND ROCKS, 17c, 60½ x 33¼ (4144/247) — 600
Anonymous, NOMADIC HUNTING SCENE, 18c, 63 x 31¾ (4223/264) — 1800
Anonymous, PAINTING THE GATE, E19c, 65½ x 16½ (4144/297) — 600
Anonymous, PALACE AND MOUNTAIN LANDSCAPE, ink, color, silk, 32½ x 17, 18c (4261/14) — 425
Anonymous, POET GAZING AT THE MOON, 42 x 18, Late Ming Dynasty (4144/249) — 1400
Anonymous, PORTRAIT OF A COURT OFFICIAL, 19c, 33½ x 20⅜, Korean (4144/305) — 1600
Anonymous, PORTRAIT OF FU HSING, 89 x 41⅝ (4223/377) — 700
Anonymous, PORTRAIT OF HSIEN KU, L18c, 39½ x 17½ (4223/306) — 750
Anonymous, PORTRAIT OF LAN TS'AI HO, 44½ x 19⅝, K'ang Hsi Per (4223/272) — 1400
Anonymous, PORTRAIT OF TIEN KUAN, K'ang Hsi Period, 60¼ x 31¼ (4144/255) — 2000
Anonymous, RIVER AND MOUNTAIN LANDSCAPE, ink, color, silk, 15 x 264, L17c (4261/3) — 1900
Anonymous, RIVER LANDSCAPE IN THE STYLE OF CH'EN YU, ink, paper, 64 x 17¾, 19c (4261/35) — 225
Anonymous, RIVER LANDSCAPE, in the style Chang Lu, 16c 6⅞ x 20 (4223/241) — 325
Anonymous, RIVER LANDSCAPE, ink, color, silk, 12 x 24¾, L16/17c (4261/2) — 1600
Anonymous, SCENE OF COURT LIFE, ink, color, silk, 52 x 104¼, L17/18c (4261/7) — 3200
Anonymous, SCENES FROM THE WESTERN PARADISE, ink, color, silk, 12½ x 149, L19c (4261/53) — *800*
Anonymous, SCHOLAR AND ATTENDANT GAZING AT AUTUMN LEAVES, 19c, 55½ x 20½ (4223/282) — 400

Anonymous
(4261/53)

Anonymous, SCHOLAR WALKING BY A RIVER, 9¼ x 7¾ (4144/293) — 80
Anonymous, SCHOLARS CONTEMPLATING THE TAO, ink, color, silk, 37½ x 17¼, 18c (4261/18) — 325
Anonymous, SCHOLARS CONVERSING, ink, color, silk, 51¾ x 22¼, L17/E18c (4261/10) — 200
Anonymous, SET FOUR BIRD AND FLOWERS PAINTING, L17-18c 87=L (4223/268) — 900
Anonymous, SET OF FOUR CONTINUOUS SCENES OF FIGURES AND GARDEN PAVILLIONS, 38 x 18¾, L18/19c (4261/30) — 1900
Anonymous, SET OF FOUR LANDSCAPES WITH FIGURES AND PAVILLIONS, 78¾ x 22, 18c (4261/16) — 600
Anonymous, SPRING PLOWING, 18c 7¼ x 68¾ (4223/259) — 300
Anonymous, TAOIST IMMORTAL, 58 x 35, E18c (4154/22) — 2700
Anonymous, THE TEN GUARDIANS OF HELL, 18c, 77 x 39½ (4144/283) — 1400
Anonymous, THE THREE RAMS SAN YANG, L17-18c, 18¼ x 11⅜ (4223/263) — 325
Anonymous, THE TORTURES IN HELL, ink, color, silk, 54 x 30½, L16/E17c (4261/9) — 1400
Anonymous, TREES, MOON AND WATER BUFFALO WITH ATTENDANT, 17c, 41¼ x 9⅜ (4223/245) — 400
Anonymous, TWO COURT OFFICIALS AND HORSE, 19c, 15 x 17¼ (4223/302) — 275
Anonymous, TWO LADIES IN GARDEN LANDSCAPE, L18-19c 57½ x 19¼ (4223/267) — 200
Anonymous, TWO WOMEN, 57 x 16¼, 18c (4154/19) — 400
Ch'a Shih Piao, style, RIVER LANDSCAPE, 9¼ x 14¼, 19c (4144/310) — 300
Ch'en Heng-K'o, CALLA LILY, 45½ x 12¼ (4153/21) — 600
Ch'en Hung-Shou, SEVEN SAGES OF THE BAMBOO GROVE, 48 x 16½, 1628 (4154/30) — 150
Ch'en Mwo, LANDSCAPE, 46½ x 17 (4223/361) — 500
Ch'en P'u, MOUNTAIN LANDSCAPE, 38 x 18¾ (4153/31) — 300
Ch'en Yun-Chang, MOUNTAINS, RIVER AND SCHOLAR, ink, color, paper, 43½ x 13¼, 1937 (4261/83) — 200
Ch'eng Chiai Tzu, COURT LADY BY A POND, dated 1975 27¼ x 12⅝ (4223/346) — 1050
Ch'eng Chiai Tzu, POETS DRINKING, dated 1948 24¾ x 31 (4223/347) — 1600
Ch'i Pai Shih, BROAD BEAN PLANT, 38¼ x 13, 1948 (4223/316) — 750
Ch'i Pai Shih, CRABS, 31¾ x 11¾ (4144/326) — 1100
Ch'i Pai Shih, GRAPEVINE AND GRASSHOPPER, 1950, 40½ x 13¼ (4144/324) — 3800
Ch'i Pai Shih, GRASSHOPPER AND AUTUMN LEAVES, 1951, 39 x 13 (4144/323) — 1800
Ch'i Pai Shih, MOUSE AND LAMP, 1944, 38¾ x 13¼ (4144/325) — 1600
Ch'i Pai Shih, attrib., FRUIT AND VEGETABLES, 34½ x 11¾ (4144/327) — 400
Ch'i Pai Shih, attrib., VEGETABLES, 32 x 11¾ (4144/328) — 100
Ch'i Pai Shih, BASKET AND CRABS, 52½ x 13⅜ (4153/46) — 2600
Ch'i Pai Shih, CALTROP FRUIT d.1922, (4153/43) — 5500
Ch'i Pai Shih, LICHEE AND GREEN FRUIT d.1952 38⅜ x 13, (4153/44) — 3000
Ch'i Pai Shih, MYNAH AND AUTUMN LEAVES d.1953, 42 x 13¼ (4153/45) — 900
Ch'i Pai Shih, OLD TRUNK ENDURING FROST d.1942, 53½ x 26¼ (4153/48) — 1000
Ch'i Pai Shih, SHRIMP d.1954, 35 x 12⅝ (4153/47) — 2600
Ch'ien Feng, style, HORSES, 19c, 25 x 12½ (4144/320) — 375
Ch'ien Hsuan, style, BIRDS, FLOWERS, AND ROCK, ink, color, silk, 60½ x 32¼, L18/19c (4261/26) — 600
Ch'ien Hsuan, style, TAOIST FAIRIES CELEBRATING A BIRTHDAY, Ch'ien Lung Period, 10¾' x 8'¼' (4144/291) — 225
Ch'ien Hui-An, FIGURE IN A LANDSCAPE, ink, color, silk, 36 x 18, 1878 (4261/47) — 275

Ch'ien Hui-An, TWO LADIES CONVERSING ON A BALCONY, ink, color, paper, 15 x 9, 19c (4261/48) 300
Ch'ien King Style, RIVER LANDSCAPE, 14 x 248¾, 18c (4154/16) 950
Ch'in Tsu-Yung, attrib., LANDSCAPE, STYLE OF HUANG KUNG-WANG d.1880, 46 x 16½ (4153/25) 1100
Ch'ing Tsai, attrib, LANDSCAPE, 48 x 15¼, 19c (4154/27) 300
Ch'ini, attrib, RIVER LANDSCAPE IN THE STYLE OF CHAO LING JAN, dated 1793, 46¼ x 18 (4223/280) 1300
Chang Chih-Wan*, LANDSCAPE IN THE STYLE OF WANG YUAN-CH'I, ink, silk, 30½ x 15⅝, M19c (4261/33) 250
Chang Fu, attrib, BIRDS, PRUNUS AND PEACH BLOSSOMS, 17c, 34½ x 17 (4223/244) 600
Chang Hsing-Chieh, CRABS AND BASKET, ink, paper, 28½ x 15, 19/20c (4261/73) 425
Chang Jui-Tu, style, LANDSCAPE, 19c, 24½ x 15¾ (4144/309) 400
Chang Nan-Sha, attrib, PHEASANTS, 45½ x 18, 1776 (4154/8) 750
Chang Shan-Tzu, LANDSCAPE AND HORSES, 41½ x 19½ (4153/20) 700
Chang Ta-Ch'ien, BUDDHIST MONASTERY IN THE HILLS, 33 x 19¼ (4223/338) 1800
Chang Ta-Ch'ien, BLUE, GREEN MOUNTAINS-RIVER LANDSCAPE d.1922, 10⅜ x 9⅜ (4153/86) 800
Chang Ta-Ch'ien, COUPLET, 52½ x 12⅝ (4153/82) 500
Chang Ta-Ch'ien, COUPLET d.1959, 68½ x 18¾ (4153/84) 850
Chang Ta-Ch'ien, COUPLET d.1959, 68½ x 18¾ (4153/83) 950
Chang Ta-Ch'ien, MOUNTAINS, SCHOLARS AND PAVILION d.1924, 35½ x 17¾ (4153/85) 3600
Chang Ta-Ch'ien, STREAM, BAMBOO AND SCHOLAR d.1922, 10¾ x 9⅛ (4153/87) 1300
Chang Wu, attrib, HAWK, ROCK AND FLOWERING BRANCH, 44 x 18, Ch'ien Lung Period (4154/6) 550
Chao Ch'eng, attrib, SCHOLAR HOLDING ROCK, dated 1645, 51¾ x 20¾ (4223/248) 2800
Chao Ch'i, NARCISSUS PRUNUS AND ROCK d.1860, 54¼ x 26¾ (4153/30) 900
Chao Meng Fu, style, HORSES, 18c, 13¼ x 130¼ (4144/280) 800
Chen Kang-Hou, INSECTS ON BLOSSOMING BRANCH, 49¾ x 12¼, 19c (4154/23) 250
Chen P' In Shan, LANDSCAPES ON THE FOUR SEASONS, dated 1905 50 x 12⅜ (4223/341) 325
Chi K'ang, CARP, 38 x 19¾ (4153/123) 400
Chia P'u, attrib, TWO SONGBIRDS AND CHRYSANTHEMUMS, dated 1822 50 x 12½ (4223/286) 650
Chiang Erh-Shih, AXTER SNOW, dated 1965 21 x 59½ (4223/351) 1100
Chiang Erh-Shih, LOTUS AND BIRD, 20¾ x 61 (4223/349) 1100
Chiang Erh-Shih, RIVER LANDSCAPE, 21 x 61 (4223/350) 1300
Chiang Erh-Shih, CLIFFS, ink, color, silk, 42¾ x 34¾, 1969 (4261/63) 1000
Chiang Erh-Shih, LOTUS, ink, paper, 70 x 37, M20c (4261/64) 2000
Chiang Hsun, attrib, LANDSCAPE, 18c, 77¼ x 35¾ (4144/274) 750
Chiang Hung, attrib, BIRD, TREE, FLOWERS AND ROCK, 19c, 60¾ x 16¾ (4223/290) 400
Chiang P'u, attrib, CAT, GRAPES AND BUTTERFLIES, 23¼ x 15 (4223/270) 750
Chiao Ping-Chen, style, COURT LADIES IN A PALACE GARDEN, 18c, 39 x 12¾ (4144/285) 700
Chiau Ping-Chen, attrib, BOYS PLAYING WITH LOQUATS, 40¼ x 21, K'ang Hsi period (4223/250) 3800
Chin Ch'eng, BIRDS AND WILLOW, 35¼ x 18 (4223/320) 425
Chin Ch'eng, COURT LADY BOATING, 39⅝ x 21¼ (4223/319) 200
Chin Ch'eng, HAWK AND PINE BRANCH, 41¼ x 17 (4153/51) 425
Chin Ch'eng, SPOTTED DEER, 40¾ x 19¼ (4153/52) 125
Chin Nung, style, ALBUM OF EIGHT LEAVES OF PRUNUS, 18c, 8¼ x 11 (4144/272) 1300
Chinese School, A VIEW OF THE HARBOR AT CANTON, 13 x 36½, M19c (4149/153) 4400
Ching Kung, attrib, MOUNTAIN LANDSCAPE WITH TRAVELERS, 77 x 40¼, K'ang Hsi Per. (4223/258) 1600
Chou Ch'uan, attrib, LANDSCAPE AFTER THE STYLE OF HI TSAN, K'ang Hsi Period, 41½ x 16 (4144/245) 3000
Chou Kuang, PRUNUS, CITRUS AND NARCISSUS d.1860, 57½ x 15¾ (4153/12) 650
Chou Lien, BIRDS, PRUNUS AND FRUIT, 48¾ x 19⅝ (4153/22) 350
Chu Lun Han, attrib, LANDSCAPE WITH SCHOLAR AND TRAVELER ON A, WATER BUFFALO, 17-18c, 45 x 13½ (4223/252) 250
Chu Te Jun, style, HUNTING SCENES, 19c 13¾ x 50⅜ (4223/301) 750
Chu Tung*, LADY AND A GENTLEMAN IN A BOAT, ink, color, paper, 56 x 14, 19c (4261/45) 225
Fei Tan Hsu, attrib, PORTRAIT OF A COURTLADY, 19c, 40 x 11¼ (4223/309) 275
Feng Hsien-Shih, MOUNTAIN LANDSCAPE, ink, color, silk, 56¼ x 19, 1775 (4261/17) 300
Folding screen, painting mounted as, Chinese landscape, 19c 95 x 126 large (4223/455) 950
Fresco, Sung style, painted with seated buddha framed, 59½ x 35½ (4223/456) 850
Fu Pao Shih, LANDSCAPE, dated 1964, 17¾ x 23¼ (4223/343) 5500
Hau Pei-Jen, LANDSCAPE, dated 1961 45½ x 18¼ (4223/354) 325
Hau Pei-Jen, MOUNTAIN LANDSCAPE, dated 1956 32¾ x 22½ (4223/353) 900
Hau Pei-Jen, FRUITING GOURDS, ink, color, paper, 42 x 13, 1961 (4261/67) 450
Hau Pei-Jen, SWALLOW AND GRAPE LEAVES, ink, color, paper, 28½ x 19½, M20c (4261/65) 250
Hsi Kang, attrib, LANDSCAPE, L18-19c, 44½ x 13 (4223/278) 650
Hsiao Chen*, SAGES ENGAGED IN SCHOLARLY PURSUITS, ink, color, silk, 74¾ x 38, 1736 (4261/13) 2800

Hsiao Chien Chung, MOUNTAIN LANDSCAPE, 34¼, 14 (4223/373) 70
Hsu Hsiang, SCHOLAR ON A RIVERBANK, ink, color, silk, 11 x 11, 1879 (4261/50) 200
Hsu Pei-Hung, CAT, ink, color, paper, 42½ x 17½, 1938 (4261/56) 5000
Hsu Pei-Hung, CATS, 45½ x 17¼ (4153/65) 7000
Hsu Pei-Hung, HORSE, 23 x 9½ (4153/66) 850
Hsu Pei-Hung, ROOSTER AND ROCK, ink, color, paper, 36 x 18⅝, 1933 (4261/57) 5500
Hsu Yang,*, SCHOLAR PLAYING THE CH'IN, ink, color, silk, 23½ x 14¾, 18c (4261/12) 600
Hu Hsi-Kuei, BOYS FLYING KITS IN A GARDEN d.1882, 48¼ x 20 (4153/14) 425
Hu Kung Shou, PRUNUS, NARCISSUS AND ROCK, 19c 92¾ x 22¼ (4223/292) 1300
Hu Pei Heng, SCHOLAR GAZING AT MOUNTAIN, dated 1933 26¼ x 13 (4223/342) 850
Hu T'ieh Mei, BAMBOO, ROCK AND WOMAN, ink, paper, 50 x 13⅝, 19c (4261/40) 850
Hua T'ing, attrib, CALLIGRAPHY, L18-19c, 63¼ x 18 (4223/276) 200
Huang Ching Hu, style, BAMBOO AND MOON, 19c 19⅛ x 27¾ (4223/296) 325
Huang Pin Hung, LANDSCAPE, dated 1891, 49 x 13½ (4144/302) 2100
Huang Pin Hung, attrib, LANDSCAPE AND SCHOLAR, 27 x 13¼ (4223/317) 500
Huang Shen, attrib, ALBUM OF THE EIGHT TAOIST IMMORTALS, 18c 8⅞ x 11¾ (4223/255) 1500
Huang Shen, style, PORTRAIT OF HSU WU MU YANG, 19c, 51 x 18½ (4144/319) 150
Huo Chi Ch'ang, attrib, RIVER AND MOUNTAIN LANDSCAPE, 19c 26½ x 13 (4223/281) 150
Jen Hsun, AUTUMN GARDEN HASTENING EVENING d.1882, 13 x 51⅜ (4153/27) 2700
Jen Po Nien, PORTRAIT OF SCHOLAR, dated 1893, 24¾ x 45⅝ (4223/312) 3200
Jen Po Nien, attrib., WILLOW AND EGRETS, 19c, 62 x 16½ (4144/299) 750
K'o P'eng, LOGUATS, dated 1944 39¾ x 13¼ (4223/344) 100
Kai Ch'i*, LADIES IN A DOORWAY, ink, color, silk 27½ x 14, 1784, (4261/34) 375
Kai Ch'i, attrib., LADY AND PARROT d.1819, 39¾ x 12⅜ (4153/1) 400
Kao Ch'i-Feng, OWL AND MOON, ink, color, paper, 34¼ x 12¼, 19/20c (4261/75) 1200
Kao Chein, attrib, LANDSCAPE IN THE STYLE OF SHEN CHOU, 83 x 37, M17/18c (4154/4) 4400
Kao Hsiang, attrib., PLUM BLOSSOMS, 18c, 58¾ x 14 (4144/268) 1050
Ku Hao-Ch'ing*, BAMBOO AND ROCK, ink, paper, 67½ x 18, L18/19c (4261/39) 400
Ku Liang Chih, attrib, FALCON AND ROCK, dated 1800, 43½ x 16 (4144/298) 700
Ku Lo, attrib, SCHOLAR WRITING BY A RIVER, dated 1800, 60¼ x 17⅝ (4223/279) 500
Ku Lo, attrib., LADY ROWING ON A RIVER, Ch'ien Lung Period, 24½ x 10⅝ (4144/286) 550
Kuan Szu, MOUNTAIN LANDSCAPE, ink, color, silk, 42¾ x 4⅝, 16/17c (4261/5) 550
Kuo Ta-Wei, BLACK CAT AND PALM TREE, ink, color, paper, 52¼ x 27, 1978 (4261/69) 650
Kuo Ta-Wei, CHICKS, ink, paper, 27 x 10½, M20c (4261/70) 650

Liu Hai-Su
(4153/70)

Kuo Ta-Wei, SHRIMPS, ink, paper, 53 x 27¼, 1978 (4261/68) 700
Kuo Ta-Wei, SIAMESE CAT, ink, color, paper, 53 x 27¼, 1978 (4261/71) 600
Li Chien, attrib., SCHOLAR GAZING AT A RIVER, L18c, 27¼ x 14 (4144/290) 1000
Li Jui Ch'ing, PRUNUS, PINE AND BAMBOO, 14⅜ x 44¼ (4153/42) 350
Li Shang-Yung, CALLIGRAPHY, 66 x 34 (4153/24) 750
Li Shih-Cho, attrib., ALBUM OF EIGHT LANDSCAPE SCENES, E18c, 9¾ x 14½ (4144/276) 3000
Li Tsao*, TWO WOMEN, ink, color, paper, 41¾ x 13, 1804 (4261/41) 160
Li Yung Yun, attrib, BAMBOO, 18c, 22¾ x 15½ (4144/273) 700
Li, Ching T'ing, GRAPE AND CHICKS, 44 x 16 (4223/363) 150
Liang Teng-Min, BODHIDHARMA CROSSING A RIVER ON A REED, 55 x 25⅛ (4153/19) 1600
Lin Liang, attrib, BIRDS AND FLOWERING BRANCHES, L15-16c, 36½ x 14 (4223/242) 1800
Liu Hai-Su, LANDSCAPE IN THE STYLE OF TAO CHI, 22¾ x 17 (4153/70) *1800*

Liu Kuo-Sung, A DREAM OF THE BLUE MOUNTAIN d.1965, 23 x 36 (4153/124) — 600
Lo Hsiao-Sung, LADY AND BANANA TREE, ink, color, paper, 28¾ x 14, 1942 (4261/84) — *350*
Lu Te Chih, attrib, BAMBOO AND ROCK, 17c, 50 x 23 (4144/243) — 3300
Ma Ch'uan, style, FISH AND FLOWERS IN A BASKET, 19c, 40⅝ x 14 (4144/322) — 275
Ma Ch'uan, style, FISH AND FLOWERS IN A BASKET, 19c 40½ x 14 (4223/295) — 250
Ma Chin, ARCHER AND HORSE d.1933, 37½ x 20½ (4153/108) — 325
Ma Chin, CAMELS AND RIDER d.1925, 38 x 20⅜ (4153/104) — 350
Ma Chin, CARP d.1938, 40¾ x 19⅞ (4153/114) — 510
Ma Chin, EWE AND RAM, 39⅜ x 19¾ (4153/103) — 425
Ma Chin, HORSES d.1938, 38 x 25½ (4153/106) — 375
Ma Chin, HUNTER AND TIGER, 68⅛ x 32½ (4153/107) — 300
Ma Chin, LION, TIGER AND WATERFALL, 53 x 25¼ (4153/109) — 325
Ma Chin, PEACOCK, ROOSTER, HEN AND GRASSHOPPERS, 48 x 25¾ (4153/105) — 700
Ma Chin, ROOSTER, HEN AND CHICKS d.1938, (4153/113) — 850
Ma Chin, ROOSTER, IRIS AND ROCK d.1938, 41½ x 20¼ (4153/110) — 275
Ma Chin, ROOSTERS d.1938, 40¾ x 19¾ (4153/112) — 325
Ma Lu, MOUNTAINS AND PAVILLION, ink, color, silk, 50½ x 19½, 18c (4261/15) — 250
Ma Meng Yung, CRAB AND CHRYSANTHEMUM, dated 1928, 23⅜ x 12⅛ (4144/333) — 450
Ma Shou-Chen style, BAMBOO, ROCK AND NARCISSUS, Ch'ien Lung Period, 49 x 11¾ (4144/269) — 300
Meng Huang-Yuan, LAN TS'AI HO, ink, color, silk, 56½ x 33⅞, 1849 (4261/42) — 1100
Nineteenth Century School, LADIES IN A PAVILLION, 18 x 23 (4161/244) — 850
P'u Hsueh-Chai, LANDSCAPE, dated 1933 26¼ x 13 (4223/336) — 950
P'u Hsueh-Chai, TREE AND BIRDS, 38⅜ x 22¼ (4223/335) — 450
P'u Hsueh-Chai, HORSES, 72 x 32 (4153/79) — 600
P'u Hsueh-Chai, MONKEY AND BEES, 41¾ x 20¼ (4153/76) — *150*
P'u Hsueh-Chai, MONKEY AND ROCKS, 41 x 19½ (4153/81) — 300
P'u Hsueh-Chai, MONKEY, BEES AND FRUITING TREE, 41¾ x 20 (4153/77) — 150
P'u Hsueh-Chai, RIVER AND MOUNTAIN LANDSCAPE, 37¼ x 20¼ (4153/78) — 175
P'u Hsueh-Chai, TIGER, 70 x 25⅜ (4153/80) — 300
P'u Ju, BUTTERFLIES AND FLOWERING BRANCH, 22¾ x 12 (4144/329) — 700
P'u Ju, CALLIGRAPHY, 13¼ x 24½ (4153/73) — *225*

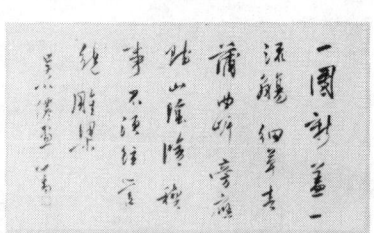

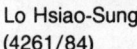

P'u Ju (4153/73)

Lo Hsiao-Sung
(4261/84)

P'u Hsueh-Chai
(4153/76)

P'u Ju, CALLIGRAPHY, ink, paper, 13 x 26½, 20c (4261/59) — 250
P'u Ju, IRIS, 22½ x 14⅝ (4153/72) — 700
P'u Ju, LANDSCAPE, 39½ x 13½ (4153/71) — 700
P'u Ju, LANDSCAPE, dated 1960 36¼ x 16⅜ (4223/329) — 475
P'u Ju, PRUNUS, ink, paper, 12½ x 35¾, 20c (4261/58) — 1800
P'u Ju, RIVER LANDSCAPE WITH FIGURE IN A BOAT, 37 x 14⅜ (4223/330) — 1600
P'u Ju, SCHOLAR GAZING, 39¼ x 12½ (4223/328) — 800
P'u Ju, SCHOLAR IN MOUNTAIN LANDSCAPE, ink, color, paper, 39½ x 13½, 20c (4261/60) — 1000
Pair of painted silk 4 fold screens, 64¾ x 18½ (4144/306) — 4200
Pan Tzu-Ju, SAGE, WATCHING BOYS AT PLAY, ink, color, silk, 11 x 11, 1881 (4261/52) — 325

Pien Shou Min, attrib., TWO GEESE BENEATH MILLET, Ch'ien Lung Period, 44½ x 21¾
(4144/263) — 850

Pien Wen-Chin, style, GEESE AND MILLET, ink, color, silk, 39 x 17, 18c (4261/21) — 400

Shen Ch'uan, attrib., BIRDS, BAMBOO AND FLOWERS, Ch'ien Lung Period, 46½ x 18¾
(4144/264) — 650

Shen Ch'uan, attrib., BUTTERFLY AND FLOWERS, Ch'ien Lung Period, 7 x 5¼ (4144/265) — 450

Shih Chung-Yu, MOTHER AND CHILD OUTSIDE A SCHOLAR'S HOUSE, silk, 11 x 11, 1824
(4261/49) — 225

Style of Ch'iu Ying, MOUNTAIN LANDSCAPE WITH PAVILIONS, 18c, 46¼ x 16 (4144/260) — 500

Style of Chang Lu, RIVER LANDSCAPE, K'ang Hsi Period, 66 x 26¾ (4144/258) — 300

Style Wen Cheng Ming, TRAVELING IN THE MOUNTAINS, L17c-E18c, 62 x 34½ (4144/259) — 600

Sun Chien Kao, IRIS FUNGUS AND ROCK, 11 3/5 x 85, Chien Lung Period (4154/15) — 600

Sung Nien, ROCKS, 6 x 6¾ (4153/18) — 300

T'ang I Fen, style, LANDSCAPE, 19c, 32¾ x 17 (4144/313) — 250

T'ang Ti, PLUM BLOSSOMS, 54½ x 18½, 1938 (4144/330) — 175

T'ang Ting Chih, attrib, LANDSCAPE, dated 1960 38½ x 13 (4223/337) — 300

T'ang Yin, style, FEMALE MUSICIAN, 19c, 24½ x 11 (4144/318) — 150

T'ing Lu*, LANDSCAPE, ink, wash on paper, 46¾ x 17, 1849 (4153/11) — 600

Tai Chin Ming, attrib, FALCON, 35½ x 12½, E18c (4154/9) — 300

Tai Hsi, attributed, SCHOLAR, BAMBOO AND MOUNTAINS, 34¼ x 16¼, 19c (4154/18) — 850

Tai T'ing Chen, PORTRAIT OF HSI WANG MU, 41¼ x 20 (4223/355) — 250

Tai T'ing Chen, PORTRAIT OF LAN TS AI-HO, 40¼ x 20¼ (4223/356) — 200

Teng T'ao, FOUR LANDSCAPE PAINTING, 1 1890, 19c, 54½ x 13 (4223/283) — 1100

Tibetan tanka, paper, painted bright colors, God of wisdom, L19c (4121/88) — 225

Ting Lu, attrib., LANDSCAPE d.1849, 46¾ x 17 (4153/10) — 600

Ting-Yun-P'eng, style, PORTRAITS OF THE 18 LOHANS, ink, silk, 9¾ x 153, 16/17c (4261/4) — 1400

To Ho Yu, attrib, ONE HUNDRED BIRDS, 19c 66¼ x 35½ (4223/291) — 800

Tung Pang Ta, style, LANDSCAPE, 19c, 43 x 10¼ (4144/316) — 175

Tzu Yi, attrib, PINE AND CHRYSANTHEMUM, 19c 54 x 15 (4223/293) — 200

Wang Ch'eng-P'ei, attrib, RUSTIC BASKET WITH GOURD AND FLOWERS, Ch'ien Lung Period,
35½ x 19⅜ (4144/271) — 1300

Wang Chen, BAMBOO AND ROCK d.1929, 53¼ x 12¾ (4153/38) — 600

Wang Chen, BLIND MAN AND DOG, 36½ x 11¼ (4223/318) — 1200

Wang Chi Ch'ien, CALLIGRAPHY d.1975, 37 x 27¼ (4153/120) — 500

Wang Chi Ch'ien, LOTUS, 54 x 27 (4153/118) — 1400

Wang Chi Ch'ien, RIVER AND MOUNTAIN LANDSCAPE d.1973, 23½ x 29⅝ (4153/117) — 950

Wang Chi Ch'ien, RUSTIC BEAUTY OF AUTUMN TREES d.1947, 16⅜ x 19¾ (4153/115) — 175

Wang Chin-Ch'ing, TAOIST IMMORTAL d.1917, 43¾ x 22⅜ (4153/36) — 400

Wang Fang Yu, attrib, NEW YEAR CELEBRATION, 51½ x 36⅜, K'ang Hsi Per (4223/262) — 600

Wang Hao, ANTIQUE AND VASES WITH FLOWERS, 37 x 19 (4223/358) — 200

Wang Hou-Nien, FLOWERS AND INSECTS, 41½ x 13 (4153/95) — 125

Wang Hou-Nien, LANDSCAPE AND SCHOLARS d.1938, 46¾ x 22½ (4153/90) — 150

Wang Hou-Nien, LOTUS, 53 x 13 (4153/92) — 275

Wang Hou-Nien, MYNAH BIRD AND NARCISSUS, 53 x 13 (4153/88) — 300

Wang Hou-Nien, PINE BRANCHES, 58½ x 16¼ (4153/94) — 150

Wang Hou-Nien, RIVER AND MOUNTAIN LANDSCAPE, 46½ x 22½ (4153/98) — 375

Wang Hou-Nien, STORMY RIVER LANDSCAPE, 46¾ x 22½ (4153/91) — 350

Wang Hui, attrib, LANDSCAPE WITH PAVILIONS, 41 x 21¾, d.1652 (4144/275) — 4200

Wang Hui, style, LANDSCAPE, ink, color, silk, 18c (4261/19) — 1250

Wang Hung, attrib., FISHING ON A WEI RIVER CREEK, 19c, 28 x 14¾ (4144/295) — 450

Wang Shih-Tzu, BIRDS AND FLOWERS, ink, color, paper, 43½ x 16, 19/20c (4261/74) — 550

Wang Shu, attrib., CROSSING THE RIVER WIND AND RAIN, 19c, 46 x 12¾ (4144/296) — 400

Wang Su, OFFERING TO KUAN YIN d.1851, 46½ x 10⅛ (4153/5) — 500

Wang Su*, LADY AND BAMBOO, ink, color, paper, 51 x 13½, 19c (4261/43) — 275

Wang Tao, PEACOCK, PEONY AND MAGNOLIA d.1881, 17½ x 10 (4153/13) — 500

Wang Wu, attrib, BIRDS AND FLOWERING PRUNUS, 48 x 15¾, 1677, sixth month (4154/5) — 850

Wang Yun, HAWK AND PINE, 51 x 13 (4153/53) — 600

Wang Yun, MONKEY AND FLY, 33 x 12⅝ (4153/54) — 275

Wang Yun, MONKEY DRINKING, 53 x 12¼ (4153/56) — 275

Wang Yun, MONKEY ON BRANCH, 35⅝ x 13⅛ (4153/57) — 275

Wang Yun, MYNAH AND PEONY BRANCH d.1928, 51¼ x 12½ (4153/55) — 275

Wang Yun, ROOSTERS d.1899, 38½ x 13⅛ (4153/58) — 275

Wang Yun, VASE WITH PRUNUS AND OIL LAMP, 36⅜ x 13 (4153/59) — 300

Wei Sung-Yeh, EIGHT ALBUM LEAVES OF LANDSCAPE PAINTINGS, 10¼ x 11¾ (4153/17) — 650

Wen Cheng Ming, attrib, PORTRAIT OF A SCHOLAR AND CALLIGRAPHY, 21¾ x 9¾, L16/17c
(4154/2) — 4000

Wen Po Jen, attrib., RIVER LANDSCAPE, 16c 6⅛ x 18¾ (4223/240) — 250

Wen Ting, attributed, LANDSCAPE, 43¼ x 17½, 1837 (4154/17) — 1300

Weng Lo, FLOWERS AND INSECTS, dated 1847, 43½ x 15½ (4144/300)	650
Weng Lo, attrib, CAT, ROCK AND FLOWERS, 19c, 48¼ x 13 (4223/285)	600
Weng Lo, attrib., CAT, ROCK AND PEONY BLOSSOMS, L18-M19c, 46 x 11 (4144/301)	700
Wu Hu Fan, BAMBOO, 26¼ x 13 (4223/327)	850
Wu Shih-Hsien, LANDSCAPE d.1857, 61¾ x 31½ (4153/34)	1600
Wu Shin Hsien, LANDSCAPE, 37½ x 16 (4223/310)	1200
Wu Shu-Pen, PARROT ON BRANCH, ink, color, silk, 50 x 14¾, 19/20c (4261/79)	100
Wu Yuh, CAT, NARCISSUS, VASE AND PRUNUS BRANCH d.1928, 49¾ x 15½ (4153/37)	350
Yen P'a Lung, BIRDS AND PINE TREES d.1938, 39¼ x 17⅝ (4153/101)	500
Yu Ch'eng-Yao, LANDSCAPE AND CALLIGRAPHY, 26¼ x 13½ and 53¼ x 13⅜ (4153/102)	150
Yu Ch'in Wang, MOUNTAIN LANDSCAPE, 45 x 25¾ (4223/365)	500
Yu Ch'in Wang, RIVER AND MOUNTAIN LANDSCAPE, 59½ x 25¾ (4223/364)	200
Yu Ch'iu style, LANDSCAPE AND SCHOLAR IN PAVILION, 46 x 14½, 19c (4154/26)	150
Yu Fei An, COURT LADY, dated 1938 35¾ x 9¾ (4223/326)	650
Yu Fei An, COURTY LADY, 33 x 10¾ (4223/322)	650
Yu Fei An, FESTIVAL, 40½ x 18½ (4223/324)	425
Yu Fei An, RIVER AND MOUNTAIN LANDSCAPE, dated 1938, 40½ x 20 (4223/321)	900
Yu Fei An, SONGBIRD ON FLOWERING BRANCH, 27¾ x 16 (4223/325)	610
Yu Fei An, SONGBIRD ON FLOWERING BRANCH, dated 1938, 35½ x 16 (4223/323)	525
Yu Fei-An, CAT AND BUTTERFLIES, 35 x 16 (4153/63)	1300
Yu Fei An, PEONIES d.1937, 40 x 19½ (4153/64)	1100
Yu Fei-An, RIVER AND MOUNTAIN LANDSCAPE d.1938, 35¾ x 16 and 25¾ x 12¼ (4153/61)	950
Yu Fei-An, SONGBIRD ON BRANCH d.1938, 42 x 20 (4153/62)	400
Yu Shao-Sung, RIVER LANDSCAPE d.1930, 26 x 16 (4153/60)	600
Yuan Chiang, attrib, RIVER AND MOUNTAIN LANDSCAPE WITH PAVILIONS, 90 x 49¼ (4223/256)	8000
Yuan Ching, attrib, ROCKS AND BANANA TREE, 52¾ x 12½, 17c (4154/1)	700
Yuan P'ei, attrib, TWO SCHOLARS, 25½ x 14½, 19c (4154/28)	250
Yung Hsing, attrib, ANCESTOR PORTRAITS OF E KANG LIEH AND WIFE, dated 1784, 52¼ x 25 (4223/275)	3600

SNUFF BOTTLES

Agate bottles

Blue chalcedony, woman holding a peony branch, small boy, (4223/95)	200
Brown, bannerman seated on a galloping horse, (4223/81)	550
Brown, carved with bat gourds leaves and tendrils, minor chip (4154/192)	120
Brown, cockerel perched on branch, (4223/85)	25
Brown, horse tethered to hitching post, (4223/79)	650
Brown and gray, two monkeys on rockwork and a bat, (4223/80)	*350*
Carnelian, perched birds, trees, rockwork, (4223/86)	*130*
Carnelian, vertical fluted pattern, (4223/94)	*325*

Brown and gray
(4223/80)

Carnelian
(4223/86)

Light gray
and brown
(4223/90)

Carnelian
(4223/94)

Embellished macaroni, carved with mask and mock ring handles, 2 boys with vase, (4154/195)	800
Gray, double gourd, branches of smaller fruit, (4223/84)	70

Gray and brown, fisherman poling this boat, mask, mock ring handles, (4154/194)　　90
Gray and brown, sage seated in a rock grotto, (4154/198)　　850
Gray and brown, two travelers on rockwork bridge, (4223/78)　　800
Gray and brown, with darker markings, well-hallowed, (4154/191)　　50
Gray and brown, woman standing beneath palm tree, gourd branch and crane, (4154/199)　　240
Grayish brown, twin fish form, (4223/82)　　300
Light gray and brown, form ear of a corn, (4223/90)　　*550*
Mottled gray and dark brown, Liu Hai standing in back 3 legged toad, (4154/197)　　130
Striated, pear shaped, (4223/87)　　90
Striped, gray, with striated, white and brown bands, (4223/88)　　225

Amber bottles

Baltic, mask and mock ring handles, opaque , honey brown, chips (4154/206)　　175
Figural, form of a Liu Hai, 3 legged toad, (4223/98)　　2100
Fruit form, prickly pear, with natural flaws, (4154/208)　　140
Honey brown, carved mask and mock ring handles, (4154/214)　　50
Mask, elongated mock ring handles, (4223/103)　　225
Pebble form, dark brown carved with sage on mule, flowering tree, (4154/207)　　250
Pebble form, flowering prunus trees, perched birds, (4223/102)　　150
Root, carved with shou Lau, peony and palm trees, rim chip (4164/211)　　225
Root, mask and mock ring handles, slight chip (4223/100)　　175
Sage ring horse, and boy attendant, (4223/99)　　900
Three goats, phoenix birds, mock ring handles, (4223/97)　　400

Amethystine Quartz

Pale, five monkeys seated in a rocky grotto, slight chip (4154/266)　　60

Aquamarine

Pale bluish green, two perched birds, lotus blossoms, pods, leafage, slight chip (4154/262)　　200

Chalcedony bottles

Dendritic, quadrangular, raised sides, (4223/91)　　250
Dendritic, three swimming goldfish, water weeds, (4223/93)　　375

Cinnabar bottles

Lacquer, landscape and pavilion settings, chip and cracking (4223/161)　　60
Lacquer, pavilions, groups of sage, attendants, chip (4223/158)　　70
Lacquer, playing boys in garden, restored (4223/152)　　275
Lacquer, sages and attendants, chip (4223/153)　　175
Lacquer, sages and attendants, chip, 1 head missing (4223/149)　　150
Lacquer, sages and attendants, mountainous landscape, (4223/150)　　225
Lacquer, sages in wooded rocky landscape, some chip (4223/160)　　90

Coral

Carved with 2 birds perched on rockwork, (4154/245)　　300
Standing robed bearded sage, hat forms stopper, (4154/244)　　175

Dendritic Chalcedony

Moss green, rust red, brown and gray, masks and mock ring handles, (4154/202)　　125
Natural gray, green markings, flattened form, brown ground, (4154/204)　　130

Enamel bottles

Canton painted, garden scene of flowering shrubs, small restoration (4223/162)　　275
Canton painted, groups of sages conversing, riverscape, slight chip rim (4223/138)　　325
Canton painted, lemon yellow ground, butterflies, flowering tree peonies, (4154/234)　　250
Canton painted, man seated amid rockwork, (4223/137)　　170
Canton painted, panels of European figures, (4223/135)　　275
Canton painted, European man and woman in garden setting, Ch'ien Lung (4154/232)　　90
Canton painted, double, design of bats amid clouds, slight chip, restored (4223/136)　　225
Canton painting, fisherman standing on bridge, (4223/157)　　90
Canton painting, pairs of dragon, slight chip, firing cracks (4223/139)　　225
Cloisonne, color-fully decorated boy riding water buffalo, Ch'ien Lung (4154/230)　　350
Cloisonne, multi-colored enamels, yellow ground, birds and trees, Ch'ien Lung (4154/236)　　250
Cloisonne, multi-colored on white ground, hundred antiques, (4154/227)　　250
Cloisonne, multicolored flowering trees and rockwork, chip and pitting (4223/156)　　100
Cloisonne, multicolored, lotus blossoms and foilage, neck reduced slightly (4223/155)　　70

Cloisonne, multicolored, 2 panel deer, landscape, (4223/146)   200
Cloisonne, red-green on white ground, lotus blossoms, chip, pitting to enamel (4223/143)   350
Cloisonne, sky blue ground with butterflies, tree peonies, asters, (4154/233)   175
Cloisonne, turquoise blue ground, 3 pandas in a bamboo grove, (4154/237)   200
Cloisonne, turquoise ground, flowers, 2 mask, ring handles, (4223/142)   425
Milk white glass, scattered sprigs of blossoms, fruit and fungus, Ch'ien Lung (4154/163)   160
Milk white glass, woman seated on horse, groom and female attendant, Ch'ien Lung seal
   (4154/156)   300
Peking painted, mountainous riverscapes, robin-egg blue floral ground, (4154/235)   50
Peking painted, woman seated with small boy, slight chip, firing crack neck (4223/134)   17000
Peking painted, European figure, enamel rubbed (4223/140)   350
Set of 4 silver and enamel, seasonal flowers, lapis, turquoise blue, (4223/145)   125

Glass bottles

Peking, flattened ovate form, (4223/25)   400
Peking, plain heart shaped flask, (4223/37)   450
Peking, simulating Jasper, carved both sides, (4223/7)   100
Peking, blue, octagonal facets, 2 circular panel, (4223/33)   150
Peking, blue, sapphire, gold flecking, (4223/28)   150
Peking, blue overlay and snowflake, carved, pair swimming gold fish, minor chip (4223/10)   *450*
Peking, brown overlay and milk white, cat perched on rock work, minor chip (4223/15)   *400*
Peking, goldstone, brown glass, gold speckling, small rim chip (4223/17)   50
Peking, green overlay and brown, cricket perched on branch, (4223/35)   110
Peking, green overlay and brown, flowering prunus trees, slight chip (4223/4)   250
Peking, lapis blue, carved archaistic dragon fret, (4223/29)   900
Peking, mottled red glass, dark red, lighter swirling striations to white, (4223/27)   325
Peking, multicolor overlay, carved, lotus plant, minor chip (4223/1)   175
Peking, multicolored overlay, carved, flowering trees, butterfly, (4223/11)   *450*
Peking, multicolored overlay, scrolling vines, (4223/5)   425
Peking, multicolored overlay and blue, peony blossoms, slight chip (4223/16)   525
Peking, multicolored overlay and frosted, flowering trees, rockwork, and waves, (4223/19)   700
Peking, overlay and snowflake, carved with a carp, (4223/13)   250
Peking, pale amber, all over intentional crackle, minor rim chip (4223/26)   150
Peking, pale yellow, fruit form, carved form fluted melon, (4223/24)   200
Peking, red, a flattened ovate flask, (4223/32)   60
Peking, red, carved with 2 shou medallions, (4223/31)   150
Peking, red, octagonal flask form, (4223/34)   475
Peking, red and yellow, double gourd, simulating realgar, (4223/38)   90
Peking, red overlay and bubble, carved with a writhing Ch'ih Lung, (4223/14)   200
Peking, red overlay and bubble, carved, 9 tripod vessels, (4223/22)   175
Peking, red overlay and milk seal, carved man and horse beside tree, minor rim chip (4223/20)   300
Peking, red overlay and milk white, bird on branch, slight chip, rings and foot (4223/2)   475
Peking, red overlay and milk white, carved with a woman, (4223/3)   650
Peking, red overlay and snowflake, carved with writhing Ch'ih Lung, (4223/6)   *200*
Peking, red overlay and white seal, carved, boy riding carp, (4223/12)   750
Peking, turquoise blue, a tapering faceted flask, (4223/30)   50
Peking, white and red overlay, carved with dragon, bird, (4223/9)   475

Gold

Wrought, two ladies standing on pavilion terrace, Ch'ien Lung (4154/229)   1500

Hair crystal

Clear, golden kutile needles, sides mask and mock handles, (4154/258)   50
Clear, with inclusions of black tourmaline needles, slight rim chip (4154/263)   200
Clear, Lohan seated on a mat, (4154/259)   400

Hardstone bottles

Jasper and soapstone, branches of leafage, dragonfly and worm, (4223/180)   130
Lapis lazuli, blue stone with gray and brown inclusions, (4223/181)   100
Lapis lazuli, bright blue stone, gray motting, (4223/178)   80
Lapis lazuli, brilliant blue stone, gray-brown inclusions, (4223/174)   70
Lapis lazuli, brilliant blue, gray mottling, gold flecking, (4223/175)   120
Lapis lazuli, mottled blue lapis with gray inclusions, (4223/173)   80
Lapis lazuli, sage riding mule, minor rim chip (4223/171)   151
Lapis lazuli, fruit form, shaped melon like fruit..fruit, leafage, (4223/167)   100
Lapis lazuli, fruit form, Buddha's hand citron branches of leafage, (4223/170)   90
Lapis lazuli, gold decorated, etched in gold, floral spray, (4223/184)   170
Malachite, melon form, 2 rodents feedin in branches, (4223/169)   300

Malachite, gold decorated, engraved in gold, woman poling boat, willow tree, (4223/186) 155
Mottled green, greenstone, with black inclusions, (4223/185) 60
Opal, dragon pursuing the 'pearl' (4223/183) 600
Sapphire, matrix, blue-gray stone, metallic veining, (4223/172) 90
Sapphire, matrix, fluted melon, chip (4223/177) 125
Turquoise, two immortals playful boys, 3 goats, (4223/164) 275
Turquoise, matrix, birds, peony trees, some chip (4223/166) 150
Turquoise, matrix, branches of smaller fruit, leafage, (4223/165) 150
Turquoise, matrix, masks above a band lotus petals, chip and cracking (4223/176) 100
Turquoise, matrix, with Liu Hai, 3 legged toad, some chip (4223/168) 100

Interior painted bottles

Glass, continuous garden landscape with group of boys, Yeh Chung-San the Younger, 1920 (4154/186) 310
Glass, five birds hovering above lotus plants, still life of vases, Yen Yu-T'ien, rubbed, 1895 (4154/180) 225
Glass, group of 8 immorals, dated 1898 (4223/60) 2700
Glass, horse standing by willow tree, riverscape, Chou Lo Yuan (4154/185) 225
Glass, landscape, and still life, dated 1895 (4223/56) 475
Glass, man standing, holding baskets of flowers, dated 1934 (4223/71) 750
Glass, rockwork, vases of flowers, (4223/73) 60
Glass, scene of numerous children, garden setting, Yeh Chung-San the Elder, 1911 (4154/183) 1550
Glass, still life rockwork, vase of flowers, slight rubbing 1896 (4223/67) 700
Glass, still life, rockwork, flowers, (4223/61) 60
Glass, two travelers and pair mules, dated 1908 (4223/58) *600*
Glass, with 2 ladies and man standing beside table, Yeh Chung San the Younger, 1916 (4154/179) 325
Gray banded agate, Chu Ko-Liang riding mule, minor rim chip 1924 (4223/65) 1100
Pale ruby red glass, eight immortals in landscape, Yung Shou T'ien (4154/187) 325
Rock crystal, continuous mountain riverscape, Yeh Chung San the Younger, 1928 (4154/181) 600
Rock crystal, fish swimming, water weeds, (4223/70) 400
Rock crystal, flowering peony shrubs, minute chip 1905 (4223/59) *1600*

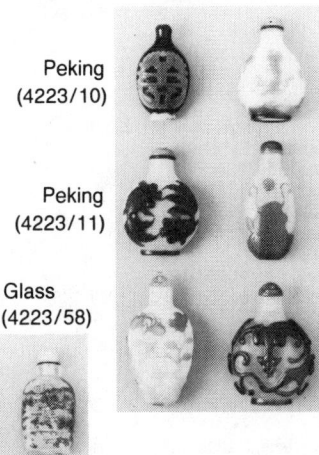

Peking
(4223/10)

Peking
(4223/15)

Peking
(4223/11)

Glass
(4223/58)

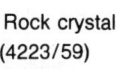

Rock crystal
(4223/59)

Peking
(4223/6)

Rock crystal, four ladies on horseback, male attendant (chip), Yeh Chung-San the Elder, 1912
(4154/182)   1500
Rock crystal, goats and willow tree, date 1899 (4223/55)   1300
Rock crystal, goldfish, carp swimming, dated 1907 (4223/62)   500
Rock crystal, marriage procession, dated 1928 (4223/63)   900
Rock crystal, young maiden standing in garden, Ting Kuei Ling (4154/184)   500
Rock crystal, double gourd, scene of children, in garden, rim chip (4223/69)   125
Smoke crystal, landscape, shephered boy seated, dated 1935 (4223/57)   1600
Smoke crystal, man conversing with woman, holding child, minor rim chip date 1913 (4223/66)   550
Smoke crystal, three equestrian, deer, snowy landscape, (4223/64)   *1400*

Ivory bottles

Baroque - rare, conical form, some pearls restuck (4223/127)   275
Double gourd, fruit, blossoms, leafage, 2 insects, (4223/113)   90
Dragon pursuing 'flaming pearl' some chip (4223/110)·   125
Eight sportive fulions, (4223/109)   650
Engraved, seven playful boys, slight chip (4223/123)   50
Figural, seated robed figure of female, (4223/131)   170
Figures at their daily pursuits, (4223/111)   125
Figures in pavilion, garden setting, (4223/114)   90
Fish form, leaping carp with dragon head, (4223/116)   8500
Green stained walrus, flattened form with rounded sides, (4223/118)   125
Hornbill, bearded man standing before 3 female attendants, (4154/215)   500
Hornbill, mask and mock ring handles, (4223/132)   340
Hornbill, twin fish form, (4223/104)   300
Hornbill, two men seated in garden, (4223/105)   500
Hornbill, two writhing dragons, (4154/220)   3400
Lotus leaf, curled lotus leaf with buds, (4223/129)   550
Scene of hundred boys, neck cracked (4223/126)   230
Seated woman and boy, (4223/125)   110
Tinted, panels of exotic birds, flowing shrubs, crack on shoulders (4223/117)   250
Tinted, scene of 8 immortals, (4223/108)   800
Tinted, stylized foliage, some cracking (4223/119)   190

Jade bottles

Black jade, incised with floral sprays, (4223/225)   200
Embellished grayish white, boy, woman beside tree, (4223/206)   475
Embellished grayish-white, two ducks swimming, (4223/219)   600
Engraved silver and jadeite, double, gourd, lotus petals, floral sprays, dragon, (4223/144)   200
Fei Ts'ui jadeite, grayish-white, emerald green and pale brown, (4223/214)   350
Fei Ts'ui jadeite, grayish-white, emerald green mottling, dragon, (4223/210)   175
Fei Ts'ui jadeite, groups of sportive Fu lions, (4223/222)   650
Fei Ts'ui jadeite, opaque grayish-white, emerald green mottling, (4223/223)   650
Fei Ts'ui jadeite, spade shape, grayish-white, emerald green, pale brown, (4223/215)   200
Fei Ts'ui jadeite, long tailed bird on tree, (4223/237)   300
Fine embellished celadon, etched in gold, Lohan seated on mat, (4223/209)   *900*
Grayish green and brown jadeite, double gourd monkey holding fruiting gourds, (4223/205)   *125*
Grayish white, incised with floral spray, chip on lip rim (4223/233)   175
Grayish white, pebble form, flying bat, (4223/227)   100
Grayish white, fruit form, Buddha's hand citron, leafage, (4223/208)   175
Grayish white and brown melon formed, (4223/234)   125
Grayish white and pale brown melon, shape, leafage, small bug, (4223/216)   130
Jadeite, crystalline pale grayish-white stone, (4223/224)   400
Lavendar and pale apple green, cluster bean pods, leafy stems, (4223/235)   350
Lavender jadeite, goldfish, water weed, (4223/204)   200
Lavender jadeite, with pale brown mottling, (4223/207)   250
Light and dark, dragon enveloped by clouds, (4223/232)   375
Mottled dark and light gray, horse striding amid waves, (4223/211)   *700*
Mottled gray, light and dark jade, (4223/212)   120
Mottled green jadeite, polished grayish stone, emerald, brown mottling, (4223/217)   110
Onion green, dragon-mask, mock ring handles, (4223/221)   250
Pale mottled green jadeite, ovate form, polished grayish-white, green, brown, (4223/218)   100
Spinach green, continuous basketry molded design, (4223/229)   450
Spinach green, dark and brighter green, black flecking, (4223/231)   100
White, rows of lotus petals, flowerhead forming foot, (4223/230)   800

Jadeite

Fei Ts'ui, boy riding water buffalo, birds, rockwork and waves, (4154/278)   600

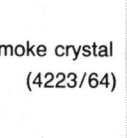

moke crystal
(4223/64)

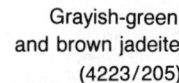

Grayish-green
and brown jadeite
(4223/205)

Fine
embellished
celadon
(4223/209)

Mottled dark
and light gray
(4223/211)

Grayish-lavender and Fei Ts'ui, branch of leafage, pale applegreen & brown mottlings, (4154/272) — 175
Lavender and Fei Ts'ui, gnarled prunus tree, plants, scrolling clouds, (4154/273) — 325
Mongolian silver, two circular plaques, carved lotus plants, (4154/288) — 100

Lacquer

Cinnabar, sages and attendants, wooded mountainous landscapes, (4154/238) — 275

Lacquer, burgaute

Butterfly, with open wings, inlaid silver-gold, mother of pearl, (4154/228) — 325

Lapis Lazuli

Animalistic, form elephant with large ears, curled trunk, short tusks, (4154/256) — 40
Black ground, inlaid, gold, silver, mother pearl floral mosaic, (4223/151) — 575
Butterfly, inlaid, gold, silver, mother of pearl, mosaic, (4223/154) — 350
Butterfly, brown ground, inlaid, gold, silver, mother pearl mosaic, (4223/148) — 100
Lady and 2 female attendants, small pavillion, (4154/246) — 150
Slender bottle, form bamboo stalk with perched bird, (4154/255) — 60

Limestone

Flattened ovate form, light gray, with black, ochre marking, (4154/250) — 90

Malachite

Cranes, a pine tree, lotus plants, matching stoppers, (4154/253) — 50
Fish form, form swimming carp, matching stopper, (4154/252) — 50

Mongolian

Jeweled silver fish form, two carp leading amid scrolling waves, bosses with glass jewels, (4154/239) — 125
Silver andd malachite tortoise form, crouching tortoise, back-shell inset with malachite, (4154/242) — 140

Mother of pearl

Embellished, young woman reading book, holding fan, matching stopper, Ch'ien Lung (4154/219) — 275

Flower filled vase, coral 'jewels' matching stopper, (4154/218)   150
Oval panels, with floral spray and bird, matching stopper, (4154/216)   80

Peking

Black overlay and milk white glass, carved with branches of plum blossoms, slight chip (4154/152)   200
Blue glass, phoenix on rockwork beside flowering tree, peonies, (4154/161)   100
Green overlay and opalescent glass, carved, 2 crabs, water plants and waves, slight chip (4154/153)   175
Green overlay and red glass, carved with peacock, (4154/141)   325
Imperial yellow glass, with swimming fish, water, weeds, (4154/157)   375
Multi-colored overlay and milk white glass, design of garden flowers and rockwork, slight chip (4154/155)   75
Multi-colored overlay and milk white glass, with flower filled vessels, chip on lip rim (4154/160)   70
Red overlay and clear glass, carved with carp, crab, aquatic plants, slight chip (4154/144)   200
Red overlay and clear glass, carved with disc and archaistic dragon, slight chip (4154/145)   125
Red overlay and opalescent glass, carved 2 carp leaping from waves, mock handles, (4154/150)   325
Red overlay and snowflake glass, carved with bat, phoenix and 3 legged toad, (4154/146)   225
Red overlay and snowflake glass, trailing gourd vine, color plantain leaves, slight chip (4154/162)   50
Red overlay and snowflake, glass, carved with blossoms, pods and leafage, slight chip (4154/142)   200
Red overlay and snowflake, glass, carved with horses and monkeys, slight chip (4154/143)   175
Rose pink, green overlay, snowflake glass, with a cockerel, flowering plants, slight chip (4154/158)   150

Porcelain bottles

Blue and white, form Pilgrim style purse, slight glaze chip on foot (4223/40)   185
Coral red, molded, with 9 Fu lions, slight chip, glaze rubbing (4154/171)   500
Enameled, molded, figural, form of the immortal Li Tieh Kuai, (4154/169)   200
Famille-rose, figural, seated boy, (4223/53)   100
Gold decorated, design of the 18 Lohan, (4223/51)   450
Molded iron red and white, five clawed dragon, probably Tao Kuang (4154/172)   120
Red and white, two flying phoenix, minor glaze chip (4223/39)   80
White glazed 'soft paste' design of 18 Lohan, small chip lip rim (4223/54)   150
White glazed 'soft paste' tree trunk, and plum blossoms, pine, bamboo, (4223/42)   850

Quartz bottles

Amethystine, bat and Show Lao seated, some chip (4223/190)   50
Amethystine, dragon amid cloud, lip rim chip (4223/194)   200
Amethystine, flowering plants, rockwork, hovering dragonfly, (4223/200)   60
Amethystine, flying bats, minor rim chip (4223/199)   210
Amethystine, woman holding branch, some chip (4223/192)   120
Amethystine, Lohan holding double gourd, (4223/191)   200
Amethystine, double, two conjoined large and small tapering flasks, (4223/193)   100
Amethystine, double gourd, branches smaller fruit, leafage, 2 bats, some chip (4223/196)   80
Aquamarine, clear crystal, inclusions of black tourm, (4223/187)   475
Aquamarine fish form, form of carp, pale bluish green stone, (4223/189)   300
Hair crystal, clear, black tourmaline needles, (4223/202)   600
Hair crystal, clear, dense inclusions, black tourmaline needles, (4223/188)   700
Tourmaline, pink, fruit form, cluster of 3 peaches with leafage, minor chip (4223/201)   350

Rock crystal

Clear, all over inclusions of cloudy net like marking, (4154/264)   150

Tourmaline

Green, figure of Shou Lao holding a staff and a peach, (4154/261)   200

TEXTILES, GARMENTS

Assorted items

Altar Frontal, K'o-Ssu, silk tapestry, crane on pierced rock, 17c (4223/404)   1700
Badges, pair, provincial, bird perched on a pierced rock, flowers, 18c unusual (4223/424)   325
Banner, Manchu, winged tiger standing striding amid clouds, 18c 49 x 50 (4223/412)   900
Blue silk informal jacket, E20c (4144/217)   125
Bolt, of brocade deep maroon, bamboo, lotus and peonies, E20c 12' x 8 (4223/411)   250

Bolt, royal blue silk, double dragons, chasing a 'Flaming Pearl' E20c 18' x 30 (4223/410) 175
Bolt, yellow stain, figured, bold circular shou characters, E20c, 26' x 30 (4223/409) 375
Buddhist Hanging, embroidered multitude of Buddhist deities, 56 x 109, Chia Ch'ing Period (4154/75) 2900
Child's dragon robe, 19c (4144/218) 200
Coat, black satin, stitched with butterflies and flowers, L19c (4223/382) 325
Coat, informal, blue-black satin embroidered with the Hundred Antiques, ca1850 (4154/61) 500
Coat, informal, bright red figured silk embroidered, blue and green, L19c (4154/64) 275
Coat, informal ceremonial, navy satin, couched silk, landscape roundels, cranes, deer, E19c (4223/381) 200
Coat, informal, navy silk, eight very fine detailed roundels, flowers, 19c fine (4223/399) 1150
Coat, lady informal, deep indigo satin, butterflies, bats and Buddhist, embroidered, M19c (4223/380) 350
Coat, lady's informal, blue, black satin, large butterflies and peonies, L19c (4223/385) 400
Coat, satin, informal, navy, mbroidered with peonies, butterflies and prunus, L19c (4154/63) 175
Costume, theatre, multicolored, embroidered with flowers, metal discs, E20c (4154/66) 400
Court vest, lady's, egret insignia, for wife of 6th rank official, ca1850-75 (4144/242) 800
Cover, throne cushion - K'o-Ssu, full face metallic gold dragon, 2 in profile, 19c 35½ x 27½ (4223/421) 475
Cut and uncut velvet runner, three male Fu lions, L19c, 23 x 88 (4144/207) 300
Door hanging, olive green satin with figures, 36½ x 37½, 19c (4154/70) 250
Dragon coat, Kun Fu, stitched satin, eight dragon medallions, L19c (4144/237) 900
Dragon robe, royal blue satin, Kuang Hsu Period (4144/215) 550
Dragon robe (Ch'i Fu) with cranes, ca1875-1900 (4144/214) 550
Embroidered satin skirt, a phoenix and dragon, ca1875-1900 (4144/223) 130
Embroidered satin theatrical skirt, ca1875-90 (4144/221) 110
Embroidery of Mandarin ducks, satin and stem stitches, multi colors, 9½, Ch'ien Period, framed (4154/55) 600
Finely embroidered jacket, 19c (4144/219) 300
Hanging, commemorative hanging, embroidered center, dedicatory, 9' 2 x 13' 11, 1836 (4223/413) 1600
Hanging, dragon, dragon embroidered in silvery beige, 40 x 28, L19c (4154/79) 125
Hanging, embroidered, (large), cream satin, stitched with flowers and birds, 80 x 116, M19c (4154/77) 500
Hanging, Taoist, Lan Ts'ai Ho carring basket, with deer, bats, L19c 5 x 10' 10 large (4223/416) 1000
Informal dragon robe Ch'i Fu, M19c (4144/222) 300
Jacket, brown silk, figured with dragon roundels and couched silver, 19c (4154/62) 150
Jacket, informal, blue, black satin, embroidered, phoenixes, deer, butterflies, flowers, L19c (4223/379) 600
Jacket, informal, magenta satin, embroidered with birds, animals, flowers, 19-20c (4223/389) 500
Jeweled kingfisher feather headdress, (4144/227) 475
K'o-ssu Ch'i Fu, nine five-clawed dragons, ca1850-75 (4144/225) 550
K'o-ssu door hanging, two panels, each with a dragon, M19c (4144/210) 300
K'o-ssu of the Taoist immortals, with children playing, woven in peach and shades of blue, 66½ x 35 (4154/71) 1000
K'o-suu panels, pair, each with warrior figures on horseback, M19c, 41 x 11¼ (4144/204) 350
K'o-ssu wall hanging large, battle scenes from Peking opera, 19c, 61 x 84½ (4144/203) 1500
Lady's court robe, white cranes and peonies, Kuang Hsu Period (4144/238) 600
Lady's informal coat, with 8 medallions, ca1875-1900 (4144/230) 325
Lady's informal robe, with gold file butterflies, ca1875-1900 (4144/224) 250
Medallion, dragon, rare, two dragons swirl in circular pattern, Tao Kuang Period, D15 (4144/195) 150
Panel, chair, cut and uncut velvet, gold, phoenixes, peony, pale peach, turquoise mauve, 18c (4223/405) 200
Panel, cut and uncut velvet, dark orange metallic gold, full face dragon, 24¾ x 72, L19c (4154/78) 450
Panel, dragon royal blue gauze, full face dragon clutching a 'Flaming Pearl' E19c 40½ x 30½ (4223/418) 175
Panel, embroidered, dragon boat festival, female figures, L19c 11' 10 x 32 (4223/414) 700
Panel, embroidered, navy silk, with 2 medallions, 33⅞ x 32½, 1825-50 (4154/74) 150
Panel, embroidered, possibly scene from Peking opera, 19c, 11' 4' x 32' (4223/415) 275
Panel, embroidered, cream satin, varieties of peonies, scrolling tendrils, 19c 54 x 36½ (4223/422) 300
Panel, with dragon medallions, embroidered gold satin dragon above waves, shade of blue, 44 x 55, Tao Kuang Period, framed (4154/76) 350
Panel, K'o-Ssu dragon, four claw dragons, clouds and bats, flowers, 18c 71 x 40 tearing (4223/417) 80
Panel, K'o-Ssu Dragon, four claw dragon, crane flying, horses prancing, rare, Ming Dynasty (4223/402) 1600
Panel, Ming silk tapestry, boys playing blind man bluff, and hunting, 16c 27 x 12 (4223/425) 1000
Priest robe, Taoist, gold satin ground with 2 official symbols, 19c (4144/240) 750
Robe, ceremonial scarlet satin, embroidered, 8 bold floral roundels, Kuang Hsu Period (4223/384) 900

Robe, dragon, bright blue satin with couched silver, gold dragon, L19c (4154/57)   175

Robe, dragon (Ch'i Fu) blue silk twill, embroidered, gold, silver dragons, clouds, cranes, Kuang Hsu Period (4223/386)   750

Robe, dragon, gold gauze ground, with silk tapestry -five claw dragon, E19c (4223/397)   850

Robe, emperor's, saffron silk, twelve symbol dragon, turquoise, blue, purple, 1875-1900 (4223/388)   1300

Robe, imperial, twelve symbol dragon, dragons, clouds, bats, rep, Tao Kuang Period (4223/400)   1300

Robe, imperial dragon navy ground, gold dragon medallions, imperial symbols, sun, moon, M19c (4223/398)   850

Robe, informal court, scarlet satin embroidered, peach, yellow, white, green, Kuang Hsu Period (4154/67)   800

Robe, informal, embroidered satin, floral sprays in Peking knot, 19c (4144/236)   475

Robe, phoenix, lavender, gauze, white, turquoise, pink peonies, 19/E20c, fine (4154/65)   2600

Robe, prince's dragon, dark blue gauze, large metallic gold dragons, Buddhist emblems, L19c (4223/392)   350

Robe, quilted K'o-Ssu, dragon, multi colored, with gold file dragon, Kuang Hsu Period (4154/59)   400

Robe, summer, dragon, royal blue gauze with 8 dragons, Kuang Hsu Period (4154/58)   400

Robe, theatrical, bright red satin, mandarin duck insignia badges, L19c (4223/390)   225

Robe, winter, black ground, embroidered, eight, medallions, bats, flowers, 18c rare (4223/387)   500

Robe, women's ceremonial, red satin, embroidered with flowers, 5 bats, Ch'ien Lung Period (4223/401)   2200

Satin informal robe, cranes carrying peaches, L19c (4144/232)   125

Silk tapestry panel, five Taoist immortals, L19c, 17¼ x 39½ (4144/205)   250

Stitched coat, orchids, peonies on navy satin, Kuang-Hsu Period (4144/229)   225

Summer robe, green gauze, 8 large roundels, (4144/231)   550

Surcoat, emperor's, navy silk 'P'u-Fu' four circular insignia, gold dragon, clouds, bats, 19c (4223/391)   400

Temple hanging, Mongolian, unusual, three sections, largest has cranes, 67¾ x 39, I Ch'ing T'ang characters (4144/211)   325

Theatrical skirt and cloud collar, L19c (4144/220)   125

Woman's informal robe, magenta silk, L19c - E20c (4144/216)   300

Woman's informal satin jacket, navy satin with bold tree peonies, 19-20c (4144/233)   80

Embroidered Hanging

Brocade, peonies, dragon border, grayish-blue ground, 56¼ x 90½, L18/E19c (4261/101)   200

Dragon, stylized waves, gold, color, 57 x 114, smoke dam, 17c (4261/95)   375

K'o-Ssu dragon, multicolors, 50 x 26½, E19c (4261/106)   325

Runner, Taoist immortals, in a garden setting, 22 x 161, L19c (4261/98)   400

Imperial Robes

Dragon, 4 imperial symbols, ca1909 (4261/122)   *550*

Dragon, prince's, blue ground, gold, 18c (4261/125)   125

Informal court, scarlet ground, peonies, flowers, E19c (4261/131)   350

Mandarin squares

Badge, leopard insignia, ca1850-75, 12½ x 12⅜ (4144/188)   225

Dragon (4261/122)

Buddhist priest (4261/132)

Badge, leopard insignia, ca1850-75, 8½ x 8½ (4144/186) — 100
Badge, lion insignia, ca1875-1900, 12¾ x 12 (4144/193) — 90
Badge, lion insignia, ca1850-75, 12¼ x 11¼ (4144/190) — 140
Badge, paradise flycatcher, ca1825-1900, 11 x 10⅞ (4144/183) — 70
Badge, tiger cat insignia, ca1900-10, 12⅜ x 12 (4144/192) — 160
Badge, Crane insignia, L18c, 13 x 12⅜, rare (4144/182) — 300
Badge, Hsi Eh Chai insignia, Tao Kuang Period, 11⅞ x 12 (4144/181) — 250
Badge, provincial, crane in lotus, embroidered, L19c, 11¼ x 11¾ (4144/197) — 60
Badges, pair, crane insignia, unusual, Ch'ien Lung Period, 12¼ x 11¾ (4144/187) — 375
Badges, pair, duck insignia, gold-silver thread, L19c, 11⅞ x 11¼, 11¾ x 11⅜ (4144/185) — 325
Badges, pair, lion insignia, ca1850-75, 11⅞ x 11¾, 11¾ x 11½ (4144/184) — 375
Badges, pair, paradise flycatcher, ca1875-1900, 11⅞ x 11⅜ (4144/194) — 225
Badges, pair, silver pheasant insignia, ca1825-75, 12¼ x 11½, 11⅜ x 11⅜ (4144/191) — 200
Badges, pair, Ko-ssu duck insignia, ca1875-1900, 11¾ x 11½ (4144/189) — 220
Early golden pheasant insignia badge, Wife of A 2nd Rank Civil Official, 11⅜ x 10⅝, Ch'ien Lung Period (4154/44) — 400
Egret insignia badges, pair, Wife of a 6th Rank Civil Official, 11½ x 11½, 1850-1900 (4154/40) — 75
Egret insignia badges, pair, 6th Rank Civil Official, 11½ x 11⅜ - 12 x 11½, 1850-75 (4154/50) — 100
Golden pheasant insignia badge, 2nd Rank Civil Official, 9¼ x 8½, L18c, rare (4154/41) — 100
Hsieh Chai ingignia badges, pair, for a Judge or Censor, 12½ x 12½ - 13⅜ x 12½, 1875-1900 (4158/48) — 150
Leopard insignia badge, 2nd Rank Military Officer, 12 x 11¾, L18c (4154/54) — 150
Leopard insignia badge, 3rd Rank Military Officer, 12¼ x 12, 1900-10 (4154/42) — 175
Lion insignia badges, pair, 2nd Rank Military Officer, 12 x 12¼ - 12⅜ x 12, 1850-75 (4154/38) — 200
Mandarin duck insignia, pair, Wife of a 7th Rank Civil Official, 12¼ x 11¾ - 1825-50 (4154/49) — 125
Mandarin duck insignia badges, pair, 7th Rank Civil Official, 12¾ x 11⅞, 1850-75 (4154/45) — 150
Paradise Flycatcher insignia badges, pair, 9th Rank Civil Official, 12½ x 11½, Tao Kuang Period (4154/39) — 150
Silver pheasant insignia badges, pair, 5th Rank Civil Official, 11⅞ x 11½ - 12 x 11½, 1850-75 (4154/43) — 100

Robes

Buddhist priest, seated figure, flanking dragons, L19c (4261/132) — *350*
Ceremonial, black ground, peonies, 19c (4261/127) — 800
Coat, ceremonial, white, lotus, butterflies, L19c (4261/117) — 700
Dragon, clouds, frayed, soil, E18c (4261/116) — 125
Dragon, clouds, aubergine, ca1900 (4261/119) — 400
Dragon, purplish-brown ground, ca1725 (4261/123) — *3000*
Dragon, embroidered, royal blue, bats, lotus, 19c (4261/121) — 300
Dragon, Coat, plum ground, gold, ca1900 (4261/124) — 200
Informal coat, light green ground, figures, L19c (4261/130) — 200
K'o-Ssu, dragon, bats, peonies, silver, ca1850 (4261/129) — 325
Priest, Taoist, orange velvet, dragon, ca1909 (4261/115) — *800*

Dragon (4261/123)

Priest (4261/115)

Libation cup (4214/41)   Lotus-form cup (4214/42)

Robe, silk dragon, Cabinet Minister, blue ground, Ming style, edged, in beaver, ca1900 (4257/41)   1000

Silk Tapestry

K'o-Ssu, Ming, 4-claw dragon, gold ground, 12 x 10¾, 17c (4261/99)   450
K'o-Ssu panel, Lan Ts'ai Ho, 37 x 18, L18c (4261/103)   425
Panel, Red satin, peonies, color, 112 x 32, fraying, 1794 (4261/100)   160
Panel, Taoist, 'shou' character, gold, color, painted, 45 x 25, E19c (4261/94)   200
Panel, Taoist, couched gold, Lao Tzu & others confronting dragons, 45 x 20, 19c (4261/97)   325

WORKS OF ART

Assorted works

Box, basketweave, large circular, cinnabar, a bar, lacquered, plain shallow form, black lacquered interior, 16½, 19c (4154/308)   375
Box, cylindrical, red lacquered pigskin, hinged cover and hinged circular hinged metal clasp, 17¾ x 14 (4154/307)   550
Boxes, gift, pair black lacquer, shallow bases with gilt scrollwork in bracket supports, 13¾, 19c (4154/306)   1600
Kuan Yin figure, rhinoceros horn, swaying figure, wood stand, 6¾ (4214/43)   325
Libation cup, rhinoceros horn, bronze-form, 18c, 5, chip (4214/41)   650
Lotus-form cup, rhinoceros horn, three rodents feeding upon branches, 18c, 6, rep, chip (4214/42)   375
Mineral plants semi precious, in cloissone enamel jardinieres, 19, chip, pcs miss (4214/100)   600
Panels, pair, jade and semi-precious stone, inlaid, lacquer, with a pair of court ladies, 56¼ x 22 (4154/304)   2500
Plaques, wall, pair, variegated marble and, wood, each with 9 variously shaped panels, ea. 15 x 19¼, 19c (4154/303)   650
Rhinoceros horn, Taoist group, two robed female Taoist figures standing on tortoise, 9 (4154/317)   325

Bamboo

Brushpot, carved, relief, lotus blossoms, 6, cracks, 19c (4261/142)   150
Brushpot, carver, relief, 7 sages, rocky landscape, 6¼, 1857 (4261/143)   225

Bronzes

Bodhisattva, figure, gilt, holding alms, surmounted by 3 deities, 3⅜, Tang (4261/176)   250
Bodhisattva, torso, hollow cast, 5½, cracked, Ming (4261/183)   150
Boy musician, figure, gilt, seated, head turned, 3, Ming (4261/182)   625
Ch'i-Lin, mythical beast, crouching, W2½, Ming (4261/179)   625

Dignitary, figure, lacquered, seated, rockwork throne, 8, chip, Ming (4261/188) — 250
Dragon, winged, crouching, turned, head raised, W2½, Ming (4261/180) — 450
Elephant and vase, group, hollow cast, reclining, pierced vase on back, 7½, late Ming (4261/185) — 375
Kuan Yin, figure, gilt, seated, lotus plinth, 3¾, dam, Tang (4261/177) — 200
Lohan, figure, gilt, standing, in prayer, 1½, Tang (4261/175) — 375
Pony, figure, gold-splashed, cast in 2 sections, 2¾, Ming (4261/181) — 300

Hardwood

Box, carved, imitation, set of books, drawers, 11¾, 8½, 4½, cracks, 18c (4261/148) — 275

Rhinoceros Horn

Cup, archaistic, faceted, octagonal, carved, 3, chip, crack, rep, 18c (4261/137) — 650
Cup, flower-form, carved, hollow magnolia blossom, 3¾, res, rep, chip, 18c (4261/136) — 400
Cup, libation, carved, fruit, leafage, W6¼, rep, 18c (4261/133) — *650*

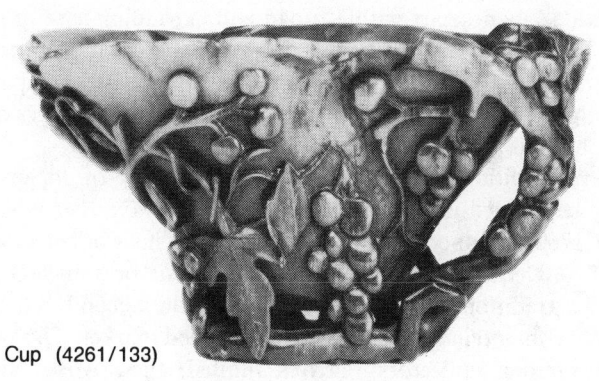

Cup (4261/133)

Cup, lotus leaf-form, carved, swirling waves, 3, chip, 18c (4261/134) — 600
Cup, lotus leaf-form, carved, swirling waves, 3, chip, 18c (4261/135) — 650

Stone

Lohan, figure, soapstone, reclining, on a sack, cat, 5⅛, L18/19c (4261/197) — 250

Wood

Kuan Ti, figure, gilt-decorated, god of War, standing, 13, flaking chip, Ming (4261/191) — 350
Lady, court, figure, gilt-decorated, seated, throne, 7½, Ming (4261/189) — 200
Lohan, figure, gilt-decorated, seated, hands later, 33, flaking, late Ming (4261/190) — 1600
Official, figure, painted, standing, god of Literature*, 12¾, Ming (4261/192) — 325

T'ang Dynasty

Stele, limestone, Carved Buddha on lotus pad throne, 16 x 9¾ x 4 (4242/252) — 5000

Yuan Dynasty

Bust of Bodhisattva, benign expression, 14½, cr (4242/247) — 1100

Ming Dynasty

Buddist lion, carved soapstone, stocky, snarling beast, 3¼, rub (4242/243) — 275
Head of Kuan Yin, cast iron, Goddess of Mercy, full round face, 20 (4242/246) — 9000
Iron, head of a deity, cast, high topnot, rusted, 21¾ (4159/41) — 1100
Lohan and cat, painted wood, 1 leg raised, loose robes, 25½ (4242/245) — 4250
Shou lao, carved soapstone, god of longevity, 10⅛, minor chip (4242/244) — 1300

Sung Dynasty

Kuan Yin, carved wood, with arms held in abhaya mudra, 17, chip (4242/250) — 950

Ch'ien Lung Period

Vase, blue glass, pear shape with flared rim, 10, chip (4242/231) — 1300

Chapter 10

Japanese Works of Art

Collectors and dealers from Japan, North America, Australia and all of Europe provide Japanese art with a broad and expanding base of support. The variety of Japanese art and the knowledge and sophistication it demands from the collector further contribute to the stability of this field. Japanese art has undergone a gradual, steady rise in values, with few of the surges and reversals brought on by fads and speculation.

Prints have traditionally been the leading category of Japanese art. This market may be divided into four segments: Primitives, artists who predate the rise around 1760 of full-color printing; Classics, who worked mostly between 1760 and 1820; Decadents, who followed the Classic printmakers who worked in the Classic tradition from about 1890 until the Second World War. The Primitives have maintained a steady if undervalued market. Though interest in these artists among collectors remains limited, their works are attracting growing scholarly notice, and the market will likely benefit from this new attention. The Classics continued their steady appreciation this past season, while the Decadents, though remaining out of favor with collectors, rose in value as decorative items. The Moderns, however, leaped enormously in value, with prices for some prints tripling or quadrupling within a year. This is due, no doubt, to the unusually large and fine selection of these items offered this past season, and to most of them being limited editions and in excellent condition, factors which are increasingly important to collectors.

Japanese pottery and porcelain maintained a solid front, though pieces of extreme rarity achieved breakthrough prices. Overall this segment showed a slow increase in value, with the ceremony pottery wares moving slightly ahead of the porcelains.

Within the field of swords and sword fittings, specialized areas showed strong trends both up and down. The Koto, "Old Sword," with the exception of the very finest examples, has diminished considerably in value. Collectors have become less sympathetic to swords which have become metallurgically "tired" and those whose authenticity is in any way questionable. Shinshinto (post-1780 revival) blades are usually metallurgically sound and bear signatures, by which they can be authenticated without question. As a result, these Shinshinto blades have risen markedly over the past two years.

Netsuke continued to advance in value, yet the field still offers beginning collectors ample opportunity to acquire moderately priced items. Tokuko, Kokuko, Ojime and Inro pieces all brought excellent prices. Lacquer items, as long as they were in excellent condition, also sold well. Decorative screens made substantial gains, due no doubt to their new popularity in interior design.

Broad international interest in Japanese art insulates the field from the kind of external pressures felt in most other areas of collectibles. The market responds mostly to internal forces such as changing evaluations of artistic merit or desirability. The field is complex and varied, yet prices on the whole have kept up at a steady rise and may be expected to continue to do so.

Despite the chapter title, a small section on other Asian works of art is included toward the end of this chapter.

CERAMICS

Agano

Bottle, part-glazed, flat ring foot, brown-bodied, 8¾, L17c (4155/239) $300

Anonymous

Chawan, black-glazed, after Kenzan, Diam 4, 19c (4257/316)   300
Model, spaniel, glazed, seated, ruffled collar, black glaze, 12¼, dam, 19c (4257/289)   50
Vase, cloisonne-on-pottery, ovid, domed feet, wide trumpet, 12⅛, L19c (4257/287)   800

Ao-kutani

Bottle, double-gourd, 6 vertical bands, waves, 6⅝, chip lip, 19c (4155/152)   100
Dish, cream crazed ground, landscape, Diam 14¼, E19c (4155/195)   600

Archaic

Jar, storage, stoneware, round-bottomed, tall mouth, flaring lip, 6¼, hc, tumulus period (4155/167)   175

Arita

Bottle, blue and white, 'grapevine', bulbous, elongated neck, 9½, 18c (4155/155)   650
Bottle, blue and white, 'grapevine', wedge ring foot, globular, 11⅝, 18c (4155/203)   425
Bottle, blue and white, globular, thick ring foot, elongated neck, 10½, 18c (4257/281)   150
Bottle, blue and white, globular, thick ring foot, elongated neck, 11, 18c (4257/280)   100
Bottle, blue and white, globular, thick ring foot, elongated neck, 10, 18c (4257/282)   125
Bottle, blue and white, globular, thick ring foot, elongated neck, 9, 18c (4257/283)   60
Bottle, blue and white, wedge ring foot, tear-form, 10, l17c/E18c (4155/202)   325
Bottle, double-gourd, blue and white, farmer, resting, waterfall, 11⅝, ca1700 (4155/154)   400
Bottle, export, globular, flared foot, elongated neck, 8⅛, E18c (4155/141)   850
Bowl, blue and white, deep, high ring foot, painted, Diam 8⅝, L17/18c (4257/301)   300
Bowl, blue and white, deep, ring foot, 2 spurs, foliage, Diam 11⅛, L17c (4155/197)   650
Bowl, bulb, blue and white, 4 stub feet, flat lip, W8¼, L17c/E18c (4155/98)   200
Bowl, kutani enamels, thin ring foot, landscape, Diam 5¼, L17c (4155/172)   125
Charger, blue and white, ring fool, scattered spurs, birds, geometrics, Diam 15⅝, L17c (4155/207)   *1400*
Charger, blue and white, ring foot, painted with roundel of birds, Diam 12⅜, L17c (4257/268)   325
Charger, blue and white, ring foot, painted with roundel of birds, Diam 15⅝, L17c (4257/267)   950
Charger, blue and white, thick ring foot, 5 spurs, Diam 18, L17c (4155/214)   *2800*
Dish, blue and white, bird amidst lotus, Diam 8⅝, L17c (4155/184)   125
Dish, blue and white, deep, fluted, blue underglaze, Diam 3½, 18c (4257/295)   350
Dish, blue and white, thick ring foot, painted, Diam 7⅞, 17c/E18c (4257/293)   1600
Dish, blue and white, thick ring foot, shallow, landscape, Diam 8, L17c (4155/187)   1100
Dish, blue and white, thin ring foot, painted with flowers, Diam 8¾, L17c (4257/264)   175
Dish, blue and white, thin ring foot, 5 spurs, Diam 13, ca1700 (4155/194)   700
Dish, blue and white, Kakiemon style, fluted, molded wide band of waves, Diam 10⅝, E18c
   (4257/279)   1100
Dish, blue and white, Kakiemon style, short ring foot, painted, Diam 14, L17c (4257/278)   *2100*
Dish, blue and white, fluted, molded with foliage, Diam 8½, ca1700 (4257/263)   150
Dishes, blue and white, pair, simple decoration, Diam 8⅞, 18c (4257/294)   150
Eagle, model, glazed pottery, perched, rocky outcrop, 14, rep, 19c (4155/100)   600
Jug, blue and white, European-form, short-flared foot, straight neck, 10½, cr handle, 1660-80
   (4257/286)   750
Jug, blue and white, European-form, short-flared foot, straight neck, 10⅜, hc mouth, 1660-80
   (4257/285)   750
Karako, polychrome, standing, holding ball, 6⅝, E18c (4155/140)   1100
Kendi, blue and white, globular body, continuous landscape, 7¾, chip, L17c (4155/198)   275
Kogo, blue and white, fish-form, simple decoration, glazed interior and foot, W3⅝, 17c (4257/306)   325
Shishi, pair, polychrome, dogs, seated, hindquarters, M10⅝, H9⅜, rep, E18c (4155/139)   3700
Vase, Kakiemon enamels, incut foot, shoulder, quatrelobed-sectioned, 10½, L17c (4155/369)   *4000*

Banko

Ewer, enamelled, elongated tear-form, ear-form handle, 9¼, res, ca1800 (4155/216)   *3250*

Bizen

Bottle, brown, molded, hexagonal, elongated neck, 5⅜, mouth res, ca1800 (4155/258)   400
Bottle, double-gourd, flat foot, lightly painted, 6⅞, 18c (4155/259)   425
Bottle, double-gourd, Imbe, concave foot, ash-glaze, 7⅛, ca1600 (4155/257)   850
Bottle, double-gourd, Kanashige Usuke*, lower lobe depressed, top tilting, 10⅛, mouth br, ca1700
   (4155/262)   300
Cat, figure, rope collar, W8, 18c (4155/252)   650

Daikoku and Ebisu, seated on launch, 7½, 19c (4155/127)   725
Daruma, standing, scowling, 11⅜, E19c (4155/253)   475
Daruma, seated figure, brown, flowing robes, scowling, unsealed, 7¼, 18/19c (4257/243)   150
Jar, storage, brown, concave foot, depressed baluster form, 7⅛, 16c (4155/261)   1800
Jar, storage, part-glazed, flat-foot, baluster-form, clotted glaze, 14⅜, 17c (4155/124)   175
Jurojin, brown-glazed, standing, god of longevity, 6¾, broken, 19c (4155/129)   125
Koro, cat-form, crouching, W5⅛, ears rep, 15c (4155/255)   *2900*
Monkey, model, part brown-glazed, seated, short coat, 5⅝, ca1800 (4155/256)   100
Nobleman, figure, by Kimura Kiyochika, seated, glazed, 6¾, cr, rep, ca1810 (4155/251)   225
Vase, flower, 'blue', finger ribbed, conical, 2 ring handles, 11, 17c (4155/250)   1700
Vase, flower, brown, concave foot, finger molded, cylindrical, 9⅞, ca1600 (4155/260)   2000

Hasami

Vase, blue and white, mallet-form, 7½, 19c (4155/210)   100

Dish (4257/278)

Ewer (4155/216)

Vase (4155/369)

Charger (4155/207)

Charger (4155/214)

Koro (4155/255)

Incense burner
(4155/336)

Tankard (4155/168)

Inkstand
(4155/150)

Hirado

Incense burner, Shiski form, seated male, paw resting on ball, 5½, 19c (4257/290)   325
Saucer, blue and white, Kiku-form, 3 stub feet, decorated, Diam 5⅛, 19c (4257/262)   100

Hizen

Kogo, double-gourd, Ato Shonsui, ring foot, 2¾, L17c (4155/234)   325

Hozan Awataguchi

Dish, covered, square, bevelled corners, flat cover, W8½, 19c (4257/255)   200

Imari

Bijin, figure, standing, flowing kimono, 17⅝, res neck, hand, 19c (4257/271)   600
Bottle, double-gourd, underglaze, blue dragon, 21½, L19c (4155/90)   900
Bottle, silver-mounted, flared foot, globular, Middle Eastern mount, 9½, 18c (4155/163)   950
Bottle, Kutani enamels, cylindrical, flared incut foot, copper mouth, 11¾, res, L17c (4155/371)   6000
Bottle, Kutani enamels, thick ring foot, tear-form, silver lip mount, 13, chip, L17c (4155/370)   8500
Bottle/stopper, sake, floral motifs, 6⅝, 18c (4155/153)   700
Bottles, sake, pair, square, plain, lightning-zag grounds, 10¼, chip, ca1700 (4155/84)   2300
Bowl, Kiku form, set of eight, molded, decorated, Diam 6⅞, 19c (4257/312)   375
Bowl, Kinrande, painted with Du'ch scenes, Diam 9⅜, 19c (4257/310)   2300
Bowl, polyheronical, multi-faceted, decorated, Diam 12½, 19c (4257/307)   800
Bowls, fluted, deep, hexagonal and decorated, Diam 6, 19c (4257/313)   450
Charger, blue and white, grapevines, shallow, landscape, Diam 22⅜, 19c (4155/80)   400
Charger, enamelled, molded, carp, waterfall, Diam 22⅝, L19c (4155/95)   1050
Dish, clam's dream, fluted, Diam 14½, 18c (4155/196)   1000
Dish, underglaze blue, overglaze gold, Diam 10⅜, ca1700 (4257/256)   125
Inkstand, low, square, floral panels, 4 x 4 x 2⅛, ca1700 (4155/150)   *500*
Jar, covered, molded, baluster-form, blue underglazed, 27½, E18c (4257/259)   1000
Kendi and stopper, globular, ribbed, peonies, 9⅛, L17c (4155/199)   1000
Shishi dancer, teapot-form, 3 boys, as shishi, W9½, 19c (4155/165)   550
Tankard, silver-mounted, thin ring foot, Dutch mounts, 8, L17c (4155/168)   *1800*
Woman, model, enamelled, standing, 11⅝, head off, ca1700 (4155/164)   750

Kakiemon

Bottle, flared ring foot, bulbous, silver lip and cover, 9¼, age cr, L17c (4155/377)   6500
Bowl, enamelled, concave foot, incised, leaves, Diam 5⅝, L17c (4155/378)   2700
Bowl, enamelled, thin ring foot, kiku cluster, waves, Diam 6, ca1700 (4155/379)   2100
Bowls, pair, rare subject, hexagonally fluted, Diam 5½, 18c (4257/265)   650
Dish, blue and white, deep, fluted, Diam 14¾, ca1700 (4155/191)   9000
Dish, enamelled, grasses, flowers, Diam 8¼, 20c (4155/188)   75
Hotei and boy, enamelled, god of felicity, laughing, W7½, E18c (4155/169)   7400
Jar, blue and white, baluster-form, low wedge foot, straight neck, 9¼, hc neck, ca1690 (4257/288)   1600
Jar, enamelled, thick flared edge-cut ring foot, bulbous, 7⅜, L17c (4155/380)   35000
Woman and child, standing, Uchiwa-form base, 6⅞, 2 figures mis, L17c (4155/376)   1800

Kameyama

Bowl, blue and white, thin ring foot, sprays of flowers, Diam 5, 18c (4155/175)   275

Karatsu

Bottle, brown-glazed, concave foot, irregularly pinched-form, 6⅞, chip, 15c (4155/241) — 400
Chaire, brown-glazed, flat string-cut foot, squat baluster-form, 2½, M16c (4155/240) — 300
Teapot, thick ring foot, globular, simple handle, 4⅝, rep, 15c (4155/242) — 1400

Ko-Imari

Bowl, enamel, Kakiemon style, wide ring foot, deep, decorated, Diam 7½, 17c (4257/318) — 375

Ko-Kutani

Dish, wedge ring irregular foot, Diam 5½, rep foot, L17c (4257/244) — 1100

Kutani

Bottle, flared ring foot, bulbous tear-form, 8, M17c (4155/338) — 17000
Bowl, deep, red, inverted bell-form, decorated, Diam 18¾, M19c (4257/258) — 950
Chawan, red, incut ring foot, flaring, Diam 4¼, ca1780 (4155/339) — 350
Dish, red, fluted, dragon, 3 ho-o, clouds, Diam 12⅞, E19c (4155/93) — 450
Incense burner, miniature, 4 ogee feet, roundels, floral, 2, 17c (4155/336) — *5500*
Incense burner, red, att Mokubei, cylindrical burner, 3 stub feet, 2⅝, ca1850 (4257/241) — 50
Saucers, set of five, rectangular, bird, plum branch, 1896 (4155/177) — 50
Stembowl, enamelled, thick trumpet foot, deep, crenellated rim, 5½, 19c (4155/130) — 125
Vase, baluster-form, wide flared mouth, painted, 14½, L19c (4257/274) — 475
Wine pourer, handled, ring foot, squat, multi colored, 5½ x 8, rep, M17c (4155/337) — 8000

Kyo

Dish, serving, blue and white, oval, high sides, painted, W8⅜, 19c (4257/317) — 125

Kyoto

Burner, enamelled, Att Hozan XVI, square section, unglazed interior, stamped, Diam 4, 19c (4257/273) — 30
Chawan, white-glazed, Rokubei*, flaring trumpet foot, conical, 2⅛, chips, 15/17c (4155/349) — 350
Hotei, Kiyomizu-yaki, standing, bulging sack, 7¾, rep, ca1800 (4155/346) — 175
Incense burner, Kiyomizu-yaki, pouch-form, 3 spurs, floral, 4⅜, rep, ca1800 (4155/347) — 550
Jar, covered, green-glazed, Eisen*, squat, baluster-form, domed, 4, 16/18c (4155/344) — 300
Teapot, enamelled, Iwakurayama, ring foot, globular, eat-form handle, 3⅝, L18c (4155/345) — 175
Vase, flower, blue-glazed, elongated, molded, 2 handles, 7¾, 19c (4155/348) — 30

Kyoto (Dohachi)

Chawan, irregular ring foot, tranparent glaze, 3⅛, 1841 (4155/360) — 650
Chawan, trumpet foot, deep, Fuji, clouds, 2⅞, M19c (4155/361) — 125
Chawan, grey-glazed, ring foot, deep, 3¼, 19/20c (4155/362) — 225
Incense burner, red and green, shaped base, square, waisted neck, 3, L18c (4155/358) — 275
Incense burner, yellow-glazed, cylindrical, 3 stub feet, 2½, 1830 (4155/359) — 150

Kyoto (Kenzan)

Bowl, enamelled, high ring foot, tree, leaves, Diam 6⅞ (4155/364) — 2000
Chawan, thin foot, cylindrical, landscape, 2⅝, hc (4155/366) — 1600
Chawan, enamelled, flat ring foot, crane in pine, 3⅜, rep (4155/365) — 125
Mizusasashi, concave string-cut foot, square, 6⅛ (4155/367) — 900
Okame, glazed, standing, plump, 8¼ (4155/363) — 275

Kyoto (Ninsei)

Bottle, double gourd, Sobokai ware, ring foot, 8⅜, 18c (4155/351) — 425
Chawan, black 'oil spot', 6 roundels, waisted squares, Diam 5 (4155/355) — 275
Chawan, brown glazed, incut ring foot, 3¾, 18c (4155/352) — 375
Chawan, Iwakurayama, flared notched floor, Rakan group, 3⅝, ca1800 (4155/353) — 350
Dish, cake, lobed, thin-walled, concave foot, W6½, ca1600 (4155/357) — 1700
Figure, white-glazed, squat, holding fan, 2½ (4155/356) — 175
Incense burner, Odoshi-form, 5⅜, 17/18c (4155/350) — 3600
Incense burner, enamelled, Iwakurayama, 3 ogee feet, incurving, 3¾, hc, 17c (4155/354) — 75

Mishima

Chawan, grey and white, concave foot, deep, incised, inlaid, Diam 5⅝, 18/19c (4155/231) — 300
Incense burner, cylindrical, ring foot, inlaid, 2⅜, 17/18c (4155/233) — 125
Incense burner, ring foot, globular, gilt pierced cover, 3⅛, 17/18c (4155/232) — 175

Ofuke

Bottle, sake, grey-green-glazed, incut concave foot, tapering, 8, 16/17c (4155/221) — 350
Chaire, grey-glazed, thick concave foot, 3 flat sand spurs, 2½, rep, ca1600 (4155/222) — 375

Ohi

Chaire, ochre-glazed, string-cut foot, ivory cover, 3½, E18c (4155/228)   950
Vase, flower, red-glazed, concave foot, twisted, 7½, E18c (4155/229)   100

Oribe

Bowl, deep, irregular flaring, 2 loop handles, Diam 19½, 19c (4155/86)   1050
Chaire, white glaze, 2¾, 19c (4155/144)   150
Chaire, brown-glazed, string-cut foot, cylindrical, 3, M18c (4155/264)   550
Chawan, black, flattened foot, compressed, 3⅛, res, ca1600 (4155/263)   1700
Chawan, green and brown glazed, Naruto, ring foot, flaring, 4½, chip, E16 (4155/265) 1000

Raku

Chaire, green and red, Chonyu, 7th gen, concave foot, globular, 2 loop handles, 2⅛, 18c (4155/269)   950
Chawan, black and red, Donyu, 3rd gen, ring foot, 5 neat spurs, Diam 5⅛ (4155/275)   2300
Chawan, green, irregular foot, named 'Nikko', Diam 4¾, rep, 19c (4155/273)   350
Chawan, green, Chonyu*, 7th gen, ring foot, swelling, 2¾, 18c (4155/270)   1500
Chawan, orange/green, Chojiro*, 1st gen, ring foot, cylindrical, 3¾ (4155/274)   900
Chawan, red, coiled foot, flaring bowl, 5⅜, 18c (4155/272)   850
Chawan, red, small foot, finger molded, Diam 4¾, 19c (4257/247)   375
Chawan, Ryonyu, 9th gen, compressed foot, melon-form, 3⅞, E19c (4155/271)   1200
Incense burner, Shishi-form, standing, open mouth, 4, 18/19c (4155/267)   175
Kogo, by Kenyo (Miura Totaro), Okame-form, seated, 2⅛, ca1880 (4155/268)   475
Kogo, green, Shishi-form, molded, carved, W2⅞, 18/19c (4155/266)   475
Mizusashi, black/red, slightly concave foot, wide mouth, black glaze, 8⅜, 18/19c (4257/236)   150
Vase, flower, double-gourd, grey, flat base, tilted, 6¾, 1789-1801 (4155/276)   125

Satsuma

Beaker, section, hexagonal, flared, samurai, 7⅛, 19c (4155/117)   200
Bottle, black-glazed, thin ring foot, elongated, flared mouth, 8⅝, 17c (4155/249)   2000
Bottle, double-gourd, many fans, 5⅝, L19c (4155/112)   300
Bottle-vase, square-section, flowers, arhats, 15¼, L19c (4155/78)   650
Bowl, flaring, enamelled designed, Diam 4⅝, M19c (4257/277)   1200
Bowl, flowers, butterflies, Diam 7⅛, 19c (4155/107)   425
Box, cylindrical, pheasants, Diam 4⅛, M19c (4155/131)   2200
Box, covered, landscape, flowers, cylindrical-form, 4, L19c (4155/111)   375
Box, cricket, pierced, barrel-form, 4⅞, L19c (4155/105)   625
Box, hexagonal, 3 stub feet, decorated with procession scene, Diam 6½, L19c (4257/252)   600
Box, rectangular, people, various pursuits, W7⅜, L19c (4155/89)   *3000*
Bucket, water, miniature, birds, flowers, Daikoku, 3⅜, L19c (4155/110)   225
Chaire, double-gourd, brown-glazed, squat, string-cut foot, 2½, E18c (4155/248)   350
Chaire, Onigara-yaki, cylindrical, string-cut foot, 3¼, 18c (4155/246)   250
Chawan, three-color, wedge-section ring foot, 3, 18c (4155/244)   325
Dish, peacock, hen, flowers, Diam 12, L19c (4155/92)   375
Incense burner, blue ground, 4 leaf feet, handles, 7, L19c (4155/106)   425
Incense burner, fan-form, scrolling foliage, 3⅞, 19c (4155/116)   225
Incense burner, hexagonal, flat shoulder, pierced cover, 3⅜, L19c (4155/114)   625
Jar, brown-painted, baluster-form, short mouth, 5¼, 17c (4155/245)   600
Jar, covered, polyhedronical, decorated surface, cylindrical cover, 4⅛, L19c (4257/254)   425
Jar, cream-glazed, squat, flared foot, baluster-form, 6⅛, 18c (4155/243)   175
Jar, molded and enamelled, baluster form, highly molded mid-section, 16⅜, hc, L19c (4257/272) *1900*
Jars, covered, miniature, baluster-form, domed, 5, 19c (4155/115)   275
Kogo, rectangular box, decorated, 2½ x 2⅛ x 1¼, 18c (4257/261)   125
Kogo, circular, manju-form box, 19c (4257/257)   125
Platter, flat, painted with a landscape, Diam 20¾, L19c (4257/314)   700
Samurai, figure, seated, rocky base, scowling, 12⅛, 19c (4155/101)   375
Vase, depressed baluster-form, cranes, plums, 11⅛, L19c (4155/88)   700
Vase, cylindrical, 3 shaped feet, elaborate enamel, 14, L19c (4257/270)   500
Vases, pair, circular-flask-form, trumpet feet, mouths, 7¼, L19c (4155/108)   225
Vases, pair, hexagonal, square feet, mouths, 8⅛, L19c (4155/109)   1200
Vases, pair, miniature, cylindrical, people, various pursuits, incut feet, 3⅞, 19c (4155/113)   300

Seto

Bottle, black, thin ring foot, elongated, 11, ca17c (4155/278)   500
Bottle, double-gourd, yellow, inset foot, glazed, 7⅛, chip, 15c (4155/290)   *225*
Bottle, double-gourd, yellow, inset ring foot, brown areas, 8¾, rep, 15c (4155/287)   *375*
Bottle, rust-glazed, string-cut foot, small neck, 6, mouth rep, E16c (4155/288)   *375*
Bottle, white and brown glazed, short spread foot, bulbous, short straight neck, 9⅝, L17c (4257/311) 150

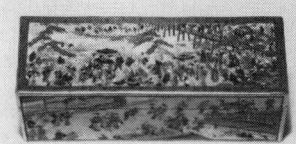

Box (4155/89)

Bottle
(4155/287)

Bottle
(4155/288)

Bottle
(4155/290)

Jar (4257/272)

Incense burner
(4155/279)

Bottle, yellow, ring foot, crazed glazed, 8½, 15c (4155/281)	475
Chaire, flat foot, flat shoulder, red-brown glaze, 2¾, 18c (4257/322)	750
Chaire, flat foot, squat, brown/black glaze, 2¼, lip res, 18/19c (4257/321)	600
Chaire, flat string-cut foot, globular, 2¾, 15c (4155/304)	950
Chaire, flat string-cut foot, inset edge, 2⅞, res, E18c (4155/305)	175
Chaire, irregular flat foot, elongated, 3¾, lip chip, 18/19c (4257/332)	1200
Chaire, string-cut foot, baluster-form, 2⅞, 18/19c (4257/325)	600
Chaire, string-cut foot, elongated, 3½, 18/19c (4257/333)	950
Chaire, string-cut foot, elongated, 3⅝, 17/18c (4257/329)	475
Chaire, string-cut foot, globular form, 3¼, 17/18c (4257/331)	500
Chaire, string-cut foot, globular-form, 2¾, 17/18c (4257/326)	450
Chaire, string-cut foot, globular-form, 3, 18/19c (4257/324)	425
Chaire, string-cut foot, globular-form, 2½, 18/19c (4257/323)	325
Chaire, brown-glazed, baluster, jar-form, string-cut foot, 2½, 16c (4155/299)	750
Chaire, brown-glazed, circularly-cut foot, inward sloping jar, 2⅝, E18c (4155/300)	1000
Chaire, brown-glazed, flat string-cut foot, 3, 16c (4155/295)	250
Chaire, brown-glazed, flat string-cut foot, baluster-form, 3, 18/19c (4155/145)	200
Chaire, brown-glazed, flat string-cut foot, cylindrical, 3⅞, E17c (4155/298)	900
Chaire, brown-glazed, flat string-cut foot, flat shoulder, 3, 18/19c (4155/148)	450
Chaire, brown-glazed, mallet-form, 2 handles, 2⅞, 16c (4155/296)	325
Chaire, brown-glazed, string-cut foot, 2⅝, mouth res, 16c (4155/297)	550
Chaire, brown-glazed, string-cut foot, angular baluster, 2¼, E18c (4155/301)	1100
Chaire, brown-glazed, string-cut foot, globular, 2¼, E18c (4155/302)	1300
Chaire, double-gourd, inset foot, deep ochre glaze, 4⅝, 19c (4155/146)	325
Chaire, handled, small string-cut foot, elongated, 4, 19c (4257/330)	650
Chaire, molded, yellow, flat foot, baluster-form, 3⅜, 15c (4155/303)	550
Chaire, red/brown-glazed, string-cut foot, swollen-form, 2⅞, E17c (4155/307)	750
Chawan, brown-glazed, irregular ring foot, Diam 5, ca1800 (4155/292)	350
Chawan, brown/green-glazed, string-cut foot, spirally grooved, 2¾, 19c (4155/306)	325
Chawan, yellow, irregular string-cut foot, flaring, Diam 5, 15c (4155/291)	950
Incense burner, green-glazed, Rakubei*, flat string-cut foot, squat, Diam 3⅞, ca1500 (4155/293)	300
Incense burner, white, Tsugumasa, No mask and Hako form, 6⅛, ca1800 (4155/279)	*1400*
Jar, storage, yellow, Toshiro manner, flat foot, baluster, 6⅞, 16c (4155/280)	325
Jar, white, flat foot, angular baluster jar, 8⅜, E16c (4155/282)	300
Mizusashi, brown, spread foot, cylindrical, 5⅞, ca1800 (4155/285)	300
Mizusashi, yellow, concave foot, cylindrical, 5¼, ca1800 (4155/284)	500
Mizusashi, yellow, inset foot, squat globular, 2 loop handles, 5¾, 15c (4155/286)	1100

Mizusashi, Uzurafi, turned/string-cut foot, cylindrical, 6⅜, E16c (4155/283)   950

Seto/Satsuma

Chaire, string-cut foot, elongated, 3, 18/19c (4257/328)   350

Seto/Takatori

Chaire, string-cut foot, globular-form, 3, 19c (4257/327)   375

Shidoro

Jar, brown-glazed, silver mounted foot, baluster, 6½, E18c (4155/238)   225

Shigaraki

Jar, red-glazed, flat-foot, baluster-form, 7¼, 18c (4155/230)   950
Jar, storage, concave foot, baluster-form, grog-imbedded body, 18, 16/17c (4155/121)   900
Jar, storage, uneven foot, irregular baluster-form, grog eruptions, 17¼, cr, 17c (4155/123)   350
Mizusashi, irregular round pocked-base, impregnated with, glassious grog, 6¼, 15/16c (4257/309)   *27000*

Mizusashi (4257/309)

Dish (4257/246)

Shino

Chawan, white-glazed, irregular ring foot, steep-walled, Diam 4¾, M17c (4155/220)   1200
Incense burner, white-glazed, thick ring foot, widely crazed, 3⅜, 16c (4155/219)   275

Shodai

Jar, storage, brown, flat foot, globular form, incut mouth, 5¾, hc, 19c (4257/237)   40

Takatori

Chaire, flat foot, baluster container, flat shoulder, 2⅞, 19c (4257/320)   950
Chaire, brown-glazed, contracted spirally-cut foot, 3⅛, M17c (4155/226)   1200
Chaire, brown-glazed, spirally-cut foot, 3¼, 17/18c (4155/227)   600

Tamba

Bottle, streak-glazed, globular, concave foot, brown, 9¾, 18c (4155/236)   125
Bottle, streak-glazed, globular, concave foot, brown, 10¼, 18c (4155/235)   100
Jar, storage, ash-glazed, flat-foot, baluster-form, wide mouth, 18½, 16/17c (4155/119)   950
Jar, storage, green-glazed, flat-foot, brown bodied, 13¾, 16c* (4155/120)   250
Jar, storage, splash-glazed, globular, wide mouth, black/brown, 10¼, 19c (4257/248)   275

Various kilns

Bottle, black-glazed, incised, flat ring foot, globular, Tokoname, 7¾, ca1700 (4155/237)   450
Bowl, covered, enamelled, birds, flowers, Diam 5¾, 19c (4155/157)   200
Box, covered, part-glazed, Arita*, elongated quatrelobed, W5¼, 18c (4155/318)   600
Chaire, green-glazed, Iga*, string-cut foot, 3½, ca1800 (4155/319)   550
Chawan, blue and white, flared notched foot, Wari Kodai Karatsu*, 3⅝, 17c (4155/158)   400
Chawan, white-glazed, flat ring foot, flaring bowl, Diam 5⅝, rep, 18c (4155/311)   350
Dish, enamelled, high ring foot, painted and decorated, Nabeshima, Diam 5¾, L18c (4257/246)   *3750*

Dishes, fan, blue and white, landscape designs, W8, L17c (4155/162) 250
Incense burner, blue and white, boat-form, molded, W4, 18c (4155/315) 30
Incense burner, blue-glazed, crane-form, compact model, 4⅛, 19c (4155/310) 400
Incense burner, Nabeshima Okochi kiln*, 4 stub feet, rectangular, 2¾, foot res, 17c (4155/314) *1400*
Jar, blue and white, ribbed, thick ring foot, squat, 3½, M17c (4155/171) 1100
Jar, footed, flat foot pierced with 4 holes, slender stem, Yayoi, 5⅜, res, 2/3c (4257/251) 400
Jar, white, soft paste, ring foot, globular, incised, 2¾, hc, 18c (4155/313) 75
Ono No Tofu, glazed, nobleman seated, 4¼, 18c (4155/312) 75
Teapot, blue-glazed, thick handle, matte, W4¼, 18c (4155/316) 40

CLOCKS

Bracket clock, moveable circular dial, shakudo hour and half-hour plates, 5⅜, 19c (4165/239) *2300*

Incense burner
(4155/314)

Bracket clock
(4165/239)

INRO

Assorted items

Brass brush holder, stylized, vines, mon, unsigned, 19c (4257/1105) 75
Embroidered, multi-colors, dragon admist clouds, 19c (4257/1100) 475
Embroidered, French knot technique, 19c (4257/1093) 75
Embroidered, French knot technique, dragon amid clouds, 19c (4257/1092) 75
Gold, circular, lacquer decorated, reverse is rogin lacquer, 'Tsunehisa, Saku', 18/19c (4201/57) 1800
Gold and Shibayama, star shape, applied with peacock and flowers, 19c (4201/61) 5000
Gold lacquer, fumibako form, rare, various tones of gold, signed 'Kansai Saku' (4201/56) 4600
Gold lacquer, lozenge section, applied with mother-of-pearl swans, 3 cases, signed 'Ryushosai'
(4201/64) 1000
Gold lacquer, oval form, 4 cases, figural scene in gold and silver, signed, 'Koryu', 19c (4201/67) 1900
Ivory, gold lacquered with geese, open fret-work runners, 19c (4201/66) 1200
Lacquer, brown, 7 cases, rabbit motifs, signed, 'Yoyusai', 19c (4201/62) 1800
Lacquer, gold, black, brown, four cases, bamboo motifs, 'Hirakawa', 19c (4201/68) 1700
Lacquer, oval form, black, H cases, signed 'Kajikawa Saku', 19c (4201/60) 1700
Lacquer, suit of armor form, multicolored, with togidashi, design, 19c (4201/59) 2600
Laquer, multicolored, Shoki form, four cases, inlay eyes, applied detail, signed, 'Kajikawa Saku' 19c
(4201/58) 2600
Lacquer and Shibayama, oval form, five cases, extremely fine, 19c (4201/63) 4200
Leather, clasp, two badgers in gilt, 19c (4257/1099) 275
Miniature, one case, metal, oval, flowering branch, Moitsu*, 19c (4191/99) 75
Miniature, one case, metal, shibuichi sheath, 19c (4191/103) 125
Miniature, one case, silver, gourd, Kojitsu, 1934 (4191/98) 150
Miniature, one case, Shibuichi, globular, gilded flowers, 19c (4191/101) 175
Miniature, Tonkotsu, silver, circular, bamboo leaves, 19c (4191/102) 250
Porcelain blue and white, three case, 2 horses, weeping willow, 19c (4257/1103) 800
Tonkotsu, woven straw, single-case, 19c (4191/108) 250
Wood, grained, applied with horn, catfish in water design, signed, 'Masanao' 19c (4201/65) 1200
Woven straw, basket-form, ojime, netsuke, 19c (4257/1091) 325

Ivory

Acrobatic octopus, 19c, (4257/1184) 475
An Islander, Bando, 18c, (4257/1206) 1300

Baby, crawling, Tomochika, 19c, (4257/1144)   375
Ball-form Shishi, 19c, (4257/1131)   300
Bathing woman, Hakuraku, 20c, (4257/1151)   450
Benjin, leaning on a box, Michigyoku, 20c, (4257/1122)   250
Boar, crouched, 19c, (4257/1155)   375
Boy and cow, 18c, (4257/1165)   225
Butterfly dancer, 20c, (4257/1149)   550
Cat, overturned bowl, Masakazu, 19c, (4257/1207)   1200
Clam shell, Yukimasa, 20c, (4257/1152)   550
Cluster of nuts, 19c, (4257/1141)   325
Cow, calf, Tomotado school, 19c, (4257/1177)   1700
Dancing figure, Tomotada, 18c, (4257/1148)   225
Deer, monkey, Kobun, E19c, (4257/1127)   275
Ebisu, seated, 19c, (4257/1192)   275
Fanciful scene, Masamitsu, 19c, (4257/1139)   500
Figure, 20c, (4257/1191)   225
Foreigner on horseback, 18/19c, (4257/1178)   550
Grazing horse, 18c, (4257/1154)   325
Handaka Sonja, standing, 19c, (4257/1193)   150
Hat with a Kakihan, 19c, (4257/1200)   450
Horse, rider, Yoshitomo, 19c, (4257/1140)   425
Hotei, lounging, 20c, (4257/1121)   275
Hotei, standing, Mitsuhiro, 19c, (4257/1180)   700
Hunter, squatting, 19c, (4257/1125)   175
Karako, seated boy with mask, 19c, (4257/1190)   300
Kwan-yu, standing, E19c, (4257/1117)   350
Lantern, Shugyokusai, 19c, (4257/1194)   275
Man, flowering log, 19c, (4257/1204)   300
Man and woman, Hyakuunsai, 19c, (4257/1136)   550
Man with monkeys, 19c, (4257/1162)   400
Manju, boy seated on ox, Koju, 19c, (4257/1199)   300
Manju, child nursing woman, Masamitsu, 19c, (4257/1198)   850
Manju, cock on drum, 18c, (4257/1150)   400
Manju, crab, brocade design, 19c, (4257/1195)   275
Manju, figure, standing, tree, 19c, (4257/1187)   175
Manju, lacquered, 3 boxes, Shibayama, 19c, (4257/1188)   400
Manju, sambaso dancer, Kosai, 19c, (4257/1135)   425
Manju, solid, map of Japan, Nantan Baisu Dai Nih, on Kuni Masasada, 19c, (4257/1186)   *500*
Manju, stained, scene of Yorimitsu, 19c, (4257/1182)   275
Manju, stained, Su She riding, 19c, (4257/1128)   50
Manju, turtle, fish in waves, Rantei, 19c, (4257/1159)   1000
Manju, vegetables, fruits, 19c, (4257/1116)   275
Manju, Yojo stabbing cloak, Kogetsusai, 19c, (4257/1185)   325
Monkey, crouching, 18c, (4257/1166)   225
Monkey, sitting, 18c, (4257/1167)   200
Monkey and goat, 18c, (4257/1201)   600
Monkeys, Masatami, 19c, (4257/1205)   2100
Monks in a bowl, stained, 19c, (4257/1161)   950
Mountain goat, 19c, (4257/1157)   425
Octopus, 2 boys, man, Shomin, 19c, (4257/1126)   450
Octopus and monkey, slight chip, 19c, (4257/1189)   325
Okame, standing, Tomomasa, 20c, (4257/1143)   300
Okimono, human skull, reptile on top, 19c, (4257/1183)   *500*
Okimono, pilgrims, Shuzan, 19c, (4257/1133)   450
Okimono, sage, Mei-ho, stained, 19c, (4257/1138)   650
Okimono, Barge, 20c, (4257/1124)   175
Okimono, Daikoku as entertainer, Shoshun (Muneharu), 19c, (4257/1137)   700
Okimono, Yoshitsune ship, Gyokkusan, 20c, (4257/1123)   *375*
Okimono, 2 horses, riders, 20c (4257/1120)   450
Puppies, side-by-side, 18c, (4257/1158)   450
Puppy, seated, 18c, (4257/1168)   750
Puppy, seated,Shingetsu, 20c, (4257/1181)   650
Quails, Masatami, 19c, (4257/1142)   1000
Rabbit eating, Ranmei, cr, 19c, (4257/1113)   400
Rabbits, 18/19c, (4257/1156)   400
Seals, 19c, (4257/1146)   425
Shishi, seated, Mitsuharu, 19c, (4257/1176)   500
Shishi & Young, 19c, (4257/1130)   200

Shoki & Oni, 19c, (4257/1114) — 250
Shoki & Oni, 19c, (4257/1163) — 175
Shoki on horseback, 19c, (4257/1179) — 450
Shoki sharpening sword, 18c, (4257/1153) — 325
Three Mystic Apes, Ryumin, 19c, (4257/1164) — 225
Tiger, seated, 19c, (4257/1160) — 1100
Tongue-cut-Sparrow legend, Yukimasa, 20c, (4257/1145) — 450
Toy Daruma, 19c, (4257/1147) — 375
Wolf with skull, Tomochika, 19c, (4257/1115) — 375

Lacquer

Case, cigar, green, bird rattle, bean vines, Keishin, 19c (4257/1095) — 1000
Five-case, bell of Dojo-ji-form, Bushu (no) ju Katsukawa, 18c (4257/1101) — 4300
Five-case, gold, pr pheasants, waterfall, Kajikawa, 19c (4257/1102) — 1100
Five-case, gold, carp in waterfall, waves, Hosensai, 19c (4191/118) — 800
Four-case, cat chasing leaves, Kajikawa Bunryusai, dam, 19c (4257/1078) — 550
Four-case, flowing river, dam, 19c (4257/1079) — 425
Four-case, Kannon standing on lotus base, Koma Kyuhaku, 18c (4257/1083) — 3800
Four-case, black, cock, hen pheasant, Toshihide, 18/19c (4257/1088) — *2400*
Four-case, brown, dark, conch shell in matsuda, Jokosai, 18c (4257/1086) — 1100
Four-case, gold, discarded drum, encroaching vines, 19c (4257/1084) — 650
Four-case, gold, roof tile, demonic head, Kwanshosai, L18c (4257/1073) — *600*
Four-case, gold, Rosei's Dream, Koma Kansai, 19c (4257/1077) — 2300
Four-case, red, children playing in garden, 19c (4257/1098) — 600
Four-case, red, dragon, swirling clouds, Chohan Takenaga, chip, 20c (4257/1081) — 850
Four-case, flowers, asa-no-ha design, 18c (4191/107) — 600
Four-case, nobleman on horse, Kansaimon Osai, 19c (4191/116) — 700
Four-case, oval, waves, clouds, 19c (4191/105) — 450
Four-case, black, cock and hen on drum, 19c (4191/117) — 700
Four-case, black, cranes in flight, clouds, 19c (4191/119) — 550
Four-case, black, deer on hill, 19c (4191/115) — 500
Four-case, brown, sages playing go, 19c (4191/120) — 350
Four-case, red, sages in a garden, 18c/19c (4191/113) — 450
Four-case, roiro, butterflies, leaves, Toyo saku, 18c (4191/111) — 725
Three-case, masses of horses, multi-toned, 18c (4257/1104) — 475
Three-case, Shibayama, animated scene, skeletons, Rohon Ksuk, uru, 19c (4257/1080) — *3500*

Four-case
(4257/1088)

Four-case
(4257/1083)

Four-case
(4257/1073)

Okimono
(4257/1183)

Three-case, 2 barges, 19c (4257/1089) — 75
Three-case, gold, night time scene, travellers, Toyo, 18c (4257/1074) — 1000
Three-case, gold, tied bundle grasses, 19c (4257/1075) — 425
Three-case, gold, continuous landscape, 19c (4191/106) — 725
Tonkotsu, textured surface, 19c (4257/1097) — 60

Tonkotsu, lacquer, lucky buddhist symbols, Taishin, 20c (4257/1094)   800
Two-case, gold, Wata Nabe no Tsuna arm wrestling, Kwansai (Koma), L18c (4257/1082)   2400
Two-case, miniature, flower-heads, Gyoku, 19c (4257/1070)   425

Wood

Four-case, Somada, figures, bridge, waterfalls, river, 19c (4257/1071)   375
Three-case, Daikoku, Fukorokojiu carved, Masayuki, 19c (4257/1069)   450
Three-case, turtle-form, Gekko, 19c (4191/114)   600
Tonkotsu, fox as a woman, gilt grass, 18c (4191/104)   550
Tonkotsu, single-case, large tied sack form, Togyokudo, 19c (4191/112)   425
Tonkotsu, stretching Daruma, 19/20c (4257/1090)   125
Two-case, pouch-form, butterflies, bird, 19c (4191/109)   150

LACQUER ITEMS

Assorted items

Box, Somada Kogo, brilliant colors, Bugaku drum with blossoms in sheet gold, 2½ x 2½, 19c (4201/72)   1700
Chest, cubic, silver mounts, foliage designs, 14 drawers, 4 x 3¾ x 3½, 19c (4201/76)   10500
Kodansu, fine gold, elaborate, landscape, aogai, 3 drawers, 8¼ x 6½ x 5½ 19c (4201/75)   *10000*
Roiro box, nashiji interior, cockrel and hen motif, 'Shoryusai', 10 7/16 x 8 x 5 9/16, E19c (4201/73)   2100

Sixteenth Century

Tiered box, Momoyama, 8 stub feet, hexagonal, H17, dam (4257/1042)   1000

Seventeenth Century

Bako, gold, trees, crane, minogame, pewter edge, 3¾ x 3½ x 2 (4191/25)   200
Buddha, gilt figure, seated, flowing robes, curled hair, 17⅞, 17/18c (4257/204)   2200
Cabinet, storage, softwood, iron-mounted, 8 shallow drawers above 1 deep, 27¾ x 19¼ x 12, 17/18c (4257/231)   1300
Hibachi, provincial, circular, copper liner, figures, Diam 12⅜ (4159/23)   575

Eighteenth Century

Box, rectangular, country scene, 6½ x 3½ x 1¾ (4257/1059)   1100
Do-Maru, gold decoration, 18/19c (4257/404)   2250
Kogo, circular, persimmon, lattice work in pewter, (4257/1058)   1200
Kogo, wood, yoshino rocks, gold, grey, ground, Ritsuo II*, (4257/1066)   750
Suzuribako, waterfall, mountain scene, fitted interior, 11½ x 10¼ x 2, 18/E19c (4191/26)   3000
Tiered box, basketwork/mother-of-pearl, Ryukyu Islands, inset high foot, 2-tiered, L15½, 18c/E19c (4257/1044)   750

Nineteenth Century

Basin, pourer, black, gold, pine seedlings, scrolling foliage, Diam 21, H8¼ (4191/22)   1400
Box, rectangular, wild flowering weeds, 4¾ x 3½ x 2 (4257/1060)   1800
Box, brown, rectangular, moths, butterflies, (4257/1049)   1700
Box, circular, flower heads, Diam 4, 18/19c (4257/1055)   1900
Box, gold, rectangular, rounded edges, rolling hills, 5¼ x 4 x 2 (4257/1065)   *2500*
Box, gold-toned, 2 overlapping rectangles-form, decorated, 8½ x 6½ x 3 (4257/1048)   3300
Box, gold/roiro, rectangular, clusters of flowers, (4257/1050)   1500
Box, miniature, rectangular, vines, flowering trees, (4257/1051)   425
Box, miniature, trunk-form, chrysanthemums, handles, 2¾ x 1¾ x 2 (4257/1067)   800

Chest (4201/75)

Box (4257/1065)

Cabinet
(4257/1068)

Box, miniature, gold, oblong, blossoming flowers, 3¼ x 1¾ x 1½ (4191/94) — 300
Box, pepper, Metsubushi, square, mouth piece, zodiac animals, (4257/1063) — 250
Cabinet, pavilion, stream, 3 drawers, silver hinges, 5½ x 6 x 4¼ (4257/1061) — 3200
Cabinet, black, various country scenes, several drawers, 16¾ x 15 x 12 (4257/1068) — *3000*
Cabinet, brass-bound, rectangular, floral engraved, gilt, black ground, 41½ x 37½ x 18, E19c (4159/178) — 4800
Case, card, gold, 2 women seated, making fans, lid cr (4257/1076) — 1000
Chest, storage, rectangular, 6 drawers, 10¼ x 12¼ x 7 (4191/24) — 600
Chest, toilette, gold, black, 4 stub feet, square, 2 drawers, 10⅝ x 10¾ x 10¾ (4191/33) — 250
Hibachi, drum-form, decorated copper liner, Diam 10⅝, 19c (4257/187) — 350
Kobako, rectangular, waterfalls, shrubbery, 3½ x 2 x 2½ (4257/1057) — 1100
Kogo, red, square, carved, birds, flowers, (4257/1047) — 150
Kojubako, two-tiered, square, indented corners, flowers, birds, 18/19c (4257/1056) — 1100
Roiro, fundame kara-bitsu, pair, circular, ribbed, flowers, 16 (4191/23) — 1900
Shrine, miniature, silver mounted, gold, opening to reveal figure of Gautama, 15¼, 19c (4257/215) — 750
Shrine, Monju Bosatsu, black, plain case, gilt wood figure, 5⅛, 19c (4257/220) — 300
Suzuribako, moonlit scene, 5 quail, fitted interior, 10¼ x 9 x 2 (4191/27) — *2800*
Suzuribako, brown, trees, fruits, 9¾ x 8½ x 1¾ (4257/1052) — 950
Suzuribako, Nashiji, gold, iris, grasses, flowing stream, 9¾ x 9 x 2 (4257/1053) — 750
Sword stand, 10 storage drawers, 3 racks, W16⅛, L19c (4257/401) — 1400
Tachi stand, dragonflies and sheaves of rice, 22⅞, 19c (4257/399) — 500
Tray, circular, brown, 4 moth-form feet, lobed, birds in flight, Diam 11 (4257/1054) — 900
Tray, serving, Mara Nashiji, rectangular, indented corners, 13⅛ x 9½ (4257/1045) — 800

Twentieth Century

Cabinet, netsuke, black, portable, 6 sections, gold, sages in garden, 13½ x 8½ x 14½ (4191/20) — 1200
Tray, clothing, black, mystical dragon-prowed barge, 21¾ x 14 x 1½ (4191/31) — 300
Trays, clothing, pair, black, shallow, oblong, fans design, 19 x 14½ x 1½ (4191/32) — 450

NETSUKE

Assorted items

Coin, bark-like fungus, grown around coin, 20c (4191/67) — 275
Compass, sundial, portable, silver, dragon amid clouds, 20c (4191/51) — 600
Horse, raised head, turned back, 'Minko', 18/19c (4201/34) — 2600
Iwami mask of bearded man, 'Sekiyo Hako Tomiharu, Chokoku', 18c (4201/7) — 1900
Kagamibuta, stagshorn, Asakusa school, wave motif, 20c (4191/50) — 75
Mask, brown pottery, smiling man, Sekino, 19c (4191/54) — 150
Reptile, frog, study, pressed horn, snaked coiled on hat, frog, 19c (4191/49) — 550
Sennin, figure, bisque, standing, carrying a gourd, L19c (4191/52) — 200
Shell cluster, stagshorn, 3 shells, 19c (4191/63) — 175
Silver, drum model, with Shakudo, solid form, golden studs, 19c (4201/23) — 350
Tortoise, horn inlaid eyes, signed 'Eibi', 19c (4201/27) — 1100

Ceramic

Drunken octopus, badger, 19c, (4257/1010) — 475
Figure with crane, Masakazu, 19c, (4257/1003) — 250

Glass

Lotus pad, ripe, Nagasaki, 19c, (4257/992) — 350

Ivory

Ashinga and Tenaga, group, holding bow on top of shoulders of other, 19c/20c (4191/181)   700
Badger, dancing, standing on 1 foot, holding a straw hat, 18c (4201/93)   450
Badger, study, 19c, (4191/173)   750
Badger in teakettle, legendary figure, compact, well-defined, signed, 'Mitsusada' (4201/135)   3400
Basket filled with leaves, small rat crouching forward, inlaid eyes, 18c (4201/105)   850
Bean group, fine and rare, with engraved leaf spray, attached to stalk, signed 'Mitsuharu' M18c
   (4191/139)   4000
Benki, marine study, seated in a shell, with Buddhist symbols, 18/19c (4201/94)   1000
Boar resting on leaves, red horn inlaid eyes, etched hair, signed, 'Mitsuharu' 18c (4201/134)   900
Boy, seated, stained, brown cap, red robe, silver trim, 'Homei', L19/E20c (4201/84)   2600
Boy, seated, stained, green robe, lacquer rondels, 'Homei', L19c (4201/85)   900
Boy playing flute and cow, on irregular base, inlaid eyes, 'Chikuyosai', 19c (4201/130)   450
Boy standing on bag, miniature, well detailed, 'Ono Ryomin', 19c (4201/98)   1500
Boy with mask, standing, inlaid eyes, moveable jaw, 'Koun', L19c (4201/81)   2200
Boy with snow-Daruma, boy rolling a snowman as Daruma, Masahiro, 19c (4191/157)   300
Cat, study, wearing bib, looks into a lantern, 19c/20c (4191/128)   475
Clam cluster, overlapping, good patina, golden hue, 'Garaku', 18c (4201/131)   850
Cockerel, study, roosting hen, Shingetsu, 20c (4191/139)   1100
Cow and calf, study, reclining, facing opposite way, Tomotadu, 19c (4191/154)   1200
Crane, model, seated, legs tucked, head back, Bishu (pupil of), 20c (4191/144)   1000
Crane figure, ballform, inlaid eyes and horn, signed, 'Bishu' contemporary (4201/83)   2100
Dog, seated, inlaid eyes, protruding ribs, 'Tomotada', L18c (4201/89)   1700
Dragon, naked, on table, cloud design base, 'Koku', M19c (4201/127)   750
Dragon around sphere, scaley body, loose ball in cloud-form sphere, 18/19c (4201/118)   1600
Ebisu with sea creature, body of a fish, face of a man, stained, signed, 'Gyokuzan' 19c (4201/110)   800
Elephant standing on base, lowered head, inlaid eyes, good patina, rep, 18/19c (4201/103)   450
Erotic group, 20c, (4191/179)   500
Fukurokoju, figure, standing next to girl, Ikkosai, M19c (4191/168)   900
Fukurokuju figure, miniature, gilt lacquer decoration, signed, 'Shogetsu', 19c (4201/91)   325
Gama Sennin, figure, leaning on tree, toad on shoulder, Masatsugu, 19c (4191/155)   800
Gourd group on branch, with caterpillar, many openings, compact, signed, 'Kiyokatsu' E19c
   (4201/136)   1400
Hanasaka Jiji figure, seated on tree stump, 'Ryuzan', L19c (4201/99)   750
Hare, study, biting its leg, loquats, Rantei, 19c (4191/130)   1100
Hare seated on grass, ball-form, inlaid with horn, 'Kwaigio', Kusai, 19c (4201/132)   3800
Head, grotesque, rare, fine, painted eyes, stippled ivory, 19c (4201/112)   2200
Horse figure, standing, lowered head, inlaid eyes, worn, 18c (4201/78)   1500
Hotei at his toilet, in oval reserve, 'Hoshin', 18c (4201/87)   1100
Hunter, study, standing, carrying sword, 18c (4191/125)   850
Icho nut group, seven, various sizes, compact group, 'Okatomo', (4201/124)   900
Icho nuts, group of seven, simple, functional form, 'Kiyokatsu', E19c (4201/82)   1900
Kanshin, portrayal, crawling through legs of a braggart, 19c (4191/122)   275
Kappa, rendition, laying down, hiding under leaf, Sozan, 19c (4191/175)   850
Karako, figure, kneeling, Daruma toy near, 19c (4191/172)   850
Karako, figure, smiling, carrying circular bell, Hidemasa, 19c (4191/176)   800
Karako, figure, standing, cockerel in arms, 19c (4191/147)   300
Kinko, study, seated on carp, swimming, Seiji, 19c (4191/185)   450
Kintaro and his mother, group, in arms of mother, Meido, Ezoc (4191/180)   1200
Kitten, sleeping on cushion, engraved with flowers, 'Garaku', 18c (4201/122)   4000
Legendary scene, stained, Watanabe no Tsuna with Rashoman oni, 19c (4201/101)   950
Macabre group, stained, skulls, toads and snakes, inlaid eyes, signed, 'Masamitsu' 19c (4201/92)   2300
Macabre scene, wolf bent over a severed head, Tomomasa, 20c (4191/174)   600
Man and boy, group, base, tied sack between them, 18c/19c (4191/165)   200
Manju, Ei, 19c, crack (4191/167)   225
Manju, marine, oval shape, hollow, 'Toryu', 19c (4201/129)   3200
Manju, unusual, square, carved with figures, birds, 'Sosei', 18/19c (4201/126)   900
Marine cluster, triangular, 2 fish, squid, octopus, huddled, 19c (4191/131)   600
Mask, Okame, in a shallow dish, Masahiro, 19c (4191/121)   300
Mask cluster, variety, No drama characters, Tomochika, 19c (4191/126)   550
Mask cluster, 7 face masks from No drama, Hakuunsai, 19c (4191/138)   500
Monkey and toads, group, monkey leaning on staff, toads on back, 19c (4191/129)   700
Monkey group, seated, stained, child climbing on back, signed, 'Masatami', 19c (4201/107)   2500
Monkey on rock, study, Gyokko, 18c/19c, heavy wear (4191/177)   500
Motei and Bijin, group, reclining, Bigin cleaning his ear, 20c (4191/183)   800
Narwhal section, with tiger, light etching, black stripes, 'Mitsuhiro', 19c (4201/114)   3800
Ox and boy group, reclining ox, inlaid horn eyes, 'Rantei', M19c (4201/120)   1900

Suzuribako (4191/27)

Penitent Oni, study, reclining, grinning, Tomomasa, 19c (4191/158)   *650*
Puppy sprawled on a scroll, inlaid horn eyes, pavilion designs, 18c (4201/88)   800
Puppy, model, playful attitude, Shingetsu, 20c (4191/140)   550
Rabbit, study, seated, Kogyoku, 19c (4191/170)   850
Rarako figure, seated, with a turtle, signed, 'Meikeisai Hoichi' M19c (4201/100)   1200
Rat group, huddled together, expertly modelled, clasped feet, 'Okatori', 18c (4201/140)   5000
Rat on umbrella, study, closed, damaged, 18c/19c (4191/148)   650
Ryujin figure, lacquered, gold robe, applied aogai, dragon headdress, 19c (4201/109)   1700
Sage, figure, holding brush, lounging, 18c (4191/161)   550
Sage, figure, seated, wearing skull cap, 18c (4191/178)   400
Sambiki-saru, group, 'see no evil, etc.', Ikkosan, 19c (4191/153)   425
Scholastic group, sage holding scroll, 2 kids, Kiyotsugu, 19c (4191/160)   400
Sennin, figure, sitting, puzzled, looking at a clam, 18c (4191/124)   375
Sennin, figure, standing, holding staff, 18c (4191/127)   450
Shishi, seated, facing left, well carved mane and tail, 18c (4201/108)   3200
Shishi, study, mythical beast holding a ball, Masanao, 19c (4191/186)   750
Shoki figure, triangular section, etched robe, good patina, 18c (4201/97)   3100
Skull and toad, toad on human skull, Munemitsu, 19c (4191/149)   750
Snail emerging from shell, very worn, pleasant texture, 'Mitsuharu', 18c (4201/86)   800
Snail on umimatsu log, rare, simulated slate, 'Sekisai', 19c (4201/35)   1800
Snake, large, coiled, carved with dots and scales, inlaid eyes, signed, 'Tomonobu', M19c (4201/137)   1100
Sparrow, study, in flight, Shingetsu, 20c (4191/141)   950
Sparrow in flight, scale-like feathers, inlaid eyes, 'Masanao', 18c (4201/123)   2400
Squirrel, study, bunch of grapes, vines, Hosai, 19c (4191/187)   400
Stags and doe group, stained, inlaid eyes, 'Masamine', 19c (4201/95)   2000
Still life group, cluster of New Year emblems, Ippo, 19c (4191/166)   375
Table, study, small Hotei figure on top, Garaku, 19c (4191/171)   550
Takaramono marine group, Buddhistic symbols, good wear, fine patina, E19c (4201/77)   500
Tengu, hatching egg shaped, smooth surface stippled and applied with leaf, 19c (4201/119)   500
Tengu, study, mythical creature emerging from shovel, Masakazu, 19c (4191/156)   *700*
Tennin, study, in flight, beating drum, Nanryu*, 20c (4191/188)   600
Tiger, model, fantastic manner, hunched, Bishu, 20c (4191/142)   1300
Toad squatting on a lotus, inlaid eyes, golden patina, 18/19c (4201/106)   550
Toy Daruma, model, 19c, (4191/163)   175
Toy Horse, Shibayama, stained, various inlays, 19/20c (4201/113)   2300
Trio in sake cup, seated back-to-back, Masahide, L19c (4191/132)   700
Wolf, study, hunched over, Yuzan, 19c (4191/123)   225
Woman at toilet, figure, bending, clipping nails, 20c (4191/164)   300
Yawning man, figure, seated, Yoshiyuki, 20c (4191/184)   800
Yojo stabbing a cloak, carriage tramples figure, well defined, signed, 'Ryo' L19c (4201/104)   1300
Zodiac group, clustered, cloud-form base, signed, 'Masamitsu', 19c (4201/90)   1500

Lacquer

Miniature log, crab in sea grass, Kogyoku, 19c, (4257/1031)   600

Optical illusion, 2 boys become 4, 19c, (4257/1025)   700

Metal

Hand Cannon, model, 19c, (4257/987)   350
Manju, geometric pattern, 19c, (4257/1004)   250
Manju, Jurojin holding an uchiwa, Sekijoken, 19c, (4257/1019)   100

Stagshorn

Asakusa School, Buddhist rosary beads with sceptre, signed, 'Masayuki' 18/19c (4201/133)   500
Extended head of Fukurokoju, 18c, (4257/998)   200
Foreigner wearing a coat, 19c, (4257/990)   400
Hat, worm eaten, lotus leaf, spider, snake decorations, 18/19c (4201/10)   700
Manju, dog, lamppost, (4257/1026)   300
Sashi, decaying fruit, Masakazu, 19c, (4257/1022)   750

Stone

Carnelian shishi, 20c, (4257/1040)   550

Tusk

Flat form, very rare, inscriptions, signed, 'Nanka To', M19c (4201/116)   1400

Wood

Actor, seated with mask, ivory inlaid, 'Tokoku', 19c (4201/19)   6500
Actor, sick, lacquered costume, ivory feet, 'Shuich', 19c (4201/46)   1200
Badger clasping lotus leaf, Tomochika, 19c, (4257/996)   900
Blind masseur, client, rubbing shoulders, seated, 18c (4191/66)   275
Boy and Cow, Gyokko, 19c, (4257/988)   550
Calico cat, sleeping, 19c, (4257/993)   400
Chestnut, study, calyx with ukibori veins, Tadatoshi, 20c (4191/44)   450
Chesnuts, ripe, loose ivory worm, Minko, 19c, (4257/999)   625
Coiled snake, horn inlaid eyes, slight split in wood, 19c (4201/15)   800
Daikoku, Shumin, (4257/1023)   1000
Daimyo's porter figure, seated, well-detailed, 19c (4201/16)   1500
Daruma, stretching, seated, signed 'Tokoku', plaque missing, L19c (4201/24)   7500
Dog, reclining, inlaid horn eyes, inscribed 'Issan', 19c (4201/17)   350
Dogs, 2 small, inlaid horn eyes, 'Itsumin to', M19c (4201/18)   750
Eagle, monkey, Masanada, 18c, (4257/1018)   1500
Ebisu and Tai, kneeling, ivory staff, 'Sokoku', 20c (4201/22)   2900
Ebony, half-egg shape, Shorusai, 18c (4257/986)   300
Farmer, seated, outstretched legs and arms, E19c (4201/13)   850
Figure of an Islander, 18c, (4257/1034)   700
Figure of Gama Sennin, 18/19c, (4257/1028)   800
Figure of Okame, dancing, (4257/1033)   600
Flower, study, ebony, open, center with silver, 19c (4191/56)   275
Fox, study, guise of a farmer, 19c (4191/57)   450
Goat, reclining, horn inlaid eyes, 'Yukisada', 18c (4201/32)   2400
Group ivory and lacquer, rare, man and 2 boys, 'Kokoku', 19/20c (4201/14)   8750
Group playing go, couple of hermits, Seizan, 19c (4191/42)   450
Hannya mask, large, glass eyes, 'Shumin', saku (Hara), L18c (4201/6)   600
Helmet, kabuto-form, 19c, (4257/1002)   200
Horse, study, standing, legs together, Kangyoku Risshisai, 20c (4191/69)   1500
Hunched monkey, 19c, (4257/1007)   1200
I No Hayata and Nuye scene, hero with dagger, ivory inlay, 'Mokusui', 18c (4201/39)   425
Karako, figure, standing, beating drum, 19c (4191/65)   350
Karako, study, holding tama, within folds, 19c (4191/36)   475
Kiyohime encircling a bell, 19c, (4257/1000)   300
Kuzunoha, fox-woman holding baby in arms, 19c (4191/40)   450
Man, seated, carving hannya mask, ivory inlay, glass eyes, 'Miwa', 18c (4201/42)   375
Man asleep over hibachi, So school, ivory inlaid, 'Sozan', L19c (4201/1)   1100
Manju, lake landscape, Kansai, 19c, (4257/1027)   250
Mask, cluster, No drama, 19c, (4257/1008)   450
Mask, face of KotObi-de, Ryumin saku, 19c, (4257/991)   325
Mask, pale boxwood, fantastic character, bulging eyes, crown, 19c (4191/48)   650
Mask, shiski-form, Ryumin saku, 19c, (4257/989)   450
Mask, Ran Ryo, freakish, fiendish, headdress, 19c (4191/46)   375
Minogame, fanciful, 19c, (4257/1029)   225
Monkey, seated, eating loquat, well-worn, 'Tomokazu', 19c (4201/31)   1600
Monkey, study, seated, 'see no evil', Koich, 19c (4191/38)   600

Monkey, study, wood, ivory, Songoku standing, holding stick, Shibayama, 19c (4191/53)	850
Mother and child, group, bare breasted, standing holding child, 19c (4191/70)	400
Mother and children, group, kneeling, holding one, the other on back, Ten, Hira, No, 20c (4191/43)	200
Monkey and young, Masanao, 19c, (4257/1036)	1900
Naked lady, standing, 19c, (4257/1012)	200
No drama mask cluster, horn eyes, 'Masakata', 19c (4201/8)	1200
Okame, figure, Ittobori, dancing, traces of paint, E19c (4191/47)	200
Oni, seated and grimacing oni, muscular figure, 'Sanko', 18c (4201/20)	1300
Ono No Komachi, seated, fine, dishevelled poetess, signed, 'Chikusai', L19c (4201/25)	2300
Rat, group, family, 2 children, eating berries, 19c, chip (4191/64)	650
Rat, seated, holding bean, horn inlaid eyes, ivory teeth, 'Tomokazu', 19c (4201/37)	5000
Rat and ricecakes, square table, inlaid horn eyes, 'Masonao', 19c (4201/41)	1300
Rat on head of dead fish, Masanao, (4257/1039)	1600
San Sukumi group, entwined, inlaid eyes, 19c (4201/30)	1100
San Sukumi group, fine, horn eyes, 'Sukeyuki', 19c (4201/9)	6250
Setsubun oni, crouched, applied ivory, 'Masakazu', 19c (4201/28)	650
Setsubun oni under straw hat, applied ivory, 'Tomokazu', L19c (4201/4)	1500
Shojo, study, drunken, sake cup on her back, 19c (4191/39)	350
Shojo sleeping figure, signed 'Tadatoshi', L19c (4201/2)	1600
Shunga Manju, oval form, 19c, (4257/1030)	600
Snail on a sandal, Masanao, 19c, (4257/1006)	500
Snake, study, ebony, coiled, 19c (4191/55)	600
Snake, toad, 19c, (4257/995)	550
Sneezer, professional, figure, seated, head back, tickler, Gyokkei, 19c (4191/41)	700
Still life on table, pottery mask, lacquer decoration, 18/19c (4201/43)	550
Tengu hatching, applied lacquer cap, 'Shumin', 19c (4201/26)	2600
Tengu peering at moon, Shishosai, 19c, (4257/1020)	1500
Theatrical box, study, ebony, hinged, Kiku-engraved, Masayoshi, 19c (4191/58)	1500
Tiger, more like a dog, Sari, 19c (4257/1016)	225
Tiger, study, seated, black staining, Hakuryu, 19c (4191/60)	650
Toad, seated, 18c, (4257/1015)	225
Turtle, group, on lotus leaf, 2 babies on back, Bazan, 19c (4191/71)	2400
Two masks, carving, open mouth, closed mouth, 20c, rep (4191/59)	300
Wolf cubs, playing, three, inlaid ivory eyes, 'Yasutada', 18c (4201/29)	2700
Zodiac group, inlaid eyes, good detailing, 'Masanao', 19c (4201/38)	3300

OJIME

Assorted materials

Bone, skull-form, human, 20c (4191/92)	60
Brass, hexagonal, copper carp, 20c (4191/81)	160
Copper, persimmon attached to stalk, 20c (4191/79)	60
Copper, pumpkin on silver leaf, 20c (4191/86)	100
Metal, flowers, butterfly, 19c (4191/72)	250
Metal, gold, silver honzogan , cylindrical, 20c (4191/78)	150
Metal, Sho-form, musical instrument, 20c (4191/75)	175
Metal, Silver, copper, snail, crab, 20c (4191/82)	300
Metal, Tsuba-form, copper, 20c (4191/85)	350
Silver, cylindrical-form, gilt, 20c (4191/87)	80
Silver, ovoid form, flowers, 20c (4191/77)	150
Silver, ovoid form, flowers, vines, 20c (4191/89)	200
Silver, Ball form, dragon, clouds, Katsomasa, 20c (4191/76)	125
Silver, copper, fox doll, 20c (4191/84)	200

Iron

Ovoid bead with perched heron, gold and silver, 'Yoshiyuki', excellent, 19c (4201/52)	1100
Owl and bird, applied golden, fine, in gold, relief, 19c (4201/53)	2100
Silver stag with golden horns molded, signed 'Hitosuyanagi Tomonaga', 19c (4201/48)	2600

Ivory

Black stained, circular bead, figures, 20c (4191/73)	50
Skull, model, human, vacant eyes, upper is intact, 19c (4191/152)	750
Sphere, carved and pierced, stylized moths in foliage, metal lined, 19c (4201/50)	425

Silver

Heron in flight, 19c (4201/49)	400

Ovoid bead molded with bird, signed 'Hidemitsu', 19c (4201/51)   500

Wood

Monkey, seated, hunched forward, inlaid eyes, well detailed, 19c (4201/54)   800

PAINTINGS

Double pencil drawing, Goyo, one side, reclining nude, reverse, standing woman, 16¾ x 11⅜
(4257/984)   2250
Drawing, Double Pencil, Goyo, bare-breasted woman, maid stroking hair, 20¼ x 13¾ (4155/576)   3100
Drawing, Hokusai school, heron, color on paper, 12 x 9⅛ (4155/489)   75
Drawing for a print, Kuniyoshi, oban, size, Tawara Oda leaving Ryu-O's palace, (4257/819)   600
Fan Drawing, Hiroshige*, oban size pa, nel, Seiro Hanami Ryaku dzu, (4257/818)   500
Kakejiku, after Jakuchu, cockrel under wisteria, 37½ x 12 (4257/832)   300
Kakejiku, after Shohaku, sage, straw, hat, staff, paper, 53¼ x 22½ (4257/831)   350
Kakejiku of a seated Bodhisattra, late Kamakura, early Muromachi Period, 32 x 15¾, 14/15c
(4257/810)   450
Kakejiku of Irises, a cluster of flowers on a plain ground, signature unread, paper, 49¼ x 11¾, E20c
(4257/812)   275
Kakemono, peasants fleeing typhoon, seal of Ninsei inscribed, 55¾ x 16⅞, L19c/E20c (4257/815)   325
Kakemono by Gyosai, Daikoku and ladder, in pursuit, paper, 40⅛ x 17 (4257/814)   750
Namban painting of a Dutch Ship, paper, 12⅛ x 17⅛, 18/19c (4257/826)   600
Namban painting of a Dutchman, paper, 20½ x 9¼, 18c (4257/825)   1700
Nanga Kakejiku, Chikuden*, strong mountain landscape, paper, 54 x 13¼, 1810 (4257/830)   900
Nanga sumi Kakejiku, Fukuhara Genso, (Gogaku)*, mountain landscape, silk, (4257/829)   700
Shijo Kakejiku, Matsmura Goshun, farmer with broom, silk, 38 x 16, 1752-1811 (4257/835)   1600
Sumi drawing, Goyo, woman in bath house, 22 x 12⅝ (4257/985)   1200
Sumi Kakejiku, after Nakanuma Shokad, o, dish with fruit, paper, 7½ x 14⅞, 18c (4257/823)   325
Sumi Kakejiku, Torei II*, three Manchurian cranes, silk, 41⅛ x 21¾ (4257/839)   1200
Sumi Kakejiku of the thirty-six poets, paper, 51¼ x 19¼, 19c (4257/813)   200
Tosa Kakejiku, Shigematsu*, Chion-in in Kyoto, 39 x 12⅜, 1738-1806 (4257/833)   200
Ukiyo-e Kakejiku, after Utamaro, courtesan with kitten, paper, 14¼ x 17¼, 19c (4257/837)   275
Ukiyo-e Kakejiku, Hokusai*, Daikoku and, Ebisu, silk, 19 x 22 (4257/822)   1200
Ukiyo-e School Kakejiku, musicians, paper, 32½ x 15⅝ (4257/840)   400
Watercolor study, Hasui, cluster of farm houses, crops, 15⅛ x 20¾ (4155/574)   1000
Watercolor study, Hasui, moonlit scene, thatch storage bin, 17¼ x 12 (4257/983)   1400
Watercolor study, Hasui, seaside village, distant hills, 10½ x 18⅝ (4155/575)   850
Watercolor study, Hasui, dusk view of, islands in Inland Sea, 14¼ x 10¼ (4155/492)   900
Watercolor study, Hasui, dusk view of, two houses, 14¼ x 10¼ (4155/491)   575
Watercolor study, Hasui, rocky coast, 14¼ x 10¼, (4155/490)   550
Watercolor study for a print, Hasui, the Inland Sea and scattered islands, 14⅛ x 10¼ (4257/821)   850
Zeshin, 2 carp, paper, watercolor, 13½ x 10¼ (4257/820)   700

PIPE CASES

Ivory, low relief carving, rare, stylized dragon under water fall, 19c (4201/70)   1500
Lacquer, blue, carved, rare, turbulant waves, edged in silver, signed, 'Shomin' 19c (4201/71)   900
Stagshorn, Chokwaro sennin, seated, expressive detail, 'Hiroyoshi', 19c (4201/69)   1200

PRINTS

Buncho

Chuban, man wearing a kimono talking to courtesan, (4257/467)   8500

Choki

Hashira, courtesan with elaborate coif, faded, slightly toned (4257/501)   1600
Hashira, parody on Chushingura, (4257/500)   500
Hashira, teahouse waitress, faded, soiled (4257/502)   1400
Oban, Yoshitsune killing the Nuye, (4257/503)   700

Eishi

Hashira, young woman after bath, faded, rub, soil, rep (4257/505)   1100
Hashira, 2 courtesans, with dog, (4257/504)   2900
Hashira, 2 young women, 1 smoking, corner torn (4257/508)   950
Oban, man, boy, 2 girls, 8 bijin, (4155/396)   1200
Oban, Furyu Yatsushi Genji, (4257/509)   6250
Oban, Furyuya Genji, (4257/506)   2200
Oban, Seiro Bijin Rokkasen, (4257/507)   4700

Oban (4155/567)

Oban
(4257/507)

Oban (4155/485)

Large panel (4155/483)

Eisho

Oban, 2 women bringing a tachi, spot wormage (4257/510) 1700

Gakutei

Surimono, carp swimming against a waterfall, (4257/583) 2300
Surimono, woman kneeling before an aged couple, soil (4257/582) 350

Gohei

Oban, Great fire of 1923, 1923 (4155/467) 200

Goyo

Hashira, woman dressing, (4257/707) 2700
Large panel, (keyblock impression) woman holding an Obi, 1921 (4257/883) 450
Large panel, woman applying cosmetics, 20⅛ x 14¼, 1919 (4155/573) 5700
Large panel, woman combing hair, 17⅜ x 12¾, 1921, faded (4155/483) *2700*
Large panel, woman combing hair, crimp, cut corner (4257/713) 3300
Large panel, woman combing hair, 1921 (4257/885) 5250
Large panel, woman holding an Obi, 1921 (4257/882) 2500
Large panel, woman holding an Obi, 20⅝ x 11½, faded, 1921 (4155/484) 1800
Large panel, Yabukei in the rain, 1919 (4257/884) 1300
Oban, nude drying after bath, crimp (4257/705) 2600
Oban, nude wringing washcloth, soil (4155/572) 6500
Oban, snowy river scene, Mt. Iki, 1920 (4155/568) 2700
Oban, woman brushing cheek, 1921 (4155/486) 1400

Oban, woman brushing cheek, 1921 (4155/570)   1300
Oban, woman brushing face with a towel, 1921 (4257/881)   1600
Oban, woman brushing face with towel, (4257/709)   2300
Oban, woman kneeling, 1921 (4257/887)   500
Oban, woman leaning on fence, 1921 (4155/485)   *1400*
Oban, woman leaning on fence, (4257/710)   1800
Oban, woman leaning on fence, 1921 (4257/889)   1600
Oban, woman seated before a mirror, faded (4257/706)   2100
Oban, Ducks, (4257/704)   2100
Oban, Ducks, 1921 (4257/888)   1400
Oban, Evening Moon over Kobe, 1921 (4155/567)   *800*
Oban, Mt. Ika, tatty edge (4257/708)   1400
Oban, O-Nao, 1921 (4155/571)   2600
Oban, O-Nao, mica spotting, 1921 (4257/886)   1300
Oban, key block, woman with handmirror, 1921 (4155/566)   550
Panel, woman holding an Obi, (4257/711)   1800
Panel, Yabakei in the Rain, faded, tatty edge (4257/712)   1300

Harunobu

Chuban, a young woman holding a lamp in the night, unsigned, minute holes (4257/457)   63000
Chuban, a young woman standing after bath, (4257/455)   8500
Chuban, man with pipe, pine, (4155/383)   *2400*

Chuban
(4155/383)

Chuban, seated young woman, unsigned, faded, poor state (4257/451)   225
Chuban, two lovers under a snow covered umbrella, slight oxidization (4257/456)   30000
Chuban, two women by the sea, moderate impression (4257/446)   750
Chuban, two young women, some rub, crease, toning (4257/449)   850
Chuban, young courtesan, standing with fan, light stains (4257/453)   5750
Chuban, Atsumori and Kumagai at the shore, (4257/450)   2600
Chuban, Furyu Edo Hakkei, slightly faded (4257/452)   6250
Chuban, Furyu Rok'kasen, (4257/454)   6000

Harushige*

Chuban, a young man making advances, unsigned, (4257/458)   3200

Hasui

Aiban, coastal village, 1923 (4257/939)   900
Aiban, spring landscape, fields, 1923 (4155/524)   600
Aiban, village in rain, 1921 (4257/946)   1400
Aiban, Hizen, Katsusa, (4257/767)   700
Aiban, Kinkakuji, toned (4257/739)   450
Aiban, Kinkakuki, (4257/738)   1400
Aiban, Okayama Uchisange, 1924 (4257/943)   450
Aiban, Senko-ji Slope, (4257/753)   1500
Aiban, Senko-ji Slope, toned (4257/752)   200
Oban, distant view of Fuji, (4257/750)   150
Oban, moonlight on a canal, 1931 (4155/537)   475

Oban, moonlit scene of a man in a boat, (4257/760) 1300
Oban, moonlit scene of 3 trees, (4257/781) 250
Oban, night scene of a lone cottage, (4257/780) 250
Oban, night scene, farmer, ox cart, 1931 (4155/534) 300
Oban, night scene, lone figure, pine, 1933 (4155/471) 300
Oban, night scene, scattered fireflies, trimmed (4257/771) 125
Oban, night view along Sumida, 1933 (4155/533) 175
Oban, night view of a fisherman, (4257/734) 300
Oban, night view of a fisherman, (4257/735) 300
Oban, night view of houses, (4257/762) 75
Oban, rainy day with a lone figure, (4257/765) 125
Oban, sailboat, wooded cliff, 1920 (4155/528) 1300
Oban, snow scene, Taish Period, (4257/926) 1900
Oban, snowscape, Tokyo back street, toned, 1926 (4257/936) 400
Oban, street scene, open market, people, (4257/782) 200
Oban, torii at Miyajima in snow, (4257/748) 200
Oban, woman passing a temple, 1926 (4155/530) 600
Oban, woman with baby in the rain, (4257/766) 1300
Oban, Arakawa on Tsuki, (4257/745) 550
Oban, Boshu, Iwaino Hama, 1921 (4155/532) 1100
Oban, Chuzenji Utagahama, (4257/746) 250
Oban, Fuji collared by clouds, (4257/770) 200
Oban, Fuyu no Arashiyama, faded, trimmed (4257/937) 175
Oban, Getsu Meiro Kamo-ko, 1920 (4155/529) 950
Oban, Hachinohe Same, (4257/758) 400
Oban, Hama Goya Etchu, 1921 (4155/525) 1200
Oban, Ichikawa no Banshu, (4257/740) 275
Oban, Inokashira no Nansetsu, (4257/779) 1300
Oban, Inokashira no Nansetsu, 1921 (4257/947) 1600
Oban, Ishi Tsumu Fune, (4257/769) 1600
Oban, Itsukushima, (4257/757) 150
Oban, Izumo Matsu-e Mizuzuki, 1925 (4155/527) 225
Oban, Izumo Matsuye Kumoribi, (4257/933) 400
Oban, Kaga Yata, (4257/761) 700
Oban, Kamakura Daibutsu, (4257/749) 175
Oban, Kanda Myojin Keidai, (4257/777) 550
Oban, Kiba no Yugure, (4257/776) 1600
Oban, Kiyomizu-dera, (4257/756) 250
Oban, Komagata Gashi, 1920 (4257/948) 1600
Oban, Kyoto Kiyomizu-dera, (4257/759) 175
Oban, Matsushima Katsura-Jima, 1920 (4155/526) 1300
Oban, May Rain on the Awakawa, (4257/744) 225
Oban, Moriqasaki no Sekiyo, 1933 (4155/535) 200
Oban, Mt Fuji, seen from the Hakone Villa of Baron K, oyata Iwasaki (4257/737) 150
Oban, Mutsu, Tsuta Onsen, trimmed (4257/772) 200
Oban, Mutsu, Tsuta Onsen, snipped corner, 1920 (4257/928) 1300
Oban, Nikko Kegon no Taki, red bleeding (4257/751) 75
Oban, Omiya, 1931 (4257/940) 300
Oban, Rain at Chihibara Canal, 1930 (4155/536) 550
Oban, Sado Kamomura, 1920 (4257/941) 1100
Oban, Sado, Nishi Mikawazaka, (4257/938) 1400
Oban, Seiten no Yuki, Miyajima, 1924 (4257/927) 1400
Oban, Senzoku Ike, toned (4257/741) 175
Oban, Senzoku Ike, (4257/742) 375
Oban, Shiba Koen no Yuki, (4257/743) 375
Oban, Shiobara Arayu no Aki, 1921 (4155/531) 1300
Oban, Shir o Hashi, (4257/768) 1100
Oban, Soshu Maekawa no Ame, (4257/763) 150
Oban, Tanjima Kinosake, 1925 (4155/522) 475
Oban, Togo no Ura, toned (4257/755) 200
Oban, Togo no Ura, (4257/754) 275
Oban, Tokyo ju-ni dai, Samidare Furo, Sanno, 1920 (4257/929) 1300
Oban, Towada Oirase no Aki, (4257/747) 100
Oban, Tsukishima no Yuki, 1931 (4257/942) 750
Oban, Yoru no Shinagawa, 1920 (4257/934) 1600
Oban, Yuki ni Kururu, Terashima-mura, 1921 (4257/935) 2250
Oban, 2 women with parasols, (4257/764) 325
Oban, 3 trees, moonlight, 1932 (4155/472) 225

Panel, circular, San-ju-ken Bori no Bosetsu, 1922 (4257/931)	4000
Panel, circular, To no seiki ei, 1922 (4257/932)	1500
Panel, circular, Tokyo Ju-ni kagetsu, 1922 (4257/930)	800
Tanzaku, arid landscape, 1920 (4155/521)	1000
Tanzaku, heavy rainstorm view, 1919 (4257/945)	2500
Tanzaku, night view at Ikao, 1920 (4155/523)	900
Tanzaku, sunset thru trees, 1920 (4257/944)	1300

Hiroshige

Fan print, 5 men and women dancing, (4257/642)	2000
Hoeido, Ishiyakushi, center fold, wormage, tear (4155/429)	325
Hoeido, Tsuchiyama, center fold, foxed (4155/428)	*1200*
Kisokaido Rokujuku tsugi no uchi, Fukaya, (4257/609)	650
Kisokaido Rokujuku tsugi no uchi, Fukushima, (4257/611)	1600
Kisokaido Rokujuku tsugi no uchi, Honjo, (4257/610)	400
Kisokaido Rokujuku tsugi no uchi, Nagakubo, (4257/612)	5000
Kisokaido Rokujuku tsugi no uchi, Seba, (4257/613)	26000
Meisho Edo Hakkei, Akasaka, Kiribatake, trimmed (4257/603)	800
Meisho Edo Hakkei, Asakusa Kannon, (4155/427)	1600
Meisho Edo Hakkei, Asakusa Tampo Tori no machi, (4257/605)	650
Meisho Edo Hakkei, Asakusa Taura, (4155/426)	*1700*
Meisho Edo Hakkei, Bikunibashi, (4257/601)	1700
Meisho Edo Hakkei, Bikunibashi, Setchu, trimmed (4257/600)	500
Meisho Edo Hakkei, Fukagawa Susaki, Juman Tsubo, (4257/604)	1200
Meisho Edo Hakkei, Masaki no hotori yori Suijin-no-Mori Uchikawa, Sekiyano-Sato, trimmed (4257/599)	850
Meisho Edo Hakkei, Ohashi, (4257/606)	5000
Meisho Edo Hakkei, Ohashi, Hiroshige ga, margin crease (4257/607)	11000
Meisho Edo Hakkei, Shoheibashi, Seido, Kandagawa, (4257/602)	325
O-tanzaku, monkey climbing a perch, (4257/649)	4000
Oban, pedestrians on a promenade, (4257/639)	600
Oban, small goose in flight, (4257/648)	550
Oban, Awa no Naruto no Fukei, faded (4155/442)	5000
Oban, Edo Meisho, Nihonbashi, (4257/637)	550
Oban, Edo Meisho, Suzaki, (4257/638)	850
Oban, Fish series, Red Snapper, soil, posthumous* (4257/633)	300
Oban, Shichi hyaku san no dzu, (4257/641)	700
Oban, Toto Meish, Surogacho, (4257/635)	500
Oban, Toto Meisho, put down (4257/645)	400
Oban, Toto Meisho, Ueno, Toeizan, (4257/636)	600
Oban, 5 women, 2 old men on a hill, (4257/640)	1800
Tanzaku, two finches and a kingfisher, (4257/646)	1100
Tanzaku, Toto Meisho no uchi Otokozaka Shiba Atago, (4257/634)	950
Tokaido gojusan tsugi, Akasaka, (4257/624)	800
Tokaido gojusan tsugi, Arai, center fold (4257/622)	750
Tokaido gojusan tsugi, Fujisawa, center fold (4257/614)	1000
Tokaido gojusan tsugi, Futagawa, (4257/623)	850
Tokaido gojusan tsugi, Hakone, faded, trimmed (4257/616)	1300
Tokaido gojusan tsugi, Kambara, (4257/619)	3100
Tokaido gojusan tsugi, Kambara, (4257/620)	3100
Tokaido gojusan tsugi, Mishima, (4257/618)	2300
Tokaido gojusan tsugi, Mishima, (4257/617)	1100
Tokaido gojusan tsugi, Mitsuke, center fold (4257/621)	650
Tokaido gojusan tsugi, Odawara, put down (4257/615)	1100
Tokaido gojusan tsugi, Okazaki, (4257/625)	1100
Tokaido gojusan tsugi, Sakanoshita, center crease (4257/630)	700
Tokaido gojusan tsugi, Seki, (4257/629)	1400
Tokaido gojusan tsugi, Seki, (4257/628)	1200
Tokaido gojusan tsugi, Shono, (4257/626)	3100
Tokaido gojusan tsugi, Shono, (4257/627)	3900
Tokaido gojusan tsugi, Tsuchiyama, trimmed, center fold (4257/631)	850
Tokaido gojusan tsugi, Tsuchiyama, put down (4257/632)	1300
60-odd views of the provinces, Hitachi, (4155/425)	325
60-odd views of the provinces, Tsushima, (4155/424)	*300*
60-odd views of the provinces, Wakasa, punctures (4155/423)	450

Hiroshige and Eisen

69 stations on the Kisokaido, Honjo, (4155/446)	*800*

Hoeido (4155/428)

Meisho Edo Hakkei
(4155/426)

69 stations on the Kisokaido
(4155/446)

69 stations on the Kisokaido, Iwamurata, (4155/443)	400
69 stations on the Kisokaido, Narai, (4155/445)	525
69 stations on the Kisokaido, Omiya, rubbing, fold (4155/444)	250

Hiroshige II

Oban, Gold Mines, (4257/652)	600
Oban, Shokoku Meisho Hakkei, (4257/651)	300
Oban, Shokoku Meisho Hakkei, Nikko Kurifuri, faded, tear (4155/447)	225

Hodaka Yoshida

Woodcut, Tea House, 22⅞ x 16½, 1956 (4257/961)	175
Woodcut, Woods, 22¾ x 16½, 1955 (4257/960)	125

Hokkei

Surimono, woman with boy lunging at toy tiger, (4257/570)	450
Surimono, Kintoki wrestling with giant carp, (4257/571)	3700

Hokuei

Oban, Arashi Rikan as Danschichi Kurobei, (4257/573)	650
Oban, Nakamura Utaemon III in a play, faded (4257/572)	325
Oban, 2 actors in a scene from a play, (4257/574)	550

Hokuju

Oban, landscape in Edo, Fuji, (4155/412)	1300

Hokusai

Oban, a group of asagao, (4257/556)	22000
Oban, a group of 3 kingfishers, center fold, faded, toned (4257/555)	1400
Oban, Shell gathered at Enoshima, center fold (4155/407)	425

Oban, 2 courtesans looking out window, (4257/554)	1100
Oban, 4 courtesans clustered in conversation, faded (4257/552)	2200
36 Views of Fuji, Bushu, Tamagawa, (4257/564)	*7000*
36 Views of Fuji, Enoshima in Soshu, toned, soiled, rub (4257/557)	600
36 Views of Fuji, Great Wave off Kanagawa, center fold, snip (4257/569)	24000
36 Views of Fuji, Great Wave off Kanagawa, faded, thin spots (4257/568)	21000
36 Views of Fuji, Koshu Kaji Kazawa, (4257/566)	11000
36 Views of Fuji, Koshu Mishima-goe, (4257/565)	5000
36 Views of Fuji, Sazai-go of the Rakkanji, faded, center crease (4257/563)	2700
36 Views of Fuji, Senju in Musashino, faded, center crease (4257/562)	2800
36 Views of Fuji, South Wind and Clear Sky, (4257/567)	13000
36 Views of Fuji, Tago no ura in Erijiri, center fold (4257/561)	3600
36 Views of Fuji, Tsukuda Island in Musashino, faded (4257/560)	2000
36 Views of Fuji, Ushibori in Hitachi, faded, foxing, 2 rep (4257/558)	1300
36 Views of Fuji, Yoshida on the Tokaido, center crease (4257/559)	1600

Hokushu

Oban, Nakamura Utaemon II as Kata Kiyomasa, (4257/575)	1100
Oban, Nakamura Utaemon III as Ishigawa Goemon, (4257/576)	1600
Oban, 2 actors as samurai, rubbed (4155/410)	100

Ishikawa Toyomasa

Chuban, Furyu Ju-ni gatsu, slightly trimmed (4257/499)	900

Junichiro Sekino

Etching, Seated Figure, 23 x 17⅛ (4257/982)	225
Lithograph, night scene, house on the water, 19 x 12⅛, 1956 (4257/980)	50
Oban, portrait, Koshira Onchi, stains (4257/971)	200
Oban, Osome Puppet, light stains (4257/968)	250
Woodblock, group portrait, 4 children, 23⅝ x 18⅛, 1956 (4257/975)	325
Woodblock, man in a blue suit, 16 x 12¼ (4257/967)	700
Woodblock, portrait of Nakamura Kichiemon, 22⅝ x 13¾ (4257/976)	800
Woodblock, portrait, Koshiro Onchi, 25¾ x 19⅝ (4257/978)	1400
Woodblock, seated man, 26 x 20⅛ (4257/970)	350
Woodblock, young boy, white cat, 28¼ x 15¼, light soil (4257/969)	500
Woodblock, Bungoro the Puppeteer, 30½ x 20 (4257/973)	750
Woodblock, Bungoro the Puppeteer, Junichiro, 30⅛ x 19¾, crease (4257/972)	800
Woodblock, Eizo and Matsuomaru, 22½ x 26⅜ (4257/977)	1100
Woodcut, fishing village in spring, 18¼ x 14⅝ (4257/979)	225
Woodcut, owl on branch, poster, 24¼ x 16½ (4257/974)	125

Kaburagi Kiyokata

Large panel, woman standing by flowers, 23⅜, 13¾ (4155/465)	1300
Large panel, woman standing next to flowers, (4257/703)	1400
Large panel, woman standing next to flowers, 2 fox spots (4257/873)	700
Oban, woman holding cloth, (4155/506)	1100

Kampo

Oban, night scene, flowers, fire baskets, 1925 (4155/565)	125
Oban, seated portrait, Hinazo, toned, 1923 (4257/952)	350
Oban, Ichikawa Sadanji as Hishikawa Gengobei, 1924 (4257/955)	150
Oban, Kataoka Gado as Miyuki, (4257/953)	300
Oban, Morning at Sanjobashi, 1925 (4257/951)	200
Oban, Nakamura Ganjiro as Kamiya Jibei, (4155/564)	275
Oban, Nakamura Ganjiro as Kamiya Jihei, (4257/954)	125

Katana

Shinto, by Kinimich (6th gen.*), signed, boy's, 19⅝ (4207/36)	500

Katsukawa Shunsen

Oban, 3 women in front of publishing house, (4155/414)	325

Kitao Masanobu

Oban, Seiro Meikun Jihitsusushu, light soil (4257/497)	1000
Oban, 2 birds on a branch, center fold (4257/498)	750

Kitao Shigemasa

Chuban, Fukurokuju seated, unsigned, slight wormage, tear (4257/466)	850

Chuban, 4 boys playing, faded and light soil (4257/465)   550

Kiyochika

Oban, moonlit view, (4257/697)	
Oban, night view, paddle wheelers, 19c, trimmed (4155/505)	350
Oban, open ferry with passengers, (4257/699)	550
Oban, sunset view, Sumida, 1881, stains (4155/504)	950
Oban, woman with 3 faces, western style, (4257/698)	150
Oban, 3 morning glories, 1880 (4155/503)	350
	4250

Oban (4155/503)

36 Views of Fuji (4257/564)

Kiyohiro

Hosoban, Nakamura Tomijuro, (4257/445)   1400

Kiyomitsu

Hosoban, Ichikawa Komazo II, torn section (4257/443)   425
Hosoban, Segawa Kikunojo, (4257/444)   1400

Kiyonaga

Aiban, Sawamura Sojuro III talking to courtesans, (4257/489)	5250
Chuban, Hai Furyu Taro, (4257/486)	1400
Chuban, 3 bijin, 2 crimps and light soil (4257/484)	1700
Hashira, woman looking from a balcony, faded (4257/487)	650
Oban, courtesan on promenade, faded and foxed (4257/485)	2000
Oban, Fuzoku Toshiba Kin, (4257/491)	7500
Oban, Minami Juni ko, (4257/490)	500
Oban, 5 woman in a bath house, faded, toned (4257/488)	375

Kiyoshi

Oban, woman wiping cheek, (4155/559)	850
Oban, woman with parasol, toning (4257/925)	425
Oban, Ichimaru, (4155/557)	425
Oban, Kami, (4155/556)	650
Oban, Shimoda no O-Kichi, rubbed (4155/558)	400

Kiyoshi Saito

Woodcut, Ancient City Nara, 16¼ x 20½, 1957 (4257/964)   225

Kobayashi Kiyochika

Large panel, Kyoto Sanjo Ohashi, 1921 (4257/880)	950
Oban, brace of mallards, slight feathering, 1880 (4257/878)	1400
Oban, kneeling man, small tear, 1885 (4257/875)	175
Oban, night conflagration, center fold, 1882 (4257/876)	600
Oban, still life, fruits, (4257/879)	700
Oban, sunset along a river, 1881 (4257/877)	750

Kogan Tabari

Large panel, nude, stained (4257/893)	4250
Large panel, Odawara no Yado, toned, 2 punctures, 1921 (4257/892)	1400

Koryusai

Aiban, Seiro Hakkei, faded (4257/462)	850
Chuban, a mitate of a play, (4257/459)	2900
Hashira, courtesan turned looking past kamuro, (4257/461)	*9000*
Oban, courtesan resting and conversing, (4257/460)	5500

Koryusai*

Oban, Shikido Torikumi Juni Bon, unsigned, center folds (4257/463)	5000

Koshiro Onchi

Woodblock, portrait of Sakutaro Hagiwara, 21½ x 17¼ (4257/965)	900
Woodblock, portrait of Sakutaro Hagiwara, different title, block, 21¾ x 17½ (4257/966)	2500

Kotondo

Oban, seated bare-breasted woman, 1931 (4155/518)	850
Oban, woman applying lip rouge, (4155/520)	950
Oban, woman brushing her shoulder against a ground, (4257/715)	750
Oban, young beauty, 1936 (4257/920)	1700
Oban, Asa Negami, (4257/922)	2500
Oban, Botan Yuki, (4257/924)	2750
Oban, Kami Suki, 1930 (4257/921)	1400
Oban, Kuchibeni, (4257/716)	1100
Oban, Nagajuban, 1930 (4155/519)	800
Oban, Nagajuban, 1930 (4257/923)	350

Kunimaru

Kakemono, bijin promenading, (4155/422)	425

Kunimitsu

Oban, people at temple entrance, (4155/420)	150

Kunisato

Oban, 2 actor in a play scene, colors toned (4155/421)	100

Kuniyoshi

O-tanzuku, 7 Gods of Felicity, (4257/659)	375
Oban, woman with bucking horse, fold, rubbed (4155/418)	2700
Oban, Hakkunin isshu no uchi, rub (4257/663)	200
Oban, Samurai attacking a giant toad, (4257/660)	800
Oban, Suikoden goketsu hyaku-hachi-nin, (4257/657)	350
Oban, Tsuzoku Suikoden goketsu hyaku-hachi-nin no h, itori (4257/662)	650
Surimono, mother walking with daughter, (4257/661)	700
24 Examples of Filial Piety, Tai Shun, wormage (4257/656)	950
24 Examples of Filial Piety, Wang Pov, light rub (4257/655)	800

Marunobu

Chuban, man reclining beside sleeping girl, center fold (4257/447)	1400

Migita Toshihide

Oban, seven gods of felicity fighting, 1888 (4155/451)	225

Okumura Masanobu

Hosoban, hand colored, Nihon Gako Okumura Masanobu sho hitsu, (4257/434)	650

Okumura Masanobu*

Hashira, two drunken shojo dancing, (4257/436)	250

Okumura Toshinobu

Hosoban, hand colored, Okumara Ichiryu Odoriko fu, (4257/437)	16000

Osaka

Oban, scene from Kagamiyama Kokyo no Nishikie, (4257/578)	550

Ryusai Shigeharu

Oban, Chinese noble with kneeling boy, (4257/585)   100

Sadahide

Oban, view of pilgrims climbing Mt. Fuji, (4155/452)   475

Sharaku

Aiban, half-length of Nakamura Nakazo II, some wormage, 1794 (4257/522)   20000
Oban, Ichikawa Omezo in a play, (4257/524)   62000
Oban, Sakata Hangoro III in a play, rep wormhole, puncture (4257/523)   32000

Shigenaga

Hashira, figure of Shoki, (4257/441)   550
Hashira, 6 Yamabushi climbing trail, (4257/442)   500

Shinsai

Chuban, Furyu Toto Hakkei, Sumidagawa in winter, (4155/404)   100

Shinsui

Aiban, The Ferry Man, (4257/789)   2000
Chuban, backpacked figure walking, 1918 (4155/552)   900
Chuban, man in boat, misty marshes, 1919 (4257/894)   2000
Chuban, Omi Hakkei no uchi Awadzu, 1918 (4155/549)   1100
Chuban, Omi Hakkei no uchi Ishiyama-ji, 1918 (4155/551)   1100
Chuban, Omi Hakkei no uchi Seta no sekisho, 1919 (4155/547)   1300
Chuban, Omi Hakkei no uchi Yabase, 1918 (4155/550)   1400
Chuban, Omi Hakkei no uchi, Karasaki, 1919 (4257/896)   750
Chuban, Omi Hakkei no uchi, Miiji, 1918 (4257/895)   800
Ko-kakemono-e, woman of ill fame, 1917 (4257/897)   4250
Large panel, woman washing hair, 19½ x 13⅝ (4155/538)   1200
Long panel, woman adjusting coif, 19½ x 9⅝, 1918 (4155/542)   2100
Oban, distant mountain, sunset, 1949 (4155/553)   200
Oban, night scene of a geisha, 1922 (4155/548)   1400
Oban, profile of a woman, 1917 (4155/540)   7000
Oban, seated woman, 1917 (4257/903)   3500
Oban, snow-covered landscape, 1922 (4257/902)   1100
Oban, willows in a heavy rain, (4257/785)   600
Oban, woman adjusting hairpin, ca1926, cut (4155/482)   425
Oban, woman applying make-up, 1923 (4155/478)   550
Oban, woman combing hair, ca1926 (4155/479)   550
Oban, woman fixing hair, 1922 (4257/899)   6000
Oban, woman holding fan with 2 hands, (4155/543)   750
Oban, woman opening umbrella, 1918 (4257/898)   3250
Oban, woman partially wrapped in a towel, 1924 (4155/546)   2000
Oban, woman sewing garment, faded (4155/480)   475

Oban
(4155/480)

Hashira
(4257/461)

Oban, woman with rouge pot, (4257/786) 1500
Oban, woman wringing out washcloth, 1918 (4155/541) 6250
Oban, After the Bath, 1930 (4155/545) 1200
Oban, Fubaki, 1933 (4155/539) 1600
Oban, Hotaru, 1935 (4155/481) 750
Oban, Hotaru, (4257/788) 800
Oban, Kotatsu, 1924 (4155/554) 1400
Oban, Kotatsu, (4257/787) 1200
Oban, Kuchibeni, 1923 (4257/901) 1800
Oban, Mayu-sumi, 1929 (4257/900) 4750
Oban, Mushi No Ne, 1924 (4257/904) 4250
Oban, Nagajuban, 1928 (4155/477) 550
Oban, Ukata, 1923 (4155/544) 1600

Shiro

Oban, Tokyo Omi Hakkei no uchi, Gyotoku Imaibashi no, shinshu, 1930 (4257/963) 275

Shoun

Oban, woman, plum tree, 1907 (4257/891) 200

Shuncho

Oban, set of 12 shunga, slightly faded, creases (4257/478) 6250
Oban, waitress holding a small tray, slightly faded, wormholes (4257/479) 16000
Oban, 3 bijin and a boy, slightly soiled, toned (4257/477) 1000

Shunei

Oban, a wrestler standing, (4257/483) *5250*

Shungyo

Hashira, teahouse waitress, rolled marks (4257/480) 1100

Shunjo

Hosoban, Nakamura Denkuro II as a porter, rub, soiled (4257/471) 800
Hosoban, Nakamura Matsue as a courtesan, (4257/472) 1700

Shunko

Hosoban, actor in front of rice sheaves, (4155/393) *1300*
Hosoban, Ichigawa Danjuro V as samurai, (4155/394) 1800
Hosoban, Nakamura Denkuro II holding a mirror, faded (4257/473) 900
Hosoban, Sakata Hangoro as a samurai, (4257/474) 2500

Shunman

Oban, from series Mu Tamagawa, faded, soil (4257/551) 1800
Surimono, white and pink peonies, (4257/549) 1600
Surimono, 3 crows in flight, rub (4257/550) 2600

Shunsen

Oban, actor holding parasol, (4257/792) 200
Oban, actor, background Sumidagawa, (4257/957) 150
Oban, Bando Shucho as Tojuro, (4155/562) 250
Oban, Ichikawa Enjaku against a curtain, (4257/791) 150
Oban, Ichikawa Sadanji as Murabashi Chuya, (4155/561) 250
Oban, Kataoka Nizaemon as Honzo, (4155/560) *900*

Shunsho

Hosoban, actor as a lord, (4155/387) *1800*
Hosoban, actor as warrior, stain (4155/384) 1200
Hosoban, actor as nobleman, Fuji behind, (4155/388) 700
Hosoban, actor as samurai, (4155/390) 1200
Hosoban, actor before stream, stains (4155/389) 450
Hosoban, Ichigawa Danjwro V as samurai, (4155/391) 1200
Hosoban, Ichikawa Danjuro V as farmer, (4155/386) 700
Hosoban, Matsumoto Koshiro II as falconer, stains (4155/385) 650
Oban, Ehon Haikai Yobukodori, unsigned, stains, 1788 (4257/468) 800

Shuntei

Oban, Soga no Guro in armour, (4257/586) 100
Oban, 2 men and 2 women at tea, faded, foxing, toned (4257/587) 150

Hosoban (4155/393)

Oban (4155/560)

Oban (4257/483)

Hosoban
(4155/387)

Shunzan

Chuban, a man and 4 women on promenade, faded, foxed, toned (4257/481) — 375
Oban, a bijin and 8 boys, (4257/482) — 1100

Sugimura Jihei

Oban, hand colored, Samurai reclining with Courtesan, wormhole, trimmed (4257/432) — 26500

Susumi Yamaguchi

Woodblock, Mt. Hotaka at Daybreak, 23⅜ x 17⅛, 1957 (4257/962) — 175

Torii Fusanobu

Hosoban, hand colored, Ichigawa as noble, (4155/381) — 900

Torii Kikyotsune

Sumizuri, Matsumoto Koshiro as TObinomono Kihei, (4155/382) — 150

Torii Kiyoshige

Large sheet, hand-colored, Bando Hikosaburo I, spot wormage (4257/440) — 20000

Toshinobu*

Hosoban, unsigned, slightly toned and trimmed (4257/439) — 550

Toyoharu

Oban, panoramic view of a boar hunt, center fold (4257/580) — 1000
Oban, panoramic view of whale hunt, center fold, rub, soil (4257/579) — 1000

Toyohiro

Hashira, 2 bijin playing, faded (4257/492)	800
Oban, Mutamagawa, (4257/494)	650
Prints, set of 6, daimyo's procession, (4257/493)	250

Toyokuni

Hosoban, Chushingura, parody on Act II, (4257/517)	800
Hosoban, 2 actors in a scene from a play, (4257/516)	450
Oban, interior of a Green House, faded, soils, stains (4257/511)	1100
Oban, scene from a play, faded, some soil (4257/514)	225
Oban, scene from Mimigatae Yoshiwara Sadachi, (4257/518)	1600
Oban, Iwai Hanshiro as a woman, (4257/513)	500
Oban, Matsumoto Koshiro seated, trimmed, thin spots (4257/515)	425
Oban, Nakayama Tomisaburo as a woman, (4257/519)	7000
Oban, Shoki with sword over an oni, trimmed, soils, put down (4257/512)	700

Toyokuni II & III

Chushingura, double faced, center creases (4257/668)	1400
Oban, wrestling match, (4257/672)	400

Toyonari

Oban, Matsusuke as Goroji, 1922 (4257/956)	750
Oban, Mitsugoro as the Dumb Man in the Play Sannin, Katawa (4257/794)	350
Oban, Nizaemon as Kakiemon, (4155/563)	850
Oban, Sonosuke as Umegawa, (4257/793)	650
Oban, Yennosuke, (4257/795)	800

Un'ichi Hiratsuka

Woodblock, seated woman, against screen, 22½ x 19½ (4257/950)	500

Unknown

Hashira, hand colored, a bijin walking with a boy, (4257/520)	325
Ishizuri, a falcon on a willow, (4257/464)	5250
Oban, western style, man with woman, (4257/890)	150

Utamaro

Chuban, courtesan holding a banner, faded (4257/525)	600
Chuban, Asazuma Fanaji no MarObine, (4257/526)	3000
Oban, a bijin dances with fan, faded (4257/539)	1400
Oban, a courtesan fanning, (4257/542)	22000
Oban, bijin with a sake cup, faded (4155/403)	1700
Oban, courtesan holding iris, faded (4155/397)	*1400*
Oban, courtesan with attendants, faded, stained (4257/544)	650
Oban, courtesan, brush, roll of paper, rubbed, soiled (4155/398)	1000
Oban, head of a woman talking to a man, soil, faded (4257/547)	2500
Oban, kei sei Kyochu Mitoshi Mitate Jyozu, slight fade (4257/531)	*4700*
Oban, man, woman, festival dress, faded (4155/400)	*700*
Oban, mother holding infant, faded (4257/535)	*5500*
Oban, Chushingura, act 5, faded, rub (4257/528)	2300
Oban, Chushingura, act 9, faded, foxed (4257/529)	1600
Oban, Furyu Kodakara Awase, (4155/401)	1400
Oban, Jitsu Kurabe Iro no minakami, (4257/541)	6750
Oban, Jitsu Kurabe Iro no Minakami, trimmed (4257/533)	*6250*
Oban, Kikojido holding a drum, soil, creasing, laid down (4257/546)	1600
Oban, Ryuko Moyo Utamaro Gata, put down, fair (4257/530)	750
Oban, Sericulture series #12, faded, wormhole (4257/527)	850
Oban, Shiki AsObi Hana no Iroka, (4257/548)	21000
Oban, Shoki seated, faded, soiled (4257/534)	700
Oban, Shunkyo Shichi Fuku AsObi, (4155/399)	1900
Oban, Yukun Go Sekku, faded (4257/537)	1700
Oban, 2 bijin at a picnic table, rep wormhole (4257/536)	3800
Oban, 2 salt maidens with a boy, faded, toned (4257/543)	550
Oban, 2 women talking while washing, faded, soiled, puncture (4257/540)	3500
Oban, 3 women and a boy on a stroll, slightly toned (4257/545)	650
Oban, 3 women around a palanquin, slight fade, tear (4257/532)	2300

Yoshida

Large panel, Asahi, Fuji, First Rays of the Sun, 21 x 28, center fold (4155/515) — 950
Large panel, Kumori Sakura, (4257/919) — 4500
Large panel, Matahorun-Yama, 20 x 14⅛, 1916 (4155/516) — 1100
Large panel, Yamanaka Ko, 24 x 18 (4155/517) — 2000
Oban, Calm Wind, (4155/510) — 300
Oban, Eboshi-dake, 1931 (4257/912) — 225
Oban, Fujiyama from Okitsu, (4257/727) — 250
Oban, Grand Canyon, 1916 (4257/908) — 700
Oban, Honoruru Suizokikan, undated (4257/906) — 150
Oban, Kashiwabara no Yuki, 1928 (4257/911) — 375
Oban, Kisogawa, (4257/723) — 400
Oban, Kura in Tomo no ura, (4257/718) — 350
Oban, Lugano, (4155/512) — 450
Oban, Lugano, (4257/717) — 650
Oban, Mitsu Kojima, (4257/722) — 400
Oban, Nabusagawa, 1927 (4257/917) — 350
Oban, Niagra Falls, 1916 (4257/909) — 850
Oban, Obutsu-en, Obatan-omu, 1917 (4257/910) — 450
Oban, Okitsu, 1929 (4257/907) — 250
Oban, Otenjo-dake Yori, 1927 (4257/915) — 550
Oban, Sumida River-Afternoon, (4257/730) — 350
Oban, Sumidagawa, 1927 (4257/916) — 350
Oban, Taguchi no Fuyu, (4257/914) — 325
Oban, Tateyama Betsuzan, 1927 (4257/913) — 300
Oban, Three Little Islands, (4155/513) — 350
Oban, Yatsuqatake, (4155/514) — 300
Oban, silk printed, Kingyo Saki, (4257/721) — 650
Panel, cottage and garden with snow, toned, tatty edges (4257/728) — 275

Yoshikazu

Oban, Oranda jin, (4257/674) — 500

Yoshikuni

Oban, Nakamura Utaemon and Ichikawa Danjuro against a, snake (4155/413) — 125

Oban (4257/531)

Oban (4155/397)

Oban
(4257/533)

Yoshitora

Oban, people around Kanagawa Bay, (4155/450)   150

Zeshin

Chuban, black brush case against plain ground, (4257/692)   350
Chuban, flowering stalks, (4155/463)   450
Chuban, sheaf of paper, bound orange, faded, rub (4257/696)   300
Chuban, stick of bamboo with fishing net, (4257/694)   350
Chuban, straw hat, bamboo stuff, bag, (4257/691)   300
Chuban, view of bonsai thru a window, (4155/462)   450
Chuban, Mishima chawan and rod, (4155/461)   400
Chuban, 3 sakura petals, (4257/693)   350
Octagonal Oban, group of travelers, around a teahouse, center crease, soil (4257/695)   200

SCREENS

Seventeenth Century

Six-fold Kano school, young prince's audience, 123 x 40¾, 17c/E18c (4257/870)   4500
Six-fold Kano school, pair, Imperial villa, Imperial Chinese audience, 124 x 47 (4257/872)   7750
Six-fold Ukiyo-e, interior of a Green House, 145 x 59½, res (4257/867)   8500
Six-fold, gold, wisteria on lattice, 142 x 60, res (4257/871)   4750

Eighteenth Century

Four-fold, Manchurian crane by rockwork, 90½ x 54¾ (4257/845)   2750
Six-fold, pair, Jakuchu School, cockrels, hens, each, 49⅞ x 19⅞ (4155/501)   5000
Six-fold gold paper, ancient pine, 139 x 63½, L17/18c (4257/843)   6250
Six-fold Kano school, sages, misty mountains, 139 x 59¾ (4257/863)   6250
Six-fold Kano school, Karaka, playing, performing, dancing, 123 x 49¼ (4257/849)   3500
Six-fold Kyoto, Kiyomitzu-dera complex, 104½ x 35¾ (4257/869)   6500
Six-fold Tosa school, gold, poetry, scenes from Genji Monogotari, (4257/868)   5500
Six-fold Tosa school, gold, 18 of the 36 Poets, 138 x 61, weak joints (4257/856)   4250
Two-fold, bamboo, color, gold, 67 x 71 (4155/498)   1600
Two-fold Tosa school, The Genji Monogotari, 67 x 59, ca1700 (4257/846)   6250
Two-fold, after Kano Yasunobu, kemori scene, Genj Monogotari, 72 x 59½, panel split (4257/865)   850

Nineteenth Century

Eight fusuma, set, extensive Chinese landscape, color, gold, each, 65 x 33½ (4155/499)   2500
Four-fold, pair, birds amidst flowers, 48½ x 80 (4155/495)   2700
Six-fold, birds, kiku, tears, 117 x 46, tears, broken joints (4257/850)   1200
Six-fold, cranes in flight above a stream, 151 x 68½, L19c (4257/847)   5500
Six-fold, Taishin o Fujin, after Soga Shohaku, 57½ x 154⅜ (4155/496)   1400
Six-fold, gold, spring flowers by stream, 139 x 60¾ (4257/861)   1700
Six-fold, gold, wisteria over a latticework, 141 x 61¾, E19c (4257/855)   10000

Six-fold, gold, Battle of Yoshima, 72½ x 61½, joints split (4257/866)   2250

Twentieth Century

Six-fold, pair, trees, flowers, stream, color, gold, 60½ x 143½ (4155/497)   2500
Six-fold, gold, cranes, wood-pigeons, ducks, 132¾ x 61 (4257/852)   1600
Six-fold, pair, birds, flowers, snowy landscape, 145 x 60½ (4257/864)   3750
Six-fold, pair, gold, Narihira's Journey, 143 x 61 (4257/862)   2100

SWORDS AND FITTINGS

Abumi

Kashu Kanazawa Shigenobu, silver, decorated, pair, 16c (4257/398)   *2500*

Kashu Kanazawa Shigenobu
(4257/398)

Kashu Nagatsugu, silver-decorated, inlaid, pair, 18/19c (4257/397)   500

Aikuchi

Bizen, by Tomomitsu, unsigned, 9¾, 1368-1370 (4207/12)   1700
Bizen Sukesada, by Yosazaemonjo*, unsigned, 9⅛, 1578 (4207/11)   1300
Koto, Tanto in Aikuchi mounts, decorated, unsigned, 9 (4207/406)   850
Meiji, by Yoshitada, dragon wood mounts, (4207/10)   200

Armour

Do-maru, red, laced, part lacquered, gilt, 18/19c (4207/8)   1600
Hachi, 6-plate, domed bowl, overlapping plates, unsigned, 18c (4207/7)   225
Mogami-do, green laced, gold lacquered, Nashiji, 18/19c (4207/9)   4750

Daisho

Ikkanshi Tadatsuna, Shakudo mounts, by Ishiguro Masayoshi and Omor, Teruhide, 28 5/16, 1692 (4257/429)   7000
Silver-mounted, after Mutsu Kaneyasu, and Shinano Noboyoshi, 22⅝, 19¾ (4207/40)   2900

Fittings

Kozura, iron, applied, gilt, silver, 19c (4207/1)   110
Tsuba, iron, by Hamano Hiroyuki, oval-form, sage, servant, crane, signed, Diam 2⅝, L18c (4207/3)   225
Tsuba, tanto, sentoku, by Ichijosai, oval-form, tiger, signed, Diam 7½, 18/E19c (4207/2)   150

Katana

Koto, by Gassan, signed, 19⅛ (4207/63)   1200
Koto, by Yamato Kaneuji*, in Shirasaya, 28¼ (4207/99)   3250
Koto, by Yasumitsu, signed, 19⅝ (4207/117)   500
Koto, Bizen, Kiyomitsu, signed, 26⅞ (4207/31)   2300
Koto, Echizen, by Uda Kunimune, cutting attestation, signed, mounts by Tsuchiya Takechika, 21 (4207/64)   8000

Koto, Gunto mounts, unsigned, 27⅜, Late (4257/416) — 400
Koto, Gunto mounts, unsigned, 27, Late (4257/417) — 550
Koto, Mumei, in Shirasaya, unsigned, 28⅜ (4207/84) — 1900
Koto, Mumei in Shirasaya, signed, 22 15/16 (4257/423) — 700
Koto, Shakudo mounts, decorated, unsigned, 20¼, Late (4257/415) — 850
Koto, Soshu Hiromasa, signed, 28⅞, Late (4257/421) — 550
Koto, Sukesada, late, signed, 26⅝, 1567 (4207/26) — 700
Koto, unsigned, 18 (4207/28) — 550
Koto, unsigned, 24⅞ (4207/29) — 1200
Koto, unsigned, in Shirasaya, 27 (4207/22) — 900
Koto Bingo Kai Mihara, by Fujiwara Masamori, late, signed, 30, 1569 (4207/111) — 8000
Koto Bitchu, by Sadatsugu (2nd or 3rd gen.*), in Shirasaya, Sayagaki by Honami Heijuro, 27½ (4207/104) — 13500
Koto Bizen, by Kiyomitsu, late, signed, from Imperial Collection, 29⅜ (4207/106) — 2250
Koto Bizen, by Nagamitsu, signed, 18⅛ (4207/67) — 3000
Koto Bizen, by Nagamitsu*, signed, 27, 1294 (4207/141) — 1250
Koto Bizen, by Nagamori, Gold attestation by Honami Koichi, silver mounts, 26¼ (4207/103) — 4750
Koto Bizen, by Tadamitsu, in Shirasaya, signed, 29½, 1393 (4207/98) — 4100
Koto Bizen, by Tadamitsu (3rd or 4th gen.*), in Shirasaya, signed, 23⅝, 1494 (4207/124) — 3500
Koto Gassan, in Shirasaya, 27 (4207/139) — 5500
Koto Hizen, by Morimitsu (3rd gen.*), signed, 26 (4207/39) — 2600
Koto Mino, by Kanenobu (Naoe Shizu), in Shirasaya, signed, 26¾ (4207/138) — 2500
Koto Mino, by Kanenori, in Shirasaya, signed, 32⅛ (4207/114) — 1900
Koto Mino, by Kanenori, signed, 27½ (4207/96) — 2000
Koto Mino, by Kanesada (1st gen.), in Shirasaya, signed, 27⅛ (4207/134) — 3250
Koto Mino, by Kaneuji, named 'Kusari Katabera', in Shirasaya, signed, 26¾ (4207/131) — 2000
Koto Mino, by Kaneyoshi, signed, 19½ (4207/27) — 1100
Koto Mino, by Magoroku Kanemoto, in Shirasaya, signed, 28⅝ (4207/74) — 2500
Koto Mino, by Seki Kanefusa*, cutting attestation, mounts by Kansai Takenori, 28¼ (4207/69) — 8500
Koto Mino Seki, by Kanemichi, in Shirasaya, signed, 30⅛ (4207/133) — 6500
Koto Mino Seki, by Kanesada (2nd gen.*), in Shirasaya, signed, 27⅞ (4207/110) — 3250
Koto Mumei, in Shirasaya, 26⅝ (4207/127) — 2300
Koto Mumei, in Shirasaya, unsigned, 27⅜ (4207/78) — 2500
Koto Mumei, 25⅜, (4207/137) — 700
Koto Mumei, 28⅞, (4207/132) — 2000
Koto Mumei Soshu, unsigned, 21¼ (4207/61) — 2500
Koto Mumei Sue Soshu, in Shirasaya, 25⅝ (4207/135) — 2000
Koto Seki, by Kanesada (3rd gen. or later), signed, 21⅜ (4207/120) — 500
Koto Shizu Kaneuji, unsigned, 27¼ (4207/82) — 2000
Koto Soshu, by Akihiro, in Shirasaya, signed, 21⅛ (4207/125) — 600
Koto Soshu, by Hiromasa (1st gen.), in Shirasaya, Sagayaki by Honami Heijuro, signed, 27⅜ (4207/83) — 3000
Koto Yamashiro, unsigned, 26¼ (4207/72) — 2800
Koto Yamashiro Rai, unsigned, 26¾ (4207/71) — 3200
Koto Yamato, by Kanenaga (6th or 7th gen.*), in Shirasaya, named 'Yakirimaru', signed, 23⅜ (4207/62) — 1000
Meiji, by Gassan Sadakazu, in Shirasaya, signed, 27¼, 1905 (4207/77) — 6250
Meiji, by Sadahiro, signed, 27⅛ (4207/34) — 1500
Shinshinto, by Hosokawa Masmori, signed, 26, 1860 (4207/70) — 4750
Shinshinto, by Joyo Masayuki, signed, 27⅜, 1868 (4207/88) — 4800
Shinshinto, by Kiyoto* or Nobuhide*, after Kiyomaro, signed, 28½ (4207/109) — 5750
Shinshinto, by Maizuro Tomohide, signed, 31⅛, 1853 (4207/107) — 7500
Shinshinto, by Sadahiro, signed, 27⅛ (4207/23) — 1400
Shinshinto, by Sanjo Munechika (16th gen.), Munetsugu, in Shirasaya, signed, 25⅞, 1819 (4207/81) — 4250
Shinshinto, by Tegarayama Masashige, iron mounts by Katsura Soei, signed, 27½, 1793 (4207/89) — 11500
Shinshinto, in Shirasaya, signed, 26⅛ (4257/419) — 700
Shinshinto, in Shirasaya, manner of Shinkai, 27¾ (4207/35) — 500
Shinshinto Musashi, by Ason Nobuhide, in Shirasaya, Sayagaki by Honami Heijuro, signed, 25⅞, 1869 (4207/76) — 8250
Shinshinto Shimosa, by Minamoto Masayuki, in Shirasaya, signed, 26⅜ (4207/129) — 1800
Shinshinto Shimotsuke, by Bakka-shi Hosokawa Masayoshi, signed, 27⅝, 1836 (4207/118) — 9000
Shinshinto Shinano, by Seishinsai Morichika, in Shirasaya, signed, 27½ (4207/93) — *4500*
Shinto, after Sukehiro, in Shirasaya, 24¼ (4207/122) — 4500
Shinto, after Tsuda Echizen Sukehiro, in Shirasaya, 22, 1675 (4207/126) — 1200
Shinto, by Bushu Kanda Kanetsune*, signed, 23¾ (4207/20) — 1300
Shinto, by Faga Kanewaka (3rd gen.*), cutting attestation, in Shirasaya, signed, 20⅛, 1662 (4207/66) — 1100
Shinto, by Harima Yoshimichi (1st gen.), in Shirasaya, signed, 30⅛ (4207/102) — 5250

Shinto, by Kunisada (1st gen.), signed by Shinkai, 20⅞, 1649 (4207/60) 3600
Shinto, by Kunisuke*, signed, 24⅝ (4207/25) 2000
Shinto, by Musashi Kaneshige, in Shirasaya, signed, 20¼ (4207/65) 4250
Shinto, by Omi Sukenao, signed, 20½ (4207/79) 11500
Shinto, by Shunshu Kanesada, signed, 21¼ (4207/21) 700
Shinto, by Vmetada Muneshige, signed, 19½, 1712 (4207/37) 3000
Shinto, Edo Seki, by Toren, signed, 22¼ (4207/59) 1700
Shinto, Kinmichi 2nd generation, cutting attestation, Gunto mounts, 27 9/16 (4257/424) *4250*

Shinshinto
Shinano
(4207/93)

Shinto
(4257/424)

Shinto, Kiyoshige, decorated, 27¼ (4257/420) 1400
Shinto, Mino Jumyo, unsigned, 21½ (4207/68) 1400
Shinto, Musashi, Shigeharu, unsigned, 26⅛ (4257/426) 2600
Shinto, Nobutaka, signed indistinctly, 26¼ (4257/425) 500
Shinto, Satsuma Mondo Masakiyo*, Gunto mounts, 26⅞ (4257/418) 1500
Shinto, Shigekuni (2nd or 3rd gen.*), signed, 29¼ (4207/113) 3250
Shinto Aki, by Harima Teruhiro (2nd gen.), signed, 26¾ (4207/73) 6250
Shinto Bunko, by Motoyuki, in Shirasaya, signed, 27 38 (4207/86) 1900
Shinto Buzen, by Heishiro Yoshimasa, signed, 27¼ (4207/91) 5000
Shinto Echigo, by Kondo Taro Kaneyuki, signed, 28¼ (4207/94) 3600
Shinto Echizen, by Shigetaka (2nd gen.), signed, 25 (4207/95) 2600
Shinto Harima, by Yoshimichi (2nd gen.), in Shirasaya, signed, 20⅝ (4207/119) 1200
Shinto Harima, by Yoshimichi (2nd gen.), in Shirasaya, signed, 20¼, 1671 (4207/123) 1400
Shinto Hizen, by Yukihiro (1st gen.), 21⅜ (4207/128) 1800
Shinto Hizen, Mumei, by Tadayoshi (3rd gen.*), silver mounts by Toryuken Naotoshi, signed, 28⅛ (4207/87) 2700
Shinto Hizen Masahiro, 6th gen.*, 21 7/16 (4257/422) 450
Shinto Inaba, by Kanesaki (3rd gen.*), signed, 27¾ (4207/130) 3400
Shinto Ise, by Muramasa (2nd gen.), in Shirasaya, signed, 27¾ (4207/140) 1700
Shinto Kaga, by Kiyomitsu (3rd gen.), in Shirasaya, signed, 27 (4207/97) 1700
Shinto Kawachi, by Kunisuke (2nd gen.), signed, 27½ (4207/108) 4000
Shinto Mino, by Yoshitoki, testing attestation, signed, 26½ (4207/100) 3500
Shinto Mino Seki, by Terukado, in Shirasaya, signed, 24⅝ (4207/92) 1600
Shinto Mino Seki, by Tokuin Iyehisa, in Shirasaya, signed, 21½ (4207/116) 1600
Shinto Mumei, in Shirasaya, 21½ (4207/121) 350
Shinto Musashi, by Yasusada, 'Five Body' cutting attestation, in Shirasaya, 29¾, 1663 (4207/85) 13000
Shinto Omi Sekido, by Zenshiro Ippo, signed, 28 (4207/112) 5000
Shinto Owari, by Nobutaka (3rd gen.*), in Shirasaya, signed, 21½ (4207/115) 1800
Shinto Rikuzen, by Kunikane (1st gen.), in Shirasaya, Sayagaki by Honami Heijuro, signed, 26⅞ (4207/80) 4500
Shinto Sesshu, by Sadanori, signed, 25¾ (4207/105) 3000
Shinto Settsu, by Kinjinmaru Kunishige, signed, Gunto mounts, 21½ (4207/24) 1000
Shinto Settsu, by Kunisuke (2nd gen.), in Shirasaya, signed, 27⅝ (4207/101) 5750
Shinto Settsu, by Sukeharu, in Shirasaya, 27½ (4207/136) 1200
Showa, unsigned, 26¼ (4207/32) 275
Showa, by Akitomo, signed, Naval Gunto mounts, 27⅞, 1936 (4207/30) 1100

Showa, by Yamagawa Yasushiki, signed, manner of Sa Nobumitsu, 26½, 1944 (4207/33)   350
Showa, in Shirasaya, signed and dated, 26¼, Showa 20 (4257/428)   425

Koshozan-Sujibachi

Saotome School, 62 plates, gilt-decorated, inscribed, 18/19c (4257/402)   750

Kozuka

Narihiro*, Shibuichi, applied, gold, copper, E19c (4257/395)   650
Nomura Masahide, Shibuichi, applied, ca1800 (4257/380)   150
Okamoto Yasuhiro, copper Ishime, molded with a boar, E19c (4257/378)   150
Omori Terumitsu, Shibuichi, molded, high relief, ca1800 (4257/381)   325
Seiunsha Toho, Shakudo Nanako, applied, 19c (4257/382)   650
Unsigned, silver Ishime, calendar, carved, 19c (4257/385)   125
Unsigned, Sentoku, applied, decorated, 18c (4257/386)   150
Unsigned, Shakudo Nanako, applied, 17/18c (4257/384)   200
Unsigned, Shakudo Nanako, bow applied, fur-covered quiver, 18c (4257/366)   200
Unsigned, Shakudo Nanako, gold applied, Chinese style halbard, L18c/E19c (4257/376)   325
Yoshioka, Shakudo Nanako, molded with a goose, 18/19c (4257/377)   850

O-Tanto

Koto Bizen, by Osafune, signed, 17¼ (4207/18)   400
Musashi Yasutsugu, unsigned, 15½ (4257/408)   600

Polearms

Koto Naga-Suyari, by Kanetoshi, 13⅛ (4207/46)   550
Shinto Nagasuyari, by Ishido Suketoshi in Shirasaya, signed, 15⅜ (4207/43)   650
Shinto Naginata, Yamashiro, by Mutsu Toshinaga (1st gen.), signed, 15⅝ (4207/42)   800
Shinto Suyari, by Mastoshi in Shirasaya, 13¼ (4207/44)   850

Tachi

Koto, by Rai Kuniyuki, signed, 27⅝ (4207/143)   4000
Koto Bitchu, by Tsuguyoshi, in Shirasaya, signed, 24¾, 1344 (4207/148)   4250
Koto Bizen Numei, by Nagamitsu, in Shirasaya, 28¼ (4207/150)   10500
Koto Echizen, by Norishige, in Shirasaya, signed, 26 (4207/157)   3250
Koto Higo, by Enju Kuniiye, in Shirasaya, signed, 27 (4207/155)   4000
Koto Mino, by Senjuin Kunishige, in Shirasaya, signed, 27⅜, ca1330 (4207/156)   3000
Koto Mino, by Shigenobu, in Shirasaya, Sayagaki by Honami Heijuro, signed, 27⅜, 1505 (4207/147)   4250
Koto Soshu, forging indistinct, unsigned, 27⅜ (4257/430)   1400
Koto Yamashiro, by Kunitomo, signed, 25⅜ (4207/159)   3900
Koto Yamashiro, by Nobukuni*, in Shirasaya, 27⅞ (4207/145)   2750
Shinshinto, by Yamato Michiharu, signed, 29¼, ca1865 (4207/152)   1700
Shinshinto, by Yokoyama Sukemitsu, signed, 31, 1858 (4207/153)   4750
Shinshinto, silver-mounted, unsigned, 27 13/16 (4257/431)   *9250*
Shinshinto Hizen, by Tadayoshi (8th gen.), in Shirasaya, signed, 27½ (4207/154)   5000
Shinto, by Hizen Yukihiro (1st gen.), signed, 26⅜ (4207/144)   3500
Shinto Hizen, by Sagami Tadamune, signed, 28 (4207/149)   3200
Shinto Hizen, by Tadayoshi (3rd gen.), signed, 26⅞ (4207/146)   2750
Shinto Mino, by Heianjo Tomohira, signed, mounts, Shakudo Nanako, 27⅜ (4207/151)   5750
Shinto Sinuki Gata, unsigned, 34⅜ (4207/142)   1600
Showa, in Shirasaya, 26¼, 1940 (4207/158)   600
Showa, signed, Gunto mounts, 26½, 1944 (4207/41)   325

Tanto

Copper, unsigned, 10¼ (4207/14)   800
Koto, by Kaneuji, in Shirasaya, signed, 11¾ (4207/47)   900
Koto, by Tomoyuki, signed in Shirasaya, 10⅜ (4207/13)   550
Koto Bizen, after Norimitsu, unsigned, 9⅜ (4207/17)   350
Koto Bizen, by Sukemitsu, in Shirasaya, signed, 13¾ (4207/49)   1400
Shinshinto Ken, unsigned, 21⅜ (4257/407)   *5000*
Shinto, unsigned, Omori Shibuichi mounts, 11⅞ (4207/15)   3300
Shinto, by Fujiwara Kuninori, in Shirasaya, signed in full, 19¼ (4207/50)   4750
Shinto, by Inaba Kanesaki, (2nd gen.*), signed, Hamano mounts by Masayuki, Masayoshi, 13
  (4207/16)   6000
Shinto, by Yamashiro Daijo Kunikane, signed, 15⅜ (4207/48)   1700
Silver mounted, decorated, unsigned, 9¼ (4257/410)   1100

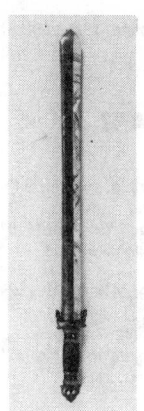

Shinshinto Ken
(4257/407)

Nomura Masayuki
(4257/360)

Tsuba

Arikawa Naomasa, iron, oval, molded in high relief, 3¼, L18c/E19c (4257/341)   650
Chohan Shunyoken, Choshu, iron, circular guard, carved, 2¾, 18/19c (4257/357)   500
Gashu Hikone, Soten, iron, molded and carved, gilt decorated, 3, 19c (4257/356)   1100
Nomura Masayuki, rounded square form, copper and gilt, 2¾, L19c (4257/360)   *2600*
Okabe Tadamasa, iron, oval, carved and molded, 3½ (4257/354)   500
Oyama Motozane III, copper, after Eijuken Motoharu, inscribed, 3⅝, L19c (4257/361)   1800
Shakudo, silver and mother-of-pearl, oval guard, thinning at the lip, 3, 19c (4257/338)   750
Tomotsune II, Choshu, iron, circular, pierced with leaves, 3, 17/18c (4257/358)   200
Unsigned, copper and gold, circular guard, carved and highlighted, 2¾, 19c (4257/339)   600
Unsigned, enamel and Sentoku, circular with lipped rim, decorated, 2½, 17c (4257/340)   250
Unsigned, iron, deeply carved circular guard, 3⅛, 19c (4257/337)   1100
Unsigned, iron, oval guard, gilt edge, 2⅝, E19c (4257/343)   375
Unsigned, iron, scene of Sato no Tadanobu, oval, 2⅜, 19c (4257/344)   150
Unsigned, Choshu, iron, oval, molded and carved with flowers, 2¾, 19c (4257/355)   225
Unsigned, Sentoku, oval, pierced marubori, decorated, 2¾, 19c (4257/347)   200
Unsigned, Shakudo Nanako Mokko, molded in brown, gilt decoration, 2¼, 18c (4257/345)   50
Unsigned, Shakudo Nanako Mokko, openwork guard, decorated, 2½, 18/19c (4257/350)   175

Wakizashi

Koto, Yamato, Mumei, by Kanenaga*, in Shirasaya, signed, 16½ (4207/56)   850
Koto Bizen, by Yoshisuke, signed, 14¾, ca1400 (4207/19)   1100
Shinshinto Hizen, by Tadayoshi (8th gen.), signed, 17⅛ (4207/53)   1700
Shinto, forging indistinct, unsigned, 14 9/16 (4257/414)   400
Shinto, by Fujiwara Kunisada (1st gen.), signed by Shinkai, in Shirasaya, 17¾ (4207/57)   2200
Shinto, by Sukesada, signed, 19½ (4207/55)   1000
Shinto, by Yamashiro Fujiwara Kunimichi, signed, 15¾ (4207/54)   4000
Shinto, Musashi, by Hankei*, silver mounts, signed, 18⅜ (4207/58)   3700
Shinto Hizen, by Tadakuni, (2nd gen.), signed, 18⅞ (4207/52)   1900
Shinto Yoshiiye in Shirasaya, signed, 16 11/16 (4257/412)   600
Yamashiro, by Tamba Yoshimichi (2nd gen.), signed, 16 (4207/51)   1400
Yamashiro, Yoshimichi* in Shirasaya, 2nd generation, 22 (4257/413)   1800

TEXTILES

Altar cloth, Ohi silk, Tendai sect, pale orange, interlocking keywork, 70, 12, 18c (4257/180)   125
Embroidered hanging, silk, depicting a sea eagle in pursuit, 68 x 15, L19c (4257/185)   900
Embroidered hanging, silk, depicting pr of cockrels, within brocade border, 78 x 50, ca1900
(4257/183)   2200
Embroidered panel, silk, mounted as a scroll, 2 wood pigeons, 19¾ x 46, ca1805 (4257/194)   550

Mantle, priest, silk, embroidered, sectioned squares of dragons, 18/19c (4257/205)   200
Robe, priest, silk, K'O-Ssu style, metallic thread, peonies and rushing stream, 45½ x 81, 17c
(4257/190)   1600
Robe, priest, silk, Kara-Ori, embroidered with stylized peonies, yellow ground, 18/19c (4257/206)   300
Robe, woven, No-Kosade, orange-red, green and white, 19c (4257/198)   375
Section, silk, embroidered, dragons, orange-red ground, 18/19c (4257/212)   60

JAPANESE WORKS OF ART

Assorted items

Ape and Pomegranate, soft metal group, ape seated atop pomegranate, incised, 11⅜, L19c
(4257/191)   900
Box, iron, foliate border, birds with bamboo, Tokyo, Yoshinobu, 4¾ x 3½, 1868-1912 (4191/17)   950
Eleven-headed Kannon, gilt figure, standing, double lotus base, architectural dias, 27⅛, 1862
(4257/195)   700
Hand warmer, gilt copper, decorated upper base, pierced domed cover, 4⅜ x 3⅜ x 4, 17/18c
(4257/218)   200
Haniwa, terracotta figure, Tumulus, skirted, vessel atop head, 22½, dam (4257/217)   2900
Haniwa, terracotta figure, Tumulus, upcurled pigtails, painted eyes, hat, man, 15¼, res (4257/216)   *1900*

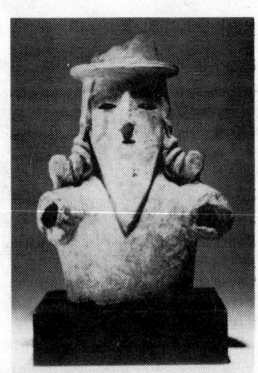

Haniwa (4257/216)

Jar, storage, Negoro, baluster-form, 4 legs attached, 22⅜, late Muromachi/Momoyama, res
(4155/75)   2600
Koro, iron, cloisonne, enamel, quatre-lobed burner, domed cover, 2 enamel pan, els, 6¼, L19c
(4155/68)   2500
Pipe, brass, silver, bamboo, 19c, (4191/13)   100
Pipe, silver, wood, L19c, (4191/14)   100
Plaques, portrait, Roiro & Fundame, European market, Edward III of England, Rousseau, of France,
4¾ ea, L18c (4257/193)   700
Pouch, tobacco, embroidered, various stitches, mountain scene, 19c (4191/15)   200
Vase, iron/soft metal, baluster-form, squash, flowers, vines, 6, L19c (4155/62)   400
Vase, soft metal and silver, ovoid, flared silver foot and elongated neck, 10⅜, L19c (4257/192)   375

Bronze

Buddha & Kannon Bosatsu, gilt figure, pair, flowing dress, 3½ each, 18/19c (4257/178)   375
Incense burner, kirin-form, standing, 8¾, 18/19c (4155/53)   200
Kannon, gilt and polychrome, standing, single lotus base, holding a lotus, 43⅜, 19c (4257/202)   1900
Pekinese, model, copper, silver, highlights, 10½, L19c (4155/56)   325
Plaque, votive, gilt, Muromachi period, incised, outer band of palmet, tes, Diam 9½ (4257/226)   500
Stands, gilt set of four, Kamakura/Muromachi, for esoteric Buddhist ritual items, Diam 4⅞
(4257/174)   550
Vase, ikebana, fan-form, hanging, molded, chased, W16⅛, L19c (4155/65)   600

Enamels

Bowl, cloisonne, dark blue ground, with peonies, Diam 11½, L19c (4257/228) 500
Box, covered, Sentoku, melon-form, silver vine entwine, gilt liner, Diam 4¾, L19c (4257/189) 1000
Charger, cloisonne, cranes, flowers, Diam 24¼, L19c (4155/58) 2300
Charger, cloisonne, shallow, circular, ring foot, Diam 36¼, L19c (4155/74) 2800
Jar, cloisonne, Yosaburo Honda, Nagoya, covered, silver-mounted, 3 stub feet, 12½, ca1890
  (4155/73) 7000
Stand, cloisonne, blue ground, millefleur base, 6¾, L19c (4155/64) 400
Vase, bronze, flaring foot, angled body, long-neck, 35½, L19c (4257/184) 950
Vase, cloisonne, black ground, ovoid, dragon, 12⅛, L19c (4155/66) 675
Vase, cloisonne, blue ground, hexagonal, leaf darts, 14¼, dam, L19c (4155/60) 125
Vase, cloisonne, blue ground, squat baluster, 9⅜, L19c (4155/69) 1900
Vase, cloisonne, grey ground, baluster-form, 23⅛, L19c (4155/70) 3400
Vase, cloisonne, grey ground, samurai, quail, 14, L19c (4155/71) 2500
Vase, cloisonne, pale green ground, elongated ovoid form, 11¾, L19c (4257/227) 375
Vase, cloisonne, silver-mounted, elongated baluster-form, 14, L19c (4155/72) 1800
Vase, worked-ground, red, elongated baluster form, dragon amidst clouds, 18¾, L19c (4257/186) 375
Vases, cloisonne, pair, sky-blue, white eagles among rocks, 9⅞, ca1900 (4257/200) 1900
Vases, pair, cloisonne, black ground, ovoid, trumpet mouths, 8¼, 19c (4155/63) 450

Ivory

Carving, Daikoku, Jushin(?)do Masayoshi, age cr, 19c (4257/1110) 700
Case, card, Shibayama, gold lacquer, couple near stream, 19c (4191/11) 425
Elephant, model, sectional, rocky wood base, L25½ (4191/7) 1900
Fan, lacquered, kiku, wild flowers, berries, 19c (4257/1106) 900
Figure, Benten, dragon at her feet, Shodo, base cr, E20c (4257/1108) 600
Figure, Hunter, 20c (4257/1112) 375
Kachi-Kachi Yama, circular base, badger saws, hare in kimono, 19c (4191/8) 800
Model, Pagoda, 14½, slight dam, L19c (4257/1109) 500
Okimono, stained, Fukurokoju & Daikoku, Sojun, 19c (4257/1107) 750
Okimono, Yajirobei and Kidahachi, irregular base, fighting blind men, Sosei, rep, dam, 19c (4191/6) *650*
Ship, treasure, 7 immortals, with attributes, Gyoku Shinsae*, L21, 19c (4191/18) *3900*

Okimono (4191/6)

Ship (4191/18)

Study, hen and rooster, separate, stylized, 24, 20c (4191/2) 950
Takarabune, model, engraved, treasure ship, 7 immortals, L15, 20c (4191/3) 900
Tusk section, carved, garden, lady dancing, men watching, 20c (4257/1111) 450
Tusks, pair, Shibayama, stained, mother-of-pearl, horn, 10⅝, 19c (4191/4) 1300
Vase, carved, cylindrical, scene from Chushingura, Yoshiaki, L19c (4191/1) 750

Wood

Box, lacquer, pottery, aquatic scene, applied pottery shells, 6¾ x 4 x 3¾, M19c, chip (4191/28)　　425
Doji, figure, polychrome, Zenzai-doji*, standing, 26½, res, 16c (4155/76)　　3400
Mask, no-style, depicting Kumasaka*, 10⅞, 19c (4257/175)　　250
Monkey, figure, half-kneeling, holding fruit, L18, 19c (4191/9)　　375
Monks, figures, pair, standing, deeply carved robes, bald, 59, 17/18c (4257/230)　　4000
Nio, head, Muromachi period, from a large statue, ferocious, face, 5¾ (4257/233)　　250
Sho-Kannon, figure, Muromachi*, standing, flowing robes, simple halo, 31⅞, 15/16c (4257/203)　　2100

Other Asian Works of Art

INDIAN　WORKS OF ART

Bronzes

Avalokites, Padmapani, Ladakh, standing, single lotus throne, 8⅝, ca14c (4155/31)　　800
Lamp, votive, fluted, ribbed, bulbous, loop handle, 6¾, 18c (4155/30)　　300
Parvati, Ceylon, standing, plain base, ivory support, 3, ca7c (4257/129)　　100
Siva, figure, Chola, rare iconography, seated, lotus throne, 13, 14c (4257/142)　　3500
Siva Nataraja, dancing, surrounded by flaming prabha, 71⅝, 17/18c (4257/157)　　20000

Stone

Apsara, grey sandstone figure, Gupta, semi-kneeling figure, 8½, ca5c (4257/151)　　2100
Bodhisattva, grey schist, Gandharan, Taxila, seated figure, preaching atttitude, 14⅝, 2/4c (4257/115)　　750
Bodhisattva Maitreya, grey schist, Gandharan, seated figure, draped base, halo, 19½, 10/12c (4257/117)　　*15500*

Bodhisattva Maitreya
(4257/117)

Buddha
(4257/116)

Gautama Buddha
(4257/154)

Buddha, buff sandstone head, Jain, full face, arched brows, curled hair, 7½, ca11c (4257/139)　　550
Buddha, grey schist figure, Gandharan, standing, elongated robes, curled hair, 21½, 2/4c, hands mis (4257/112)　　2800
Buddha, grey schist figure, Gandharan, standing, square pedesttal, wavy hair, 30, 2/3c (4257/116)　　*4600*

Siva (4257/122)

Parvati (4257/120)

Buddha, grey schist figure, Gandharan, Taxila, part, static, banded curly hair, 8⅝, 2/4c (4257/113) 375
Buddha, grey schist figure, Gandharan, seated, headless, 16¼,¾c (4155/32) 700
Buddha, stucco figure, Gandharan, seated, dressed in monastic robes, 7⅜,¾c (4257/111) 300
Buddha, stucco head, Gandharan, ovoid face, curled hair, traces of pigment, 6⅜,¾c (4257/110) 700
Deity, head, red sandstone, round face, tiered coif, 9, ca2c (4155/28) 325
Deva & Devi, red sandstone group, part, upper halves of both, elaborate dress, 16½, 10/12c (4257/145) 650
Devi, grey sandstone figure, bare-breasted, elaborate jewels, 20¼, 10/12c (4257/126) 700
Diety, red sandstone head, weather-worn face, deeply carved, 15½, 9/10c (4257/148) 1400
Gautama Buddha, stone stele, Pala, seated, lion throne, flowing robes, 22, 10/12c (4257/154) *7250*
Gomatesvara, white marble stele, Jain, standing, within architectural frame, 11⅛, 10/12c (4257/156) 550
Head, Stucco, Gandharan,¾ view, simplified face, rolled hair,   5½, 2/4c (4257/109) 450
Khasarpana-Lokesvara, black chlorite, stele, Pala, seated, single lotus throne, 24, 10/12c (4257/125) 2400
Lakshmi, grey sandstone figure, part, full-breasted, elaborate dress, 15¾, ca10c (4257/149) 9750
Lakshmi, red sandstone figure, seated, low cushion, infant on knee, 17½, 11/13c (4257/134) 800
Nandi, green stone model, recumbent bull, carved, W25, 14/16c (4257/130) 5400
Parvati, grey sandstone stele, manifestation of, seated, she holds an infant, 15, 13/15c (4257/133) 650
Parvati, red sandstone, swaying figure, elaborate jewelry, 25½, 10/12c (4257/120) *2500*
Siva, granite figure, Chola, standing, elaborate dress, 47, 12/14c, hand missing (4257/122) *1800*
Siva, grey sandstone figure, as Dakshinamurti, partial, ferocious face, 12, 10/12c (4257/131) 500
Siva, red sandstone figure, standing, small square base, 25¼, 10/12c (4257/121) 1800
Surya, red sandstone figure, part, standing, large foliate halo, 14½, 10/12c (4257/155) 1000
Surya, red sandstone figure, serene figure, elaborate jewels, 9¼, 9/11c (4257/150) 375
Surya, red sandstone stele, standing figure, simple dress, holding lotus, 29, 8/12c (4257/136) 1800
Trithankara, buff sandstone, Jain, seated figure, rounded cushion, headless, 19½, 10/12c (4257/118) 650
Uma-Mahesvara, grey sandstone stele, standing, square plinth, Siva, Parvati, embrace, 25½, 10/12c (4257/138) 2000
Uma-Mahesvara, red sandstone, seated, low cushion, Siva supports Parvati, 12½, ca12c (4257/137) 700
Unknown, black stone figure, standing, square base, ivory-eyed, 22⅝, arms missing, 17c* (4257/123) 300
Unknown, red sandstone figure, standing, elaborate jewels, 24, 10/11c (4257/153) 1000
Vishnu, black chlorite stele, Pala-Sena, standing, double lotus base, 16½, 10/12c (4257/146) 1700
Vishnu, black chorite stele, Pala, standing, single lotus base, elaborate dress, 29½, res, 10/11c (4257/124) 2300
Vishnu, buff sandstone head, well-carved face, crowned, 10½, res, ca10c (4257/152) 1500
Vishnu, grey sandstone figure, part, serene face, elaborate dress, 10⅜, ca12c (4257/132) 3800
Vishnu & Lakshmi, red sandstone, standing group, holding hands, with attributes, 24, 8c (4257/127) 1000
Yakshi, grey schist figure, Gandharan, standing, cross-legged, metal stand, 18½, 2/4c (4257/114) 4200
Yakshi, red sandstone figure, Mathura, standing, her hair swept up, 17½, 10/12c (4257/128) 500
Yakshi, red sandstone post, Gupta, swaying figure, hand to coif, 28½, 6/8c (4257/135) 2900

KOREAN   WORKS OF ART

Bronzes

Mirror of the Pao-Tien palace, cast with Taoist saints, attendants, diam8⅜, 12c, casting hole
  (4257/21)   200
Vase, thin ring foot, tear-form, flaring mouth, 11⅜, ca12c (4257/29)   *750*

Ceramics

Bottle, blue and white, thick ring foot, dragon, clouds, 11¼, 18/19c (4155/9)   425
Bottle, carved celadon, ovoid, flared foot, vertical grooves, Yueh-type, glaze, 9¼, ca11c (4257/31)   450
Bottle, celadon, baluster form, vertical grooves oxidized c, eladon glaze, 10⅛, ca12c (4257/3)   175
Bottle, celadon, Baluster form, vertical grooves sea-green, glaze, 10⅞, ca12c (4257/2)   375
Bottle, inlaid celadon, thick ring foot, tear-form, white inlay, lappet, collar, 12½, 13c, mouth res
  (4257/9)   400
Bottle, oil, Sang'gam, inlaid, 6-pointed, collar, sea-green glaze, Diam 2⅞, 12/13c (4155/7)   850
Bowl, celadon molded, Kangjin*, thick ring foot with 3 spurs, deep, even sea-green glaze, Diam 7½,
  12c (4257/14)   1400
Bowl, celadon, incised, short ring foot, 3 spurs, shallow, Diam 6¾, E12c (4155/6)   1300
Bowl, celadon, painted black and white, short straight foot, deep, 5 vertical, bands, Diam 7, 13c
  (4257/19)   750
Bowl, celadon, Sang'gam, ring foot, flaring, Diam 7, 12/13c (4155/333)   500
Bowl, celadon, Sang'gam, ring foot, 3 spurs, cranes, clouds, Diam 6¼, rep, 12c (4155/335)   950
Bowl, celadon, Sang'Gam, short ring foot, shallow, roundel of lappet, s, crazed glaze, Diam 7⅝, 13c
  (4257/8)   300
Bowl, incised celadon, Kangjin*, 3 spurs, exterior lotus petals, pale sea-green, glaze, Diam 6½, 12c
  (4257/24)   275
Bowl, inlaid celadon, short ring foot, shallow, white inlay of cranes, lappet circle, Diam 7⅜, 13c
  (4257/10)   150
Bowl, inlaid celadon, Cholla-Do*, ring foot, deep, white inlay concentric bands leaves, Diam 7⅜,
  14/15c (4257/13)   325
Bowl, stoneware, Silla, grey, trumpet-form foot, pierced, 10⅜, res, 6/8c (4155/10)   1650
Bowl, white, high ring foot, flared, blue-white glaze, diam 5⅝, 18/19c (4257/26)   150
Box, covered, Sang'gam, ring foot, flat, cylindrical, Diam 3¾, 13c (4155/334)   475
Chawan, 'Ido', deep ring foot, matte ochre glaze, Diam 5⅜, 16c (4155/331)   1600
Chawan, tan, high notched flaring foot, Diam 5⅝, rep, 15/19c (4155/330)   450
Chawan, tan-glazed, deep ring foot, swelling bowl, Diam 5½, 15/19c (4155/332)   300
Cup, wine, celadon, crude cut foot, flaring bowl, Diam 3¾, 13/14c (4155/329)   150
Dish, saucer, Sang'gam, hexagonal, molded, sea-green glaze, Diam 4⅜, 13c (4155/5)   175
Ewer, wine, inlaid celadon, ring foot, swan spout, ear handle, white and, black inlay, 11⅞, ca13c
  (4257/33)   *2600*

Vase (4257/29)

Ewer (4257/33)

Head rest, celadon, 2 seated lion-form, flat base, concave cushion, W7⅝, chip, 12c (4155/14)   10500

Jar, white storage, shouldered baluster form, high neck, pale blue-white glaze, 16, 18/19c (4257/16)   1100
Pot, wine, celadon, melon-form, handle, spout, sea-green glaze, 8¼, res, ca13c (4159/11)   1000
Water sprinkler, celadon, baluster form, flat shoulder, elongated neck se, a-green glaze, 12¼, ca12c (4257/5)   300

Lacquer

Cup, Lo-lang, irregular oval, ear-form handles, deep red, W5, res,½c (4155/13)   2000

Paintings

Anonymous, KOREAN ANCESTOR PORTRAIT, ink, color, silk, 58½ x 36, 17c (4261/11)   1800

SOUTH EAST ASIAN WORKS OF ART

Buddha, figure, bronze, seated, double lotus throne, shaped base, 12½, 17/18c (4155/43)   225
Buddha, figure, bronze, standing, single lotus base, 28⅞, 17/18c (4155/39)   700
Buddha, figure, bronze, Thai, elongated face, 7½, partial, 15/16c (4155/38)   375
Buddha, figure, gilt bronze, Thai, torso, serene face, traces of polychroming, 11½, L15c (4155/40)   800
Buddha, figure, gilt wood, Thai, seated, tiered architectural base, 14¼, 18/19c (4155/44)   200
Buddha, head, grey sandstone, Khmer, square face, diadem, 8⅝, 12/14c (4155/36)   900
Buddha, head, grey sandstone, Thai, downcast eyes, 11, nose res, 15c (4155/34)   600

Bronzes

Buddha, gilt figure, Thai, standing, tiered base, elaborate dress, 21, 18/12c (4257/169)   450
Buddha, hand, Thai, bejeweled, gilding traces, arc W9¼, 17/18c (4257/164)   175
Buddha, head, Sukhothai, degraded head and shoulders, curled hair, 10¼, 15c (4257/171)   500
Buddha, head, Thai, serene face, formal diadem, 4⅞, 16/17c (4257/170)   200
Buddha, head crowned, Ayudhya, serene face, low diadem, stone base, 5⅝, 16/17c (4257/160)   425
Buddha, head, Thai, elongated face, tightly curled hair, 5½, 15/16c (4257/165)   350
Buddha subduing Maya, Khmer, seated on coils of Naga, 8¼, 12/14c (4257/172)   1200

Stone

Buddha, grey sandstone figure, Khmer, Lopburi, upper torso, head and shoulders, 16½, ca12c (4257/173)   2000
Buddha, grey sandstone head, Thai, rounded face, black lacquer, gilding traces, 8½, 15c (4257/163)   800
Buddha & Naga, grey sandstone head, Khmer, Buddha surrounded by multiple heads of, Naga, 16¼, 12/13c (4257/167)   2500
Lintel, red sandstone, Khmer, deeply carved block, mask of Kala, 42 x 21 x 10, 11/12c (4257/161)   1500
Mahishasura-Mardini, volcanic stone, Javanese figure, standing on buffalo demon, 48, 10/14c (4257/166)   7750

TIBETAN WORKS OF ART

Bronzes

Amitabha, gilt, seated, separate double gilt bronze prahha, 5, 18/19c (4257/78)   700
Arapacana Manjusri, Nepalese, seated, separated double lotus throne, 7¾, L17c (4257/92)   500
Avalokitesvara Padmapani Triad, North Indian-Nepalese, standing, two attendants, stepped base, 7, 16/18c (4257/81)   375
Avalokitesvara Padnapani, gilt, Sino-Tibetan, seated, double lotus base, 10¼, 17c (4257/105)   1200
Bhaisajyaguru, gilt, Tibetan, seated, elaborate double lotus throne, 8⅞, 18c (4155/18)   1400
Bhaisajyaguru, Tibetan, seated, double lotus throne, painted, 8, ca15c (4155/20)   2000
Bodhisattva, gilt, Sino-Tibetan, standing, single lotus throne, tilted head, 7, 18c (4257/74)   650
Bodhisattva, gilt, Tibetan, usntsavijaya*, seated dhyanasana, double lotus throne, 3⅛, L18c (4257/66)   425
Buddha, gilt, Nepalese, seated, low cushion, 4⅞, 14/16c (4155/26)   600
Buddha, Sino-Tibetan, seated, double lotus throne, tightly curled hair, 4⅛, 17/18c (4257/90)   200
Dharmaraja, gilt, Mongolo-Tibetan, seated on horse, battle dress, skull diadem, 9⅜, 18c (4257/103)   1800
Dhayanibuddha Amitayus, gilt, Nepalese, seated, double lotus throne, turquoise, set jewelry, 17, L16/17c (4257/85)   11000
Dhayanibuddha Amitayus, gilt, Sino-Tibetan, seated, architectural support, 8, L18c (4257/86)   400
Dhayanibuddha Amitayus, gilt, Sino-Tibetan, seated, engraved Ch'ien Lung, 1769, 7½, 18c (4257/87)   600
Dhyanibuddha Amitayus, gilt, Sino-Tibetan, seated, architectural base, Ch'ien, Lung, 8¼, 1761 (4257/89)   700
Dhyanibuddha Amitayus, gilt, Sino-Tibetan, seated, double lotus throne, 6¾, 18c (4257/77)   500
Figure, gilt, Tibetan, unusual, single lotus throne, Greco-Asiatic blouse, 5⅞, 18/19c (4257/73)   650
Gururimpoche as Padmas Ambhava, gilt, seated, Yeshe-Tsogyal, double lotus base, 3½, ca15c (4155/17)   1700

Indra mask, gilt, Nepalese, serene face, large circular traces of red pigment, 9, 17/18c (4257/101)   1600
Jambhala, Tibetan/Western Himmalayan, standing on Kubera, 4, 19c (4155/16)   500
Krakucchadra, gilt, crowned, seated, double lotus throne, downturned head, 5⅜, 17/18c (4257/80)   425
Lion, Guardian, gilt plaque, Sino-Tibetan, rampant, holding two cintamani aloft, 5, 18c (4257/100)   1200
Manjusri, gilt, Sino-Tibetan, seated dhyanasana, double lotus throne, 4⅜, 18c (4257/71)   425
Manjusri Vajranangamanjughosa, gilt, Tibetan, seated, double lotus base, 7⅛, 18c (4257/88)   350
Sadaksari Avalokitesvara, Nepalese, seated, set with garnets, turquoise, emeralds, 8⅛, 12/14c
   (4257/107)   16500
Stupa, gilt, double lotus base, stepped and tiered, dec caboch, on turquoises, 7⅞, 17/18c (4257/48)   850
Stupa, gilt, standard form, four of five Tathagatas under monster arches, 5⅞, 15/17c (4257/47)   800
Syamatara, gilt, seated dhayanasana, single lotus throne, Bodhis, attva garment, 4⅜, 18c (4257/67)   375
Syamatara, gilt, seated lalitasana, double lotus throne, 4½, 17/18c (4257/83)   500
Usnisavijaya, gilt, Tibetan, seated dhyanasana, double lotus throne, 6⅛, 18/19c (4257/72)   550
Vasudhara, gilt, seated lalitasana, separate double lotus throne, 7¼, 15/17c (4257/76)   *1900*
Vasurara, gilt, Nepalese, seated lalitasana, softly worn, gilt traces, 3¼, 13/14c (4257/95)   1100
Yi-dam, Hevajra, gilt, Sino-Tibetan, treading on bodies, 8 heads, 16 arms, 7¼, 15/16c (4155/21)   *3000*
Yi-Dam Samvara, gilt, Tibetan, stepping on 2 figures, separate single lotus throne, 8⅛, 18c
   (4257/94)   1400

Gilt copper

Bhairava, gilt copper head, face highlighted with lapis lazuli, turquoise, carnelian, W5¾, 18/19c
   (4257/98)   1000
Dhyanibuddha Amitayus, gilt copper, Sino-Tibetan, seated, double lotus throne, 7⅞, 18/19c
   (4257/75)   375
Dhyanibuddha Amitayus, gilt copper, Sino-Tibetan, seated, double lotus throne, 7⅝, 18/19c
   (4257/79)   400
Halo, gilt copper, Nepalese, part, 3 sections, Garuda figure, lower parts with lions, 8½, 18c (4257/84)   1700
Padmasambhava, copper or bronze, seated, single lotus throne, cap with sapphires, reverse base,
   13½, 18c* (4257/99)   2500

Metals

Mandala, repousse copper, Tibetan, astrological diagram, Wheel of Life, the 8 Trig, rams, 12 x 10¾,
   19c (4257/50)   600
Sakyamuni, gilt copper, Tibetan, seated, double lotus throne, 9⅞, 18c (4257/104)   1000

Stone

Umamahesvara, sandstone stele, Nepal, depicting Siva, Parvati, single lotus throne, 16¼, 17/18c
   (4257/91)   *1700*

Vasudhara   (4257/76)

Yi-dam   (4155/21)

Koto (4257/405)

Textiles

Mandala, Aryavalokitesvara, Tibetan, color on cloth, 20¼ x 13¼, 19c (4257/59)   350
Mandala, Chandamaharoshana, Nepalese, color and gold on cloth, 11¾ x 11¾, 17/18c (4257/57)   4400
Mandala, Tibetan, color, gold, cloth, eight trigrams, 17⅜, 13 (4155/15)   375
Mandala, Yi-Dam Hevajra, Nepalese, color 8 gilt on cloth, blue foliate ground, 16½ x 13⅝, 18/19c
  (4257/63)   *5800*
Tanka, Aryavalokitesvara, Tibetan, color on cloth, 30¾ x 19½, 19c (4257/60)   850
Tanka, Buddha, Tibetan, color on cloth, 17¾ x 12¼, 19c (4257/62)   200
Tanka, Dharmapala Yamantaka, Tibetan, color on cloth, 20⅝ x 13⅜, 18/19c (4257/61)   300
Tanka, Mahasiddha, Tibetan, color on cloth, seated on elephant treading on, 2 humans, 21⅝ x 15½,
  19c (4257/55)   900
Tanka, Syamatara, color on cloth, seated, single lotus throne, 62¼ x 39⅝, 18c (4155/25)   1900
Vestment, black hat ceremony, central black ground, yellow brocade, red band, yoke, 34¾ x 34¼,
  L18c/E19c (4257/46)   500

Wood Figures

Tara, Nepalese, seated Dhyanasana, single lotus base, 14⅜, 18c (4257/64)   700
Koto, Oei, indistinctly signed, 8¼, 1399 (4257/405)   275

Chapter 11

Russian Works of Art

Enamels, porcelain, silver, icons and bronzes of the Imperial era make up the field of Russian works of art. Production, and the export from Russia, of most of these items ceased at the time of the Russian Revolution and has never resumed; the supply of these works has therefore remained relatively fixed. The field is further distinguished by there being few collectors from the country of origin.

Collectors of Russian material tend to be unusually dedicated, most of them having started buying because of an overwhelming enthusiasm for the period and its art. These factors have contributed to rising prices in recent years. Russian works of art enjoyed a spectacular season last year, with prices up across the board, and new highs recorded in several areas.

Religious art in Russia is limited to icons. Because of export restrictions, high-quality early examples are scarce, but excellent eighteenth- and nineteenth-century examples are available at reasonable prices.

Prices for items by Faberge, the most famous name in Russian works of art, continued to be strong. Enamels form an important aspect of the Russian market, and they continued to sell well.

The failure of Western-style representational painting to take root in Russia until the mid-nineteenth century explains in part the great number and variety of Russian bronzes, and the prices vary accordingly.

Most Russian art, especially the much sought-after products of the Faberge studios, is relatively high-priced. The enthusiasm of the collectors in this field will certainly cause further increases for top-quality works. Beginning collectors can, however, find excellent opportunities among bronzes and icons, all but the finest of which remain undervalued.

Bear (4137/231)

Troika group with 3 figures
(4137/226)

BRONZES

Assorted items

A cossack, H11½, L19c (4137/223)	$475
Alexander I, silvered, bust, H13¼, 19c (4137/225)	450
American Indian chieftain, Troubetzkoy, standing holding staff, 18, 1916 (4271/63)	3000
Anonymous, horses pulling a sled with 2 men, rectangular base, 11⅝, L19c (4186/81)	1100
Antokolski, Markus, Mephistopheles, nude male figure seated on rock, 67¾, 19c (4233/18)	27000
Bear, mounted on quartz simulating ice, L14, L19c (4137/231)	*1500*
Bear, figure, reclining on an oval rocky base, 15, L19c (4233/51)	1000
Boy with donkeys, group, branch in hand driving 2 donkeys, 9, inscribed Lanceray (4233/7)	1200
Equestrian group, mounted soldier bidding farewell to sweetheart, 9, inscribed Gratchev (4233/10)	1200
Equestrian group, Lanceray, officer astride his walking horse, 10¼, L19c (4271/70)	1000
Gratchev, a mounted soldier embracing a woman, 8½, L19c, Gratcher (4186/69)	1100
Gratchev, harness racing, marble base, 9⅝, L19c (4186/71)	1600
Gratchev, mounted hunter smoking pipe, 2 dogs, 15½, L19c (4233/5)	1700
Gratchev, three figures, oval malachite base, 8¾, L19c (4186/78)	1800
Gratchev, group, lady and gentleman in sled, 13¼, L19c (4233/11)	1500
Gratchev, group, Cossack bidding farewell to wife, horse waiting, 13, L19c (4233/13)	2400
Gratchev, Troika group, three horses pulling sled with 3 figures, 9, L19c (4233/6)	1800
Gratchev, Troika group, gilt-bronze, three horses pulling sled with 3 figures, 9, L19c (4233/8)	2000
Group of a peasant family, Lanceray, boy riding horse pulling cart, 3 women seated, 22½, 1871 (4271/60)	3500
Karpova, Ye., troika with 3 figures, 29, L19c (4186/77)	5000
Lanceray, Evgenie, the Tzar's falconer, 6¼, L19c (4233/3)	900
Lanceray, Evgenie, equestrian, horsebreaking, oval base, 23½, 1874 (4186/75)	3300
Lanceray, Evgenie, mounted Cossack galloping across rough terrain, 7¼, L19c (4186/83)	1650
Lanceray, Evgenie, of a mounted Tartar soldier, 11, L19c (4186/76)	2100
Lanceray, Evgenie, two mounted Cossacks, oval base, 21, L19c (4186/72)	1800
Lanceray, Evgenie, Cossack firing while standing on horseback, 11¼, L19c (4186/82)	1600
Naps, Ye, Troika group, Izvoshchik standing in the sled, woman and man seated, boy, 15½, L19c (4233/4)	2500
Safonov, mounted soldier driving 3 Turkish prisoners, 10, 1882 (4186/80)	1100
Tartar warrior, figure mounted on a rearing horse, 11¼, inscribed Lanceray (4233/14)	900
Three Cossacks resting, group, gathered around campfire, 13, L19c (4233/16)	1200
Troubetzkoy, Prince Paul, of a cowboy on horseback, 20¾, 1911 (4186/73)	1400
Turgueneff, shepherd dog, alert posture, 15½, L19c (4233/1)	650
Wolf, group, Cossack embracing his sweetheart, 10¼, L19c (4233/12)	2600
Wolf, M., two oxen pulling a cart, peasant on yoke, 13½, 1894 (4233/15)	1600

Gratchev

Troika group with 3 figures, L9¼, L19c (4137/220)	1100
Troika group with 3 figures, L9½ (4137/226)	*1600*
Troika group with 3 figures, L9, L19c (4137/234)	1000

Lanceray, Evgenie

Equestrian group of ancient warrior, H30, 1885 (4137/224)	5750
Equestrian group, cossack, woman, H15, L19c (4137/235)	*2300*
Group, boy on donkey, 2 pack horses, H8½, L19c (4137/232)	*1500*
Troika group with 3 figures, L11, 1880 (4137/230)	2000

Naps,

Equestrian group, mounted boy, dog, L8⅛, L19c (4137/228)	*950*

Tourgueneff, Pierre

A mounted soldier, H24, ca1900 (4137/229)	1600
Group of a mounted soldier, H24, ca1900 (4137/233)	1600

ENAMELS

Assorted artists and localities

Badge, silver-gilt, enamel, arms of the cross, eagles, 2½, 1883 (4233/428)	170
Beaker and stand, silver and enamel, faceted hammered finish, 5¼, 1895 (4271/322)	1300
Beaker silver-gilt and plique a jour, enamel, tapered shape on circular foot, 3⅛, ca1890 (4233/523)	1900

Beaker, silver and champleve enamel, band of stylized plants in green, red and blue, 2¾, 1877 (4186/578) 375

Beaker, silver and champleve enamel, tapered form, crosses and paterac, mosaic design, 2, 1889 (4186/446) 300

Beaker, silver and shaded enamel, colorful flowers, 2⅜, ca1900 (4233/486) 1400

Beaker, silver-gilt and enamel, borders of blue beads, 2⅝, 1893 (4233/472) 1400

Beaker, silver-gilt and enamel, circular shape, flaring circular foot, flowers, 3⅛, 1879 (4186/496) 1700

Beaker, silver-gilt and enamel, 2 reserves, courting couple, rural landscape, 3, M19c (4271/189) 750

Beaker, silver-gilt and plique a jour, tapered form, stylized foliage, 2⅜, 1896 (4271/227) *3500*

Beaker, silver-gilt and shaded enamel, slightly tapered cyl shape, bands of waves, grapevine scrolls, 2⅞, ca1910 (4271/349) 1400

Beakers, pair, silver-gilt, shaded enamel, tapered cyl shape, on circular foot, geometric design, 4¾, 1908-17 (4271/347) 5750

Belt silver-gilt and enamel, flowers in multi-colors, dagger form clasp, 26½, ca1900 (4233/459) *2000*

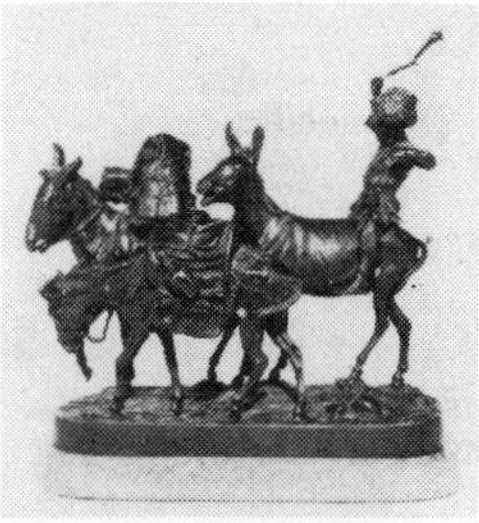

Group (4137/232)

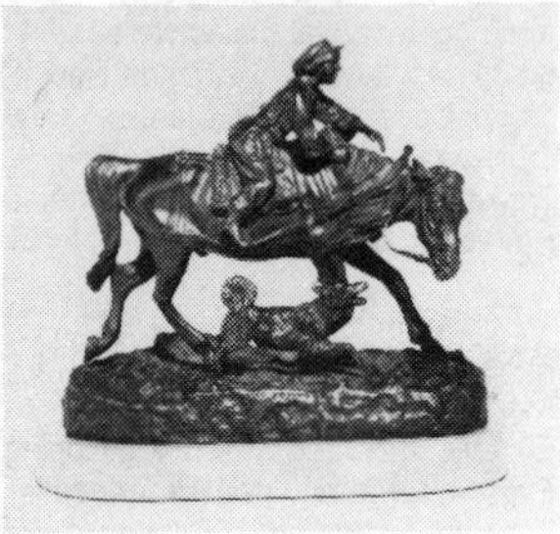

Equestrian group (4137/228)

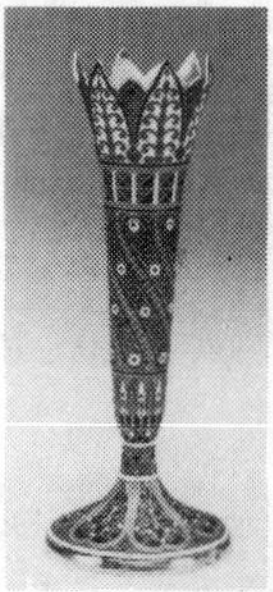

Bud vase (4233/484)

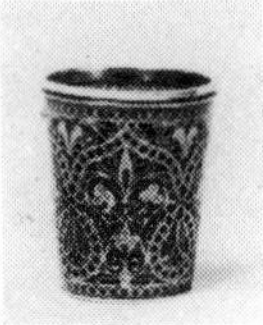

Beaker (4271/227)

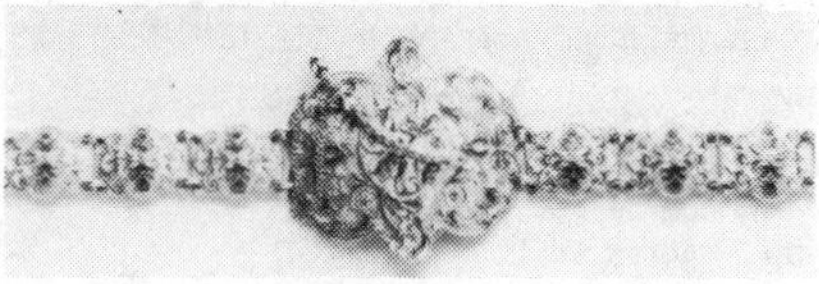

Belt silver-gilt and enamel (4233/459)

Bowl, silver and shaded enamel, multi-colored flowers, 3⅝, 1896-1908, mark N.A. (4186/590) 5000

Bowl, silver and plique a jour enamel, oval boat shape, 5, ca1900 (4186/598) 1700

Bowl, silver-gilt and champleve enamel, circular, geometric, 3 ring supports, 2¾, ca1880 (4271/266) 425

Bowl, silver-gilt and enamel, multi-colored geometric bands foliage, 3¼, 1887 (4186/437) 850

Bowl, silver-gilt and enamel, sides lobed, flowers, 2¾, 1908-17 (4271/239) 700

Bowl and cover, silver, retailed by Tiffany and Co., 4⅜ (4233/500) *1300*

Bowl and cover, silver-gilt and enamel, inverted pear shape, 3⅜, ca1900 (4271/283) 1300

Bowls, pair, silver-gilt and enamel, 17c style, formal foliage on 3 ball feet, 3½, ca1910 (4271/335) 1400

Box, circular silver and enamel, hinged cover, multi-colored scrolling foliage, 2¼, ca1890 (4233/454) 600

Box, circular silver-gilt and enamel, hinged cover, over all scrolling, 2⅜ (4233/424) 600

Box, circular, silver and enamel, hinged cover, stylized foliage, 2, ca1890 (4233/504) 450

Box, circular, silver and shaded enamel, hinged cover, flowering foliage, 2¼, 1908-17 (4233/535) 1900

Box, circular, silver-gilt, enamel, multi-colored flowers, 2, ca1910 (4186/547) 1000

Box, circular, silver-gilt and enamel, hinged cover, multi-colored stylized foliage, 2, 1887 (4233/539) 600

Box, circular, silver-gilt and enamel, stylized flowerheads, 2 ca1890 (4271/291) 600

Box, circular, silver-gilt and enamel, stylized foliage, 5, 1908-17 (4271/274) 475

Box, circular, silver-gilt and enamel, stylized foliage, mirror inside cover, 2⅛, ca1890 (4271/272) 550

Cigar box
(4233/521)

Bowl and cover
(4233/500)

Equestrian group
(4137/235)

Box, pill, silver and translucent enamel, lilac over sun-ray ground, 2½, ca1910 (4186/519)	275
Box, round, silver-gilt and shaded enamel, hinged cover, 2, 1908-17 (4271/292)	1500
Box, silver and shaded enamel, flowering foliage, hinged top, 1⅝, 1908-17 (4271/278)	425
Box, silver-gilt and shaded enamel, tapered square section with hinged dome cover, 5, 1895 (4271/342)	6000
Box, silver-gilt, shaded enamel, cut corners, enamel roses, royal blue, pink ground, 2⅞, 1908-17 (4271/355)	4750
Buckle, shaped oval form, dagger form clasp, 2¾, ca1890 (4233/532)	200
Buckle, silver-gilt and enamel, dagger form clasp, 3, ca1900 (4271/192)	275
Buckle, silver-gilt and enamel, multi-colored scrolling foliage, 3, ca1890 (4233/416)	400
Bud vase, silver-gilt and enamel, tapered, arched top, circular foot, 5½, L19c (4233/484)	*1700*
Caddy shovel, silver and champleve enamel, enamel in a simulated mosaic design, 4⅛, 1891 (4271/287)	325
Caddy shovel, silver-gilt and enamel, sea green, filigree scrolls, 5⅝, 1896 (4233/503)	400
Cake basket, matching sugar bowl, silver, oval basket, both with cartouches, L8¼, H4½, Moscow, 1888-9 (4137/161)	500
Cane handle, silver-gilt, geometric designs, L2¾, Moscow, ca1900 (4137/43)	375
Card case, silver-gilt and enamel, enamel with colorful foliage, L3⅛, Moscow, ca1910 (4137/31)	750
Case, silver-gilt and enamel, multi-colored scrolling foliage, 2¾, ca1885 (4233/497)	550
Casket, jewel, silver and enamel, raised on 4 leaf and ball feet, 5⅜, 1892 (4233/495)	1000
Casket, silver-gilt, champleve enamel, hinged cover, applied deck of cards, 7½, 1877 (4186/562)	8500
Casket, silver-gilt, four bracket feet, hinged cover, 6½, ca1900 (4233/444)	1700
Casket, silver-gilt and enamel, square, slip on cover, raised on 4 claw and ball feet, 2⅛, 1879, fine, unusual (4186/524)	3750
Casket, silver-gilt and shaded enamel, foliage, bracket feet, hinged cover, 6, 1908-17, fine (4233/415)	15000
Caster, silver and enamel, form of a temple with emerald green roof, 3½, ca1900 (4233/438)	800
Chalice, silver-gilt and enamel, four ovals high relief with Deesis group, 13⅜, 1908-17 (4186/587)	2500
Change box, silver-gilt and enamel, three spring loaded compartments, 2½, ca1910 (4233/462)	275
Change purse, silver and enamel, multi-colored scrolling, flowering foliage, (4186/466)	300
Charka, silver and enamel, circular bowl, 6¾, ca1890 (4233/449)	1700
Charka, silver-gilt and enamel, hemispherical bowl on circular foot, c scroll handle, 2⅜, 1893 (4186/556)	475
Charka, silver-gilt and enamel, translucent, red, white, blue design, 3½ over handles, 1877 (4271/230)	750
Cigar box, silver and enamel, hinged cover simulating trade label, 5⅞, ca1900 (4233/521)	*1900*
Cigarette case, gold and enamel, zig zag pattern, cupid enamel, 3⅞, ca1910, mark K.F. (4186/486)	2400
Cigarette case, gold, enamel and jeweled, rectangular, hinged cover, blue ground, 3¾, ca1890 (4271/200)	5000
Cigarette case, silver, simulated mosaic design, gilt interior, 3⅝, 1887 (4186/442)	450
Cigarette case, silver, stylized foliage, L4⅛, ca1910 (4137/108)	675
Cigarette case, silver, with a female profile, L4½, Moscow, ca1910 (4137/114)	550
Cigarette case, silver and enamel, art nouveau style, embossed male profile, 4⅛, ca1900 (4186/514)	550

Cigarette case, silver and enamel, multi-colored stylized foliage, 4, ca1890 (4233/526)   800

Cigarette case, silver and shaped enamel, in muted tones with a Pan Slavic design, 4½, 1908-17 (4233/482)   1400

Cigarette case, silver-gilt, both sides geometric designs, 3¾, 1885 (4233/423)   475

Cigarette case, silver-gilt, champleve enamel, stylized foliate designs, 4⅛, ca1890 (4186/552)   450

Cigarette case, silver-gilt, cover enamel with a lily of the valley, 4⅛, ca1890 (4233/432)   1600

Cigarette case, silver-gilt, each side swan floating on pond, 3⅞, ca1900 (4186/439)   2100

Cigarette case, silver-gilt, enamel both sides, Czar's Falconer, 4½, ca1910, mark D.S. (4186/441)   950

Cigarette case, silver-gilt, exotically plumed birds, border blue beads, 4⅜, ca1900 (4186/579)   1900

Cigarette case, silver-gilt, narrow rectangular shape, colorful foliage, 4⅛, 1908-10 (4233/430)   2300

Cigarette case, silver-gilt, shaded enamel swans, butterflies, 3¾, ca1900, fine (4186/513)   1200

Cigarette case, silver-gilt, with flowers on a cream ground, 3⅞, ca1900, fine (4233/429)   2300

Cigarette case, silver-gilt and enamel, birds in foliage, geometric borders, 3⅝, 1889 (4271/276)   900

Cigarette case, silver-gilt and enamel, borders of blue beads, 3⅝, ca1890 (4271/286)   400

Cigarette case, silver-gilt and enamel, decorated with stylized foliage, 3⅜, ca1900, small (4233/530)   225

Cigarette case, silver-gilt and enamel, multi-colored scrolling flowering foliage, 4⅛, 1908-17 (4186/464)   550

Cigarette case, silver-gilt and enamel, peasant girl, 4⅝, 1908-17, mark P.M. (4186/530)   2100

Cigarette case, silver-gilt and enamel, rectangular shape, rounded sides, 3⅝, 1892 (4233/524)   750

Cigarette case, silver-gilt and enamel, scrolling, foliage within geometric borders, 3½, ca1890 (4233/506)   550

Cigarette case, silver-gilt, enamel, enamel Japanese style, cream color, 3⅜, ca1900 (4271/215)   1100

Cigarette case, silver-gilt, shaded enamel, colorful flowers, border of blue beads, 3¾, ca1900 (4271/275)   1100

Cigarette case, silver-gilt, rectangular with flowering scrolling foliage, L4⅜, Moscow, ca1885 (4137/37)   1100

Cigarette case, silver-gilt, rectangular with geometric designs, birds, L4⅜, Moscow, 1895 (4137/117)   800

Cigarette case, silver-gilt, rectangular, reserves of scrolls, L4⅜, St. Petersburg, ca1885 (4137/113)   650

Cigarette case, silver-gilt, shaded, enamel with colorfully plumed peacock, L4½, Moscow, ca1910 (4137/101)   1700

Cigarette case, silver-gilt, shaded, pastel flowers and geometric designs, L4⅛, Moscow, ca1910 (4137/70)   900

Cigarette case, silver, gold, engraved with panel of flowers, signatures, L4¼, Moscow, ca1910 (4137/64)   400

Cigarette case, silver, champleve enamel rounded sides, hinged cover, flower arrangement, (4186/471)   400

Cigarette case, gold mounted silver-gilt, enamel, upright, two color gold, 3⅝, ca1910 (4186/554)   1600

Cigarette holder, gold mounted, ivory mouthpiece, 3¼, ca1900 (4186/563)   200

Cigarette holder, silver-gilt and enamel, bone mouthpiece, multi-color foliage, 3½, ca1925 (4233/544)   150

Clock, desk, swiss silver, miniature, arched top, cupids and flowers, 1⅞, ca1910 (4186/481)   1600

Coin holder, three conjoined cylinders, stylized foliage, L2¾, ca1910 (4137/106)   275

Cream jug, silver-gilt and enamel, border of blue beads, 3, 1895 (4271/258)   600

Cream mug, silver-gilt, cylindrical shape, reserves of flowers, H2, Moscow, ca1900 (4137/165)   350

Creamer, silver and enamel, raised on 3 ball feet, 2¼, 1895 (4233/440)   625

Creamer, silver-gilt, champleve enamel, foliage, geometric designs, 3, 1891 (4186/550)   1000

Crucifix, enamel, multi-colored foliage, applied body of Christ, 7¾, 18c (4271/329)   325

Crucifix, silver-gilt and enamel, figure of Christ, flanked by 2 Marys', 13⅞, ca1900 (4186/592)   1600

Crucifix pendant, gold, red and blue, L2, Moscow, ca1885 (4137/95)   550

Cup, bird-form, silver-gilt and enamel, multi-colors with detachable liner, 2½, ca1890 (4271/254)   1700

Cup, child's, silver and enamel, square base, circular lip, scrolling foliage, (4233/460)   325

Cup, silver-gilt, enamel and scroll handle, ring foot, 2⅜, ca1900 (4233/553)   400

Cup, silver and champleve enamel, cyl body, multi-colored strapwork, c-scroll handle, 3¼, 1883 (4186/453)   600

Cup, silver and enamel, bulbous body, foliage, scroll handle, circular foot, 2⅝, ca1900, mark I.G.T. (4186/489)   550

Cup, silver-gilt and champleve enamel, simulated mosaic design 3 ball feet, 2½, 1887 (4186/451)   350

Cup, silver-gilt enamel, border of anthemion and acanthus leaves, 3½, ca1890 (4233/468)   800

Cup, silver-gilt and enamel, c scroll handle, stylized flower, 3½, 1896-1908, mark S. Sch. (4186/555)   400

Cup, silver-gilt and enamel, stylized, multi-colored foliage, blue beaded border, 2⅝, 1886 (4271/216)   500

Cup and saucer, multi-colored stylized scrolling foliage, 4½, ca1910 (4233/473)   450

Cups, demi tasse pair, with paterae and foliage, 2⅛, 1892 (4233/471)   1400

Cups, pair, silver-gilt and enamel, cylindrical, foliage, leaf from handles, 1¼, ca1900 (4271/219)   1500

Cups, vodka, pair, silver-gilt and enamel, slightly tapered, foliage, 2 ca1900 (4271/238)   1600

Cups, vodka, set of twelve, silver-gilt, multi-colored scrolling foliage, 1⅝, ca1890, Gratchev (4233/498)   *11500*

Cups (4233/498)

Flagon (4137/99)

Desk portfolio, leather, silver, chased with an ancient warrior, H17¾, Moscow, ca1910 (4137/63) — 4500
Dish, oval, silver-gilt and enamel, scrolling foliage, 5¾, ca1890 (4233/447) — 800
Dish, oval, silver-gilt, enamel, central circular medalion with griffin, 4¾, ca1885 (4233/455) — 1600
Dish, silver and shaded enamel, multi-colored flowers, 4¾, ca1900, mark S.G. (4186/529) — 550
Dish, silver and shaded enamel, shells at intervals, 7½, ca1912 (4186/553) — 5250
Dish, silver-gilt enamel, small, domed base, multi-colored foliage, 2⅞, 1880 (4233/427) — 500
Easter egg, foliage, white beads, screw in egg cup bases, 2½, ca1900 (4186/576) — 2500
Easter egg, miniature enamel, translucent pale green, with gold ring,½, ca1900 (4271/320) — 500
Easter egg, pendant, silver-gilt and enamel, miniature, red enamel,¾ (4186/549) — 400
Easter egg, silver-gilt and enamel, band of simulated mosaic, multi-colored scrolling foliage, 2¾, ca1890 (4271/353) — 2900
Easter egg, silver-gilt and enamel, multi-colored, foliage on blue ground, 3¾ (4233/481) — 1400
Easter egg, silver-gilt and enamel, stylized foliate design, geometric bands, 2, ca1885 (4186/488) — 2100
Easter egg, silver-gilt, silver filigree scrolls, L1½, Moscow, ca1890 (4137/86) — 1200
Ewer, silver-gilt and enamel, bulbous body, elongated neck, domed circular foot, 14¼, L19c (4271/244) — *4500*
Flagon, silver-gilt, shaded, fine, cylindrical shape with signs of zodiac, H10⅛, L19c (4137/99) — 10000
Flask, scent, silver, pansy within border, white beads on chain, 2¾, 1896-1908 (4186/461) — 2300
Fork, pickle, silver-gilt and enamel, multi-colored foliage, borders of blue beads, 4¾, ca1890 (4271/268) — 275
Fork, savory, silver-gilt and enamel, stylized foliage, 4¼, ca1910 (4233/446) — 125
Glass holder, silver-gilt and enamel, open work sides, 3, 1899 (4233/514) — 225
Goblet, silver-gilt, plique-a-jour, decorated with peacocks, H5, Moscow, ca1910 (4137/164) — 4500
Holder, tea glass, pair, Soviet, silver-gilt, enamel, 4, modern (4271/207) — 180
Holder, tea glass, silver-gilt, enamel, multi-colored flowers, gilded· stippled ground, 4, 1893 (4271/310) — 1150
Holder, tea glass, silver-gilt, shaded enamel, swans, flowers, 3⅝, 1896-1908 (4271/194) — 4000
Icon, miniature, silver-gilt and enamel, St. George slaying the dragon, scrolling foliage, 2¼, ca1900 (4271/327) — 600
Inkwell, silver, enamel and cut glass, square section cut with diamond shape, 3¼, some chip, L19c (4186/479) — 375
Jug, cream, silver, gilt and enamel, baluster shape, 2¾, 20c (4186/548) — 50
Kovsh, silver-gilt and enamel, pair of exotically plumed fanciful birds, back peacock, 8, 1891 (4186/444) — 6500
Kovsh, silver-gilt and shaded enamel, 'Jeweled' flowers on alternating ground, 9½, ca1910 (4186/436) — 14000
Kovsh, silver-gilt and shaded enamel, border of blue beads, 3, 1908-17 (4233/488) — 1100
Kovsh, silver-gilt and shaded enamel, colorful foliage with geometric reserves, 3, 1908-17 (4233/490) — 1100

Kovsh, plique a jour, champleve enamel silver, engraved sea horse, 6¼, ca1900 (4186/564) — 2000

Kovsh, silver and enamel, multi-colored, foliage, border blue-white beads, 5, 1895 (4186/528) — 1400

Kovsh, silver and enamel, small, multi-colored scrolling, foliage, border of blue beads, 3½, ca1890 (4233/485) — 450

Kovsh, silver and shaded enamel, colorful flowers on a cream ground, 5½, ca1910 (4233/542) — 1900

Kovsh, silver and shaded enamel, colorful flowers on a gilded stippled ground, blue beads, 5½, ca1900 (4271/306) — 2750

Kovsh, silver and shaded enamel, flowering foliage, 6⅛, ca1900 (4233/463) — 1600

Kovsh, silver and shaded enamel, multi-colored flowers, 4¼, ca1910, good (4186/532) — 1700

Kovsh, silver and shaded enamel, peacocks, geometric forms, 5, 1908-17 (4271/271) — 3500

Kovsh, silver and plique a jour enamel, foliate design, 4⅞, L19c (4186/569) — 3400

Kovsh, silver-gilt, flowers on apple green and aubergine, 3⅝, ca1910 (4233/465) — 1200

Kovsh, silver-gilt, plique a jour enamel, butterfly, birds, flowering plants, 5, 1896-1908 (4186/595) — 9000

Kovsh, silver-gilt and champleve enamel, enamel with multi-colored strapwork, 10¾, ca1890 (4271/253) — 800

Kovsh, silver-gilt and champleve enamel, interior enamel with a cock, 4, 1877 (4233/550) — 1250

Kovsh, silver-gilt and enamel, colorful flowers on stippled ground, 6¾, 1896-1908 (4233/480) — 5600

Kovsh, silver-gilt and enamel, colorful foliage with border of blue beads, 3, 1908-17 (4271/285) — 1100

Kovsh, silver-gilt and enamel, exotically plumed bird, sky blue ground, 3⅝, 1908-17 (4271/354) — 1400

Kovsh, silver-gilt and enamel, flat shaped handle, flowering foliage, 5¼, 1908-17 (4233/517) — 1700

Kovsh, silver-gilt and enamel, flowers and leaves within border of blue beads, 3½, ca1910, mark N.A. (4186/538) — 700

Kovsh, silver-gilt and enamel, flowers on ground of sea green and aubergine, 3¼, 1908-17 (4271/217) — 900

Kovsh, silver-gilt and enamel, front back, with fanciful birds with strapwork, 6⅛, 1889 (4186/463) — 2400

Kovsh, silver-gilt and enamel, interior, multi-colored flowers, on aubergine field, 8½, ca1900 (4271/346) — 7750

Kovsh, silver-gilt and enamel, multi-colored birds and flowers, 5¾, ca1900, mark Ye.P.R. (4186/506) — 2400

Kovsh, silver-gilt and enamel, multi-colored foliage, blue beads border, 4¼, ca1890 (4271/263) — 1000

Kovsh, silver-gilt and enamel, scrolling foliage apple green ground, 6, ca1900 (4233/474) — 2400

Kovsh, silver-gilt and enamel, scrolling foliage, blue beads, 3¾, ca1890 (4271/284) — 850

Kovsh, silver-gilt and enamel 'jeweled', multi-colored wave form design open work handle, seahorse, 7¼, 1908-17 (4271/324) — 4250

Kovsh, silver-gilt and enamel, small, multi-colored flowers on a gilded stippled ground, 2⅞, ca1900 (4233/554) — 1100

Kovsh, silver-gilt and shaded enamel, body lobed, colorful foliage, gilded stippled ground, 11¼, 1908-17 (4271/344) — 11500

Kovsh, silver-gilt and shaded enamel, colorful flowers, 3⅝, 1908-17, fine (4186/533) — 2300

Kovsh, silver-gilt and shaded enamel, flowering scrolling foliage, sea green ground, 5, ca1900 (4271/312) — 2800

Kovsh, silver-gilt and shaded enamel, flowers on ground of ivory, blue, green, 4¾, 1908-17 (4186/500) — 2200

Kovsh, silver-gilt and shaded enamel, foliage on avocado ground, 5, ca1900 (4233/509) — 3500

Kovsh, silver-gilt and shaded enamel, lobed and multi-colored flowers, ground of sky blue, 5½, ca1900 (4271/348) — 4250

Kovsh, silver-gilt and shaded enamel, milti-colored flowers and leaves, 3⅝, 1908-17 (4233/547) — 1600

Kovsh, silver-gilt and shaded enamel, multi-colored, 3⅞, 1908-17 (4281/211) — 1800

Kovsh, silver-gilt and shaded enamel, multi-colored flower, sea green and cream ground, 4¾, 1908-17 (4271/352) — 3250

Kovsh, silver-gilt and shaded, enamel, flowering foliage, handle and base, border blue beads, 2½, ca1900, small (4186/581) — 1300

Kovsh, silver-gilt and Plique a Jour, swans and flowering foliage, border of red beads, 6, ca1910 (4271/350) — 10000

Kovsh, silver-gilt and Plique a Jour enamel, swan floating on a pond, flowering plants, 6⅛, ca1910 (4271/351) — 9500

Kovsh, silver-gilt, stylized foliage on gilded stippled ground, L3¾, Moscow, ca1885 (4137/61) — 850

Kovsh, silver-gilt, stylized foliage, gilded stippled ground, L3⅜, Moscow, ca1900 (4137/59) — 1000

Kovsh, silver-gilt, shaded enamel, enamel with colorful flowers, L4⅜, Moscow, 1908-17 (4137/25) — 1600

Kovsh, silver, jeweled, enamel with a pomegranate, L10½, Moscow, ca1910 (4137/92) — *1350*

Kovsh, silver, plique a jour enamel, eagle grasping a monogram, 7⅛, ca1900 (4233/507) — 7250

Kovsh, small, silver-gilt and enamel, multi-colored foliage, blue beads, 3, ca1910, mark M.Z. (4186/497) — 650

Kovshi, pair, silver-gilt and shaded enamel, flowering vines, border of blue beads, 3¼, ca1900 (4271/229) — 2200

Ladle sauce, silver-gilt and shaded enamel, multi-colored flowers, 7½, c1900 (4186/516) — 850

Letter opener, silver-gilt and enamel, mounted birchwood, handle, 9¾, ca1900 (4186/512) — 225

Lighter case, gold, silver-gilt and enamel, gold mount chased with leaves, 2⅜, ca1910 (4233/425) — 1500

Kovsh (4137/92)

Liquer set, Soviet silver-gilt, enamel, carafe, 6 cups, grey and white flowers, green ground, 8, 20c (4186/537) — 600

Match box holder, silver-gilt, colorful flowers, gilded stripped ground, 1¾, ca1910 (4186/577) — 475

Match box holder, silver-gilt, gilded stippled ground, blue beads, 1¾, ca1885 (4186/460) — 200

Match box holder, silver-gilt, shaded enamel, multi-colored flowers, 2¼, 1908-17 (4271/224) — 450

Match box holder, silver and enamel, foliage on ground of ivory and pale blue, blue, white beads, 2⅜, ca1900 (4271/317) — 325

Match case, silver-gilt and enamel, upright, base with striker, hinged cover, 2⅜, L19c (4271/195) — 350

Mirror, hand, silver-gilt and shaded enamel, flowering foliage, 9, ca1900 (4271/190) — 3000

Mug, silver-gilt and enamel, multi-colored cockerels with geometric borders, 2¾, 1875 (4271/345) — 2100

Napkin ring, silver and enamel, border blue beads, multi-colored foliage, 1 1/16, 1908-17 (4271/222) — 250

Napkin ring, silver and enamel, multi-colored stylized foliage, border, blue beads, 1½, ca1900 (4186/505) — 200

Napkin ring, silver and enamel, stylized flower beads, 1½, ca1900 (4186/483) — 175

Napkin ring, silver and shaded enamel, oval shape, flowers, 1½, 1908-17 (4271/225) — 750

Napkin ring, silver-gilt and champleve, enamel, buds and flowers, inc. French, 2 December 1881, 1 9/16, ca1881 (4186/450) — 225

Napkin ring, silver-gilt and enamel, multi-colored foliage, blue beads, 1⅝, ca1900 (4271/330) — 550

Napkin ring, silver-gilt and enamel, multi-colored foliage, blue beads, 1⅝, ca1900 (4271/331) — 550

Napkin ring, silver-gilt and enamel, multi-colored foliage, borders of blue beads, 1⅜, ca1900 (4271/294) — 250

Napkin ring, silver-gilt and enamel, multi-colored, scrolling foliage, 1⅝, ca1910, mark S.K. (4186/448) — 300

Napkin ring, silver-gilt and enamel, oval shape, turquoise blue reserves, 2⅛, ca1890 (4233/537) — 200

Napkin ring, silver-gilt and enamel, stylized foliage, 1½, ca1900 (4271/247) — 300

Napkin ring, silver-gilt and enamel, stylized foliage, blue beads, 1⅝, 1908-17 (4271/332) — 550

Napkin ring, silver-gilt and enamel, turquoise blue, 1½, ca1885 (4186/591) — 325

Napkin ring, silver-gilt and shaded enamel, oval, flowers, 1¾, 1908-17 (4271/193) — 375

Napkin ring, silver-gilt, enamel, multi-colored foliage, blue beads, 1908-17 (4271/333) — 550

Napkin ring, silver-gilt, foliage on gilded stippled ground, H1½, Moscow, ca1910 (4137/54) — 275

Napkin ring, silver-gilt, scrolling foliage, H1½, Moscow, ca1900 (4137/52) — 250

Napkin ring, silver-gilt, stylized foliage on gilded ground, H1⅝, Moscow, ca1910 (4137/55) — 400

Napkin ring, silver-gilt, shaded, flowers, geometric borders, H1 15/16, Moscow, ca1910 (4137/45) — 400

Napkin ring, silver, gilt and shaded, enamel, multi-colored flowers, 1 9/16, ca1910, mark S.K.
(4186/447)   425
Napkin rings, pair, silver-gilt and enamel, reserves of foliage on gilded stippled ground, 1⅝, ca1890
(4186/449)   475
Nosegay holder, silver-gilt, trumpet shape with foliage, H6¼, L19c (4137/71)   1500
Oval dish, silver-gilt, center with Catherine the Great coin, 10½, ca1890 (4233/515)   6500
Paper knife, dagger form, mounted with bloodstone, 8½, L19c (4233/464)   650
Parasol handle, mushroom shape, translucent pink, Russian*, L2⅜, ca1900 (4137/89)   1000
Pencil holder, silver, mauve and purple over engine turned ground, 3⅛, ca1900 (4233/520)   200
Pendant, gold, marking the coronation of Nicholas II, L1⅛, ca1896 (4137/62)   300
Pendant and fob chain, gold, sunray design, set with diamond, L5½, St. Petersburg, ca1910
(4137/91)   225
Pin, silver and shaded enamel, oval, brightly plumed, griffins, 2⅞, ca1900, mark S.V. (4186/445)   400
Pin, silver-gilt, scrolls on stippled ground, L2¼, ca1900 (4137/58)   250
Plaque, silver-gilt and enamel, form of a photograph frame, multi-colored foliage, 5¼, ca1886
(4186/523)   900
Punch set, heavy Russian silver partly gilt, and enamel, bowl, stand, 12 cups and ladle, 19¼,
ca1910, fine (4186/468)   15500
Purse, change, silver-gilt, geometric designs, multi-colored foliage, 3, ca1900 (4233/422)   475
Purse, silver and champleve enamel, enamel with a spray of roses, 3 (4233/549)   350
Round box, silver-gilt and shaded enamel, stippled ground, 2, 1908-17 (4271/293)   1000
Salt, cellar silver and enamel, formal foliage, blue beaded border-three ball feet, 1½, ca1900
(4186/544)   175
Salt cellar, silver-gilt flowers on ground of ivory, blue, green, chartreuse, 1⅝, 1908-17 (4186/582)   500
Salt cellar, silver and enamel, circular shape, multi-colored foliage, 1¾, 1893 (4233/458)   250
Salt cellar, silver and enamel, foliage, blue beads, 2, ca1890, mark V.R. (4186/501)   275
Salt cellar, silver and enamel, geometric design, white beads, 3 ball feet, 2, ca1910 (4186/493)   300
Salt cellar, silver and enamel, multi-colored, foliage, border blue beads, 2, ca1900, mark, Ye.S.
(4186/487)   250
Salt cellar, silver and enamel, scrolling foliage, three ball feet, 1 9/16, ca1910, mark G.P. (4186/491)   175
Salt cellar, silver and shaded enamel, foliage on cream ground, 2, ca1900 (4233/461)   600
Salt cellar, silver and shaded enamel, pastel stylized flowers, 1⅝, ca1910, mark G.S. (4186/499)   350
Salt cellar, silver-gilt and champleve, geometric designs, raised on 3 feet, D2⅝, ca1890 (4233/510)   275
Salt cellar, silver-gilt and enamel, colorful foliage and a gilded ground, 1⅝, ca1900 (4233/538)   375
Salt cellar, silver-gilt and enamel, compressed circular shape, 1⅞, ca1910 (4186/568)   475
Salt cellar, silver-gilt and enamel, multi-colored, 1⅜, ca1900 (4233/543)   800
Salt cellar, silver-gilt and enamel, three shaped feet, 2, ca1910 (4186/495)   475
Salt cellars, pair, silver-gilt, circular with 4 panels, (4233/527)   2200
Salt cellars, pair, silver-gilt and enamel, stylized flowers, 1¾, ca1900 (4271/245)   550
Salt cellars, pair, silver-gilt shaded enamel, flowers, white borders beads, 3 ball feet, 1¾, 1908-17
(4271/261)   700
Salt throne, silver-gilt, fantastic birds and animals, 7, 1889, mark N.Ya (4186/597)   3000
Salt throne, silver-gilt and enamel, shaped back, monogram, hinged cover with date, 5¾, 1881
(4186/526)   3200
Salt throne, silver-gilt, shaded, multi-colored foliage, H5¾, Moscow, ca1910 (4137/74)   7500
Scent flask pendant, silver and enamel, multi-colored stylized foliage, hung from chain, 1⅛, ca1900
(4271/299)   200
Serving spoon, silver-gilt, shaded enamel, fig shaped bowl, enamel foliage, 7¾, 1908-17 (4271/328)   900
Serving spoon, silver-gilt, fig-shaped bowl enamel with flowers, L6⅝, Moscow, ca1900 (4137/21)   275
Serving spoon, silver-gilt, hearts and foliage, L6⅞, Moscow, ca1900 (4137/152)   325
Serving spoon, silver-gilt, multi-colored flowers, L7½, ca1900 (4137/151)   500
Serving spoon, silver-gilt, shaded, flowering garden in pastel shades, L7¼, Moscow, ca1910
(4137/67)   850
Small bowl, silver-gilt, bombe sides, stylized foliage, D2¼, Moscow, ca1910 (4137/42)   500
Small bowl, silver-gilt, shaded, bombe sides with flowers, D2⅝, Moscow, ca1910 (4137/131)   1200
Small bowl, silver, shaded, colorful flowers, 3 ball feet, D1¾, Moscow, ca1910 (4137/47)   850
Snuff box, gold and enamel, cover mounted hardstone - cameo of bearded warrior, 3⅝, 1801-25,
fine (4186/435)   6750
Snuff box, silver-gilt and enamel, hinged cover, multi-colored foliage, 2½, ca1900 (4186/517)   375
Snuff box, silver-gilt, shaded, rectangular with scrolling foliage, L2¾, Moscow, 1896-1908 (4137/41)   1200
Spoon, caviar, silver-gilt and plique-ajour, enamel, stylized foliage, 5⅜, ca1900 (4233/420)   225
Spoon, serving, blue bead border, foliage, (4233/443)   450
Spoon, serving, fig shaped bowl, handle tapered square section, 7⅜, ca1890 (4233/492)   1600
Spoon, serving silver-gilt, champleve, enamel, geometric design twist stem, 6, 1875 (4186/473)   225
Spoon, serving, mounted in birchwood, silver-gilt and enamel, multi-colored foliage, 7¼, ca1890
(4271/323)   75
Spoon, serving, silver-gilt, colorful flowers, 7, ca1900 (4233/502)   1200

Spoon, serving, silver-gilt and enamel, back of circular bowl, 8 point star, formal foliage, 8⅜, ca1890 (4271/295) — 650

Spoon, serving, silver-gilt and enamel, circular bowl, colorful foliage, 7⅜, ca1910 (4233/491) — 600

Spoon, serving, silver-gilt and enamel, circular bowl, flat shaped handle, stylized foliage, 7½, 1893 (4271/296) — 450

Spoon, serving, silver-gilt and enamel, colorful foliage, 7½, ca1900 (4271/237) — 250

Spoon, serving, silver-gilt and enamel, fig shaped, monogrammed, enamel foliage, 6½, 1889 (4271/202) — 250

Spoon, serving, silver-gilt and enamel, fish shaped bowl, foliage, border of white beads, 6⅞, 1900 (4271/280) — 400

Spoon, serving, silver-gilt and enamel, multi-colored foliage, border white beads, 6⅝, ca1900 (4271/235) — 250

Spoon, serving, silver-gilt and enamel, oval bowl, multi-colored foliage, border of white beads, 8½, 1910 (4271/297) — 475

Spoon, serving, silver-gilt and enamel, stylized foliage, blue bead border, ca1900 (4233/445) — 800

Spoon, serving, silver-gilt and enamel, translucent red, 6¾, ca1900 (4271/270) — 425

Spoon, serving, silver-gilt, enamel, circular bowl, 7½, 1895 (4271/201) — 400

Spoon, serving, silver-gilt, enamel, hook terminal, 7¼, ca1900 (4271/279) — 1400

Spoon, serving, silver-gilt, shaded enamel, circular bowl, flowers on a gilded stippled ground, 6¾, ca1910 (4271/316) — 475

Spoon, serving, silver-gilt, Champleve, enamel, fig shaped bowl, foliage, royal blue ground, 8, ca1890 (4271/298) — 325

Spoon, strawberry, flowers on pale green ground, 7½, ca1910, fine (4233/470) — 1800

Spoon, strawberry, twist and knopped stem, 7⅛, ca1900, fine (4233/469) — 2100

Spoons, demi tasse set six, silver, gilt enamel, twist stems, 4¼, ca1900, mark S.SH. (4186/490) — 600

Spoons, demi tasse, set six, silver-gilt, fig shaped bowls with flowers, 4⅜, ca1900 (4186/520) — 900

Spoons, demi tasse, set six, design in 3 shades, blue, red, white, 4⅜, ca1893 (4233/494) — 550

Spoons, serving, pair, with views of cathedrals, 7½, ca1880 (4233/487) — 600

Sugar basket, silver-gilt and enamel, flowers, swing handle, 4⅜, ca1890 (4271/242) — *2500*

Sugar basket
(4271/242)

Sugar basket, silver-gilt and enamel, swing handle, ring foot, 4⅜, ca1885 (4186/484) — 2100

Sugar bowl, creamer, silver-gilt, enamel with stylized foliage, H4⅛ and H3, 1896-1908 (4137/7) — 2100

Sugar bowl, silver and enamel, circular, swing handle, stylized foliage, 4, 1908-17 (4186/539) — 2200

Sugar scoop, silver and enamel, flower heads, turquoise blue enamel, 4¼, 1891 (4271/228) — 350

Sugar shovel, silver and enamel, engraved Columbia Exposition deep blue, flowers, ca1890 (4186/527) — 100

Sugar shovel, silver-gilt and enamel, flat shaped handle, scrolling foliage, 4½, ca1890 (4233/489) — 300

Sugar shovel, silver-gilt and enamel, foliage, geometric border, 4½, 1891 (4271/203) — 425

Sugar shovel, silver-gilt and enamel, multi-colored foliage, blue beads, 4½, 1891 (4271/289) — 425

Sugar shovel, silver-gilt and enamel, multi-colored foliage, turquoise blue reserves, 4⅝, ca1900 (4271/231) — 350

Sugar shovel, silver-gilt and enamel, multi-colored geometric forms, 5⅜, ca1910 (4271/220) — 550

Sugar shovel, silver-gilt and enamel, multi-colored, foliage, 4⅜, ca1890 (4233/508) — 275

Sugar shovel, silver-gilt and plique a jour, geometric design, flat handle, 4⅞, ca1890 (4271/288) — 1000

Sugar shovel, silver-gilt and plique a jour, multi-colored stylized flowers, 4⅞, ca1890 (4271/199) — 850

Sugar shovel, silver-gilt and Champleve, enamel, multi-colored stylized foliage, 5½, 1908-17 (4271/338)   300
Sugar shovel, silver and enamel, multi-color foliage with geometric border, 4⅜, ca1890 (4233/483)   325
Sugar shovel, silver-gilt, plique a jour, scrolling foliage, blue beads, 5½, ca1890 (4271/334)   1100
Sugar shovel, silver, enamel, turquoise blue between filigree scroll, 4⅛, 1891 (4233/435)   425
Sugar tongs, pair, silver-gilt, multi-colored foliage on a gilded ground, 4¾, ca1890 (4233/466)   400
Sugar sifter, bowl with geometric design flat handle, 6½, 1889 (4233/534)   300
Sugar sifter, silver and enamel, flat handle, 6⅜, ca1900 (4271/269)   325
Sugar sifter, silver-gilt and enamel, multi-colored stylized foliage, 7¼, 1891 (4271/249)   550
Sugar sifter, silver-gilt and shaded enamel, multi-colored foliage on a sky blue ground, 5⅞, 1908-17 (4271/259)   500
Sugar tongs, pair silver and enamel, pan-slavic, geometric designs, 4, ca-1910 (4186/541)   300
Sugar tongs, pair silver and enamel, turquoise reserve with flower heads, 2⅞, ca1910 (4233/479)   175
Sugar tongs, pair, silver-gilt and enamel, borders of blue beads, 5¼, ca1890 (4271/281)   275
Sugar tongs, pair, silver-gilt and enamel, multi-colored stylized foliage, 4¼, 1908-17 (4271/282)   250
Sugar tongs, pair, silver-gilt and shaded enamel, multi-colored stylized foliage, 4⅛, ca1900 (4271/255)   275
Sugar tongs, pair, silver, gilt and enamel, arms with foliage, 3½, ca1900 (4186/546)   300
Sugar tongs, pair, silver, shaded, multi-colored flowers, L4⅛, Moscow, ca1910 (4137/154)   400
Sugar tongs, silver-gilt, enamel with geometric foliate designs, L5½, ca1910 (4137/10)   450
Tazza, silver, hemispherical bowl with scrolling foliage, H5¼, Moscow, ca1900 (4137/66)   3000
Tazza, silver and enamel, shallow circular bowl, domed base, 8, L19c (4271/240)   *900*
Tea and coffee set, silver, enamel, yellow and black on green ground, 8¼, 22 pcs, modern (4271/319)   800
Tea glass holder, multi-color peacock flowering scrolling foliage, 4¾, 1908-17, mark, Ye.S. (4186/455)   1200
Tea glass holder, turquoise blue between silver filigree, 3⅜, ca1900 (4233/439)   700
Tea glass holder, silver and enamel, octagonal shape, date 1859-1884, 4⅞, 1884 (4186/509)   700
Tea glass holder, silver-gilt, flowering plants on a gilded stippled ground, 3½, 1896 (4186/454)   1500
Tea glass holder, silver-gilt, ivory and aubergine ground, 4, 1894 (4186/456)   950
Tea glass holder, silver-gilt, multi-colored foliage, 4, 1908-17, mark A.L. (4186/584)   2200
Tea glass holder, silver-gilt and enamel, presentation, Imperial, 3¾, 1888 (4186/498)   1200
Tea set, 3 pieces and tongs, silver-gilt, shaded enamel, tea pot, sugar, creamer, ca1900 (4186/502) 12500
Tea strainer, silver-gilt and enamel, circular stylized foliage, blue beads, 5½, 1895 (4271/248)   500
Teaspoon, pair, silver-gilt and enamel, multi-colored foliage, borders of blue beads, 4¾ (4271/321) 310
Teaspoon, silver-gilt, plique a jour enamel, multi-color scrolling foliage, 5½, ca1891 (4186/559)   500
Teaspoons, five, matching, stylized foliage, (4233/528)   450
Teaspoons, set of six, silver-gilt, multi-colored, scrolling foliage, 5½, ca1885 (4186/494)   1000
Teaspoons, set of six, silver-gilt, stylized foliage, strapwork, twist stems, 4½, 1891 (4186/475)   750
Teaspoons, set of six, silver-gilt and enamel, stylized foliage, geometric design, 4⅜, ca1890 (4186/534)   850
Teaspoons, set of twelve, fig shape bowls, colorful flowers, (4233/476)   2900
Teaspoons, set of twelve, silver-gilt, fig-shaped bowls, 5½, 1885 (4233/453)   1000
Teaspoons, set of 6 silver-gilt, enamel, stylized foliage, enamel stems, 4½, 1887 (4186/531)   650
Teaspoons, set of 6, silver-gilt and enamel, borders of white beads, 4½, ca1900 (4186/503)   750
Teaspoons, set of 6, silver-gilt enamel, multi-colored foliage, blue beads, 4½, ca1890 (4271/267)   800
Teaspoons, set twelve, fig shaped bowls, colorful flowers, 4¼, ca1900 (4233/467)   1800
Teaspoons, silver-gilt and enamel (five), multi-colored foliage, twist stems, 5½, ca1910 (4186/515) 550
Teaspoons, six, silver-gilt and enamel, fig-shaped bowls, 5½, ca1900 (4233/448)   850
Teaspoons, 3 matching, flatshape handles, geometric designs, 5⅜, ca1890 (4233/477)   375
Toilet box, circular silver-gilt, geometric designs and foliage, 4⅜, ca1900 (4233/442)   1600
Toilet box and cover, silver and enamel, turquoise blue between filigree scrolls, 3¼, ca1890 (4233/519)   1400
Tray, liqueur, silver-gilt and enamel, circular form, 11⅝, 1894 (4233/496)   *2500*
Tray, rectangular, silver-gilt and enamel, shaped corners and recessed center, 8⅝, 1895 (4233/451)   900
Tray, silver and plique a jour enamel, rounded sides, 5⅛, ca1885 (4186/600)   3250
Tumbler cup, silver, plique a jour enamel, stylized foliage, 1⅜, L19c (4186/566)   2400
Vase, flower, silver-gilt and enamel, foliage, red and white stripes, 5⅞, 1891 (4186/536)   2600
Vesta case, silver-gilt and enamel, circular form, pink enamel striker on base, 1¾, ca1900 (4186/452)   200
Vodka cup, silver-gilt, cylindrical shape, scrolling foliage, H1¾, Moscow, ca1885 (4137/168)   450
Vodka cup, silver-gilt, cylindrical shape, scrolling foliage, H1¾, Moscow, 1894 (4137/169)   700
Vodka cup, silver-gilt, cylindrical, multi-colored scrolling foliage, H2¼, Moscow, ca1900 (4137/170) 700

Agafanov, Vasili

Napkin ring, silver-gilt, oval shape, stylized foliage, H1⅜, Moscow, ca1885 (4137/50)   300
Tea set, 3 pc, silver-gilt, flowering foliage on gilded stippled ground, (4137/98)   8500

Teapot, silver-gilt and enamel, cylindrical shape with bands of reeding, H6, Moscow, ca1900 (4137/27) 2000

Gratchev

Sugar basket, silver-gilt, royal blue interlaced strapwork, D3¾, St. Petersburg, ca1885 (4137/68) 2300
Sugar bowl and stand, silver-gilt, stylized foliage, D7¼, St. Petersburg (4137/82) 1100
Vase, silver-gilt, tapered body, enamel with geometric designs, H6⅞, St. Petersburg, ca1885 (4137/18) *2300*

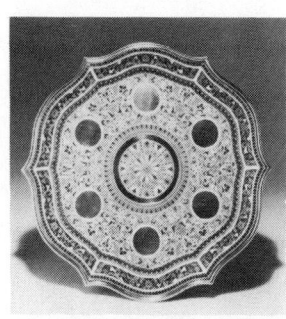

Tray (4233/496)

Vase (4137/18)

Tazza (4271/240)

Sugar bowl and creamer
(4137/143)

Khlebnikov, Ivan

Easter egg, silver-gilt, champleve, geometric bands, L2¼, Moscow, 1889 (4137/85) 2500
Kovsh, silver-gilt, plique-a-jour, with a fire-breathing fantastic creature, L6⅛, Moscow, ca1900 (4137/119) 2500
Strawberry spoon, silver-gilt, Pan-Slavic geometric design, L6, Moscow, ca1900 (4137/150) 650
Sugar bowl, tongs, matching, silver, champleve, circular, panel simulates napkin, D5, Moscow, ca1900 (4137/158) 600
Sugar sifter, silver-gilt, enamel with colorful stylized foliage, L6¼, Moscow, ca1910 (4137/19) 275
Sugar tongs, pair, silver-gilt, Pan-Slavic geometric designs, L4¼, Moscow, ca1900 (4137/155) 300
Tea caddy, sugar bowl, silver-gilt, octagonal shape, engraved chinoiserie figures, H4¼, Moscow, 1894-5 (4137/127) 9500
Tea glass holder, spoon, silver, champleve, 5 hoops, Pan-Slavic design, H2⅞, Moscow, ca1900 (4137/80) 325

Klingert, Gustav

Beaker, silver-gilt, cylindrical shape, multi-colored flowers, H3, Moscow, 1892 (4137/172) 1200
Cigarette case, silver-gilt, rectangular with scrolling flowering foliage, L4¾, Moscow, ca1885 (4137/38) 1500
Cigarette case, silver-gilt, scrolling foliage, L4⅜, Moscow, 1895 (4137/118) 900
Circular box, silver-gilt, bombe sides, foliage designs, D2, Moscow, 1892 (4137/163) 1100
Cream jug, silver-gilt, flowering foliage, H3½, Moscow, 1896 (4137/115) 1200
Cup, saucer and spoon, silver-gilt, foliage on gilded stippled ground, D3⅝ (saucer), Moscow, 1894 (4137/125) 1300
Egg cup, silver-gilt, stylized foliage, H2⅞, Moscow, 1890 (4137/44) 375
Inkwell, silver-gilt, enamel, glass, enamel with multi-colored foliage, H3¼, Moscow, ca1880 (4137/28) 450
Inkwell, silver-gilt, glass, stylized foliage, H3⅛, Moscow, 1895 (4137/123) 1400
Liquer cup, silver-gilt, champleve, cylindrical body enamel simulating mosaic, H2¾, Moscow, ca1900 (4137/49) 400
Napkin ring, silver-gilt, scrolling foliage on gilded stippled ground, H1½, Moscow, ca1900 (4137/56) 400

Napkin ring, silver-gilt, scrolling foliage on gilded stippled ground, H1½, Moscow, ca1900 (4137/57)   400
Small bowl, silver-gilt and enamel, bombe, gilded stippled ground, D2¼, 1894 (4137/8)   300
Small bowl on foot, scrolling foliage, H1⅝, Moscow, 1886 (4137/53)   350
Sugar bowl and creamer, silver-gilt, multi-colored foliage, gilded stippled ground, H4¾, 3¼, Moscow, 1892 (4137/143)   *3000*
Sugar bowl and creamer, silver-gilt, scrolling foliage, gilded stippled ground, H4⅛, 3¼, Moscow, ca1900 (4137/141)   2300
Tea glass holder, silver, champleve, mosaic design, H3¾, Moscow, 1890 (4137/126)   750
Tea set, 3 pieces, silver-gilt, opaque blue, gilded stippled ground, H5¾ (tpt), Moscow, ca1885 (4137/90)   *6000*
Teaspoons, set of 12, fig-shaped bowls, backs have stylized foliage, Moscow, 1889 (4137/15)   *1700*

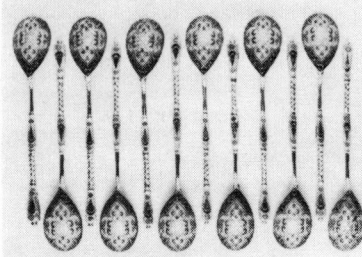

Teaspoons (4137/15)

Tea set (4137/90)

Kurliukov, Orest

Napkin ring, silver-gilt, gilded stippled ground, blue beaded borders, H1 7/16, Moscow, ca1900 (4137/51)   300

Kuzmichev, Anton

Buckle, silver-gilt, escutcheon shape with geometric designs, W2½, Moscow, ca1890 (4137/104)   200
Kovsh, silver-gilt, engraved with lovebirds, scrolling foliage, L5¾, Moscow, ca1900 (4137/135)   2800
Pill box, silver-gilt, champleve, enamel with lady, retailed by Tiffany & Co., D2, Moscow, 1887 (4137/147)   1000
Pitcher, fine, silver-gilt, helmet shape, retailed by Tiffany & Co., N.Y., H4⅜, Moscow, ca1900 (4137/137)   2400
Teaspoons, set of 6, silver-gilt, scrolling foliage, L4⅜, Moscow, ca1900 (4137/87)   1100

Nicholaev, Dmitri

Bowl and 4 salt cellars, bombe sides, foliage, gilded stippled ground, D2, 1⅜, Moscow, ca1900 (4137/111)   1400
Vodka cup, silver-gilt, cylindrical shape, scrolling foliage, H1¾, Moscow, ca1900 (4137/167)   450

Saltykov, Ivan

Beaker, silver-gilt, shaded, cylindrical shape with colorful flowers, H2¼, Moscow, ca1885 (4137/139)   1300
Card case, silver-gilt and enamel, enamel with scrolling foliage, L2⅞, Moscow, 1885 (4137/33)   600
Demi-tasse spoons, 12, silver-gilt, fig-shaped bowls with foliage, L3⅝, Moscow, ca1890 (4137/102)   1400
Enamel casket, silver-gilt, shaded, rectangular with multi-colored flowers, L2¾, Moscow, ca1900 (4137/107)   4750
Kovsh, large and matching ladle, silver-gilt with flowers, L9¾, 7⅝, Moscow, ca1885 (4137/144)   8500
Kovsh, silver-gilt, foliage on gilded stippled ground, L3, Moscow, 1895 (4137/60)   750
Kovsh, silver-gilt, 17c style, shaded with flowering foliage, L4⅛, Moscow, ca1900 (4137/73)   2600
Small bowl, silver-gilt, bombe sides, multi-colored foliage, D2⅛, Moscow, 1894 (4137/153)   400

Sugar sifter, silver, decorated with formal foliage, Moscow, ca1890 (4137/97) 200
Sugar tongs, pair, silver-gilt, stylized foliage, L4⅜, Moscow, ca1885 (4137/156) 225
Vodka mug, silver-gilt, scrolls, H2¼, Moscow, 1887 (4137/166) 600

Semenova, Maria

Beaker, silver and shaded enamel, cylindrical, enamel with flowering plants, H2⅛, Moscow, ca1900 (4137/16) 1100
Bowl, silver, shaded, lobed sides, colorful flowers, D4½, Moscow, ca1900 (4137/94) 4250
Kovsh, silver-gilt, shaded, flowering foliage, L5¾, Moscow, ca1910 (4137/133) 3500
Kovsh, silver, shaded, flowering scrolling foliage, L5½, Moscow, ca1900 (4137/83) 3000
Kovsh and spoon, silver-gilt, shaded flowers on gilded stippled ground, L5, Moscow, ca1910 (4137/105) 2400
Tea utensils, silver-gilt, sugar tong and shovel, jam spreader, fork, L3½-5, Moscow, ca1910 (4137/109) 1400

Zverev and Klingert

3 teaspoons, silver-gilt, enamel terminals, L4⅛, Moscow, ca1900-10 (4137/24) 450

Zverev, Nicholai

Card case, silver-gilt and enamel, enamel with scrolling foliage, L2⅝, Moscow, ca1910 (4137/32) 700
Cigarette case, silver-gilt, scrolling foliage, L4, Moscow, ca1900 (4137/116) 1000
Serving spoon, pair, silver-gilt, foliage and scrolls, L7½, Moscow, ca1910 (4137/129) 900
Serving spoon, silver-gilt, fig-shaped bowl, stylized flowering foliage, L7⅞, Moscow, ca1900 (4137/149) 700

FABERGE

Anemone, gold, enamel and nephrite, red and white enamel petals, nephrite leaf, 5⅛, ca1900 (4271/375) 10000
Basket, sweetmeat, silver mounted cut glass, square shape, geometric designs, gadroon silver border, 4½, ca1900 (4271/381) 1600
Basket, sweetmeat, cut glass and silver, bulbous body cut in geometric pattern, silver cover, handle, 5½, ca1900 (4271/361) 1900
Bellpush, silver and enamel, rectangular, silver applied horses heads at ends, 6¾, 1908-17 (4271/385) *7500*
Bellpush, silver and translucent enamel, circular, rose pink, swags of ribbon tied laurel, 2, ca1910 (4271/359) 3000
Bonbonniere, carved agate, acorn form, with diamond set gold mounts, 1¾, ca1890 (4186/417) 11000
Bowl, form swan, silver, eyes set with red stones, 6½, 1908-17 (4186/426) 3100
Bowl, mounted with coin, silver, reeded panel sides, gilt interior, 3⅜, ca1890 (4186/425) 1600
Bowl, silver-gilt and enamel, small, multi-colored flowers, 2½, ca1900 (4233/401) 2100
Bowl, silver-gilt and shaded enamel, lobed, panel of flowers in ivory, turquoise blue ground, 3⅞, ca1910 (4186/410) 5000
Box, demi-lune, rock crystal, gold-mounted, thumbpiece with diamonds, ruby, L2½, St. Petersburg, ca1900 (4137/374) 4750
Box, form boar head, mounted in gold and, enamel, ivory tusks, white enamel eyes set with emeralds, 3, ca1910 (4271/402) 15000
Box, presentation imperial, gold mounted, circular gold coronation inscription, 1, ca1885 (4271/407) 19000
Box, presentation, gold, enamel, diamonds, center miniature of Nicholas II, W3¼, L19c (4271/358) 65000
Box, silver-gilt and shaded enamel, 2 peasant women, 1 carrying water, sky blue ground, 2, 1908-17 (4271/356) 8500
Box, silver-gilt and shaded enamel, small, troika scene, 2¾, 1908-17 (4233/403) 11000
Box, triangular, silver-gilt, enamel lilac over a sunburst ground, W1⅝, St. Petersburg, ca1910, Perchin (4137/365) *2700*

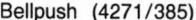

Bellpush (4271/385)

Box
(4137/365)

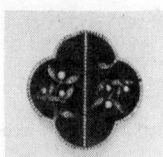

Buckle
(4137/351)

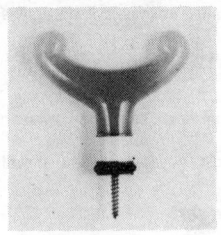

Cane handle
(4137/366)

Buckle, silver-gilt and shaded enamel, colorful flowers, 2¼, 1 half lacking (4233/409)   550
Buckle, silver, gold, enamel, oval, pale green, L2⅝, St. Petersburg, ca1900, Wigstrom (4137/363)   1100
Buckle, silver, gold, enamel, cartouche shape, diamond and pearl flowers, W2½, St. Petersburg,
   ca1900, Perchin (4137/351)   *1200*
Caddy shovel, silver-gilt and shaded enamel, multi-colored muted tones with Pan Slavic design of
   insects, 4½, 1908-17 (4271/372)   1200
Cane handle, bowenite, gold, enamel, head of a cockatoo, H2⅜, St. Petersburg, ca1900, Perchin
   (4137/373)   3200
Cane handle, bowenite, jeweled, enamel ivory over guilloche ground, L3, St. Petersburg, ca1900,
   Perchin (4137/366)   *1700*
Centerpiece, silver, stem with globe, foliate monogram, berried leafage, 9⅞, 1894 (4186/428)   1400
Centerpiece, silver, three naked infants arms raised, 4 scroll supports, 6⅝, ca1885 (4186/408)   3600
Centerpiece, silver and cutglass, oval, dec flowerheads and anthemion, 4 paw feet, 14½, 35 ozs,
   1908-17 (4271/394)   *6250*
Centerpieces, pair, silver and cut glass, three fluted column supports, leaves and foliage, 15, ca1890
   (4186/415)   4750
Charka silver, handle in form of a peacock head, 5, ca1910 (4233/408)   *2600*
Cigarette box, silver-gilt, enamel, scene after Vasnetsov's 'Prophecy to Oleg', L4½, Moscow,
   ca1910 (4137/344)   *9500*
Cigarette case, gold, rectangular shape, rounded sides, reeded all over, 3¾, ca1910 (4271/378)   2750

Centerpiece (4271/394)

Cigarette case
(4271/387)

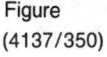

Figure
(4137/350)

Etui
(4137/349)

Cigarette case, gold and enamel, rectangular, curved sides, opaque white stripes, 3¼, 1908-17
(4271/387) 4000
Cigarette case, nephrite, rectangular, gold mount enamel, L3⅞, St. Petersburg, ca1890, Perchin
(4137/367) 2900
Cigarette case, samorodok gold, set with diamonds and sapphires, 3⅜, ca1890 (4233/399) 4000
Cigarette case, silver-gilt, sunburst design, 3½, ca1900 (4233/410) 5000
Cigarette case, two color gold, rectangular, reeded with red and yellow gold, 4, ca1900 (4271/368) 2100
Cigarette case, viatka birch, gold mounted, cover with border of running leaf tips, initial 'N', 4,
ca1900 (4271/384) 4250
Clock, desk, silver translucent enamel, shield shape, apple green over a guilloche ground, 4¼,
ca1900 (4271/397) 7250
Clock, gold, silver-gilt, enamel, square, 4 ball feet, 3⅛, ca1890, fine (4186/414) 14000
Cup, miniature, gold mounted nephrite, cyl body, gold base mount, gold handle with coin, 1½,
ca1910 (4271/388) 2300
Cup, 3-handled, fine and important, silver-gilt, lobed, shaded enamel swan, H5, Moscow, ca1900,
Ruckert (4137/360) 15000
Cup, 3-handled, silver, lobed, shaded enamel flowers, H4, Moscow, ca1900, Ruckert (4137/361) 7000
Cup and cover, silver-gilt and shaded enamel, with falconer, antelope, plumed eagle, 14½, ca1890
(4233/414) 23000
Desk, seal gold mounted rock crystal, mushroom form, border of acanthus leaves, 3½, ca1910
(4186/432) 2100
Desk clock, form of rose, silver, molded in bloom, leaves on stem, white enamel dial, 5⅛, ca1885
(4271/401) 5000
Dish, oval silver, incurved sides decorated with pilasters, 9, ca1900 (4233/392) 1350
Dish, silver-gilt and shaded enamel, Pan Slavic design of stylized foliage, 4, 1908-17 (4233/405) 2300
Dish, silver-gilt and translucent, enamel, circular, border chased leaf tips, 3½, ca1900 (4186/431) 3000
Dish, sweetmeat, silver, enamel, miniature, apple green, beaded border, 3, ca1900 (4233/398) 4900
Easter egg, gold and malachite, chased yellow gold foliage, reeded bands interspaced, 3½, ca1910
(4271/357) 40000
Easter egg, gold mounted jasper miniature, within a gold 'cage' of vine,⅝, ca1890 (4271/366) 1200
Easter egg, miniature, gold cap, translucent red enamel,⅝, ca1900 (4233/394) 950
Easter egg, silver-gilt and shaded enamel, jeweled, painted pansies set with diamonds, 2½, ca1900
(4271/413) 16000
Easter egg, silver-gilt and shaded enamel, multi-colored, stylized flowering foliage, cream ground, 3,
ca1900 (4271/411) 9500
Etui, silver-gilt, gold-mounted, with jewels, dark blue enamel, H3⅛, St. Petersburg, ca1910, Wigstrom
(4137/349) *3000*
Figure, hippopotamus, carved bowenite, eyes, red stones, 2⅞, ca1900 (4186/420) 7000
Figure, Imp'l Horse Guards officer, H7½, St. Petersburg, ca1900, Wigstrom (4137/350) *25000*

Fish knives and forks, set, 12 each, engraved with foliage, Moscow, ca1900 (4137/352)   1100
Flatware, dessert set, silver-gilt, leafage and strapwork, monogrammed, 87 ozs excluding knives, 54
   pcs, 1896-1908 (4271/373)   6000
Flatware, silver, handles dec with swans surmounting cornucopia, 4 pcs, ca1910 (4271/380)   1000
Flower in rock crystal tub, gold, nephrite leaves, fired sapphires, ruby, 5⅛, ca1900 (4233/413)   5000
Frame, miniature, gold and enamel, rectangular, onion dome top, strut support, 2⅜, ca1900
   (4271/382)   3500
Frame, double jeweled, gold mounted enamel, gold bow knot centered by cabochon ruby, 3¼,
   ca1900 (4271/406)   18000
Frame, miniature, silver-gilt and enamel, triangle shape, salmon over a guilloche ground, 2⅝, ca1900
   (4271/379)   5000
Frame, silver and enamel, miniature, form 8 pointed star, 2, ca1890 (4186/422)   1300
Hat pin, gold and enamel, finial of mushroom shape, translucent strawberry red, 8⅜, ca1900
   (4271/369)   1100
Hippopotamus, obsidian carved, standing position with cabochon ruby eyes, 2, ca1900 (4271/416)   18000
Horn bill bowenite, bird seated, bill raised in the air, gold set cabochan ruby eyes, 1¾, ca1900
   (4271/418)   2500
Icon Pendant, depicting resurrection, silver frame, 2⅛, 1896-1903, fine (4186/416)   4500
Inkwell, gold and rock crystal, octagonal shape, mount fluted, 4 bun feet, 4⅝, 1908-17 (4271/403)   15000
Jugs, claret, pair, silver mounted glass, bodies Dec. with Griffins, oval cartouches, cover, 12¼,
   ca1903 (4186/419)   5250
Kiwi, carved agate and gold, diamond set eyes, chased gold legs and beak, 1896-1908 (4271/415)   20000
Kovsh, Art Nouveau style, H5, St. Petersburg, 1900 (4137/375)   1600
Kovsh, miniature, silver-gilt, shaded enamel, Pan Slavic designs in muted colors, 1¼, 1908-1917
   (4271/393)   1500
Kovsh, silver-gilt, chased scalework, handle pierced, dec with heads of satyrs, 5¼, ca1890
   (4271/390)   3700
Kovsh, silver-gilt and shaded enamel, enamel foliage on ground of sea green, openwork handle, 2⅞,
   1908-17 (4271/363)   2750
Kovsh, silver-gilt and shaded enamel, muted colors, green, aubergine, blue, yellow, high handle, 2½,
   1908-17 (4271/412)   4250
Kovsh, silver-gilt and shaded enamel, Pan Slavic design, 7¾, 1908-1917, fine and large (4233/397)   *13500*

Raspberry plant
(4271/360)

Letter rack   (4137/345)

Kovsh   (4233/397)

Kovsh, silver-gilt and shaded enamel, with stylized chicken in Pan Slavic style, blue ground, 13⅝,
   1908-17 (4271/362)   3200
Kovsh, silver-gilt and shaded enamel fine, stylized foliage in Pan Slavic shaped handle, 7½, ca1900
   (4186/434)   12000

Letter opener, silver-gilt, enamel, tortoise shell, Pan-Slavic design on handle, L12¾, Moscow, ca1910 (4137/347)   2250

Letter rack, silver-gilt, rectangular with etched glass divisions, L9, Moscow, ca1900, Rappaport (4137/345)   5000

Match holder, silver mounted ceramic, bulbous blue ceramic body, mount chased, entwined ribbon, 2½, ca1890 (4271/389)   1150

Model of elephant, carved nephrite, diamond-set eyes, L1, St. Petersburg, 1887-90 (4137/356)   3300

Pen, rock crystal, gold and enamel, translucent apple green, opaque white borders, 6, ca1890 (4271/370)   1300

Pencil holder, gold and translucent enamel, diamonds, moonstones, 2¼, ca1890 (4233/412)   2000

Pendant, gold and enamel, Russian imperial eagle, 1 side chased with flowers, 1¾, ca1910 (4186/430)   800

Pin tray, silver, rectangular, ball feet, L5⅝, Moscow, ca1900, Wakeva (4137/354)   700

Pitcher, silver and cut-glass, bulbous body with geometric patterns, H8¾, Moscow, ca1890 (4137/355)   1800

Raspberry plant, gold, hardstone, gold stem, gold flower set with diamond, 5¾, ca1900 (4271/360)   5500

Salt cellar, silver-gilt and shaded enamel, circular, band multi-colored flowers, sky blue ground, (4186/411)   1500

Salver, silver, circular anthemion and beading border, 45 ozs, 15¾, ca1900 (4271/386)   2000

Scoring set, preference, silver-gilt, translucent enamel, two chalk holders, two brushes, ca1900 (4271/374)   1600

Seal, hand, rhodenite, carved as weeping monk, 2¾, ca1900 (4271/391)   4250

Seal, palisander wood, gold and silver, square section with incurved corners, monogrammed, 3⅛, 27 ozs, ca1910 (4271/396)   1700

Sedan chair, gold and eosite, eosite body with gold mounts, scrolls, foliate swags, flowers, 3¾, ca1890 (4271/399)   60000

Sphinx, silver, on a Rhodenite base, 6⅜, ca1910 (4186/423)   1500

Spoon, serving silver-gilt and shaded, enamel, multi-colored, stylized foliage, 8½, ca1900, fine (4186/427)   1900

Stamp moistener, nephrite, gold, cylindrical, H3¾, St. Petersburg, ca1900, Perchin (4137/372)   4250

Stick pin, gold, enamel and jeweled, cabouchon sapphire, surrounded by diamonds, 2¾, ca1900 (4233/395)   1300

Table cigarette box, silver, Russian Imperial Eagle, L5¾, Moscow, ca1910, Nevalainen (4137/368)   1500

Tankard, miniature, silver,gilt, enamel, with 18c coins, H2⅝, St. Petersburg, ca1890, Nevalainen (4137/371)   5000

Tankard, silver, slightly tapered cyl shape, form of barrel, two fluted bands, 5⅝, 1891 (4271/367)   1400

Tea and coffee set, silver, 7 pc, chased with neo rococo scrolls and shellwork, 9⅜ coffee pot, 211 ozs, 1896-1908 (4271/398)   9000

Tea and coffee set, 4 pc, silver, Dec. with girdles of berried foliage festoons, 6¾, 1896-1908 (4186/429)   4000

Tea and coffee set, 8 pcs, silver-gilt, faceted hammered surface, 25 ozs, 1887-90 (4271/377)   4000

Tea caddy, ceramic, silver-mounted, body simulates shagreen, H9½, Moscow, ca1900 (4137/369)   1600

Stamp
moistener
(4137/372)

Tea caddy
(4137/369)

Tankard
(4137/371)

Tea caddy, silver-gilt and shaded enamel, winged dragons, 4⅞, 1896-1908, fine (4233/402)   10500

Tea glass holder, silver, border waves, ribbon tied berries foliage, handle, 3¼, ca1910 (4186/418)   1600

Toilet box, silver and cut-glass, Russian Imperial Eagle, L5⅜, Moscow, ca1910 (4137/348) 700
Tumbler cup, silver-gilt and shaded enamel, four circular medallions, depicting swans, 1½, 1908-7
 (4233/404) 2900
Vase, silver-gilt, shaded enamel, cylindrical, flared rim, flowers, H5¼, Moscow, ca1910, Ruckert
 (4137/364) 2000
Waiter, circular, D9½, St. Petersburg, ca1890, Wakeva (4137/358) 1000

ICONS

Assorted localities

Apparition of the Virgin to St. Sergi, with contemporary repousse and chased silver riza, 12¼ x 10,
 L18c (4271/597) 650
Biographical of St. Elijah, 12¼ x 10, 18c, (4271/514) 1000
Biographical of St. Elijah, 7 x 6, M19c, (4271/613) 400
Biographical of St. Elijah, 8¾ x 7½, 19c, (4271/577) 400
Christ Named Holy Silence, brass and enamel, surrounded by the Apostles, 6 x 5¼, 19c
 (4271/558) 250
Christ Pantocrator, chased silver-gilt riza, robes sewn with seed pearls, 12½ x 10½, ca1900
 (4271/590) 1400
Christ Pantocrator, metal riza, 15¼ x 12½, 19c (4271/455) 350
Christ Pantocrator, painted with Holy Virgin and St. John Forerunner, 13¼ x 10¾, 19c (4271/450) 350
Christ Pantocrator, silver-gilt and enamel riza, 7¼ x 6 (4271/527) 450
Christ Pantocrator, with chased metal riza, 12½ x 10½ (4271/428) 325
Christ Pantocrator, with metal riza, 8¾ x 7, ca1900 (4271/537) 160
Christ Pantocrator, with silver-gilt and enamel riza, 9 x 7, ca1900 (4271/433) 1100
Christ Pantocrator, with silver, partly gilt riza, 8⅞ x 7⅛, ca1900 (4271/595) 250
Christ Pantocrator, 12 x 9½, 19c, (4271/499) 225
Christ Pantocrator, 12½ x 10½, 17c, (4271/533) 5000
Christ Pantocrator, 12¼ x 10½, 19c, (4271/493) 400
Christ Pantocrator, 21 x 18, 19c, (4271/554) *650*
Christ the Saviour, painted with the Mother God and St. John the Forerunner, 14 x 12⅛, 19c
 (4271/578) 650
Christ the Saviour, 21 x 17½, 19c, (4271/440) 425
Complete Resurrection, 20½ x 16½, E19c, (4271/581) 700
Crucifix, brass and enamel, 13¾, 19c, (4271/531) 325
Crucifix, bronze, 15, 19c, (4271/574) 375
Dormition of the Holy Virgin, 10¼ x 12, 19c, (4271/582) 700
I am the Vine, Christ surrounded by 12 Apostles, 22 x 16, E18c (4271/596) 1500
Intercession of the Holy Virgin, hold veil above St. Romanus the Hymnwriter, 20⅝ x 17½, E19c
 (4271/591) 700
Intercession of the Holy Virgin, 12 x 10¼, 18c, (4271/542) 650
Marriage of SS. John Chrysostom and, Elizabeth, 14 x 11¼, L19c (4271/565) 450
Mother of God, from a Deesis group, 20¼ x 16¼, 19c (4271/560) 1200
Mother of God, from a Deesis group, 19¾ x 16½, 19c (4271/594) 500
Mother of God, joy to those who grieve, 12⅜ x 10¾, 18c, (4271/541) 350
Mother of God, joy to those who grieve, 8¾ x 6⅞, 19c, (4271/538) 225
Mother of God Iverskaya, 10⅝ x 8¾, 18c, (4271/539) 450
Nativity of the Holy Virgin, 14 x 11¾, border res, E17c (4271/543) 8000
Nativity of the Virgin, 7 x 6¼, 19c, (4271/579) 375
Our Lady of Joy to Those Who Grieve, 12¼ x 10⅜, ca1900 (4186/395) 4500
Panagia, silver, partly gilded, circular, hinged each side, icon origin and child, 3⅜, L19c (4271/586) 600
Polyptych, bronze and enamel, depicting the 16 Cardinal Feast Days of Orthodox Church, 7¼ x
 16½, 19c (4271/571) 375
Quadripartite, four representations of Virgin, 14 x 12¼, 19c (4271/498) 375
Quadripartite, painted with crucifixion at the center, 13¾ x 12, 19c (4271/490) 500
Quadripartite, 14 x 12¼, 19c, (4271/509) 700
Resurrection of Christ, surrounded by 12 Orthodox feast days, 28 x 21¾, 19c (4271/551) 950
Selected saints, metal riza, 14¼ x 12½, 19c (4271/452) 500
Selected saints, Christ in clouds above, border painted simulate enamel, 14 x 12¼, 19c (4271/609) 550
Selected saints, 17½ x 15, 19c, (4271/496) 300
Six registers of selected saints and, feasts, 12 x 10 (4271/483) 700
Smolensk Mother of God, with fine silver and enamel riza, 4½ x 3½, L19c (4271/614) 1600
St. Alexander Nevsky, fine silver, partly gilded riza, 14 x 9¾, L19c (4271/494) 2100
St. Anastasius, 11¼ x 8½, 18c, (4271/434) 175
St. Andrew Stratilat, fine repousse and chased gilt and shaded enamel riza, 12¼ x 10¼, ca1900
 (4271/587) 6250
St. Dmitri, painted with patron saints in border, Christ above, 15 x 13, 19c (4271/458) 400

St. George slaying the dragon, with Christ in clouds above, 17½ x 15¾, E19c (4271/427)	1900
St. John the Baptist and selected saints, 14½ x 12, 18c, (4271/555)	300
St. John the Evangelist in Silence, border gilded with vine on blue ground, 8¾ x 6⅞, ca1900 (4271/515)	150
St. John the Forerunner, with silver metal riza, 17½ x 13¾, 19c (4271/521)	600
St. John the Forerunner, 17½ x 14¼, 19c, (4271/544)	350
St. Luke, 21 x 17¼, E17c (4186/355)	4000
St. Makari, with engraved and chased silver metal okhlad, 12¼ x 10½, 18c (4271/460)	950
St. Mitrophan, fine repousse and chased silver-gilt riza, 21½ x 16, 19c (4271/491)	4000
St. Nicholas and the Archangel Michael, with silver-gilt and enamel riza, arched top, 16⅛, ca1900 (4271/588)	3500
St. Nicholas Mozhaysky, with silver okhlad, L18c (4271/420)	450
St. Nicholas the Miracleworker, flanked by Christ and the Holy Virgin, 14 x 12, 19c (4271/442)	800
St. Nicholas the Miracleworker, flanked by Christ and the Holy Virgin, 31 x 20¾, 19c (4271/548)	1050
St. Nicholas the Miracleworker, flanked by Christ and the Holy Virgin, 28 x 22½, 19c (4271/563)	2250
St. Nicholas the Miracleworker, painted with saints in border, 15 x 12, 19c (4271/507)	550
St. Nicholas the Miracleworker, silver-gilt riza, 8⅞ x 7, L19c (4271/547)	425
St. Nicholas the Miracleworker, 14 x 12, 18c, (4271/419)	750
St. Nil Stolbinski, 12½ x 10¼, ca1800, (4271/540)	*1900*
St. Paraskeva, 17½ x 13¾, E19c, (4271/429)	475
Sts. Andrew and Anna, border painted with foliage on blue ground, 8¾ x 7, ca1900 (4271/513)	175
Sts. Joachim and Anna, silver okhlad, border decorated with grapevines, 12½ x 10½, E19c (4271/482)	550
Sts. John Damoskin and Agripina, chased silver riza, 19c (4271/552)	400
Sts. Sergi and Alexander, with silver and enamel halos, framed, 15½ x 12 (4271/526)	*700*

Christ Pantocrator (4271/554)

St. Nil Stolbinski (4271/540)

Sts. Sergi and Alexander (4271/526)

The crucifixion, 12½ x 10½, 18c, (4271/423)	250
The Annunciation, with repousse and chased silver okhlad, 14¼ x 12¼, 19c (4271/463)	650
The Annunciation, with silver metal riza, 12½ x 10¾, 19c (4271/495)	450
The Archangel Michael, signed by Michael Damaskinos, 39⅜ x 29½, 16c, rare (4186/379)	56000
The Archangel Michael, 12½ x 10⅝, E17c, (4271/532)	4000
The Chin Mother of God, from Deesis group, 12¼ x 10¼, 19c (4271/500)	800
The Complete Resurrection, chased silver okhlad, 14⅛ x 12⅛, L18c (4271/485)	1900
The Complete Resurrection, with gilt metal okhlad, 12¼ x 10⅜, E19c (4271/467)	800
The Complete Resurrection, 13½ x 10¼, 19c, (4271/468)	500
The Complete Resurrection, 15¾ x 14, 19c, (4271/456)	475
The Complete Resurrection, 20¾ x 17¾, 19c, (4271/506)	1000
The Complete Resurrection, 21 x 18, 19c, (4271/437)	650
The Council of the Archangel Michael, 12¼ x 10½, M19c, (4271/451)	600
The Fiery Ascension of St. Elijah, 12 x 10, (4271/444)	600
The Holy Virgin, painted with patron saints on border, 17¼ x 14, 19c (4271/519)	400
The Kazan Mother of God, oval silver riza with ring, 2¾, L19c (4271/464)	500
The Kazan Mother of God, painted with patron saints in border, 21 x 17, 19c (4271/459)	700
The Kazan Mother of God, painted with patron saints in borders, 14¼ x 12½, 19c (4271/466)	1200
The Kazan Mother of God, painted with saints in border, 14 x 12¼, 19c (4271/508)	400
The Kazan Mother of God, with silver-gilt and shaded enamel risa, 10¾ x 8¾, ca1900 (4271/472)	950
The Mother of God, from a Deesis group, 15¾ x 13¼, 19c (4271/511)	600
The Mother of God, joy to those who grieve, chased silver riza, 19c (4271/446)	650
The Mother of God, joy to those who grieve, 10½ x 8¾, ca1800, (4271/501)	325
The Mother of God, joy to those who grieve, 12 x 9¾, 19c, (4271/504)	425
The Mother of God of the Sign, with gilded metal riza, 8⅞ x 7, ca1900 (4271/530)	325
The Mother of God Sporutchnitza, with repousse and chased silver, gilt riza, 10½ x 8¾ (4271/480)	550
The Mother of God Umilenie, silver-gilt and enamel riza, 5½ x 4⅝, L19c (4271/528)	620
The Nativity of the Holy Virgin, 12⅜ x 10¼, L18c, (4271/536)	800
The Nativity of the Virgin, double arched top, 19 x 20¾ (4271/488)	850
The Nativity of the Virgin, 13¼ x 11½, 18c, (4271/453)	350
The Old Testament Trinity, with repousse and chased silver, gilt and enamel riza, 12¼ x 10½, L19c (4271/584)	4750
The St. Princess Olga, fine silver, partly gilded riza, 14 x 9¾, L19c (4271/454)	1900
The Tichvin Mother of God, fine silver-gilt repousse and chased riza, 7½ x 5½, 19c (4271/462)	500
The Tolga Mother of God, 12 x 10½, 19c, (4271/502)	375
The Virgin of Consolation, 13½ x 11¼, 17c, (4271/448)	1400
The Virgin of Tenderness, silver-gilt basma decorated with key pattern design, 10½ x 8¾, L19c (4271/469)	2400
The Virgin of the Sign, 10½ x 8¾, E19c, (4271/449)	600
Tichvin Mother of God, 8¾ x 7, 19c, (4271/600)	425
Triptych, 4 x 10⅜, 18c (4186/400)	800
Triptych, 4¾ x 11¾, E18c (4186/343)	2900
Triptych, brass, panel depicting St. Nicholas Mozhaysky, 2¾ x 4, 19c (4271/470)	100
Triptych, brass and enamel, 5¾ x 15¾, 19c (4186/314)	200
Triptych, silver, 2¼ x 3½ (4186/390)	600
Two registers, The Annunciation and Three Church Fathers, 13¾ x 13 (4271/549)	1100
Two registers, The Transfiguration and Presentation of Virgin in Temple, 10¼ x 9, 19c (4271/443)	600
Two registers, The Virgin, Lower Archangel Michael, 14 x 12, 19c (4271/473)	600
Two Male Saints, depicted before a monastery, 8¾ x 7, ca1900 (4271/516)	225
Virgin and Child, with beaded okhlad mounted with pastes, 7¼ x 6¼, 19c (4271/598)	500
Virgin of Kazan, 12 x 10½, 19c, (4271/559)	375
Virgin of Tenderness, with metal and enamel riza, 12¾ x 10⅝ (4271/546)	350
Virgin Sporutchnitza, 19 x 15, 19c, (4271/553)	475

Balkan

St. George slaying the dragon, 12 x 9¼, 19c, (4271/422)	475

Greek

A Female Saint, 9½ x 8, 18c (4137/568)	80
An Apostle, 13 x 10, (4271/479)	375
An Apostle, 13 x 10, 18c, (4271/477)	325
Mother of God Eleousa, 12½ x 9¾, 18c (4233/353)	1000
Nativity of Christ, 12½ x 10, 18c (4233/373)	500
Nativity of the Holy Virgin, 21 x 15¼, 18c, (4271/599)	1000
New Testament Trinity, 9¾ x 7¾, 17c (4137/513)	400
Resurrection and Descent, 4⅞ x 8, 18c (4233/289)	300
St. Andrew, with shadow box, 10½ x 7½, 17c (4186/248)	1000
St. Dmitri, 18½ x 13 (4233/322)	350

St. George slaying the dragon, 10¼ x 7, (4271/604) 325
St. John Chrysostom, 14¼ x 11⅜, 18c (4233/235) 850
St. Marina, 9¼ x 6½, 18c, (4271/556) 450
St. Menas, 11⅛ x 7⅞, 19c (4137/557) 70
St. Nicholas the Miracleworker, 10 x 6, 19c (4233/362) 200
St. Nicholas the Miracleworker, 6⅛ x 4¾, 17/18c, (4271/484) 400
The Adoration of the Magi, 13 x 9⅝, 19c (4137/558) 225
The Forty Martyrs of Sebastia, 20½ x 15¼, 18c (4137/564) 350
The Virgin Enthroned, 13¼ x 11¼, 19c (4137/555) 100
The Virgin Hodegetria, 12 x 7½, 19c (4137/559) 175
Triptych, central panel depicting flight into Egypt, 10½ x 15½, L18c (4271/562) 800
Virgin and Child, 40 x 27¾, 19c, (4271/605) 2300
Virgin of Tenderness, Christ holding a scroll (the spirit of God is in me), 17¾ x 14, L18c (4271/567) 450

Italo-Cretan

The Virgin and Child, 11⅜ x 9¾, 17c (4137/430) 225
The Virgin of Consolation, frame carved with pillars, 8 x 6½, 17c (4271/445) 1600

Middle Eastern

The Virgin from a Deesis group, repousse silver riza, 18⅛ x 14, L19c (4137/536) *1300*

The Virgin from a Deesis group (4137/536)

Polish

St. Barbara, 5⅞ x 4¾, M19c (4233/220) 400

Russian

Adoration of the Magii, 12⅜ x 10⅜, 19c (4233/333) 1400
Archangels Michael and Gabriel, two icons, 31⅜ x 12¾, cent. Rus., M18c (4137/431) 1500
Baptism of Christ (Epiphary), John Baptist hand on head of Christ, 17¼ x 14⅛, 18c (4186/263) 400
Biographical, of St. N. Mozhaysky, 21¾ x 17⅜, March 1879 (4137/531) 1700
Biographical Icon of St. Elijah, 14 x 12¼, E19c (4233/254) 375
Brass and enamel Icon Polyptych, 6½, 19c (4233/316) 275
Brass Icon Triptych, 5⅝ x 15½, 19c (4233/331) 250
Bronze and enamel icon with crucifix, with blue, white, and red enamel, 15½, 19c (4186/268) 325
Christ before Herod the King, 12¼ x 10¼, 19c (4233/308) 300
Christ enthroned, 47½ x 23½, 19c (4137/540) 900
Christ in the Garden of Gethsemane, 12¼ x 10¼, 19c (4137/447) 250
Christ in Majesty, with 12 feast days of the Orthodox Church, 17⅜ x 14¾, ca1900 (4137/493) 700
Christ Panocrator, miniature, silver and enamel frame, Moscow, Mark S.G., H2, ca1900 (4137/425) 375
Christ Pantocrator, 17¾ x 14½, L18c (4186/261) 375
Christ Pantocrator, 12½ x 10½, 19c (4137/419) 400
Christ Pantocrator, 17⅝ x 14½, 19c (4186/260) 300

Christ Pantocrator, 16 x 14, 19c (4233/232) 400
Christ Pantocrator, 21 x 17½, 19c (4233/276) 550
Christ Pantocrator, 8⅞ x 7, L19c (4233/234) 425
Christ Pantocrator, 10⅝ x 8¾, L19c (4233/311) 175
Christ Pantocrator, 11½ x 9½, 19c (4233/284) 225
Christ Pantocrator, 33 x 34½, E17c (4233/208) 3250
Christ Pantocrator, 12⅜ x 10⅝, ca1900 (4233/306) 1500
Christ Pantocrator, 8¾ x 7, ca1900 (4233/236) 350
Christ Pantocrator, 7⅛ x 5⅝, L19c (4233/293) 300
Christ Pantocrator, 27¾ x 21¾, 18c (4233/360) 550
Christ Pantocrator, border, decorated to simulate enamel, 12⅜ x 10½, 19c (4186/269) 275
Christ Pantocrator, chased silver riza, Moscow, 1839, 9 x 7, 19c (4137/385) 900
Christ Pantocrator, comteporary silver partially gilded riza, 8¾ x 7½, ca1910, mark N.G. (4186/270) 425
Christ Pantocrator, fine silver-gilt and enamel riza, 21 x 17½, ca1910 (4186/253) 6500
Christ Pantocrator, gilded metal riza, 14 x 11¾, 19c (4137/490) 650
Christ Pantocrator, gilded metal riza, 6⅝ x 5, L19c (4137/444) 375
Christ Pantocrator, gilt-metal riza, 10½ x 8¾, 19c (4137/512) 550
Christ Pantocrator, parcel-gilt riza, Moscow, 12¼ x 11, ca1800 (4137/485) 850
Christ Pantocrator, silver and enamel riza, Moscow, 1896-1908, 12¼ x 10½, L19c (4137/461) 3200
Christ Pantocrator, silver and gilded metal riza, 6½ x 5¼, L19c (4137/445) 350
Complete Resurrection, 21⅛ x 17⅜, E19c (4186/265) 800
Complete Resurrection, 17½ x 15, E19c (4233/288) 475
Complete Resurrection, 12½ x 10, 19c (4233/262) 325
Complete Resurrection, 21 x 17½, E19c (4233/291) 700
Complete Resurrection, 12¼ x 10½, 19c (4233/226) 550
Complete Resurrection, 14 x 12¼, 18c (4233/258) 550
Complete Resurrection, 17½ x 14¾, 19c (4233/282) 425
Complete Resurrection, 12¼ x 10½, E19c (4233/327) 1000
Complete Resurrection, 14 x 12 (4233/342) 400
Complete Resurrection, South Russian, 14 x 12, 19c (4137/397) 700
Crucifix, brass and enamel, H10⅛, 19c (4137/455) 175
Crucifix, bronze, H6, 18/19c (4137/470) 175
Crucifix, bronze and enamel, H6¼, 18c (4137/534) 200
Crucifix, silver and enamel, 15¼, ca1910 (4186/372) 1000
Crucifixion, 14 x 12⅜, L18c/E19c (4137/386) 650
Crucifixion, 21¼ x 17½, M19c (4186/304) 2100
Crucifixion, 20 x 17¾, 19c (4233/279) 800
Crucifixion, 12⅛ x 10¼, 19c (4233/229) 300
Crucifixion, 20 x 16, 19c (4233/270) 475
Crucifixion, 21 x 17¾, E19c (4233/273) 1400
Decollation of St. John the Baptist, 12¼ x 10½, 19c (4137/506) *700*
Decollation of St. John the Baptist, 12 x 10⅝, 18c (4137/502) 700
Decollation of St. John the Baptist, 7⅜ x 6¼, 19c (4233/290) 200
Deesis, 14 x 12¼, 19c (4186/284) 270
Deesis, 17 x 13¾, E19c (4186/283) 450
Deesis, 21 x 17½, 19c (4233/261) 950
Descent into Hell, 13⅜ x 11, 18c (4186/257) 300
Diptych, silver, H1¾, Moscow, ca1910 (4137/454) 650
Dormition of the Holy Virgin, 14 x 12¼, E19c (4233/267) 600
Dormition of the Holy Virgin, 13½ x 11, 18c (4233/355) 700
Dormition of the Virgin, 21 x 18¼, 19c (4233/361) 650
Dormition of the Virgin, large, brass, 10¾ x 9, 19c (4137/457) 300
Five metal icons, mounted on a panel, 1⅞ to 2¾, 18/19c (4137/535) 70
Group of saints, 42½ x 36½, 19c (4186/273) 850
Guardian Angel, 12¼ x 10¼, 19c (4186/278) 250
Guardian Angel SS Alex, Ander Nevsky and Maria, 12½ x 10¼, 19c (4233/376) 300
Holy Virgin, 13½ x 12, 19c (4233/253) 250
Icon, Weep not for me mother, 12⅜ x 10⅜, E18c (4233/222) 800
Icon, 3 saints, 12½ x 10¼, 19c (4186/300) 200
Icon Diptych, 6½ x 11¼, 19c (4233/317) 150
Icon Diptych, 3, 18c (4233/341) 275
Icon in 2 parts, depicts Baptism and Transfiguration of Christ, 22¾ x 27½ (4137/497) ... 750
Icon in 2 registers, 13¾ x 12¼, E19c (4233/246) 475
Icon in 2 registers, 14 x 12⅜, 19c (4233/263) 450
Icon in 2 registers, 13¾ x 12⅜, 19c (4233/295) 250
Icon in 3 registers, 9⅛ x 7¼, 17c (4233/219) 2000
Icon in 3 registers, 14 x 12¼, E19c (4233/265) 250
Icon in 3 registers, 12¼ x 9⅞, 19c (4233/242) 225

Icon in 3 registers, 10¾ x 9, 19c (4233/201) — 375
Icon of Saints Zosima and Savati, 11¾ x 9½, L16c (4186/287) — 950
Icon Triptych, 6⅜ x 14 (4233/287) — 1000
Icon Triptych, 2½ x 6¾, E18c (4233/283) — 550
Icon Triptych, bronze, 3 x 4⅜, 18c (4233/352) — 75
Icon Triptych, carved wood, 6¼ x 6½, 19c (4233/344) — 150
Icon Triptych, silver-gilt and enamel, 1⅝ x 5 (4186/293) — 850
Icon with crucifix, brass and enamel, H10½, 19c (4137/533) — 175
Icon with crucifix, brass, enamel, H15½, 19c (4137/458) — 600
Icon with Crucifix, brass and enamel, 15⅝, 19c (4233/335) — 300
Iconostasis panel of Prophet Elijah, 28 x 13, 19c (4137/388) — 550
Intercession of the Virgin, (Pokrov), 12⅛ x 10½, 18c (4233/247) — 550
Intercession of the Virgin, bronze and enamel (Pokrov), 6¾ x 3¾ (4233/338) — 75
Kazan Mother of God, 10⅝ x 8⅞, ca1900 (4233/238) — 1600
Kazan Mother of God, 7 x 6, L19c (4233/266) — 350
Kazan Mother of God, 14¼ x 12¼, 19c (4233/244) — 725

Decollation of St. John the
Baptist (4137/506)

Kazan Mother of God, 8¾ x 7¼, L19c (4233/274) — 375
Kazan Mother of God, 12¾ x 9⅝, 19c (4233/302) — 325
Korsun Mother of God, 10½ x 9, 19c (4233/374) — 250
Menological, of the full year, 20¾ x 17, 18c (4137/484) — 1300
Menological, of Month of June, 12¼ x 10½, L18c (4137/442) — 500
Menological, of Month of December, 14 x 11⅞, E19c (4233/348) — 325
Miraculous Image of St. Nicholas, silver basma, Moscow, 1880, 5¾ x 4½, L19c (4137/565) — 400
Mother of God, Feodorovskaya, 12 x 11, 19c (4186/254) — 400
Mother of God, Feodorovskaya, with silver partially gilded riza, 10½ x 8¾, ca1910 (4186/251) — 1000
Mother of God, Skorbashchix, with silver-gilt okhlad, 10½ x 8¾, ca1900, marker's mark G.P. (4186/252) — 800
Mother of God of the Burning Bush, 14 x 12⅛ (4233/318) — 400
Mother of God, Akhtyrskaya, 12¼ x 11, 18c (4186/288) — 450
Nativity of the Holy Virgin, 16½ x 17¾, 19c (4233/230) — 425
Nativity of the Virgin, 17¼ x 13, 19c (4233/259) — 325
Old Testament Trinity, 12½ x 10½, 19c (4186/277) — 1000
Our Lady Akhtyrskaya, 9¼ x 8¾, 19c (4233/368) — 70
Our Lady Console Our Sorrow, 21 x 17, 18c (4186/276) — 450
Our Lady Feodorovskaya, 10½ x 8⅝, 19c (4137/410) — 550
Our Lady Iverskaya, 8¾ x 7, M19c (4233/292) — 400
Our Lady Kazanskaya, silver riza, robes of filigree silver, multicolor enamel, 12½ x 10¾, ca1900, mark S.G. (4186/259) — 2600

Our Lady Kazanskaya, silver-gilt riza, St. Petersburg, 1842, 11 x 9½, 18c (4137/384)   900
Our Lady of Bogolubskaya, 15¾ x 13, 19c (4137/378)   700
Our Lady of Bogolubskaya, with metal riza, 12½ x 10½, 19 (4137/390)   650
Our Lady of Consolation of Sorrow, 11 x 9½, 18c (4137/566)   800
Our Lady of Feodorovskaya, 8⅞ x 7, 19c (4137/389)   525
Our Lady of Joy to Those Who Suffer, 13¾ x 12¼, 19c (4233/307)   300
Our Lady of Joy to Those Who Suffer, 12¼ x 10½, 18c (4137/569)   700
Our Lady of Joy to Those Who Suffer, 28⅜ x 21⅛ (4186/301)   1100
Our Lady of Joy to Those Who Suffer, gilt-metal riza, 12¾ x 11, 19c (4137/514)   600
Our Lady of the Fountain, silver-gilt riza, Moscow, 1765, 8⅜ x 7, 18c (4137/383)   550
Our Lady of the Passion, brass and enamel, 4 x 3½, 19c (4137/532)   175
Our Lady of the Sign, 12½ x 10⅛, 18c (4233/205)   450
Our Lady of Unexpected Joy, 12 x 10, 18c (4137/480)   425
Our Lady Pochayevskaya, 21 x 17, L19c (4233/370)   850
Our Lady Smolenskaya, 8¾ x 6½, L19c (4186/285)   450
Our Lady Smolenskaya, with shadow box, enamel halo, multicolor foliage, pale blue ground, 8¾ x
   7⅛, ca1910 (4186/262)   1600
Our Lady Tichvinskaya, 10½ x 8¾, L19c (4233/216)   450
Our Lady Troyarushitsa, 4½ x 3⅝, L19c (4186/306)   325
Polyptyeh brass and enamel, 7 x 16, 19c (4186/354)   375
Presentation of the Holy Virgin, in the Temple, 8⅞ x 7, L19c (4233/269)   175
Presentation of Virgin in Temple, 37 x 27¾, 18c (4137/416)   *1300*
Protection of the Mother, of God (Pokrov), 12⅜ x 10⅜, E19c (4186/289)   1500
Protection of the Mother, of God (Pokrov), 17¾ x 15½, 18c (4186/286)   1300
Quadrapartite, 14 x 12¼, 19c (4137/475)   650
Quadrapartite icon, 17¼ x 15, 19c (4137/408)   650
Quadrapartite icon, Palekh school, crucifixion in center, 12⅛ x 10¼, 19c (4137/401)   *1000*
Quadrapartite Icon, gilt metal okhlad, visit of Magii, 14 x 12½, 18c (4186/274)   1200
Quadripartite icon, 15⅞ x 13⅛, 18c (4233/206)   900
Quadripartite icon, 35 x 27½, 19c (4233/299)   350
Resurrection and Descent, into Hell, 12¼ x 10½ (4233/330)   1600
Selected saints, 12½ x 11½, E19c (4233/271)   425
Selected saints, 12½ x 10¼, 19c (4233/260)   300
Small Icon, an extended Deesis, Crucifiction Greek, 3½ x 3¼, 18c (4186/291)   200
St. Abraham, 27 x 16 (4186/279)   550
St. Alexander Nevsky, 12½ x 10½, L19c (4233/379)   850
St. Basil, painted on canvas and mounted, 20½ x 14¾, 19c (4137/550)   75
St. Basil, silver frame, Moscow, 1887, H4⅜, L19c (4137/427)   550
St. Basil, silver-gilt and enamel riza, Moscow, 1892, 12¼ x 10½, 19c (4137/511)   4500
St. Dmitri, 13¾ x 12¼, 19c (4137/391)   900
St. Elijah, biographical, 15½ x 13, E19c (4233/371)   2300
St. Elizabeth, 12½ x 10⅝, L19c (4233/369)   700
St. Ermogeni, border, strapwork and stylized foliage, simulate enamel, 12¼ x 10½, L19c (4186/266)   200
St. George slaying the dragon, 12¼ x 10⅜, L18c (4233/250)   650
St. George slaying the dragon, princess, parents on balcony, four saints, 12⅛ x 10⅝, L18c
   (4186/292)   1300
St. George slaying the dragon, with selected saints, 13⅝ x 12¼, 19c (4233/213)   650
St. George slaying the dragon, bronze, 3⅜ x 3, 19c (4233/337)   100
St. George slaying the dragon, bronze, 5½ x 4¾, 18c (4233/332)   275
St. George slaying the dragon, 12¼ x 10½, 19c (4137/381)   *1000*
St. John the Baptist in Wilderness, 10 x 8, 17c (4137/526)   6250
St. John the Evangelist in Silence, 14 x 12¼, E19c (4137/508)   750
St. John the Evangelist in Silence, 17½ x 15⅜, 19c (4137/521)   *550*
St. John the Evangelist in Silence, South Russian, 12 x 10½, 18c (4137/394)   700
St. John the Forerunner, 20¾ x 17, 19c (4137/412)   500
St. John the Forerunner, 28 x 22¼, 19c (4137/415)   500
St. John the Forerunner, 38¼ x 15, 18c (4137/464)   700
St. John the Forerunner, 14 x 11¾, 19c (4138/402)   575
St. John the Forerunner, 14 x 12⅜, 19c (4233/257)   275
St. John the Forerunner, with selected saints, 12¼ x 10¼, 18c (4137/503)   650
St. Nicholas Mozhaysky, 12¼ x 10½, L18/E19c (4137/406)   700
St. Nicholas Mozhaysky, 14 x 12¼, 18c (4137/515)   300
St. Nicholas Mozhaysky, 47 x 32½, 19c (4137/494)   700
St. Nicholas the Miracleworker, 8¾ x 7⅛, 18c (4137/382)   200
St. Nicholas the Miracleworker, 38 x 31½, 18c (4137/405)   2000
St. Nicholas the Miracleworker, 31½ x 12¼, cent. Rus., M18c (4137/436)   1200
St. Nicholas the Miracleworker, 14¼ x 11¾, 18c (4137/422)   600

Quadrapartite icon
(4137/401)

Presentation of Virgin in Temple
(4137/416)

St. John the Evangelist
in Silence (4137/521)

St. George slaying
the dragon
(4137/381)

St. Nicholas the Miracleworker, 14 x 12¼, 19c (4137/418)	600
St. Nicholas the Miracleworker, 7 x 5¾, 19c (4137/505)	350
St. Nicholas the Miracleworker, 11⅜ x 9¼, 18c (4137/495)	225
St. Nicholas the Miracleworker, 12¼ x 10¼, 19c (4137/510)	175
St. Nicholas the Miracleworker, 14 x 12, 19c (4186/299)	250
St. Nicholas the Miracleworker, 12½ x 10, 18-19c (4186/282)	850
St. Nicholas the Miracleworker, 13½ x 11½, 18c, mark. P.S. Tver (4186/298)	1100
St. Nicholas the Miracleworker, 12¼ x 10¾, 19c (4186/295)	1600
St. Nicholas the Miracleworker, 12⅜ x 11¼, 19c (4233/227)	275
St. Nicholas the Miracleworker, 13⅞ x 11¼, E19c (4233/212)	750
St. Nicholas the Miracleworker, 8⅝ x 6¾, ca1900 (4233/240)	300
St. Nicholas the Miracleworker, 20½ x 16½, L19c (4233/209)	1600
St. Nicholas the Miracleworker, 10⅝ x 8¾, L19c (4233/221)	300
St. Nicholas the Miracleworker, 22 x 17⅝, 17c (4233/381)	1700
St. Nicholas the Miracleworker, 12⅛ x 10½, ca1900 (4233/305)	350
St. Nicholas the Miracleworker, 12 x 10⅜, 19c (4233/349)	700
St. Nicholas the Miracleworker, 12½ x 10⅝, 19c (4233/312)	625

St. Nicholas the Miracleworker, 14¼ x 12, 19c (4233/264) 300
St. Nicholas the Miracleworker, contemporary silvered brass riza, 13 x 9½, E19c (4137/539) 700
St. Nicholas the Miracleworker, gilded metal riza, 12⅛ x 10⅛, 19c (4137/380) 425
St. Nicholas the Miracleworker, silver riza, Moscow, ca1910, 10¾ x 9, 18c (4137/395) 550
St. Nicholas the Miracleworker, silver-gilt okhlad, Moscow, 1888, 12½ x 10½, 19c (4137/501) 900
St. Nicholas the Miracleworker, silver-gilt riza, Moscow, 1858, 12¼ x 10¾, 18c (4137/561) 1400
St. Nicholas the Wonderworker, 12½ x 10⅝, 18c (4186/280) 1300
St. Pantelemon, with silver partly gilt, enamel riza, 8¾ x 7, ca1900, mark A.S. (4186/256) 1500
St. Peter Metropolitan of, Moscow, 4 x 3¼, L19c (4186/290) 300
St. Simeon, with silver riza, 2¾ x 2¼, ca1900 (4137/519) 200
St. Simeon Verkhotoursky, 27 x 22¼, 18c (4233/203) 1000
St. Sophia with her three daughters, enamel plaque by Igor Antipev, 8½ x 6½, M19c (4186/249) 950
St. Xenia, robes sewn with seed pearls and mounted with colored stones, 8¾ x 7, M19c (4186/272) 350
The Annunciation, 15⅞ x 13, 18c (4137/492) 550
The Annunciation, 12¼ x 10⅞, ca1700 (4137/488) 550
The Archangel Michael, 12¼ x 10½, 19c (4137/489) 325
The Archangel Michael, silver and enamel riza, ca1900, 12⅜ x 10¾, L17c (4137/496) 2500
The Complete Resurrection, 14 x 12¼, 19c (4137/417) 750
The Crucifixion, 34½ x 25½, 18c (4137/424) 950
The Crucifixion, 12¼ x 10½, 18c (4137/473) 700
The Deesis, 19½ x 16½, 19c (4137/404) 950
The Deesis, 14¼ x 11⅛, 18c (4137/400) 550
The Deesis, 13⅞ x 12⅜, 19c (4137/530) 450
The Deesis, metal riz, 8¾ x 7, E19c (4137/465) 425
The Descent into Hell, 12¼ x 10, 18c (4137/546) 1400
The Eucharist, 12⅜ x 10½, 17c (4137/491) 1500
The Guardian Angel, silver frame, St. Petersburg, ca1910, H3⅝, ca1910 (4137/437) 250
The Intercession of the Virgin, brass and enamel, H6½, ca1800 (4137/499) 175
The Last Supper, 12⅜ x 10½, 17c (4137/486) 1700
The Mother of God, 14 x 11¾, 19c (4137/399) 475
The Mother of God Iverskaya, silvered-metal rica, 5⅜ x 4⅜, L19c (4137/443) 425
The Old Testament Trinity, 14 x 12⅛, 18c (4137/476) 650
The Old Testament Trinity, 7 x 5⅝, 19c (4137/403) 200
The Pokrov, 21 x 18¼, 19c (4137/409) 1000
The Resurrection, with 12 Festivals of the Orthodox Church, 14 x 12, 19c (4137/538) 550
The Transfiguration, 12¼ x 10⅜, L19c (4137/448) 475
The Transfiguration, 34½ x 28, 17c (4137/411) 2900
The Virgin, 14⅛ x 11⅞, 19c (4137/453) 350
The Virgin Kievo Percherskaya, silver-gilt and shaded enamel riza, ca1900, 10½ x 8¾, L19c (4137/432) 4000
The Virgin of Kazan, 12½ x 10½, 19c (4137/407) 475
The Virgin of Kazan, silver parcel-gilt riza, 8¾ x 7½ (4137/517) 750
The Virgin of Korsun, 12⅜ x 9⅞, 17c (4137/556) 1900
The Virgin of Tenderness, 11⅞ x 10⅛, 18c (4137/528) 750
The Virgin of Tichvin, 12¼ x 10⅛, 18c (4137/554) 850
The Virgin of Tichvin, 4½ x 3¾, 19c (4137/518) 150
The Virgin of Tichvin, silver-gilt okhlad, Moscow, 1868, 14 x 12¼, 19c (4137/516) 900
Three Saints, 13 x 10⅜, 18c (4137/483) 425
Three selected saints, 12⅛ x 10½, 19c (4233/224) 375
Tichvin Mother of God, 28¼ x 23¾, ca1800 (4233/383) 2100
Tolga Mother of God, 20 x 16, 19c (4137/379) 425
Transfiguration (Metamorphosis), 13¼ x 11¼, 19c (4233/336) 1100
Triptych, silver parcel-gilt riza, by Sazikov, 9 x 12¼, St. Petersburg, 1882 (4137/387) 1900
Triptych, brass and enamel, the Deesis flanked by selected saints, 2⅜ x 6⅝, 18/19c (4137/498) 250
Triptych, brass, and Diptych, bronze, enamel diptych, H2⅝, 3⅞, 19c (4137/549) 180
Triptych, silver and enamel, Gustav Klingert, 3¾ x 6⅜, Moscow, ca1900 (4137/456) *2200*
Two enamel icons, H2½, 2⅛, 19c (4137/547) 275
Vernicle, with engraved brass basma, 12 x 10½, 18c (4186/255) 300
Virgin, from a Deesis group, 17⅝ x 14¾, 19c (4186/258) 450
Virgin and Child with selected, saints, 13¾ x 12¼, 19c (4233/248) 425
Virgin of Kazan, 12 x 10⅜, 18c (4137/414) 450
Virgin of Kazan, 12½ x 10½, L19c (4186/307) 1250
Virgin of Kazan, silver parcel-gilt and enamel riza, Moscow, 12 x 10¼, ca1910 (4137/451) 2600
Virgin of Smolensk, with metal okhlad, 12¾ x 10½, 18c (4137/377) 450
Virgin of Tenderness, 12½ x 10½ (4233/378) 350
Virgin of the Don, 14 x 12¼, 19c (4137/396) 900
Virgin of the Sign, 25¼ x 18½, 17c (4137/421) 1800
Virgin of Tichrin, 13⅜ x 10¾, 19c (4137/393) 450

Virgin of Vladimir, 11 x 9, L16c (4137/481)	6400
Virgin Pecherskaya, 12½ x 10¾, 19c (4233/211)	500
Virgin Tichvinskaya, 8¾ x 7, L19c (4233/218)	400
Virgin Vladimirskays, 8¾ x 7, L19c (4233/237)	400
Vladimir Mother of God, 12¼ x 10¾, L19c (4233/296)	300
Vladimir Mother of God, 9 x 7¼, L19c (4233/347)	250
Vladimir Mother of God, 12¼ x 10½, 19c (4233/301)	250
Vladimir Mother of God, 10½ x 8¾, ca1900 (4233/324)	1900
Vladimir Mother of God, 11 x 9, E18c (4233/243)	450
Vladimir Mother of Holy Virgin, 13½ x 11, 18c (4233/354)	250

PORCELAIN

Assorted factories

Compotes, pair, imperial, the Golden Service, gilded border of acanthus leaves, 8½, 1903 (4233/112)	400
Cup and saucer, cup portrait Michael Mikhailovich, 5' saucer, ca1831 (4186/101)	275
Cups and saucers, 5 matching, gilt foliage on royal blue ground, 5¾, ca1900 (4233/116)	100
Dish, oval, with pointed ends with Pan-Slavic strapwork, 10, ca1900 (4233/110)	200
Dish, leaf form from the Order of St. Andrew, First Called service, 10¼, ca1780 (4233/118)	3000
Easter egg, flowers, inscription 'Christ is Risen', 3, L19c (4271/73)	200
Easter egg, painted alternating panels of flower sprays, 4, ca1900 (4233/109)	300
Easter egg, painted sprays of flowers, butterflies, 3¾, ca1900 (4186/114)	100
Easter egg, painted with sprays of flowers, sky blue ground, 4, L19c (4271/84)	275
Easter egg, painted with 2 soldiers and gilt scrollwork, 3¼, L19c (4186/123)	250
Figures, pair, man and woman, entitled Kalmic and Kalmichka, 10¼ and 10 (4233/107)	375
Plaque, St. the Great Princess Olga, wearing jewelled crown and rich robes, silver frame, 10¼, ca1900 (4271/75)	725
Plaques, painted with the image of Christ, 6 7/9, ca1900 (4271/83)	75
Plate from the banquet service, with Russian Imperial Eagle, 8¾, 1825-55 (4233/117)	425
Plates, dinner set of twelve, imperial, the Golden Service, gilded border, 9½ (4233/113)	1400
Plates, dinner, pair, Meissen, circular, gilded edges, sprays of flowers, 9¾, 19c (4271/80)	800

Triptych (4137/456)

Plates (4271/88)

Basket-form dish (4137/239)

Plates, service set of twelve, center black roundel, flowering vines, 9⅜, under glaze blue mark (4186/108)	2200
Plates, soup set of twelve, Imperial, shaped borders gilded anthemion and shells, 9, ca1835 (4271/88)	*2300*
Soup plates, set of six, matching, D9⅛, ca1900 (4137/242)	350
Tazze, pair, imperial, the Golden Service, shallow bowls with gilded borders, 7½, 1907 (4233/111)	600
Yakut woman, in regional costume, furcoat and hood, 8, 1913, green factory mark (4186/92)	450

Berlin

Plate, view of Novodivichy Monastery, Cyrillic monogram, 10, L19c (4271/79)	400

Gardner

Cobbler, working on shoe, 5, L19c (4186/88)	375
Country man, dressed in white tunic, 10, L19c, res (4186/85)	250

Dancing Coachman, 9½, L19c (4186/84)	375
Debtor pleading his case, man standing at table, green cover, 5½, L19c (4186/94)	250
Milkmaid, yoek on shoulder carrying milk pails, 9⅜, L19c, res (4186/89)	175
Peasant girl, white apron over blue skirt, bare footed, 9, L19c, res (4186/86)	250
Peasant girl picking berries, seated on tree stump, 9¾, L19c, res (4186/87)	225
Peasant woman and child, woman seated on bench holding child, 6⅝, L19c (4186/95)	550
Tea and coffee set complete, gilded with foliage, oval reserves enclosing portraits, 30 pcs, ca1820 (4271/71)	3800
Teaset, fifteen pcs, all gilded, painted with flowers, tea pot 5¼, L19c, 15 pcs. (4186/112)	1000
Tug-O'-War, man and boy facing each other, straining on baton, 7, L19c (4186/93)	250
Two children ladling milk, one kneeling, 1 seated, saucer of milk, 5, L19c (4186/96)	500

Gardner Factory

Basket, Order of St. George service, both sides with Badge of Order, D9½, 1775-1800 (4137/247)	1300

Figure of a dancing country girl (4137/258)

Figure of a lady playing a spinet (4137/257)

Basket-form dish, St. George service, both sides with badge of order, L13¾, 1775-1800 (4137/239)	*1700*
Bowl, hemispherical shape with puce shading, D7¼, L19c (4137/265)	75
Bowl and stand, matching, with sprays of flowers, D9¼ (stand), L19c (4137/241)	125
Bowl and stand, 4 smaller bowls, sprays of flowers, D9⅛ (stand), L19c (4137/236)	250
Cup, saucer and jam dish, decorated with courting couples in landscape, D5¾ (saucer), L19c (4137/259)	110
Cups and saucers, set of six, reserves of fashionably dressed ladies, D5⅝ (saucers), 1850-1900 (4137/256)	350
Figure of a country man, white tunic, wearing black boots, H10⅛, L19c (4137/252)	*350*
Figure of a dancing country girl, with 1 hand on her hip, H7⅝, L19c (4137/258)	*275*
Figure of a peasant girl, with a yoke over shoulders, H9⅛, 1850-75 (4137/237)	350
Figure of a woman, dressed in long skirt, H9½, L19c (4137/253)	*275*
Figures of a farm boy and girl, bird's nest, lamb, H11, L19c (4137/262)	*800*

Figure of a woman (4137/253)

Figure of a country man (4137/252)

German

Easter egg, painted with castle within a gilded border, 3⅞, ca1900 (4186/119)	500

Imperial Factory

Charger, center view within Kremlin, inscription, 14, ca1900 (4271/76)	500
Easter egg, crowned monogram of Alexandra Feodorovna, H2½, ca1900 (4137/266)	350
Easter egg, crowned monogram of Alexandra Feodorovna, H2½, ca1900 (4137/272)	180
Easter egg, crowned monogram of Alexandra Feodorovna, H2½, ca1915 (4137/269)	300
Easter egg, crowned monogram of Nicholas II, H2½, ca1900 (4137/267)	475
Easter egg, cyrillic initials 'X B', for Christ is risen, date 1915, 2½, 1915 (4186/120)	350
Easter egg, gilded cypher Alexandra Feodorovna, 2½, ca1900 (4186/111)	250
Easter egg, gilded, crowned cypher, Anastasia Nicholaevna, 2½, ca1900-10 (4186/113)	500
Easter egg, gilded, crowned cypher Alexandra Feodorovna, 2½, ca1915 (4186/118)	400
Easter egg, gilded, side red cross other monogram, 2½, ca1900 (4271/86)	450
Easter egg, gilded, Imperial monogram of Alexander Feodorovna, 2½, ca1900 (4271/87)	400
Easter egg, gilded, Imperial monogram of Alexander Feodorovna, 2⅝, ca1900 (4271/89)	450
Easter egg, painted with country estate, within oval, 3¼, ca1900 (4186/117)	600
Easter egg, peachbloom red egg, crowned monogram M. Feodorovna, 3½, L19c (4186/116)	425
Easter egg, peachbloom, gilded, monogram of Maria Feodorovna, 4⅛, L19c (4271/74)	550
Plate, dinner, simulated basketweave, sprays of summer flowers, 10, 1762-96 (4271/72)	350
Plate, soup, border painted, black Imperial eagle, gilded borders, 9⅞, d.1883 (4271/77)	180
Plate from Guryev service, deep red border, stylized plants central roundel, 9⅝, E19c (4186/103)	200
Platter from the Elizabeth service, D12⅝, period of 1741-62 (4137/244)	1000

Kornilov

Charger, tercentenary, gilded border, entwined foliage, red ground, eagle, 18¾, ca1913 (4186/100)	1700
Dessert dishes, pair, decorated in Pan-Slavic style, D9½, St. Petersburg, ca1900 (4137/260)	775
Plate, border gilded, painted geometric designs, blue and white, 9½, ca1900 (4186/98)	100
Plate, dessert, center stylized Russian Imperial Eagle, proverb, 9⅝, ca1900 (4186/97)	210

Kuznetsov Factory

Box in the form of a ram, L6¾, L19c (4137/238)	175
Dessert dishes, pair, Chinoiserie, Chinese figures ascending a rope ladder, D9⅛, Moscow, L19c (4137/248)	200
Platter, fish and game, circular with wildfowl and fish, D12¼, Moscow, L19c (4137/249)	200

Popov Factory

Boy Gardener, spade, basket of grapes at feet, 6½, M19c (4186/90)	600
Cups and saucers, set of six, with bands of deep blue, 2¾, E19c, one saucer repaired (4186/102)	500
Figure of a lady playing a spinet, in mid-18th century French taste, H7¼, L19c (4137/257)	450
Model, of a lioness and her cub, protective attitude, seated on her haunches, 5¼, L19c (4186/104)	850
Peasant man, brown tunic and blue pants, 6, L19c (4186/91)	250
Tea set, 4 pcs, 6 cups, saucers, flower sprays, white ground, H5⅜ (tea pot), L19c (4137/263)	700
Teapot, cream mug, 4 cups, saucers, with sprays of flowers, L19c (4137/254)	425

SILVER

Album cover, silver, rectangular shape, Art Nouveau foliate cartouche, 11¼, ca1896 (4271/93)	300
Bachelor's set, silver parcel-gilt, knife, fork, spoon, teaspoon, and vodak cup, engraved, flowers, maker's mark M.S., 1891 (4186/139)	260
Baptismal horn, silver-gilt and niello, Guardian Angel and Cyrillic inscription, 4½, 1815 (4233/140)	1100
Basket, basket-weave platter, depiction of Kremlin, L16, Moscow, 1874 (4137/339)	1700
Basket, tapered circular shape, scrolling foliage, leaves, 6⅛, 1871, fine and heavy (4186/153)	900
Basket, cake, lobed oval shaped on shaped oval foot, 10¼, 1844, Stahle (4233/139)	300
Basket, silver, with fleurs de lis, swing handles, 5, ca1900, 7 ozs (4271/181)	200
Basket, sugar, circular form, engraved with flowers, landscape, 4, 1879 (4233/145)	130
Beaker, chased with birds, scrolling foliage, 3½, 1774 (4233/178)	300
Beaker, chased with eagle and basket of flowers, 3⅛, 1786 (4233/170)	350
Beaker, chased with hearts on pricked scalework ground, 3½, 1733, 2 ozs, 5 dwts (4160/69)	800
Beaker, chased with scroll, shellwork and scalework, 3⅛, 1756, Semenov (4233/190)	550
Beaker, embossed and chased with birds perched on scrolls and shells, 3¼, L18c (4186/239)	250
Beaker, tapered shape, flowersprays, drapery swags, 3¼, 1790, S. Savelev (4186/156)	400
Beaker, coronation enamel copper, Nicholas II imperial monograms, eagle, 4, 1896 (4233/33)	100
Beaker, coronation, partly gilded and niello, imperial monograms, 4⅛, 1896 (4233/133)	*1700*
Beaker, niello, with an architectural view, H2¾, Moscow, 1889 (4137/329)	250

Beaker (4271/146)

Beaker, parcel-gilt and niello, with everted molded rim, scrolling foliage, 3, 1844, 6 ozs, 10 dwts
(4160/79)   400
Beaker, parcel-gilt, foliate and drapery shield, H3½, Moscow, 1890, A. Fuld (4137/330)   300
Beaker, silver, chased with 2 oval reserves, lion and antelope, 3¼, 1735, 2 ozs (4271/167)   275
Beaker, silver, interlaced strapwork, engraved, 2⅜, 1860 (4233/200)   150
Beaker, silver and niello, flowering foliage and roundels, gilt interior, 3⅞, 1858 (4271/146)   *550*
Beaker, silver-gilt and niello, continuous landscape and with a gadroon lip, 1⅞, 1834 (4271/99) 225
Beaker, silver-gilt and niello, monument to Minin and Pozharsky, in Red Square, 4⅛, 1956
(4233/183)   1200
Beaker, silver-gilt and niello, scrolling grapevine with birds, 3¾, 1853 (4233/182)   *425*
Beaker, silver-gilt and niello, two oval reserves, monument, Alexander column, 3¾, 1835 (4271/171) 1000
Beaker, silver-gilt, with chain hung swags of fruit and flowers, 3⅜, 1779, 3 ozs, 10 dwts (4160/76) 400
Beaker, silver-gilt and niello, flared lip nielloed oval each side, 4⅜, 1839 (4186/188)   1900
Beaker, silver, parcel-gilt, interlaced strapwork and flowering vine matted ground, 3½, 1856, G.
Simonsson (4186/235)   475
Beaker, silver, partly gilded, Cyrillic inscription, 4 ball feet, 2⅞, 1881 (4271/176)   75
Beakers, pair, tapered cylindrical shape, with Napoleon Bonaparte, 5, 1908-17 (4233/124)   600
Beakers, pair, parcel-gilt, cylindrical shape, H4½, Moscow, 1872, A. Muchin (4137/311)   250
Belt, silver-gilt, seven rectangular sections, silver filigree scrolls, 31½ (4186/142)   500
Belt, Caucasian silver-gilt and niello, thirty 8 rectangular sections, foliage, openwork, 29½, L19c,
maker's mark TSE CH. (4186/140)   700
Belt, Georgian, silver and niello, interlocking panels, nielloed with foliage, 31, L19c (4186/179) 550
Belt, Georgian, silver and niello, interlocking rectangular pcs, 32½, L19c (4186/169)   425
Belt, Georgian, silver and niello, numerous shaped interlocking sections, stylized foliage, 27, L19c
(4186/154)   625
Belt, Georgian, silver-gilt and niello, interlocking sections, stylied foliage, 33, ca1885 (4186/160) 725
Belt, silver-gilt, mounted with turquoise, seven sections, filigree scrolls and domes, 31½, ca1900
(4186/149)   550
Bowl, square, rim of flowerheads, gryphons, helmets, 6¼, 1835, 10 ozs (4271/133)   300
Bowl, lobed sides, rim scroll and shellwork, gilt interior, 6¾, 1846, Schelaputin (4186/211)   200
Bowl, silver, baluster shape, engine turned, beaded borders, 3¼, L19c, 3 ozs (4271/97)   100

Beaker
(4233/182)

Box (4233/197)

Bowl, sugar, plain, circular shape, monogram below royal crown, 5⅞, 1894, mark. M.S. (4186/212) 175
Bowl, sugar, silver, bands of neo-classical ornament, openwork handles, 6, 1908-17 (4271/141) 500
Box, cigar, chased to simulate wood grain, rectangular shape, 8¼, 1896 (4233/197) *3600*
Box, circular, silver-gilt and niello, equestrian group, 3⅞, ca1815 (4271/122) 1400
Box, form loaf of bread, silver, oval, hinged cover, 5⅜, 1866, 5 ozs (4271/125) 950
Box, spice, decked with bells and pennants, 9, 1890, 4 ozs, 10 dwts (4160/77) 450
Butter dish & stand, form hooped barrel, engraved to stimulate wood grain, 6⅝, 1878, Khlebnikov
  (4186/213) 950
Caddy, tea, silver-gilt, monogram below a crown, slip-on cover, 4¼, Johan Henrik Blom, 1776-83
  (4186/194) 4250
Candlestick, pair, table, chased with grapevine, 13½ (4233/162) 275
Candlesticks, pair, table, decorated with foliage, Goldman, 14, 1874 (4233/160) 575
Casket, jewel, chased to simulate basketweave, 4 pad feet, 5¼, ca1894, maker's mark, T.G.L.
  (4186/173) 1200
Casket, silver, filigree, semi-dome cover, 4 ball feet, arches, scrollwork, 3⅜, 1835 (4186/208) 550
Caviar pail, tub shape, simulated wood grain, twist lock cover, 5½, 1864 (4186/234) 400
Censor, silver filigree, globe shape, hinged at center, 4 1/3, ca1900 (4186/184) 150
Centerpiece, silver and ruby glass, H10¼, St. Petersburg, ca1890, Gratcher, (4137/286) 550
Chalice, silver-gilt and enamel, four plaques with Christ of the Crown of Thorns, 12½, ca1910
  (4186/163) 1900
Champagne flute, cyl. body, flowering foliage, with ovals, 7⅝, 1845, mark. Ye.   (4186/215) 650
Change purse, rectangular shape, L2¾, Moscow, ca1885 (4137/294) 100
Cigar box, with simulated overall wood grain, tax bands, 5½, 1885, 14 ozs (4271/178) 300
Cigar box, fine, niello, rectangular, flowering foliage, L8⅛, Moscow, ca1900,   M.F. Sokolov
  (4137/304) 1600
Cigar case, silver and niello, top opening, compartments, foliage with birds, 4¾, ca1900 (4271/91) 500
Cigar case, silver and niello, view of St. Petersburgh, 4⅝, 1876 (4271/159) 250
Cigarette case, embossed with playful bears, woodland setting, 4¼, ca1910 (4186/228) 75
Cigarette case, embossed with woman and child, L4¼, Moscow, ca1930 (4137/333) 110
Cigarette case, hinged cover with gold monogram, 3⅝, 1879, Klingert (4233/134) 175
Cigarette case, rectangular shape, rounded sides, reeded all over, 4⅜, ca1890 (4186/151) 70
Cigarette case, rectangular, gold Russian Imperial Eagle, L4½, Moscow, ca1910 (4137/315) 200
Cigarette case, reeded all over, match compartment, laurel wreath, 4, ca1890 (4186/240) 175
Cigarette case, scroll work and geometric designs, 4¼, 1894, 5 ozs (4271/151) 150
Cigarette case, sunburst design, gilt interior, blue stone thumbpiece, 3¾, 1907-17 (4186/217) 150
Cigarette case, gold and silver, alternating panels of polished red gold and silver, 3 15/16, ca1900
  (4186/182) 375
Cigarette case, gold Samorodok, thumbpiece set with a cabochon sapphire, 3¼, ca1910
  (4271/136) 1500
Cigarette case, niello, depicting monument to Minin and Pozharzsky, L4⅛, Moscow, 1874
  (4137/338) 190
Cigarette case, niello, nielloed with rural landscape, L4½, Moscow, 1883 (4137/336) 220
Cigarette case, silver and niello, basketweave design, simulated tax bands, 4¼, ca1900 (4271/183) 190
Cigarette case, silver and niello, checker design, L3¾, Moscow, 1886 (4137/279) 300
Cigarette case, silver and niello, rounded sides, simulate basket weave, 3⅝, 1879 (4186/193) 300
Cigarette case, silver and niello, top, troika scene, 4⅛, 1908-17 (4271/182) 175

Cigarette case, silver and niello, troika scene in a snowy landscape, 4⅛, ca1890, Klingert
(4233/137)   325
Cigarette case, silver-gilt, flowering branch, red stone thumb pc, 4½, ca1910 (4186/190)   100
Coffee pot, baluster shape, girdle of flowering foliage, scroll handle, 9⅜, L19c (4186/222)   475
Coffee pot, baluster shape, matted finish, gilt interior, 6½, 1895, 16 ozs (4271/157)   300
Coffee pot, tapered circular shape, drapery & strapwork, Pan-Slavic style, 8½, 1889 (4186/203)   600
Creamer, border of basket of flowers, bone handle, gilt interior, 4¼, 1839 (4233/144)   275
Creamer, bulbous body, flower sprays and scrolls, 6¼, ca1885 (4233/179)   350
Crucifix, silver-gilt, the reverse chased with rococo ornament, 16¾, 1766, 25 ozs (4271/110)   1500
Crucifix, silver-gilt, Christ nailed to Cross, flanked by 2 Marys, 14, ca1900, Dmitri Schelaputin
(4186/168)   1000
Crucifix, silver, niello and partly gilt, the reverse repousse and chased with flowers, 13½, 1801
(4271/107)   1300
Crucifix pendant, cypher of Nicholas II, H5¼, Moscow, ca1900 (4137/320)   650
Cup, footed, silver, engraved with stylized foliage and a landscape, 5½, 1882, 3 ozs (4271/100)   125
Cup, stirrup, form of fox's head with silver ring, 6¾, 19c (4233/138)   800
Cup, vodka, chased with a band scrolling foliage, 1½, 1767, 1 oz, 5 dwts (4160/78)   275
Cup, vodka, oval, ribbed, engraved foliage, scroll handle, 1⅜, 1786, 1 oz (4271/170)   200
Cup, vodka, oval, ribbed, scroll handle, chased with arches, 1¾, 1797, 1 oz (4271/173)   200
Cup, vodka, with 2 circular mythological reserves, 2⅜, 1825, 1 oz (4271/174)   275
Cup, vodka, silver-gilt and niello, view of the Moscow Kremlin, 2⅛, 1872 (4271/175)   550
Cups, vodka, four, landscapes and foliage, engraved, 2 (4233/189)   375
Cups, vodka, four, flared rim, landscape and flower sprays, 2 (4233/174)   525
Cups, vodka, six, partly gilded, tapered circular form, engraved with plants, 2½, ca1900 (4233/135)   175
Cups, vodka, 6 trumpet-shaped foot, engraved with foliage and landscape, 2½, ca1900 (4233/184)   350
Desk set, traveling, borders of acanthus leaves, Gratcher, ca1900, (4233/154)   2100
Dish, cake, shell form, chased with flowers, 4 shell feet, 10, ca1903 (4186/189)   200
Easter Egg, engraved with waterflowers, 2½, ca1900 (4186/155)   275
Easter Egg, geometric patterns, conversion to egg cups, 2¾, ca1895 (4186/147)   375
Evening purse, mesh, hung with pendants, Moscow, ca1910 (4137/317)   225
Evening purse, silver, with gold signatures and charms, hung for chain, 4⅞, L19c (4271/154)   375
Ewer, silver mounted and cut glass, geometric designs, 17, ca1900, Gratchev (4186/223)   600
Flatware, 24 pcs, with swags of flowers, all monogrammed, ca1910, Gratchev (4186/159)   325
Flute, champagne, scrolling foliage with flower sprays, 8½, ca1815 (4233/171)   300
Holder, tea glass, openwork form, semidraped female, figures, flowers, 3⅝, ca1910 (4186/141)   250
Holder, tea glass, sides pierced, strapwork handle, 4⅜, ca1900, mark. A.I. (4186/216)   175
Holder, tea glass, silver-gilt, applied 3 horse heads, set with jewels, 4⅞, 1883, holder 8 ozs
(4271/144)   550
Holder, tea glass, silver Art Nouveau, pierced with foliage, dragonfly, 3⅞, ca1900, 8 ozs holder
(4271/156)   275
Ice bucket, barrel shape, gilt interior, H8⅝, Moscow, ca1890, V. Baladanov (4137/306)   475
Inkstand, border with berried foliage, four-toupee feet, Carl Palm, 10⅞, 1827 (4186/167)   350
Inkwell, double, gilt and niello, oval, landscapes, L4½, 1804, Shilin and Ustyug (4137/318)   2600
Jug, claret, silver mounted etched, glass, bulbous body, plain silver mount, hinged cover, 9½, 1893
(4186/424)   1800
Jug, claret, silver mounted etched glass, ca1905, 12⅛, Nemirov-Kolodkin (4186/225)   700
Jug, hot milk, imperial, silver-gilt, engraved with an imperial monogram, 6¼, 1880, Ovchinnikov
(4186/198)   1300
Jug, milk, plain pear shape, short spout, carved bone handle, 5½, 1866, Adolf Seipel (4186/196)   375

Desk set   (4233/154)

Kovsh
(4271/140)

Jug, mug, silver, plain bulbous body, gilded interior, scroll handle, 2½, 1871, 6 ozs (4271/123)	150
Jug, wine, silver mounted cut glass, tapered body with flaring base, 12¾, ca1911 (4186/226)	650
Kovsh, border with a Cyrillic inscription, body engraved, 6, 1875, 3 ozs (4271/120)	350
Kovsh, silver, flat shaped handle and oval foot, 13¾, 30 ozs (4271/168)	1400
Kovsh, silver, with foliage and hard stone cabochons, 8¼, ca1900, 11 ozs (4271/140)	*1200*
Kovsh, silver partly gilt and jeweled, oval, Pan Slavic motifs, hardstone, 7¼, E19c, 7 ozs (4271/118)	140
Kovsh, silver, Art Nouveau, chased with flowers, 5¼, 5 ozs, 1908-17 (4271/101)	400
Kovsh, Art Nouveau, repousse with waterflowers, H3⅜, Moscow, ca1910 (4137/331)	400
Lampatka, Engraved with scrolling foliage, pierced gallery, 20, ca1900, Adrian Ivanov (4186/171)	825
Lampatka, filagree, baluster shape, H18½, Moscow, 1857 (4137/283)	325
Lampatka, silver-gilt, with flowersprays and scrolls, H21½, Moscow, 1889 (4137/282)	400
Letter opener, silver mounted and ivory, handle, silver, lion and lioness, 13¼, ca1910, original fitted case (4186/174)	475
Liqueur set, silver and niello, tray, pierced gallery, baluster carafe and 6 cups, L19c, 8 pcs (4271/137)	1000
Liqueur set, tray, 6 glasses, carafe, engraved with patera and trelliswork, Tula, carafe 8½, 1882 (4186/195)	375
Medal, for the inauguration of Kronshtadt Cathedral by the Sea, 2⅝, ca1913 (4186/128)	125
Medal, in Commemoration of the Conquest in 1829 of the Fort of Erevan, 2⅝, 1839 (4186/137)	800
Mezuzah, chased with columns below crown supported by lions, 8, 1864 (4233/192)	1000
Mirror, dressing, oval shape raised on 2 shell and scroll supports, 21½, ca1894 (4233/120)	1500
Mug, frieze of eastern women, circular foot, H5¼, Moscow, 1847 (4137/326)	275
Mug, silver and cut-glass, classical figures, H3¼, St. Petersburg, 1833, Peter Madsen (4137/278)	250
Napkin ring, silver, embossed with a bogatyr, 1⅝, 1908-17 (4271/142)	100
Note pad holder, silver mounted, with a bogatyr and decorative column, 8, ca1910 (4271/139)	350
Pail, caviar, chased to simulate bark, slip-on cover, 6⅜, 1883, Khlebnikov (4233/168)	950
Pen, silver-gilt, in the form of a feather, 7½, ca1890 (4233/167)	120
Pendant, engraved 1 side with St. Mitrophan, 1¼, ca1900, Kostroma (4186/175)	200
Pitcher, syrup, silver and cut glass, cut with facets, plain silver mount, hinged cover, 7⅝, ca1900 (4233/172)	175
Pitcher, water, silver mounted cut glass, body geometric patterns, mount-handle Pan-Slavic design, 12, ca1900 (4186/224)	425
Portfolio, desk, silver mounted, cover applied with large silver plaque, 16⅞, ca1910 (4186/181)	775
Portfolio, silver mounted, and leather, mounts, enamel, armorials within laurel wreath, 13¾, ca1900 (4186/180)	600
Presentation Kovsh, imperial, rare, inscription from Alexei Mikhailovich, L9½, ca1645-76 (4137/332)	3000
Presentation vase, parcel-gilt, enamel, cylindrical, Order of St. George, H9½, ca1900 (4137/325)	1200
Punch bowl and ladle, cut-glass, Pan-Slavic style, H12½, Moscow, ca1910 (4137/305)	1100
Purse, evening, applied with gold Cyrillic signatures, Hebrew inscription, 8⅞ (4233/195)	275
Purse, evening, mesh, shaped border hung with drops, 1896-1908 (4186/197)	150
Purse, silver and niello, cartouche shape, view of a mansion, 3, L19c (4271/132)	100
Salad servers, pair, silver & bone, silver handles decorated with vine, fitted case, ca1910 (4186/221)	250
Salt cellar, baluster shaped, domed cover, 3 dolphin feet, 4⅜, 1793-95 (4186/183)	2600
Salt throne, silver-gilt, with fantastic birds and animals, H7, St. Petersburg, 1889 (4137/299)	225
Salt throne, silver, partly gilt, shaped and pierced back, 3¼, 1876 (4186/233)	300

Salver, partially gilded and niello, view of St. Basil's Cathedral in Red Square, 10⅞, 1868, fine (4186/143)	1000
Seal, desk, form of couple courting, 3⅜, 1875 (4233/161)	570
Seal box, with imperial land grant, signed by Czar Paul I, 5⅜, 1796/7 (4186/162)	3500
Snuff box, rectangular, nielloed with foliage, lozenges, L3¾, Moscow, 1790 (4137/313)	175
Snuff box, gilt and niello, equestrian figure of Peter the Great, L3¼, Moscow, 1817 (4137/335)	350
Snuff box, niello, architectural views on cover and base, L2¾, Moscow, 1847 (4137/307)	275
Snuff box, silver and niello, nielloed with architectural views, L2½, Moscow, 1853 (4137/280)	200
Snuff box, silver and niello, view of a city by a river, 3½, ca1891 (4271/105)	200
Snuff box, silver-gilt and niello, rectangular shape, checker design, 3⅛, 1873 (4271/186)	125
Spice tower, silver filigree, box and foot with filigree scrolls, 9¼, ca1900, 8 ozs (4271/180)	1600
Spoon, serving, silver-gilt, birds and foliage, terminal form of knight, 8⅞, 1875, 4 ozs (4271/124)	325
Sugar and creamer, matching, vacant reserves flanked by strapwork, 3 ball feet, 4 x 3¼, ca1890 (4186/178)	275
Sugar bowl and cover silver, circular body, engraved, oval foliate cartouches, 5¼, 1886, 10 ozs (4271/115)	225
Sweetmeat basket, oval shape, sides pierced with trellis design, L6⅝, Moscow, 1790 (4137/314)	375
Sword, short, Caucasian silver and niello, scrolling leafage, 20¾, L19c (4233/148)	450
Sword, Caucasian silver, partly gilt, niello, filigree scrolls, stylized foliage, 19⅝, L19c (4186/232)	650
Sword, Caucasian silver, partly gilt, niello, scrolling foliage, birds and insects, 23⅛, L19c (4186/231)	600
Table bell, foliate scrolls, 5 ozs, H3⅝, St. Petersburg, 1857, Joseph Nordberg (4137/289)	900
Tankard, engraved with bands of geometric decorations, 5½, 1873, Ivanov (4233/147)	500
Tankard, silver parcel-gilt, the barrel chased with grapevine, twig form handle, 6½, 1857, Carl Adolf Seipel (4186/166)	1000
Tankard, silver, partially gilded, tapered barrel, strapwork, 2 reeded bands, 6½, 1860, Nordberg (4186/218)	1000
Tankard, silver, partly gilt, cyl. barrel, Bacchanalian scene, caryatid handle, 7¾, ca1700 (4186/245)	5000
Tea and coffee set, 4 piece, silver, initials 'O.S.', tapered, gilt interiors, 6½ coffee pot, 1885, 49 ozs (4271/98)	900
Tea glass holder, basketweave design with loop handle, 3⅝, 1881 (4233/164)	300
Tea glass holder, cyl. barrel, chased continuous scene, hook, scroll handle, 4¾, 1887, Fuld (4186/237)	350
Tea glass holder, flowering vine, gilt interior, 4½, ca1900 (4186/150)	100
Tea glass holder, gilt interior, handle bird's head, 3¾, 1894, Ovchinnikov (4186/230)	250
Tea glass holder, simulated basektweave, with scene, 3⅞, 1874, Ovchinnikov (4186/236)	550
Tea set, 3 piece, chased with flowering plants, 6½, ca1900, 35 ozs (4271/161)	950
Tea tray, rectangular, niello, L16¾, Caucasian, 19c (4137/284)	1100
Teapot, chased with bands of scrolls and shells, 4⅝, 1760, Klushin (4233/175)	850
Teaspoons, set of six, niello, fiddle pattern, Moscow, 1854, M. Dmitriev (4137/298)	220
Teaspoons, set of six, silver-gilt, fig shaped bowls, of niello, 5⅜, 1864, 4 ozs (4271/148)	100
Teaspoons, set of ten, silver-gilt and niello, twist and knob stems, 5⅛, 1866, Vassili Semenov (4233/132)	300
Teaspoons, set of twelve, silver-gilt, backs of bowls engraved with flowers, 5½, 1896 (4186/238)	170
Teaspoons, set six, silver and niello, architectural views, twist stems, 5, 1874, Khlebnikov (4233/166)	400
Toilet set, 8 piece silver and cut glass, 3 boxes, bottle, 4 jars, with monogram, ca1890 (4271/92)	2500
Tray, oval, raised border, molded edge, engraved with amorials, A. Bragin, ca1890 (4186/157)	1900
Tray, silver, partly gilded, circular, key pattern border, loop handles, 17¾, 1860, 75 ozs (4271/119)	1000
Tray, tea, 2 handle, silver plated, rectangular, decorated with grapevine, 32½, L19c (4271/127)	100
Tray, two-handled, oval shape, raised oval handles, L20¼, Moscow, 1791 (4137/281)	1500
Tumbler, cup, silver-gilt and niello, lower section nielloed to simulate scales, 2, 1876, Semenor (4186/227)	550
Vase, engraved and enamel with flowers, inscription, 6¾, 2 ozs (4271/162)	175
Vase, engraved with flowers, 5, ca1900 (4233/180)	125
Vase, bud, double gourd shape, swirl fluted, 8½, 1842, Wennerstrom (4186/185)	225
Vase, silver mounted, cut glass, mount dec. with scrolling foliage, scroll handles, 12, ca1910, German control mark (4186/172)	300
Vodka cups, pair, silver-gilt, niello, H1⅞, Moscow, 1864 (4137/276)	275
Vodka cups, set of four, with rococo shellwork, H1⅜, M18c (4137/301)	225

WORKS OF ART

Assorted items

Album cover, papier mache and lacquer, a courting couple, by Lukutin, 11½ x 9⅜, L19c (4233/48)	525
Album cover, papier mache and lacquer, painted with girl leaving house, 12, L19c (4186/60)	375
Badge, gold and enamel, Imperial Order of St. Stanislaus with swords, 1⅞, ca1910 (4271/51)	800
Badge, gold and enamel, Marian Insignia of Distinction, 1⅞, ca1900 (4186/5)	550

Badge, gold and enamel, The Imperial Order of St. Anne, 2⅛, ca1900 (4186/1)   600
Badge, gold and enamel, The Imperial Order of St. Anne, 1⅝, ca1910 (4186/8)   175
Badge, gold and enamel, The Imperial Order of St. Stanislaus, 2⅛, ca1890 (4186/2)   450
Badge, gold and enamel, The Imperial Order of St. Vladimir, 1 9/16, ca1900 (4186/6)   400
Badge, gold and bronze, The Imperial Order of St. Anne, 1⅜, ca1900 (4233/20)   400
Badge, gold and enamel, The Imperial Order of St. Stanislaus, 1⅝, ca1910 (4233/22)   650
Beaker, coronation enamelled copper, for Nicholas II with Pan-Slavic strapwork, 4, 1896 (4233/28)   100
Bear, model silvered bronze, playful pose, malachite base, 6, L19c (4233/29)   275
Bishop's mitre, gold and silver threads, cyrillic inscription, 8, L19c (4186/26)   400
Bowl, ceramic silver mounted, narrow oval shape, loop handles, ram's masks, 6⅝, ca1890
(4271/21)   650
Bowl, footed, ormolu and malachite, three dolphins tail supports, 5⅜, ca1900 (4233/72)   1000
Box, circular, papier mache and lacquer, grooved sides, cover, 7⅞, L19c (4233/37)   360
Box, circular, papier mache and lacquer, cover painted with troika scene, 3⅝, L19c (4271/13)   150
Box, gold, enamel and diamond pendant, oval, Imperial monogram of Nicholas II, blue enamel, 3½
(4271/59)   14000
Box, jade, gold-mounted, circular, inscribed 'Russia' in Cyrillic, D2¼, ca1900 (4137/186)   1600
Box, papier mache and lacquer, rectangular cover, girl in woodland setting, 4, 1925 (4233/46)   75
Box, papier mache and lacquer, round, form of a barrel, painted peasant couple, 4¾, L19c (4271/19)   240
Box, papier mache and lacquer, round, slip on cover, painting, 7⅞, L19c (4271/17)   325
Box, snuff, lacquer, scene of concubine before 2 men, 3¾ (4186/54)   150
Box, stamp, palisander wood, silver, enamel mount, rectangular, hinged cover, 3¾, ca1900
(4271/30)   500
Bracelet, gold, ruby, and peridot, form as 10 gold links, 1908-17 (4271/5)   500
Brocade dalmatic, gold and silver, for the coronation of Nicholas II, ca1896 (4186/27)   450
Brooch, gold, enamel and jeweled flower, three ruby and diamond drops, 2⅛, ca1900 (4271/11)   750
Brooch, gold, enamel, and jeweled, rectangular shape, with pearls and diamond, 1⅜, ca1900
(4271/10)   2200
Brooch, Art Nouveau, gold amethyst, leaves and diamond set flowers, 1½, ca1900-10 (4271/25)   500
Bust of a young woman, gilt-metal, H11½, L19c (4137/212)   150
Bust of Nicholas II, metal, 10, L19c, (4271/1)   225
Candelabra, pair, malachite, bronze, seven light, females holding candleholders, 44, L19c (4186/29)   10000
Candelabra, pair, malachite, ormolu and crystal, square base, porcelain stems, form of fountain, 16,
19c (4186/23)   500
Candelabra, 4 light, pair, ormolu, malachite and rock crystal, 33½, L19c (4233/76)   3000
Candelabrum, 4 light, silver plate, circular base, 3 branches, 19½, ca1865, F.N. Sereb (4233/32)   250
Candle sticks, pair, cut glass and ormolu, circular domed bases, 9¼, ca1835 (4271/24)   *600*

Candle sticks
(4271/24)

Cane handle, 4-color gold, nephrite, L8¾, St. Petersburg, ca1890 (4137/217)   2000
Casket, jewel, malachite, rectangular shape, raised on 4 block feet, hinged top, 5¼, 19c (4186/19)   800
Casket, jewel, ormolu and malachite, Rectangular shape, flat hinged cover, well figured, 6½, L19c
(4186/17)   1350
Casket, jewel, walrus ivory, pinched hinged cover, with lion, birds, hounds, 5, 18c (4186/25)   750

Casket, ormolu and malachite, cover and sides veneered, with leaves, bracket feet, 10½, L19c (4233/70) — 1300

Cassolette, malachite and ormolu, hemispherical bowl, 3 slender supports, 8⅝, 19c (4233/71) — 500

Cassolettes, pair, malachite and ormolu, Louis XVI style, egg shape, 7⅞, ca1900 (4233/61) — 2100

Charger, silvered copper, center embossed with Russian Imperial Eagle, 16¾, M19c (4186/16) — 375

Clock, globe, malachite and ormolu, held aloft by 3 semidraped female figures, 30½, L19c, fine (4186/30) — 7500

Clock, mantle, malachite and ormolu, woman in chariot pulled by swan, 13, L19c (4186/24) — *6000*

Column, decorative, malachite, ormolu, surmounted by an eagle, H9⅞, 1850-75 (4137/205) — 1100

Coronation beaker, enamel, cylindrical shape with Russian Imperial Eagle, H4⅛, ca1896 (4137/209) — 175

Coronation beaker, enamel, cylindrical shape with Russian Imperial Eagle, H4⅛, ca1896 (4137/214) — 110

Cross, tercentenary Russian silver-gilt, white, blue and green enamel, 2½, ca1913 (4186/4) — 550

Cufflinks, gold and chrysoprase, mounted within gold free standing circles, ½, ca1910 (4233/27) — 500

Cufflinks, gold and enamel, circular shape, strawberry red, green stone, sunray ground, ca1900 (4233/26) — 800

Cufflinks, gold, diamond, sapphire, mounted with crowns, D9/16, St. Petersburg, ca1900 (4137/188) — *1500*

Clock (4186/24)

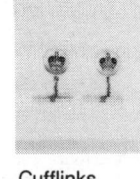

Cufflinks
(4137/188)

Desk set, silver and nephrite, with 2 bears, candlesticks, match holder, 8⅞, ca1900 (4186/58) — 3500

Dinner menu, period of Alexander II, inscribed in French, dated, H12¾, 26 August 1856 (4137/216) — 400

Dish, malachite, shallow circular bowl, veneered, well figured, 5¼, 19c (4186/18) — 400

Easter egg, glass, painted with flowerheads, 'Christ is Risen', 3⅛, L19c (4271/31) — 225

Easter egg, lacquer, with resurrection and a cathedral, 2½, L19c (4233/41) — 200

Easter egg, miniature, form chick hatching from egg, inscribed 'X.B.', ⅞, ca1900 (4271/8) — 500

Easter egg, miniature, silver, lapus lazuli, mounted with oval cabochon of lapus lazuli, ⅝, ca1900 (4271/7) — 100

Easter egg, old believers, papier mache, one half, descent into Hell, other half, Guardian Angel, 6½, L19c (4186/52) — 800

Easter egg, papier mache and lacquer, one side, Resurrection, other, with chalice, 2⅝ (4186/53) — 375

Easter egg, papier mache and lacquer, with painting, inscription, 4, L19c (4271/41) — 1100

Encrier, marble, 2 inkwells with hinged covers, pen rest, 2 candle holders, 17¼, L19c (4271/54) — 125

Flask, ceramic, form money bag, inscribed, 8, ca1900 (4271/44) — 800

Flask, silver-gilt and mother pearl, mounted with turquoise, fine and rare, 14½, ca1907, mark. P. Ye (4186/64) — 3750

Frame, photograph, gilt metal, laurel and foliage, strut back, 16, ca1900 (4271/37) — 550

Glass, wine, faceted stem, plain circular foot, Russian Imperial Eagle, 8¼, ca1915 (4186/11) — 1100

Group, F. Gural, ormolu, peasant man and woman dancing, malachite base, 5, L19c (4271/29) — 450

Inkstand, malachite and ormolu, rectangular with curved pen tray, L15¾, L19c (4137/192) — 525

Inkstand, marble, rectangular, with blotter, stamp moistener, pen holder, L14¾, L19c (4137/190) — 200

Jewel casket malachite, rectangular shape, stepped domed top on 4 paw feet, 5¾, 19c (4271/12) — 1100

Kovsh, Nephrite, silver mounted, spinach green, seahorse handle, 12½, ca1900 (4233/35) — 8000

Lamp, bouillotte, ormolu, 4 curved candle shades, Russian landscape, 30, ca1830 (4271/36) — 3600

Medallion, bronze, commemorating Crimean War, Imperial Eagle, D2⅜, Paris Mint, ca1955 (4137/218) — 90

Medallion, gold, ox and plow below an oak tree, Klepikov, A., D3½, St. Petersburg, ca1825-50 (4137/191) — 2600

Miniature, peasant couple, 4⅜, 1858 (4186/68) — 275

Table (4137/213)

Seal
(4137/184)

Urns (4137/176)

Miniature on ivory of Nicholas II, in uniform, contained in silver frame, 2, ca1909 (4271/9)	1100
Mirror, cheval, karelian birch and ormolu, four-carved sphinxes, ceramic medallions, 89, E19c, rare (4233/74)	12000
Necklace, gold and enamel, chain links enamel blue and white, pendant 2 tassles, locket, 15½, ca1920 (4271/14)	850
Obelisk, malachite and ormolu, square base with acanthus leaves, 41½, L19c (4271/18)	5000
Obelisks, pair, malachite, tapered square section on 4 balls, square bases, 10¾, L19c (4233/66)	1450
Painting, oil, of a Bishop, bearded wearing jeweled icon, 34½ x 26¾, Lukitsch Borovikovsky (4233/55)	5500
Painting, oil, portrait of Nicholas I, in military uniform, 36½ x 28¼ (4233/47)	3300
Panel, papier mache and lacquer, young peasant woman standing in a garden, 11¾, L19c (4233/30)	850
Pendant, gold and enamel, circular, flower set with cabochon ruby,¾, ca1910 (4271/52)	700
Pendant, Easter egg, miniature, enamel, gold, 8 diamonds, royal blue ground,⅝, ca1890 (4233/25)	2200
Pin, cameo, set with diamond, gold mounted, oval, female profile, edged by diamonds, 1⅝, L19c (4186/15)	2100
Plaque, bronze, Alexander II, bust, profile, on drapery mantle, 8½, ca1885 (4186/67)	425
Plaque, gilt copper, entry of Ivan IV into Kazan in 1552, 22, ca1880 (4233/42)	300
Plaque, papier mache and lacquer, troika scene cart, 3 horses, 3 girls, 11⅝, L19c (4186/61)	375
Plate, bread and salt, carved wood, Imperial Arms of Russia, 18½, ca1909 (4186/32)	550
Plate, bread and salt, presentation, carved wood, border monograms of Nicholas II, 17, ca1896 (4186/34)	900
Ring, cameo, gold mount, black enamel, carving of Catherine the Great, Ins., 1801 (4186/14)	400
Samovar, brass, almost cylindrical, H18¾, Tula, L19c (4137/185)	175
Samovar and tray, brass, cylindrical body, scroll handles with medallions, 28¼, 19c (4233/34)	200
Seal, agate, H3¾, Ekaterinburg, 19c (4137/194)	375
Seal, large, crystal, flared neck, ovoid body, oval base, H4, Ekaterinburg*, 19c (4137/179)	375
Seal, malachite, octagonal seal on giltmetal baluster, H4, Ekaterinburg*, 19c (4137/183)	300
Seal, rock crystal, Atlas holding globe, Imperial lapidary, H3⅛, Ekaterinburg, 19c (4137/184)	*1400*
Silver sculpture, woodchopper on lapis lazuli base, 6¼, ca1890 (4186/62)	4250
Silver sculpture, wounded Cossack falling from horse, 5, ca1885 (4186/59)	2100
Snuff box, gold mounted composition, circular cover with profile medallion, 3, L18c (4271/34)	600
Stickpin gold and carnelian, twist stem, egg shaped, 2¾, ca1900 (4233/23)	80
Table, circular, malachite, ormolu, supports headed by eagles, trilateral base, H29¾, 19c (4137/213)	*16000*
Table lamps, pair, malachite, columns veneered on tripod feet, with ormolu, H35½, 19c (4137/208)	*7250*
Tables, pair, malachite and ormolu, Circular tops, beveled legs, 27½, L19c (4186/31)	12000
Tzar, Kolokol, miniature, replica of a famous bell at the Kremlin, 5¼, 19c (4233/56)	125
Tzar, Kolokol, miniature, replica of bell at the Kremlin, 4⅞, 19c (4233/57)	150
Urn, nephrite and rhodenite, three slender supports, paw feet, 10½, L19c (4271/38)	1600
Urns, pair, green quartz, mounted on gray kalgan jasper plinths on square section, 10¼, 20c (4233/53)	350
Urns, pair, red jasper, ormolu-mounted, flared neck, ovoid bodies, H10, 20c (4137/176)	*500*
Water jug, cut glass and silver, tapered cylindrical shape, hinged cover, 14, ca1900 (4271/27)	1300

Watches

Hunting case, 14 karat gold, engine turned subsidiary dial with seconds, 2, by V. Gabja (4233/58)	700

Chapter 12

Oriental Miniatures and Islamic Works of Art

American interest in Oriental miniatures and Islamic works of art has grown steadily in recent years, with particular focus on Indian, Persian and Turkish miniature paintings, Oriental manuscripts and calligraphic items. The pattern of sales this past season indicates that there are both a market for this material in the United States and opportunities for the collector.

In the popular category of Indian miniatures, prices hinge on quality rather than on date or region. Persian manuscripts and early Arabic calligraphy were in demand. Collectors vied for examples by well-known scribes.

In ceramics, Kashan pieces from Persia were strong, and Arab pottery from Syria, Egypt and Turkey was also popular. Metalwork from all periods and all parts of Islam found buyers at a variety of prices. Large pieces like an engraved fifteenth-century Egyptian basin and Mamluk brass candlesticks of the same period brought high prices. On the other hand, Iranian bronze pendants, dated hundreds of years before Christ, sold for modest amounts. Beginning collectors might well consider them for investment purposes and for their decorative value.

Price swings were apparent in almost every category of Islamic art. Dozens of pieces of tenth- and eleventh-century pottery brought eight to ten times as much as others, and the same was true of textiles, which were frequently fragments of early carpets and nineteenth-century Turkish Ottoman pieces.

The uncertainty of the market is, in part, due to the recent turmoil in the Islamic world. Iranian dealers, for example, are usually the principal buyers of Qajar art, the oil paintings, enamels and laquerwork of nineteenth-century Persia; and their absence recently has resulted in prices in many areas that were lower than had been anticipated. In truth, however, the fluctuations predated the unrest; firm price levels have simply not yet been established for Indian and Islamic art.

It is a rich field, then, for the investor interested in building a new and relatively inexpensive collection. Tenth- and eleventh-century pottery and the early Iranian bronze pendants offer this kind of opportunity. Or collectors might specialize in early-nineteenth-century Indian miniatures; the humorous (in one of which tigers stalk their human hunters) or those showing Europeans tend to sell for less than the more traditional miniatures. Whatever the choice, it is clear that the growing interest in these pieces and the chances that now exist to buy them at modest prices combine to create a favorable climate for the collector. Certainly there is every reason to believe that the market for Indian and Islamic art will show substantial gains in the future.

CALLIGRAPHY AND ILLUMINATION

Arabic

Qur'an leaf, kufic, 5 lines of script, on vellum, 5⅜ x 7⅞, def, 9-10c (4197/191) $1800

Bihari

Qur'an leaf, fifteen lines of Bihari script, 14⅜ x 7¾, stains, framed, 18c (4264/166)   250
Qur'an leaf, fifteen lines of Bihari script, 19 x 11, rep, stains, 18c (4264/167)   175

Kufic

Kufic Qur'an leaf, fourteen lines of kufic script, 7⅜ x 4½, rep, framed, 9/10c (4264/160)   300
Kufic Qur'an leaf, sixteen lines of kufic script, red diacritics, 7⅝ x 10⅛, tear, 9/10c (4264/159)   600
Large Kufic Qur'an leaf, sixteen lines of kufic script, 13¼ x 11¾, stains, 9/10c (4264/161)   850

Persia

Calligraphy, Nasta'liq, 4 diagonal lines of gold script, 4⅞ x 2½, rub, framed, E16c (4197/202)   950

Tabriz

Calligraphy, Nasta'liq, by Shah Mahmud al Nishapuri, 6⅞ x 2¾, framed, L16c (4197/203)   2800

INDIAN MINIATURES

Amber

A formal garden with fountains, 2 pairs of ascetics, panel of nagri script, 9½ x 7¾, imp, ca1760
(4197/60)   250
The lustration of a holy man, on a stool, pavilion behind, 9 x 15, fla, disc, ca1740 (4197/59)   800

Antarda

4 devotees worshipping Brahma, Krishna to the left, nagri inscription, 7⅝ x 7¼, disc, ca1760
(4197/62)   300

Bandralta

A seated portrait of Raja Indra Dev of Bandralta, holds the mouthpiece of a hookah, 7⅝ x 10¼,
fraying, ca1750 (4264/126)   3750

Basohli

A maiden standing upon a gold stool, a stork nearby, 4¾ x 2¼, disc, ca1720-30 (4197/173)   600
Krishna addresses Radha, yellow ground, red border, 8¾ x 6¾, rub, M18c (4264/125)   *2750*
Varaha Avatar, he walks upon a river, one foot on a demon, 5¼ x 3, L17c (4264/123)   200

Bikaner

A lady holding a vase of flowers, gold turban upon her head, on a green ground, 5⅞ x 3¾, red
border, E18c (4264/105)   650
A lady holding a vase of flowers, wearing orange bodice, 6⅛ x 4⅛, rub, rep, ca1700 (4197/117)   600
A lady smoking a hookah, on a terrace, a green shawl on her shoulders, 7¼ x 4⅝, rub, E18c
(4264/108)   450
A raja at a balcony, 3 ladies in attendance, 11⅞ x 7⅜, mounted, L18c (4197/119)   400
A sad lady with a garland, dressed in red and green on a green ground, 3⅜ x 6¼, red border,
ca1720 (4264/103)   350
An illustration to the Rasikapriya, Ruinuddin*, silver flecked orange border, 7⅜ x 5⅛, ca1685
(4264/101)   4250
Durga attacking the buffalo demon, she astride a yellow tiger, red border, 7 x 5¼, 1850
(4197/127)   850
Durga attacking the buffalo demon, she pulls his tongue, 8⅛ x 5⅝, ca1800 (4197/123)   800
Durga fighting the buffalo demon, seated on lion, green ground, 7¾ x 4⅞, flaking, M19c
(4264/111)   600
Kamod Ragini, girl kneels beside a pond, 4 6/8 x 6, framed, E18c (4264/104)   700
Khambhavati Ragini, Brahma cross-legged on a terrace, 7¾ x 5½, rub, ca1800 (4197/124)   300
Krishna kneels upon a lotus flower, 2 gopis, white cows on riverbank, 8⅛ x 6⅛, rub, imp, E19c
(4197/126)   400
Krishna standing upon a lotus flower, he plays a flute, 7⅝ x 5⅝, disc, worn, E19c (4197/125)   425
Maidservant stands, arms outstretched, before her mistress, pink border, 7⅝ x 5, ca1760-80
(4197/122)   1400

Bikaner*

The figure of Shiva, on a tiger skin, the Ganges springing from his forehead, 3¾ x 5⅞, L17c (4264/106) — 250

Bilaspur

Krishna standing behind herd of cattle, on light green ground, 7⅞ x 5⅜, rub, ca1760-70 (4197/174) — 900

Bundi

A lady pouring a cup of wine, upon a terrace, 8⅛ x 7, fla, retouch, ca1770-80 (4197/148) — 350
A man shooting a lion, an attendant and a horse wait behind, 6⅜ x 4¾, L18c (4264/94) — 400
A Raji holding a lotus blossom in one hand, facing a maiden, weapons before him, 11⅝ x 9⅛, dis, E19c (4264/96) — 250
Camel drinks from a pool, with 3 maidens, 11¼ x 7⅞, mount, ca1760 (4197/139) — 375
Cowgirls enact Krishna's life, standing in groups enacting incidents, 15½ x 7¾, crease, disc, M18c (4197/138) — 900
Desakahya Ragini, with 2 acrobats, 6¾ x 4½, worn, ca1740 (4197/140) — 300
Krishna and Radha seated, within a bower, 10 x 6⅛, sta, repaint, ca1760 (4197/142) — 1100
Krishna and Radha seated in forest, river in foreground, 9¾ x 6¼, sta, ca1760 (4197/146) — 4750
Krishna kneeling before Radha, beside a riverbank with hands outspread, 9¾ x 6¼, sta, repaint, ca1760 (4197/145) — 4500
Malkos Raga, a prince and his lady seated on a stool, 7⅜ x 4⅜, ca1680, rub (4264/90) — 2750
Portrait of a Mughal emperor, holding a sword and a flywhisk, 7¾ x 5⅞, M18c, flaking (4264/92) — 500
Radha kneels before Krishna, upon a white platform, dense vegetation, 9¾ x 6¼, retouch, ca1760 (4197/143) — 5500
Radha standing before Krishna, halo about his head, 9¾ x 6¼, sta, frame, ca1760 (4197/144) — 5000
Two maidens surprised whilst bathing, prince appearing from behind a hill, 8¾ x 6¼, rub, L18c (4264/93) — 1200
Vibhasa Ragini, lady seated in prince's arms, 7 x 4⅝, rub, ca1700 (4197/135) — 950

Krishna addresses Radha
(4264/125)

3 Maidens seated beside a pool, partially clad, 7¾ x 5, sta, rub, ca1760 (4197/147) — 500
5 gopis in search of Krishna, from a set, 10 x 6¼, sta, retouch, ca1760 (4197/141) — 4250

Calcutta

Green hummingbird, inscribed in English, 8½ x 7½, framed, E19c (4197/16) — 170
Hummingbird, uncolored ground, inscribed in English, 8¾ x 9, framed, E19c (4197/15) — 170

Central India

A princess making a garland in a garden, a pool with a fountain and maidservants behind, 14¼ x 10, stain, L18c (4264/45) — 750
A ruler receiving two princes, seated on a throne, red border with decoration, 10 x 6, def, L18c (4264/46) — 250
An ascetic sits cross-legged, sits within a green oval line, 9¼ x 6½, worn, L18c (4264/44) — 350
Bakhtawar Singh hunting pig, nagri inscription on reverse, 7 x 9¾, rep, ca1800 (4197/70) — 300
Bangal Ragini, a young maiden with a tamed tiger by her side, 5½ x 9, rub, 18c (4264/49) — 250
Bhairava Ragini, yellow panel with six lines of nagri script, 7½ x 5⅞, framed, L18c (4264/47) — 400

Kamoda Ragini, lady before a shrine, 9 x 7½, fla, ca1760 (4197/63)   450
Portrait of the Raja of Bundelkhand, a green halo about his head, 9½ x 6½, L19c (4264/50)   275
Todi Ragini, lady beneath a tree, 9 x 5⅞, rub, L18c (4197/68)   750

Datia

A prince in conversation with a lady, yellow panel with nagri script, 11 x 7, fla, ca1780 (4197/66)   400
Krishna and the river demon, white nagri inscriptions above the figures, 9 1/3 x 16, L18c (4264/48)   400
Krishna in conversation with a king, nagri script above figures, 6¾ x 6⅞, L18c (4197/67)   250
Krishna kneeling upon a terrace, messenger before him, 7 x 7⅝, ca1770 (4197/64)   300

Deccan

A blossoming shrub, on uncolored ground with orange border, 12 x 7½, dis, M18c (4264/25)   1200
A lady kneeling beside a bookstand, on a golden crutch, nasta'lig script, 4½ x 2⅝, E19c (4197/50)   125
A lady standing alone, against a tree, 6¼ x 6½, crease, frame, ca1760 (4197/46)   *800*
A prince hawking, astride his mount, a falcon upon his hand, 6⅜ x 5¼, mounted, L18c (4264/34)   1400
A young lady smoking a hookah, dressed in robes of green, red and gold, 9¼ x 5½, def, E18c (4264/23)   50
Basant Ragini, Ragamala series, a lord celebrates a holy festival, 9¼ x 5¾, L18c (4264/28)   1500
Desakh Ragini, Ragamala series, three acrobats on maroon ground, 9¼ x 5¾, L18c (4264/32)   900
Devgandhar Ragini, Ragamala series, mounted on an album page with gilt border, 9¼ x 5¾, L18c (4264/33)   1500
Dipak Ragini, Ragamala series, a seated couple listens to musicians, 9¼ x 5¾, sta, L18c (4264/27)   650
Gavri Ragini, holding pink blossoms, 8¾ x 5⅝, framed, ca1780 (4197/48)   *1100*

Gavri Ragini
(4197/48)

A lady standing
alone (4197/46)

Portrait of a nobleman
(4197/53)

Radha turning away from
Krishna (4264/153)

Hindola Ragini, a prince and his lady on a gold swing, 8⅛ x 4¼, def, E18c (4264/22)   400
Kanada Ragini, soldiers, white elephant before him, 8¾ x 5⅝, ca1780 (4197/49)   1000
Khambavati Ragini, Ragamala series, Brahma sits cross-legged on a terrace, 9¼ x 5¾, L18c (4264/31)   750
Lalit Ragini, Ragamala series, a seated lord greets a lady, 9¼ x 5¾, L18c (4264/29)   650
Malkos Ragini, Ragamala series, two ladies discourse on a terrace, 9¼ x 5¾, L18c (4264/30)   550
Portrait of a nobleman, holding the mouthpiece of a hookah, 13 x 9⅜, fla, ca1870 (4197/53)   *5000*
Rustam holding an opponent, with green landscape, nasta'liq script, 10¼ x 8, crease, rub, E19c (4197/51)   225

Seated portrait of Timur, a green halo about his head, 6⅜ x 3⅝, E19c (4264/36) — 100
Sohini Ragini, Ragamala series, a lady in a meadow with peacocks, trees, ducks, 9¼ x 5¾, L18c
(4264/26) — 900

Delhi

A lady presenting a garland of flowers, in a howdah, 12 x 9, framed, L18c (4197/42) — 2100
A lady taking refreshment, seated in a garden, 11⅜ x 8⅛, res, E19c (4264/20) — 400
A prince receiving refreshment at a well, three lines of Nagri script at top, 9⅞ x 7, def, L18c
(4264/19) — 550
Figure of a half-beast half-man, the figure walking on a green ground, 3 x 3, rub, E19c (4264/21) — 150
Firoz shah's cotlah, path in foreground, 4¾ x 6¾, mounted, M19c (4197/21) — 125

Devgarh

A faqir, beneath a tree, sitting, 6⅝ x 5⅝, ca1800 (4197/134) — 150

Garwhal

A lady smoking a hookah, 3 maidservants, 8¾ x 6⅝, rub, M19c (4197/175) — 1200
An illustration to the Mahabharta, white nagri inscriptions, 12⅛ x 17, ca1800 (4197/180) — 4750
An illustration to the Ramayana, depicting the holy family, Brahma, Shiva, Parvati, 9 x 13⅜,
mounted, E19c (4264/128) — 2500
An illustration to the Ramayana, monkey prince overcomes a demon, 11¼ x 16½, framed, ca1850
(4264/129) — 1000

Gujerat

A view of the pantheon in Rome, some color, 8½ x 15⅛, dis, E19c (4264/1) — 250
Krishna dancing in the forest, musicians, yellow ground, 6 x 4, imp, L17c (4197/1) — 160

Guler

Krishna prostrates himself before Radha, she against a gold bolster, 8¾ x 12, ca1870 (4197/178) — 400

Hindur

Rama shoots 7 trees with 1 arrow, monkey-king kneeling before him, 8 x 11⅞, retouch, ca1820
(4197/177) — 1800
Vishvamitra conducts Rama and Lakshmana, to the hermitage of Guatama, folio 22, 17 x 23¾, red
border, M19c (4264/148) — 700

Jaipur

A kneeling man stabs a lady, soldiers in foreground, 6¾ x 9¼, E19c (4197/130) — 250
A lady kneeling upon a terrace, one maidservant before her, one to her right, 5⅛ x 7⅝, 19c
(4264/59) — 150
A princely hunting party, two mounted noblemen with falcons, 11⅜ x 8¾, colored border, L19c
(4264/61) — 250
A princess smoking a hookah at night, kneeling on gold throne, 9¾ x 6¾, rub, disc, L18c
(4197/129) — 1200
Ancestral portrait, succeeding rulers of the House of Jaipur, 17⅞ x 13½, mounted, ca1810
(4197/128) — 3100
Krishna as Vishnu, with gopis, Radha, 16½ x 10¼, def, E19c (4197/131) — 650
The child Krishna, seated naked on a couch, gold border, 4⅞ x 4, L18c (4264/85) — 250

Jodhpur

Vasudeva carrying Krishna, 10 avatars of Vishnu at top, 9¼ x 22, creased, framed, L19c
(4197/111) — 175

Kalighat

Krishna overcoming the stork-demon, on uncolored ground, 16 x 10½, 19c (4264/4) — 325
Siva and Parvati face half-left, holding Ganesa in his arms, 8¾ x 61/6, L19c (4264/7) — 175
Two youths holding a bow and arrow, couple in dispute nearby, 17 x 11, dis, L19c (4264/5) — 150

Kangra

A lady casting off her jewelry, beside the bank of a river, in the moonlight, 7¾ x 5, fla, ca1800
(4197/189) — 3750
A lady proffering 3 blades of grass, young ascetic before her, 7⅝ x 5½, worn, ca1800 (4197/190) — 5250
A prince and his mistress, lie entwined upon a terrace, 7½ x 4⅝, def, E19c (4197/176) — 1200
Krishna embracing Radha, oval, blue spandrels, gilt scrolling, 6⅝ x 4¾, E19c (4264/155) — 2750
Radha turning away from Krishna, two maidservants stand in conversation in front, 9⅝ x 12, E19c
(4264/153) — *1600*

A raja hunting wild boar (4197/99)

Two European ladies in conversation (4264/99)

Kishangarh

A horse facing to the right, green saddle, uncolored ground, 9 x 12⅜, mounted, E19c (4197/115)   500
Portrait of a maiden, some color, flecked, 11¾ x 8¾, ca1830 (4264/119)   1500
Portrait of an ugly lady, drawing with some color, uncolored ground, 9½ x 8½, E19c (4197/116)   150
Portrait of Raja Bir Singh, in white jama, pearl necklace, 8 x 3½, rub, ca1760 (4197/113)   800
Radha and Krishna among herd of cows, river in foreground, 9 x 6, imp, ca1820 (4197/121)   4000
The view from a palace, pool, flanked by two arcades, 13⅜ x 16¾, frayed, E19c (4264/120)   850

Kotah

A blue-skinned prince receives two soldiers, forested landscape, yellow panel at top, 10¼ x 7, rub, M18c (4264/98)   500
A chained elephant, on uncolored ground, 10¼ x 13¼, M18c (4197/154)   500
A portrait of Ram Singh II hunting tigers, seated in a howdah upon an elephant, 12 x 16¼, flaking, L19c (4264/102)   1000
A raja wounding a wild boar, astride a rearing horse, 8 x 7, in case, 19c (4197/166)   500
Bhairava Raga, Shiva seated on a lotus, 8 x 4½, fla, worn, M18c (4197/159)   700
Drawing of Ram Singh II hunting lion, amongst a wooded landscape, 9⅞ x 15, def, mount, 19c (4197/165)   2100
Patmanjari Ragini, a girl kneels before her mistress, 7½ x 5¾, fla, mount, ca1690 (4197/153)   300
Ram Singh hunting a tiger, hilly yellow landscape, 8½ x 11⅜, fla, M19c (4197/155)   *1100*
Tigers in pursuit of their hunters, seven tigers after four hunters, with color, 13½ x 21⅝, stain, E19c (4264/100)   1900
Two European ladies in conversation, upon a terrace, palace and trees in background, 9⅞ x 6¼, M18c (4264/99)   *800*
Yellow cock, on uncolored ground, nagri inscription above, 6¾ x 8½, E19c (4197/157)   100

Kulu

Rama shoots a crescent tipped arrow at Ravana, illustration from the Ramayana, 7¼ x 10⅞, E18c (4264/146)   5000

Kulu*

A blue-skinned prince being rebuked by a lady, green ground, orange border, 6¾ x 4¼, crease, flaked, L18c (4264/145)   800

Lucknow

A bungalow, steward with hookah, 5¾ x 10¾, framed E19c (4197/7)   140
A man with facial markings, in landscape, 6¾ x 5, mounted, ca1815 (4197/11)   160
The celebration of a holy festival, a ruler amongst a circle of ladies, 10¾ x 7⅞, rub, L18c (4264/18)   325

Malpura

Madhumadavi Ragini, a lady rushes into a palace from a storm, 11 x 8½, M18c (4264/54)   300

A lady cajoling Krishna
(4264/41)

Ram Singh hunting a tiger (4197/155)

Malwa

A lady cajoling Krishna, yellow panel at top and bottom, 7¾ x 6⅛, fla, L17c (4264/41)	*650*
A prince grasping his mistress, standing naked in a chamber, 7 x 5½, imp, ca1660 (4197/54)	1000
A young ascetic with long hair, sitting within a pavilion holding a text, 9¼ x 6½, worn, L17c (4264/42)	600
Episodes from the visit of Krishna, nagri text on reverse, 6⅞ x 10½, L17c (4197/55)	1000
Gunakari Ragini, blue ground, yellow panel, nagri script, 6¼ x 5¼, rub, ca1680 (4197/57)	500
Lalit Ragini, a prince and his mistress in a chamber, 8½ x 6¼, framed, M17c (4264/40)	475
Set Mallar Ragini, 2 panels, orange border, 11½ x 10, imp, ca1680 (4197/56)	800
Vamana Avatar, a crowned prince and his consort on a throne, 7⅛ x 5⅝, dis, L17c (4264/43)	150

Mandi

A Prince and his mistress, with fingers entwined, beneath a tree, 8⅛ x 4½, rub, L18c (4197/183)	375
Hanuman makes obeisance to a king, attendant with a morchal behind, 6⅞ x 4½, def, L18c (4264/122)	200
Portrait of Raja Sukma Sen, he kneels, holding a falcon, 8⅛ x 5⅞, crease, ca1785 (4197/182)	450
Varaha Avatar, Vishnu standing in a lilypond, 4⅞ x 7⅛, fla, ca1760 (4197/179)	300

Mankot

Shiva and Paruati with a female companion, drawing, some color, 8½ x 12⅛, crease, flaked, ca1720 (4264/152)	1600

Marwar

A raja hunting wild boar, astride brown mount, 7⅝ x 10⅞, imp, ca1800 (4197/99)	*325*

Mewar

A blue skinned prince before a lady, yellow panel with nagri inscriptions, 7¼ x 5⅞, trim, def, ca1680 (4197/79)	350
A lady flying a kite, within a courtyard, 10¾ x 7½, disc, mounted, ca1780 (4197/83)	300
A Maharaja entertained in a garden, seated with his consort on a terrace, 14 x 9⅞, ca1825, res (4264/87)	800
A Raja holding a flywhisk, dressed in a white jama on a green ground, 8¾ x 6, red border, ca1810 (4264/71)	250
A Raja in procession, smoking a hookah borne by an attendant, 18 x 14⅞, fray, E19c (4264/76)	350
A Raja riding with attendants, seated on a horse, attendants walk on foot, 17 x 14⅛, ca1800 (4264/73)	400
A view of the palace, white stone, blue pillars, 20 x 15¼, imp, framed, ca1780 (4197/84)	425
An equestrian portrait, a groom upon a brown stallion on a green ground, 9¼ x 8⅝, mounted, L18c (4264/66)	550
An illustration to a Rasikapriya, a variety of scenes depicting Krishna and Radha, 13 x 9⅝, red border (4264/67)	800

An illustration to the Siva Sakti, 2 devotee before an image of Krishna, 8½ x 8⅛, rep, 1780
    (4197/81)   350
Equestrian portrait, dappled white stallion, red border, 7⅞ x 9⅛, L18c (4197/87)   250
Gauri Ragini, with 2 peacoc. ᴊ, 8⅜ x 6⅝, rub, L18c (4197/86)   275
Portrait of a ruler, holding flower, sword, 8¾ x 6¼, fla, ca1780 (4197/82)   100
Standing portrait of Arsingh-Ji, by the artist Nath-Ji, 8½ x 5¾, def, L19c (4264/84)   250
Two Rajas in conversation, one offers pan, a halo about his head, 8 x 4⅞, red border, ca1800
    (4264/72)   225
Vishnu seated upon a lotus, he wears a yellow dhoti, 7¾ x 15, ca1720 (4197/80)   100

Mughal

A blue skinned prince clubbing a tiger, Krishna*, 11¾ x 9½, imp, E17c (4197/40)   275
A lady with a burning lamp, dressed in red bodice and skirt, 8¾ x 7⅛, def, L18c (4264/13)   225
A lady, possibly Rupmati, upon a horse, an album page, in frame, 7 x 11½, E19c (4264/14)   200
A leaf from the 'Chester Beatty' Tutinama, with nasta' liq script, 4 x 4¼, ca1580 (4197/36)   6000
A prince making love, figures in intimate embrace, 7 x 5⅛, def, L17c (4264/8)   300
A ruler sits astride an elephant, provincial, 6⅛ x 8⅞, flaking, M17c (4264/11)   3000
A youth asleep in the lap of an angel, white jama, red trousers, 7¾ x 4⅜, fla, ca1600 (4197/35)   2300
An elephant with mahout, seated astride his neck, 3⅝ x 3⅝, trim, disc, ca1650 (4197/38)   1100
Drawing of a lion, a soldier slicing the lion with his sword, 9 x 5, L17c (4264/9)   900
Portrait of a child, pale blue ground, panel of script, 5½ x 3⅛, ca162C 30 (4197/39)   500
Portrait of a courtier facing right, holding sword, green ground, 7 x 4¼, rub, rep, mounted, ca1620
    (4197/37)   325

Murshihabad

A mendicant, in a landscape, 9½ x 7½, framed, L18c (4197/5)   120

Nepal

A couple making love upon a terrace, red border, erotic, 17¾ x 14, creased, L19c (4197/24)   500

North India

An illustration from a series, Rajput Bhagauata Purana, 6⅞ x 9, fla, imp, ca1540 (4197/73)   3000

Orissa

Palm leaf painting, Hanuman beneath arch, each 1¾ x 8, mounted, L18c (4197/4)   150

Oudh

A lady visiting a Yogini at night, sitting within a pavilion with a quest, 9 x 6¼, L18c (4264/16)   600

Pahari

A lady seated upon a European-style chair, maidservant before and behind her, 8⅜ x 6¼, pink
    border, L19c (4264/137)   800
A Prince seated within a pavilion, reading a letter, 7 x 11, L19c (4197/185)   800
A Raja dressed in a green jama, kneeling, holding the mouthpiece of a hookah, 6⅞ x 6⅜, rub, E19c
    (4264/132)   450
A ruler leaning against a purple bolster, attendant with a whisk behind, 7⅛ x 5⅜, red and blue
    border, M19c (4264/136)   350
An illustration to the Bhagavata Purana, an immolation, 13¾ x 19⅝, M19c (4264/141)   1500
Ganfsh seated upon a lotus, a snake coiled around him, blue ground, 9⅛ x 7⅜, yellow border, E19c
    (4264/131)   350
Lady seated within a pavilion, oval, decorated yellow spadrels, 8⅜ x 5½, rub, ca1830 (4264/134)   *700*
Saraswati worshiped by Brahma, she, seated cross-legged upon a lotus, 5⅞ x 10⅜, crease, M18c
    (4264/130)   1100
Vishnu and his consort Lakshmi, seated upon a lotus, 7⅝ x 3⅝, def, L19c (4197/172)   250

Raghogarh

A Raja on horseback, in white jama mauve turban, 9 x 6¼, fla, M18c (4264/115)   550
An Abyssinian on horse, dressed in a coat of chain-mail, 9⅞ x 7⅜, rubbed, 18c (4264/116)   1450

Raghogarh*

Madhumadaviragini, lady rushes into a pavilion from the rain, 6⅞ x 4¾, rub, ca1700 (4264/114)   450

Rajasthan

A lady wearing a diaphanous sari, wearing jewelry, 9⅞ x 6, rub, worn, 18c (4197/77)   375
A prince kneeling before his mistress, she lies upon a patterned orange rug, 5¾ x 4½, def, L18c
    (4264/55)   80
Bazbahadur and Rupmati, seated together on a galloping mount, 6⅝ x 10⅛, L18c (4264/52)   750
Ganesh attended by 2 ladies, he sits cross-legged beneath an umbrella, 8⅜ x 9, imp, mounted, 19c
    (4197/76)   100

Portrait of Maharaja Sri Kesu Das-ji, kneels against a bolster, 14 x 16⅝, imp, L18c (4197/74)   475
2 princes stand before a city gate, with 2 chariots, 10⅜ x 8⅛, rub, M18c (4197/95)   100

Ratlam

Portrait of 2 rajas, on uncolored ground, 8 x 6¼, ca1840 (4197/69)   250

Sawar

Drawing of an elephant, chains about two legs, on uncolored ground, 13¼ x 18¼, rep, stains, E18c (4264/117)   1200

Sirohi

A nobleman making love, within a pavilion, erotic, 6¼ x 6½, worn, E18c (4197/92)   250
An illustration from a Devimahatmya manuscript, Devi on tiger, warriors in combat, 4 4/8 x 6, def, L17c (4264/112)   500
Asavari Ragini, a maiden, cobra on her wrist, 8 x 6, with border, ca1660-70 (4197/89)   1500
Bilawal Ragini, maiden kneels on a stool, 6½ x 4½, ca1670 (4197/90)   700
Dhanasri Ragini, lady draws a portrait of her lover, 11 x 8 with border, ca1680-90 (4197/91)   1200

South India

A portrait of Raja Wadiyar III, richly dressed, a blossom in one hand, 18 x 14½, stain, L19c (4264/38)   *650*

Lady seated
within a pavilion
(4264/134)

A portrait of Raja
Wadiyar III
(4264/38)

Sultanate

Faridun receiving a prisoner, rocky landscape, with text, 4⅞ x 4¾, M16c (4197/34)   400

Tanjore

A bangle seller, in a landscape with wife, 11 x 8⅛, imp, mounted, ca1800-20 (4197/8)   40
The figure of Rama, in a gold costume, 10¼ x 7, fla, 18c (4197/2)   125

Udaipur

Desakh Ragini, a warrior and two acrobats watched by a Raja, 9⅛ x 8, split, L18c (4264/68)   450

Uniara

Bhairavi Ragini, lady kneeling before a shrine, 9½ x 6¼, rub, ca1780 (4197/65)   300

West Bengal

A seated brahma, Bankura district, in the gesture of exposition, 8⅝ x 7, def, L19c (4264/3)   300

ISLAMIC CERAMICS

Assorted items

Bowl, lustre, carinated bowl, feathered guilloche band, diam. 6½, 12/13c A.D. (4123/262)   200
Bowl, lustre-painted, human central motif, diam. 19⅞, 13c A.D. (4123/237)   900
Bowl, lustre-painted, rounded sides, central foliate arabesque decor, diam. 7, 13c A.D. (4123/260)   325

Bowl, lustre-painted, carinated sides, inscription, diam. 8⅜, 13c A.D. (4123/254) 850
Bowl, lustre-painted, carinated sides, seated prince, diam. 8¾, 12/13c A.D. (4123/253) 1800
Bowl, lustre-painted, convex sides, central figures, geometric design, diam. 19¾, 13c A.D. (4123/255) 2000
Bowl, lustre-painted, large, convex sides, peacock, diam. 13½, 13c A.D. (4123/251) 3300
Bowl, minai, fragmentary, foliate, interior design, diam. 8, 13c A.D. (4123/246) 400
Bowl, minai, painted, molded, interior relief, diam. 8⅛, 13c A.D. (4123/248) 325
Bowl, minai, repainted interior scene of figures, diam. 8⅛, 13c A.D. (4123/247) 400
Bowl, minai, rounded body, interior painted equestrians, diam. 7⅞, 13c A.D. (4123/245) *2100*
Bowl, polychrome, bird painted incised interior, diam. 11¼, 13c A.D. (4123/250) 500
Bowl, polychrome, painted, incised interior, diam. 8, 13c A.D. (4123/249) 550
Bowl, turquoise glaze, flaring sides, painted interior, diam. 8¼, 12c A.D. (4123/241) 1000
Bowl, turquoise glaze, foliate ground, reserved tondo, diam. 8, 12c A.D. (4123/242) *900*
Bowl, turquoise glaze, money bowl with relief frieze, diam. 8, 13c A.D. (4123/243) 750
Bowl, white-glazed, thin convex sides, incised underglaze interior, diam. 7½, 12c A.D. (4123/244) 275
Bronze, bowl, shallow, chased, engraved foliate interior, diam. 12¼, 12c A.D. (4123/270) 1800
Bronze, dove, hollow cast, spouted, pendant loop, length 8¼, 12/13c A.D. (4123/269) 325
Bronze, incense burner, square, zoomorphic feet, 9¼, 12/13c A.D. (4123/275) 200
Bronze, lamp, spouted lamp, pedestal foot, 7⅛, 12/13c A.D. (4123/274) 300
Bronze, stand, openwork base, tripod paw feet, 26¾, 12/13c A.D. (4123/273) 275
Bronze, stand, tripod, lobed base, 1 26½, 12/13c A.D. (4123/271) 900
Candlestick, brass, tapering concave drum, 15½, 13/14c A.D. (4123/277) 4300
Dish, lustre-painted, large convex, with birds, diam. 18½, 13c A.D. (4123/256) 700
Dish, lustre-painted, convex sides, arabesque roundel, diam. 12½, 13c A.D. (4123/259) 400
Dish, lustre-painted, rounded sides, arabesque roundel, diam. 14¾, 13c A.D. (4123/258) 350
Dish, polychrome, fragmentary, Chinese Eddy pattern, diam. 11¼, 17c A.D. (4123/268) 125
Dish, polychrome, Chinese Eddy pattern, diam. 10, 17c A.D. (4123/267) *650*
Ewer, turquoise glaze, beaked spout, flat handle, 13¼, 13c A.D. (4123/232) 850
Ewer, turquoise glaze, globular body, cylindrical spout, indentations, 7, 11/12c A.D. (4123/236) 350
Ewer, turquoise glaze, pyriform, flat handle, head form spout, H7¼, ca12/13c (4123/234) 275
Ewer, turquoise glaze, pyriform, pinched mouth, handle, 7⅝, 12/13c A.D. (4123/233) 900
Ewer, turquoise glaze, cock's head, Kufic inscription, 9½, 13c A.D. (4123/228) 1500
Jar, aquamarine-glazed, Egypt, floral motifs, 10, 18/19c (4159/43) 130
Jug, turquoise glaze, ovoid body, cylindrical neck, 11½, 13c (4123/231) 900
Jug, white-ware, pear-shaped, splay foot, finely carved design, 6, 12c A.D. (4123/225) 475
Jug, white-ware, pyriform body, underglaze black arabesques, 6¾, 13c A.D. (4123/240) 225
Koran stand, wood, inlaid borders, tortoise shell, 11¾, 19c A.D. (4123/281) 225
Scent flask, hard stone, Ottoman, pale green Arab inscription, Eros design, 3⅛, AH1309 (1892 A.D.) (4123/282) 1800
Vase, enameled, Qajar, ovoid form, enameled medallions, 19¼, 19c A.D. (4123/278) 6800
Vase, turquoise glaze, globular body, cup mouth, carved frieze relief, (4123/230) 750
Vessel, polychrome, globular vessel, painted foliation, 7¾, 17c A.D. (4123/266) 600

Damascus

Tile, polychrome, green and blue medallions, scrolling foliage, 9¾ x 9¾, framed, M16c (4264/265) 200
Tiles, panel of, composed of twelve tiles, 9½ x 9¼ each, 2 fragmentary, M16c (4264/266) 850

Garrus

Bowl, champleve, convex sides, 7¾, 12c (4264/259) 1100
Bowl, green-glaze champleve, green-glaze, depicting an eagle, 6½, 12c (4264/231) 325

Glass

Beaker, colorless, cylindrical cup applied foot, iridescent, 4⅛, 13/14c A.D. (4123/128) 175
Rosewater sprinkler, aubergine, twin handles, marvered opaque feather pattern, 3½, 13c A.D. (4123/124) 900
Rosewater sprinkler, clear, tapering spout, eliptical body, 7⅛, 13/14c A.D. (4123/126) 250
Rosewater sprinkler, greenish, eliptical body, slender neck, iridescent, 7⅝, 13/14c A.D. (4123/125) 275

Gurgan 'Nawruz'

Shrine, Iran, oblong form, glazed turquoise, 4 x 5⅞, 13c (4197/247) *350*

Hispano Moresque

Tile, luster-ware, luster-ware, in wooden frame, 7½ x 7½, 11c (4264/224) 325
Tile, luster-ware, Andalusia*, yellow, white, wood frame, 7½ x 7½, 11c (4197/236) 800

Indian

Dish, blue and white, central medallion of Nasta'liq script, 12¾, L19c (4264/268) 225

Dish (4264/270)

Bowl (4123/242)

Bowl (4123/245)

Shrine (4197/247)

Iznik

Dish, painted in two shades of blue on white ground, 12¼, L16c (4264/270)	1600
Dish, blue and white, flaring sides and everted rim, 11½, L16c (4264/271)	1800
Dish, blue and white, floral motif, two shades of blue and white, 12, L16c (4264/269)	4100
Dish, polychrome, border pattern of blue and two shades of green, 11¾, crack, 17c (4264/272)	425
Dish, polychrome, floral motif, white ground, 11½, L16c (4264/273)	1600
Dish, polychrome, Turkey, green, blue ground, 12¾, 17c (4197/272)	800
Dish, polychrome, Turkey, palmette decoration, Diam 10, E17c (4197/270)	800
Jug, polychrome, Turkey, tulips, foliage, 6½, 17c (4197/273)	600
Tankard, polychrome, Turkey, frieze of saz leaves, 8, E17 (4197/271)	1300
Tile, polychrome border, white and turquoise on blue ground, 4⅞ x 9⅞, L16c (4264/274)	225

Kirman

Plate, blue and white, depicts two musicians in a landscape, 9, ca1700 (4264/252)	325

Kubachi

Plate, turquoise-glazed, red earthenware, black, turquoise glaze, 13¾, E16c (4264/246)	850

Mamluk

Beaker, painted, with red bands of decoration, 6⅜, rub, 13/14c (4264/264)	275

Nishapur

Bowl, white slip, white slip, rounded body, figure of a leopard, 6⅝, 11c (4264/230)	350

Persian

Tile, turquoise-glazed, Persia, naskhi inscription, 8 x 9½, 14c (4197/254)	375

Safavid

Base, blue and white Kalian, Mashad, 2 dragons, floral band, 6½, E17c (4197/262)	1400
Dish, blue and white, fragmentary base, flaring sides, 13¾, E18c (4264/254)	500
Dish, blue and white, Yazd or Isfahan, Diam 14, 18c (4197/267)	1000
Dish, luster-ware, flaring sides, painted in brown luster, 8¾, L17c (4264/249)	250
Plate, blue and white, Kirman*, foliated rim, Diam 6¾, 18c (4197/266)	350

Samanid

Bowl, buff slip, straight sides, painted stylized doves, D6⅝, 10c A.D. (4123/192)	500
Bowl, buff-ware, bird and palmettes in interior, 7⅜, 10c A.D. (4123/204)	150
Bowl, buff-ware, stylized bird, Kufic inscription, D9, 10c (4123/199)	200

Bowl, color splashed, scrolled, incised lozenge pattern, 3 colors, D9⅞, 10c A.D. (4123/197)   325
Bowl, cream slip, stylized birds, circular motifs, 7¾, 10c A.D. (4123/203)   325
Bowl, cream slip, Kufic inscription, central motif, D7½, 10c A.D. (4123/201)   150
Bowl, cream slip, Kufic inscription, fleur de lis, D5¼, 10c (4123/200)   350
Bowl, polychrome, stylized figures on elephant, D10¾, 10c A.D. (4123/202)   425
Bowl, slip-painted, straight sides, fantastic birds, D9⅛, 10c (4123/188)   850
Bowl, splash-glaze, Nishapur, beveled foot, incurving rim, Diam 6⅞, 9-10c (4197/232)   125
Bowl, white slip, convex sides, painted black caligraphic birds, D14½, 10c A.D. (4123/190)   500
Bowl, white slip, shallow, sloping sides, lozenge painted interior, D5⅝, 10c A.D. (4123/193)   425
Bowl, white slip, straight sides, painted stylized band interior, D5¼, 10c A.D. (4123/194)   175
Bowl, white slip, straight sides, painted Kufic inscription, D8¾, 10c A.D. (4123/191)   1300
Bowl, white slip, straight sides, Kufic inscription, brown stain, D11¾, 10c A.D. (4123/187)   1300
Bowl, white slip, beveled base and flaring sides, 7½, 9/10c (4264/227)   425
Jug, white slip, globular body, flaring neck, 4½, 10c (4264/228)   *2300*

Bowl (4264/256)

Jug (4264/228)

Ewer (4197/253)

Lamp, white slip, Samarkand or Nishapur, Kufic script, L12 7/I6, 9-10c (4197/234)   400

Seljuk

Bowl, splayed foot, flaring sides, incurring rim, 7½, foot chip, 13/14c (4264/262)   500
Bowl, luster-ware, central medallion, a seated man, 8½, E13c (4264/255)   1300
Bowl, luster-ware, straight sides, high foot, 8⅜, E13c (4264/256)   *4400*
Bowl, turquoise, convex sides, flattened rim, 8, iridescent, E13c (4264/236)   350
Bowl, turquoise-glazed, deep, low foot, Herat*, Diam 4, 13c (4197/239)   850
Bowl, turquoise-glazed, high foot, flaring sides, 7¼, iridescent, 13c (4264/241)   1100
Bowl, turquoise-glazed, Iran, flaring sides, everted rim, Diam 9½, 13c (4197/238)   275
Bowl, turquoise-glazed, Sultanabad, molded decoration, on a stand, Diam 10⅝, 13-14c (4197/257)   1100
Capital, luster-ware, Kashan, rectangular, gold luster overglaze, 16¼, 13-14c (4197/259)   4800
Dish, luster-ware, raised foot, shallow sides, everted rim, 7¾, 13c (4264/237)   250
Ewer, luster-ware, Kashan*, molded in relief, 9, 13c (4197/253)   *1100*
Ewer, turquoise-glazed, pear-shaped form, pinched mouth, 8¼, fragmentary, stand, 13c (4264/240)   200
Head, stucco, with some turquoise glaze, Iran, 15⅛, fragmentary, 13c (4197/252)   125
Jar, blue-glazed, squat globular body, Rayy or Nishapur, Diam 7½, E13c (4197/237)   550
Jar, turquoise-glazed, low splayed foot, high straight sides, neck, 12½, res, 12/13c (4264/233)   250
Jar, turquoise-glazed, Syria, Rakka, cross hatch decoration, 8¼, L12/E13c (4197/250)   2400
Vase, luster-ware, Kashan, octagonal, 13¼, 13c (4197/260)   1900
Vessel, lion, white-glazed, fragmentary, 7⅜, res, 12/13c (4264/232)   250

Sgraffiato

Bowl, convex sides, glaze, 7½, chip, 11/12c (4264/258)   800
Bowl, turquoise-glazed, flaring sides, 6, 13c (4264/238)   100
Bowl, 'Amol', convex sides, continuous row of animals, 7, 11/12c (4264/260)   *1100*

Candlestick (4264/287)

Persian astrolabe
(4264/298)

Timurid

Bowl, flaring sides, painted in blue, black, 8½, 15c (4264/244) 100

ISLAMIC METALWORK

Brass

Astrolabe, Qajar, engraved, 4, 19c (4264/307) 250
Candlestick, Mamluk, chased and engraved tapering drum, 7¼, shoulder replaced, 13/14c (4264/289) 900
Chandelier, circular domed body, six additions, 27, 19c (4264/308) 550
Dish, large inlaid Saracenic, engraved with knotted kufic script, 16¼, traces of silver inlay, E16c (4264/294) 3200
Persian astrolabe, engraved with various inscriptions, 7¼, E18c (4264/298) *2900*

Bronze

Bowl, Talismanic, engraved with two rows of Naskhi inscriptions, 7¼, 15c (4264/290) 500
Bowl and cover, Saracenic, arabesques, silver inlay, 6½, 16c (4264/295) 1600
Candlestick, Mamluk, band of thulth script, 9½, traces of silver inlay, E14c (4264/287) *3600*
Candlestick, Timurid column, engraved trefoil and geometric decoration, 11, 15c (4264/291) 450
Faucet, Iran, short cylindrical pipe, 7¼, 13/14c (4264/286) 200
Oil-lamp, Seljuk, double spouts, lid and handle topped with a bird, 6, 12c (4264/281) *425*

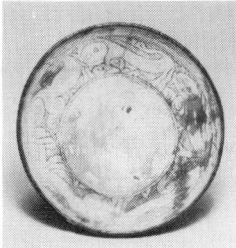

Bowl (4264/260)

Oil-lamp (4264/281)

Panel
(4264/352)

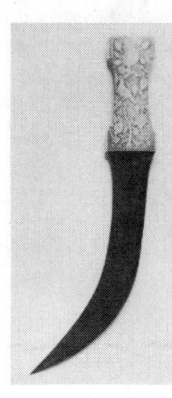

Qajar dagger
(4264/299)

Protome of a hare, head with large ears, rounded cheeks, pointed nose, 6, standed, 11/13c
(4264/284)   1000
Protome of a hare, pointed chin, nose, ears, bulbous cheeks, 7¼, 11/13c (4264/283)   300
Tray, Seljuk, small tay, sloping sides, 3⅜, 12c (4264/278)   100

Copper

Cup, large 'Hamman', long spout, bulbous body, everted rim, 5½, 16/17c (4264/296)   275

Mamluk

Basin, brass, Egypt, sides repousse with 24 lobes, Diam 13½, 15c (4197/286)   3200
Candlestick, brass, Egypt, flared pan, concave drum, cylindrical neck, 8, 14c (4197/285)   3300
Candlestick Base, brass, Egypt, tapering concave drum, thulth script, 8¾, 13-14c (4197/283) 950
Cup, bronze 'Hammon', Egypt, inlaid, engraved with silver, 2⅜, 14c (4197/284)   1300

Ottoman

Inkwell and pen-case, ebony with gilt, Turkish seal, L9, 18c (4197/291)   550
Mounts on a 16th century Ming vase, Turkey, chased with panels, medallions, 11¾, ca17c
(4197/287)   400
Shield, with iron boss, struts, Turkey, Diam 11⅝, 17c (4197/290)   325

Seljuk

Basin, bronze, Khurasan, scalloped form, inlaid in copper, Diam 20⅛, 13c (4197/281)   700
Dish, silver, Iran, convex base, flaring sides, 9½, 10c (4197/274)   350
Mirror, bronze, Iran, circular, engraved, chased, Diam 14¼, 13c (4197/278)   150
Stand, bronze, tripod, lobed base, chased, engraved, 20, 12-13c (4197/282)   700

Steel

Horse's chanfron, Turkish, engraved with mark of St. Irene Arsenal, 23, 15c (4264/292)   8000
Horse's chanfron, Turkish, pierced around edges for mail links, 20½, ca1500 (4264/293)   6000
Indian Shamshir, steel blade, green jade carved hilt, 33¼, def, 18c (4264/300)   400
Qajar dagger, watered steel blade, carved ivory handle, 7½, E19c (4264/299)   *1500*
Shamshir, steel blade, horn grip, guard with silver inlay, 35, worn, 19c (4264/302)   75

ISLAMIC TEXTILES

Embroidery

Kashmiri, central medallion composed of botehs, 74 x 68, fringed, 19c (4264/342)   200
Panel, repeating bands of composite leaf motif, 96 x 49½, L19c (4264/344)   425
Panel, Kirman, crimson ground, central cusped medallion, 59½ x 38, 19c (4264/358)   375
Panel, Ottoman gold and silver thread, smaller panels of blue, crimson, beige, 118 x 70, 19c
(4264/352)   *850*

Silk

Banner, Ottoman, with a large central 'sword zulfikar', 120 x 130, 17c (4264/339)   3000
Fragment, Ottoman textile, olive green ground, 10½ x 21¼, framed, L16c (4264/345)   600
Panel, cream, broad border at each end of floral motif, 96 x 51, fringed, 19c (4264/343)   175
Panel, Ottoman gold and metal thread, oblong blue ground, gold foliate design, 26 x 42½, 18c (4264/347)   350
Panel, Ottoman velvet, octagonal medallions, red ground, 25 x 21½, 17c (4264/346)   70
Panel, Qajar, aubergine colored ground, 70 x 51, 19c (4264/359)   700
Panel, Safavid, crimson ground, repeating parrot pattern, 14⅛ x 15, 17c (4264/354)   325
Panel, Safavid, yellow field, green lattice and blue flowers, 26 x 25½, 17c (4264/355)   250
Prayer cloth, Ottoman, green velvet, gold metal thread, red border, 61 x 36, 19c (4264/350)   150
Prayer rug, Mughal embroidered, silk and velvet, ground of silver thread, 72 x 48, 18c (4264/341)   2300
Saddle-cloth, Mughal, silver thread, field of orange, 32¾ x 42, slight def, E18c (4264/340)   1400
Sash with silver threads, silk, depicting flowering plants, 38 x 19½, 17c (4197/312)   375

ISLAMIC WORKS OF ART

Alabaster

Three chess pieces, slight carved decoration, 1¼, 12c (4264/318)   60

Glass

Beaker, green, indented base, flaring sides, 4¾, iridescent, 12/14c (4264/328)   50
Bottle, amber, conically indented base, 2⅝ x 9, 10c (4197/297)   400
Bottle, green, indented base, mold-blown squat body, 3, iridescent, 4/7c (4264/323)   150
Bottle, green, indented base, straight neck, rounded shoulder, 3½, 10/11c (4264/326)   75
Bottle, green, slender neck, coiled collar, 7⅜, chip, 12c (4264/327)   300
Bottle, greenish, pincer form decoration, Diam 3½, 7-9c (4197/296)   425
Bowl, blue, footering, 2½, 18c (4264/329)   100
Carafe, cobalt blue, spiral thread, coiling collar, 6 5/16, 18/19c (4264/330)   50
Jug, greenish yellow, conically indented base, rounded body, 4⅝, iridescent, 10/12c (4264/325)   150

Gold

Filigree belt, gold buckle, strip of blue silk, 31, ca1900 (4264/320)   950

Horn

Figure of Garuda, folded wings, kneeling position, Dutch inscribed, 4¾, 19c (4264/331)   75

Ivory

Mortar, Hispano Moresque, with lobed arcades, kufic script, 4, rim broken (4197/310)   *3000*
Powder horn, Safavid, Iran, trefoil motif, L7½, 17c (4197/307)   1200

Jade

Dagger hilt, India, carved with floral foliate decorations, 5⅜, 19c (4197/309)   600

Limestone

Head, rounded face, pointed nose and lips, 3½, 11c (4264/317)   250

Marble

Fatamid wash-basin and stand, basin decorated with band of kufic script, 17¼, res, 11c (4264/316)   *750*

Mortar
(4197/310)

Fatamid wash-basin
and stand   (4264/316)

Window-shutter
(4197/319)

Portrait of Nasir
Ud-Din Shah
(4264/189)

Steel

Knife dagger, Mughal, India, steel blade, gold inscriptions, L14¾, 19c (4197/308)   550

Stone

Stele, with Kufic inscription, 12 lines of Kufic script, 26¾ x 21, 869 A.D. (4197/294)   1600

Wood

Bowl, Qalian, inlaid with turquoises, semi-precious stones, three feet, 3½, 19c (4264/333)	40
Cross-beams, pair, carved, bold thulth inscription, 39, 14c (4264/335)	800
Kashkul, top, sides carved with floral decoration, 10, L19c (4264/337)	250
Kashkul, carved, Persia, 2 clasps with chain attached, 13½ x 19, M19c (4197/321)	950
Lintel, carved, Marrakesh, carved kufic inscription, 79, 12c (4197/315)	1200
Panel, Safavid, carved, geometric design, 12½ x 8½, def, 16c (4264/334)	375
Window-shutter, Turkey*, kufic script, 45¾ x 26, 15c (4197/319)	*2500*

ORIENTAL MANUSCRIPTS

Arabic

Qur'an, India, manuscript on paper, 12¾ x 7½, rep, soiled, 19c (4264/205)	500
Qur'an, India, manuscript on paper, gold discs in between verses, 6⅝ x 4, stains, E19c (4264/204)	400
Qur'an, Turkey, manuscript on paper, naskhi script, 14¼ x 9½, worn, rebacked, 19c (4264/213)	550

Persian

A fine gilt-stamped Persian binding, central panel, monkeys in a tree, 10¼ x 7¼, worn, rebacked, 15c (4264/217)   2600

Gilt-stamped Persian binding, central panels, pair of herons, 14¾ x 9⅝, rub, rebacked, L16c (4264/218)   3000

Unidentified poetical text, manuscript on paper, blind stamped brown morocco, 8⅞ x 5¼, def, rep, M16c (4264/219)   450

PERSIAN AND TURKISH MINIATURES

Bukhara

King Zahhak enthroned, maiden, three ministers, guard, 7½ x 6¼, dis, rub, L16c (4264/180)   1600

Isfahan

Drawing of a youth, panel of Nasta'liq script below, 10 x 6⅛, M17c, (4264/181)   600

Horsemen skirmish on a gold hillside, illustration on a manuscript leaf, 7⅛ x 5⅜, framed, M17c (4264/182)   350

Horsemen skirmish upon a hillside, 2 trumpeters on horizon, 6½ x 5¼, fla, res, L17c (4197/210)   1000

Khurusan

Two princes being entertained, two musicians seated in foreground, 7 x 4, flaked, mounted, L16c
(4264/178) *1200*

Persia

Drawing of a dragon, upon a rocky hillside, 3 x 6⅞, 16c (4197/206) 400
Two two-winged dragons, drawing with some color, on uncolored ground, 5⅜ x 3, framed, L16c
(4264/175) 700

Qajar

A maiden holding a parrot, blue dress, on uncolored ground, 10⅞ x 7½, dis, crease (4264/187) 600
A standing youth, wearing hawking glove, uncolored ground, 8⅝ x 6¼, dis, frayed, M19c
(4264/188) 300
Painting on glass, three-quarter length portrait of Nur'Ali Shah, 10¼ x 8⅜, def, E19c (4264/193) 550
Portrait of Nasir Ud-Din Shah, inscribed 'Nasser-Eddin Shah de la Perse', 12¾ x 9, frayed, ca1860
(4264/189) *3750*

Two princes being
entertained
(4264/178)

2 bearded men
in discussion
(4197/204)

Kay Ka'us in his flying
machine (4264/173)

Shiraz

A ruler in conversation with his ministers, he sits cross-legged on a throne, 6 x 4, def, on card,
L16c (4264/177) 300
An attendant standing without a gate, two women above, a servant to the left, 4¼ x 3⅛, oxidation,
L16c (4264/176) 200
Angels kneeling about a naked body, dressed in multi-color robes, 6¾ x 5, rub, framed, L16c
(4197/2005) 3500
Kay Ka'us in his flying machine, from a manuscript of Firdausi's Shahnama, 5¾ x 5⅛, framed,
M16c (4264/173) *900*
Khusraw espies Shirin bathing, from a manuscript of Nizami's Khamsa, 4½ x 2¾, crease, dis,
M16c (4264/174) 800
Rustam kicking rock thrown by Bahman, beside a stream, green valley, 10 x 7½, fla, M16c
(4197/207) 3600
2 bearded men in discussion, within a chamber, 8⅛ x 5¼, ca1550-60 (4197/204) *1600*
2 youths before their teacher, Mihr and Mushtari*, 5⅞ x 4, ca1570 (4197/208) 350

Turkey

A page with decoupe decoration, falcon, several animals, flowering tree, 6 x 3½, framed, L18c
(4264/186) 130
Book of Prayers, 82 leaves, 6⅜ x 3½, 19c (4197/224) 125
Portrait of a youth, light-blue coat bulbous turban, 4½ x 2⅞, uncolored ground, ca1700 (4264/185) 300

QAJAR ENAMEL AND LAQUERWORK

Assorted items

Mirror, Qajar, painted glass border, 30¼ x 17½, L19c (4264/391) 400

Qur'an holder, enameled gold, symetric designs in enamel, precious stones, 4⅛, L19c (4264/395)   11000

Enamel

Bowl, Qajar Qalian, Persia, polychrome enamel, 6, chip, ca1860-70 (4197/338)   5000
Bowl, Qajar Qalian, Persia, 4 figural medallions, 7¼, chip, M19c (4197/342)   4250
Bowl, Qajar Qalian, 2 oval portraits, polychrome enamels, 2, chip, ca1870 (4197/339)   2800
Dagger, Qajar, 2 blades, gold koftgari decoration, L17⅝, L19c (4197/325)   1100
Hookah base, Qajar, Persia, sides with 4 oval medallions, 11, 19c (4197/341)   4500

Lacquer

Casket, Qajar, scenes of horsemen, Persia, 4⅞ x 7, ca1840 (4197/331)   300
Doors, pair, Qajar, nightingales, floral decoration, Persia, miniature, 6¼ x 17, L19c (4197/322)   1600
Mirror, Qajar, Persia, foliate border, 30½ x 17½, M19c (4197/320)   300
Mirror-case, Persian, mirrors lacking, Qajar, 9 x 6, chip, ca1840 (4197/336)   2000
Mirror-case, Persian, Qajar, mirrors, metal hinges intact, 11¾ x 8, chip, ca1840 (4197/335)   3000
Pen-box, Persian, in the style of Abu Talib, Qajar, L8, chip, ca1840-60 (4197/328)   200
Pen-box, Persian, Qajar, gilt floral decoration underneath, L9½, ca1840 (4197/327)   *950*
Pen-box, Persian, Qajar, on black ground, L8¾, chip, ca1860-70 (4197/330)   750
Persian lacquer box, by Ahmad Ibn Abdul Wahhab, 9⅜, 1886 (4264/369)   *2300*
Persian lacquer box, fallaciously inscribed 'Ya Sahib al-Zaman', 9, M19c (4264/382)   900
Persian lacquer box, inscribed with gold nasta'liq script, 8⅞, L19c (4264/362)   400
Persian lacquer box, panels depicting hazel nuts, foliage, birds, 9⅜, L19c (4264/378)   2000
Persian lacquer box, the sides with four landscape scenes, 8⅞, L19c (4264/374)   650
Persian lacquer box, top and sides with gilt arabesques, 8¾, L19c (4264/372)   700
Persian lacquer box, top panel depicts a child asleep in a lady's lap, 8⅝, L19c (4264/379)   1600
Persian lacquer box, underside red, gilt floral decoration, 8¾, M19c (4264/368)   700

Panels

Group of Europeans feasting, food on a green carpet, two musicians playing, 13¼ x 20, L19c (4264/384)   400
Persian lacquer panel, a prince seated on a rug, attendant before him, 13¼ x 17⅜, L19c (4264/387)   150
Persian, lacquer panel, depicting a hunting scene, 11⅝ x 15, framed, 19c (4264/385)   750
Repousse copper and gilt, four nightingales perched in a rosebush, 18½ x 13½, L19c (4264/389)   800

Qalian bowl

Qalian bowl, gold, Qajar, portraits of a prince and a maiden, 2¼, chip, M19c (4264/396)   2500

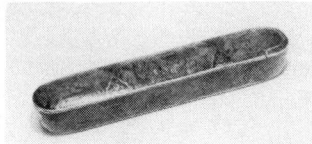

Pen-box (4197/327)

Persian lacquer box (4264/369)

Persian lacquer box (4264/382)

Chapter 13

Ethnological Works of Art

The market for ethnological art has grown rapidly in the last few years. Values vary widely in the four major categories—African, Oceanic, pre-Columbian and American Indian—of this relatively new, volatile field. Well-documented pieces, thoroughly researched and unquestionably authenticated, reach high levels, but many items are still available at reasonable prices.

Prices are generally lowest in the area of African art, though the growing knowledge of Africa's early history and increased awareness of its varied cultures will surely stimulate interest and drive values upward. Because most African art is damaged, workmanship and rarity count for more than condition in determining value.

The least expensive pieces of Oceanic art are utensils like New Guinea Sago pounders and double bowls. Carvings such as a canoe figurehead from the Solomon Islands are higher. More intricate work, like a hair-and-ivory necklace from Hawaii and an imposing carved Easter Island figure, bring the highest prices, in the thousands of dollars.

As prices for American Indian art skyrocket, the quality, number and variety of works coming on the market have increased dramatically. Prices have climbed as much as one hundred percent in a year in some categories. Painted buffalo hides, beaded blanket strips and other colorful items brought high prices, as did pottery from the Southwest. The distinctive carvings of the Pacific Northwest were particularly prized.

Though prices for pre-Columbian art have risen with every sale, much of the overall increase is due to the enormous rise in the value of gold. Pottery, stone carvings and other artifacts have appreciated, but not at the rate of gold, perhaps in part because of questions about the age and authenticity of some of the items which are offered in the market. However, pottery figures from the east coast of Mexico sold at double the prices of a few years ago, and particularly fine examples sold for considerably more.

The beginning collector can still find fine pieces of pre-Columbian art available at relatively small amounts. Utensils provide excellent opportunities to acquire interesting examples. Nazca polychrome dishes and Vicus vessels are attractive and reasonably priced, as are many American Indian artifacts like moccasins, tomahawks and beaded hunting shirts. Small baskets and pots are within modest budgets.

The field of ethnological art holds great potential for collectors. It is a relatively new field, and museums are just beginning to enter it. American

Indian and pre-Columbian art have already made substantial gains. Presumably African and Oceanic art will follow in the near future.

Bakongo ivory tusk
(4227/135)

Agni female figure
(4227/67)

Akan equestrian
figure (4227/70)

AFRICAN WORKS OF ART

Agni clay female figure, krinjabo, rudimentary arms, black pigment, 13¼ (4227/63)	*$1000*
Agni clay figure, splayed arms, legs, smiling mouth, 11⅞ (4227/68)	300
Agni clay male figure, krinjabo, seated, extended arms, black pigment, 13½ (4227/64)	500
Agni clay woman's head, krinjabo, incised neck, cicatrice marks, 8½ (4227/65)	1300
Agni female figure, crouching posture, venetian trade beads, 26 (4227/67)	*1900*
Agni woman's head, krinjabo, incised neck, asymetric features, 8½ (4227/66)	850
Akan equestrian figure, small horse, man wearing belt, 13½ (4227/70)	*900*
Ashanti comb, seven teeth, dentate bands, 8⅛ (4227/72)	200
Ashanti female doll, akua'ba, typical form, red pigment, 13¼ (4227/71)	450
Ashanti goldweight, figure with European hat, 2 smaller figures, 3⅛ (4227/74)	500
Ashanti maternity figure, seated, holding 2 children, brown patina, 12⅛ (4227/73)	900
Babinji helmet mask, feather, fur, horsehair attachments, 13 (4227/150)	800
Bajkwe lintel, five mask carved relief, L24 (4227/149)	950
Bajokwe composite mask, fiber headdress, canvas face, feathers, 20 (4227/146)	150
Bajokwe staff, surmounted by seated female, 18⅛ (4227/147)	500
Bakongo fetish figure, mirror covered fetish cavity, rich patina, 7⅞ (4227/134)	1200
Bakongo ivory tusk, European figure and zoomorphic forms, 13⅛ (4227/135)	*2100*
Bakota reliquary figure, mbulu-ngulu, brass neck ring, 20⅞ (4227/125)	8750
Bakota reliquary figure, mbulu-ngulu, lozenge shaped body, brass sheeted coiffure, 20⅞ (4227/126)	2000
Bakuba composite helmet mask, cowrie shell eyes, canvas headdress, 14 (4227/151)	225
Balega turtle shell hand mask, gaping mouth, flat nose, oval eyes, 5½ (4227/175)	125
Baluba chief's scepter, copper sheathed shaft, 61¾ (4227/168)	700
Baluba chief's scepter, slender shaft, 65 (4227/167)	800
Baluba shaker, two gourds with feathers, female form handle, (4227/172)	300
Baluba stool, circular base and seat, 14⅝ (4227/170)	2000
Baluba-Hemba janus figure, kabeja, 9½ (4227/162)	900
Baluba-Hemba male figure, hand on hips, long neck, 14⅝ (4227/161)	750
Baluba-Wazali stool, stepped oval base, concave seat, 15⅝ (4227/169)	1000
Bambara antelope headdress, chiwara, cylindrical neck, patina, length 23 (4227/6)	750
Bambara antelope headdress, chiwara, rectangular legs, cylindrical body, 40 (4227/9)	900
Bambara elephant mask, abstract form, large ears, trunk, 28¾ (4227/11)	400
Bambara female fetish figure, cicatrice marks, brass neckring, 5⅝ (4227/127)	1500
Bambara female figure, angular build, bent knees, 25¾ (4227/1)	300
Bambara fetish figure, deep brown patina, 4⅝ (4227/128)	500
Bambara kono society helmet mask, bared jaws, rectangular nose, horns, L43¼ (4227/13)	300
Bambara kore society mask, souroukow, curving forehead, bared teeth, 18 (4227/14)	650
Bambara male figure of iron, attenuated form, splayed hands, feet, 18¼ (4227/2)	550
Bamum helmet, smiling mouth, cowrie shell eyes, 15¼ (4227/118)	325
Bapende ivory head pendant, large lips, wedge nose, 1⅞ (4227/143)	150
Basonga male fetish figure, cowrie shell eyes, beads, 13⅝ (4227/158)	600
Basonga male fetish figure, large head, grooved beard, 30⅛ (4227/156)	1200
Basundi fetish figure, bent legs, fetish material encrusted, 27½ (4227/129)	2400
Bateke male fetish figure, body enclosed in fetish material, 12¼ (4227/132)	800
Bateke male fetish figure, fetish cavity, glass inlay, 18 (4227/133)	650
Baule birds head finial, brass tack studding, 6¾ (4227/61)	100
Baule face mask, oval face, surmounting female figure, 16⅞ (4227/54)	800
Baule face mask, short beard, pointed teeth, 13⅛ (4227/53)	2000
Baule face mask, small size, oval face, black ornamentation, 8½ (4227/59)	200
Baule female figure, cicatrization mark overall, 16¼ (4227/51)	650
Baule goli society mask, horned, circular face, bared teeth, 17½ (4227/57)	325
Baule heddle pulley, square shoulders, human head, oval face, tall ears, 8¼ (4227/62)	450
Baule heddle pulley, with linear and dentate ornament, 6⅝ (4227/49)	125
Baule helmet mask, ox head, black details, length 26½ (4227/58)	550
Baule horsehair fly whisk, surmounted by human head, 8½ (4227/60)	400
Baule mask, oval face, striated beard, 15 (4227/55)	1300
Baule monkey god, gbekre, raffia shirt, bent legs, cup, 24 (4227/52)	175
Bayaka fetish figure, angular legs, fetish covered torso, 11¼ (4227/140)	200
Bayaka initiation mask, grip, slit eyes, basketry cap, 17 (4227/141)	1300
Bayaka slit drum, oval eyes, cicatrization, 16½ (4227/142)	400
Bekom elephant head helmet, ears, trunk, black patina, length 35½ (4227/119)	700
Bena lulua guardian figure, legless, oval eyes, pigmented forehead, 13⅛ (4227/154)	300
Bena lulua janus figure, four faced head, patina, 12½ (4227/153)	1200
Bena-Kanioka bowl, human figure beneath bowl, diam. 8 (4227/171)	200
Benin bronze bell, rectangular form with arched handle, 8¾ (4227/99)	300

Benin bronze female figure, beaded belt, collar, pointed eyes, 6⅝ (4227/97)   1600
Benin head of oba, domed headdress, 14 (4227/98)   600
Benin iron staff shrine, bird finial, quadrupeds climbing staff, 63¾ (4227/89)   375
Benin iron staff shrine, bird seated on quadruped finial, 52 (4227/91)   250
Benin ivory leopard plaque, stalking posture, bared teeth, L9⅞ (4227/100)   2100
Bobo antelope mask, conical eyes, carved face, eyes, 23¼ (4227/27)   300
Bobo do society owl mask, circular face, concentric ornaments, 39½ (4227/26)   250
Bobo helmet mask, beard, gaping mouth, pigmentation traces, 16 (4227/25)   325
Bobo-Fing helmet mask, convex face, short nose, painted designs, 19 (4227/28)   1100
Buteke fetish figure, angular legs, high crest, 12½ (4227/130)   450
Dagger with hide sheath, steel blade, brass hilt, length 16 (4227/181)   600
Dan face mask, beak on chin, studded with metal, 17½ (4227/36)   450
Dan face mask, slender oval form, protruding lips, 8¾ (4227/34)   275
Dan face mask, tin rimmed eyes, chevron horns, 10½ (4227/35)   400
Dan passport mask, oval face, pointed chin, lug ears, 3⅝ (4227/40)   150
Dan-Yakouba miniature fetish mask, geometric features, 8¼ (4227/38)   400
Dogon antelope face mask, angular facial plane, fine patina, 20 (4227/21)   1400
Dogon face mask, median crest, polychrome ornament, 17⅛ (4227/22)   125
Dogon female figure, holding long implement in hands, 12⅜ (4227/19)   200
Dogon figure, bent legs, projecting buttocks, small breasts, 39¾ (4227/15)   900
Dogon hornbill face mask, eyes over projecting beak, surmounted female, 23¼ (4227/20)   *600*

Ibo-Koba ikenga
figure (4227/101)

Lower niger bronze
potentate figure
(4227/92)

Dogon hornbill face mask
(4227/20)

Dogon iron staff, slender, surmounted by human form, 41½ (4227/23)   200
Dogon male figure, elongated form, bent legs, clasped hand, 36 (4227/17)   325
Enzapo-Zapo male figure, stocky form, oval eyes, 12¾ (4227/155)   300
Fang figure, geometric incised head and body, 13¼ (4227/124)   100
Fanti male figure, touching cheek, black pigment, 17¼ (4227/75)   100
Fon bronze mother and child, seated, child clinging to back, 5 (4227/77)   75
Fon fetish figure, slender figure, heavy encrustation, 13¾ (4227/76)   600
Fon table, circular top supported by 3 couples, 27 x 30 (4227/78)   300
Giryama ancestor figure, kaya, stylized flat human form, 58½ (4227/183)   200
Guro female figure, arms at side, rich red patina, 14½ (4227/47)   650
Guro female figure, arms at side, slender waist, patina, 23½ (4227/48)   550
Ibibio female figure, stout legs, hip rings, spiral braids, 24¾ (4227/108)   2500
Ibo white maiden mask, grinning mouth, 14½ (4227/103)   175
Ibo white maiden mask, mmwo society, grinning mouth, 14½ (4227/102)   425
Ibo-Koba ikenga figure, abstract form, compressed facial features, red pigment, 13 (4227/101) *175*
Idoma alijeru face mask, oval face, small beard, inlaid coins, 8¾ (4227/106)   200
Ife clay shrine figure, rotund, cowrie shells on waist, circa 1300, 11 (4227/79)   1200
Ishan male figure, abdominal cicatrization, 38 (4227/95)   900
Koro-Ache helmet mask, headdress with red seeds, 35 (4227/109)   1100
Kotoko gray clay figure, stylized form, bowed legs, uplifted face, 6⅝ (4227/112)   75
Lobi female figure, slender forms, arms at side, 21⅜ (4227/29)   325
Lower niger bronze potentate figure, seated, 7¼ (4227/92)   *800*

Yoruba lid with mother
and child (4227/85)

Yoruba gelede mask
(4227/82)

Madagascan equestrian figure, small horse, feet reaching ground, extended hand, 17¾ (4227/187)	450
Madagascan erotic couple, male embracing female, head on breast, 36 (4227/192)	1200
Madagascan female figure, standing, knopped coiffure, 58¾ (4227/193)	450
Madagascan female figure, large, slender stylized form, vessel on head, 47½ (4227/191)	600
Madagascan grave post, elaborate openwork shaft surmounted by two, figures with airplane, 56¼ (4227/188)	370
Madagascan grave post, figure in loincloth, European above, (4227/185)	1400
Madagascan grave post, shaft surmounted by European equestrian, 56¼ (4227/189)	475
Madagascan male in European dress, holding book, tunic, cap, 30 (4227/186)	375
Madagascan warriors, six warriors with carved rifles, 13½ (4227/194)	325
Mambila crow-totem headdress, long open mouth, stubby horns, L13¼ (4227/113)	350
Maou komo society helmet mask, zoomorphic form, triple beak, horns, length 36½ (4227/12)	600
Mende sande society helmet mask, bundu form, braids fetish bundle, 15¼ (4227/31)	375
Minianka female figure, hands on abdomen, conical breasts, 11⅝ (4227/24)	600
Mumuye figure, large, abstract angular form, black patina, 56½ (4227/107)	700
Nigerian ancestor figure, simplified form, carved features, 20 (4227/110)	550
Ogoni goat's head mask, grooved mouth, drilled nostrils, horns, L11⅝ (4227/104)	200
Senufo equestrian figure, long legged horse, black pigment overall, 14 (4227/45)	550
Senufo female figure, heart shaped face, large breasts, 15½ (4227/41)	1200
Senufo male figure, short legs, facial scarification, 9 (4227/42)	125
Senufo maternity figure, seated holding 2 children, 18 (4227/44)	1300
Senufo rhythm pounders, matched pair, korhogo, male and female, 54 each (4227/46)	1900
Sherbro steatite male figure, nomoli, squatting, large head, 5¾ (4227/32)	350
Tikar seated figure, flaring torso, squared shoulders, 28½ (4227/114)	1000
Tiv female figure, conical breasts, fine natural patina, 41 (4227/105)	400
Western grasslands brass pipe, elephant head form, 2 tusks, L6¾ (4227/122)	350
Yoruba agere ifa bowl, man on lid, 11¾ (4227/86)	275
Yoruba egungun mask, cheek, forehead scarification, red and black pigment, L21 (4227/83)	350
Yoruba equestrian figure, stoutly built horse and rider, patina, 11⅜ (4227/81)	700
Yoruba gelede mask, pierced pupils, cicatrized cheeks, 17½ (4227/82)	*2300*
Yoruba ibeji twin, hands on hips, traces of pigment, 11⅛ (4227/87)	150
Yoruba iron and brass poker, flattened shaft, 38 (4227/90)	400
Yoruba iron staff shrine, bird finial, bells, lizard on staff, 36 (4227/88)	200
Yoruba lid with mother and child, mother with child on back, 14 (4227/85)	*425*
Yoruba male shrine figure, holding attributes, tunic, pigmentation, 16 (4227/80)	1800
Yoruba oshe shango staff, large, kneeling figure holding flute, 24 (4227/84)	500
Zaire clay elephant, stylized form, baby hippo in trunk, 8¾ (4227/180)	125
Zaire walking stick, surmounted by human head, 39¾ (4227/179)	100

AMERICAN INDIAN WORKS OF ART

Acoma

Jar, pottery, striped triangle decoration, Diam 9 (4166/116) 275

Algonkian

Basket, plaited, decorated with rows of potato-stamped rosettes, H11 (4166/11)   425

Apache

Basket, burden, twined, high flaring sides, H13 (4166/178)   750
Basket, coiled, flat base and flaring sides, Diam 15 (4166/176)   550
Basket, coiled, spiraling pattern of triangle columns, Diam 14⅞ (4166/177)   650
Basket, storage, coiled, rounded body and flaring neck, H12½ (4166/174)   _950_

Basket (4166/174)

Basket, storage, coiled, rounded body and flaring rim, H16¾ (4166/175)   850
Dress, lavender cloth with geometric ornament, L39 (4166/54)   200
Pouch, beaded hide, rectangular, 2 beaded crescents and 2 'X' motifs on front, L9¾ (4166/63)   375

Arapaho

Bag, hide, medicine, composed of a desiccated skunk's body, L33 (4166/58)   200

Athabaskan

Pouch, sealskin, red panels beaded with floral motifs, L31 (4166/309)   300

Attu

Basket, lidded, twined, double-wedge motifs with zig-zag lines, Diam 7¼ (4166/312)   800
Basket, lidded, twined, friezes of crosses with panels of rectangles, Diam 13⅝ (4166/313)   450
Basket bottle, twined, tiny geometric motifs, H7⅝ (4166/311)   3400
Wallet, rectangular, twined, large diamond with rows of butterflies, L5 5/16 (4166/314)   850

Bella Coola

Figure, wood, form of a killer whale, L16 (4166/269)   700
Mask, face, wood, pierced downcast mouth, hooked nose, H9¾ (4166/291)   2100

Blackfoot

Pouch, beaded hide, rectangular, 2 long diamond and triangle motifs on front, L9¼ (4166/62)   175

California Mission

Basket, coiled, alternating panels of stylized birds, Diam 6 (4166/211)   325
Basket, coiled, encircling panel of stylized trees, Diam 21¼ (4166/207)   500
Basket, coiled, radiating pattern of stepped zig-zag lines, Diam 9⅛ (4166/209)   200
Basket, coiled, shades of ochre, dark brown, Diam 12 (4237/274)   525
Basket, coiled, vertical diamond columns, Diam 19⅜ (4237/276)   225
Basket, coiled, American desert palm motifs woven on side, Diam 12¼ (4166/208)   600

Californian

Basket, California coiled, Chemehuveve*, birds, swastikas, Diam 5½ (4237/273)   1800
Basket, Hupa twined, flaring cylindrical body, Diam 13½ (4237/299)   100
Basket, Hupa twined, globular body, pale yellow ground, Diam 5½ (4237/300)   750

Basket, Pomo coiled, boat shaped body, red feathers at shoulder, Diam 4¼ (4237/287)   1200
Basket, Pomo coiled, boat shaped body, seam of repair at rim, L20½ (4237/293)   400
Basket, Pomo coiled, encircling panels of zig-zag ornament, Diam 6 (4237/289)   800
Basket, Pomo coiled, flat base, rounded sides, blackish-brown, Diam 10½ (4237/294)   425
Basket, Pomo coiled, form of small storage jar, Diam 6¾ (4237/295)   600
Basket, Pomo coiled, rosette, triangular motifs, Diam 5 (4237/288)   2600
Basket, Pomo coiled, squat rounded body, Diam 6½ (4237/290)   450
Basket, Pomo coiled, triangular decorations overall, Diam 7 (4237/291)   300
Basket, Pomo coiled miniature, pattern of stepped motifs, Diam 1⅝ (4237/286)   150
Basket, Tulare coiled, flaring sides, zig-zag lines, Diam 6⅛ (4237/281)   225
Basket, Washo coiled, stepped diamond, triangular motifs, Diam 8½ (4237/271)   200
Basket, Yokut coiled, 'rattlesnake' panels of diamonds, triangles, Diam 7½ (4237/282)   350
Basket, Yokut coiled, checkered rosette on flat base, Diam 7½ (4237/284)   500
Basket, Yokut coiled 'pride', cylindrical body, triangle decoration, Diam 3 15/16 (4237/278)   600
Basket, Yokut coiled bottleneck, frieze of double-diamond motifs, Diam 6 (4237/280)   900
Basket, Yokut coiled bottleneck, slanted columns of triangles, Diam 7 (4237/279)   425
Basket cap, Hupa twined, bowl shaped body, Diam 6⅞ (4237/303)   80
Basket cap, Hupa twined, three hooked motifs around base, Diam 7 (4237/301)   275
Basket cap, Yurok-Karok twined, shades of brown, pale yellow ground, Diam 7 (4237/302)   100

Canadian

Gorgettes, silver, engraved with figure of a beaver, L3¾ (4166/235)   1300

Cherokee

Pipe, black stone, seated bear and bear standing on all fours, L6⅛ (4166/4)   675
Pipe, black stone, seated woman facing a small standing bear, L6⅜ (4166/3)   500

Cheyenne

Bag, beaded and fringed hide, rectangle decoration, L26 (4166/77)   1100
Bag, beaded and fringed hide, pipe, striped decoration, L32 (4166/76)   1600

Chippewa

Bag, beaded cloth bandoleer, contour beaded with flowers and leaves, L48 (4166/17)   _700_

Bag
(4166/17)

Knife sheath, beaded cloth, flower and leaf spray on white beaded ground, L13½ (4166/21)   225
Shoulder strap and panel, cloth, form of a bandoleer bag, contour beaded, L41½ (4166/16)   350

Cochiti

Figure, pottery, man figure with elaborate costume, H19½ (4166/97)   1300

Crow

Hair ornament, beaded hide, tapering rectangular panel with motifs, L30 (4166/78)   300

Eastern Woodlands

Box, rectangular birchbark, zig-zag ornament on body, L5⅛ (4166/6)   400

Case, birchbark, embroidered with flowers and leaves, H5¼ (4166/5)   400
Case, birchbark, frieze of figures on lid, H5⅝ (4166/7)   *400*
Container, birchbark, decorated with sun and leaf motifs, H8⅝ (4166/10)   *450*
Pipe, stone, form of a human head, H2 (4166/1)   175

Eskimo

Animal, ivory, possibly a bear, black inlays, L4⅜ (4237/373)   175
Basket, beehive, coiled, whirling pattern of stepped checkered lines, Diam 8¼ (4166/310)   175
Basket, coiled cylindrical, raised lid, ivory bear's head, Diam 6 (4237/370)   425
Basket, coiled whale baleen, globular body, ivory disk at base, Diam 3½ (4237/371)   750
Bear, ivory, standing on all fours, L3¼ (4237/377)   1200
Bolas, six bone, ivory weights on a string, (4237/379)   200
Canoe, women's model, 6 wood dolls seated inside, L23¾ (4166/316)   1100
Cribbage board, ivory, carvings of seal, sea-lion, L16⅞ (4237/382)   750
Cribbage board, ivory, decoration darkened in black pigment, L27¼ (4237/381)   *1800*
Cribbage board, ivory, with map of Alaska, L23 (4237/380)   1600
Cribbage board, ivory, drilled gameboard flanked by a bear's head, L22⅜ (4166/304)   1300
Cribbage board, ivory, form of a whale, L18 5/16 (4166/303)   2900
Cribbage board, ivory, miniature, incised decoration darkened in black pigment, L9⅝ (4166/305)   375
Doll, ivory, arms held close to body, H5⅛ (4166/306)   275
Fragment, tusk, ivory, incised scenes darkened in black pigment, L13⅞ (4166/302)   1300
Fragment, tusk, ivory, striding animal carved on 1 side, L11¼ (4166/301)   1200
Kayak, model, wood frame, wood doll and paddle, L20½ (4237/384)   300
Kayak, model, 3 wood figures seated inside, L14⅞ (4166/317)   800
Knife, ivory story, decoration darkened in black pigment, L11 (4237/372)   650
Moccasins, hide, beaded rosette on the front, L7¾ (4166/308)   40
Necklace, beaded rectangle decoration and bone pendant, L20 (4166/307)   300·
Seal, ivory swimming, decoration darken in black pigment, L2⅝ (4237/374)   375;
Toggle, ivory, form of a seal head, H1 11/32 (4237/376)   150
Toggle, ivory, probably used with a lure hook, L3 5/16 (4237/375)   100

Great Lakes

Bag, beaded cloth bandoleer, loom-beaded panels containing floral motifs, L41 (4166/19)   475
Bag, beaded cloth bandoleer, with flowerheads and leaves, L42 (4166/18)   500
Club, ball-headed, wood, metal tack decoration on tapering handle, L15¾ (4166/13)   500

Haida

Bowl, rectangular, carved wood, stylized totemic face on each end, L12½ (4166/274)   950
Box, bentwood, rectangular form with animal motifs, 15 x 12⅛ x 6⅛ (4166/273)   2600
Box, lidded, argillite, bear's head carved on front, 9⅞ x 5⅛ x 4 13/16 (4166/254)   2100
Figure, wood, form of a shaman, H17¼ (4166/270)   3900
Ladle, horn, mountain sheep, handle carved with a raven's head, L13⅞ (4166/238)   850
Pendant, shaman's, bone, form of an arched killer whale, L5⅜ (4166/244)   1900
Plate, argillite, decorated with totemic bird motifs, L11½ (4166/252)   *1500*

Case (4166/7)

Container (4166/10)

Cribbage board
(4237/381)

Plate (4166/252)

Rattle, wood, form of a raven holding the sun in its beak, L13⅛ (4166/281)	1900
Spoon, horn, mountain goat, 3 totemic heads carved in handle, L11⅛ (4166/237)	800
Totem pole, argillite, bear holding a fish in his teeth, H10¼ (4166/249)	550
Totem pole, argillite, sea mammal devouring its own tail, H15⅛ (4166/247)	1200
Totem pole, argillite, sea mammal devouring its own tail, H10⅛ (4166/250)	750
Totem pole, argillite, seated bear holding frog in forepaws, H18⅜ (4166/246)	2000
Totem pole, argillite, seated beaver holding a log in forepaws, H10 (4166/248)	625
Totem pole, argillite, seated beaver surmounted by a raven, a bear, H7⅝ (4166/251)	550
Totem pole, argillite, seated beaver surmounted by whale, face, bear, H18⅝ (4166/245)	4000
Vessel, wood, form of a swimming seal, L15½ (4166/278)	950

Hopi

Basket, coiled, flaring cylindrical form, Diam 10½ (4166/190)	125
Basket, coiled, rectangular body, L15½ (4166/191)	125
Blanket, banded design, 56½ x 42 (4166/168)	350
Doll, Kachina, wood, feather attachments on ears and top of head, H7½ (4166/142)	300
Doll, Kachina, wood, head with red semi-circular ears and snout, H12 (4166/132)	750
Doll, Kachina, wood, large helmet head with tubular snout, H12 (4166/133)	650
Doll, Kachina, wood, long black beard with rectangle decoration, H7¾ (4166/146)	225
Doll, Kachina, wood, pointed projection attached at each side, H6⅝ (4166/147)	225
Doll, Kachina, wood, protruding cylindrical eyes, feathered ears, H12 (4166/134)	850
Doll, Kachina, wood, rainbow decoration radiating from the mouth, H10¾ (4166/144)	400
Doll, Kachina, wood, spool of red wool on mouth, black wool hair, H10 (4166/148)	325
Doll, Kachina, wood, tubular mouth and red protruding ears, H8⅞ (4166/141)	250
Doll, Kachina, wood, wearing white kilt, H8¼ (4166/128)	125
Doll, Kachina, wood insect, black and white stripes on the upper torso, H8 (4166/143)	350
Doll, Kachina, wood Hemis, wearing red moccasins, white skirt, H25¾ (4166/131)	1900
Doll, Kachina, wood, wearing tall conical cap with feathers, H12⅛ (4166/145)	375
Instrument, hollowed out gourd speaker with wood insert, L10¼ (4166/125)	1300
Jar, pottery, squat body with panels of birds and feathers, Diam 12½ (4166/117)	4000

Hupa

Bowl, utility, twined, panels of zig-zag decorations encircling body, Diam 11½ (4166/224)	450
Cap, basket, twined, stripes and double-parallelograms, L21¾ (4166/225)	125
Cap, woman's, a network of beads sewn in a lattice design, (4166/297)	275

Jemez

Shield, circular, rawhide, narrow panel between 2 curving horns, Diam 25½ (4166/124)	2400

Klamath

Cap, basket, twined, band of connected diamonds, Diam 8 (4166/223)	100

Klikitat

Basket, coiled, imbricated pattern of zig-zag lines, H12½ (4166/227)	375

Kwakiutl

Frontlet, rectangular, wood, face of an eagle, H7 1/16 (4166/288)	225
Mask, bird, wood and fibre, long hooked beak, L36 (4166/289)	15000
Mask, face, wood, flattened chin, pierced eyes, hooked nose, H10⅜ (4166/295)	650
Rattle, wood, form of a raven holding the sun in its beak, L12⅛ (4166/280)	5750
Rattle, wood, head of a hawk and the head of a shark, H12¼ (4166/282)	750
Totem pole, wood, bear holding a human before him, H17¼ (4166/260)	750

Maidu

Basket, coiled, encircling stylized flame motif, Diam 4½ (4166/217)	550
Basket, coiled, pairs of stylized foxes, Diam 6⅜ (4166/218)	375

Mexican

Blanket, fringed, double column of serrated diamonds, 71 x 32¼ (4166/165)	350

Mono

Basket, coiled, flat oval base, Diam 5¾ (4166/197)	600

Navajo

Blanket, wearing, coalesced serrated diamonds, 74 x 44½ (4166/153)	1300
Blanket, wearing, handspun, red rectangles enclosing checkered lines, 61 x 49 (4166/151)	650
Blanket, wearing, Germantown, terraced diamonds, striped background, 84 x 50¼ (4166/152)	*1400*
Rug, central panel of converging serrated angles, 81 x 64 (4166/157)	*750*
Rug, double-hooked lozenge and crossed-bar motifs, 106½ x 53 (4166/158)	700
Rug, interlocking stepped rectangles, 51½ x 47¾ (4166/166)	300
Rug, 6 horizontal columns of triangles, 67½ x 48½ (4166/167)	350
Rug, chief's blanket style, rectangles enclosing geometric motifs, 75¼ x 66½ (4166/156)	900
Rug, eyedazzler, overall serrated design, 82 x 56½ (4166/154)	900
Rug, eyedazzler, serrated zig-zag panels, 50 x 33½ (4166/155)	850
Rug, large, central hooked lozenge between 2 diamonds, 46 x 128 (4166/159)	*3600*

Rug (4166/157)

Intricate multi-colored
symbolic motifs
(654/218)

Rug (4166/159)

Rug, yei, log pattern of 8 small skirted figures, 72 x 72 (4166/161) — 1900
Rug, yei, 7 skirting figures holding feathers, 80 x 44½ (4166/160) — 650

Navajo mat

Serrated diamonds on grayish-white ground, 50½ x 30 (654/212) — 100

Navajo rug

Diamond pattern, black, white, maroon, 54 x 35¾ (654/210) — 200
Diamonds, swastikas, crabs, 82 x 59, torn, frayed edges (654/216) — 150
Diamonds, triangles on gray field, 86 x 56, torn (654/215) — 200
Diamonds on striped ground, multi-colored, 79¼ x 55, worn (654/214) — 175
Intricate multi-colored symbolic motifs, 87 x 44½ (654/218) — *400*
Lizards, vines, gray and black on white, 62 x 39 (654/213) — 125
Serrated diamonds, white, black, red on gray, 59½ x 37 (654/211) — 100

Nez Perce

Bag, cornhusk, twined, crosses within hexagon columns, L16½ (4166/219) — 150
Bag, cornhusk, twined, symbolic stepped triangle and arrow motifs, L20½ (4166/220) — 250
Dress, fringed hide, graduated triangles in black against white, L47½ (4166/52) — 950

Nootka

Rattle, wood, form of bird with short beak and rounded body, L9 (4166/283) — 125

Northern California

Bowl, utility, twined, zig-zag lines between columns of triangles, Diam 9¾ (4166/221) — 250

Northern Plains

Moccasins, beaded hide, contour beaded with floral motifs, L10 (4166/41) — 350

Northwest

Basket, Attu twined, cylindrical body, floral motifs, H4⅛ (4237/364) — 650
Basket, Attu twined, encircling panel of parallelograms, H4⅜ (4237/366) — 1300
Basket, Attu twined, encircling panel of wedge motifs, H3 (4237/368) — 425
Basket, Attu twined, finely embroidered, H4¼ (4237/365) — 1200
Basket, Attu twined, tiny open crosses between zig-zag lines, H4½ (4237/367) — 850
Basket, Nootka twined, cylindrical form, row of ducks, Diam 4¾ (4237/311) — 100
Basket, Tlingit twined spruce root, flaring cylindrical body, cross, stepped motifs, Diam 5½ (4237/312) — 350
Basket bottle, Attu twined, pear-shaped body, long slender neck, H11 (4237/369) — 1100
Battle, Kwakiutl, wood, globular head carved with 2 bear faces, L11 (4237/341) — 4000
Board, wood pattern, possibly for a Chilkat blanket, 25½ x 17½ (4237/354) — 750
Bowl, wood, boat shaped body, carved in relief, L8½ (4237/344) — 1600
Bowl, wood, carved in the form of a raven, L12½ (4237/345) — 950
Bowl, Haida argillite, in form of a small crouching beaver, L2¼ (4237/318) — 1700
Box, rectangular wood storage, stylized bear faces on front, back, inlay of shells, 21½ x 18½ x 14⅛ (4237/343) — 1600
Canoe, Kwakiutl, wood model, carved with 2 running figures, movable head, on one, L34 (4237/353) — *2000*
Canoe paddle, Haida, wood, carved with a killer whale, totemic motifs, L48 (4237/350) — 475
Carving, Haida argillite, probably illustrating the Bear Mother story, 6¼ x 7¼ (4237/321) — 550
Drum, hexagonal wood and hide, Tlingit*, painted stylized bear's head, H15¾ (4237/363) — 350
Face panel, Kwakiutl Sisiutl, broad mouth, wide nose, articulated lower jaw, W21 (4237/360) — 6250
Figure, wood, seated, arms and knees hugging body, H10 (4237/338) — 350
Fish creel, twined, hooked motifs, pale yellow ground, (4237/306) — 850
Grease dish, wood, Haida*, stylized totemic face, L3 9/16 (4237/346) — 1400
Halibut club, Nootka, wood, globular head, spiral-ribbed grip, L14½ (4237/342) — 400
Hat, Haida twined basket, domed shape, stylized faces, eyes, Diam 14¼ (4237/316) — 300
Hat, Nootka twined basket, domed body, onion shaped finial, Diam 11⅜ (4237/315) — 650
Hat, Tsimshian twined spruce root, of truncated conical form, painted in red, black, Diam 18⅞ (4237/314) — 8500
Headdress, wood raven, long beak, articulated lower jaw, L26¼ (4237/357) — 2000
Headdress, Kwakiutl wood eagle, short hooked beak, sea mammel encircling eyes, L20¼ (4237/362) — 1600
Headring, Kwakiutl Hamatsa cedarbark, narrow panels of red cloth, (4237/359) — 400
Knife, Tlingit slave, steel blade, carved yellow bone handle, L14⅞ (4237/332) — 26000
Ladle, wood, deep oval bowl, L7⅜ (4237/347) — 100
Ladle, wood, elongated shallow pear-shaped bowl, L13 (4237/348) — 1400
Ladle, wood potlatch, in the form of a raven, L19 (4237/349) — *33000*

Figure (4166/268)

Ladle, Haida mountain sheep horn, nearly pointed oval bowl, animal head, L13¼ (4237/324)	250
Mask, wood miniature, in the form of a human face, pieces of ivory, 2⅝ (4237/355)	600
Mask, Kwakiutl, wood and fibre, carved, crooked beak, cedar bark at crown, L38 (4237/358)	11500
Mask, Tlingit circular wood face, face combining human, beaver attributes, 9 11/16 (4237/356)	23000
Paddle, wood, carved in low relief, animal face, eye motif, L37½ (4237/352)	450
Paddle, wood, painted on both sides, L48 (4237/351)	350
Panel, Haida wood, probably used as a head decoration, H12¼ (4237/337)	200
Pipe, antler, Tlingit*, form of a killer whale, L4½ (4237/327)	4000
Shaman's charm, bone, carved on front with a bears head, concave back, L4 29/32 (4237/333)	300
Shaman's charm, ivory, form of a voracious sea mammal, L2⅞ (4237/329)	250
Shamon's charm, ivory, Haida*, carved with a fish, a human, L2⅞ (4237/328)	1700
Spoon, coast horn, mountain-sheep horn bowl, copper plaque, L11 11/16 (4237/322)	2200
Spoon, coast mountain goat horn, flattened oval bowl, handle carved with mouth of, bear, L8¾ (4237/323)	1400
Totem pole, wood, figure surmounted by 4 graduated heads, H27¼ (4237/340)	1000
Totem pole, Haida argillite, carved with a beaver, human face, sea creature, H13⅜ (4237/319)	1600
Totem pole, Haida argillite, concave back, beaver, human mask, wolf, H17⅛ (4237/320)	1600
Totem pole, Kwakiutl wood model, a human figure holding a halibut, thunderbird, H16⅞ (4237/339)	500
Whistle, Kwakiutl wood twin chambered, three pieces of wood bound with string, L10½ (4237/336)	275

Northwest Coast

Basket, twined, band of angular and 'tatoo' motifs, Diam 11 (4166/233)	550
Basket, twined, 2 butterflies between 2 encircling bands, Diam 6¼ (4166/232)	200
Canoe, model, wood, stylized totemic motifs on sides, L51 (4166/261)	650
Carving, wood and horn, form of human head, frog projecting at mouth, H12¼ (4166/239)	600
Figure, wood, wearing bear headdress, clenching a staff, H17 (4166/268)	*650*
Hook, halibut, wood, carved on 1 side with a standing bear, H12¼ (4166/263)	300
Hook, halibut, wood, one side carved with stylized predatory bird, H13 (4166/265)	150
Hook, halibut, wood, one side carved with 2 confronted birds, H11¾ (4166/264)	*300*
Key, totem, wood, carved in form of a seal's head, L12¾ (4166/266)	175
Mask, face, wood, pierced wide mouth, large hooked nose, H11⅝ (4166/290)	1800
Stone, 'slave-killer', of zoomorphic form, short ears, flat back, 14 1/16 (4237/15)	950
Totem, model, wood, stylized sea mammal surmounted by an eagle, H14⅜ (4166/257)	150
Totem, wood, stands in a frog bowl, H22⅝ (4166/256)	900
Totem pole, wood, bear with long tongue and human face mask, H63 (4166/258)	2500
Totem pole, wood, eagle with backspread wings perched at top, H18½ (4166/259)	600
Totem pole, wood, seated raven holding animal between wings, H35 (4166/255)	3000
Vessel, wood, form of a bear standing on all fours, L15 (4166/279)	2000

Ojibwa

Pouch, loom-beaded rectangular, decorated rows of geometric floral motifs, L6 (4166/15)	30

Osage

Shawl, blue trade cloth, stitched with 5 silk hands, motifs on side, 70½ x 57½ (4166/32)	1600

Paiute

Basket, trinket, coiled, flat base and carinated body, Diam 5⅝ (4166/193) — 350
Cap, woman's, twined, 2 encircling bands of diamonds, Diam 7½ (4166/196) — 125

Panamint

Basket, coiled, flat base and high rounded sides, Diam 13¼ (4166/199) — 1600
Basket, coiled, flat oval base, flaring sides curving inward, Diam 6 (4166/198) — 650

Papago

Basket, coiled, cylindrical body with encircling bands, Diam 11⅝ (4166/171) — 250
Basket, coiled, flaring cylindrical body, flattened lid, H14½ (4166/170) — 300

Pima

Basket, coiled, circle in the tondo and crosses in the field, Diam 9¼ (4166/186) — 100
Basket, coiled, flat base and flaring cylindrical body, Diam 11¼ (4166/185) — 300

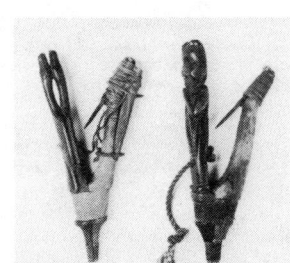

Hook (4166/264)

Basket, gift, coiled, flat base and flaring sides, Diam 5⅞ (4166/187) — 350
Basket, storage, coiled, rows of human figures, H15¼ (4166/179) — 1100

Pitt River

Basket, twined, 2 undulating lightning panels, Diam 12 (4166/215) — 300

Plains

Awl case, beaded hide, flap ornamented in butterfly motifs, L7¼ (4237/192) — 175
Awl case, beaded hide, trimmed with metal cone, red feather suspensions, L17¼ (4237/193) — 125
Awl case, beaded hide, with a linear pattern in white, yellow blue, L13 (4237/194) — 125
Backrest, child's triangular, Blackfoot, of a column of graduated wood rod, 25⅜ (4237/150) — 150
Backrest, wood, composed of graduated wood rods, 51½ (4237/156) — 700
Bag, beaded hide 'possible', stepped diamond motifs on white beaded ground, L17¾ (4237/218) — 450
Bag, beaded hide 'possible', trimmed with metal cones and red horsehair, L19¼ (4237/214) — 475
Bag, beaded hide 'possible', with rows of metal cones, green wool suspensions, L19½ (4237/217) — 525
Bag, beaded hide, medicine, composed of a skunk's body, L37 (4166/57) — 750
Bag, quilled hide 'possible', with bright red dyed quillwork, L19 (4237/215) — 475
Bag, Nez Perce twined cornhusk, embroidered, 'bow-tie' motifs, 21 (4237/269) — 325
Bag, Nez Perce twined cornhusk, embroidered, a bird, geometric motif, 11½ (4237/266) — 375
Bag, Nez Perce twined cornhusk, embroidered, a cross within a star, 12⅛ (4237/267) — 200
Bag, Nez Perce twined cornhusk, embroidered, black, red, pale blue wool, 8 (4237/264) — 325
Bag, Nez Perce twined cornhusk, embroidered, lime green, purple wool, 8 (4237/263) — 350
Bag, Nez Perce twined cornhusk, embroidered, pink, red, black, green, 10 (4237/265) — 300
Bag, Nez Perce twined cornhusk, embroidered, red, brown, green, black, beige, 9¾ (4237/268) — 125
Belt, beaded leather, decorated with stepped checkered diamonds, L43⅛ (4237/171) — 175
Belt, beaded leather, Cheyenne, with 3 diamond and angle motifs, L33⅞ (4237/172) — 150
Belt, quilled hide, Cheyenne, stitched with fleur-de-lis, pinched rectangles, L26½ (4237/174) — 425
Blanket, beaded hide, stars and linear decoration, Diam 59 x 53¾ (4166/60) — 900
Blanket strip, beaded hide, with rectangular and triangular motifs, L65¼ (4237/221) — 300

Blanket strip, Crow beaded hide, composed of 4 panels, overlaid with red wool, L74⅜ (4237/220)   6600
Bonnet, beaded hide baby, bull's eye motif at the top of the head, (4237/165)   200
Boot leggings, fringed hide, pair, mustard-dyed decoration overall, L22 (4237/240)   250
Breast ornament, man's, four rows of slender vertical hairpipes, L10 (4237/255)   250
Breast ornament, man's, two columns of slender vertical hairpipes, L15⅜ (4237/256)   *550*
Breast ornament, woman's, rectangular, strands of glass beads, slender hairpipes, L36¼ (4237/257)   225
Catlinite flute, carved in relief with Dakota on 1 side, 21½ (4237/12)   1600
Clay, rectangular pipe, ornamented with a deer and a feathered arrow, 2 9/16 x 2 (4237/5)   150
Club, war, handle bound with hide, bi-conical stone head, 24⅝ (4237/153)   400
Cradle cover, cloth and hide, Sioux, with silver metallic crosses, 23¾ (4237/159)   1100
Cradleboard, beaded hide, mounted on 2 wood slats, metal stud decor, L16½ (4166/61)   *600*
Cradleboard, fringed hide model, black and red cloth hood, silver metal buttons, L20½ (4237/162)   350
Cuffs, pair of beaded hide, each stitched in translucent blue and red, L6½ (4237/222)   200
Decoration, beaded hide, narrow tube, wound in multi-color glass beads, L15¼ (4237/252)   60
Deerskin, Shoshone painted, depicting a buffalo hunt, 47½ x 36 (4237/107)   2500
Doll, beaded hide, hide moccasins, fringed leggings and shirt, H11½ (4237/164)   150
Doll, hide, beaded moccasins, fringed dress, H10 (4237/163)   175
Dress, beaded and fringed hide, trimmed with cylindrical white glass, L45 (4237/232)   1300
Drum, wood and hide, cylindrical, painted in red and turquoise, Chief George Bullchild, Diam 12⅞ (4237/149)   400
Drum, wood and hide, Blackfoot, in orange, encircling row of dots, Diam 16¼ (4237/148)   275
Flute, love, catlinite, small bird bound with hide over vent holes, L20 1/16 (4166/84)   225
Gauntlets, beaded hide, pair, striding horse, multi-color parallelograms, L13 (4237/224)   300
Gauntlets, fringed quilled hide, stepped wedge and rectangular motif, L14 (4166/45)   550
Headdress, feather, hide cap with red painted decoration, H13 (4166/82)   125
Knife sheath, beaded, with 3 crosses in shades of green, red, L8⅞ (4237/212)   150
Knife sheath, beaded hide, white beaded panels with light, dark blue, L9¼ (4237/213)   350
Leggings, beaded hide, woman's, with crosses, angular motifs, L15¾ (4237/251)   350
Leggings, beaded hide, woman's, pair, stitched with crosses, diamonds, triangles, L14½ (4237/249)   300
Leggings, beaded hide, woman's, pair, with track, angular motifs, L13⅛ (4237/250)   350
Leggings, fringed hide, pair, yellow, red, green, white, L30½ (4237/248)   350
Mittens, beaded hide, pair, wool lining, red velvet, black silk, L13⅞ (4237/223)   300
Moccasins, beaded hide, beaded on front with rectangular motif, L10 (4166/43)   75
Moccasins, beaded hide, stitched with geometric decoration, L10¼ (4166/38)   150
Moccasins, beaded hide, child's, green triangular motifs, L4¾ (4166/35)   100
Moccasins, beaded hide, pair, checkered, striped, L9½ (4237/242)   200
Moccasins, beaded hide, pair, large cross on fronts, L10½ (4237/244)   *250*

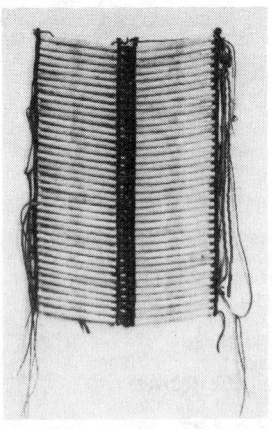

Breast ornament
(4237/256)

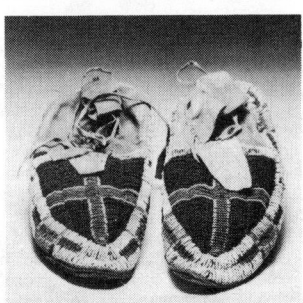

Moccasins (4237/244)

Moccasins, hide, Winnebago, pair, green, red cloth, silk, L9⅜ (4237/247)   100
Moccasins, quilled hide, strips of red quillwork, L10 (4166/34)   250
Parfleche, Blackfoot rectangular, of Chief George Bull Child, L16½ (4237/167)   300
Parfleche container, cylindrical, diamond and triangle decorations, L20¾ (4237/170)   450
Parfleche container, cylindrical, painted in red, yellow, green, blue, L28 with fringe (4237/169)   425

Pipe bag, beaded and fringed hide, with stepped diamond and rectangle motif, L38 (4237/209) 850
Pipe bag, beaded, fringed hide, beaded panel of stepped diamonds, angular motifs, L35 (4237/204) 750
Pipe bag, beaded, fringed hide, rectangle and triangle decoration, L38 with twisted fringe (4237/203) 2100
Pipe bag, beaded, fringed hide, Blackfoot, in yelow, red, white, light blue, L37 (4237/210) 400
Pipe bag, beaded, fringed hide, Sioux, decorated with a warrior and 4 thunderbirds, L29 (4237/205) 1400
Pipe bag, beaded, fringed hide, Sioux, in blue, green, red, white and purple, L29 (4237/207) 700
Pipe bag, fringed, quilled hide, Sioux, with 3 quilled flower buds, L34 (4237/208) 1000
Pottery, effigy jar, in the form of a kneeling human, 4½ (4237/14) 175
Pouch, beaded hide, long triangular flap with triangle motifs, L8¾ (4166/66) 75
Pouch, beaded hide 'strike-a-light', diamond and triangle motifs, row of metal cones, L4⅝ (4237/188) 175
Pouch, beaded hide 'strike-a-light', geometric decoration on front and flap, L6⅜ (4166/67) 225
Pouch, beaded hide oval, with 4 crescent motifs, L7⅛ (4237/202) 250
Pouch, beaded hide triangular, floral motifs, horseshoes and 2 pipes, L12 (4237/190) 125
Pouch, beaded hide, rectangular, green beaded squares within diamond network, L7⅝ (4166/69) 375
Pouch, beaded hide, triangular, rows of short fringes, L8¼ (4166/73) 325
Pouch, fringed and beaded hide, with contour floral motifs on front, L8¼ (4237/195) 150
Pouch, fringed hide, with yellow pigment overall, L24 (4237/219) 200
Pouch, hide 'strike-a-light', triangle motifs, row of metal cones, L5 (4237/187) 150
Pouch, hide flask, of circular form, beaded in white and blue, L6½ (4237/186) 200
Pouch, parfleche medicine, green, red, diamonds on front, flap, Chief George Bull Child, L7⅜ (4237/166) 325
Pouch, rectangular parfleche, diamond and triangle pattern, L14½ (4166/59) 225
Purse, Nez Perce twined cornhusk, embroidered, cross, hourglass motifs, 4⅝ (4237/270) 80
Robe, buffalo hide, painted warriors on horseback, L91 x 64 (4166/79) 7750
Shawl, blue trade cloth, stitched with 5 floral panels, 64½ x 58 (4237/200) 550
Shawl, blue, red trade cloth, with 2 panels of stylized flowers, arrows, 84 x 56 (4237/201) 550
Sheath, beaded parfleche, panel of stepped triangles along side, L14⅜ (4166/74) 700
Shirt, fringed hide, cape-like style, L20¼ (4237/228) 2600
Shirt and leggings, hide, green, yellow painted linear ornament, shirt 29⅜, leggings 26¼ (4237/229) 1600
Stone, frog pipe, with conical hole drilled at top and on back, 3½ (4237/4) 375
Tomahawk, pipe, metal head with incised geometric ornament, 24½ (4237/151) 500
Vest, beaded hide child's, cotton cloth lining, green, ochre, white, red, L12½ (4237/227) 450
Wood and black stone pipe, with elbow pipehead, probably not belonging, 30 (4237/11) 300
Wood and catlinite pipe, elbow pipehead, lead inlaid decoration, (4237/10) 325
Wood and catlinite pipe, red-dyed horsehair, blue ribbon, feathers, 31⅞ (4237/9) 1200
Wood and catlinite pipe, with elbow pipehead, probably not belonging, 28 3/16 (4237/8) 525

Pomo

Basket, coiled, rectangle panel between 2 zig-zag bands, Diam 6¾ (4166/214) 300
Basket, gift, coiled, rosette motif with shell beads and feathers, Diam 7½ (4166/212) 950

Pueblo

Bowl, pottery, stylized floral motifs, Diam 13 (4166/110) 450

Rio Grande

Rug, serrated zig-zag panels, diamond in center, 69 x 42 (4166/164) 800
Rug, fringed, 2 horizontal sections, arrowfeather motifs, 94½ x 51 (4166/163) 900

Salish

Basket, lidded, coiled, imbricated stepped zig-zag band, Diam 11½ (4166/230) 350

Santo Domingo

Jar, pottery, curvilinear motifs in a network of triangles, H10⅛ (4166/111) 700
Jar, pottery, rounded body and outward flaring rim, H6½ (4166/112) 150

Sauk

Awl, fox, form of horse's head, H6⅝ (4166/12) 150

Shastan

Basket, trinket, twined, horizontal and vertical decorations, Diam 4¼ (4166/216) 250

Sioux

Bag, beaded hide, pipe, 4 crosses and elaborate geometric motif, L23 (4166/75) 375
Dress, black trade cloth, dentalium shell decoration, L51½ (4166/53) 1100
Knife, catlinite, floral ornament on blade, L16½ (4166/85) 175
Leggings, beaded and fringed hide, decorated with triangular motifs, L31¼ (4166/46) 200

Moccasins, beaded hide, ceremonial, pattern of lines, squares and step motifs, L8 (4166/36)   350
Shirt, beaded and fringed hide, stepped diamonds and checkered wedges, L32 (4166/56)   *650*

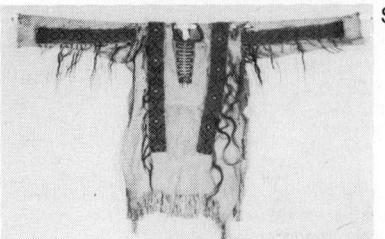

Shirt (4166/56)

Jar (4237/113)

Basket (4237/124)

Vest, beaded and fringed hide, crosses within stepped triangle and diamonds, L17⅝ (4166/51)   375
Vest, beaded and fringed hide, symbolic geometric motifs, L21 (4166/50)   750
Vest, beaded hide, Indians on horseback, 1 kneeling in combat, L20⅞ (4166/49)   1200

Southeast Woodlands

Pipe, bird effigy, form of a predatory bird, L8 (4166/2)   325

Southern California

Basket, coiled, long and short panels of zig-zag lines, Diam 15¼ (4166/204)   1600
Basket, coiled, 3 encircling meander bands on body, Diam 6½ (4166/206)   1400

Southern Plains

Pouch, beaded hide, pattern of concentric arches, L6⅝ (4166/68)   175
Shirt, fringed hide ghost dance, cluster of feathers, 2 crosses, L30 (4166/55)   475

Southwest

Basket, coiled, in reddish brown, radiating trefoil pattern, Diam 18¾ (4237/136)   900
Basket, coiled storage, straight sides, sloping shoulder, dark brown, H9 1/16 (4237/131)   200
Basket, coiled, Jicarilla Apache*, two handles at rim, Diam 23⅝ (4237/123)   950
Basket, storage, coiled, flaring sides and inward-curving shoulder, H27 (4166/169)   800
Basket, Apache coiled, boat shaped body, 2 rows of triangles on base, W18½ (4237/132)   375
Basket, Apache coiled, flattened base, a rosette in the tondo, Diam 11¾ (4237/133)   475
Basket, Apache coiled, of shallow form, checkered panels radiating out, Diam 10⅜ (4237/135)   300
Basket, Apache coiled storage, dark brown with checkered diamond panels, H28 (4237/128)   2100
Basket, Apache coiled storage, fields of horses within negative diamonds, H39 (4237/125)   16000
Basket, Apache coiled storage, in dark brown, 4 open crosses near the base, H9½ (4237/130)   200
Basket, Apache coiled storage, small animals and human figures in the field, H22¼ (4237/126)   1100
Basket, Apache coiled storage, small crosses and animals in the field, H21 (4237/127)   600
Basket, Apache coiled storage, zig-zag decoration radiating from the base, H14¼ (4237/129)   600
Basket, Apache coiled, western, flat base, squat body, small crosses at neck, field, Diam 7½
     (4237/134)   350
Basket, Apache twined burden, sides and rim with hide fringes, H9½ (4237/121)   121
Basket, Hopi coiled storage, thickly coiled flaring cylindrical body, Diam 21½ (4237/111)   1600
Basket, Jicarilla Apache coiled, flaring sides, 4 pointed star motif, Diam 14¾ (4237/122)   300
Basket, Paiute coiled, made for use by the Navajo, Diam 13¼ (4237/139)   200
Basket, Paiute coiled bottleneck, row of stepped diamonds on the border, Diam 18¾ (4237/137)   375
Basket, Papago coiled storage, with 5 vertical checkered panels, animals, H15⅛ (4237/120)   200
Basket, Pima coiled, whirling pattern of angular meander motifs, Diam 15¾ (4237/116)   275
Basket, Pima coiled storage, angular decorations on body, triangles on rim, H11½ (4237/117)   325
Basket, Pima coiled storage, dark brown, encircling pattern of double diamonds, H14¾ (4237/115)   200
Basket, Yavapai coiled, flat base, high rounded sides, animals in the field, Diam 20¾ (4237/124)   *3300*
Blanket, Hopi fringed, narrow white stripes, blue with brown background, 59 x 44 (4237/68)   1100

Blanket, Mexican fringed, in black, white, orange, purple, green, red, 88 x 43 (4237/105)   425
Blanket, Navajo, narrow stripes of parallelograms, banded design, 77 x 52½ (4237/69)   600
Blanket, Navajo, with a Chief's 3rd Phase, 9 spot pattern, 79½ x 68 (4237/73)   1500
Blanket, Navajo saddle, white ground, red stripes, brown border, 37⅛ x 28½ (4237/66)   275
Blanket, Navajo woman's, with a second phase 9 spot pattern, 52¾ x 44 (4237/67)   850
Blanket, Navajo Germantown, bright red ground, black, blue, white crosses, 79 x 55 (4237/71)   6400
Blanket, Navajo Germantown, of a stylized Chief's pattern, 68¾ x 53¼ (4237/70)   3800
Blanket, Navajo Moki style, serrated zig-zag columns, overlaying 5 panels, 75 x 49½ (4237/74)   4800
Blanket, Rio Grande, woven in 2 horizontal sections, 85 x 46 (4237/103)   200
Canteen, pottery, flattened circular body, H7¼ (4166/100)   950
Drum, wood and hide, painted in black and red with a sun, trees, Diam 10 (4237/146)   100
Jar, coiled storage, with triangular and angular fret motifs, Diam 9½ (4237/118)   150
Jar, Pima coiled storage, woven overall in dark brown, Diam 7 (4237/113)   *575*
Moccasins, Navajo orange dyed, pair, silver repousee butterfly buttons at ankle, L9⅝ (4237/241)   60
Pottery, acoma jar, flaring rounded sides, curving in at shoulder, Diam 8¼ (4237/59)   500
Pottery, canteen, twin loop handles, stylized smiling human face, 6¾ (4237/46)   600
Pottery, fish flask, Casas Grandes, black and red, 6⅝ (4237/39)   450
Pottery, jar, San Juan pueblo, polished redware base and rim, Diam 13½ (4237/65)   600
Pottery, pueblo jar, Acoma*, 4 diamond panels, floral motifs, Diam 12 (4237/60)   850
Pottery, rattle, form of a 2 legged zoomorphic creature, 5½ (4237/45)   150
Pottery, Acoma jar, globular body, twin loop handles, scalloped rim, (4237/61)   900
Pottery, Navajo ladle, hollow cylindrical handle, gourd-shaped bowl, 8⅞ (4237/43)   225
Pottery, Santo Domingo bowl, decorated with a panel of star rosettes, Diam 11¾ (4237/62)   450
Pottery, Santo Domingo jar, two panels of zig-zag decoration, rosettes below, Diam 9 (4237/63)   *1000*
Pottery, Santo Domingo Jar, neckband of leaf motifs, Diam 10 (4237/64)   650
Pottery, Zuni bowl, seated owl applied in relief at the center, Diam 11¼ (4237/57)   *850*
Pottery, Zuni dough bowl, painted with stylized bird motifs, Diam 15¾ (4237/53)   *1000*

Pottery (4237/57)

Pottery (4237/63)

Pottery (4237/53)

Pottery, Zuni jar, three spotted frogs molded in relief to the body, Diam 6 (4237/54)   450
Pottery, Zuni jar, with a band of 'dagger' motifs at the neck, Diam 10½ (4237/56)   1100
Pottery, Zuni jar, with 4 molded spotted frogs, 1 missing head, Diam 11¼ (4237/55)   300
Pottery, Zuni kiva bowl, painted in alternating dragonflies, frogs, Diam 10 (4237/58)   500
Rawhide, Apache playing cards, deck of, based on Spanish cards, in 4 suits, 39 cards (4237/108)   3200
Rug, Navajo, angle border around 2 Maltese crosses, 85 x 47½ (4237/100)   500
Rug, Navajo, deep red ground, black, white, serrated border, 57½ x 40¾ (4237/83)   400
Rug, Navajo, gray-brown ground, with red, black, gray, white, 80 x 56½ (4237/96)   350
Rug, Navajo, light brown and red, stepped triangular border, 66 x 37¼ (4237/89)   400
Rug, Navajo, natural gray-brown ground, double triangle motif, 81¼ x 53½ (4237/87)   300
Rug, Navajo, natural shaded gray-brown, small central cross, 79 x 47½ (4237/98)   500
Rug, Navajo, of a central square, bordered by angular scrolls, 104½ x 57½ (4237/99)   650
Rug, Navajo, on natural shaded gray ground, border of triangles, 95 x 63 (4237/85)   700
Rug, Navajo, on white ground, pink, brown-black, tan, brown, 92½ x 59 (4237/102)   1600
Rug, Navajo, red, gray-black, pink, pale green on natural ground, 77 x 39¼ (4237/97)   600
Rug, Navajo, shaded red ground, 2 rectangular borders, 65 x 49½ (4237/91)   500
Rug, Navajo, softly-woven on light brown ground, 76 x 55 (4237/95)   1000

Rug, Navajo, tightly-woven in black, white, gray, red, 78½ x 51¾ (4237/92) — 250
Rug, Navajo, with a border of crosses around a field, 96 x 68 (4237/94) — 3200
Rug, Navajo, with a border of double-hooked motifs, 82 x 53½ (4237/93) — 2000
Rug, Navajo, with an American flag design, fifty stars, 57½ x 36¼ (4237/106) — 400
Rug, Navajo, woven in white, brown, red, swastika star motif, 95 x 68 (4237/88) — 4600
Rug, Navajo, woven in white, deep red, shaded black, brown, 71 x 41 (4237/90) — 375
Rug, Navajo, woven on natural shaded light brown, 108 x 63 (4237/84) — 1400
Rug, Navajo, woven on shaded red ground, black, orange, green, 84½ x 50½ (4237/77) — 1700
Rug, Navajo, zig-zag border around 2 hooked diamond motifs, 86 x 45 (4237/101) — 1000
Rug, Navajo eyedazzler, bright red ground, striped panel at either end, 85 x 55½ (4237/80) — 600
Rug, Navajo eyedazzler, shaded red ground, white, yellow, orange, black, 71 x 51¼ (4237/79) — 650
Rug, Navajo eyedazzler, woven in red, white, orange, yellow, rust, blue, gray, 91 x 55½ (4237/81) — 1000
Rug, Navajo Germantown, tightly woven, red ground, white, yellow, green, 95 x 64 (4237/72) — 2000
Rug, Navajo Germantown eyedazzler, central column of serrated diamonds, fringed, 70 x 39¼ (4237/76) — 850
Rug, Navajo Germantown eyedazzler, on shaded bright red ground, 57⅜ x 32⅝ (4237/75) — 850
Rug, Navajo, deep red ground, orange, purple, shades of green, 67¾ x 45 (4237/82) — 750
Silver, Navajo band bracelet, stamped decoration with swastika, diamond motif, 2⅝ (4237/28) — 150
Silver, Navajo band bracelet, stamped with thunderbird motif, raincloud symbols, W⅜ (4237/31) — 350
Silver, Navajo squash blossom necklace, globular beads, 14 simple 'blossoms', 28½ (4237/25) — 550
Silver, Zuni necklace, single chain, 7 pendants of Knife Winged God, 17 (4237/27) — 200
Silver, Zuni pin, in the form of the Knife Wing God, 3⅝ (4237/21) — 200
Textile, horizontal rows of serrated diamonds, 56 x 41 (4166/162) — 150
Wood, Apache fiddle and bow, hollow cylindrical body, in yellow, black, purple, 22½ (4237/109) — 250
Wood, Hopi female Kachina doll, white shawl over a black dress, 9⅝ (4237/37) — 600
Wood, Hopi Kachina doll, representing Heheya, in white kilt, 7⅞ (4237/35) — 550
Wood, Hopi Kachina doll, representing Holi, red body, blue helmet, 7¼ (4237/36) — 275
Wood, Hopi Kachina doll, spotted decoration on arm and legs, white shawl, 16 (4237/34) — 1500

Tlingit

Bag, octopus, cloth, foliate and geometric decoration, L19¾ (4166/298) — 900
Basket, twined spruce root, encircling band of spread-winged eagles, Diam 5½ (4166/231) — 475
Basket, twined spruce root, zig-zag decoration, Diam 5 (4166/234) — 400
Bowl, food, wood, form of a swimming seal or sea lion, L13¾ (4166/275) — 700
Bowl, oval, wood, stylized totemic faces encircling body, 14 1/16 (4166/276) — 400
Frontlet, wood, large puffin bird head, H8⅛ (4166/285) — *2500*

Tsimshian

Headdress, chief's, wood, form of a winged insect, H11⅛ (4166/284) — 6000
Mask, face, wood, pierced open mouth and everted lips, H8½ (4166/293) — 4800
Mask, wood, combination of human and eagle traits, H10⅝ (4166/294) — 6000
Wand, shaman's, wood, carved with 2 addorsed crouching bears, L13½ (4166/267) — 1600

Tulare

Basket, coiled, rounded body with encircling bands, Diam 5⅛ (4166/202) — 650
Basket, coiled, 2 encircling rattlesnake bands, Diam 14¼ (4166/200) — 1300
Tray, gambling, coiled, concentric rattlesnake bands of triangles, Diam 18½ (4166/201) — *700*

Washo

Basket, coiled, flat base and flaring sides curving inward, Diam 7½ (4166/195) — 500
Basket, trinket, coiled, parallelograms and arrowfeather motifs, Diam 4¼ (4166/194) — 150

Woodlands

Bag, beaded cloth bandoleer, contour beaded on the shoulder strap, L43 (4237/181) — 650
Bag, cloth octopus, stitched with 2 red cloth rosettes, L17 (4237/185) — 550
Bag, cloth octopus, with profuse scrolling foliate motifs, L14½ (4237/184) — 400
Box, birchbark, cylindrical, decorated with triangle motifs on lid, 3 (4237/141) — 300
Box, birchbark, cylindrical, quillwork of red, purple, blue, white, 3¾ (4237/142) — 225
Box, birchbark, rectangular, divided into 3 panels on the sides, L4¾ (4237/140) — 175
Box, elmbark, rectangular, a moose striding on the lid, L10½ (4237/144) — 200
Cap, beaded, Iroquois, in the form of a Scottish bonnet, L10½ (4237/178) — 225
Cloth decoration, beaded, in the form of a bandoleer bag, L51¼ (4237/182) — 600
Coat, fringed hide, of European style, lined, L38 (4237/238) — 4200
Doll, cloth and hide, flowered cotton blouse, brown wool apron, H19¾ (4166/14) — 300
Gauntlets, beaded and fringed hide, curvilinear floral decoration, L14¼ (4166/27) — 75
Gauntlets, beaded and fringed hide, decorated with contour-beaded flowers, leaves, L16¼ (4166/26) — 250
Jacket, fringed hide, long sleeves, short collar, L29⅜ (4237/239) — 500

Knife, crooked, handle carved with a moose head, 9⅜ (4237/145) — 75
Pouch, cloth and hide, drawstring through top, metal cones, red horsehair, L12½ (4237/180) — 125
Pouch, slipper-form cloth, stitched on red wool in white, yellow, blue, L9 7/16 (4237/179) — 75

Frontlet (4166/285)

Jar (4166/104)

Pouch (4237/179)

Tray (4166/201)

Powderhorn, decorated with 2 black velvet panels, L24¾ (4237/183) — 375

Yokut

Basket, coiled, 3 panels of checkered rectangles, Diam 10¼ (4166/205) — 200
Tray, circular, coiled, a 'rattlesnake' band of connected hexagons, Diam 18¼ (4166/203) — 500

Zia

Jar, pottery, a field of birds and floral motifs, Diam 9 (4166/115) — 250
Jar, pottery, encircling panel of stylized flowers, Diam 12½ (4166/114) — 1500

Zuni

Bracelet, silver openwork, inlaid plaque, Knife Wing God, Juan Calavaza, W2⅜, 1938 (4166/91) — 650
Fetish, animal, brown stone, bound with shell and turquoise beads, L3 (4166/121) — 200
Jar, pottery, diamond motifs alternating with splayed frogs, Diam 8 (4166/108) — 750
Jar, pottery, fragmentary band of spotted deer, Diam 10½ (4166/105) — 700
Jar, pottery, neckband of 'dagger' motifs, Diam 10 (4166/103) — 1200
Jar, pottery, stylized 'daggers' and curvilinear motifs, Diam 12 (4166/104) — *1600*
Pin, circular, silver, in form of the sun mask, Diam 2¼ (4166/93) — 375
Pin, silver butterfly, inlaid in mosaic technique, Dan Simplico, H2½, 1948 (4166/92) — 600
Vessel, pottery, form of a fetish jar, H6½ (4166/120) — 400

OCEANIC WORKS OF ART

Aborigine boomerang, typical shape, incised hardwood, L24 (4227/221) — 325
Aborigine spear thrower, leaf shape form, small tooth hook, length 24½ (4227/222) — 50
Batak human figure amulet, man standing holding spiral to chest, 5, Indonesian (4227/236) — 175
Cook Island adze, unusually long handle, L65 (4227/201) — 450
Easter island male figure, curving slender form, ribs showing, 13½ (4227/204) — 2500
Fijian whale teeth necklace, twenty 3 curving graduated teeth, (4227/234) — 700
Hawaiian basalt food pounder, concave conical form, 9 (4227/203) — 100
Hawaiian dog tooth leg rattle, twenty-five rows on olona fiber, L12 (4227/200) — 750

Hawaiian ivory and hair necklace, ivory hook pendant, human hair cord, L4½ (4227/202)	2900
Iban human figure amulet, standing, circular eyes, Indonesian (4227/235)	225
Maori jade pendant, drop shape form, pierced at end, 1⅝ (4227/198)	75
Maori nephrite tiki pendant, hei-tiki figure, worn features, cord, 4 13/16 (4227/196)	2600
Maori nephrite tiki pendant, hei-tiki grotesque figure, 4⅜ (4227/197)	650
Maori whalebone hand club, spatulate blade, grooved grip, L14⅞ (4227/199)	200
New Caledonian roof spire, highly stylized mythological creature, 37¾ (4227/233)	3600
New Guinea ceremonial ladle, paddle form, L50½ (4227/218)	100
New Guinea dance shield, intricate scrolls with central grip, L24½ (4227/217)	*575*
New Guinea double bowl, oval vessels connected by human figure, L26 (4227/213)	150
New Guinea face mask, sepik, oval form, cicatrization, painted patina, 17 (4227/207)	650
New Guinea flute stopper, sepik, human form, eagle head, pigmentation, 10⅞ (4227/210)	400
New Guinea flute stopper, sepik, male figure, cormorant head, 16⅞ (4227/212)	100
New Guinea food bowl, boat form, carved exterior, L31 (4227/220)	2000
New Guinea head ornament, sepik, grooved smiling face, 10¾ (4227/208)	100
New Guinea human figure, sepik, oversized head, short beard, 17 (4227/206)	225
New Guinea male figure, polychrome decoration, 44¾ (4227/205)	700
New Guinea mortar, supported by stylized human form, 8¼ (4227/219)	125
New Guinea plaque figure, elaborate carved motifs, 30½ (4227/215)	175
New Guinea sago pounder, sepik, swelling cylindrical shaft, 14¼ (4227/211)	100
New Guinea standing figure, brown-black patina, 6⅛ (4227/216)	850
New Hebrides canoe prow ornament, pig on notched runners, length 30¼ (4227/231)	*900*
New Hebrides slit-gong terminal, highly stylized head, 66 (4227/230)	350
New Hebrides temes nevinbur, paste modeled janus headed figure, conical eyes, 14 (4227/229)	125
Santa Cruz boat shaped club, elaborately painted geometric ornament, L41 (4227/232)	125
Solomon Island boomerang dance club, boomerang form, inlaid haliotis shells, L55 (4227/227)	325
Solomon Island canoe prow figure, with hands under, facial scarification, 5⅛ (4227/224)	*900*
Solomon Island model canoe, mother of pearl inlaid exterior, L35¼ (4227/225)	250
Solomon Island tortoise shell form, human figure, fish's tail, fish head, 7¼ (4227/226)	75

PRE-COLUMBIAN WORKS OF ART

Aztec stone goddess A.D.1400-1520, heavy headdress, arms at side, knotted sash, 14¾ (4181/134)	1000
Central coast figure A.D.1100-1400, standing female, raised arms, pierced nose, 15¼ (4181/34)	250
Chancay cloth head A.D.1100-1400, rectangular form sewn with metal facial design, 18½ (4181/30)	175
Chancay female figure A.D.1100-1400, standing, raised arms, large head, cream, black, 24¼ (4181/29)	425
Chancay female figure A.D.1100-1400, standing, raised arms, large head, cream, black, 22¼ (4181/27)	*1300*
Chancay female figure A.D.1100-1400, standing, raised arms, large head, cream, black, 21½ (4181/26)	1100
Chancay female figure A.D.1100-1400, standing, raised arms, large head, cream, black, 17 15/16 (4181/28)	*700*
Chancay lace textile A.D.1100-1400, square fragment of pale tan with woven condor, 20 x 19½ (4181/33)	300
Chancay whistle vessel A.D.1100-1400, double body with perched bird and strap handle, 10⅝ (4181/32)	250
Chavin bottle, tembladera 700-400B.C., brown, bi-conical body with geometric design, 8⅛ (4181/36)	375
Chavin vessel, tembladera 700-400B.C., seated old man figure with traces of paint, 10¾ (4181/35)	*4500*
Chimu copper knife A.D.900-1400, lozenge blade, llama head finial, pointed ears, 5 15/16 (4181/105)	125
Chimu copper roundel A.D.900-1400, openwork form, molded birds, dot decoration, diameter 4⅝ (4181/109)	150
Chimu erotic bottle A.D.900-1400, erotic couple, central spout, grayware pottery, 7⅝ (4181/102)	400
Chimu fish vessel A.D.900-1400, open mouth, incised fins, moulded step design, 9¼ (4181/104)	1000
Chimu head vessel A.D.900-1400, llama form, widely set eyes, grayware pottery, 7⅝ (4181/103)	325
Chimu silver beaker A.D.900-1400, flaring cylindrical body, low relief panels, 7 (4181/101)	800
Chimu squash pot A.D.900-1400, dark grayware, flattened base, 8 11/16 (4181/108)	375
Chimu wood figure A.D.900-1400, standing, raised hands, inlaid shell eyes, 13½ (4181/107)	275
Chinesco figure 100B.C.-A.D.250, standing, short torso, incised facial features, 9 1/16 (4181/139)	600
Chinesco squash pot 100B.C.-A.D.250, molded, scalloped body, flaring neck, 7¾ (4181/140)	300
Colima female figure 350-100B.C., standing, hands on abdomen, short coiffure, 7½ (4181/152)	150
Colima gadrooned jar 100B.C.-A.D.250, tripod feet incised with parrots, painted red, diameter 14½ (4181/154)	1300
Colima jar 100B.C.-A.D.250, molded row of seed pods, outward flaring rim, 10½ (4181/155)	325

New Guinea dance shield (4227/217)

Chavin vessel
(4181/35)

Solomon Island
canoe prow figure
(4227/224)

Chancay female figure
A.D.1100-1400 (4181/27)

Chancay female
figure A.D.1100-1400
(4181/28)

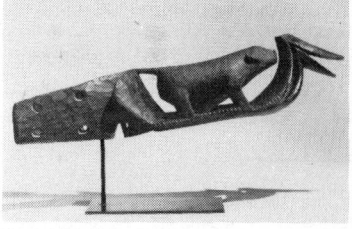

New Hebrides canoe prow ornament
(4227/231)

Colima male figure 100B.C.-A.D.250, seated holding long cylindrical vessel, 14¾ (4181/156)	800
Colonial wood beaker A.D.1500-1600, kero incised with diamonds and rectangles, 7¼ (4181/116)	325
Costa Rican tripod vessel A.D.800-1500, narrow tapering legs of stylized human figure, 11¼ (4181/186)	800
Guerro four-legged bowl 300-100B.C., bulbous legs, incised, banded body, diameter 8¼ (4181/136)	200
Guerro stone mask 300-100B.C., perforated eyes and mouth, ridged eyebrows, 6 7/16 (4181/135)	600
Honduran female figure 300-100B.C., squatting with hands resting on thighs, 11¼ (4181/183)	500
Honduran tripod jar A.D.550-950, polychrome feline head and curled serpent, 5½ (4181/174)	1000
Huari polychrome bottle A.D.800-1000, stylized condors of orange, grey, cream, black, 13¾ (4181/25)	650
Huari polychrome bowl A.D.700-100, cream, dark brown, orange with linear design, diameter 5⅞ (4181/17)	200
Inca avial vessel A.D.1400-1532, large central spout, pedestal foot, brown paint, 7½ (4181/114)	750
Inca double-bodied vessel A.D.1400-1532, one cup, one gourd surmounted by human figure, 9 (4181/115)	325
Inca head flask A.D.1400-1532, polychrome, close set eyes, lug handles, spout, 7⅞ (4181/113)	750
Inca head vessel A.D.1400-1532, llama form, pointed snout, small ears, tan paint, length 9 (4181/111)	175
Inca polychrome vase A.D.1400-1532, pear shape, geometric design, cream, black, orange, 12½ (4181/112)	325
Jalisco figure 100B.C.-A.D.250, seated female holding vessel, raised arm, 8⅝ (4181/151)	400
Jalisco warrior 100B.C.-A.D.250, seated, criss-cross headband, upraised arm, 16¾ (4181/148)	2000
Jalisco warrior 100B.C.-A.D.250, standing, holding club, wearing armor, 14½ (4181/150)	900

Jalisco warrior 100B.C.-A.D.250, standing, holding club, wearing armor, 15⅜ (4181/149)   1200
Lambayegue erotic vessel A.D.900-1250, erotic couple with strap handle, tapering spout, 7½
   (4181/98)   400
Mayan carved emblem vase A.D.550-950, sides carved with sunken roundels of warriors, diameter
   6¼ (4181/171)   4500
Mayan carved vase A.D.550-950, waisted form with incised seated personage, diameter 6
   (4181/181)   1100
Mayan figure whistle A.D.550-950, mold-made, seated, skirted, headdress, 6 9/16 (4181/178)   250
Mayan glyph bowl A.D.550-950, round body, band of glyphs below linear bands, 7 (4181/180)   600
Mayan jaina warrior A.D.550-950, standing in elaborately decorated dress, 7 (4181/176)   700
Mayan molded vase A.D.600-900, cylindrical ridged body, molded monkey motif, 7 (4181/184)   200
Mayan olychrome vase A.D.550-950, tall slender shape, serenading woman depicted, 8 5/16
   (4181/170)   11500
Mayan painted vase A.D.550-950, tall form on ringed foot, geometric motif, 7 9/16 (4181/175)   950
Mayan polychrome plate A.D.550-950, tondo with fox and geometric design banding, diameter 15
   (4181/182)   850
Mayan polychrome vase A.D.550-950, tall cylindrical form, ceremonial motif, 9 1/16 (4181/169)   13000
Mayan standing priest A.D.550-950, extended arms, long cape, incised beard, 6⅝ (4181/179)   500
Mixtec gold disc A.D.1200-1500, small rounded form, diameter 2¾ (4181/131)   800
Mixtec necklace A.D.1200-1500, thirty-four gld rectangular pieces and bells, length 9¾ (4181/130)   6250
Mixtec stone figure A.D.1200-1500, seated tlaloc, crossed arms, glyph scrolls, 5 5/16 (4181/132)   850
Mixtec stone figure A.D.1200-1500, seated tlaloc, crossed arms, janiform headdress, 4 5/16
   (4181/133)   850
Mochica avial vessel A.D.100-500, curving beak, painted tan and reddish-brown, (4181/78)   650
Mochica bat vessel A.D.100-500, squash form body surmounted by bat, 8⅞ (4181/79)   800
Mochica death effigy vessel A.D.100-500, protruding tongue, recessed eyes, wearing cap, 9⅛
   (4181/59)   *2900*
Mochica drum vessel A.D.100-500, llama form with tall cylindrial neck, 11 (4181/82)   450
Mochica feline effigy jar A.D.100-500, seated, cross-legged figure, growling expression, 16¾
   (4181/64)   2300
Mochica feline vessel A.D.100-500, crouching figure, curling tail, black and cream, 7½ (4181/81)   275
Mochica figural bottle, standing with heavy hood and cape, 8⅝ (4181/75)   550
Mochica figural jar A.D.100-500, hand over right eye, wearing earrings, cream, 7 (4181/91)   175
Mochica figural jar A.D.100-500, standing with hands to chest, feline headdress, 10⅞ (4181/67)   725
Mochica figural vessel A.D.100-500, figure with dipper and vessel in hands, 8¼ (4181/63)   525
Mochica figural vessel A.D.100-500, kneeling mutilated dwarf, stump feet, cap, 7¼ (4181/84)   400
Mochica figural vessel A.D.100-500, mutilated reclining figure with headdress, 8 (4181/72)   *950*

Mochica death effigy
vessel A.D.100-500
(4181/59)

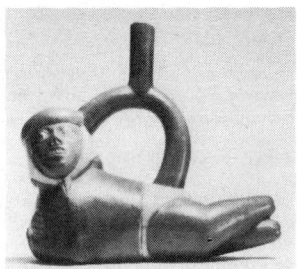

Mochica figural vessel
A.D.100-500 (4181/72)

Mochica figural vessel A.D.100-500, robed figure holding feline, geometric designs, 7¾ (4181/83)   300
Mochica figural vessel A.D.100-500, rotund seated figure with hands on stomach, 8⅛ (4181/69)   950
Mochica figural vessel A.D.100-500, standing in prayer, long robes, earrings, cap, 8⅞ (4181/74)   850
Mochica figural vessel A.D.100-500, standing with pouch at side, 8⅝ (4181/86)   375
Mochica figural vessel A.D.200-500, seated with hands holding headdress, 9 (4181/70)   325
Mochica figural vessel 400B.C.-100A.D., seated figure in cream, orange and red, 7⅛ (4181/55)   550
Mochica figural vessel A.D.100-500, human figure emerging from squash, raised hand, 6⅞
   (4181/92)   400

Mochica figure vessel A.D.100-500, bound prisoner with rope around neck, painted, 9⅜ (4181/88)	250
Mochica figure vessel 400B.C.-A.D.500, seated figure with headdress in cream, ochre, 6½ (4181/54)	225
Mochica fish vessel A.D.100-500, round body, lug handles, low marine life relief, 7⅞ (4181/89)	200
Mochica fox vessel A.D.100-500, standing growling figure painted brown, cream, 10½ (4181/80)	1200
Mochica head jar A.D.100-500, molded cheeks, forelock and moustache, 7¾ (4181/95)	300
Mochica head jar A.D.300-600, nose ornament, ear spools, feline headdress, 7¼ (4181/62)	750
Mochica head vessel A.D.100-500, human face emerging from potato, geometric, designs 9 5/16 (4181/90)	
Mochica head vessel A.D.100-500, Ai-Apec form with cap and fringe, 10⅞ (4181/73)	375
Mochica head vessel 200B.C.-500A.D., skull form painted cream and orange-brown, 9 (4181/57)	325
Mochica head vessel 400-100B.C., small feet under chin, painted orange, cream, 8½ (4181/56)	500
Mochica incised vessel 400B.C.-100A.D., chavin influenced zoomorphic design on tan, 8⅝ (4181/53)	1600
Mochica otter vessel A.D.100-500, recumbent otter eating shellfish, curled tail, 11 (4181/85)	400
Mochica painted vessel 400B.C.-100A.D., recuay influenced squat body, light brown paint, length 11 (4181/52)	250
Mochica portrait head cups A.D.100-500, molded forelock, ear ornaments, painted brown, 4 9/16 one pair (4181/77)	500
Mochica portrait jar A.D.100-500, janiform with feline ear ornaments, 6⅛ (4181/87)	375
Mochica seal head bottle A.D.200-600, ridged eyes, lug ears, tall spout, round handle, 7½ (4181/71)	250
Mochica seated vessel A.D.100-500, beggar with hand extended, wearing hooded cape, 7⅜ (4181/93)	375
Mochica seated vessel A.D.100-500, Ai-Apec figure with mountain, smaller figures, 8¼ (4181/76)	800
Mochica standing amputee jar A.D.100-500, severed arms, broad collar, ear spools, headdress, 10⅞ (4181/65)	750
Mochica vessel A.D.100-500, standing woman with child on back, 8⅛ (4181/94)	150
Mochica vessel A.D.100-700, crouching deer with geometric design, 10½ (4181/96)	300
Mochica war club vessel A.D.100-500, molded club in form of Ai-Apec praying, 11 (4181/60)	500
Mochica warrior jar A.D.100-500, rotund stand figure with club, shield, headdress, (4181/66)	900
Mochica warrior jar A.D.100-700, standing dressed as owl with club and shield, 7½ (4181/97)	175
Mochica warrior vessel A.D.100-500, molded with two combating warriors and clubs, 7⅝ (4181/61)	1400
Mochica warrior vessel A.D.100-500, sleeping with crossed arms, crested helmet, 7 15/16 (4181/68)	1300
Nayarit couple 100B.C.-A.D.250, seated, woman with bowl, man with club, painted, 10½ each (4181/142)	1200
Nayarit figure 100B.C.-A.D.250, seated female, ear and nose ornaments, skirted, 10¾ (4181/145)	500
Nayarit figurine 100B.C.-A.D.250, seated female, hands on abdomen, headdress, skirt, 6 15/16 (4181/147)	150
Nayarit squash bottle 100B.C.-A.D.250, three graduating squash form tiers, blackened, 8⅞ (4181/146)	225
Nayarit warrior 100B.C.-A.D.250, seated on stool holding club with helmet, 11 (4181/141)	650
Nayarit warrior 100B.C.-A.D.250, seated, holding club in hand, with helmet, 10¼ (4181/144)	450
Nayarit warrior 100B.C.-A.D.250, standing on heavy legs and feet with club, 17 1/16 (4181/143)	1500
Nazca avial vessel A.D.100-300, round body of grey, red, brown, cream and orange, length 7¼ (4181/5)	300
Nazca bridge spout vessel A.D.1-300, round polychrome body with demon figures, (4181/9)	450
Nazca head jar A.D.300-600, purple, grey, orange with molded nose and hat, 6⅛ (4181/11)	375
Nazca painted beaker, beige, red, brown, grey, demon figures on white, diameter 4 3/16 (4181/6)	150
Nazca painted bowl A.D.100-300, polychrome band of lozenge motif on brown, diameter 6¾ (4181/7)	225
Nazca polychrome beaker A.D.100-300, waisted form with band of polychrome monkeys, 5¼ (4181/8)	225
Nazca polychrome dish A.D.100-300, cream, reddish-brown on brown with 'S' design, diameter 5⅞ (4181/12)	175
Nazca polychrome dish A.D.100-300, red, purple, orange avial figures on cream, diameter 8¼ (4181/4)	350
Nazca polychrome dish A.D.100-300, red, tan, brown on white with sea creatures, 6½ (4181/13)	125
Nazca polychrome dish A.D.100-300, tan, cream, black feline head with serpent body, 7⅝ (4181/10)	275
Nazca polychrome dish 100B.C.-A.D.100, grey, tan, red, brown avial figures on cream, diameter 7⅝ (4181/2)	275
Nazca vase, early 100B.C.-A.D.200, llama hoof form, painted overall dark brown, 4 3/16 (4181/1)	150
Olmec stone mask 1150-550B.C., greenstone, pronounced jaguar mouth, pigment, 5¼ (4181/118)	7750
Peruvian necklace A.D.900-1400, shells, gold bead, turquoise, coral, quartz, length 31 (4181/100)	250
Preclassic figure 1150-550B.C., female, incised headdress, hands at waist, 10 (4181/122)	250
Preclassic figurine 1150-550B.C., female, swollen abdomen, incised hair, features, 6⅞ (4181/124)	700

Preclassic figurine 1150-550B.C., standing, raised arms, large head, headdress, 7⅝ (4181/125)   425
Preclassic vessel 1150-550B.C., standing zoomorphic figure, incised features, length 9 (4181/127)   175
Salinar feline vessel 500-300B.C., recumbent, fangs, tapering spout, red-dish brown, 9 (4181/39)   450
Salinar whistle vessel 500-300B.C., male figure in grayware with bowl to mouth, 8 (4181/40)   *650*
Salinar-viru feline vessel 500-300B.C., round head, fangs, curling tail, brownish-orange, 8 (4181/38)   600
South coast textile A.D.1100-1400, rectangular, multi-color avial design in bands, 29 x 14¾ fragment (4181/22)   300
South coast textile A.D.1100-1400, rectangular, woven multi-color avial designs, 49 x 15¾ fragment (4181/19)   1100
South coast textiles A.D.1100-1400, two pieces from multi-color figural panel, 14½ x 7½ and 14½ x 8¾ (4181/21)   700
South coast woven panel A.D.700-1000, multi-color animal motifs in squares, 35 x 19⅝ fragment (4181/18)   1200
Tiahuanaco bottle A.D.700-1100, sea turtle form with central spout, incising, 8¼ (4181/15)   125
Tiahuanaco vase A.D.700-1100, feline form with geometric designs in brown, length 8¾ (4181/14)   250
Tlatilco bottle 1150-550B.C., incised squat-shaped body, cylindrical spout, 10⅞ (4181/126)   250
Tlatilco figurine 1150-550B.C., type D-1 standing female, incised hair, 4 13/16 (4181/121)   275
Tlatilco figurine 1150-550B.C., type D-1, standing, long hair, traces pigment, 4 (4181/120)   600
Veracruz dancer A.D.550-950, standing with arms thrown out, skirted, bowed, 21¼ (4181/161)   1300
Veracruz death-head hacha A.D.550-950, stone, recessed eyes, crested forehead, carved, 9¼ (4181/158)   3600
Veracruz female figure A.D.550-950, mold-made, standing, raised arms, striated hair, 8⅞ (4181/163)   300
Veracruz figure A.D.550-950, standing, smiling, articulated arms, necklace, 13 (4181/162)   *500*
Veracruz head fragment A.D.550-950, parted lips, close-set eyes, headdress, 5¼ (4181/165)   400
Veracruz head A.D.550-950, wearing helmet with chin strap, paint traces, 5½ (4181/166)   175
Veracruz laughing boy A.D.550-950, seated, raised arms with rattles, headband, 13¼ (4181/160)   2750
Veracruz seated dwarf A.D.550-950, hunchbacked figure wearing goatee, ridged hat, 4 15/16 (4181/167)   *500*
Veracruz seated dwarf A.D.550-950, short bent arms, knotted skirt, headdress, 4⅝ (4181/168)   *500*

Veracruz seated figure A.D.250-950
(4181/157)

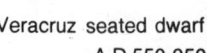

Veracruz seated dwarf
A.D.550-950

(4181/167)   (4181/168)

Veracruz seated figure A.D.250-950, monumental size, loin cloth belt with bow, 30¼ (4181/157)   *3000*
Veracruz smiling head A.D.550-950, rectangular headdress, low relief decoration, 6 (4181/164)   475

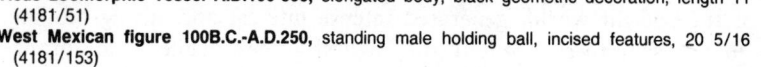

Veracruz tripod dish A.D.900-1300, polychromed tondo with stylized serpent head, diameter 9½ (4181/159) — 3200

Vicus duck vessel A.D.100-500, geometric design of brown, black and cream, length 9¼ (4181/46) — 600

Vicus erotic vessel A.D.100-500, round body surmounted by two extended phallus, diameter 9¾ (4181/43) — 250

Vicus erotic vessel A.D.100-500, round body with fox head and phallus spout, diameter 7 (4181/45) — 500

Vicus feline vessel A.D.100-500, bared fangs, erect ears, cream-black resist decor, length 11½ (4181/42) — 700

Vicus figure vessel A.D.100-500, early mochica style with resist decoration, 8¼ (4181/50) — 250

Vicus figure vessel A.D.100-500, seated male of orange, cream, black, 9⅛ (4181/48) — 200

Vicus figure vessel A.D.100-500, stylized human form, perforation, brown paint, length 8⅛ (4181/49) — 200

Vicus whistle vessel A.D.100-500, ring body with crouching monkey handle, black, diameter 8 (4181/44) — 250

Vicus whistle vessel A.D.100-500, tubular form with molded upturned rodent form, 8¼ (4181/47) — *400*

Vicus zoomorphie vessel A.D.100-500, elongated body, black geometric decoration, length 11 (4181/51) — 325

West Mexican figure 100B.C.-A.D.250, standing male holding ball, incised features, 20 5/16 (4181/153) — 800

Vicus whistle vessel
A.D.100-500 (4181/47)

Chapter 14

Antiquities

Recently, after several dull years, every category of antiquities, the art and artifacts of the ancient world, generated intense interest and strong bidding. Museum-quality sculptures brought the highest prices, while small bronze figures were relatively plentiful and reasonably priced. Household utensils in glass and ceramics sold for under a thousand dollars.

Spurred by recent publicity, Egyptian works of art led the price rise. Old Kingdom sculpture and relief sold in six figures, double and triple their presale estimates. At a more moderate level, the low five figures, a number of other Egyptian objects, such as an alabaster jar, a stone figure of a man and a marble head of the child Horus, sold for as much as five to seven times the prices for which they were purchased at previous sales within the last ten years.

Objects from the classical Mediterranean world of Rome and Greece proved popular also. Roman bronzes, including a number of portraits of the emperors and members of their families, sold well above their estimated value.

Those who wished to purchase beautiful objects made more than two thousand years ago for under a thousand dollars concentrated on glass items—vases, bowls and other utensils. Some remarkable examples which anticipated many of the techniques and forms used more than a thousand years later sold in the low hundreds of dollars. Ceramic jars and other containers sold at comparable prices.

The few pieces of the finest-quality ancient sculpture which reach the market are monopolized by museums. However, the age of lesser objects, the smaller figures and household utensils ensures the value of each piece, no matter how humble its origin. Many items are collectible for the technology they represent. In particular, the glass items which combine primitive technique with beautiful design are well worth collector attention.

Growing popular interest in Ancient Egypt and its art will undoubtedly make for an expanding market in works from that region. Strong showings by Hellenistic and Roman objects in every category point to excellent gains in this field in future years.

EGYPTIAN

Assorted items

Amulet, faience, blue-green, Pataek, standing on crocodiles, 2½, 712-30 B.C. (4082/243) — $550
Amulet, faience, blue, cat, crouching supported by 4 kittens, 2, 712-30 B.C. (4082/246) — 375
Amulet, faience, green, goddess, fragmentary, striding, holding scroll, 1¾, 712-30 B.C. (4082/245) — 375
Blue crown, bronze, depicts Horus, 2¾, 712-30 B.C. (4260/1064) — 650
Braclet, gold and glass, serpents' heads, D3 15/16, 1/2c A.D. (4082/52) — 700
Bronze figure, cat, seated, small head, gold earring, 5¼, 946-342 B.C. (4123/162) — 1600
Bronze figure, Isis and Horus, seated wearing dress, horns sundisk, 6½, 712-30 B.C. (4123/164) — 550
Bronze figure, Uraeus, fragmentary pendant, gold inlay, 1 5/16, 1196-655 B.C. (4123/161) — 125
Bronze Head, cat, angular features, pierced ears, engraved, 2 11/16, 946-342 (4123/163) — 200
Canopic jar, Alabaster, inscriptions, Hapy head lid, 13, 664-525 B.C. (4082/198) — 3300
Canopic jar lid, clay, human head stopper, smooth wig, painted, 5½, 1305-1080 B.C. (4082/197) — 1700
Coffin lid, wood, polychromed, anthropomorphic lid depicting deceased, 61½, 712-30 B.C. (4082/203) — 3100
Cup, Blue faience, Egypto-Phoenician, double ring handle, painted, 3⅞, 1900-1700 B.C. (4082/196) — 17500
Face mask, wood, coffin mask, traces pigment, 7, 1554-1080 B.C. (4082/271) — 450
Face panel, faience, beaded, human face form, colored beads, 8¾, 100 B.C.-100 A.D. (4123/160) — 300
Faience, blue-green, figure girl, seated, elbows on knees, painted sidelocks, 1⅞, 1305-1080 B.C. (4082/242) — 300
Faience head, green, Pataek, shaven head with pendant loop, 1⅛, 712-30 B.C. (4082/249) — 250
Faiyum portrait, woman, on panel, jewelry, wavy hair, 15¾,¾c A.D. (4082/272) — 4800
Feldspar, green, figure of frog, large eyes, long mouth, flat back, L1.6cm. 1554-1080 B.C. (4082/239) — 200
Figure of a goddess, bronze, lion-headed, 6¾, 664-341 B.C. (4260/1065) — 1100
Figure of a man, wood, pleated kilt, 6⅝ (4260/1063) — 200
Figure of a woman, limestone, long, close-fitting dress, 7⅛, ca1850-1785 B.C. (4260/1058) — 5000
Glass paste inlay, Isis knot of glass in jasper, 2 9/16, 305-30 B.C., Ptolemaic (4123/157) — 350
Hand of a god or king, limestone, clenched position, L8, 712-30 B.C. (4260/1061) — 850
Handles, pair, bronze, kitten, hanging tail forms loop, 3⅛ ea., 712-30 B.C. (4082/263) — 650
Head, limestone Coptic, full features, incised eyebrows, 4¾, 5/6c A.D. (4123/149) — 425
Head of a king, limestone, wearing crown, 12¾ (4260/1062) — 650
Ibis, bronze and wood, squatting, cross-hatched legs, engraved, L7¾, 712-30 B.C. (4082/240) — 2700
Jar, stone, miniature, ovoid form, flat rim, twin handles, 2 5/16, ca3500-3000 B.C. (4082/192) — 1000
Jar, Alabaster, ovoid jar, short neck, wide flat rim, 3¾, 1554-1305 B.C. (4082/193) — 550
Mask, plaster, portrait, woman with necklace, earrings, l0 2c A.D. (4123/148) — 2000
Mummiform figure, wood, Divinity, smooth wig, 22¾, 305-30 B.C. Ptolemaic (4123/153) — 800
Mummiform figure, wood, Ptah-Soker, polychromed, 29½, 664-525 B.C. 26th Dyn (4123/152) — 5500
Mummy mask, wood, finely carved, painted red, 15, 712-30 B.C. (4123/154) — 275
Mummy portrait, plaster, elaborate coiffure, 5½, 1st half 2c A.D. (4260/1067) — 350
Necklace, amethyst, rock crystal, globular/gold rock crystal, L19, Dynastic Period (4123/138) — 225
Necklace, faience and gold, faience disks, gold beads and amulets, L19, 712-30 B.C. (4082/217) — 325
Necklace, faience and stone, tiny disk beads, tiny stone, amulets, 18¼, New Kingdom (4082/215) — 550
Necklace, millefiori, rock crystal, cylindrical, faceted, L16, 200-100 B.C. (4082/221) — 300

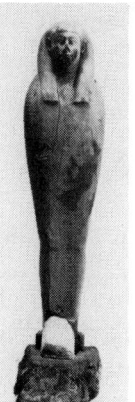

Mummiform figure
(4123/153)

Faience figure
(4123/158)

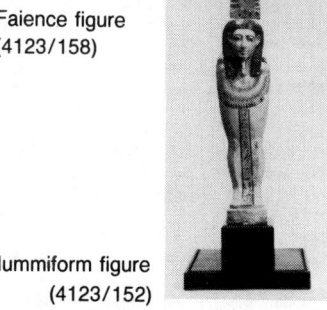

Mummiform figure
(4123/152)

Pendant, ibis, gold, flat, standing on bar, applied eye, ca½, 1991-1785 B.C. (4082/214)	1450
Portrait mask, plaster, glass eyes, modeled wavy locks, 7¼, 2c A.D. (4082/273)	2300
Portrait mask, plaster, lady with painted and glass eyes, 6½, 2c A.D. (4082/275)	1100
Portrait mask, plaster, man, fragmentary glass eyes, 9½, 2c A.D. (4082/274)	750
Relief, limestone fragment, buff colored, head Amenhotep III, 6¾ x 7⅝, 1403-1365 B.C. (4123/145)	600
Relief, limestone fragment, seated baboon with moon disk, 13½ x 10¾, 712-30 B.C. (4123/147)	250
Relief, limestone fragment, Coptic, head of nymph, 10 x 12½, 5/6c A.D. (4123/150)	650
Relief, limestone, fragment, Coptic, arch carved with animals, 6 x 19, 5/6c A.D. (4123/151)	200
Ring, faience, green, oblong bezel with King's prenomen, bezel, 2.1 cm, 1403-1365 B.C. (4082/241)	275
Schist Bust, dark green, King, Ptolemy wearing nemes headcloth, 3⅞, 200-100 B.C. (4082/201)	3200
Schist Head, black, goddess, small, striated curled wig, relief, features, 1¼, 1305-720 B.C. (4082/200)	1800
Shrine of Sais, bronze, goddess Neith enthroned, 4½, 712-30 B.C. (4260/1066)	700
Steatite, black, figure of Lion, couchant, stylized incised mane, inscription, 3 11/16, 305-100 B.C. (4082/235)	1000
Terracotta torso, youthful diety, reddish clay hollow cast, 11, 1c B.C. (4082/73)	900
Ushabti, wood, polychromed, holding hoes, tripartite wigs, 8¾, 1305-1080 B.C. (4082/202)	850
Ushabti, Blue faience, Neskhonsu, holding hoes, seadsack, wig, 6½, 1080-946 B.C. (4082/204)	1900
Ushabti, Green faience, broad face, holding hoe, seed, sack, 6¼, 664-342 B.C. (4082/205)	700
Vase, Alabaster, small, broad shoulders, short neck, flat rim, 3⅛, 1900-1700 B.C. (4082/195)	700
Votive bust of a king, limestone, face with full, soft features, 10, ca305-200 B.C. (4260/1060)	2300
Votive head of a king, limestone, nemes headcloth without Uraeus, 3¼, ca305-250 B.C. (4260/1059)	1100
Votive relief, limestone, divine beard and royal nemes headcloth, 12⅜ x 7, ca305-280 B.C. (4260/1057)	16000
Wood figure, polychromed, Isis, kneeling, painted, surmounted, wig, 14⅜, 305-30 B.C. (4082/199)	2800

Bronze

Aegis, Khnum-headed, incised broad collar, 3, 712/30 B.C. (4253/245)	450
Anubis, figure, holding his clenched hands to his sides, 3⅞, 712/30 B.C. (4253/239)	900
Anubis, jackal form, alert posture, standing on coffin, L3½, 712-30 B.C. (4082/236)	1200
Anubis, pendant amulet, jackal headed god striding, rectangular base, 2⅛, 712/30 B.C. (4253/238)	500
Aphrodite-Hathor, standing, jewlery, diadem, curls, inlaid eyes, base, 16, 1/3c A.D. (4082/116)	6000
Apis bull, figure, wearing the sun disk with uraeus, 3, 712/30 B.C. (4253/247)	1200
Apis bull, small, striding on a sled-like base, 2⅛, 664/525 B.C. (4253/248)	250
Bastet, feline-headed, striing, wearing royal dress, 5½, 712-30 B.C. (4082/264)	800
Bastet, figure, cat headed goddess standing, 3¾, 664/342 B.C. (4253/234)	1350
Bes, figure, striding, 6⅜, headress and arms res, 745/655 B.C. (4253/51)	*1200*
Cat, fragmentary neck, engraved collar, long ears, 2½, 946-342 B.C. (4082/257)	500
Cat, life size, engraved features, scarab relief, 4⅜, 946-342 B.C. (4082/256)	3000
Cat, seated wearing aegis, incised and pierced, 8, 946-342 B.C. (4082/207)	3500
Cat, seated, body thrust forward, incised collar, 5⅜, 946-342 B.C. (4082/261)	1800
Cat, seated, curling tail, wearing panther aegis and, scarab, 7, 946-342 B.C. (4082/206)	12000
Cat, seated, large eyes, pierced ears, incised collar, 5⅝, 946-342 B.C. (4082/209)	3600
Cat, seated, small reworked head, gold earring, 5¼, 946-342 (4082/262)	1500
Cat, seated, stocky build, round face, brown patina, 5⅛, 946-342 B.C. (4082/208)	4400
Cat, slid cast, seated, wearing collar, incised marks, 4⅜, 946-342 B.C. (4082/260)	3000
Cat, small, separately cast, broad face, incised, markings, 2¼, 664-342 B.C. (4082/259)	700
Cat, small, solid cast, smooth brown patina, 1⅝, 946-342 B.C. (4082/211)	500
Cat, strong angular features, engraved markings, 2 11/16, 946-342 B.C. (4082/258)	650
Cat, unpierced ears, inlaid eyes, reddish patina, 3 11/16, 946-342 B.C. (4082/255)	2800
Cat, figure, seated, tail curled to the front, 4, 664/525 B.C. (4253/233)	*4000*
Cat, large, sleekly-modeled, drilled nostrils, engraved scarab, 5, 946-342 B.C. (4082/212)	3200
Cat, small, engraved whiskers and ears, 1⅝, 946-342 B.C. (4082/213)	650
Cat, small, incised body markings, collar, wearing aegis, 3 1/16, 946-342 B.C. (4082/210)	1500
Child, figure, squatting on a tenon, holding a scepter, uraeus, 1⅞, 664/342 B.C. (4253/38)	400
Coffin with Mongoose, fragmentary coffin surmounted by ichneumon, L5½, 664-342 B.C. (4082/237)	1600
Divinity, figure, holding an eye of Horus to his chest, 4⅛, 664/342 B.C. (4253/45)	800
Falcon, Horus, realistic, engraved feathers, wearing crown, 3 11/16, 712-30 B.C. (4082/233)	1000
Falcon, Horus, standing hollow cast figure, extensive, engraving, 3⅝, 664-342 B.C. (4082/231)	1600
Falcon, Horus, standing on coffin wearing collar and crown, 5 1/16, 664-342 B.C. (4082/232)	1800
Falcon, Horus, standing, fragmentary hollow cast, engraved, feathers, 6⅜, 664-342 B.C. (4082/230)	1800
Goddess, cow-headed figure, Hathor*, trapazoidal base, 5, 664/342 B.C. (4253/246)	1500
Goddess, figure, Mut*, traces of metal inlay, 3 9/16, 664/525 B.C. (4253/23)	600
Harmerty, figure, hawk-headed god of Pharbaithos in the Delta, 8⅝, 712/30 B.C. (4253/254)	3100
Harmiysis, pendant figure, striding lion-head god wearing a royal kilt, 3⅜, 745/342 B.C. (4253/241)	550
Harpocrates, figure, seated, his feet on a trapezoidal base, 3⅝, 712/30 B.C. (4253/40)	300

Harpocrates, figure, seated, lifting fragmentary hand to his mouth, 5½, 305 B.C./100 A.D. (4253/34)	750
Harpocrates, figure, striding, rectangular base, 4⅛, 712/30 B.C. (4253/35)	550
Harpocrates, pendant, child god sits in a lotus blossom, 3¾, 712/30 B.C. (4253/36)	1050
Harpocrates, pendant figure, seated on a lion throne, 3¾, 712/30 B.C. (4253/37)	1000
Harpocrates, pendant figure, seated, holding his right forefinger to his mouth, 3½, 712/30 B.C. (4253/39)	350
Hathor, head of, molded in relief, broad collar, wide wig, 2, 664/342 B.C. (4253/24)	425
Ibis, large wood and bronze, grooved beak, circular eyes once inlayed, 15¾, 712/30 B.C. (4253/250)	*3000*
Isis with Horus, child on lap, crowned, 8⅜, 664-342 B.C. (4082/267)	4200
Isis with Horus, seated, child on lap, crowned, 5⅛, 664-525 B.C. (4082/268)	1800
Isis-Selket, figure, from the top of a papyrus scepter, 3½, 712/30 B.C. (4253/240)	600
Isis/Horus, figure, both deities standing, rectangular base, 2 9/16, 712/30 B.C. (4253/30)	275
Isis/Horus, figure, sits holding Horus in her lap, 8¼, 712/30 B.C. (4253/26)	1000
Isis/Horus, figure, sits holding Horus in her lap, black patina, 4⅛, 664/632 B.C. (4253/28)	1300
Isis/Horus, figure, sits holding Horus in her lap, brown patina, 9⅜, 712/30 B.C. (4253/27)	1600
Isis/Horus, figure, sits holding Horus in her lap, green patina, 3⅝, 712/30 B.C. (4253/29)	400
Jah, figure of the moon-god, seated, clenched hand on his knee, 4, 712/30 B.C. (4253/46)	700
Khnum, pendant figure, ram-headed god wearing a kilt, 4 without tenons, 664/341 B.C. (4253/244)	600
Kneeling king, figure, hands extended to hold an offering, 4½, 664/342 B.C. (4253/47)	1900
Kneeling man, wearing rounded wig, back inscription, 2⅛, 712-30 B.C. (4082/265)	275
Lion Headed God, striding, holding attribute, 7⅜, 664-342 B.C. (4082/234)	3300
Menant pendant, engraved with the goddess Mehyt, 3⅝, 712/30 B.C. (4253/253)	350
Menant pendant, surmounted by heads of Onuris and Mehyt, 5⅜, 712/30 B.C. (4253/252)	1200
Mongoose, small, fur incised, green patina, 2⅞, 664/341 B.C. (4253/249)	*550*
Mut, figure of, striding, rectangular base, 6¾, 664/525 B.C. (4253/22)	3900
Nefertum, pendant figure, striding, rectangular base, 6¾, 712/30 B.C. (4253/43)	550
Neith, figure, striding, rectangular base, 8½, 664/525 B.C. (4253/25)	*6800*

Bes (4253/51)

Ibis (4253/250)

Cat (4253/233)

Mongoose (4253/249)

Neith (4253/25)

Nile perch, figure, supported by a narrow rectangular base, 4⅝, 712/30 B.C. (4253/237)	2200
Osiris, solid-cast, standing, clenched fists, attributes, 7⅝, 745-655 B.C. (4082/266)	600
Osiris, figure, standing, clenched hands on his chest, 7, 946/720 B.C. (4253/31)	1600
Osiris, figure, standing, hands grasping the crook and flail, 18⅛, 712/30 B.C. (4253/33)	7500
Osiris, figure, standing, hands holding the crook and flail, 7⅛, 664/525 B.C. (4253/32)	*3000*

Priest, figure, kneeling, hands palms downward on his thighs, 2⅜, 664/342 B.C. (4253/48) *1400*

Ptah, figure, standing, holding a scepter to his chest, 2 13/16, 664/525 B.C. (4253/41) 1000

Shrine with Thoth, ibis-headed god, wearing a short kilt, 8⅛, 712/30 B.C. (4253/251) 2400

Situla, cast with a frieze of gods and goddesses, 5⅜, 946/525 B.C. (4253/258) 450

Triad, Isis, Osiris, Horus, family of Osiris standing, 3 5/16, 712-30 B.C. (4082/269) 1100

Uraeus, a snake with flaring hood, 6½, 712/30 B.C. (4253/243) 1400

Uraeus, flat pendant, serpent form, inlaid hood, modeled, both sides, 4, 712-30 B.C. (4082/238) 450

Uraeus, lioness-headed figure, the goddess Uto*, 4⅝, 712/30 B.C. (4253/242) 800

Faience

Ape, amulet, bright blue, squatting, paws gripping the knees, 1⅜, 305 B.C./50 A.D. (4253/343) 325

Ape, fragment, squatting, sacred to Toth, wearing a pectoral, 2⅜, 712/30 B.C. (4253/339) 275

Fragment, blue war crown, incised dotted concentric circle ornament overall, 6¼ x 5, 1365/1347 B.C. (4253/331) 600

Girl, figure, turquoise blue, standing, hands to her thighs, 5⅞, 1991/1785 B.C. (4253/328) 1100

Harmiysis, amulet, pale blue, the lion-headed god striding, 2½, 305 B.C./50 A.D. (4253/344) 250

Isis enthroned fragment, blue-green, sides of the throne each with a Nile god, 4⅜, 946/525 B.C. (4253/335) 1000

Isis with Horus, pale green figure, seated on a throne, Horus in her lap, 4⅞, 305/30 B.C. (4253/336) 800

Jar, turquoise, flat base, flaring cylindrical body, 4⅞, 712/30 B.C. (4253/348) 500

Knot of Isis, bright blue, tapering forms, small knot on top, 4⅜, 305 B.C./50 A.D. (4253/347) 375

Lion-headed goddess, fragment, pale green, holding the papyrus sceptor to her breast, 2⅝, 712/30 B.C. (4253/338) 300

Pataek, amulet, turquoise, holding knives against his abdomen, 2¼, 305 B.C./50 A.D. (4253/342) 300

Pataek, pendant figure, protector of small children, 3, 712/30 B.C. (4253/341) 900

Ram-headed sphinx, figure, deep blue, couchant on an oblong base, 1¾, 745/655 B.C. (4253/340) 150

Ring, blue-green, hoop of semi-circular section, bezel, 1¾, 1347/1337 B.C. (4253/282) 650

Shu, torso of, pale green, god of the vacuum between earth and sky, 3, 664/342 B.C. (4253/337) 500

Sistrum fragment, pale blue-green, form of head of goddess Hathor, 3¾, 946/525 B.C. (4253/334) 2100

Ushabti, blue, holding 2 sets of hoes, 1 behind, 4¼, 1196/946 B.C. (4253/100) 600

Ushabti, bright blue, holding hoes, seedsacks, implements, 8¼, 1305/1080 B.C. (4253/98) 1200

Ushabti, brilliant blue, stock form, details in black, 6, 1080/946 B.C. (4253/99) 1000

Ushabti, green, six lines of inscription, 6⅝, 664/342 B.C. (4253/307) 450

Ushabti, green figure, divine beard, smooth tripartite wig, 5⅛, 380/250 B.C. (4253/311) 275

Ushabti, pale blue, inscribed for a grand priest of Mendes, 7, 380/342 B.C. (4253/304) 900

Ushabti, pale blue, slender form, holding hoe, pick, seed sack, 6½, 380/342 B.C. (4253/305) 1000

Ushabti, turquoise figure, holding the hoe, pick, seed sack, 4⅞, 380/30 B.C. (4253/308) 650

Glass

Queen or Goddess, bust, traces of right hand visible on breast, 2½, 946/720 B.C. (4253/330) 2600

Unguentarium, aquamarine, heavy, spool-shaped, repairs, 2¼, 2/3c. A.D. (4123/12) 200

Jewelry

Collar, beaded, amber, lapis-lazuli, carnelian, turquoise beads, dynastic period and later (4253/64) 550

Necklace, bead, faience, 12 pendants of Bes with disk beads, 18, 712/30 B.C. (4253/65) 475

Scaraboid, steatite, head of Hathor mounted in a gold stickpin,⅜, 1554/1080 B.C. (4253/68) 125

Miscellaneous objects

Carving, Coptic bone, St. Christopher carrying the Christ Child, 2¾, ca5/6c A.D. (4253/88) 150

Jar lid fragment, clay canopic, molded in form of a head, probably Hapy, 3⅜, 1439/1403 B.C. (4253/332) 2800

Mask of a woman, stucco funerary, wide triangular face, globular earring, 7¾, 2nd Century A.D. (4253/85) 1800

Mask of a woman, stucco funerary, young, slightly smiling face, 8, 2nd Century A.D. (4253/84) *3800*

Mummy mask, cartonnage, painted in blue, purple, red, pink, green, yellow ground, 12¾, 150 B.C./50 A.D. (4253/86) *2400*

Mummy ornament, cartonnage, painted in numerous colors, 15, 11½, 200/30 B.C. (4253/80) 2000

Spoon, alabaster, form of a highly stylized fish, 5, 2134/1650 B.C. (4253/20) 275

Ushabti of an overseer, clay, inscribed for Wep-wawet-nakht, 5¼, 1305/1080 B.C. (4253/101) *350*

Woman, clay head, from a doll or servant figurine, 3¾, 2134/1550 B.C. (4253/329) 200

Painting

Portrait of a woman, funerary, painted in encaustic on thin panel, 15⅜, 2nd Century A.D. (4253/83) 12000

Wall fragment, figure of Horus falcon between 2 signs, 8⅜, 10⅜, 305 B.C./100 A.D. (4253/87) 400

Scarabs

Faience, turquoise glassy, smooth wingcase, legs without detail,⅞, 1991/1785 B.C. (4253/285) 600

Faience, winged, bright blue, pierced for attachment, 6, 712/30 B.C. (4253/345) 1600

Steatite
(4253/281)

Falcon-headed God
(4253/319)

Priest (4253/48)

Osiris (4253/32)

Faience, Tuthmosis III, with divided wingcase, striated legs,⅜ (4253/290) — 800
Feldspar, green, heart, base incised with eleven lines of inscription, 3, 1554/1080 B.C. (4253/298) — 2000
Hardstone, mottled green, heart, carved, realistic detail, base inscribed, 2, 1554/1080 B.C. (4253/299) — 1900
Lapis lazuli, scaraboid, head of a falcon, 1⅛, 1554/1080 B.C. (4253/302) — 450
Steatite, blue glazed, wingcase divided by 3 lines,⅞, 1991/1785 B.C. (4253/286) — 700
Steatite, dark green-glazed, commemorative scarab of Amenhotep III, 2¾, 1393 B.C. (4253/281) — *13500*
Steatite, Amenirdas, blue-green glazed, back inscribed for the divine consort,⅝, 715/700 B.C. (4253/297) — 550
Steatite, Rameses I, green-glazed, base carved with cartouche, prenomen Rameses I,⅝, 1305/1303 B.C. (4253/292) — 2000
Steatite, Rameses II, green-glazed, carved with the figure of Rameses II,¾, 1290/1294 B.C. (4253/293) — 1500
Steatite, Takelot II, turquoise-glazed, divided wingcase, finely striated legs,¾, 866/840 B.C. (4253/295) — 2600
Steatite, Tuthmosis III, green-glazed, divided wingcase, notches at prothorax,⅝ (4253/291) — 900

Stone

Alabastron, stout tapering cylindrical form, 5⅛, 664/525 B.C. (4253/269) — 500
Anubis, limestone figure, in recumbent pose, stylized shoulder markings, 6¾, 712/30 B.C. (4253/323) — 400
Boy, granite head, broad shaven cranium, black, 4⅜, 1305/1080 B.C. (4253/280) — 3600
Cup, alabaster, deep rounded form, single ear-shaped lug, 2⅞, 1554/1080 B.C. (4253/265) — 200
Falcon-headed deity, bust, carved in hard white crystalline stone, 3⅞, 664/342 B.C. (4253/320) — 550
Falcon-headed God, limestone bust, Horus or Harmerty*, 11½, 380/30 B.C. (4253/319) — *2800*
Fragment, limestone relief, bust of a man, facing right, 7⅛, 2134/1991 B.C. (4253/273) — 800
Fragment, limestone relief, carved with torsos of 2 prisoners, 7, 14, 1360:1347 B.C. (4253/278) — 7000
Fragment, quartzite relief, four fragmentary columns of inscription, red, 4¼, 8¼, 1554/1080 B.C. (4253/279) — 250

Fragment, sandstone relief, figure of a Roman Emperor as king of Egypt, 15½ x 13, ca1c A.D. (4253/327)   650

Frog, white limestone figure, highly simplified form, bulbous eyes, 2½, 2955/2635 B.C. (4253/270)   250

God or king, staetite head, wearing the cap of Amun, 3 5/16, L3c B.C. (4253/321)   1700

Hathor, limestone head, cow-eared goddess, 2⅞, 664/342 B.C. (4253/333)   *2800*

Coffin lid (4253/77)

Hathor (4253/333)

Vase (4253/13)

Horus falcon, pendant, deep circular eyes once inlaid, 1¾, 712/30 B.C. (4253/346)   150

Isis, magnesite marble figure, she on a throne, Horus in her lap, 6⅜, 664/342 B.C. (4253/312)   4200

Jar, alabaster, pear-shaped cosmetic, incised with nomen, prenomen of King Tuthmosis III, 8⅜, 1490/1436 B.C. (4253/260)   4600

Jar, alabaster, splayed foot, concave underneath, wide neck, 2⅝, 1554/1305 B.C. (4253/262)   600

Jar, alabaster, canopic, surmounted by head of a deity, 18½, 1305/1080 B.C. (4253/267)   4500

Jar, alabaster, of Merenptah, pyriform body, twin arched handles, 14, 1224/1214 B.C. (4253/266)   7000

Jar, serpentine pear-shaped cosmetic, fitted conical lid, 3⅝, 1490/1365 B.C. (4253/261)   1200

King, limestone head, perhaps Nectanebo II or Ptolemy I, 3¼, 380/280 B.C. (4253/316)   4400

Lion, steatite, black figure, couchant, rectangular base, 3¾, 305/30 B.C. (4253/322)   1300

Man, basalt head, mature face, smooth wig, black stone, 4⅞, 1878/1842 B.C. (4253/274)   4800

Queen, granite figure, striding, clenched hands, 15¾, 200/100 B.C. (4253/317)   4500

Stele, limestone, round-topped, carved in sunk relief, 9¾, 305 B.C./50 A.D. (4253/326)   1300

Stele, limestone, round-topped, inscribed for Iret-hor-ru, son of Hetires, 20, 305/30 B.C. (4253/325)   2000

Ushabti, limestone, holding an adze and hoe, 11¼, 1305/1080 B.C. (4253/96)   4200

Ushabti, limestone, inscribed for Amun, clenched hands on abdomen, 9, 1332/1305 B.C. (4253/94)   4000

Ushabti, limestone, inscribed for Iy-nefer-ti, wife of Sennedjem, 7½, 1305/1080 B.C. (4253/95)   2200

Ushabti fragment, holding hoes and seedsack, 8¼, 1305/1080 B.C. (4253/97)   600

Woman, steatite, brown, standing, tapering black pillar, 5⅝, 1785/1650 B.C. (4253/275)   2000

Vessels

Flask, stone, oval lentoid form, grayish-black, 2⅜, 3500/3000 B.C. (4253/6)   200

Flask, stone, pointed ovoid form, striated black greenish-yellow, 2¾, 3400/3000 B.C. (4253/7)   75

Jar, alabaster, flat base, disk rim, flanged cover, 2⅛, 1991/1785 B.C. (4253/15)   350

Jar, alabaster, ovoid form, flattened base, flanged rim, 3⅝, 2134/1650 B.C. (4253/14)   275

Jar, alabaster kohl, flat base, disk rim, without cover, 2⅜, 1991/1785 B.C. (4253/16)   550

Jar, alabaster kohl, flat base, flat flanged rim, 1¾ without lid, 1991/1785 B.C. (4253/18)   550

Jar, alabaster kohl, with flat base, disk rim, without cover, 2¼, 1991/1785 B.C. (4253/17)   375

Jar, anaydrite, polished, blue marble, globular body, 3, 1991/1785 B.C. (4253/19)   2000

Jar, buff clay, ovoid body, flat everted rim, 4½, ca3400 B.C. (4253/1)   250

Jar, copper spouted, fragmentary hammered body, cast double spout, 4⅝, 2780/2635 B.C. (4253/11)   200

Jar, stone, hard olive-greenish, black striations, 2⅞, 3500/3000 B.C. (4253/4)   550

Jar, stone, hard, creamy-white, red veining, black, speckling, 3, 3500/3000 B.C. (4253/2)   400

Vase, alabaster, ovoid form, flattened base, rounded rim, 9⅜, 2134/1650 B.C. (4253/13)   *1800*

Vase, alabaster, slender, slightly concave form, 11, 2880/2820 B.C. (4253/9)   1400

Wood

Coffin lid, childs anthropoid, body painted overall with numerous deities, 35, 712/30 B.C. (4253/77)   *2400*

Deity, figure of, perhaps Ptah-Soker, white over black ground, 11, 1305/720 B.C. (4253/92) 1600
Face mask, from an inner coffin, 'sfumato' eyes, 4¾, 1305/1080 B.C. (4253/82) *5400*
Isis, figure, seated on a throne, right hand to her breast, 13¾, 712/30 B.C. (4253/74) 1200
Man, figure, standing, his hands clasped to his breast, 4⅛, 2134/1785 B.C. (4253/272) 1200
Mummy case of a falcon, mummy of the bird inside, 21, 305 B.C./50 A.D. (4253/79) *1000*
Ptah-Soker-Osiris, figure, wearing a broad collar, smooth wig, divine beard, 14¾, 712/30 B.C. (4253/76) 1800
Sarcophagus post, wood inscribed, inscribed for Pen-amun, Master of the Sculptors, 27¼, 1554/1305 B.C. (4253/73) 800
Ushabti, black inscription on yellow ground in front, 7¼, 1305/1196 B.C. (4253/93) 950
Ushabti, holding hoes and seed sacks, 8⅝, 1305/1196 B.C. (4253/91) 800
Ushabti, slender form holding hoes in front, 9⅜, 1290/1224 B.C. (4253/90) *5200*

Ushabti (4253/90)

Head (4253/184)

Helmet (4253/214)

ETRUSCAN

Bronze

Hand mirror, Etruscan, notched rim, equine-head handle, 9⅜, 5, 3c B.C. (4253/212) 550
Hand mirror, Etruscan, tongues on rim, palmettes above equine handle, 11½, 6, 3c B.C. (4253/213) 900
Handle, Etruscan, two wrestlers, flat plinth, 3⅛, 325/250 B.C. (4253/193) 4250
Helmet, Etruscan, of 'jockey' type, small finial at domed top, 12¼, 3c B.C. (4253/214) *5500*
Herakles, figure, slender fragmentary figure, 4, ca2c B.C. (4253/198) 150
Priest, Etruscan figure, standing on a forked tenon, holding a patera, 4¾, ca3/1c B.C. (4253/196) 625
Warrior, Etruscan, highly simplified attenuated form, 2⅝, ca5/3c B.C. (4253/194) 225

Jewelry

Scarab, agate, Etrusco-Phoenician, brown and white stone with smooth wing case,½ ca3/2c B.C. (4253/136) 1000
Scarab, calcedony, Etrusco-Phoenician, set in modern gold mount,¾, ca3c B.C. (4253/135) 450

Pottery

Antefix, Etruscan terracotta, molded in relief, head of Achelous, 8, 4c B.C. (4253/180) 800
Head, woman, Etruscan terracotta votive, remains of red and black pigment, 11, ca3c B.C. (4253/185) 350
Head, youth, Etruscan terracotta votive, fragmentary himation drawn over his head, 11¾, 3c B.C. (4253/184) *3250*
Head, youth, Etruscan terracotta votive, idealized face, somber expression, 8⅝, ca2c B.C. (4253/186) 500

GREEK AND ROMAN

Assorted items

Alabastron, glass, sandcore, cobalt-blue, twin handles, L3¾, 4/3c B.C. (4083/281) 300
Amphora, bail, red figure, Campanian, seated maenad, 15⅞, ca340-325 B.C. (4082/96) 850

Amphora, bail, red figure, Campanian, Capua painter pc, heavy woman, 13, ca350-325 B.C.
(4082/97) 850
Amphora, black figure, Attic, belly amphora, Taleides Painter pc, 16½, ca540 B.C. (4082/77) *5000*

Amphora (4082/77)

Lamp (4082/130)

Amphora, red figure, Apulian, small, youth, chiton clad girl, 5⅞, 4c B.C. (4082/87) 400
Amphora, Nolan, black glaze, Attic, disk foot, twin central handles, 6⅜, 470-450 B.C. (4082/15) 1500
Aryballos, terracotta, warrior in Corinthian helmet, 2¾, E6c B.C. (4260/1011) 2450
Askos, black glaze, Attic, circular, arched handle, flaring mouth, D3¼, 5c B.C. (4082/18) 325
Bottle, aubergine, slender conical body, 9,¾c A.D. (4123/98) 2000
Bottle, red figure, Apulian, seated woman, 5¾, ca330-320 B.C. (4082/92) 900
Bottle, red figure, Apulian, Eros among foliage, 5 11/16, ca330-320 B.C. (4082/91) 950
Bowl, black glaze, high foot ring, everted rim, stamped interior, D10⅛, 4c B.C. (4082/28) 500
Bowl, black glaze, reserved foot ring, palmette stamped interior, D7, 4c B.C. (4082/29) 125
Bowl, red ware, Cypriot, high wishbone handle, fragmentary, D6, bronze age (4082/7) 100
Bracelet, gold, faceted, rounded beryls with gold link, L14, 2c A.D. (4082/53) 650
Bust of Artemis, marble, , 16½,½c A.D. (4260/1043) 7250
Cameo, onyx, high relief, child, gold mount, L½, 3c A.D. (4082/64) 700
Cup, black glaze, Boeotian, horizontal fluting, twin strap, handles, D5⅛, 4c (4082/19) 400
Dish, black glaze, Attic, shallow, rounded bowl, splayed foot, D8, 5c B.C. (4082/21) 700
Dish, stemmed, black glaze, Attic, rounded profile, splayed foot, D8, 5c B.C. (4082/20) 800
Dish, teano-ware, Campanian, high foot, rounded sides, stamped interior, D9¾, 4c B.C. (4082/27) 400
Earring, gold, bull's head, fragmentary loop, ca3c, B.C. (4082/54) 275
Earrings, gold pair, oval, spiral wire, cabachon garnets, L1½, 2c A.D. (4082/57) 1200
Epichysus, gnathia-ware, Apulian, domed shoulder, painted body, 6 11/16, ca350-300 B.C.
(4082/98) 900
Figure of a dancer, terracotta, hand raised, traces of pigment, 10¾, E4c B.C. (4260/1022) 1500
Figure of a dog, terracotta, stocky with curled tail, 3¼,½c A.D. (4260/1020) 175
Figure of a dwarf, terracotta, holding spherical object, 4¾, ca1c B.C. (4260/1019) 650
Figure of a fish-tailed goddess, marble, arms outstretched, L7¼, ca4/3c B.C. (4260/1039) 1700
Figure of a fox, terracotta, in an alert position, L4½, caE5c A.D. (4260/1016) 1016
Figure of a goat, terracotta, standing, beard, 1 horn remaining, L3¾, E5c B.C. (4260/1014) 1200
Figure of a goddess, terracotta, extended arms, traces of paint, 10⅝, L6c B.C. (4260/1012) 325
Figure of a ram, terracotta, forward-curving horns, 3½, caE5c B.C. (4260/1015) 300
Figure of a woman, elaborate coiffure, 15¼ (4260/1033) 425
Figure of a woman, holding a flask in her right hand, 7⅛ (4260/1034) 225
Figure of a woman, terracotta, gazing downward, 6½, 3c B.C. (4260/1028) 450
Figure of a woman, terracotta, long chiton, himation, 8⅛, 3c B.C. (4260/1027) 450
Figure of a woman, terracotta, long chiton, himation, finely-modeled, 10, 3c B.C. (4260/1023) 3250
Figure of a woman, terracotta, reaching back to fix sandal, 6¼, 3c B.C. (4260/1030) 1700
Figure of a woman, terracotta, relaxed position, chignon, 11, 3c B.C. (4260/1025) 1900
Figure of a woman, terracotta, rock support, figure of Eros, 10, caL4/3c B.C. (4260/1024) 1500
Figure of a woman, terracotta, with a fan, 7⅛ (4260/1029) 350
Figure of a woman, terracotta, with fan, 10¼, 3c B.C. (4260/1026) 800

Figure of Demeter, terracotta, reclining on the back of a striding lion, 9¼, E4c B.C. (4260/1021) 1200
Fragment, terracotta, slightly turned head, centrally-parted hair, 4¾, 3c B.C. (4260/1031) 225
Fragment, terracotta, tassel falling over the shoulders, 5¾, 3c B.C. (4260/1032) 950
Goddress, seated, terracotta, Greek, enthroned, long chiton, low polos, 6⅜, 5c B.C. (4082/6) 225
Guttus, black glaze, Campanian, , D3⅞, 3c B.C. (4082/23) 350
Guttus, black glaze, Campanian, incised perimeter, relief molded female head, D3⅞, 3c B.C. (4082/25) 325
Guttus, black glaze, Campanian, relief molded satyr, 3⅞, 3c B.C. (4082/24) 350
Guttus, black glaze, Campanian, three-quarter Medusa, head, D3⅝, 3c B.C. (4082/22) 325
Hand, bronze, child's, black patina, L7, ca2/3c A.D. (4260/1009) 1800
Head fragment, terracotta, Greek, idealized female features, 5⅞, 5c B.C. (4082/5) 1100
Head fragment, terracotta, Greek, micaceous orange clay, smiling, black, 6⅜, 6/5c B.C. (4082/4) 850
Head of a goddess, marble, , 5¼, ca1c B.C. (4260/1053) 900
Head of a goddess, marble, chignon, diadem, 5¼, L2/3c A.D. (4260/1052) 1600
Head of a goddess, marble, inspired by Praxiteles, 6½, ca1c A.D. (4260/1050) 15500
Head of a herm, marble, curly hair, beard, 7¾, ca1c B.C./1c A.D. (4260/1051) 2900
Head of a horse, marble, divided mane, lower jaw missing, 6¼, ca1c A.D. (4260/1041) 4400
Head of a lion, marble, from end of a sarcophagus, 15, ca250-300 A.D. (4260/1042) 19000
Head of a woman, marble, gazing upward, 9¾ (4260/1056) 1200
Head of a young hero, marble, manner of Skopas, 11, 1c A.D. (or earlier) (4260/1049) 3250
Intaglio, Carnelian, oval engraved Fortuna, silver ring, 2/3c A.D. (4082/67) 125
Intaglio, Carnelian, oval, carved bust of Mars, fold, L½, 2c A.D. (4082/65) 500
Jar, red ware, Etruscan, massive ovoid body, flaring, rim, 28½, 7/6c B.C. (4082/10) 1400
Jug, buff ware, Cypriot, globular body, short neck, painted red, 9½, 6/5c B.C. (4082/9) 525
Kantheros, black glaze, heavily potted, twin handles, interior banding, W8½, 4c B.C. (4082/30) 275
Kantheros, gnathia-ware, Apulian, carinated body, high echinus foot, D4⅞, 350-300 B.C. (4082/104) 525
Krater, bell, red figure, large, Apollo in chariot, D16, ca375-325 B.C. (4082/86) 1200
Krater, bell, red figure, Apulian, plain-style, dancing, youths, satyrs, D14⅜, E4c B.C. (4082/85) 1300
Krater, bell, red figure, Apulian, Apollo, divinities, satyrs, D18, ca350-325 B.C. (4082/89) 1700
Krater, bell, red figure, Campanian, Painter of The Louvre Sacrifice pc, 12⅜, E4c B.C. (4082/84) 1400
Krater, bell, red-figure, Campanian, small, seated maenad, 8⅝, ca340-320 B.C. (4082/88) 650
Kylix, black figure, small, reserved lip, D5⅛, 560-530 B.C. (4082/16) 1300
Kylix, black figure, Attic, stemmed foot, chariot race, D10, ca500 B.C. (4082/78) 4400
Kylix, stemless, black glaze, spreading foot, handles, impressed interior, D7⅜, 4c B.C. (4082/32) 275
Kylix, stemless, red figure, ring foot in two degrees, lady, D5⅞, 4c B.C. (4082/94) 300
Lamp, bronze, Byzantine, form of sandaled human foot, 5¼, 5c A.D. (4082/129) 1500
Lamp, bronze, Byzantine, stallion with nozzle projecting from, chest, L5⅛, 5c A.D. (4082/130) *700*
Lekanis, Hellenistic, high foot ring, concave handle, D4⅞, 3c B.C. (4082/90) 325
Lekythos, black figure, Attic, cock group pc, warrior scenes, 5, ca520-510 B.C. (4082/81) 1350
Lekythos, black figure, Attic, Class of Athens 581, Dionysus, 5⅞, ca5c B.C. (4082/82) 450
Lekythos, squat, gnathia-ware, Apulian, painted zig-zag, band, 8⅜, ca350-300 B.C. (4082/101) 275
Lekythos, squat, red figure, Attic, L.M. Painter Style, 6⅜, 5c B.C. (4082/83) 450
Male head, terracotta, Etruscan, reddish-buff, drilled curls, beard, 4⅞, 6c B.C. (4082/3) 300
Mesomphalos, bronze, phiale, with Dionysus reclining on a panther, D6¼, ca2c B.C./2c A.D. (4260/1008) 900
Mesomphalos, Phiale, black glaze, interior relief of winged dieties, figures and, hares, D7⅜, 3c B.C. (4082/31) 325
Mug, Bucchero Sottile, Etruscan, polished globular body, lidded, 4½, 6c B.C. (4082/13) 450
Necklace, gold and beryl, links with beryl, gold, glass, L16, 1c A.D. (4082/51) 950
Oinochoe, black figure, Attic, wedding procession, details red, 9½, L6c B.C. (4082/80) 3800
Oinochoe, gnathia-ware, Apulian, squat pyriform body, 4 1/3, 4c B.C. (4082/102) 225
Oinochoe, gnathis-ware, Apulian, large, red, white, yellow, grapevine, 12¼, ca350-300 B.C., res (4082/99) 400
Oinochoe, pottery, Attic, geometric, buff slip, black line, 8⅜, 725-700 B.C. (4082/76) 600
Oinochoe, Bucchero Pesante, Etruscan, ovoid body, human figure handle, 12⅜, 6c B.C. (4082/12) 1600
Oinochoe, Bucchero Sottile, Etruscan, pyriform body, flat handle, 9⅛, 6c B.C. (4082/11) 350
Oinochoe, Chous, red figure, small, ribbed handle, woman near stele, 3 15/16, 4c B.C. (4082/95) 150
Olpe, pottery, Italo-Corinthian, incised body, animal friezes, fugg, 12¼, 6c B.C. (4082/75) *1400*

Aphrodite
(4253/207)

Aphrodite (4082/119)

Ornochoe, gnathia-ware, Apulian, white, red, yellow, grapevine, 7½, 350-300 B.C. (4082/100)	525
Pelike, black figure, Attic, panel painting both sides, red, 13⅝, ca500 B.C. (4082/79)	4000
Prochous, black glaze, Etruscan, pyriform body, painted with female figure, 10, 4/3c B.C. (4082/14)	250
Protome, terracotta, Greek, goddess with stephane, 10¾, 5c B.C. (4082/2)	1600
Pyxis, marble, knopped lid, rounded form, D4½, 4/3c B.C. (4260/1038)	950
Ring, gold and agate, white cabochon agate, ca1c B.C. (4082/63)	450
Ring, gold and intaglio, jasper, carnelians, L½, 1c B.C. (4082/62)	650
Ring, gold, Byzantine, convex hoop, circular bezel, L1, 5/6c A.D. (4082/66)	1300
Schist, figurine, Sphinx, winged figure couchant on base, 4¼, 2/3c A.D. (4123/222)	400
Seal, Steatite, cylinder, animal motifs, L1, 3/E2c B.C. (4260/1037)	275
Skyphos, lead glaze, Roman Asia Minor, copper green glaze, handles, D6, 1c B.C. (4082/105)	1650
Skyphos, red figure, running, satyr, D5 5/16, 4c B.C. (4082/93)	550
Snake, Hellenistic, scales in relief, missing tongue, L11 5/16, 4/3c B.C. (4082/38)	1400
Spout, marble, in the form of a head of a goat, 9, ca2c B.C. (4260/1054)	800
Steelyard weight, bronze, lead filled bust of Attis, Phrygian cap, 4⅛, 3c A.D. (4082/128)	1650
Table support, marble, panther's head form, 18¼, ca2c A.D. (4260/1044)	2800
Terracotta head, votive, Etruscan, youth wearing himation, 6¼, 2c B.C. (4082/72)	325
Terracotta head, votive, Etruscan, youth with himation, 8½, 2c B.C. (4082/71)	550
Theater mask, terracotta, grotesque face, thick beard, moustache, 7¾, ca2c B.C. (4260/1018)	1700
Torso of a goddess, marble, , 7⅞, ca2c A.D. (4260/1047)	800
Torso of a goddess, marble, , 10½, ca3c A.D. (4260/1046)	1300
Torso of Aphrodite, marble, , 10½, 1c B.C. (4260/1045)	5000
Toy, terracotta, in the form of a saddle horse on wheels, 6¾, ca3c B.C. (4260/1017)	850
Woman, Roman silver figure, holding a pitcher in her left hand, 4 1/16, 1c A.D. (4253/208)	5000
Wreath, gold, Etruscan, with stamped laurel leaves, L11, 3c B.C. (4082/50)	2500

Black figure

Lekythos, Attic, disk foot Heracles in combat, 6⅜, 5c B.C. (4123/49)	350

Black-glaze

Bottle, Apulian, pear shaped, over glaze painting, 4⅝, L4c B.C. (4123/61)	150
Bottle, Hellenistic, pear shape, twin convex handles, 3⅞, ca3/1c B.C. (4123/60)	150
Guttus, Campanian, large, high footed, 7 ca300-250 B.C. (4123/57)	125
Hydria, Apulian, reserved ogee foot, 5¼, 4c B.C. (4123/54)	200
Jug, Campanian, bulbous body, cup mouth, concave handle, unusual form, 8¾, ca4c B.C. (4123/59)	200
Kantharos, Boeotian, hollow foot, twin handles, 3 3/16, M4c B.C. (4123/55)	275
Krater, bell, small, painted, 7¾, L4c B.C. (4123/50)	150
Lekythos, torus fooot, flaring mouth, 5⅞, 4c B.C. (4123/56)	175

Bronze

Aphrodite, nude, removing sandals, long torso, fine patina, 4,½c A.D. (4082/118)	1200
Aphrodite, large, looking at mirror in hand,, nude, 10⅛,½c A.D. (4082/119)	*3200*

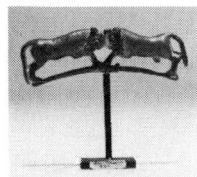

Bulls (4082/37)

Eros-Harpocrates
(4253/201)

Hippocamp
(4082/39)

Aphrodite, Hellenistic figure, standing slender figure, arms fragmentary, 5¾, ca2/1c B.C. (4253/209)	5000
Aphrodite, Roman figure, slender figure, standing, high circular pedestal, 6⅞ without base, 1c B.C./1c A.D. (4253/207)	*18000*
Apollo, standing nude with paetera quiver, 5,½c A.D. (4123/79)	600
Applique, bull's head, hollow cast head, pierced nostrils, 1⅝, 1/3c A.D. (4082/43)	200
Athena, standing, relaxed pose, fragmentary forearms, 6¼, 2/3c A.D. (4082/117)	1700
Attis, standing, lively attitude, upraised arm, patina, 4 3/16, 3c A.D. (4082/124)	800
Balsamarium, bust form, chalmys clad youth, lid missing, 3⅛, 2/3c A.D. (9123/82)	100
Balsamarium, fragmentary vessel in bust of Dionysus form, 7¼, 2c A.D. (4082/126)	1000
Balsamarium, small in form of pygmy head, lid missing, 2 5/16, 1c B.C. (4082/127)	150
Bull, figure, high rump and massive head, 3, 700/600 B.C. (4253/190)	200
Bull, head, small, head broken from larger pc, L1, 3/2c B.C. (4082/40)	300
Bull, humped, head to right, deep green patina, 2⅜,½c A.D. (4082/41)	700
Bull, Aegean, standing, thick cylindrical body, tapering head, 1⅞, 1400-1000 B.C. (4082/34)	275
Bulls, two, fighting, buttin heads, L3⅛, 5c B.C. (4082/37)	*750*
Diety, Hermanubis holding winged kerykeion, fine patina, 3/38, 1c B.C. (4082/111)	1900
Eagle, Byzantine, simplified form, wings spread in flight, 4¾, 6/8c A.D. (4253/217)	3200
Eros, based on Eros of Praxiteles, goosehead cap, 4, 1c B.C./1c A.D. (4082/110)	2000
Eros, smiling, curly hair, headdress missing, 8¼, ca1c A.D. (4123/80)	450
Eros, weeping Hellenistic figure, body resting against a square pillar, 6⅞, ca1c B.C. (4253/204)	37000
Eros, winged figure of child holding alabastron, 5⅛, 2/1c B.C. (4082/113)	650
Eros-Harpocrates, small, relaxed standing pose, wearing himation, 2⅞, 1c A.D. (4082/114)	250
Eros-Harpocrates, Hellenistic figure, standing, lively attitude, deep green patina, 5, ca2c B.C. (4253/201)	*10000*
Fortuna, standing on spool base, 6, 2c A.D. (4123/78)	500
Goddess, Roman figure, clad in finely pleated chiton, 4⅝, ca1c A.D. (4253/206)	5000
Head of youth, 4c B.C. style, drilled pupils, 3⅛, 2c A.D. (4123/81)	300
Hephaistos, Hellenistic figure, god of fire, clad in blacksmith's tunic, 2⅝, ca3c B.C. (4253/205)	5000
Herakles, figure, muscular figure, wielding a club, 4 3/16, ca1c B.C. (4253/199)	225
Hercules, Etruscan, elongated figure, relaxed posture, patinaed, 4 3/16, 3/2c B.C. (4082/106)	700
Hercules, Etruscan, stout disproportionate figure, encrustations, 3¼, 4/3c B.C. (4082/107)	300
Herm, youth emerging from rectangular pillar, 12⅞, 2/3c A.D. (4082/123)	2800
Hermes, standing nude, engraved hair, 4½, 1/3c A.D. (4123/77)	750
Hippocamp, forequarters of horse, tail of fish, L4½, 3/2c B.C. (4082/39)	*1050*
Horse, geometric, Greek, alert posture, flat mane, 2½, 8c B.C. (4082/36)	1500
Lady, Roman bust, Antonia*, green and brown patina, 4¾ with pedestal, 20/30 A.D. (4253/202)	24000
Libation dish handle, lion mask, tapering tongue, L7⅛, 5c B.C. (4082/44)	950
Lion, Etruscan, realistically molded, stylized mane, L4, 5c B.C. (4082/35)	3400
Mirror, Roman, repousse Europa and Zeus, traces of gilding, D5¾, 2c A.D. (4082/47)	1700
Oikoumene, Roman figure, seated on a rocky hilltop, green and red patina, 8⅝, 2c A.D. (4253/203)	46000
Oinochoe, fragmentary, trefoil mouth, ribbed handle, 9⅜, 6c B.C., res (4082/45)	1100
Patera handle, springing lion form, deep green patina, L8 3/16, 6c B.C. (4082/42)	1400
Patera handle, Roman, form of a protome of a panther, 9½, 1c B.C. (4253/216)	2600

Priest, Etruscan, standing, elongated, protruding, corroded, patina, 11⅝, 4/3c B.C. (4082/108)   2100
Protome, Roman dog's head, from a ship's prow*, 9½, 5½, 3c A.D. (4253/215)   13000
Ram, pendant, form of a double-headed ram, 3½, ca7c B.C. (4253/189)   750
Seated athlete, stocky, bearded figure, hands on knees, 3, 1/3c A.D. (4123/76)   225
Serapis, bust, thick wavy beard, long engraved hair, modius, 3, 2/3c A.D. (4082/125)   650
Steelyard, Roman, two parts of unequal length, 41½, 3c A.D. (4253/218)   4500
Steelyard weight, Byzantine, form of a bust of Athena, 9½, 4/5c A.D. (4253/219)   2000
Stirgil, scraper with acute ribbed blade, looped handle, L7½,½c A.D. (4082/48)   200
Tyche, hollow cast, standing, wearing diadem, himation, 7⅛, 1/3c A.D. (4082/120)   1800
Votive figure, Iberian, stylized form, himation falling across 1 shoulder, 3½, ca5/4c B.C. (4253/192)   300
Votive figure, Iberian, stylized, projecting arms, tunic, 3¼, 4c B.C. (4123/74)   150
Wing from large figure, projecting busts of deities, 4, 3c A.D. (4082/122)   1300
Winged goddess, seated, 4¾,½c A.D. (4082/121)   650
Youth, athlete standing in Polycleitan manner, patina, 6, 3c B.C. (4082/109)   1600
Youth, figure, standing in a Polycleitan attitude, 5⅛, L5/4c B.C. (4253/195)   3000
Youth, figure, standing in an awkward posture, 5, ca¼c A.D. (4253/211)   450
Youth, figure, standing in lively attitude, 4⅞, ca4c B.C. (4253/191)   1350
Youth, Greek figure, weight on his right leg, right hand lifted, 6⅝, 4c B.C. (4253/197)   6000
Zeus, standing, wearing chalmys, wreath, raised arm, 3 3/16, ca½c A.D. (4082/112)   850

Buff-ware

Apulian, Askos, globular Messapian Ware, 2 spouts, 5½, 4c B.C. (4123/47)   225
Jug, Cypriot, sloping shoulders, red banding, 6½, ca1200-800 B.C. (4123/44)   150

Clay

Equestrian figure, Boeotian, typical stylized figure, pigment, 4⅛, M6c B.C. (4123/62)   100
Votive figure, Cypriot, flat shaft figure, pinched nose, 7½, ca1100-1000 B.C. (4123/64)   125

Daunian-ware

Askos, Apulian, handmade waterbird type, 4⅛, 6c B.C. (4123/48)   100

Glass

Alabastron, cobalt blue, sandcore vessel, ribbed body, 5 7/16, 6/4c B.C (4123/1)   850
Alabastron, cobalt blue sandcore, cylindrical form, lug handles, 3⅞, 4/3c B.C. (4253/355)   500
Alabastron, translucent blue, sandcore vessel, 5⅛, 2/1c B.C., rest (4123/2)   750
Amphorikos, cobalt blue sandcore, pale blue lip and base, 3, 6/4c B.C. (4253/352)   700
Amphoriskos, cobalt blue sandcore, yellow lip, handles, base, 3⅛, 6/4 B.C. (4253/351)   700
Armband, aubergine, six ribs, oval ornament, D3½, 3/5c A.D. (4123/95)   475
Aryballos, glass, globular, opaque, flaring lip, twin handles, 1¾, 5/3c B.C. (4082/280)   275
Aryballos, green, wheel-cut bands, strap handles, 5¼, 2/3c A.D. (4123/104)   400
Aryballos, olive green, twin suspension handles, 3¼, L½c A.D. (4253/367)   1100
Balsamarium, aquamarine, double tubular body, 7⅞, 1 rim and handle rep, 4/5c A.D. (4253/380)   300
Balsamarium, colorless, slender tapering body, twin loop handles, 4, 1/3c A.D. (4253/368)   100
Balsamarium, glass, greenish, spiral thread decoration, 4½, 2/3c A.D. (4082/285)   325
Balsamarium, greenish, double tubular body, highly iridescent, 6½, 3/5c A.D. (4253/375)   450
Balsamarium, olive green, thread decoration, chip rim, rep, 5⅝, 6c A.D. (4123/90)   200
Balsarium, greenish, cosmetic vessel, thread decor, rep, 5¾, 4/6c A.D. (4123/89)   175
Beaker, bluish-green, cylindrical body, highly iridescent, 1, 4c A.D. (4253/379)   325
Beaker, greenish, body encircled by 2 flanges, 3⅝, 2/3c (4253/373)   100
Beaker, greenish, splayed foot, iridescent, 4½, 2/3c A.D. (4123/35)   200
Bottle, amber, ribbed melon shaped body, 2½, 2c A.D. (4253/372)   200
Bottle, aubergine splashed, indented base, twin handles, 4⅞, 1c A.D. (4253/361)   600
Bottle, blue, pyriform, conical vase, long neck, 5 14/16, 4/5c A.D. (4123/103)   325
Bottle, bluish twin-handled, twin ribbon handles, silver iridescent, 2⅞, 3c A.D. (4253/370)   350
Bottle, bluish-green, flaring cylindrical neck, 10¼,¾c A.D. (4123/105)   300
Bottle, brown, pyriform body, narrow neck, threads, missing foot, 3¾,¾c A.D. (4123/107)   100
Bottle, colorless, neck encircled by an aquamarine collar, 4⅛, 6/9c A.D. (4253/387)   175
Bottle, colorless, ovoid body, carinated shoulder, 6⅛, 2/3c A.D. (4123/109)   625
Bottle, deep green, heavy, squat molded form, vertical ribs, flaring neck, 2⅝, 8/10c A.D. (4123/114)   75
Bottle, glass, aquamarine, depressed body, vertical ribbing, 2¼,¾c A.D. (4082/276)   475
Bottle, glass, aubergine, mold blown bunch of grapes form, 5½, 2c A.D. (4082/289)   1500
Bottle, glass, clear, cylindrical neck, flaring mouth, 3¼, 1c A.D. (4082/283)   450
Bottle, glass, greenish, globular vessel, tapering neck, indented base, 8⅝, 2/3c A.D. (4082/292)   300
Bottle, glass, greenish, round body, indented base, sunk shoulder, 7⅞, 2/3c A.D. (4082/291)   350
Bottle, greenish, globular body, cylindrical neck, 6¼, 2/3c (4123/99)   *200*
Bottle, greenish, globular body, tall flaring neck, 7¼, 2/3c A.D. (4123/97)   175
Bottle, greenish, slender bell shaped body, 10¼, 3/5c A.D. (4253/376)   550
Bottle, greenish-blue, round body, flaring neck, 4⅝,¾c A.D. (4123/102)   200

Bottle, marbled amber, indented base, iridescent, 4⅛, 1c A.D., cracks (4123/22) 800
Bottle, marbled aubergine, globular body, 5, cracked, rim restored, 1c A.D. (4253/362) 500
Bottle, marbled aubergine, translucent matrix decor, 4¼, 1c A.D. (4123/23) 200
Bottle, olive-greenish, heavy globular body, short wide neck, iridescent, 3½, 7/9c A.D. (4123/113) 225
Bottle, sprinkler, greenish, mold blown, lozenge pattern, chip, 4 7/16, 3/4c A.D. (4123/108) 375
Bowl, amber, ribbed, deep bowl, wheel-cut grooves, 4¾, 1c A.D. (4123/7) 320
Bowl, bluish ribbed, flat base, vertical rim, 5⅛, 1c A.D. (4253/358) 600
Bowl, bluish, ribbed, wheel-cut lines, short ribs, 5⅛, 1c A.D. (4123/8) 400
Bowl, glass, bluish, deep bowl, swelling body, folded lip, D3½,¾c A.D. (4082/277) 200
Bowl, glass, bluish, splayed foot ring, flaring sides, iridescent, D5⅝, 2/3c A.D. (4082/294) 275
Bowl, glass, clear, deep, folded splayed foot, vertical sides, D5⅝, 2/3c A.D. (4082/293) 600
Bowl, glass, greenish, large, round body, wheel cut circles, 9⅞, 1c A.D. (4082/290) 300
Bowl, greenish, conical, wheel-cut grooves, 5⅝, 2/1c B.C. (4123/3) 800
Bowl, greenish, rounded, wheel-cut grooves, 4⅝, 1c A.D. (4123/4) 200
Bowl, yellowish green, spiral ribbing, splayed foot, 8⅝,¾c A.D. (4123/33) 550
Bowl, Hellenistic amber, hemispherical form, 5, 2/1c B.C. (4253/357) 600
Bowl, Hellenistic greenish amber, rounded conical profile, 6⅛, 2/1c B.C. (4253/356) 500
Bowl fragment, cobalt blue ribbed, wheel cut grooves inside, 5⅞, res, E1c A.D. (4253/359) 150
Cinerarium, greenish, indented base, ovoid body, flaring neck, 12⅜, 1c A.D. (4253/360) *1600*

Bottle (4123/99)

Cinerarium (4253/360)

Cup, greenish, carinated vessel, 2 9/16, 1c A.D. (4123/6) 320
Cup, greenish, iridescent, wheel-cut lines, 3¾, Ic A.D. (4123/5) 300
Fish vessel, glass, amber, mold-blown, fins, impressed pattern, L4, 4/5c A.D. (4082/278) 1000
Flask, amber date, mold blown body, solid silver iridescent, 2¾, 2c A.D. (4253/365) 125
Flask, aquamarine phallic, corrugated ribbon, details applied, 9⅜,¾c A.D. (4253/371) 2800
Flask, fragmentary, amber, pear shape, opaque blue handles, 3,½c A.D. (4123/24) 125
Flask, greenish, handleless amphorisk, flaring mouth, 6½, 2/3c A.D. (4123/91) 800
Flask, opaque white, mold blown, relief decorated, 3, 1c A.D., repair (4123/19) 1100
Flask, sprinkler, glass, olive green, mold-blwn globular body, iridescent, 2⅞, 2c (4082/287) 125
Flask, sprinkler, yellowish, pronged foot, pinched ribs, small hole, iridescent, 4⅛,¾c A.D. (4123/110) 350
Flask, yellowish head, mold blown body, form of head of Bacchus, 2⅝, 2c A.D. (4253/366) 375
Glass melt, highly iridescent blue green chunk, L14, 4/6c A.D. (4082/306) 2200
Head flask, greenish, Janus head form, iridescent, rep, 3 3/16, 1/3c A.D. (4123/21) 600
Jar, amber, decorated, pinched ribs, 3⅝, 3/5c A.D. (4253/381) 75
Jar, amber, globular body, pinched vertical ribs, rep, 3⅝,¾c (4123/85) 275
Jar, aubergine, flat base, round body, diagonal ribs, iridescent, 3½,¾c A.D. (4123/101) 225
Jar, aubergine, pale green handles, fine surface, 2⅝, 3c A.D. (4123/34) 1000
Jar, aubergine, three handles, muted iridescent, 2⅝, 4c A.D. (4123/38) 325
Jar, colorless, globular body, flaring mouth, faintmold pattern, cracked, 3⅜, 5/6c A.D. (4123/112) 125
Jar, colorless, miniature, brilliant iridescent, 1 11/16, 3/5c A.D. (4123/36) 1000
Jar, glass, aubergine, indented base, round body, sunk shoulder, 3⅞, 3c A.D. (4082/304) 550
Jar, glass, greenish, broad slightly convex body, wide mouth, 3⅞, 3c A.D. (4082/297) 275
Jar, greenish, aquamarine spiral thread, 3 15/16, 4/5c A.D. (4123/37) 700
Jar, greenish, globular body, a folded bulge below the rim, 3⅛, 4/5c A.D. (4253/383) 225
Jar, greenish, ribbed body, broad mouth, 4 3/16, 3/4c A.D. (4123/100) 450

Jar, greenish, slightly lopsided, 3½,¾c A.D. (4123/86)   *225*

Jar, greenish-yellow, molded globular body, 2 handles, 3, 2/4c, damage (4123/39)   225

Jar, olive green, globular body encircled by indentations, thread, 3⅜, 4/5c A.D. (4253/377)   400

Jar, olive green, tapering body, twin loop handles, 4⅜, 3/5c A.D. (4253/384)   225

Jar, pale green, globular body, traces of spiral thread, 3⅞, 3/5c A.D. (4253/382)   400

Jar, twin-handled, greenish, with pyriform body, twin cylindrical handles, (4253/385)   225

Jug, aubergine, slender neck ribbed handle, 5, 3/5c A.D. (4123/31)   450

Jug, colorless, pear shaped, cylindrical handle, 5½, 4/6c A.D. (4123/32)   150

Jug, double, greenish, two separate flasks pressed glass, 6¾, 1/3c A.D. (4123/10)   1400

Jug, glass, greenish, ribbed, sunk shoulder, ringed rim, 6¼,¾c A.D. (4082/302)   750

Jug, glass, olive-greenish, indented base, domed body, molded fluting, 5, 3c A.D. (4082/300)   600

Jug, greenish, broad cylindrical body, handle, 5⅛, 2c A.D. (4123/15)   300

Jug, greenish, cobalt handle, opaque blue rim, 6⅛, 3/5c A.D. (4123/29)   400

Jug, greenish, concave base, ribbed handle, 5¼, 1/3c A.D. (4123/17)   350

Jug, greenish, cylindrical body, sloping shoulder, 7⅛, 2/3c A.D. (4253/374)   350

Jug, greenish, cylindrical neck, flaring rim, handle, 3¼, 2c A.D. (4123/16)   225

Jug, large, greenish, cylindrical body, ribbed handle, 9½, 3c A.D. (4123/14)   550

Jug, olive green, twisted handle, applied, foot, 8¾, 3/6c A.D. (4123/106)   *1000*

Oinochoe, cobalt blue sandcore, elongated form, blue matrix, yellow, white thread, 5⅜, 3/2c B.C. (4253/354)   400

Patella cup, glass, yellowish green, vertical collar rim, D2¾,½c A.D. (4082/295)   450

Pitcher, aubergine, globular body, coiled collars around neck, 4⅝,¾c A.D. (4253/369)   325

Pitcher, colorless, conical base, thread decoration, 4⅜, 2c A.D. (4123/28)   600

Pitcher, glass, amber, ballooning body, iridescent, 5⅞, 3c A.D. (4082/299)   1250

Pitcher, glass, clear, rounded shoulder, pinched mouth, 6, 4/6c A.D. (4082/279)   850

Pitcher, glass, greenish, Egypt, pyriform body, pinched mouth, 10½,¾c A.D. (4082/305)   1100

Pitcher, glass, olive green, thread decoration, handle, 5, 2c A.D. (4082/288)   200

Pitcher, greenish, coiled foot, ribbed body, 6⅛, ca4c A.D. (4123/30)   1300

Pitcher, tinted aubergine, globular body, shallow fluting, 4⅜,½c A.D. (4123/27)   550

Pyxis, amber, folded foot, conical lid, 3¾,½c A.D., rest (4123/26)   550

Sprinkler bottle, colorless, spiral fluting, short neck, 5⅛,¾c A.D. (4123/40)   425

Sprinkler bottle, glass, clear, globular, mold blown, 3½, 4c A.D. (4082/298)   100

Sprinkler bottle, glass, clear, mold blown globular body with chevron pattern, 3½, 2c A.D. (4082/296)   225

Unguentarium, bluish-green, heavy conical body, flat base, 4¾, 2/3c (4123/11)   300

Unguentarium, engraved, colorless, inward folded rim, 3 1/16, 2c A.D. (4123/9)   500

Unguentarium, glass, bluish-green, candlestick, tall neck, iridescent, 9, 2/3c A.D. (4082/286)   375

Unguentarium, glass, millefiori, pyriform, matrix ornamentation, 2⅛, 1c A.D. (4082/284)   2400

Urn, pale aquamarine, globular body, massive handles, cover 13¾,½c A.D. (4123/18)   2800

Vase, amber, splayed foot silver iridescent, 6⅛, 4/5c A.D. (4123/96)   650

Vase, cobalt blue sandcore, cobalt blue matrix with yellow thread, 4⅝, 3/2c B.C. (4253/353)   500

Vase, colorless, tapering body, flaring mouth, 4⅝, 2/3c A.D. (4123/25)   200

Vase, glass, greenish, pyriform body, ribbon ornament, handle, collar, 7, 3c A.D. (4082/303)   650

Vase, greenish, broad shallow fluting, iridescent, 7⅝,¾c A.D. (4123/94)   950

Vase, olive green, spreading foot, 20 handles, 6⅝, 5/6c A.D. (4123/87)   *2300*

Jug   (4123/106)

Vase   (4123/87)

Jar   (4123/86)

Cup (4253/172)

Amphora
(4253/157)

Gnathia-ware

Kylix, Apulian, small cup, twin handle, D3½, c.350-300 B.C. (4123/51) 125

Gold

Wreath, Hellenistic, fragmentary, laurel leaves, Medusa head, L13, 1/3c A.D. (4123/84) 500

Jewelry

Intaglio, carnelian, Roman oval, engraved with a leaping lion, in modern ring,⅜, ca½c A.D. (4253/141) 275
Intaglio, carnelian, Roman oval, engraved with a youthful male deity,½, ca½c A.D. (4253/143) 175
Intaglio, carnelian, Roman oval,⅜, ca2c A.D., (4253/142) 200
Ring, gold, Byzantine, form of a flat, rimmed ornamented band,¾, 10/12c A.D. (4253/145) 450
Ring, gold, Roman intaglio, oval bezel set with green jasper, 7, 2/3c A.D. (4253/140) 1000
Ring, gold, Roman intaglio, oval bezel set with red jasper,⅝, 2/3c A.D. (4253/139) 1200
Roundel, silver, Hellenistic, ornamented with a mounted, armed warrior, 1½, ca3/2c B.C. (4253/147) 1100

Limestone

Figure fragment, Cypriot, upper half of figure in tunic, 8⅞, 5c B.C. (4123/66) 200
Votive head, Cypriot, priest, curled hair, head wreath, 4⅝, 5c B.C. (4123/67) 400

Marble

Aphrodite, fragments of himation clad figure on base, 12, 1/3c A.D. (4082/141) 550
Aphrodite, Roman, from 4c B.C. prototype, 46¾, 1c A.D. (4123/69) 6500
Aphrodite torso, lower half of Knidian type torso, 5¼,½c A.D. (4082/140) 400
Dionysus, Hellenistic, figure, square column, arms missing, 26¼,½c B.C. (4123/71) 4200
Dionysus head, of Praxitelian prototype, incised, hair, 4⅛,½c A.D. (4082/135) 3000
Goddess figure, Roman, seated, head missing, 29¼, ca2c A.D. (4123/72) 700
Goddess head, Sappho type, beautifully carved, hair, 12¾, 1c A.D. (4082/137) 12000
Head, Aphrodite, Indo-Greek, strong Gandharan influence, 5⅝, 2c A.D. (4123/73) 2600
Relief, Attic, worn, relief of female diety on horse, 9¼ x 11½, 4c B.C. (4123/70) 1600
Roman head, centrally partd hair, reworked face, 5½,½c A.D. (4082/142) 650
Woman's head, idealized features, 3⅝, 2/1c B.C. (4082/139) 425
Woman's head, smiling expression, wavy hair, 2½, 1c B.C. (4082/138) 650

Pottery

Amphora, Campanian red-figure bail, low ridged handle, figure of a maenad, 12½, 350/325 B.C. (4253/158) 600
Amphora, Campanian red-figure neck, twisted handles, echinus mouth, figures of 2, youths, 11, 475/425 B.C. (4253/157) *1800*
Bull, Mycenaean clay, cylindrical body, hand made figure, 4¼, 1400/1200 B.C. (4253/175) 800
Bust of a woman, Greek terracotta, short coiffure, back unworked, 6, L6c B.C. (4253/177) 150
Cup, Apulian Daunian-ware, shallow carinated form, flaring rim, 5⅜, 4c B.C. (4253/172) *450*

Goddess (4253/187)

Kotyle (4253/159)

Cheekpiece (4082/177)

Deity, bust, Roman terracotta, Helios*, beardless face, 7, ca2c A.D. (4253/188) 250

Dish, Campanian black-glaze, interior painted over the glaze in red, 5⅝, caL4c B.C. (4253/165) 100

Figure, dancer, Hellenistic terracotta, stepping lightly on a tapering oval base, 8⅝, 3c B.C. (4253/181) 1200

Goddess, terracotta figure, standing, high rectangular base, 14⅞, ca1c B.C./1c A.D. (4253/187) *1000*

Head, youth, terracotta, modeled in the severe style, 8¾, 475/450 B.C. (4253/183) 8500

Hydria, Apulian red-figure, splayed foot, mouth in 2 degrees, 10¾, 4c B.C. (4253/166) 500

Kotyle, Campanian red-figure, figure of winged Eros before a woman, 7½, 350/320 B.C. (4253/159) *1600*

Krater, Campanian red-figure bell, figure of a chiton-clad lady, 7⅛, 360/330 B.C. (4253/162) 700

Kylix, South Italian red-figure, torus foot, up-curved handles, male, female profile, heads, 5½, 350/325 B.C. (4253/168) 300

Lamp, Roman buff clay, center depicts harbor of Ostia or Alexandria, 5⅝, Ic A.D. (4253/174) 800

Lamp, Roman buff clay, center in relief, figure of Christ, 5⅝, 4/5c A.D. (4253/173) 800

Lekanis, Campanian red-figure, torus foot, concave strap handles, knopped cover, 4¾, 350/325 B.C. (4253/163) *400*

Lekythos, Apulian red-figure, foot in 3 degrees, figure of a woman, youth, 8¾, 350/325 B.C. (4253/167) *1000*

Lekythos, South Italian black-glaze, foot in 3 degrees, trumpet-shaped mouth, 9⅛, 4c B.C. (4253/156) 750

Oinochoe, Apulian red-figure chous, trefoil mouth, figure of a youth, 5¾, 360/340 B.C. (4253/164) 250

Oinochoe, Attic black-glaze, echinus foot, trefoil mouth, 9, partially res, ca500 B.C. (4253/154) 1300

Oinochoe, Campanian red-figure trefoil, spear/carrying maenad pursuing a satyr, 11½, 360/340 B.C. (4253/161) 750

Pelike, Apulian red-figure, figures of Eros and himation clad lady, 9⅜, 350/325 B.C. (4253/160) 500

Skyphos, attic black-glaze, reserved band above foot painted in black, 5¾, 475/425 B.C. (4253/152) 2000

Skyphos, Apulian red-figure, horizontal handles beneath rim, 3⅞, 400/350 B.C. (4253/171) 950

Skyphos, Apulian red-figure, twin up-turned handles, details in red, yellow, white, 3¾, 350/320 B.C. (4253/170) 400

Skyphos, Attic red figure, torus foot, horizontal handles at the rim, 7⅛, M5c B.C. (4253/155) 1000

Thymiaterion, Apulian Gnathia-ware, three concave, cylindrical sections, 8⅜, L4c B.C. (4253/169) 600

Red figure

Krater, bell, seated youth, dancing satyr on reverse, 9 L4c B.C. (4123/53) 700

Krater, bell, Campanian, farewell scene, D13¾, C.340-320 B.C. (4123/52) 1900

Red-slip

Jug, Cypriot, ovoid body short neck, banding, 8⅛, 9/7c B.C. (4123/45) 225

Stone

Aphrodite, marble, Greco-Roman torso, after Praxiteles' Aphrodite of Knidos, 13½, ca1c A.D. (4253/225) 11000

Aphrodite, marble, Syrian figure, broad rounded hips, eyes recessed, 7½, ca½c A.D. (4253/231) 1000

Asclepios, marble, Greco-Roman head, long moustache, thick beard, 4⅝, ca1c B.C. (4253/227) 2200

Boy, marble, bust, turned to his right, 8½, neck restored incorrectly, 2/1c B.C. (4253/230) 900
Female, marble, cycladic female, slender tapering form, blade-like shoulders, 8⅛, 2700/2500 B.C. (4253/220) 1400
God or priest, limestone, Cypriot head, over life-size head, slightly smiling mouth, 15, L5c B.C. (4253/222) 17500
Goddess, marble, Greco-Roman head, one of the muses*, 10¼, L2c A.D. (4253/228) 13000
Grave stele, limestone, Hellenistic, carved in relief, central niche recessed, 17, 14¾, 3/2c B.C. (4253/223) 225
Grave stele, limestone, Hellenistic, carved in high relief, 16, 12½, 3/2c B.C. (4253/224) 400
Head, Basalt, Celtic, emaciated face, rectangular mouth, 5, 4/3c B.C. (4253/232) 900
Votary, limestone, Cypriot head, hair surmounted by a laurel wreath, 4½, 5c B.C. (4253/221) 450

WESTERN ASIATIC

Assorted items

Applique, bronze, mythical beast of equine type, 4⅞, ca1000/1500 B.C. (4253/119) 1000
Beaker, white slip, Tepe Sialk, fragmentary, horned animal design, 5¾, 4th mil. B.C. (4123/167) 750
Bowl, buff-ware spouted, burnished bowl glat base, broad spout, beveled rim, L8 1/3, 1000 B.C. (4123/172) 300
Bowl, orange-ware, mountain peak design, 10½, 4th mil. B.C. (4123/168) 350
Bowl, pottery Persian, stylized bird, D9⅛, 10c (4260/1073) 550
Bowl, pottery, Persian, cursive inscriptions, D5⅛, 10c (4260/1075) 700
Bowl, pottery, Persian, geometric, D6⅞, 10c (4260/1074) 525
Bowl, red-ware, plant and geometric motifs, 9¾, 4th mil. B.C. (4123/169) 300
Bracelet, gold, hollow circular sections swelling out, 3⅜, 600/200 B.C. (4253/125) 11000
Bust of Zeus Serapis, alabaster, emerging from a lotus blossom, 7,½c A.D. (4260/1055) 2600
Cheekpiece, bronze, Luristan, in the form of a striding horse, 3⅛, ca800/700 B.C. (4260/1005) 1050
Cheekpiece, Luristan, bronze, openwork form of leonine figures, 4⅜, ca800-600 B.C. (4082/177) *1050*

Lekythos
(4253/167)

Lekanis (4253/163)

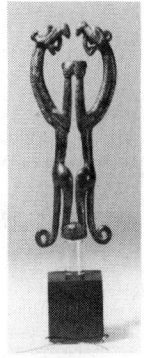

Finial
(4253/108)

Clay figure, horse and rider, hand-modeled whistle form, Persian, 4⅞, 13/14c A.D. (4123/223) 250
Clay figure, votive, Syro-Hittite, stylized figue, knotted girdle, beaked head, 7¾, 1000-1500 B.C. (4123/217) 350
Dagger, bronze, Iranian, ridged midrib, domed openwork panel, 9, ca1000/2000 B.C. (4253/105) 350
Dish, enameled polychrome, Qajar, in Chinese export style, diam. 12, 1298 (1880) (4123/265) 250
Dish, enameled polychrome, Qajar, in Chinese export style, diam. 13⅞, ca1820-60 (4123/264) 200
Dish, lustre-painted Safavid, peacock in white, diam. 9⅝, 17c A.D. (4123/263) 250
Dish, polychrome, Turkish, animals, Isnik, D11⅛, 17c (4260/1079) 6750
Dish, polychrome, Turkish, profusion of foliage, Isnik, D14, 17c (4260/1081) 1700
Dish, tripod, lustre-painted, Ilkhanid, fantastic bird, diam. 6¾, 13c A.D. (4123/261) 250
Ewer, turquoise glaze, Ilkhanid, pyriform body, cock's head spout, guilloche band, 9¾, 13c A.D. (4123/229) 1600
Figure, Iranian clay female, steotopygous body with conical legs, 6⅝, ca1000 B.C. (4253/124) 1400
Figure of a man, bronze, bent knees, palms up, 2 15/16 (4260/1070) 225
Figure of a stag, clay, Iranian, massive horns, 5, ca1300/1000 B.C. (4260/1004) 550
Finial, bronze, Luristan, form of rampant confronted leopards, 5¾, ca900/700 B.C. (4253/108) *2000*

Finial, bronze, Luristan, standing goddess, hands raised to her breasts, 9⅛, 900/700 B.C. (4253/112)   525

Head of a boy, Palmyrene limestone, from a high relief, 5½, 2c A.D. (4253/132)   *1200*

Head of a goddess, bronze, profile, wavy hair in sakkos, 8 (4260/1010)   450

Horse, clay, hand molded red-ware, applied features, H7⅛, 8/7c B.C. (4123/179)   450

Idol, marble, Anatolian, disk head, trapezoidal idol, 5¼, ca2700 B.C. (4260/1035)   750

Incense shovel, Byzantine, bronze, leaping boar, lion, terminal, ibex, L11½,¼c A.D. (4082/181)   500

Incense shovel, Parthian bronze, terminal in the form of a cloven hoof, 11⅝, ca½c A.D. (4253/133)   375

Instrument, bronze, Etruscan, pierced socket, spiraling shaft, 14, ca5c B.C. (4260/1007)   1300

Jar, clay, Iranian spouted, twisted handle ending in ram's head, D8½, ca1000 B.C. (4260/1006)   250

Jar, gray-ware, cylindrical, animal head mount, incised banding, 8½, 1100-900 B.C. (4123/175)   125

Jar, gray-ware, spouted, flaring mouth with horse head, L11¾ 1000-800 B.C. (4123/173)   350

Jar, marble, cycladic, covered, double-loop handles, D3½, ca2700-2400 B.C. (4260/1036)   2800

Jar, neolithic, clay, lozenge form body, festoons, zig-zag ornament, 4⅛, 5800/5300 B.C. (4253/121)   1300

Jar, turquoise glaze, underglaze black design, 7½, 13c A.D. (4123/238)   200

Jar, turquoise glaze, Ilkhanid, pyriform body cursive inscriptions, 13½, 13c A.D. (4123/239)   500

Jar, Iranian reddish clay, globular body, flaring neck, small loop handle, 16, 1300/800 B.C. (4253/128)   550

Jug, cobalt-blue glaze, Ilkhanid*, pear shaped, flat handle, 9½, 13c A.D. (4123/235)   375

Jug, polychrome, Turkish, Armenian bole, Isnik, 9½, 17c (4260/1080)   1080

Man riding a ram, Syro-Hittite clay, rider holding ram's horns, 3¼, 2000/1500 B.C. (4253/123)   225

Mask, basketry, New Guinea, bird-headed form, 5½ (4260/1072)   350

Mortar, Betel-nut, wood, New Guinea, , 6 (4260/1071)   100

Mother and child, Syro-Hittite clay, goddess holding infant to her breast, 7⅝, 2000/1500 B.C. (4253/122)   1300

Necklace, bead, agate, fifty graduated globular agates, L32, 3/6c A.D. (4082/187)   200

Necklace, beryl and glass, gold glass, rock crystal, L21, Roman Period (4123/140)   150

Pendant, bronze jingle, form of a bird, 2, ca9/6c B.C. (4253/116)   400

Pendant, quartz, Gnostic*, tear drop shape, figure of Bes, 1½ (4082/70)   300

Pendant, Iranian bronze deer, standing in a breaking attitude, 3⅛, ca1000 B.C. (4253/115)   700

Relief, Achaemenid, limestone fragment from Persepolis of servant, 8⅛, 5c B.C. (4123/220)   7500

Relief fragment, Assyrian limestone, from palace of Sennacherib at Nineveh, 7½, 6¼, 705/681 B.C. (4253/134)   8500

Rhyton, clay, bird form, spouted, applied eyes, L8¼, 1000-800 B.C. (4123/176)   700

Rhyton, clay, cylindrical body, cream slip, camel form, L8¼, 8/7c B.C. (4123/180)   375

Rhyton, clay, horse form, pierced nose, 8½, 8c B.C. (4123/177)   650

Rhyton, clay, polished red-ware, bull head form, spout, W7¼, ca8c B.C. (4123/182)   600

Rhyton, clay, recumbent bull red clay, incised features, 10, ca8c B.C. (4123/181)   1200

Rhyton, clay, 2 handled, handles mounted with ram heads, base spouts, 8½, 8/7c B.C. (4123/183)   300

Rhyton, Iranian blackware, form of a human foot wearing stippled shoe, 4¼, ca9c B.C. (4253/131)   700

Rhyton, Iranian, Seleucid, clay, trumpet shape, forequarters of couchant horse, L12, 4/3c B.C. (4082/184)   3100

Ring, gold, Erurtria*, with harpy intaglio, L½, 7c B.C. (4082/59)   1900

Standard, bronze Luristan, rampant confronting felines, 5¾, 900/700 B.C. (4253/109)   375

Standard, bronze, Luristan, two confronted ibexes, 5⅞, 800/600 B.C. (4253/111)   650

Standard, bronze, Luristan, 2 confronted gnome-like figures, 11¾, 900/700 B.C. (4253/110)   500

Standard, Luristan, bronze, rampant ibexes on bottle shaped, sockle, 12, 800-600 B.C. (4082/179)   575

Terracotta, figurine, Syrian, mother and child seated on camel, 8¼, 2c A.D. (4123/221)   200

Tripod jar, clay, Iranian, buff colored slip painted with red and brown, D4½, ca2000/1500 B.C. (4260/1003)   125

Vessel, clay, hand molded, carinated, mounted on horse, 8¾, 8/7c B.C. (4123/184)   950

Votive goddess, clay, syro-hittite, , 5⅜, ca2000/1500 B.C. (4260/1002)   300

Votive goddess, clay, syro-hittite, pierced coiffure, 5, ca2000/1500 B.C. (4260/1001)   550

Bronze

Clasp, Celtic, zoomorphic form, horsehead hook, L3 7/16, 400-350 B.C. (4082/46)   175

Heracles, Etruscan, slender figure, lionskin, 3½, 3/2c B.C. (4123/75)   200

Pendant, Luristan, two horse forequarters back to back, 3 5/16, 800-600 B.C. (4123/216)   200

Pendant, Luristan, two horse forequarters back to back, 2¾, 800-600 B.C. (4123/215)   250

Pinhead, Luristan, circular, openwork, central demonic figure, 3 15/16, 800-600 B.C. (4123/213)   400

Pinhead, Luristan, rampant ibexes, horned diety, circular, 2 1/16, 800-600 B.C. (4123/214)   350

Stag, horns, bird on back, 3¼, 1200-900 B.C. (4123/205)   400

Stag, Parthian, leaping figure, stylized face, massive horns, L4 1/16, 100 B.C. - 100 A.D. (4082/180)   1800

Standard, Luristan, short sockle, rampant equine and diety finial, 8¾, 800-600 B.C. (4123/212)   375

Standard, Luristan, short sockle, rampant ibex finial, 5⅝, 800-600 B.C. (4123/211)   200

Standard, Luristan, tall sockle, rampant leopard finial, 5⅝, 800-600 B.C. (4123/210)   900

Glass

Amphorisk, glass, sandcore, phoenician, cobalt-blue, band decoration, 3⅛, 5/4c B.C. (4082/282) 1000
Bottle, amber, relief molded body, cut at shoulder, 8¾, 11/12c A.D. (4123/118) 1000
Bottle, colorless, heavy glass, faint abrasions, iridescent, 9, 10c A.D. (4123/122) 600
Bottle, colorless, mold-blown relief vessel, 5¼, 11/12c A.D. (4123/119) 300
Bottle, green, engraved Kufic characters, dots, restored, 5, 9/10c A.D. (4123/123) 800
Bottle, greenish, mold blown gurgan type, cellular rosettes, 7⅛, 11/12c A.D. (4123/117) 600
Bottle, greenish-yellow, globular molded body with 10 ribs, long neck, 8 5/16, 11/12c A.D. (4123/116) 700
Flask, molar, colorless, four sided, cut facets, 3, 9/10c A.D. (4123/120) 625
Flask, molar, greenish, small, ledge feet, engraved palmettes, 2¼, 9/10c A.D. (4123/121) 125
Flask, tinted aubergine, mold blown, twin handles, 2⅞,½c A.D. (4123/20) 650
Rosewater sprinkler, Shiraz, ovoid body, mold blown, 19, 17/18c A.D. (4123/127) 2200

Marble

Cowroid seal, Sumerian, engraved with 2 couchant lions, Lca½, 4 mil. B.C. (4082/145) 300
Goddess, Cycladic, keros-syros type, incised features, 26½, ca2700-2500 B.C. (4082/133) 65000

Seljuk

Ewer, pottery, Persian, , 6⅞, 13c (4260/1078) 150
Jug, turquoise-glazed, Persian, , 4¾, 13c (4260/1077) 275
Vase, turquoise-glazed, Persian, , 16¾, 13c (4260/1076) 375

Head of a boy
(4253/132)

Chapter 15

Books, Manuscripts and Autographs

Books and manuscripts continued to attract many collectors, and prices were consistently high. American historical manuscripts and documents showed renewed vigor after the lackluster seasons of recent years, while interest in first editions by modern writers continued to grow.

Signatures of Presidents and other famous individuals frequently sell for a few hundred dollars or less when the document involved has little significance, but when there is historical importance, values soar. A letter from Lincoln to Grant requesting that Lincoln's son be attached to Grant's staff at Lincoln's expense brought $32,000, a record for a Lincoln letter. The signed log kept during the atom-bombing of Hiroshima sold for double what it brought in 1972, and a copy of key phrases from President Kennedy's inaugural address, signed and dated, reached a record for Kennedy items.

Historically important books and documents also sell at a premium. Morton's *New Englands Memoriall,* 1669, an early statement of the Colonial position, brought a good price, as did the first map to show Indian claimed territory in detail, published in 1775. Thomas Jefferson's letter outlining plans for the Lewis and Clark expedition was an important document for which collectors competed.

Literary items continue to attract strong bidders. First editions and letters were sought after. Special editions of well-known authors' works with hand-colored illustrations and unusual typefaces sold in the hundreds of dollars.

Other collectors specialized in musical items. Here too, letters and documents signed by classical composers were valued more than modern signatures. Letters by Mozart, Beethoven and Bach brought ten to twenty times as much as the Wagners and more modern composers.

Medical and scientific books were valued for their contributions to knowledge and the quality of their illustrations. A rarity like Antonio Pigafetta's account of Spanish exploration published in 1525 sold for one hundred thousand dollars, but many handsome volumes published in the nineteenth century sold in the hundreds of dollars. These contained fascinating illustrations printed with a care that seems possible no longer.

Books and manuscripts offer an opportunity to own a share of history. Anyone who is interested in the arts or in an historical episode can accumulate documents relating to his specialty and often the signatures of participants. A wide variety of books which significantly enhanced human knowledge or were the first publications of soon-to-be-famous authors is available. If a collector specializes in American related themes, autographs of those involved in the arts, or volumes which contain early scientific thought, his collection is almost certain to increase in value.

BOOKS AND PRINTED MATERIALS

Agricola, Georgius, De Re Metallica Libri XII, 1st ed., Basel, 1556 (4184/275) $2750
Agricola, Georgius, De Re Metallica, inscribed Herbert Hoover as translator, London, 1912
(4184/276)   275
Ainsworth, William Harrison, The Tower of London, 1st ed., London, 1840, very good (4109/1)   475

Ainsworth (4109/1)

Aldington, Richard, Ezra Pound and T.S. Eliot, A Lecture, 1st ed., Peacocks, 1954 (4109/592)   250
Aleyn, Charles, The Historie of That Wise and Fortunate Prince, Henrie VII, London, 1638 (4109/4) 125
Allerton, R.G., Brook Trout Fishing, presentation inscription, N.Y., 1869 (4184/125)   325
Amory, Thomas, The Life of John Buncle, 1st ed., London, 1756 (4109/5)   150
Anderson, Hans C., Stories, color plates after Dulac, 1 of 250, signed Dulac, London, 1911
(4184/19)   350
Anderson, Sherwood, The Modern Writer, 1st ed., 8 vols., cloth case, Lantern, 1925, inscribed
(4109/595)   325
Apperley, Charles James, Memoirs of Life of Late John Mytton, 1st ed., London, Ackermann, 1835
(4184/128)   325
Aristophanes, Lysistrata, 6 etchings, 35 lithos by Picasso, signed, N.Y., 1934 (4184/24)   950
Arrowsmith, Aaron and S. Lewis, A New and Elegant Atlas, Philadelphia, 1804 (4158/3)   325
Ascham, Roger, The Schoolemaster, London, 1589 (4109/6)   750
Ashley, William H., Morgan Dale, ed., The West of William H. Ashley, Denver, 1964 (4158/5)   225
Audubon, John J. and Bachman, John, The Quadrupeds of North America, 3 vols., N.Y., 1851-4
(4158/6)   1800
Bacon, Edward, Dimensions of Fire Bricks, Welch Lumps, Files, London, 1822 (4184/283)   600
Bacon, Sir Francis, Essayes, 1st issue, London, 1625 (4109/9)   650
Bacon, Sir Francis, The Two Bookes of the advancement of learning, 1st ed., London, 1605 (4109/8) 650
Bardon, Dandre, Costume De Anciens Peuples, 3 vols., 1st ed., Paris, 1722 (4184/197)   350
Beaumont, Francis and John Fletcher, Comedies and Tragedies never before printed, 1st ed.,
London, 1647 (4109/12)   750
Beaumont, Sir John, Bosworth-Field, ... other poems 1st ed., London, 1629 (4109/13)   125
Benet, Stephen V., The Drug Shop, 1st ed., Yale University, 1917 (4109/599)   250
Berenson, Bernard, The Drawings of the Florentine Painters, Chicago, 1938, 3 vols. (4184/1)   225
Berthoud, Ferdinand, Essai Sur L'Horlogerie, 2 vols. second ed., Paris, 1786 (4184/286)   1400
Blair, Robert, The Grave, a poem, 'subscribers copy', London, 1818 (4109/15)   1400
Bloch, Marc Elieser, Ichtyologie, vols. 1-6 of 12, 1st French ed., Berlin, 1786-88 (4184/160)   7500
Bonaparte, Charles Lucien, American Ornithology..., 3 vols. of 4, plates, Philadelphia, 1825-28
(4184/161)   450
Borelli, Giovanni Alfonso, De Vi Percussionis, 1st ed., Bologna, 1667 (4184/289)   800
Borrow, George, The Bible in Spain, 1st ed., London, 1843 (4109/17)   125
Boswell, James, Journal Of Hebrides Tour With Samuel Johnson, 1st ed., London, 1785 (4184/95)   450

Boswell, James, The Life of Samuel Johnson, 2 vols., 1st ed., London, 1791 (4109/18)	1900
Boswell, James, The Life Of Samuel Johnson, 2 vols, 1st ed., London, 1791 (4184/96)	850
Brant, Sebastian, Stultifera Navis ... The Ship of Fooles, 1st ed., London, 1570 (4109/19)	1800
Bronte, Charlotte, Jane Eyre, 1st ed., London, 1847 (4109/20)	500
Brookes, Samuel, Introduction to Study of Conchology, 1st ed., 11 plates, London, 1815 (4184/162)	350
Brookshaw, George, Pomona Britannica, second ed., 2 vols., London, 1817 (4184/163)	1700
Browne, Sir Thomas, Pseudodoxia Epidemica, 1st ed., London, 1646 (4109/21)	325
Browning, Robert, Men and Women, 1st ed., London, 1855 (4109/22)	375
Bryce, James, The American Commonwealth, T.S. Eliot's copy, N.Y., 1907 (4109/637)	300
Buchanan, George, Ane Detectioun of the Duinges of Marie Quene, of Scottes, 1st ed., London, 1571 (4109/23)	350
Bunyan, John, The Holy War, 1st ed., London, 1682 (4109/24)	500
Byron, George Gordon, Lord, The Bride of Abydos, 1st ed., London, 1813 (4109/26)	1400
Carey, David, Life In Paris, 1st ed., 21 handcolored plates, London, 1822 (4184/133)	350
Carlyle, Thomas, Sartor Resartus, 1st ed., cropped signature, London, 1834 (4184/97)	550
Cartwright, William, Comedies, Tragi-Comedies, 1st ed., London, 1651 (4109/30)	650
Catesby, Mark, The Natural History Of Carolina, Fla., Bahama, 2 vols., London, 1771 (4184/164)	21000
Caulfield, James, Portraits, memoirs, and characters, 1st ed., 7 vol., London, 1813-20 (4109/31)	225
Cervantes Saavedra, Miguel De, The History of Don-Quichote, 1st ed., London, 1620 (4109/32)	1200
Chapman, (Frederik Henrik), Architectura Navalis Mercatoria, 1st ed., Stockholm 1768 (4184/296)	3100
Char, Rene, Dent prompte, color lithos after Max Ernst, signed (both), Paris, 1969 (4184/20)	400
Chatterton, Thomas, Miscellanies in Prose and Verse, 1st ed., London, 1779 (4109/34)	175
Choiseul-Gouffier, Marie, Comte De, Voyage Pittoresque De La Grece, 3 vols., Paris, 1782-1822 (4184/203)	3500
Chronicles, The Cronycles of Englonde, London, Wynkyn de, Worde, 1515 (4109/36)	1400
Clark, Jonas, A Sermon at Lexington, April 4, 1776, 1st ed., Boston, 1776, disbound (4158/14)	400
Cleland, William, A collection of several poems and verses, NP, 1699 (4109/37)	400
Coleridge, Samuel Taylor, Sibylline Leaves, 1st ed., London, 1817 (4109/38)	400
Collins, Wilkie, The Woman in White, 1st ed., London, 1860 (4109/40)	650
Combe, William, The Second Tour Of Dr. Syntax, 1st ed., London, Ackermann, 1820 (4184/138)	500
Congreve, William, The Double-Dealer, 1st ed., London, 1694 (4109/41)	350
Continental Congress, Articles of Confederation, printed by Francis, Bailey, Lancaster, 1777 (4158/4)	2100
Cornwallis, Sir William, Essayes, 1st ed. of Part 1, London, 1600, rare (4109/44)	200
Coryate, Thomas, Coryats Crudities, 1st ed., London, 1611 (4109/45)	500
Crane, Hart, The Bridge, 1st ed., Paris, Black Sun Press, 1930 (4109/605)	850
Davenant, Sir William, Works, 1st ed., London, 1673 (4109/47)	300
Davy, Sir Humphry, On The Safety Lamp For Coal Miners..., 1st., ed., London, 1800 (4184/303)	75
Dee, John, ... what passed ... between Dr. John Dee ... and some, spirits, 1st ed., London, 1659 (4109/48)	600
Dekker, Thomas, The Second Part of the Honest Whore, 1st ed., London, 1630 (4109/56)	450
Denham, Sir John, Poems and Translations, 1st ed., London, 1668 (4109/57)	125
DeQuincey, Thomas, Confessions of an English Opium-Eater, 1st ed., London, 1822 (4109/58)	400
Dibdin, Thomas Frognall, The Bibliographical Decameron, 1st ed., uncut, London, W. Bulmer, 1817 (4184/2)	200
Dickens, Charles, A Christmas Carol, 1st ed., 2nd issue, London, 1843 (4109/608)	475
Dickens, Charles, A Christmas Carol, color illus. after Rackham, signed, London, 1915 (4184/28)	550
Dickens, Charles, A Tale of Two Cities, 1st ed., London, 1859 (4109/62)	1200
Dickens, Charles, David Copperfield, 1st ed., original wrappers, London, 1849-50 (4109/609)	1000
Dickens, Charles, Master Humphrey's Clock, 1st ed., London, 1840-41 (4109/61)	275
Dickens, Charles, Mystery of Edwin Drood, 1st ed., cloth case, London, 1870 (4109/610)	175
Dickens, Charles, Nicholas Nickleby, 1st ed., London, 1838-39 (4109/60)	350
Dodgson, Charles L., Lewis Carroll, Alice's Adventures ..., illus. and signed, Dali, N.Y., 1969 (4184/17)	900
Dolet, Etienne, Commentariorum Linguae Latinae, 1st ed., Lyons, 1536-38 (4184/421)	425
Dubourg, Matthew, Views Of Remains Of Ancient Buildings Of Rome, 1st ed., London, 1820 (4184/209)	650
Dutton, John, The Dublin Scuffle, 1st ed., London, 1699 (4109/76)	450
Edwards, Johnathan, Essay on Freedom of Will, 1st ed, Boston, 1754 (4158/22)	90
Egan Imitation, Real Life In London, 1st ed., 2nd issue, London, 1821-22 (4184/141)	325
Eliot, George, Scenes of Clerical Life, 1st ed., 2 vols., London, 1858 (4109/617)	500
Eliot, T.S., Animula, 1st ed., inscribed, London, 1929 (4109/622)	900
Eliot, T.S., Four Quartets, 1st ed., inscribed, London, 1944 (4109/625)	475
Eliot, T.S., Geoffrey Faber 1889-1961, 1st ed., London, 1961 (4109/628)	400
Eliot, T.S., Journey of the Magi, 1st ed., inscribed, London, 1927, fine (4109/620)	475
Eliot, T.S., Poems, handprinted, 1st ed., 1st state, Richmond, Hogarth Press, 1919 (4109/618)	1300
Eliot, T.S., Poems, 1st ed., 1st state text, 2nd state bind., Richmond, Hogarth Press, 1919 (4109/619)	400

Eliot, T.S., The Classics and the Man of Letters, 1st ed., London, 1942, inscribed (4109/624)	375
Eliot, T.S., The Cocktail Party, 1st ed., inscribed, London, 1950, very good (4109/626)	250
Eliot, T.S., The Confidential Clerk, 1st ed., London, 1954 (4109/627)	375
Elliot, Daniel Giraud, A Monograph of the Pittadae, 1st ed., N.Y., 1861-63 (4184/170)	2500
Elliot, Daniel Giraud, A Monograph Of The Bittidae, second ed., N.Y., 1861-6? (4184/171)	2400
Elliot, Daniel Giraud, A Monograph Of The Paradiseidae, large folio, plates, N.Y., 1873 (4184/168)	13500
Elliot, Daniel Giraud, A Monograph Of The Tetraoninae, 27 plates, N.Y., 1864-65 (4184/172)	5250
Elliot, Daniel Giraud, The New...Species Of Birds Of North America, N.Y., 1866-69 (4184/169)	6000
Evelyn, John, Memoirs, 1st ed., London, 1818 (4109/86)	400
Evelyn, John, Sculptura, 1st ed., London, 1662 (4109/85)	650
Exquemelin, Alexandre, Bucaniers of America, 1st English ed., London, 1684-85 (4109/87)	800
Fabyan, (Robert), The Chronicle (with continuation to May 8, 1559), London, 1559 (4184/423)	375
Faulkner, William, Absalom, Absalom, 1st ed., inscribed, N.Y., 1936, dust jacket (4109/640)	2250
Faulkner, William, Intruder in the Dust, 1st ed., inscribed, N.Y., 1948 (4109/641)	*950*

Faulkner (4109/641)

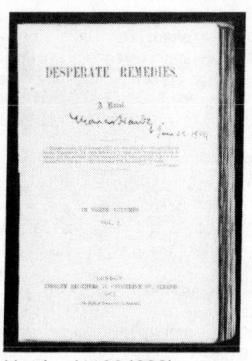

Hardy (4109/680)

Faulkner, William, The Marionettes, 1st ed., facsimile, illus., Charlottesville, 1975 (4109/644)	150
Faulkner, William, The Reivers, 1st ed., N.Y., 1962 (4109/642)	375
Fielding, Henry, An inquiry intow ... the late increase of, robbers, 1st ed., London, 1751 (4109/92)	150
Fielding, Henry, Miscellanies, 1st ed., London, 1743 (4109/91)	400
Fitzgerald, F. Scott, The Great Gatsby, inscribed, May, 1935, N. York, Modern Lib., 1934 (4184/100)	500
Fletcher, John, Monsieur, Thomas. A comedy, 1st ed., 1st issue, London, 1639 (4109/94)	400
Florio, John, Florios Second Frutes ... 1st ed., London, 1639 (4109/95)	1300
Fourcroy, A(ntoine)-F(rancois) De., Systeme Des Connaissances Chimiques, 10 vols., Paris, an IX-X (1801-02) (4184/315)	325
Franklin, Benjamin, Printing, Law of Library Company of Philadelphia, Phila., 1764 (4158/26)	400
Frost, Robert, A Boy's Will, 1st Am. ed., dust jacket, N.Y., 1915, superb (4109/652)	1375
Frost, Robert, A Way Out, a 1 act play, 1st ed., inscribed, N.Y., 1929 (4109/655)	900
Frost, Robert, Come In and Other Poems, 1st ed., inscribed, N.Y., 1943, very fine (4109/660)	600
Frost, Robert, Hard Not To Be King, 1st ed., House of Books, N.Y., 1951 (4109/665)	200
Frost, Robert, Mountain Interval, 1st ed., 1st state, N.Y., 1916, fine (4109/653)	600
Frost, Robert, The Complete Poems, Limited Editions Club, N.Y., 1950 (4109/664)	200
Galilei, Galileo, Discorsi E Dimostrazioni Matematiche, 1st, ed., Leyden, 1638 (4184/277)	3250
Galilei, Galileo, Opere, 2 vols., 1st collected ed. of Galilei', s works, bologna, 1655-56 (4184/318)	400
Galilei, Galileo, Systema, Cosmicum 1st Latin ed., Strasbourg, 1635 (4184/425)	1000
Galland, Isaac, Galland Iowa Immigrant, containing map, 1st ed, Chillicothe, 1840 (4158/27)	1300
Gallois, Jean, Seneuze, Laurent, Biblioteca D. Joannis Galloys, library catalog, ue, Paris, 1710 (4184/5)	100
Gay, John, The Beggar's Opera, 1st ed., London, 1728 (4109/97)	500
Gerarde, John, The Herbal Or Gen. Histry Of Plants, folio, London, 1636 (4184/174)	650
Goldsmith, Oliver, Retaliation, A Poem, 1st ed., London, 1774 (4109/101)	300
Goldsmith, Oliver, She Stoops to Conquer, 1st ed., London, 1773 (4109/100)	450
Goldsmith, Oliver, The Vicar of Wakefield, 1st ed., Salisbury, 1766 (4109/99)	850
Gould, John, A Monograph Of The Frogonidae, 36 plates, London, 1838 (4184/176)	2100
Gould, John, A Monograph Of The Odon Tophorinae...of America, London, (1844-50) (4184/175)	6250
Gower, John, De Confessio Amantis, 3rd ed., T. Fox copy, London, 1554 (4109/106)	550

Gower, Lord Ronald S., Sir Thomas Lawrence, 1 of 200 extra,, illustrated, uncut, London, 1812 (4184/6) — 300

Grandi, Guido, Instituzioni Meccaniche, 1st ed., Florence, 1739 (4184/322) — 175

Graves, Algernon, A Century of Loan Exhibitions, 5 vols., uncut, 1 of 250, London, 1913-15 (4184/8) — 150

Graves, Algernon and Wm. V. Cronin, A History Of The Works Of Sir Joshua Reynolds, 1 of 200, London, 1885 (4184/7) — 275

Guglielmini, Domenico, Della Natura De' Fiumi, 1st ed., Bologna, 1697 (4184/325) — 110

Hakluyt, Richard, The Principal Navigations ... of the English, Nation, 1st enlarged ed., Lon., 1599-1600 (4109/107) — 1900

Hall, Capt. Basil, Account of Voyage...to West Coast of Corea, London, 1818 (4184/218) — 100

Hall, John, Horae Vacivae, or Essays, 1st ed., London, 1646 (4109/108) — 150

Hamerton, Philip G., Etching And Etchers, orig. works including, Rembrandt, London, 1868 (4184/11) — 600

Hardy, Thomas, Desperate Remedies, 1st ed., London, 1871, rare (4109/680) — *1200*

Harrington, James, The Commonwealth of Oceana, 1st ed., London, 1656 (4109/109) — 200

Harrison, (John), The Principles Of Mr. Harrison's Time-Keeper, 1st ed., London, 1767 (4184/328) — 2300

Head, Richard, Proteus Redivivus, 1st ed., London, 1675 (4109/110) — 150

Hemingway, Ernest, A Farewell To Arms, 1st ed., signed, large, paper, N.Y., 1929 (4184/101) — 850

Hemingway, Ernest, Across the River and Into the Trees, advance, N.Y., 1950 (4109/697) — 450

Hemingway, Ernest, Across the River and Into the Trees, galleys, N.Y., 1950 (4109/696) — 550

Hemingway, Ernest, For Whom The Bell Tolls, advance proof, N.Y., 1940, Book Club ed. (4109/692) — 250

Hemingway, Ernest, For Whom The Bell Tolls, galley proofs for 1st, N.Y., 1940 (4109/691) — 1100

Hemingway, Ernest, For Whom The Bell Tolls, Limited Editions Club, Princeton, 1942 (4109/695) — 300

Hemingway, Ernest, For Whom The Bell Tolls, 1st ed., dust jacket, N.Y., 1940, inscribed (4109/694) — 1400

Hemingway, Ernest, For Whom The Bell Tolls, 1st ed., inscribed, N.Y., 1940 (4109/693) — 1200

Hemingway, Ernest, Green Hills of Africa, 1st Eng. ed., inscribed, London, 1936 (4109/686) — 1000

Hemingway, Ernest, In Our Time, 1st ed., inscribed, Paris, 1924 (4109/681) — 4250

Hemingway, Ernest, In Our Time, 2nd Am. ed., revised, inscribed, N.Y., 1930 (4109/684) — 700

Hemingway, Ernest, Introduction to Kiki of Montparnasse, 1st ed., Paris, Black Manikin, 1929 (4184/102) — 550

Hemingway, Ernest, Men Without Women, dust jacket, 1st ed., N.Y., 1927, inscribed (4109/683) — 1000

Hemingway, Ernest, The Fifth Column, a play, 1st separate ed., N.Y., 1940 (4109/689) — 650

Hemingway, Ernest, Today is Friday, 1st ed., Englewood, N.J., fine (4109/682) — 375

Heywood, Thomas, The English Traveller, 1st ed., London, 1633 (4109/111) — 250

Heywood, Thomas, The Life of Merlin, 1st ed., London, 1641 (4109/112) — 300

Hogarth, William, Works, folio, 114 plates, edited by Nichols, London, 1822 (4184/221) — 700

Hogarth, William, Works, limited ed., Philadelphia, 1900 (4109/113) — 350

Holcroft, Thomas, Alwyn, or the Gentleman Comedian, 1st ed., London, 1780 (4109/114) — 400

Hooke, Robert, Micrographia Restaurata..., 33 copperplates, London, 1745 (4184/269) — 375

Huddy, William H., editor, Militiary Magazine, record of the Philadelphia Volunteers, Philadelphia, 1839-40 (4158/49) — 1000

Huygens, Christian, Opera Varia, 2 vols., 56 engraved plates, Leiden, 1724 (4184/344) — 375

Irving, Washington, Astoria, 1st ed. with map, 2 vols., Phila., 1836 (4158/33) — 225

Irving, Washington, Life of George Washington, 68 parts, illustrated, 1857-1861 (4267/718) — 225

Jefferys, Thomas, The American Atlas, London, 1776 (4158/35) — 5500

Jenkins, James, The Naval Achievements Of Grt. Britain, 1st e, d., London, 1812-16 (4184/223) — 3800

Jerrold, Douglas, A Man Made of Money, 1st ed., London, 1849 (4109/116) — *550*

Johnson, Samuel, A Dictionary of the English Language, 1st ed., London, 1755 (4109/120) — 1600

Johnson, Samuel, A Dictionary Of The English Language, 1st ed., London, 1755 (4184/103) — 1300

Johnson, Samuel, A Journey to the Western Isles of Scotland, 1st ed., 1st issue, London, 1775 (4109/121) — 500

Johnson, Samuel, Sermon Written ... for the Burial of His Wife, 1st ed., London, 1788 (4109/122) — 350

Johnson, Samuel, The Idler, 1st collected ed., 2 vols., London, 1761 (4184/105) — 325

Johnson, Samuel, The Rambler, 1st ed., 2 vols., London, 1751 (4109/119) — 750

Jonson, Benjamin, Workes, 1st ed., 2 vols., London, 1616-40 (4109/124) — 950

Joyce, James, Chamber Music, 1st ed., London, 1907, fine (4109/734) — 375

Joyce, James, Exiles, 2nd Eng. ed., inscribed, London, 1921 (4109/735) — 650

Joyce, James, Finnegan's Wake, 1st ed., London & N.Y., 1939, nearly fine (4109/745) — 1300

Joyce, James, Pomes Penyeach, unusual 1st ed. burned by Lucia, Joyce, Paris, 1932 (4109/741) — 3500

Joyce, James, Pomes Penyeach, 1st ed., Paris, 1927 (4109/740) — 450

Joyce, James, Ulysses, 1st ed. in French, Paris, 1929 (4109/738) — 650

Joyce, James, Ulysses, 1st ed., 'Press Copy', Shakespeare & Co., Paris, 1922, rare (4109/736) — 900

Joyce, James, Ulysses, 8th printing, inscribed Shakespeare & Co., Paris, 1926 (4109/737) — 1500

Kaempfer, Engelbert, The History of Japan, 1st English ed., London, 1728 (4184/224) — 1200

Kennedy, John F., Editor, As We Remembered Joe, private printing, Cambridge, Mass., 1945 (4158/36) — 1000

Kerouac, Jack, On the Road, 1st ed., advance issue, N.Y., 1957 (4109/756) — 750

Kerouac, Jack, The Town and the City, 1st ed., inscribed, N.Y., 1950 (4109/755) 2500
Kippis, Andrew, attributed to, Consideration on Provisional Treaty with America, London, 1783
 (4158/37) 250
Landor, Walter Savage, Imaginary Conversations, 1st ed., London, 1824-28 (4109/129) 200
Langbaine, Gerard and Charles Gildon, The Lives and Characters of the English Dramatick, Poets,
 1st ed., London, 1699 (4109/130) 250
Lawrence, D.H., Bay, a book of poems, 1st ed., Beaumont Press, Westminster, 1919, very good
 (4109/762) 950
Lawrence, T.E., Crusader Castles, Golden Cockrel Press, 1st ed., 1936 (4109/769) 350
Lawrence, T.E., Men in Print, Golden Cockrel Press, 1st ed., 1940, very good (4109/771) 250
Lawrence, T.E., Secret Despatches from Arabia, 1st ed., Golden Cockrel, 1939 (4109/770) 400
Lawrence, T.E., Seven Pillars of Wisdom, 1st ed., private print, London, 1926, inscribed (4109/766) 5750
Lawrence, T.E., translator, The Odyssey of Homer, 1st ed., London, 1932, fine (4109/767) 950
Ledyard, John, Journal of Captain Cook's Last Voyage, 1st ed., Hartford, 1783 (4158/39) 4750
Lee, Samuel, Joy of Faith, 1st ed., Boston, 1687 (4158/40) 600
Levinson, Andre, I7L'oevre de Leon Bakst ..., 1 of 500, by, Bakst, folio, Paris, 1922 (4184/16) 550
Lewis, Mathew Gregory, The Monkia Romance, 1st ed., London, 1796 (4109/773) 450
Lewis, Matthew Gregory, Tales of Wonder, 1st ed., London, 1801 (4109/131) 225
Lewis, Meriwether and William Clark, Original journals, limited reprint of 1904-05, ed. N.Y., 1959
 (4158/41) 225
Lewis, Sinclair, Our Mr. Wrenn, 1st ed., inscribed twice, dust jacket, N.Y., 1914 (4109/775) 850
Lewis, Sinclair, The Innocents, 1st ed., dust jacket, N.Y., 1917, fine (4109/776) 500
Lewis, Sinclair as Tom Graham, Hike and the Aeroplane, 1st ed., inscribed, N.Y., 1912 (4109/774) 850
Lilford, (Thomas Powys), Lord, Colored Figures Of Bivas Of The British Islan, ds, London, 1885-97
 (4184/179) 1600
Linnaeus, Carolus, Genera Plantarum, 8 vols., second ed., Leiden, 1742 (4184/180) 150
Linperch, Pieter, Architectura Mechanica Of Moole-boek, folio, Amsterdam, 1727 (4184/354) 150
Lloyd, Lodowick, The Pilgrimage of Princes, London, 1586 (4109/132) 250
Lopez de Sigura, Ruy, Il Guiuoco De Gli Scacchi, 1st Italian ed., Venice, 1584 (4184/435) 475
Lovecraft, H.P., The Shunned House, The Recluse Press, 1st ed., Athol, Mass., 1928 (4109/780) 600
Lucian, Dialogues Des Courtesanes, 35 illus. after, Maillol, Paris, 1948 (4184/21) 500
Macchiavelli, Niccolo, Discourses, 1st ed. in English, London, 1636 (4109/134) 250
Mace Thomas, Musick's Monument, London, 1676 (4184/439) 650
MacNiece, Louis, Blind Fireworks, 1st ed., London, 1929 (4109/781) 250
Mallarme, Stephane, Poesies, 29 etchings by Matisse, 1 of 145, Lausanne, A. Skira, 1932 (4184/22) 11750
Markwell, Marmaduke (pseud.), Advice To Sportsmen, 1st ed., London, 1809 (4184/147) 375
Marlowe, Christopher, attributed to, Lusts Dominion, 1st ed., 1st issue, London, 1657 (4109/135) 1100
Martin, F.R., A History of Oriental carpets before 1800, Court Printing, Vienna 1908 (4198/1) 10000
Mather, Cotton, Ecclesiastees-Life of Rev. Jon. Mitchel, Mass. Green and Allen 1697 (4158/44) 900
Mather, Cotton, Maqualia Christ. Americana, 1st ed., London, 1702 (4158/46) 800
Maupertius, (Pierre Louis Moreau De), Oeuvres, 4 vols., Lyon, 1768 (4184/366) 350
McCracken, Harold, Catlin and the Old Frontier, signed, N.Y., 1959 (4158/13) 100
McKenney, Thomas L. and James Hall, The Indian Tribes of North America, Edinburgh, 1933-34
 (4158/43) 200
Melanchthon, (Franz Anton), Initia Doctrina Physica, Wittenberg, 1559 (4184/369) 325
Mercatus, Michael, Mettallotheca (-appendix), 2 vols., Rome, 1717-19 (4184/440) 325
Merriman, Henry Seton, Hugh S. Scott, With Edged Tools, 1st ed., London, 1894, fine (4109/138) 150
Miller, Henry, Order and Chaos Chez Hans Riechel, 1st ed., New Orleans, 1966 (4109/784) 200
Milne, A.A., When We Were Very Young, 1st ed., London, 1924 (4109/787) 800
Milton, John, Paradise Lost, 1st ed., fourth state, London, 1668 (4184/107) 1800
Mitchell, Johnathan, Nehemiah on the Wall in Troublesome Times, Cambridge, 1671 (4158/50) 2000
Moore, Marianne, A Talisman, 1st ed., Cambridge, 1963 (4109/793) 500
Moore, Marianne, Collected Poems, 1st Am. issue, N.Y., Macmillan, 1951 (4109/790) 225
Moore, Marianne, Predilections, galley proofs, N.Y., 1955 (4109/791) 750
Morse, Jedidah, Geography Made Easy, Boston, 1790 (4158/52) 250
Morse, Jedidah, The American Geography, Elizabethtown, 1789 (4158/51) 750
Morton, Nathaniel, New Englands Memoriall, Cambridge, 1669 (4158/53) 6500
Munnings, Sir Alfred, Pictures of Horses and English Life, uncut 1, of 250, signed, Lon., 1927
 (4184/9) 475
Neal, Daniel, The History of New-England, London, 1720 (4158/54) 150
Nin, Anais, House of Incest, 1 of 50 copies, N.Y., Gemor, 1947 (4184/109) 375
O'Neill, Eugene, Anna Christie, 1st sep. ed., signed, N.Y., 1930, very good (4109/798) 650
Ogilby, John, America,being the latest and most Accurate Description, London, 1671 (4158/58) 2950
Ovid, Les Metamorphoses, 15 Picasso etchings, signed, Lausanne, A. Skira, 1931 (4184/26) 8000
Parke-Bernet Galleries, Collection of Americana-Thomas W. Streeter, 1960-69, 7 vols., lacks vol. 5
 (4158/69) 225

Parke-Bernet Galleries, Collection of Americana, Thomas W., Streeter, 1966-69, 7 vols. lacks index (4158/2) — 225
Paxton, (Sir Joseph), Paxton's Magazine Of Botany..., 7 vols., London, 1834-40 (4184/187) — 1000
Pecchius, Franciscus Maria, Tractatus De Aquaeductu, 1st ed., Pavia, 1670-76 (4184/383) — 275
Pennington, John H., Aerostation, or steam Aerial Navigation, rare, 1st ed., (Baltimore, 1838) (4184/384) — 650
Pennsylvania, Proclamation, to preserve the observation of the Sabbath, 1782 (4267/801) — 150
Pennsylvania, Proclamation, Associators call to arms, signed in print, 1776 (4267/803) — 7000
Pepys, Samuel, Memoires Relating to the State of the Royal, Navy, 1st ed., 1st issue, 1690 (4109/152) — *450*

Pepys
(4109/152)

O'Neill (4109/798)

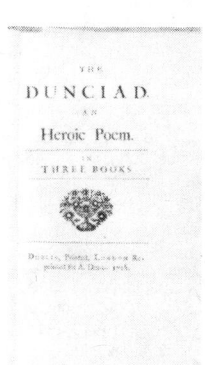

Pope (4109/155)

Marlowe
(4109/135)

Piranesi, Giovanni Battista, Lapides Capitolini, Rome, 1762 (4184/235) — 600
Pope, Alexander, Miscellaneous Poems and Translations, 1st ed., London, 1712 (4109/154) — 650
Pope, Alexander, The Dunciad, An Heroic Poem, 1st octavo ed., Dublin, London, 1728 (4109/155) — *1300*
Porter, Katherine Anne, Flowering Judas, 1st ed., 1 of 600 copies, N.Y., 1930 (4184/111) — 100
Porter, Lieut. and Mrs. Whitworth, Views in the Island of Dominica, 1849 (4158/62) — 250
Pound, Ezra, typed letter, signed, to O.R. Orage, 1930's, (4109/811) — 700
Pound, Ezra, Antheil And The Treatise On Harmony, 1st ed., in, scribed, Paris, 1924, fine (4109/805) — 450
Pound, Ezra, ABC Of Reading, 1st ed., inscribed, London, 1934 (4109/806) — 500
Pound, Ezra, Dyptych Rome, London, 1st ed., signed, N.Y., 1958, mint (4109/807) — 500
Pound, Ezra, Le Cahiers De L'Herne, 2 vols., unopened, Paris, 1965 (4109/810) — 400
Pound, Ezra, Lustra, 1st ed., 1st impression, inscribed, N.Y., 1917, spine dam. (4109/809) — 550
Pound, Ezra, Redondellas, Or Something Of That Sort, 1st ed., signed, N.Y., 1967, mint (4109/808) — 500
Prince, Thomas, A Chronological History of N.Eng., Boston, 1736 (4158/63) — 250
Raucourt De Charleville, A Manual of Lithography, 1st English ed., London, 1820 (4184/393) — 475
Revere's Copy, Paul, Muller's Treatise on Artillery, 4 times, by Revere (4158/125) — 3000
Ricci, Corrado, Antonio Allegri da Correddio, 1 of 100 copies, 3 vols., London, 1896 (4184/12) — 125
Roberts, David, Egypt and Nubia, 3 vols., 125 plates and maps, London, 1846-49 (4184/236) — 6500
Rojas, Fernando De, La Celestine, 66 Picasso etchings, 1 of 400, signed, Paris, 1971 (4184/25) — 2600
Rose, John Holland, The Life Of Napoleon, letters, extra illustra, tions, London, 1902 (4184/231) — 750
Rosetti, Christina, Goblin Market, illus. after Arther Rackham, signed, London, 1933 (4184/29) — 350
Roth, Henry, Call It Sleep, 1st ed., N.Y., 1934 (4109/812) — *850*

Roth
(4109/812)

Ruskin, John, The King Of The Golden River, illus after A., Rackham, London, 1932 (4184/30) — 350
Sabartes, Jaime, Dans L'Atelier de Picasso, 6 lithos, 4 color, artist signed, Paris, 1957 (4184/27) — 1400
Schott, Kaspar, Tecnica Curiosa, Siva Mirabilia Artis, 1st, ed., Nuremberg, 1664 (4184/399) — 700
Scrope, William, The Art Of Deer Stalking, 8 vols., 1st ed., London, 1838 (4184/190) — 175
Shakespeare, William, Plays, notes by Samuel Johnson, 1st ed., edited, by Johnson, London, 1765 (4109/172) — 500
Shakespeare, William and John Fletcher, The Two Noble Kinsmen, 1st ed., London, 1634 (4109/171) — 2600
Shaw, G.B., Cymbeline Refinished, 1st ed., notes and revis., on N.p., private printing, 1937, fine (4109/817) — 650
Shaw, G.B., Fanny's First Play, rough proof, unpublished, 1st ed., London, 1911, soiled (4109/814) — 550
Shaw, G.B., The Simpleton Or The Unexpected Isles, proofs, or 1st printing, N.p., 1935 (4109/816) — 550
Shelley, Percy Bysshe, Adonais, 1st ed., Pisa, 1821 (4109/173) — 375
Shelley, Percy Bysshe, The Cenci. A Tragedy, In Five Acts, 1st ed., London, 1819 (4109/174) — 550
Sheridan, Richard Brinsley, The Rivals, A Comedy, 1st ed., London, 1775 (4109/179) — 250
Sitwell, Sacheverell, William Blunt, Great Flower Books, 1 of 295 copies, Folio, London, 1956 (4184/13) — 475
Smith, Joseph, The Book of Mormon, Palmyra, 1830 (4158/66) — 900
Southey, Robert, editor, The Annual Anthology, Bristol, 1799-1800 (4109/186) — 400
Spinoza, Benedict De, Tractatus Theologico-Politicus, 1st ed., Hamburg, 1670 (4109/216) — 1300
Starbuck, Alexander, History of the American Whale Fishery, signed, N.Y., 1964, limited ed. (4158/67) — 125
Stein, Gertrude, Chicago Inscriptions, private printing, 1st ed., Chicago, 1934, very fine (4109/844) — 300
Stein, Gertrude, Dix Portraits, 1st ed., signed, Paris, 1930, very good (4109/842) — 400
Stein, Gertrude, Lucy Church Amiably, 1st ed., Paris, 1930, pristine (4109/841) — 352
Stein, Gertrude, Morceaux De La Fabrication Des Americains, 1st, French ed., inscribed, 1929 (4109/840) — 350
Stein, Gertrude, Three Lives, 1st ed., inscribed, London 1920, spine, faded (4109/839) — 550
Stein, Gertrude, with Virgil Thomson, Four Saints And Three Acts (Opera), 1st ed., Thomson, signed, N.Y., 1934 (4109/845) — 650
Stevens, Wallace, Three Academic Pieces, 1st ed., Cummington Press, 1947 (4184/114) — 500
Stokes, I. W. Phelps, The Iconography of Manhattan Island, 1498-1909, 6 vols., N.Y., 1915-28 (4158/69) — 1000
Surtees, Robert Smith, The Analysis of The Hunting Field, 1st ed., London, Ackermann, 1846 (4184/154) — 250
Taconet, Maurice, Par Les Sentiers, Etchings, Rudaux, Leandre, japon paper, Paris, 1894 (4184/31) — 50
Thackeray, William Makepeace, The Adventures of Philip, 1st ed., London, 1862 (4109/191) — 150
Thomas, Dylan, Portrait Of Artist As Young Dog, 1st U.S. ed., inscribed, Norfolk, 1940 (4184/115) — 650
Thomas, Dylan, 18 Peoms, second ed., later issue, London, 1942 (4184/117) — 225
Thomson, Charles, Autograph memorandum book, political observations, 1782 (4158/80) — 1500
Tipping, H. Avray, C. Hussey, English Homes, 2 vols. in 8, folio, London, 1920-28 (4184/14) — 650
Tortellius, Joannes, De Orthographia Dictionum e Graecis Tractarum, Viceuza, Koblinger, 1479 (4184/449) — 2000
Trew, Christoph Jakob, Plantae Selectae, large folio, 100 plates, 1s, t ed., Augsburg, 1750-53 (4184/192) — 8500
Walpole, Horace, The Castle of Otranto, Parma, 1791 (4109/201) — 201

Walpole, Hugh, Harmer, John, corrected proofs, inscribed twice, London, 1926 (4109/857)	250
Walton, Izaak, The Compleat Angler, 1st ed., London, 1653 (4109/202)	3800
Walton, Izaak, The Compleat Angler, 2nd ed., London, 1655 (4109/203)	1100
Walton, Izaak, The Life of John Donne, 1st separate ed., London, 1658 (4109/205)	1100
Walton, Izaak, The Universal Angler, 1st ed., London, 1658 (4109/204)	900
Washington, George, official letters to the Hon. American Congress, Boston, 1795 (4158/72)	175
Westmacott, Charles Molloy, The English Spy, 1st ed., London, 1825-26 (4184/157)	650
Wilder, Thornton, Bridge Of San Luis Rey, 1st ed., true, N.Y., 1927, rare (4109/859)	850
Williams, Tennessee, Battle Of Angels, 1st ed., Utah, 1945, fine (4109/860)	450
Williamson, Geo. G., H. Engleheart, George Engleheart, uncut, 1 of 360 copies, London, 1902 (4184/15)	100
Wise, John, A System Of Aeronautics, 1st ed., extremely, rare, Philadelphia, 1850 (4184/411)	450
Wiseman, Richard, Eight Chirurgical Treatises, folio, London, 1705 (4184/274)	175
Wolfe, Thomas, From Death To Mourning, 1st ed., inscribed, N.Y., 1935, very good (4109/862)	800
Wolfe, Thomas, The Web And The Rock, galley proofs, N.Y., 1939, fine, rare (4109/863)	550
Wolfe, Thomas, To Rupert Brooke, 1st ed., private printing, Paris, 1948 (4109/864)	125
Wood, William, New England's Prospect, London, 1634 (4158/74)	300
Zukofsky, Louis, First Half Of 'A', 1st ed., inscribed, N.Y., 1940, very good, rare (4109/867)	800

MANUSCRIPTS AND AUTOGRAPHS

Assorted items

Adams, John, autograph letter to Ben. Rush, N.Y. 19 June, 1789, fine (4158/75)	2250
Adams, John, printed document signed, Philadelphia , 9 March 1798, (4158/76)	400
Adams, John, printed document signed, Washington, 24 June 1828, (4158/78)	200
Adams, John Quincy, 6th Pres., autographed letter, 25 Feb. 1788, to N. Freeman, comment on Constitution (4267/601)	1450
Adams, John Quincy, 6th Pres., document signed, led to Indian treaty, 1828 (4267/602)	1900
American Revolution, broadside, last Thursday in April is day of, fasting, 1782 (4267/607)	425
American Revolution, broadside, Definitive Peace Treaty, Annapolis, 1784 (4267/661)	2600
American Revolution, broadside, Sandwich Town Meeting, 1774, (4267/605)	800
American Revolution, instructions to John Jay in code, Congress, 1781 (4267/606)	16500
American Revolution, Broadside, Boston Committee of Correspondence, 1773 (4267/604)	950
Andros, Sir Edmund, autograph document signed, 17 June 1687, (4158/107)	625
Anthony, Susan B., three checks with her signature, (4158/85)	225
Arnold, Benedict, autograph will disposing of money and land, 1781 (4267/616)	6750
Arnold, Benedict, draft of autograph letter about pay at West Point, 1780 (4267/615)	1900
Arnold, Ten Eyck, Capt. John, autograph letter, describes Arnold's treason, 1780 (4267/617)	2200
Articles of Confederation, Boston, 1777 Folio, (4267/618)	600
Avery, John, signed document, certifying Massachusetts Bay Congress delegates, 1776 (4267/782)	350
Bach, Johann Sebastian, autograph receipt, 4 lines, signed, framed, Leipzig, 29 July 1747 (4184/33)	14500
Beauregard, Gen. Pierre G. T., autograph letter about design of artillery, 1855 (4267/621)	275
Beethoven, Ludwig Van, autograph letter, 4 pages, no place or date, (Vienna, ca 5 Nov. 1825) (4184/34)	18500
Benjamin, Judah P., autograph letter to Gen. Breckenridge introducing, Col. Norris, 1864 (4267/624)	600
Benjamin, Judah P., autograph letter to Gen. Wise concerning, munitions, 1862 (4267/622)	850
Benjamin, Judah P., autograph letter to Jefferson Davis about, molasses for troops, 1862 (4267/623)	850
Berlioz, Hector, autograph letter signed, 3 pages, 'Sunday morning' (London, 1853) (4184/35)	650
Bizet, Georges, autograph letter signed, 3 pages, to composer, Puget, no date or place (4184/36)	550
Black military recruitment, lithograph, United States Soldiers at Camp, 19 x 11½, 1863 (4267/627)	450
Black military recruitment, poster on linen, wooden rollers, Philadelphia, 90 x 44, 1862 (4267/628)	1000
Brahms, Johannes, autograph card signed, no place (Vienna?), no date (4184/38)	650
Brahms, Johannes, autograph musical quotation (12 bars), on card (4184/39)	1200
Brahms, Johannes, autograph musical quotation, 1 page, signed, dated 12 September 1872 (4184/37)	2300
Brahms, Johannes, autograph note signed, 1 page, on verso, 23 April 1876 (4184/40)	475
Bryant, William Cullen, autograph manuscript, 'Death of Slavery', 1866 (4267/631)	2500
Buchanan, James, printed document signed, Washington, 1 Oct. 1858, (4158/152)	200
Bunker Hill, broadside, British account of events, 14 x 8½, 1775 (4267/632)	1300
Butler, Benjamin, printed broadside, martial law in New Orleans, 1862 (4267/798)	400
California, Captain E.O.D. Ord, contract for survey of Los Angeles, 1849 (4267/634)	3600
Carlyle, Thomas, autograph letter signed, 4 pages, Chelsea, September 27, 1844 (4184/80)	450
Caruso, Enrico, large and bold autograph self-caricature, signed, 27 February 1910 (4184/41)	400
Chase, Salmon P., autograph document, oath of office for Andrew, Johnson, 1865 (4267/725)	11000
Civil War, broadside, Fall of Richmond, Philadelphia, 19¼ x 25, 1865 (4267/640)	2100
Civil War, colored engraving, Grant and Lee before surrender, 22¼ x 28, 1866 (4267/641)	200
Civil War, political broadside, Elect M'Clellan, anti-democratic, 26 x 22, 1864 (4267/639)	325

Civil War, Stephen D. Lee, autograph copy of ultimatum to Fort Sumter, copy dated 1905 (4267/638)	500
Clay, Henry, autograph letter signed, Ashland, 30 Oct. 1841, to N.P. Tallmadge (4158/108)	275
Clementi, Muzio, autograph letter signed, 1 page, London, 27 January 1816 (4184/42)	600
Clinton, George, autograph letter signed, Poughkeepsie, 30 Dec. 1777, (4158/153)	225
Confederate, Charleston Mercury Extra, broadside, dissolution ordinance passed, 1860 (4267/652)	3600
Coolidge, Calvin, and cabinet, signed, photograph, second cabinet, 12½ x 17½, 1925-28 (4267/655)	700
Cruikshank, George, pencil drawing for etching, the gin-'juggarn, ath', 7½ x 9¼ (4184/81)	325
Custis, G.W.P., autograph letter signed, 17 Oct. 1834, to William, Nelson (4158/96)	120
Dali, Salvador, sheet of heavy oriental paper with sketches, autographs, N. York, ca1955 (4184/18)	550
Davis, Jefferson, autograph letter giving away wife's cat, 1864 (4267/657)	1100
Davis, Jefferson, autograph letter to Pres. Pierce, to introduce, Sen. Summer, 1853 (4267/660)	750
Davis, Jefferson, broadside, captured in wife's dress, advertising Wanamaker's, 1865 (4267/659)	600
Davis, Jefferson, printed document, Davis's last pay voucher, signed, 1865 (4267/658)	3250
Davis, Jefferson, as Secretary of War, endorsement of letter to army officers, 1856 (4267/656)	450
Decatur, Susan, autograph letter signed, Wash. 15 Jan. 1821, (4158/110)	350
Donizetti, Gaetano, autograph musical manuscript, 1½ pages, framed with portrait (4184/44)	400
Doubleday, Gen. Abner, autograph manuscript account of Battle of Gettysburg, 1863 (4267/690)	5000
Drake, Sir Francis, autographed deed of sale of Grayhurst Manor, 1582 (4267/662)	10500
Dubuque, Julien, French pioneer, autograph letter about provisions for Iowa, mines, 1809 (4267/663)	650
Dvorak, Antonin, autograph card signed, framed, Prague, 18 April 1887 (4184/45)	500
Eliot, T.S., Typed letter signed, London Nov. 8, 1926, (4109/635)	425
Emancipation Proclamation, exact facsimile with photo of Lincoln, 30 x 23½, 1863 (4267/665)	500
Evans, Lewis, Essays, 1st has map of U.S., 1st engraved in, U.S. to show Ohio country, 1755 (4267/671)	3700
Franklin, Benjamin, autograph letter to Mrs. Katherine Green, 1762 (4267/675)	4800
Franklin, Benjamin, printed document signed, Philadelphia , 20 Jan. 1786, (4158/100)	1100
Franklin, Benjamin, printed document signed, 13 May 1786, (4158/101)	800
Franklin, Benjamin, printed document, signed, order to pay money, 1786 (4267/677)	1000
Franklin, Benjamin, signed document, certified power of attorney, 1779 (4267/676)	700
Frontenac, Louis, autograph letter, letter to his uncle, 1644 (4267/680)	1100
Frost, Robert, Autograph letter to Joseph Margolies, 3/3/45, (4109/675)	750
Frost, Robert, Autograph letter to Van Wyck Brooks, 2/11/37, very fine (4109/674)	1700
Frye, Maj. Frederick, autograph letter, military situation in front of Vicksburg, 1862 (4267/842)	300
Fulton, Robert, autograph letter to Secretary of Navy, 1813 (4267/681)	2100
Garfield, James, autograph letter to job applicant, 1881 (4267/686)	5750
Garfield, James, documents signed directing U.S. seal be affixed to envelope, 1881 (4267/685)	2400
Garfield, James A., autograph letter to Secretary Chase about wartime conditions, 1863 (4267/684)	1200
George III, King of England, appointment of Sir Henry Clinton as Major, Gen., 1772 (4267/688)	1500
George III, King of England, document signed authorizing Sir Henry Clinton to maintain discipline, 1778 (4267/689)	1000
Gounod, Charles, autograph letter signed, 3 pages, 4 July 1871 (4184/51)	100
Grant, Ulysses, autograph document to Gen. Ord ordering, advance, 1865 (4267/696)	1700
Grant, Ulysses, autograph endorsement recommending Gen. Meagher, be dismissed, 1865 (4267/694)	750
Grant, Ulysses, autograph letter to Gen. Meade suggesting, headquarters guard, 1865 (4267/695)	1600
Grant, Ulysses, autograph letter to Gen. Halleck about, Gen. Sherman, 1864 (4267/693)	600
Grant, Ulysses, autograph letter to Gen. Quimby about Western Army affairs, 1862 (4267/692)	1200
Grant, Ulysses, autograph letter to Gov. Smith of Mont., 1867 (4267/698)	275
Grant, Ulysses S., autograph letter signed, Executive Mansion, 20 May, 1874 (4158/154)	325
Greene, Nathaniel, autograph letter to Count Rochambeau, 1782 (4267/700)	850
Greene, Nathaniel, autograph letter to Gen. Washington at end of war, 1783 (4267/701)	4000
Greene, Nathaniel, autograph letter to Mr. Weiss ordering rations for Pa. troops, 1779 (4267/699)	600
Grieg, Edvard, autograph letter signed, 2 pages, Kristiana, 26 Nov. 1906 (4184/52)	375
Hale, Nathan, autograph sentiment sending love to mother, May 24, (no year) (4267/703)	1700
Hamilton, Alexander, autograph letter to widow of Nathaniel Greene, 1793 (4267/704)	700
Hanami, Kohei, autograph note from commander of destroyer, which sank PT 109, 1963 (4267/738)	200
Hancock, John, appointment signed, (4158/131)	275
Hancock, John, autograph letter signed, 'Congress Cham.', 20 Aug., 1776, to G. Washington (4158/129)	1300
Hancock, John, document signed, 'In Congress', 30 Dec. 1776, (4158/113)	850
Hancock, John, document signed, 1 July 1789, fine signature, (4158/130)	600
Harding, Warren G., autograph manuscript, speech at Dayton, Ohio, 1921 (4267/705)	750
Harding, Warren G., printed check, signed, one cent only, 1921 (4267/706)	800
Harrison, Anna, First Lady, autograph letter to cousin about social affairs, 3 September (no year) (4267/711)	800
Harrison, William H., autograph letter to nephew on family matters, 1841 (4267/709)	7000

Harrison, William Henry, document signed, 12 March 1795, (4158/114)	200
Haydn, Joseph, autograph letter signed, 1 page to M.B. Veltm, ann, Vienna, 20 July 1799 (4184/53)	7000
Haydn, Michael, autograph letter signed, 1 page, framed, Salzburg, 7 October 1799 (4184/54)	1100
Haynes, John, Colonial Gov. of Conn., autograph letter to John Winthrop, 1649 (4267/713)	2600
Hemingway, Ernest, autograph letter, 8/18/28, to Bill Smith, (4109/715)	1600
Hemingway, Ernest, typed letter signed, 5/16/36 to Harry Saltpeter, (4109/719)	500
Hemingway, Ernest, typescript of autographical sketch, N.Y., 1936 (4109/720)	350
Hemingway, Ernest, typescript signed, 'On the Am. Dead in Spain', N.p. 1939 (4109/721)	1300
Hemingway, Ernest, 2 autograph letters to Edward Titus, Key West, Jan., Mr., 20, 1931 (4184/86)	1300
Hemingway, Ernest, 32 letters to his son John, 20 holographs, (4109/725)	15000
Hoover, Herbert C., ornate illuminated leaf with signatures of state governors, 1931 (4267/714)	800
Houston, Samuel, letter signed, Wash., 10 Aug. 1852 to Z. Kayler, (4158/133)	400
Howe, Julia Ward, autograph copy of the first 12 words of the 'Battle 'Hymn' signed, 1899 (4158/134)	500
Humperdinck, Engelbert, autograph musical quotation,½ page, dated 11 December 1910 (4184/55)	175
Illinois and Wabash Land Companies, bound copy of all requests for compensation, 1802 (4267/717)	150
Jackson, Andrew, autograph letter signed, Northville, 8 Oct. 1819, to J.C. Calhoun (4158/115)	650
Jackson, Andrew, autograph receipt for doctor's care and coffin, for Rachel Jackson, 1829 (4267/719)	4800
Jackson, Andrew, printed document signed, 8 Oct. 1830, (4158/138)	375
Jay, John, P. Livingston and Gov. Morris, document signed, N.Y., 23 June 1776, (4158/116)	375
Jefferson, Thomas, autograph letter (third person), 16 Nov. 1825, to Dr. Thom. Sewall (4158/141)	750
Jefferson, Thomas, autograph letter (3rd person) Monticello, 8 Feb. 1805 (4158/159)	425
Jefferson, Thomas, autograph letter sending copy of 12th amendment, 1803 (4267/722)	2100
Jefferson, Thomas, autograph letter signed, Wash., 4 March 1803, to Dr. Bollman (4158/117)	2600
Jefferson, Thomas, autograph letter to London bookseller, 1785 (4267/720)	1500
Jefferson, Thomas, autograph letter, a translation of letter, from Louis XVI, 1791 (4267/721)	3000
Jefferson, Thomas, autograph manuscript to church in Conn. about religious freedom, 1809 (4267/723)	10500
Jefferson, Thomas, document signed, Wash., 1 Jan. 1806, (4158/140)	700
Jefferson, Thomas, document signed, Wash., 5 April 1803, (4158/157)	550
Jefferson, Thomas, printed document signed, Wash., 8 Feb., 1805, (4158/158)	450
Johnson, Andrew, letter signed, Executive Mansion, 5 Feb. 1863, to Gideon Welles (4158/118)	3500
Johnson, Andrew, printed check, signed, payable to Thomas Cooper, 1867 (4267/726)	3000
Johnson, Andrew, printed document, signed, affix seal of U.S., to proclamation, 1868 (4267/728)	550
Johnson, Thomas, autograph letter signed, Frederick Town, 21 April 1776, (4158/142)	160
Johnston, Gen. Joseph E., autograph letter to Gen. Beauregard about war, plans, 1861 (4267/730)	600
Johnston, Gen. Joseph E., autograph letter to Gen. Beauregard about war, plans, 1861 (4267/731)	650
Kennedy, John F., autograph letter signed, Hyannisport, n.d., to, Dr. Williamson (4158/119)	800
Kennedy, John F., autograph quotation signed on typescript of speech, 1956 (4267/733)	1200
Kennedy, John F., signed commemorative envelope of Vatican visit, 1963 (4267/734)	400
Kennedy, John F., signed photograph 'with best wishes', 12¾ x 10¾, (no year) (4267/737)	600
Kennedy, John F., signed photograph at inauguration with four presidents (4267/735)	1100
Kennedy, John F., signed photograph of president with cabinet, 10½ x 16, 1961-63 (4267/736)	2100
Kosciuszko, Tadeusz, autograph letter from Polish patriot, 26 January (no year) (4267/740)	550
Lafayette, Gilbert, Marquis De, autograph letter discussing war plans, 1781 (4267/741)	750
Lafayette, Gilbert, Marquis De, autograph letter praising George Washington, 1825 (4267/742)	475
Lafayette, Marquis De, autograph note (English), Paris, 5 May 1827, (4158/160)	85
Lamb, Charles, Authograph letter signed, Nov. 3, 1825, to his friend Thomas Allsop (4109/128)	350
Lee, Gen. Robert E., autograph letter to Col. Imboden about war, plans, 1863 (4267/743)	1700
Lee, Gen. Robert E., autograph letter to Gen. Bragg about artillery, 1864 (4267/744)	1500
Lee, Gen. Robert E., autograph letter to Governor of Va. about, free negroes, 1864 (4267/745)	1300
Lee, Gen. Robert E., printed check, signed, payable to J.G. Pole, 1868 (4267/747)	350
Lee, Gen. Robert E., printed document, signed, reporting student's grades, 1867 (4267/746)	350
Lee, Robert E., autograph letter signed, Lexington, 1 Oct. 1866, to Mrs. Mary Nearly (4158/145)	600
Lee, Robert E., letter signed, portion, 'Headquarters', 10 Sept. 1863, to Louis T. Wigkall (4158/144)	900
Lincoln, Abraham, autograph document signed, 1864, (4158/147)	450
Lincoln, Abraham, autograph letter signed, Springfield, 19 Jan. 1858, Hon. G. Koerner (4158/146)	2250
Lincoln, Abraham and others, A. Lincoln and His Cabinet - A Collection, 1861-65, bound (4158/120)	1200
Lincoln, Mary Todd, autograph letter, pension request to U.S. Senate, 1870 (4267/778)	1300
Lincoln, Mary Todd, autograph letter, request for visit to friend, not dated (4267/779)	650
Liszt, Franz, autograph letter signed, framed, no place, 'dimanche matin' (4184/57)	425
Longfellow, Henry Wadsworth, autograph letter signed, 4 page, Cambridge, Mass., 18 November 1851 (4184/87)	450
Madison, James, printed check, Wash., 19 June 1815, (4158/161)	350
Madison, James, signed letter, about Constitutional amendments to J. Millhouse, 1830 (4267/781)	1900
Mahler, Gustav, autograph card signed, verso of Court Theatre, stationary, no date, place (4184/59)	450

Massenet, Jules, autograph letter signed, 4 pages, On Thais, Paris, 11 September 1911 (4184/60)	250
McKinley, William, signed photograph, with first cabinet members and signatures, 21¾ x 24¾, 1898-1901 (4267/785)	1100
Mendelssohn-Bartholdy, Felix, autograph note signed, framed, Leipzig, 10 February 1843 (4184/61)	550
Monroe, James, document signed, July 1819, (4158/172)	400
Monroe, James, autograph letter, to James Madison about mission to England, 1806 (4267/786)	2200
Montcalm, L.J., manuscript report, victory over Lord Abercrombie in Canada, 1758 (4267/788)	1100
Montgomery, Gen. Richard, broadside, Articles of Capitulation of Montreal, 1775 (4267/789)	4500
Morris, Gouverneur, autograph manuscript, Independence Day Address, 1794 (4267/791)	450
Mozart, Wolfgang Amadeus, autograph letter signed, 3 pgs., to dying father, Vienna, 4 April 1787 (4184/63)	47000
Napoleon I, 2-line note with 2-line autograph subscription, 'Nap', 24 January 1809 (4184/89)	450
Pendleton, Edmund, signed document, early draft of Va. Resolution to add Bill of, Rights, 1788 (4267/843)	2300
Penn, Thomas, autograph check, payable to Ebenezer Tomlinson, 1733 (4267/800)	275
Philidor, Andre Danican, autograph letter signed, 1 page, Paris, 29 May 1786 (4184/64)	300
Poe, Edgar Allan, letter signed, 2¼ closely-written pages to F., Wm. Thomas, 3 Feb. 1842 (4184/90)	17000
Polk, James K., autograph letter signed, April 1844, (4158/186)	1900
Puccini, Giacomo, large, bold autograph musical quotation, 'La Bo, heme', Paris, 9 June 1910 (4184/66)	600
Revere, Paul, autograph memorandum signed, Dec. 1813, (4158/189)	1000
Revere, Paul, printed document signed, N.P., N.D., (4158/190)	1000
Roosevelt, Franklin, typed letter signed, The White House, 20 April, 1938, to George Northrop (4158/127)	600
Roosevelt, Franklin D., inscribed card, D-Day prayer printed as Christmas card, 1944 (4267/817)	2400
Roosevelt, Theodore, typed manuscript of speech, corrections, Oct. 1912, (4158/191)	400
Roosevelt, Theodore, typewritten manuscript for article, extensively, annotated, 1910 (4158/126)	300
Roosevelt, Theodore, autograph, manuscript of book review, 1910 (4267/821)	1750
Roosevelt, Theodore, autograph letter, to son Archie, with pen and ink sketches, 1907 (4267/820)	2300
Roosevelt, Theodore, typescript, speech in Galesburg, Illinois, 1914 (4267/823)	325
Rush, Benjamin, autograph letter signed, 29 Aug. 1799, (4158/164)	150
Schonberg, Arnold, autograph letter signed, 1 page, no place or, date (?Berlin 1912) (4184/68)	600
Schubert, Franz, autograph musical manuscript signed, 4 pages, dated March 1817 (4184/69)	18000
Schubert, Franz, autograph musical manuscript, signed, 2 half, quart. pgs., 3 July 1813 (4184/70)	3400
Schumann, Robert, autograph letter signed, 1 page, no place, 29 January 1850 (4184/71)	950
Seward, William H., signed, document, 15th amendment, 1869 (4267/673)	1100
Shaw, G.B., typed letter to editor, Feb. 1901, London, (4109/832)	700
Shaw, G.B., typed letter to Kate Pervgini (Dickens) 6/2/03, London (4109/833)	3500
Sheeran, Rev. James, Father Sheeran's War Journal, autograph manuscript, 1862-66 (4158/92)	1400
Sherman, William T., autograph letter signed, (4158/165)	400
Simcoe, John Graves, document signed, April 1796, (4158/196)	325
Stevenson, Robert Louis, Hoster Noble's Mistake, 3 page sketch for un, published play (4184/92)	2300
Strauss, Johann, the younger, autograph letter signed, 4 pages, Vienna, no date (4184/73)	500
Strauss, Richard, autograph letter signed, 1 page, Berlin, 3 January 1909 (4184/74)	175
Streeter, Thomas W., Celebrated Collection of Americana, 8 vols., Parke Bernet, 1966-69 ,(4267/831)	250
Thomson, Charles, Concerning the Stamp Act, autograph manuscript, (4158/198)	3250
Thomson, Charles, signed document, resolution convening Constitutional Convention, 1787 (4267/835)	15000
Thomson, Charles and Hannah, document signed, marriage license, Dec. 1744, (4158/201)	600
Tonti, Henri de, and F. De La Forest, signed document concerning furs, 1693 (4267/836)	1600
Truman, Harry S., autograph letter to Paul Patterson, signed, Aug. 1945, (4158/202)	7500
Tyler, John, printed document signed, June 1851, (4158/203)	250
Tyler, John, autograph letter, discussing politics in Va. and S.C., 1834 (4267/839)	950
Tyler, John, autograph letter, Christmas message to 15 year old daughter, 1835 (4267/838)	750
Van Buren, Martin, autograph letter signed, N.P., N.D., (4158/205)	200
Van Buren, Martin, document signed, Oct. 1840, (4158/166)	160
Van Buren, Martin, printed document signed, Feb. 15, 1840, (4158/204)	190
Washington, Bushrod, autograph letter signed, to Peter Wager, Feb. 15 1829 (4158/207)	150
Washington, George, autograph docket (4158/214)	800
Washington, George, autograph note signed, Mount Vernon, May 12 1798 (4158/213)	900
Washington, George, document signed, Wash., 11 April 1796, (4158/212)	2250
Washington, George, letter signed, N.Y., Aug. 10 1789, (4158/210)	350
Washington, George, letter signed, 2 pages to Lt. Col. J. Laurens, White Plains, 8 Aug. 1778 (4184/93)	3000
Washington, George, letter to Major Henry Lee, July 24 1780, (4158/208)	2500

Wayne, Anthony, autograph letter, seeks to organize his Georgia lands, 1784 (4267/861)	600
Weber, Carl Maria Von, 4 page letter to Director-Gen'l, Berlin opera, Dresden, April 12, 1824 (4184/75)	2400
Wentworth, John, proclamation, public fast to pray for privileges, N.H., 1773 (4267/793)	500
Wesley, John, autograph letter, discussion of Methodist doctrine, 1772 (4267/863)	1100
Whittier, John, autograph letter of thanks for cane, wood from Barbara Fritchie's house, 1865 (4267/679)	450
Wilde, Oscar, letter signed, 4 pages, 9 Charles Stree Lon, don, (May 1883-May1884) (4184/94)	1200
Wilkinson, Gen. James, autograph letter signed, to Gen. Anthony Wayne, July 12, 1796 (4158/216)	250
Wolf, Hugo, autograph card (closely written) signed, Vienna, 30 March 1895 (4184/76)	800

Lincoln, Abraham

Autograph book, 97 cabinet and congressional signatures, 1862-63 (4267/765)	1400
Document, signed, appointing chaplain to U.S. hospital, 1862 (4267/760)	800
Document, signed, appointing Assistant Adjutant Gen., with Seward's signature, 1862 (4267/761)	1000
Duplicate of 13th Amendment Resolution, signed, with 39 other signatures, 1864 (4267/764)	30000
Land survey, autograph manuscript, for Jesse Gum in New Salem, Ill., 1834 (4267/749)	3500
Legal brief, autograph, land case in Sangamon County, 1854 (4267/750)	2500
Letter to Gen. Butler, autograph, about wages to negroes, 1862 (4267/7662)	6000
Letter to Gen. Sanford, autograph, declining to review 1st N.Y. Guards Division, 1863 (4267/763)	4000
Letter to Jackson Grimshaw, autograph, asking to settle case, 1858 (4267/752)	2000
Letter to M.L. Bishop, autograph, regarding patent law, 1858 (4267/753)	1700
Letter to M.W. Delahay, autograph, about Republican Convention in Kansas, 1859 (4267/754)	4000
Letter to William Kellogg, autograph, about Kellogg-Horace Greeley controversy, 1859 (4267/755)	5500
Order for removal of body, permitting passage of Pres. Lincoln's body, 1865 (4267/772)	1300
Pardon for Sudan A. Bargie, signed, with seal and part of Seward's, signature, 1861 (4267/758)	900
Playbill, Ford's Theatre, original, April 14, 1865, evening of assassination, (4267/769)	3800
Reward for capture of assasins, broadside, without photos at top, 1865 (4267/771)	1700
Roster of Illinois legislature, manuscript in hand of Lincoln, voting record, 1854 (4267/751)	6250
Telegram to Gen. Grant, informing him of assassination, 1865 (4267/770)	2300

Washington, George

Copy of surveys made by John Saunders, autograph, 1783 (4267/849)	550
Lafayette, Marquis de, transmitting Brevet Commission, autograph, 1790 (4267/853)	4250
Letter offering to repay expenses, autograph, 1784 (4267/850)	1600
Letter to Mr. Nisbet, autograph, declining gift of a hat, 1783 (4267/848)	1400
Military order announcing death, broadside, specifies honors to be paid, 1799 (4267/858)	200
Order of battle for Light Infantry, autograph plan, Gen. Lafayette commanding, 1780 (4267/847)	28000
Receipt for payment of expenses, autograph document concerning Ohio lands, 1774 (4267/846)	500
Secy of War, autograph letter, nomination is confirmed, 1796 (4267/854)	4000
Secy of War, autograph letter, organization the army in view of French War, 1798 (4267/856)	8500
Secy of War, autograph postscript, asking about final accounting of Federal money, 1797 (4267/855)	1600
State of Acct. with Capt. Crawford, autograph document relating to surveying, 1773 (4267/845)	900
Thanksgiving Day, proclamation printed in Philadelphia, 1789 (4267/852)	275

Chapter 16
Carpets

Rugs and carpets have become an important part of the art and antiques market, with both volume and prices on the rise. Research and scholarship have been instrumental in this expansion. By studying the weaving methods employed in their production, experts are able to date and determine the place of origin of many of these carpets. Discerning collectors, familiar with the full range available to them, have tended in recent years to specialize in the products of one particular region or style.

Much of the recent demand for Persian rugs and carpets came from the oil-producing states of the Middle East, especially Iran, where these items had originally been produced. Political turmoil in that country first resulted in a weakening of the premium part of the market. Later there were signs that American buyers had begun to bid more actively, and some Iranians appeared to have reentered the market.

The rugs, carpets and other woven items of the nomadic tribes of Russia, Turkey and Afghanistan still offer the beginning collector an opportunity to purchase at relatively low price levels. Almost more than in any other area of the art and antiques market, condition is crucial in determining the value of carpets. They are subject not only to ordinary wear and tear but to various forms of rot, mildew, and damage caused by excessive dryness. rugs are often trimmed and patched in ways not obvious to casual inspection. Collectors should consult experts both to authenticate rugs and to judge their condition.

Chinese rugs, which are in relatively short supply, bring extremely high prices if they date from before 1850, but later Chinese rugs are often quite reasonable. European carpets drew increased attention from American buyers, perhaps because of uncertainties about the Middle Eastern situation. Many American collectors, though, seem to be confident that the sag in the Middle Eastern Market was temporary, and have taken advantage of the opportunity to buy fine carpets at depressed prices.

CAUCASIAN

Baku, long, midnight blue field, border of stylized crabs, 120 x 48 (4138/24)	$1500
Borchalou Kazak prayer rug, red prayer field, 3 latchhook medallions, dragon border, 101 x 66 (4106/17)	6500
Caucasian, Kelim, unusual, tan field, polychrome medallions, 47 x 40, minor rep (4138/31)	1100
Caucasian bag, red field, green spandrels, blue border, 52 x 22 (626/256)	300
Caucasian Silk Embroidery, Antique, dark brown field, blossoms, moth dam, 41 x 28½ (4106/61)	2200
Caucasian Verneh Embroidered Cover, solid red field, camels, Soumak stitch, 92 x 72 (4106/67)	3500
Chelaberd rug, red field, 2 eagle sunburst medallions, crab, border, 90 x 55 (4106/42)	2700
Daghestan, blue field, leaf tendril medallion border, 90 x 48 (4138/67)	2600
Daghestan, blue field, dragon border, 48 x 39 (4138/100)	800
Daghestan, dark mustard field, flowerhead ivory border, 61 x 46 (4138/2)	850
Daghestan, midnight blue field, 2 star guard borders, 68 x 43 (4138/115)	1400
Daghestan prayer rug, flowerhead guard borders, 58 x 46 (626/192)	950
Daghestan prayer rug, ivory field, leaves, flowers, borders reduced, 48 x 46 (4205/10)	1100
Daghestan prayer rug, midnight blue prayer niche, botehs, moth dam, 60 x 44 (4106/82)	3750
Daghestan rug, blue central panel with animal, human figures, 127 x 62 patches (626/223)	350
Daghestan rug, brown field, ivory border, 66 x 40 (4074/29)	850
Daghestan rug, central midnight blue field, 60 x 41 (626/187)	1500
Daghestan rug, midnight blue field, animals, 89 x 37 (626/1)	950
Daghestan square rug, gold field, ivory border, 64 x 61 (4074/85)	1600
Derbend mat, blue field with stylized flower design, 38 x 30 (626/23)	1200
Derbend rug, blue field, Cuenca design, 56 x 42 (626/78)	450
Derbend rug, midnight blue field, barber pole border, 63 x 41 (4074/27)	1100
Eagle Kazak rug, red field, snowflakes, sunburst medallion, 119 x 69 (4106/59)	3000
Gashgai rug, blue field, red medallion, patched, repaired, 82 x 62 (4205/9)	1300
Gashgai rug, floral sprigs, scorpion border, rewoven, 123 x 58 (4205/57)	1300
Gashgai rug, serrated medallions, flowerhead border, 60 x 36 (4205/80)	1000
Gendje bagfaces pair, made into a pillow, 24 x 20 (626/25)	550
Gendje long rug, blue field, striped diagonal bars, 116 x 43 (626/5)	200
Gendje long rug, diagonal polychrome stripes, 101 x 38 (626/43)	550
Gendje rug, box tendrils, serrated leaf, fold cut, 71 x 47 (4205/64)	750
Gendje rug, gold field, 84 x 48 (626/189)	1500
Gendje rug, latchhook medallions, dragon border, repairs, glue, reduced, 108 x 36 (4205/88)	950
Gendje rug, yellow field, 5 latchhook medallions, 100 x 34, guard border missing (626/246)	1000
Gendje rug, long, midnight ground, polychrome boteh, 118 x 20 (4074/50)	1100
Karabagh, blue field, cows, goats, blue green primary border, 97 x 54, repair (4138/81)	1300
Karabagh, corridor, midnight blue field, guard border, 216 x 84, rep (4138/152)	2200
Karabagh, long, brown field, blue border of scorpion design, 104 x 44 (4138/49)	550
Karabagh, long, midnight blue field, blue primary border, 120 x 46 (4138/36)	1000
Karabagh, red field within orange field, 122 x 51 (4138/10)	500
Karabagh, red field, ivory border, 100 x 40 (4138/4)	550
Karabagh, runner, blue field, polychrome barber pole border, 147 x 38, rewoven, moth dam (4138/37)	1000
Karabagh chelaberd rug, sunburst medallions, crab border, holes, folds, 96 x 60 (4205/94)	1900
Karabagh chelaberd rug, sunburst medallions, flowerhead border, 87 x 63 (4205/68)	5500
Karabagh Long rug, brown flower-filled field, medallions, birds, 112 x 46 (4106/104)	1300
Karabagh Long rug, red field, rows of flowers, dated, restored, 132 x 60 (4106/26)	1500
Karabagh prayer rug, tan field, blue prayer arch, 2 camels, 40 x 34, sm patch on guard (4074/66)	1100
Karabagh rug, blue field, latch-hook diamonds, 76 x 54, repair, restoration (626/68)	900
Karabagh rug, bouquets in pole medallion, greek key border, 81 x 54 (4074/47)	500
Karabagh rug, four orange medallions, 114 x 58, small repairs (626/210)	1400
Karabagh rug, lobed medallion, dragon spandrels, 95 x 48 (4205/29)	2100
Karabagh rug, red field, latchhook medallions, 86 x 55, repairs (626/165)	3800
Karabagh rug, red field, star filled medallions, polygons, 60 x 42 (4205/41)	850
Karabagh rug, red ground, dragon border on gold ground, 70 x 45 (4074/51)	850
Karabagh rug, stylized geometric flowerheads, 74 x 38, repairs (626/186)	150
Karabugh rug, red field, 3 sunburst medallions, crab border, 95 x 35 (4106/95)	850
Karachoo Kazak, green field, 2 winged medallions, 66 x 49, silver fish dam. (626/50)	2000
Karachopt rug, double ram's horn motifs flanked by medallions, 72 x 41 (626/235)	500
Karatchoph Kazak prayer rug, prayer arch, chalice border, 79 x 53 (4205/55)	1300
Karatchoph Kazak rug, brick field, octagonal medallion, blue border, 99 x 69 (4205/16)	10000
Kashmir embroidered rug, Aubusson style, rococo medallion, celadon field, 162 x 121 (619/437)	1500
Kazak, trefoil design, ivory ground, 102 x 36 (4138/41)	700
Kazak, blue field, ivory border of polychrome dragon design, 90 x 53 (4138/44)	1200
Kazak, prayer, red field, brown border, 58 x 42, signed (4138/61)	*2200*
Kazak, prayer, double-ended, ivory field, red spandrels, brown border, 66 x 41 (4138/62)	6500

Kazak, prayer, red field, ivory trefoil border, 64 x 50 (4138/92)   5750
Kazak, red field, ascending rosebud primary border, 100 x 68 (4138/110)   2400
Kazak, red field, double-ended prayer niche, 62 x 47 (4138/108)   *6500*
Kazak, red ground, ivory border of stylized dragon design, 68 x 56 (4138/69)   4000
Kazak, Karachopt, red field, checkerboard spandrels, 80 x 51, res (4138/65)   800
Kazak Long rug, gold field, stylized frog, star flower, fold cut, 124 x 48 (4205/26)   2400
Kazak Long rug, midnight blue field, winged medallions, 115 x 57, restorations (626/60)   2600
Kazak prayer rug, brick red field with flowerheads, 60 x 36, small hole, fold ware (626/242)   600
Kazak prayer rug, central latchhook medallion, 64 x 36 (626/181)   1800
Kazak prayer rug, ivory medallion on brick red panel, 60 x 48 (626/232)   900
Kazak prayer rug, red, latchhook medallions, 127 x 48 (4205/42)   7250
Kazak prayer rug, green niche, geometric motifs, red border, ivory guard, 66 x 42 (4106/98)   1700
Kazak rug, blue field, ivory medallion, 3 guard borders, 85 x 54 (4074/62)   2600
Kazak rug, blue field, polychrome squares, ivory border, 74 x 45, 1 ragged guard bor (4074/67)   700
Kazak rug, floral spray, umbrella motif, repairs, 84 x 57 (4205/39)   2300
Kazak rug, garden design, slant leaf, reduced border, wear, 80 x 51 (4205/48)   1400
Kazak rug, garden design, stylized scorpion, 89 x 64 (4205/58)   2600
Kazak rug, ivory border with oak leaf and chalice design, 75 x 46 (626/236)   700
Kazak rug, ivory octagon, hooked medallions, repairs, 72 x 48 (4205/74)   1900
Kazak rug, ivory umbrella border, medallions, patch, 106 x 49 (4205/90)   3500
Kazak rug, red field with animals, 81 x 60, dry, fold cut (626/86)   1100
Kazak rug, red field, 6 winged medallions, 83 x 40 (626/216)   900
Kazak rug, red ground, 3 medallions, 63 x 43, rewoven and restored (626/211)   350
Kazak rug, three rows of stylized scorpions, 94 x 50 (626/118)   450
Kazak rug, Lesghi star medallions, umbrella design, 69 x 43 (4205/76)   3750

Kazak (4138/61)

Kazak (4138/108)

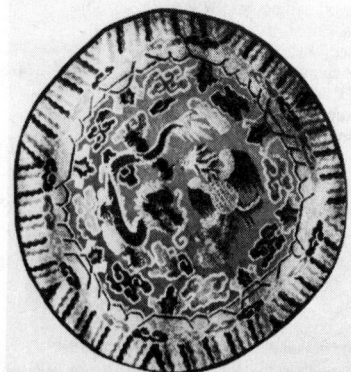

Chinese circular (4138/86)

Kazak rug, blue field, ascending flower, tree design, ivory border, 90 x 46 (4106/12) — 1400
Kazak rug, deep blue field, stepped medallions, crab, flower motif, 74 x 49 (4106/35) — 2400
Kazak rug, field of 4 radiating latchhook polychrome, medallions, 84 x 60 (4106/22) — 1500
Kazak rug, ivory field, latchhook medallions, rewoven, 94 x 54 (4106/77) — 3000
Kazak rug, mint green fields, geometric stars, oak leaf border, 70 x 58 (4106/20) — 4250
Kazak rug, red field, 5 latchhook medallions, crab border, 96 x 48 (4106/49) — 1400
Kazak rug, slate blue field with latchhook medallions, holes, 110 x 53 (4106/21) — 2000
Kazak rug, Central field latchhook medallions, ivory border, 84 x 60 (4106/19) — 3250
Kazak rug, Redfield with stylized candelabras, dragon, minor rep., 98 x 44 (4106/40) — 2100
Konagend rug, all over trellis design, star motif, 72 x 42 (4205/72) — 1300
Kuba rug, blue field, 2 barber pole guard borders, 74 x 36, small patch (4074/55) — 3100
Kuba rug, blue flower-filled field, ivory border, 67 x 50, sm rewoven areas (4074/72) — 2800
Kuba rug, blue stylized flower-filled field, 57 x 46 (4074/78) — 1400
Kuba rug, ivory ground, stylized floral medallions, 61 x 40 (626/80) — 2000
Lesghi rug, five star Lesghis, scorpion border, small hole, 87 x 49 (4205/69) — 2500
Lesghi rug, red starret-filled field, star Leghis, 68 x 43 (4106/101) — 1200
Lori-pambak rug, latchhook medallion, guard borders, 120 x 72 (4205/67) — 11500
Seychour rug, blue field, 3 turtle medallions, 63 x 41 (626/208) — 700
Sharistan, garden design, cypress trees, 264 x 176, reduced (4265/160) — 4000
Sharistan carpet, fabulous beasts, Greek key border, 183 x 132 (4205/105) — 1800
Shirdan rug, royal blue central field, garden design, 58 x 39, end guard borders missing (626/184) — 700
Shirvan, red field, brown spandrels, ivory border, 93 x 47 (4138/59) — 1300
Shirvan long rug, medallion filled trellis work, 96 x 42, small fold cut (626/110) — 2600
Shirvan Marajala prayer rug, ivory field, floral sprigs, 54 x 42 (626/180) — 1600
Shirvan Marajala prayer rug, ivory prayer niche, 39 x 57 (626/170) — 2500
Shirvan Perpedil rug, central blue panel with perpedrils, 48 x 36 (626/233) — 800
Shirvan prayer rug, 40 x 28 (626/172) — 1100
Shirvan prayer rug, ivory prayer field, dragon border on red grnd, 75 x 45, 2 patches, restor (4074/7) — 950
Shirvan prayer rug, ivory prayer niche containing trellis work, 72 x 36 (626/130) — 3400
Shirvan rug, dark blue field, camel's hair border, 56 x 43 (4074/88) — 850
Shirvan rug, eight panels, star Lesghi, candelabra motifs, 70 x 90 (4205/27) — 1600
Shirvan rug, flower-filled blue field, 84 x 54½, reduced, repaired (626/215) — 500
Shirvan rug, ivory Lesghi star medallions, flower border, 56 x 45 (4205/91) — 1500
Shirvan runner, serrated polygons, crab border, 100 x 36 (4205/77) — 2300
Shirvan throne rug, mustard field, 3 rows of flower faces, 60 x 49, hole, fold cuts (626/24) — 2600
Soumak, panel, embroidered, horizontal panels, 54 x 39 (4138/116) — 400
Soumak bags, pair, made into pillows, 23 x 22 (626/156) — 450
Soumak embroidered rug, blue field with serrated medallions, 115 x 60 (626/138) — 750
Soumak rug, dual brick red panels, 70 x 42 (626/266) — 650
Soumak rug, mustard field, star flowerhead, dated 2 places, 99 x 46 (4205/34) — 1600
Talish long rug, blue field, latchhook medallions, (626/141) — 1500
Talish prayer rug, blue field filled with diagonal rows of stars, 60 x 36 (4106/72) — 2300
Talish rug, central blue panel, ivory primary border, 100 x 44, cuts, painted (626/245) — 1400
Zazak, cloudband, field, flower, latchhook, ivory border, 96 x 46 (4138/7) — 3200

CHINESE

Chinese, beige field of birds & urns, lotus border, 216 x 144 (4138/173) — 2400
Chinese, blue field, urns, mocha floral spray, butterfly, 106 x 72 (4222/104) — 2000
Chinese, buff, phoenix bird above flowering tree, 67 x 48 (4222/28) — 1600
Chinese, embossed savonnerie, acanthus leaf, flower border, 137 x 108 (4222/150) — 2100
Chinese, ivory field floral sprigs, butterflies lotus, 139 x 74 (4222/93) — 2600
Chinese, sky blue bat-filled field, 140 x 107 (4138/129) — 1100
Chinese, Floral wreath, dragon, round shou border, stain, 75 x 48 (4205/63) — 800
Chinese, blue field, peony vines, 228 x 136 (4265/158) — 3250
Chinese, central pagoda, birds in flight, 90 x 58 (4265/67) — 800
Chinese, column, cocoa brown field, Chinese characters, 95 x 64 (4138/33) — 2000
Chinese, floral sprigs, lotus design, 240 x 144 (4265/206) — 2900
Chinese, floral-spray medallion, Greek key spandrels, 192 x 129 (4265/145) — 4000
Chinese, green field, floral sprigs, 137 x 97 (4265/168) — 1600
Chinese, mat, gold field, rust border, 38 x 23 (4138/82) — 450
Chinese, royal blue field, cloudband border, 162 x 130 (4265/119) — 3250
Chinese, silk, gold field, lavender border, 139 x 137 (4138/148) — 3750
Chinese, Savonnerie style, acanthus leaves, 144 x 120 (4265/134) — 2000
Chinese aubusson style carpet, floral sprigs, wreath, scrolling leaf, stains, 173 x 129 (4205/126) — 1100
Chinese blue field, dk. blue primary border, 138 x 138, stains (4138/176) — 1000
Chinese carpet, blue field, 2 birds, surrounding buff field, 115 x 94 (4074/145) — 2200

Isphahan (4265/156)

Chinese carpet, brown salt and pepper field, midnight border, 117 x 99 (4074/105)   850

Chinese carpet, celadon field, Chinese motifs, vines, stained, 176 x 141 (4205/184)   1100

Chinese carpet, ivory field surrounded by meandering vine, 161 x 85 (626/3)   1300

Chinese carpet, lavender field, sea green border, 138 x 106 (4074/114)   650

Chinese carpet, midnight blue field, grey border, 138 x 107 (4074/135)   900

Chinese carpet, oblong medallion, plywhisks, vine border, 143 x 108 (4205/121)   550

Chinese carpet, phoenix, reindeer wreath medallions, bats, unusual 136 x 109 (4205/172)   3800

Chinese carpet, rose field with blossom, leaves, bat border, 256 x 173 (4074/120)   2250

Chinese carpet, rose field, 3 abstract floral sprays, 132 x 109 (626/56)   1400

Chinese carpet, scrolling vine, pheasant, lotus, 139 x 108 (4205/182)   2100

Chinese carpet, taupe field, delicate floral sprigs, 139 x 108 (626/29)   650

Chinese circular, silk, metallic, red field, dragon, phoenix, diameter 47 (4138/86)   550

Chinese mat., ivory field, floral medallion, 58 x 36 (626/254)   700

Chinese mat., ivory ground with lotus design, 54 x 30 (626/36)   300

Chinese mat., scrolling vines and flowers, 64 x 30 (626/255)   450

Chinese mats, pair, purple field, 2 butterflies, 47 x 24 (626/61)   400

Chinese palace rug, gold field with central dragon, 96 x 63 (626/71)   2800

Chinese palace rug, midnight blue field, dragon spandrels, 84 x 63 (626/101)   2400

Chinese palace rug, midnight blue field, dragons, 84 x 63 (626/100)   1900

Chinese palace rug, orange field, dragon medallion, 96 x 63 (626/197)   2300

Chinese pictorial rug, a reindeer and dove in rocky landscape, 61 x 37 (626/243)   450

Chinese pictorial rug, blue field with eleven noble figures, 74 x 30, moth damage border (4074/86)   750

Chinese pictorial rug, landscape design, rose sky, 79 x 48 (4074/89)   900

Chinese pillar, Taoist scene, 2 Tantric Buddhist priests, 86 x 50 (4265/20)   3250

Chinese pillar rugs, pair, dragon facing flaming pearl, 82 x 48 (626/10)   4200

Chinese rug, blue dragon, fiery pearls, landscape border, 84 x 50 (4205/78)   1500

Chinese rug, blue rug, floral design, 96 x 60 (4074/45)   600

Chinese rug, camel's hair ground, 2 stylized dragons, 49 x 24½ (4074/34)   200

Chinese rug, ivory field, floral sprigs, 113 x 97 (626/153)   1100

Chinese rug, maze mocha medallion, flowers, key border, 81 x 70 (4205/20)   1800

Chinese rug, royal blue field, mauve border, 104 x 83 (4074/71)   800

Chinese rugs, round, pair, blue field, foo dogs, cloudband design, D48 (4074/40)   950

Chinese rugs, round, pair, blue field, foo dogs, cloudband design, D48 (4074/41)   900

Chinese runner, bat and cloudband design, 220 x 29, rewoven areas (4265/70)   1700

Chinese runner, beige field, greek key border, 134 x 31, made of 2 borders (4074/82)   200

Chinese runner, ivory field, lotus palmettes, ivory border, 136 x 26 (4074/81)   600

Chinese Nichols, ivory flowering urn border, 141 x 109 (4265/100)   1100

Silk and metallic pictorial rug, Chinese, landscape scene, 94 x 65, at 1 end (626/120)   2000

INDIAN

Indian, ivory field of scrolling pink vine, 206 x 150, stains (4138/178)   2000

Indian, blue field, flower sprays, 204 x 162 (4265/154)   1800

Indo-Kirman, millefleurs field, cypress trees, blossom trees, birds, 236 x 142 (4265/121)   7000

Indo-Serabend, boteh design within ivory border, 183 x 157 (4265/140)   1600

Manchester Indo-Kashan, flower-filled border, 258 x 117 (4265/113)   4500

PERSIAN, SILK

Fereghan silk, eggplant medallion, lance head palmettes, 81 x 49, stains (4222/50)	6250
Hereke Prayer, silk and metallic, ivory mirab, flowering urn, fluted columns, 58 x 39 (4222/44)	4500
Hereke rug, Silk, gold field, vines, birds, central medallion, 103 x 78 (4106/134)	18500
Hereke rug, Silk, ivory field, palmette and vine, 57 x 46 (4106/172)	5250
Hereke rug, Silk, wine field, Isphahan vines, birds, flowers, dry, rep, 72 x 52 (4106/150)	15500
Heriz, antique, archaic forked-leaf border, 80 x 56, fragile (4265/87)	700
Heriz Prayer, silk, Tree of Life, columns, blue prayer arch borders, 67 x 47 (4222/89)	20000
Heriz rug, Silk, ivory flower filled field, burgundy, medallion, 77 x 56 (4106/131)	21000
Isphahan, salmon spandrels, ivory border, 136 x 114 (4265/156)	*10000*
Isphahan prayer rug, silk, wool, flowering tree, lotus, leaf border, 83 x 46 (4205/54)	1200
Kashan, floral spray design, gold borders, 83 x 55 (4265/56)	4750
Kashan, floral spray design, gold borders, 83 x 52 (4265/55)	5000
Kashan Animal rug, Silk, brick-red ground, urn, leaf design, animals, 81 x 52 (4106/148)	4000
Kashan Meditation rug, Silk, ivory field, bird filled trees, dogs, deer, 78 x 50 (4106/167)	12000
Kashan pictorial rug, landscapes, historical importance, 60 x 40, small rep (4265/66)	4000
Kashan prayer rug, Silk, Hereke style, sultan head's prayer arch, clouds, 80 x 53 (4106/170)	10500
Kashan rug, Silk, ivory field, central blue medallion, 78 x 50 (4106/118)	8750
Kashan rug, Silk, ivory ground, brown trees, purple boteh, slightly ddry, 83 x 52 (4106/136)	2200
Kashan rug, Silk, ivory ground, midnight blue medallion, 78 x 50 (4106/117)	9750
Kashan Tree of Life rug, Silk, ivory field, tree, urns, palmettes, dry, 80 x 52 (4106/180)	7500
Nain, central light brown medallion, forked spandrels, 129 x 86 (4265/175)	*7500*

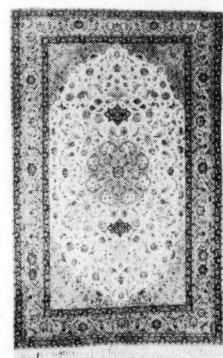

Nain (4265/175)

Qum, flowerhead design, green guard borders, 78 x 53 (4265/74)	2750
Sevas Meditation rug, Silk, cocoa brown niche, vine, spandrels, dry, 74 x 53 (4106/149)	2700
Sevas multiple prayer arch silk, 8 prayer arches blue scrolling vines, mosque, 115 x 40 (4222/51)	3000
Sevas prayer rug, Silk, blue-grey field with flowers, golden, columns, 66 x 47 (4106/120)	2000
Silk Kaijeric saph, prayer arches surrounded by architectural border, 162 x 45 (626/106)	550
Silk Kashan rug, ivory field, cloudband spandrals, dry, repairs, 84 x 55 (4205/35)	2000
Silk Kashan rug, sky blue field, vines, palmettes, leaves, dry, 85 x 52 (4106/115)	4000
Silk rug, copper field, blue vines, rep, tear, 78 x 54 (4106/121)	2000
Souf Kashan, silk and metallic, magenta and blue boteh, carnation border, 78 x 52 (4222/78)	18000
Tabriz Hunt, silk and metallic, salmon birds, hunting equestrian figures, 76 x 54 (4222/49)	5750
Tabriz Medallion rug, Silk, ivory field, palmettes, animals, inscribed, 70 x 51 (4106/175)	5500
Tabriz prayer, silk, salmon prayer field, mosque lamp, columns, 64 x 50 (4222/46)	5250
Tabriz rug, Silk, ivory field, flower borders, rep, 71 x 55 (4106/137)	950
Tabriz silk, green field, scrolling vine, fan and pomegranate, 96 x 76 (4222/20)	8000
Teheran Hunt Silk, buff field with equestrian figures, (4222/18)	7250
Turkish rug, silk, blue field, ivory ground, 64 x 52 (4074/37)	550
Turkish Silk, metallic thread mosque rug, a mosque with floral spandrels, 63 x 42 (626/13)	100
Turkish Silk, Metallic Thread rug, light blue field, animal, spandrels, fringe adds, 106 x 62 (4106/178)	8000

PERSIAN, WOOL

Afshar, camel cover, midnight blue ground, stylized animals, 34 x 25 (4138/63) — 250
Afshar, ivory field, midnight blue primary border, 60 x 46 (4138/47) — 2900
Afshar, rose field, midnight blue spandrels, 99 x 63 (4138/79) — 1500
Afshar rug, over-all trellis, crab border, 79 x 56 (4205/59) — 1200
Afshar rug, three blue crab-filled octagons, 105 x 67 (626/18) — 650
Afshar rug, blue field, rows of botch, bright floral border, 85 x 54 (4106/7) — 1300
Afshar rug, three part midnight blue medallion, snowflake motif, rep., 67 x 51 (4106/74) — 2600
Agra, herati design, cream ground, 173 x 143 (4265/170) — 1400
Agra, ivory field, ivory acanthus leaf border, 132 x 84 (4138/162) — 1400
Agra, lime green field, ivory border of vine & rosette design, 144 x 136, rep (4138/158) — 2100
Agra, prayer, red prayer niche, midnight blue border, 76 x 52 (4138/75) — 750
Agra carpet, gold field with repeating flower-filled urn, 234 x 174 (4074/130) — 3250
Agra carpet, stylized boteh, meander vines, birds, 168 x 135 (4205/128) — 1200
Agra prayer rug, ivory field, polychrome leaves, red, guard border, 69 x 48 (4106/151) — 1000
Antique, Gashgai fragment, red field, diagonal rows of boteh, 109 x 67, cut and pcd (626/35) — 800
Bakshaish, blue field, ivory border, 192 x 144, moth damage (4138/155) — 1700
Bakshaish, rust crab palmette border, 222 x 144 (4265/161) — 4000
Bakshaish, corridor, midnight blue field, 3 floral borders, 216 x 78 (4138/124) — 1400
Bakshaish, midnight blue field, red border of flowers & vines, 228 x 138 (4138/131) — 3900
Baktiari, long, cabbage roses and lions within ivory spandrels, 193 x 74 (4265/92) — *5000*
Baktiari, midnight blue field, gold leaf & flower borders, 232 x 97 (4138/189) — 2300
Baktiari Embroidered Bagface, various animal figures in field, 39 x 29 (4106/5) — 1400
Baktiari garden carpet, polychrome cartouches, trees, sunflowers, 134 x 162 (4205/113) — 4750
Baktiari rug, red field floral sprigs, 69 x 42 (626/98) — 500

Bidjar   (4138/23)

Belouchistan saddle bag, olive field, rust ground, 28 x 19 (4205/7) — 350
Beshir, Ersari, 3 rows of stylized flowers, 75 x 46 (4138/19) — 600
Bessarabian, floral clusters, lobed medallions, 245 x 156 (4265/133) — 10000
Bidjar, burgundy abstract flowers, blue carnations, 109 x 62 (4222/27) — 4250
Bidjar, lancehead palmettes, 178 x 116 (4265/180) — 2300
Bidjar, red field Herati design, anchor palmette, 216 x 152 (4222/95) — 9000
Bidjar, waterbug palmette border, 73 x 53 (4265/4) — 2000
Bidjar, ivory field, midnight blue border, 88 x 56 (4138/23) — *3000*
Bidjar, brick red field, cabbage leaf border, reindeer-form palmettes, 147 x 101 (4265/153) — 6000
Bidjar, flower medallion, fan palmettes, 312 x 177 (4265/167) — *5000*
Bidjar, midnight blue field, rows of cabbage roses, 128 x 84 (4265/172) — 2200
Bidjar, midnight-blue field, rose cluster design, 175 x 80 (4265/146) — 5000
Bidjar, navy blue field, red guard borders, 75 x 49, dam (4138/95) — 1000
Bidjar, runner, midnight blue field, ivory border of double E & dragon design, 211 x 41 (4138/106) — 2000
Bidjar, warwig, red field, multi-design border, 64 x 46 (4138/43) — 350
Bidjar, Kurdistan, gold field, salmon border, 100 x 55 (4138/90) — 650
Bidjar carpet, flowerheads, floral sprigs, moth damage, 139 x 108 (4205/139) — 3250
Bidjar carpet, gold field, floral cartouches, 140 x 97 (626/150) — 4750
Bidjar carpet, stylized herati, bat palmette border, stains, 175 x 112 (4205/165) — 3000

Bidjar (4265/167)

Bidjar Corridor, flowerhead guard borders, 137 x 67 (4265/151)	2250
Bidjar long, red field, blue pole medallions, flower borders, 117 x 57 (4222/53)	2100
Bidjar mat, flower-filled blue field, 33 x 27, moth damage (626/103)	300
Bidjar Medallion rug, red flower, bird filled field, medallion, spandrels, 103 x 66 (4106/173)	3200
Bidjar rug, red field, ivory sprigs, 84 x 53, moth damage, breaks (626/85)	500
Bidjar rug, red field, red border, 110 x 67 (4138/85)	600
Bidjar rug, blue field, abstract vines, rose designs, red, border, 122 x 56 (4106/153)	1000
Bidjar rug, blue field, floral cartouche, flower border, 77 x 55 (4106/139)	2800
Bidjar runner, three rows of star flowers, 134 x 42, patches, holes (626/28)	150
Bidjar Warwig rug, red field, multi-design border, 64 x 46 (4074/63)	400
Borlou carpet, grey ground, aqua border, 216 x 182 (4074/121)	1600
Cashgai bagface, blue ground, polychrome flowerheads, 25 x 18 (626/114)	425
Dhurrie, grey serrated latticework field, 137½ x 100 (4138/127)	850
Dhurrie, maize field, Greek key border, 72 x 48 (4138/25)	400
Dhurrie, peach field, Greek key border, 113 x 73 (4138/126)	650
Embossed Sarouk mat., midnight blue field, gold leaf sprays, 30 x 26, moth damage (626/89)	650
Ersari beshir corridor carpet, compartments, flowers, star block, reduced, 235 x 94 (4205/163)	1800
Fereghan, cloudband design, dragon and barberpole border, 75 x 46 (4265/78)	4000
Fereghan, corridor, dk. brown field, floral border, 180 x 82 (4138/144)	800
Fereghan, herati-filled medallion, palmette border, 78 x 51 (4265/28)	2500
Fereghan carpet, lerati design, flowerhead spandrels, reduced, 214 x 185 (4205/181)	2500
Fereghan Corridor, herati design, rust field, 228 x 91 (4265/104)	1300
Fereghan long rug, green medallion center with inscribed panel, 202 x 69 (626/190)	4400
Fereghan rug, blue field with Herati, 3 flower borders, 60 x 38 (4074/36)	750
Fereghan rug, long, dark brown field, multiple floral borders, 180 x 82 (4074/52)	750
Fereghan Sarouk rug, blue Herati field, ivory border, 78 x 36 (4074/13)	2000
Fereghan Sarouk rug, antique, ivory field, palmette and vine border, 59 x 39 (4074/38)	550
Fereghan Senna rug, Herati filled red field, gold border, 72 x 53, small repairs (4074/73)	2500
Gashgai, ivory field, dragon border on brown ground, 72 x 51, rewoven, stains (4138/87)	1700
Gashgai, long, red field, 3 crab medallions, barber pole border, 104 x 47, rewoven (4138/111)	650
Gashgai, red field, 3 geometric medallions, 96 x 63½ (4138/8)	300
Gashgai Bags, Pair, red field, stepped medallions, ornate, matched, complete, 39 x 23 (4106/43)	750
Gashgai Long rug, midnight blue field, abstract carnations, 127 x 67 (4106/73)	2600
Gashgai rug, blue field, snowflake and flowerhead design, 63 x 42 (4106/89)	1100
Gashgai rug, midnight blue field, herati design, botch spandrels, rep., run, 86 x 36½ (4106/56)	2600
Gashgai rug, ivory field, polychrome boteh, dark rust border, 72 x 56 (4074/64)	1900
Gorevan, ivory bat palmette spandrels, 149 x 111 (4265/181)	2750
Gorevan, corridor, blue field of herati, red border, 213 x 87 (4138/190)	1200
Gorevan, dark blue field, red border of cartouche & flower design, 140 x 104 (4138/146)	1900
Gorevan, red field, waterbug palmette, 131 x 98 (4265/95)	1700
Gorevan carpet, red vine and palmette field, midnight border, 123 x 108 (4074/93)	1000
Hamadan, red ground, midnight blue border, 55 x 39 (4138/48)	700
Hamadan carpet, herati design, boteh border, touched, 192 x 84 (4205/143)	1100
Hamadan carpet, potted flower design, ziz zag, bat border, repairs, 236 x 141 (4205/101)	1100
Hamadan corridor carpet, herati design, zigzag, boteh border, hole, 191 x 89 (4205/108)	750

Hamadan mat., brown field, floral motifs, 47 x 29 (626/179) — 125
Hamadan rug, blue field, herati design, 93 x 97 (626/149) — 950
Hamadan rug, rose ground, arabesque-floral design, 85 x 60, minor repairs, dry (626/49) — 1000
Hamadan rug, tan field within red spandrels, 81 x 49 (626/214) — 350
Hamadan runner, boteh design, floral design, 228 x 39 (4205/56) — 1700
Hamadan runner, pole medallions, guard borders, signed, dated, 188 x 41 (4205/65) — 650
Hamadan runner, solid orange field, 216 x 48 (626/84) — 550
Hereke silk and metallic, gold ground, equestrian figures, wild boar, 108 x 72, dry and powdering (4222/22) — 8750
Heriz, aqua field, serrated-leafs, 129 x 110, touched (4265/187) — 3250
Heriz, central blue medallion, crab palmette border, 121 x 97, slightly reduced (4265/143) — 3500
Heriz, central red medallion, inscription cartouches, 222 x 158 (4265/155) — 11000
Heriz, fan palmettes, ivory field within blue-green spandrels, 165 x 144 (4265/120) — 7000
Heriz, ivory field, scarab anchors, 120 x 84 (4265/109) — *5250*
Heriz, red field, arabesque medallion, red border, 198 x 145 (4138/150) — 6250
Heriz, red field of stylized flower, sky blue border, 131 x 116 (4138/171) — *4000*
Heriz, waterbug palmette border, 156 x 122 (4265/150) — 4000
Heriz carpet, anchor palmette, spandrels, 161 x 125 (4205/151) — 2500
Heriz carpet, flowerheads, forked leaves, damage, touched, 141 x 108 (4205/156) — 1700
Heriz carpet, herati design, flowerheads, patch, repair, 144 x 120 (4205/180) — 1100
Heriz carpet, medallion, sunburst, palmettes, 179 x 132 (4205/162) — 6000
Heriz carpet, midnight blue field, vines, floral medallion, 183 x 151, repairs, patches (626/42) — 3500
Heriz carpet, minor patches, restoration, 180 x 139, guard borders missing (626/90) — 5000
Heriz carpet, red field with trelliswork floral design, 263 x 132, minor moth dam. (626/27) — 3400
Heriz carpet, red ground, stylized flowers, 166 x 108, painted, restorations (626/54) — 1500
Heriz carpet, red stylized vine, flower field, dark blue brdr, 168 x 112, brown painted (4074/99) — 1700
Heriz carpet, salmon grnd, ivory medallion, blue spandrel, 213 x 138, slight moth dmge (4074/101) — 14500
Heriz carpet, serrated leaf, spandrels, leaf, vine, painted, 136 x 99 (4205/173) — 1900
Heriz carpet, stepped medallion, palmettes, flowerheads, 151 x 103 (4205/147) — 2000
Heriz carpet, stylized flower-filled field, 144 x 116, painted (626/64) — 1400
Heriz carpet, stylized flower, vine field, palmettes, 147 x 105 (4205/176) — 3250
Heriz carpet, silk, rose field, border with palmetts and vines, 220 x 149, very worn (4074/131) — 2250
Heriz rug, blue field, dark red border, 77 x 60 (4074/4) — 550
Heriz rug, orange field within blue border, 66 x 62 (626/263) — 600
Heriz rug, red field, stylized flowers, 77 x 61 (626/112) — 450
Heriz prayer rug, Silk, ivory ground, spandrels, columns, medallion, dry, 74 x 54 (4106/130) — 5500
Heriz prayer rug, ivory field, Tree of Life, 76 x 49 (4265/36) — 5500

Heriz (4138/171)

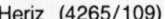

Heriz (4265/109)

Indo-Isphahan, cloudband design, aqua field, palmette border, 209 x 190 (4265/93) — 2200
Indo-Isphahan carpet, light burgundy field, interconnected palmettes, 176 x 120 (626/30) — 3200
Indo-Kashan carpet, mustard field, repeating trefoils on border, 288 x 188, reduced (4074/137) — 6750
Indo-Kashan carpet, flower-filled lattice design, reduced, repairs, 327 x 163 (4205/167) — 3000
Indo-Kirman carpet, blossom trees, rose and floral borders, 299 x 192 (4205/100) — 8750
Indo-Kirman carpet, blossoming tree design, moth damage, 215 x 139 (4205/154) — 8000

Indo-Kirman, dark blue field, gold primary border, 228 x 146, rep (4138/156)	2200
Indo-Persian runner, navy field, mustard border, 199 x 45, moth damage (4074/77)	450
Indo-Tabriz carpet, arabesque vine, palmette, damage, stains, 301 x 102 (4205/152)	4750
Indo-Tabriz carpet, blue field, border on a magenta ground, 273 x 124 (4074/95)	800
Indo-Tabriz carpet, vase design, flowerhead, vine design, 210 x 142 (4205/175)	2500
Isphahan, magenta medallion blue field, spandrels, 94 x 56 (4222/23)	6750
Isphahan, red palmette field, vine design, blue border, 46 x 36 (4222/24)	1800
Isphahan, scroll vines, red sunburst medallion, spandrels, 84 x 57 (4222/26)	8750
Isphahan, blue field, red lobed medallion, beige spandrels, 61 x 41½, silk warp (4138/57)	2750
Isphahan, blue scrolling vine, green sprandrels, 66 x 40 (4265/84)	2750
Isphahan, corridor, antique, magenta field, brown field, 164 x 67½, res (4138/182)	3750
Isphahan, cream silk field, signed Serafian, 70 x 41 (4265/10)	6000
Isphahan, ivory field, boteh design, 138 x 90 (4265/126)	2700
Isphahan, ivory field, forked leaves, 82 x 56, silk warp (4265/44)	5250
Isphahan, ivory field, red border, 94 x 57 (4138/3)	4500
Isphahan, sky blue field, nine flowering urns, parading birds, 73 x 53 (4265/18)	2500
Isphahan carpet, meander vine pattern, 139 x 106 (4205/149)	2600
Isphahan prayer rug, ivory fields, blue arch, red border, silk warp, 87 x 52 (4106/116)	3250
Isphahan rug, cream field with vines, palmettes, 84 x 57 (4106/123)	1600
Isphahan rug, ivory field, beige border, 71 x 44 (4074/49)	1750
Isphahan rug, ivory vine field, red border, 85 x 59 (4074/48)	3000
Jabriz rug, russet field, floral medallion, leaf, florals, 67 x 48 (4205/13)	550
Josah Sarouk, flower medallion, vines, palmette, urn, cartouche, 206 x 145 (4222/133)	10000
Josan Sarouk rug, midnight blue field, palmete design, 51 x 76 (626/161)	1300
Joshaghan carpet, antique, garden design, patched, rewoven areas, 208 x 104 (4205/179)	1000
Karadja carpet, herati design, signed, dated, repairs, damage, 341 x 102 (4205/133)	6000
Karadja runner, midnight blue field, interconnected medallions, 76 x 43 (626/16)	700
Karaja rug, 5 animal filled polygons, slant leaf border, 109 x 41 (4074/75)	750
Karaja runner, brown field, multi-colored hour-glass border, 126 x 41 (4074/61)	600
Karaja runner, midnight blue field, diagonal rows of floral sprigs, 204 x 48 (626/55)	900
Karaja Triclinium carpet, rare, midnight blue field with animals, medallions, 273 x 197 (4074/115)	2100
Kashan, blue field, arabesque medallion, fan palmette, 81 x 53, slight moth damage (4222/14)	3250
Kashan, blue, dense floral decoration, medallion, border, 81 x 52 (4222/74)	8000
Kashan, flower field, urns, wine border, tree cartouches, 174 x 149, slightly dry (4222/124)	6500
Kashan, flowers and vines with blue lobed medallion, 60 x 42 (4222/10)	2000
Kashan, scrolling vine field, carnation, anchor, borders, 82 x 53 (4222/86)	8000
Kashan, 12 rows of ascending florals, vine border, 182 x 142, minor reweaving (4222/126)	8000
Kashan, central arabesque-formed, medallion, 82 x 52 (4265/72)	2000
Kashan, central blue medallion, cypress trees, 144 x 101 (4265/178)	3400
Kashan, flower-filled field, ivory spandrels, 112 x 73 (4265/190)	3000
Kashan, flowerhead design, scrolling vine, 141 x 107, dry (4265/211)	3250
Kashan, forked leaf design, ivory field, scrolling vines, 82 x 52 (4265/19)	2000
Kashan, meditation, silk, ivory field, Tree of Life, wine border, 72 x 48, dry, breaks (4138/91)	12000
Kashan, midnight blue field, burgundy primary border, 264 x 138 (4138/184)	2500
Kashan, midnight blue field, ivory spandrels, 60 x 42 (4265/60)	2250
Kashan, red vine & flower field, midnight blue border, 169 x 125, rewoven (4138/174)	3250
Kashan, red vine & palmette field, midnight blue border, 147 x 104 (4138/195)	4000
Kashan, silk mat, ivory field, midnight blue ground, 54 x 30 (4138/84)	2300
Kashan, silk, ivory vine field, red primary border of vines & palmettes, 144 x 96 (4138/147)	53500
Kashan, vase, ivory field, midnight blue ground, 78 x 52 (4138/29)	6000
Kashan, vase, ivory field, midnight blue ground, 78 x 52 (4138/28)	*6250*
Kashan, Manchester, midnight blue field, wine primary border, 222 x 138 (4138/132)	11000
Kashan, Manchester, garden, ivory field, arched border, 144 x 96, dry, moth damage (4138/133)	10000
Kashan, Manchester, millefleur, midnight blue field, red border, birds, 81 x 53, stains (4138/73)	2750
Kashan, Souf, meditation, silk, metallic thread, Trees of Life, 84 x 52 (4138/17)	10000
Kashan carpet, deep wine field, blue medallion, blue border, 137 x 103, small repair (4074/124)	4500
Kashan carpet, floral sprays, fan palmette, boteh border, 168 x 126 (4205/107)	4500
Kashan carpet, floral sprays, forked leaves, palmettes, 276 x 168 (4205/177)	8500
Kashan carpet, ivory field, blue and cocoa scrolling vine, 249 x 150 (4074/97)	3600
Kashan carpet, red scrolling design field, dark blue border, 142 x 103 (4074/110)	5000
Kashan carpet, repetitive floral sprays, vine and palmette, 144 x 100 (4205/110)	2800
Kashan carpet, vine-filled field, meander vine, 142 x 105 (4205/153)	4600
Kashan carpet, vine, flowerhead field, lotus palmettes, 142 x 104 (4205/120)	3200
Kashan Garden rug, gold field, meandering vines, birds, red border, 84 x 48 (4106/171)	2900
Kashan mat, rose ground, Tree of Life, 61 x 29 (626/34)	800
Kashan Medallion carpet, blue field, spandrels, and border, 168 x 116 (4106/133)	4250
Kashan Pictorial, 3 female equestrian figures, blacksmith, border, 81 x 50 (4222/13)	3750
Kashan Pictorial mat, ivory field depicting birds among iris, 112 x 12 (4106/152)	250

Kashan Pictorial mats, silk and wool, matched pair, 24 x 24 ea. (4106/179) — 1300
Kashan prayer rug, Silk, magenta flower filled field, vase, 75 x 45 (4106/125) — 14000
Kashan rug, burgundy field, urns and scrolling vines, 104 x 72 (626/167) — 1000
Kashan rug, dark rose field, dark blue spandrels, 80 x 53 (4074/9) — 1500
Kashan rug, palmette and cream white field, 85 x 52½ (626/9) — 650
Kashan rug, rose field, floral sprigs, boteh border, 78 x 60 (626/38) — 1100

Kashan (4138/28)

Kashan rug, Silk, magenta field, vines, animals, ivory border, 76 x 52 (4106/159) — 6250
Kashan rugs, Matched Pair, brick red medallion, spandrels, borders, 86 x 52 (4106/176) — 6250
Kashan tree of life carpet, pomegranates, roses, birds, 135 x 101 (4205/157) — 6500
Kazak rug, red field, light blue border, 88 x 57, fold cuts, rest'n. (4074/76) — 650
Kazvin carpet, blue field, primary border on green ground, 197 x 158, patches, cut (4074/140) — 4200
Kazvin carpet, flower-filled spandrels, flower border, 144 x 109 (4205/168) — 2400
Kazvin Pictorial, village water scene, trees, animals, houses, 32 x 24 (4222/15) — 1100
Kazvin rug, red flower filled field, blue, medallion, 60 x 53 (4106/129) — 1400
Khorassan, red field, midnight blue border, 324 x 198 (4138/181) — 1000
Khorassan carpet, ivory field, midnight blue border, 122 x 84, moth damage (4074/91) — 1700
Khorassan corridor, orange field, queen cypress, repeating borders, 161 x 85 (4222/102) — 3100
Khorassan prayer, midnight blue border, 65 x 46 (4265/41) — 2500
Khotan rug, orange border, border with polychrome designs, 106 x 55 (4074/1) — 1400
Kirman, blue field, arabesque design on red border, 135 x 106 (4138/177) — 3200
Kirman, blue lobed medallion, millefleur beige field, floral border, 199 x 128 (4138/149) — 1000
Kirman, hanging mosque lamps, Trees of Life, cypress trees, 174 x 128 (4265/202) — 2300
Kirman, ivory ground, 4 colored floral guard borders, 80 x 50 (4138/191) — 1600
Kirman, ivory ground, floral design, floral border, (4138/196) — 2400
Kirman, laver, pictorial, architectural field, great rulers of world, 84 x 61 (4138/78) — 16500
Kirman, medallion, red scroll vine, wide navy border, 261 x 220 (4138/194) — 1300
Kirman, midnight blue field, Ardebil design, 153 x 108 (4265/107) — 4250
Kirman, pictorial, ivory field, trellis support of birds, ducks, 76 x 56 (4138/42) — 3200
Kirman, red millefleurs field, rows of cypress trees, 204 x 132 (4265/210) — 3000
Kirman, rose field, Trees of Life, blossom trees, rose, ivory midnight, blue, 194 x 121 (4265/116) — 20000
Kirman carpet, arabesque palmette on ivory field, 143 x 105 (619/425) — 2250
Kirman carpet, beige field with scrolling arabesque vine, 177 x 108 (4074/151) — 4250
Kirman carpet, beige fld, flower borders in blue, red, ivory, 143 x 141, sm repair 1 side (4074/104) — 2400
Kirman carpet, central medallion on a red ground, 242 x 117 (619/435) — 1300
Kirman carpet, concentric floral designs, 228 x 140 (4205/103) — 4500
Kirman carpet, floral spray, urns, palmettes, moth damage, 281 x 139 (4205/142) — 2800
Kirman carpet, flower-formed medallion in ivory field, 197 x 144 (619/421) — 2000
Kirman carpet, garden design, vines, flowers, 185 x 132 (4205/150) — 2100
Kirman carpet, ivory field with millefleur design in pastels, 142 x 104 (4074/111) — 1000
Kirman carpet, ivory field with stylized blossom design, 139 x 106 (619/450) — 2200
Kirman carpet, ivory field, medallion, 146 x 106 (619/449) — 800
Kirman carpet, ivory ground with a millefleur design, 204 x 139 (619/436) — 2500
Kirman carpet, ivory ground with vases, blue border, 180 x 108 (4074/119) — 2400
Kirman carpet, lozenge design in gold, brown, skyblue, 270 x 161, at 1 end (4074/102) — 1600

Kirman carpet, red field, floral sprigs, blue border, 168 x 117 (619/448) — 1100
Kirman carpet, rows of urns, birds, flowers, small repair, 143 x 141 (4205/122) — 2400
Kirman carpet, royal palmette cloudband design, 306 x 162 (4205/137) — 6750
Kirman carpet, vine, cloudband design, at 1 end, 127 x 96 (4205/174) — 3600
Kirman carpet, woven with floral scrolls, 142 x 106 (619/434) — 650
Kirman carpet, Ivory field with floral vine, 114 x 95 (619/433) — 2250
Kirman carpet, medallion, red scrolling vine, palmette grnd, navy border, 261 x 220, outer borders gone (4074/94) — 1800
Kirman laver prayer rug, ivory field of flowering tree of life, 78 x 53 (4074/83) — 500
Kirman mat, flowers on a beige ground, 58 x 36 (619/430) — 450
Kirman mat, ivory ground with floral decoration, 48 x 23 (619/431) — 200
Kirman mat., floral sprigs on ivory field, 49 x 25 (626/121) — 150
Kirman medallion rug, central floral medallion on navy blue field, 32 (626/201) — 350
Kirman medallion rug, millefleur field, sunburst medallion, 91 x 57, at 1 end (626/48) — 1600
Kirman meditation, Tree of Life, 84 x 50 (4265/51) — 1700
Kirman Millefleur prayer rug, ivory ground, bird filled border, trees, 86 x 54 (4106/155) — 3000
Kirman Millefleur prayer rug, ivory ground, trees, birds, moth dam, 86 x 54 (4106/154) — 2750
Kirman Pictorial, blue field with animals and figures, borders, 88 x 52 (4222/12) — 2500
Kirman pictorial, blossoming tree, birds, seashore motif, borders, 169 x 129 (4222/146) — 9500
Kirman pictorial fragment, portrait of a Persian king, signed in 2 places (626/104) — 375
Kirman pictorial meditation rug, Tree of Life, 88 x 52 (626/15) — 850
Kirman pictorial rug, crimson field, flowering trees, repairs, reweave, 77 x 52 (4205/18) — 1800
Kirman picture mat, Abraham sacrificing his son Ishmael, (4074/23) — 425
Kirman prayer, Tree of Life, 85 x 55 (4265/7) — 2300
Kirman prayer, Tree of Life flanked by 2 deer, 87 x 54 (4265/77) — 2250
Kirman prayer rug, blue arch, ivory field, 76 x 53 (4074/3) — 1500
Kirman rug, ivory palmette-filled field, midnight-blue, medallion, 87 x 54 (4106/147) — 3750
Kirman rug, midnight blue field, directional medallion, 84 x 48 (619/432) — 900
Kirman rug, blue field, all over floral design, 56 x 37 (626/124) — 750
Kirman rug, flower formed field, flower border in pastels, 80 x 55 (4074/79) — 750
Kirman rug, millefleur design, cartouche border, 88 x 53 (4205/49) — 2600
Kirman saddlecover, Tree of Life, 41 x 21 (4265/1) — *1600*
Kirman square rug, green sunburst medallion, beige millefleur field, 61 x 60 (626/99) — 1800

Kirman saddlecover
(4265/1)

Korassan rug, ivory field, boteh, purple, border, 51 x 40 (4106/145) — 2200
Korassan rug, sky blue field, floral scrolling design, 81 x 63 (4106/128) — 3250
Kurd, bagface, blue ground, ivory border, 38 x 27 (4138/89) — 350
Kurd, runner, ivory ground, red border, 265 x 43 (4138/34) — 1500
Kurd, runner, unusual, dk. blue field, ivory border, rewoven areas, 142 x 38, moth damage (4138/11) — 1100
Kurd bagface, green medallion, black flowerhead border, 43 x 32 (4074/19) — 150
Kurd Karabagh rug, russet field, rhombs, scorpions, diamond border, 99 x 55 (4205/23) — 1900
Kurd long rug, blue field, rows of boteh, 105 x 32, repairs, 1 border missing (626/46) — 550
Kurd rug, brick red field, medallion with flowerheads, animals, 78 x 46, repair (626/237) — 275
Kurd rug, brown field, stepped diamonds, 88 x 54, moth damage (626/94) — 300
Kurd rug, tan field, serrated leafs, umbrella design, 84 x 41 (4205/37) — 1100
Kurd rug, unusual, midnight blue field, medallions, ivory border, 120 x 60 (4074/84) — 750
Kurd runner, flowered octagonal medallions, plum border, 149 x 47 (4074/42) — 1400

Kurd runner, red field, gold border, 145 x 46 (4074/16) 1100
Kurd runner, rust field, dark border, 144 x 30, no side guard (4074/14) 650
Kurd runner, unusual, dark blue field, ivory border, 142 x 38, 2 reweaves (4074/6) 650
Kurd runner, deep blue field, winged medallions, flowers and animals, repairs, 144 x 46 (4106/36) 900
Kurdistan Long rug, red field, floral sprigs, oak leaf border, 122 x 48 (626/65) 350
Kurdistan runner, midnight blue field, diagonal floral sprays, 173 x 42 (626/32) 700
Kurdistan runner, midnight blue field, stylized blossoming trees, 138 x 40, patch (626/53) 800
Laver Kirman carpet, trelliswork, fan palmette, 150 x 135 (4205/109) 5750
Lenkoran rug, blue snowflake filled field, ivory border, 69 x 48 (4074/70) 1600
Lillihan runner, red field, ascending vine, 132 x 27 (626/63) 550
Mahal, midnight blue field, blue flowerhead guard borders, 156 x 120 (4138/143) 1000
Mahal, midnight-blue field, stylized crab medallion, 195 x 149 (4265/149) 1700
Mahal, red field, palmette border, 231 x 147 (4265/102) 2500
Mahal, red field, rosette border, flowerhead and floral clusters, 202 x 127 (4265/142) 2100
Mahal, red ground, dark blue border, 194 x 128 (4138/185) 3500
Mahal carpet, herati field, palmette border, 142 x 106 (4205/158) 1700
Mahal carpet, strap work design, cartouche, flower head design, 132 x 114 (4205/102) 6500
Mahal carpet, Herati filled border in aqua, midnight field, 162 x 130 (4074/118) 3000
Mahtashem Kashan, 5 rows arabesque medallions, multiple borders, 156 x 123 (4222/105) 8500
Malayer, lattice-work design, waterbug palmette border, 216 x 132 (4265/94) 4250
Malayer rug, midnight blue Herati filled field, 60 x 56 (4074/74) 2100
Malayer Sarok rug, ivory field, 80 x 58 (626/117) 1900
Malayer Sarouk, blue field, stylized flowering vine, 82 x 60, dry (626/52) 1400
Malayer Sarouk, cloudband design, 78 x 48, moth dam (4265/83) 3500
Malayer Sarouk, flower-filled ivory field, 82 x 52 (626/134) 1300
Malayer Sarouk, red and brown stylized flowers, 84 x 53, dry (626/79) 700
Malayer Sarouk mat., rose field, flowering vines, 28 x 21 (626/231) 175
Malayer Sarouk rug, arabesque medallion, meander vine, 83 x 50 (4205/43) 1800
Malayer Sarouk rug, blue field, stylized flowers, 78 x 51, dry (626/51) 600
Malayer Sarouk rug, central floral medallion, 79 x 50 (626/174) 1100
Malayer Sarouk rug, ivory field, medallion, red border, 81 x 58, dry (626/154) 1800
Malayer Sarouk rug, midnight blue field with flowering vines, 81 x 50, dry (626/225) 600
Malayer Sarouk rug, ruby red field, floral sprigs, 120 x 105 (626/31) 2400
Malayer Sarouk rug, rust field, pulled medallion, 63 x 38 (626/155) 650
Manchester Kashan, floral sprays, flowering urns and palmettes, 175 x 140, reduced (4265/141) 3250
Manchester Kashan, red field, scrolling vine border, (4265/165) 6000
Manchester Kashan Tree of Life rug, dark blue field, bird filled tree, 80 x 48 (4106/119) 6600
Meshed, blue medallion, smaller sunflower medallion, 196 x 136, rewoven area (4265/112) 2000
Meshed, cypress tree, meander vine design, 258 x 108 (4265/122) 800
Meshed, flower filled blue field, red border, 229 x 165 (4138/161) 1300
Meshed, magenta border, palmette design, 207 x 145 (4265/147) 1900
Meshed carpet, floral spray, cloudband, fan palmette, 116 x 86 (4205/170) 2200
Meshed carpet, foliate scrolls and palmettes on wine ground, 167 x 120 (619/424) 650
Meshed carpet, plum ground with scrolling vine, 171 x 124 (619/427) 650
Meshed carpet, red field, midnight spandrels, blue border, 205 x 142 (4074/125) 1600
Meshed carpet, salmon field, midnight blue flowerhead border, 155 x 121 (4074/112) 900
Meshed carpet, star medallion, bat spandrels, numbered, stained, 144 x 108 (4205/148) 1300
Meshed carpet, vine field, midnight blue border, 144 x 104 (4074/98) 1700
Mir Serabend carpet, red field, ivory border with vines, boteh, 191 x 85, repair, reweaving (4074/144) 850
Moghan rug, garden design on blue field, 89 x 39, primary border missing 1 end (626/92) 700
Moghan rug, midnight blue field, dragon border, 69 x 47, moth damage (626/102) 600
Mohtashem kaghan square carpet, rose field, vines and flowers, padding residue, 150 x 150 (4205/131) 10500
Mohtashem Kashan, blue field, vine, lily design, sunburst, flowers, 140 x 88 (4222/129) 28000
Mohtashem Kashan, blue flowered, red lobed medallion, borders, 82 x 55 (4222/21) 5000
Mohtashem Kashan, flower field, unusual arabesque field, flowers, 176 x 127, slightly dry (4222/108) 8500
Mohtashem Kashan, salmon field, garden design, trees, trellises, 456 x 154, minor moth damage (4222/106) 11500
Mohtashem Kashan, 4 petal medallion, scrolling vine, 2 color border, 81 x 50 (4222/45) 4500
Mosul rug, blue field, 2 floral borders, 74 x 46, repairs (626/205) 500
Mosul rug, midnight blue field containing 3 diamonds, 73 x 55 (626/97) 450
Mosul rug, midnight blue field, herati design, 61 x 42 (626/91) 525
Mosul rug, red field, blue medallion, 57 x 40 (626/202) 325
Moustasha Kashan rug, beige ground, stylized flowers, 79 x 52, dry (626/164) 2500

Moustasha Kashan rug, ivory field, flowering vines, 78 x 52, dry, inscribed (626/239) — 1700
Mudjar prayer rug, red prayer arch, 3 hanging lamps, 70 x 49 (626/111) — 300
Mudjar rug, red double-ended prayer arch, 63 x 42 (626/129) — 175
Nain, central blue medallion, fork leaf design, 101 x 65 (4265/16) — 9750
Nain, concentric sunflower, red field, 109 x 68 (4265/79) — 5250
Nain, silk, wool, buff field, sky blue border, 101½ x 68 (4138/21) — 2800
Nain rug, green field, ivory border, both vine filled, 94 x 59 (4074/53) — 3000
Nain rug, stylized animals, flowerhead border, 106 x 67 (4205/95) — 1100
North Persian rug, central latchhook medallion, 60 x 48 (626/195) — 900
Perpedil rug, blue field, perpedil motifs, 69 x 48 (626/126) — 1900
Persian brocade, array of sinuous boteh with unusual skirts, 130 x 54 (4265/21) — 500
Persian Turcoman rug, red field, rows of guls, sunburst border, 96 x 63 (4205/15) — 550
Qum, maroon field, blue border with animals, 80 x 66 (4138/114) — 1400
Qum, midnight blue medallion, flowering scroll design, 64 x 42 (4265/8) — 1700
Qum, rust field, inscribed cartouche, 62 x 41 (4265/47) — 2750
Qum hunt, red field, animals, 159 x 90 (4265/125) — 5500
Qum rug, midnight blue central medallion, 102 x 52 (626/222) — 1300
Qum rug, sky blue field with flowering vines, 91 x 56 (626/258) — 1000
Qum rug, ivory fields, cloudbands, bat palmettes, birds, vines, boteh, 82 x 56 (4106/156) — 2200
Sarouk, boteh design on ivory field, 130 x 100 (4265/207) — 1700
Sarouk, burgundy flower field, blue palmette border, 137 x 102 (4222/97) — 4000
Sarouk, floral sprigs, cabbage leaves, blue border, 195 x 129, small hole and stains (4222/125) — 4750
Sarouk, flowerhead palmettes, 190 x 156, minor rep (4265/182) — 8250
Sarouk, flowers and vines, reds and blues, iris border, 82 x 51 (4222/16) — 3000
Sarouk, ivory flower-filled field, 81 x 50, stains (4265/90) — 2750
Sarouk, red field, yellow & blue medallion, spandrels, 176 x 133, dry rot (4222/103) — 7750
Sarouk, red ground, floral sprigs, blue border, 180 x 124 (4222/91) — 5500
Sarouk, scrolling vine, 4 spandrels, blue border, 142 x 103 (4222/148) — 5500
Sarouk, vine border, 60 x 41 (4265/2) — 1600
Sarouk, blue field, floral sprays, 115 x 95, 1 torn selvage (4265/111) — 2500
Sarouk, blue 8-petal medallion, palmette border, 82 x 52 (4265/46) — 3250
Sarouk, cartouches in blue, rose field, rose border, 216 x 132, dry (4138/169) — 4250
Sarouk, deep red field, midnight blue border, 213 x 153, rep (4138/180) — *15500*
Sarouk, directional medallion, bat palmettes, 149 x 112 (4265/205) — *5750*
Sarouk, embossed, mat, blue field, red border, 36 x 24 (4138/30) — 1300
Sarouk, fereghan, beige field, midnight blue border, 84 x 54, dry (4138/104) — 4300
Sarouk, fereghan, ivory field, midnight blue border, 56 x 39, dam (4138/93) — 650
Sarouk, fereghan, ivory field, midnight blue border, 80 x 50½ (4138/101) — 2000
Sarouk, flowerhead medallion, ivory spandrels, 139 x 118 (4265/98) — 1800
Sarouk, green and blue spandrels, palmette border, 139 x 110 (4265/195) — 2800
Sarouk, green flower-filled, medallion, 145 x 107 (4265/186) — 3000
Sarouk, ivory flower field, dk. brown border, 78 x 46 (4138/54) — 1100
Sarouk, ivory medallion, salmon spandrels, 58 x 42, slightly dry (4265/73) — 1900
Sarouk, josan, blue field, midnight blue border, 82 x 52, repair, rewoven (4138/74) — 1000
Sarouk, malayer, red field, stylized flowers, blue spandrels, 80 x 50 (4138/112) — 1800
Sarouk, red field, blue floral border, 164 x 124, dry (4138/136) — 2300
Sarouk, red field, floral spray design, 239 x 122 (4265/123) — 5000
Sarouk, red field, flowerhead border, all over floral spray design, 210 x 104 (4265/132) — 2000
Sarouk, red field, all-over flowers, flowerhead border, 252 x 144 (4265/208) — 2000
Sarouk, red ground, blue floral border, 217 x 139, stains (4138/175) — 2500
Sarouk, red ground of boteh, ivory border of cypress tree, 210 x 144 (4138/121) — 4000
Sarouk, rose ground, midnight blue border, 118 x 91 (4138/138) — 3000
Sarouk, ruby red field, midnight blue border of palmettes & vines, 300 x 144 (4138/141) — 5500
Sarouk, runner, rose field, midnight blue border, 276 x 34 (4138/39) — 2750
Sarouk, sea blue field, red border of palmette & vine design, 252 x 138, dry (4138/137) — 3100
Sarouk, mat, blue flower-filled, red medallion, 29 x 27 (4106/143) — 750
Sarouk carpet, arabesque, blue spandrels, rewoven, patch, 160 x 126 (4205/115) — 4500
Sarouk carpet, blood red field, ivory rococo style border, 137 x 107 (4074/108) — 3250
Sarouk carpet, blue field, red medallion, both Herati filled, 144 x 108 (4074/100) — 2750
Sarouk carpet, blue field, 2 tan borders with meander vine, 254 x 152 (4074/132) — 7250
Sarouk carpet, burgundy field, mauve primary border, 168 x 125 (4074/117) — 6000
Sarouk carpet, central medallion, spandrels, dry, reduced, 146 x 105 (4205/161) — 3350
Sarouk carpet, deep wine flowered field, border on midnight, 246 x 144 (4074/136) — 2500
Sarouk carpet, diamond medallion, waterbug palmettes, 139 x 118 (4205/124) — 2000
Sarouk carpet, floral medallion centered by a copper field, 204 x 122 (626/250) — 4500
Sarouk carpet, floral sprays, palmettes, 222 x 129 (4205/132) — 2500

Sarouk carpet, floral sprigs covering a red field, 174 x 142 (626/268)   4500
Sarouk carpet, floral sprigs, palmette border, 253 x 129 (4205/169)   1700
Sarouk carpet, floral sprigs, pinwheel medallions, dry, repairs, 141 x 105 (4205/164)   2200
Sarouk carpet, forked leaf design, rose border, 168 x 120 (4205/117)   2000
Sarouk carpet, magenta field, midnight blue border, 144 x 105 (4074/133)   2500
Sarouk carpet, midnight blue field, black border, 138 x 106 (4074/109)   3000
Sarouk carpet, midnight blue field, deep red border, 148 x 101 (4074/147)   2000
Sarouk carpet, midnight field, red border with palmettes, 128 x 104 (4074/134)   2750
Sarouk carpet, midnight field, red border, foliate designs, 122 x 84 (4074/148)   2900
Sarouk carpet, plum field, midnight border with meander vine, 122 x 84 (4074/150)   2600
Sarouk carpet, pulmette and flower-filled field, 142 x 110 (626/6)   600
Sarouk carpet, red field with flowers, dark border, 195 x 129 (4074/92)   3250
Sarouk carpet, red field, flowering vines, 180 x 124 (626/221)   1800
Sarouk carpet, red flower-filled carpet, dark border, 139 x 107 (4074/106)   3000
Sarouk carpet, serrated leaf, palmette border, reduction, 228 x 132 (4205/123)   2700
Sarouk carpet, stretched medallion, flowering urns, damage, 132 x 96 (4205/144)   1800
Sarouk carpet, wine red field, midnight blue ground, 137 x 106 (4074/146)   2000
Sarouk embroidery, red ground, geometric border, 71 x 66, cttn, wool embroid (4074/17)   600
Sarouk Fereghan, ascending boteh design, fish hook vine design, 77 x 49, small hole (4222/77)   6000
Sarouk Fereghan, flowerhead midnight-blue border, 60 x 40 (4265/85)   *4750*
Sarouk Fereghan, cartouche design, 76 x 49, (4265/12)   1500
Sarouk Fereghan, flowerhead design, red fan palmette and meandering vine border, 76 x 50 (4265/15)   4000

Sarouk Fereghan
(4265/5)

Sarouk Fereghan, red field, flower filled urn, flowerhead border, 76 x 49 (4222/80)   2100
Sarouk Fereghan, sunflower border, 58 x 43, dry (4265/86)   1800
Sarouk Fereghan, Mustafi design, 75 x 56, minor rep (4265/5)   *4000*
Sarouk Fereghan rug, ivory field, flowering vines, 77 x 49, dry, patch (626/238)   1900
Sarouk Fereghan rug, red field, stylized flowers, 75 x 47 (626/160)   3000
Sarouk Fereghan rug, red field, flower design, blue, medallion, rep, 84 x 48 (4106/141)   4500
Sarouk mat, 48 x 26 (626/7)   225
Sarouk mat., bright red field, floral sprigs, 46 x 25 (626/59)   450
Sarouk mat., red field, floral sprays, 48 x 22 (626/107)   600
Sarouk mat., red field, stylized flowers, 31 x 22 (626/88)   200
Sarouk mat., ruby red field, floral sprigs, 57 x 30 (626/39)   600
Sarouk mats, pair, magenta field, floral sprigs, 31 x 24 (626/58)   400
Sarouk mats, pair, midnight blue fields, blossoming trees, 31 x 19 (626/57)   650
Sarouk medallion rug, midnight blue field with flowering vines, 83 x 53, dry (626/267)   1200
Sarouk rug, black-lined flower and urn filled ground, 76 x 55 (4106/157)   4500
Sarouk rug, flower filled red field, midnight blue border, 61 x 43 (4106/174)   950
Sarouk rug, ivory flower-filled field, blue medallion, slightly dry, 54 x 40 (4106/161)   1300
Sarouk rug, ivory ground, boteh, blue meander, 81 x 49 (4106/142)   5000
Sarouk rug, midnight blue field enlarged boteh, vine motif, glue on border, 60 x 39 (4106/181)   3500

Senna
(4138/56)

Sarouk rug, blue field, floral medallion, 83 x 57 (626/73)	1000
Sarouk rug, blue field, floral sprays, palmettes, vines, 77 x 52 (4205/22)	2200
Sarouk rug, burgundy field, flower-filled urns, 60 x 42 (626/173)	600
Sarouk rug, central medallion and complimentary spandrels, 113 x 76 (626/8)	400
Sarouk rug, dark magenta field, midnight blue border, 57 x 40 (4074/87)	700
Sarouk rug, flower field, blue spandrels, blue border, 52 x 41 (4205/66)	1700
Sarouk rug, ivory flower-filled field, blue border, 75 x 50 (4074/65)	1800
Sarouk rug, ivory, floral field, 58 x 36, silverfish dam, dry rot (626/75)	600
Sarouk rug, midnight blue field with floral sprigs, 80 x 30, dry (626/37)	1300
Sarouk rug, midnight blue field, deep red border, 82 x 52 (4074/26)	1500
Sarouk rug, midnight blue field, gold and red floral medallion, 80 x 36 (626/76)	1100
Sarouk rug, pink field, flower filled urns, 81 x 50 (626/247)	1300
Sarouk rug, red field with flowers, dark border, 78 x 52 (4074/43)	400
Sarouk rug, red field, blue fan palmette, repairs, 80 x 54 (4205/1)	1700
Sarouk rug, red field, dark border, 80 x 50 (4074/15)	1600
Sarouk rug, red field, midnight border with palmettes, 82 x 48, slight dryness (4074/90)	750
Sarouk rug, red lobed medallion, flowering trees, reduced border, 82 x 54 (4205/32)	2400
Sarouk rug, rose field with flowering vines, 52 x 26 (626/251)	500
Sarouk rug, rose field, floral sprigs, 62 x 39 (626/74)	1200
Sarouk rug, royal blue, flower-head medallion, 78 x 49 (4205/24)	1900
Sarouk rug, beige field, herati design, reduced border at, one end, 57 x 40 (4205/4)	1100
Sarouk runner, two runner pcd together, 2 end borders cut, 40 x 34 (626/93)	1800
Senna, ivory field, red border, 79 x 37 (4138/27)	2500
Senna, red waterbug palmette border, 77 x 55 (4265/54)	3750
Senna, Herati field red, gold, blue, Herati spandrels, 73 x 52 (4222/19)	3000
Senna, Herati-blue, red borders leaf, vine design, 78 x 58 (4222/47)	17000
Senna, dark brown field, ivory border, 75 x 47 (4138/14)	2900
Senna, herati filled ground, 73 x 52, rewoven border, (4265/62)	2100
Senna, kelim, saddle cover, 72 x 58, rep, holes (4138/113)	1900
Senna, malayer, herati-filled field, red border, 144 x 80, rep, fold cut (4138/122)	3500
Senna, salmon field, herati design, 77 x 52 (4265/37)	2750
Senna, Kelim, blue field, small ivory border, 66 x 49 (4138/56)	*2500*
Senna Kelim rug, black ground, central orange medallion, 73 x 48 (626/241)	700
Senna Kelim rug, copper red field within olive green border, 76 x 53, repairs (626/234)	750
Senna Malayer rug, ivory field, stylized crab and palmette border, 75 x 53 (626/139)	1500
Senna rug, blue field, herati design, dry, color runs, 76 x 50 (4205/17)	6000
Senna rug, midnight blue, turtle palmette, multicolor silk, 80 x 51 (4205/25)	6000
Senna rug, six stepped medallions, bat design, ivory field, torn, repaired, 75 x 51 (4205/12)	1800
Senna rug, ivory field, heruti-filled medallions, 50 x 40 (4106/113)	3500
Senna rug, ivory field, polychrome botehs, 78 x 59 (4106/122)	7500
Senna rug, red field, blue-green herati, filled diamond, rep, 75 x 50 (4106/146)	4000
Senna rug, red herati-filled field, green spandrels, cut on end, 79 x 53 (4106/140)	3250
Senna rug, red field, botch and vines, green border, rep, 62 x 48 (4106/114)	3250

Serab Camel Hair runner, Camel's Hair field, oak leaf medallions, 146 x 55 (4106/99)	1900
Serab carpet, camel's hair field, herati design, 204 x 162 (4205/138)	2000
Serab carpet, trellis design, medallions, repairs, 240 x 150 (4205/160)	4750
Serab carpet, trelliswork, palmette border, vine guard border, 288 x 148 (4205/118)	11500
Serab runner, 113 x 34, inscribed at end (626/17)	700
Serab runner, brown field, floral primary border, 165 x 43, patch, foldwear (626/69)	650
Serab runner, vine border, camel's hair field, 180 x 47 (4265/32)	2750
Serapi, 5 rows of 5 arches, vine tendril, 153 x 110 (4222/149)	5250
Serapi, sawtooth red field, sky blue border of crab palmettes, 214 x 132, rep, moth damage (4138/164)	*12500*
Serapi, 8-petal medallion, lancehead palmettes, 286 x 209 (4265/166)	16000

Serapi (4138/164)

Seychour, long, blue field, stylized bat design, red border, 160 x 47 (4138/72)	1700
Seychour, midnight blue field, sky blue border, 132 x 58 (4138/45)	2400
Shiraz, bird & flower blue field, diamond medallions, 76 x 58 (4138/60)	1100
Shiraz, blue field, red border of oak leaf & chalice, 78 x 51 (4138/99)	1300
Shiraz bagface, blue field, central medallion, 24 x 20 (626/162)	250
Shiraz long rug, midnight field with chickens, blue border, 104 x 68, slight fold cut (4074/11)	750
Shiraz rug, blue field within stylized leaf and flowerhead design, 64 x 47 (626/133)	250
Shiraz rug, blue field with diagonal rows of boteh, 98 x 58 (626/132)	350
Shiraz rug, blue field with serrated leaves, 96 x 60 (626/131)	850
Shiraz rug, blue field, barber pole border, 70 x 64, repair, reweaving (626/123)	650
Shiraz rug, blue field, large abstract crab medallion, 68 x 51, blue, painted (626/77)	450
Shiraz rug, midnight blue field with polychrome boteh, 44 x 31, striped Kelim skirt at ends (626/176)	300
Shiraz rug, midnight blue field, stylized cypress trees, 101 x 60 (626/96)	250
Shiraz rug, navy blue field, stylized animals, 53 x 46 (626/198)	550
Shiraz rug, navy ground, multiple guard borders, 98 x 60 (4074/21)	650
Shiraz rug, red field with blue medallions, 75 x 53 (626/135)	1100
Shirvan prayer rug, black field with rows of boteh, 57 x 38 (4074/44)	750
Souf Mohal antique, Tree of Life in Jerdiniere, serpents, dogs, 128 x 98 (4222/127)	14500
Tabriz, ivory field Herati-medallion, spandrels, 178 x 129 (4222/130)	14000
Tabriz, Dragon design, serrated leaves, birdds, animals, 113 x 79 (4222/99)	4500
Tabriz, aqua blue field of palmette, leaf, lilybud, vine, coral border, 182 x 132 (4138/140)	10000
Tabriz, central red-lobed medallion, fan palmettes, 150 x 112 (4265/152)	3000
Tabriz, flower-filled medallion, rust spandrels, 96 x 71 (4265/58)	3000
Tabriz, garden, windowpane design filled with flowers, 216 x 142 (4138/128)	9000
Tabriz, herati medallion, rust spandrels, 164 x 128 (4265/191)	*8000*
Tabriz, herati-filled medallion, meander vine, 68 x 48 (4265/9)	2500
Tabriz, ivory field, scrolling vine, 221 x 147 (4265/101)	5000
Tabriz, millefleur, exotic birds, midnight blue field, tan border, 78 x 56 (4138/71)	*4000*
Tabriz, possibly Hajiyalil, magenta field, serrated leaves, birds, bellflower, 192 x 174, moth damage, ragged selvage, repairs (4222/107)	18500

Tabriz, prayer, silk, rose field, midnight border, 63 x 40 (4138/13) 4400
Tabriz, rust field, midnight blue border, 184 x 133, reduced (4138/192) 3250
Tabriz, rust field, herati design, rosette border, 163 x 111 (4265/196) 3250
Tabriz, silk, prayer, lavender field, green primary border, 63 x 47 (4138/35) 15000
Tabriz, silk, red field, forked leaf medallion, red border, 167 x 116 (4138/170) 5000
Tabriz, Moustafi design, flowerhead border, 167 x 133 (4265/135) 4000
Tabriz carpet, arabesques, spandrels, flowerhead, 177 x 146 (4205/159) 2500
Tabriz carpet, geometric medallions, repairs, patch, cut, 197 x 158 (4205/116) 5500
Tabriz carpet, ivory field with rust flower blossom, 165 x 120 (4074/123) 4500
Tabriz carpet, ivory field with vine, palmette, red border, 238 x 158 (4074/107) 4000
Tabriz carpet, plum ground, palmettes, vines, 129 x 90 (4205/134) 1100
Tabriz carpet, red field, border with palmette on blue field, 245 x 152 (4074/143) 2250
Tabriz carpet, vase design, flowerheads, stain, 230 x 150 (4205/140) 5250

Tabriz (4265/191)

Tabriz (4138/71)

Tabriz Medallion rug, Silk, ivory field, polychrome medallions, rep, dry, 69 x 49 (4106/127) 4500
Tabriz prayer rug, salmon niche, pale primary border, some cuts, dry, 65 x 47 (4106/144) 1800
Tabriz rug, Shirvan style, blue field, 3 star lesghis, 63 x 40 (4106/138) 3500
Tabriz rug, olive ground centering on orange field, 67 x 46, moth damage (626/226) 250
Tabriz rug, blue field, red border, 74 x 54, guards and borders reduced (626/204) 1000
Tabriz rug, blue floral garden field, 76 x 54, minor moth damage (626/207) 1200
Tabriz rug, ivory Herati field, blue border, 48 x 67 (4074/12) 900
Teheran, brick red field within midnight blue field, 85 x 55 (4138/12) *4000*
Teheran, millefleur field, lt. blue floral border, 29 x 24, holes, ragged ends (4138/77) 275
Teheran, millefleurs, central flowering urn flanked by similar urns, 164 x 116 (4265/139) 5500
Teheran, prayer, silk, gold field, tree of birds, serpents, leopards, deer, 78 x 57, signed (4138/97) 10000

Teheran (4138/12)

Teheran mat., 29 x 24, moth damage (626/87)   350
Teheran millefleurs meditation, cypress trees, 85 x 53 (4265/75)   *5250*
Teheran prayer, ivory ground, flower filled urn, 2 peacocks, 85 x 55 (4222/82)   6500
Teheran rug, millefleur prayer field, urn, cypress trees, blue border, 88 x 58 (4106/169)   4750
Teheran rug, millefleur prayer field,urn, cypress tree, blue border, 88 x 58 (4106/168)   4750
Teheran Sarouk rug, ivory ground, stylized leaves, 78 x 52, breaks, repairs (626/148)   550

TURCOMAN

Afghan Ersari rug, brick red field, stepped flowerhead border, 79 x 62 (626/45)   2200
Afghan Hatchli rug, double prayer arch, brown field, 63 x 46, holes (626/178)   800
Afghan rug, six guls rows, star motif, torn, repaired, 114 x 42 (4205/71)   700
Afghan runner, magenta field with eleven guls, 125 x 41 (4074/69)   200
Afghan Turcoman bagface, red field, floral skirt at end, 58 x 38 (626/163)   225
Afghan Turcoman carpet, brown field within complementary border, 162 x 93 (626/194)   950
Afghan Turcoman carpet, red field within trellis work primary border, 134 x 77 (626/196) 1000
Afghanistan fragment, orange field with geometric motifs, 88 x 36, repairs (626/175)   175
Afghanistan Turcoman carpet, red field, flowerhead border, 114 x 97 (4074/126)   1500
Afghanistan Turcoman rug, red field, checkerboard zig-zag border, 110 x 80 (4074/35)   650
Armenian prayer rug, mosque lamp, urn, pedestal, flower border, 87 x 56 (4205/81)   2250
Belouchistan, olive field, rust border, kelim skirt, 60 x 36 (4138/70)   450
Belouchistan, prayer, rust field, geometric floral border, 43 x 34 (4138/88)   300
Beloughistan, geometric flowerheads, 35 x 28 (626/229)   350
Beloughistan Bag, rust red field, guls, floral guard borders, complete, 70 x 32 (4106/34) 800
Beloughistan Bagface, standard, 30 x 18 (4106/11)   550
Belouchistan prayer rug, blue field, red tree of life, 2 hand arch, 66 x 24 (4106/47)   1000
Belouchistan rug, blue field, rust and ivory flowerheads, 52 x 27, minor holes, ragged ends
(626/213)   250
Belouchistan rug, central column, running dog borders, with silk, 84 x 42 (4205/85)   3500
Belouchistan rug, geometric design, running dog guard border, 72 x 48 (4205/82)   550
Belouchistan rug, navy blue field, latchhook medallions, 62 x 34, small hole (626/70)   1500
Belouchistan rug, rust field, diagonal rows of blue and salmon, 73 x 38 (626/14)   400
Belouchistan rug, rust ground with flowerhead design, 39 x 35 (626/142)   1000
Beloughistan rug, blue field overall Latchhook design, 48 x 30 (4106/80)   500
Beloughistan rug, cocoa field, sunburst flowerheads, S, design border, 67 x 41 (4106/83) 1900
Bokhara, embroidery, ivory field of trellis work, ivory border, 85½ x 64 (4138/109)   550
Chodor rug, rust brown, flattened guls, ivory border, medallions, 98 x 50 (4106/70)   3000

Ersari Beshir bagface, brick red ground, checkerboard primary border, 64 x 19 (4074/8) — 2400
Ersari Beshir bagface, brown field with trellis work, 59 x 37 (626/185) — 650
Ersari Beshir bagface, striped field, geometric motifs, 59 x 39 (626/143) — 500
Ersari Beshir door hanging, red, 6 guls, thunderbird border, 56 x 12 (4205/30) — 550
Ersari Beshir long rug, brown field, red stylized leaves, 156 x 53 (626/166) — 350
Ersari Beshir Namasilk rug, blue blossom filled prayer arch, ivory, dam, 41 x 84 (4106/62) — 22000
Konya prayer rug, Antique, red prayer niche, meander vines, ivory arches, rep., 55 x 53 (4106/45) — 4750
Kotan Square rug, ivory field, vase and pomegranate design, 36 x 33 (4106/109) — 2700
Pakistani Bokhara, ivory ground, 5 rows of guls, 100 x 72 (626/125) — 650
Panderman prayer rug, ivory field, stylized flowers, chandelier, 72 x 52 (4106/4) — 1300
Pendi Hatchli rug, cruciform design, chandeliers, 68 x 60 (4106/112) — 9500
Perpedil rug, midnight blue field with perpedil figures, 61 x 48, cuts (626/12) — 850
Salor Bagface, deep red field, 6 magenta guls, floral skirt, 48 x 29 (4106/41) — 2300
Salor rug, blood red central field, row of guls, magenta border, 106 x 75 (4106/8) — 3500
Salor Turcoman rug, ragged end borders, 78 x 56, silverfish damage (626/240) — 1500
Samarkand carpet, buff and gold field with skeletal designs, 128 x 81 (4074/127) — 550
Samarkand carpet, stylized flower-filled field, central medallion, 180 x 90 (626/2) — 500
Seychour rug, dark blue field with trellis work, 70 x 37, borders removed, 1 missing (626/41) — 500
Seychour rug, blue field with flowerbuds, running dogs, 57 x 38 (4106/84) — 1500
Seychour rug, ivory field, diagomals of floral sprigs, 72 x 49 (4106/2) — 3000
Sharistan, pale green field, 5 dragons above seascape, 190 x 188, small patch (4138/139) — 4750
Sharistan carpet, beige field with lotus formed medallions, 280 x 168 (4074/116) — 2700
Sharistan mat, lotus blossom and vine design, gold ground, 59 x 30 (4106/111) — 300
Tekke Turcoman, brick red field, 5 rows of guls, 71 x 48, repairs, cuts (626/261) — 900
Tekke Turcoman, red field with guls, 57 x 36 (626/248) — 250
Tekke Turcoman carpet, brick red field, sunburst border, 126 x 78 (626/40) — 1300
Tekke Turcoman carpet, red ground within sunburst border, 126 x 90 (626/83) — 1100
Tekke Turcoman carpet, red-ground, sunburst border, 123 x 85 (626/82) — 900
Tekke Turcoman mat, brick red field, sunburst border, 50 x 39 (626/44) — 250
Tekke Turcoman mat, magenta field within sunburst border, 47 x 39 (626/19) — 175
Tekke Turcoman rug, brick field, geometric flowerheads, 48 x 38, silverfish damage (626/191) — 250
Tekke Turcoman rug, brick red field, 30 x 23 (626/67) — 300
Tekke Turcoman rug, brick red field, guls, sunburst border, 48 x 72 (626/152) — 750
Tekke Turcoman rug, brown field, brown sunburst border, 65 x 42 (626/199) — 400
Tekke Turcoman rug, burgundy field, 3 rows of guls, 82 x 49 (626/116) — 2200
Tekke Turcoman rug, magenta field, 42 x 42, moth damage (626/95) — 150
Tekke Turcoman rug, red field within sunburst border, 57 x 45, small paint stain (626/136) — 250
Tekke Turcoman rug, red ground, sunburst border, 41 x 36, moth damage, restorations (626/212) — 600
Tekke Turcoman rug, rose prayer niche flanked by inscribed columns, 63 x 48 (626/21) — 250
Tekke Turcoman rug, rust field, guls, sunburst border, 66 x 44 (626/188) — 700
Turcoman Kelim rug, rose field with navy flowerheads, 56 x 32, rewoven areas (626/249) — 300
Turcoman, bag, orange field, double ram's horn border, 21 x 14 (4138/64) — 225
Turcoman, bagface, embroidered, red ground, 4 rows of gulls, 45 x 32 (4138/96) — 200
Turcoman, red ground, sunburst border, serrated leaf skirt, 76 x 52 (4138/119) — 850
Turcoman, saryk, plum field, directional border, 133 x 93 (4138/118) — 2600
Turcoman, tekke, burgundy field, geometric borders, 57 x 47 (4138/98) — 500
Turcoman, tekke, red field, stepped border, 56 x 42 (4138/22) — 450
Turcoman, tekke, burgundy ground, sunburst border, 124 x 71, rep (4138/166) — 800
Yomud, red brick field, geometric flower border, 108 x 72, res (4138/125) — *3000*
Yomud Bagface, cinnamon field within directional border, 48 x 30 (626/177) — 950
Yomud Bagface, red field, floral skirt at 1 end, 46 x 37 (626/157) — 200
Yomud Bagface, rust field, ivory border, 46 x 38 (626/26) — 150
Yomud Bagface, rust field, ivory primary border, 46 x 28 (626/183) — 250
Yomud Bag, plum field with 3 rows guls, flowerhead, border, complete, 45 x 31 (4106/9) — 750
Yomud Bagface, brown field, 3 guls, ivory trefoil border, 43 x 34 (4106/97) — 500
Yomud Bagface, burgundy ground with 3 rows of guls, 42 x 30 (4106/78) — 650
Yomud Bagface, red field, 3 rows of 4 guls, 64 x 39 (4106/16) — 450
Yomud Bagface, red ground, 4 rows guls, flowertree skirt, 48 x 30 (4106/10) — 800
Yomud carpet, aubergine ground, kespe Guls, tendrils, 143 x 74 (4106/68) — 3000
Yomud Hatchli, brown field, candlelabra, tree design, 55 x 42 (4106/69) — 1200
Yomud Hatchli, cruciform design, candlelabra filled squares, 62 x 48 (4106/85) — 2000
Yomud Hatchli rug, cruciform design, 'E' guard border, 68 x 53 (4205/53) — 1200
Yomud Hatchli rug, cruciform design, candelabra, split-hair border, 62 x 45 (4205/11) — 1200
Yomud Hatchli rug, cruciform design, sunburst border, 59 x 44 (4074/57) — 650
Yomud Hatchli rug, salmon field, double prayer niche, 63 x 54, repairs (626/220) — 1700
Yomud rug, dark brown field, blue, green urns, repairs, stains, 67 x 59 (4106/6) — 750

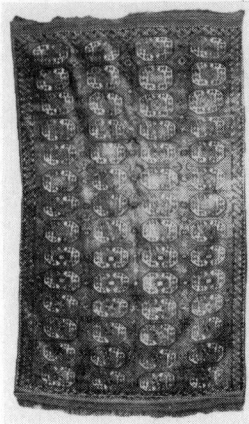

Yomud (4138/125)

TURKISH

Beloughistan prayer rug, camel field with tree of life, flowers, silk, 40 x 31 (4106/37)   600
Bergamo, antique, green field, Holbein border, 89 x 65, res, rewoven (4138/40)   5000
Bergamo Column rug, ivory double trefoil-filled ground, star filled columns, 40 x 30 (4106/53)   1500
Bergamo prayer rug, narrow red arch, latchhook design, rep., 68 x 41 (4106/38)   1800
Bergamo prayer rug, red field, ascending geometric tree of life, rep., 46 x 40 (4106/50)   1700
Bergamo prayer rug, red field,latchhook diamond design, (4106/106)   5500
Bergamo rug, blue field, diamond star design, embroidered eye, 48 x 36 (4106/91)   2700
Bergamo rug, Antique, red field, star medallion, 3 chandeliers, minor repairs, 133 x 62 (4106/15)   3000
Bergamo rug, stepped medallion, starflower, repairs, holes, unusual (4205/96)   2400
Ghiordes, prayer, antique, maroon urn, brown & maroon border, 76 x 53 (4138/103)   2000
Ghiordes prayer rug, Antique, blue arch within 2 burgundy flower, leaf borders, 71 x 53 (4106/57)   2000
Hereke prayer rug Silk, gold arch, scrolling flower Tree of Life, guard, borders, 66 x 44 (4106/158)   12000
Karachopt rug, Rare, light brown with ram's horn motif, lesghi, res., 101 x 56 (4106/31)   4000
Kirsehir prayer rug, red prayer arch centered with Tree of Life, minor rep., 51 x 41 (4106/76)   2600
Konya, antique, red field, midnight blue border, 115 x 87, rewoven (4138/26)   125
Kula Graveyard rug, Antique, green field, cypress trees, edifices, rep., 76 x 51 (4106/23)   3500
Kula rug, antique, red field, blue border with palmettes, vines, 115 x 87 (4074/22)   400
Ladik prayer rug, red prayer niche ending in tulip panel, 72 x 41 (626/127)   100
Ladik prayer rug, antique, stepped prayer arch, dragon border, rewoven, 77 x 50 (4205/83)   8000
Ladik prayer rug, Antique, red field, ivory flower form arch, tulips, reweaving, 75 x 43 (4106/33)   8000
Melas prayer rug, rust, floral spriigs, mirab, 59 x 44 (4205/28)   1100
Melas prayer rug, fragment, 54 x 40, cut and pcd (626/47)   150
Melas rug, green field, abstract meander leaf pattern, 64 x 44 (4106/71)   1600
Mudjar prayer rug, red prayer arch in ivory, lavender, red borders, 63 x 37 (4106/60)   450
Mudjar rug, ivory field with starettes, 53 x 42 (626/259)   200
Oushak, celadon field, concentric blue medallion, 215 x 164 (4138/135)   4500
Oushak, leaf green ground, octagonal medallion, tree border, 138 x 100, rewoven, damage (4138/165)   1300
Oushak, peach field, arabesque border, peach and yellow guard borders, 97 x 70 (4265/129)   3500
Oushak, sky blue field, salmon border of blossoms & flowerheads, 182 x 136 (4138/142)   3000
Oushak carpet, arabesque medallion, 137 x 98 (4205/183)   1500
Oushak carpet, arabesque spandrels, Kufic border, 159 x 120 (4205/99)   1500
Oushak carpet, blossom tree design, 204 x 104 (4205/112)   2000
Oushak carpet, crimson field, sky blue border, 212 x 158 (4074/129)   2750
Oushak carpet, flowerheads, palmettes, vines, rewoven, 174 x 128 (4205/166)   5100
Oushak carpet, garden design, leaf, palmettes, inscription, hole, dated 1888, 238 x 135 (4205/111)   5000
Oushak carpet, light blue field, checkered border, 216 x 216, rewoven area (4074/141)   2750
Oushak carpet, red field with crab-like medallions, 182 x 149 (4074/113)   650
Oushak carpet, red field, slant leaf and floral border, 218 x 130 (4074/103)   900

Oushak carpet, salmon field, green medallion, salmon border, 265 x 152 (4074/128)	3000
Oushak Small rug, Salmon field, stylized flowers, stepped vines, tear, 72 x 72 (4106/32)	750
Sevas prayer rug, 76 x 47 (626/20)	600
Sevas prayer rug, ivory prayer niche with flower-filled urns, 71 x 47 (626/253)	950
Sevas rug, ivory field with flower-filled urns at each end, 67 x 46 (626/244)	400
Sevas rug, lavendar ground, Kufic inscriptions, 108 x 72 (626/151)	1100
Single Turkish Kelim door surround, horizontally striped, 154 x 31 (626/158)	700
Sparta carpet, plum field, floral sprigs, 129 x 70 (626/62)	650
Turkish Bergamo rug, stylized Holbein border, 117 x 65, moth damages, holes (626/224)	500
Turkish Bergamo rug, Antique, blue field, 2 red flowerhead columns, guard missing, 79 x 44 (4106/25)	1800
Turkish Kazak rug, three stepped central medallions, 108 x 74, minor reweaving, new fringe (626/200)	1100
Turkish Kelim double panel door surround, 140 x 69, holes, rep. (626/33)	350
Turkish Kilim door surrounds, pair, ladder design, serrated flower-filled border, 168 x 61 (4074/18)	800
Turkish Kilim prayer rug, blue arch ending in tree flanked by rose borders, metallic thread, 60 x 45 (4106/86)	3750
Turkish Kilim rug, horizontal polychrome panels, small tears, 132 x 66 (4106/44)	750
Turkish prayer rug, red field, red polygon and primary border, 60 x 24 (4074/46)	500
Turkish Verneh Embroidered Long rug, two burgundy, 1 blue panels, latchhooks, 129 x 72 (4106/30)	2600
Turkish wool and cotton prayer rug, two tree of life motifs, 84 x 32, small holes, repairs (626/140)	1300
Yomud Hatchli rug, cruciform design flower, double E, guard, skirt, repairs, 60 x 46 (4106/28)	2800
Yomud Namasilk rug, Central ivory field, pomegranate design, 42 x 40 (4106/27)	2300
Yuruk, brown field, green border, 77 x 49 (4138/107)	1000
Yuruk, ivory prayer niche, polychrome zigzag borders, 52 x 42, res (4138/6)	700
Yuruk, Angora, aqua blue medallion, brown flowerhead border, 61 x 41 (4138/20)	1100
Yuruk prayer rug, Magenta arch, stylized geometric design, blue field, 49 x 39 (4106/87)	1300
Yuruk rug, blue field, 3 octagonal medallions, salmon border, 84 x 48 (4106/88)	1000

VARIOUS OTHER RUGS AND CARPETS

Afgan Turcoman carpet, burgundy red field, medallion border, 205 x 132 (4089/113)	1900
Afshar, ivory field, 3 meander vine and flower borders, 66 x 49 (4130/76)	1700
Agra carpet, celadon ground, leaf and palmette border, 191 x 137 repaired (4089/117)	2400
Agra carpet, cream field containing bellflower sprigs, 154 x 119 restored (4089/114)	3800
Agra carpet, light blue field, Herati design, 158 x 151 (4089/106)	1600
Agra carpet, light blue ground, palmette, leaf design, 184 x 141 restored (4089/137)	2600
Agra prayer rug, green prayer arch, ivory border, 72 x 52 (4089/3)	1100
Amritzer carpet, beige medallion on blue field, 173 x 134 (4074/683)	750
Amritzer carpet, beige field with stylized floral groupings, 240 x 144 (4074/142)	4500
Amritzer rug, ivory field, border on a yellow field, 106 x 72 (4074/5)	900
Antique Aubusson carpet, tan field, diagonal flowerhead, cocoa border, 198 x 163, much res (4168/175)	600
Antique Cuenca rug, shades of green and blue with central medallion, 109 x 82 (626/260)	2100
Aubusson, directoire, tapestry, octagonal, coral field, diameter 178, imperfection (4148/300)	1000
Aubusson, panel, beige field, celadon border, 86 x 50 (4148/301)	250
Aubusson, rose center, fleur de lis border, 182 x 166 (4265/97)	3750
Aubusson, serpentine flowering vases, 209 x 146 (4265/179)	6500
Aubusson carpet, 216 x 135, holes (669/672)	100
Aubusson carpet, 204 x 144 (4142/188)	800
Aubusson carpet, buff field with oval medallion, 252 x 183 (4142/194)	1800
Aubusson carpet, central floral medallion on beige ground, 160 x 161 (631/441)	600
Aubusson carpet, floral cluster on magenta field, 117 x 106 (669/678)	325
Aubusson carpet, green field, a canthus leaves, 170 x 113(669/691)	2600
Aubusson carpet, ivory field, flower-formed medallion, 164 x 142 (4142/198)	650
Aubusson carpet, olive field, rococo cartouche, ivory border, 264 x 258 (4168/172)	550
Aubusson carpet, oval reserve, frame-like border, 160 x 114, res (4168/167)	350
Aubusson carpet, rococo floral medallion in plum field, 133 x 94 (619/423)	400
Aubusson carpet, wine red field, acanthus medallion, 218 x 180, 19c (4168/173)	1000
Aubusson carpet, wine red field, floral cartouche, 137 x 103, restorations, reweaving (4142/199)	275
Aubusson carpet, antique, cocoa field, floral wreath, 130 x 112, major restorations (4142/200)	275
Aubusson carpet, antique, cocoa field, ornate floral wreath, 192 x 163, major restorations (4142/202)	650
Aubusson rug, acanthus medallion in burgundy/beige field, 75 x 56 (631/446)	100
Aubusson rug, ivory field within purple border, 128 x 54 (669/675)	100
Aubusson rug, wreath medallion on green ground, 103 x 78 (669/674)	100
Aubusson rug-circular, beige field, floral wreath, centered by acanthus, D72 (4142/190)	650
Aubusson runner, beige with floral sprigs, 228 x 59 (631/440)	400

Backtari long, black field within blue trellis border, 172 x 86, signature panel at 1 end touched (4222/6)   3750
Bakshuish carpet, red field, large medallion, blue border, 175 x 131 (4089/132)   5750
Belouchistan prayer rug, tan prayer niche, stylized tree of life, 48 x 32 (4089/9)   800
Belouchistan rug, tan field, tree of life motif, 75 x 46 (4089/7)   600
Bessarabian carpet, floral wreath surrounded by peacocks, 120 x 108, stains (631/443)   550
Bessarabian carpet, spring green field with floral sprays, 168 x 142 (4142/204)   5000
Bessarabian rug, olive ground, flowered border, 115 x 111, res (4168/165)   350
Bidjar, herati field, palmettes, vines, 6' 1' x 4' 9', ragged border, minor damage (4198/26)   3000
Bidjar, ivory medallion, spearhead palmettes, Herati, 137 x 92 (4222/137)   3250
Bidjar, mustafi design, vines, leaves, 7' x 4' 6' (4198/16)   *3500*
Bidjar, red field, blue Herati, red palmette border, 56 x 40, minor moth damage (4222/42)   2600
Bidjar, repeating Herati design, fan palmettes & vines, 286 x 168 (422/136)   4500
Bidjar, repeating Herati design, fan palmettes & vines, 286 x 168 (4222/136)   4500
Bidjar, mat, herati design, vines, flowerheads, 4' 2' x 3' (4198/17)   1500
Bidjar, runner, stylized herati design, 18' 10' x 4' 10' (4198/12)   2000

Bidjar (4198/16)

Bidjar carpet, cypress trees, medallion, spandrels, 13' x 9' 6', ragged border, moth damage (4198/117)   3750
Bidjar carpet, medallion, vines, flowerheads, 12' 7' x 9' 3' (4198/151)   8000
Bidjar carpet, moustafi design, 6' 7' x 11' 2', slightly dry (4198/153)   9500
Bidjar carpet, ornate vines, floral sprays, cabbage leaf des., 23' 9' x 12' 3', stains (4198/114)   13000
Bidjar carpet, repetitive herati design, 11' 7' x 7' 7', repairs (4198/161)   3000
Bidjar long rug, midnight blue field, red border, repaired, 144 x 69 (4089/99)   1100
Bidjar Medallion rug, red flower-filled field, spandrels, 102 x 67 (4106/165)   3000
Bokhara, lozenge-shaped medallions, 73 x 40¼ (4148/297)   300
Caucasian, midnight-blue field, stylized floral rosettes, 98 x 57½ (4148/293)   2000
Caucasian, prayer, midnight-blue mihrab, 53 x 39½ (4148/289)   80
Chinese, ivory field, floral sprigs, flowering vines, 115 x 98 (4222/138)   3500
Chinese, mustard ground, trees, lotus, urn, incense burner, 139 x 106, minor rust stains (4222/112)   2800
Chinese carpet, black field, green border, pheasants, 138 x 108 (4089/125)   950
Chinese carpet, cream field, midnight blue border, 136 x 99 (4089/146)   2600
Chinese carpet, dragon, thunderhead spandrels, 12' x 9' (4198/131)   3500
Chinese carpet, ivory field, blue medallion, blue border, 138 x 110 (4089/131)   950
Chinese carpet, ivory field, lotus, greek key spandrels, 139 x 108 (4089/143)   2200
Chinese carpet, midnight blue field, 137 x 109 (4089/152)   1400
Chinese carpet, salmon field with lotus blossoms, 126 x 84 (4089/154)   1900
Chinese column rug, ivory field, thunder borders, 89 x 64 (4089/52)   1500
Chinese round rug, beige field, butterflies, blossoms, D101 (4089/53)   1100
Chinese rug, blue lattice work, field, lotus, vine border, 113 x 73 (4089/36)   2800
Chinese rug, burgundy field, stylized blossom tree, 103 x 71 (4089/38)   650
Chinese rug, ivory field, royal pheasant design, 59 x 31 (4089/34)   250
Chinese runner, 10 gold panels, arabesque circular medallions, 229 x 24 (4222/67)   2200

Chinese runner, symbols of the literati, flowers, 24' 1' x 3' 1' (4198/54)   4000
Chinese square rugs, pair, bronze field, rose medallion, inter-connected, 53 x 27 (4089/16)   250
Daghastan, prayer, deep brown mihrab, ivory border, 63½ x 41, wear (4148/292)   150
Daghastan rug, beige field, blue spandrels, ivory border, 62 x 44 (4089/94)   800
Dalmatian prayer rug, embroidery, applique, flowers surround green velvet field, 66 x 43 (4074/10)   400
Derbend rug, blue field, snowflake design, ivory border, 60 x 43 (4089/72)   850
English Needlepoint, floral cluster border, 220 x 130 (4265/203)   5000
Fereghan, midnight-blue field, red palmette border, 217 x 100 (4148/298)   5500
Fereghan, silk, medallion, stylized flowers, 6' 9' x 4' 7' (4198/37)   27000
Ferraghan carpet, blue field, meander vine border, 338 x 192 slight repairs (4089/136)   4500
Gashgai Millefleur, prayer niche, urn, cypress tree, 8' 4' x 5' 6' (4198/74)   14000
Gendje rug, blue checkered field, geometric border, 69 x 35 (4089/46)   500
Gendje rug, red field, animals and trefoil designs, 84 x 48 (4089/83)   750
Gendje rug, red field, trefoil border, 79 x 40 (4089/87)   450
Ghiordes, antique prayer rug, mosque lamp, dragon panel, 6' x 4' 8', repairs (4198/7)   *3500*

Hereke silk prayer rug
(4198/60)

Ghiordes
(4198/7)

Ghiordes, prayer rug, mosque lamp, minarets, 5' 4' x 3' 5', ragged edges, moth damage (4198/28)   700
Gorevan carpet, blue field, flower medallion, red border, 141 x 100 (4089/123)   1200
Greek Island prayer rug, silk embroidered flowered arch and border, 62 x 42 (4074/30)   750
Greek Island prayer rug, silk embroidered, double prayer niche, 45 x 36 (4089/86)   450
Greek Island prayer rug, silk embroidered, Isnik filled arch, tree panel, 60 x 36 (4074/28)   650
Grospoint, carpet, ivory field, 7 rows of 3 medallions, 228 x 130, stains (4218/201)   11000
Grospoint, rug, ivory ground, 4 ascending columns, bouquets, 132 x 66 (4218/203)   2000
Hamadan runner, boteh design, 18' 5' x 3' 5', moth damage (4198/67)   1900
Hamadan runner, brown field, border of flowerheads, leaves, 168 x 53 (4089/22)   600
Hamadan runner, navy field, midnight blue guard border, 196 x 38 (4089/80)   750
Hereke prayer rug, silk and metallic thread, inscribed with poetry and signed, vines, leaves, 5' 9' x 3' 11' (4198/48)   15000
Hereke silk prayer rug, leaf design, cloud bands, inscribed cartouches, 5' 5' x 3' 8' (4198/60)   *10000*
Heriz, blue & salmon medallion, leaf, flowerheads, animal, 146 x 104 (4222/115)   4250
Heriz carpet, cinnamon field, large medallion, ivory border, 171 x 126 (4089/151)   3100
Heriz carpet, red field with palmettes, blue border, 142 x 116 (4089/100)   2300
Heriz carpet, red field, blue medallion, border, 128 x 94 (4089/147)   1000
Heriz carpet, red field, ivory medallions, blue border, 160 x 113 (4089/96)   5000
Heriz carpet, red stylized flower-filled field, blue border, 154 x 105 painted (4089/144)   2500
Heriz carpet, salmon field, flower-formed medallion, 147 x 118 (4089/148)   3100
Heriz carpet, stylized vine and palmette design, 14' 2' x 10' 5', slight border reduction (4198/136)   6750
Heriz carpet, stylized vines and palmettes, medallions, 10' 7' x 7' 6' (4198/109)   13500
Heriz silk prayer rug, tree of life issuing from urn, 5' 5' x 4' 1' (4198/84)   *12500*

Heriz silk prayer rug
(4198/84)

Indian palace carpet, Isphahan style, 22' x 22', repaired, reduced (4198/142)	12500
Indo-Isphahan antique carpet, palmettes, vines, animals, 23' 8' x 11' 10' (4198/111)	4100
Indo-Kashan carpet, blue field with flowering trees, 228 x 156 (631/445)	1000
Indo-Kashan carpet, flowerhead and cloudband design, 15' 8' x 10' (4198/137)	3000
Indo-Kashan carpet, wine red field containing blossom trees, 153 x 231 (4089/108)	1100
Iraqi coat of arms, silk, hanging, black field, coat of arms of the state, 64 x 49 (4074/80)	800
Isphahan, concentric circle design, inscribed serafian, 9' 6' x 9', silk warp, stain (4198/91)	40000
Isphahan, flower heads, palmettes medallions, 7' 2' x 4' 7' (4198/34)	3500
Isphahan, fork leaf, flowering vine, blue spandrels, 79 x 51 (4222/57)	3000
Isphahan, ivory field, prayer arch Tree of Life, peacocks, 88 x 55 (4222/85)	4250
Isphahan, pictorial directional medallion, 6' 9' x 4' 7' (4198/11)	3400
Isphahan, scrolling vine, inscribed Serafian, 7' 4' x 5', silk warp (4198/19)	10500
Isphahan, similar to preceding, 7' 4' x 5 (4198/20)	9500
Isphahan, tree of life, bird and flower filled urn and trees, 6' 10' x 4' 6' (4198/45)	4250
Isphanan, ivory trellis within blue trellis border, 77 x 64, silk warp and weft (4222/5)	3000
Isphahan carpet, scrolling Isphahan design, palmettes, flowers, 15' 4' x 10' 1' (4198/139)	21000
Isphahan carpet, similar to the preceding, 15' 1' x 10' 2' (4198/140)	23000
Isphahan Hunt, grey field, equestrian figures, hunt scene, 98 x 60 (4222/43)	7500
Josan Sarouk carpet, vines, palmettes, leaves, flowerheads, 20' 7' x 72' 4' (4198/108)	20000
Joshagan, flowers and palmettes, 6' 1' x 4' 4' (4198/36)	4750
Joshagan garden carpet, floral sprigs, lattice design, 20' x 12', rewoven area (4198/118)	9500
Joshagan garden rug, formal garden design, waterbug palmette, 7' x 4' 5' (4198/40)	4500
Joshagan garden rug, similar to preceding, 7' x 4' 5' (4198/41)	4500
Kaghan mats, pair, magenta field, ivory floral border, 26 x 22 (4089/10)	700
Karabagh double panel embroid. rug, polychrome latchhook design, double 'E' border, 64 x 64 (4089/43)	2000
Karabagh rug, red ground, star-filled guard border, 79 x 52 (4089/81)	900
Karabagh rug, rust field, ivory border, 92 x 46 (4089/4)	800
Karabagh runner, brown field, floral cartouches, 216 x 38 (4142/205)	2100
Karadja runner, blue ground, 152 x 42 (4089/58)	700
Kashan, boteh, vines, flowers, 6' 8' x 4' 4' (4198/62)	3250
Kashan, burgundy, flowering tree, yellow bird, borders, 80 x 52 (4222/33)	10000
Kashan, floral sprig design, 6' 5' x 4' 3' (4198/32)	4000
Kashan, garden design, bird of paradise, 7' 1' x 4' 3' (4198/5)	2200
Kashan, pictorial rug, depicting a forest, tree and deer, 41 x 23 (4089/8)	650
Kashan, prayer rug, flower and bird filled trees, 7' 1' x 4' 5' (4198/25)	*7000*
Kashan, silk, arabesque medallion, vine design, 6' 7' x 4' 7' (4198/6)	4000
Kashan, silk, flowers and palmettes, 7' 5' x 4' 8' (4198/58)	7000
Kashan, Moustasha, rug, red vine filled field, dark blue medallion, 81 x 51 (4089/59)	1400
Kashan carpet, arabesque medallion, anchor palmettes, 17' x 12' (4198/141)	7500
Kashan carpet, midnight blue flower-filled field, blue border, 138 x 96 (4089/149)	7250
Kashan carpet, vines, flowers, medallion, 10' 1' x 7' 1', moth damage (4198/143)	7750
Kashan carpet, vines, palmettes, cloudbands, 15' 6' x 10' 5' (4198/157)	13500
Kashan carpet, vines, urns, medallion, 11' 10' x 8' 7' (4198/146)	13000

Kashan carpet, wine red field, midnight blue border, 134 x 222 (4089/115)   5000
Kashan carpet, silk and wool, Isphahan vine, palmette and forked leaf design, 13' 9' x 10' 6'
(4198/145)   22000
Kashan carpet, Manchester, rose field, midnight blue border, 117 x 83 small repairs (4089/119)   5500
Kashan corridor carpet, vine and flowerhead design, 20' x 9' (4198/122)   7000
Kashan prayer rugs, pair, deep red field, midnight blue border, 63 x 42 (4089/37)   4000
Kashan rug, midnight blue field, border of flowerheads, 42 x 30½ (4089/2)   900
Kashan rug, midnight blue field, red border, 78 x 49 (4089/97)   3400
Kashan rug, wine red field, cartouche border, 77 x 48 (4089/92)   1700
Kashan rug, Manchester, ivory field, midnight blue border, 115 x 84 (4089/6)   4750
Kashan rug, Manchester, rose field, midnight blue signature panel, 41 x 39 (4089/56)   2500
Kashan rug, Manchester, tree of life, fish and bird-filled pond, 78 x 48 (4089/76)   4250
Kashan silk, cream field, crimson medallion blue spandrels, 82 x 52 (4222/2)   2300
Kashan silk, cream, blue medallion, flowering urns, peacocks, 70 x 43 (4222/58)   2400
Kashan silk carpet, blossoming trees, animals and birds, 12' 2' x 8' 7' (4198/115)   36000
Kashan silk pictorial, historic landscapes, blue borders, 60 x 40 (4222/31)   5250

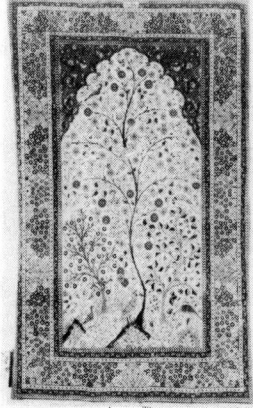

Kashan (4198/25)

Kashmir rug, green central reserve, 60 x 36 (669/664)   25
Kasvin runner, ivory floral field, blue flowerhead border, 264 x 26 (669/666)   650
Kayserie silk carpet, medallion, spandrels, trees, 13' x 9' 3' (4198/113)   4750
Kazak, sapphire-blue field, 3 octagon medallions, ivory border, 84 x 61½ (4148/287)   3600
Kazak long rug, blue field, latchhook, flowerhead border, 91 x 46 (4089/54)   1550
Kazak long rug, mustard field, trefoil design, ivory border, 125 x 53 (4089/82)   1000
Kazak prayer rug, ivory geometric prayer niche, meander border, 60 x 39 (4089/85)   1300
Kazak rug, blue field, double prayer niche, 89 x 54 (4089/55)   650
Kazak rug, blue field, geometric latchhook design, 73 x 50 (4089/65)   700
Kazak rug, four latchhook medallions, ivory border, 84 x 60 (4089/69)   475
Kazak rug, gold field, latticework, star design, 72 x 44 (4089/44)   750
Kazak rug, red field, trefoil motifs, antelope figures, (4089/40)   1100
Kazak rug, red ground, 2 animals, ivory border, 58 x (4089/67)   1100
Kazak runner, red field, ivory border, 54 x 37 (4089/32)   1000
Kirman, beige field, floral trellis, vine border, 72 x 51¼ (4148/290)   1300
Kirman, midnight blue field, ardebil design, midnight blue border, 290 x 166 (4138/120)   7000
Kirman, silk, vines, flowers, spandrels, palmettes, 6' x 4' 6' (4198/39)   6000
Kirman, stylized floral motifs, beige field, 74½ x 5l (4148/296)   1150
Kazvin carpet, arabesque boteh, 10' 10' x 8' 2' (4198/95)   8000
Keshan rugs, pair, midnight blue field, brick red floral medal, 84 x 52 (4089/13)   1500
Khatan carpet, rust and gold geometric field, thunder border, 279 x 149 (4089/103)   6750
Khorassan carpet, red field, sunburst medallion, blue border, 210 x 162 (4089/107)   3750
Khotam rug, flower, orange field with flowering vase, 45 x 25 (4089/57)   200
Kirman, arabesque floral design, 6' 10' x 4' 3' (4198/73)   2000
Kirman, garden design, vine, palmettes, leaf borders, 330 x 168 (4222/145)   4500
Kirman, medallions, palmette, 6' 7' x 4' 2' (4198/52)   2400
Kirman carpet, burgundy field, rose flower-filled border, 167 x 125 (4089/110)   3800
Kirman carpet, celadon field, alternating cartouche border, 127 x 93 (4089/135)   3000
Kirman carpet, deep burgundy field, dark blue border, 132 x 107 (4089/109)   1700
Kirman carpet, dragon, flying fish, star medallion, 13' 7' x 11' 7' (4198/150)   4750
Kirman carpet, floral sprays in ivory field, 157 x 137 (631/448)   3200

Kirman carpet, floral sprigs on rose field, 160 x 120 (631/450)   2600
Kirman carpet, ivory field surrounded by floral sprays, 197 x 126 (669/687)   2300
Kirman carpet, ivory field, blue arabesque medallion, 144 x 101 (669/699)   3100
Kirman carpet, ivory field, floral medallion, 198 x 122 (669/673)   1800
Kirman carpet, ivory field, flower primary border, 147 x 103 (4089/145)   1500
Kirman carpet, lobed control medallion on ivory field, 144 x 117 (669/663)   450
Kirman carpet, millefleur design on blue field, 206 x 150 (669/686)   1100
Kirman carpet, millefleur design, ivory field, 240 x 116 (669/665)   3000
Kirman carpet, vine palmette, lanceolate, leaf design, 14' x 8' 9' (4198/121)   3200
Kirman carpet fragment, millefleur field, cartouches in yellow, 201 x 161 (4089/129)   1400
Kirman medallion rug, millefleur field on rose ground, 106 x 71 (4089/15)   2100
Kirman medallion rug, ivory field, salmon sunburst medallion, 111 x 71 (4089/33)   2200
Kirman Millefleur tree of life carpet, crown medallion, 15' 9' x 9' 3' (4198/100)   6500
Kirman rug, wine field, star-shaped medallion, 73 x 50 (669/698)   325
Konya Kilim, two rectangles, brown and ivory border, 65 x 43 (4089/91)   1000
Konya prayer rug, antique, red field, gold arch, 62 x 47 (4074/24)   850
Kuba, antique dragon rug fragment, 18C, leaf medallions, cypress trees, flowers, 14' 9' x 6', major restoration (4198/107)   1600
Kuba rug, geometric floral design, Holbein border, 60 x 36 (4089/41)   1400
Kula, antique prayer rug, pomegranate tree, arches, 5' 10' x 4', rewoven areas (4198/4)   *1900*

Kula (4198/4)

Mohtashem Kashan
(4198/75)

Kurd long rug, brown field, boteh interspersed w/animals, 100 x 48 (4089/42)   650
Kurd rug, blue field with floral sprays, brown border, 71 x 48 (4089/73)   900
Kurd runner, blue field with Herati design, red border, 450 x 40 (4089/70)   425
Kurd runners, pair, blue field with Herati design, red border, 450 x 40 (4089/71)   550
Kurdish runner, medallions and flowers, 14' 6' x 3' 5' (4198/43)   1700
Kurdistan carpet, midnight blue field, primary ivory border, 192 x 168 slight repair (4089/111)   2300
Lenkoran rug, blue snowflake filled field, oak leaf border, 70 x 47 (4074/25)   1600
Machine Art Deco rug, 63 x 36, small tear (4230/850)   175
Machine made Art Deco carpet, 142 x 106, stains (4230/849)   1000
Machine made carpet, rust field, all over lozenge pattern, 189 x 128, torn (669/684)   100
Mahal carpet, blue field, gold border, 138 x 102 (4089/130)   800
Mahal carpet, blue field, rust border, 224 x 123 (4089/134)   2000
Mahal carpet, ivory ground, Herati design, 125 x 90 (4089/138)   1100
Mahal carpet, red ground, midnight blue medallion, 126 x 102 (4089/128)   1700
Malayer, Herati pattern, blue and rust, 74 x 54 (4222/3)   1300
Malayer carpet, abstract floral design, 10' 10' x 10, small patches (4198/92)   *11000*
Manchester Indo-Kashan, overall garden design, 2 geometric borders, 362 x 170, stairs, slight repairs (4222/131)   16000
Manchester Kashan, blue ground repetitive vine & leaf, borders, 206 x 120, torn and repaired (4222/121)   17000

Manchester Kashan, directional medallion, flowers, 5' 2' x 3' 6' (4198/61) — 3250
Manchester Kashan, flowering urn, floral spray, fan palmette, 182 x 123 (4222/144) — 10000
Manchester Kashan, magenta pictorial field, floral sprigs, urns, 78 x 54 (4222/56) — 5750
Manchester Kashan, vines, leaves, 5' x 3' 5' (4198/70) — 3750
Manchester Kashan Meditation, red field, flower filled urn, bird filled shrub, 78 x 50 (4222/39) — 5500
Manchester Kashan prayer, brown mirab woven, Hereke cloudband, colors, 58 x 41 (4222/65) — 6500
Manchester Kashan tree of life, deer, birds, flowers, 6' 6' x 4' 2' (4198/77) — 7250
Marasali, prayer rug, dark brown field, ivory border, 46 x 46 (4089/23) — 4100
Maylayer rug, blue field, Herati design, red border, 85 x 57 (4089/75) — 1200
Melas prayer rug, salmon prayer niche, oak leaf border, 66 x 44 (4089/18) — 450
Meshed carpet, dark blue field with scrolling vine, 324 x 126 (4089/112) — 550
Meshed rug, red field, arabesque vines, birds of Paradise, 84 x 50 (4106/163) — 3500
Meshed rug, red field, cypress trees, 3 floral borders, vines, 84 x 50 (4106/164) — 3250
Mhtashem Kashan, Joshegan garden design, flowers, 6' 9' x 4' 6', rewoven fringe (4198/18) — 8000
Millefleur Kirman, flora medallion on wine ground, 177 x 140 (631/449) — 1400
Millefleur Kirman carpet, 211 x 142 (669/693) — 1400
Mohtashem Kashan, birds, flowers, vines, 6' 1' x 4' 1' (4198/76) — 6000
Mohtashem Kashan, flowers, palmettes, spandrels, 13' 6' x 10', slight moth damage (4198/135) — 25000
Mohtashem Kashan, medallion, spandrels, 6' 5' x 4' 2' (4198/90) — 10000
Mohtashem Kashan, medallion, spearhead palmettes, 6' 10' x 4' 5' (4198/75) — *13000*
Mohtashem Kashan, medallions, spandrels, flowers, 7' 2' x 4' 3' (4198/24) — 6250
Mohtashem Kashan carpet, vines, flowers, leaves, 13' 5' x 10', slightly dry (4198/123) — 19000
Mohtashem Kashan hunt rug, 2 scenes from Shahnama, inscribed cartouche, 6' 5' x 4' 6' (4198/35) — *6500*
Mohtashem Kashan pictorial, cartouche of Shah Ahmad, 6' 6' x 4' 5' (4198/23) — *8000*

Mohtashem Kashan hunt rug
(4198/35)

Mohtashem Kashan
pictorial (4198/23)

Mohtashem Kashan prayer rug, flowering urn, palmettes, birds, 6' 7' x 4' 6' (4198/38) — 4250
Mongolian flat woven blanket, brown field, 5 ibis, 95 x 48 (626/105) — 275
Needlepoint fragment English, 97 x 81 (4142/195) — 550
Oushak carpet, beige field, red border, 187 x 156 restored (4089/141) — 1900
Perpedil rug, blue field, floral primary border, 58 x 45 (4074/39) — 650
Persian, Fereghan design, blue field, red trellis corners, 39 x 34 (4148/294) — 200
Persian crown carpet, 4 pictorial cartouches, 20' x 16' 2' (4198/128) — 7000
Persian Resht Embroidery, silk scrolling vine, black background, double, red border, 99 x 58 (4106/182) — 2300
Portuguese needlepoint carpet, red and yellow surrounded by a rose cluster border, 181 x 117 (669/671) — 350
Qum carpet, wool, silk, arabesque vine design, boteh, 10' 9' x 7', unravelled fringe (4198/99) — 6500
Ravar Kirman carpet, Zil-I-Soltan design, 21' 6' x 12' 4' (4198/101) — 5000

Rescht embroidered saddle cover, millefleur field, flower filled urn, 6' x 5' 3', pc replaced (4198/68)   1200
Rescht embroidery, green ground, red border, 79 x 54 (4074/2)   450
Roumanian Kilim prayer rug, red field, tree, latchhook archigold border, 66 x 45 (4106/108)   1600
Samarkand, brick-red key-fret field, 77 x 43½, imperfections (4148/291)   850
Samarkand antique, buff field, flowers, spandrels, compliment, border, 165 x 84 (4222/114)   2100
Sarouk, blue field, floral drapery, lobsters, borders, 204 x 144 (4222/117)   10000
Sarouk, blue field, overall floral sprig design, 77 x 49 (4222/64)   3000
Sarouk, central medallion, spandrels, cypress trees, 6' 5" x 4' 6' (4198/27)   *4500*

Sarouk (4198/27)

Tapriz carpet (4198/126)

Sarouk, long, dark blue field, floral sprays, fan palmettes, 144 x 66 (4222/84)   3000
Sarouk, flowers, medallion, waterbug palmette, 6' 10' x 4' 4', stained, dry (4198/47)   2600
Sarouk, herati filled pole medallions, 6' 4' x 4' (4198/31)   8750
Sarouk, medallion, spandrels, vines, 6' 7' x 4' 4', extremely dry (4198/65)   4500
Sarouk, medallions, locust palmettes, spandrels, vines, 7' x 4' 6' (4198/15)   3750
Sarouk, stylized flowers and trees, 4' 10' x 3' 6' (4198/78)   1200
Sarouk, stylized urns, flowers, 7' 5' x 5' 7' (4198/87)   3250
Sarouk, vine medallion, 4 spandrels, flower palmettes, 164 x 128 (4222/143)   8500
Sarouk carpet, deep red ground, midnight blue border, 137 x 102 (4089/133)   2700
Sarouk carpet, floral sprigs within red border, 121 x 90 (626/209)   1300
Sarouk carpet, floral sprigs, trees, 26' x 11' 8' (4198/132)   6000
Sarouk carpet, medallions, vines, flowers, 15' 10' x 9' 10' (4198/98)   11500
Sarouk carpet, midnight blue field, burgundy border, 168 x 82 (4089/124)   1000
Sarouk carpet, red field, blue border with palmettes, vines, 141 x 103 (4089/105)   1700
Sarouk carpet, red flower filled field, blue border, 198 x 120 (4089/122)   4500
Sarouk carpet, red with floral sprigs, blue border, 138 x 108 (4089/153)   2100
Sarouk carpet, vases, floral sprays, 18' 2' x 12' 5' (4198/102)   8000
Sarouk carpet, vines, 10' x 7' 4' (4198/127)   1900
Sarouk Fereghan, ivory carnation field, feathered medallion, 77 x 51, slightly dry (4222/68)   3500
Sarouk Fereghan, ivory field, blue and salmon designs, 58 x 40, slightly dry (4222/8)   1800
Sarouk Fereghan, ivory medallion, salmon and blue design, 60 x 41 reduced guard borders (4222/4)   2000
Sarouk Fereghan, medallion, palmettes, spandrels, 5' x 3' 4' (4198/63)   2000
Sarouk prayer rug, jardiniere, flanked by trees of life, 6' 10' x 4' 6', border patch (4198/46)   3500
Sarouk rug, ivory flower-filled field, brown border, 54 x 27 (4089/88)   700
Sarouk rug, red field with scrolling arabesque design, 81 x 55 (4089/29)   1200
Sarouk rug, red field, 2 vases at either end, 79 x 52 (4089/24)   1800
Sarouk rug, stylized flower-filled ivory field, fold cuts (626/128)   450
Sarouk rug, maylayer, midnight blue field, large red medallion, 81 x 53 (4089/63)   1500
Sarouk rug, maylayer, salmon field, midnight blue border, 81 x 51 (4089/98)   950
Sarouk runner, gold field with floral sprays, blue border, 79 x 30 (4198/63)   1200
Sarouk runner, wine red field, midnight blue border, dry 79 x 30 (4089/90)   1100
Saryk, Bagface, red field, multiple guls, cotton highlights, 48 x 31 (4106/14)   1600
Savonnerie carpet, rose formed cartouche on ivory ground, 156 x 136, slightly dry (4168/174)   1900
Savonnerie long rug, Portuguese, brown field, cabbage rose border, dated, 182 x 68 (4205/98)   1200

Savonnerie style carpet, central brown oblong medallion, ivory field, 174 x 137 (669/689)   1800
Savonnerie style Spanish carpet, flower filled ivory field, 298 x 235 (4218/207)   3500
Senna, boteh design, flowers, vines, 6' 2' x 4' 4', patch, repairs (4198/30)   2750
Senna, flowers and bat palmette design, 6' 3' x 4' 5' (4198/29)   7000
Senna, herati design, 6' 6' x 4' 4', silk warp, border reductions (4198/33)   13500
Senna, pinwheel boteh design, 6' 10' x 4' 5', reduced border, silk warp (4198/57)   8500
Senna, red waterbug palmette, vine border, 6' 7' x 4' 6' (4198/8)   2200
Senna, rows of boteh, 6' 5' x 4' 5' (4198/89)   4000
Senna, Herati, hexagonal medallion, green spandrels, 56 x 42 (4222/62)   3000
Senna carpet, herati design, 14' 4' x 8' 6' (4198/155)   6000
Senna Kilim rug, dark brown field, 3 flower borders, 75 x 54 (4089/39)   1000
Serab, latticework design, leaves, flowers, 6' 5' x 4' 11' (4198/83)   2200
Serab carpet, beige field, blue border, 305 x 172 stains (4089/116)   2300
Serebend, long, boteh, vines, 19' 11' x 3', ragged borders, nail holes (4198/56)   2000
Serebend, brick red field, pear motif, ivory border, 77 x 46½ (4148/286)   1050
Serebend, brick red field, pear motifs, ivory border, 77 x 49 (4148/288)   1100
Sevas carpet, blue field, Herati pattern, red border, 228 x 192 (4089/120)   2100
Sevas carpet, silk, vines, birds, leaves, medallion, 9' 5' x 6' 5' (4198/159)   4750
Sevas silk carpet, vines, medallions, cartouches, 11' 6' x 8' 4' (4198/112)   3000
Seychour rug, midnight blue field, ivory primary border, 107 x 51 (4089/66)   2000
Seychour runner, midnight blue field, star meander border, 132 x 44 (4089/51)   1100
Sharistan carpet, in the Chinese style, 5 dragons, 6' 2' x 15' 4' (4198/144)   3000
Shirvan prayer rug, blue field, oak leaf border, 72 x 36 (4089/19)   800
Shirvan prayer rug, ivory field, dragon border, 48 x 48 (4089/5)   1100
Shirvan prayer rug, ivory field, scorpion design border, 68 x 36 (4089/50)   1000
Shirvan rug, blue field filled with snowflake design, 72 x 44 (4089/68)   1000
Shirvan rug, blue field, ivory border, 60 x 46 torn (4089/64)   850
Shirvan rug, midnight blue field, 4 winged medallions, 72 x 43 (4089/14)   1300
Souf Kashan silk and metallic, vine and flower design, spandrels, fan palmette, 77 x 50 (4222/30)   33000
Soumak carpet, red field containing 4 medallions, 122 x 96 (4089/121)   1200
Soumak carpet, red field, zig zag border, brown ground, 96 x 82 (4089/118)   1100
Soumak carpet, red ground, 3 medallions, 108 x 88 (4089/150)   2000
South Russian rug, red ground, snowflakes, 42 x 29 (626/108)   400
South Russian rug, yellow field within brick red border, 65 x 48 (626/252)   600
Spanish carpet, blue floral pattern on ivory field, 143 x 107 (619/426)   300
Sperta carpet, flower-filled lozenges, red border, 114 x 101 (4089/139)   1400
Tabriz, aqua field, trellis pattern, spandrels, border, 132 x 83 (4222/113)   3250
Tabriz, flower, vine ground, floral motifs, gold flowers, 213 x 149 (4222/123)   5500
Tabriz, herati design, 5' 8' x 4' (4198/69)   1500
Tabriz, medallion, spandrels, 5' 9' x 4' 1' (4198/50)   1600
Tabriz, of the herati design, 5' 11' x 4' 4' (4198/72)   3250
Tabriz, prayer design, 6 x 4' 1 (4198/2)   *4500*
Tabriz, Herati-salmon field, medallion, reindeer border, 75 x 55 (4222/40)   2900
Tabriz, Moss field, lattice, spiderweb design, Isphahan, 168 x 114 (4222/142)   11000
Tabriz, silk, compartmental design, 6' 1' x 4' 4' (4198/81)   16000
Tabriz, silk, medallion, spandrels, 5' 4' x 4, slightly dry (4198/49)   10000
Tabriz, silk, poetry from Hafiz, medallion, flowers, vines, 5' 8' x 4' 5', slightly dry (4198/160)   15000
Tabriz, silk hunt rug, animals, birds and clouds, 6' x 4' 2', numbered (4198/22)   23000
Tabriz, silk prayer rug, mosque lamp, columns, vines palmettes, 5' 4' x 3' 9' (4198/9)   20000
Tabriz, silk prayer rug, spandrels, medallions, leaves, flowers, 6' 2' x 4' 6' (4198/3)   6500
Tabriz, tree of life, tulips, vines, 6' 1' x 4' 5', dry, small repair (4198/14)   3100
Tabriz carpet, arabesque vine and bat palmette design, 25' 10' x 18' 4½', moth damage (4198/103)   16500
Tabriz carpet, medallion, mosque lamps, cloudband design, 15' 6' x 11' 6' (4198/156)   13000
Tabriz carpet, medallion, stylized flowers, 12' 5' x 8' 3' (4198/96)   6500
Tabriz carpet, saw-tooth herati medallion, 13' 6' x 9' 8' (4198/129)   9250
Tabriz carpet, wine field, blue border, 198 x 131 (4089/102)   5250
Tabriz carpet, important 19c, depicting Persepolis during the Achaemenid pd., 19' 7' x 14' (4198/130)   35000
Tabriz carpet, possibly Hajiyalil, arabesque medallion, spandrels, leaves, 11' x 10' (4198/134)   15000
Tabriz carpet, possibly Hajiyalil, forked leaf, vine and palmette design, 15' 9' x 10' 9' (4198/154)   7000
Tabriz carpet, possibly Hajyalil, vines, medallion, flowers, pictorial cartouches, 40' x 22' 6' (4198/93)   40000
Tabriz hunt, blue field, palmette, animals, Good & Evil fig., 164 x 127, small repairs, fol weak (4222/119)   11000
Tabriz prayer rug, Silk, copper field, red niche with hanging lamp, 63 x 48 (4106/162)   11000
Tapriz carpet, medallion, arabesque design, 11' x 8' 2' (4198/126)   *10000*
Teheran carpet, flower and bird filled urns, 18' 10' x 11' 8' (4198/124)   18000
Teheran carpet, silk and wool, interconnected garden design, 12' 9' x 8' 5', ragged borders (4198/158)   8500

Teheran Millefleur, millefleur field, medallion, spandrels, palmette, 6' x 4' 3' (4198/66)   4000
Teheran Millefleur, flowers, trees, urn, 6' 4' x 4' 4' (4198/80)   5000
Teheran rug, palmette-formed medallions, burgundy border, 81 x 54 (4089/84)   1800
Tekke Turcoman rug, wine field, sunburst border, 78 x 48 (4089/78)   850
Turcoman embroidered bag, burgundy field, geometric border, 49 x 30 (4089/20)   200
Turkistan rug, polychrome field, various geometric figures, 103 x 54 (4089/79)   550
Verdure tapestry fragment, Brussels, flora and fauna, 96 x 72, 18c (631/439)   900
Verneh embroidery, central kilim, stylized crab border, 72 x 50 (4205/92)   8250
Yomud animal trapping, latchhook guls, 28 x 16 (4089/47)   3400
Yomud bags, pair (complete), moth damage, 37 x 18 (4089/77)   150
Yomud embroidered bagface, red field with blue guls, 51 x 29 (4089/12)   300
Yomud saddle cover, Geometric and solid striped field, 50 x 49 (4089/48)   2500
Yomud Turcoman rug, red field, checkered medallion border, 99 x 74 (4089/74)   600
Yoruk rug, burgundy field, 4 medallions, 96 x 46 (4089/45)   450
Zil-I-Soltan, flowers, 6' 4' x 4' 7' (4198/79)   7000

Chapter 17

Photographic Images

Being relatively new, the market in photography often behaves erratically, but interest in the field is without question strongly on the rise. The price of a print is affected by a number of factors, including the importance of the photographer and the subject, and the age and any historical significance of the print. However, perhaps the most important factor and the most difficult for the layman to evaluate is the condition and quality of the print itself. Thus, two prints from the same negative frequently sell for widely differing amounts.

All these factors appear to have been at work in recent sales. A Thomas Eakins portrait and a print of the *The Vanishing Race* by Edward Curtis sold well. A series of celebrity portraits by Cecil Beaton and his private snapshot albums also were well received—a good example of a great photographer matched with interesting subjects. Similarly, Lewis Carroll's portrait *Alice and Lorinna Liddell* and Steichen's *Portrait of Greta Garbo* both received high prices.

It was disappointing, however, to see a series of rare studies, *Gettysburg,* by the studio of Mathew Brady receive little attention and to see a splendid portrait series, *American Statesmen,* and a *Sequence 17,* both by Minor White, go unbought, although they were sold privately several days after the SPB sale.

Among current photographers, Richard Avedon and Ansel Adams prints sold well. On the negative side, four studies of *The Interior of the Arensberg Apartment* failed to sell.

Photography's sales strength continues to lie with high-quality nineteenth- and twentieth-century works by leading photographers. The number of buyers and their sophistication is increasing dramatically. Prices will certainly keep rising as more and more people enter the field and the scarcity of fine material becomes more widely appreciated.

NINETEENTH CENTURY

Anonymous, WOODLANDS INDIAN, PORTRAIT OF, 1840's, daguerreotype, sixth plate (4175/18)   *$325*

Anonymous (Jackson?), DEVIL'S GATE, albumen, 7½ 5¼, d1870's (684/1112)   30

Anonymous Photographer, FRENCH STEAM ENGINE, 1884, 10½ x 14½, albumen (4175/169)   100

Anonymous Photographer, WATERFALLS, half-plate daguerreotype, case, scratched, d.1850s (684/1011)   425

Anonymous Royal Engineer Photog, SPOKANE CHIEF AND WIFE, 1860, 7¾ x 9½, albumen (4175/71)   500

Anschutz, Thomas, MOTHER AND CHILD, 1895, 7⅛ x 5⅜, silver (4175/52)   175

Aubry, Charles, IRIS, 1860, 14¼ x 10¾, albumen (4175/164)   175

Baldus, Eduoard Denis, PALAIS DU LUXEMBOURG A PARIS, 7⅞ x 10¼, salt print (4175/153)   100

Barnard, George N., Photographic views of Sherman's Campaign, 61, albumen prints, 10 x 14, 1866 (4267/619)   9750

Bisson Freres, DEPART DES GRANDS MULETS, 1861, 9½ x 15½, albumen (4175/152)   250

Bisson Freres, NOTRE DAME, 1854, 18 x 10⅛, heliogravure (4175/151)   *375*

Brady, Mathew, ABRAHAM LINCOLN, PORTRAIT OF, 1863, carte de visite, albumen (4175/6)   125

Brady, Mathew or associate, WOODS ON LEFT, CUPOLA IN DISTANCE, 6⅛ x 8¼, albumen (4175/9)   250

Brady, Mathew, or associatae, CEMETERY HILL, DR. HOLMES TENT, 1863, 6⅜ x 8⅞, albumen (4175/11)   175

Brady, Mathew, or associate, CEMETERY, 1863, 6¾ x 9¼, albumen (4175/14)   100

Brady, Mathew, or associate, PENNSYLVANIA COLLEGE, 1863, 5⅞ x 8⅞, albumen (4175/10)   50

Brady, Mathew, or associate, SUGAR LOAF MOUNTAIN, 1863, 6⅜ x 9¼, albumen (4175/13)   150

Brady, Mathew, studio of, ULYSSES S. GRANT, PORTRAIT OF, 1869, cabinet card, albumen (4175/7)   70

Brady, Mathew, PORTRAIT OF A GENTLEMAN,¼ plate daguerreotype (684/988)   80

Brady, Mathew attributed to, GROUP PORTRAIT OF COURT OF COMMISSIONERS, albumen print, 15¾ x 18, d.1885 (684/989)   125

Brady, Mathew studio of, PORTRAIT OF ABRAHAM LINCOLN, copy print, post 1863 (684/995)   80

Carjat, Etienne, PORTRAIT OF AUGUSTE BARBIER, 1860's, 9¾ x 7¼, albumen (4175/186)   75

Carjat, Etienne, PORTRAIT OF CHARLES BAUDELAIRE, 1860's, 9 x 7¼, woodbury type (4175/184)   400

Carjat, Etienne, PORTRAIT OF VICTOR HUGO, 1860, 8 x 6, albumen (4175/187)   75

Cheney, R.H., BURLINGTON HOUSE ARCADE, 1853, 7 x 8¾, albumenized salt (4175/76)   325

Cheney, R.H., BURLINGTON HOUSE, COURTYARD, 1853, 7 x 8¾, albumenized salt (4175/75)   325

Clifford, Charles, PHILLIP II'S SPANISH SUIT OF ARMOUR, 1857, 17½ x 8¾, albumen (4175/78)   275

Collard, JARDIN DES PLANTES IN SERRES, albumen, 9 x 13, stamped, 1860's (684/1038)   125

Collard, JARDIN DES PLANTES, 1860's, 9 x 13, albumen (4175/154)   275

Curtis, Edward S., PORTRAIT OF AN INDIAN WOMAN, silver print, 7 x 6 (684/1007)   175

Curtis, Edward S. after, NAVAHO MEDICINE MAN, photogravure, matted but unframed, 7¼ x 5¼ (684/1003)   30

Eakins, Thomas, MARGARET EAKINS AND 'HARRY', 1880, 2½ x 2, albumen (4175/50)   2900

Eakins, Thomas, WILL, 'HARRY', MARGARET AND ARTIE CROWELL, 1883, 3⅝ x 3¼, albumen (4175/51)   *1500*

Famin, C., STUDY OF TREES, 1870's, 13¼ x 10, albumen (4175/163)   500

Frith, Francis, THE MOSQUE OF THE EMEER AKHOOR, CAIRO, albumen, mammoth plate, 1858 (684/1042)   550

Gardner, Alexander, Photographic sketch book of war, 100 albumen, prints, 1865-66 (4267/683)   13000

Gardner, Alexander, CAMP OF THE 3rd CORPS NEAR CULPEPER, inscribed on reverse (684/990)   150

Gardner, Alexander, PORTRAIT OF ABRAHAM LINCOLN, silver print, 14 x 10½, ca1861 (684/993)   700

Genthe, Arnold, CHINATOWN, silver print, unfr., 11⅜ x 7¼ (684/1086)   225

Genthe, Arnold, MARKETING IN OLD CHINATOWN, silver print, unfr., 8⅛ x 11¾ (684/1087)   225

Genthe, Arnold, VEGETABLE PEDDLER, OLD CHINATOWN, SAN FRAN., silver print, unfr., 8½ x 12½ (684/1085)   225

Hill, D.O., and Adamson, Robert, PORTRAIT OF PROFESSOR JOHN WILSON, 1843, 48 x 5¾, calotype (4175/72)   *600*

Huffman, Laton, THE BADLANDS, 5¾ x 7½, gelatin (4175/65)   75

Huffman, Laton, TWO YOUNG CHEYENNES IN WAR COSTUME, 1858, 7¾ x 5¾, gelatin (4175/64)   100

Jackson, William Henry, TRAIL IN WEST GALLATIN CANYON, 1873, Survey print, albumen (4175/33)   125

Jarger, H., LITTLE FALLS BRIDGE, PATTERSON,N.J., 1885, 13¾ x 16¼, albumen (4175/39)   100

Langenheim, F., LIEUT. GENERAL (WINFIELD) SCOTT AT WEST POINT, glass stereo slide, ca1865 (684/1069)   60

MacPherson, Robert, ETRUSCAN GATEWAY AT PERUGIA, 1850's, 9⅝ x 16⅛, albumen (4175/107)   250

MacPherson, Robert, FALLS OF TERNI, 1850's, 9⅝ x 16⅛, albumen (4175/106)   175
MacPherson, Robert, TEMPLE OF VENUS AND ROME, 1850's, 11 x 15¾, albumen (4175/105)   175
McAllister, T.H., A GROUP OF SIXTY GLASS NEGATIVES, location, inscribed, some unlabeled
(684/1027)   60
Muybridge, Eadweard, WOMAN THROWING AWAY WATER FROM DISH, 1887, collotype
locomotion plate (4175/48)   200
Muybridge, Eadweard, GIRL WITH BASKET AND ROD STEPPING, 1887, collotype locomotion plate
(4175/47)   100
Muybridge, Eadweard, WILDCAT FALL,YOSEMITE VALLEY, 1870's, mammoth plate #30, albumen
(4175/41)   1300
Nadar, Gaspard Felix Tournachon, PORTRAIT OF A SIAMESE DIPLOMAT, carte de visite, 1861
(4175/175)   200
O'Sullivan, Timothy, ANCIENT RUINS, CANYON DE CHELLY, N.M.,1871, 11 x 8, albumen
(4175/29)   1000
Petit, Pierre, PORTRAIT OF GARIBALDI, 1860's, 10 x 7½, albumen (4175/182)   50
Savage and Ottinger, BRIGHAM YOUNG, PORTRAIT OF, 1860's, carte de visite, albumen
(4175/24)   400
Stewart, John, PONT SUR LA ROUTE DE GABAS, 1858, 8⅞ x 10½, Blanquart-Evrard (4175/150)   500
Stieglitz, Alfred, A WET DAY ON THE BOULEVARD, PARIS, 1897, 6 x 11, photogravure (4175/255)   1100
Stieglitz, Alfred, GLOW OF NIGHT, NEW YORK, 1897, 4¾ x 9¼, photogravure (4175/256)   225
Stieglitz, Alfred, REFLECTIONS VENICE, 1897, 8⅜ x 11½, photogravure (4175/258)   500
Stoddard, AUSABLE CHASM-GRAND FLUME FROM THE NARROWS, 1874, 13⅝ x 9 (654/457)   80
Teynard, Felix, EGYPTIAN RUIN, 1851-52, 9 x 11⅜, salt print (4175/143)   125
Thomson, John, LONDON BOARDMAN, 1887, 4½ x 3¼, woodbury type (4175/92)   *150*

Anonymous
(4175/18)

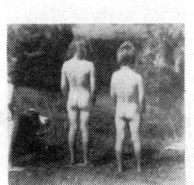

Eakins (4175/51)

Bisson Freres (4175/151)

Thomson (4175/92)

Hill (4175/72)

Thomson, John, STRAWBERRIES, ALL RIPE, ALL RIPE, 1887, 3½ x 4½, woodbury type (4175/93)   130
Warren, Henry F. PORTRAIT OF ABRAHAM LINCOLN, albumen, 7½ x 5½ oval, d.1865 (684/994)   175
Watkins, Carl, EL CAPITAN, 3,300 FEET, YOSEMITE, CAL., 1870'S, mammoth plate, albumen
(4175/30)   300
Watkins, Carl, PARROT ESTATE, SAN MATEO, CAL., 1870's, mammoth plate, albumen (4175/31)   350
White, Clarence, WOMAN BLOWING A BUBBLE, 1898, 8 X 5⅛, platinum (4175/250)   650
Williams, James Leon, TWO VILLAGERS, STRATFORD ON AVON, 1891, 13½ x 17, carbon
(4175/103)   200

TWENTIETH CENTURY

Abbot, Bernice, A WET DAY ON THE BOULEVARD, PARIS, 1897, 9⅝ x 7⅝, silver (4175/301)   *450*
Abbot, Bernice, JAY STREET #115, 1936, 9⅛ x 7¼, silver (4175/302)   200
Abbot, Bernice, RADIO ROW, COURTLANDT STREET, 1936, 7½ x 9¾, silver (4175/299)   250
Adams, Ansel, ASPENS, NEW MEXICO, 1958, 20 x 15½, silver (4175/411)   2500
Adams, Ansel, AT CHINESE CAMP, CALIFORNIA, silver print, 9½ x 7½ (684/1125)   300

Adams, Ansel, EUCALYPTUS TREE, FOG, FORT ROSS, CA. 1954, 19 x 14, silver (4175/413) 750
Adams, Ansel, EVENING CLOUD, SIERRA NEVADA, OWENS VALLEY, 1960, 19½ x 15¼, silver (4175/406) 1100
Adams, Ansel, FERN SPRING, DUSK, silver print, 12½ x 9 ca1961, printed later (684/1111) 225
Adams, Ansel, FERNS, HAWAII NATIONAL PARK, silver print, 15½ x 19½ (684/1126) 800
Adams, Ansel, FOREST AND STREAM, NORTHERN CALIFORNIA, 1959, 15¼ x 19¼, silver (4175/412) *850*
Adams, Ansel, GATE-CORDOVA, NEW MEXICO, silver print, 3⅛ x 4¼ (654/481) 225
Adams, Ansel, INDIAN GRAVESTONE CARVING, 1948, 10 x 12½, silver (4175/410) 350
Adams, Ansel, JULIAN MARTINEZ, SAN ILDEFONSO PUEBLO, 1928, 13¼ x 10, silver (4175/404) 300
Adams, Ansel, LEAVES, GLACIER NATIONAL PARK, silver print, 14⅜ x 18½ (684/1127) 800
Adams, Ansel, MADONNA AND CHILD, TRAMPAS, NEW MEXICO, 1966, 12½ x 10, silver (4175/416) 300
Adams, Ansel, MOON AND CLOUDS, NORTHERN CALIFORNIA, 1959, 15½ x 99½, silver (4175/418) 2100
Adams, Ansel, MOONRISE, HERNANDEZ, NEW MEXICO, 1941, 15⅜ x 19¼, silver (4175/407) 5200
Adams, Ansel, OLD FAITHFUL GEYSER, YELLOWSTONE, 19½ x 14½, silver (4175/419) 750
Adams, Ansel, WHITE STUMPS,MONO LAKE, CALIFORNIA, 7⅜ x 9⅜, silver (4175/415) 300
Anonymous Photographer, MARGARET BOURKE-WHITE IN RUSSIA, 6 x 7¼, silver (4175/293) 100
Atget, Eugene, ST. CLOUD, 1900, #1212, 6⅞x 8¾, albumen (4175/201) 800
Atget/Abbot, VEGETABLE MARKET, PARIS, 9 x 6⅝, Sepia-toned silver (4175/200) 300
Baron Von Gloeden, SEATED YOUTH AND CHILD WITH ROSES, 1900's, 15¼ x 11⅜, pigment print (4175/202) 550
Beaton, Cecil, ALAN WEBB, 9 x 9, Bromide (4178/469) 125
Beaton, Cecil, ANDRE COURREGES IN HIS ALL WHITE SALON, 1968, 9¼ x 9¼, Bromide (4178/426) 150
Beaton, Cecil, ANDY WARHOL, 1969, 9 5/16 x 9 7/16, Bromide (4178/595) 400
Beaton, Cecil, ANITA LOOS, 7½ x 6, Bromide (4178/512) 225
Beaton, Cecil, ANYA LINDER, 10 x 8, Bromide (4178/546) 100
Beaton, Cecil, AUDREY HEPBURN, 10⅛ x 9⅝, Bromide (4178/586) 450
Beaton, Cecil, AUGUSTUS JOHN, 8¼ x 7⅛, Bromide (4178/526) 150
Beaton, Cecil, BABA BEATON IN FANCY DRESS, 9½ x 7¼, Bromide (4178/475) 375
Beaton, Cecil, BALLET-BACKSTAGE, 1937, 7⅜ x 8¼, Bromide (4178/545) 200
Beaton, Cecil, BARANOVA BACKSTAGE, 9½ x 7½, Bromide (4178/544) 275
Beaton, Cecil, BEATRICE LILLIE, 9½ x 8¼, Bromide (4178/515) 150
Beaton, Cecil, BENJAMIN BRITTEN, 9½ x 7, Bromide (4178/537) 125
Beaton, Cecil, BOWERY DESIGN, 1937, 10¼ x 10¼, Bromide (4178/556) 250
Beaton, Cecil, BROADWAY ABSTRACTS, 1937, 8¾ x 10¼, Bromide (4178/555) 175
Beaton, Cecil, CAROLINE KENNEDY, 9⅞ x 7⅛, Bromide (4178/593) 175
Beaton, Cecil, CECIL BEATON IN NEW YORK, SUNDAY MORNING, 1937, 6⅞ x 8¼, Bromide (4178/434) 300
Beaton, Cecil, CHARLES FORD, 10½ x 10, Bromide (4178/514) 300
Beaton, Cecil, COBINA WRIGHT MODELLING AN EVENING DRESS, 1930, 7½ x 9½, Bromide (4178/403) 75
Beaton, Cecil, DANILOVA AT CURTAIN CALL, 1937, 10 x 8, Bromide (4178/543) 325
Beaton, Cecil, DAVID HOCKNEY, 12¼ x 18, Bromide (4178/599) 175
Beaton, Cecil, DOMIVA, HEAD AND SHOULDERS, 1950's, 7⅞ x 7⅝, Bromide (4178/424) 125
Beaton, Cecil, DORIEN LEIGH MODELLING AN EVENING DRESS, 1950, 10 x 8, Bromide (4178/401) 125
Beaton, Cecil, DOUBLE EXPOSURE STUDY, mid 1930's, 9 x 8, Bromide (4178/413) 125
Beaton, Cecil, DRUGSTORE SERVICE, 1937, 10¼ x 10¼, Bromide (4178/563) 325
Beaton, Cecil, DUCHESS OF WINDSOR, BOULEVARD SUCHET, 1939, 8 x 6½, Bromide (4178/492) 200
Beaton, Cecil, EDITH SITWELL, 1927, 10 x 8, Bromide (4178/507) 475
Beaton, Cecil, EISENHOWER, 7⅝ x 7 11/16, Bromide (4178/569) 200
Beaton, Cecil, ERTE, 1967, 5 x 7, Bromide (4178/541) 275
Beaton, Cecil, EVELYN WAUGH, 1955, 8 x 7½, Bromide (4178/511) 150
Beaton, Cecil, FASHION ALBUM, 1965-70, Bromide prints-170 (4178/554) 500
Beaton, Cecil, FASHION STUDY AGAINST DRAPED NET, 1930, 9 5/16 x 7, Bromide (4178/402) 175
Beaton, Cecil, FASHION STUDY IN WHITE PAPER, late 1930's, 9½ x 6¾, Bromide (4178/406) 225
Beaton, Cecil, GARY COOPER, 10 x 8, Bromide (4178/453) 1200
Beaton, Cecil, GEORGE LYNES, 9¼ x 7, Bromide (4178/533) 225
Beaton, Cecil, GEORGIA O'KEEFE, 1966, 9¼ x 9½, Bromide (4178/535) 500
Beaton, Cecil, GERTRUDE LAWRENCE, 1930, 10 x 8, Bromide (4178/447) 400
Beaton, Cecil, GERTRUDE STEIN, 9½ x 8, Bromide (4178/522) 225
Beaton, Cecil, GIACOMETTI, 1957, 10 x 9¾, Bromide (4178/532) 350
Beaton, Cecil, GRAND ENGLISH INTERIOR, 9 x 7, Bromide (4178/575) 225
Beaton, Cecil, GRETA GARBO, 10 x 8, Bromide (4178/455) 200

Beaton, Cecil, GROUP IN TANGIER, 1950, 10 x 9½, Bromide (4178/531)   300
Beaton, Cecil, ICE DELIVERY CART, 1937, 10¼ x 10¼, Bromide (4178/558)   200
Beaton, Cecil, IRVING PENN, 10 x 8, Bromide (4178/534)   250
Beaton, Cecil, IVY COMPTON BURNETT, 1949, 8 x 7, Bromide (4178/516)   175
Beaton, Cecil, JACK WARNER, 13 x 8, Bromide (4178/460)   200
Beaton, Cecil, JAPAN IN WINTER, 14 x 11, Bromide (4178/573)   200
Beaton, Cecil, JAPAN-GEISHA, 10 x 8, Bromide (4178/572)   100
Beaton, Cecil, JEAN COCTEAU, 9⅜ x 9⅞, Bromide (4178/519)   600
Beaton, Cecil, JEAN SHRIMPTON, 1960's, 13⅞ x 11, Bromide (4178/427)   300
Beaton, Cecil, JOAN BENNETT, 1930's, 8 x 10, Bromide (4178/449)   125
Beaton, Cecil, JOAN CRAWFORD, 8 x 7¾, Bromide (4178/466)   200
Beaton, Cecil, JOHNNIE WEISSMULLER, 9 x 8, Bromide (4178/452)   300
Beaton, Cecil, KATHERINE HEPBURN, 10 x 8, Bromide (4178/463)   225
Beaton, Cecil, KAY FRANCIS IN VICE SQUAD, 1931, 10 x 8⅛, Bromide (4178/448)   200
Beaton, Cecil, KAY THOMPSON, 8 x 7, Bromide (4178/464)   50
Beaton, Cecil, LADY LOUIS MOUNTBATTEN, 13 x 10½, Bromide (4178/481)   850
Beaton, Cecil, LADY MENDL IN A WINTERHALTER DRESS CHEZ ELLE, 10 x 8, Bromide (4178/505)   275
Beaton, Cecil, LILY LANGTRY IN OLD AGE, late 1920's, 8 x 6, Bromide (4178/456)   300
Beaton, Cecil, LOELIA DUCHESS OF WESTMINSTER, 13½ x 9¾, Bromide (4178/487)   225
Beaton, Cecil, LORD AND LADY PEMBROKE, 10 x 9¾ (4178/496)   225
Beaton, Cecil, MAE MURRAY, 10 x 8, Bromide (4178/461)   100
Beaton, Cecil, MAE WEST, 9 x 9, Bromide (4178/468)   175
Beaton, Cecil, MARGOT FONTEYN, 1967, 9¾ x 10⅜, Bromide (4178/548)   225
Beaton, Cecil, MARILYN MONROE, 1956, 8⅛ x 7⅞, Bromide (4178/589)   600
Beaton, Cecil, MARKEVITCH, 1937, 10 x 8, Bromide (4178/513)   200
Beaton, Cecil, MARLENE DIETRICH, 10 x 8, Bromide (4178/454)   550
Beaton, Cecil, MARLON BRANDO, 9 x 8, Bromide (4178/457)   850
Beaton, Cecil, MARY TAYLOR, 10 x 8, Bromide (4178/488)   150
Beaton, Cecil, MICK JAGGER, 1970, 7¾ x 11½, Bromide (4178/598)   325
Beaton, Cecil, MISS CLARA DI URIBURU, 11½ x 9¼, Bromide (4178/480)   250
Beaton, Cecil, MME COLLETTE, 1929, 6 x 7, Bromide (4178/524)   600
Beaton, Cecil, MR & MRS ROBERT KENNEDY, 9½ x 9½, Bromide (4178/592)   200
Beaton, Cecil, MR. AND MRS. JOHN BARRY-RYAN, 8 x 10, Bromide (4178/539)   100
Beaton, Cecil, MRS ASTOR, 1970, 9½ x 9½, Bromide (4178/588)   250
Beaton, Cecil, MRS DUDELY WARD, 9½ x 11½, Bromide (4178/479)   400
Beaton, Cecil, MRS HARRISON WILLIAMS AND DOG THROUGH PAPER, 10 x 8, Bromide (4178/503)   175
Beaton, Cecil, MRS JAMES IN DRESS CREATED BY MR. JAMES, 1955, 9⅛ x 9⅜, Bromide (4178/420)   275
Beaton, Cecil, NANCY CUNARD, 9¼ x 8½, Bromide (4178/521)   550
Beaton, Cecil, NATALIE PALEY AND FRIEND, 10 x 8, Bromide (4178/502)   300
Beaton, Cecil, NOEL COWARD, 1942, 8½ x 6, Bromide (4178/510)   450
Beaton, Cecil, NORA HOLT, 1930, 10 x 8, Bromide (4178/508)   175
Beaton, Cecil, NUREYEV-HEAD AND SHOULDERS, 1972, 17⅜ x 17⅜, Bromide (4178/549)   400
Beaton, Cecil, ORSON WELLES, 10 x 8, Bromide (4178/459)   225
Beaton, Cecil, PHOTO ALBUM-EARLY YEARS, Bromide prints-600 (4178/551)   2100
Beaton, Cecil, PICASSO, 1965, 9½ x 7¾, Bromide (4178/540)   600
Beaton, Cecil, PRINCESS LEE RADZIWELL, 1967, 9½ x 9½, Bromide (4178/591)   250
Beaton, Cecil, RAOUL DUFY, 8¼ x 10½, Bromide (4178/527)   100
Beaton, Cecil, ROYAL BALLET SCHOOL AT RICHMOND, 7⅜ x 7⅜, Bromide (4178/550)   150
Beaton, Cecil, SALVADOR DALI, 9⅜ x 7½, Bromide (4178/520)   275

Adams (4175/412)

Beaton, Cecil, SCRAP BOOK ALBUM-MISC, 1960, Bromide prints (4178/553) 150

Beaton, Cecil, SELF PORTRAIT WITH PABLO PICASSO, 11 5/16 x 9 5/16, Bromide (4178/436) 1100

Beaton, Cecil, SIR MAX BEERBOHM, 1930, 9 x 7, Bromide (4178/509) 175

Beaton, Cecil, SNAPSHOT ALBUM, 1930's, Bromide prints-860 (4178/552) 2500

Beaton, Cecil, SYLVIA SYDNEY, 10 x 8, Bromide (4178/451) 75

Beaton, Cecil, TALULLAH BANKHEAD, 13⅞ x 10¾, Bromide (4178/445) 600

Beaton, Cecil, TEHELITCHEW, 9 x 10, Bromide (4178/517) 225

Beaton, Cecil, THE MAHARANEE OF COOCH BEHAR, 8 x 10, Bromide (4178/491) 175

Beaton, Cecil, VIVIEN LEIGH AS ANNA KARENINA, 10 x 9, Bromide (4178/462) 300

Beaton, Cecil, WILLIAM POWELL, 10 x 8, Bromide (4178/450) 200

Beaton, Cecil, YUL BRENNER, 9 x 10, Bromide (4178/458) 175

Beaton, Cecil, 10 DOWNING STREET-CHURCHILL'S BEDROOM, 10⅜ x 9½, Bromide (4178/574) 100

Beaton,Cecil, DUCHESS OF WINDSOR, 10½ x 7¾, Bromide (4178/493) 200

Berrard, Christian, FASHION STUDY, 1930's, 14¾ x 11⅞ (4178/444) 350

Blumenfeld, Erwin, MULTIPLE IMAGE PROFILE, 11½ x 8½, Bromide (4178/443) 300

Blumenfeld, Erwin, PHOTO-DISTORTION, 1950, 13⅜ x 8¾, Colour Print (4178/442) 250

Blumenfield, Erwin, HEAD AND SHOULDERS OF CECIL BEATON, 1940's, 9 x 13, solarized Bromide (4178/433) 300

Bravo, Manuel Alvarez, EL SISTEMA NERVIOSO DEL GRAN SIMPATICO, 1974, 9½ x 7½, silver (4175/358) 175

Bravo, Manuel Alvarez, LA QUEMA, 1974, 6½ x 9¼, silver (4175/357) 100

Breitenbach, Joseph, PORTRAIT OF MAX ERNST, PARIS, 1939, 13¾ x 11, silver (4175/352) *250*

Bruguiere, Francis, LADY IN BLUE, 5 x 7, autochrome (4175/216) 450

Bruguiere, Francis, LANDSCAPE BY SEA, TREE IN FOREGROUND, 5 x 7, autochrome (4175/215) 150

Bullock, John, PORTRAIT OF A YOUNG WOMAN, 7⅜ x 5½, platinum (4175/254) 225

Callahan, Harry, REEDS, numbered EM88, 5½ x 7½, silver (4175/386) 425

Caponigro, Paul, MT. MINGUS, ARIZONA, 6 x 9¾, silver (4175/393) 300

Caponigro, Paul, PEBBLE BEACH, CALIFORNIA, 1970, 7 x 9, silver (4175/394) 150

Caponigro, Paul, WOODS, REDDING, CONN, 1968, 13¾ x 19, silver (4175/395) 475

Carillo, Manuel, BOY WITH HORSES, 7½ x 9¾, silver (4175/360) 100

Cartier-Bresson, Henri, THE POET C.H. FORD IN A FRENCH PISSOIR, 1930's, 6⅜ x 9⅜, Bromide (4178/441) 550

Clark, Larry, YOUNG MAN IN CAR (PROFILE), 5½ x 8¼, silver (4175/403) 150

Clark, Larry, YOUNG MAN WITH PISTOL, 11¼ x 7½, silver (4175/402) 250

Coburn, Alvin Langdon, ROAD TO ALGECIRES, photogravure-camera work, 21, dJanuary, 1908 (684/1113) 40

Cunningham, Imogen, DENNIS, 1972, 7¾ x 6¾, silver (4175/325) 125

Cunningham, Imogen, MAN RAY VERSION OF MAN RAY, 1961, 9⅜ x 6½, silver (4175/322) 400

Cunningham, Imogen, MY FATHER, MOTHER AND BOSSY, 1923, 9 x 12, silver (4175/320) 450

Cunningham, Imogen, PORTRAIT OF GERTRUDE STEIN, 8 x 6¾, silver (4175/323) *700*

Cunningham, Imogen, PORTRAIT OF MINOR WHITE, 1963, 6⅜ x 6⅜, silver (4175/324) 425

Cunningham, Imogen, TRIANGLES, 1928, 4 x 2⅝, silver (4175/321) 850

Curtis, Edward, PORTRAIT OF ALDEN SAMPSON, 1910, 5 x 3½, platinum (4175/55) 275

Curtis, Edward, SIGNAL FIRE TO MOUNTAIN GOD, 13½ x 10½, orotone (4175/59) 1200

Curtis, Edward, THE FISHERMAN, 7⅜ x 9¾, orotone (4175/56) 850

Curtis, Edward, THE VANISHING RACE, 1904, 12½ x 16, sepia-toned silver (4175/61) 650

Curtis, Edward, THE VANISHING RACE, 1904, 15¼ x 21, sepia-toned silver (41475/57) 1800

Curtis, Edward, THREE INDIANS ON HORSEBACK, 1905, 13⅜ x 18⅛, silver (4175/62) 500

Evans, Walker, FARMER'S KITCHEN, HALE COUNTY, ALABAMA, 1936, 9½ x 6⅜, silver (4175/305) *725*

Evans, Frederick, BORROWDALE, 1900, 3⅞ x 2½, platinum (4175/212) 400

Evans, Frederick, CARCASSONE, 1900, 3¼ x 5⅛, platinum (4175/213) 550

Evans, Frederick, CHATEAU LE LUDEJ THE FOSSE, 9½ x 7¾, platinum (4175/209) 600

Evans, Frederick, ELY CATHEDRAL, SOUTH CHOIR AISLE TO EAST, 1900, 9½ x 6⅛, platinum (4175/211) 700

Evans, Frederick, PORTRAIT OF GEORGE BERNARD SHAW, 1902, 9¼ x 4½, platinum (4175/208) 450

Evans, Frederick, WEST TOWER FROM MOAT, 1900's, 9½ x 7¼, platinum (4175/210) *700*

Evans, Walker, GRAVESTONE AND GRAVE OF CHILD, ALABAMA, 1936, 7¼ x 9¼, 1936 (4175/304) 425

Evans, Walker, MARY FRANK'S BEDROOM, 1959, 10¼ x 10½, silver (4175/306) 450

Evans, Walker, SUBWAY PORTRAIT, 1941, 7 x 10, silver (4175/308) 250

Evans, Walker, SUBWAY PORTRAIT, 1941, 7 x 10, silver (4175/307) 350

Genthe, Arnold, AINOU CHILDREN, 1908, 8¾ x 6⅞, silver (4175/222) 100

Genthe, Arnold, CHINATOWN, GROUP OF FOUR CHILDREN, 1905, 8 x 9⅞, silver (4175/220) 350

Genthe, Arnold, CHINATOWN, GROUP OF FOUR CHILDREN, 1905, 10 x 8, silver (4175/217) 350

Genthe, Arnold, CHINATOWN, TWO CHILDREN, 1905, 10 x 7 3/9, silver (4175/218) 250

Genthe, Arnold, CHINATOWN, TWO MEN SELLING WARES, 1905, 7⅞ x 9⅞, silver (4175/219) 250

Genthe, Arnold, CHINATOWN YOUNG GIRL, 1905, 10 x 8, silver (4175/221) 350

Genthe, Arnold, ELDERLY AINOU COUPLE, 1908, 8⅝ x 7⅜, silver (4175/223)   125
Genthe, Arnold, PORTRAIT OF AN ELDERLY AINOU MAN, 1908, 10 x 8, silver (4175/226)   125
Genthe, Arnold, PORTRAIT OF AN ELDERLY AINOU MAN, 1908, 10 x 8, silver (4175/225)   300
Genthe, Arnold, TWO BIRDS, ISLAND OF YEZE, JAPAN, 1908, 7¼ x 8⅝, silver (4175/224)   100
Gloeden, Baron von, MEDITERRANEAN YOUTH, 1900, 8⅝ x 6½, Albumen (4178/437)   400
Greene, Milton, PORTRAIT OF MARILYN MONROE, 1952, 15½ x 19½, silver (4175/385)   400
Greene, Milton, PORTRAIT OF MARLENE DIETRICH, 1952, 16 x 19½, silver (4175/383)   225
Greene, Milton, PORTRAIT OF MARLENE DIETRICH, 1952, 15½ x 15½, silver (4175/384)   450
Grotz, Paul, PORTRAIT OF WALKER EVANS, 1929, 8 x 5¼, silver (4175/303)   350
Hausmann, Raoul, MELANOGRAPHIE, 1931, 7¾ x 11¾, silver (4175/351)   175
Hausmann, Raoul, MELANOGRAPHIE, 1931, 7¾ x 11¾, silver (4175/349)   200
Henri, Florence, SELF PORTRAIT, 1928, 11 x 7½, silver (4175/328)   200
Hesse, Edwin Bower, PORTRAIT OF A MODEL, ca1920, 16¼ x 13¼ (654/469)   10
Huene, George Hoyningen, GARY COOPER, 10⅛ x 8 (4178/440)   600
Huene, George Hoyningen, HALF FIGURE PORTRAIT OF BEATON, 1933, 8½ x 6½, Bromide (4178/432)   350
Hurrell, GRETA GARBO, 12⅞ x 10, Bromide (4178/439)   100
Kasebier, Gertrude, PORTRAIT OF MARTINE MC CULLOCH, 8 x 6 platinum (4175/253)   525
Kasebier, Gertrude, THE READERS, 1908, 5⅞ x 4, platiinum (4175/252)   350
Kertesz, Andre, CHAGALL AND HIS FAMILY, 1933, 7¾ x 9¾, silver (4175/330)   500
Kertesz, Andre, CHEZ MONDRIAN, 1926, 14 x 11, silver (4175/329)   850
Kertesz, Andre, DISTORTION 5', 1933, 9½ x 6, silver (4175/331)   275
Leigh-Hunt, Jocelyn, PORTRAIT OF ALFRED ALOYSIUS HORN, 1927, 6 x 8¼, silver (4175/327)   75
Lynnes, George Platt, FULL FIGURE PORTRAIT OF BEATON, 1930's, 8⅞ x 6⅞, Bromide (4178/429)   250

Breitenbach (4175/352)

Evans (4175/210)

Greene (4175/384)

Evans (4175/305)

Tiffany (4175/195)

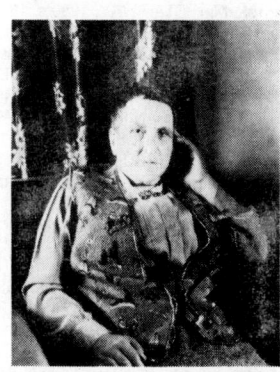
Cunningham (4175/323)

Man Ray, GERTRUDE STEIN AND ALICE B. TOKLAS, 1923, 3¾ x 4⅝, silver (4175/337)	2200
Man Ray, RAYOGRAPH, 8½ x 6¾, silver (4175/339)	375
Man Ray, SELF PORTRAIT, 1960, 6½ x 8¼, silver (4175/338)	225
Martensen, William, PORTRAIT OF MYRDITH, 1927, 7½ x 5¾, silver (4175/275)	300
Mather, Margarithe, BLANCHE SWEET'S BEDROOM, 1927, 9 x 6⅞, silver (4175/271)	350
Mather, Margarithe, PORTRAIT OF HAROLD GRIEVE AND JETTA GOODALL, 1930, 7 x 9, silver (4175/270)	400
McBean, Angus, SYDNEY HOWARD AND ARTHUR RISCOE, 1938, 19½ x 14¼, silver (4175/335)	150
Meatyard, Ralph, CHINA DOLL AND FLOWERS, silver print, 7½ x 7⅜, d1950's, printed later (684/1124)	60
Mortensen, William, PREPARATION FOR THE SABBOTH, 1926, 14¼ x 11¾, pigment (4175/276)	500
North, Peter, HEAD AND SHOULDERS OF CECIL BEATON, 11⅜ x 9, Bromide (4178/428)	50
Notman, William, HARVARD 36-YALE O, 1914, 14½ x 53, gelatin panorama (4175/227)	375
Penn, Irving, BEATON AND ARTIST FRIENDS, 1947, 8 x 10, Bromide (4178/430)	350
Reed, Roland, INDIANS WORSHIPPING, 19 x 15¼, silver (4175/70)	350
Reed, Roland, PIGEON HUNTING GROUND, 1913, 15¾ x 20½, sepia toned silver (4175/69)	350
Rothstein, Arthur, CLOSED BANK, HAVERHILL, IOWA, silver print, 7 x 9½, ca1939 (684/1017)	40
Sander, August, PORTRAIT OF GERMAN PEASANT, 1930's, 11½ x 8¾, silver (4175/347)	225
Smith, W. Eugene, SCHWEITZER BUILDING PORTABLE RAILROAD, 1954, 9 x 12½, silver (4175/391)	325
Smith, W. Eugene, SPANISH WAKE, 1951, 8¾ x 13, silver (4175/389)	850
Sommer, Frederick, DEAD RABBIT, 1940, 7½ x 9½, silver (4175/362)	1300
Steichen, Edward, ANATOLE FRANCE, photogravure-camera work 42/, 43, d1913 (684/1101)	50
Steichen, Edward, BALZAC-THE SILHOUETTE, A.M., photogravure, camera work, 42/43, d1913 (684/1098)	100
Steichen, Edward, BALZAC-THE OPEN SKY, photogravure-camera, work 34/35, d.1911 (684/1095)	110
Steichen, Edward, BALZAC-TOWARDS THE LIGHT, MIDNIGHT, photogravure-camera work, d.1911 (684/1094)	140
Steichen, Edward, CYCLAMEN-MRS. PHILIP LYDIG, photogravure- camera work 34/35, d.1913 (684/1096)	80
Steichen, Edward, HENRY W. TAFT, photogravure-camera work 42/43, d1913 (684/1103)	50
Steichen, Edward, LATE AFTERNOON-VENICE, photogravure-camera, work, 42/43, d1913 (684/1099)	160
Steichen, Edward, MARY LEARNS TO WALK, photogravure-camera work, 42/43, d1913 (684/1102)	50
Steichen, Edward, NOCTURNE-ORANGERIE STAIRCASE, photogravure- camera work, 42/43, d1913 (684/1097)	120
Steichen, Edward, PASTORAL-MOONLIGHT, hardtoned photogravure- camera work 19, d.July 1907 (684/1115)	140
Steichen, Edward, VITALITY-YVETTE GUILBERT, photogravure- camera work, 42/43, d1913 (684/1093)	150
Stieglitz, Alfred, PORTRAIT OF FARMER WITH DAUGHTER, 4½ x 3½, silver mounted (4175/264)	450
Stieglitz, Alfred, THE FERRY BOAT, 1910, photogravure (4175/261)	500
Stieglitz, Alfred, THE NEW YORK CENTRAL YARDS, 1903, photogravure (4175/260)	375
Stieglitz, Alfred, THE STEERAGE, 12⅝ x 10⅝, photogravure (4175/262)	1600
Stoumen, Lou, TIMES SQUARE IN RAIN, 1940, 16¾ x 12⅝, silver (4175/369)	175
Thorek, Max, JUDITH, 1930's, 15¾ x 12⅞, toned silver (4175/282)	350
Thorek, Max, STAIRWAY, 1930's, 13 x 10¼, toned silver (4175/283)	200
Tice, George A., PETIT MOBIL STATION AND WATER TOWER, 1974, 10½ x 13, silver (4175/399)	250
Tiffany, Louis Comfort, PUMPKINS, silver print, 7⅜ x 9½ (684/1119)	100
Tiffany, Louis Comfort, STALK OF LILIES, 9¾ x 8 (684/1118)	100
Tiffany, Louis Comfort, STUDY OF IRISES, 9½ x 7⅜, albumen (4175/195)	375
Vane, Caleb D., SAN FRANCISCO EARTHQUAKE, silver prints, 1906, 7¾ x 9¾ (654/467)	50
Weegee, MRS. VANDERBILT, 1940, 13⅜ x 10⅝, silver (4175/375)	175
Weegee, MURDERED MAN HELL'S KITCHEN, 13⅞ x 10⅝, silver (4175/372)	300
Weegee, NEW YORK (three photographs), silver prints, 1940's/50's (684/1128)	50
Weegee, TENEMENT PENTHOUSE, 1940, 13⅜ x 10⅝, silver (4175/374)	400
Weegee, THE CIRCUS (three photographs), silver prints, 1940's (684/1129)	30
Weegee, THE CRITIC, 1940, 10⅝ x 13⅜, silver (4175/376)	650
Weegee, WOMAN DRIVER JUST AFTER FATAL COLLISION, 1940, 10⅝ x 13⅜, silver (4175/373)	250
Weston, Brett, NEW YORK GARBAGE CAN, 1945, 10¼ x 13½, silver (4175/370)	400
Weston, Edward, CAT IN BASKET, 1934, 7¾ x 9½, silver (4175/317)	700
Weston, Edward, KELP, 1936, 7½ x 9⅜, silver (4175/319)	850
Weston, Edward, NUDE, 1934, 4½ x 3¾, silver (4175/316)	450
Weston, Edward, PORTRAIT OF NAHUI OLIN, 1926, 9⅛ x 7, silver (4175/314)	1300

Chapter 18

Old Master Paintings, Drawings and Sculpture

The market for Old Master paintings is rapidly changing. A new wave of American collectors, most of them young and middle-class, have become active at auctions, purchasing perhaps half of all items sold in this field. Knowledgeable and shrewd, they have stimulated interest and rising prices in several areas relatively neglected until recent years, particularly Dutch and Flemish works and English portraiture.

Though all Dutch and Flemish paintings sell well, those of indisputable authorship, relatively small size and good condition sell for far more than works that fail of those criteria. Though the lesser lights of this field have enjoyed the steepest climb in prices, the great names never fail to generate strong bidding.

Eighteenth-century French painting, always popular, remained strong. There were even indications of increased interest in post-Revolution works.

Seeking an area where attractive paintings are available and undervalued, young American collectors have siezed on eighteenth-century English portraits. Although prices are still modest, high-quality works now command sums many times higher than just a few years ago. And interest seems to be spreading from portraiture into collateral areas like sporting scenes.

New collectors are continually entering the Old Master market and will doubtless push the field on to further gains. Dutch and Flemish works should maintain their strong rate of appreciation, while English portraits and early drawings seem poised for a dramatic surge. Increased interest in one segment of the market almost always spills over into related areas, so collectors should watch the whole of the market for signs of activity in currently undervalued fields.

Abbott, Lemuel Francis, circle of, PORTRAIT OF ARCHIBALD·TROTTER, 29 x 23, (4224/36) $600
After Peter Bruegel the elder, A MAN OF WAR BETWEEN TWO ARMED GALLEYS, 8½ x 11½
(4078/11)   600
After Peter Bruegel the elder, INSIDIOSUS AUCHEPS, 12 x 17, stained (4078/10)   200
Albrici, Enrico, A GROTESQUE, AN ELEGANT COUPLE IN A CHARIOT, 10 x 14½ (4258/65)   2300
Allori, Christofanco, THE HOSPITALITY OF SAINT JULIEN, 64½ x 48 (633/170)   1100
Anderson, William, SHIPPING SCENES, pr, on panel, 5 x 7 (4068/7)   4750
Anguisciola, Sofonisba School, PORTRAIT OF A BOY, 52 x 31 (4068/101)   1600
Antwerp School, THE ADORATION OF THE MAGI, 15 x 12, ca1515, on panel (4224/29)   7000
Antwerp School, 2nd half 16c, SAINT JOSEPH OF ARIMATHEA, on panel, 23½ x 12 (4068/81)   5500
Aviani, Francesco, circle of, AN ARCHITECTURAL CAPRICCIO WITH AMORS AT PLAY, 27½ x 38
(4224/134)   1600
Aviani, Francesco, School, AN ARCHITECTURAL CAPRICCIO, 27 x 36¼, (4224/135)   650
Bachelier, Jean-Jacques, A STILL LIFE OF FLOWERS, 28¼ x 31 (4258/284)   6500
Bachelier, Nicolas, after, STILL LIFES OF FLOWERS, 33 x 26 (4224/25)   4500
Backhuysen, Lodolf, School of, SHIPPING OFF A COAST, 7 x 10½, on panel (4258/185)   550
Balding, H., THE LAST JUDGEMENT, 10⅛ x 6⅞ (4078/3)   175
Balen, Hendrick van and Brueghel, Jan, THE FEAST OF THE GODS, on metal, 18 x 27 (4068/68)   15000
Bally, Alexandre, PORTRAIT OF LADY, 1811, 22½ x 18½ (4068/11)   1100
Barbarini, G.F. (Il Guercino), after, VENUS BORNE ALOFT BY PUTTI, 32 x 25½ (633/24)   300
Barocci, Federico, THE CIRCUMCISION OF CHRIST, 26 x 21¾ (633/175)   950
Bassano, Francesco follower, THE PRODIGAL SON EXPELLED FROM HARLOT'S HOUSE, 49 x
65½ (4068/40)   1500
Bassano, Jacopo, attrib. (1510-92), THE PURIFICATION OF THE TEMPLE, 29 x 37 (633/177)   500
Bassano, Jacopo, School of, THE ADORATION OF THE MAGI, 35¼ x 47½ (633/5)   200
Bassano, Leandro, circle of, ADAM AND EVE, 23¾ x 29½, (4224/44)   700
Bassi, Giambattista, THE FALLS OF TIERNEY, 39 x 28½, d.1820, (4224/127)   2200
Beach, Thomas*, PORTRAIT OF A LADY, 35½ x 27¼ (4258/199)   650
Beck, Leonhard, ROLANDUS, 9⅜ x 8½ (4078/4)   40
Beechey, R.A., William, Attrib., PORTRAIT OF A MEMBER OF THE GREGORY FAMILY, 29½ x
24½ (4224/122)   750
Beeldemaker, Adriaen Cornelisz, A ROCKY LANDSCAPE WITH SPANIELS, 16¾ x 21½,   d.16-0
(4224/195)   2300
Beert, Osias, A STILL LIFE, 18¾ x 25¾ (4258/104)   20000
Bega, Cornelis, A TAVERN INTERIOR, on panel, 12½ x 9 (4068/118)   5000
Benaschi Giovanni Battista, CHRIST AT SUPPER WITH SIMON THE PHARISEE, 88 x 122½
(4068/95)   8500
Bergmuller, Johannes Georg, THE GUARDIAN ANGEL, 96½ x 70¼, unframed (4258/129)   6750
Bernart, Francois, A MILITARY ENCAMPMENT, 12¾ x 17¾, on panel (4258/215)   3600
Beuckelaer, Joachim, A MARKETPLACE, 48 x 75, unframed (4258/280)   7000
Bison, Giuseppe-Bernardino, A STORMY SOUTHERN RIVER LANDSCAPE, 24½ x 29½, unframed
(4258/162)   800

Boilly (4224/61)

Abbott (4224/36)

Bol (4258/56)

Bloemart, Ábraham, Attrib., A SEATED CLERIC, 7 x 6½, chalk on paper, (4224/90)	800
Boeckhorst, Johannes, A CAVALRY SKIRMISH, 27 x 36½ (4258/230)	1700
Bogdani, Jacob, A STILL LIFE OF FRUIT, canvas on panel, 7¼ x 8½ (4068/4)	3500
Boilly, Louis Leopold, School of, PORTRAIT OF A YOUNG WOMAN, 12 x 9 (4258/59)	900
Boilly, Louis-Leopold, PORTRAIT OF A YOUNG WOMAN, 8½ x 6½ (4258/82)	2000
Boilly, Louis-Leopold, PORTRAITS OF A GENTLEMAN AND A LADY, A PAIR, 8½ x 6½ (4224/61)	*1500*
Bol, Ferdinand, A YOUNG MAN AT A WINDOW, 35 x 26¾ (4258/56)	*2000*
Bol, Ferdinand, OLD MAN WITH FLOWERING BEARD AND VELVET CAP, 4¾ x 3⅜ (4078/9)	275
Bol, Ferdinand, PORTRAIT OF A GENTLEMAN, 35 x 29 (4068/107)	3750
Bol, Ferdinand, School of, PORTRAIT OF A MAN IN A FEATHERED CAP, 30 x 25, (4224/88)	1000
Bol, Hans Follower, THE REST ON THE FLIGHT INTO EGYPT, parchment, 4 x 6¼ (4068/8)	8500
Bolognese school, DIANA AND ACTAEON 17c, 27¾ x 38¾ (633/178)	800
Bolognese school, THE HOLY FAMILY, 17c, 12 x 16 (633/11)	325
Bonechi, Matteo, Attrib., THE PRESENTATION OF THE VIRGIN IN THE TEMPLE, 38 x 22½ (4224/50)	1800
Boonen, Arnold, FIGURES IN AN INTERIOR, 19 x 25¼, unframed (4258/297)	2300
Boucher, Francois, THE HEAD OF A YOUNG WOMAN WEARING A CAP, 8¼ x 6½, chalk, pastel, paper (4258/221)	8000
Boucher, Francois, After, THE CHARMS OF SPRING, 14½ x 17¾ (4258/259)	700
Boucher, Francois, School of, THE BATHERS, 15¾ x 39½ (666/34)	1900
Brand, Johann Christian, circle, A SOUTHERN PORT SCENE, 16½ x 24, (4224/185)	1600
Bronzino, Agnolo, circle of, PORTRAIT OF A LADY, 26 x 22, on panel, (4224/17)	3400
Brouwer, Adriaen, school of, PORTRAIT OF A MAN, 9¼ x 7¼, on panel (633/166)	1400
Brueghel, Jan the elder, FLOWERS IN A GLASS VASE, on panel, 16¼ x 13¼ (4068/127)	560000
Buesen, Jan Jansz, PEASANTS IN AN INTERIOR, 14¾ x 11½, on panel (4258/3)	3600
Burler, Gaspar, VESUVIUS ERUPTING, 8 x 15¾, on metal (4258/163)	1300
Bylert, Jan van, circle of, CAVALIERS AND LADIES IN AN INTERIOR, on panel, 23½ x 31½ (4068/46)	3500
Campi,Giulo, circle of, PORTRAIT OF A YOUNG GENTLEMAN, 34 x 27 (4258/93)	7750
Campidoglio, manner of, A STILL LIFE OF FLOWERS IN A PARKLAND SETTING, 98 x 44 (4224/38)	2200
Carree, Michiel, A SOUTHERN LANDSCAPE, 9¾ x 12¼, on panel, unframed (4258/38)	2200
Casissa, Nicola*, A STILL LIFE OF FLOWERS, 60¼ x 50, unframed (4258/15)	3700
Casteels, Pieter, School, A STILL LIFE OF FLOWERS, 27 x 45, (4224/118)	2300
Castiglione, Giovanni B., circle, A WOODED LANDSCAPE, 24½ x 29¼, (4224/183)	1600
Cellot, J., THE PARTING OF THE RED SEA, 4⅞ x 9⅛ (4078/17)	525
Cignani,Carlo, HAGAR AND ISHMAEL, 37½ x 48 (4258/296)	2400
Cimaroli, Giovanni Battista, circle of, A SOUTHERN RIVER LANDSCAPE, 23½ x 33 (4258/160)	1400
Cipriani, Giovanni B. , attrib.. (1727-85), FLORA, 30 x 17, ovoid, on panel (633/1)	250
Cittadini, Gaetano, WOODED MOUNTAIN LANDSCAPES WITH A PORT, PAIR, 21 x 30 ea., d.1728, panel (4224/173)	5000

Claesz, Pieter, A STILL LIFE, 1640, 21 x 34¾ (4068/111)	50000
Clowes, Daniel, PREPARING FOR RACE AT CHESTER RACECOURSE, 33½ x 42½ (4068/36)	7000
Codazzi, Niccolo Viviani, TRAVELLERS RESTING IN A CLASSICAL RUIN, 28 x 22½ (4258/154)	5500
Coello, Alonso Sanchez, PORTRAIT OF A YOUNG NOBLEMAN, 51¼ x 36 (4068/102)	9000
Coques, Gonzalez, DE MEER FAMILY IN A RIVER LANDSCAPE, PORTRAIT, 27 x 32½ (4068/71)	14500
Cotes, Francis, PORTRAIT OF A LADY, 48½ x 38½, (4224/60)	1700
Cotes, Francis*, A PORTRAIT OF A LADY SAID TO BE MISS KITTY STARR, 23¾ x 19¾, within a painted oval (4258/206)	1600
Cotes, Francis, Attrib., PORTRAIT OF A LADY, 24 x 19¾, (4224/123)	900
Coypel, Noel, AN ALLEGORY OF NIGHT AND DAY, oval, 27 x 22 (4068/70)	3500
Craesbeeck, Joos van, THE READER, paper laid on panel, 4¾ x 4¼ (4068/74)	3000
Cranach, Lucas, manner of, GENTLEMAN ON HIS DEATH BED, (MARTIN LUTHER), on panel, 16 x 11½ (4068/73)	900
Croos, Anthony Jansz van, A RIVER LANDSCAPE AT RHENEN, on panel, 20¼ x 30¾ (4068/25)	18000
Cuyp, Aelbert, follower, A PORT SCENE, 36 x 54 (4068/112)	4250
Cuyp, Benjamin Gerritsz, THE NATIVITY, on panel, 33 x 45 (4068/29)	7000
D'Arellano, Juan, circle of, A STILL LIFE WITH FLOWERS, 26 x 20½, (4224/23)	1800
Da Cadore, Antonio Rosso, circle of, SAINT GEORGE AND THE DRAGON, 21¼ x 19½, on panel (4258/224)	1800
Da Lanciano, Polidoro, circle of, THE MYSTIC MARRIAGE OF SAINT CATHERINE, 23 x 27, on panel (4258/270)	1800
Da Pontormo, Jacopo Carrucci, School of, PORTRAIT OF A NOBLEMAN, 24 x 18½, on panel (4258/288)	5250
Da Vercelli, Giovanni Antonio Bazzi, circle of, VIRGIN AND CHILD WITH SAINTS JOHN AND ELIZABETH, 30, on panel, circular (4258/269)	6250
Daddi, Bernardo, after, THE MADONNA AND CHILD, A TRIPTYCH, center 30½ x 21, w. 30½ x 10½, on panel (4224/131)	2500
Daniell, Thomas, THE WELLINGTON PILLAR AT SEZINCOTE, 1811, 50 x 39½ (4068/124)	12000

De Gryeff (4224/21)

Dutch School (4224/35)

De Keyser (4224/15)

Duck (4224/108)

De Beel, Cornelius, STILL LIFE WITH GRAPES, MELON, PEACHES AND ROSES, 13½ x 16, on panel (4258/41) 1200

De Gelder, Aert, PORTRAIT OF A GENTLEMAN, 36 x 29, arched top (4258/289) 3000

De Gryeff, Adriaen, ANIMALS IN A PARKLAND SETTING, 12½ x 16, on, panel (4224/21) *5000*

De Gyselaer, Nicholas, THE RETURN OF THE PRODIGAL SON, 30¾ x 44½, on panel (4258/196) 4000

De Hooch, Pieter, School of, A COUPLE IN AN INTERIOR, 20 x 15, on panel, (4224/149) 900

De Keyser, Thomas, School of, PORTRAIT OF A YOUNG BOY, 9¼ x 7½, d.1636, on, metal (4224/15) *2800*

De Marne, Jean Louis, FIGURES IN A TAVERN, 8¼ x 10¼, on panel (4258/191) 5000

De Marne, Jean Louis, MOTHER AND CHILD IN A TAVERN INTERIOR, 8¼ x 10¼, on panel (4258/192) 4500

De Momper, Joost, AN EXTENSIVE RIVER LANDSCAPE, on panel, 26 x 56½ (4068/14) 60000

De Moor, Karel, School of, PORTRAIT OF A MAN PLAYING A VIOLIN, 6¼ x 5, on panel (4224/71) 550

De Roy, Jean-Baptiste, A WOODED RIVER LANDSCAPE, 18 x 22¼, on panel, unframed (4258/161) 3750

De Troy, Jean Francois, circle of, VENUS AND ADONIS BEFORE A TENT, 15 x 9 (4258/130) 1200

De Vlieger, Simon, FISHERMAN BESIDE AN ESTUARY, on panel, 16 x 23¼ (4068/24) 29000

De Wit, Jacob, AN ALLEGORY OF ABUNDANCE, 7 x 8½, pen and black ink and black wash, paper (4224/64) 500

Del Garbo, Raffaellino, THE LAMENTATION, on panel 18 x 24 (4068/31) 10000

Del Sarto, Andrea, After, THE ASSUMPTION OF THE VIRGIN, 51 x 30½, arched top (4258/21) 1100

Del Sarto, Andrea, School of, THE HOLY FAMILY, 28 x 21½, on panel, (4224/19) 1600

Dell' Abbate, Nicolo, Studio of, THE VIRGIN ANNUNCIATE, D8½, mixed inks and wash (4224/67) 600

Devis, Arthur, PORTRAIT OF GENTLEMAN, 23½ (4068/19) 10000

Diegonza, THE EXPULSION, on metal (4258/186) 550

Diepraam, Abraham, circle of, A PEASANT COUPLE MAKING MERRY, 8¾ x 6¾, on panel (4224/144) 1300

Dionijs Ver Burgh*, A LANDSCAPE ALONG THE RHINE, 35 x 52½, signed with monogram DVB (4258/251) 4750

Diziani, Antonio, TOBIAS AND THE ANGEL IN A RIVER LANDSCAPE, 16½ x 25, canvas on board (4224/137) 4000

Diziani, Gasparo, School of, A SURRENDER BEFORE A CASTLE, 27½ x 37, (4224/94) 1000

Dodd, Robert, SHIPPING IN COASTAL WATERS, 35 x 47 (4068/76) 6500

Dolci, Carlo, circle of, THE MUSE OF LITERATURE, 21¾ x 16¾ (4258/134) 1000

Dou, Gerard attributed to, PORTRAIT OF A GENTLEMAN, on panel, oval, 7½ x 5¾ (4068/88) 3250

Dou, Gerrit, PORTRAIT OF A GENTLEMAN IN ORIENTAL COSTUME, 16 x 13¼, on panel (4258/157) 16000

Drolling, Martin, A PORTRAIT OF A LADY, 12½ x 9 (4258/301) 1400

Droochsloot, Joost Cornelisz, A VILLAGE STREET SCENE, 1645, on panel, 31 x 47 (4068/91) 23000

Duck, Jacob, manner, GENTLEMAN AND A LADY IN AN INTERIOR, 21 x 29, on panel (4224/108) *2300*

Dughet, Gaspard, (Poussin), school of, AN EXTENSIVE LANDSCAPE WITH TRAVELLERS, 38½ x 53 (633/159) 2500

Durer, A., CHRIST BEFORE ANNAS, 5 x 7⅞ (4078/33) 200

Durer, A., CHRIST BEFORE CAIAPHAS, 4⅝ x 2⅞ (4078/22) 750

Durer, A., DEATH OF THE VIRGIN, 11½ x 8, corners missing (4078/41) 250

Durer, A., FREDERICK THE WISE, ELECTOR OF SAXONY, 7⅝ x 5 (4078/31) 325

Durer, A., LADY ON HORSEBACK AND LANSQUENET, 4⅛ x 3 (4078/29) 800

Durer, A., MELANCOLIA I, 9½ x 7⅜ (4078/28) 3750

Durer, A., PHILIPP MELANCHTON, 7 x 5⅛ (4078/32) 325

Durer, A., SAINTS STEPHED, SIXTUS AND LAWRENCE, 8¼ x 5⅝ (4078/44) 110

Durer, A., ST CHRISTOPHER WITH THE FLIGHT OF BIRDS, 8⅝ x 5¾ (4078/43) 400

Durer, A., ST. JEROME IN HIS STUDY, 9⅝ x 7⅜ (4078/27) 3100

Durer, A., THE FLAGELLATION, 5 x 7¾ (4078/35) 325

Durer, A., THE FOUR HORSEMAN, 15½ x 11 (4078/38) 4300

Durer, A., THE HOLY FAMILY WITH FIVE ANGELS, 8½ x 5¾ (4078/42) 350

Durer, A., THE LAST JUDGEMENT, 5 x 3⅞ (4078/37) 350

Durer, A., THE PRESENTATION IN THE TEMPLE, 11⅝ x 8¼ (4078/40) 550

Durer, A., THE SUDARIUM HELD BY ONE ANGEL, 7¼ x 5¼ (4078/23) 700

Durer, A., THE VIRGIN AND CHILD WITH MONKEY, 7⅜ x 4¾ (4078/26) 550

Durer, A., THE VIRGIN ON THE CRESCENT, 4⅛ x 2¾ (4078/24) 425

Durer, A., THE VIRGIN ON THE CRESCENT, WITH SCEPTRE, CROWN, 4½ x 2⅞ (4078/25) 800

Durer, A., THE VISITATION, 11¾ x 8¼ (4078/39) 375

Durer, A., THE LARGE HORSE, 6½ x 4¾ (4078/30) 850

Dusart, Cornelis, PEASANTS MAKING MERRY IN A TAVERN, 1695, 13¼ x 15 (4068/99) 14000

Dusart, Cornelis, Attrib., PEASANTS DRINKING OUTSIDE A TAVERN, 10 x 14¾, on panel (4224/2) 3200

Dutch School, 'A FOOL AND HIS MONEY ARE SOON PARTED', D7½, on panel (4224/165) 1500

Dutch School, A STORMY LANDSCAPE WITH MILLS, 15 x 11, E19c (4224/73) 1100

Dutch School, PEASANTS BRAWLING OUTSIDE AN INN, 22¾ x 28½, 17c, on panel (4224/35) *6750*

Engelbrechtsz (4258/53)

Flemish School (4258/6)

Dutch School, THE HUNT, 18c, on panel, 24½ x 18½ (666/17)   1700
Dutch School, ca1630, PORTRAIT OF A WOMAN, 28 x 21½ on panel (4258/78)   1900
Dutch School, ca1640, PORTRAIT OF A WOMAN, 25½ x 20, on panel (4258/175)   1600
Dutch School, 17th Century, PORTRAIT OF HILLEGONDA VAN VIERSSEN, 28 x 21½ (4258/77)   1500
Dutch School, 18th Century, A RIVER LANDSCAPE, 18½ x 30, on panel (4258/203)   3600
Dutch School, 18th Century, A STILL LIFE OF FLOWERS, 33 x 24, L18c (4258/87)   2000
Engelbrechtsz, Cornelis, LOT AND HIS DAUGHTERS, 21 x 16, on panel (4258/53)   *4500*
English School, A WOODED LANDSCAPE WITH A WATERFALL,' 20 x 26¾ (4224/126)   1100
English School, PORTRAIT OF A GENTLEMAN, 18c, 30 x 25 (666/39)   225
English School, PORTRAIT OF A LADY SAID TO BE MARY BURDEN, ca12700, 30 x 25 (633/23)   375
English School, PORTRAIT OF A YOUNG WOMAN, 23¾ x 30¾, d.1594, on panel (4224/12)   600
English School, 18th Century, PORTRAIT OF SIR JOHN AND ELIZABETH, 94 x 71 (4258/275)   4000
Fabritius, Barent, SELF-PORTRAIT, 25½ x 20½ (4258/290)   27000
Fargue, Paulus Constantin la, Circle, A VIEW OF AMSTERDAM WITH WESTERKERK, on panel, 11 x 15 (4068/34)   2100
Flemish School, A BATTLE, 4½ x 7, on copper (4258/229)   4500
Flemish School, A WOODED RIVER LANDSCAPE, ca1700, 57 x 51 (4068/77)   4000
Flemish School, AUTUMN, 17c, 8½ x 11¼, on copper (633/165)   24000
Flemish School, NYMPH AND SATYR, L18c, 25½ x 21⅛ (666/15)   500
Flemish School, PORTRAIT OF A LADY AS CERES, 41¼ x 33½ (4219/10)   1900
Flemish School, SUMMER, 17c, 8½ x 11¼, on copper (633/164)   19500
Flemish School, THE BATTLE OF THE AMAZONS, 40 x 48, (4224/117)   600
Flemish School, THE MADONNA AND CHILD APPEARING TO A BISHOP, 66½ x 46¼, L16c, panel (4224/74)   500
Flemish School, THE VIRGIN ANNUNCIATE, en grisaille, E17c, 43 x 29¾, on panel (633/22)   100
Flemish School, first quarter 17c, PORTRAIT OF A YOUNG LADY, 26¼ x 21½ (4068/59)   3500
Flemish School, Early 19th Century, A HEN WITH A BROOD, 24 x 29 (4258/6)   1800
Flemish School, 17th Century, THE TOWER OF BABEL, 21½ x 34½, on panel (4258/90)   3250
Flemish School, 18th Century, A VILLAGE WITH A POND, 7½ x 10, on panel (4258/89)   3500
Florentine School, 16th century, THE HOLY FAMILY AND THE INFANT ST. JOHN, circular, on panel, D33 (4068/48)   6000
Forte, Luca, School of, A STILL LIFE OF FRUIT, 19 x 26, unframed (4258/211)   2100
Fragonard, Jean-Honore, School of, TWO PUTTI IN A CARTOUCHE DECORATED WITH FLOWERS, 17¼ x 14, oval (4258/11)   800
Franceschini, Marc Antonio*, THE CALYDONIAN BOAR HUNTER, 13½ x 25, unframed (4258/264)   800
French School, A COUPLE EMBRACING IN A GARDEN, 13½ x 10½, 18c, on panel (4224/80)   1100
French School, A FETE CHAMPETRE, 38½ x 43, 18c, (4224/189)   3100
French School, A HARBOR SCENE, 18c, 18 x 34¾ (666/33)   1100
French School, A WOODED LANDSCAPE WITH A COUNTRY PALACE, 39 x 49 (4224/114)   2000

French School, ALLEGORY OF THE ELEMENTS, 18c, 18 x 21 (666/32) 2000
French School, PORTRAIT OF A GENERAL, L18c, 8¾ x 7 (666/31) 650
French School, PORTRAIT OF A GENTLEMAN, 45½ x 35¼ (666/35) 225
French School, PORTRAIT OF A LADY, 18c, 30 x 23, ovoid (633/113) 300
French School, PORTRAIT OF A LADY, 11 x 8½, 16c, on panel, (4224/184) 3100
French School, PORTRAIT OF A NOBLEMAN, 18C, 30 x 22 (633/25) 350
French School, PORTRAIT OF A NOBLEWOMAN, 28 x 22½, M17c (4224/39) 850
French School, PORTRAIT OF GABRIELLE DESTREE, 14 x 10½, on panel (4224/113) 750
French School, VENUS AND ADONIS, 20¼ x 47½, 18c, (4224/103) 900
French School, VENUS AND APOLLO, 17¼ x 13½, L17c, (4224/188) 1100
French School, WOMAN RECLINING IN A GARDEN, D9¾, M17c, pen and brown ink, paper (4224/66) 450
French School, ca1700, PORTRAIT OF A YOUNG MAN, 74 x 52 (4258/181) *6250*

French School (4258/181)

German School (4224/76)

French School, ca1820, A FEAST OF THE GODS, gouache, paper, 17¼ x 23½, unframed (4258/240) 300
French School, Late 18th Century, THE HEAD OF A WOMAN, 11 x 9¼, chalks, paper (4258/101) 750
French School, M18th Century, A RECLINING YOUTH, 8⅞ x 12¾, chalk, paper (4258/217) 400
French School, 18th Century, PORTRAIT OF A GENTLEMAN, 9 x 7½, within a painted octagon, L18c (4258/309) 350
French School, 18th Century, THE COQUETTE, 41 x 34, unframed (4258/271) 1100
Fyt, Jan, attrib. (1609-1661), A STILL LIFE WITH DEAD GAME, 32 x 24¾, on panel (633/173) 1800
Gainsborough, R.A., Thomas, School, THE HARVEST WAGON, 32 x 38, (4224/89) 5250
Gainsborough, Thomas, School, GEORGIANA, COUNTESS SPENCER, 29 x 24, (4224/132) 1000
Gainsborough, Thomas, School of, A SHEPHERD IN A WOODED LANDSCAPE, 39 x 45, d.1764 (4224/45) 4750
Gelder, Aert de, School of, PORTRAIT OF A MAN IN A TURKISH COSTUME, on panel, 13 x 9⅛ (666/10) 325
Gellee, Claude (Le Lorraine) manner, LANDSCAPE WITH CATTLE, PEASANTS, FORTRESS, 29 x 40 (666/5) 800
Genga, Girolomo*, BERNARDINO DA FELTRE STANDING WITHIN A COLONNADE, 11¼ x 8¾, on panel (4258/222) 2500
Genoese School, PEASANTS GAMBLING, 35½ x 48, E17c, (4224/54) 800
Genoese School, THE CORONATION OF THE VIRGIN, 26 x 21, (4224/168) 1300
German School, A MOUNTAINOUS LANDSCAPE WITH A WATERFALL, 15 x 22½ (4224/115) 1000
German School, PORTRAIT OF A YOUNG PRINCE, 39 x 30, L18c, canvas laid down on board (4224/76) *500*
German School, PORTRAIT OF FRANC FORG, 30 x 27, 18c, (4224/41) 600
German School, TRAVELLERS IN A STORMY RIVER LANDSCAPE, 6¾ x 8½, 18c, mixed media on panel (4224/91) 800
German School, TRAVELLERS IN A WOODED LANDSCAPE, 13 x 16, 18c,(4224/175) 1300
Ghisi, G., PERSICHA, 22¾ x 17½ (4078/49) 40
Ghisolfi, Giovanni, School, AN ARCHITECTURAL CAPRICCIO WITH TWO FIGURES, 19¾ x 14 (4224/191) 1000
Gibson, Thomas, Attrib., PORTRAIT OF A YOUNG GIRL WITH A BASKET, 43 x 34, (4224/77) 1300

Giordano, Luca, A PHILOSOPHER, 44½ x 33½ (4258/294) — 3250
Giordano, Luca, circle of, DIANA AND ACTEON, 29 x 37¾, (4224/49) — 1000
Glauber, Johannes*, A WOODEN LANDSCAPE WITH A HERDSMAN AND HIS ANIMALS, 30 x 43
(4258/201) — 1600
Goes, Hugo van der, follower, THE DESCENT FROM THE CROSS, on panel, 26½ x 34 (4068/84) — 8000
Goltzius, H., NEPTUNUS, NEPTUNE AND AMPHITRITE, 14 x 8⅞, 12½ x 8½ (4078/52) — 175
Gordon, John Watson (1790-1864), PORTRAIT OF AN OFFICER, 36 x 28 (666/42) — 1400
Goyen, Jan van, A RIVER LANDSCAPE, on panel, 1639, 11¾ x 17¼ (4068/62) — 31000
Goyen, Jan van manner of, A RIVER LANDSCAPE, monogram, on panel, 22½ x 32½ (4068/121) — 4250
Griffier, Jan, the Elder, A LANDSCAPE WITH A WATERFALL, 16 x 26½ (4258/246) — 2750
Grimmer, Abel Circle, A WOODED RIVER LANDSCAPE, JOURNEY TO EMMAUS, on panel, 20 x 26
(4068/15) — 8000
Grund, Norbert, FIGURES AMID THE RUINS OF A ROMAN BUILDING, 14 x 18 (4224/86) — 700
Hackert, Jan, A SOUTHERN RIVER LANDSCAPE, 27 x 33¼ (4258/95) — 3900
Hals, Dirck, A MERRY COMPANY, on panel, 11 x 13¾ (4068/18) — 12000
Hals, Dirck, A MUSICAL COMPANY, 1624, 15 18½ (4068/100) — 21000
Hals, Frans, manner of, LAUGHING BOY, 8 x 6½, on panel, (4224/78) — 2500
Hamilton, Hugh Douglas, School of, PORTRAIT OF A LADY WITH A CHILD, 35½ x 27½ (4258/45) — 1300
Hamilton, William, PORTRAIT OF DAVID GARRICK IN A THEATRICAL PERFORMANCE, 81¼ x 52
(4224/143) — *3000*

Lawrence (4224/95)

Lawrence (4258/225)

Hamilton (4224/143)

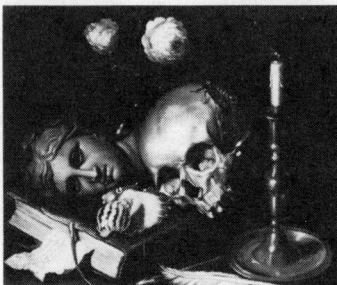

Ihle (4224/75)

Hanneman, Adriaen, A PORTRAIT OF A YOUNG GIRL WITH FLOWERS, 35 x 27¾, unframed
(4258/303) — 1900
Haringh, Daniel, TWO CHILDREN BEFORE A WINDOW, 27 x 22, (4224/161) — 3400
Haughton, Matthew, AN ALLEGORY OF VANITAS, 10¼ x 8¼ (4258/42) — 150
Heda, William Claesz, A BREAKFAST STILL LIFE, 1640, 14½ x 19 (4068/12) — 20000
Heeremans, Thomas, BEFORE THE CITY GATES OF HAARLEM, 1691, 19 x 24¼ (4068/22) — 6250
Herrera, Francesco (1576-1656), VANITAS, 29 x 39¾ (633/171) — 3500
Highmore, Joseph, PORTRAIT OF MRS. JOSHUA IREMONGER, 49 x 39, d.1742 (4224/180) — 7000
Highmore, Joseph, manner of, PORTRAIT OF A LADY WITH FLOWER, 50 x 40½, (4224/20) — 700
Hobbema, Meindert, circle of, A LANDSCAPE AT THE OUTSKIRTS OF A VILLAGE, 28 x 39, on
panel (4258/144) — 7250
Hoet, Gerard, THE MARRIAGE OF ALEXANDER AND ROXANE, 18½ x 27, on metal (4224/68) — 2800
Hoet, Gerard, THE RAPE OF EUROPA, 25 x 21½, (4224/8) — 900

Holbein, Hans, after, PORTRAIT OF ERASMUS OF ROTTERDAM, 10¼ x 7¾, on panel (4224/56) — 1400
Hopfer, H., ERASNUS OF ROTTERDAM, 9⅝ x 14 (4078/55) — 125
Hoppner, John, A PORTRAIT OF J.H. SMYTH, 29¼ x 24½ (4258/46) — 3000
Hoppner, John, PORTRAIT OF LADY FRANCES WYNDHAM, 35 x 27½ (4258/120) — 2500
Hoppner, R.A. John, COL. W.G. BRADDYLL OF CONISHEAD PRIORY, PORTRAIT, (4068/10) — 1200
Hoppner, R.A., John, circle, A CHILD FEEDING HER PET PIGEONS, 42 x 36, (4224/167) — 3600
Hoppner, R.A., John, circle, PORTRAIT OF BARON GRENVILLE, 30 x 25, (4224/96) — 1400
Hoppner, R.A., John, Attrib., PORTRAIT OF W. JAMES, ESQ., 29½ x 24½, (4224/133) — 1100
Horemans, Jan Josef the Elder, STUDIES OF A YOUNG HORSEMAN, 10¼ x 6⅞, chalk, paper (4258/51) — 1300
Howitt, S. attributed to (1765-1822), HUNTERS IN A HILLY LANDSCAPE, on panel, 12 x 18 (666/150) — 750
Hudson, Thomas*, PORTRAIT OF MR JENNINGS, 48 x 39 (4258/113) — 2400
Hue, Jean-Francois, A SHIPWRECK, L'ORAGE, 49 x 66 (4258/286) — 4100
Huet, Jean-Baptiste, CHILDREN FROLICKING IN A LANDSCAPE, 31¼ x 25 (4258/266) — 27000
Huet, Jean-Baptiste, School, CHILDREN PLAYING IN A PARKLAND SETTING, 40 x 35 (4224/147) — 2500
Hulk, Jacobsz, SHIPPING IN A CALM SEA, 15½ x 20½ (4068/113) — 2200
Huysmans, Jacob, A STILL LIFE OF FRUIT AND FLOWERS, 46 x 67½, 1653 (4258/57) — 8500
Ihle, Daniel Friedrich, A VANITAS, 16¾ x 19½, d.1760, (4224/75) — *7500*
Il Borgognone, School of, A CALVARY ENGAGEMENT, 20 x 33, (4224/93) — 2300
Il Guercino, School, HERCULES, 5¼ x 7½, brown pen on paper, (4224/192) — 1500
Il Sassoferrato, School, THE MADONNA IN PRAYER, 16¼ x 12, (4224/174) — 1000
Il Todeschini, School, PORTRAIT OF A MAN HOLDING A GLASS, 27½ x 21, (4224/157) — 400
Italian School, A STILL LIFE WITH FRUIT AND FLOWERS, 18c, 19¾ x 28 (666/23) — 275
Italian School, A STILL LIFE WITH ROOSTER IN A LANDSCAPE, 17c, 41 x 74 (633/162) — 2250
Italian School, AN ELEGANT COURTYARD WITH FIGURES, 18c, 25¼ x 35½ (666/20) — 1100
Italian School, BIRTH OF SAINT JOHN THE BAPTIST, 10½ x 8½, 17c, paper laid down on canvas (4224/79) — 1100
Italian School, FLOWERS BY A POOL, 18c, 29½ x 38½ (666/25) — 2500
Italian School, LANDSCAPE WITH PEASANTS AND A RUINED ABBEY, 18c, 18¾ x 22¼ (666/22) — 550
Italian School, SERGIUS GALBA, d.1592, 54½ x 44½ (633/13) — 125
Italian School, THE ANNUNCIATION, 17c, 59 x 44½ (666/21) — 600
Italian School, THE INFANTA DONNA MARIA GIUSEPPA, 40 x 29¾, (4224/176) — 1400
Italian School, THE MADONNA AND CHILD, 13 x 10, on panel (633/10) — 275
Italian School, THE PENITENT MAGDALEN IN THE WILDERNESS, L17c, 12 x 16¾ (633/17) — 225
Italian School, THE VIRGIN IN PRAYER, 19c, 23 x 14, on panel (633/20) — 550
Italian School, VERTUMNUS AND POMONA, L17c, 24 x 30 (633/2) — 400
Italian School, YOUNG BOY WITH POMEGRANATE, 18c, laid on board, 19 x 15¼ (666/24) — 275
Italian School, Early 19th Century, A WINTER LANDSCAPE, 24 x 30, unframed (4258/2) — 400
Italian School, L15c, SAINTS CATHERINE OF ALEXANDRIA, SEBASTIAN, on panel, 36 x 31½, L15c (666/1) — 2250
Italian School, 17th Century, STUDY OF A KNEELING NUDE MALE, 11 x 15½, chalk, paper (4258/216) — 800
Italian School, 18th Century, A STILL LIFE IN A SOUTHERN LANDSCAPE, 35¼ x 42 (4258/165) — 900
Italian School, 18th Century, STUDIES OF ANGELS, 9¼ x 6¾, pencil, paper (4258/293) — 450
Jackson, John, PORTRAIT OF A GENTLEMAN, 30 x 25 (4258/205) — 500
Johnson, Cornelis, circle of, PORTRAIT OF A NOBLEMAN, 33½ x 25, (4224/179) — 3500
Juel, Jens, A CHILD PICKING A ROSE, 31 x 25 (4068/32) — 3000
Kauffmann, R.A., Angelica, circle, ATHENA AND MELPOMENE, PAIR, 16¾ x 13 ea., on copper (4224/193) — 1600
Kessel, Ferdinand van, THE MUSIC PARTY, on metal, 11 x 14¼ (4068/115) — 3000
Key, Adriaen Thomasz, PORTRAIT OF A LADY, on panel, 14 x 12 (4068/89) — 5500
Kneller, Geoffrey, PORTRAIT OF A GENTLEMAN, 18c, 50 x 40 (633/181) — 800
Kneller, Geoffrey, PORTRAIT OF A LADY, 18c, 50 x 40 (633/180) — 750
Kobell, Franz, A WOODED RIVER LANDSCAPE, 4 x 6⅜, wash, paper (4258/62) — 450
Kobell, Franz*, PEASANTS WITH A HORSE AND A DOG IN A LANDSCAPE, 12 x 14, pen, ink, wash, paper (4258/238) — 700
Krug, L., ADORATION OF THE MAGI, 6½ x 4⅞ (4078/56) — 130
Labille-Guiard, Adelaide, PORTRAIT OF THE MARQUISE DE SABLE, 21½ x 18, oval (4258/300) — 7500
Lagrenee, Louis Jean Francois, the Elder, VENUS AND ADONIS, 47 x 67¼ (4258/91) — 30000
Lampi, Giovanni Battista, PORTRAIT OF COMTE ARTEME LAZAREFF, 27 x 21½, within a painted oval (4258/197) — 1000
Lautensack, H.S., PAUL LAUTENSACK, 8½ x 6⅜ (4078/57) — 50
Lavreince, Nicolas, LE BILLET DOUX, 21½ x 18¼ (4068/49) — 3500
Lawrence, P.R.A., Sir Thomas, circle, PORTRAIT OF GEORGIANA, DUCHESS OF BEDFORD, 29½ x 24 (4224/95) — *1300*
Lawrence, Sir Thomas*, PORTRAIT OF KING GEORGE IV, 36 x 28 (4258/256) — 5500
Lawrence, Sir Thomas*, PORTRAIT OF SIR ROBERT DUNDAS, 30 x 25 (4258/225) — *2500*

North Italian School (4224/62)

Lawrence, Sir Thomas, circle of, PORTRAIT OF MARGUERITE, COUNTESS OF BLESSINGTON, 35¼ x 27¼ (4258/247)　　2500

Lawrence, Sir Thomas, School of, PORTRAIT OF A LADY SAID TO BE MRS SIDDONS, 43 x 33½ (4258/119)　　1600

Lawrence, Sir Thomas, School of, PORTRAIT OF A YOUNG GIRL READING HAMLET, 31½ x 26½, on panel (4224/151)　　1000

Lawrence, Sir Thomas, School of, PORTRAIT OF LADY BEAUCLERK, 23¼ x 18½ (4258/226)　　1000

Lawrence, Thomas, attributed (1769-1830, PORTRAIT OF MISS O'NEIL, paper, laid on canvas, 17 x 13 (666/44)　　225

Le Marchand, Guillaume, FAMILY PORTRAIT OF HENRI DE BOULAINVILLIERS, 47½ x 55½, 1676 (4258/235)　　7500

Le Prince, Jean-Baptiste, HOME FROM MARKET, 8, circular (4258/220)　　4500

Ledoux, Jeanne Philiberte, Attrib., A YOUNG GIRL, 17½ x 14½, (4224/171)　　1700

LeNain, Louis, school of, BLOWING A BUBBLE, 10⅜ x 9½ (633/158)　　750

Lepicie, Nicholas Bernard*, A YOUNG BOY HOLDING A BASKET OF APPLES, 20¼ x 16¾, unframed (4258/84)　　1900

Lesuer, Eustache, attrib. (1616-95), CORIOLANUS' MOTHER INTERCEDING....ROME, 54 x 35 (633/179)　　2000

Lombard, Lambert, School of, THE DEATH OF THE VIRGIN, 42 x 43¼, on panel (4258/295)　　1700

Longhi, Pietro, A VENETIAN COFFEE HOUSE, 7¾ x 11¼, brush, wash, paper (4258/177)　　5000

Longhi, Pietro, A VENETIAN WINESHOP, 7⅞ x 11, brush, wash, paper (4258/178)　　3000

Luini, Bernardo, Circle of, ANGELS MAKING MUSIC, 47 x 35 (4258/108)　　5000

Machy, Pierre Antoine de, A RIVER VIEW, on metal, 26¾ x 49 (4068/126)　　15000

Maes, Nicholas, School of, PORTRAIT OF MARY BUTLER, 41¾ x 32 (4258/187)　　600

Maes, Nicolas, PORTRAIT OF A YOUNG BOY, canvas on panel, 17 x 12¾ (4068/75)　　7250

Magliolo, SOLDIERS IN A CLASSICAL RUIN, 13¾ x 17½ (4258/115)　　1000

Maltese, Enrico, A STILL LIFE, 27 x 37½ (4258/164)　　1000

Maratta, Carlo, School of, CHRIST AND THE WOMAN OF SAMARIA, 52 x 38 (4258/232)　　3500

Martin, Elias, A ROCKY LANDSCAPE, pencil and watercolor, 5 x 9 (4068/53)　　300

Mazzone, Sebastiano, circle, A WOMAN HOLDING A SHEET OF MUSIC, 24½ x 20, (4224/100)　　200

Mehus, Livio, THE OPENING OF THE RED SEA, 46 x 48½, (4224/69)　　4400

Meinz, Domenicus, A SOUTHERN HARBOR, 27½ x 37½ (4258/195)　　1300

Mercier, Philippe, circle of, THE SWING, 18 x 24½ (666/29)　　1600

Mercier, Philippe, School of, A FETE CHAMPETRE, 31 x 37½, (4224/152)　　1300

Mercier, Philippe, School of, PORTRAIT OF A YOUNG GIRL, 22¼ x 18, (4224/43)　　2200

Mercier, Phillippe, attributed to, YOUNG GIRL PORTRAIT, 42 x 39 (4068/33)　　2300

Metsu, Gabriel, School of, A YOUNG WOMAN DRAWING FROM A PLASTER CAST, 15½ x 11½, on panel (4224/47)　　900

Metsu, Gabriel, School of, THE VEGETABLE MARKET AT AMSTERDAM, 14 x 18¾, on panel (4224/34)　　1700

Meulen, A. Fivan, School of, THE PRISONERS, 29¼ x 39¾ (666/18)   1750
Meulener, Pieter, CAVALRY ON THE OUTSKIRTS OF A TOWN, 32¾ x 46, 1653 (4258/73)   *13500*
Michau, Theobald, Circle of, A VILLAGE SCENE, 12½ x 16, on panel (4258/69)   21000
Millet, Jean Francois*, called Francisque, A SOUTHERN LANDSCAPE, 15¾ x 24¾ (4258/255)   1600
Millet, Jean Francois, called Francisque, MERCURY DISCOVERS HERSE RETURNING FROM A FESTIVAL, 26 x 45¾ (4258/265)   5000
Moeyaert, Claes Cornelisz, JOSEPH SELLING CORN IN EGYPT, 53½ x 70 (4258/110)   15000
Mola, Pier Francesco, School of, A BIBLICAL SCENE, 48¾ x 39¼ (666/14)   550
Molenaer, Bartholomeus, BOORS CAROUSING, 6½ x 6¾, on panel, (4224/124)   2600
Molenaer, Jan Miense, THREE PEASANTS SINGING, circular on panel, D7½ (4068/45)   9500
Molenaer, Jan Miense, Attrib., MERRYMAKING IN A TAVERN, 19 x 23, on panel, (4224/107)   4800
Molenaer, Klaes, A WOODED LANDSCAPE, on panel, 18 x 25 (4068/103)   11500
Moni, Louis de, THE CONSULTATION, on panel, 11¼ x 9½ (4068/105)   11500
Monnoyer, Antoine, circle, STILL LIFES WITH FLOWERS, A PAIR OF PAINTINGS, 38½ x 29, canvas laid down (4224/120)   11000
Monnoyer, Jean-Baptiste, A STILL LIFE WITH FLOWERS, 35¼ x 25½ (4258/75)   10000
Morin, T., JEAN-PIERRE CAMUS, EVEQUE DE BELLAY, 11⅞ x 9½ (4078/69)   40
Morland, George, A WINTER LANDSCAPE, 27¼ x 35 (4258/34)   *3000*

Morland (4258/34)

Meulener (4258/73)

Morland, George, THE HUNT, 19½ x 25½, (4224/153)   20000
Morland, George, THE TRAVELLERS HALT, 14½ x 11½, d.1790, (4224/102)   3200
Morland, George, School of, THE LANDING, 16¾ x 23¼ (666/38)   175
Morland, George, School of, PREPARING THE BOATS, 14 x 17½ (666/37)   275
Moro, Antonio, after, PORTRAIT OF QUEEN MARY OF ENGLAND, 26 x 21 (633/184)   300
Mostaert, Gillis, CHRIST HEALING THE EPILEPTIC, 13½ x 17, on metal (4258/274)   4000
Munoz, Johannes, A STILL LIFE OF FLOWERS, 32 x 24, unframed (4258/17)   1400
Murillo, Bartolome Esteban, School of, THE MADONNA AND CHILD, 24½ x 19¾ (4258/152)   325
Muziano, Girolamo, Attrib., SAINT JEROME, 9 x 6¾, on metal, (4224/63)   2400
Mytens, Jan, School of, PORTRAIT OF A FAMILY, 34¼ x 40½ (4258/234)   1800
Nattier, Jean Marc, School of, PORTRAIT OF LADY WITH A CUPID, 50½ x 40 (4258/272)   2500
Neapolitan School, A STILL LIFE OF FLOWERS AND FRUIT, 28¾ x 38¼,   17c (4224/130)   3400
Neefs, Peter School, A CHURCH INTERIOR, on panel, 9¾ x 13 (666/4)   400
Netherland School, ADORATION OF THE MAGI, M16c, on panel, 21½ x 16 (4068/82)   6000
Netscher, Caspar, A YOUNG BOY AT A BUTCHER'S SHOP, 1662, 14½ x 12 (4068/122)   5500
Netscher, Caspar, circle, COUPLE IN A PARKLAND SETTING, 12½ x 10½ (4068/110)   4500
Nigg, Joseph, circle, A STILL LIFE WITH FLOWERS, 32 x 25½, (4224/170)   4800
Nollekens, Josef Frans, School of, FIGURES IN AN INTERIOR, 20 x 19½ (4258/298)   1500
North Italian School, A RIVER LANDSCAPE, 12¾ x 16½, L18c, on metal (4224/62)   *1800*
North Italian School, AN EXTENSIVE SOUTHERN LANDSCAPE, E18c, 29½ x 40 (4068/85)   2100
North Italian School, ST. GREGORY AND ST. AMBROSE, pair, 16c, 12¾ x 5 (4068/93)   3250
North Italian School, THE FOUR EVANGELISTS, PAIR, 11¾ x 19¾, on panel, (4224/178)   1800
North Italian School, 15th Century, THE MADONNA AND CHILD, arched top, on panel, 29¼ x 17¼ (4068/58)   22000
Novelli, Pietro, SAINT FRANCIS, 11¾ x 8¼ (4258/24)   500

Ochtervelt, Jacob, YOUNG COUPLES IN AN INTERIOR, 32½ x 26½ (4068/6) 10000
Oosterwyck, Maria van, A STILL LIFE OF FLOWERS AND FRUIT, 21 x 18 (4068/98) 26000
Opie, R.A., John, PORTRAIT OF JOHN VIVIAN OF PENCALEWICK, 29½ x 25 (4224/13) *900*
Opie, R.A., John, PORTRAIT OF MRS. DEERING, 36 x 28, (4224/166) 3000
Orizzonte, School of Bloemen, A SOUTHERN LANDSCAPE WITH WOODS, 63¾ x 44, (4224/116) 2200
Ostade, Adriaen van, School of, PORTRAIT OF A MAN, on panel, 5 x 4 (4068/50) 1700
Ostade, Isaac van, A TAVERN INTERIOR, monogram, on panel, 9½ x 12¾ (4068/119) 20000
Ostade, Isaac van, SKATERS ON A FROZEN RIVER, on panel, 21 x 29½ (4068/78) 45000
Oudry, Jean-Baptiste, circle of, A RIVER LANDSCAPE, 12½ x 16½ (4258/94) 1700
Pagano, Matteo, THE ENTOMBMENT, 39 x 49½, d.1669, (4224/82) 3000
Palamedesz, Palamedes, A SKIRMISH, on panel, 31½ x 45 (4068/42) 5500
Palamedsz, Antonie, School of, GENTLEMEN AND LADIES IN AN INTERIOR, 13 x 16, on panel (4224/72) 2000
Palmeri, Pietro, A PEASANT AND TWO HORSES, ink and wash, 12x 15¼ (4068/20) 750
Pannini, Giovanni Paolo, School, ALEXANDER VISITING THE TOMB OF ACHILLES, 27½ x 35¾ (4068/86) 6250
Paolino, Fra, studio of, SAINT VINCENT FERRER, 11½ x 9½, on panel, (4224/9) 600
Parentino, Bernardo, A SCENE FROM THE TRAJAN SAGA, 18 x 20, on panel (4258/249) 16500
Parrocel, Charles*, A MILITARY SKIRMISH, 10½ x 12 (4258/111) 800
Pater, Jean-Baptiste, School of, ELEGANT FIGURES IN A PARKLAND SETTING, 28½ x 23 (4258/61) 1900
Pellegrini, Giovanni Antonio, circle of, APOLLO, VENUS AND FAME, 23½ x 17½, within a painted oval (4258/183) 3100
Pensionante Del Saraceni, JOB MOCKED BY HIS WIFE, 38¾ x 50½ (4258/190) 52500
Pernet, J.H.A. (after), RUINS OF A VILLA WITH FIGURES AND A FOUNTAIN, 12⅛ x 14⅜ (4078/75) 80
Petitot, Jean the Elder*, PORTRAIT OF KING LOUIS XIV, 9½ x 8, on panel (4258/9) 1600
Piranesi, G.B., VEDUTE DI ROMA INTERIOR OF THE COLOSSEUM, 17⅞ x 27 (4078/79) 175
Piranesi, G.B., VEDUTE DI ROMA, VEDUTA DELLA CURIA OSTILIA, 16 x 23⅞ (4078/77) 225
Pittoni, Giovanni Battista, School, SAINT CATHERINE OF ALEXANDRIA, 25 x 19½, (4224/182) 1500
Poelenburgh, Cornelis V., manner of, AN ELEGANT PARTY AMONG RUINS, (633/167) 1100
Poussin, Nicolas, school of, THE FESTIVAL OF VENUS, 35 x 54 (633/172) 1200
Quast, Pieter, School of, A PEASANT DRINKING, 5¼ x 4½, on panel (4258/105) 800
Querfurt, August, A MILITARY ENCAMPMENT, 12½ x 17, on metal (4258/214) 2200
Raeburn, R.A., Sir Henry, PORTRAIT OF JAMES WARDROP OF TORBANEHILL, 29¼ x 24¼ (4224/32) *5200*
Raeburn, R.A., Sir Henry, School of, PORTRAIT OF HENRY DUNDAS, VISCOUNT MELVILLE, 15¾ x 12½ (4224/26) 600
Raeburn, Sir Henry, PORTRAIT OF CHARLES HENRY KERR, 29 x 24 (4258/117) *2000*
Raeburn, Sir Henry, PORTRAIT OF JOHN LAMONT OF LAMONT, 29 x 24 (4258/118) 7750
Raeburn, Sir Henry, PORTRAIT OF SIR WILLIAM FORBES, 29 x 24½, (4224/155) 1600
Raeburn, Sir Henry, School of, THE HAIG, 70 x 56½ (4258/276) 4750
Ramsay, Allan, COMPTON, LADY ELISABETH, PORTRAIT, 49½ x 39½ (4068/64) 7000
Ramsay, Allan, PORTRAIT OF ELIZABETH LOVE ROBERTSON, 29¼ x 24¼, d.1757 (4224/37) *6500*
Reattu, Jacques, THE TRIUMPH OF CIVILIZATION, 57½ x 77, unframed (4258/128) 7000
Reinagle, Ramsey Richard (1775-1862), PORTRAIT OF ADMIRAL CHARLES HAMILTON, 30 x 25 (666/41) 1600
Reni, Guido, THE RAPE OF EUROPA, 47 x 64 (4258/291) 6000
Reni, Guido, manner of, THE PREMONITION OF THE VIRGIN, 36 x 46¾ (633/6) 275
Repton, Humphrey, THE PUMP ROOM, BATH, pen, ink, watercolor, 17¼ x 23¾ (4068/60) 4500
Reymerswaele, Marinus van, circle, SAINT JEROME IN HIS STUDY, on panel, 38½ x 49½ (4068/83) 5500
Reynolds, P.R.A. Sir Joshua, Attrib., PORTRAIT OF SIR GILBERT ELLIOT, 30 x 24¼, (4224/51) *2300*
Reynolds, Sir Joshua, WILLIAM BOUVERIE PORTRAIT, EARL OF RADNOR, 29 x 24 (4068/21) 1300
Reynolds, Sir Joshua P.R.A., SACKVILLE, LORD GEORGE, PORTRAIT, 29 x 24 (4068/108) 10000
Ricci, Marco, School of, A SOUTHERN RIVER LANDSCAPE, 21 x 17¼ (4258/33) 1900
Ridolfi, Michele, FORTUNA, 29 x 24¾, on panel, unframed (4258/126) 2400
Rigaud, Hyacinthe, School of, PORTRAIT OF A LADY, 24 x 18 (666/30) 350
Rigaud, John Francis, circle of, PORTRAIT OF AN OFFICER, 23½ x 22½, (4224/40) 1100
Robert, Hubert, A PYRAMID, 14¼ x 11⅜ (4258/218) 3000
Robert, Hubert, A RIVER LANDSCAPE WITH A WATERFALL, 14 x 17½ (4258/233) 28000
Robert, Hubert, School of, PEASANTS IN A PALACE GARDEN, A PAIR, 26½ x 22, on panel (4224/92) 3000
Robert, Hubert, School of, THE TEMPLE OF LOVE, 68 x 48 (4258/60) 2300
Roman School, ca1700, CUPID AND THE MUSE OF PAINTING, 49¾ x 40¼ (4258/302) 800
Roman School, Late 17th Century, VENUS AND MARS, 18¾ x 29¼, unframed (4258/12) 2750
Rombouts, Theodore, AN ALLEGORY OF TEMPTATION, 45½ x 64½ (4258/71) 4750

Raeburn
(4258/117)

Opie (4224/13)

Raeburn
(4224/32)

Ramsay (4224/37)

Reynolds (4224/51)

Romney, George, after, THE PARSON'S DAUGHTER, 20 x 18, watercolor and, pencil on paper
(4224/27) 600
Rosa, Carlo, CHRIST BLESSING CHILDREN, 50 x 38 (4258/143) 3200
Rosa, Salvatore, A RIVER LANDSCAPE, 19 x 23 (4258/285) 1200
Roslin, Alexander, School of, AN ELEGANT COUPLE, 41 x 33 (4068/51) 500
Rottenhammer, Hans, School, THE LAST JUDGEMENT, on panel, 25½ x 29 (4068/23) 1500
Rottenhammer, Johann, VENUS AND MARS, oval on metal, 4¾ x 7 (4068/67) 1800
Rubens, Peter Paul, School, THE HORSES OF ACHILLES, 22 x 30 (4068/39) 13000
Rubens, Peter Paul, after, EXPULSION FROM THE TEMPLE, on copper, 27 x 34½ (666/11) 475
Rubens, Peter Paul, School of, A COUPLE EMBRACING, 25 x 19 (4258/76) 2300
Rubens, Peter Paul, School of, SAINT BARTHOLOMEW, 24 x 20, on panel (4258/142) 1200
Rubens, Sir Peter Paul, circle of, THE JUDGEMENT OF PARIS, 18 x 25½, on metal, (4224/3) 14000
Ruisdael, Jacob, School of, A COUNTRY WATERFALL, 33 x 29¾ (666/13) 650
Russell, John, A STILL LIFE OF GAME IN A MOUNTAINOUS LANDSCAPE, 41½ x 65¾, unframed
(4258/7) 2000
Ruthart, Carl Borromaeus Andreas, Attrib., THE KILL, 12½ x 16, (4224/22) 2100
Ruysdael, Solomon van, A RIVER LANDSCAPE, on panel, 5¾ x 8 (4068/61) 20000

Rysbrack, Pieter Andreas, the Younger, RICHMOND FERRY AT KEW GARDENS, 35 x 46
  (4258/184)   12500
Sacchi, Andrea, Studio of, THE BAPTISM OF CHRIST, 30½ x 24½, unframed (4258/31)   600
Salvi, G.B. (I Sassoferrato), manner of, THE HOLY FAMILY, 29¼ x 39⅛ (666/16)   275
Salvi, Giovanni Battista, THE MADONNA AND CHILD, 27½ x 36½, oval (4258/68)   7500
Salviati, Francesco, School of, PORTRAIT OF A GENTLEMAN, 27½ x 21¼, on panel, (4224/59)   *4000*
Santa Croce, Francesco da, CHRIST AT THE SEPULCHRE, panel, 10¾ x 8 (4068/30)   2000
Sanzio, Raphael, workshop of, HOLY FAMILY WITH SAINTS ELIZABETH AND JOHN THE
  BAPTIST, 53 x 42, 1516 (4258/123)   15000
Sartorius, John Nott, MR. G. MOORE'S HAMPSTEAD, 1780, 13¼ x 17 (4068/37)   2900
Savery, Roelandt, A WOODED LANDSCAPE, on panel, 8½ x 11 (4068/80)   12500
Schall, Jean Frederick, School of, THE INTERIOR OF A BROTHEL, 34¼ x 27¼ (4068/52)   600
Schoevaerdts, Math, TRAVELLERS IN A LANDSCAPE, canvas on metal, 6 x 8½ (4068/2)   5000
Schongaver, M., THE FLAGELLATION FROM THE PASSION, 6½ x 4⅝ (4078/103)   750
School of Seville, A STILL LIFE WITH FRUIT, 29½ x 21, 17c, (4224/24)   5250
Schooten, Floris van, A STILL LIFE, on panel, 12¾ x 21½ (4068/66)   28000
Schouman, Aert, A PARK LANDSCAPE, 35 x 31¼ (4068/123)   1600
Schutz, Christian Georg, AN EXTENSIVE RIVER LANDSCAPE, 9½ x 13, on panel (4258/252)   4000
Seton, Thomas*, AN ARTIST PAINTING A PORTRAIT OF A YOUNG WOMAN, 33½ x 29½
  (4258/169)   1500
Shee, Sir Martin Archer*, A YOUNG WOMAN HOLDING A SKETCHBOOK, 33 x 25½ (4258/36)   *2700*

Salviati (4224/59)

Van Heemskerck
(4258/4)

Shee (4258/36)

Simonini, Francesco, A CAVALRY ENGAGEMENT BETWEEN CHRISTIANS AND TURKS, 23¾ x
  38¾, unframed (4258/231)   3500
Sole, Giovan Gioseffo dal, SAINT BENEDICT RETRIEVING WOODCUTTERS AXE, 42 x 71
  (4068/87)   700
Son, Joris van, A STILL LIFE OF FLOWERS AND FRUIT, 34 x 28.5 (4068/55)   8000

Spanish School, THE ADORATION OF THE MAGI AND THE ASSUMPTION, OF THE VIRGIN, 23½ x 21½ ea (4224/121) — 2000

Steen, Jan, A PEASANT FAMILY LEAVING AN INN, on panel, 12 x 10½ (4068/120) — 7500

Steen, Jan, A VILLAGE WEDDING, 26 x 33½ (4068/94) — 60000

Steen, Jan, School of, PEASANTS CAROUSING BEFORE A TAVERN, 19¼ x 23½ (4258/72) — 2300

Storck, Jacobus, SHIPPING IN A CHOPPY SEA, on panel, 9½ x 10¼ (4068/104) — 5000

Streek, Juriaen van, A STILL LIFE, on panel, 22½ x 16 (4068/116) — 5250

Strozzi, Bernardo, circle of, PORTRAIT OF A YOUNG MAN IN A FEATHERED HAT, 16¼ x 14, on panel (4224/14) — 800

Strozzi, Bernardo, School of, SAINT JOHN THE BAPTIST PREACHING, 27½ x 38 (4258/98) — 1500

Sustermans, Justus, PORTRAIT OF A LADY, 21 x 17¼ (4258/86) — 8750

Sweerts, Jeronimus, A STILL LIFE, on panel, 8 x 6½ (4068/65) — 15000

Teniers, Abraham, PEASANTS GATHERED BEFORE AN INN, on panel, 10 x 13¾ (4068/1) — 11000

Teniers, David the Younger, A GYPSY BAND, on panel, 12¼ x 18¼ (4068/26) — 14000

Teniers, David the Younger, BOORS AT AN INN, on panel, 14½ x 18¼ (4068/27) — 20000

Teniers, David the Younger, PEASANTS IN AN INTERIOR, on panel, 8¾ x 7¼ (4068/114) — 8000

Teniers, David the Younger, School, PEASANTS PLAYING BOWLS OUTSIDE A TAVERN, 10½ x 13, on metal (4224/1) — 2200

Teniers, David, School of, PEASANTS BEFORE A COTTAGE, 6½ x 8¾, on panel, (4224/28) — 1300

Teniers, David, School of, THE TEMPTATION OF SAINT ANTHONY, 9½ x 12, on, panel (4224/142) — 1800

Terborch, Gerard circle, A LADY WRITING A LETTER, 16 x 13 (4068/106) — 4500

Tiepolo, Giovanni Battista*, TWO STUDIES OF A RECLINING BOY, 6¼ x 8⅞, pen, ink, wash, paper (4258/50) — 4500

Tischbein, Johann Friedrich August, BOODE, JACOB HENDRICK AND WIFE, PORTRAIT, 49½ x 37 (4068/109) — 3250

Trinquesse, Louis Rolland, A WOMAN SEATED AT A TABLE, 8¼ x 11⅛, chalk, ink, wash, gouache, paper (4258/219) — 1900

Troyen, Rombout van, JEHU PUNISHING THE FOLLOWERS OF BAAL, 1652, 48 x 45½ (4068/28) — 4500

Utrecht School, A VANITAS, A WOMAN WITH A LUTE, 46 x 36, (4224/160) — 1800

Uytenbroeck, M. van School (1590-1648), THE NURTURING OF BACCHUS, on panel, 9¼ x 7 (666/3) — 800

Valkenburg, Dirk, Circle of, A STILL LIFE OF GAME, 17 x 15, unframed (4258/16) — 700

Van de Velde, Willem, school of, UNLOADING THE SHIPS, 23 x 28 (633/163) — 1200

Van der Ast, Balthasar, A STILL LIFE OF FLOWERS, 22¾ x 17¼, on panel (4258/100) — 145000

Van der Heyden, Jan, THE RETURN FROM THE HUNT, 16 x 22, on panel (4258/258) — 18000

Van der Lamen, Christoph Jacobsz., After, LADIES AND GENTLEMAN ON A TERRACE, 23 x 33¼, on panel (4258/19) — 5000

Van der Meer, Barend, A CLUSTER OF GRAPES, 21 x 16½ (4258/14) — *1600*

Van der Neer, Aert, manner of, A MOONLIGHT RIVER LANDSCAPE, 7 x 9, on metal, (4224/83) — 650

Van der Smissen, PEASANTS SHOEING A HORSE IN A VILLAGE LANDSCAPE, (4258/25) — 300

Van Antum, Aert, WHALING SHIPS IN A STORM TOSSED SEA, 8½ x 13, on metal (4224/58) — 2000

Van Balen, Hendrick, Keirincx, Alexander, A WOODED RIVER LANDSCAPE, 21 x 32, on panel (4258/20) — 21000

Van Beyren, Abraham, A STILL LIFE, 22¼ x 28¼ (4068/13) — 67500

Van Bloemen, Pieter, A LANDSCAPE WITH A SLEEPING HERDSMAN AND HIS ANIMALS, 14 x 18 (4258/39) — 2000

Van Coninxloo, Gillis, Attrib., TRAVELLERS IN A WOODED LANDSCAPE, 8¼ x 7¼, on metal (4224/57) — 4200

Van Diest, Adriaen, THE BATTLE OF LOWESTOFT, 1665, 29¼ x 53½ (4258/124) — 3100

Van Dyck, Anthony, School of, CHRIST AT THE COLUMN, 25 x 15, on panel (4258/228) — 700

Van Dyck, Anthony, School of, PORTRAIT OF CHARLES I, 78 x 46½, (4224/145) — 2300

Van Dyck, Sir Anthony, School of, SAINT PETER, 25½ x 19¼, on panel (4258/168) — 4750

Van Eertvelt, Andries, SHIPPING IN A ROUGH SEA, 18 x 31½, on panel (4258/141) — 8500

Van Everdingen, Caesar, CHRIST BLESSING CHILDREN, 30 x 50, on panel (4258/147) — 25000

Van Falens, Karel, A HUNTING PARTY, 16 x 22½, on panel, (4224/164) — 3000

Van Gorp, Nicholas, A LADY AND TWO YOUNG BOYS IN A LANDSCAPE, 15½ x 12½ (4224/125) — 1600

Van Goyen, Jan, A CITY TOWER BESIDE A RIVER, 1642, 28 x 24 (4068/38) — 47500

Van Goyen, Jan, School of, A VILLAGE SCENE WITH TRAVELLING PLAYERS, 7 x 10¾, chalk and wash on paper (4224/98) — 600

Van Heemskerck, Egbert, A TAVERN INTERIOR, 15¼ x 12½, on panel (4258/4) — 7000

Van Kessel, Jan*, THE MADONNA AND CHILD SURROUNDED BY FLOWERS, 21¼ x 15½, on metal (4258/135) — 13500

Van Leuden, L., CAIN KILLING ABEL, 6½ x 4⅝ (4078/58) — 650

Van Leuden, L., THE ADORATION OF THE MAGI, 12 x 17¼ (4078/59) — 950

Van Leudenil, THE POET VIRGIL SUSPENDED IN A BASKET, 9½ x 7⅜ (4078/65) — 175

Van Loo, Charles Andre, THE STERN OF THE FRENCH SHIP 'LE TRIOMPHAM', 31¾ x 23¼, gouache, paper (4258/103) — 13500

Van Loo, Jacob, BACCHUS AND ARIADNE, 65 x 55½, (4224/181) — 2000

Van Loo, Jacob, PORTRAIT OF A BOY IN A BLACK VELVET CAP, 20¾ x 16, on panel (4258/85) — 6500

Van Mieris, Willem, A PEASANT FAMILY IN AN INTERIOR, 16¾ x 13¾, on panel (4258/260) — 3000

Van Minderhout, Hendrick, circle, A SHIPPING SCENE, 31½ x 46, (4224/186) — 4200

Van Nieulandt, Willem, Manner of, PEASANTS AT THE OUTSKIRTS OF A TOWN, 5 x 7½, on panel (4258/32) — 600

Van Ostade, A., THE DANCE IN THE INN, 10 x 12⅝ (4078/74) — 1300

Van Ostade, A., THE FAMILY, 7⅛ x 6¼ (4078/73) — 350

Van Ostade, A., THE SMOKER AND THE DRINKER, 2⅜ x 3 (4078/72) — 70

Van Ostade, A., VILLAGE ROMANCE, 6¼ x 5⅛ (4078/71) — 275

Van Rijn, Rembrandt, CHRIST AND THE WOMEN OF SAMARIA, 4⅞ x 6¼ (4078/89) — 500

Van Rijn, Rembrandt, CHRIST PREACHING, 11 x 15⅝ (4078/90) — 12000

Van Rijn, Rembrandt, JAN LUTMA, GOLDSMITH, 7¾ x 5⅞ (4078/97) — 2600

Van Rijn, Rembrandt, REMBRANDT IN A FLAT CAP, AND EMBROIDERED DRESS, 3⅜ x 2⅜ (4078/83) — 750

Van Rijn, Rembrandt, SHEET OF STUDIES, HEAD OF ARTIST AND BEGGARS, 3⅞ x 4⅛ (4078/100) — 1600

Van Rijn, Rembrandt, STUDIES OF A MOTHER AND CHILD, 5½ x 5¼, pen, ink, wash, paper (4258/81) — *22000*

Van Rijn, Rembrandt, STUDIES OF THE HEAD OF SASKIA AND OTHERS, 6 x 5 (4078/101) — 1100

Van Rijn, Rembrandt, THE DESCENT FROM THE CROSS BY TORCHLIGHT, 8¼ x 6⅜ (4078/91) — 650

Van Rijn, Rembrandt, THE PRESENTATION IN THE TEMPLE, 8½ x 11½ (4078/86) — 450

Van Rijn, Rembrandt, THE STAR OF THE KINGS, A NIGHT PIECE, 3¾ x 5⅝ (4078/92) — 1250

Van Rijn, Rembrandt, THE STAR OF THE KINGS, A NIGHT PIECE, 3⅝ x 5⅝ (4078/93) — 450

Van Rijn, Rembrandt, THE STROLLING-MUSICIANS, 5½ x 4½ (4078/95) — 2400

Van Rijn, Rembrandt, THE TRIUMPH OF MORDECAI, 6⅞ x 8⅜ (4078/85) — 450

Van Rijn, Rembrandt, THREE ORIENTAL FIGURES, 5½ x 4½ (4078/94) — 850

Van Rijn, Rembrandt, VIRGIN AND CHILD IN THE CLOUDS, 6⅝ x 4¼ (4078/87) — 650

Van Rijn, Rembrandt, WOMAN BATHING HER FEET, 6¼ x 3½ (4078/96) — 650

Van Rijn, Rembrandt, WOMAN READING, 4⅞ x 4 (4078/99) — 950

Van Rijn, Rembrandt, manner, PORTRAIT OF A GENTLEMAN, 7½ x 5½, on panel, (4224/148) — 450

Van Rijn, Rembrandt, School of, THE CARDPLAYERS, 6½ x 8, on paper (4258/80) — 3000

Van Rijn, Rembrandt, School of, VERTUMNUS AND POMONA, 4½ x 3½, brush, ink, paper (4258/79) — 1900

Van Roestraten, Pieter Gerritsz, A STILL LIFE, 24¾ x 29½ (4258/166) — 7250

Van Ruysdael, Salomon, manner, A RIVER LANDSCAPE, 24 x 39, (4224/112) — 1700

Van Schooten, Floris, SAINT JOHN THE BAPTIST PREACHING TO THE MULTITUDES, 20½ x 36, on panel (4258/273) — 3250

Van Tilborch, Gillis, PEASANTS GATHERED OUTSIDE A TAVERN, 22½ x 27½ (4258/145) — 12000

Van Troyen, Rombout, LANDSCAPE WITH FIGURES, 10 x 15, 1648 (4258/244) — 2250

Van Vries, Roelof, A RIVER LANDSCAPE, 18¾ x 26¾, on panel, unframed (4258/204) — 3500

Vanni, Francesco, THE TRINITY ADORED BY TWO SAINTS, 14½ x 8⅞, chalk, pen, wash, ink, paper (4258/179) — 650

Vasari, Giorgio, School of, A SYMBOLIC FIGURE IN A MEDALLION, 65 x 64, (4224/84) — 2500

Vasari, Giorgio, School of, AN ANGEL HOLDING A LILY AND A WREATH, 41½ x 34, (4224/106) — 450

Vasari, Giorgio, School of, SYMBOLIC FIGURES IN MEDALLIONS, A PAIR, 64 x 64 (4224/85) — 2500

Vecellio, Tiziano, School of, called Titian, BUST OF CHRIST, 30¼ x 21½, on panel (4258/106) — 4500

Venetian School, A VIEW OF THE PIAZZA SAN MARCO, VENICE, 25¼ x 36¼ (4224/150) — 3300

Verbruggen, Gaspar Pieter, School, A STILL LIFE OF FLOWERS, 29½ x 19½, (4224/104) — 800

Verbrugghen, Gaspar Pieter, Attrib., A STILL LIFE OF FLOWERS, 37¾ x 28, (4224/196) — 3800

Verbrugghen, Gaspar Pieter, School, A STILL LIFE OF FLOWERS, 40½ x 31, (4224/169) — 4500

Verbrugghen, Gasper Pieter, the Younger, A STILL LIFE WITH FLOWERS, 33¼ x 26 (4258/74) — 8000

Verendael, Nicolaes van, A VASE OF FLOWERS IN A NICHE, on panel, 10⅜ x 7⅞ (4068/117) — 57500

Verkolje, Jan, A MERRY COMPANY, 21¾ x 17¾ (4068/5) — 13500

Vernet, Claude Joseph, circle of, A SOUTHERN RIVER LANDSCAPE, 15¾ x 21, (4224/46) — 1400

Veronese School, THE MADONNA AND CHILD ENTHRONED, 35½ x 23½, ca1600 (666/2) — 300

Verschuier, Lieve, SHIPS AT SEA, 25 x 28 (4258/140) — 6500

Victoryns, Anthonie, THE FOOT OPERATION, 9¼ x 13¼, on panel (4258/18) — 5750

Vigee-Lebrun, Elizabeth, after, PORTRAIT OF THE DAUPHIN AND HIS SISTER, 47 x 35 (633/182) — 900

Vigee-Lebrun, Elizabeth, attrib., THE MADONNA AND CHILD WITH SAINT ANN, 12 x 9½, on panel (633/198) — 275

Vigee-Lebrun, Elizabeth, school of, PORTRAIT OF THE ARTIST, 24 x 19 (633/183) — 750

Vincent, Francois Andre, THE FIRE OF LOVE, 17¼ x 13¾, oval (4258/131) — 2500

Vinck, Jan, A RIVER LANDSCAPE, on panel, 17¼ x 25¾ (4068/35) — 6250

Vitale, Candido, A GATHERING OF BIRDS IN A RIVER LANDSCAPE, 13½ x 20½ (4258/5) — 1400

Vleughels, Nicolas, JUPITER AND ANTIOPE, on panel, 20¼ x 25 (4068/69) — 1600

Voet, Jacob Ferdinand, School of, AN ACTRESS OF THE COMMEDIA DELL'ARTE, 24½ x 18½, (4224/52) — 500

Vouet, Simon, circle of, PORTRAIT OF A YOUNG ARTIST, 24 x 18, (4224/163)   1000

Vrancx, Sebastian, A WOODED RIVER LANDSCAPE, 31¼ x 45 (4068/90)   6500

Wheatley, Francis, R.A., attributed, THE FATHER'S ADMONITION, 13 x 15¾, dated 1798, watercolor (4068/57)   850

Wilson, Richard, School of, TWO BOYS FISHING BY A LAKE, 24 x 35 (666/40)   425

Wintter, Joseph Georg, DEER IN A WOODED LANDSCAPE, A PAIR OF PAINTINGS, 18 x 13½ ea., d.1782 (4224/111)   7250

Wolffsen, Aleida, PORTRAIT OF A LADY, 15 x 12, (4224/48)   *2000*

Wouwermans, Jan, A DUNE LANDSCAPE, on panel, 25 x 40 (4068/41)   14000

Wright, Joseph of Derby, HALL, H.B., PORTRAIT, painted oval, 29¼ x 24¼ (4068/63)   9500

Zais, Giuseppe, School of, A SOUTHERN RIVER LANDSCAPE, 24½ x 56, (4224/33)   1800

Zais, Giuseppe, School of, FIGURES BY A STREAM, 39½ x 32¾ (666/27)   1800

Zucarelli, Francesco, AN EXTENSIVE RIVER LANDSCAPE WITH TRAVELLER, 21¾ x 28 (633/169)   400

Zucarelli, Francesco, circle, A SOUTHERN RIVER LANDSCAPE, 24 x 36, (4224/138)   1100

Zucarelli, Francesco, manner of, A LANDSCAPE WITH DIANA AND HER MAIDENS, 40¼ x 50 (633/160)   650

Wolffsen (4224/48)

Chapter 19

Nineteenth Century Paintings, Drawings and Sculpture

Nineteenth-century European paintings have seen five years of steady gains. Prices were up in almost all the various national schools, with some, particularly French Barbizon and German paintings, showing spectacular increases. Strong bids by European dealers sent prices soaring to record levels in many categories. These dealers usually pursued works by their compatriots, though French paintings were the subject of broad competition.

German paintings have shown a particularly strong rise in the past five years. Led by landscapes and pictures with animal subjects, works by Munich painters attained world record prices at every auction. Genre scenes of taverns and kitchens in country surroundings also sold well.

Paintings of children have traditionally been the most popular among nineteenth-century paintings, but prices for these works rose to unprecedented levels last season. However, the amazing strength of the German market shows best in the high prices paid for paintings by little-known artists.

Dutch paintings again realized excellent prices. The spectacular boom in works of the later-nineteenth-century Hague School—prices have risen as much as five hundred percent in five years—showed no signs of abating, and Belgian paintings also brought in more than expected. Street scenes of both schools were especially popular.

American and Spanish bidders confirmed that Joaquin Sorolla y Bastida is the most sought-after Spanish artist of the period, and decorative Spanish paintings also found a ready market.

There is a current surge of interest in Barbizon artists. American museums and Continental dealers have been joined by Japanese collectors in bidding for these works, further driving up prices for these newly popular artists. World record prices were set for works by Jules Dupre and Charles-Emile Jacque. Prices for the work of Adolphe-William Bouguereau have risen dramatically with the revival of interest in academic painting. Bouguereau suffered an eclipse in the thirties and forties, but his highly finished canvases are now in great demand.

Prices for English painting held solid, without showing the kinds of breakthroughs seen in other areas.

Intense international competition for works in this field points to a solid future for almost every category of nineteenth-century European painting.

French academic and German painting will probably continue as the star performers in this field, with the Dutch, Belgian and Spanish schools only slightly behind.

Achenbach, Oswald, MEDITERRANEAN COAST, TWILIGHT, 28 x 39, 1886 (4241/6) — $10000

Achenbach, Oswald (1827-1905), MEDITERRANEAN BEACH WITH FISHERFOLK, 16¼ x 30¼ (4208/3) — 3250

Adam, Julius, 1852-1913, THE HUNGRY QUARTET, 12¾ x 17 (4161/33) — 26000

Aerni, Franx T., 1853-1918, FISHERMEN PREPARING THEIR NETS, 13½ x 20½ (4122/25) — 2000

After, Joseph Desire Court (1797-1865), RIGOLETTE, 45¼ x 35½ (4071/173) — 2500

Aivasovsky, Ivan, BEACH SCENE BY MOONLIGHT, 12½ x 18 (4241/157) — 5500

Aivasovsky, Ivan (1817-1900), SUNSET OVER CONSTANTINOPLE, 9 x11, on board (4208/101) — 4500

Ajdukiewicz, Zygmunt, 1861-1917, BRINGING HOME THE WILD BOAR, 1888, Polish, 20½ x 32½ (4161/115) — 7250

Akkersdyk, Jacob (1815-62), READING THE NEWS, d.1843, 19¼ x 16, on panel (4208/54) — 5000

Albori, V., READING 'LA CHIACCHERA', 18½ x 23¾ (633/208) — 650

Alenza Y Nieta, Leonardo (1807-1845), FIGURES CONVERSING ON THE OUTSKIRTS OF A TOWN, 5¼ x 7¼, brown ink (4260/639) — 900

Alfieri, Guiliano, THE NEW PET, 29 x 39½ (4241/170) — 2600

Alken, Henry, manner of, A HORSE DRAWN GIG IN A WINTER LANDSCAPE, 19¼ x 15¼ (666/147) — 325

Alken, Henry, Jr. attributed (19c), A PAIR OF HUNTING SCENES, each 12 x 20 (4208/208) — 2400

Allenroth, J., after J. van Bremen, CHILD READING (LITTLE MONA LISA), 16¼ X 13¼ (4240/13) — 1600

Alma-Tadema, Lawrence (1836-1912), A LAKE IN BAVARIA, 9 x 14 (633/193) — 1700

Alvarez, Luis (1841-1901), THE CARDINAL'S RECEPTION, d.1877, 26¼ x 47¼ (4208/129) — 24000

Amerling, Friedrich, Von, A WOMAN WITH A RED KERCHIEF, 20½ x 13¾ (4241/44) — 2600

Anastasi, Auguste P.C., 1820-89, COURTYARD OF CONVENT OF ST. BONAVENTURE, 1867, 14 x 24 (4122/178) — 1700

Andreotti, Federigo (1847-1930), THE FLIRTATION, 41½ x 31¼ (4208/122) — 8500

Anker, Albert (1831-1910), THE OLDER SISTER, d.1879, 9 x 11 (4208/30) — 34000

Anrooy, Anton van (1870-1949), PATH ALONG THE CANAL, 20½ x 30½ (4208/65) — 1800

Ansdell, Richard, attributed to (1815-85), HORSE AND DOG IN A STABLE, 1830, 20 x 25½ (666/146) — 1200

Ansdell, Richard, R.A. (1815-85), CROSSING THE MOOR, d.1866, 30 x 54 (4208/212) — 5000

Aranda, Jose Jimenez, 1837-1903, DON QUIXOTE & SANCHO PANZA RETURNING, 1900, 16½ x 22 (4161/127) — 14500

Armand-Dumaresq, E.C. (1826-95), THE GENEVA CONFERENCE-FOUNDING OF RED CROSS, 50¾ x 78¾ (4240/70) — 3750

Aron, Antal, BY THE LAKE, 12 x 9, on panel (4241/57) — 1800

Assmus, Robert (b.1837-), A RESOUNDING CALL, 29¼ x 42¼ (4071/11) — 3250

Attanasio, Natale, 1846-1923, VISITING DAY, 14 x 24 (4122/162) — 1200

Aubusson, GRENADIER, 11 x 7¾, watercolor (4208/202) — 1900

Austrian School, VIEW OF SALZBURG, 13 x 25¾ (4241/21) — 4000

Bachrach-Baree, Emmanuel (b.1863), AN ADMIRING GLANCE, 8½ x 6, on panel (4208/50) — 900

Bakalowicz, L. 1833-1903, Polish, BEHIND THE ARRAS, 39¼ x 27½ (4122/123) — 2600

Bachrach-Baree
(4208/50)

Bakalowicz (4122/123)

Benoit (4208/167)

Berne-Bellecour (4208/196)

Bakker-Korff, Alexander Hugo (1824-82), SERVING THE SOUP, 6½ x 4, on panel (4208/70)   6250
Ballesio, F., A FAVORITE OF THE HAREM, 29½ x 21¼ (4122/154)   1250
Ballesio, F., FAREWELL, 38½ x 25½ (4241/182)   700
Barbarini, Emil (1855-1930), AFTER THE THUNDERSTORM, 20⅝ x 16⅝ (666/191)   3250
Barbarini, Franz (1804-73), BY THE WATERFALL, 22¾ x 31 (633/203)   1600
Barillot, Leon (1844-1929), PEASANT WOMAN WITH COWS BY A POND, 10½ x 13¾, on
panel (4208/161)   850
Barker, Thomas Jones, 1815-82, THE MOSS TROOPER, 36¼ x 28 (4122/293)   750
Barland, Adam (19c), THE OLD BRIDGE AND COUNTRY ROAD, pair, d.1887, 20 x 30
(4208/217)   2750
Barnes, Samuel J. (1884-6 fl.), WEST MALVERN, WORCESTERSHIRE, dated '8, 46 x 36
(666/181)   800
Baro, Jose Tapiro Y, 1830-1913, THE AMBUSH, 20 x 15 (4264/404)   3000
Bartolini, Francesco, 19-20c, THE CARPET MERCHANTS, 20½ x 14¾ (4197/349)   5250
Barucci, Pietro, b.1845, LOADING THE HAYWAGONS, 28 x 52 (4122/148)   2100
Barye, Antoine Louis (1796-1875), TIGER DEVOURING A HORSE, 4⅛ x 9¼, black chalk
(4260/607)   2200
Barzanti, L., THE ROSE BUSH, 40 x 28 (633/41)   350
Baudit, Amedee, Swiss, 1825-90, LOW TIDE, MOONLIGHT, 1888, 39¾ x 61¼ (4122/208)   1500
Baumgartner, Peter, SEE THE FINE DUCK?, 26 x 33¼ (4241/70)   25000
Baumgartner, Peter, SEE THE FINE PIG?, 26 x 33¼ (4241/69)   29000
Becker, Carl Ludwig, Friedrich, 1820-1900, WOMAN IN RED VELVET, 1879, 25½ x 19¼
(4161/55)   4500
Beernaert, Euphrosine, WINDMILL BY A CANAL, 19½ x 13½ (4241/133)   1000
Beers, Jacob van (1852-1927), LADY WITH POODLE, on panel, 13 x 9½ (666/199)   1800
Begas, Karl Joseph (1794-1854), FANNY ELSSLER, 82 x 59½ (4240/1)   5750
Begas, Oscar (1828-83), BEGGAR GIRL, 1850, 31½ x 26½ (4240/2)   1700
Bellet, A. (19c), A COSTUME BALL, 25¼ x 31½ (666/164)   800
Benoit, V.P.F.L. attributed to (19c), HOT AIR BALLOONING, 28 x 36 (4208/167)   2400
Beraud, Jean (1849-1936), LE BOULEVARD ST. DENIS, PARIS, 15¼ x 22 (4208/191)   70000
Berg, Reinierus Carolus Van Den, FEEDING THE CAT, 15 x 19 (4241/117)   1800
Bernard, Emile, 1868-1941, ODALISQUES, 1898, 47¼ x 71 (4161/234)   16500
Berne-Bellecour, Etienne P., 1838-1910, BUGLERS IN A FIELD, 1877, 4¾ x 8¼ (4122/242)   1600
Berne-Bellecour, Etienne P., 1838-1910, LETTER FROM HOME, 13¾ x 10½ (4161/227)   3200
Berne-Bellecour, Etienne P. (1838-1910), CAVALRY OFFICER LIGHTING A CIGARETTE,
d.1901, 14½ x 10¼, on panel (4208/198)   1400
Berne-Bellecour, Etienne P. (1838-1910), CAVALRY OFFICER WARMING HIS HANDS,
d.1896, 14¾ x 10¼, on panel (4208/196)   *2100*
Berne-Bellecour, Etienne P. (1838-1910), ON GUARD, d.1903, 15 x 10¾, on panel
(4208/197)   1400

Berne-Bellecour, Etienne P. (1838-1910), THE CARD GAME, d.1890, 13¾ x 18½, on panel
(4208/200)   4000
Berne-Bellecour, Etienne P. (1838-1910), THE ZOUAVE, 14¾ x 10¼ on panel (4208/195)   2300
Berne-Bellecour, Jean J., b.1874, A SKITTISH MOUNT, 14¾ x 18¼ (4122/243)   2750
Beul, Frans de, PEASANT WITH SHEEP AND CHICKENS IN A STABLE, 19¾ x 13½
(4241/132)   2000
Bilbao y Martinez, Gonzalo (1860-1938), CIGARETTE GIRLS OF SEVILLE, 42 x 64 (666/259)   1600
Binder, Alois, A GOOD GAME OF CARDS, 22½ x 18 (4241/60)   2700
Biseo, Cesare, 1843-1909, EVENING IN AN ARAB VILLAGE, 39½ x 29½ (4197/368)   1300
Bjorck, Gustav Oscar (1860-1929), THE NAILMAKERS, 53 x 59 (4240/26)   18000
Blaas, Eugen von, 1843-1931, Aust., THE WATER CARRIER, 1907, 47 x 27¼ (4122/38)   *45000*

Blaas (4122/38)

Blas, G. (19c), THE RETURN FROM FLANDERS, on panel, 26 x 15½ (666/138)   100
Blommers, Bernardus Johannes, BUYING MILK, 23 x 26 (4241/119)   12500
Blommers, Bernardus Johannes, LEARNING TO SHARE, 19 x 14¼, watercolor on paper
(4241/120)   12000
Bocion, Francois L.D., 1828-90, BY THE LAKE, 1883, 10½ x 8¼ (4122/201)   1600
Bock, T. E. A. de (1851-1904), THE POUDON COMMONS, 32 x 56 (4240/20)   11000
Bock, T.E.A. de, 1851-1904, FARMHOUSE, COTTAGE BY EDGE OF MEADOW, 13 x 18¾
(4122/69)   3500
Boddington, Henry John (1811-1865), CROSSING A STREAM, 32 x 39½ (666/144)   550
Boehme, Karl Theodor (b.1866-), A SUNNY DAY, 29½ x 22¾ (4071/18)   1600
Boggs, Frank, attrib., (1855-1926), OFF THE COAST, 12 x 17½ (633/49)   450
Boldini, Giovanni (1842-1931), TEASING THE PARROT, 18 x 13 (4208/124)   34000
Boldini, Giovanni (1845-1931), EDGAR DEGAS AT A CAFE TABLE, d.1883, 11¼ x 8, black
crayon (4260/633)   8000
Boldini, Giovanni (1845-1931), PORTRAIT OF JACQUES EMILE BLANCHE, d.1884, 12 x 8¼,
pencil (4260/638)   7000
Boldini, Giovanni (1845-1931), STUDY OF A LADY TAKING TEA, 21¼ x 17, charcoal
(4260/636)   4000
Boldini, Giovanni (1845-1931), TWO DANCERS, 14 3/16 x 10 9/16, mixed media (4260/635)   12500
Boldini, Giovanni, 1842-1931, THE GOSSIPERS, 8½ x 14 (4122/165)   15000
Bonheur, Rosa, BULL IN A LANDSCAPE, 15 x 18 (4240/52)   1700
Bonheur, Rosa, After, 1822-90, LABOURAGE NIVERNAIS, LE SOMBRAGE, 1850, 33 x 65
(4122/215)   2500
Bonheur, Rosa, 1822-99, TEAM OF CHAROLAIS OXEN, 12¾ x 17 (4161/235)   600
Bonington, Richard P.,manner (1802-28), ON THE SEA COAST, 10¾ x 13¾ (4240/77)   700
BoniFazi, Adriano, SLEEPING GRANDMOTHER, 28½ x 19½ (4241/172)   850
Bonnard, Pierre, GROUPE DE FEMMES, 1895, Watercolor, pencil, 7¾ x 10¼ (4170/110)   11000
Bonnat, Leon Joseph F., 1883-1922, YOUNG ROMAN GIRL, 36½ x 28¼ (4122/273)   1300

Bortignoni, Giuseppe, THE TRAVELLING MUSICIAN, d.1901, 20½ x 28 (4208/123) — 3000
Bos, G. Van Den, TEN ON THE TERRACE, 23¼ x 36¼ (4241/121) — 6500
Bosch, E.M.T. (1863-1933), SUNDOWN, pastel on paper, 19¼ x 21 (666/206) — 800
Bossuet, Francois A., 1800-89, A SPANISH HILL TOWN, 1850, 29½ x 37 (4161/99) — 15000
Bostock, John, 1808-69, PORTRAIT OF ROSA BRADWARDINE, 18 x 13¼ (4122/298) — 1400
Bough, Samuel (1822-78), AT THE TOP OF A LAKE, 20 x 28¼ (666/230) — 1000
Bouguereau, William Adolphe (1825-1905), L'ORAGE, d.1874, 63 x 35½ (4208/176) — 57500
Bouquet, Michel (1807-90), HALT OF THE HUNTERS AT FONTAINEBLEAU, 16 x 22¾ (4240/37) — 5250
Bourlard, A. (19c), AN ITALIAN OXCART, 1860, 38½ x 32½ (4240/54) — 750
Boussuet, Francois Antoine, 1800-89, MOSQUE D'AL-GEBER, ARSILLE, MOROCCO, 17½ x 13½ (4197/357) — 2400
Bouter, Cornelis Wouter, BENEATH THE APPLE TREE, 24 x 36 (4241/111) — 4000
Bouter, Cornelis Wouter, FEEDING THE BABY, 20 x 24 (4241/112) — 3400
Boutibonne, C.E., 1816-97, Hungarian, SHOWING A PREFERENCE, 1874, 23¼ x 18¼ (4122/121) — *7000*

Boutibonne
(4122/121)

Brabazon, Hercules B. (1821-1906), PORTRAIT OF AN ELDERLY LADY, AFTER REMBRANDT, 8¼ x 5⅞, pastel (4260/650) — 450
Braekeleer, Ferdinand de (1792-1883), LE MENAGE HEUREUX AND LE MENAGE MALHEUREUX, pair, on panel, 1853, 28 x 22½ (4240/14) — 60000
Braekeleer, Ferdinand de, 1792-1883, GRANDFATHER'S FAVORITE, 1839, 14¼ x 11¼ (4122/101) — 10000
Braith, Anton, 1836-1905, CALVES IN A FIELD, 17 x 22 (4122/7) — 16000
Brangwyn, Sir Frank (1867-1956), SELF PORTRAIT, 8½ x 5½, black chalk (4260/657) — 1300
Breanski, Alfred F. de (d.1893), MORNING MIST IN BORROWDALE, 24¼ x 36 (633/232) — 1100
Breanski, Alfred F. de, (19c), THAMES, EAST MOLESY, 20 x 30 (666/219) — 950
Bremen, Johann Georg M. von (l813-86), A GOOD DINNER, d.1856, 9¾ x 8¼ (4208/28) — 13000
Bremen, Johann Georg M. von (1813-86), THE FIRST PRAYER (Gottvertrauen), d.1883, 21¾ x 15¾ (4208/29) — 25000
Breton, Jules Adolphe (1827-1905), BRITTANY WIDOW, 1886, 37 x 30¾ (4240/61) — 3750
British School, SUSANNAH AND THE ELDERS, 8½ x 9¾ (4264/414) —
British School, 19c, FIGURES IN A TAVERN INTERIOR, 24¾ x 29½ (4208/232) — 1500
Bromley, William, III (d.1888), RIDING THE SOW, 28 x 36½ (4208/225) — 7000
Brown, Henriette (1829-1901), PORTRAIT OF A YOUNG WOMAN, 1877, 45¾ x 35¼ (666/179) — 475
Brozik, Wenceslas (1851-1901), COLUMBUS AT THE COURT OF SPAIN, 36 x 60 (4208/108) — 5000
Bruckman, Lodewyk (b.1903), TO LOUISE, 1945, 19½ x 16 (4240/25) — 600
Brunery, Francois, NAUGHTY MAIDS, 22 x 18 (4241/181) — 7000
Brunner, Leopold, 1788-1866, FLORAL STILL LIFES, pair, 34½ x 24¼ (4161/2) — 11000
Bryan, Alfred (1852-99), TWO CARICATURES, CARLYLE AND DISRAELI, each, 16½ x 10¾, pastel (4260/658) — 2200

Buchlinder, S. (19c), PORTRAIT OF THE ARTIST, on panel, 7⅛ x 5¼ (666/173) — 550

Buhler, Fritz Zuber, MORNING GLORIES IN HER HAIR, 21½ x 18 (4241/59) — 5500

Bundy, Edgar (1862-1922), A GOOD SMOKE, d.1888, 14 x 18 (4208/230) — 1900

Burne-Jones, Sir Edward C. (1833-98), HEAD OF A SLAVE, 8⅝ x 7 6/8, black crayon (4260/653) — 4600

Burne-Jones, Sir Edward C. (1833-98), STUDIES OF A DRAPED FEMALE FIGURE DOUBLE-SIDED, 15 x 10, black chalk (4260/648) — 500

Burne-Jones, Sir Edward C. (1833-98), STUDIES OF ANDROMEDA, 13¼ x 19⅜, charcoal (4260/654) — 7200

Burne-Jones, Sir Edward C. (1833-98), STUDY OF THE ARTIST'S SON, PHILIP, ca1875, 8¾ x 7, pencil (4260/646) — 2300

Burnier, Richard (1826-84), CATTLE ON THE SEASHORE NEAR SCHEVENINGEN, 41 x 63 (4240/21) — 5000

Burrows, Robert, 1851-71, LANDSCAPE WITH COTTAGE AND FIGURES, 1871, 14 x 18 (4122/297) — 1700

Burt, Charles-Thomas (1823-1902), HAYING, d.1892, 30 x 48 (633/132) — 650

Bylandt, A.E.A. van (1829-1890), IN THE BRUNNER PASS, on panel, 16 x 12¾ (666/171) — 850

Cabanel, Alexandre (1824-89), THE DEATH OF MOSES, 1851, 112 x 120 (4240/57) — 70000

Cachoud, Francois-Charles (b.1853), DRIVING THE HERD BY MOONLIGHT, 27½ x 31½ (4208/156) — 1100

Cachoud, Francois-Charles (b.1853), SUMMER EVENING, 25½ x 32 (4208/157) — 1300

Calamata, Josephine, d.1893, THREE GENERATIONS, 15 x 18 (4161/233) — 1100

Calame, A., and VerboeckHoven, GOATHERD AND GOATS RESTING BY A MOUNTAIN STREAM, 23½ x 16½ (4241/131) — 9500

Calbet, Antoine (1860-1944), AMONG THE ROSES, 46 x 32½ (666/252) — 2000

Callow, J., THE VALE OF CLWYD, 1863, 12 x 8 (633/66) — 600

Camphausen, Wilhelm, 1818-85, PRUSSIAN SOLDIER GUARDING A ZOUAVE, 1879, 15½ x 18½ (4161/37) — 3000

Canton, Gustav Jacob, Austrian, GYPSY CARAVAN, 21¾ x 42 (4161/22) — 1750

Capeinick, Jean (1838-1890), A STILL LIFE WITH ROSES, 21½ x 14½ (633/79) — 800

Capone, Gaetano, 1845-1920, LA SPIAGGIA DI MAIORI DURANTE L'IMBARCO, 1891, 25 x 58 (4122/144) — 3250

Carbo, Mariano Fortuny Y, 1838-74, ARABS OUTSIDE A GROTTO, 12¼ x 17½ (4197/360) — 800

Carelli, Giuseppe, 1858-1921, FISHING BOATS OFF THE COAST, 7½ x 14¼ (4122/146) — 350

Carmichael, James Wilson, 1800-68, A STIFF BREEZE, 1859, 24 x 36 (4161/249) — 2500

Carolus-Duran, C.E.A. (1838-1917), TEMPTATION, 23 x 28 (666/190) — 1400

Carolus, Jean, LE CONTEMPLATION, 20½ x 16 (4241/123) — 1700

Carpeaux, Jean Baptiste (1827-75), PORTRAIT OF CHARLES GOUNOD, 1871, H25½, terra cotta (4260/1441) — 7000

Carpeaux, Jean Baptiste (1827-75), SELF-PORTRAIT, 5 3/16 x 4 15/16, charcoal (4260/611) — 1100

Carpentero, H. Joseph Gommarus, KITCHEN CHORES, 12 x 9½ (4241/139) — 1700

Carriere, Eugene, 1849-1906, PORTRAIT OF A WOMAN, 13¾ x 10¾ (4122/263) — 1300

Cazin, J.C. (1841-1901), LANDSCAPE WITH HAYSTACKS, 18 x 21½ (4240/50) — 4500

Cazin, J.C. (1841-1901), MOONLIGHT IN HOLLAND, 26 x 32 (4240/49) — 3250

Celli, Lelio(?), THE BERRY GATHERER, 87 x 32 (633/201) — 1200

Ceramano, Charles-Ferdinand, (1829-1909), SHEPHERD AND SHEEP, 25½ x 32 (633/33) — 1400

Cerri, Giulio, 19c, ARRIVAL AT THE PORT OF CAPRI, 1883, 31¼ x 23½ (4161/140) — 11000

Cezanne, Paul (1839-1906), PAGE OF STUDIES, INCLUDING MME CEZANNE SEWING, ca1877-80, 7¾ x 9⅛, pencil (4260/1430) — 27000

Chabas, Paul (1869-1937), L'ALGUE, 83 x 63 (4208/184) — 17000

Chalon, Henry B., 1770-1849, THE DUKE OF HAMILTON ON CHESTNUT HUNTER, 1800, 34 x 47½ (4161/245) — 3000

Charlemont, Hugo, 1850-1939, Aust., AT THE FORGE, 14½ x 18 (4122/31) — 1100

Charles, Frantz (1862-1928), MAKING THE TOY BOAT, 25 x 32 (4208/90) — 3300

Chasseriau, Theodore (1819-56), PORTRAIT OF LOUIS MARCOTTE DE QUIVIERES, d.1841, 13⅛ x 10, pencil (4260/608) — 102000

Chelmonski, Jozef (1850-1914), OBEREK (UN DANSE POLOGNE), 1878, 27 x 51½ (666/261) — 20000

Cheret, Jules (1836-1933), A WOMAN, SEEN FROM THE BACK, ca1890, 14⅜ x 9⅝, sanguine crayon (4260/1433) — 900

Chevilliard, Vincent J.B. (1841-1904), SELECTING THE MEAL, 7¼ x 5¾, on panel (4208/192) — 2900

Chialiva, Luigi (1842-1914), THE OLD SHEPHERD, 30½ x 45½ (4240/9) — 6250

Chialiva, Luigi (1842-1914), THE SHEPHERDESS, 30½ x 43½ (4240/10) — 5000

Chinese school (E19c), THE HONGS AT CANTON, 16 x 23½ (666/195) — 7000

Chinnery, George, attributed (1748-1847), VIEW OF HONG KONG HARBOR, 15¾ x 24 (4208/206) — *1900*

Costa (4122/152)

Chinnery (4208/206)

Chwala, Adolf, MOONLIGHT ON A CASTLE BY THE SEA, 35¼ x 48¾ (4241/158)	2400
Ciardi, Gugliemo, (1842-1917), A VENETIAN FISHING BOAT, 14 x 10 (633/60)	475
Clairin, Georges, 1843-1919, SARAH BERNHARDT DIRECTING BATTLE AT WAGRAM, 33½ x 43½, 1900 (4161/231)	3500
Clarion, J., FISHING BOATS, 21 x 27¾ (633/116)	325
Clays, Paul Jean, CALME, OUDE MAAS, DORDRECHT, 21x 29¼, on panel (4241/134)	5000
Clays, Paul Jean (1819-1900), A HARBOR BY MOONLIGHT, 30½ x 43½ (4208/97)	6250
Coccorante, Leonardo, circle of, A VIEW OF RUINS, 18c, 46 x 55½ (4148/197)	2200
Codina Y Langlin, Victoriano, OFF TO SCHOOL, 23 x 30 (4241/187)	2750
Col, Jan David, THE WINE TASTERS, 5 x 4½ (4241/140)	1600
Cole, George (1810-83), SHEPHERD AND HIS FLOCK, SUNSET, d.1873, 17 x 24, on board (4208/213)	2400
Coleman, Charles, d.1874, A ROMAN STREET SCENE, d.1872, 17½ x 40½ (633/34)	1200
Colkett, Samuel D., attributed (1806-63), CHILDREN FISHING BY A POND NEAR A FARMHOUSE, 21¼ x 31¼, on panel (4208/220)	8500
Collins, Anthony, LANDSCAPE WITH FIGURES, 15¾ x 22 (4122/299)	1800
Constable, John, manner of, HOUSE BY A STREAM, 14 x 18½ (633/42)	500
Constable, John, school of, DEDHAM LOCK AND MILL, 8 x 11, on panel (633/80)	425
Constant, Jean Joseph B. (1845-1902), PORTRAIT OF A LADY, 21¾ x 17¾, on panel (633/228)	700
Constantin, Auguste Aristide F., 1824-95, 16 x 13 (4161/212)	2000
Constantini, G., THE OLD SMOKER, d.1883, 8¼ x 6 (633/76)	225
Conti, Tito (1824-1924), COURTLY LOVE, 30½ x 24 (633/195)	3500
Cooke, Edward William (1811-80), BOULOGNE FROM THE SOUTH PIER, 4 x 11 9/16, pencil (4260/665)	450
Coomans, Diana, 19c, LES COLOMBRES, 17½ x 13½ (4122/106)	4500
Coomans, Heva & Diana, 19c, ANTICIPATION, 12½ x 9¾ (4122/107)	650
Coomans, Pierre Oliver Joseph, A LANGUID BEAUTY, 7 x 8¾ (4241/122)	800
Cooper, Abraham, 1787-1868, MR. FELLOWES ON HIS FAVORITE HUNTER FALSTAFF, 33¾ x 44 (4122/285)	3000
Cooper, Thomas S., attrib. to, 1803-1902, CATTLE WATERING, 1846, 24 x 28 (4122/295)	1500
Corot, Jean Baptiste C. (1796-1875), FONTAINEBLEAU-LA VALLEE DE LA SOLLE, ca.1865, (4208/142)	15000
Corot, Jean Baptiste C., 1796-1875, LES ROCHES BOISEES AU PATRE SOLITAIRE, 1850, 15 x 10½ (4161/154)	35000
Corrodi, Hermann David Salomon, 1844-1905, AN ARAB STREET, 39½ x 22 (4197/358)	5750

Cosenza, Giuseppe, 1847-1922, PAIR, FISHING BY SHORE, FISHING BY NAPLES BAY, 1884, 11 x 7 (4122/149) — 800

Costa, Emanuele, FEEDING DOVES, 22½ x 17 (4241/180) — 1200

Costa, Giovanni (1833-1903), TURKISH SLAVE GIRL, 47 x 26½ (4208/117) — 5000

Costa, Oreste, b.1851, HUNTSMAN'S STILL LIFE, 1873, 32 x 25, oval (4122/152) — 1200

Couder, Jean A. R., 1848-1912, POULTRY FEEDING OUTSIDE A STABLE DOOR, 32 x 25½ (4122/212) — 1400

Courbet, Gustave, attrib. to (1819-77), DEER GRAZING IN A CLEARING, 19¾ x 24⅞ (666/209) — 1000

Courbet, Gustave, LE CHEMINEAU, 13 x 9¾ (4241/203) — 19000

Courbet, Gustave (1819-77), ANATOLE, 9¾ x 8, pencil (4260/603) — 6250

Courbet, Gustave, 1819-77, MOUNTAIN STREAM, 27¾ x 36¼ (4122/187) — 22000

Court, Joseph Desire, 1797-1865, TRIUMPHAL SCENE, 15¼ x 23 (4122/249) — 2500

Couture, Thomas (1815-47), PORTRAIT OF THE ARTIST'S MOTHER, 19 x 15, charcoal (4260/621) — 1900

Couture, Thomas (1815-70), FEMALE HEAD, 21¾ x 20½ (4240/58) — 13500

Couture, Thomas (1815-79), PORTRAIT OF A YOUNG BOY, 14¼ x 11 (4208/181) — 4000

Couturier, Philbert-Leon, DUCKS AND CHICKENS IN A FARMYARD, 12¼ x 15¾ (4241/215) — 1400

Creswick, Thomas (1811-1869), CHILDREN BY A POND, 1850, 18¼ x 21¾ (666/152) — 700

Creswick, Thomas, 1811-69, RIVER LANDSCAPE WITH CASTLE RUIN, 21 x 28 (4161/254) — 1000

Culverhouse, Johann M., 1820-ca91, MARKET SCENE BY MOONLIGHT, 1850, 16¼ x 20 (4161/63) — 4000

Culverhouse, Johann M. (1820-ca91), FLEMISH SEAPORT, MOONLIGHT, 1849?, 29½ x 36 (4240/18) — 2750

Dahl, Hans Andreas, WINDY HILLSIDE ABOVE THE FJORD, 38 x 62 (4241/151) — 8000

Dalph, J. H., PORTRAIT OF A SEATED BOY HOLDING A STICK, 41 x 33, 1862 (4149/152) — 1300

Danger, Henri-Camille (1857-1937), PORTRAIT OF A YOUNG GIRL, 13½ x 11 (633/48) — 650

Dansaert, L. Marie Constant, A DOMESTIC CHAT, 13 x 9¼ (4241/142) — 1800

Dansaert, L.M.C. (1830-1909), A DANDY, 1882, on panel, 10½ x 8½ (666/185) — 900

Darnaut, Hugo, 1851-1937, Austrian, PATH TO THE FIELDS, 43¾ x 33 (4161/13) — 5000

Daubigny, Charles Francois, LA MOISSON, 11½ x 20½ (4241/205) — 14000

Daubigny, Charles Francois, 1817-78, RIVER LANDSCAPE, 1873, 16 x 26 (4161/156) — 3000

Daubigny, Charles Francois, 1817-78, WINDMILLS ON A CANAL, 1872, 8½ x 15¾, on board (4161/155) — 4250

Daumier, Honore, L'AVOCAT SALUANT, bronze, 6¼, 1840-45 (4252/602) — 6250

Daumier, Honore, SPECTATORS AND COUPLE (double sided drawing) pen and ink, 5¾ x 6¾ (4250/403) — 17500

Daumier, Honore (1807-79), AMATEURS EN CONTEMPLATION, pair of sculptures, H7¼ each, bronze (4164/3) — 9000

Daumier, Honore (1807-79), STUDY OF HEADS (THE SPECTATORS), 6⅝ x 7¾, mixed media (4260/1405) — 8000

Daumier, Honore (1807-79), TARTUFFE (FULCHIRON), H6⅜, bronze (4260/1404) — 18000

David, Jacques Louis, school of, THE BATTLE OF THERMOPOLAE, 18 x 22, on paper (633/197) — 1300

David, Jules, 1808-92, FASHION DESIGNS, 4 WATERCOLORS, 1871-78, 10½ x 8½ (4122/268) — 750

Dawson, Montague, 1895-1973, NEARING THE LAND, 1867, 36 x 24¼ (4161/276) — 16000

De Beul, Franz, 1849-1919, SHEEP & CHICKENS IN A STABLE, 1881, 27½ x 21½ (4161/94) — 2300

De Bruine, 19c, RUSTICS BY THE WAYSIDE, 1841, 26¼ x 23½ (4122/71) — 2400

De Cool, Gabriel, b.1854, A YOUNG WOMAN WITH A BOOK, 24¾ x 20½ (4122/261) — 500

De Cuvillon, Louis, Robert, b.1848, THE TAMBOURINE PLAYER, 8¾ x 5½, 1886 (4264/418) — 800

Debat-Ponson, E.B., 1847-1913, A PLEASANT INTERRUPTION, 1889, 26 x 36½ (4122/221) — 4250

Defaux, Alexandre, 1826-1900, FISHING BOATS IN A HARBOUR, 1859, 16 x 21 (4161/171) — 1500

Defregger, Franz von (1835-1921), SUNDAY AFTERNOON, 25 x 19½ (4208/34) — 29000

Degas, Edgar, FEMME SORTANT DU BAIN, FRAGMENT, bronze, 16¼, ca1896-1911 (4252/606) — 9500

Deiters, Heinrich, 1840-1916, THE OLD MILL, 1880, 24¾ x 38 (4161/7) — 1700

Del Campo, Federico, 19c, THE FLOWER VENDOR, 1880, 8¾ x 14¾ (4161/139) — 17000

Delacroix, Eugene, ETUDE DE FEMMES ARABES, pen, ink, 6¾ x 10⅝ (4170/104) — 3300

Delacroix, Eugene (1798-1863), L'APOTHEOSE DU DUC DE BUCKINGHAM, ca1825, 25¼ x 25¼ (4169/5) — 35000

Delacroix, Eugene (1798-1863), MERE ET ENFANT, 5 x 3⅞, pencil (4164/2) — 550

Delacroix, Eugene (1798-1863), STUDY OF A SEATED WOMAN, 9½ x 7, mixed media (4260/604) — 11000

Delacroix, H., ARAB MARKET SCENE, 18 x 30 (4122/224) — 1300

Delaroche, Paul, attrib. to (1797-1856), NAPOLEON IN EGYPT, 1837, 27 x 21¾ (666/216) — 1800

Delart, Charles, 1841-95, THE DEFENSE OF THE CASTLE, 24 x 19½ (4161/218) — 3500

Delattre, Henri (1801-76), LOADING THE WAGON, d.1848, 31 x 50 (4208/162) — _3000_

Delobbe (4208/173)

Delattre (4208/162)

Delessard, Auguste J., 1827-90, CHICKS & HEN, 1858, 36 x 48 (4122/213)	1500
Delobbe, Francois Alfred (1835-1920), A DEMURE MAIDEN, d.1870, 38 x 28 (4208/173)	*4000*
Delort, Charles-Edouard, 1841-95, AT THE WELL, 1874, 37 x 51 (4122/248)	6750
Delpy, Hippolyte Camille, WOMAN WASHING ON A RIVERBANK, 12 x 19¾ (4241/224)	2600
Delpy, Hippolyte Camille (1842-1910), SUNSET OVER A POND, 6¼ x 8½, on panel (633/62)	950
Demeur-Charton, LE CHEMIN INONDE, 21½ x 15¼ (4241/214)	1800
Derain, Andre, BATHERS, 13 x 16⅛, ca1908 (4252/623)	6000
Derain, Andre, BATHERS, 11¾ x 12½ (4252/622)	6500
Desboutin, Marcelllin (1823-1902), SELF-PORTRAIT, ca1892-98, 13¾ x 10¼ (4260/632)	4200
Dessoulavy, Thomas (1829-48), A SCENE IN THE ROMAN CAMPAGNA, 1842, 30 x 45 (666/227)	1300
Desvarreaux, Raymond, 1876-1961, THE CHARGE, 1904, 34½ x 26¾ (4122/241)	1500
Detaille, Jean B.E. (1848-1912), GENERAL OF THE FIRST EMPIRE, 1892, 31½ x 25½ (4240/66)	14000
Detaille, Jean B.E. (1848-1912), LE REGIMENT QUI PASSE, PARIS, 1875, 60 x 50 (4240/65)	30000
Detti, Cesare, 1847-1914, THE HALT AT THE CABARET, 26 x 49¾ (4122/158)	39000
Deveria, Achille (1800-57), LADY WITH A MANTILLA, 12¼ x 17½, pencil (4260/601)	3200
Di Chirico, Giacomo, 1845-84, A PROCESSION, WINTER, 29 x 23 (4122/161)	10000
Diaz de la Pena, Narcisse V., 1807-76, REVERIE, 10½ x 8 (4161/199)	3000
Diaz de la Pena, Narcisse V. (1807-76), A WOODLAND POOL, 7¼ x 10, on panel (4208/144)	6250
Diaz de la Pena, Narcisse V. (1807-76), PLAYING BOWLS, 6¾ x 9¾, on board (4208/143)	5500
Diaz de la Pena, Narcisse V., 1807-76, CLEARING IN THE FOREST, 1872, 10¼ x 7¾ (4122/182)	3500
Diaz de la Pena, Narcisse V., 1807-76, ROCKY LANDSCAPE, 8¾ x 15½ (4122/190)	2800
Diaz de la Pena, Narcisse V., 1807-76, WOMAN IN RED BESIDE A FOREST POOL, 7½ x 9½ (4161/153)	3750
Diddaert, Henri (fl. 1845-66), CAVALIERS STOPPING AT AN INN, d.1860, 10½ x 13½, on panel (4208/91)	2200
Dirks, Andreas, 1866-1922, SHIPPING OFF A COASTAL TOWN, 5½ x 7 (4122/26)	1200
Doll, Anton, SKATING OUTSIDE AN INN, 36 x 60½ (4241/14)	14000
Dollmann, John Charles, 1851-1934, AT THE CAB STAND, 1894, 15 x 24½ (4122/319)	2500
Domingo Y Marques, Francisco, GOYA AND MAJA, 23 x 37 (4241/194)	3500
Dommerson, William, VILLAGE MARKET, 36 x 28 (4241/95)	2500
Dore, Gustav, MOUNTAIN GOATS CROSSING A RAVINE, 15½ x 25 (4241/201)	1400
Dore, Gustav, 1832-83, CINDERELLA TRYING ON THE SLIPPER, 29 x 17¾ (4161/190)	3250

Dore, Gustav, 1832-83, PEASANTS BOWING TO PUSS-IN-BOOTS, 29 x 45 (4161/196)	8500
Dore, Gustav, 1832-83, PUSS-IN-BOOTS, 29¾ x 18 (4161/194)	6500
Dore, Gustav, 1832-83, PUSS-IN-BOOTS BEFORE THE OGRE, 29½ x 18 (4161/195)	5000
Dore, Gustav, 1832-83, REST ON THE FLIGHT INTO EGYPT, 32½ x 55½ (4161/229)	2200
Dore, Gustav, 1832-83, THE GALLOP TOWARD THE CASTLE, 20½ x 18 (4161/192)	1750
Dore, Gustav, 1832-83, THE PRINCESS ON THE STAIRS, (4161/191)	1500
Dore, Gustav, 1832-83, TOM THUMB AND THE GIANT, 28 x 44½ (4161/193)	9500
Douzette, Louis, BEACH SCENE BY MOONLIGHT, 6¾ x 9½, on panel (4241/24)	1500
Dr. Fregger, Franz von, attrib. to, JOHANNES BRAHMS, 1889, on copper, 18½ x 14⅜ (666/256)	400
Drathmann, Johann-Christoffer, MATING CALL, 31½ x 47½ (4241/34)	850
Drouin, D., BY THE BANKS OF A CANAL, 16 x 21¼ (4122/173)	600
Du Chene de Vere, H., PEASANT GIRL WITH A BASKET, 1882, 13¼ x 9¼ (4122/271)	1500
Dubowskoi, Nicholas, 1859-1918, A FISHING BOAT, 1898, 21 x 28 (4161/105)	2500
Duffield, William L., fl.1873-81, THE DAY'S BAG, 1881, 19 x 30¼ (4122/309)	2750
Dulverger, Theophile E., b.1821, A PAUSE AT THE PIANO, 10 x 8 (4161/214)	3000
Dumont (?), Francois (19c), THE CONTRIBUTION, d.1872, 25½ x 35½, on panel (4208/89)	2100
Duntze, Johannes B., 1823-95, WINTER LANDSCAPE, 1875, 24 x 36 (4161/11)	8000
Dupre, Jules, FEEDING THE CHICKENS, 13 x 18 (4241/211)	3600
Dupre, Jules, 1811-89, A PUNT ON A POND, SUMMER, 14½ x 21, on panel (4208/135)	10000
Dupre, Jules, 1811-89, A WOODLAND POOL, 29 x 36 (4122/191)	4750
Dupre, Jules, 1811-89, BRIDGE OVER A WOODLAND STREAM, 16 x 12 (4161/166)	3500
Dupre, Jules, 1811-89, COWS WATERING AT SUNSET, 20¼ x 32¼ (4208/134)	4250
Dupre, Jules, 1811-89, FARMHOUSES BY A POND, 13 x 16½ (4208/139)	1500
Dupre, Jules, 1811-89, MOONLIGHT BY THE SEA, ca1870, 32 x 39½ (4240/42)	3750
Dupre, Jules, 1811-89, STORMY LANDSCAPE, on panel, 7½ x 10 (4240/41)	6000
Dupre, Jules, 1811-89, THE OAK TREE, 34 x 50½ (4122/192)	10000
Dupre, Jules, 1811-89, THE POND OF THE GREAT OAK, ca1865, 38 x 30 (4240/40)	18000
Dupre, Julien, 1851-1910, FEEDING THE COWS, 35½ x 43½ (4161/168)	3000
Dupre, Julien, 1851-1910, HARVESTING WHEAT, 21¾ x 26 (4122/219)	4500
Dupre, Julien, 1851-1910, HAYMAKERS, 1886, 31 x 25 (4161/167)	5250
Dupre, Julien, 1851-1910, MILKING THE COW, 25¾ x 32 (4161/169)	3750
Dupre, Julien, 1851-1910, MILKING TIME, 19 x 26 (4122/216)	3750
Dupre, Julien, 1851-1910, THE BROKEN TETHER, 34¾ x 49 (4122/220)	2500
Dupre, Julien, 1851-1910, THE HARVESTERS, 1881, 25¾ x 32 (4122/218)	5000
Dupre, Julien, 1851-1910, THE MILKMAID, 22 x 26¼ (4122/217)	3250
Dupre, Julien, 1851-1910, WATERING THE COWS, 18¼ x 24 (4161/170)	4500
Dupre, Leon Victor (1816-79), CATTLE WATERING IN A MARSHY FIELD, 10½ x 18, on panel (4208/138)	3750
Dutch School, A WINTER LANDSCAPE WITH SKATES, 20 x 30 (666/244)	550
Dutch School, SKATERS ON A FROZEN LAKE, 9½ x 7¼, on panel (4241/97)	2100
Duverger, Theophile Emmanuel, b.1821, SISTERLY AFFECTION, 12¾ x 16¼ (4122/272)	13500
Eastern European School, A RIVERSIDE TOWN, 14½ x 21 (4241/154)	1200
Eberle, Adolf, 1843-1914, AFTER THE HUNT, 21 x 26 (4161/43)	21000
Eckenfelder, Friedrich, 1861-1938, FEEDING THE POULTRY, 6½ x 9 (4161/31)	4000
Edelfelt, Albert Gustav A. (1854-1905), THE PROPOSAL, d.1880, 19¾x 28½ (4208/106)	23000
Eeckhault, C., THE YOUNG SHEPHERD, d.1867, 18 x 15 (633/210)	1700
Eerelman, Otto, 1839-1926, A TOAST TO THE FAIR MAID, 1880, 22¼ x 16 (4122/59)	4750
Ehrmann, Theodor F. Von, (1846-?), A MOUNTAINOUS LANDSCAPE, 29 x 39½ (633/40)	500
Eichinger, Erwin, Austrian, PIPE SMOKER, WINE CONNOISSEUR, 10¼ x 8, on board (4122/39)	1200
Eickelberg, Willem H., 1845-1920, CANAL SCENE, ZAANDAM, 12 x 15¼ (4122/83)	1600
Einsle, Anton (1801-71), PORTRAIT OF A LADY, 1869, 31¼ x 24¾ (666/180)	600
Elsley, Arthur J., 1878-1919, PICKING APPLES, 1919, 37½ x 27 (4161/268)	15000
Elten, H.D.K. van (1829-1904), AN EXTENSIVE SUMMER LANDSCAPE, 15½ x 25 (666/238)	900
Elten, H.D.K. van (1829-1904), APPROACHING A TOWN, 13½ x 20 (666/237)	950
Engel, Otto Heinrich, AT SUNSET, 59 x 74½ (4241/64)	3100
Engelhardt, Georg Hermann, b.1855, EXTENSIVE ALPINE SCENE, 27½ x 38 (4161/16)	3250
English School (19c), THE LOVERS SERENADE, 20 x 25 (666/182)	500
Enjolras, Delphin (b.1857), IN THE BOUDOIR, 21½ x 15 (4208/189)	2900
Epp, Rudolf (1834-1910), FEEDING THE RABBITS, d.1878 (?), 35 x 28 (4208/33)	22000
Epp, Rudolf, 1834-1910, PEASANT CHILD WITH FEATHERED HAT, 1875, 10½ x 8 (4161/50)	5000
Epp, Rudolf, 1834-1910, TYROLIAN PEASANT WOMAN, 1877, 23½ x 18¼ (4161/49)	8000
Etty, William, attrib. to, 1787-1849, THE ARTIST'S MODEL, 28¾ x 18½ (4122/312)	2000
Etty, William, 1787-1849, THE HESPERIDES, FROM COMUS, A LUNETTE, 34½ x 69, gouache & chalk (4122/311)	1800
Eversen, Adrianus, 1818-97, STREET SCENE IN HOLLAND, 1885, 15 x 21½ (4161/75)	18000
Eckout, Jakob J. (1793-1861), AN OUTDOOR CONCERT, on panel, 26 x 22 (4240/24)	550

Fabbi, Fabbio, 1861-1946, HAREM DANCER, 21¾ x 16 (4161/149) 3750
Fabbi, Fabbio, 1861-1946, SLAVE AUCTION, 30 x 19 (4197/372) 5000
Fabbi, Fabbio, 1861-1946, THE FAVORITES, 23½ x 31½ (4197/370) 6000
Faed, John (1820-1902), SHAKESPEARE AND HIS CONTEMPORARIES, 53 x 68 (4240/73) 6250
Fantin-Latour, Henri, VISION, pastel, 17 x⅛ x 11½ (4250/401) 6750
Fantin-Latour, Henri (1856-1904), SELF-PORTRAIT, 1860, 10 6/16 x 8¼ (4260/617) 25000
Fantin-Latour, Henri, 1836-1904, NOLI ME TANGERE, A L'ITALIENNE, 1871, 5 x 8¾ (4122/202) 1000
Farrer, Thomas Charles (1838-91), SELF PORTRAIT WITH VIOLIN, d.1859, 9⅞ x 7¾, pencil (4260/662) 2200
Faustner, Luitpold, 1845-1925, THE DACHSTEIN, 1915, 36½ x 28 (4122/14) 2900
Feitbauer, Leopold, PORTRAIT OF A LADY, 24 x 18¾ (4241/42) 1100
Felix, Eugene (1837-1906), A COASTAL SCENE, 18 x 34 (633/69) 750
Ferneley, John Jr., attributed (ca1815-62), A DAPPLE GREY AND A BAY HUNTER, 26 x 36 (4208/209) *1000*
Ferrari, A., EGYPTIAN BAZAAR, 1887, 25 x 18 (4122/156) *3500*
Ferrari, Giuseppe, 1840-1905, THE GYPSY CAVALIER, 19 x 14¾ (4122/157) 1500
Feuerbach, Anselm, attrib. to, 1829-80, MUSICIANS BY THE WELL SIDE, 9½ x 13 (4161/35) 900
Fichel, Benjamin Eugene (1826-95), THE PRESENT, d.1857, 16 x 12½, on panel (4208/188) 1000
Fildes, Luke (1844-1927), THE JEWEL CASKET, laid on board, 24 x 20 (666/249) 1300
Fines, Eugene Francois (1826-82?), CONTRIBUTIONS FOR THE FEAST, 22 x 26½ (4208/187) 3000
Fischer, Paul Gustav, A BALLET LESSON IN THE COPENHAGEN ROYAL, THEATRE, 20¼ x 40 (4241/149) 11000
Fischer, Paul Gustav, BATHERS AT HUMLEBACK, 14¾ x 20¼ (4241/153) 2300
Fischer, Paul Gustav, THE FISH MARKET ON THE GAMMELSTRAND, 22 x 28¾ (4241/150) 9000
Flandrin, Jean Hippolyte, 1809-64, PORTRAIT OF A WOMAN IN A RED SHAWL, 1834, 21¾ x 18¼ (4122/274) 2000
Flint, Sir William R. (1880-1969), 'AMONG MISTY ISLES', 21½ x 30¼, watercolor (4208/234) 7000
Flint, Sir William R. (1880-1969), LEARNERS, GRIMMIALP, 1925, 19½ x 26, watercolor (4208/235) 6250
Flint, Sir William R. (1880-1969), SPANISH WOMEN UNDER AN ARCHWAY, 12½ x 20, watercolor (4208/236) *4250*

Ferrari (4122/156)

Ferneley (4208/209)

Flint (4208/236)

Garrido (4122/131)

Flint, William R., 1880-1969, APPEAL, 1928-30, 21 x 30, watercolor (4161/280) 3500
Fontana, Ernesto (1837-1918), FLIRTATION IN THE PANTRY, d.1882, 51 x 40 (4208/116) 3000
Forti, Eduardo, WELL-SIDE GOSSIP, 19½ x 30½ (4122/164) 4000
Fortuny y Carbo, M., 1838-74, BEGGAR IN A TURBAN, 6¾ x 4¾, paper (4122/130) 900
Fortuny y Carbo, M., 1838-74, SLEEPING ARAB, 5½ x 11¾ (4122/135) 1900
Frances Y Pascual, FEEDING THE FLAMINGOS, 11¼ x 18 (4241/197) 5000
Frappa, Joseph, 1854-1905, THE MORNING SHAVE, 13½ x 10½ (4161/204) 2400
French School, MOTHER, DAUGHTER AND GRANDDAUGHTER IN AN INTERIOR, 19c,
    12⅛ x 11, pencil (4260/602) 2000
French School, PORTRAIT OF A BEARDED MAN, 19c, 25¾ x 21¾ (4260/624) 950
French School, THE PAINTER AND HIS MODEL, ca1900, 28¾ x 23¾ (666/250) 325
French School, THE PAINTER AND HIS PATRON, 10 x 11¾, on panel (633/81) 600
French School, WARMING BY THE FIRE, on panel, 10½ x 8½ (666/188) 350
Frere, Charles Theodore, 1814-88, ARAB CARAVAN, 6¾ x 14¼ (4197/361) 2800
Frere, Charles Theodore, 1814-88, VUE DE JERUSALEM, PRISE DE LA VALLEE DE
    JOSAPHAT, 15¾ x 24½ (4197/362) 6600
Frere, Pierre E., 1819-86, SPINNING WOOL, 1863, 20¼ x 26 (4161/232) 2750
Frey, Johann Jakob (1813-65), THE ROME OF THE POPES, 1859, 39 x 54 (4240/5) 8500
Frey, Johann Jakob (1813-65), TIVOLI, 11860, 39 x 54 (4240/6) 7000
Fricke, Longin C., 1816-93, SHEPHERD BY A LAKESIDE, 1850, 18½ x 26½ (4161/104) 1600
Friedlander, Alfred, b.1860, Aust., TRAVELERS RESTING, 5¼ x 8½ (4122/44) 950
Friedrich, Waldemar, VILLAGE GOSSIP, 12½ x 8¼, on panel (4241/37) 2100
Fromentin, Eugene, 1820-76, ARAB CAMP, 1850, 10¾ x 16 (4122/230) 1200
Fromentin, Eugene, 1820-76, FEMMES ARABES AU BAIN, 40 x 56 (4122/233) 9000
Fromentin, Eugene, 1820-76, LE SIMOUN, 19 x 27½ (4197/369) 5250
Fromentin, Eugene, 1820-76, ON THE BANKS OF THE NILE, 20 x 26¼, 1875 (4264/400) 250
Fuechsel, Hermann, 1833-1915, THE WATERFALL, 1895, 30¼ x 22¼ (4122/13) 1200
Funk, Heinrich, 1807-77, MOUNTAIN LAKE, 1851, 16 x 22¾ (4161/15) 2500
Gailliard, Francois (1861-1932), STREET SCENE, BRUSSELS, d.1884, 35½ x 26 (4208/96) 11500
Gaisser, Jakob Emanuel, CARD PLAYER'S, 13¾ x 17¾, on panel (4241/74) 1000®
Gallait, Louis, 1810-87, LE PRISONNIER A ROME, 1862, 20¾ x 16¾ (4122/102) 3750
Gallait, Louis, 1810-87, THE MINSTREL BOY, 52 x 41 (4161/102) 3000
Gallegos Y Arnosa, Jose, A CHOIR OF NUNS, 24 x 16 (4241/193) 4500
Gallegos Y Arnosa, Jose, THE CARDINAL AND HIS SECRETARY, 8 x 13 (4241/185) 6000

Gallegos Y Arnosa, Jose, VENETIAN FESTIVAL, 18 x 25¾ (4241/189) — 24000

Garcia y Hispaleto, R., 1833-54, PRIMER CUADRO DE COMPOSICION, 1854, 36 x 66 (4122/129) — 600

Garcia y Mencia, Antonio, THROUGH THE BINOCULARS, 16 x 13 (4122/137) — 5250

Garcia y Ramos, Jose, b.1825, THE CASTANET PLAYER, 25½ x 15¼ (4161/126) — 1400

Garcia y Rodriguez, M., b.1863, GETTING OUT, MORNING, 1897, 15¾ x 29½ (4122/141) — 700

Garcia y Rodriguez, M., b.1863, WAITING ON THE DOCK, 16 x 29½ (4122/140) — *1100*

Garrido, Eduardo L., 1856-1906, A STROLL IN THE PARK, 16 x 12¼ (4122/131) — 2700

Garcia y Rodriguez (4122/140)

Garrido, Fernando, 19c, THE CHESS PLAYERS, 17¼ x 22¼ (4161/122) — 2000

Gaudefroy, Alphonse, UN ECART-A MOMENT ASIDE, 23 x 28 (4122/245) — 2800

Gauermann, Friedrich (1807-62), GASTHAUS FROHNWIES, paper on canvas, 12½ x 17 (4071/4) — 9750

Gauguin, Paul (1848-1903), HEAD OF A YOUNG WOMAN, ca1884, 10½ x 8, charcoal (4260/1423) — 2500

Gauguin, Paul (1848-1903), PROFILE OF MAN IN A SKULLCAP-HEAD OF MIMI, ca1888, 6⅜ x 7⅝, mixed media (4260/1424) — 7500

Gavarni, Paul (1804-1866), THALIE, 11 x 8, watercolor (4260/618) — 2000

Gegerfelt, Wilhelm von (1844-1920), CANAL SCENE BY MOONLIGHT, d.1876, 23½ x 38 (4208/98) — 2600

Gelder, Lucia Mathilde von (1865-99), GRANDPARENT'S DELIGHT, d.1897, 32¼ x 25¾ (4208/35) — 2600

Gerard, Theodore, 1829-95, CAT NAP, 12¾ x 10½ (4122/99) — 1300

Gerard, Theodore, 1829-95, THE HUNTSMAN'S BAG, 1878, 26¾ x 17½ (4161/95) — 4750

Gerasch, August, ON THE WAY TO THE PASTURE, 10¼ x 14¼, on panel (4241/2) — 2100

Gerhard, George (1830-1902), FEEDING THE PUPPIES, 1875, 16 x 12 (4208/31) — 1800

Gerhart, Aloys, 1837-89, Hungarian, THE MARKET IN TIFLIS, 7 x 12½ (4161/110) — 2500

Gericault, Theodore, 1791-1824, attrib. to, L'ECURIE, 4¾ x 6½ (4161/223) — 700

Germain, V., CHATEAU INTERIOR, 1884, 16 x 25¾ (4122/251) — 750

German School, BLIND MAN'S BLUFF, 15¾ x 21¾ (666/198) — 750

German School, PORTRAIT OF A PRUSSIAN GENERAL, 19½ x 17¾ (4241/66) — 2000

German School, THE ARMORER'S WORKSHOP, 20 x 24 (4241/50) — 4750

Gerome, Jean Leon, attrib. to, 1824-1904, LES DEUX MAJESTES, 19 x 34¼ (4122/226) — 5000

Gerome, Jean Leon, 1824-1904, CHESTNUT HORSE IN A LANDSCAPE, 6 x 8¾ (4122/281) — 800

Gerome, Jean Leon, 1824-1904, FELLAHEEN DRAWING WATER, 17¼ x 24½ (4122/225) — 10000

Gerome, Jean Leon, 1824-1904, L'ARRIVEE AU CAIRE, 22¾ x 36 (4122/234) — 4000

Gessnitzer, J.C., CITYSCAPES, A PAIR OF PAINTINGS, 27 x 22 (633/214) — 1300

Gilbault, Eugene (19c), FRUIT STILL LIFE, d.1883, 24 x 31½ (4208/179) — 3500

Gilbert, Victor Gabriel, b.1847, LE MARCHE, b.1847, 18 x 24 (4122/280) — 1200

Giordano, A RUSHING RIVER, 42 x 75 (4241/173)   3250
Girardet, Karl, 1813-71, Swiss, LAC A GENEVE, 7½ x 10½ (4122/196)   3500
Girardet, Karl, 1813-71, Swiss, VUE DE LA MARNE, PRES CHARLY, 7 x 9½ (4122/197)   4000
Girardet, Leon, 1857-95, THE PET PARROT, 22 x 15 (4122/269)   2800
Girardot, Ernest Gustave (fl.1860-93), THE GRAPE PICKERS, d.1865, 39 x 30 (4208/227)   2300
Gleason, J. (19c), 'OLD IRON' Bridge, on panel, 13 x 17½ (666/145)   650
Gloag, Isabel Lilian, 1865-1917, THE ENCHANTED CLOAK, 60¼ x 78½ (4122/316)   15000
Gogh, Vincent van (1853-90), MAN STANDING, TOP HAT IN HAND, 1882, 19¼ x 9¼, pencil (4260/1429)   30000
Goodall, Frederick, 1822-1904, A BEDOUIN ARRIVING AT A WELL, 17½ x 14, 1864 (4197/367)   2000
Goubie, Jean Richard, 1842-99, A SUMMER RIDE, 1896, 19¾ x 15 (4161/206)   4750
Grailly, Victor de, 1804-89, DUTCH RIVER SCENE, 1843, 16¼ x 21¼ (4122/174)   4000
Grailly, Victor de, 1804-89, FISHING IN THE CANAL, 1843, 16¼ x 21¼ (4122/175)   4250
Greaves, Walter (1841-1930), PORTRAIT OF THOMAS CARLYLE, d.1871, 14 3/16 x 11½, mixed media (4260/663)   6200
Greaves, Walter (1846-1930), PORTRAIT OF JAMES H. McNEILL WHISTLER, 30 x 24 (4240/74)   1700
Green, E.F. (19c), AN ARAB SERVANT GIRL CARRYING A BARDAK, 1839, 36 x 28 (666/229)   600
Greuze, Jean-Baptiste, school of, INNOCENCE, 13 x 12 (633/53)   475
Grimshaw, John Atkinson (1836-93), THE SUN'S FAREWELL, d.1882, 19½ x 29½ (4208/219)   6000
Groenewegen, A.J. (1874-1963), CATTLE FEEDING AT DUSK, watercolor, 13½ x 20 (666/204)   1400
Grolleron, Paul Louis N., 1848-1901, STORMING THE GATE, (4161/226)   2200
Gruppe, Charles Paul, LOW TIDE AT SCHEVENINGEN, 16 x 24 (4241/109)   1700
Gruppe, Charles Paul, WOODCUTTER BY A RIVERSIDE, 16½ x 24½ (4241/108)   1600
Guaccimanni, Vittorio, 1859-1938, AN ARAB GUARD, 22½ x 16 (4264/403)   900
Guay, Gabriel (b.1848), A GIRL AND HER KITTEN, 44 x 35½ (633/204)   1500
Guigou, Paul C., 1834-71, THE BANKS OF THE RIVER DURANCE, 1864, 24½ x 58¼ (4122/179)   60000
Guillaumin, Jean Baptiste A. (1841-1927), SEATED PEASANT, ca1870, 21½ x 17¾ (4260/1411)   15000
Guillemet, Jean Baptiste, A PONT ON A RIVER NEAR A VILLAGE, 28¾ x 21½ (4241/227)   2100
Guys, Constantin (1802-92), attrib., SOLDIERS AND THEIR LADIES, mixed media, 4¼ x 6¼ (4071/132)   1300
Guys, Constantin (1805-92), AFTER THE THEATER, 8¾ x 13, sepia ink (4260/1401)   2600
Guys, Constantin (1805-92), ONLOOKERS AT THE PROMENADE, 11¼ x 8⅝, sepia ink (4260/1402)   1800
Guys, Constantin (1805-92), TWO SPANISH WOMEN, 6½ x 4¾, sepia ink (4260/1403)   1200
Gyselinckx, Joseph (19c), THE THREE CHILDREN, d.1869, 23¼ x 17¾, on panel (4208/95)   2750
Haanen, Cecil van, 1844-85, YOUNG VENETIAN GIRL, 12½ x 8½ (4122/64)   1500
Haase, C. Von, THE EAVESDROPPER, 15¾ x 12½ (4241/67)   1100
Hackl, Gabriel von (1843-c.1919), IN GOOD CARE, d.1869, 31 x 25½ (4208/47)   6250
Haddon, Arthur Trevor, 1864-1941, ARABS BENEATH AN ARCHWAY, 16 x 11½ (4264/397)   1100
Haddon, Arthur Trevor, 1864-1941, GATEWAY IN FEZ, MOROCCO, 25 x 20¾ (4197/353)   1800
Hafer, Heinrich, 1825-78, DRIVING THE HERD TO WATER, 1859, 10¾ x 13¾ (4161/17)   4500
Hagborg, August, FISHERMAN'S FAMILY, 69½ x 52 (4241/156)   7500

Hardy   (4208/226)

Herzog (4208/13)

Hagborg, August, THE DANCE, 26¾ x 38 (4241/152)	11000
Halberg-Krauss, Fritz (1874-1951), LANDSCAPE WITH CATTLE, 28 x 44 (633/64)	1300
Hamza, Johann, 1850-1927, A HELPFUL FRIEND, 14 x 10¾ (4161/60)	15000
Haquette, Georges - Jean M. (1854-1906), FATHER AND DAUGHTER, 18 x 22 (666/245)	1100
Hardy, David (fl.1855-70), THE LOVE LETTER, 10 x 12¼ (4208/231)	1000
Hardy, Heywood (1843-1933), THE MORNING RIDE, d.1906, 24 x 33¼ (4208/226)	*11000*
Harpignes, Henri Joseph, 1819-1916, A FARM IN SUMMER, 1869, 12 x 18 (4161/158)	14000
Harpignies, Henri Joseph, RIVERSCAPE, SUMMER, 11¼ x 14¼ (4241/222)	10000
Harpignies, Henri Joseph (1819-1916), A WOODED RIVER LANDSCAPE, 1901, 16 x 37¾ (4208/146)	22000
Harpignies, Henri Joseph (1819-1916), ETANG DE GRAND-RUE, d.1910, 11½ x 17, charcoal (4260/615)	2900
Harpignies, Henri Joseph (1819-1916), LA BOURBOULE, d.1881, 9⅛ x 11¾ (4260/616)	2800
Harpignies, Henri Joseph (1819-1916), WOODLAND POOL, d.1907, 15 x 21¾ (4208/149)	6750
Harpignies, Henri Joseph, 1819-1916, SOUVENIR DE CAP MARTIN, 1907, 25½ x 32 (4161/159)	8500
Harpseau, C., attrib., FISHING AT DUSK, 25½ x 19¼ (633/36)	375
Hartmann, Ludwig, 1835-1902, ARRIVAL AT THE INN, 1871, 15½ x 30¾ (4122/9)	55000
Hartwich, Herman (1853-1926), TILLING THE FIELD, 12¼ x 18 (4071/12)	1500
Hasselbach, Wilhelm, b.1846, SURPRISE, 43½ x 33½ (4161/45)	6000
Havell, Charles R., attrib. to, 1858-66, HARVESTER'S NOONTIME, 36 x 60 (4122/290)	3000
Hawkins, Louis Welden, 1849-1910, SPINNING, 14 x 10, watercolor (4161/263)	700
Hayllar, James, b.1829, THE BRIDE, 1863, 10¼ x 8 (4161/270)	1000
Heckel, August von, 1824-83, HE LOVES ME, HE LOVES ME NOT, 27¼ x 19½ (4122/54)	1500
Heilmayer, Karl (1829-1908), MORNING ON THE TIBER, d.1892, 21½ x 29½ (4208/9)	1000
Heim, Francois Joseph (1787-1865), PORTRAIT OF BARON FRANCOIS GERARD, 1827, 13 1/3 x 16¾, blackchalk (4260/605)	2900
Hein, Hendrik J., 1822-66, STILL LIFE OF PEACHES, PLUMS & GRAPES, 16 x 13¾ (4122/66)	6000
Heine, Johann A., 1885-1900, AN ALPINE MELODY, 10¾ x 8¼ (4122/32)	2100
Henner, Jean Jacques, 1829-1905, IDEAL HEAD, 10½ x 8½ (4122/265)	6000
Henner, Jean Jacques, 1829-1905, IDEAL HEAD, 13 x 8¾ (4161/200)	3250
Henner, Jean Jacques, 1829-1905, YOUNG WOMAN WITH RED HAIR, 18¼ x 13¼ (4122/264)	6000
Hereau, Jules (1839-79), A SHEPHERD AND HIS FLOCK, 10 x 18 (4208/160)	800
Herman, Phillip Ludwig, LANDING THE BOAT, 6¼ x 8¼, on panel, 1880 (4241/23)	5200
Hermann, Hans (1813-90), SPRINGTIME, 24½ x 32½ (4071/7)	5000
Hermann, Hans, 19c, THE FRUIT VENDOR, 11¾ x 9¼ (4122/34)	1100
Hernault, Justine L., PAINTER AND PATRON, 18½ x 15 (633/212)	1000
Herpfer, Carl, SWEET THOUGHTS, 42¾ x 28 (4241/58)	3500
Herpfer, Carl (1836-97), MOTHERHOOD, 32½ x 25¼ (4208/36)	2100
Herring, John Frederick, 1795-1865, STABLE INTERIOR, 1851, 22 x 30 (4122/287)	17000
Herring, John Frederick, 1815-1907, BARNYARD SCENE, 1852, diameter 16 (4122/289)	4000
Herzog, Hermann (1832-1932), A STORM OFF A ROCKY COAST, 20 x 27¼ (4071/1)	600
Herzog, Hermann (1832-1932), COWS ON A HILLSIDE, 11 x 15 (4208/13)	2600
Herzog, Hermann (1832-1932), FISHING OFF THE BEACH, 13 x 17 (4208/1)	2200
Herzog, Hermann (1832-1932), HARBOR SCENE BY MOONLIGHT, 13 x 19 (4208/2)	1300

Herzog,Hermann (1832-1932), DEER IN A LANDSCAPE, 22 x 29 (4208/14)	2200
Hetzel, George (1826-1906), MOUNTAIN STREAM, 1881, 30 x 45 (666/226)	250
Heydendahl, Friedrich J.N. (1844-1906), A WINTER SUNSET, 32 x 42 (4071/16)	4000
Heyn, August (b.1837), A MERRY PARTY, 11 x 13½, on panel (4208/40)	5750
Heyn, August, b.1837, BORED WITH LESSONS, 18 x 14¾ (4161/40)	8750
Heyn, August, b.1837, THE YOUNG SMOKERS, 1876, 18 x 14¾ (4161/39)	10000
Hider, F. (19c), A ROCKY SHORE, 1907, 30 x 20 (666/167)	325
Hilda, E.B., Austrian, NIGHT STALKERS, ca1895, 18 x 21¾ (4122/5)	1300
Hildebrandt, Eduard (1818-69), MOONRISE IN MADEIRA, 35½ x 47 (4240/7)	3500
Hilder, Richard, 1830-51, WOODED RIVER LANDSCAPE WITH FIGURES, (4161/252)	9500
Hofer, Heinrich, BY A FROZEN LAKE, 1877, 6¾ x 10 (4122/18)	5000
Hofer, Heinrich (1825-78), ALPINE TRAVELLER STOPPING BY A MILL, d.1868, 21½ x 17 (4208/7)	7500
Hofer, Heinrich, 1825-78, BLACKSMITH'S COTTAGE IN WINTER, 1865, 16½ x 20½ (4161/18)	8500
Hoff, Conrad, FISHING BOATS, VENICE, 12½ x 23½ (4241/19)	1400
Hofner, Johann B., 1832-1913, SUMMER LANDSCAPE, 11½ x 17½, on board (4122/1)	1600
Hoog, Bernard de (1866-1943), PEELING POTATOES, 39¼ x 49¼ (4208/73)	7000
Hoog, Bernard de (1866-1943), SPINNING BY THE WINDOW, 31 x 39½ (4208/72)	10000
Hook, James Clarke, 1819-1907, UNLOADING THE CATCH, 1866, 27½ x 42½ (4122/308)	500
Horner, Friedrich, 1800-64, Swiss, VIEW OF THE ROMAN FORUM, 1846, 12¼ x 17¾ (4122/22)	700
Houben, Henri, fl.1885-98, MARKET DAY, 28½ x 44 (4122/95)	3000
Hove, Bartholomeus J. van (1790-1880), A CHURCH INTERIOR, d.1873, 10¼ x 14, on panel (4208/58)	1100
Howard, W. (19c), VIEW OF TWICKERSHAM ON THE THAMES, 24 x 36 (666/153)	1400
Huet, Paul (1803-69), A SHEPHERD AND HIS FLOCK, 25¾ x 32 (4208/133)	1400
Hughes, Edward R. (1851-1941), THE CARNIVAL, 23¼ x 17⅛ (666/165)	800
Huguet, Victor Pierre, 1835-1902, WASHERWOMEN OUTSIDE THE VILLAGE WALLS, 24 x 32½ (4264/398)	3600
Huguet, Victor Pierre (1835-1902), AN ARAB STREET SCENE, 15 x 18¼ (633/225)	1700
Hulk, Abraham, FISHING BOATS AT LOW TIDE, 12 x 18 (4241/82)	7000
Hulk, Abraham, 1813-97, FISHING BOATS IN AN ESTUARY, 15¾ x 26 (4161/79)	7500
Hulk, John Frederik, 1855-1913, A PAIR OF TOWN HOUSES, 11¾ x 8¼ (4161/68)	6000
Hulme, Frederick William (1816-84), SHEEP RESTING ALONG A SHADY PATH, 28 x 32 (4208/211)	4000
Humborg, Adolf, b.1847, Austrian, CLOISTER ANTICS, 1894, 24¾ x 20 (4122/36)	4750
Humborg, Adolf, b.1847, Austrian, MONK PREPARING BREAKFAST, 14¾ x 11¾ (4161/57)	6000
Hunt, Charles, THE PRISONER, 1880, 30 x 50 (4161/264)	5500
Hunt, William Henry (1790-1864), HEAD OF A YOUNG WOMAN, oval, 6¼ x 5⅜, charcoal (4260/651)	450
Huygens, Francois J., 1820-1908, STILL LIFE OF FLOWERS ON STONE LEDGE, 1853, 15¼ x 12 (4161/100)	7000

Isabey (4208/165)

Joris (4208/126)

Igler, Gustav, b.1842, Hungarian, OFF TO SCHOOL, 47½ x 35 (4161/46)	12000
Indoni, Filippo, TWO FISHWIVES, 21 x 14½, watercolor (633/73)	275
Ingres, Jean-Auguste D. (1780-1867), PORTRAIT OF M. AND MME. EDMOND RAMEL, d.1855, 13½ x 10⅝, pencil (4260/609)	145000
Innoceli, Camilio, A CAVALIER, 18 x 14¾ (4241/166)	900
Irolli, Vicenzo, 1860-1942, PEASANT GIRL WITH TAMBOURINE, 21¼ x 13½ (4122/172)	5000
Isabey, Louis Gabriel E. (1803-86), UNLOADING THE CATCH, 25½ x 36¾ (4208/164)	8250
Isabey, Louis Gabriel E. (1803-86), VIEW OF LE HAVRE, d.1854, 21½ x 32¼ (4208/165)	*5000*
Israels, Josef (1824-1911), SELF PORTRAIT IN TOP HAT, 15½ x 10¾ (4260/644)	12500
Israels, Josef (1824-1911), THE COAL CARRIER, 8¾ x 6¼, on panel (4208/69)	2200
Israels, Josef, attributed to, ON THE BEACH, 25 x 30¼ (4208/76)	1500
Israels, Josef, 1824-1911, MOTHERHOOD, 36½ x 31½ (4161/67)	25000
Issupoff, Alessio, A WINTER FARMYARD, 13 x 23¾ (4161/111)	1000
Italian School, THE APPROACH TO THE MOSQUE, 14¼ x 9¼ (4264/402)	550
Jacque, Charles Emile, RETURN OF THE FLOCK, 7¼ x 15 (4241/213)	2000
Jacque, Charles Emile, SHEPERD WITH HIS FLOCK, 34 x 44 (4241/218)	5500
Jacque, Charles Emile, SHEPHERDESS WITH FLOCK IN A MEADOW, 11¼ x 16 (4241/209)	3500
Jacque, Charles Emile, TWO HENS, 7¼ x 10¾ (4241/210)	1600
Jacque, Charles Emile (1813-94), HENS IN A BARN, 4⅝ x 6⅛, on panel (633/186)	1300
Jacque, Charles Emile (1813-94), RETURN TO THE FOLD, 32 x 26 (4240/43)	19000
Jacque, Charles Emile(1813-94), AT THE STABLE DOOR, 26 x 21½ (4208/159)	14500
Jacque, Charles Emile, 1813-94, RUFFLED ROOSTER, 9½ x 12¾ (4161/176)	1100
Jacque, Charles Emile, 1813-94, STABLE INTERIOR WITH SHEPHERD AND FLOCK, 13 x 18 (4161/160)	12000
Jacque, Charles Emile, 1813-94, THE PLOUGHMAN'S REST, 25¾ x 21¼ (4161/161)	7750
Jacquet, Gustave Jean, 1846-1909, THE CRIMSON BERET, 18 x 15¼ (4122/258)	4700
Jaeckel, Henry, A VILLA ON THE ITALIAN LAKES, 27¼ x 35 (4241/20)	1900
James, David, 1881-98, A STIFF BREEZE, 1896, 20 x 30 (4161/250)	3000
Jardines, J.M., 19c, A DRIVE THROUGH TOWN, 10½ x 13¾ (4122/134)	750
Jentzen, Friedrich, THE ROMAN FORUM, 46 x 68¾ (4241/22)	5250
Jettel, Eugene, 1845-1901, Austrian, CHILDREN BATHING IN A WOODLAND POOL, 26 x 40½ (4161/14)	11000
Jimenez y Aranda, Luis, 1845-1928, STUDENTS OF GALLANTRY, 29¼ x 24½ (4122/136)	8250
Jongkind, Johan Barthold (1819-91), BOATS IN A HARBOR, 1882, 6½ x 10¾, watercolor, crayon (4161/84)	2750
Jongkind, Johan Barthold (1819-91), A COUNTRY ROAD, 6¾ x 20, mixed media (4260/1407)	4500
Jongkind, Johan Barthold (1819-91), COTE ST. ANDRE, HOTEL DE VILLE, d.1890, 6 1/16 x 8¾, oil on panel (4260/1408)	9500
Jony, Jacobus Sterre de, READING THE PAPER, 13 x 10¾ (4241/115)	1700
Joris, Pio (1843-1921), THE ROAD TO MARKET, 32¾ x 69 (4208/126)	*9500*

Kern (4208/107)

Jourdain, Roger-Joseph, (1845-1918), THE TRAVELLERS BESEIGED, 28½ x 23½ (4197/351)	3750
Junghauns, Julius Paul, HORSE DRAWN CART, 14½ x 12 (4241/30)	2200
Kaemmerer, Frederik H., (1839-1902), AFTER THE MASQUERADE, 13¾ x 8½ (4122/65)	2600
Kampf, Eugen (1861-1933), THE ROAD HOME, 19½ x 23½ (4208/11)	2300
Kannemans, Christian C., (1812-84), FISHING BOATS ASHORE, 1851, 14½ x 20¾ (4161/77)	4000
Karlovsky, Bertalan de (1858-1912), STILL LIFE WITH FRUIT AND FLOWERS, 39½ x 31, oil on panel (4208/23)	2100
Karlovsky, Bertalan de (1858-1939), A STILL LIFE WITH FRUITS AND FLOWERS, 39½ x 30¾, on panel (633/189)	650
Kauffman, Hermann, 1808-89, BY THE WOODPILE, WINTER, 26¼ x 37 (4161/12)	19000
Kauffmann, Hugo (1844-1915), MAKING A SALE, d.1878, 8 x 10, on panel (4208/48)	23000
Kaufmann, Adolf (1848-1916), FISHERMEN UNLOADING, 20¾ x 16½ (666/166)	1700
Kaufmann, Adolf, 1848-1916, TANA FJORD, Austrian, 27 x 41½ (4161/5)	2100
Kaulbach, Friedrich A. von (1850-1920), SAPPHO, 26 x 22½, pastel (633/199)	800
Keene, Charles S. (1823-91), ICE SKATING IN REGENT'S PARK, 13 x 12½, black crayon (4260/667)	500
Kels, Franz, 1828-93, THE YOUNG ARTIST, 1853, 24½ x 30 (4161/61)	11500
Kemm, Robert, THE QUEEN OF HEARTS, 24 x 15 (633/68)	850
Kemm, Robert, attrib., THE GOAT ATTACK, 16 x 21 (633/110)	400
Kern, Hermann, A PROFITABLE WEEK, 18 x 11½ (4241/161)	5250
Kern, Hermann (1839-1912), THE VIOLIN TUNER, 19 x 12½ (4208/107)	*6500*
Kern, Hermann, 1839-1912, Hungarian, DRESSING UP, 1883, 28¼ x 22¾ (4122/127)	14000
Kern, Hermann, 1839-1912, Hungarian, THE JOLLY FIDDLER, 1906, 19 x 12½ (4122/125)	4500
Kever, Jacob Simon Hendrik (1854-1922), BROTHER AND SISTER, 18 x 21 (4208/75)	5250
Kiesslung, Paul Johann Adolf, DIANA AND THE SLEEPING ENDYMION, 24¾ x 30¼ (4241/48)	2100
King, Henry John Y., 1855-1924, THE OLD STONE BRIDGE, 24 x 36 (4122/303)	1200
Kirchner, Otto, IN THE LIBRARY, 19¾ x 23½ (4241/72)	2000
Klein, Johann A., 1792-1875, HITCHING UP THE HORSES, 1857, 13¾ x 19 (4161/32)	15000
Klever, Julius S. von, 1850-1924, PEASANT IN A WINTER LANDSCAPE, 13¾ x 21 (4122/114)	1800
Kluyver, Pieter L.F., 1816-1900, HORSEMAN IN STORMY LANDSCAPE, 20½ x 26 (4161/81)	7500
Knaus, Ludwig, 1829-1910, PORTRAIT OF A YOUNG BOY, 1884, 11 x 9 (4161/56)	2000
Knebel, Franz, Jr., 1809-77, Swiss, EXTENSIVE VIEW OF CASCADE AT TIVOLI, 29¼ x 39½ (4161/9)	3500
Kockert, Julius (1827-1912), THE SIGNAL, 38 x 30 (4208/25)	1600
Koekkeck, Hendrick B., 1849-1909, HORSEMAN ON A SNOWY PATH, 34¼ x 28 (4161/83)	2750
Koekkoek, Aendnk (1843-90), A COUNTRY ROAD, 24 x 18 (633/209)	1200
Koekkoek, Barend Cornelis (1803-62), BEFORE THE STORM, 8 x 10, mixed media (4208/56)	2750
Koekkoek, Hermanus, Snr., HAY BARGE IN A QUIET BAY, 19 x 25, oil on panel (4241/81)	5500

Koekkoek, Johannes H.B., 1840-1912, KELP GATHERER ON THE BEACH, 13 x 19 (4161/78)   5750

Koekkoek, Willem, VILLAGE STREET SCENE, 21½ x 27 (4241/98)   29000

Koekkoek, William, 1839-95, TOWN OF HOORN ON THE ZUYDER ZEE, 15¼ x 23¼ (4161/70)   25000

Koerner, Ernst Karl Eugen, b.1846, ON THE NILE, 26 x 41, 1873 (4197/345)   2200

Kosler, Franz Xaver, b.1864, Aust., PAIR, YOUNG EGYPTIANS, 1903, 23½ x 16 (4122/41)   1500

Kossok, J.F. von, 1857-1942, Polish, THE HORSE TRAINER, 15¼ x 17¾ (4122/111)   *1600*

Kossok (4122/111)

Lambert (4122/278)

Kotowski, Jan, RETURN FROM THE HORSE MARKET, 26 x 51 (4241/155)   1300

Krafft, Albert, THE EXPULSION OF HAGAR, 34 x 28 (633/44)   425

Kraus, August, 1852-1917, BACK FROM MARKET, 15 x 18 (4122/46)   2300

Kummer, Julius Hermann (b.1817), EXTENSIVE ALPINE SCENE, d.1854, 20 x 30 (4208/5)   750

Kunz, Ludwig Adam, FISH, PRAWNS AND A BLUE AND WHITE JUG, still life, 11 x 4, on panel (4241/25)   1700

Kurzweil, Maximillian (1867-1916), THE CONNOISSEUR, on panel, 23⅝ x 15¼ (666/197)   850

Kuwasseg, Charles E., 1838-1904, A STORM OVER NAPLES, 1869, 22 x 39¼ (4161/174)   4000

Lafite, Ernst (1826-85), WOMAN IN A GOLD HEADDRESS, d.1875, 23½ x 17 (4208/51)   1700

Lahalle, Charles D.O. (d.1909), LEGIONNAIRES RESTING, d.1891, 12¾ x 10½, on panel (4208/201)   550

Lambert, Louis Eugene, LAFONTAINE'S FABLE, 20½ x 27 (4122/279)   1300

Lambert, Louis Eugene, 1825-1900, CURIOUS KITTENS, 18 x 15 (4161/208)   2750

Lambert, Louis Eugene, 1825-1900, THE PROUD MOTHER, 35¾ x 29 (4122/278)   *3000*

Lambinet, Emile, PICKING APPLES, 35½ x 57 (4241/204)   4000

Lambinet, Emile (1815-77), UNLOADING A RIVERBOAT, d.1857, 13¾ x 25¾ (4208/140)   1700

Lambrichs, Edmond A.C. (1830-87), THE LATEST FASHION, 18 x 14 (633/192)   900

Lamoriniere, Jean P.F., 1828-1911, RIVER LANDSCAPE WITH FIGURE, 16 x 28½ (4161/98)   3000

Landseer, Sir Edwin Henry (1802-73), NOT BROTHERS, 4⅜ x 4, sepia ink (4260/674)   400

Lapostolet, Charles, 1824-90, THE HARBOUR AT DUNKIRK, 42 x 48 (4161/172)   4500

Lasch, Carl, 1822-88, THE LETTER, 16 x 14½ (4161/54)   3750

Laszlo, Philip A. de (1869-1937), HEAD OF AN INDIAN PRINCE, 1906, 32½ x 20 (4240/79)   1800

Laszlo, Philip A. de (1869-1937), PAIR OF PORTRAITS OF MR. AND MRS. F. KELLOGG, 1925 & 1929, 37 x 30, 36 x 28 (4240/80)   1000

Laubmann, Paul, THE COOK'S STORY, 27 x 34½ (4241/77)   9000

Lauer, Josef, 1818-81, Austrian, AZALEA, BELL FLOWERS IN A MOUNTAIN CRAG, 1871, 30¼ x 25 (4122/30)   11500

Launstein, Heinrich, 1835-1910, YOUNG WOMAN HOLDING A CARNATION, 1890, 25¾ x 19½ (4122/55) — 2300

Laurent-Desrousseaux, Henri A.L., 1862-1906, FISHERFOLK DIGGING CLAMS, 25¾ x 36¼ (4122/246) — 3200

Lazerges, Jean R. Hippolyte, 1817-87, FATIMA LA CHANTEUSE, 48½ x 33 (4122/236) — 2500

Lazerges, Paul Jean Baptiste, 1845-1902, ARAB CAMP AT SUNSET, 18 x 21¾, 1899 (4197/347) — 850

Le Duc, Victor Viollet, 1848-1901, SHIPPING ON THE SEINE, 10¾ x 16 (4161/178) — 4750

Leader, Benjamin W. (1831-1923), EVENING NEAR WORCESTER, d.1910, 14 x 20 (4208/222) — 1700

Leader, Benjamin W. (1831-1923), THE END OF THE DAY, d.1899, 24 x 40 (4208/221) — 1600

Lear, Edward, 1812-88, COAST OF LEBANON, MT. SANNINE, 1861, 29 x 57½ (4122/310) — 45000

Lebref, Frans, SHEEP GRAZING, SUMMER'S AFTERNOON, 30½ x 39¼ (4241/90) — 4200

Lecomte, Victor, 1856-1920, READING BY LAMPLIGHT, 1887, 12 x 9 (4161/202) — 2000

Lecomte du Nouy, Jean J.A., 1842-1923, THE SMOKER, 1876, 18¾ x 13½ (4161/230) — 15000

Leech, John (1817-64), DAVIE GOING TO THE BALL, 7 x 5¼, pencil (4260/666) — 550

Leemputten, Frans van, 1850-1914, A SHEPHERD WITH HIS FLOCK, 26½ x 32 (4122/94) — 2400

Leemputten, Frans van, 1850-1914, CROSSING THE BRIDGE, 19¾ x 28 (4122/93) — 4500

Lefebvre, Jules Joseph (1836-1911), ITALIAN PEASANT GIRL, 12½ x 8½, on panel (4208/174) — 3500

Legrande, Rene (1847-?), WATERING THE FLOWERS, 1872, 16 x 12¾ (666/187) — 300

Legros, Alphonse (1837-1911), PROFILE PORTRAIT OF MICHEL CAZIN, 9½ x 7⅞, sanguine (4260/610) — 420

Legros, Alphonse, 1837-1911, LE PLAIN CHANT, 1863, 20 x 27¼ (4122/254) — 2500

Leickert, Charles Henri Joseph, A MARKET STREET IN AMSTERDAM, 7 x 9, on panel (4241/99) — 10500

Leickert, Charles Henri Joseph, 1816-1907, SKATERS ON A FROZEN RIVER, 30 x 43½ (4161/72) — 40000

Leighton, Frederick (1830-96), THE CAPTIVE ANDROMACHE, 5¼ x 15, black chalk (633/50) — 300

Leloir, Maurice (1853-1940), AT THE FAIR, d.1877, 15½ x 12¼, on panel (4208/194) — 7250

Lemmer, August (1862-?), VENETIAN FISHING BOATS, 4 x 18¾, on board (633/52) — 300

Lemoine-Benoit, Victor P.F., HOT AIR BALLOONING, 28 x 36 (4122/283) — 1900

Lemoine-Benoit, Victor P.F., HOT AIR BALLOON RISING FROM ITS PLATFORM, 24 x 19¾ (4122/284) — 850

Leon y Escosura, Ignacio, 19c, THE LETTER, 1865, 9¼ x 12¾ (4161/123) — 2800

Leon y Escosura, 19c, SANS INVITATION, 1871, 19¼ x 23¾ (4161/124) — 5750

Lepine, Stanislas (1835-92), NOTRE DAME DE PARIS, 13⅛ x 18, oil on panel (4260/1410) — 15000

Lerch, Leo, 1856-92, Czech., YOUNG WOMAN IN A JEWELED HEADDRESS, 16 x 12½ (4161/117) — 2500

Lerolle, Henry (1848-1929), DUSK, 44¼ x 18½ (633/202) — 1200

Leroux, P. (19c), FEEDING THE CHICKENS, 18 x 14¾ (666/257) — 1100

Lesrel, Adolphe Alexandre, 1839-90, THE STANDARD BEARER, 1878, 24¾ x 17¾ (4122/257) — 2700

Lessieux, Ernest Louis, 1848-1925, A HAREM BEAUTY, 20½ x 29 (4264/415) — 900

Levis, Maurice, LE CHAFEAU DE LAROCHE, 14 x 10 (4241/232) — 1100

Lewis, John Frederick, 1805-76, WAITING FOR THE FERRY, UPPER EGYPT, 13 x 31¾, 1859 (4197/355) — 15000

Lezcano, Carlos, TOLEDO, OVERLOOKING THE RIVER TAGUS, 35½ x 39½ (4241/188) — 3000

Lhermitte, Leon A., 1844-1925, LE CLOCHER DE PRIMELLE, 18 x 21 (4122/198) — 3500

Linder, Philippe, J. (19c), THE BUTTERFLY, 20 x 14 (4240/62) — 3000

Lindsay, Norman A.W., 1879-1969, THE BULL FIGHT, 9 x 10, watercolor (4161/279) — 3000

Linnell, John, 1792-1882, COLLECTING THE FLOCK, 28 x 39¼ (4122/302) — 4000

Lintott, Bernard (1875-1951), AT THE THEATRE, 10 3/16 x 11¾, ink and wash (4260/659) — 1000

Lobrichon, Timoleon Marie, 1831-1914, THE MASQUE, 10½ x 8¾, oval (4161/201) — 2000

Loder, James (fl.1820-57), CHALLENGER, ETC., 27 x 36 (4071/200) — 40710

Loeffler, A., A MOUNTAIN POOL, 17 x 30, 1886 (4241/7) — 600

Loir, Luigi (1845-1916), EFFECT OF SNOW, 22½ x 30 (4240/53) — 23000

Loir, Luigi (1845-1916), LA PLACE DE LA REPUBLIQUE, mixed media, 13¼ x 20¾ (4071/133) — 2500

Loir, Luigi (1845-1916), LA SEINE A ATHIS-MONS, mixed media, 7 x 16¾ (4071/134) — 1900

Loir, Luigi, 1845-1916, THE HOMECOMING, 17½ x 11¾, on board (4161/205) — 3100

Loos, Friedrich, Circle of, DEER JUMPING A MOUNTAIN, 9½ x 13, on paper (4241/1) — 600

Lorenz, Carl, b1871, Austrian, A PATH BY THE EDGE OF THE FOREST, 29 x 39½ (4122/11) — 1700

Lourbet, Gustave (1819-77), PORTRAIT OF ALPHONSE BON, 1849, 17⅝ x 12¼, oil on panel (4260/613) — 11000

Lowith, Wilhelm, Tea Time, 5½ x 7½ (4241/73) — 2400

Lucas y Villaamil, 19c, THE CHRISTENING, 26½ x 16¾ (4161/125) 3000
Lucas Y Padilla, Eugenio (1824-70), SCENE FROM THE WAR OF INDEPENDENCE, 16¼ x 24⅛ (4260/640) 11500
Luminais, Evariste V., 1822-96, THE WRECKERS, 59¾ x 81½ (4122/209) 500
Maaten, Jacob Jan van der (1820-79), CATTLE GRAZING ALONG A WOODED ROAD, 16½ x 21¼ (4208/64) 3000
Macco, Georg, AN ARAB MARKET SCENE, 1907, 19 x 28½ (666/248) 2750
Madrazo y Garreta, R. de, (1841-1920), PORTRAIT OF MRS. JAMES LEIGH COLEMAN, 1886, 57¾ x 38 (4240/36) 4500
Maes, H., A HARBOR SCENE, 8 x 11¾, on panel (633/226) 1300
Magni, Giuseppe, b.1869, NOCTURNAL AFFECTION, 19¾ x 24½ (4161/143) 1700
Malbon, William (fl.1834-53), BIRD'S EYE, BEDLAM BESS, ETC., unframed, 39½ x 66½ (4071/199) 3300
Malderelli, Federico, attrib. to, 1826-93, TWO WOMEN OF POMPEII, 61 x 54 (4122/169) 2700
Mali, Christian Friedrich, CATTLE AND SHEEP BY A MOUNTAIN LAKE, 29 x 22 (4241/35) 21000
Mali, Christian Friedrich (1832-1906), THE CHRISTENING, d.1868, 25 x 22½ (4208/16) 6000
Mancini, Antonio, 1852-1930, HEAD OF A BEARDED MAN, diameter 13½ (4122/171) 1100
Marais, Adolphe Charles, COWS IN A SUNNY GROVE, 26 x 32 (4241/216) 900
Marchal, Charles F., 1825-77, EVENING IN ALSACE, 36½ x 57¾ (4122/189) 500
Marchal, Charles F., 1825-77, MORNING IN ALSACE, 36½ x 57¾ (4122/188) 500
Marchand, Charles, A CAPRICCIO OF ROME, 1868, 27 x 42 (4161/173) 2200
Maris, Jacob, VILLA ON A HILLSIDE, 14½ x 9½ (4241/106) 1200
Maris,Jacob (1837-99), BEACHED FISHING BOAT, d.1871, 12 x 9¼ (633/231) 4250
Marko, Andreas, 1824-95, Austrian, SHEPHERDESS WITH HER FLOCK, 1877, 45½ x 38¾ (4161/24) 4250
Markos, Lajos, 1867-1942, Hungarian, THE LESSON, 36¼ x 30¼ (4122/126) 6750
Markos, Lajos, 1867-1942, Hungarian, THE SLEIGH, 24 x 30 (4122/115) 1600
Marscke de Lummen, Emile van, (1827-90) COWS IN A MEADOW, 23 x 33 (4240/51) 2500
Marshall, H., FOUR COACHING SCENES, 8¼ x 16 (4122/288) 1600
Mastenbroek, J.H. van, 1875-1945, SLOOTJE, 1900, 14½ x 20 (4122/84) 6250
Masters, E. (l9c), VILLAGE SCENE IN DEVONSHIRE, 20 x 30 (4208/215) 3500
Mattenheimer, Andreas T. (1787-1856), STILL LIFE WITH FRUIT AND A BIRD'S NEST, d.1832, 12½ x 15¼ (4208/21) 4000
Mattenheimer, Andreas T. (1787-1856), STILL LIFE WITH FRUIT AND NUTS, d.1832, 12½ x 15½ (4208/22) *2500*

Mattenheimer (4208/22)

Lemoine-Benoit (4122/284)

Meyer-Waldeck (4122/28)

Mattenheimer, Andreas T., 1787-1856, STILL LIFE OF PEARS, GRAPES, PLUMS, 1849, 10 x 8 (4122/29) 2700
Maurin, Charles (1856-1914), A SEATED SOLDIER, 9¾ x 12, charcoal (4260/623) 800
Mauve, Anton, AN OLD COTTAGE, OSTERBECK, HOLLAND, 12½ x 16, on panel (4241/102) 1700
Mauve, Anton (1838-88), THE RETURN OF THE FAGGOT GATHERER, 10 x 16½, ink and wash (4260/641) 2600
May, Gabriel (1840-1915), A CHRISTIAN MARTYR, 24 x 20 (633/190) 400
McCloy, Samuel (1831-1904), READING THE PAPER, 11½ x 9½, on board (633/61) 425
McColvin, John (19c), THE FORTUNE TELLER, 30 x 20 (666/223) 300
Meadows, James E. (1828-1888), A SUMMER LANDSCAPE, 24 x 42 (666/177) 1500
Meinert, F., COSSACS RESTING, 18 x 13½, on panel (4241/29) 950
Meissonier, Jean Louis E., 1815-91, GENERAL DESAIX & THE PEASANT, 1867, 12½ x 16 (4161/219) 45000
Meissonier, Jean Louis E., 1815-91, STUDY OF A HORSE, 1879, 5¼ x 5¼ (4161/222) 1500
Meissonier, Jean Louis E., 1815-91, THE SMOKER, 1879, 7¼ x 5½ (4161/220) 5000
Menpes, Mortimer L. (b.1860), VENETIAN BALCONY, on panel, 8½ x 11 (4240/76) 2400
Mesag Hendrik Willem (1831-1915), FISHING VESSELS ON CALM SEAS AT SUNSET, d.1908, 19¼ x 31¼ (4208/80) 12000
Mesdag, Hendrik Willem, TWILIGHT AT SCHEVENINGEN, 15 x 18, on panel (4241/110) 7750
Mesgrigny, Frank de (1836-84), ALONG THE RIVERBANKS AT DUSK, 19¾ x 29¼ (4208/168) 2000
Messonier, Jean Louis E., 1815-91, A STUDY OF A HORSE, 1878, 11¾ x 5¾ (4161/221) 2500
Mettling, Louis (1847-94), A YOUNG MAN IN A WHITE RUFF, 30 x 21 (4240/72) 700
Meyer-Waldeck, Kunz, 1859-1953, LAUNCHING THE FISHING BOAT, 23¾ x 35¾ (4122/28) *3250*
Meyer, Ernst L. (1848-?), ARRANGING THE FLOWERS, 1886, 27 x 22 (666/174) 1600
Meyer, J.H.L., 1809-66, RESCUE IN A STORMY SEA, 16 x 23 (4122/85) 7750
Meyerheim, Hermann, b.1840, VIEW OF GERMAN RIVERSIDE TOWN, 26 x 37½ (4161/4) 9500
Meyerheim, Wilhelm A., 1815-82, HAY BARGES, A RIVERSIDE TOWN, 26¾ x 37¾ (4122/24) 8750
Meyerheim, Wilhelm A. (1815-82), LOADING HAY, A MARKET TOWN, 27 x 38½ (4071/2) 9500
Michel, Georges, THE ROAD UP THE HILLSIDE, 20 x 32 (4241/202) 6500
Michel, Georges (1763-1843), LANDSCAPE WITH A GROVE OF TREES, 29 x 39¼ (4208/137) 7500
Michel, Georges (1763-1843), LANDSCAPE, TWILIGHT, 16 x 21 (4240/48) 1400
Michel, Georges, (1763-1843), GOATS AND SHEEP IN AN EXTENSIVE LANDSCAPE, 19¾ x 26 (4208/136) 10500
Michel, Marius (b.1853), THE ARTIST'S STUDIO, d.1892, 50 x 32 (4208/190) 7500
Michie, John D., 1864-88, DAYDREAMING, 1888, 26½ x 32 (4161/266) 1800
Migliaro, Vicenzo, 1858-1938, THE VANITY TABLE, 40½ x 30 (4122/170) 2000
Miles, Thomas Rose, EBBING TIDE, NORTH DEAL, 20 x 30 (633/84) 425
Millais, Sir John E. (1829-96), TWO STUDIES OF A WOMAN CARRYING A BASKET, 7 7/16 x 4⅞, pencil (4260/647) 1600
Millet, Jean Francois, 1814-75, LA VANNEUR, 1847-48, 40½ x 28 (4161/179) 600000
Millet, Jean Francois, 1814-75, NU ASSIS CONTRE UN ARBE, 1848-50, 11½ x 8, drawing (4161/181) 6000

Millet, Jean Francois, 1814-75, PORTRAIT PRESUME D'EMELIE MILLET, 8¾ x 6½ (4161/180) 3250

Miralles, Francisco, THE LETTER, 36 x 28¼ (4241/192) 5750

Moimile, Gaetano, DRIVING THE TURKEYS, 25 x 14¼ (4241/179) 900

Monchablon, Jean F., 1855-1905, RIVES DE LA SAONE, 10½ x 15¾ (4161/177) 1900

Monchablon, Jean F., 1855-1905, VIEW OF A COUNTRY TOWN, 1889, 9¾ x 13¾ (4122/200) 1900

Monsted, Peder (1859-1941), SPRINGTIME ALONG THE RIVER, d.1912, 15 x 20¾, on academy board (4208/102) 5000

Monsted, Peder, 1859-1941, Danish, VIEW OVER MENTON, 1906, 14¾ x 22¼ (4161/106) 2000

Monticelli, Adolphe J.T., 1824-86, AFTERNOON IN THE PARK, 15½ x 21¼ (4161/183) 3500

Monticelli, Adolphe J.T., 1824-86, IN THE PARK, 1875, 17¼ x 21¾ (4161/182) 9500

Monticelli, Adolphe J.T., 1824-86, LADIES IN THE PARK, 15½ x 22 (4161/184) 3500

Monticelli, Adolphe J.T., 1824-86, LES DAMES DE LA REINE, 1868, 25¾ x 21¼ (4122/262) 5000

Morbelli, Angelo (1863-1919), THE RICE GLEANERS, d.1901, 71 x 51 (4208/127) 57500

Mordt, Gustav A., 1826-56, Norweg., NORWEGIAN SUMMER, 1853, 15 x 20¾ (4122/118) 1500

Moreau de Tours, Georges, A DREADFUL EDICT, 1878, 45 x 67¼ (4122/247) 1000

Morel, Jan Evert, The Younger, BESIDE A STREAM, SUMMER, 12½ x 17¼, on panel (4241/83) 4250

Morel, Jan Evert, The Younger, SHEEP ON PATH, 8 x 6 on panel (4241/84) 2000

Morel, Jan Evert, The Younger, THE PATH TO THE VILLAGE and THE RETURN HOME, Pair, 8 x 6¼ each (4241/85) 6250

Morin, Gustave-Francois (1809-86), SONGS FOR A HAPPIER FUTURE, 12½ x 15½ (633/55) 600

Morisot, Berthe, ENFANTS AU BORD DU LAC, oil on paper, 21⅛ x 25½ (4250/410) 13000

Moro, Ferrucio, b.1859, THE TOAST, 32 x 43½ (4161/138) 6250

Morot, Aime Nicholas (1850-1913), EL BRAVO TORO, 1884, 60 x 31 (4240/68) 16000

Moser, Ernst C., 1815-67, Austrian, INCRIMINATING EVIDENCE, 1853, 24¾ x 19½ (4122/52) 4250

Mucke, Carl Emile, 1847-1923, MOTHERHOOD, 1878, 23½ x 20½ (4161/59) 2800

Muhlig, Albert Ernst, (b.1862), AN EXTENSIVE SUMMER LANDSCAPE, 22 x 31½ (644/56) 700

Muhlig, Hugo, SUNDAY MORNING, SPRING, 23 x 19 (4241/28) 16000

Muhlig, Hugo, TARGET PRACTICE, 9 x 15, on panel (4241/27) 14000

Muhlig, Meno, 1823-73, THE HUNTER'S PORTRAIT, 13½ x 15½ (4161/41) 3000

Muller, August, SAYING GRACE, 29½ x 23¼ (4241/55) 5000

Muller, August, THE ANGLER, 17¼ x 14¼ (4241/79) 2500

Muller, August (1836-85), THE COURTING COUPLE, 36¾ x 29½ (4208/17) *5500*

Muller, Charles Louis (1815-92), CHARLOTTE CORDAY IN PRISON, 41 x 33 (4240/60) 3250

Muller, Moritz (1841-99), DEER SURPRISING DUCKS AT SUNSET, d.1875, 21½ x 28 (4208/15) 4000

Muller, Moritz, 1841-99, A FAMILY OF DEER, 1877, 11¼ x 14¼ (4122/4) *2600*

Muller (4122/4)

Muller (4208/17)

Munkacsy, Michael Von Lieb, THE PAWNBROKER'S SHOP, 64 x 86¼ (4241/148) 23000

Munkacsy, Michel L., 1844-1909, THE TWO FAMILIES, Hungarian, 34¾ x 46 (4122/124) 43000

Munkacsy, Michel L., 1844-1909, WOMAN IN WHITE, 1884, Hungarian, 21¾ x 18¼
(4122/122)   3000
Munthe, Ludwig (1841-96), LANDSCAPE, 28 x 36 (666/240)   8250
Murillo, Bartholome, E., Manner of, MADONNA AND CHILD, 35 x 27½ (633/57)   250
Murray, Charles Fairfax (1849-1917), THREE STUDIES OF A WOMAN'S HEAD, 9⅜ x 7½,
charcoal (4260/649)   600
Musin, Francois E., 1820, FISHING OFF A COAST, I6½ x 29 (4122/86)   6000
Naysmyth, Alexander, 1758-1840, PORTRAIT OF A FAMILY, 43 x 59 (4148/198)   12000
Neubert, Ludwig (1846-92), AN OLD CASTLE IN BAVARIA, 29½ x 54 (4240/8)   1600
Neuhuys, Albert, 1844-1914, COTTAGE INTERIOR, 1878, 23 x 30¾ (4122/63)   4500
Neustatter, Ludwig (1820-99), PLAY HORSIE, 22 x 16½ (4208/32)   *3500*
Neustatter, Ludwig, 1820-99, GIDDYUP HORSIE, 13¾ x 10¼ (4161/47)   8000
Neustatter, Ludwig, 1820-99, THE SEESAW, 1876, 13¾ x 10¼ (4161/48)   8000
Neuville, Alfred A.B. de (19c), THREE KITTENS PLAYING WITH A FAN, 15 x 18 (4208/177)   *2500*

Neustatter (4208/32)

Neuville (4208/177)

Neuville, Alphonse Marie de (1835-85), A FRENCH DRAGOON OF THE SECOND EMPIRE,
1877, 18¾ x 14¾ (4161/225)   2500
Neuville, Alphonse Marie de (1835-85), CHAMPIGNY, 1882, 54 x 77 (4240/67)   4000
Nichol, Erskine (1825-1904), PADDY'S MARK, 1869, 24 x 32 (4240/75)   9000
Nicolet, Gabriel Emile E. (1856-1921), LETTER TO A FRIEND, 36 x 28½ (4208/26)   2400
Nitsch, Richard, b.1866, PAIR, WOMAN WITH BASKET, MAN WITH PIPE, 7 x 5½ (4122/40)   2500
Noel, Jules Achille, (1815-81), THE TEMPEST, 1858, 22½ x 29½ (4122/207)   1500
Nordenberg, Bengt, (1822-1902), A DIFFICULT MOMENT, 1867, Swedish, 14 x 17¼
(4161/113)   14000
Nordgren, Anna, 1847-1916, Swedish, YOUNG GIRL WITH PARASOL, 1890, 35 x 42
(4161/120)   1100
Norio, Orlando, AN OFFICER, 8¾ x 7, watercolor (633/126)   75
Norwich School, (19c), WOODSMEN IN A CLEARING, 24 x 20 (666/143)   700
O'Neill, George Bernard (1828-1917), LET ME THINK, 12 x 17 (4208/229)   8500
Oeder, Georg, CHILDREN PLAYING IN A CLEARING, 25½ x 39, 1881 (4241/9)   5250
Oliveri, A., PLAYING MOMMY, 20 x 26 (4241/168)   1200
Olivier de Penne, Charles, THREE SETTERS IN A FIELD, 12 x 9 (4161/209)   950
Orazi, A.P., COLD HANDS, WARM HEARTS, 29½ x 18¼ (4241/171)   2100
Ortlieb, Friedrich, (1839-1909), THE FLIRT, 25½ x 20½ (4161/42)   5250
Ostersetzer, C., PREPARING THE MEAL, 12½ x 8¼, on panel (4241/75)   2000
Ostersetzer, C. (19/20c), LOCAL POLITICIANS, 1905, on panel, 20 x 15¾ (666/242)   1600
Oudinot, Achille, (1820-91), THE YOUNG WATER CARRIER, 28¾ x 23½ (4161/213)   2100
Outin, Pierre, (1840-99), ON THE CLIFF, 24 x 39¼ (4161/210)   20000
Papperitz, Gustav Friedrich, (1813-61), LANDSCAPE WITH A MUSICAL PARTY, d.1841, 6 x
9½, on board (633/28)   300
Paredes, Vincenta de (1808-97), THE BULL FIGHT, 10½ x 16, on panel (4208/128)   1700
Parsons, Alfred (1847-1920), BREDON-ON-THE-AVON, 1913, 47½ x 72 (4240/78)   8000

Pascal, Paul, (1832-1903), ON THE NILE, 12 x 17¼, 1889 (4197/343) 325
Pascal, Paul, (1832-1903), PAIR, AT THE OASIS, JOURNEY THE DESSERT, 21¼ x 27½, gouaches (4122/222) 2100
Pascal, Paul, (1832-1903), PASSING THROUGH AN ARAB VILLAGE, 18 x 26, 1899 (4197/352) 1500
Pascucci, A., A LANDSCAPE WITH TRAVELLERS, d.1875, 25 x 29 (633/250) 650
Pasini, Alberto, A COURTYARD IN CONSTANTINOPLE, 10 x 18 (4241/176) 8500
Pasini, Alberto, Manner of, ARABS AT THE VILLAGE GATE, 15¾ x 25½ (4197/359) 700
Pasini, Alberto, (1826-99), GATEWAY TO THE MOSQUE, 10¾ x 8½ (4197/375) 3000
Pasmore, John F., (1838-81), FEEDING TIME, 28 x 36 (4122/296) 1700
Payne, David, SHEPHERD AND SHEEP AT A CLEARING, 18 x 39 (633/119) 425
Pedretti, Vittore (1799-1868), THE PRINT COLLECTOR, 13 x 18 (666/212) 1200
Peel, James (1811-1906), BROOK IN WEARDALE, YORKSHIRE, 26 x 36 (4208/218) 2900
Pelligrini, Riccardo, b.1866, FISHING BOATS ON A MOUNTAIN LAKE, 23¼ x 39 (4161/141) 1000
Pelouse, Leon Germain, A MISTY MORNING ON A MEADOW, 23¾ x 36½ (4241/219) 2800
Pelouse, Leon Germain, THE OPEN GATE, 27½ x 39⅜ (4241/220) 1800
Pena, Narcisse Virgile De La, GATHERING FAGGOTS, 8½ x 11½ (4241/200) 2200
Perboyre, Paul E.L., THE BUGLER, 10¼ x 8¼ (4161/228) 2000
Percy, Sidney R., (1821-86), VALLEY OF THE DONGELLY, 30 x 50 (4161/256) 2000
Peretti, Bernardo (1828-89), INDIAN CORN AND GRAPES, 20½ x 17¼ (4240/32) 1600
Perez, Alonso, fl.1892-1914, A RAINY WEDDING, 1892, 22¾ x 28½ (4122/139) 4000
Perrier, Emilio Sanchez, (1855-1907), LE JOUR TOMBE, 6 x 10 (4161/130) 2000
Petit, Eugene (1839-86), ROSES IN A VASE, 32 x 25½ (4208/169) 2600
Petruolo, Salvatore, A PAIR OF BATTLE SCENES, 28½ x 59 (4241/174) 1800
__Pezant,__ Aymar (b.1846), DRIVING THE HERD, 15 x 21¾ (4208/158) *1500*
Pfyffer, Eduard (1836-99), PEASANT WOMAN RETURNING FROM MARKET, d.1880, 30x 22 (4208/49) *3250*

Pezant (4208/158)

Pfyffer (4208/49)

Picault, C. (19c), FONTAINEBLEAU, on panel, 10⅜ x 14⅜ (666/221) 1100
Pickersgill, F.R. (1820-1900), SAMPSON AND DELILAH, on panel, 12¼ x 10 (666/258) 1800
Picou, Henri Pierre, (1824-95), MOLIERE A VERSAILLES, 1868, 25 x 30 (4122/253) 1500
Pieler, Franz Xaver, (1897-1952), STILL LIFE WITH FLOWERS & PEACHES, 20½ x 6¼ (4161/3) 3750
Pieters, Evert, FEEDING BABY BY THE HEARTH, 30 x 24¾ (4241/114) 13500
Piloty, Carl T., (1826-86), BEDSIDE VIRGIL, 21¾ x 26¾ (4122/57) 2200
Pinchart, Auguste Emile, b.1842, CONSULTING CUPID, 1872, 24 x 15 (4122/267) 1900
Pinchart, Auguste Emile, b.1842, LOVE'S ENTREATY, 1875, 30 x 22¾ (4122/266) 1800
Piot, Adolphe Etienne, (1850-1910), SPRINGTIME, THE ROSES, 32 x 23 (4122/259) 8000
Piot, Adolphe Etienne, (1850-1910), THE YOUNG READER, 18¼ x 15 (4122/260) 4900
Pissarro, Camille (1830-1903), HEAD OF A BOY, YOUNG WOMAN DOZING, DOUBLE SIDED, 11⅝ x 8¾, chalk (4260/1415) 5500
Pitzner, Max Joseph, (1855-1910), A PASSING FLIRTATION, 1883, 6 x 8¼ (4161/29) 2000

Poggenbeek George (1853-1903), CATTLE BESIDE A STREAM, SPRINGTIME, d.1879,
18½ x 34 (4208/63)   3400
Portaels, J.F., (1818-95), THE TAMBORINE GIRL, 35 x 26 (4122/105)   2750
Portieje, Gerard, (1856-1929), PORTRAIT OF A MAN WITH RED CAP, 8½ x 6¼ (4122/100)   1000
Portielie, Edward, (1861-1949), THE CONNOISSEUR, 1882, 39¾ x 32½ (4161/88)   3500
Portielje, Jon F.P., (1829-95), AN EASTERN BEAUTY, 23¼ x 19 (4122/104)   4250
Powell, C.M. 1824, FISHING BOATS IN A HARBOR, 24½ x 29 (4208/204)   2750
Pratt, Jonathan, (1871-93), THE YOUNG ARTIST, 20 x 30¾ (4122/318)   1000
Preston, Thomas, THE TRAVELLER, d.1848, 25 x 30½ (633/58)   400
Preyer, Johann Wilhelm, STILL LIFE OF FRUIT ON A STONE LEDGE, 9½ x 12½ (4241/38)   18000
Priechonfied, Alois Heinrich, AN ENGAGING LETTER, 19 x 12¼, on panel (4241/61)   2000
Prouve, Victor Emile, (1858-1943), LA MORT DE JEZEBEL, 1880, 53½ x 40½ (4122/239)   2000
Pyne, James B., attrib. to, (1800-70), RIVER AVON & PULTNEY BRIDGE, BATH, 25 x 30
(4161/259)   950
Pyne, James B., (1800-70), CASTLE IN A RIVER LANDSCAPE, 19 x 28, watercolor
(4161/258)   1100
Pyne, James B., (1800-70), SUNDAY AFTERNOON ON THE RIVER, 1861, 19 x 26, watercolor
(4161/257)   1300
Quitton, Edouard, b.1842, STILL LIFE OF SONG BIRDS, 1885, 10½ x 8½ (4122/109)   1400
Quitton, Edouard, b.1842, STILL LIFE WITH SONG BIRDS, 1881, 12 x 9 (4122/108)   1500
Quloaga Y Zabaleta, Ignacio (1870-1945), WOMEN ON THE BALCONY, 72 x 52 (4208/130)   32000
Ranzoni, Gustav, 1826-1900, Austria, DRIVING THE FLOCK, 1897, 10½ x 18½ (4161/23)   2200
Rasch, Heinrich (1840-1913), WATERING THE COWS, 15¾ x 26¼ (4208/10)   *3250*
Redon, Odilon, IRISES IN A VASE, pastel, 14 x 10¼ (4250/407)   7000
Redon, Odilon, LE GUERRIER, oil on board, 12½ x 9 (4252/612)   10000
Reggianini, Vittorio, THE RECITAL, 30 x 40 (4241/178)   8500
Reggianini, Vittorio, b.1853, TEASING AMOR, 38½ x 51½ (4161/144)   41610
Regnault, Henri (1843-71), A LADY IN A MANTILLA, 1968, on board, 12¾ x 10½ (4240/71)   500
Rehbenitz, T.M., attrib. to (1791-1861), AFTER THE SERVICE, on panel, 10 x 7¾ (666/189)   1000
Reich, Albert, b.1881, LAST MINUTE RESERVATIONS, 19¾ x 15½ (4122/51)   2000
Reich, Albert, b.1881, THE CURIO CABINET, 19¾ x 15½ (4122/50)   *2100*
Rein, Johan Eimerich (1827-1900), HARBOR BY MOONLIGHT, d.1878, 29½ x 48 (4208/103)   1200
Reinert, A. (19c), A MOONLIT BAY, 22 x 36 (666/236)   600
Remde, Friedrich, GATHERING HAY, 19 x 25½ (4241/63)   700
Renoir, Pierre Auguste (1841-1919), YOUNG WOMAN IN A LANDSCAPE, 8 1/16 x 12¼,
mixed media (4260/1426)   33000
Repin, Ilya, 1844-1930, ACCOUTREMENTS, 1904, 52 x 47 (4161/109)   12000
Reyntjens, Hendrik Engelbert (1817-59), BEHIND THE GARDEN WALL, d.1857, 8¼ x 11, on
panel (4208/57)   2200
Rhomberg, Hanno, A NEW LITTER, 42½ x 42½, 1866 (4241/53)   31000
Ribot, G.T.C. (1823-93), STILL LIFE OF FRUIT, on panel, 5½ x 11¼ (666/208)   900
Ribot, Theodore, Augustin, 1823-91, HEAD OF A WOMAN IN BLACK, 8¾ x 6 (4161/197)   700
Ricci, Pio, b.1919, THE PROPOSAL, 20½ x 14¾ (4122/168)   1200
Ricciardi, Oscar (1864-?), THE MARKET PLACE, on panel, 13½ x 9 (666/210)   425
Richet, Leon, COTTAGES BY A WINDMILL, (4241/229)   6500
Richet, Leon, PEASANT WOMAN ON A PATH BY A RIVER, 21¼ x 28¾ (4241/230)   5750
Richet, Leon, SUNSET OVER A POOL, 17 x 25½ (4241/231)   5500
Richet, Leon (1847-1907), A PATH THROUGH THE FOREST, d.1885, 26 x 32 (4208/148)   3500
Richet, Leon (1847-1907), PEASANT WOMAN ON A PATH BY A FARMHOUSE, d.1882, 48½
x 64½ (4208/147)   *7500*

Richet (4208/147)

Riegen (4122/82)

Reich (4122/50)

Rasch (4208/10)

Richet, Leon (1847-1907), REST BY A WATERFALL, 25 x 19½ (4208/172)   3500
Richet, Leon (1847-1907), YOUNG GIRLS FETCHING WATER, d.1880, 32 x 24½, on panel
(4208/171)   7000
Richet, Leon, 1847-1907, Diaz de la Pena, 1808-76, PATH THROUGH FOREST, 1877, 35½ x
46 (4122/184)   8000
Richet, Leon, 1847-1907, GATHERING WOOD AT EDGE OF FOREST, 26¾ x 35¾
(4122/193)   3500
Richet, Leon, 1847-1907, MEADOW'S EDGE, 16¼ x 20 (4122/195)   2250
Richet, Leon, 1847-1907, PUNTING ON THE RIVER, 18¼ x 24 (4122/194)   4500
Richet, Leon, 1847-1907, RIVER LANDSCAPE WITH STORMY SKY, 21 x 30½ (4161/162)   6000
Richet, Leon, 1847-1907, WOODLAND POOL AT SUNSET, 25½ x 36½ (4161/163)   4000
Richter, Carl Adolph (1812-52), THREE JOLLY FRIARS, 19 x 27 (633/238)   1200
Richter, Edouard Frederic Wilhelm, 1844-1913, WOMAN IN ORIENTAL HEADDRESS, 21 x
15¼, 1880 (4197/364)   950
Richter, Edouard Frederic Wilhelm, 1844-1913, WOMAN IN ORIENTAL HEADRESS, 21 x
15¼, 1880 (4264/411)
Rico y Ortega, M., 1833-1908, THE BANKS OF THE ADIGE, 18¾ x 31¾ (4122/143)   12000
Riegen, Nicolaas, 1827-89, A DANGEROUS COASTLINE, 19¾ x 31½ (4122/82)   2000
Rieger, Albert (b.1834), A RIVER TOWN, 20¾ x 31¼ (633/216)   1400
Risse, Roland (b. 1835), BLIND MAN'S BLUFF, d.1836, 13¾ x 17¼ (4208/27)   2900
Rivas, A., 19c, THE VEIL DANCER, 14¼ x 22¾, on panel (4264/416)   1500
Rizzo, E. (19/20c), DELICACIES, 13 x 18 (666/213)   800
Robbe, Louis (1806-87), LANDSCAPE AND CATTLE, 34½ x 49 (4240/15)   12000
Robbe, Louis (1806-87), SHEPHERD AND HIS FLOCK, 34 x 49 (4240/16)   14000
Robert-Fleury, Tony, attrib., PORTRAIT OF A BEARDED MAN, 16¼ x 13¼ (4260/626)   1300
Robert-Fleury, Tony, 1837-1912, REMBRANDT IN HIS STUDIO, 1865, 33½ x 39½
(4161/216)   1600
Robert-Fleury, Tony, 1837-1912, THE CARDINAL'S CONCERT, 33¾ x 46 (4122/252)   2800
Roberts, David, attrib. (1796-1864), ST. STEPHEN'S VIENNA, d.1851, 13½ x 18, on panel
(633/75)   750
Roberts, David, 1796-1864, INTERIOR OF A CATHEDRAL, 1851, 18¼ x 16½ (4122/313)   1500
Robie, Jean Baptiste, ROSES IN A GLASS VASE, 12 x 10 (4161/101)   3500
Rodin, Auguste, small study for IRIS, MESSAGERE DES DIEUX, bronze, 6¼, 1890-91
(4252/601)   4500
Rodin, Auguste, EVE AU ROCHER, white marble, 30½, ca1883 (4249/209)   75000
Rodin, Auguste, HOMME AU NEZ CASSE, bronze, 10¾, 1864 (4252/605)   10000
Rodin, Auguste, JEUNE FILLE A LA COURONNE ROSES, terra cotta, 13⅜, ca1868
(4249/202)   19000
Rodin, Auguste, L'ETERNEL PRINTEMP, bronze, 15¼, 1884 (4252/603)   14000

Rodin, Auguste, STUDY FOR FIGURE OF ANDRIEU D'ANDRES, bronze, black patina, 24, 1973 (4249/214)	27000
Rodin, Auguste, STUDY FOR FIGURE OF EUSTACHE DE SAINT-PIERRE, bronze, black patina, 27¼, 1973 (4249/213)	22000
Rodin, Auguste, STUDY FOR FIGURE OF JACQUES DE WIESSANT, bronz, e, black patina, 27, 1973 (4249/215)	22000
Rodin, Auguste, STUDY FOR FIGURE OF JEAN D'AIRE, bronze, black pati, na, 27, 1973 (4249/212)	19000
Rodin, Auguste, STUDY FOR FIGURE OF JEAN DE FIENNES, bronze, black patina, 28½, 1973 (4249/210)	21000
Rodin, Auguste, STUDY FOR FIGURE OF PIERRE DE WIESSANT, bronze, black patina, 28, 1973 (4249/211)	20000
Rodin, Auguste (1840-1917), HANDS (STUDY FOR 'THE SECRET'), 1910, H4¾, bronze (4260/1427)	8000
Rodin, Auguste (1840-1917), LE MARTYRE, 1885, L24, bronze (4164/10)	9000
Rodin, Auguste (1840-1917), RIGHT HAND, HALF-CLOSED, H4⅜, bronze (4260/1428)	5500
Roessler, W.R., 19-20c, pair, THE SMOKER, THE DRINKER, 9½ x 7¼ (4161/119)	2900
Roessler, W.R., 19-20c, PAIR, THE SMOKER, THE DRINKER, 9½ x 7¼ (4122/128)	1900
Roffianen, J.F.X., 1820-98, BY A LAKESIDE, SUMMER, 19¼ x 32 (4122/88)	4000
Rolfe, Alexander F. (19c), HORSE AND DOG IN A LANDSCAPE, 1843, 28 x 36 (666/142)	2500
Romako, Anton, THE LAST CONFESSION OF BEATRICE CENCI, 29½ x 39½ (4241/49)	2500
Roman, Max Wilhelm (1810-1849), A VENETIAN CANAL, 11 x 17 (633/223)	325
Ronner, Henriette, DOGCART ON THE DUNES, 7 x 9½, on paper (4241/88)	700
Ronner, Henriette and J.D. Col, THE DOG CART, 18 x 27½ (4241/91)	3200
Roosenboom, Albert, HIDE AND SEEK, 25½ x 9½ (4241/144)	5750
Roosenboom, Nicolaas Johannes, 1805-80, SKATERS ON A FROZEN ESTUARY, 12¼ x 18 (4161/71)	9500
Roqueplan, Camille (1803-55), A SPRING DAY'S OUTING, d.1840, 22 x 16½ (633/35)	600
Rosati, Giulio, 1853-1917, BUYING A BRIDE, 18¾ x 13¾, watercolor (4122/153)	700
Rose, Julius (1828-1911), PEASANTS BY A MOUNTAIN LAKE, 45¼ x 58½ (4071/13)	1400
Rosetti, Dante Gabriel (1828-82), PORTRAIT OF ELIZA HARRIET POLIDORI, d.1858, 8⅞ x 7⅛, pencil (4260/645)	4800
Rosierse, Johannes (1818-1901), THE FRUIT SELLER, 18¼ x 14½ (4208/55)	3250
Rosierse, Johannes, 1818-1901, VEGETABLE SELLER, MOONLIGHT, 19½ x 15 (4161/65)	3250
Rosseau, Theodore (1812-67), A RIVER LANDSCAPE, 5⅜ x 7⅝, sepia ink (4260/614)	3500
Rossignol, Ferdinand, STILL LIFE WITH FLOWERS & FRUIT, 1848, 23¼ x 19 (4122/277)	5000
Rothenstein, Sir William (1872-1945), A STUDY OF SARGENT, STEER AND TONKS, d.1903, 30½ x 25⅛ (4260/656)	5200
Rothenstein, Sir William (1872-1945), PORTRAIT OF GEORGE BERNARD SHAW, d.1897, 14¾ x 10, pencil (4260/661)	650
Rousseau, Henri, 1844-1910, ARAB WARRIORS CROSSING THE DESERT, 21¼ x 29 (4197/348)	6500
Rousseau, Pierre Etienne ᵢ (1812-67), A BREAK IN THE CLOUDS, 16¾ x 20, on panel (4208/145)	26000
Rousseau, Pierre Etienne, 1812-67, A BARBIZON VILLAGE, ca1850, 12¼ x 18, on paper (4161/152)	12000
Rousseau, Pierre Etienne, 1812-67, MINUIT, 7¾ x 12 (4161/150)	5000
Roux, Carl, 1826-94, HERD WATERING AT ALPINE LAKE, 16 x 31 (4161/21)	4250
Roux, Louis Eugene le (1833-1905), ALEXANDER II OF RUSSIA GIVING AUDIENCE, 40½ x 58¾ (4240/69)	1600
Roy, Marius, b.1883, POLISHING HIS HELMET, 9½ x 5 (4122/240)	850
Roybet, Ferdinand, THE BROKEN DOLL, 18¼ x 15¼ (4260/628)	3200
Roybet, Ferdinand (1840-1920), THE MODEL, 16 x 13 (633/217)	1700
Roybet, Ferdinand 1840-1920, THE LUTE PLAYER, 16¼ x 12¾ (4122/255)	2100
Royten, Jan, STREET SCENE IN ANTWERP, 9 x 11¼ (4241/145)	5250
Rozier, Dominique Hubert, 1840-1901, PAIR, STILL LIFE WITH FISH, WITH LOBSTER, 24 x 20 (4161/237)	2500
Rugendas, Johann Morritz, GAUCHOS RESCUING A HOSTAGE, 31½ x 41 (4241/31)	35000
Ruppert, Otto von (1841-?), VENICE FROM LIDO, d.1894, 5⅞ x 16½, on panel (633/224)	750
Ruyten, Jan (1813-81), THE MARKET AT ANTWERP, d.1865, 31½ x 39 (4208/92)	25000
Rychen, Y. (19c), AN ALPHINE CITY, on panel, 5⅜ x 7⅜ (666/196)	800
Ryland, Henry, 1856-1924, PAIR, BIRDS OF A FEATHER, AUTUMN FRUITS, 23 x 15½, watercolors (4122/314)	1000
Sadler, Walter D., 1854-1923, THE CONFERENCE, 22 x 32¼ (4161/267)	1500
Saint Pierre, Gaston C. (1833-1916), Nedjma-Odalisque, 43 x 60½ (4240/64)	16500
Salentin, Hubert, 1822-1910, IN THE CHURCHYARD, 1869, 33 x 26 (4122/33)	4250
Salinas, A., FISHING OFF COAST, 15½ x 21½ (4241/186)	1200
Salinas, Juan Pablo, 1871-1946, THE COURTSHIP, 11½ x 14¾ (4161/133)	16000

Salomon, Hermann D., 1844-1905, VIEW OF THE TIBER, 34 x 65 (4122/147)   4500
Sandrucci, G., A FINE VINTAGE, 33½ x 24 (4241/167)   1000
Sani, Alessandro, IDLE PLEASURES, 1881, 16 x 12¼ (4122/166)   2300
Sani, Alessandro, SEE THE PRETTY PARROT, 13 x 9¼ (4122/167)   1900
Sant, James R.A., 1820-1916, CHILDHOOD, 36½ x 48 (4161/265)   1700
Santoro, Rubens (1859-1942), PORTRAIT OF A YOUNG BOY, 24½ x 17¼ (4208/118)   1500
Sartorio, Giulio, 1860-1932, MARE DEL PERU, 22¾ x 28¾ (4122/145)   2000
Sartorio, Giulio, 1860-1932, ISOLOTTO A PUNTARENAS, 10½ x 22, gouache, pastel (4161/147)   600
Savry, Hendrick (1823-1907), CATTLE AND SHEEP IN A LANDSCAPE, 24 x 42½ (4208/60)   3250
Schaeffels, Hendrik Frans, THE ROYAL BARGE, 43 x 46 (4241/137)   10000
Schaep, H.A., 1826-70, FISHING BOATS IN THE SHALLOWS, 10¼ x 13 (4122/89)   1800
Schafer, Hermann, MARKET IN ANTHWERP, 32 x 25¾ (4241/5)   3700
Scheffer, Ary, (1795-1858), JACOB AND RACHEL, 22½ x 16½, on panel (633/196)   750
Schenck, August F.A., 1828-1901, SHEEP STRANDED IN A BLIZZARD, Danish, 16 x 23½ (4122/112)   900
Schendel, Petrus Van, THE ADORATION OF THE CHILD, 51 x 36½ (4241/136)   8000
Scheurer, Julius (1859-1913), CHICKENS AT FEED, 7¼ x 9¼, on panel (633/200)   1600
Schiertz, Franz Wilhelm (1813-87), SEAL HUNTERS ON AN ICE FLOE, GREENLAND, 29½ x 45½ (4071/17)   5250
Schirmer, August W., 1802-66, VIEW OF CAPRI THROUGH A GROTTO, 10¼ x 13¾ (4122/27)   1100
Schleich, Robert (1845-1934), WINTER SKATING SCENE, on panel, 9 x 12¾ (4071/10)   14500
Schlesinger, Felix, THE FIRST SNOW, 21 x 24 (4241/65)   36000
Schlesinger, Felix, 1833-1910, KINDER-GARTEN, 27½ x 39 (4122/48)   65000
Schlesinger, Felix, 1833-1910, WEDDING CONGRATULATIONS, 1857, 31½ x 41½ (4122/49)   17000
Schmidt, A., A COUNTRY ROAD, 12¼ x 16⅛ (633/83)   300
Schmidt, A., COWS GRAZING IN A LANDSCAPE, 9½ x 13⅜ (633/82)   375
Schodl, Max (1834-1921), STILL LIFE WITH ORIENTAL OBJECTS, 1886, on panel, 13⅜ x 9⅜ (666/207)   4750
Schotel, Anthonie Pieter (1890-1958), DUTCH CANAL SCENE, 26 x 20¼ (666/159)   500
Schreyer, Adolf, 1828-1899, BEDOUINS ON THE MARCH, 33½ x 45 (4161/34)   38000
Schreyer, Adolf, 1828-99, FORDING A RIVER, WALLACHIANS ON THE MOVE, 20 x 32¾ (4122/8)   18000
Schroder, Albert Friedrich, THE PIPE SMOKER, 11 x 8, on panel (4241/80)   5000
Schrodl, Anton, 1823-1906, SUNSET, RETURN OF THE FLOCK, 40½ x 29½ (4161/25)   5000
Schrotter, Alfred von (1856-1935), THE GUNSMITH, 15 x 11¾, on panel (4208/44)   *5000*
Schuetze, Wilhelm, 1840-98, ADORABLE KITTENS, 29½ x 24¼ (4122/47)   *16000*
Schumaker, C.J., CASTLE RHINESTEIN, d.1881, 22 x 16¼ (633/213)   500
Schweninger, Carl, Jr., 1854-1903, THE DUET, Austrian, 39 x 30 (4122/53)   4250
Sckell, Ludwig, 1833-1912, MOUNTAIN LANDSCAPE, 15¾ x 25½ (4122/10)   41220
Seben, Henri Van, YOUNG SKATERS, 32½ x 26¼ (4241/143)   1100
Seben, Henri Van, (1825-1913), THE SKATERS, 16¾ x 14½ (666/203)   2250
Seitz, Anton (1829-1900), THE PORTRAIT PAINTER, 12½ x 17½, on cradled panel (4208/41)   *19000*
Seitz, Georg Johann, 1810-70, STILL LIFE WITH FRUIT AND A ROSE, 21¾ x 26¾ (4161/1)   1100
Sellmayr, Ludwig, A FOX AND A SQUIRREL, 10¼ x 8½, on panel (4241/36)   800
Senet, Rafael, b.1856, CHILDREN PLAYING ON A BEACH, 8 x 13½ (4161/128)   2700
Serusier, Paul (1863-1927), YOUNG BRETON WOMAN, 8 x 4⅜, mixed media (4260/1421)   1500
Seurat, Georges (1859-91), PROMENADE, ca1881-82, 12¼ x 9¼, conte crayon (4260/1413)   82000
Seurat, Georges (1859-91), STANDING MALE NLUDE, d.1877, 23¾ x 18¼, black crayon (4260/1412)   30000
Severdonck, Francois van, 1809-89, SHEEP and DUCKS BY A POND, 1885, 18 x 25½ (4122/96)   5250
Severdonck, Francois Van, CHICKENS AND BIRDS FEEDING, 19¾ x 29½ (4241/128)   5250
Severdonck, Francois Van, 1809, ANIMALS RESTING BY POOL AT DUSK, 1880, 19 x 26¾ (4161/89)   7000
Shayer, William Jnr., b.1811, FARMYARD SCENE, 1846, 16½ x 29 (4161/246)   750
Shayer, William, attrib. to, 1788-1879, BY THE BANKS OF A STREAM, 25¾ x 36½ (4122/294)   2400
Shayer, William, attrib. to, 1788-1879, RUSTICS BY THE WAYSIDE, 30 x 25¼ (4122/292)   1800
Shayer, William, (1788-1879), FISHERFOLK UNDER A PORTICO, 40¼ x 52½ (4208/224)   7000
Shayer, William, 1788-1879, A GYPSY ENCAMPMENT, 14¼ x 12¼ (4122/291)   3500
Sicialiano, attrib. to (19c), ROCKY LANDSCAPE, 18 x 25½ (4240/45)   1000
Sickert, Walter Richard (1860-1942), STUDIES OF WOMEN, CAMDENTOWN, 13½ x 10⅛, mixed media (4260/660)   2400
Siegen, August, 19-20c, MAMLUK MOSQUE OF SULTAN HASSAN, CAIRO, 38½ x 56 (4122/21)   2000

Sinding
(4208/105)

Siegen
(4122/21)

Schrotter (4208/44)

Seitz
(4208/41)

Schuetze (4122/47)

Simonetti, Attilio, 1843-1925, THE LOVE LETTER, 26 x 20 (4161/135)   1600
Simoni, Gustavo, b.1846, A CEREMONY IN THE COURTYARD, 31 x 44½, 1904 (4264/406)   3800
Simons, Jan Frans (1855-1919), DEVOTION, dated '81, on panel, 12¾ x 8¾ (666/202)   400
Sinding, Otto Ludvig (1842-1909), BATHING IN THE FJORD, d.1889(?), 38 x 55½ (4208/105)   7000
Skutezky, Dome (1850-1921), A GARLAND OF FLOWERS, d.1874 (?), 23¾ x 16¾ (4208/24)   2400
Sluiter, Willy, SELF PORTRAIT, 20 x 15¾ (4241/116)   406
Smith-Hald, Frithjof, GATHERING MUSSELS BY MOONLIGHT, 18½ x 29¾ (4241/159)   3100
Solomon, Simeon (1840-1905), STUDY OF A BEARDED MAN, d.1861, 11½ x 8½, charcoal
(4260/652)   2300
Somm, Henry, FOURTEEN ASSORTED SKETCHES, overall,15¾ x 22½, mixed media
(4260/629)   1400
Sommer, Ferdinand Johann A. (1822-1901), AN ALPINE INN, d.1875, 17¼ x 26 (4208/4)   2000
Sondermann, Hermann, SIGNING THE MARRIAGE CONTRACT, 26¾ x 33½ (4241/68)   12000
Sorkau, Albert (b.1874), LADIES AT A TABLE, 25½ x 32 (666/200)   700
Sorolla y Bastida, Joaquin, 1863-1923, COLUMBUS INN AT CORDOBA, 41½ x 32
(4161/132)   31000
Sorolla y Bastida, Joaquin (1863-1923), ON THE BEACH, 1906, on panel, 12 x 15½
(4240/33)   32000
Sospatak, Lazlo P., 1857-1912, MARKET DAY, 1887, Hungarian, 19¾ x 31¾ (4122/116)   2000
Spaendonck, Gerard V., attrib. (1746-1822), A STUDY OF FLOWERS, 10½ x 15, on panel
(633/194)   1600

Spiridon, Ignace, 19c, THE CONVALESCENCE, 16 x 12½ (4161/134) — 4000
Spitzweg, Carl (1808-85), GETTING SOME SHADE, 9 x 5, pencil (633/46) — 550
Spohler, Jan J.C., 1837-1923, BARGES ON A CANAL, HOLLAND, 17 x 26 (4161/76) — 3500
Spohler, Johannes Franciscus, FOOTBRIDGE OVER A CANAL, 8 x 6, on panel (4241/96) — 5250
Spoilum, attributed to, PORTRAIT OF FRANCIS ELLIOT, 9½ x 8 (666/194) — 850
Spring, Alfons (1843-1908), AN EXCITING STORY, 10¼ x 13½, on panel (4208/45) — 7500
Spring, Alfons (1843-1908), THE POACHER'S VISIT, 9½ x 12½ on panel (4208/46) — 6250
Stademann, Adolf, att. to (1824-95), A WINTER LANDSCAPE WITH SKATERS, 15¼ x 19 (666/183) — 2500
Stademann, Adolph, PEASANTS ON A PATH, 10¼ x 14, on paper (4241/17) — 1000
Stademann, Adolph, SKATERS ON A FROZEN POND AT SUNSET, 14 x 17¼ (4241/18) — 9500
Stadler, Toni von (1850-1917), EARLY EVENING, on panel, 5⅜ x 7 (666/205) — 2000
Stahl, Friedrich, 1863-1940, AT THE BALL, 1902, 26¾ x 24¼ (4122/56) — 13000
Stanfield, George Clarkson, 1828-78, NAMUR ON THE MEUSE, BELGIUM, 1869, 20 x 30 (4122/306) — 1800
Stanley, Caleb Robert, 1795-1868, FRENCH STREET SCENE, 28½ x 36¼ (4122/300) — 5250
Starkenborgh Stachouwer, J.N.T. van, 1822-95, LANDSCAPE WITH CATTLE GRAZING, 36¼ x 50¾ (4122/68) — 2200
Starkenborgh Stachouwer, J.N.T. van, 1822-95, LANDSCAPE WITH HAYWAGON, 36¼ x 50¾ (4122/67) — 2100
Steinheil, Louis August (1814-85), CONSULTATION, d.1880, 8½ x 5½, on panel (4208/193) — 1100
Steinlen, Theophile A. (1859-1923), PORTRAIT OF CHARLES DEBUSSY, 15 x 11⅛, conte crayon (4260/1442) — 4200
Stevens, Alfred, 1823-1906, READY FOR THE FANCY DRESS BALL, 1879, 35 x 45½ (4161/96) — 80000
Stevens, Alfred, 1825-1906, FISHING BOATS OFF A ROCKY COAST, 17½ x 28 (4161/97) — 1900
Stevens, Joseph Edovard, THE VIGILANT HERD DOG, 15 x 18¼ (4241/129) — 400
Sticks, G.B. (1843-1930), A MOUNTAIN LANDSCAPE,d.1898, 28 x 36 (633/191) — 650
Stiepevich, V.G. (19c), THE IMPORTUNATE VISITOR, on board, 7 x 9 (666/136) — 1600
Stifter, Moritz (1857-1905), A HAREM SCENE, 7¾ x 10, on panel (633/188) — 1200
Stillman, Marie S., 1844-1927, GIRL WITH PEACOCK FEATHER, 27¼ x 21¼, watercolor (4161/269) — 4250
Strang, William (1859-1921), PORTRAIT OF D.H. LAWRENCE, 22 x 17 (633/70) — 1000
Struys, A.T.H. (1852-1941), KNITTING, 1871, on panel, 21½ x 16½ (666/243) — 500
Stuck, Franz Von, A LADY HOLDING A BOOK, 94 x 94 (4241/46) — 4100
Tamburini, Arnaldo, b.1843, COUNTING CHANGE, 1882, 12¼ x 10 (4122/160) — 2100
Tamburini, Arnaldo, b.1843, THE PET OF THE MONASTERY, 9¾ x 7 (4161/136) — 1000
Tamburini, Arnaldo, b.1843, THE POOR BOX, 12¼ x 10¼ (4122/159) — 1400
Tanzi, Leon L.A. (1846-1913), AMONG THE FLOWERS, 21 x 29 (666/251) — 2750
Tarenghi, Enrico (1848-?), TIPSY FRIAR AND FRIEND, watercolor, 19½ x 13½ (666/139) — 450
Tavernier, Jules (19c), THE FLIRTATION, d.1871, 20¼ x 14¼ (4208/170) — 2000
Temburini, Arnold, AN OLD MONK, 9 x 7 on panel (4241/165) — 2200
Ten Cate, Johannes, 1859-96, LA PLACE DE LA REPUBLIQUE, 1888, 13¾ x 10½ (4161/74) — 1600
Ten Kate, Herman F.C. (1822-91), DEVASTATING NEWS, 6½ x 9½, watercolor (633/65) — 1400
Ten Kate, Johan M.H., 1831-1910, IN THE ARTIST'S ABSENCE, 18¾ x 27 (4122/70) — 24000
Thaulow, Frits, RIVER BANKS IN AUTUMN, 29 x 36½ (4241/160) — 14000
Thaulow, Frits, THE MILL STREAM IN WINTER, 21½ x 25¾ (4208/104) — 11000
Thoma, Hans, 1839-1924, FLIGHT INTO EGYPT, 1874, 12 x 14 (4161/38) — 7000
Thomassin, Desire, 1858-1933, Austrian, HAYMAKING, Austrian, 27½ x 39½ (4122/15) — 9250
Thomassin, Desire, 1858-1933, TRAVELERS ON A MARSHY PATH, WINTER, 14 x 21¼ (4122/16) — 4250
Thors, Joseph (19c), FEEDING THE HENS, 10¼ x 8, on panel (4208/223) — 1300
Thors, Joseph, 1863-84, RUSTICS ON A COUNTRY PATH, 1867, 25¼ x 30¼ (4122/304) — 1300
Tissot, James Jacques J., AT THE LOUVRE, 29 x 20 (4260/631) — 23000
Tissot, James Jacques J., THE COMEDIAN, 10¾ x 6¾, oil on panel (4260/630) — 10500
Tissot, James Jacques J. (1836-1902), PORTRAIT OF A SEATED WOMAN, d.1891, 22 x 11, pencil (4260/620) — 3600
Tjarda Van Starkenborgh Stachouwer, 1823-95, HORSEMAN WITH HERD BESIDE RIVER, 26½ x 37 (4161/80) — 4500
Tom, Jan Bedys (1813-94), CATTLE, on panel, 9¾ x 14½ (4240/19) — 1800
Touche, G. de la, 1854-1913, THE PROCESSION, 38½ x 32½ (4161/238) — 1500
Toulouse-Lautrec, Henri de (1864-1901) CUNARD STEAMSHIP ABYSSINIA, c.1880, mixed media, 5⅞ x 9⅜ (4170/101) — 1600
Toulouse-Lautrec, Henri de (1864-1901) FEMME AU MIROIR, 1896, charcoal, 20 x 12⅞ (4170/105) — 15500
Toulouse-Lautrec, Henri de (1864-1901) THREE MASTED SCHOONER DIANA, c.1880, mixed media, 4⅝ x7⅜ (4170/102) — 1800

Toulouse-Lautrec, Henri de (1864-1901) YAWL, c.1880, mixed media, 4½ x 5¾ (4170/103) 650
Toulouse-Lautrec, Henri de (1864-1901), HUNTER WITH HOUND, 1880, 10⅛ x 6¼, mixed media (4260/1431) 12000
Toulouse-Lautrec, Henri de (1864-1901), STUDIES OF A HORSE, DOUBLE SIDED, ca1879-81, 10¼ x 6¼, pencil (4260/1432) 7500
Toulouse-Lautrec, Henri de (1864-1901), TETES D'HOMMES, 1892, 6¾ x 4, pencil (4164/5) 550
Triebel, Carl (1823-85), MILL IN A MOUNTAIN LANDSCAPE, d.1849, 27 x 37 (4241/4) 3750
Tromp, Jan Zoetelief, A WALK THROUGH A MEADOW, 16 x 19½ (4241/113) 8500
Trouillebert, Paul D., 1829-1900, GNARLED TREES BESIDE A LAKE, 25½ x 32 (4161/164) 5250
Trouillebert, Paul D. (1829-1900), PEASANT WOMAN WITH A COW BY A LAKE, 26 x 32½ (4208/155) 12500
Troyon, Constant (1810-65), A PEASANT WITH CATTLE, 26 x 40 (633/29) 1400
Troyon, Constant (1810-65), BEACHED BOATS, 9¼ x 14, on panel (4208/152) 2000
Troyon, Constant (1810-65), ON THE BANKS OF A POND, 9½ x 7, on panel (4208/151) 5000
Troyon, Constant, attributed to (1810-65), LANDSCAPE WITH SHEEP, 10¾ x 15¾ (666/137) 1100
Troyon, Constant, 1810-65, A YOUNG SHEPHERD BOY, 18¾ x 15¼ (4122/270) 5250
Tseregoty, N.G., 19-20c, WHITE NIGHT AT ST. PETERSBURG, 24¼ x 40½ (4122/120) 800
Turner, George (1843-1910), THE WAY TO THE VILLAGE, 20 x 30 (4208/214) 2200
Unterberger, Franz R., 1838-1902, A VIEW TOWARDS SAN GIORGIO MAGGIORE, 32½ x 27½ (4122/97) 23000
Ury, Lesser, PORTRAIT OF A LADY IN BLUE, 18¾ x 13, 1895 (4241/45) 2700
Vaarberg, Johannes Christofel, 1825-71, THE PRISONER, 1865, 15¼ x 20¼ (4161/64) 3750
Van der Venne, 1828-1911, Austrian, DRIVING THE HORSES TO MARKET, 1867, 21 x 28¼ (4122/3) 7500
Van Elten, Hendrik, D.K., 1829-1904, WINTER SUNSET, 12¼ x 19¼ (4161/82) 3250
Van Severdonck, Francois, 1809-89, FAMILY OF CHICKENS, 7 x 10¼ (4161/90) 3500
Van Severdonck, Francois, 1809-89, SHEEP ON A HILLSIDE, 1874, 18½ x 27 (4161/93) 7750
Van Severdonck, Francois, 1809-89, SHEEP, CHICKS, DUCKS IN LANDSCAPE, 1888, 7 x 10 (4161/92) 1800
Van Severdonck, Francois, 1809-89, SHEEP, CHICKS, DUCKS IN MEADOW, 1861, 9¼ x 12 (4161/91) 2250
Van Wijngaerdt, Petrus Theodorus, 1816-93, MOTHER & CHILD PLAYING WITH DOG, 9¾ x 7½ (4161/66) 2000
Vantier, Benjamin (1829-98), YOUNG SHEPHERD WITH A FLUTE, 12¼ x 16 (4071/5) 9250
Velde, J. van der (b.1814?), THE ARTIST'S SKETCH,d.1850, 25½ x 34¼ (4208/93) 700
Venneman, Charles Ferdinand, THE FARMYARD, 18 x 22 (4241/127) 17000
Verboeckhoven, Eugene J. (1799-1881), IN THE STABLE, d.1877, 10½ x 14 (4208/83) 6250
Verboeckhoven, Eugene J. (1799-1881), SHEEP AND A GOAT RESTING BY A POOL, d.1874, 21¼ x 26¾, on panel (4208/85) 6000
Verboeckhoven, Eugene J. (1799-1881), SHEEP AND POULTRY IN A BARN, d.1867, 29½ x 40 (4208/84) 15000
Verboeckhoven, Eugene J. (1799-1881), SHEEP, A GOAT AND DUCKS IN A LANDSCAPE, d.1864, 22 x 29½ (4208/82) 21000
Verboeckhoven, Eugene J., 1799-1881, CATTLE IN A LANDSCAPE, 13 x 14¾ (4161/86) 12000
Verboeckhoven, Eugene J., 1799-1881, PEASANT CHILDREN BY MOUNTAIN LAKE, 1830, 27½ x 38½ (4161/85) 62500
Verboeckhoven, Eugene J., 1799-1881, TWO COWS IN A LANDSCAPE, 1838, 26½ x 31½ (4161/87) 6000
Vergeses, Hippolyte de, b.1847, SALOME, 51½ x 35 (4197/366) 5000
Vermorcken, Frederic, M., b.1860, THE BELLOWS, 10¾ x 17¾ (4161/103) 600
Vernet, Horace, 1789-1863, A MILITARY ENCAMPMENT AT NIGHT, 1835, 11¼ x 14½ (4161/224) 1100
Vernokken, Dutch or Flemish School, PORTRAIT OF A MAN SEATED AT A TABLE, 15¼ x 13½ (4149/151) 1400
Verschuur, Wouterus (1812-74), AT THE BLACKSMITH'S, 17½ x 25½, on panel (4208/59) 14500
Vertin, Pieter Gerardus, 1819-93, DUTCH STREET SCENE, 1867, 14½ x 11¼ (4161/69) 4250
VerHoesen, Albertus, COWS RESTING BY A FENCE, 9½ x 10¾, on panel (4241/87) 2700
Veyrassat, Jules Jacques (1828-93), OUTSIDE THE INN, 11½ x 15¾, on panel (4208/163) 4750
Vezzani, F., THE LOVE LETTER, 16½ x 22 (4241/177) 4000
Vickers, Alfred, attrib. to, 1786-1868, BLOWING FRESH OFF DOVER, 25 x 36 (4161/248) 2600
Villalobos, M. (19c), COURTYARD WITH ORANGE TREES, on panel, 6¾ x 4⅜ (666/184) 650
Villegas y Cordero, Jose, 1848-1922, CHERUBS IN THE REEDS, 17 x 23¾ (4161/129) 1000
Villeneuve, Julien Vallou de (1795-1866), THE LOCKED DOOR, 10 x 8, on panel (633/222) 450
Voight, August, BEFORE THE STORM, 26½ x 40 (4161/28) 1100
Volkers, Emil (1831-1905), A WAYSIDE ENCOUNTER, 19¾ x 28 (4071/6) 4750
Vollon, Antoine, 1833-1900, A CATHEDRAL CITY, 13 x 16 (4161/175) 6000
Vollon, Antoine, 1833-1900, STILL LIFE WITH FISH & CRAYFISH, 21¼ x 25¾ (4161/236) 2600
Vollon, Antoine, 1833-1900, THE OLD MILL, 16 x 22, on panel (4208/154) 2200

Volpe, Allesandro La, BAY OF NAPLES, 28 x 52 (4241/175)	1000
Voltz, Friedrich, 1817-86, CATTLE WATERING, 1871, 18 x 46½ (4122/20)	62500
Voltz, Friedrich, 1817-86, GOATS AND COWS IN A LANDSCAPE, 31¼ x 29¾ (4071/15)	34000
Voltz, Ludwig, 1825-1911, CATTLE BY A BRIDGE, 7¾ x 15¾ (4161/26)	8500
Voltz, Ludwig, 1825-1911, OXEN TEAM PLOWING, 7½ x 12½ (4161/27)	3250
Von Bremen, Johann G.M., 1813-86, MEDITATION, 1872, 14½ x 11¾ (4122/37)	11500
Von Defregger, Franz, 1835-1921, YOUNG GIRL IN TYROLEAN COSTUME, 26½ x 21½ (4161/51)	29000
Von Eckenbrecher, Themistocles, 1842-1921, BOATING ON THE FJORD, 1913, 21½ x 12¼ (4161/6)	1500
Von Horrmann, Theodor (1840-95), PEASANTS AT THE EDGE OF A FIELD, 31¼ x 25 (4071/9)	12500
Von Meckel, Adolf, 1856-1893, ABSOLOM'S TOMB, 1889, 35½ x 47¾ (4122/23)	2600
Von Muller, Emma, b.1859, Austrian, TYROLEAN GIRL READING, 13 x 8¾ (4161/53)	3250
Vostagh, Geza, 1866-1919, Hungarian, A LIONESS WITH HER CUBS, 32 x 52¾ (4161/114)	3500
Wagner, Alexander Von, GATE OF JUSTICE, GRANADA, 40 x 28 (4241/146)	6250
Wagner, Franz, A GOOD SMOKE, 10½ x 7½ (4241/76)	1500
Wagner, H., 19c, THE PICTURE BOOK, 27 x 20 (4122/42)	1700
Wainwright, John, PAIR OF STILL LIFES, SUMMER, WINTER, 1869, 24 x 20, oval (4161/261)	7250
Waldmuller, Ferdinand Georg, Attrib, PORTRAIT OF A YOUNG GIRL WITH FLOWERS, 8¼ x 6¼, oval, on panel (4241/43)	6250
Ward, James, school of, GATHERING BLACKBERRIES, initials, 1794, 17 x 14 (666/246)	550
Washington, Georges, 1827-1910, ARABS ON HORSEBACK, 20 x 24 (4197/346)	4200
Washington, Georges, 1827-1910, ON THE MOVE, 17¾ x 26 (4122/227)	2800
Waterhouse, John W., 1849-1917, AT CAPRI, 1890, 33½ x 19¼ (4161/271)	29000
Watts, Frederick W., 1800-62, THE WAINWRIGHT, 25 x 30 (4161/253)	4000
Weber, Gottlieb D.P. (1823-1916), FISHERMEN ON THE BANKS OF LOCH LEWIS, 24¼ x 37 (4071/3)	2200
Weber, Gottlieb D.P., CATTLE GRAZING BELOW A SNOWY PEAK, 27 x 38½, 1868 (4241/10)	8000
Weber, Gottlieb D.P., CATTLE WATERING BY A MILL, 20 x 30, 1859 (4241/11)	6250
Weber, Gottlieb D.P., CHILDREN FEEDING DUCKS BY A RIVER, 24 x 33½, 1872 (4241/12)	6250
Weber, Gottlieb, D.P., 1823-1916, THE HUNTER'S RETURN, AUTUMN, 1875, 35 x 48 (4161/8)	5750
Weber, Maria (19c), LITTLE GIRL POUTING, 26 x 14 (666/172)	950
Weber, Otto (1832-1888), THE OTHER SIDE OF THE FENCE, on panel, 13 x 19 (666/154)	500
Weeks, Edwin Lord, 1849-1903, MOSQUE OF THE KAID BEG, TOMBS OF THE MAMELUKES, 20¾ x 15¾ (4197/356)	3750
Weiland, Johannes, 1856-1909, THE READING LESSON, 26¼ x 21½ (4122/61)	3500
Weiss, Carl, IN THE ANTIQUE SHOP, 10¾ x 14 (4241/71)	900
Weiss, Jose, b.1859, BY THE BANKS OF THE RIVER, SUMMERTIME, 16 x 24 (4122/305)	800
Weiss, R. (19c), VILLAGE ON AN ALPINE LAKE, d.1905, 24 x 35½ (4208/12)	2200
Wells, Henry Tanworth (1828-1903), PORTRAIT OF A LADY, 1876, 36½ x 29⅜ (666/178)	950
Wenglein, Joseph (1845-1919), A MOUNTAIN LANDSCAPE WITH WILDFLOWERS, 11 x 16¾ (4071/8)	1500
Wenglein, Joseph, 1845-1919, CATTLE WATERING, SUMMER DAY, 10 x 17¾ (4161/19)	25000
Weretshagin, Vassilij, A MOUNTAIN PASS, 12¼ x 15½ (4241/162)	1600
Westerbeek, Cornelis, SHEEP GRAZING ON A HILLSIDE, 15½ x 31½ (4241/101)	1700
Wex, Willibald (1831-92), SUNDOWN, 16 x 21¾ (666/262)	1600
Wierusz-Kowalski, Alfred von (1849-1915), READY FOR THE MORNING RIDE, d.1880, 22 x 29 (4208/20)	31000
Wierusz-Kowalski, Alfred von, A LITHUANIAN SLEIGH RIDE, Polish, 28¾ x 46¾ (4122/113)	67500
Wilkie, David (1785-1841), FAREWELL, 1823, ink, watercolor, 9 x 11½ (666/151)	3500
Willems, Florent, THE ACCOUNTANT, 29 x 21½ (4241/141)	4500
Willems, Florent (1823-1905), FEEDING THE PARROT, 13¾ x 10¾, on panel (4208/94)	2150
Williams, Penry (1798-1885), IDYLLIC PASTTIMES, 1855, 24¼ x 36¼ (4208/216)	1900
Willis, Henry B., 1810-84, WOODSMAN'S DAUGHTER, 1852, 21 x 17 (4161/262)	1600
Wilson, George (1848-90), A RIVER LANDSCAPE WITH SAIL BOATS, 30 x 50½ (666/231)	325
Winterhatter, Franz Xavier, Attrib, PORTRAIT OF PRINCESS CATHERINE ORLOFF, 45¾ x 39, oval (4241/41)	2300
Woutermaertens, Edouard (1819-97), A SHEEP DOG WITH HIS FLOCK, 9¾ x 12¾, on panel (4208/87)	1000
Woutermaertens, Edouard (1819-97), WATCHING THE FLOCK, 10¾ x 17¾, on panel (4208/86)	1400
Zamacois Y Zabala, Eduardo, (1842-71), THE SMOKING DRUMMER, 10¾ x 8¼, watercolor (633/31)	400
Zampighi, Eugenio (1859-1944), AN UNEXPECTED LUNCH GUEST, 28½ x 47 (4208/111)	14000
Zampighi, Eugenio (1859-1944), MUSIC MAKERS, 22 x 30 (4208/114)	10000

Zampighi, Eugenio, THE PLAYFUL PARROT, 35½ x 25¼ (633/207)   2700
Zampighi, Eugenio (1859-1944), FEEDING HER PET, 22 x 30 (4208/115)   *5750*
Zampighi, Eugenio (1859-1944), GIRL WITH A MANDOLIN, 19 x 15 (4208/113)   3250
Zampighi, Eugenio (1859-1944), HE LOVES ME, HE LOVES ME NOT, 24½ x 18 (4208/112)   5250
Zandomeneghi, Federico (1841-1917), FEMME TENANT UN BOUQUET, 22 x 18¼ (4208/125)   36000
Zandomeneghi, Federico (1841-1917), HEAD OF A YOUNG GIRL, 17¼ x 12⅛, pastel (4260/637)   2300
Ziem, Felix (1821-1911), BOARDING THE GONDOLA, 21 x 26 (4208/166)   2750
Ziem, Felix (1821-1911), VENICE, 16¾ x 26½, on panel (633/211)   2000
Ziem, Felix, (1821-1911), BACINO WITH A VIEW TO DOGE'S PALACE, 13 x 20¼ (4122/204)   2000
Ziem, Felix, (1821-1911), SHIPPING IN THE GRAND CANAL, 28¼ x 39½ (4122/203)   4000
Ziem, Felix, (1821-1911), VIEW OF TEMPLE OF SATURN IN FORUM, ROME, 12 x 8⅜ (4122/205)   700
Zorn, Anders (1860-1920), PORTRAIT OF DR. IRA DE VER WARNER, d.1901, 40 x 34 (4208/109)   *5750*
Zorn, Anders (1860-1920), PORTRAIT OF HONORABLE DAVID J. HILL, 1911, 38 x 30 (4240/27)   14000
Zorn, Anders (1860-1920), PORTRAIT OF MRS. EVA DE VER WARNER, d.1901, 40 x 34 (4208/110)   9000
Zorn, Anders, (1860-1920), PORTRAIT OF HONORABLE DAVID J. HILL, 1910, 49 x 35¾ (4240/28)   6000
Zugel, Heinrich Von, AT THE TROUGH, C¼ x 10 (4241/32)   26000

Zorn   (4208/109)

Zampighi   (4208/115)

Chapter 20

Impressionist Paintings, Drawings and Sculpture

The zest for life and joyful celebration of the everyday caught by the Impressionist painters have brought them worldwide fame. And, as the supply of these canvases dwindles, the demand continues to rise. Today, an Impressionist painting is beyond the reach of all but the most affluent collector.

During the 1970s, eager buyers led by the Japanese pushed Impressionist prices to new highs. By and large, they have sustained those levels; the few paintings that do come on the market each year usually go to museums, which means, of course, that they're permanently retired from the marketplace. The fact that five Renoirs failed to sell last season says more about the sky-high expectations of their owners than it does about any weakening in the demand for Renoirs or the French Impressionist School.

This art comes so high that it is clearly the province of the very few. The average collector has no choice, then, but to consider those lesser artists whose work appears influenced by the Impressionists or paintings of the lower-priced but still highly desirable American Impressionists.

Bonnard, Pierre, SCENE DE RUE (VIADUL D'AUTEUIL), 24¼ x 18¼, ca1910 (4249/245) $57500
Boudin, Eugene, DEAUVILLE LES DUNES, 14 x 22⅞, ca1888-95 (4249/218)   20000
Boudin, Eugene, ENVIRONS D'ANTIBES, 19⅝ x 29½, 1893 (4249/219)   22000
Boudin, Eugene (1824-98), LA PLAGE DE TROUVILLE, d.1863, 13⅝ x 22⅞, oil on panel (4169/11)   170000
Boudin, Eugene (1824-98), PATURAGE, VALLEE DE LA TOUQUES, 1881, 25⅝ x 35½ (4124/41)   20000
Boudin, Eugene (1824-98), PLOUGASTEL. LE PASSAGE DU Bac, d.1870, 9¼ x 13½, oil on panel (4169/9)   26000
Boudin, Eugene (1824-98), TROUVILLE, LES JETEES, MAREE BASSE, 1879, 12¼ x 18¼ (4124/7)   21000
Boudin, Eugene (1824-98), TROUVILLE, MARCHE AUX POISSONS, 1884, 14 x 17⅛ (4124/8)   35000
Boudin, Eugene, (1824-90), TROUVILLE, LES JETEES, MAREE HAUTE, 1892-96, 12⅛ x 15¼ (4124/9)   25000
Boudin, Eugene, (1824-98), ENVIRONS DU FAOU, 12¾ x 18¼ (4124/4)   16000
Braque, Georges, NU COUCHE AU GUERIDON, 9½ x 16¼, 1931 (4249/283)   40000
Cezanne, Paul, DOUBLE-SIDED SHEET FROM A SKETCHBOOK, pencil, 6⅝ x 10⅝ (4263/3)   2400
Cezanne, Paul, LES ARBRES, watercolor, 8¼ x 5 (4250/422)   11500
Cezanne, Paul, PAYSAGE, 8⅞ x 11⅛, ca1863-65 (4249/205)   25000
Cezanne, Paul, SUR LES FLANC DE LA SAINTE-VICTOIRE, pencil, watercolor, 14 x 21⅜, ca1900-06 (4249/233)   125000
Corot, Jean-Baptiste Camille, LE COURS D'EAU A LA TOUR CARREE (PAYSANNE DEBOU, T AU PREMIER PLAN), 12⅝ x 15¾, ca1865-70 (4249/206)   52500
Corot, Jean-Baptiste Camille, LES DEUX JEUNES VACHERES DANS LA PRAIRIE AU, BORD DE L'EAU, 16⅜ x 18½, ca1850-55 (4249/204)   65000
Courbet, Gustave (1819-77), PAYSAGE-LE PECHEUR, 23½ x 28¾ (4169/7)   47500
Degas, Edgar, ETUDE DE DANSEUSE, charcoal, 21⅜ x 13⅝ (4250/411)   *12000*

Degas
(4250/411)

Degas, Edgar, FEMME EN PEIGNOIR JAUNE SE COIFFANT, pastel on joined buff paper, 43¼ x 39½, ca1894 (4249/224)   250000
Degas, Edgar, JEUNE HOMME VU DE PROFILE, sanguine, 11 x 8¼ (4250/404)   11500
Degas, Edgar, LE PETIT DEJEUNER APRES LE BAIN, pastel on joined buff paper, 47 x 41½, ca1889 (4249/225)   190000
Degas, Edgar (1834-1917), AU SALON, ca1879, 6½ x 4¾, pastel over monotype (4169/14)   100000
Degas, Edgar (1834-1917), GRANDE ARABESQUE, PREMIER TEMPS, ca1882-85, H19¼, bronze (4225/177)   42000
Degas, Edgar (1834-1917), QUATRE DANSEUSES A MI-CORPS, 1899, 27½ x 28⅜, pastel (4124/14)   140000
Degas, Edgar, (1834-1917), DANSEUSES RUSSES, 1895, 25 x 17⅝, pastel (4124/15)
Degas, Edgar, (1834-1917), DEUX DANSEUSES EN MAILLOT, 17⅝ x 21¼, charcoal (4125/109)   11500
Degas, Edgar, (1834-1917), TROIS DANSEUSES, 28½ x 22 1/1, charcoal, pastel (4124/13)   19000
Fantin-latour, Henri (1836-1904), VASE DE PIVOINES ET BOULES DE NIEGE, 1878, 17⅜ x 14 (4124/6)   45000
Gauguin, Paul, AUTOUR DES HUTTES, 34¾ x 21½, 1887 (4249/222)   350000
Gauguin, Paul, STUDY OF A CHILD, pencil, charcoal, on paper, 10½ x 8, ca1884 (4263/47)   2400
Gauguin, Paul (1848-1903), LE BASSIN CARRE, d.1884, 21 x 25 (4169/6)   70000
Guillaumin, Jean-Baptiste Armand, LA ROCHE DE L'ECHO, 21¼ x 25⅝, ca1905 (4249/239)   20000

Lepine, Stanislas (1835-92), BORDS D'UNE RIVIERE, 11 x 14⅜ (4124/3) — 16000
Lepine, Stanislas, (1835-92), LE PONT DE BERCY, 14¾ x 23 (4124/2) — 24000
Lepine, Stanislas, (1835-92), ROUTE DE VILLAGE, 12¾ x 18½ (4124/1) — 7500
Loiseau, Gustave, LES BERGES DE LA SEINE, PORT JOIE, 32½ x 24½, 1902 (4249/238) — 21000
Loiseau, Gustave, RUE DANS LA VILLE, 21½ x 25¾, 1919 (4249/252) — 28000
Luce, Maximilien, HAYMAKERS RESTING, wash, pencil, paper, 8½ x 11 (4263/5) — 550
Manet, Edouard, JEUNE FILLE DANS LA VERDURE, 59 x 45¾, 1882 (4249/220) — 85000
Matisse, Henri, BOUQUET SUR FAUTEUIL VENETIEN, colored crayons, white paper, 20¾ x 15⅞, ca1943 (4249/268) — 22000
Matisse, Henri, LYDIA SEATED, pencil, 10 x 6½ (4250/466) — *9500*

Pissarro (4250/406)

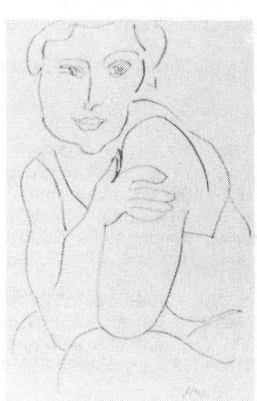

Matisse (4250/466)

Matisse, Henri, NUDE IN AN INTERIOR, pencil, 9⅜ x 12⅜ (4250/445) — 7000
Matisse, Henri, PETITE TETE, bronze, gold, patina, 3¾, ca1906-07 (4249/299) — 9000
Matisse, Henri, VASE DE GLAIEULS SUR UNE CHAISE, 60½ x 40, 1928 (4249/265) — 340000
Matisse, Henri, WOMAN WITH A NECKLACE, pen and ink, 21 x 16¼ (4250/465) — 18000
Monet, Claude (1840-1926), FALAISES A POURVILLE, MAREE BASSE, d.1882, 23½ x 32¼ (4169/13) — 115000
Monet, Claude (1840-1926), L'EGLISE DE VARENGEVILLE ET LA GORGE DE, MOUTIERS, 1882, 22⅜ x 31⅞ (4124/44) — 75000
Monet, Claude (1840-1926), LA SEINE PRES DE GIVERNY, d.1888, 26 x 36½ (4169/15) — 290000
Monet, Claude (1840-1926), MATINEE SUR LA SEINE, TEMPS NET, 1897, 33½ x 38 (4124/43) — 330000
Monet, Claude (1840-1926), POMMIERS EN FLEUR, d.1881, 31½ x 39½ (4169/12) — 250000
Monet, Claude (1840-1926), PRAIRIE A GIVERNY, ca1889, 32 x 36¼ (4169/29) — 90000
Picabia, Francis, LES OLIVIERS AUX MARTIGUES, EFFET DU SOLEIL, 28¾ x 36¼, 1905 (4263/17) — 7000
Pissarro, Camille, FEMME ET ENFANT COUSANT (PONTOISE), 19⅞ x 16⅛, 1877 (4249/207) — 62500
Pissarro, Camille, GARDEUSE D'OIES AU BORD DE L'EPTE, eragny, gouache, 8 x 6¾ (4250/409) — 9000
Pissarro, Camille, LA CARRIERE A L'HERMITAGE, PONTOISE, 21⅞ x 18⅛, 1878 (4249/208) — 65000
Pissarro, Camille, MME. PISSARRO AND HER DAUGHTER, charcoal, 14⅝ x 10¾ (4250/406) — *10500*
Pissarro, Camille, PORTRAIT OF A MAN, charcoal on paper, 10⅛ x 9 (4263/24) — 1200
Pissarro, Camille, ROAD THROUGH THE WOODS, crayon, pencil, paper, (4263/4) — 3400
Pissarro, Camille, STANDING PEASANT, charcoal on paper, 12⅜ x 9⅝ (4263/23) — 1700
Pissarro, Camille (1830-1903), LA SAVOIE, 7¾ x 10, pencil (4140/2) — 300
Pissarro, Camille (1830-1903), LA SEINE A PARIS, PONT ROYAL, 1903, 21½ x 25¾ (4124/54) — 145000
Pissarro, Camille (1830-1903), LES ARBRES, 9⅜ x 6¼, pencil (4140/4) — 450
Pissarro, Camille (1830-1903), PAYSANNES, 9½ x 12¼, charcoal (4204/5) — 3400
Pissarro, Camille (1830-1903), ROUTE DE VILLAGE, 6 x 7¾, pencil (4140/1) — 1300
Pissarro, Camille (1830-1903), ROUTE DU FOND DE L'HERMITAGE, PONTOISE, 1877, 25½ x 21¼ (4124/11) — 90000
Pissarro, Camille (1830-1903), SCENE DE MARCHE, 9⅝ x 7⅜, mixed media (4140/11) — 2500
Pissarro, Camille (1830-1903), STUDY OF TWO MEN, SEEN FROM THE BACK, 4⅛ x 6⅝, pencil (4260/1414) — 1100

Pissarro, Camille, (1830-1903), COURS DU HAVRE, GARE SAINT LAZARE, 1893, 15½ x 18½ (4124/12) 135000

Pissarro, Camille, (1830-1903), ETUDE, PAYSANNE RAMASSANT DE L'HERBE, 1881, 26 x 19, charcoal (4125/104) 5500

Pissarro, Camille, (1830-1903), PORTAIL DE L'EGLISE ST. JACQUES A DIEPPE, 1901, 30½ x 26½ (4124/17) 82500

Redon, Odilon, L'APPARITION D'UNE FEMME NUE, board, 16 x 13, ca1900 (4249/232) 45000

Renoir, Pierre Auguste, CLASSICAL COMPOSITION, 7¼ x 14⅝ (4263/25) 10500

Renoir, Pierre Auguste, DANSEUSE A LA VOILE, bronze, 25½, 1964 (4263/26) 14000

Renoir, Pierre Auguste, STUDY FOR LA LOGE, charcoal, 18¼ x 23 (4250/414) 50000

Renoir, Pierre Auguste (1841-1919), JEUNE FEMME AU CHIEN, 1876, 18⅛ x 14⅞ (4124/36) 125000

Renoir, Pierre Auguste (1841-1919), SHEET OF STUDIES, HEADS OF YOUNG WOMEN, SEATED GIRL, HEAD OF A MAN, 1883, 20⅜ x 12½, ink (4260/1425) 26000

Renoir, Pierre Auguste (1841-1919), VASE DE ROSES ET DAHLIAS, ca1883-84, 16 x 12½ (4124/42) 55000

Renoir, Pierre Auguste (1841-1919), JEUNE FEMME REGARDANT UNE ESTAMPE, 25⅞ x 21⅜ (4169/21) 360000

Renoir, Pierre Auguste (1841-1919), PORTRAIT DE JACQUES-EUGENE SPULLER, 1871, 18¼ x 15 (4169/10) 95000

Rousseau, Henri, PORTRAIT DE MONSIEUR S, 16⅛ x 13, 1898 (4249/230) 40000

Signac, Paul, ALONG THE QUAIS, watercolor, crayon, graph paper, 6¾ x 4¼ (4263/11) 1400

Signac, Paul, RAINBOW, watercolor, crayon, graph paper, 4⅜ x 6¾ (4263/12) 800

Sisley, Alfred (1839-99), LA BAIE DE LANGLAND, d.1897, 21½ x 25 (4169/28) 90000

Toulouse-Lautrec, Henri de, MADAME LILI GRENIER, board, 17 x 14¼, 1888 (4249/221) 150000

Toulouse-Lautrec, Henri de, PRINCETEAU DANS SON ATELIER, 28¾ x 21⅜, ca1881-82 (4249/217) 190000

Utrillo, Maurice, RUE GIRARDON, 23⅝ x 18⅛, ca1915 (4249/246) 50000

Valtat, Louis, ANTIBES, watercolor, pencil, paper, 8⅞ x 10¾, 1898 (4263/13) 2100

Valtat, Louis, PAYSAGE DU MIDI, watercolor, paper, 9⅞ x 12⅞ (4263/10) 2300

Valtat, Louis (1869-1952), LA SOURIS BLANCHE, d.1893, 32 x 39½ (4169/18) 24000

Chapter 21

Modern Paintings, Drawings and Sculpture

Sales of modern paintings have continued their steady growth. Foreign buyers, benefiting from the dollar exchange, paid high prices, as did domestic collectors anxious to find a hedge against inflation. More significant was the development of specialized auctions of Russian, Mexican and German modernists designed to respond to special interests of collectors.

Drawings have increased notably as an area for collecting in the past few years. While few collectors can afford important Impressionist and Modern paintings, it is still possible to find watercolors and drawings by major artists in a reasonable price range.

Prices for Mexican art have risen dramatically over the past two seasons. Two paintings by Tamayo broke all previous auction records for this artist.

Long considered a relatively undervalued area—as compared, for example, with the French Impressionists—the market for German Expressionism has turned around in the last two years. The entry of Japanese bidders into this area of collecting has contributed to rising values, as has changing public taste, which has moved to greater acceptance of the frank eroticism of Schiele, Klimt and Nolde.

The Surrealists and the Modern masters—among them Picasso, Magritte and Miro—recovered strongly from the sharp reversal that followed the boom years of 1973 and 1974.

The outlook in modern paintings is for steady appreciation in all segments of the market. German and Mexican paintings are just beginning to be revived after spells of relative obscurity, and they promise to make even more spectacular advance in the future. The scarcity of good Russian work and the growing appeal of drawings of all types promise to keep prices of those works growing at a steady clip. Surrealists and Modern painters once again seem poised to make strong gains after a period of market weakness, as new international buyers join established collectors in the competition for these works.

Abelard, Gesner, BIRDS SURROUNDED BY FOLIAGE, 23½ x 40, on masonite (691/109)   160
Abelard, Gesner, TWO PEACOCKS AMONG FLOWERS AND BUTTERFLIES, 12 x 14, on masonite
(691/29)   150
Adler, Jankel (1895-1949), BIRD AND LAMP, 1945, 37 x 31½ (4096/78)   8000
Adler, Jankel (1895-1949), BIRDS, 8 x 10, watercolor (4096/77)   850
Adler, Jankel (1895-1949), GIRL WITH STILL LIFE, 1946, 34 x 44 (4140/89)   7500
Adler, Jankel (1895-1949), PEASANT WOMAN WITH COW, 1943, 44 x 34 (4140/88)   8500
Adrion, Lucien (1889-1953), CARREFOUR RICHELIEU DROUOT, d.1927, 24 x 32 (4204/27)   1500
Adrion, Lucien (1889-1953), LAFE ROTUNDE, 7¼ x 9⅝, pencil (4260/1438)   900
Afro (Balsadella), (b.1912), COMPOSIZIONE, d.1952, 7⅛ x 11½, mixed media (4140/111)   700
Agam, Yaacov (b.1928), ARC EN CIEL DE MINUIT, d.1966, 13 x 14, oil on aluminum (4164/139)   3000
Alechinsky, Pierre, b.1927, LES FAMILLIERS, 1959, 51 x 76½ (4127/397)   18000
Alix, Gabriel, BOY AT WELL, 20 x 24, on masonite (691/106)   170
Alix, Gabriel, THE DANCERS, 19¾ x 16, on board (691/124)   130
Alix, Gabriel, THREE WOMEN WASHING IN RIVER, 20 x 24, on masonite (691/3)   200
Andre, Albert (1869-1954), PETITE PLACE AU GROS DU ROI, 1908, 12⅞ x 16⅛ (4204/19)   2000
Andreou, LA JEUNESSE, ca1972, H75, bronze (4225/228)   3600
Annenkov, Yuri (b.1889), COMPOSITION, early 1920's, 14¾ x 10⅝, photomontage (4172/363)   1000
Antoine, Montas, COURTYARD, ca1953, 20 x 16, on masonite (691/60)   225
Appel, Karel, 'I FIND THREE PEOPLE', BEACH SERIES #8, mixed media, 22 x 30, 1957 (4263/113)   1100
Appel, Karel, BEACH SERIES #7, mixed media, 22 x 30, 1957 (4263/111)   1400
Appel, Karel, SMALL ACRYLIC NO. 2, acrylic on paper, 25 x 19⅜, 1969 (4263/112)   2600
Appel, Karel (b.1921), COMPOSITION, ca1963-64, 12⅞ x 20⅞, acrylic on board (4228/104)   2000
Appel, Karel (b.1921), CONSTANT LISTENER, d.1971, 36 x 18 (4164/126)   4500
Appel, Karel (b.1921), TETE, 1962, 15 x 10¼, colored crayons (4096/129)   800
Appel, Karel, (b.1921), COMPOSITION, 18⅞ x 24, mixed media (4173/583)   3600
Appel, Karel, (b.1921), HEAD, 10¾ x 10, mixed media (4173/584)   350
Archipenko, Alexander, (1887-1964), FLAT TORSO, bronze, marble base, 14½, 1914 (4249/277)   18000
Archipenko, Alexander, (1887-1964), HEAD (MARLENE DIETRICH), bronze, 16, 1922 (4263/51)   6000
Archipenko, Alexander, (1887-1964), KING SOLOMON, bronze, 52¾, 1963 (4252/648)   18000
Archipenko, Alexander, (1887-1964), WOMAN WITH FAN, bronze, 34, 1914 (4252/649)   23000
Archipenko, Alexander (1887-1964), THE PAST, 1926, H14¼, bronze (4140/31)   4200
Archipenko, Alexander (1887-1964), TWO WOMEN, H14, bronze (4140/21)   4800
Archipenko, Alexander, (1887-1964), WOMAN WITH FAN, d.1914, H34, bronze relief (4172/318)   31000
Archipenko, Alexander, (1887-1964), DEUX NUS DEBOUT, ca1920-23, H20, bronze (4173/530)   *7000*ET]
Archipenko, Alexander, (1887-1964), REPOSE, 1911, 13½ x 14½ (4127/348)   *7500*
Arp, Jean, COLLAGE,CHARTRES, mixed media, 13 x 14¾ (4250/517)   *2600*

Arp
(4250/517)

Arp, Jean, COMPOSITION, collage, 14⅜ x 39¼ (4250/518)   3750
Arp, Jean, GUELE DE FLEUR, white marble, 19, 1960 (4249/319)   27000

Arp, Jean, JOAILLERIE DE CAMPAGNE, bronze, 18⅞, 1962 (4252/680)	9000
Arp, Jean, TETE COQUILLE, bronze, 9¾, 1958 (4263/131)	9000
Arp, Jean (1887-1966), AMPHORE D'UN PHILOSOPHE, 1964, H22½, white marble (4225/217)	25000
Arp, Jean (1887-1966), BOURGEON D'ECLAIR, 1965, H23, marble (4169/73)	16000
Arp, Jean (1887-1966), COMPOSITION, 11⅜ x 7⅞, mixed media (4204/103)	600
Arp, Jean (1887-1966), COMPOSITION, ca1963, 16⅛ x 12⅜, pencil (4140/115)	1600
Arp, Jean (1887-1966), DEUX PROFILS (RELIEF), 1959, 18 x 19, oil on pavatex (4140/117)	4500
Arp, Jean (1887-1966), EVOCATION HUMAINE LUNAIRE SPECTRALE, 1960, H15½, polished bronze (4169/53)	25000
Arp, Jean (1887-1966), SQUELETTE D'OISEAU, 1947, H42 (4124/85)	45000
Arp, Jean, (1887-1966), SCULPTURE A ETRE PERDUE DANS LA FORET, 1932, L8¾, polished bronze (4173/536)	8250
Arp, Jean, 1887-1966, FIGURE-GERME DITE L'APRES-MIDINETTE, H32½, polished bronze (4127/405)	15000
Arp, Jean, 1887-1966, PISTIL, 1950, 3/5, H13⅜, polished bronze (4127/407)	6000
Atl, Dr., PAISAJE CON VOLCAN, charcoal, 8⅞ x 11¾ (4105/30)	1500
Atlan, Jean (1913-1960), COMPOSITION, d.1959, 20⅝ x 31¼, oil on burlap (4228/110)	6500
Auguste, Toussaint, BIRDS NESTING IN A TREE, d.1951, 16 x 20, on masonite (691/17)	200
Auguste, Toussaint, MARKET DAY, d.1951, 20¼ x 24¼, on board (691/53)	700
Auguste, Toussaint, THE MIRACULOUS DRAUGHT OF FISH, 20 x 24, on masonite (691/34)	475
Aumborg, Adolf (1847-?), THE MOURNERS, d.1921, 10¾ x 16¾ (633/218)	650
Ayrton, Michael (b.1921), DEMETER AND KORE, 1965, H5½ bronze (4260/1506)	2500
Ayrton, Michael (b.1921), PORTRAIT OF WYNDHAM LEWIS, d.1955, 9⅞ x 14 pencil (4260/1503)	1600
Ayrton, Michael (b.1921), STUDY OF A MAN (ZOOMORPHIC FORM), d.1961, 17⅞ x 12 pencil (4260/1508)	1000
Ayrton, Michael (b.1921), TURNING MALE FIGURE, 1966, H9½ bronze (4260/1507)	2800
Balla, Giacomo (1871-1958), FIORE FUTURISTICO, 1968, H51¼, polychromed wood (4096/137)	1000
Balthus, NATURE MORTE AU VASE DE FLEURS, 1954, pencil, 21½ x 17⅛ (4170/170)	4500
Balthus, Jean, B.K. (1908-), LANDSCAPE, 1956, 25⅝ x 31⅞ (4124/87)	25000
Barlach, Ernst (1870-1938), HEAD OF TILLA DURIEUX III, ca1912, H7¼, bronze (4260/1479)	9000
Bauchant, Andre (1873-1958), PAYSAGE, d.1953, 15 x 18 (4204/78)	2000
Bauer, Rudolf (1889-1953), ALLEGRETTO, 1923, 17¼ x 12½, mixed media (4172/383)	3700
Bauer, Rudolf (1889-1953), KOMPOSITION 27 (SPITZEN), 1917, 40 x 27½, oil on board (4172/343)	9000
Bauer, Rudolf (1889-1953), PRESTO, 1926, 19¾ x 12¾, mixed media (4172/384)	4900
Baumeister, Willi (1889-1950), EIDOS ABSCHIED I, on board, 1940, 25¾ x 21½ (4247/135)	18500
Baumeister, Willi (1889-1950), ZWEI WELTALTER, 1947, 18⅛ x 25⅝ (4247/134)	10000
Bazaine, Jean, (b.1904), ROCHETAILLIE, d.1958, 15¾ x 10½, pencil (4173/587)	100
Beaudin, Andre (b.1895), L'OISEAU, 1947, H7⅞, bronze (4096/53)	850
Beaudin, Andre (b.1895), LE ROCHER, d.1967, 12½ x 21 (4140/124)	1100
Beckmann, Max (1884-1950), SCHWIMMBAD CAP MARTIN, 1944, 23⅝ x 37⅜ (4247/129)	75000
Beckmann, Max, (1884-1950), FISCHSTILLEBEN MIT NETZ, 1941, 29⅝ x 19⅜ (4173/548)	37000
Beckmann, Max, (1884-1950), KLEINE ITALIENISHE LANDSCHAFT, 1938, 25¾ x 41½ (4173/549)	38000
Beerbohm, Sir Max (1872-1956), JOSEPH CONRAD AND HIS CIRCLE, d.1935, 10 x 8, mixed media (4260/673)	4200
Beerbohm, Sir Max (1872-1956), THE EDWARDYSSEY, SUITE OF NINE CARICATURES, each, 12 x 7, mixed media (4260/676)	13000
Bellmer, Hans (1902-75), LA DEMIE POUPEE, 1971, L45½, painted wood (4164/165)	5750
Benoit, Rigaud, VOODOO CEREMONY, before 1958, 24 x 30, on masonite (691/108)	1100
Benoit, Rigaud, WEDDING PROCESSION, 23½ x 29½, on masonite (691/146)	4500
Berlewi, Henryk (1894-1967), COMPOSITION, 1920-25, 10 x 6, India ink (4172/398)	550
Berrocal, Miguel Ortiz (b.1933), CRIME IN CUENCA, LOVERS, 1961, L40, bronze (4096/154)	3100
Bigaud, Wilson, ADAM AND EVE, 24 x 36 (691/92)	350
Bigaud, Wilson, FISH SELLER, d.1964, 24¼ x 14, on masonite (691/31)	800
Bigaud, Wilson, MON COUSIN BROWN, 17¼ x 15½, on masonite (691/82)	275
Bigaud, Wilson, PARADIS, before 1973, 30 x 36, on masonite (691/24)	400
Bigaud, Wilson, PEASANTS TRAVELLING TO MARKET, 24 x 30, on masonite (691/83)	300
Bigaud, Wilson, STILL LIFE WITH FRUIT, 18 x 24, on masonite (691/130)	200
Bigaud, Wilson, STILL LIFE WITH PINEAPPLE, 24 x 31½ (691/91)	225
Bigaud, Wilson, STILL LIFE WITH ROSES AND HIBISCUS, d.1962, 16 x 12, on masonite (691/32)	400
Bigaud, Wilson, VILLAGE MARKETPLACE, 24 x 48 (691/93)	325
Bigaud, Wilson, VOODOO CEREMONY, 18 x 24, on masonite (691/102)	250
Bigaud, Wilson, WEDDING PARTY, 24 x 36, on masonite (691/104)	500
Bigaud, Wilson, WOMEN GOING TO THE VILLAGE MARKET, d.1966, 15½ x 24, on masonite (691/144)	200
Birchall, William Minshall, U.S. FOUR MASTER GOLDEN GATE, 15 x 22, gouache (633/114)	200
Bissier, Jules, (1893-), COMPOSITION, 1959, 6½ x 9 (4125/187)	3250

Bissier, Julius, MONTI, 1960(?), egg tempera, gold leaf, 7 x 8½ (4170/165)   7500
Bissier, Julius, 13.FEBR.62MO, egg tempera, 18 x 22½ (4170/166)   17500
Blanchard, Sisson, BIRD PECKING AT A FRUIT, 21¼ x 18½, on maso,nite (691/44)   50
Blanchard, Sisson, BIRDS BECKING AT AN EAR OF CORN, 24 x 16, on masonite (691/73)   90
Blanchard, Sisson, THREE OWLS, 24 x 32, on masonite (691/128)   160
Bogomazov, Alexander (1880-1930), FUTURIST COMPOSITION, d.1915, 16 x 12¾, charcoal
(4172/329)   1000
Bogomazov, Alexander (1880-1930), STILL LIFE WITH JUG AND BOWL, d.1915, 15½ x 13½,
charcoal (4172/328)   900
Bolotowsky,Ilya, DIAMOND 1947 ('ARCTIC WINDOW'), gouache, 6 x 6 (4250/509)   2400
Bomberg, David (1890-1956), DANCER, 1919, 25¼ x 20, watercolor (4172/324)   4500
Bombois, Camille, SANNOIS, LE VIEUX MOULIN, 31½ x 23¼, 1929 (4252/664)   11000
Bombois, Camille (1883-1963), LES LAVEUSES VILLAGEOISES, 1947, 10⅞ x 16⅜ (4204/76)   3750
Bombois, Camille, (1883-1963), LES LAVANDIERES, ca1926-28, 15 x 18⅛ (4173/543)   6000
Bombois, Camille, (1883-1963), NATURE MORTE AUX FRUITS, ca1920, 9⅛ x 13 (4173/526)   2500
Bombois, Camille, 1883-1963, BORDS DE LA RIVIERE, 7⅝ x 10¾ (4127/362)   2250
Bombois, Camille, 1883-1963, ENFANTS DANS UN PARC, 10¼ x 13½ (4127/363)   2750
Bonhomme, Leon, WOMAN IN A BAR, d.1906, 5½ x 4, watercolor (633/91)   175
Bonhomme, Leon (1870-1924), WOMAN'S HEAD, 10¾ x 8, watercolor (633/90)   225
Bonnard, Pierre, JARDIN PUBLIC, ETUDE POUR UN DECOR DE THEATRE, pastel, 25⅜ x 16⅝
(4250/418)   5000
Bonnard, Pierre (1867-1947), DEUX FEMMES NUES DANS UN PAYSAGES, ca1914-15, 20⅞ x
27½ (4124/26)   50000
Bonnard, Pierre (1867-1947), FEMME AU CORSAGE BLEU (ETUDE), 1915, 31⅞ x 13⅛ (4124/27)   60000
Bonnard, Pierre (1867-1947), JEUNE FEMME AU CHAPEAU NOIR, ca1910, 23⅝ x 21¼ (4124/45)   80000
Bonnard, Pierre (1867-1947), NA AU PEIGNOIR, 1906, 22⅞ x 17½ (4124/22)   75000
Bonnard, Pierre (1867-1947), NU, 6¼ x 4, mixed media (4140/5)   800
Bonnard, Pierre (1867-1947), PAYSAGE, HARMONIE VERTE, ca1915, 16 x 12¾, oil on panel
(4169/22)   27000
Bonnard, Pierre (1867-1947), PAYSAGE DU CANNET, 1938, 20¾ x 28¾ (4124/46)   150000
Bonnard, Pierre (1867-1947), THE BATH, 8⅝ x 5⅜, pencil (4260/1467)   5000
Bonnard, Pierre (1867-1947), VOILIER AU COUCHANT, ca1921, 15¾ x 19¼ (4169/24)   75000
Bonnard, Pierre, attrib. (1867-1947), HEAD OF A YOUNG GIRL, 6½ x 4½, on panel (633/105)   425
Bores, Francisco, NATURE MORTE, 1926, watercolor, pencil, 6¼ x 6¾ (4170/119)   1600
Bores, Francisco, STILL LIFE, 18 x 21½, 1944 (4263/97)   3000
Bores, Francisco (1898-1972, DRAPERIE MAUVE, d.1948, 18⅛ x 24¼ (4096/66)   1200
Bores, Francisco (1898-1972), ANIMAUX DOMESTIQUES, d.1952, 14¾ x 18 (4096/67)   850
Bores, Francisco (1898-1972), FIGURES ET CHEVAUX, 25½ x 19⅝, mixed media (4096/43)   400
Bores, Francisco (1898-1972), INTERIEUR, d.1942, 15 x 18⅛ (4096/64)   800
Bortynik, Sandor (b.1893), CONSTRUCTIVIST COMPOSITION, 1921-23, 12½ x 9⅜, watercolor
(4172/355)   3000
Bottex, J.B., THE COCK FIGHT, d.1968, 15⅞ x 20 (691/89)   350
Bottex, Seymour, BULL AND TWO BIRDS, 20 x 24, on masonite (691/74)   225
Bottex, Seymour, CHRIST BEFORE PONTIUS PILATE, 20 x 16, on masonite (691/111)   500
Botton, Jean de, LE CIRQUE MEDRANO, 47½ x 47¾, 1930 (4263/29)   5000
Boudin, Eugene (1824-1898), BERCK, PECHEUSES SUR LA PLAGE, ca1875-78, 7 x 10, oil on
panel (4228/15)   5750
Boudin, Eugene (1824-98), CAMERET, BATEAUX DANS LA RADE, 1871-73, 14¼ x 22¾ (4124/35)   35000
Boudin, Eugene (1824-98), TROUVILLE. VUE PRISE DES HAUTEURS, d.1897, 19⅞ x 29¼
(4169/33)   62500
Boudin, Eugene Louis, (1824-98), FEMME ASSISE, 4⅜ x 3½, mixed media (4173/540)   1300
Bourdelle, Antoine, (1861-1929), CHEVAL COMPLET SANS SELLE, ca1915, H18, bronze
(4173/504)   *12000*
Bourdelle, Emile Antonine, BAIGNEUSE ACCROUPIE, bronze, 20, 1907 (4252/604)   16000
Boureau, Paul, JUNGLE SCENE, 30 x 24 (691/56)   60
Brangwyn, Frank (1867-1943), IN THE CASHON panel, 13½ x 10¼, (666/49)   700
Braque, Georges, COUPE DE MARGUERITES, oil on paper, 8 x 14 (4252/665)   17000
Braque, Georges, LA BICYCLETTE, 52⅜ x 30½, 1952 (4249/313)   95000
Braque, Georges (1882-1963), FEMME NUE COUCHEE, d.1924, 10½ x 25¾, oil and sand
(4169/47)   50000
Braque, Georges, (1882-1963), VERRE ET COMPOTIER, 1922, 8 x 25½ (4124/49)   65000
Brauner, Victor, DRAGOSTEA, wax, oil on board, 28¾ x 20, 1948 (4249/295)   23000
Brauner, Victor, ORIGINES DE L'IMAGINATION DE LA MATIERE, encaustic, on board, 35¾ x 28⅝,
1958 (4249/297)   40000
Bravo, Manual A., BARDA DE PANTEON, 49⅝ x 7⅛ (4105/53)   150
Bravo, Manual A., OBRERO EN HUELGA, ASESINADO, 7⅝ x 9⅝ (4105/41)   150
Bravo, Manual A., PARABOLA OPTICA, 9¼ x 7⅛ (4105/52)   150

Brever, Noor Jade, SEATED GIRL (ARABESQUE), H9¼ bronze (4260/1487) — 1000
Brianchon, Maurice (b.1899), LE BASSIN, 32 x 39⅜ (4164/60) — 5250
Buffet, Bernard, LE TOREADOR, 63 x 19¾, 1958 (4252/668) — 14000
Buffet, Bernard, MOULIN ROUGE, 18¼ x 25⅜, 1958 (4263/88) — 7750
Buffet, Bernard, STILL LIFE WITH FRIED EGGS, pen, ink, watercolor, pencil, 19¾ x 25¼, 1958 (4263/98) — 4000
Buffet, Bernard (b.1928), LE PORT DU GUILDO, d.1968, 28¾ x 39¼ (4164/72) — 11500
Buffet, Bernard (b.1928), LE SACRE-COEUR, d.1958, 25¾ x 18⅛ (4096/97) — 10500

Bourdelle (4173/504)

Buffet, Bernard (b.1928), NATURE MORTE AU CITRON, d.1952, 10¾ x 16¼ (4164/71) — 3200
Buffet, Bernard (b.1928), NATURE MORTE AUX CRABES, d.1948, 22 x 25 (4204/119) — 7750
Buffet, Bernard (b.1928), NATURE MORTE AUX FRUITS, 13 x 21¾ (4096/96) — 6250
Buffet, Bernard (b.1928), PIERROT, d.1955, 42½ x 29¼, mixed media (4204/116) — 5250
Buffet, Bernard (b.1928), PORTRAIT DE JEUNE HOMME, d.1959, 25½ x 18⅛ (4204/117) — 7000
Buffet, Bernard (b.1928), SKYSCRAPERS, NEW YORK, d.1958, 64¾ x 31½ (4228/103) — 12000
Buffet, Bernard (b.1928), VASE DE FLEURS, d.1952, 23⅞ x 28⅞ (4228/101) — 8000
Buffet, Bernard, (b.1928), CABINES PRES DE LA MER, d.1949, 19½ x 25¼ (4173/556) — 6000
Buffet, Bernard, (b.1928), NATURE MORTE AUX CERISES, d.1950, 18¼ x 25¾ (4173/555) — 8500
Buffet, Bernard, (b.1928), NATURE MORTE AUX VASES DE LIS, d.1955, 38⅜ x 51⅜ (4173/557) — 25000
Burliuk, David, THE YELLOW COW, 9⅛ x 12¼, 1942 (4263/34) — 1300
Bury, Pol (b.1922), UNTITLED, ca1965, 20½ x 20½ x 8, wood and nylon (4164/102) — 2000
Butler, Reg, MUSEE IMAGINAIRE, DISPLAY CASE WITH 39 SCULPTURES, case 30¾ x 48½ x 5, sculptures 2¾ x 7½ (4252/685) — 7000
Butler, Reg (b.1913), JAPANESE GIRL, 1968, H14⅝, bronze (4140/125) — 1500
Butler, Reg (b.1913), STANDING FEMALE NUDE, H21½, bronze (4164/96) — 1300
Butler, Reg (b.1913), STUDY FOR 'FIGURE BENDING', 1954, H16¾, bronze (4096/141) — 1300
Butler, Reg (b.1913), TORSO OF A WOMAN, H17¼, bronze (4140/126) — 1300
Butler, Reg (b.1913), WOMAN IN STAYS, 1956, H20¼, bronze (4096/142) — 1900
Caffe, Nino (b.1909), PRETI E SCOPE, 10⅝ x 19⅝, oil on panel (4096/83) — 1800
Caillebotte, Gustave (1848-94), SOLEILS AU BORD DE LA SEINE, 1885-86, 36⅜ x 28¾ (4169/30) — 70000
Camoin, Charles, WOMAN READING, 26¼ x 22 (4252/619) — 16000
Camoin, Charles (1879-1965), BOUQUET DE FLEURS, 13 x 9½ (4228/38) — 1200
Camoin, Charles (1879-1965), PORTRAIT D'HOMME, 9½ x 6, oil on paper (4096/10) — 900
Campendonck, Heinrich (1889-1957), AKT MIT ZIEGEN, d.1919, 38 x 20⅞ (4172/312) — 41000
Campigli, Massimo, (b.1895), DONNA AL BALCONE, d.1930, 21¾ x 12 (4173/547) — 5250
Cantu, Federico, RETRATO DE UNA MUJER, green chalk, 18½ x 14 (4105/24) — 250
Capogrossi, Guiseppe (1900-72), SUPERFICIE, d.1950, 27⅞ x 19⅞ (4164/82) — 5750
Capuletti, Jose Manuel (b.1925), LA MARCHE EN AVANT, 29 x 19⅞ (4228/74) — 650
Carrington, Leonora, PURA FIRMA, pen, ink, 22¾ x 14⅛, 1969 (4263/82) — 800
Cascella, Pietro (b.1921), ULYSSES, 1963, H13, L12½, W10½, marble (4096/155) — 2100
Casimir, Laurent, MASS OF VILLAGERS DANCING, d.1970, 24 x 30 (691/114) — 170
Casimir, Laurent, VILLAGE CROWD, 15¼ x 23½, on masonite (691/75) — 300
Casimir, Laurent, VILLAGE CROWD WALKING TO MARKET, 24 x 32, on masonite (691/127) — 170
Casimir, Laurent, VILLAGE CROWD, d.1974, 19 x 23½'00 (691/76) — 175

Cesar, SEATED NUDE, bronze, 25½ (4252/687) 7000
Cesar, STANDING FIGURE, welded metal, 41 (4252/686) 7500
Cesar Baldaccini, (b.1921), ABSTRACT SCULPTURE, H17, welded steel (unique) (4173/575) 2100
Cezanne, Paul (1839-1906), LA ROUTE TOURNANTE A LA ROCHE-GUYON, ca1885, 25¼ x 31¾ (4096/17) 30000
Chadwick, Lynn (b.1914), BIRD, 1954, L27, bronze (4096/147) 2600
Chadwick, Lynn (b.1914), INQUISITOR II, d.1964, H15, bronze (4096/144) 1550
Chadwick, Lynn (b.1914), MAQUETTE FOR 'BEAST', L9½, bronze (4164/93) 750
Chadwick, Lynn (b.1914), STANDING FIGURE, d.1962, 24½ x 18⅞, mixed media (4228/125) 500
Chadwick, Lynn (b.1914), TWO WATCHERS II, H55¾, bronze (4164/95) 14000
Chadwick, Lynn (b.1914), WINGED FIGURES, H8¼, bronze (4164/94) 1400
Chadwick, Lynn, (b.1914), SEATED ELECTRA, d.1968, H23, bronze (4173/581) 4500
Chadwick, Lynn, (b.1914), STANDING ELECTRA, d.1969, H25½, bronze (4173/580) 4500
Chadwick, Lynn, (b.1914), STANDING FIGURE, d.1968, H28½, bronze (4173/578) 2900
Chadwick, Lynn, (b.1914), STANDING FIGURE, d.1968, H28¾, bronze (4173/579) 3600
Chagall, Marc, FEMME A LA JUPE VERTE, 1930, gouache, watercolor, 19 1/16 x 24⅞ (4170/130) 67500
Chagall, Marc, L'ANGE ET LA FIANCEE, 31½ x 25, ca1940 (4249/249) 190000
Chagall, Marc, LA PENDULE, 1963, monotype, 19¼ x 15½ (4170/180) 22000
Chagall, Marc (1887-), LES AMOUREUX AUX MARGERITES, 1949-50, 28¾ x 18½ (4124/90) 80000
Chagall, Marc, (1887-), DEUX TETES, 1950, 21¼ x 18⅞, gouache (4125/179) 32500
Chagall, Marc, (1887-), LA MUSE D'ARTISTE, 1958-9, 24¼ x 19, pastel, gouache (4125/181) 30000
Chagall, Marc, (1887-), LE VIEIL MUSICIEN, 1925, 14¼ x 11, gouache (4125/124) 25000
Chagall, Marc, (1887-), LES AMANTS, 12¾ x 9½, watercolor (4125/131) 15500
Chagall, Marc, (1887-), VILLAGE ENNEIGE, 9 x 8½, watercolor (4125/125) 5000
Charchoune, Serge (b.1888), COMPOSITION INSPIRE PAR UNE SUITE DE BACH, d.1958, 25½ x 36¼ (4164/80) 950
Charchoune, Serge (b.1888), COMPOSITION, 1921, 12 x 13¼ (4172/361) 3000
Charchoune, Serge (b.1888), CONCERTO POUR VIOLIN N.4, EN RE DE MOZART, d.1956, 15¾ x 31¼ (4164/79) 650
Charlot, Jean, FRED DAVIS' GARDEN IN CUERNAVACA, color pencils, 12 x 9, 1946 (4263/75) 400
Charlot, Jean, GIRL WITH BUNDLE, 1937, oil on canvas, 54 x 31 (4105/27) 6750
Charlot, Jean, LA TORMENTA, 1935, oil on canvas, 46¼ x 26⅛ (4105/26) 7500
Charlot, Jean, MALINCHE, 1926, oil on canvas, 16 x 11⅞ (4105/14) 4250
Charlot, Jean, MUSICIAN, 14⅛ x 19, 1940 (4263/65) 3300
Charlot, Jean, WASHERWOMAN, 10⅛ x 8⅛ (4263/67) 2000
Charlot, Jean, WOMAN WITH CRADLE, fresco, 20½ x 26½, 1940 (4263/69) 3750
Charlot, Jean (b.1898), TALI IBE (WEAVING MATS), d.1978, 24 x 20 (4204/86) 2500
Charlot, Jean (b.1898), VAKATAGI DERUA (MUSICAL BAMBOO), d.1978, 20 x 24¼ (4204/87) 2750
Charreton, Victor (1864-1937), PAYSAGE DE NEIGE, 21⅛ x 25⅛ (4228/66) 1500
Chattaway, William, TORSO OF A FEMALE NUDE, H7 bronze (4260/1510) 500
Chavannes, E., GARAGE MECANIQUE, 20 x 24¼, on masonite (691/50) 125
Chery, Jean Rene, PEASANT MEAL, ca1965, 19¾ x 23¾, on masonite (691/35) 325
Chirico, Giorgio di, ELECTRE CONSOLANT ORESTE, 1924, pencil, watercolor, 11¾ x 8¼ (4170/157) 9500
Chirico, Giorgio di, SKETCH FOR LE MYSTERE LAIC, pencil, 12⅝ x 9¾ (4250/473) *5500*
Corinth, Louis (1858-1925), DAMENBILDNIS, 11⅞ x 8⅞, pastel (4096/13) 2200
Cortes, Edouard (b.1882), APPROACHING LA PLACE DE LA CONCORDE, 13 x 18 (633/230) 2750
Cortes, Edouard (b.1882), LA RUE ROYALE, 18 x 22 (4204/10) 6500
Cortes, Edouard (b.1882), PECHEURS SUR LE QUAI, d.1914, 51½ x 76¾ (4228/16) 11000
Cortes, Edouard (b.1882), SOIR DE NEIGE, Paris, 13 x 18 (4204/11) 4250
Cortes, Edouard (b.1882), THEATRE DE VAUDEVILLE, 18 x 22 (4204/12) 5750
Covarrubias, Miguel (1904-1957), PORTRAIT OF CALVIN COOLIDGE, 13¾ x 9¾, mixed media (4228/96) 500
Cross, Henri Edmond (1856-1910), LANDSCAPE AT ST. CLAIR, 6⅞ x 9⅞, mixed media (4260/1446) 4500
Cross, Henri Edmond (1856-1910), MAN CARRYING A JUG (STUDY FOR 'PECHEUR PROVENCAL'), 11¾ x 9, conte crayon (4260/1447) 2400
Cross, Henri Edmond (1856-1910), STANDING NUDE, 13⅜ x 10⅝, black crayon (4260/1448) 1600
Cross, Henri Edmond (1856-1910), VUE DE LA MER, 4⅝ x 5⅝, watercolor (4228/32) 500
Cross, Henri Edmond, (1856-1910), VIEILLE BLANCHISSEUSE, 15 x 11½, pencil (4173/537) *750*
Csaky, Joseph, FEMME, bronze, 34½, 1928 (4252/647) 14000
Cuevas, Jose Luis, AUTORETRATO NO. 8, 1968, watercolor, 26 x 39½ (4105/77) 3100
Cuevas, Jose Luis, JUSTINE Y LE MARQUIS DE SADE, mixed media, 8½ x 6¼ (4105/74) 1100
Cuevas, Jose Luis, MAN SEATED IN ARMCHAIR, 1953-54, mixed media, 11⅜ x 9 (4105/75) 1100
Cuevas, Jose Luis, MUCHACHA CATALANA, ink, wash on paper, 3⅝ x 3½, 1963 (4263/80) 300
Cuevas, Jose Luis, TECHNICA DE LA PERSECUCION, 1968, mixed media, 12 x 9 (4105/76) 1100
Cuevas, Jose Luis, 3 FIGURES, ink, 11 x 17 (4105/78) 500
Cuevas, Jose Luis (b.1934), ASESINO DE MUJERES, d.1968, 8⅛ x 5½, mixed media (4164/74) 500

Cuevas, Jose Luis (b.1934), AUTORETRADO CON SANTO, d.1969, 11 x 14, mixed media (4228/93) — 400

Cuevas, Jose Luis (b.1934), AUTORETRADO EN UN PROSTIBULO, d.1969, 13½ x 10, mixed media (4228/94) — 400

Cuevas, Jose Luis (b.1934), AUTORETRATO CON MODELO, d.1965, 8⅝ x 10¾, mixed media (4096/118) — 800

Cuevas, Jose Luis (b.1934), AUTORETRATO CON MUJER AGRESIVA, 9⅞ x 13¾, watercolor (4140/99) — 1000

Cuevas, Jose Luis (b.1934), DELINCUENTE PISTOLERA, d.1968, 8 x 5, mixed media (4228/92) — 350

Cuevas, Jose Luis (b.1934), MISTERIO EN TANGER, d.1968, 10⅝ x 6⅞, mixed media (4096/119) — 450

D'Espagnat, Georges (1874-1946), PAYSAGE, 21¼ x 28¾ (4225/182) — 3000

D'Espagnat, Georges (1874-1946), RUE DU VILLAGE, 25⅝ x 31⅞ (4225/181) — 11000

Dali, Salvador, HORSE AND RIDER, pen and ink, 5⅝ x 3⅝ (4250/494) — 3500

Dali, Salvador, HOW SKYSCRAPERS WILL LOOK IN 1987, 1937, pen, ink, 11½ x 14½ (4170/155) — 7750

Dali, Salvador, LA CAVALIERE, 1935, inks, 22½ x 17⅞ (4170/154) — 4000

Dali, Salvador, LA MELACOLIE 'AERODINAMIQUE', 1937, pencil, ink, 10⅝ x 8 (4170/150) — 3600

Dali, Salvador, PORTRAIT OF TWO LITTLE GIRLS, 1945, pencil, 28½ x 22½ (4170/159) — 13000

Dali, Salvador, PORTRAITS OF GALA, mixed media, 20 x 30 (4250/495) — *13000*

Dali, Salvador, RECLINING NUDE, 6½ x 7¼ (4250/474) — 3000

Dali, Salvador, SPHINX, pen, ink on paper, 10⅜ x 7⅝, 1942 (4263/56) — 3100

Dali, Salvador, SURREALIST FIGURE, pencil, 17⅜ x 21½ (4170/151) — 3500

Dali, Salvador, UNTITLED, 1952, colored inks, 30⅛ x 22⅜ (4170/152) — 6250

Dali, Salvador (b.1904), THE QUEEN OF PORT LLIGAT, d.1956, 19¾ x 29⅝ ballpoint pen (4260/1483) — 5500

Dali, Salvador (b.1904), UNTITLED, 1969, 11½ x 9, mixed media (4228/121) — 600

Dali, Salvador, after, THE PERSISTENCE OF MEMORY, 54½ x 65, tapestry (633/102) — 750

Dali, Salvador, b.1904, MADAME BUTTERFLY, 1955, 13¾ x 10⅞, watercolor (4127/387) — 6000

Daumier, Honore (1807-79), LE BON VIVANT, H6¼, bronze (4228/3) — 4200

Daumier, Honore (1807-79), LE SUBTIL (M. Lecomte), H6¾, bronze (4096/14) — 6250

Daumier, Honore, 1807-79, DUBOIS, 7/25, H7⅞, bronze, dark brown (4127/316) — 3750

Daumier, Honore, 1807-79, HARLE PERE, 28/30, H4⅞, bronze, dark brown (4127/315) — 4000

Cross
(4173/537)

Chirico
(4250/473)

Delaunay (4250/534)

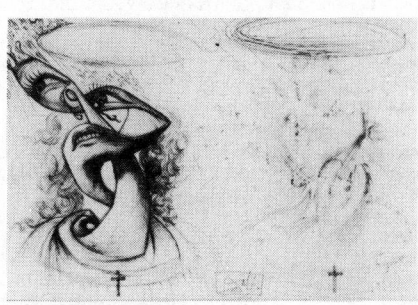

Dali (4250/495)

Daumier, Honore, 1807-79, LE BON VIVANT, 8/30, H6¼, bronze, blk. patina (4127/317) 3750
Daumier, Honore, 1807-79, LE BOURGEOIS EN ATTENTE, 29/30, H6⅛, bronze, blk. patina (4127/319) 7250
Daumier, Honore, 1807-79, LE MONSIEUR QUI RICANE, 23/30, H7⅜, bronze, dark brown (4127/318) 3500
De la Fresnaye, Roger, (1885-1925), ETUDES, 7⅛ x 4½, ink, paper (4125/144) 650
De la Fresnaye, Roger, (1885-1925), LE MATELOT, 1921, 10 x 6½ (4125/147) 1600
De Stael, Nicolas, (1914-55), COMPOSITION, 1944, 12⅜ x 9⅝ (4125/190) 1500
De Stael, Nicolas, 1914-55, French, COMPOSITION, 1944, 9½ x 13⅛ (4127/392) 5000
Delaunay, Sonia, RYTHME COULEUR-NO.1646, gouache and crayons, 27½ x 20⅞ (4250/534) 4000
Demette, A MODERN HAITIAN HOUSE, 22 x 30 (691/49) 100
Derain, Andre, NATURE MORTE, watercolor, pencil, 19 x 24⅝ (4170/118) 6500
Derain, Andre (1880-1954), HOMME NU, VU DE DOS, 24¾ x 18¾, sanguine (4164/11) 800
Derain, Andre (1880-1954), ITALIENNE BLONDE, 1922-24, 31¼ x 26½ (4096/33) 17000
Derain, Andre (1880-1954), LES BAIGNEUSES, 10⅜ x 11 (4228/44) 4000
Derain, Andre (1880-1954), NU ALLONGE, 19¼ x 24¾, sanguine (4204/38) 600
Derain, Andre (1880-1954), PROFILE DE JEUNE FEMME, 19 x 25, sanguine (4204/39) 400
Derain, Andre (1880-1954), TETE DE FEMME, 15½ x 13⅝ (4096/32) 2500
Derain, Andre (1880-1954), TETE DE FEMME, 15½ x 13⅝ (4228/42) 2500
Derain, Andre (1880-1954), THREE HEADS, ca1910-12, 9¼ x 7⅞, pencil (4260/1474) 800
Derain, Andre, 1880-1954, NATURE MORTE AUX POIRES, 1924, 11¼ x 15⅜ (4127/335) 5250
Derain, Endre (1880-1954), PAYSAGE A ETAPLES, 1930, 29⅛ x 36¼ (4124/68) 25000
Dix, Otto (1891-1969), PAGE OF STUDIES, ink, 1913, 20⅝ x 14⅝ (4247/101) 2750
Dix, Otto (1891-1969), SEATED WOMAN, 1931, sanguine, chalk, 25⅛ x 18⅛ (4247/47) 1600
Dix, Otto (1891-1969), SPELUNKE, gouache, pencil, 1925, 19¾ x 26½ (4247/109) 17000
Dodd, Francis (1874-1949), MISS VIRGINIA STEPHEN, d.1908, 14⅜ x 11 charcoal (4260/1490) 6500
Dodd, Francis (1874-1949), PORTRAIT OF JACOB EPSTEIN, d.1910, 15 x 11 charcoal (4260/1491) 3500
Dongen, Kees van (1877-1968), STUDY OF A WOMAN, 6⅞ x 4, black crayon (4260/1434) 1200
Dongen, Kees Van (1877-1968), LES JOUEUSES DE CARTES, 10 x 11⅜, mixed media (4096/46) 3250
Dorce, Jacque, VOODOO CEREMONY UNDER A LARGE TREE, 23¾ x 18⅜, on masonite (691/30) 100
Dubic, Abner, FERMIERS DANS LES PROVINCES, ca1975, 48 x 18 (691/25) 1600
Dubic, Abner, HAITIAN VILLAGE, 36 x 48 (691/69) 900
Dubic, Abner, LES TRAVAILS DU PAYSANT, ca1975, 48 x 18 (691/26) 950
Dubic, Abner, THE GARDEN OF EDEN, 16 x 24, on masonite (691/126) 325
Dubuffet, Jean, AUTOMOBILE, 1973, felt markers, 13¾ x 20½ (4170/187) 6000
Dubuffet, Jean, CHIEN, 1954, pen, ink, 9¾ x 12¾ (4170/181) 3000
Dubuffet, Jean, DEUX MECANOS, 28¾ x 23⅝, 1944 (4249/306) 97500
Dubuffet, Jean, DEUX PERSONNAGES SUR FOND NOIR, 1963, gouache, 19¾ x 26⅜ (4170/184) 12000
Dubuffet, Jean, LE PRUNEAU, papier mache, 13⅜, 1959 (4252/677) 16000
Dubuffet, Jean, PORTRAIT D'HOMME, mixed media on metal, board, 13⅞ x 10⅞, 1952 (4249/314) 20000
Dubuffet, Jean, PROMENEUR A L'ARBRE, assemblage d'empreintes, 28 x 23⅝ (4250/519) 12500
Dubuffet, Jean, PROMENEURS DU DESERT, peintare a la colle on paper, 14¾ x 21 (4250/520) 13500
Dubuffet, Jean, RUE MONTMARTRE (LA PALTOQUE), 1962, gouache, 19⅝ x 26⅜ (4170/182) 28000
Dubuffet, Jean (b.1901), PERSONNAGE MI-CORPS, d.1967, 18 x 12, polychrome relief (4164/101) 3000
Dubuffet, Jean (b.1901), PERSONNAGE S.12, d.1963, 8¼ x 5¼, ball-point pens (4096/134) 1700
Dubuffet, Jean (b.1901), PERSONNAGE S.2, d.1963, 8¼ x 5¼, ball-point pens (4096/132) 1700
Dubuffet, Jean (b.1901), PERSONNAGE S.21, d.1963, 8¼ x 5¼, ball-point pens (4096/135) 1300
Dubuffet, Jean (b.1901), PERSONNAGE S.3, d.1963, 8¼ x 5¼, ball-point pens (4096/133) 1600
Dubuffet, Jean (b.1901), ROBINET, d.1965, 10¼ x 8⅞, mixed media (4140/118) 2500
Dubuffet, Jean (b.1901), TROIS ARBRES, d.1971, 13⅛ x 11¾, mixed media (4140/119) 2000
Dubuffet, Jean (b.1901), LE CAMPAGNARD, d.1961, 39¾ x 32 (4169/54) 65000
Dubuffet, Jean (b.1901), PAYSAGE AVEC CORNES ET ELANCEMENTS, d.1953, 28¾ x 36¼ (4169/56) 30000
Dubuffet, Jean, (b.1901), PROMENEUSE EN VILLE, d.1974, 70⅝ x 55⅛, vinyl on canvas (4169/68) 55000
Dubuffet, Jean, (1901-), JARDIN DES ILES, 1955, 9 x 12½, collage, butterfly (4125/183) 15000
Dubuffet, Jean, (1901-), OBSCUR THEATRE AU PIED DU MUR, 1957, 51¾ x 26¼, mixed media (4125/189) 9000
Duchamp, Marcel, FEMME NUE AGENOUILLEE, pen and ink, 20¼ x 13 1/l6 (4250/429) 3200
Duchamp, Marcel, FEMME NUE AGENOUILLEE, pen and ink, 20¼ x 13 1/l6 (4250/428) 2000
Duchamp, Marcel (1887-1968), FONTAINE (FOUNTAIN), d.1917, 14 x 19 x 24, porcelain (4172/368) 18500
Duchamp, Marcel (1887-1968), FROM OR BY MARCEL DUCHAMP (BOITE EN VALISE), H15¾, W11¾, D3¼, cardboard box (4140/58) 2600
Duffault, Prefete, A LOA WITH FEMALE HEAD AND VOODOO SYMBOLS, 1977, 24 x 16, on masonite (691/129) 300
Duffaut, Prefete, BATEAUX A VOILE DANS LES DEUX BAIES, ca1975, 14 x 22 (691/95) 250
Duffaut, Prefete, CITY WITH RIVER INLET AND BRIDGE, 16 x 19⅞, on masonite (691/113) 300
Duffaut, Prefete, COASTAL VILLAGE, d.1956, 15½ x 19½, on masonite (691/1) 275
Duffaut, Prefete, FANTASTIC CITY, 20 x 30 (691/143) 300

Duffaut, Prefete, FANTASTIC CITY WITH ISLAND AND SAILBOATS, 24 x 48 (691/47) — 550
Duffaut, Prefete, HAITIAN VILLAGE WITH RIVER AND BRIDGE, D.1958, 14¾ x 18, on masonite (691/20) — 250
Duffaut, Prefete, IMAGINARY CITY WITH WATERFALL, 48 x '15½, on masonite (691/65) — 275
Duffaut, Prefete, IMAGINARY TOWN WITH HARBOR, d.1966, 24 x 16½, on masonite (691/125) — 325
Duffaut, Prefete, IMAGINARY VILLAGE, 16 x 20 (691/13) — 200
Duffaut, Prefete, IMAGINARY VILLAGE BY THE SEA, 20 x 30 (691/15) — 250
Duffaut, Prefete, THREE WORLDS, 24 x 8 (691/123) — 190
Duffaut, Prefete, TOWN WITH HARBOR AND SAILING BOATS, 7½ x 9½, on masonite (691/67) — 150
Duffaut, Prefete, VIEW OF COASTAL CITY, 5½ x 9½ (691/68) — 140
Dufy, Jean, LES CHAMPS ELYSEES, gouache, pencil on paper, 15½ x 19½ (4263/91) — 4400
Dufy, Jean, PORT SCENE, 25¼ x 31, ca1917 (4263/27) — 6250
Dufy, Jean, THE BULL RING, gouache on paper, 19¼ x 25 (4263/89) — 5750
Dufy, Jean, VASE OF FLOWERS, 7 x 11⅛, 1924 (4263/28) — 2900
Dufy, Jean (1888-1964), AU BOIS DE BOULOGNE, 18 x 23½, mixed media (4164/62) — 2400
Dufy, Jean (1888-1964), BOUQUET DE FLEURS, 10¼ x 10¼, watercolor (4140/79) — 450
Dufy, Jean (1888-1964), BOUQUET DE FLEURS, d.1917, 24⅜ x 19, mixed media (4204/44) — 2100
Dufy, Jean (1888-1964), GLASGOW, 19 x 25, gouache (4164/63) — 4600
Dufy, Jean (1888-1964), GRAND BOUQUET DE FLEURS, 17⅜ x 16⅛, mixed media (4228/87) — 600
Dufy, Jean (1888-1964), HOMMAGE A RUDYARD KIPLING, d.1924, 21⅞ x 19, watercolor (4164/20) — 1900
Dufy, Jean (1888-1964), LE PONT ALEXANDRE III, 10½ x 13½ (4225/179) — 4500
Dufy, Jean (1888-1964), LE PORT, d.1925, 19¼ x 21¼, mixed media (4096/38) — 2000
Dufy, Jean (1888-1964), LES ARBRES, 28¾ x 23¾ (4096/35) — 6000
Dufy, Jean (1888-1964), LES USINES PRES DU PORT, d.1926, 17¼ x 22⅛, mixed media (4228/52) — 1700
Dufy, Jean (1888-1964), MUSICIENS, d.1954, 6 x 9¾, gouache (4140/83) — 600
Dufy, Jean (1888-1964), NATURE MORTE AUX FRUITS ET AU BOUQUET DE, FLEURS, 17¾ x 25⅜, mixed media (4228/82) — 1900
Dufy, Jean (1888-1964), NATURE MORTE AUX VASE DE FLEURS, AUX FRUITS ET, AUX COQUILLES, 8¾ x 14 (4140/82) — 850
Dufy, Jean (1888-1964), NATURE MORTE, d.1922, 12¾ x 20¾, oil on panel (4228/49) — 3100
Dufy, Jean (1888-1964), ROUTE DE VILLAGE, d.1920, 17⅝ x 22, watercolor (4140/26) — 1200
Dufy, Jean (1888-1964), SCENE DE PARIS, ca1938, 12⅞ x 19⅛, gouache (4204/45) — 2600
Dufy, Jean (1888-1964), VASE DE DLEURS, 21½ x 17⅞ (4228/81) — 2100
Dufy, Jean (1888-1964), VASE DE FLEURS, 14 x 8¾ (4164/21) — 1700
Dufy, Jean (1888-1964), VUE DE PARIS, 14½ x 27, gouache (4228/75) — 2700
Dufy, Jean (1888-1964), VUE DE VENISE, 13 x 16 (4140/87) — 3000
Dufy, Raoul, L'HINDOUE, 18¼ x 21⅝, ca1929 (4249/267) — 41000
Dufy, Raoul, L'HOTEL SUISSE A NICE ET LE TOURNANT 'RAUBA, CAPEU', 15 x 18⅛, ca1928 (4249/266) — 40000
Dufy, Raoul, LA FONTAINE, 21¼ x 25¾ (4249/276) — 34000
Dufy, Raoul, LA PLAGE AUX NAIADES, 1931, watercolor, 19¾ x 25¾ (4170/131) — 21000
Dufy, Raoul, LA PLAGE DE SAINT-ADRESSE, 25⅝ x 31⅞, 1906 (4249/242) — 95000
Dufy, Raoul, LANDSCAPE, painted linen, 186 x 206, 1924 (4263/30) — 6250
Dufy, Raoul, LE PESAGE A DEAUVILLE, 1929-31, gouache, 19½ x 25⅜ (4170/132) — 37500
Dufy, Raoul, PARADE DES MANNEQUINS A LONGCHAMPS, mixed media, 9 x l7 (4250/462) — 13000
Dufy, Raoul, PAYSAGE EN SICILE, 1922, pencil, 17½ x 22 (4170/126) — 3100
Dufy, Raoul, ROWING AT HENLEY, gouache, 19¾ x 25¾ (4250/469) — 31000
Dufy, Raoul, THE PADDOCK, gouache, 20½ x 25⅞ (4250/464) — 27000
Dufy, Raoul (1877-1953), ARRIVEE A NEW YORK, 1937, 20 x 26, mixed media (4225/205) — 14000
Dufy, Raoul (1877-1953), BOUQUET DE FLEURS, d.1922, 21⅝ x 17⅛, mixed media (4225/190) — 11500
Dufy, Raoul (1877-1953), BROOKLYN BRIDGE, 1951, 6¾ x 25⅝, watercolor (4225/178) — 4250
Dufy, Raoul (1877-1953), CARNAVAL A NICE, 11⅛ x 21¾ (4225/188) — 28000
Dufy, Raoul (1877-1953), COUP DE VENT, 1907, 21¼ x 25½ (4124/55) — 60000
Dufy, Raoul (1877-1953), LA PROMENADE A TROUVILLE, 1922, 24¾ x 31½ (4124/28) — 35000
Dufy, Raoul (1877-1953), LE PADDOCK, 19⅞ x 26⅛, mixed media (4225/203) — 30000
Dufy, Raoul (1877-1953), PORTRAIT OF ADOLPHE BASLER, ca1929, 22¾ x 15, pencil (4260/1477) — 1800
Dufy, Raoul, (1877-1953), LA FAVORI, 19⅝ x 25½, gouache (4125/117) — 5500
Dufy, Raoul, (1877-1953), LA REGATTE, 13⅝ x 17⅝, gouache (4125/126) — 23000
Dufy, Raoul, (1877-1953), LES YACHTS A DEAUVILLE, ca1935, 19 x 24⅝, pencil (4173/538) — 2300
Dufy, Raoul, 1877-1953, LA FENETRE OUVERTE, SAINTE-ADRESSE, 16½ x 13 (4127/336) — 17000
Duranchamps, Rafael (b.1891), PUERTO DE LA SELVA (HAVEN OF THE FOREST), 35 x 31 (4204/71) — 9000
Dyf, Marcel, RECLINING NUDE, 21 x 25 (633/94) — 800
Edzard, Dietz, YOUNG WOMAN BEFORE A MIRROR, 36⅜ x 23¾ (4252/628) — 4250
Edzard, Dietz (1893-1963), CAROLINE, 18⅜ x 15⅛ (4228/89) — 1800
Edzard, Dietz (1893-1963), DEUX JEUNES FILLES, 8⅛ x 7⅛ (4164/56) — 600

Edzard, Dietz (1893-1963), LE LOUP ROSE, 18⅛ x 14⅞ (4096/82)	1200
Edzard, Dietz (1893-1963), NATURE MORTE AU VIOLON, 25¾ x 32 (4204/54)	3750
Edzard, Dietz (1893-1963), TETE DE JEUNE FEMME, ca1912-14, 9½ x 7¼, oil on panel (4140/17)	900
Eisendieck, Suzanne (b.1908), LA CHANTEUSE, 32 x 23¾ (4140/18)	900
Eisendieck, Suzanne (b.1908), LA SEINE A MARLY, 18⅛ x 21¾ (4228/90)	1700
Eisendieck, Suzanne (b.1908), LES CONFIDENCES, 26 x 32 (4164/58)	2200
Eisendieck, Suzanne (b.1908), LES TONNELLES A JUMIEGES, 28½ x 39¼ (4204/51)	3500
Eisendieck, Suzanne (b.1908), ROSES DANS UN VERRE, 9½ x 6¼ (666/57)	400
Epstein, Jacob, PORTRAIT OF JACKIE, pencil, 22⅜ x 17⅛, 1935 (4263/48)	700
Epstein, Jacob, VICTOR, bronze, 6¾ (4263/50)	2000
Epstein, Jacob (1880-1959), FIFTH PORTRAIT OF KATHLEEN, 1935, H30, bronze (4164/38)	2100
Epstein, Jacob (1880-1959), NEPTUNE, 1946, H13¾, bronze (4140/48)	2800
Epstein, Jacob (1880-1959), SELF-PORTRAIT WITH BEARD, 1918, H14, bronze (4096/52)	2300
Epstein, Jacob (1880-1959), SUNITA RECLINING (RECLINING GODDESS), 1931, L30, bronze (4096/51)	2000
Epstein, Jacob, 1880-1959, MASK OF MEUM, 1918, H11½, bronze, brown (4127/351)	1500
Epstein, Jacob, 1880-1959, SECOND PORTRAIT OF ANNABEL FREUD, 1954, H8¼, bronze, brown (4127/353)	3250
Epstein, Jacob, 1880-1959, SEVENTH PORTRAIT OF KATHLEEN, 1948, H27½, bronze, brown (4127/354)	2500
Epstein, Sir Jacob (1880-1959), BERTRAND RUSSELL, 1953, H16½ bronze (4260/1505)	5000
Epstein, Sir Jacob (1880-1959), SOMERSET MAUGHAM, 1951, H16½ bronze (4260/1504)	3500
Erni, Hans (b.1909), JEUNE FILLE, d.1956, 38 x 17¼ (4228/88)	2250
Ernst, Max, COMPOSITION, 25½ x 31½ (4249/291)	47500
Ernst, Max, DEUX OISEAUX, 1928-29, gouache, oil, paper, 9 x 12⅛ (4170/160)	21000
Ernst, Max, FLEUR-COQUILLE, 18⅛ x 15, 1928 (4249/287)	32500
Ernst, Max, LA TABLE EST MISE, bronze, black patina, W23½, 1944 (4249/316)	28000
Ernst, Max, PORTRAIT OF CARESSE CROSBY, gouache and pencil, 9½ x 7½ (4250/472)	*11500*
Ernst, Max, SUN OVER THE SEA, gouache, 9¾ x 14¼ (4250/484)	18000
Ernst, Max, UNTITLED, pastel, 18 x 14 (4250/475)	9000
Ernst, Max (1891-1976), FLAMINGOS, d.1920, 10⅞ x 9, mixed media (4172/364)	18000
Ernst, Max (1891-1976), GYPSY ROSE LEE, d.1943, 17¾ x 23½ (4169/65)	110000
Ernst, Max (1891-1976), JEUNE FEMME EN FORME DE FLEUR, 1957, H14⅛, bronze (4169/61)	15000
Ernst, Max (1891-1976), TORTUE, 1944, H10¼ (4124/79)	14000
Ernst, Max, 1891-1976, LA TOURANGELLE, 1960, H10½, bronze, black (4127/404)	6500
Esteue, Maurice (b.1904), NATURE MORTE, d.1938, 12¼ x 19¾ (4096/65)	6500
Etrog, Sorel (b.1933), LEITZAN, H25½, bronze (4228/130)	3600
Etrog, Sorel (b.1933), STANDING FIGURE, H25⅝, bronze (4228/129)	2000
Etrog, Sorel (b.1933), STUDIES FOR SCULPTURE, 9½ x 12½, pencil on buff board (4204/105)	3500
Evans, Powys (B.1899), PORTRAITS OF SIR MAX BEERBOHM, 10¼ x 8¼, pencil (4260/671)	800
Exter, Alexandra (1882-1949), CASTLES UNDER THE SEA, ca1930, 35½ x 43¾ (4172/393)	5500
Exter, Alexandra (1882-1949), CUBIST NUDE and THEATRICAL COMPOSITION, 57 x 44, double-sided (4172/322)	7500
Exter, Alexandra (1882-1949), PERSONNAGE, ca1924-25, 19 x 8⅝, gouache (4172/388)	1800
Exter, Alexandra (1882-1949), WOMAN WITH BIRD, ca1925, 32 x 25½ (4172/390)	3250
Falk, Robert (1886-1958), HARBOR SCENE, 23½ x 31½ (4204/21)	3400
Fantin-Latour, Henri, 1836-1904, BOUQUET DE ROSES, 1890, 8⅜ x 12¾ (4127/301)	18000
Fautrier, Jean, FLOWERS, 31¾ x 25 (633/104)	800
Feininger, Lyonel, AT SEA, mixed media, 6½ x 9½ (4250/481)	*5500*
Feininger, Lyonel, BAUERNHAUS IN LOBBE, 15 x 24¾, 1907 (4263/37)	4400
Feininger, Lyonel, FIVE GHOSTIES, ink, watercolor, 4⅛ x 6⅛ (4170/147)	2400
Feininger, Lyonel, FOUR GHOSTIES, ink and watercolor, 4¾ x 5¾ (4250/479)	2000
Feininger, Lyonel, FOUR GHOSTIES, 1955, mixed media, 3 x 6 (4170/146)	2200
Feininger, Lyonel, NEPPERMIN I, 1914, charcoal, pen, ink, 9¼ x 12⅛ (4170/142)	5250
Feininger, Lyonel, THE SMOKE CLOUD, watercolor, 12 x 18 (4250/482)	9500
Feininger, Lyonel, THREE GHOSTIES, ink, watercolor, 6½ x 3½ (4170/148)	2700
Feininger, Lyonel, THREE GHOSTIES, ink and watercolor, 6 x 4⅛ (4250/478)	2000
Feininger, Lyonel, TWO GHOSTIES, ink, watercolor, 6⅛ x 3½ (4170/149)	1900
Feininger, Lyonel (1871-1956), BARQUE, watercolor, ink, 1936, 12⅜ x 18½ (4247/128)	12000
Feininger, Lyonel (1871-1956), DER GRUTZTURM, 16.8.30, ink, watercolor, 14¾ x 11 (4247/99)	5750
Feininger, Lyonel (1871-1956), FOUR GHOSTIES, d.1953, 4¾ x 6, mixed media (4204/98)	2100
Feininger, Lyonel (1871-1956), HARBOR SCENE, 1940, ink, watercolor, 12⅜ x 14 (4247/100)	19000
Feininger, Lyonel (1871-1956), MANHATTAN, DUSK, 23⅛ x 36⅛ (4124/88)	27500
Feininger, Lyonel (1871-1956), SEATED FIGURE, 4 x 2¾, mixed media (4164/76)	450
Feininger, Lyonel (1871-1956), THREE GHOSTIES WITH DOG, 3¼ x 6, mixed media (4140/77)	1600
Feininger, Lyonel (1871-1956), THREE GHOSTIES, d.1953, 5⅜ x 4¼, mixed media (4140/76)	1600
Feininger, Lyonel (1871-1956), TWO GHOSTIES, d.1954, 6⅛ x 3¼, mixed media (4204/97)	1800
Feininger, Lyonel (1871-1956), TWO GHOSTIES, d.1955, 5¼ x 3⅛, mixed media (4140/78)	1200

Feininger, Lyonel, (1871-1956), FIGURE BY THE SEA, 9⅛ x 11⅝, ink, paper (4125/156)	4500
Feininger, Lyonel, (1871-1956), LANDSCAPES WITH FIGURES, 1948, 11⅝ x 18¼, watercolor (4125/158)	2250
Feininger, Lyonel, (1871-1956), THE SCHOONER FROM BREMEN, 1935, 10⅜ x 10½, watercolor (4125/157)	7000
Feininger, Lyonel, (1871-1956), THREE GHOSTIES, 1954, 3 x 6⅛, ink, gouache (4125/159)	3250
Ferat, Serge, NATURE MORTE NO.2, gouache, 10⅞ x 7¼ (4250/436)	1500
Ferat, Serge, (1881-1958), NATURE MORTE AU COMPOTIER, 1918, 9¼ x 6⅜, gouache (4125/139)	1200
Ferat, Serge, 1881-1958, Russian, NATURE MORTE, 15½ x 11 (4127/332)	4000
Ferriera, Jesus R. (Chucho), CABALLO ROJIZO, gouache on tissue, 29¾ x 19½ (4105/86)	600
Ferriera, Jesus R. (Chucho), FIGURA FANTASTICA, gouache on red tissue, 19⅜ x 29½ (4105/84)	375
Ferriera, Jesus R. (Chucho), UN ANGEL, 1964, gouache on tissue, 29¼ x 19¼ (4105/85)	900
Filonov, Pavel (1883-1941), THE CITY AND ITS INHABITANTS, 1927-28, 13 x 13¾, mixed media (4172/310)	2200
Folon, Jean-Michel (b.1934), LES FOOTBALLEURS, 8⅛ x 10¼, mixed media (4228/95)	600
Fontana, Lucio, CONCETTO SPAZIALE, ATTESA, water paint on canvas, 21½ x 18, 1967 (4252/695)	3750
Fontana, Lucio (1899-1968), AURIGA, 1941, H11½, bronze (4164/35)	900
Forain, Jean Louis, TWO STUDIES OF A WOMAN LEANING AGAINST A CUSHION, charcoal, 9⅜ x 16 (4250/417)	1200
Forain, Jean Louis (1852-1931), COURT SCENE, d.1921, 7¾ x 11⅜, mixed media (4260/1462)	1800

Feininger (4250/481)

Foujita (4250/463)

Forain
(4125/102)

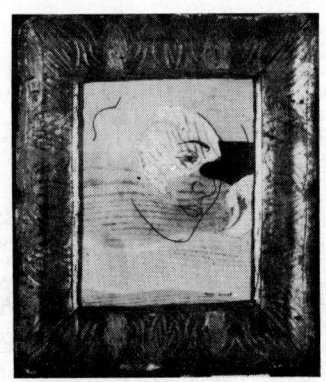

Ernst (4250/472)

Foujita (4250/460)

Forain, Jean Louis (1852-1931), HEAD AND SHOULDERS OF A YOUNG GIRL, 7 x 7½, watercolor (4260/1461) 950
Forain, Jean Louis (1852-1931), LE MERCANTI, ca1915, 14 x 21⅞, mixed media (4204/1) 900
Forain, Jean Louis (1852-1931), THE CONNOISSEUR, ca1900, 15⅞ x 10¼, mixed media (4260/1460) 1600
Forain, Jean Louis (1852-1931), YOUNG WOMAN IN A BLUE HAT, ca1883, 17¼ x 12⅛, watercolor (4260/1459) 7800
Forain, Jean Louis, (1852-1931), DANS LES COULISSES, 29 x 23¾ (4173/505) 3200
Forain, Jean Louis, (1852-1931), L'ATELIER DE L'ARTIST, 9¼ x 6⅝, watercolor (4125/102) *2200*
Forain, Jean-Louis (1852-1931), SORTIE DES FOLIES BERGERES, 1895, 45½ x 31½ (4124/51) 40000
Foujita, Tsuguharu, AMOROUS COUPLE, CAFE SCENE, WRESTLERS, ink on rice, paper, 9⅝ x 13½ (4263/43) 950
Foujita, Tsuguharu, AT THE RACES, pen an ink, 14⅛ x 11⅛ (4250/463) *2700*
Foujita, Tsuguharu, CAT, Sepia and ink, 11⅝ x 15 (4250/460) *10000*
Foujita, Tsuguharu, LA CHAT, d.1953, 9 x 6¾, mixed media (4164/53) 3300
Foujita, Tsuguharu, PORTRAIT OF A YOUNG GIRL, 9½ x 7½, 1961 (4252/666) 34000
Foujita, Tsuguharu, PORTRAIT OF MME GEORGES ENESCO, PRINCESS CANTACUZENE, 32 x 23¾, 1921 (4263/32) 16500
Foujita, Tsuguharu, SEATED WOMAN, charcoal, 42½ x 16 (4250/461) 23000
Foujita, Tsuguharu, THREE DOGS, pen, ink, 20 x 14⅝ (4263/107) 3000
Foujita, Tsuguharu, TWO JAPANESE DOLLS, watercolor and ink, 13⅝ x 12½ (4250/459) 9000
Foujita, Tsuguharu, YOUNG WOMAN READING IN BED, pencil, 12⅜ x 17⅛ (4263/45) 4000
Foujita, Tsuguharu (1886-1968), AUTO-PORTRAIT, d.1952, 7¼ x 5½ (4096/69) 22000
Foujita, Tsuguharu (1886-1968), BUSTE DE FEMME, 10⅛ x 8¾, mixed media (4164/54) 4400
Foujita, Tsuguharu (1886-1968), CHAT TIGRE, d.1939, 15 x 17⅞ (4204/49) 15000
Foujita, Tsuguharu (1886-1968), COPIE DE GOETHE PAR TISCHBEIN, 18 x 15 (4164/55) 600
Foujita, Tsuguharu (1886-1968), CRUCIFIXION, 1920, 13¼ x 17¾, mixed media (4228/61) 2100
Foujita, Tsuguharu (1886-1968), FEMME EN PROFIL, 13⅛ x 9¾, mixed media (4140/24) 2600
Foujita, Tsuguharu (1886-1968), FIGHTING ANIMALS, 19¾ x 15, mixed media (4096/40) 1500
Foujita, Tsuguharu (1886-1968), JEUNE FEMME AVEC UN CHAT, d.1950, 13⅛ x 9⅝ (4096/70) 42000
Foujita, Tsuguharu (1886-1968), LE CHAT, d.1932, 7½ x 6⅝, watercolor (4096/41) 3000
Foujita, Tsuguharu (1886-1968), NU ASSIS, 16½ x 9, pencil (4140/22) 1100
Foujita, Tsuguharu (1886-1968), PORTRAIT DE JEUNE FILLE, 9⅝ x 7½, mixed media (4228/62) 4250
Foujita, Tsuguharu (1886-1968), PORTRAIT DE JEUNE FILLE, d.1928, 13⅝ x 11⅞, pen, India ink (4096/39) 4000
Foujita, Tsuguharu (1886-1968), PORTRAIT DE MADAME FOUJITA, d.1932, 17 x 13, mixed media (4140/23) 7500
Foujita, Tsuguharu (1886-1968), SANTA CLAUS CAT, 5⅛ x 3¼, mixed media (4140/74) 650
Foujita, Tsuguharu (1886-1968), TETE DE FEMME, d.1930, 16¼ x 12¾, mixed media (4140/25) 6500
Foujita, Tsuguharu (1886-1968), VASE DE ROSES, d.1961, 13 x 9½ (4096/71) 31000
Foujita, Tsuguharu, (1886-1968), LE CHAT, 1949, 12 x 15, ink, wash, paper (4125/128) 8500
Foujita, Tsuguharu, (1886-1968), LE PETIT CHAT ENDORMI, d.1956, 6¼ x 8⅝ (4173/553) 15500
Fous, Jean (1901-71), METRO BARBES, 14¾ x 23¾, oil on panel (4204/75) 900
Fresnaye, Roger de la (1885-1925), MAN WITH A MONOCLE, ca1918, 10⅜ x 7½, mixed media (4260/1476) 600
Fresnaye, Roger de la (1885-1925), SELF PORTRAIT WITH CAPE, ca1921-22, 8⅛ x 4⅞, india ink (4260/1475) 700
Friesz, Emile Othon, BY THE BANKS OF THE SEINE, pencil, paper, 9⅛ x 11¾, ca1935 (4263/8) 150
Friesz, Emile Othon, NOGENT SUR SEINE, pencil, paper, 8¼ x 10¾ (4263/7) 150
Friesz, Emile Othon, SEATED NUDE, 18⅛ x 15, ca1934 (4252/624) 6500
Friesz, Emile Othon, STANDING FEMALE NUDE, watercolor, pencil, paper, 19 x 11¼, 1924 (4263/19) 1000
Friesz, Emile Othon, STUDY OF A GARDEN, pencil, paper, 8¼ x 11 (4263/6) 150
Friesz, Emile Othon (1879-1949), LE PORT DE TOULON, d.1928, 29 x 36¼ (4096/29) 4500
Friesz, Emile Othon (1879-1949), MODELE ASSIS, d.1931, 9½ x 5½ (4096/28) 550
Friesz, Emile Othon (1879-1949), PAYSAGE A LA ROCCA PARVERA (PIEMONTE), 21½ x 25½ (4225/185) 10000
Galien-Laloue, Eugene (1854-1941), BOULEVARD DE PARIS, 12⅜ x 7½, mixed media (4096/2) 2600
Galien-Laloue, Eugene (1854-1941), PARIS, LA PLACE CLICHY, 7½ x 12⅜, mixed media (4096/3) 2600
Galvan, Jesus G., MOTHER AND CHILD, 1944, watercolor, 19½ x 15⅜ (4105/28) 900
Galvan, Jesus G., NINA CON VESTIDO ROSADO, 1939, ink, watercolor, 11⅛ x 9⅛ (4105/29) 950
Garcia, Joaquin Torres, CONSTRUCTIVO 926, on panel, 15¾ x 7⅝, 1931 (4263/60) 3000
Garcia, Joaquin Torres, FORMAS EN NEGRO Y ROJO, on board, 21½ x 16⅝, 1938 (4263/63) 4000
Garcia, Joaquin Torres, PAIVOS, 28⅝ x 23½, 1942 (4263/62) 6000
Gauguin, Paul (1848-1903), CROQUIS, 9 x 11½, mixed media (4140/10) 2100

Gauguin, Paul (1848-1903), ETUDE D'ENFANT, ca1884, 10½ x 8, mixed media (4228/12) 1800
Gauguin, Paul (1848-1903), VIOLONCELLISTE ET CROQUIS DE TETES, a double-, sided drawing,
11½ x 9, charcoal (4140/9) 2500
Gen Paul (b.1895), LE COURSE DE CHEVAUX, ca1948, 22⅞ x 29⅛, gouache (4096/72) 2500
Gen Paul (b.1895), LE DUET, 16½ x 12½, pastel (4164/64) 750
Gen Paul (b.1895), LE JOUEUR DE SAXOPHONE, 18⅝ x 13⅝, mixed media (4164/66) 1100
Gen Paul (b.1895), LE VIOLONISTE, 13¾ x 8⅝, oil on masonite (4164/67) 1700
Gen Paul (b.1895), LES COURSES A LONGCHAMP, 1952, 19½ x 25½, gouache (4164/65) 2000
Gen Paul (b.1895), MONTFORT L'AMAURY, ca1960-70, 19½ x 25½, gouache (4096/73) 2000
Gen Paul (b.1895), MOULIN ROUGE, 19½ x 25⅝, gouache (4140/85) 1800
Gernez, Paul-Elie (1889-1948), NUS SUR LA PLAGE, d.1925, 15 x 18¼ (4096/34) 2250
Gerzso, Gunther, EL MAGO, 1948, tempera, 13¼ x 17½ (4105/59) 3000
Gerzso, Gunther, MORADA, 1964, oil on canvas, 28¾ x 23¾ (4105/61) 5250
Gerzso, Gunther, PAISAJE AMARILLO, 1965, oil on canvas, 21½ x 32⅛ (4105/60) 6000
Giacometti, Alberto, ANNETTE DORMANT, 1946, pencil, 10⅞ x 14½ (4170/169) 3500
Giacometti, Alberto, DEUX ETUDES, A DOUBLE SIDED PORTRAIT, 1946, pencil, 19¾ x 12½
(4170/168) 4250
Giacometti, Alberto, LA MERE LISANT, A DOUBLE SIDED DRAWING, pencil, 19⅝ x 12⅞
(4170/167) 3500
Giacometti, Alberto, LAMP BASE, bronze, 61⅛ (4252/652) 4500
Giacometti, Alberto (1901-1966), BUST OF DIEGO, d.1953, H13¼ bronze (4260/1484) 77000
Giacometti, Alberto (1901-1966), DEUX SCULPTURES, 4½ x 5¼, ball-point pen (4140/36) 1100
Giacometti, Alberto (1901-1966), TETE DE PROFIL, 7¼ x 5½, pencil (4140/35) 1000
Giacometti, Alberto (1901-66), A PAIR OF MEDALLIONS, diam. 2½, bronze (4096/49) 1400
Giacometti, Alberto (1901-66), ETUDES DE TETES ET DE FIGURES, 10⅛ x 6½, pencil (4164/27) 1100
Giacometti, Alberto (1901-66), NU DEBOUT IV, 1953, H13⅛ (4124/78) 20000
Giacometti, Alberto, (1901-66), PIED DE LAMPE, ca1930-33, H59⅞, bronze (4173/534) *6500*

Giacometti
(4173/534)

Giacometti, Alberto, (1901-66), PIED DE LAMPE, ca1930-33, H19¼, bronze (4173/535) 5000
Giacometti, Alberto, (1901-66), TETE DE PIERRE LOEB, 9 x 7½, pencil (4125/175) 1200
Giacometti, Alberto, 1901-66, Swiss, PETIT MONSTRE, 1953, H4, bronze, green (4127/400) 9500
Giacometti, Diego, TABLE BASE, bronze, 15 x 16¼ x 44, 1945 (4252/653) 5250
Gilioli, Emilio, L'HOMME DE L'ESPACE, bronze, 34 (4263/132) 1500
Gilioli, Emilio (b.1911), COUPLE, H20½, bronze (4164/92) 500
Gilioli, Emilio (b.1911), LYS, H8½, polished bronze (4164/91) 750
Gilioli, Emilio (b.1911), SCULPTURE, H8¾, white marble (4204/112) 1000
Gilioli, Emilio (b.1911), SCULPTURE, H8¾, white marble (4228/128) 800

Gilioli, Emilio (b.1911), SCULPTURE, H14, marble (4173/573)	1500
Gilioli, Emilio (b.1911), SCULPTURE, H9½, polished bronze (4173/572)	1000
Gilioli, Emilio b.1911, LA COLOMBE, 6/6, H8½ (4127/406)	1400
Gilles, Joseph-Jean, FARM LANDSCAPE WITH HARVESTERS, 30 x 36 (691/64)	1200
Gilles, Werner (?), DER WURGENGEL AGNES, 1945, watercolor, 12 x 16¼ (4247/132)	1200
Gleizes, Albert (1881-1953), COMPOSITION ABSTRAIT, 1925-29, 11¾ x 2½, gouache (4172/391)	4000
Gleizes, Albert (1881-1953), ETUDE POUR 'FEMMES COUCHANT', d.1913, 16 x 13 (4172/321)	12500
Gleizes, Albert (1881-1953), VAUDEVILLE, BROADWAY, d.1916, 9¼ x 7⅜, mixed media (4172/325)	1100
Gleizes, Albert, (1881-1953), VAUDEVILLE, BROADWAY, 1916, 9¼ x 7⅜, ink (4125/137)	1300
Goldberg, Michael (b.1924), ROSES, 1965, 18 x 24 (666/70)	250
Gontcharova, Natalia (1881-1962), ABSTRACT COMPOSITION, ca1912, 12¾ x 9, pencil (4172/335)	1300
Gontcharova, Natalia (1881-1962), ABSTRACT COMPOSITION, ca1918-20, 11 x 7½, watercolor (4172/337)	1900
Gontcharova, Natalia (1881-1962), DEUX PERSONAGES FACE A FACE, d.1912, 14¼ x 10, mixed media (4172/313)	2000
Gontcharova, Natalia (1881-1962), FEMME GEOMETRIQUE, 1912, 14 x 10, mixed media (4172/314)	2750
Gontcharova, Natalia (1881-1962), FOREST POOL, 15¾ x 10, black crayon (4172/333)	1900
Gontcharova, Natalia (1881-1962), PURPLE SPHERES, ca1917, 12¼ x 8½, watercolor (4172/336)	1700
Gontcharova, Natalia (1881-1962), RAYONIST COMPOSITION, ca1912-13, 8¼ x 5¾, charcoal (4172/332)	1500
Gontcharova, Natalia, (1881-1962), HOMME AUX BRETELLES, 1918-20, 16 x 11⅜, watercolor (4125/145)	2250
Gonzalez, Julio (1881-1942), HOMME CACTUS NO. 2, ca1939-40, H30¼ (4124/80)	34000
Gonzalez, Julio, 1881-1942, PETITE DANSEUSE, 1935, 1/6, H6⅛, bronze, dark brown (4127/350)	2200
Gorky, Arshile, BULL IN THE SUN, A PRELIMINARY STUDY, mixed media, 22 x 28 (4250/505)	13500
Gourgue, Jean Enguerrand, BLACK MAGIC SYMBOLS, 49½ x 12 (691/10)	100
Gourgue, Jean Enguerrand, DUSK, BOATMAN SLEEPING, 23½ x 34½, on masonite (691/77)	600
Gourgue, Jean Enguerrand, EVENING, VILLAGE SCENE, 18 x 36 (691/27)	450
Gourgue, Jean Enguerrand, FIGURE STANDING IN FRONT OF HUT, 24 x 8, on masonite (691/9)	100
Gourgue, Jean Enguerrand, FIGURE STANDING NEAR THREE BOATS, 19¾ x 23½ (691/120)	375
Gourgue, Jean Enguerrand, FLOWER POTS, 16½ x 22, on masonite (691/69)	475
Gourgue, Jean Enguerrand, FUNERAL PROCESSION, 17½ x 47½, on masonite (691/117)	325
Gourgue, Jean Enguerrand, MARCHE, 1953, 24 x 36, on masonite (691/58)	1400
Gourgue, Jean Enguerrand, MYSTICAL LANDSCAPE, 28 x 36, on masonite (691/145)	700
Gourgue, Jean Enguerrand, STARVING CHILD, 24 x 16, on masonite (691/11)	250
Gourgue, Jean Enguerrand, VOODOO CEREMONY, 48 x 72 (691/112)	1400
Gourgue, Jean Enguerrand, ZOMBIS, ca1947, 16 x 19¾, on cardboard (691/59)	550
Grau Sala, Emilio (1911-75), CLOWN, 20½ x 8⅝, oil on panel (4140/91)	700
Grau Sala, Emilio (1911-75), GIRL WITH BOWL OF FRUIT AND PLAYING CARDS, 15 x 18⅛ (4140/93)	1500
Grau Sala, Emilio (1911-75), SCENE DE CIRQUE, 13 x 16⅛ (4140/92)	1600
Grau Sala, Emilio (1911-75), SCENE DE CIRQUE, 20⅛ x 14, mixed media (4140/90)	650
Grau Sala, Emilio (1911-75), JEUNE FILLE A LA NATURE MORTE, 13¼ x 16⅛ (4164/68)	2500
Grau Sala, Emilio (1911-75), LES DANSEUSES, 19¾ x 23⅞, mixed media (4164/69)	1400
Grau Sala, Emilio (1911-75), PORTRAIT DE JEUNE FEMME, d.1936, 35½ x 27½ (4204/52)	6500
Greenwood, Marion, MUJER PENSATIVA, gouache, 9¾ x 12⅞ (4105/22)	125
Gregoire, Alexandre, FAMILY ACTIVITY, 24 x 36, on masonite (691/84)	130
Gregoire, Alexandre, PLAYGROUND, 24 x 24, on masonite (691/28)	175
Gregoire, Alexandre, REST AND RECREATION, 24 x 36, on masonite (691/85)	170
Grigorieff, Boris D. (1866-1939), FACES OF RUSSIA, 1918-20, 19¾ x 22⅛, mixed media (4172/311)	2700
Gris, Juan (1887-1927), UNTITLED, 1905-12, 16⅛ x 12⅝, mixed media (4096/6)	2100
Gromaire, Marcel (1892-1971), NU ALLONGE, d.1950, 10⅛ x 13, mixed media (4228/60)	550
Gromaire, Marcel (1892-1971), NU ALLONGE, d.1952, 10 x 13, mixed media (4140/33)	*700*
Gromaire, Marcel (1892-1971), NU ASSIS, d.1947, 12⅞ x 10, mixed media (4096/45)	1400
Gromaire, Marcel (1892-1971), NU ASSIS, JAMBE REPLIE, d.1952, 32 x 25½ (4096/58)	10500
Gromaire, Marcel (1892-1971), NU DEBOUT, d.1924, 12¾ x 9⅞, pen, India ink (4096/44)	275
Gromaire, Marcel (1892-1971), PETITE NU SUR FOND GRENAT, d.1922, 13 x 16¼ (4096/57)	3250
Grosz, George, DAS DUELL, 1919, pen, ink, 14⅝ x 12 (4170/138)	3200
Grosz, George, ZWEI SIMPLE SCHAECHTER-HINDENBERG & NOSKE, 1920, brush, ink, 21¾ x 18⅛ (4170/137)	3250
Grosz, George (1893-1959), LIEGENDER AKT, ca1914-15, 15⅝ x 23⅛, mixed media (4228/59)	1600
Grosz, George, (1893-1959), JUDGES, 1912, 23 x 18, watercolor (4125/174)	8000
Gruber, Francis (1912-48), L'AMOUR ENDORMI, d.1942, 25½ x 32, oil on masonite (4140/65)	2800

Gruber (4140/63)

Gromaire (4140/33)

Gruber, Francis (1912-48), NATURE MORTE, L'ATELIER, d.1940, 51¼ x 32 (4140/66) 3300
Gruber, Francis (1912-48), NU AU DIVAN ROUGE, d.1948, 28¾ x 36¼ (4140/63) *2600*
Gruber, Francis (1912-48), VENUS ET L'AMOUR RENCONTRANT UNE DE LEUR, VICTIMES, d.1934, 39½ x 32 (4140/64) 1800
Guerin, Armand, PLACE DU TERTRE, PARIS, 21¼ x 25⅝ (4263/87) 400
Guerin, Armand (b.1913), L'ECHAFAUDAGE, 36 x 23⅝, oil on masonite (4228/72) 600
Guerin, Armand (b.1913), NOTRE DAME, 31¾ x 39¼, oil on masonite (4164/31) 400
Guillaumin, Jean Baptiste (1841-1927), ARBRES AU BORD DE LA MER, ca1903, 25⅝ x 21¼ (4225/200) 15000
Guillaumin, Jean Baptiste (1841-1927), BORDS DE RIVIERE, d.1901, 21½ x 25¾ (4225/220) 19000
Guillaumin, Jean Baptiste (1841-1927), LA CORNICHE A ST. PALAIS, ca1892, 15⅜ x 25⅜ (4225/180) 6500
Guillaumin, Jean Baptiste (1841-1927), PAYSAGE DE CROZANT, VALLEE DE LA FOLIE, ca1894, 28¾ x 36⅝ (4225/213) 20000
Guillaumin, Jean Baptiste (1841-1927), PAYSAGE, 1905, 21¼ x 23¾ (4096/19) 12250
Guillaumin, Jean Baptiste (1841-1927), LES ROCHES ROUGES A AGAY, ca1910, 10¾ x 13⅞ (4228/21) 4000
Guillaumin, Jean Baptiste (1841-1927), PAYSAGE DE PRINTEMPS, 24 x 29¼ (4228/25) 19000
Guillaumin, Jean Baptiste, (1841-1927), DAMIETTE, LES POMMIERS, 17 x 20½ (4173/514) 14000
Guillaumin, Jean Baptiste, (1841-1927), LE MOULIN DE BOUCHARDON, CROZANT, AU PRINTEMPS, ca1903, 25⅝ x 32 (4173/511) 30000
Guillaumin, Jean Baptiste, (1841-1927), LE PUY BARIOU A CROZANT, ca1903, 23⅞ x 29 (4173/509) 16000
Guillaumin, Jean Baptiste, (1841-1927), LE TRAYAS, MAI, 1907, 25⅝ x 32 (4173/510) 20000
Guillaumin, Jean Baptiste, (1841-1927), CROZANT, 20 x 24 (4127/307) 28000
Guillaumin, Jean Baptiste, (1841-1927), CHAUMIERE A CROZANT, 1900, 23¾ x 28⅞ (4124/60) 23000
Guys, Constantin (1805-92), FEMME AU FENETRE, 7¾ x 6½, mixed media (4228/2) 375
Guys, Constantin (1805-92), FEMME CORPULENTE, 11¼ x 7⅜, mixed media (4228/1) 700
Guys, Constantin (1805-92), UNE DAME, 5⅜ x 3⅞, watercolor (4096/1) 450
Hajdu, Etienne, JEUNE FILLE AU CHAPEAU, marble, 24¾, 1957 (4252/690) 7000
Hajdu, Etienne, TETE DE FEMME, slate, 25¾, 1965 (4252/691) 3000

Hartung, Hans (b.1904), COMPOSITION, 10½ x 7¾, black and yellow crayons (4228/126) — 700
Hartung, Hans (b.1904), UNTITLED, d.1960, 25½ x 19¾, charcoal (4164/89) — 1800
Hartung, Hans, (1904-), COMPOSITION, 1958, 19⅝ x 25¾, pastel (4125/191) — 3250
Hartung, Hans, (1904-), UNTITLED, 1960, 19 x 28¾, pastel, crayon (4125/194) — 2000
Hayden, Henri, 1883-1970, NATURE MORTE, 1917, 18¼ x 25¾ (4127/333) — 6500
Hayter, Stanley (b.1901), INTRODUCTION, 29⅛ x 34¼, oil on panel (4204/109) — 1900
Heckel, Erich (1883-1970), SELF-PORTRAIT, India ink, 1919, 18 x 12¼ (4247/76) — 2100
Heckel, Erich (1883-1970), SONNENBLUMEN, 1924, 25¾ x 21⅞, ink, wash, laid on board (4247/102) — 2750
Heckel, Erich, (1883-1970), ZWEI SCHLAFENDES, 18½ x 25⅞, watercolor (4125/135) — 6000
Helion, Jean, FIGURES JUMELLES, 50 x 65 (4252/663) — 23000
Helion, Jean (b.1904), COMPOSITION ABSTRAITE AU CARRE ROUGE, d.1932, 25½ x 19½ (4172/399) — 8500
Hepworth, Barbara, 1903-75, FIGURE (MERRYN), 1962, H13¾, alabaster (4127/403) — 14500
Hepworth, Barbara, 1903-75, SCULPTURE WITH COLORS & STRINGS, 1961, L9⅞, bronze, dark brown (4127/402) — 5250
Herbin, Auguste (1882-1960), NATURE MORTE AUX POISSONS, d.1937, 19¾ x 24 (4164/42) — 1100
Herbin, Auguste, (1882-1960), PREMIERE COMPOSITION SUR BOUCHE, 13¾ x 10⅜ (4125/154) — 2500
Hilbert, Jaro, SACRED LANDSCAPE, 9/1927, 27¼ x 34 (666/67) — 600
Hoech, Hannah (1889-1977), COMPOSITION, d.1923, 11½ x 7⅝, pen and India ink (4172/348) — 3300
Hofer, Carl (1878-1955), TWO STANDING MEN, pencil, 1928, 21¾ x 15⅛ (4247/46) — 1600
Hofmann, Hans, UNTITLED, oil on paper, 17 x 14 (4250/532) — 4000
Hyppolite, Hector, ST. JOHN SURROUNDED BY FLOWERS, before 1948, 30 x 24, on masonite (691/147) — 11500
Ipousteguy, Jean (b.1920), LE BON DIEU, d.1959, H16, bronze (4096/152) — 2200
Ipousteguy, Jean (b.1920), TORSE DE FEMME, H6½, bronze (4228/113) — 600
Jaenisch, Hans (b.1907), VERTIKALE BRECHUNG, 12½ x 7½, mixed media (4140/112) — 300
Jansem, Jean, STILL LIFE WITH PITCHERS, gouache, watercolor, ink, 21½ x 18 (4263/96) — 1200
Jansem, Jean (b.1920), CONVERSATION DANS LE PARC, 51 x 63½ (4140/97) — *2200*

Jansem
(4140/97)

Jansem, Jean (b.1920), DEUX JEUNES FILLES, 25⅝ x 39⅜ (4096/88) — 2600
Jansem, Jean (b.1920), LE MONDE, 10¾ x 6¼ (633/95) — 425
Jansem, Jean (b.1920), LE REPAS, 19⅝ x 25¾ (4140/96) — 1100
Jansem, Jean (b.1920), MERE ET ENFANT, 19¾ x 10 (4140/95) — 700
Jansem, Jean (b.1920), NATURE MORTE, d.1957, 45 x 68 (4096/89) — 6000
Jansem, Jean (b.1920), PORTRAIT OF AN OLD WOMAN, H3¾, bronze (633/96) — 200
Jansem, Jean (b.1920), SCENE DOMESTIQUE, 102½ x 55½ (4204/118) — 6500
Jansem, Jean (b.1920), VIEILLE FEMME, LES MAINS SUR LES HANCHES, d.1963, 57½ x 38 (4096/91) — 3500
Jawlensky, Alexej (1867-1941), HEAD (WARME DAMMERUNG), oil on board, 1933, 16⅞ x 13 (4247/55) — 33000
Jawlensky, Alexej (1867-1941), INNERES SCHAUEN, 1928, 16⅝ x 17⅞ (4124/65) — 21000
Jawlensky, Alexej (1867-1941), SCHMERZ, d.1927, 13¼ x 9¾ (4169/43) — 33000
Jawlensky, Alexej (1867-1941), HEAD, 1928, laid on board, 13⅜ x 10¼ (4247/67) — 30000
Joachim, Guy F., THE ARITHMETIC LESSON, 19¾ x 24, on masonite (691/36) — 275

John, Augustus, (1878-1961), THE MARCHESA ORIGO, ca1937, 20 1/16 x 14 Pencil (4260/1500) 2000

John, Augustus, SWEET WILLIAM, oil on board, 24⅛ x 20 (4252/642) 2000

John, Augustus (1878-1961), LADY OTTOLINE MORRELL, ca1908, 14⅜ x 11⅝ mixed media (4260/1494) 19000

John, Augustus (1878-1961), LINNERARIA IN A CLAY POT, ca1930, 39¾ x 32¼ (4260/1497) 17000

John, Augustus (1878-1961), PORTRAIT OF A LADY, 14 x 9 pencil (4260/1496) 2400

John, Augustus (1878-1961), PORTRAIT OF TRELAWNEY DAYREEL REED, ca1918, 24⅛ x 16⅛ (4260/1495) 34000

John, Augustus (1878-1961), SEATED NUDE, LIFE STUDY, 14⅝ x 11⅛ pencil (4260/1499) 1400

John, Augustus (1878-1961), SEATED NUDE, LIFE STUDY, 14⅞ x 11 pencil (4260/1498) 1400

John, Augustus (1878-1961), SELF PORTRAIT, ac1923, 35⅝ x 24½ oil on panel (4260/1501) 36000

John, Augustus (1878-1961), SELF PORTRAIT, ca1901, 4¼ x 3¾ pencil (4260/1493) 4000

John, Gwen (1876-1939), PORTRAIT OF ARTHUR SYMONS, early 1920s, 10⅜ x 10 charcoal (4260/1492) 3000

Jongkind, Johan Barthold (1819-91), LA MEUSE, 1868, 22¾ x 31¾ (4124/34) 40000

Kadar, Bela (1877-1956), CONSTRUCTION, ca1927, 23½ x 17¼, gouache (4172/392) 4000

Kadar, Bela (1877-1956), CONSTRUCTIVIST COMPOSITION, 1920-25, 26¾ x 20, gouache (4172/357) 4250

Kadar, Bela (1877-1956), MODEL WITH CAT, 40 x 27¼ (4172/389) 1900

Kadar, Bela (1877-1956), SELF-PORTRAIT, ca1928, 17⅞ x 13½, watercolor (4172/309) 1300

Kandinsky, Wassily, DUMPFES ROT, 1927, 26 x 30, 1927 (4249/281) 150000

Kandinsky, Wassily, DUNKEL ZACHEN, 1931, watercolor, ink, 15⅜ x 19⅝ (4170/144) 21000

Kandinsky, Wassily (1866-1944), KUHLE ENERGIE, d.1926, 23⅝ x 28¾ (4169/44) 150000

Kandinsky, Wassily (1866-1944), STUDY FOR AUF WEISS, watercolor, ink, 1920, 15⅜ x 20½ (4247/60) 77500

Kandinsky, Wassily (1866-1944), VERTICAL, d.1928, 19 x 12¾, mixed media (4172/386) 34000

Kandinsky, Wassily, (1866-1944), FROEHLICH, 1924, 13½ x 8⅞ (4125/150) 35000

Kandinsky, Wassily, (1866-1944), IMPROVISATION MIT PFERDEN, 1911, 28 x 38⅞ (4124/48) 365000

Kassak, Lajos (1887-1967), COMPOSITION FOR 'MA', 1921-22, 12¼ x 8¾, gouache (4172/349) 2100

Kaus, Max (1891-1977), COUPLE, 12½ x 13⅝, watercolor, laid, paper, 1921 (4247/78) 1400

Kienbusch, William (b.1914), CORRIDOR, PHAISTOS, casein on paper, 1959, 26¾ x 39 (666/69) 300

Kirchner, Ernst Ludwig, SHEET OF STUDIES, pen ink on paper, 9¼ x 13½ (4263/42) 1100

Kirchner, Ernst Ludwig (1880-1938), FIVE BATHERS (FEHMARN), 1912, 18 x 23¼, India ink, laid on paper (4247/77) 6000

Kisling, Moise, LANDSCAPE, 15 x 21¾, 1950 (4252/641) 16000

Kisling, Moise, PORT SCENE, 10⅞ x 16¼, ca1933 (4252/640) 7000

Kisling, Moise (1891-1953), BOUQUET DE FLEURS, 21½ x 14⅞ (4228/80) 12000

Kisling, Moise (1891-1953), BOUQUET DE PAVOTS, 21¾ x 15⅛ (4225/183) 16500

Kisling, Moise (1891-1953), JEUNE HOMME LISANT, ca1910, 30⅛ x 25¼ (4204/48) 2000

Kisling, Moise (1891-1953), NU ASSIS, 1919, 14½ x 10⅝ (4204/47) 7000

Kisling, Moise, (1891-1953), BOUQUET VARIE, 1918, 32 x 24 (4173/516) 16000

Kisling, Moise, (1891-1953), PAYSAGE PROVENCAL, 1918, 21¼ x 25⅝ (4173/515) 17000

Kisling, Moise, 1891-1953, Polish, BUSTE DE JEUNE FEMME, 1943, 16¼ x 13¼ (4127/361) 8250

Kisling, Moise, 1891-1953, Polish, LIS, 1943, 7 x 5⅝ (4127/360) 4000

Kisling, Moise, 1891-1953, Polish, NU ASSIS A LA DRAPERIE ROUGE, 1920, 21¾ x 18¼ (4127/359) 10000

Klee, Paul, ADAM UND EVCHEN, mixed media, 12⅜ x 8¾ (4170/141) 100000

Klee, Paul, BEGEGNUNG, 1929, brush, ink, 11⅞ x 17¾ (4170/143) 8750

Klee, Paul, BERG-WILD, A DOUBLE SIDED DRAWING, 1940, gouache, 12 x 18¾ (4170/145) 52500

Klee, Paul, BOTANISCHE SYMBOLE, on burlap, 7½ x 11¾, 1938 (4249/305) 50000

Klee, Paul, DIE KLAERUNG, 27½ x 37⅞, 1932 (4249/285) 435000

Klee, Paul (1879-1940), MIT DEM EINGANG, 1931, numbered S5, 17⅞ x 13¾ (4247/69) 72500

Klee, Paul (1879-1940), MYSTISCH PHYSIOGNOMISCH, numbered 31, watercolor on mount, 1924, 5¼ x 5¼ (4247/57) 33000

Klee, Paul (1879-1940), ROTES UND BLAUES X, laid on board, 1914, watercolor, gouache, 8 x 4¾ (4247/59) 37000

Klee, Paul (1879-1940), VOGELSAMMLUNG, numbered 28, laid on board, ink, watercolor, 1917, 7⅝ x 5½ (4247/56) 30000

Klee, Paul, (1879-1940) Swiss, DAS KIND, 1924, 8⅞ x 8¾ (4125/161) 7500

Kleinschmidt, Paul (1883-), LANDSCAPE, watercolor, 1938, 9⅞ x 7 (4247/79) 800

Kleinschmidt, Paul (b.1883), CIRCUS RIDER, watercolor, pencil, 1936, 22¼ x 17⅞ (4247/105) 900

Kleinschmidt, Paul (b.1883), COCKTAIL PARTY, 1934, 26 x 19, watercolor, laid on board (4247/104) 1200

Klimt, Gustav (1862-1918), HEAD OF AN OLD MAN, LIEBE study, pencil, ink, ca1894, 15 x 9½ (4247/48) 10500

Klimt, Gustav (1862-1918), KNEELING NUDE, pencil, 1901-2, 19⅛ x 12⅝ (4247/61) 3000

Klimt, Gustav (1862-1918), SEATED FEMALE FIGURE, pencil, crayon, 1906-8, 22 x 14½ (4247/62) 15000

Kliun, Ivan (1873-1943), ARCHITECTONIC COMPOSITION, ca1923, 5¾ x 5, mixed media (4172/352) 4000
Kliun, Ivan (1873-1943), COMPOSITION, d.1922, 11¼ x 9, watercolor (4172/353) 8750
Koch, Gerard, RECLINING FIGURE, ca1969, L28, bronze (4225/243) 1200
Kokoschka, Oskar (b.1886), PORTRAIT OF WOMAN, crayons, 1952, 18¾ x 23¾ (4247/121) 2750
Kokoschka, Oskar, (1886-) Austrian, BILDNIS EINER DAME, 1921, 27 x 20¼, waterclor (4125/136) 6250
Kolar, Jiri (b.1919), FLIEGENDER HOLLANDER, 16 x 12 x 5, chiasmage (4164/178) 1400
Kolar, Jiri (b.1919), LAGUNA, d.1968, 10¾ x 18½, collage (4164/177) 750
Kolbe, Georg (1876-1945), ALLEGRO, 1929, H28½ (4124/30) 10000
Kollwitz, Kathe, FRAU IM KRANKENBETT, 1920, charcoal, 24⅝ x 18¾ (4170/136) 5250
Kollwitz, Kathe, STUDIEN ZU IN DER SPRECHSTUNDE, 1920, pen, ink, 9¼ x 12⅝ (4170/135) 2200
Kollwitz, Kathe (1867-1945), DER ABSCHIED, 1940, H7, bronze (4096/56) 3750
Kollwitz, Kathe (1867-1945), DIE KLAGE, 1938, 10⅝ x 10, bronze relief (4096/55) 3600
Kollwitz, Kathe (1867-1948), DEATH WITH WOMAN IN LAP, 16⅝ x 23½, 1921, charcoal, laid paper (4247/49) 6000
Kollwitz, Kathe (1867-1948), PIETA, 1937-8, bronze, H15 (4247/52) 9000
Kollwitz, Kathe (1867-1948), SELF-PORTRAIT, foundry mark H. Noack Berlin, bronze, H14½, 1926-36 (4247/51) 6750
Krauskopf, Bruno (b.1892), RECLINING WOMAN, on pressed board, 19⅝ x 23¾ (4247/122) 250
Kremegne, Pinchus, PYRENEES ORIENTALES, 24 x 29¼ (4252/637) 4000
Kremegne, Pinchus (b.1890), DANS L'ATELIER, 32 x 25¾ (4164/30) 3100
Kromka, Frederico (1890-1942), CONSTRUCTIVIST COMPOSITION, d.1922, 8½ x 6½, watercolor (4172/356) 1100
Kupka, Frank (1871-1957), ETUDE 'POUR EQUATION DES BLEUS EN MOUVEMENT', 1929, 11¼ x 11⅛, gouache (4172/373) 8500
Kupka, Frank (1871-1957), LEVERS, 1929, 35⅝ x 43⅜ (4124/69) 55000
La Baptiste, Lucas, WOMEN WASHING IN A RIVER, 24 x 24, on masonite (691/21) 70
La Fortune, Felix, A LOA (?), D.1978, 23½ x 23½, on masonite (691/46) 120
Lachaise, Gaston, NUDE, pencil, 18 x 11⅞ (4250/427) 2300
Lam, Wifredo, UNTITLED, mixed media, 23¾ x 18 (4250/492) 4000
Lancaster, Mark (b.1938), 14TH STREET SERIES #11, d.1972, 34 x 50, mixed media (4164/134) 550
Lanskoy, Andre, LA NEIGE ROSE, 23¾ x 28¾, 1951 (4252/681) 4250
Lanskoy, Andre, LE NOEUD INVISIBLE, 39½ x 28½ (4252/682) 9500
Lanskoy, Andre (b.1902), LE CANAL, 21¼ x 32 (4164/59) 850
Lanskoy, Andre (b.1902), PAYSAGE DE NEIGE, 23½ x 31½ (4228/67) 2000
Lanskoy, Andre (b.1902), RUSH HOUR, 1955, 39½ x 29 (4096/99) 6000
Lardera, Berto, (b.1911), CATHEDRAL OF SORROW I, 1952-53, H39½, iron and copper (4173/565) 1600
Lardera, Berto, (b.1911), SPELL OF THE NIGHT I, d.1955, 37⅜ x 37⅜, iron, copper and wood (4173/567) 1000
Larionov, Mikhail (1881-1964), BAKERS, ca1907, 28½ x 23¾ (4172/303) 17500
Larionov, Mikhail (1881-1964), BLUE RAYONISM, 10¼ x 2, gouache (4172/331) 1100
Larionov, Mikhail (1881-1964), RAYONIST FIGURE, d.1907, 10⅜ x 7⅞, mixed media (4172/330) 1200
Larionov, Mikhail (1881-1964), VENUS, 1912, 22 x 29, tempera on burlap (4172/302) 12000
Latortue, Marie Claude, ANIMALS IN A LANDSCAPE, 24 x 48, on masonite (691/19) 425
Latortue, Marie Claude, JUNGLE SCENE, 30 x 40 on masonite (691/99) 275
Latortue, Philton, VILLAGE SCENE, 24 x 36, on masonite (691/81) 225
Laurencin, Marie, PORTRAIT OF A WOMAN SEATED, mixed media, 7⅛ x 4⅞ (4250/416) 1500
Laurencin, Marie, PORTRAIT OF A WOMAN WITH BROWN HAT, 17 x 14, 1937 (4252/635) 8000
Laurencin, Marie, PORTRAIT OF A YOUNG WOMAN, 25¾ x 21⅜ (4252/634) 33000
Laurencin, Marie, WOODLAND SCENE, 10⅝ x 16⅛, 1930 (4252/630) 21000
Laurencin, Marie, YOUNG BOY SEATED IN AN ARMCHAIR, DOUBLE-DRAWING, crayon, 6⅝ x 7¾ (4263/22) 1000
Laurencin, Marie, YOUNG WOMAN WITH A MANDOLIN, 13 x 16¼ (4252/636) 16000
Laurencin, Marie (1885-1956), JEUNE FEMME AU RUBAN ROSE, 23⅞ x 19¾ (4169/40) 37000
Laurencin, Marie (1885-1956), JEUNE FEMME AU RUBAN ROSE, d.1944, 16¼ x 13 (4096/31) 13500
Laurencin, Marie (1885-1956), JEUNE FEMME, d.1921, 18 x 14⅜ (4096/30) 11500
Laurencin, Marie, (1885-1956), JEUNES FILLES SUR LE BALCON, 57⅞ x 36⅜ (4173/519) 48000
Laurencin, Marie, (1885-1956), PORTRAIT DE JEUNE FILLE, 24¼ x 19⅞ (4173/517) 21000
Laurencin, Marie, (1885-1956), PORTRAIT DE JEUNE FILLE, ca1930, 16¼ x 13 (4173/518) 16000
Laurencin, Marie, 1885-1956, BUSTE DE JEUNE FEMME, 18⅛ x 15 (4127/344) 21000
Laurencin, Marie, 1885-1956, PORTRAIT DE JEUNE FEMME, 16⅛ x 13 (4127/343) 17000
Laurencin, Marie, 1885-1956, TROIS FEMMES DANS UN LOGE, 1949, 8½ x 10⅝ (4127/342) 16000
Laurens, Henri, HEAD, gouache and crayon, 11 1/l6 x 7⅜ (4250/438) 4200
Laurens, Henri (1885-1954), ETUDE DE FEMME, 13 x 9¾, pencil (4140/20) *350*
Laurens, Henri, (1885-1954), FEMME COUCHEE, 1920, 9 x 14, gouache (4125/142) 8000
Laurens, Henri, (1885-1954), FEMME DEBOUT A LA DRAPERIE AU BRAS LEVE, 1928, H14⅞, bronze (4173/531) 7500
Laurens, Henri, (1885-1954), LA PETITE NUIT, 1949, L9¼, bronze (4173/532) 7000

Laurent, Jean-Joseph, MAN WITH PIPE AND YOUNG GIRL ON A PATH, 24⅛ x 15, on masonite (691/38) — 170

Laurent, Jean-Joseph, MAN AND WOMAN DANCING, 24 x 16, masonite (691/37) — 80

Laurent, Jean-Joseph, SIX FIGURES IN A LANDSCAPE, 16 x 24, on masonite (691/131) — 300

Lazo, Augustin, CASERO Y ARBOLEDA, colored crayons, 10⅝ x 14¾ (4105/31) — 1000

Lazo, Augustin, LOS DESIGNIOS DE LA PROVIDENCIA, collage, 9¾ x 9⅞ (4105/54) — 1500

Lazo, Augustin, UNTITLED COMPOSITION, collage, 9¼ x 12 (4105/55) — 1500

Le Sidaner, Henri (1862-1939), LE PAVILLON DE MUSIQUE SOUS LA NEIGE A VERSAILLES, 29 x 23½ (4164/17) — 5250

Le Sidaner, Henri (1862-1939), MAISON SUR LA RIVIERE AU CLAIR-DE-LUNE, 1920, 29¼ x 36½ (4204/31) — 8000

Le Sidaner, Henri (1862-1939), NATURE MORTE AU PLAT D'ETAIN, 1931, 18½ x 22 (4204/32) — 2000

Le Sidaner, Henri, (1862-1939), LA MAISON DE CAMPAGNE, 26 x 32¼ (4173/513) — 16000

Le Sidaner, Henri, 1862-1939, L'EVECHE, 1903, 26 x 38 (4127/313) — 7000

Le Sidaner, Henri, 1862-1939, LA BOUTIQUE A CHARTRES, 1903, 11¾ x 14¾ (4127/311) — 3500

Le Sidaner, Henri, 1862-1939, LA CATHEDRAL A TREGUIER, 1913, 12¼ x 15⅜ (4127/312) — 3000

Le Sidaner, Louis, CREPUSCULE A NEMOURS, 25¾ x 32 (4252/621) — 13000

Lebasque, Henri, AMANDIERS EN FLEURS, COLLIOURE, 25 x 29¾, 1921 (4252/625) — 10000

Lebasque, Henri (1865-1937), LE CLOCHER, 1911, 25½ x 21¼ (4164/13) — 2800

Lebasque, Henri (1865-1937), LE JARDIN DE LAGNY, 1904, 26 x 21½ (4164/14) — 2400

Lebenstein, Jan (b.1930), AXIAL FIGURE #48, d.1960, 51 x 38 (4140/129) — 1200

Lebourg, Charles Albert (1849-1928), BORDS DU CANAL, ca1902, 29 x 20 (4204/14) — 2000

Lebourg, Charles Albert (1849-1928), LE MOULIN, d.1896, 26 x 20 (4228/14) — 3300

Lebourg, Charles Albert (1849-1928), MONTREUIL, LES ANCIENS REMPARTS, 16 x 25½ (4140/12) — *6500*

Laurens (4140/20)

Lebourg (4140/12)

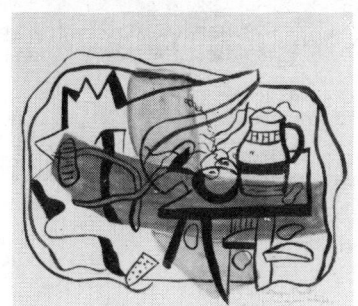

Leger (4250/467)

Lebourg, Charles Albert (1849-1928), NOTRE DAME ET LE PONT DE LA TOURNELLE, 12⅜ x 18⅜ (4204/17) — 2000

Lebourg, Charles Albert (1849-1928), PAYSAGE, 19¾ x 25⅝ (4228/22) — 2500

Leeb, Nat (b.1906), FORET DE CRISTAL, d.1937, 28¾ x 39⅜ (4172/397) — 10000

Leger, Fernand, COMPOSITION JAUNE, 21¼ x 25½, 1937 (4252/662) — 29000

Leger, Fernand, COMPOSITION WITH PITCHER AND FRUIT, mixed media, 22½ x 15¾ (4250/468) — 16000

Leger, Fernand, COMPOSITION, gouache and ink, 12⅞ x 14¾ (4250/467) — *8000*

Leger, Fernand, COMPOSITION, mixed media, 17¾ x 11⅞ (4250/471) — 5500

Leger, Fernand, LA DANSEUSE BLEUE, 28¾ x 34¼, 1928 (4249/282) — 80000

Leger, Fernand, LA FLEUR NOIRE, 25¾ x 21⅜, 1949 (4249/311) — 57500

Leger, Fernand, MARINE FORMS, A PAIR OF WATER COLORS, watercolor and pencil, 12 x 8½
(4250/441)   5750
Leger, Fernand, MARINE FORMS, A PAIR OF WATERCOLORS, watercolor and pencil, 8½ x 12
(4250/443)   5000
Leger, Fernand, MARINE, FORMS, A PAIR OF WATERCOLORS, watercolor and pencil, 8½ x 12
(4250/442)   5750
Leger, Fernand, PAYSAGE A L'ARBRE (CALIFORNIE), 16 x 20, 1940 (4252/661)   16000
Leger, Fernand, STUDY FOR LA FEMME AU COLLIER, 1921, crayon, 15 x 11 (4170/124)   12000
Leger, Fernand, UNE FIGURE ET UNE FLEUR, 19¾ x 25½, 1950 (4249/312)   40000
Leger, Fernand (1881-1955), COMPOSITION (LA DANSEUSE AU TRIANGLE JAUNE), d.1930, 25 x
21¾ (4169/50)   45000
Leger, Fernand (1881-1955), COMPOSITION A LA ROUE, 11½ x 9, mixed media (4204/56)   2500
Leger, Fernand (1881-1955), COMPOSITION A LECHELLE ET AUX FLEURS, 11 x 8½, mixed media
(4204/57)   2700
Leger, Fernand (1881-1955), ETUDE DE MAINS, d.1943, 11⅝ x 8¾, mixed media (4140/38)   1100
Leger, Fernand (1881-1955), FEMME ET ELEPHANTS, 1952, 10⅝ x 8⅜, mixed media (4225/208)   5750
Leger, Fernand (1881-1955), LES TRAPEZISTES, d.1953, 17½ x 22⅞, mixed media (4225/207)   23000
Leger, Fernand (1881-1955), NATURE MORTE, 1928, 36¼ x 25½ (4124/66)   65000
Leger, Fernand, (1881-1955), PERSONNAGES ET PERROQUET, 1951, 19¾ x 25⅝, gouache
(4125/155)   14000
Leloir, Maurice (1853-1940), VIEW FROM THE BALCONY, 37 x 20¾ (633/92)   1000
Lempicka, Tamara de (b.1898), NATURE MORTE AUX CITRONS, 13⅞ x 18 (4204/53)   1300
Lempicka, Tamara de (b.1898), NU DEBOUT, VU DE DOS, 18 x 14 (4204/50)   1300
Lentulov, Artistarkh (1882-1943), THE CHURCH, 11⅝ x 9¼, watercolor (4172/306)   3000
Leontus, Adam, BIRDS IN AN EXOTIC FOREST, 24 x 19¾, on masonite (691/79)   550
Leontus, Adam, LE MAGICIEN, 15½ x 19½, on masonite (691/18)   250
Lewis, Percy Wyndham (1882-1957), FROANNA - PORTRAIT OF THE ARTIST'S WIFE, d.1940,
19⅝ x 13 1/6 mixed media (4260/1502)   7800
Lhote, Andre (1885-1962), TETE D'HOMME, 19 x 12½, mixed media (4140/29)   850
Lhote, Andre, (1885-1962), MIRMANDE, 1925, 19¾ x 24 (4173/528)   *5750*
Lhote, Andre, 1885-1962, LA CUEILLEUSE DE SIMPLES, 1906, 31 x 25 (4127/327)   9000
Lhote, Andre, 1885-1962, LE CHATEAU, 1912, 18 x 15 (4127/326)   2700
Lieberman, Max, (1847-1935), LANDSCHAFT, 12 x 9¼, pastel (4125/107)   1500
Lipchitz, Jacques, RAPE OF EUROPA, bronze, dark brown patina, 15¾ x 20⅛, 1938 (4249/308)   20000
Lipchitz, Jacques, SKETCH FOR FIGURE, bronze, 9¾, 1926 (4252/645)   4000
Lipchitz, Jacques (1891-1973), PORTRAIT SKETCH, GERTRUDE STEIN, 1938, H11½, bronze
(4260/1480)   10000
Lissitzky, El (1890-1941), PROUN 4B, ca1920, 5⅜ x 4⅞, mixed media (4172/354)   26000
Lobo, Balthazar (b.1911), RECLINING NUDE, L8¾, bronze (4096/145)   750
Loiseau, Gustave, LE QUATORZE JUILLET A PARIS, LA RUE DE CLIGNANCOURT, 24¼ x 19⅞
(4252/620)   30000
Loiseau, Gustave (1865-1935), L'AVANT PORT DE DIEPPE, 1903, 18¼ x 21¾ (4204/22)   13000
Loiseau, Gustave (1865-1935), L'AVENUE DE ST-OVEN APRES LA PLUIE, d.1903, 21½ x 25⅝
(4204/18)   13000
Loiseau, Gustave (1865-1935), LA MAISON DU PECHEUR, 1927, 28¾ x 23¾ (4225/201)   14000
Loiseau, Gustave (1865-1935), PONT AVEN, LE MARCHE, d.1923, 28 1'/2 x 23½ (4169/34)   20000
Loiseau, Gustave, (1865-1935), RUE A SAINT LUNAIRE, 1904, 20¼ x 23½ (4124/20)   10000
Loiseau, Gustave, 1865-1935, PECHES, 1902, 11½ x 17 (4127/304)   2500
Lorjou, Bernard (b.1908), ALLEE DES ARBRES, 1955, 51½ x 38 (4096/90)   3500
Lorjou, Bernard (b.1908), NATURE MORTE, 13 x 21½ (4096/85)   1400
Lorjou, Bernard (b.1908), NATURE MORTE AUX FRUITS ET AU PICHET, 31 x 25⅝ (4140/108)   2100
Lorjou, Bernard (b.1908), NATURE MOTRE AU FAISAN, d.1957, 57 x 45 (4096/87)   5250
Lorjou, Bernard (b.1908), VASE DE TULIPES, 28½ x 21¼ (4096/86)   3500
Lucchesi, Bruno (b.1926), BOYS ON A SWING, H35, bronze (4164/49)   2000
Lucchesi, Bruno (b.1926), RECLINING WOMAN, L21, bronze (4228/114)   800
Lucchesi, Bruno (b.1926), WOMAN COMBING HER HAIR, H31½, bronze (4228/116)   1600
Lucchesi, Bruno (b.1926), WOMAN HOLDING A GOAT, H15, bronze (4228/115)   750
Luce, Maximilien, WOMAN SEWING, 12⅞ x 9⅝ (4252/618)   4500
Luce, Maximilien (1858-1941), BATHERS, 11¼ x 15⅝, mixed media (4260/1449)   1900
Luce, Maximilien (1858-1941), BORDS DE LA SEINE A MERICOURT, 21⅜ x 28¾ (4228/23)   4000
Luce, Maximilien (1858-1941), LA SEINE, 24 x 19⅝ (4124/61)   21000
Luce, Maximilien (1858-1941), OUVRIERS, 12⅞ x 19¾, oil on paper (4228/13)   1300
Luce, Maximilien (1858-1941), PORTRAIT OF HENRI EDMOND CROSS, 9¾ x 6¾, black crayon
(4260/1451)   1400
Luce, Maximilien (1858-1941), PORTRAIT OF PAUL SIGNAC, 8⅝ x 6¾, crayon (4260/1453)   1600
Lurcat, Jean (b.1892), LE DESERT, d.1936, 28¾ x 39½ (4096/62)   750
Lurcat, Jean (b.1892), NATURE MORTE AUX FRUITS, d.1927, 15¼ x 23, pastel on sandpaper
(4096/61)   450

Lurcat, Jean (б.1892), LA PECHEUSE AU FILET, d.1931, 12¼ x 9, qouache (4140/40)   425

Lurcat, Jean (b.1892), PAYSAGE SURREALISTE, 13¼ x 25¾, mixed media (4140/41)   *500*

Lurcat, Jean (B.1892), PAYSAGE SURREAVISTE, 32 x 45¾ (4140/46)   800

Maclet, Elisee, LA MAISON OU NAPOLEON EST DESCENDU A GOLFE-JUAN, 19¾ x 25¾, ca1926 (4263/36)   1800

Maclet, Elisee, LE MOULIN DANS LE MARQUIS, 18¼ x 21½ (4263/84)   2000

Maclet, Elisee, LE MOULIN ROUGE, 18¼ x 21½ (4263/85)   2000

Maclet, Elisee, STREET SCENE, 21½ x 18 (4263/86)   1500

Maclet, Elisee (1881-1962), LA MAISON DE BALZAC, 11⅞ x 14½, mixed media (4228/71)   900

Maclet, Elisee (1881-1962), LE PORT DE LA ROCHELLE, 12 x 14½, mixed media (4228/70)   550

Maclet, Elisee (1881-1962), LES BORDS DE LA BIEVRE, ca1920, 21¾ x 18⅛ (4228/69)   1300

Maclet, Elisee (1891-1962), LA RUE SAINT VINCENT, 1935, 18⅛ x 21½ (4096/26)   1600

Maclet, Elisee (1891-1962), LE MOULIN, 13¾ x 10¾ (4096/27)   1000

Maclet, Elisee (1891-1962), RUE ST. VINCENT, MONTMARTRE, 21¾ x 15 (4096/76)   2500

Magritte, Rene, FEUILLE D'ETUDES, A DOUBLE SIDED DRAWING, ballpoint pen, paper, 8 x 5¼ (4170/158)   1200

Magritte, Rene, L'ART DE LA CONVERSATION, 31⅞ x 24¼, 1961 (4249/296)   110000

Magritte, Rene, STUDY FOR LE SOURIRE DU DIABLE, gouache, 16½ x 11⅝ (4250/497)   16000

Magritte, Rene (1898-1967), CECI N'EST PAS UNE PIPE, 1928-29, 23⅝ x 32 (4124/70)   115000

Magritte, Rene (1898-1967), L'EVIDENCE ETERNELLE, 1930, 8¾ x 6⅜, 8¾ x 4½(4124/72)   135000

Magritte, Rene, (1898-1967), L'ENJOLEUSE, 1946, 19¾ x 13¾, gouache (4125/164)   30000

Maillol, Aristide, LES DEUX LUTTEUSES, bronze, dark brown, mottled, green patina, 7½, 1900 (4249/234)   16000

Maillol, Aristide (1861-1944), FEMME ASSISE, 1910, H7¾, terra cotta (4204/40)   7000

Maillol, Aristide (1861-1944), NUDE, BENDING TO THE RIGHT, 11⅝ x 9¼, sanguine (4260/1470)   4000

Maillol, Aristide (1861-1944), STUDY FOR 'LA MEDITERRANEE', L7½ H 6¾, terra cotta (4260/1469)   6000

Maillol, Aristide (1861-1944), TORSE DE FEMME, 12 x 8⅞, charcoal (4140/6)   *800*

Lhote   (4173/528)

Maillol, Aristide, (1861-1944), EVE A LA POMME, 1899, H22⅝, bronze (4173/503)   25000

Malevich, Kasimir (1879-1935), CONGRESS OF COMMITTEES OF PEASANT POVERTY, 1918, 17¾ x 12¾, lithograph (4172/341)   19000

Malevich, Kasimir (1879-1935), SUPREMATIST COMPOSITION, ca1917-20, 6½ x 4⅜, pencil (4172/338)   1900

Malevich, Kasimir (1879-1935), SUPREMATIST COMPOSITION, 1916, 7¼ x 9⅛, pencil (4172/340)   8500

Mandel, Lydia (d.1976), ABSTRACT COMPOSITION, 1922, 10½ x 7, watercolor (4172/339)   450

Mane-Katz, HORSES, 36 x 29, ca1955-60 (4252/639)   9500

Mane-Katz, VILLAGE STREET SCENE, 20 x 24 (4252/638)   6250

Mane-Katz, 1894-1962, DEUX MUSICIENS, 13⅞ x 10⅝ (4127/357)   5250

Mane-Katz, 1894-1962, TROIS MUSICIENS, 39 x 32 (4127/358)   15000

Manessier, Alfred (b.1911), LA PASSION, d.1949, 12⅞ x 9⅞, oil on paper (4096/103)   1000

Manessier, Alfred, b.1911, LE TORRENT I, 1959, 38 x 51 (4127/396)   4500

Mansouroff, Paul (b.1896), CONTRASTING FORMS, d.1928, 8¼ x 5¼, mixed media (4172/377)   700

Mansouroff, Paul (b.1896), MOON IN TRIANGLE, d.1928, 8¼ x 5¼, mixed media (4172/378)	1000
Manzu, Giacomo, CARDINALE, bronze, golden brown patina, 93, 1950-72 (4249/318)	65000
Manzu, Giacomo (b.1908), SEDIA CON ARAGOSTA, 1966, H47, bronze (4225/219)	15000
Manzu, Giacomo (B.1908), CARDINALE SEDUTO, 1964, H19, bronze (unique) (4169/52)	31000
Manzu, Giacomo (1908-), CARDINALE, 1958, H12¾ (4124/83)	25000
Manzu, Giacomo, (1908-), CRUCIFIXION WITH CENTURION, 1942, 27½ x 19⅛, ink (4125/172)	1500
Manzu, Giacomo, (1908-), STANDING NUDE & KNEELING FIGURE, 26⅞ x 19¼, ink (4125/173)	1200
Marchand, Andre, LE SOLEIL QUI SOMBRE, 18⅛ x 21⅝, 1948 (4263/94)	800
Marchand, Jean Hippolyte (1883-1940), NATURE MORTE DEVANT UNE PORTE OUVERTE, 31¾ x 21⅛ (4204/55)	1000
Marcks, Gerhard (b.1889), Cenerentola, numbered IV, bronze, 1941, H16 (4247/125)	5250
Marcks, Gerhard (b.1889), Zopfhaltende, 1938, bronze, H21½ (4247/126)	5000
Marcks, Gerhard (1889-1965), KLEINE STEHENDE, RECHTE HAND AUF DER BRUST, 1960, H16⅜, bronze (4164/50)	2600
Marcoussis, Louis, LA GUITARE, oil on panel, 37½ x 16¾, 1922 (4252/659)	14000
Marcoussis, Louis, THE BOTTLE OF MARC, 25¾ x 36⅜, 1928 (4252/660)	11000
Marcoussis, Louis (1883-1941), DEUX HOMMES AU CAFE, d.1930, 6⅜ x 8¼, mixed media (4140/39)	1900
Marini, Marino, HORSE AND RIDER, ink and gouache, 17¼ x 14 (4250/502)	*1500*
Marini, Marino, PORTRAIT OF GASPAR DE MIGUEL, bronze, 10¾ (4252/650)	3500
Marini, Marino, RIDER ON HORSE, 1952, brush, ink, pastel, 24½ x 17 (4170/179)	6000
Marini, Marino, SMALL FIGURE, bronze, 12⅞, ca1942-45 (4252/646)	8000
Marini, Marino (b.1901), LA MODELLA, d.1928, 18⅛ x 22, mixed media (4164/26)	900
Marini, Marino (b.1901), THE DANCER, 15 x 10⅞, mixed media (4260/1482)	1500
Marini, Marino, (b.1901), CAVALLO, H15¼, bronze (4173/564)	12500
Marino, Marini, (1901-), CAVALLO E CAVALIERE, 1947, 20⅛ x 15⅛, gouache, pastel (4125/168)	4500
Marquet, Albert (1875-1947), BY THE BANKS OF THE RIVER, ca1900, 6½ x 9¾, mixed media (4260/1456)	4000
Marquet, Albert (1875-1947), ETUDES DE NU, A DOUBLE-SIDED DRAWING, 10¾ x 6⅛, mixed media (4164/12)	350
Marquet, Albert (1875-1947), FEMMES ASSISES, LE BASIN D'ARCACHON, ca1895, 8½ x 10⅝, oil on panel (4260/1457)	8000
Marquet, Albert (1875-1947), HEAD OF A WOMAN, ca1900, 8 x 7½, oil on panel (4260/1458)	2800
Marquet, Albert (1875-1947), VUE DE LA MEDITERANEE, 13 x 16 (4096/23)	5750
Martin-Ferrieres, Jac (1893-1972), LE PORT, d.1918, 15 x 18¼, oil on panel (4228/31)	1800
Martin, Henri, YOUNG WOMAN SEATED ON A BED, oil on burlap, 36⅜ x 28¾ (4252/617)	10000
Martin, Henri (1860-1943), LA FEMME DE L'ARTISTE, 17¾ x 21¼ (4204/34)	4750
Martin, Henri (1860-1943), LA PERGOLA, 26¼ x 28¼, oil on panel (4204/34)	5250
Martin, Henri (1860-1943), LE SULPHATEUR DE RAISINS, 35½ x 21¼ (4204/33)	6500
Martin, Henri, (1860-1943), JEUNE FILLE AU CHAPEAU, 16⅛ x 13¼ (4173/507)	*7000*
Martin, Henri, 1860-1943, LE PORT DE COLLIOURE, 1904, 12⅝ x 16¼ (4127/309)	2800
Martinez, Ricardo, DOS PERSONAJES, 1961, oil on canvas, 33½ x 45¼ (4105/93)	6500
Martinez, Ricardo (b.1892), CARA MAYA, d.1960, 11¾ x 9⅞ (4096/124)	850
Masereel, Frans (b.1889), GREEN SMOKESTACK, 1929, 28¾ x 36¼ (4247/110)	3000
Masson, Andre, LES POISSONS, 15 x 21½, 1923 (4252/656)	11000
Masson, Andre, MOUVEMENT, pastel on canvas, 25¾ x 19¾ (4250/493)	5000
Masson, Andre (b.1896), LES METEORES, 1925, 28¾ x 21¼ (4172/381)	25000
Masson, Andre (b.1896), SEATED FIGURE, 14¾ x 11, mixed media (4228/122)	1300
Masson, Andre (b.1896), SORTIE DE BAIN, d.1946, 33 x 27 (4140/68)	*7000*
Masson, Andre (1896-), CORTEGE D'INSECTES, 1934, 27½ x 39½ (4124/76)	45000
Masson, Andre, (b.1896), AUGURING SIBYL, 31⅞ x 37⅛, oil and sand on canvas (4173/552)	31000
Mathieu, Georges, MATIN DE SOLEIL, 1963, mixed media, 22½ x 30¼ (4170/164)	1700
Mathieu, Georges (b.1921), COMPOSITION (RED AND WHITE ON BLACK), 38 x 51 (4164/83)	6000
Mathieu, Georges (b.1921), COMPOSITION, d.1957, 38¼ x 51¼ (4096/108)	15500
Matisse, Henri (1869-1954), FAUNE DANSANT, ca1907, 5 x 4¾, ceramic tile (4204/36)	3000
Matisse, Henri (1869-1954), MIMOSA, 58 x 36¼, wool tapestry (4096/136)	3000
Matisse, Henri (1869-1954), MIMOSA, 58½ x 36, wool tapestry (4164/78)	2300
Matisse, Henri (1869-1954), NATURE MORTE AUX POMMES, 15⅜ x 18½ (4124/21)	60000
Matta, COMPOSITION, pencil, 9⅛ x 12¾ (4250/488)	2000
Matta, L'ORIENT, 40⅛ x 37, 1968 (4252/683)	10000
Matta, SUN, TARGET, 1937, crayons, pencil, 9¾ x 12⅞ (4170/162)	4250
Matta, UNTITLED, Pencil and crayon, 9½ x 12¼ (4250/487)	2500
Matta, UNTITLED, pencil and crayon, 14⅜ x 19⅜ (4250/489)	3250
Matta, UNTITLED, pencil and crayon, 22 x 27¾ (4250/490)	5000
Matta, b.1911, Chilean, COMPOSITION, 1955, 16⅜ x 14½, watercolor (4127/388)	2400
Maufra, Maxime (1861-1918), LE MATIN, L'OUED D'EL KANTARA, d.1913, 29 x 36½ (4164/15)	3700

Masson (4140/68)

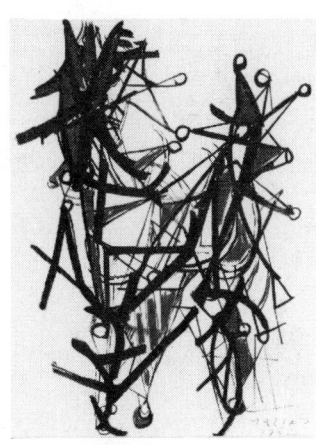

Marini (4250/502)

Martin (4173/507)

Maufra, Maxime (1861-1918), PRINTEMPS AU BORD DU CRACH (BRETAGNE), d.1911, 29 x 36¼
(4225/187)   8500
Maufra, Maxime, 1861-1918, APRES-MIDI A PORT-MARIN, LES ANDELYS, 1902, 21½ x 28¾
(4127/306)   5600
Menkes, Sigismund (b.1896), COUNTRY ROAD, 25½ x 32 (666/51)   850
Menkes, Sigismund (b.1896), YOUNG GIRL IN A LACE DRESS, 32 x 25¾ (666/54)   1700
Merelus, C., HAITIAN VILLAGE SCENE, before 1949, 16 x 20, on cardboard (691/54)   160
Merida, Carlos, COMPOSITION IN BLUE, gouache with pencil, 8¾ x 5½, 1949 (4263/83)   1600
Merida, Carlos, DIALOGO SILENTE, 1968, mixed media, masonite, 17¼ x 13 (4105/57)   6750
Merida, Carlos, FLOTANDO EN EL ESPACIO, 1948, gouache, pencil, 16½ x 12½ (4105/56)   1900
Merida, Carlos, LA REINA XIL, 1961, casein on parchment, 24 x 18 (4105/58)   11500
Merida, Carlos, b.1891, Guatemalan, 1964, 19 x 14½, gouache (4127/393)   2700
Messagier, Jean (b.1920), A MEME LA MER, 1955, H14, bronze (4164/98)   700
Metzinger, Jean, 1883-1956, LA FENETRE DANS LE MIROIR, ca1925, 21¾ x 15 (4127/334)   3000
Meza, Guillermo, ARRIEROS SOMOS, 1944, oil on canvas, 19⅞ x 23¾ (4105/50)   2500
Meza, Guillermo, MUJER CON PANUELO, 1941, oil on canvas, 23¾ x 23¾ (4105/37)   1400
Meza, Guillermo, SEATED FIGURE OF A MAN, 1962, pastel, 36 x 26½ (4105/94)   1000
Meza, Guillermo, SURREALIST STREET SCENE, gouache, 18 x 15¼ (4105/51)   500
Michel, Charles (1763-1843), LA RADE DE PERROS, COTES DU NORD, 13 x 16, oil on board
(4228/27)   1000
Michel, Robert (b.1897), THE BLACK OPA YALE, d.1927, 13¾ x 16¾, mixed media (4172/375)   2000
Minaux, Andre (b.1923), VASE DE FLEURS, 1953, 25⅝ x 19⅝ (4096/95)   1100
Miro, Joan, COMPOSITION, pencil, 9⅛ x 6 (4250/477)   6750
Miro, Joan, COMPOSITION, 21¼ x 15¾, 1968 (4263/137)   5800
Miro, Joan, COMPOSITION, burlap, 19¾ x 24⅛, 1927 (4249/286)   35000
Miro, Joan, COMPOSITION, on sandpaper, 14⅛ x 9, 1935 (4249/303)   26000

Miro, Joan, LES DEUX SOEURS JUMELLES NUES DANS LA FORET A, L'HEURE DU CREPUSCULE, 23¾ x 25½, 1931 (4249/288)　115000

Miro, Joan, PERSONNAGE DEVANT LA LUNE, on burlap, 12½ x 5, 1944 (4249/304)　31000

Miro, Joan (b.1893), DESIGNS FOR A POEM BY RUTHVEN TODD, d.1970, 15½ x 10¾, mixed media (4204/100)　1500

Miro, Joan (b.1893), DESIGNS FOR A POEM BY RUTHVEN TODD, d.1970, 15½ x 10⅞, mixed media (4204/102)　1300

Miro, Joan (b.1893), DESIGNS FOR A POEM BY RUTHVEN TODD, d.1970, 15½ x 11, mixed media (4204/101)　1000

Miro, Joan (b.1893), PERSONNAGES IMAGINAIRES II, 1956, 12⅜ x 9¼, mixed media (4096/131)　3300

Miro, Joan (1893-), LA PORTE (OBJET), 1931, 44⅞ x 28¾ (4124/71)　145000

Miro, Joan, (b.1893), COMPOSITION, d.1956, 7¾ x 9¾, mixed media (4173/550)　6500

Miro, Joan, (1893-), COMPOSITION ABSTRAIT, 1957, 14¾ x 11⅛, mixed media (4125/188)　3250

Miro, Joan, (1893-), PERSONNAGE, 1936, 16¼ x 12⅞ (4125/162)　3600

Miro
(4125/162)

Miro, Joan, (1893-), PERSONNAGES, 1949, (4125/163)　3750

Miro, Joan, b.1893, COMPOSITION, 1959, 16¼ x 12½, crayons, paper (4127/390)　2600

Modersohn-Becker, Paula, 1876-1907, OSTFRIESLAND, 1902, 20¾ x 15¾, on board (4127/328)　11000

Modigliani, Amadeo, NU AU DIVAN, 1909, Crayon, paper, 16⅞ x 10½ (4170/113)　10000

Modigliani, Amadeo, TETE DE FEMME AU CHAPEAU, 1907, watercolor, crayon, 13⅞ x 10⅝ (4170/111)　11000

Modigliani, Amedeo, CARYATID, watercolor, 24½ x 17⅛ (4250/430)　67500

Modigliani, Amedeo, MINOUTCHA, 21¾ x 13, ca1917 (4249/250)　210000

Modigliani, Amedeo, PORTRAIT OF A WOMAN, mixed media, 12 x 9 (4250/423)　19000

Modigliani, Amedeo (1884-1920), PORTRAIT OF M. KOHLER, ca1908-09, 17 x 10½, mixed media (4260/1471)　15500

Modigliani, Amedeo (1884-1920), PORTRAIT OF MICHEL, ca 1916, 16¾ x 10⅛, sepia ink (4260/1472)　3500

Modigliani, Amedeo (1884-1920), TESTA DI DONNA, 16⅛ x 10⅝ (4169/48)　100000

Modigliani, Amedeo, (1884-1920), PORTRAIT DE GARCON, DOUBLE SIDED DRAWING, 8½ x 7¼, pencil (4125/132)　3500

Moholy-Nagy, Laszlo, COMPOSITION, mixed media, 4 x 8½ (4250/508)　1400

Moholy-Nagy, Laszlo (1895-1946), COMPOSITION, d.1941, 8⅝ x 11, mixed media (4204/107)　1700

Moholy-Nagy, Laszlo (1895-1946), UNTITLED, 11 x 15, mixed media (4172/358)　2100

Mondrian, Piet (1872-1944), GEIN FARMHOUSE III, 1905, 15¾ x 18⅝ (4124/53)　16000

Montenegro, Roberto, ESCULTURA, 1949, brush, ink, 19⅞ x 13⅛ (4105/35)　700

Montenegro, Roberto, THE MOURNING, 1946, ink, colored washes, 12½ x 19¼ (4105/38)　600

Monti, Cesare (1891-1952), LA PLUMA VERDE, d.1932, 28½ x 19½ (633/86)　600

Moore, Henry, FOUR SEATED FIGURES, mixed media, 12⅞ x 21¾ (4250/501)　25000

Moore, Henry, HEADS, FIGURES, FORMS, AND WOMEN WITH CHILDREN, watercolor and ink, 8⅝ x 6¼ (4250/500)　13500

Moore, Henry, RECLINING FIGURE, bronze, gold patina, W8½, 1939 (4249/300)　33000

Moore, Henry, SQUARE HEAD, bronze, 11, 1960 (4252/676)　8500

Moore, Henry, UNTITLED, 1939, mixed media, 12⅛ x 19½ (4170/171)	16000
Moore, Henry, UPRIGHT MOTIVE A, bronze, 11¼, 1968 (4252/675)	9250
Moore, Henry, WOMAN SEATED, 1959, charcoal, pink crayon, 11⅜ x 9⅝ (4170/172)	7500
Moore, Henry, WORKING MODEL FOR TWO PIECE RECLINING FIGURE POINTS, bronze, golden brown patina, 48 x 30¾, 1969-70 (4249/322)	115000
Moore, Henry (b.1898), SEATED NUDE and STANDING NUDE, double-sided, d.1925, 16½ x 11, mixed media (4096/47)	2500
Moore, Henry (b.1898), WOMAN, 1961, H7, bronze (4204/114)	3750
Moore, Henry (1898-), SEATED WOMAN IN CHAIR, 1956, H10⅞ (4124/31)	42000
Moore, Henry, (b.1898), HALF FIGURE, 1952, H6¾, bronze (4173/559)	7000
Moore, Henry, (b.1898), SMALL HEAD, STRATA, 1960, H4¾, bronze (4173/558)	4000
Moore, Henry, (b.1898), TWO PIECE RECLINING FIGURE, MAQUETTE NO. 5, 1962, L6, bronze (4173/560)	8000
Moore, Henry, (1898-), RECLINING FIGURES, 1841, 14¼ x 21⅝ (4125/171)	10000
Moore, Henry, b.1898, FAMILY GROUP, 1944, H6⅜, bronze, dark brown (4127/377)	40000
Moore, Henry, b.1898, TIME/LIFE SCREEN, 1952, L12¾, bronze, green (4127/401)	9000
Morandi, Giorgio, NATURA MORTA, 11⅞ x 17¾, 1958 (4249/310)	47500
Morandi, Giorgio, STILL LIFE, watercolor and pencil, 6½ x 8¼ (4250/514)	7500
Morandi, Giorgio, STILL LIFE, watercolor and pencil, 6⅜ x 8¼ (4250/515)	6500
Moret, Henry (1856-1913), UN VALON PRES DE PONT-AVEN, d.1901, 24 x 29 (4204/15)	4250
Morris, Robert (b.1931), untitled, mixed media, 12 x 9 (666/68)	1400
Mucha, Alphonse (1860-1939), HEAD OF A WOMAN, d.1908, 23 x 14, blue pencil (4096/7)	1100
Music, Antonio (b.1909), CAVALLI E CAVALIERI, 8¾ x 12¾, mixed media (4164/75)	500
Nadelman, Elie, HEAD IN PROFILE NO.2, pen and ink, 7¾ x 3 (4250/426)	500
Nadelman, Elie, MOTHER AND CHILD, pen and ink, 7⅛ x 5⅞ (4250/425)	1500
Nadelman, Elie, SUPPLIANT FEMALE NUDE, pen and ink, 11 x 4¾ (4250/424)	1000
Nadelman, Elie (1882-1946), HEAD OF A WOMAN, 12⅜ x 7⅞, sepia ink (4260/1473)	1900
Nemerov, Renee (b.1903), EMERGENCE, ca1967, H67, bronze (4225/236)	1000
Nicholson, Ben, RUM BOTTLE & GOBLET, 1953, oil wash, pencil, 19⅛ x 10¾ (4170/173)	13000
Niermann, Leonardo, untitled, dated 1963, on masonite, 24 x 32 (666/52)	650
Noguchi, Isamu, WEDLOCK, marble, 13½ x 11¼, 1967 (4252/692)	9500
Nolde, Emil, HALLIGLANDSCHAFT, 1919, watercolor, ink 13 x 18½ (4170/140)	24000
Nolde, Emil (1867-1956), TWO WOMEN, watercolor, 8¼ x 6¾ (4247/70)	24000
Nolde, Emil (1867-1956), TWO WOMEN, 23 x 18, watercolor, gouache, 1925 (4247/98)	75000
Normil, Andre, PATIENCE, 36½ x 24 (691/12)	1800
Normil, Andre, THE DICE GAME, before 1954, 16 x 20, on masonite (691/87)	400
Noyer, Philippe (b.1917), MODEL IN THE STUDIO, d.1967, 25½ x 21 (633/93)	950
O'Gorman, Juan, RECUERDO DE CUERNAVACA, 1943, tempera on masonite, 12⅝ x 23⅝ (4105/34)	7250
Obin, Auguste, FESTIVAL OF FRUITS AND FLOWERS, before 1960, 15¾ x 20, on masonite (691/96)	250
Obin, J.M., LE SNEM EN ACTION CHEZ BOSS DJO, d.1946, 20 x 24, on masonite (691/94)	110
Obin, Philome, DESSALINES ET BOISRONDTONNERRE, d.1971, 23½ x 29¼, on masonite (691/133)	1700
Obin, Philome, LES CACOS DE LECONTE JUILLET, 1911, d.1946, 24 x 36, on bagasse board (691/80)	5250
Obin, Philome, PAYSANS SUR LA ROUTE DE QUARTIER-MORIN, d.1971, 23½ x 29, on masonite (691/132)	1700
Obin, Philome, UN CORDIAL ENTRETIEN ENTRE BOTTEX ET MONDESIR, 1901, d.1970, 23½ x 29¼, on masonite (691/135)	1900
Obin, Seneque, MARCHE POISSONS, before 1957, 16¾ x 21, on masonite (691/121)	2100
Obin, Telemaque, FAMILY ACTIVITY, 20 x 24, on masonite (691/2)	350
Obin, Telemaque, HAITIAN VILLAGE SCENE, 20 x 24 on masonite (691/71)	200
Obin, Telemaque, MENAGE CREOLE, ca1974, 20 x 24, on masonite (691/66)	325
Orozco, Jose Clemente, DRAWING FROM 'LOS TEVLES', 11⅜ x 14½, gouache (4096/125)	1800
Orozco, Jose Clemente, EL ENTIERRO, mixed media, 14⅛ x 18⅞ (4105/39)	9000
Orozco, Jose Clemente, STRIKE, brush, ink, 12⅛ x 17⅛ (4263/74)	1800
Orozco, Jose Clemente, STUDY OF ARMS AND TORSO, charcoal on paper, 18 x 26¼ (4263/76)	800
Orozco, Jose Clemente, STUDY OF ARMS, charcoal on paper, 18½ x 23½ (4263/73)	700
Orozco, Jose Clemente (1883-1949), DIABLOS, d.1945, 17⅝ x 11⅝, pen, India ink (4096/120)	1300
Orozco, Jose Clemente (1883-1949), GRUPO DE FIGURAS, d.1945, 11⅝ x 17½, pen, India ink (4096/121)	900
Orozco, Jose Clemente (1883-1949), LA PIE, DETAIL STUDY FOR A MURAL, 15⅝ x 10, mixed media (4204/83)	500
Otto, Waldemar, EVE 64, 1964, H60, bronze (4225/241)	1600
Oudot, Roland (b.1897), MOISSON DANS L'EURE, 25¾ x 36¼ (4164/34)	1500
Paalen, Wolfgang, VENT D'EST, 16¼ x 13, 1937 (4263/78)	3800

Paolozzi, Edouardo (b.1924), BLACK DEVIL, 1957, H18¾, bronze (unique) (4096/151) 1400
Paolozzi, Edouardo (b.1924), MONKEY EATING A NUT, 1956, H17, bronze (unique) (4096/150) 1000
Pascin, Jules, CREOLE FAMILY, watercolor, 8 1/16 x 7⅞ (4250/433) *1500*
Pascin, Jules, DEUX FEMMES NUES, 29½ x 24¼, ca1919 (4249/251) 25000
Pascin, Jules, ELIENA KRYLENKO, 38 x 25¼, ca1927-28 (4249/257) 48000
Pascin, Jules, FOUR WOMEN IN AN INTERIOR, pen and ink, 10¾ x 10¾ (4250/431) 1500
Pascin, Jules, JEUNE FEMME SE CHAUSSANT, 25⅜ x 21⅜, ca1916 (4249/247) 23000
Pascin, Jules, ON THE BEACH, pen and ink, 6½ x 8¼ (4250/432) 1500
Pascin, Jules, STANDING FEMALE NUDE IN PROFILE, pencil, 12½ x 8 (4263/15) 325
Pascin, Jules, STANDING FEMALE NUDE, brush, ink, paper, 12½ x 8 (4263/16) 550
Pascin, Jules (1885-1930), NU ASSIS, 12½ x 8, mixed media (4164/22) 300
Pascin, Jules (1885-1930), THE CARD GAME, panal on paper, 6 x 9 (666/47) 600
Pascin, Jules (1885-1930), YOUNG WOMAN WITH A BLACK BOW TIE, ca1914, 12⅝ x 10, mixed media (4260/1478) 9500
Pattison, Abbott, BOUNTIFUL HARVEST, ca1966, H72, bronze (4225/235) 3000
Pattison, Abbott, THE FRUIT PICKERS, ca1966, H55, bronze (4225/237) 2200
Pattison, Abbott, THE SWIMMERS, ca1966, L32, bronze (4225/242) 600
Paupelet, Jane, ROOSTER, H6½ bronze (4260/1489) 750
Pechstein, Max (1881-1955), BICYCLE RACE, 5¼ x 8⅛, crayon, ink, laid on paper (4247/84) 1600
Pechstein, Max (1881-1955), BOXING MATCH, watercolor, 1910, 6½ x 8¼ (4247/83) 1600
Pechstein, Max (1881-1955), CABARET SCENE, watercolor, pencil, 6½ x 7⅞ (4247/86) 2000
Pechstein, Max (1881-1955), CAFE SCENE, watercolor, pencil, 1910, 6⅞ x 8⅝ (4247/87) 1900
Pechstein, Max (1881-1955), KURISCHE HAUSER, 1911, 20½ x 28⅜ (4247/89) 50000
Pechstein, Max (1881-1955), LANDSCAPE WITH TRAIN, watercolor, pencil, 6¾ x 8 (4247/85) 2200
Pechstein, Max (1881-1955), MORGENSONNE, 1921-46, 39¾ x 31¾ (4247/90) 27500
Pechstein, Max (1881-1955), RESTAURANT SCENE, 6¾ x 8½, watercolor, pencil, 1911 (4247/88) 2100
Pechstein, Max (1881-1955), SEATED WOMAN, PUTTING ON HER STOCKING, ink, 1910, 16½ x 12¾ (4247/75) 1600
Pechstein, Max (1881-1955), STILLEBEN MIT FRUCHTEN, KRUG UND KACHEL, d.1913, 35⅝ x 35¾ (4169/41) 31000
Pechstein, Max (1881-1955), ZIRKUS PAUSE, 1935, 31 x 27 (4247/106) 20000
Pechstein, Max (1881-1955), BALTIC COAST, d.1911, 6½ x 8, colored crayons (4096/12) 1800
Petitjean, Hippolyte (1854-1929), LA MAISON DE CAMPAGNE, 14⅞ x 21¼, mixed media (4228/30) 1600
Petitjean, Hippolyte (1854-1929), LE CHEMIN, 9¼ x 6½ (4164/16) 425
Philippe-Auguste, Jean-Robert, BOUQUET, d.1969, 24 x 18, on masonite (691/141) 425
Philippe-Auguste, Salnave, JUNGLE SCENE, before 1965, 20 x 30, on masonite (691/7) 1000
Philippe-Auguste, Salnave, TREE OF LIFE, 26½ x 16, on masonite (691/4) 500
Picabia, Francis, ROMARIN, 1929, 17¾ x 21½ (4225/194) 10500
Picabia, Francis (1879-1953), ETUDE POUR 'UDINE', d.1913, 10 x 7¾, pencil (4172/370) 1200
Picasso, Pablo, AU CIRQUE, 1954, colored crayons, 9⅜ x 12⅝ (4170/175) 11000
Picasso, Pablo, BAIGNEUSES AU BALLON, 6¼ x 8⅝, 1928 (4249/302) 85000
Picasso, Pablo, BUSTE D'HOMME, oil on corrugated board, 37⅝ x 25⅝, 1969 (4252/669) 29000
Picasso, Pablo, BUSTE DE FEMME ASSISE, oil, sand, on canvas, 25½ x 19⅝, 1938 (4249/307) 250000
Picasso, Pablo, FAUNE ET CHEVRE, 1963, gouache, linogravure, 29½ x 24⅜ (4170/186) 9000
Picasso, Pablo, FEMME DEBOUT, bronze, 5¾, 1945 (4252/670) 5500
Picasso, Pablo, FEMME ET CHAT, 1954, brush, ink, 12⅝ x 9½ (4170/177) 10500
Picasso, Pablo, FIGURE AND TROIS TETES, DOUBLE SIDED, 1967, ink, colored crayons, 19⅝ x 23⅞ (4170/178) 14000
Picasso, Pablo, GUITARE ET COMPOTIER SUR UNE TABLE CARREE, pastel, (4250/439) 25000
Picasso, Pablo, HOMME, A LA PIPE, 51¼ x 31⅞, 1968 (4249/324) 140000
Picasso, Pablo, LA CHOUETTE, painted ceramic, 13¾, ca1953 (4249/315) 31000
Picasso, Pablo, LES GENS DU CIRQUE, 1954, brush, ink, 9½ x 12¾ (4170/176) 14000
Picasso, Pablo, MERE ET ENFANT, 1951, brush, ink, 10½ x 8¼ (4170/174) 19000
Picasso, Pablo, PETITE FEMME ENCEINTE, bronze, 12¾, 1948 (4252/672) 14000
Picasso, Pablo, PORTRAIT D'UN ARTISTE AU SALON D'AUTOMNE, 1911, watercolor, ink, 11⅞ x 6 (4170/112) 19000
Picasso, Pablo, TETE D'HOMME, pen, ink, paper, 10⅜ x 8¼, 1969 (4263/109) 13500
Picasso, Pablo, TETE D'HOMME, 1964, watercolor, wash, 25⅛ x 19¾ (4170/185) 8000
Picasso, Pablo, TROIS DANSEURS, pen and ink, 14⅜ x 10½ (4250/448) *19000*
Picasso, Pablo (1881-1973), CHANTEUR AVEUGLE, 1903, H6, bronze (4169/37) 10000
Picasso, Pablo (1881-1973), FEMME ASSISE, 1949, 24 x 19¾ (4124/91) 52500
Picasso, Pablo (1881-1973), FEMME DEBOUT, d.1953, H20¼, bronze (4169/62) 25000
Picasso, Pablo (1881-1973), FEMME DEBOUT, 1947, H8, bronze (4225/176) 7000
Picasso, Pablo (1881-1973), HOMME AU BATON, 1961, H15, bronze (4169/60) 15000
Picasso, Pablo (1881-1973), LA PIQUE, d.1960, 15 x 18⅛ (4225/211) 49000

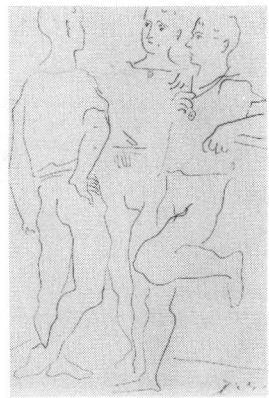

Picasso (4250/448)

Pascin (4250/433)

Picasso, Pablo (1881-1973), LE BAISER, d.1967, 13 x 19, pencil on paper (4164/166)   10500
Picasso, Pablo (1881-1973), NU COUCHE, d.1968, 44⅞ x 63⅝ (4169/58)   140000
Picasso, Pablo (1881-1973), TETE D'HOMME II, d.1965, 24⅛ x 19¾ (4225/215)   57000
Picasso, Pablo (1881-1973), TETE DE FEMME COURONNE DE FLEURS, d.1969, 25¾ x 19⅞, mixed media (4169/57)   42500
Picasso, Pablo (1881-1973), TETE DE FEMME, d.1962, 28¾ x 21⅝ (4160/59)   52000
Picasso, Pablo, (1881-1973), FEUILLE D'ETUDES, 1960, 20¼ x 26, ink, wash, paper (4125/178)   13500
Picasso, Pablo, (1881-1973), FIGURE FEMININE, 1951, H4½, bronze (4173/561)   2400
Picasso, Pablo, (1881-1973), FIGURE FEMININE, 1951, H3⅝, bronze (4173/563)   2300
Picasso, Pablo, (1881-1973), GUITARE ET COMPOTIER, 1920, 11 x 8¼, pastel (4125/143)   15000
Picasso, Pablo, (1881-1973), HOMME ASSIS, 1922, 15¾ x 20, watercolor, ink (4125/134)   37000
Picasso, Pablo, (1881-1973), LA PIQUE III, 1959, 19½ x 25½, watercolor (4125/169)   13000
Picasso, Pablo, (1881-1973), TETE D'HOMME, HOMME NU DEBOUT, DOUBLE SIDED, 1966, 24 x 19¾, ink, crayon (4125/180)   10000
Picasso, Pablo, (1881-1973), TETE DE TAUREAU, d.1950, H2¼, bronze (4173/562)   5250
Picasso, Pablo, 1881-1973, FEMME ASSISE, 1947, 9/10, H4⅞, bronze, dark brown (4127/369)   3000
Picasso, Pablo, 1881-1973, FEMME DEBOUT, 1945, 8/10, H7⅞, bronze, dark brown (4127/374)   7250
Picasso, Pablo, 1881-1973, FEMME DEBOUT, 1945, 9/10, H9⅛, bronze, dark brown (4127/376)   7750
Picasso, Pablo, 1881-1973, FEMME DEBOUT, 1945, 9/10, H9⅛, bronze, dark brown (4127/375)   5250
Picasso, Pablo, 1881-1973, FEMME DEBOUT, 1947, 5/10, H6⅞, bronze, dark brown (4127/368)   6250
Picasso, Pablo, 1881-1973, FEMME DEBOUT, 1947, 5/10, H3⅜, bronze, dark brown (4127/370)   2200
Picasso, Pablo, 1881-1973, FEMME DEBOUT, 1947, 7/10, H5⅜, bronze, dark brown (4127/371)   4250
Picasso, Pablo, 1881-1973, FEMME DEBOUT, 1947, 8/10, H7¾, bronze, brown (4127/372)   7250
Picasso, Pablo, 1881-1973, NATURE MORTE SUR UNE SPHERE, 1948, H16½, ceramic, wood base (4127/382)   4750
Picasso, Pablo, 1881-1973, NU DEBOUT, 1945, 10/10, H10, bronze, dark brown (4127/373)   7000
Picasso, Pablo, 1881-1973, PLAT A LA TETE DE FAUNE, 1947, 12⅜ x 14¾, ceramic (4127/380)   2500
Picasso, Pablo, 1881-1973, PLAT A LA TETE DE FAUNE, 1949, 12⅝ x 15⅛, ceramic (4127/381)   3000
Picasso, Pablo, 1881-1973, POT AUX DEUX VISAGES ET AUX BRANCHES, 1952, H11¾, bronze, dark brown (4127/379)   6250
Picasso, Pablo, 1881-1973, POT DE FLEURS, 1958, 10¾ x 8⅝, pastel (4127/389)   4500
Picasso, Pablo, 1881-1973, TAUREAU, 1957, L6½, bronze, dark brown (4127/378)   5250
Pierre, Andre, LINGLINSSOU BASSIN SANG, 40 x 50, on masonite (691/142)   750
Pierre, Andre, VOODOO CEREMONY IN A CEMETERY, 20 x 16, on masonite (691/8)   550
Pierre, Andre , LA COURE MYSTE BIEU, 24 x 32, on masonite (691/115)   650
Pierre, Fernand, JUNGLE SCENE, ca1974, 20 x 24 on masonite (691/78)   160
Pierre, Fernand, TREE BEARING FRUITS AND VEGETABLES, 24 x 20, on masonite (691/6)   100
Pignon, Edouard (b.1905), PAYSAGE AUX ARBRES, d.1957, 23⅝ x 39½ (4096/98)   1300

Pissarro, Lucien (1863-1944), L'HERMITAGE PONTOISE, 18⅝ x 26⅝ (4228/26)	2500
Pissarro, Lucien (1863-1944), RABBIT HILL, BROUGH, d.1914, 21 x 25⅝ (4096/21)	3000
Pissarro, Lucien (1863-1944), TOWER HILL CHAPEL, 19¾ x 25½ (4096/22)	2800
Pissarro, Paulemile (b.1884), L'ORNE A LA CHAIZE, 23½ x 28¾ (4228/64)	1700
Pissarro, Paulemile (b.1884), LA LIEURE, d.1929, 23⅝ x 28¾ (4204/29)	3000
Pissarro, Paulemile (b.1884), POMMIERS EN FLEUR, 15 x 18 (4164/57)	850
Pluviose, Dieudonne, BEACH SCENE, 24 xc 35¾, on masonite (691/41)	200
Poindujour, Serge, JUNGLE SCENE, ca1973 24 x 36, on masonite (691/122)	425
Poliakoff, Serge, b.1906, French, SANS TITRE, 36¼ x 26⅝, tempera (4127/391)	5600
Pomodoro, Arnaldo, MOVIMENTO E SOLE, silver relief, 22⅜ x 33¾, 1957 (4263/129)	2500
Pomodoro, Arnaldo, ROTANTE CON SFERA INTERIORE, bronze, 3 1/16 x 5⅝, 1968 (4252/688)	3200
Pomodoro, Arnaldo (b.1930), UNTITLED, H10⅜, silvered bronze (4096/156)	1700
Pomodoro, Gio, COMPOSIZIONE N 44, lead relief, 21¾ x 11¾, 1957 (4263/130)	1400
Popova, Livbov (1889-1924), STUDIES FOR BOOK COVER, ca1920, 8¾ x 5¾, collage (4172/350)	10500
Pottex, Seymour, ESTHER (A LOA), d.1966, 24 x 20, on masonite (691/33)	175
Puni, Ivan (1892-1956), DESIGN FOR A CONSTRUCTION, d.1916, 21¼ x 16¼, mixed media (4172/351)	13500
Quizet, Alphonse (1885-1955), LE LONG DE LA RIVIERE, 21⅝ x 18⅛, oil on masonite (4204/28)	1400
Raetz, Markus (Contemporary), 3-2-1, 1967-68, 55 x 67, acrylic on wood (4140/132)	600
Redon, Odilon (1840-1916), FEUILLE D'ETUDES, 12½ x 9½, mixed media (4228/10)	2300
Renard, STILL LIFE WITH FRUIT, 17¼ x 23¾ (4263/99)	1500
Renoir, Pierre Auguste, 1841-1919, PAYSAGE A CAGNES, 1914-19, 9½ x 15 (4127/314)	25000
Richier, Germaine, FIGURE, bronze, 24½ (4252/684)	10500
Richier, Germaine (1904-1959), FEMME, 1952, H7⅞, bronze (4096/149)	700
Richier, Germaine (1904-1959), PETITE SCULPTURE, H12½, bronze (4096/148)	1000
Richier, Germaine, 1904-59, LA FOURMI, 1953, H39¼, bronze, gray-green (4127/399)	18500
Richier, Germaine, 1904-59, LA MANTE, H25, bronze, dark brown (4127/398)	11500
Rivera, Diego, BACK FROM ERONGARICUARO IN LAKE FATZCUARO, 1948, watercolor, ink, 18⅞ x 23⅝ (4105/19)	8250
Rivera, Diego, CABESA DE MUJER, charcoal, 15⅜ x 10⅞ (4105/9)	5500
Rivera, Diego, FEMME EN VERTE, 1913, Pencil, watercolor, 13 x 10¼ (4105/6)	7250
Rivera, Diego, MURAL STUDY, 1927, Charcoal, 8½ x 12½ (4105/10)	6500
Rivera, Diego, NATURE MORTE AU CIGARE, 1916, oil on canvas, 13 x 8¾ (4105/7)	22000
Rivera, Diego, NINO CON ARO, brush, India ink, 15 x 10⅜ (4105/15)	1700
Rivera, Diego, NINO, 1938, Tempera on masonite, 23⅞ x 16¼ (4105/16)	28000
Rivera, Diego, PAISAJE, 1928, watercolor, charcoal, 12½ x 18½ (4105/17)	5250
Rivera, Diego, PEASANT, brush, ink on rice paper, 11 x 15½, 1934 (4263/77)	1200
Rivera, Diego, PORTRAIT OF JOHN DUNBAR, 1931, oil on canvas, 78½ x 62⅜ (4105/12)	19000
Rivera, Diego, RETRATO DE ANITA, Charcoal, 15⅜ x 11¾ (4105/8)	7000
Rivera, Diego, VENDEDORA DE FLORES, 1948, watercolor, ink, 15⅜ x 11 (4105/18)	3250
Rivera, Diego (1886-1957), EL SOPLADOR DE VIDREO, 15½ x 10¾, brush, India ink (4096/122)	1400
Rivera, Diego (1886-1957), LA VENDEDORA DE FLORES, 8½ x 10⅝, black crayon (4204/82)	2200
Rodin, Auguste (1840-1917), BELLONE, 1879, H26, marble (4169/8)	95000
Rodin, Auguste (1840-1917), DEUX MAINS, ca1909-10, H35 (4124/62)	125000
Rodin, Auguste (1840-1917), FIGURE DEBOUT, 7 x 4½, pencil (4096/5)	500
Rodin, Auguste (1840-1917), LE FRERE ET LA SOEUR, 1890, H15¼ (4124/63)	21000
Rodin, Auguste (1840-1917), LE LION QUI PLEURE, 1881, L13, bronze (4096/16)	3700
Rodin, Auguste (1840-1917), MODELE DEBOUT, 13 x 9⅞, mixed media (4096/4)	700
Rodin, Auguste (1840-1917), TORSO D'HOMME, H11⅛, bronze (4225/175)	11500
Rodin, Auguste (1840-1917), TORSO D'HOMME, ca1910, 48, marble (4169/2)	15500
Rodin, Auguste (1840-1917), TROIS FAUNESSES, 1882, 49½, bronze (4169/1)	17000
Rodin, Auguste (1840-1917), VICTOR HUGO, 1883, H19, bronze (4169/4)	22000
Rodin, Auguste, (1840-1917), SUZON, 1872, H16, gilt bronze (4173/501)	13500
Rodin, Auguste, (1840-1917), TORSE DE FEMME AGENOUILLEE, LA JAMBE DROITE, LEVEE, ca1890, H8¼, bronze (4173/502)	8500
Rodin, Auguste, 1840-1917, PREMIERES FUNERAILLES, 7/12, H9, bronze, dark brown (4127/323)	8000
Romero, Carlos Orozco, CABEZA DE MUJER, 1937, watercolor, 10⅜ x 9 (4105/20)	550
Romero, Carlos Orozco, MUJER, 1929, oil on canvas, 31½ x 23½ (4105/21)	1800
Rosai, Ottone, (1895-1957), INCONTRO, 27½ x 19¾, oil on board (4173/544)	3750
Rosso, Medardo (1858-1928), IL MALATO ALL'OSPEDALE, 1889, H7¾, bronze (unique) (4169/3)	13500
Rothenstein, Sir William (1872-1945), PORTRAIT OF WILLLAM BUTLER YEATS, 12¾ x 10⅝, charcoal (4260/668)	3000
Rouault, Georges, JESUS ET LES DOCTEURS, oil on paper mounted on, canvas, 13 x 17½, 1920 (4249/270)	41000
Rouault, Georges, LE PARISIEN, 20¼ x 15¾, 1937 (4249/269)	80000
Rouault, Georges (1871-1958), LE LUTTEUR, 1913, 41⅛ x 28¾ (4124/57)	50000
Rouault, Georges (1871-1958), PIERROT, 1935-38, 39½ x 25 (4124/77)	115000
Rouault, Georges, (1871-1958), NU (LE BAS-BLEU), 12⅛ x 7⅞, crayon (4125/120)	8500

Rouault, Georges, (1871-1958), SCENE DE BALLET, 8½ x 10, on celluloid (4125/122)   4750
Rouault, Georges, 1871-1958, VIEIL ARABE, 1937, 11⅞ x 14⅜ (4127/341)   18500
Roussel, Ker Xavier (1867-1944), NYMPHE ET FAUNE, d.1919, 67½ x 87 (4204/35)   3600
Roussel, Pierre (b.1927), AU BORD DE LA MER, 16¼ x 24⅝, mixed media (4204/7)   700
Rubin, Reuven (1893-1974), DELPHINA, 1942, 32 x 26 (4204/79)   13500
Rubin, Reuven (1893-1974), FLUTE PLAYER, d.1940, 19¾ x 14½, mixed media (4140/75)   *1600*

Rubin
(4140/75)

Ruelas, Julio, LA BELLA OTERO, 1906, pen, India ink, tan paper, 8 x 10 (4105/5)   2750
Ruelas, Julio, LA CRITICA, red pencil, 9⅞ x 7⅞ (4105/3)   4000
Ruelas, Julio, LA ESFINGE, 1906, Pencil, tan paper, 7 x 9⅞ (4105/4)   1200
Saint Phalle, Niki de (b.1930), NANA, 20 x 28¼, mixed media (4164/164)   600
Sala, Emilio Grau, CHESS PLAYERS, 36¼ x 28¾ (4263/103)   7500
Sala, Emilio Grau, FILLETTE AUX FLEURS, 18 x 21, 1963 (4263/100)   3500
Salemme, Attilio, TIME OF DECISION, 13 x 33, 1945 (4263/64)   3500
Santomaso, Guiseppe (b.1907), PAESAGGIO GIALLO, d.1953, 47¼ x 59¼ (4140/114)   2500
Saul, Audes, DOG AND CHICKEN WITH CACTI, 24 x 48 (691/45)   350
Saul, Charles, AVOCADO TREE WITH FLOWERS, ca1976, 24 x 20, on masonite (691/5)   100
Saura, Antonio, (b.1930), RETRATO #109, d.1960, 23½ x 28¾ (4173/585)   1500
Scheiber, Hugo (1873-1950), WALKING FIGURE, ca1925, 26 x 19½, gouache (4172/347)   2700
Schiele, Egon, LIEGENDE AKT, 1918, pencil, gouache, 17⅞ x 11½ (4170/134)   45000
Schiele, Egon, MADCHEN MIT SCHWARTZEN STRUMPFEN, 1911, gouache, pencil, 22¼ x 15⅛ (4170/133)   57500
Schiele, Egon (1890-1918), BOY AND GIRL, black chalk, 1918, 12¼ x 19½ (4247/94)   21000
Schiele, Egon (1890-1918), FEMALE NUDE, 1912, pencil, watercolor, 12½ x 19 (4247/64)   33000
Schiele, Egon (1890-1918), GIRL WITH SCARF, 1913, watercolor, 19 x 12⅜ (4247/73)   37500
Schiele, Egon (1890-1918), MOTHER AND CHILD, ca1908, colored crayons, 5¾ x 2⅝ (4247/34)   18000
Schiele, Egon (1890-1918), PREGNANT WOMAN, watercolor, 17⅝ x 12¼ (4247/96)   47500
Schiele, Egon (1890-1918), RECLINING NUDE, pencil, 1912, 12½ x 18⅞ (4247/63)   17000
Schiele, Egon (1890-1918), STANDING MALE NUDE WITH CROSSED ARMS, watercolor, ink, 1912, 18¼ x 11¾ (4247/74)   40000
Schiele, Egon (1890-1918), WOMAN IN YELLOW, 1914, tempera, pencil, 19 x 12¼ (4247/65)   62500
Schuffenecker, Claude Emil (1851-1934), LES FALAISES, 5⅜ x 8½, pastel (4096/8)   250
Schuffenecker, Emile (1851-1934), SHEET OF STUDIES, 8¼ x 6, black crayon (4260/1422)   1100
Schwitters, Kurt (1887-1948), Z.i.3 NEU AUSGESTATTET, d.1920, 5¾ x 4¾, mixed media (4172/365)   8000
Schwitters, Kurt, (1887-1948), MERZ 275, 1921, 7 x 5¾, fabric collage (4125/149)   18000
Schwitters, Kurt, (1887-1948), MERZ, 1939, 13 x 11½ (4125/148)   9000
Scott, Peter, (b.1909), RED BREASTED GEESE IN FLIGHT, d.1966, 48 x 72, on masonite (633/100)   1500
Segonzac, Andre Dunoyer de, LANDSCAPE, pen and ink, 14⅛ x 19½ (4250/455)   2600
Segonzac, Andre Dunoyer de, LANDSCAPE, pen and ink, 14¼ x 19¼ (4250/453)   2800
Segonzac, Andre Dunoyer de, LE PONT-NEUF, 25¾ x 32⅛, 1947 (4252/632)   10000
Segonzac, Andre Dunoyer de, NATURE MORTE A L'ALCARAZAS, 19⅞ x 24⅛, 1947 (4252/633)   10000
Segonzac, Andre Dunoyer de, PARSAGE DE L'ILE DE FRANCE, mixed media, 18⅛ x 29⅞ (4170/127)   8000
Segonzac, Andre Dunoyer de, STILL LIFE WITH CABBAGE AND CARROTS, watercolor, pen and ink, 22⅞ x 31 (4250/456)   15000

Segonzac, Andre Dunoyer de, STILL LIFE WITH FRUIT AND FLOWERS, watercolor and ink, 23 x 31⅜ (4250/454)	18000
Segonzac, Andre Dunoyer de, VASE DE FLEURS, 32 x 25¾, 1925 (4252/631)	28000
Segonzac, Andre Dunoyer de, VILLAGE CHURCH, pen, ink, 10⅜ x 14⅜ (4263/106)	750
Segonzac, Andre Dunoyer de, 1884-1974, LA SOIREE, ST. TROPEZ, 9⅝ x 24½, watercolor (4125/112)	2750
Segonzac, Andre Dunoyer de, 1884-1974, LE MATIN, ST. TROPEZ, 9⅝ x 24½, watercolor (4125/111)	*2750*
Segonzac, Andre Dunoyer de (1884-1974), BORDS DE RIVIERE, 13½ x 19¾, mixed media (4140/34)	*950*

Segonzac (4125/111)

Segonzac (4140/34)

Segonzac, Andre Dunoyer de (1884-1974), JEUNE FEMME COUCHEE, 9 x 13⅛, mixed media (4228/58)	650
Segonzac, Andre Dunoyer de (1884-1974), NATURE MORTE - LES OEUFS, 1929, 25½ x 20½ (4225/195)	10500
Segonzac, Andre Dunoyer de (1884-1974), PORTRAIT D'HOMME, 8¾ x 8¾, India ink (4228/63)	350
Segonzac, Andre Dunoyer de, (1884-1974), NATURE MORTE AU BOUQUET DE FLEURS, 19½ x 25, mixed media (4173/554)	14500
Segonzac, Andre Dunoyer de, (1884-1974), PAYSAGE D'HIVER, 1923-24, 15¼ x 21⅞ (4173/508)	6500
Segonzac, Andre Dunoyer de, (1884-1974), VENUS AU COLLIER, 12½ x 10⅛, mixed media (4204/41)	650
Seligmann, Kurt (1900-62), PERSONNAGE SURREALISTE, 14⅛ x 8, mixed media (4140/57)	550
Senatus, SUGAR CANE AND SISAL FIELDS, d.1974, 7½ x 9½, on masonite (691/23)	350
Severe, Jean Claude, LA SORTIE DE RECRETION, ca1975-76, 20 x 24, on masonite (691/63)	275
Severe, Jean Claude, LE JEU DE L'ENFANT EN VACANCE, 16 x 20, on masonite (691/107)	275
Severe, Jean Claude, MORT DE DESSALINES DANS UNE EMBUSCADE, ca1975, 24 x 32, on masonite (691/88)	400
Severini, Gino, DANCERS, mixed media, 6⅞ x 4⅜, 1957 (4263/104)	1900
Severini, Gino, DEUX MUSICIENS, pastel on grey paper, 25¾ x 19⅞, 1917 (4249/278)	25000
Severini, Gino, STILL LIFE, oil on board, 15 x 18¼, 1946 (4252/657)	8000
Severini, Gino (1883-1966), MAN IN SPACE, A MURAL IN SIX PANELS, d.1955, 161½ x 94½, gouache on panel (4204/111)	19500
Shahn, Ben (1898-1969), COUPLE, pencil on paper, 16 x 10 (666/66)	1000
Shterenberg, David, COMPOSITION, ca1920-21, 9½ x 12⅞, mixed media (4172/382)	2000
Signac, Paul, LA ROCHELLE, watercolor and crayon, 11⅜ x 16⅜ (4250/449)	9500
Signac, Paul, LEZARDRIEUX, mixed media, 10¾ x 17 (4250/450)	7500
Signac, Paul, THE LIGHTHOUSE AT LOCTUDY, crayon, watercolor, graph paper, 10½ x 6¾ (4263/9)	800
Signac, Paul, UNE CALANQUE A ST. TROPEZ, 25⅝ x 32⅛, 1926 (4249/264)	125000
Signac, Paul (1863-1934), COASTAL LANDSCAPE WITH TREES, d.1894, 9 1/16 x 11⅞, mixed media (4260/1445)	14000
Signac, Paul (1863-1934), LA TURBALLE, d.1930, 9⅝ x 17¼, mixed media (4260/1444)	7000
Signac, Paul (1863-1934), LEZARDRIEUX, d.1927, 11 x 18¼, mixed media (4260/1443)	10000

Signac, Paul (1863-1934), PORTRAIT OF MAXIMILIEN LUCE, 10¾ x 7⅞, black crayon (4260/1450)	1800
Signac, Paul (1863-1934), PORTRAIT OF MAXIMILIEN LUCE, 5 1/16 x 5⅛, black crayon (4260/1452)	1300
Sigueiros, David Alfaro, PORTRAIT OF IONE ROBINSON, 1931, oil on burlap, 34 x 22⅞ (4105/43)	20000
Sigueiros, David Alfaro (b.1898), COLOR STUDY, d.1963, 22¾ x 31, acrylic on paper (4096/128)	1400
Sintenis, Renee (1888-1965), Bucking Foal, stamped with initials, bronze, H4¾, 1923 (4247/41)	3250
Sintenis, Renee (1888-1965), Foal Grooming Itself, bronze, 1928, H3¾ (4247/39)	2800
Sintenis, Renee (1888-1965), Kneeling Doe, patinated silver, H3⅛, 1915 (4247/44)	1800
Sintenis, Renee (1888-1965), Nurmi, numbered II, bronze, H16¾ (4247/130)	4750
Sintenis, Renee (1888-1965), Polo Player, bronze, H17 (4247/131)	14000
Sintenis, Renee (1888-1965), Sleeping Ram on marble base, patinated silver, L4¾ (4247/43)	1600
Sintenis, Renee (1888-1965), Standing Foal, bronze, H4¾ (4247/40)	1600
Sintenis, Renee (1888-1965), Standing Foal on marble base, patinated silver, H4¾ (4247/42)	2200
Sironi, Mario (1885-1961), LA CONVERSAZIONE, 8½ x 11½, mixed media (4228/98)	475
Sironi, Mario (1885-1961), LANDSCAPE, watercolor and ink on paper, 13½ x 19½ (666/56)	900
Sironi, Mario (1885-1961), PAESAGGIO, 7¾ x 9⅜, gouache (4228/97)	800
Soudeikine, Serge (1886-1946), HARLEM NIGHT CLUB, 14½ x 17¼, mixed media (4096/59)	500
Soudeikine, Serge (1886-1946), LANDSCAPE, 62 x 51 (4096/60)	1300
Soutine, Chaim (1894-1943), LE GARCON BOUCHER, 25⅝ x 21¼ (4169/39)	52500
St. Brice, Robert, A FEMALE LOA, 19¾ x 17, on masonite (691/40)	325
St. Brice, Robert, BOTANICAL FORMS, 13⅝ x 24⅛, on masonite (691/39)	150
Stael, de Nicholas, LE NU ROSE, collage, 14½ x 10⅜ (4170/183)	2600
Steinberg, Saul, MASK WITH RUBBER STAMPS, mixed media, 16 x 7¾ (4250/531)	*2750*

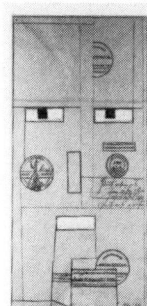

Steinberg (4250/531)

Signac (4250/449)

Steinlen, Theophile Alexandre, Swiss, 1859-1923, CHAT ASSIS, H2¾, bronze, gold-brown (4127/322)	1400
Steinlen, Theophile Alexandre, SEATED CHILD, conte crayon, 12⅛ x 9⅝ (4263/1)	600
Stephane, Micius, THE ORANGE HOUSE, 20 x 24, on masonite (691/57)	200
Stephen, A CHURCH WEDDING, d.1967, 17 x 24, on board (691/119)	180
Storel, Sergio (contemporary), PRISONER, d.1968, H22½, bronze (4164/99)	350
Supris, Remy, NOAH'S ARK, d.1976, 36 x 48, on masonite (691/119)	350
Survage, Leopold (1879-1968), VISAGES, d.1950, 34¼ x 23⅜, mixed media (4204/108)	950
Sutherland, Graham, STANDING FORM AGAINST A WALL, mixed media, 22⅜ x 9⅜ (4250/504)	3500
Suzuki, James (b.1933), MY LAST AFFAIR III, d.1957, 32 x 30 (4140/136)	300
Tal Coat, Pierre (b.1905), PEINTURE, 1956-57, 35⅛ x 51⅜ (4096/106)	2450

Tal Coat, Pierre, (b.1905), DANS LE CHAMPS, 1959, 14¾ x 18, oil on burlap (4173/588) 550
Tamayo, Rufino, ACROBATS, 1947, oil, sand on canvas, 40 x 29¾ (4105/49) 40000
Tamayo, Rufino, CABEZA DE MUJER, watercolor, 21⅞ x 17 (4105/45) 6000
Tamayo, Rufino, FIGURA, 1971, oil on canvas, 39½ x 31¾ (4105/63) 35000
Tamayo, Rufino, MUJER, colored pencils, 15¾ x 10 (4105/79) 2200
Tamayo, Rufino, MUJER CON GUITARRA, 1941, oil on canvas, 50⅛ x 36⅛ (4105/46) 40000
Tamayo, Rufino, MUJER INDIA, 1942, oil on canvas, 46½ x 36⅜ (4105/47) 47000
Tamayo, Rufino, QUATRO MUJERES CON REBOZOS AZULES, 1931, watercolor, 10½ x 8 (4105/44) 4700
Tamayo, Rufino, RECLINING NUDE FIGURE, 1953, oil, sand, masonite, 11⅜ x 31¼ (4105/80) 20000
Tamayo, Rufino, SANDIAS, 1958, oil on canvas, 51¼ x 76¾ (4105/81) 37500
Tamayo, Rufino (b.1899), SANDIAS NO. 10, d.1967, 9 x 12½, mixed media (4204/80) 2200
Tanguy, Yves, COMPOSITION, ink, 5¾ x 5⅝ (4250/486) 1100
Tanguy, Yves, COMPOSITION, pen and ink, 10 x 3½ (4250/485) 1900
Tanguy, Yves (1900-55), LA LUMIERE DE L'OMBRE, 1939, 25½ x 21 (4169/64) 85000
Tappert, Georg (1880-1952), GREEN NUDE AND WOMAN WITH CROSSED ARMS, 2-sided, 1905, 35 x 30½ (4247/66) 15000
Tappert, Georg (1880-1952), NUDE WITH MONKEY, ca1910, 25⅝ x 26½ (4247/82) 9000
Tchelitchew, Pavel, THE HAMMOCK, watercolor, 14½ x 20¾, 1929 (4263/105) 900
Tchelitchew, Pavel (1898-1957), SAILOR AT A CONCERT AT THE GRAND CAFE, LYON, 5⅝ x 3⅝ blue ink (4260/1486) 1000
Tchelitchew, Pavel, (1898-1957), THE DAHLIAS OF GUERMANTES, 1927, 25½ x 19½, watercolor (4125/133) *1200*
Thialy, HAITIAN COUNTRYSIDE, 41½ x 27¾ (691/98) 150
Toledo, Francesco (b.1940), FANTASTIC, 16¼ x 20⅛, mixed media (4140/100) 500
Toledo, Francisco, BURRO, pen, ink, 5¼ x 8⅛ (4105/67) 850
Toledo, Francisco, COLUMPIO, 1975, bronze, H7¼ (4105/71) 900
Toledo, Francisco, DIBUJO EROTICO, 1965, gouache, ink, 14¾ x 18⅛ (4105/90) 900
Toledo, Francisco, DOS FIGURAS CON CABEZA INDIA, 1965, mixed media, 19½ x 25¼ (4105/88) 1800
Toledo, Francisco, EL HOMBRE MALO, 1965, mixed media, 9¼ x 12⅛ (4170/189) 1300
Toledo, Francisco, EL MONO, gouache, 9⅜ x 12⅞ (4105/68) 1300
Toledo, Francisco, ESCANES IMAGINARIAS, 1962, mixed media, 18⅝ x 24⅜ (4105/87) 1800
Toledo, Francisco, FIGURAS FANTASTICAS, 1965, gouache, ink, 23 x 17⅜ (4105/92) 1600
Toledo, Francisco, FIGURAS Y ANIMALES, mixed media, 21 x 16¼ (4105/89) 1500
Toledo, Francisco, FIGURAS Y GATO, 1965, mixed media, 9¾ x 11½ (4170/188) 1300
Toledo, Francisco, FIGURE IN HOUSE, watercolor, 20 x 12 (4263/71) 350
Toledo, Francisco, MUJER AHORCADA, 1974, bronze, H11½ (4105/70) 3300
Toledo, Francisco, THREE FIGURES, watercolor, 13⅞ x 11⅛ (4263/70) 700
Toledo, Francisco, TOROS, gouache, 10 x 13 (4105/66) 900
Toledo, Francisco, TORTUGA, 1975, bronze, H5½ (4105/72) 1600
Toledo, Francisco (b.1940), CABALLO MARINO, 9⅞ x 21, mixed media (4096/115) 400
Toledo, Francisco (b.1940), CARA DE PAYASO, 12⅞ x 9⅜, mixed media (4204/90) 600
Toledo, Francisco (b.1940), COMPOSICION, 17½ x 20½, mixed media (4096/110) 425
Toledo, Francisco (b.1940), COMPOSICION, A DOUBLE-SIDED DRAWING, d.1959, 17¼ x 25½, mixed media (4204/95) 600
Toledo, Francisco (b.1940), EL BARRENDERO, A DOUBLE-SIDED DRAWING, 9½ x 12¼, mixed media (4204/93) 450
Toledo, Francisco (b.1940), ESCENA FANTASTICA, 15½ x 20⅜, mixed media (4096/112) 275
Toledo, Francisco (b.1940), ESCENA FANTASTICA, 16½ x 21⅛, mixed media (4096/111) 275
Toledo, Francisco (b.1940), FANTASTIC, 16¼ x 20⅛, mixed media (4096/114) 550
Toledo, Francisco (b.1940), FIGURA FANTASTICA, 9¾ x 12⅝, mixed media (4204/89) 450
Toledo, Francisco (b.1940), FIGURA INDIA, d.1963, 15½ x 11⅜, collage (4204/88) 700
Toledo, Francisco (b.1940), FIGURA, ca1960, 18⅞ x 24¾, pastel (4096/109) 400
Toledo, Francisco (b.1940), FIGURA, d.1960, 16¾ x 11½, mixed media (4204/94) 600
Toledo, Francisco (b.1940), PERSONAJE AZUL Y NEGRO, d.1960, 24 x 17, mixed media (4204/96) 450
Topolski, Feliks (B.1907), PORTRAIT OF SIR JACOB EPSTEIN, 19 x 12¼, black chalk (4260/669) 1700
Topolski, Feliks (B.1907), STUDY OF E. M. FORSTER AND BENJAMIN BRITTEN, 10⅛ x 8⅛, brown ink (4260/672) 1000
Topolski, Feliks (B.1907), STUDY OF SIR OSBERT AND DAME EDITH SITWELL, d.1947, 7⅛ x 5½, mixed media (4260/675) 1000
Torres-Garcia, Joaquin, COMPOSICION, 18⅛ x 15, 1940 (4252/655) 7000
Torres-Garcia, Joaquin (1874-1949), CIUDAD CON PUENTEY PUERTO CONSTRUCTIVO, d.1942, 31⅞ x 34¾, oil on board (4204/69) 8000

Torres-Garcia, Joaquin (1874-1949), COMPOSICION, 11⅛ x 7, gouache (4140/55) 850
Torres-Garcia, Joaquin (1874-1949), CONSTRUCTINO CINCO COLORES, d.1943, 19¾ x 28, oil on board (4140/50) 8000
Torres-Garcia, Joaquin (1874-1949), CONSTRUCTIVO EN CINCO TONOS, d.1943, 20 x 27¼, oil on board (4140/51) 7000
Torres-Garcia, Joaquin (1874-1949), CONSTRUCTIVO EN CINCO TONOS, d.1943, 16⅝ x 17⅜, oil on board (4204/70) 3000
Torres-Garcia, Joaquin (1874-1949), ESTRUCTURA CON GRAN PEZ, 1943, 10¾ x 16⅜, oil on board (4140/53) 5000
Torres-Garcia, Joaquin (1874-1949), TG 759, d.1943, 16¾ x 20¼, oil on board (4204/68) 4500
Torres-Garcia, Joaquin, 1874-1949, ARTE CONSTRUCTIVO, 1943, 20¼ x 29⅝, on board (4127/384) 7000
Torres-Garcia, Joaquin, 1874-1949, Uruguayan, CONSTRUCTIVO 539, 1937, 31¾ x 39½, on board (4127/383) 10000
Ubac, Rudolphe Raoul (b.1910), FORMES PLEINES II, d.1959, 25⅝ x 20, gouache (4096/104) 1400
Utrillo, Maurice, CHATEAU DE NERONDE, (AUVERGNE), gouache, 19⅛ x 24¾ (4250/452) 19000
Utrillo, Maurice, EGLISE SAINT-JEAN-DE-MONTMARTRE, RUE DES ABBESSES, 23⅜ x 19⅜, ca1919-20 (4249/253) 30000
Utrillo, Maurice, L'EGLISE DE SAINT-BERNARD, oil on board, 8⅛ x 10¾ (4252/626) 14500
Utrillo, Maurice, LA CHAPELLE DE L'ARDON A CHATILLON DE MICHAILLE, gouache, 19¾ x 14½ (4250/451) 13000
Utrillo, Maurice, LE MOULIN DE LA GALETTE A MONTMARTRE, cradled, panel, 14¼ x 16½, ca1942-44 (4249/273) 26000
Utrillo, Maurice, RUE DE FAUBOURG, 18 x 21½ (4249/275) 29000
Utrillo, Maurice, SANNOIS (SEINE ET OISE), 18 x 21⅝ (4249/274) 27500
Utrillo, Maurice (1883-1955), LA CASERNE DE COMPIEGNE (OISE), ca1933, 18⅛ x 21⅝ (4225/196) 26000
Utrillo, Maurice (1883-1955), LE LAPIN AGILE, 5⅞ x 7⅜, mixed media (4225/198) 8500
Utrillo, Maurice (1883-1955), LES USINES, BANLIEUX DE PARIS, ca1950, 18 x 23½, oil on board (4225/197) 26000
Utrillo, Maurice (1883-1955), ROUTE AUX ENVIRONS DE MONTMAGNY, ca1907, 30¾ x 22⅛, oil on wood (4169/36) 40000
Utrillo, Maurice (1883-1955), VIEUX PORCHE A ST. BERNARD, 1927, 28⅜ x 23⅝ (4124/67) 30000
Utrillo, Maurice (1883-1955), VUE DE MONTMARTRE, ca.1931-32, 15 x 18⅛ (4169/76) 45000
Utrillo, Maurice, (1883-1955), BONNE ANNEE, 1922, 10½ x 8¼, gouache, paper (4125/116) 9000
Utrillo, Maurice, (1883-1955), EGLISE ST.-SEVERIN A PARIS, 1909, 25¼ x 19¼ (4124/23) 72500
Utrillo, Maurice, (1883-1955), LIANCOURT, 1923, 10⅛ x 13⅝, gouache (4125/118) 8500
Utrillo, Maurice, (1883-1955), MONTMARTRE, PARIS, 1923, 15 x 11 (4125/119) 18500
Utrillo, Maurice, 1883-1955, BANLIEU DE PARIS, 1936-37, 15 x 18 (4127/338) 27000
Utrillo, Maurice, 1883-1955, LA RUE SAINT-RUSTIQUE, ca1926, 23⅞ x 19⅞ (4127/337) 31000
Utrillo, Maurice, manner of (1883-1955), STREET SCENE, on board, 9 x 12 (4240/47) 1000
Vagnetti, Giovanni (b.1898), IN PARTORIENTE, d.1932, 32½ x 29 (633/87) 700
Valcin, Gerard, CEREMONY, d.1971, 20 x 24 (691/48) 550
Valmier, Georges, COMPOSITION, gouache, 6⅛ x 4¼ (4250/435) 850
Valmier, Georges, COMPOSITION, mixed media, 19⅝ x 7⅞ (4250/437) 4000
Valtat, Louis, CRUCHE, GROSEILLES ROUGES ET BLANCHES, 25⅝ x 31⅞, 1927 (4249/260) 13000
Valtat, Louis, PIVOINES A LA CRUCHE BEIGE, 32¼ x 26 (4252/643) 21000
Valtat, Louis, VASE, ANEMONES ET TETE EN BRONZE, 23⅝ x 28¾, 1927 (4249/261) 12000
Valtat, Louis (1869-1952), AZALEES ET POMMES, 1932, 28⅞ x 21⅜ (4228/56) 18000
Valtat, Louis (1869-1952), CRUCHE, ANEMONES, TULIPES ET POMMES, 1937, 21¼ x 28¾ (4225/193) 18000
Valtat, Louis (1869-1952), GRAND BOUQUET DE FLEURS ET FRUITS SUR FOND, rouge, 1921, 32 x 25¾ (4228/57) 25000
Valtat, Louis (1869-1952), GRAND BOUQUET DE FLEURS, 1936, 28¾ x 21¼ (4225/214) 17000
Valtat, Louis (1869-1952), IN THE PARK, 8⅝ x 11, watercolor (4260/1455) 3600
Valtat, Louis (1869-1952), PAYSAGE DE NORMANDIE, 1930, 15 x 18⅛ (4228/55) 9000
Valtat, Louis (1869-1952), SCENE DE PARC, ca1904, 10¾ x 13¾ (4096/20) 2750
Valtat, Louis (1869-1952), VASE D'ANEMONES, 13 x 18⅛ (4225/189) 13000
Valtat, Louis, (1869-1952), LES QUAIS ET LE PONT NEUF, 1929, 14⅞ x 21¾ (4173/529) *9500*
Valtat, Louis, (1869-1952), VASE, ANEMONES, ET CITRONS, DRAPERIE, 1934, 25⅜ x 32 (4173/523) 22000
Valtat, Louis, (1869-1952), VASE, TULIPES ROUGES, 1922, 21¾ x 15 (4173/522) 23000
Valtat, Louis, 1869-1952, BOUQUET DE FLEURS, 11⅜ x 9, on board (4127/330) 3500

Tchelitchew
(4125/133)

Valtat, Louis, 1869-1952, BOUQUET DE FLEURS, 15 x 21¾ (4127/331)　　　　　13000
Van Doesburg, Theo (1883-1931), COVER DESIGN FOR 'ARCHITECTURE VIVANTE', 11½ x 9¼,
mixed media (4172/400)　　　　　20000
Van Dongen, Kees, LE CHEVAL BLANC, 19⅞ x 25½ (4249/262)　　　　　17000
Van Dongen, Kees, PAYSAGE, LA PETITE EGLISE, 19¾ x 25½ (4249/263)　　　　　27000
Van Dongen, Kees (1877-1968), AU RESTAURANT SHEPHEARDS, CAIRO, d.1928, 39⅜ x 31¾
(4169/38)　　　　　115000
Van Dongen, Kees (1877-1968), LUISA, 1920, 21¾ x 18¼ (4225/206)　　　　　32000
Van Dongen, Kees (1877-1968), VASE DE FLEURS, 16¼ x 13 (4124/29)　　　　　26000
Van Rysselberghe, Theo, (1862-1926), PORTRAIT DE KARIN VON BODENHAUSEN, LISANT,
d.1910, 25⅝ x 19¾ (4173/506)　　　　　5000
Vasarely, Victor, BELLE ISLE NO. 2, oil on panel, 32¼ x 27¼, 1952-56 (4252/696)　　　　　2750
Vasarely, Victor (b.1908), (C-35)NB-2, 1954, 16 x 12½, oil on paper (4164/107)　　　　　2500
Vasarely, Victor (b.1908), CAJIS OUY, ca1955, 13 x 12, tempera on board (4164/106)　　　　　2600
Vasarely, Victor (b.1908), UNTITLED, 13 x 8¼, mixed media (4140/141)　　　　　2800
Vasarely, Victor (b.1908), UNTITLED, 14½ x 13¼, metal plate (4164/104)　　　　　400
Vassilieff, Marie (1884-1957), FEMME A L'EVENTAL, 1910, 23½ x 28⅝ (4172/315)　　　　　15000
Venard, Claude, COMPOSITION WITH GREEN SOFA, 28¾ x 23⅝ (4263/101)　　　　　700
Venard, Claude, LAVENDER PICKERS IN THE SOUTH OF FRANCE, acrylic, 29½ x 29½ (4263/93)　　　　　1000
Venard, Claude, PORT SCENE, 18⅛ x 21⅝ (4263/92)　　　　　750
Venard, Claude, STILL LIFE, 15 x 18⅛ (4263/95)　　　　　400

Valtat
(4173/529)

Venard
(4140/107)

Venard, Claude, WOMAN PLAYING THE PIANO, 39¼ x 39⅜ (4263/102)	2300
Venard, Claude (b.1913), BATEAUX A VOILES AU CLAIR DE LUNE, 18⅛ x 21¾ (4140/105)	550
Venard, Claude (b.1913), COMPOSITION, d.1963, 12 x 23½ (4228/108)	450
Venard, Claude (b.1913), FEMME ASSISE DEVANT LA FENETRE, 47 x 81 (4140/107)	*1600*
Venard, Claude (b.1913), L'ARLEQUIN, 29 x 23½ (4096/94)	2100
Venard, Claude (b.1913), LA JETEE, 29½ x 29⅜ (4228/109)	800
Venard, Claude (b.1913), NATURE MORTE, 39⅜ x 39⅜ (4204/120)	650
Venard, Claude (b.1913), NATURE MORTE A LA PASTEQUE, d.1956, 29½ x 29⅝ (4096/93)	950
Venard, Claude (b.1913), SCENE DE VILLE, 29½ x 29½ (4140/106)	850
Venard, Claude (b.1913), STUDIO INTERIOR, 15 x 18¼ (666/58)	450
Venard, Claude (b.1913), THE BEDROOM, 19¾ x 25' (666/59)	600
Vertes, Marcel (1895-1962), THE CLOWNS, A THREE PART FOLDING SCREEN, 90 x 60 (633/97)	800
Viera da Silva, Maria Elena (B.1908), CHANDELEUR, 1969, 38½ x 51⅛ (4169/67)	18000
Vignon, Victor (1847-1909), LES ARBRES ETETES, 10½ x 16, oil on panel (4204/30)	1000
Villon, Jacques, LE COQUILLAGE, 28¾ x 36¼, 1933 (4249/284)	20000
Villon, Jacques (1875-1963), BEACH SCENE WITH FIGURES, d.1902, 9 x 7⅝, mixed media (4260/1435)	3800
Villon, Jacques (1875-1963), FEMME AU MANTEAU GRIS, c.1918, 7¾ x 5, watercolor (4204/4)	1600
Villon, Jacques (1875-1963), L'AVENTURE, d.1935, 10⅝ x 8, pen, India Ink (4096/42)	650
Villon, Jacques (1875-1963), STUDY FOR 'DANSEUSE ESPAGNOLE', d.1899, 20⅛ x 15, mixed media (4260/1439)	20000
Villon, Jacques (1875-1963), THE POET, 1899, 19 x 12½, mixed media (4204/2)	3500
Vital, Pauleus, CEREMONY FOR AGOUE, d.1978, 20 x 24, on masonite (691/97)	600
Vital, Pauleus, VOODOO CEREMONY UNDERGROUND, d.1975, 43¾ x 33½ (691/42)	800
Vivancos, Georges (b.1895), FLEURS, d.1953, 18⅛ x 14⅞ (4140/81)	500
Vivancos, Georges (b.1895), POT ET FLEURS, d.1957, 18⅛ x 15 (4096/80)	700
Vladon, Suzanne (1865-1938), AFTER THE BATH, d.1895, 9⅜ x 11, black crayon (4260/1468)	1800
Vlaminck, Maurice de, CANAL BORDANT LE VILLAGE, 21½ x 25⅝, ca1925 (4249/259)	35000
Vlaminck, Maurice de, L'EGLISE A HAMEAU, 18¼ x 21¾, 1927 (4252/627)	35000
Vlaminck, Maurice de, LA ROUTE DU VILLAGE, 21½ x 25⅝, ca1945 (4249/272)	36000
Vlaminck, Maurice de (1876-1958), LA PLACE DE MARCHE, ca1920, 28⅝ x 36¼ (4225/216)	27000
Vlaminck, Maurice de (1876-1958), LE CARGO, 1926, 32¼ x 39¾ (4169/77)	47500
Vlaminck, Maurice de (1876-1958), LE VILLAGE, ca1911-12, 24½ x 29½ (4124/24)	42500
Vlaminck, Maurice de (1876-1958), MAISONS A BOUGIVAL, 1913, 15⅝ x 19½ (4124/59)	19000
Vlaminck, Maurice de (1876-1958), NATURE MORTE AUX FLEURS, ca1912, 28½ x 23¾ (4169/45)	40000
Vlaminck, Maurice de (1876-1958), NATURE MORTE-LES FLEURS, 21⅝ x 18⅛ (4169/75)	32000
Vlaminck, Maurice de (1876-1958), NATURE MORTE, 1914, 23¾ x 28¾ (4228/47)	11000
Vlaminck, Maurice de (1876-1958), PATSAGE DE POISSY, 1909, 24 x 32¼ (4124/58)	36000
Vlaminck, Maurice de (1876-1958), ROUTE DE VILLAGE, 21½ x 25¾ (4140/28)	19000
Vlaminck, Maurice de (1876-1958), RUE ENNEIGEE, 15 x 18⅛ (4225/212)	30000
Vlaminck, Maurice de, (1876-1958), LE MUR, ca1920, 25¾ x 32¼ (4173/512)	10000
Vlaminck, Maurice de, (1876-1958), NATURE MORTE, ca1928, 27¼ x 28 (4173/527)	26000
Vlaminck, Maurice de, VILLAGE ROAD, gouache and ink, 15¼ x 21⅛ (4250/457)	11000

Vlaminck, Maurice de, VILLAGE SCENE, gouache and watercolor, 18⅛ x 21⅝ (4250/458) — 21000

Vogler, Paul (1852-1904), PAYSAGE D'HIVER, d.1903, 23¾ x 32 (4228/28) — 1500

Vuillard, Edouard, LE PARC DES CLAYES, pastel, 36¼ x 58¾ (4250/419) — 25000

Vuillard, Edouard, MME. HESSEL ET ROMAIN COOLUS DANS LE SALON, oil on paper, 34½ x 33¾, 1935 (4252/610) — 18000

Vuillard, Edouard (1868-1940), PORTRAIT OF MMS ALEXANDRE NATANSON, 5⅛ x 5¾, pencil (4260/1465) — 1800

Vuillard, Edouard (1868-1940), PORTRAIT OF PRINCESS BIBESCO, NEE ELIZABETH ASQUITH, ca1935-37, 16⅞ x 12⅛, pastel (4260/1466) — 19000

Vuillard, Edouard (1868-1940), PORTRAIT OF THADEE NATANSON, ca1895, 4½ x 3⅜, pencil (4260/1464) — 1700

Vuillard, Edouard (1868-1940), SCENE D'INTERIEUR AU BOUQUET DE FLEURS, 8⅜ x 5, mixed media (4228/17) — 1400

Vuillard, Edouard (1868-1940), UN COIN DE LA PLACE VINTIMILLE, ca1905, 16¼ x 10⅝ (4204/16) — 5500

Vuillard, Edouard (1868-1940), YOUNG WOMAN SEATED BEHIND A TABLE, 4¾ x 8⅛, pencil (4260/1463) — 600

Vuillard, Edouard, (1868-1940), FILLETTES SE PROMENANT, ca1891, 32 x 25⅝ (4124/47) — 190000

Vuillard, Edouard, (1886-1940), AUX CLAYES, LA SALLE DE BILLARD, 19½ x 25½, pastel (4125/110) — 11000

Vuillard, Edouard, 1886-1940, FEMME SE COIFFANT, 1900-05, 23 x 18½, on board (4127/303) — 10000

Weber, Max (1881-1961), COASTAL LANDSCAPE, 1909, 14 x 19¾ (666/63) — 200

Weber, Max (1881-1961), Venice, 17½ x 23¼ (666/62) — 400

Weininger, Andor (b.1899), COMPOSITION, 12½ x 15½, colored crayons (4172/395) — 350

Winter, Fritz (b.1905), FIGURE IN RED AND GREEN, on board, 1929, 18 x 25⅛ (4247/136) — 1750

Wols Wolfgang Schulze (1912-51), ANIMAUX SOU-MARINS, 6¾ x 8½, mixed media (4140/56) — 3000

Wotruba, Fritz (1907-1975), WALKING MAN, 1952, H16¾, bronze (4096/153) — 4000

Wotruba, Fritz (1907-75), LIEGENDER AKT, 1931, L21¾, bronze (4164/97) — 4000

Wynne, David (b.1926), FEMALE TORSO NO.1, H22 bronze (4260/1509) — 1800

Yeats, John Butler (1839-1922), PORTRAIT OF PADRAIC COLUM, 13¾ x 10, pencil (4260/670) — 1800

Zadkine, Ossip, PORTRAIT OF RUTH STEPHAN, pen, ink on paper, 24⅞ x 18¾, 1944 (4263/54) — 275

Zadkine, Ossip, SURREALIST PORTRAIT OF RUTH STEPHAN, pen, ink on, paper, 18⅝ (4263/53) — 600

Zadkine, Ossip, TROIS HOMMES, 1921, charcoal, pastel, 25¼ x 19½ (4170/125) — 3250

Zadkine, Ossip (1890-1967), ARLEQUIN HURLANT, d.1956, H78, bronze (4225/239) — 18000

Zadkine, Ossip (1890-1967), LA COUPLE, 13⅞ x 9⅞, lavender pencil (4204/58) — 275

Zadkine, Ossip (1890-1967), LA FEMME MADREPORE, d.1943, 23¾ x 17⅝, mixed media (4140/37) — 750

Zadkine, Ossip (1890-1967), TETE D'HOMME, 1943, H13¾, quartz (4096/50) — 5250

Zadkine, Ossip, (1890-1967) Russian, HOMME ASSIS AU BOUTEILLE DE VIN, 1927, 17½ x 13, gouache (4125/146) — 3500

Zao Wou-Ki, b.1921, Chinese-French, LA MERE PERDUE, 1952, 30 x 44 (4127/394) — 2300

Zao Wou-Ki, b.1921, Chinese-French, PAYSAGE AUX AMOUREUX, 1928, 45 x 50½ (4127/395) — 6250

Zdanevich, Kiril (1892-1970), COMPOSITION, 47¼ x 47¼ (4172/344) — 20000

Zdanevich, Kiril (1892-1970), CONTRAST OF FORMS, d.1917, 8½ x 6¼, mixed media (4172/326) — 750

Zovach, William (1887-1966), MAN AND WOMAN, pair of bronzes, gold patina, H's, 7⅛, 7⅜ (666/64) — 1000

Zovach, William (1887-1966), MOTHER AND CHILD, gold patina, bronze, H8 (666/65) — 1700

Zuniga, Francisco, DESNUDO ACOSTADO, 1976, bronze, L20¾ (4105/101) — 8000

Zuniga, Francisco, DESNUDO RECLINADO, 1974, pastel, 19¾ x 25⅝ (4105/99) — 1500

Zuniga, Francisco, DESNUDO RECLINADO, 1975, pastel, 19¾ x 27½ (4105/98) — 1800

Zuniga, Francisco, JOVEN ACURRUCADA, 1975, pastel, 19½ x 27½ (4105/100) — 1500

Zuniga, Francisco, DOS MUJERES, 1963, pen, ink, watercolor, 19½ x 25 (4105/95) — 4000

Zuniga, Francisco, GRUPO DES TEHUAMAS, 1972, bronze, 12¼ x 15½ (4105/97) — 7750

Zuniga, Francisco, YALALTECA SENTADA, 1975, bronze, H14 (4105/96) — 7250

Zuniga, Francisco (b.1913), MUJER SENTADA, d.1965, H14, bronze (4225/224) — 4750

Zuniga, Francisco (b.1913), MUJER SENTADA, d.1969, 13½ x 10½, brown pastel (4204/81) — 1200

Zuniga, Francisco (b.1913), VIRGINIA SENTADA, d.1972, 19¾ x 25¾, brown pastel (4225/226) — 2000

Zuniga, Francisco, b.1913, Mexican, DESNUDO EN CUCLILLAS, 1971, H9½, bronze, brown (4127/410) — 5500

Zuniga,Francisco (b.1913), EL ABRAZO, d.1974, L14, bronze (4225/225) — 4200

Archipenko
(4173/530)

Maillol
(4140/6)

Chapter 22

Contemporary Paintings, Drawings and Sculpture

The market in contemporary art tends to move in cycles, with prices leveling off after strong surges, then gathering momentum again. Following the boom years of 1973-74, economic recession contributed to stagnation in prices, but this past season prices resumed their upward movement.

Few examples of work by the acknowledged masters of the forties and fifties came up for sale last season. With these "blue chip" artists becoming scarcer and more expensive, buyers entering the market have turned to the still relatively available and affordable works of artists of the early sixties, showing a preference for Pop and Color Field painters. In Pop, Oldenburg, Warhol, Lichtenstein and Ruscha led the way. Morris Louis and Kenneth Noland paintings brought high prices in the Color Field category.

The market in contemporary art is necessarily speculative. And in comparison to 1973-74, buying was more selective, from among a broader spectrum of artists by a more informed public. But tremendous gains are possible in the contemporary market.

Marking specific investment choices is difficult in such a volatile market as contemporary painting, but the continuing entry of new buyers, mostly young Americans and corporations, promises to keep prices for the favored artists strongly on the rise.

Agam, Yaacov, SOLFEGE, gouache, 1970, 27 x 27 (4226/124)	$2200
Agostini, Peter, BURLESQUE QUEEN, numbered 1/6, plaster, 1950, 11½ x 4 (4226/80)	450
Albers, Josef, HOMAGE TO THE SQUARE, SENTINEL, board, 48 x 48, 1968 (4249/341)	35000
Albers, Josef, COMPOSITION, gouache, 16½ x 23 (4263/133)	2600
Alechinsky, Pierre, LE QUATRE COIN, acrylic, 38¼ x 59¾ (4249/358)	12500
Alf, Martha, RED, WHITE AND BLUE, 1973, acrylic oon canvas, 28 x 28 (4226/144)	1200
Altoon, John, untitled, 1968, watercolor, ink, wash, 30 x 40 (4226/125)	1200
Antonakos, Steven, (Small) NEON, pen and ink, 6/7/67, 14 x 22 (4226/138)	250
Antonakos, Steven, 3 SMALL TALL NEONS, 14 x 22, pencil and ink, 12/27/70 (4226/139)	150
Appel, Karen, DEUX PERSONNAGES, dated '57, 26 x 32 (4226/38)	5250
Arakawa, Shusaku, UNTITLED, mixed media, 84 x 53, 1964 (4249/361)	12000
Arakawa, Shusaku, b.1936, SEPARATED CONTINUUMS, d.1966, 62½ x 90½ (4171/234)	14500
Arman, COLERE DE VIOLIN, 1967, 9¾ x 9¾ x 9¾, smashed violin, polyester (4226/79)	3750
Ay-o, FORMS, THREE RELIEFS, 1966, acrylic and foam, 12 x 16 (4226/141)	450
Baber, Alice, JAGUAR FOREST, acrylic, 1977, 32 x 28 (4226/90)	700
Banard, Walter Derby, NAVAHO, 1971, alkyd resin on canvas, 96 x 51 (4226/102)	1400
Bauermeister, Mary, b.1934, CHINESE FLOWERS WITH CLOUDS, 30 x 29½ x 15, mixed media (4171/229)	3000
Baumeister, Willi, UNTITLED, mixed media, 18⅝ x 25½ (4250/512)	3000
Bissier, Julius, ARTE VITAE FINEM, egg oil on linen, 17¼ x 19 (4250/513)	19000
Bladen, Ronald, untitled, 38 x 28½, paper and ink collage (4226/127)	500
Bogoshian, Varujan, AT THE GATE OF HELL, wood, 1965, 39½ x 15¾ x 15½ (4226/81)	4500
Botero, Fernando, THE OLD BISHOP, gouache on cardboard, 45 x 37, 1962 (4249/354)	18000
Boxer, Stanley, untitled, '71, acrylic, 66½ x 66½ (4226/57)	1500
Capp, Al, b.1909, THE QUESTION, d.1976, 48 x 58, acrylic on canvas (4171/264)	5000
Chevas, Jose Luis, PROSTIBULO, mixed media, 22¾ x 18 (4250/523)	2600
Christo, RUNNING FENCE (PROJECT FOR SONOMA COUNTY, CALIFORNIA), mixed media, 14 x 22 (4250/536)	*2250*

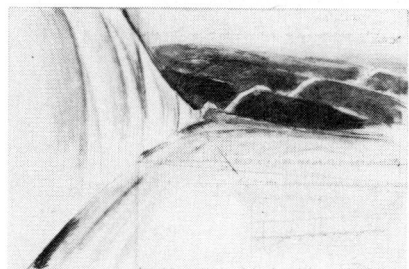

Christo
(4250/536)

Christo, RUNNING FENCE (PROJECT FOR THE WEST COAST OF USA), 28 x 22 (4250/537)	6250
Christo, VALLEY CURTAIN, RIFLE, GRAND HOGBACK, chalk, pencil, 28 x 22, 1971 (4226/130)	3200
Christo, WRAPPED BRIDGE, collage, pencil, crayon, 46½ x 28 (4249/356)	10500
Christo, WRAPPED TABLE WITH A PACKAGE, 1976, chalk, mixed media, 21½ x 28 (4226/131)	5000
Christo, b.1935, PACKED COAST, NEW SOUTH WALES, AUSTRALIA, d.1969, 28¼ x 22½, mixed media (4171/262)	6250
Copley, William, WOMAN, charcoal, 1973, 23 x 17½ (4226/128)	400
Cornell, Joseph, SIRIUS, box construction, 8¼ x 15, ca1950 (4249/330)	14000
Cornell, Joseph, SOAP BUBBLE SET, box construction, 9 x 13 x 3, 1947 (4249/332)	29000
Davie, Alan, ALTAR OF THE SNAKE, on board, dated '56, 60 x 48 (4226/49)	2400
De Rivera, Jose, BLUE AND BLACK #20, aluminum on wood, 16 x 16 x 6½ (4226/77)	1700
Di Suvero, Mark, untitled, 1966, welded iron, 15 x 19 x 21 (4226/72)	7000
Diao, David, BLUEPRINT, acrylic, 1971, 84 x 108 (4226/98)	500

Dine, Jim, A.R. AT OBERLIN #7 (THE SAME CURTAIN) enamel, rubber, aluminum, 84 x 48, 1966 (4249/352)	20000
Dine, Jim, COMING HOME HEARTS FOR N #3, 1969, 18¾ x 23½ (4226/108)	3750
Dubuffet, Jean, LE CONJECTURAL, vinyl, acrylic on klegecell, 74 x 44, 1972 (4249/325)	27500
Dubuffet, Jean, PERSONNAGE, marker on board, 1971, 13 x 7 (4226/122)	2900
Dubuffet, Jean, PERSONNAGE COSTUME, 1971, marker on board, 17½ x 10½ (4226/123)	4500
Dubuffet, Jean, b.1901, PRACTICABLE MASSIS A L'HOMME, d.1971, 84½ x 106 x 1½, mixed media (4171/226)	61000
Dzubas, Friedel, untitled, 1963, 17¾ x 12¾ (4226/63)	1000
Estes, Richard, WOMAN IN NEW YORK STREET, 1966, 25½ x 31½ (4226/87)	3000
Ferber, Herbert, STUDY FOR PASADENA MUSEUM OF MODERN ART, gouache, 9/1970, 10 x 29 (4226/126)	750
Ferren, John, FLEUR DU MAL, '52, watercolor on paper, 26 x 20 (4226/4)	550
Flack, Audrey L., AIX EN PROVENCE, Florence, pair drawings, watercolor, 1956, 11¾ x 14¼ (4226/5)	650
Folon, Jean Michel, RED DEVIL, watercolor, ink, 7 x 9 (4226/136)	1600
Francis, Sam, BRIGHT RING, acrylic, 64 x 44¼, 1966 (4249/350)	13000
Francis, Sam, b.1923, UNTITLED, d.1960, 20¼ x 14 (4171/248)	3750
Francis, Sam, b.1923, UNTITLED, d.1960-65, 9¾ x 13¼, Gouache (4171/203)	3000
Francis, Sam, b.1923, UNTITLED, d.1973, 22 x 29½, acrylic on paper (4171/261)	6500
Frank, Mary, NUDE, 1964, charcoal on paper, 17½ x 22¼ (4226/26)	350
Frankenthaler, Helen, untitled, on paper, 12½ x 9 (4226/61)	3750
Frankenthaler, Helen, COPPER AFTERNOON II, acrylic, 41½ x 71, 1973 (4249/340)	30000
Freen, John, RED SPOT, dated '64, 84 x 64 (4226/42)	1000
Goodnough, Robert, red, blue, gray, acrylic, 1973, 57 x 59 (4226/100)	1400
Goodnough, Robert, untitled, dated '55, 36 x 36¼ (4226/50)	1500
Goodnough, Robert, ABDUCTION, ca1959, 24 x 24 (4226/51)	1100
Goodnough, Robert, BEIGE-TAN, acrylic, 40 x 60 (4226/101)	1200
Gorky, Arshile, CROOKED RUN, 18⅞ x 28, 1944 (4249/326)	90000
Gottlieb, Adolph, b.1903, DIVISIONS OF DARKNESS, d.1945, 23½ x 29½ (4171/208)	9500
Graham, Robert, PANTIES, assemblage, 12½ x 10¾ (4226/73)	1200
Hare, David, FIGURE IN THE FOREST, 1958, steel wire mesh, 13 x 19 x 15 (4226/74)	800
Hartigan, Grace, b.1922, DUN LAOGHAIRE, d.1958, 70¾ x 39 (4171/223)	3500
Held, Al, yellow (untitled), 1968, acrylic, 18½ x 24½ (4226/88)	4000
Held, Al, b.1928, WEST-SOUTHWEST, d.1973, 69 x 60 (4171/253)	10000
Hepworth, Barbara, SLIM FORMS, slate, 1965, H10¾ (4226/67)	8000
Hofmann, Hans, 1880-1965, VARIATIONS ON A THEME IN GREEN NO. I, d.1956, 36 x 48 (4171/255)	35000
Hofmann, Hans, untitled, 1958, 10¾ x 13¾ (4226/52)	2500
Hofmann, Hans, 1880-1965, PROVINCETOWN, d.1937, 24½ x 29½, oil on board (4171/224)	13000
Hofmann, Hans, FLUSE NO. VI, board, 26 x 15½, 1962 (4249/327)	8000
Hofmann, Hans, 1880-1965, HOUSE AND STUDIO, d.VIII.15.43, 17¼ x 24, watercolor (4171/204)	5000
Hofmann, Hans, 1880-1965, UNTITLED, d.VIII.9.43, 17¼ x 24, watercolor (4171/205)	7000
Hundertwasser, Friedrich, SMOKING SEAMANS SUNSET, watercolor, silver paint, composition board, 24½ x 17, 1968 (4249/336)	25000
Indiana, Robert, COMPOSITION, acrylic on canvas, 12 x 12 (4252/699)	2750
Jenkins, Paul, PHENOMENA AUDUBON FIND, watercolor, 1972, 42 x 30¼ (4226/119)	1200
Jenkins, Paul, PHENOMENA 3 IN STEP, watercolor, 1968, 30¼ x 22 (4226/120)	1600
Johns, Jasper, NUMBER 2, encaustic, collage, 3 x 2⅝ (4249/331)	19000
Johnson, Ben, WOMAN WITH PEAR, 1966, 34¼ x 36½ (4226/86)	1700
Johnson, Lester, GRAND STREET, 1963, 66 x 44 (4226/55)	1100
Kelly, Ellsworth, BROOKLYN BRIDGE, 30 x 13, 1958 (4249/342)	9000
Kelly, Ellsworth, b.1923, 4 x 38, (4171/212)	12000
Klemann, Ronald, INTERNATIONAL HARVEST . . ER, acrylic, 1971, 48 x 48 (4226/93)	3500
Kooning, Elaine, de, untitled, charcoal on paper, ca1957, 16½ x 13½ (4226/13)	250
Kooning, Willem de, untitled, gouache on paper, 18¾ x 23½ (4226/83)	3750
Kooning, Willem de, WOMAN, 29½ x 22¼, watercolor, crayon on paper (4226/82)	13500
Lewitt, Sol, ALTERNATE NOT-STRAIGHT AND BROKEN LINES, ink, Dec. 7, 1972, 10 x 10 (4226/137)	1400
Lewitt, Sol, VARIATIONS OF INCOMPLETE OPEN CUBES, painted aluminium, 42 x 42 x 42, 1974 (4252/698)	6000
Lewitt, Sol, 1 PART SET A5, 8 x 32 x 32, baked enamel on steel, ca'70 (4226/68)	5500
Lichtenstein, Roy, b.1923, BRUSHSTROKE, d.1958, 21 x 29, pencil and tusche (4171/241)	10500
Lichtenstein, Roy, b.1923, MODULAR PAINTING WITH FOUR PANELS No. 5, d.1969, 54 x 54 (4171/220)	47500
Liberman, Alexander, untitled, ca1965, on enamel on aluminum, 48 x 48 (4226/45)	1000
Liberman, Alexander, b.1912, SYNTHESIS, d.1952, 40 x 80, enamel on aluminum (4171/214)	2000
Lindner, Richard, 1901-1978, GIRL IN SAILOR BLOUSE, d.1967, 20 x 28, mixed (4171/247)	7500

Lindner, Richard, 1901-1978, WOMAN, d.1967, 22½ x 17¼ (4171/245)	16000
Louis, Morris, 1912-1962, GAMMA RHO, d.1960, 102½ x 164¼, acrylic (4171/217)	115000
Lukin, Sven, VOTARY, dated 1961 (4226/43)	1200
Mallory, Ronald, untitled, '71, mercury, glass, mirror, 23 x 23 (4226/71)	350
Mangold, Robert, W SERIES DIAGONAL I, acrylic on masonite, 48 x 72, 1968 (4252/700)	4200
Marca-Relli, Conrad, b.1913, UNTITLED, d.1958, 21¼ x 27¼, oil and collage (4171/227)	4000
Martin, Agnes, b.1912, BROWN COMPOSITION, d.1962, 12 x 12 (4171/228)	6000
McCracken, John, #23, 1964, 60½ x 60 (4226/44)	850
McLaughlin, John, 1898-1976, #3, 48 x 60 (4171/259)	4000
Mitchell, Joan, untitled, ca1960, 21½ x 18 (4226/36)	2400
Mitchell, Joan, b.1926, UNTITLED d.1959, 45½ x 35 (4171/210)	7000
Motherwell, Robert, untitled, 1965, 14½ x 11¼ (4226/64)	2100
Motherwell, Robert, DRAWING 1944, watercolor, 13½ x 10¾ (4250/503)	3750
Motherwell, Robert, GAULOISES, watercolor and collage, 11¾ x 8¾ (4250/535)	*3750*
Motherwell, Robert, LANDSCAPE OF THE INNER MIND, watercolor, 9 x 12 (4250/506)	2300
Motherwell, Robert, OPEN #96, 54 x 40, 1969 (4249/344)	28000
Motherwell, Robert, RED OPEN #3, acrylic, 84 x 42, 1973 (4249/348)	26000
Motherwell, Robert, UNTITLED, watercolor, 8½ x 11½ (4250/507)	2500
Motherwell, Robert, b.1915, THE AFRICAN PLATEAU #2, d.1975, 24 x 36, acrylic polymer (4171/219)	12000
Natkin, Robert, untitled, 1969, 12¾ x 9½ (4226/65)	1300
Nevelson, Louise, BLACK EXCURSION 13, 1969, painted wood, formica, 37½ x 47½ (4226/69)	10000
Nevelson, Louise, UNIT OF SEVEN, gold painted wood, 78 x 62, 1960 (4249/345)	25000
Nice, Don, BLUEJAY, watercolor, 1976, 18 x 18 (4226/135)	400
Nice, Don, RADISHES, watercolor, 1971, 24 x 18 (4226/134)	550
Noguchi, Isamu, SOLITUDE, bronze, 68, 1962 (4249/333)	24000
Nolan, Sidney, NED KELLY, board, 48¼ x 36, 1956 (4249/337)	13000
Noland, Kenneth, ANOTHER WORLD, acrylic, 68½ x 68½, 1963 (4249/339)	23000
Noland, Kenneth, FILE LINE, acrylic, 5½ x 102, 1969 (4249/347)	5000
Noland, Kenneth, PENDULUM, 33½ x 33½, 1962 (4249/346)	16000
Noland, Kenneth, TURN LIGHT, 1972, acrylic, 92 x 15 (4226/99)	9000
Noland, Kenneth, b.1924, HIGH EASTER, d.1960-61, 64⅝ x 66½, acrylic on canvas (4171/231)	37000
Noland, Kenneth, b.1924, SOLAR THRUST, d.1963, 67 x 70 (4171/256)	14500
Oldenberg, Claes, STRANGE GEOMETRIC MICKEY MOUSE, ink on paper, 1966, 14 x 14 (4226/111)	2500
Oldenberg, Claes b.1929, PICASSO'S CUFFLINK, 28 x 24 x 19, mixed media (4171/235)	10000
Oldenburg, Claes, b.1929, CHANTILLY DESSERT, d.1964, 12 x 17¼, watercolor, crayon (4171/201)	2600
Oliveira, Nathan, STONE, 1974, 13½ x 15½ (4226/89)	1000
Oliveira, Nathan, SUMMER DRAWING SEATED WOMAN BY THE SEA, gouache on paper, 12¼ x 9½ (4226/15)	850
Parker, Raymond, b.1922, 72 P 35, d.1959, 73 x 70 (4171/222)	1750
Pearlstein, Philip, TWO NUDES, pencil, 13½ x 11 (4226/117)	1500
Pepper, Beverly, TURNING KNIGHT, ca1969, stainless steel, H73¼ (4226/66)	8000
Pistoletto, Michelangelo, b.1933, PERSONE ALLA BALCONATA, d.1964, 78¾ x 78¾, oil on steel (4171/216)	8000

Motherwell
(4250/535)

Pollock, Jackson, 1912-1956, UNTITLED, ca.1943, 14½ x 11, mixed media, collage (4171/206)   21000
Poons, Larry, b.1937, WILDCAT ARRIVAL, d.1967, 116 x 190, acrylic on canvas (4171/232)   7000
Poons, Larry, b.1937, WILMA, d.1973, 90 x 101½ (4171/260)   6500
Rauschenberg, Robert, b.1925, EARLY EGYPTIAN A, d.1973, 45 x 30¼, mixed media (4171/263)   4250
Rauschenberg, Robert, b.1925, HOUSE PARTY, d.1965, 40 x 27½ (4171/242)   11000
Rauschenberg, Robert, b.1925, TRAVELING PIECE, d.1966, 8½ x 11, mixed media (4171/244)   12500
Resnick, Milton, untitled, '57, on board, 25¾ x 19¼ (4226/46)   850
Resnick, Milton, OULU, '58, on board, 27 x 27 (4226/48)   850
Resnick, Milton, RED FOX, dated '58, 23 x 19 (4226/47)   1350
Rickey, George, b.1907, HORIZONTAL III, d.1973, 96½ x 63½, stainless steel (4171/251)   12500
Rivera, Jose de, CONSTRUCTION NO. 99, bronze on motorized base, 7½ (4249/334)   8500
Rivers, Larry, untitled, ca1960, 23 x 32 (4226/53)   2400
Rivers, Larry, ACCORDION PLAYER, Pencil, 13½ x 15¼ (4250/538)   *1100*

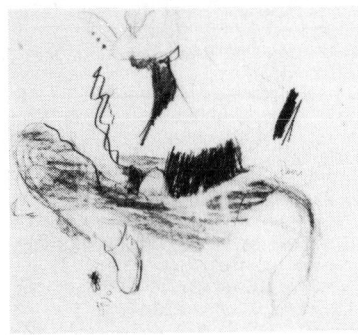

Rivers
(4250/538)

Rivers, Larry, LIONS ON THE DREYFUS FUND II, oil, collage, 63 x 40, 1964 (4249/338)   34000
Rivers, Larry, b.1923, GIRL,DRAWING FROM PLAYBOY CENTERFOLD, d.1966, 56¾ x 52, mixed media (4171/246)   10000
Rosenquist, James, PERCENTAGES AND EQUILATERAL TRIANGLE, mixed media, paper, 22 x 43 (4226/110)   3000
Rosenquist, James, TOASTER, mixed media, 12 x 7 x 12, 1963 (4252/693)   6000
Rosenquist, James, b.1933, STAR SPOONS, d.1968, 17¼ x 29¾, watercolor, pencil (4171/202)   2100
Ruscha, Edward, SURGICAL, 1967, 20 x 24 (4226/92)   1400
Ruscha, Edward, b.1937, 20TH CENTURY FOX WITH SEARCHLIGHTS, d.1962, 132 x 67 (4171/257)   57500
Ryan, Anne, UNTITLED, collage, 12 x 9½ (4250/533)   2000
Salemme, Attilio, LOVERS, '51, oil, 30 x 23 (4226/31)   5000
Shields, Alan, MY ASS HURTS, paint and cloth, 1973, 30 x 30 (4226/143)   1800
Smith, David, untitled, with initials, 1-10-19-57, gouache on paper, 19½ x 25¼ (4226/20)   4000
Smith, David, AT THE BAR, bronze, wood base, 7½ x 7¾ x 4¼, 1941 (4249/335)   9500
Sonnenstern, Friedrich, DER WETTLAUF ZWISCHEN TOD UND LEBEN, Crayon and pencil, 18½ x 27 (4250/540)   *5500*
Soto, Jesus Raphael, DOS METALES, brass, silver rods, string, black pa, int, wood, 31½ x 31½, 1970 (4249/343)   5000
Soto, Jesus Raphael, b.1923, PLANS VIRTUEL BLANC ET NOIR d.1965, 42 x 42, mixed media (4171/215)   6250
Stamos, Theodoros, BEYOND EMPERORS, ca1962, 28 x 32 (4226/32)   1500
Stamos, Theodoros, CORNISH SUN-BOX, 1967, acrylic, 13½ x 9¾ (4226/62)   1100
Stamos, Theodoros, INFINITY FIELD, 1969-70, 52 x 56 (4226/103)   2200
Stella, Frank, b.1923, ABRA III, 120 x 120, fluorescent acrylic (4171/252)   14000
Tanning, Dorothea, untitled, '49, ink, gouache, collage, 10 x 7¼ (4226/3)   650
Tapies, Antoni, VELOURS ROUGE, mixed media, 25¾ x 32, 1972 (4249/360)   13000
Tapis, Antoni, untitled, gouache, 1968, 16¾ x 14 (4226/129)   1200
Thompson, Bob, NUDE, '60, mixed media on paper, 24 x 18 (4226/27)   850
Tinguely, Jean, META-MATIC #4, 60, watercolor on paper, 17¼ x 13½ (4226/17)   500
Tobey, Mark, untitled, '58, tempera, pen, 6¾ x 10 (4226/21)   1800
Tobey, Mark, YOUNG WOMAN PORTRAIT, pencil on paper, 1918, 18½ x 14 (4226/1)   1500

Toledo, Francisco, BLUE HEAD, mixed media, 30 x 22 (4250/529)   2200
Toledo, Francisco, EMBRACE, gouache and paint, 8¼ x 10⅝ (4250/528)   900
Toledo, Francisco, FIGURE WITH TWO BEASTS, mixed media, 9½ x 12½ (4250/526)   1200
Toledo, Francisco, FIGURE, mixed media, 9½ x 12¼ (4250/525)   1200
Toledo, Francisco, HEAD, mixed media, 24⅛ x 19¾ (4250/530)   *2200*
Toledo, Francisco, MAN WITH BIRDS, mixed media, 9¼ x 12½ (4250/524)   950
Toledo, Francisco, THREE FIGURES, mixed media, 9½ x 12½ (4250/527)   1200
Trova, Ernest, NEW YORK SERIES, NO. 6, collage, 9 x 12½, 1970 (4263/134)   1100
Tworkov, Jack, FIGURE, ca1958, mixed media on paper, 22 x 7 (4226/29)   650
Vasarely, Victor, O U R C C, casein on rag board, 26¾ x 24½,1963 (4249/328)   5250
Vasarely, Victor, PENGO 2, 1966, acrylic on board, 31½ x 31½ (4226/84)   3750
Vasarely, Victor, b.1908, HYSSAR d.1949-1953, 25½ x 23¾, tempera on board (4171/213)   4000
Vicente, Esteban, untitled, 1962, charcoal, 20 x 15½ (4226/23)   400
Warhol, Andy, A CHRISTMAS BOY, ca1955, watercolor, 21¾ x 27¾ (4226/12)   1100
Warhol, Andy, BIRDS AND BEES, ca1955, paper collage, 24 x 22 (4226/7)   1000
Warhol, Andy, CAT, ca1955, ink on paper, 17¾ x 14 (4226/10)   900
Warhol, Andy, DOUBLE ONE DOLLAR BILL, silkscreen on canvas, 8½ x 9¾ (4252/697)   4500
Warhol, Andy, FABRIC DESIGN, paper collage, 1953-55, 18 x 22½ (4226/9)   200
Warhol, Andy, FLOWER, silkscreen, 77 x 74, 1965 (4249/353)   12000
Warhol, Andy, HAPPY BUG DAY, watercolor over print, 14 x 9½, ca1955 (4263/135)   800
Warhol, Andy, INTERIORS, pair of watercolors, on paper, ca1955, 22½ x 28⅛ (4226/8)   950
Warhol, Andy, MAO-TSE-TUNG, pencil, 40 x 30 (4226/140)   2000
Warhol, Andy, MAO, acrylic, silkscreen, 12 x 10, 1970 (4263/136)   2200
Warhol, Andy (b.1930), MAO-TSE-TUNG (TRIPTYCH), d.1973, each 12 x 10, mixed media (4164/154)   7250
Warhol, Andy, b.1930, MAO-TSE-TUNG, d.1973, 26 x 22, acrylic silkscreen (4171/265)   5250
Wesselmann, Tom, EMBOSSED NUDE #9, 1967, liquitex, pencil, 14⅞ x 17¾ (4226/115)   2700
Wesselmann, Tom, GREAT AMERICAN NUDE #78, pencil, 1977, 4 x 9 (4226/114)   2600
Wesselmann, Tom, NUDE #64, 1974, watercolor, 4 x 9 (4226/116)   2100
Wesselmann, Tom, b.1931, STILL LIFE #37, d.1964, 48 x 60 x 4, mixed media (4171/237)   18000
Wiley, William T., THE NEW KID, 1972, 27 x 33, mixed media on chamois (4226/142)   1200
Zao-Wou-Ki, untitled, dated 17-12-60, 63¼ x 51 (4226/41)   3100

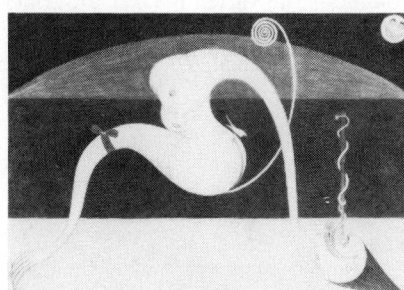

Sonnenstern (4250/540)

Toledo (4250/530)

Chapter 23

American Paintings, Drawings and Sculpture

During the past season the market for American paintings, watercolors, drawings and sculpture soared to new highs. Dealers, collectors and museums competed for works in all categories.

Western artists such as Farny, Hennings, Sharp and Seltzer proved as popular as ever. Led by works of Proctor, Russell and Remington, bronzes were particularly strong. American Impressionists continued their surge. Childe Hassam, Reed and Redfield provoked spirited bidding. Landscapes and outdoor scenes commanded strong prices. Twentieth-century American painters like Georgia O'Keeffe also did well, and watercolors and drawings by Burchfield, Bellows and Hopper were well received, while works by Demuth and Sheeler brought particularly strong prices.

The tastes of American collectors seem broader and more adventurous in the art of their own country than in most other fields. The past season saw vigorous activity and strong gains throughout the varied market for American art. The outlook for this field is strongly optimistic, with broad competition bidding up prices for top-quality pieces, and specialized collectors in each category actively seeking works for purchase.

American School (4076/701)

Akeley, Carl E. (1864-1926), WATER BUFFALO DOWNED BY A LION, H12, bronze (4268/310) — 2200

Albers, Josef (1880-1976), HOMMAGE TO THE SQUARE, ca1960, 3½ x 3½, oil on paper (4164/135) — 1100

Albers, Josef (1880-1976), HOMMAGE TO THE SQUARE, ca1960, 4 x 4, oil on paper (4164/136) — 1300

Albright, Ivan Le Lorraine (b.1897), STARLIGHT IN HER EYES, mixed media, 13¼ x 18 (4236/206) — 6500

Alonso-Rochi, Alexander, A STILL LIFE WITH FRUIT, 32 x 39½ (633/103) — 500

American Primitive School, 19c, A MYTHOLOGICAL SCENE, 29 x 36 (684/885) — 125

American Primitive School, 19c, THE CIVIL WAR VETERAN, 28 x 20 (684/852) — 150

American School, A MOUNTAINOUS LANDSCAPE, 19c, 24 x 32 (633/274) — 450

American School, A SUMMER LANDSCAPE, d.1874, 19c, 7½ x 13½ (633/256) — 350

American School, DAKOTA INDIAN OF THE PLAINS, 6¼ x 6½, d.1906, watercolor (684/865) — 30

American School, FARMERS ALONG THE HUDSON, 19c, 24 x 31 (633/117) — 225

American School, HAYING IN THE COUNTRY, ca1820 (684/863) — 300

American School, HUSBAND AND WIFE, A PAIR OF PORTRAITS, 19c, 36 x 29 (633/260) — 700

American School, LANDSCAPE NEAR LAKE GENEVA, ca1870, 17½ x 24¼, on artist's board (633/137) — 400

American School, MEMORIAL PICTURE ON VELVET, 20 x 24 (684/899) — 120

American School, PANNING FOR GOLD, 32 x 60 (4180/548) — 1200

American School, PORTRAIT OF A GIRL IN PROFILE, 30 x 23½ (4180/461) — 2300

American School, PORTRAIT OF A LADY WITH A SPANIEL, 18c, 35 x 34 (633/241) — 950

American School, PORTRAIT OF A WOMAN, 28 x 24¼, ca1845 (684/892) — 150

American School, PORTRAIT OF A WOMAN, E20C, 45½ x 35 (4260/686) — 1200

American School, PORTRAIT OF A WOMAN, on reverse, 30 x 25, Ammi Phillips 1884 (684/858) — 300

American School, PORTRAIT OF RICHARD A. MARSHALL, 15 x 11¾ (4180/462) — 800

American School, SEATED GENTLEMAN, 19c, 6½ x 4, pencil (4260/682) — 750

American School, STILL LIFE WITH FRUIT AND ORIENTAL BOTTLE, 12 x 15½ (4076/714) — 850

American School, TWO MAIDENS IN A FIELD, L19c, 24 x 36 (633/252) — 325

American School, YOUNG BOY WITH A DOG, 55¼ x 29¼ (4180/466) — 5000

American School, 19c, A BOY AND A GIRL, A PAIR OF PORTRAITS, each 23¾ x 18½ (684/896) — 400

American School, 19c, A CLIPPER SHIP OFF THE COAST, 18¼ x 23⅝ (684/810) — 650

American School, 19c, A RIVER LANDSCAPE, 10 x 13½, on panel (684/841) — 60

American School, 19c, BABY CHICKS IN A BOX, 11 x 14, on panel (684/845) — 190

American School, 19c, BROWN HOMESTEAD, HAMBURG, CT., 34½ x 48½ (4076/701) — *7250*

American School, 19c, CLASSICAL LANDSCAPE, 30 x 40 (4076/699) — 1100

American School, 19c, COUNTRY LIFE, 32½ x 44¼ (684/901) — 350

American School, 19c, GIRL IN A RED DRESS, 26 x 21 (684/879) — 275

American School, 19c, HUDSON HIGHLANDS FROM WEST POINT, 8 x 9½, inscribed on reverse (684/884) — 350

American School, 19c, HUSBAND AND WIFE, A PAIR OF PORTRAITS, 30 x 25 (684/825) — 150

American School, 19c, LANDSCAPE WITH A STAG, 26 x 36 (684/869) — 125

American School, 19c, MOUNTAINOUS LANDSCAPE, 23½ x 32 (684/894) — 80

American School, 19c, MOURNING PICTURE, 6¼ x 8, ovoid, watercolor (684/830) — 125

American School, 19c, PORTRAIT OF A GENTLEMAN, 30 x 24¼ (4076/706) — *500*

American School, 19c, PORTRAIT OF A GENTLEMAN, 36½ x 29, canvas on masonite (4076/708) — *600*

American School, 19c, PORTRAIT OF A MAN, 30 x 27¼, unframed (684/813) — 550

American School, 19c, PORTRAIT OF A YOUNG BOY WITH BIRD, 30 x 25 (684/817) — 400

American School, 19c, PORTRAIT OF A YOUNG GIRL, 30 x 22 (684/846) — 175

American School (4076/708)

American School (4076/706)

American School, 19c, PORTRAIT OF ADMIRAL PERRY, 24 x 19½, on board (684/816)   100
American School, 19c, PORTRAIT OF E.G. MINOR, 5½ x 4⅝, d.1848, watercolor (684/832)   200
American School, 19c, PORTRAIT OF HARRISON PENNY, 10½ x 8, pastel on paper (684/895)   400
American School, 19c, RIVER SCENE, 6¼ x 8¼ (684/829)   120
American School, 19c, THE CLIPPER SHIP NIGHTINGALE, 16 x 20 (684/809)   200
American School, 19c, THE STEAMSHIP EMERALD, on zinc, 11 x 15¼, W.H.H. (684/839)   325
American School, 20c, AERIAL, FERRY, DULUTH TO MINNESOTA, 19½ x 28¼, d.1905 (684/806)   250
Ames, Daniel F., fl. 1837-58, HESTER WESTERWELD HUNT, 24 x 20 (4268/186)   400
Amick, Robert W. (1879-1970), ON THE TOP OF LOOKOUT ROCK, 40 x 30 (4236/156)   2700
Anshutz, Thomas Pollack (1851-1912), THE FARMER AND HIS SON AT HARVESTING, d.1879, 24¼ x 17¼ (4236/42)   110000
Anuskiewicz, Richard (b.1930), UNTITLED, d.1968, 60 x 60, acrylic on canvas (4164/183)   3400
Artschwager, Richard (b.1924), DESTRUCTION #4, 1972, 40 x 48, acrylic on celotex (4164/174)   3800
Ary, Henry (1802-59), HUDSON RIVER LANDSCAPE, 30 x 44 (4268/216)   5750
Auerbach-Levy, William (1889-c.1963), WOMAN SEATED ON STONE WALL, 30 x 40 (4180/613)   600
Ault, George (1867-1933), PORTSMOUTH, NEW HAMPSHIRE d.1922, 17¼ x 22 (4167/204)   1500
Ault, George CAP GRIS NEZ, HAYSTACKS IN THE DUNES, 1911, 14 x 18 (666/131)   550
Ault, George (1867-1933), MOONLIGHT AND DESERT LANDSCAPE d.1921, 8¼ x 6, pencil, pr. drawings (4167/201)   *2100*
Avery, Milton (1893-1964), BEACH UMBRELLAS d.1944, 22 x 30, gouache (4167/178)   8500
Avery, Milton (1893-1964), HARBOR AT NIGHT, gouache, 17¼ x 24 (4112/200)   1900
Avery, Milton (1893-1964), HEN AND COCK, d.1950-51, 34 x 38 (4112/180)   22000
Avery, Milton (1893-1964), HEN, pastel, d.1962, 11 x 8¼ (4236/236)   2600
Avery, Milton (1893-1964), NUDE ON A RED COUCH, d.1950, 14 x 22 (4112/163)   7500
Avery, Milton (1893-1964), PORCH SITTER, d.1943, 36 x 28 (4236/227)   15000
Avery, Milton (1893-1964), RECLINING WOMAN, gouache, 8¼ x 11¾ (4112/161)   1700
Avery, Milton (1893-1964), RED ROOSTER, BLUE HEN, d.1956, 12 x 15¾ (4112/211)   2750
Avery, Milton (1893-1964), RIDERS IN THE PARK, watercolor, 14¾ x 21¾ (4112/189)   2000
Avery, Milton (1893-1964), SEATED GIRL, 28 x 36 (4112/162)   3500
Avery, Milton (1893-1964), SEATED NUDE, felt pen on paper, d.1960, 11 x 8½ (4112/173)   950
Avery, Milton (1893-1964), STANDING FEMALE NUDE, 11 x 7½, oil on board (4167/218)   2600

Ault (4167/201)

Bacon (4167/211)

Avery, Milton (1893-1964), TWO TREES, d.1955, 58 x 30 (4112/199)   21000
Avery, Milton (1893-1964), WADING GOAT, gouache, d.1960, 17 x 22½ (4236/238)   4500
Babbidge, J.G. (19c), THE FANNIE WHITMORE, 25 x 36¼, 1883 (4076/763)   3500
Bachman, Max, 1921, ABRAHAM LINCOLN, H28, bronze (4268/318)   2400
Bacon, Henry (1839-1912), WOMAN PEELING APPLES, 19¾ x 28½ (4180/484)   3800
Bacon, Peggy, (b.1895), HEAVENLY DAY d.1964, 11¼ x 15, gouache (4167/211)   *1600*
Balink, Henry Cornelius (1882-1962), SHIVERING INDIAN BOY, 8½ x 8½ (4167/60)   1750
Ball, Thomas (1819-1911), BUST OF A YOUNG GIRL, marble, d.1868, H16 (4236/29)   3500
Bannister, Edward M. (1833-1901), THE YOUNG SHEPHERDESS, 22 x 29¾ (4180/537)   2500
Barnes, Gertrude, b.1865, EXPECTATION, 18¼ x 14¼ (4268/349)   1200
Barse, George R. Jr. (1861-1938), STAMPEDING HORSES, 37 x 54½, 1881(?) (4076/751)   2800
Bascom, Ruth H., PORTRAIT OF A CHILD, 15½ x 11½ (4211/619)   1200

Baskerville, Charles (b.1896), CIRCUS BACK LOT d.1942, 22 x 30½ (4167/231) — 1300

Beal, Gifford (1879-1956), GARDEN IN SUMMER, oil on masonite, 16 x 20 (4112/60) — 5500

Beal, Gifford (1879-1956), THE FISHERMEN, 1922, 30 x 42 (666/120) — 2250

Beal, Gifford (1879-1956), VIEW OF THE TOWN, oil on board, 15¾ x 19¾ (4112/67) — 5000

Beard, E., DINNER TIME, 25 x 30, d.1862 (684/854) — 1700

Beckwith, James Carroll, 1852-1917, IN THE GARDENS OF LUXOR, 13¾ x 10¼, on panel, 1893 (4264/419) — 700

Bellows, George (1882-1924), ARTILLERY TRAIN d.1917, 9 x 14¼, pencil on paper (4167/202) — *1000*

Bellows, George (1882-1925), PARTY SCENE, STREET FIGHT, double drawing, mixed media, 20¾ x 22 (4236/182) — 14000

Bellows, George (1882-1925), PIGS, 8 x 11¾, oil on board (4167/226) — 3300

Bellows, George (1882-1925), PORTRAIT OF MARY MCKINNON, 44 x 34, 1922 (4098/51) — 18000

Bellows, George (1882-1925), WHITEHEAD, MONHEGAN, MAINE, oil on panel, d.1911, 10½ x 14½ (4112/87) — 5500

Bellows, George (1882-1925), WINTER MORNING, mixed media, d.1908, 5¾ x 9 (4112/89) — 1800

Benson, Frank W. (1862-1951), PORTRAIT OF MRS. DANIEL DOUGHERTY, 40 x 30, 1891 (4076/759) — 1100

Benton, Thomas Hart (1889-1975), COUNTRY PATH, watercolor, 11 x 7¾ (666/122) — 2500

Benton, Thomas Hart (1889-1975), FLOWERS AND FRUIT, oil temper, d.'47, 27½ x 16½ (4112/185) — 13000

Benton, Thomas Hart (1889-1975), INSTRUCTION, 33 x 40, tempera on canvas (4167/185) — 105000

Benton, Thomas Hart (1889-1975), PROFILE OF AN OLD MAN, tempera, 24 x 18 (4236/202) — *18000*

Benton, Thomas Hart (1889-1975), STILL LIFE WITH LETTER d.1957, 23¼ x 16, tempera on masonite (4167/209) — 13000

Bellows (4167/202)

Benton (4236/202)

Benton, Thomas Hart (1889-1975), STILL LIFE, oil on board, 9½ x 8 (4112/133) — 3500

Benton, Thomas Hart (1889-1975), STUDY FOR 'THE CHANGING WEST', tempera, d.1929, 13 x 17 (4236/200) — 19000

Berninghaus, Oscar Edmund (1847-1952), MARKET PLACE, OAXACA, MEXICO, 18 x 13¼, watercolor (4167/68) — 3500

Betts, Louis (1873-1961), 'HE PAUSED...AND CLUTCHED HIS BOW', oil on, board, 24½ x 18½ (4236/154) — 3250

Betts, Louis (1873-1961), CAPTURED INDIANS, 18 x 11 (4236/153) — 1000

Betts, Louis (1873-1961), INDIAN GIRL, oil on board, 24½ x 18½ (4236/157) — 2700

Betts, Louis (1873-1961), PORTRAIT OF FRANCIS-INNOCENCE, 30 x 25 (4076/783) — 750

Betts, Louis (1873-1961), TEA PARTY, 24 x 18 (4236/72) — 5000

Biddle, George (1885-1965), PORTRAIT OF EDMUND WILSON, d.1956, 12½ x 10¾, silverpoint on paper (4260/695) — 1300

Biddle, George (1885-1965), PORTRAIT OF GEORGE SANTAYANA, d.1952, 13 x 9¼, silverpoint on paper (4260/694) — 1000

Bierstadt, Albert (1830-1902), CAPTAIN GEORGES CANYON, oil on paper on canvas, 14 x 19
(4167/65)   8000
Bierstadt, Albert (1830-1902), CATHEDRAL FOREST, 39¾ x 30½ (4112/40)   52500
Bierstadt, Albert (1830-1902), CLOUDS IN THE MOUNTAINS, 14 x 19, oil on paper (4076/768)   2800
Bierstadt, Albert (1830-1902), DEER IN LANDSCAPE, oil on paper on board, 12 x 19½ (4112/33)   35000
Bierstadt, Albert (1830-1902), DOG'S HEAD d.1882, 7 x 7½, Watercolor on Paper (4167/45)   1100
Bierstadt, Albert (1830-1902), FIGURE ON THE BEACH AT NASSAU, 11¼ x 18½ (4180/574)   6500
Bierstadt, Albert (1830-1902), FIGURES IN A HUDSON RIVER LANDSCAPE, 4¼ x 6¼, oil on paper
(4112/14)   4750
Bierstadt, Albert (1830-1902), INDIAN ENCAMPMENT ON A RIVER, oil on paper on, masonite, 14 x
18 (4236/128)   8000
Bierstadt, Albert (1830-1902), INDIAN ENCAMPMENT, oil on paper on masonite, 13¾ x 18½
(4236/129)   10500
Bierstadt, Albert (1830-1902), LANDSCAPE, NEW HAMPSHIRE, 11 x 15, oil on paper mounted
(4098/15)   8000
Bierstadt, Albert (1830-1902), LONG PEAK, ESTES PARK, COLORADO, 15 x 19, mounted on board
(4167/59)   *19000*
Bierstadt, Albert (1830-1902), MOUNTAINOUS RIVER LANDSCAPE, 4½ x 5¾ (633/121)   800
Bierstadt, Albert (1830-1902), STORM IN THE ROCKIES, oil on paper on board, 14 x 20 (4112/42)   3500
Bierstadt, Albert (1830-1902), STORM OVER YOSEMITE, 20 x 26½ (4112/27)   6000
Bierstadt, Albert (1830-1902), THE WETTERHORN, 36 x 47 (4112/28)   23000
Bierstadt, Albert (1830-1902), RIVER VIEW, 6 x 9, oil on board (4268/225)   7000
Biestadt, Albert (1830-1902), AN ALPINE SCENE, 19 x 13½, paper laid on canvas (666/93)   4500
Birch, Thomas (1779-1851), SHIP AT SEA d.1802, 31 x 43¼ (4167/8)   *6000*
Birney, William V. (1858-1909), PLEASANT THOUGHTS, 23½ x 35½ (4180/488)   1000
Birney, William V. (1858-1909), THE LETTER, 14 x 16 (4180/480)   850
Birney, William V. (1858-1909), THE WOOER WOOED, 18¼ x 24 (4236/34)   2400
Blakelock, Ralph Albert (1847-1919), DEER ON RIVERBANK, 12 x 20 (4167/15)   5250
Blakelock, Ralph Albert (1847-1919), FOREST POOL, 12 x 20 (4167/14)   5250
Blakelock, Ralph Albert (1847-1919), LANDSCAPE WITH TWO FIGURES, 4¾ x 6⅛ (633/235)   700
Blashfield, Edwin H. (1898-1936), RED-HAIRED BEAUTY, 20 x 16 (666/100)   3000
Blauvelt, Charles F. (1824-1900), PREPARING VEGETABLES, 10 x 8 (4180/479)   1100
Blenner, Carle J. (1864-1952), STILL LIFE WITH LILACS AND DOGWOOD BLOSSOMS, 25 x 36
(666/123)   800
Bluemner, Oscar (1867-1934), FARM AT RIDEFIELD, NEW JERSEY, mixed media, d.1910, 10 x 15
(4112/129)   1300
Blum, Robert (1857-1903), JAPANESE GARDENS, watercolor, 11½ x 17 (4236/75)   3250
Boggs, Frank (1855-1926), BASIN AT HONFLEUR, 15 x 21¾ (4167/154)   2500
Boggs, Frank (1855-1926), CROSSING THE RIVER, 21¾ x 15 (4236/80)   3250
Boggs, Frank (1855-1926), VIEW OF AMIENS, 21¼ x 25½ (4112/64)   5000
Boggs, Frank   (1855-1926), LANDSCAPE WITH RESTING CATTLE, 12 x 20 (666/121)   750
Boghosian, Varujan (b.1926), EURYDICE IN THE FOREST, 1963, 13 x 5 x 2¼, wooden box
(4140/130)   1200
Bohrod, Aaron (b.1907), BEAUTIFUL CHICAGO, gouache on board, d.1939 (4236/232)   2100
Bohrod, Aaron (b.1907), CUPID AND ROSES, tempera on panel, 9¾ x 8 (4236/230)   1500
Bohrod, Aaron, b.1907, VIEW OF PROVINCETOWN, 14 x 19½, gouache on board (4268/360)   1300
Boice, Bruce (b.1942), UNTITLED, d.1974, 3 panels, 31½ x 91¼, acrylic on canvas (4164/180)   600
Bonfield, William V. De V. (fl 1860-80), HORSE AND RIDER IN SNOWSTORM, 8 x 14 (4180/516)   850
Bontecou, Lee (b.1931), UNTITLED, d.1973, 18½ x 25, pencil (4164/150)   300

Bierstadt (4167/59)

Borein, Edward (1873-1945), ROUNDING UP THE HERD, watercolor, 11 x 15 (4236/143) 20000
Borein, Edward (1873-1945), THREE MEXICAN RIDERS, 9¼ x 12, ink on paper (4112/30) 1300
Borglum, John Gutzon (1867-1941), THREE SOCCER PLAYERS, 21, bronze (4167/99) 3500
Botke, Jesse A. (1883-), WHITE PEACOCKS AND DELPHINIUM, 29¾ x 22½ (4180/540) 1300
Botke, Jesse A. (1883-), CROWNED CRANES, 40¼ x 32½, oil on masonite (4076/776) 1500
Botke, Jesse A. (1883- }, THE JOURNEY, on masonite, 12 x 16 (666/125) 150
Bouche, Louis (1896-1969), BITS AND BRIDLES, 20 x 24 (4236/234) 800
Bouche, Louis (1896-1969), NEW YORK CITY STREET SCENE-WINTER, 24 x 20 (4167/234) 41670
Boughton, George Henry (1830-1905), FALLING LEAVES, 18½ x 36 (4180/483) 1300
Boughton, George Henry attrib. to, THE SEA BREEZE, 6 x 4, on panel (684/867) 175
Boxer, Stanley (b.1926), NIGHTSTONIGHTSDARKLY, d.1975, 12 x 80 (4164/179) 1000
Boyer, Ralph L. (1879-1952), PORTRAIT OF A WOMAN, 34 x 26¾ (4076/761) 750
Bradford, William (1823-1892), ROCKY MOUNTAIN LANDSCAPE, oil on board, 13½ x 20¾ (4236/122) 3100
Bradford, William (1823-92), FISHING AT DAWN, 13¼ x 19 (4076/742) 10000
Brett, Harold M. (1880-), THE DEPARTURE, 24 x 36 (4180/592) 1000
Bricher, Alfred Thompson (1837-1908), A SUMMER LANDSCAPE WITH POND, watercolor on paper, 14 x 20 (666/107) 850
Bricher, Alfred Thompson (1837-1908), NEAR MOUNT DESERT, MAINE, 21 x 14¾ (4180/568) 900
Bricher, Alfred Thompson (1837-1908), SAILING OFF THE COAST, 15 x 33 (4180/571) 3500
Bricher, Alfred Thompson (1837-1908), IN MY NEIGHBOR'S GARDEN d.1883, 24 x 44 (4167/42) 22000

Birch
(4167/8)

Bricher, Alfred Thompson (1837-1908), INDIAN SUMMER, MASSACHUSETTS d.1864, 22 x 36 (4167/9) 10500
Bricher, Alfred Thompson (1837-1908), LOOKING OUT TO SEA, 20 x 38 (4167/28) 9000
Bricher, Alfred Thompson (1837-1908), ON THE HUDSON, 10 x 20 (4076/724) 2000
Bricher, Alfred Thompson (1837-1908), AUTUMN RIVER SCENE, 9 x 19½, oil on board (4268/220) 2200
Bricher, Alfred Thompson (1837-1908), BOATING ON THE LAKE, 9 x 18, oil on board (4268/219) 2600
Bricher, Alfred Thompson (1837-1908), INCOMING TIDE, MONHEGAN ISLAND, MAINE, 15 x 32 (4268/279) 2000
Bricher, Alfred Thompson (1837-1908), SAILBOATS OFF A SHORE, 10¼ x 26¼, watercolor (4268/282) 900
Bridgman, Frederick A. (1847-1928), A PAUSE AT THE OASIS, 20½ x 29 (4197/354) 1800
Bridgman, Frederick A. (1847-1928), BAB EL OUED, 19¾ x 27¾ (4122/232) 1100
Bridgman, Frederick A. (1847-1928), DIVERTISSEMENT D'UN ROI ASSYRIEN, 44½ x 92 (4122/235) 9500
Bridgman, Frederick A. (1847-1928), HAREM INTERIOR, 1879, 21½ x 29 (4122/231) 3750
Bridgman, Frederick A. (1847-1928), PORTRAIT OF ZORA, 20 x 16, unframed, 1886 (4264/412)
Briscoe, Franklin D. (1844-1903), AFTER THE STORM, 1887, en grisaille, 17 x 26¾ (666/94) 275
Bristol, John Bunyan (1826-1909), CONNECTICUT LANDSCAPE, 16¼ x 30 (4076/736) 1100
Brooks, James (b.1906), FAALON, 1968, 28 x 32 (4164/124) 1800
Browere, A.D.O., CAPTURE OF FORT CASIMIR, 27 x 34 (4076/698) 1250
Browere, A.D.O. (1814-1887), PETER STUYVESANT AT THE RECAPTURE OF FORT CASIMIR, 27 x 34 (4076/697) 1100
Browere, A.D.O. (1814-1887), RECRUITING PETER STUYVESANT'S ARMY, 24 x 28¾, 1838 (4076/696) 1250

Brown*, Harrison B. (1831-1915), VILLAGE LANDSCAPE, 20 x 32½ (4180/511) 2800
Brown, F.G., after Bartlett 19c, G. WASHINGTON'S TOMB AT MOUNT VERNON, 25¼ x 30¼, 1868
(4076/700) 400
Brown, George Loring (1814-89), A FRENCH COASTAL SCENE,d.1834, 25 x 30 (633/263) 650
Brown, John George (1831-1913), THE TRANSIT OF VENUS, 30 x 25, d.1883 (4098/24) 24000
Brown, John George (1831-1913), EUCHRED SURE, 25 x 20¼ (4268/337) 12500
Brown, John George (1831-1913), READING BY THE WINDOW, 35 x 40½ (4268/336) 5000
Brown, John George (1831-1913), SHOESHINE BOY AND HIS DOG, 24 x 17 (4268/338) 10500
Browne, Byron, THE GREEN BRANCHES, N.Y., 27½ x 23½ (4219/2) 1500
Browne, Byron, 20c, COMPOSITION, 26 x 20½, gouache (633/88) 375
Browne, George Elmer (1871-1946), OLD SAW MILL, SILVERMINE, 23½ x 28½ (4268/361) 1400
Bruestle, George M. (1872-1939), ARCHES OF CAPISTRANO MISSION, CALIFORNIA, 26 x 34
(4180/551) 650
Bunker, Dennis M. (1861-90), SHIP'S BOW, oil on paper on board, 7 x 9 (4236/52) *7500*
Bunner, Andrew Fisher (1841-97), FISHING ON THE RIVER, 16 x 26 (4268/223) 3100
Burchfield, Charles, LOCOMOTIVE, watercolor and pencil, d.1916, 14 x 20 (4236/181) 13500
Burchfield, Charles (1893-1967), DREAM OF A STORM AT DAWN, watercolor, d.(1963) 1966, 30 x
40 (4112/194) 30000
Burchfield, Charles (1893-1967), HAUNTED EVENING, watercolor, d.1919, 16 x 25 (4112/125) 19000
Burchfield, Charles (1893-1967), HORIZON SUNLIGHT d.1916, 14 x 10, watercolor (4167/195) 4000
Burchfield, Charles (1893-1967), HOUSE THROUGH TREES d.1916, 14 x 10, watercolor and pencil
(4167/193) 4500
Burchfield, Charles (1893-1967), INSECTS AT TWILIGHT, mixed media, d.1917, 10¾ x 8½
(4112/122) 5250
Burchfield, Charles (1893-1967), MOON IN MIDWINTER, mixed media, d.1960, 12¾ x 18¾
(4112/124) 11100
Burchfield, Charles (1893-1967), PIGEONS FLYING d.1916, 14 x 10, watercolor and pencil
(4167/194) *5750*

Burchfield (4167/194)

Bunker (4236/52)

Burchfield, Charles (1893-1967), RAINY SUN, watercolor, d.1916, 8¾ x 11¾ (4112/158) 2100
Burchfield, Charles (1893-1967), SEPTEMBER, watercolor, d.1949-56, 22 x 48 (4112/164) 34000
Burchfield, Charles (1893-1967), STORM AFTER SUNSET d.1916, 14 x 20, watercolor and pencil
(4167/196) 7000
Burchfield, Charles (1893-1967), SUNFLOWER AND NEW MOON, mixed media, d.1917, 15½ x 8
(4112/123) 4250
Burchfield, Charles (1893-1967), WILD SWEET PEAS IN A SUMMER RAIN, 47 x 30½, (1961) 1965,
watercolor (4098/63) 45000
Burliuk, David (1882-1967), NEW MEXICAN LANDSCAPE, 12 x 24 (4180/614) 700
Burliuk, David (1882-1967), PORTRAIT OF MARUSSIA, d.1922, ink (4260/698) 500
Burroughs, Bryson (1869-1934), AN ITALIAN GARDEN, d.1912, 18 x 24 (633/26) 150
Buttersworth, James E., SAILING NEAR THE INLET, 7½ x 11¼, oil on panel (4268/290) 2500
Buttersworth, James E. (1817-1894), THE YACHT 'MAGIC' OFF CASTLE GARDEN, 14 x 24
(4236/4) 18000
Buttersworth, James E. (1817-1894), YACHTING IN NEW YORK BAY, oil on millboard, 6 x 10
(4236/1) *9500*

Buttersworth, James E. (1817-94), RACING ALONG THE COAST, 8¼ x 10¼ (4180/566) 7250
Buttersworth, James E. (1817-94), SAILING OFF THE BATTERY, NEW YORK HARBOR, 8 x 12 (4180/565) 6000
Buttersworth, James E. (1817-94), SCHOONER RACE IN NEW YORK HARBOR, 8¼ x 14 (4098/3) 12000
Buttersworth, James E. (1817-94), RACING, 7 x 12 (4268/278) 7000
Buttersworth, James E. (1817-94), SAILING IN PHILADELPHIA HARBOR, 5¾ x 9½ (4268/275) 4000
Cadmus, Paul (b.1904), ABOARD THE YACHT 'LUXURXIA', mixed media, 5¼ x 8¾ (4236/225) 2800
Caesar, Doris (1893-1977), VISION, H25, bronze (4164/52) 1100
Caesar, Doris (1893-1977), STANDING WOMAN, 1956, H26, bronze (4164/51) 1700
Calder, Alexander, ACROBATS, d.1969, 29⅜ x 43⅛, mixed media (4204/123) 3500
Calder, Alexander, AIR MAIL, d.1974, 43¼ x 29½, mixed media (4173/593) 3500
Calder, Alexander, BLACK PIERCED ON RED POST, d.1968, L29, H18, painted metal (4173/570) 13000
Calder, Alexander, BLACK TRIANGLE, gouache and ink, 22½ x 31 (4250/510) 3250
Calder, Alexander, BOLLARDS AND BLUE SUN, gouache, ink on paper, 22⅝ x 31⅜, 1944 (4263/126) 2500
Calder, Alexander, BOOMERANGS, d.1971, 29½ x 43¼, gouache (4173/591) 3400
Calder, Alexander, COGWHEELS, d.1971, 22¾ x 30¾, mixed media (4173/590) 2500
Calder, Alexander, COMPOSITION IN BLACK AND BLUE, watercolor and ink, 23 x 31¼ (4250/511) *2750*

Buttersworth (4236/1)

Calder (4250/511)

Calder, Alexander, COMPOSITION WITH SPIRAL, RED SPHERE AND BLACK REEDS, gouache, 30¾ x 22¾, 1966 (4263/125) 2000
Calder, Alexander, COMPOSITION ON YELLOW GROUND, 29 x 39 (4263/128) 6500
Calder, Alexander, COMPOSITION WITH BLUE HEART, ink, gouache, 23 x 30⅞, 1949 (4263/121) 1700
Calder, Alexander, COMPOSITION WITH SPIRAL AND SNAKE, brush, ink, 22⅝ x 31¼, 1946 (4263/119) 1000
Calder, Alexander, COMPOSITION WITH SPIRAL, RED SPHERE AND BLACK, FORMS, gouache, 30¾ x 22¾, 1966 (4263/127) 2000
Calder, Alexander, COMPOSITION IN BLACK, BLUE, RED AND YELLOW, d.1946, 11⅜ x 10½, mixed media (4164/45) 1200
Calder, Alexander, COMPOSITION IN BLACK, RED, YELLOW AND BLUE, d.1947, 11⅜ x 15½, mixed media (4164/47) 1600
Calder, Alexander, COMPOSITION IN BLUE, ORANGE AND YELLOW, d.1946, 11⅜ x 10½, mixed media (4164/44) 1700
Calder, Alexander, COMPOSITION IN RED, ORANGE, BLUE, YELLOW AND BLACK, d.1949, 10¼ x 13, mixed media (4164/46) 1500
Calder, Alexander, COMPOSITION WITH BUTTERFLY
Calder, Alexander, COMPOSITION, d.1968, 26 x 19¾, mixed media (4204/122) 3250
Calder, Alexander, COMPOSITION, 55 x 81, hand woven rug (633/101) 750
Calder, Alexander, DANCING COUPLE, 19¾ x 12¾, mixed media (4204/64) 3000
Calder, Alexander, FLYING BOOMERANGS, 1961, L118⅛ (4124/89) 37500
Calder, Alexander, HANGING SPIRAL, d.1969, 29½ x 42½, gouache (4096/138) 2000
Calder, Alexander, HAPPY AS LARRY, H46, painted metal (4169/71) 42500
Calder, Alexander, HORIZON WEEDS, d.1963, L60, painted metal (4169/78) 24000
Calder, Alexander, ILLUSTRATIONS FOR A POEM BY RUTHVEN TODD, 1947, 15½ x 10⅞, mixed media (4204/99) 800

Calder, Alexander, KNOBS & CURLICUES, 1963, H74⅝ (4124/82)	30000
Calder, Alexander, MOBILE, metal and wire, 13½, ca1952 (4252/674)	11000
Calder, Alexander, MOBILE, ca1965, L17, painted metal (4173/568)	7500
Calder, Alexander, MODEL FOR 'THE Y', ca1960, L36, painted metal (4173/571)	27000
Calder, Alexander, MOUNTAIN RANGE, gouache, 31¼ x 44¼, 1965 (4263/123)	3500
Calder, Alexander, PALM FRONDS, d.1965, 29½ x 42½, gouache (4140/120)	3200
Calder, Alexander, PORTRAITS OF A MAN AND A WOMAN, TWO CARICATURES, 8⅛ x 10¼, 1928 (4263/55)	1000
Calder, Alexander, RED SPHERE, BLACK SPIRALS, brush, ink, watercolor, 22¾ x 31, 1947 (4263/120)	2400
Calder, Alexander, SERPOLET, d.1974, 29½ x 43¼, mixed media (4173/592)	2600
Calder, Alexander, SPIRALS AND SERPENTINES, d.1951, 15½ x 11⅜, mixed media (4164/43)	1600
Calder, Alexander, STUDIES FOR SCULPTURE, 11 x 8½, mixed media (4140/59)	850
Calder, Alexander, STUDY FOR SCULPTURE, 5⅝ x 4¼, mixed media (4140/60)	550
Calder, Alexander, THE CONVERSATION, 16⅝ x 14⅜, mixed media (4204/65)	3750
Calder, Alexander, THE NOSE, MAQUETTE FOR STABILE, metal, 12½ x 17¼, 1968 (4252/678)	6500
Calder, Alexander, THREE BLACK EGGS, d.1967, 22¾ x 30¾, gouache (4140/122)	1800
Calder, Alexander, UNTITLED, 43½ x 29½, gouache (4140/121)	1700
Calder, Alexander, UNTITLED, d.1948, 11⅜ x 15⅜, mixed media (4164/48)	1900
Calder, Alexander, WHITE DISCS, painted metal, W120, 1955 (4249/317)	58000
Calder, Alexander, YELLOWS IN THE AIR, d.1961, L48, painted metal (4169/79)	31000
Calder, Alexander, 3 LITTLE CHILDREN SITTING ON THE SAND, 11¼ x 10⅜, ink (4125/184)	1500
Califano, John (b.1864), A MOUNTAINOUS LANDSCAPE, 29 x 42 (633/242)	800
Callery, Mary (b.1903), MAQUETTE FOR 'FREE FORM', L8½, bronze (4096/157)	500
Campus, Peter (b.1937), RAY DRAWING FOR INTERFACE OF VIDEO AND REFLEC-, TED IMAGE, 15 x 23, ink (4164/132)	150
Carles, Arthur B. (1876-1952), LUNCHEON IN THE GARDEN, 18¼ x 21¾ (4112/61)	2750
Carlin, John (1813-91), OUTSIDE A DUTCH TAVERN, d.1860, 18 x 24 (633/259)	1100
Carlsen, Emil (1853-1932), IRON KETTLE AND CLAMS, d.1926, 25 x 24 (4236/111)	42000
Carlsen, Emil (1853-1932), PEONIES AND KANG HSI VASE, 56 x 38½ (4236/87)	8000
Carlsen, Emil (1853-1932), PINK ROSES AND BRASS BOWL, 18¾ x 15 (4236/86)	9500
Carlsen, Emil (1853-1932), POND IN SPRINGTIME, 19¾ x 23¾ (4167/128)	*5500*
Carlson, John E., 1875-1945, WINTER QUIET, 16 x 20 (4268/362)	1100
Carmiencke, Johann H. (1810-67), NEW YORK LANDSCAPE, 25 x 36 (4180/519)	1900
Carr, S.S. (1837-1908), BOY FISHING, 12 x 10 (4180/481)	900
Carr, S.S. (1837-1908), BUYING ORANGES AT THE BEACH d.1877, 16¼ x 20¼ (4167/43)	15000
Carr, S.S. (1837-1908), THE YACHT RACE, d.1881, 14 x 24 (4236/35)	29000
Carr, S.S. (1837-1908), WALKING IN THE RAIN, 12 x 16 (666/84)	2250
Carr, S.S. (1837-1908), YOUNG GIRL AT SEASHORE d.1887, 15 x 12¼ (4167/44)	7000
Carr, S.S. (1837-1908), SHEEP IN A LANDSCAPE, 16 x 24 (4268/346)	1000
Carreno, Mario, ISLAND OF SHELLS, watercolor, 15¾ x 19½ (4219/3)	300
Casilear, John William (1811-93), FIGURE IN A LANDSCAPE, 12 x 10 (4167/11)	3750
Cassatt, Mary, ETUDE D'ENFANT NU, 1914, watercolor, 18½ x 13 (4170/107)	4750
Cassatt, Mary, ETUDE DE FEMME ET D'ENFANT, 1908, watercolor, 18¾ x 12¾ (4170/106)	5500
Cassatt, Mary, SKETCH OF A YOUNG BOY, pastel, 17½ x 13⅜ (4250/415)	*6500*
Cassatt, Mary (1844-1926), DRAWING FOR 'PORTRAIT OF KATHERINE KELSO CASSATT', ca1905, 9½ x 6¼, pencil (4260/1418)	7000
Cassatt, Mary (1844-1926), HALF-LENGTH PROFILE OF A BABY HOLDING A DOLL, ca1876, 4½ x 4⅜, pencil (4260/1417)	3200
Cassatt, Mary (1844-1926), MOTHER AND CHILD, ca1890, 12½ x 9½, pencil (4140/7)	4800
Cassatt, Mary (1844-1926), SKETCH OF VERNON LEE WEARING A PINCE-NEZ, 1895, 10¼ x 7¼, mixed media (4260/1419)	11000
Cassatt, Mary (1844-1926), STUDY OF A MOTHER'S HEAD, 1913, 17½ x 14, watercolor (4260/1420)	6000
Chambers, Thomas, attrib. (1806-66), LANDSCAPE AT SUNSET, 22¼ x 30 (4211/601)	3000
Chandler, Joseph Goodhue, 1813-84, ABIGAIL TAPPAN EMMERY, 30 x 25 (4268/187)	800
Chapman, John Gadsby (1808-89), SLEEPING BOY WITH DOG, 66 x 48 (4268/350)	1700
Chase, William M. (1849-1916), GOWANUS BAY, oil on panel, 10 x 15½ (4236/45)	10500
Chase, William M. (1849-1916), LANDSCAPE, oil on panel, 10¼ x 14¾ (4236/55)	8500
Chase, William M. (1849-1916), PORTRAIT OF LOUIS BETTS, 20 x 16 (4167/136)	*5750*
Chase, William M. (1849-1916), PORTRAIT OF MR. LESLIE PEASE BARNUM, 21½ x 17½ (4260/689)	8800
Chatterton, Clarence K. (1880-1973), CHADEAYNE PLACE, CORNWALL, d.1917, 28¼ x 36 (4236/90)	6250
Christensen, Dan (b.1924), BRIGHT BEAR, d.1970, 113 x 37, mixed media (4140/143)	550
Christensen, Dan (b.1924), ORANGE CHASER, d.1972, 89 x 54½, acrylic on canvas (4164/105)	500
Christy, Howard Chandler (1873-1952), SPRINGTIME FROLIC d.1928, 66 x 149, unframed (4167/113)	8000

Chryssa (b.1933), STUDY FOR 'THE GATES TO TIMES SQUARE', ca1965, 36¾ x 23½ x 18½,
neon tubing (4140/131)   1500

Church, Frederic Edwin (1826-1900), IN THE ANDES, oil on academy board, 10¼ x 9¼ (4112/16)   16000

Church, Frederic Edwin (1826-1900), JULY SUNSET, BERKSHIRE COUNTY, MASS., d.1847, 29 x
40 (4167/16)   210000

Church, Frederic Edwin (1826-1900), NEW ENGLAND LANDSCAPE, 25 x 36 (4167/23)   230000

Church, Frederic Edwin (1826-1900), SOUTH AMERICAN LANDSCAPE c.1874, 15 x 22 (4167/31)   35000

Clapp, William H. (1879-1954), PORTRAIT OF A SEATED LADY, on masonite, 22 x 18 (666/116)   500

Clark, Benton (1895-1964), ILLUSTRATION FOR 'ARIZONA', d.1939, 25 x 36 (4236/159)   2600

Clark, F. Myron (1876-1965), THE YACHT 'PAOLA', 26 x 30 (633/266)   325

Coffin, William A. (1855-1925), A STROLL BY THE RIVER, oil on panel, d.1882, 16¼ x 12¾
(4236/67)   13500

Coffin, William A. (1855-1925), HILLSIDE LANDSCAPE, 48 x 60 (4180/517)   2100

Cole, Joseph Foxcroft (1837-92), BY THE STREAM, 11½ x 19¼ (4268/252)   900

Cole, Joseph Foxcroft (1837-92), SAN JUAN MISSION, 18¼ x 26 (4268/304)   1400

Cole, Thomas (1801-48), STUDY FOR 'THE OX BOW' CONNECTICUT RIVER, 5¾ x 9½, oil on
panel (4112/18)   1600

Cole, Thomas (1801-48), TORRE DI SCHIAVI, CAMPAGNA DI ROMA, 14¾ x 24, 1842 (4098/13)   20000

Colman, Samuel (1832-1920), LANDSCAPE, 16 x 28¾ (4180/528)   950

Colman, Samuel (1832-1920), SOLOMON'S TEMPLE, COLORADO, casein on paper, d.1888, 20¾ x
26 (4236/123)   *28000*

Colman, Samuel (1832-1920), THE EFFECT OF CLOUD SHADOWS, YOSEMITE VALLEY, 9½ x
13½, gouache (4167/54)   1600

Coman, Charlotte B. (1833-1924), OLD WINDMILLS, 19 x 15 (4180/527)   700

Cope, George (1855-1929), STRAWBERRIES AND CREAM, 20¼ x 16¼ (4180/501)   4600

Carlsen (4167/128)

Cassatt (4250/415)

Chase (4167/136)

Colman (4236/123)

Cope, George (1855-1929), UNION MOMENTOES ON A DOOR, d.1889, 52 x 32 (4236/60)   19000

Copeland, Alfred B., (1840-1909), MILL AT CHARENTON, d.1876, 9¼ x 6¾ (633/27)   150

Copley, William (b.1919), LOLA PULCO, 29¼ x 23¾ (4164/167)   500

Copley, William (b.1919), UNTITLED, d.1931, 30 x 51 (4164/163)   1300

Cornoyer, Paul (1864-1923), WASHINGTON SQUARE, 22 x 26 (666/124)   10500

Corwin (4167/72)

Corwin, Charles Abel (1857-1938), INDIAN'S BREAKING HORSES, 20 x 16 (4167/72)   *1000*

Costigan, John Edward (1888-1972), BROOK IN WINTER, 20 x 26, mixed media (633/153)   400

Cote, Alan (b.1937), UNTITLED, d.1973, 84 x 60, acrylic on canvas (4164/125)   350

Couse, Eanger I. (1866-1936), A QUIET DAY, 8½ x 10½ (4236/131)   6500

Couse, Eanger I. (1866-1936), BY THE EVENING FIRE, 18 x 15 (4236/133)   13500

Couse, Eanger, I. (1866-1936), INDIAN ENCAMPMENT AT DUSK, 12 x 16 (4236/126)   5000

Craig, Thomas Bigelow (1849-1924), AFTER A SUMMER SHOWER, 10 x 14 (666/92)   400

Craig, Thomas Bigelow (1849-1924), LANDSCAPE WITH WATERING COWS, 16 x 24 (633/118)   475

Crane, Rovbert Bruce (1857-1934), YELLOW ROSES, 16¼ x 12¾, watercolor (633/134)   275

Criss, Francis (b.1901), THIRD AVENUE L, 25 x 19 (4236/193)   5000

Crocker, John Denison, 1823-c.1879, THAMES RIVER, NEW LONDON, 23¼ x 37 (4268/222)   5250

Cropsey, Jasper Francis, (1823-1900), RIVER LANDSCAPE, 7¾ x 6½ (4180/523)   3500

Cropsey, Jasper Francis, (1823-1900), SUNSET AT GREENWOOD LAKE, d.1888, 36 x 59½
(4112/26)   31000

Cropsey, Jasper Francis, (1823-1900), CATTLE IN A RIVER LANDSCAPE d.1881, 12 x 20
(4167/20)   *7500*

Cropsey, Jasper Francis, (1823-1900), MONK AT A WELL, 18 x 14¾ (4180/503)   3250

Cropsey, Jasper Francis, (1823-1900), MOUNT WASHINGTON FROM LAKE SEBAGO, MAINE, 20 x
33, 1867 (4098/19)   28000

Culverhouse, Johann Mongles, (1825-95), MARKETPLACE AT NIGHT, 36 x 50¼ (4268/324)   3500

Curran, Charles C., THE ENCHANTED SHORE d.1895, 17¾ x 32 (4167/119)   3250

Curran, Charles C. (1861-1942), THE GARDEN WALK, 23½ x 13½ (4236/98)   4750

Curran, Charles C. (1861-1942), THE LANTERNS, d.1913, 30¼ x 30¼ (4236/99)   17500

Curry, John S. (1897-1946), THE REIFFENBACH SISTERS, mixed media, d.1932, 22 x 24
(4112/121)   3750

Cushing, Lily, CENTRAL PARK, gouache, 19¾ x 25 (4219/4)   400

Chapman, John G. (1809-89), YOUNG SHEPHERD WITH FLUTE, 30 x 25¼ (4122/151)   3250

D'Arcangelo, Allan (b.1930), CONSTELLATION #6, d.1970, 60 x 60, acrylic on canvas (4164/158)   1600

Dabo, Leon (1868-1960), A LANDSCAPE, d.1918, 14 x 10 (633/125)   200

Dallin, Cyrus E., (1861-1944), APPEAL TO THE GREAT SPIRIT, bronze, d.1913, H8¾ (4236/140)   2600

Dallin, Cyrus E., (1861-1944), APPEAL TO THE GREAT SPIRIT, bronze, d.1913, H8¾ (4236/142)   2600

Dallin, Cyrus E., (1861-1944), THE SCOUT, bronze, d.1910, H8½ (4236/141)   1800

Dallin, Cyrus E., (1861-1944), APPEAL TO THE GREAT SPIRIT, d.1913, 8¾, bronze (4167/92)   3000

Dallin, Cyrus E., (1861-1944), ON THE WARPATH, 8¾, bronze (4167/93)   2100

Dallin, Cyrus E., 1861-1944, APPEAL TO THE GREAT SPIRIT, H8¾, bronze (4268/311) — 2300
Dana, William Parsons W. (1833-1927), THE RESCUE, d.1861, 30 x 25 (633/146) — 800
Danton, F. Jr., FATHER TIME INTRODUCING AMERICA, 1901, 27 1/2 x 34¼ (4180/499) — 4500
Daphnis, Nassos, (b.1914), 7-76, 40 x 37½, enamel on canvas (4164/173) — 550
Darley, Felix Octavius, 1822-88, DEATH OF LEATHERSTOCKING, 9½ x 16, unframed (4268/301) — 900
Daveneck, Frank (1848-1919), PORTRAIT OF MAGGIE WILSON, oil on panel, 15 x 12 (4236/62) — 10500
Davey, Randall (1887-1964), STEEPLE CHASERS LEAVING THE PADDOCK, 18 x 22, oil on masonite (4167/237) — 1700
Davidson, Jo, ABRAHAM LINCOLN, H11¼, d.1943 (684/890) — 900
Davies, Arthur B. (1862-1928), CANYON OVERTONES, 26 x 40 (4112/110) — 4250
Davies, Arthur B. (1862-1928), DAWN, d.1926, 36 x 66 (4236/190) — 12000
Davies, Arthur B. (1862-1928), ITALY BY TOWN BY TOWER, d.1922, 26 x 40 (4112/111) — 2500
Davies, Arthur B. (1862-1928), REQUIEM, 18½ x 30 (4112/97) — 2250
Davies, Arthur B. (1862-1928), THE GOATHERD, 22 x 17¼ (4236/188) — 4500
Davies, Arthur B., (1862-1928), SHEPHERDESS, 20¼ x 20¼ (4112/96) — 2250
Davis, Stuart (1894-1964), RED BRICK BUILDINGS, gouache, 11½ x 17 (4236/212) — 20000
Davis, Warren B. (1865-1928), NUDE, 16 x 12 (4098/43) — 2750
Davis, Warren B. (1865-1928), WOMAN IN WHITE d.1906, 14 x 10 (4167/143) — 2800
Davis, Warren B. (1865-1928), WOODLAND N.Y.MPHS, 12¼ x 8 (4167/133) — 700
Dearth, Henry G. (1864-1918), LANDSCAPE WITH HOUSES, 20 x 30 (4180/531) — 600
Dehn, Adolph (1895-1968), NEW ORLEANS - SATURDAY NIGHT, watercolor, d.1941, 20 x 29 (4112/190) — 1300
Deming, Edward W. (1860-1942), BIG HORNED SHEEP, bronze, d.1905, H13 (4112/48) — 1700
Deming, Edward W. (1860-1942), INDIAN ENCAMPMENT, unframed, 30½ x 75 (4236/125) — 7000
Deming, Edward W. (1860-1942), PRONGHORN ANTELOPE ON THE PLAINS, unframed, oil on masonite, 24 x 60 (4236/124) — 4500
Demuth, Charles (1883-1935), 'PARROTS', ca1911-12, 8¼ x 6½, mixed media (4260/700) — 1200
Demuth, Charles (1883-1935), ACROBATS, watercolor and pencil, d.1917, 13 x 8 (4236/172) — 34000
Demuth, Charles (1883-1935), BOY WITH BOXING POSTER, 10¼ x 7¾, watercolor and ink (4167/176) — 2000
Demuth, Charles (1883-1935), DANCING SAILORS 1917, 8 x 10, watercolor on paper (4167/175) — *17000*

Cropsey (4167/20)

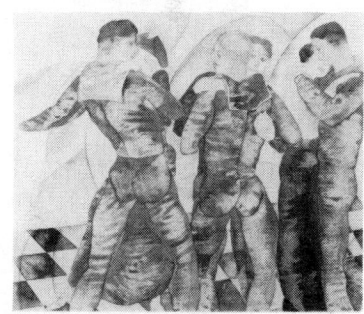

Demuth (4167/175)

Demuth, Charles (1883-1935), FOUR MALE FIGURES, watercolor, 13 x 8 (4112/140) — 3500
Demuth, Charles (1883-1935), IN VAUDEVILLE, TWO DANCERS, watercolor, d.1920, 13 x 8 (4236/191) — 37500
Demuth, Charles (1883-1935), LANDSCAPE #4, oil on board, 12 x 16 (4236/164) — 5250
Demuth, Charles (1883-1935), MEN SWIMMING, 8 x 10¼, watercolor and ink (4167/177) — 2750
Demuth, Charles (1883-1935), SAILS, gouache, .1921, 19¾ x 23¾ (4112/145) — 57500

Demuth, Charles (1883-1935), THREE ACROBATS, watercolor, d.1916, 13 x 8 (4236/173) 33000
Demuth, Charles (1883-1935), TUMBLERS, watercolor and pencil, d.1917, 13 x 8 (4236/167) 42500
Demuth, Charles (1883-1935), TREES, ROOFTOP, LANDSCAPE, watercolor/double sides, d.1916 and 1922 (4112/143) 15000
DeHaas, Mauritz F.H. (1832-95), BOATS OFF A LONG ISLAND BEACH, 14¼ x 24 (4076/737) 1700
DeHaas, Mauritz F.H. (1832-95), FISHING AT SUNSET, 12 x 9¾, 1875 (4076/740) 1400
DeHaas, Mauritz F.H. (1832-95), SAILING, 12 x 19 (4076/738) 1700
Diao, David (b.1943), TURN BUCKLE, d.1968, 88 x 88, acrylic on canvas (4164/112) 350
Diao, David, (b.1943), UNTITLED-OPEN, d.1972, 84½ x 66¼, acryllic on canvas (4164/111) 460
Dickinson, Preston (1891-1930), STILL LIFE WITH COMPOTE, 15½ x 18½, pastel on paper (4098/58) 3250
Dickinson, Preston (1891-1930), STILL LIFE WITH VEGETABLES, 18½ x 24½, pastel on paper (4167/188) 1100
Diebenkorn, Richard (b.1922), UNTITLED, d.1953, 9 x 12, ink on paper (4164/147) 650
Diebenkorn, Richard (b.1922), UNTITLED, d.1954, 10¼ x 11¼, ink on paper (4164/145) 500
Dine, Jim (b.1935), LARGE BOOT LYING DOWN, 1965, L39, metal (4164/133) 2500
Dixon, Maynard Lafayette, WESTERN STREET SCENE, 16¼ x 20 (4167/58) 3000

Du Bois (4167/187)

Dixon, Maynard Lafayette (1875-1946), LATE AFTERNOON, EAST SHORE OF THE SIERRAS
  d.1934, 20 x 26 (4167/64) — 4000
Dolph, John Henry, 1835-1903, DOG , DUCK AND DUCKLINGS, 18 x 24 (4268/347) — 1800
Donati, Enrico (b.1909), ROUGE ET NOIR, d.1967, 25 x 30, mixed media (4164/122) — 400
Donoghue, John T. (1853-1903), THE YOUNG SOPHOCLES, bronze, H44¾ (4236/109) — 8000
Doughty, Thomas, BOATS ON A LAKE, 14 x 20 (4268/221) — 2500
Dove, Arthur G. (1880-1946), BEYOND ABSTRACTION, d.1946, 12 x 9 (4236/197) — 8000
Dove, Arthur G. (1880-1946), BUILDINGS, watercolor, d.1938, 5 x 7 (4112/147) — 3000
Dove, Arthur G. (1880-1946), DERRICK, watercolor, d.1933, 3½ x 5 (4112/148) — 1500
Dove, Arthur G. (1880-1946), HARVEST TIME, watercolor and charcoal, 5 x 7 (4236/196) — 1800
Dove, Arthur G. (1880-1946), ITALIAN CHILD COMBING HAIR, watercolor, d.1933, 5 x 7 (4112/149) — 1700
Dove, Arthur G. (1880-1946), SWITCH ENGINES, watercolor, d.1937, 5 x 7 (4112/146) — 2000
Drew, Clement (attrib) (C.1807-89), THE BRIG WAKULLA IN A STORM, 21 x 28½ (4180/562) — 1000
Drew, Clement (C.1807-89), SAILING OFF MARBLEHEAD, 9 x 12 (4180/563) — 1300
Drew, Clement (1807-89), PLYMOUTH HARBOR, MASSACHUSETTS, 18 x 26 (4076/772) — 1700
Drew, George W. (b.1875), BY THE POND, CONNECTICUT, 24 x 36 (633/262) — 800
Drew, George W. (1875-), GIANT OAK NEW ENGLAND, 20 x 29¾ (4076/770) — 650
Drew, George W. (1875-), HOUSE IN THE COUNTRY, 20 x 30½ (4180/534) — 850
Driggs, Elsie (b.1898), AEROPLANE, d.1928, 44 x 38 (4236/194) — 16000
Drysdale, Alexander J. (b.1870), A MISTY MORNING, 20 x 13½, watercolor on board (633/139) — 650
Du Bois, Guy Pene (1880-1946), ART LOVERS, 20 x 16 (4236/210) — 8750
Du Bois, Guy Pene (1880-1946), CARNIVAL INTERLUDE d.1935, 57¾ x 45 (4167/187) — *24000*
Du Bois, Guy Pene (1880-1946), THE BASHFUL NUDE, 31 x 23 (4112/175) — 5000
Du Bois, Guy Pene (1880-1946), THE CAFE, oil on panel, 21½ x 18 (4112/113) — 3500
Du Bois, Guy Pene, 1880-1946, SEATED NUDE, 20 x 15, oil on board (4268/389) — 1200
Dubreuil, Victor (19c-20c), STILL LIFE WITH FRUIT AND FIFTY DOLLAR BILL, 10¼ x 12¼
  (4098/1) — 2750
Dubreuil, Victor, 19-20c, BARRELS OF MONEY, 25 x 30 (4268/207) — 24000
Dufner, Edward (1872-1957), THREE NUDES IN A LANDSCAPE, oil on panel, 15¾ x 20 (4112/70) — 1800
Dunack, Ola, INDIAN BY THE SHORES OF A LAKE, 11½ x 19⅞ (684/828) — 100
Dunning, Robert S. (1829-1905), STILL LIFE WITH FRUIT AND HONEYCOMB, d.1876, 12¾ x 9
  (4236/57) — 6000
Durand, Asher B. (1796-1886), STREAM IN LANDSCAPE, 14 x 20 (4236/14) — 4500
Durand, Asher B. (1796-1886), NEW JERSEY LANDSCAPE d.1867, 15 x 24¼ (4167/19) — 6000
Durrie, George H. (1820-63), WINTER SCENE, CHILDREN SKATING, 6½ x 11¼, oil on board
  (4112/17) — 8500
Duveneck, Frank (1848-1919), ITALIAN VILLA d.1887, 25 x 30 (4167/115) — 8500
Duveneck, Frank (1848-1919), MAN WITH BLACK HAT, 22 x 18¼ (4260/688) — 7000
Duveneck, Frank (1848-1919), VENETIAN WOMEN, 23 x 15, d.1884 (4098/23) — 12000
Duveneck, Frank (1849-1919), PORTRAIT OF MISS WESTLAKE 1890, 21¾ x 16 (4167/137) — 3750
Dzubas, Friedl (b.1915), UNTITLED, d.1960, 36 x 31 (4164/127) — 950
Eakins, Thomas (1844-1916), PORTRAIT OF FLORENCE EINSTEIN, d.1905, 20 x 24 (4236/64) — 50000
Eakins, Thomas (1844-1916), THE ARCHBISHOP WILLIAM HENRY ELDER, d.1903, 66½ x 45½
  (4112/99) — 265000
Eaton, Charles Harry, 1850-1901, ROWBOAT ON A LILY POND, 28 x 44¼ (4268/255) — 1000
Edmonds, Francis W. (1806-63), STUDY FOR THE THIRSTY DROVER, 9¼ x 13¼, oil on board
  (4112/12) — 7000
Eggenhofer, Nick (b.1897), MEXICAN HORSEMAN, 9 x 14¾, ink on paper (4167/50) — 1300
Eggleston, Benjamin O. (1867-?), A STROLL IN THE COUNTRY, 22 x 16, 1897 (4076/749) — 600
Eichelberger, Robert A., A WATCHFUL EYE, 41½ x 35½ (4122/256) — 2500
Eilshemius, Louis Michel (1864-1941), NUDE IN INTERIOR, 39 x 24½ (4180/618) — 1300
Eliscu, Frank (b. 1912), NAIAD, 22½, bronze on marble base (4167/98) — 2200
Elliot, Charles Loring, 1812-68, THE REVEREND RUSSELL COOKE, 36 x 29¼ (4268/191) — 1800
Elwell, Farrington (1874-1962), DISRUPTING CAMP, 30 x 39¼ (4167/77) — 3000
Emerson, Charles Chase (d.1922), FINDING THE WAY, canvas laid on board, 16 x 20 (666/113) — 850
Emerson, Charles Chase (1874-1962), BEFORE THE STORM, 23¾ x 29¾ (4167/78) — 1000
Hassam, Frederick C. (1858-1935), MOONRISE AT SUNSET d.1900, 27 x 27 (4167/147) — 30000
Hassam, Frederick C. (1859-1935), CHURCH OF THE PAULIST FATHERS, NEW YORK, 22 x 24
  (4098/35) — 70000
Hassam, Frederick C. (1859-1935), ON THE BOAT DECK d.1885, 9 x 8, watercolor on paper
  (4167/123) — *12000*
Hassam, Frederick C. (1859-1935), STREET SCENE d.1883, 14¾ x 10¼, pen and ink (4167/124) — 2250
Hassam, Frederick C. (1859-1935), THE ENGLISH GIRL, 30 x 20, d.1919 (4098/37) — 22000
Hassam, Frederick C. (1859-1935), STILL LIFE WITH SHELLS AND BOTTLE, 11½ x 10¼, oil on
  panel (4268/385) — 3000

Enneking, John J. (1841-1916), AUTUMN LANDSCAPE, 20¼ x 24¼ (4236/76)   2800
Enneking, John J. (1841-1916), HYDE PARK WITH FIGURE AND RIVER, 10 x 16 (4076/722)   750
Estes, Richard (b.1936), UNTITLED, ca1962, 6½ x 6½, watercolor (4164/144)   500
Evergood, Philip (1901-1973), DAVID AND THE WIFE OF URIAH, THE HITTITE, 32 x 21½ (4236/214)   10500
Evergood, Phillip (1901-73), ILLUSTRATIONS FOR OLD RUSSIAN STORIES, 15 x 9½ pair of watercolors (4167/232)   1600
Eyre, Louisa (1872-1953), FAUN WITH URN, bronzed, 1936, H43½, (4112/108)   2300
Farny, Henry F. (1847-1910), SUSPENSE d.1890, 14 x 10, gouache (4167/56)   35000
Farny, Henry F. (1847-1916), SIOUX CHIEF d.1897, 9½ x 7½, gouache on paper (4167/67)   20000
Farny, Henry F. (1847-1916), CROSSING THE DIVIDE, d.1907, 28¼ x 18¼ (4112/52)   195000
Farny, Henry F. (1847-1916), INDIAN WITH HIS HORSE, gouache, d.1899, 11¼ x 8¼ (4236/130)   50000
Farny, Henry F. (1847-1916), INDIANS ON THE PLAIN, oil on board, d.1902, 13 x 24¼ (4236/150)   37500
Farny, Henry F. (1847-1916), PUEBLO MAIDEN, gouache, 14¼ x 10¼ (4236/139)   52500
Farny, Henry F. (1847-1916), LAST STAND OF THE PATRIARCH, gouache, d.1906, 13¾ x 22 (4112/44)   120000
Farrer, Henry, SEASCAPE, 6¼ x 10⅜, pencil and wash (684/893)   100
Faulker, John, 19c, VIEW OF THE SHENANDOAH WATER GAP, 14¼ x 22 (4268/251)   2200
Fechin, Nicolai (1881-1955), WESTERN LANDSCAPE, 14¾ x 24¼, mounted on board (4167/57)   20000
Feke, Robert (ca1705-50), PORTRAIT OF CAPTAIN WILLIAM STODDARD, 30 x 25 (4098/5)   12500
Field, E. Loyal (1856-1914), A COUNTRY ROAD, 12 x 18 (633/111)   225
Fiene, Ernest (b.1894), BEFORE THE ACT, 28 x 28, oil on masonite (4167/230)   650
Fisher, Alvin, 1792-1863, COASTAL SCENE, NAHANT, MASS., 14¼ x 18¼ (4268/217)   1500
Flannagan, John B. (1895-1942), FIGURES, wood relief, 23¼ x 8½ (4112/177)   1200
Flannagan, John B. (1895-1942), STANDING CHILD, brown sandstone, H16¼ (4112/178)   1900
Francis, John F. (1808-86), FRUIT AND WINE, 25 x 30, 1858 (4098/4)   65000
Frankenberg, H., THE EMPTY POCKETS, 22 x 17, cop. (abbrev.) (684/868)   60
Frankenthaler, Helen, (1928-), UNTITLED, 1968, 18 x 23¾, oil, wash, paper (4125/192)   4500
Frieseke, Frederick C. (1874-1939), HOLLYHOCKS, 31¾ x 31¾ (4236/69)   22000
Frieseke, Frederick C. (1874-1939), LADY ON A BEACH, oil on panel, 14¾ x 18 (4236/70)   18000
Frieseke, Frederick C. (1874-1939), WOMAN WITH A MIRROR, oil on panel, 13¾ x 10½ (4236/73)   *8000*

Frieseke
(4236/73)

Frieseke, Frederick C. (1874-1939), SEATED WOMAN, 13½ x 10½ (4167/141)   2750
Frishmuth, Harriet W. (b.1880), PLAYDAYS, bronze, H52½ (4112/109)   10500
Frishmuth, Harriet W. (b.1880), SOARING FIGURE, bronze, d.1921, H6 x L12 (4112/104)   1700
Frishmuth, Harriet W. (1880-), WOMAN AND FROG (ASHTRAY), L6¾, bronze, 1910 (4076/796)   1000
Frismuth, Harriet W. (b.1880), THE CREST OF THE WAVE 1925, 21, bronze (4167/102)   3000
Frost, Albert, b.1843, ESKIMO DEPARTURE, 20 x 30 (4268/230)   2100
Frost, Arthur B. (1851-1928), THE AUCTION LIST, 14½ x 11 (4180/591)   1000
Frost, Arthur B., PORTRAIT STUDY OF A MAN, 6 x 4⅜, pen and ink (684/886)   100
Frost, Arthur B. (1851-1928), CAP N.Y.E PLAYING CARDS, 11¼ x 9¼, gouache (633/124)   475
Frost, George A. (1843-), THE SLEIGH TEAM, 20 x 34 (4180/535)   1500
Frosthingham, James (1786-1864), PORTRAIT OF GEORGE WASHINGTON, 26¾ x 18¾, oil on panel (4076/694)   1300
Fuertes, Louis A. (1874-1927), BIRDS OF MASSACHUSETTS, 19½ x 14½ (4180/541)   1900

Fuller, George (1822-84), COWS WATERING AT A RIVER BANK, 1880, 18 x 32 (666/95)   375
Gallatin, Albert E. (1882-1952), COMPOSITION, d.1940, 10 x 6½ (4236/195)   3400
Garber, Daniel (1880-1958), TANIS, 60 x 46¼ (4167/146)   55000
Garber, Daniel (1880-1958), THE RIVER BRIDGE, 50¼ x 60 (4236/108)   26000
Garber, Daniel, 1880-1958, SEPTEMBER, 9½ x 12¾, oil on board (4268/371)   1600
Garland*, Francis, THE BATTLE OF FORT SUMTER, 24 x 36 (4180/556)   1800
Gaspard, Leon (1882-1964), TAOS INDIANS, oil on panel, d.1920, 11 x 5½ (4236/148)   2750
Gaudens, Augustus S. (1848-1907), PORTRAIT OF FRANCIS D. MILLET, bronze plaque, 10½ x 6¾ (4180/545)   1300
Gaudens, Augustus S. (1848-1907), BUST OF ABRAHAM LINCOLN, H16½, bronze (4076/797)   4250
Gaul, Gilbert (1855-1919), INDIAN ENCAMPMENT-SOUTH DAKOTA, oil on board, 21 2/3 x 27¾ (4112/37)   11000
Gay, George Howell, A COASTAL SCENE WITH SAILBOATS, 14 x 27, watercolor (684/881)   300
Gay, George Howell, BIRCHES BY A RIVER, 9¾ x 16⅝, watercolor (684/824)   125
Gay, George Howell, COUNTRY ROAD, 9¾ x 16⅝, watercolor (684/823)   100
Gay, George Howell, SEASCAPE, 9¼ x 19¼, watercolor (684/834)   300
Gay, George Howell, SEASCAPE, 13½ x 23½, watercolor (684/851)   225
Gay, George Howell (1858-1931), VESSELS OFF A LIGHTHOUSE, d.1881, 18 x 27 (633/265)   650
Gay, Walter (1856-1937), INTERIOR, 18 x 21¾ (4180/497)   1200
Genth, Lillian (1876-?), NUDE IN A FOREST, 20 x 16 (666/130)   400
Gerry, Samuel L. (1813-91), CATTLE WATERING, 18 x 34¼ (4180/522)   1300
Geuth, Lillian Mathilde, 1876-1934, A DESERT GAME, 18 x 23 (4264/401)   400
Geyer, Herman, WINTER LANDSCAPE, 22 x 36 (4180/507)   1700
Geyer, Herman, WOODED LANDSCAPE, 24 x 32 (4180/508)   500
Gifford, Sanford Robinson (1840-1905), ROCKY COAST, 16½ x 26¾, watercolor on panel (633/133)   350
Gignoux, Regis, 1816-82, AUTUMN SUNRISE, 21 x 17 (4268/215)   1300
Gihon, Clarence M. (1871-1929), SAILBOATS ON A COUNTRY LAKE, 32 x 39¼ (4180/602)   3100
Gihon, Clarence M. (20c), SUR LE QUAIS LA ROCHELLE, 38½ x 51 (4076/781)   1100
Gillespie, Dorothy (contemporary), ANTICIPATED JOURNEY, 1974, 48 x 40 (4164/181)   400
Glackens, William J. (1870-1938), CALENDULA AND FREESIA, 12¼ x 9½ (4112/132)   4500
Glackens, William J. (1870-1938), GIRL ARRANGING TULIPS, 24 x 18 (4112/118)   29000
Glackens, William J. (1870-1938), MOTHER AND CHILD, oil on board, 12½ x 10½ (4112/131)   5000
Glackens, William J. (1870-1938), NEGRESS IN ORIENTAL COSTUME, 32 x 26 (4112/139)   21000
Glackens, William J. (1870-1938), THE CAPTAIN'S PIER, 26 x 32 (4098/42)   115000
Goldberg, Michael (b.1924), COMPOSTE HEAP, d.1964, 78 x 98, oil and pastel (4164/130)   1500
Gollings, Elling W. (1878-1932), LET 'ER RAIN, 26½ x 19¾ (4180/552)   4000
Golub, Leon (b.1922), HEAD (XXXIV), d.1959, 24½ x 23½, mixed media (4164/119)   1200
Goodnough, Robert (b.1917), ABSTRACTION LYZ, d.1963, 18 x 24 (4140/133)   650
Goodnough, Robert (b.1917), THE NOMADS I, d.1960, 36¼ x 40 (4164/123)   800
Goodwin, Arthur Clifton (1866-1927), BOSTON HARBOR, 53¾ x 96½ (4167/155)   *8500*
Gorky, Arshile, COMBINATIONS, pen, ink, 11⅞ x 8⅜ (4170/161)   4250
Gorky, Arshile (1904-48), untitled, composition of abstract shapes, 10 x 15 (4140/42)   200
Graham, Charles (1852-1911), GRAND COURT OF THE COLUMBIAN EXPOSITION, 16½ x 24½ (4180/594)   1700
Graham, John, 1890-1961, STILL LIFE WITH SAW, 16 x 22 (4268/383)   2000
Graham, William, 1841-1910, A STREET SCENE IN CAIRO, 31½ x 19¾ (4197/363)   1800
Grant, Gordon (1875-1960), CONCARNEAU, d.1927, 11½ x 16¼, watercolor (633/257)   425
Graves, Morris (b.1910), BIRD AND THE SEA, 22½ x 26¾, watercolor (4167/198)   8000
Graves, Morris (b.1910), BIRD STUDIES, 2 wash drawings, on brown paper, 21½ x 27 (4236/218)   2200

Goodwin (4167/155)

Graves (4236/217)

Graves, Morris (b.1910), BOUQUET, tempera, d.1910, 17½ x 13½ (4112/203)	2400
Graves, Morris (b.1910), NESTING, ink wash, 16 x 23½ (4236/217)	*1200*
Graves, Morris (b.1910), SURF SOUND, gouache, 26 x 30 (4236/216)	2500
Greenwood, Ethan Allen (1779-1856), PORTRAIT OF A MAN, 1815, on panel, 26¼ x 19 (666/73)	750
Grooms, Red (b.1937), MAN AND WOMAN IN CAR, 10¼ x 13½, ink on paper (4164/146)	175
Gropper, William (1897-1977), QUOTES, ink and gouache, 25½ x 19½ (4236/219)	1500
Gross, Chaim (b.1904), ACROBATS, TWO SCULPTURES, 7¼ and 8¼ bronze on wood (4167/233)	2000
Gross, Chaim (b.1904), RECLINING NUDE, d.1937, 11¼ x 17¼, pencil (633/150)	125
Gross, Chaim (b.1904), SEATED NUDE, d.1925, 16½ x 10, pastel (633/149)	175
Grosvenor, Robert (b.1937), UNTITLED, d.1970, 15 x 22, pencil on paper (4164/131)	300
Grosz, George, A MAN WITH HIS DOG, pen, ink, on paper, 8¾ x 7¾, ca1912 (4263/40)	1100
Grosz, George, PISSENDER HUND, charcoal, pencil on paper, 18⅛ x 22¾ (4263/38)	1200
Grosz, George, THE MASSAGE, ink, brush, 19¼ x 24⅞, ca1930-32 (4263/41)	1500
Grosz, George (1893-1959), A GLASS OF WINE, 1929, India ink, 19¾ x 18¼ (4247/117)	2000
Grosz, George (1893-1959), BERLIN BARRICADE, watercolor, 19¼ x 15 (4247/115)	2500
Grosz, George (1893-1959), BURLESQUE SCENE, watercolor, 1933, 19 x 12¼ (4247/114)	2750
Grosz, George (1893-1959), DIE LIEBENDEN, 15⅛ x 19⅞, India ink (4204/66)	2800
Grosz, George (1893-1959), GEMEINER SOLDAT (#64), d.1937, 23½ x 18¼, mixed media (4204/67)	5500
Grosz, George (1893-1959), I WOKE UP ONE NIGHT AND I SAW A BURNING HOUSE, on panel, 1942, 26 x 20¼ (4247/119)	10000
Grosz, George (1893-1959), NEW YORK CITY SKYLINE, 24¼ x 17¼ (4180/593)	3250
Grosz, George (1893-1959), THE UNAVOIDABLE CIRCLE OF CRISIS, charcoal, ink, 1922, 23½ x 17¾ (4247/118)	2500
Grosz, George (1893-1959), TWO NUDES, oil wash, 19½ x 15⅜ (4247/113)	3000
Grosz, George (1893-1959), ZUGTIERE (BEASTS OF BURDEN), watercolor, 18¾ x 26¼ (4247/116)	3000
Gruppe, Charles Paul, FISHER FOLK ON THE BEACH, 15¾ x 11¼, on board (4241/104)	1200
Gruppe, Charles Paul, ON THE CANAL, 16 x 13¼ (4241/105)	800
Gruppe, Emile A. (1896-), NEW HAMPSHIRE SNOW, 23 x 30, oil on masonite (4076/786)	900
Gruppe, Emile A., b.1896, PROVINCETOWN, 30¼ x 36¼ (4268/259)	1600
Guglielni, Louis O. (1906-1956), ABINGDON SQUARE, tempera on masonite, 30¼ x 24 (4236/192)	4500
Gumpert, C.L., IN THE CLOUDS, 11¾ x 11¾, d.1870, watercolor (684/889)	100
Hale, Phillip Leslie (1865-1931), RIDERS ON A BEACH, 48 x 76¼ (4167/114)	2000
Hall, George Henry (1825-1913), THE WATER CARRIERS, d.1878, 48 x 35 (633/261)	600
Halpert, Samuel T. (1884-1930), NOTRE DAME, 25½ x 32 (4180/598)	1300
Hamilton, Hamilton (1847-1928), ROCKY MOUNTAIN LANDSCAPE 1874, 27 x 45 (4167/63)	1500
Hamilton, James (1819-78), A SIDE-WHEELER SHIPPING OUT, 14 x 23 (633/258)	1200
Hamilton, James (1819-78), ROCKY SHORE AT SUNSET, 14½ x 20 (4180/564)	750

Hansen, Herman Wendelborg (1854-1924), MEXICAN VAQUEROS, 12¼ x 11, pen and ink (4167/52)
2000

Hansen, Herman Wendelborg (1854-1924), PONY EXPRESS RIDER, 25½ x 19½, Watercolor on Paper (4167/55)
6000

Harnett, William M. (1848-92), AN EVENING'S COMFORT, oil on panel, d.1888, 7½ x 9½ (4236/56) 62500

Harnett, William M. (1848-92), STILL LIFE, d.1878, 12¼ x 10 (4236/32) 40000

Hart, George O.P. (1868-1933), MARKET PLACE, WEST INDIES, watercolors, 11¾ x 17½ (4112/192)
1500

Hart, James M. (1828-1901), CATTLE WATERING BY THE RIVER, d.1869, 10½ x 20 (4236/16) 4250

Hart, James M. (1828-1901), WINTER ON THE HUDSON, d.1869, 34½ x 71½ (4236/11) 24000

Hart, James M. (1828-1901), WATERING COWS, d.1882, 21 x 21 (633/135) 850

Hart, James M., 1823-1901, THE FORDING PLACE, 16 x 12 (4268/241) 2200

Hart, James M., 1828-1901, FARMINGTON RIVER CONNECTICUT, 22 x 34 (4268/240) 1400

Hart, James M. (1828-1901), LANDSCAPE WITH COWS, 12 x 14½ (4269/236) 900

Hart, William M., CATTLE WATERING, 10¼ x 8¼, 1887 (4076/732) 1300

Hart, William M. (1823-1894), CATTLE IN A LANDSCAPE, 9¼ x 14 (4076/733) 850

Hart, William M. (1823-1894), LANDSCAPE ON HILLSIDE, 11½ x 19½ (4180/533) 1000

Hart, William M. (1823-1894), LANDSCAPE WITH COWS AND COWHERD, 12 x 10 (666/82) 900

Hart, William M. (1823-1894), WOODED ·LANDSCAPE WITH A BROOK, 17¼ x 14¾, 1875 (4076/729)
1800

Hart, William M. (1823-94), CATTLE BY A RIVER, 23½ x 33½ (4180/521) 2500

Hart, William M. (1823-94), RUINS IN A LANDSCAPE, 14¼ x 21 (4236/20) 3750

Hartley, Marsden (1877-1943), LANDSCAPE WITH TREE TRUNKS, 23 x 41¼ (4098/50) 14000

Hartley, Marsden (1877-1943), HANDS, oil on masonite, 27¾ x 22 (4112/182) 3700

Hartley, Marsden (1877-1943), LITTLE RIVER AFTER RAIN 1929, 16 x 13 (4167/205) 3750

Hartley, Marsden (1877-1943), PANSY, 16 x 12 (4167/206) 2300

Hartley, Marsden (1877-1943), PINK FLOWERS WITH BLUE AND YELLOW BUTTERFLIES, 34 x 15 d.1942 (4167/207)
5000

Hartley
(4167/207)

Hartley, Marsden (1877-1943), ROCKS IN WATER (LANDSCAPE #40), oil on board, d.1928, 18 x 21¾ (4236/166)
5250

Hartley, Marsden (1877-1943), THE AXE MAN, d.1908, 11¾ x 8¾, pencil (633/152) 200

Hartley, Marsden (1877-1943), VASE OF FLOWERS, 10¾ x 8¾ (4167/184) 2200

Hartley, Marsden (1877-1943), SELF PORTRAIT, 11½ x 8½, charcoal pencil (4260/697) 1600

Hassam, Frederick C. (1859-1935), GOLF COURSE AT EAST HAMPTON, oil on panel, d.1926, 9 x 11¾ (4112/116)
6250

Hassam, Frederick C. (1859-1935), IN A CENTRAL AMERICAN FOREST, mixed media, d.1895, 21½ x 14 (4236/97)
5750

Hassam, Frederick C. (1859-1935), MOUNT BEACON IN SPRING, oil on panel, d.1915, 6½ x 9½ (4236/78)
4500

Hassam, Frederick C. (1859-1935), TWO GOLFERS, oil on panel, 10½ x 11¼ (4112/115) 4500

Hauser, John (1858-1913), AMBUSH, 12 x 12½ (4268/305) 900
Hawthorne, Charles (1872-1930), VENETIAN CANAL SCENE, 21 x 19, oil on panel (4098/22) 4750
Hawthorne, Charles (1872-1930), VENETIAN GIRL WITH FAN, d.1906, 50 x 40 (4260/693) 18000
Heade, Martin Johnson (1819-1904), HAYSTACKS, 10¼ x 19¾ (4112/22) 21000
Heade, Martin Johnson (1819-1904), RED ROSE IN A TUMBLER, 14 x 10 (4112/24) 6000
Heade, Martin Johnson (1819-1904), SUNSET, MARSHLAND, NEW JERSEY, 15½ x 30 (4167/29) 23000
Heade, Martin Johnson (1819-1904), TWO HUMMINGBIRDS AND TWO VARIETIES OF ORCHIDS,
12 x 19¾ (4098/21) 37500
Healy, George P. A. (1813-94), PORTRAIT OF CARDINAL JOHN McCLOSKEY, 30 x 25 (4180/476) 1200
Heliker, John Edward (b.1909), MAINE STUDIO, 32 x 26¼, oil on board (4167/238) 2400
Heliker, John Edward, b.1909, LANDSCAPE, 12¼ x 19¼, oil on masonite (4268/388) 650
Hennings, Ernest Martin (1886-1956), IN THE MOUNTAIN FOOTHILLS, 30½ x 25 (4112/55) 8500
Henri, Robert (1865-1925), CORI LOOKING OVER CHAIR, d.1907, 24 x 20 (4112/117) 10000
Henri, Robert (1865-1929), A NORMANDY FIREPLACE, 25¾ x 32 (4236/66) 8250
Henri, Robert (1865-1929), A PLACE TO READ, pastel, 20 x 12¼ (4236/168) 2100
Henri, Robert (1865-1929), A SKETCH IN THE WOODS, pastel, 12 x 19½ (4236/170) 3250
Henri, Robert (1865-1929), ATLANTIC CITY, 18 x 24 (4236/65) 14500
Henri, Robert (1865-1929), IRISH FARM LANDSCAPE, oil on panel, d.1913, 12½ x 16 (4236/174) 5000
Henri, Robert (1865-1929), LITTLE GIRL IN RED, 24 x 20 (4236/176) 23000
Henri, Robert (1865-1929), MAINE SEASCAPES, TWO PAINTINGS, 8 x 10, oil on panel, pair
(4167/166) 3750
Henri, Robert (1865-1929), MARY PATTON IN ROSE SMOCK, 24 x 20, 1926 (4098/38) 21000
Henri, Robert (1865-1929), NUDE ON A COUCH, 7½ x 9¾, pencil (633/154) 275
Henri, Robert (1865-1929), PORTRAIT OF A YOUNG GIRL, 22 x 18 (4076/784) 4500
Henri, Robert, attributed to (1865-1929), PORTRAIT OF A YOUNG LADY, 22 x 18 (666/126) 2150
Henry, Edward Lamson (1841-1919), BEAR HILL d.1908, 22 x 26 (4167/41) *9500*

Henry (4167/41)

Hassam (4167/123)

Henry, Edward Lamson (1841-1919), ST. JOHN'S CHURCH, NEW YORK CITY, 6½ x 4¼ oil on
board (4112/11) 5500
Henry, Edward Lamson, 1841-1919, GOSSIPS, 6¾ x 8½, watercolor on paper (4268/353) 5000
Herron, Jane Rathbone, HANGING GRAPES, 20 x 9, on board (684/891) 15
Herzog, Herman (1832-1932), DEER IN A LANDSCAPE, 21 x 26½ (4076/734) 1200

Herzog, Herman attrib. to, A STORMY COAST, 18 x 24, unframed (684/882) — 225
Herzog, Herman, 1832-1932, EVENING ON THE SUSQUEHANNA, 12 x 17 (4268/224) — 2600
Herzog, Herman, 1832-1932, NEAR STONE HARBOR, NEW YORK, 14¼ x 20¼ (4180/573) — 3200
Heynertz, F.D.G. (Dutch, 19th Cent), THE BARK 'MARBLEHEAD', 16½ x 21 (4180/555) — 1900
Higgins, Eugene (1874-1958), WEARY, 30 x 21¾ (666/117) — 850
Hill, Edward, THE FISHERMEN, d.1898, 24 x 36 (633/245) — 850
Hill, J.W., MOUNTAINOUS LANDSCAPE WITH A COTTAGE, 5¾ x 8⅞, d.1870, watercolor (684/850) — 125
Hill, Thomas, FLOWER FANTASY, 30 x 24½ (4268/209) — 3750
Hill, Thomas (1829-1908), WESTERN LANDSCAPE, YOSEMITE, 24 x 20 (4180/554) — 3500
Hirsch, Joseph (b.1910), LUNCH COUNTER, d.1941, 15¾ x 38 (4236/233) — 9500
Hitchcock, George (1850-1913), MARKEN PEASANT GIRL, 32 x 24 (633/270) — 2200
Hitchcock, George, 1850-1913, FOR THE FLOWER MARKET, 32 x 26 (4268/381) — 2800
Hofmann, Hans (1880-1965), ORNIT, d.1944, 17⅝ x 23¾, watercolor (4140/67) — 3400
Homer, Winslow (1836-1910), DAY IS DONE, 13¾ x 19⅞, d.1878, watercolor (4098/25) — 57500
Homer, Winslow (1836-1910), SCARBOROUGH BEACH, wolfe pencil, d.1882, 8½ x 9¾ (4236/49) — 9500
Homer, Winslow (1836-1910), TWO BOYS ROWING, watercolor, 10 x 13¾ (4236/51) — 150000
Hooper, Elizabeth, INTERIOR, watercolor, 20¾ x 16½ (4219/8) — 400
Hope, James (1818-92), CASTLETON FALLS, CASTLETON, VERMONT, d.1856, 20 x 26 (633/249) — 1700
Hope, T.H., 19c, PIPE AND MUG, 8 x 9¾ (4268/213) — 550
Hopper, Edward, LOCOMOTIVE, pencil, 13¼ x 19½ (4236/180) — 14500
Horsfall, R. Bruce, BLUE JAYS, 13¾ x 9¾, d.1915, watercolor (684/827) — 70
Horton, William S. (1865-1936), SNOW IN THE MOUNTAINS, oil on board, 25 x 30 (4236/95) — 6250
Hudson River School, 19c, A PAIR OF MOUNTAINOUS LANDSCAPES, 17¾ x 23¾, unframed (684/807) — 30
Hudson River School, 19c, LANDSCAPE WITH WADING COWS, 22 x 36 (684/808) — 100
Hunt, William M. (1824-1879), PORTRAIT OF JANE MARIA L. HUNT, 50 x 35¾, 1850 (4076/743) — 2250
Hunt, William M. (1824-79), TEMPLE OF HERCULES, TIVOLI, oil on panel, 10½ x 13¾ (4236/19) — 3250
Huntington, Anna Hyatt, GUARDING THE NEST, 1955, H16½, aluminum alloy (654/389) — 550
Huntington, Daniel (1816-1906), PORTRAIT OF DR. OLIVER WALCOTT GIBBS, 30 x 25 (4180/475) — 1600
Huntington, Daniel attrib. to, PORTRAIT OF MRS. CHARLES BURGESS, 36 x 28 (684/888) — 450
Inman, John O'Brien, 1828-96, THE SWING, 8½ x 5½, oil on board (4268/340) — 1600
Inness, George (1825-1894), IN THE BERKSHIRES, 24 x 22 (4236/10) — 17000
Inness, George (1825-94), AFTER THE SHOWER, 12¼ x 18½ (4098/18) — 52000
Inness, George (1825-94), GLIMPSE OF LAKE, ALBANO, ITALY, 18 x 26 (4236/24) — 12000
Inness, George (1825-94), MOONLIGHT LANDSCAPE, 16 x 24 (4167/24) — *30000*

Inness (4167/24)

Inness, George (1825-94), ON THE HUDSON ca.1875, 16 x 13¾ (4167/27) — 30000
Inness, George (1825-94), SKETCH OF BIRCHES, oil on board, d.1847, 15¼ x 12 (4112/9) — 4500
Inness, George (1825-94), SUNSET AT MONTCLAIR d.1892, 30 x 45 (4167/33) — 28000
Inness, George (1825-94), THE ELM TREE c.1860-64, 11¾ x 9¾ (4167/32) — 6500
Inness, George (1825-94), THE OLIVE GROVE, 17¾ x 25¾ (4236/23) — 20000
Inness, George, attrib. (1825-94), AN EXTENSIVE RIVER LANDSCAPE, 25 x 36 (633/127) — 800
Inness, George, attributed to (1825-94), THE ROMAN CAMPAGNA, 25 x 37 (666/77) — 600

Inukai, Kyohei, 20c, THE BROTHERS, d.1921, 60 x 50½ (633/30)   700
Irving, J. Beaufain (1826-77), M.O. RHINELANDER AS A CHILD, 20½ x 16, 1873 (4076/750)   3000
Jackson, Harry (b.1924), HAZIN' THE LEADER, bronze, d.1959, H12¼ (4112/47)   3250
Jackson, John A. (1825-79), BUST OF A GREEK WOMAN, marble, H25 (4236/30)   1000
Jacobsen, Antonio (1850-1921), A REGOTTA IN NEW YORK HARBOR, 1886, 28 x 48 (666/88)   5500
Jacobsen, Antonio (1850-1921), LA PROVENCE, 27¾ x 48 (4180/582)   1700
Jacobsen, Antonio (1850-1921), SAILING SHIP IN UPPER N.Y. HARBOR, 10 x 16, 1886 (4076/771)   1900
Jacobsen, Antonío (1850-1921), STEAMSAILER, 'ABANA', 22 x 36, 1894 (4076/773)   2500
Jacobsen, Antonio, 1850-1921, CUSTOM TENDER, 18 x 30 (4268/266)   3250
Jacobsen, Antonio, 1850-1921, ISLAND 22 x 36, (4268/268)   3100
Jacobsen, Antonio, 1850-1921, YEMASEE, 22 x 36, unframed (4268/267)   2500
Jacobson, Antonio, 1850-1921, CLIPPER SHIP, 16 x 12, oil on board (4268/289)   1700
James, Frederick, 1845-1907, THE INTRODUCTION, 13 x 16 (4268/342)   3000
Jameson, John S. (1842-1864), SARANAC WATERS, 21 x 36, 1863 (4076/739)   3750
Jamison, Philip (b.1925), CHRIS SANDERSON'S WREATH, watercolor, 17¾ x 28¾ (4236/223)   2500
Jamison, Philip (b.1925), DAISIES BY CARVERS POND, mixed media, 17¼ x 29¼ (4236/224)   1200
Jansson, Alfred (1863-1931), WINTER SCENE, d.1926, 30 x 25 (4236/93)   1700
Jarvis, John Wesley (1770-1840), PORTRAIT OF A LADY, 9¼ x 7¼ (4260/683)   1700
Jefferson, Joseph, 1829-1905, SWAMP SCENE, FLORIDA, 34 x 48 (4268/244)   1100
Jenkins, Paul (b.1923), PHENOMENA SHADOW OF AFTER, d.1969, 33 x 34, acrylic on canvas (4140/134)   2800
John, Augustus, RECLINING NUDE, charcoal, on paper, 8½ x 10½, 1912 (4263/21)   750
Johnson, David (1827-1908), A SPRING LANDSCAPE, 8 x 9½ (633/130)   200
Johnson, David (1827-1908), FIGURE IN A LANDSCAPE, oil on board, d.1865, 5½ x 8½ (4112/15)   2000
Johnson, David (1827-1908), SCENERY AT GEORGETOWN CONNECTICUT, 12 x 18 (4236/13)   2300
Johnson, David (1827-1908), WEST COMPTON, NEW HAMPSHIRE, d.1867, 14 x 20 (4236/15)   5250
Johnson, David (1827-1908), WEST CORNWALL, CONNECTICUT 1875, 17 x 13¾ (4167/10)   *5250*
Johnson, David, 1827-1908, NARROWS OF LAKE GEORGE, 5½ x 7¾, oil on board (4268/226)   1700
Johnson, David, 1827-1908, NEAR WARWICK, NEW YORK, 14½ x 12½ (4268/227)   8750
Johnson, Eastman (1824-1906), GIRL WITH SKATES, d.1880, 52½ x 30 (4236/59)   31000
Johnson, Eastman (1824-1906), HEAD OF A NEGRO WOMAN, 19½ x 13¾, oil on board (4112/25)   4500
Johnson, Eastman (1824-1906), PORTRAIT OF AN OFFICER, 22¼ x 26, 1876 (4076/745)   4250
Johnson, Eastman (1824-1906), READING THE NEWSPAPER, 10 x 13¼, oil on board (4167/39)   18000
Johnson, Eastman (1824-1906), STUDY FOR CRANBERRY PICKERS, 13¼ x 22¾, oil on board (4112/19)   15000
Johnson, Eastman (1824-1906), THE BLACKSMITH SHOP, oil on board, 18 x 24 (4236/58)   4000
Johnson, Eastman (1824-1906), WASHINGTON CROSSING THE DELAWARE, d.1851, 40½ x 68 (4236/28)   370000
Johnson, Eastman (1825-1906), RUSTIC VIOLINIST WITH LITTLE GIRL, 15½ x 13, '68, oil on panel (4098/20)   30000
Johnson, Frank T. (1874-1939), SHERIFF IN THE MOONLIGHT, d.1930, 20 x 16 (4112/43)   12000
Johnson, Frank T. (1874-1939), THROUGH THE FOOTHILLS, d.1931, 20 x 24 (4236/149)   19000
Johnson, Frank T. (1874-1939), THE BRIDAL PATH, watercolor on board, 20¾ x 14½ (4236/135)   2250
Johnson, Lester (b.1919), FIVE SITTING FIGURES WITH HATS, d.1969, 22 x 22 (4164/110)   1300
Jones, Francis Coates (1857-1932), ADMIRING THE CHILD, 20 x 30 (633/244)   2250
Jones, Hugh Bolton (1848-1927), LANDSCAPE WITH CATTLE, 16 x 24 (4076/728)   1200
Jones, Hugh Bolton, 1848-1927, A SUMMER'S BLAZE, 16 x 24 (4268/256)   2100
Kallos, Paul (b.1925), UNTITLED, d.1959, 45¾ x 35¼ (4096/105)   450
Kalmbach, E.R.,AMERICAN EGRET, 7¾ x 11½, d.1924, watercolor (684/826)   40
Katz, Alex (b.1927), MADISON SQUARE, d.1964, 9¾ x 11¾, oil on masonite (4164/121)   600
Katz, Alex (b.1927), MAN AND WOMAN, 65½ x 50 (4164/115)   2300
Kauba, Carl (1865-1922), FRIEND IN NEED, 21½, bronze (4167/90)   14000
Kauba, Carl (1865-1922), HOW-KOLA, 24¼, bronze (4167/89)   13000
Kauba, Carl (1865-1922), TAKING AIM, 11¾, bronze on marble base (4167/86)   4750
Kelly, James Edward (b.1855), SHERIDAN'S RIDE 1879, H18 bronze (633/255)   2000
Kemeys, Edward (1843-1907), THE STILL HUNT, 19, painted in terra cotta (4167/100)   800
Kensett, John F. (1816-1872), COASTLINE AT SUNSET, d.1868, 14 x 24 (4236/8)   8500
Kensett, John F. (1816-1872), LANDSCAPE, 14 x 24 (4236/26)   6000
Kensett, John F. (1816-72), LANDSCAPE WITH DEER, 48 x 72½ (4236/25)   90000
Kensett, John F. (1816-72), LAKE GEORGE d.1871, 20 x 36¼ (4167/17)   7500
Kensett, John F. (1816-72), PATH THROUGH THE WOODS, 13¼ x 10 (4076/735)   1700
Kensett, John F. (1816-72), SCENE IN CONWAY, NEW HAMPSHIRE, 12 x 18½ (4098/14)   7000
Key, John Ross (1837-1920) SUMMER LANDSCAPE WITH GRACING COWS, on board, 18½ x 24½ (666/74)   1100
Keyser, Ernest W. (1875-1959), THE WIRELESS (BOOKENDS), H8¼, bronze, 1914 (4076/795)   650
King, John, SHIP NANCY, 25 x 30 (4180/558)   2300

King, 19c, VIEW OF PHILLIPSTOWN, N.Y., 24 x 36½, 1863 (4076/702)	800
Kingman, Dong, VIEW OF CAPITOL, WASHINGTON, D.C., watercolor, d.'45, 15½ x 22¼ (4112/201)	800
Kingman, Dong (b.1911), CHINATOWN, watercolor, 29 x 21 (4236/222)	2400
Kingman, Dong (b.1911), CITYSCAPE, watercolor, 21 x 29 (4236/221)	1900
Kline, Franz, (1910-1962), UNTITLED, 2¼ x 3½, ink on paper (4164/138)	3200
Knaths, Karl (1891-1971), DUCK AND PAPER 1960, 30 x 42 (4167/239)	3600
Knight, Daniel R. (1839-1924), AN AUTUMN STROLL, 22 x 18 (4161/239)	4500
Knight, Louis Aston (1873-1934), COTTAGE AT HATTONVILLE, 25¾ x 33 (4161/240)	2700
Knight, Louis Aston (1873-1948), LES BORDS D'UN VILLAGE, 31¾ x 25¼ (4122/206)	950
Koch, Gerard, ACROBATS, ca1971, H75, bronze (4225/232)	1600
Koeniger, Walter, b.1881, RIVER IN WINTER, 34 x 37 (4268/378)	1200
Koerner, William H.D. (1878-1938), BOLD PROMISES, 22½ x 30¼, oil on board (4167/80)	2200
Koerner, William H.D. (1878-1938), STAYIN' OUT OF IT, 21½ x 16½, oil on board (4167/79)	1100
Kroll, Leon (1884-1975), RIVER LANDSCAPE, 32¼ x 26, 1916 (4076/790)	1200
Kronberg, Louis (1872-1964), REPOSE, 29¾ x 25 (4167/144)	2300
Kronberg, Louis (1872-1964), REPOSE, pastel, d.1914, 15 x 21½ (4236/121)	3300
Kronberg, Louis, 1872- 1964, THE SLIPPER, 18¼ x 14 (4268/382)	1400
Kuhn, Walt (1880-1949), CIRCUS SCENE, gouache on panel, 10¾ x 7¾ (4112/120)	1300
Kuhn, Walt (1880-1949), JOADY THE CLOWN, d.1946, 10¾ x 8 (4260/691)	2200
Kuhn, Walt (1880-1949), PORTRAIT OF A WOMAN, 15 x 12 (4268/386)	2500
Kuhn, Walt (1880-1949), PORTRAIT OF A WOMAN, 15 x 12 (4268/387)	2000
Kuniyoshi, Yasuo (1893-1953), COW AND SCARECROW, 24 x 20 (4236/179)	12000
Kuniyoshi, Yasuo (1893-1953), GIRL WITH HANDKERCHIEF, 30 x 20 (4236/178)	10000
Kuniyoshi, Yasuo (1893-1953), GIRL WITH HAT, 18 x 15 (4167/224)	7500
L'Engle, MEXICAN PEASANTS, watercolor, 13 x 19 (4219/6)	200
La Farge, John (1835-1910), CLASSICAL FIGURES, 9 x 7¾, watercolor on paper (4098/27)	2500
La Farge, John (1835-1910), STILL LIFE WITH ROSE, oil on board, 6 x 10 (4236/37)	3100
La Forge, John (1835-1910), ST. LAURENT FAISANT L'AUMONE, pencil, charcoal, laid on board, 69 x 26 (666/110)	50
Lachaise, Gaston, FEMME NUE DEBOUT, ink, pencil, 13⅝ x 9½ (4170/123)	1800
Lachaise, Gaston (1886-1935), BUSTE DE FEMME, 12½ x 9¾, sanguine (4140/19)	200
Lachaise, Gaston (1886-1935), STANDING NUDE, d.1933, 19 x 12, pencil (4204/42)	1300
Lachaise, Gaston, 1886-1935, MASK, 1925, H6¾ (4127/352)	4750
Lambdin, George Cochran (1830-96), BIDDLE CHILDREN FISHING ON THE SCHUYKILL d.1869, 20¼ x 16 (4167/34)	8000
Lambdin, James Reid (1807-89), GENERAL WILLIAM HARRISON, 30 x 25, 1835 (4076/707)	15000
Lanman, Charles, 1819-95, TROUTING IN NEW HAMPSHIRE, 18 x 16 (4268/233)	2400
Latoix, Gaspard (19-20c), LOADING THE HORSES WITH FIREWOOD, 22 x 30 (4167/62)	6000
Latoix, Gaspard, 19/20 century, TWO HORSES, 13¾ x 18, watercolor (4268/299)	2500
Laurence, Sydney (1858-1940), THE WELCOME LIGHT ALONG THE TRAIL, 36 x 40 (633/277)	16000

Lambdin (4167/34)

Johnson (4167/10)

Laurent, Robert (1890-1970), FEMALE NUDE, alabaster, H13 (4236/189) 2100
Laux, August (1847-1921), YOUNG BOY READING, 16 x 12, 1864 (4076/755) 700
Lawrence, Jacob (b.1917), DRAMA-HALLOWEEN PARTY, 21½ x 29½, d.1950, gouache (4098/61) 7000
Lawrence, Jacob (b.1917), NAPLES, 1944, 16 x 20, d.1947, mixed media (4098/62) 3250
Lawrence, Jacob (b.1917), THE WEDDING, tempera on gessoed board, d.1948, 20 x 24 (4236/213) 7000
Lawson, Ernest (1873-1939), MORET-SUR-LOING, 16¼ x 20¼ (4167/158) 7500
Lawson, Ernest (1873-1939), SUMMER LANDSCAPE, 16 x 20, canvas on board (4167/161) 9500
Lawson, Ernest (1873-1939), UNIVERSITY HEIGHTS, NEW YORK, 25 x 30 (4098/46) 35000
Lawson, Ernest (1873-1939), WINTER LANDSCAPE, 22 x 26, canvas on aluminum (4167/159) 17000
Lawson, Ernest, 1873-1939, EVENING BY A RIVER, 14 x 20 (4268/375) 4750
Lazarus, Jacob H., YOUNG GIRL IN THE FOREST, 35½ x 28½ (4076/744) 600
Lebduska, Lawrence (1894-1966), AWAKENING, d.1960, 23¼ x 18⅞, oil on masonite (4228/73) 500
Lebduska, Lawrence (1894-1966), PINK HORSES, d.1958, 16¼ x 20 (4204/77) 500
Lebduska, Lawrence (1894-1966), THE WATERING HOLE, d.1952, 18½ x 24½, oil on panel
(4096/79) 800
Lee, Arthur (b.1881), RHYTHYM, 36½, bronze (4167/101) 1600
Leigh, William R. (1866-1955), WOMAN GRINDING CORN, TAOS, oil on board, 11¾ x 16
(4236/132) 25000
Leland, Henry (1850-1877), MISCHIEF, 11½ x 8½ (4180/489) 1700
Lever, Hayley (1866-1958), GLOUCESTER, 20 x 24 (4236/101) 2800
Lever, Hayley (1866-1958), IMPRESSIONS OF LONDON BRIDGE, 18 x 24 (4112/65) 1900
Lever, Hayley (1866-1958), LOWER MANHATTAN, 25 x 30 (4112/66) 6500
Lever, Hayley (1866-1958), MONHEGAN ISLAND, 25 x 30 (4236/100) 4250
Lever, Hayley (1866-1958), ST. IVES HARBOR, 30¼ x 36¼ (4112/138) 4250
Lever, Hayley (1866-1958), VIEW OF NEW YORK, d.1933, 25 x 30 (4236/102) 6250
Lever, Hayley (1866-1958), WOODSTOCK, NEW YORK, 16 x 20 (4236/104) 2300
Lever, Hayley (18₹6-1958), GLOUCESTER HARBOUR, 16 x 20 (4167/157) *3200*
Levine, Jack (b.1915), LADY WITH RED SLIPPER, oil on board, 20¾ x 29¼ (4236/204) 7000
Levine, Jack (b.1915), PAWNSHOP NO. 2, d.1949, 17¾ x 24 (4112/186) 2000
Levine, Jack (b.1915), TWO WOMEN d.1956, 17½ x 11¼, gouache on paper (4167/221) 1400
Lewandoski, Edmund D. (b.1914), R.R. DIESELS 1948, 20¼ x 16¼, gouache (4167/213) 3250
Lewandoski, Edmund D. (b.1914), WISCONSIN 1948, 13 x 13, gouache (4167/214) 1600
Lewis, Edmund Darch, A SUMMER LANDSCAPE WITH WATERING COWS, d.1884, 50 x 30
(633/109) 650
Lewis, Edmund Darch (1837-1910), A SEASCAPE, d.1897, 47 x 37 (633/248) 1100
Lewis, Edmund Darch (1837-1910), COWS WATERING AT A LAKE, 1887, 39¾ x ⁇⁇¾ (666/83) 2500
Lewis, Edmund Darch (1837-1910), LAKE CHAMPLAIN, 15 x 25 (633/219) 750
Lewis, Edmund Darch, (1837-1910), NARRAGANSETT BAY, d.1901, 22 x 34, watercolor (633/59) 475
Leyendecker, Frank X. (1877-1924), AT THE CIRCUS, ILLUSTRATION FOR LIFE, 32 x 25½
(4236/231) 4000
Lichtenstein, Roy, untitled HEAD I (Gemini 209) 36/75, brass object, 1970, 25⅝ x 10¼ (4226/287) 5800
Lichtenstein, Roy (b.1923), AZURE OCEAN MOTION, d.1966, motorized, 18½ x 22½, mixed media
(4164/161) 1400
Lie, Jonas (1880-1940), DOUARNENEZ BAY, 25 x 36 (4180/576) 1500
Lie, Jonas (1880-1940), WINTER LANDSCAPE, 30 x 25 (4236/92) 3100
Lindner, Richard (1901-78), OFFENBACH, d.1941, 26¾ x 20, watercolor (4164/108) 5500
Linford, Charles (1846-97), THE BIG BIRCHES, d.1889, 12 x 17 (633/47) 400
Linnig, Egidas, 1821-60, THE JACOB STAMMLER, 21 x 29¼ (4268/263) 1900
Lipchitz, Jacques (1891-1973), THE EMBRACE, d.1939, 19⅝ x 25⅝, mixed media (4140/43) 1700
Lipchitz, Jacques (1891-1973), HAGAR, L6½, cast stone (4140/47) 2000
Lipchitz, Jacques (1891-1973), PORTRAIT SKETCH, MARSDEN HARTLEY SLEEPING, 1942, H11,
terra cotta (4260/1481) 3500
Lipchitz, Jacques (1891-1973), STUDY FOR 'PROMETHEUS STRANGLING THE VULTURE',
d.1936, H17½, bronze (4204/63) 7000
Lipchitz, Jacques (1891-1973), STUDY FOR SCULPTURE, 8 x 10⅞, mixed media (4204/61) 950
Lipchitz, Jacques, 1891-1973, THESEUS & THE MINOTAUR, 1943, 24¼ x 22½, on board
(4127/345) 7500
Lippincott, William H. (1849-1920), LOVE'S AMBUSH, 29 x 43½ (4180/485) 8000
Lippincott, William H. (19c), YOUNG GIRL WITH AN ORANGE, 10¾ x 8¾, 1878 (4076/758) 950
Loewy, Amelia, COWS AND FARMHANDS IN A PASTURE BY A, STEAMBOAT DOCK, 18 x 23
(684/818) 650
Lucioni, Luigi (b.1900), STILL LIFE WITH FRUIT AND PORCELAIN DOG 1934, 16 x 23 (4167/225) *1100*
Lucioni, Luigi, b.1900, STILL LIFE, 17 x 20 (4268/384) 2600
Luks, George (1867-1933), BREAD WOMAN, 30 x 25, 1921 (4076/782) 4250
Luks, George (1867-1933), CUNNER'S ROCK, MAINE, d.1922, 16 x 20 (4112/86) 6000
Luks, George (1867-1933), ENTRANCE TO FARM, 12 x 15 (4167/169) 3750
Luks, George (1867-1933), GILBERTON COW, watercolor, 14 x 20 (4236/237) 1800

Luks, George (1867-1933), PORTRAIT OF A WOMAN, 34 x 26 (4112/112)   3500
Luks, George (1867-1933), RICHMOND ISLAND, MAINE d.1922, 16 x 20 (4167/168)   2750
Luks, George (1867-1933), SHOW FOLKS, 18 x 22 (4112/119)   4000
Luks, George (1867-1933), THE BRIDGE, 7½ x 10, watercolor, pencil (4167/203)   *2900*

Lever (4167/157)

Luks (4167/203)

Lucioni (4167/225)

Luks, George (1867-1933), THE LEDGE CAPE ELIZABETH MAINE d.1922, 16 x 20 (4167/167)   3250
Luks, George (1867-1933), UPPER MANHATTAN, 16¼ x 20 (4236/106)   5000
Macdonall, Angus P. (1876-1927), GETTING EVEN, 15 x 25½ (4180/588)   700
MacMonnies, Frederick W. (1863-1937), BACCHANTE AND INFANT FAUN, bronze, d.1898, H15¾ (4112/107)   1500
MacMonnies, Frederick W. (1863-1937), BACCHANTE WITH AN INFANT FAUN d.1894, 34, bronze (4167/94)   3000
MacMonnies, Frederick W. (1863-1937), BACCHANTE WITH AN INFANT FAUN d.1894, 33¾, bronze (4167/95)   3000
MacMonnies, Frederick W. (1863-1937), DIANA, bronze, d.1890, H18½ (4112/106)   1400
MacMonnies, Frederick W. (1863-1937), PAN OF ROHALLION, H14½ (4180/543)   1300
MacMonnies, Frederick W. 1863-1937, BACCMANTE WITH AN INFANT FAUN, H33, bronze (4268/316)   2400
MacMonnies, Frederick W., 1863-1937, DIANA, 18½, bronze (4268/315)   1000
MacNeil, Herman Atkins (1863-1947), EARLY TOIL, 11¼, bronze (4167/85)   1700
Man-Ray, ARTIFICIAL FLORIST, artificial rose, 24 x 30, 1943 (4249/293)   16000
Man-Ray (1890-1976), COMPOSITION, ca1960, 9⅜ x 12⅞, oil on masonite (4140/123)   1300
Manship, Paul Howard (1885-1966), DIANA 1921, 27, bronze on wood base (4167/103)   20000
Manship, Paul Howard (1885-1966), FLIGHT OF EUROPA 1925, 20½ x 31¾, bronze on marble (4167/104)   16000
Manship, Paul Howard (1885-1966), HEAD OF JOHN BARRYMORE, d.1920, H13, alabaster (4260/692)   25000
Marin, John (1870-1953), ADIRONDACK LAKE NO. 10 1911, 14 x 16½, watercolor (4167/173)   5250
Marin, John (1870-1953), DEER LAKE 1927, 16¾ x 14¼, watercolor (4167/174)   7000

Marin, John (1870-1953), FROM NEW YORK HOSPITAL, watercolor, d.1952, 10½ x 14½
(4236/226)   5000
Marin, John (1870-1953), HUTS AND TREES, pastel on paper, 11½ x 15 (4112/127)   850
Marin, John (1870-1953), PARIS STREET SCENE - THE COLUMN, mixed media, 11¼ x 14¼
(4112/126)   550
Marin, John (1870-1953), SEA, ISLAND AND TREE, MAINE, watercolor, d.1923, 17 x 13¾
(4112/144)   10000
Marin, John (1870-1973), LATE SUMMER, CASTORLAND, NEW YORK, ca1913, 14 x 15⅞,
watercolor (4225/221)   6000
Marsh, Reginald (1898-1954), BRIDGE OVER THE EAST RIVER, d.1931, 10½ x 29½ (4236/186)   3000
Marsh, Reginald (1898-1954), FROM PIER II, BROOKLYN, watercolor, d.9/9/31, 6½ x 20
(4112/134)   1400
Marsh, Reginald (1898-1954), GIRL WALKING d.1944, 10 x 7½, ink and watercolor (4167/220)   *4000*

Marsh
(4167/220)

Marsh, Reginald (1898-1954), GIRLS AT CONEY ISLAND, tempera on masonite, d.1951, 18 x 23¾
(4236/185)   15000
Marsh, Reginald (1898-1954), HAT DISPLAY, 40 x 26½, d.1939, watercolor (4098/56)   16000
Marsh, Reginald (1898-1954), VIEW FROM COENTIES SLIP, watercolor, d.'32, 13¾ x 19¾
(4112/137)   3000
Marsh, Reginald (1898-1954), VIEW OF NEW YORK, NEW YORK SKYLINE - watercolor, 9¼ x 13¼,
12 x 17¾ (4112/136)   1600
Marsh, Reginald (1898-1954), WATERSPORTS, double-sided watercolor 1944, 26½ x 36¼, Chinese
ink (4167/212)   8500
Marsh, Reginald (1898-1954), 14TH STREET, watercolor, d.1945, 38 x 25 (4112/169)   18500
Martin, Agnes (b.1912), BLUE-GREY COMPOSITON, 1962, 12 x 12 (4164/137)   2800
Martin, Homer Dodge (1836-97), LAKE ONTARIO, 14 x 22, 1875 (4076/726)   4000
Martin, Homer Dodge (1836-97), MOUNTAIN BROOK, 13¼ x 20, 1894 (4076/727)   1700
Martin, Knox (b.1923), RECLINING WOMAN (RED NUDE), 1972, 59 x 79¾, acrylic on canvas
(4164/160)   3000
Mason*, Benjamin Franklin, THE BUGBEE FAMILY, November 1826 on reverse, 18 x 24 (4180/458)   5500
Mason*, William Sanford (1824-64), FIGURES IN A COUNTRY LANDSCAPE, pair, 9¼ x 12
(4180/494)   1600
Mason, Sanford, attrib, A GENTLEMAN AND A LADY, a pair of portraits, 14 x 11 (4211/614)   1100
Matta (b.1911), COMPOSITION, 16¾ x 13¾, mixed media (4204/104)   1300
Matta (b.1911), THE THIRD CONTRADICTION, ca1953, 19⅞ x 25¾, mixed media (4228/117)   1700
Matta (b.1911), UNTITLED, ca1942, 15 x 20½, mixed media (4228/118)   3500
Matta (b.1911), UNTITLED, ca1950, 6½ x 31, mixed media (4228/119)   2000
Matta (b.1911), UNTITLED, 1965, 25¼ x 19¼, pastel (4096/107)   1350
Maurer, Alfred H., PORTRAIT OF MISS ROSELLE FITZPATRICK, 32½ x 26½ (4236/61)   9000
Maurer, Alfred H. (1868-1932), GIRL WITH BLUE HAT, gouache on board, 26 x 18¼ (4236/184)   3100
Maurer, Alfred H. (1868-1932), HEAD OF A GIRL, oil on gessoed board, 35¾ x 25½ (4236/183)   8000
Maurer, Alfred H. (1868-1932), HEAD WITH BROWN DRAPE d.1929, 38¾ x 24 (4167/186)   8250
Maurer, Alfred H. (1868-1932), JEANNE, 74¾ x 39⅜ (4098/36)   115000

Maurer, Alfred H. (1868-1932), SAILBOATS IN PORTS, oil on board, 14¼ x 17¾ (4236/165) — 3000
Maurer, Alfred H. (1868-1932), TIGER LILY, 26¼ x 18, gouache (4167/208) — 2100
Maurer, Alfred H., (1868-1932), HEAD, gouache, 21 x 17½ (4112/160) — 1500
Mayer, Francis Blackwell, 1827-99, THUNDER DANCE, 7¼ x 14¼ (4268/303) — 1700
McAuliffe, James J. (1848-1921), A SHIP AT SEA, d.1913, 20 x 30 (633/264) — 700
McCord, George Herbert (1849-1909), A COASTAL LANDSCAPE, 12 x 16 (633/240) — 450
McCord, George Herbert (1849-1909), CABIN BY A POND, 1878, 14 x 22 (666/109) — 500
McFarlane, D. (fl.1840-1866), BARQUE BRAZILIRO, 24 x 36 (4076/764) — 11500
Meade, Martin Johnson, 1819-1904, BLACK ROCK, CONNECTICUT, 9 x 12¼ (4268/253) — 6500
Menkes, Sigmund (b.1896), FRUITS ON TABLE WITH VIOLIN, 26½ x 21½ (4167/240) — 1600
Metcalf, Willard L. (1858-1925), COASTAL SCENE, d.1877, 10 x 14 (4236/54) — 4500
Metcalf, Willard L. (1858-1925), THE THAWING POOL, d.1922, 33¾ x 35¾ (4236/96) — 47500
Metcalf, Willard L. (1858-1925), BOOTHBAY HARBOR, d'04, 26 x 29 (4112/80) — 29000
Metcalf, Willard L. (1858-1925), SPRING LANDSCAPE, d.1889, 10¾ x 18½ (4112/78) — 3500
Metcalf, Willard L. (1858-1925), SPRINGTIME FESTIVAL, 26 x 29, 1910 (4098/47) — 17000
Metcalf, Willard L. (1858-1925), THE HILLS IN FEBRUARY d.1922, 28½ x 33 (4167/129) — *32000*
Mignot, Louis Remy (1831-70), LATE SUMMER LANDSCAPE, d.1854, 16 x 24 (633/220) — 900
Millar, Addison T. (1860-1913), ON THE BEACH, 4½ x 7½ (4180/609) — 2100
Miller, Harriette G. (20th Century), CROUCHING NUDE, marble, d.1930, H19 (4236/110) — 1400
Miller, Kenneth Hayes (1876-1952), SUPRISED BY THE HUNT, 1942-43, 62 x 53½ (666/127) — 1600
Miller, Richard E. (1875-1943), TWO LADIES IN THE GARDEN, 25½ x 31¾ (4236/71) — 18000
Miller, William Rickaby, 1818-93, HANGING GRAPES, 16¾ x 13½ (4268/210) — 1700
Millet, Francis Davis (1846-1912), ARTIST AND NUN, 28¼ x 20½ (4268/327) — 1000
Monbray, Harry Siddons (1858-1928), THE ALCHEMIST, 22 x 18 (4268/328) — 3300
Moore*, Nelson A (1824-1902), ON THE HUDSON RIVER, 24 x 38 (4180/520) — 750
Mora, Francis L. (1874-1940), (4236/50) — 1200
Moran, E. Percy (1867-1935), Venice, 26 x 36 (666/89) — 750
Moran, Edward (1829-1901), A SHEPHERD AND HIS FLOCK, 21¼ x 31¼ (4076/723) — 1200
Moran, Paul N. (1864-1907), RELAXING AFTER TEA, 20 x 16 (4180/487) — 1700
Moran, Thomas (1837-1926), MOUNTAIN PEAKS, watercolor, 6 x 13½ (4112/32) — 7000
Moran, Thomas (1837-1926), A SUMMER SHOWER d.1878, 14 x 19½ (4167/25) — *27000*

Metcalf (4167/129)

Moran (4167/25)

Moran, Thomas (1837-1926), LONG ISLAND COAST, d.1919, 16¼ x 20½ (4236/27) — 25000
Moran, Thomas (1837-1926), THE OLD WINDMILL, LONG ISLAND d.1890, 15¾ x 14 (4167/26) — 16000
Moran, Thomas (1837-1926), VENICE AT SUNSET d.1897, 20 x 30, mounted on board (4167/116) — 13500
Moran, Thomas (1837-1926), VIEW OF HUDSON RIVER FROM PALISADES, 11½ x 8, oil on panel
(4112/20) — 6000

Morse, Samuel, F.B. (1791-1872), PORTRAIT OF ROBERT YOUNG HAYNE, 30 x 25 (4098/12)	19000
Mosca, August (b.1909), WOMAN IN THE WOODS, 1945, 32 x 28 (666/128)	375
Moses, Anna M. R. 'Grandma' (1860-1961), SUGARING TIME d.1954, 18 x 24, oil on masonite (4167/199)	18000
Moses, Anna M.R. 'Grandma' (1860-1961), OLD OAKEN BUCKET IN SUMMER 1952, 18 x 24, oil on masonite (4167/200)	*12000*
Moses, Anna M.R., 'Grandma' (1860-1961), HARPER'S FERRY, 20½ x 28 (4180/615)	17000
Mosler, Henry (1841-1920), THE FAREWELL, 36 x 27 (4208/322)	2400
Mote, Marcus (19c), SANTA BARBARA FROM THE FOOT HILLS LOOKING SOUTH, 14 x 24 (4211/446)	1700
Mount, William Sidney (1807-64), CHILD'S FIRST RAMBLE, 8½ x 6¼, oil on board (4268/341)	17000
Mowbray, H. Siddons (1858-1928), IRIDESCENCE, 16 x 22¼ (4236/113)	18000
Mowbray, H. Siddons (1858-1928), STUDY FOR CEILING AT GUNN MEMORIAL LIBRARY, 24½ x 48 (4236/114)	2500
Muller, Dan, b.1888, ROPING, 30 x 36 (4268/307)	1400
Murphy, James Francis (1853-1921), FIGURES IN A COUNTRY LANDSCAPE, 13¾ x 19 (4268/246)	2900
Myers, Jerome (1867-1940), LOWER EAST SIDE, d.1930, 16 x 20 (4236/119)	18000
Myers, Jerome (1867-1940), PARK CONCERT, NEW YORK, 30 x 25, d.1919 (4098/52)	26000
Nadelman, Elie, STUDY FOR SCULPTURE, pen, ink wash, 6½ x 5 (4170/122)	550
Nadelman, Elie (1882-1946), LA TOILETTE, ca1935-40, H13⅛, polychrome, ceramic (4140/32)	2500
Nast, Thomas, MARCHING THROUGH GEORGIA, 49½ x 79½ (4268/329)	60000
Natkin, Robert (b.1930), UNTITLED, d.1967, 22 x 15½, watercolor (4164/184)	500
Neagle, John (1799-1865), PORTRAIT OF A GENTLEMAN, 29½ x 24¾, 1823 (4076/692)	900
Neagle, John, (1799-1865), LANDSCAPE WITH FARM, 7¾ x 12 (4180/506)	3500
Nehlig, Victor (1830-1909), CUBAN SCENE, MAN WITH A ROOSTER, 10 x 8, 1861 (4076/747)	600
Nell, T. (1936-1953), PORTRAIT OF A BOY, 30 x 24 (666/129)	250
Nevelson, Louise (b.1900), END OF DAY XXX, 1972, 34½ x 18¾, black painted wood (4164/103)	7750
Nichols, Burr H. (1848-1915), AN ARAB SCENE, 25 x 30 (666/78)	800
Nichols, Henry H., JANUARY THAW, 25 x 30 (4180/604)	5500
Nicholson, George W. (1832-1912), LANDSCAPE WITH APPROACHING STORM, on panel, 12 x 16 (666/96)	550
Nicoll, James, SHIP AT SEA, 18 x 29¾ (684/853)	300
Noble, William C. (1858-1938), OLD TIME SALT, H26½, bronze, 1840 (4076/798)	1100
Noguchi, Isamu (b.1904), MOTHER AND CHILD, 1930, 96 x 43¾, mixed media (4096/48)	4600
Noguchi, Isamu (b.1904), TWO SEATED NUDES, d.1930, 20⅜ x 16, mixed media (4228/86)	600
Noguchi, Isamu, (b.1904), TIGER'S EYE, 1962, L32, makabe granite (4127/408)	6500
Norton, William E. (1843-1916), BEATING TO OPEN SEA, 22 x 30¼ (4180/561)	1400
O'Keeffe, Georgia (b.1887), GREEN-GREY ABSTRACTION, d.1931, 36 x 24 (4112/168)	90000
O'Keeffe, Georgia (b.1887), RED POPPY, d.1927, 7 x 9 (4236/177)	82500
O'Kelly, Aloysius (1850-), A BRITTANY INN, 28¾ x 36¼ (4076/753)	650
Oddie, Walter M., ca1805-65, LANDSCAPE, 36 x 50¼, arched frame (4268/239)	1800
Oliveira, Nathan (b.1928), FIGURE, d.1963, 20 x 16 (4164/114)	1700
Olson, Herb, (20c), A DAY OF FISHING, 21 x 28, watercolor (633/141)	150
Onderdonk, Julian, 1882-1922, SWAMPLANDS, 12¼ x 18 (4268/243)	2100
Ongley, W., LANDSCAPE WITH BOATERS, 18 x 30, unframed (684/811)	100
Osthaus, Edmund H. (1858-1928), THE CHAMPIONS, 21¾ x 31¾ (4076/756)	3500
Parker, Ray (b.1922), UNTITLED, 1967, 32 x 32, acrylic on canvas (4140/137)	400
Parrish, Maxfield (1870-1966), AIR CASTLES, oil on paper, 29 x 20 (4112/85)	28000
Parrish, Maxfield (1870-1966), EVENING BY THE RIVER, oil on panel, 15 x 17¼ (4112/98)	10000
Parrish, Maxfield (1870-1966), HOUSE IN A LANDSCAPE, 23½ x 19 (4167/111)	14000
Parrish, Maxfield (1870-1966), KNAVE OF HEARTS, illustration, oil on board, d.1924, 20 x 16¼ (4112/90)	22000
Parrish, Maxfield (1870-1966), SKETCH FOR A HOUSE IN A LANDSCAPE, 11½ x 9¼ (4167/110)	5750
Parrish, Maxfield (1870-1966), YOUNG GIRL IN A LANDSCAPE 1918, 10 x 8 (4167/109)	11000
Parton, Arthur, FISHING BY A STREAM, 6¼ x 8, oil on board (4268/228)	1600
Parton, Arthur, 1842-1914, A POOL IN THE ADIRONDACKS, 48½ x 40 (4268/234)	6750
Pascin Jules, PORTRAIT OF WALT KUHN, pencil, crayon, 19 x 15½ (4170/115)	1800
Pascin, Jules, AUX BORDS DE LA RIVIERE, 1917, mixed media, 13⅛ x 19¾ (4170/117)	3500
Pascin, Jules (1885-1930), CUBAINS, d.1916, 8 9/16 x 10 5/16, mixed media (4225/191)	2100
Pascin, Jules (1885-1930), ETUDES and FEMME ASSISE, double-sided drawing, 7⅞ x 12, mixed media (4164/24)	300
Pascin, Jules (1885-1930), HERMINE DAVID METTANT SON SOULIER, 1918, 26⅛ x 22 (4169/26)	34000
Pascin, Jules (1885-1930), LE PIQUE-NIQUE DE CANDIDE, d.1922, 17 x 19⅞, oil on board (4169/23)	28000
Pascin, Jules (1885-1930), MARIE-CLAIRE, d.1922, 10½ x 13⅛, mixed media (4225/192)	1500
Pascin, Jules (1885-1930), MODELE ASSIS, 9¼ x 7½, pen and ink (4164/23)	700
Pascin, Jules (1885-1930), NU DEBOUT, 12½ x 8, brush, India ink (4096/36)	425
Pascin, Jules (1885-1930), SCENE DE RUE, 14 x 19¼, mixed media (4204/43)	2000

Pascin, Jules (1885-1930), WALT KUHN SKETCHING, 12⅜ x 7⅞, India ink (4164/25) — 375
Pascin, Jules, (1885-1930), DEUX MODELES, 31¾ x 25⅝ (4173/525) — 25000
Paxson, Edgar S. (1852-1919), LAST OF THE HERD, watercolor, d.1915, 20½ x 14 (4112/41) — 4500
Paxson, Edgar S. (1852-1919), LOLO TRAIL, HEAD OF BITTER ROOT RIVER, d.1917, 40½ x 26 (4112/35) — 10000
Peale, Charles Wilson (1741-1827), PORTRAIT OF A LADY IN BLUE, 30 x 25 (4098/7) — 16000
Peale, James (1749-1831), GRAPES, APPLES AND A BOWL OF PEACHES, 19¾ x 26, 1828 (4098/6) — 18000
Peale, James (1749-1831), STILL LIFE, ARRANGEMENT OF GRAPES, d.1829, 20 x 26¾ (4236/5) — 23000
Peale, Raphaelle (1774-1825), STRAWBERRIES AND CREAM, oil on panel, d.1816, 13 x 19½ (4112/5) — 170000
Peale, Rembrandt (1778-1860), GEORGE WASHINGTON, portrait, d.1857, 36 x 29 (4236/7) — 21000
Peale, Rembrandt (1778-1860), LADY WITH A TURBAN, 25 x 30 (4112/3) — 6000
Peale, Rembrandt (1778-1860), SELF PORTRAIT, 30 x 25 (4098/16) — 50000
Peale, Rubens (1784-1865), SILVER BASKET OF FRUIT, 18 x 24 (4112/4) — 2000
Pearce, Charles S. (1851-1914), AFTERNOON TEA, 34¼ x 42½ (4112/63) — 13500
Peck, Sheldon (1797-1868), A LADY AND A GENTLEMAN, A PAIR OF PORTRAITS, 28¾ x 23¾, oil on board (4167/1) — *27000*

Moses (4167/200)

Peck (4167/1)

Penalba, Alicia (b.1918), FAUNE DES MERS, 1959, L33½, bronze (4096/146) — 3750
Penalba, Alicia, (b.1918), ABSTRACT SCULPTURE, H16¼, bronze (4173/577) — 1200
Pendergrast, Maurice Brazil (1859-1924), MOUNTAIN LANDSCAPE, 9¾ x 13¾, watercolor (4167/152) — 9000
Pendergrast, Maurice Brazil (1859-1924), PARK SCENE, 13¾ x 19¾, watercolor (4167/151) — 20000
Pennington, Harper (1854-1920), PORTRAIT OF A YOUNG WOMAN, 40 x 30 (4076/760) — 1700
Perkins, Granville, ROCKY COAST, 11¼ x 18½, 1894, watercolor (684/864) — 150

Perkins, Granville, 1830-95, ON THE SPANISH COAST, 10½ x 18 (4268/276)   1500
Perry, Enoch Wood, 1831-1915, DUTCH GIRL, 24 x 20, oil on panel (4268/339)   1600
Peto, John F., (1854-1907), STILL LIFE ON GREEN CLOTH, 10¼ x 8 (4112/23)   3250
Peto, John F. (1854-1907), CANDLESTICK, PIPE AND BOOKS, 8 x 10 (4180/502)   3500
Peto, John F. (1854-1907), STILL LIFE WITH FRUIT, VASE AND STATUETTE, 28¼ x 24¼ (4112/6)   2000
Peto, John F. (1854-1907), WINE AND BRASS STEWING KETTLE, 22 x 29¾ (4112/7)   5000
Peto, John F., 1854-1907, MUG, PIPE, BOOK AND BISCUITS, 6 x 9, oil on board (4268/208)   3500
Pettet, William (b.1942), BOW TIE, d.1969-70, 82 x 75, acrylic on canvas (4164/128)   350
Pettet, William, d.1970, RAGTIME, d.1970, 66 x 114 (4140/135)   450
Phillips, Ammi, 1787-1865, A LADY AND A GENTLEMAN, portraits, pair, 33½ x 27¾ (4268/199)   4000
Phillips, Ammi, 1787-1865, A WOMAN, 33½ x 27¼ (4268/188)   2500
Phillips, Bert G. (1868-1956), HUSKING CORN, TAOS PUEBLO, oil on board, 7¼ x 10 (4112/38)   4750
Phillips, Bert G. (1868-1956), THE GOLDEN ASPENS, 16½ x 28¼ (4236/127)   4750
Phillips, Gordon, b.1927, BRINGING IN THE SADDLE STOCK, 22 x 30 (4268/308)   3800
Potthast, Edward H. (1857-1927), HOURTIDE, 24 x 30 (4112/95)   36000
Potthast, Edward H. (1857-1927), PICNICKERS ON THE BEACH, oil on panel, 12 x 16 (4112/71)   17000
Potthast, Edward H. (1857-1927), ROCKAWAY BEACH, oil on panel, 12 x 16 (4112/68)   22000
Potthast, Edward H. (1857-1927), STAR GAZING, 7¾ x 9½ (4180/610)   1400
Powers, Hiram (1805-73), THE GREEK SLAVE, marble, H15½ (4236/31)   4750
Pratt, Amos, SAILING INTO PORT, 19¼ x 30 (684/857)   1000
Pratt, Bela Lyon, 1867-1917, GEORGE WASHINGTON ON HORSEBACK, H21¼, bronze (4268/317)   1300
Prendergast, Maurice B. (1859-1924), NEW ENGLAND BEACH SCENE, watercolor, 13¾ x 19¾ (4112/84)   40000
Prendergast, Maurice B. (1859-1924), RIVA SAN BIAGIO, VENICE, 12 x 10½, 1898, mixed media (4098/41)   72500
Prendergast, Maurice B. (1859-1924), ST. MALO, oil on panel, 8½ x 6¼ (4112/62)   6500
Prendergast, Maurice B. (1859-1924), SUMMER DAY, 32 x 37, 1918 (4098/45)   160000
Prentice, Levi W. (1851-1935), ADIRONDACK LAKE, 7½ x 15 (4180/514)   600
Price, Alan (20c), DOCK, d.1962, 10 x 14, on masonite (633/140)   600
Prior*, M. B. (19c), MR. AND MRS. T. FORD, (pair), 31½ x 24½ (4211/592)   3250
Prior*, William M. (1806-1873), PORTRAIT OF JOSEPH PINKHAM, 13½ x 9¾ (4180/465)   1600
Proctor, Alexander P. (1860-1950), PURSUED, 18¾, bronze (4167/83)   *28000*
Proctor, Alexander P. (1860-1950), THE INDIAN WARRIOR, bronze, d.1899, H19½ (4112/49)   24000
Proctor, Alexander P. (1860-1950), THE SURPRISE, 20 x 28 (4180/549)   2250
Pushman, Hovsep T. (1877-1966), ARABIAN STREET BARBER, 10 x 16 (4180/585)   1100
Raffael, Joseph (b.1933), HEART, FACE, SMILE, 22½ x 30, watercolor (4164/175)   425
Raleigh*, Charles S. (1830-1925), THE NANCY ANN OF FAIRHAVEN, 21¾ x 30 (4180/557)   1900
Ranger, Henry Ward, 1858-1916, LANDSCAPE WITH HAYSTACK, 12 x 14, oil on board (4268/258)   1100
Rattner, Abraham (1895-1978), CITY SKY, d.1956, 13 x 22 (4112/187)   1800
Read, F.W. (19/20c), RIGHT OF WAY, charcoal, pastel on paper, 21½ x 18 (666/111)   100
Read, Thomas B. (1822-72), SHERIDAN'S RIDE, 29¼ x 24 (4180/536)   1100
Ream*, Carducius I. (1837-1917), COUNTING UP, 14 x 10 (4180/482)   1500
Ream, Carducius I . (1837-1917), STILL LIFE WITH APPLES, 11 x 17 (4076/715)   1600
Redfield, Edward W. (1869-1965), THE BROOKLYN BRIDGE AT NIGHT, d.1909, 36 x 50 (4236/103)   7000

Proctor (4167/83)

Remington
(4167/88)

Redfield, Edward W. (1869-1965), WINTER LANDSCAPE, 20¼ x 24 (4076/785)	2000
Redfield, Edward W. (1869-1965), PARADISE VALLEY, 50 x 56 (4098/54)	12000
Redfield, Edward W. (1869-1965), THE ROCK GARDEN, MONHEGAN ISLAND d.1928, 38 x 50¼ (4167/140)	*12000*
Reedy, Leonard Howard, 1899-1956, SHELTER IN THE STORM, 22¼ x 30 (4268/306)	1000
Rehn, Frank K.M. (1848-1914), COASTAL SCENE, 14 x 24 (4076/765)	650
Reid, Robert (1862-1929), FOREST BROOK, 26½ x 30½ (4112/75)	16000
Reid, Robert (1862-1929), REVERIE, 12 x 20, d.'90 (4098/30)	37500
Remington, Frederic (1861-1909), A DAKOTA CHICKEN WAGON, mixed media, 12 x 28 (4236/137)	16500
Remington, Frederic (1861-1909), HORSES AT A MOUNTAIN STREAM, 24 x 20 (4236/145)	62500
Remington, Frederic (1861-1909), ILLUSTRATION - FOR SONG OF HIAWATHA, 15 x 12, ink on paper (4112/31)	6500
Remington, Frederic (1861-1909), ON THE IOWA, pen and ink, 12½ x 14 (4236/136)	6500
Remington, Frederic (1861-1909), SONG OF HIAWATHA, FIVE DRAWINGS, mixed media, 30 x 36¼ - framed as one (4112/31)	6000
Remington, Frederic (1861-1909), THE BRONCO BUSTER, bronze, H22¼ (4236/146)	45000
Remington, Frederic (1861-1909), THE CHARGE ON THE SUN POLE, oil on board, 18 x 24 (4236/138)	130000
Remington, Frederic (1861-1909), THE MOUNTAIN MAN, bronze, H28¾ (4236/134)	90000
Remington, Frederic (1861-1909), THE RATTLESNAKE d.1905, 24, bronze (4167/88)	*82500*

Redfield (4167/140)

Rungius (4167/49)

Remington, Frederic, after, INDIAN ON HORSEBACK, on marble base, H17 (666/112)   2500
Remington, Frederic, after, THE COWBOY, H10¼ bronze (633/268)   1000
Remington, Frederic, after, THE SERGEANT, H10½, bronze (654/414)   300
Remington, Frederic, attrib., (1861-1909), INDIAN AND WHITE MAN, 16½ x 14, ink on paper
  (633/108)   750
Renard, HARVESTING IN THE BERKSHIRE HILLS, 14¼ x 24 (684/855)   275
Reusswig, William (b.1902), THE CUSTER BATTLE, 27 x 40 (4167/82)   7000
Reusswig, William (b.1902), THE DINNER PARTY, en grisalle, 27 x 42 (666/134)   175
Reusswig, William (1902-78), BATTLE OF FRENCH AND MEXICAN TROOPS, gouache, 15½ x 33
  (4236/144)   2800
Rhodes, W.B., THE EVENING PIPE, 19c, 24 x 20 (633/115)   375
Richards, Thomas Addison (1820-1900), RIVER PLANTATION, 21¼ x 30 (4076/731)   3250
Richards, William Trost, CLOVELLY, on panel, 4⅝ x 7 (684/821)   800
Richards, William Trost, NEAR HARTLAND PT., DEVONSHIRE, on board, 4¾ x 7⅛ (684/819)   750
Richards, William Trost, TINTAGEL HEAD, CORNWALL, ENGLAND, 4½ x 7¼, on panel (684/820) 700
Richards, William Trost, attributed to, WATERFALL, 14 x 10 (666/90)   200
Riopelle, Jean Paul (b.1923), SNOW ISLAND, d.1963, 28⅝ x 45⅝, acrylic on canvas (4164/88) 7000
Rivers, Larry (b.1923), JOSEPHINE HERST HOUSE IN BUCKS COUNTY, d.1951, 28 x 36
  (4164/120)   2000
Rivers, Larry (b.1923), PORTRAIT OF JOHN PORTER, d.1953, 16¼ x 13¾, pencil (4164/149) 1000
Robbins, Ellen (1828-1905), FLOWERS IN A WOOD, 18 x 28 (4180/539)   8500
Robbins, Horace W. (1842-1903), SUMMER DAY, 17½ x 30 (4180/512)   2100
Robinson, Boardman (1876-1952), PORTRAIT OF THE ARTIST GEORGE BIDDLE, d.1937, 9 x 7¾,
  ink and wash (4260/696)   400
Robinson, Charles Dorman (1847-?), SUNSET OVER THE SEA, 9 x 16 (666/102)   100
Robinson, Theodore (1852-1896), GIRL IN RED AT PIANO, 12½ x 8¼ (4112/57)   4250
Robinson, Theodore (1852-1896), VALLEY OF THE SEINE, oil on board, 8¼ x 10 (4112/79) 2800
Robinson, Theodore (1852-1896), YELLOW APPLES d.1892, 18 x 22 (4167/135)   50000
Robinson, Theodore (1852-1896), A TROUT STREAM, NORMANDY, 18⅛ x 22, d.1892 (4098/33) 55000
Robinson, Theodore (1852-1896), GIRL IN RED SEWING, 16 x 12¾ (4112/56)   6000
Rockwell, Norman (b.1894), SINGING COWBOY, FRED HILDEBRANDT, oil on board, 19½ x 12½
  (4112/209)   12000
Rockwell, Norman (b.1894), STUDY FOR FREEDOM OF WORSHIP, mixed media, d.'43, 21½ x
  17¾ (4112/210)   13000
Rockwell, Norman (b.1894), THE TOY MAKER, 28¼ x 24 (4112/170)   35000
Rockwell, Norman (1894-), THE BUCCANEER, 14 x 9¾ (4180/616)   8500
Rockwell, Norman (1894-1978), PARDON ME, 23 x 19 (4236/187)   40000
Rockwell, Norman (1894-1978), THE BOOKWORM, 32 x 26 (4236/207)   65000
Rockwell, Norman (1894-1978), TRIPLE SELF-PORTRAIT, charcoal pencil, 44 x 34½ (4236/241) 50000
Rockwell, Norman (1894-1978), THE COMMON COLD, drawing, 8¾ x 6½, ink on board (4268/352) 4250
Rockwell, Norman (1894-1978), WATCHING FOR SANTA CLAUS, 31 x 27 (4268/370)   42500

Roesen, Severin (fl c.1846-70), STILL LIFE WITH FRUIT, 21½ x 26½ (4167/4) — 8000
Roesen, Severin (fl. c. 1846-70), STILL LIFE WITH FLOWERS d.1848, 40 x 30 (4167/6) — 22000
Roesen, Severin (fl. c.1846-70), STILL LIFE WITH FLOWERS, 30 x 25 (4167/2) — 25000
Roesen, Severin (fl. c.1850-70), STILL LIFE WITH FRUIT, and BIRDS NEST - pair, 30¼ x 25 (4112/2) — 24000
Roesen, Severin (fl. c. 1850-70), STILL LIFE WITH FRUIT, 21 x 27 (4098/8) — 26000
Rogers, Randolf (1825-92), NYDIA, BLIND FLOWER GIRL OF POMPELL, marble, H55 (4112/102) — 22500
Rollins, Warren E. (1861-1962), APACHE INDIAN, 29 x 23¼ (4076/794) — 1200
Roseland, Harry, (1867-1950), IN MAMMY'S PLACE, 11¼ x 9 (4268/330) — 3000
Roseland, Harry, (1867-1950), THE GYPSY, 58 x 40 (4268/344) — 4000
Rosenquist, James (b.1937), LIGHTBULB, d.1975, 35½ x 74½, mixed media (4164/159) — 3800
Ross, H. (19c), A MOUNTAINOUS LANDSCAPE, 1878, 30 x 50 (666/79) — 600
Rosseau, Percival L. (1859-1937), OVERHILLS, d.1928, 24½ x 40¼ (4236/89) — 11000
Rosseau, Percival L. (1859-1937), SETTERS IN A WOODLAND STREAM, d.1921, 18¼ x 26 (4236/88) — 7000
Rosseau, Percival Leonard, 1859-1937, POINTER IN A FIELD, 10 x 14¼ (4268/348) — 2000
Rungius, Carl (1869-1959), MOOSE IN A LANDSCAPE, 8½ x 11½, pencil on paper (4167/49) — *1900*

Russel (4167/84)

Rungius, Carl (1869-1959), SADDLED HORSE, 23 x 19 (4167/51) — 2000
Ruscha, Edward (b.1937), 3 FORKS, d.1967, 14¼ x 22¾, gunpowder on paper (4164/142) — 1300
Russel, Charles, Marion (1864-1926), AIN'T NO LADYS' JOB, 29, bronze (4167/84) — *10000*
Ryder, Chauncey F. (1868-1949), THE COMING OF WINTER, 20 x 30 (4076/788) — 2900
Ryder, Chauncey F. (1868-1949), THE HOUSE AT THE CROSSROADS, unf. 22 x 28 (4180/605) — 1700
Sage, Kay (1898-1963), POINT OF INTERSECTION, d.1951-52, 38⅞ x 32⅛ (4169/66) — 19000
Saint-Gaudens, Augustus, 1848-1907, ROBERT LOUIS STEVENSON, Diam 17½, bronze (4268/88) — 2800
Salisbury, Paul (1903-1976), HUNTERS IN WOODS, 30 x 40 (4167/76) — 3200
Salmon, Robert (c.1775-1845), VIEW OF GREENOCK, SCOTLAND, 16 x 25½, oil on panel (4112/1) — 7500
Sandzen, Sven Birger (1879-1954), TWILIGHT EARLY FALL, 16 x 12, oil on board (4076/780) — 1500
Sargent, John Singer (1856-1925), DOORWAY OF A VENETIAN PALACE, 23 x 18, watercolor, pencil (4098/29) — 27000
Sargent, John Singer (1856-1925), ETHEL BARRYMORE, 1903, 14 x 9½, pencil (4260/687) — 20500
Sargent, John Singer (1856-1925), GIRGENTI, 12¼ x 18, watercolor, pencil (4098/26) — 5250
Sargent, John Singer (1856-1925), ITALIAN STREET SCENE, watercolor, 11 x 7½ (4112/72) — 3250
Sargent, John Singer (1856-1925), PERSEUS BY NIGHT, watercolor, 21½ x 15½ (4112/74) — 6500
Sargent, John Singer (1856-1925), PORTRAIT OF CHARLES STUART FORBES, 28¾ x 21¼ (4098/28) — 110000
Sargent, John Singer (1856-1925), PORTRAIT OF MARY TURNER AUSTIN, 18 x 15, 1878 (4098/32) — 60000
Sargent, John Singer (1856-1925), PORTRAIT OF MILLICENT, DUCHESS OF SUTHERLAND, d.1904, 100 x 57½ (4260/690) — 210000

Sargent, John Singer (1856-1925), PORTRAIT OF MRS. JOSHUA MONTGOMERY SEARS, d.1896, 58¼ x 38¼ (4260/685) — 185000

Sargent, John Singer, 1856-1925, MRS. GRACE ELLISON, 24 x 18, charcoal on paper (4268/358) — 2000

Sargent, John Singer, 1856-1925, MRS. THEODORE FROTHINGHAM, JR, 24 x .18, charcoal on paper (4268/357) — 6000

Sauerwen, Frank P. (1871-1910), BRYCE CANYON, UTAH, d.1901, 22 x 24 (4236/152) — 4250

Sax, G., HARBOR VIEW, ROCKAWAY BEACH, 24 x 20 (684/856) — 300

Schafer, F. (19c), THE YOSEMITE VALLEY, 30 x 50 (666/106) — 2250

Schofield, Walter Elmer (1867-1944), McLEGRENOW FARM 1920, 30 x 36 (4167/162) — 8500

Schofield, Walter Elmer (1867-1944), SUMMER HOUSE, 25 x 30 (4268/365) — 3000

Schoonover, Frank E. (1877-1972), HOPALONG TAKES COMMAND, d.1906, 36¼ x 24¼ (4112/45) — 10000

Schoonover, Frank E. (1877-1972), KEEP TWO YARDS AHEAD-DON'T TURN YOUR BEEZER, 24 x 37 (4112/46) — 4000

Schreyrogel, Charles (1861-1912), CATSKILL SCENE, mounted on masonite, 18¾ x 14½ (4236/162) — 5250

Schuessele, Christian (1824-79), LAGER BEER SALOON, d.1851, 21 x 25 (4112/13) — 17000

Seltzer, Olaf Carl (1877-1957), FRONTIER WOMAN, watercolor, 12 x 6 (4236/147) — 6000

Shahn, Ben (1898-1969), CARNIVAL, tempera on masonite, d.1946, 22 x 29¾ (4236/215) — 36000

Shahn, Ben (1898-1969), CHATEAU, tempera on board, d.1957, 25½ x 19½ (4112/202) — 6000

Shahn, Ben (1898-1969), MY FRIEND THE PHOTOGRAPHER, tempera on board, d.1945, 22 x 30 (4112/184) — 23000

Shahn, Ben (1898-1969), STUDY FOR THE LABYRINTH, watercolor and ink, d.1952, 13 x 10 (4236/239) — 5500

Sharp, Joseph Henry (1859-1953), COUNCIL, 25¼ x 30½ (4167/73) — 26000

Sharp, Joseph Henry (1859-1953), EARLY WINTER ON CROW RESERVATION, 17¾ x 25½ (4167/61) — 20000

Sharp, Joseph Henry (1859-1953), THE SIGNAL d.1932, 25¼ x 25¼ (4167/71) — 8000

Sharp, Joseph Henry, 1859-1953, PASADENA BRIDGE, 20 x 30 (4268/377) — 4000

Shattuck, Aaron D. (1832-1928), LAKE CHAMPLAIN, 26¼ x 45 (4236/12) — 12000

Sheeler, Charles (1883-1965), COMPOSITION AROUND REO PENNSYLVANIA, tempera, d.1958, 6 x 8 (4112/166) — 4250

Sheeler, Charles (1883-1965), CONVOLUSIONS, d.1952, 36 x 26 (4236/220) — 120000

Sheeler, Charles (1883-1965), SUN, ROCKS, TREES, NO.2, tempera, d.1959, 6¾ x 9½ (4112/167) — 9000

Sheets, Millard Owen (b. 1907), MEXICAN LANDSCAPE d.1952, 21¼ x 29¼, watercolor (4167/69) — 1100

Shinn
(4167/145)

Sloan
(4236/118)

Shepherd, J. Clinton (b.1888), THE BULLDOGGER, bronze, d.1928, H12½ (4236/161) 5000
Sheppard, Warren (1874-1960), SEASCAPE AT SUNSET, 24 x 36 (4180/572) 2700
Sheppard, Warren W., b.1859, SAILING AT SEA, 30 x 36 (4268/295) 1400
Shikler, Aaron (b.1922), AFTER THE BATH, 50 x 40 (4112/206) 6000
Shikler, Aaron (b.1922), MEDITATION, d.'60, 35 x 29 (4112/207) 4750
Shinn, Everett (1875-1953), MRS. A. STEWART WALKER d.1910, 27½ x 13½, pastel (4167/145) *9000*
Shinn, Everett (1876-1953), 'IS HE HOME', pastel, d.1903, 10¼ x 15¾ (4236/120) 5250
Shinn, Everett (1876-1953), CONCERT SINGER, 10 x 8 (4112/59) 8000
Shinn, Everett (1876-1953), DANCERS, 3⅜ x 4, mixed media (633/155) 125
Shinn, Everett (1876-1953), GREEN PARK, LONDON d.1908, 8 x 13, pastel and watercolor
(4167/125) 10000
Shinn, Everett (1876-1953), MAID DRESSING NUDE, 17 x 12, pastel on paper (4098/48) 5250
Shinn, Everett (1876-1953), PARIS STREET SCENE, d.1912, 12 x 9 (4112/82) 6500
Shinn, Everett (1876-1953), THE CHRIST STORY, d.1945, 10½ x 18, India ink (633/156) 275
Shinn, Everett (1876-1953), THEATRE STAGE AND AUDIENCE, 4½ x 6, pencil and wash
(4260/699) 1000
Shinn, Everett (1876-1953), TWO GIRLS DRESSING FOR A PARTY, pastel, d.1914, 29½ x 27½
(4112/94) 8000
Silva, Francis A. (1835-86), BEACH AT SEABRIGHT, 10½ x 20 (4076/720) 3600
Silva, Francis A. (1835-86), FLAT ROCK, NARAGANSETT d.1876, 20¼ x 30¼ (4167/18) 8500
Silva, Francis A. (1835-86), SUNRISE, BOSTON HARBOR, 15 x 18 (4076/741) 2750
Silva, Francis A., attrib., 1835-86, SUNSET ON A MOUNTAIN LAKE, 5 x 10 (4268/286) 850
Singer, William H. (1868-1943), OCTOBER AFTERNOON, HOLLAND, 1933 (4076/775) 800
Sloan, John, TURQUOISE BAY, 20 x 24, 1914 (4098/40) 19000
Sloan, John (1871-1951), HOUSE ACROSS THE FENCE, 20 x 16⅛ (4112/130) 6000
Sloan, John (1871-1951), PLAYING ON THE PALISADES, COYTSVILLE, 9 x 11 (4112/88) 4250
Sloan, John (1871-1951), SALLY STANTON PLAYING, GLOUCESTER, 20 x 24 (4236/175) 7500
Sloan, John (1871-1951), THE RED LANE, 30 x 26 (4167/165) 14000
Sloan, John (1871-1951), WOMAN SEATED BY A RIVER, d.1908, 9¼ x 11¼ (4236/118) *10500*
Smillie, George H. (1840-1921), HUDSON RIVER LANDSCAPE, 12 x 18 (4076/725) 700
Smillie, George Henry, LANDSCAPE, 11¼ x 17¼ (4268/257) 2600
Smillie, George Henry (1840-1921), OFF MARBLEHEAD NECK, 19¼ x 27¼ (4180/505) 4750
Smillie, George Henry, 1840-1921, DISTANT VIEW OF CAMPBELL'S LODGE, 8¾ x 6¾, arched
frame (4268/242) 1600
Smith, Archibald Cary, 1837-1911, OFF CUTLYHUNK, 10 x 18 (4268/287) 900
Smith, Henry Pember, 1854-1907, EARLY SPRING, 20 x 24 (4268/247) 2700
Smith, Henry Pember, 1854-1907, LATE AFTERNOON WATERFORD CONNECTICUT, 12 x 16
(4268/248) 1100
Smith, Henry Pember, 1854-1907, MORNING ON DEAL LAKE, NEW JERSEY, 20 x 28¼ (4268/249) 4500

Smithson, Robert (1938-73), URINATION MAP ON THE CONSTELLATION HYDRA, d.1969, 17 x 36, mixed media (4164/176) — 2000

Snydam, James Augustus, 1819-65, MOONLIT SCENE, 6¼ x 10¼ (4268/285) — 2750

Snydam, James Augustus, 1819-65, RIVER SCENE, 5½ x 10¼ (4268/284) — 6250

Sonntag, William L., LANDSCAPE AT DUSK, 4¾ x 7, watercolor (684/859) — 450

Sonntag, William Louis (1822-1900), A RIVER LANDSCAPE, 36 x 56 (633/237) — 3250

Sonntag, William Louis (1822-1900), MOUNTAIN LANDSCAPE, 36¼ x 56¼ (4167/21) — 6000

Soyer, Moses (1899-1974), NUDE, on panel, 13¼ x 11 (666/132) — 325

Soyer, Moses (1899-1974), SEATED WOMAN, 18½ x 12, mixed media (633/147) — 250

Soyer, Moses (1899-1974), WOMAN IN YELLOW, 24 x 20 (4268/356) — 1100

Soyer, Moses (1899-1974), SEATED NUDE 1955, 24 x 18 (4167/219) — *1800*

Soyer, Raphael (b.1899), GIRL WITH RED HAT, 30¼ x 17 (4112/174) — 3750

Soyer, Raphael (b.1899), INTERIOR WITH NUDE, 20 x 14 (4112/172) — 3100

Soyer, Raphael (b.1899), MODEL, 34 x 26 (4236/235) — 6750

Soyer, Raphael (B.1899), DOUBLE PORTRAIT, THE ARTIST AND HIS FATHER, 9 x 12, pencil (4260/701) — 3000

Soyer, Raphael, (b.1899), DRRESSED AND UNDRESSED, 18½ x 12, mixed media (633/148) — 750

Speicher, Eugene (b.1883), STANDING NUDE, d.1923, 13½ x 9, charcoal (633/151) — 125

Speicher, Eugene (1883-1962), BOUQUET IN WHITE VASE, 20 x 16 (4098/49) — 2300

Spencer, Frederick (1806-75), TWO YOUNG BOYS, 34¼ x 27¼ (4180/468) — 2100

Spencer, Lilly Martin (1847-1902), CUPID, 15½ x 12¼ (633/239) — 450

Spencer, Niles (1893-1952), FALL RIVER, d.1938, 11¾ x 17¾ (4112/165) — 5500

Spencer, Niles (1893-1952), STUDY FOR THE TWO BRIDGES, d.1948, 9 x 14¼ (4236/201) — 23000

Sprague, Howard F., THE 'U.S.S. GLOUCESTER' AT SANTIAGO, 22 x 36 (4180/583) — 750

Stamos Theodoros, (b.1922), UNTITLED, d.1947, 30 x 24, on masonite (633/99) — 800

Stearns, Junius Brutus, attrib. 1810-85, THE VOLUNTEER'S DEPARTURE, 26¾ x 36 (4268/323) — 8000

Stearns, Junius Brutus, 1810-85, WASHINGTON AND LAFAYETTE AT BRANDYWINE, 23½ x 42½ (4268/321) — 7000

Steinberg, Saul (b.1914), DO YOU KNOW THE MILKY WAY, ca1945, 22½ x 27½, ink on paper (4164/169) — 2400

Steinberg, Saul (b.1914), OBELISK RIDER, 14 x 22½, pen and ink (4167/228) — 3250

Steinberg, Saul (b.1914), TWENTY POSTCARDS (LONG ISLAND), ink-watercolor, d.1968, 22½ x 28½ (4236/240) — 6500

Steinberg, Saul, (1914-), VIOLIN RECITAL, 1932, 11⅝ x 14½, ink (4125/185) — 3000

Stella, Joseph (1876-1946), TREE TRUNK, 18 x 23, pastel on paper (4167/191) — 1700

Stella, Joseph (1879-1946), PEARS, 9 x 12¾ (4112/152) — 1500

Stella, Joseph (1879-1946), PORTRAIT OF GIOVANNI PETROCCONE, mixed media, 21 x 16 (4112/181) — 800

Stella, Joseph (1879-1946), STILL LIFE WITH GLADIOLA, colored pencil, 24¾ x 18½ (4112/151) — 5000

Stella, Joseph (1879-1946), STILL LIFE, pastel, 24¾ x 18½ (4112/150) — 5000

Stella, Joseph (1879-1946), TREES, pastel, 19¼ x 23¾ (4236/171) — 1200

Stella, Joseph (1879-1946), TWILIGHT THROUGH THE TREES, pastel, d.1942, 24½ x 18½ (4236/169) — 3100

Stella, Joseph (1879-1946), VASE OF FLOWERS, 10½ x 10 (4236/211) — 3400

Stella, Joseph (1879-1946), WOMAN WITH WHITE PARASOL, d.1896, 30¼ x 12¼ (4112/77) — 18000

Sterne, Maurice (1877-1957), WOMAN WITH A PARASOL, oil on panel, 15 x 7¾ (4112/58) — 2000

Sterner, Albert (1863-1946), OLIVIA IN PINK DRESS, 28¾ x 21½ (4180/617) — 900

Stevens, William Lester (1888-1969), EARLY SPRING, 24 x 30, on masonite (633/253) — 1100

Stevens, William Lester (1888-1969), THE DARLING HOME, 24 x 36, on masonite (633/254) — 1100

Stewart, Julius L. (1855-1920), READY FOR THE BALL, oil on panel, d.1877, 39¼ x 27 (4236/38) — 20000

Stick, Frank (20c), FORDING THE RIVER, 24 x 35 (4167/75) — 2100

Stock, Ernest (20th Century), MARATHON DANCERS, mixed media, 20½ x 17 (4112/191) — 1000

Stoops, Herbert Morton (1887-1948), THE CONFRONTATION, 32¼ x 36 (4167/81) — *1700*

Storer, Charles, 19c, ORCHIDS, 10½ x 8¼, 1896 (4076/777) — 400

Story, William W. (1819-95), CLEOPATRA, marble, d.1858, H55 x L49 (4112/100) — 40000

Story, William W. (1819-95), LIBYAN SIBYL, marble, d.1861, H53 x L43 (4112/101) — 13000

Stuart, Alexander, SHIP IN A STORM, 30 x 50, indistinctly (684/815) — 500

Stuart, Gilbert (1755-1828), CAPTAIN JAMES T. GERRY, portrait, 27 x 23 (4236/6) — *10000*

Stuart, Gilbert (1755-1828), PORTRAIT OF DANIEL WEBSTER d.1825, 36 x 28 (4167/7) — 42000

Stuart, Gilbert (1755-1828), PORTRAIT OF OZIAS HUMPHREY, R.A., 30 x 25, 1787 (4098/9) — 6500

Stuart, Gilbert, after, PORTRAIT OF GEORGE WASHINGTON, 30 x 26, ovoid frame (684/883) — 500

Stuart, Gilbert, School of, PORTRAIT OF A MAN, 30 x 24¾, unframed (684/814) — 125

Stuart, Gilbert, School of, PORTRAITS OF GEORGE AND MARTHA WASHINGTON (2), each 24¼ x 20⅜, ovoid (684/876) — 300

Stubbs, William P., BOSTON PILOT BOAT, 20¼ x 30 (4268/262) — 2300

Stubbs, William P., 1842-1909, THE KEARSARGE AND THE ALABAMA, 22 x 36 (4268/264) — 2000

Stuempfig, Walter (1914-1970), NOON CANVAS, 24 x 36½ (666/119) — 1900

Stuempfig, Walter (1914-70), FATIGUE, 19¼ x 25⅛ (666/118) — 750

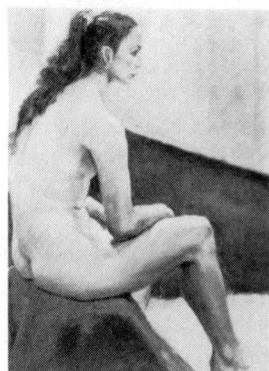

Soyer (4167/219)

Stuart (4236/6)

Stoops (4167/81)

Sully, Thomas (1783-1872), FIGURE STUDIES, DOUBLE SIDED DRAWING, 8½ x 11¼, mixed media (4260/679) — 1600

Sully, Thomas (1783-1872), FIGURE STUDIES, DOUBLE SIDED DRAWING, 8¼ x 10¾, mixed media (4260/680) — 1200

Sully, Thomas (1783-1872), FIGURE STUDIES, DOUBLE SIDED DRAWING, 8½ x 11¼, sepia ink (4260/678) — 1200

Sully, Thomas (1783-1872), PEASANT GIRL d.1857, 30 x 25 (4167/5) — 7000

Sully, Thomas (1783-1872), THE SPANISH MANTILLA, 36¼ x 28, 1840 (4098/11) — 32000

Sully, Thomas, 1783-1872, MRS. MIDDLETON SMITH, 27½, 21¼, oval (4268/184) — 3100

Sully, Thomas, 1783-1872, PETER VAN BRUGH LIVINGSTON, 30 x 25 (4268/183) — 3200

Sully, Thomas, 1783-1872, YOUNG WOMAN IN A LANDSCAPE, 16 x 13¼ (4268/205) — 1000

Swenarton, M.M., PORTRAIT OF A DOG, 20 x 15½, d.1887 (684/877) — 30

Swope, Kate F., THE FLOWER GARDEN, unf. 27 x 22 (4180/607) — 500

Sword, James Brade (1839-1915), LAKE GEORGE, 18 x 30 (633/131) — 275

Symons, George G., HILLSIDE IN AUTUMN, 25 x 30 (4236/94) — 3250

Symons, George G. (1863-1930), RIVER IN WINTER, 20 x 25 (4180/599) — 3500

Symons, George G. (1863-1930), THE FIRST SNOWFALL, 20 x 25, oil on board (4076/787) — 4250

Symons, George G. (1863-1930), THE OLD MILL, 25 x 30¼ (4236/81) — 5000

Symons, George G. (1863-1930), WINTER IN THE BERKSHIRES, 20 x 25 (4236/82) — 5500

Symons, George G. (1863-1930), WINTER LANDSCAPE, 18 x 24½ (4180/600) — 5250

Tait, Arthur Fitzwilliam (1819-1905), A SUMMER NOON,d.1901, 8 x 12, on panel (633/273) — 1400

Tait, Arthur Fitzwilliam (1819-1905), RUFFED GROUSE, 11⅛ x 16⅛, 1863 (4098/2) — 13000

Tait, Arthur Fitzwilliam (1819-1905), SHEEP IN A MEADOW, 13¾ x 22 (4076/757) — 2600

Tallman, H. Weaver, THE WATERMILL, 16 x 22, d.1897 (684/842) — 100

Taylor, Henry Fitch, 1853-1925, SOUVENIR OF NORMANDY, 20 x 24 (4268/367) — 1400

Teichman, Sabina (b.1905), ODE TO MOVEMENT, 1973, 50 x 60 (4164/90) — 5000

Thom, James Crawford (1835-98), JOYFUL SPRING, 27 x 37 (633/236) — 1300

Thom, James Crawford, 1835-98, AFTERNOON BATH, 16½ x 26, oil on panel (4268/326)   2300

Thompson, Alfred Wordsworth (1840-96), A RIVER LANDSCAPE WITH BOYS FISHING, 14 x 24 (666/76)   800

Thompson, Bob, HORSEBACK RIDER WITH FIGURES, '60, mixed media on paper, 25½ x 39½ (4226/25)   1000

Thompson, Robert (b.1937), THE ENTOMBMENT, d.1964, 20 x 16 (4164/116)   1500

Thon, William (1906-), ADRIATIC MIST, 20½ x 26¾ (4180/611)   600

Tobey, Mark (b.1890), COMPOSITION, d.1957, 34¼ x 24⅜, sumi ink on paper (4140/116)   *2300*

Tobey, Mark (1890-1976), UNTITLED, d.1967, 5¾ x 5¾, mixed media (4164/140)   650

Tonk, Ernest, b.1889, THE GETAWAY, 21¼ x 29 (4268/309)   2600

Tooker, George (b.1920), THE CHESS GAME, tempera on masonite, d.1956, 30 x 14½ (4112/208)   18000

Torres-Garcia, Joaquin (1874-1949), CONSTRUCTIVO 924, d.1913, 19 x 5⅝, painted wood (4172/374)   3000

Trego, Johnathan, PORTRAIT OF FRANCES DAVIS BODINE, 26¼ x 21, d.1855, ovoid (684/873)   175

Trotter, Newbold Hough (1827-98), RIVAL BULLS, 28 x 42 (666/99)   1200

Twachtman, John H. (1853-1902), L'ETANG, 19½ x 24 (4236/41)   13000

Twachtman, John H. (1853-1902), LANDSCAPE, 15 x 18 (4236/77)   5250

Twachtman, John H. (1853-1902), LANDSCAPE, oil on panel, 9¼ x 14 (4236/39)   7250

Twachtman, John H. (1853-1902), NEW YORK HARBOR, d.1979, 14 x 24¼ (4236/44)   *8750*

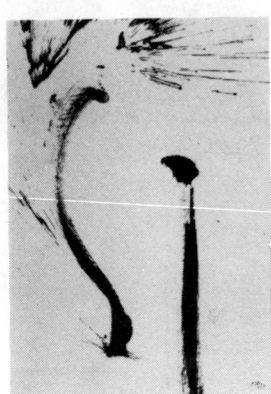

Tobey (4140/116)

Ufer (4167/70)

Twachtman (4236/44)

Twachtman, John H. (1853-1902), VILLAGE STREET SCENE, d.1889, 14 x 20 (4236/43)   8500

Twachtman, John H. (1853-1902), WINTER LANDSCAPE, oil on panel, unframed, 8¼ x 9½ (4236/40)   5000

Twachtman, John Henry (1853-1902), THE CABBAGE PATCH, 25 x 25 (4098/34)   25000

Tyler, Bayard, VASE WITH THREE ROSES, 16 x 12, d.1902 (684/835)   110

Tyler, James Gale, SHIP AT SEA, 32¼ x 22 (4268/288)   2750

Tyler, James Gale, 1855-1931, POUNDING SURF, 18 x 30¼ (4268/294)   850

Tyler, James Gale, 1855-1931, SHIP OFF A ROCKY COAST, 20 x 30 (4268/292)   900

Ufer, Walter (1876-1936), WESTERN TOWN, 25 x 25 (4167/70)   *3000*

Van Gorder, Luther E. (1861-1931), WORKING IN THE GARDEN, d.1896, 20 x 16 (4236/68)	3000
Van Zandt, W.C., attribute to 19-20c, LADY MOSCOW, 19 x 26 (4076/716)	1000
Vedder, Elihu (1836-1923), SARACEN GIRL, d.1868, 13¼ x 6 (4236/18)	2400
Volkman, Charles (1841-1914), CATTLE AND GEESE WATERING, pair of paintings, inscribed Paris, 17 x 28 (666/91)	475
Vonnoh, Bessie P. (1872-1955), MOTHER AND CHILD, H10¼ (4180/542)	2300
Vonnoh, Robert W. (1858-1933), EARLY SPRING, 24 x 30 (4112/76)	11000
Vonnoh, Robert W. (1858-1933), MOIST WEATHER, FRANCE, d.1890, 25½ x 21¼ (4236/79)	7250
Vonnoh, Robert W., (1858-1933), MRS. E.G. LE FAVOR, 40 x 30 (4268/355)	450
Waldo, Samuel Lovett, PORTRAIT OF THE ARTIST'S SON, 16¾ x 14, on panel (684/849)	325
Waldo, Samuel Lovett (1783-1861), MAJOR GENERAL ANDREW JACKSON, 33¼ x 26½ (4167/3)	33000
Walker, William Aiken, CABIN SCENE, 6 x 12½ (4180/496)	2900
Walker, William Aiken (1838-1921), COTTON PICKERS, 9 x 12 (4180/495)	4250
Walker, William Aiken, 1838-1921, CABIN SCENE, 9 x 12, oil on board (4268/332)	5750
Wandesforde, Juan B. (fl. 1850-69), LITTLE GIRL WITH A HOOP, 25 x 19 (4180/486)	1900
Warhol, Andy (b.1930), MAO-TSE-TUNG, 40 x 30, pencil on paper (4164/155)	3500
Watkins, Franklin C. (b.1894), CLOWN WITH BOUQUET, d.'31, 25 x 30 (4112/193)	2100
Waugh, Frederick J. (1861-1940), GREAT MANAN COAST, 25 x 30 (4236/163)	6250
Waugh, Frederick J. (1861-1940), LAND'S END, MAINE, 16¼ x 19¾ (4180/578)	1400
Waugh, Frederick J. (1861-1940), LIGHT. SKY, 24 x 32 (4180/577)	3500
Waugh, Frederick J. (1861-1940), SEASCAPE, 25 x 30¼ (4076/779)	2500
Weber, C. Philipp (1849-?), BRIDAL VEIL FALLS, d.1880, 30 x 22 (633/271)	650
Weber, Carl, FIGURES BY THE SHORE, 12¼ x 24, watercolor (684/836)	275
Weber, Max (1881-1961), ARTIST'S STUDIO, d.1956, 16¼ x 20 (4112/196)	3250
Weber, Max (1881-1961), CONVERSATION, gouache, d.1955, 23 x 17¾ (4112/195)	3750
Weber, Max (1881-1961), FIGURE IN ROTATION, bronze, H24½ (4112/142)	13000
Weber, Max (1881-1961), STANDING NUDE, sterling silver, H5⅞ (4112/176)	1000
Weber, Max (1881-1961), STILL LIFE, 25¼ x 20¼ (4112/154)	2600
Weber, Max (1881-1961), THE LAKE, 10½ x 13¼ (4236/105)	2700
Weber, Max (1881-1961), THE RED COMB, d.1942, 13 x 16¼ (4236/205)	4000
Weeks, Edwin Lord, 1849-1903, CAMEL CARAVAN RESTING BEFORE A GATE, 1880, 35½ x 61 (4122/229)	5500
Weeks, Edwin Lord, 1849-1903, THE SNAKE CHARMER, 20 x 29½ (4122/228)	1600
Weir, Julian Alden (1852-1919), PEONIES, 16¼ x 25¼, watercolor on paper (4167/122)	7500
Weir, Julian Alden (1852-1919), PEONIES, 32¼ x 36 (4167/121)	10000
Weir, Julian Alden (1852-1919), STILL LIFE WITH FRUIT, 17¼ x 14¼ (4167/148)	5250
Weir, Julian Alden (1852-1919), WINTER LANDSCAPE d.1897, 12 x 18 (4167/118)	2100
Weir, Julien Alden (1852-1919), MIDDAY, 34 x 2¼, d.'91 (4098/31)	13000
Wells, Lynton (b.19400, UNTITLED, 1973, 84 x 72, acrylic (4164/113)	350
Wesselman, Tom (b.1931), STUDY FOR BEDROOM PAINTING, 3 x 4, mixed media (4164/151)	1300
Wheelock, Warren F. (1880-1960), ABRAHAM LINCOLN ON HORSEBACK, H20½ (4180/544)	850
Whistler, James Abbott McNeil, (1834-1903), MULE STANDING IN STREET, AJACCIO, mixed media, 5½ x 3¼ (4112/73)	2600
Whistler, James Abbott McNeil, (1834-1903), SELF PORTRAIT, 6¾ x 5½, black chalk (4260/681)	10000
Whittredge*, Thomas Worthington (1820-1910), AUTUMN LANDSCAPE, 16¾ x 14¾ (4180/504)	3200
Whittredge, Thomas, Johnson, Eastman, SUNDAY MORNING, NEW ENGLAND c.1860-70, 15½ x 23½ (4167/38)	10000
Whorf, John (1903-1959), CAROLINA CABIN, 17 x 21, d.'17, watercolor (4098/57)	2200
Whorf, John (1903-1959), GYPSY WAGONS, unframed, 11 x 15, watercolor on paper (4167/227)	500
Wieghorst, Olaf, b.1899, HORSE IN A PASTURE, 24 x 30 (4268/300)	4700
Wier, Julian A., (1852-1919), STILL LIFE, oil on panel, d.1885, 7½ x 6 (4236/36)	4250
Wiggins, Guy (1883-1962), EARLY MORNING, ESSEX, 25 x 30¼ (4180/575)	3400
Wiggins, Guy (1883-1962), GOLDEN DAYS, 20 x 24 (4180/603)	950
Wiggins, Guy (1883-1962), HILLS IN AUTUMN, 12 x 16 (4180/601)	3250
Wiles, Irving R. (1862-1948), MODEL'S DRESSING ROOM, oil on masonite, 12 x 16 (4236/117)	1800
Wiles, Irving R. (1862-1948), WOMAN READING ON A BENCH, 14 x 16¾, oil on panel (4167/131)	7000
Wiles, Irving R. (1862-1948), YACHT BASIN, GREENPORT, LONG ISLAND, d.1902, 18¼ x 22¼ (4236/53)	7750
Willard, Archibald, DEACON JONES' EXPERIENCE, 20 x 30¼ (4076/754)	1900
Williams, Micah, attrib (1782-1837), PORTRAIT OF A YOUNG LADY, 23½ x 18¼ (4211/616)	1600
Williamson, John (1826-85), ARABIAN STALLION, 14 x 21 (4180/584)	1000
Williamson, John (1826-85), VIEW OF LAKE GEORGE, 28 x 50 (4180/509)	3750
Wilson, Jane, (b.1924), FRESH SEASON, 1961, 80 x 60 (633/89)	425
Winter, Charles A. (b.1869), A SPHINX, d.1921, 24¼ x 20¼ (4236/116)	4000
Wollaston, John after, ANN DE LANCEY WATTS, 30¼ x 25 (684/878)	50
Wood, George Bacon, Jr. (1832-1910), FEEDING TIME, 12 x 12 (4180/493)	750
Wood, Grant (1891-1942), GRANDMA MENDING, mixed media, d.1935, 26¼ x 19½ (4236/199)	52500

Wood, Grant (1891-1942), GRANDPA EATING POPCORN, mixed media, d.1935, 26¼ x 19½ (4236/198) — 48000

Wright, Charles Lennon (b.1876), ROAD TO PECONIC BATHING BEACH d.1891, 19¾ x 30 (4167/117) — 3100

Wuermer, Carl (1900-), DAISY FIELD, 28 x 30 (4180/606) — 1200

Wyant, Alexander Helwig (1836-92), LAKE SCENE d.1872, 14½ x 20 (4167/12) — *6000*

Wyant, Alexander Helwig (1836-92), NEWPORT LANDSCAPE d.1859, 8 x 14 (4167/13) — 3000

Wyant, Alexander Helwig, 1836-92, INDIAN SUMMER IN ARKVILLE, 18½ x 25 (4268/250) — 3500

Wyant, Alexander Helwig, 1836-92, SUNSET LANDSCAPE, 15½ x 12 (4268/245) — 2200

Wydeveld, Arnoud, fl. 1855-67, FLOWERS, 16 x 18, oil on panel (4268/212) — 3300

Wyeth, Andrew (b.1917), BEAMS END d.1954, 21¼ x 29¼, watercolor (4167/229) — 20000

Wyeth, Andrew (b.1917), BUILDING, MARINE COAST d.1944, 25 x 30 (4167/192) — 25000

Wyeth, Andrew (b.1917), CANOE BIRCH, watercolor, 29¼ x 21¼ (4112/198) — 16000

Wyeth, Andrew (b.1917), KELP AND SEAWEED, watercolor, d.1938, 17½ x 21½ (4236/208) — 13500

Wyeth, Andrew (b.1917), SEAL FARM, watercolor, d.1961, 21½ x 29 (4236/209) — 24000

Wyeth, Andrew (b.1917), SILVER DUNES, watercolor, d.1944, 15¼ x 19¾ (4112/197) — 13000

Wyeth, Andrew (b.1917), SUNDAY MEETING, 22 x 30, 1945 (4098/59) — 31000

Wyeth, Andrew (b.1917), THE RABBIT HUNTER d.1939, 16 x 25½ grisaille watercolor (4167/197) — *17000*

Wyeth, Andrew (b.1917), WINFIELD 1977, 21½ x 30, watercolor on paper (4167/217) — 39000

Wyeth, Newell C. (1882-1945), GOLD SEEKERS, 30 x 40 (4236/158) — 5750

Wyeth, Newell C. (1882-1945), HEADLONG HE LEAPED ON THE BOASTER, 40¾ x 30 (4112/50) — 13000

Wyeth, Newell C. (1882-1945), HOMEWARD BOUND O'ER THE SEA, 40½ x 30 (4112/51) — 6750

Wyeth, Newell C. (1882-1945), WHY DON'T YOU SPEAK FOR YOURSELF, JOHN, 40½ x 30 (4112/53) — 10000

Yewell, George Henry (1830-1923), THE HUDSON RIVER FROM WEST POINT, 1855, 24 x 34¼ (666/98) — 825

Zerbe, Karl (b.1903), THE BEAUTY SHOP 1951, 31½ x 21, mixed media (4167/241) — 450

Zorach, William (1887-1966), PIGEON, bronze, H6 (4112/141) — 2000

Wyant (4167/12)

Wyeth (4167/197)

Chapter 24

Prints

The past season produced a dramatic surge of activity in the sale of prints. Price gains in all areas were sparked by Old Masters, new records in Americana and steady development of the market in modern printmakers, American as well as European. European and Japanese buyers took advantage of the dollar's decline to purchase prints in New York. Growing numbers of private collectors have joined dealers and museums in the competition for quality works. Several record prices and general strength throughout the field proved that the market for prints had recovered from the downturn that followed the peak years of 1973-74.

Picasso, whose work is always heavily represented at print sales, seemed to be returning to favor with collectors. Other modern and contemporary printmakers also rebounded from the slump of the past few years with strong prices across the board. Nineteenth-century artists remained solid. In recent years collectors in search of undervalued areas have begun to seek out American artists of the early twentieth century. Prices have risen accordingly.

The Old Master market was relatively unhurt by the slump of the recent years, as speculators tend to stick to the more volatile area of modern and contemporary prints. Prices for Old Master Works, having held steady through the market downturn, soared to new highs with last season's surge.

Competition for high-quality works was stiff, but buyers were extremely selective this past season. Quality and condition are paramount in determining the value of a print. Only an expert is qualified to authenticate prints and determine which impression a particular examples represents. Prints of all types promise to continue their gains, but collectors should choose carefully and make certain that the quality of each purchase justifies its price.

AMERICAN PRINTS

Agam, Yaacov, COMPOSITION, silkscreen, 24⅞ x 27⅝ (4203/1)	$225
Albers, Josef, EA, 4/100, good condition, 1973, silkscreen, 10⅛ x 13¾ (4226/211)	125
Albers, Josef, I-S LXXLA, 1971, silkscreen, 15 x 15 (4067/2)	275
Albers, Josef, I-SD, 100/125, good condition, 1969, silkscreen, 13¾ x 13¾ (4226/210)	450
Albers, Josef, VARIANT I-S VA3, 58/150, good condition, silkscreen, 1969, 24 x 27½ (4226/207)	250
Albers, Josef, VARIANT I-S VA5, 61/150, good condition, silkscreen, 1969, 24 x 27½ (4226/208)	350
Albers, Josef, VARIANT I-S VA6, 58/150, good condition, 1969, 24 x 27½ (4226/209)	250
Albers, Josef, VARIANT II, 144/200, good condition, silkscreen, 11 x 11⅜ (4226/203)	250
Albers, Josef, WHITE LINE SQUARE IV, 1966, lithograph, 15¾ x 15¾ (4067/1)	475
Albert, Josef, VARIANT IV, 114/200, mat stain, 1966, silkscreen, 10¾ x 11¾ (4226/204)	275
Albright, Ivan, SELF-PORTRAIT AT 55 E. DIVISION ST., lithograph 14⅛ x 10¼, 1947 (4203/2)	1500
Albright, Ivan ., FOLLOW ME, lithograph, 13¾ x 8⅞ (4118/65)	350
Alechinsky, Pierre, CREVETTE ET SALADE, lithograph, 19⅞ x 28¾, 1969 (4147/7)	150
American School, 19c, MAP OF CORTLANDT MANOR, pen & ink with wash, 29 x 47 (684/913)	300
American School, 19c, MIDNIGHT RACE ON THE MISSISSIPPI, lithograph, 17¾ x 24¾ (684/908)	400
Anuskiewicz, Richard, COMPOSITION, silkscreen, 29 x 22¼, 1973 (4147/8)	80
Appel, Karel, COMPOSITION, lithograph, 17¾ x 21⅞, 1960 (4147/9)	125
Appel, Karel, COMPOSITION, lithograph, 15⅜ x 19⅝ (4147/19)	100
Appel, Karel, COMPOSITION, lithograph, 18¼ x 22⅞, 1962 (4147/10)	125
Appel, Karel, FIGURE AND ANIMAL, lithograph, inscribed 'e.a.', 26¼ x 40⅛, 1971 (4147/14)	175
Appel, Karel, HAPPY MORNING SUITE, six lithograph with collage, 1974 (4147/15)	1600
Appel, Karel, TETES, lithograph, slight stain, 26⅜ x 40, 1971 (4147/12)	175
Ara Kawa, EVENING ON WHICH, edition of 60, good condition, lithograph, 31⅛ x 62¼ (4226/212)	625
Arms, John Taylor, ORVIEDO THE HOLY, etching, 12¼ x 4⅜, 1937 (4203/12)	175
Audubon, J.J., after, AMERICAN BITTERN, engraving, aquatint, 25¼ x 38, imp, 1838 (4211/393)	*1400*
Audubon, J.J., after, AMERICAN GOLDFINCH, engraving, aquatint, 19½ x 12⅛, imp, 1832 (4211/363)	*700*
Audubon, J.J., after, AMERICAN PTARMIGAN, WHITETAILED GROUSE, engraving, aquatint, 16¾ x 23, imp, 1838 (4211/404)	950
Audubon, J.J., after, AMERICAN REDSTART, engraving, aquatint, 19¾ x 12¼, imp, 1828 (4211/364)	*600*
Audubon, J.J., after, AMERICAN WIDGEON, engraving, aquatint, 15 x 12, imp, 1837 (4211/394)	900
Audubon, J.J., after, BAND-TAILED PIGEON, engraving, aquatint, 29¼ x 21⅝, imp, 1837 (4211/400)	1400
Audubon, J.J., after, BARNACLE GOOSE, engraving aquatint, 25 x 38, imp, 1836 (4211/389)	1400
Audubon, J.J., after, BEWICK'S LONG TAILED WREN, engraving, aquatint, 19¾ x 12¼, imp, 1827 (4211/361)	400
Audubon, J.J., after, BLACK TERN, engraving, aquatint, 19⅝ x 12⅜, imp, 1835 (4211/385)	425
Audubon, J.J., after, BLUE JAY, engraving, aquatint, 25⅝ x 20½, imp, 1830 (4211/376)	1800
Audubon, J.J., after, BLUE WINGED YELLOW WARBLER, engraving, aquatint, 19¾ x 12¼, imp, 1827 (4211/362)	425
Audubon, J.J., after, BLUE YELLOW BACK WARBLER, engraving, aquatint, 19¾ x 12¼, imp, 1827 (4211/360)	425
Audubon, J.J., after, BRANT GOOSE, engraving, aquatint, 25 x 37⅞, imp, 1837 (4211/401)	1200
Audubon, J.J., after, CANADA PORCUPINE, lithograph, 22½ x 16¾, imp, 1844 (4211/409)	500
Audubon, J.J., after, CEDAR BIRD, engraving, aquatint, 19½ x 12⅜, imp, 1828 (4211/366)	1100
Audubon, J.J., after, CERULEAN WARBLER, engraving, aquatint, 19½ x 12¼, imp, 1828 (4211/368)	650
Audubon, J.J., after, FISH HAWK, OSPREY, chromolithograph, 39½ x 26½, imp, 1860 (4211/414)	325
Audubon, J.J., after, GREAT AMERICAN COCK MALE, engraving, aquatint, 39⅜ x 26⅜, imp, 1829 (4211/357)	13500
Audubon, J.J., after, GREAT WHITE HERON, VIEW OF KEY WEST, engraving, aquatint, 24¾ x 37¾, imp, 1835 (4211/387)	3100
Audubon, J.J., after, HERRING GULL, engraving, aquatint, 37⅜ x 25¾, imp, 1836 (4211/388)	850
Audubon, J.J., after, ICELAND, chromolithograph, 35⅞ x 23⅜, imp, 1860 (4211/412)	675
Audubon, J.J., after, ICELAND'S FALCON, engraving, aquatint, 38½ x 25⅝, imp, 1837 (4211/399)	2700
Audubon, J.J., after, MACGILLIVRAY'S FINCH, engraving, aquatint, 19⅝ x 12⅜, 1837 (4211/397)	425
Audubon, J.J., after, OWLS GROUP, engraving, aquatint, 21¾ x 26, imp, 1838 (4211/407)	800
Audubon, J.J., after, PAINTED BUNTING, engraving, aquatint, 19¾ x 12¼, imp, 1829 (4211/369)	950
Audubon, J.J., after, PIGEON HAWK, chromolithograph, 23½ x 18, imp, 1860 (4211/413)	275
Audubon, J.J., after, POLAR BEAR, lithograph, 17⅛ x 24, imp, 1846 (4211/408)	600
Audubon, J.J., after, PURPLE FINCH, etching, engraving, 20⅜ x 12⅜, imp, 1827 (4211/358)	425
Audubon, J.J., after, PURPLE GALLINULE, engraving, aquatint, 12⅜ x 19½, imp, 1836 (4211/390)	550
Audubon, J.J., after, PURPLE HERON, engraving, aquatint, 25½ x 38⅜, imp, 1835 (4211/383)	2900
Audubon, J.J., after, RATHBONE'S WARBLER, engraving, aquatint, 19⅜ x 12¼, imp, 1829 (4211/372)	425

Audubon, J.J., after, RED SHOULDERED HAWK, engraving, aquatint, 19⅜ x 12¼, imp, 1829 (4211/371) — 1900

Audubon, J.J., after, RICE BUNTING, engraving, aquatint, 19¾ x 12¼, imp, 1829 (4211/370) — 500

Audubon, J.J., after, ROCKY MOUNTAIN PLOVER, engraving, aquatint, 12¼ x 19⅜, imp, 1836 (4211/395) — 325

Audubon, J.J., after, ROUGH LEGGED FALCON, engraving, aquatint, 38⅛ x 25, imp, 1833 (4211/382) — 1100

Audubon, J.J., after, ROUGH-LEGGED FALCON, engraving, aquatint, 38 x 25⅛, imp, 1838 (4211/405) — 750

Audubon, J.J., after, RUFFED GROUSE, engraving and aquatint, 25⅝ x 38¼, 1828 (4211/365) — 2200

Audubon, J.J., after, SAVANNAH FINCH, engraving, aquatint, 19¾ x 12½, imp, 1831 (4211/377) — 525

Audubon, J.J., after, SEMIPALMATED SNIPE OR WILLET, engraving, aquatint, 14¾ x 20⅝, imp, 1835 (4211/384) — 900

Audubon, J.J., after, SLENDER-BILLED GUILLEMONT, engraving, aquatint, 12¼ x 19½, imp, 1838 (4211/406) — 375

Audubon, J.J., after, SNOWY OWL, engraving, aquatint, 37¾ x 25⅛, imp (4211/378) — 2700

Audubon, J.J., after, SUMMER RED BIRD, engraving, aquatint, 19¾ x 12¼, imp, 1828 (4211/367) — 950

Audubon, J.J., after, TELL-TALE GODWIT OR SNIPE, engraving, aquatint, 14¾ x 21⅛, imp, 1836 (4211/391) — 700

Audubon, J.J., after, THE BLACK WARRIOR, engraving, aquatint, 38¼ x 25⅛, imp, 1830 (4211/374) — 1100

Audubon, J.J., after, THE BLUE-EYED YELLOW WARBLER, engraving, aquatint, 19⅝ x 12¼, imp, 1830 (4211/375) — 450

Audubon, J.J., after, THE LITTLE SANDPIPER, engraving, aquatint, 14¾ x 20⅜, imp, 1836 (4211/392) — 550

Audubon, J.J., after, THE PINE CREEPING WARBLER, engraving, aquatint, 19⅝ x 12⅜, imp, 1832 (4211/379) — 425

Audubon, J.J., after, THE REDWINGED STARLING, engraving, aquatint, 26 x 20⅞, imp, 1832 (4211/373) — 1000

Audubon, J.J., after, TOWNSEND'S WARBLER, ARCTIC AND WESTERN BLUE-BIRD, engraving, aquatint, 19¼ x 12¼, imp, 1837 (4211/402) — 750

Audubon (4211/393)

Audubon (4211/363)

Audubon (4211/364)

Audubon, J.J., after, WHITE AMERICAN WOLF, lithograph, 17½ x 24¼, imp, 1845 (4211/411)   450

Audubon, J.J., after, WHITE-WINGED SILVERY GULL, engraving, aquatint, 20¾ x 25¾, imp, 1835 (4211/386)   650

Audubon, J.J., after, WILD TURKEY, engraving, aquatint, 5⅝ x 38⅝, imp (4211/359)   2600

Audubon, J.J., after, YELLOW BILL MAGPIE, STELLERS AND ULTRAMARINE JAYS, CLARK'S CROW, 26¼ x 21⅝, imp, 1837 (4211/398)   850

Audubon, J.J., after, ZENAIDA DOVE, engraving, aquatint, 25⅞ x 20¾, imp, 1833 (4211/381)   1100

Audubon, J.J, after, THE TENNESSEE WARBLER, engraving, aquatint, 19¼ x 12¼,imp, 1932 (4211/380)   425

Avery, Milton, BATHERS, drypoint, 4¼ x 8⅜ (4203/15)   325

Avery, Milton, FLIGHT, 1953, woodcut, 7⅛ x 9¼ (4215/11)   450

Avery, Milton, ROOSTER, 1953, woodcut, 9⅝ x 7¼ (4215/10)   325

Avery, Milton, THREE BIRDS, woodcut, 9½ x 25, 1952 (4203/16)   950

Bacon, Francis, METROPOLITAN MUSEUM POSTER, 98/200, lithograph, 45¼ x 33¾ (4226/213)   900

Bacon, Peggy, THE PROMENADE DECK, drypoint, 6 x 8½ (4147/23)   200

Bacon, Peggy, CONGENIAL SCENE, drypoint, 8¾ x 12 (4270/29)   450

Baskin, Leonard, (WINGED MAN), etching, 17⅝ x 17½ (4270/36)   125

Baskin, Leonard, AGONIZED, woodcut, 31⅞ x 21¾ (4270/37)   125

Baskin, Leonard, BARTHELBY, DEAD, lithograph 22⅝ x 30¾ (4203/19)   150

Baskin, Leonard, BETRAYAL, woodcut, 23¼ x 29½ (4270/38)   125

Baskin, Leonard, CALLOT, etching, 17¾ x 17½ (4270/33)   200

Baskin, Leonard, CHILD AND STILL LIFE, woodcut, Diam12¼ (4118/77)   125

Baskin, Leonard, CHILDREN & STILL LIFE, woodcut, D12¼ (4147/35)   150

Baskin, Leonard, DE HOOGUE, woodcut, 26¼ x 13¾ (4270/32)   200

Baskin, Leonard, HIDATSA-MEDICINE MAN, lithograph, 32¼ x 19, 1972 (4147/30)   160

Baskin, Leonard, MAN AND SLOTH, woodcut, 3¼ x 7½, 1952 (4203/18)   130

Baskin, Leonard, MAN OF PEACE, 1952, woodcut, 39½ x 30¾ (4067/10)   250

Baskin, Leonard, POET LAUREATE, 1952, woodcut, 23 x 47⅝ (4067/9)   225

Baskin, Leonard, SHARP NOSE-ARAPAHO, lithograph, 31½ x 20⅞, 1972 (4147/33)   125

Baskin, Leonard, SITTING BULL, lithograph (4147/31)   125

Baskin, Leonard, THE APPLE TREE, etching and aquatint, 13½ x 17¾ (4270/34)   125

Baskin, Leonard, THE SHERIFF, etching, 17¾ x 17½ (4270/35)   150

Baskin, Leonard, WHITE HORSE, lithograph, 31¾ x 20½, 1972 (4147/34)   150

Baskin, Leonard, WOLF-ROBE-CHEYENNE, lithograph, 31½ x 21⅞, 1972 (4147/32)   125

Baskin, Leonardd, GRUENEWALD, etching, (4215/13)   250

Bearden, Romare, THE TRAIN, XXIV/XXV, good condition, etching, intaglio, 17¾ x 22⅛ (4226/215)   250

Beauve, E.W. (lithographer), BATTLE OF THE THAMES, 13¾ x 20⅜, print, discolored, 1842 (4076/806)   1000

Bellows, George, ANNE IN A BLACK HAT, lithograph 14½ x 11¾, 1924 (4203/30)   550

Bellows, George, ANNE IN A SPOTTED DRESS, lithograph, 9⅞ x 8⅝, 1921 (4203/32)   700

Bellows, George, ANNE, lithograph 8¾ x 8⅝, 1921 (4203/26)   425

Bellows, George, ARTISTS JUDGING WORKS OF ART, 1916, lithograph, 14¾ x 19¼ (4215/22)   1700

Bellows, George, BENEDICTION IN GEORGIA, lithograph, 16⅛ x 20⅛, 1916 (4118/83)   750

Bellows, George, BENEDICTION IN GEORGIA, lithograph, 16 x 20 (4270/48)   700

Bellows, George, BENEDICTION, 1916, lithograph, 16¼ x 20 (4215/21)   800

Bellows, George, BILLY SUNDAY, lithograph, 8⅞ x 16, 1923 (4118/82)   1300

Bellows, George, BILLY SUNDAY, lithograph, 9 x 16¼ (4270/46)   1200

Bellows, George, EDITH CAVELL, 1918, lithograph, 19 x 24⅞ (4215/15)   800

Bellows, George, ELSIE READING TO EMMA, lithograph, 10⅜ x 8½ (4270/47)   350

Bellows, George, HEAD OF ANNE, lithograph 9¾ x 8¼, 1923 (4203/23)   275

Bellows, George, HEAD OF JEAN, lithograph 7¼ x 5⅞, 1921 (4203/34)   250

Bellows, George, INTRODUCING JOHN L. SULLIVAN, 1916, lithograph, 20¾ x 20⅝ (4215/18)   2200

Bellows, George, JEAN IN A BLACK HAT, lithograph, 10⅝ x 9¼, 1924 (4203/31)   650

Bellows, George, JEAN, HEAD, lithograph 5¼ x 4¼, 1921 (4203/29)   200

Bellows, George, NUDE STUDY, GIRL STANDING WITH HAND RAISED TO MOUTH, lithograph, 12 x 4⅛ (4270/50)   250

Bellows, George, PORTRAIT OF MRS HERB ROTH, lithograph, 14 x 12⅝, 1924 (4203/28)   200

Bellows, George, PORTRAIT OF MRS. HERB ROTH, 1924, lithograph, (4215/19)   100

Bellows, George, PRAYER MEETING, 1916, lithograph, 18½ x 22¼ (4215/17)   600

Bellows, George, PUNCHINELLO IN THE HOUSE OF DEATH, lithograph, 16¼ x 19¼ (4270/45)   500

Bellows, George, REDUCING, lithograph, 18 x 16⅝ (4270/49)   600

Bellows, George, SPRING, CENTRAL PARK, lithograph, 8½ x 7⅛, 1921 (4203/25)   450

Bellows, George, STUDY OF B.P., lithograph 4¾ x 7¼, 1924 (4203/33)   150

Bellows, George, STUDY OF MARY, lithograph, 11⅜ x 10 (4270/44)   250

Bellows, George, STUDY OF MY MOTHER, NO. 2, lithograph, 11⅜ x 8, 1921 (4203/22)   250

Bellows, George, SUNDAY GOING TO CHURCH, 1921, lithograph, 16 x 18¾ (4215/23)   900

Bellows, George, TENNIS AT NEWPORT, lithograph, 14¾ x 18⅛, 1920 (4203/27)   1900

Bellows, George, THE APPEAL TO THE PEOPLE, 1924, lithograph, 14⅛ x 18¼ (4215/20)   500

Bellows, George, THE IRISH FAIR, lithograph, 18⅞ x 20¾, 1923 (4203/24)	600
Bellows, George, WORKMAN'S KITCHEN, lithograph, 6⅜ x 7½ (4270/51)	225
Benecke, Thomas, after, SLEIGHING IN NEW YORK, chromolithograph, (4211/302)	800
Benjamin, Russell (After), SPERM WHALING WITH ITS VARIETIES, 15½ x 32⅜, print, repairs, 1870 (4076/813)	350
Benton, Thomas Hart, A DRINK OF WATER, lithograph, 10⅜ x 14⅜, 1937 (4203/41)	900
Benton, Thomas Hart, AFTER THE BLOW, lithograph, 9⅞ x 14, 1946 (4118/85)	550
Benton, Thomas Hart, ARRON, lithograph, 12¾ x 9½, 1941 (4203/43)	750
Benton, Thomas Hart, BACK FROM THE FIELDS, 1945, lithograph, 9¾ x 12⅞ (4067/28)	375
Benton, Thomas Hart, CRADLING WHEAT, lithograph, 9⅝ x 12, 1939 (4203/42)	900
Benton, Thomas Hart, FIRE IN THE BARNYARD, lithograph, 8⅝ x 13⅜ (4270/57)	550
Benton, Thomas Hart, FIRE IN THE BARNYARD, lithograph, 8½ x 13¼ (4270/58)	850
Benton, Thomas Hart, FRANKIE AND JOHNNIE, lithograph, 16⅜ x 22¼, 1936 (4244/25)	3600
Benton, Thomas Hart, FRANKIE AND JOHNNIE, lithograph, 16⅜ x 22¼ (4270/55)	3600
Benton, Thomas Hart, GATESIDE CONVERSATION, lithograph, 9⅞ x 14, 1946 (4244/29)	750
Benton, Thomas Hart, HUCK FINN, lithograph, 16½ x 22⅞, 1936 (4203/40)	3100
Benton, Thomas Hart, I GOT A GIRL ON SOURWOOD, 1938, lithograph, 12½ x 9¼ (4067/21)	625
Benton, Thomas Hart, INVESTIGATION, 1937, lithograph, 9½ x 12¾ (4067/20)	400
Benton, Thomas Hart, ISLAND HAY, lithograph, 9⅜ x 12⅝, 1945 (4203/47)	800
Benton, Thomas Hart, ISLAND HAY, lithograph, 10 x 12⅝, sta, frame, 1945 (4244/28)	850
Benton, Thomas Hart, ISLAND HAY, 1945, lithograph, 10⅛ x 12¾ (4067/29)	425
Benton, Thomas Hart, LOADING CORN, lithograph, 9½ x 12⅞, 1945 (4118/84)	675
Benton, Thomas Hart, LOADING CORN, 1945, lithograph, 9⅝ x 12⅞ (4215/27)	850
Benton, Thomas Hart, MISSOURI FARMYARD, lithograph, 10¼ x 16, 1936 (4203/39)	750
Benton, Thomas Hart, MORNING TRAIN, 1943, lithograph, 9¼ x 3⅝ (4067/26)	650
Benton, Thomas Hart, PLOUGHING IT UNDER, lithograph, 8 x 9⅝, 1934 (4203/38)	300
Benton, Thomas Hart, RUNNING HORSES, lithograph, 12½ x 16½, 1955 (4118/86)	950
Benton, Thomas Hart, SPRING TRYOUT, lithograph, 9½ x 13¾, sta, 1943 (4244/26)	1100
Benton, Thomas Hart, SUNDAY MORNING, 1939, lithograph, 9⅝ x 12⅝ (4215/24)	650
Benton, Thomas Hart, THE BOY, 9½ x 13¾ (4270/56)	625
Benton, Thomas Hart, THE BOY, lithograph, 9½ x 13¾, 1948 (4244/30)	850
Benton, Thomas Hart, THE BOY, 1948, lithograph, 9⅝ x 13¾ (4067/30)	550
Benton, Thomas Hart, THE FENCE MENDER, 1940, lithograph, 10 x 18 (4215/25)	650
Benton, Thomas Hart, THE FENCE MENDER, 1940, lithograph, 10 x 14 (4067/24)	525
Benton, Thomas Hart, THE HYMN' SINGER, 1950, lithograph, 16 x 12¼ (4067/31)	250
Benton, Thomas Hart, THE MEETING, 1941, lithograph, 8⅞ x 11⅝ (4067/25)	525
Benton, Thomas Hart, THE MUSIC LESSON, 1943, lithograph, 10⅛ x 12⅞ (4067/27)	475
Benton, Thomas Hart, THE MUSIC LESSON, 1943, lithograph, 10⅛ x 12⅞ (4215/26)	900
Benton, Thomas Hart, THE RACE (HOMEWARD BOUND) lithograph, 9 x 13¼, 1942 (4203/45)	1500
Benton, Thomas Hart, THE WHITE CALF, lithograph, 9⅞ x 12¾, 1945 (4244/27)	400
Benton, Thomas Hart, THRESHING, lithograph, 9¼ x 13¾, 1941 (4203/44)	1000
Benton, Thomas Hart, WHITE CALF, lithograph, 10 x 12¾, 1945 (4203/46)	750
Benton, Thomas Hart, WHITE CALF, 1935, lithograph, 10 x 12¾ (4215/28)	400
Bertin, F. Sala & Co., SCENE ON THE LOWER MISSISSIPPI, lithograph, 10½ x 15¼, imp (4211/329)	150
Bill, Max, 7 SCARIONS, silkscreen, 10¾ x 10¾, 1967 (4203/51)	75
Bingham, George Caleb, after, THE JOLLY FLAT BOATMAN, engraving, 18¾ x 24, imp, 1847 (4211/327)	2100
Birch, William, PENNSYLVANIA HOSPITAL, etching, engraving, 11 x 12⅞, imp, 1804 (4211/318)	375
Birch, William, THE CITY AND PORT OF PHILADELPHIA, etching, engraving, 11 x 13¼, imp, 1800 (4211/317)	575
Blake, Peter, STUDIO TACK-BOARD, 85/100, good condition, silkscreen, 1972, 34 x 54 (4226/216)	225
Bolatowsky,Irya, COMPOSITION, silkscreen, 26½ x 26¾ (4203/54)	100
Bufford, J.H., lithograph, 11 x 33¾, imp (4211/311)	1000
Calder, Alexander, (BIRD AND CLOCK), etching, 9¼ x 6⅛ (4270/92)	75
Calder, Alexander, ACROBATS, lithograph, 22 x 12⅜ (4067/47)	275
Calder, Alexander, AFFICHE AV ARTIG, lithograph, in colors, 21⅞ x 15⅜, 1975 (4147/67)	275
Calder, Alexander, AFFICHE AV ARTIG. 1975, color lithograph, 20¾ x 16⅛, 1975 (4118/103)	175
Calder, Alexander, AFFICHE, lithograph, 30¼ x 26 (4270/86)	150
Calder, Alexander, ALBI, lithograph, in colors, 35 x 23⅝ (4147/61)	300
Calder, Alexander, ALBI, lithograph, 35 x 23½ (4067/50)	375
Calder, Alexander, BALLOONS, lithograph, 40 x 48¼ (4067/51)	475
Calder, Alexander, BIRTH OF THE UNEXPECTED, lithograph, 20½ x 28⅜ (4270/89)	300
Calder, Alexander, BLACK SUN AND RED MOON, lithograph, in colors, 23½ x 31½ (4147/59)	350
Calder, Alexander, CANDY CANE, lithograph, 29¼ x 20½ (4270/88)	250
Calder, Alexander, CAPTIVE BUTTERFLY, lithograph, 25¼ x 38⅞ (4270/90)	350
Calder, Alexander, CARREFOUR, lithograph, in colors, 19¼ x 17½ (4147/69)	250
Calder, Alexander, CIRCUS, lithograph, 26¼ x 38, frame (4244/56)	700

Calder, Alexander, COMPOSITION, lithograph, in colors, 28⅜ x 21⅛ (4147/63) 250

Calder, Alexander, COMPOSITION, lithograph, in colors, 28⅜ x 20¾ (4147/62) 325

Calder, Alexander, COMPOSITION, lithograph, in colors, 20½ x 29¼ (4147/68) 275

Calder, Alexander, COMPOSITION IN ORANGE, BLUE, BLACK, lithograph, 17½ x 22¼ (4244/54) 550

Calder, Alexander, COMPOSITION, color lithograph, 29 x 43, 1971 (4118/100) 275

Calder, Alexander, COMPOSITION, color lithograph, 20¾ x 16⅛, 1975 (4118/105) 350

Calder, Alexander, COMPOSITION, color lithograph, 22 x 29¾ (4118/108) 300

Calder, Alexander, COMPOSITION, lithograph, 22 x 29⅞ (470/81) 300

Calder, Alexander, COMPOSITION, lithograph, 26½ x 20⅛ (4067/52) 250

Calder, Alexander, COMPOSITION, lithograph, 21⅜ x 15¾ (4203/76) 150

Calder, Alexander, DARK PYRAMID, lithograph, 28¼ x 20½ (4270/84) 250

Calder, Alexander, FIESTA, lithograph, 28¼ x 20¼ (4270/83) 375

Calder, Alexander, FLAT WORLD, 1969, lithograph, 28⅜ x 42⅝ (4067/48) 850

Calder, Alexander, GALACTIC SYSTEM, color lithograph, 20½ x 28⅜, 1976 (4118/106) 325

Calder, Alexander, GALACTIC SYSTEM, lithograph, in colors, 20½ x 28⅜, 1976 (4147/71) 175

Calder, Alexander, GREY OVAL, 1969, lithograph, 29¼ x 45¼ (4067/49) 850

Calder, Alexander, LE NOBLE CHEVALIER, lithograph, in red and black, 14¾ x 10½ (4147/57) 225

Calder, Alexander, LE NOBLE CHEVALIER, lithograph, in red and black, 14¾ x 10½ (4147/58) 175

Calder, Alexander, LES OIGNONS, lithograph, 20½ x 28¼ (4270/87) 250

Calder, Alexander, MAGIE AEOLIENNE, color lithograph, 25⅜ x 19½, 1972 (4118/101) 300

Calder, Alexander, MAMA CITRON, lithograph, in black and yellow, 15 x 11⅛ (4147/64) 175

Calder, Alexander, MANHOLE COVERS, lithograph, in colors, 29½ x 43½ (4147/60) 425

Calder, Alexander, MCGOVERN FOR MCGOVERNMENT, color silkscreen, 30⅛ x 22⅞, slight scuffs (4118/102) 75

Calder, Alexander, MCGOVERN FOR MCGOVERNMENT, silkscreen, 34⅝ x 24 (4270/93) 150

Calder, Alexander, MES ETOFFES, lithograph, in colors, 20½ x 28⅜ (4147/65) 225

Calder, Alexander, NEZ ET OREILLE TRES GAI, lithograph, 28⅝ x 36⅝ (4244/59) 1000

Calder, Alexander, NEZ ET OREILLE TRES GAI, lithograph, 29½ x 39½ (4215/47) 1000

Calder, Alexander, OUR UNFINISHED REVOLUTION, lithographs, ten, 22 x 30, complete portfolio, 1976 (4244/62) 3000

Calder, Alexander, POEME, lithograph, 24 x 13 (4270/94) 175

Calder, Alexander, PYRAMIDS AND SPIRALS, lithograph, 29½ x 43¾ (4270/95) 450

Calder, Alexander, PYRAMIDS AND SUN, lithograph, 26 x 39¼ (4203/75) 500

Calder, Alexander, RED DOLPHIN, lithograph, 26⅜ x 38⅜, frame (4244/57) 450

Calder, Alexander, RED NOSE, lithograph, 29½ x 42⅞ (4244/60) 1100

Calder, Alexander, RED SUN, lithograph, 24¾ x 35⅜ (4244/61) 550

Calder, Alexander, RIBICOFF, lithograph, 30½ x 22⅛ (4067/55) 300

Calder, Alexander, RIBICOFF, lithograph, 31⅛ x 23¼ (4203/77) 225

Calder, Alexander, SPIRALE MULTICOLORE, lithograph, 43⅛ x 29½, 1969 (4244/53) 600

Calder, Alexander, SPIRALE, lithograph, 25½ x 19⅜ (4203/78) 300

Calder, Alexander, SPIRO, 1972, lithograph, 41⅜ x 29⅜ (4067/58) 375

Calder, Alexander, SUN, MOON, STARS, SPIRAL AND PYRAMID, lithograph, 29½ x 41½ (4270/96) 400

Calder, Alexander, THE PUPPET MAN, lithograph, 4½ x 14¼ (4244/58) 600

Calder, Alexander, THE ROCK AND THE SPIRAL, color lithograph, 26 x 37⅜ (4118/109) 650

Calder, Alexander, TROIS OIGNONS, lithograph, 21½ x 29½ (4270/97) 375

Calder, Alexander, TWO DISCS AND HALF, color lithograph, 30 x 43¼, 1975 (4118/104) 450

Calder, Alexander, VIOLIN, lithograph, 21⅝ x 29½ (4067/60) 375

Calder, Alexander, WATERGATE, lithograph, in colors, 29½ x 43⅛, 1973 (4147/66) 375

Calvert, Edward, THE FLOOD, pen lithograph, 1¾ x 3, 1829 (4203/80) 250

Calvert, Edward, THE LADY WITH THE ROOKS, wood engraving, 1⅝ x 3, 1893 (4203/81) 100

Cameron, David Young, PONTE DELLA TRINITA, etching and drypoint, 6⅝ x 8⅝, 1902-7 (4203/82) 70

Carmi, Eugenio, CHROMO-SYNCLASMA, suite of six, 105/200, silkscreens, 1971, 34⅝ x 24⅜ (4226/217) 150

Cary, John, ENGINEER, A NEW MAP OF N. AMERICA, 1806, engraving, 18 x 20¼ (654/428) 85

Cassatt, Mary, HEAD OF A MODEL LOOKING DOWN, drypoint in sepia, 7⅞ x 5½, ca1889 (4203/84) 700

Cassatt, Mary, JEANNETTE WEARING A BONNET, NO. 1, drypoint, reprint, 9½ x 6½, 1904 (4203/85) 275

Cassatt, Mary, JENNETTE WEARING A BONNET, 1904, drypoint, 9¼ x 6¾ (4067/63) 400

Cassatt, Mary, JENNETTE WEARING A BONNET, 1904, drypoint, 9 x 6⅛ (4067/62) 500

Chagall, Marc, DAPHNIS AND CHLOE, ARRIVAL OF DIONYSOPHANES, 1961, lithograph 16¼ x 12½ (4067/68) 375

Cockburn, James Pattison, THE FALL OF NIAGRA, aquatint, 20¼ x 27⅝, imp, 1833 (4211/307) 550

Cozzens, Frederick, after, TEN SAILING PRINTS, lithograph, 14¼ x 20½ (654/437) 600

Currier & Ives, A CHANCE FOR BOTH BARRELS, lithograph, 19 x 27, 1857 (4211/350) 1100

Currier & Ives, BLACKWELLS ISLAND, lithograph, 10¾ x 15½, imp, 1862 (4211/296) 800

Currier & Ives, BURNING OF THE CLIPPER SHIP GOLDEN LIGHT, lithograph, 8¼ x 12¼ (684/917) 110

Currier & Ives, BURNING OF THE STEAMSHIP GOLDEN GATE, lithograph, 8 x 12¼ (684/918) 150
Currier & Ives, CITY OF NEW YORK & ENVIRONS, 1875, lithograph, 8½ x 13 (654/440) 225
Currier & Ives, CLIPPER SHIP 'RED JACKET', lithograph, 8⅝ x 13¾, imp (4211/337) 375
Currier & Ives, CLIPPER SHIP IN A SNOW SQUALL, 8½ x 12½ (4156/268) 225
Currier & Ives, EARLY WINTER, lithograph, 9½ x 11⅞, imp, 1869 (4211/346) 1600
Currier & Ives, NEW ENGLAND WINTER SCENE, lithograph, 16⅜ x 23⅝, imp, 1861 (4211/349) 1700
Currier & Ives, NEW ENGLAND WINTER SCENE, lithograph, 16⅜ x 23⅝, imp, 1861 (4211/348) 3300
Currier & Ives, NEW YORK BAY, FROM BAY RIDGE, L.I., lithograph, 14⅞ x 20⅛, imp, 1860 (4211/290) 1000
Currier & Ives, PIGEON SHOOTING, lithograph, 19⅛ x 27⅝, imp, 1862 (4211/351) 2100
Currier & Ives, PLACID LAKE, ADIRONDACKS, lithograph, 8 x 12½, imp (4211/299) 225
Currier & Ives, SKATING SCENE-MOONLIGHT, lithograph, small folio, 1868 (4156/267) 225
Currier & Ives, SLOOP YACHT POCHOHANTIS OF NEW YORK, 19⅛ x 27½ (4156/269) 175
Currier & Ives, STATEN ISLAND AND THE NARROWS, lithograph, 14¾ x 20¼, imp, 1861 (4211/293) 1000
Currier & Ives, SUMMER SHADES, lithograph, 15⅜ x 22¾ (684/984) 300
Currier & Ives, THE GRAND PACER KINGSTON, BY SPENDTHRIFT, lithograph, 19⅞ x 27, d.1891 (684/968) 425
Currier & Ives, THE GREAT EAST RIVER SUSPENSION BRIDGE, chromolithograph, 18⅛ x 36¾, imp, 1883 (4211/294) 550
Currier & Ives, THE LEADERS, JAY EYE SEE, 2,10, MAUD S., lithograph, 18 x 27, d.1888, unfr. (684/969) 300
Currier & Ives, THE MOUNTAIN SPRING, lithograph, 10½ x 15⅛, d.1862 (684/937) 90
Currier & Ives, THE MOUNTAIN SPRING, lithograph, 14¾ x 19⅝, imp, 1862 (4211/300) 300
Currier & Ives, THE NIGHT AFTER THE BATTLE, lithograph, 7½ x 12¼, d.1862 (684/923) 30
Currier & Ives, THE PIONEER'S HOME, lithograph, 18¾ x 26⅞, imp, 1867 (4211/342) 1250

Calder
(4147/58)

Currier & Ives, THE PORT OF NEW YORK FROM THE BATTERY, chromolithograph, 20½ x 33¼, imp, 1892 (4211/292) 425
Currier & Ives, THE PORT OF NEW YORK, FROM THE BATTERY, chromolithograph, 20⅞ x 33¼, imp, 1892 (4211/291) 900
Currier & Ives, THE RETURN FROM THE WOODS, lithograph, 11 x 15⅜, imp (4211/352) 300
Currier & Ives, THE SKATING POND, lithograph, 18⅛ x 26¾, imp, 1861 (4211/295) 2500
Currier & Ives, THE YACHT SQUADRON AT NEWPORT, chromolithograph, 20⅜ x 32⅛, imp, 1872 (4211/340) 300
Currier & Ives, TRASH TO WINDWARD, chromolithograph, 16 x 24¼, imp, 1893 (4211/338) 400
Currier & Ives, VIEW IN DUTCHESS COUNTY, lithograph, 15 x 20⅛, imp (4211/298) 650
Currier & Ives (Pub.), CAMPING IN THE WOODS, 18⅞ x 27⅝, hand colored lithograph discolored, 1863 (4076/830) 325
Currier & Ives (Pub.), CLIPPER SHIP 'OCEAN EXPRESS', 16⅛ x 24½, print, tears, creases, 1856 (4076/815) 250
Currier & Ives (Pub.), LIFE IN THE WOOD, STARTING OUT, 18⅞ x 27⅜, hand colored lithograph fox, discolored, 1860 (4076/832) 900

Currier, C., after George Holland, VIEW OF FEDERAL HALL OF NEW YORK CITY, lithograph, 13¼ x 20 (654/426) — 100

Currier, N., AMERICAN COUNTRY LIFE, MAY MORNING, lithograph, 16¾ x 23⅞, imp, 1855 (4211/343) — 550

Currier, N., AMERICAN COUNTRY LIFE, PLEASURES OF WINTER, lithograph, 16¾ x 23⅞, imp, 1855 (4211/344) — 650

Currier, N., AMERICAN FARM SCENES #3, lithograph, 17 x 22¼, imp, 1853 (4211/345) — 375

Currier, N., PEYTONA AND FASHION, lithograph, 17¾ x 28⅜, imp (4211/353) — 2800

Currier, N., QUAIL SHOOTING, lithograph, 13 x 20¼, d.1852 (684/956) — 550

Currier, N., THE HIGH BRIDGE AT HARLEM,1849, lithograph., 8 x12½ (654/431) — 120

Currier, N., U.S. SHIP OF THE LINE PENNA., 140 GUNS, lithograph, 8¾ x 12¾ (654/442) — 225

Currier, N., U.S. SHIP OF THE LINE PENNSYLVANIA, 140 GUNS, lithograph, 8¾ x 12¾ (684/906) — 150

Currier, N., VIEW OF SAN FRANCISCO, CALIFORNIA, lithograph, 15 x 30, imp, 1850 (4211/331) — 6250

Currier, N. (Pub.), AMERICAN COUNTRY LIFE, PLEASURES OF WINTER, 16¾ x 23⅞, hand colored, lithograph tear, 1855 (4076/821) — 1100

Currier, N. (Pub.), AMERICAN FARM SCENES (AUTUMN), 17 x 24, hand colored lithograph foxed, waterstain, 1853 (4076/823) — 350

Currier, N. (Pub.), HIGH PRESSURE STEAMBOAT 'MAYFLOWER', 16¼ x 28, hand colored lithograph paper loss, 1855 (4076/816) — 1800

Currier, N. (Pub.), THE CARES OF A FAMILY, 18½ x 23¾, hand colored lithograph tears, stains, 1856 (4076/825) — 800

Currier, N. (Pub.), THE PURSUIT, 17⅞ x 25⅜, hand colored lithograph discolored, 1856 (4076/819) — 850

Currier, N. after L. Maurer, THE CELEBRATED HORSE LEXINGTON, lithograph, 19⅜ x 26½ (684/946) — 650

Currier & Ives (Pub.), LIFE IN THE WOODS, RETURNING TO CAMP, 11¾ x 27½, hand clored lithograph foxed, stained, 1860 (4076/831) — 1000

Currier & Ives (Pub.), LIFE ON THE PRAIRIE, 18½ x 27⅛, hand colored lithograph discolored, 1862 (4076/818) — 2200

Currier & Ives (Pub.), MIDNIGHT RACE ON THE MISSISSIPPI, 9 x 13¼, hand colored lithograph tears, 1875 (4076/817) — 150

Currier & Ives (Pub.), MISTER BONNER'S HORSE, 17 x 26¾, print, mat stain, soiled, 1873 (4076/833) — 600

Currier & Ives (Pub.), THE BEAUTIES OF BILLIARDS, 16⅛ x 24¾, hand colored lithograph laid down, 1869 (4076/829) — 800

Currier & Ives (Pub.), THE CARES OF A FAMILY, 18½ x 23¾, hand colored lithograph discolored, 1856 (4076/826) — 1200

Currier & Ives (Pub.), THE FARMER'S HOME-SUMMER, 16⅜ x 23⅝, hand colored lithograph discolored, 1864 (4076/827) — 1000

Currier & Ives (Pub.), THE FARMER'S HOME-WINTER, 16⅜ x 23¾, print, discolored, 1863 (4076/828) — 2200

Currier & Ives (Pub.), THE LIGHTNING EXPRESS TRAINS, 17¾ x 27⅞, hand colored lithograph discolored, 1863 (4076/820) — 6200

Currier & Ives (Pub.), VIEW ON THE HARLEM RIVER, 14¾ x 20¼, hand colored lithograph foxing, tears, 1852 (4076/839) — 650

Curry, John Stuart, JOHN BROWN, lithograph, 14¾ x 10⅞ (4270/139) — *1200*

Curry, John Stuart, MANHUNT, lithograph, 9¾ x 12⅞ (4270/138) — 250

Curry, John Stuart, THE PLAINSMAN, lithograph, 15¾ x 9⅝ (4270/140) — 600

D'Arcangelo, Alan, FROM SPEED TO TENSION, suite of 7 silkscreens, 43/120, plexiglass box (4226/219) — 1500

Davies, Arthur B., DREAM STRIFE, lithograph, 7⅛ x 11¾, 1920 (4203/118) — 150

Davies, Arthur B., PRELUDE, lithograph, 12¾ x 17⅞, 1920 (4203/117) — 150

Davies, Arthur B., PSYCHE, lithograph 5¾ x 9⅛, 1919 (4203/120) — 175

Davies, Arthur B., SHIPS, lithograph and lithotint, 15⅝ x 10½, 1921 (4118/153) — 125

Davies, Arthur B., VENUS, mezzotint, 9⅞ x 5¾, 1927 (4203/121) — 150

Davis, Gene, COMPOSITION, 77/150, scuffs, silkscreen, 1974, 76¾ x 42 (4226/220) — 500

Davis, Ronald, FIVE BLOCK ROW, 35/50, good condition, silkscreen, 1974, 11½ x 25⅜ (4226/221) — 275

Davis, Stuart, BASS ROCKS, silkscreen, 8⅜ x 11¾, 1939 (4203/122) — 1100

Davis, Stuart, TEN WORKS/TEN PAINTERS, COMPOSITION, silkscreen, 11 x 14⅛, pub. 1964 (4203/123) — 300

Dehn, Adolphe, CENTRAL PARK NIGHT, 1946, lithograph, 12½ x 17½ (4067/82) — 90

Dickinson, John, THE PATRIOTIC AMERICAN FARMER, engraving, 1768, oval (4158/21) — 1600

Dine, Jim, A TOOL BOX (Galerie Mikro 42), 10 work portfolio, silkscreens, 76/150, 1966 (4226/240) — 1000

Dine, Jim, CALICO, silkscreen, 39½ x 29½ (4270/171) — 200

Dine, Jim, DELUXE CATALOGUE, book, edition of 200, 1970, 1970, mixed media, 8⅛ x 8⅝ (4226/242) — 500

Dine, Jim, HANDS, lithograph, 31¼ x 22⅜ (4270/173) — 425

Dine, Jim, RIMBAUD AT HARAR IN 1893, 1973, etching, aquatint and drypoint, 4⅛ x 3¼ (4067/90) — 150

Dine, Jim, SELF PORTRAIT HEAD 3, STATE, drypoint with aquatint, 11¾ x 8¾ (4067/89) — 425

Dine, Jim, SELF PORTRAIT, 1971, drypoint, 7¾ x 5⅞ (4067/86) — 225

Dine, Jim, TOOLS (Williams College 10) 1970, 39/63, creases, offset lithograph, 33½ x 50¼ (4226/241) — 700

Dine, Jim, WHITE TEETH, 2/24, lithograph, 11⅜ x 9⅞ (4226/239) — 1050

Doney, T. after George C. Bingham, THE JOLLY FLATBOAT MEN, published 1847, 18¾ x 34, engraving, color (654/417) — 275

Dufresne, Charles, WILD BOAR, lineoleum cut, 11¾ x 8 (4203/139) — 375

Durand, Asher B. after John Trumbull, THE DECLARATION OF INDEPENDENCE, engraving, 20⅜ x 30⅜, d.1820 (684/945) — 60

Eddy, Don, WILLIAM'S BAR-B-QUE, lithograph, 23¼ x 17½ (4203/144) — 325

Endicot & Co., COLONEL KANE'S COACH, lithograph, 25½ x 35¼, d.1876 (684/987) — 225

Endicott & Co., ALBANY OF THE HUDSON RIVER DAY LINE, chromolithograph, 17½ x 26⅝, imp, 1880 (4211/341) — 300

Endicott & Co., NEW BEDFORD, lithograph, 15¾ x 23⅝, imp, 1858 (4211/310) — 625

Curry
(4270/139)

Endicott, George, CLIPPER SHIP 'RACER' OF NEW YORK, chromolithograph, 16½ x 22½, imp, 1834-40 (4211/336) — 175

Ensor, James, LECOMBAT, 1896, etching, 4¾ x 7¼ (4067/92) — 650

Estes, Richard, URBAN LANDSCAPE, THE ST LOUIS ARCH, 20/75, silkscreen, 1972, 14¾ x 24 (4226/248) — 750

Estes, Richard, URBAN LANDSCAPES, portfolio of 8 silkscreens, 19¾ x 27⅜, 1972 (4118/171) — 4750

Estes, Richard, URBAN LANDSCAPES, DANBURY TILE, 25/75, silkscreen, 1972, 15 x 20 (4226/249) — 900

Estes, Richard, URBAN LANDSCAPES, MAURICE FRENCH ICE CREAM, 25/75, silkscreen, 1972, 13⅜ x 20 (4226/250) — 950

Estes, Richard, URBAN LANDSCAPES, TEN DOORS, 20/75, silkscreen, 1972, 14½ x 21⅜ (4226/252) — 750

Estes, Richard, URBAN LANDSCAPES, 50/75, soiled, 8 silkscreens, 1972, 19¾ x 27⅜ (4226/247) — 6750

Feininger, Lyonel (1871-1956), DAS TOR, 1912, edition of 125, etching, drypoint, 10⅝ x 7¾ (4247/142) — 3750

Fiene, Ernest, SEATED FEMALE NUDE, lithograph, 15 x 10⅞, 1929 (4203/148) — 90

Forester, Edmund & Co. (Pub.), SCENE ON THE UPPER MISSISSIPPI, 16¾ x 23¼, hand colored lithograph discolored (4076/814) — 700

Foujita, Tsughouharu, DEUX NUS, lithograph, 12¼ x 15⅜, 1929 (4118/177) — 950

Foujita, Tsughouharu, NU, lithograph, 16⅛ x 12¼, 1929 (4118/176) — 950

Francis, Sam, UNTITLED (Blue Bone), edition of 101, lithograph, 1964, 17¾ x 13⅜ (4226/254) — 400

Francis, Sam, UNTITLED, lithograph, 24 x 19 (4203/154) — 200

Francis, Sam, WEB (Gemini 408), 16/50, silkscreen, 1972, 42⅜ x 54⅜ (4226/255) — 1100

Frankenthaler, Helen, AIR FRAME, silkscreen, 21⅞ x 16⅞ (4270/198) — 375

Frankenthaler, Helen, AIR FRAME, 190/200 from N.Y. 10 portfolio, silkscreen, 1965, 21⅞ x 16⅞ (4226/256) — 400

Frankenthaler, Helen, WHAT RED LINES CAN DO, suite of 5, 72/75, silkscreens, 1970, 38 x 26⅛ (4226/257) — 1700

Friedlander, Johnny, CHATS II, soft ground, etching, 18⅝ x 17¼, 1953 (4203/155)   400
Friedlander, Johnny, HAARLEM, lithograph, in colors, 30⅛ x 22⅞ (4147/118)   250
Friedlander, Johnny, OISEAU DANS LE CERCLE, etching, aquatint, intaglio, 29¾ x 22¼, 1970
   (4203/156)   475
Geller, W.O. after Baron Jolly, FRANKLIN AT THE COURT OF FRANCE, engraving, 27½ x 39½,
   d.1853 (684/915)   30
Goode, Joe, UNTITLED, numbered A P 3, lithograph, pastel, 1973, 8 x 14 (4226/258)   125
Gould, J. and Richter, H.C., TWO ORNITHOLOGICAL PRINTS, lighographs, 18⅛ x 13½ (684/941)   70
Grooms, Red, (GANGSTER AND MOLL), silkscreen, 40¼ x 28½ (4270/213)   250
Grooms, Red, BICENTENNIAL BANDWAGON, silkscreen, 26¼ x 34¾ (4270/214)   250
Gwathmey, Robert, TIN OF LARD, lithograph, 17½ x 13½ (4270/217)   150
Hagter, William S., L'ESCOUTAY, engraving, aquatint, 7¾ x 12, 1951 (4147/132)   180
Hamaguchi, Yozo, PINK, AND SHELL, two mezzotints, 3⅞ x 3 and 3 x 3⅞, 1960 (4118/183)   750
Hamilton, Richard, LA SCALA MILANO (Davidson Art Center 25), 13/65, photo etching, silkscreen,
   '68 (4226/260)   500
Hartung, Hans, COMPOSITION, lithograph, 20⅛ x 12⅝ (4203/165)   100
Haskell & Allen, A BRUSH FOR THE LEAD, lithograph, 17¾ x 26, imp, 1875 (4211/354)   375
Hassam, Childe, A NEW ENGLAND BARROOM, etching, 5 x 5⅝, 1917 (4203/167)   500
Hassam, Childe, AN EASTHAMPTON IDYLL, etching with drypoint, 9⅛ x 7½ (4270/227)   *950*
Hassam, Childe, CALVARY CHURCH IN SNOW, etching, 7 x 4¾ (4270/231)   325
Hassam, Childe, COS COB DOCK, etching, 8¼ x 6½, 1915 (4203/166)   200
Hassam, Childe, HOME SWEET HOME COTTAGE, etching, 8⅞ x 11 (4270/230)   1400
Hassam, Childe, THE CABILDO NEW ORLEANS, 1927, etching, 10¾ x 8¼ (4067/105)   1000
Hassam, Childe, THE CHASE HOUSE, 1929, etching, 7 x 8⅜ (4067/106)   500
Hassam, Childe, THE CHIMNEYS, PORTSMOUTH, etching, 5 x 8¼, 1915 (4147/131)   425
Hassam, Childe, THE CHURCH ACROSS THE WAY, 1916, etching, 8⅛ x 4½ (4215/143)   325
Hassam, Childe, THE HIGH POOL, etching, 4⅝ x 3 (4203/168)   300
Hassam, Childe, THE LITTLE CHURCH AROUND THE CORNER, etching, drypoint, 7⅞ x 11½, 1923
   (4118/184)   600
Hassam, Childe, THE OLD TOLL BRIDGE, etching, 6⅞ x 5½ (4270/228)   350
Hassam, Childe, UPPER MANHATTAN, drypoint, 6 x 9 (4203/169)   300
Hassam, Childe, VILLAGE ELMS, EASTHAMPTON, etching, 6⅞ x 8⅞, 1923 (4203/170)   700
Haugg, L. after J.L. Krimmel, WHITE'S GREAT CATTLE SHOW, lithograph, 14⅛ x 23½, imp, 1850-
70 (4211/323)   150

Hassam
(4270/227)

Havell, Robert after J.J. Audubon, WANDERING SHEARWATER, engraving, 10 6/8 x 17¾, d.1835
   (684/902)   600
Havell, Robert, after J.J. Audubon, 4 hand colored engravings, aquatint, 19½ x 12¼ (654/421)   700
Havell, Robert, after J.J. Audubon, 4 hand colored engravings, aquatint, 19½ x 12¼ (654/422)   1100
Havell, Robert, after J.J. Audubon, 4 hand colored engravings, aquatint, 19½ x 12¼ (654/420)   700
Havell, Robert, after J.J. Audubon, 4 hand colored engravings, aquatint, 19¼ x 12¼ (654/418)   800
Havell, Robert, after J.J. Audubon, 4hand colored engravings, aquatint, 19½ x 12¼ (654/423)   900
Hayter, Stanley Wm., AMAZON, engraving, soft ground, intaglio, 24⅝ x 15⅝, 1945 (4203/173)   1400
Hayter, Stanley Wm., PAVANE, engraving and intaglio, 11⅝ x 7¾, 1935 (4203/171)   425
Hayter, Stanley, Wm., MIROIR, embossed etching and engraving, 7½ x 4¾, 1941 (4203/172)   300

Hill, John W. (After), NEW YORK, 34⅜ x 55⅞, engraving, aquatint, repairs, 1855 (4076/837) — 1600

Hill, John W. (After), NEW YORK AND BROOKLYN, 24½ x 38⅛, etching, aquatint, repairs, 1855 (4076/838) — 2800

Homer, Winslow, EIGHT BELLS, etching, 19⅜ x 25, 1887 (4203/178) — 4100

Hopper, Edward, LES POILUS, etching, 6 x 6¾ (4270/245) — 2250

Hopper, Edward, LES POILUS, 1915-18, etching, 5⅞ x 6⅞ (4215/163) — 3200

Hopper, Edward, NIGHT SHADOWS, etching, 7 x 8¾, 1921 (4203/179) — 1800

Hopper, Edward, NIGHT SHADOWS, 1921, etching, 7 x 8¼ (4067/110) — 850

Huggins, William J. (After), SOUTH SEA WALE FISHERY, 17½ x 30½, print, laid down, 1825 (4076/808) — 500

Hurd, Peter, SERMON FROM REVELATIONS, 1938, lithograph, 9⅞ x 13⅝ (4067/111) — 250

Hurd, Peter, THE SHEPHERDERS CHRISTMAS, lithograph, 6⅛ x 8 (4270/247) — 140

Indiana, Robert, POSTER FOR THE SANTA FE OPERA, silkscreen, 31⅛ x 22⅛ (4270/250) — 175

Indiana, Robert, PURIM, THE FOUR FACES OF ESTHER (II), silkscreen, 26½ x 21½, 1967 (4203/181) — 300

Indiana, Robert, PURIM, THE FOUR FACETS, 26⅜ x 21½ (4067/112) — 300

Indiana, Robert, PURIM, THE FOUR FACETS OF ESTHER, 1967, silkscreen, 26⅜ x 21½ (4067/113) — 225

Indiana, Robert, SKID ROW, silkscreen, 10½ x 10½ (4203/180) — 125

Indiana, Robert, SKID ROW, silkscreen, 10⅝ x 10⅝ (4270/251) — 125

Indiana, Robert, SKID ROW, 1969, lithograph, 10⅝ x 10⅝ (4215/164) — 200

Jansen, BALLERINA, lithograph, 23⅝ x 16½ (4067/114) — 110

Jansen, BALLET CLASS, lithograph, 16½ x 23⅝ (4067/115) — 80

Jenkins, Paul, AVIARY, 27/100, lithograph, 1971, 30⅜ x 22⅝ (4226/268) — 175

Johns, Jasper, DEVICE (Gemini 345) 56/62, crinkling, lithograph, 1972, 26⅜ x 20¼ (4226/272) — 750

Johns, Jasper, FEET, 1974, lithograph, 14⅜ x 15¾ (4067/116) — 600

Johns, Jasper, FIGURE 1 (Field 13), artist's proof B/D, lithograph, 1963, 9 x 6½ (4226/269) — 1200

Johns, Jasper, FIGURE 6 (Field 100, Gemini 93) 47/70, lithograph, 1968, 27⅜ x 21¼ (4226/270) — 1900

Johns, Jasper, FOOL'S HOUSE (Gemini 348), 7/67, lithograph, 1972, 40½ x 20 (4226/273) — 3100

Johns, Jasper, KNEE, 1974, lithograph, 14⅝ x 14⅜ (4067/117) — 450

Johns, Jasper, NUMERALS (0-9), 92/100, aquatint, etching, 1974, 16⅞ x 13⅝ (4226/275) — 1800

Johns, Jasper, PAINTING WITH TWO BALLS, 20/66, silkscreen, 1971, 29½ x 24⅜ (4226/274) — 2700

Johns, Jasper, SOUVENIR (Field 127), 50/50, lithograph, 1970, 24⅛ x 17¾ (4226/271) — 3400

Johnston, Inez, BRIDGE OF THE SARACENS, woodcut, 18⅛ x 26 (4203/183) — 350

Johnston, Inez, LION IN THE FOREST, woodcut, 16⅜ x 26, 1953 (4203/182) — 400

Johnston, Inez, THE ISTHMUS, etching, 21⅝ x 4½ (4270/257) — 360

Katz, Alex, (BUST OF A WOMAN LOOKING DOWN), lithograph, 28½ x 21¾ (4270/264) — 250

Katz, Alex, ADA FROM BELOW, etching and aquatint, 8¾ x 11¾ (4270/261) — 200

Katz, Alex, GIRL WITH EARRING, lithograph, 28⅝ x 22 (4203/184) — 275

Katz, Alex, HEAD OF A MAN, etching and aquatint, 5⅛ x 8⅞ (4270/263) — 150

Katz, Alex, THE SWIMMER, aquatint, 28⅛ x 35⅞, 1974 (4147/140) — 500

Kelly, Ellsworth, FOUR PANELS, 1971, silkscreen, 28¾ x 54 (4067/119) — 900

Kelly, Ellsworth, RED AND BLUE, 25/75, silkscreen, 16 x 27⅜ (4226/279) — 325

Kelly, Ellsworth, RED/BLACK/GREEN/BLUE, numbered A.P. 8/20, lithograph, 22 x 19½ (4226/278) — 400

Kelly, Ellsworth, YELLOW/ORANGE (Gemini 239) 20/75, lithograph, 1970, 22⅞ x 29½ (4226/277) — 550

Kent, Rockwell, FAIR WIND, wood engraving, 5½ x 6⅞ (4270/265) — 250

Kent, Rockwell, NORTHERN LIGHT, wood engraving, linoleum block, 5⅝ x 8⅛, 1930 (4203/186) — 350

Knirsch, O. after A.F. Tait, AMERICAN FEATHERED GAME, PARTRIDGES, lithograph, 16¼ x 13½, d.1854 (684/965) — 150

Kokoschka, Oskar, SELBSTBILDNIS VON ZWEISEITENALS MALER, 1923, lithograph 50½ x 36 (4067/121) — 800

Kooning, Willem de, (TWO WOMEN), lithograph, 14 x 10¾, 1973 (4118/154) — 400

Kooning, Willem de, BEACH SCENE, 1970, lithograph, 10/39, 29½ x 22½ (4226/232) — 475

Kooning, Willem de, BIG, 1970, lithograph, 8/10, 31½ x 23⅝ (4226/228) — 650

Kooning, Willem de, CLAM DIGGER, 9/34, lithograph, 1970, 22¼ x 23⅝ (4226/238) — 950

Kooning, Willem de, FIGURE AT GERARD BEACH, 8/32, lithograph, 1970, 31⅞ x 23⅝ (4226/235) — 600

Kooning, Willem de, JAPANESE VILLAGE, 8/58, lithograph, 1970, 20⅞ x 30¼ (4226/227) — 450

Kooning, Willem de, LANDING PLACE, 8/54, lithograph, 1970, 23⅝ x 31¾ (4226/224) — 475

Kooning, Willem de, LOVE TO WAKAKO, 8/58, lithograph, 41⅛ x 25¾ (4226/236) — 500

Kooning, Willem de, MOTHER AND CHILD, 8/44, good condition, lithograph, 1970, 22 x 32¼ (4226/223) — 625

Kooning, Willem de, REFLECTIONS, TO KERMIT FOR OUR TRIP TO JAPAN, lithograph, 1970, 8/28, 45⅜ x 31½ (4226/234) — 700

Kooning, Willem de, SOUVENIR OF MONTAUK, 1970, lithograph, 8/43, 33⅞ x 23⅝ (4226/229) — 550

Kooning, Willem de, STINGRAY, 1970, tattered, lithograph, 9/48, 42⅞ x 31½ (4226/233) — 550

Kooning, Willem de, TABLE AND CHAIR, 8/66, lithograph, 1970, 22¼ x 31 (4226/226) — 550

Kooning, Willem de, THE MARSHES, 1970, lithograph, 8/20, 32 x 23½ (4226/230) — 1400

Kooning, Willem de, TROIS MONUMENTS, 244/250, good condition, silkscreen, 1972, 10½ x 27¾
(4226/201) — 275

Kooning, Willem de, VALENTINE, 9/47, lithograph, 1970, 27 x 23⅝ (4226/237) — 350

Kooning, Willem de, WOMAN AT CLEARWATER BEACH, 8/44, lithograph, 1970, 22⅝ x 31½
(4226/222) — 525

Kooning, Willem de, WOMAN IN AMAGANSETT, 8/49, lithograph, 1970, 23 x 31⅛ (4226/225) — 425

Kooning, Willem de, WOMAN WITH CORSET AND LONG HAIR, 1970, lithograph, 9/61, 31⅞ x 22⅞
(4226/231) — 500

Krimmel, John L. (After), PROCESSION OF VICTUALLERS, 19⅞ x 25⅝, hand colored etching,
foxed (4076/834) — 450

Krushenick, Nicholas, COMPOSITION, 12/30, silkscreen, 1965, 35¾ x 30⅞ (4226/280) — 100

Kuniyoshi, Yasuo, BURLESQUE QUEEN, lithograph, 11¾ x 9⅝, 1933 (4244/193) — 2000

Kuniyoshi, Yasuo, CAFE, 1934, lithograph, 10 x 7¾ (4215/176) — 2300

Kuniyoshi, Yasuo, CIRCUS GIRL WITH PLUMED HAT, 1933, lithograph, 12⅝ x 9½ (4215/175) — 1600

Kuniyoshi, Yasuo, GIRL IN FEATHERED HAT, lithograph, 7¾ x 5⅞ (4270/276) — 1200

Kuniyoshi, Yasuo, NUDE AT DOOR, lithograph, 13¼ x 7½, 1928 (4244/192) — 1900

Kuniyoshi, Yasuo, PEARS AND GRAPES, 1928, lithograph, 8¼ x 10¾ (4215/174) — 700

Kuniyoshi, Yasuo, SCULPTURE MOLD AND GRAPES, lithograph, 9⅞ x 11⅝ (4244/194) — 700

Kuniyoshi, Yasuo, SEATED EROTIC WOMAN, lithograph, 9½ x 7¾, 1935 (4244/195) — 700

Kuniyoshi, Yasuo, SOUTH BERWICK, MAINE, 1934, lithograph, 9 x 12½ (4215/177) — 1000

Kuniyoshi, Yasuo, SUMMER, 1927, lithograph, 14⅜ x 10 (4215/173) — 1800

Kuniyoshi, Yasuo, THE ACROBAT, lithograph, 11½ x 8¾, frame, 1928 (4244/191) — 1800

Kurz & Allison, THE BATTLE OF GETTYSBURGH, 1884, lithograph, 17½ x 25 (654/439) — 200

Laing, Gerald, DMT 42, book of 23 silkscreens, 17 x 13⅜, 1969 (4147/149) — 200

Laing, Gerald, PARACHUTES, set of 6 silkscreens, 35 x 23, 1968 (4147/148) — 175

Leroux, after Ary Scheffer, PORTRAIT OF LAFAYETTE, engraving, 21½ x 14½, d.1824 (684/919) — 15

Levine, Jack, HOMMAGE A WATTEAU, lithograph, 'artist's proof', 19⅞ x 26 (4147/154) — 200

Levine, Jack, LA FUMEURE, lithograph, 14 x 16 (4147/157) — 425

Levine, Jack, MAYOR DALEY'S GESTURE, drypoint and aquatint, 8⅞ x 11¾ (4147/155) — 375

Levine, Jack, ON THE CONVENTION FLOOR, lithograph, 19¼ x 25¼ (4147/156) — 50

Levine, Jack, TIGER BROWN, etching, 11¾ x 8¾ (4067/129) — 100

Lewis, Martin, BEACHING THE BOAT (JAPAN), drypaint, 7 x 10 (4270/286) — 250

Lewis, Martin, BOSS OF THE BLOCK, 1928, etching, 11¼ x 7½ (4067/130) — 130

Lewis, Martin, CHANCE MEETING, drypoint, 10½ x 7½ (4270/289) — 1100

Lewis, Martin, CLEARING RAIN-EVENING, JAPAN, drypoint, sandpaper ground, 14¾ x 9⅜, 1927
(4203/203) — 375

Lewis, Martin, DAY'S END, drypoint, 9¾ x 13½, 1937 (4203/205) — 900

Lewis, Martin, DOWN TO THE SEA AT NIGHT, drypoint, sandpaper ground, 8⅛ x 13 (4203/204) — 1200

Lewis, Martin, EAST SIDE NIGHT, etching, 9⅞ x 12 (4270/287) — 250

Lewis, Martin, ROUTE 6, 1933, drypoint, 9 x 14⅝ (4215/198) — 675

Lewis, Martin, SHADOW MAGIC, drypoint, 13⅜ x 9⅜, 1939 (4203/206) — 800

Lewis, Martin, SNOW ON THE EL, drypoint, 14 x 9 (4270/288) — 1300

Lewis, Martin, SUN BATH, ca1935, lithograph, 10⅛ x 13⅞ (4215/200) — 1400

Lewis, Martin, THE GREAT SHADOW, drypoint, 10 x 7, 1925 (4203/202) — 500

Lewis, Martin, TWIN SILOS, 1933, drypoint and aquatint, 7½ x 8½ (4215/199) — 325

Lichtenstein, Roy, BRUSHSTROKES (Bianchini 20), 42/300, silkscreen, 1967, 21⅞ x 30
(4226/282) — 1100

Lichtenstein, Roy, CRAK, lithograph, 18⅝ x 27 (4270/292) — 650

Lichtenstein, Roy, FISH IN THE SKY, silkscreen, 11 x 16 (4270/293) — 250

Lichtenstein, Roy, FOOT AND HAND, lithograph, 16½ x 20⅞ (4270/291) — 400

Lichtenstein, Roy, FOOT AND HAND, 1962, lithograph, 16½ x 20⅞ (4067/133) — 500

Lichtenstein, Roy, FOOT MEDICATION, 1963, lithograph, 15⅝ x 15¾ (4067/134) — 150

Lichtenstein, Roy, HAYSTACK #5 (B.33-E, G.154), 59/100, lithograph, silkscreen, 1969
(4226/285) — 975

Lichtenstein, Roy, INDUSTRY AND MELODY, 162/250, silkscreen, 1969, 17⅛ x 14¼ (4226/283) — 850

Lichtenstein, Roy, LITHO-LITHO, lithograph, 28 x 43½ (4270/295) — 225

Lichtenstein, Roy, MIRROR #5 (G. 386) 7⅛0, silkscreen, 1972, 34¼ x 24⅜ (4226/288) — 550

Lichtenstein, Roy, MIRROR #5, silkscreen, 34¼ x 24⅜, 1972 (4244/208) — 300

Lichtenstein, Roy, MIRROR #6 (G. 387), 5⅝0, scuffs, soiling, silkscreen, 1972, 32⅛ x 22⅛
(4226/289) — 550

Lichtenstein, Roy, MIRROR #6, silkscreen, 32⅛ x 22⅛ (4270/300) — 475

Lichtenstein, Roy, MIRROR #7 (G. 388), 58/80, silkscreen, 1972, 29⅞ x 17½ (4226/290) — 300

Lichtenstein, Roy, MIRROR #7, silkscreen, 29⅞ x 17½, 1972 (4244/209) — 275

Lichtenstein, Roy, MODERN PRINT, lithograph and silkscreen, 23¾ x 24 (4270/297) — 550

Lichtenstein, Roy, PEACE THROUGH CHEMISTRY II (Gemini 241), 15/43, lithograph, silkscreen,
1970 (4226/286) — 5000

Lichtenstein, Roy, PORTRAIT GIRL, 50/100, silkscreen, 1974, 38¼ x 28½ (4226/291) — 700

Lichtenstein, Roy, SHIPBOARD GIRL, lithograph, in colors, 26 x 19¼, 1965 (4147/160) — 325

Lewis
(4270/287)

Lichtenstein (4270/294)

Lozowick (4270/310)

Lichtenstein, Roy, SHIPBOARD GIRL (Bianchini 12) 1965, soiling, offset lithograph, 1965
(4226/281) · · · 1000
Lichtenstein, Roy, STILL LIFE, silkscreen, 36 x 36 (4270/294) · · · *500*
Lichtenstein, Roy, TEMPLE, lithograph, blue and black, 22⅞ x 16⅞, 1964 (4147/159) · · · 100
Lichtenstein, Roy, TEMPLE, 1964, lithograph 23¾ x 17⅝ (4067/135) · · · 150
Lidner, Richard, ON, lithograph, collotype in colors, 24¼ x 20⅛, 1971 (4203/207) · · · 300
Linder, Richard, FIRST AVENUE, lithograph and collotype, 24¼ x 20⅛ (4270/306) · · · 400
Linder, Richard, FUN CITY, ST. MARK'S PLACE, lithograph and collotype, 25¼ x 19¾ (4270/304) · · · 350
Linder, Richard, ON, lithograph and collotype, 24¼ x 20⅛ (4270/307) · · · 200
Linder, Richard, REDHEAD, lithograph, 29⅛ x 22 (4270/305) · · · 250
Lindner, Richard, BANNER #2, 1966, edition of 20, felt collage banner, 84 x 48 (4226/292) · · · 1200
Lindner, Richard, BANNER #3, numbered XVIII, edition of 20, vinyl collage, zipper, 1968 (4226/294) · · · 1350
Lindner, Richard, FUN CITY, 24 HOUR SELF-SERVICE, 93/175, 1971, lithograph, collotype, 23⅞ x
19¾ (4226/296) · · · 550
Lindner, Richard, ROOM FOR RENT, 100/150, silkscreen, 1971, 39 x 27¾ (4226/297) · · · 600
Lindner, Richard, THE KISS, 35/49V, on Japan nacre, 1970, lithograph, collotype, 23⅞ x 20
(4226/295) · · · 475
Littleford (After), THE HONBLE. JOHN HANCOCK OF BOSTON, 14⅛ x 19¼, print, foxing, 1775
(4076/802) · · · 750
Lozowick, Louis, STEEL VALLEY, lithograph, 9¼ x 13½ (4147/161) · · · 225
Lozowick, Louis, STILL LIFE #1 (Guitar, Telephone and Ashtray), lithograph, 9 x 11⅞ (4270/310) · · · *550*
Lozowick, Louis, SWANS CENTRAL PARK, lithograph, 10⅜ x 10½ (4270/311) · · · 300
Lozowick, Louis, UNDER THE EL (TWO CARS AND TWO STRIDING FIGURES), lithograph, 13¼ x
8¾ (4270/309) · · · 1300
Man-Ray, JULIE, lithograph, in colors, 18½ x 14⅝, 1968 (4203/300) · · · 275
Man-Ray, MONUMENT, lithograph, silkscreen, 22¾ x 17½, 1968 (4147/258) · · · 125
Marden, Brice, ADRIATICS GRIDS III, 1973, etching, 23⅝ x 14 (4067/141) · · · 175
Marden, Brice, GRID ETCHING SECOND STATE, etching, 14⅜ x 23⅝ (4270/316) · · · 175
Marden, Brice, UNTITLED, lithograph, 13⅜ x 19⅞, 1969 (4147/164) · · · 100

Marin, John, BAL BULLIER, PARIS, etching and drypoint, 5½ x 7⅞ (4270/318)	350
Marin, John, BROOKLYN BRIDGE, 1911, etching, 10⅞ x 8½ (4215/209)	1800
Marin, John, DELLA FAVA VENICE, 1907, etching, 9½ x 6⅞ (4067/144)	475
Marin, John, DOWNTOWN, THE EL, etching, 6¾ x 8¾, 1921 (4147/165)	550
Marin, John, NOTRE DAME, PARIS, etching and drypoint, 12⅝ x 10¾ (4270/317)	*800*
Marin, John, SANTA MARIA DELLA SALUTE VENICE, 1907, etching, 5¼ x 7⅛ (4067/143)	250
Marsh, Reginald, BETTS, etching with engraving, 4⅞ x 4, 1931 (4147/168)	175
Marsh, Reginald, CONEY ISLAND BEACH, etching, 9 x 12, 1935 (4147/170)	1050
Marsh, Reginald, CONEY ISLAND BEACH, etching, 9 x 12 (4270/325)	2100
Marsh, Reginald, FROZEN CUSTARD, etching, 7 x 9⅞, 1939 (4147/171)	550
Marsh, Reginald, GAIETY BURLESK, etching, hand-colored, 1929 (4203/215)	1500
Marsh, Reginald, GIRL WALKING (ELEVATED), lithograph, 10⅝ x 8 (4270/324)	500
Marsh, Reginald, GIRL WALKING (ELEVATED), lithograph, 10⅝ x 8 (4270/323)	1000
Marsh, Reginald, LA POULE, 1932, lithograph, 9¼ x 6¼ (4215/220)	700
Marsh, Reginald, MERRY-GO-ROUND, engraving, 10 x 8, 1943 (4147/172)	400
Marsh, Reginald, ST JEAN de LUZ, 1928, lithograph, 8¼ x 12⅝ (4067/146)	425
Marsh, Reginald, THE BARKER, etching, 10 x 8, 1931 (4147/169)	*1100*
Martin, David, THOMAS PENN ESQ., mezzotint, 12⅞ x 9, imp, 1766 (4211/316)	325
Matta, Roberto, HOM'MERE (L'EAUTRE), etching and aquatint, 15 x 19½, 1974 (4147/179)	175
Matta, Roberto, JAZZ BANDE, etching and aquatint, 14⅞ x 19½, 1973 (4147/178)	200
Mayer, Ferdinand & Co., VASSAR FEMALE COLLEGE, 17 x 31⅞, hand colored lithograph discolored (4076/842)	650
McArdle, James after Parsous, THE INDIAN CHIEF, 13⅞ x 10¼, print, 1766 (4076/801)	325
McBey, James, DAWN, CAMEL PATROL SETTING OUT, etching, in sepia, 9 x 15, 1919 (4203/210)	600
Meyers, Jerome, REHEARSAL, lithograph, 5½ x 7½ (4147/180)	125
Meyers, Jerome, THE MARKET WOMAN, etching, 7⅞ x 2¾ (4147/181)	125
Milton, Peter, JULIA PASSING, lift ground, aquatint, etching, engraving, 17½ x 23¾, 1968 (4203/226)	1100

Marin (4270/317)

Marsh (4147/169)

Morlin, J.F., PLAN OF CITY OF N.Y. & OF ISLAND, 1828, engraving, 23¾ x 15½ (654/435)   80
Motherwell, Robert, AUTOMATISM, inscribed 'Trial Proof', lithograph, 1965, 18⅜ x 13⅜ (4226/302)   300
Motherwell, Robert, AUTOMATISM, lithograph, 18⅜ x 13⅜ (4270/375)   300
Motherwell, Robert, COMPOSITION, lithograph, 18¾ x 14 (4270/376)   275
Motherwell, Robert, HARVEST, WITH BLUE SHADOW (Gemini 479), 44/55, lithograph collage,
   1973, 29⅞ x 12 (4226/306)   1100
Motherwell, Robert, LITHOGRAPHIC, 1973, lithograph, 12¼ x 9¼ (4067/163)   150
Motherwell, Robert, MADRID SUITE, COMPOSITION, lithograph, 19⅞ x 25¾ (4270/378)   100
Motherwell, Robert, WEST ISLIP, 1½0, 1970, hard colored lithograph, 29 x 41 (4226/304)   1300
Munakata, Shiko, CALLIGRAPHY, 1959, 15⅛ x 19¼, (4067/280)   110
Munakata, Shiko, FIGURE IN PATTERNED ROBE, woodcut, washes, 17¾ x 12¾ (4147/193)   350
Munakata, Shiko, NUDE, 1959, lithograph, 15 x 20½ (4067/278)   140
Munakata, Shiko, OWLS, 1959, lithograph, 14¾ x 20⅛ (4067/279)   110
Munakata, Shiko, SELF PORTRAIT, 1960, lithograph, 18¾ x 15¾ (4067/277)   200
Munakata, Shiko, THREE FIGURES, woodcut, artist's seal, 15⅛ x 14⅝ (4147/194)   550
Munakata, Shiko, TWO NUDES, 1959, lithograph, 21¾ x 15¾ (4067/281)   140
Nevelson, Louise, COMPOSITION, 22/100, with gold, 1976, offset print collage, 34⅝ x 24¾
   (4226/307)   250
Oakley, Francis F., LEWISTON FALLS MAINE, lithograph, 11⅞ x 18⅝, imp, 1857-63 (4211/314)   400
Oldenburg, Claes, COLOSSAL MONUMENT FOR BATTERSEA PARK, DRUM SET, photo-offset
   lithograph, 228/300 (4226/309)   425
Oldenburg, Claes, COLOSSAL STRUCTURE, CLOTHESPIN, 77/200, silkscreen, 1972, 21¼ x 13¾
   (4226/312)   375
Oldenburg, Claes, GIANT 3-WAY PLUG, lithograph, 32 x 24¼ (4270/384)   300
Oldenburg, Claes, GIANT 3-WAY PLUG, photo-offset lithograph, in colors, 32 x 24¼, 1965
   (4203/235)   200

Oldenburg, Claes, INJUN POSTER, silkscreen, 18 x 14 (4270/385) — 125
Oldenburg, Claes, INVERTED FIREPLUG-AS SKYSCRAPER, lithograph, 29¾ x 20⅛, 1969 (4147/201) — 125
Oldenburg, Claes, INVERTED FIREPLUG-AS SKYSCRAPER, 80/100, lithograph, 1969 (4226/311) — 125
Oldenburg, Claes, NOTES, litho. and collage, 20⅞ x 11¾, 1968 (4147/203) — 160
Oldenburg, Claes, PROPOSAL FOR COLOSSAL STRUCTURE, silkscreen, 21¼ x 13¾ (4270/386) — 350
Oldenburg, Claes, SOFT DRUM SET-ON CHALK BOARD, silkscreen, 29 x 39 (4270/387) — 500
Oldenburg, Claes, WAR MEMORIAL (Gemini 108), 55/100, 1968, lithograph, embossing, 22⅝ x 15¾ (4226/310) — 400
Orozeo, Jose Clemente, MAGUAYES Y NOPALES, lithograph, 12⅛ x 17 (4203/238) — 750
Palmer, Samuel, THE EARLY PLOUGHMAN, etching, 7 x 10⅝, ca1861 (4203/239) — 200
Palmer, Samuel, THE MORNING OF LIFE, etching, 5¾ x 8½, 1860-61 (4203/240) — 200
Papprill, H., VIEW OF HER MAJESTY'S STEAM FRIGATE CYCLOPS, 1857, aquatint, 19¼ x 27¾ (654/434) — 400
Parsons, Endicott & Co., after, THE U.S. GUNBOAT METACOMET, lithograph., 15¾ x 30 (654/433) — 400
Pearlstein, Philip, GIRL ON EMPIRE SOFA, numbered X, lithograph, 1971, 32⅛ x 24 (4226/314) — 500
Pearlstein, Philip, GIRL ON STRIPED RUG, 22/70, lithograph, 21 x 24 (4226/315) — 550
Pearlstein, Philip, NUDE ON EAMES STOOL, 86/125, lithograph, 1977, 19¾ x 27¾ (4226/316) — 650
Pearlstein, Philip, TWO NUDES, lithograph, 22 x 30⅛ (4270/398) — 500
Pennel, Joseph, THE CLOCK, GRAND CENTRAL, NEW YORK, etching, 11¾ x 10⅛, 1919 (4203/256) — 250
Pennel, Joseph, THE STOCK EXCHANGE, etching, 11⅞ x 7⅝, 1904 (4203/245) — 175
Pennel, Joseph, THE TICKET OFFICE, PENN. STATION, N.Y., etching, 11¾ x 8⅞ (4203/258) — 275
Pennel, Joseph, WARSHIP COMING IN, NEW YORK, etching, in sepia, 9⅞ x 6⅞ (4203/259) — 175
Pennell, Joseph, HAIL AMERICA, mezzotint, 8½ x 14⅞, 1908 (4203/247) — 650
Pennell, Joseph, NEW YORK, FROM BROOKLYN BRIDGE, etching, 11 x 8½, 1908 (4203/246) — 250
Pennell, Joseph, NEW YORK, FROM GOVERNOR'S ISLAND, etching in sepia, 7½ x 12, 1915 (4203/250) — 100
Pennell, Joseph, ON THE RIVA, FROM PENNELL'S WINDOW, etching, 7¾ x 10⅛, 1883 (4203/241) — 150
Pennell, Joseph, PANAMA CANAL, BUILDING THE LOCKS, lithograph, 22¼ x 17, 1912 (4147/217) — 125
Pennell, Joseph, THE ARCADE, PENN. STATION, etching, 11¾ x 6⅞ (4203/257) — 250
Pennell, Joseph, THE FLATIRON BUILDING, etching, 10 x 7½, 1904 (4203/243) — 200
Pennell, Joseph, THE GOLDEN CORNICE, NO. II, etching, 10⅞ x 8⅜, 1915 (4203/254) — 150
Pennell, Joseph, UNION SQUARE AND BANK OF METROPOLIS, etching, 11¾ x 18½, 1904 (4203/244) — 175
Pennell, Joseph, UP TO THE WOOLWORTH, 1915, etching, 12 x 7½ (4215/295) — 150
Peterdi, Gaber, CLAWS OF THE SEA, etching, in greenish black, 30¼ x 40, 1977 (4203/261) — 250
Pfahler, Karl, NEUN SERIGRAPHIEN KPp 16 (9-i), suite of 16, 36/100, silkscreens, in plexiglass box (4226/318) — 400
Piper, John, DEATH IN VENICE, suite of 8, 28/70, silkscreens, 1973 (4226/317) — 1600
Pond, Clayton, THE KITCHEN SINK IN MY STUDIO, silkscreen, 26¾ x 19½ (4147/253) — 90
Pond, Clayton, THINGS IN MY STUDIO, suite of 8 silkscreens, 1972-73, 52/100, 29¼ x 23 (4226/320) — 700
Rauschenberg, Robert, AUTOBIOGRAPHY, lithograph, 66¼ x 48¾ (4270/444) — 175
Rauschenberg, Robert, BANNER (Foster 77), 29/40, lithograph, 1969, 54½ x 36 (4226/330) — 2300
Rauschenberg, Robert, BRAKE (Foster 76) 50/60, lithograph, 1969, 42 x 29 (4226/331) — 400
Rauschenberg, Robert, EARTH TIE (Foster 75) 44/48, lithograph, 1969, 48 x 34 (4226/334) — 400
Rauschenberg, Robert, LOOP (Foster 78), 50/79, lithograph, 1969, 33 x 28 (4226/336) — 450
Rauschenberg, Robert, MARSH (Foster 76) 50/60, lithograph, 1969, 33 x 28 (4226/335) — 350
Rauschenberg, Robert, MOON ROSE (Foster 80), 4¼7, lithograph, 1969, 51 x 35 (4226/337) — 450
Rauschenberg, Robert, POSTER FOR PEACE, lithograph, 27⅛ x 20 (4270/442) — 175
Rauschenberg, Robert, POSTER FOR THE BENEFIT OF CONGRESSMAN JOHN BRADEM, silkscreen, 28 x 20¼ (4270/443) — 175
Rauschenberg, Robert, RACK, lithograph, in brown, 27¾ x 21½, 1969 (4147/256) — 400
Rauschenberg, Robert, SACK (Foster 82), 50/60, lithograph, 1969, 40 x 28 (4226/339) — 500
Rauschenberg, Robert, SHELL (Foster 81), 50/70, lithograph, 1969, 32⅛ x 26 (4226/338) — 350
Rauschenberg, Robert, SKY GARDEN (Foster 74), 27/35, lithograph, 1969, 89 x 42 (4226/329) — 5000
Rauschenberg, Robert, TEST STONE #4 (Foster 43), 24/46, lithograph, 1967, 24 x 33⅝ (4226/328) — 400
Rauschenberg, Robert, TEST STONE 2 (Foster 41) 51/76, lithograph, 1967, 31½ x 24⅜ (4226/326) — 650
Rauschenberg, Robert, TEST STONE 3 (Foster 42) 59/71, lithograph, 1967, 21⅞ x 28½ (4226/327) — 500
Rauschenberg, Robert, TRUST ZONE (Foster 86) 50/60, lithograph, 1969, 40 x 33 (4226/341) — 400
Rauschenberg, Robert, UNTITLED, lithograph, in colors, 33 x 24⅝, 1968 (4147/255) — 200
Rauschenberg, Robert, VEILS IV, lithograph, 17½ x 19¼, 1974 (4147/257) — 275
Rauschenburg, Robert, HORN (Foster 72) 50/58, lithograph, 1969, 44½ x 34 (4226/333) — 1300

Reinhardt, Ad, TEN SCREEN PRINTS, 234/250, 1966, 21⅞ x 17 (4226/342) 600

Revere, Paul (Engraver), THE BOSTON MASSACRE, some tears, 10½ x 19½, engraving, 1770 (4076/799) 3250

Richards, Joseph B., AMERICAN WATCH COMPANY, lithograph, 11¼ x 9⅞, imp (4211/313) 175

Rivers, Larry, DOUBLE FRENCH MONEY, 1965, 30⅛ x 32, silkscreen, plexiglass collage (4226/345) 1800

Rivers, Larry, LIVING AT THE MOVIES, 1974, offset and silkscreen, 21¼ x 26⅛ (4067/202) 150

Rivers, Larry, LUCKY STRIKE IN MIRROR, artist's proof, lithograph, 1961, 19½ x 14⅛ (4226/344) 650

Rivers, Larry, SMITHSONIAN, lithograph, in colors, 29⅞ x 21¼ (4147/268) 250

Rivers, Larry, THE WEDDING, lithograph, in colors, 7¾ x 14⅞, 1959 (4147/267) 300

Robertson, William, A HOME IN THE COUNTRY (SUMMER), lithograph, 18 x 24¾, d.1867 (684/960) 130

Rogers, F.K., PROVINCETOWN, 1877, lithograph, 13½ x 25⅜ (654/436) 40

Root & Tinker, LIBERTY ENLIGHTENING THE WORLD, chromolithograph, 29⅛ x 20⅛, imp, 1883 (4211/304) 275

Rosenquist, James, FEAST-FEAST, 21/38, etching, aquatint, 1976, 6 x 12 (4226/349) 325

Rosenquist, James, HORIZON BAR, 1973, lithograph, 20⅞ x 29 (4067/204) 175

Rosenquist, James, MY MIND IS A GLASS OF WATER, lithograph, in colors, 22¾ x 17⅞, 1972 (4147/270) 225

Rosenquist, James, OFF THE CONTINENTAL DIVIDE, 29/43, 1973-74, lithograph, 36¼ x 77⅜ (4226/346) 4500

Rosenquist, James, PALE TENT II, 2¼2, etching, aquatint, 1976, 5½ x 11⅞ (4226/348) 350

Rosenquist, James, POT OF GOLD, etching, 21 x 14⅜ (4270/490) 325

Rosenquist, James, SPINNING FACES IN SPACE, lithograph, 32⅞ x 23¼ (4270/489) 250

Ruscha, Edward, DISH, lithograph, 3½ x 7⅞, 1973 (4147/281) 50

Ruscha, Edward, DOCUMENTA 5, silkscreen, 33¼ x 23⅝, 1972 (4147/280) 50

Ruscha, Edward, DROPS, lithograph, 20 x 80, 1971 (4147/279) 100

Ruscha, Edward, LISP, lithograph, 20⅛ x 28, 1970 (4147/278) 100

Ruscha, Edward, LISP (Ruscha 42) 17/90, 1970, lithograph, 20 x 28 (4226/351) 300

Ruscha, Edward, SIN, silkscreen, 13 x 21⅝, 1970 (4147/277) 175

Russell, Benjamin (After), A SHIP ON THE NORTH WEST, 17 x 26½, hand colored lithograph foxed and stained (4076/810) 400

Russell, Benjamin (After), RIGHT WHALING IN ITS VARIETIES, 15⅞ x 32⅛, print, discoloration, foxed (4076/811) 750

Russell, Benjamin (After), SPERM WHALING NO. 1 - THE CHASE, 16¾ x 26⅜, hand colored lithograph 1859 (4076/809) 500

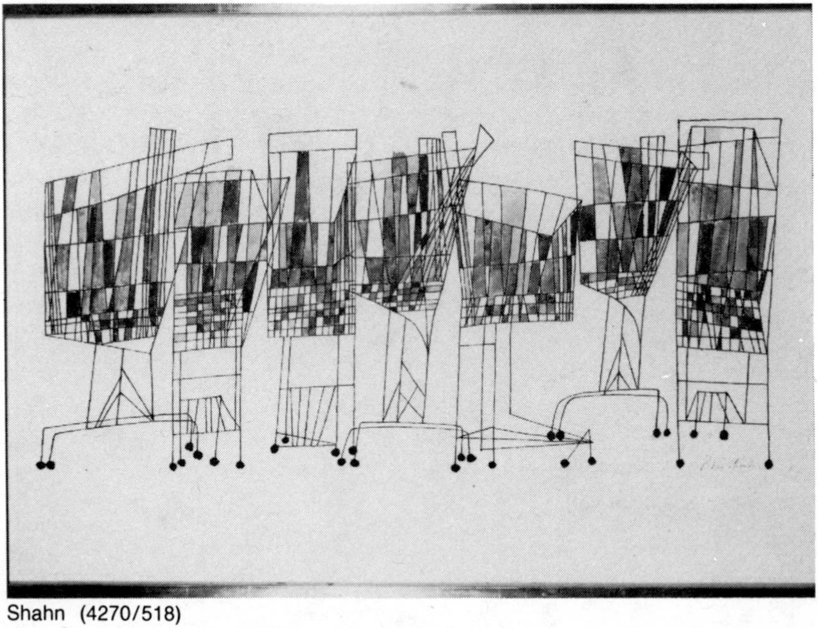

Shahn (4270/518)

Russell, Benjamin (After), SPERM WHALING WITH ITS VARIETIES, 16 x 32½, print, foxed, 1870
    (4076/812)   550
Scholder, Fritz, BIRD INDIAN, lithograph, 20½ x 28⅛ (4270/510)   450
Scholder, Fritz, HOPI DANCERS, lithograph, 22¼ x 30¼ (4270/508)   500
Scholder, Fritz, PORTRAIT OF A MASSACRED INDIAN 3, lithograph, 40⅛ x 30⅛ (4270/509)   400
Scholder, Fritz, PORTRAIT OF AN AMERICAN INDIAN #2, lithograph, 35/50, 30 x 22½, 1973
    (4203/319)   550
Segal, George, GIRL MEDITATING, plaster multiple, 18⅞ x 8⅛ x 5⅛ (4270/511)   1200
Shahn, Ben, ANDANTE, silkscreen, ed. of 50, 16⅞ x 22⅛, 1966 (4203/321)   900
Shahn, Ben, LUTE AND MOLECULE, NO 2, silkscreen, 28½ x 36 (4215/429)   1700
Shahn, Ben, MANY MEN, lithograph, 16¾ x 14¾, 1968 (4147/287)   500
Shahn, Ben, MAXIMUS OF TYRE, 1963, silkscreen, 36⅛ x 26⅝ (4215/430)   900
Shahn, Ben, MINE BUILDING, silkscreen, 17 x 28½ (4270/517)   600
Shahn, Ben, OWL NO. 2, lithograph, 22¼ x 12⅝, 1968 (4147/286)   400
Shahn, Ben, SUPERMARKET, silkscreen, 16⅞ x 37⅝ (4270/518)   *2000*
Shahn, Ben, SUPERMARKET, 1957, silkscreen, 16½ x 37 (4215/428)   2200
Shahn, Ben, TO CHILDHOOD ILLNESSES, lithograph, 20¼ x 16⅞ (4270/519)   100
Shaw, Joshua (After), HELLGATE, 11¾ x 15, hand colored aquatint, torn, foxed, 1820 (4076/835)   175
Sheeler, Charles, YACHTS, 1924, lithograph, 11¾ x 13¾ (4215/431)   *5750*
Simon, John after Verelst, John, KING OF THE MAQUAS, 14⅜ x 10⅝, print, 1710 (4076/800)   1500
Sloan, John, A THIRST FOR ART, 1939, etching, 8 x 6⅛ (4215/438)   550
Sloan, John, BANDIT'S CAVE, 1920, etching, 6⅞ x 5⅛ (4067/208)   350
Sloan, John, BOB CAT WINS, etching, 2¼ x 3¾ (4147/293)   300
Sloan, John, BOB CAT WINS, etching, 2⅜ x 3¾ (4270/534)   175
Sloan, John, BONFIRE, etching, 5¼ x 7¼ (4270/533)   600
Sloan, John, BUSSES IN WASHINGTON, 1925, etching, 7⅞ x 9⅞ (4067/209)   1000
Sloan, John, FIFTH AVENUE CRITICS, 1905, etching, 5⅛ x 7 (4067/207)   375

Sheeler (4215/431)

Sloan (4270/528)

Sloan, John, FOURTEEN STREET, THE WIGWAM, 1928, etching, 9¾ x 6⅞ (4215/435) — 900
Sloan, John, JEWELRY STORE WINDOW, 1906, etching, 5¾ x 3¾ (4215/434) — 300
Sloan, John, MEMORY, etching, 7½ x 8⅞ (4270/528) — *800*
Sloan, John, NUDE ON CHAISE LOUNGE BY WINDOW, etching, engraving, inscribed, 100 proofs, 6 x 11⅜, 1933 (4203/326) — 275
Sloan, John, RAG PICKERS, etching, 2¾ x 3¾ (4270/532) — 200
Sloan, John, THE LAFAYETTE, etching, 5 x 6⅞, 1928 (4147/292) — 950
Sloan, John, THE PICTURE BUYER, etching, 5¼ x 7 (4270/530) — 450
Sloan, John, THE WAKE ON THE FERRY, etching, 4⅞ x 6⅞ (4270/536) — 500
Sloan, John, THE WAKE ON THE FERRY, etching, 5 x 7⅛ (4270/537) — 500
Sloan, John, THE WOMEN'S PAGE, etching, 5 x 7, 1905 (4147/290) — 550
Sloan, John, TWENTY-FIFTH ANNIVERSARY, etching, 4 x 4⅞, 1926 (4147/291) — 200
Sloan, John, WAKE ON THE FERRY, 1949, etching, 5 x 7⅛ (4067/211) — 475
Soyer, Moses, DEFENSE WORKERS, lithograph, 10 x 15 (4147/295) — 130
Soyer, Raphael, GIRLS WITH PARTED LIPS, etching, 9⅞ x 7¾ (4270/539) — 200
Soyer, Raphael, HEAD OF A GIRL, lithograph, 16 x 12 (4270/543) — 75
Soyer, Raphael, HEAD OF A GIRL, lithograph, 16⅛ x 12 (4270/542) — 75
Soyer, Raphael, STUDIES WITH SELF PORTRAIT, lithograph, 20⅞ x 23¼ (4270/540) — 150
Soyer, Raphael, UNEMPLOYED, lithograph, in colors, 19/150, 14½ x 12¾, 1969 (4203/330) — 150
Spalatin, Marko, FIGURE VII, silkscreen, in colors, 24½ x 20 (4203/331) — 150
Spruance, Benton, AMERICAN PATTERN - BARN, lithograph, in colors, 11⅝ x 14 (4203/332) — 750
Steinberg, Saul, COMPOSITION, silkscreen, 21 x 22⅛ (4147/297) —
Stella, Frank, BLACK SERIES II, Jill, lithograph, in black and gray, 10 x 8¾, 1967 (4203/336) — 175
Stella, Frank, DOUBLE GREY SCRAMBLE (Gemini 491) 93/100, silkscreen, 1973, 23½ x 46⅞ (4226/356) — 3900
Stella, Frank, EMPRESS OF INDIA II (Gemini 82), 99/100, lithograph, 1968, 11⅛ x 32 (4226/352) — 800
Stella, Frank, PASTEL STACK (Gemini 227) 68/100, silkscreen, 1970, 39¾ x 26¾ (4226/353) — 1200
Stella, Frank, RIVER OF PONDS II (Gemini 271), 35/78, lithograph, 1971, 31¾ x 31¾ (4226/354) — 3750
Stella, Frank, STAR OF PERSIA II, lithograph, 22½ x 26 (4270/548) — 1800
Stella, Frank, YORK FACTORY I (Gemini 303) 51/100, silkscreen, 1971, 13½ x 41 (4226/355) — 3100
Strang, William, BOOK SALE, etching, 11⅝ x 15⅛, 1889 (4203/337) — 150
Summers, Carol, LA TERRA TREMA, woodcut, 35¾ x 36⅝ (4270/550) — 500
Sutherland, Thomas, after Huggins, SOUTH SEA WHALE FISHERY,1825, 17¼ x 22½, aquatint (654/416) — 250
Tamayo, Rufino, EXTASIS COSMICO, mixograph, 29⅜ x 21¼, 1974 (4147/299) — 450
Thomas & Eno (Lithographers), UNION POND, 16⅞ x 27⅛, print, discoloration (4076/840) — 1500
Tobey, Mark, ANIMAL BLANCO, lithograph, 15⅜ x 20⅝ (4270/567) — 50
Tobey, Mark, EL CAIMAN, lithograph, 20⅛ x 17⅝ (4270/570) — 50
Tobey, Mark, EL CIEGO Y SU PERRO, etching, 9½ x 12 (4270/571) — 50
Tobey, Mark, EN EL CAMPO, lithograph, 13¾ x 18⅛ (4270/572) — 50
Tobey, Mark, FALL, 1964, lithograph 6¼ x 3⅞ (4067/214) — 175

Tobey, Mark, LA FAMILIA, lithograph, 12⅜ x 10¾ (4270/573)   50
Tooker, George, SLEEP, molded paper relief, 7 x 9⅞, 1975 (4203/341)   800
Trova, Ernest, FALLING MAN MANSCAPE, 1969, silkscreen, 26 x 26 (4067/230)   200
Trova, Ernest, SHADOWS, PLANES AND TARGETS, 1971, silkscreen, 23 x 23 (4067/232)   150
Trova, Ernest, SHADOWS, PLANES, TARGETS, silkscreen, in colors, 23 x 23, 1971 (4203/349)   275
Vasarely, Victor, AIX-MC, silkscreen, in colors, 25¾ x 13⅛ (4203/356)   375
Vasarely, Victor, AIX, silkscreen, in colors, 18¼ x 18⅛ (4203/352)   300
Vasarely, Victor, COMPOSITION, silkscreen, in colors, 23⅝ x 23⅝, 1968 (4203/354)   350
Vasarely, Victor, COMPOSITION, 100/125, silkscreen, 26 x 13¼ (4226/360)   250
Vasarely, Victor, KEZDI, silkscreen, in colors, 18⅛ x 18⅛, 1977 (4203/358)   300
Vasarely, Victor, PERMUTATIONS, silkscreen, in colors, 23¾ x 23½ (4203/357)   200
Vasarely, Victor, PURPLE AND YELLOW, silkscreen, in colors, 22½ x 22½ (4203/353)   150
Walker, George H. & Co., PORTLAND STAR MATCH FACTORY, lithograph, 14 x 19¾, imp
(4211/315)   375
Wall, W.G. (After), VIEW NEAR HUDSON, 17⅞ x 24¼, hand colored aquatint, stained, 1822
(4076/836)   750
Ward, Lynn, CUP OF SKY, linoleum cut, 19⅞ x 11¾ (4147/333)   70
Warhol, Andy, CAMPBELL'S TOMATO SOUP SHOPPING BAG, silkscreen, 16½ x 9¼ (4270/610)   175
Warhol, Andy, ELECTRIC CHAIRS, 184/250, suite of 10, silkscreens, 1971, 35⅜ x 48 (4226/363)   1400
Warhol, Andy, FLOWERS (Crone 626) 74/250, silkscreen, 1970, 36 x 36 (4226/362)   600
Warhol, Andy, JACKIE, 1969, silkscreen on canvas, 20 x 16 (4226/105)   2000
Warhol, Andy, MAO-TSE-TUNG (triptych), 1973, acrylic silkscreen, 12 x 10 (4226/106)   5250
Warhol, Andy, MAO, silkscreen, 36 x 36 (4270/612)   450
Warhol, Andy, MAO, 1972, silkscreen, 36 x 36 (4067/246)   250
Warhol, Andy, MERCE CUNNINGHAM, silkscreen, 19 x 16⅛ (4270/613)   300
Warhol, Andy, MERCE CUNNINGHAM, silkscreen, 29⅞ x 20⅛ (4270/614)   400
Warhol, Andy, MICK JAGGER, SUITE OF TEN, silkscreen, 43¾ x 28⅞ (4270/615)   *3500*

Warhol (4270/615)

Whistler (4244/462)

Warhol, Andy, TRANSVESTITES, suite of 10, 35/125, silkscreens, 1975, 43¾ x 29 (4226/366)   1400
Warner, W. after John Trumbull, GENERAL WASHINGTON, engraving and mezzotint, 24½ x 17⅝
(684/924)   15
Weber, Max, STILL LIFE WITH APPLES, lithograph, 12⅜ x 16⅛, ca1938-30 (4203/371)   550
Weber, Max, FRENCH JUG, lithograph, 9⅛ x 7⅛, 1928-30 (4147/334)   100
Weber, Max, PEWTER CUP, lithograph, 8½ x 9⅞ (4270/617)   100
Weber, Paul, after, PHILADELPHIA, etching, engraving, 16 x 26¼, imp, 1860 (4211/324)   375
Wesselmann, Tom, STILL LIFE, 190/200, embossing, pencil, 1965, 15½ x 20⅝ (4226/369)   225
Wesselmann, Tom, SEASCAPE, silkscreen, 18 x 17⅞ (4270/620)   550
Whistler, James Abbott McNeil, BILLINGSGATE, etching, drypoint, 6 x 9 (4203/377)   575
Whistler, James Abbott McNeil, CHELSEA RAGS, transfer lithograph, on Chine applique, 7⅛ x 6¼,
1888 (4203/382)   350
Whistler, James Abbott McNeil, DROUET, etching, drypoint, 9 x 6 (4203/378)   325
Whistler, James Abbott McNeil, LES BONNES DU LUXEMBOURG, lithograph, pub. in Art Journal, 8
x 6¼, 1894 (4203/380)   150
Whistler, James Abbott McNeil, MAUNDER'S FISH SHOP, CHELSEA, lithograph, 7⅜ x 6¾, 1890
(4203/379)   700

Whistler, James Abbott McNeil, READING BY LAMPLIGHT, etching, drypoint, 6⅜ x 4⅞ (4203/375) 500
Whistler, James Abbott McNeil, THE UNSAFE TENEMENT, etching, fourth state, 6⅛ x 9 (4203/373) 600
Whistler, James Abbott McNeil, BIBI LALOUETTE, etching and drypoint, 9 x 6 (4147/336) 750
Whistler, James Abbott McNeil, FULHAM, etching with drypoint, 5¼ x 8⅛ (4147/338) 325
Whistler, James Abbott McNeil, LA MARCHANDE DE MOUTARDE, etching with drypoint, 6¼ x 3½ (4147/335) 375
Whistler, James Abbott McNeil, ST GILES-IN-THE-FIELDS, lithograph, ed. of 100, reprinted, 8⅝ x 5⅜, 1896 (4147/342) 250
Whistler, James Abbott McNeil, THE 'ADAM AND EVE' OLD CHELSEA, etching, second state, sepia, backed, 7 x 12 (4147/337) 750
Whistler, James Abbott McNeil, WHEELWRIGHT, etching, 5 x 6⅞ (4147/339) 1100
Whistler, James Abbott McNeil, BIBI LALOUETTE, etching, 9 x 6⅛ (4067/250) 650
Whistler, James Abbott McNeil, DROUET, etching and drypoint, 9 x 6 (4067/251) 300
Whistler, James Abbott McNeil, LE MARCHANDE DE MOUTARDE, etching and drypoint, 6⅛ x 3½ (4067/248) 275
Whistler, James Abbott McNeil, SOUPE A TROIS SOUS, etching, 6⅛ x 9 (4067/249) 450
Whistler, James Abbott McNeil, BIBI LA LOUETTE, etching and drypoint, 9⅛ x 6⅛ (4270/630) 550
Whistler, James Abbott McNeil, BIBI LALOUETTE, etching and drypoint, 9 x 6 (4215/492) 700
Whistler, James Abbott McNeil, BILLINGSGATE, etching and drypoint, 6¼ x 9⅛ (4215/490) 750
Whistler, James Abbott McNeil, BILLINGSGATE, 1879, etching and drypoint, 6⅛ x 8¾ (4215/491) 375
Whistler, James Abbott McNeil, CONFIDENCES IN THE GARDEN, lithograph, 8⅜ x 6¼ (4215/509) 450
Whistler, James Abbott McNeil, DRAPED MODEL STANDING BY A SOFA, lithograph, 8⅛ x 8¼ (4215/526) 2000
Whistler, James Abbott McNeil, DRURY LANE RAGS, lith, 5⅞ x 6½ (4215/503) 500
Whistler, James Abbott McNeil, EARLY MORNING, 1878, lithograph, 6½ x 10¼ (4215/499) 850
Whistler, James Abbott McNeil, EVENING, LITTLE WATERLOO BRIDGE, lithograph, 4¾ x 7⅝ (4215/522) 800
Whistler, James Abbott McNeil, FIRELIGHT (MRS. PENNELL), lithograph, 7½ x 5⅞ (4215/519) 425
Whistler, James Abbott McNeil, FIRELIGHT (MRS. PENNELL), lithograph, 7½ x 5⅞ (4244/463) 350
Whistler, James Abbott McNeil, GANTS DE SUEDE, lithograph, 8½ x 4 (4215/505) 500
Whistler, James Abbott McNeil, GANTS DE SUEDE, lithograph, 8½ x 4 (4215/504) 950
Whistler, James Abbott McNeil, GIRL WITH BOWL, lithograph, ⅜ x 2⅝ (4215/517) 125
Whistler, James Abbott McNeil, LA BELLE JARDINIERE, lithograph, 8⅝ x 6¼ (4215/511) 800
Whistler, James Abbott McNeil, LA FRUITIERE DE LA RUE DE GRENELLE, lithograph, 9⅛ x 16 (4215/512) 600
Whistler, James Abbott McNeil, LA RETAMEUSE, etching, 4⅜ x 3½ (4270/621) 225
Whistler, James Abbott McNeil, LA JOLIE NEW YORKAISE, lithograph, 8⅞ x 6⅛ (4215/510) 300
Whistler, James Abbott McNeil, LINDSAY ROW CHELSEA, lithograph, 4⅞ x 8 (4215/502) 250
Whistler, James Abbott McNeil, LINDSAY ROW, CHELSEA, lithograph, 5 x 8⅛ (4270/637) 225
Whistler, James Abbott McNeil, LITTLE DOROTHY, lithograph, 7½ x 5¼ (4270/643) 325
Whistler, James Abbott McNeil, LITTLE EVELYN, lithograph, 6⅞ x 4½ (4215/520) 350
Whistler, James Abbott McNeil, LITTLE LONDON MODEL, lithograph, 6¾ x 5 (4215/524) 200
Whistler, James Abbott McNeil, LITTLE VENICE, etching, 7½ x 10⅜ (4215/495) 1300
Whistler, James Abbott McNeil, LIVERDUN, etching, 4⅛ x 6 (4215/488) 375
Whistler, James Abbott McNeil, LONG VENICE, etching and drypoint, 5 x 12¼ (4215/498) 2400
Whistler, James Abbott McNeil, MAUNDER'S FISH SHOP, CHELSEA, lithograph, 7½ x 6⅞ (4270/638) 200
Whistler, James Abbott McNeil, MAUNDER'S FISH SHOP CHELSEA, lithograph, 7½ x 6¾ (4215/506) 850
Whistler, James Abbott McNeil, MODEL DRAPING, lithograph, 7½ x 4¼ (4270/639) 150
Whistler, James Abbott McNeil, MOTHER AND CHILD NO 1, lithograph, 7¼ x 7½ (4215/516) 350
Whistler, James Abbott McNeil, MOTHER AND CHILD NO 2, lithograph, 6¾ x 11¾ (4215/518) 500
Whistler, James Abbott McNeil, MOTHER AND CHILD, lithograph, 7⅞ x 6⅞ (4270/642) 375
Whistler, James Abbott McNeil, NEEDLEWORK, lithograph, 7¾ x 5¾ (4215/521) 600
Whistler, James Abbott McNeil, OLD BATTERSEA BRIDGE, lithograph, 5¾ x 13⅛ (4215/501) 500
Whistler, James Abbott McNeil, PONTE DEL PIOVAN, etching and drypoint, 8⅞ x 5⅞ (4215/497) 1100
Whistler, James Abbott McNeil, PORTRAIT STUDY, lithograph, 7¼ x 4⅜ (4270/644) 200
Whistler, James Abbott McNeil, ROTHERHITHE, etching and drypoint, 11 x 8 (4215/493) 2500
Whistler, James Abbott McNeil, SOUPE ATROIS SOUS, etching and drypoint, 6 x 9 (4270/629) 500
Whistler, James Abbott McNeil, SAN BIAGIO, etching and drypoint, 8⅜ x 12⅛ (4215/496) 2700
Whistler, James Abbott McNeil, STUDY OF A HORSE, lithograph, 3½ x 4½ (4270/641) 250
Whistler, James Abbott McNeil, THE ADAM AND EVE, OLD CHELSEA, etching, 7 x 12 (4270/631) 450
Whistler, James Abbott McNeil, THE ADAM AND EVE, OLD CHELSEA, etching and drypoint, 7 x 12 (4270/632) 450
Whistler, James Abbott McNeil, THE BEGGARS, etching, drypoint, 12 x 8¼ (4244/462) *3000*
Whistler, James Abbott McNeil, THE CAP, lithograph, 8¼ x 5⅛ (4215/525) 800
Whistler, James Abbott McNeil, THE GIRL, lithograph, 8⅞ x 4½ (4215/527) 275
Whistler, James Abbott McNeil, THE GIRL, lithograph, 8½ x 5 (4270/646) 250

Whistler, James Abbott McNeil, THE HOROSCOPE, lithograph, 6⅜ x 6⅛ (4215/508)   325

Whistler, James Abbott McNeil, THE LIME BURNER, etching and drypoint, 10 x 7 (4215/489)   2000

Whistler, James Abbott McNeil, THE LITTLE PUTNEY NO. 1, etching and drypoint, 5¼ x 8⅛ (4270/633)   225

Whistler, James Abbott McNeil, THE MEDICI COLLAR, lithograph, 7 x 5 (4270/645)   400

Whistler, James Abbott McNeil, THE POOL, etching and drypoint, 5⅜ x 8½ (4270/626)   500

Whistler, James Abbott McNeil, THE PRIEST'S HOUSE, lithograph, 9½ x 6¼ (4215/515)   550

Whistler, James Abbott McNeil, THE SISTERS, lithograph, 5⅞ x 9¼ (4215/514)   1300

Whistler, James Abbott McNeil, THE THAMES, lithotint, 10½ x 7¾, 1896 (4244/464)   1900

Whistler, James Abbott McNeil, TWO SHIPS, etching and drypoint, 8¼ x 5¼ (4215/494)   3100

Whistler, James Abbott McNeil, VICTORIA CLUB, lithograph, 8¼ x 5⅜ (4270/635)   175

Wood, Grant, APPROACHING STORM, 1942, lithograph, 11⅞ x 9 (4067/257)   850

Wood, Grant, JANUARY, lithograph, 9⅛ x 12 (4067/254)   475

Wood, Grant, JANUARY, lithograph, 9 x 12 (4270/649)   950

Wood, Grant, JULY FIFTEENTH, lithograph, 9 x 11⅞ (4270/650)   1050

Wood, Grant, JULY FIFTEENTH, 1938, lithograph, 9⅛ x 12 (4067/255)   500

Wood, Grant, SEED TIME AND HARVEST, 1937, lithograph, 7½ x 12¼ (4067/253)   500

Wood, Grant, SEEDTIME AND HARVEST, lithograph, 7½ x 12¼, 1937 (4203/386)   750

Wood, Grant, SEEDTIME AND HARVEST, lithograph, 7½ x 12⅛ (4270/647)   1100

Wood, Grant, SULTRY NIGHT, lithograph, 9 x 11¾ (4270/651)   1500

Wood, Grant, TREE PLANTING GROUP, lithograph, 8⅜ x 10¾ (4270/648)   *1100*

Wood, Grant, TREE PLANTING GROUP, 1937, lithograph, 8½ x 11 (4067/252)   550

Woodville, R. Caton (after), MEXICAN NEWS, 25 x 22, print, foxing, discoloration, 1853 (4076/807)   225

Wunderlich, Paul, EVA I, lithograph, 25¾ x 20 (4147/343)   225

Wyllie, Harold, after W.L. Wyllie, U.S. 44-GUN FRIGATE CONSTITUTION, aquatint, 13¼ x 20¼ (654/429)   100

Youngerman, Jack, IMAGES, 1974, silkscreen, 25½ x 25½ (4067/259)   75

Zorn, Anders, ANATOLE FRANCE, etching, fourth state, 8¼ x 6⅜, 1906 (4203/390)   225

Zorn, Anders, AUGUSTE RODIN, etching, third state, 8⅜ x 6⅛, 1906 (4203/391)   350

Zorn, Anders, BEFORE THE STOVE, etching, drypoint, fifth state, 7⅛ x 4¾, 1903 (4203/389)   650

Zorn, Anders, CABIN, etching, in brown, third state, 11¾ x 7⅞, 1917 (4203/400)   800

Zorn, Anders, DAL RIVER, etching, 7 x 4⅝, 1919 (4203/401)   300

Zorn, Anders, ELIN, etching, drypoint, second state, 7⅞ x 11¾, 1913-14 (4203/397)   700

Zorn, Anders, GOPSMOR COTTAGE, etching, third state, 11⅜ x 7⅞, 1917 (4203/399)   450

Zorn, Anders, MADONNA, etching, drypoint, third state, 9⅝ x 7¾, 1900 (4203/393)   700

Zorn, Anders, PROFESSOR JOHN BERG, etching, third state, 7⅛ x 4¾, 1912 (4203/395)   200

Zorn, Anders, SELF-PORTRAIT, etching, drypoint, 7⅛ x 4¾, 1916 (4203/398)   450

Zorn, Anders, SKERIKULLA, etching, drypoint, second state, 9¾ x 7⅞, 1912 (4203/392)   375

Wood (4270/648)

Zorn, Anders, SUNDAY MORNING, etching, 10¾ x 7¾, 1894 (4203/388)	600
Zorn, Anders, THREE SISTERS, etching, drypoint, third state, 9⅝ x 7⅛, 1913 (4203/396)	400
Zorn, Anders, VALKULLA, etching, drypoint, second state, 11¾ x 7¾, 1912 (4203/394)	500
Zorn, Anders, VENUS DE LA VILLETTE, etching, 5⅜ x 4, 1893 (4203/387)	400
Zox, Larry, COMPOSITION, silkscreen, 15¾ x 17¾ (4270/673)	100
Zox, Larry, COMPOSITION, silkscreen, in colors, 12 x 24 (4203/402)	100
Zox, Larry, PURPLE, silkscreen, 15 x 26 (4270/672)	125
Zox, Larry, PURPLE, silkscreen, in colors, 15 x 26 (4203/403)	75

ASSORTED 19TH AND 20TH CENTURY PRINTS

Afro, ABSTRACT COMPOSITION, aquatint, 50¾ x 20⅜ (4270/1)	175
Agam, Yaacov, BOUT A BOUT, silkscreen, plate 2, 22⅝ x 23¾, 1974 (4147/4)	200
Agam, Yaacov, HOMMAGE A G.B., ENGAGEMENT, silkscreen, 14⅞ x 9⅜, 1972 (4244/1)	625
Agam, Yaacov, THORA MANTAL, silkscreen, 18½ x 22¼ (4270/2)	225
Agam, Yaacov, TROIS MOUVEMENTS, silkscreen, 10½ x 28 (4270/3)	250
Agam, Yaacov, TROIS MOVEMENTS, silkscreen, 10½ x 28⅛, 1972 (4244/2)	225
Agam, Yaacov, UNTITLED, silkscreen, 9¾ x 28⅜ (4244/3)	275
Albers, Josef, TEN VARIANTS, complete suite, 10 silkscreens, initialed, 17 x 17, 1966 (4118/64)	3250
Albers, Josef, WHITE EMBOSSING ON GREY 2, 23 x 15½ (4270/6)	200
Albright, Ivan Le Lorraine, FLEETING TIME THOU HAST LEFT ME OLD, lithograph, 13¾ x 9⅝ (4270/7)	900
Alechinsky, Pierre, CHUTE BLANCHE, lithograph, 23½ x 33⅞ (4270/9)	90
Alechinsky, Pierre, FEUILLE OREE DE VERBE, lithograph, 30¼ x 23 (4270/10)	120
Aman, Edmond Jean, MADEMOISELLE MORENO, ca1890, lithograph, 13½ x 14½ (4215/3)	800
Appel, Karel, APPEL CIRCUS, silkscreen, 33⅜ x 23⅞, 1978 (4203/8)	200
Appel, Karel, CIRQUE, lithograph, 33¼ x 9¼ (4270/18)	150
Appel, Karel, COMPOSITION, color lithograph, 17½ x 26¾ (4118/69)	225
Appel, Karel, COMPOSITION, lithograph, 8¼ x 15½ (4270/12)	60
Appel, Karel, COMPOSITION, 1971, lithograph, 27⅞ x 40 (4215/5)	275
Appel, Karel, COUPLE IN WOOD, 17¾ x 24¾ (4215/7)	1600
Appel, Karel, COUPLE IN WOOD, wood sculpture, 17¾ x 24¾ (4270/17)	1150
Appel, Karel, DEUX TETES, lithograph, 19½ x 29¼ (4270/11)	175
Appel, Karel, FIGURE, lithograph 40 x 26, 1971 (4203/5)	225
Appel, Karel, GOLDEN GATE SUITE, THE KISS, lithograph, 26 x 38 (4244/5)	250
Appel, Karel, HOMMAGE A'MOURLOT, lithograph, 23¾ x 18 (4270/15)	125
Appel, Karel, L'HOMME SOURIANT, lithograph 25¾ x 20, 1969 (4203/4)	175
Appel, Karel, LAUGHING PEOPLE, color lithograph, 25⅝ x 19¼, 1974 (4118/71)	275
Appel, Karel, LES AMOUREUX, 1959, lithograph, 18⅛ x 23¾ (4215/4)	275
Appel, Karel, PERSON WITH FISH, lithograph, 25¼ x 18⅞ (4270/13)	175
Appel, Karel, PERSONNAGE, color lithograph, 28½ x 20¾, 1974 (4118/74)	300
Appel, Karel, PERSONNAGES, (Tete), color lithograph, framed, 19⅝ x 25¼, 1969 (4118/70)	300
Appel, Karel, SEEING EYES, color lithograph, 24⅝ x 17½, 1975 (4118/72)	275
Appel, Karel, THE CHILD PRODIGY, color lithograph, 26⅛ x 20¼, 1976 (4118/73)	275
Appel, Karel, THE CHILD PRODIGY, lithograph 26¼ x 20⅛, 1976 (4203/6)	250
Appel, Karel, THE DONKEY, lithograph, 26⅛ x 40⅛ (4270/14)	200
Appel, Karel, TOI ET MOI, color lithograph, 25⅜ x 19¼ (4118/68)	450
Appel, Karel, TWO HEADS IN THE WILDERNESS, lithograph 29½ x 42, 1976 (4203/7)	200
Appel, Karel, DONKEY, 1971, lithograph 23¼ x 33⅛ (4067/6)	275
Archipenko, Alexander, TWO FEMALE NUDES, lithograph, 14½ x 11½, 1921-22 (4244/6)	850
Arms, John Taylor, CAVENDISH COMMON, etching, 6⅜ x 14⅝ (4270/22)	275
Arms, John Taylor, THIRTY KNOTS OR BETTER, etching and aquatint, 4½ x 9½ (4270/21)	175
Arp, Hans, GRIS-NOIR, lithograph, 27⅜ x 19¾ (4270/25)	250
Arp, Hans, PRESQUE VASE ET FLEUR, lithograph, 19⅝ x 17 (4270/24)	150
Arp, Jean, COMPOSITION, color linoleum cut, 14⅛ x 10⅝, 1965 (4118/76)	250
Arp, Jean, COMPOSITION, lithograph in colors, 19⅝ x 13¾, 1954 (4203/14)	100
Arp, Jean, FIGURATIONER, color lithograph, 12⅜ x 9⅞, 1962 (4118/75)	175
Asselin, Maurice, LA TOILETTE, lithograph, 11¼ x 9⅞ (4215/8)	100
Auriol, George, (YOUNG WOMAN AT WINDOW), lithograph, 18⅛ x 9⅞ (4244/468)	650
Auriol, George, BOIS FRISSONANTS, lithograph, 19½ x 12¾, 1893 (4244/467)	850
Auriol, George, SCHEHERAZADE, lithograph, 9¼ x 5⅞ (4244/469)	100
Avati, Mario, LES OIGNONS DE SYRACUSE, mezzotint, 10 x 12 (4270/27)	225
Baj, Enrico, GREEN EYES, lithograph, 23 x 18¾ (4147/27)	40
Baj, Enrico, LADY JANE GREY, QUEEN OF ENGLAND FOR NINE DAYS, etching, 11¾ x 9¾ (4270/30)	150
Baj, Enrico, MECCANO, book of 17 silkscreens, 76/194, good condition, soiled, 7⅝ x 20⅞ (4226/214)	125
Baj, Enrico, PERSONNAGGIO, silkscreen, 23½ x 19⅜, 1969 (4147/26)	150
Bannard, Walter Darby, SPRING #1, silkscreen, 24 x 22 (4270/31)	100

Baumeister, Willi, OHNE TITEL (GRUPPE MIT RITZFIGUR), drypoint, 6¼ x 8, 1943 (4244/12)	175
Beckmann, Max, BILDNES FRAU H.M., woodcut, 13½ x 13, sta, 1923 (4244/22)	600
Beckmann, Max, DAY AND DREAM, DERMORGEN, lithograph, 11¾ x 9½ (4270/42)	250
Beckmann, Max, DIE FURSTIN, drypoint, 7 x 5½, 1917 (4244/15)	275
Beckmann, Max, FASTNACHT, drypoint, 12¾ x 9¾, frame, 1922 (4244/20)	*650*
Beckmann, Max, GESELLSCHAFT, drypoint, 10¼ x 12⅜, 1915 (4244/14)	800
Beckmann, Max, GESICHTE, AUFERSTEHUNG, drypoint, 9⅝ x 13, 1918 (4244/16)	600
Beckmann, Max, GESICHTE, FRUHLING, drypoint, 11¾ x 7¾ (4244/17)	375
Beckmann, Max, GESICHTE, SPIELENDE KINDER, drypoint, 10¼ x 12 (4244/18)	600
Beckmann, Max, MAINLANDSCHAFT MIT REGENBOGEN, 9½ x 8, 1923 (4244/21)	800
Beckmann, Max, TANZENDE, woodcut, 7⅛ x 4, frame, 1922 (4244/19)	450
Beckmann, Max, THEATERLOGE, drypoint, 11¾ x 9⅜, 1918 (4118/79)	550
Beckmann, Max, VIERTE KLASSE 11, etching, 7⅝ x 5⅝, 1913 (4244/13)	300
Beckmann, Max (1884-1950), DIE ENTTAUSCHTEN II, 95/100, mat stain, lithograph, 1922, 18⅞ x 15 (4247/139)	1600
Beckmann, Max (1884-1950), IN DER TRAMBAHN, IV/XX, 2nd state, drypoint, 1922, 11¼ x 16⅞ (4247/140)	1100
Beckmann, Max (1884-1950), JAHRMARKT, DAS KARUSSELL, drypoint, edition 75, 1921, 11½ x 10⅛ (4247/138)	1000
Bellmer, Hans, BONJOUR MAX ERNST, etching, aquatint in black, taupe, white, 10 x 10, 1975 (4118/81)	200
Bellmer, Hans, SOUTERRAIN, lithograph, 15⅜ x 22⅞ (4270/43)	200
Berthon, Paul, LE LIVRE DE MAGDA, lithograph, 22¼ x 14⅞, frame, 1898 (4244/471)	700
Berthon, Paul, LE LIVRE DE MAGDA, 1898, lithograph, 22½ x 15 (4215/29)	450
Berthon, Paul, LES BOULES DE NEIGE, lithograph, 15½ x 21⅛ (4215/30)	450
Berthon, Paul, LES BOULES DE NEIGE, lithograph, 15⅜ x 21, frame, 1900 (4244/470)	400
Berthon, Paul, NORTRE DAME DE PARIS, ca1900, lithograph, 22¼ x 16¾ (4215/31)	450
Besnard, Paul-Albert, CLAIRE, etching and drypoint, 11¾ x 7⅞, 1887 (4147/38)	125
Besnard, Paul-Albert, LA MORTE, etching, (4203/48)	80
Besnard, Paul-Albert, LE FEMME AU VASE, etching and aquatint, in sepia, 7¾ x 5½, 1894, ed of 75 (4203/50)	275
Bonnard, Pierre, AFFICHE POUR L'EXPOSITION DES P.-G., lithograph 25½ x 19, 1896 (4203/56)	350
Bonnard, Pierre, DANS LA RUE, lithograph, in colors, 10⅜ x 5¼, 1900 repairs (4147/46)	700
Bonnard, Pierre, LA COUPE ET LE COMPOTIER, lithograph 7⅜ x 10¼ (4203/57)	475
Bonnard, Pierre, LA PETITE BLANCHISSEUSE, color lithograph, 11⅝ x 7⅞, 1896 (4118/88)	20000
Bonnard, Pierre, PAYSAGE DU MIDI, lithograph, 8½ x 11⅜, 1925 (4147/47)	1000
Bonnard, Pierre, POSTER FOR THE FIGARO, brown and black, lithograph, 17¾ x 14⅛, 1904 (4118/90)	205
Brackhurst, Gerald, LA TRESSE, etching, 8¼ x 6⅞ (4203/67)	450
Bracquemond, Felix, JANOT LAPIN, etching with drypoint, 9⅜ x 13¼, 1894 (4147/49)	70
Bracquemond, Felix, LES MOUETTES (SEAGULLS), etching, 11⅝ x 18¼ (4270/65)	*650*
Braque, Georges, AOUT, ECRITS ET GRAVURES VII, aquatint, 9⅞ x 12⅝, 1958 (4203/60)	475
Braque, Georges, CANARD SAUVAGE, lithograph 13½ x 17⅞ (4203/61)	1500

Beckmann (4244/20)

Bracquemond (4270/65)

Braque, Georges, FEMME ASSISE, etching, 9½ x 7⅛, 1934 (4118/91) — 2100
Braque, Georges, L'OISEAU DE FEU, OU OISEAU XIII, color, aquatint, 15½ x 15, 1958 (4118/95) — 3000
Braque, Georges, L'OISEAU DEVANT LA LUNE, lithograph, 6¾ x 9¼ (4270/66) — 750
Braque, Georges, L'ORDRE DES OISE, aux., 1962, aquatint, 8⅞ x 8⅞ (4067/35) — 250
Braque, Georges, LA VERRE ET LA POMME, color lithograph, 6¼ x 9⅞, 1963 (4118/97) — 800
Braque, Georges, LE GUITARE, 1953, lithograph, 22⅜ x 29½ (4215/39) — 1200
Braque, Georges, LE TIR L'ARC, PROFIL, lithograph, 8¼ x 5¾, 1960 (4244/37) — 800
Braque, Georges, LETTERA AMOROSA LE LISERON, 1963, lithograph 4⅜ x 7¼ (4067/37) — 525
Braque, Georges, LETTERA AMOROSA LES, 1963, lithograph 8⅞ x 8⅞ (4067/36) — 1200
Braque, Georges, LETTERA AMOROSA, COUPLE D'OISEAUX, color, lithograph, 6¾ x 7¾, 1963 (4118/98) — 1600
Braque, Georges, LETTERA AMOROSA, L'ETANG, lithograph 7 x 6¾ (4203/63) — 325
Braque, Georges, LETTERA AMOROSA, L'ETANG, lithograph, 4¾ x 6⅞ (4270/67) — 300
Braque, Georges, LETTERA AMOROSA, LA NUIT, lithograph (4203/62) — 400
Braque, Georges, LETTERA AMOROSA, LE LISERON VERT, lithograph, 4⅜ x 6⅞ (4270/69) — 600
Braque, Georges, LETTERA AMOROSA, LE TREFLE, lithograph 4¾ x 6⅞, 1963 (4203/64) — 750
Braque, Georges, LETTERA AMOROSA, METAMORPHOSE, lithograph, 10½ x 7⅛ (4270/68) — 800
Braque, Georges, MIGRATION, aquatint, 9¼ x 7 (4215/45) — 2000
Braque, Georges, MIGRATION, 1963, lithograph, 9¼ x 7 (4215/44) — 750
Braque, Georges, OISEAU BLEU SUR FOND DE SABLE, color aquatint, 11⅝ x 14⅜, 1963 (4118/96) — 2100
Braque, Georges, SI JE MOURAIS LA BAS, LA MUSIQUE, woodcut, 8 x 12¾, 1962 (4244/41) — 1400
Braque, Georges, SI JE MOURAIS LA'BAS, BOUQUET, 1962, woodcut, 15¾ x 12⅜ (4215/42) — 1600
Braque, Georges, SI JE MOURAIS LA'BAS, 1962, woodcut, 13⅜ x 13¼ (4215/41) — 1300
Braque, Georges, STILL LIFE, etching printed with plate tone, 13½ x 8⅝, frame (4244/33) — 5500
Braque, Georges, THEIERE ET POMMES, color lithograph, 11½ x 25⅝, 1946 (4118/94) — 11500
Braque, Georges, THEOGENIE, etching, some stains, rep, 14½ x 11¾, 1932 (4118/93) — 700
Braque, Georges, THEOGONIE, etching, 14⅜ x 11¾ (4215/37) — 1400
Braque, Georges, THEOGONIE, etching, 14½ x 11¾ (4215/36) — 1300
Braque, Georges, THEOGONIE, etching, 14½ x 11¾ (4215/35) — 1900
Braque, Georges, THEOGONIE, etching, 14⅝ x 18⅛, sta, crease, frame (4244/31) — 700
Braque, Georges, URANIE, 1958, lithograph, 9⅜ x 12⅝ (4215/40) — 3500
Braque, Georges, L'OISEAU D'OCTOBRE, lithograph, 10⅝ x 19¼, 1962 (4244/39) — 2400
Braque, Georges, L'OISEAU ET SON OMBRE, 1959, 23 x 33⅛, lithograph (4225/152) — 6500
Braque, Georges, LES AMARYLLIS, 1958, 21½ x 17¾, aquatint (4225/151) — 14500
Braque, Georges, OISEAU BLEU ET JAUNE, 1960, 13 x 20, lithograph (4225/153) — 5000
Braquemond, Felix, AU JARDIN D'ACCLIMATATION, etching and aquatint, 7⅞ x 8¼, 1873 (4203/58) — 700
Braquemond, Felix, JEANNOT, LAPIN, etching, 9⅝ x 13¼, 1897 (4203/59) — 425
Brauner, Victor, CODEX D'UNE VISAGE, PLATE I, 1962, 18⅝ x 14⅜ (4244/43) — 400
Brauner, Victor, CODEX D'UNE VISAGE, PLATE VII, etching, plate tone, 18⅝ x 14⅜ (4244/44) — 350
Brauner, Victor, PERSONNAGES, etchings, aquatint, 6⅝ x 5, 1947 (4244/42) — 1900

Bresdin, Rodolphe, INTERIEVRE FLAMAND, etching, 9 x 5½ (4244/45)   550
Bresdin, Rodolphe, LE COURSE D'EAU, 1880, etching, 5¼ x 8¼ (4215/46)   425
Brockhurst, Gerald, ADOLESCENCE, etching, 14½ x 10½, 1932 (4244/46)   2400
Brockhurst, Gerald, NADEJDA, etching, 5⅞ x 4½, 1924 (4203/66)   300
Brockhurst, Gerald, NOEMIE, etching, 7¼ x 4¼ (4147/51)   160
Brockhurst, Gerald, THE BLACK SILK DRESS, etching, 8¾ x 6¼, 1927 (4203/68)   450
Buffet, Bernard, BALLERINA, lithograph, 27 x 18⅞ (4067/46)   150
Buffet, Bernard, HOG-FISH, 1964, lithograph, 19⅛ x 26⅜ (4067/44)   225
Buffet, Bernard, NEW YORK, 1965, lithograph, 19½ x 19¼ (4067/45)   275
Buffet, Bernard, PARIS, L'ILE SAINT-LOUIS, lithograph, in colors, 20¼ x 26, 1962 (4147/53) 475
Buffet, Bernard, PARIS, LA PLACE DES VOSGES, 1962, lithograph 20½ x 25¾ (4067/39)   300
Buffet, Bernard, PARIS, LA PORTE, SAINT MARTIN, 1962, lithograph 20½ x 25¾ (4067/41)   300
Buffet, Bernard, PARIS, LE PONT DES ARTS, lithograph, in colors, 21 x 27⅛, 1962 (4147/54) 450
Buffet, Bernard, PARIS, LE SACRE'COEUR, 1962, lithograph, 20½ x 25¾ (4067/43)   300
Buffet, Bernard, PARIS, PONT-DU-JOUR, 1962, lithograph 16⅜ x 21¼ (4067/40)   375
Buffet, Bernard, PARIS, THE EIFFEL TOWER, 1962, lithograph, 20½ x 25¾ (4067/42)   350
Buffet, Bernard, STILL-LIFE A LA COFFE-POT, lithograph, in colors, 27⅛ x 19½, 1955 (4147/52) 225
Buhot, Felix, L'HIVER A PARIS, 9⅜ x 13⅞ (4270/77)   500
Buhot, Felix, L'HIVER A PARIS, etching, aquatint, roulette, 9½ x 13¾, frame (4244/47)   450
Buhot, Felix, LA FALAISE-BAIE DE SAINT-MALO, etching, aquatint, drypoint, 11¾, 15½, 1889-90
    (4244/48)   1200
Buhot, Felix, LE PETIT ENTERREMENT, mixed media, 3½ x 4½ (4270/79)   275
Buhot, Felix, LE RETOUR DES ARTISTES, etching and aquatint, 8 x 12⅜, 1877 (4203/71)   750
Buhot, Felix, LES OIES, etching and aquatint, 6⅛ x 10⅛, 1887 (4203/79)   325
Buhot, Felix, LES OIES, mixed media, 6⅛ x 10¼ (4270/78)   225
Buhot, Felix, UN DEBARQUEMENT EN ANGLETERRE, etching and aquatint, 11¾ x 7⅛, 1879
    (4203/72)   650
Buhot, Felix, UN GRAIN A TROUVILLE, etching and aquatint, 6⅜ x 9½, 1874 (4203/69)   800
Buhot, Felix, UN GRAIN A TROUVILLE, mixed media, 6⅜ x 9½ (4270/76)   350
Buhot, Felix, UNE MATINEE D'HIVER, etching with drypoint, 9¼ x 16½, 1876 (4203/70)   400
Campigi, Massimo, FENETRES, lithograph, 18¾ x 24 (4270/99)   225
Castellon, Federico, LANDSCAPE IN SPAIN, lithograph, 9⅞ x 13¾ (4270/102)   225
Castellon, Federico, OF LAND AND SEA, lithograph, 10⅜ x 9⅞ (4270/103)   400
Cezanne, Paul, PORTRAIT DE CEZANNE PAR LUI-MEME, ca1898-1900, lithograph, 12⅞ x 11⅛
    (4215/50)   1400
Cezanne, Paul, PORTRAIT DE CEZANNE PAR LUI-MEME, lithograph, 12¾ x 10⅝ (4244/65)   850
Cezanne, Paul, PORTRAIT DE CEZANNE, lithograph in gray, 12¾ x 11, 1896-97 (4118/111)   700
Chagall, Marc, ADAM AND EVE AND FORBIDDEN FRUIT, lithograph 14 x 10⅜, 1958 (4203/106)   250
Chagall, Marc, ANGEL WITH SWORD, lithograph 14¾ x 10⅝, 1956 (4203/104)   2100
Chagall, Marc, ARABIAN NIGHTS, plate 4, color lithograph, 14⅝ x 11, 1948 (4118/123)   5500
Chagall, Marc, ARABIAN NIGHTS, plates 4 and 7, color litho's, (2), 14½ x 11, 1948 (4118/124) 1000
Chagall, Marc, ARABIAN NIGHTS, PLATE XI, lithograph, 14¾ x 11, frame (4244/77)   550
Chagall, Marc, ARABIAN NIGHTS, PLATE 1, 14¾ x 11 (4270/110)   275
Chagall, Marc, ARABIAN NIGHTS, PLATE 1, lithograph 14¾ x 11⅛, 1948 (4203/99)   1000
Chagall, Marc, ARABIAN NIGHTS, PLATE 3, lithograph, 14⅜ x 11 (4244/76)   450
Chagall, Marc, ARABIAN NIGHTS, PLATE 3, lithograph, 14½ x 11 (4270/111)   300
Chagall, Marc, ARABIAN NIGHTS, PLATE 5, lithograph 14⅝ x 11⅛, 1948 (4203/100)   500
Chagall, Marc, ARABIAN NIGHTS, PLATE 8, lithograph 14⅝ x 11⅛, 1948 (4203/101)   500
Chagall, Marc, ARABIAN NIGHTS, PLATE 9, lithograph 14¾ x 11⅜, 1948 (4203/102)   550
Chagall, Marc, AYANT APPRIS LA MORT DE JONATHON, hand colored, etching, 12⅜ x 9¼
    (4244/71)   1500
Chagall, Marc, BATEAU-MOUCHE WITH BOUQUET, lithograph 15⅜ x 11¾, 1960 (4203/109)   1100
Chagall, Marc, BOUQUET WITH EIFFEL TOWER, lithograph, 24⅜ x 18¾, 1958 (4244/81)   9000
Chagall, Marc, CHRIST IN THE CLOCK, color lithograph, 9⅝ x 8½ (4118/125)   1200
Chagall, Marc, CHRIST IN THE CLOCK, 1957, lithograph, 9½ x 8⅜ (4215/70)   2100
Chagall, Marc, COUPLE AGAINST A BLACK BACKGROUND, 1973, lithograph, 12⅞ x 10 (4215/84)   2750
Chagall, Marc, DAPHNIS & CHLOE, CHLOE IS CARRIED OFF, 1961, lithograph, 16¾ x 25⅜
    (4215/74)   10500
Chagall, Marc, DAPHNIS & CHLOE, DORCON'S STRATEGY, 1961, lithograph, 16¾ x 12¾
    (4215/73)   6000
Chagall, Marc, DAPHNIS & CHLOE, MEGACLES RECOGNIZES HIS DAUGHTER, 1961, lithograph,
    16¾ x 25¼ (4215/75)   12500
Chagall, Marc, DAPHNIS AND CHLOE, BRYAXIS'S DREAM, color, lithograph, 16⅝ x 25⅜, 1961
    (4118/127)   5500
Chagall, Marc, DAPHNIS AND CHLOE, CHLOE IS DRESSED AND BRAIDED BY CLEARISTE, 1961,
    lithograph 16¼ x 12½ (4067/69)   475
Chagall, Marc, DAPHNIS AND CHLOE, CHLOE, 1961, 16¾ x 12⅝, lithograph (4225/158)   10000

Chagall, Marc, DAPHNIS AND CHLOE, DEAD DOLPHIN, lithograph, in colors, 16⅝ x 12¾, 1961 (4147/81) — 550

Chagall, Marc, DAPHNIS AND CHLOE, DEATH OF DORCON, 1961, 16¾ x 12¼, lithograph (4225/155) — 15000

Chagall, Marc, DAPHNIS AND CHLOE, ECHO, lithograph, in colors, 16½ x 25, 1961 (4147/82) — 1300

Chagall, Marc, DAPHNIS AND CHLOE, LAMON DISCOVERS DAPHNIS, 1961, 16¾ x 12¾, lithograph (4225/154) — 8500

Chagall, Marc, DAPHNIS AND CHLOE, LAMON'S AND DRYAS'S DREAMS, 1961, lithograph 16¼ x 12½ (4067/66) — 425

Chagall, Marc, DAPHNIS AND CHLOE, LEMON'S AND DRYAS'S DREAM, lithograph, 16¾ x 12⅝, 1961 (4118/126) — 5000

Chagall, Marc, DAPHNIS AND CHLOE, MEAL AT DRYAS'S color, lithograph, 16⅝ x 25⅛, 1961 (4118/133) — 700

Chagall, Marc, DAPHNIS AND CHLOE, PAN'S BANQUET, color, lithograph, 16¾ x 12¾, 1961 (4118/132) — 650

Chagall, Marc, DAPHNIS AND CHLOE, SACRIFICES MADE color, lithograph, 16⅝ x 25⅛, 1961 (4118/129) — 5000

Chagall, Marc, DAPHNIS AND CHLOE, SPRINGTIME ON THE MEADOW, lithograph, 16⅝ x 25¼, 1961 (4118/130) — 850

Chagall, Marc, DAPHNIS AND CHLOE, SPRINGTIME ON THE MEADOW, lithograph, 16¾ x 25⅜, frame, 1961 (4244/82) — 11500

Chagall, Marc, DAPHNIS AND CHLOE, THE BIRD CHASE, color, lithograph, 16½ x 25¼, 1961 (4118/128) — 8500

Chagall, Marc, DAPHNIS AND CHLOE, THE MEAL AT DRYAS'S HOUSE, 1961, 16¾ x 25⅜, lithograph (4225/156) — 12000

Chagall, Marc, DAPHNIS AND CHLOE, THE NYMPH'S CAVE, lithograph, 17 x 25¼, frame (4244/83) — 13000

Chagall, Marc, DAPHNIS AND CHLOE, THE ORCHARD, lithograph, in colors, 16½ x 25¼, 1961 (4147/83) — 1100

Chagall, Marc, DAPHNIS AND CHLOE, THE WINE HARVEST, color, lithograph, 16¾ x 12¾, 1961 (4118/131) — 600

Chagall, Marc, DAPHNIS AND CHLOE, THE WOLF PIT, 1961, lithograph 16¼ x 12½ (4067/67) — 550

Chagall, Marc, DAPHNIS AND CHLOE, YOUNG METHYMNEAN, lithograph, in colors, 16½ x 12¾, 1961 (4147/80) — 550

Chagall, Marc, DIE GROSSMUTTER, drypoint, plate 4 from Mein, Leben, 8⅛ x 6⅜, 1922 (4118/112) — 1650

Chagall, Marc, DIE LIEBENDEN, etching, drypoint, an ex. Mein, Leben plate, 11 x 8½, 1922 (4118/114) — 2600

Chagall, Marc, DIE VERLIEBTE III, etching, 9 x 15¾, 1954-5 (4203/103) — 1800

Chagall, Marc, ELIE DU HAUT DU MONT CARMEL, etching, 11⅜ x 9⅞, 1956 (4203/107) — 300

Chagall, Marc, ELIE RESSUSCITE LE FILS etching, plate 84, of the Bible, 11⅞ x 9½, 1956 (4118/120) — 1000

Chagall, Marc, FABLES OF LA FONTAINE, etching, 11½ x 9⅜, c.1927-30 (4147/75) — 450

Chagall, Marc, FABLES OF LE FONTAINE, LA TORTUE, etching and drypoint, 11⅝ x 9½, 1927-30 (4203/98) — 500

Chagall, Marc, FABLES, LA FONTAINE, L'ANE ET CHIEN, etching, 11⅝ x 9⅜, 1927-30, pub. 1952 (4118/118) — 350

Chagall, Marc, FAMILY WITH COCK, 1969, lithograph, 24¼ x 16 (4215/79) — 5500

Chagall, Marc, FOUR TALES FROM THE ARABIAN NIGHTS, lithograph, 15 x 11¼, frame (4244/75) — 5100

Chagall, Marc, FOUR TALES FROM THE ARABIAN NIGHTS, lithograph, 14¾ x 11¼, frame (4244/74) — 5000

Chagall, Marc, FOUR TALES FROM THE ARABIAN NIGHTS, lithograph, 14¾ x 11⅛ (4244/73) — 6000

Chagall, Marc, GOAT IN THE NIGHT, lithograph, 16⅛ x 10⅜, frame, 1922-23 (4244/67) — *3500*

Chagall, Marc, GOOD MORNING OVER PARIS, lithograph, 16⅛ x 20⅞, frame, 1952 (4244/78) — 5750

Chagall, Marc, GRAND AUTOPORTRAIT NOIR, 1975, lithograph, 25⅝ x 18⅞ (4215/88) — 3250

Chagall, Marc, HARLEQUIN'S FAMILY, lithograph, 26⅜ x 20, frame, 1965 (4244/85) — 4000

Chagall, Marc, ILE. SAINT LOUIS, 1959, lithograph, 19⅞ x 26 (4215/72) — 7500

Chagall, Marc, IN THE LAND OF THE GODS, 1967, lithograph, 17½ x 14⅝ (4215/78) — 4200

Chagall, Marc, JEREMIE JETE DANS UNE CITERNE etching, plate 102, 13 x 10½, 1956 (4118/122) — 1200

Chagall, Marc, JOSUE, SUCCESSEUR DE MOISE A LA TETE D'ISRAEL, etching, hand colored, 11⅝ x 9⅛ (4244/70) — 1400

Chagall, Marc, L'ACROBATE ROUGE, 1974, lithograph, 27 x 20⅜ (4215/86) — 6500

Chagall, Marc, L'INSPIREE, lithograph, 13 x 10 (4270/114) — 3000

Chagall, Marc, LA FEMME EN CHRIST, etching and aquatint, 5¼ x 7 (4203/110) — 1200

Chagall, Marc, LA PIROUETTE BLEUE, lithograph, 14⅝ x 10⅝ (4215/76) — 3750

Chagall, Marc, LA VOCATION D'EZECHIEL, etching, hand colored, 12¾ x 9¾, 63/100, pub. 1956 (4147/76) — 750

Chagall, Marc, LE CONCERT, lithograph, in colors, 15½ x 22⅛, 1957 (4147/79) — 2100

Chagall (4244/67)

Chagall, Marc, LE MARIAGE, 1968, etching and aquatint, 24¼ x 17⅜ (4215/89)	4750
Chagall, Marc, LECIRQUE, lithograph 16½ x 25½ (4067/70)	600
Chagall, Marc, LITHOGRAPH FOR A CATALOGUE, lithograph 8 x 12½, 1959 (4203/105)	650
Chagall, Marc, LITHOGRAPH FOR A CATALOGUE, lithograph, 8 x 12½, 1959 (4244/80)	875
Chagall, Marc, MEIN LEBEN, LIEBENDE AUF BER BANK, 5 x 6⅞ (4244/68)	900
Chagall, Marc, MOISE SAUVE DES EAUX DU NIL, etching plate 26, of the Bible, 11¼ x 9, 1956 (4118/119)	1500
Chagall, Marc, MOISE, AU SINAI, RECOIT DES MAINS DE DIEO LES TABLES, DE LA LOT, etching, 11¼ x 9⅛ (4244/69)	1400
Chagall, Marc, PAINTER AND MODEL, lithograph, 12⅝ x 9¾, frame, 1963 (4244/84)	1500
Chagall, Marc, PARIS BOUQUET, color lithograph, 16½ x 13⅜, 1971 (4118/137)	2500
Chagall, Marc, PEASANT WITH A CLOCK, 1968, lithograph, 14⅛ x 10 (4215/80)	3750
Chagall, Marc, POKROWSKAJA IN WITE BSK, 1922, drypoint, 7 x 8¼ (4215/51)	2700
Chagall, Marc, PROPHETE REBELLE A L'ETERNAL TUE PAR UN LION, etching, 12⅝ x 8½ (4244/72)	1400
Chagall, Marc, REBECCA AT THE WELL, lithograph, 13¾ x 11¼, 1972 (4244/89)	4500
Chagall, Marc, REGARDS SUR PARIS, lithograph, in colors, 15½ x 11⅞, 1960 (4147/84)	750
Chagall, Marc, REVERIE, lithograph, 12 x 16⅛, 1969 (4244/88)	3750
Chagall, Marc, REVERIE, 1969, lithograph, 12 x 16⅛ (4215/83)	3100
Chagall, Marc, S'ETANT ATTARDE A GAZA CHEZ UNE COURTISANE, etching, 11⅜ x 8⅞ (4270/109)	1000
Chagall, Marc, SALOMON PROCLAME ROI D'ISRAEL, 1956, etching, 12⅜ x 9 (4215/66)	1600
Chagall, Marc, SAUL RECIT DE SAMUEL, 1956, etching, 12½ x 8⅝ (4215/65)	1700
Chagall, Marc, SPELL, lithograph, 24¾ x 17½, frame, 1973 (4244/91)	3250
Chagall, Marc, STORY OF EXODUS, set of 24 lithographs, 19⅞ x 14½, 1966 (4118/136)	9000
Chagall, Marc, THE ARTIST AT THE VILLAGE I, 1969, lithograph, 16⅛ x 11 (4215/82)	4000
Chagall, Marc, THE BASTILLE, 1954, lithograph, 20¼ x 26⅛ (4215/69)	13500
Chagall, Marc, THE BLACK MOON, color lithograph, 9⅞ x 13, 1965 (4118/135)	1600
Chagall, Marc, THE BLUE COW, lithograph, 13 x 9⅞, frame, 1967 (4244/86)	5500
Chagall, Marc, THE FABLES OF FONTAINE, plate 7, etching, 11⅝ x 9⅜, 1927-30, pub. 1952 (4118/116)	450
Chagall, Marc, THE FABLES OF FONTAINE, LA MORT ET LE BUCHERON, etching, 11¾ x 9⅝ (4270/108)	250
Chagall, Marc, THE FABLES OF LA FONTAINE, etching, 11½ x 9⅜, 1927-30, pub. 1952 (4118/117)	500
Chagall, Marc, THE FABLES OF LA FONTAINE, LA GRENOUILLE, drypt, 11⅝ x 9¼, 1927-30, pub. 1952 (4118/115)	275
Chagall, Marc, THE FABLES OF LA FONTAINE, LE SINGE ET LE LEOPARD, etching, 11¾ x 9⅝ (4270/106)	225

Chagall, Marc, THE FABLES OF LA FONTAINE, 1927-30, etching, 11⅝ x 9½ (4067/65) 650
Chagall, Marc, THE FABLES OF LA FONTAINE, 1927-30, etching, 11⅝ x 9½ (4215/63) 450
Chagall, Marc, THE FUNERAL, etching, 8¼ x 11 (4270/107) 150
Chagall, Marc, THE LITTLE HARLEQUINS, color lithograph, 9⅝ x 13⅝, 1962 (4118/134) 700
Chagall, Marc, THE MAGICIAN OF PARIS II, 1970, lithograph, 34⅞ x 26⅝ (4215/81) 8000
Chagall, Marc, THE PAINTER'S DREAM, 1967, lithograph, 28¼ x 22⅛ (4215/77) 4750
Chagall, Marc, THE PASSION, 1975, lithograph, 15¾ x 9⅞ (4215/85) 2300
Chagall, Marc, THE PROPHET, color lithograph, 27½ x 21, 1974 (4118/138) 4750
Chagall, Marc, VOR DEM TORE, etching, plate 14 from Mein, Leben, 8⅛ x 6⅜, 1922 (4118/113) 1850
Chagall, Marc, WOMAN CIRCUS RIDER, lithograph, 14⅜ x 21, framed, 1956 (4244/79) 3500
Chasseriau, Theodore, DAPHNE ET APOLLEN AGENOUILLE, lithograph 8⅞ x 6¼, 1844 (4203/112) 175
Chasseriau, Theodore, DAPHNE ET APOLLON AGENOUILLE, 1844, lithograph, 8⅞ x 6¼ (4215/90) 500
Chasseriau, Theodore, VENUS ANADYOMENE, lithograph 11¼ x 9, 1839 (4203/111) 375
Cheret, Jules, ALCAZAR D'ETE (LIDIA), 48⅛ x¾ (4270/119) 300
Cheret, Jules, L'ETANDARD FRANCAIS, lithograph, 47¼ x 33¾, 1891 (4244/473) 400
Cheret, Jules, PAVILLON DE LA VILLE DE PARIS (CHAMPS-ELYSEES), lithograph, 47¾ x 33½ (4270/118) 300
Cheret, Jules, SAXOLEINE, lithograph, 49 x 34⅛, 1890 (4244/472) 300
Cheret, Jules, SAXOLEINE, lithograph, 49 x 33¾, 1893 (4244/474) 400
Christiansen, Hans, L'ART DE CORATIE, lithograph, 22⅝ x 15½ (4270/120) 500
Clave, Antoni, BONJOUR DU ROI, lithograph, 22⅜ x 30⅛ (4270/127) 225
Clave, Antoni, COMPOSITION, aquatint, 31⅞ x 24¾ (4270/128) 225
Clave, Antoni, COMPOSITION, etching, 30 x 22½ (4270/124) 175
Clave, Antoni, COMPOSITION, etching, 28¾ x 24½ (4270/129) 200
Clave, Antoni, NATURE MORTE, etching, 23½ x 15½ (4270/126) 200
Clave, Antoni, ROI A LA PIPE, lithograph, 26⅜ x 20⅞ (4270/125) 150
Corbusier, Le, AUTREMENT QUE SUR TERRE, 1963, etching, 19⅜ x 25⅝ (4215/193) 200
Corbusier, Le, LA FEMME ROSE, 1961, lithograph, 25½ x 37⅝ (4215/190) 700
Corbusier, Le, LA MAIN OUVERTE, 1963, lithograph, 23¼ x 18½ (4215/191) 450
Corbusier, Le, MAINS CROISEES, 1964, lithograph, 25 x 19¾ (4215/192) 250
Corbusier, Le, PORTRAIT, 1960, lithograph, 28 x 23⅝ (4215/189) 500
Corbusier, Le, TAUREAU, 1964, lithograph, 23 x 20⅝ (4215/194) 350
Corbusier, Le, UNITE 4A, 1963-65, aquatint, 16⅜ x 12⅜ (4215/188) 325
Corinth, Louis, SELBSTBILDNIS, lithograph, 12¼ x 9⅝, frame, 1920 (4244/97) 800
Corinth, Louis, SELF PORTRAIT IN ARMOUR, drypoint, 10⅛ x 4⅞, frame (4244/95) 300
Corinth, Louis, UMARMUNG, etching, drypoint, 7⅛ x 6¼, 1915 (4244/96) 175
Corinth, Louis (1858-1925), DER WALCHENSEE, HOTEL AM WALCHENSEE, ed. of 40, drypoint, 1923, 9⅞ x 12⅝ (4247/141) 1500
Corinth, Lovis, BILDNIS ANDREAS WEISSGAERBER II, drypoint, minor flaws, 11¾ x 8⅝, 1919 (4118/139) 250
Cornell, Joseph, HOTEL DU NORD, silkscreen, 14⅞ x 11¼, frame (4244/98) 900
Corot, LE DORMOIR DES VACHES, lithograph, 1st state, 6¼ x 5⅛, 1871 (4147/93) *1200*

Corot (4147/93)

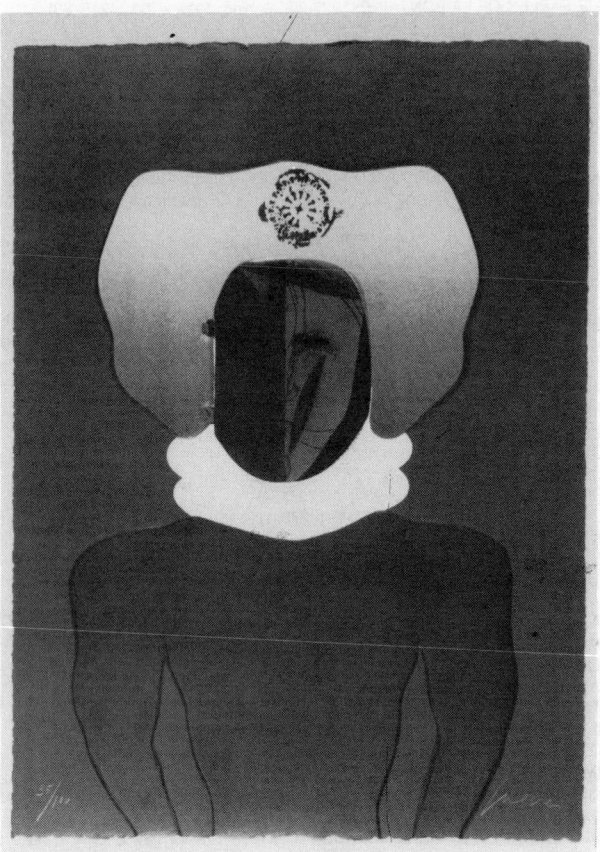

Cuevas (4244/101)

Corot, Camille, ENVIRONS DE ROME, 1866, etching and drypoint, 12¼ x 9 (4215/96)   375
Corot, Camille, LE PETIT CAVALIER SOUS BOIS, 1854, impression, 7¾ x 5⅞ (4215/97)   1800
Corot, Camille, SOUVENIR D'ITALIE, 1866, etching and drypoint, 12⅝ x 9½ (4215/95)   900
Corot, Camille, SOUVENIR DU LAC DE NEMI, cliche verre, brown, ink, 4¾ x 6½, 1871 (4118/141)   325
Cuevas, Jose Luis, CRIME BY CUEVAS, lithograph, 29⅞ x 21⅞ (4270/137)   100
Cuevas, Jose Luis, CRIME, BORGIA, color lithograph, 21⅞ x 29⅞, 1968 (4118/143)   175
Cuevas, Jose Luis, CRIME, BORGIA, lithograph, 21⅞ x 29¾, frame, 1968 (4244/100)   400
Cuevas, Jose Luis, CUEVAS COMEDIES, complete set of lithographs, 30¼ x 22⅝ (4244/103)   2100
Cuevas, Jose Luis, HOMMAGE A QUEVEDO, lithograph, 30⅛ x 22¼, frame (4244/102)   275
Cuevas, Jose Luis, HOMMAGE A QUEVEDO, set of twelve lithographs, 30⅛ x 22½ (4244/101)   *3000*
Cuevas, Jose Luis, HOMMAGE TO QUEVEDO, EL VIAJE, color lithograph, 30 x 22¼, 1969
  (4118/144)   125
Cuevas, Jose Luis, LA MAGA, lithograph, 22½ x 10⅛, 1972 (4244/104)   200
Cuevas, Jose Luis, RECOLLECTIONS OF CHILDHOOD, lithograph, in colors, 17⅛ x 10½, 1962
  (4147/95)   100
Cuevas, Jose Luis, THE POET IN THE DINING ROOM, lithograph, 22⅝ x 30 (4244/105)   200
Cuevas, Jose Luis, WANTED, lithograph, 22⅛ x 7¾ (4270/136)   175
D'Arcangelo, Alan, COMPOSITION, silkscreen, 25¼ x 25¼ (4270/145)   100
Dali, Salador, DYONISOS, 1967, etching, 14½ x 18¾ (4215/99)   700
Dali, Salvador, AMOURS JAUNES, set, 10 drypoints, aquatint, gilt, 11⅝ x 8½, 1974 (4118/151)   1400
Dali, Salvador, CIRQUE, LE FOU, etching, 14⅛ x 20½ (4270/142)   300
Dali, Salvador, CLEOPATRA, drypoint, 16¼ x 20¼ (4270/143)   225

Dali, Salvador, KING OF ARAGON, etching and aquatint, 14 x 10⅝ (4147/103) — 175
Dali, Salvador, L'ACADEMIE, sepia drypoint, 16⅞ x 23½, 1975 (4118/152) — 300
Dali, Salvador, MARGUERITE, 1967, etching, 23 x 15¼ (4067/78) — 550
Dali, Salvador, MEMORIES OF SURREALISM, portfolio of 12 works, 29⅞ x 21, 1971 (4118/150) — 2200
Dali, Salvador, SAN FRANCISCO, complete suite, drypoints, lithograph, 20¼ x 14⅜, 1970 (4118/149) — 1500
Dali, Salvador, ST. GEORGE AND THE DRAGON, etching, 17¾ x 11¼ (4270/141) — 2000
Dali, Salvador, TRISTAN AND ISEULT, complete portfolio of 21, color drypt, 17⅞ x 13, 1970 (4118/145) — 2250
Dali, Salvador, TRISTAN AND ISEULT, two color drypoints, 15¾ x 10⅝, 1969 (4118/146) — 350
Dali, Salvador, TRISTAN AND ISEULT, two color drypoints, 15¾ x 10⅝, 1969 (4118/147) — 325
Damoye, Pierre Emmanuel, WINTER THAW, 26¼ x 43½ (4241/221) — 1800
Daubigy, Charles Francois, LEBERGER ET LA BERGERE, 1874, etching, 11½ x 8¾ (4067/79) — 160
Daumier, Honore, BAISSEZ LE RIDEAU LA FARCE EST JOUEE, 1834, lithograph, 7⅞ x 11 (4215/101) — 425
Daumier, Honore, LEVENTRE LEGISLATIF, 1834, lithograph, 11⅛ x 17⅛ (4215/104) — 2100
Daumier, Honore, MORDERNE GALILEE, 1834, lithograph, 8¾ x 10⅞ (4215/102) — 75
Daumier, Honore, QUELLE SALE, 1835, lithograph, 9 x 15⅜ (4215/103) — 125
De Chirico, Giorgio, AUTORITRATTO IN COSTUME, lithograph 25¼ x 19¾ (4067/73) — 360
De Chirico, Giorgio, AUTORITRATTO IN COSTUME, lithograph 25¼ x 19¾ (4067/74) — 260
De Chirico, Giorgio, CAVALLI ANTICHI, lithograph, 18¼ x 13⅜ (4270/151) — 300
De Chirico, Giorgio, CAVALLI, ANTICHI, lithograph, 23¾ x 17⅞ (4270/153) — 350
De Chirico, Giorgio, GLI ARCHEOLOGI, lithograph, 15⅞ x 11⅞ (4270/150) — 900
De Chirico, Giorgio, IL RITORNO DEL FIGLIUOL, lithograph, 16¼ x 12¼ (4270/149) — 650
De Chirico, Giorgio, LA PARTENZA DI GIASONE, 1966, lithograph, 12 x 16 (4215/92) — 650
De Chirico, Giorgio, LA SPONDA MISTERIOSA, lithograph, 15¾ x 19⅞ (4270/152) — 350
De Chirico, Giorgio, MANICHINO, lithograph, 15⅛ x 10¾, frame, 1964 (4244/93) — 375
De Chirico, Giorgio, METAMORPHOSIS, GIL ARCHEOLOGI IV, 1929, lithograph, 16 x 11⅞ (4215/91) — 850
Degas, Edgar, DANSEUSES DANS LA COULISSE, pastel over etching, 5⅝ x 4¼ (4244/114) — 18000
Delacroix, Eugene, JEUNE TIGRE JOUANT AVEC SA MERE, lithograph, first state, 4⅜ x 7½, 1831 (4147/110) — 950
Delacroix, Eugene, UN FORGERON, aquatint, sixth state, foxed, 9⅛ x 6½, 1833 (4118/155) — 250
Delacroix, Eugene, UN FORGERON, 1833, aquatint, 8¾ x 6¼ (4215/107) — 325
Delacroix, Eugene, UN FORGERON, 1833, aquatint, 9 x 6⅜ (4215/106) — 1000
Delaunay, Sonia, AVEC MOI MEME I, etching and aquatint, 19¼ x 15⅝ (4215/108) — 275
Delaunay, Sonia, AVEC MOI MEME I, etching and aquatint, 19¼ x 15⅝ (4215/109) — 250
Delaunay, Sonia, AVEC MOI-MEME I, etching and aquatint, 19¼ x 15⅝, pub. 1970 (4203/127) — 225
Delaunay, Sonia, AVEC MOI-MEME VIII, etching and aquatint, 19¼ x 15⅝, 1970 (4203/128) — 125
Delaunay, Sonia, AVEC MOI-MEME X, etching and aquatint, 19¼ x 15⅝, pub. 1970 (4203/129) — 235
Delaunay, Sonia, AVEC MOI-MEME, plate 3, aquatint, 19⅜ x 15⅝, 1970 (4244/126) — 250
Delaunay, Sonia, AVEC MOI-MENE, plate 10, etching, 19½ x 15⅝, frame (4244/127) — 250
Delaunay, Sonia, COMPOSITION, color etching and aquatint, 19¼ x 14, 1970 (4118/157) — 225
Delaunay, Sonia, COMPOSITION, lithograph in colors, 18⅛ x 17⅞, 1971 (4203/130) — 325
Delaunay, Sonia, LE RYTHME VI, etching, 16⅛ x 14⅜ (4203/126) — 150
Delaunay, Sonia, LES DAMIERS, lithograph, 16½ x 13¼ (4270/165) — 200
Delvaux, Paul, HALF-LENGTH PORTRAIT OF A WOMAN II, etching, 5⅞ x 4½ (4270/166) — 650
Delvaux, Paul, LADY WITH THE CANDLE, lithograph, 12¾ x 9⅞, 1966 (4244/129) — 1050
Delvaux, Paul, MIRRORS, lithograph, 22¾ x 30⅝, 1966 (4244/128) — 2100
Delvaux, Paul, THE BEACH, lithograph, 19⅝ x 26, 1972 (4244/130) — 1300
Derain, Andre, LA CENE, etching, 19½ x 13¾ (4203/131) — 100
Derain, Andre, PAYSAGE DU MIDI, lithograph, 15⅝ x 22½ (4270/169) — 200
Dix, Otto, MADCHEN MIT HUT, lithograph, 19¼ x 11⅝, frame, 1948 (4244/132) — 350
Dix, Otto, SITZENDES KIND, lithograph, 23⅝ x 17⅞, frame, 1964 (4244/134) — 1200
Dubuffet, Jean, CADASTRE, AMENITE, color lithograph, 18½ x 14½, 1959 (4118/164) — 350
Dubuffet, Jean, CADASTRE, JEUX ET CONGRES, lithograph in colors, 19½ x 15 (4203/136) — 225
Dubuffet, Jean, CHARS ET CHEVAUX CELESTES, lithograph, 12¾ x 19, 1953 (4118/161) — 250
Dubuffet, Jean, CHEMINEMENT, lithograph, 19⅝ x 15⅛ (4270/176) — 150
Dubuffet, Jean, DEUX PERSONNAGES, 1973, silkscreen, 10 x 7¾ (4215/115) — 900
Dubuffet, Jean, FESTIVAL D'AUTOMNE A. PARIS, 1973, lithograph, 25¾ x 17¾ (4067/91) — 450
Dubuffet, Jean, FESTIVAL D'AUTOMNE A PARIS, lithograph, 26¼ x 17¾ (4270/178) — 250
Dubuffet, Jean, FESTIVAL D'AUTOMNE, A PARIS, lithograph, 26¼ x 18¼ (4270/179) — 250
Dubuffet, Jean, FESTIVAL D AUTOMNE A PARIS, 1973, lithograph, 25¾ x 17¾ (4215/113) — 500
Dubuffet, Jean, FESTIVAL D AUTOMNE A PARIS, 1973, lithograph, 25¾ x 19⅛ (4215/114) — 300
Dubuffet, Jean, GEOGRAPHIE, FRAICHEUR, color lithograph, 20 x 13¾, 1959 (4118/163) — 275
Dubuffet, Jean, L'ARPENTEUR ESPRIT DE TERRE, 1959, lithograph, 20 x 15⅛ (4215/111) — 200
Dubuffet, Jean, LE SURINTENDENT, 1972, lithograph, 20 x 12¼ (4215/112) — 850
Dubuffet, Jean, L'ENFLE-CHIQUE II, lithograph, 23¼ x 14½, frame, 1963 (4244/136) — *4000*

Dubuffet, Jean, L'HOURLOUPE-CARTES A JOUER ET A TIRER, ed. of 350, 52 playing cards, 1967,
9⅞ x 6½ (4226/243) — 550
Dubuffet, Jean, LE CIEL ENTRANGER, lithograph, 37 x 24⅜ (4270/175) — 225
Dubuffet, Jean, LES MURS, 10 lithographs of suite of 15, 15 x 11¼, 1945 (4118/160) — 950
Dubuffet, Jean, PEUPLEMENT DES TERRES, color lithograph, 25⅝ x 19¾, 1953 (4118/162) — 900
Dubuffet, Jean, SAMEDI TANTOT, lithograph, 21⅝ x 16, frame, 1964 (4244/137) — 3250
Dubuffet, Jean, SERENITE, lithograph, 17½ x 14⅜ (4270/177) — 250
Dubuffet, Jean, TERRITOIRES ATTENTE, 1959, lithograph, 18½ x 16⅛ (4215/110) — 150
Dubuffet, Jean, VACHE NO. 1, lithograph, 7⅛ x 5¾, frame, 1944 (4244/135) — 900
Duchamp, Marcel, SELF-PORTRAIT IN PROFILE, 18/30 silkscreen, 1959, 25½ x 19⅝ (4226/244) — 1300
Duchamp, Marcel, ROTORELIEFS, 6 cardboard discs, 105/150, offset lithographs, 1935 (4226/246) — 500
Duchamp, Marcel, TIRE A 4 EPINGLES, 2½ x 2½ (4270/180) — 400
Dufresne, Charles, CONCARNEAU, etching, drypoint and lavis, 9 x 11¾ (4203/140) — 250
Dufy, Raoul, (MEXICAN BAND), etching, 7½ x 9⅞ (4270/185) — 300
Dufy, Raoul, LE DOCTEUR, etching, 5⅞ x 4¼ (4203/143) — 275
Dufy, Raoul, LE HAVRE, lithograph, 18½ x 26 (4270/182) — *1700*
Dufy, Raoul, MARINE (HORSE WITH SEASHELLS), lithograph, 10 x 13¾, frame (4244/140) — 200
Dufy, Raoul, NUDE IN THE SEA, etching and aquatint, 8½ x 12¼ (4203/142) — 125
Dufy, Raoul, PECHEURS ET PECHEUSES, lithograph, 13½ x 17¾ (4270/183) — 700
Dufy, Raoul, AMPHITRITE, etching, 6⅝ x 4⅛ (4203/141) — 275
Dumont, Henri, TOUS LES SOIRS AUX AMBASSADEURS, lithograph, 78 x 29½ (4270/186) — 600
English School (19c), THE HUNT, 13 x 16⅛ (666/148) — 650
Engravings, set of six, McLean, London, 21½ x 26 1819 framed (4216/50) — 1900
Engravings, set of six, McLean, London, ENGLISHMEN ON HUNT IN INDIA, 21½ x 26 1819 framed
(4216/51) — 1700
Ensor, James, GRAND VIEW OF MARIAKERKE, 1887, etching, 8½ x 10⅝ (4215/116) — 1700
Ensor, James, L'AVARICE, etching, 3⅞ x 5⅞, 1904 (4244/141) — 2400
Ensor, James, THE CATHEDRAL, etching, second plate, trial, proof, 13⅞ x 20¼ (4118/165) — 2250
Ernst, Max, A NOUVEAU LOP-LOP, color etching, 18⅝ x 12⅜, 1975 (4118/167) — 400
Ernst, Max, ETOILE DE MER, 1950, lithograph, 16¾ x 10½ (4215/118) — 1000
Ernst, Max, ETOILE DE MER, 1950, lithograph, 16¾ x 10⅝ (4215/117) — 1300
Ernst, Max, LES CHIENS ONT SOIF, etching, 13¼ x 8½ (4270/188) — 300
Ernst, Max, LES CHIENS ONT SOIF, etching and softground, 13¼ x 8⅝ (4215/121) — 400
Ernst, Max, LES CHIENS ONT SOIF, etching and softground, 13¼ x 8⅝ (4215/120) — 400
Ernst, Max, LIEBESPAAR, 1966, etching, 16½ x 12⅝ (4067/93) — 650
Ernst, Max, OHNE TITEL, etching, aquatint, collage, 16¼ x 12¼, 1971 (4244/143) — 750
Ernst, Max, PAR DESSUS LES MOULINS, 1974, aquatine, 10½ x 8 (4215/122) — 300
Ernst, Max, PAROLES PEINTES, etchings, (4067/94) — 325
Ernst, Max, RHYTHMES, 1950, lithograph, 16⅞ x 10⅝ (4215/119) — 650
Escher, Maurits Cornelis, DRAGON, 1952, wood engraving, 12⅝ x 9½ (4215/124) — 2300
Escher, Maurits Cornelis, ST. PETER'S ROME, 1935, wood engraving, 9⅝ x 12½ (4215/123) — 2100
Escher, Maurits Cornelis, UP AND DOWN, lithograph, 19⅝ x 8, 1947 (4244/144) — 4000
Esteve, Maurice, COMPOSITION, lithograph 19⅝ x 13½ (4203/145) — 250
Fallon, Andre, COMPOSITION, engraving and aquatint, 11¾ x 8⅞ (4203/146) — 850
Fantin-Latour, ANDROMEDE, lithograph 17¼ x 12½ (4203/147) — 300
Feininger, Lyonel, DAS TOR, etching and drypoint, fine, 10⅝ x 7⅞, 1912 (4118/172) — 2600
Feininger, Lyonel, MANHATTAN I, lithograph, second, published, state, 11¼ x 8⅝, 1951 (4118/174) — 800
Feininger, Lyonel, MANHATTAN 2, lithograph, second, published, state, 10⅞ x 8⅛, 1951
(4118/175) — 800
Feininger, Lyonel, OLD TARS, 1907, woodcut, 5⅛ x 7⅜ (4067/95) — 350
Feininger, Lyonel, VILLAGE CHURCH, woodcut, 5¼ x 5¾ (4270/189) — *650*
Feininger, Lyonel, WALDKIRCHE, woodcut, first state, 5¾ x 4½, 1920 (4118/173) — 325
Fini, Leonar, LE CHAT, lithograph 21 x 17⅛ (4203/149) — 250
Flint, William Russel, GLEAMING SANDS, drypoint, 13½ x 8½ (4270/190) — 275
Forain, Jean-Louis, 1ER SALON DE LA SOCIETE DES DESSINATEURS HUMORISTES, lithograph,
45¾ x 34 (4270/192) — 100
Foujita, Tsouguharu, (THREE STANDING FEMALE FIGURES), lithograph, 21¼ x 15¾ (4270/195) — 850
Foujita, Tsouguharu, (WOMAN WITH CHILD HOLDING CAT), lithograph, 17½ x 11¾ (4270/193) — 600
Foujita, Tsouguharu, DANCING NUDE AND HARLEQUIN, lithograph, 38⅛ x 26¾ (4215/125) — 1700
Foujita, Tsouguharu, FEMMES, DEUX FEMMES NUES ASSISES, etching, 23½ x 15⅞ (4215/126) — 3500
Foujita, Tsouguharu, MOTHER AND CHILD WITH CATS, lithograph, 17¼ x 11¾ (4215/130) — 850
Foujita, Tsouguharu, MOTHER AND CHILD, 1964, lithograph, 21⅝ x 18 (4215/131) — 700
Foujita, Tsouguharu, NU DEVANT L'OPERA, etching, 9¼ x 11½ (4215/127) — 1600
Foujita, Tsouguharu, SLEEPING NUDE, LEFT ARM BEHIND HEAD, ca1929, lithograph, 13¾ x 13
(4215/128) — 1350
Foujita, Tsouguharu, STREET SCENE, lithograph, 12½ x 19¼ (4270/197) — 300
Foujita, Tsouguharu, SURREALIST COMPOSITION WITH NUDE AND ANIMALS, lithograph, 19¾ x
26 (4215/129) — 1000

Dufy (4270/182)

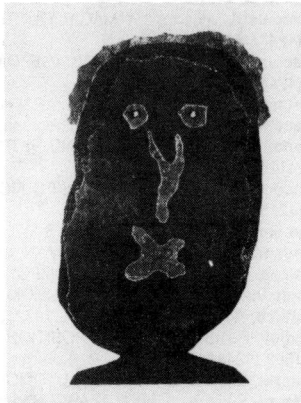

Dubuffet (4244/136)

Feininger
(4270/189)

Foujita, Tsouguharu, YOUNG GIRL WITH CAT, lithograph, 16⅞ x 7⅞ (4270/194)   900
Foujita, Tsuguharu, (YOUNG GIRL HOLDING CAT), lithograph, 16¾ x 7⅞ (4244/154)   450
Foujita, Tsuguharu, CHOW DOG, lithograph, 14⅜ x 16½ (4244/152)   600
Foujita, Tsuguharu, FEMMES, NUDE RECLINING ON HER STOMACH, etching, roulette, 16 x 23
(4244/148)   5000
Foujita, Tsuguharu, LES ENFANTS, BABY WITH BOWS IN HIS HAIR, etching, roulette, 14¾ x 11¼
(4244/145)   2500
Foujita, Tsuguharu, LES ENFANTS, LITTLE GIRL HOLDING A BIRD, etching, roulette, 14⅝ x 11⅜
(4244/147)   2600
Foujita, Tsuguharu, LES ENFANTS, TWO BOYS, etching, roulette, 14½ x 11¼ (4244/146)   2600
Foujita, Tsuguharu, SLEEPING CAT, etching, roulette, 12¼ x 14¾ (4244/151)   4250
Foujita, Tsuguharu, WOMAN RESTING HER CHIN ON RIGHT HAND, roulette, soft ground, 15¼ x
13½ (4244/150)   2000
Frelaut, Jean, LE PONT DE VENSIN, drypoint, 5½ x 7⅛ (4270/200)   250
Friedlander, Johnny, COMPOSITION, lithograph, 30⅛ x 22½ (4270/202)   275
Gauguin, Paul, MAHANA ATUA, woodcut, 7⅛ x 8⅝, 1921 (4203/157)   1750
Gauguin, Paul, TE ARII VAHINE, woodcut, 6½ x 12⅜, ca1896 (4203/158)   375
Gauguin, Paul, TITRE DU SOURIRE (DECEMBER 1899), woodcut, 5½ x 8¾ (4270/204)   1500
Gauguin, Paul, TITRE DU SOURIRE, woodcut, 3¾ x 6½ (4270/203)   1300
Gavarni, Paul, PORTRAIT OF ALFRED DE MUSSET, lithograph, 13⅝ x 8¾ (4270/205)   80

Gerzso, Gunther, MUJER DE LA JUNGLA, 1974, lithograph, 27 x 20¾ (4105/161)   150
Gerzso, Gunther, T-4, color lithograph, 20 x 28½, 1974 (4118/178)   300
Gerzso, Gunther, T-4, 1974, lithograph, 20 x 28½ (4105/160)   250
Giacometti, Alberto, BUST I, lithograph, 14⅛ x 9⅛ (4270/206)   1600
Giacometti, Alberto, BUSTE II, lithograph, slight discoloration, 12⅝ x 8, 1960 (4118/179)   1900
Giacometti, Alberto, FIGURINES IN THE STUDIO, etching, 16½ x 11¾ (4270/209)   200
Giacometti, Alberto, INTERIOR WITH THE STOVE, etching, 8⅛ x 5⅝, frame, 1956 (4244/156)   600
Giacometti, Alberto, INTERIOR WITH THE STOVE, 1956, etching, 8⅛ x 5⅝ (4215/137)   700
Giacometti, Alberto, LA MAGIE QUOTIDIENNE, FIGURINES DANS L'ATELIER, etching, 16½ x 11,
    1966 (4244/158)   275
Giacometti, Alberto, LA MAGIE QUOTIDIENNE, YOUNG WOMAN, etching, 16½ x 11, 1966
    (4244/157)   300
Giacometti, Alberto, PERSONNAGE DANS L'ATELIER, lithograph, 21½ x 14⅛, frame, 1954
    (4244/155)   *2400*
Giacometti, Alberto, RIMBAUD VU PAR LES PEINTRES, 1962, etching, 11¾ x 9¾ (4215/138)   750
Giacometti, Alberto, STAMPA, lithograph, 18¼ x 16 (4270/207)   800
Giacometti, Alberto, STOOL AND PICTURE, etching, from LA DOUBLE VUE, 10 x 7⅞, 1964
    (4118/180)   1100
Giacometti, Alberto, THE ARTIST'S MOTHER AT THE WINDOW, 1964, lithograph, 22 x 14⅜
    (4215/134)   1300
Giacometti, Alberto, THE ARTIST'S MOTHER SEATED II, 1964, lithograph, 11⅛ x 8¾ (4215/136)   1000
Giacometti, Alberto, YOUNG WOMAN, etching, 16½ x 11 (4270/208)   150
Gleizes, Albert, KUBISTISCHE KOMPOSITION, lithograph, 14⅛ x 10½, 1921 (4244/159)   200
Gogh, Vincent Van, LE FUMEUR-L'HOMME A LA PIPE, etching, 7⅛ x 5⅞, 1890 (4118/181)   16500
Gottlieb, Adolph, COMPOSITION, 1972, aquatint, 23½ x 17¾ (4067/98)   375
Gottlob, Fernand Louis, 2e EXPOSITION DES PEINTRES LITHOGRAPHS, lithograph, 46¾ x 30⅝,
    1899 (4244/475)   700
Grasset, Eugene, CYCLES ET AUTOMOBILES, lithographic poster, 14½ x 20⅛ (4244/477)   650
Grasset, Eugene, JEANNE D'ARC, lithograph, 47 x 30⅜, 1889-90 (4244/476)   500
Griggs, Frederick L., STEPPING STONES, drypoint, 7¼ x 9¼ (4270/212)   300

Giacometti
(4244/155)

Helleu (4244/479)

Heckel (4244/165)

Guillaumin, Jean Baptiste Armand, LA CHARETTE, 1889, lithograph 10⅜ x 14⅝ (4067/102) — 450
Guston, Philip, THE STREET, 1970, lithograph, 19⅞ x 26⅜ (4215/141) — 175
Haden, Sir Francis Seymour, A SUNSET IN IRELAND, drypoint, 5½ x 8½ (4270/221) — 550
Haden, Sir Francis Seymour, KENSINGTON GARDENS, etching with drypoint, 8 x 5 (4270/220) — 110
Hamaguchi, Yozo, RED PIPE, lithograph 23⅞ x 18⅛, 1971 (4203/164) — 650
Hamaguchi, Yozo, TWENTY SIX CHERRIES, lithograph 23¾ x 18¼, 1971 (4203/163) — 700
Hartung, Hans, GRUNSCHWARZ, lithograph, 29⅞ x 22⅛ (4270/225) — 100
Hayter, Stanley William, COMPOSITION, engraving, 13½ x 13⅛, 1952 (4244/161) — 200
Hayter, Stanley William, COMPOSITION, engraving, 7¾ x 12⅛ (4270/233) — 150
Hayter, Stanley William, COMPOSITION, engraving, etching, aquatint, 13½ x 13⅛, 1952 (4244/160) — 300
Hayter, Stanley William, DIPTYCH, engraving, 13¾ x 8, 1968 (4244/162) — 375
Hayter, Stanley William, FLIGHT, engraving, 14⅞ x 9¾ (4270/232) — 550
Heckel, Eric, AM STAND, impression in third state, 16 x 10⅛ (4244/163) — 325
Heckel, Eric, DREIFRAVEN AM WASSER, woodcut, 15¾ x 12⅝, 1923 (4244/164) — 940
Heckel, Eric, REITER IN DEN BERGEN, woodcut, 25¼ x 18¾, 1960 (4244/165) — *350*
Heckel, Eric (1883-1970), BADENDE JUNGLINGE, lithograph, 18⅞ x 14½ (4247/144) — 1000
Heckel, Eric (1883-1970), GESCHWISTER, 2nd state from edition of 40, woodcut, 1913, 16⅜ x 12¼ (4247/146) — 1800
Heckel, Eric (1883-1970), MANNLICHES BILDNIS, lithograph, 1919, 14¾ x 12¾ (4247/145) — 1200
Helleu, Paul Cesar, (LADY WITH A BOA), drypoint, 21¼ x 13¼ (4244/480) — 750
Helleu, Paul Cesar, (LADY WITH PLUMED HAT), drypoint, 21½ x 13¼ (4244/478) — 750
Helleu, Paul Cesar, (PROFILE OF A LADY WITH FUR COLLAR AND HAT), drypoint, 22½ x 12 (4244/479) — *700*
Helleu, Paul Cesar, COMTESSE DE SAN MARTINO, drypoint, 22 x 13¾ (4215/156) — 700
Helleu, Paul Cesar, ED. SAGOT-ESTAMPES ET AFFICHES ILLUSTREES, lithograph, 41¾ x 29⅝ (4244/483) — 450
Helleu, Paul Cesar, GIRL WITH BLACK HAT AND FUR COLLAR, drypoint, 14⅞ x 9⅝ (4215/145) — 450
Helleu, Paul Cesar, GIRL WITH GREY PLUMED HAT, 1907, drypoint, 21½ x 13¼ (4215/144) — 650
Helleu, Paul Cesar, LADY IN FUR HAT AND STOLE, drypoint, 21½ x 13¼ (4215/153) — 500
Helleu, Paul Cesar, LADY WITH FUR BOA AND MUFF, 21⅞ x 13⅜, drypoint (4215/152) — 500
Helleu, Paul Cesar, LADY WITH HIGH LACE, drypoint, 21⅝ x 13¼ (4215/146) — 300
Helleu, Paul Cesar, LADY WITH PLUMED HAT, drypoint, 21½ x 13¼ (4067/107) — 200
Helleu, Paul Cesar, LITTLE SAILOR BOY, drypoint, 15¾ x 11⅞ (4215/155) — 575
Helleu, Paul Cesar, MEDITATION, drypoints, 21⅝ x 13⅝ (4215/148) — 225
Helleu, Paul Cesar, MLLE. TAYLOR, drypoint, 22½ x 13¼ (4215/150) — 400
Helleu, Paul Cesar, PORTRAIT OF A YOUNG WOMAN WITH FUR COLLAR, drypoint, 15½ x 11⅝ (4215/151) — 400
Helleu, Paul Cesar, RECLINING LADY IN FUR HAT, drypoint, 10⅞ x 15⅝ (4215/154) — 650
Helleu, Paul Cesar, SEATED LADY FACING RIGHT, drypoint, 23 x 13½ (4215/159) — 350
Helleu, Paul Cesar, SEATED LADY, drypoint, 16 x 10¼ (4215/158) — 325
Helleu, Paul Cesar, SEATED LADY, drypoint, 15½ x 11¾ (4215/157) — 275
Helleu, Paul Cesar, YOUNG GIRL WITH BOW, drypoint, 21¼ x 13⅜ (4215/162) — 525

Helleu, Paul Cesar, YOUNG GIRL WITH CLASPED HANDS, drypoint, 15⅝ x 11⅜ (4215/147) 225
Helleu, Paul Cesar, (WOMAN IN HIGH COLLAR FACING LEFT), drypoint, 21⅝ x 13¼ (4270/236) 300
Helleu, Paul Cesar, (WOMAN WITH FEATHERED BOA), drypoint, 20⅛ x 16⅛ (4270/237) 150
Helleu, Paul Cesar, (YOUNG WOMAN IN FEATHERED HAT AND LONG CAPE), drypoint, 16⅞ x 9⅛ (4270/238) 400
Helleu, Paul Cesar, TETE DE FEMME, drypoint, 14⅜ x 9⅞ (4270/239) 150
Helleu, Paul Cesar, WOMAN IN FEATHERED HAT AND HIGH NECK BLOUSE, drypoint, 22 x 13¾ (4270/235) 300
Herbin, Auguste, COMPOSITION, silkscreen, 18⅞ x 15 (4203/176) 175
Hernandz, Mateo, (MONKEY, CAMEL, ELEPHANT AND ZEBRA), lithograph, 14 x 10 (4270/241) 60
Hoch, Hannah, MINIATUREN, (set of sixteen), linoleum cuts, 12½ x 9 (4067/108) 450
Hockney, David, ARTIST AND MODEL, 98/100, etching, aquatint, 1974 (4226/266) 1700
Hockney, David, CAVAFY POEM ILLUSTRATIONS, OSSY AND MO, 4/75, etching, aquatint, 1966 (4226/263) 400
Hockney, David, CAVAFY POEM ILLUSTRATIONS, READY CLEANERS, 4/75, etching, aquatint, 1966 (4226/264) 275
Hockney, David, FRENCH SHOP, etching, 21⅛ x 18⅛ (4244/166) 725
Hockney, David, GRIMM'S FAIRY TALES ILLUSTRATIONS, THE LAKE, 77/100, etching, aquatint, 1964 (4226/265) 650
Hockney, David, JOE McDONALD (Gemini 717) 34/99, lithograph, 1976, 63 x 29½ (4226/267) 1300
Hockney, David, JUNGLE BOY, artist's proof, etching, aquatint, 1964, 15¾ x 19¼ (4226/262) 1800
Hockney, David, JUNGLE BOY, etching, 15¾ x 19¼ (4270/243) 1700
Holder, Ferdinand, FRUHLING, lithograph 26¾ x 17⅛ (4067/109) 650
Hundertwasser, Friedensreich, GOOD MORNING CITY BLEEDING TOWN, silkscreen, 33⅜ x 22⅛ (4244/172) 600
Hunt, William Holman, MOTHER AND CHILD, etching, 7½ x 10 (4270/246) 140
Isabey, Eugene, SOUVENIR DE BRETAGNE, lithograph, 10⅞ 7¾ (4270/252) 175
Jongkind, Joan Barthold, SORTIE DE LA MAISON COCHIN, etching, 6⅜ x 9⅝ (4270/259) 250
Kandinsky, Wassily, KLEINE WELTEN II, lithograph, 9⅞ x 8¼, 1922 (4244/174) 3200
Kandinsky, Wassily, KLEINE WELTEN II, 1922, lithograph, 9⅞ x 8¼ (4215/167) 4750
Kandinsky, Wassily, KLEINE WELTEN VII, 1922, lithograph, 10¾ x 9¼ (4215/168) 5000
Kandinsky, Wassily, KLEINE WELTON IX, drypoint, 9⅜ x 7¾ (4270/260) 1700
Kandinsky, Wassily (1866-1944), KLEINE WELTEN IX, edition of 230, drypoint, 1922, 9⅜ x 7¾ (4247/151) 1900
Kandinsky, Wassily (1866-1944), SCHWARZE LINIEN, 6/50, lithograph, 1924, 9¾ x 8½ (4247/152) 2200
Kirchner, Ernst Ludwig (1880-1938), DAME IM REGEN, lithograph, 1914, 16¼ x 12⅜ (4247/158) 6000
Kirchner, Ernst Ludwig (1880-1938), LEUCHTTURMZIMMER, second state, etching, 1913, 9⅞ x 8⅛ (4247/156) 1250
Kirchner, Ernst Ludwig (1880-1938), MARDERSTEIG, spotting, lithograph, 1920, 23½ x 20⅛ (4247/159) 8000
Kirchner, Ernst Ludwig (1880-1938), RUF DES TODES, before edition of 100, lithograph, 1934-5, 14⅝ x 15⅝ (4247/160) 2100
Klinger, Max, AMORUND PSYCHE, 1880, (Book), 13¾ x 9⅞ (4215/171) 1000
Klinger, Max, BRAMSPHANTASIE, DER BAUER DESSEN SAAT IN UNHEIL, AUFGEHT, etching, drypoint, 10⅜ x 3⅛ (4244/180) 500
Klinger, Max, BRAMSPHANTASIE, DIE KALTE HAND, etching, 6⅞ x 5¼ (4244/176) 2600
Klinger, Max, BRAMSPHANTASIE, FEST, etching, drypoint, 10 x 13¾ (4244/179) 3800
Klinger, Max, BRAMSPHANTASIE, IM GRASE, etching, aquatint, 10¾ x 5⅞ (4244/178) 1050
Klinger, Max, BRAMSPHANTASIE, LIEBESPAAR IM GEMACH, etching, aquatint, 10¾ x 7 (4244/177) 1000
Klinger, Max, VOM TODE-2 THEIL, ZEIT UND RUHM, etching, 17⅞ x 10⅞ (4244/182) 225
Kokoschka, Oscar, CHRISTUS AM OLBERG, lithograph, sheet 19⅞ x 15, 1916 (4147/144) 125
Kokoschka, Oskar, DAS PRINZIP, lithograph, 27½ x 17¼, framed (4244/184) 450
Kollwitz, Kathe, ARBEITEFRAU (MIT DEM OHRRING), etching, 13 x 9¾ (4270/271) 400
Kollwitz, Kathe, BROT, lithograph, 13¾ x 10¾ (4244/189) 1100
Kollwitz, Kathe, EIN WEBERAUFSTAND WEGERZUG, etching, 8⅜ x 11¾ (4270/268) 325
Kollwitz, Kathe, ENDE, etching, 9⅝ x 12 (4270/269) 400
Kollwitz, Kathe, KLEINES SELBSTBILDNIS, lithograph, 9 x 8¼, 1920 (4244/188) 2100
Kollwitz, Kathe, LOSBRUCH, etching, 20½ x 23½ (4270/270) 550
Kollwitz, Kathe, MUTTER MIT KIND AUF DEM ARM, lithograph, 13⅛ x 7⅜, frame, 1916 (4244/187) 3100
Kollwitz, Kathe, NACHDENKENDE FRAU, lithograph, 11⅜ x 10½ (4270/274) 800
Kollwitz, Kathe, SELBSTBILDINS, etching, 5½ x 4 (4270/273) 900
Kollwitz, Kathe, SELBSTBILDNIS, etching, soft ground, 5¼ x 4 (4244/186) 1100
Kollwitz, Kathe, SITZENDER MANNLICHER AKT, etching, 6¼ x 5 (4270/267) 375
Kollwitz, Kathe, TOD UND FRAU, etching, soft ground, 17½ x 17¼, framed, 1910 (4244/185) 2050
La Bisse, Felix, LASAINTE HERMANDAD, 1973, lithograph 23 x 18½ (4067/124) 50
Lange, Otto, CITYSCAPE, etching, 22 x 15⅛ (4244/196) 275
Lasansky, Mauricio, ESPANA, 1956, etching, 31⅞ x 20⅞ (4215/179) 1100

Lasansky, Mauricio, MY SON LEONARDO, etching, aquatint, engraving, 25½ x 16½, frame, 1959 (4244/197) 950
Laurencin, Marie, (BUSTE DE FEMME), lithograph, 8¼ x 5½ (4270/277) 400
Laurencin, Marie, (HEAD OF A WOMAN WITH PEARL NECKLACE), lithograph, 16½ x 12⅜ (4270/279) 550
Laurencin, Marie, (OUTDOOR SCENE WITH BIRDS AND DOG), lithograph, 7½ x 6¾ (4270/278) 225
Laurencin, Marie, (THREE WOMAN), lithograph, 13¼ x 10¾ (4270/280) 700
Laurencin, Marie, ALICE IN WONDERLAND, (6), lithograph, 9⅝ x 11⅜ (4215/180) 850
Laurencin, Marie, BALS DES PETITS LITS BLANCS, lithograph poster, 20 x 14¼, 1931 (4244/198) 700
Laurencin, Marie, MERMAID, etching, 4¾ x 6⅞ (4203/193) 325
Laurencin, Marie, PETIT BESTIAIRE, the book, eight etchings, 10¼ x 6⅛ (4244/199) 750
Laurencin, Marie, THE HUNT (AMAZONS), lithograph, 9⅞ x 13⅜, frame (4244/200) 1100
Laurencin, Marie, WOMAN WEARING HAT AND FUR COLLAR, lithograph, 12 x 7½ (4215/186) 450
Laurencin, Marie, YOUNG GIRL IN PLUMED HAT, PEARL NECKLACE WITH, PUPPYDOG, lithograph, 15⅜ x 11¼ (4215/184) 700
Laurencin, Marie, YOUNG GIRL WITH WREATH IN HER HAIR, lithograph, 12¼ x 9⅞ (4215/182) 700
Laurencin, Marie, YOUNG GIRL WITH WREATH IN HER HAIR, lithograph, 12⅝ x 9⅞ (4215/181) 1100
Laurencin, Marie, YOUNG WOMAN WITH HORSE AND DOG, lithograph, 11¼ x 8⅛ (4215/185) 500
Laurencin, Marie, YOUNG WOMAN WITH LONG HAIR, PINK BOW AND SCARF, lithograph, 13¼ x 10 (4215/183) 900
Leandre, Charles Lucien, LE ROI DE ROME, lithograph, 50¾ x 37 (4244/484) 350
Leger, Fernand, COMPOSITION SUR FOND, 1954, lithograph 17⅜ x 21⅝ (4067/128) 750
Leger, Fernand, FEMME SUR FOND JAUNE, lithograph, 16¼ x 13⅛ (4270/282) 550
Leger, Fernand, LES CONSTRUCTEURS, lithograph, 17 x 23⅛, frame, 1955 (4244/204) 1100
Leger, Fernand, TETE DE FEMME, lithograph, 22⅞ x 14, frame, 1949 (4244/202) 1700
Leger, Fernand, TETE DE FEMME, 1949, lithograph, 22⅞ x 14 (4215/196) 2100
Lehmbruck, Wilhelm, BRUSTBILD EINER FRAU, etching, 9½ x 7½, 1912 (4244/206) 400
Lepere, Auguste, BELLE MATINEE' D' AUTOMNE, etching, onion skin paper, 7⅜ x 11⅜, 1910 (4203/195) 100
Lepere, Auguste, LE PONT-NEUF, lithograph, on chine volant, 14⅛ x 18, 1913 (4203/196) 90
Lepere, Auguste, THE FARM WITH THE DUTCH POPLARS, etching, 11¾ x 14⅛, 1914 (4203/197) 130
Lewis, Martin, SPORTING GENTLEMAN, ca1929, drypoint, 5⅞ x 4⅞ (4215/197) 200
Libermann, Max, SELF-PORTRAIT, lithograph, 14¾ x 11⅝ (4270/302) 300
Lipchitz, Jacques, STANDING FIGURE, lithograph, in black on green-grey paper, 22¾ x 13⅝ (4203/208) 500
Lissitsky, El, COVER DESIGN FOR DUTCH PERIODICAL WENDINGEN, lithograph, 26⅜ x 13, 1921-22 (4244/210) 800
Lozowick, Louis, CITY ON A ROCK, 1931, lithograph 8¼ x 13 (4067/137) 225
Luce, Maximilien, LE PERCEMENT DE LA RUE REAUMUR, lithograph, 12¼ x 15⅞ (4244/212) 275
Luce, Maximilien, LE PORT DE ST-TROPEZ, lithograph, 10⅜ x 15¾ (4244/211) 800
Lurcat, Jean, (HARLEQUINADE), drypoint, 10 x 7⅞, ca1921 (4203/200) 175
Lurcat, Jean, ARLEQUIN DIPLOMATE, aquatint, 10¼ x 7 (4270/312) 175
Magritte, Rene, LES MOYENS D'EXISTENCE, 1967, etching and aquatint, 6⅜ x 4⅜ (4215/201) 400
Maillol, Aristide, BACCHANTE, soft ground etching, 6⅞ x 5¼, 1926 (4203/213) 200
Maillol, Aristide, DEUX FEMMES S'ETREIGNANT, lithograph, 7¾ x 9¼ (4244/213) 600
Manet, Edouard, JEANNE, LE PRINTEMPS, etching and aquatint, 6⅛ x 4¼ (4270/314) 400
Manet, Edouard, LES PETITS CAVALIERS, etching, 10⅞ x 15⅜ (4270/313) 400
Manet, Edouard, LES PETITS CAVALIERS, 1860, etching and drypoint, 9⅝ x 15⅛ (4215/202) 1500
Manet, Edouard, ODALISQUE, 1884, etching and aquatint, 5 x 7⅞ (4215/203) 375
Marcoussis, Louis, EAUX-FORTES POUR ALCOOLS, SIGNE, etching, 6⅛ x 3¾ (4244/220) 500
Marcoussis, Louis, ENFANCE, etching, 9⅜ x 8, 1930 (4244/216) 600
Marcoussis, Louis, GABY, 1912, drypoint, 7⅜ x 5½ (4215/204) 4000
Marcoussis, Louis, IGOR MARKEVITCH, drypoint, 15⅜ x 9¾, framed (4244/221) 250
Marcoussis, Louis, LA TABLE, etching, 9½ x 7⅛, 1930 (4244/215) 2900
Marcoussis, Louis, LES DEVINS, L'ASTROLOGUE, 1940, drypoint, 7⅞ x 7¾ (4215/205) 325
Marcoussis, Louis, LES DEVINS, LE NUMERALISTE, 1940, drypoint, 7⅞ x 7¾ (4215/208) 400
Marcoussis, Louis, LES DEVINS, LE PENDULE, 1940, drypoint, 8 x 7⅞ (4215/206) 1100
Marcoussis, Louis, LES DEVINS, LES OSSELETS, 1940, drypoint, 8 x 7¾ (4215/207) 350
Marden, Brice, ADRIATICS GRIDS II, 1973, etching, 23 x 13¾ (4067/139) 150
Marden, Brice, ADRIATICS GRIDS IV, 1973, etching, 23¾ x 28 (4067/140) 175
Marini, Marino, ACROBAT, lithograph, 24 x 18½, frame (4244/223) 1100
Marini, Marino, CAVALIER AU BONNET POINTU, etching, 14¼ x 17⅜, frame (4244/226) 300
Marini, Marino, CAVALIER NOIR, lithograph, 22⅝ x 18¾ (4270/322) 250
Marini, Marino, CAVALIER SUR FOND OCRE, lithograph, 24⅝ x 18 (4270/319) 200
Marini, Marino, CHENALIER ROUGE ET NOIR, 1955, lithograph, 23½ x 16⅝ (4215/213) 450
Marini, Marino, CHEVAUX ET CAVALIERS PLATE, 1972, lithograph, 15 x 19½ (4215/217) 350
Marini, Marino, COMPOSITION (THREE FIGURES), 1950, etching and drypoint, 17⅜ x 15⅜ (4215/211) 250

Marini (4244/225)

Marini, Marino, GUERRIERO, 1968, lithograph, 12⅞ x 19½ (4215/216)   270
Marini, Marino, HOMMAGE TO MARINI, lithograph, 12¾ x 19¾ (4147/166)   100
Marini, Marino, HORSE AND RIDER ON VIOLET GROUND WITH RED BORDER, 1954, lithograph,
    24½ x 17 (4215/212)   475
Marini, Marino, HORSE AND RIDER, lithograph, 12¾ x 19⅞ (4215/219)   325
Marini, Marino, HORSE AND RIDER, 1956, lithograph, 15½ x 12¼ (4215/214)   425
Marini, Marino, IDEA E SPAZIO GUERRIERO, 1963, aquatint, 15⅝ x 11¾ (4215/215)   475
Marini, Marino, IL GRIDO, lithograph, 21¼ x 30¼ (4270/321)   500
Marini, Marino, LE SACRE DU PRINTEMPS, lithograph, 12⅜ x 9⅞, 1973 (4244/225)   *200*
Marini, Marino, PERSONNAGES DU SACRE DU PRINTEMPS, lithograph, 20½ x 15½ (4147/167)   225
Marini, Marino, PERSONNAGES DU SACRE DU PRINTEMPS, 1974, lithograph, 20⅝ x 15½
    (4215/218)   400
Marini, Marino, RECLINING HORSE, lithograph 12¾ x 19¾ (4067/145)   250
Marini, Marino, TETE D'HOMME, ca1950, aquatint, 17⅛ x 13¾ (4215/235)   2400
Marini, Marino, TETE D'HOMME, TOURNEE A GAUCHE, ca1950, aquatint, 17⅛ x 13¾ (4215/233)   2300
Marini, Marino, TETE DE FACE, ca1950, aquatint, 17¼ x 13¾ (4215/234)   2600

Marisol, PNOM PENH, ONE, etching, 23¼ x 17¾, frame, 1970 (4244/227)	150
Masson, Andre, (COMPOSITION WITH TOWER OF BABEL), etching, 17⅞ x 13¾ (4244/231)	250
Masson, Andre, (FIGURE WITH HEAVENS), etching, 19⅝ x 12¾ (4244/232)	175
Masson, Andre, COMPOSITION, aquatint, 13½ x 10, 1960 (4244/228)	125
Masson, Andre, COMPOSITION, lithograph, 12¼ x 9½ (4270/327)	125
Masson, Andre, COMPOSITION, lithograph, 24½ x 18½ (4270/326)	125
Masson, Andre, COMPOSITION,drypoint, 11¾ x 13¼ (4244/229)	200
Masson, Andre, LE RUISSEAU, lithograph 22⅝ x 12 (4067/148)	175
Masson, Andre, THE COUPLE, lithograph, 19¾ x 13½ (4244/234)	100
Matisse, Henri, (FEMME NUE ASSISE), drypoint, 8 x 4¾, frame (4244/243)	4250
Matisse, Henri, BUSTE DE FEMME A'LA FRANGE, 1914, lithograph, 19¾ x 12⅞ (4215/221)	2900
Matisse, Henri, BUSTE DE JEUNE FILLE AUX CHEVEUX LONG'S, lithograph, 7⅜ x 5 (4270/329)	1200
Matisse, Henri, DANSEUSE AU TABOURET, 1927, lithograph, 18 x 11 (4215/225)	3720
Matisse, Henri, FIGURE SUR FOND TAPIS AFRICAIN, lithograph, 21 x 17, frame, 1935 (4244/241)	4750
Matisse, Henri, JEUNE FILLE REGARDANT UN AQUARIUM, 1929, etching, 4⅞ x 6⅝ (4215/227)	3250
Matisse, Henri, LE REPOS DU MODELE, lithograph, 8⅝ x 12, 1924 (4147/175)	1000
Matisse, Henri, LE REPOS DU MODELE, lithograph, 8¾ x 12¾, framed, 1924 (4244/236)	3000
Matisse, Henri, NU ALLONGE AU COLLIER, etching, 5 x 7, frame, 1929 (4244/242)	2000
Matisse, Henri, NU ALLONGE LA TETE LEVEE, 1925, lithograph, 10 x 18⅝ (4215/224)	3250
Matisse, Henri, NU RENVERSE ET TABLE I, lithograph, 21⅝ x 17⅞, frame, 1929 (4244/238)	5750
Matisse, Henri, ODALISQUE SUR UN BANQUETTE, lithograph, 17¾ x 21½, frame, 1929 (4244/240)	10000
Matisse, Henri, STANDING NUDE WITH ARMS FOLDED, lithograph, 17¾ x 11, 1906, frame (4244/235)	3000
Matisse, Henri, TETE D'ODALISQUE, lithograph, 20⅛ x 13⅝, framed, 1929 (4244/239)	3000
Matisse, Henri, TETE DE FACE, aquatint, 17⅛ x 13¾, frame (4244/247)	1700
Matisse, Henri, TETE DE FEMME, TOURNEE A GAUCHE, ca1950, aquatint, 17½ x 13¾ (4215/231)	4000
Matisse, Henri, TETE DE JEUNE FILLE DE FACE, 1923, lithograph, 8 x 5¾ (4215/222)	2300
Matisse, Henri, TETE TOURNEE A DROITE, aquatint, 12⅜ x 9¾ (4215/230)	2400
Matisse, Henri, VASE DE FLEURS, 1938, linoleum cut, 7⅞ x 9 (4215/228)	4000
Matisse, Henri, VISAGE, aquatint, 17⅛ x 13¾ (4215/232)	2300
Matisse, Henri, WOMAN WITH SCALLOPPED COLLAR, lithograph, 14 x 8⅞ (4215/229)	1800
Matta, Roberto, AFTER THE NUREMBERG TRIAL, etching and aquatint, 16½ x 21⅝ (4270/331)	100
Matta, Roberto, COMPOSITION, lithograph, 19⅞ x 25 (4270/342)	125
Matta, Roberto, EMOSPHERAL, etching, aquatint, 14⅛ x 21¼, 1973 (4244/252)	250
Matta, Roberto, FEUILLES OUVERTES, etching aquatint, 22½ x 16⅜, 1971, framed (4244/249)	300
Matta, Roberto, FIGURE 1, 1968, etching and aquatint, 21½ x 13⅞ (4215/239)	175
Matta, Roberto, FLUTE ET FLUTISTES, 1969, etching and aquatint, 21⅛ x 16⅜ (4215/240)	325
Matta, Roberto, JAZZ BANDE, etching, aquatint, 14¾ x 19¼, frame, 1973 (4244/251)	450
Matta, Roberto, L'EXCITATEUR, lithograph, 17⅞ x 22⅞ (4270/340)	125
Matta, Roberto, LES PARNNOS, 1967, etching and aquatint, 19¼ x 25⅜ (4215/238)	300
Matta, Roberto, LES SUISSIDES, aquatint, 16¼ x 21¾ (4270/333)	100
Matta, Roberto, PASSAGE ET SAGE DU COUPLE, 1964, aquatint, 11 x 14½ (4215/236)	200
Matta, Roberto, PERSONNAGE VERTE, 1972, etching and aquatint, 9⅝ x 7¼ (4215/241)	175
Matta, Roberto, PERSONNAGES, 1966, aquatint, 16⅞ x 19½ (4215/237)	200
Matta, Roberto, SI NON TI TUMBO TI MASO, 1974, etching, 14 x 11¾ (4067/153)	175
Matta, Roberto, UN AUTRE APRES, 1973, etching and aquatint, 14⅛ x 11 (4215/242)	325
Matta, Roberto, VA-RIANTE, etching, aquatint, 19¾ x 14¾, framed (4244/253)	325
Matta, Roberto, VIVANTE MORTALITE, etching and aquatint, 11¾ x 8½ (4270/336)	125
McBey, James, VENICE HARBOR, etching, 7 x 14⅞ (4270/343)	275
Mecksepper, Friedrich, SECHS KUGELN, mixed media, 19½ x 15⅜ (4270/344)	325
Merida, Carlos, DANCES OF MEXICO (Portfolio of 10), lithographs, each 16¾ x 12½ (4105/134)	1100
Merida, Carlos, MEXICAN COSTUME (Portfolio of 25), 1941, silkscreens, each 16 x 13 (4105/135)	950
Merida, Carlos, POPUH-VUH (Portfolio of 10), 1943, lithographs, each 15⅜ x 12⅜ (4105/136)	1100
Meryon, Charles, LA MORGUE, 1854, etching, 9⅛ x 8⅛ (4215/243)	3000
Meryon, Charles, LA POMPE NOTRE-DAME, PARIS, etching, 6⅞ x 10, framed, 1852 (4244/258)	500
Meryon, Charles, LE MINISTERE DE LA MARINE, PARIS, etching, drypoint, 6⅝ x 5¾, 1865 (4203/220)	550
Meryon, Charles, LE STRYGE, etching, drypoint, 6⅞ x 5⅛, 1853 (4203/219)	500
Meryon, Charles, LE TOUR DE L'HORLOGE, PARIS, etching and drypoint, 10½ x 7½ (4270/345)	550
Meyers, Jerome, STANDING PEASANT WOMAN, etching in clors, 8 x 2¾ (4203/222)	250
Millet, Jean Francois, LA BOUILLIE, etching, 8⅜ x 6¼ (4270/350)	450
Millet, Jean Francois, LA COUSEUSE, etching, 4¼ x 3 (4270/348)	450
Millet, Jean Francois, LA FILEUSE AUVERGNATE, etching, 7⅞ x 5¼, 1869 (4203/225)	650
Millet, Jean Francois, LA FILEUSE AUVERGNATE, etching, 7¾ x 5⅛ (4244/259)	550
Millet, Jean Francois, LE DEPART POUR LE TRAVAIL, etching and drypoint, 15⅛ x 12 (4270/351)	3700
Millet, Jean Francois, LES BECHEURS, etching, 9¼ x 13¼ (4215/244)	1900
Millet, Jean Francois, LES GLANEUSES, etching, 7½ x 10 (4270/349)	2900

Millet, Jean Francois, LES GLANEUSES, etching, in bistre, 7½ x 10 (4203/223) — 1500
Milton, Peter, COLLECTING WITH RUDI, mixed media, 19¾ x 29¼ (4270/353) — 800
Milton, Peter, RETURN, etching, 12 x 17½ (4270/352) — 300
Milton, Peter, THE FIRST GATE, photosensitive-ground etching, aquatint, 19 x 30⅞, 1974 (4244/262) — 750
Milton, Peter, THE JOLLY CORNER, PLATE 1, etching, aquatint, 10 x 14¾, 1971 (4244/261) — 225
Miro, Joan, AFFICHE POUR L'EXPOSITION MIRO, lithograph, 23¼ x 17¾, 1962 (4244/274) — 750
Miro, Joan, ALBUM 19, PLATE 9, lithograph, 26¼ x 20⅛, 1961 (4147/183) — 300
Miro, Joan, ANTHOLOGIE DE L'HUMOUR NOIR, 1950, lithograph, 9 x 6¼ (4215/246) — 1800
Miro, Joan, BAGUE D'AURORE, TABLE DES EAUX-FORTES, etching, 11⅞ x 8, 1958 (4203/227) — 700
Miro, Joan, BETHSABEE, aquatint, 26⅞ x 21⅛, frame, 1972 (4244/286) — 2000
Miro, Joan, BOUQUET DE REVES POUR NEILA, lithograph, 6⅛ x 9¼ (4270/363) — 450
Miro, Joan, BOUQUET DE REVES POURNEILA, lithograph, 12 x 8½ (4270/362) — 450
Miro, Joan, CERCLE FRANCHI, lithograph, 20⅞ x 28¼ (4270/357) — 750
Miro, Joan, CHAVAUCHEE-BRUN, lithograph, 33½ x 23⅝ (4270/359) — 900
Miro, Joan, COMPOSITION, lithograph, 23 x 18⅛ (4147/188) — 1000
Miro, Joan, COMPOSITION, lithograph, 35¼ x 24¼, 1969 (4147/184) — 800
Miro, Joan, COMPOSITION FOR MIRO LITHOGRAPHE II, lithograph, 12 x 9½, 1974 (4244/292) — 700
Miro, Joan, COMPOSITION FOR MIRO LITHOGRAPHE II, 1974, lithograph, 17¾ x 14½ (4215/274) — 600
Miro, Joan, COMPOSITION FOR MIRO LITHOGRAPHE II, 1974, lithograph, 17¾ x 24¼ (4215/275) — 900
Miro, Joan, COMPOSITION FROM ALBUM, 1948, lithograph, 15 x 7⅛ (4215/245) — 1400
Miro, Joan, COMPOSITION WITH MAN WALKING, 1970, lithograph, 29⅞ x 22 (4215/269) — 1000
Miro, Joan, COMPOSITION, aquatint, 17½ x 25¾ (4215/278) — 950
Miro, Joan, COMPOSITION, lithograph, 34⅞ x 24⅜ (4215/273) — 900
Miro, Joan, COMPOSITION, lithograph, 17½ x 14¼ (4244/293) — 750
Miro, Joan, COMPOSITION, lithograph, 60 x 12¾ (4270/356) — 400
Miro, Joan, CORTESAN GROTESQUE, aquatint, drypoint, 16⅜ x 22⅞, 1974 (4203/229) — 450
Miro, Joan, COUPLE D'OISEUX I, 1966, etching and aquatint, 22¾ x 36¼ (4215/259) — 2100
Miro, Joan, COURTISAN GROTESQUE, aquatint and drypoint, 16⅜ x 22⅞ (4270/365) — 500
Miro, Joan, COURTISAN GROTESQUE, aquatint and drypoint, 16⅜ x 22⅞ (4270/366) — 450
Miro, Joan, COURTISAN GROTESQUE, aquatint, drypoint, 16⅜ x 22⅞, 1974 (4203/228) — 550
Miro, Joan, DEFILE DE MANNEQUINS A BAHIA, ca1969, lithograph, 47¼ x 31⅝ (4215/267) — 2800
Miro, Joan, EL PI DE FORMENTOR PLATE 1, 1976, aquatint, 34⅞ x 29½ (4215/279) — 2600
Miro, Joan, EXPOSITION 'CARTONS', lithograph, 25¼ x 18½, 1965 (4147/186) — 400
Miro, Joan, EXPOSITION SOBRETEIXIMAS, lithograph, 33¾ x 23¼ (4270/367) — 1100

Miro (4215/259)

Miro, Joan, EXPOSITION XXII SALON DE MAI, lithograph, 26⅝ x 20½ (4270/368) — 1000
Miro, Joan, FEMME AU MIROIR, 1956, lithograph, 15⅜ x 22¼ (4215/248) — 6500
Miro, Joan, FEMME-OISEAU I, softground, aquatint, 13½ x 18¼, 1960 (4244/272) — 900

Miro, Joan, FIGURE WITH A RED SUN II, 1950, lithograph, 25¼ x 19¾ (4215/247) — 2600
Miro, Joan, FUSEE (COMPOSITION V), aquatint, 5¾ x 16¼, 1959 (4244/270) — 950
Miro, Joan, FUSEE, aquatint, 5⅛ x 7⅛, frame, 1959 (4244/271) — 850
Miro, Joan, FUSEE, 1959, aquatint, 5⅛ x 7 (4215/252) — 1100
Miro, Joan, GRAND DUC I, 1965, etching and aquatint, 35⅜ x 25 (4215/257) — 2600
Miro, Joan, GRAND DUC II, 1965, etching, 26⅞ x 20¾ (4215/258) — 1900
Miro, Joan, HAI-KU, TOUTE NUIT DESORMAIS, lithograph, 10½ x 7¾, 1967 (4244/279) — 800
Miro, Joan, HOMAGE A PISCASSO, 1972, aquatint, 9⅜ x 17¼ (4215/270) — 1100
Miro, Joan, HOMENTAGE A JOAN PRATS, PLATE 15, lithograph, 21½ x 29⅜, frame, 1971 (4244/285) — 1100
Miro, Joan, HOMENTAGE A JOAN PRATS, PLATE 9, frame, 21½ x 29⅜, frame, 1971 (4244/284) — 2100
Miro, Joan, HOMMAGE A JOAN PRATS, 1972, lithograph 29½ x 22⅞ (4067/160) — 850
Miro, Joan, JAILLIE DU CALCAIRE, lithograph, 12⅝ x 9⅞, frame, 1972 (4244/288) — 700
Miro, Joan, L'ENFANCE D 'UBU, lithograph in colors, 9⅞ x 14⅝, 1976 (4203/232) — 400
Miro, Joan, L'ENFANCE D'UBU I, 1975, lithograph, 10¼ x 16 (4215/276) — 500
Miro, Joan, L'ENFANCE D'UBU VIII, 1975, lithograph, 11 x 15⅜ (4215/277) — 550
Miro, Joan, L'EXILE VERT, 1969, etching and carborundum, 40⅝ x 27⅝ (4215/262) — 2900
Miro, Joan, L'INVITEE DU DIMANCHE, FOND NOIR, etching, 23½ x 39 (4244/281) — 2000
Miro, Joan, LA BAGUE D'AURORE, 1957, aquatint, 4½ x 5½ (4067/156) — 900
Miro, Joan, LA BAQUE D'AURORE, aquatint, 5½ x 4½, frame, 1957 (4244/269) — 1200
Miro, Joan, LA CALEBASSE, aquatint, carborundum, 39¾ x 27¾, frame, 1969 (4244/280) — 3250
Miro, Joan, LA FEMME ANGORA, 1969, etching, aquatint, carborundum, 41½ x 27⅜ (4215/263) — 4500
Miro, Joan, LA NUIT, lithograph, 15⅜ x 11, frame, 1953 (4244/267) — 2200
Miro, Joan, LE COURTISAN GROTESQUE, 1974, 16⅜ x 20¼, drypoint, aquatint (4225/162) — 1700
Miro, Joan, LE COURTISAN GROTESQUE, 1974, 16½ x 22⅝, drypoint, aquatint (4225/163) — 2200
Miro, Joan, LE GRAND CARNASSIER, etching, aquatint, carborundum, 40 x 27⅜ (4215/264) — 2600
Miro, Joan, LE JOUR, lithograph, 15¼ x 11, frame, 1953 (4244/266) — 2000
Miro, Joan, LE LEZARD AUX PLUMES D'OR, lithograph, 13¾ x 19½, frame (4244/278) — 1800
Miro, Joan, LE MAGNETISEUR FOND BLANC, lithograph, 31½ x 23 (4270/361) — 1600
Miro, Joan, LE PELER IN DE COMPOSTELLE, lithograph, 20⅞ x 17 (4270/360) — 1500
Miro, Joan, LE PORTEUR D'EAU II, 1962, aquatint, 22¼ x 29¼ (4215/254) — 1000
Miro, Joan, LE PROPHETE LA NUIT, etching, 27 x 20¾, 1965 (4244/276) — 1600
Miro, Joan, LE SAMOURAI, 1968, aquatint and carborundum, 30 x 17⅜ (4215/261) — 4750
Miro, Joan, LEDAME AUX DAMIERS, 1969, lithograph, 27½ x 18¾ (4215/265) — 1400
Miro, Joan, LEJARDIN DE MOUSSEE, 1968, aquatint and carborundum, 15¾ x 18¼ (4215/260) — 2800
Miro, Joan, LES COQUILLAGES, 1969, lithograph, 30¾ x 45¼ (4215/266) — 2500
Miro, Joan, LITHOGRAPH FOR THE COUNTY MUSEUM OF ART, L.A., lithograph, 24½ x 18¼, frame, 1969 (4244/283) — 1350
Miro, Joan, LITTLE GIRL SKIPPING ROPE, etching, aquatint, 11¾ x 8⅞, 1947 (4244/264) — 2500
Miro, Joan, MIRO A L'ENCRE II, 1972, lithograph, 14 x 10 (4215/271) — 800
Miro, Joan, MURDEROUS LANDSCAPE, etching, 16 x 11½, frame, 1938 (4244/263) — 2800
Miro, Joan, OISEAU LUNE JAUNE, aquatint, 22½ x 31⅛, 1963 (4147/189) — 1100

Miro
(4215/257)

Moore (4244/296)

Miro, Joan, OISEAU MONGOL, aquatint, carborundum, 41⅜ x 27½, frame (4244/282)   3250
Miro, Joan, OUVRAGE DU VENT III, 8½ x 22⅞ (4067/157)   850
Miro, Joan, PARTIE DE CAMPAGNE III, etching and aquatint, 22⅞ x 36⅜, 1967 (4147/190)   1700
Miro, Joan, POSTER FOR THE MUSEE NATIONALE D'ART MODERNE, lithograph, 23½ x 17¾
(4270/355)   650
Miro, Joan, ROUGE ET BLEU, 1960, lithograph, 22⅞ x 14¾ (4215/253)   1200
Miro, Joan, SCARABEE, lithograph 13⅞ x 19½ (4067/161)   650
Miro, Joan, SCULPTURESQUE, lithograph in colors, 7½ x 15, 1975 (4203/231)   550
Miro, Joan, SERIE BARCELONE, PLATE 7, aquatint, 41⅜ x29½, frame, 1972-73 (4244/287)   3000
Miro, Joan, SERIE II FOUGE ET VERT, lithograph, 17½ x 23¾ (4270/354)   750
Miro, Joan, SIGNES ET METEORES, 1958, lithograph, 17 x 19¼ (4215/249)   2000
Miro, Joan, SOLEIL NOYE II, 1962, aquatint, 8⅝ x 23 (4215/255)   1200
Miro, Joan, TERRE ATTEINTE ET SOLEIL INTACT, 1973, aquatint, 26¾ x 21 (4215/272)   2500
Miro, Joan, TERRES DE GRAND FEU, lithograph, 26¾ x 20⅛, 1956 (4147/185)   450
Miro, Joan, TRACE SUR LA PAROI I, aquatint, 23 x 36½, frame, 1967 (4244/277)   4250
Miro, Joan, TRACE SUR PAROI II, 1967, etching, 23 x 36½ (4067/159)   3100
Miro, Joan, UBU AUX BALEARES X, lithograph in colors, 18¾ x 24¾, 1974 (4203/230)   550
Miro, Joan, UBU AUX BALEARES, lithograph, 19¾ x 26 (4270/364)   550
Moore, Henry, FOUR MOTHERS, etching, 12 x 9¼ (4270/371)   700
Moore, Henry, FOUR STANDING WOMEN, 9⅛ x 15⅞ (4270/373)   400
Moore, Henry, IDEAS FOR SCULPTURE, etching, 12¼ x 9½ (4270/370)   325
Moore, Henry, INTERIOR SETTING I, RECLINGING FIGURE, lithograph, 9½ x 12⅜ (4244/296)   *700*
Moore, Henry, MINERVA PROMETHEUS AND PANDORA, 1950, lithograph, 11¾ x 9⅜ (4215/282)   950
Moore, Henry, SEATED FIGURE, lithograph, in colors, 11⅜ x 8½, 1950 (4203/233)   1100
Moore, Henry, STANDING AND RECLINING, 1950, lithograph, 11⅝ x 9½ (4215/281)   1300
Moore, Henry, THREE RECLINING FIGURES, WITH WATER IN THE BACKGROUND, lithograph, 15
x 19¼, 1973 (4244/295)   700
Moore, Henry, THREE STANDING FIGURES, 1966, lithograph, 8 x 7¼ (4215/283)   325
Moore, Henry, TWO BLACK FORMS, METAL FIGURES, lithograph, 12⅝ x 10¼ (4270/372)   200
Morandi, Giorgio, NATURA MORTA CON LA TAZZINA BIANCA A SINISTRA, etching, 7⅜ x 11⅜,
frame (4244/297)   *6000*
Morandi, Giorgio, NATURA MORTA CON VASETTO E TRE BOTTIGLIE, etching, 6⅞ x 5¼, frame,
1945 (4244/298)   5750
Mucha, Alphonse, LA TOSCA, lithograph, 38⅜ x 12⅝, frame, 1899 (4244/486)   1400
Mueller, Otto (1874-1930), SITZENDES UND ZWEI LIEGENDE MADCHEN IM GRAS, lithograph,
1922, 23/70, 12½ x 17¼ (4247/161)   3900
Muller, Albert, L'ESCAR POLLETE, 1904, drypoint and roulette, 25⅜ x 17⅜ (4215/284)   250
Munakata, Shiko, (NUDE WITH PET BIRD), woodcut, inkwash, 16 x 12⅜, frame, 1958 (4244/299) 1800
Munakata, Shiko, (SEATED BUDDHA AND TWO SAINTS), woodcut, 18⅛ x 18½, frame (4244/300) 2800
Munakata, Shiko, NUDE WITH PET BIRD, 1958, woodcut, 16 x 12⅜ (4215/285)   1700
Munch, Edvard, MUTTERGLUCK, 1902, drypoint, 15 x 10¾ (4067/164)   2500

Morandi (4244/297)

Munch, Edvard (1863-1944), ALFA AND OMEGA, DER BAR, crease, lithograph, 1909, 9½ x 16⅛ (4247/168) — 1200

Munch, Edvard (1863-1944), DAS MADCHEN UND DER TOD, mat stain, drypoint, 12 x 8¾ (4247/162) — 8500

Munch, Edvard (1863-1944), DAS WEIB-DIE SPHINX, lithograph, 1899, 18⅛ x 23½ (4247/165) — 23000

Munch, Edvard (1863-1944), DER GARTEN BEI NACHT, tears, etching, aquatint, 1902, 19½ x 25⅜ (4247/166) — 1600

Munch, Edvard (1863-1944), DER KUSS, tear, creases, woodcut, 1902, 18¾ x 18¼ (4247/164) — 40000

Munch, Edvard (1863-1944), LOWENGRUPPE, scratches, 11¼ x 19½, hand colored lithograph, 1912 (4247/170) — 4000

Munch, Edvard (1863-1944), MADCHEN AUF EINER LANDUNGSBRUCKE, third state, etching, 1903, 7⅜ x 10¼ (4247/167) — 8500

Munch, Edvard (1863-1944), THE WEDDING OF THE BOHEMIAN, tear, lithograph, after 1920, 13½ x 19½ (4247/169) — 5000

Munch, Edvard (1863-1944), TRIAL BY FIRE-THE ORDEAL, woodcut, 1927-31, 18⅛ x 14¾ (4247/171) — 10500

Nevelson, Louise, COLLEGIATE SCHOOL, plexiglass, 9⅛ x 8½ (4270/383) — 500

Nevelson, Louise, THE GREAT WALL, collage, 23½ x 17½ (4270/382) — 500

Nolde, Emil (1867-1956), DOPPELBILDNIS, 115/150, mat stain, woodcut, 1937, 12⅜ x 9 (4247/175) — 3500

Nolde, Emil (1867-1956), FRAUENKOPF, numbered 3, edition of 20, 7⅞ x 6⅛, etching, aquatint, 1905-6 (4247/172) — 1800

Nolde, Emil (1867-1956), IM SCHAUKELSTUHL, numbered 8, edition 20, foxing, etching, aquatint, 1906, 6 x 7¾ (4247/174) — 2000

Nolde, Emil (1867-1956), NACH DEM PFERDEMARKT, first state of three, aquatint, etching, 1906, 6 x 7⅝ (4247/173) — 1600

Nuillard, Edouard, PORTRAIT DE CEZANNE, lithograph 9⅞ x 9½ (4067/244) — 225

O'Higgins, Pablo, DOCKWORKERS, lithograph, 11¾ x 14¾ (4105/132) — 175

Orozco, Jose Clemente, BROTHEL, 1935, lithograph, 12 x 15½ (4215/290) — 800

Orozco, Jose Clemente, CASA ARRUINADA, 1928, lithograph, 12⅝ x 17½ (4105/109) — 400

Orozco, Jose Clemente, DEMENTED, 1944, aquatint, 10⅜ x 6¾ (4215/291) — 300

Orozco, Jose Clemente, DESOCUPADO (THE UNEMPLOYED), lithograph, 14⅜ x 10½, 1932 (4244/308) — 400

Orozco, Jose Clemente, EL CAMPESINO, lithograph, 11⅞ x 9⅞, 1926 (4244/305) — 550

Orozco, Jose Clemente, LA FAMILIA, 1926, lithograph, 10½ x 14¾ (4105/108) — 1200

Orozco, Jose Clemente, MAGUAYES Y NOPALES, lithograph, 12 x 17, 1928 (4147/204) — 650

Orozco, Jose Clemente, MANOS, 1928, lithograph, 16¾ x 8½ (4105/107) — 475

Orozco, Jose Clemente, PAISAJE MEXICANA, lithograph, 12¾ x 17¼, frame, 1930 (4244/307) — *550*

Orozco, Jose Clemente, PROMETEO, drypoint, 8⅞ x 6½, 1935 (4147/205) — 75

Orozco, Jose Clemente, PULQUERIA (MASKED DANCERS), lithograph, 12¾ x 16⅜ (4270/390) — 400

Orozco, Jose Clemente, PULQUERIA, 1928, lithograph, 12¾ x 16⅛ (4105/110) — 900

Orozco, Jose Clemente, REQUIEM, 1928, lithograph, 11⅞ x 15⅞ (4215/288) — 1200

Orozco, Jose Clemente, SOLDADERA (SOLDIER'S WIFE), lithograph, 15¾ x 10, 1926 (4244/304) — 650

Orozco, Jose Clemente, SOLDADERA (SOLDIER'S WIFE), lithograph, 15¾ x 10 (4270/389) — 450

Orozco, Jose Clemente, SOLDADERAS (MEXICAN ·SOLDIERS), lithograph, 11 x 17⅞, 1928
  (4244/306)   700
Orozco, Jose Clemente, THE UNEMPLOYED - PARIS 1932, 1932, lithograph, 14½ x 10½
  (4215/289)   450
Orozco, Jose Clemente, THREE GENERATIONS, 1926, lithograph, 10½ x 14¾ (4215/286)   900
Orozco, Jose Clemente, ZAPATISTAS, lithograph, 13 x 16⅜, 1936 (4244/309)   1000
Palmer, Samuel, THE EARLY PLOUGHMAN, 1861, etching, 5¼ x 7⅞ (4215/292)   200
Palmer, Samuel, THE MORNING LIFE, 1860, etching, 5¾ x 8⅜ (4215/293)   1200
Panko, Otto, LEUCHTTURM, etching, 9 x 12¼ (4270/394)   80
Pascin, Jules, BROTHEL SCENE, drypoint, roulette and aquatint, 12¾ x 9⅝ (4147/212)   375
Pascin, Jules, ENCORE L'ENFANT PRODIGUE, drypoint, 13¼ x 18¾ (4270/397)   375
Pascin, Jules, L'ENFANT PRODIGUE, drypoint and roulette, 12 x 18¾ (4147/213)   275
Pascin, Jules, YOUNG WOMAN IN A GREEN SHIFT, etching, aquatint, drypoint, 20¾ x 16⅜
  (4147/211)   1500
Pasmore, Victor, COMPOSITION, aquatint, in colors, 25 x 17¾, 1971 (4147/214)   175
Pearlstein, Philip, TWO RECLINING NUDES, 1971, lithograph, 22⅛ x 30⅛ (4215/294)   450
Pechstein, Max, BATHERS BY A BRIDGE, lithograph 5½ x 7⅞ (4067/168)   250
Pechstein, Max (1881-1955), AM MEER II, mat stain, drypoint, 1912, 10¼ x 10 (4247/177)   600
Penfield, Edward, HARPER'S MARCH, lithograph, 13⅞ x 19 (4270/399)   175
Pennell, Joseph, WASHINGTON, THE STATION FROM THE CAPITOL, etching, 11¾ x 9⅞
  (4270/403)   325
Peterdi, Gabor, HEAVY WEATHER, 1963, etching and engraving, 21⅞ x 27½ (4215/297)   80
Peterdi, Gabor, TRIUMPH OF WEED, etching and engraving, 17¾ x 23½ (4270/407)   110
Petitjean, Hippolite, PORTRAIT MAURICE MAETERLINCK, lithograph, in sanguine, 10¼ x 7⅞, 1898
  (4203/262)   100
Picasso, Pablo, AFFICHE EXPOSITION DE CERAMIQUES, lithograph, 23¼ x 16⅛ (4270/423)   375
Picasso, Pablo, ALEX MAGUY EXPOSE 7 TABLEAUX MAJEURS, litho. poster in colors, 21¼ x 13⅜
  (4203/277)   850
Picasso, Pablo, APRES LA PIQUE, 1959, linoleum cut, 20⅞ x 25⅛ (4215/358)   7000
Picasso, Pablo, BACCHANALE, lithograph, 22⅜ x 30, 1957 (4203/268)   1600
Picasso, Pablo, BACCHANALE AU TAUREAU, linoleum cut, 20¾ x 25, frame, 1959 (4244/344)   4750
Picasso, Pablo, BACCHANALE AU TAUREAU, 1959, linoleum cut, 20¾ x 25¼ (4215/360)   12000
Picasso, Pablo, BUFFON, LE SINGE, etching and aquatint, 12½ x 8⅞ (4270/416)   300
Picasso, Pablo, BUFFON, 1941-42, aquatint and etching, 15⅝ x 10½ (4215/337)   2200
Picasso, Pablo, BUSTE DE FEMME D'APRES CRANACH LE JEUNE, 1958, linoleum cut, 25⅜ x
  21⅛ (4215/356)   85000
Picasso, Pablo, CARNAVAL, linoleum cut, brown, 25⅜ x 20⅞, 1967 (4147/236)   1000
Picasso, Pablo, CENTAURE ET BACCHANTE AVEC UNE FAUNE, lithograph, 19¾ x 25⅝
  (4244/334)   3200
Picasso, Pablo, CHEVAL MOURANT, etching, 8 x 12, 1931 (4244/330)   2100
Picasso, Pablo, CHRONIQUE DES TEMPS HEROIQUES, drypoint, 7¾ x 5¾, frame, 1956
  (4244/339)   600
Picasso, Pablo, COLOMBE VOLANT 'AL'ARCEN-CIEL', lithograph, in colors, 19⅝ x 25½, 1952
  (4147/232)   1000
Picasso, Pablo, COMPOSITION AU VASE DE FLEURS, lithograph, 17¾ x 23¾, 1947 (4244/335)   5000
Picasso, Pablo, COQUILLAGES ET OISEAUX, 1946, lithograph 9½ x 13⅜ (4067/180)   550
Picasso, Pablo, DANSEURS ET MUSICIEN, 1959, linoleum cut, 20⅞ x 25¼ (4215/361)   4250
Picasso, Pablo, DEUX FIGURES LINEAIRES, 1939, engraving, 9¾ x 5⅛ (4215/336)   2600

Orozco (4244/307)

Picasso, Pablo, DEUX PETITS TAUREAUX, lithograph, 5⅝ x 10⅜, 1945 (4147/237) 225

Picasso, Pablo, DEUX PETITS TAUREAUX, lithograph, 10⅜ x 5½ (4270/426) 500

Picasso, Pablo, DIURNES, linoleum cut, in brown, 15½ x 11⅞, 1962 (4203/270) 1600

Picasso, Pablo, DORMEUSE ET SCULPTURES, etching, 10½ x 7¾, frame, 1933 (4244/331) 2600

Picasso, Pablo, ETREINTE, 1963, etching and drypoint, 16¾ x 22⅜ (4215/363) 3000

Picasso, Pablo, ETUDE DE PROFILS, lithograph, 29⅞ x 22¼, 1948 (4147/229) 1700

Picasso, Pablo, EXPOSITION CERAMIQUE VALLAURIS, linoleum cut, in brown and black, 25¼ x 21, 1959 (4203/274) 500

Picasso, Pablo, EXPOSITION 1958 VALLAURIS, linoleum cut, 25 x 21 (4270/424) 500

Picasso, Pablo, FAUNE DE VOILANT UNE FEMME, 1936, aquatint and etching, 12½ x 16⅜ (4215/320) 11500

Picasso, Pablo, FAUNES ET CHEVRE, linoleum cut, 20⅞ x 25¼, frame, 1959 (4244/345) 6300

Picasso, Pablo, FEMME ASSISE AU CHAPEAU, 1934, etching, 10⅞ x 7¾ (4215/315) 2500

Picasso, Pablo, FEMME ASSISE DANS UN FAUTEUIL, aquatint, 14¾ x 10⅝, frame, 1966 (4244/358) 1300

Picasso, Pablo, FEMME ASSISE, lithograph, 11⅜ x 8¼, 1924 (4244/318) 1300

Picasso, Pablo, FEMME AU BALCON AFFICHE, 1959, lithograph 23⅝ x 18½ (4067/189) 750

Picasso, Pablo, FEMME AU BALCON, lithograph, poster, 23¾ x 18¼, 1960 (4203/275) 800

Picasso, Pablo, FEMME AU CHAPEAU, linoleum cut, 13⅝ x 10⅝, frame, 1962 (4244/348) 7700

Picasso, Pablo, FEMME AU CHAPEAU, 1962, 13⅝ x 10⅝, linoleum (4225/169) 7500

Picasso, Pablo, FEMME AU CHIGNON, lithograph, 21⅞ x 17¼, frame, 1957 (4244/340) 6000

Picasso, Pablo, FEMME AU FAUTEUI NO.4, 1949, lithograph, 27⅜ x 21½ (4215/346) 17000

Picasso, Pablo, FEMME NU A LA SOURCE, 1962, linoleum cut, 20⅞ x 25¼ (4215/362) 4500

Picasso, Pablo, FEMME NUE ASSISE ET TROIS TETES BARBUES, etching, engraving, 5⅛ x 7⅛, frame, 1934 (4244/327) 1700

Picasso, Pablo, FEMME NUE ASSISE ET TROIS TETES BARBUES, mixed media, 5⅛ x 7⅛ (4270/414) 1600

Picasso, Pablo, FEMME NUE COURONNEE DE FLEURS ACCROUPIE, 1930, etching, 12⅜ x 8¾ (4215/326) 2500

Picasso, Pablo, FEMME NUE COURONNEE DE FLEURS, 1929, etching, 11 x 7¾ (4215/324) 4700

Picasso, Pablo, FEMME NUE COURONNEE DE FLEURS, 1930, etching, 12⅜ x 8¾ (4215/325) 3200

Picasso, Pablo, FEUILLE D'ETUDES A'DEUX TETES, 1939, aquatint and drypoint, 15⅝ x 7¾ (4215/335) 2400

Picasso, Pablo, FIGURE, lithograph, 25½ x 19⅝, 1949 (4147/231) 1500

Picasso, Pablo, FIGURE, lithograph, 9⅛ x 5¼, 1929 (4147/220) 1300

Picasso, Pablo, FLEURS, (for U.C.L.A.), lithograph, poster, in color, 22⅞ x 18⅛, 1961 (4203/276) 1050

Picasso, Pablo, FLEURS, lithograph, 22⅝ x 17¾ (4270/425) 1100

Picasso, Pablo, FLUTISTE ET FEMME NUE, 1932, engraving, 11¾ x 7¼ (4215/328) 2600

Picasso, Pablo, FLUTISTE, 1932, engraving, 11¾ x 7⅛ (4215/327) 2000

Picasso, Pablo, FUMEUR, etching, 16½ x 12½, frame, 1964 (4244/357) 2900

Picasso, Pablo, GARCON ET DORMEUSE A LA CHANDELLE, etching, aquatint, 9¼ x 11¾, frame, 1934 (4244/328) 4250

Picasso, Pablo, GARCON ET DORMEUSE A LA CHANDELLE, 1934, 9¼ x 11¾, etching, aquatint (4225/166) 4250

Picasso, Pablo, GRANDE TETE DE FEMME AU CHAPEAU ORNE, linoleum cut, 25¼ x 20⅞, frame, 1962 (4244/349) 9800

Picasso, Pablo, HIBOU AU CRAYON, lithograph, 25⅝ x 19⅞ (4270/418) 1400

Picasso, Pablo, HOMME DEVOILANT UNE FEMME, drypoint, 14⅝ x 11, 1931 (4147/221) 1700

Picasso, Pablo, HOMME ET FEMME, etching, 7⅝ x 11 (4270/408) 1400

Picasso, Pablo, HOMME ET FEMME, 1966, etching and aquatint, 9⅝ x 15 (4067/190) 650

Picasso, Pablo, JACQUELINE DE PROFIL A DROITE, lithograph, 21¾ x 17⅜, frame, 1958 (4244/341) 7000

Picasso, Pablo, JEUNE FILLE AUX GRANDS CHEVEUX, lithograph, 15⅜ x 12⅞ (4147/224) 650

Picasso, Pablo, L'ATELIER DU VIEUX PEINTRE, 1954, lithograph, 13¼ x 21¼ (4215/354) 3800

Picasso, Pablo, L'ECUYERE, lithograph, 21½ x 27⅛ (4270/420) 300

Picasso, Pablo, L'ETRIENTE, etching, 16¾ x 22½, frame, 1963 (4244/353) 2500

Picasso, Pablo, L'ITALIENNE, 1953, lithograph, 17½ x 15 (4215/350) 8500

Picasso, Pablo, Le REPOS DU SCULPTEUR ET LE MODELE AU MASQUE, 1933, etching, 10½ x 7½ (4215/305) 3600

Picasso, Pablo, LA CELESTINE, 1971, etching, 8¼ x 6½ (4215/365) 4250

Picasso, Pablo, LA DANSE, 1905, drypoint, 11¼ x 9¼ (4215/301) 1800

Picasso, Pablo, LA DANSE DES FAUNES, lithograph, ochre, 16⅛ x 20¾, 1957 (4147/234) 200

Picasso, Pablo, LA FAMILLE DE SALTIMBANQUES AU MACAQUE, drypoint, 9¼ x 7, 1905 (4244/311) 2500

Picasso, Pablo, LA FEMME AU CHAPEAU, linoleum cut, 20⅞ x 15⅜, frame, 1963 (4244/355) 17500

Picasso, Pablo, LA MERE ET LES ENFANTS, 1953, lithograph, 18⅝ x 9⅛ (4215/349) 3900

Picasso, Pablo, LA MINOTAUROMACHIE, 1935, pen and ink, 19½ x 27⅛ (4215/323) 125000

Picasso, Pablo, LA TABLE, etching, 7⅝ x 5½, frame, 1910 (4244/314) 1800

Picasso, Pablo, LE BAIN, drypoint, 13½ x 11¼, 1905 (4244/312) 3500
Picasso, Pablo, LE BAIN, 1905, drypoint, 13½ x 11¼ (4215/299) 2500
Picasso, Pablo, LE CHAPEAU A FLEURS, linoleum cut, 20⅞ x 15⅜, frame, 1963 (4244/356) 10000
Picasso, Pablo, LE COUPLE, etching, 8⅝ x 6 11/16 (4067/181) 250
Picasso, Pablo, LE DANSEUR, linoleum cut, 25¼ x 20⅞ (4270/438) 2400
Picasso, Pablo, LE FAMILLE DU SALTIMBANQUE, 1954, lithograph, 19¾ x 25⅝ (4215/351) 5000
Picasso, Pablo, LE HIBOU NOIR, lithograph, 24¾ x 18¾, frame, 1947 (4244/333) 3300
Picasso, Pablo, LE MODELE, drypoint and aquatint, 15 x 10⅞ (4270/422) 1000
Picasso, Pablo, LE MODELE, 1965, etching and aquatint, 15⅛ x 10⅞ (4067/188) 650
Picasso, Pablo, LE PEINTRE A LA PALETTE, linoleum cut, 25¼ x 20⅞, 1963 (4203/272) 2150
Picasso, Pablo, LE PEINTRE ET SON MODELE, etching, 4½ x 9⅜, 1963 (4203/271) 1350
Picasso, Pablo, LE PEINTRE ET SON MODELE, lithograph, 9¼ x 15⅜ (4270/409) 1600
Picasso, Pablo, LE PEINTRE ET SON MODELE, 1964, etching, 9¼ x 13⅛ (4067/185) 1100
Picasso, Pablo, LE PICADOR, aquatint, 18⅛ x 21⅞, frame, 1952 (4244/338) 3250
Picasso, Pablo, LE REPOS DU SCULPTEUR, etching, 7⅞ x 10⅝ (4147/222) 1800
Picasso, Pablo, LE REPOS DU SCULPTEUR ET LA SCULPTURE SURREALISTE, 1933, etching, 7¾x 10½ (4215/307) 2200
Picasso, Pablo, LE REPOS DU SCULPTEUR ET LE MODELE AU MASQUE, etching, 10½ x 7½, frame, 1933 (4244/321) 2800
Picasso, Pablo, LE SCULPTEUR, 1965, drypoint and aquatint, 15 x 10¾ (4067/187) 1000
Picasso, Pablo, LE VASE DE FLEURS, 1959, linoleum cut, 25¼ x 21⅛ (4215/359) 3500
Picasso, Pablo, LE VERRE SOUS LA LAMPE, linoleum cut, 13¾ x 10⅝, frame, 1962 (4244/352) 2800
Picasso, Pablo, LE VIEUX ROI, lithograph, 25½ x 19½, 1959 (4147/235) 950
Picasso, Pablo, LE VIOL II, 1933, drypoint, 11¾ x 14⅜ (4215/310) 1500
Picasso, Pablo, LE VIOL VIII, 1933, engraving and etching, 7⅞ x 10⅞ (4215/330) 2700
Picasso, Pablo, LES BAIGNEUSES SURPRISES, etching, drypoint, 7¾ x 10⅝, 1933 (4203/264) 450
Picasso, Pablo, LES BANDERILLES, lithograph, 18½ x 19½, 1949 (4203/267) 1550
Picasso, Pablo, LES DEUX FEMMESNUES, 1946, lithograph 13 x 17⅜ (4067/179) 850
Picasso, Pablo, LES DEUX SALTIMBANQUES, drypoint, 4¾ x 3⅝, 1905 (4147/219) 1300
Picasso, Pablo, LES MAINS LIEES, II, lithograph, 19⅞ x 26 (4270/419) 950
Picasso, Pablo, LES PAUVRES, etching, 9⅜ x 7⅛, 1905 (4244/310) 2100
Picasso, Pablo, LES SALTIMBANQUES, 1905, drypoint, 14¼ x 13 (4215/298) 2500
Picasso, Pablo, LES TROIS AMIES, etching, 16¼ x 11⅝, 1898 (4203/263) 1500
Picasso, Pablo, LES TROIS FEMMES ET LE TORERO, 1954, lithograph, 19⅞ x 25¾ (4215/353) 4750
Picasso, Pablo, LES TROIS GRACES II, 12¾ x 7⅞, 1922-23, frame (4244/317) 2700
Picasso, Pablo, LES TROIS GRACES II, 1923, etching, 12¾ x 7¾ (4215/302) 3900
Picasso, Pablo, MINOTAUR CARESSANT UNE DORMEUSE, drypoint, 11¾ x 14⅜, frame, 1933 (4244/326) 6250
Picasso, Pablo, MINOTAUR, BUVEUR ET FEMMES, etching, drypoint, 11⅝ x 14⅜, frame, 1933 (4244/325) 4250
Picasso, Pablo, MINOTAUR ATTAQUANT UNE AMAZONE, etching, 7½ x 10½, frame, 1933 (4244/324) 1600
Picasso, Pablo, MINOTAUR AVEUGLE GUIDE PAR UNE FILLETTE DANS LA NUIT, 1934, aquatint, 9¾ x 13⅝ (4215/318) 9000
Picasso, Pablo, MINOTAUR AVEUGLE GUIDE PAR UNE FILLETTE III, 1934, etching, 8⅞ x 12⅜ (4215/317) 2800
Picasso, Pablo, MINOTAUR BLESSE VI, 1933, etching, 7⅝ x 10½ (4215/312) 1600
Picasso, Pablo, MINOTAUR CARESSANT UNE DORMEUSE, 1933, drypoint, 11⅝ x 14⅜ (4215/313) 7000
Picasso, Pablo, MINOTAUR CARESSANT UNE FEMME, 1933, 11⅝ x 14½, etching (4225/165) 3600
Picasso, Pablo, MINOTAUR CARESSANT UNE FEMME, 1933, etching, 11¾ x 14⅜ (4215/311) 4000
Picasso, Pablo, MINOTAUR UNE COUPE A LA MAIN, ET JEUNE FEMME, 1933, 7⅝ x 10⅝, etching (4225/164) 2250
Picasso, Pablo, MODELE ET SCULPTEUR SURREALISTE, etching, 10½ x 7½, frame, 1933 (4244/323) 2600
Picasso, Pablo, MUSEE MUNICIPAL D'ART MODERNE CERET, linoleum cut in colors, 23⅝ x 17¾, 1958 (4203/273) 700
Picasso, Pablo, NATURE MORTE SOUS LA LAMPE, linoleum cut, 25¼ x 20⅞, frame, 1962 (4244/351) 22000
Picasso, Pablo, NATURE MORTE SOUS LA LAMPE, linoleum cut, 20⅞ x 25¼, 1962 (4244/350) 42000
Picasso, Pablo, NEUF TETES, 1934, aquatint and drypoint, 12½ x 8⅞ (4215/331) 1800
Picasso, Pablo, NU DEBOUT ET CHEVAL, 1938, drypoint, 9⅝ x 13¾ (4215/333) 3000
Picasso, Pablo, NU DEBOUT FLUTISTE ET JEUNE FILLE ACCROUPIS, 1938, drypoint, 9¾ x 13⅝ (4215/334) 5000
Picasso, Pablo, NU DEBOUT, 1935, aquatint and drypoint, 9⅜ x 4¾ (4215/332) 2600
Picasso, Pablo, PABLO PICASSO, 1945, etching, 11¼ x 8¾ (4215/338) 1800
Picasso, Pablo, PEINTRE AU TRAVAIL, etching, 12¼ x 16¼, frame, 1963 (4244/354) 1300
Picasso, Pablo, PEINTRE AU TRAVAIL, etching and aquatint, 13 x 10⅞ (4270/421) 850

Picasso, Pablo, PEINTRE ET MODELE TRICOTANT, 1927, etching, 7¾ x 11 (4067/175) — 1400
Picasso, Pablo, PEINTRE ET MODELE, 1964, aquatint, 15⅛ x 10¾ (4067/186) — 1300
Picasso, Pablo, PEINTRE ET MODELE, 1965, aquatint and drypoint, 8¾ x 12⅝ (4215/364) — 1300
Picasso, Pablo, PEINTRE RAMASSANT SON PINCEAU, 1927, etching, 7¾ x 11 (4067/177) — 700
Picasso, Pablo, PERSONNAGE ASSIS , 1956, lithograph 19¾ x 26 (4067/182) — 650
Picasso, Pablo, PERSONNAGES MASQUES ET FEMME OISEAU, aquatint, etching, 9⅝ x 13⅝, frame, 1934 (4244/329) — 1700
Picasso, Pablo, PICADOR ET TAUREAU, 1959, linoleum cut, 20⅞ x 25¼ (4215/357) — 6000
Picasso, Pablo, PIQUE, linoleum cut, 20⅞ x 25¼, frame, 1959 (4244/342) — 8500
Picasso, Pablo, PIQUE, 1959, 20⅞ x 25¼, linoleum (4225/167) — 8000
Picasso, Pablo, SALOME, drypoint, 15¾ x 13⅝, 1905 (4244/313) — 6500
Picasso, Pablo, SALOME, 1905, drypoint, 15¾ x 13¾ (4215/300) — 5000
Picasso, Pablo, SCENE MYTHOLOGIQUE, 1966, drypoint, 10⅝ x 14⅞ (4067/191) — 950
Picasso, Pablo, SCULPTEUR A MI CORPS AU TRAVAIL, 1933, etching, 10½ x 7⅝ (4215/304) — 1800
Picasso, Pablo, SCULPTEUR DEVANT SA SCULPTURE, 1927, etching, 7¾ x 11 (4067/174) — 1250
Picasso, Pablo, SCULPTEUR ET MODELE ADMIRANT UNE TETE SCULPTE, etching, 10½ x 7⅝ (4270/412) — 2400
Picasso, Pablo, SCULPTEUR ET MODELE AGENOUILLE, etching, 14⅜ x 11⅝, frame, 1933 (4244/322) — 7000
Picasso, Pablo, SCULPTEUR ET MODELE AGENOUILLE, 1933, etching, 14½ x 11¾ (4215/309) — 6000
Picasso, Pablo, SCULPTEUR ET SON MODELE DEVANT UNE FENETRE, etching, 7⅝ x 10⅝ (4270/413) — 850
Picasso, Pablo, SCULPTEUR MODELANT, 1927, etching, 7¾ x 11 (4067/176) — 600
Picasso, Pablo, SCULPTEUR, MODELE COUCHEE ET SCULPTEUR, etching, 10½ x 7⅝ (4270/411) — 1700
Picasso, Pablo, SIX CONTES FANTASQUES, engraving, 13½ x 10½ (4270/417) — *1500*
Picasso, Pablo, SUENO Y MENTIRA DE FRANCO, two aquatints with text, 15⅛ x 22⅜, 1937 (4147/223) — 1300
Picasso, Pablo, SUENO Y MENTIRA DE FRANCO, 1937, aquatint, (Book 2), 15⅛ x 22½ (4215/322) — 1500
Picasso, Pablo, TAUREAU ATTAQUANT UN CHEVAL, etching, 6⅞ x 9¼, frame, 1921 (4244/315) — 1600
Picasso, Pablo, TAUREAU ET CHEVAUX DANS L'ARENE, 1933, etching, 7½ x 10½ (4215/314) — 1300

Picasso
(4270/417)

Picasso, Pablo, TAUREAU, 1946, lithograph, 10¼ x 14⅜ (4215/341)	2000
Picasso, Pablo, TETE DE FEMME DE TROIS QUARTS, 1953, lithograph, 21½ x 17¾ (4215/348)	1700
Picasso, Pablo, TETE DE FEMME DE TROIS QUARTS, lithograph, 21½ x 17¾, 1953 (4147/233)	1100
Picasso, Pablo, TETE DE FEMME, 1945, lithograph, 12⅜ x 9⅝ (4215/339)	3500
Picasso, Pablo, TETE DE FEMME, 1962, 25¼ x 20¾, linoleum (4225/168)	12500
Picasso, Pablo, TETE DE JEUNE FILLE, lithograph, fourth state, 12⅝ x 10⅜, 1945 (4147/226)	500
Picasso, Pablo, TETES DE BELIERS, lithograph, trial proof, 9⅜ x 13⅜, 1945 (4147/225)	250
Picasso, Pablo, TETES ET FIGURES EMMELEES, 1934, etching, 11⅛ x 7⅞ (4067/178)	500
Picasso, Pablo, TROIS FEMMES NUES PRES D'UNE FENETRE, 1933, etching, 14½ x 11¾ (4215/308)	3900
Picasso, Pablo, TROIS TETES D'HOMMES, etching, 12⅝ x 9⅞, frame, 1931 (4244/319)	1000
Picasso, Pablo, TROUPE D'ACTEURS, 1954, lithograph, 19¾ x 25⅝ (4215/352)	3900
Picasso, Pablo, VENUS ET L'ARMOUR, lithograph, 26¾ x 19⅝, frame, 1949 (4244/336)	3750
Picasso, Pablo, VISAGE GEOMETRIQUE, faience plate, 14⅜ x 14⅛ (4270/410)	650
Picasso, Pablo, VISAGE, 1928, lithograph, 8⅛ x 5⅝ (4215/303)	4000
Picasso, Pablo, 347 SERIES, etching, 12⅜ x 16⅜, 1968 (4203/283)	1400
Picasso, Pablo, 347 SERIES, etching, 12½ x 15⅜, 1968 (4203/282)	1800
Picasso, Pablo, 347 SERIES, aquatint, 8¼ x 6, 1968 (4203/287)	1100
Picasso, Pablo, 347 SERIES NO 1, 1968, etching, 15⅛ x 22⅛ (4215/366)	9500
Picasso, Pablo, 347 SERIES NO 123, 1968, aquatint, 19½ x 13¼ (4215/371)	4150
Picasso, Pablo, 347 SERIES NO 144, 1968, aquatint, 16⅜ x 19½ (4215/372)	1300
Picasso, Pablo, 347 SERIES NO 159, 1968, etching, 16⅜ x 19½ (4215/373)	2400
Picasso, Pablo, 347 SERIES NO 165, 1968, etching, 8⅛ x 5⅞ (4215/374)	1200
Picasso, Pablo, 347 SERIES NO 173, 1968, aquatint, 8⅛ x 5⅞ (4215/375)	1100
Picasso, Pablo, 347 SERIES NO 182, 1968, etching and drypoint, 8⅛ x 5⅞ (4215/376)	850
Picasso, Pablo, 347 SERIES NO 198, 1968, aquatint, 5⅞ x 8⅛ (4215/377)	1300
Picasso, Pablo, 347 SERIES NO 2, 1968, etching, 15½ x 22 (4215/367)	2150
Picasso, Pablo, 347 SERIES NO 221, 1968, etching, 12⅜ x 12⅜ (4215/378)	1300
Picasso, Pablo, 347 SERIES NO 241, 1968, etching, 6¾ x 10⅜ (4215/379)	800
Picasso, Pablo, 347 SERIES NO 258, 1968, etching, 8⅛ x 6⅛ (4215/380)	1000
Picasso, Pablo, 347 SERIES NO 301, 1968, etching, 11¾ x 20⅛ (4215/381)	2300
Picasso, Pablo, 347 SERIES NO 82, 1968, etching, 10⅞ x 14¾ (4215/369)	1700
Picasso, Pablo, 347 SERIES NO 92, 1968, etching and aquatint, 6¾ x 8⅛ (4215/370)	800
Picasso, Pablo, 347 SERIES, etching, 8⅞ x 11⅜, 1968 (4203/286)	900
Picasso, Pablo, 347 SERIES, etching, aquatint, drypoint, 6⅝ x 8¼, 1968 (4203/284)	1300
Picasso, Pablo, 347 SERIES, etching, drypoint, 7⅞ x 10, 1968 (4203/285)	1100
Picasso, Pablo, 347 SERIES, NO. 15, etching, 12⅜ x 16⅜, frame, 1968 (4244/360)	1800
Picasso, Pablo, 347 SERIES, NO. 152, aquatint, 8¾ x 12½, 1968 (4147/239)	1000
Picasso, Pablo, 347 SERIES, NO. 154, etching, 8¾ x 11¼, 1968 (4147/240)	1500
Picasso, Pablo, 347 SERIES, NO. 160, etching, 16⅜ x 19½, 1968 (4244/365)	2100
Picasso, Pablo, 347 SERIES, NO. 168, etching, 5¾ x 8⅛ (4270/427)	1100
Picasso, Pablo, 347 SERIES, NO. 205, 16⅛ x 19½, frame, 1968 (4244/369)	2500
Picasso, Pablo, 347 SERIES, NO. 220, drypoint, 5¾ x 8¾ (4270/428)	900
Picasso, Pablo, 347 SERIES, NO. 223, aquatint, 13⅜ x 12⅜, 1968 (4203/288)	1350
Picasso, Pablo, 347 SERIES, NO. 224, etching, 5¾ x 8¾ (4270/429)	850
Picasso, Pablo, 347 SERIES, NO. 225, etching, 8¾ x 5¾ (4270/430)	850
Picasso, Pablo, 347 SERIES, NO. 229, etching, 7 x 8¾, 1968 (4147/241)	1000
Picasso, Pablo, 347 SERIES, NO. 231, etching, 8¾ x 5¾ (4270/431)	850
Picasso, Pablo, 347 SERIES, NO. 233, etching, 6¾ x 10¼, 1968 (4147/242)	1100
Picasso, Pablo, 347 SERIES, NO. 261, etching, 12¾ x 7¾, 1968 (4147/247)	1300
Picasso, Pablo, 347 SERIES, NO. 262, etching, 10½ x 8¼, 1968 (4203/289)	1500
Picasso, Pablo, 347 SERIES, NO. 263, aquatint, drypoint, 12¾ x 7⅞, 1968 (4203/290)	1050
Picasso, Pablo, 347 SERIES, NO. 288, etching, 11 x 15⅜, frame, 1968 (4244/370)	1700
Picasso, Pablo, 347 SERIES, NO. 294, etching and drypoint, 6½ x 8 (4270/432)	750
Picasso, Pablo, 347 SERIES, NO. 30, etching, 12⅜ x 16⅜, 1968 (4203/279)	1150
Picasso, Pablo, 347 SERIES, NO. 302, etching, 5¾ x 8⅛ (4270/436)	1000
Picasso, Pablo, 347 SERIES, NO. 302, etching, 5¾ x 8⅛ (4270/433)	1100
Picasso, Pablo, 347 SERIES, NO. 306, etching, 5¾ x 8⅛ (4270/434)	700
Picasso, Pablo, 347 SERIES, NO. 308, etching, 5¾ x 8⅛ (4270/435)	900
Picasso, Pablo, 347 SERIES, NO. 321, etching 5¾ x 8⅛, (4270/437)	1100
Picasso, Pablo, 347 SERIES, NO. 325, etching, 8¼ x 10½, 1968 (4147/248)	1000
Picasso, Pablo, 347 SERIES, NO. 325, etching, 8¼ x 10½, 1968 (4203/291)	1250
Picasso, Pablo, 347 SERIES, NO. 335, etching, 8¼ x 10½, 1968 (4203/292)	950
Picasso, Pablo, 347 SERIES, NO. 337, aquatint and etching, 8¼ x 10⅝, 1968 (4203/293)	1000
Picasso, Pablo, 347 SERIES, NO. 340, aquatint, 8¼ x 10½, 1968 (4147/249)	850
Picasso, Pablo, 347 SERIES, NO. 40, etching, aquatint, drypoint, 8¾ x 12⅝, 1968 (4203/281)	1250
Picasso, Pablo, 347 SERIES, NO. 41, etching, aquatint, drypoint, 8¾ x 12⅝, 1968 (4203/280)	1200
Picasso, Pablo, 347 SERIES, NO. 48, etching, 12⅜ x 15½, 1968 (4147/238)	2000

Picasso, Pablo, 347 SERIES, NO. 86, aquatint, 6¾ x 8, 1968 (4244/362) — 1400
Picasso, Pablo, 347 SERIES, NO. 97, etching, drypoint, 13¼ x 19¼, frame, 1968 (4244/364) — 4000
Picasso, Pablo, 347 SERIES, 235, aquatint, 6¾ x 10¼, 1968 (4147/243) — 1100
Picasso, Pablo, 347 SERIES, 236, etching, 6¾ x 10¼, 1968 (4147/244) — 1100
Picasso, Pablo, 347 SERIES, 237, etching, 6¾ x 10¼, 1968 (4147/245) — *1200*

Picasso (4147/245)

Picasso, Pablo, 347 SERIES, 241, etching, 6¾ x 10¼, 1968 (4147/246) — 1000
Picasso, Pablo (1881-1973), GRANDE TETE, 1962, 25¼ x 20¾, linoleum (4225/170) — 16000
Pissarro, Camille, GROUPE DE PAYSANS, lithograph, 5⅛ x 4⅛, frame (4244/375) — 750
Pissarro, Camille, LA CHARRUE, lithograph, in colors, 8⅞ x 6, 1901 (4147/250) — 950
Pissarro, Camille, LA CHARRUE, lithograph, 9 x 6, 1901 (4244/376) — 1600
Pissarro, Camille, LA CHARRUE, 1901, lithograph, 8¾ x 5⅞ (4215/383) — 1200
Pissarro, Camille, LES FANEUSES, 1890, etching, 7¾ x 5¼ (4215/382) — 450
Pissarro, Camille, LES QUATRE BAIGNEUSES, etching, aquatint, 8½ x 7⅛, 1895 (4244/374) — 700
Pissarro, Camille, MARCHE A VOLAILLE, A GISORS, etching, aquatint, 10 x 7⅝, 1891 (4244/373) — 550
Pissarro, Camille, MARCHE AUX LEGUMES A PONTOISE, etching, aquatint, 10 x 8, 1891 (4203/295) — 200
Pissarro, Camille, PAYSAN PORTANT DU FOIN, etching, 4¾ x 3⅛, 1900 (4203/296) — 200
Porter, Fairfield, THE DOG AT THE DOOR, 1971, lithograph, 30 x 22⅛ (4215/384) — 475
Raffaelli, Jean, LA PETIT PLAGE, drypoint, equatint, in colors, 16⅛ x 24¾, 1909 (4203/298) — 900
Raffaelli, Jean, LE TERRASSIER DE LA PLAINE S. DENIS, lithograph, in colors, 12 x 17⅞, 1896 (4203/299) — 300
Raffaelli, Jean, MOVING DAY, etching, in colors, 6¼ x 7⅝ (4203/297) — 300
Raffaelli, Jean Francois, LES RAPINS, etching and drypoint, 7⅞ x 5⅝ (4270/439) — 160
Ray, Man, AEROGRAPH, silkscreen, 19¼ x 16¼ (4270/445) — 200
Ray, Man, BALLADE DES DAMES HORS DU TEMPS, portfolio, etching, 26¾ x 20 (4244/378) — 1400
Ray, Man, LA DANZATRICE, lithograph, 19¾ x 27⅝ (4270/447) — 275
Ray, Man, LES TROIS NUS, silkscreen, 17¼ x 21⅛ (4270/446) — 200
Ray, Man, SEGUIDILLA, silkscreen, 15¾ x 20¼, frame, 1971 (4244/380) — 400
Ray, Man, SELF PORTRAIT, silkscreen, 20 x 14¼, frame, 1970 (4244/379) — 350
Redon, Odilon, CHRIST, lithograph, 13¼ x 10⅝ (4270/449) — 250
Redon, Odilon, LA MAISON HANTEE DES LARVES SI HIDEUSES, 1896, lithograph, 5 x 6¾ (4215/389) — 400
Redon, Odilon, PROFILE DE LUMIERE, lithograph, 13¼ x 9⅜ (4270/448) — 1700
Redon, Odilon, TENTATION DE SAINT ANTOINE HELENE, lithograph, 3⅝ x 3¼ (4270/451) — 200
Redon, Odilon, TENTATION DE SAINT ANTOINE, ELLE TIRE, lithograph, 7⅝ x 6⅛ (4270/450) — 275
Redon, Odilon, TENTATION DE SAINT ANTOINE, LA VIEILLE, lithograph, 6½ x 4⅜ (4270/454) — 300
Redon, Odilon, TENTATION DE SAINT ANTOINE, LE DIABLE, lithograph, 12¼ x 10 (4270/453) — 300
Redon, Odilon, TENTATION DE SAINT ANTOINE, lithograph, 1896, 12 x 9 (4215/387) — 225
Redon, Odilon, TENTATION DE SAINT ANTOINE, lithograph, 1896, 10⅜ x 7⅛ (4215/388) — 325
Redon, Odilon, TENTATION DE SAINT ANTOINE, lithograph, 12⅜ x 8½, 1896 (4244/386) — 325
Redon, Odilon, TENTATION DE SAINT ANTOINE, lithograph, 10¼ x 8, 1896 (4244/388) — 425
Redon, Odilon, TENTATION DE SAINT ANTOINE, lithograph, 8½ x 5⅛, 1896 (4244/384) — 450
Redon, Odilon, TENTATION DE SAINT ANTOINE, lithograph, 11⅝ x 8⅝, 1896 (4244/385) — 450
Redon, Odilon, TENTATION DE SAINT ANTOINE, lithograph, 10¼ x 8¼, 1896 (4244/382) — 225
Redon, Odilon, TENTATION DE SAINT ANTOINE, lithograph, 5⅞ x 5⅛, 1896 (4244/387) — 225
Redon, Odilon, TENTATION DE SAINT ANTOINE, lithograph, 1896, 5⅞ x 5 (4215/386) — 200
Redon, Odilon, YEUX CLOS, lithograph, trial proof, 8⅝ x 7¼, frame (4244/381) — 13000

Renoir
(4270/472)

Renoir, Pierre Auguste, AMBROISE VOLLARD, ca1904, lithograph, 9¼ x 6¾ (4215/403)   850
Renoir, Pierre Auguste, AMBROISE VOLLARD, lithograph, 9¼ x 6¾ (4270/472)   *700*
Renoir, Pierre Auguste, BAIGNEUSE ASSISE, ca1897, soft ground etching, 8⅝ x 5¼ (4215/392)   1400
Renoir, Pierre Auguste, BAIGNEUSE ASSISE, etching, 8¾ x 5¼, frame (4244/391)   1200
Renoir, Pierre Auguste, BAIGNEUSE DEBOUT A MI-JAMBE, ca1910, etching, 6⅝ x 4½ (4215/397)   150
Renoir, Pierre Auguste, BAIGNEUSE DEBOUT A MI-JAMBE, etching, 6⅝ x 4½ (4244/394)   250
Renoir, Pierre Auguste, BAIGNEUSE DEBOUT, A MI-JAMBES, etching, 6¾ x 4½, ca1910
(4147/264)   275
Renoir, Pierre Auguste, CLAUDE RENOIR, LA TETE BAISEE, ca1904, lithograph, 8¼ x 7½
(4215/404)   750
Renoir, Pierre Auguste, CLAUDE RENOIR, TOURNE A GAUCHE, ca1904, lithograph, 5 x 4⅝
(4215/405)   750
Renoir, Pierre Auguste, CLAUDE RENOIR, DE TROISQUARTS, etching and roulette, 6⅜ x 5⅛,
ca1908 (4147/263)   500
Renoir, Pierre Auguste, CLAUDE RENOIR, TOURNE A GAUCHE, lithograph, 5⅛ x 4½, frame
(4244/401)   700
Renoir, Pierre Auguste, ENPANTS JOUANT A LA BALLE, 1900, lithograph, 23¼ x 20⅛ (4215/402)   33000
Renoir, Pierre Auguste, ETUDE DE FEMME NUE ASSISE, ca1904, lithograph, 7⅝ x 6½ (4215/407)   800
Renoir, Pierre Auguste, ETUDE DE FEMME NUE ASSISE, lithograph, 7½ x 6⅜ (4244/403)   900
Renoir, Pierre Auguste, ETUDE POUR UNE BAIGNEUSE, ca1906, etching and drypoint, 8¾ x 6½
(4215/396)   1300
Renoir, Pierre Auguste, ETUDE POUR UNE BAIGNEUSE, drypoint, 8⅝ x 6½, frame (4244/393)   1100
Renoir, Pierre Auguste, FEMME COUCHEE, etching, 5½ x 7¾, frame (4244/392)   800
Renoir, Pierre Auguste, FEMME NUE ASSISE, ca1906, soft ground etching, 7⅜ x 5¾ (4215/393)   1300
Renoir, Pierre Auguste, FEMME NUE COUCHEE TOURNEE A DROITE, ca1906, etching, 5½ x 7⅞
(4215/394)   1300
Renoir, Pierre Auguste, FEMME NUE COUCHEE TOURNEE A GAUCHE, ca1906, etching, 5½ x 7⅞
(4215/395)   1300
Renoir, Pierre Auguste, JEUNE FILLE EN BUSTE ET ETUDES DE TETES, lithographs, 10⅝ x 7¾
(4244/407)   450
Renoir, Pierre Auguste, L'ENFANT AU BISCUIT, CHARLES RENOIR, lithograph, 12¾ x 10½. 1898-
99 (4244/398)   6600
Renoir, Pierre Auguste, LA DANSE A LA CAMPAGNE, etching, 8¾ x 5⅜, frame (4244/389)   2400
Renoir, Pierre Auguste, LA DANSE A LA CAMPAGNE, 1890, etching, 8¾ x 5⅜ (4215/390)   2400
Renoir, Pierre Auguste, LA DANSE A LA CAMPAGNE, 1890, etching, 8¾ x 5⅜ (4067/201)   1800
Renoir, Pierre Auguste, LA FLEUVE SCAMANDRE, etching, 8⅝ x 6⅞, ca1900 (4147/266)   400
Renoir, Pierre Auguste, LA PIERRE AUX TROIS CROQUIS, lithograph, 8¾ x 11¼, frame (4244/402)   1000
Renoir, Pierre Auguste, LE CHAPEAU EPINGLE, etching, 4¾ x 3½, ca1894 (4147/262)   300
Renoir, Pierre Auguste, LE CHAPEAU EPINGLE 2E PLANCHE, lithograph, 23⅞ x 11¼ (4215/400)   22000
Renoir, Pierre Auguste, LE CHAPEAU EPINGLE, ca1894, etching, 5¼ x 3⅝ (4215/391)   2400
Renoir, Pierre Auguste, LE CHAPEAU EPINGLE, drypoint, 5 1/3 x 3⅝ (4244/390)   750

Renoir, Pierre Auguste, LE CHAPEAU EPINGLE, 2E PLANCHE, lithograph, 23⅞ x 11¼, frame
(4244/396)   18000
Renoir, Pierre Auguste, LE FLEUVE SCAMANDRE 2E PLANCHE, ca1900, etching, 10 x 7½
(4215/398)   600
Renoir, Pierre Auguste, LE FLEUVE SCAMANDRE, IRE PLANCHE, etching, 9 x 7¼ (4244/395)   650
Renoir, Pierre Auguste, LE PIERRE AUX TROIS CROQUIS, ca1904, lithograph, 8⅞ x 11⅜
(4215/406)   1200
Renoir, Pierre Auguste, LOUIS VALTAT, lithograph, 11¾ x 9½ (4244/400)   900
Renoir, Pierre Auguste, MATERNITE, GRANDE PLANCHE, lithograph, 20¼ x 19¼, frame
(4244/406)   3300
Renoir, Pierre Auguste, SUR LA PLAGE, A BERNEVAL, etching, 13¼ x 3¾, ca1892 (4147/261)   700
Renoir, Pierre Auguste (1841-1919), FEMME NUE COUCHEE (TOURNEE A DROITE), 1re
PLANCHE, ca1906, 5 x 7⅞, etching (4225/174)   1200
Renoir, Pierre Auguste, BAIGNEUSE ASSISE, etching, 8⅝ x 5½ (4270/459)   *1200*

Renoir
(4270/459)

Renoir, Pierre Auguste, CLAUDE RENOIR, etching, 6½ x 5⅛ (4270/466)   350
Renoir, Pierre Auguste, CLAUDE RENOIR, etching, 6½ x 5⅛ (4270/465)   450
Renoir, Pierre Auguste, CLAUDE RENOIR, lithograph, 7¾ x 7⅛ (4270/473)   500
Renoir, Pierre Auguste, ETUDE DE FEMME NUE ASSISE, lithograph, 7⅝ x 6½ (4270/475)   600
Renoir, Pierre Auguste, ETUDE DE FEMME NUE ASSISE, lithograph, 7½ x 6½ (4270/477)   550
Renoir, Pierre Auguste, ETUDE DE FEMME NUE ASSISE, Variante, lithograph, 6⅜ x 6¼
(4270/478)   300
Renoir, Pierre Auguste, FEMME COUCHEE, etching, 5⅜ x 7⅞ (4270/462)   1000
Renoir, Pierre Auguste, FEMME NUE ASSISE, etching, 7⅜ x 5⅝ (4270/460)   950
Renoir, Pierre Auguste, FEMME NUE COUCHEE, etching and drypoint, 5⅛ x 7⅞ (4270/461)   600
Renoir, Pierre Auguste, LA PIERRE AU TROIS CROQUIS, lithograph, 8⅞ x 11¼ (4270/474)   600
Renoir, Pierre Auguste, LE CHAPEAU EPINGLE, drypoint, 5¼ x 3¾ (4270/457)   400
Renoir, Pierre Auguste, LE CHAPEAU EPINGLE, etching, 4½ x 3⅛ (4270/458)   225
Riopelle, FEUILLES, lithograph, 23 x 33¾ (4270/481)   75
Rivera, Diego, AUTORETRATO, 1930, lithograph, 15 x 11¼ (4105/125)   1600
Rivera, Diego, SEATED NUDE WITH RAISED ARMS, 1930, lithograph, 16½ x 10⅞ (4105/124)   1000
Rivera, Diego, ZAPATA, 1932, lithograph, 16¼ x 13⅛ (4105/123)   1900
Riviere, Henri, HARBOR VIEW, 9 x 14 (4270/483)   350
Robbe, Manuel, (WOMAN PINNING HER HAT), aquatint, 19½ x 13¾ (4244/488)   1000
Robbe, Manuel, AUX CHAMPS ELYSEES, ca1900, aquatint, 12⅞ x 19½ (4215/417)   1200
Robbe, Manuel, BOOK STALLS ON THE SEINE, aquatint, in colors, 11⅝ x 15½ (4203/310)   475
Robbe, Manuel, CHILDREN PLAYING ON A RIVERBANK, aquatint, 16⅛ x 21⅛ (4215/415)   600
Robbe, Manuel, CLAUDINE, aquatint, drypoint, 12 x 9¾ (4244/489)   250
Robbe, Manuel, DOG DRINKING FROM A DISH, drypoint, 13¾ x 19½ (4270/485)   150
Robbe, Manuel, ETUDE DE FEMME NUE ASSISE VARIANTE, ca1904, lithograph, 6⅜ x 6¼
(4215/411)   450
Robbe, Manuel, FEMME DANS UN PARC, drypoint, 19⅝ x 13 (4244/490)   600
Robbe, Manuel, IN THE PARK, aquatint, 11¼ x 15½ (4215/413)   550
Robbe, Manuel, L'ECLATANTE, lithograph, 51⅜ x 36¾ (4244/494)   550

Robbe, Manuel, LE DERNIER ROMAN, ca1900, aquatint, 20½ x 14⅞ (4215/419)   850
Robbe, Manuel, LE MODELE, drypoint, 19½ x 13 (4215/412)   1450
Robbe, Manuel, LE PECHEUR, aquatint, 13¾ x 19½ (4244/491)   650
Robbe, Manuel, LES FOINS, ca1900, aquatint, 9½ x 15½ (4215/418)   550
Robbe, Manuel, MIDINETTES, aquatint, 19½ x 13⅝ (4244/487)   1100
Robbe, Manuel, NOCTURNE, aquatint, 13¼ x 17⅝ (4215/416)   750
Robbe, Manuel, NU A LA NATUR, aquatint, 11⅝ x 8⅜ (4244/493)   600
Robbe, Manuel, PLASSON CYCLES, lithograph, 46½ x 33, frame (4244/495)   750
Robbe, Manuel, REVERIE, equatint, in colors, 19⅞ x 13⅜ (4203/311)   550
Robbe, Manuel, SUR LA TERRACE, drypoint, 19½ x 14⅛ (4215/414)   400
Robbe, Manuel, WOMAN IN ARTIST'S STUDIO, drypoint, 19¾ x 14⅛ (4270/486)   500
Rodin, Auguste, LE PRINTEMPS, drypoint, 5⅝ x 3⅝ (4203/312)   900
Rodin, Auguste, VICTOR HUGO, DE FACE, drypoint, 9 x 7⅛, ca1886 (4203/313)   650
Rops, Felicien, LA PAUPEE DE SATYR, etching, 6 x 5 (4203/314)   175
Rouault, Georges, AIDE BORREAU PORTANT, 1936, aquatint, 12⅜ x 8⅝ (4067/205)   175
Rouault, Georges, AIDE-BOURREAU PORTANT UN DES BOIS DE LA CROIX, 1936, 12 x 8½,
    aquatint (4215/427)   1000
Rouault, Georges, AUGUSTE, aquatint, 12⅜ x 8¼, 1934 (4147/276)   1200
Rouault, Georges, CELUI QUI CROIT EN MOI, FUT-IL MORT, aquatint, plate 28 of Miserere, 22⅝ x
    17, 1923 (4203/315)   200
Rouault, Georges, CHRIST AU FAUBOURG, 1935, aquatint, 12 x 8⅛ (4215/425)   1100
Rouault, Georges, CHRIST DE FACE, aquatint, 11¾ x 8¼, 1938, frame (4244/416)   *2000*

Rouault
(4244/416)

Rouault, Georges, DOUCE AMER, 1934, aquatint, 12 x 8⅛ (4215/424)   1400
Rouault, Georges, EN TANT D'ORDERS DIVERS LE BEAU METIER, aquatint, 23¼ x 16⅞
    (4270/495)   325
Rouault, Georges, FEMME AU COLLIER, etching, roulette, plate 19 from Reincarnations, 9¾ x 6⅜,
    1928 (4203/318)   125
Rouault, Georges, FEMME FIERE, aquatint, 12⅜ x 8⅜, 1938, frame (4244/415)   1300
Rouault, Georges, FILLE AU GRAND CHAPEAU, aquatint, 11⅝ x 7¾ (4270/494)   100
Rouault, Georges, GUSTAVE MOREAU A LA BARBE BLANCHE, lithograph, 9⅛ x 6¾ (4270/500)   350
Rouault, Georges, HOMO HOMINI LUPUS, aquatint, 23 x 16⅝ (4270/497)   200
Rouault, Georges, HOMO HOMINI LUPUS, aquatint, plate 37 of Miserere, 22¾ x 16⅜, 1948
    (4203/317)   200
Rouault, Georges, LA MORT LA PRIS COMME IL SORTAIT DU LIT D'ORTIEN, aquatint, 21¼ x
    13¼ (4270/498)   175
Rouault, Georges, LE CHRIST ET MAMMON, aquatint, 12¼ x 8⅝, 1936, frame (4244/414)   750
Rouault, Georges, LE CLOWN A LA GROSSE CAISSE, 1930, aquatint, 12¼ x 8⅜ (4215/421)   1200
Rouault, Georges, LE CLOWN JAUNE, aquatint, 13¾ x 10, frame, 1930 (4244/410)   1400
Rouault, Georges, LE CLOWN JAUNE, 1930, aquatint, 13¾ x 11 (4215/422)   1200

Rouault, Georges, LE CONDAMNE S'EN EST ALLE, aquatint, 19¾ x 13⅝, 1922 (4147/271) 300
Rouault, Georges, LE JONGLEUR, aquatint, 12¼ x 8½, 1930 (4147/275) 750
Rouault, Georges, LE JONGLEUR, 1930, aquatint, 12¼ x 8½ (4215/420) 900
Rouault, Georges, LES USINES ELLES-MEMES ONT PERI, aquatint, plate 34 of Miserere, 22¾ x 17½, 1926 (4203/316) 200
Rouault, Georges, MADAME LOUISON, 1935, aquatint, 12⅛ x 4½ (4215/423) 1200
Rouault, Georges, MISERERE, set of 58 aquatints, 25¾ x 20, 1922-27 (4244/409) 24000
Rouault, Georges, PAYSANS, aquatint, 13⅛ x 9¼, frame, 1939 (4244/413) 800
Rouault, Georges, PIERROT, aquatint, 12⅜ x 8½, 1938, frame (4244/411) 1600
Rouault, Georges, RENCONTRE, 1936, aquatint, 12⅜ x 8¾ (4215/426) 1000
Rouault, Georges, SELF PORTRAIT, lithograph, 9 x 6¾, 1927 (4147/273) 150
Rouault, Georges, SOUVENIR IN TIMES, ANDRE SUARES, lithograph, 9½ x 6⅞ (4270/501) 175
Rouault, Georges, SUNT LACRYMAE RERUM, aquatint, 22¾ x 16⅜, 1926 (4147/272) 375
Ruelas, Julio, LA CRITICA, etching, dry paint, 7 x 5¾ (4105/102) 1600
Ruelas, Julio, LA ESFINGE, 1906, etching, 5⅛ x 7½ (4105/103) 650
Ruelas, Julio, LA ESFINGE, 1907, soft, ground etching, 5⅛ x 7¼ (4105/104) 700
Schiele, Egon (1890-1918), MANNLICHER AKT, nail hole, tiny nicks, lithograph, 1912, 17⅝ x 15¾ (4247/180) 5750
Schiele, Egon (1890-1918), SECESSION 49, AUSSTELLUNG, tear, laid down, lithograph, 1918, 25¾ x 19 (4247/181) 5500
Schmidt-Rotluff, Karl (1884-1976), PETRI FISCHZUG, edition of 75, mat stain, woodcut, 1918, 15⅝ x 19⅝ (4247/182) 3100
Segonzac, Andre, LE PANIER A SABLE, etching, 3½ x 6⅛, 1930-2 (4147/284) 225
Seguin, Armand, LA FEMME AUX FIGUES, etching, 10½ x 16⅜ (4147/285) 75
Seguin, Armand, LA FEMME AUX FIGUES, etching, 1½ x 16⅜ (4270/514) 100
Seguin, Armand, LA FEMME AUX FIGUES, etching, 10½ x 5¾ (4270/513) 150
Severini, Gino, ABSTRACT COMPOSITION, lithograph, 24¼ x 18¼ (4270/515) 700
Severini, Gino, LA FAMIGLIA DEGLI ARLECCHINI, lithograph, 12 x 8⅛, 1922 (4244/418) 600
Shalom of Safed, EXODUS, lithograph, 22¼ x 16½ (4270/503) 225
Sheeler, Charles, YACHTS, lithograph, 8⅛ x 10, frame, 1924 (4244/419) 5600
Signac, Paul, LE SOIR, lithograph, 8 x 10⅜, frame, 1898 (4244/421) 1000
Signac, Paul, PARIS, LE PONT DES ARTS AVEC REMORQUEURS, 1927, etching and, aquatint, 5 x 7½ (4215/433) 150
Siqueiros, David Alfaro, BROWN DANCER, lithograph, 26¼ x 19¾ (4147/288) 250
Siqueiros, David Alfaro, MADREY NINA, lithograph, 30¼ x 23 (4270/520) 600
Siqueiros, David Alfaro, SELF-PORTRAIT, lithograph, 21¼ x 16⅛, 1930 (4244/423) 700
Siqueiros, David Alfaro, ZAPATA, lithograph, 20¼ x 15½, 1930 (4244/422) 1400
Smith, R., after Morland, pair, INNOCENCE ALARM'D, SPORTSMEN RETURN, 1792, 18¾ x 23¾, mezzotints (4148/184) 425
Steinlen, Theophile Alexandre, AU BORD DE LA MER, etching, drypoint, 15 x 15½, 1880 (4244/498) 400
Steinlen, Theophile Alexandre, BERTHE, etching, drypoint, 14⅛ x 11⅛, 1883 (4244/501) 550
Steinlen, Theophile Alexandre, BLANCHISSEUSES, 1896, lithograph, 14¾ x 11¾ (4215/442) 450
Steinlen, Theophile Alexandre, HISTOIRE ENNUYEUSE, etching, drypoint, 12½ x 8 (4244/497) 450
Steinlen, Theophile Alexandre, LE BANC DE JARDIN, mezzotint, 16½ x 22¼, 1883 (4244/502) 700
Steinlen, Theophile Alexandre, LE JOURNAL, etching, drypoint, 15 x 11⅝, 1883 (4244/500) 1400
Steinlen, Theophile Alexandre, LE MAIN, mezzotint, 16½ x 22¼, 1886 (4244/503) 300
Steinlen, Theophile Alexandre, RACAHOUT DES ARABES, lithograph, 22½ x 15⅛, frame (4244/496) 600
Summers, Carol, MEZZOGIORNO, 1960, woodcut, 35⅝ x 36⅛ (4215/443) 1100
Summers, Carol, THE CREATION OF MALWA, 1970, woodcut, 36¾ x 33⅛ (4215/444) 1600
Tamayo, Rufino, AFICHE AVANT LETTRE, lithograph, 33¼ x 24 (4105/140) 450
Tamayo, Rufino, CABEZA, lithograph, 29¼ x 21⅞ (4105/139) 650
Tamayo, Rufino, CARNAVALESQUE, 1969, lithograph, 27⅛ x 21⅛ (4105/146) 600
Tamayo, Rufino, COMPOSITION, lithograph, 22¼ x 30 (4270/553) 500
Tamayo, Rufino, DEMI-POISSON, lithograph, 20⅞ x 27½ (4270/554) 400
Tamayo, Rufino, DEUX TETES, 1969, lithograph, 27⅛ x 21⅛ (4105/145) 750
Tamayo, Rufino, DOS NINAS MEXICANAS, 1925, woodcut, 3¼ x 3½ (4105/137) 600
Tamayo, Rufino, EL PERRO MUEVE LA COLA, 1974, mixograph, 22 x 30 (4105/151) 600
Tamayo, Rufino, FEMME AU COLLANT NOIR, lithograph, 27½ x 20⅞ (4270/555) 300
Tamayo, Rufino, FEMME EN MAUVE, lithograph, 26¾ x 20¾ (4270/556) 400
Tamayo, Rufino, FEMME EN ROUGE, lithograph, 27½ x 20⅞ (4270/557) 300
Tamayo, Rufino, FEMME GRIS, 1969, lithograph, 26 x 19¼ (4105/144) 350
Tamayo, Rufino, GREEN CAT, lithograph, 18¾ x 25½ (4270/558) 500
Tamayo, Rufino, HEAD, lithograph, 16½ x 12, frame (4244/431) 300

Tamayo, Rufino, HOMBRE BLANCO, lithograph, 29¾ x 22 (4270/559)   650
Tamayo, Rufino, HOMBRE CONTEMPLANDO LA LUNA, etching, aquatint, 7⅞ x 5⅞ (4105/138)   700
Tamayo, Rufino, HORSEMAN OF THE APOCALYPSE-CONQUEROR, 1961, lithograph, 13 x 20⅛ (4105/143)   900
Tamayo, Rufino, HORSEMAN OF THE APOCALYPSE-DEATH, 1961, lithograph, 13 x 20⅛ (4105/141)   700
Tamayo, Rufino, HORSEMAN OF THE APOCALYPSE-FAMINE, 1961, lithograph, 13 x 20⅛ (4105/142)   950
Tamayo, Rufino, JACKAL, lithograph, 22½ x 30¼, 1973 (4244/432)   400
Tamayo, Rufino, LA NEGRESSE, 1969, lithograph, 27⅛ x 21⅛ (4105/148)   500
Tamayo, Rufino, LA PAYSANNE, 1969, lithograph, 27⅛ x 21⅛ (4105/147)   450
Tamayo, Rufino, MAN AND WOMAN, woodcut, 9⅞ x 9⅞, ca1925 (4244/429)   450
Tamayo, Rufino, NINO BAILANDO, 1974, mixograph, 29¼ x 21¼ (4105/152)   700
Tamayo, Rufino, PASTEQUE NO. 2, 1969, lithograph, 27⅛ x 21⅛ (4105/150)   550
Tamayo, Rufino, VENUS NOIR, 1969, lithograph, 27⅜ x 21 (4105/149)   275
Tissot, James Jacques, BERTHE, 1883, etching and drypoint, 14⅛ x 11⅛ (4215/451)   600
Tissot, James Jacques, LA SOEUR AINEE, etching and drypoint, 11⅝ x 6 (4270/564)   425
Tissot, James Jacques, LE FOYER DE LA COMEDIE - FRANCAISE, 1877, etching, 15 x 10⅞ (4215/447)   450
Tissot, James Jacques, LE HAMAC, etching, 11 x 7¼ (4270/561)   350
Tissot, James Jacques, LE HAMAC, 1880, etching and drypoint, 11 x 7⅛ (4215/449)   750
Tissot, James Jacques, LE JOURNAL, etching and drypoint, 14⅛ x 11½ (4270/565)   1150
Tissot, James Jacques, PRINTEMPS, 1878, etching and drypoint, 15 x 5⅜ (4215/448)   750
Tissot, James Jacques, PROMENADE DANS LA NEIGE, etching and drypoint, 22⅛ x 10½ (4270/562)   *1500*

Toulouse-Lautrec
(4270/582)

Tissot (4270/562)

Utrillo
(4147/308)

Tissot, James Jacques, REVERIE, etching, 8⅞ x 4½ (4270/563) — 400
Tissot, James Jacques, SOIREE D'ETE, 1882, etching and drypoint, 9¼ x 15⅝ (4215/450) — 750
Toledo, F., FUNCION DE MAGO 1972, etching and aquatint, 7⅞ x 9⅞ (4105/156) — 250
Toledo, F., GATO Y MANZANA, 1975, etching, aquatint, 19½ x 13¼ (4105/159) — 950
Toledo, F., LADRONES DE COCHINOS 1975, etching, aquatint, 12⅛ x 17 (4105/158) — 500
Toledo, F., PESCADO, 1973, etching, aquatint, 14¾ x 11⅛ (4105/157) — 375
Toledo, Francisco, LOS DEL MECATE, 1976, drypoint, aquatint, 19¼ x 26⅝ (4105/155) — 750
Toorop, Jan, DEUTSCHE KUNST UND DEKORATION, 1902, woodcut, 9⅝ x 7¾ (4215/453) — 175
Toorop, Jan, JEUGD EN OUDERDOM DER UROUW, 1895, drypoint, 7⅞ x 9⅞ (4215/452) — 375
Toulouse - Lautrec, Henri de, PAUVRE PIERREUSE, lithograph, 10¾ x 6⅞ (4270/579) — 400
Toulouse-Lautrec, Henri de, AFFICHE POUR LES ELLES, 1896, lithograph 24 x 18⅞ (4067/217) — 1500
Toulouse-Lautrec, Henri de, COUVERTURE POUR LES COURTES TOIES, 1897, lithograph 7¼ x 9¾ (4067/219) — 250
Toulouse-Lautrec, Henri de, EMILIENNE d'ALENCON, 1895, lithograph 11¼ x 9⅛ (4067/216) — 900
Toulouse-Lautrec, Henri de, L'ARTISAN MODERNE, 1894, lithograph 34⅝ x 24⅜ (4067/227) — 1100
Toulouse-Lautrec, Henri de, LA TROUPE DE MLLE EGLANTINE, 1896, lithograph 24½ x 31½ (4067/228) — 1200
Toulouse-Lautrec, Henri de, LE DIVAN JAPONAIS, 1892, lithograph 30¾ x 23¼ (4067/226) — 3500
Toulouse-Lautrec, Henri de, LE MARCHAND DE MARRONS, ca1897, lithograph 10¼ x 7 (4067/225) — 400
Toulouse-Latrec, Henri de, MAY MILTON, lithograph, 31¼ x 27⅜, frame, 1895 (4244/444) — 7250
Toulouse-Lautrec, H., CARNAVAL, lithograph, 10 x 6, 1894 (4147/301) — 3600
Toulouse-Lautrec, H., DECLARATION, lithograph, 10½ x 9⅛, ca1930 (4203/346) — 650
Toulouse-Lautrec, H., L'HARNEG SAUR, lithograph, 9¼ x 8¼, 1895 (4147/303) — 275
Toulouse-Lautrec, H., LE CAFE-CONCERT, Edmee Lescot, lithograph, in black and grey, 10½ x 7¼, 1893 (4203/345) — 950
Toulouse-Lautrec, H., LE DIVAN JAPONAIS, lithograph, in colors, laid down, 32 x 24, 1892 (4203/347) — 3600
Toulouse-Lautrec, H., LE MARCHAND DE MARRONS, lithograph, 10⅛ x 6⅞, 1897 (4147/306) — 1000
Toulouse-Lautrec, H., LENDER DANSANT LE PAS DU BOLERO, lithograph, 14½ x 10½, 1895 (4147/302) — 1300
Toulouse-Lautrec, H., LES VIEILLES HISTOIRES, Nuit Blanche, lithograph, second style, 10⅛ x 7⅛, 1893 (4203/343) — 500
Toulouse-Lautrec, H., MME. REJANE, lithograph, 11⅝ x 9¼, 1899 (4147/305) — 650
Toulouse-Lautrec, H., YVETTE GUILBERT, lithograph, 12¾ x 10½, 1898 (4147/304) — 600
Toulouse-Lautrec, Henri de, COUVERTURE DE L'ESTAMPE ORIGINALE, lithograph, 23¼ x 32⅝ frame, 1895 (4244/442) — 3250
Toulouse-Lautrec, Henri de, L'ARGENT, lithograph, 12½ x 9⅜, 1895 (4244/438) — 4300
Toulouse-Lautrec, Henri de, LA PARTIE DE CAMPAGNE, lithograph, 15⅞ x 20½, 1897 (4244/441) — 51000
Toulouse-Lautrec, Henri de, PAN, MLLE. MARCELLE LENDER, lithograph, 14½ x 11, 1895 (4244/440) — 8500
Toulouse-Lautrec, Henri de, TROUPE DE MLLE. EGLANTINE, lithograph, 24½ x 31½, 1896 (4244/443) — 6250
Toulouse-Lautrec, Henri de, ARISTIDE BRUANT, 1893, lithograph, 10½ x 8¼ (4215/455) — 1600
Toulouse-Lautrec, Henri de, CARNOR MALADE, lithograph, 9⅝ x 7⅜ (4270/578) — 400
Toulouse-Lautrec, Henri de, CONFETTI, 1895, lithograph, 22½ x 17½ (4215/457) — 5750
Toulouse-Lautrec, Henri de, EROSE UANNE, lithograph, 10¾ x 13½ (4270/581) — 500
Toulouse-Lautrec, Henri de, LA LOGE AU MASCARON DORE, 1894, lithograph, 12⅛ x 9½ (4215/454) — 3500
Toulouse-Lautrec, Henri de, LATIGE, 1894, lithograph, 11⅜ x 9⅞ (4215/456) — 2800
Toulouse-Lautrec, Henri de, LE PETIT TROTTIN, lithograph, 11 x 7¼ (4270/580) — 1500
Toulouse-Lautrec, Henri de, LE REVUE BLANCHE, 1895, lithograph, 49¼ x 35½ (4215/458) — 5500
Toulouse-Lautrec, Henri de, LENDER DAN SANT LE PAS DU BOLERO, lithograph, 14¾ x 10⅜ (4270/582) — *1300*
Toulouse-Lautrec, Henri de, PORTRAITS D'ACTEURS ET D'ACTRICES, lithograph, 11½ x 9¾ (4270/584) — 700
Toulouse-Lautrec, Henri de, PROSPECTUS-PROGRAMME DE L'OEUVRE, lithograph, 8⅜ x 13½ (4270/583) — 400
Toulouse-Lautrec, Henri de, LA LOGE AU MASCARON DORE, lithograph, 14⅜ x 11⅜ (4244/439) — 8000
Uillon, Jaques, COMPOSITION, 1954, lithograph 12⅜ x 16¼ (4067/240) — 250
Utrillo, Maurice, LA PLACE DU TERTRE, lithograph, 7½ x 10⅝ (4270/585) — 600
Utrillo, Maurice, LE LAPIN AGILE, lithograph, 7½ x 10¾, frame (4244/445) — 675
Utrillo, Maurice, NOTRE-DAME DE PARIS, lithograph, 6⅞ x 8⅞ (4147/308) — 850
Valadon, Suzanne, PORTRAIT D'UTRILLO, 1928, lithograph, 8¾ x 7 (4215/459) — 900
Vallotton, Felix, C'EST LA GUERRE I, LA TRANCHEE, woodcut, 7 x 8¾, 1915-16 (4147/311) — 400
Vallotton, Felix, C'EST LA GUERRE II, L'ORGIE, woodcut, 7 x 8¾, 1915-16 (4147/312) — 400
Vallotton, Felix, C'EST LA GUERRE III, LES FILS DE FER, woodcut, 7 x 8⅞, 1915-16 (4147/313) — 175

Vallotton, Felix, C'EST LA GUERRE IV, DANS LES TENEBRES, woodcut, 7 x 8¾, 1915-16 (4147/314) 225
Vallotton, Felix, C'EST LA GUERRE V, LE GUETTEUR, woodcut, 7 x 8¾, 1915-16 (4147/315) 175
Vallotton, Felix, C'EST LA GUERRE VI, LES CIVILS, woodcut, 6⅞ x 8¾, 1915-16 (4147/316) 175
Vallotton, Felix, C'EST LA GUERRE, complete set, 6 woodcuts, 10⅛ x 13, 1915-16 (4244/447) 1600
Vallotton, Felix, CINQ HEURES, 1901, woodcut, 6½ x 4¾ (4215/462) 350
Vallotton, Felix, INSTRUMENTS DE MUSIQUE LE PISTON, 1897, woodcut, 8⅞ x 7 (4215/461) 850
Vallotton, Felix, L'ASSASSINAT, woodcut, cream wove paper, 5¾ x 9¾ (4203/350) 350
Vallotton, Felix, LES TROIS BAIGNEUSES, 1894, woodcut, 7¼ x 4½ (4215/460) 650
Vasarely, Victor, AIX, silkscreen, 26 x 13¼ (4244/450) 250
Vasarely, Victor, ANTARES, silkscreen, 18¼ x 12¼, 1970 (4147/317) 150
Vasarely, Victor, BABEL III, silkscreen, 19¾ x 19¾ (4270/587) 250
Vasarely, Victor, CLARITES IX, silkscreen, 18¼ x 14¼ (4067/235) 225
Vasarely, Victor, COMPOSITION, silkscreen, 22½ x 22½ (4147/321) 250
Vasarely, Victor, COMPOSITION, silkscreen, 22½ x 22⅜ (4147/320) 100
Vasarely, Victor, COMPOSITION, silkscreen, 22⅜ x 22½ (4147/319) 100
Vasarely, Victor, COMPOSITION, silkscreen, 22½ x 22½ (4147/322) 125
Vasarely, Victor, COMPOSITION, silkscreen, 22½ x 22½ (4147/318) 125
Vasarely, Victor, COMPOSITION, silkscreen, 26 x 13¼ (4215/465) 250
Vasarely, Victor, COMPOSITION, silkscreen, 23½ x 17½ (4270/589) 200
Vasarely, Victor, COMPOSITION, silkscreen, 21 x 19⅞ (4270/590) 250
Vasarely, Victor, COMPOSITION, silkscreen, 12¼ x 10⅝ (4270/591) 200
Vasarely, Victor, DIAGO CF, silkscreen, 23⅝ x 23⅝ (4147/325) 250
Vasarely, Victor, DIAGO, C.F., silkscreen, 23½ x 23½ (4067/238) 350
Vasarely, Victor, DIAGO, C.G., silkscreen, 23⅝ x 23⅝ (4067/239) 300
Vasarely, Victor, DIAX, silkscreen, 23½ x 23½ (4067/237) 575
Vasarely, Victor, DICE I, silkscreen, 26 x 21½ (4215/463) 250
Vasarely, Victor, JINDEY, silkscreen, 23⅝ x 23⅝ (4147/324) 250
Vasarely, Victor, KEZDI-GA, silkscreen, 20⅛ x 20⅛ (4270/592) 275
Vasarely, Victor, KEZDI, silkscreen, 18¼ x 18 (4244/451) 325
Vasarely, Victor, LAPIDAIRE, silkscreen, 27¼ x 25⅜, frame, 1966 (4244/449) 500
Vasarely, Victor, MA-TA-FA, silkscreen, 28⅜ x 21¼ (4270/594) 350
Vasarely, Victor, OETKA, silkscreen, 36¼ x 27½ (4270/595) 250
Vasarely, Victor, OR VAR, silkscreen, 36¼ x 27½ (4270/596) 200
Vasarely, Victor, POKOL BC, silkscreen, 23⅝ x 23⅝ (4147/327) 225
Vasarely, Victor, POKOL BF, silkscreen, 23⅝ x 23⅝ (4147/326) 200
Vasarely, Victor, YAK, silkscreen, 19 x 19 (4147/323) 250
Vasarely, Victor, ZETT, silkscreen, 23⅝ x 23⅝ (4147/328) 275
Vertes, Marcel, OMBRE DE MON AMOUR, drypoint, hand colored, 11½ x 8¾ (4203/359) 60
Villon, Jacques, (HARVEST SCENE), etching, 10⅝ x 16½ (4203/364) 400
Villon, Jacques, ABSTRACT COMPOSITION, lithograph, 10⅝ x 18 (4270/606) 275
Villon, Jacques, Composition, lithograph, 12½ x 16¼ (4270/607) 400
Villon, Jacques, COMPOSITION, 1953, lithograph, 7½ x 18¾ (4215/468) 175
Villon, Jacques, DANSEUSE AU MOULIN-ROUGE, 1899, lithograph, 11½ x 8⅞ (4215/467) 800
Villon, Jacques, L'ENLEVEMENT OU LE RAVISSEUR, 1903, aquatint, 19½ x 15½ (4215/466) 1000
Villon, Jacques, LA VASE JAUNE, lithograph, in colors, 11½ x 16½ (4203/361) 125
Villon, Jacques, LE BAIN DE MINNE, MINNE ETENDUE ... , etching, drypoint, signed, 'epreuve a pres.', 6¾ x 9⅞, 1907 (4203/360) 700
Villon, Jacques, PAYSAGE, lithograph, in colors, 11⅝ x 19⅝ (4203/362) 525
Villon, Jacques, PETITE PEINTURE CUBISTE, silkscreen, in colors, 18⅝ x 12⅝ (4203/363) 375
Villon, Jacques, PORTRAIT DE MELLE, etching, 8⅝ x 6¼ (4270/602) 250
Villon, Jacques, TAIRE, silkscreen, 30¾ x 17⅛ (4270/599) 550
Villon, Jacques After Modigliani, L'ITALIENNE, aquatint, 19⅝ x 12⅛ (4270/603) 3200
Villon, Jacques After Paul Cezanne, LES JOUEURS DE CARTES, aquatint, 19¼ x 23⅝ (4270/604) 1500
Villon, Jacques, after Amedeo Modigliani, L'ITALIENNE, aquatint, 19¾ x 12¼, frame, 1927 (4244/456) 2000
Villon, Jacques, after Bonnard, LA FEMME AU CHIEN, 1925, aquatint, 19¾ x 9¾ (4215/473) 2200
Villon, Jacques, after Braque, NATURE MORTE, 1922, aquatint, 23 x 8⅝ (4215/470) 950
Villon, Jacques, after Derain, BUSTE DE FEMME, 1922, aquatint, 23½ x 19⅛ (4215/471) 750
Villon, Jacques, after Laurencin, LA FEMME AU HAMAC, 1924, aquatint, 17 x 21½ (4215/472) 1600
Villon, Jacques, after Modigliani, L'ITALIENNE, 1927, aquatint, 19⅝ x 12⅛ (4215/474) 1800
Villon, Jacques, after Picasso, LES SALTIMBANQUES, 1922, aquatint, 23½ x 16½ (4215/469) 2000
Villon, Jacques, after Van Gogh, LES ROSES, aquatint, 15 x 19⅝, frame, 1927 (4244/457) 800
Vlaminck, Maurice de, CREPUSCULE, lithograph, second state, 8⅞ x 12¾ (4203/366) 325
Vlaminck, Maurice de, LA ROUTE, lithograph, 24⅝ x 19⅜, frame, 1958 (4244/461) 1000
Vlaminck, Maurice de, LE PONT SUR L'OISE A MERY II, lithograph, 9⅝ x 13¾ (4147/331) 950
Vlaminck, Maurice de, MARINE, L'EGLISE, lithograph, 8⅞ x 12, frame (4244/459) 550

Zorn
(4270/663)

Vlaminck, Maurice de, PAYSAGES DES MAISONS, LE CAFE DE PARIS, 1927, etching, 4 x 6⅝ (4067/242) 425
Vlaminck, Maurice de, TOURNANT DANGEREUX, LES BORDS DU SAUSSERON, lithograph, 6⅜ x 5⅞, frame, 1930 (4244/460) 275
Vlaminck, Maurice de, MAREIL, 1913, woodcut, 10⅛ x 13¼ (4215/475) 1600
Vuillard, Edouard, FRONTISPICE POUR LES NOUVELLES PASS., lithograph, 7½ x 3, 1893 (4147/332) 150
Vuillard, Edouard, UNE GALERIE AU GYMNASE, lithograph, in colors, third state, 9⅞ x 7¾, ca1900 (4203/367) 275
Ward, W., after Morland, 1803, HARD BARGAIN, THE LAST LITTER, 17¾ x 23½ (4148/185) 375
Wengenroth, Stow, BIRD OF FREEDOM, 1942, lithograph 15¾ x 11¾ (4067/247) 250
Wood, Grant, MIDNIGHT ALBUM, 1939, lithograph, 12 x 7 (4215/478) 450
Wunderlich, Paul, DIE FUSSE, lithograph, 29⅞ x 22⅛, 1968 (4147/344) 200
Wunderlich, Paul, FEMME AU FAUTEUIL, etching, 19½ x 14¾ (4270/656) 275
Wunderlich, Paul, JOANA BEI KARIN, 1968, lithograph, 22⅝ x 19⅞ (4215/480) 200
Wunderlich, Paul, JOANA DREAMING OF BISMARCK, 1968, lithograph, 19¾ x 25¾ (4215/481) 200
Wunderlich, Paul, JOANA IM STUHL, 1968, lithograph, 22⅝ x 19¾ (4215/479) 200
Wunderlich, Paul, LA TETE, lithograph, 22⅛ x 19⅞ (4270/652) 75
Zadkine, Ossip, LE COMBAT ANTIQUE, 1964, etching, 32½ x 10½ (4067/261) 50
Zorn, Anders, AT THE PIANO, etching and drypoint, 7⅞ x 5⅞ (4270/661) 500
Zorn, Anders, BEADLE, etching, 6¼ x 4¾ (4270/664) 250
Zorn, Anders, CABIN, etching, 11¾ x 7¾, 1917 (4244/465) 550
Zorn, Anders, CABIN, etching, 11¾ x 7¾ (4270/668) 650
Zorn, Anders, CABIN, 1917, etching, 11¾ x 7⅞ (4067/266) 650
Zorn, Anders, ELIM, etching, 7¾ x 11¾ (4270/667) 425
Zorn, Anders, FISHERMAN AT SAINT IVES, 1891, etching, 10⅞ x 7⅞ (4067/263) 1800
Zorn, Anders, IDA, etching, 9¼ x 6¼ (4270/663) *500*
Zorn, Anders, J.B. FAURE, 1891, etching, 9¼ x 6¼ (4215/482) 360
Zorn, Anders, KING OSCAR II, etching and aquatint, 9¾ x 7 (4270/660) 450
Zorn, Anders, KING OSCAR II, 1898, etching and aquatint, 9¾ x 7⅛ (4215/485) 250
Zorn, Anders, MAJA VON HEIJNE, etching, 9¾ x 7⅞, 1900 (4147/347) 425
Zorn, Anders, MME, ARMAND DAYOT, etching and drypoint, 9⅜ x 6¼ (4270/658) 400
Zorn, Anders, MR. AND MRS. ATHERTON, 1906, etching, 9½ x 7¼ (4067/265) 900
Zorn, Anders, OLS MARIA, 1919, etching, 7¾ x 11¾ (4215/487) 300
Zorn, Anders, READING, etching, 9½ x 6¼ (4270/659) 550
Zorn, Anders, ROSITA MAURI, etching (4147/345) 500
Zorn, Anders, ROSITA MAURI, etching, 9¼ x 6, 1889 (4147/346) 150
Zorn, Anders, SEAWARD SKERRIES, etching, 7 x 9¾ (4270/665) 800
Zorn, Anders, SHALLOW, etching, 11⅝ x 7⅞ (4270/666) 300
Zorn, Anders, STORM, 1891, etching, 7⅞ x 5½ (4067/264) 1600
Zorn, Anders, VICKE, 1918, etching and drypoint, 7⅞ x 11¾ (4215/486) 300
Zorn, Anders, WICKE, etching, 7¾ x 11½ (4270/669) 385
Zorn, Anders, ZORN AND HIS WIFE, 1890, etching, 12 x 7⅞ (4067/262) 1700

Zuniga, Francisco, LA SEMBRADORA, 1976, lithograph, 25 x 34⅝ (4105/165)   1300
Zuniga, Francisco, MADRE CON NINO, 1973, lithograph, 19⅝ x 25¾ (4105/164)   1100
Zuniga, Francisco, MUJER, lithograph, 16½ x 13 (4270/674)   550
Zuniga, Francisco, YUCATECA CON FRUTA, 1974, lithograph and silkscreen, 27 x 19¼ (4067/271) 800

OLD MASTER PRINTS

Aldegrever, Heinrich, TITUS MANCIUS HAVING SON BEHEADED, engraving, 4½ x 2⅞, few spots
(4118/1)   130
Altdorfer, Albrecht, ALLEGORICAL FIGURE, TRUTH FLOATING OVER THE EARTH, engraving,
3¾ x 1⅞ (4215/533)   3700
Altdorfer, Albrecht, HERCULES AND A MUSE, 2⅝ x 1¾ (4215/551)   700
Altdorfer, Albrecht, HERCULES AND THE NEMEAN LION, engraving, 1¾ x 1⅜ (4215/544)   475
Altdorfer, Albrecht, HORATIUS COCLES LEAPING INTO THE RIVER, engraving, 2⅝ x 1½
(4215/549)   1100
Altdorfer, Albrecht, NEPTUNE RIDING ON A SEA SERPENT, 1 x 1¾ (4215/552)   1300
Altdorfer, Albrecht, ORNAMENT WITH A CHERUB'S HEAD, engraving, 2⅜ x 1⅝ (4215/558)   750
Altdorfer, Albrecht, PYRAMUS AND THISBE, engraving, 2⅜ x 1⅝ (4215/538)   900
Altdorfer, Albrecht, RAPE OF A NYMPH, engraving, 1¾ x 3⅛ (4215/553)   850
Altdorfer, Albrecht, SAMSON AND DELILAH, engraving, 1¾ x 1⅜ (4215/545)   325
Altdorfer, Albrecht, SAMSON BEARING THE GATES OF GAZA, engraving, 1⅝ x 1⅜ (4215/542)   325
Altdorfer, Albrecht, SOLOMON'S IDOLATRY, engraving, 2⅜ x 1⅝ (4215/540)   275
Altdorfer, Albrecht, ST. CHRISTOPHER, engraving, 2½ x 2⅜ (4215/534)   575
Altdorfer, Albrecht, ST. GEORGE AND THE DRAGON, engraving, 2⅜ x 1⅝ (4215/536)   2800
Altdorfer, Albrecht, ST. JEROME IN THE GROTTO, engraving, 4½ x 2⅜ (4215/539)   700
Altdorfer, Albrecht, ST. SEBASTIAN BOUND TO A COLUMN, engraving, 3½ x 1⅞ (4215/529)   250
Altdorfer, Albrecht, THE CARPENTER, engraving, 1⅜ x 1⅛ (4215/546)   450
Altdorfer, Albrecht, THE DEATH OF DIDO, engraving, 2½ x 1⅜ (4215/550)   575
Altdorfer, Albrecht, THE INFANT CHRIST ON THE RAINBOW, engraving, 3 x 1¾ (4215/531)   250
Altdorfer, Albrecht, THE JUDGEMENT OF PARIS, engraving, 2⅜ x 1⅝ (4215/537)   2800
Altdorfer, Albrecht, THE KNIGHT WITH THE BREAD AND WINE, engraving, and etching, 3½ x 1⅞
(4215/530)   950
Altdorfer, Albrecht, THE REST ON THE FLIGHT TO EGYPT, engraving, 3¾ x 1⅞ (4215/535)   4900
Altdorfer, Albrecht, THE REVENGE OF THE SORCERER VIRGIL, engraving, 3 x 1¾ (4215/548)   800
Altdorfer, Albrecht, THE VIRGIN AND CHILD ON AN ALTER, engraving, 2⅜ x 1⅝ (4215/541)   4200
Altdorfer, Albrecht, THE VIRGIN WITH THE CHILD IN A LANDSCAPE, engraving, 6⅜ x 4½
(4215/532)   2200
Altdorfer, Albrecht, TRITON AND NEREID, engraving, 2⅜ x 1⅝ (4215/555)   700
Altdorfer, Albrecht, TWO SATYRS FIGHTING OVER A NYMPH, engraving, 2⅜ x 1⅝ (4215/554)   450
Altdorfer, Albrecht, VENUS AFTER THE BATH, engraving, 2⅜ x 1⅝ (4215/557)   1500
Altdorfer, Albrecht, VENUS CROUCHING, engraving, 2⅜ x 1⅝ (4215/556)   425
Altdorfer, Albrecht, VIRGIN WITH THE CHILD AND TWO BOYS, engraving, 2¾ x 2 (4215/528)   450
Altdorfer, Albrecht, WOMAN BATHING HER FEET, engraving, 1½ x 1⅛ (4215/547)   700
Baldung, Hans, GROUP OF SEVEN HORSES, woodcut, 8½ x 12¾, some damage (4118/3)   1250
Bartolozzi, Francesco, WILLIAM PITT, engraving, 20¼ x 15¼ (4215/564)   70
Beham, Hans Sebald, CHRIST CROWNED WITH THORNS SPEAKING WITH HIS MOTHER,
engraving, 2⅝ x 1⅝ (4215/563)   1800
Beham, Hans Sebald, THE FOUNTAIN OF YOUTH, wood cut, 14½ x 31⅞ (4215/565)   270
Blake, William, SO THE LORD BLESSED THE LATTER END OF JOB, engraving, 8⅝ x 6¾
(4215/576)   300
Blake, William, THEN WENT SATAN FORTH FROM THE PRESENCE OF THE LORD, engraving,
8⅝ x 6½ (4215/569)   650
Blake, William, THOU HAST FULFILLED THE JUDGEMENT OF THE WICKED, engraving, 7⅞ x 6½
(4215/573)   275
Blake, William, THY SONS AND THY DAUGHTERS WERE EATING AND DRINKING WINE,
engraving, 8⅝ x 6¾ (4215/567)   700
Bol, Ferdinand, THE YOUNG MAN WEARING A PLUMED CAP, etching, 3½ x 3⅛ (4118/5)   200
Callot, Jacques, LE DEBARQUEMENT DES TROUPES, etching, 5⅜ x 12¾, trimmed (4118/7)   110
Callot, Jacques, VUE DE LOUVRE, etching, 6⅜ x 13⅜ (4215/579)   800
Canal, Antonio, called Canaletto, LE PROCURATIE NIOVE E.S. ZIMINIAN, etching, 5⅝ x 8¼
(4215/582)   600
Canal, Antonio, called Canaletto, MESTRE, etching, 11¾ x 17 (4215/580)   2750
Canal, Antonio, called Canaletto, THE BISHOP'S TOMB, etching, 8⅝ x 5⅛ (4215/583)   475
Canal, Antonio, called Canaletto, VIEW OF A TOWN ON A RIVER BANK, etching, 11⅝ x 17
(4215/581)   1500
Dujardin, Karel, THE RESTING GOAT AND THE TWO SHEEP, etching, 5¾ x 5¼ (4118/8)   175
Durer, Albrecht, APOLLO AND DIANA, engraving, 4⅜ x 2¾ (4215/589)   2200
Durer, Albrecht, COAT OF ARMS WITH A SKULL, engraving, 8⅝ x 6⅛ (4215/595)   1400